WILEY
CPA
EXAM
REVIEW

WILEY
CPA
EXAM
REVIEW

2010-2011

37th Edition

Volume 2
Problems and Solutions

O. Ray W

Patrick R.

WILEY

JOHN WILEY & SONS, INC.

CONTENTS

---

* *As explained in Chapter 1, this volume is organized into 45 modules (manageable study units). Volume 1 is organized in a parallel fashion.*

PREFACE

Passing the CPA exam upon your first attempt is possible! The *Wiley CPA Examination Review* preparation materials provide you with the necessary materials (visit our Web site at www.wiley.com/cpa for more information). It's up to you to add the hard work and commitment. Together we can beat the first-time pass rate of less than 20%. All Wiley CPA products are continuously updated to provide you with the most comprehensive and complete knowledge base. Choose your products from the Wiley preparation materials and you can proceed confidently. You can select support materials that are exam-based and user-friendly. You can select products that will help you pass!

The first purpose of Volume 2 is to provide CPA candidates with sample examination problems/questions organized by topic (e.g., internal control, consolidations, etc.). This text includes over 2,600 multiple-choice questions. These questions provide an effective means of studying the material tested on past exams; however, it is also necessary to work with simulation style questions to develop the solutions approach (the ability to solve CPA questions and problems efficiently).

The second objective of this volume is to explain the AICPA unofficial answers and author question answers to the examination problems/questions included in this text. The AICPA published all CPA examinations and unofficial answers through the November 1995 exam and selected questions and answers since then. No explanation is made, however, of the procedures that should have been applied to the examination problem to obtain the unofficial answers. Relatedly, the unofficial answers to multiple-choice questions provide no justification and/or explanation. This text provides explanations of both how to work problems and the unofficial answers to multiple-choice questions.

This text is designed to be used in conjunction with Volume 1, *Outlines and Study Guides,* but may be used with or without any other study source. Both volumes are organized into 45 manageable study units (modules) to assist candidates in organizing their study programs. The multiple-choice questions in this volume are grouped into topical categories (submodules) that correspond to the sequencing of material as it appears in Volume 1.

New author-constructed questions have been added to this Thirty-Seventh Edition. As new questions and problems are added, older ones are deleted. New problems have been added to address the new content of the computerized exam.

A Sample Examination for each of the four parts of the exam is included in the Appendix at the end of this volume.

The CPA exam is one of the toughest exams you will ever take. It will not be easy. But if you follow our guidelines and focus on your goal, you will be thrilled with what you can accomplish.

Ray Whittington
April 2010

Don't forget to visit our Web site at www.wiley.com/cpa

for supplements and updates.

ABOUT THE AUTHORS

Ray Whittington, PhD, CPA, CMA, CIA, is the dean of the College of Commerce at DePaul University. Prior to joining the faculty at DePaul, Professor Whittington was the Director of Accountancy at San Diego State University. From 1989 through 1991, he was the Director of Auditing Research for the American Institute of Certified Public Accountants (AICPA), and he previously was on the audit staff of KPMG. He previously served as a member of the Auditing Standards Board of the AICPA and as a member of the Accounting and Review Services Committee and the Board of Regents of the Institute of Internal Auditors. Professor Whittington has published numerous textbooks, articles, monographs, and continuing education courses.

Patrick R. Delaney, deceased, was the dedicated author and editor of the *Wiley CPA Exam Review* books for twenty years. He was the Arthur Andersen LLP Alumni Professor of Accountancy and Department Chair at Northern Illinois University. He received his PhD in Accountancy from the University of Illinois. He had public accounting experience with Arthur Andersen LLP and was coauthor of *GAAP: Interpretation and Application*, also published by John Wiley & Sons, Inc. He served as Vice President and a member of the Illinois CPA Society's Board of Directors, and was Chairman of its Accounting Principles Committee; was a past president of the Rockford Chapter, Institute of Management Accountants; and had served on numerous other professional committees. He was a member of the American Accounting Association, American Institute of Certified Public Accountants, and Institute of Management Accountants. Professor Delaney was published in *The Accounting Review* and was a recipient of the Illinois CPA Society's Outstanding Educator Award, NIU's Excellence in Teaching Award, and Lewis University's Distinguished Alumnus Award. He was involved in NIU's CPA Review Course as director and instructor.

ABOUT THE CONTRIBUTORS

Anita L. Feller, PhD, CPA, is a Lecturer in Accountancy at the University of Illinois at Urbana-Champaign. She is the recipient of the Commerce Council Excellence in Teaching Award. Formerly a staff accountant in the tax department at KPMG Peat Marwick, she teaches courses in financial accounting and applied professional research. Professor Feller also teaches financial and managerial topics in the University of Illinois CPA Review Course. She is also the author of *Mastering Accounting Research for the CPA Exam* and *Wiley CPA Exam Review Impact Audios* (both published by Wiley).

Edward C. Foth, PhD, CPA, is the Administrator of the Master of Science in Taxation Program at DePaul University. He is a member of the American Accounting Association, the American Institute of Certified Public Accountants, the Illinois CPA Society, and the American Taxation Association. He has been a recipient of the Ledger & Quill Faculty Excellence Award, and is the author of CCH Incorporated's *Federal Tax Study Manual, Federal Taxation Refresher Course,* and is coauthor of their *S Corporations Guide*. He prepared Chapter 6.

Mark L. Frigo, PhD, CPA, CMA, is Director of The Center for Strategy, Execution and Valuation in Kellstadt Graduate School of Business and Eichenbaum Foundation Distinguished Professor of Strategy and Leadership in the School of Accountancy at DePaul University. Professor Frigo authored the Performance Measures module for the Business Environment and Concepts section of this manual.

Patricia L. McQueen, MBA, CPA, is an instructor in the School of Accountancy at DePaul University. She has a background in auditing and financial accounting. She has audit experience with KPMG. She contributed to the auditing modules.

Kurt Pany, PhD, CPA, is a Professor of Accounting at Arizona State University. Prior to entering academe, he worked as a staff auditor for Deloitte and Touche LLP. He is a former member of the AICPA's Auditing Standards Board and has taught in the Arizona State University CPA Review Course.

1 HOW TO USE THIS BOOK

This volume is a collection of CPA problems and solutions. The text is designed and organized to be used in conjunction with Volume 1, *CPA Examination Review: Outlines and Study Guides*, but may be used with or without any other study source. Each module in this volume corresponds to a module in Volume 1. In this volume, a module consists of

1. Multiple-choice questions
2. Simulation problems
3. Unofficial answers for the multiple-choice questions with the author's explanations
4. Answers for simulation problems

The sources of the problem material in each module are, of course, the four sections of the CPA Exam. The modules are grouped together into chapters, which correspond with the four sections of the exam. The following table shows how the modules are organized in Volume 2.

If you take the CPA examination after December 31, 2010, you should also review Appendix E for changes in the content and format of the exam.

CPA EXAM SECTION AND CORRESPONDING MODULES

Auditing and Attestation	CH 2	Modules 1-6
Financial Accounting and Reporting	CH 3	Modules 7-20
Regulation	CH 5 & 6	Modules 21-37
Business Environment and Concepts	CH 7	Modules 38-45

The material in Volume 2 allows candidates to work CPA exam questions, some of which have appeared on previous examinations. This provides candidates with an effective method of studying the material tested on the exam. However, candidates should also realize that the CPA has new material. Therefore, candidates should use the study guides and outlines included in Volume 1 as a means of bridging this gap.

Also included at the end of this volume are sample exams for all four sections. They are included to enable candidates to gain experience in taking a "realistic" exam. While working through the modules, the candidate can become accustomed to concentrating on a fairly narrow range of topics. By taking the sample examinations near the end of their study program, candidates will be better prepared for taking the actual examination.

Before you begin working the CPA problems in this volume, peruse the table of contents and scan through the book, noting the manner in which the chapters and modules are organized. The schedule at the beginning of each chapter provides an index to the simulations and problems appearing in each module. Some questions have been modified to reflect recent changes in law or practice. For a complete analysis of recent examinations and the AICPA Uniform CPA Examination Content Specification Outlines of future examinations, see the beginning of each chapter starting with Chapter 5 in Volume 1, Outlines and Study Guides.

Multiple-Choice Questions

The multiple-choice questions and answer explanations can be used in many ways. First, they may be used as a diagnostic evaluation of your knowledge. For example, before beginning to review audit sampling you may wish to answer every fourth multiple-choice question to determine your ability to answer CPA examination questions on audit sampling. The apparent difficulty of the questions and the correctness of your answers will allow you to determine the necessary breadth and depth of your review. Additionally, exposure to examination questions prior to review and study of the material should provide motivation. You will develop a feel for your level of proficiency and an understanding of the scope and difficulty of past examination questions.

Second, the multiple-choice questions can be used as a poststudy or postreview evaluation. You should attempt to understand all concepts mentioned (even in incorrect answers) as you answer the questions. Refer to the explanation of the answer for discussion of the alternatives even though you selected the correct response. Thus, you should read the explanation of the unofficial answer unless you completely understand the question and all of the alternative answers.

Third, you may wish to use the multiple-choice questions as a primary study vehicle. This is probably the quickest, but least thorough, approach. Make a sincere effort to understand the question and to select the correct reply before referring to the answer and explanation. In many cases the explanations will appear inadequate because of your unfamiliarity with the topic.

The multiple-choice questions in Volume 2 are grouped into study sets. The study sets include a smaller amount of related material than the study modules, which provides greater flexibility in the individual candidate's study strategy. The answer explanations for the multiple-choice questions in Volume 2 also include headings which provide cross-references to the text material in Volume 1. For example, in Module 9, Fixed Assets, the heading "F. Depreciation" appears above the answers to those questions dealing with depreciation. The topical coverage of depreciation in Volume 1 can then be found by referring to the corresponding heading within Module 9.

One of the benefits of working through multiple-choice questions is that it helps you to identify your weak areas. Once you have graded your answers, your strong areas and weak areas should be clearly evident. Yet, the important point here is that you should not stop at a simple percentage evaluation. The percentage only provides general feedback about your knowledge of the material contained within that particular module. The percentage **does not** give you any specific feedback regarding the concepts which were tested. In order to get this feedback, you should look at the questions missed on an individual basis because this will help you gain a better understanding of **why** you missed the question. This feedback process has been facilitated by the fact that within each module where the multiple-choice answer key appears, two blank lines have been inserted next to the multiple-choice answers. As you grade the multiple-choice questions, mark those questions which you have missed. However, instead of just marking the questions right and wrong, you should now focus on marking the questions in a manner which identifies **why** you missed the question. As an example, a candidate could mark the questions in the following manner: ✓ for math mistakes, x for conceptual mistakes, and ? for areas which the candidate was unfamiliar with. The candidate should then correct these mistakes by reworking through the marked questions. The objective of this marking technique is to help you identify your weak areas and thus, the concepts which you should be focusing on. While it is still important for you to get between 75% and 80% correct when working multiple-choice questions, it is more important for you to understand the concepts. This understanding applies to both the questions answered correctly and those answered incorrectly. Remember, most of the questions on the CPA exam will be different from the questions in the book; however, the concepts will be the same. Therefore, your preparation should focus on understanding concepts, not just getting the correct answer.

The multiple-choice questions substantially outnumber the simulation problems in this book. This is similar to what can be expected on the CPA exam. The multiple-choice questions make up about 75% of the total examination.

One difficulty with so many multiple-choice questions is that you may overemphasize them. Candidates generally prefer to work multiple-choice questions because they are shorter and less time consuming and solvable with less effort.

Simulations require the ability to organize and compose a solution, as well as knowledge of the subject matter. Remember, working simulations from start to finish is just as important as, if not more important than, working multiple-choice questions.

Another difficulty with the large number of multiple-choice questions is that you may tend to become overly familiar with the questions. The result may be that you may begin reading the facts and assumptions of previously studied questions into the questions on your examination. Guard against this potential problem by reading each multiple-choice question with **extra** care.

Although not as critical as for simulations, the solutions approach (a systematic problem-solving methodology) is relevant to multiple-choice questions.

Multiple-Choice Screen Layout

The following is a computer screenshot that illustrates the manner in which multiple-choice questions will be presented:

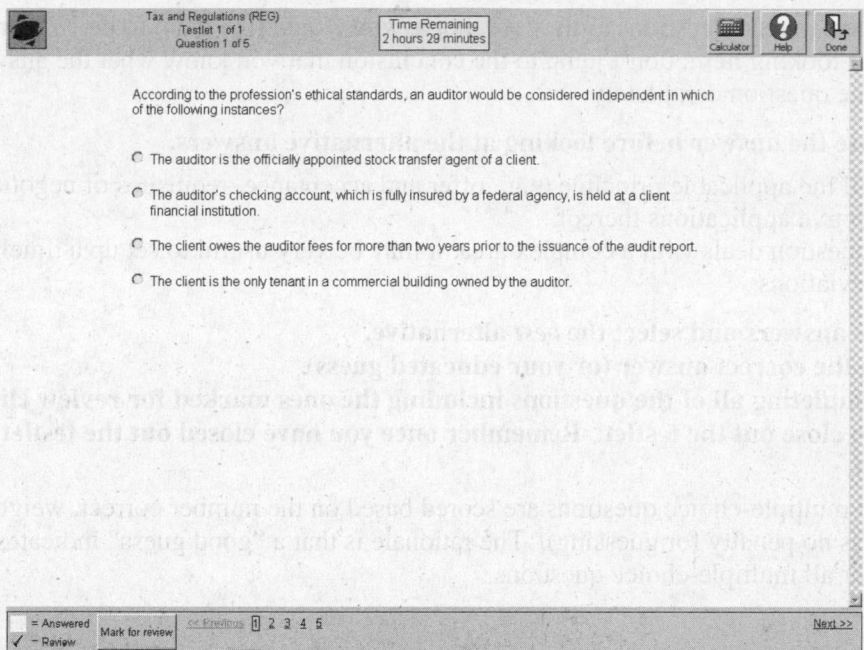

As indicated previously, multiple-choice questions will be presented in three individual testlets of 24 to 30 questions each. Characteristics of the computerized testlets of multiple-choice questions include the following:

1. You may move freely within a particular testlet from one question to the next or back to previous questions until you click the "Done" button. Once you have indicated that you have finished the testlet by clicking on the "Done" button, you can never return to that set of questions.
2. A button on the screen will allow you to mark a question for review if you wish to come back to it later.
3. A computer calculator is available as a tool.
4. The time remaining for the entire exam section is shown on the screen.
5. The number of the questions out of the total in the testlet is shown on the screen.
6. The "Help" button will provide you with help in navigating and completing the testlet.

The screenshot above was obtained from the AICPA's tutorial at www.cpa-exam.org. Candidates are urged to complete the tutorial and other example questions on the AICPA's Web site to obtain additional experience with the computer-based testing.

Multiple-Choice Questions Solutions Approach Algorithm

1. **Work individual questions in order.**

    a. If a question appears lengthy or difficult, skip it until you can determine that extra time is available. Mark it for review to remind you to return to it later.

2. **Read the stem of the question without looking at the answers.**

    a. The answers are sometimes misleading and may cause you to misread or misinterpret the question.

3. **Read each question *carefully* to determine the topical area.**

    a. Study the requirements **first** so you know which data are important
    b. Note keywords and important data
    c. Identify pertinent information
    d. Be especially careful to note when the requirement is an **exception** (e.g., "Which of the following is **not** an effective disclaimer of the implied warranty of merchantability?").
    e. If a set of data is the basis for two or more questions, read the requirements of each of the questions before beginning to work the first question (sometimes it is more efficient to work the questions out of order)

    f.   Be alert to read questions as they are, not as you would like them to be. You may encounter a familiar looking item; don't jump to the conclusion that you know what the answer is without reading the question completely.

4. **Anticipate the answer before looking at the alternative answers.**

    a.   Recall the applicable principle (e.g., offer and acceptance, requisites of negotiability, etc.) and the respective applications thereof.

    b.   If a question deals with a complex area, it may be very useful to set up a timeline or diagram using abbreviations.

5. **Read the answers and select the *best* alternative.**

6. **Click on the correct answer (or your educated guess).**

7. **After completing all of the questions including the ones marked for review click on the "Done" button to close out the testlet. Remember once you have closed out the testlet you can never return to it.**

Currently, all multiple-choice questions are scored based on the number correct, weighted by a difficulty rating (i.e., there is no penalty for guessing). The rationale is that a "good guess" indicates knowledge. Thus, you should answer all multiple-choice questions.

Simulations

The simulations have multiple parts separated by computer tabs. Typically they begin with directions and a situation and continue with various tabs requiring responses and a resource tab. An example of simulation instructions is shown below.

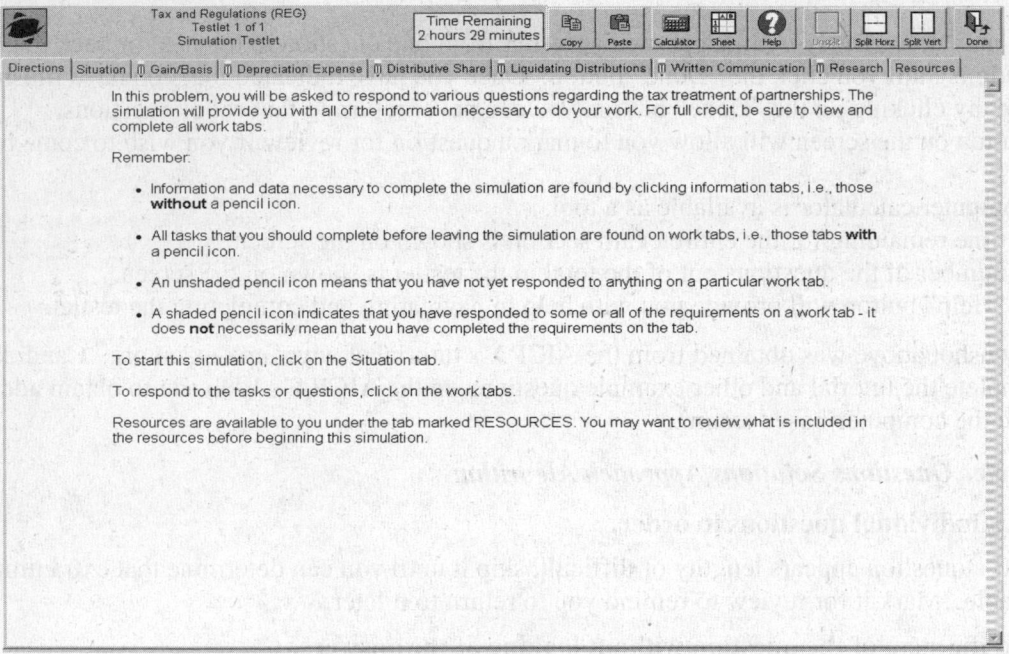

While the tabs without the pencils are informational in nature, the tabs with pencils require a response. The responses may involve checking a list, selecting from a pull-down menu, inputting words or a quantity, researching an issue, or writing a memo.

To complete the simulations, candidates are provided with a number of tools, including

- Calculator
- The ability to split windows to show two tabs on the screen (e.g., you can examine the situation tab in one window and a particular requirement in a second window)
- Access to professional literature databases to answer research requirements
- Scratch spreadsheet

In addition, the resource tab provides other resources that may be needed to complete the problem. For example, a resource tab might contain a present value table for use in answering a lease problem.

A window on the screen shows the time remaining for the entire section and the "Help" button provides instructions for navigating the simulation and completing the requirements.

The screenshots above were obtained from the AICPA's tutorial at www.cpa-exam.org. You are urged to complete the tutorial and sample exams that are on the AICPA's Web site to obtain additional experience with the computer-based testing.

Simulations Solutions Approach Algorithm

The following solutions approach is suggested for answering simulations:

1. **Review the entire problem.** Tab through the problem in order to get a feel for the topical area and related concepts that are being tested. Even though the format of the question may vary, the exam continues to test your understanding of applicable principles or concepts. Relax, take a deep breath, and determine your strategy for conquering the simulation.
2. **Identify the requirements of the problem.** This step will help you focus in more quickly on the solution(s) without wasting time reading irrelevant material.
3. **Study the items to be answered.** As you do this and become familiar with the topical area being tested, you should recall the concepts of that area. This will help you organize your thoughts so that you can relate logically the requirements of the simulation with the applicable concepts.
4. **Answer each tab requirement one at a time.** If the requirements don't build on one another, don't be afraid to answer the tab requirements out of order. Also, if the scenario is long or complex, you may wish to use the split screen function to enable you to view the simulation data while answering a requirement.
5. **Use scratch paper (which will be provided) and the spreadsheet and calculator tools to assist you in answering the simulation.**

Research Requirements of Simulations

Research tabs of simulations require candidates to search the professional literature and income tax code and regulations in electronic format and interpret the results. The table below describes the research material that will be available for each section of the exam that includes simulations.

Section	*Potential research resources*
Auditing and Attestation	• Statements on Auditing Standards and Interpretations • Statements on Attestation Standards and Interpretations • Statements on Standards for Accounting and Review Services and Interpretations
Financial Accounting and Reporting	• FASB Current Text and Original Pronouncements
Regulation	• Internal Revenue Code

Diagnose Your Weaknesses prior to the Exam

This volume of problems and solutions provides you with an opportunity to diagnose and correct any exam-taking weaknesses prior to your taking the examination. Continuously analyze the contributing factors to incomplete or incorrect solutions to CPA questions prepared during your study program. General categories of candidates' weaknesses include

1. Failure to understand the exam question requirements
2. Misunderstanding the supporting text of the problem
3. Lack of knowledge of material tested, especially recently issued pronouncements
4. Failure to develop proficiency with practice tools such as electronic research databases and spreadsheets
5. Inability to apply the solutions approach
6. Lack of an exam strategy (e.g., allocation of time)
7. Sloppiness and computational errors
8. Failure to proofread and edit

Time Management

Each section of the CPA exam will contain a number of multiple-choice testlets, and all of the sections except Business Environment and Concepts will contain two simulations. As you complete each testlet keep track of how you performed in relation to the AICPA suggested times. After you finish the multiple-choice testlets, budget your time for the simulations based on your remaining time and the AICPA suggested times.

For example, if you have two hours remaining to complete two simulations that each have the same AICPA suggested time, budget one hour for each simulation. Remember that you alone control watching your progress towards successfully completing this exam.

Additional Study Aids

A more complete discussion of the solutions approach, including illustrations thereof, appears in Chapter 3 of Volume 1, Outlines and Study Guides. Additionally, use of "note cards" as an integral part of your study program is discussed and illustrated in Chapter 1 of Volume 1. Chapter 4 of Volume 1 includes a detailed checklist to assist candidates with their last-minute preparation and to provide guidance concerning the actual taking of the exam.

NOW IS THE TIME

TO MAKE A COMMITMENT

2 AUDITING AND ATTESTATION PROBLEMS AND SOLUTIONS

The Auditing and Attestation Exam is scheduled for four and one-half hours. Based on information released by the AICPA, candidates should expect three multiple-choice testlets of approximately thirty questions each, and two simulations.

The Uniform CPA Examination Content Specifications appear in *Volume 1, Outlines and Study Guides.*

MULTIPLE-CHOICE QUESTIONS (1-131)

1. Financial statement assertions are established for account balances,

	Classes of transactions	Disclosures
a.	Yes	Yes
b.	Yes	No
c.	No	Yes
d.	No	No

2. Which of the following is **not** a financial statement assertion relating to account balances?
   a. Completeness.
   b. Existence.
   c. Rights and obligations.
   d. Valuation and competence.

3. As the acceptable level of detection risk decreases, an auditor may
   a. Reduce substantive testing by relying on the assessments of inherent risk and control risk.
   b. Postpone the planned timing of substantive tests from interim dates to the year-end.
   c. Eliminate the assessed level of inherent risk from consideration as a planning factor.
   d. Lower the assessed level of control risk from the maximum level to below the maximum.

4. The risk that an auditor will conclude, based on substantive tests, that a material misstatement does **not** exist in an account balance when, in fact, such misstatement does exist is referred to as
   a. Sampling risk.
   b. Detection risk.
   c. Nonsampling risk.
   d. Inherent risk.

5. As the acceptable level of detection risk decreases, the assurance directly provided from
   a. Substantive tests should increase.
   b. Substantive tests should decrease.
   c. Tests of controls should increase.
   d. Tests of controls should decrease.

6. Which of the following audit risk components may be assessed in nonquantitative terms?

	Control risk	Detection risk	Inherent risk
a.	Yes	Yes	No
b.	Yes	No	Yes
c.	Yes	Yes	Yes
d.	No	Yes	Yes

7. Inherent risk and control risk differ from detection risk in that they
   a. Arise from the misapplication of auditing procedures.
   b. May be assessed in either quantitative or nonquantitative terms.
   c. Exist independently of the financial statement audit.
   d. Can be changed at the auditor's discretion.

8. On the basis of the audit evidence gathered and evaluated, an auditor decides to increase the assessed level of control risk from that originally planned. To achieve an overall audit risk level that is substantially the same as the planned audit risk level, the auditor would

a. Decrease substantive testing.
b. Decrease detection risk.
c. Increase inherent risk.
d. Increase materiality levels.

9. Relationship between control risk and detection risk is ordinarily
   a. Parallel.
   b. Inverse.
   c. Direct.
   d. Equal.

10. Which of the following would an auditor most likely use in determining the auditor's preliminary judgment about materiality?
    a. The anticipated sample size of the planned substantive tests.
    b. The entity's annualized interim financial statements.
    c. The results of the internal control questionnaire.
    d. The contents of the management representation letter.

11. Which of the following statements is **not** correct about materiality?
    a. The concept of materiality recognizes that some matters are important for fair presentation of financial statements in conformity with GAAP, while other matters are **not** important.
    b. An auditor considers materiality for planning purposes in terms of the largest aggregate level of misstatements that could be material to any one of the financial statements.
    c. Materiality judgments are made in light of surrounding circumstances and necessarily involve both quantitative and qualitative judgments.
    d. An auditor's consideration of materiality is influenced by the auditor's perception of the needs of a reasonable person who will rely on the financial statements.

12. Which of the following elements underlies the application of generally accepted auditing standards, particularly the standards of fieldwork and reporting?
    a. Internal control.
    b. Corroborating evidence.
    c. Quality control.
    d. Materiality and relative risk.

13. In considering materiality for planning purposes, an auditor believes that misstatements aggregating $10,000 would have a material effect on an entity's income statement, but that misstatements would have to aggregate $20,000 to materially affect the balance sheet. Ordinarily, it would be appropriate to design auditing procedures that would be expected to detect misstatements that aggregate
    a. $10,000
    b. $15,000
    c. $20,000
    d. $30,000

14. Which of the following would an auditor most likely use in determining the auditor's preliminary judgment about materiality?
    a. The results of the initial assessment of control risk.
    b. The anticipated sample size for planned substantive tests.

c. The entity's financial statements of the prior year.
d. The assertions that are embodied in the financial statements.

15. Holding other planning considerations equal, a decrease in the amount of misstatement in a class of transactions that an auditor could tolerate most likely would cause the auditor to

a. Apply the planned substantive tests prior to the balance sheet date.
b. Perform the planned auditing procedures closer to the balance sheet date.
c. Increase the assessed level of control risk for relevant financial statement assertions.
d. Decrease the extent of auditing procedures to be applied to the class of transactions.

16. When issuing an unqualified opinion, the auditor who evaluates the audit findings should be satisfied that the

a. Amount of known misstatement is documented in the management representation letter.
b. Estimate of the total likely misstatement is less than a material amount.
c. Amount of known misstatement is acknowledged and recorded by the client.
d. Estimate of the total likely misstatement includes the adjusting entries already recorded by the client.

17. Which of the following is an example of fraudulent financial reporting?

a. Company management changes inventory count tags and overstates ending inventory, while understating cost of goods sold.
b. The treasurer diverts customer payments to his personal due, concealing his actions by debiting an expense account, thus overstating expenses.
c. An employee steals inventory and the "shrinkage" is recorded in cost of goods sold.
d. An employee steals small tools from the company and neglects to return them; the cost is reported as a miscellaneous operating expense.

18. Which of the following best describes what is meant by the term "fraud risk factor?"

a. Factors whose presence indicates that the risk of fraud is high.
b. Factors whose presence often have been observed in circumstances where frauds have occurred.
c. Factors whose presence requires modification of planned audit procedures.
d. Material weaknesses identified during an audit.

19. Which of the following is correct concerning requirements about auditor communications about fraud?

a. Fraud that involves senior management should be reported directly to the audit committee **regardless** of the amount involved.
b. Fraud with a material effect on the financial statements should be reported directly by the auditor to the Securities and Exchange Commission.
c. Fraud with a material effect on the financial statements should ordinarily be disclosed by the auditor through use of an "emphasis of a matter" paragraph added to the audit report.
d. The auditor has no responsibility to disclose fraud outside the entity under any circumstances.

20. When performing a financial statement audit, auditors are required to explicitly assess the risk of material misstatement due to

a. Errors.
b. Fraud.
c. Illegal acts.
d. Business risk.

21. Audits of financial statements are designed to obtain assurance of detecting misstatement due to

	Errors	Fraudulent financial reporting	Misappropriation of assets
a.	Yes	Yes	Yes
b.	Yes	Yes	No
c.	Yes	No	Yes
d.	No	Yes	No

22. An auditor is unable to obtain absolute assurance that misstatements due to fraud will be detected for all of the following **except**

a. Employee collusion.
b. Falsified documentation.
c. Need to apply professional judgment in evaluating fraud risk factors.
d. Professional skepticism.

23. The most difficult type of misstatement to detect is fraud based on

a. The overrecording of transactions.
b. The nonrecording of transactions.
c. Recorded transactions in subsidiaries.
d. Related-party receivables.

24. When considering fraud risk factors relating to management's characteristics, which of the following is **least likely** to indicate a risk of possible misstatement due to fraud?

a. Failure to correct known reportable conditions on a timely basis.
b. Nonfinancial management's preoccupation with the selection of accounting principles.
c. Significant portion of management's compensation represented by bonuses based upon achieving unduly aggressive operating results.
d. Use of unusually conservative accounting practices.

25. Which of the following conditions identified during fieldwork of an audit is most likely to affect the auditor's assessment of the risk of misstatement due to fraud?

a. Checks for significant amounts outstanding at year-end.
b. Computer generated documents.
c. Missing documents.
d. Year-end adjusting journal entries.

26. Which of the following is most likely to be a response to the auditor's assessment that the risk of material misstatement due to fraud for the existence of inventory is high?

a. Observe test counts of inventory at certain locations on an unannounced basis.
b. Perform analytical procedures rather than taking test counts.

c. Request that inventories be counted prior to year-end.

d. Request that inventory counts at the various locations be counted on different dates so as to allow the same auditor to be present at every count.

27. Which of the following is most likely to be an example of fraud?

a. Defalcations occurring due to invalid electronic approvals.

b. Mistakes in the application of accounting principles.

c. Mistakes in processing data.

d. Unreasonable accounting estimates arising from oversight.

28. Which of the following characteristics most likely would heighten an auditor's concern about the risk of intentional manipulation of financial statements?

a. Turnover of senior accounting personnel is low.

b. Insiders recently purchased additional shares of the entity's stock.

c. Management places substantial emphasis on meeting earnings projections.

d. The rate of change in the entity's industry is slow.

29. Which of the following statements reflects an auditor's responsibility for detecting misstatements due to errors and fraud?

a. An auditor is responsible for detecting employee errors and simple fraud, but **not** for discovering fraud involving employee collusion or management override.

b. An auditor should plan the audit to detect misstatements due to errors and fraud that are caused by departures from GAAP.

c. An auditor is **not** responsible for detecting misstatements due to errors and fraud unless the application of GAAS would result in such detection.

d. An auditor should design the audit to provide reasonable assurance of detecting misstatements due to errors and fraud that are material to the financial statements.

30. Disclosure of fraud to parties other than a client's senior management and its audit committee or board of directors ordinarily is not part of an auditor's responsibility. However, to which of the following outside parties may a duty to disclose fraud exist?

	To the SEC when the client reports an auditor change	To a successor auditor when the successor makes appropriate inquiries	To a government funding agency from which the client receives financial assistance
a.	Yes	Yes	No
b.	Yes	No	Yes
c.	No	Yes	Yes
d.	Yes	Yes	Yes

31. Under Statements on Auditing Standards, which of the following would be classified as an error?

a. Misappropriation of assets for the benefit of management.

b. Misinterpretation by management of facts that existed when the financial statements were prepared.

c. Preparation of records by employees to cover a fraudulent scheme.

d. Intentional omission of the recording of a transaction to benefit a third party.

32. What assurance does the auditor provide that misstatements due to errors, fraud, and direct effect illegal acts that are material to the financial statements will be detected?

	Errors	Fraud	Direct effect illegal acts
a.	Limited	Negative	Limited
b.	Limited	Limited	Reasonable
c.	Reasonable	Limited	Limited
d.	Reasonable	Reasonable	Reasonable

33. Because of the risk of material misstatement, an audit of financial statements in accordance with generally accepted auditing standards should be planned and performed with an attitude of

a. Objective judgment.

b. Independent integrity.

c. Professional skepticism.

d. Impartial conservatism.

34. Which of the following most accurately summarizes what is meant by the term "material misstatement?"

a. Fraud and direct-effect illegal acts.

b. Fraud involving senior management and material fraud.

c. Material error, material fraud, and certain illegal acts.

d. Material error and material illegal acts.

35. Which of the following statements best describes the auditor's responsibility to detect conditions relating to financial stress of employees or adverse relationships between a company and its employees?

a. The auditor is required to plan the audit to detect these conditions on all audits.

b. These conditions relate to fraudulent financial reporting, and an auditor is required to plan the audit to detect these conditions when the client is exposed to a risk of misappropriation of assets.

c. The auditor is required to plan the audit to detect these conditions whenever they may result in misstatements.

d. The auditor is not required to plan the audit to discover these conditions, but should consider them if he or she becomes aware of them during the audit.

36. When the auditor believes a misstatement is or may be the result of fraud but that the effect of the misstatement is not material to the financial statements, which of the following steps is required?

a. Consider the implications for other aspects of the audit.

b. Resign from the audit.

c. Commence a fraud examination.

d. Contact regulatory authorities.

37. Which of the following statements is correct relating to the auditor's consideration of fraud?

a. The auditor's interest in fraud consideration relates to fraudulent acts that cause a material misstatement of financial statements.

b.   A primary factor that distinguishes fraud from error is that fraud is always intentional, while errors are generally, but not always, intentional.

c.   Fraud always involves a pressure or incentive to commit fraud, and a misappropriation of assets.

d.   While an auditor should be aware of the possibility of fraud, management, and not the auditor, is responsible for detecting fraud.

38. Which of the following factors or conditions is an auditor least likely to plan an audit to discover?

a.   Financial pressures affecting employees.

b.   High turnover of senior management.

c.   Inadequate monitoring of significant controls.

d.   Inability to generate positive cash flows from operations.

39. At which stage(s) of the audit may fraud risk factors be identified?

	Planning	Obtaining understanding	Conducting fieldwork
a.	Yes	Yes	Yes
b.	Yes	Yes	No
c.	Yes	No	No
d.	No	Yes	Yes

40. Management's attitude toward aggressive financial reporting and its emphasis on meeting projected profit goals most likely would significantly influence an entity's control environment when

a.   External policies established by parties outside the entity affect its accounting practices.

b.   Management is dominated by one individual who is also a shareholder.

c.   Internal auditors have direct access to the board of directors and the entity's management.

d.   The audit committee is active in overseeing the entity's financial reporting policies.

41. Which of the following is **least** likely to be required on an audit?

a.   Test appropriateness of journal entries and adjustment.

b.   Review accounting estimates for biases.

c.   Evaluate the business rationale for significant unusual transactions.

d.   Make a legal determination of whether fraud has occurred.

42. Which of the following is most likely to be an overall response to fraud risks identified in an audit?

a.   Supervise members of the audit team less closely and rely more upon judgment.

b.   Use less predictable audit procedures.

c.   Only use certified public accountants on the engagement.

d.   Place increased emphasis on the audit of objective transactions rather than subjective transactions.

43. Which of the following is **least** likely to be included in an auditor's inquiry of management while obtaining information to identify the risks of material misstatement due to fraud?

a.   Are financial reporting operations controlled by and limited to one location?

b.   Does it have knowledge of fraud or suspect fraud?

c.   Does it have programs to mitigate fraud risks?

d.   Has it reported to the audit committee the nature of the company's internal control?

44. Individuals who commit fraud are ordinarily able to rationalize the act and also have an

	Incentive	Opportunity
a.	Yes	Yes
b.	Yes	No
c.	No	Yes
d.	No	No

45. What is an auditor's responsibility who discovers management involved in what is financially immaterial fraud?

a.   Report the fraud to the audit committee.

b.   Report the fraud to the Public Company Oversight Board.

c.   Report the fraud to a level of management at least one below those involved in the fraud.

d.   Determine that the amounts involved are immaterial, and if so, there is no reporting responsibility.

46. Which of the following is most likely to be considered a risk factor relating to fraudulent financial reporting?

a.   Domination of management by top executives.

b.   Large amounts of cash processed.

c.   Negative cash flows from operations.

d.   Small high-dollar inventory items.

47. Which of the following is most likely to be presumed to represent fraud risk on an audit?

a.   Capitalization of repairs and maintenance into the property, plant, and equipment asset account.

b.   Improper revenue recognition.

c.   Improper interest expense accrual.

d.   Introduction of significant new products.

48. An auditor who discovers that a client's employees paid small bribes to municipal officials most likely would withdraw from the engagement if

a.   The payments violated the client's policies regarding the prevention of illegal acts.

b.   The client receives financial assistance from a federal government agency.

c.   Documentation that is necessary to prove that the bribes were paid does **not** exist.

d.   Management fails to take the appropriate remedial action.

49. Which of the following factors most likely would cause a CPA to **not** accept a new audit engagement?

a.   The prospective client has already completed its physical inventory count.

b.   The CPA lacks an understanding of the prospective client's operation and industry.

c.   The CPA is unable to review the predecessor auditor's working papers.

d.   The prospective client is unwilling to make all financial records available to the CPA.

50. Which of the following factors would most likely heighten an auditor's concern about the risk of fraudulent financial reporting?

a.   Large amounts of liquid assets that are easily convertible into cash.

b.   Low growth and profitability as compared to other entities in the same industry.

c. Financial management's participation in the initial selection of accounting principles.

d. An overly complex organizational structure involving unusual lines of authority.

51. An auditor who discovers that a client's employees have paid small bribes to public officials most likely would withdraw from the engagement if the

a. Client receives financial assistance from a federal government agency.

b. Evidence that is necessary to prove that the illegal acts were committed does not exist.

c. Employees' actions affect the auditor's ability to rely on management's representations.

d. Notes to the financial statements fail to disclose the employees' actions.

52. Which of the following illegal acts should an audit be designed to obtain reasonable assurance of detecting?

a. Securities purchased by relatives of management based on knowledge of inside information.

b. Accrual and billing of an improper amount of revenue under government contracts.

c. Violations of antitrust laws.

d. Price fixing.

53. Which of the following relatively small misstatements most likely could have a material effect on an entity's financial statements?

a. An illegal payment to a foreign official that was **not** recorded.

b. A piece of obsolete office equipment that was **not** retired.

c. A petty cash fund disbursement that was **not** properly authorized.

d. An uncollectible account receivable that was **not** written off.

54. During the annual audit of Ajax Corp., a publicly held company, Jones, CPA, a continuing auditor, determined that illegal political contributions had been made during each of the past seven years, including the year under audit. Jones notified the board of directors about the illegal contributions, but they refused to take any action because the amounts involved were immaterial to the financial statements. Jones should reconsider the intended degree of reliance to be placed on the

a. Letter of audit inquiry to the client's attorney.

b. Prior years' audit programs.

c. Management representation letter.

d. Preliminary judgment about materiality levels.

55. The most likely explanation why the auditor's examination **cannot** reasonably be expected to bring all illegal acts by the client to the auditor's attention is that

a. Illegal acts are perpetrated by management override of internal control.

b. Illegal acts by clients often relate to operating aspects rather than accounting aspects.

c. The client's internal control may be so strong that the auditor performs only minimal substantive testing.

d. Illegal acts may be perpetrated by the only person in the client's organization with access to both assets and the accounting records.

56. If specific information comes to an auditor's attention that implies the existence of possible illegal acts that could have a material, but indirect effect on the financial statements, the auditor should next

a. Apply audit procedures specifically directed to ascertaining whether an illegal act has occurred.

b. Seek the advice of an informed expert qualified to practice law as to possible contingent liabilities.

c. Report the matter to an appropriate level of management at least one level above those involved.

d. Discuss the evidence with the client's audit committee, or others with equivalent authority and responsibility.

57. An auditor who discovers that client employees have committed an illegal act that has a material effect on the client's financial statements most likely would withdraw from the engagement if

a. The illegal act is a violation of generally accepted accounting principles.

b. The client does not take the remedial action that the auditor considers necessary.

c. The illegal act was committed during a prior year that was not audited.

d. The auditor has already assessed control risk at the maximum level.

58. Under the Private Securities Litigation Reform Act of 1995, Baker, CPA, reported certain uncorrected illegal acts to Supermart's board of directors. Baker believed that failure to take remedial action would warrant a qualified audit opinion because the illegal acts had a material effect on Supermart's financial statements. Supermart failed to take appropriate remedial action and the board of directors refused to inform the SEC that it had received such notification from Baker. Under these circumstances, Baker is required to

a. Resign from the audit engagement within ten business days.

b. Deliver a report concerning the illegal acts to the SEC within one business day.

c. Notify the stockholders that the financial statements are materially misstated.

d. Withhold an audit opinion until Supermart takes appropriate remedial action.

59. Which of the following would be **least** likely to be considered an audit planning procedure?

a. Use an engagement letter.

b. Develop the overall audit strategy.

c. Perform risk assessment.

d. Develop the audit plan.

60. Which of the following factors would most likely cause a CPA to decide not to accept a new audit engagement?

a. The CPA's lack of understanding of the prospective client's internal auditor's computer-assisted audit techniques.

b. Management's disregard of its responsibility to maintain an adequate internal control environment.

c. The CPA's inability to determine whether related-party transactions were consummated on terms equivalent to arm's-length transactions.

d. Management's refusal to permit the CPA to perform substantive tests before the year-end.

61. Before accepting an engagement to audit a new client, a CPA is required to obtain
- a. An understanding of the prospective client's industry and business.
- b. The prospective client's signature to the engagement letter.
- c. A preliminary understanding of the prospective client's control environment.
- d. The prospective client's consent to make inquiries of the predecessor auditor, if any.

62. Before accepting an audit engagement, a successor auditor should make specific inquiries of the predecessor auditor regarding
- a. Disagreements the predecessor had with the client concerning auditing procedures and accounting principles.
- b. The predecessor's evaluation of matters of continuing accounting significance.
- c. The degree of cooperation the predecessor received concerning the inquiry of the client's lawyer.
- d. The predecessor's assessments of inherent risk and judgments about materiality.

63. Before accepting an audit engagement, a successor auditor should make specific inquiries of the predecessor auditor regarding the predecessor's
- a. Opinion of any subsequent events occurring since the predecessor's audit report was issued.
- b. Understanding as to the reasons for the change of auditors.
- c. Awareness of the consistency in the application of GAAP between periods.
- d. Evaluation of all matters of continuing accounting significance.

64. An auditor is required to establish an understanding with a client regarding the services to be performed for each engagement. This understanding generally includes
- a. Management's responsibility for errors and the illegal activities of employees that may cause material misstatement.
- b. The auditor's responsibility for ensuring that the audit committee is aware of any significant deficiencies in internal control that come to the auditor's attention.
- c. Management's responsibility for providing the auditor with an assessment of the risk of material misstatement due to fraud.
- d. The auditor's responsibility for determining preliminary judgments about materiality and audit risk factors.

65. Which of the following matters is generally included in an auditor's engagement letter?
- a. Management's responsibility for the entity's compliance with laws and regulations.
- b. The factors to be considered in setting preliminary judgments about materiality.
- c. Management's vicarious liability for illegal acts committed by its employees.
- d. The auditor's responsibility to search for significant internal control deficiencies.

66. During the initial planning phase of an audit, a CPA most likely would
- a. Identify specific internal control activities that are likely to prevent fraud.
- b. Evaluate the reasonableness of the client's accounting estimates.
- c. Discuss the timing of the audit procedures with the client's management.
- d. Inquire of the client's attorney as to whether any unrecorded claims are probable of assertion.

67. Which of the following statements would **least** likely appear in an auditor's engagement letter?
- a. Fees for our services are based on our regular per diem rates, plus travel and other out-of-pocket expenses.
- b. During the course of our audit we may observe opportunities for economy in, or improved controls over, your operations.
- c. Our engagement is subject to the risk that material misstatements or fraud, if they exist, will **not** be detected.
- d. After performing our preliminary analytical procedures we will discuss with you the other procedures we consider necessary to complete the engagement.

68. Which of the following documentation is **not** required for an audit in accordance with generally accepted auditing standards?
- a. A written audit plan setting forth the procedures necessary to accomplish the audit's objectives.
- b. An indication that the accounting records agree or reconcile with the financial statements.
- c. A client engagement letter that summarizes the timing and details of the auditor's planned fieldwork.
- d. The assessment of the risks of material misstatement.

69. An engagement letter should ordinarily include information on the objectives of the engagement and

	CPA responsibilities	Client responsibilities	Limitation of engagement
a.	Yes	Yes	Yes
b.	Yes	No	Yes
c.	Yes	No	No
d.	No	No	No

70. Arrangements concerning which of the following are **least** likely to be included in engagement letter?
- a. A predecessor auditor.
- b. Fees and billing.
- c. CPA investment in client securities.
- d. Other services to be provided in addition to the audit.

71. The auditor should document the understanding established with a client through a(n)
- a. Oral communication with the client.
- b. Written communication with the client.
- c. Written or oral communication with the client.
- d. Completely detailed audit plan.

72. Which of the following factors most likely would influence an auditor's determination of the auditability of an entity's financial statements?
    a.   The complexity of the accounting system.
    b.   The existence of related-party transactions.
    c.   The adequacy of the accounting records.
    d.   The operating effectiveness of control procedures.

73. Which of the following is most likely to require special planning considerations related to asset valuation?
    a.   Inventory is comprised of diamond rings.
    b.   The client has recently purchased an expensive copy machine.
    c.   Assets costing less than $250 are expensed even when the expected life exceeds one year.
    d.   Accelerated depreciation methods are used for amortizing the costs of factory equipment.

74. A CPA wishes to determine how various publicly held companies have complied with the disclosure requirements of a new financial accounting standard. Which of the following information sources would the CPA most likely consult for information?
    a.   AICPA Codification of Statements on Auditing Standards.
    b.   AICPA *Accounting Trends and Techniques*.
    c.   SEC Quality Control Review.
    d.   SEC Statement 10-K Guide.

75. An auditor should design the written audit program so that
    a.   All material transactions will be selected for substantive testing.
    b.   Substantive tests prior to the balance sheet date will be minimized.
    c.   The audit procedures selected will achieve specific audit objectives.
    d.   Each account balance will be tested under either tests of controls or tests of transactions.

76. The audit program usually **cannot** be finalized until the
    a.   Consideration of the entity's internal control has been completed.
    b.   Engagement letter has been signed by the auditor and the client.
    c.   Reportable conditions have been communicated to the audit committee of the board of directors.
    d.   Search for unrecorded liabilities has been performed and documented.

77. Audit programs should be designed so that
    a.   Most of the required procedures can be performed as interim work.
    b.   Inherent risk is assessed at a sufficiently low level.
    c.   The auditor can make constructive suggestions to management.
    d.   The audit evidence gathered supports the auditor's conclusions.

78. In designing written audit programs, an auditor should establish specific audit objectives that relate primarily to the
    a.   Timing of audit procedures.
    b.   Cost-benefit of gathering evidence.
    c.   Selected audit techniques.
    d.   Financial statement assertions.

79. With respect to planning an audit, which of the following statements is always true?
    a.   It is acceptable to perform a portion of the audit of a continuing audit client at interim dates.
    b.   An engagement should not be accepted after the client's year-end.
    c.   An inventory count must be observed at year-end.
    d.   Final staffing decisions must be made prior to completion of the planning stage.

80. The element of the audit planning process most likely to be agreed upon with the client before implementation of the audit strategy is the determination of the
    a.   Evidence to be gathered to provide a sufficient basis for the auditor's opinion.
    b.   Procedures to be undertaken to discover litigation, claims, and assessments.
    c.   Pending legal matters to be included in the inquiry of the client's attorney.
    d.   Timing of inventory observation procedures to be performed.

81. To obtain an understanding of a continuing client's business, an auditor most likely would
    a.   Perform tests of details of transactions and balances.
    b.   Review prior year working papers and the permanent file for the client.
    c.   Read current issues of specialized industry journals.
    d.   Reevaluate the client's internal control environment.

82. An auditor obtains knowledge about a new client's business and its industry to
    a.   Make constructive suggestions concerning improvements to the client's internal control.
    b.   Develop an attitude of professional skepticism concerning management's financial statement assertions.
    c.   Evaluate whether the aggregation of known misstatements causes the financial statements taken as a whole to be materially misstated.
    d.   Understand the events and transactions that may have an effect on the client's financial statements.

83. Which of the following procedures would an auditor **least** likely perform while obtaining an understanding of a client in a financial statement audit?
    a.   Coordinating the assistance of entity personnel in data preparation.
    b.   Discussing matters that may affect the audit with firm personnel responsible for nonaudit services to the entity.
    c.   Selecting a sample of vendors' invoices for comparison to receiving reports.
    d.   Reading the current year's interim financial statements.

84. Ordinarily, the predecessor auditor permits the successor auditor to review the predecessor's working paper analyses relating to

	Contingencies	*Balance sheet accounts*
a.	Yes	Yes
b.	Yes	No
c.	No	Yes
d.	No	No

85. In auditing the financial statements of Star Corp., Land discovered information leading Land to believe that Star's prior year's financial statements, which were audited by Tell, require substantial revisions. Under these circumstances, Land should
- a. Notify Star's audit committee and stockholders that the prior year's financial statements **cannot** be relied on.
- b. Request Star to reissue the prior year's financial statements with the appropriate revisions.
- c. Notify Tell about the information and make inquiries about the integrity of Star's management.
- d. Request Star to arrange a meeting among the three parties to resolve the matter.

86. A successor auditor should request the new client to authorize the predecessor auditor to allow a review of the predecessor's

	Engagement letter	Working papers
a.	Yes	Yes
b.	Yes	No
c.	No	Yes
d.	No	No

87. Which of the following procedures would an auditor most likely perform in planning a financial statement audit?
- a. Inquiring of the client's legal counsel concerning pending litigation.
- b. Comparing the financial statements to anticipated results.
- c. Examining computer generated exception reports to verify the effectiveness of internal control.
- d. Searching for unauthorized transactions that may aid in detecting unrecorded liabilities.

88. Analytical procedures used in planning an audit should focus on
- a. Reducing the scope of tests of controls and substantive tests.
- b. Providing assurance that potential material misstatements will be identified.
- c. Enhancing the auditor's understanding of the client's business.
- d. Assessing the adequacy of the available evidence.

89. The objective of performing analytical procedures in planning an audit is to identify the existence of
- a. Unusual transactions and events.
- b. Illegal acts that went undetected because of internal control weaknesses.
- c. Related-party transactions.
- d. Recorded transactions that were **not** properly authorized.

90. Which of the following nonfinancial information would an auditor most likely consider in performing analytical procedures during the planning phase of an audit?
- a. Turnover of personnel in the accounting department.
- b. Objectivity of audit committee members.
- c. Square footage of selling space.
- d. Management's plans to repurchase stock.

91. The in-charge auditor most likely would have a supervisory responsibility to explain to the staff assistants
- a. That immaterial fraud is **not** to be reported to the client's audit committee.

- b. How the results of various auditing procedures performed by the assistants should be evaluated.
- c. What benefits may be attained by the assistants' adherence to established time budgets.
- d. Why certain documents are being transferred from the current file to the permanent file.

92. The audit work performed by each assistant should be reviewed to determine whether it was adequately performed and to evaluate whether the
- a. Auditor's system of quality control has been maintained at a high level.
- b. Results are consistent with the conclusions to be presented in the auditor's report.
- c. Audit procedures performed are approved in the professional standards.
- d. Audit has been performed by persons having adequate technical training and proficiency as auditors.

93. While assessing the risks of material misstatement auditors identify risks, relate risk to what could go wrong, consider the magnitude of risks and
- a. Assess the risk of misstatements due to illegal acts.
- b. Consider the complexity of the transactions involved.
- c. Consider the likelihood that the risks could result in material misstatements.
- d. Determine materiality levels.

94. Which of the following are considered further audit procedures that may be designed after assessing the risks of material misstatement?

	Substantive tests of details	Risk assessment procedures
a.	Yes	Yes
b.	Yes	No
c.	No	Yes
d.	No	No

95. Which of the following is **least** likely to be considered a risk assessment procedure?
- a. Analytical procedures.
- b. Confirmation of ending accounts receivable.
- c. Inspection of documents.
- d. Observation of the performance of certain accounting procedures.

96. In an audit of a nonissuer (nonpublic) company, the auditors identify significant risks. These risks often
- a. Involve routine, high-volume transactions.
- b. Do not require special audit attention.
- c. Involve items with lower levels of inherent risk.
- d. Involve judgmental matters.

97. The "Special Committee on Assurance Services" defined assurance services as independent professional services that
- a. Include a written communication that expresses a conclusion.
- b. Improve the quality of information, or its context, for decision makers.
- c. Include audit services, attest services, and consulting services.
- d. Involve the examination of the credibility of a written assertion that is the responsibility of another party.

98. The group that was established in 1994 by the American Institute of Certified Public Accountants to analyze and report on the current state and future of the audit/assurance function and trends shaping its environment is the
- a. Commission on Auditors' Responsibilities.
- b. Committee of Sponsoring Organizations (COSO).
- c. Special Committee on Assurance Services.
- d. Accountancy Future Task Force (AFTF).

99. Which of the following is **not** a type of attest engagement?
- a. Agreed-upon procedures.
- b. Compilation.
- c. Examination.
- d. Review.

100. Which of the following is a conceptual difference between the attestation standards and generally accepted auditing standards?
- a. The attestation standards do not apply to audits of historical financial statements, while the generally accepted auditing standards do.
- b. The requirement that the practitioner be independent in mental attitude is omitted from the attestation standards.
- c. The attestation standards do **not** permit an attest engagement to be part of a business acquisition study or a feasibility study.
- d. **None** of the standards of fieldwork in generally accepted auditing standards are included in the attestation standards.

101. Which of the following is **not** an attestation standard?
- a. Sufficient evidence shall be obtained to provide a reasonable basis for the conclusion that is expressed in the report.
- b. The report shall identify the subject matter on the assertion being reported on and state the character of the engagement.
- c. The work shall be adequately planned and assistants, if any, shall be properly supervised.
- d. A sufficient understanding of internal control shall be obtained to plan the engagement.

102. On an audit engagement performed by a CPA firm with one office, at the minimum, knowledge of the relevant professional accounting and auditing standards should be held by
- a. The auditor with final responsibility for the audit.
- b. All professionals working upon the audit.
- c. All professionals working upon the audit and the partner in charge of the CPA firm.
- d. All professionals working in the office.

103. An attitude that includes a questioning mind and a critical assessment of audit evidence is referred to as
- a. Due professional care.
- b. Professional skepticism.
- c. Reasonable assurance.
- d. Supervision.

104. Professional skepticism requires that an auditor assume that management is
- a. Honest, in the absence of fraud risk factors.
- b. Dishonest until completion of audit tests.
- c. Neither honest nor dishonest.
- d. Offering reasonable assurance of honesty.

105. An unqualified attestation report ordinarily may refer to
- a. Only the assertion.
- b. Only the subject matter to which the assertion relates.
- c. Either the assertion or the subject matter to which the assertion relates.
- d. Neither the assertion nor the subject matter to which the assertion relates.

106. Which of the following is most likely to be unique to the audit work of CPAs as compared to work performed by practitioners of other professions?
- a. Due professional care.
- b. Competence.
- c. Independence.
- d. Complex body of knowledge.

107. The third general standard states that due care is to be exercised in the performance of an audit. This standard is ordinarily interpreted to require
- a. Thorough review of the existing safeguards over access to assets and records.
- b. Limited review of the indications of employee fraud and illegal acts.
- c. Objective review of the adequacy of the technical training and proficiency of firm personnel.
- d. Critical review of the judgment exercised at every level of supervision.

108. After fieldwork audit procedures are completed, a partner of the CPA firm who has not been involved in the audit performs a second or wrap-up working paper review. This second review usually focuses on
- a. The fair presentation of the financial statements in conformity with GAAP.
- b. Fraud involving the client's management and its employees.
- c. The materiality of the adjusting entries proposed by the audit staff.
- d. The communication of internal control weaknesses to the client's audit committee.

109. Which of the following statements is correct concerning an auditor's responsibilities regarding financial statements?
- a. Making suggestions that are adopted about the form and content of an entity's financial statements impairs an auditor's independence.
- b. An auditor may draft an entity's financial statements based on information from management's accounting system.
- c. The fair presentation of audited financial statements in conformity with GAAP is an implicit part of the auditor's responsibilities.
- d. An auditor's responsibilities for audited financial statements are **not** confined to the expression of the auditor's opinion.

110. Which of the following is an authoritative body designated to promulgate attestation standards?
- a. Auditing Standards Board.
- b. Governmental Accounting Standards Board.
- c. Financial Accounting Standards Board.
- d. General Accounting Office.

111. Which of the following best describes what is meant by the term generally accepted auditing standards?
- a. Procedures to be used to gather evidence to support financial statements.
- b. Measures of the quality of the auditor's performance.
- c. Pronouncements issued by the Auditing Standards Board.
- d. Rules acknowledged by the accounting profession because of their universal application.

112. The auditor with final responsibility for an engagement and one of the assistants have a difference of opinion about the results of an auditing procedure. If the assistant believes it is necessary to be disassociated from the matter's resolution, the CPA firm's procedures should enable the assistant to
- a. Refer the disagreement to the AICPA's Quality Review Committee.
- b. Document the details of the disagreement with the conclusion reached.
- c. Discuss the disagreement with the entity's management or its audit committee.
- d. Report the disagreement to an impartial peer review monitoring team.

113. The objective of an accountant's compilation of the financial statements of a nonissuer (nonpublic company) is to provide what type of assurance?
- a. Absolute assurance.
- b. Limited assurance.
- c. No assurance.
- d. Reasonable assurance.

114. When engaged to compile the financial statements of a nonissuer (nonpublic) entity, an accountant is required to possess a level of knowledge of the entity's accounting principles and practices. This requirement most likely will include obtaining a general understanding of the
- a. Stated qualifications of the entity's accounting personnel.
- b. Design of the entity's internal controls placed in operation.
- c. Risk factors relating to misstatements arising from illegal acts.
- d. Internal control awareness of the entity's senior management.

115. An accountant is required to comply with the provisions of Statements on Standards for Accounting and Review Services when

I. Reproducing client-prepared financial statements, without modification, as an accommodation to a client.
II. Preparing standard monthly journal entries for depreciation and expiration of prepaid expenses.

- a. I only.
- b. II only.
- c. Both I and II.
- d. Neither I nor II.

116. If requested to perform a review engagement for a nonissuer in which an accountant has an immaterial direct financial interest, the accountant is
- a. Not independent and, therefore, may **not** be associated with the financial statements.
- b. Not independent and, therefore, may **not** issue a review report.
- c. Not independent and, therefore, may issue a review report, but may **not** issue an auditor's opinion.
- d. Independent because the financial interest is immaterial and, therefore, may issue a review report.

117. Kell engaged March, CPA, to submit to Kell a written personal financial plan containing unaudited personal financial statements. March anticipates omitting certain disclosures required by GAAP because the engagement's sole purpose is to assist Kell in developing a personal financial plan. For March to be exempt from complying with the requirements of Statements on Standards for Accounting and Review Services. Kell is required to agree that the
- a. Financial statements will **not** be presented in comparative form with those of the prior period.
- b. Omitted disclosures required by GAAP are **not** material.
- c. Financial statements will **not** be disclosed to a non-CPA financial planner.
- d. Financial statements will **not** be used to obtain credit.

118. An accountant has been engaged to review a nonissuer's financial statements that contain several departures from GAAP. If the financial statements are **not** revised and modification of the standard review report is **not** adequate to indicate the deficiencies, the accountant should
- a. Withdraw from the engagement and provide **no** further services concerning these financial statements.
- b. Inform management that the engagement can proceed only if distribution of the accountant's report is restricted to internal use.
- c. Determine the effects of the departures from GAAP and issue a special report on the financial statements.
- d. Issue a modified review report provided the entity agrees that the financial statements will **not** be used to obtain credit.

119. Statements on Standards for Accounting and Review Services (SSARS) require an accountant to report when the accountant has
- a. Typed client-prepared financial statements, without modification, as an accommodation to the client.
- b. Provided a client with a financial statement format that does **not** include dollar amounts, to be used by the client in preparing financial statements.
- c. Proposed correcting journal entries to be recorded by the client that change client-prepared financial statements.
- d. Generated, through the use of computer software, financial statements prepared in accordance with a comprehensive basis of accounting other than GAAP.

120. Statements on Standards for Accounting and Review Services establish standards and procedures for which of the following engagements?
- a. Assisting in adjusting the books of account for a partnership.
- b. Reviewing interim financial data required to be filed with the SEC.

c.   Processing financial data for clients of other accounting firms.

d.   Compiling an individual's personal financial statement to be used to obtain a mortgage.

121. The authoritative body designated to promulgate standards concerning an accountant's association with unaudited financial statements of an entity that is **not** required to file financial statements with an agency regulating the issuance of the entity's securities is the

a.   Financial Accounting Standards Board.
b.   General Accounting Office.
c.   Accounting and Review Services Committee.
d.   Auditing Standards Board.

122. Which of the following accounting services may an accountant perform **without** being required to issue a compilation or review report under the Statements on Standards for Accounting and Review Services?

I.   Preparing a working trial balance.
II. Preparing standard monthly journal entries.

a.   I only.
b.   II only.
c.   Both I and II.
d.   Neither I nor II.

123. An examination of a financial forecast is a professional service that involves

a.   Compiling or assembling a financial forecast that is based on management's assumptions.
b.   Limiting the distribution of the accountant's report to management and the board of directors.
c.   Assuming responsibility to update management on key events for one year after the report's date.
d.   Evaluating the preparation of a financial forecast and the support underlying management's assumptions.

124. An accountant may accept an engagement to apply agreed-upon procedures to prospective financial statements provided that

a.   Use of the report is restricted to the specified parties.
b.   The prospective financial statements are also examined.
c.   Responsibility for the adequacy of the procedures performed is taken by the accountant.
d.   Negative assurance is expressed on the prospective financial statements taken as a whole.

125. The nature and extent of a CPA firm's quality control policies and procedures depend on

	The CPA firm's size	The nature of the CPA firm's practice	Cost-benefit considerations
a.	Yes	Yes	Yes
b.	Yes	Yes	No
c.	Yes	No	Yes
d.	No	Yes	Yes

126. A CPA firm may communicate its quality control policies and procedures to its personnel in which manner(s):

	Orally	Written
a.	No	No
b.	No	Yes
c.	Yes	No
d.	Yes	Yes

127. Which of the following is **not** an element of quality control?

a.   Acceptance and continuance of client relationships and specific engagements.
b.   Human resources.
c.   Internal control.
d.   Monitoring.

128. Quality control for a CPA firm, as referred to in Statements on Quality Control Standards, applies to

a.   Auditing services only.
b.   Auditing and management advisory services.
c.   Auditing and tax services.
d.   Auditing and accounting and review services.

129. One of a CPA firm's basic objectives is to provide professional services that conform with professional standards. Reasonable assurance of achieving this basic objective is provided through

a.   A system of quality control.
b.   A system of peer review.
c.   Continuing professional education.
d.   Compliance with generally accepted reporting standards.

130. Which of the following is correct concerning PCAOB guidance that uses the term "should"?

a.   The auditor must fulfill the responsibilities.
b.   The auditor must comply with requirements unless s/he demonstrates that alternative actions were sufficient to achieve the objectives of the standard.
c.   The auditor should consider performing the procedure; whether the auditor performs depends on the exercise of professional judgment in the circumstances.
d.   The auditor has complete discretion as to whether to perform the procedure.

131. Which of the following sets of standards does the Public Company Accounting Oversight Board not have the authority to establish for audits of public companies?

a.   Auditing standards.
b.   Quality control standards.
c.   Accounting standards.
d.   Independence standards.

SIMULATION PROBLEMS

Simulation Problem 1   (50 to 60 minutes)

Situation			
	Audit and Fraud Risk	**Fraud Discussion**	**Research**	**Communication**

Green, CPA, is considering audit risk, including fraud risk, at the financial statement level in planning the audit of National Federal Bank (NFB) Company's financial statements for the year ended December 31, 2005. Audit risk at the financial statement level is influenced by the risk of material misstatements, which may be indicated by a combination of factors related to management, the industry, and the entity. In assessing such factors Green has gathered the following information concerning NFB's environment.

Company profile

NFB is a federally insured bank that has been consistently more profitable than the industry average by marketing mortgages on properties in a prosperous rural area, which has experienced considerable growth in recent years. NFB packages its mortgages and sells them to large mortgage investment trusts. Despite recent volatility of interest rates, NFB has been able to continue selling its mortgages as a source of new lendable funds.

NFB's board of directors is controlled by Smith, the majority stockholder, who also acts as the chief executive officer. Management at the bank's branch offices has authority for directing and controlling NFB's operations and is compensated based on branch profitability. The internal auditor reports directly to Harris, a minority shareholder, who also acts as chairman of the board's audit committee.

The accounting department has experienced little turnover in personnel during the five years Green has audited NFB. NFB's formula consistently underestimates the allowance for loan losses, but its controller has always been receptive to Green's suggestions to increase the allowance during each engagement.

Recent developments

During 2005, NFB opened a branch office in a suburban town thirty miles from its principal place of business. Although this branch is not yet profitable due to competition from several well-established regional banks, management believes that the branch will be profitable by 2007.

Also, during 2005, NFB increased the efficiency of its accounting operations by installing a new, sophisticated computer system.

	Audit and Fraud Risk			
Situation		**Fraud Discussion**	**Research**	**Communication**

Based only on the information above, indicate by marking the appropriate button whether the following factors indicate an increased or decreased audit risk. Also, indicate whether the factor is a fraud risk factor.

Factor	*Increased audit risk*	*Decreased audit risk*	*Fraud risk factor*
1. Branch management authority	O	O	O
2. Government regulation	O	O	O
3. Company profitability	O	O	O
4. Demand for product	O	O	O
5. Interest rates	O	O	O
6. Availability of mortgage funds	O	O	O
7. Involvement of principal shareholder in management	O	O	O
8. Branch manager compensation	O	O	O
9. Internal audit reporting relationship	O	O	O
10. Accounting department turnover	O	O	O
11. Continuing audit relationship	O	O	O
12. Internal controls over accounting estimates	O	O	O
13. Response to proposed accounting adjustments	O	O	O
14. New unprofitable branch	O	O	O
15. New computer system	O	O	O

Situation	Audit and Fraud Risk	Fraud Discussion	Research	Communication

Assume you are preparing for the audit personnel discussion of potential risks of material misstatement due to fraud for the NFB audit. While any matters below might be discussed, indicate by marking the appropriate **four** highest risks based on the information contained in the simulation description and requirements of professional standards.

	Risk	*High risk item*
1.	Computer fraud risk	○
2.	Risk related to management override of internal control	○
3.	Fraud by branch management	○
4.	Fraud by accounting personnel	○
5.	Misstatement of accounting estimates	○
6.	Fraud by loan processing clerks	○
7.	Fraud by internal auditors	○
8.	The risk of fraudulent misstatement of revenues	○

Situation	Audit and Fraud Risk	Fraud Discussion	Research	Communication

Research the professional standards and locate the requirements regarding the required audit documentation of your consideration of fraud for the NFB audit. Excerpt the appropriate paragraphs.

Situation	Audit and Fraud Risk	Fraud Discussion	Research	Communication

Professional standards require auditors to have a staff discussion regarding fraud when planning the audit. Write a memorandum describing the purpose of this discussion.

REMINDER: Your response will be graded for both technical content and writing skills. Technical content will be evaluated for information that is helpful to the intended reader and clearly relevant to the issues. Writing skills will be evaluated for development, organization, and the appropriate expression of ideas in professional correspondence. Use a standard business memo or letter format with a clear beginning, middle, and end. Do not convey information in the form of a table, bullet point list, or other abbreviated presentation.

To: Audit Working Papers
From: CPA Candidate
Re: Staff discussion regarding fraud

Simulation Problem 2   (50 to 60 minutes)

Situation				
	Nonattest Services	Auditing Standards	Research	Communication

The director of the audit committee of Hanmei Corp., a nonissuer (nonpublic) company, has indicated that the company may be interested in engaging your firm to perform various professional services. Consider each of the following potential services **by itself**, and determine whether a CPA firm may provide such a service. If a CPA firm may provide the service, fill in the circle under the first or second column of replies based upon whether independence is required. If the service may not be provided, fill in the circle under "May Not Provide." For each service you should have only one reply.

Situation	Nonattest Services	Auditing Standards	Research	Communication

Service	May provide, independence *is required*	May provide, independence is *not required*	May *not provide*
1. Provide an opinion on whether financial statements are prepared following the cash basis of accounting	○	○	○
2. Compile a forecast for the coming year.	○	○	○
3. Compile the financial statements for the past year and issue a publicly available report.	○	○	○
4. Apply certain agreed-upon procedures to accounts receivable for purposes of obtaining a loan, and express a summary of findings relating to those procedures.	○	○	○
5. Review quarterly information and issue a report that includes limited assurance.	○	○	○
6. Perform an audit of the financial statements on whether they are prepared following generally accepted accounting principles.	○	○	○
7. Perform a review of a forecast the company has prepared for the coming year.	○	○	○
8. Compile the financial statements for the past year, but not issue a report since the financial statements are only for the company's use.	○	○	○
9. Calculate the client's taxes and fill out the appropriate tax forms.	○	○	○
10. Design a new payroll system for Hanmei and base billings on Hanmei's actual savings for the next three years.	○	○	○

Situation	Nonattest Services	Auditing Standards	Research	Communication

Now assume that you have been hired to perform the audit of Hanmei's financial statements. When planning such an audit, you often may need to refer to various of the profession's auditing standards. For each of the following circumstances in Column A, select the topic from the Professional Standards that is likely to provide the most guidance in the planning of the audit. A topic may be selected once, more than once, or not at all.

Topic

A. Analytical Procedures
B. Audit Risk and Materiality
C. Communications between Predecessor and Successor Auditors
D. Consideration of Fraud in a Financial Statement Audit
E. Understanding the Entity and Its Environment and Assessing the Risks of Material Misstatement

F. Illegal Acts by Clients
G. Management Representations
H. Part of the Audit Performed by Other Independent Auditors
I. Related Parties

Transactions	(A)	(B)	(C)	(D)	(E)	(F)	(G)	(H)	(I)
1. Possible risk factors related to misappropriation of assets.	○	○	○	○	○	○	○	○	○
2. The relationship between materiality used for planning versus evaluation purposes.	○	○	○	○	○	○	○	○	○
3. Hanmei Corp. has transactions with the corporation president's brother.	○	○	○	○	○	○	○	○	○
4. Comparing a client's unaudited results for the year with last year's audited results.	○	○	○	○	○	○	○	○	○
5. Auditing and reporting guidance on the possible need to reaudit previous year results due to the disbanding of the firm that performed last year's audit.	○	○	○	○	○	○	○	○	○

	Transactions	(A)	(B)	(C)	(D)	(E)	(F)	(G)	(H)	(I)
6.	Requirements relating to identifying violations of occupational safety and health regulations.	○	○	○	○	○	○	○	○	○
7.	Audit report considerations when audit of a subsidiary of the client will be performed by Williams & Co., CPAs.	○	○	○	○	○	○	○	○	○
8.	The need to "brainstorm" among audit team members about how accounts could be intentionally misstated.	○	○	○	○	○	○	○	○	○
9.	Details on considering design effectiveness of controls.	○	○	○	○	○	○	○	○	○
10.	The importance of considering the possibility of overstated revenues (for example, through premature revenue recognition).	○	○	○	○	○	○	○	○	○

Situation	Nonattest Services	Auditing Standards	Research		Communication

An auditor must establish an understanding with the client regarding the nature of the services to be provided. Research the Professional Standards for the information that an understanding with the client generally includes. You may simply paste the appropriate material to your solution.

Situation	Nonattest Services	Auditing Standards	Research	Communication

Write a memorandum to Caroline Smith, the Chairperson of Hanmei's audit committee, describing why independence is required to perform an audit.

REMINDER: Your response will be graded for both technical content and writing skills. Technical content will be evaluated for information that is helpful to the intended reader and clearly relevant to the issues. Writing skills will be evaluated for development, organization, and the appropriate expression of ideas in professional correspondence. Use a standard business memo or letter format with a clear beginning, middle, and end. Do not convey information in the form of a table, bullet point list, or other abbreviated presentation.

To: Ms. Caroline Smith, Chairperson of the Audit Committee
From: CPA Candidate
Re: Independence

MULTIPLE-CHOICE ANSWERS*

1. a __ __	24. d __ __	47. b __ __	70. c __ __	93. c __ __	116. b __ __
2. d __ __	25. c __ __	48. d __ __	71. b __ __	94. b __ __	117. d __ __
3. b __ __	26. a __ __	49. d __ __	72. c __ __	95. b __ __	118. a __ __
4. b __ __	27. a __ __	50. d __ __	73. a __ __	96. d __ __	119. d __ __
5. a __ __	28. c __ __	51. c __ __	74. b __ __	97. b __ __	120. d __ __
6. c __ __	29. d __ __	52. b __ __	75. c __ __	98. c __ __	121. c __ __
7. c __ __	30. d __ __	53. a __ __	76. a __ __	99. b __ __	122. c __ __
8. b __ __	31. b __ __	54. c __ __	77. d __ __	100. a __ __	123. d __ __
9. b __ __	32. d __ __	55. b __ __	78. d __ __	101. d __ __	124. a __ __
10. b __ __	33. c __ __	56. a __ __	79. a __ __	102. a __ __	125. c __ __
11. b __ __	34. c __ __	57. b __ __	80. d __ __	103. b __ __	126. d __ __
12. d __ __	35. d __ __	58. b __ __	81. b __ __	104. c __ __	127. c __ __
13. a __ __	36. a __ __	59. c __ __	82. d __ __	105. c __ __	128. d __ __
14. c __ __	37. a __ __	60. b __ __	83. c __ __	106. c __ __	129. a __ __
15. b __ __	38. a __ __	61. d __ __	84. a __ __	107. d __ __	130. b __ __
16. b __ __	39. a __ __	62. a __ __	85. d __ __	108. a __ __	131. c __ __
17. a __ __	40. b __ __	63. b __ __	86. c __ __	109. b __ __	
18. b __ __	41. d __ __	64. b __ __	87. b __ __	110. a __ __	
19. a __ __	42. b __ __	65. a __ __	88. c __ __	111. b __ __	
20. b __ __	43. a __ __	66. c __ __	89. a __ __	112. b __ __	
21. a __ __	44. a __ __	67. d __ __	90. c __ __	113. c __ __	
22. d __ __	45. a __ __	68. c __ __	91. b __ __	114. a __ __	1st: __/131 = __%
23. b __ __	46. c __ __	69. a __ __	92. b __ __	115. d __ __	2nd: __/131 = __%

MULTIPLE-CHOICE ANSWER EXPLANATIONS

A.1. Financial Statement Assertions

1. **(a)** The requirement is to identify the categories of financial statement assertions. Answer (a) is correct because the professional standards establish financial statement assertions for account balances, classes of transactions and disclosures. Answer (b) is incorrect because financial statement assertions are established for disclosures. Answer (c) is incorrect because financial statement assertions are established for classes of transactions. Answer (d) is incorrect because financial statement assertions are established for both classes of transactions and disclosures.

2. **(d)** The requirement is to identify the item that is **not** a financial statement assertion relating to account balances. Answer (d) is correct because valuation and allocation is an account balance assertion, not valuation and *competence*. Answer (a) is incorrect because completeness is an assertion relating to account balances. Answer (b) is incorrect because existence is an assertion relating to account balances. Answer (c) is incorrect because rights and obligations is an assertion relating to account balances.

A.2. Audit Risk

3. **(b)** The requirement is to determine a likely auditor reaction to a decreased acceptable level of detection risk. Answer (b) is correct because postponement of interim substantive tests to year-end decreases detection risk by reducing the risk for the period subsequent to the performance of those tests; other approaches to decreasing detection risk include changing to more effective substantive tests and increasing their extent. Answer (a) is incorrect because increased, not reduced, substantive testing is required. Answer (c) is incorrect because inherent risk must be considered in planning, either by itself or in combination with

control risk. Answer (d) is incorrect because tests of controls must be performed to reduce the assessed level of control risk.

4. **(b)** The requirement is to identify the risk that an auditor will conclude, based on substantive tests, that a material error does **not** exist in an account balance when, in fact, such error does exist. Answer (b) is correct because detection risk is the risk that the auditor will not detect a material misstatement that exists in an assertion. Detection risk may be viewed in terms of two components (1) the risk that analytical procedures and other relevant substantive tests would fail to detect misstatements equal to tolerable misstatement, and (2) the allowable risk of incorrect acceptance for the substantive tests of details. Answer (a) is incorrect because sampling risk arises from the possibility that, when a test of controls or a substantive test is restricted to a sample, the auditor's conclusions may be different from the conclusions he or she would reach if the tests were applied in the same way to all items in the account balance or class of transactions. When related to substantive tests sampling risk is only a part of the risk that the auditor's substantive tests will not detect a material misstatement. Answer (c) is incorrect because nonsampling risk includes only those aspects of audit risk that are not due to sampling. Answer (d) is incorrect because inherent risk is the susceptibility of an assertion to a material misstatement, assuming that there are no related controls.

5. **(a)** The requirement is to identify an effect of a decrease in the acceptable level of detection risk. Answer (a) is correct because as the acceptable level of detection risk decreases, the assurance provided from substantive tests should increase. To gain this increased assurance the auditors may (1) change the **nature** of substantive tests to more

---

Explanation of how to use this performance record appears on page 1.

effective procedures (e.g., use independent parties outside the entity rather than those within the entity), (2) change the **timing** of substantive tests (e.g., perform them at year-end rather than at an interim date), and (3) change the **extent** of substantive tests (e.g., take a larger sample). Answer (b) is incorrect because the assurance provided from substantive tests increases, it does not decrease. Answers (c) and (d) are incorrect because the acceptable level of detection risk is based largely on the assessed levels of control risk and inherent risk. Accordingly, any tests of controls will already have been performed.

6.   **(c)**   The requirement is to determine whether inherent risk, control risk, and detection risk may be assessed in nonquantitative terms. Answer (c) is correct because all of these risks may be assessed in either quantitative terms such as percentages, **or** nonquantitative terms such as a range from a minimum to a maximum.

7.   **(c)**   The requirement is to determine a manner in which inherent risk and control risk differ from detection risk. Answer (c) is correct because inherent risk and control risk exist independently of the audit of the financial statements as functions of the client and its environment, whereas detection risk relates to the auditor's procedures and can be changed at his or her discretion. Answer (a) is incorrect because inherent risk and control risk are functions of the client and its environment and do not arise from misapplication of auditing procedures. Answer (b) is incorrect because inherent risk, control risk and detection risk may each be assessed in either quantitative or nonquantitative terms. Answer (d) is incorrect because inherent risk and control risk are functions of the client and its environment, they cannot be changed at the auditor's discretion. However, the assessed levels of inherent and control risk (not addressed in this question) may be affected by auditor decisions relating to the cost of gathering evidence to substantiate assessed levels below the maximum.

8.   **(b)**   The requirement is to determine the best way for an auditor to achieve an overall audit risk level when the audit evidence relating to control risk indicates the need to increase its assessed level. Answer (b) is correct because a decrease in detection risk will allow the auditor achieve an overall audit risk level substantially the same as planned. Answer (a) is incorrect because a decrease in substantive testing will increase, not decrease, detection risk and thereby increase audit risk. Answer (c) is incorrect because an increase in inherent risk will also increase audit risk. Answer (d) is incorrect because there appears to be no justification for increasing materiality levels beyond those used in planning the audit.

9.   **(b)**   The requirement is to determine the relationship between control risk and detection risk. Inverse is correct because as control risk increases (decreases) detection risk must decrease (increase).

A.3.   Materiality

10.   **(b)**   The requirement is to identify the information that an auditor would most likely use in determining a preliminary judgment about materiality. Answer (b) is correct because many materiality measures relate to an annual figure (e.g., net income, sales). Answer (a) is incorrect because the preliminary judgment about materiality is a factor used in determining the anticipated sample size, not the reverse as

suggested by the reply. Answers (c) and (d) are incorrect because materiality will not normally be affected by the results of the internal control questionnaire or the contents of the management representation letters.

11.   **(b)**   The requirement is to identify the statement that is **not** correct concerning materiality. Answer (b) is the proper reply because the auditor considers materiality for planning purposes in terms of the **smallest,** not the **largest,** aggregate amount of misstatement that could be material to any one of the financial statements. Answers (a), (c), and (d) all represent correct statements about materiality.

12.   **(d)**   The requirement is to identify the elements which underlie the application of generally accepted auditing standards, particularly the standards of fieldwork and reporting. Answer (d) is correct because AU 150 states that materiality and relative risk underlie the application of all the standards. Answer (a) is incorrect because a consideration of internal control is one of the field standards, not an element underlying the standards. Answer (b) is incorrect because the second fieldwork standard, on evidence, relates most directly to corroborating evidence. Answer (c) is incorrect because while it is accurate that quality control standards encompass the firm's policies and procedures to provide reasonable assurance of conforming with professional standards, the standards are not related more directly to the fieldwork and reporting standards than to the general group of generally accepted auditing standards.

13.   **(a)**   The requirement is to determine the appropriate level of materiality for planning purposes when $10,000 would have a material effect on an entity's income statement, but $20,000 would materially affect the balance sheet. AU 312 states that the audit should be designed to obtain reasonable assurance about whether the financial statements are free of material misstatement. Because it will ordinarily be difficult to anticipate during the planning stage of an audit whether all misstatements will affect only one financial statement, the auditor is generally required to use the lower financial statement figure for most portions of planning. Therefore, answer (a), $10,000, is correct. Answers (b), (c), and (d) are all incorrect because they are dollar amounts which exceed the lowest level of materiality.

14.   **(c)**   The requirement is to identify the information that an auditor would be most likely to use in making a preliminary judgment about materiality. Answer (c) is correct because auditors often choose to use a measure relating to the prior year's financial statements (e.g., a percentage of total assets, net income, or revenue) to arrive at a preliminary judgment about materiality. Answer (a) is incorrect because materiality is based on the magnitude of an omission or misstatement and not on the initial assessment of control risk. Answer (b) is incorrect because while an auditor's materiality judgment will affect the anticipated sample size for planned substantive tests, sample size does not affect the materiality judgment. Answer (d) is incorrect because the assertions embodied in the financial statements remain the same from one audit to another.

15.   **(b)**   The requirement is to identify the most likely effect of a decrease in the tolerable amount of misstatement (tolerable misstatement) in a class of transactions. Answer (b) is correct because auditing standards state that decreasing the tolerable amount of misstatement will require the auditor to do one or more of the following: (1) perform auditing procedures closer to the balance sheet date (answer [b]); (2) select a more effective auditing procedure; or (3) increase the extent of a particular auditing procedure. Answer (a) is incorrect because in such a circumstance substantive tests are more likely to be performed at or after the balance sheet date than prior to the balance sheet date. Answer (c) is incorrect because decreasing the tolerable amount of misstatement will not necessarily lead to an increase in the assessed level of control risk. Answer (d) is incorrect because the extent of auditing procedures will be increased, not decreased.

16. (b) The requirement is to identify the necessary condition for an auditor to be able to issue an unqualified opinion. Answer (b) is correct because if the estimate of likely misstatement is equal to or greater than a material amount a material departure from generally accepted accounting principles exists and thus AU 508 requires either a qualified or adverse opinion in such circumstances. Answer (a) is incorrect because the amount of known misstatement (if any) need not be documented in the management representation letter. Answer (c) is incorrect because it ordinarily is not necessary for the client to acknowledge and record immaterial known misstatements. Answer (d) is incorrect because the total likely misstatement need not include the adjusting entries already recorded by the client.

A.4. Errors and Fraud

17. (a) The requirement is to identify the example of fraudulent financial reporting. Answer (a) is correct because fraudulent financial reporting involves intentional misstatements or omissions of amounts or disclosures in financial statements to deceive financial statement users and changing the inventory count tags results in such a misstatement. Answers (b), (c), and (d) are all incorrect because they represent the misappropriation of assets. See AU 316 which divides fraudulent activities into misstatement arising from fraudulent financial reporting and misstatements arising from misappropriation of assets (sometimes referred to as defalcation).

18. (b) The requirement is to identify the best description of what is meant by a "fraud risk factor." Answer (b) is correct because AU 316 suggests that while fraud risk factors do not necessarily indicate the existence of fraud, they often have been observed in circumstances where frauds have occurred. Answer (a) is incorrect because the risk of fraud may or may not be high when a risk factor is present. Answer (c) is incorrect because the current audit program may in many circumstances appropriately address a fraud risk factor. Answer (d) is incorrect because a fraud risk factor may or may not represent a material weakness.

19. (a) The requirement is to identify the reply which represents an auditor communication responsibility relating to fraud. Answer (a) is correct because all fraud involving senior management should be reported directly to the audit committee. Answer (b) is incorrect because auditors are only required to report fraud to the Securities and Exchange Commission under particular circumstances. Answer (c) is incorrect because auditors do not ordinarily disclose fraud through use of an "emphasis of a matter" paragraph added to their report. Answer (d) is incorrect because under certain circumstances auditors must disclose fraud outside the entity.

20. (b) The requirement is to identify the risk relating to material misstatement that auditors are required to assess. Answer (b) is correct because SAS 109 and AU 316 require auditors to specifically assess the risk of material misstatements due to fraud and consider that assessment in designing the audit procedures to be performed. Answer (a) is incorrect because while SAS 109 also requires an assessment of the overall risk of material misstatement (whether caused by error or fraud) there is no requirement to explicitly assess the risk of material misstatement due to errors. Answer (c) is incorrect because the auditor need not explicitly assess the risk of misstatement due to illegal acts (see AU 317 for information on illegal acts). Answer (d) is incorrect because no assessment of business risk is required.

21. (a) The requirement is to determine whether audits are designed to provide reasonable assurance of detecting misstatements due to errors, fraudulent financial reporting, and/or misappropriation of assets. Answer (a) is correct because AU 110 and AU 316 require that an audit obtain reasonable assurance that material misstatements, whether caused by error or fraud, be detected. Fraudulent financial reporting and the misappropriation of assets are the two major types of fraud with which an audit is relevant.

22. (d) The requirement is to identify the reply which is not a reason why auditors are unable to obtain absolute assurance that misstatements due to fraud will be detected. Answer (d) is correct because while an auditor must exercise professional skepticism when performing an audit it does not represent a limitation that makes is impossible to obtain absolute assurance. Answers (a), (b), and (c) are all incorrect because they represent factors considered in the professional literature for providing reasonable, and not absolute assurance.

23. (b) The requirement is to identify the type of fraudulent misstatement that is most difficult to detect. Answer (b) is correct because transactions that have not been recorded are generally considered most difficult because there is no general starting point for the auditor in the consideration of the transaction. Answers (a), (c), and (d) all represent recorded transactions which, when audited, are in general easier to detect.

24. (d) The requirement is to identify the **least likely** indicator of a risk of possible misstatement due to fraud. Answer (d) is correct because one would expect unusually aggressive, rather than unusually conservative accounting practices to indicate a risk of misstatement due to fraud. Answers (a), (b), and (c) are all incorrect because they represent risk factors explicitly included in AU 316, which provides guidance on fraud.

25. (c) The requirement is to determine the reply which represents information most likely to affect the auditor's assessment of the risk of misstatement due to fraud. Answer (c) is correct because AU 316 states that missing documents may be indicative of fraud. Answer (a) is incorrect because checks for significant amounts are normally expected to be outstanding at year-end. Answer (b) is incorrect because almost all audits involve computer generated documents and their existence is not considered a condition indicating possible fraud. Answer (d) is incorrect because while last-minute adjustments that significantly affect financial results may be considered indicative of possible fraud, year-end adjusting journal entries alone are to be expected.

26. **(a)** The requirement is to identify the most likely response to the auditor's assessment that the risk of material misstatement due to fraud for the existence of inventory is high. Answer (a) is correct because observing test counts of inventory on an unannounced basis will provide evidence as to whether record inventory exists. Answer (b) is incorrect because replacing test counts with analytical procedures is not likely to be particularly effective. Answers (c) and (d) are incorrect because the inventories might well be counted at year-end, all on the same date, rather than prior to year-end and at differing dates.

27. **(a)** The requirement is to identify the reply that is most likely to be an example of fraud. Answer (a) is most likely, since "defalcation" is another term for misstatements arising from misappropriation of assets, a major type of fraud. Answers (b), (c), and (d) are all incorrect because mistakes in the application of accounting principles or in processing data, and unreasonable accounting estimates arising from oversight are examples of misstatements rather than fraud.

28. **(c)** The requirement is to identify the characteristic most likely to heighten an auditor's concern about the risk of intentional manipulation of financial statements. Answer (c) is correct because the placement of substantial emphasis on meeting earnings projections is considered a risk factor. Answer (a) is incorrect because high turnover, not low turnover, is considered a risk factor. Answer (b) is incorrect because insider purchases of additional shares of stock are less likely to be indicative of intentional manipulation of the financial statements than is undue emphasis on meeting earnings projections. Answer (d) is incorrect because a rapid rate of change in an industry, not a slow rate, is considered a risk factor.

29. **(d)** The requirement is to identify an auditor's responsibility for detecting errors and fraud. Answer (d) is correct because AU 110 requires that an auditor design the audit to provide reasonable assurance of detecting misstatements due to errors and fraud that are material to the financial statements. Answer (a) is incorrect because audits provide reasonable assurance of detecting material errors and fraud. Answer (b) is incorrect because it doesn't restrict the responsibility to material errors and fraud. Answer (c) is incorrect because it is less precise than answer (d), which includes the AU 110 responsibility on errors and fraud.

30. **(d)** The requirement is to identify the circumstances in which an auditor may have a responsibility to disclose fraud to parties other than a client's senior management and its audit committee or board of directors. Answer (d) is correct because AU 316 states that such a responsibility may exist to the SEC when there has been an auditor change to a successor auditor or to comply with SEC 1995 Private Securities Reform Act communication requirement, when the successor auditor makes inquiries, and to a government agency from which the client receives financial assistance. In addition, that section states that an auditor may have such a disclosure responsibility in response to a subpoena, a circumstance not considered in this question.

31. **(b)** Errors refer to unintentional mistakes in financial statements such as misinterpretation of facts. Answers (a), (c), and (d) all represent fraud which are defined as intentional distortions of financial statements.

32. **(d)** The requirement is to identify the level of assurance an auditor provides with respect to detection of material errors, fraud, and direct effect illegal acts. Answer (d) is correct because AU 110 requires the auditor to design the audit to provide **reasonable assurance** of detecting material errors, fraud and direct effect illegal acts. (A "direct effect" illegal act is one that would have an effect on the determination of financial statement amounts.)

33. **(c)** The requirement is to identify the proper attitude of an auditor who is performing an audit in accordance with generally accepted auditing standards. Answer (c) is correct because the auditor should plan and perform the audit with an attitude of professional skepticism, recognizing that the application of the auditing procedures may produce evidence indicating the possibility of misstatements due to errors or fraud. Answer (a) is incorrect because while the CPA must exhibit objective judgment, "professional skepticism" more accurately summarizes the proper attitude during an audit. Answer (b) is incorrect because while a CPA must be independent and have integrity, this is not the "attitude" used to plan and perform the audit. Answer (d) is incorrect because the audit is not planned and performed with impartial conservatism.

34. **(c)** The requirement is to identify the meaning of the term "material misstatement" when used in the professional standards. Answer (c) is correct because SAS 107 and AU 316 state that a material misstatement may occur due to errors, fraud, and illegal acts with a direct effect on financial statement amounts.

35. **(d)** The requirement is to identify an auditor's responsibility for detecting financial stress of employees or adverse relationships between a company and its employees. Answer (d) is correct because AU 316 states that, while the auditor is not required to plan the audit to discover information that is indicative of financial stress of employees or adverse relationships between the company and its employees, such conditions must be considered when an auditor becomes aware of them. Answers (a), (b), and (c) are all incorrect because the auditor does not plan the audit to detect these conditions.

36. **(a)** The requirement is to identify an auditor's responsibility when he or she believes that a misstatement is or may be the result of fraud, but that the effect of the misstatements is immaterial to the financial statements. Answer (a) is correct because AU 316 states that in such circumstances the auditor should evaluate the implications of the fraud, especially those dealing with the organizational position of the person(s) involved.

37. **(a)** The requirement is to identify the correct statements relating to the auditor's consideration of fraud. Answer (a) is correct because AU 316 states that the auditor's interest relates to fraudulent acts that cause a material misstatement of financial statements. Answer (b) is incorrect because errors are unintentional. Answer (c) is incorrect because fraud does not necessarily involve the misappropriation of assets (it may involve fraudulent financial reporting). Answer (d) is incorrect because an auditor must design an audit to obtain reasonable assurance of detecting misstatements, regardless of whether they are caused by errors or fraud.

38. **(a)** The requirement is to identify the factor or condition that an audit is least likely to be planned to discover. Answer (a) is correct because it represents a financial stress, and auditors are not required to plan audits to discover information that is indicative of financial stress of employees or adverse relationships between the entity and its employees. Answers (b), (c), and (d) are all incorrect because they represent examples of risk factors that should be considered in an audit and are included in AU 316.

39. **(a)** The requirement is to determine when audit risk factors may be identified. Answer (a) is correct because AU 316 states that fraud risk factors may be identified during planning, obtaining an understanding, or while conducting fieldwork; in addition, they may be identified while considering acceptance or continuance of clients and engagements.

40. **(b)** The requirement is to identify the circumstance in which it is most likely that management's attitude toward aggressive financial reporting and toward meeting projected profit goals would most likely significantly influence an entity's control environment. Answer (b) is correct because when management is dominated by one individual, that individual may be able to follow overly aggressive accounting principles.

41. **(d)** The requirement is to identify the procedure **least** likely to be required on an audit. Answer (d) is correct because fraud is a broad legal concept and auditors do not make legal determinations of whether fraud has occurred. Answers (a), (b), and (c) are incorrect because considering journal entries, estimates, and unusual transactions are ordinarily required audit procedures to address the risk of management override of controls. See AU 316 for information on the auditor's responsibility for the consideration of fraud in a financial statement audit.

42. **(b)** The requirement is to identify the most likely response when a risk of fraud has been identified on an audit. Answer (b) is correct because AU 316 indicates that overall responses to the risk of material misstatements due to fraud include (1) assigning personnel with particular skills relating to the area and considering the necessary extent of supervision to the audit, (2) increasing the consideration of management's selection and application of accounting principles, and (3) making audit procedures less predictable. Answer (a) is incorrect because closer supervision, not less close supervision, is more likely to be appropriate. Answer (c) is incorrect because individuals with specialized skills may be needed who are not CPAs. Answer (d) is incorrect because subjective transactions (e.g., accounting estimates) often provide more risk than objective transactions.

43. **(a)** The requirement is to identify the **least** likely inquiry of management relating to identifying the risk of material misstatement due to fraud. Answer (a) is correct because financial operations of many companies are not ordinarily controlled by and limited to one location. Answers (b), (c), and (d) are all incorrect because they are included in AU 316 as inquiries that should be made of management.

44. **(a)** The requirement is to identify the attributes ordinarily present when individuals commit fraud. Answer (a) is correct because AU 316 suggests that the three conditions generally present when fraud occurs are that individuals have an (1) incentive or pressure, (2) opportunity, and (3) ability to rationalize. Answers (b), (c), and (d) are all incorrect because they suggest that one of the three elements is not ordinarily present.

45. **(a)** The requirement is to determine an auditor's reporting responsibility when he or she has discovered that management is involved in a financially immaterial fraud. Answer (a) is correct because AU 316 requires that all management fraud, regardless of materiality, be reported to the audit committee. Answer (b) is incorrect because fraud is not directly reported to the Public Company Accounting Oversight Board. Answer (c) is incorrect because if anything, in addition to the audit committee, the fraud is reported to a level of management at least one level above those involved in a fraud. Answer (d) is incorrect because there is a reporting responsibility for financially immaterial management fraud.

46. **(c)** The requirement is to identify the most likely risk factor relating to fraudulent financial reporting. Answer (c) is correct because negative cash flows from operations may result in pressure upon management to overstate the results of operations. Answer (a) is incorrect because one would expect a company's top executives to dominate management—domination by one or a few might be considered a risk factor. Answers (b) and (d) are incorrect because large amounts of cash being processed and small high-dollar inventory items are more directly related to the misappropriation of assets than they are to fraudulent financial reporting.

47. **(b)** The requirement is to identify the most likely fraud risk factor on an audit. Answer (b) is correct because the possibility of improper revenue recognition is ordinarily presumed on audits. Answers (a), (c), and (d) all represent potential risks, but risks that are not ordinarily presumed on an audit. See AU 316 for information on the auditor's responsibility for the consideration of fraud in a financial statement audit.

48. **(d)** The requirement is to identify the circumstances relating to the discovery of the payment of small bribes to municipal officials that is most likely to cause an auditor to withdraw from an engagement. Answer (d) is correct because AU 317 states that management failure to take the appropriate remedial action is particularly problematical since it may affect the auditor's ability to rely on management representation and may therefore lead to withdrawal. Answers (a), (b), and (c) all represent circumstances which the auditor will consider, but are not ordinarily considered as serious as failure to take the appropriate remedial action.

49. **(d)** The requirement is to identify the factor most likely to cause a CPA **not** to accept a new audit engagement. Answer (d) is correct because a part of the understanding an auditor must obtain with a client is that management is responsible for making all financial records and related information available (see SAS 108). Accordingly, if the client refuses to make such information available the auditor is unlikely to accept the audit client. Answer (a) is incorrect because a circumstance-imposed scope limitations such as completion of the physical inventory count results in a situation in which the auditor may consider using alternative procedures (including making some test counts) to determine whether inventory counts are proper. Answer (b) is incorrect because an auditor may obtain an understanding of the client's operations and industry while performing the audit. Answer (c) is incorrect because while a review of the predecessor auditor's working papers is ordinarily desirable, it is not required.

50. (d) The requirement is to identify the factor most likely to heighten an auditor's concern about the risk of fraudulent financial reporting. Answer (d) is correct because AU 316, which presents a variety of risk factors, suggests that an overly complex organizational structure is such a risk factor. Answer (a) is incorrect because large amounts of liquid assets that are easily convertible into cash represent more of a risk relating to misappropriation of assets rather than to fraudulent financial reporting. Answer (b) is incorrect because high growth, rather than low growth, is considered a risk factor. Answer (c) is incorrect because one would expect financial management's participation in the initial selection of accounting principles.

A.5. Illegal Acts

51. (c) The requirement is to identify the situation in which an auditor would be most likely to withdraw from an engagement when he or she has discovered that a client's employees have paid small bribes to public officials. Answer (c) is correct because AU 317 states that resignation should be considered when an illegal act does not receive proper remedial action, because such inaction may affect the auditor's ability to rely on management representations and the effects of continued association with the client. Answer (a) is incorrect because the receipt of federal funds in such a situation is not as likely to result in auditor withdrawal as is answer (c). Answer (b) is incorrect because it seems inconsistent with the premise of the question in that, if no evidence exists, the auditor is unlikely to know that bribes have been paid. Answer (d) is incorrect because such small bribes will not ordinarily need to be disclosed. Alternatively, if the auditor believes that there is such a need, the lack of such disclosure represents a departure from generally accepted accounting principles and either a qualified or adverse opinion is appropriate.

52. (b) The requirement is to identify the illegal act that an audit should be designed to obtain reasonable assurance of detecting. Answer (b) is correct because the accrual and billing of an improper amount of revenue under government contracts is an illegal act with a direct effect on the determination of financial statement amounts, and audits are designed to detect such illegal acts. Answers (a), (c), and (d) are all incorrect because they represent illegal acts with an indirect financial statement effect and an audit provides no assurance that such acts will be detected or that any contingent liabilities that may result will be disclosed. See AU 317 for detailed guidance on auditor responsibility with respect to direct and indirect illegal acts.

53. (a) The requirement is to identify the small misstatement that is most likely to have a material effect on an entity's financial statements. Answer (a) is correct because an illegal payment of an otherwise immaterial amount may be material if there is a reasonable possibility that it may lead to a material contingent liability or a material loss of revenue.

54. (c) The requirement is to determine what an auditor might reconsider when a client's board of directors has refused to take any action relating to an auditor's disclosure that the company has made immaterial illegal contributions. Answer (c) is correct because in such a circumstance the failure to take remedial action may cause an auditor to decrease reliance on management representations. Answer (a) is incorrect because the reply by the attorney is likely to disclose any claims, litigation or assessments that the client has improperly omitted from the letter of audit inquiry. Answer (b) is incorrect because the prior years' audit programs are not being relied upon for this year's audit. Answer (d) is incorrect because the preliminary judgment about materiality levels would not be expected to change.

55. (b) The requirement is to identify a reason why audits cannot reasonably be expected to bring all illegal acts to the auditor's attention. Answer (b) is correct because illegal acts relating to the operating aspects of an entity are often highly specialized and complex and often are far removed from the events and transactions reflected in financial statements. Answer (a) is partially correct since management override represents a limitation of the effectiveness of internal control. Yet, auditors are more likely to identify such transactions because they relate to events and transactions reflected in the financial statements. Answer (c) is incorrect because many illegal acts are not subject to the client's internal control. Answer (d) is incorrect because illegal acts may be perpetrated without access to both assets and accounting records.

56. (a) The requirement is to determine an auditor's responsibility when information comes to his/her attention that implies the existence of possible illegal acts with a material, but indirect effect on the financial statements. Answer (a) is correct because AU 317 requires the auditor to apply audit procedures specifically designed to determine whether an illegal act has occurred when such information comes to his/her attention. Answers (b), (c), and (d) are all incorrect because they represent procedures the auditor would perform after initial procedures had confirmed the existence of the possible illegal act(s).

57. (b) The requirement is to determine the circumstance in which it is most likely that a CPA would withdraw from an audit engagement after having discovered that client employees have committed an illegal act. Answer (b) is correct because the auditor may conclude that withdrawal is necessary when the client does not take the remedial action, even when the illegal act is not material to the financial statements. Answers (a) and (c) are incorrect because whether generally accepted accounting principles have been violated and whether the illegal act occurred during a prior year that was not audited may or may not have an effect on the decision to withdraw from the engagement. Answer (d) is incorrect because the assessed level of control risk will not have a direct relationship on the decision to withdraw from the engagement.

58. (b) The requirement is to identify a CPA's responsibility under the Securities Litigation Reform Act of 1995 for uncorrected illegal acts which have been communicated to the board of directors which refuses to inform the SEC of their existence. Answer (b) is correct because CPAs are required under the law to deliver a report on those illegal acts to the SEC within one business day in such circumstances. Answer (a) in incorrect because there is no requirement to resign, although the auditor may decide to do so. Answer (c) is incorrect because the Act sets up reporting to the SEC, not to the stockholders. Answer (d) is incorrect because withholding of the audit opinion is not suggested in the Act.

B. Audit Planning

59. (c) The requirement is to identify the procedure **least** likely to be considered an audit planning procedure. Answer (c) is correct because performing the risk assessment occurs subsequent to audit planning. Answer (a) is incorrect because an engagement letter is used to establish an understanding with the client, and this is a planning procedure. Answer (b) is incorrect because auditors develop the overall audit strategy during audit planning. Answer (d) is incorrect because the audit plan is developed during planning.

60. (b) The requirement is to identify the factor most likely to cause a CPA to decide not to accept a new audit engagement. Answer (b) is correct because a certain level of internal control is essential for financial statement reporting, and management's disregard in this area may lead the CPA to reject the engagement. Answer (a) is incorrect both because a CPA may not need an understanding of the prospective client's internal auditor's computer-assisted audit technique to form an opinion on the financial statements, and because if such understanding is necessary, it can be obtained subsequent to engagement acceptance. Answer (c) is incorrect because AU 334 indicates that a CPA often will be unable to determine whether related-party transactions were consummated on terms equivalent to arm's-length transactions. Answer (d) is incorrect because while management's refusal to permit the performance of substantive tests before the year-end may present a problem, the auditor may be able to effectively perform such tests after year-end.

B.1. Communicate with Predecessor Auditors (Prior to Engagement Acceptance)

61. (d) The requirement is to identify a requirement prior to accepting an engagement to audit a new client. Answer (d) is correct because AU 315 requires that an auditor attempt to obtain client permission to contact the predecessor prior to accepting a new engagement. Answers (a), (b), and (c) are incorrect because they may all be obtained subsequent to accepting an engagement.

62. (a) The requirement is to determine the nature of the inquiries that a successor auditor should make of the predecessor auditor prior to accepting an audit engagement. Answer (a) is correct because the inquiries should include specific questions to management on (1) disagreements with management as to auditing procedures and accounting principles (reply [a]), (2) facts that might bear on the integrity of management and (3) the predecessor's understanding as to the reasons for the change of auditors. Answers (b), (c), and (d) are incorrect because, if made at all, they will be after the engagement has been accepted.

63. (b) The requirement is to identify the correct statement regarding a successor auditor's inquiries of the predecessor auditor. Answer (b) is correct because the successor should request information such as (1) facts that might bear on the integrity of management, (2) disagreements with

management as to accounting principles, auditing procedures, or other significant matters, and (3) the predecessor's understanding of the reasons for the change of auditors. Answers (a), (c), and (d) all relate to matters not required to be discussed prior to accepting an audit engagement.

B.2. Establishing an Understanding with the Client (Engagement Letters)

64. (b) The requirement is to identify the item ordinarily included when an auditor establishes an understanding with a client regarding the services to be performed. Answer (b) is correct because auditing standards require that an auditor ensure that the audit committee is aware of any significant deficiencies which come to the CPA's attention. Answer (a) is incorrect because while an understanding will include a statement that management is responsible for the entity's financial statements, an explicit statement about errors and illegal activities of employees is not ordinarily included. Answer (c) in incorrect because management does not provide the auditor with an assessment of the risk of material misstatement due to fraud. Answer (d) is incorrect because no such statement about an auditor's responsibility for determining preliminary judgments about materiality and audit risk factors is ordinarily included in establishing an understanding. See SAS 108 for information on establishing an understanding with a client.

65. (a) The requirement is to identify the matter generally included in an auditor's engagement letter. Answer (a) is correct because AU 310, which outlines requirements for engagement letters, indicates that an engagement letter should include an indication that management is responsible for identifying and ensuring that the company complies with the laws and regulations applicable to its activities. Answer (b) is incorrect because such detailed information on materiality is not generally included in an engagement letter. Answer (c) is incorrect because management liability (if any) for illegal acts committed by employees is not generally included in an engagement letter. Answer (d) is incorrect because while an auditor is required to obtain an understanding of internal control, he or she is not required to search for significant internal control deficiencies.

66. (c) The requirement is to identify the most likely procedure during the initial planning phase of an audit. Answer (c) is correct because during initial planning the timing of procedures will be discussed due to the need for client assistance with many of these procedures. Answer (a) is incorrect because the timing of audit procedures will occur subsequent to the **initial** planning stage of an audit. Answer (b) is incorrect because the evaluation of reasonableness of the client's accounting estimates will occur after planning (see AU 342). Answer (d) is incorrect because the inquiry of a client's attorney will occur subsequently to initial planning (see AU 337). See SAS 108 for information on planning.

67. (d) The requirement is to identify the statement that is **least** likely to appear in an auditor's engagement letter. Answer (d) is correct because auditors ordinarily will not discuss with management the details of procedures that are necessary to perform the audit. Answers (a), (b), and (c) are incorrect because engagement letters **will** include a statement on the risk of not detecting material errors and fraud, and **may** include information on fees and observed opportunities for economy.

68. (c) The requirement is to identify the item for which the generally accepted auditing standards do not require documentation. Answer (c) is correct because while a CPA firm will include an engagement letter in the working papers, it will not detail the auditor's planned fieldwork. Answer (a) is incorrect because SAS 108 requires a written audit plan. Answer (b) is incorrect because SAS 103 requires that the working papers document the agreement or reconciliation of the accounting records with the financial statements. Answer (d) is incorrect because SAS 109 requires the auditor to document the assessment of the risks of material misstatement.

69. (a) The requirement is to determine what types of items are ordinarily included in an engagement letter in addition to the objectives of the engagement. Answer (a) is correct because SAS 108 also requires inclusion of information on CPA responsibilities, client responsibilities, and limitations of the engagement.

70. (c) The requirement is to determine the reply which is least likely to be included in an engagement letter. Answer (c) is correct because AU 311, which provides information on obtaining an understanding with the client, does not suggest any arrangement concerning CPA investment in client securities; indeed such investments are prohibited by the Code of Professional Conduct. Answers (a), (b), and (d) all represent arrangements which AU 311 suggests may be included in an engagement letter (or other form of understanding with a client).

B.3. Preliminary Engagement Activities

71. (b) The requirement is to identify form(s) of documentation of the understanding obtained with a client. Answer (b) is correct because the professional standards require that an auditor document the understanding through a written communication with the client. Answer (a) is incorrect because an oral communication is not sufficient. Answer (c) is incorrect because the communication should be in writing. Answer (d) is incorrect because the understanding is not documented in a *completely detailed audit plan*—a term of questionable meaning.

72. (c) The requirement is to identify the factor that most likely would influence an auditor's determination of the auditability of an entity's financial statements. Answer (c) is correct because inadequate accounting records may cause an auditor to conclude that it is unlikely that sufficient appropriate evidence will be available to support an opinion on the financial statements; accordingly, an auditor may determine that the financial statements are not auditable. Answer (a) is incorrect because an auditor should be able to obtain the knowledge necessary to audit a complex accounting system. Answer (b) is incorrect because while related-party transactions may raise transaction valuation issues due to the lack of an "arm's-length transaction," the problem is normally not so severe as to make the entity not auditable. Answer (d) is incorrect because a lack of operating effectiveness of controls may often be overcome through an increase in the scope of substantive tests.

B.4. Developing an Overall Strategy

73. (a) The requirement is to identify the area that is most likely to require special audit planning considerations. Answer (a) is correct because an inventory comprised of

diamond rings is likely to require that the auditor plan ahead to involve a specialist to assist in valuation issues. Answer (b) is incorrect because valuation of an asset such as a new copy machine is not ordinarily expected to provide valuation difficulties. Answer (c) is incorrect because the expensing purchases of such small assets is ordinarily acceptable due to the immateriality of the transactions. Answer (d) is incorrect because accelerated depreciation methods are ordinarily acceptable.

74. (b) The requirement is to identify the information source that a CPA would most likely consult for information on how various publicly held companies have complied with the disclosure requirements of a new financial accounting standard. Answer (b) is correct because AICPA *Accounting Trends and Techniques*, which is issued annually, summarizes such disclosures of 600 industrial and merchandising corporations. Answer (a) is incorrect because the AICPA Codification of Statements on Auditing Standards codifies the various Statements on Auditing Standards and does not include information on individual company compliance with disclosure requirements. Answer (c) is incorrect because Quality Control Review standards are established by the AICPA and because they do not include information on individual company compliance with disclosure requirements. Answer (d) is incorrect because Form 10-K itself provides information on preparing Form10-K and this form does not include information on individual company compliance with disclosure requirements.

B.5. The Audit Plan

75. (c) The requirement is to determine why an auditor should design a written audit program. Answer (c) is correct because an audit program sets forth in detail the audit procedures that are necessary to accomplish the objectives of the audit. Answer (a) is incorrect because audit programs address topics beyond selecting material transactions and this is not their primary focus. Answer (b) is incorrect because a program may include numerous substantive tests to be performed prior to the balance sheet date. Answer (d) is incorrect because immaterial accounts often are not tested and because tests of transactions, tests of balances, and analytical procedures are used to test account balances; account balances are not directly tested through tests of controls.

76. (a) The requirement is to determine a point at which an audit program may be finalized. Answer (a) is correct because the consideration of internal control helps the auditor to assess control risk and to plan the audit: accordingly, the audit program is not generally finalized prior to the consideration of internal control. Answer (b) is incorrect because, while generally desirable, engagement letters are not required on audits. Answer (c) is incorrect because reportable conditions may be communicated at various times subsequent to finalization of the audit program. Answer (d) is incorrect because audit programs are often finalized prior to the performance of the search for unrecorded liabilities.

77. (d) The requirement is to determine the manner in which audit programs should be designed. Answer (d) is correct because an audit program should be designed so that the audit evidence gathered is sufficient to support the auditor's conclusions. Answer (a) is incorrect because, often, most audit procedures will not be performed as interim work. Answer (b) is incorrect because inherent risk need not be assessed at a low level. Answer (c) is incorrect because while providing constructive suggestions to management is desirable, the audit program is not based on developing constructive suggestions.

78. (d)   The requirement is to determine what specific audit objectives are addressed when designing an audit program. Answer (d) is correct because in obtaining evidence in support of financial statement assertions, the auditor develops specific audit objectives in the light of those assertions. Answers (a), (b), and (c) are all incorrect because these replies do not relate specifically to the audit objectives as do the financial statement assertions.

B.7.   Timing of Audit Procedures

79. (a)   The requirement is to identify the statement that is always true with respect to planning an audit. Answer (a) is correct because it is acceptable for an auditor to perform a certain portion of the audit at an interim date; for example, performing a portion of planning prior to year-end is always acceptable for a continuing client. Also, when a new client has engaged an auditor prior to year-end, a portion of the audit may be conducted prior to year-end. Answer (b) is incorrect because an engagement may be accepted after the client's year-end. Answer (c) is incorrect because alternative procedures may be possible when an inventory count was not observed at year-end. Answer (d) is incorrect because final staffing decisions need not be made prior to completion of the planning stage of audits.

80. (d)   The requirement is to identify the element of the audit planning process most likely to be agreed upon with the client before implementation of the audit strategy. Answer (d) is correct because the auditor will ordinarily observe the counting of inventory and this will require a degree of coordination between the performance of audit procedures and client count procedures. Answer (a) is incorrect because the client will not determine the evidence to be gathered to provide a sufficient basis for the auditor's opinion. Answers (b) and (c) are incorrect because these procedures will be determined subsequent to implementation of the audit strategy.

C.   Obtain an Understanding of the Entity and Its Environment

81. (b)   The requirement is to determine the manner in which an auditor plans an audit of a continuing client. Answer (b) is correct because a review of prior year working papers and the permanent file may provide useful information about the nature of the business, organizational structure, operating characteristics, and transactions that may require special attention. Answer (a) is incorrect because tests of details of transactions and balances occur subsequent to planning. Answer (c) is incorrect because while reading specialized industry journals will help the auditor to obtain a better understanding of the client's industry, it is likely to be less helpful than reviewing the working papers. Answer (d) is incorrect because a reevaluation of the client's internal control environment occurs subsequent to the ordinal planning of the audit.

82. (d)   The requirement is to determine why an auditor obtains knowledge about a new client's business and its industry. Answer (d) is correct because obtaining a level of knowledge of the client's business and industry enables the CPA to obtain an understanding of the events, transactions,

and practices that, in the CPA's judgment, may have a significant effect on the financial statements. Answer (a) is incorrect because providing constructive suggestions is a secondary, and not the primary, reason for obtaining knowledge about a client's business and industry. Answer (b) is incorrect because while a CPA must develop an attitude of professional skepticism concerning a client, this attitude is not obtained by obtaining knowledge about the client's business and industry. Answer (c) is incorrect because information on the business and industry of a client will provide only limited information in determining whether financial statements are materially misstated, and numerous other factors are considered in evaluating audit findings.

83. (c)   The requirement is to identify the **least** likely procedure to be performed in planning a financial statement audit. Answer (c) is correct because selecting a sample of vendors' invoices for comparison to receiving reports will occur normally as a part of the evidence accumulation process, not as a part of the planning of an audit. Answer (a) is incorrect because coordination of the assistance of entity personnel in data preparation occurs during planning. Answer (b) is incorrect because while planning the audit, CPAs may discuss matters that affect the audit with firm personnel responsible for providing nonaudit services to the entity. Answer (d) is incorrect because any available current year interim financial statements will be read during the planning stage.

C.1.   Communicate with Predecessor Auditors (Subsequent to Engagement Acceptance)

84. (a)   The requirement is to identify whether a predecessor auditor should permit a successor auditor to review working paper analyses relating to contingencies, balance sheet accounts, or both. Answer (a) is correct because AU 315 states that a predecessor auditor should ordinarily permit the successor to review working papers, including documentation of planning, internal control, audit results, and other matters of continuing accounting and auditing significance, such as the working paper analysis of balance sheet accounts and those relating to contingencies.

85. (d)   The requirement is to determine a successor auditor's responsibility when financial statements audited by a predecessor auditor are found to require substantial revisions. Answer (d) is correct because when a successor auditor becomes aware of information that indicates that financial statements reported on by the predecessor may require revision, the successor should request that the client arrange a meeting among the three parties to discuss and attempt to resolve the matter. Answer (a) is incorrect because the successor is not required to notify the audit committee and stockholders. Answer (b) is incorrect because the client should first communicate with the predecessor before revising the financial statements. Answer (c) is incorrect because a meeting of the three parties is arranged by the client and because the situation may or may not have anything to do with the integrity of management.

86. (c)   The requirement is to determine whether a successor auditor should request a new client to authorize the predecessor auditor to allow a review of the predecessor's engagement letter, working papers, or both. Answer (c) is correct because AU 315 states that it is advisable that a successor auditor request to be allowed to review the predecessor's working papers.

C.2. Perform Analytical Procedures

87. (b)   The requirement is to identify the audit procedure that an auditor will most likely perform in planning a financial statement audit. Answer (b) is correct because AU 329 requires that an auditor perform analytical procedures such as comparing the financial statements to anticipated results during the planning stage of an audit. Answers (a), (c), and (d) are all incorrect because these procedures will all occur subsequent to planning.

88. (c)   The requirement is to determine the proper focus of analytical procedures used in planning an audit. Answer (c) is correct because analytical procedures used in planning should focus on (1) enhancing the auditor's understanding of the client's business and the transactions and events that have occurred since the last audit date, and (2) identifying areas that may represent specific risks relevant to the audit. Answer (a) is incorrect because while analytical procedures performed as substantive tests may affect the scope of other substantive tests and of tests of controls, analytical procedures used in planning generally do not. Answer (b) is incorrect because the general nature of analytical procedures used in planning provide only very limited assurance that potential misstatements will be identified; analytical procedures used as substantive tests provide a level of assurance that potential misstatements will be identified. Answer (d) is incorrect because analytical procedures performed at the review stage of audits more directly relate to assessing the adequacy of the available evidence.

89. (a)   The requirement is to identify the objective of performing analytical procedures in planning an audit. Answer (a) is correct because AU 329 states that the objective of such procedures during planning is to identify such things as the existence of unusual transactions and events, amounts, ratios and trends that might indicate matters that have financial statement and audit planning ramifications. Answers (b), (c), and (d) are all incorrect because while analytical procedures may lead to the discovery of illegal acts, related-party transactions, and unauthorized transactions, this is not the primary objective.

90. (c)   The requirement is to identify the type of nonfinancial information an auditor would most likely consider in performing analytical procedures during the planning phase of an audit. Answer (c) is correct because the square footage of selling space may be used in considering the overall reasonableness of sales. Answer (a) is incorrect because while the turnover of personnel in the accounting department may provide a measure of risk relating to the accounting function, it is not ordinarily used in performing analytical procedures. Similarly, answer (b) is incorrect because while the objectivity of audit committee members is an important consideration, it is not ordinarily used in performing analytical procedures. Answer (d) is also incorrect because management's plans to repurchase stock is not directly related to analytical procedures. See AU 329 for information on analytical procedures.

C.4. Supervision Requirements

91. (b)   The requirement is to identify the information that is most likely to be communicated by a supervisor to staff assistants. Answer (b) is correct because staff assistants must be aware of how their procedures should be evaluated in order to perform these procedures effectively.

Answer (a) is incorrect because some immaterial fraud may be reported to the client's audit committee. Answer (c) is incorrect because the emphasis in an audit must be on performing the audit effectively and not merely on adhering to time budgets. Answer (d) is incorrect because decisions regarding transferring documents from the current file to the permanent file are generally of less importance than the procedure suggested by answer (b).

92. (b)   The requirement is to determine why the work of each assistant should be reviewed. Answer (b) is correct because AU 311 suggests that the work performed by each assistant should be reviewed to determine whether it was adequately performed and to evaluate whether the results are consistent with the conclusions to be presented in the auditor's report. Answer (a) is incorrect because CPA firms, not individual auditors within the firms, have systems of quality control. Answer (c) is incorrect because the professional standards do not in general approve specific audit procedures. Answer (d) is incorrect because while determining that the audit has been performed by persons having adequate technical training and proficiency as auditors is important, it should be addressed prior to the commencement of fieldwork.

D.   Assess the Risks of Material Misstatement and Design Further Audit Procedures

93. (c)   The requirement is to identify the next step in assessing the risks of material misstatement after auditors identify risks, relate risks to what could go wrong, and consider the magnitude of risks. Answer (c) is correct because the professional standards suggest that auditors should then consider the likelihood that risks involved could result in material misstatements. Answer (a) is incorrect because the assessment is not limited to illegal acts. Answer (b) is incorrect because the complexity of transactions is not next to be considered. Answer (d) is incorrect because determining materiality levels occurs prior to this stage of the audit.

94. (b)   The requirement is to identify whether substantive tests of details and/or risk assessment procedures are considered further audit procedures that may be designed after assessing the risks of material misstatement. Further audit procedures are composed of substantive procedures (tests of details and analytical procedures) and tests of controls. Answer (b) is correct because while substantive tests of details are further audit procedures, risk assessment procedures are not. Answer (a) is incorrect because risk assessment procedures are not further audit procedures. Answer (c) is incorrect because substantive tests of details are further audit procedures and because risk assessment procedures are not. Answer (d) is incorrect because substantive tests of details are further audit procedures.

95. (b)   The requirement is to identify the procedure that is **least** likely to be considered a risk assessment procedure. Answer (b) is correct because confirmation is a substantive test, rather than a risk assessment procedure. Answers (a), (b), and (c) are all risk assessment procedures, as are certain inquiries of others outside the entity.

96. (d)   Answer (d) is correct because significant risks often involve accounting estimates or complex accounting that involves significant judgments. Answer (a) is incorrect because routine, high-volume transactions typically have lower risk. Answer (b) is incorrect because significant risks do require special audit attention. Answer (c) is incorrect because significant risks involve items with high levels of inherent risk.

E.1.   Other Responsibilities

97.   (b)   The requirement is to identify the definition of assurance services. Answer (b) is correct because the Special Committee on Assurance Services, also referred to as the Elliott Committee, defined assurance services as independent professional services that improve the quality of information, or its context, for decision makers. Answer (a) is incorrect because the definition does not include a statement on a written communication or a conclusion. Answer (c) is incorrect because not all consulting services are included as assurance services, and because the definition differs. Answer (d) is incorrect because it abstracts a portion of the definition of an attest engagement that is not included in the definition of an assurance service.

98.   (c)   The requirement is to identify the organization that was formed to analyze and report on the current state and future of the audit/assurance function and trends shaping its environment. Answer (c) is correct because it was the Special Committee on Assurance Services, also referred to as the "Elliott Committee," that was established to analyze and report on the current state and future of the audit/assurance function and trends shaping its environment. Answer (a) is incorrect because the Commission on Auditors' Responsibilities, a similar but much earlier committee, was charged with developing conclusions and recommendation regarding the appropriate responsibilities of independent auditors in 1974. Answer (b) is incorrect because the Committee of Sponsoring Organizations is primarily concerned with internal control. Answer (d) is incorrect because no committee with that name has been established.

99.   (b)   The requirement is to identify the service that is **not** a type of attest engagement. Answer (b) is correct because compilations are not considered attest engagements. Answers (a), (c), and (d) are incorrect because AT 101 establishes agreed-upon procedures for engagements, examinations, and reviews as the three basic types of attest engagements.

100.   (a)   The requirement is to identify a conceptual difference between the attestation standards and generally accepted auditing standards. Answer (a) is correct because AT 101 states that the attestation standards do not apply to audits of historical financial statements. Answer (b) is incorrect because an independent mental attitude is required for attestation engagements. Answer (c) is incorrect because an attest engagement may be related to a business acquisition study or a feasibility study. Answer (d) is incorrect because while there is no internal control fieldwork standard under the attestation standards, both a planning and an evidence standard of fieldwork are included.

101.   (d)   The requirement is to identify the reply which is **not** an attestation standard. Answer (d) is correct because the attestation standards do not include a requirement that a sufficient understanding of internal control be obtained to plan the engagement. There is no internal control standard because the concept of internal control may not be relevant to certain assertions on which a CPA may be engaged to report (e.g., aspects of information about computer software). Answers (a), (b), and (c) are all incorrect because

standards exist for evidence, reporting on the assertion or subject matter, and proper planning.

102.   (a)   The requirement is to determine who, at a minimum, must have knowledge of the relevant professional accounting and auditing standards when an audit is being performed. Answer (a) is correct because AU 230 requires that, at a minimum, the auditor with final responsibility have such knowledge. Answers (b), (c), and (d) are all incorrect because they suggest a higher minimum requirement.

103.   (b)   The requirement is to determine which concept requires an attitude that includes a questioning mind and a critical assessment of audit evidence. Answer (b) is correct because AU 230 states that professional skepticism includes these qualities. Answer (a) is incorrect because due professional care is a broader concept that concerns what the independent auditor does and how well he or she does it. Answer (c) is incorrect because reasonable assurance is based on the concept that an auditor is not an insurer and his or her report does not provide absolute assurance. Answer (d) is incorrect because supervision involves the directing of the efforts of assistants who are involved in accomplishing the objectives of the audit and determining whether those objectives were accomplished.

104.   (c)   The requirement is to determine what presumption concerning management's honesty that professional skepticism requires. Answer (c) is correct because professional skepticism requires that an auditor neither assume dishonesty nor unquestioned honesty. Answers (a) and (b) are incorrect because neither honesty in the absence of fraud risk factor nor dishonesty are assumed. Answer (d) is incorrect because the concept of reasonable assurance is not directed towards management's honesty.

105.   (c)   Answer (c) is correct because AT 101 indicates that an unqualified may ordinarily refer to that assertion or to the subject matter to which the assertion relates. Answer (a) is incorrect because it suggests reporting only on the assertion. Answer (b) is incorrect because it suggests reporting only on the subject matter. Answer (d) is incorrect because it suggests that reporting on neither the assertion nor the subject matter is appropriate. Note, however, that AT 101 also states that when a deviation from the criteria being reported upon exists (e.g., a material weakness in internal control) the CPA should report directly upon the subject matter and not upon the assertion.

E.2.   Audit

106.   (c)   The requirement is to identify the characteristic that is most likely to be unique to the audit work of CPAs as compared to work performed by practitioners of other professions. Answer (c) is correct because independence is absolutely required for the performance of audits; other professions do not in general require such independence. Answers (a), (b), and (d) are incorrect because the various professions require due professional care and competence and have a complex body of knowledge.

107.   (d)   The requirement is to determine what is meant by the third general standard's requirement of due care in the performance of an audit. Answer (d) is correct because due care requires critical review at every level of supervision of the work done and the judgment exercised by those assisting in the audit. Answer (a) is incorrect because the due care standard does not directly address safeguards over access to assets and records. Answer (b) is incorrect because due care does not relate to a limited review of employee fraud and illegal acts. Answer (c) is incorrect because the first general standard addresses technical training and proficiency as an auditor.

108. (a) The requirement is to identify the focus of a final wrap-up review performed by a second partner who has not been involved in the audit. Answer (a) is correct because this second or "cold" review aims at determining whether the financial statements result in fair presentation in conformity with GAAP and with whether sufficient appropriate evidence has been obtained. Answer (b) is incorrect because most frequently fraud involving the client's management and its employees have not been discovered and, even if they have been, the focus of the review is still on the fairness of presentation of the financial statements. Answers (c) and (d) are incorrect because decisions on materiality and communications with the audit committee are only two of the many matters the review may address in an effort to address fairness of presentation of the financial statements.

109. (b) The requirement is to identify the correct statement concerning an auditor's responsibilities regarding financial statements. Answer (b) is correct because an auditor may draft an entity's financial statements based on information from management's accounting system. Answer (a) is incorrect because making suggestions does not necessarily impair an auditor's independence. Answer (c) is incorrect because fair presentation of financial statements is an implicit part of management's, not the auditor's, responsibilities. Answer (d) is incorrect because an auditor's responsibilities for the audited financial statements is confined to the expression of an opinion on them.

110. (a) The requirement is to identify the listed authoritative body designated to promulgate attestation standards. Answer (a) is correct because only the Auditing Standards Board, the Accounting and Review Services Committee, and the Management Advisory Services Executive Committee have been authorized to promulgate attestation standards.

111. (b) The requirement is to identify the statement that best describes the meaning of generally accepted auditing standards. Answer (b) is correct because generally accepted auditing standards deal with measures of the quality of the performance of audit procedures. Answer (a) is incorrect because procedures relate to acts to be performed, not directly to the standards. Answer (c) is incorrect because generally accepted auditing standards have been issued by predecessor groups, as well as by the Auditing Standards Board. Answer (d) is incorrect because there may or may not be **universal** compliance with the standards.

112. (b) The requirement is to determine the proper method for handling a difference of opinion between auditors concerning interpretation of the results of an auditing procedure. Answer (b) is correct because the quality control standards require documentation of the considerations involved in the resolution of differences of opinion. Answer (a) is incorrect because the AICPA does not, in general, rule on disagreements of this nature. Answer (c) is incorrect because the disagreement relates to an auditing procedure

and therefore in most such circumstances the entity's management or its audit committee will have no particular expertise. Answer (d) is incorrect because the disagreement need not necessarily be reported to a peer review "monitoring" team.

E.3. Compilation and Review

113. (c) The requirement is to identify the type of assurance (if any) provided in a financial statement compilation report. Answer (c) is correct because the objective of a compilation is to present in the form of financial statements information that is the presentation of management (owners) without undertaking to express any assurance on the statements. Answer (a) is incorrect because accountants never provide absolute assurance. Answer (b) is incorrect because reviews result in limited (negative) assurance. Answer (d) is incorrect because audits, not compilations, provide reasonable assurance.

114. (a) The requirement is to determine an accountant's responsibility relating to knowledge of the client's accounting principles and practices when performing a compilation. Answer (a) is correct because to compile financial statements the accountant should possess a general understanding of the nature of the entity's business transactions, the form of its accounting records, the stated qualifications of its accounting personnel, the accounting basis on which the financial statements are to be presented, and the form and content of the financial statements. Answer (b) is incorrect because the accountant need not have a general understanding of the entity's controls. Answer (c) is incorrect because no such consideration of risk factors is envisioned in a compilation. Answer (d) is incorrect because no such consideration of internal control awareness of senior management is made.

115. (d) The requirement is to determine whether reproducing client-prepared financial statements without modification and preparing standard monthly journal entries are included in the provisions of Statements on Standards for Accounting and Review Services. Answer (d) is correct because AR 100 allows these services as long as the accountant's name is not associated with the financial statements.

116. (b) The requirement is to determine the effect of an immaterial direct financial interest on accountant independence. Answer (b) is correct because even immaterial direct financial interests impair the independence that is required for the performance of reviews and other attestation services. Answer (a) is incorrect because a CPA who lacks independence may compile those financial statements when this lack of independence is disclosed in the compilation report. Answer (c) is incorrect because a review report may not be issued. Answer (d) is incorrect because the CPA is not independent.

117. (d) The requirement is to identify the correct statement about unaudited personal financial statements included in a personal financial plan. Answer (d) is correct because AT 600 requires that the financial statements be used solely to assist the client and the client's advisor and not be used to obtain credit. Answer (a) is incorrect because financial statements may be presented in comparative form. Answer (b) is incorrect because omitted disclosures may be material. Answer (c) is incorrect because such financial statements may be disclosed to a non-CPA financial planner.

118. (a) The requirement is to determine a CPA's responsibilities when performing a review of a nonissuer's financial statements that contain uncorrected departures from GAAP and the CPA believes that the review report is not adequate to indicate the deficiencies. Answer (a) is correct because AR 100 states that in such circumstances the CPA should withdraw from the engagement and provide no further services with respect to those financial statements. Answers (b) and (d) are incorrect because restricting distribution is not adequate or appropriate in such a circumstance. Answer (c) is incorrect because the standards on special reports do not apply in this circumstance.

119. (d) The requirement is to identify the circumstance in which Statements on Standards for Accounting and Review Services require an accountant to prepare a report. A report is required when a CPA submits unaudited financial statements of a nonissuer (nonpublic) entity to his or her client or others. Accordingly, answer (d) is correct because when a CPA prepares financial statements a compilation report (assuming that neither a review nor an audit has been performed) is required. Answers (a), (b), and (c) are all incorrect because they are all included as services that do not constitute a submission of financial statements to a client.

120. (d) The requirement is to identify the engagement for which Statements on Standards for Accounting and Review Services establish standards and procedures. Answer (d) is correct because the Statements apply when a CPA either compiles or reviews the financial statements of a nonissuer. Answer (a) is incorrect because the Statements do not apply when the CPA is assisting in adjusting the books of account for a partnership or other organization. Answer (b) is incorrect because the Statements only apply to nonissuer (nonpublic) entities. Answer (c) is incorrect because the Statements do not apply when processing the financial data for clients of other accounting firms.

121. (c) The requirement is to identify the authoritative body designated to promulgate standards concerning an accountant's association with unaudited financial statements of an entity that is **not** required to file financial statements with an agency regulating the issuance of the entity's securities. Answer (c) is correct because the Accounting and Review Services Committee is so designated. Answer (a) is incorrect because the Financial Accounting Standards Board is the authoritative body designated to promulgate financial accounting standards. Answer (b) is incorrect because Government Accountability Office is not one of the bodies designated by the AICPA to promulgate technical standards. Answer (d) is incorrect because the Auditing Standards Board is the authoritative body designated to promulgate statements on auditing standards. ET Appendix A presents the bodies designated to promulgate technical standards.

122. (c) The requirement is to determine which of the two listed accounting services an accountant may perform **without** being required to issue a compilation or review report under the Statements on Standards for Accounting and Review Services. Answer (c) is correct because the Statements on Standards for Accounting and Review Services do not apply to preparing a working trial balance or to preparing standard monthly journal entries. See AR 100 for these and additional circumstances in which the standards do not apply. Accordingly, no compilation or review report needs to be issued when these services are provided.

E.4. Prospective Financial Statements

123. (d) The requirement is to identify what is included in the examination of a financial forecast. Answer (d) is correct because an examination of a forecast includes an evaluation of its preparation and the support underlying management's assumptions. As discussed in AT 301, an examination also includes evaluating the representation of the prospective financial statements for conformity with AICPA presentation guidelines and the issuance of an examination report. Answer (a) is incorrect because the service need not include the compiling or assembling of the financial forecast. Answer (b) is incorrect because distribution of financial forecasts need not be limited. Answer (c) is incorrect because the CPA assumes no responsibility to update management on key events. See AT 301 for information on prospective financial information.

124. (a) The requirement is to identify the circumstance in which an accountant may accept an engagement to apply agreed-upon procedures to prospective financial statements. Answer (a) is correct because AT 301 states that an accountant may accept an engagement to apply agreed-upon procedures to prospective financial statements provided that (1) the specified parties involved have participated in establishing the nature and scope of the engagement and take responsibility for the adequacy of the procedures to be performed, (2) use of the report is to be restricted to the specified parties involved, and (3) the prospective financial statements include a summary of significant assumptions. Answer (b) is incorrect because the prospective financial statements need not be examined. Answer (c) is incorrect because responsibility for the adequacy of the procedures is taken by the specified parties. Answer (d) is incorrect because a summary of findings may be provided based on the agreed-upon procedures.

E.5. Quality Control

125. (a) The requirement is to determine the factors that affect the nature and extent of a CPA firm's quality control policies and procedures. Answer (a) is correct because the nature and extent of a firm's quality control policies and procedures depend on a number of factors, including its size, the degree of operating autonomy allowed to its personnel and practice offices, the nature of its practice, its organization, and appropriate cost-benefit considerations.

126. (d) The requirement is to identify the manners in which a CPA firm may communicate its quality control policies and procedures to its personnel. Answer (d) is correct because the requirements relating to quality control standard documentation state that either orally or written are acceptable. Answers (a), (b) and (c) all include one or more inappropriate "no" replies.

127. (c) The requirement is to identify the reply that is **not** one of the elements of quality control. Answer (c) is correct because there is no quality control element on internal control. Acceptance of client relationships and specific engagements (a), human resources (b), and monitoring (d) are all elements of quality control. In addition, the following also are elements of quality control: leadership responsibilities for engagement performance, quality within the firm, and relevant ethical requirements.

128. (d) The requirement is to determine the types of services to which Statements on Quality Control Standards apply. Answer (d) is correct because the standards explicitly limit application to auditing and accounting and review services. Although the quality control standards may be applied to other segments of a firm's practice (e.g., management advisory services and tax), the standards do not require it.

129. (a) The requirement is to determine how a CPA firm obtains reasonable assurance of providing professional services that conform with professional standards. Answer (a) is correct because a system of quality control is designed to provide a CPA firm with reasonable assurance of meeting its responsibility to provide professional services that conform with professional standards. Answer (b) is incorrect because a peer review provides information on whether a CPA firm is following an appropriate system of quality control. Answer (c) is incorrect because it is less complete than answer (a) since continuing professional education helps achieve the specific quality control element of professional development. Answer (d) is incorrect because complying with generally accepted reporting standards is only one part of the basic objective of providing professional services that conform with professional standards.

E.6. Public Company Accounting Oversight Board Requirements

130. (b) The requirement is to identify the correct statement concerning PCAOB guidance that uses the term "should." Answer (a) is correct because the term "should" means that the auditor must comply with the requirements unless he or she can demonstrate that alternative actions were sufficient to achieve the objectives of the standards. Answer (a) is incorrect because terms such as "must," "shall," and "is required to" are used to indicate that the auditor must fulfill the responsibilities. Answer (c) is incorrect because terms such as "may," "might," and "could" are used when the auditor should consider performing the audit procedure. Answer (d) is incorrect because no particular terms are used for the situation in which the auditor has complete discretion whether to perform the procedure.

131. (c) The requirement is to determine the set of standards that the PCAOB does *not* have authority to establish. Answer (c) is correct because the FASB establishes accounting standards for both public and nonpublic companies. Answer (a) is incorrect because the PCAOB has authority to issue auditing standards. Answer (b) is incorrect because the PCAOB has the authority to issue quality control standards. Answer (d) is incorrect because the PCAOB has the authority to issue independence standards.

SOLUTION TO SIMULATION PROBLEMS

Simulation Problem 1

Situation	Audit and Fraud Risk	Fraud Discussion	Research	Communication

	Factor	Increased audit risk	Decreased audit risk	Fraud risk factor
1.	Branch management authority	●	○	●
2.	Government regulation	○	●	○
3.	Company profitability	○	●	○
4.	Demand for product	○	●	○
5.	Interest rates	●	○	○
6.	Availability of mortgage funds	○	●	○
7.	Involvement of principal shareholder in management	○	●	○
8.	Branch manager compensation	●	○	●
9.	Internal audit reporting relationship	○	●	○
10.	Accounting department turnover	○	●	○
11.	Continuing audit relationship	○	●	○
12.	Internal controls over accounting estimates	●	○	●
13.	Response to proposed accounting adjustments	○	●	○
14.	New unprofitable branch	●	○	●
15.	New computer system	●	○	○

Situation	Audit and Fraud Risk	Fraud Discussion	Research	Communication

	Risk	High risk item
1.	Computer fraud risk	○
2.	Risk related to management override of internal control[1]	●
3.	Fraud by branch management	●
4.	Fraud by accounting personnel	○
5.	Misstatement of accounting estimates	●
6.	Fraud by loan processing clerks	○
7.	Fraud by internal auditors	○
8.	The risk of fraudulent misstatement of revenues[1]	●

Situation	Audit and Fraud Risk	Fraud Discussion	Research	Communication

To get the appropriate guidance you could search on Statement on Auditing Standards No. 99, or AU Section 316 and then scan the documentation requirements. Alternatively, a word search with "fraud" and "documenting" would get you right to the appropriate place in the literature. The excerpt from the literature is shown below.

---

[1] *Required points for these types of discussions.*

83. The auditor should document the following:

- The discussion among engagement personnel in planning the audit regarding the susceptibility of the entity's financial statements to material misstatement due to fraud, including how and when the discussion occurred, the audit team members who participated, and the subject matter discussed. (See paragraphs 14 through 17.)
- The procedures performed to obtain information necessary to identify and assess the risks of material misstatement due to fraud. (See paragraphs 19 through 34.)
- Specific risks of material misstatement due to fraud that were identified (see paragraphs 35 through 45), and a description of the auditor's response to those risks. (See paragraphs 46 through 56.)
- If the auditor has not identified in a particular circumstance, improper revenue recognition as a risk of material misstatement due to fraud, the reasons supporting the auditor's conclusion. (See paragraph 41.)
- The results of the procedures performed to further address the risk of management override of controls. (See paragraphs 58 through 67.)
- Other conditions and analytical relationships that caused the auditor to believe that additional auditing procedures or other responses were required and any further responses the auditor concluded were appropriate, to address such risks or other conditions. (See paragraphs 68 through 73.)
- The nature of the communications about fraud made to management, the audit committee, and others. (See paragraphs 79 through 82.)

Situation	Audit and Fraud Risk	Fraud Discussion	Research	Communication

To: Audit Working Papers
From: CPA Candidate
Re: Staff discussion regarding fraud

This memorandum is designed to explain the requirements and purpose of the required staff discussion about fraud. SAS No. 99, *Consideration of Fraud in a Financial Statement Audit*, requires the staff to have a discussion of how and where fraud might be perpetrated. The discussion must also emphasize the importance of maintaining professional skepticism during the audit. Participants to the discussion should include the partner in charge of the audit, along with other members of the audit staff. The purpose of the discussion is to focus the audit team on those areas that might have a higher risk of fraud.

If you have any additional questions, please talk to your supervisor.

Simulation Problem 2

Situation	Nonattest Services	Auditing Standards	Research	Communication

Service	May provide, independence is required	May provide, independence is not required	May not provide
1. Provide an opinion on whether financial statements are prepared following the cash basis of accounting.	●	○	○
2. Compile a forecast for the coming year.	○	●	○
3. Compile the financial statements for the past year and issue a publicly available report.	○	●	○
4. Apply certain agreed-upon procedures to accounts receivable for purposes of obtaining a loan, and express a summary of findings relating to those procedures.	●	○	○
5. Review quarterly information and issue a report that includes limited assurance.	●	○	○
6. Perform an audit of the financial statements on whether they are prepared following generally accepted accounting principles.	●	○	○
7. Perform a review of a forecast the company has prepared for the coming year.	○	○	●
8. Compile the financial statements for the past year, but not issue a report since the financial statements are only for the company's use.	○	●	○

	Service	*May provide, independence is required*	*May provide, independence is not required*	*May not provide*
9.	Calculate the client's taxes and fill out the appropriate tax forms.	○	●	○
10.	Design a new payroll system for Hanmei and base billings on Hanmei's actual savings for the next three years.	○	●	○

Situation	Nonattest Services	Auditing Standards	Research	Communication

Transactions

		(A)	(B)	(C)	(D)	(E)	(F)	(G)	(H)	(I)
1.	Possible risk factors related to misappropriation of assets.	○	○	○	●	○	○	○	○	○
2.	The relationship between materiality used for planning versus evaluation purposes.	○	●	○	○	○	○	○	○	○
3.	Hanmei Corp. has transactions with the corporation president's brother.	○	○	○	○	○	○	○	○	●
4.	Comparing a client's unaudited results for the year with last year's audited results.	●	○	○	○	○	○	○	○	○
5.	Auditing and reporting guidance on the possible need to reaudit previous year results due to the disbanding of the firm that performed last year's audit.	○	○	●	○	○	○	○	○	○
6.	Requirements relating to identifying violations of occupational safety and health regulations.	○	○	○	○	○	●	○	○	○
7.	Audit report considerations when audit of a subsidiary of the client will be performed by Williams & Co., CPAs.	○	○	○	○	○	○	○	●	○
8.	The need to "brainstorm" among audit team members about how accounts could be intentionally misstated.	○	○	○	●	○	○	○	○	○
9.	Details on considering design effectiveness of controls.	○	○	○	○	●	○	○	○	○
10.	The importance of considering the possibility of overstated revenues (for example, through premature revenue recognition).	○	○	○	●	○	○	○	○	○

Situation	Nonattest Services	Auditing Standards	Research	Communication

SAS 109, para 9 and 10 provides the necessary information.

1. Information generally included

9. An understanding with the client regarding an audit of the financial statements generally includes the following matters:

- The objective of the audit is the expression of an opinion on the financial statements.
- Management is responsible for the entity's financial statements and the selection and application of the accounting policies.
- Management is responsible for establishing and maintaining effective internal control over financial reporting.
- Management is responsible for designing and implementing programs and controls to prevent and detect fraud.
- Management is responsible for identifying and ensuring that the entity complies with the laws and regulations applicable to its activities.
- Management is responsible for making all financial records and related information available to the auditor.
- At the conclusion of the engagement, management will provide the auditor with a letter that confirms certain representations made during the audit.
- The auditor is responsible for conducting the audit in accordance with generally accepted auditing standards. Those standards require that the auditor obtain reasonable rather than absolute assurance about whether the financial statements are free of material misstatement, whether caused by error or fraud. Accordingly, a material misstatement may remain undetected. Also, an audit is

not designed to detect error or fraud that is immaterial to the financial statements. If, for any reason, the auditor is unable to complete the audit or is unable to form or has not formed an opinion, he or she may decline to express an opinion or decline to issue a report as a result of the engagement.

- An audit includes obtaining an understanding of the entity and its environment, including its internal control, sufficient to assess the risks of material misstatement of the financial statements and to design the nature, timing, and extent of further audit procedures. An audit is not designed to provide assurance on internal control or to identify significant deficiencies. However, the auditor is responsible for ensuring that those charged with governance are aware of any significant deficiencies that come to his or her attention.
- Management is responsible for adjusting the financial statements to correct material misstatements and for affirming to the auditor in the management representation letter that the effects of any uncorrected misstatements aggregated by the auditor during the current engagement and pertaining to the latest period presented are immaterial, both individually and in the aggregate, to the financial statements taken as a whole.

These matters should be communicated in the form of an engagement letter.

10. An understanding with the client may also include other matters, such as the following:

- The overall audit strategy
- Involvement of specialists or internal auditors, if applicable
- Arrangements involving a predecessor auditor
- Involvement of specialists or internal auditors, if applicable
- Involvement of a predecessor auditor
- Fees and billing
- Any limitation of or other arrangements regarding the liability of the auditor or the client, such as indemnification to the auditor for liability arising from knowing misrepresentations to the auditor by management (regulators may restrict or prohibit such liability limitation arrangements)
- Conditions under which access to audit documentation may be granted to others
- Other services to be provided in connection with the engagement, for example, nonattest services, such as accounting assistance and preparation of tax returns subject to the limitation of Ethics Interpretation No. 101-3, "Performance of Nonattest Services," under Rule 101, *Independence*

Situation	Nonattest Services	Auditing Standards	Research	Communication

To: Ms. Caroline Smith, Chairperson of the Audit Committee
From: CPA Candidate
Re: Independence

You have asked why independence is required to perform an audit in accordance with generally accepted auditing standards. This memorandum is designed to answer that question.

The purpose of an audit is to lend credibility to your company's financial statements by acquiring an audit opinion. Only by maintaining our independence will users, such as stockholders and financial institutions, believe that our opinion is objective and not subject to bias. We must not only maintain independence; in fact, we must also avoid relationships and investments that would cause others to question our independence.

If you need any additional information about these requirements, please contact me.

MULTIPLE-CHOICE QUESTIONS (1-166)

1. Which of the following most likely would **not** be considered an inherent limitation of the potential effectiveness of an entity's internal control?
a. Incompatible duties.
b. Management override.
c. Mistakes in judgment.
d. Collusion among employees.

2. When considering internal control, an auditor should be aware of the concept of reasonable assurance, which recognizes that
a. Internal control may be ineffective due to mistakes in judgment and personal carelessness.
b. Adequate safeguards over access to assets and records should permit an entity to maintain proper accountability.
c. Establishing and maintaining internal control is an important responsibility of management.
d. The cost of an entity's internal control should **not** exceed the benefits expected to be derived.

3. Proper segregation of functional responsibilities calls for separation of the functions of
a. Authorization, execution, and payment.
b. Authorization, recording, and custody.
c. Custody, execution, and reporting.
d. Authorization, payment, and recording.

4. An entity's ongoing monitoring activities often include
a. Periodic audits by the audit committee.
b. Reviewing the purchasing function.
c. The audit of the annual financial statements.
d. Control risk assessment in conjunction with quarterly reviews.

5. The overall attitude and awareness of an entity's board of directors concerning the importance of internal control usually is reflected in its
a. Computer-based controls.
b. System of segregation of duties.
c. Control environment.
d. Safeguards over access to assets.

6. Management philosophy and operating style most likely would have a significant influence on an entity's control environment when
a. The internal auditor reports directly to management.
b. Management is dominated by one individual.
c. Accurate management job descriptions delineate specific duties.
d. The audit committee actively oversees the financial reporting process.

7. Which of the following factors are included in an entity's control environment?

	Audit committee	Integrity and ethical values	Organizational
a.	Yes	Yes	No
b.	Yes	No	Yes
c.	No	Yes	Yes
d.	Yes	Yes	Yes

8. Which of the following is **not** a component of an entity's internal control?

a. Control risk.
b. Control activities.
c. Monitoring.
d. Control environment.

9. Which of the following is a provision of the Foreign Corrupt Practices Act?
a. It is a criminal offense for an auditor to fail to detect and report a bribe paid by an American business entity to a foreign official for the purpose of obtaining business.
b. The auditor's detection of illegal acts committed by officials of the auditor's publicly held client in conjunction with foreign officials should be reported to the Enforcement Division of the Securities and Exchange Commission.
c. If the auditor of a publicly held company concludes that the effects on the financial statements of a bribe given to a foreign official are **not** susceptible of reasonable estimation, the auditor's report should be modified.
d. Every publicly held company must devise, document, and maintain internal control sufficient to provide reasonable assurances that internal control objectives are met.

10. An auditor suspects that certain client employees are ordering merchandise for themselves over the Internet without recording the purchase or receipt of the merchandise. When vendors' invoices arrive, one of the employees approves the invoices for payment. After the invoices are paid, the employee destroys the invoices and the related vouchers. In gathering evidence regarding the fraud, the auditor most likely would select items for testing from the file of all
a. Cash disbursements.
b. Approved vouchers.
c. Receiving reports.
d. Vendors' invoices.

11. Which of the following procedures most likely would provide an auditor with evidence about whether an entity's internal control activities are suitably designed to prevent or detect material misstatements?
a. Reperforming the activities for a sample of transactions.
b. Performing analytical procedures using data aggregated at a high level.
c. Vouching a sample of transactions directly related to the activities.
d. Observing the entity's personnel applying the activities.

12. Which statement is correct concerning the relevance of various types of controls to a financial audit?
a. An auditor may ordinarily ignore a consideration of controls when a substantive audit approach is taken.
b. Controls over the reliability of financial reporting are ordinarily most directly relevant to an audit, but other controls may also be relevant.
c. Controls over safeguarding of assets and liabilities are of primary importance, while controls over the reliability of financial reporting may also be relevant.
d. All controls are ordinarily relevant to an audit.

13. In an audit of financial statements in accordance with generally accepted auditing standards, an auditor is required to
    a. Document the auditor's understanding of the entity's internal control.
    b. Search for significant deficiencies in the operation of internal control.
    c. Perform tests of controls to evaluate the effectiveness of the entity's internal control.
    d. Determine whether controls are suitably designed to prevent or detect material misstatements.

14. In obtaining an understanding of an entity's internal control relevant to audit planning, an auditor is required to obtain knowledge about the
    a. Design of the controls pertaining to internal control components.
    b. Effectiveness of controls that have been implemented.
    c. Consistency with which controls are currently being applied.
    d. Controls related to each principal transaction class and account balance.

15. An auditor should obtain sufficient knowledge of an entity's information system to understand the
    a. Safeguards used to limit access to computer facilities.
    b. Process used to prepare significant accounting estimates.
    c. Controls used to assure proper authorization of transactions.
    d. Controls used to detect the concealment of fraud.

16. When obtaining an understanding of an entity's internal control, an auditor should concentrate on the substance of controls rather than their form because
    a. The controls may be operating effectively but may **not** be documented.
    b. Management may establish appropriate controls but **not** enforce compliance with them.
    c. The controls may be so inappropriate that **no** reliance is contemplated by the auditor.
    d. Management may implement controls whose costs exceed their benefits.

17. Decision tables differ from program flowcharts in that decision tables emphasize
    a. Ease of manageability for complex programs.
    b. Logical relationships among conditions and actions.
    c. Cost benefit factors justifying the program.
    d. The sequence in which operations are performed.

18. During the consideration of internal control in a financial statement audit, an auditor is **not** obligated to
    a. Search for significant deficiencies in the operation of the internal control.
    b. Understand the internal control and the information system.
    c. Determine whether the control activities relevant to audit planning have been implemented.
    d. Perform procedures to understand the design of internal control.

19. A primary objective of procedures performed to obtain an understanding of internal control is to provide an auditor with
    a. Knowledge necessary to assess the risks of material misstatements.
    b. Evidence to use in assessing inherent risk.
    c. A basis for modifying tests of controls.
    d. An evaluation of the consistency of application of management's policies.

20. Which of the following statements regarding auditor documentation of the client's internal control is correct?
    a. Documentation must include flowcharts.
    b. Documentation must include procedural write-ups.
    c. No documentation is necessary although it is desirable.
    d. No one particular form of documentation is necessary, and the extent of documentation may vary.

21. In obtaining an understanding of an entity's internal control, an auditor is required to obtain knowledge about the

	Operating effectiveness of controls	Design of controls
a.	Yes	Yes
b.	No	Yes
c.	Yes	No
d.	No	No

22. Which of the following may not be required on a particular audit of a nonissuer (nonpublic) company?
    a. Risk assessment procedures.
    b. Tests of controls.
    c. Substantive procedures.
    d. Analytical procedures.

23. Control risk should be assessed in terms of
    a. Specific controls.
    b. Types of potential fraud.
    c. Financial statement assertions.
    d. Control environment factors.

24. After assessing control risk, an auditor desires to seek a further reduction in the assessed level of control risk. At this time, the auditor would consider whether
    a. It would be efficient to obtain an understanding of the entity's information system.
    b. The entity's controls have been implemented.
    c. The entity's controls pertain to any financial statement assertions.
    d. Additional audit evidence sufficient to support a further reduction is likely to be available.

25. Assessing control risk at a low level most likely would involve
    a. Performing more extensive substantive tests with larger sample sizes than originally planned.
    b. Reducing inherent risk for most of the assertions relevant to significant account balances.
    c. Changing the timing of substantive tests by omitting interim-date testing and performing the tests at year-end.
    d. Identifying specific controls relevant to specific assertions.

26. An auditor assesses control risk because it
    a. Is relevant to the auditor's understanding of the control environment.

b. Provides assurance that the auditor's materiality levels are appropriate.

c. Indicates to the auditor where inherent risk may be the greatest.

d. Affects the level of detection risk that the auditor may accept.

27. When an auditor increases the assessed level of control risk because certain control activities were determined to be ineffective, the auditor would most likely increase the

a. Extent of tests of controls.

b. Level of detection risk.

c. Extent of tests of details.

d. Level of inherent risk.

28. An auditor uses the knowledge provided by the understanding of internal control and the assessed level of the risk of material misstatement primarily to

a. Determine whether procedures and records concerning the safeguarding of assets are reliable.

b. Ascertain whether the opportunities to allow any person to both perpetrate and conceal fraud are minimized.

c. Modify the initial assessments of inherent risk and preliminary judgments about materiality levels.

d. Determine the nature, timing, and extent of substantive tests for financial statement assertions.

29. An auditor may compensate for a weakness in internal control by increasing the

a. Level of detection risk.

b. Extent of tests of controls.

c. Preliminary judgment about audit risk.

d. Extent of analytical procedures.

30. Which of the following statements is correct concerning an auditor's assessment of control risk?

a. Assessing control risk may be performed concurrently during an audit with obtaining an understanding of the entity's internal control.

b. Evidence about the operation of internal control in prior audits may not be considered during the current year's assessment of control risk.

c. The basis for an auditor's conclusions about the assessed level of control risk need not be documented unless control risk is assessed at the maximum level.

d. The lower the assessed level of control risk, the less assurance the evidence must provide that the control procedures are operating effectively.

31. Regardless of the assessed level of control risk, an auditor would perform some

a. Tests of controls to determine the effectiveness of internal control policies.

b. Analytical procedures to verify the design of internal control.

c. Substantive tests to restrict detection risk for significant transaction classes.

d. Dual-purpose tests to evaluate both the risk of monetary misstatement and preliminary control risk.

32. How frequently must an auditor test operating effectiveness of controls that appear to function as they have in past years and on which the auditor wishes to rely in the current year?

a. Monthly.

b. Each audit.

c. At least every second audit.

d. At least every third audit.

33. Before assessing control risk at a level lower than the maximum, the auditor obtains reasonable assurance that controls are in use and operating effectively. This assurance is most likely obtained in part by

a. Preparing flowcharts.

b. Performing substantive tests.

c. Analyzing tests of trends and ratios.

d. Inspection of documents.

34. An auditor generally tests the segregation of duties related to inventory by

a. Personal inquiry and observation.

b. Test counts and cutoff procedures.

c. Analytical procedures and invoice recomputation.

d. Document inspection and reconciliation.

35. The objective of tests of details of transactions performed as tests of controls is to

a. Monitor the design and use of entity documents such as prenumbered shipping forms.

b. Determine whether controls have been implemented.

c. Detect material misstatements in the account balances of the financial statements.

d. Evaluate whether controls operated effectively.

36. After obtaining an understanding of internal control and assessing the risk of material misstatement, an auditor decided to perform tests of controls. The auditor most likely decided that

a. It would be efficient to perform tests of controls that would result in a reduction in planned substantive tests.

b. Additional evidence to support a further reduction in the risk of material misstatement is **not** available.

c. An increase in the assessed level of the risk of material misstatement is justified for certain financial statement assertions.

d. There were many internal control weaknesses that could allow misstatements to enter the accounting system.

37. In assessing control risk, an auditor ordinarily selects from a variety of techniques, including

a. Inquiry and analytical procedures.

b. Reperformance and observation.

c. Comparison and confirmation.

d. Inspection and verification.

38. Which of the following types of evidence would an auditor most likely examine to determine whether controls are operating as designed?

a. Confirmations of receivables verifying account balances.

b. Letters of representations corroborating inventory pricing.

c. Attorneys' responses to the auditor's inquiries.

d. Client records documenting the use of computer programs.

39. Which of the following is **not** a step in an auditor's assessment of control risk?
- a. Evaluate the effectiveness of internal control with tests of controls.
- b. Obtain an understanding of the entity's information system and control environment.
- c. Perform tests of details of transactions to detect material misstatements in the financial statements.
- d. Consider whether controls can have a pervasive effect on financial statement assertions.

40. To obtain audit evidence about control risk, an auditor selects tests from a variety of techniques including
- a. Inquiry.
- b. Analytical procedures.
- c. Calculation.
- d. Confirmation.

41. Which of the following is **least** likely to be evidence the auditor examines to determine whether controls are operating effectively?
- a. Records documenting usage of computer programs.
- b. Canceled supporting documents.
- c. Confirmations of accounts receivable.
- d. Signatures on authorization forms.

42. Which of the following procedures concerning accounts receivable would an auditor most likely perform to obtain evidence in support of an assessed level of control risk below the maximum?
- a. Observing an entity's employee prepare the schedule of past due accounts receivable.
- b. Sending confirmation requests to an entity's principal customers to verify the existence of accounts receivable.
- c. Inspecting an entity's analysis of accounts receivable for unusual balances.
- d. Comparing an entity's uncollectible accounts expense to actual uncollectible accounts receivable.

43. The internal control provisions of the Sarbanes-Oxley Act of 2002 apply to which companies in the United States?
- a. All companies.
- b. SEC registrants.
- c. All issuer (public) companies and nonissuer (nonpublic) companies with more than $100,000,000 of net worth.
- d. All nonissuer companies.

44. The framework most likely to be used by management in its internal control assessment under requirements of the Sarbanes-Oxley Act of 2002 is the
- a. COSO internal framework.
- b. COSO enterprise risk management framework.
- c. FASB 37 internal control definitional framework.
- d. AICPA internal control analysis manager.

45. Which of the following is correct concerning the level of assistance auditors may provide in assisting management with its assessment of internal control?
- a. No assistance of any type may be provided.
- b. No limitations on assistance exist.
- c. Only very limited assistance may be provided.
- d. As less risk is assumed by the auditors, a higher level of assistance is appropriate.

46. Which of the following need **not** be included in management's report on internal control under Section 404a of the Sarbanes-Oxley Act of 2002?
- a. A statement that the company's auditor has issued an attestation report on management's assertion.
- b. Identification of the framework for evaluating internal control.
- c. Management's assessment of the effectiveness of internal control.
- d. Management's statement of responsibility to establish and maintain internal control that has no significant deficiencies.

47. Which of the following is an accurate statement about internal control weaknesses?
- a. Material weaknesses are also control deficiencies.
- b. Significant deficiencies are also material weaknesses.
- c. Control deficiencies are also material weaknesses.
- d. All control deficiencies must be communicated to the audit committee.

48. In an integrated audit, which of the following is defined as a weakness in internal control that is less severe than a material weakness but important enough to warrant attention by those responsible for oversight of the financial reporting function?
- a. Control deficiency.
- b. Unusual weakness.
- c. Unusual deficiency.
- d. Significant deficiency.

49. A material weakness is a significant deficiency (or combination of significant deficiencies) that results in a reasonable possibility that a misstatement of at least what amount will not be prevented or detected?
- a. An amount greater than zero.
- b. An amount greater than zero, but at least inconsequential.
- c. An amount greater than inconsequential.
- d. A material amount.

50. The minimum likelihood of loss involved in the consideration of a control deficiency is
- a. Remote.
- b. More than remote.
- c. Probable.
- d. Not explicitly considered.

51. Assume that a company has a control deficiency regarding the processing of cash receipts. Reconciliation of cash accounts by a competent individual otherwise independent of the cash function might make the likelihood of a significant misstatement due to the control deficiency remote. In this situation, reconciliation may be referred to as what type of control?
- a. Compensating.
- b. Preventive.
- c. Adjustive.
- d. Nonroutine.

52. According to Public Company Accounting Oversight Board Standard 5, what type of transaction involves establishing a loan loss reserve?
- a. Substantive transaction.
- b. Routine transaction.

c. Nonroutine transaction.
d. Estimation transaction.

53. A procedure that involves tracing a transaction from its origination through the company's information systems until it is reflected in the company's financial report is referred to as a(n)
a. Analytical analysis.
b. Substantive procedure.
c. Test of a control.
d. Walk-through.

54. For purposes of an audit of internal control performed under Public Company Accounting Oversight Board standards, the "as of date" is ordinarily
a. The first day of the year.
b. The last day of the fiscal period.
c. The last day of the auditor's fieldwork.
d. The average date for the entire fiscal period.

55. Consider an issuer (public) company whose purchases are made through the Internet and by telephone. Which of the following is correct?
a. These types of purchases represent control objectives for the audit of internal control.
b. These purchases are the assertions related to the purchase class of transactions.
c. These types of purchases represent two major classes of transactions within the purchases process.
d. These two types of transactions represent routine transactions that must always be investigated in extreme detail.

56. For an issuer (public) company audit of internal control, walkthroughs provide the auditor with *primary evidence* to

	Evaluate the effectiveness of the design of controls	Confirm whether controls have been placed in operation
a.	Yes	Yes
b.	Yes	No
c.	No	Yes
d.	No	No

57. Which is **most** likely to be a question asked of employee personnel during a walk-through in an audit of the internal control of an issuer (public) company?
a. Have you ever been asked to override the process?
b. Do you believe that you are underpaid?
c. What do you do when you find a fraudulent transaction?
d. Who trained you for this job?

58. How large must the *actual loss identified by the auditor* be for a control deficiency to possibly be considered a material weakness?

	Immaterial	Material
a.	Yes	Yes
b.	Yes	No
c.	No	Yes
d.	No	No

59. For purposes of an audit of internal control performed under Public Company Accounting Oversight Board requirements, an account is significant if there is more than a
a. Reasonably possible likelihood that it could contain immaterial or material misstatements.

b. Reasonably possible likelihood that it could contain material misstatements.
c. Remote likelihood that it could contain material misstatements.
d. Remote likelihood that it could contain more than inconsequential misstatements.

60. A control deficiency that is more than a significant deficiency is most likely to result in what form of audit opinion relating to internal control?
a. Adverse.
b. Qualified.
c. Unqualified.
d. Unqualified with explanatory language.

61. Which of the following is most likely to be considered a material weakness in internal control for purposes of an internal control audit of an issuer (public) company?
a. An ineffective oversight of financial reporting by the audit committee.
b. Restatement of previously issued financial statements due to a change in accounting principles.
c. Inadequate segregation of recordkeeping from accounting.
d. Weaknesses in control activities.

62. Inability to evaluate internal control due to a circumstance-caused scope limitation relating to a significant account in a Sarbanes-Oxley 404 internal control audit is most likely to result in a(n)
a. Adverse opinion.
b. Qualified opinion.
c. Unqualified opinion with explanatory language.
d. All of the above are equally likely.

63. Which of the following is most likely to indicate a significant deficiency relating to a client's antifraud programs?
a. A broad scope of internal audit activities.
b. A "whistle-blower" program that encourages anonymous submissions.
c. Audit committee passivity when conducting oversight functions.
d. Lack of performance of criminal background investigations for likely customers.

64. An auditor identified a material weakness in December. The client was informed and corrected it shortly after the "as of date" (December 31); the auditor agrees that the correction eliminates the material weakness as of January 31. The appropriate report under a PCAOB Standard 5 audit of internal control is
a. Adverse.
b. Unqualified.
c. Unqualified with explanatory language relating to the material weakness.
d. Qualified.

65. In an integrated audit, which of the following lead(s) to an adverse opinion on internal control?

	Material weaknesses	Significant deficiencies
a.	Yes	Yes
b.	Yes	No
c.	No	Yes
d.	No	No

66. In an integrated audit, what must the auditor communicate to the audit committee?

	Known material weaknesses	All control deficiencies
a.	Yes	Yes
b.	Yes	No
c.	No	Yes
d.	No	No

67. In which manner are significant deficiencies communicated by the auditors to the audit committee under Public Company Accounting Oversight Board Standard 5?

    a. The communication may either be orally or in written form.

    b. The communication must be oral, and not in written form.

    c. The communication must be in written form.

    d. No such communication is required as only material weaknesses must be communicated.

68. Which is correct concerning the external auditors' use of the work of others in an audit of internal control performed for a public company?

    a. It is not allowed.

    b. The work of internal auditors may be used, but only when those internal auditors report directly to the audit committee.

    c. Ordinarily the work of internal auditors and others is used primarily in low-risk areas.

    d. There is no limitation and is likely to reduce auditor liability since the auditors will then share legal responsibility with those who have performed the service.

69. In an integrated audit, which must the auditor communicate in writing to management?

    a. Only material weaknesses.

    b. Material weaknesses and significant deficiencies.

    c. Material weaknesses, significant deficiencies and other control deficiencies.

    d. Material weaknesses, significant deficiencies, other control deficiencies, and all suspected and possible employee law violations.

70. Which of the following is correct when applying a top-down approach to identify controls to test in an integrated audit?

    a. For certain assertions, strong entity-level controls may allow the auditor to omit additional testing beyond those controls.

    b. Starting at the top—controls over specific assertions—the auditor should link to major accounts and reporting items.

    c. The goal is to focus on details of accounting controls, while avoiding consideration of overall entity-level controls.

    d. The goal is to focus on all controls related to assertions, omitting consideration of controls related to the financial statements.

71. Which of the following is not included in a standard unqualified opinion on internal control over financial reporting performed under PCAOB requirements?

    a. Because of inherent limitations, internal control over financial reporting may not prevent or detect misstatements.

    b. In our opinion, [company name] maintained, in all material respects, effective internal control over financial reporting.

    c. Our audit included obtaining an understanding of internal control over financial reporting.

    d. The [company name] management and audit committee is responsible for maintaining effective internal control over financial reporting.

72. Walk-throughs ordinarily provide evidence that helps the auditor to

	Evaluate design effectiveness of controls	Confirm whether controls have been placed in operation
a.	Yes	Yes
b.	Yes	No
c.	No	Yes
d.	No	No

73. Which of the following procedures would an auditor most likely perform to test controls relating to management's assertion about the completeness of cash receipts for cash sales at a retail outlet?

    a. Observe the consistency of the employees' use of cash registers and tapes.

    b. Inquire about employees' access to recorded but undeposited cash.

    c. Trace deposits in the cash receipts journal to the cash balance in the general ledger.

    d. Compare the cash balance in the general ledger with the bank confirmation request.

74. Sound internal control dictates that immediately upon receiving checks from customers by mail, a responsible employee should

    a. Add the checks to the daily cash summary.

    b. Verify that each check is supported by a prenumbered sales invoice.

    c. Prepare a duplicate listing of checks received.

    d. Record the checks in the cash receipts journal.

75. Tracing shipping documents to prenumbered sales invoices provides evidence that

    a. No duplicate shipments or billings occurred.

    b. Shipments to customers were properly invoiced.

    c. All goods ordered by customers were shipped.

    d. All prenumbered sales invoices were accounted for.

76. Which of the following controls most likely would reduce the risk of diversion of customer receipts by an entity's employees?

    a. A bank lockbox system.

    b. Prenumbered remittance advices.

    c. Monthly bank reconciliations.

    d. Daily deposit of cash receipts.

77. An auditor suspects that a client's cashier is misappropriating cash receipts for personal use by lapping customer checks received in the mail. In attempting to uncover this embezzlement scheme, the auditor most likely would compare the

    a. Dates checks are deposited per bank statements with the dates remittance credits are recorded.

    b. Daily cash summaries with the sums of the cash receipts journal entries.

c. Individual bank deposit slips with the details of the monthly bank statements.
d. Dates uncollectible accounts are authorized to be written off with the dates the write-offs are actually recorded.

78. Upon receipt of customers' checks in the mailroom, a responsible employee should prepare a remittance listing that is forwarded to the cashier. A copy of the listing should be sent to the
a. Internal auditor to investigate the listing for unusual transactions.
b. Treasurer to compare the listing with the monthly bank statement.
c. Accounts receivable bookkeeper to update the subsidiary accounts receivable records.
d. Entity's bank to compare the listing with the cashier's deposit slip.

79. Which of the following procedures most likely would **not** be a control designed to reduce the risk of misstatements in the billing process?
a. Comparing control totals for shipping documents with corresponding totals for sales invoices.
b. Using computer programmed controls on the pricing and mathematical accuracy of sales invoices.
c. Matching shipping documents with approved sales orders before invoice preparation.
d. Reconciling the control totals for sales invoices with the accounts receivable subsidiary ledger.

80. Which of the following audit procedures would an auditor most likely perform to test controls relating to management's assertion concerning the completeness of sales transactions?
a. Verify that extensions and footings on the entity's sales invoices and monthly customer statements have been recomputed.
b. Inspect the entity's reports of prenumbered shipping documents that have **not** been recorded in the sales journal.
c. Compare the invoiced prices on prenumbered sales invoices to the entity's authorized price list.
d. Inquire about the entity's credit granting policies and the consistent application of credit checks.

81. Which of the following controls most likely would assure that all billed sales are correctly posted to the accounts receivable ledger?
a. Daily sales summaries are compared to daily postings to the accounts receivable ledger.
b. Each sales invoice is supported by a prenumbered shipping document.
c. The accounts receivable ledger is reconciled daily to the control account in the general ledger.
d. Each shipment on credit is supported by a prenumbered sales invoice.

82. An auditor tests an entity's policy of obtaining credit approval before shipping goods to customers in support of management's financial statement assertion of
a. Valuation or allocation.
b. Completeness.
c. Existence or occurrence.
d. Rights and obligations.

83. Which of the following controls most likely would help ensure that all credit sales transactions of an entity are recorded?
a. The billing department supervisor sends copies of approved sales orders to the credit department for comparison to authorized credit limits and current customer account balances.
b. The accounting department supervisor independently reconciles the accounts receivable subsidiary ledger to the accounts receivable control account monthly.
c. The accounting department supervisor controls the mailing of monthly statements to customers and investigates any differences reported by customers.
d. The billing department supervisor matches prenumbered shipping documents with entries in the sales journal.

84. Which of the following controls most likely would be effective in offsetting the tendency of sales personnel to maximize sales volume at the expense of high bad debt write-offs?
a. Employees responsible for authorizing sales and bad debt write-offs are denied access to cash.
b. Shipping documents and sales invoices are matched by an employee who does not have authority to write off bad debts.
c. Employees involved in the credit-granting function are separated from the sales function.
d. Subsidiary accounts receivable records are reconciled to the control account by an employee independent of the authorization of credit.

85. Proper authorization of write-offs of uncollectible accounts should be approved in which of the following departments?
a. Accounts receivable.
b. Credit.
c. Accounts payable.
d. Treasurer.

86. Employers bond employees who handle cash receipts because fidelity bonds reduce the possibility of employing dishonest individuals and
a. Protect employees who make unintentional misstatements from possible monetary damages resulting from their misstatements.
b. Deter dishonesty by making employees aware that insurance companies may investigate and prosecute dishonest acts.
c. Facilitate an independent monitoring of the receiving and depositing of cash receipts.
d. Force employees in positions of trust to take periodic vacations and rotate their assigned duties.

87. During the consideration of a small business client's internal control, the auditor discovered that the accounts receivable clerk approves credit memos and has access to cash. Which of the following controls would be most effective in offsetting this weakness?
a. The owner reviews errors in billings to customers and postings to the subsidiary ledger.
b. The controller receives the monthly bank statement directly and reconciles the checking accounts.

c.   The owner reviews credit memos after they are re-
     corded.
d.   The controller reconciles the total of the detail ac-
     counts receivable accounts to the amount shown in
     the ledger.

88. When a customer fails to include a remittance advice
with a payment, it is common practice for the person opening the mail to prepare one. Consequently, mail should be
opened by which of the following four company employees?
a.   Credit manager.
b.   Receptionist.
c.   Sales manager.
d.   Accounts receivable clerk.

89. To provide assurance that each voucher is submitted
and paid only once, an auditor most likely would examine a
sample of paid vouchers and determine whether each
voucher is
a.   Supported by a vendor's invoice.
b.   Stamped "paid" by the check signer.
c.   Prenumbered and accounted for.
d.   Approved for authorized purchases.

90. In testing controls over cash disbursements, an auditor
most likely would determine that the person who signs
checks also
a.   Reviews the monthly bank reconciliation.
b.   Returns the checks to accounts payable.
c.   Is denied access to the supporting documents.
d.   Is responsible for mailing the checks.

91. In assessing control risk for purchases, an auditor
vouches a sample of entries in the voucher register to the
supporting documents. Which assertion would this test of
controls most likely support?
a.   Completeness.
b.   Existence or occurrence.
c.   Valuation or allocation.
d.   Rights and obligations.

92. Which of the following controls is **not** usually performed in the vouchers payable department?
a.   Matching the vendor's invoice with the related re-
     ceiving report.
b.   Approving vouchers for payment by having an au-
     thorized employee sign the vouchers.
c.   Indicating the asset and expense accounts to be
     debited.
d.   Accounting for unused prenumbered purchase or-
     ders and receiving reports.

93. With properly designed internal control, the same employee most likely would match vendors' invoices with receiving reports and also
a.   Post the detailed accounts payable records.
b.   Recompute the calculations on vendors' invoices.
c.   Reconcile the accounts payable ledger.
d.   Cancel vendors' invoices after payment.

94. An entity's internal control requires for every check
request that there be an approved voucher, supported by a
prenumbered purchase order and a prenumbered receiving
report. To determine whether checks are being issued for
unauthorized expenditures, an auditor most likely would
select items for testing from the population of all
a.   Purchase orders.
b.   Canceled checks.

c.   Receiving reports.
d.   Approved vouchers.

95. Which of the following questions would most likely be
included in an internal control questionnaire concerning the
completeness assertion for purchases?
a.   Is an authorized purchase order required before the
     receiving department can accept a shipment or the
     vouchers payable department can record a
     voucher?
b.   Are purchase requisitions prenumbered and inde-
     pendently matched with vendor invoices?
c.   Is the unpaid voucher file periodically reconciled
     with inventory records by an employee who does
     not have access to purchase requisitions?
d.   Are purchase orders, receiving reports, and vouch-
     ers prenumbered and periodically accounted for?

96. For effective internal control, the accounts payable department generally should
a.   Stamp, perforate, or otherwise cancel supporting
     documentation after payment is mailed.
b.   Ascertain that each requisition is approved as to
     price, quantity, and quality by an authorized em-
     ployee.
c.   Obliterate the quantity ordered on the receiving de-
     partment copy of the purchase order.
d.   Establish the agreement of the vendor's invoice
     with the receiving report and purchase order.

97. Internal control is strengthened when the quantity of
merchandise ordered is omitted from the copy of the purchase order sent to the
a.   Department that initiated the requisition.
b.   Receiving department.
c.   Purchasing agent.
d.   Accounts payable department.

98. A client erroneously recorded a large purchase twice.
Which of the following internal control measures would be
most likely to detect this error in a timely and efficient manner?
a.   Footing the purchases journal.
b.   Reconciling vendors' monthly statements with sub-
     sidiary payable ledger accounts.
c.   Tracing totals from the purchases journal to the
     ledger accounts.
d.   Sending written quarterly confirmations to all ven-
     dors.

99. With well-designed internal control, employees in the
same department most likely would approve purchase orders, and also
a.   Reconcile the open invoice file.
b.   Inspect goods upon receipt.
c.   Authorize requisitions of goods.
d.   Negotiate terms with vendors.

100. In obtaining an understanding of a manufacturing entity's internal control over inventory balances, an auditor
most likely would
a.   Analyze the liquidity and turnover ratios of the in-
     ventory.
b.   Perform analytical procedures designed to identify
     cost variances.
c.   Review the entity's descriptions of inventory poli-
     cies and procedures.

d. Perform test counts of inventory during the entity's physical count.

101. Which of the following controls most likely would be used to maintain accurate inventory records?
a. Perpetual inventory records are periodically compared with the current cost of individual inventory items.
b. A just-in-time inventory ordering system keeps inventory levels to a desired minimum.
c. Requisitions, receiving reports, and purchase orders are independently matched before payment is approved.
d. Periodic inventory counts are used to adjust the perpetual inventory records.

102. A client maintains perpetual inventory records in both quantities and dollars. If the assessed level of control risk is high, an auditor would probably
a. Insist that the client perform physical counts of inventory items several times during the year.
b. Apply gross profit tests to ascertain the reasonableness of the physical counts.
c. Increase the extent of tests of controls of the inventory cycle.
d. Request the client to schedule the physical inventory count at the end of the year.

103. Which of the following controls most likely addresses the completeness assertion for inventory?
a. Work in process account is periodically reconciled with subsidiary records.
b. Employees responsible for custody of finished goods do **not** perform the receiving function.
c. Receiving reports are prenumbered and periodically reconciled.
d. There is a separation of duties between payroll department and inventory accounting personnel.

104. Sound internal control dictates that defective merchandise returned by customers should be presented initially to the
a. Salesclerk.
b. Purchasing clerk.
c. Receiving clerk.
d. Inventory control clerk.

105. Alpha Company uses its sales invoices for posting perpetual inventory records. Inadequate controls over the invoicing function allow goods to be shipped that are not invoiced. The inadequate controls could cause an
a. Understatement of revenues, receivables, and inventory.
b. Overstatement of revenues and receivables, and an understatement of inventory.
c. Understatement of revenues and receivables, and an overstatement of inventory.
d. Overstatement of revenues, receivables, and inventory.

106. Which of the following is a question that the auditor would expect to find on the production cycle section of an internal control questionnaire?
a. Are vendors' invoices for raw materials approved for payment by an employee who is independent of the cash disbursements function?
b. Are signed checks for the purchase of raw materials mailed directly after signing without being returned to the person who authorized the invoice processing?
c. Are all releases by storekeepers of raw materials from storage based on approved requisition documents?
d. Are details of individual disbursements for raw materials balanced with the total to be posted to the appropriate general ledger account?

107. The objectives of internal control for a production cycle are to provide assurance that transactions are properly executed and recorded, and that
a. Production orders are prenumbered and signed by a supervisor.
b. Custody of work in process and of finished goods is properly maintained.
c. Independent internal verification of activity reports is established.
d. Transfers to finished goods are documented by a completed production report and a quality control report.

108. An auditor vouched data for a sample of employees in a payroll register to approved clock card data to provide assurance that
a. Payments to employees are computed at authorized rates.
b. Employees work the number of hours for which they are paid.
c. Segregation of duties exist between the preparation and distribution of the payroll.
d. Controls relating to unclaimed payroll checks are operating effectively.

109. Which of the following is a control that most likely could help prevent employee payroll fraud?
a. The personnel department promptly sends employee termination notices to the payroll supervisor.
b. Employees who distribute payroll checks forward unclaimed payroll checks to the absent employees' supervisors.
c. Salary rates resulting from new hires are approved by the payroll supervisor.
d. Total hours used for determination of gross pay are calculated by the payroll supervisor.

110. In determining the effectiveness of an entity's controls relating to the existence or occurrence assertion for payroll transactions, an auditor most likely would inquire about and
a. Observe the segregation of duties concerning personnel responsibilities and payroll disbursement.
b. Inspect evidence of accounting for prenumbered payroll checks.
c. Recompute the payroll deductions for employee fringe benefits.
d. Verify the preparation of the monthly payroll account bank reconciliation.

111. An auditor most likely would assess control risk at a high level if the payroll department supervisor is responsible for
a. Examining authorization forms for new employees.
b. Comparing payroll registers with original batch transmittal data.

   c.   Authorizing payroll rate changes for all employees.
   d.   Hiring all subordinate payroll department employees.

112. Which of the following controls most likely would prevent direct labor hours from being charged to manufacturing overhead?
   a.   Periodic independent counts of work in process for comparison to recorded amounts.
   b.   Comparison of daily journal entries with approved production orders.
   c.   Use of time tickets to record actual labor worked on production orders.
   d.   Reconciliation of work-in-process inventory with periodic cost budgets.

113. In meeting the control objective of safeguarding of assets, which department should be responsible for

	Distribution of paychecks	*Custody of unclaimed paychecks*
a.	Treasurer	Treasurer
b.	Payroll	Treasurer
c.	Treasurer	Payroll
d.	Payroll	Payroll

114. Proper internal control over the cash payroll function would mandate which of the following?
   a.   The payroll clerk should fill the envelopes with cash and a computation of the net wages.
   b.   Unclaimed pay envelopes should be retained by the paymaster.
   c.   Each employee should be asked to sign a receipt.
   d.   A separate checking account for payroll be maintained.

115. The purpose of segregating the duties of hiring personnel and distributing payroll checks is to separate the
   a.   Authorization of transactions from the custody of related assets.
   b.   Operational responsibility from the recordkeeping responsibility.
   c.   Human resources function from the controllership function.
   d.   Administrative controls from the internal accounting controls.

116. To minimize the opportunities for fraud, unclaimed cash payroll should be
   a.   Deposited in a safe-deposit box.
   b.   Held by the payroll custodian.
   c.   Deposited in a special bank account.
   d.   Held by the controller.

117. The auditor may observe the distribution of paychecks to ascertain whether
   a.   Pay rate authorization is properly separated from the operating function.
   b.   Deductions from gross pay are calculated correctly and are properly authorized.
   c.   Employees of record actually exist and are employed by the client.
   d.   Paychecks agree with the payroll register and the time cards.

118. Which of the following departments most likely would approve changes in pay rates and deductions from employee salaries?

   a.   Personnel.
   b.   Treasurer.
   c.   Controller.
   d.   Payroll.

119. Which of the following questions would an auditor most likely include on an internal control questionnaire for notes payable?
   a.   Are assets that collateralize notes payable critically needed for the entity's continued existence?
   b.   Are two or more authorized signatures required on checks that repay notes payable?
   c.   Are the proceeds from notes payable used for the purchase of noncurrent assets?
   d.   Are direct borrowings on notes payable authorized by the board of directors?

120. The primary responsibility of a bank acting as registrar of capital stock is to
   a.   Ascertain that dividends declared do **not** exceed the statutory amount allowable in the state of incorporation.
   b.   Account for stock certificates by comparing the total shares outstanding to the total in the shareholders subsidiary ledger.
   c.   Act as an independent third party between the board of directors and outside investors concerning mergers, acquisitions, and the sale of treasury stock.
   d.   Verify that stock is issued in accordance with the authorization of the board of directors and the articles of incorporation.

121. Where no independent stock transfer agents are employed and the corporation issues its own stocks and maintains stock records, canceled stock certificates should
   a.   Be defaced to prevent reissuance and attached to their corresponding stubs.
   b.   Not be defaced but segregated from other stock certificates and retained in a canceled certificates file.
   c.   Be destroyed to prevent fraudulent reissuance.
   d.   Be defaced and sent to the secretary of state.

122. Which of the following is **not** a control that is designed to protect investment securities?
   a.   Custody over securities should be limited to individuals who have recordkeeping responsibility over the securities.
   b.   Securities should be properly controlled physically in order to prevent unauthorized usage.
   c.   Access to securities should be vested in more than one individual.
   d.   Securities should be registered in the name of the owner.

123. Which of the following controls would a company most likely use to safeguard marketable securities when an independent trust agent is **not** employed?
   a.   The investment committee of the board of directors periodically reviews the investment decisions delegated to the treasurer.
   b.   Two company officials have joint control of marketable securities, which are kept in a bank safe-deposit box.

c. The internal auditor and the controller independently trace all purchases and sales of marketable securities from the subsidiary ledgers to the general ledger.

d. The chairman of the board verifies the marketable securities, which are kept in a bank safe-deposit box, each year on the balance sheet date.

124. A weakness in internal control over recording retirements of equipment may cause an auditor to

a. Inspect certain items of equipment in the plant and trace those items to the accounting records.

b. Review the subsidiary ledger to ascertain whether depreciation was taken on each item of equipment during the year.

c. Trace additions to the "other assets" account to search for equipment that is still on hand but **no** longer being used.

d. Select certain items of equipment from the accounting records and locate them in the plant.

125. Which of the following questions would an auditor **least** likely include on an internal control questionnaire concerning the initiation and execution of equipment transactions?

a. Are requests for major repairs approved at a higher level than the department initiating the request?

b. Are prenumbered purchase orders used for equipment and periodically accounted for?

c. Are requests for purchases of equipment reviewed for consideration of soliciting competitive bids?

d. Are procedures in place to monitor and properly restrict access to equipment?

126. Which of the following controls would be most effective in assuring that the proper custody of assets in the investing cycle is maintained?

a. Direct access to securities in the safe-deposit box is limited to only one corporate officer.

b. Personnel who post investment transactions to the general ledger are **not** permitted to update the investment subsidiary ledger.

c. The purchase and sale of investments are executed on the specific authorization of the board of directors.

d. The recorded balances in the investment subsidiary ledger are periodically compared with the contents of the safe-deposit box by independent personnel.

127. A company holds bearer bonds as a short-term investment. Responsibility for custody of these bonds and submission of coupons for periodic interest collections probably should be delegated to the

a. Chief Accountant.

b. Internal Auditor.

c. Cashier.

d. Treasurer.

128. Which of the following controls would an entity most likely use to assist in satisfying the completeness assertion related to long-term investments?

a. Senior management verifies that securities in the bank safe-deposit box are registered in the entity's name.

b. The internal auditor compares the securities in the bank safe-deposit box with recorded investments.

c. The treasurer vouches the acquisition of securities by comparing brokers' advices with canceled checks.

d. The controller compares the current market prices of recorded investments with the brokers' advices on file.

129. Which of the following controls would an entity most likely use in safeguarding against the loss of marketable securities?

a. An independent trust company that has no direct contact with the employees who have recordkeeping responsibilities has possession of the securities.

b. The internal auditor verifies the marketable securities in the entity's safe each year on the balance sheet date.

c. The independent auditor traces all purchases and sales of marketable securities through the subsidiary ledgers to the general ledger.

d. A designated member of the board of directors controls the securities in a bank safe-deposit box.

130. When there are numerous property and equipment transactions during the year, an auditor who plans to assess control risk at a low level usually performs

a. Tests of controls and extensive tests of property and equipment balances at the end of the year.

b. Analytical procedures for current year property and equipment transactions.

c. Tests of controls and limited tests of current year property and equipment transactions.

d. Analytical procedures for property and equipment balances at the end of the year.

131. In general, material fraud perpetrated by which of the following are most difficult to detect?

a. Cashier.

b. Keypunch operator.

c. Internal auditor.

d. Controller.

132. Which of the following is **not** an accurate statement about communication of internal control related matters to management on a nonissuer (nonpublic) company?

a. The auditor must communicate both material weaknesses and significant deficiencies.

b. The auditor must communicate in writing.

c. Previously communicated weaknesses that have not been corrected need not be recommunicated.

d. A communication indicating that no significant deficiencies were identified should not be issued.

133. Which of the following matters would an auditor most likely consider to be a material weakness to be communicated to those charged with governance of an audit client?

a. Management's failure to renegotiate unfavorable long-term purchase commitments.

b. Recurring operating losses that may indicate going concern problems.

c. Ineffective oversight of financial reporting by those charged with governance.

d. Management's current plans to reduce its ownership equity in the entity.

134. Which of the following statements is correct concerning significant deficiencies in an audit?

a. An auditor is required to search for significant deficiencies during an audit.

b. All significant deficiencies are also considered to be material weaknesses.

c. An auditor may communicate significant deficiencies during an audit or after the audit's completion.

d. An auditor may report that **no** significant deficiencies were noted during an audit.

135. An auditor's letter issued on significant deficiencies relating to an entity's internal control observed during a financial statement audit should

a. Include a brief description of the tests of controls performed in searching for significant deficiencies and material weaknesses.

b. Indicate that the significant deficiencies should be disclosed in the annual report to the entity's shareholders.

c. Include a paragraph describing management's assertion concerning the effectiveness of internal control.

d. Indicate that the audit's purpose was to report on the financial statements and **not** to express an opinion on internal control.

136. Which of the following statements is correct concerning an auditor's required communication of significant deficiencies?

a. A significant deficiency previously communicated during the prior year's audit that remains uncorrected causes a scope limitation.

b. An auditor should perform tests of controls on significant deficiencies before communicating them to the client.

c. An auditor's report on significant deficiencies should include a restriction on the distribution of the report.

d. An auditor should communicate significant deficiencies after tests of controls, but before commencing substantive tests.

137. Which of the following statements is correct concerning significant deficiencies noted in an audit?

a. Significant deficiencies are material weaknesses in the design or operation of specific internal control components.

b. The auditor is obligated to search for significant deficiencies that could adversely affect the entity's ability to record and report financial data.

c. Significant deficiencies need not be recommunicated each year if management has acknowledged its understanding of such deficiencies.

d. The auditor should separately communicate those significant deficiencies considered to be material weaknesses.

138. Which of the following representations should **not** be included in a report on internal control related matters noted in an audit?

a. Significant deficiencies related to internal control exist.

b. There are no significant deficiencies in the design or operation of internal control.

c. Corrective follow-up action is recommended due to the relative significance of material weaknesses discovered during the audit.

d. The auditor's consideration of internal control would not necessarily disclose all significant deficiencies that exist.

139. Which of the following statements concerning material weaknesses and significant deficiencies is correct?

a. An auditor should not identify and communicate material weaknesses separately from significant deficiencies.

b. Compensating controls may limit the severity of a material weakness or significant deficiency.

c. Upon discovery an auditor should immediately report all material weaknesses and significant deficiencies identified during an audit.

d. All significant deficiencies are material weaknesses.

140. During the audit the independent auditor identified the existence of a weakness in the client's internal control and communicated this finding in writing to the client's senior management and those charged with governance. The auditor should

a. Consider the weakness a scope limitation and therefore disclaim an opinion.

b. Consider the effects of the condition on the audit.

c. Suspend all audit activities pending directions from the client's audit committee.

d. Withdraw from the engagement.

141. In identifying matters for communication with those charged with governance of an audit client, an auditor most likely would ask management whether

a. The turnover in the accounting department was unusually high.

b. It consulted with another CPA firm about accounting matters.

c. There were any subsequent events of which the auditor was unaware.

d. It agreed with the auditor's assessed level of control risk.

142. Which of the following statements is correct concerning an auditor's required communication with those charged with governance of an audit client?

a. This communication is required to occur before the auditor's report on the financial statements is issued.

b. This communication should include discussion of any significant disagreements with management concerning the financial statements.

c. Any significant matter communicated to the audit committee also should be communicated to management.

d. Significant audit adjustments proposed by the auditor and recorded by management need **not** be communicated to those charged with governance.

143. An auditor would **least** likely initiate a discussion with those charged with governance of an audit client concerning

a. The methods used to account for significant unusual transactions.

b. The maximum dollar amount of misstatements that could exist without causing the financial statements to be materially misstated.

c. Indications of fraud and illegal acts committed by a corporate officer that were discovered by the auditor.

d. Disagreements with management as to accounting principles that were resolved during the current year's audit.

144. Which of the following statements is correct about an auditor's required communication with those charged with governance of an audit client?

a. Any matters communicated to the entity's audit committee also are required to be communicated to the entity's management.

b. The auditor is required to inform those charged with governance about significant misstatements discovered by the auditor and subsequently corrected by management.

c. Disagreements with management about the application of accounting principles are required to be communicated in writing to those charged with governance.

d. Weaknesses in internal control previously reported to those charged with governance need not be re-communicated.

145. Which of the following matters is an auditor required to communicate to an entity's audit committee?

I. Disagreements with management about matters significant to the entity's financial statements that have been satisfactorily resolved.

II. Initial selection of significant accounting policies in emerging areas that lack authoritative guidance.

a. I only.
b. II only.
c. Both I and II.
d. Neither I nor II.

146. Should an auditor communicate the following matters to those charged with governance of an audit client?

	Significant audit adjustments recorded by the entity	Management's consultation with other accountants about significant accounting matters
a.	Yes	Yes
b.	Yes	No
c.	No	Yes
d.	No	No

147. In reporting on an entity's internal control over financial reporting, a practitioner should include a paragraph that describes the

a. Documentary evidence regarding the control environment factors.
b. Changes in internal control since the prior report.
c. Potential benefits from the practitioner's suggested improvements.
d. Inherent limitations of any internal control.

148. Which of the following best describes a CPA's engagement to report on an entity's internal control over financial reporting?

a. An attestation engagement to form an opinion on the effectiveness of its internal control.
b. An audit engagement to provide negative assurance on the entity's internal control.

c. A prospective engagement to project, for a period of time **not** to exceed one year, and report on the expected benefits of the entity's internal control.

d. A consulting engagement to provide constructive advice to the entity on its internal control.

149. An engagement to examine internal control will generally

a. Require procedures that duplicate those already applied in assessing control risk during a financial statement audit.
b. Increase the reliability of the financial statements that have already been audited.
c. Be more extensive in scope than the assessment of control risk made during a financial statement audit.
d. Be more limited in scope than the assessment of control risk made during a financial statement audit.

150. How do the scope, procedures, and purpose of an examination of internal control compare to those for obtaining an understanding of internal control and assessing control risk as part of an audit?

	Scope	Procedures	Purpose
a.	Similar	Different	Similar
b.	Different	Similar	Similar
c.	Different	Different	Different
d.	Different	Similar	Different

151. When an independent auditor reports on internal control based on criteria established by governmental agencies, the report should

a. Not include the agency's name in the report.
b. Indicate matters covered by the study and whether the auditor's study included tests of controls with the procedures covered by the study.
c. Not express a conclusion based on the agency's criteria.
d. Assume responsibility for the comprehensiveness of the criteria established by the agency and include recommendations for corrective action.

152. When an examination has been performed on the effectiveness of entity's internal control over financial reporting and a material weakness has been noted, the practitioner's report should express an opinion on

a. The assertion.
b. The subject matter to which the assertion relates.
c. Neither of the above.
d. Both of the above.

153. In assessing the competence of an internal auditor, an independent CPA most likely would obtain information about the

a. Quality of the internal auditor's working paper documentation.
b. Organization's commitment to integrity and ethical values.
c. Influence of management on the scope of the internal auditor's duties.
d. Organizational level to which the internal auditor reports.

154. For which of the following judgments may an independent auditor share responsibility with an entity's internal auditor who is assessed to be both competent and objective?

	Assessment of inherent risk	Assessment of control risk
a.	Yes	Yes
b.	Yes	No
c.	No	Yes
d.	No	No

155. The work of internal auditors may affect the independent auditor's

I. Procedures performed in obtaining an understanding of internal control.
II. Procedures performed in assessing the risk of material misstatement.
III. Substantive procedures performed in gathering direct evidence.

  a: I and II only.
  b.   I and III only.
  c.   II and III only.
  d.   I, II, and III.

156. An internal auditor's work would most likely affect the nature, timing, and extent of an independent CPA's auditing procedures when the internal auditor's work relates to assertions about the
  a.   Existence of contingencies.
  b.   Valuation of intangible assets.
  c.   Existence of fixed asset additions.
  d.   Valuation of related-party transactions.

157. During an audit an internal auditor may provide direct assistance to an independent CPA in

	Obtaining an understanding of internal control	Performing tests of controls	Performing substantive tests
a.	No	No	No
b.	Yes	No	No
c.	Yes	Yes	No
d.	Yes	Yes	Yes

158. When assessing the internal auditor's competence, the independent CPA should obtain information about the
  a.   Organizational level to which the internal auditors report.
  b.   Educational background and professional certification of the internal auditors.
  c.   Policies prohibiting the internal auditors from auditing areas where relatives are employed.
  d.   Internal auditors' access to records and information that is considered sensitive.

159. In assessing the competence and objectivity of an entity's internal auditor, an independent auditor would **least** likely consider information obtained from
  a.   Discussions with management personnel.
  b.   External quality reviews of the internal auditor's activities.
  c.   Previous experience with the internal auditor.
  d.   The results of analytical procedures.

160. If the independent auditors decide that the work performed by the internal auditor may have a bearing on their own procedures, they should consider the internal auditor's
  a.   Competence and objectivity.
  b.   Efficiency and experience.
  c.   Independence and review skills.
  d.   Training and supervisory skills.

161. In assessing the objectivity of internal auditors, an independent auditor should
  a.   Evaluate the quality control program in effect for the internal auditors.
  b.   Examine documentary evidence of the work performed by the internal auditors.
  c.   Test a sample of the transactions and balances that the internal auditors examined.
  d.   Determine the organizational level to which the internal auditors report.

162. Dunn, CPA, is auditing the financial statements of Taft Co. Taft uses Quick Service Center (QSC) to process its payroll. Price, CPA, is expressing an opinion on a description of the controls implemented at QSC regarding the processing of its customers' payroll transactions. Dunn expects to consider the effects of Price's report on the Taft engagement. Price's report should contain a(n)
  a.   Description of the scope and nature of Price's procedures.
  b.   Statement that Dunn may assess control risk based on Price's report.
  c.   Assertion that Price assumes no responsibility to determine whether QSC's controls are suitably designed.
  d.   Opinion on the operating effectiveness of QSC's internal controls.

163. Payroll Data Co. (PDC) processes payroll transactions for a retailer. Cook, CPA, is engaged to express an opinion on a description of PDC's internal controls implemented as of a specific date. These controls are relevant to the retailer's internal control, so Cook's report may be useful in providing the retailer's independent auditor with information necessary to plan a financial statement audit. Cook's report should
  a.   Contain a disclaimer of opinion on the operating effectiveness of PDC's controls.
  b.   State whether PDC's controls were suitably designed to achieve the retailer's objectives.
  c.   Identify PDC's controls relevant to specific financial statement assertions.
  d.   Disclose Cook's assessed level of control risk for PDC.

164. The auditor who audits the processing of transactions by a service organization may issue a report on controls

	Implemented	Operating effectiveness
a.	Yes	Yes
b.	Yes	No
c.	No	Yes
d.	No	No

165. Computer Services Company (CSC) processes payroll transactions for schools. Drake, CPA, is engaged to report on CSC's policies and procedures implemented as of a specific date. These policies and procedures are relevant to the schools' internal control, so Drake's report will be useful in providing the schools' independent auditors with information necessary to plan their audits. Drake's report expressing an opinion on CSC's policies and procedures implemented as of a specific date should contain a(n)
  a.   Description of the scope and nature of Drake's procedures.
  b.   Statement that CSC's management has disclosed to Drake all design deficiencies of which it is aware.

    c.   Opinion on the operating effectiveness of CSC's policies and procedures.

    d.   Paragraph indicating the basis for Drake's assessment of control risk.

166. Lake, CPA, is auditing the financial statements of Gill Co. Gill uses the EDP Service Center, Inc. to process its payroll transactions. EDP's financial statements are audited by Cope, CPA, who recently issued a report on EDP's internal control. Lake is considering Cope's report on EDP's internal control in assessing control risk on the Gill engagement. What is Lake's responsibility concerning making reference to Cope as a basis, in part, for Lake's own opinion?

    a.   Lake may refer to Cope only if Lake is satisfied as to Cope's professional reputation and independence.

    b.   Lake may refer to Cope only if Lake relies on Cope's report in restricting the extent of substantive tests.

    c.   Lake may refer to Cope only if Lake's report indicates the division of responsibility.

    d.   Lake may **not** refer to Cope under the circumstances above.

SIMULATION PROBLEMS

Simulation Problem 1   (35 to 40 minutes)

Directions				
	Situation	Internal Control	Research	Communication

An auditor's working papers include the narrative description (situation tab) of the cash receipts and billing portions of Southwest Medical Center's internal control.

Evaluate the information in the situation on the worksheet (internal control tab) as being either (1) a strength, (2) a weakness, (3) not a strength or a weakness.

	Situation			
Directions		Internal Control	Research	Communication

Southwest is a health care provider that is owned by a partnership of five physicians. It employs eleven physicians, including the five owners, twenty nurses, five laboratory and X-ray technicians, and four clerical workers. The clerical workers perform such tasks as reception, correspondence, cash receipts, billing, accounts receivable, bank deposits, and appointment scheduling. These clerical workers are referred to in the situation as office manager, clerk #1, clerk #2, and clerk #3. Assume that the narrative is a complete description of the system.

		Internal Control		
Directions	Situation		Research	Communication

About two-thirds of Southwest's patients receive medical services only after insurance coverage is verified by the office manager and communicated to the clerks. Most of the other patients pay for services by cash or check when services are rendered, although the office manger extends credit on a case-by-case basis to about 5% of the patients.

When services are rendered, the attending physician prepares a prenumbered service slip for each patient and gives the slip to clerk #1 for pricing. Clerk #1 completes the slip and gives the completed slip to clerk #2 and a copy to the patient.

Using the information on the completed slip, clerk #2 performs one of the following three procedures for each patient:

- Clerk #2 files an insurance claim and records a receivable from the insurance company if the office manager has verified the patient's coverage, or
- Clerk #2 posts a receivable from the patient on clerk #2's PC if the office manager has approved the patient's credit, or
- Clerk #2 receives cash or a check from the patient as the patient leaves the medical center, and clerk #2 records the cash receipt.

At the end of each day, clerk #2 prepares a revenue summary.

Clerk #1 performs correspondence functions and opens the incoming mail. Clerk #1 gives checks from insurance companies and patients to clerk #2 for deposit. Clerk #2 posts the receipt of patients' checks on clerk #2's PC patient receivable records and insurance companies' checks to the receivables from the applicable insurance companies. Clerk #1 gives mail requiring correspondence to clerk #3.

Clerk #2 stamps all checks "for deposit only" and each day prepares a list of checks and cash to be deposited in the bank. (This list also includes the cash and checks personally given to clerk #2 by patients.) Clerk #2 keeps a copy of the deposit list and gives the original to clerk #3.

Clerk #3 personally makes the daily bank deposit and maintains a file of the daily bank deposits. Clerk #3 also performs appointment scheduling for all of the doctors and various correspondence functions. Clerk #3 also maintains a list of patients whose insurance coverage the office manager has verified.

When insurance claims or patient receivables are not settled within sixty days, clerk #2 notifies the office manager. The office manager personally inspects the details of each instance of nonpayment. The office manger converts insurance claims that have been rejected by insurance companies into patient receivables. Clerk #2 records these patient receivables on clerk #2's PC and deletes these receivables from the applicable insurance companies. Clerk #2 deletes the patient receivables that appear to be uncollectible from clerk #2's PC when authorized by the office manager. Clerk #2 prepares a list of patients with uncollectible balances and gives a copy of the list to clerk #3, who will not allow these patients to make appointments for future services.

Once a month an outside accountant posts clerk #2's daily revenue summaries to the general ledger, prepares a monthly trial balance and monthly financial statements, accounts for prenumbered service slips, files payroll forms and tax returns, and reconciles the monthly bank statements to the general ledger. This accountant reports directly to the physician who is the managing partner.

All four clerical employees perform their tasks on PCs that are connected through a local area network. Each PC is accessible with a password that is known only to the individual employee and the managing partner. Southwest uses a standard software package that was acquired from a software company and that cannot be modified by Southwest's employees. None of the clerical employees have access to Southwest's check writing abilities.

	Condition	Strength	Weakness	Neither
1.	Southwest is involved only in medical services and has not diversified its operations.	○	○	○
2.	Insurance coverage for patients is verified and communicated to the clerks by the office manager before medical services are rendered.	○	○	○
3.	The physician who renders the medical services documents the services on a prenumbered slip that is used for recording revenue and as a receipt for the patient.	○	○	○
4.	Cash collection is centralized in that Clerk #2 receives the cash (checks) from patients and records the cash receipt.	○	○	○
5.	Southwest extends credit rather than requiring cash or insurance in all cases.	○	○	○
6.	The office manager extends credit on a case-by-case basis rather than using a formal credit search and established credit limits.	○	○	○
7.	The office manager approves the extension of credit to patients and also approves the write-offs of uncollectible patient receivables.	○	○	○
8.	Clerk #2 receives cash and checks and prepares the daily bank deposit.	○	○	○
9.	Clerk #2 maintains the accounts receivable records and can add or delete information on the PC.	○	○	○
10.	Prenumbered service slips are accounted for on a monthly basis by the outside accountant who is independent of the revenue generating and revenue recording functions.	○	○	○
11.	The bank reconciliation is prepared monthly by the outside accountant who is independent of the revenue generating and revenue recording functions.	○	○	○
12.	Computer passwords are only known to the individual employees and the managing partner who has no duties in the revenue recording functions.	○	○	○
13.	Computer software cannot be modified by Southwest's employees.	○	○	○
14.	None of the employees who perform duties in the revenue generating and revenue recording are able to write checks.	○	○	○

Directions	Situation	Internal Control	Research	Communication

An auditor may discover certain audit adjustments, material and immaterial, that relate to the financial statements. Search the Professional Standards to determine auditor responsibility for communicating these adjustments to the audit committee. Select the appropriate paragraph(s) from the professional standards.

Directions	Situation	Internal Control	Research	Communication

Assume that in your audit of Southwest you assessed control risk at a low level for accounts receivable. However, your substantive procedures have detected a large number of errors in the accounts. Write a memorandum to the audit working papers describing the implications of this situation.

REMINDER: Your response will be graded for both technical content and writing skills. Technical content will be evaluated for information that is helpful to the intended reader and clearly relevant to the issues. Writing skills will be evaluated for development, organization, and the appropriate expression of ideas in professional correspondence. Use a standard business memo or letter format with a clear beginning, middle, and end. Do not convey information in the form of a table, bullet point list, or other abbreviated presentation.

To: Audit Working Papers
From: CPA Candidate
Reportable: Implications of errors discovered in accounts receivable

Simulation Problem 2   (25 to 35 minutes)

The following flowchart (Flowchart tab) depicts part of a client's purchases and cash disbursements cycle. Some of the flowchart symbols are labeled to indicate operations, controls, and records. For each symbol numbered 1 through 12, select one response from the answer lists below. Each response in the lists may be selected once or **not** at all.

Operations and controls	*Connectors, documents, departments, and files*	
A. Approve receiving report	J. Accounts payable	O. Purchase order No. 5
B. Prepare and approve voucher	K. Canceled voucher	P. Receiving report No. 1
C. Prepare purchase order	package	Q. Stores
D. Prepare purchase requisition	L. From purchasing	R. To vendor
E. Prepare purchases journal	M. From receiving	S. Treasurer
F. Prepare receiving report	N. From vouchers	T. Unpaid voucher file,
G. Prepare sales journal	payable	filed by due date
H. Prepare voucher		
I. Sign checks and cancel voucher package documents		

The Professional Standards state that internal control provides reasonable and not absolute assurance of achieving a client's control objectives. Relatedly, the Professional Standards acknowledge that internal control has certain limitations. Search the Professional Standards to find the location at which a number of limitations are discussed together. Select the paragraphs that provide this guidance.

![Communication tab]

Internet controls either (1) prevent misstatements, or (2) detect material misstatements of financial statements. Write a memorandum to the audit staff describing these two types of controls.

To: Audit Staff
From: CPA Candidate
Re: Types of controls

```
[blank response box]
```

REMINDER: Your response will be graded for both technical content and writing skills. Technical content will be evaluated for information that is helpful to the intended reader and clearly relevant to the issues. Writing skills will be evaluated for development, organization, and the appropriate expression of ideas in professional correspondence. Use a standard business memo or letter format with a clear beginning, middle, and end. Do not convey information in the form of a table, bullet point list, or other abbreviated presentation.

Simulation Problem 3   (40 to 50 minutes)

![Situation tab]

You are working for Smith & Co. CPAs. The following partially completed flowchart depicts part of Welcore Inc., your client's revenue cycle. Some of the flowchart symbols are labeled to indicate controls and records. For each symbol numbered **1** though **13**, select one response from all the answer lists below. Each response in the lists may be selected once or **not** at all.

	Operations and controls		Documents, journals, ledgers, and files
A.	Enter shipping data	P.	Shipping document
B.	Verify agreement of sales order and shipping document	Q.	General ledger master file
C.	Write off accounts receivable	R.	General journal
D.	To warehouse and shipping department	S.	Master price file
E.	Authorize account receivable write-off	T.	Sales journal
F.	Prepare aged trial balance	U.	Sales invoice
G.	To sales department	V.	Cash receipts journal
H.	Release goods for shipment	W.	Uncollectible accounts file
I.	To accounts receivable department	X.	Shipping file
J.	Enter price data	Y.	Aged trial balance
K.	Determine that customer exists	Z.	Open order file
L.	Match customer purchase order with sales order		
M.	Perform customer credit check		
N.	Prepare sales journal		
O.	Prepare sales invoice		

Now assume that the flowchart was originally prepared as a part of the necessary documentation for an audit of Welcore's financial statements. Very early in the audit of the financial statements, the president of Welcore asked you about the possibilities of your issuing a publicly available report on its internal control over financial reporting (in addition to the financial statement audit report). Select the excerpts from Professional Standards that illustrate an appropriate report on internal control over financial reporting.

NOTE: If you do not have access to professional standards indicate the keywords or section numbers that you would use to do your search. Then go to the solution which has excerpts from professional standards to complete the requirement.

			Communication
Situation	Flowchart	Research	

Assume that Bill Warren, CFO of Welcore Inc., wants an explanation of how improvements in internal control will affect the audit of the company. Write a brief memorandum explaining how the audit might change based on improved internal control.

REMINDER: Your response will be graded for both technical relevance and writing skills. Technical content will be evaluated for information that is helpful to the intended reader and clearly relevant to the issue. Writing skills will be evaluated for development, organization, and the appropriate expression of ideas in professional correspondence. Use a standard business memo or letter format with a clear beginning, middle, and end. Do not convey information in the form of a table, bullet point list, or other abbreviated presentation.

To: Bill Warren, CFO
       Welcore Inc.
From: CPA Candidate
Re: Effect of improvements in internal control

1._____   8._____

2._____   9._____

3._____   10._____

4._____   11._____

5._____   12._____

6._____   13._____

7._____

Simulation Problem 4   (45 to 50 minutes)

Situation			
	Internal Control Evaluation	**Purpose of Internal Control**	**Research and Communication**

The following flowchart depicts the activities relating to the purchasing, receiving, and accounts payable departments of Model Company, Inc. Assume that you are a supervising assistant assigned to the Model Company audit.

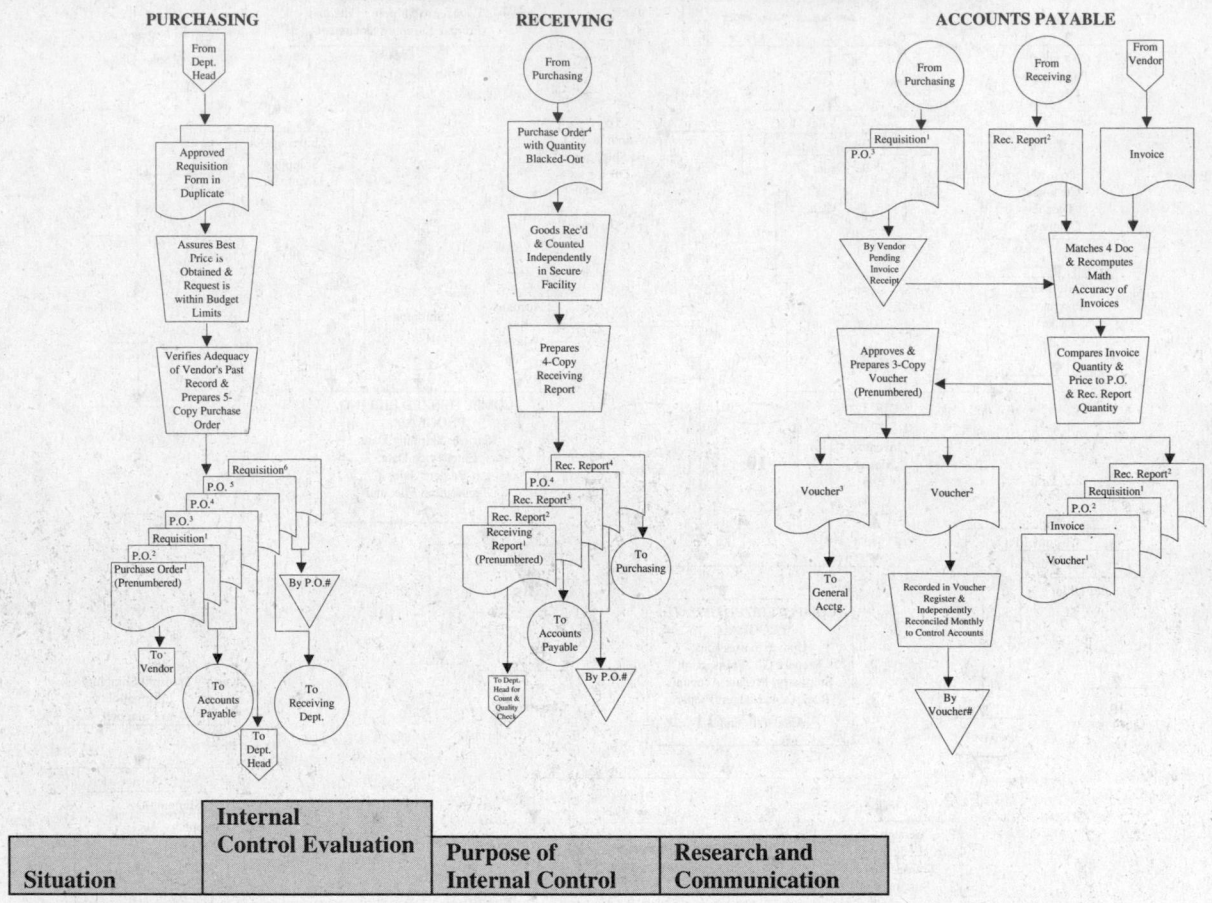

	Internal Control Evaluation		
Situation		**Purpose of Internal Control**	**Research and Communication**

Joe Werell, a beginning assistant, analyzed the flowchart and has supplemented the flowchart by making certain inquiries of the controller. He has concluded that the internal control over purchasing, receiving, and accounts payable is strong and has provided the following list of what he refers to as internal control strengths. Review his list and for each internal control strength indicate whether you agree or disagree that each represents a strength. For those in which you disagree briefly explain why.

Internal Control Strengths
Prepared by Joe Werell

		Agree	*Disagree*
Purchasing			
1.	The department head of the requisitioning department selects the appropriate supplier.	○	○
2.	Proper authorization of requisitions by department head is required before purchase orders are prepared.	○	○
3.	Purchasing department makes certain that low-cost supplier is always chosen.	○	○
4.	Purchasing department assures that requisitions are within budget limits before purchase orders are prepared.	○	○
5.	The adequacy of each vendor's past record as a supplier is verified.	○	○
Receiving			
6.	Secure facilities limit access to the goods during the receiving activity.	○	○
7.	Receiving department compares its count of the quantity of goods received with that listed on its copy of the purchase order.	○	○

	Agree	Disagree
8. A receiving report is required for all purchases, including purchases of services.	○	○
9. The requisitioning department head independently verifies the quantity and quality of the goods received.	○	○
10. Requisitions, purchase orders, and receiving reports are matched with vendor invoices as to quantity and price.	○	○

Accounts Payable

	Agree	Disagree
11. Accounts payable department recomputes the mathematical accuracy of each invoice.	○	○
12. The voucher register is independently reconciled to the control accounts monthly by the originators of the related vouchers.	○	○
13. All supporting documentation is marked "paid" by accounts payable immediately prior to making it available to the treasurer.	○	○
14. All supporting documentation is required for payment and is made available to the treasurer.	○	○
15. The purchasing, receiving, and accounts payable functions are segregated.	○	○

Situation	Internal Control Evaluation	Purpose of Internal Control	Research and Communication

Another assistant has been working in the revenue cycle area and has compiled a list of possible errors and fraud that may result in the misstatement of Model Company's financial statements, and a corresponding list of controls that, if properly designed and implemented, could assist in preventing or detecting the errors and fraud.

For each possible error and fraud numbered **1 through 15,** select one internal control from the answer list below that, if properly designed and implemented, most likely could assist management in preventing or detecting the errors and fraud. Each response in the list of controls may be selected once, more than once, or not at all.

Controls

A. Shipping clerks compare goods received from the warehouse with the details on the shipping documents.

B. Approved sales orders are required for goods to be released from the warehouse.

C. Monthly statements are mailed to all customers with outstanding balances.

D. Shipping clerks compare goods received from the warehouse with approved sales orders.

E. Customer orders are compared with the inventory master file to determine whether items ordered are in stock.

F. Daily sales summaries are compared with control totals of invoices.

G. Shipping documents are compared with sales invoices when goods are shipped.

H. Sales invoices are compared with the master price file.

I. Customer orders are compared with an approved customer list.

J. Sales orders are prepared for each customer order.

K. Control amounts posted to the accounts receivable ledger are compared with control totals of invoices.

L. Sales invoices are compared with shipping documents and approved customer orders before invoices are mailed.

M. Prenumbered credit memos are used for granting credit for goods returned.

N. Goods returned for credit are approved by the supervisor of the sales department.

O. Remittance advices are separated from the checks in the mailroom and forwarded to the accounting department.

P. Total amounts posted to the accounts receivable ledger from remittance advices are compared with the validated bank deposit slip.

Q. The cashier examines each check for proper endorsement.

R. Validated deposit slips are compared with the cashier's daily cash summaries.

S. An employee, other than the bookkeeper, periodically prepares a bank reconciliation.

T. Sales returns are approved by the same employee who issues receiving reports evidencing actual return of goods.

Possible Errors and Fraud

1. Invoices for goods sold are posted to incorrect customer accounts.
2. Goods ordered by customers are shipped, but are **not** billed to anyone.
3. Invoices are sent for shipped goods, but are **not** recorded in the sales journal.
4. Invoices are sent for shipped goods and are recorded in the sales journal, but are **not** posted to any customer account.
5. Credit sales are made to individuals with unsatisfactory credit ratings.
6. Goods are removed from inventory for unauthorized orders.
7. Goods shipped to customers do **not** agree with goods ordered by customers.
8. Invoices are sent to allies in a fraudulent scheme and sales are recorded for fictitious transactions.
9. Customers' checks are received for less than the customers' full account balances, but the customers' full account balances are credited.
10. Customers' checks are misappropriated before being forwarded to the cashier for deposit.
11. Customers' checks are credited to incorrect customer accounts.
12. Different customer accounts are each credited for the same cash receipt.
13. Customers' checks are properly credited to customer accounts and are properly deposited, but errors are made in recording receipts in the cash receipts journal.
14. Customers' checks are misappropriated after being forwarded to the cashier for deposit.
15. Invalid transactions granting credit for sales returns are recorded.

Situation	Internal Control Evaluation	Purpose of Internal Control	Research and Communication

Assume that in Internal Control Evaluation you have identified some circumstances that may be considered deficiencies in internal control—indeed some might be considered significant deficiencies or even material weaknesses. Write a memorandum addressed to Bill Jones, the job's senior, that abstracts from the professional standards the following:

1. Definition of material weakness and significant deficiency.
2. Whether a preference exists in the standards on whether any communication need be in writing versus presented orally to the audit committee.
3. Whether deficiencies of which an audit committee is already aware must be communicated to the audit committee.

Assume that this is the audit of a nonissuer (nonpublic) company for which no overall public reporting responsibility relating to internal control is required under the requirements of the Sarbanes-Oxley Act of 2002. Also, identify the paragraph(s) of the professional standards in which you find the guidance.

NOTE: If you do not have access to professional standards indicate the keywords or section numbers that you would use to do your search. Then, go to the solution which has excerpts from professional standards to complete the requirement.

REMINDER: Your response will be graded for both technical content and writing skills. Technical content will be evaluated for information that is helpful to the intended reader and clearly relevant to the issues. Writing skills will be evaluated for development, organization, and the appropriate expression of ideas in professional correspondence. Use a standard business memo or letter format with a clear beginning, middle, and end. Do not convey information in the form of a table, bullet point list, or other abbreviated presentation.

To: Mr. Bill Jones
From: CPA Candidate
Re: Reporting on internal control

MODULE 2 INTERNAL CONTROL 65

MULTIPLE-CHOICE ANSWERS

1. a __ __	35. d __ __	69. c __ __	103. c __ __	137. d __ __
2. d __ __	36. a __ __	70. a __ __	104. c __ __	138. b __ __
3. b __ __	37. b __ __	71. d __ __	105. c __ __	139. b __ __
4. b __ __	38. d __ __	72. a __ __	106. c __ __	140. b __ __
5. c __ __	39. c __ __	73. a __ __	107. b __ __	141. b __ __
6. b __ __	40. a __ __	74. c __ __	108. b __ __	142. b __ __
7. d __ __	41. c __ __	75. b __ __	109. a __ __	143. b __ __
8. a __ __	42. a __ __	76. a __ __	110. a __ __	144. b __ __
9. d __ __	43. b __ __	77. a __ __	111. d __ __	145. a __ __
10. a __ __	44. a __ __	78. c __ __	112. c __ __	146. a __ __
11. d __ __	45. c __ __	79. d __ __	113. a __ __	147. d __ __
12. b __ __	46. d __ __	80. b __ __	114. c __ __	148. a __ __
13. a __ __	47. a __ __	81. a __ __	115. a __ __	149. c __ __
14. a __ __	48. d __ __	82. a __ __	116. c __ __	150. d __ __
15. b __ __	49. d __ __	83. d __ __	117. c __ __	151. b __ __
16. b __ __	50. d __ __	84. c __ __	118. a __ __	152. b __ __
17. b __ __	51. a __ __	85. d __ __	119. d __ __	153. a __ __
18. a __ __	52. d __ __	86. b __ __	120. d __ __	154. d __ __
19. a __ __	53. d __ __	87. c __ __	121. a __ __	155. d __ __
20. d __ __	54. b __ __	88. b __ __	122. a __ __	156. c __ __
21. b __ __	55. c __ __	89. b __ __	123. b __ __	157. d __ __
22. b __ __	56. a __ __	90. d __ __	124. d __ __	158. b __ __
23. c __ __	57. a __ __	91. b __ __	125. d __ __	159. d __ __
24. d __ __	58. a __ __	92. d __ __	126. d __ __	160. a __ __
25. d __ __	59. c __ __	93. b __ __	127. d __ __	161. d __ __
26. d __ __	60. a __ __	94. b __ __	128. b __ __	162. a __ __
27. c __ __	61. a __ __	95. d __ __	129. a __ __	163. a __ __
28. d __ __	62. b __ __	96. d __ __	130. c __ __	164. a __ __
29. d __ __	63. c __ __	97. b __ __	131. d __ __	165. a __ __
30. a __ __	64. a __ __	98. b __ __	132. c __ __	166. d __ __
31. c __ __	65. b __ __	99. b __ __	133. c __ __	
32. d __ __	66. b __ __	100. c __ __	134. c __ __	
33. d __ __	67. c __ __	101. d __ __	135. d __ __	1st: __/166= __%
34. a __ __	68. c __ __	102. d __ __	136. c __ __	2nd: __/166= __%

MULTIPLE-CHOICE ANSWER EXPLANATIONS

A.1. Definition of Internal Control

1. **(a)** The requirement is to identify the reply that most likely would **not** be considered an inherent limitation of the potential effectiveness of an entity's internal control. Answer (a) is correct because incompatible duties may generally be divided among individuals in such a manner as to control the problem. Answers (b), (c), and (d) are all incorrect because management override, mistakes of judgment, and collusion among employees are all inherent limitations of internal control.

2. **(d)** The requirement is to identify the meaning of the concept of reasonable assurance. Answer (d) is correct because reasonable assurance recognizes that the cost of internal control should not exceed the benefits expected to be derived.

3. **(b)** The requirement is to identify the functions that should be segregated for effective internal control. Answer (b) is correct because authorizing transactions, recording transactions, and maintaining custody of assets should be segregated.

A.2. Major Components of Internal Control

4. **(b)** The requirement is to identify the most likely type of *ongoing* monitoring activity. Answer (b) is correct

because ongoing monitoring involves assessing the design and operation of controls on a timely basis and taking necessary corrective actions and such an approach may be followed in reviewing the purchasing function. Answer (a) is incorrect because periodic audits are not ordinarily performed by the audit committee, a subcommittee of the Board of Directors. Answer (c) is incorrect because the audit of the annual financial statements is not ordinarily considered monitoring as presented in the professional standards. Answer (d) is incorrect because the meaning of the reply, control risk assessment in conjunction with quarterly reviews, is uncertain.

5. **(c)** The requirement is to identify where the overall attitude and awareness of an entity's board of directors concerning the importance of internal control is normally reflected. Answer (c) is correct because the control environment reflects the overall attitude, awareness, and actions of the board of directors, management, owners, and others concerning the importance of control and its emphasis in the entity.

6. **(b)** The requirement is to identify the circumstance in which management philosophy and operating style would have a significant influence on an entity's control environment. Answer (b) is correct because management philosophy and operating style, while always important, is particularly so when management is dominated by one or a few individuals because it may impact numerous other factors. Answer (a) is incorrect because the impact of the internal auditor reporting directly to management is likely to be less than that of answer (a). Answer (c) is incorrect because while accurate management job descriptions are desirable, they do not have as significant of an effect on management philosophy and operating style as does domination by an individual. Answer (d) is incorrect because an active audit committee might temper rather than lead to a more significant influence of management philosophy and operating style.

7.   (d)   The requirement is to determine which of the factors listed are included in an entity's control environment. Answer (d) is correct because the audit committee, integrity and ethical values, and organization structure are all included.

8.   (a)   The requirement is to identify the reply that is **not** a component of an entity's internal control. Answer (a) is correct because while auditors assess control risk as a part of their consideration of internal control, it is not a component of an entity's internal control. Answers (b), (c), and (d) are incorrect because the control environment, risk assessment, control activities, information and communication, and monitoring are the five components of an entity's internal control (SAS 109).

A.3.   Related Topics

9.   (d)   The Foreign Corrupt Practices Act makes payment of bribes to foreign officials illegal and requires publicly held companies to maintain systems of internal control sufficient to provide reasonable assurances that internal control objectives are met.

B.1.   Obtain Understanding of the Client and Its Internal Control

10.   (a)   The requirement is to determine the most likely population from which an auditor would sample when vendors' invoices and related vouchers relating to purchases made by employees have been destroyed. Answer (a) is correct because the disbursement will be recorded and the auditor may thus sample from that population. Answers (b) and (d) are incorrect because the related vouchers and vendors' invoices are destroyed. Answer (c) is incorrect because there is no recording of the receipt of the merchandise.

11.   (d)   The requirement is to identify the procedure an auditor would perform to provide evidence about whether an entity's internal control activities are suitably designed to prevent or detect material misstatements. Answer (d) is correct because SAS 109 indicates an auditor will observe the entity's personnel applying the procedures to determine whether controls have been implemented. Answer (a) is incorrect because reperforming the activities is a test of control to help assess the operating effectiveness of a control. Answer (b) is incorrect because analytical procedures are not performed to determine whether controls are suitably designed. Answer (c) is incorrect because vouching a sample of transactions is a substantive test not directly aimed at determining whether controls are suitably designed. See SAS 109 for a discussion of an auditor's responsibility for determining whether controls have been implemented vs. their operating effectiveness.

12.   (b)   The requirement is to identify the correct statement relating to the relevance of various types of controls to a financial statement audit. Answer (b) is correct because, generally, controls that are relevant to an audit pertain to the entity's objective of preparing financial statements for external purposes. Answer (a) is incorrect because SAS 109 makes clear that an auditor may not ignore consideration of controls under any audit approach. Answer (c) is incorrect because control over financial reporting are of primary importance. Answer (d) is incorrect because many operational and compliance related controls are not ordinarily relevant to an audit.

13.   (a)   The requirement is to identify the statement that represents a requirement when an audit of financial statements in accordance with generally accepted accounting principles is performed. Answer (a) is correct because SAS 109 requires that the auditor document the understanding of the entity's internal control. Answer (b) is incorrect because while an auditor might find significant deficiencies in the operation of internal control, no such search is required. Answer (c) is incorrect because an auditor might use a substantive approach in performing an audit and thereby perform few (if any) tests of controls. Answer (d) is incorrect because while auditors must obtain knowledge of internal control sufficiently to identify types of potential misstatements, they are not required to obtain the detailed knowledge of internal control suggested by this reply.

14.   (a)   The requirement is to identify the knowledge that an auditor must obtain when obtaining an understanding of an entity's internal control sufficient for audit planning. Answer (a) is correct because an auditor must obtain an understanding that includes knowledge about the design of relevant controls and records and whether the client has placed those controls in operation. Answers (b) and (c) are incorrect because auditors may choose not to obtain information on operating effectiveness of controls and their consistency of application. Answer (d) is incorrect because there is no such explicit requirement relating to controls; see SAS 109 for the necessary understanding of internal control.

15.   (b)   SAS 109 states that the auditor should obtain sufficient knowledge of the information (including accounting) system to understand the financial reporting process used to prepare the entity's financial statements, including significant accounting estimates and disclosures. It also states that this knowledge is obtained to help the auditor to understand (1) the entity's classes of transactions, (2) how transactions are initiated, (3) the accounting records and support, and (4) the accounting processing involved from initiation of a transaction to its inclusion in the financial statements.

16.   (b)   The requirement is to determine why an auditor should concentrate on the substance of procedures rather than their form when obtaining an understanding of an entity's controls. Answer (b) is correct because management may establish appropriate controls but not act on them, thus creating a situation in which the form differs from the substance. Answer (a) is incorrect because documentation is not directly related to the issue of substance over form. Answer (c) is incorrect because inappropriate controls is only a part of an auditor concern; for example, a control may be appropriate, but it may not be operating effectively. Answer (d) is incorrect because while an auditor might suggest to management that the cost of certain controls seems to exceed their likely benefit, this is not the primary reason auditors are concerned with the substance of controls.

17. **(b)** Decision tables include various combinations of conditions that are matched to one of several actions. In an internal control setting, the various important controls are reviewed and, based on the combination of answers received, an action such as a decision on whether to perform tests of controls is determined. Program flowcharts simply summarize the steps involved in a program. Answer (a) is incorrect because decision tables do not emphasize the ease of manageability for complex programs. Answer (c) is incorrect because while decision tables may be designed using various cost benefit factors relating to the various conditions and actions, they do not justify the program. Answer (d) is incorrect because program flowcharts, not decision tables, emphasize the sequence in which operations are performed.

18. **(a)** The requirement is to identify the procedure that is not required to be included in an auditor's consideration of internal control. Answer (a) is correct because the auditor need not obtain evidence relating to operating effectiveness when control risk is to be assessed at the maximum level. Answer (b) is incorrect because an auditor must obtain an understanding of the internal control environment and the information system. Answers (c) and (d) are incorrect because an auditor is obligated to obtain information on the design of internal control and on whether control activities have been implemented.

19. **(a)** The requirement is to identify the primary objective of procedures performed to obtain an understanding of internal control. Answer (a) is correct because the auditor obtains a sufficient understanding of internal control to assess the risks of material misstatement and to design the nature, timing, and extent of further audit procedures. Answer (b) addresses inherent risk, the susceptibility of an assertion to material misstatement, assuming that there are no related controls. Answer (b) is incorrect since the concept of inherent risk assumes **no** internal control and is therefore not the primary objective. Answer (c) is incorrect because answer (a) is more complete and because decisions on modifying tests of controls are often made at a later point in the audit. Answer (d) is incorrect because the consistency of application of management's policies relates more directly to tests of controls than to obtaining an understanding of internal control.

20. **(d)** The requirement is to determine the correct statement with respect to the auditor's required documentation of the client's internal control. An auditor may document his/her understanding of the structure and his/her conclusions about the design of that structure in the form of answers to a questionnaire, narrative memorandums, flowcharts, decision tables, or any other form that the auditor considers appropriate in the circumstances. Answers (a) and (b) are, thus, incorrect because they suggest restrictions which do not exist in practice. Answer (c) is incorrect since at a minimum a list of reasons for nonreliance must be provided.

21. **(b)** In obtaining an understanding of internal control, the auditor should perform procedures to provide sufficient knowledge of the design of the relevant controls and whether they have been implemented. Information on

operating effectiveness need not be obtained unless control risk is to be assessed at a level below the maximum.

B.2. Assess the Risk of Material Misstatement and Design Further Audit Procedures

22. **(b)** Answer (b) is correct because tests of controls are only required when the auditor relies on the controls or substantive tests alone are not sufficient to audit particular assertions. Answers (a), (c), and (d) are incorrect because these procedures are required on every audit.

23. **(c)** The requirement is to identify the terms in which control risk should be assessed. Answer (c) is correct because SAS 109 requires that control risk be assessed in terms of financial statement assertions.

24. **(d)** The requirement is to identify a situation in which an auditor may desire to seek a further reduction in the assessed level of control risk. Answer (d) is correct because such a reduction is only possible when additional evidence, evaluated by performing additional tests of controls, is available. Answer (a) is incorrect because auditors at this point will ordinarily already have obtained the understanding of the information system to plan the audit. Furthermore, an understanding of internal control is needed on all audits. Answer (b) is incorrect because auditors must determine that controls have been implemented in all audits. Answer (c) is incorrect because a significant number of controls always pertain to financial statement assertions.

25. **(d)** Assessing control risk at a low level involves (1) identifying specific controls relevant to specific assertions that are likely to prevent or detect material misstatements in those assertions, and (2) performing tests of controls to evaluate the effectiveness of such controls. Answer (a) is incorrect because assessing control risk at a low level may lead to less extensive, not more extensive substantive tests. Answer (b) is incorrect because the actual level of inherent risk is not affected by the level of control risk. Also, one would not expect a change in the assessed level of control risk to result in a change in the assessed level of inherent risk. Answer (c) is incorrect because assessing control risk at a low level may lead to interim-date substantive testing rather than year-end testing.

26. **(d)** The requirement is to determine why an auditor assesses control risk. Answer (d) is correct because the assessed levels of control risk and inherent risk are used to determine the acceptable level of detection risk for financial statement assertions.

27. **(c)** Increases in the assessed level of the risk of material misstatement lead to decreases in the acceptable level of detection risk. Accordingly, the auditor will need to increase the extent of substantive tests such as tests of details. Answer (a) is incorrect because tests of controls are performed to reduce the assessed level of control risk only when controls are believed to be effective. Answer (b) is incorrect because the level of detection risk must be decreased, not increased. Answer (d) is incorrect because the level of inherent risk pertains to the susceptibility of an account to material misstatement independent of related controls.

28. **(d)** The requirement is to determine the primary purpose for which an auditor uses the knowledge provided by the understanding of internal control and the assessed level of the risk of material misstatement. Answer (d) is correct because the auditor uses such knowledge in determining the nature, timing, and extent of substantive tests for financial statement assertions. Answer (a) is incorrect because it is incomplete. For example, while auditors are concerned with the safeguarding of assets, they also need to determine whether the financial statement information is accurate. Answer (b) is incorrect for reasons similar to (a) in that determining whether opportunities are available for committing and concealing fraud is incomplete since this knowledge is also used to ascertain whether the chance of errors is minimized. Answer (c) is incorrect because knowledge provided by the understanding of internal control and the assessed level of control risk is not used to modify initial assessments of inherent risk and preliminary judgments about materiality levels. This knowledge is unrelated to those processes.

29. (d) The requirement is to identify a way that an auditor may compensate for a weakness in internal control. Answer (d) is correct because increasing analytical procedures decreases detection risk in a manner which may counterbalance the condition in internal control. In effect, the weakness in internal control is compensated for by increased substantive testing. See the outline of SAS 107 for the relationships among audit risk and its component risks—inherent risk, control risk, and detection risk. Answer (a) is incorrect because increasing both control risk (through a weakness in internal control) and detection risk increases audit risks. In addition, control risk and detection risk do not compensate for one another. Answer (b) is incorrect because increasing the extent of tests of controls is unlikely to be effective since the condition is known to exist. Answer (c) is incorrect because it is not generally appropriate to increase the judgment as to audit risk based on the results obtained.

30. (a) The requirement is to identify the correct statement concerning an auditor's assessment of control risk. Answer (a) is correct because SAS 109 indicates that assessing control risk may be performed concurrently during an audit with obtaining an understanding of internal control. Answer (b) is incorrect because evidence about the operation of internal control obtained in prior audits may be considered during the current year's assessment of control risk. Answer (c) is incorrect because the basis for an auditor's conclusions about the assessed level of control risk needs to be documented when control risk is assessed at levels **other than** the maximum level. Answer (d) is incorrect because a lower level of control risk requires more assurance that the control procedures are operating effectively.

31. (c) The requirement is to determine the correct statement concerning the assessed level of control risk. Answer (c) is correct because ordinarily the assessed level of control risk **cannot** be sufficiently low to **eliminate** the need to perform any substantive tests to restrict detection risk for significant transaction classes. Answer (a) is incorrect because tests of controls are unnecessary when control risk is assessed at the maximum level. Answer (b) is incorrect because analytical procedures are not designed to verify the design of internal control. Answer (d) is incorrect because dual-purpose tests (i.e., those that serve as both substantive tests and tests of controls) are not required to be performed, and because the term "preliminary control risk" is unclear.

B.3. Perform Further Audit Procedures—Tests of Controls

32. (d) The requirement is to identify how frequently controls that the auditor wishes to rely upon must be tested. Answer (d) is correct because the professional standards require auditors to test controls at least every third year. Answer (a) is incorrect because controls need not be tested monthly. Answer (b) is incorrect because ordinarily controls need not be tested with each audit. Answer (c) is incorrect because auditors may test such controls every third year, not every second year.

33. (d) The requirement is to identify the type of audit test most likely to provide assurance that controls are in use and operating effectively. Answer (d) is correct because inspection of documents is a form of a test of controls, and such tests are used to obtain reasonable assurance that controls are in use and operating effectively. Answer (a) is incorrect because auditors prepare flowcharts to document a company's internal control, not to obtain assurance that controls are in use and operating effectively. Answer (b) is incorrect because substantive tests relate to the accuracy of accounts and assertions rather than testing controls directly. Answer (c) is incorrect because analyzing tests of trends and ratios is an analytical procedure that does not directly test controls.

34. (a) The requirement is to identify the appropriate procedures for testing the segregation of duties related to inventory. Answer (a) is correct because SAS 109 suggests that when no audit trail exists (as is often the case for the segregation of duties) an auditor should use the observation and inquiry techniques.

35. (d) The requirement is to identify the objective of tests of details of transactions performed as tests of controls. Answer (d) is correct because the purpose of tests of controls is to evaluate whether internal control operates effectively. Answer (a) is incorrect because while monitoring the design and use of entity documents may be viewed as a test of controls, it is not the objective. Answer (b) is incorrect because determining whether internal control is implemented is not directly related to tests of controls; see SAS 109 for the distinction between "implemented" and "operating effectiveness." Answer (c) is incorrect because substantive tests, not tests of controls, are focused on detection of material misstatements in the account balances of the financial statements.

36. (a) The requirement is to identify a circumstance in which an auditor may decide to perform tests of controls. Answer (a) is correct because tests of controls will be performed when they are expected to result in a cost effective reduction in planned substantive tests. Answer (b) is incorrect because tests of controls are only performed when they are likely to support a further reduction in the assessed level of the risk of material misstatement. Answer (c) is incorrect because tests of controls are designed to decrease the assessed level of the risk of material misstatement, not increase it. Answer (d) is incorrect because internal control weaknesses normally result in more substantive testing and less tests of controls.

37. (b) The requirement is to identify the most appropriate procedures for assessing control risk. Auditors perform tests of controls to obtain evidence on the operating effectiveness of controls to assess control risk. Answer (b) is correct because tests of controls include inquiries of appropriate entity personnel, inspection of documents and reports, observation of the application of the policy or procedure, and reperformance of the application of the policy or procedure.

38. **(d)** The requirement is to identify the type of evidence an auditor most likely would examine to determine whether controls are operating as designed. Answer (d) is correct because inspection of client records documenting the use of computer programs will provide evidence to help the auditor evaluate the effectiveness of the design and operation of internal control; the client's control over use of its computer programs in this case is documentation of the use of the programs. In order to test this control, the auditor will inspect the documentation records. See SAS 110 for information on the nature of tests of controls. Answer (a) is incorrect because the confirmation process is most frequently considered a substantive test, not a test of a control. Answer (b) is incorrect because letters of representations provide corroborating information on various management representations obtained throughout the audit and therefore only provides limited evidence on internal control. Answer (c) is incorrect because attorneys' responses to auditor inquiries most frequently pertain to litigation, claims, and assessments.

39. **(c)** The requirement is to identify the procedure that is **not** a step in an auditor's assessment of control risk. Answer (c) is correct because performing tests of details of transactions to detect material misstatements pertains more directly to detection risk rather than inherent or control risk. Answer (a) is incorrect because auditors evaluate the effectiveness of internal control with tests of controls. Answer (b) is incorrect because obtaining an understanding of the entity's information system and control environment is a preliminary step for considering control risk. Answer (d) is incorrect because auditors will consider the effect of internal control on the various financial statement assertions.

40. **(a)** The requirement is to identify an approach that auditors use to obtain audit evidence about control risk. Answer (a) is correct because auditors test controls to provide evidence for their assessment of control risk through inquiries of appropriate personnel, inspection of documents and records, observation of the application of controls, and reperformance of the application of the policy or procedure. Answers (b), (c), and (d) are incorrect because analytical procedures, calculation, and confirmation relate more directly to substantive testing and are not primary methods to test controls for purposes of assessing control risk.

41. **(c)** The requirement is to identify the **least** likely type of evidence the auditor will examine to determine whether controls are operating effectively. Answer (c) is correct because confirmation of accounts receivable is a substantive test, not a test of a control. Answer (a) is incorrect because records documenting the usage of computer programs may be tested to determine whether access is appropriately controlled. Answer (b) is incorrect because examining canceled supporting documents may help the auditor to determine that the structure will not allow duplicate billing to result in multiple payments. Answer (d) is incorrect because proper signatures will help the auditor to de-

termine whether the authorization controls are functioning adequately.

42. **(a)** The requirement is to identify the accounts receivable auditing procedure that an auditor would most likely perform to obtain support for an assessed level of control risk below the maximum. Since an auditor uses the results of tests of controls to support an assessed level of control risk below the maximum, we are attempting to identify a test of a control. Answer (a) is correct because observing an entity's employee prepare the schedule of past due accounts receivable is a test of a control to evaluate the effectiveness the process of preparing an accurate schedule of past due accounts; if the process is found to be effective it may lead to a reduction in the assessed level of control risk. Answer (b) is incorrect because the confirmation of accounts receivable is a substantive test, not a test of a control. Answer (c) is incorrect because the inspection of accounts receivable for unusual balances and comparing uncollectible accounts expense to actual accounts expense is ordinarily an analytical procedure performed as a substantive test. Answer (d) is incorrect because comparing uncollectible accounts expense to actual uncollectible accounts is ordinarily a substantive test.

C.1. Management's Responsibility

43. **(b)** The requirement is to identify the type of companies to which the internal control provisions of the Sarbanes-Oxley Act of 2002 apply. Answer (b) is correct because the provisions apply to public companies that are registered with the Securities and Exchange Commission. Answer (a) is incorrect because nonissuer companies are not directly affected by the control provisions. Answer (c) is incorrect; there is no $100,000,000 requirement. Answer (d) is incorrect because nonissuer companies are not directly affected by the internal control provisions of the Act.

44. **(a)** The requirement is to identify the most likely framework to be used by management in its internal control assessment. Answer (a) is correct as the COSO internal control framework is by far the most frequently used one. Answer (b) is incorrect because while a COSO enterprise risk management framework does exist, it is not ordinarily used by management in its internal control assessment. Answers (c) and (d) are incorrect because there is no such thing as a "FASB 37 internal control definitional framework" or an "AICPA internal control analysis manager."

C.2. Management's Assessment

45. **(c)** The requirement is to identify the correct statement concerning the level of assistance that auditors may provide in assisting management with its assessment of internal control. Answer (c) is correct since only limited assistance may be provided so as not to create a situation in which the auditors are auditing their own work. Answer (a) is incorrect since some assistance may be provided. Answer (b) is incorrect because there are limitations on the level of assistance. Answer (d) is incorrect because the tie between risk and assistance seems inappropriate and in the wrong direction; also, this type of tradeoff between risk and assistance is not included in PCAOB Standard 5.

46. **(d)** The requirement is to identify which of the following need **not** be included in management's report on internal control under Section 404a of the Sarbanes-Oxley Act of 2002. Answer (d) is correct because, while the report must indicate that it is management's responsibility to establish and maintain adequate internal control, it need not also indicate that such control has no significant deficiencies. Answers (a), (b), and (c) are all incorrect because they include information that must be contained in management's report.

C.3. Control Definitions

47. **(a)** Answer (a) is correct because all material weaknesses are control deficiencies. Answer (b) is incorrect because a significant deficiency may or may not be a material weakness. Answer (c) is incorrect because not all control deficiencies are material weaknesses. Answer (d) is incorrect because only significant deficiencies and material weaknesses must be communicated.

48. **(d)** The requirement is to identify the term that is defined as a weakness in internal control that is less severe than a material weakness but important enough to warrant attention by those responsible for oversight of the financial reporting function. Answer (d) is correct because this is the definition of a significant deficiency. Answer (a) is incorrect because a *control deficiency* exists when the design or operation of a control does not allow management, or employees, in the normal course of performing their functions to prevent or detect misstatements on a timely basis. Answer (b) is incorrect because an *unusual weakness* is not used in the standards for integrated audits. Answer (c) is incorrect because the term unusual deficiency is not used in the standards for integrated audits.

49. **(d)** The requirement is to identify the amount involved with a material weakness. Answer (d) is correct because a material amount is involved. Answers (a), (b), and (c) are all incorrect because they suggest smaller amounts.

50. **(d)** The requirement is to identify the minimum likelihood of loss involved in the consideration of a control deficiency. Answer (d) is correct because a control deficiency is a condition in which the operation of a control does not allow management, or employees, in the normal course of performing their functions to prevent or detect misstatements on a timely basis—it does not explicitly consider likelihood of loss. Answer (a) is incorrect because the minimum likelihood of loss is not considered. Answer (b) is incorrect because the control deficiency occurrence of loss need not be more than remote. Answer (c) is incorrect because whether the minimum likelihood of loss is probable is not considered.

C.4. Evaluating Internal Control

51. **(a)** The requirement is to identify the type of control that reconciliation of cash accounts represents. Answer (a) is correct in that it is a compensating control which supplements a basic underlying control, in this case basic information processing controls related to cash. Answer (b) is incorrect because a preventive control prevents errors or fraud from occurring. Answer (c) is incorrect because the term "adjustive" control is not ordinarily used. Answer (d) is incorrect because "nonroutine" is ordinarily considered a type of transaction (e.g., the year-end close process), not a type of control.

52. **(d)** The requirement is to identify the type of transaction that establishing loan loss reserves is. An-

swer (d) is correct because *estimation transactions* are activities involving management's judgments or assumptions, such as determining the allowance for doubtful accounts, establishing warranty reserves, and assessing assets for impairment. Answer (a) is incorrect because the term substantive transaction is not used in PCAOB standards. Answer (b) is incorrect because routine transactions are those for recurring activities, such as sales, purchases, cash receipts and disbursements, and payroll. Answer (c) is incorrect because nonroutine transactions occur only periodically, such as the taking of physical inventory, calculating depreciation expense, or adjusting for foreign currencies; nonroutine transactions generally are not a part of the routine flow of transactions.

C.5. The Audit of Internal Control

53. **(d)** The requirement is to identify the procedure that involves tracing a transaction from origination through the company's information systems until it is reflected in the company's financial report. Answer (d) is correct because this is the approach followed in a walk-through. Answer (a) is incorrect because analytical analysis is a general term that simply suggests a general analysis. Answer (b) is incorrect because a substantive procedure addresses the correctness of a particular financial statement amount or disclosure. Answer (c) is incorrect because a test of a control addresses the operating effectiveness of a control.

54. **(b)** The requirement is to identify the "as of date" for purposes of an audit of internal control performed under PCAOB standards. Answer (b) is correct because the "as of date" is the last day of the fiscal period; it is this date on which the auditor concludes as to the effectiveness of internal control. Answers (a) and (c) are incorrect because neither the first day of the year nor the last day of the auditor's fieldwork is the appropriate date on which to evaluate internal control. Answer (d) is incorrect because the "as of date" is a particular date, not an average.

55. **(c)** The requirement is to identify the correct statement concerning a company that makes purchases both through the Internet and by telephone. Answer (c) is correct because both types of purchases are a part of the purchases process and represent major classes of transactions, as per PCAOB Standard 5. Answer (a) is incorrect because the purchase types themselves are not control objectives for internal control (control objectives address issues such as the completeness of the recording of sales). Answer (b) is incorrect because purchases are not assertions. Answer (d) is incorrect because purchase transactions may or may not be investigated in extreme detail.

56. **(a)** The requirement is to identify the circumstance(s) in which walk-throughs provide the auditor with primary evidence. A walk-through involves literally tracing a transaction from its origination through the company's information systems until it is reflected in the financial reports. Answer (a) is correct because a walk-through provides evidence to (1) confirm the auditor's understanding of the flow of transactions and the design of controls, (2) evaluate the effectiveness of the design of controls, and (3) to confirm whether controls have been placed in operation. Answer (b) is incorrect because walk-throughs provide the auditors with primary evidence to confirm whether controls have been placed in operation. Answer (c) is incorrect because walk-throughs provide primary evidence to evaluate the effectiveness of design in internal control. Answer (d) is incorrect both because walk-throughs provide primary evidence to (1) evaluate the effectiveness of the design of controls and (2) confirm whether the controls have been placed in operation.

57. **(a)** The requirement is to identify the most likely question to be asked of employee personnel during a walk-through. Answer (a) is correct because a question on whether an employee has ever been asked to override the process is included in the example questions to be asked by the auditor. Answer (b) is incorrect because auditors do not in general ask whether the employee believes he or she is underpaid. Answer (c) is incorrect because a direct question on fraudulent transactions like this, while possible, ordinarily is not suggested. Answer (d) is incorrect because the auditor will not usually ask who trained the person. Note that all four questions might be asked, but only one is among those recommended in Standard 5.

58. **(a)** The requirement is to identify how large the actual loss identified must be for a control deficiency to possibly be considered a material weakness. Answer (a) is correct because a material weakness is determined by whether there is more than a remote likelihood of a material loss occurring due to the control deficiency; the actual loss identified need not be material. Answer (b) is incorrect because it suggests that a material amount identified will not be considered a material weakness. Answer (c) is incorrect because it states that when the identified amount is immaterial it is never a material weakness. Answer (d) is incorrect because it suggests that when an immaterial or material actual loss is discovered, the situation would not be assessed as a possible material weakness.

59. **(c)** The requirement is to identify the circumstance that makes an account significant for purposes of a PCAOB audit of internal control. Answer (c) is correct because Standard 5 requires only more than a remote likelihood of material misstatement. Answer (a) is incorrect because the standard requires only a remote likelihood and because it is limited to material misstatements. Answer (b) is incorrect because the standard requires more than a remote likelihood, not more than a reasonably possible likelihood. Answer (d) is incorrect because material misstatements are involved, not misstatements that are more than inconsequential.

60. **(a)** The requirement is to identify the appropriate report when a control deficiency that is more than a significant deficiency is identified. Answer (a) is correct because a control deficiency that is more than a significant deficiency is a material weakness, and because a material weakness leads to an adverse opinion on internal control. Answer (b) is incorrect because qualified opinions are not issued when a material weakness exists. Answer (c) is incorrect because an unqualified opinion is not issued when a material weakness exists. Answer (d) is incorrect because explanatory language added to an unqualified report is not appropriate when a material weakness exists.

61. **(a)** The requirement is to identify the deficiency that is most likely to be considered a material weakness in internal control for purposes of an internal control audit of a public company. Answer (a) is correct because ineffective oversight of financial reporting by the audit committee is among the list of circumstances that PCAOB Standard 5 suggests are strong indicators of the existence of a material weakness. Restatement of previously issued financial statements as a result of a *change in accounting principles* is ordinarily not considered even a significant deficiency. Answer (c) is incorrect because the reply "inadequate segregation of recordkeeping from accounting" makes no real sense because accounting is involved with recordkeeping. Answer (d) is incorrect because control activity weaknesses often do not represent material weaknesses.

62. **(b)** The requirement is to identify the most appropriate report when a circumstance-caused scope limitation results in inability to evaluate internal control for a significant account involved in the audit. Answer (b) is correct because PCAOB Standard 5 indicates that either a qualified opinion or a disclaimer is appropriate, and because the disclaimer is not listed as an option. Answer (a) is incorrect because an adverse opinion is not appropriate. Answer (c) is incorrect because an unqualified opinion with explanatory language is not appropriate when the auditor is unable to evaluate internal control for a significant account. Answer (d) is incorrect because answers (a) and (c) are not appropriate.

63. **(c)** The requirement is to identify the most likely significant deficiency relating to a client's antifraud programs. Answer (c) is correct because an active audit committee, not a passive audit committee is needed. Answer (a) is incorrect because a broad scope of internal audit activities is ordinarily a strength, not a deficiency. Answer (b) is incorrect because a whistle-blower program that encourages anonymous submissions is required. Answer (d) is incorrect because it is not ordinarily necessary to perform criminal background investigations for likely customers.

64. **(a)** The requirement is to identify the appropriate audit report when a material weakness is corrected subsequent to year-end, but before the audit report is issued. Answer (a) is correct because PCAOB Standard 5 requires an adverse audit report when a material weakness exists at year-end, the "as of date." Answer (b) is incorrect because an unqualified opinion is not appropriate. Answer (c) is incorrect because an unqualified opinion with explanatory language is not adequate. Answer (d) is incorrect because a qualified opinion is not appropriate when a material weakness exists at year-end.

65. **(b)** The requirement is to specify whether material weaknesses and/or significant deficiencies lead to an adverse opinion on internal control in an integrated audit. Answer (b) is correct because only material weaknesses lead to an adverse opinion. Answer (a) is incorrect because significant deficiencies do not result in an adverse opinion. Answer (c) is incorrect because material weaknesses do result in adverse opinions but significant deficiencies do not. Answer (d) is incorrect because material weaknesses do result in adverse opinions.

66. **(b)** The requirement is to specify what types of deficiencies must be communicated by the auditor to the audit committee. Answer (b) is correct because the auditor must communicate material weaknesses and other significant deficiencies, but not all control deficiencies. Answer (a) is incorrect because control deficiencies that are not significant need not be communicated to the audit committee (unless the auditor has made an agreement to communicate them).

Answers (c) and (d) are incorrect because known material weaknesses must be communicated to the audit committee and control deficiencies that are not significant deficiencies need not be communicated.

67. (c) The requirement is to determine the manner in which significant deficiencies are communicated by the auditor to the audit committee under PCAOB Standard 5. Answer (c) is correct because the Standard requires a written communication. Answer (a) is incorrect because a written communication is required. Answer (b) is incorrect because the communication must be in a written form, not in an oral form. Answer (d) is incorrect because both material weaknesses and significant deficiencies must be communicated.

68. (c) The requirement is to identify the correct statement concerning the external auditors' use of the work of others when performing an audit of internal control of a public company. Answer (c) is correct because, after assuring themselves as to the competence and objectivity of the internal auditors and others, the external auditors may use their work—particularly in low-risk areas and when that work is supervised and/or reviewed. Answer (a) is incorrect because using the work of internal auditors and others is allowed. Answer (b) is incorrect because there is no such requirement of reporting to the audit committee, although this is one indication of internal auditor objective. Answer (d) is incorrect because there are limitations, and because it is uncertain whether liability will be shared.

69. (c) The requirement is to identify the information that must be communicated in writing to management. Answer (c) is correct because in an integrated audit all material weaknesses, significant deficiencies, and other control deficiencies must be reported to management. Answers (a) and (b) are incorrect because they are incomplete. Answer (d) is incorrect because "all suspected and possible employee law violations" need not be communicated.

70. (a) The requirement is to identify a correct statement about applying a top-down approach to identify controls to test in an integrated audit. Answer (a) is correct because certain effective entity-level controls may allow the auditor to omit additional testing beyond those controls. Answer (b) is incorrect because starting with assertions does not represent starting at the top (starting at the top includes consideration of the financial statements and entity-level controls first). Answer (c) is incorrect because consideration of entity-level controls cannot be avoided. Answer (d) is incorrect because not all controls related to assertions need to be focused upon, and because one may not omit controls related to the financial statements.

71. (d) The requirement is to identify the statement not included in a standard unqualified opinion on internal control performed under PCAOB requirements. Answer (d) is correct because the report indicates that management is responsible for maintaining effective internal control over financial reporting, not management and the audit committee. Answers (a), (b) and (c) are all incorrect because they represent statements included in the audit report.

72. (a) The requirement is to identify the correct statement relating to walk-throughs. Answer (a) is correct because walk-throughs—literally tracing transactions from their origination through the company's information system until they are reflected in the company's financial reports—

are often effective procedures for evaluating both the design effectiveness of controls and whether those controls have been placed in operation. Answer (b) is incorrect because walk-throughs help auditors to confirm whether controls have been placed in operation. Answer (c) is incorrect because walk-throughs help auditors to evaluate the design effectiveness of controls. Answer (d) is incorrect because walk-throughs help auditors evaluate the design effectiveness of controls and to confirm whether controls have been placed in operation.

D.1. Sales, Receivables, and Cash Reciepts

73. (a) The requirement is to identify the procedure an auditor most likely would perform to test controls relating to management's assertion about the completeness of cash receipts for cash sales at a retail outlet. Answer (a) is correct because the use of cash registers and tapes helps assure that all such sales are recorded. Answer (b) is incorrect because the cash has already been recorded. Answer (c) is incorrect because the procedure only deals with recorded deposits, and therefore the completeness assertion is not addressed as directly as in answer (a). Answer (d) is incorrect because one would not expect the cash balance in the general ledger to agree with the bank confirmation request amount due to items in transit and outstanding at the point of reconciliation.

74. (c) The requirement is to identify the proper procedure to be performed immediately upon receipt of checks by mail. Sound internal control requires the use of adequate documentation to ensure that all transactions are properly recorded. This helps the company attain the financial statement assertion of completeness. Answer (c) is correct because the preparation of a duplicate listing of checks received provides the company with a source document of all the checks received that day. One list is then forwarded to the employee responsible for depositing the checks at the end of the day and the other list is sent to the accounting department so that they can post the amount to the cash receipts journal. Answer (a) is incorrect because the daily cash summary will ordinarily be prepared at the end of the day when all checks have been received. Answer (b) is incorrect because checks need not be compared to a sales invoice. Answer (d) is incorrect because the employee opening the mail should not also perform the recordkeeping function of recording the checks in the cash receipts journal.

75. (b) The requirement is to determine the type of evidence obtained when tracing shipping documents to prenumbered sales invoices. Answer (b) is correct because the shipping documents relate to shipments to customers, and tracing them to sales invoices will provide evidence on whether sales invoices were prepared. Answer (a) is incorrect because duplicate shipments or billings will not in general be detected by tracing individual shipping documents to prenumbered sales invoices. Answer (c) is incorrect because an auditor will trace from customer orders to shipping documents to determine whether all goods ordered were shipped. Answer (d) is incorrect because an auditor will account for the sequence of sales invoices to determine whether all sale invoices were accounted for.

76. (a) The requirement is to identify the control most likely to reduce the risk of diversion of customer receipts by an entity's employees. Answer (a) is correct because a bank lockbox system eliminates employee contact with cash receipts, and thereby greatly reduces the risk of diversion by employees. Answer (b) is incorrect because remittance advices are ordinarily prenumbered using the numbering schemes of the various customers and not of the client; also, even if a prenumbering system is instituted, difficulties remain in assuring that all receipts are recorded. Answer (c) is incorrect because a monthly bank reconciliation is only likely to be effective when receipts are deposited and then abstracted. Answer (d) is incorrect because while the daily deposit of cash receipts may reduce the risk of employee diversion of receipts, the procedure is not as effective as the bank lockbox system, which eliminates employee contact with the receipts.

77. (a) The requirement is to identify the best listed procedure for detecting the lapping of cash receipts by the client's cashier through use of customer checks received in the mail. Answer (a) is correct because lapping will result in a delay in the recording of specific remittance credits on the financial records, but the checks will be deposited in the bank as they are received. Answer (b) is incorrect because the daily cash summaries will include the same sums as the cash receipts journal entries. Answer (c) is incorrect because the bank deposit slips will be identical to any details included in the monthly bank statements. Answer (d) is incorrect because while the write-off of a receivable may help the individual involved in the lapping to avoid repayment, no lag is to be expected between authorization of the write-off and the date it is actually recorded.

78. (c) The requirement is to determine the individual or organization to which a list of remittances should be forwarded to in addition to the cashier. Answer (c) is correct because the accounts receivable bookkeeper will use the listing to update the subsidiary accounts receivable records. Answer (a) is incorrect because internal auditors will not normally investigate each day's listing of remittances for unusual transactions. Answer (b) is incorrect because the treasurer will not in general compare daily listings to the monthly bank statement. Answer (d) is incorrect because the list will not be sent to the bank.

79. (d) The requirement is to identify the procedure that most likely would **not** be a control designed to reduce the risk of errors in the billing process. Answer (d) is correct because the reconciliation of the control totals for sales invoices with the accounts receivable subsidiary ledger will follow billing; thus billing errors will have already occurred. Answer (a) is incorrect because identification of differences in shipping documents and sales invoices will allow for a correction of any errors and proper billing. Answer (b) is incorrect because computer programmed controls will assure the accuracy of the sales invoice. Answer (c) is incorrect because the matching of shipping documents with the approved sales orders will allow the preparation of a correct invoice.

80. (b) The requirement is to identify the audit procedure an auditor most likely would perform to test controls relating to management's assertion concerning the completeness of sales transactions. Answer (b) is correct because inspection of shipping documents that have **not** been recorded in the sales journal will possibly reveal items that have been sold (as evidenced by a shipping document) but for some reason have not been recorded as sales. Answers (a), (c), and (d) are all incorrect because verification

of extension and footings, comparing invoiced prices, and inquiring about credit granting policies all relate more directly to the valuation assertion than to the completeness assertion.

81. (a) The requirement is to identify the control that most likely would assure that all billed sales are correctly posted to the accounts receivable ledger. Answer (a) is correct because the daily sales summary will include all "billed" sales for a particular day. Comparing this summary to the postings to the accounts receivable ledger will provide evidence on whether billed sales are correctly posted. Answer (b) is incorrect because comparing sales invoices to shipping documents provides evidence on whether invoiced sales have been shipped. Answer (c) is incorrect because reconciling the accounts receivable ledger to the control account will not provide assurance that all billed sales were posted in that both the receivable ledger and the control account may have omitted the sales. Answer (d) is incorrect because comparing shipments with sales invoices provides evidence on whether all shipments have been invoiced, not on whether all billed sales are correctly posted.

82. (a) The requirement is to determine the financial statement assertion being most directly tested when an auditor tests an entity's policy of obtaining credit approval before shipping goods to customers. Answer (a) is correct because testing credit approval helps assure that goods are shipped to customers who are likely to be able to pay; accordingly the valuation assertion for receivables is being directly tested. Answer (b) is incorrect because completeness deals with whether all transactions and accounts are recorded. Answer (c) is incorrect because existence deals with whether assets exist at a given date and whether recorded transactions have occurred during a given period. Answer (d) is incorrect because rights and obligations deal with whether assets are the rights of the entity and liabilities are the obligations of the entity at a given date.

83. (d) The requirement is to identify the control that most likely would help ensure that **all** credit sales transactions are recorded. Answer (d) is correct because the matching of shipping documents with entries in the sales journal will provide assurance that all shipped items (sales) have been completely recorded. Answer (a) is incorrect because comparison of approved sales orders to authorized credit limits and balances will help ensure that customer credit limits are not exceeded, rather than the complete recording of credit sales. Answer (b) is incorrect because reconciliation of the accounts receivable subsidiary ledger to the accounts receivable control account will provide only a limited amount of control over the complete recording of sales. The control is incomplete since, for example, a sale that has not been recorded in either the subsidiary or control accounts will not be detected. Answer (c) is incorrect because monthly statements generally will not be sent to customers to whom no sales have been recorded.

84. (c) The requirement is to identify the control that will be most effective in offsetting the tendency of sales personnel to maximize sales volume at the expense of high bad debt write-offs. Answer (c) is correct because segregation of the authorization of credit from the sales function will allow an independent review of the creditworthiness of customers. Answer (a) is incorrect because while denying access to cash by employees responsible for sales and bad debt write-offs may deter embezzlements, the problem of high bad debt write-offs is likely to remain. Answer (b) is incorrect because while so segregating the matching of shipping documents and sales invoices may help assure that items are shipped properly and subsequently recorded, it will not significantly affect bad debts. Answer (d) is incorrect because while independent reconciliation of control and subsidiary accounts receivable records may defer embezzlements, bad debt write-offs will not be affected.

85.   (d)   The requirement is to determine the department that should approve bad debt write-offs. The department responsible for bad debt write-offs should be independent of the sales, credit, and the recordkeeping for that function, and should have knowledge relating to the accounts. Answer (d) is correct because, in addition to being independent of the various functions, the treasurer's department is likely to have knowledge to help make proper decisions of this nature. Answers (a) and (b), accounts receivable and the credit department, are incorrect because neither department is independent of this function. Answer (c) is incorrect because while accounts payable is independent of the function, its personnel are less likely than those of the treasurer's department to have the necessary information relating to the accounts that should be written off.

86.   (b)   The requirement is to identify a reason that employers bond employees who handle cash receipts. Answer (b) is correct because employee knowledge that bonding companies often prosecute those accused of dishonest acts may deter employees' dishonest acts. Answer (a) is incorrect because bonding protects the employer from dishonest acts, not the employee from unintentional errors. Answer (c) is incorrect because the bonding company does not serve the role of independent monitoring of cash. Answer (d) is incorrect because while rotation of positions and forcing employees to take periodic vacations are effective controls for preventing fraud, they are not accomplished through bonding.

87.   (c)   The requirement is to identify the control which would offset a weakness that allowed the accounts receivable clerk to approve credit memos and to have access to cash. Note that such a weakness may lead to a fraud in which the accounts receivable clerk receives and keeps cash payments while issuing a fraudulent credit memo as the basis for a credit to the customer's account. Answer (c) is correct because the owner's review of credit memos could help establish that fraudulent memos had not been issued for receivables which had in actuality been collected by the clerk; for example, when reviewing credit memos the owner would expect to see a receiving report for sales returns for which credit memos have been generated. Answer (a) is incorrect because the bookkeeper may be able to maintain the records in such a manner as to avoid billing errors related to the fraud, and therefore a review of billings and postings may not reveal such fraud. Answer (b) is incorrect because month-end reconciliation of checking accounts with the monthly bank statement will not reflect cash that has been improperly diverted by the accounts receivable clerk. Answer (d) is incorrect because the accounts receivable clerk should be able to maintain the detail and ledger amount in balance and thereby avoid detection.

88.   (b)   The requirement is to determine who should prepare a remittance advice when the customer fails to in-

clude one with a remittance. Remittances should be opened by an individual such as a receptionist who is independent of the sales function. That individual will prepare any needed remittance advices. The credit manager [answer (a)], and the sales manager [answer (c)], are incorrect because they perform an authorization function related to sales. Answer (d) is incorrect because the accounts receivable clerk performs a recordkeeping function for sales.

D.2.   Purchases, Payables, and Cash Disbursements

89.   (b)   The requirement is to identify the audit procedure relating to paid vouchers that will provide assurance that each voucher is submitted and paid only once. Answer (b) is correct because when the check signer stamps vouchers "paid" it is unlikely to be paid a second time since that individual will notice the stamp on the voucher the second time it is submitted for payment.

90.   (d)   The requirement is to determine the appropriate responsibility for the person who signs checks. Answer (d) is correct because the individual who signs checks should be responsible for mailing them so as to avoid a variety of fraud in which the checks are improperly converted into cash by company employees. Answer (a) is incorrect because the individual who reconciles the bank accounts should have no other responsibilities with respect to cash. Answer (b) is incorrect because accounts payable does not need the checks and, if they receive them, those checks may be converted into cash which is then stolen. Answer (c) is incorrect because the person who signs the checks should determine that proper supporting documents exist and should cancel that documentation after the payment is made.

91.   (b)   The requirement is to determine the financial statement assertion that a test of controls of vouching a sample of entries in the voucher register to the supporting documents most directly addresses. Answer (b) is correct because the existence or occurrence assertion addresses whether recorded entries are valid and the direction of this test is from the recorded entry in the voucher register to the supporting documents. Answer (a) is incorrect because completeness addresses whether all transactions and accounts are included and would involve tests tracing from support for purchases to the recorded entry. Answers (c) and (d) are incorrect because vouching the entries provides only limited evidence on valuation and rights.

92.   (d)   The requirement is to determine the control that is **not** usually performed in the vouchers payable department. Answer (d) is correct because the vouchers payable department will not in general have access to unused prenumbered purchase orders and receiving reports. Answer (a) is incorrect because the vouchers payable department will match the vendor's invoice with the related receiving report to determine that the item for which the company has been billed has been received. Answer (b) is incorrect because the vouchers payable department will approve vouchers for payment when all documentation is proper and present. Answer (c) is incorrect because the vouchers payable department will code the voucher with accounts to be debited.

93.   (b)   The requirement is to identify the function that is consistent with matching vendors' invoices with receiving reports. Answer (b) is correct because while matching invoices and receiving reports, the employee might effectively recompute the calculations on the vendors' invoices to determine that the amounts are proper. Answers (a) and (c) are incorrect. The individual who matches the invoices and receiving reports will often also approve them for payment. Therefore, this individual should not also post accounts payable records or reconcile the accounts payable ledger. Answer (d) is incorrect because the individual who controls the signing of the checks should cancel the invoices after payment.

94.   (b)   The requirement is to identify the population from which items should be selected to determine whether checks are being issued for unauthorized expenditures. Answer (b) is correct because a sample of canceled checks should be selected and compared with the approved vouchers, a prenumbered purchase order and prenumbered receiving reports. A canceled check that does not have such support may have been unauthorized. Answers (a), (c), and (d) are all incorrect because selecting items from purchase orders, receiving reports, or approved vouchers will not reveal circumstances in which a check was issued without that supporting document. For example, when selecting a sample from purchase orders, one would not discover a situation in which a check had been issued without a purchase order.

95.   (d)   The requirement is to determine which question would most likely be included in an internal control questionnaire concerning the completeness assertion for purchases. Answer (d) is correct because prenumbering and accounting for purchase orders, receiving reports, and vouchers will allow a company to determine that purchases are completely recorded. For example, in examining a receiving report the client might discover that the purchase was not recorded. Answer (a) is incorrect because requiring a purchase order before a shipment is accepted will address whether or not the shipment has been ordered. Answer (b) is incorrect because matching purchase requisitions with vendor invoices does not directly address whether the purchase is recorded. Answer (c) is incorrect because the unpaid voucher file represents items that have already been recorded, and thus will not directly address the completeness of the recording of purchases.

96.   (d)   The requirement is to identify the proper control pertaining to the accounts payable department. Answer (d) is correct because the accounts payable department should establish the agreement of the vendor's invoice with the purchase order and receiving report to provide assurance that the item was both ordered and received. Answer (a) is incorrect because the individual signing the check (e.g., the treasurer), not the accounts payable department, should stamp, perforate, or otherwise cancel supporting documentation after a check is signed. Answer (b) is incorrect because purchase requisitions will not normally include detailed price information. Answer (c) is incorrect because the quantity ordered on the receiving department copy of the purchase order will already be obliterated when the purchase order is completed by the purchasing department.

97.   (b)   The requirement is to determine which copy of the purchase order should omit indication of the quantity of merchandise ordered. Answer (b) is correct because if the receiving department personnel are unaware of the quantities ordered, they will provide an independent count of quantities received. Answer (a) is incorrect because the department

that initiated the requisition needs the merchandise, and therefore, should know what has been ordered. Answer (c) is incorrect because the purchasing agent is involved with purchasing the items and therefore must be aware of the quantity involved. Answer (d) is incorrect because the accounts payable department must reconcile the quantity received and the quantity billed to the quantity that was authorized to be purchased per the purchase order.

98.   (b)   The requirement is to identify the audit procedure which would most likely detect a client error in recording a large purchase. Answer (b) is correct because reconciling the vendors' monthly statements with the subsidiary ledger for payables should disclose a difference in the month following the error. Answer (a), footing the purchases journal, is unlikely to detect the error since the journal's totals will have been mathematically accumulated properly. Answer (c) is incorrect because the incorrect total will be reflected in both the purchases journal and in the ledger accounts. Answer (d) is incorrect because such confirmations will only detect the error quarterly which is neither timely nor efficient.

99.   (d)   The requirement is to identify a function that is compatible with the approval of purchase orders. Answer (d) is correct because the purchases department will normally approve purchase orders (generated from user departments or stores) and negotiate terms of purchase with vendors. Answer (a) is incorrect because while the purchases department may reconcile the open invoice file, this is primarily a recordkeeping function that will often be performed by the accounting department. Answer (b) is incorrect because most frequently the receiving department will inspect goods upon receipt. Answer (c) is incorrect because user groups or stores will authorize requisitions of goods. Keep in mind the principle of segregation of functions. Recordkeeping, authorization, and custodial functions should all be segregated.

D.3.   Inventories and Production

100.   (c)   The requirement is to identify the most likely procedure an auditor would perform in obtaining an understanding of a manufacturing entity's internal control for inventory balances. Answer (c) is correct because a review of the entity's descriptions of inventory policies and procedures will help the auditor to obtain the necessary understanding about the design of relevant policies, procedures, and records, and whether they have been implemented by the entity. Answers (a) and (b) are incorrect because analyses of liquidity and turnover ratios are analytical procedures designed to identify cost variances that will help the auditor primarily to determine the nature, timing and extent of auditing procedures that will be used to obtain evidence for specific account balances or classes of transactions. Answer (d) is incorrect because test counts of inventory are generally obtained as a substantive procedure.

101.   (d)   The requirement is to identify the control that most likely would be used to maintain accurate inventory records. Answer (d) is correct because periodic inventory counts will assure that perpetual inventory records are accurate and, because employees will know that inventory differences are investigated, they will be less likely to steal any inventory. Answer (a) is incorrect because comparing the perpetual inventory records with current costs of items will reveal situations in which costs have changed, but is unlikely to help in the maintenance of accurate inventory records. Answer (b) is incorrect because while a just-in-time inventory ordering system may help assure that inventory records are accurate (as well as kept at low levels), such a system generally also requires periodic inventory counts to maintain accurate inventory records. Answer (c) is incorrect because matching requisitions, receiving reports, and purchase orders only helps assure that items received are paid for; the matching process does not assure accurate inventory records.

102. (d) The requirement is to determine a likely effect on the audit of inventory if the assessed level of control risk is high. Answer (d) is correct because a high assessed level of control risk may result in changing the timing of substantive tests to year-end rather than at an interim date. If the assessed level of control risk is low, the auditor could perform interim substantive tests and rely upon internal control to provide valid year-end records. However, because the assessed level of control risk is high, the controls cannot be relied upon. Also, the nature of substantive tests may change from less effective to more effective procedures (e.g., use of independent parties outside the entity rather than internal) and an increase in the extent of procedures (e.g., larger sample sizes). Answer (a) is incorrect because, as indicated, an auditor will generally seek a year-end count of inventory. Answer (b) is incorrect because gross profit tests will not in general have the required precision when control risk is high. Answer (c) is incorrect because tests of controls are likely to substantiate an auditor's view that control risk is high, and it is therefore unlikely that their performance will be cost-effective.

103. (c) The requirement is to identify the control which is most likely to address the completeness assertion for inventory. Answer (c) is correct because by prenumbering receiving reports and by reconciling them with inventory records, one is able to test completeness by determining whether all receipts have been recorded. Answer (a) is incorrect because reconciling the subsidiary records with the work in process will only identify discrepancies between the records, it will not identify whether all transactions that should be in the inventory records are represented in the records. Answer (b) is incorrect because while the segregation of receiving from custody of finished goods is important, it less directly addresses completeness than does answer (a). Answer (d) is incorrect because separating the duties between the payroll department and inventory accounting personnel does not directly address completeness of inventory.

104. (c) The requirement is to determine the proper internal control for handling customer returns of defective merchandise. Answer (c) is correct because the receiving department can count the goods, and list them on a sales return notice to determine that all such returns are properly recorded. This serves as a control because the normal procedures of the receiving function include establishing the original accountability and recordkeeping for items received. Answers (a), (b), and (d) all represent functions not typically involved in the receiving function and thus involve a higher risk relating to establishing accountability.

105. (c) The requirement is to identify the effect on revenues, receivables, and inventory of inadequate controls over the invoicing function that allows goods to be shipped without being invoiced. Items shipped without invoicing will result in a situation in which the accounting department is unaware of the sale. Therefore, debits to accounts receivable and credits to sales will not be recorded, resulting in an understatement of both revenues and receivables. Similarly, because accounting is unaware of the sale, no entry to reduce inventory will be made, resulting in an overstatement of inventory.

106. (c) The requirement is to identify the question that an auditor would expect to find on the **production** cycle section of an internal control questionnaire. Answer (c) is correct because approved requisitions will help maintain control over raw materials released to be used in the production cycle. Answers (a), (b), and (d) are all incorrect because approval of vendors' invoices for payment, mailing of checks after signing, and comparing individual disbursements to totals all pertain more directly to the disbursement cycle.

107. (b) The requirement is to determine an objective of internal control for a production cycle in addition to providing assurance that transactions are properly executed and recorded. Answer (b) is correct because, in addition to providing assurance as to proper execution and recording, an objective for the production cycle (as well as other cycles) is the safeguarding of assets, here work in process and finished goods. Answers (a), (c), and (d) are incorrect because they represent detailed controls established to help achieve the overall objectives. They are all much more specific than the overall objectives.

D.4. Personnel and Payroll

108. (b) The requirement is to identify a purpose of vouching data for a sample of employees in a payroll register to approved clock card data. Answer (b) is correct because the clock card data provides the auditor with evidence on whether employees worked the number of hours for which the payroll register indicates they were paid. Answer (a) is incorrect because clock card data often does not include authorized pay rates. Answer (c) is incorrect because the procedure does not directly address the segregation of duties since no information is provided concerning the distribution of the payroll. Answer (d) is incorrect because unclaimed payroll checks are not being analyzed.

109. (a) The requirement is to identify the control that most likely could help prevent employee payroll fraud. Answer (a) is correct because prompt notification of the payroll supervisor concerning terminations will lead to timely removal of terminated employees from the payroll. Accordingly, no payroll checks will be prepared for such terminated employees. Answer (b) is incorrect because unclaimed payroll checks should not be returned to the supervisors who might inappropriately cash them. Answer (c) is incorrect because since the payroll department is involved in recordkeeping, it should not approve salary rates. Answer (d) is incorrect because calculation of total hours by the payroll supervisor is unlikely to prevent employee payroll fraud.

110. (a) The requirement is to determine the best procedure for determining the effectiveness of an entity's controls relating to the existence or occurrence assertion for payroll transactions. Answer (a) is correct because proper segregation of duties between personnel and payroll disbursement eliminates many frauds in which "phantom" employees are being paid. Answer (b) is incorrect because accounting for the prenumbered payroll checks addresses completeness more directly than it does existence or occurrence. Answer (c) is incorrect because recomputing payroll deductions for employee fringe benefits, without additional analysis, provides only a very limited test of existence or occurrence. Answer (d) is incorrect because verifying the preparation of the monthly payroll account bank reconciliation is unlikely to provide evidence on the existence or occurrence assertion, although some possibility does exist if signatures on checks are analyzed in detail.

111. (c) The requirement is to identify the situation in which it is most likely that an auditor would assess control risk for payroll at a high level. Answer (c) is correct because the payroll department, which is essentially a recordkeeping function, should not also authorize payroll rate changes. Under strong internal control recordkeeping, authorization, and custody over assets should be segregated. Answer (a) is incorrect because examining authorization forms for new employees is consistent with the payroll department's recordkeeping function. Answer (b) is incorrect because comparing payroll registers with original batch transmittal data is a control relating to recordkeeping. Answer (d) is incorrect because while the actual hiring of employees is normally done in the personnel department, allowing the payroll department supervisor to hire subordinates, with proper approval, is not as inconsistent with payroll's recordkeeping function as is authorizing rate changes for all employees.

112. (c) The requirement is to identify the control most likely to prevent direct labor hours from being charged to manufacturing overhead. Answer (c) is correct because time tickets may be coded as to whether direct labor on various projects was involved. Accordingly, using time tickets will help identify direct labor costs. Answer (a) is incorrect because while periodic counts of work in process may provide a control over physical units of production, the counts will not in general provide assurance that direct labor hours are properly charged to the product rather than to manufacturing overhead. Answer (b) is incorrect because comparing daily journal entries with production orders will not in general identify costs that have been omitted from direct labor due to the level of aggregation of the entries. Answer (d) is incorrect because the reconciliation of work in process inventory with budgets will provide only very limited detection ability relating to the charging of direct labor to manufacturing overhead.

113. (a) The requirement is to determine the individual(s) who should distribute paychecks and have custody of unclaimed paychecks. Answer (a) is correct because these custody functions should not be performed by the payroll department which is a recordkeeping function. Under proper internal control recordkeeping, custody, and authorization of transactions should be segregated.

114. (c) If payment of wages were to be in cash, each employee receiving payment should be required to sign a receipt for the amount of pay received. Thus, there would be control over the total amount disbursed as well as amounts disbursed to each individual employee. Answer (a) is incorrect because if a signed receipt is not received from each employee paid, there would be no proof of payment. Even though the pay envelopes include both cash and a

computation of net wages, the employees should have the opportunity to count the cash received before signing a payroll receipt. Answer (b) is incorrect because unclaimed pay envelopes should not be retained by the paymaster, but rather deposited in a bank account by the cashier. Answer (d) is incorrect because the wage payment will be made in cash and not by check. Accordingly, a receipt must be obtained for each cash payment.

115. (a) The requirement is to identify the purpose of segregating the duties of hiring personnel and of distributing payroll checks. Answer (a) is correct because the hiring of personnel is an authorization function while the distribution of checks is a custody function. Thus, in order to properly segregate authorization from custody, these duties should not be performed by the same individual. The combination of these two functions in the same position would create the possibility of the addition of a fictitious employee to the payroll and subsequent misappropriation of paychecks. Answer (b) is incorrect because the functions involved are not primarily operational or recordkeeping. Answer (c) is incorrect because the treasury function, and not the controllership function, will normally be responsible for distributing payroll checks. Answer (d) is incorrect because segregation of duties does not directly address administrative controls vs. internal accounting controls.

116. (c) The requirement is to determine the best method to minimize the opportunities for fraud for unclaimed cash in a **cash** payroll system. For a **cash** payroll the best control is to get the unclaimed cash out of the firm's physical control and into the bank. Answer (a) is incorrect because maintaining the accountability for cash which is in a safe-deposit box is difficult. Answers (b) and (d) are incorrect because the cash need not be kept by the firm.

117. (c) The requirement is to identify a reason why an auditor may observe the distribution of paychecks. Answer (c) is correct because an employee's presence to collect the paycheck provides evidence that the employee actually exists and is currently employed by the client. Answer (a) is incorrect because the distributions of payroll checks would not reveal whether payrate authorization is properly separated from the operating function. Answer (b) is incorrect because the paycheck distribution does not provide information on whether deductions from gross pay have been calculated properly. Answer (d) is incorrect because observation of the paycheck distribution process does not of itself provide assurance that the paychecks agree with the related payroll register and time cards.

118. (a) The requirement is to determine the department most likely to approve change in pay rates and deductions from employee salaries. Answer (a) is correct because the personnel department, which has the primary objective of planning, controlling and coordinating employees, will determine that proposed salary increases (often recommended by supervisors of employees) are consistent with the company's salary guidelines and will approve changes in deductions. Answers (b) and (c) are incorrect because the treasurer and controller will in general initiate the pay rate change process for only those employees within their departments and will not generally approve changes for employees outside their departments. Answer (d) is incorrect because the payroll functions is a recordkeeping function which will modify employee pay rates based on approved changes from personnel. Payroll should not have authority regarding pay rates and deductions.

D.5. Financing

119. (d) The requirement is to determine the most likely question that would be included on an internal control questionnaire for notes payable. Answer (d) is correct because companies frequently require that direct borrowings on notes payable be authorized by the board of directors; accordingly, auditors will determine whether proper policy has been followed. Answer (a) is incorrect because internal control questionnaires do not in general include questions on whether assets that collateralize notes payable are critically needed. Answer (b) is incorrect because the internal control questionnaire for disbursements is more likely to address the required authorized signatures on checks than will the internal control questionnaire for notes payable. Answer (c) is incorrect because while it is often good business practice to use proceeds from long-term notes to purchase noncurrent assets, this is not required and is not included on an internal control questionnaire.

120. (d) The requirement is to identify the primary responsibility of a bank acting as registrar for capital stock. Answer (d) is correct because the primary responsibility of the stock registrar is to prevent any overissuance of stock, and thereby verify that the stock is issued properly. Answer (a) is incorrect because registrar will not in general determine that the dividend amounts are proper. Answer (b) is incorrect because the transfer agent will maintain records of total shares outstanding as well as detailed stockholder records, and carry out transfers of stock ownership. Answer (c) is incorrect because registrars do not perform the role described relating to mergers, acquisitions, and the sale of treasury stock.

121. (a) Canceled stock certificates should be defaced and attached to corresponding stubs as is done with voided checks. The objective of the control is to prevent reissuance. Answer (b) is incorrect because failure to deface permits reissuance. Answer (c) is incorrect because destruction of the certificates would preclude their control (i.e., their existence after defacing provides assurance that they cannot be reissued). If the certificates were destroyed, one or more might be reissued without any proof that such occurred. Answer (d) is incorrect because the Secretary of State has no interest in receiving defaced and canceled stock certificates.

D.6. Investing

122. (a) The requirement is to identify the reply which is **not** a control that is designed to protect investment securities. Answer (a) is not a control since the custody of securities should be assigned to individuals who **do not** have accounting responsibility for securities; as with other assets, authorization, recordkeeping, and custody should be separated. Answer (b) is incorrect because securities should be properly controlled physically in order to prevent unauthorized usage. Answer (c) is incorrect because access to securities should ordinarily be vested in two individuals so as to assure their safekeeping. Answer (d) is incorrect because securities should be registered in the name of the owner.

123. (b) The requirement is to identify the best control for safeguarding marketable securities when an independent trust agent is not employed. Answer (b) is correct because

requiring joint control over securities maintained in a safe-deposit box assures that, absent collusion, assets are safeguarded. Answer (a) is incorrect because a review of investment decisions by the investment committee will have a very limited effect on *safeguarding* marketable securities. Answer (c) is incorrect because the simple tracing of marketable securities from the subsidiary ledgers to the general ledger does not directly safeguard marketable securities since, for example, unrecorded transactions may occur. Answer (d) is incorrect because, even if the chairman of the board did verify marketable securities on the balance sheet date, the control will only be effective at that point in time.

124. (d) The requirement is to identify the best audit procedure when a weakness in internal control over reporting of retirements exists. Answer (d) is correct because selecting certain items of equipment from the accounting records and attempting to locate them will reveal situations in which the accounting records still have them recorded subsequent to their retirement. Answer (a) is incorrect because inspecting items that still exist is not likely to lead to discovery of unrecorded retirements. Answer (b) is incorrect because depreciation may continue to be taken on equipment that has been retired, but not recorded. Answer (c) is incorrect because it is doubtful that such retirements have been reclassified as "other assets."

125. (d) The requirement is to identify the question that is **least** likely to be included on an internal control questionnaire concerning the initiation and execution of equipment transactions. Answer (d) is correct because procedures to monitor and properly restrict access to equipment do not relate directly to the initiation and execution of equipment transactions. Answer (a) is incorrect because requests for major repairs relate to initiation of a transaction which should be controlled. Answer (b) is incorrect because prenumbered purchase orders may be used to control all purchases, including purchases of equipment. Answer (c) is incorrect because the significant amounts of money involved with purchases of equipment suggest the need for the solicitation of competitive bids.

126. (d) The requirement is to identify the control that would be most effective in assuring that the proper custody of assets in the investing cycle is maintained. Answer (d) is correct because comparing recorded balances in the investment subsidiary ledger with physical counts will help assure that recorded assets are those over which the company has custody. This is an example of the control activity of comparison of assets with recorded accountability. Answer (a) is incorrect because internal control is improved when two individuals, not one, must be present for entry to the safe-deposit box. Answer (b) is incorrect because while the segregation of duties within the recordkeeping may in certain circumstances be desirable, it does not directly address custody over assets. Answer (c) is incorrect because only extremely major investments generally need be authorized by the board of directors.

127. (d) The requirement is to determine who should have responsibility for custody of short-term bearer bond investments and the submission of coupons for periodic collections of interest. The treasurer authorizes such transactions. Answer (a) is incorrect because the chief accountant, who is in charge of the recordkeeping function, should not also maintain custody of the bonds. Answer (b) is incorrect because the internal auditor should not be directly involved as such involvement would make an independent review of the system impossible. Answer (c) is incorrect because the cashier function is more directly involved with details such as endorsing, depositing, and maintaining records of cash receipts.

128. (b) The requirement is to identify the control that would be most likely to assist an entity in satisfying the completeness assertion related to long-term investments. Answer (b) is correct because completeness deals with whether all transactions are recorded, and the comparison of securities in the bank safe-deposit box with recorded investments may reveal securities which are in the safe-deposit box but are not recorded. Answer (a) is incorrect because verification of security registration helps establish the rights assertion not the completeness assertion. Answer (c) is incorrect because vouching the acquisition of securities by comparing brokers' advices with canceled checks helps to establish the existence assertion not the completeness assertion. Answer (d) is incorrect because a comparison of the current market prices of recorded investments with brokers' advices addresses the valuation assertion not the completeness assertion.

129. (a) The requirement is to identify the best control for safeguarding marketable securities against loss. Answer (a) is correct because use of an independent trust company allows the effective separation of custody and recordkeeping for the securities. Answer (b) is incorrect because a verification of marketable securities at the balance sheet date may have only a limited effect on safeguarding the securities throughout the year. Answer (c) is incorrect because tracing all purchases and sales of marketable securities will not affect securities that have disappeared for which no entries have been made. Also, it is unlikely that an entity will rely upon the independent auditor in this manner. Answer (d) is incorrect because maintenance of control over custody by a member of the board of directors may provide less complete control than the use of an independent trust company.

130. (c) The requirement is to determine the appropriate combination of audit tests when there are numerous property and equipment transactions during the year and the auditor plans to assess control risk at a low level. Answer (c) is correct because, to justify an assessment of control risk at a low level, tests of controls will be required. This will allow auditors to perform only limited tests of current year property and equipment transactions. Answer (a) is incorrect because tests of controls will be performed to allow the auditor to perform limited, not extensive, tests of property and equipment balances at the end of the year. Answers (b) and (d) are incorrect because analytical procedures on either year-end balances or transactions will not justify a low assessed level of control risk.

D.7.   Overall Internal Control Questionnaires (Check-
     lists)

131. (d) The requirement is to determine the type of fraud which is most difficult to detect. Answer (d), a fraud committed by the controller, is most difficult to detect because the controller is in control of the recordkeeping function and thus may be able to commit a fraud and then manipulate the accounting records so as to make its discovery unlikely. Answer (a) is incorrect because while a cashier

may be able to embezzle funds, s/he will not have access to the accounting records and thus discovery of the embezzlement will be likely. Answer (b) is incorrect because a keypunch operator will not in general have access to assets. Answer (c) is incorrect because an internal auditor will not generally be able to manipulate the accounting records and generally has limited access to assets.

E.1.a.   Communication of Internal Control Related
     Matters

132. (c) Answer (c) is correct because weaknesses that were communicated in the past and not corrected must be recommunicated to management and those charged with governance. Answers (a), (b), and (d) are all accurate statements about audit requirements.

133. (c) The requirement is to identify the matter an auditor would most likely consider to be a material weakness to be communicated to those charged with governance. Answer (c) is correct because ineffective oversight of financial reporting by those charged with governance is an indicator of a material weakness (AU 325). Answers (a), (b), and (d) are all incorrect because a failure to renegotiate unfavorable long-term purchase commitments, recurring operating losses, and plans to reduce ownership equity do not fall within the definition of a material weakness.

134. (c) The requirement is to identify the correct statement concerning significant deficiencies identified in an audit. Answer (c) is correct because an auditor may communicate significant deficiencies either during an audit or after the audit's completion. Answer (a) is incorrect because an auditor need not search for significant deficiencies. Answer (b) is incorrect because all significant deficiencies are not also material weaknesses. Answer (d) is incorrect because an auditor may not issue a written report that **no** significant deficiencies were noted during an audit.

135. (d) The requirement is to identify the statement that should be included in an auditor's letter on significant deficiencies. Answer (d) is correct because AU 325 indicates that such a letter to the audit committee should (1) indicate that the audit's purpose was to report on the financial statements and **not** to express an opinion on internal control, (2) include the definition of a significant deficiency, and (3) restrict distribution of the report.

136. (c) The requirement is to identify the correct statement concerning an auditor's required communication of significant deficiencies. Answer (c) is correct because distribution of an auditor's report on significant deficiencies should be restricted to management and the audit committee. Answer (a) is incorrect because lack of correction of a significant deficiency does not necessarily result in a scope limitation. Answer (b) is incorrect because tests of controls need not be performed relating to significant deficiencies. Answer (d) is incorrect because although timely communication of significant deficiencies may be important, depending upon the nature of the significant deficiency identified, the auditor may choose to communicate it either after the audit is concluded or during the course of the audit.

137. (d) The requirement is to identify the correct statement about significant deficiencies noted in an audit. Answer (d) is correct because the auditor should separately identify and communicate material weaknesses and significant deficiencies (AU 325). Answer (a) is incorrect because significant deficiencies are less severe than material weaknesses. Answer (b) is incorrect because the auditor is not obligated to search for significant deficiencies. Answer (c) is incorrect because such deficiencies should be recommunicated.

138. (b) The requirement is to determine the representation that should **not** be included in a report on internal control related matters noted in an audit. Answer (b) is correct because the auditors should not issue a report on internal control stating that no significant deficiencies were identified during the audit. Answer (a) is incorrect because significant deficiencies should be disclosed. Answer (c) is incorrect because an auditor may recommend corrective follow-up action. Answer (d) is incorrect because an auditor may disclose the fact that the consideration of internal control would **not** necessarily disclose all significant deficiencies that exist.

139. (b) The requirement is to identify the correct statement regarding material weaknesses and significant deficiencies. Answer (b) is correct because a compensating control is a control that lessens the severity of a deficiency (AU 325). Answer (a) is incorrect because material weaknesses should be reported separately from significant deficiencies. Answer (c) is incorrect because while the auditor may choose to communicate material weakness and significant deficiencies immediately, the communication may occur at other times. Answer (d) is incorrect because significant deficiencies are less severe than material weaknesses.

140. (b) The requirement is to determine an auditor's responsibility after s/he has discovered and orally communicated information on a weakness in internal control to the client's senior management and those charged with corporate governance. Answer (b) is correct because the auditor, as outlined throughout AU 318, considers and documents his/her understanding of internal control to assist in planning and determining the proper nature, timing, and extent of substantive tests. Answer (a) is incorrect because no scope limitation is indicated although an internal control condition does exist. Similarly, answers (c) and (d) are incorrect because audit activities need not be suspended and the auditor need not withdraw from the engagement.

E.1.b   The Auditor's Communication with Those Charged with Governance

141. (b) The requirement is to determine the matter that an auditor would communicate to those charged with governance. Answer (b) is correct because AU 380 requires that when the auditor is aware of such consultation with another CPA, s/he should discuss with the audit committee his/her views about significant matters that were the subject of such consultation; accordingly, such a discussion with management is to be expected. While the information suggested in answers (a), (c), and (d) may all be communicated to the audit committee, they are not included as required disclosures under AU 380. See AU 380 for the various matters that must be communicated to those charged with governance.

142. (b) The requirement is to identify the correct statement concerning an auditor's required communication with those charged with governance. Answer (b) is correct be-

cause the communication should include such information on disagreements. See AU 380 for this and other required communications with those charged with governance. Answer (a) is incorrect because the communication may occur before or after issuance of the auditor's report. Answer (c) is incorrect because not all matters need be communicated to management. Answer (d) is incorrect because significant adjustments need to be communicated to those charged with governance.

143. (b) The requirement is to identify the discussion that it is least likely that an auditor will initiate with those charged with governance. Answer (b) is correct because auditors do not generally initiate a discussion on materiality, although they do occasionally respond to such questions. See AU 380 for auditor communications with those charged with governance.

144. (b) The requirement is to identify the correct statement about an auditor's required communication with those charged with governance. Answer (b) is correct because the communication must include significant misstatements discovered, even if corrected by management. Answer (a) is incorrect because while such communications may be communicated to management, there is no such requirement. Answer (c) is incorrect because disagreements with management, as well as the other required disclosures, may be communicated either orally or in writing. Answer (d) is incorrect because an auditor must recommunicate such weaknesses in internal control. Also, see AU 380 for the matters communicated to those charged with governance.

145. (a) The requirement is to determine whether disagreements with management and initial selection of significant accounting policies need to be communicated to those charged with corporate governance. Answer (a) is correct because disagreements should be communicated directly to those charged with corporate governance. Answer (b) is incorrect because direct communication by the auditor is not required for selection of accounting principles. Management may engage in this communication with those charged with corporate governance. Answer (c) is incorrect because the auditor only needs to make sure that management has communicated with the committee concerning initial selection of significant accounting policies in emerging areas that lack authoritative guidance. Answer (d) is incorrect because disagreements should be communicated directly to those charged with corporate governance.

146. (a) The requirement is to determine the information that an auditor should communicate to those charged with corporate governance. Answer (a) is correct because both significant audit adjustments and management's consultation with other accountants about significant accounting matters should be communicated to an audit committee. See AU 380 for these and other matters that should be so communicated.

E.2.   Reporting on Internal Control

147. (d) The requirement is to identify the statement that should be included in a CPA's report on a client's internal control over financial reporting. Answer (d) is correct because AT 501 requires that the report include a comment on the inherent limitations of any internal control.

148. (a) The requirement is to identify the statement that best describes a CPA's engagement to report on an entity's internal control over financial reporting. Answer (a) is correct because the objective of an attestation engagement is to form an opinion on the effectiveness of internal control. Answer (b) is incorrect because no such negative assurance is provided based on an "audit" of the entity's internal control. Answer (c) is incorrect because such engagements do not project expected benefits of the entity's internal control. Answer (d) is incorrect because such engagements are attestation engagements, not consulting engagements.

149. (c) The requirement is to determine the correct statement regarding an engagement to examine internal control. Answer (c) is correct because the procedures relating to internal control will be more extensive when reporting on internal control as compared to procedures performed for a financial statement audit. This difference occurs because during financial statement audits the auditor may decide not to perform tests of controls and may simply assess control risk at the maximum level. Conversely, in an engagement to report on internal control an auditor must perform additional tests of controls. Answer (a) is incorrect because such duplication of procedures may not be necessary. Answer (b) is incorrect because a report on internal control will not in general increase the reliability of the financial statements. Answer (d) is incorrect because, as indicated, the scope of procedures relating to internal control is more extensive, not more limited, than the assessment of control risk made during a financial statement audit.

150. (d) The requirement is to identify the relationship between an examination of internal control and obtaining an understanding of internal control and assessing control risk as part of an audit. Answer (d) is correct because, while the scope and purpose differ between the two types of engagements, the procedures followed are similar. See AT 501 (or PCAOB Standard 5) for information on reporting on an audit of internal control.

151. (b) The requirement is to describe the contents of a report on the study of internal control that is based on criteria established by governmental agencies. Answer (b) is correct because the report should indicate matters covered by the consideration and whether the auditor's consideration included tests of controls with the procedures covered by his/her consideration. Additionally, the report should describe the objectives and limitations of internal control and the accountant's evaluation thereof; state the accountant's conclusion, based on the agency's criteria; and describe the purpose of the report and state that it should not be used for any other purpose. Answer (a) is incorrect because the agency's name should be included. Answer (c) is incorrect because a conclusion may be made relative to the agency's criteria. Answer (d) is incorrect because the accountant should not assume responsibility for the comprehensiveness of the criteria.

152. (b) AT 501 states that when a deviation from the control criteria being reported upon exists (here a material weakness in internal control) the CPA should report directly upon the subject matter and not upon the assertion.

E.3. Effects of an Internal Audit Function

153. (a) The requirement is to identify the most likely information a CPA would obtain in assessing the competence of an internal auditor. Answer (a) is correct because in assessing competence, an internal auditor will consider the quality of working paper documentation as well as a variety

of other factors outlined in AU 322. Answer (b) is incorrect because an organization's commitment to integrity and ethical values, while important, does not bear as directly upon internal auditor competence. Answers (c) and (d) are incorrect because the influence of management and the organizational level to which the internal auditor reports are factors used to assess internal auditor objectivity. AU 322 provides overall guidance on the use of internal auditors.

154. (d) The requirement is to determine whether the independent auditor may share responsibility with an entity's internal auditor for assessing inherent risk and control risk. AU 322 requires that judgments about inherent and control risk always be those of the independent auditor. It also requires that judgments about the materiality of misstatements, the sufficiency of tests performed, the valuation of significant accounting estimates, and other matters affecting the auditor's report should always be those of the independent auditor. See AU 322 for information on the external auditor's consideration of the internal audit function.

155. (d) The work of internal auditors may affect the nature, timing and extent of the audit, including (1) procedures the auditor performs when obtaining an understanding of the entity's internal control, (2) procedures the auditor performs when assessing risk, and (3) substantive procedures the auditor performs.

156. (c) The requirement is to identify the circumstance in which an internal auditor's work would most likely affect the nature, timing, and extent of a CPA's auditing procedures. When considering the effect of the internal auditors' work, the CPA considers (1) the materiality of financial statement amounts, (2) the risk of material misstatement of the assertions, and (3) the degree of subjectivity involved in the evaluation of the audit evidence. Answer (c) is correct because the existence of fixed asset additions involves little subjectivity. Answers (a) and (b) are incorrect because the existence of contingencies and the valuation of intangible assets are subjective and the risk of misstatement may be high. Answer (d) is incorrect because the valuation of related-party transactions may be very subjective due to the lack of an "arm's-length" transaction.

157. (d) AU 322 states that internal auditors may assist the CPA in obtaining an understanding of internal control, in performing tests of controls, and in performing substantive tests.

158. (b) The requirement is to identify the type of information used by a CPA to assess the competence of internal auditors. Answer (b) is correct because, along with various other factors, AU 322 indicates that the CPA should obtain evidence on the educational background and professional certification of the internal auditors when considering competence. Answers (a) and (c) are incorrect because analysis of organizational level to which the internal auditors report and policies on relatives are considered when assessing internal auditor objectivity. Answer (d) is incorrect because access to sensitive records will not provide a CPA with information on competence.

159. (d) The requirement is to identify the **least** likely source of information to the CPA on an entity's internal auditor's competence and objectivity. Answer (d) is correct because analytical procedures do not ordinarily provide information on the internal auditor. See AU 329 for information on analytical procedures.

160. **(a)** The requirement is to identify the characteristics of an internal auditor which must be considered by an independent auditor who decides that the internal auditor's work might have a bearing on his/her procedures. Answer (a) is correct because independent auditors must consider internal auditor competence, objectivity, and work performance. Answer (b) is incorrect because an independent auditor is less concerned about internal auditor efficiency, although internal auditor experience will be considered in the assessment of competence. Answers (c) and (d), while partially correct, are less complete than answer (a).

161. **(d)** The requirement is to determine how a CPA should assess the objectivity of an internal auditor. Answer (d) is correct because when assessing the objectivity of an internal auditor the CPA should consider organizational status and policies for maintaining objectivity. Answers (a), (b), and (c) are all incorrect because evaluating the quality control program, and examining and testing an internal auditor's work all relate more directly to assessing internal auditor competence rather than to objectivity. See AU 322 for these and other factors considered when assessing internal auditor competence.

E.4. Reports on the Processing of Transactions by Service Organizations

162. **(a)** The requirement is to identify the information provided in a service auditor's report which includes an opinion on a description of controls implemented. Answer (a) is correct since such a report includes a description of the scope and nature of the CPA's procedures. Answers (b), (c), and (d) are all incorrect because they suggest information not included in such a report. See AU 324 for information on the audit of service organizations.

163. **(a)** The requirement is to identify a CPA's reporting responsibility when reporting on internal control implemented for a service organization that processes payroll transactions. Answer (a) is correct because since the CPA is only expressing an opinion on whether controls have been implemented, a disclaimer should be provided on operating effectiveness. Answer (b) is incorrect because no specific statement is made with respect to earlier objectives. Answer (c) is incorrect because controls relevant to financial statement assertions are not so identified. Answer (d) is incorrect because the assessed level of control risk is not disclosed. See AU 324 for information on processing of transactions by service organizations.

164. **(a)** The requirement is to determine whether an auditor who audits the processing of transactions by a service organization may issue a report on either, or both, of whether controls have been implemented and control operating effectiveness. Answer (a) is correct because AU 324 indicates that such "service auditors" may issue either of the two types of reports.

165. **(a)** The requirement is to identify the proper information to be included in a service auditor's report on whether a client's controls have been implemented. Answer (a) is correct because such a report should include a description of the scope and nature of the client's procedures.

166. **(d)** The requirement is to determine the propriety of a computer "user" auditor (Lake) making reference to a service auditor's (Cope) report. Answer (d) is correct because the user auditor should not make reference to the report of the service auditor. See AU 324 for reports on the processing of transactions by service organizations.

SOLUTIONS TO SIMULATION PROBLEMS

Simulation Problem 1

Directions	Situation	Internal Control	Research	Communication

Condition	Strength	Weakness	Neither
1. Southwest is involved only in medical services and has not diversified its operations.	○	○	●
2. Insurance coverage for patients is verified and communicated to the clerks by the office manager before medical services are rendered.	●	○	○
3. The physician who renders the medical services documents the services on a prenumbered slip that is used for recording revenue and as a receipt for the patient.	●	○	○
4. Cash collection is centralized in that Clerk #2 receives the cash (checks) from patients and records the cash receipt.	○	●	○
5. Southwest extends credit rather than requiring cash or insurance in all cases.	○	○	●
6. The office manager extends credit on a case-by-case basis rather than using a formal credit search and established credit limits.	○	●	○
7. The office manager approves the extension of credit to patients and also approves the write-offs of uncollectible patient receivables.	○	●	○
8. Clerk #2 receives cash and checks and prepares the daily bank deposit.	○	●	○
9. Clerk #2 maintains the accounts receivable records and can add or delete information on the PC.	○	●	○
10. Prenumbered service slips are accounted for on a monthly basis by the outside accountant who is independent of the revenue generating and revenue recording functions.	●	○	○
11. The bank reconciliation is prepared monthly by the outside accountant who is independent of the revenue generating and revenue recording functions.	●	○	○
12. Computer passwords are only known to the individual employees and the managing partner who has no duties in the revenue recording functions.	●	○	○
13. Computer software cannot be modified by Southwest's employees.	●	○	○
14. None of the employees who perform duties in the revenue generating and revenue recording are able to write checks.	●	○	○

Directions	Situation	Internal Control	Research	Communication

AU 380.09-.10 provides requirements with respect to communication of audit adjustments to the audit committee as follows:

Audit Adjustments	**AU380.09**

The auditor should inform the audit committee about adjustments arising from the audit that could, in his judgment, either individually or in the aggregate, have a significant effect on the entity's financial reporting process. For purposes of this section, an audit adjustment, whether or not recorded by the entity, is a proposed correction of the financial statements that, in the auditor's judgment, may not have been detected except through the auditing procedures performed. Matters underlying adjustments proposed by the auditor but not recorded by the entity could potentially cause future financial statements to be materially misstated, even though the auditor has concluded that the adjustments are not material to the current financial statements.

AU380.10

> The auditor also should inform the audit committee about uncorrected misstatements aggregated by the auditor during the current engagement and pertaining to the latest period presented that were determined by management to be immaterial, both individually and in the aggregate, to the financial statements taken as a whole.

Directions	Situation	Internal Control	Research	Communication

To: Audit Working Papers
From: CPA Candidate
Re: Implications of errors discovered in accounts receivable

    The memorandum is designed to document the implications of the errors discovered in accounts receivable. In the course of performing our substantive audit procedures for the audit of Southwest's accounts receivable, we detected a large number of errors. Having assessed control risk at a low level, we should reassess control risk for the assertions regarding accounts receivable and then reevaluate the sufficiency of our substantive procedures. This will allow us to control audit risk at the appropriate level.
    If you have any additional questions about the implications of this matter, please contact me.

Simulation Problem 2

Directions	Flowchart		Research	Communication

  1. (**C**) *Prepare purchase order*—A trapezoid represents a manual operation. Here, a purchase order enters the flowchart after this step; accordingly, a purchase order is being prepared.

  2. (**R**) *To vendor*—A circle represents a connector, a symbol indicating that a document is entering or leaving that portion of the flowchart. Here a copy of the purchase order is sent to the vendor to order the goods. This must be the case because, otherwise, the vendor would not be informed of the order.

  3. (**F**) *Prepare receiving report*—A trapezoid represents a manual operation. Here, a receiving report enters the flowchart after this step; accordingly, a receiving report is being prepared. Also, note above this step that goods are received, the point at which one would expect preparation of a receiving report.

  4. (**L**) *From purchasing*—A circle represents a connector, a symbol indicating that a document is entering or leaving that portion of the flowchart. The document here is from purchasing because below the connector is requisition No. 1, which purchasing has sent with the purchase order No. 5 to vouchers payable, as evidenced by the connector in the bottom far right under purchasing.

  5. (**M**) *From receiving*—A circle represents a connector, a symbol indicating that a document is entering or leaving that portion of the flowchart. The document here is from receiving because under the receiving portion of the flowchart, approximately 3/4 of the way down, we see a connector indicating that receiving report No. 1 is being sent to vouchers payable. Also, toward the bottom under the vouchers payable portion of the flowchart, we see that receiving report No. 1 is indeed in the system.

  6. (**O**) *Purchase order No. 5*—We know from item 4 that this document was sent from purchasing, and we know that purchasing has sent to vouchers payable requisition No. 1 and purchase order No. 5. Since requisition No. 1 is labeled on the flowchart, this must be purchase order No. 5.

  7. (**P**) *Receiving report No. 1*—We know from item 5 that this document was sent from receiving, and since we know that receiving has sent receiving report No. 1 to vouchers payable this must be that document.

  8. (**B**) *Prepare and approve voucher*—A trapezoid represents a manual operation. Here, an approved voucher enters the flowchart after this step; accordingly, a voucher is being prepared and approved in this step.

  9. (**T**) *Unpaid voucher file, filed by due date*—The triangle symbol represents a file. Entering this file are the approved but unpaid vouchers with the support of their invoices, receiving reports, purchase orders and purchase requisitions. Because these vouchers are sent to the treasurer in order of due date (the bottom, right symbol under vouchers payable) this file is the unpaid voucher file, filed by due date.

10. (**S**) *Treasurer*—Because the unpaid vouchers (the "voucher package") was sent from vouchers payable to the treasurer, this is the treasurer.

11. (**I**) *Sign checks and cancel voucher package documents*—A trapezoid represents a manual operation. Here, the operation prior to 11 involves a review of documents and preparation of a check and a remittance advice. After this operation the documents changed are a "canceled voucher package file" and a "signed check"; accordingly, checks are being signed and the voucher package is being canceled.

12. **(K)** *Canceled voucher package*—After step 11, the check copy, remittance advice No. 1, the signed check, and remittance advice No. 2 exit on the far right. Accordingly, item 12 is the voucher package, now canceled as evidenced by the description below the triangular file symbol.

Directions	Flowchart	Research		Communication

SAS 109, para 64.-66. provides a discussion of limitations of an entity's internal control as follows:

Limitations of an Entity's Internal Control

64. Internal control, no matter how well designed and operated, can provide an entity with reasonable assurance, but not absolute assurance, about achieving an entity's objectives. The likelihood of achievement is affected by limitations inherent to internal control. These include the realities that human judgment in decision making can be faulty and that breakdowns in internal control can occur because of human failures such as simple errors or mistakes. For example, if an entity's information system personnel do not sufficiently understand how an order entry system processes sales transactions, they may design changes to the system that will erroneously process sales for a new line of products. On the other hand, such changes may be correctly designed but misunderstood by individuals who translate the design into program code. Errors also may occur in the use of information produced by IT. For example, automated controls may be designed to report transactions over a specified amount for management review, but individuals responsible for conducting the review may not understand the purpose of such reports and, accordingly, may fail to review them or investigate unusual items.

65. Additionally, controls, whether manual or automated, can be circumvented by the collusion of two or more people or inappropriate management override of internal control. For example, management may enter into undisclosed agreements with customers that alter the terms and conditions of the entity's standard sales contracts which may result in improper revenue recognition. Also, edit checks in a software program that are designed to identify and report transactions that exceed specified credit limits may be overridden or disabled.

66. Smaller entities often have fewer employees, which may limit the extent to which segregation of duties is practicable. However, for key areas, even in a very small entity, it can be practicable to implement some degree of segregation of duties or other form of unsophisticated but effective controls. The potential for override of controls by the owner-manager depends to a great extent on the control environment and, in particular, the owner-manager's attitudes about the importance of internal control.

Directions	Flowchart	Research		Communication

To: Audit Staff
From: CPA Candidate
Re: Types of controls

    This memorandum is designed to describe the types of internal controls. Financial reporting controls may be viewed as having a function of either (1) preventing misstatements, or (2) detecting and correcting misstatements. Preventive controls are usually more effective because they reduce the possibility of a misstatement occurring. While detective controls are generally less expensive, they may be ineffective if they detect misstatements too late.

    If you have any additional questions about the nature of these two types of controls, please contact me.

Simulation Problem 3

1.   **(M)** *Perform customer credit check*—The customer credit file is being accessed, making it likely that a credit check is occurring.

2.   **(Z)** *Open order file*—The processing to the right of #2 begins with "open orders," making this an open order file.

3.   **(L)** *Match customer purchase order with sales order*—Two copies of the sales order are being combined with the customer purchase order through a manual operation (the trapezoid).

4.   **(B)** *Verify agreement of sales order and shipping document*—This manual operation (trapezoid) includes two copies of the shipping document being combined with the sales order.

5.   **(H)** *Release goods for shipment*—The department is the warehouse and shipping department, and out of this operation is "shipping information"; accordingly goods are being released for shipment.

6.   **(S)** *Master price file*—The operation below #6 includes entering price data; since the first two files being accessed are the accounts receivable master file and the shipping file, this third file must include prices.

7.   **(O)** *Prepare sales invoice*—Since a document is being prepared through this computerized billing program, it is the sales invoice.

8.   **(U)** *Sales invoice*—A sales invoice is normally sent to the customer.

9.   **(I)** *To accounts receivable department*—This copy of the sales invoice informs accounts receivable that the sale has been both processed and shipped.

10.   **(Q)** *General ledger master file*—Because the processing step below includes updating of master files, this is the general ledger master file.

11.   **(N)** *Prepare sales journal*—Sales transactions are being processed; accordingly a sales journal is prepared.

12.   **(T)** *Sales journal*—From above, a sales journal was prepared; the accounting department will receive the sales journal.

13.   **(Y)** *Aged trial balance*—In the processing step above, an aged trial balance of accounts receivable is prepared; the credit department will receive such a report.

Situation	Flowchart	Research	Communication

The first step is to determine the manner in which you wish to identify the pertinent research in the area. Since this is not an audit report on whether a company's financial statements follow generally accepted accounting principles, the approach outlined in the Reporting Module for preparing a report is not used. If a keyword or index search is to be used, words such as "internal control report" or "illustration internal control report" may be helpful. But in reviewing the requirements for the question watch for hints—you find such hints to include "internal control over financial reporting" and "examination on internal control over financial reporting" which may be helpful. But internal control is a difficult area to research in that the term occurs frequently throughout the standards. If you know that reporting on internal control is included in the attestation standards, you have a significant head start in either a keyword search or in searching sections, since the attestation standards have few sections. Here AT 501 involves reporting on internal control. It provides the following report illustration:

SSAE 15, Exhibit A—Illustrative Reports, paragraph 3.

Example 1: Unqualified Opinion on Internal Control

3. The following is an illustrative report expressing an unqualified opinion directly on internal control.

Independent Accountant's Report

[*Introductory paragraph*]

We have examined W Company's internal control over financial reporting as of December 31, 20XX, based on [*identify criteria*]. W Company's management is responsible for maintaining effective internal control over financial reporting, and for its assertion of the effectiveness of internal control over financial reporting, included in the accompanying [*title of management's report*]. Our responsibility is to express an opinion on W Company's internal control over financial reporting based on our examination.

[*Scope paragraph*]

We conducted our examination in accordance with attestation standards established by the American Institute of Certified Public Accountants. Those standards require that we plan and perform the examination to obtain reasonable assurance about whether effective internal control over financial reporting was maintained in all material respects. Our examination included obtaining an understanding of internal control over financial reporting, assessing the risk that a material weakness exists, and testing and evaluating the design and operating effectiveness of internal control based on the assessed risk. Our examination also included performing such other procedures as we considered necessary in the circumstances. We believe that our examination provides a reasonable basis for our opinion.

[*Definition paragraph*]

An entity's internal control over financial reporting is a process effected by those charged with governance, management and other personnel, designed to provide reasonable assurance regarding the preparation of reliable financial statements in accordance with [*applicable financial reporting framework, such as accounting principles generally accepted in the United States of America*]. An entity's internal control over financial reporting includes those policies and procedures that (1) pertain to the maintenance of records that, in reasonable detail, accurately and fairly reflect the transactions and disposition of the assets of the entity; (2) provide reasonable assurance that transactions are recorded as necessary to permit preparation of financial statements in accordance with [*applicable financial reporting framework, such as accounting principles generally accepted in the United States of America*], and that receipts and expenditures of the entity are being made only in accordance with authorizations of management and those charged with governance; and (3) provide reasonable assurance regarding prevention, or timely detection and correction of unauthorized acquisition, use, or disposition of the entity's assets that could have a material effect on the financial statements.

[*Inherent limitations paragraph*]

Because of inherent limitations, internal control over financial reporting may not prevent, or detect and correct misstatements. Also, projections of any evaluation of effectiveness to future periods are subject to the risk that controls may become inadequate because of changes in conditions, or that the degree of compliance with the policies or procedures may deteriorate.

[*Opinion paragraph*]

In our opinion, W Company maintained, in all material respects, effective internal control over financial reporting as of December 31, 20XX, based on [*identify criteria*]

[*Audit of financial statements paragraph*]

We also have audited, in accordance with auditing standards generally accepted in the United States of America, the [*identify financial statements*] of W Company and out report dated [*date of report, which should be the same as the date of the report on the examination of internal control*] expressed [*include nature of opinion*].

[*Signature*]

[*Date*]

Situation	Flowchart	Research	Communication

To: Bill Warren, CFO
        Welcore Inc.
From: CPA Candidate
Re: Effect of improvements in internal control

You have requested a description of the effects of improved internal control on our audit. Improved internal control may affect the audit in at least two related ways. First, it may change the combination of audit tests performed and thereby lead to a more efficient audit. In auditing the financial statements of a company, auditors perform two types of tests: tests of the effectiveness of internal control (referred to as test of controls) and substantive tests of financial statement balances and transactions. As internal control improves, more reliance can be placed on tests of controls and a result may be a more efficient audit. Second, because an improvement in internal control is likely to decrease the occurrence of material misstatements, there may be a reduction in the required overall scope of audit procedures that may also lead to a more efficient audit.

If you would like additional explanation regarding the relationship of internal control to the audit, please contact me.

Simulation Problem 4

Situation	Internal Control Evaluation	Purpose of Internal Control	Research and Communication

1.   Disagree. Someone independent of requisitioning should select the supplier.

2.   Agree.

3.   Disagree. Often, factors in addition to cost are considered (e.g., quality, dependability).

4.   Agree.

5.   Agree.

6.   Agree.

7.   Disagree. A comparison of quantities is not possible because quantity is blacked out on the purchase order provided to receiving.

8.   No receiving report is ordinarily necessary for purchases of services.

9.   Agree.

10. Agree.

11. Agree.

12. Disagree. The reconciliation should be performed by an independent party.

13. Disagree. Documentation should be marked "paid" by the individual making the payment.

14. Agree.

15. Agree.

Situation	Internal Control Evaluation	Purpose of Internal Control	Research and Communication

1.   (C) Invoices posted to incorrect customer accounts will be detected by analyzing customer responses to monthly statements that include errors, particularly statements with errors not in favor of the customer.

2.   (G) The comparison of shipping documents with sales invoices will detect goods that have been shipped but not billed when no sales invoice is located for a particular shipping document.

3.   (F) To provide assurance that all invoiced goods that have been shipped are recorded as sales, daily sales summaries should be compared with invoices. For example, a sale that has not been recorded will result in a sales summary that does not include certain sales invoices.

4.   (K) A comparison of the amounts posted to the accounts receivable ledger with the control total for invoices will provide assurance that all invoices have been posted to a customer account.

5.   (I) Comparing customer orders with an approved customer list will provide assurance that credit sales are made only to customers that have been granted credit.

6.   (B) Requiring an approved sales order before goods are released from the warehouse will provide assurance that goods are not removed for unauthorized orders.

7.   (D) A comparison by shipping clerks of goods received from the warehouse with the approved sales orders will provide assurance that goods shipped to customers agree with goods ordered by customers.

8.   (L) A comparison of sales invoices with shipping documents and approved sales orders will detect invoices that do not have the proper support. Accordingly, it will help prevent the recording of fictitious transactions.

9.   (P) Comparing amounts posted to the accounts receivable ledger with the validated bank deposit will detect improper postings to accounts receivable since any differences in amounts will be investigated.

10. (C) Misappropriations of customers' checks will be detected when customers indicate that they have made payments for items shown as payable on their monthly statement. Note that replies O and P will only detect this misappropriation in the unlikely event that the perpetrator does not dispose of the remittance advice.

11. (C) Mispostings of payments made will be detected when customers indicate that they have made payments for items shown as payable on their monthly statement.

12. (P) Crediting more than one account for a cash receipt will be detected when the total of amounts posted to the accounts receivable ledger is compared with the validated bank deposit slip.

13. (S) An independent reconciliation of the bank account will reveal improper total recording of receipts in the cash receipts journal because unlocated differences between bank and book balances will occur and be investigated.

14. (P) Comparing total amounts posted to the accounts receivable ledger with the validated bank deposit slip will detect a difference between total cash receipts and the amount credited to the accounts receivable ledger.

15. (N) Requiring the approval of the supervisor of the sales department for goods received will provide assurance that invalid transactions granting credit for sales returns are not recorded. Note that using prenumbered credit memos (reply M) will only be effective if the sequence is accounted for and if credit memos may be compared in some form to actual returns.

Situation	Internal Control Evaluation	Purpose of Internal Control	Research and Communication

The first step is to determine the manner in which the candidate wishes to identify the pertinent research in the area. If a keyword or index search is to be used, words such as "internal control report" or "significant deficiency" may be helpful. But internal control is a difficult area to research in that the term occurs frequently throughout the standards. Concerning internal control it is probably best to memorize the fact that the auditor's responsibility for reporting on internal control significant deficiencies is included in AU 325 (also, know that other communications to the audit committee are included in AU 380). Attest reports on internal control over financial reporting (not an issue in this question) are in AT 501.

1. AU 325 includes the following definition for a significant deficiency and a material weakness:

    .06 A material weakness is a deficiency, or combination of deficiencies in internal control, such that there is a reasonable possibility that a material misstatement of the entity's financial statements will not be prevented, or detected and corrected on a timely basis.

    .07 A significant deficiency is a deficiency, or a combination of deficiencies, in internal control that is less severe than a material weakness, yet important enough to merit attention by those charged with governance.

2. AU 325 establishes a presumptively mandatory requirement that the communication be in writing.

3. AU 325 also establishes a presumptively mandatory requirement that such matters be recommunicated. It states:

    .17 Deficiencies identified during the audit that upon evaluation are considered significant deficiencies or material weaknesses under this section should be communicated, in writing, to management and those charged with governance as a part of each audit, including significant deficiencies and material weaknesses that were communicated to management and those charged with governance in previous audits and have not yet been remediated. Significant deficiencies and material weaknesses that previously were communicated and have not yet been remediated may be communicated, in writing, by referring to the previously issued written communication and the date of that communication.

Given the above information, one may write a memorandum as follows:

To: Mr. Bill Jones
From: CPA Candidate
Re: Reporting on internal control
Date: [*Today's date*]

At your request, I researched the Professional Standards on the following three issues:

a. Definitions of material weaknesses and significant deficiencies.
b. Whether a communication on significant deficiencies must be in writing.
c. Whether a significant deficiency must be communicated when the audit committee is already aware of it.

The guidance for all three of these matters is included in AU section 325.

Definitions of material weaknesses and significant deficiencies

The definitions for a significant deficiency and a material weakness are presented in AU section 325 as

A material weakness is a deficiency, or combination of deficiencies, in internal control, such that there is a reasonable possibility that a material misstatement of the entity's financial statements will not be prevented, or detected and corrected on a timely basis.

A significant deficiency is a deficiency, or a combination of deficiencies, in internal control that is less severe than a material weakness, yet important enough to merit attention by those charged with governance.

Must a communication on significant deficiencies be in writing?

Yes. Control deficiencies noted by the auditor that are considered to be significant deficiencies or material weaknesses should be communicated in writing to management, and those charged with governance as a part of each audit, even if they previously have been communicated to these parties in connection with previous audits.

Must a significant deficiency of which the audit committee is aware be communicated?

Yes. As indicated above, even if previously communicated, it should again be communicated.

If you have additional questions about internal control, please contact me.

MULTIPLE-CHOICE QUESTIONS (1-190)

1. Which of the following is **not** an assertion relating to classes of transactions?
    a.   Accuracy.
    b.   Consistency.
    c.   Cutoff.
    d.   Occurrence.

2. Which of the following is a general principle relating to the reliability of audit evidence?
    a.   Audit evidence obtained from indirect sources rather than directly is more reliable than evidence obtained directly by the auditor.
    b.   Audit evidence provided by copies is more reliable than that provided by facsimiles.
    c.   Audit evidence obtained from knowledgeable independent sources outside the client company is more reliable than audit evidence obtained from nonindependent sources.
    d.   Audit evidence provided by original documents is more reliable than audit evidence generated through a system of effective controls.

3. Which of the following types of audit evidence is the most persuasive?
    a.   Prenumbered client purchase order forms.
    b.   Client work sheets supporting cost allocations.
    c.   Bank statements obtained from the client.
    d.   Client representation letter.

4. Which of the following presumptions is correct about the reliability of audit evidence?
    a.   Information obtained indirectly from outside sources is the most reliable audit evidence.
    b.   To be reliable, audit evidence should be convincing rather than persuasive.
    c.   Reliability of audit evidence refers to the amount of corroborative evidence obtained.
    d.   Effective internal control provides more assurance about the reliability of audit evidence.

5. Which of the following statements relating to the appropriateness of audit evidence is always true?
    a.   Audit evidence gathered by an auditor from outside an enterprise is reliable.
    b.   Accounting data developed under satisfactory conditions of internal control are more relevant than data developed under unsatisfactory internal control conditions.
    c.   Oral representations made by management are **not** valid evidence.
    d.   Evidence gathered by auditors must be both valid and relevant to be considered appropriate.

6. Which of the following types of audit evidence is the **least** persuasive?
    a.   Prenumbered purchase order forms.
    b.   Bank statements obtained from the client.
    c.   Test counts of inventory performed by the auditor.
    d.   Correspondence from the client's attorney about litigation.

7. In evaluating the reasonableness of an entity's accounting estimates, an auditor normally would be concerned about assumptions that are

    a.   Susceptible to bias.
    b.   Consistent with prior periods.
    c.   Insensitive to variations.
    d.   Similar to industry guidelines.

8. Which of the following is not a basic procedure used in an audit?
    a.   Risk assessment procedures.
    b.   Substantive procedures.
    c.   Tests of controls.
    d.   Tests of direct evidence.

9. Which of the following procedures would an auditor ordinarily perform first in evaluating management's accounting estimates for reasonableness?
    a.   Develop independent expectations of management's estimates.
    b.   Consider the appropriateness of the key factors or assumptions used in preparing the estimates.
    c.   Test the calculations used by management in developing the estimates.
    d.   Obtain an understanding of how management developed its estimates.

10. In evaluating the reasonableness of an accounting estimate, an auditor most likely would concentrate on key factors and assumptions that are
    a.   Consistent with prior periods.
    b.   Similar to industry guidelines.
    c.   Objective and **not** susceptible to bias.
    d.   Deviations from historical patterns.

11. In evaluating an entity's accounting estimates, one of an auditor's objectives is to determine whether the estimates are
    a.   Not subject to bias.
    b.   Consistent with industry guidelines.
    c.   Based on objective assumptions.
    d.   Reasonable in the circumstances.

12. In testing the existence assertion for an asset, an auditor ordinarily works from the
    a.   Financial statements to the potentially unrecorded items.
    b.   Potentially unrecorded items to the financial statements.
    c.   Accounting records to the supporting evidence.
    d.   Supporting evidence to the accounting records.

13. A client uses a suspense account for unresolved questions whose final accounting has not been determined. If a balance remains in the suspense account at year-end, the auditor would be most concerned about
    a.   Suspense debits that management believes will benefit future operations.
    b.   Suspense debits that the auditor verifies will have realizable value to the client.
    c.   Suspense credits that management believes should be classified as "Current liability."
    d.   Suspense credits that the auditor determines to be customer deposits.

14. Which of the following would **not** be considered an analytical procedure?
    a.   Estimating payroll expense by multiplying the number of employees by the average hourly wage rate and the total hours worked.

b. Projecting an error rate by comparing the results of a statistical sample with the actual population characteristics.
c. Computing accounts receivable turnover by dividing credit sales by the average net receivables.
d. Developing the expected current year sales based on the sales trend of the prior five years.

15. What type of analytical procedure would an auditor most likely use in developing relationships among balance sheet accounts when reviewing the financial statements of a nonpublic entity?
a. Trend analysis.
b. Regression analysis.
c. Ratio analysis.
d. Risk analysis.

16. An auditor may achieve audit objectives related to particular assertions by
a. Performing analytical procedures.
b. Adhering to a system of quality control.
c. Preparing auditor working papers.
d. Increasing the level of detection risk.

17. An entity's income statements were misstated due to the recording of journal entries that involved debits and credits to an unusual combination of expense and revenue accounts. The auditor most likely could have detected this fraudulent financial reporting by
a. Tracing a sample of journal entries to the general ledger.
b. Evaluating the effectiveness of internal control.
c. Investigating the reconciliations between controlling accounts and subsidiary records.
d. Performing analytical procedures designed to disclose differences from expectations.

18. Auditors try to identify predictable relationships when using analytical procedures. Relationships involving transactions from which of the following accounts most likely would yield the highest level of evidence?
a. Accounts receivable.
b. Interest expense.
c. Accounts payable.
d. Travel and entertainment expense.

19. Analytical procedures used in the overall review stage of an audit generally include
a. Gathering evidence concerning account balances that have not changed from the prior year.
b. Retesting control procedures that appeared to be ineffective during the assessment of control risk.
c. Considering unusual or unexpected account balances that were not previously identified.
d. Performing tests of transactions to corroborate management's financial statement assertions.

20. Which of the following tends to be most predictable for purposes of analytical procedures applied as substantive tests?
a. Relationships involving balance sheet accounts.
b. Transactions subject to management discretion.
c. Relationships involving income statement accounts.
d. Data subject to audit testing in the prior year.

21. A basic premise underlying the application of analytical procedures is that
a. The study of financial ratios is an acceptable alternative to the investigation of unusual fluctuations.
b. Statistical tests of financial information may lead to the discovery of material misstatements in the financial statements.
c. Plausible relationships among data may reasonably be expected to exist and continue in the absence of known conditions to the contrary.
d. These procedures cannot replace tests of balances and transactions.

22. For all audits of financial statements made in accordance with generally accepted auditing standards, the use of analytical procedures is required to some extent

	In the planning stage	As a substantive test	In the review stage
a.	Yes	No	Yes
b.	No	Yes	No
c.	No	Yes	Yes
d.	Yes	No	No

23. An auditor's analytical procedures most likely would be facilitated if the entity
a. Segregates obsolete inventory before the physical inventory count.
b. Uses a standard cost system that produces variance reports.
c. Corrects material weaknesses in internal control before the beginning of the audit.
d. Develops its data from sources solely within the entity.

24. Analytical procedures performed in the overall review stage of an audit suggest that several accounts have unexpected relationships. The results of these procedures most likely would indicate that
a. Irregularities exist among the relevant account balances.
b. Internal control activities are not operating effectively.
c. Additional tests of details are required.
d. The communication with the audit committee should be revised.

25. Which of the following comparisons would an auditor most likely make in evaluating an entity's costs and expenses?
a. The current year's accounts receivable with the prior year's accounts receivable.
b. The current year's payroll expense with the prior year's payroll expense.
c. The budgeted current year's sales with the prior year's sales.
d. The budgeted current year's warranty expense with the current year's contingent liabilities.

26. To be effective, analytical procedures in the overall review stage of an audit engagement should be performed by
a. The staff accountant who performed the substantive auditing procedures.
b. The managing partner who has responsibility for all audit engagements at that practice office.

    c.   A manager or partner who has a comprehensive knowledge of the client's business and industry.

    d.   The CPA firm's quality control manager or partner who has responsibility for the firm's peer review program.

27. Which of the following is the best example of a substantive test?

    a.   Examining a sample of cash disbursements to test whether expenses have been properly approved.

    b.   Confirmation of balances of accounts receivable.

    c.   Comparison of signatures on checks to a list of authorized signers.

    d.   Flowcharting of the client's cash receipts system.

28. The objective of tests of details of transactions performed as substantive tests is to

    a.   Comply with generally accepted auditing standards.

    b.   Attain assurance about the reliability of the accounting system.

    c.   Detect material misstatements in the financial statements.

    d.   Evaluate whether management's policies and procedures operated effectively.

29. In the context of an audit of financial statements, substantive tests are audit procedures that

    a.   May be eliminated under certain conditions.

    b.   Are designed to discover significant subsequent events.

    c.   May be either tests of transactions, direct tests of financial balances, or analytical tests.

    d.   Will increase proportionately with the auditor's reliance on internal control.

30. The auditor will most likely perform extensive tests for possible understatement of

    a.   Revenues.

    b.   Assets.

    c.   Liabilities.

    d.   Capital.

31. Which of the following procedures would an auditor most likely perform in auditing the statement of cash flows?

    a.   Compare the amounts included in the statement of cash flows to similar amounts in the prior year's statement of cash flows.

    b.   Reconcile the cutoff bank statements to verify the accuracy of the year-end bank balances.

    c.   Vouch all bank transfers for the last week of the year and first week of the subsequent year.

    d.   Reconcile the amounts included in the statement of cash flows to the other financial statements' balances and amounts.

32. In determining whether transactions have been recorded, the direction of the audit testing should be from the

    a.   General ledger balances.

    b.   Adjusted trial balance.

    c.   Original source documents.

    d.   General journal entries.

33. Which statement is correct concerning the deletion of audit documentation?

    a.   Superseded audit documentation should always be deleted from the audit file.

    b.   After the audit file has been completed, the auditor should not delete or discard audit documentation.

    c.   Auditors should use professional skepticism in determining which audit documentation should be deleted.

    d.   Audit documentation should never be deleted from the audit file.

34. Ignoring any particular legal or regulatory requirement, audit documentation should be retained

    a.   A minimum of five years.

    b.   As long as lead schedules have relevance to forthcoming audits.

    c.   Until 3 years after the client selects another auditor.

    d.   Working papers must be maintained indefinitely.

35. Which of the following pairs of accounts would an auditor most likely analyze on the same working paper?

    a.   Notes receivable and interest income.

    b.   Accrued interest receivable and accrued interest payable.

    c.   Notes payable and notes receivable.

    d.   Interest income and interest expense.

36. An auditor's working papers serve mainly to

    a.   Provide the principal support for the auditor's report.

    b.   Satisfy the auditor's responsibilities concerning the Code of Professional Conduct.

    c.   Monitor the effectiveness of the CPA firm's quality control procedures.

    d.   Document the level of independence maintained by the auditor.

37. The permanent file of an auditor's working papers generally would **not** include

    a.   Bond indenture agreements.

    b.   Lease agreements.

    c.   Working trial balance.

    d.   Flowchart of internal control.

38. An auditor ordinarily uses a working trial balance resembling the financial statements without footnotes, but containing columns for

    a.   Cash flow increases and decreases.

    b.   Audit objectives and assertions.

    c.   Reclassifications and adjustments.

    d.   Reconciliations and tick marks.

39. Which of the following is least likely to be a factor in the auditor's decision about the extent of the documentation of a particular audit area?

    a.   The risk of material misstatement.

    b.   The extent of the judgment involved in performing the procedures.

    c.   The nature and extent of exceptions identified.

    d.   Whether or not the client has an internal audit function.

40. Which of the following is required documentation in an audit in accordance with generally accepted auditing standards?

    a.   A flowchart or narrative of the accounting system describing the recording and classification of transactions for financial reporting.

b. An audit program setting forth in detail the procedures necessary to accomplish the engagement's objectives.
c. A planning memorandum establishing the timing of the audit procedures and coordinating the assistance of entity personnel.
d. An internal control questionnaire identifying controls that assure specific objectives will be achieved.

41. Which of the following factors most likely would affect an auditor's judgment about the quantity, type, and content of the auditor's working papers?
a. The assessed level of control risk.
b. The likelihood of a review by a concurring (second) partner.
c. The number of personnel assigned to the audit.
d. The content of the management representation letter.

42. The audit working paper that reflects the major components of an amount reported in the financial statements is the
a. Interbank transfer schedule.
b. Carryforward schedule.
c. Supporting schedule.
d. Lead schedule.

43. Which of the following documentation is required for an audit in accordance with generally accepted auditing standards?
a. A flowchart or an internal control questionnaire that evaluates the effectiveness of the entity's controls.
b. A client engagement letter that summarizes the timing and details of the auditor's planned fieldwork.
c. An indication in the working papers that the accounting records agree or reconcile with the financial statements.
d. The basis for the auditor's conclusions when the assessed level of control risk is at the maximum level for all financial statement assertions.

44. No deletions of audit documentation are allowed after the
a. Client's year-end.
b. Documentation completion date.
c. Last date of significant fieldwork.
d. Report release date.

45. Under the requirements of the PCAOB, audit documentation must contain sufficient information to allow what type of auditor to understand the nature, timing, extent, and results of procedures performed?
a. An experienced audit team member.
b. An experienced auditor having no previous connection with the engagement.
c. Any certified public accountant.
d. An auditor qualified as a peer review specialist.

46. Audit documentation for audits performed under the requirements of the Public Company Accounting Oversight Board should be retained for
a. The shorter of five years, or the period required by law.
b. Seven years.
c. The longer of seven years, or the period required by law.
d. Indefinitely.

47. Which of the following sets of information does an auditor usually confirm on one form?
a. Accounts payable and purchase commitments.
b. Cash in bank and collateral for loans.
c. Inventory on consignment and contingent liabilities.
d. Accounts receivable and accrued interest receivable.

48. The usefulness of the standard bank confirmation request may be limited because the bank employee who completes the form may
a. Not believe that the bank is obligated to verify confidential information to a third party.
b. Sign and return the form without inspecting the accuracy of the client's bank reconciliation.
c. Not have access to the client's cutoff bank statement.
d. Be unaware of all the financial relationships that the bank has with the client.

49. An auditor most likely would limit substantive audit tests of sales transactions when control risk is assessed as low for the occurrence assertion concerning sales transactions and the auditor has already gathered evidence supporting
a. Opening and closing inventory balances.
b. Cash receipts and accounts receivable.
c. Shipping and receiving activities.
d. Cutoffs of sales and purchases.

Items 50 and 51 are based on the following:

The information below was taken from the bank transfer schedule prepared during the audit of Fox Co.'s financial statements for the year ended December 31, 2005. Assume all checks are dated and issued on December 30, 2005.

Check no.	Bank accounts		Disbursement date		Receipt date	
	From	To	Per books	Per bank	Per books	Per bank
101	National	Federal	Dec. 30	Jan. 4	Dec. 30	Jan. 3
202	County	State	Jan. 3	Jan. 2	Dec. 30	Dec. 31
303	Federal	American	Dec. 31	Jan. 3	Jan. 2	Jan. 2
404	State	Republic	Jan. 2	Jan. 2	Jan. 2	Dec. 31

50. Which of the following checks might indicate kiting?
- a. #101 and #303.
- b. #202 and #404.
- c. #101 and #404.
- d. #202 and #303.

51. Which of the following checks illustrate deposits/transfers in transit at December 31, 2005?
- a. #101 and #202.
- b. #101 and #303.
- c. #202 and #404.
- d. #303 and #404.

52. An auditor should trace bank transfers for the last part of the audit period and first part of the subsequent period to detect whether
- a. The cash receipts journal was held open for a few days after the year-end.
- b. The last checks recorded before the year-end were actually mailed by the year-end.
- c. Cash balances were overstated because of kiting.
- d. Any unusual payments to or receipts from related parties occurred.

53. To gather evidence regarding the balance per bank in a bank reconciliation, an auditor would examine all of the following **except**
- a. Cutoff bank statement.
- b. Year-end bank statement.
- c. Bank confirmation.
- d. General ledger.

54. Which of the following cash transfers results in a misstatement of cash at December 31, 2005?

Bank Transfer Schedule

	Disbursement		Receipt	
Transfer	Recorded in books	Paid by bank	Recorded in books	Received by bank
a.	12/31/05	1/4/06	12/31/05	12/31/05
b.	1/4/06	1/5/06	12/31/05	1/4/06
c.	12/31/05	1/5/06	12/31/05	1/4/06
d.	1/4/06	1/11/06	1/4/06	1/4/06

55. A cash shortage may be concealed by transporting funds from one location to another or by converting negotiable assets to cash. Because of this, which of the following is vital?
- a. Simultaneous confirmations.
- b. Simultaneous bank reconciliations.
- c. Simultaneous verification.
- d. Simultaneous surprise cash count.

56. The primary purpose of sending a standard confirmation request to financial institutions with which the client has done business during the year is to
- a. Detect kiting activities that may otherwise **not** be discovered.
- b. Corroborate information regarding deposit and loan balances.
- c. Provide the data necessary to prepare a proof of cash.
- d. Request information about contingent liabilities and secured transactions.

57. An auditor observes the mailing of monthly statements to a client's customers and reviews evidence of follow-up on errors reported by the customers. This test of controls most likely is performed to support management's financial statement assertion(s) of

	Presentation and disclosure	Existence occurrence
a.	Yes	Yes
b.	Yes	No
c.	No	Yes
d.	No	No

Items 58 and 59 are based on the following:

Miles Company
BANK TRANSFER SCHEDULE
December 31, 2005

Check no.	Bank accounts From	To	Amount	Date disbursed per Books	Bank	Date deposited per Books	Bank
2020	1st Natl.	Suburban	$32,000	12/31	1/5◆	12/31	1/3•
2021	1st Natl.	Capital	21,000	12/31	1/4◆	12/31	1/3•
3217	2nd State	Suburban	6,700	1/3	1/5	1/3	1/6
0659	Midtown	Suburban	5,500	12/30	1/5◆	12/30	1/3•

58. The tick mark ◆ most likely indicates that the amount was traced to the
- a. December cash disbursements journal.
- b. Outstanding check list of the applicable bank reconciliation.
- c. January cash disbursements journal.
- d. Year-end bank confirmations.

59. The tick mark • most likely indicates that the amount was traced to the
- a. Deposits in transit of the applicable bank reconciliation.
- b. December cash receipts journal.
- c. January cash receipts journal.
- d. Year-end bank confirmations.

60. Which of the following statements is correct concerning the use of negative confirmation requests?

a. Unreturned negative confirmation requests rarely provide significant explicit evidence.

b. Negative confirmation requests are effective when detection risk is low.

c. Unreturned negative confirmation requests indicate that alternative procedures are necessary.

d. Negative confirmation requests are effective when understatements of account balances are suspected.

61. When an auditor does **not** receive replies to positive requests for year-end accounts receivable confirmations, the auditor most likely would

a. Inspect the allowance account to verify whether the accounts were subsequently written off.

b. Increase the assessed level of detection risk for the valuation and completeness assertions.

c. Ask the client to contact the customers to request that the confirmations be returned.

d. Increase the assessed level of inherent risk for the revenue cycle.

62. In confirming a client's accounts receivable in prior years, an auditor found that there were many differences between the recorded account balances and the confirmation replies. These differences, which were not misstatements, required substantial time to resolve. In defining the sampling unit for the current year's audit, the auditor most likely would choose

a. Individual overdue balances.

b. Individual invoices.

c. Small account balances.

d. Large account balances.

63. Confirmation is most likely to be a relevant form of evidence with regard to assertions about accounts receivable when the auditor has concerns about the receivables'

a. Valuation.

b. Classification.

c. Existence.

d. Completeness.

64. An auditor should perform alternative procedures to substantiate the existence of accounts receivable when

a. No reply to a positive confirmation request is received.

b. No reply to a negative confirmation request is received.

c. Collectibility of the receivables is in doubt.

d. Pledging of the receivables is probable.

65. Which of the following procedures would an auditor most likely perform for year-end accounts receivable confirmations when the auditor did **not** receive replies to second requests?

a. Review the cash receipts journal for the month prior to the year-end.

b. Intensify the study of internal control concerning the revenue cycle.

c. Increase the assessed level of detection risk for the existence assertion.

d. Inspect the shipping records documenting the merchandise sold to the debtors.

66. In which of the following circumstances would the use of the negative form of accounts receivable confirmation most likely be justified?

a. A substantial number of accounts may be in dispute and the accounts receivable balance arises from sales to a few major customers.

b. A substantial number of accounts may be in dispute and the accounts receivable balance arises from sales to many customers with small balances.

c. A small number of accounts may be in dispute and the accounts receivable balance arises from sales to a few major customers.

d. A small number of accounts may be in dispute and the accounts receivable balance arises from sales to many customers with small balances.

67. To reduce the risks associated with accepting e-mail responses to requests for confirmation of accounts receivable, an auditor most likely would

a. Request the senders to mail the original forms to the auditor.

b. Examine subsequent cash receipts for the accounts in question.

c. Consider the e-mail responses to the confirmations to be exceptions.

d. Mail second requests to the e-mail respondents.

68. To reduce the risks associated with accepting fax responses to requests for confirmations of accounts receivable, an auditor most likely would

a. Examine the shipping documents that provide evidence for the existence assertion.

b. Verify the sources and contents of the faxes in telephone calls to the senders.

c. Consider the faxes to be nonresponses and evaluate them as unadjusted differences.

d. Inspect the faxes for forgeries or alterations and consider them to be acceptable if none are noted.

69. In auditing accounts receivable, the negative form of confirmation request most likely would be used when

a. The total recorded amount of accounts receivable is immaterial to the financial statements taken as a whole.

b. Response rates in prior years to properly designed positive confirmation requests were inadequate.

c. Recipients are likely to return positive confirmation requests without verifying the accuracy of the information.

d. The combined assessed level of inherent risk and control risk relative to accounts receivable is low.

70. Under which of the following circumstances would the use of the blank form of confirmations of accounts receivable most likely be preferable to positive confirmations?

a. The recipients are likely to sign the confirmations without devoting proper attention to them.

b. Subsequent cash receipts are unusually difficult to verify.

c. Analytical procedures indicate that few exceptions are expected.

d. The combined assessed level of inherent risk and control risk is low.

71. In confirming accounts receivable, an auditor decided to confirm customers' account balances rather than individual invoices. Which of the following most likely would be included with the client's confirmation letter?

    a. An auditor-prepared letter explaining that a nonresponse may cause an inference that the account balance is correct.

    b. A client-prepared letter reminding the customer that a nonresponse will cause a second request to be sent.

    c. An auditor-prepared letter requesting the customer to supply missing and incorrect information directly to the auditor.

    d. A client-prepared statement of account showing the details of the customer's account balance.

72. Which of the following statements would an auditor most likely add to the negative form of confirmations of accounts receivable to encourage timely consideration by the recipients?

    a. "This is **not** a request for payment; remittances should **not** be sent to our auditors in the enclosed envelope."

    b. "Report any differences on the enclosed statement directly to our auditors; **no** reply is necessary if this amount agrees with your records."

    c. "If you do **not** report any differences within fifteen days, it will be assumed that this statement is correct."

    d. "The following invoices have been selected for confirmation and represent amounts that are overdue."

73. Which of the following strategies most likely could improve the response rate of the confirmation of accounts receivable?

    a. Including a list of items or invoices that constitute the account balance.

    b. Restricting the selection of accounts to be confirmed to those customers with relatively large balances.

    c. Requesting customers to respond to the confirmation requests directly to the auditor by fax or e-mail.

    d. Notifying the recipients that second requests will be mailed if they fail to respond in a timely manner.

74. An auditor most likely would make inquiries of production and sales personnel concerning possible obsolete or slow-moving inventory to support management's financial statement assertion of

    a. Valuation.
    b. Rights.
    c. Existence.
    d. Presentation.

75. While observing a client's annual physical inventory, an auditor recorded test counts for several items and noticed that certain test counts were higher than the recorded quantities in the client's perpetual records. This situation could be the result of the client's failure to record

    a. Purchase discounts.
    b. Purchase returns.
    c. Sales.
    d. Sales returns.

76. To gain assurance that all inventory items in a client's inventory listing schedule are valid, an auditor most likely would trace

    a. Inventory tags noted during the auditor's observation to items listed in the inventory listing schedule.

    b. Inventory tags noted during the auditor's observation to items listed in receiving reports and vendors' invoices.

    c. Items listed in the inventory listing schedule to inventory tags and the auditor's recorded count sheets.

    d. Items listed in receiving reports and vendors' invoices to the inventory listing schedule.

77. To measure how effectively an entity employs its resources, an auditor calculates inventory turnover by dividing average inventory into

    a. Net sales.
    b. Cost of goods sold.
    c. Operating income.
    d. Gross sales.

78. Which of the following auditing procedures most likely would provide assurance about a manufacturing entity's inventory valuation?

    a. Testing the entity's computation of standard overhead rates.

    b. Obtaining confirmation of inventories pledged under loan agreements.

    c. Reviewing shipping and receiving cutoff procedures for inventories.

    d. Tracing test counts to the entity's inventory listing.

79. A client maintains perpetual inventory records in both quantities and dollars. If the assessed level of control risk is high, an auditor would probably

    a. Increase the extent of tests of controls of the inventory cycle.

    b. Request the client to schedule the physical inventory count at the end of the year.

    c. Insist that the client perform physical counts of inventory items several times during the year.

    d. Apply gross profit tests to ascertain the reasonableness of the physical counts.

80. An auditor concluded that no excessive costs for idle plant were charged to inventory. This conclusion most likely related to the auditor's objective to obtain evidence about the financial statement assertions regarding inventory, including presentation and disclosure and

    a. Valuation.
    b. Completeness.
    c. Existence.
    d. Rights.

81. An auditor selected items for test counts while observing a client's physical inventory. The auditor then traced the test counts to the client's inventory listing. This procedure most likely obtained evidence concerning management's assertion of

    a. Rights.
    b. Completeness.
    c. Existence.
    d. Valuation.

82. An auditor most likely would analyze inventory turn-over rates to obtain evidence concerning management's assertions about
   a. Existence.
   b. Rights.
   c. Presentation.
   d. Valuation.

83. An auditor usually examines receiving reports to support entries in the
   a. Voucher register and sales returns journal.
   b. Sales journal and sales returns journal.
   c. Voucher register and sales journal.
   d. Check register and sales journal.

84. When auditing inventories, an auditor would **least** likely verify that
   a. The financial statement presentation of inventories is appropriate.
   b. Damaged goods and obsolete items have been properly accounted for.
   c. All inventory owned by the client is on hand at the time of the count.
   d. The client has used proper inventory pricing.

85. An auditor who physically examines securities should insist that a client representative be present in order to
   a. Detect fraudulent securities.
   b. Lend authority to the auditor's directives.
   c. Acknowledge the receipt of securities returned.
   d. Coordinate the return of securities to the proper locations.

86. In establishing the existence and ownership of a long-term investment in the form of publicly traded stock, an auditor should inspect the securities or
   a. Correspond with the investee company to verify the number of shares owned.
   b. Inspect the audited financial statements of the investee company.
   c. Confirm the number of shares owned that are held by an independent custodian.
   d. Determine that the investment is carried at the lower of cost or market.

87. When an auditor is unable to inspect and count a client's investment securities until after the balance sheet date, the bank where the securities are held in a safe-deposit box should be asked to
   a. Verify any differences between the contents of the box and the balances in the client's subsidiary ledger.
   b. Provide a list of securities added and removed from the box between the balance sheet date and the security-count date.
   c. Confirm that there has been **no** access to the box between the balance sheet date and the security-count date.
   d. Count the securities in the box so the auditor will have an independent direct verification.

88. In testing long-term investments, an auditor ordinarily would use analytical procedures to ascertain the reasonableness of the
   a. Completeness of recorded investment income.
   b. Classification between current and noncurrent portfolios.

   c. Valuation of marketable equity securities.
   d. Existence of unrealized gains or losses in the portfolio.

89. Analysis of which account is **least** likely to reveal evidence relating to recorded retirement of equipment?
   a. Accumulated depreciation.
   b. Insurance expense.
   c. Property, plant, and equipment.
   d. Purchase returns and allowances.

90. Which of the following explanations most likely would satisfy an auditor who questions management about significant debits to the accumulated depreciation accounts?
   a. The estimated remaining useful lives of plant assets were revised upward.
   b. Plant assets were retired during the year.
   c. The prior year's depreciation expense was erroneously understated.
   d. Overhead allocations were revised at year-end.

91. In testing for unrecorded retirements of equipment, an auditor most likely would
   a. Select items of equipment from the accounting records and then locate them during the plant tour.
   b. Compare depreciation journal entries with similar prior year entries in search of fully depreciated equipment.
   c. Inspect items of equipment observed during the plant tour and then trace them to the equipment subsidiary ledger.
   d. Scan the general journal for unusual equipment additions and excessive debits to repairs and maintenance expense.

92. An auditor analyzes repairs and maintenance accounts primarily to obtain evidence in support of the audit assertion that all
   a. Noncapitalizable expenditures for repairs and maintenance have been recorded in the proper period.
   b. Expenditures for property and equipment have been recorded in the proper period.
   c. Noncapitalizable expenditures for repairs and maintenance have been properly charged to expense.
   d. Expenditures for property and equipment have **not** been charged to expense.

93. The auditor is most likely to seek information from the plant manager with respect to the
   a. Adequacy of the provision for uncollectible accounts.
   b. Appropriateness of physical inventory observation procedures.
   c. Existence of obsolete machinery.
   d. Deferral of procurement of certain necessary insurance coverage.

94. Treetop Corporation acquired a building and arranged mortgage financing during the year. Verification of the related mortgage acquisition costs would be least likely to include an examination of the related
   a. Deed.
   b. Canceled checks.
   c. Closing statement.
   d. Interest expense.

95. In testing plant and equipment balances, an auditor may inspect new additions listed on the analysis of plant and equipment. This procedure is designed to obtain evidence concerning management's assertions of

	Existence or occurrence	Presentation and disclosure
a.	Yes	Yes
b.	Yes	No
c.	No	Yes
d.	No	No

96. In auditing intangible assets, an auditor most likely would review or recompute amortization and determine whether the amortization period is reasonable in support of management's financial statement assertion of
    a.   Valuation or allocation.
    b.   Existence or occurrence.
    c.   Completeness.
    d.   Rights and obligations.

97. When auditing prepaid insurance, an auditor discovers that the original insurance policy on plant equipment is not available for inspection. The policy's absence most likely indicates the possibility of a(n)
    a.   Insurance premium due but **not** recorded.
    b.   Deficiency in the coinsurance provision.
    c.   Lien on the plant equipment.
    d.   Understatement of insurance expense.

98. Which of the following procedures would an auditor most likely perform in searching for unrecorded liabilities?
    a.   Trace a sample of accounts payable entries recorded just before year-end to the unmatched receiving report file.
    b.   Compare a sample of purchase orders issued just after year-end with the year-end accounts payable trial balance.
    c.   Vouch a sample of cash disbursements recorded just after year-end to receiving reports and vendor invoices.
    d.   Scan the cash disbursements entries recorded just before year-end for indications of unusual transactions.

99. When using confirmations to provide evidence about the completeness assertion for accounts payable, the appropriate population most likely would be
    a.   Vendors with whom the entity has previously done business.
    b.   Amounts recorded in the accounts payable subsidiary ledger.
    c.   Payees of checks drawn in the month after the year-end.
    d.   Invoices filed in the entity's open invoice file.

100. Auditor confirmation of accounts payable balances at the balance sheet date may be unnecessary because
    a.   This is a duplication of cutoff tests.
    b.   Accounts payable balances at the balance sheet date may not be paid before the audit is completed.
    c.   Correspondence with the audit client's attorney will reveal all legal action by vendors for nonpayment.
    d.   There is likely to be other reliable external evidence to support the balances.

101. Which of the following is a substantive test that an auditor most likely would perform to verify the existence and valuation of recorded accounts payable?
    a.   Investigating the open purchase order file to ascertain that prenumbered purchase orders are used and accounted for.
    b.   Receiving the client's mail, unopened, for a reasonable period of time after the year-end to search for unrecorded vendors' invoices.
    c.   Vouching selected entries in the accounts payable subsidiary ledger to purchase orders and receiving reports.
    d.   Confirming accounts payable balances with known suppliers who have zero balances.

102. In auditing accounts payable, an auditor's procedures most likely would focus primarily on management's assertion of
    a.   Existence.
    b.   Presentation and disclosure.
    c.   Completeness.
    d.   Valuation.

103. When a CPA observes that the recorded interest expense seems to be excessive in relation to the balance in the bonds payable account, the CPA might suspect that
    a.   Discount on bonds payable is understated.
    b.   Bonds payable are understated.
    c.   Bonds payable are overstated.
    d.   Premium on bonds payable is overstated.

104. An auditor most likely would inspect loan agreements under which an entity's inventories are pledged to support management's financial statement assertion of
    a.   Presentation and disclosure.
    b.   Valuation or allocation.
    c.   Existence or occurrence.
    d.   Completeness.

105. In auditing long-term bonds payable, an auditor most likely would
    a.   Perform analytical procedures on the bond premium and discount accounts.
    b.   Examine documentation of assets purchased with bond proceeds for liens.
    c.   Compare interest expense with the bond payable amount for reasonableness.
    d.   Confirm the existence of individual bond holders at year-end.

106. The auditor can best verify a client's bond sinking fund transactions and year-end balance by
    a.   Confirmation with individual holders of retired bonds.
    b.   Confirmation with the bond trustee.
    c.   Recomputation of interest expense, interest payable, and amortization of bond discount or premium.
    d.   Examination and count of the bonds retired during the year.

107. An auditor usually obtains evidence of stockholders' equity transactions by reviewing the entity's
    a.   Minutes of board of directors meetings.
    b.   Transfer agent's records.
    c.   Canceled stock certificates.
    d.   Treasury stock certificate book.

108. When control risk is assessed as low for assertions related to payroll, substantive tests of payroll balances most likely would be limited to applying analytical procedures and

a. Observing the distribution of paychecks.
b. Footing and crossfooting the payroll register.
c. Inspecting payroll tax returns.
d. Recalculating payroll accruals.

109. Which of the following circumstances most likely would cause an auditor to suspect an employee payroll fraud scheme?

a. There are significant unexplained variances between standard and actual labor cost.
b. Payroll checks are disbursed by the same employee each payday.
c. Employee time cards are approved by individual departmental supervisors.
d. A separate payroll bank account is maintained on an imprest basis.

110. In auditing payroll, an auditor most likely would

a. Verify that checks representing unclaimed wages are mailed.
b. Trace individual employee deductions to entity journal entries.
c. Observe entity employees during a payroll distribution.
d. Compare payroll costs with entity standards or budgets.

111. In performing tests concerning the granting of stock options, an auditor should

a. Confirm the transaction with the Secretary of State in the state of incorporation.
b. Verify the existence of option holders in the entity's payroll records or stock ledgers.
c. Determine that sufficient treasury stock is available to cover any new stock issued.
d. Trace the authorization for the transaction to a vote of the board of directors.

112. During an audit of an entity's stockholders' equity accounts, the auditor determines whether there are restrictions on retained earnings resulting from loans, agreements, or state law. This audit procedure most likely is intended to verify management's assertion of

a. Existence or occurrence.
b. Completeness.
c. Valuation or allocation.
d. Presentation and disclosure.

113. When a client company does **not** maintain its own stock records, the auditor should obtain written confirmation from the transfer agent and registrar concerning

a. Restrictions on the payment of dividends.
b. The number of shares issued and outstanding.
c. Guarantees of preferred stock liquidation value.
d. The number of shares subject to agreements to repurchase.

114. An audit program for the examination of the retained earnings account should include a step that requires verification of the

a. Market value used to charge retained earnings to account for a two-for-one stock split.
b. Approval of the adjustment to the beginning balance as a result of a write-down of an account receivable.
c. Authorization for both cash and stock dividends.
d. Gain or loss resulting from disposition of treasury shares.

115. An auditor most likely would perform substantive tests of details on payroll transactions and balances when

a. Cutoff tests indicate a substantial amount of accrued payroll expense.
b. The assessed level of control risk relative to payroll transactions is low.
c. Analytical procedures indicate unusual fluctuations in recurring payroll entries.
d. Accrued payroll expense consists primarily of unpaid commissions.

116. An auditor usually tests the reasonableness of dividend income from investments in publicly held companies by computing the amounts that should have been received by referring to

a. Dividend record books produced by investment advisory services.
b. Stock indentures published by corporate transfer agents.
c. Stock ledgers maintained by independent registrars.
d. Annual audited financial statements issued by the investee companies.

117. The most likely risk involved with a bill and hold transaction at year-end is a(n)

a. Accrued liability may be overstated as of year-end.
b. Buyer may have made an absolute purchase commitment.
c. Sale may inappropriately have been recorded as of year-end.
d. Buyer may have assumed the risk and reward of the purchased product.

118. Which of the following accounts is the practice of "channel stuffing" for sales most likely to most directly affect, and thereby result in additional audit procedures?

a. Accrued liabilities.
b. Allowance for sales returns.
c. Cash.
d. Marketable investments.

119. Recorded entries in which of the following accounts are most likely to relate to the property, plant, and equipment completeness assertion?

a. Allowance for doubtful accounts.
b. Marketable securities.
c. Property, plant, and equipment.
d. Repairs and maintenance expense.

120. For which of the following matters should an auditor obtain written management representations?

a. Management's cost-benefit justifications for **not** correcting internal control weaknesses.
b. Management's knowledge of future plans that may affect the price of the entity's stock.

c. Management's compliance with contractual agreements that may affect the financial statements.

d. Management's acknowledgment of its responsibility for employees' violations of laws.

121. To which of the following matters would materiality limits **not** apply in obtaining written management representations?

a. The availability of minutes of stockholders' and directors' meetings.

b. Losses from purchase commitments at prices in excess of market value.

c. The disclosure of compensating balance arrangements involving related parties.

d. Reductions of obsolete inventory to net realizable value.

122. The date of the management representation letter should coincide with the date of the

a. Balance sheet.

b. Latest interim financial information.

c. Auditor's report.

d. Latest related-party transaction.

123. Which of the following matters would an auditor most likely include in a management representation letter?

a. Communications with the audit committee concerning weaknesses in internal control.

b. The completeness and availability of minutes of stockholders' and directors' meetings.

c. Plans to acquire or merge with other entities in the subsequent year.

d. Management's acknowledgment of its responsibility for the detection of employee fraud.

124. The current chief executive and financial officers have only been employed by ABC Company for the past five months of year 2. ABC Company is presenting comparative financial statements on Years 1 and 2, both of which were audited by William Jones, CPA. For which year(s) should Jones obtain written representations from these two individuals?

	Year 1	Year 2
a.	No	No
b.	No	Yes
c.	Yes	No
d.	Yes	Yes

125. Which of the following statements ordinarily is included among the written client representations obtained by the auditor?

a. Compensating balances and other arrangements involving restrictions on cash balances have been disclosed.

b. Management acknowledges responsibility for illegal actions committed by employees.

c. Sufficient audit evidence has been made available to permit the issuance of an unqualified opinion.

d. Management acknowledges that there are **no** material weaknesses in the internal control.

126. When considering the use of management's written representations as audit evidence about the completeness assertion, an auditor should understand that such representations

a. Complement, but do **not** replace, substantive tests designed to support the assertion.

b. Constitute sufficient evidence to support the assertion when considered in combination with reliance on internal control.

c. Are **not** part of the audit evidence considered to support the assertion.

d. Replace reliance on internal control as evidence to support the assertion.

127. A written representation from a client's management which, among other matters, acknowledges responsibility for the fair presentation of financial statements, should normally be signed by the

a. Chief executive officer and the chief financial officer.

b. Chief financial officer and the chairman of the board of directors.

c. Chairman of the audit committee of the board of directors.

d. Chief executive officer, the chairman of the board of directors, and the client's lawyer.

128. A limitation on the scope of the auditor's examination sufficient to preclude an unqualified opinion will always result when management

a. Prevents the auditor from reviewing the working papers of the predecessor auditor.

b. Engages the auditor after the year-end physical inventory count is completed.

c. Fails to correct a significant deficiency of internal control that had been identified during the prior year's audit.

d. Refuses to furnish a management representation letter to the auditor.

129. A purpose of a management representation letter is to reduce

a. Audit risk to an aggregate level of misstatement that could be considered material.

b. An auditor's responsibility to detect material misstatements only to the extent that the letter is relied on.

c. The possibility of a misunderstanding concerning management's responsibility for the financial statements.

d. The scope of an auditor's procedures concerning related-party transactions and subsequent events.

130. "There have been no communications from regulatory agencies concerning noncompliance with, or deficiencies in, financial reporting practices that could have a material effect on the financial statements." The foregoing passage is most likely from a

a. Report on internal control.

b. Special report.

c. Management representation letter.

d. Letter for underwriters.

131. Which of the following statements is correct concerning an auditor's use of the work of a specialist?

a. The work of a specialist who is related to the client may be acceptable under certain circumstances.

b.   If an auditor believes that the determinations made by a specialist are unreasonable, only a qualified opinion may be issued.

c.   If there is a material difference between a specialist's findings and the assertions in the financial statements, only an adverse opinion may be issued.

d.   An auditor may **not** use a specialist in the determination of physical characteristics relating to inventories.

132. In using the work of a specialist, an auditor may refer to the specialist in the auditor's report if, as a result of the specialist's findings, the auditor

a.   Becomes aware of conditions causing substantial doubt about the entity's ability to continue as a going concern.

b.   Desires to disclose the specialist's findings, which imply that a more thorough audit was performed.

c.   Is able to corroborate another specialist's earlier findings that were consistent with management's representations.

d.   Discovers significant deficiencies in the design of the entity's internal control that management does **not** correct.

133. Which of the following statements is correct about the auditor's use of the work of a specialist?

a.   The specialist should **not** have an understanding of the auditor's corroborative use of the specialist's findings.

b.   The auditor is required to perform substantive procedures to verify the specialist's assumptions and findings.

c.   The client should **not** have an understanding of the nature of the work to be performed by the specialist.

d.   The auditor should obtain an understanding of the methods and assumptions used by the specialist.

134. In using the work of a specialist, an auditor referred to the specialist's findings in the auditor's report. This would be an appropriate reporting practice if the

a.   Client is **not** familiar with the professional certification, personal reputation, or particular competence of the specialist.

b.   Auditor, as a result of the specialist's findings, adds an explanatory paragraph emphasizing a matter regarding the financial statements.

c.   Client understands the auditor's corroborative use of the specialist's findings in relation to the representations in the financial statements.

d.   Auditor, as a result of the specialist's findings, decides to indicate a division of responsibility with the specialist.

135. In using the work of a specialist, an understanding should exist among the auditor, the client, and the specialist as to the nature of the specialist's work. The documentation of this understanding should cover

a.   A statement that the specialist assumes **no** responsibility to update the specialist's report for future events or circumstances.

b.   The conditions under which a division of responsibility may be necessary.

c.   The specialist's understanding of the auditor's corroborative use of the specialist's findings.

d.   The auditor's disclaimer as to whether the specialist's findings corroborate the representations in the financial statements.

136. Which of the following is **not** a specialist upon whose work an auditor may rely?

a.   Actuary.

b.   Appraiser.

c.   Internal auditor.

d.   Engineer.

137. A lawyer's response to an auditor's inquiry concerning litigation, claims, and assessments may be limited to matters that are considered individually or collectively material to the client's financial statements. Which parties should reach an understanding on the limits of materiality for this purpose?

a.   The auditor and the client's management.

b.   The client's audit committee and the lawyer.

c.   The client's management and the lawyer.

d.   The lawyer and the auditor.

138. The refusal of a client's attorney to provide information requested in an inquiry letter generally is considered

a.   Grounds for an adverse opinion.

b.   A limitation on the scope of the audit.

c.   Reason to withdraw from the engagement.

d.   Equivalent to a significant deficiency.

139. Which of the following is an audit procedure that an auditor most likely would perform concerning litigation, claims, and assessments?

a.   Request the client's lawyer to evaluate whether the client's pending litigation, claims, and assessments indicate a going concern problem.

b.   Examine the legal documents in the client's lawyer's possession concerning litigation, claims, and assessments to which the lawyer has devoted substantive attention.

c.   Discuss with management its policies and procedures adopted for evaluating and accounting for litigation, claims, and assessments.

d.   Confirm directly with the client's lawyer that all litigation, claims, and assessments have been recorded or disclosed in the financial statements.

140. The primary reason an auditor requests letters of inquiry be sent to a client's attorneys is to provide the auditor with

a.   The probable outcome of asserted claims and pending or threatened litigation.

b.   Corroboration of the information furnished by management about litigation, claims, and assessments.

c.   The attorneys' opinions of the client's historical experiences in recent similar litigation.

d.   A description and evaluation of litigation, claims, and assessments that existed at the balance sheet date.

141. Which of the following is **not** an audit procedure that the independent auditor would perform concerning litigation, claims, and assessments?

a.   Obtain assurance from management that it has disclosed all unasserted claims that the lawyer has

advised are probable of assertion and must be disclosed.
b. Confirm directly with the client's lawyer that all claims have been recorded in the financial statements.
c. Inquire of and discuss with management the policies and procedures adopted for identifying, evaluating, and accounting for litigation, claims, and assessments.
d. Obtain from management a description and evaluation of litigation, claims, and assessments existing at the balance sheet date.

142. The scope of an audit is **not** restricted when an attorney's response to an auditor as a result of a client's letter of audit inquiry limits the response to
a. Matters to which the attorney has given substantive attention in the form of legal representation.
b. An evaluation of the likelihood of an unfavorable outcome of the matters disclosed by the entity.
c. The attorney's opinion of the entity's historical experience in recent similar litigation.
d. The probable outcome of asserted claims and pending or threatened litigation.

143. A CPA has received an attorney's letter in which no significant disagreements with the client's assessments of contingent liabilities were noted. The resignation of the client's lawyer shortly after receipt of the letter should alert the auditor that
a. Undisclosed unasserted claims may have arisen.
b. The attorney was unable to form a conclusion with respect to the significance of litigation, claims, and assessments.
c. The auditor must begin a completely new examination of contingent liabilities.
d. An adverse opinion will be necessary.

144. Which of the following statements extracted from a client's lawyer's letter concerning litigation, claims, and assessments most likely would cause the auditor to request clarification?
a. "I believe that the possible liability to the company is nominal in amount."
b. "I believe that the action can be settled for less than the damages claimed."
c. "I believe that the plaintiff's case against the company is without merit."
d. "I believe that the company will be able to defend this action successfully."

145. When auditing the fair value of an asset or liability, valuation issues ordinarily arise at the point of

	Initial recording	Subsequent to initial recording
a.	Yes	Yes
b.	Yes	No
c.	No	Yes
d.	No	No

146. Which of the following is **least** likely to be an approach followed when auditing the fair values of assets and liabilities?
a. Review and test management's process of valuation.

b. Confirm valuations with audit committee members.
c. Independently develop an estimate of the value of the account.
d. Review subsequent events relating to the account.

147. Which of the following auditing procedures most likely would assist an auditor in identifying related-party transactions?
a. Inspecting correspondence with lawyers for evidence of unreported contingent liabilities.
b. Vouching accounting records for recurring transactions recorded just after the balance sheet date.
c. Reviewing confirmations of loans receivable and payable for indications of guarantees.
d. Performing analytical procedures for indications of possible financial difficulties.

148. After determining that a related-party transaction has, in fact, occurred, an auditor should
a. Add a separate paragraph to the auditor's standard report to explain the transaction.
b. Perform analytical procedures to verify whether similar transactions occurred, but were **not** recorded.
c. Obtain an understanding of the business purpose of the transaction.
d. Substantiate that the transaction was consummated on terms equivalent to an arm's-length transaction.

149. When auditing related-party transactions, an auditor places primary emphasis on
a. Ascertaining the rights and obligations of the related parties.
b. Confirming the existence of the related parties.
c. Verifying the valuation of the related-party transactions.
d. Evaluating the disclosure of the related-party transactions.

150. Which of the following statements is correct concerning related-party transactions?
a. In the absence of evidence to the contrary, related-party transactions should be assumed to be outside the ordinary course of business.
b. An auditor should determine whether a particular transaction would have occurred if the parties had **not** been related.
c. An auditor should substantiate that related-party transactions were consummated on terms equivalent to those that prevail in arm's-length transactions.
d. The audit procedures directed toward identifying related-party transactions should include considering whether transactions are occurring, but are **not** being given proper accounting recognition.

151. An auditor most likely would modify an unqualified opinion if the entity's financial statements include a footnote on related-party transactions
a. Disclosing loans to related parties at interest rates significantly below prevailing market rates.
b. Describing an exchange of real estate for similar property in a nonmonetary related-party transaction.

c. Stating that a particular related-party transaction occurred on terms equivalent to those that would have prevailed in an arm's-length transaction.

d. Presenting the dollar volume of related-party transactions and the effects of any change in the method of establishing terms from prior periods.

152. Which of the following conditions or events most likely would cause an auditor to have substantial doubt about an entity's ability to continue as a going concern?

a. Significant related-party transactions are pervasive.

b. Usual trade credit from suppliers is denied.

c. Arrearages in preferred stock dividends are paid.

d. Restrictions on the disposal of principal assets are present.

153. Cooper, CPA, believes there is substantial doubt about the ability of Zero Corp. to continue as a going concern for a reasonable period of time. In evaluating Zero's plans for dealing with the adverse effects of future conditions and events, Cooper most likely would consider, as a mitigating factor, Zero's plans to

a. Discuss with lenders the terms of all debt and loan agreements.

b. Strengthen controls over cash disbursements.

c. Purchase production facilities currently being leased from a related party.

d. Postpone expenditures for research and development projects.

154. Which of the following conditions or events most likely would cause an auditor to have substantial doubt about an entity's ability to continue as a going concern?

a. Cash flows from operating activities are negative.

b. Research and development projects are postponed.

c. Significant related-party transactions are pervasive.

d. Stock dividends replace annual cash dividends.

155. Which of the following auditing procedures most likely would assist an auditor in identifying conditions and events that may indicate substantial doubt about an entity's ability to continue as a going concern?

a. Inspecting title documents to verify whether any assets are pledged as collateral.

b. Confirming with third parties the details of arrangements to maintain financial support.

c. Reconciling the cash balance per books with the cutoff bank statement and the bank confirmation.

d. Comparing the entity's depreciation and asset capitalization policies to other entities in the industry.

156. Which of the following audit procedures would most likely assist an auditor in identifying conditions and events that may indicate there could be substantial doubt about an entity's ability to continue as a going concern?

a. Review compliance with the terms of debt agreements.

b. Confirmation of accounts receivable from principal customers.

c. Reconciliation of interest expense with debt outstanding.

d. Confirmation of bank balances.

157. Davis, CPA, believes there is substantial doubt about the ability of Hill Co. to continue as a going concern for a reasonable period of time. In evaluating Hill's plans for dealing with the adverse effects of future conditions and events, Davis most likely would consider, as a mitigating factor, Hill's plans to

a. Accelerate research and development projects related to future products.

b. Accumulate treasury stock at prices favorable to Hill's historic price range.

c. Purchase equipment and production facilities currently being leased.

d. Negotiate reductions in required dividends being paid on preferred stock.

158. The adverse effects of events causing an auditor to believe there is substantial doubt about an entity's ability to continue as a going concern would most likely be mitigated by evidence relating to the

a. Ability to expand operations into new product lines in the future.

b. Feasibility of plans to purchase leased equipment at less than market value.

c. Marketability of assets that management plans to sell.

d. Committed arrangements to convert preferred stock to long-term debt.

159. Which of the following procedures would an auditor most likely perform in obtaining evidence about subsequent events?

a. Determine that changes in employee pay rates after year-end were properly authorized.

b. Recompute depreciation charges for plant assets sold after year-end.

c. Inquire about payroll checks that were recorded before year-end but cashed after year-end.

d. Investigate changes in long-term debt occurring after year-end.

160. Which of the following events occurring after the issuance of an auditor's report most likely would cause the auditor to make further inquiries about the previously issued financial statements?

a. An uninsured natural disaster occurs that may affect the entity's ability to continue as a going concern.

b. A contingency is resolved that had been disclosed in the audited financial statements.

c. New information is discovered concerning undisclosed lease transactions of the audited period.

d. A subsidiary is sold that accounts for 25% of the entity's consolidated net income.

161. Zero Corp. suffered a loss that would have a material effect on its financial statements on an uncollectible trade account receivable due to a customer's bankruptcy. This occurred suddenly due to a natural disaster ten days after Zero's balance sheet date, but one month before the issuance of the financial statements and the auditor's report. Under these circumstances,

	The financial statements should be adjusted	The event requires financial statement disclosure, but no adjustment	The auditor's report should be modified for a lack of consistency
a.	Yes	No	No
b.	Yes	No	Yes
c.	No	Yes	Yes
d.	No	Yes	No

162. After an audit report containing an unqualified opinion on a nonissuer (nonpublic) client's financial statements was issued, the client decided to sell the shares of a subsidiary that accounts for 30% of its revenue and 25% of its net income. The auditor should

a. Determine whether the information is reliable and, if determined to be reliable, request that revised financial statements be issued.

b. Notify the entity that the auditor's report may **no** longer be associated with the financial statements.

c. Describe the effects of this subsequently discovered information in a communication with persons known to be relying on the financial statements.

d. Take **no** action because the auditor has **no** obligation to make any further inquiries.

163. A client acquired 25% of its outstanding capital stock after year-end and prior to completion of the auditor's fieldwork. The auditor should

a. Advise management to adjust the balance sheet to reflect the acquisition.

b. Issue pro forma financial statements giving effect to the acquisition as if it had occurred at year-end.

c. Advise management to disclose the acquisition in the notes to the financial statements.

d. Disclose the acquisition in the opinion paragraph of the auditor's report.

164. Which of the following procedures would an auditor most likely perform to obtain evidence about the occurrence of subsequent events?

a. Confirming a sample of material accounts receivable established after year-end.

b. Comparing the financial statements being reported on with those of the prior period.

c. Investigating personnel changes in the accounting department occurring after year-end.

d. Inquiring as to whether any unusual adjustments were made after year-end.

165. Which of the following procedures should an auditor generally perform regarding subsequent events?

a. Compare the latest available interim financial statements with the financial statements being audited.

b. Send second requests to the client's customers who failed to respond to initial accounts receivable confirmation requests.

c. Communicate material weaknesses in internal control to the client's audit committee.

d. Review the cutoff bank statements for several months after the year-end.

166. On February 25, a CPA issued an auditor's report expressing an unqualified opinion on financial statements for the year ended January 31. On March 2, the CPA learned that on February 11, the entity incurred a material loss on an uncollectible trade receivable as a result of the deteriorating financial condition of the entity's principal customer that led to the customer's bankruptcy. Management then refused to adjust the financial statements for this subsequent event. The CPA determined that the information is reliable and that there are creditors currently relying on the financial statements. The CPA's next course of action most likely would be to

a. Notify the entity's creditors that the financial statements and the related auditor's report should **no** longer be relied on.

b. Notify each member of the entity's board of directors about management's refusal to adjust the financial statements.

c. Issue revised financial statements and distribute them to each creditor known to be relying on the financial statements.

d. Issue a revised auditor's report and distribute it to each creditor known to be relying on the financial statements.

167. An auditor is considering whether the omission of a substantive procedure considered necessary at the time of an audit may impair the auditor's present ability to support the previously expressed opinion. The auditor need **not** apply the omitted procedure if the

a. Financial statements and auditor's report were not distributed beyond management and the board of directors.

b. Auditor's previously expressed opinion was qualified because of a departure from GAAP.

c. Results of other procedures that were applied tend to compensate for the procedure omitted.

d. Omission is due to unreasonable delays by client personnel in providing data on a timely basis.

168. On March 15, 2002, Kent, CPA, issued an unqualified opinion on a client's audited financial statements for the year ended December 31, 2001. On May 4, 2002, Kent's internal inspection program disclosed that engagement personnel failed to observe the client's physical inventory. Omission of this procedure impairs Kent's present ability to support the unqualified opinion. If the stockholders are currently relying on the opinion, Kent should first

a. Advise management to disclose to the stockholders that Kent's unqualified opinion should **not** be relied on.

b. Undertake to apply alternative procedures that would provide a satisfactory basis for the unqualified opinion.

c. Reissue the auditor's report and add an explanatory paragraph describing the departure from generally accepted auditing standards.

d. Compensate for the omitted procedure by performing tests of controls to reduce audit risk to a sufficiently low level.

169. Six months after issuing an unqualified opinion on audited financial statements, an auditor discovered that the engagement personnel failed to confirm several of the client's material accounts receivable balances. The auditor should first

a. Request the permission of the client to undertake the confirmation of accounts receivable.

b. Perform alternative procedures to provide a satisfactory basis for the unqualified opinion.

c. Assess the importance of the omitted procedures to the auditor's ability to support the previously expressed opinion.

d. Inquire whether there are persons currently relying, or likely to rely, on the unqualified opinion.

170. Which of the following procedures is **least** likely to be performed before the balance sheet date?

a. Testing of internal control over cash.

b. Confirmation of receivables.

c. Search for unrecorded liabilities.

d. Observation of inventory.

171. Which of the following most likely would be detected by an auditor's review of a client's sales cutoff?

a. Shipments lacking sales invoices and shipping documents.

b. Excessive write-offs of accounts receivable.

c. Unrecorded sales at year-end.

d. Lapping of year-end accounts receivable.

172. Cutoff tests designed to detect credit sales made before the end of the year that have been recorded in the subsequent year provide assurance about management's assertion of

a. Presentation.

b. Completeness.

c. Rights.

d. Existence.

173. Which of the following procedures would an auditor most likely perform during an audit engagement's overall review stage in formulating an opinion on an entity's financial statements?

a. Obtain assurance from the entity's attorney that all material litigation has been disclosed in the financial statements.

b. Verify the clerical accuracy of the entity's proof of cash and its bank cutoff statement.

c. Determine whether inadequate provisions for the safeguarding of assets have been corrected.

d. Consider whether the results of audit procedures affect the assessment of the risk of material misstatement due to fraud.

174. Which of the following procedures is ordinarily performed by an accountant in a compilation engagement of a nonissuer (nonpublic) entity?

a. Reading the financial statements to consider whether they are free of obvious mistakes in the application of accounting principles.

b. Obtaining written representations from management indicating that the compiled financial statements will **not** be used to obtain credit.

c. Making inquiries of management concerning actions taken at meetings of the stockholders and the board of directors.

d. Applying analytical procedures designed to corroborate management's assertions that are embodied in the financial statement components.

175. Davis, CPA, accepted an engagement to audit the financial statements of Tech Resources, a nonissuer. Before the completion of the audit, Tech requested Davis to change the engagement to a compilation of financial statements.

Before Davis agrees to change the engagement, Davis is required to consider the

	Additional audit effort necessary to complete the audit	Reason given for Tech's request
a.	No	No
b.	Yes	Yes
c.	Yes	No
d.	No	Yes

176. May an accountant accept an engagement to compile or review the financial statements of a not-for-profit entity if the accountant is unfamiliar with the specialized industry accounting principles, but plans to obtain the required level of knowledge before compiling or reviewing the financial statements?

	Compilation	Review
a.	No	No
b.	Yes	No
c.	No	Yes
d.	Yes	Yes

177. Which of the following statements is correct concerning both an engagement to compile and an engagement to review a nonissuer's financial statements?

a. The accountant does not contemplate obtaining an understanding of internal control.

b. The accountant must be independent in fact and appearance.

c. The accountant expresses no assurance on the financial statements.

d. The accountant should obtain a written management representation letter.

178. One of the conditions required for an accountant to submit a written personal financial plan containing unaudited financial statements to a client without complying with the requirements of Statements on Standards of Accounting and Review Services, is that the

a. Client agrees that the financial statements will **not** be used to obtain credit.

b. Accountant compiled or reviewed the client's financial statements for the immediate prior year.

c. Engagement letter acknowledges that the financial statements will contain departures from generally accepted accounting principles.

d. Accountant expresses limited assurance that the financial statements are free of any material misstatements.

179. Which of the following is not generally considered a procedure followed by an accountant in obtaining a reasonable basis for the expression of limited assurance for a review of financial statements?

a. Apply analytical procedures.

b. Assess fraud risk.

c. Make inquiries of management.

d. Obtain written representations from management.

180. When providing limited assurance that the financial statements of a nonissuer (nonpublic entity) require **no** material modifications to be in accordance with generally accepted accounting principles, the accountant should

a. Assess the risk that a material misstatement could occur in a financial statement assertion.

b. Confirm with the entity's lawyer that material loss contingencies are disclosed.

c. Understand the accounting principles of the industry in which the entity operates.

d. Develop audit programs to determine whether the entity's financial statements are fairly presented.

181. Which of the following procedures would an accountant **least** likely perform during an engagement to review the financial statements of a nonissuer?

a. Observing the safeguards over access to and use of assets and records.

b. Comparing the financial statements with anticipated results in budgets and forecasts.

c. Inquiring of management about actions taken at the board of directors' meetings.

d. Studying the relationships of financial statement elements expected to conform to predictable patterns.

182. Which of the following procedures should an accountant perform during an engagement to review the financial statements of a nonissuer?

a. Communicating significant deficiencies discovered during the assessment of control risk.

b. Obtaining a client representation letter from members of management.

c. Sending bank confirmation letters to the entity's financial institutions.

d. Examining cash disbursements in the subsequent period for unrecorded liabilities.

183. Smith, CPA, has been asked to issue a review report on the balance sheet of Cone Company, a nonissuer, and not on the other related financial statements. Smith may do so only if

a. Smith compiles and reports on the related statements of income, retained earnings, and cash flows.

b. Smith is **not** aware of any material modifications needed for the balance sheet to conform with GAAP.

c. The scope of Smith's inquiry and analytical procedures is **not** restricted.

d. Cone is a new client and Smith accepts the engagement after the end of Cone's fiscal year.

184. An accountant should perform analytical procedures during an engagement to

	Compile a nonissuer's financial statements	Review a nonissuer's financial statements
a.	No	No
b.	Yes	Yes
c.	Yes	No
d.	No	Yes

185. Which of the following inquiry or analytical procedures ordinarily is performed in an engagement to review a nonissuer's financial statements?

a. Analytical procedures designed to test the accounting records by obtaining corroborating audit evidence.

b. Inquiries concerning the entity's procedures for recording and summarizing transactions.

c. Analytical procedures designed to test management's assertions regarding continued existence.

d. Inquiries of the entity's attorney concerning contingent liabilities.

186. Which of the following procedures would most likely be included in a review engagement of a nonissuer?

a. Preparing a bank transfer schedule.

b. Inquiring about related-party transactions.

c. Assessing internal control.

d. Performing cutoff tests on sales and purchases transactions.

187. Which of the following would the accountant most likely investigate during the review of financial statements of a nonissuer if accounts receivable did **not** conform to a predictable pattern during the year?

a. Sales returns and allowances.

b. Credit sales.

c. Sales of consigned goods.

d. Cash sales.

188. When performing an engagement to review a nonissuer's financial statements, an accountant most likely would

a. Confirm a sample of significant accounts receivable balances.

b. Ask about actions taken at board of directors' meetings.

c. Obtain an understanding of internal control.

d. Limit the distribution of the accountant's report.

189. Operational auditing is primarily oriented toward

a. Future improvements to accomplish the goals of management.

b. The accuracy of data reflected in management's financial records.

c. The verification that a company's financial statements are fairly presented.

d. Past protection provided by existing internal control.

190. A typical objective of an operational audit is to determine whether an entity's

a. Internal control is adequately operating as designed.

b. Operational information is in accordance with generally accepted governmental auditing standards.

c. Financial statements present fairly the results of operations.

d. Specific operating units are functioning efficiently and effectively.

SIMULATION PROBLEMS

Simulation Problem 1   (30 to 35 minutes)

Directions				
	Audit Objectives—Investments	Audit Objectives—Accounts Receivable	Research	Communication

To support financial statement assertions, an auditor develops specific audit objectives. The auditor then designs substantive tests to satisfy or accomplish each objective.

Items 1 through 7 represent audit objectives for the investments and accounts receivable. To the right of each set of audit objectives is a listing of possible audit procedures for that account. For each audit objective, select the audit procedure that would primarily respond to the objective. Select only one procedure for each audit objective. A procedure may be selected only once, or not at all.

	Audit Objectives—Investments			
Directions		Audit Objectives—Accounts Receivable	Research	Communication

Audit procedures for investments

A. Trace opening balances in the subsidiary ledger to prior year's audit working papers.
B. Determine that employees who are authorized to sell investments do not have access to cash.
C. Examine supporting documents for a sample of investment transactions to verify that prenumbered documents are used.
D. Determine that any impairments in the price of investments have been properly recorded.
E. Verify that transfers from the current to the noncurrent investment portfolio have been properly recorded.
F. Obtain positive confirmations as of the balance sheet date of investments held by independent custodians.
G. Trace investment transactions to minutes of the Board of Directors meetings to determine that transactions were properly authorized.

Audit objectives for investments	(A)	(B)	(C)	(D)	(E)	(F)	(G)
1. Investments are properly described and classified in the financial statements.	○	○	○	○	○	○	○
2. Recorded investments represent investments actually owned at the balance sheet date.	○	○	○	○	○	○	○
3. Trading investments are properly valued at fair market value at the balance sheet date.	○	○	○	○	○	○	○

		Audit Objectives—Accounts Receivable		
Directions	Audit Objectives—Investments		Research	Communication

Audit procedures for accounts receivable

A. Analyze the relationship of accounts receivable and sales and compare it with relationships for preceding periods.
B. Perform sales cutoff tests to obtain assurance that sales transactions and corresponding entries for inventories and cost of goods sold are recorded in the same and proper period.
C. Review the aged trial balance for significant past due accounts.
D. Obtain an understanding of the business purpose of transactions that resulted in accounts receivable balances.
E. Review loan agreements for indications of whether accounts receivable have been factored or pledged.
F. Review the accounts receivable trial balance for amounts due from officers and employees.
G. Analyze unusual relationships between monthly accounts receivable balances and monthly accounts payable balances.

Audit objectives for accounts receivable	(A)	(B)	(C)	(D)	(E)	(F)	(G)
4. Accounts receivable represent all amounts owed to the entity at the balance sheet date.	○	○	○	○	○	○	○
5. The entity has legal right to all accounts receivable at the balance sheet date.	○	○	○	○	○	○	○
6. Accounts receivable are stated at net realizable value.	○	○	○	○	○	○	○
7. Accounts receivable are properly described and presented in the financial statements.	○	○	○	○	○	○	○

Directions	Audit Objectives— Investments	Audit Objectives— Accounts Receivable	Research	Communication

Your client has suggested to you that his previous auditor did not confirm accounts receivable. Search the Professional Standards to determine whether there are any circumstances in which an auditor need not request the confirmation of accounts receivable. Select the appropriate paragraph.

Directions	Audit Objectives— Investments	Audit Objectives— Accounts Receivable	Research	Communication

Assume that you are preparing accounts receivable confirmations for a client. You are concerned that some of the companies whose accounts were selected from the client's records may be fictitious. Write a memorandum to the audit files describing how you will detect fictitious companies.

REMINDER: Your response will be graded for both technical content and writing skills. Technical content will be evaluated for information that is helpful to the intended reader and clearly relevant to the issue. Writing skills will be evaluated for development, organization, and the appropriate expression of ideas in professional correspondence. Use a standard business memo or letter format with a clear beginning, middle, and end. Do not convey information in the form of a table, bullet point list, or other abbreviated presentation.

To: Audit Working Papers
From: CPA Candidate
Re: Procedures to detect fictitious companies

Simulation Problem 2   (40 to 50 minutes)

Directions	Audit Implications	Confirmations	Inventory Observation	Research	Communication

In the following simulation you are asked to reply to various statements concerning situations that may arise in an audit.

Directions	Audit Implications	Confirmations	Inventory Observation	Research	Communication

In applying audit procedures and evaluating the results of those procedures, auditors may encounter specific information that may raise a question concerning the existence of illegal acts and related-party transactions. Indicate whether each of the following is more likely related to an illegal act (IA) or a related-party transaction (RP).

	Statement	IA	RP
1.	A note payable has an interest rate well below the market rate at the time at which the loan was obtained.	○	○
2.	The company has a properly documented loan but the loan has no scheduled repayment terms.	○	○
3.	Unexplained payments have been made to government officials.	○	○
4.	The company exchanged certain real estate property for similar real estate property.	○	○
5.	Large cash receipts near year-end have been received based on cash sales for which there is no documentation.	○	○

Directions	Audit Implications	Confirmations	Inventory Observation	Research	Communication

An auditor may use confirmations of accounts receivable. Reply as to whether the following statements are correct or incorrect with respect to the confirmation process when applied to accounts receivable.

Statement	Correct	Incorrect
1. The confirmation requests should be mailed to respondents by the CPAs.	○	○
2. A combination of positive and negative request forms must be used if receivables are significant.	○	○
3. Second requests are ordinarily sent for positive form confirmations requests when the first request is not returned.	○	○
4. Confirmations address existence more than they address completeness.	○	○
5. Confirmation of accounts receivable is a generally accepted auditing standard.	○	○
6. Absent a few circumstances, there is a presumption that the auditor will confirm accounts receivable.	○	○
7. Auditors should always confirm the total balances of accounts rather than individual portions (e.g., if the balance is made up of three sales, all three should be confirmed).	○	○
8. Auditors may ignore individually immaterial accounts when confirming accounts receivable.	○	○
9. The best way to evaluate the results of the confirmation process is to total the misstatements identified and to compare that total to the account's tolerable error amounts.	○	○
10. Accounts receivable are ordinarily confirmed on a standard form developed by the American Institute of Certified Public Accountants and the Financial Executives Institute.	○	○

Directions	Audit Implications	Confirmations	Inventory Observation	Research	Communication

Auditors often observe the counting of their clients' inventories. Reply as to whether the following statements are correct or incorrect with respect to the inventory observation.

Statement	Correct	Incorrect
1. With strong internal control, the inventory count may be at the end of the year or at other times.	○	○
2. When a client has many inventory locations, auditors ordinarily need not be present at each location.	○	○
3. All auditor test counts must be documented in the working papers.	○	○
4. Auditors' observation of the counting of their clients' inventories addresses the existence of inventory, and not the completeness of the count.	○	○
5. When the client manufactures a product, direct labor and overhead ordinarily become a part of inventory item costs.	○	○
6. Inventory is ordinarily valued at the lower of standard cost or market.	○	○
7. Inventory items present as "consigned in" should not be included in the clients' inventory value.	○	○
8. Auditor recording of test counts ordinarily replaces the need for client "tagging" of inventory.	○	○
9. Ordinarily, an auditor need not count all items in the inventory.	○	○
10. At the completion of the count, an auditor will ordinarily provide the client with copies of his or her inventory test counts to help assure inventory accuracy.	○	○

Directions	Audit Implications	Confirmations	Inventory Observation	Research	Communication

When audit clients may become involved with financial derivative transactions, auditors need to determine that client financial statements meet the completeness assertion with respect to determining that all of the client's derivatives are properly reported. Search the Professional Standards to identify suggested substantive procedures for completeness as it relates to financial derivatives.

	Audit		Inventory		Communication
Directions	Implications	Confirmations	Observation	Research	

Write a memorandum to the audit working papers about the importance of controlling the mailing of confirmations.

REMINDER: Your response will be graded for both technical content and writing skills. Technical content will be evaluated for information that is helpful to the intended reader and clearly relevant to the issue. Writing skills will be evaluated for development, organization, and the appropriate expression of ideas in professional correspondence. Use a standard business memo or letter format with a clear beginning, middle, and end. Do not convey information in the form of a table, bullet point list, or other abbreviated presentation.

To: Audit Working Papers
From: CPA Candidate
Re: Audit confirmations

Simulation Problem 3   (40 to 50 minutes)

Audit			
Procedures	Assessing		
	Audit Risk	Research	Communication

Items 1 through 6 represent the items that an auditor ordinarily would find on a client-prepared bank reconciliation. The accompanying **List of Auditing Procedures** represents substantive auditing procedures. For each item, select one or more procedures, as indicated, that the auditor most likely would perform to gather evidence in support of that item. The procedures on the **List** may be selected once, more than once, or not at all.

Assume

- The client prepared the bank reconciliation on 10/2/05.
- The bank reconciliation is mathematically accurate.
- The auditor received a cutoff bank statement dated 10/7/05 directly from the bank on 10/11/05.
- The 9/30/05 deposit in transit, outstanding checks #1281, #1285, #1289, and #1292, and the correction of the error regarding check #1282 appeared on the cutoff bank statement.
- The auditor assessed control risk concerning the financial statement assertions related to cash at the maximum.

List of Auditing Procedures

A. Trace to cash receipts journal.
B. Trace to cash disbursements journal.
C. Compare to 9/30/01 general ledger.
D. Confirm directly with bank.
E. Inspect bank credit memo.

F. Inspect bank debit memo.
G. Ascertain reason for unusual delay.
H. Inspect supporting documents for reconciling item **not** appearing on cutoff statement.
I. Trace items on the bank reconciliation to cutoff statement.
J. Trace items on the cutoff statement to bank reconciliation.

General Company
BANK RECONCILIATION
1ST NATIONAL BANK OF US BANK ACCOUNT
September 30, 2005

1.	Select 2 Procedures	—	Balance per bank		$ 28,375
2.	Select 5 Procedures	—	Deposits in transit		
			9/29/05	$4,500	
			9/30/05	1,525	6,025
					34,400
3.	Select 5 Procedures	—	Outstanding checks		
			# 988 8/31/05	2,200	
			#1281 9/26/05	675	
			#1285 9/27/05	850	
			#1289 9/29/05	2,500	
			#1292 9/30/05	7,225	(13,450)
					20,950

4.	Select 1 Procedure	—	Customer note collected by bank	(3,000)
5.	Select 2 Procedures	—	Error: Check #1282, written on 9/26/05 for $270 was erroneously charged by bank as $720; bank was notified on 10/2/05	450
6.	Select 1 Procedure	—	Balance per books	$ 18,400

Audit Procedures	Addressing Audit Risk		
		Research	Communication

Items 1 through 12 represent possible errors and fraud that you suspect may be present at General Company. The accompanying *List of Auditing Procedures* represents procedures that the auditor would consider performing to gather evidence concerning possible errors and fraud. For each item, select one or two procedures, as indicated, that the auditor most likely would perform to gather evidence in support of that item. The procedures on the list may be selected once, more than once, or not at all.

List of Auditing Procedures

A. Compare the details of the cash receipts journal entries with the details of the corresponding daily deposit slips.
B. Scan the debits to the fixed asset accounts and vouch selected amounts to vendors' invoices and management's authorization.
C. Perform analytical procedures that compare documented authorized pay rates to the entity's budget and forecast.
D. Obtain the cutoff bank statement and compare the cleared checks to the year-end bank reconciliation.
E. Prepare a bank transfer schedule.
F. Inspect the entity's deeds to its real estate.
G. Make inquiries of the entity's attorney concerning the details of real estate transactions.
H. Confirm the terms of borrowing arrangements with the lender.
I. Examine selected equipment repair orders and supporting documentation to determine the propriety of the charges.
J. Send requests to confirm the entity's accounts receivable on a surprise basis at an interim date.
K. Send a second request for confirmation of the receivable to the customer and make inquiries of a reputable credit agency concerning the customer's creditworthiness.

L. Examine the entity's shipping documents to verify that the merchandise that produced the receivable was actually sent to the customer.
M. Inspect the entity's correspondence files for indications of customer disputes for evidence that certain shipments were on consignment.
N. Perform edit checks of data on the payroll transaction tapes.
O. Inspect payroll check endorsements for similar handwriting.
P. Observe payroll check distribution on a surprise basis.
Q. Vouch data in the payroll register to documented authorized pay rates in the human resources department's files.
R. Reconcile the payroll checking account and determine if there were unusual time lags between the issuance and payment of payroll checks.
S. Inspect the file of prenumbered vouchers for consecutive numbering and proper approval by an appropriate employee.
T. Determine that the details of selected prenumbered vouchers match the related vendors' invoices.
U. Examine the supporting purchase orders and receiving reports for selected paid vouchers.

Possible misstatements due to errors and fraud

1. The auditor suspects that a kiting scheme exists because an accounting department employee who can issue and record checks seems to be leading an unusually luxurious lifestyle. (**Select only 1 procedure**)

2. An auditor suspects that the controller wrote several checks and recorded the cash disbursements just before year-end but did not mail the checks until after the first week of the subsequent year. (**Select only 1 procedure**)

3. The entity borrowed funds from a financial institution. Although the transaction was properly recorded, the auditor suspects that the loan created a lien on the entity's real estate that is not disclosed in its financial statements. (**Select only 1 procedure**)

4. The auditor discovered an unusually large receivable from one of the entity's new customers. The auditor suspects that the receivable may be fictitious because the auditor has never heard of the customer and because the auditor's initial attempt to confirm the receivable has been ignored by the customer. (**Select only 2 procedures**)

5. The auditor suspects that fictitious employees have been placed on the payroll by the entity's payroll supervisor, who has access to payroll records and to the paychecks. (**Select only 1 procedure**)

6. The auditor suspects that selected employees of the entity received unauthorized raises from the entity's payroll supervisor, who has access to payroll records. (**Select only 1 procedure**)

7. The entity's cash receipts of the first few days of the subsequent year were properly deposited in its general operating account after the year-end. However, the auditor suspects that the entity recorded the cash receipts in its books during the last week of the year under audit. (**Select only 1 procedure**)

8. The auditor suspects that vouchers were prepared and processed by an accounting department employee for merchandise that was neither ordered nor received by the entity. (**Select only 1 procedure**)

9. The details of invoices for equipment repairs were not clearly identified or explained to the accounting department employees. The auditor suspects that the bookkeeper incorrectly recorded the repairs as fixed assets. (**Select only 1 procedure**)

10. The auditor suspects that a lapping scheme exists because an accounting department employee who has access to cash receipts also maintains the accounts receivable ledger and refuses to take any vacation or sick days. (**Select only 2 procedures**)

11. The auditor suspects that the entity is inappropriately increasing the cash reported on its balance sheet by drawing a check on one account and not recording it as an outstanding check on that account and simultaneously recording it as a deposit in a second account. (**Select only 1 procedure**)

12. The auditor suspects that the entity's controller has overstated sales and accounts receivable by recording fictitious sales to regular customers in the entity's books. (**Select only 2 procedures**)

| Audit Procedures | Addressing Audit Risk | Research | Communication |

Now assume that the note collected by the bank is from a "related party." Search the Professional Standards to determine procedures that should be performed concerning a related-party transaction that has been identified.

NOTE: If you do not have access to professional standards indicate the keywords or section numbers that you would use to do your search.

| Audit Procedures | Addressing Audit Risk | Research | Communication |

General Company wishes to put a note in the company's financial statements indicating that the terms of the related-party loan is comparable to those between unrelated parties. Write a brief memorandum to Joe Smith, the CEO of General Company, explaining the implications of this proposed action.

REMINDER: Your response will be graded for both technical content and writing skills. Technical content will be evaluated for information that is helpful to the intended reader and clearly relevant to the issue. Writing skills will be evaluated for development, organization, and the appropriate expression of ideas in professional correspondence. Use a standard business memo or letter format with a clear beginning, middle, and end. Do not convey information in the form of a table, bullet point list, or other abbreviated presentation.

To: Joe Smith, CEO
       General Company
From: CPA Candidate
Re: Related-party loan disclosure

Additional Simulations

Appendix A—Simulation 4 involves Evidence
Appendix A—Simulation 5 involves Evidence
Appendix A—Simulation 6 involves Evidence
Appendix A—Simulation 7 involves Evidence

MULTIPLE-CHOICE ANSWERS

1. b __ __	33. b __ __	65. d __ __	97. c __ __	129. c __ __	161. d __ __
2. c __ __	34. a __ __	66. d __ __	98. c __ __	130. c __ __	162. d __ __
3. c __ __	35. a __ __	67. a __ __	99. a __ __	131. a __ __	163. c __ __
4. d __ __	36. a __ __	68. b __ __	100. d __ __	132. a __ __	164. d __ __
5. d __ __	37. c __ __	69. d __ __	101. c __ __	133. d __ __	165. a __ __
6. a __ __	38. c __ __	70. a __ __	102. c __ __	134. b __ __	166. b __ __
7. a __ __	39. d __ __	71. d __ __	103. b __ __	135. c __ __	167. c __ __
8. d __ __	40. b __ __	72. c __ __	104. a __ __	136. c __ __	168. b __ __
9. d __ __	41. a __ __	73. a __ __	105. c __ __	137. d __ __	169. c __ __
10. d __ __	42. d __ __	74. a __ __	106. b __ __	138. b __ __	170. c __ __
11. d __ __	43. c __ __	75. d __ __	107. a __ __	139. c __ __	171. c __ __
12. c __ __	44. b __ __	76. c __ __	108. d __ __	140. b __ __	172. b __ __
13. a __ __	45. b __ __	77. b __ __	109. a __ __	141. b __ __	173. d __ __
14. b __ __	46. c __ __	78. a __ __	110. d __ __	142. a __ __	174. a __ __
15. c __ __	47. b __ __	79. b __ __	111. d __ __	143. a __ __	175. b __ __
16. a __ __	48. d __ __	80. a __ __	112. d __ __	144. b __ __	176. d __ __
17. d __ __	49. b __ __	81. b __ __	113. b __ __	145. a __ __	177. a __ __
18. b __ __	50. b __ __	82. d __ __	114. c __ __	146. b __ __	178. a __ __
19. c __ __	51. b __ __	83. a __ __	115. c __ __	147. c __ __	179. b __ __
20. c __ __	52. c __ __	84. c __ __	116. a __ __	148. c __ __	180. c __ __
21. c __ __	53. d __ __	85. c __ __	117. c __ __	149. d __ __	181. a __ __
22. a __ __	54. b __ __	86. c __ __	118. b __ __	150. d __ __	182. b __ __
23. b __ __	55. c __ __	87. c __ __	119. d __ __	151. c __ __	183. c __ __
24. c __ __	56. b __ __	88. a __ __	120. c __ __	152. b __ __	184. d __ __
25. b __ __	57. c __ __	89. d __ __	121. a __ __	153. d __ __	185. b __ __
26. c __ __	58. b __ __	90. b __ __	122. c __ __	154. a __ __	186. b __ __
27. b __ __	59. a __ __	91. a __ __	123. b __ __	155. b __ __	187. b __ __
28. c __ __	60. a __ __	92. d __ __	124. d __ __	156. a __ __	188. b __ __
29. c __ __	61. c __ __	93. c __ __	125. a __ __	157. d __ __	189. a __ __
30. c __ __	62. b __ __	94. a __ __	126. a __ __	158. c __ __	190. d __ __
31. d __ __	63. c __ __	95. b __ __	127. a __ __	159. d __ __	1st: __/190 = __%
32. c __ __	64. a __ __	96. a __ __	128. d __ __	160. c __ __	2nd: __/190 = __%

MULTIPLE-CHOICE ANSWER EXPLANATIONS

A.1. Sufficient Appropriate Audit Evidence

1.   (b)   The requirement is to identify the reply that is **not** an assertion for classes of transactions. The assertions for classes of transactions are occurrence, completeness, accuracy, cutoff and classification. Answer (b) is correct since consistency is not an assertion for classes of transactions. Answer (a), (c), and (d) are all incorrect because accuracy, cutoff and occurrence are class of transaction assertions.

2.   (c)   The requirement is to identify the type of evidence that is generally most reliable. Answer (c) is correct because audit evidence obtained from knowledgeable independent sources outside the client company is more reliable than audit evidence obtained from nonindependent sources (e.g., company sources who may be biased). Answer (a) is incorrect because audit evidence obtained from direct sources is more reliable. Answer (b) is incorrect because it is not clear as to whether copies or facsimile copies are more reliable. Answer (d) is incorrect because it is unclear whether audit evidence provided by original documents is more reliable than that provided through a system of effective controls—indeed, they may be one and the same.

3.   (c)   The requirement is to identify the most persuasive type of evidence. Answer (c) is correct because a bank statement represents evidence prepared outside of the entity

and is considered an audit evidence source which provides the auditor with a high level of assurance. Answers (a), (b), and (d) are incorrect because prenumbered client purchase order forms, client work sheets and a representation letter all represent internally generated documents, generally considered less persuasive than externally generated documents. See SAS 106 for information on the persuasiveness of audit evidence.

4.   (d)   The requirement is to identify a correct presumption about the reliability of audit evidence. Answer (d) is correct because SAS 106 indicates that effective internal control provides more assurance about the reliability of audit evidence than ineffective control. Answer (a) is incorrect because information obtained directly is considered more reliable than that obtained indirectly. Answer (b) is incorrect because audit evidence is normally persuasive rather than convincing. Answer (c) is incorrect because reliability of audit evidence relates to the appropriateness of audit evidence.

5.   (d)   The requirement is to determine the correct statement with respect to the appropriateness of audit evidence. To be appropriate, evidence must be both reliable and relevant. Answer (a) is incorrect because while externally generated evidence is generally considered to provide greater assurance of reliability, there are important exceptions, (e.g., the confirmation is erroneously returned with no exception when one actually exists). Answer (b) is incorrect because while evidence so gathered is typically considered to provide greater assurance concerning reliability, no similar generalization can be made about its relevance. Answer (c) is incorrect because oral representations from management, when corroborated by other forms of evidence, are considered valid evidence.

6.   (a)   The requirement is to identify the **least** persuasive type of evidence. Answer (a) is correct because evidence secured solely from within the entity, here prenumbered purchase order forms, is considered less persuasive than evidence obtained from independent sources. Answer (b) is incorrect because a bank statement (even though received from the client) is externally created and therefore more persuasive than audit evidence secured solely from within the entity. Answer (c) is incorrect because evidence obtained directly by the auditor through observation is considered relatively persuasive. Answer (d) is incorrect because correspondence from the client's attorney about litigation is obtained directly from independent sources and is therefore more persuasive than audit evidence secured from within the entity.

7.   (a)   The requirement is to identify an area of concern to auditors when evaluating the reasonableness of an entity's accounting estimates. Answer (a) is correct because AU 342 states that in evaluating the reasonableness of estimates auditors normally concentrate on assumptions that are subjective and susceptible to bias. Answer (b) is incorrect because all things being equal, an auditor would expect assumptions that are consistent with prior periods. Answer (c) is incorrect because assumptions that are insensitive to variations in underlying data have little predictive ability. Answer (d) is incorrect because, often, one would expect assumptions similar to industry guidelines.

A.2.   Types of Evidence

8.   (d)   The requirement is to identify the reply that is not a basic procedure used in an audit. Answer (d) is correct because the term "test of direct evidence" is not used in the professional standards. Answer (a) is incorrect because risk assessment procedures are used while obtaining an understanding of the client. Answer (b) is incorrect because substantive procedures test account balances. Answer (c) is incorrect because tests of controls test the operating effectiveness of controls.

9.   (d)   The requirement is to identify the procedure an auditor would perform first in evaluating management's accounting estimates for reasonableness. Answer (d) is correct because in evaluating reasonableness, the auditor should first obtain an understanding of how management developed the estimate. Answers (a), (b), and (c) are all incorrect because developing independent expectations, considering appropriateness of key factors or assumptions, and testing calculations occur after obtaining the understanding. See AU 342 for information on auditing accounting estimates.

10.   (d)   The requirement is to identify a factor that an auditor would concentrate upon when evaluating the reasonableness of an accounting estimate. Answer (d) is correct because AU 342 states that the auditor normally concentrates on key factors and assumptions that are deviations from historical patterns, as well as those that are significant to the accounting estimate, sensitive to variations, and subjective and susceptible to misstatement and bias. Answer (a)

is incorrect because deviations from historical patterns, not consistent patterns, are concentrated upon. Answer (b) is incorrect because factors and assumptions that are similar to industry guidelines are often reasonable. Answer (c) is incorrect because subjective factors and assumptions that are susceptible to bias are concentrated upon, not objective ones that are **not** susceptible to bias. See AU 342 for information on the manner in which auditors consider accounting estimates.

11.   (d)   The requirement is to identify one of an auditor's objectives when evaluating an entity's accounting estimates. Answer (d) is correct because when evaluating accounting estimates an auditor's objectives are to obtain sufficient appropriate audit evidence that (1) all material accounting estimates have been developed, (2) those accounting estimates are reasonable, and (3) those accounting estimates are in conformity with GAAP.

12.   (c)   The requirement is to determine the proper test for the existence assertion of an asset. Answer (c) is correct because testing **from** accounting records **to** the supporting evidence discloses whether recorded transactions occurred and whether the asset exists. Answer (a) is incorrect because testing for the completeness assertion addresses whether there are unrecorded items. Also, the aggregated nature of the financial statements makes the use of potentially unrecorded items unlikely as a method of identifying unrecorded items. Answer (b) is incorrect because testing potentially unrecorded items to the financial statements addresses the completeness assertion. Answer (d) is incorrect because testing from the supporting evidence to the accounting records addresses the completeness assertion. See the outline of SAS 106 for information on the financial statement assertions.

13.   (a)   The requirement is to determine which balance remaining in a "suspense" account would be of most concern to an auditor. Answer (a) is correct because suspense debits that management believes will benefit future operations must be audited carefully to determine whether they have value and should be classified as an asset. Answer (b) is incorrect because when an auditor has already determined that a suspense debit has value it becomes a relatively straightforward issue of the item's proper classification. Answer (c) is incorrect because the conservative approach taken in audits is likely to cause the auditor to have somewhat more concern about suspense purported to be assets [i.e., answer (a)], than for those classified as current liabilities. Answer (d) is incorrect because when the auditor determines that the suspense credits represent customer deposits, establishing a proper accounting will ordinarily be relatively simple.

B.1.a.   Analytical Procedures

14.   (b)   The requirement is to identify the procedure that would **not** be considered an analytical procedure. Analytical procedures consist of evaluations of financial information made by a study of plausible relationships among both financial and nonfinancial data. Answer (b) is correct because projecting an error rate from a statistical sample to an actual population is not a comparison of a plausible relationship. Answers (a), (c), and (d) are all incorrect because they all include a study of plausible relationships.

15. **(c)** The requirement is to identify the type of analytical procedure an auditor would most likely use in developing relationships among balance sheet accounts when reviewing the financial statements of a nonpublic entity. Answer (c) is correct because balance sheet accounts may be analyzed through a number of ratios (e.g., current ratio). Answer (a) is incorrect because trend analysis is often more appropriate for income statement analysis. Answer (b) is incorrect because regression analysis, while used in practice, is not used as frequently as is ratio analysis. Answer (d) is incorrect because risk analysis in and of itself is not a type of analytical procedure. See AR 100 for information on reviews of nonissuer (nonpublic) entities.

16. **(a)** The requirement is to identify how an auditor may achieve audit objectives related to particular assertions. Answer (a) is correct because an auditor may perform analytical procedures to achieve an audit objective related to a particular assertion. Answer (b) is incorrect because a system of quality control provides the CPA firm with reasonable assurance of conforming with professional standards. Answer (c) is incorrect because while working papers provide support for the audit report and aid in the conduct and supervision of the audit, they do not in and of themselves achieve audit objectives (see SAS 103 for information on audit working papers). Answer (d) is incorrect because increasing the level of detection risk does not in and of itself achieve audit objectives.

17. **(d)** The requirement is to identify the procedure most likely to detect a fraud involving misstatement of income statements due to the recording of journal entries with unusual combinations of debits and credits to expense and revenue accounts. Answer (d) is correct because an objective of analytical procedures is identification of unusual transactions and events, and amounts, ratios and trends that might indicate misstatements. Answer (a) is incorrect because the limited number of journal entries traced to the general ledger in a sample is unlikely to include the erroneous journal entries. Answer (b) is incorrect because while an evaluation of the effectiveness of internal control might help detect such misstatements, it is somewhat doubtful due to the fact that it is likely that few journal entries are involved. Answer (c) is incorrect because there is no indication that the fraud involves differences between controlling accounts and subsidiary records.

18. **(b)** The requirement is to identify the account that would yield the highest level of evidence through the performance of analytical procedures. As higher levels of assurance are desired from analytical procedures, more predictable relationships are required to develop the auditor's expectation. Relationships involving income statement accounts tend to be more predictable than relationships involving only balance sheet accounts, and relationships involving transactions not subject to management discretion are generally more predictable. Answer (b) is correct because interest expense relates to the income statement, and because interest expense is subject to only limited management discretion, given the existence of the related debt. Answers (a) and (c) are incorrect because accounts receivable and accounts payable are balance sheet accounts. Answer (d) is incorrect because travel and entertainment expense is normally subject to management discretion. See AU 329 for more information on the use of analytical procedures.

19. **(c)** The requirement is to determine what is included when analytical procedures are used in the overall review stage of an audit. Answer (c) is correct because the overall review stage includes reading the financial statements and notes and considering the adequacy of evidence gathered in response to unusual or unexpected balances. Answer (a) is incorrect because analytical procedures are not particularly aimed at gathering evidence on account balances that have not changed. Answer (b) is incorrect because analytical procedures do not directly test control procedures. Answer (d) is incorrect because tests of transactions to corroborate management's financial statement assertions are performed when considering internal control and for substantive tests of transactions. See AU 329 for information on analytical procedures.

20. **(c)** The requirement is to determine the most predictable relationship for purposes of analytical procedures applied as substantive tests. Answer (c) is correct because AU 329 indicates that relationships involving income statement accounts tend to be more predictable than relationships involving only balance sheet accounts. Answer (a) is incorrect because, as indicated, relationships involving income statements are considered more predictable. Answer (b) is incorrect because relationships involving transactions subject to management discretion are often less predictable. For example, management might incur maintenance expense rather than replace plant and equipment, or they may delay advertising expenditures. Answer (d) is incorrect because prior year data is sometimes not a reliable predictor of subsequent year's data.

21. **(c)** The requirement is to identify a basic premise underlying the application of analytical procedures. Answer (c) is correct because, as indicated in AU 329, a basic premise underlying the application of analytical procedures is that plausible relationships among data may reasonably be expected to exist and continue in the absence of known conditions to the contrary. Answer (a) is incorrect because the study of financial ratios is an approach to identifying unusual fluctuations, not an acceptable alternative to investigating them. Answer (b) is incorrect because analytical procedures may be either statistical or nonstatistical. Answer (d) is incorrect because analytical procedures may be used as substantive tests, and may result in modification of the scope of tests of balances and transactions.

22. **(a)** The requirement is to identify the stages of an audit for which the use of analytical procedures is required. AU 329 requires the use of analytical procedures at both the planning and overall review stages of the audit, but not as a substantive test.

23. **(b)** The requirement is to determine the reply that would facilitate an auditor's analytical procedures. Answer (b) is correct because use of a standard cost system (a form of budgeting) produces variance reports that will allow the auditor to compare the financial information with the standard cost system data to identify unusual fluctuations. See AU 329 for the approach used. Answer (a) is incorrect because segregating obsolete inventory before the inventory count is related to the auditor's physical inventory observation and will not necessarily affect analytical procedures. Answer (c) is incorrect because correcting a material weakness in internal control before the beginning of the audit generally will have minimal, if any, effect on the historical information used for analytical procedures. Answer (d) is incorrect because data from independent sources outside the entity is more likely to be reliable than purely internal sources.

24. **(c)** The requirement is to identify the most likely effect on an audit of having performed analytical procedures in the overall review stage of an audit which suggest that several accounts have unexpected relationships. Answer (c) is correct because when unexpected relationships exist, additional tests of details are generally required to determine whether misstatements exist. Answer (a) is incorrect because irregularities (fraud) may or may not exist. Answer (b) is incorrect because internal control activities may or may not be operating effectively. Answer (d) is incorrect because ordinarily the situation need not be communicated to the audit committee.

25. **(b)** The requirement is to identify the comparison an auditor most likely would make in evaluating an entity's costs and expenses. Answer (b) is correct because payroll expense is an income statement expense and because it may be expected to have a relationship with that of the prior year. Answer (a) is incorrect because the accounts receivable account is not a cost or expense. Answer (c) is incorrect because comparing budgeted sales with actual sales of the current year is more likely to be performed than comparing budgeted sales with those of prior years. Answer (d) is incorrect because comparing the budgeted current year's warranty expense with the current year's contingent liabilities is less direct than that in answer (b), and because one would be more likely to compare current year budgeted warranty expense with actual warranty expense.

26. **(c)** The requirement is to identify the best individual to perform analytical procedures in the overall review stage of an audit. At this stage of an audit the objective of analytical procedures is to assist the auditor in assessing the conclusions reached and in the evaluation of the overall financial statement presentation. Answer (c) is correct because an experienced individual with business and industry knowledge is likely to be able to fulfill this function. Answer (a) is incorrect because a staff accountant who has performed the substantive auditing procedures may not be able to objectively perform the analytical procedure and may not have the necessary experience to perform the function. Answer (b) is incorrect because the managing partner of the office may not be close enough to the audit to perform the function effectively. Answer (d) is incorrect because the individual in charge of quality control and the peer review program should be as independent as possible of the audits he or she is considering. See AU 329 for guidance on analytical procedures.

B.1.b. Tests of Details of Transactions and Balances

27. **(b)** The requirement is to identify the best example of a substantive test. Answer (b) is correct because confirmation of balances of accounts receivable will provide a test of the ending account balance and is therefore a detailed test of a balance, a type of substantive test. Answers (a) and (c) are incorrect because examining approval of cash disbursements and comparison of signatures on checks to a list of authorized check signers are tests of controls. Answer (d) is incorrect because flowcharting a client's cash receipts system is a method used to document the auditor's understanding of internal control.

28. **(c)** The requirement is to identify the objective of tests of details of transactions performed as substantive tests. Answer (c) is correct because SAS 110 states that the objective of tests of details of transactions performed as substantive tests is to detect material misstatements in the financial statements. Answer (a) is incorrect because while performing tests of details of transactions as substantive tests complies with generally accepted auditing standards, this is not their objective. Answers (b) and (d) are incorrect because neither attaining assurance about the reliability of the accounting system nor the evaluation of the operating effectiveness of management's policies and procedures are the objective of tests of details of transactions performed as substantive tests.

29. **(c)** The requirement is to find the statement which describes substantive audit tests. Answer (c) is correct because substantive tests are defined as tests of transactions, direct tests of financial balances, or analytical procedures. Answer (a) is incorrect because substantive tests may not be eliminated due to the limitations of internal control. Answer (b) is incorrect since substantive tests primarily directly test ending financial statement balances, not subsequent events. Answer (d) is incorrect because substantive tests **decrease** with increased reliance on internal control.

30. **(c)** The requirement is to determine the account for which the auditor is most likely to perform extensive tests for possible understatement. An analysis of past audits, in which existing financial statement errors were not discovered prior to the issuance of the financial statements, reveals that the great majority of the errors resulted in overstated profits. Therefore, the risk to a CPA is that the client is overstating profits. Answer (c) is correct because it is the only item whose understatement results in overstated profits. Answers (a), (b), and (d) are incorrect because understatement of these items would result in understated profits.

B.2. Preparing Substantive Test Audit Programs

31. **(d)** The requirement is to determine the most likely approach for auditing the statement of cash flows. Answer (d) is correct because the statement of cash flows includes accounts considered during the audit of the balance sheet and income statements and, accordingly, the most frequent approach is to reconcile amounts. Answers (a), (b), and (c) are all incorrect because they suggest approaches not typically followed when auditing the statement of cash flows.

32. **(c)** The requirement is to determine the direction of audit testing to determine whether transactions have been recorded. Answer (c) is correct because to determine whether transactions have been recorded the auditor will test **from** the original source documents **to** the recorded entries. Answers (a), (b), and (d) are incorrect because when testing from the general ledger, the adjusted trial balance, or from general journal entries the auditor is dealing with the entries that have been recorded, not whether all transactions have been recorded.

B.3. Documentation

33. **(b)** The requirement is to identify the correct statement concerning the deletion of audit documentation. Answer (b) is correct because after the audit file has been completed (ordinarily 60 days or less after the issuance of the audit report), no portions of audit documentation should be deleted. Answer (a) is incorrect because after completion of the audit file no documentation should be deleted or discarded. Answer (c) is incorrect because professional skepticism is not the basis for determining deletions. Answer (d) is incorrect because prior to the file completion date most superseded documentation may be deleted (an exception is that information that reflects a disparate point of view should be retained).

34.   (a)   The requirement is to determine how long audit documentation must be retained. Answer (a) is correct because SAS 103 requires that they be maintained a minimum of five years. Answers (b), (c) and (d) all present other, incorrect time periods.

35.   (a)   The requirement is to identify the most likely pair of accounts to be analyzed on the same working paper. Answer (a) is correct because an auditor will often consider interest income with notes receivable because the interest is earned on those notes and therefore closely related. Answer (b) is incorrect because interest receivable relates to an asset account (notes receivable) while accrued interest payable relates to a liability account (notes payable) and accordingly one would expect separate working papers. Answer (c) is incorrect because notes payable and receivable are entirely separate accounts. Answer (d) is incorrect because interest income relates to interest-bearing securities while interest expense relates to debt accounts.

36.   (a)   The requirement is to identify a primary purpose of an auditor's working papers. SAS 103 states that working papers serve mainly to provide the principal support for the auditor's report and to aid the auditor in the conduct and supervision of the audit.

37.   (c)   The requirement is to identify the **least** likely item to be included in the permanent file of an auditor's working papers. Answer (c) is correct because permanent files include information affecting a number of years' audits, and the working trial balance relates most directly to the current and, to a limited extent, the subsequent year's audit. Answers (a), (b), and (d) are all incorrect because bond indenture agreements, lease agreements, and a flowchart of internal control affect more years' audits than does a specific year's working trial balance.

38.   (c)   The requirement is to determine a difference between an auditor's working trial balance and financial statements without footnotes. Answer (c) is correct because a working trial balance includes columns for reclassification and adjustments. Answers (a), (b), and (d) are all incorrect because while they suggest information that might be included on a working trial balance, they will not be included in the form of additional columns.

39.   (d)   SAS 103 states that the degree of documentation for a particular audit area should be affected by (1) the risk of material misstatement, (2) extent of judgment, (3) nature of the auditing procedures, (4) significance of the evidence obtained, (5) nature and extent of the exceptions identified, and (6) the need to document a conclusion that is not obvious from the documentation of the work.

40.   (b)   The requirement is to identify the required documentation in an audit. Answer (b) is correct because SAS 108 requires a written audit program setting forth in detail the procedure necessary to accomplish the engagement's objectives. Answer (a) is incorrect because while flowcharts and narratives are acceptable methods of documenting an auditor's understanding of internal control, they are not required. Answer (c) is incorrect because a planning memorandum is not required. Answer (d) is incorrect because completion of an internal control questionnaire is not required.

41.   (a)   The requirement is to identify a factor that would most likely affect the auditor's judgment about the quantity, type, and content of the working papers. Answer (a) is correct because the Professional Standards state that the assessed level of control risk will affect the quantity, type and content of working papers. SAS 103 provides a listing of this and other factors. For example, the quantity, type and content of working papers will be affected by whether tests of controls have been performed.

42.   (d)   The requirement is to identify the type of audit working paper that reflects the major components of an amount reported in the financial statements. Answer (d) is correct because lead schedules aggregate the major components to be reported in the financial statements. Answer (a) is incorrect because an interbank transfer schedule summarizes transfers between banks among accounts. Answer (b) is incorrect because the term "carryforward schedule" is not frequently used. Answer (c) is incorrect because supporting schedules present the details supporting the information on a lead schedule. For example, a detailed bank reconciliation for a cash account might serve as a supporting schedule for an account on the cash lead schedule.

43.   (c)   The requirement is to identify the documentation that is required for an audit in accordance with generally accepted auditing standards. Answer (c) is correct because SAS 103 requires that the working papers show that the accounting records agree or reconcile with the financial statements. Answer (a) is incorrect because neither a flowchart nor an internal control questionnaire is required. Answer (b) is incorrect because the *Professional Standards* do not require the use of an engagement letter. Answer (d) is incorrect because when control risk is assessed at the maximum level, the auditor's understanding of internal control needs to be documented, but the basis for the conclusion that it is at the maximum level need not be documented.

44.   (b)   The requirement is to identify the point at which no deletions of audit documentation are allowed. Answer (b) is correct because the professional standards indicate that audit documentation may not be deleted after the documentation completion date. Answer (a) is incorrect because documentation may be deleted between the client's year-end date and the documentation completion date. Answer (c) is incorrect because the last date of significant fieldwork is prior to the documentation completion date. Answer (d) is incorrect because the report release date is up to 60 days prior to the documentation completion date; 45 days for issuer (public) company audits.

45.   (b)   The requirement is to determine the type of auditor that should be able to understand audit documentation of the nature, timing, extent, and results of audit procedures performed. Answer (b) is correct because PCAOB Standard 3 requires that audit documentation be understandable to an experienced auditor having no prior connection with the engagement. Answer (a) is incorrect because the requirement is not limited to audit team members. Answer (c) is incorrect because the requirement is more limited than to any certified public accountant. Answer (d) is incorrect both because there is no certification of a peer review specialist and because this is not a requirement.

46. (c) The requirement is to identify the period for which audit documentation should be retained for issuer (public) company audits. Answer (c) is correct because PCAOB Standard 3 requires that audit documentation be retained for the longer of seven years or the period required by law. Answer (a) is incorrect both because of the seven-year requirement, and because it is the longer of seven years or the period required by law. Answer (b) is incorrect because while seven years is the general requirement, a longer period may be required by law. Answer (d) is incorrect because audit documentation need not be retained indefinitely.

C.1. Evidence—Cash

47. (b) The requirement is to identify the information that an auditor usually confirms on one form. Answer (b) is correct because the standard form to confirm account balance information with financial institution requests information on both the cash in bank and collateral for loans. Answers (a), (c), and (d) are all incorrect because they suggest pairs of information that are not usually confirmed on one form.

48. (d) The requirement is to determine a reason that the usefulness of the standard bank confirmation request may be limited. Answer (d) is correct because the bank employee who completes the form often will not have access to all the financial relationships that the bank has with the client. Answer (a) is incorrect because bank employees who complete the form realize that they may verify confidential information with the auditor. Answer (b) is incorrect because while it is correct that the employee who completes the confirmation form will not generally inspect the accuracy of the bank reconciliation, this does not limit the confirmation's usefulness. Answer (c) is incorrect because the employee who completes the form does not need to have access to the client's cutoff bank statement to complete the confirmation.

49. (b) The requirement is to determine the type of evidence that is likely to result in an auditor limiting substantive audit tests of sales transactions when control risk is assessed as low for the occurrence assertion for sales. Answer (b) is correct because an auditor may analyze the completeness of sales using cash receipts and accounts receivable (for example, an auditor may add year-end receivables to cash receipts and subtract beginning receivables to obtain an estimate of sales). Answer (a) is incorrect because the opening and closing inventory balances will only provide indirect evidence on sales through calculation of the cost of goods sold. Answer (c) is incorrect because while shipping as of year-end will help assure an accurate cutoff of sales, the receiving activity has no necessary relationship to the sales figure. Answer (d) is incorrect because while the cutoff of sales will provide evidence on the completeness of sales, the purchases portion of the reply is not appropriate.

50. (b) The requirement is to determine the two checks that might indicate kiting, a form of fraud that overstates cash by simultaneously including it in two or more bank accounts. Answer (b) is correct because checks #202 and #404 include cash in two accounts at year-end. The cash represented by check #202 is included in both State Bank and County Bank cash as of December 31. This is because its receipt is recorded prior to year-end, but its disbursement is recorded after year-end. (For the cash receipts journal to remain in balance prior to year-end, some account must have been credited on December 30 to offset the debit to cash.) Check #404 also represents a situation in which the cash is included in two accounts as of year-end; the check may represent a situation in which a shortage in the account is concealed through deposit of the check that is not recorded on the books at year-end. Check #101 does not result in a misstatement of cash since the books recorded both the debit and credit portions of the entry before year-end, while both banks recorded them after year-end. Check #303 represents a situation in which funds are disbursed on the Federal account as of year-end, but not received into the American account (per bank or per books) until after year-end; check #303 accordingly understates cash and the nature of the debit for the entry on December 31 is unknown. Answer (a) is incorrect because neither check #101 nor #303 overstates cash. Answer (c) is incorrect because check #101 does not overstate cash. Answer (d) is incorrect because check #303 understates cash.

51. (b) The requirement is to determine the checks which represent deposits in transit at December 31, 2001. Deposits in transit are those that have been sent to the bank prior to year-end, but have not been received by the bank as of year-end. Answer (b) is correct because both check #101 and check #303 have been disbursed per books as of year-end, but have not yet been received by the bank as of December 31. Checks #202 and #404 have been received by the bank as of year-end and accordingly are not in transit. Answer (a) is incorrect because check #202 has been received before year-end. Answer (c) is incorrect because both checks #202 and #404 have been received before year-end. Answer (d) is incorrect because check #404 has been received before year-end.

52. (c) The requirement is to identify why auditors trace bank transfers for the last part of the audit period and the first part of the subsequent period. Answer (c) is correct because auditors use a bank transfer schedule to analyze transfers so as to detect kiting that overstates cash balances. Answers (a) and (b) are incorrect because the process of analyzing transfers is not an efficient way to determine whether the cash receipts journal was held open or when the year's final checks were mailed. Auditors use a bank cutoff statement rather than a bank transfer schedule to help detect these situations. Answer (d) is incorrect because the process of analyzing transfers is unlikely to identify any unusual payments or receipts from related parties.

53. (d) The requirement is to determine the source of evidence which does **not** contain information on the balance per bank in a bank reconciliation. Answer (d) is correct because the general ledger contains only the client's cash balance, not the balance per bank. Answer (a) is incorrect because the beginning balance on a cutoff statement represents the year-end bank balance. Answer (b) is incorrect because the primary purpose of a year-end bank statement is to present information on the balance per bank. Answer (c) is incorrect because the first question on a standard bank confirmation form requests information on the year-end balance per bank.

54. (b) The requirement is to identify the cash transfer which will result in a misstatement of year-end cash. Answer (b) is correct because the receipt is recorded on the books prior to year-end, while the disbursement is recorded subsequent to year-end. Therefore, the cash on the books is overstated. Answers (a), (c), and (d) are incorrect because they do not reveal a cutoff error. Answer (a) is incorrect because both the disbursement and receipt are recorded on the books prior to year-end; note that one would expect to see an outstanding check on the disbursing bank reconciliation as of year-end. Answer (c) is incorrect because both the disbursement and receipt are recorded on the books prior to year-end; one would expect the disbursing bank reconciliation to show an outstanding check and the receiving bank to show a deposit in transit as of year-end. Answer (d) is incorrect because the entire transaction is recorded after year-end.

55. (c) The requirement is to determine an approach for detecting the concealing of a cash shortage by transporting funds from one location to another or by converting negotiable assets to cash. Answer (c) is correct because the timing of the performance of auditing procedures involves the proper synchronizing of their application and thus comprehends the possible need for simultaneous examination of, for example, cash on hand and in banks, securities owned, bank loans, and other related items.

56. (b) The requirement is to identify the primary purpose of sending a standard confirmation request to financial institutions with which the client has done business during the year. Answer (b) is correct because CPAs generally provide the account information on the form and ask for balance corroboration. The form explicitly states that the CPAs do not request, nor expect, the financial institution to conduct a comprehensive, detailed, search of its records for other accounts. Answer (a) is incorrect because a standard confirmation request will not detect kiting, a manipulation causing an amount of cash to be included simultaneously in the balance of two or more bank accounts. Answer (c) is incorrect because bank statements available from the client allow the CPA to prepare a proof of cash. Answer (d) is incorrect because the standard form does not request information about contingent liabilities and secured transactions.

57. (c) The requirement is to determine the assertion (or assertions) being tested by a test of a control in which an auditor observes the mailing of monthly statements to a client's customers and reviews evidence of follow-up on errors reported by the customers. Answer (c) is correct because observing the mailing of monthly statements and follow-up of errors will provide evidence to the auditor as to whether the receivables **exist** at a given date; the tests do not directly address the presentation and disclosure assertion since little evidence is obtained about whether financial statement components are properly classified, described, and disclosed. See SAS 106 for a discussion of the various financial statement assertions. Answer (a) is incorrect because the presentation and disclosure assertion is not addressed. Answer (b) is incorrect because the presentation and disclosure assertion is not addressed and because the existence or occurrence assertion is addressed. Answer (d) is incorrect because the existence or occurrence assertion is addressed.

58. (b) The requirement is to determine the most likely audit step summarized by the tick mark placed under "date disbursed per bank." Answer (b) is correct because the checks were written in December but cleared in January and should therefore be listed as outstanding on the year-end outstanding check list of the applicable bank reconciliation. Answer (a) is incorrect because the tick marks are beside the date per bank, and not per books. Answer (c) is incorrect because the December cash disbursements journal, and not the January cash disbursements journal, will include these disbursements. Answer (d) is incorrect because the year-end bank confirmations do not include information on outstanding checks.

59. (a) The requirement is to determine the most likely audit step summarized by the tick mark placed under "date deposited per bank." Answer (a) is correct because deposits recorded on the books as of 12/31 should be included as deposits in transit on the applicable bank reconciliation. Answer (b) is incorrect because the tick mark is placed beside the "bank" column, and not the books column. Answer (c) is incorrect because the December cash receipts journal, and not the January cash receipts journal should include the deposit. Answer (d) is incorrect because the year-end bank confirmations will not include deposits in transit.

C.2. Evidence—Receivables

60. (a) The requirement is to identify the correct statement concerning the use of negative confirmation requests. Answer (a) is correct because AU 330 states that unreturned negative confirmation requests rarely provide significant evidence concerning financial statements assertions other than certain aspects of the existence assertion. Answer (b) is incorrect because positive, not negative, confirmation requests are normally used when a low level of detection risk is to be achieved. Answer (c) is incorrect because alternative procedures are not generally performed on unreturned negative confirmation requests since it is assumed that the respondent did not reply because of agreement with the balance on the confirmation request. Answer (d) is incorrect because respondents may not reply when misstatements are in their favor.

61. (c) The requirement is to identify the most likely action taken by an auditor when no reply is received to positive confirmation requests. Answer (c) is correct because asking the client to contact customers to ask that confirmation requests be returned may increase response rates. Answer (a) is incorrect because the lack of a reply to a confirmation request does not necessarily indicate that the account needs to be written off. Answer (b) is incorrect because accounts receivable confirmations deal more directly with existence than with valuation or completeness and because alternative procedures may provide the auditor with the desired assurance with respect to the nonrespondents. Answer (d) is incorrect because the assessed level of inherent risk will not normally be modified due to confirmation results.

62. (b) The requirement is to determine the best sampling unit for confirmation of accounts receivable when many differences between the recorded account balances and the confirmation replies have occurred in the past. Answer (b) is correct because the misstatements may have occurred because respondents are not readily able to confirm account balances. AU 330 suggests that in such circumstances certain respondents' accounting systems may facilitate the confirmation of single transactions (individual invoices) rather than of entire account balances.

63. (c) The requirement is to identify the assertion most directly addressed by accounts receivable confirmations. SAS 106 presents information on financial statement assertions. Answer (c) is correct because a confirmation addresses whether the entity replying to the confirmation believes that a debt exists. Answer (a) is incorrect because while confirmations provide limited information on valuation, they do not directly address whether the entity replying will pay the debt (or whether the account has been factored). Answer (b) is incorrect because limited classification information is received via confirmations. Answer (d) is incorrect because confirmations are generally sent to recorded receivables, and are of limited assistance in the determination of whether all accounts are recorded (completeness).

64. (a) The requirement is to determine when alternative procedures should be performed in order to substantiate the existence of accounts receivable. Answer (a) is correct because the auditor should employ alternative procedures for nonresponses to positive confirmations to satisfy himself/herself as to the existence of accounts receivable. Those procedures may include examination of evidence of subsequent cash receipts, cash remittance advices, sales and shipping documents, and other records. Answer (b) is incorrect because with negative confirmations the debtor is asked to respond only if s/he disagrees with the information on the confirmation; thus, no reply is assumed to indicate agreement. Answers (c) and (d) are incorrect because while **additional** procedures may be required when collectibility is questionable, **alternative** procedures are those used in lieu of confirmation.

65. (d) The requirement is to identify the most likely alternate procedure when replies have not been received to either first or second accounts receivable confirmation requests. Answer (d) is correct because the inspection of shipping records will provide evidence that the merchandise was actually shipped to the debtor. Answer (a) is incorrect because, a review of the cash receipts journal **prior** to year-end is unlikely to provide evidence on account recorded as unpaid as of year-end. Also, the procedure would only detect one specific type of misstatement, that in which payments were recorded in the cash receipts journal, but not credited to the customers' accounts. Answer (b) is incorrect because the lack of a reply to the confirmation provides no particular evidence that the scope of procedures related to internal control should be modified. Answer (c) is incorrect because the lack of a reply need not necessarily lead to a presumption that the account is misstated. See AU 330 for procedures typically performed for year-end accounts receivable confirmation requests for which no reply is received.

66. (d) The requirement is to identify the circumstances in which use of the negative form of accounts receivable confirmation most likely would be justified. Negative confirmations are used when (1) the combined assessed level of inherent and control risk is low, (2) a large number of small balances is involved, and (3) the auditor has no reason to believe that the recipients of the requests are unlikely to give

them consideration. Positive confirmations are used when those conditions are not met as well as in other circumstances in which it seems desirable to request a positive response, such as when accounts are in dispute. Answer (d) is best because small balances are involved and few accounts are in dispute. Answer (a) is incorrect because it refers to a substantial number of accounts in dispute and sales are to a few major customers. Answer (b) is incorrect because it refers to a substantial number of accounts in dispute. Answer (c) is incorrect because it refers to sales to a few major customers.

67. (a) The requirement is to identify a method to reduce the risk associated with accepting e-mail responses to accounts receivable confirmation requests. Answer (a) is correct because a response by mail will confirm the e-mail response. Answer (b) is incorrect because while such subsequent cash receipts will ordinarily be examined, this represents an alternative, complementary approach to confirmation. Answer (c) is incorrect because the auditor need not consider e-mail responses to be confirmations with exception. Answer (d) is incorrect because a second request is more likely to elicit either no response or another e-mail response.

68. (b) The requirement is to determine the most likely procedure to reduce the risks associated with accepting fax responses to requests for confirmations of accounts receivable. Answer (b) is correct because verification of the sources and contents through telephone calls will address whether the information on the fax (which may have been sent from almost anywhere) is correct. Answer (a) is incorrect because an examination of the shipping documents is less complete than is verification of the entire balance. Answer (c) is incorrect because such faxes need not be treated as nonresponses. Answer (d) is incorrect because inspection of the faxes is unlikely to reveal forgeries or alterations, even when such circumstances have occurred.

69. (d) The requirement is to identify the circumstance in which the negative form of confirmation request most likely would be used. Answer (d) is correct because AU 330 states that negative confirmations may be used when (1) the combined assessed level of inherent and control risk is low [answer (d)], (2) a large number of small balances is involved, and (3) the auditor has no reason to believe that the recipients of the requests are unlikely to give them consideration. Answer (a) is incorrect because when the accounts receivable are immaterial, a decision may be made to send no confirmations. Answer (b) is incorrect because an inadequate rate is not an acceptable reason to send negative confirmations. Answer (c) is incorrect because negative confirmations are only of value when the auditor has no reason to believe that the recipients of the requests are unlikely to give them consideration.

70. (a) The requirement is to identify the circumstance in which an auditor would use the blank form of confirmations (one which includes no amount and asks the respondent to supply the amount due) rather than positive confirmations. Answer (a) is correct because if a recipient simply signs a blank confirmation and returns it the confirmation will have no amount on it and the auditor will know that additional procedures are necessary. Answers (b) and (c) are incorrect because there is no necessary relationship between the use of blank confirmations and subsequent cash receipt verification difficulty and analytical procedures results. Answer (d) is incorrect because when the combined assessed level of inherent risk and control risk is low it is unlikely to lead to the blank form of confirmation. In fact, when that risk is low, and when adequate other substantive tests of details, no confirmation may be necessary. See AU 330 for information on the confirmation process.

71.   (d)   The requirement is to identify the most likely information that would be included in a client's confirmation letter that is being used to confirm accounts receivable balances rather than individual invoices. Answer (d) is correct since including details of the account is likely to make it easier for the customer to respond in a meaningful manner. Answer (a) is incorrect because no such auditor-prepared letter will be included and because only in the case of the negative form of confirmation does a nonresponse lead to an inference that the account balance is correct. Answer (b) is incorrect because confirmation requests do not ordinarily include a letter suggesting that a second request will be sent. Answer (c) is incorrect because the auditor does not enclose a letter requesting that the information be supplied. See AU 330 for information on the confirmation process.

72.   (c)   The requirement is to identify a statement that an auditor would be most likely to add to the negative form of confirmation of accounts receivable to encourage a timely consideration by the recipient. Answer (c) is correct because providing such information might increase timely consideration in that the recipient may realize the importance of a reply when the information is incorrect. Answers (a) and (b) are incorrect because while a confirmation request may include these statements, the statements are unlikely to encourage timely consideration of the request. Answer (d) is incorrect because many accounts that are not overdue are sampled, and because even for those overdue such a statement is not ordinarily included with the confirmation request.

73.   (a)   The requirement is to identify the strategy most likely to improve the response rate for confirmation of accounts receivable. Answer (a) is correct because including a list of items or invoices that constitute the account balance makes it easier for the potential respondent to reply. Answer (b) is incorrect because customers with relatively large balances may or may not be more likely to reply. Answers (c) and (d) are incorrect because there is no research available indicating that requesting a fax or e-mail reply, or threatening a second request is likely to improve response rate.

C.3.   Evidence—Inventory

74.   (a)   The requirement is to determine the financial statement most directly related to the procedure of making inquiries concerning possible obsolete or slow-moving inventory. Answer (a) is correct because inquiries concerning possible obsolete or slow-moving inventory deal with whether the inventory is being carried at the proper value and this is most directly related to the valuation assertion. The other assertions are less directly related. Answer (b) is incorrect because the rights assertion deals with whether assets are the rights of the entity and liabilities are the obligations of the entity at a given date. Answer (c) is incorrect because the existence assertion deals with whether assets exist at a given date. Answer (d) is incorrect because the

presentation assertion deals with whether particular components of the financial statements are properly classified. See SAS 106 for information on the financial statement assertions.

75.   (d)   The requirement is to identify the type of omitted journal entry that would result in inventory test counts that are higher than the recorded quantities in the client's perpetual records. Answer (d) is correct because a failure to record sales returns results in a situation in which the item is returned by a customer and included in the inventory count, but not recorded in the perpetual records; accordingly the test counts are higher than the recorded quantities. Answer (a) is incorrect because purchase discounts do not affect quantities in inventory. Answers (b) and (c) are incorrect because a failure to record purchase returns or sales result in a situation in which less inventory will be counted (since the items are no longer physically in inventory) than is recorded on the perpetual records.

76.   (c)   The requirement is to identify a procedure that will provide assurance that all inventory items in a client's inventory listing schedule are valid. Answer (c) is correct because tracing **from** the inventory listing schedule **to** inventory tags and **to** the auditor's recorded count sheets will provide assurance that the listed items actually exist. Answer (a) is incorrect because tracing from inventory tags to items in the inventory listing schedule tests the completeness of the inventory listing sheet, not whether all of the items it lists are valid. Answer (b) is incorrect because it does not directly test the client's inventory listing schedule. Answer (d) is incorrect because tracing items listed in receiving reports and vendors' invoices to the inventory listing schedule will provide assurance on the completeness of the inventory listing sheet; it will also be a difficult procedure to accomplish due to the fact that a number of these items will not be in inventory due to sales. See SAS 106 for information on the testing of the various financial statement assertions.

77.   (b)   The requirement is to identify the factor that average inventory is divided into to calculate inventory turnover. Answer (b) is correct because the average inventory is divided into the cost of goods sold to calculate the inventory turnover.

78.   (a)   The requirement is to identify the auditing procedure that most likely would provide assurance about a manufacturing entity's inventory valuation. Answer (a) is correct because testing the overhead computation will provide evidence on whether inventory has been included in the financial statements at the appropriate amount. Answer (b) is incorrect because obtaining confirmation of inventories pledged under loan agreements relates more directly to the presentation assertion. Answers (c) and (d) are incorrect because reviewing shipping and receiving cutoff procedures for inventories and tracing test counts to the inventory listing relate more directly to the existence and completeness assertions.

79.   (b)   The requirement is to identify an action that an auditor might take when the assessed level of control risk is high for inventory. Answer (b) is correct because a high level of control risk will generally result in a low acceptable level of detection risk, which may be achieved by changing the timing of substantive tests to year-end, changing the nature of substantive tests to more effective procedures, and/or by changing the extent of substantive tests. Answer (a) is incorrect because control risk has been assessed and tests of controls, if any, will already have been completed. Answer (c) is incorrect because a year-end count of inventory is more appropriate when control risk is high. Answer (d) is incorrect because gross profit tests will generally provide less assurance than is required in circumstances such as this when control risk is assessed at a high level.

80. (a) The requirement is to identify the financial statement assertion (other than presentation and disclosure) most directly related to an auditor's conclusion that no excessive costs for idle plant were charged to inventory. Answer (a) is correct because the assertion deals with whether the inventory has been included in the financial statements at the appropriate amount, and therefore that no excessive costs were charged to inventory. Answer (b) is incorrect because the completeness assertion deals with whether all inventory items that should be presented are so included. Answer (c) is incorrect because existence deals with whether the inventory actually exits at the given date. Answer (d) is incorrect because rights deal with whether the inventory is owned by the client. For more information on management's financial statement assertions, see SAS 106.

81. (b) The requirement is to identify the financial statement assertion most directly related to an auditor's tracing of inventory test counts to the client's inventory listing. Answer (b) is correct because the completeness assertion deals with whether all transactions are included. Tracing from the inventory items observed to the inventory listing will help determine whether all the transactions are included and the inventory listing is complete. Answer (a) is incorrect because the rights assertion deals with whether assets are the rights of the entity and this is not being tested when an auditor traces test counts to an inventory listing. Answer (c) is incorrect because existence deals with whether the inventory existed at the date of the count. To test existence the auditor would sample from the inventory listing and compare quantities to the test counts. Answer (d) is incorrect because valuation deals with whether the inventory is properly included in the balance sheet at the appropriate dollar amount and this is not being tested here. See SAS 106 for more information on management's financial statement assertions.

82. (d) The requirement is to determine the assertion most directly related to an auditor's analysis of inventory turnover rates. Answer (d) is correct because an analysis of inventory turnover rates will provide the auditor with evidence on slow-moving, excess, defective, and obsolete items included in inventories. These items may be improperly valued.

83. (a) The requirement is to determine which types of entries will be supported when the auditor examines receiving reports. Answer (a) is correct because receiving reports will be prepared when goods are received through purchase (as recorded in the voucher register) and when goods are received through sales returns (as recorded in the sales returns journal). Answers (b), (c), and (d) are incorrect because entries in sales journals result in items being shipped, not received. Note, however, that answers (b), (c), and (d) are partially correct because the sales returns journal,

voucher register, and check register all result from transactions related to the receipt of goods.

84. (c) The requirement is to identify the response which does **not** represent one of the independent auditor's objectives regarding the examination of inventory. Answer (c) is correct because verifying that all inventory owned by the client is on hand at the time of the count is not an objective. For example, purchased items in transit at year-end, for which title has passed, should be included in inventory. Similarly, inventory out on consignment should also be included in inventory. Answer (a) is incorrect because proper presentation of inventory pertains to the presentation and disclosure assertion and therefore would be subject to auditor verification. Answers (b) and (d) are incorrect because proper accounting for damaged and obsolete items and proper inventory pricing pertain to the valuation assertion and therefore would be subject to auditor verification. See SAS 106 for details on financial statement assertions.

C.4.   Evidence—Investment Securities

85. (c) The requirement is to determine why an auditor should insist that a client representative be present when he or she physically examines securities. Answer (c) is correct because requiring that a client representative acknowledge the receipt of the securities will eliminate any question concerning the CPA's responsibility for any subsequent misplacement or misappropriation of the securities. Answer (a) is incorrect because the client's representative will not in general help the CPA to detect fraudulent securities. Answers (b) and (d) are incorrect because while the client's representative will help the CPA to gain access to the securities and may coordinate their return, these are not the auditor's primary purpose.

86. (c) The requirement is to identify the best procedure other than inspection to establish the existence and ownership of a long-term investment in a publicly traded stock. Answer (c) is correct because confirmation of the number of shares owned that are held by an independent custodian is effective at testing existence. Answer (a) is incorrect because auditors do not in general correspond with the investee company and because that company may or may not have detailed information on the identity of shareholders at any point in time. Answer (b) is incorrect because while inspection of the audited financial statements of the investee company may provide limited information on valuation of the investment, it does not directly address existence; note that this procedure is of limited use here since the stock is publicly traded and obtaining its value through stock price quotations should not be difficult. Answer (d) is incorrect because this procedure addresses the valuation of the securities. In addition, under SFAS 115, investments are no longer carried at the lower of cost or market. See SAS 106 for more information on management's financial statement assertions.

87. (c) The requirement is to determine the best procedure when an auditor has been unable to inspect and count a client's investment securities (held in a safe-deposit box) until after the balance sheet date. Answer (c) is correct because banks maintain records on access to safe-deposit boxes. Thus, the confirmation of no access during the period will provide the auditor with evidence that the securities in the safe-deposit box at the time of the count were those available at year-end. Answers (a) and (b) are incorrect because the bank will not generally be able to provide a list of securities added and removed from the box (typically, only records on access are maintained by the bank). Therefore, the bank will have no information on reconciling items between the subsidiary ledger and the securities on hand. Answer (d) is incorrect because it is the responsibility of the auditor and the client, not the bank, to count the securities maintained in a safe-deposit box.

88. (a) The requirement is to determine the most likely use of analytical procedures when testing long-term investments. Answer (a) is correct because the predictable relationship between long-term investments and investment income creates a situation in which analytical procedures may provide substantial audit assurance. Answer (b) is incorrect because the classification between current and noncurrent portfolios may be expected to fluctuate in an unpredictable manner as investment goals and the environment change. Answers (c) and (d) are incorrect because the valuation of marketable equity securities at the lower of cost or market and unrealized gains or losses do not result in a predictable relationship on which analytical procedures may provide effective results.

C.5. Evidence—Property, Plant, and Equipment

89. (d) The requirement is to identify the account whose analysis is **least** likely to reveal evidence relating to **recorded** retirements of equipment. Answer (d) is correct because the purchase returns and allowances account deals with returns and allowances for purchases of merchandise, not equipment. Answer (a) is incorrect because analysis of accumulated depreciation will reveal the retirement through charges made to the accumulated depreciation account. Answer (b) is incorrect because companies will ordinarily modify insurance coverage when assets are retired. Answer (c) is incorrect because the property, plant, and equipment account will reflect the retirement.

90. (b) The requirement is to identify a likely explanation for a situation in which significant debits have been posted to the accumulated depreciation expense. Answer (b) is correct because debits to accumulated depreciation are properly recorded upon retirement of a plant asset. Answer (a) is incorrect because changing the useful lives of plant assets does not affect accumulated depreciation. Answer (c) is incorrect because understatement of the prior year's depreciation expense does not result in an adjustment to accumulated depreciation. Answer (d) is incorrect because overhead allocations do not ordinarily affect accumulated depreciation.

91. (a) The requirement is to identify the best procedure for testing unrecorded retirements of equipment. Answer (a) is correct because selecting items from the accounting records and attempting to locate them will reveal unrecorded retirements when the item cannot be located. Answer (b) is incorrect because depreciation entries will continue when retirements have not been recorded. Answer (c) is incorrect because the direction of the test is incorrect since beginning with the item is unlikely to reveal a situation in which an unrecorded retirement has occurred. Answer (d) is incorrect because scanning the general journal for **recorded** entries is unlikely to reveal **unrecorded** retirements of equipment.

92. (d) The requirement is to determine why an auditor analyzes repairs and maintenance accounts. Answer (d) is correct because clients often erroneously charge expenditures for property and equipment acquisitions as expenses rather than capitalize them as assets. An analysis of repairs and maintenance accounts will reveal such errors. Answer (a) is incorrect because while auditors will want to determine that noncapitalizable expenses for repairs and maintenance have been recorded in the proper period, analyzing only the recorded entries is an incomplete test since entries occurring after year-end will also need to be examined. Answer (b) is incorrect because procedures relating to the property and equipment account will be performed to determine whether such entries have been recorded in the proper period. Answer (c) is incorrect because analyzing the repairs and maintenance accounts only considers recorded entries and not whether all noncapitalizable expenditures for repairs and maintenance have been properly charged to expense.

93. (c) The requirement is to determine the information an auditor is most likely to seek from the plant manager. The plant manager comes into day-to-day contact with the machinery when producing a product; that contact is likely to provide information on its condition and usefulness. Answers (a) and (d) are incorrect because the plant manager will generally not have detailed knowledge as to the adequacy of the provision for uncollectible accounts or the amount of insurance which is desirable. Answer (b) is incorrect because the plant manager will have limited knowledge concerning physical inventory observation procedures and their appropriateness.

94. (a) The requirement is to identify the document least likely to provide evidence regarding mortgage acquisition costs. Deeds generally consist of a legal conveyance of rights to use real property. Frequently the sales price is not even specified and the related mortgage acquisition costs are much less likely to be stated in a deed. Answer (b) is incorrect because cancelled checks would provide verification of mortgage acquisition costs. Answer (c) is incorrect because the closing statement would provide a detailed listing of the costs of acquiring the real property, including possible mortgage acquisition costs. Answer (d) is incorrect because examination of interest expense would also relate to the mortgage acquisition costs.

95. (b) The requirement is to determine the assertion(s) involved when an auditor is inspecting new additions on a list of property, plant, and equipment. Answer (b) is correct because an auditor who inspects new additions relating to property and equipment balances addresses existence or occurrence, but not presentation and disclosure; presentation and disclosure relates more directly to proper classification and note disclosures rather than account balances.

C.6. Evidence—Prepaid Assets

96. (a) The requirement is to determine the financial statement assertion most directly related to the procedure of reviewing or recomputing amortization of intangible assets. Answer (a) is correct because the amortization of intangible assets deals with whether the accounts are properly valued, the valuation assertion. The other assertions are less directly related. Answer (b) is incorrect because the existence or occurrence assertion deals with whether assets or liabilities exist at a given date and whether recorded transactions have occurred during a given period. Answer (c) is incorrect because the completeness assertion deals with whether all transactions and accounts that should be presented in the financial statements are so included. Answer (d) is incorrect because the rights and obligations assertion deals with whether assets are the rights of the entity and liabilities are the obligations of the entity at a given date. See SAS 106 for information on the financial statement assertions.

97. (c) The requirement is to determine the most likely reason for the absence of the original insurance policy on plant equipment. Answer (c) is correct because the holder of the lien may also in certain circumstances maintain the original insurance policy. Answer (a) is incorrect because an insurance premium which is due but not recorded is unlikely to account for the lack of the original insurance policy. Answer (b) is incorrect because while coinsurance provisions are outlined in the policy, they are unlikely to be a reason that the policy is not available for inspection. Answer (d) is incorrect because there is no obvious relationship between the understatement of insurance expense and the presence or absence of an insurance policy.

C.7. Evidence—Payables (Current)

98. (c) The requirement is to identify the best audit procedures for identifying unrecorded liabilities. Answer (c) is correct because unrecorded liabilities eventually become due and must be paid. Accordingly, a review of cash disbursements after the balance sheet date is an effective procedure for detecting unrecorded payables. Answer (a) is incorrect because tracing a sample of accounts payable that have been recorded is not likely to result in identification of unrecorded liabilities. Answer (b) is incorrect because purchase orders issued after year-end will not result in liabilities as of year-end. Answer (d) is incorrect because disbursement entries recorded before year-end generally relate to accounts payable that have been paid before year-end.

99. (a) The requirement is to identify the appropriate population when using accounts payable confirmations directed towards obtaining evidence on the completeness assertion. Answer (a) is correct because to address completeness the auditor attempts to determine that all accounts payable are reflected, and a company potentially may be liable to any of its vendors. Answer (b) is incorrect because confirming based on recorded amounts addresses existence more directly than completeness. Answer (c) is incorrect because basing the sample on payees after year-end only deals with those payables that have been paid as of that point. Answer (d) is incorrect because open invoices are a less complete population than are vendors. See AU 330 for information on the confirmation process, and SAS 106 for information on management's financial statement assertions.

100. (d) The requirement is to determine why confirmation of accounts payable is unnecessary. Accounts payable are usually not confirmed because there is better evidence available to the auditor, (i.e., examination of cash payments subsequent to the balance sheet date). If the auditor reviews all cash payments for a sufficient time after the balance sheet date for items pertaining to the period under audit and finds no such payments which were not recorded as liabilities at year-end, the auditor is reasonably assured that accounts payable were not understated. Answer (a) is a non-

sense answer. Answer (b) is incorrect because AP balances could be paid during year-end audit work after the balance sheet date. Answer (c) is incorrect because whether or not legal action has been taken against the client is irrelevant to the confirmation procedure.

101. (c) The requirement is to identify the substantive test to be performed to verify the existence and valuation of recorded accounts payable. Answer (c) is correct because the vouching of various payable accounts to purchase orders and receiving reports will provide evidence that the debt was incurred and the related goods received, thereby providing evidence on the existence of the debt and its amount, or valuation. Answer (a) is incorrect because determining whether prenumbered purchase orders are used and accounted for relates more directly to the completeness with which purchases and accounts payable were recorded. Answers (b) and (d) are incorrect because the question addresses the existence and valuation of **recorded** accounts payable, not unrecorded payables or payables with a zero balance.

102. (c) The requirement is to determine management's accounts payable assertion that an auditor will primarily focus on. Experience has indicated that overstated income is more of a risk than is understated income. Answer (c) is correct because the completeness assertion focuses upon whether payables have been omitted, thereby overstating income. Answer (a) is incorrect because the existence assertion deals with whether recorded accounts payable are overstated, thereby understating income. Answer (b) is incorrect because payables often require no particularly troublesome presentations and disclosures. Answer (d) is incorrect because payables are most frequently simply valued at the cost of the related acquisition. See SAS 106 for more information on management's financial statement assertions.

C.8. Evidence—Long-Term Debt

103. (b) The requirement is to identify a likely reason for a recorded interest expense that seems excessive in relation to the balance in the bonds payable account. Answer (b) is correct because understated bonds payable will result in a lower account balance than is proper and thereby create a situation in which the interest expense appears excessive. Answers (a) and (d) are incorrect because an understated discount or an overstated premium on bonds payable result in situations in which the recorded interest expense seems lower than expected since the net bonds payable are overstated. Answer (c) is incorrect because understatements, not overstatements, of bonds payable will result in what appears to be an excessive rate of interest expense.

104. (a) The requirement is to determine the financial statement assertion most directly related to an auditor's inspection of loan agreements under which an entity's inventories are pledged. Answer (a) is correct because the presentation and disclosure assertion deals with whether particular components of the financial statements—such as loan agreement covenants—are properly classified, described, and disclosed. The other assertions are less directly related. Answer (b) is incorrect because the valuation or allocation assertion deals with whether asset, liabilities, revenue, and expense components have been included in the financial statements at the appropriate amounts. Answer (c) is incorrect because the existence or occurrence assertion deals with whether assets or liabilities exist at a given date and whether recorded transactions have occurred during a given period. Answer (d) is incorrect because the completeness assertion deals with whether all transactions and accounts that should be presented in the financial statements are so included. See SAS 106 for information on the financial statement assertions.

105. (c) The requirement is to identify a procedure an auditor would perform in auditing long-term bonds payable. Answer (c) is correct because comparing interest expense with the bond payable amount will provide evidence as to reasonableness. Such a procedure may reveal either interest not expensed or debt not properly recorded. Answer (a) is incorrect because analytical procedures will not in general be performed on bond premiums and discounts since these accounts may easily be verified by examining details of the entry recording the debt issuance and any subsequent amortization. Answer (b) is incorrect because an examination of the documentation of assets purchased with bond proceeds is only necessary when such a use of the funds is a requirement of the debt issuance. Answer (d) is incorrect because confirmation of bonds outstanding will often be with the trustee rather than with individual bondholders.

106. (b) The requirement is to determine how an auditor can best verify a client's bond sinking fund transactions and year-end balance. Answer (b) is correct because confirmation with the bond trustee represents externally generated evidence received directly by the auditor. Such evidence is considered very reliable. Answer (a) is incorrect because individual holders of retired bonds will have no information on actual bond sinking fund transactions or year-end balances. Answer (c) is incorrect because, while recomputing interest expense, interest payable, and amortization of bond discount or premiums are desirable procedures, they do not directly address bond sinking fund transactions and year-end balances. Answer (d) is similar to answer (c) in that it is desirable but does not address the actual bond sinking fund transactions and year-end balance.

C.9. Evidence—Owners' Equity

107. (a) The requirement is to determine how an auditor ordinarily obtains evidence of stockholders' equity transactions. Answer (a) is correct because the board of directors will, in general, authorize changes in stockholders' equity. Answer (b) is less complete in that for small clients there may be no transfer agent, and because the transfer agent deals most directly with transfers of outstanding stock. Answer (c) is incorrect because canceled stock certificates are ordinarily available only for small clients. Answer (d) is incorrect because companies do not ordinarily have a "treasury stock certificate book."

108. (d) The requirement is to identify the most likely audit procedure, in addition to analytical procedures, when control risk for payroll is assessed as low. Answer (d) is correct because accrual of payroll at year-end is not an entry made frequently throughout the year and accordingly recording of the entry is often not controlled by the payroll portion of the internal control structure. Answers (a), (b), and (c) are incorrect because observing the distribution of paychecks, the footing and crossfooting of the payroll register, and inspection of payroll tax returns are recurring op-

erations that will have been considered when assessing control risk at a low level.

109. (a) The requirement is to identify the circumstance that most likely would cause an auditor to suspect an employee payroll fraud scheme. Answer (a) is correct because significant unexplained variances between standard and actual labor cost may lead an auditor to suspect fraud. Answer (b) is incorrect because one would expect payroll checks to be distributed by the same employees each payday. Answer (c) is incorrect because time cards are ordinarily approved by individual departmental supervisors. Answer (d) is incorrect because the maintenance of a separate payroll bank account is considered a control, not an indication of fraud.

110. (d) The requirement is to identify the procedure that an auditor most likely would perform when auditing payroll. Answer (d) is correct because a comparison of payroll costs with entity standards or budgets will generally be included in the audit program as a test of overall payroll reasonableness. Answer (a) is incorrect because unclaimed wages will not be mailed unless an employee so requests and this often will not be tested by an auditor. Answer (b) is incorrect because total employee deductions will be traced to journal entries. Answer (c) is incorrect because observing entity employees during a payroll distribution is generally only included in an audit program when internal control is weak; accordingly, it is more likely that a comparison of payroll costs with entity standards or budgets [answer (d)] will be included.

111. (d) The requirement is to identify the procedure that is most likely when an auditor is performing tests concerning the granting of stock options. Answer (d) is correct because authorizing the issuance of stock options is ordinarily a decision made by the board of directors. Answer (a) is incorrect because the Secretary of State of the state of incorporation will not have this information on stock options. Answer (b) is incorrect because the existence of the option holders is not ordinarily a significant question. Answer (c) is incorrect because stock to be issued relating to options may be either from treasury stock or new issuances; accordingly, sufficient treasury stock need not be available.

112. (d) The requirement is to identify the assertion to which determining whether there are restrictions on retained earnings relates most directly. Answer (d) is correct because such restrictions will result in disclosures and thus the presentation and disclosure assertion is most directly being verified. Answer (a) is incorrect because the existence or occurrence assertion addresses whether assets or liabilities of the entity exist at a given date and whether recorded transactions have occurred during a given period. Answer (b) is incorrect because the completeness assertion addresses whether all transactions and accounts that should be presented in the financial statements are so included. Answer (c) is incorrect because the valuation or allocation assertion addresses whether asset, liability, revenue, and expense components have been included in the financial statements at appropriate amounts. See SAS 106 for a discussion of financial statement assertions.

113. (b) The requirement is to identify the information an auditor should confirm with a client's transfer agent and registrar. Answer (b) is correct because when a client employs a transfer agent and registrar, there will be no stock certificate book to examine, and accordingly, information on shares issued and outstanding should be confirmed. Answers (a), (c), and (d) are incorrect because the transfer agent and registrar often will not have information on dividend restrictions, guarantees of preferred stock liquidation values, and the number of shares subject to agreements to repurchase.

114. (c) The requirement is to determine a likely step in the audit program for retained earnings. The legality of a dividend depends in part on whether it has been properly authorized (state laws differ on specific requirements). Thus, the auditor must determine that proper authorization exists, as both cash and stock dividends affect retained earnings. Answer (a) is incorrect since only a memo entry is required for a stock split. Answer (b) is incorrect because the write-down of an account receivable will not, in general, be recorded in retained earnings. Answer (d) is incorrect because gains from the disposition of treasury shares are recorded in paid-in capital accounts.

115. (c) The requirement is to determine when an auditor would be most likely to perform substantive tests of details on payroll transactions and balances. Answer (c) is correct because analytical procedures result in further investigation when unexpected differences occur. This investigation will generally involve substantive tests of details of transactions and balances. AU 329 provides detailed information on analytical procedures. Answer (a) is incorrect because a substantial amount of accrued payroll expense as indicated by a cutoff test will not necessarily result in additional substantive tests. Answer (b) is incorrect because a low assessed level of control risk is likely to result in less substantive testing. Answer (d) is incorrect because the nature of accrued payroll expense being unpaid commissions need not necessarily result in more substantive testing.

116. (a) The requirement is to determine a source an auditor uses to test the reasonableness of dividend income from investments in publicly held companies. Answer (a) is correct because dividend record books produced by investment advisory services provide summaries of dividends paid for various securities, and an auditor is able to compare the reasonableness of a client's recorded dividend income from investments with this information. Answers (b) and (c) are incorrect because auditors do not, in general, determine the reasonableness of dividend income by examining stock "indentures" or "stock ledgers." Answer (d) is incorrect because while annual financial statements of investee companies may include such information, examining such financial statements is not generally an efficient approach for testing the reasonableness of dividend income. Also, the current year financial statements of the investees often are not available when the auditor is performing the current audit.

C.10. Revenue

117. (c) The requirement is to identify the most likely risk involved with a bill and hold transaction at year-end. Answer (c) is correct because a bill and hold transaction results in the recording of a sale prior to delivery of the goods—accordingly, sales may be inappropriately recorded. Answer (a) is incorrect because accrued liabilities are not ordinarily affected by bill and hold transactions. Answers (b) and (d) are incorrect because an absolute purchase

commitment and the assuming of risk and reward relating to the product represent conditions which increase the likelihood that recording of a sale for such a transaction is appropriate.

118. (b) The requirement is to identify the most likely listed effect of "channel stuffing." Answer (b) is correct because channel stuffing is a marketing practice that suppliers sometimes use to boost sales by inducing distributors to buy substantially more inventory than they can promptly resell; accordingly, increased sales returns in the future are likely. Answers (a), (c) and (d) are incorrect because accrued liabilities, cash, and marketable investments are less likely to be affected by channel stuffing, which results in entries increasing accounts receivable, cost of good sold, and sales, while decreasing inventory.

C.11. Expenses

119. (d) The requirement is to identify the account in which a recorded entry is most likely to relate to the property, plant, and equipment completeness assertion. The completeness assertion addresses whether all transactions have been recorded in an account (here, property, plant, and equipment). Answer (d) is correct because the purchase of property, plant, and equipment may inappropriately have been recorded in the repairs and maintenance account rather than in property, plant, and equipment; this is a frequent bookkeeping error since the individual recording the entry may frequently see similar invoices which do represent repairs and maintenance expense. Answers (a), (b), and (c) are all incorrect because the allowance for doubtful accounts, marketable securities, and sales has no apparent relationship to the completeness of recording of property, plant, and equipment.

C.12. Client Representation Letters

120. (c) The requirement is to identify the matter on which an auditor should obtain written management representations. Answer (c) is correct because written representations are ordinarily obtained on noncompliance with aspects of contractual agreements that may affect the financial statements. Answer (a) is incorrect because auditors do not ordinarily obtain a cost-benefit justification from management related to internal control weaknesses. Answer (b) is incorrect because written representations are not ordinarily obtained on such future plans. Answer (d) is incorrect because management may or may not be responsible for employee violations of laws, and because such a representation is not ordinarily obtained. See AU 333 for information on client representations.

121. (a) The requirement is to determine a matter to which materiality limits do **not** apply in obtaining written management representations. Answer (a) is correct because materiality considerations do not apply to management's acknowledgment of its responsibility for fair presentation of financial statements, the availability of all financial records, the completeness and availability of all minutes and meetings of stockholders, directors, and committees of directors, and communication from regulatory agencies. Answers (b), (c), and (d) are all incorrect because materiality considerations relate to losses from purchase commitments, compensating balances, and obsolete inventory. AU 333 discusses client representations.

122. (c) The requirement is to determine the proper date for a client's representation letter. AU 333 states that the representation letter should be dated as of the date of the auditor's report.

123. (b) The requirement is to identify the matter that an auditor most likely would include in a management representation letter. Auditors will generally request assurance as to the completeness and availability of minutes of stockholders' and directors' meetings. See AU 333 for written representations ordinarily obtained by the auditor.

124. (d) The requirement is to determine the year(s) on which a CPA must obtain written representations from management, when comparative financial statements are being issued, but current management has only been employed for a portion of one of those years. AU 333 states that if current management was not present during all periods reported upon, the auditor should nevertheless obtain written representations from current management on all such periods.

125. (a) The requirement is to identify the information ordinarily included among the written client representations obtained by the auditor. Answer (a) is correct because AU 333 includes information on compensating balances in the list of representations normally obtained. Answer (b) is incorrect because management need not acknowledge a responsibility for employee illegal actions. Answer (c) is incorrect because the auditor, not the client, determines whether sufficient audit evidence has been made available. Answer (d) is incorrect because, for purposes of a financial statement audit, management need not attempt to determine whether material weaknesses in internal control exist.

126. (a) The requirement is to determine the correct statement with respect to the use of a management representation letter as audit evidence about the completeness assertion. Answer (a) is correct because such written representations are meant to complement, but not replace, substantive tests. Answer (b) is incorrect because the complementary nature of such representations is **not** considered sufficient, even when combined with reliance upon internal control. The inherent limitations of internal control do not permit the auditor to **replace** substantive tests with complete reliance on internal control. Answer (c) is incorrect because the written representations are considered complementary evidence in support of various assertions. Answer (d) is incorrect because such written representations are not considered to be replacements for reliance upon internal control.

127. (a) The requirement is to determine who should sign a letter of representation. AU 333 states that, normally, the chief executive officer and the chief financial officers should sign the letter of representation.

128. (d) The requirement is to identify the scope limitation which **in all cases** is sufficient to preclude an unqualified opinion. Answer (d) is correct because the professional standards state that management refusal to furnish written representations constitutes a limitation on the scope of the auditor's examination sufficient to preclude an unqualified opinion. Answer (a) is incorrect because management's refusal to allow the auditor to review the predecessor's work may not necessarily result in report modification. Answer (b) is incorrect because alternate procedures may be available that will make report modification unnecessary when the auditor has been engaged after completion of the

year-end physical count. Answer (c) is incorrect because management may choose not to correct a significant deficiencies in internal control without a resulting limitation on the scope of the audit.

129. (c) The requirement is to identify a purpose of a management representation letter. Answer (c) is correct because a management representation letter is meant to reduce the possibility of a misunderstanding concerning management's responsibility for the financial statements. Answer (a) is incorrect because reducing audit risk to an aggregate level of misstatement that could be considered material is not a logically sound statement. Answer (b) is incorrect because the management representation letter does not modify an auditor's responsibility to detect material misstatements. Answer (d) is incorrect because management representation letters are not a substitute for other procedures.

130. (c) The requirement is to identify the most likely source of a statement suggesting that there have been no communications from regulatory agencies. Answer (c) is correct because information such as this is ordinarily included in a management representation letter. Answers (a), (b), and (d) are incorrect because such a disclosure is not ordinarily included in a report on internal control, a special report, or a letter for an underwriter. See AU 333 for guidance on representation letters.

C.13. Using the Work of a Specialist

131. (a) The requirement is to identify the correct statement concerning an auditor's use of the work of a specialist. Answer (a) is correct because the work of a specialist who is related to the client may be acceptable under certain circumstances. Answer (b) is incorrect because if the auditor believes that the findings of the specialist are unreasonable, it is generally appropriate to obtain the findings of another specialist. Answer (c) is incorrect because a material difference between a specialist's findings and those included in the financial statements may result in the need for an explanatory paragraph, a qualified opinion, a disclaimer, or an adverse opinion. Answer (d) is incorrect because an auditor may use a specialist in the determination of various physical characteristics of assets.

132. (a) The requirement is to identify a circumstance in which an auditor may refer to the findings of a specialist in the auditor's report. Answer (a) is correct because the auditor may refer to the specialist when the specialist's findings result in inclusion of an explanatory paragraph to an audit report, in this case on going concern status. Answers (b), (c), and (d) are all incorrect because a specialist is only referred to in an audit report when that specialist's findings identify a circumstance requiring modification of the audit report. Auditors do not modify audit reports to simply inform the user that a specialist was involved.

133. (d) The requirement is to identify the statement that is correct about the auditor's use of the work of a specialist. Answer (d) is correct because the auditor should obtain an understanding of the nature of the work performed by the specialist. Answer (a) is incorrect because ordinarily a specialist will have a basic understanding of the auditor's corroborative use of the findings. Answer (b) is incorrect because the auditor need not perform substantive procedures to verify the specialist's assumptions and findings. Answer (c) is incorrect because the client may have an understanding of the nature of the work performed by the specialist. See AU 336 (revised in 1994 by SAS 73) for information on the auditor's use of the work of a specialist.

134. (b) The requirement is to identify the circumstance in which an auditor may appropriately refer to the findings of a specialist. Answer (b) is correct because an auditor may refer to a specialist when the report is being modified due to the specialist's findings. Answers (a) and (c) are incorrect because a client's familiarity with a specialist or understanding of the auditor's use of the findings of a specialist does not result in modification of the audit report. Answer (d) is incorrect because an auditor does not divide responsibility with a specialist.

135. (c) The requirement is to identify the statement that an auditor must document when using the work of a specialist. Answer (c) is correct because the specialist's understanding of the auditor's corroborative use of his or her findings must be documented. See AU 336 for this and other documentation requirements. Answer (a) is incorrect because no statement concerning an update of the specialist's report is required to be documented. Answer (b) is incorrect because a division of responsibility relates to circumstances in which other auditors, not specialists, are involved. Answer (d) is incorrect because an auditor will not normally issue a disclaimer related to whether the specialist's findings corroborate the representations in the financial statements. The specialist's report is only referred to when there is a material difference between the specialist's findings and the representations in the financial statements. See AU 336 for information on the effect of a specialist's work on an auditor's report.

136. (c) The requirement is to determine which individual is **not** considered a **specialist** upon whose work an independent auditor may rely. The professional standards relating to using the work of a specialist do not apply to using the work of an internal auditor. Answers (a), (b), and (d), actuary, appraiser, and engineer, respectively, are all examples of specialists per the professional standards. Note here that the question and its reply do not imply that a CPA cannot use the work of an internal auditor. What is being suggested is that an internal auditor is not considered a specialist under the professional standards.

C.14. Inquiry of a Client's Lawyer

137. (d) The requirement is to identify which parties should reach an understanding on the limits of materiality for purposes of a lawyer's response to an auditor's inquiry concerning litigation, claims, and assessments. Answer (d) is correct because AU 337 states that a lawyer's response to an inquiry may be limited to material items, provided the lawyer and the auditor have reached an understanding on the limits of materiality for this purpose. Answer (a) is incorrect because it includes the client's management. Answer (b) is incorrect because it includes the client's audit committee and omits the auditor. Answer (c) is incorrect because it includes the client's management and omits the auditor.

138. (b) The requirement is to identify the correct statement concerning the refusal of a client's attorney to provide information requested in an inquiry letter. Answer (b) is correct because AU 337 indicates that this is a limitation on

the scope of the audit. Answer (a) is incorrect because the lack of information is unlikely to lead to an adverse opinion since no information has been provided indicating that the financial statements are misstated. Answer (c) is incorrect because withdrawal is not generally necessary due to the client's attorney's failure to provide information. Answer (d) is incorrect because significant deficiencies pertain to weaknesses in internal control.

139. (c) The requirement is to identify the audit procedure that an auditor most likely would perform concerning litigation, claims, and assessments. Answer (c) is correct because auditors must discuss with management its policies and procedures for evaluating and accounting for litigation, claims and assessments. See AU 337 for this and other requirements. Answer (a) is incorrect because the client's lawyer is not ordinarily asked to make an assessment about whether the client has a going concern problem (see AU 341 for information on an auditor's consideration of a client's ability to continue as a going concern). Answer (b) is incorrect because an auditor will not ordinarily examine legal documents in the client's lawyer's possession. Answer (d) is incorrect because an auditor will not ordinarily confirm with the client's lawyer that all litigation, claims, and assessment have been recorded.

140. (b) The requirement is to identify the primary reason that an auditor should request a client to send a letter of inquiry to its attorneys. Answer (b) is correct because a letter of audit inquiry to the client's attorney is the auditor's primary means of obtaining corroboration of the information furnished by management concerning litigation, claims, and assessments. Answer (a) is incorrect because it will often be impossible to determine the probable outcome of asserted claims and pending or threatened litigation. Answer (c) is incorrect because no such opinions on historical experiences are generally available. Answer (d) is incorrect because the description of litigation, claims, and assessments is generally prepared by the client.

141. (b) The requirement is to identify the procedure that is **not** performed regarding litigation, claims, and assessments. Answer (b) is correct because the CPA does not confirm directly with the client's lawyer that all claims have been recorded in the financial statements. Answers (a), (c), and (d) are all incorrect because they represent information obtained from management regarding litigation, claims, and assessments as summarized in AU 337.

142. (a) The requirement is to identify the appropriate limitation for an attorney's response to a client's letter of audit inquiry. Answer (a) is correct because AU 337 states that an attorney may appropriately limit his response to matters to which s/he has given substantive attention in the form of legal consultation or representation. Answers (b), (c), and (d) are incorrect because AU 337 presents a variety of other requests in addition to information on the likelihood of an unfavorable outcome of the matters disclosed by the entity, similar litigation, and probable outcomes.

143. (a) If a client's lawyer resigned shortly after the receipt of an attorney's letter which indicated no significant disagreements with the client's assessment of contingent liabilities, the auditor should inquire why the attorney resigned. The auditor's concern is whether any undisclosed unasserted claims have arisen. Per AU 337, a lawyer may be required to resign if his advice concerning reporting for litigation, claims, and assessments is disregarded by the client. Accordingly, the resignation shortly after issuance of an attorney's letter may indicate a problem. Answer (b) is incorrect because the attorney issued a letter indicating no significant disagreement with the client's assessment of contingent liabilities. Answers (c) and (d) are incorrect because AU 337 only suggests that the auditor should consider the need for inquiries (i.e., AU 337 does not require a complete new exam of contingent liabilities or an adverse opinion).

144. (b) The requirement is to identify the lawyer's letter comment that is most likely to cause the auditor to request clarification. Answer (b) is correct because a statement that the action can be settled for less than the damages claimed is unclear as to the details of the attorney's belief. Answers (a), (c), and (d) are all incorrect because they represent responses that may be clearly interpreted by the auditor. See AU 337, interpretation 7, for information on assessing lawyer's evaluations of the likely outcome of litigation.

C.15. Fair Values

145. (a) The requirement is to determine whether valuation issues arise at initial recording, subsequent to initial recording, or at both times when considering fair value of an asset or liability. Answer (a) is correct because AU 328 makes clear that valuation issues arise at both times. Answers (b), (c), and (d) are all incorrect because they suggest that there are no valuation issues at one or both of these time periods.

146. (b) The requirement is to identify the **least** likely approach for auditing the fair values of assets and liabilities. Answer (b) is correct because it is doubtful that audit committee members will have information on the valuation. Answers (a), (c), and (d) are all incorrect because they represent the three approaches presented for auditing fair values (as well as other estimates).

C.16. Related-Party Transactions

147. (c) The requirement is to identify the auditing procedure that would most likely assist an auditor in identifying related-party transactions. Answer (c) is correct because reviewing confirmations of loans receivable and payable for indications of guarantees may reveal unusual transactions that involve related parties. See AU 334 for procedures related to identifying transactions with related parties. Answer (a) is incorrect because inspecting the correspondence with lawyers for evidence of unreported contingent liabilities does not generally relate directly to related-party transactions. Answer (b) is incorrect because nonrecurring transactions are more indicative of related-party transactions. Answer (d) is incorrect because analytical procedures performed to identify possible financial difficulties do not relate directly to related-party transactions.

148. (c) The requirement is to determine an auditor's responsibility after having determined that a related-party transaction has occurred. Answer (c) is correct because after identifying the existence of such an act, the auditor should obtain an understanding of the business purpose of the transaction. See AU 334 for this and other responsibilities. Answer (a) is incorrect because the mere existence of a related-party transaction may or may not lead to audit report

modification. Answer (b) is incorrect because the performance of analytical procedures is not required. Answer (d) is incorrect because except for routine transactions, it will generally not be possible to determine whether the transaction would have taken place, or whether it was consummated on terms equivalent to an arm's-length transaction.

149. (d) The requirement is to identify the correct statement concerning related-party transactions. Answer (d) is correct because AU 334 requires that the auditor should place primary emphasis on the adequacy of disclosure. Answer (a) is incorrect because ascertaining rights and obligations is only part of the auditor's total responsibility and not the primary emphasis. Answer (b) is incorrect because while auditors attempt to determine the existence of related parties, this is not the primary emphasis. Answer (c) is incorrect because verifying the valuation of related-party transactions will often not be possible.

150. (d) The requirement is to identify the correct statement concerning related-party transactions. Answer (d) is correct because AU 334 requires that procedures directed toward identifying related-party transactions should be performed, even if the auditor has no reason to suspect their existence. Answer (a) is incorrect because, in the absence of evidence to the contrary, related-party transactions need not be assumed to be outside the ordinary course of business. Answer (b) is incorrect because the auditor will not in general be able to determine whether a particular transaction would have occurred if the parties had **not** been related. Answer (c) is incorrect because, if proper disclosures are made, the related-party transactions are not required to be recorded on terms equivalent to arm's-length transactions.

151. (c) The requirement is to identify the circumstance in which an auditor most likely would modify an unqualified opinion if the entity's financial statements include a footnote on related-party transactions. Answer (c) is correct because it generally will not be possible to determine whether a particular transaction was consummated on terms equivalent to those with unrelated parties. Therefore, the auditor may be required to express a qualified or an adverse opinion when such an unsubstantiated disclosure is included. Answers (a), (b), and (d) are all incorrect because they represent situations that may be disclosed in related-party transaction disclosures.

C.17. Going Concern Considerations

152. (b) The requirement is to identify the condition or event most likely to cause an auditor to have substantial doubt about an entity's ability to continue as a going concern. Answer (b) is correct because denial of usual trade from suppliers is ordinarily an indicator that the company is in weak financial condition. Answer (a) is incorrect because while such related-party transactions may be considered risky, there is less likely to be a question concerning going concern status than suggested by answer (a). Answer (c) is incorrect because the payment of such stock dividends does not indicate financial weakness. Answer (d) is incorrect because restrictions on the disposal of principal assets is a condition often present in various loan agreements.

153. (d) The requirement is to identify the most likely mitigating factor a CPA would consider when a client's ability to continue as a going concern is in question. Answer (d) is correct because the ability to postpone expenditures for research and development projects may mitigate the circumstance. See AU 341 for this and other mitigating factors. Answer (a) is incorrect because there is no guarantee that Zero's discussions with its lenders will lead to a restructuring of the debt and loan agreements. Only existing or committee agreements to restructure the debt would be considered a mitigating factor. Answer (b) is incorrect because weak internal control over cash disbursements may or may not have caused the going concern problem. Answer (c) is incorrect because an entity with a going concern problem is unlikely to be able to purchase such production facilities.

154. (a) The requirement is to identify the condition or event that is most likely to cause an auditor to have substantial doubt about an entity's ability to continue as a going concern. Answer (a) is correct because AU 341 includes negative cash flows as one of its examples of such conditions and events. Answer (b) is incorrect because while the postponement of research and development projects may sometimes be due to extreme financial difficulties, often it is not. Answers (c) and (d) are incorrect because neither significant related-party transactions nor stock dividends need not indicate substantial doubt about an entity's ability to continue as a going concern. See AU 341 for information on an auditor's consideration of an entity's ability to continue as a going concern.

155. (b) The requirement is to identify the condition or event that might indicate to an auditor substantial doubt about an entity's ability to continue as a going concern. Answer (b) is correct because confirmation with related and third parties of the details of arrangements to provide or maintain financial support is a procedure that would assist an auditor in identifying a question concerning going concern status. See AU 341 for this and other such conditions and events indicating doubt about an entity's ability to continue as a going concern. Answer (a) is incorrect because the pledging of assets as collateral is a normal business transaction and it need not necessarily indicate a question of going concern status. Answer (c) is incorrect because reconciling the cash balances with the cutoff bank statement is an acceptable audit procedure, but will not normally identify a going concern question. Answer (d) is incorrect because comparing an entity's depreciation and asset capitalization policies will not normally indicate a question of going concern status.

156. (a) The requirement is to identify the audit procedure most likely to assist an auditor in identifying conditions and events that may indicate there could be substantial doubt about an entity's ability to continue as a going concern. Answer (a) is correct because a review of compliance with terms of debt and loan agreements may reveal conditions of non-compliance due to poor financial condition. See the outline of AU 341 for a list of procedures that may identify such conditions and events. Answers (b), (c), and (d) are all incorrect because, while they might in some circumstances reveal a question concerning the company's ability to continue as a going concern, they are not considered to be as effective as answer (a).

157. (d) The requirement is to identify the factor which a CPA would most likely consider as mitigating substantial doubt about the ability of an entity to continue as a going concern. Answer (d) is correct because management's abil-

ity to negotiate reductions of required dividends will decrease required cash outflows, and thereby increase the likelihood that the entity will be able to continue as a going concern. AU 341 provides examples of information that might mitigate such concern. Answers (a), (b), and (c) are all incorrect because they involve spending cash, rather than reducing outflows of cash.

158. (c) The requirement is to identify the circumstance most likely to mitigate an auditor's substantial doubt about an entity's ability to continue as a going concern. Answer (c) is correct because the marketable assets that management intends to sell may potentially provide the necessary financial resources to mitigate the substantial doubt about the entity's ability to continue as a going concern. Answer (a) is incorrect because the ability to expand operations into new product lines is a suspect circumstance, given the substantial doubt about the entity's ability to continue as a going concern. Answer (b) is incorrect because it also requires cash resources which may not be available. Answer (d) is incorrect because converting preferred stock to long-term debt will not generally alleviate a question concerning an entity's ability to continue as a going concern.

C.18. Subsequent Events

159. (d) The requirement is to identify the most likely procedure to be performed in obtaining evidence about subsequent events. Answer (d) is correct because changes in long-term debt occurring after year-end may require note disclosure. Answers (a) and (b) are incorrect because auditors will not generally test changes in employee pay rates after year-end or recompute depreciation expense for plant assets sold. Answer (c) is incorrect because payroll checks issued near year-end may frequently be cashed after year-end and their investigation will not in general be directly related to obtaining evidence about subsequent events. See AU 560 for the responsibilities of auditors with respect to subsequent events.

160. (c) The requirement is to identify the event occurring after the issuance of an auditor's report that would most likely cause the auditor to make further inquiries about the previously issued financial statements. Answer (c) is correct because when an auditor becomes aware of information which relates to the financial statements previously reported upon, but which was not known at the date of the report, he or she should undertake to determine whether the information is reliable and whether the facts existed at the date of the audit report; in this circumstance it seems that the lease transactions existed as of the date of the audit report. Answer (a) is incorrect because the natural disaster occurred subsequent to the issuance of the audit report. Answer (b) is incorrect because the contingency had been properly disclosed. Answer (d) is incorrect because the sale of the subsidiary occurred subsequent to the issuance of the audit report.

161. (d) The requirement is to determine proper accounting and auditing treatment of uncollectibility of an account receivable resulting from a customer's bankruptcy due to a natural disaster occurring after a client's balance sheet date. Answer (d) is correct because a customer's major casualty loss after year-end will result in a financial statement note disclosure with no adjustment and no audit report modification due to consistency.

162. (d) The requirement is to determine an auditor's responsibility when subsequent to issuance of an audit report a client sells the shares of a major subsidiary. Answer (d) is correct because no action need be taken since the event arose after the issuance of the auditor's report. Answers (a), (b), and (c) are all incorrect because they outline responsibilities which are not appropriate in this circumstance. See AU 561 for a discussion of auditor responsibility when subsequent to the issuance of the auditor's report the auditor becomes aware of a fact that **existed at the date of the auditor's report**.

163. (c) The requirement is to determine the auditor's responsibility with respect to a client acquisition of 25% of its outstanding capital stock after year-end and prior to the completion of the auditor's fieldwork. Answer (c) is correct because the transaction described is a type 2 subsequent event (since the acquisition provided evidence of a condition which came into existence after year-end) and therefore the proper accounting approach would be note disclosure rather than adjustment. Answer (a) is incorrect because adjustments are only appropriate for type 1 subsequent events (events which provide evidence that the condition was in existence at year-end). Answer (b) is incorrect because the auditor does not issue financial statements for the client. Answer (d) is incorrect because the opinion paragraph of the report need not be modified; if any report modification were considered necessary, it would be an explanatory paragraph emphasizing the matter.

164. (d) The requirement is to identify a procedure that an auditor would perform to obtain evidence about the occurrence of subsequent events. Answer (d) is correct because an auditor will inquire of officers and other executives having responsibility for financial and accounting matters whether any unusual adjustments have been made during the period from the balance sheet date to the date of inquiry. See AU 560 for auditing procedures performed to identify subsequent events.

165. (a) The requirement is to determine a procedure that an auditor should generally perform regarding subsequent events. Answer (a) is correct because the *Professional Standards* state that the auditor generally should compare the latest available interim financial statements with the financial statements being audited. See AU 560 for this and other requirements. Answer (b) is incorrect because second accounts receivable confirmation requests will be sent well before the auditor's review of subsequent events. Answer (c) is incorrect because the communication of material weaknesses is not a subsequent event procedure. See AU 325 for the required communication of **significant deficiencies**. Answer (d) is incorrect because auditors generally only receive cutoff statements for the period immediately after year-end, not for multiple months.

C.19. Omitted Procedures Discovered After the Report Date

166. (b) The requirement is to identify an auditor's responsibility when a client refuses to adjust recently issued financial statements for a subsequent event related to the bankruptcy of the entity's principal customer. Answer (b) is correct because if the client refuses to make disclosures, AU 561 requires the auditor to notify each member of the board of directors of such refusal and that he or she will take steps

to prevent future reliance upon the audit report. Ordinarily the auditor will then notify the clients and regulatory agencies that the report should no longer be associated with the financial statements, and when possible, notify persons known to be relying upon the financial statements. Answer (a) is incorrect because it is less likely that all of the creditors will be informed. Answer (c) is incorrect because the financial statements are the responsibility of management, and the auditor will not revise or distribute them. Answer (d) is incorrect because no revised report will be issued.

167. (c) The requirement is to identify the circumstance in which an auditor who finds that he or she has omitted a substantive procedure at the time of an audit may decide not to apply that procedure. Answer (c) is correct because when results of other procedures tend to compensate for the procedure it may be omitted. Answer (a) is incorrect because, even when distribution of the financial statement has been limited to management and the board of directors, it may be necessary to perform the procedure. Answer (b) is incorrect because the type of report issued does not affect the need to perform the procedure. Answer (d) is incorrect because delays by the client in providing data are not an acceptable reason not to perform that procedure.

168. (b) The requirement is to determine professional responsibility when, subsequent to issuance of an audit report, an auditor has determined that a necessary audit procedure has been omitted. Answer (b) is correct because an auditor must apply procedures that would provide a satisfactory basis for the opinion issued. Answer (a) is incorrect because stockholders need not be informed at this point that the audit report should **not** be relied upon. Answer (c) is incorrect because the auditor's report will not be reissued unless the financial statements are restated. Answer (d) is incorrect because tests of controls will not compensate for the omitted procedure. See AU 390 for overall procedures relating to considering omitted procedures after an audit report has been issued.

169. (c) The requirement is to identify an auditor's first responsibility upon discovering six months after completion of an audit that engagement personnel failed to confirm several of the client's material accounts receivable balances. Answer (c) is correct because the auditor must first assess the importance of the omitted procedures to the auditor's ability to support the previously expressed opinion. Answers (a) and (b) are incorrect because prior to attempting any such confirmation or performing alternative procedures, an assessment of whether the procedures are needed is to be performed. Answer (d) is incorrect because a consideration of whether anyone is relying on, or is likely to rely on, the unqualified opinion is made after assessing the importance of the omitted procedure.

D. Completing the Audit

170. (c) The requirement is to determine the procedure **least** likely to be performed before the balance sheet date. Answer (c) is correct because the search for unrecorded liabilities relies upon a review of documents unrecorded at year-end, as well as inspection of purchases and disbursements recorded after year-end, to determine whether a proper cutoff of transactions between periods has occurred. Answer (a) is incorrect because auditors are able to test internal control over cash prior to year-end. Answers (b) and (d) are incorrect because in cases of good internal control, receivables may be confirmed and inventory observed prior to year-end.

171. (c) The requirement is to determine the most likely type of transaction that would be detected by an auditor's review of a client's sales cutoff. Answer (c) is correct because the auditor's review will include a study of sales recorded late in December and early in January. This will be accomplished by reviewing the period when the revenue was earned by shipment of goods or performance of services, as compared to the period in which the revenue was recorded. Accordingly, the review of sales recorded in January may reveal unrecorded sales for the preceding year. Answer (a) is incorrect because shipments lacking sales invoices and shipping documents will be very difficult to identify; also, this reply is more limited than answer (c). Answer (b) is incorrect because excessive write-offs of accounts receivable will not usually be detected when testing the sales cutoff. Answer (d) is incorrect because it is unlikely that lapping in the application of cash receipts will be detected by sales cutoff testing. More frequently, procedures such as confirmations, analytical procedures, and an analysis of deposit tickets reveal lapping.

172. (b) The requirement is to identify the assertion being tested by cutoff tests designed to detect credit sales made before the end of the year that have improperly been recorded in the subsequent year. Answer (b) is correct because the completeness assertion deals with whether all transactions have been included in the proper period. Answer (a) is incorrect because the presentation or disclosure assertion deals with whether particular components of the financial statements are properly classified, described, and disclosed. Answer (c) is incorrect because the rights and obligations assertion deals with whether assets are the rights of the entity and liabilities are the obligations of the entity at a given date. Answer (d) is incorrect because the existence or occurrence assertion deals with whether assets or liabilities of the entity exist at a given date and whether recorded transactions have occurred during a given period. In this question, the existence assertion would be tested if the auditor sampled from sales recorded prior to year-end to determine whether the sale occurred before or after year-end.

D.1. Procedures Completed near the End of the Audit

173. (d) The requirement is to identify the procedure an auditor would most likely perform during the overall review stage of formulating an opinion on an entity's financial statements. Answer (d) is correct because a consideration of results relating to the assessment of the risk of material misstatement due to fraud may reveal that the audit has inadequately addressed that risk; in such a case additional procedures would be required. Answer (a) is incorrect because such assurance from the entity's attorney is ordinarily obtained prior to the overall review stage of an audit. Answer (b) is incorrect because the verification of the accuracy of the proof of cash is ordinarily performed prior to the overall review and because little verification of the bank cutoff statement is usually necessary since it is ordinarily received directly by the auditor from the bank. Answer (c) is incorrect because such provisions for the safeguarding of

assets may be corrected well after the conclusion of the audit.

E.1. Compilation Procedures

174. (a) The requirement is to identify the procedure an accountant ordinarily performs in a compilation engagement of a nonissuer. Answer (a) is correct because the accountant is required, at a minimum, to read the financial statements to consider whether they are free from obvious material errors.

175. (b) The requirement is to determine whether either or both of (1) the additional audit effort necessary to complete the audit and (2) the reason for the change in the engagement should be considered by a CPA whose client has requested that an audit engagement be changed to a compilation. Answer (b) is correct because AR 100 states that additional necessary audit effort and the reason for the change—as well as the additional cost to complete the audit—be considered.

176. (d) The requirement is to determine whether an accountant can accept a compilation or a review engagement when s/he is unfamiliar with a prospective client's specialized industry accounting principles, but s/he plans to obtain the required level of knowledge prior to the engagement. Answer (d) is correct because an accountant may accept either a compilation or a review engagement in such circumstances.

177. (a) The requirement is to determine the correct statement concerning both an engagement to compile and an engagement to review a nonissuer's financial statements. Answer (a) is correct because neither a compilation nor a review contemplates obtaining an understanding of internal control. Answer (b) is incorrect because when performing a compilation the accountant need not be independent; independence is required for reviews. Answer (c) is incorrect because a review provides limited assurance. Answer (d) is incorrect because the accountant is not required to obtain a written management representation letter for a compilation; a management representation letter is required for a review.

178. (a) The requirement is to identify a condition required for an accountant to submit a written personal financial plan containing unaudited financial statements to a client without complying with the compilation and review requirements presented in SSARS 1. Answer (a) is correct because AR 600 allows such an exception when the plan (1) is to be used to assist the client and the client's advisors in developing financial goals and objectives, (2) will not be used to obtain credit, and (3) when nothing comes to the accountant's attention that would lead him/her to believe that the statements will be used for credit or for any other purposes. Answer (b) is incorrect because any work performed on the prior year statements is not applicable to the statements of the current year. Answer (c) is incorrect because the engagement letter need not acknowledge departures from GAAP. Answer (d) is incorrect because no assurance is provided in such reports.

E.2. Review Procedures

179. (b) The requirement is to identify the procedure not followed by an accountant in obtaining a reasonable basis for the expression of limited assurance for a review of financial statements. Answer (b) is correct because reviews ordinarily do not include an assessment of the risk of fraud. Answer (a) is incorrect because reviews include analytical procedures. Answer (c) is incorrect because a review includes inquiries of management. Answer (d) is incorrect because auditors obtain written representation from management when performing a review.

180. (c) The requirement is to determine the listed requirement when an accountant is providing limited assurance that the financial statements of a nonissuer require **no** material modifications to be in accordance with generally accepted accounting principles. Accountants perform reviews to provide such limited assurance. Answer (c) is correct because obtaining an understanding of the accounting principles in the industry is required for reviews. See AR 100 for this and other requirements. Answer (a) is incorrect because reviews do not require the accountant to assess the risk of material misstatement. Answer (b) is incorrect because reviews generally do not include any communication with the entity's lawyer. Answer (d) is incorrect because an "audit" program is not required since a review is being performed.

181. (a) The requirement is to identify the procedure **least** likely to be performed in a review of the financial statements of a nonissuer. Answer (a) is correct because a review of a nonissuer financial statements does not specifically address observing the safeguards over access to and use of assets and records. Answers (b), (c), and (d) are all incorrect because they are included in the procedures suggested for a review by AR 100.

182. (b) The requirement is to identify the procedures that an accountant would perform during an engagement to review the financial statements of a nonissuer. Answer (b) is correct because AR 100 requires that the CPA obtain a representation letter. Answers (a), (c), and (d) are incorrect because they are not included in AR 100 which presents a list of procedures performed during a review.

183. (c) The requirement is to identify the circumstances in which a CPA may issue a review report on the balance sheet of a nonissuer, and not report on the related financial statements. Answer (c) is correct because an accountant may issue a review report on one financial statement and not on the other related statements if the scope of the inquiry and analytical procedures has not been restricted. Answer (a) is incorrect because the CPA need not compile or report on the related statements of income, retained earnings, and cash flows when reviewing only the balance sheet. Answer (b) is incorrect because, when material modifications are needed, a CPA may still report on the balance sheet, but must indicate the modifications in the review report. Answer (d) is incorrect because the client need not be new.

184. (d) The requirement is to determine whether analytical procedures need to be performed on a compilation and/or a review engagement. Answer (d) is correct because a compilation does not require performance of analytical procedures, while a review does.

185. (b) The requirement is to determine the type of inquiry or analytical procedures ordinarily performed in an engagement to review a nonissuer's financial statements. Answer (b) is correct because an accountant will make inquiries concerning the entity's procedures for recording, classifying, and summarizing transactions, and accumulating information for disclosure in the financial statements. Answer (a) is incorrect because the analytical procedures and other procedures involved in a review do not in general obtain corroborating audit evidence as do the procedures of an audit. Answer (c) is incorrect because the procedures for reviews are not specially designed to test management's assertion regarding continued existence. Answer (d) is incorrect because inquiries of the entity's attorney are not normally required when a review is being performed.

186. (b) The requirement is to determine the most likely procedures to be included in a review engagement of a nonissuer. Answer (b) is correct because a review consists primarily of inquiries and analytical procedures. Answer (a) is incorrect because a bank transfer schedule is generally not prepared for a review engagement. Answer (c) is incorrect because a review does not include assessing the control structure. Answer (d) is incorrect because cutoff tests on sales and purchases are not normally performed on a review. Note that the procedures included in answers (a), (c), and (d) are typically performed in an audit.

187. (b) The requirement is to determine the type of transaction the accountant is most likely to investigate during a review when the year's accounts receivable did **not** conform to a predictable pattern. Answer (b) is correct because accounts receivable are generated from credit sales and an accountant would therefore investigate them. Answer (a) is incorrect because sales returns and allowances would be less likely to cause large shifts in accounts receivable than credit sales. Answer (c) is incorrect because it is less complete than answer (b) since sales of consigned goods represent only one possible type of sale that might impact accounts receivable. Answer (d) is incorrect because cash sales do not affect accounts receivable.

188. (b) The requirement is to identify the most likely procedure to be included in a review of a nonissuer's financial statements. Answer (b) is correct because AR 100 states that reviews ordinarily include inquires concerning actions taken at board of directors' meetings. Answer (a) is incorrect because reviews consist primarily of inquiry and analytical procedures and do not generally include confirmation of accounts receivable. Answer (c) is incorrect because a review of a nonpublic entity does not normally include obtaining an understanding of internal control or assessing control risk. Answer (d) is incorrect because distribution of a review report need not be limited. See AR 100 for specific procedures included in reviews.

F. Operational Auditing

189. (a) The requirement is to identify the correct statement with respect to the primary orientation of operational auditing. Answer (a) is correct because operational audits deal primarily with evaluating the efficiency and effectiveness with which operations function, often with the intention of making improvements to accomplish the goals of management. Answers (b) and (c) are incorrect because financial statement audits are oriented toward such determinations, not operational audits. Answer (d) is incorrect because examinations of internal control are not performed on operational audits.

190. (d) The requirement is to identify a typical objective of an operational audit. Answer (d) is correct because operational audits typically address efficiency and effectiveness. Answer (a) is incorrect because while the adequacy of internal control design may be addressed during an operational audit, this is less complete than answer (d). Answer (b) is incorrect because operational audits may or may not be related to compliance with generally accepted governmental auditing standards. Answer (c) is incorrect because financial statement audits, not operational audits, address whether results of operations are fairly presented.

SOLUTIONS TO SIMULATION PROBLEMS

Simulation Problem 1

Directions	Audit Objectives—Investments	Audit Objectives—Accounts Receivable	Research	Communication

Audit objectives for investments   (A) (B) (C) (D) (E) (F) (G)

1. Investments are properly described and classified in the financial statements.   ○ ○ ○ ○ ● ○ ○

2. Recorded investments represent investments actually owned at the balance sheet date.   ○ ○ ○ ○ ○ ● ○

3. Trading investments are properly valued at fair market value at the balance sheet date.   ○ ○ ○ ● ○ ○ ○

Explanation of solutions

1. **(E)** The verification of transfers from the current to the noncurrent investment portfolio will provide assurance that the investments are properly classified in the financial statements.

2. **(F)** Positive confirmation replies as of the balance sheet date for investments held by independent custodians will provide assurance that the recorded investments are in fact owned by the audit client.

3. **(D)** Because trading investments should be valued at fair market value, determining whether any impairments in the price of investments have been recorded will provide assurance that investments are properly valued.

Directions	Audit Objectives—Investments	Audit Objectives—Accounts Receivable	Research	Communication

Audit objectives for accounts receivable   (A) (B) (C) (D) (E) (F) (G)

4. Accounts receivable represent all amounts owed to the entity at the balance sheet date.   ○ ● ○ ○ ○ ○ ○

5. The entity has legal right to all accounts receivable at the balance sheet date.   ○ ○ ○ ○ ● ○ ○

6. Accounts receivable are stated at net realizable value.   ○ ○ ● ○ ○ ○ ○

7. Accounts receivable are properly described and presented in the financial statements.   ○ ○ ○ ○ ○ ● ○

Explanation of solutions

4. **(B)** Performance of ~~...~~ will provide assurance that sales transactions and the related receivables are recorded in the proper period. Thus, sales cutoff tests will provide assurance that all amounts ~~...~~ at the balance sheet date are recorded in that period.

5. **(E)** A review of loan agreements, paying special attention to accounts receivable that have been factored, will provide assurance as to whether the entity has a legal right to all accounts receivable at the balance sheet date.

6. **(C)** An analysis of the aged trial balance for significant past due accounts will provide evidence with respect to accounts that may be uncollectible. Accordingly, the procedure will address the net realizable value of accounts receivable.

7. **(F)** Because material amounts due from officers and employees should be segregated from other receivables, a review of the trial balance for amounts due from officers and employees will provide assurance that accounts receivable are properly described and presented in the financial statements.

Directions	Audit Objectives—Investments	Audit Objectives—Accounts Receivable	Research	Communication

AU 330.34 states that

Confirmation of accounts receivable is a generally accepted auditing procedure. As discussed in paragraph .06, it is generally presumed that evidence obtained from third parties will provide the auditor with higher-quality audit evidence than is typically available from within the entity. Thus, there is a presumption that the auditor will request the confirmation of accounts receivable during an audit unless one of the following is true:

- Accounts receivable are immaterial to the financial statements
- The use of confirmations would be ineffective.[4]
- The auditor's combined assessed level of inherent and control risk is low, and the assessed level, in conjunction with the evidence expected to be provided by analytical procedures or other substantive tests of details is sufficient to reduce audit risk to an acceptably low level for the applicable financial statement assertions. In many situations both confirmation of accounts receivable and other substantive tests of details are necessary to reduce audit risk to an acceptably low level for the applicable financial statement assertions.

.35 An auditor who has not requested confirmations in the examination of accounts receivable should document how he or she overcame this presumption.

[4] *For example, if, based on prior years' audit experience or on experience with similar engagements, the auditor concludes that response rates to properly designed confirmation requests will be inadequate, or if responses are known or expected to be unreliable, the auditor may determine that the use of confirmations would be ineffective.*

Directions	Audit Objectives—Investments	Audit Objectives—Accounts Receivable	Research	Communication

To: Audit Working Papers
From: CPA Candidate
Re: Procedures to detect fictitious companies

     This memorandum is designed to address a risk with respect to accounts receivable. We have discovered that there is a risk that some of the accounts receivable on the company's financial statements may be from fictitious companies. To detect such companies, we are going to verify names and addresses in telephone directories or on Web sites. If we detect even one fictitious company, we will reassess fraud risk for the engagement. This will require that we redesign our planned audit procedures. If any issues arise regarding these accounts, please contact me immediately.

Simulation Problem 2

Directions	Audit Implications	Confirmations	Inventory Observation	Research	Communication

	Statement	IA	RP
1.	A note payable has an interest rate well below the market rate at the time at which the loan was obtained.	○	●
2.	The company has a properly documented loan but the loan has no scheduled repayment terms.	○	●
3.	Unexplained payments have been made to government officials.	●	○
4.	The company exchanged certain real estate property for similar real estate property.	○	●
5.	Large cash receipts near year-end have been received based on cash sales for which there is no documentation.	●	○

Directions	Audit Implications	Confirmations	Inventory Observation	Research	Communication

	Statement	Correct	Incorrect
1.	The confirmation requests should be mailed to respondents by the CPAs.	●	○
2.	A combination of positive and negative request forms must be used if receivables are significant.	○	●
3.	Second requests are ordinarily sent for positive form confirmations requests when the first request is not returned.	●	○
4.	Confirmations address existence more than they address completeness.	●	○
5.	Confirmation of accounts receivable is a generally accepted auditing standard.	○	●
6.	Absent a few circumstances, there is a presumption that the auditor will confirm accounts receivable.	●	○
7.	Auditors should always confirm the total balances of accounts rather than individual portions (e.g., if the balance is made up of three sales, all three should be confirmed).	○	●
8.	Auditors may ignore individually immaterial accounts when confirming accounts receivable.	○	●
9.	The best way to evaluate the results of the confirmation process is to total the misstatements identified and to compare that total to the account's tolerable error amounts.	○	●
10.	Accounts receivable are ordinarily confirmed on a standard form developed by the American Institute of Certified Public Accountants and the Financial Executives Institute.	○	●

Directions	Audit Implications	Confirmations	Inventory Observation	Research	Communication

	Statement	Correct	Incorrect
1.	With strong internal control, the inventory count may be at the end of the year or at other times.	●	○
2.	When a client has many inventory locations, auditors ordinarily need not be present at each location.	●	○
3.	All auditor test counts must be documented in the working papers.	○	●
4.	Auditors' observation of the counting of their clients' inventories addresses the existence of inventory, and not the completeness of the count.	○	●
5.	When the client manufactures a product, direct labor and overhead ordinarily become a part of inventory item costs.	●	○
6.	Inventory is ordinarily valued at the lower of standard cost or market.	○	●
7.	Inventory items present as "consigned in" should not be included in the client's inventory value.	●	○
8.	Auditor recording of test counts ordinarily replaces the need for client "tagging" of inventory.	○	●
9.	Ordinarily, an auditor need not count all items in the inventory.	●	○
10.	At the completion of the count, an auditor will ordinarily provide the client with copies of his or her inventory test counts to help assure inventory accuracy.	○	●

Directions	Audit Implications	Confirmations	Inventory Observation	Research	Communication

AU 332.22 discusses completeness as it relates to derivative instruments

.22 Completeness assertions address whether all of the entity's derivatives and securities are reported in the financial statements through recognition or disclosure. They also address whether all derivatives and securities transactions are reported in the financial statements as a part of earnings, other comprehensive income, or cash flows or through disclosure. The extent of substantive procedures for completeness may properly vary in relation to the assessed level of control risk. In addition, the auditor should consider that since derivatives may not involve an initial exchange of tangible consideration, it may be .... of derivatives to an acceptable level with an assessed level of control risk at the maximum. Paragraph .19 provides guidance on the auditor's determination of the nature, timing, and extent of substantive procedures to be performed. Examples of substantive procedures for completeness assertions about derivatives and securities are

- Requesting the counterparty to a derivative or the holder of a security to provide information about it, such as whether there are any side agreements or agreements to repurchase securities sold.
- Requesting counterparties or holders who are frequently used, but with whom the accounting records indicate there are presently no derivatives or securities, to state whether they are counterparties to derivatives with the entity or holders of its securities. [fn 13]
- Inspecting financial instruments and other agreements to identify embedded derivatives.
- Inspecting documentation in paper or electronic form for activity subsequent to the end of the reporting period.
- Performing analytical procedures. For example, a difference from an expectation that interest expense is a fixed percentage of a note based on the interest provisions of the underlying agreement may indicate the existence of an interest rate swap agreement.
- Comparing previous and current account detail to identify assets that have been removed from the accounts and testing those items further to determine that the criteria for sales treatment have been met.
- Reading other information, such as minutes of meetings of the board of directors or finance, asset/liability, investment, or other committees.

(You might have chosen to paste paragraphs 332.23-.24 also.)

Directions	Audit Implications	Confirmations	Inventory Observation	Research	Communication

To: Audit Working Papers
From: CPA Candidate
Re: Audit confirmations

This memorandum describes the risks related to confirming balances and transactions. In preparing audit confirmations, it is very important for the audit staff to control the mailing of the confirmations. If client officers or employees are allowed to intercept the confirmations, they could mitigate any evidence that could be derived from the audit procedure. If you discover any unusual confirmation issues, please notify the audit manager.

Simulation Problem 3

Audit Procedures			
	Assessing Audit Risk	Research	Communication

1. **(D, I)** The balance per bank may be traced to a standard form used to confirm account balance information with financial institutions and to the cutoff statement (on which will appear the beginning balance).

2. **(A, G, H, I, J)** One of the deposits in transit does not appear on the cutoff bank statement (the 9/29/05 deposit for $4,500). Accordingly, that deposit should be traced to the cash receipts journal (procedure A), the reason for the delay should be investigated (procedure G), and supporting documents should be inspected (procedure H). Both deposits should be traced to and from the bank reconciliation and the cutoff statement (procedures I and J).

3. **(B, G, H, I, J)** One of the checks does not appear on the cutoff statement (check #988 dated 8/31/05 for $2,200). Accordingly, that check should be traced to the cash disbursements journal (procedure B), the reason for the delay should be investigated (procedure G), and supporting documents should be inspected (procedure H). All checks should be traced to and from the bank reconciliation and cutoff statement (procedures I and J).

4. **(E)** The credit memo from the bank for the note collected should be investigated.

5. **(E, I)** The credit for the check that was charged by the bank for an incorrect amount should be investigated on both the bank credit memo and on the cutoff statement.

6. **(C)** The only source of the balance per books is the cash general ledger account as of 9/30/05.

Audit Procedures	Addressing Audit Risk		
		Research	Communication

1. **(E)** Kiting involves manipulations causing an amount of cash to be included simultaneously in the balance of two or more bank accounts. Kiting schemes are based on the float period—the time necessary for a check deposited in one bank to clear the bank on which it was drawn. To detect kiting, a bank transfer schedule is prepared to determine whether cash is improperly included in two accounts.

2. **(D)** A comparison of the cleared checks to the year-end bank reconciliation will identify checks that were not mailed until after the first week of the subsequent year because most of those checks will not be returned with the cutoff statement and will appear to remain outstanding an abnormally long period of time.

3. **(H)** Among the terms confirmed for such a borrowing arrangement will be information on liens.

4. **(K, L)** A reply to the second request, or information from the credit agency, may confirm the existence of the new customer. Also, examination of shipping documents will reveal where the goods were shipped, and ordinarily to which party.

5. **(P)** Observing the payroll check distribution on a surprise basis will assist in detection since the auditor will examine details related to any paychecks not picked up by employees.

6. **(Q)** Vouching data in the payroll register to document authorized pay rates will reveal situations in which an employee is earning income at a rate that differs from the authorized rate.

7. **(A)** A comparison of the details of the cash receipts journal to the details on the daily deposit slips will reveal a circumstance since the details will have been posted to accounts during the last week of the year under audit.

8. **(U)** When vouchers are processed for merchandise not ordered or received, there will be no supporting purchase orders and receiving reports and this will alert the auditor to the problem.

9. **(B)** Scanning the debits to the fixed asset accounts and vouching selected amounts will reveal repairs that have improperly been capitalized.

10. **(A, J)** Lapping involves concealing a cash shortage by delaying the recording of journal entries for cash receipts. Since lapping includes differences between the details of postings to the cash receipts journal and corresponding deposit slips, comparing these records will reveal it. Also, confirmation requests may identify lapping when payments of receivables (as indicated by confirmation replies) appear to have taken too much time to be processed.

11. **(E)** Increasing cash by drawing a check in this manner is a form of kiting (see answer 1). Preparation of a bank transfer schedule will assist the auditor in identifying such transactions.

12. **(J, L)** Confirmations will identify overstated accounts receivable when customers disagree with the recorded balance due. Also, the related overstated sales will not have shipping documents indicating that a shipment has occurred.

Audit Procedures	Addressing Audit Risk	Research	Communication

The first step is to determine the manner in which the candidate wishes to identify the pertinent research in the area. If a keyword or index search is to be used, words such as "identified related-party transactions" or "identified related-party" may be helpful. Even using "related party" will get the candidate to AU 334 which provides the needed information. AU 334 indicates the following with respect to identified related-party transactions:

.09   After identifying related-party transactions, the auditor should apply the procedures he considers necessary to obtain satisfaction concerning the purpose, nature, and extent of these transactions and their effect on the financial statements. The procedures should be directed toward obtaining and evaluating sufficient appropriate audit evidence and should extend beyond inquiry of management. Procedures that should be considered include the following:

    a.   Obtain an understanding of the business purpose of the transaction.

    b.   Examine invoices, executed copies of agreements, contracts, and other pertinent documents, such as receiving reports and shipping documents.

    c.   Determine whether the transaction has been approved by the board of directors or other appropriate officials.

    d.   Test for reasonableness the compilation of amounts to be disclosed, or considered for disclosure, in the financial statements.

    e.   Arrange for the audits of intercompany account balances to be performed as of concurrent dates, even if the fiscal years differ, and for the examination of specified, important, and representative related-party transactions by the auditors for each of the parties, with appropriate exchange of relevant information.

    f.   Inspect or confirm and obtain satisfaction concerning the transferability and value of collateral.

.10   When necessary to fully understand a particular transaction, the following procedures, which might not otherwise be deemed necessary to comply with generally accepted auditing standards, should be considered.

    a.   Confirm transaction amount and terms, including guarantees and other significant data, with the other party or parties to the transaction.

    b.   Inspect evidence in possession of the other party or parties to the transaction.

    c.   Confirm or discuss significant information with intermediaries, such as banks, guarantors, agents, or attorneys, to obtain a better understanding of the transaction.

    d.   Refer to financial .... credit agencies, and other information sources when there is reason to believe that unfamiliar customers, suppliers, or other business enterprises with whom a material amounts of business have been transacted may lack substance.

    e.   With respect to material uncollected balances, guarantees, and other obligations, obtain information about the financial capability of the other party or parties to the transaction. Such information may be obtained from audited financial statements, unaudited financial statements, income tax returns, and reports issued by regulatory agencies, taxing authorities, financial publications, or credit agencies. The auditor should decide on the degree of assurance required and the extent to which available information provides such assurance.

Audit Procedures	Addressing Audit Risk	Research	Communication

To: Joe Smith, CEO
       General Company
From: CPA Candidate
Re: Related-party loan disclosure

This memorandum is designed to describe the implications of related-party transactions. By their nature, related-party transactions are not at arm's length—they do not involve independent bargaining. Except for routine transactions, it is generally not possible to determine whether a particular transaction would have occurred if the parties were not related, or assuming it would have occurred, what the terms would have been. Therefore, it is difficult to support representations that the transaction's terms are similar to those that would have occurred between unrelated parties. Accordingly, we do not recommend that this representation be included in the notes to the financial statements.

If you have any additional questions about this issue, please contact me.

MULTIPLE-CHOICE QUESTIONS (1-180)

1. The existence of audit risk is recognized by the statement in the auditor's standard report that the auditor
   a. Obtains reasonable assurance about whether the financial statements are free of material misstatement.
   b. Assesses the accounting principles used and also evaluates the overall financial statement presentation.
   c. Realizes some matters, either individually or in the aggregate, are important while other matters are not important.
   d. Is responsible for expressing an opinion on the financial statements, which are the responsibility of management.

2. When an accountant performs more than one level of service (for example, a compilation and a review, or a compilation and an audit) concerning the financial statements of a nonissuer (nonpublic) entity, the accountant generally should issue the report that is appropriate for
   a. The lowest level of service rendered.
   b. The highest level of service rendered.
   c. A compilation engagement.
   d. A review engagement.

3. Which of the following is **least** likely to be a restricted use report?
   a. A report on internal control significant deficiencies noted in an audit.
   b. A required communication with the audit committee.
   c. A report on financial statements prepared following a comprehensive basis of accounting other than generally accepted accounting principles.
   d. A report on compliance with aspects of contractual agreements.

4. Which of the following statements is correct concerning an auditor's responsibility for controlling the **distribution by the client** of a restricted-use report?
   a. An auditor must inform the client that a restricted-use report is not intended for distribution to non-specified parties.
   b. When an auditor is aware that a client has distributed a restricted-use report to inappropriate third parties, the auditor should immediately inform the client to cease and desist.
   c. An auditor controls distribution through insisting that the client not duplicate the restricted-use report for any purposes.
   d. An auditor is not responsible for controlling the distribution of such reports.

5. Which of the following statements is a basic element of the auditor's standard report?
   a. The disclosures provide reasonable assurance that the financial statements are free of material misstatement.
   b. The auditor evaluated the overall internal control.
   c. An audit includes assessing significant estimates made by management.
   d. The financial statements are consistent with those of the prior period.

6. In May 2009, an auditor reissues the auditor's report on the 2007 financial statements at a continuing client's request. The 2007 financial statements are not restated and the auditor does not revise the wording of the report. The auditor should
   a. Dual date the reissued report.
   b. Use the release date of the reissued report.
   c. Use the original report date on the reissued report.
   d. Use the current period auditor's report date on the reissued report.

7. Which paragraphs of an auditor's standard report on financial statements should refer to generally accepted auditing standards (GAAS) and generally accepted accounting principles (GAAP)?

	GAAS	GAAP
a.	Opening	Scope
b.	Scope	Scope
c.	Scope	Opinion
d.	Opening	Opinion

8. An auditor expressed a qualified opinion on the prior year's financial statements because of a lack of adequate disclosure. These financial statements are properly restated in the current year and presented in comparative form with the current year's financial statements. The auditor's updated report on the prior year's financial statements should
   a. Be accompanied by the auditor's original report on the prior year's financial statements.
   b. Continue to express a qualified opinion on the prior year's financial statements.
   c. Make **no** reference to the type of opinion expressed on the prior year's financial statements.
   d. Express an unqualified opinion on the restated financial statements of the prior year.

9. An auditor's responsibility to express an opinion on the financial statements is
   a. Implicitly represented in the auditor's standard report.
   b. Explicitly represented in the opening paragraph of the auditor's standard report.
   c. Explicitly represented in the scope paragraph of the auditor's standard report.
   d. Explicitly represented in the opinion paragraph of the auditor's standard report.

10. Which of the following phrases should be included in the opinion paragraph when an auditor expresses a qualified opinion?

	When read in conjunction with Note X	With the foregoing explanation
a.	Yes	No
b.	No	Yes
c.	Yes	Yes
d.	No	No

11. How does an auditor make the following representations when issuing the standard auditor's report on comparative financial statements?

	Examination of evidence on a test basis	Consistent application of accounting principles
a.	Explicitly	Explicitly
b.	Implicitly	Implicitly
c.	Implicitly	Explicitly
d.	Explicitly	Implicitly

12. The fourth standard of reporting requires the auditor's report to contain either an expression of opinion regarding the financial statements taken as a whole or an assertion to the effect that an opinion cannot be expressed. The objective of the fourth standard is to prevent

a. An auditor from expressing different opinions on each of the basic financial statements.

b. Restrictions on the scope of the audit, whether imposed by the client or by the inability to obtain evidence.

c. Misinterpretations regarding the degree of responsibility the auditor is assuming.

d. An auditor from reporting on one basic financial statement and **not** the others.

13. Which of the following **best** describes the reference to the expression "taken as a whole" in the fourth generally accepted auditing standard of reporting?

a. It applies equally to a complete set of financial statements and to each individual financial statement.

b. It applies only to a complete set of financial statements.

c. It applies equally to each item in each financial statement.

d. It applies equally to each material item in each financial statement.

Abco's December 31, 2009 financial statements on March 6, 2010. A subsequent event requiring adjustment to the 2009 financial statements occurred on April 10, 2010, and came to Wilson's attention on April 24, 2010. If the adjustment is made without disclosure of the event, Wilson's report ordinarily should be dated

a. March 6, 2010.

b. April 10, 2010.

c. April 24, 2010.

d. Using dual dating.

15. An auditor issued an audit report that was dual dated for a subsequent event occurring after the completion of fieldwork but before issuance of the auditor's report. The auditor's responsibility for events occurring subsequent to the completion of fieldwork was

a. Extended to subsequent events occurring through the date of issuance of the report.

b. Extended to include all events occurring since the completion of fieldwork.

c. Limited to the specific event referenced.

d. Limited to include only events occurring up to the date of the last subsequent event referenced.

16. A financial statement audit report issued for the audit of an issuer (public) company concludes that the financial statements follow

a. Generally accepted accounting principles.

b. Public Company Accounting Oversight Board standards.

c. Generally accepted auditing standards.

d. International accounting standards.

17. Which of the following is not correct concerning information included in an audit report of financial statements issued under the requirements of the Public Company Accounting Oversight Board?

a. The report should include the title "Report of Independent Registered Public Accounting Firm."

b. The report should refer to the standards of the PCAOB.

c. The report should include a paragraph referring to the auditor's report on compliance with laws and regulations.

d. The report should contain the city and state or country of the office that issued the report.

18. A principal auditor decides not to refer to the audit of another CPA who audited a subsidiary of the principal auditor's client. After making inquiries about the other CPA's professional reputation and independence, the principal auditor most likely would

a. Add an explanatory paragraph to the auditor's report indicating that the subsidiary's financial statements are **not** material to the consolidated financial statements.

b. Document in the engagement letter that the principal auditor assumes no responsibility for the other CPA's work and opinion.

c. Obtain written permission from the other CPA to omit the reference in the principal auditor's report.

d. Contact the other CPA and review the audit programs and working papers pertaining to the subsidiary.

19. The introductory paragraph of an auditor's report contains the following sentences:

> We did not audit the financial statements of EZ Inc., a wholly owned subsidiary, which statements reflect total assets and revenues constituting 27% and 29%, respectively, of the related consolidated totals. Those statements were audited by other auditors whose report has been furnished to us, and our opinion, insofar as it relates to the amounts included for EZ Inc., is based solely on the report of the other auditors.

These sentences

a. Indicate a division of responsibility.

b. Assume responsibility for the other auditor.

c. Require a departure from an unqualified opinion.

d. Are an improper form of reporting.

20. In which of the following situations would an auditor ordinarily issue an unqualified audit opinion without an explanatory paragraph?

a. The auditor wishes to emphasize that the entity had significant related-party transactions.

b. The auditor decides to make reference to the report of another auditor as a basis, in part, for the auditor's opinion.

c. The entity issues financial statements that present financial position and results of operations, but omits the statement of cash flows.

d. The auditor has substantial doubt about the entity's ability to continue as a going concern, but the circumstances are fully disclosed in the financial statements.

21. An auditor may issue the standard audit report when the
   a. Auditor refers to the findings of a specialist.
   b. Financial statements are derived and condensed from complete audited financial statements that are filed with a regulatory agency.
   c. Financial statements are prepared on the cash receipts and disbursements basis of accounting.
   d. Principal auditor assumes responsibility for the work of another auditor.

22. In the auditor's report, the principal auditor decides not to make reference to another CPA who audited a client's subsidiary. The principal auditor could justify this decision if, among other requirements, the principal auditor
   a. Issues an unqualified opinion on the consolidated financial statements.
   b. Learns that the other CPA issued an unqualified opinion on the subsidiary's financial statements.
   c. Is unable to review the audit programs and working papers of the other CPA.
   d. Is satisfied as to the independence and professional reputation of the other CPA.

23. When financial statements of a company that follows GASB standards would be misleading due to unusual circumstances depart from those standards, the auditor should explain the unusual circumstances in a separate paragraph and express an opinion that is
   a. Unqualified.
   b. Qualified.
   c. Adverse.
   d. Qualified or adverse, depending on materiality.

24. An auditor concludes that there is substantial doubt about an entity's ability to continue as a going concern for a reasonable period of time. If the entity's financial statements adequately disclose its financial difficulties, the auditor's report is required to include an explanatory paragraph that specifically uses the phrase(s)

	"Reasonable period of time, not to exceed 1 year"	*"Going concern"*
a.	Yes	Yes
b.	Yes	No
c.	No	Yes
d.	No	No

25. Mead, CPA, had substantial doubt about Tech Co.'s ability to continue as a going concern when reporting on Tech's audited financial statements for the year ended June 30, 2009. That doubt has been removed in 2010. What is Mead's reporting responsibility if Tech is presenting its financial statements for the year ended June 30, 2010, on a comparative basis with those of 2010?
   a. The explanatory paragraph included in the 2010 auditor's report should **not** be repeated.
   b. The explanatory paragraph included in the 2010 auditor's report should be repeated in its entirety.
   c. A different explanatory paragraph describing Mead's reasons for the removal of doubt should be included.
   d. A different explanatory paragraph describing Tech's plans for financial recovery should be included.

26. When an auditor concludes there is substantial doubt about a continuing audit client's ability to continue as a going concern for a reasonable period of time, the auditor's responsibility is to
   a. Issue a qualified or adverse opinion, depending upon materiality, due to the possible effects on the financial statements.
   b. Consider the adequacy of disclosure about the client's possible inability to continue as a going concern.
   c. Report to the client's audit committee that management's accounting estimates may need to be adjusted.
   d. Reissue the prior year's auditor's report and add an explanatory paragraph that specifically refers to "substantial doubt" and "going concern."

27. Green, CPA, concludes that there is substantial doubt about JKL Co.'s ability to continue as a going concern. If JKL's financial statements adequately disclose its financial difficulties, Green's auditor's report should

	Include an explanatory paragraph following the opinion paragraph	*Specifically use the words "going concern"*	*Specifically use the words "substantial doubt"*
a.	Yes	Yes	Yes
b.	Yes	Yes	No
c.	Yes	No	Yes
d.	No	Yes	Yes

28. In which of the following circumstances would an auditor most likely add an explanatory paragraph to the standard report while **not** affecting the auditor's unqualified opinion?
   a. The auditor is asked to report on the balance sheet, but **not** on the other basic financial statements.
   b. There is substantial doubt about the entity's ability to continue as a going concern.
   c. Management's estimates of the effects of future events are unreasonable.
   d. Certain transactions **cannot** be tested because of management's records retention policy.

29. After considering an entity's negative trends and financial difficulties, an auditor has substantial doubt about the entity's ability to continue as a going concern. The auditor's considerations relating to management's plans for dealing with the adverse effects of these conditions most likely would include management's plans to
   a. Increase current dividend distributions.
   b. Reduce existing lines of credit.
   c. Increase ownership equity.
   d. Purchase assets formerly leased.

30. For which of the following events would an auditor issue a report that omits any reference to consistency?
   a. A change in the method of accounting for inventories.
   b. A change from an accounting principle that is **not** generally accepted to one that is generally accepted.
   c. A change in the useful life used to calculate the provision for depreciation expense.
   d. Management's lack of reasonable justification for a change in accounting principle.

31. An auditor would express an unqualified opinion with an explanatory paragraph added to the auditor's report for

	An unjustified accounting change	A material weakness in the internal control
a.	Yes	Yes
b.	Yes	No
c.	No	Yes
d.	No	No

32. Under which of the following circumstances would a disclaimer of opinion **not** be appropriate?

a. The auditor is unable to determine the amounts associated with an employee fraud scheme.
b. Management does **not** provide reasonable justification for a change in accounting principles.
c. The client refuses to permit the auditor to confirm certain accounts receivable or apply alternative procedures to verify their balances.
d. The chief executive officer is unwilling to sign the management representation letter.

33. Digit Co. uses the FIFO method of costing for its international subsidiary's inventory and LIFO for its domestic inventory. Under these circumstances, the auditor's report on Digit's financial statements should express an

a. Unqualified opinion.
b. Opinion qualified because of a lack of consistency.
c. Opinion qualified because of a departure from GAAP.
d. Adverse opinion.

34. In the first audit of a new client, an auditor was able to extend auditing procedures to gather sufficient evidence about consistency. Under these circumstances, the auditor should

a. Not report on the client's income statement.
b. Not refer to consistency in the auditor's report.
c. State that the consistency standard does **not** apply.
d. State that the accounting principles have been applied consistently.

35. When management does **not** provide reasonable justification that a change in accounting principle is preferable and it presents comparative financial statements, the auditor should express a qualified opinion

a. Only in the year of the accounting principle change.
b. Each year that the financial statements initially reflecting the change are presented.
c. Each year until management changes back to the accounting principle formerly used.
d. Only if the change is to an accounting principle that is **not** generally accepted.

36. When an entity changes its method of accounting for income taxes, which has a material effect on comparability, the auditor should refer to the change in an explanatory paragraph added to the auditor's report. This paragraph should identify the nature of the change and

a. Explain why the change is justified under generally accepted accounting principles.
b. Describe the cumulative effect of the change on the audited financial statements.
c. State the auditor's explicit concurrence with or opposition to the change.

d. Refer to the financial statement note that discusses the change in detail.

37. An entity changed from the straight-line method to the declining balance method of depreciation for all newly acquired assets. This change has no material effect on the current year's financial statements, but is reasonably certain to have a substantial effect in later years. If the change is disclosed in the notes to the financial statements, the auditor should issue a report with a(n)

a. "Except for" qualified opinion.
b. Explanatory paragraph.
c. Unqualified opinion.
d. Consistency modification.

38. When reporting on comparative financial statements, an auditor ordinarily should change the previously issued opinion on the prior year's financial statements if the

a. Prior year's financial statements are restated to conform with generally accepted accounting principles.
b. Auditor is a predecessor auditor who has been requested by a former client to reissue the previously issued report.
c. Prior year's opinion was unqualified and the opinion on the current year's financial statements is modified due to a lack of consistency.
d. Prior year's financial statements are restated following a pooling of interests in the current year.

39. Jewel, CPA, audited Infinite Co.'s prior year financial statements. These statements are presented with those of the current year for comparative purposes without Jewel's auditor's report, which expressed a qualified opinion. In drafting the current year's auditor's report, Crain, CPA, the successor auditor, should

I. Not name Jewel as the predecessor auditor.
II. Indicate the type of report issued by Jewel.
III. Indicate the substantive reasons for Jewel's qualification.

a. I only.
b. I and II only.
c. II and III only.
d. I, II, and III.

40. Before reissuing the prior year's auditor's report on the financial statements of a former client, the predecessor auditor should obtain a letter of representations from the

	Former client's management	Successor auditor
a.	Yes	Yes
b.	Yes	No
c.	No	Yes
d.	No	No

41. When single-year financial statements are presented, an auditor ordinarily would express an unqualified opinion in an unmodified report if the

a. Auditor is unable to obtain audited financial statements supporting the entity's investment in a foreign affiliate.
b. Entity declines to present a statement of cash flows with its balance sheet and related statements of income and retained earnings.
c. Auditor wishes to emphasize an accounting matter affecting the comparability of the financial statements with those of the prior year.

d. Prior year's financial statements were audited by another CPA whose report, which expressed an unqualified opinion, is **not** presented.

42. A client is presenting comparative (two-year) financial statements. Which of the following is correct concerning reporting responsibilities of a continuing auditor?

    a. The auditor should issue one audit report that is on both presented years.

    b. The auditor should issue two audit reports, one on each year.

    c. The auditor should issue one audit report, but only on the most recent year.

    d. The auditor may issue either one audit report on both presented years, or two audit reports, one on each year.

43. The predecessor auditor, who is satisfied after properly communicating with the successor auditor, has reissued a report because the audit client desires comparative financial statements. The predecessor auditor's report should make

    a. Reference to the report of the successor auditor only in the scope paragraph.

    b. Reference to the work of the successor auditor in the scope and opinion paragraphs.

    c. Reference to both the work and the report of the successor auditor only in the opinion paragraph.

    d. No reference to the report or the work of the successor auditor.

44. Unaudited financial statements for the prior year presented in comparative form with audited financial statements for the current year should be clearly marked to indicate their status and

I. The report on the prior period should be reissued to accompany the current period report.

II. The report on the current period should include as a separate paragraph a description of the responsibility assumed for the prior period's financial statements.

    a. I only.

    b. II only.

    c. Both I and II.

    d. Either I or II.

45. What is an auditor's responsibility for supplementary information, such as segment information, which is outside the basic financial statements, but required by the FASB?

    a. The auditor has **no** responsibility for required supplementary information as long as it is outside the basic financial statements.

    b. The auditor's only responsibility for required supplementary information is to determine that such information has **not** been omitted.

    c. The auditor should apply certain limited procedures to the required supplementary information, and report deficiencies in, or omissions of, such information.

    d. The auditor should apply tests of details of transactions and balances to the required supplementary information, and report any material misstatements in such information.

46. If management declines to present supplementary information required by the Governmental Accounting Standards Board (GASB), the auditor should issue a(n)

    a. Adverse opinion.

    b. Qualified opinion with an explanatory paragraph.

    c. Unqualified opinion.

    d. Unqualified opinion with an additional explanatory paragraph.

47. What is an auditor's reporting responsibility concerning information accompanying the basic financial statements in an auditor-submitted document?

    a. The auditor should report on all the accompanying information included in the document.

    b. The auditor should report on the accompanying information only if the auditor participated in its preparation.

    c. The auditor should report on the accompanying information only if the auditor did **not** participate in its preparation.

    d. The auditor should report on the accompanying information only if it contains obvious material misstatements.

48. If information accompanying the basic financial statements in an auditor-submitted document has been subjected to auditing procedures, the auditor may include in the auditor's report on the financial statements an opinion that the accompanying information is fairly stated in

    a. Accordance with US generally accepted auditing standards.

    b. Conformity with US generally accepted accounting principles.

    c. All material respects in relation to the basic financial statements taken as a whole.

    d. Accordance with attestation standards expressing a conclusion about management's assertions.

49. An auditor concludes that there is a material inconsistency in the other information in an annual report to shareholders containing audited financial statements. If the auditor concludes that the financial statements do **not** require revision, but the client refuses to revise or eliminate the material inconsistency, the auditor may

    a. Revise the auditor's report to include a separate explanatory paragraph describing the material inconsistency.

    b. Issue an "except for" qualified opinion after discussing the matter with the client's board of directors.

    c. Consider the matter closed since the other information is **not** in the audited financial statements.

    d. Disclaim an opinion on the financial statements after explaining the material inconsistency in a separate explanatory paragraph.

50. When audited financial statements are presented in a client's document containing other information, the auditor should

    a. Perform inquiry and analytical procedures to ascertain whether the other information is reasonable.

    b. Add an explanatory paragraph to the auditor's report without changing the opinion on the financial statements.

    c. Perform the appropriate substantive auditing procedures to corroborate the other information.

    d. Read the other information to determine that it is consistent with the audited financial statements.

51. An auditor includes a separate paragraph in an otherwise unmodified report to emphasize that the entity being reported on had significant transactions with related parties. The inclusion of this separate paragraph
   a. Is considered an "except for" qualification of the opinion.
   b. Violates generally accepted auditing standards if this information is already disclosed in footnotes to the financial statements.
   c. Necessitates a revision of the opinion paragraph to include the phrase "with the foregoing explanation."
   d. Is appropriate and would **not** negate the unqualified opinion.

52. An auditor concludes that a client's illegal act, which has a material effect on the financial statements, has not been properly accounted for or disclosed. Depending on the materiality of the effect on the financial statements, the auditor should express either a(n)
   a. Adverse opinion or a disclaimer of opinion.
   b. Qualified opinion or an adverse opinion.
   c. Disclaimer of opinion or an unqualified opinion with a separate explanatory paragraph.
   d. Unqualified opinion with a separate explanatory paragraph or a qualified opinion.

53. Which of the following phrases would an auditor most likely include in the auditor's report when expressing a qualified opinion because of inadequate disclosure?
   a. Subject to the departure from US generally accepted accounting principles, as described above.
   b. With the foregoing explanation of these omitted disclosures.
   c. Except for the omission of the information dis-
   d. Does **not** present fairly in all material respects.

54. In which of the following circumstances would an auditor be most likely to express an adverse opinion?
   a. The chief executive officer refuses the auditor access to minutes of board of directors' meetings.
   b. Tests of controls show that the entity's internal control is so poor that it **cannot** be relied upon.
   c. The financial statements are **not** in conformity with the FASB Statements regarding the capitalization of leases.
   d. Information comes to the auditor's attention that raises substantial doubt about the entity's ability to continue as a going concern.

55. When an auditor qualifies an opinion because of inadequate disclosure, the auditor should describe the nature of the omission in a separate explanatory paragraph and modify the

	Introductory paragraph	Scope paragraph	Opinion paragraph
a.	Yes	No	No
b.	Yes	Yes	No
c.	No	Yes	Yes
d.	No	No	Yes

56. If a publicly held company issues financial statements that purport to present its financial position and results of operations but omits the statement of cash flows, the auditor ordinarily will express a(n)

   a. Disclaimer of opinion.
   b. Qualified opinion.
   c. Review report.
   d. Unqualified opinion with a separate explanatory paragraph.

57. In which of the following situations would an auditor ordinarily choose between expressing an "except for" qualified opinion or an adverse opinion?
   a. The auditor did not observe the entity's physical inventory and is unable to become satisfied as to its balance by other auditing procedures.
   b. The financial statements fail to disclose information that is required by generally accepted accounting principles.
   c. The auditor is asked to report only on the entity's balance sheet and not on the other basic financial statements.
   d. Events disclosed in the financial statements cause the auditor to have substantial doubt about the entity's ability to continue as a going concern.

58. In which of the following situations would an auditor ordinarily choose between expressing a qualified opinion or an adverse opinion?
   a. The auditor did **not** observe the entity's physical inventory and is unable to become satisfied about its balance by other auditing procedures.
   b. Conditions that cause the auditor to have substantial doubt about the entity's ability to continue as a going concern are inadequately disclosed.
   c. There has been a change in accounting principles that has a material effect on the comparability of the entity's financial statements.
   d. The auditor is unable to apply necessary procedures concerning an investor's share of an investee's earnings recognized on the equity method.

59. In the first audit of a client, an auditor was not able to gather sufficient evidence about the consistent application of accounting principles between the current and the prior year, as well as the amounts of assets or liabilities at the beginning of the current year. This was due to the client's record retention policies. If the amounts in question could materially affect current operating results, the auditor would
   a. Be unable to express an opinion on the current year's results of operations and cash flows.
   b. Express a qualified opinion on the financial statements because of a client-imposed scope limitation.
   c. Withdraw from the engagement and refuse to be associated with the financial statements.
   d. Specifically state that the financial statements are **not** comparable to the prior year due to an uncertainty.

60. In which of the following circumstances would an auditor **not** express an unqualified opinion?
   a. There has been a material change between periods in accounting principles.
   b. Quarterly financial data required by the SEC has been omitted.
   c. The auditor wishes to emphasize an unusually important subsequent event.
   d. The auditor is unable to obtain audited financial statements of a consolidated investee.

61. Due to a scope limitation, an auditor disclaimed an opinion on the financial statements taken as a whole, but the auditor's report included a statement that the current asset portion of the entity's balance sheet was fairly stated. The inclusion of this statement is
  a. Not appropriate because it may tend to over-shadow the auditor's disclaimer of opinion.
  b. Not appropriate because the auditor is prohibited from reporting on only one basic financial statement.
  c. Appropriate provided the auditor's scope paragraph adequately describes the scope limitation.
  d. Appropriate provided the statement is in a separate paragraph preceding the disclaimer of opinion paragraph.

62. Park, CPA, was engaged to audit the financial statements of Tech Co., a new client, for the year ended December 31, 2009. Park obtained sufficient audit evidence for all of Tech's financial statement items except Tech's opening inventory. Due to inadequate financial records, Park could not verify Tech's January 1, 2009 inventory balances. Park's opinion on Tech's 2009 financial statements most likely will be

	Balance sheet	Income statement
a.	Disclaimer	Disclaimer
b.	Unqualified	Disclaimer
c.	Disclaimer	Adverse
d.	Unqualified	Adverse

63. An auditor who qualifies an opinion because of an insufficiency of evidential matter should describe the limitations in an explanatory paragraph. The auditor should also refer to the limitation in the

	Scope paragraph	Opinion paragraph	Notes to the financial statements
a.	Yes	No	Yes
b.	No	Yes	No
c.	Yes	Yes	No
d.	Yes	Yes	Yes

64. Harris, CPA, has been asked to audit and report on the balance sheet of Fox Co. but not on the statements of income, retained earnings, or cash flows. Harris will have access to all information underlying the basic financial statements. Under these circumstances, Harris may
  a. Not accept the engagement because it would constitute a violation of the profession's ethical standards.
  b. Not accept the engagement because it would be tantamount to rendering a piecemeal opinion.
  c. Accept the engagement because such engagements merely involve limited reporting objectives.
  d. Accept the engagement but should disclaim an opinion because of an inability to apply the procedures considered necessary.

65. When disclaiming an opinion due to a client-imposed scope limitation, an auditor should indicate in a separate paragraph why the audit did not comply with generally accepted auditing standards. The auditor should also omit the

	Scope paragraph	Opinion paragraph
a.	No	Yes
b.	Yes	Yes
c.	No	No
d.	Yes	No

66. An auditor decides to issue a qualified opinion on an entity's financial statements because a major inadequacy in its computerized accounting records prevents the auditor from applying necessary procedures. The opinion paragraph of the auditor's report should state that the qualification pertains to
  a. A client-imposed scope limitation.
  b. A departure from generally accepted auditing standards.
  c. The possible effects on the financial statements.
  d. Inadequate disclosure of necessary information.

67. A scope limitation sufficient to preclude an unqualified opinion always will result when management
  a. Prevents the auditor from reviewing the working papers of the predecessor auditor.
  b. Engages the auditor after the year-end physical inventory is completed.
  c. Requests that certain material accounts receivable **not** be confirmed.
  d. Refuses to acknowledge its responsibility for the fair presentation of the financial statements in conformity with GAAP.

68. An auditor may **not** issue a qualified opinion when
  a. An accounting principle at variance with GAAP is used.
  b. The auditor lacks independence with respect to the audited entity.
  c. A scope limitation prevents the auditor from completing an important audit procedure.
  d. The auditor's report refers to the work of a specialist.

69. An auditor may express an opinion on an entity's accounts receivable balance even if the auditor has disclaimed an opinion on the financial statements taken as a whole provided the
  a. Report on the accounts receivable discloses the reason for the disclaimer of opinion on the financial statements.
  b. Distribution of the report on the accounts receivable is restricted to internal use only.
  c. Auditor also reports on the current asset portion of the entity's balance sheet.
  d. Report on the accounts receivable is presented separately from the disclaimer of opinion on the financial statements.

70. March, CPA, is engaged by Monday Corp., a client, to audit the financial statements of Wall Corp., a company that is not March's client. Monday expects to present Wall's audited financial statements with March's auditor's report to 1st Federal Bank to obtain financing in Monday's attempt to purchase Wall. In these circumstances, March's auditor's report would usually be addressed to
  a. Monday Corp., the client that engaged March.
  b. Wall Corp., the entity audited by March.
  c. 1st Federal Bank.
  d. Both Monday Corp. and 1st Federal Bank.

71. When an auditor expresses an adverse opinion, the opinion paragraph should include
  a. The principal effects of the departure from generally accepted accounting principles.

b. A direct reference to a separate paragraph disclosing the basis for the opinion.
c. The substantive reasons for the financial statements being misleading.
d. A description of the uncertainty or scope limitation that prevents an unqualified opinion.

72. An auditor should disclose the substantive reasons for expressing an adverse opinion in an explanatory paragraph
a. Preceding the scope paragraph.
b. Preceding the opinion paragraph.
c. Following the opinion paragraph.
d. Within the notes to the financial statements.

73. When an independent CPA assists in preparing the financial statements of a publicly held entity, but has **not** audited or reviewed them, the CPA should issue a disclaimer of opinion. In such situations, the CPA has **no** responsibility to apply any procedures beyond
a. Documenting that internal control is **not** being relied on.
b. Reading the financial statements for obvious material misstatements.
c. Ascertaining whether the financial statements are in conformity with GAAP.
d. Determining whether management has elected to omit substantially all required disclosures.

74. When an independent CPA is associated with the financial statements of a publicly held entity but has **not** audited or reviewed such statements, the appropriate form of report to be issued must include a(n)
a. Regulation S-X exemption.
b. Report on pro forma financial statements.
c. Unaudited association report.
d. Disclaimer of opinion.

75. Green, CPA, is aware that Green's name is to be included in the interim report of National Company, a publicly held entity. National's quarterly financial statements are contained in the interim report. Green has not audited or reviewed these interim financial statements. Green should request that

I. Green's name not be included in the communication.
II. The financial statements be marked as unaudited with a notation that **no** opinion is expressed on them.

a. I only.
b. II only.
c. Both I and II.
d. Either I or II.

76. While performing a compilation of financial statements, information indicating that the entity whose information is being compiled may lack the ability to continue as a going concern has come to the accountant's attention. The client agrees that such a situation does exist, but refuses to add disclosures relating to it. What effect is this most likely to have on the accountant's review report?
a. No effect, a standard unqualified report is appropriate.
b. The report should indicate a departure from generally accepted accounting principles, with modification of the report's third paragraph and addition of an explanatory paragraph.

c. An adverse opinion should be issued, with modification of the opinion paragraph and addition of an explanatory paragraph.
d. A qualified opinion should be issued, with modification of the opinion paragraph and addition of an explanatory paragraph.

77. When compiled financial statements are accompanied by an accountant's report, that report should state that
a. A compilation includes assessing the accounting principles used and significant management estimates, as well as evaluating the overall financial statement presentation.
b. The accountant compiled the financial statements in accordance with Statements on Standards for Accounting and Review Services.
c. A compilation is substantially less in scope than an audit in accordance with GAAS, the objective of which is the expression of an opinion.
d. The accountant is not aware of any material modifications that should be made to the financial statements to conform with GAAP.

78. Miller, CPA, is engaged to compile the financial statements of Web Co., a nonissuer (nonpublic) entity, in conformity with the income tax basis of accounting. If Web's financial statements do **not** disclose the basis of accounting used, Miller should
a. Disclose the basis of accounting in the accountant's compilation report.
b. Clearly label each page "Distribution Restricted— Material Modifications Required."
c. Issue a special report describing the effect of the incomplete presentation.
d. Withdraw from the engagement and provide **no** further services to Web.

79. When an accountant is engaged to compile a nonissuer's financial statements that omit substantially all disclosures required by GAAP, the accountant should indicate in the compilation report that the financial statements are
a. Not designed for those who are uninformed about the omitted disclosures.
b. Prepared in conformity with a comprehensive basis of accounting other than GAAP.
c. Not compiled in accordance with Statements on Standards for Accounting and Review Services.
d. Special-purpose financial statements that are **not** comparable to those of prior periods.

80. An accountant may compile a nonissuer's financial statements that omit all of the disclosures required by GAAP only if the omission is

I. Clearly indicated in the accountant's report.
II. Not undertaken with the intention of misleading the financial statement users.

a. I only.
b. II only.
c. Both I and II.
d. Either I or II.

81. When unaudited financial statements of a nonissuer are presented in comparative form with audited financial statements in the subsequent year, the unaudited financial statements should be clearly marked to indicate their status and

I. The report on the unaudited financial statements should be reissued.

II. The report on the audited financial statements should include a separate paragraph describing the responsibility assumed for the unaudited financial statements.

    a.   I only.
    b.   II only.
    c.   Both I and II.
    d.   Either I or II.

82. Clark, CPA, compiled and properly reported on the financial statements of Green Co., a nonissuer, for the year ended March 31, 2008. These financial statements omitted substantially all disclosures required by generally accepted accounting principles (GAAP). Green asked Clark to compile the statements for the year ended March 31, 2009, and to include all GAAP disclosures for the 2009 statements only, but otherwise present both years' financial statements in comparative form. What is Clark's responsibility concerning the proposed engagement?

    a.   Clark may **not** report on the comparative financial statements because the 2008 statements are **not** comparable to the 2009 statements that include the GAAP disclosures.
    b.   Clark may report on the comparative financial statements provided the 2009 statements do **not** contain any obvious material misstatements.
    c.   Clark may report on the comparative financial statements provided an explanatory paragraph is added to Clark's report on the comparative financial statements.
    d.   Clark may report on the comparative financial statements provided Clark updates the report on the 2008 statements that do **not** include the GAAP disclosures.

83. Which of the following statements should **not** be included in an accountant's standard report based on the compilation of an entity's financial statements?

    a.   A statement that the compilation was performed in accordance with standards established by the American Institute of CPAs.
    b.   A statement that the accountant has **not** audited or reviewed the financial statements.
    c.   A statement that the accountant does **not** express an opinion but expresses only limited assurance on the financial statements.
    d.   A statement that a compilation is limited to presenting, in the form of financial statements, information that is the representation of management.

84. How does an accountant make the following representations when issuing the standard report for the compilation of a nonissuer's financial statements?

	The financial statements have not been audited	The accountant has compiled the financial statements
a.	Implicitly	Implicitly
b.	Explicitly	Explicitly
c.	Implicitly	Explicitly
d.	Explicitly	Implicitly

85. An accountant's compilation report should be dated as of the date of

    a.   Completion of fieldwork.
    b.   Completion of the compilation.

    c.   Transmittal of the compilation report.
    d.   The latest subsequent event referred to in the notes to the financial statements.

86. An accountant has compiled the financial statements of a nonissuer in accordance with Statements on Standards for Accounting and Review Services (SSARS). Does SSARS require that the compilation report be printed on the accountant's letterhead and that the report be manually signed by the accountant?

	Printed on the accountant's letterhead	Manually signed by the accountant
a.	Yes	Yes
b.	Yes	No
c.	No	Yes
d.	No	No

87. Which of the following is correct relating to compiled financial statements when third-party reliance upon those statements is anticipated?

    a.   A compilation report must be issued.
    b.   Omission of note disclosures is unacceptable.
    c.   A written engagement letter is required.
    d.   Each page of the financial statements should have a restriction such as "Restricted for Management's Use Only."

88. Which communication option(s) may be used when an accountant submits compiled financial statements to be used only by management?

	Compilation report	Written engagement letter
a.	Yes	Yes
b.	Yes	No
c.	No	Yes
d.	No	No

89. A compilation report is **not** required when compiled financial statements are expected to be used by

    a.   Management only.
    b.   Management and third parties.
    c.   Third parties only.
    d.   A compilation report is required whenever financial statements are compiled.

90. In reviewing the financial statements of a nonissuer, an accountant is required to modify the standard report for which of the following matters?

	Inability to assess the risk of material misstatement due to fraud	Discovery of significant deficiencies in the design of the entity's internal control
a.	Yes	Yes
b.	Yes	No
c.	No	Yes
d.	No	No

91. Moore, CPA, has been asked to issue a review report on the balance sheet of Dover Co., a nonissuer. Moore will not be reporting on Dover's statements of income, retained earnings, and cash flows. Moore may issue the review report provided the

    a.   Balance sheet is presented in a prescribed form of an industry trade association.
    b.   Scope of the inquiry and analytical procedures has not been restricted.
    c.   Balance sheet is not to be used to obtain credit or distributed to creditors.

d.   Specialized accounting principles and practices of Dover's industry are disclosed.

92. Baker, CPA, was engaged to review the financial statements of Hall Co., a nonissuer. During the engagement Baker uncovered a complex scheme involving client illegal acts that materially affect Hall's financial statements. If Baker believes that modification of the standard review report is **not** adequate to indicate the deficiencies in the financial statements, Baker should

a.   Disclaim an opinion.
b.   Issue an adverse opinion.
c.   Withdraw from the engagement.
d.   Issue a qualified opinion.

93. Each page of a nonissuer's financial statements reviewed by an accountant should include the following reference:

a.   See Accompanying Accountant's Footnotes.
b.   Reviewed, No Material Modifications Required.
c.   See Accountant's Review Report.
d.   Reviewed, No Accountant's Assurance Expressed.

94. Financial statements of a nonissuer that have been reviewed by an accountant should be accompanied by a report stating that a review

a.   Provides only limited assurance that the financial statements are fairly presented.
b.   Includes examining, on a test basis, information that is the representation of management.
c.   Consists principally of inquiries of company personnel and analytical procedures applied to financial data.
d.   Does **not** contemplate obtaining corroborating evidential matter or applying certain other procedures ordinarily performed during an audit.

95. An accountant who had begun an audit of the financial statements of a nonissuer was asked to change the engagement to a review because of a restriction on the scope of the audit. If there is reasonable justification for the change, the accountant's review report should include reference to the

	Scope limitation that caused the changed engagement	Original engagement that was agreed to
a.	Yes	No
b.	No	Yes
c.	No	No
d.	Yes	Yes

96. Gole, CPA, is engaged to review the 20X8 financial statements of North Co., a nonissuer. Previously, Gole audited North's 20X7 financial statements and expressed an unqualified opinion. Gole decides to include a separate paragraph in the 20X8 review report because North plans to present comparative financial statements for 20X8 and 20X7. This separate paragraph should indicate that

a.   The 20X8 review report is intended solely for the information of management and the board of directors.
b.   The 20X7 auditor's report may **no** longer be relied on.
c.   No auditing procedures were performed after the date of the 20X7 auditor's report.

d.   There are justifiable reasons for changing the level of service from an audit to a review.

97. An accountant's standard report on a review of the financial statements of a nonissuer should state that the accountant

a.   Does **not** express an opinion or any form of limited assurance on the financial statements.
b.   Is **not** aware of any material modifications that should be made to the financial statements for them to conform with GAAP.
c.   Obtained reasonable assurance about whether the financial statements are free of material misstatement.
d.   Examined evidence, on a test basis, supporting the amounts and disclosures in the financial statements.

98. Financial statements of a nonissuer that have been reviewed by an accountant should be accompanied by a report stating that

a.   The scope of the inquiry and analytical procedures performed by the accountant has not been restricted.
b.   All information included in the financial statements is the representation of the management of the entity.
c.   A review includes examining, on a test basis, evidence supporting the amounts and disclosures in the financial statements.
d.   A review is greater in scope than a compilation, the objective of which is to present financial statements that are free of material misstatements.

99. During a review of the financial statements of a nonissuer, an accountant becomes aware of a lack of adequate disclosure that is material to the financial statements. If management refuses to correct the financial statement presentations, the accountant should

a.   Issue an adverse opinion.
b.   Issue an "except for" qualified opinion.
c.   Disclose this departure from generally accepted accounting principles in a separate paragraph of the report.
d.   Express only limited assurance on the financial statement presentations.

100. An accountant who reviews the financial statements of a nonissuer should issue a report stating that a review

a.   Is substantially less in scope than an audit.
b.   Provides negative assurance that internal control is functioning as designed.
c.   Provides only limited assurance that the financial statements are fairly presented.
d.   Is substantially more in scope than a compilation.

101. The objective of a review of interim financial information of a public entity (issuer) is to provide an accountant with a basis for reporting whether

a.   Material modifications should be made to conform with generally accepted accounting principles.
b.   A reasonable basis exists for expressing an updated opinion regarding the financial statements that were previously audited.

   c. Condensed financial statements or pro forma financial information should be included in a registration statement.

   d. The financial statements are presented fairly in accordance with generally accepted accounting principles.

102. An independent accountant's report is based on a review of interim financial information. If this report is presented in a registration statement, a prospectus should include a statement clarifying that the

   a. Accountant's review report is **not** a part of the registration statement within the meaning of the Securities Act of 1933.

   b. Accountant assumes **no** responsibility to update the report for events and circumstances occurring after the date of the report.

   c. Accountant's review was performed in accordance with standards established by the Securities and Exchange Commission.

   d. Accountant obtained corroborating evidence to determine whether material modifications are needed for such information to conform with GAAP.

103. A modification of the CPA's report on a review of the interim financial statements of a publicly held company would be necessitated by which of the following?

   a. An uncertainty.

   b. Lack of consistency.

   c. Reference to another accountant.

   d. Inadequate disclosure.

104. Which of the following procedures ordinarily should be applied when an independent accountant conducts a review of interim financial information of a publicly held entity?

   a. Verify changes in key account balances.

   b. Read the minutes of the board of directors' meetings.

   c. Inspect the open purchase order file.

   d. Perform cut-off tests for cash receipts and disbursements.

105. Which of the following is **least** likely to be a procedure included in an accountant's review of interim financial information of a public entity?

   a. Compare disaggregated revenue data by month to that of the previous interim period.

   b. Read available minutes of meetings of stockholders.

   c. Observe counting of physical inventory.

   d. Inquire of management concerning significant journal entries and other adjustments.

106. An accountant's review report on interim financial information of a public entity is most likely to include a

   a. Statement that the interim financial information was examined in accordance with standards of the Public Company Accounting Oversight Board.

   b. Statement that the interim financial information is the responsibility of the entity's shareholders.

   c. Description of the procedures for a review.

   d. Statement that a review of interim financial information is less in scope than a compilation conducted in accordance with AICPA standards.

107. An auditor may report on condensed financial statements that are derived from complete financial statements if the

   a. Condensed financial statements are distributed to stockholders along with the complete financial statements.

   b. Auditor described the additional procedures performed on the condensed financial statements.

   c. Auditor indicates whether the information in the condensed financial statements is fairly stated in all material respects in relation to the complete financial statements from which it has been derived.

   d. Condensed financial statements are presented in comparative form with the prior year's condensed financial statements.

108. An auditor is engaged to report on selected financial data that are included in a client-prepared document containing audited financial statements. Under these circumstances, the report on the selected data should

   a. Be limited to data derived from the audited financial statements.

   b. Be distributed only to senior management and the board of directors.

   c. State that the presentation is a comprehensive basis of accounting other than GAAP.

   d. Indicate that the data are **not** fairly stated in all material respects.

109. Before reporting on the financial statements of a US entity that have been prepared in conformity with another country's accounting principles, an auditor practicing in the US should

   a. Understand the accounting principles generally accepted in the other country.

   b. Be certified by the appropriate auditing or accountancy board of the other country.

   c. Notify management that the auditor is required to disclaim an opinion on the financial statements.

   d. Receive a waiver from the auditor's state board of accountancy to perform the engagement.

110. The financial statements of KCP America, a US entity, are prepared for inclusion in the consolidated financial statements of its non-US parent. These financial statements are prepared in conformity with the accounting principles generally accepted in the parent's country and are for use only in that country. How may KCP America's auditor report on these financial statements?

  I. A US style report (unqualified).

  II. A US-style report modified to report on the accounting principles of the parent's country.

  III. The report form of the parent's country.

	I	*II*	*III*
a.	Yes	No	No
b.	No	Yes	No
c.	Yes	No	Yes
d.	No	Yes	Yes

111. Field is an employee of Gold Enterprises. Hardy, CPA, is asked to express an opinion on Field's profit participation in Gold's net income. Hardy may accept this engagement only if

   a. Hardy also audits Gold's complete financial statements.

b.   Gold's financial statements are prepared in conformity with GAAP.
c.   Hardy's report is available for distribution to Gold's other employees.
d.   Field owns controlling interest in Gold.

112. When an auditor reports on financial statements prepared on an entity's income tax basis, the auditor's report should
a.   Disclaim an opinion on whether the statements were examined in accordance with generally accepted auditing standards.
b.   Not express an opinion on whether the statements are presented in conformity with the comprehensive basis of accounting used.
c.   Include an explanation of how the results of operations differ from the cash receipts and disbursements basis of accounting.
d.   State that the basis of presentation is a comprehensive basis of accounting other than GAAP.

113. Helpful Co., a nonprofit entity, prepared its financial statements on an accounting basis prescribed by a regulatory agency solely for filing with that agency. Green audited the financial statements in accordance with generally accepted auditing standards and concluded that the financial statements were fairly presented on the prescribed basis. Green should issue a
a.   Qualified opinion.
b.   Standard three-paragraph report with reference to footnote disclosure.
c.   Disclaimer of opinion.
d.   Special report.

114. An auditor's special report on financial statements prepared in conformity with the cash basis of accounting should include a separate explanatory paragraph before the opinion paragraph that
a.   Justifies the reasons for departing from generally accepted accounting principles.
b.   States whether the financial statements are fairly presented in conformity with another comprehensive basis of accounting.
c.   Refers to the note to the financial statements that describes the basis of accounting.
d.   Explains how the results of operations differ from financial statements prepared in conformity with generally accepted accounting principles.

115. An auditor's report would be designated a special report when it is issued in connection with
a.   Interim financial information of a publicly held company that is subject to a limited review.
b.   Compliance with aspects of regulatory requirements related to audited financial statements.
c.   Application of accounting principles to specified transactions.
d.   Limited use prospective financial statements such as a financial projection.

116. Delta Life Insurance Co. prepares its financial statements on an accounting basis insurance companies use pursuant to the rules of a state insurance commission. If Wall, CPA, Delta's auditor, discovers that the statements are **not** suitably titled, Wall should

a.   Disclose any reservations in an explanatory paragraph and qualify the opinion.
b.   Apply to the state insurance commission for an advisory opinion.
c.   Issue a special statutory basis report that clearly disclaims any opinion.
d.   Explain in the notes to the financial statements the terminology used.

117. A CPA is permitted to accept a separate engagement (**not** in conjunction with an audit of financial statements) to audit an entity's

	Schedule of accounts receivable	Schedule of royalties
a.	Yes	Yes
b.	Yes	No
c.	No	Yes
d.	No	No

118. Financial information is presented in a printed form that prescribes the wording of the independent auditor's report. The form is not acceptable to the auditor because the form calls for statements that are inconsistent with the auditor's responsibility. Under these circumstances, the auditor most likely would
a.   Withdraw from the engagement.
b.   Reword the form or attach a separate report.
c.   Express a qualified opinion with an explanation.
d.   Limit distribution of the report to the party who designed the form.

119. A registration statement filed with the SEC contains the reports of two independent auditors on their audits of financial statements for different periods. The predecessor auditor who audited the prior period financial statements generally should obtain a letter of representation from the
b.   Client's audit committee.
c.   Principal underwriter.
d.   Securities and Exchange Commission.

120. Which of the following statements is correct concerning letters for underwriters, commonly referred to as comfort letters?
a.   Letters for underwriters are required by the Securities Act of 1933 for the initial public sale of registered securities.
b.   Letters for underwriters typically give negative assurance on unaudited interim financial information.
c.   Letters for underwriters usually are included in the registration statement accompanying a prospectus.
d.   Letters for underwriters ordinarily update auditors' opinions on the prior year's financial statements.

121. Comfort letters ordinarily are signed by the client's
a.   Independent auditor.
b.   Underwriter of securities.
c.   Audit committee.
d.   Senior management.

122. Comfort letters ordinarily are addressed to
a.   Creditor financial institutions.
b.   The client's audit committee.
c.   The Securities and Exchange Commission.
d.   Underwriters of securities.

123. When an accountant issues to an underwriter a comfort letter containing comments on data that have **not** been audited, the underwriter most likely will receive

    a. Negative assurance on capsule information.
    b. Positive assurance on supplementary disclosures.
    c. A limited opinion on pro forma financial statements.
    d. A disclaimer on prospective financial statements.

124. When an independent audit report is incorporated by reference in a SEC registration statement, a prospectus that includes a statement about the independent accountant's involvement should refer to the independent accountant as

    a. Auditor of the financial reports.
    b. Management's designate before the SEC.
    c. Certified preparer of the report.
    d. Expert in auditing and accounting.

125. Which of the following matters is covered in a typical comfort letter?

    a. Negative assurance concerning whether the entity's internal control procedures operated as designed during the period being audited.
    b. An opinion regarding whether the entity complied with laws and regulations under Government Auditing Standards and the Single Audit Act of 1984.
    c. Positive assurance concerning whether unaudited condensed financial information complied with generally accepted accounting principles.
    d. An opinion as to whether the audited financial statements comply in form with the accounting requirements of the SEC.

126. When unaudited financial statements are presented in comparative form with audited financial statements in a document filed with the Securities and Exchange Commission, such statements should be

	Marked as "unaudited"	Withheld until audited	Referred to in the auditor's report
a.	Yes	No	No
b.	Yes	No	Yes
c.	No	Yes	Yes
d.	No	Yes	No

127. In connection with a proposal to obtain a new audit client, a CPA in public practice is asked to prepare a report on the application of accounting principles to a specific transaction. The CPA's report should include a statement that

    a. The engagement was performed in accordance with Statements on Standards for Accounting and Review Services.
    b. Responsibility for the proper accounting treatment rests with the preparers of the financial statements.
    c. The evaluation of the application of accounting principles is hypothetical and may **not** be used for opinion-shopping.
    d. The guidance is provided for management's use only and may **not** be communicated to the prior or continuing auditor.

128. In connection with a proposal to obtain a new client, an accountant in public practice is asked to prepare a written report on the application of accounting principles to a specific transaction. The accountant's report should include a statement that

    a. Any difference in the facts, circumstances, or assumptions presented may change the report.
    b. The engagement was performed in accordance with Statements on Standards for Consulting Services.
    c. The guidance provided is for management use only and may **not** be communicated to the prior or continuing auditors.
    d. Nothing came to the accountant's attention that caused the accountant to believe that the accounting principles violated GAAP.

129. Blue, CPA, has been asked to render an opinion on the application of accounting principles to a specific transaction by an entity that is audited by another CPA. Blue may accept this engagement, but should

    a. Consult with the continuing CPA to obtain information relevant to the transaction.
    b. Report the engagement's findings to the entity's audit committee, the continuing CPA, and management.
    c. Disclaim any opinion that the hypothetical application of accounting principles conforms with generally accepted accounting principles.
    d. Notify the entity that the report is for the restricted use of management and outside parties who are aware of all relevant facts.

130. Which of the following statements is **not** included in an accountant's report on the application of accounting principles?

    a. The engagement was performed following standards established by the American Institute of Certified Public Accountants.
    b. The report is based on a hypothetical transaction not involving facts or circumstances of this particular entity.
    c. The report is intended solely for the information and use of specified parties.
    d. Responsibility for the proper accounting treatment rests with the preparers of the financial statements.

131. Which of the following services would be most likely to be structured as an attest engagement?

    a. Advocating a client's position in tax matter.
    b. A consulting engagement to develop a new database system for the revenue cycle.
    c. An engagement to issue a report addressing an entity's compliance with requirements of specified laws.
    d. The compilation of a client's forecast information.

132. A practitioner is issuing a standard unqualified examination report under the attestation standards. The CPA's conclusion may be on

	Subject matter	Management's written assertion
a.	Yes	Yes
b.	Yes	No
c.	No	Yes
d.	No	No

133. Conditions exist that result in a material deviation from the criteria against which the subject matter was evaluated during an examination. The CPA's conclusion may be on

	Subject matter	Written assertion
a.	Yes	Yes
b.	Yes	No
c.	No	Yes
d.	No	No

134. When performing an attestation engagement, which of the following is **least** likely to be present?
   a. Assertion.
   b. Practitioner independence.
   c. Subject matter.
   d. Suitable criteria.

135. Suitable criteria in an attestation engagement may be available

	Publicly	In CPA's report
a.	Yes	Yes
b.	Yes	No
c.	No	Yes
d.	No	No

136. Which of the following is **least** likely to result in a restricted use attest report?
   a. Criteria suitable only for a limited number of parties.
   b. Subject matter available only to specified parties.
   c. A written assertion has not been obtained.
   d. Criteria developed by an industry association.

137. Which of the following is **least** likely to be included in an agreed-upon procedures attestation engagement report?
   a. The specified party takes responsibility for the sufficiency of procedures.
   b. Use of the report is restricted.
   c. Limited assurance on ...
   d. A summary of procedures performed.

138. A summary of findings rather than assurance is most likely to be included in
   a. Agreed-upon procedures report.
   b. Compilation report.
   c. Examination report.
   d. Review report.

139. Which of the following is **not** correct concerning "specified parties" of an agreed-upon procedures report under either the auditing or attestation standards?
   a. They must agree on the procedures to be performed.
   b. They must take responsibility for the adequacy of the procedures performed.
   c. They must sign an engagement letter.
   d. After completion of the engagement, another party may be added as a specified user.

140. When an accountant examines projected financial statements, the accountant's report should include a separate paragraph that
   a. Describes the limitations on the usefulness of the presentation.
   b. Provides an explanation of the differences between an examination and an audit.
   c. States that the accountant is responsible for events and circumstances up to one year after the report's date.

   d. Disclaims an opinion on whether the assumptions provide a reasonable basis for the projection.

141. An accountant's compilation report on a financial forecast should include a statement that
   a. The forecast should be read only in conjunction with the audited historical financial statements.
   b. The accountant expresses only limited assurance on the forecasted statements and their assumptions.
   c. There will usually be differences between the forecasted and actual results.
   d. The hypothetical assumptions used in the forecast are reasonable in the circumstances.

142. Accepting an engagement to examine an entity's financial projection most likely would be appropriate if the projection were to be distributed to
   a. All employees who work for the entity.
   b. Potential stockholders who request a prospectus or a registration statement.
   c. A bank with which the entity is negotiating for a loan.
   d. All stockholders of record as of the report date.

143. A CPA in public practice is required to comply with the provisions of the Statements on Standards for Attestation Engagements (SSAE) when

	Testifying as an expert witness in accounting and auditing matters given stipulated facts	Compiling a client's financial projection that presents a hypothetical course of action
a.	Yes	Yes
b.	Yes	No
c.	No	Yes
d.	No	No

144. An accountant's compilation ... forecast should include a statement that the
   a. Compilation does **not** include evaluation of the support of the assumptions underlying the forecast.
   b. Hypothetical assumptions used in the forecast are reasonable.
   c. Range of assumptions selected is one in which one end of the range is less likely to occur than the other.
   d. Prospective statements are limited to presenting, in the form of a forecast, information that is the accountant's representation.

145. Which of the following is a prospective financial statement for general use upon which an accountant may appropriately report?
   a. Financial projection.
   b. Partial presentation.
   c. Pro forma financial statement.
   d. Financial forecast.

146. Given one or more hypothetical assumptions, a responsible party may prepare, to the best of its knowledge and belief, an entity's expected financial position, results of operations, and changes in financial position. Such prospective financial statements are known as
   a. Pro forma financial statements.
   b. Financial projections.
   c. Partial presentations.
   d. Financial forecasts.

147. An accountant may accept an engagement to apply agreed-upon procedures to prospective financial statements provided that
   a. The prospective financial statements are also examined.
   b. Responsibility for the adequacy of the procedures performed is taken by the accountant.
   c. Negative assurance is expressed on the prospective financial statements taken as a whole.
   d. Distribution of the report is restricted to the specified parties.

148. When an accountant examines a financial forecast that fails to disclose several significant assumptions used to prepare the forecast, the accountant should describe the assumptions in the accountant's report and issue a(n)
   a. "Except for" qualified opinion.
   b. "Subject to" qualified opinion.
   c. Unqualified opinion with a separate explanatory paragraph.
   d. Adverse opinion.

149. An accountant's report on a review of pro forma financial information should include a
   a. Statement that the entity's internal control was not relied on in the review.
   b. Disclaimer of opinion on the financial statements from which the pro forma financial information is derived.
   c. Caveat that it is uncertain whether the transaction or event reflected in the pro forma financial information will ever occur.
   d. Reference to the financial statements from which the historical financial information is derived.

150. Which of the following is **not** an objective of a CPA's examination of a client's management discussion and analysis (MD&A) prepared pursuant to Securities and Exchange Commission rules and regulations?
   a. The historical amounts have been accurately derived, in all material respects, from the entity's financial statements.
   b. The presentation is in conformity with rules and regulations adopted by the Securities and Exchange Commission.
   c. The underlying information, determinations, estimates and assumptions of the entity provide a reasonable basis for the disclosures contained herein.
   d. The presentation includes the required elements of MD&A.

151. Which of the following is an assertion embodied in management's discussion and analysis (MD&A)?
   a. Valuation.
   b. Reliability.
   c. Consistency with the financial statements.
   d. Rights and obligations.

152. Which of the following statements is correct relating to an auditor's review engagements on an entity's management discussion and analysis (MD&A)?
   a. A review consists principally of applying analytical procedures and search and verification procedures.
   b. The review report of a public entity should be restricted to the use of specified parties.

   c. No consideration of internal control is necessary.
   d. The report issued will ordinarily include a summary of findings, but no negative assurance.

153. Which of the following is a term for an attest engagement in which a CPA assesses a client's commercial Internet site for predefined criteria such as those over online privacy?
   a. ElectroNet.
   b. EDIFACT.
   c. TechSafe.
   d. WebTrust.

154. Trust Service engagements are performed under the provisions of
   a. Statements on Assurance Standards.
   b. Statements on Standards for Attestation Engagements.
   c. Statements on Standards for Trust Engagements
   d. Statements on Auditing Standards.

155. The WebTrust seal of assurance relates most directly to
   a. Financial statements maintained on the Internet.
   b. Health care facilities.
   c. Risk assurance procedures.
   d. Web sites.

156. A CPA's examination report relating to a WebTrust engagement is most likely to include
   a. An opinion on whether the site is "hackproof."
   b. An opinion on whether the site meets the WebTrust criteria.
   c. Negative assurance on whether the site is electronically secure.
   d. No opinion or other assurance, but a summary of findings relating to the Web site.

157. An engagement in which a CPA considers security, availability, processing integrity, online privacy, and/or confidentiality over any type of defined electronic system is most likely to considered which of the following types of engagements?
   a. Internal control over financial reporting.
   b. SysTrust.
   c. Web siteAssociate.
   d. WebTrust.

158. A client's refusal to provide a written assertion in a Trust Services engagement is most likely to result in which of the following types of opinions?
   a. Adverse.
   b. Disclaimer.
   c. Qualified.
   d. Unqualified with explanatory language.

159. Which of the following types of engagements is **not** permitted under the professional standards for reporting on an entity's compliance?
   a. Agreed-upon procedures on compliance with the specified requirements of a law.
   b. Agreed-upon procedures on the effectiveness of internal control over compliance with a law.
   c. Review on compliance with specified requirements of a law.
   d. Examination on compliance with specified requirements of a law.

160. Mill, CPA, was engaged by a group of royalty recipients to apply agreed-upon procedures to financial data supplied by Modern Co. regarding Modern's written assertion about its compliance with contractual requirements to pay royalties. Mill's report on these agreed-upon procedures should contain a(n)

   a. Disclaimer of opinion about the fair presentation of Modern's financial statements.

   b. List of the procedures performed (or reference thereto) and Mill's findings.

   c. Opinion about the effectiveness of Modern's internal control activities concerning royalty payments.

   d. Acknowledgment that the sufficiency of the procedures is solely Mill's responsibility.

161. A CPA's report on agreed-upon procedures related to an entity's compliance with specified requirements should contain

   a. A statement of limitations on the use of the report.

   b. An opinion about whether management's assertion is fairly stated.

   c. Negative assurance that control risk has not been assessed.

   d. An acknowledgment of responsibility for the sufficiency of the procedures.

162. When reporting on an examination of a company's compliance with requirements of specified laws, the practitioner has identified an instance of material noncompliance. Management has agreed to include this instance in its written assertion. The examination report should include

   a. No modification from the standard form.

   b. An opinion paragraph that is unqualified, and an explanatory paragraph.

   c. A qualified or adverse opinion.

   d. A disclaimer of opinion.

163. In auditing a not-for-profit entity that receives governmental financial assistance, the auditor has a responsibility to

   a. Issue a separate report that describes the expected benefits and related costs of the auditor's suggested changes to the entity's internal control.

   b. Assess whether management has identified laws and regulations that have a direct and material effect on the entity's financial statements.

   c. Notify the governmental agency providing the financial assistance that the audit is **not** designed to provide any assurance of detecting misstatements and fraud.

   d. Render an opinion concerning the entity's continued eligibility for the governmental financial assistance.

164. Hill, CPA, is auditing the financial statements of Helping Hand, a not-for-profit organization that receives financial assistance from governmental agencies. To detect misstatements in Helping Hand's financial statements resulting from violations of laws and regulations, Hill should focus on violations that

   a. Could result in criminal prosecution against the organization.

   b. Involve significant deficiencies to be communicated to the organization's trustees and the funding agencies.

   c. Have a direct and material effect on the amounts in the organization's financial statements.

   d. Demonstrate the existence of material weaknesses.

165. A governmental audit may extend beyond an examination leading to the expression of an opinion on the fairness of financial presentation to include

	Program results	Compliance	Economy & efficiency
a.	Yes	Yes	No
b.	Yes	Yes	Yes
c.	No	Yes	Yes
d.	Yes	No	Yes

166. When auditing an entity's financial statements in accordance with Government Auditing Standards (the "yellow book"), an auditor is required to report on

  I. Noteworthy accomplishments of the program.

  II. The scope of the auditor's testing of internal controls.

   a. I only.

   b. II only.

   c. Both I and II.

   d. Neither I nor II.

167. When auditing an entity's financial statements in accordance with Government Auditing Standards (the "yellow book"), an auditor is required to report on

  I. Recommendations for actions to improve operations.

  II. The scope of the auditor's tests of compliance with laws and regulations.

   a. I only.

   b. II only.

   c. Both I and II.

   d. Neither I nor II.

168. Which of the following statements is a standard applicable to financial statement audits in accordance with Government Auditing Standards (the "yellow book")?

   a. An auditor should report on the scope of the auditor's testing of compliance with laws and regulations.

   b. An auditor should assess whether the entity has reportable measures of economy and efficiency that are valid and reliable.

   c. An auditor should report recommendations for actions to correct problems and improve operations.

   d. An auditor should determine the extent to which the entity's programs achieve the desired results.

169. Which of the following statements is a standard applicable to financial statement audits in accordance with Government Auditing Standards (the "yellow book")?

   a. An auditor should report on the scope of the auditor's testing of internal controls.

   b. All instances of abuse, waste, and mismanagement should be reported to the audit committee.

   c. An auditor should report the views of responsible officials concerning the auditor's findings.

   d. Internal control activities designed to detect or prevent fraud should be reported to the inspector general.

170. In reporting under Government Auditing Standards, an auditor most likely would be required to report a falsification of accounting records directly to a federal inspector general when the falsification is

    a.   Discovered after the auditor's report has been made available to the federal inspector general and to the public.

    b.   Reported by the auditor to the audit committee as a significant deficiency in internal control.

    c.   Voluntarily disclosed to the auditor by low-level personnel as a result of the auditor's inquiries.

    d.   Communicated by the auditor to the auditee and the auditee fails to make a required report of the matter.

171. Although the scope of audits of recipients of federal financial assistance in accordance with federal audit regulations varies, these audits generally have which of the following elements in common?

    a.   The auditor is to determine whether the federal financial assistance has been administered in accordance with applicable laws and regulations.

    b.   The materiality levels are lower and are determined by the government entities that provided the federal financial assistance to the recipient.

    c.   The auditor should obtain written management representations that the recipient's internal auditors will report their findings objectively without fear of political repercussion.

    d.   The auditor is required to express both positive and negative assurance that illegal acts that could have a material effect on the recipient's financial statements are disclosed to the inspector general.

172. An auditor most likely would be responsible for communicating significant deficiencies in the design of internal control

    a.   To the Securities and Exchange Commission when the client is a publicly held entity.

    b.   To specific legislative and regulatory bodies when reporting under Government Auditing Standards.

    c.   To a court-appointed creditors' committee when the client is operating under Chapter 11 of the Federal Bankruptcy Code.

    d.   To shareholders with significant influence (more than 20% equity ownership) when significant deficiencies are deemed to be material weaknesses.

173. Wolf is auditing an entity's compliance with requirements governing a major federal financial assistance program in accordance with Government Auditing Standards. Wolf detected noncompliance with requirements that have a material effect on the program. Wolf's report on compliance should express

    a.   No assurance on the compliance tests.

    b.   Reasonable assurance on the compliance tests.

    c.   A qualified or adverse opinion.

    d.   An adverse or disclaimer of opinion.

174. Which of the following is a specific documentation requirement that an auditor should follow when auditing in accordance with Government Auditing Standards?

    a.   The auditor should obtain written representations from management acknowledging responsibility for correcting instances of fraud, abuse, and waste.

    b.   Before the report is issued, evidence of supervisory review of the audit.

    c.   The auditor should document the procedures that assure discovery of all illegal acts and contingent liabilities resulting from noncompliance.

    d.   The auditor's working papers should contain a caveat that all instances of material misstatements and fraud may **not** be identified.

175. In performing a financial statement audit in accordance with Government Auditing Standards, an auditor is required to report on the entity's compliance with laws and regulations. This report should

    a.   State that compliance with laws and regulations is the responsibility of the entity's management.

    b.   Describe the laws and regulations that the entity must comply with.

    c.   Provide an opinion on overall compliance with laws and regulations.

    d.   Indicate that the auditor does **not** possess legal skills and **cannot** make legal judgments.

176. In reporting under Government Auditing Standards, an auditor most likely would be required to communicate management's misappropriation of assets directly to a federal inspector general when the fraudulent activities are

    a.   Concealed by management by circumventing specific internal controls designed to safeguard those assets.

    b.   Reported to the entity's governing body and the governing body fails to make a required report to the federal inspector general.

    c.   Accompanied by fraudulent financial reporting that results in material misstatements of asset balances.

    d.   Perpetrated by several levels of management in a scheme that is likely to continue in future years.

177. In auditing compliance with requirements governing major federal financial assistance programs under the Single Audit Act, the auditor's consideration of materiality differs from materiality under generally accepted auditing standards. Under the Single Audit Act, materiality is

    a.   Calculated in relation to the financial statements taken as a whole.

    b.   Determined separately for each major federal financial assistance program.

    c.   Decided in conjunction with the auditor's risk assessment.

    d.   Ignored, because all account balances, regardless of size, are fully tested.

178. Kent is auditing an entity's compliance with requirements governing a major federal financial assistance program in accordance with the Single Audit Act. Kent detected noncompliance with requirements that have a material effect on that program. Kent's report on compliance should express a(n)

    a.   Unqualified opinion with a separate explanatory paragraph.

    b.   Qualified opinion or an adverse opinion.

    c.   Adverse opinion or a disclaimer of opinion.

    d.   Limited assurance on the items tested.

179. When performing an audit of a city that is subject to the requirements of the Uniform Single Audit Act of 1984, an auditor should adhere to

    a.   Governmental Accounting Standards Board *General Standards.*

b. Governmental Finance Officers Association *Governmental Accounting, Auditing, and Financial Reporting Principles.*
c. General Accounting Office Government Auditing Standards.
d. Securities and Exchange Commission *Regulation S-X.*

180. A CPA has performed an examination of the general-purpose financial statements of Big City. The examination scope included the additional requirements of the Single Audit Act. When reporting on Big City's internal accounting and administrative controls used in administering a federal financial assistance program, the CPA should
a. Communicate those weaknesses that are material in relation to the general-purpose financial statements.
b. Express an opinion on the systems used to administer major federal financial assistance programs and express negative assurance on the systems used to administer nonmajor federal financial assistance programs.
c. Communicate those weaknesses that are material in relation to the federal financial assistance program.
d. Express negative assurance on the systems used to administer major federal financial assistance programs and express **no** opinion on the systems used to administer nonmajor federal financial assistance programs.

SIMULATION PROBLEMS

Simulation Problem 1   (20 to 25 minutes)

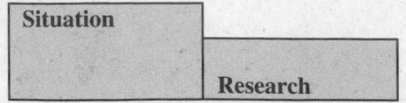

The audit of Park Publishing Co., for the year ended September 30, 20X2, is near completion. Your senior, Dave Moore, at Tyler & Tyler CPAs, has asked you to draft the audit report, considering the following:

- During fiscal year 20X2, Park changed its depreciation method. The engagement partner concurred with this change in accounting principle and its justification, and Moore wants it properly reflected in the auditors' report; the change is discussed in Note 7 to the financial statements.
- The 20X2 financial statements are affected by an uncertainty concerning a lawsuit over patent infringement, the outcome of which cannot presently be estimated. Moore has suggested the need for an explanatory paragraph in the auditors' report related to this matter which is discussed in Note 4 to the financial statements.
- The financial statements for the year ended September 30, 20X1, are to be presented for comparative purposes. Wilson & Wilson previously audited these statements and expressed a standard unqualified opinion.

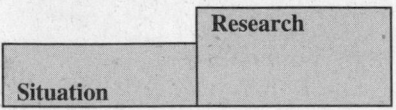

1. Identify the paragraphs in the professional standards that provide guidance regarding the modification of the audit report for the change in accounting principle.
2. Identify the paragraph in professional standards that provides the guidance regarding the modification of the audit report for the uncertainty.
3. Identify the paragraphs in the professional standards that provide the guidance regarding the effect of Wilson & Wilson's opinion on the 20X1 financial statements on Tyler & Tyler's audit report on the 20X2 financial statements.

Simulation Problem 2   (30 to 40 minutes)

Assume that items 1 through 8 are situations that Jones, CPA, has encountered during his audit of Welles Incorporated. List A represents the types of opinions the auditor ordinarily would issue and List B represents the report modifications (if any) that would be necessary. For each situation, select one response from List A and one from List B. Select as the **best** answers for each item the action the auditor would normally take. The types of opinions in List A and the report modifications in List B may be selected once, more than once, or not at all.

Assume

- The auditor is independent.
- The auditor previously expressed an unqualified opinion on the prior year's financial statements.
- Only single-year (not comparative) statements are presented for the current year.
- The conditions for an unqualified opinion exist unless contradicted by the facts.
- The conditions stated in the items to be answered are material, unless otherwise indicated.
- Each item to be answered is independent of the others
- No report modifications are to be made except in response to the factual situation.
- The auditor will not treat a situation as an "emphasis of a matter" in what remains an unqualified audit report unless it is one of those circumstances specifically illustrated in the Professional Standards as an example of a matter an auditor may wish to emphasize.

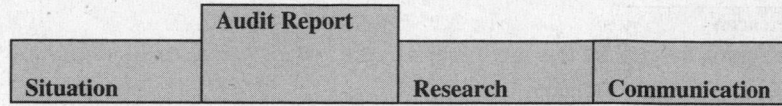

	List A		List B
	Types of opinions		*Report modifications*

List A
Types of opinions

A. Either an "except for" qualified opinion or an adverse opinion
B. Either a disclaimer of opinion or an "except for" qualified opinion
C. Either an adverse opinion or a disclaimer of opinion
D. An "except for" qualified opinion
E. An unqualified opinion
F. An adverse opinion
G. A disclaimer of opinion

List B
Report modifications

H. Describe the circumstances in an explanatory paragraph **without modifying** the three standard paragraphs.
I. Describe the circumstances in an explanatory paragraph and **modify** the **opinion** paragraph.
J. Describe the circumstances in an explanatory paragraph and **modify** the **scope** and **opinion** paragraphs.
K. Describe the circumstances in an explanatory paragraph and **modify** the **introductory, scope,** and **opinion** paragraphs.
L. Describe the circumstances within the **scope** paragraph without adding an explanatory paragraph.
M. Describe the circumstances within the **opinion** paragraph without adding an explanatory paragraph.
N. Describe the circumstances within the **scope** and **opinion** paragraphs without adding an explanatory paragraph.
O. Describe the circumstances within the **introductory, scope,** and **opinion** paragraphs without adding an explanatory paragraph.
P. Issue the standard auditor's report **without modification.**

	Types of opinions (A-G)	*Report Modifications* (H-P)

1. Jones hired an actuary to assist in corroborating Welles' complex pension calculations concerning accrued pension liabilities that account for 25% of the client's total liabilities. The actuary's findings are reasonably close to Welles' calculations and support the financial statements.

2. Welles holds a note receivable consisting of principal and accrued interest payable in 20X4. The note's maker recently filed a voluntary bankruptcy petition, but Welles failed to reduce the recorded value of the note to its net realizable value, which is approximately 20% of the recorded amount.

3. Jones was engaged to audit a client's financial statements after the annual physical inventory count. The accounting records were not sufficiently reliable to enable him to become satisfied as to the year-end inventory balances.

4. Jones found an immaterial adjustment relating to inventory. Welles has refused to adjust the financial statements to reflect this immaterial item.

5. Welles' financial statements do not disclose certain long-term lease obligations. Jones determined that the omitted disclosures are required by FASB.

6. Jones decided not to take responsibility for the work of another CPA who audited a wholly owned subsidiary of Welles. The total assets and revenues of the subsidiary represent 27% and 28%, respectively, of the related consolidated totals.

7. Welles changed its method of accounting for the cost of inventories from FIFO to LIFO. Jones concurs with the change although it has a material effect on the comparability of the financial statements.

8. Due to losses and adverse key financial ratios, Jones has substantial doubt about Welles' ability to continue as a going concern for a reasonable period of time. The client has adequately disclosed its financial difficulties in a note to its financial statements, which do **not** include any adjustments that might result from the outcome of this uncertainty. Also, Jones has ruled out the use of a disclaimer of opinion.

Situation	Audit Report	Research		Communication

Research the Professional Standards and identify the matters that are ordinarily the subjects of a successor auditor's inquiry of the predecessor auditor prior to accepting the new engagement. Select the appropriate paragraphs from the Professional Standards as your solution.

Situation	Audit Report	Research	Communication

The CEO of Welles is concerned about the audit report modification due to a change in accounting principle. Write a memorandum to her explaining the purpose of this modification of the audit report.

REMINDER: Your response will be graded for both technical content and writing skills. Technical content will be evaluated for information that is helpful to the intended reader and clearly relevant to the issue. Writing skills will be evaluated for development, organization, and the appropriate expression of ideas in professional correspondence. Use a standard business memo or letter format with a clear beginning, middle, and end. Do not convey information in the form of a table, bullet point list, or other abbreviated presentation.

To: CEO, Welles Inc.
From: CPA Candidate

Additional Simulations

Appendix A—Simulation 4 (Part b.) involves Reporting
Appendix A—Simulation 5 (item 8) involves Reporting
Appendix A—Simulation 6 (item 8) involves Reporting

MULTIPLE-CHOICE ANSWERS

1. a	38. a	75. d	112. d	149. d
2. b	39. d	76. b	113. d	150. b
3. c	40. a	77. b	114. c	151. c
4. d	41. d	78. a	115. b	152. b
5. c	42. a	79. a	116. a	153. d
6. c	43. d	80. c	117. a	154. b
7. c	44. d	81. d	118. b	155. d
8. d	45. c	82. a	119. a	156. b
9. b	46. d	83. c	120. b	157. b
10. d	47. a	84. b	121. a	158. b
11. d	48. c	85. b	122. d	159. c
12. c	49. a	86. d	123. a	160. b
13. a	50. d	87. a	124. d	161. a
14. a	51. d	88. a	125. a	162. c
15. c	52. b	89. a	126. a	163. b
16. a	53. c	90. d	127. b	164. c
17. c	54. c	91. b	128. a	165. b
18. d	55. d	92. c	129. a	166. b
19. a	56. b	93. c	130. b	167. b
20. b	57. b	94. c	131. c	168. a
21. d	58. b	95. c	132. a	169. a
22. d	59. a	96. c	133. b	170. d
23. a	60. d	97. b	134. a	171. a
24. c	61. a	98. b	135. a	172. b
25. a	62. b	99. c	136. d	173. c
26. b	63. c	100. a	137. c	174. b
27. a	64. c	101. a	138. a	175. a
28. b	65. d	102. a	139. c	176. b
29. c	66. c	103. d	140. a	177. b
30. c	67. d	104. b	141. c	178. b
31. d	68. b	105. c	142. c	179. c
32. b	69. d	106. c	143. c	180. c
33. a	70. a	107. c	144. a	
34. b	71. b	108. a	145. d	
35. b	72. b	109. a	146. b	
36. d	73. b	110. d	147. d	1st: __/180 = __%
37. c	74. d	111. a	148. d	2nd: __/180 = __%

MULTIPLE-CHOICE ANSWER EXPLANATIONS

A.1. Overall Issues

1. **(a)** The requirement is to identify the statement in the standard audit report that indicates the existence of audit risk. Answer (a) is correct because the existence of audit risk is recognized by the statement in the auditor's standard report that the auditor obtained "reasonable assurance." Answer (b) is incorrect because while the standard report does indicate that the CPA assesses the accounting principles used and the overall financial statement presentation, this does not indicate the existence of audit risk. Answer (c) is incorrect because while the standard report does indicate that the audit relates to whether the financial statements are free of material misstatement, it does not discuss materiality and the audit risk associated with materiality. Answer (d) is incorrect because while the financial statements are the responsibility of management and the CPA's responsibility is to express an opinion, the indication that the CPA expresses an opinion does not address audit risk and is less precise than the statement that the auditor obtains reasonable assurance.

2. **(b)** The requirement is to determine an accountant's reporting responsibility when more than one level of service concerning the financial statements of a nonissuer (nonpublic) entity has been performed. Answer (b) is correct because AR 100 requires that the accountant report on the highest level of service rendered. Answer (a) is incorrect because the highest, and not the lowest, level is reported on. Answer (c) is incorrect because regardless of the other type of service performed, the compilation level is always the lowest level and therefore should not be the basis of the report. Answer (d) is incorrect because in circumstances in which an audit has been performed, an audit report, not a review report, is appropriate.

3. **(c)** The requirement is to identify the report that is **least** likely to be a restricted-use report. Answer (c) is correct because AU 623 indicates that reports on most comprehensive basis financial statements are not restricted. Answers (a) and (b) are incorrect because reports on significant deficiencies and reports to audit committees are restricted under AU 325 and AU 380, respectively. Answer (d) is incorrect because AU 623 restricts such reports on compliance. Also, see AU 532 for information on restricting the use of an audit report.

4. (d) The requirement is to determine an auditor's responsibility for controlling the distribution by the client of a restricted-use report. Answer (d) is correct because AU 532 states that an auditor is not responsible for controlling the distribution of such reports. Answer (a) is incorrect because while an auditor should consider informing a client that restricted-use reports are not intended for such distribution, there is no such requirement. Answer (b) is incorrect because the auditor need not inform the client to cease and desist. Answer (c) is incorrect because an auditor need not insist that the client not duplicate the restricted-use report.

A.2. Financial Statement Audit Reports—Nonissuer (Nonpublic) Companies

5. (c) The requirement is to identify the statement that is included in the auditor's standard report. Answer (c) is correct because the auditor's standard report states that an audit includes assessing significant estimates made by management; see AU 508 for this and other required elements included in a standard report.

6. (c) The requirement is to determine the proper date of a reissued audit report on financial statements that have **not** been restated. Answer (c) is correct because use of the original date on the reissued audit report removes any implication that records, transactions or events after the date of the audit report have been examined or reviewed.

7. (c) The requirement is to identify which paragraph of an auditor's standard audit report should refer to generally accepted auditing standards and generally accepted accounting principles. Answer (c) is correct because the scope paragraph indicates that generally accepted auditing standards have been followed, while the opinion paragraph indicates that the financial statements follow generally accepted accounting principles.

8. (d) The requirement is to determine auditor reporting responsibility when prior period financial statements which received a qualified opinion due to a lack of adequate disclosure have been restated to eliminate the lack of disclosure. Answer (d) is correct because AU 508 states that an auditor should express an unqualified opinion on the restated financial statements of the prior year (with an explanatory paragraph describing the circumstance). Answer (a) is incorrect because the auditor's original report is not reissued. Answer (b) is incorrect because the qualified opinion is eliminated. Answer (c) is incorrect because reference to the type of opinion expressed is included in the reissued report's explanatory paragraph.

9. (b) The requirement is to identify the correct statement concerning an auditor's responsibility to express an opinion on the financial statements. Answer (b) is correct because the opening (introductory) paragraph of the auditor's standard report states that the auditor's responsibility is to express an opinion on the financial statements based on the audit. Answer (a) is incorrect because of the explicit statement in the introductory paragraph. Answers (c) and (d) are incorrect because the introductory paragraph, not the scope or opinion paragraphs, includes the statement on the auditor's responsibility.

10. (d) The requirement is to determine whether the terms "when read in conjunction with Note X," and "with the foregoing explanation" should be included in the opinion paragraph of a qualified opinion. AU 508 states that an audit report with a qualified opinion should **not** include either phrase in the opinion paragraph.

11. (d) The requirement is to determine the representations made explicitly and implicitly when issuing the standard auditor's report on comparative financial statements. Answer (d) is correct because the standard audit report explicitly states that the examination of evidence is made on a test basis and implicitly assumes consistent application of accounting principles. Answer (a) is incorrect because consistency of application of accounting principles is not indicated explicitly. Answer (b) is incorrect because examination of evidence on a test basis is referred to explicitly. Answer (c) is incorrect because examination of evidence on a test basis is explicitly referred to and because consistent application of accounting principles is not explicitly referred to.

12. (c) The requirement is to determine the objective of the fourth reporting standard which requires either an opinion regarding the financial statements taken as a whole or an assertion to the effect that an opinion cannot be expressed. Answer (c) is correct because the standard states that the objective is to prevent misinterpretation of the degree of responsibility that the auditor is assuming when his/her name is associated with financial statements. Answer (a) is incorrect because differing opinions may be issued on each of the financial statements (e.g., if the count of the beginning inventory has not been observed, an auditor may disclaim an opinion on the income statement and yet express an unqualified opinion on the balance sheet). Answer (b) is incorrect because the objective does not relate directly to scope limitations. Answer (d) is incorrect because an auditor may report on only one statement.

13. (a) The requirement is to determine the meaning of the expression "taken as a whole" in the fourth generally accepted auditing standard of reporting. AU 508 states that "taken as a whole" applies equally to a complete set of financial statements and to an individual financial statement.

14. (a) The requirement is to determine the appropriate date for an audit report when a subsequent event requiring adjustment of financial statements, without disclosure of the event, comes to the auditor's attention. AU 530 states that the date of completion of fieldwork should be used in such circumstances.

15. (c) The requirement is to determine an auditor's responsibility for subsequent events when an audit report has been dual dated for a subsequent event. Answer (c) is correct because, when dual dating is used, auditor responsibility for events subsequent to the completion of fieldwork is limited to the specific event referred to in the notes to the financial statement. Answers (a), (b), and (d) are all incorrect because they establish more responsibility than required by the professional standards. Note, however, that if the auditor chooses to date the report as of the date of the subsequent event, his/her responsibility for other subsequent events extends to the date of the audit report.

A.3. Financial Statement Audit Reports—Issuer (Public) Companies

16. (a) The requirement is to determine the accounting principles that an issuer (public) company audit report refers to. Answer (a) is correct because the financial statements follow generally accepted accounting principles. Answer (b) is incorrect because, while the audit is performed in accordance with PCAOB standards, the financial statements do not follow those standards. Answer (c) is incorrect because the financial statements do not follow generally accepted auditing standards. Answer (d) is incorrect because the financial statements ordinarily follow generally accepted accounting principles, not International Accounting Standards.

17. (c) The requirement is to identify the incorrect statement concerning information included in an audit report of financial statements issued under the requirements of the PCAOB. Answer (c) is correct since the report should refer to the auditor's report on internal control, not on compliance with laws and regulations. Answer (a) is incorrect because the report should include the title "Report of Independent Registered Public Accounting Firm." Answer (b) is incorrect because the report should refer to the standards of the PCAOB. Answer (d) is incorrect because the report should contain the city and state or country of the office that issued the report.

B.1.a. Opinion Based, in Part, on Report of Another Auditor

18. (d) The requirement is to determine a principal auditor's responsibility, in addition to making inquiries of the other auditor's reputation and independence, after having decided **not** to refer to the audit of the other auditor. Answer (d) is correct because when a decision is made **not** to make reference to the other audit—that is, to take responsibility for that auditor's work—the principal auditor should consider (1) visiting the other auditor, (2) reviewing the audit programs of the other auditor, (3) reviewing the work-
...., and (4) performing additional audit procedures. Answer (a) is incorrect because no explanatory paragraph is added to the audit report. Answer (b) is incorrect because the principal auditor is assuming responsibility for the other auditor's work when a decision is made not to refer to the other auditor's report. Answer (c) is incorrect because written permission is not required when the principal auditor is taking responsibility for the work of the other auditor.

19. (a) The requirement is to determine the meaning of sentences added to an introductory paragraph of an auditor's report that states that another auditor audited a portion of the entity. Answer (a) is correct because AU 508 provides that such a statement indicates a division of responsibility. Answer (b) is incorrect because when the other auditor is referred to the CPA, the CPA is not assuming responsibility for the other auditor. Answer (c) is incorrect because an unqualified opinion may be issued. Answer (d) is incorrect because the sentences are proper.

20. (b) The requirement is to determine the situation in which an auditor would ordinarily issue an unqualified audit opinion without an explanatory paragraph. Answer (b) is correct because when an auditor makes reference to the report of another auditor, each of the three standard paragraphs of the report are modified, but no additional paragraph is added to the report. Answer (a) is incorrect because emphasizing that the entity had significant related-party transactions is normally accomplished through the addition of an explanatory paragraph. Answer (c) is incorrect because the

omission of a statement of cash flows when an entity issues financial statements that present financial position and result of operations results in a qualified audit opinion with an explanatory paragraph. Answer (d) is incorrect because substantial doubt about the entity's ability to continue as a going concern normally results in either an unqualified opinion with an explanatory paragraph or a disclaimer of opinion.

21. (d) The requirement is to identify the situation in which an auditor may issue the standard audit report. Answer (d) is correct because a standard report may be issued in circumstances in which the principal auditor assumes responsibility for the work of another auditor. Answer (a) is incorrect because the standard report does not include reference to a specialist. Thus, reference to a specialist within a report by definition causes modification of the standard report. Answer (b) is incorrect because the auditor is required to issue a modified report on condensed financial statements per AU 552. Answer (c) is incorrect because audit reports on financial statements prepared on a comprehensive basis other than GAAP are considered to be "special reports" which require departures from the standard form.

22. (d) The requirement is to determine a principal auditor's reporting responsibility when a decision has been made to not make reference to another CPA who has audited a client's subsidiary. Answer (d) is correct because, regardless of whether the other auditor is referred to, the principal auditor must be satisfied as to the independence and professional reputation of the other CPA. Answer (a) is incorrect because the principal auditor need not issue an unqualified opinion on the consolidated financial statements. Answer (b) is incorrect because it is not necessary that the other CPA issue an unqualified opinion on the subsidiary's financial statements. Answer (c) is incorrect because the principal auditor should consider reviewing the audit programs and working papers of the other CPA when a decision is made to not make reference to that CPA.

B.1.b. Unusual Circumstances Requiring a Departure from Promulgated GAAP

23. (a) The requirement is to determine the type of opinion to be issued when financial statements of an entity that follows GASB standards include a justified departure from GAAP. Answer (a) is correct because the auditor should issue an unqualified opinion and should include a separate explanatory paragraph explaining the departure from GAAP. Answers (b), (c), and (d) are incorrect because when the auditor believes that the departure is justified, neither a qualified nor adverse opinion is appropriate.

B.1.c. Substantial Doubt about Ability to Remain a Going Concern

24. (c) The requirement is to determine whether the term "reasonable period of time, not to exceed one year" and/or "going concern" is included in an explanatory paragraph relating to going concern status. Answer (c) is correct because while the term "going concern" must be included, the first term is not included in such a report.

25. (a) The requirement is to determine an auditor's reporting responsibility when reporting on comparative financial statements in which the first year presented originally received a going concern modification on a matter that has now been resolved, thus removing the auditor's substantial doubt. Answer (a) is correct because if substantial doubt has been removed in the current period, the explanatory paragraph included in the auditor's report on the financial statements of the prior period should not be repeated. Answers (b), (c), and (d) are all incorrect because they suggest the need for an explanatory paragraph.

26. (b) The requirement is to determine the auditor's responsibility when s/he concludes that there is substantial doubt about an entity's ability to continue as a going concern for a reasonable period of time. Answer (b) is correct because when the auditor concludes there is substantial doubt, s/he should consider the possible effects on the financial statements, and the adequacy of the related disclosures. Answer (a) is incorrect because either an unqualified opinion with an explanatory paragraph or a disclaimer is generally appropriate, not a qualified or adverse opinion. Answer (c) is incorrect because the substantial doubt of going concern status does not require adjusting accounting estimates. Answer (d) is incorrect because the prior year's audit report need not be reissued with an explanatory paragraph.

27. (a) The requirement is to determine an auditor's reporting responsibility when there is substantial doubt about a client's ability to continue as a going concern. Answer (a) is correct because the audit report must include an explanatory paragraph following the opinion paragraph, and must use the terms "going concern" and "substantial doubt."

28. (b) The requirement is to identify the situation in which an explanatory paragraph may be added to an unqualified report. Answer (b) is correct because substantial doubt about the entity's ability to continue as a going concern leads to either an unqualified report with an explanatory paragraph or a disclaimer of opinion. Answer (a) is incorrect because an auditor may issue an opinion on a balance sheet without reporting on the other basic financial statements. Answer (c) is incorrect because unreasonable estimates lead to either a qualified or an adverse opinion. Answer (d) is incorrect because inadequate management record retention policies are a scope limitation that may result in a qualified opinion or a disclaimer.

29. (c) The requirement is to identify the management plan an auditor would most likely positively consider when a question concerning an entity's ability to continue as a going concern exists. Answer (c) is correct because increasing the ownership equity will bring in funds to possibly overcome the negative trends and financial difficulties. Answers (a), (b), and (d) are all incorrect because increasing dividend distributions, reducing lines of credit, and purchasing assets will all use funds, they will not provide funds. See AU 341 for guidance on an auditor's consideration of an entity's ability to continue as a going concern.

B.1.d. Inconsistency in Application of GAAP

30. (c) The requirement is to identify the circumstances in which an auditor would issue a report that omits any reference to consistency. Answer (c) is correct because, as discussed in AU 508, a change in the useful life of assets is a change in estimate, and a change in estimate does not result in a consistency modification. Answers (a) and (b) are incorrect because they both represent a change in accounting principle, and a change in accounting principle requires a consistency modification. Answer (d) is incorrect because

management's lack of reasonable justification for a change in accounting principle is a departure from generally accepted accounting principles, and the description of the departure will discuss the inconsistency.

31. (d) The requirement is to determine whether an unjustified accounting change, a material weakness in internal control, or both, would cause an auditor to express an unqualified opinion with an explanatory paragraph. Answer (d) is correct because an unjustified accounting change will result in either a qualified or an adverse opinion and a material weakness will ordinarily result in no report modification (see AU 325 for information on the treatment of material weaknesses); accordingly, an unqualified opinion with an explanatory paragraph added to the auditor's report is not appropriate in either case.

32. (b) The requirement is to identify the circumstance in which a disclaimer of opinion is **not** appropriate. Answer (b) is correct because when management does **not** provide reasonable justification of a change in accounting principles either a qualified or an adverse opinion is appropriate, not a disclaimer. Answers (a), (c), and (d) are all incorrect because they represent scope limitations that lead to either a qualified opinion or a disclaimer of opinion.

33. (a) The requirement is to determine the effect on an audit report of a client's decision to use differing inventory costing methods for various portions of its inventory. Answer (a) is correct because a standard unqualified opinion may ordinarily be issued (see AU 420 for a discussion of the consistency standard). Answer (b) is incorrect because there is no lack of consistency between accounting periods. Answer (c) is incorrect because there is no departure from GAAP. Answer (d) is incorrect because adverse opinions are only issued when a departure from GAAP exists that makes the financial statements misleading.

34. (b) The requirement is to identify an auditor's reporting responsibility when performing a first audit of a new client and when the auditor was able to extend auditing procedures to gather sufficient evidence about consistency. Answer (b) is correct because, when the auditor has obtained assurance as to the consistency of application of accounting principles between the current and preceding year, no mention of consistency is included in the audit report. Answer (a) is incorrect because the auditor may report on the client's income statement. Answer (c) is incorrect because the consistency standard does apply. Answer (d) is incorrect because the auditor does not refer to consistency when accounting principles have been applied consistently.

35. (b) The requirement is to determine auditor reporting responsibility when management does not provide reasonable justification for a change in accounting principle and presents comparative financial statements. Answer (b) is correct because the auditor should continue to express his/her exception with the financial statements for the year of change as long as they are presented and reported on. Answer (a) is incorrect because the auditor must express his/her exception for as long as the financial statements for the year of change are presented and reported on. Answer (c) is incorrect because the auditor need not qualify the report until management changes back to the accounting principle formerly used. Answer (d) is incorrect because the qualification is necessary despite the fact that the principle is generally accepted.

36. **(d)** The requirement is to determine the information that must be presented when a client has changed accounting principles. Answer (d) is correct because in addition to identifying the nature of the change, the auditor must refer to the financial statement note that discusses the change in detail. Answer (a) is incorrect because while the auditor must believe that the change is justified, it is not necessary to explain it in the report. Answer (b) is incorrect because the cumulative effect of the change need not be described in the audit report. Answer (c) is incorrect because the auditor need not make explicit concurrence with the change.

37. **(c)** The requirement is to determine the proper reporting option for a change in accounting principles with an immaterial current year effect, but which is expected to have a substantial effect in subsequent years. Answer (c) is correct because the auditor need not recognize the change in the audit report and may issue a standard unqualified opinion.

B.1.e. Certain Circumstances Affecting Comparative Financial Statements

38. **(a)** The requirement is to identify the circumstance in which an auditor reporting on comparative financial statements would ordinarily change the previously issued opinion on the prior year's financial statements. Answer (a) is correct because when an auditor has previously expressed a qualified or an adverse opinion on financial statements of a prior period and those financial statements have been restated, the auditor's updated report is changed. Answer (b) is incorrect because, ordinarily, the reissued report by a predecessor auditor will be the same as that originally issued. Answer (c) is incorrect because the prior year's opinion will remain qualified if the current year's audit report is modified due to a lack of consistency. Answer (d) is incorrect because restatement of prior year's financial statements following a pooling of interest will not lead to a change in the previously issued opinion.

39. **(d)** The requirement is to determine the information to be included in an audit report on comparative financial statements when a predecessor auditor's report is not being reissued. Answer (d) is correct because the introductory paragraph of the successor's report should indicate (1) that the financial statements of the prior period were audited by another auditor (whose name is not presented), (2) the date of the predecessor's report, (3) the type of report issued by the predecessor, and (4) if the report was other than a standard report, the substantive reasons therefor.

40. **(a)** The requirement is to determine whether the predecessor auditor should obtain a representation letter from management, the successor auditor, or both, before reissuing the prior year's audit record. Answer (a) is correct because the predecessor auditor should obtain a representation letter from both management (AU 333) and the successor auditor (AU 508).

41. **(d)** The requirement is to identify the circumstance in which a standard unqualified report may be issued when single-year financial statements are presented. Answer (d) is correct because when the prior year's financial statements are not being presented, the CPA need not refer to them or include the predecessor auditor's report. See AU 508 for information on reissuance of a predecessor's report when comparative financial statements are being issued. Answer (a) is incorrect because inability to audit an investment in a foreign affiliate is a scope limitation that is likely to result in either a qualified opinion or a disclaimer. Answer (b) is incorrect because a qualified opinion is appropriate when an entity declines to present a statement of cash flows with its balance sheet and related statements of income and retained earnings. Answer (c) is incorrect because the emphasis of an accounting matter by an auditor results in inclusion of an explanatory paragraph to the unqualified audit report.

42. **(a)** The requirement is to identify the correct form of an audit report on comparative financial statements when a continuing auditor has audited the two years of financial statements being presented. Answer (a) is correct because one audit report should be issued that includes the years involved. Answer (b) is incorrect because one report, not two reports, should be issued. Answer (c) is incorrect because both years should be reported upon. Answer (d) is incorrect because auditors do not have the option of issuing two audit reports in this circumstance.

43. **(d)** The requirement is to determine the manner in which a predecessor auditor who has reissued a report for comparative financial statements should refer to the successor auditor. AU 508 indicates that the predecessor auditor should not refer in the reissued report to the report or work of the successor auditor.

44. **(d)** The requirement is to determine the proper reporting procedure for comparative financial statements for which the prior year is unaudited, and the current year is audited. AU 504 states that when unaudited financial statements are presented in comparative form with audited financial statements, the report on the prior period may be reissued to accompany the current period report. In addition, the report on the current period may include a separate paragraph describing responsibility assumed for the prior period financial statements. If these statements are filed with the SEC, the statements should be clearly marked as "unaudited" but should not be referred to in the auditor's report.

B.1.g. Supplementary Information Required by FASB or GASB

45. **(c)** The requirement is to identify an auditor's responsibility for supplementary information required by the FASB that is placed outside the basic financial statements. Answer (c) is correct because AU 558 requires that the auditor apply limited procedures to the information and report deficiencies in, or the omission of, the information. Answer (a) is incorrect because the auditor does have some responsibility for the supplementary information. Answer (b) is incorrect because the auditor must apply limited procedures to information presented and report deficiencies in the information in addition to determining whether it has been omitted. Answer (d) is incorrect because tests of details of transactions and balances need not be performed.

46. **(d)** The requirement is to determine the proper audit report when management declines to present supplementary information required by the Governmental Accounting Standards Board. Answer (d) is correct because omission of required supplementary information, which when presented is not considered audited, leads to an unqualified opinion with an explanatory paragraph. Answers (a) and (b) are incorrect because neither an adverse opinion nor a qualified opinion is appropriate since the supplementary information is not audited. Answer (c) is incorrect because it is incomplete since an unqualified opinion with an additional explanatory paragraph is required.

B.1.h.   Other Information in a Document Containing Audited Financial Statements

47.   (a)   The requirement is to identify the auditor's reporting responsibility concerning information accompanying the basic financial statements in an auditor-submitted document. Answer (a) is correct because the auditor should report on all the information included in the document. Answers (b) and (c) are incorrect because the auditor should report on the accompanying information regardless of whether he or she participated in its preparation. Answer (d) is incorrect because the auditor should report on the accompanying information regardless of whether it contains misstatements. See AU 551 for information on auditor-submitted documents.

48.   (c)   The requirement is to identify the correct statement that may be included in an auditor's report when information accompanying the basic financial statements in an auditor-submitted document has been subjected to auditing procedures. Answer (c) is correct because the report indicates whether the accompanying information is fairly stated in all material respects in relation to the basic financial statements taken as a whole. Answer (a) is incorrect because the information is not presented in accordance with generally accepted auditing standards. Answer (b) is incorrect because the information is in addition to that required by generally accepted accounting principles. Answer (d) is incorrect because it is not in accordance with attestation standards.

49.   (a)   The requirement is to identify the auditor's reporting responsibility for a material inconsistency between the audited financial statements and the other information in an annual report to shareholders containing audited financial statements. Answer (a) is correct because AU 550 states that if a material inconsistency exists and the client refuses to revise the other information, the auditor should include an explanatory paragraph that explains the inconsistency. The auditor may also withhold the use of the audit report or the auditor may withdraw from the engagement. Answer (b) is incorrect because the financial statements are not misstated. Answer (c) is incorrect because the auditor must review the other information to ensure that it is consistent with the financial statements. Answer (d) is incorrect because the financial statements are not misstated and therefore a disclaimer of opinion is inappropriate.

50.   (d)   The requirement is to determine an auditor's responsibility when audited financial statements are presented in a client's document containing other information. Answer (d) is correct because the auditor is required to read the other information to determine that it is consistent with the audited financial statements. Answers (a) and (c) are incorrect because no such inquiry, analytical procedures, or other substantive auditing procedures are required. Answer (b) is incorrect because, unless the information seems incorrect or inconsistent with the audited financial state-

ments, no explanatory paragraph needs to be added to the auditor's report.

B.1.i.   Emphasis of a Matter

51.   (d)   The requirement is to identify the proper statement about an audit report that includes a separate paragraph in an otherwise unmodified report that emphasizes that the entity being reported on had significant transactions with related parties. Answer (d) is correct because AU 508 allows such emphasis of a matter and states that it does not negate the unqualified opinion. Answer (a) is incorrect because the report is considered unqualified. Answer (b) is incorrect because such emphasis of a matter does not violate generally accepted auditing standards if this information is disclosed in notes to the financial statements. Answer (c) is incorrect because the report should **not** include the phrase "with the foregoing explanation."

B.1.j.   Departures from GAAP

52.   (b)   The requirement is to identify the appropriate types of audit reports when an illegal act with a material effect on the financial statements has not been properly accounted for or disclosed. Answer (b) is correct because omission of required disclosures, a departure from generally accepted accounting principles, leads to either a qualified or an adverse opinion. Answer (a) is incorrect because a disclaimer of opinion is not appropriate when the auditor knows of such misstatements. Answer (c) is incorrect because neither a disclaimer of opinion nor an unqualified opinion with a separate explanatory paragraph is appropriate. Answer (d) is incorrect because an unqualified opinion with a separate explanatory paragraph is not appropriate.

53.   (c)   The requirement is to identify the phrase that an auditor would include in an audit report with a qualified opinion because of inadequate disclosure. AU 508 indicates that the phrase "except for the omission of the information discussed in the opinion paragraph" is the proper phrase. Answers (a), (b), and (d) are all incorrect because they are phrases not allowed in reports with qualified opinions.

54.   (c)   The requirement is to identify the circumstance that would most likely result in an auditor expressing an adverse opinion. Answer (c) is correct because departures from GAAP, such as inappropriately reporting leases, result in either a qualified or an adverse opinion. Answer (a) is incorrect because client refusal to provide access to minutes is a client imposed scope limitation that will normally result in a disclaimer of opinion. Answer (b) is incorrect because weak internal control will not in general result in an adverse opinion; if controls are so weak that an audit cannot effectively be completed, a disclaimer of opinion or withdrawal may be appropriate. Answer (d) is incorrect because substantial doubt about going concern status results in either an unqualified opinion with an explanatory paragraph or a disclaimer of opinion.

55.   (d)   The requirement is to identify the paragraphs of an audit report that are modified when an auditor qualifies an opinion because of inadequate disclosure. In addition to requiring the inclusion of a separate explanatory paragraph, AU 508 indicates that only the opinion paragraph should be modified.

56.   (b)   The requirement is to determine the appropriate report modification that results when the management of a publicly held company issues financial statements that purport to present its financial position and results of operations but omits the statement of cash flows. Answer (b) is correct because failure to include a statement of cash flows will lead the auditor to qualify the opinion.

57. (b) The requirement is to identify the circumstance in which an auditor will choose between expressing an "except for" qualified opinion and an adverse opinion. Answer (b) is correct because omissions of required information, a departure from generally accepted accounting principles, leads to either a qualified or an adverse opinion. Answer (a) is incorrect because a scope limitation such as the failure to observe a client's physical inventory leads to either a qualified opinion or a disclaimer of opinion. Answer (c) is incorrect because an auditor may issue an unqualified opinion on one statement. Answer (d) is incorrect because substantial doubt about an entity's ability to continue as a going concern leads to either an unqualified report with explanatory language or a disclaimer of opinion.

58. (b) The requirement is to identify the situation in which an auditor will ordinarily choose between expressing a qualified opinion or an adverse opinion. Answer (b) is correct because departures from generally accepted accounting principles result in either a qualified opinion or an adverse opinion—such lack of disclosure is a departure from generally accepted accounting principles. Answer (a) is incorrect because the inability to observe the physical inventory and inability to become satisfied about its balance represents a scope limitation that will result in either a qualified opinion or a disclaimer of opinion. Answer (c) is incorrect because a change in accounting principles leads to an unqualified opinion with an explanatory paragraph added to the report. Answer (d) is incorrect because inability to apply ~~procedures to one area represents a scope limitation that will~~ result in either a qualified opinion or a disclaimer of opinion. See AU 508 for information on audit reports.

B.1.k. Scope Limitations

59. (a) The requirement is to identify the type of opinion that should be issued on the financial statements when an auditor has been unable to obtain sufficient evidence relating to the consistent application of accounting principles between the current and prior year. Answer (a) is correct because the scope limitation will affect the year's beginning balances and thereby affect the current year's results of operations and cash flows. Answer (b) is incorrect because the year-end balance sheet will be unaffected by the scope limitation (any retained earnings misstatement of the preceding year will be offset in the current year). Answer (c) is incorrect because the auditor need not withdraw in such circumstances. Answer (d) is incorrect because this situation represents a scope limitation, and not an uncertainty.

60. (d) The requirement is to identify the circumstance in which an auditor would **not** express an unqualified opinion. Answer (d) is correct because an inability to obtain the audited financial statements of a consolidated investee represents a scope limitation, and a significant scope limitation results in either a qualified opinion or a disclaimer of opinion. Answer (a) is incorrect because a material change between periods in accounting principles will result in an explanatory paragraph being added to a report with an unqualified opinion. Answer (b) is incorrect because the omis-

sion of the SEC required quarterly financial data, which is considered "unaudited," results in a report with an unqualified opinion with an explanatory paragraph. Answer (c) is incorrect because an auditor's emphasis of an unusually important subsequent event results in a report with an unqualified opinion with an explanatory paragraph.

61. (a) The requirement is to determine the propriety of including a statement that the current asset portion of an entity's balance sheet was fairly stated in an audit report that disclaims an opinion on the overall financial statements. Answer (a) is correct because expressions of opinion as to certain identified items in financial statements (referred to as "piecemeal opinions") should not be expressed when the auditor has disclaimed an opinion or has expressed an adverse opinion. Such opinions tend to overshadow or contradict the disclaimer or adverse opinion. Answer (b) is incorrect because an auditor may report on one basic financial statement. Answers (c) and (d) are incorrect because providing such assurance is **not** appropriate.

62. (b) The requirement is to identify the type of opinion that should be issued on the balance sheet and the income statement when an auditor did not observe a client's taking of the beginning physical inventory and was unable to become satisfied about its accuracy by using other auditing procedures. Answer (b) is correct because the scope limitation will not affect the year-end balance sheet account balances. However, because evidence with respect to the beginning inventory is lacking, verification of cost of goods sold, an income statement element, is impossible. Although year-end retained earnings will not be affected, both the current and prior years' retained earnings statements will be affected (by an offsetting amount) by the cost of goods sold misstatement. If no other problems arise, the auditor will be able to issue an unqualified opinion on the balance sheet and a disclaimer on the income statement (and on the retained earnings statement). Answer (a) is incorrect because an unqualified opinion may be issued on the balance sheet. Answer (c) is incorrect because an unqualified opinion may be issued on the balance sheet with a disclaimer on the income statement. Answer (d) is incorrect because a disclaimer should be issued on the income statement.

63. (c) The requirement is to determine whether the scope paragraph, opinion paragraph, and/or notes to the financial statements should refer to an audit scope limitation. Answer (c) is correct because the suggested report presented for a scope limitation includes modification of both the scope and opinion paragraphs. In addition, it is not appropriate for the scope of the audit to be explained in a note to the financial statements.

64. (c) The requirement is to identify a CPA's responsibility when asked to report on only one financial statement. Answer (c) is correct because the auditor may accept the engagement because the situation involves limited reporting objectives, not a limitation on the scope of audit procedures. Answers (a), (b), and (d) are incorrect because the auditor is able to accept such an engagement and because the auditor is able to apply the procedures considered necessary.

65. (d) The requirement is to determine whether either the scope paragraph, the opinion paragraph, or both should be deleted when an auditor is disclaiming an opinion due to a client-imposed scope limitation. Answer (d) is correct because the scope paragraph is omitted in this situation and the opinion paragraph is modified to disclaim an opinion. Answer (a) is incorrect because it suggests that the scope paragraph is not omitted but that the opinion paragraph is omitted. Answer (b) is incorrect because it states that the opinion paragraph is omitted. Answer (c) is incorrect because it states that the scope paragraph is not omitted.

66. (c)   The requirement is to identify the information included in the opinion paragraph of an auditor's report that is qualified due to a major inadequacy in the computerized accounting records. Answer (c) is correct because the opinion paragraph indicates that the exception is due to the possible effects on the financial statements. Answer (a) is incorrect because the opinion paragraph will not include a reference to client-imposed scope limitations. Answer (b) is incorrect because no indication of a departure from generally accepted auditing standards is provided in the opinion paragraph and this situation is not a departure from GAAS. Answer (d) is incorrect because there is no indication that there is inadequate disclosure of necessary information.

67. (d)   The requirement is to identify the circumstance in which a scope limitation is sufficient to preclude an unqualified opinion. Answer (d) is correct because AU 333 states that management's refusal to furnish such a written representation constitutes a limitation on the scope of an audit sufficient to preclude an unqualified opinion. Answers (a), (b), and (c) are all incorrect because while they represent scope limitations, they may sometimes not result in a report that is other than unqualified.

B.1.l.   Lack of Independence

68. (b)   The requirement is to identify the situation in which an auditor may **not** issue a qualified opinion. Answer (b) is correct because the auditor who lacks independence must disclaim an opinion, not qualify an opinion. Answer (a) is incorrect because a departure from GAAP will result in either a qualified opinion or an adverse opinion. Answer (c) is incorrect because scope limitations result in either a qualified opinion or a disclaimer of opinion. Answer (d) is incorrect because a specialist may be referred to when an auditor is issuing a qualified opinion, an adverse opinion, or a disclaimer of opinion.

B.2.   Report Preparation

69. (d)   The requirement is to identify the manner in which an auditor may express an opinion on an entity's accounts receivable when that auditor has disclaimed an opinion on the financial statements taken as a whole. Answer (d) is correct because such a report is considered a "specified elements, accounts, or items report," and should include the opinion on the accounts receivable separately from the disclaimer of opinion on the financial statement. Answer (a) is incorrect because reason for the disclaimer of opinion need not be provided. Answer (b) is incorrect because distribution of such a report is not restricted to internal use only. Answer (c) is incorrect because the auditor need not report on the current asset portion of the entity's balance sheet to issue such a report.

70. (a)   The requirement is to determine the proper addressee of a report in a circumstance in which one company has hired a CPA to audit another company's financial statements. Answer (a) is correct because while audit reports are ordinarily addressed to the company whose financial statements are being audited, when a CPA audits the financial statements of a company that is not his or her client (as is the case here) the report is addressed to the company that hired the CPA.

71. (b)   The requirement is to identify the information that should be included in the opinion paragraph of an audit report with an adverse opinion. Answer (b) is correct because the opinion paragraph should include a direct reference to a separate paragraph disclosing the basis for the opinion. Answer (a) is incorrect because the principal effects, if available, should be described in a separate explanatory paragraph, and not in the opinion paragraph. Answer (c) is incorrect because while a separate explanatory paragraph provides a description of the substantive reasons for the adverse opinion, the opinion paragraph does not. Answer (d) is incorrect because neither an uncertainty nor a scope limitation leads to an adverse opinion.

72. (b)   The requirement is to determine the proper placement of an explanatory paragraph disclosing the substantive reasons for expressing an adverse opinion. AU 508 requires that such paragraphs precede the opinion paragraph.

C.1.a.   Unaudited Statements

73. (b)   The requirement is to determine the CPA's responsibility when s/he assists in preparing financial statements of a publicly held entity, but has **not** audited or reviewed them. Answer (b) is correct because the CPA must, at a minimum, read the financial statements for obvious material misstatements. Answer (a) is incorrect because no documentation with respect to internal control is necessary. Answer (c) is incorrect because the limited scope of procedures being performed does not allow the CPA to ascertain whether the financial statements are in conformity with generally accepted accounting principles. Answer (d) is incorrect because omitting all required disclosures is not expected for a publicly held entity in these circumstances.

74. (d)   The requirement is to identify the appropriate form of report to issue when the CPA is associated with the financial statements of a publicly held entity but has **not** audited or reviewed such statements. Answer (d) is correct because the standards require the CPA to disclaim an opinion on the financial statements when the accountant has not audited or reviewed such statements. Answer (a) is incorrect because Regulation S-X exemption is not a form of audit report. Answer (b) is incorrect because pro forma information is not involved. Answer (c) is incorrect because there is no such report as an unaudited association report.

75. (d)   The requirement is to identify a CPA's responsibility when his/her name is to be included in the interim report of a publicly held entity and the CPA has not audited or reviewed the interim financial statements. Answer (d) is correct because when an accountant is aware that his/her name is to be included in a client-prepared written communication of a public entity containing financial statements that have not been audited or reviewed, he/she should request (1) that his/her name not be included in the communication **or** (2) that the statements be marked as unaudited and note that there is no opinion expressed on them.

C.1.b. Compilations

76. (b) The requirement is to identify an accountant's reporting responsibility when performing a compilation and he or she determines that a going concern uncertainty has not been properly disclosed by a client. Answer (b) is correct because this is a departure from GAAP and results in modification of the report's third paragraph and addition of an explanatory paragraph. Answer (a) is incorrect because the information on the client's ability to continue as a going concern should be included in the financial statements; if it is not, a departure from GAAP exists. Answer (c) is incorrect because adverse opinions are not issued based on compilations. Answer (d) is incorrect because qualified opinions are not issued based on compilations.

77. (b) The requirement is to identify the statement that should be included in a compilation report. Answer (b) is correct because compilation reports indicate that the accountant compiled the financial statements in accordance with Statements on Standards for Accounting and Review Services.

78. (a) The requirement is to determine how a CPA should indicate that a client's compiled financial statements were prepared in conformity with the income tax basis of accounting when the financial statements provide no such disclosure. Answer (a) is correct because if the basis of accounting is not disclosed in the financial statements, the accountant should disclose the basis in the compilation report. Answer (b) is incorrect because each page of the financial statements should only include the reference "See Accountant's Compilation Report." Answer (c) is incorrect because the auditor is not required to issue a special report. See AU 623 for information on special reporting. Answer (d) is incorrect because the auditor does not have to withdraw from the engagement.

79. (a) The requirement is to determine how the compilation report should be modified to indicate that the entity's financial statements do not include all disclosures required by GAAP. Answer (a) is correct because AR 100 states that while the accountant may compile such financial statements, the accountant must clearly indicate in the compilation report that substantially all disclosures required by GAAP have been omitted. Answer (b) is incorrect because the financial statements are not compiled on a comprehensive basis other than GAAP. Answer (c) is incorrect because a compilation may be performed on financial statements lacking such disclosures. Answer (d) is incorrect because these financial statements are not considered "special-purpose financial statements."

80. (c) The requirement is to determine when a CPA may compile and be associated with financial statements that omit disclosures required by GAAP. Answer (c) is correct because the CPA may compile such financial statements provided that the omission of substantially all disclosures (1) is clearly indicated in the audit report and (2) is not, to the CPA's knowledge, undertaken with the intention of misleading those who might reasonably be expected to use the financial statements.

81. (d) The requirement is to determine the proper reporting procedure for comparative financial statements for which the prior year is unaudited, and the current year is audited. AU 504 states that when unaudited financial state-

ments are presented in comparative form with audited financial statements, the report on the prior period may be reissued to accompany the current period report. In addition, the report on the current period may also include a separate paragraph describing responsibility assumed for the prior period financial statements. If these statements are filed with the SEC, the statements should be clearly marked as "unaudited" but should not be referred to in the auditor's report.

82. (a) The requirement is to determine a CPA's responsibility when the first year of compiled comparative financial statements omit substantially all disclosures required by generally accepted accounting principles, while the second year's statements include such disclosures. Answer (a) is correct because the CPA may **not** report on the comparative financial statements because of a lack of comparability. Answers (b), (c), and (d) are all incorrect because they allow such reporting to occur under certain circumstances.

83. (c) The requirement is to identify the statement that should **not** be included in a CPA's financial statement compilation report. Answer (c) is correct because a compilation report provides no assurance on the financial statements.

84. (b) The requirement is to determine the representations made explicitly and implicitly when issuing a standard compilation report on a nonissuer's financial statements. Answer (b) is correct because the report explicitly states that the financial statements have not been audited and that the accountant has compiled them.

85. (b) The requirement is to determine the appropriate date for an auditor's compilation report. AR 100 requires that the date of completion of the compilation should be

86. (d) The requirement is to determine whether an accountant's compilation report must be printed on the accountant's letterhead, manually signed by the accountant, or both. Answer (d) is correct because the professional standards require neither that the report be printed on the accountant's letterhead, nor that it be manually signed by the accountant. Answers (a), (b), and (c) are all incorrect because they include an inappropriate "yes" to one or both issues. See AR 100 for information on reporting on a compilation of financial statements.

87. (a) The requirement is to identify the correct statement concerning compiled financial statements that are to be made available to third parties. Answer (a) is correct because a compilation report must be issued when third-party reliance upon compiled financial statements is anticipated. Answer (b) is incorrect because note disclosures may be omitted. Answer (c) is incorrect because while advisable, use of an engagement letter is not required in such circumstances. Answer (d) is incorrect because no such restriction is necessary.

88. (a) The requirement is to identify the correct statement concerning appropriate communication option(s) when compiled financial statements are only going to be used by management. Answer (a) is correct because when an accountant submits to a client compiled financial statements that are not expected to be used by a third party, either a compilation report or a written engagement letter (or both) may be used. Answer (b), (c), and (d) are all incorrect because they suggest that either a compilation report, a written engagement letter, or both are unacceptable.

89. (a) The requirement is to identify the circumstance in which a compilation report is not required. Answer (a) is correct because when financial statements are only for management, no compilation report is required. Answers (b) and (c) are incorrect because when third parties are expected to use compiled financial statements, a compilation report is required. Answer (d) is incorrect because a compilation report is not always required.

C.1.b. Reviews

90. (d) The requirement is to identify whether a review report is modified due to either inability to assess the risk of material misstatement due to fraud, a discovery of internal control deficiencies, or both. Answer (d) is correct because neither of these circumstances requires modification of a review report. Answers (a), (b), and (c) are all incorrect because they suggest that one or the other of these circumstances results in modification of a review report. A departure from GAAP is the primary cause of a review report modification. AR 100 provides guidance on review reports.

91. (b) The requirement is to identify the circumstance in which a CPA may issue a review report on a single financial statement. Answer (b) is correct because an accountant may issue a review report on a financial statement, such as a balance sheet, and not report on the other related financial statements if the scope of his or her inquiry and analytical procedures has not been restricted. Answer (a) is incorrect because the balance sheet need not be presented in prescribed form. Answer (c) is incorrect because the balance sheet may be used to obtain credit or to distribute to creditors. Answer (d) is incorrect because specialized accounting principles and practices in an industry may or may not need to be disclosed depending upon the circumstances.

92. (c) The requirement is to identify a CPA's responsibility when he or she believes that modification of the standard review report is **not** adequate to indicate deficiencies in financial statements affected by illegal acts. Answer (c) is correct because whenever a CPA believes that modification of the standard report is not adequate to indicate the deficiencies in the financial statements, he or she should withdraw from the review engagement and provide no further services with respect to those financial statements.

93. (c) The requirement is to identify the reference that should be included in each page of a nonissuer's reviewed financial statements. AR 100 requires that each page of the financial statements include a reference such as "See Accountant's Review Report."

94. (c) The requirement is to identify the statement that is included in an accountant's review report on the financial statements of a nonissuer. Answer (c) is correct because a review report includes a statement that a review consists principally of inquires of company personnel and analytical procedures applied to financial data. See AR 100 for information that should be included in a review report.

95. (c) The requirement is to determine a CPA's reporting responsibility when an audit engagement for a nonissuer has been changed to a review engagement because of what the CPA believes to be a reasonable restriction on the scope

of the audit. Answer (c) is correct because in such circumstances the CPA should neither include reference to the original engagement nor to the scope limitation.

96. (c) The requirement is to identify the correct statement relating to a CPA's report on comparative statements when the current year has been reviewed and the previous year has been audited. Answer (c) is correct because when a separate paragraph is being added to the CPA's review report the CPA should clearly indicate the difference in the levels of assurance for the two years. In this situation, AR 200 requires the auditor to indicate that the previous year's financial statements were audited, the date of the report, the type of opinion expressed and if the opinion was other than unqualified, the substantive reasons for that opinion, and that no auditing procedures were performed after the date of the previous report. Answer (a) is incorrect because the review report is not solely intended for management or the board of directors. Answer (b) is incorrect because the prior year's audit report may still be appropriate. Answer (d) is incorrect because this statement does not need to be included within the review report.

97. (b) The requirement is to identify the statement included in the standard report issued by an accountant after reviewing the financial statements of a nonissuer. Answer (b) is correct because the report states that the accountant is not aware of any material modifications that should be made to the financial statements in order for them to be in conformity with generally accepted accounting principles. AR 100 presents the required disclosures for a review report.

98. (b) The requirement is to identify the information presented in a review report of financial statements of a nonissuer. Answer (b) is correct because the report indicates that all information included in the financial statements is the representation of the management of the entity.

99. (c) The requirement is to determine an accountant's reporting responsibility when associated with a nonissuer's reviewed statements which contain a material departure from generally accepted accounting principles. Answer (c) is correct because AR 100 requires the inclusion of a separate paragraph describing the departure. Answers (a) and (b) are incorrect because an adverse opinion or an "except for" qualified opinion may only be issued when an audit has been performed. Answer (d) is incorrect because expressing limited assurance (as is normally provided in reviews) on the financial statements is not adequate to disclose the departure.

100. (a) The requirement is to identify the reply which is correct concerning the content of a review report. Answer (a) is correct because a review report indicates that a review is substantially less in scope than an audit. Answer (b) is incorrect because a review report provides no information on internal control. Answer (c) is incorrect because while a review report states that the accountant is not aware of any material modifications that should be made to the financial statements, it does not provide limited assurance that the financial statements are fairly presented. Answer (d) is incorrect because while a review report does state that a review is substantially less in scope than an audit, it does not refer to a compilation.

C.1.c.   Reviewed Interim (Quarterly) Statements

101. (a)   The requirement is to identify the objective of a review of interim financial information. Answer (a) is correct because AU 722 states that the objective of a review of interim financial information is to provide a basis for reporting on whether material modification should be made for such information to conform with generally accepted accounting principles. Answer (b) is incorrect because no updated opinion is being issued. Answer (c) is incorrect because condensed statements or pro forma financial information are not being considered in this question. Answer (d) is incorrect because the statements may or may not be presented in conformity with generally accepted accounting principles.

102. (a)   The requirement is to identify the correct statement with respect to an independent accountant's review report on interim financial information presented in a registration statement. Answer (a) is correct because an accountant's review report is **not** a part of the registration statement within the meaning of Section 11 of the Securities Act of 1933. Answer (b) is incorrect because under certain conditions an accountant is required to update the report. Answers (c) and (d) are incorrect because the prospectus includes neither a statement that the review was performed in accordance with SEC standards, nor a statement that the accountant obtained corroborating evidence.

103. (d)   The requirement is to determine the circumstances which will lead to a modification of an interim report. Departures from generally accepted accounting principles, which include adequate disclosure, require modification of the accountant's report. Normally neither an uncertainty [answer (a)] nor a lack of consistency [answer (b)] would cause a report modification. Reference to another accountant [answer (c)] is not considered a modification.

104. (b)   The requirement is to identify the procedure that would ordinarily be applied when an accountant conducts a review of the interim financial information of a publicly held entity. Answer (b) is correct because the accountant will ordinarily read the minutes of meetings of stockholders, the board of directors, and committees of the board of directors to identify actions that may affect the interim financial information. AU 722 describes the nature of procedures for conducting a review of interim financial information. Answers (a), (c), and (d) are all incorrect because they represent verification procedures typically beyond the scope of a review of interim financial information.

105. (c)   The requirement is to identify the least likely procedure to be included in an accountant's review of interim financial information of an issuer (public) entity. Answer (c) is correct because a review consists principally of performing analytical procedures and making inquiries, not procedures such as observation, inspection, and confirmation. Answers (a), (b), and (d) are all incorrect because they include review procedures, as presented in AU 722.

106. (c)   The requirement is to identify the most likely information included in a review report. Answer (c) is correct because AU 722 requires that the report include a description of procedures performed. Answer (a) is incorrect because the information was reviewed, not examined, in accordance with standards of the PCAOB. Answer (b) is incorrect because the interim financial information is the responsibility of the entity's management, not the shareholders. Answer (d) is incorrect because a review is less in scope than an audit, not than a compilation.

C.1.d.   Condensed Financial Statements

107. (c)   The requirement is to determine the circumstance under which an auditor may report on condensed financial statements that are derived from complete audited financial statements. Answer (c) is correct because a report may be issued when the information in the condensed financial statements is fairly stated in all material respects in relation to the financial statements. Answer (a) is incorrect because the condensed financial statements need not be distributed with the complete financial statements. Answer (b) is incorrect because the report need not indicate the nature of any additional procedures. Answer (d) is incorrect because prior year condensed financial information is not necessary. See AU 552 for information on condensed financial statements.

108. (a)   The requirement is to determine the appropriate response relating to selected financial data that are included in a client's prepared document containing audited financial statements. Answer (a) is correct because the selected data should be limited to data derived from the audited financial statements. Answer (b) is incorrect because distribution of the report need not be limited to senior management and the board of directors. Answer (c) is incorrect because the selected data need not follow a comprehensive basis of accounting other than GAAP. Answer (d) is incorrect because the report will ordinarily state that the selected data are fairly stated in all material respects in relation to the consolidated financial statements.

C.1.e.   Financial Statements Prepared for Use in Other Countries

109. (a)   The requirement is to identify audit reporting requirements when reporting on financial statements of a US entity prepared in accordance with another country's accounting principles. Answer (a) is correct because AU 534 states that the auditor should understand the accounting principles generally accepted in the other country. Answer (b) is incorrect because the auditor does not have to obtain certification outside of the United States. Answer (c) is incorrect because the auditor does not have to disclaim an opinion. Answer (d) is incorrect because the auditor does not have to receive a waiver from the auditor's State Board of Accountancy.

110. (d)   The requirement is to determine the appropriate types of reports that may be issued when the financial statements of a US subsidiary are prepared following the principles of a non-US parent company's country for inclusion in that parent company's non-US consolidated financial statements. AU 534 allows either a modified US style report or the report form of the parent's country. A US style unmodified report is not appropriate.

C.2.a.   Special Reports

111. (a)   The requirement is to identify a requirement for a CPA to express an opinion on a profit participation plan relating to an entity's net income. Answer (a) is correct because if a specified element is, or is based upon, an entity's net income or stockholders' equity, the CPA should have audited the complete financial statements in order to express an opinion on the element. Answer (b) is incorrect because the financial statements need not be prepared in conformity with GAAP, as other bases of accounting may be followed. Answer (c) is incorrect because the report need not be made available for distribution to other employees. Answer (d) is incorrect because the individual in the profit participation plan need not own a controlling interest in the company.

112. (d) The requirement is to determine the information that should be included in an audit report on financial statements prepared on the income tax basis of accounting. AU 623 presents the form of the report to be issued. Answer (d) is correct because AU 623 requires that the report indicate that the income tax basis of accounting is a comprehensive basis of accounting other than GAAP.

113. (d) The requirement is to identify the appropriate type of audit report to be issued for a nonprofit entity's financial statements prepared following an accounting basis prescribed by a regulatory agency solely for filing with that agency. Answer (d) is correct because audit reports for such financial statements are considered special reports. Answer (a) is incorrect because an unqualified report may be issued if there are no departures from the prescribed basis. The report would not be qualified because the financial statements were prepared using an accounting basis prescribed by a regulatory agency. Answer (b) is incorrect because the report issued has five paragraphs. Answer (c) is incorrect because a disclaimer of opinion need not be issued.

114. (c) The requirement is to identify the disclosure included in a separate explanatory paragraph of an auditor's special report on financial statements prepared in conformity with the cash basis of accounting. Answer (c) is correct because the explanatory paragraph refers to the note to the financial statements that describes the basis of accounting. AU 623 presents complete details on such special reports. Answer (a) is incorrect because the report need not justify the reasons for following a basis other than generally accepted accounting principles. Answer (b) is incorrect because the explanatory paragraph contains no statement on fair presentation, and because the opinion paragraph states whether the presentation is in conformity with the basis described in the appropriate financial statement note. Answer (d) is incorrect because no explanation of how the results of operations differ from financial statements prepared in conformity with generally accepted accounting principles is necessary.

115. (b) The requirement is to identify the example of a "special report." AU 623 defines reports on compliance with aspects of regulatory requirements related to audited financial statements as special reports. [The other types of special reports include (1) other comprehensive basis financial statements, (2) specified elements, (3) financial presentations to comply with contracts, and (4) financial information presented in prescribed forms.]

116. (a) The requirement is to determine the type of report to issue when a client who uses a comprehensive basis of accounting has not appropriately titled its financial statements. Answer (a) is correct because any such exceptions or reservation should be described in an explanatory paragraph and possibly a qualified (or adverse) opinion should be issued. Answer (b) is incorrect because no such application to

the state insurance commission is necessary. Answer (c) is incorrect because a disclaimer of opinion is not appropriate when known misstatements exist. Answer (d) is incorrect because, as indicated, more than describing the terminology is necessary.

117. (a) The requirement is to determine whether a CPA is permitted to accept an engagement to audit either a schedule of accounts receivable, a schedule of royalties, or both. Answer (a) is correct because auditors may audit "specified elements, accounts or items of a financial statement," including either a schedule of accounts receivable or a schedule of royalties. Answer (b) is incorrect because an auditor may audit a schedule of royalties. Answer (c) is incorrect because an auditor may audit a schedule of accounts receivable. Answer (d) is incorrect because an auditor may audit both a schedule of accounts receivable and a schedule of royalties.

118. (b) The requirement is to identify an auditor's reporting responsibility when a printed form prescribes the wording of the independent auditor's report that will accompany it, but that wording is not acceptable to the auditor. AU 623 suggests that the auditor reword the report (or attach a separate report) when involved with this type of "special report."

C.2.b. Letters for Underwriters

119. (a) The requirement is to determine a predecessor auditor's responsibility when the financial statements he or she audited are being included in an SEC registration statement filing. Answer (a) is correct because AU 711 requires that the predecessor (1) read pertinent portions of the document, and (2) obtain a letter of representation from the successor auditor.

120. (b) The requirement is to identify the statement that is correct concerning letters for underwriters. Answer (b) is correct because letters for underwriters typically provide negative assurance on unaudited interim financial information. Answer (a) is incorrect because letters for underwriters are not required by the Securities Act of 1933. Answer (c) is incorrect because letters for underwriters are not included in registrations statements. Answer (d) is incorrect because auditors' opinions on the prior year's financial statement are not updated.

121. (a) The requirement is to determine who ordinarily signs a comfort letter. Answer (a) is correct because a comfort letter (also known as letter to an underwriter) is sent by the independent auditor to the underwriter.

122. (d) The requirement is to identify to whom comfort letters are ordinarily addressed. Answer (d) is correct because comfort letters, also referred to as letters for underwriters, are ordinarily addressed to underwriters.

123. (a) The requirement is to determine the type of opinion or assurance provided by an accountant who issues a comfort letter containing comments on data that have **not** been audited. Answer (a) is correct because when procedures short of an audit are applied to information such as capsule information, a comfort letter will generally provide negative assurance. Answer (b) is incorrect because CPAs do not provide positive assurance on supplementary disclosures. Answer (c) is incorrect because no "limited opinion" is issued on pro forma or other information. Answer (d) is incorrect because no disclaimer will be included on the prospective financial statements.

124. (d) The requirement is to determine the appropriate reference to an independent accountant in a prospectus (relating to an SEC registration statement) that includes a statement about his/her involvement with an independent audit report. AU 711 indicates that the independent accountant is an expert in auditing and accounting.

125. (d) The requirement is to identify the information included in a typical comfort letter. Answer (d) is correct because in a comfort letter auditors provide an opinion as to whether the audited financial statements comply in form with the accounting requirements of the SEC. Answer (a) is incorrect because negative assurance concerning whether the entity's internal control procedures operated as designed during the period is not provided. Answer (b) is incorrect because a comfort letter does not include an opinion on whether the entity complied with Government Auditing Standards and the Single Audit Act. Answer (c) is incorrect because negative, not positive, assurance is provided on unaudited condensed financial information.

126. (a) The requirement is to determine the proper treatment of unaudited financial statements presented in comparative form with audited financial statements in a document filed with the Securities and Exchange Commission. Answer (a) is correct because those statements should be marked "unaudited," not withheld until they are audited, and not referred to in the auditor's report.

127. (b) The requirement is to identify the requirement relating to a CPA's report when reporting on the application of accounting principles to a specific transaction. Answer (b) is correct because AU 625 requires that the report include a statement that responsibility for the proper accounting treatment rests with the preparers of the financial statements. Answer (a) is incorrect because the report states that the engagement was performed in accordance with applicable AICPA standards, not Statements on Standards for Accounting and Review Services. Answer (c) is incorrect as no such statement about opinion-shopping is included. Answer (d) is incorrect because the information may be communicated to a prior or continuing auditor.

C.2.c. Application of Accounting Principles

128. (a) The requirement is to determine an auditor's reporting responsibility when asked by a prospective client to render an opinion on the application of accounting principles to a specific transaction. Answer (a) is correct because AU 625 indicates that the report must include a statement that any difference in the facts, circumstances, or assumptions presented may change the report, as well as various other disclosures. Answer (b) is incorrect because the report indicates that the engagement was performed in accordance with AICPA standards, not Statements on Standards for Consulting Services. Answer (c) is incorrect because the report need **not** indicate that the guidance is for management use only and may not be communicated to the prior or continuing auditors. Answer (d) is incorrect because the report does not include negative assurance ("nothing came to our attention"). See AU 625 for performance and reporting standards relating to reports on the application of accounting principles.

129. (a) The requirement is to determine an auditor's responsibility when asked to render an opinion on the application of accounting principles to a specific transaction by an entity that is audited by another CPA. Answer (a) is correct because the accountant must consult with the continuing CPA to attempt to obtain information relevant to the transaction. Answer (b) is incorrect because the engagement's findings need not be reported to all of the groups listed—the entity's audit committee, the continuing CPA, and management. Answer (c) is incorrect because the accountant need not disclaim an opinion. Answer (d) is incorrect because the report's distribution need not be restricted to management and outside parties who are aware of all relevant facts.

130. (b) Answer (b) is correct because AU 625 indicates that an accountant should not undertake such an engagement when the report would be based on such a hypothetical transaction. Answers (a), (c), and (d) are all incorrect because they include information included in an accountant's report on the application of accounting principles.

C.3.a. Attestation Engagements—General

131. (c) The requirement is to select the service that is most likely to be structured as an attest engagement. Answer (c) is correct because CPAs may provide assurance as to compliance with requirements of specified laws through a variety of services, including agreed-upon procedures engagements and various compliance audits. Answers (a) and (b) are incorrect because advocating a client's tax position and consulting on a new database system are examples of professional services **not** typically structured as attest services. Answer (d) is incorrect because compilations are not a form of attest engagement.

132. (a) The requirement is to identify the correct statement. When a standard unqualified examination report is being issued, that report may be upon the subject matter or the written assertion. Answers (b), (c), and (d) are all incorrect because they suggest that the report may not be upon either the subject matter, the written assertion, or both.

133. (b) The requirement is to determine whether a CPA's conclusion may be upon the subject matter, the written assertion, or both when conditions exist that result in a material deviation from the criteria against which the subject matter was evaluated during an examination. Answer (b) is correct because in such circumstances the conclusion should be directly upon the subject matter. Answer (a) is incorrect because it suggests that the conclusion may be upon the written assertion. Answer (c) is incorrect because it states that the conclusion may not be upon the subject matter and may be upon the written assertion. Answer (d) is incorrect because it states that the conclusion may not be upon the subject matter.

134. (a) The requirement is to determine the element that is **least** likely to be present when a practitioner performs an attest engagement. Answer (a) is correct because while an assertion is generally present, it is not ordinarily required. Answers (b), (c), and (d) are all incorrect because practitioner independence, subject matter, and suitable criteria are all required.

135. (a) The requirement is to determine whether suitable criteria in an attestation engagement may be available publicly, and/or in the CPA's report. Answer (a) is correct because suitable criteria may be available publicly in the CPA's report, included with the subject matter or in the assertion, well understood by users (e.g., the distance between A and B is twenty feet) or available only to specified parties. Answers (b), (c), and (d) are all incorrect because they suggest that suitable criteria may not be available publicly, in the CPA's report, or both.

136. (d) The requirement is to identify the situation that is **least** likely to result in a restricted use attest report. Answer (d) is correct because criteria developed by an industry association may or may not result in a restricted use attest report. Answers (a), (b), and (c) always result in a restricted use report.

137. (c) The requirement is to identify the information that is **least** likely to be included in an agreed-upon procedures attestation report. Answer (c) is correct because an agreed-upon procedures report provides a summary of procedures performed and findings, not limited assurance. Answer (a) is incorrect because the specified party does not take responsibility for the sufficiency of procedures. Answer (b) is incorrect because the report's use is restricted. Answer (d) is incorrect because a summary of procedures performed is included.

138. (a) The requirement is to identify the type of report that is most likely to include a summary of findings rather than assurance. Answer (a) is correct because agreed-upon procedures reports include a summary of findings. Answer (b) is incorrect because a compilation report does not provide a summary of findings. Answer (c) is incorrect because an examination report includes positive assurance and not a summary of findings. Answer (d) is incorrect because a review report includes limited (negative) assurance, not a summary of findings.

C.3.b.   Agreed-Upon Procedures Engagements

139. (c) The requirement is to identify the statement that is **not** correct concerning "specified parties" of an agreed-upon procedures report under either the auditing or attestation standards. Answer (c) is correct because while a practitioner should establish a clear understanding regarding the terms of the engagement, preferably in an engagement letter, no such engagement letter is required. Answers (a) and (b) are incorrect because the specified parties must agree on the procedures to be performed and take responsibility for their adequacy. Answer (d) is incorrect because an additional party may be added as a specified party after completion of the engagement.

C.3.c.   Financial Forecasts and Projections

140. (a) The requirement is to determine the information to be included in a separate paragraph included in an accountant's report on the examination of projected financial statements. Answer (a) is correct because AT 301 requires that such a report include a separate paragraph that describes the limitations on the usefulness of the presentation. See AT 301 for information that should be included in an examination report of prospective financial statements. Answer (b) is incorrect because the report includes no such statement attempting to distinguish between an examination and an audit. Answer (c) is incorrect because the report includes no such disclosure and because the accountant is **not** responsible for events and circumstances up to one year

after the report's date. Answer (d) is incorrect because the report suggests that the assumptions do provide a reasonable basis.

141. (c) The requirement is to identify the statement which should be included in an accountant's compilation report on financial forecasts. Answer (c) is correct because when the accountant is preparing a standard compilation report on prospective financial statements, AT 301 requires that the accountant include a statement indicating that the prospective results may not be achieved.

142. (c) The requirement is to identify the appropriate distribution of an entity's financial projection. A financial projection is sometimes prepared to present one or more hypothetical courses of action for evaluation in response to a question such as "What would happen if...?" It is based on a responsible party's assumptions reflecting conditions it expects would exist and the course of action it expects would be taken, given one or more hypothetical assumptions. Projections are "limited use" financial statements meant for the responsible party (generally management) and third parties with whom the responsible party is negotiating directly. Answer (c) is correct because a bank might be expected to receive such a projection. Answers (a), (b), and (d) are all incorrect because projections are meant for "limited use" and not to be broadly distributed to groups such as all employees or potential or current stockholders. AT 301 provides overall guidance on the area of financial forecasts and projections.

143. (c) The requirement is to determine whether either testifying as an expert witness, compiling a financial projection, or both are engagements governed by the provisions of the Statement on Standards for Attestation Statements. Answer (c) is correct because the attestation standards explicitly exclude expert witness work, but include the compilation of a financial projection; note that in most areas compilations are not included in attestation standard coverage, but in the area of prospective financial statement (forecasts as well as projections) coverage is included. Answer (a) is incorrect because it states that expert witness work is included. Answer (b) is incorrect both because it states that expert witness work is included and that compiling a projection is not included. Answer (d) is incorrect because it states that compilations of projections are not included.

144. (a) The requirement is to identify the statement that should be included in a compilation report on a financial forecast. Answer (a) is correct because the report should state that the compilation does **not** include evaluation of the support of the assumptions underlying the forecast. Answer (b) is incorrect because no such statement is included in a compilation report, and because hypothetical assumptions pertain to financial projections, not financial forecasts. Answer (c) is incorrect because the report makes no statement concerning the range of assumptions. Answer (d) is incorrect because the statement is not included in the report, and because the prospective statements are management's, not the accountant's, representation.

145. (d) The requirement is to identify the type of general use prospective financial statement on which the accountant may appropriately report. Answer (d) is correct because financial forecasts are considered prospective financial statements, and they are appropriate for general use. Answer (a) is incorrect because financial projections are only appropriate for the party responsible for preparing them or for third parties with whom the responsible party is negotiating directly. Answers (b) and (c) are incorrect because partial presentations and pro forma financial statements are not considered prospective financial statements.

146. (b) The requirement is to identify the type of prospective financial statement that includes one or more hypothetical ("what if?") assumptions. Answer (b) is correct because financial projections include one or more hypothetical assumptions. Answer (a) is incorrect because pro forma financial presentations are designed to demonstrate the effect of a future or hypothetical transaction by showing how it might have affected the historical financial statements if it had been consummated during the period covered by those statements. Answer (c) is incorrect because partial presentations are presentations that do not meet the minimum presentation guidelines of AT 301. Answer (d) is incorrect because financial forecasts present, to the best of the responsible party's knowledge and belief, an entity's expected financial position, results of operations, and changes in financial information.

147. (d) The requirement is to determine an accountant's responsibility when he or she accepts an engagement to apply agreed-upon procedures to prospective financial statements. Answer (d) is correct because distribution of such a report is to be restricted to the specified parties involved. AT 301 also requires that the specified parties participate in establishing and taking responsibility for the adequacy of the procedures, and that the prospective financial statements include a summary of significant assumptions. Answer (a) is incorrect because the prospective financial statements need not be examined. Answer (b) is incorrect because responsibility for the adequacy of the procedures is taken by the specified parties, not by the accountant. Answer (c) is incorrect because when the accountant reports on the results of applying agreed-upon procedures he or she should not express any form of negative assurance on the prospective financial statements taken as a whole.

148. (d) The requirement is to determine the appropriate type of audit report to be issued when an accountant examines a financial forecast that fails to disclose several significant assumptions used to prepare the forecast. AT 301 states that an adverse opinion is appropriate when significant assumptions are not disclosed.

C.3.d.   Pro Forma Financial Information

149. (d) The requirement is to determine the statement that should be included in an accountant's report on a review of pro forma financial information. Answer (d) is correct because the report must include a reference to the financial statements from which the historical financial information is derived and a statement as to whether such financial statements were audited or reviewed.

C.3.e.   Management Discussion and Analysis

150. (b) The requirement is to determine the reply that is **not** an objective of a CPA's examination of a client's MD&A. Answer (b) is correct because an examination of a client's MD&A does not directly address overall conformity with such rules and regulations. Answers (a), (c), and (d)

are the three objectives of an MD&A examination agreement.

151. (c) The requirement is to identify an assertion embodied in MD&A. Answer (c) is correct because the attestation standards on MD&A indicate that consistency with the financial statements is an assertion—in addition, occurrence, completeness, and presentation and disclosure are embodied assertions. Answers (a), (b), and (d) are all incorrect because valuation, reliability, and rights and obligations are not considered to be assertions embodied in the MD&A.

152. (b) Answer (b) is correct because the MD&A review of an issuer (public) entity should be restricted to the use of specified parties. Answer (a) is incorrect because a review consists principally of applying analytical procedures, rather than also including search and verification procedures. Answer (c) is incorrect because a consideration of relevant portion of internal control is necessary to identify types of potential misstatements and to select the inquiries and analytical procedures. Answer (d) is incorrect because a review report ordinarily provides negative assurance, not a summary of findings.

C.3.f.   Trust Services

153. (d) The requirement is to identify the proper term for an attest engagement in which a CPA assesses a client's commercial Internet site for predefined criteria such as those over online privacy. Answer (d) is correct because the AICPA's Trust Services Principles relate to this area, and WebTrust is the most likely product—see www.aicpa.org. Answers (a), (b), and (c) all represent names of products not included in the professional standards.

154. (b) The requirement is to identify the standards under which Trust Services engagements are performed. Answer (b) is correct because the Statements on Standards for Attestation engagements address such engagements. More information on Trust Services engagements (WebTrust and SysTrust) is available on the AICPA's Web site—www.aicpa.org. Answers (a) and (c) are incorrect because such standards do not exist. Answer (d) is incorrect because Statements on Auditing Standards do not address Trust Services engagements.

155. (d) The requirement is to identify what the WebTrust seal of assurance relates most directly to. Answer (d) is correct because the WebTrust seal is designed to provide assurance on Web site security, availability, processing integrity, online privacy and confidentiality. Answers (a), (b), and (c) are all incorrect since WebTrust isn't specially aimed at financial statements, health care facilities, or risk assurance procedures.

156. (b) The requirement is to determine the type of opinion or assurance most likely to be included in a CPA's report relating to WebTrust engagements. Answer (b) is correct because the WebTrust examination report provides an opinion on whether the site meets the Trust Services criteria for one or more of the Trust Services Principles. Answer (a) is incorrect because no opinion on being "hackproof" is issued. Answer (c) is incorrect because negative assurance is not provided. Answer (d) is incorrect because an agreed-upon procedures engagement, not an examination engagement results in a summary of findings.

157. (b) The requirement is to identify the type of engagement that considers security, availability, processing integrity, online privacy and/or confidentiality over any type of defined electronic system. Answer (b) is correct because SysTrust engagements consider any type of defined electronic system. Answer (a) is incorrect because an engagement to consider internal control over financial reporting does not directly address these attributes. Answer (c) is incorrect because there is no such engagement as a Web site Associate. Answer (d) is incorrect because WebTrust deals more directly with company Web sites.

158. (b) The requirement is to identify the most likely report when a client refuses to provide a written assertion in a Trust Services engagement. Answer (b) is correct because this represents a scope limitation, and client imposed scope limitations are most likely to result in a disclaimer of opinion. Answer (a) is incorrect because an adverse opinion is appropriate when a CPA believes that the information is so misstated as to be misleading. Answer (c) is incorrect because client imposed scope limitations generally result in disclaimers, not qualified opinions. Answer (d) is incorrect because an unqualified opinion is most likely not appropriate in such a circumstance.

D.1.a.   Compliance Attestation Engagements—Agreed-Upon Procedures Engagements

159. (c) The requirement is to identify the type of association **not** permitted under the compliance attestation standards. AT 601 does not allow the CPA to perform a review over compliance.

160. (b) The requirement is to identify the information provided in an agreed-upon procedures report on compliance with contractual requirements to pay royalties. Answer (b) is correct because agreed-upon procedures reports include a list of the procedures performed (or reference thereto) and findings. Answer (a) is incorrect because no such disclaimer of opinion is provided in an agreed-upon procedures report. Answer (c) is incorrect because no opinion is included in an agreed-upon procedures report. Answer (d) is incorrect because an agreed-upon procedures report includes a statement disclaiming an opinion on the sufficiency of procedures, not an acknowledgement of the sufficiency of the procedures. See AT 201 for guidance on agreed-upon procedures engagements.

161. (a) The requirement is to identify the statement that is included in a CPA's report on agreed-upon procedures on management's assertion about an entity's compliance with specified requirements. Answer (a) is correct because such an agreed-upon procedures report includes a statement of limitations on the use of the report because it is intended solely for the use of specified parties. See AT 601 for information that should be included in such an agreed-upon procedures report. Answer (b) is incorrect because no "opinion" is included. Answer (c) is incorrect because a summary of findings, not negative assurance is provided. Answer (d) is incorrect because the CPA makes no representation regarding the sufficiency of procedures.

D.1.b.   Compliance Attestation Engagements—Examination Engagements

162. (c) The requirement is to identify the correct statement concerning an examination report when management

has properly disclosed an instance of material noncompliance. AT 601 states that the opinion should be qualified or adverse. Note that AT 601 requires the CPA's report to relate directly to the subject matter when the opinion is modified.

D.2.a.   Compliance Auditing of Federal Financial Assistance Programs—GAAS Audits

163. (b) The requirement is to determine an auditor's responsibility when auditing a not-for-profit entity that receives governmental financial assistance. Answer (b) is correct because AU 801 requires that the auditor assess whether management has identified laws and regulations that have a direct and material effect on the entity's financial statements; AU 801 also presents procedures to be followed in assessing such laws and regulations. Answer (a) is incorrect because such a separate report describing expected benefits and costs does not need to be issued. Answer (c) is incorrect because the CPA will not notify the governmental agency that the audit is not designed to provide assurance. Answer (d) is incorrect because the CPA does not express an opinion on the entity's continued eligibility for governmental financial assistance. AU 801 presents requirements relating to compliance auditing for governmental entities and recipients of governmental financial assistance.

164. (c) The requirement is to determine the focus of an auditor's attention in detecting misstatements resulting from violations of laws and regulations when auditing a not-for-profit organization that receives financial assistance from governmental agencies. Answer (c) is correct because the focus of such procedures should be on violations that have a direct and material effect on the amounts in the organization's financial statements (AU 801). Answers (a), (b), and (d) all represent a focus that is not as accurate as that provided in answer (c).

165. (b) The requirement is to determine the proper scope of a governmental audit. The General Accounting Office's "yellow book" suggests that in addition to financial statements, such an audit may include consideration of (1) program results, (2) compliance with laws and regulations, and (3) economy and efficiency.

166. (b) The requirement is to identify whether an auditor performing an audit in accordance with Government Auditing Standards (the "yellow book") is required to report on noteworthy accomplishments of the program, the scope of the auditor's testing of internal controls, or both. Answer (b) is correct because the "yellow book" requires reporting only upon the scope of the auditor's testing of internal controls. Answers (a), (c), and (d) all include an incorrect combination of reporting replies.

167. (b) The requirement is to identify whether an auditor performing an audit in accordance with Government Auditing Standards (the "yellow book") is required to report on recommendations for actions to improve operations, the scope of tests of compliance with laws and regulations, or both. Answer (b) is correct because the "yellow book" requires reporting upon the scope of the auditor's tests of compliance with laws and regulations. Answers (a), (c), and (d) all include an incorrect combination of reporting replies.

D.2.b. Compliance Auditing of Federal Financial Assistance Programs—GAGAS Audits

168. (a) The requirement is to identify the correct statement with respect to a financial statement audit conducted in accordance with Government Auditing Standards (the "yellow book"). Answer (a) is correct because the auditor issues a report on compliance with laws and internal control, and a report on the financial information. Answer (b) is incorrect because a financial statement audit does not address economy and efficiency in the manner suggested. Answer (c) is incorrect because recommendations for actions to correct problems and improve operations are not ordinarily included. Answer (d) is incorrect because a financial statement audit does not address whether programs are achieving the desired results.

169. (a) The requirement is to identify the correct statement with respect to a financial statement audit conducted in accordance with Government Auditing Standards (the "yellow book"). Answer (a) is correct because the auditor issues a report on compliance with laws and internal control, and a report on the financial information. Answer (b) is incorrect because not all instances of abuse, waste and mismanagement are so reported. Answer (c) is incorrect because the views of officials are not reported. Answer (d) is incorrect because internal control activities designed to detect or prevent fraud are not reported to the inspector general.

170. (d) The requirement is to identify the circumstance in which an auditor is required to report a falsification of accounting records directly to a federal inspector general. Answer (d) is correct because under Government Auditing Standards a falsification of accounting records must ordinarily be communicated by the auditor to the auditee and, if the auditee fails to make appropriate disclosure, by the

(c) all provide inaccurate descriptions of auditor reporting responsibility. See Government Auditing Standards (the "yellow book") for information on reporting under Government Auditing Standards.

171. (a) The requirement is to identify a common aspect of various types of audits of recipients of federal financial assistance in accordance with federal audit regulations. Answer (a) is correct because audits of recipients of federal financial assistance include reports on (1) the financial statements, and (2) a separate or combined report on internal control and on compliance with laws and regulations. Answer (b) is incorrect because materiality levels are not ordinarily lower or always determined by the governmental entity. Answer (c) is incorrect because the auditor need not obtain such written management representations. Answer (d) is incorrect because requirements for reporting illegal acts may vary depending upon the type of audit being performed. AU 801 provides requirements related to auditing entities that have received governmental financial assistance. In addition, guidance is provided by Government Auditing Standards (GAS), also referred to as the "yellow book," published by the Comptroller General of the United States.

172. (b) The requirement is to identify to whom an auditor most likely would be responsible for communicating significant deficiencies in the design of internal control. Answer (b) is correct because in audits under Government

Auditing Standards, significant deficiencies in the design of internal control are communicated to legislative and regulatory bodies (AU 801). Answer (a) is incorrect because the Securities and Exchange Commission does not ordinarily receive information on such deficiencies. Answer (c) is incorrect because while a court-appointed creditors' committee might in some circumstances receive information on such deficiencies, this practice is not as frequent as is done under Government Auditing Standards. Answer (d) is incorrect because shareholders do not normally receive reports on significant deficiencies or material weaknesses (see AU 325).

173. (c) The requirement is to determine the opinion which an auditor should express in a report on compliance when s/he has detected material instances of noncompliance within the program. AU 801 defines these instances of material noncompliance as failures to follow requirements, or violations of regulations or grants which cause the auditor to conclude that the total of the misstatements resulting from these failures or violations is material to the financial statements. Therefore, answer (c) is correct because the auditor should issue a qualified or an adverse opinion. Answer (a) is incorrect because the auditor is required under Governmental Auditing Standards to provide reasonable assurance on the entity's compliance with the applicable laws and regulations. Answer (b) is incorrect because the auditor must disclose the instances of noncompliance. Answer (d) is incorrect because the auditor should not disclaim an opinion as a result of noncompliance.

174. (b) The requirement is to determine a documentation requirement that an auditor should follow when auditing in accordance with (also referred to as the "yellow book"). Answer (b) is correct because Government Auditing Standards require documentation of supervisory review

175. (a) The requirement is to identify the statement that should be included in an auditor's report on an entity's compliance with laws and regulations when performing an audit in accordance with Government Auditing Standards. Answer (a) is correct because such compliance reports require a statement that management is responsible for compliance with laws, regulations, contracts, and grants. See AU 801 for this requirement and others.

176. (b) The requirement is to determine when an auditor reporting under would most likely be required to communicate management's misappropriation of assets directly to a federal inspector general. Answer (b) is correct because Government Auditing Standards requires that when a governing body fails to make a required report on such acts the auditors should communicate the matter to the external body specified in the law or regulation. Answer (a) is incorrect because such concealment will not necessarily lead to communication to a federal inspector general. Answer (c) is incorrect because material misstatement does not necessarily lead to such communication. Answer (d) is incorrect because the expected duration of the scheme is not what leads to reporting to a federal inspector general.

D.2.c. Compliance Auditing of Federal Financial Assistance Programs—Single Audit Act

177. (b) The requirement is to identify the auditor's proper measure of materiality for major federal financial

assistance programs under the Single Audit Act. AU 801
requires that it be determined separately for each major program.

178. (b)   The requirement is to identify the appropriate
compliance report under the Single Audit Act when a CPA
has detected noncompliance with requirements that have a
material effect on that program. AU 801 states that under
such circumstances the auditor should express a qualified or
adverse opinion.

179. (c)   The requirement is to identify the source of authoritative guidance for performing audits of a city that is
subject to the requirements of the Uniform Single Audit Act
of 1984. Answer (c) is correct because while the AICPA's
generally accepted auditing standards must be followed to
the extent they are pertinent, the General Accounting Office
Government Auditing Standards must also be adhered to.
The other replies all relate to standards not directly related to
the Uniform Single Audit Act.

180. (c)   The requirement is to identify the correct statement which would communicate weaknesses in internal
control used in administering a federal financial assistance
program when a CPA has examined the general purpose
financial statements of a municipality. The AICPA Accounting and Audit Guide, *Audits of State and Local Governmental Units*, requires the communication of weaknesses
that are material in relation to the federal financial assistance
program.

SOLUTIONS TO SIMULATION PROBLEMS

Simulation Problem 1

| | Research |
| Situation | |

1. The appropriate guidance regarding reporting on consistency is found in AU 508.16-.18:

Lack of Consistency

.16   The auditor's standard report implies that the auditor is satisfied that the comparability of financial statements between periods has not been materially affected by changes in accounting principles and that such principles have been consistently applied between or among periods because either (a) no change in accounting principles has occurred, or (b) there has been a change in accounting principles or in the method of their application, but the effect of the change on the comparability of the financial statements is not material. In these cases, the auditor should not refer to consistency in the report. If, however, there has been a change in accounting principles or in the method of their application that has a material effect on the comparability of the company's financial statements, the auditor should refer to the change in an explanatory paragraph of the report. Such explanatory paragraph of the report. Such explanatory paragraph (following the opinion paragraph) should identify the nature of the change and refer the reader to the note in the financial statements that discusses the change in detail. The auditor's concurrence with a change is implicit unless he or she takes exception to the change in expressing his or her opinion as to fair presentation of the financial statements in conformity with generally accepted accounting principles. When there is a change in accounting principles, there are also other matters that the auditor should consider (see paragraphs .50 through .57). [Paragraph renumbered by the issuance of Statement on Auditing Standards No. 79, December 1995.]

.17   Following is an example of the appropriate explanatory paragraph: As discussed in Note X to the financial statements, the Company changes its method of computing depreciation in 20X2. [Paragraph renumbered by the issuance of Statement on Auditing Standards No. 79, December 1995.]

.18   The addition of this explanatory paragraph in the auditor's report is required in reports on financial statements of subsequent years as long as the year of the change is presented and reported on. However, if the accounting change is accounted for by retroactive restatement of the financial statements affected, the additional paragraph is required only in the year of the change since, in subsequent years, all periods presented will be comparable. [Paragraph renumbered by the issuance of Statement on Auditing Standards No. 79, December 1995.]

2. The appropriate guidance regarding emphasis of a matter is found in AU 508.19:

Emphasis of a Matter

.19   In any report on financial statements, the auditor may emphasize a matter regarding the financial statements. Such explanatory information should be presented in a separate paragraph of the auditor's report. Phrases such as "with the foregoing [following] explanation" should not be used in the opinion paragraph if an emphasis paragraph is included in the auditor's report. Emphasis paragraphs are never required; they may be added solely at the auditor's discretion. Examples of matters the auditor may wish to emphasize are

- That the entity is a component of a larger business enterprise.
- That the entity has had significant transactions with related parties.
- Unusually important subsequent events.
- Accounting matters, other than those involving a change or changes in accounting principles, affecting the comparability of the financial statements with those of the preceding period.

3. The appropriate guidance is regarding reporting on comparative financial statements is found in AU 508.65-.66

Reports on Comparative Financial Statements

.65   The fourth standard of reporting requires that the auditor either express an opinion regarding the financial statements taken as a whole or an assertion to the effect that an opinion cannot be expressed, in the auditors report. Reference in the fourth reporting standard to the financial statements taken as a whole applies not only to the financial statements of the current period but also to those of one or more prior periods that are presented on a comparative basis with those of the current period. Therefore, a continuing auditor should update the report on the individual financial statements of the one or more prior periods presented on a comparative basis with those of the current period. Ordinarily, the auditor's report on comparative financial statements should not be dated earlier than the date on which the auditor has obtained sufficient appropriate audit evidence on which to support the opinion for the most recent audit. (See Section 530, *Dating of the Independent Auditor's Report,* paragraph .01.) [Paragraph renumbered by the issuance of Statement on Auditing Standards No. 79, December 1995. As amended, effective September 2002, by Statement on Auditing Standards No. 98 Revised December 2005, to reflect conforming changes necessary due to the issuance of Statement on Auditing Standards No. 103.]

.66   During the audit of the current-period financial statements, the auditor should be alert for circumstances or vents that affect the prior-period financial statements presented (see paragraph .68) or the adequacy of informative disclosures concerning those statements. (See Section 431, *Adequacy of Disclosure in Financial Statements,* and ARB No. 43, Chapter 2A [AC section F43].) In updating his or her report on the prior-period financial statements the auditor should consider the effects of any such circumstances or events coming to his or her attention. [Paragraph renumbered by the issuance of Statement on Auditing Standards No. 79, December 1995.]

Simulation Problem 2

| Situation | Audit Report | Research | Communication |

#		Assets *(A-G)*	Liabilities *(H-P)*
1.	Jones hired an actuary to assist in corroborating Welles' complex pension calculations concerning accrued pension liabilities that account for 35% of the client's total liabilities. The actuary's findings are reasonably close to Welles' calculations and support the financial statements.	E	P
2.	Welles holds a note receivable consisting of principal and accrued interest payable in 20X4. The note's maker recently filed a voluntary bankruptcy petition, but Welles failed to reduce the recorded value of the note to its net realizable value, which is approximately 20% of the recorded amount.	A	I
3.	Jones was engaged to audit a client's financial statements after the annual physical inventory count. The accounting records were not sufficiently reliable to enable him to become satisfied as to the year-end inventory balances.	B	J
4.	Jones found an immaterial adjustment relating to inventory. Welles has refused to adjust the financial statements to reflect this immaterial item.	E	P
5.	Welles' financial statements do not disclose certain long-term lease obligations. Jones determined that the omitted disclosures are required by FASB.	A	I
6.	Jones decided not to take responsibility for the work of another CPA who audited a wholly owned subsidiary of Welles. The total assets and revenues of the subsidiary represent 27% and 28%, respectively, of the related consolidated totals.	E	O
7.	Welles changed its method of accounting for the cost of inventories from FIFO to LIFO. Jones concurs with the change although it has a material effect on the comparability of the financial statements.	E	H
8.	Due to losses and adverse key financial ratios, Jones has substantial doubt about Welles' ability to continue as a going concern for a reasonable period of time. The client has adequately disclosed its financial difficulties in a note to its financial statements, which do **not** include any adjustments that might result from the outcome of this uncertainty. Also, Jones has ruled out the use of a disclaimer of opinion.	E	H

Explanation of solutions

1. (**E, P**) When an auditor hires a specialist to assist in corroborating a client estimate (here complex pension calculations), and that specialist's findings are reasonably close to those of the client, no report modification is required or permitted. Since the specialist's findings support the financial statements in this situation, a standard unqualified audit report is appropriate. When major unresolved differences between the findings of management and the specialist exist, report modification is appropriate.

2. (**A, I**) When the client's financial statements materially depart from generally accepted accounting principles, either a qualified opinion or an adverse opinion is appropriate, depending on the magnitude of the misstatement. The value of the client's note receivable has been impaired and therefore the client should write the note receivable down to its net realizable value. The auditor will have to determine whether to issue a qualified opinion or an adverse opinion on the basis of the materiality of the misstatement. Factors the auditor will consider include the significance of the account, the pervasiveness of the misstatement and the misstatement's effect on the financial statement taken as whole. The audit report, for either opinion, will include an explanatory paragraph to describe the substantive reasons for the modification, and the opinion paragraph will be modified.

3.   **(B, J)** A situation where the auditor is unable to obtain sufficient competent evidential matter is referred to as a scope limitation. A scope limitation may require the auditor to either qualify his or her opinion or to disclaim an opinion altogether. Since the auditor was unable to observe the inventory count or to obtain evidence through alternative procedures, the auditor will have to decide whether to issue a qualified opinion or a disclaimer of opinion. The decision will be based on the auditor's judgment as to the nature and magnitude of the potential effects of the matters in question and by their significance to the financial statements. A qualified opinion will describe the circumstances in an explanatory paragraph and will modify the scope and opinion paragraphs. A disclaimer of opinion will omit the scope paragraph and will include modification of the opinion paragraph.

4.   **(E, P)** An auditor need not modify a report for an immaterial item that the client declines to reflect.

5.   **(A, I)** Since the client's financial statements omitted required disclosures on certain long-term lease obligations, they are not prepared in accordance with generally accepted accounting principles. As a result, the auditor should express either a qualified opinion or an adverse opinion. The decision to express either a qualified or adverse opinion is based on the significance of the lack of disclosure, the pervasiveness of the misstatement, and the overall effect the lack of disclosure has on the financial statements. The audit report, for either opinion, will include an explanatory paragraph to describe the substantive reasons for the modification, and the opinion paragraph will be modified.

6.   **(E, O)** When a principal auditor decides not to take responsibility for the work of another auditor, the principal auditor should make reference to the work of the other auditor in the audit report. The audit report should clearly indicate the division of responsibility between the two auditors in the introductory, scope, and opinion paragraphs. Reference to the other auditor in the audit report does not prevent the principal auditor from issuing an unqualified opinion. The reference to the other auditor is designed to emphasize the divided responsibilities between the two auditors.

7.   **(E, H)** When an auditor agrees with a change in accounting principles, a lack of consistency results in an unqualified opinion with an explanatory paragraph following the opinion paragraph. There is no modification of the three standard paragraphs.

8.   **(E, H)** The auditor has substantial doubt about the client's ability to remain a going concern for a reasonable period of time. The audit report should emphasize this concern to the financial statement users. As a result, the auditor's report will include an unqualified opinion with an explanatory paragraph following the opinion paragraph.

Situation	Audit Report	Research		Communication

The necessary information, presented in AU 315.09, is as follows:

The successor auditor should make specific and reasonable inquiries of the predecessor auditor regarding matters that will assist the successor auditor in determining whether to accept the engagement. Matters subject to inquiry should include

- Information that might bear on the integrity of management.
- Disagreements with management as to accounting principles, auditing procedures, or other similarly significant matters.
- Communications to audit committees or others with equivalent authority and responsibility regarding fraud, illegal acts by clients, and internal control related matters.
- The predecessor auditor's understanding as to the reasons for the change of auditors.

The successor auditor may wish to consider other reasonable inquiries.

Situation	Audit Report	Research		Communication

To: CEO, Welles Inc.
From: CPA Candidate

You have requested an explanation of the audit report modification for a change in accounting principle. This modification to our report is merely a one-sentence paragraph that emphasizes the fact that the company has changed accounting principles and gives our concurrence with the change. It in no way affects our unqualified opinion on your company's financial statements.

If you have any additional questions please contact us.

MULTIPLE-CHOICE QUESTIONS (1-58)

1. An advantage of using statistical over nonstatistical sampling methods in tests of controls is that the statistical methods
   a. Can more easily convert the sample into a dual-purpose test useful for substantive testing.
   b. Eliminate the need to use judgment in determining appropriate sample sizes.
   c. Afford greater assurance than a nonstatistical sample of equal size.
   d. Provide an objective basis for quantitatively evaluating sample risk.

2. An advantage of statistical sampling over nonstatistical sampling is that statistical sampling helps an auditor to
   a. Eliminate the risk of nonsampling errors.
   b. Reduce the level of audit risk and materiality to a relatively low amount.
   c. Measure the sufficiency of the evidential matter obtained.
   d. Minimize the failure to detect errors and fraud.

3. The likelihood of assessing control risk too high is the risk that the sample selected to test controls
   a. Does **not** support the auditor's planned assessed level of control risk when the true operating effectiveness of the control structure justifies such an assessment.
   b. Contains misstatements that could be material to the financial statements when aggregated with misstatements in other account balances or transactions classes.
   c. Contains proportionately fewer monetary errors or deviations from prescribed controls than exist in the balance or class as a whole.
   d. Does **not** support the tolerable error for some or all of management's assertions.

4. The risk of incorrect acceptance and the likelihood of assessing control risk too low relate to the
   a. Allowable risk of tolerable misstatement.
   b. Preliminary estimates of materiality levels.
   c. Efficiency of the audit.
   d. Effectiveness of the audit.

5. Which of the following best illustrates the concept of sampling risk?
   a. A randomly chosen sample may **not** be representative of the population as a whole on the characteristic of interest.
   b. An auditor may select audit procedures that are **not** appropriate to achieve the specific objective.
   c. An auditor may fail to recognize errors in the documents examined for the chosen sample.
   d. The documents related to the chosen sample may **not** be available for inspection.

6. In assessing sampling risk, the risk of incorrect rejection and the risk of assessing control risk too high relate to the
   a. Efficiency of the audit.
   b. Effectiveness of the audit.
   c. Selection of the sample.
   d. Audit quality controls.

Items 7 and 8 are based on the following information:

The diagram below depicts the auditor's estimated deviation rate compared with the tolerable rate, and also depicts the true population deviation rate compared with the tolerable rate.

	True State of Population	
	Deviation rate exceeds tolerable rate	**Deviation rate is less than tolerable rate**
Auditor's estimate based on sample results **Deviation rate exceeds tolerable rate**	I.	II.
Deviation rate is less than tolerable rate	III.	IV.

7. In which of the situations would the auditor have properly concluded that control risk is at or below the planned assessed level?
   a. I.
   b. II.
   c. III.
   d. IV.

8. As a result of tests of controls, the auditor assesses control risk too high and thereby increases substantive testing. This is illustrated by situation
   a. I.
   b. II.
   c. III.
   d. IV.

9. While performing a test of details during an audit, an auditor determined that the sample results supported the conclusion that the recorded account balance was materially misstated. It was, in fact, not materially misstated. This situation illustrates the risk of
   a. Assessing control risk too high.
   b. Assessing control risk too low.
   c. Incorrect rejection.
   d. Incorrect acceptance.

10. The size of a sample designed for dual purpose testing should be
   a. The larger of the samples that would otherwise have been designed for the two separate purposes.
   b. The smaller of the samples that would otherwise have been designed for the two separate purposes.
   c. The combined total of the samples that would otherwise have been designed for the two separate purposes.
   d. More than the larger of the samples that would otherwise have been designated for the two separate purposes, but less than the combined total of the samples that would otherwise have been designed for the two separate purposes.

11. The expected population deviation rate of client billing errors is 3%. The auditor has established a tolerable rate of 5%. In the review of client invoices the auditor should use

a. Stratified sampling.
b. Variable sampling.
c. Discovery sampling.
d. Attribute sampling.

12. Which of the following sampling methods would be used to estimate a numerical measurement of a population, such as a dollar value?
a. Attribute sampling.
b. Stop-or-go sampling.
c. Variables sampling.
d. Random-number sampling.

13. For which of the following audit tests would an auditor most likely use attribute sampling?
a. Making an independent estimate of the amount of a LIFO inventory.
b. Examining invoices in support of the valuation of fixed asset additions.
c. Selecting accounts receivable for confirmation of account balances.
d. Inspecting employee time cards for proper approval by supervisors.

14. An underlying feature of random-based selection of items is that each
a. Stratum of the accounting population be given equal representation in the sample.
b. Item in the accounting population be randomly ordered.
c. Item in the accounting population should have an opportunity to be selected.
d. Item must be systematically selected using replacement.

15. Which of the following statistical selection techniques is **least** desirable for use by an auditor?
a. Systematic selection.
b. Stratified selection.
c. Block selection.
d. Sequential selection.

16. Which of the following statistical sampling plans does **not** use a fixed sample size for tests of controls?
a. Dollar-unit sampling.
b. Sequential sampling.
c. PPS sampling.
d. Variables sampling.

17. If certain forms are not consecutively numbered
a. Selection of a random sample probably is not possible.
b. Systematic sampling may be appropriate.
c. Stratified sampling should be used.
d. Random number tables cannot be used.

18. When performing a test of a control with respect to control over cash receipts, an auditor may use a systematic sampling technique with a start at any randomly selected item. The biggest disadvantage of this type of sampling is that the items in the population
a. Must be systematically replaced in the population after sampling.
b. May systematically occur more than once in the sample.
c. Must be recorded in a systematic pattern before the sample can be drawn.

d. May occur in a systematic pattern, thus destroying the sample randomness.

19. What is the primary objective of using stratification as a sampling method in auditing?
a. To increase the confidence level at which a decision will be reached from the results of the sample selected.
b. To determine the occurrence rate for a given characteristic in the population being studied.
c. To decrease the effect of variance in the total population.
d. To determine the precision range of the sample selected.

20. As a result of tests of controls, an auditor assessed control risk too low and decreased substantive testing. This assessment occurred because the true deviation rate in the population was
a. Less than the risk of assessing control risk too low, based on the auditor's sample.
b. Less than the deviation rate in the auditor's sample.
c. More than the risk of assessing control risk too low, based on the auditor's sample.
d. More than the deviation rate in the auditor's sample.

21. Which of the following factors is(are) considered in determining the sample size for a test of controls?

	Expected deviation rate	*Tolerable deviation rate*
a.	Yes	Yes
b.	No	No
c.	No	Yes
d.	Yes	No

22. Which of the following statements is correct concerning statistical sampling in tests of controls?
a. Deviations from control procedures at a given rate usually result in misstatements at a higher rate.
b. As the population size doubles, the sample size should also double.
c. The qualitative aspects of deviations are **not** considered by the auditor.
d. There is an inverse relationship between the sample size and the tolerable rate.

23. In determining the sample size for a test of controls, an auditor should consider the likely rate of deviations, the allowable risk of assessing control risk too low, and the
a. Tolerable deviation rate.
b. Risk of incorrect acceptance.
c. Nature and cause of deviations.
d. Population size.

24. Which of the following combinations results in a decrease in sample size in a sample for attributes?

	Risk of assessing control risk too low	*Tolerable rate*	*Expected population deviation rate*
a.	Increase	Decrease	Increase
b.	Decrease	Increase	Decrease
c.	Increase	Increase	Decrease
d.	Increase	Increase	Increase

25. An auditor is testing internal control procedures that are evidenced on an entity's vouchers by matching random numbers with voucher numbers. If a random number matches the number of a voided voucher, that voucher ordinarily should be replaced by another voucher in the random sample if the voucher
  a.   Constitutes a deviation.
  b.   Has been properly voided.
  c.   Cannot be located.
  d.   Represents an immaterial dollar amount.

26. An auditor plans to examine a sample of twenty purchase orders for proper approvals as prescribed by the client's control procedures. One of the purchase orders in the chosen sample of twenty cannot be found, and the auditor is unable to use alternative procedures to test whether that purchase order was properly approved. The auditor should
  a.   Choose another purchase order to replace the missing purchase order in the sample.
  b.   Consider this test of control invalid and proceed with substantive tests since internal control **cannot** be relied upon.
  c.   Treat the missing purchase order as a deviation for the purpose of evaluating the sample.
  d.   Select a completely new set of twenty purchase orders.

27. When assessing the tolerable rate, the auditor should consider that, while deviations from control procedures increase the risk of material misstatements, such deviations do not necessarily result in errors. This explains why
  a.   A recorded disbursement that does **not** show evidence of required approval may nevertheless be a transaction that is properly authorized and recorded.
  b.   Deviations would result in errors in the accounting records only if the deviations and the errors occurred on different transactions.
  c.   Deviations from pertinent control procedures at a given rate ordinarily would be expected to result in errors at a higher rate.
  d.   A recorded disbursement that is properly authorized may nevertheless be a transaction that contains a material error.

28. The objective of the tolerable rate in sampling for tests of controls of internal control is to
  a.   Determine the probability of the auditor's conclusion based upon reliance factors.
  b.   Determine that financial statements taken as a whole are not materially in error.
  c.   Estimate the reliability of substantive tests.
  d.   Estimate the range of procedural deviations in the population.

29. The tolerable rate of deviations for a test of a control is generally
  a.   Lower than the expected rate of errors in the related accounting records.
  b.   Higher than the expected rate of errors in the related accounting records.
  c.   Identical to the expected rate of errors in related accounting records.
  d.   Unrelated to the expected rate of errors in the related accounting records.

30. If the auditor is concerned that a population may contain exceptions, the determination of a sample size sufficient to include at **least** one such exception is a characteristic of
  a.   Discovery sampling.
  b.   Variables sampling.
  c.   Random sampling.
  d.   Dollar-unit sampling.

31. In determining the number of documents to select for a test to obtain assurance that all sales have been properly authorized, an auditor should consider the tolerable rate of deviation from the control activity. The auditor should also consider the

  I. Likely rate of deviations.
  II. Allowable risk of assessing control risk too high.

  a.   I only.
  b.   II only.
  c.   Both I and II.
  d.   Either I or II.

32. An auditor should consider the tolerable rate of deviation when determining the number of check requests to select for a test to obtain assurance that all check requests have been properly authorized. The auditor should also consider

	The average dollar value of the check requests	The allowable risk of assessing control risk too low
a.	Yes	Yes
b.	Yes	No
c.	No	Yes
d.	No	No

33. Which of the following statements is correct concerning statistical sampling in tests of controls?
  a.   As the population size increases, the sample size should increase proportionately.
  b.   Deviations from specific internal control procedures at a given rate ordinarily result in misstatements at a lower rate.
  c.   There is an inverse relationship between the expected population deviation rate and the sample size.
  d.   In determining tolerable rate, an auditor considers detection risk and the sample size.

34. What is an auditor's evaluation of a statistical sample for attributes when a test of fifty documents results in three deviations if tolerable rate is 7%, the expected population deviation rate is 5%, and the allowance for sampling risk is 2%?
  a.   Modify the planned assessed level of control risk because the tolerable rate plus the allowance for sampling risk exceeds the expected population deviation rate.
  b.   Accept the sample results as support for the planned assessed level of control risk because the sample deviation rate plus the allowance for sampling risk exceeds the tolerable rate.
  c.   Accept the sample results as support for the planned assessed level of control risk because the tolerable rate less the allowance for sampling risk equals the expected population deviation rate.
  d.   Modify the planned assessed level of control risk because the sample deviation rate plus the allowance for sampling risk exceeds the tolerable rate.

Items 35 and 36 are based on the following:

An auditor desired to test credit approval on 10,000 sales invoices processed during the year. The auditor designed a statistical sample that would provide 1% risk of assessing control risk too low (99% confidence) that not more than 7% of the sales invoices lacked approval. The auditor estimated from previous experience that about 2 1/2% of the sales invoices lacked approval. A sample of 200 invoices was examined and 7 of them were lacking approval. The auditor then determined the achieved upper precision limit to be 8%.

35. In the evaluation of this sample, the auditor decided to increase the level of the preliminary assessment of control risk because the
  a. Tolerable rate (7%) was less than the achieved upper precision limit (8%).
  b. Expected deviation rate (7%) was more than the percentage of errors in the sample (3 1/2%).
  c. Achieved upper precision limit (8%) was more than the percentage of errors in the sample (3 1/2%).
  d. Expected deviation rate (2 1/2%) was less than the tolerable rate (7%).

36. The allowance for sampling risk was
  a. 5 1/2%
  b. 4 1/2%
  c. 3 1/2%
  d. 1%

37. Which of the following statements is correct concerning statistical sampling in tests of controls?
  a. The population size has little or **no** effect on determining sample size except for very small populations.
  b. The expected population deviation rate has little or **no** effect on determining sample size except for very small populations.
  c. As the population size doubles, the sample size also should double.
  d. For a given tolerable rate, a larger sample size should be selected as the expected population deviation rate decreases.

38. When an auditor has chosen a random sample and is using nonstatistical attributes sampling, that auditor
  a. Need not consider the risk of assessing control risk too low.
  b. Has committed a nonsampling error.
  c. Will have to use discovery sampling to evaluate the results.
  d. Should compare the deviation rate of the sample to the tolerable deviation rate.

39. How would increases in tolerable misstatement and assessed level of control risk affect the sample size in a substantive test of details?

	Increase in tolerable misstatement	Increase in assessed level of control risk
a.	Increase sample size	Increase sample size
b.	Increase sample size	Decrease sample size
c.	Decrease sample size	Increase sample size
d.	Decrease sample size	Decrease sample size

40. Which of the following courses of action would an auditor most likely follow in planning a sample of cash disbursements if the auditor is aware of several unusually large cash disbursements?
  a. Set the tolerable rate of deviation at a lower level than originally planned.
  b. Stratify the cash disbursements population so that the unusually large disbursements are selected.
  c. Increase the sample size to reduce the effect of the unusually large disbursements.
  d. Continue to draw new samples until all the unusually large disbursements appear in the sample.

41. Which of the following sample planning factors would influence the sample size for a substantive test of details for a specific account?

	Expected amount of misstatements	Measure of tolerable misstatement
a.	No	No
b.	Yes	Yes
c.	No	Yes
d.	Yes	No

42. When planning a sample for a substantive test of details, an auditor should consider tolerable misstatement for the sample. This consideration should
  a. Be related to the auditor's business risk.
  b. Not be adjusted for qualitative factors.
  c. Be related to preliminary judgments about materiality levels.
  d. Not be changed during the audit process.

43. A number of factors influences the sample size for a substantive test of details of an account balance. All other factors being equal, which of the following would lead to a larger sample size?
  a. Greater reliance on internal control.
  b. Greater reliance on analytical procedures.
  c. Smaller expected frequency of errors.
  d. Smaller measure of tolerable misstatement.

44. In estimation sampling for variables, which of the following must be known in order to estimate the appropriate sample size required to meet the auditor's needs in a given situation?
  a. The qualitative aspects of errors.
  b. The total dollar amount of the population.
  c. The acceptable level of risk.
  d. The estimated rate of misstatements in the population.

45. An auditor established a $60,000 tolerable misstatement for an asset with an account balance of $1,000,000. The auditor selected a sample of every twentieth item from the population that represented the asset account balance and discovered overstatements of $3,700 and understatements of $200. Under these circumstances, the auditor most likely would conclude that
  a. There is an unacceptably high risk that the actual misstatements in the population exceed the tolerable misstatement because the total projected misstatement is more than the tolerable misstatement.
  b. There is an unacceptably high risk that the tolerable misstatement exceeds the sum of actual overstatements and understatements.

c. The asset account is fairly stated because the total projected misstatement is less than the tolerable misstatement.

d. The asset account is fairly stated because the tolerable misstatement exceeds the net of projected actual overstatements and understatements.

46. Which of the following statements is correct concerning probability-proportional-to-size (PPS) sampling, also known as dollar unit sampling?

a. The sampling distribution should approximate the normal distribution.

b. Overstated units have a lower probability of sample selection than units that are understated.

c. The auditor controls the risk of incorrect acceptance by specifying that risk level for the sampling plan.

d. The sampling interval is calculated by dividing the number of physical units in the population by the sample size.

47. Hill has decided to use probability-proportional-to-size (PPS) sampling, sometimes called dollar-unit sampling, in the audit of a client's accounts receivable balances. Hill plans to use the following PPS sampling table:

TABLE
Reliability Factors for Overstatements

Number of over-	Risk of incorrect acceptance				
statements	1%	5%	10%	15%	20%
0	4.61	3.00	2.31	1.90	1.61
1	6.64	4.75	3.89	3.38	3.00
2	8.41	6.30	5.33	4.72	4.28
3	10.05	7.76	6.69	6.02	5.52
4	11.61	9.16	8.00	7.27	6.73

Additional information

Tolerable misstatements (net of effect of expected misstatements)	$ 24,000
Risk of incorrect acceptance	20%
Number of misstatements	1
Recorded amount of accounts receivable	$240,000
Number of accounts	360

What sample size should Hill use?

a. 120
b. 108
c. 60
d. 30

48. In a probability-proportional-to-size sample with a sampling interval of $5,000, an auditor discovered that a selected account receivable with a recorded amount of $10,000 had an audit amount of $8,000. If this were the only error discovered by the auditor, the projected error of this sample would be

a. $1,000
b. $2,000
c. $4,000
d. $5,000

49. An auditor is determining the sample size for an inventory observation using mean-per-unit estimation, which is a variables sampling plan. To calculate the required sample size, the auditor usually determines the

	Variability in the dollar amounts of inventory items	Risk of incorrect acceptance
a.	Yes	Yes
b.	Yes	No
c.	No	Yes
d.	No	No

50. In statistical sampling methods used in substantive testing, an auditor most likely would stratify a population into meaningful groups if

a. Probability-proportional-to-size (PPS) sampling is used.

b. The population has highly variable recorded amounts.

c. The auditor's estimated tolerable misstatement is extremely small.

d. The standard deviation of recorded amounts is relatively small.

51. The use of the ratio estimation sampling technique is most effective when

a. The calculated audit amounts are approximately proportional to the client's book amounts.

b. A relatively small number of differences exist in the population.

c. Estimating populations whose records consist of quantities, but **not** book values.

d. Large overstatement differences and large understatement differences exist in the population.

52. In the application of statistical techniques to the estimation of dollar amounts, a preliminary sample is usually taken primarily for the purpose of estimating the population

a. Variability.
b. Mode.
c. Range.
d. Median.

53. Using statistical sampling to assist in verifying the year-end accounts payable balance, an auditor has accumulated the following data:

	Number of accounts	Book balance	Balance determined by the auditor
Population	4,100	$5,000,000	?
Sample	200	$ 250,000	$300,000

Using the ratio estimation technique, the auditor's estimate of year-end accounts payable balance would be

a. $6,150,000
b. $6,000,000
c. $5,125,000
d. $5,050,000

54. Use of the ratio estimation sampling technique to estimated dollar amounts is **inappropriate** when

a. The total book value is known and corresponds to the sum of all the individual book values.

b. A book value for each sample item is unknown.

c. There are some observed differences between audited values and book values.

d. The audited values are nearly proportional to the book values.

55. An auditor is performing substantive tests of pricing and extensions of perpetual inventory balances consisting of a large number of items. Past experience indicates numerous pricing and extension errors. Which of the following statistical sampling approaches is most appropriate?

    a.   Unstratified mean-per-unit.
    b.   Probability-proportional-to-size.
    c.   Stop or go.
    d.   Ratio estimation.

56. The major reason that the difference and ratio estimation methods would be expected to produce audit efficiency is that the

    a.   Number of members of the populations of differences or ratios is smaller than the number of members of the population of book values.
    b.   Beta risk may be completely ignored.
    c.   Calculations required in using difference or ratio estimation are less arduous and fewer than those required when using direct estimation.
    d.   Variability of the populations of differences or ratios is less than that of the populations of book values or audited values.

57. Which of the following statements is correct concerning the auditor's use of statistical sampling?

    a.   An auditor needs to estimate the dollar amount of the standard deviation of the population to use classical variables sampling.
    b.   An assumption of PPS sampling is that the underlying accounting population is normally distributed.
    c.   A classical variables sample needs to be designed with special considerations to include negative balances in the sample.
    d.   The selection of zero balances usually does **not** require special sample design considerations when using PPS sampling.

58. Which of the following most likely would be an advantage in using classical variables sampling rather than probability-proportional-to-size (PPS) sampling?

    a.   An estimate of the standard deviation of the population's recorded amounts is **not** required.
    b.   The auditor rarely needs the assistance of a computer program to design an efficient sample.
    c.   Inclusion of zero and negative balances generally does **not** require special design considerations.
    d.   Any amount that is individually significant is automatically identified and selected.

SIMULATION PROBLEMS

Simulation Problem 1   (30 to 35 minutes)

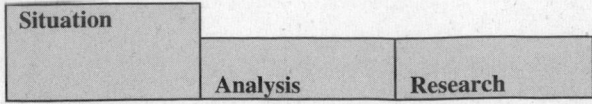

The following is a computer printout generated by audit software using probability-proportional-to-size (PPS) sampling:

Winz Corporation
Receivable Sampling Evaluation Results
December 31, 20X2

Population book value = $2,400,00;   Tolerable misstatement = $280,000

Projected Misstatement

Book value	Audited value	Misstatement	Tainting percentage	Sampling interval	Projected misstatement
$1,000	$ 0	$1,000	100%	$80,000	$ 1,000
750	600	150	20%	$80,000	16,000
85,000	60,000	25,000	NA	NA	25,000
					$42,000

Basic Precision = 3.0 * $80,000 $240,000

Incremental Allowance

Reliability factor	Increment	(Increment −1)	Projected misstatement	Incremental allowance
3.00				
4.75	1.75	.75	$16,000	$12,000
6.30	1.55	.55	1,000	550
				$12,550

The software uses factors from the following PPS sampling table:

TABLE
Reliability Factors for Overstatements

Number of overstatements	Risk of incorrect acceptance				
	1%	5%	10%	15%	20%
0	4.61	3.00	2.31	1.90	1.61
1	6.64	4.75	3.89	3.38	3.00
2	8.41	6.30	5.33	4.72	4.28
3	10.05	7.76	6.69	6.02	5.52
4	11.61	9.16	8.00	7.27	6.73

Answer the following questions relating to the above worksheet:

Questions	Answers
1. What was the planned sample size?	A. 30 items
	B. 60 items
2. What is the total misstatement in the sample?	C. 76 items
3. What is the most likely total misstatement in the population?	D. 90 items
	E. 0
4. Calculate the upper limit on misstatement.	F. $ 12,550
	G. $ 26,150
5. Calculate the allowance for sampling risk.	H. $ 42,000
6. Would one "accept" or "reject" the population as being materially correct?	I. $ 54,550
	J. $ 80,000
7. What is the risk of incorrect acceptance?	K. $252,550
	L. $280,000
	M. $294,550
	N. $354,550
	O. Accept
	P. Reject
	Q. 5%
	R. 20%
	S. 100%

Situation	Analysis	Research

Audit risk includes both sampling and nonsampling risk. Search the Professional Standards to identify the nature of sampling risk versus nonsampling risk. You should select the appropriate paragraph(s).

Simulation Problem 2   (35 to 45 minutes)

Situation	Characteristics	Calculation	Spreadsheet	Research	Communication

Edwards has decided to use probability-proportional-to-size (PPS) sampling, sometimes called dollar-unit sampling, in the audit of his client Jane2 Inc.'s accounts receivable balance. Few, if any, misstatements of account balance overstatement are expected.

Situation	Characteristics	Calculation	Spreadsheet	Research	Communication

Reply as to whether you believe the following statements are correct or incorrect concerning PPS sampling:

		Correct	*Incorrect*
1.	Size of a PPS sample is not based on the estimated variation of audited amounts.	○	○
2.	PPS sampling results in a stratified sample.	○	○
3.	Individually significant items are automatically identified.	○	○
4.	PPS sampling results in a smaller sample size when numerous small misstatements are expected.	○	○
5.	If no misstatements are expected, PPS sampling will usually result in a smaller sample size than classical variables sampling methods.	○	○
6.	One does not need a book value for individual items to evaluate a PPS sample.	○	○
7.	A PPS sample eliminates the need to project results to the overall population.	○	○
8.	PPS sampling is "preferred" by the professional standards.	○	○

Situation	Characteristics	Calculation	Spreadsheet	Research	Communication

Calculate the sampling interval Edwards should use given the following information:

Tolerable misstatements	$ 50,000
Sample size	100
Number of misstatements allowed	$ 10,000
Recorded amount of accounts receivable	$300,000

Sampling interval =

- A. $ 1,000
- B. $ 3,000
- C. $ 2,500
- D. $ 4,200
- E. $ 10,000
- F. $ 62,000
- G. $300,000

Situation	Characteristics	Calculation	Spreadsheet	Research	Communication

Complete the spreadsheet to calculate total projected misstatement if the following three misstatements were discovered in a PPS sample:

	Recorded amount	Audit amount	Sampling interval
1st misstatement	$ 400	$ 320	$1,000
2nd misstatement	500	0	1,000
3rd misstatement	3,000	2,500	1,000

Projected misstatement =

- a. $ 723
- b. $ 1,080
- c. $ 1,533
- d. $ 1,700
- e. $ 2,169
- f. $16,200
- g. $18,234
- h. $32,520

	A	B	C	D	E	F	G
1	Jane2 Inc.						
2	Accounts Receivable						
3	December 31, 20X2						
4							
5		Recorded amount	Audited amount	Difference	Tainting %	Sampling interval	
6	1st misstatement	400	320			1,000	
7	2nd misstatement	500	0			1,000	
8	3rd misstatement	3,000	2,500			1,000	

Situation	Characteristics	Calculation	Spreadsheet	Research	Communication

Auditors must consider both the concepts of materiality and tolerable misstatement. Search the Professional Standards to identify the relationship between tolerable misstatement and materiality. Select the appropriate material for your solution.

Situation	Characteristics	Calculation	Spreadsheet	Research	Communication

Write a memorandum to the audit working papers describing the importance of projection sample results to the population.

REMINDER: Your response will be graded for both technical content and writing skills. Technical content will be evaluated for information that is helpful to the intended reader and clearly relevant to the issue. Writing skills will be evaluated for development, organization, and the appropriate expression of ideas in professional correspondence. Use a standard business memo or letter format with a clear beginning, middle, and end. Do not convey information in the form of a table, bullet point list, or other abbreviated presentation.

To:　　　Audit Working Papers
From:　　CPA Candidate

MULTIPLE-CHOICE ANSWERS

1. d		13. d		25. b		37. a		49. a	
2. c		14. c		26. c		38. d		50. b	
3. a		15. c		27. a		39. c		51. a	
4. d		16. b		28. d		40. b		52. a	
5. a		17. b		29. d		41. b		53. b	
6. a		18. d		30. a		42. c		54. b	
7. d		19. c		31. a		43. d		55. d	
8. b		20. d		32. c		44. c		56. d	
9. c		21. a		33. b		45. a		57. a	
10. a		22. d		34. d		46. c		58. c	
11. d		23. a		35. a		47. d		1st: ___/58 = ___%	
12. c		24. c		36. b		48. b		2nd: ___/58 = ___%	

MULTIPLE-CHOICE ANSWER EXPLANATIONS

A.2. General Approaches to Audit Sampling— Nonstatistical and Statistical

1.   (d)   The requirement is to identify an advantage of statistical sampling over nonstatistical sampling. Answer (d) is correct because statistical sampling helps the auditor to: (1) design an efficient sample, (2) measures the sufficiency of the evidential matter obtained, and (3) evaluate the sample results (AICPA *Audit Sampling Guide*). Answer (a) is incorrect because dual-purpose tests, which both test a control and serve as substantive test, may be performed with either a statistical or a nonstatistical sample. Answer (b) is incorrect because both statistical and nonstatistical sampling require the use of judgment, although that judgment is quantified when statistical sampling is used. Answer (c) is incorrect because either statistical or nonstatistical sampling may provide equal assurance to the auditor.

2.   (c)   The requirement is to identify an advantage of statistical sampling over nonstatistical sampling. Answer (c) is correct because statistical sampling helps the auditor to: (1) design an efficient sample, (2) measure the sufficiency of the evidential matter obtained, and (3) evaluate the sample results (AICPA *Audit Sampling Guide*). Answer (a) is incorrect because the risk of nonsampling errors is not directly affected by whether statistical or nonstatistical sampling is used. Answer (b) is incorrect because either statistical or nonstatistical sampling can be used to reduce the level of audit risk to a low level; the materiality level should not be affected by the type of sampling used. Answer (d) is incorrect because either statistical or nonstatistical sampling may be used to minimize the failure to detect errors and fraud.

A.3. Uncertainty and Audit Sampling

3.   (a)   The requirement is to determine the meaning of the likelihood of assessing control risk too high in a test of controls. Answer (a) is correct because the risk of assessing control risk too high is the risk that the sample does **not** support the auditor's planned assessed level of control risk when the true operating effectiveness of the control structure justifies such an assessment. Answer (b) is incorrect because the risk of assessing control risk too high relates to the deviation rate from a control procedure in a population, not to monetary misstatements. Answer (c) is incorrect because the risk of assessing control risk too high does not directly relate to monetary misstatements. Answer (d) is incorrect because tolerable error (misstatement) relates to variables

sampling applied to substantive testing and not to tests of controls and because the meaning of "support the tolerable error" is uncertain.

4.   (d)   The requirement is to determine the nature of the risk of incorrect acceptance and the risk of assessing control risk too low. Answer (d) is correct because the risk of incorrect acceptance and the risk of assessing control risk too low relate to the effectiveness of an audit in detecting an existing material misstatement or deviation. Answer (a) is incorrect because the term "allowable risk of tolerable misstatement" is not used in the professional standards. Answer (b) is incorrect because preliminary estimates of materiality levels relate most directly to the risk of incorrect acceptance, and only indirectly to the risk of assessing control risk too low. Answer (c) is incorrect because the risk of incorrect rejection and the risk of assessing control risk too high relate to the efficiency of the audit.

5.   (a)   The requirement is to determine which answer represents the concept of sampling risk. Sampling risk arises from the possibility that an auditor's conclusions based upon a sample would differ from the conclusions which would be drawn from examining the entire population (i.e., the risk that the sample examined is not representative of the population). Answers (b), (c), and (d) are all incorrect because they relate to errors which could occur even if 100% of the population were examined, that is, nonsampling risk.

6.   (a)   The requirement is to determine what is related to the risk of incorrect rejection and the risk of assessing control risk too high. Answer (a) is correct because AU 350 states that the risk of incorrect rejection and the risk of assessing control risk too high relate to the efficiency of the audit. These two errors generally result in an auditor performing unnecessary additional procedures. Answer (b) is incorrect because the risk of incorrect acceptance and the risk of assessing control risk too low relate to the effectiveness of an audit. Answer (c) is incorrect because the risks do not relate directly to the actual selection of the sample. Answer (d) is incorrect because the audit quality controls do not directly mention either of these risks.

7.   (d)   The requirement is to determine the situation in which an auditor has properly concluded that control risk is at or below the planned assessed level. Answer (d) is correct because to support the planned level, the deviation rate must be less than the tolerable rate and the auditor must conclude that the deviation rate is less than the tolerable rate. Answer (a) is incorrect because it represents a situation in which the auditor appropriately decides that the deviation rate exceeds the tolerable rate. Answer (b) is incorrect because it represents a situation in which an auditor erroneously concludes that the deviation rate exceeds the tolerable rate when it actually does not. Answer (c) is incorrect because the auditor erroneously concludes that the deviation rate is less than the tolerable rate when it actually exceeds it.

8. (b) The requirement is to determine the situation in which the auditor assesses control risk too high and thereby increases substantive testing. Answer (b) is correct because to assess control risk too high, an auditor must estimate that the deviation rate exceeds the tolerable rate when it actually is less than the tolerable rate. Answer (a) is incorrect because it represents a situation in which the auditor appropriately decides that the deviation rate exceeds the tolerable rate. Answer (c) is incorrect because the auditor erroneously concludes that the deviation rate is less than the tolerable rate when it actually exceeds the tolerable rate. Answer (d) is incorrect because to properly rely on internal control, the deviation rate must be less than the tolerable rate and the auditor must conclude that the deviation rate is less than the tolerable rate.

9. (c) The requirement is to determine the type of risk demonstrated when an auditor concludes that an account is misstated when in fact it is not. Answer (c) is correct because the risk of incorrect rejection is the risk that the sample supports the conclusion that the recorded account balance is materially misstated when the account is not misstated. Answers (a) and (b) are incorrect because the risk of assessing control risk too high and the risk of assessing control risk too low relate to tests of controls, and not to substantive tests of details. Answer (d) is incorrect because the risk of incorrect acceptance is the risk that the sample support the conclusion that the account is not misstated when in fact it is misstated.

A.4. Types of Audit Tests in Which Sampling May Be Used

10. (a) The requirement is to identify the correct statement with respect to the size of a sample required for dual purpose testing. Answer (a) is correct because the auditor should select the larger of the required sample sizes.

A.5. Types of Statistical Sampling Plans

11. (d) The requirement is to identify the type of sampling involved in a review of client invoices in which an expected population deviation rate and an established tolerable rate are provided. Answer (d) is correct because attribute sampling is used to reach a conclusion about a population in terms of a rate of occurrence (*Audit Sampling Guide*). Answer (a) is incorrect because stratified sampling is generally used to reach a dollar-based conclusion in variables sampling approaches. Answer (b) is incorrect because, as indicated, variables sampling deals with a dollar amount conclusion, not deviation rates. Answer (c) is incorrect because discovery sampling is only used in cases in which the auditor expects deviation rates to be extremely low (approaching zero).

12. (c) The requirement is to identify the sampling method that would be used to estimate a numerical measurement such as a dollar value of a population. Answer (c)

is correct because sampling for variables addresses such numerical measurements. Answer (a) is incorrect because attributes sampling deals with deviation rates. Answer (b) is incorrect because stop-or-go sampling (also referred to as sequential sampling) is a form of attributes sampling. Answer (d) is incorrect because random-number sampling is simply a sample selection technique that may be used with either an attributes or a variables form of sampling; accordingly, a numerical measurement such as a dollar value is not necessary for random-number sampling.

13. (d) The requirement is to determine the audit test for which an auditor would most likely use attribute sampling. Answer (d) is correct because attribute sampling is used to reach a conclusion about a population in terms of a rate of occurrence. Here the rate of occurrence will be the rate of (un)approved time cards. Answers (a), (b), and (c) are all incorrect because they all relate more directly to variables sampling which is generally used to reach conclusion about a population in terms of a dollar amount. See the AICPA Audit and Accounting Guide, *Audit Sampling* and AU 350 for more information on audit sampling.

General Sampling Questions

14. (c) The requirement is to determine the correct statement with respect to random sampling. Answer (c) is correct because every item in the accounting population should have an opportunity to be selected. Answer (a) is incorrect because with stratified random sampling, each stratum need not be given equal representation. Answer (b) is incorrect because while sample units should be randomly selected, there is no requirement that the accounting population be randomly ordered. Answer (d) is incorrect because random sampling, by its very nature, is not systematic. Additionally, random sampling may be performed without replacement.

15. (c) The requirement is to determine the least desirable statistical selection technique. Answer (c), block selection, is correct because, ideally, a sample should be selected from the entire set of data to which the resulting conclusions are to be applied. When block sampling is used, the selection of blocks often precludes items from being so selected. In most cases, systematic [answer (a)], stratified [answer (b)], and sequential [answer (d)] selection techniques all provide a better representation of the entire population than does block selection.

16. (b) The requirement is to identify the type of sampling plan that does **not** use a fixed sample size for tests of controls. Answer (b) is correct because sequential sampling results in the selection of a sample in several steps, with each step conditional on the result of the previous steps. Therefore, sample size will vary depending upon the number of stages that prove necessary. Answers (a), (c), and (d) are all incorrect because dollar-unit sampling, PPS sampling, and variables sampling all use a fixed sample size.

17. (b) The requirement is to identify the correct statement concerning a statistical sampling application where the population consists of forms which are not consecutively numbered. Answer (b) is correct because systematic sampling is a procedure where a random start is obtained and then every n*th* item is selected. For example, a sample of forty from a population of a thousand would require selecting every 25th item after obtaining a random start between items 1 through 25. Answer (a) is incorrect because selection of a random sample is possible even though the population is not consecutively numbered. Answer (c) is incorrect because there is no special reason for using stratified sampling. Stratified sampling breaks down the population into subpopulations and applies different selection methods to each subpopulation. This selection method is used when the population consists of different types of items (e.g., large balances and small balances). Answer (d) is incorrect because random number tables can be used even though the forms are not consecutively numbered. If random numbers are selected for which there are no forms, they are ignored. This is the same as if there were 86,000 items in a consecutively numbered population and random numbers selected between 86,000 and 99,999 are ignored.

18.   (d)   Answer (d) is correct because systematic items occurrence in a population **may** destroy a sample's randomness. Answer (a) is incorrect because items need not be replaced in the population, and therefore is not a disadvantage of systematic sampling. Answer (b) is incorrect because an individual item will not occur more than once in a sample when systematic sampling is being used (because the auditor selects every nth item). Answer (c) is incorrect because systematic sampling refers to the type of sampling selection plan used and not the manner in which items in the population are recorded. Also, as indicated in (d) above, a systematic pattern in the population is a hindrance to systematic sampling.

19.   (c)   Stratified sampling is a technique of breaking the population down into subpopulations and applying different sample selection methods to the subpopulations. Stratified sampling is used to minimize the variance within the overall population [answer (c)]. Recall that as variance increases, so does the required sample size (because of the extreme values). Thus, stratification allows the selection of subpopulations to reduce the effect of dispersion in the population.

B.1.   Tests of Controls—Sampling Risk

20.   (d)   The requirement is to identify the circumstance that would cause an auditor to assess control risk too low and decrease substantive testing inappropriately. Answer (d) is correct because when the true deviation rate in the population exceeds that in the sample, the auditor may assess control risk too low. The AICPA *Audit Sampling Guide* discusses tests of controls and attributes sampling in its second chapter. Answers (a) and (c) are incorrect because the true deviation rate and the risk of assessing control risk too low do not have such a relationship, either positive or negative. Answer (b) is incorrect because a deviation rate in the population that is less than the deviation rate in the auditor's sample may lead the auditor to assess control risk too high.

21.   (a)   The requirement is to determine whether the expected deviation rate, the tolerable deviation rate, or both affect the sample size for a test of controls. Answer (a) is correct because attribute sampling formulas and tables used in auditing generally require the auditor to specify an expected deviation rate, a tolerable deviation rate and the risk of assessing control risk too low. See AICPA *Audit Sampling Guide* and AU 350 for more information on audit sampling.

22.   (d)   The requirement is to identify the correct statement about sampling for attributes. Answer (d) is correct because the sample size increases as the tolerable rate decreases, an inverse relationship. Answer (a) is incorrect because many deviations do not necessarily result in a misstatement. Answer (b) is incorrect because a doubling of the population size will result in less than a doubling of the required sample size. Answer (c) is incorrect because auditors must consider the qualitative aspects of deviations.

23.   (a)   The requirement is to identify the information needed in addition to the likely rate of deviations and the allowable risk of assessing control risk too low to determine the sample size for a test of controls in an attributes sampling plan. Answer (a) is correct because the tolerable deviation rate is also needed. Answer (b) is incorrect because the risk of incorrect acceptance relates to variables sampling applied to substantive testing, not attributes sampling applied to tests of controls. Answer (c) is incorrect because the auditor will examine the nature and cause of deviations after the sample has been selected. Answer (d) is incorrect because auditors often do not consider population size when performing attributes sampling applied to tests of controls.

24.   (c)   The requirement is to determine when a sample size would be decreased when sampling for attributes. Answer (c) is correct because the sample size will decrease when the risk of assessing control risk too low is increased, the tolerable rate is increased, and the expected population deviation rate is decreased (Audit and Accounting Guide *Audit Sampling*). Answers (a), (b), and (d) are all incorrect because they include combinations of changes that would not necessarily decrease sample size.

25.   (b)   The requirement is to identify the correct statement with respect to treatment of a voided voucher that has been selected in a sample. Answer (b) is correct because the AICPA *Audit Sampling Guide* states that the auditor should obtain reasonable assurance that the voucher has been properly voided, and should then replace it with another voucher. Answer (a) is incorrect because the voided voucher is not normally considered to be a deviation. Answer (c) is incorrect because the auditor must obtain reasonable assurance that the misplaced voucher has been voided. Answer (d) is incorrect because the level of materiality normally does not directly affect the decision.

26.   (c)   The requirement is to determine the proper method of handling a sample item which cannot be located for evaluation purposes. Answer (c) is correct because an auditor would ordinarily consider the selected item to be a deviation. Answers (a) and (d) are incorrect since a possible cause for the missing purchase order could be a breakdown in one of the controls of the system. Thus, in selecting a new sample item(s) the auditor may be ignoring a portion of the population which is in error and may be artificially skewing the results of the tests performed on the sample. Answer (b) is incorrect because there is no reason to believe that the entire test is invalid and cannot be relied upon.

27.   (a)   The requirement is to determine why deviations from control procedures do not necessarily result in errors. Answer (a) is correct because it provides an example of a situation in which a deviation from a control procedure exists (lack of documentation of transaction approval), although the entry was authorized and proper. Thus, such a deviation does not necessarily result in an error in the financial statements. Answer (b) is incorrect because a deviation from control procedure and an error may occur in the same transaction. Answer (c) is incorrect since the fact that all deviations do not lead to errors will result in a lower error rate. Answer (d) is incorrect because while it represents a correct statement, it does not follow from the point of the question which is based on the idea that deviations do not directly result in errors.

28. (d) The requirement is to determine the objective of the tolerable rate in sampling. Tolerable rate is calculated to determine the range of procedural deviations in the population. Answer (a) is incorrect because probabilities relate more directly to reliability. Answer (b) is incorrect because errors on financial statements in materiality terms relate to variables sampling. Answer (c) is incorrect because the tolerable rate does not relate directly to substantive tests.

29. (b) The requirement is to determine the correct relationship between the tolerable rate of deviations and the expected rate of deviations for a test of a control. The tolerable rate of deviations is the maximum rate of deviations from a prescribed control procedure that an auditor would be willing to accept and, unless the expected error rate is lower, reliance on internal control is not justified. Answer (a) is incorrect because if the tolerable rate of deviations is less than the expected rate, the auditor would not plan to rely on internal control and would therefore omit tests of controls. Answer (c) is incorrect because testing of controls is inappropriate if the expected rate of errors equals the tolerable rate of deviations (mathematically, the precision of zero makes the sample size equal to population size). Answer (d) is incorrect because, as indicated above, to perform tests of controls one must assume that the tolerable rate of deviations is more than the expected error rate.

30. (a) The requirement is to determine the type of sampling which is most directly related to finding at least one exception. Discovery sample sizes and related discovery sampling tables are constructed to measure the probability of at least one error occurring in a sample if the error rate in the population exceeds the tolerable rate. Answer (b) is incorrect because variables sampling need not include at least one exception (mean per unit sampling, for example, needs no errors). Answer (c) is incorrect since random sampling only deals with the technique used to select items to be included in the sample. Answer (d) is incorrect because dollar-unit sampling results are not directly related to finding at least one exception.

31. (a) The requirement is to determine whether an auditor should consider the likely rate of deviation, the allowable risk of assessing control risk too high, or both, when performing a test of a control. Answer (a) is correct because an auditor will consider the likely rate of deviations, but will not ordinarily consider the allowable risk of assessing control risk too high when following the approach outlined in the AICPA *Audit Sampling Guide*.

32. (c) The requirement is to determine whether an auditor would consider the average dollar value of check requests, the allowable risk of assessing control risk too low, or both, when testing whether check requests have been properly authorized. Answer (c) is correct because a test of authorization such as this is an attributes test which requires

the auditor to determine an allowable risk of assessing control risk too low, but does not deal directly with dollar values. Answers (a), (b) and (d) are all incorrect because they include incorrect combinations of the replies. See AU 350 and the AICPA *Audit Sampling Guide* for information on sampling.

B.2. Statistical (Attributes) Sampling for Tests of Controls

33. (b) The requirement is to identify the correct statement concerning statistical sampling in tests of controls. Answer (b) is correct because while deviations from pertinent control procedures increase the risk of material misstatements, any specific deviation need not necessarily result in a misstatement. For example, a recorded disbursement that does not show evidence of required approval might nevertheless be a transaction that is properly authorized and recorded (AICPA *Audit Sampling Guide*). Answer (a) is incorrect because increases in population size result in small increases in sample size. Answer (c) is incorrect because a direct relationship, not an inverse relationship, exists between the expected population deviation rate and the sample size—that is, increases in the expected population deviation rate result in an increase in the required sample size. Answer (d) is incorrect because when determining the tolerable rate, the auditor does not yet have the required sample size.

34. (d) The requirement is to determine the proper evaluation of a statistical sample for attributes when a test of 50 documents results in 3 deviations, given a tolerable rate of 7%, an expected population deviation rate of 5%, and an allowance for sampling risk of 2%. Answer (d) is correct because when the deviation rate plus the allowance for sampling risk exceeds the tolerable rate, the assessed level of control risk may increase. Here the deviation rate of 6% (3 deviations/50 documents) plus the allowance for sampling risk of 2% equals 8% and exceeds the tolerable rate of 7%. Answer (a) is incorrect because the tolerable rate plus the allowance for sampling risk will always exceed the expected population deviation rate when tests of controls are being performed. Answer (b) is incorrect because when the sample deviation rate plus the allowance for sampling risk exceeds the tolerable rate the sample results do not support the planned assessed level of control risk. Answer (c) is incorrect because the tolerable rate less the allowance for sampling risk should be compared with the actual deviation rate.

35. (a) The requirement is to determine the circumstance in which an auditor would decide to increase the level of the preliminary assessment of control risk. Answer (a) is correct because the assessment of control risk will increase when the achieved upper precision limit (here 8%) exceeds the tolerable rate (here 7%). Answer (b) is incorrect because the expected deviation rate was 2 1/2%, not 7%. Also, if the expected deviation rate is higher than the percentage of error in the sample, the preliminary assessment does not need to be increased. Answer (c) is incorrect because the achieved upper precision limit will always exceed the percentage of errors in the sample. Answer (d) is incorrect because, in circumstances in which the auditor decides to sample the population, the expected deviation rate will always be less than the tolerable rate.

36. (b) The requirement is to determine the allowance for sampling risk of the presented sample. When considering the allowance for sampling risk, one may consider both the planned allowance for sampling risk or the adjusted allowance based on the sample results. Answer (b) is correct because both the planned and adjusted allowance for sampling risk are 4 1/2% (7% – 2.5% for planning purposes, and 8% – 3.5% [7/200] as adjusted).

37. (a) The requirement is to identify the correct statement concerning statistical sampling for tests of controls. Answer (a) is correct because population size has little or **no** effect on sample size. Answer (b) is incorrect because the population deviation rate has a significant effect on sample size. Answer (c) is incorrect because sample size increases to a much lesser extent than doubling as the population size doubles. Answer (d) is incorrect because for a given tolerable rate, a smaller, and not a larger, sample size should be selected as the expected population deviation rate decreases.

B.3. Nonstatistical Sampling for Tests of Controls

38. (d) The requirement is to identify the proper statement concerning a random sample when nonstatistical attributes sampling is being used. Answer (d) is correct because the deviation rate of the sample should be compared to the tolerable deviation rate regardless of whether statistical or nonstatistical sampling is being used. Answer (a) is incorrect because the risk of assessing control risk too low should be considered, although it may be done judgmentally. Answer (b) is incorrect because nonsampling error relates to "human" type errors such as not identifying a deviation, and not specifically to the use of nonstatistical sampling. Answer (c) is incorrect because discovery sampling will not be used to evaluate the results.

C.1. Tests of Details—Sampling Risk

39. (c) The requirement is to determine whether either or both of an increase in tolerable misstatement and an increase in the assessed level of control risk increase sample size in a substantive test of details. Answer (c) is correct because while an increase in tolerable misstatement decreases sample size for a substantive test of details, an increase in the assessed level of control risk increases the sample size for a substantive test of details because a lower level of detection risk is required.

40. (b) The requirement is to determine the proper course of action when an auditor is planning a sample of cash disbursements and he or she is aware of several unusually large cash disbursements. Given the description of the several disbursements as "unusually large," an auditor will generally test them. Answer (b) is therefore correct because stratifying the population will allow the auditor to ensure inclusion of the disbursements. The sampling procedure (selecting less than all items) will then be applied only to the smaller disbursements. Answer (a) is incorrect because the existence of the large disbursements will have no necessary relationship to the tolerable rate of deviation when attributes sampling is being used. Answer (c) is incorrect because while increasing the sample size might be appropriate in some variables sampling applications (we are not told in this problem whether attributes or variables sampling is being followed), the fact that the disbursements are described as "unusually large" leads one to include them. Answer (d) is incorrect because an auditor will not draw numerous samples to assure inclusion of the large disbursements.

41. (b) The requirement is to determine whether either or both of the expected amount of misstatement and the measure of tolerable misstatement influence sample size for a substantive test of details. Answer (b) is correct because both the expected amount of misstatement and the tolerable misstatement affect sample size (AICPA *Audit Sampling Guide*). Increases in the expected amount of misstatements increase sample size, while increases in the tolerable misstatement decrease sample size.

42. (c) The requirement is to determine the correct statement concerning the auditor's consideration of tolerable misstatement. Answer (c) is correct because the consideration of tolerable misstatement is related to preliminary judgments in a manner such that when the auditor's preliminary judgments about tolerable misstatement levels for accounts or transaction types are combined for the entire audit plan, the preliminary judgments about materiality levels for the financial statements are not exceeded. Answer (a) is incorrect because the auditor's judgment of business risk related to a client is not directly related to tolerable misstatement. Answer (b) is incorrect because tolerable misstatement may be adjusted for qualitative factors. Answer (d) is incorrect because tolerable misstatement may be changed during the audit process, especially as misstatements are identified and the auditor considers the nature of the misstatements.

43. (d) The requirement is to determine the factor that would lead to larger sample size in a substantive test of details. Answer (d) is correct because the sample size required to achieve the auditor's objective at a given risk of incorrect acceptance increases as the auditor's assessment of tolerable misstatement for the balance or class decreases. Answer (a) is incorrect because a greater reliance on internal control will lead to a smaller sample size in a substantive test of details. Answer (b) is incorrect because greater reliance upon analytical procedures will result in a need for less reliance on substantive tests of details and therefore will result in a smaller sample. Answer (c) is incorrect because a smaller expected frequency of errors will generally include properly functioning internal control and will therefore result in a smaller sample for substantive tests of details.

44. (c) The requirement is to identify the factor which must be known in order to estimate the appropriate sample size when using variables sampling. Answer (c) is correct because the auditor must set an acceptable level of risk for both variables sampling and attribute sampling. Answer (a) is incorrect because while the auditor will consider the qualitative aspects of errors when evaluating the sample, they need not be considered in determining an appropriate sample size. Answer (b) is incorrect because a primary objective of variables sampling is to estimate the audited dollar amount of the population. Also, in some forms of variables sampling, knowledge of book values is not necessary (e.g., mean-per-unit). Answer (d) is incorrect because a rate of error in the population relates to attribute sampling.

45. (a) The requirement is to identify an auditor's most likely response to a circumstance in which there is a tolerable misstatement of $60,000, and the auditor has discovered misstatement of a net overstatement of $3,500 ($3,700 – $200) when 1/20 of the account has been included in the sample. Because auditors must project the misstatements to the entire population, one would expect a misstatement of approximately $70,000 (20 times the misstatement of $3,500). Since this exceeds the tolerable misstatement, there is little question that the risk of material misstatement is too high and that the misstatement in the population exceeds the tolerable misstatement, therefore answer (a) is correct. Answer (b) is incorrect because it seems that the sum of actual overstatement and understatement is likely to exceed the tolerable misstatement. Also, answer (b) makes little sense since there probably is no such thing as "an unacceptably high risk" that the tolerable misstatement exceeds the sum of actual overstatements and understatements; in such a circumstance the auditor simply accepts the population as being materially correct. Answers (c) and (d) are incorrect because the total projected misstatement must be calculated as indicated above. See AU 350 and the *Audit Sampling Guide* for information on sampling.

C.2. Probability-Proportional-to-Size (PPS) Sampling

46.   (c)   The requirement is to identify the correct statement regarding probability-proportional-to-size (PPS) sampling. Answer (c) is correct because when using PPS sampling, the auditor controls the risk of incorrect acceptance by specifying a risk level when planning the sample. Answer (a) is incorrect because PPS sampling does not assume a normal distribution. Answer (b) is incorrect because the book value of the unit determines how probable it is that it will be included in the sample, not whether it is over or understated. Answer (d) is incorrect because the sampling interval is calculated by dividing the book value of the population by the sample size.

47.   (d)   The requirement is to determine the sample size that should be used in a probability-proportional-to-size (PPS) sample. One approach is to first calculate a sampling interval and use it to determine an appropriate sample size. Using this approach, when provided with the tolerable misstatement already adjusted for expected misstatements (as is the situation in this problem), one divides that total by the number of expected misstatements column for the appropriate risk of incorrect acceptance (the fact that some overstatements are expected is not used). Here that computation is $24,000/1.61 = $14,906.83. Sample size is computed by dividing the recorded amount by the sampling interval, here $240,000/14,906.83, for a sample size of 16. An alternate approach is to use the reliability factor for the expected number of overstatements. In that case the computations become $24,000/3.00 = $8,000. Sample size is $240,000/$8,000 = 30. In either case answer (d) is the closest and therefore the correct reply.

48.   (b)   The requirement is to determine the projected error (misstatement) of a probability-proportional-to-size (PPS) sample with a sampling interval of $5,000, when an auditor has discovered that an account with a recorded amount of $10,000 had an audit amount of $8,000. Answer (b) is correct since, when an account's recorded amount exceeds the sampling interval, the projected error equals the actual misstatement, here $2,000 ($10,000 – $8,000).

C.3. Classical Variables Sampling

49.   (a)   The requirement is to determine whether an auditor uses the variability in dollar values, the risk of incorrect acceptance, or both, in a mean-per-unit estimation variables sampling plan. Answer (a) is correct because both

factors are included in a sampling plan. Answers (b), (c) and (d) are all incorrect because they suggest that one or both factors are not considered. See AU 350 and the AICPA *Audit Sampling Guide* for information on sampling.

50.   (b)   The requirement is to identify the circumstance in which an auditor most likely would stratify a population into meaningful groups. Answer (b) is correct because stratified sampling is used to minimize the effect on sample size of variation within the overall population and results in the largest savings for populations with high variability. Answer (a) is incorrect because while PPS sampling may in essence stratify a population, the items selected, other than those larger than the sampling interval, are not in "meaningful groups." Answer (c) is incorrect because the tolerable misstatement in and of itself will not lead to stratification. Answer (d) is incorrect because stratification is used primarily when there is a relatively large standard deviation, not a relatively small standard deviation.

51.   (a)   The requirement is to determine when ratio estimation sampling is most effective. The ratio estimation sampling technique uses the ratio between the audited to book amounts as a measure of standard deviation in its sample size computation. Answer (a) is correct because when audit differences are approximately proportional to account size the standard deviation of the ratio is small and this results in a relatively small required sample size. Answer (b) is incorrect because a relatively large number of differences between book and audited values must exist to calculate a reliable standard deviation under the ratio method. Answer (c) is incorrect because while the ratio estimation sampling technique may be used with quantities, it offers no particular advantage over other methods. Answer (b) is incorrect because the absolute size of differences does not make the ratio estimation method most effective.

52.   (a)   The requirement is to determine the purpose of taking a preliminary sample when one uses statistical techniques. It is necessary to obtain an estimate of a population's standard deviation (variability) when calculating the required sample size and when using sampling techniques. Answers (b), (c), and (d) are incorrect because, in most statistical techniques used by auditors, the mode (most frequent balance), the median (middle balance) and the range (difference between the highest and lowest values) are not used.

53.   (b)   The requirement is to determine the estimated audited accounts payable balance using the ratio estimation technique. Answer (b) is correct because the ratio estimation technique estimates the audited value by multiplying the audited value/book value of the sample times the population book value. In this case, ($300,000/$250,000) × $5,000,000 = $6,000,000.

54.   (b)   The ratio estimation sampling technique is based on comparing the ratio of the book value to the audited value of the sampled items. Answer (b) is correct because this method cannot be used when there is no book value to make the comparison. The circumstances described in answers (a) and (c) are necessary for ratio point and interval estimation. Answer (d) describes the circumstances in which the use of ratio estimation will be efficient in terms of required sample size.

55.   (d)   The requirement is to determine the most appropriate sampling approach for substantive tests of pricing and extensions of perpetual inventory balances consisting of a large number of items for which past experience indicates numerous expected pricing and extension errors. Answer (d) is correct because ratio estimation is appropriate when testing a population for which a large number of errors of this nature is expected (Audit and Accounting Guide, *Audit Sampling*). Answer (a) is incorrect because the unstratified mean-per-unit method will typically provide a larger sample size than the ratio estimation method to achieve the same level of sampling risk. Thus, the ratio estimation method would be more appropriate. Answer (b) is incorrect because probability-proportional-to-size sampling is most efficient for testing populations with relatively low expected error rates. Answer (c) is incorrect because "stop or go" or "sequential" sampling is most frequently used in attribute sampling.

56. **(d)** Difference and ratio estimation methods are statistical sampling methods. They measure the difference between audit and book values or the ratio of audit to book values. As these differences should not be great, the population of these differences will have little variance. In statistical sampling, the less variation in a population, the smaller the required sample to provide an estimate of the population. In other words, difference and ratio estimation methods are more efficient because the differences between audit and book values are expected to vary less than the actual items in the population. Answer (a) is incorrect because the number of members in the population for differences or ratio methods would be the same as the number of items in the population for a direct estimation method. In difference sampling, many items would be zero because audit and book are the same, and in ratio sampling, many of the members would be one for the same reason. Answer (b) is incorrect because beta risk can never be ignored, as beta risk is the risk of accepting an incorrect (unacceptable) population. Answer (c) is incorrect because the calculations required in difference and ratio sampling are similar to those used in direct estimation sampling.

57. **(a)** The requirement is to identify the correct statement concerning the auditor's use of statistical sampling. Answer (a) is correct because an estimate of the variation of the population, the standard deviation, is needed to use classical variables sampling (AICPA Audit and Accounting Guide, *Audit Sampling*). Answer (b) is incorrect because PPS sampling does not make an assumption that the underlying population is normally distributed. Answers (c) and (d) are incorrect because classical variables sample selected accounts and therefore need not include special considerations to those with a negative balance.

C.4. Comparison of PPS Sampling to Classical Variables Sampling

58. **(c)** The requirement is to identify an advantage in using classical variables sampling rather than probability-proportional-to-size sampling. Answer (c) is correct because the inclusion of zero and negative balances generally does **not** require special design considerations when using classical sampling, while it does when using probability-proportional-to-size sampling (AICPA *Audit Sampling Guide*). Answer (a) is incorrect because classical variables sampling does require an estimate of the standard deviation of the population's recorded amounts. Answer (b) is incorrect because the computational process involved with classi-

cal variables sampling may make use of a computer program desirable. Answer (d) is incorrect because probability-proportional-to-size sampling, not classical sampling, automatically stratifies individually significant items.

SOLUTIONS TO SIMULATION PROBLEMS

Simulation Problem 1

	Analysis	
Situation		Research

1. **(A)** Thirty items. Calculated by dividing the population book value ($2,400,000) by the sampling interval size ($80,000). Accordingly $2,400,000/80,000 = 30 items.

2. **(G)** $26,150. Calculated by summing the misstatements ($1,000 + $150 + $25,000 = $26,150).

3. **(H)** $42,000. Projected misstatement represents the most likely total misstatement in the population ($42,000).

4. **(M)** $294,550. The upper limit on misstatement is the sum of projected misstatement, basic precision, and the incremental allowance ($42,000 + $240,000 + $12,550 = $294,550).

5. **(K)** $252,550. The allowance for sampling risk is the sum of basic precision and the incremental allowance ($240,000 + $12,550 = $252,550).

6. **(Reject)** Reject because the upper limit on misstatement ($294,550) exceeds the tolerable misstatement ($280,000).

7. **(5%)** Because basic precision uses a 3.0 factor, the test is being performed at 5%.

		Research
Situation	Analysis	

AU 350.09-.11 discusses sampling and nonsampling risk as follows:

.09 Audit risk includes both uncertainties due to sampling and uncertainties due to factors other than sampling. These aspects of audit risk are sampling risk and nonsampling risk, respectively.

.10 Sampling risk arises from the possibility that when a test of controls or a substantive test is restricted to a sample, the auditor's conclusions may be different from the conclusion he would reach if the test were applied in the same way to all items in the account balance or class of transactions. That is, a particular sample may contain proportionately more or less monetary misstatements or deviations from prescribed controls than exist in the balance or class as a whole. For a sample of a specific design, sampling risk varies inversely with sample size: the smaller the sample size, the greater the sampling risk.

.11 Nonsampling risk includes all the aspects of audit risk that are not due to sampling. An auditor may apply a procedure to all transactions or balances and still fail to detect a material misstatement. Nonsampling risk includes the possibility of selecting audit procedures that are not appropriate to achieve the specific objective. For example, confirming receivables cannot be relied on to reveal unrecorded receivables. Nonsampling risk also arises because the auditor may fail to recognize misstatements included in documents that he examines, which would make that procedure ineffective even if he were to examine all items. Nonsampling risk can be reduced to a negligible level through such factors as adequate planning and supervision.

Simulation Problem 2

	Characteristics				
Situation		Calculation	Spreadsheet	Research	Communication

	Correct	Incorrect
1. Size of a PPS sample is not based on the estimated variation of audited amounts.	●	○
2. PPS sampling results in a stratified sample.	●	○
3. Individually significant items are automatically identified.	●	○
4. PPS sampling results in a smaller sample size when numerous small misstatement are expected.	○	●
5. If no misstatements are expected, PPS sampling will usually result in a smaller sample size than classical variables sampling methods.	●	○
6. One does not need a book value for individual items to evaluate a PPS sample.	○	●
7. A PPS sample eliminates the need to project results to the overall population.	○	●
8. PPS sampling is "preferred" by the professional standards.	○	●

		Calculation				
Situation	Characteristics			Spreadsheet	Research	Communication

(B) $3,000. Sampling interval is equal to the recorded amount of accounts receivable ($300,000) divided by sample size (100). Accordingly, $300,000 ÷ 100 = $3,000.

			Spreadsheet			
Situation	Characteristics	Calculation			Research	Communication

(D) $1,700. The projected misstatement is calculated as

	Recorded amount	Audit amount	Sampling interval	Difference	Tainting %	Projected misstatement
1st misstatement	$ 400	$ 320	$1,000	$80	20%	$ 200
2nd misstatement	500	0	1,000	500	100%	1,000
3rd misstatement	3,000	2,500	1,000	1,000	N/A	500
						$1,700

	A	B	C	D	E	F	G
1	Jane2 Inc.						
2	Accounts Receivable						
3	December 31, 20X2						
4							
5		Recorded amount	Audited amount	Difference	Tainting %		Sampling interval	Projected misstatement
6	1st misstatement	$ 400	$ 320	$ 80	20%	$	1,000	$ 200
7	2nd misstatement	500	--	500	100%		1,000	1,000
8	3rd misstatement	3,000	2,500	500	N/A		1,000	500
9								$ 1,700

				Research		
Situation	Characteristics	Calculation	Spreadsheet			Communication

AU 350.18 discusses the relationship between tolerable misstatement and materiality as follows:

.18 Evaluation in monetary terms of the results of a sample for a substantive test of details contributes directly to the auditor's purpose since such an evaluation can be related to his judgment of the monetary amount of misstatements that would be material. When planning a sample for a substantive test of details, the auditor should consider how much monetary misstatement in the related account balance or class of transactions may exist without causing the financial statements to be materially misstated. This maximum monetary misstatement for the balance or class is called tolerable misstatement for the sample. Tolerable misstatement is a planning concept and is related to the auditor's preliminary judgments about materiality levels in such a way that tolerable misstatement, combined for the entire audit plan, does not exceed those estimates.

					Communication
Situation	Characteristics	Calculation	Spreadsheet	Research	

To: Audit Working Papers
From: CPA Candidate

This memorandum is designed to describe the nature of audit sampling. When audit sampling is used, a sample from a population is selected to make a conclusion about some characteristic of the population. Accordingly, to make a conclusion about the population, the results of the sample must be extended or projected to the population. This provides us with an estimate of the relevant characteristic of the population. If you have any additional questions, ask the audit manager.

MULTIPLE-CHOICE QUESTIONS (1-33)

1. An advantage of using systems flowcharts to document information about internal control instead of using internal control questionnaires is that systems flowcharts

    a.   Identify internal control weaknesses more prominently.

    b.   Provide a visual depiction of clients' activities.

    c.   Indicate whether control procedures are operating effectively.

    d.   Reduce the need to observe clients' employees performing routine tasks.

2. A flowchart is most frequently used by an auditor in connection with the

    a.   Preparation of generalized computer audit programs.

    b.   Review of the client's internal control.

    c.   Use of statistical sampling in performing an audit.

    d.   Performance of analytical procedures of account balances.

3. Matthews Corp. has changed from a system of recording time worked on clock cards to a computerized payroll system in which employees record time in and out with magnetic cards. The computer system automatically updates all payroll records. Because of this change

    a.   A generalized computer audit program must be used.

    b.   Part of the audit trail is altered.

    c.   The potential for payroll-related fraud is diminished.

    d.   Transactions must be processed in batches.

4. Which of the following is correct concerning batch processing of transactions?

    a.   Transactions are processed in the order they occur, regardless of type.

    b.   It has largely been replaced by on-line real-time processing in all but legacy systems.

    c.   It is more likely to result in an easy-to-follow audit trail than is on-line transaction processing.

    d.   It is used only in nondatabase applications.

5. An auditor would be most likely to assess control risk at the maximum level in an electronic environment with automated system-generated information when

    a.   Sales orders are initiated using predetermined, automated decision rules.

    b.   Payables are based on many transactions and large in dollar amount.

    c.   Fixed asset transactions are few in number, but large in dollar amount.

    d.   Accounts receivable records are based on many transactions and are large in dollar amount.

6. In a highly automated information processing system tests of control

    a.   Must be performed in all circumstances.

    b.   May be required in some circumstances.

    c.   Are never required.

    d.   Are required in first year audits.

7. Which of the following is **least** likely to be considered by an auditor considering engagement of an information technology (IT) specialist on an audit?

    a.   Complexity of client's systems and IT controls.

    b.   Requirements to assess going concern status.

    c.   Client's use of emerging technologies.

    d.   Extent of entity's participation in electronic commerce.

8. Which of the following strategies would a CPA most likely consider in auditing an entity that processes most of its financial data only in electronic form, such as a paperless system?

    a.   Continuous monitoring and analysis of transaction processing with an embedded audit module.

    b.   Increased reliance on internal control activities that emphasize the segregation of duties.

    c.   Verification of encrypted digital certificates used to monitor the authorization of transactions.

    d.   Extensive testing of firewall boundaries that restrict the recording of outside network traffic.

9. Which of the following is **not** a major reason for maintaining an audit trail for a computer system?

    a.   Deterrent to fraud.

    b.   Monitoring purposes.

    c.   Analytical procedures.

    d.   Query answering.

10. Computer systems are typically supported by a variety of utility software packages that are important to an auditor because they

    a.   May enable unauthorized changes to data files if **not** properly controlled.

    b.   Are very versatile programs that can be used on hardware of many manufacturers.

    c.   May be significant components of a client's application programs.

    d.   Are written specifically to enable auditors to extract and sort data.

11. An auditor would most likely be concerned with which of the following controls in a distributed data processing system?

    a.   Hardware controls.

    b.   Systems documentation controls.

    c.   Access controls.

    d.   Disaster recovery controls.

12. Which of the following types of evidence would an auditor most likely examine to determine whether internal control is operating as designed?

    a.   Gross margin information regarding the client's industry.

    b.   Confirmations of receivables verifying account balances.

    c.   Client records documenting the use of computer programs.

    d.   Anticipated results documented in budgets or forecasts.

13. An auditor anticipates assessing control risk at a low level in a computerized environment. Under these circumstances, on which of the following activities would the auditor initially focus?

    a.   Programmed control activities.

    b.   Application control activities.

    c.   Output control activities.

    d.   General control activities.

14. After the preliminary phase of the review of a client's computer controls, an auditor may decide not to perform tests of controls (compliance tests) related to the controls within the computer portion of the client's internal control. Which of the following would **not** be a valid reason for choosing to omit such tests?

    a.   The controls duplicate operative controls existing elsewhere in the structure.

    b.   There appear to be major weaknesses that would preclude reliance on the stated procedure.

    c.   The time and dollar costs of testing exceed the time and dollar savings in substantive testing if the tests of controls show the controls to be operative.

    d.   The controls appear adequate.

15. Auditing by testing the input and output of a computer system instead of the computer program itself will

    a.   Not detect program errors which do **not** show up in the output sampled.

    b.   Detect all program errors, regardless of the nature of the output.

    c.   Provide the auditor with the same type of evidence.

    d.   Not provide the auditor with confidence in the results of the auditing procedures.

16. Which of the following client electronic data processing (EDP) systems generally can be audited without examining or directly testing the EDP computer programs of the system?

    a.   A system that performs relatively uncomplicated processes and produces detailed output.

    b.   A system that affects a number of essential master files and produces a limited output.

    c.   A system that updates a few essential master files and produces no printed output other than final balances.

    d.   A system that performs relatively complicated processing and produces very little detailed output.

17. An auditor who wishes to capture an entity's data as transactions are processed and continuously test the entity's computerized information system most likely would use which of the following techniques?

    a.   Snapshot application.

    b.   Embedded audit module.

    c.   Integrated data check.

    d.   Test data generator.

18. Which of the following computer-assisted auditing techniques processes client input data on a controlled program under the auditor's control to test controls in the computer system?

    a.   Test data.

    b.   Review of program logic.

    c.   Integrated test facility.

    d.   Parallel simulation.

19. To obtain evidence that on-line access controls are properly functioning, an auditor most likely would

    a.   Create checkpoints at periodic intervals after live data processing to test for unauthorized use of the system.

    b.   Examine the transaction log to discover whether any transactions were lost or entered twice due to a system malfunction.

    c.   Enter invalid identification numbers or passwords to ascertain whether the system rejects them.

    d.   Vouch a random sample of processed transactions to assure proper authorization.

20. An auditor most likely would introduce test data into a computerized payroll system to test controls related to the

    a.   Existence of unclaimed payroll checks held by supervisors.

    b.   Early cashing of payroll checks by employees.

    c.   Discovery of invalid employee I.D. numbers.

    d.   Proper approval of overtime by supervisors.

21. When an auditor tests a computerized accounting system, which of the following is true of the test data approach?

    a.   Several transactions of each type must be tested.

    b.   Test data are processed by the client's computer programs under the auditor's control.

    c.   Test data must consist of all possible valid and invalid conditions.

    d.   The program tested is different from the program used throughout the year by the client.

22. Which of the following statements is **not** true of the test data approach when testing a computerized accounting system?

    a.   The test need consist of only those valid and invalid conditions which interest the auditor.

    b.   Only one transaction of each type need be tested.

    c.   The test data must consist of all possible valid and invalid conditions.

    d.   Test data are processed by the client's computer programs under the auditor's control.

23. Which of the following is **not** among the errors that an auditor might include in the test data when auditing a client's computer system?

    a.   Numeric characters in alphanumeric fields.

    b.   Authorized code.

    c.   Differences in description of units of measure.

    d.   Illogical entries in fields whose logic is tested by programmed consistency checks.

24. Which of the following computer-assisted auditing techniques allows fictitious and real transactions to be processed together without client operating personnel being aware of the testing process?

    a.   Integrated test facility.

    b.   Input controls matrix.

    c.   Parallel simulation.

    d.   Data entry monitor.

25. Which of the following methods of testing application controls utilizes a generalized audit software package prepared by the auditors?

    a.   Parallel simulation.

    b.   Integrated testing facility approach.

    c.   Test data approach.

    d.   Exception report tests.

26. In creating lead schedules for an audit engagement, a CPA often uses automated work paper software. What client information is needed to begin this process?

    a.   Interim financial information such as third quarter sales, net income, and inventory and receivables balances.

b. Specialized journal information such as the invoice and purchase order numbers of the last few sales and purchases of the year.

c. General ledger information such as account numbers, prior year account balances, and current year unadjusted information.

d. Adjusting entry information such as deferrals and accruals, and reclassification journal entries.

27. Using microcomputers in auditing may affect the methods used to review the work of staff assistants because

a. The audit fieldwork standards for supervision may differ.

b. Documenting the supervisory review may require assistance of consulting services personnel.

c. Supervisory personnel may **not** have an understanding of the capabilities and limitations of microcomputers.

d. Working paper documentation may not contain readily observable details of calculations.

28. An auditor would **least** likely use computer software to

a. Access client data files.

b. Prepare spreadsheets.

c. Assess computer control risk.

d. Construct parallel simulations.

29. A primary advantage of using generalized audit software packages to audit the financial statements of a client that uses a computer system is that the auditor may

a. Access information stored on computer files while having a limited understanding of the client's hardware and software features.

b. Consider increasing the use of substantive tests of transactions in place of analytical procedures.

c. Substantiate the accuracy of data through self-checking digits and hash totals.

d. Reduce the level of required tests of controls to a relatively small amount.

30. Auditors often make use of computer programs that perform routine processing functions such as sorting and merging. These programs are made available by electronic data processing companies and others and are specifically referred to as

a. Compiler programs.

b. Supervisory programs.

c. Utility programs.

d. User programs.

31. Smith Corporation has numerous customers. A customer file is kept on disk storage. Each customer file contains name, address, credit limit, and account balance. The auditor wishes to test this file to determine whether credit limits are being exceeded. The best procedure for the auditor to follow would be to

a. Develop test data that would cause some account balances to exceed the credit limit and determine if the system properly detects such situations.

b. Develop a program to compare credit limits with account balances and print out the details of any account with a balance exceeding its credit limit.

c. Request a printout of all account balances so they can be manually checked against the credit limits.

d. Request a printout of a sample of account balances so they can be individually checked against the credit limits.

32. An auditor most likely would test for the presence of unauthorized computer program changes by running a

a. Program with test data.

b. Check digit verification program.

c. Source code comparison program.

d. Program that computes control totals.

33. An entity has the following invoices in a batch:

Invoice #	Product	Quantity	Unit price
201	F10	150	$ 5.00
202	G15	200	$10.00
203	H20	250	$25.00
204	K35	300	$30.00

Which of the following numbers represents the record count?

a. 1

b. 4

c. 810

d. 900

SIMULATION PROBLEM

Simulation Problem 1   (40 to 45 minutes)

Situation				
	Technology	Controls	Research	Communication

Computer processing has become the primary means used to process financial accounting information in most businesses. Consistent with this situation, CPAs must have knowledge of audit techniques using computers and of computer terminology.

	Technology			
Situation		Controls	Research	Communication

Select the type of audit technique being described in **items 1 through 5**. Computer audit techniques may be used once, more than once, or not at all.

<u>Computer audit technique</u>

A. Auditing "around" the computer	E. Processing output control
B. I/O audit approach	F. Test data
C. Integrated test facility	G. Write extract routine
D. Parallel simulation	

<u>Description</u>	(A)	(B)	(C)	(D)	(E)	(F)	(G)
1. Auditing by manually testing the input and output of a computer system.	○	○	○	○	○	○	○
2. Dummy transactions developed by the auditor and processed by the client's computer programs, generally for a batch processing system.	○	○	○	○	○	○	○
3. Fictitious and real transactions are processed together without the client's operating personnel knowing of the testing process.	○	○	○	○	○	○	○
4. May include a simulated division or subsidiary into the accounting system with the purpose of running fictitious transactions through it.	○	○	○	○	○	○	○
5. Uses a generalized audit software package prepared by the auditors.	○	○	○	○	○	○	○

		Controls		
Situation	Technology		Research	Communication

For **items 1 through 5** select the type of computer control that is described in the definition that is presented. Each control may be used once, more than once, or not at all.

<u>Control</u>

H. Backup and recovery	M. Hash total
I. Boundary protection	N. Missing data check
J. Check digit	O. Personal identification codes
K. Control digit	P. Visitor entry logs
L. File protection ring	

<u>Description</u>	(H)	(I)	(J)	(K)	(L)	(M)	(N)	(O)	(P)
1. A control that will detect blanks existing in input data when they should not.	○	○	○	○	○	○	○	○	○
2. A control to ensure that jobs run simultaneously in a multiprogramming environment cannot change the allocated memory of another job.	○	○	○	○	○	○	○	○	○
3. A digit added to an identification number to detect certain types of data transmission or transposition errors.	○	○	○	○	○	○	○	○	○
4. A terminal control to limit access to programs or files to authorized users.	○	○	○	○	○	○	○	○	○
5. A total of one field for all the records of a batch where the total is meaningless for financial purposes.	○	○	○	○	○	○	○	○	○

Situation	Technology	Controls	Research	Communication

The use of sophisticated information technology may provide both benefits and risks relating to internal control. Find one place in the Professional Standards that lists IT benefits and risks relating to internal control. You should select the appropriate paragraph(s) of The Professional Standards.

Situation	Technology	Controls	Research	Communication

Write a memorandum to the audit working paper describing the risk of "auditing around the computer."

REMINDER: Your response will be graded for both technical content and writing skills. Technical content will be evaluated for information that is helpful to the intended reader and clearly relevant to the issue. Writing skills will be evaluated for development, organization, and the appropriate expression of ideas in professional correspondence. Use a standard business memo or letter format with a clear beginning, middle, and end. Do not convey information in the form of a table, bullet point list, or other abbreviated presentation.

To: Audit Working Papers
From: CPA Candidate

1. b __ __	7. b __ __	13. d __ __	19. c __ __	25. a __ __	31. b __ __
2. b __ __	8. a __ __	14. d __ __	20. c __ __	26. c __ __	32. c __ __
3. b __ __	9. c __ __	15. a __ __	21. b __ __	27. d __ __	33. b __ __
4. c __ __	10. a __ __	16. a __ __	22. c __ __	28. c __ __	
5. c __ __	11. c __ __	17. b __ __	23. a __ __	29. a __ __	1st: __/33 = __%
6. b __ __	12. c __ __	18. d __ __	24. a __ __	30. c __ __	2nd: __/33 = __%

MULTIPLE-CHOICE ANSWER EXPLANATIONS

A. Auditor's Consideration of Internal Control When a Computer Is Present

1. **(b)** The requirement is to identify an advantage of using systems flowcharts to document information about internal control instead of using internal control questionnaires. Answer (b) is correct because flowcharts provide a visual depiction of clients' activities which make it possible for auditors to quickly understand the design of the system. Answer (a) is incorrect because while the flow of operations is visually depicted, internal control weaknesses are not as obvious. Answer (c) is incorrect because while a flowchart describes a system, the flowchart alone does not indicate whether that system is operating effectively. Answer (d) is incorrect because auditors still need to determine whether the system has been placed in operation and therefore the need to observe employees performing routine tasks remains.

2. **(b)** The requirement is to determine when a flowchart is most frequently used by an auditor. Answer (b) is correct because flowcharts are suggested as being appropriate for documenting the auditor's consideration of internal control. Answer (a) is incorrect because auditors do not frequently write their own generalized computer audit programs, the most likely time a flowchart would be used with respect to such software. Answers (c) and (d) are incorrect because statistical sampling and analytical procedures do not in general require the use of flowcharts.

3. **(b)** The requirement is to identify the correct statement with respect to a computerized, automatically updating payroll system in which magnetic cards are used instead of a manual payroll system with clock cards. Answer (b) is correct because the automatic updating of payroll records alters the audit trail which, in the past, included steps pertaining to manual updating. Answer (a) is incorrect because although an auditor may choose to use a generalized computer audit program, it is not required. Answer (c) is incorrect because no information is presented that would necessarily indicate a change in the likelihood of fraud. Answer (d) is incorrect because given automatic updating, a large portion of the transactions are not processed in batches.

4. **(c)** The requirement is to identify the correct statement concerning the batch processing of transactions. Batch processing involves processing transactions through the system in groups of like transactions (batches). Answer (c) is correct because the similar nature of transactions involved with batch processing ordinarily makes it relatively easy to follow the transactions throughout the system. Answer (a) is incorrect because transactions are processed by type, not in the order they occur regardless of type. Answer (b) is incorrect because many batch applications still exist and might be expected to exist well into the future. Answer (d) is incor-

rect because batch processing may be used for database applications.

5. **(c)** The requirement is to determine when an auditor would be most likely to assess control risk at the maximum level in an electronic environment with automated system-generated information. Answer (c) is correct because the few transactions involved in fixed assets make it most likely to be one in which a substantive approach of restricting detection risk is most likely to be effective and efficient. Answer (a) is incorrect because an auditor might be expected to perform tests of controls to assess control risk below the maximum when automated decision rules are involved for an account (sales) which ordinarily has many transactions. Answers (b) and (d) are incorrect because the numerous transactions in payables and receivables make it likely that control risk will be assessed below the maximum.

6. **(b)** The requirement is to identify the most accurate statement with respect to tests of controls of a highly automated information processing system. Answer (b) is correct because SAS 110 states that in some such circumstances substantive tests alone will not be sufficient to restrict detection risk to an acceptable level. Answer (a) is incorrect because tests of controls need not be performed in all such circumstances. Answer (c) is incorrect because such tests are sometimes required. Answer (d) is incorrect because tests of controls are not in such circumstances in all first year audits.

7. **(b)** The requirement is to identify the least likely circumstance in which an auditor would consider engagements of an IT specialist on an audit. Answer (b) is correct because the requirement to assess going concern status remains the same on all audits, and thus does not directly affect engagement of an IT specialist. Answers (a), (c), and (d) are all incorrect because complexity, the use of emerging technologies, and participation in electronic commerce are all factors which SAS 110 suggests make it more likely that an IT specialist will be engaged.

8. **(a)** The requirement is to identify a strategy that a CPA most likely would consider in auditing an entity that processes most of its financial data only in electronic form. Answer (a) is correct because continuous monitoring and analysis of transaction processing with an embedded audit module might provide an effective way of auditing these processes—although some question exists as to how many embedded audit modules CPAs have actually used in practice. Answer (b) is incorrect because there may well be a decrease in reliance on internal control activities that emphasize this segregation of duties since so many controls are in the hardware and software of the application. Answer (c) is incorrect because digital certificates deal with electronic commerce between companies, a topic not directly addressed by this question, and because such certificates provide limited evidence on authorization. Answer (d) is incorrect because while firewalls do control network traffic, this is not the most significant factor in the audit of electronic form financial data.

9.   (c)   The requirement is to identify the reply that is **not** a major reason for maintaining an audit trail for a computer system. Answer (c) is correct because analytical procedures use the outputs of the system, and therefore the audit trail is of limited importance. Answer (a) is incorrect because an audit trail may deter fraud since the perpetrator may realize that his or her act may be detected. Answer (b) is incorrect because an audit trail will help management to monitor the computer system. Answer (d) is incorrect because an audit trail will make it much easier to answer queries.

10.   (a)   The requirement is to identify a reason that utility software packages are important to an auditor. Answer (a) is correct because client use of such packages requires that the auditor include tests to determine that no unplanned interventions using utility routines have taken place during processing (Audit and Accounting Guide, *Computer Assisted Audit Techniques*). Answer (b) is incorrect because a client's use of such programs implies that they are useful on his/her computer hardware, and therefore any flexibility is not of immediate relevance to the auditor. Answer (c) is incorrect because the primary purpose of utility programs is to support the computer user's applications (*Computer Assisted Audit Techniques*). Answer (d) is incorrect because utility software programs have a variety of uses in addition to enabling auditors to extract and sort data (*Computer Assisted Audit Techniques*).

11.   (c)   The requirement is to identify the types of controls with which an auditor would be most likely to be concerned in a distributed data processing system. A distributed data processing system is one in which there is a network of remote computer sites, each having a computer connected to the main computer system, thus allowing access to the computers by various levels of users. Accordingly, answer (c) is correct because numerous individuals may access the system, thereby making such controls of extreme importance. Answers (a), (b), and (d), while requiring concern, are normally considered less critical than proper access controls for this situation.

12.   (c)   The requirement is to identify the type of evidence an auditor would examine to determine whether internal control is operating as designed. Answer (c) is correct because the inspection of documents and records such as those related to computer programs represents an approach for obtaining an understanding of internal control. Answer (a) is incorrect because examining gross margin information is more likely to be performed during the performance of analytical procedures. Answer (b) is incorrect because confirming of receivables is a substantive test. Answer (d) is incorrect because anticipated results documented in budgets or forecasts are much more frequently used in the performance of analytical procedures.

13.   (d)   The requirement is to determine the procedures on which the auditor would initially focus when anticipating assessing control risk at a low level. Answer (d) is correct because auditors usually begin by considering general control procedures. Since the effectiveness of specific applica-

tion controls is often dependent on the existence of effective general controls over all computer activities, this is usually an efficient approach. Answers (a), (b), and (c) are all incorrect because they represent controls that are usually tested subsequent to the general controls.

14.   (d)   The requirement is to determine an **inappropriate** reason for omitting tests of controls related to computer control procedures. Answer (d) is correct because the fact that the controls **appear** adequate is not sufficient justification for reliance; tests of controls must be performed before the auditor can actually rely upon a control procedure to reduce control risk. Answer (a) is incorrect because when controls duplicate other controls the auditor who wishes to rely upon internal control need not test both sets. Answer (b) is incorrect because if weak controls are not to be relied upon, the auditor need not test their effectiveness. Answer (c) is incorrect because tests of controls may be omitted if their cost exceeds the savings from reduced substantive testing resulting from reliance upon the controls.

15.   (a)   The requirement is to determine the correct statement with respect to testing inputs and outputs of a computer system instead of testing the actual computer program itself. Answer (a) is correct because portions of the program which have errors not reflected on the output will be missed. Thus, if a "loop" in a program is not used in one application, it is not tested. Answer (b) is incorrect because the lack of an understanding of the entire program precludes the detection of all errors. Answer (c) is incorrect because while auditing inputs and outputs can provide valuable evidence, it will often be different than the evidence obtained by testing the program itself. Answer (d) is incorrect because such auditing of inputs and outputs may well satisfy the auditor.

16.   (a)   The requirement is to identify the type of computer system that can be audited without examining or directly testing computer programs (i.e., auditing around the system). Auditing around the system is possible if the system performs uncomplicated processes and produces detailed output (i.e., is a fancy bookkeeping machine). Answers (b), (c), and (d) all describe more complicated computer systems that produce only limited output. In these more complicated systems, the data and related controls are within the system, and thus the auditor must examine the system itself. Auditors must identify and evaluate the accounting controls in all computer systems. Further, complex computer systems require auditor specialized expertise to perform the necessary procedures.

17.   (b)   The requirement is to determine an audit technique to determine whether an entity's transactions are processed and to continuously test the computerized information system. Answer (b) is correct because an embedded audit module is inserted within the client's information system to continuously test the processing of transactions. Answer (a) is incorrect because a snapshot application analyzes the information system at one point in time. Answer (c) is incorrect because an integrated data check simply tests data at one point in time. Answer (d) is incorrect because a test data generator provides a sample of possible circumstances in which data might be improperly processed.

18.   (d)   The requirement is to identify the computer-assisted audit technique that processes client input data on a controlled program under the auditor's control to test controls in a computer system Answer (d) is correct because parallel simulation processes actual client data through an auditor's generalized audit software program. Answer (a) is incorrect because test data is a set of dummy transactions developed by the auditor and processed by the client's programs to determine whether the controls which the auditor intends to test are operating effectively. Answer (b) is incorrect because a review of program logic is an approach in which an auditor reviews the steps by which the client's program processes data. Answer (c) is incorrect because an integrated test facility introduces dummy transactions into a client's system in the midst of live transactions.

B. Computerized Audit Tools

19. (c) The requirement is to determine the best way to obtain evidence that on-line access controls are properly functioning. Answer (c) is correct because entering invalid identification numbers or passwords will provide the auditor with evidence on whether controls are operating as designed. Answer (a) is incorrect because directly testing access controls is more direct than testing data through checkpoints at intervals. Answer (b) is incorrect because a transaction log will not in general, by itself, identify whether transactions were lost or entered twice. Answer (d) is incorrect because vouching proper authorization is only one measure of whether controls are properly functioning.

20. (c) The requirement is to identify the situation in which it is most likely that an auditor would introduce test data into a computerized payroll system. Test data is a set of dummy transactions developed by the auditor and processed by the client's computer programs. These dummy transactions are used to determine whether the controls which the auditor tests are operating effectively. Answer (c) is correct because test data with invalid employee I.D. numbers could be processed to test whether the program detects them. Answer (a) is incorrect because the unclaimed payroll checks are held by the supervisors and no testing of the computer program is involved. Answer (b) is incorrect because no computer processing is generally involved when payroll checks are "cashed early" by employees. Answer (d) is incorrect because to test whether the approval of overtime is proper, one must determine what criteria are used for the decision and must then determine whether supervisors are following those criteria; it is less likely that this will all be included in a computer program than a test for invalid employee ID numbers.

21. (b) The requirement is to identify the correct statement regarding the test data approach. Answer (b) is correct because the test data approach consists of processing a set of dummy transactions on the client's computer system. The test data approach is used to test the operating effectiveness of controls the auditor intends to rely upon to assess control risk at a level lower than the maximum. Answer (a) is incorrect because only one transaction of each type is generally tested. Answer (c) is incorrect because it is not possible to include **all** possible valid and invalid conditions. Answer (d) is incorrect because the program that should be tested is the client's program which is used throughout the year.

22. (c) The requirement is to identify the statement which is **not** true of the test data approach. Answer (c) is

correct (not true) because it is impossible or not cost beneficial to test **all** possible valid and invalid conditions. Answer (a) is incorrect because the auditor should test those valid and invalid conditions in which s/he is interested. Answer (b) is incorrect because only one transaction of each type need be tested in a computer control system in which the controls either work or do not work. Answer (d) is incorrect because test data is run using the client's computer programs under the auditor's control.

23. (a) The requirement is to determine which reply is not among the errors which are generally detected by test data. An auditor uses test data to determine whether purported controls are actually functioning. Answer (a) is correct because one would not use test data to test numeric characters in alphanumeric fields; numeric characters are accepted in alphanumeric fields and thus do not represent error conditions. Answer (b) is incorrect because authorization codes may be tested by inputting inappropriate codes. Answer (c) is incorrect because differing descriptions of units of measure may be inputted to test whether they are accepted. Answer (d) is incorrect because illogical combinations may be inputted to test whether they are detected by the system.

24. (a) The requirement is to identify the computer-assisted auditing technique which allows fictitious and real transactions to be processed together without client operating personnel being aware of the testing process. Answer (a) is correct because the integrated test facility approach introduces dummy transactions into a system in the midst of live transactions. Accordingly, client operating personnel may not be aware of the testing process. Answer (b) is incorrect because an input control matrix would simply indicate various controls in the form of a matrix. Answer (c) is incorrect because the parallel simulation technique requires the processing of actual client data through an auditor's software program. In this case, the client would be aware of the testing process since the auditor would need to request copies of data run on the actual system so that the data could then be run on the auditor's software program. Additionally, only valid transactions would be tested under parallel simulation. Answer (d) is incorrect because the client would generally be aware of an auditor using a data entry monitor (screen) to input transactions.

25. (a) The requirement is to determine the auditing technique which utilizes generalized audit software. Answer (a) is correct because the parallel simulation method processes the client's data using the CPA's software. Answers (b) and (c) are incorrect because the client's hardware and software are tested using test data designed by the CPA. Answer (d) is incorrect because although a CPA may test a client's exception reports in various manners, generalized software is unlikely to be used. Exception reports are generally tested via CPA-prepared test data containing all the possible error conditions. The test data are then run on the client's hardware and software to ascertain whether the exception reports are "picking up" the CPA's test data.

26. (c) The requirement is to identify the information that must be available to begin creating automated lead schedules. A lead schedule is used to summarize like accounts (e.g., if a client has five cash accounts those accounts may be summarized on a lead schedule). Answer (c) is correct because lead schedules include information such as account numbers, prior year account balances, and current year unadjusted information. Answer (a) is incorrect because interim information is not necessary. Answer (b) is incorrect because invoice and purchase order numbers are not summarized on lead schedules. Answer (d) is incorrect because adjusting entry information is identified subsequent to the creation of lead schedules.

27. (d) The requirement is to identify an effect on audit work review methods of using microcomputers in auditing. Answer (d) is correct because microcomputers typically produce a number of the "working papers" in computer disk form and because many computations, etc. will be performed directly by the computer with few details of the calculations conveniently available. Answer (a) is incorrect because the fieldwork standards remain the same regardless of whether or not computers are being utilized. Answer (b) is incorrect because one would not normally expect consulting services personnel to help with documentation. Answer (c) is incorrect because supervisory personnel must have an understanding of the capability and limitations of microcomputers before they are utilized on audits. •

28. (c) The requirement is to determine an auditor's **least** likely use of computer software. Answer (c) is correct because an auditor will judgmentally assess control risk related to both the computer and manual systems after having performed the various tests of controls. Answer (a) is incorrect because computer software will be used to access client data files. Answers (b) and (d) are incorrect because software is used to prepare spreadsheets and to perform parallel simulations.

29. (a) The requirement is to identify a primary advantage of using generalized audit software packages to audit the financial statements of a client that uses a computer system. Answer (a) is correct because generalized audit software allows an auditor to perform audits tests on a client's computer files. Answer (b) is incorrect because generalized audit software packages may assist the auditor with either substantive tests of transactions or analytical procedures. Answer (c) is incorrect because while generalized audit software might be used to perform such operations, this is not their primary advantage. Answer (d) is incorrect because generalized audit software packages have no direct relationship to the performance of tests of controls.

30. (c) The requirement is to determine the type of computer programs which auditors use to assist them in functions such as sorting and merging. Answer (c) is correct because a utility program is a standard routine for performing commonly required processing such as sorting, merging, editing, and mathematical routines. Answer (a) is incorrect because compiler programs translate programming languages such as COBOL or FORTRAN to machine language. Answer (b) is incorrect because supervisory programs or "operating systems" consist of a series of programs that perform functions such as scheduling and supervising the application programs, allocating storage, controlling peripheral devices, and handling errors and restarts. Answer (d) is incorrect because user or "application programs" perform specific data processing tasks such as general ledger, accounts payable, accounts receivable, and payroll. Application programs make use of utility routines.

31. (b) The requirement is to determine the best approach for determining whether credit limits **are being exceeded** when accounts receivable information is stored on disk. Answer (b) is correct because a program to compare actual account balances with the predetermined credit limit and thereby prepare a report on whether any actual credit limits are being exceeded will accomplish the stated objective. Answer (a) is incorrect because while test data will indicate whether the client's program **allows** credit limits to be exceeded, it will not indicate whether credit limits **are actually being exceeded**. Answer (c) is incorrect because a manual check of all account balances will be very time consuming. Answer (d) is incorrect because a sample will provide less complete information than the audit of the entire population which is indicated in answer (b).

32. (c) The requirement is to identify how an auditor would test for the presence of unauthorized computer program changes. Answer (c) is correct because comparing source code of the program with a correct version of the program will disclose unauthorized computer program changes. Answer (a) is incorrect because test data is generally used to test specific controls and it will generally be less effective for detecting unauthorized changes than will source code comparison. Answer (b) is incorrect because check digits are primarily used as an input control to determine that input data is proper. Answer (d) is incorrect because properly computing control totals is only one possible unauthorized change that might be made to a program.

33. (b) The requirement is to identify the number that represents the record count. Answer (b) is correct because the record count represents the number of records in a file, in this case 4.

SOLUTION TO SIMULATION PROBLEM

Simulation Problem 1

Situation	Technology	Controls	Research	Communication

Description	(A)	(B)	(C)	(D)	(E)	(F)	(G)
1. Auditing by manually testing the input and output of a computer system.	●	○	○	○	○	○	○
2. Dummy transactions developed by the auditor and processed by the client's computer programs, generally for a batch processing system.	○	○	○	○	○	●	○
3. Fictitious and real transactions are processed together without the client's operating personnel knowing of the testing process.	○	○	●	○	○	○	○
4. May include a simulated division or subsidiary into the accounting system with the purpose of running fictitious transactions through it.	○	○	●	○	○	○	○
5. Uses a generalized audit software package prepared by the auditors.	○	○	○	●	○	○	○

Explanation of solutions

1. **(A)** Auditing "around" the computer involves examining inputs into and outputs from the computer while ignoring processing, as contrasted to auditing "through" the computer which in some manner directly utilizes the computer's processing ability.

2. **(F)** Test data is a set of dummy transactions developed by the auditor and processed by the client's computer programs to determine whether the controls that the auditor intends to rely upon are functioning as expected.

3. **(C)** An integrated test facility introduces dummy transactions into a system in the midst of live transactions and is often built into the system during the original design.

4. **(C)** An integrated test facility approach may incorporate a simulated division or subsidiary into the accounting system with the sole purpose of running test data through it.

5. **(D)** Parallel simulation involves processing actual client data through an auditor's software program to determine whether the output equals that obtained when the client processed the data.

Situation	Technology	Controls	Research	Communication

Description	(H)	(I)	(J)	(K)	(L)	(M)	(N)	(O)	(P)
1. A control that will detect blanks existing in input data when they should not.	○	○	○	○	○	○	●	○	○
2. A control to ensure that jobs run simultaneously in a multiprogramming environment cannot change the allocated memory of another job.	○	●	○	○	○	○	○	○	○
3. A digit added to an identification number to detect certain types of data transmission or transposition errors.	○	○	●	○	○	○	○	○	○
4. A terminal control to limit access to programs or files to authorized users.	○	○	○	○	○	○	○	●	○
5. A total of one field for all the records of a batch where the total is meaningless for financial purposes.	○	○	○	○	○	●	○	○	○

Explanation of solutions

1. **(N)** A missing data check tests whether blanks exist in input data where they should not (e.g., an employee's division number). When the data is missing, an error message is output.

2. **(I)** Boundary protection is necessary because most large computers have more than one job running simultaneously (a multiprogramming environment). To ensure that these simultaneous jobs cannot destroy or change the allocated memory of another job, the systems software contains boundary protection controls.

3. **(J)** A check digit is an extra digit added to an identification number to detect certain types of data transmission or transposition errors. It is used to verify that the number was entered into the computer system correctly; one approach is using a check digit that is calculated as a mathematical combination of the other digits.

4. **(O)** Personal identification codes require individuals to in some manner identify themselves to determine that only authorized users access programs or files.

5. (M) A hash total is the total of one field for all the records of a batch where the total is a meaningless total for financial purposes, such as a mathematical sum of employee social security numbers to determine that all employees have been processed.

Situation	Technology	Controls	Research		Communication

SAS 110.18-.19 provides lists of benefits and risks relating to internal control and the use of information technology as follows:

.18 IT provides potential benefits of effectiveness and efficiency for an entity's internal control because it enables an entity to

- Consistently apply predefined business rules and perform complex calculations in processing large volumes of transactions or data.
- Enhance the timeliness, availability, and accuracy of information.
- Facilitate the additional analysis of information.
- Enhance the ability to monitor the performance of the entity's activities and its policies and procedures.
- Reduce the risk that controls will be circumvented.
- Enhance the ability to achieve effective segregation of duties by implementing security controls in applications, databases, and operating systems.

.19 IT also poses specific risks to an entity's internal control including

- Reliance on systems or programs that are inaccurately processing data, processing inaccurate data, or both.
- Unauthorized access to data that may result in destruction of data or improper changes to data, including the recording of unauthorized or nonexistent transactions or inaccurate recording of transactions.
- Unauthorized changes to data in master files.
- Unauthorized changes to systems or programs.
- Failure to make necessary changes to systems or programs.
- Inappropriate manual intervention.
- Potential loss of data.

Situation	Technology	Controls	Research	Communication	

To: Audit Working Papers
From: CPA Candidate

     This memorandum is designed to describe the nature and use of auditing around the computer. Auditing around the computer is a phrase used to describe a situation in which we do not test the controls in the system itself. Instead we focus on the input and output.

     Auditing around the computer can only be justified in a situation in which the client has an unsophisticated computer system with no effective controls. When this technique is used there is a risk that we will not identify how errors or fraud could occur. Accordingly, we should never use the technique when we do not understand the system and its risks.

     If you have any other questions, please contact me.

3 FINANCIAL ACCOUNTING AND REPORTING PROBLEMS AND SOLUTIONS

The Financial Accounting and Reporting Exam is scheduled for four hours. Based on information released by the AICPA, candidates should expect three multiple-choice testlets of approximately thirty questions each, and two simulations.

The Uniform CPA Examination Content Specifications appear in *Volume 1, Outlines and Study Guides*.

MULTIPLE-CHOICE QUESTIONS (1-70)

1. What are the Statements of Financial Accounting Concepts intended to establish?
a. Generally accepted accounting principles in financial reporting by business enterprises.
b. The meaning of "Present fairly in accordance with generally accepted accounting principles."
c. The objectives and concepts for use in developing standards of financial accounting and reporting.
d. The hierarchy of sources of generally accepted accounting principles.

2. According to the FASB conceptual framework, the objectives of financial reporting for business enterprises are based on
a. Generally accepted accounting principles.
b. Reporting on management's stewardship.
c. The need for conservatism.
d. The needs of the users of the information.

3. According to the FASB conceptual framework, the usefulness of providing information in financial statements is subject to the constraint of
a. Consistency.
b. Cost-benefit.
c. Reliability.
d. Representational faithfulness.

4. During a period when an enterprise is under the direction of a particular management, its financial statements will directly provide information about
a. Both enterprise performance and management performance.
b. Management performance but not directly provide information about enterprise performance.
c. Enterprise performance but not directly provide information about management performance.
d. Neither enterprise performance nor management performance.

5. According to Statements of Financial Accounting Concepts, neutrality is an ingredient of

	Reliability	*Relevance*
a.	Yes	Yes
b.	Yes	No
c.	No	Yes
d.	No	No

6. According to the FASB conceptual framework, which of the following relates to both relevance and reliability?
a. Comparability.
b. Feedback value.
c. Verifiability.
d. Timeliness.

7. According to the FASB conceptual framework, the process of reporting an item in the financial statements of an entity is
a. Allocation.
b. Matching.
c. Realization.
d. Recognition.

8. Under FASB Statement of Financial Accounting Concepts 5, which of the following items would cause earnings to differ from comprehensive income for an enterprise in an industry **not** having specialized accounting principles?

a. Unrealized loss on investments classified as available-for-sale securities.
b. Unrealized loss on investments classified as trading securities.
c. Loss on exchange of similar assets.
d. Loss on exchange of dissimilar assets.

9. Under FASB Statement of Financial Accounting Concepts 5, comprehensive income excludes changes in equity resulting from which of the following?
a. Loss from discontinued operations.
b. Prior period error correction.
c. Dividends paid to stockholders.
d. Unrealized loss on securities classified as available-for-sale.

10. According to the FASB conceptual framework, which of the following situations violates the concept of reliability?
a. Data on segments having the same expected risks and growth rates are reported to analysts estimating future profits.
b. Financial statements are issued nine months late.
c. Management reports to stockholders regularly refer to new projects undertaken, but the financial statements never report project results.
d. Financial statements include property with a carrying amount increased to management's estimate of market value.

11. According to the FASB conceptual framework, which of the following statements conforms to the realization concept?
a. Equipment depreciation was assigned to a production department and then to product unit costs.
b. Depreciated equipment was sold in exchange for a note receivable.
c. Cash was collected on accounts receivable.
d. Product unit costs were assigned to cost of goods sold when the units were sold.

12. What is the underlying concept that supports the immediate recognition of a contingent loss?
a. Substance over form.
b. Consistency.
c. Matching.
d. Conservatism.

13. What is the underlying concept governing the generally accepted accounting principles pertaining to recording gain contingencies?
a. Conservatism.
b. Relevance.
c. Consistency.
d. Reliability.

14. FASB's conceptual framework explains both financial and physical capital maintenance concepts. Which capital maintenance concept is applied to currently reported net income, and which is applied to comprehensive income?

	Currently reported net income	*Comprehensive income*
a.	Financial capital	Physical capital
b.	Physical capital	Physical capital
c.	Financial capital	Financial capital
d.	Physical capital	Financial capital

15. According to the FASB conceptual framework, an entity's revenue may result from
- a. A decrease in an asset from primary operations.
- b. An increase in an asset from incidental transactions.
- c. An increase in a liability from incidental transactions.
- d. A decrease in a liability from primary operations.

16. According to the FASB conceptual framework, which of the following is an essential characteristic of an asset?
- a. The claims to an asset's benefits are legally enforceable.
- b. An asset is tangible.
- c. An asset is obtained at a cost.
- d. An asset provides future benefits.

17. According to the FASB conceptual framework, which of the following attributes would **not** be used to measure inventory?
- a. Historical cost.
- b. Replacement cost.
- c. Net realizable value.
- d. Present value of future cash flows.

18. According to SFAC 7, *Using Cash Flow Information and Present Value in Accounting Measurements*, the most relevant measurement of an entity's liabilities at initial recognition and fresh-start measurements should always reflect
- a. The expectations of the entity's management.
- b. Historical cost.
- c. The credit standing of the entity.
- d. The single most-likely minimum or maximum possible amount.

19. Which of the following is **not** covered by SFAC 7, *Using Cash Flow Information and Present Value in Accounting Measurements*?
- a. Measurements at initial recognition.
- b. Interest method of amortization.
- c. Expected cash flow approach.
- d. Determining when fresh-start measurements are appropriate.

20. In calculating present value in a situation with a range of possible outcomes all discounted using the same interest rate, the expected present value would be
- a. The most-likely outcome.
- b. The maximum outcome.
- c. The minimum outcome.
- d. The sum of probability-weighted present values.

21. A cash flow of $200,000 may be received by Lydia Nickels, Inc. in one year, two years, or three years, with probabilities of 20%, 50%, and 30%, respectively. The rate of interest on default risk-free investments is 5%. The present value factors are

PV of 1, at 5%, for 1 year is	.95238
PV of 1, at 5%, for 2 years is	.90703
PV of 1, at 5%, for 3 years is	.86384

What is the expected present value of Lydia Nickels' cash flow (in whole dollars)?
- a. $181,406
- b. $180,628
- c. $ 90,703
- d. $ 89,925

22. Which of the following statements regarding interest methods of allocations is **not** true?
- a. The term "interest methods of allocation" refers both to the convention for periodic reporting and to the several approaches to dealing with changes in estimated future cash flows.
- b. Interest methods of allocation are reporting conventions that use present value techniques in the absence of a fresh-start measurement to compute changes in the carrying amount of an asset or liability from one period to the next.
- c. Interest methods of allocation are grounded in the notion of current cost.
- d. Holding gains and losses are generally excluded from allocation systems.

23. Which of the following is **not** an objective of using present value in accounting measurements?
- a. To capture the value of an asset or a liability in the context of a particular entity.
- b. To estimate fair value.
- c. To capture the economic difference between sets of future cash flows.
- d. To capture the elements that taken together would comprise a market price if one existed.

24. On December 31, 2009, Brooks Co. decided to end operations and dispose of its assets within three months. At December 31, 2009, the net realizable value of the equipment was below historical cost. What is the appropriate measurement basis for equipment included in Brooks' December 31, 2009 balance sheet?
- a. Historical cost.
- b. Current reproduction cost.
- c. Net realizable value.
- d. Current replacement cost.

25. Which of the following accounting literature is not included in the FASB Accounting Standards Codification?
- a. AICPA Statements of Position.
- b. FASB Statements.
- c. Accounting Research Bulletins.
- d. Statements of Auditing Standards.

26. On October 1, 2009, Acme Fuel Co. sold 100,000 gallons of heating oil to Karn Co. at $3 per gallon. Fifty thousand gallons were delivered on December 15, 2009, and the remaining 50,000 gallons were delivered on January 15, 2010. Payment terms were: 50% due on October 1, 2009, 25% due on first delivery, and the remaining 25% due on second delivery. What amount of revenue should Acme recognize from this sale during 2009?
- a. $ 75,000
- b. $150,000
- c. $225,000
- d. $300,000

27. Amar Farms produced 300,000 pounds of cotton during the 2009 season. Amar sells all of its cotton to Brye Co., which has agreed to purchase Amar's entire production at the prevailing market price. Recent legislation assures that the market price will not fall below $.70 per pound during the next two years. Amar's costs of selling and distributing the cotton are immaterial and can be reasonably estimated. Amar reports its inventory at expected exit value. During 2009, Amar sold and delivered to Brye 200,000 pounds at the market price of $.70. Amar sold the remaining 100,000 pounds during 2010 at the market price of $.72. What amount of revenue should Amar recognize in 2009?

a. $140,000
b. $144,000
c. $210,000
d. $216,000

28. Lin Co., a distributor of machinery, bought a machine from the manufacturer in November 2009 for $10,000. On December 30, 2009, Lin sold this machine to Zee Hardware for $15,000, under the following terms: 2% discount if paid within thirty days, 1% discount if paid after thirty days but within sixty days, or payable in full within ninety days if not paid within the discount periods. However, Zee had the right to return this machine to Lin if Zee was unable to resell the machine before expiration of the ninety-day payment period, in which case Zee's obligation to Lin would be canceled. In Lin's net sales for the year ended December 31, 2009, how much should be included for the sale of this machine to Zee?

a. $0
b. $14,700
c. $14,850
d. $15,000

29. Under a royalty agreement with another company, Wand Co. will pay royalties for the assignment of a patent for three years. The royalties paid should be reported as expense

a. In the period paid.
b. In the period incurred.
c. At the date the royalty agreement began.
d. At the date the royalty agreement expired.

30. Clark Co.'s advertising expense account had a balance of $146,000 at December 31, 2009, before any necessary year-end adjustment relating to the following:

• Included in the $146,000 is the $15,000 cost of printing catalogs for a sales promotional campaign in January 2010.
• Radio advertisements broadcast during December 2009 were billed to Clark on January 2, 2010. Clark paid the $9,000 invoice on January 11, 2010.

What amount should Clark report as advertising expense in its income statement for the year ended December 31, 2009?

a. $122,000
b. $131,000
c. $140,000
d. $155,000

31. An analysis of Thrift Corp.'s unadjusted prepaid expense account at December 31, 2009, revealed the following:

• An opening balance of $1,500 for Thrift's comprehensive insurance policy. Thrift had paid an annual premium of $3,000 on July 1, 2008.
• A $3,200 annual insurance premium payment made July 1, 2009.
• A $2,000 advance rental payment for a warehouse Thrift leased for one year beginning January 1, 2010.

In its December 31, 2009 balance sheet, what amount should Thrift report as prepaid expenses?

a. $5,200
b. $3,600
c. $2,000
d. $1,600

32. Roro, Inc. paid $7,200 to renew its only insurance policy for three years on March 1, 2009, the effective date of the policy. At March 31, 2009, Roro's unadjusted trial balance showed a balance of $300 for prepaid insurance and $7,200 for insurance expense. What amounts should be reported for prepaid insurance and insurance expense in Roro's financial statements for the three months ended March 31, 2009?

	Prepaid insurance	Insurance expense
a.	$7,000	$300
b.	$7,000	$500
c.	$7,200	$300
d.	$7,300	$200

33. Aneen's Video Mart sells one- and two-year mail order subscriptions for its video-of-the-month business. Subscriptions are collected in advance and credited to sales. An analysis of the recorded sales activity revealed the following:

	2008	2009
Sales	$420,000	$500,000
Less cancellations	20,000	30,000
Net sales	$400,000	$470,000
Subscriptions expirations:		
2008	$120,000	
2009	155,000	$130,000
2010	125,000	200,000
2011		140,000
	$400,000	$470,000

In Aneen's December 31, 2009 balance sheet, the balance for unearned subscription revenue should be

a. $495,000
b. $470,000
c. $465,000
d. $340,000

34. Regal Department Store sells gift certificates, redeemable for store merchandise, that expire one year after their issuance. Regal has the following information pertaining to its gift certificates sales and redemptions:

Unredeemed at 12/31/08	$ 75,000
2009 sales	250,000
2009 redemptions of prior year sales	25,000
2009 redemptions of current year sales	175,000

Regal's experience indicates that 10% of gift certificates sold will not be redeemed. In its December 31, 2009 balance sheet, what amount should Regal report as unearned revenue?

a. $125,000
b. $112,500
c. $100,000
d. $ 50,000

35. Wren Corp.'s trademark was licensed to Mont Co. for royalties of 15% of sales of the trademarked items. Royalties are payable semiannually on March 15 for sales in July through December of the prior year, and on September 15 for sales in January through June of the same year. Wren received the following royalties from Mont:

	March 15	September 15
2008	$10,000	$15,000
2009	12,000	17,000

Mont estimated that sales of the trademarked items would total $60,000 for July through December 2009. In Wren's 2009 income statement, the royalty revenue should be

a. $26,000
b. $29,000
c. $38,000
d. $41,000

36. In 2008, Super Comics Corp. sold a comic strip to Fantasy, Inc. and will receive royalties of 20% of future revenues associated with the comic strip. At December 31, 2009, Super reported royalties receivable of $75,000 from Fantasy. During 2010, Super received royalty payments of $200,000. Fantasy reported revenues of $1,500,000 in 2010 from the comic strip. In its 2010 income statement, what amount should Super report as royalty revenue?

a. $125,000
b. $175,000
c. $200,000
d. $300,000

37. Rill Co. owns a 20% royalty interest in an oil well. Rill receives royalty payments on January 31 for the oil sold between the previous June 1 and November 30, and on July 31 for oil sold between December 1 and May 31. Production reports show the following oil sales:

June 1, 2008 - November 30, 2008	$300,000
December 1, 2008 - December 31, 2008	50,000
December 1, 2008 - May 31, 2009	400,000
June 1, 2009 - November 30, 2009	325,000
December 1, 2009 - December 31, 2009	70,000

What amount should Rill report as royalty revenue for 2009?

a. $140,000
b. $144,000
c. $149,000
d. $159,000

38. Decker Company assigns some of its patents to other enterprises under a variety of licensing agreements. In some instances advance royalties are received when the agreements are signed, and in others, royalties are remitted within sixty days after each license year-end. The following data are included in Decker's December 31 balance sheet:

	2008	2009
Royalties receivable	$90,000	$85,000
Unearned royalties	60,000	40,000

During 2009 Decker received royalty remittances of $200,000. In its income statement for the year ended December 31, 2009, Decker should report royalty income of

a. $195,000
b. $215,000
c. $220,000
d. $225,000

39. Cooke Company acquires patent rights from other enterprises and pays advance royalties in some cases, and in others, royalties are paid within ninety days after year-end. The following data are included in Cooke's December 31 balance sheets:

	2008	2009
Prepaid royalties	$55,000	$45,000
Royalties payable	80,000	75,000

During 2009 Cooke remitted royalties of $300,000. In its income statement for the year ended December 31, 2009, Cooke should report royalty expense of

a. $295,000
b. $305,000
c. $310,000
d. $330,000

40. The premium on a three-year insurance policy expiring on December 31, 2011, was paid in total on January 1, 2009. The original payment was initially debited to a prepaid asset account. The appropriate journal entry has been recorded on December 31, 2009. The balance in the prepaid asset account on December 31, 2009, should be

a. Zero.
b. The same as it would have been if the original payment had been debited initially to an expense account.
c. The same as the original payment.
d. Higher than if the original payment had been debited initially to an expense account.

41. On January 1, 2009, Sip Co. signed a five-year contract enabling it to use a patented manufacturing process beginning in 2009. A royalty is payable for each product produced, subject to a minimum annual fee. Any royalties in excess of the minimum will be paid annually. On the contract date, Sip prepaid a sum equal to two years' minimum annual fees. In 2009, only minimum fees were incurred. The royalty prepayment should be reported in Sip's December 31, 2009 financial statements as

a. An expense only.
b. A current asset and an expense.
c. A current asset and noncurrent asset.
d. A noncurrent asset.

42. A retail store received cash and issued gift certificates that are redeemable in merchandise. The gift certificates lapse one year after they are issued. How would the deferred revenue account be affected by each of the following transactions?

	Redemption of certificates	*Lapse of certificates*
a.	No effect	Decrease
b.	Decrease	Decrease
c.	Decrease	No effect
d.	No effect	No effect

43. Jersey, Inc. is a retailer of home appliances and offers a service contract on each appliance sold. Jersey sells appliances on installment contracts, but all service contracts must be paid in full at the time of sale. Collections received for service contracts should be recorded as an increase in a

a. Deferred revenue account.
b. Sales contracts receivable valuation account.
c. Stockholders' valuation account.
d. Service revenue account.

44. Ward, a consultant, keeps her accounting records on a cash basis. During 2009, Ward collected $200,000 in fees from clients. At December 31, 2008, Ward had accounts receivable of $40,000. At December 31, 2009, Ward had accounts receivable of $60,000, and unearned fees of $5,000. On an accrual basis, what was Ward's service revenue for 2009?

a. $175,000
b. $180,000
c. $215,000
d. $225,000

45. Zeta Co. reported sales revenue of $4,600,000 in its income statement for the year ended December 31, 2009. Additional information is as follows:

	12/31/08	12/31/09
Accounts receivable	$1,000,000	$1,300,000
Allowance for uncollectible accounts	(60,000)	(110,000)

Zeta wrote off uncollectible accounts totaling $20,000 during 2009. Under the cash basis of accounting, Zeta would have reported 2009 sales of
    a. $4,900,000
    b. $4,350,000
    c. $4,300,000
    d. $4,280,000

46. Marr Corp. reported rental revenue of $2,210,000 in its cash basis federal income tax return for the year ended November 30, 2009. Additional information is as follows:

Rents receivable—November 30, 2009	$1,060,000
Rents receivable—November 30, 2008	800,000
Uncollectible rents written off during the fiscal year	30,000

Under the accrual basis, Marr should report rental revenue of
    a. $1,920,000
    b. $1,980,000
    c. $2,440,000
    d. $2,500,000

47. The following information pertains to Eagle Co.'s 2009 sales:

Cash sales	
Gross	$ 80,000
Returns and allowances	4,000
Credit sales	
Gross	120,000
Discounts	6,000

On January 1, 2009 customers owed Eagle $40,000. On December 31, 2009, customers owed Eagle $30,000. Eagle uses the direct writeoff method for bad debts. No bad debts were recorded in 2009. Under the cash basis of accounting, what amount of net revenue should Eagle report for 2009?
    a. $ 76,000
    b. $170,000
    c. $190,000
    d. $200,000

48. The following balances were reported by Mall Co. at December 31, 2009 and 2008:

	12/31/09	12/31/08
Inventory	$260,000	$290,000
Accounts payable	75,000	50,000

Mall paid suppliers $490,000 during the year ended December 31, 2009. What amount should Mall report for cost of goods sold in 2009?
    a. $545,000
    b. $495,000
    c. $485,000
    d. $435,000

49. Class Corp. maintains its accounting records on the cash basis but restates its financial statements to the accrual method of accounting. Class had $60,000 in cash-basis

pretax income for 2009. The following information pertains to Class's operations for the years ended December 31, 2009 and 2008:

	2009	2008
Accounts receivable	$40,000	$20,000
Accounts payable	15,000	30,000

Under the accrual method, what amount of income before taxes should Class report in its December 31, 2009 income statement?
    a. $25,000
    b. $55,000
    c. $65,000
    d. $95,000

50. On February 1, 2010, Tory began a service proprietorship with an initial cash investment of $2,000. The proprietorship provided $5,000 of services in February and received full payment in March. The proprietorship incurred expenses of $3,000 in February, which were paid in April. During March, Tory drew $1,000 against the capital account. In the proprietorship's financial statements for the two months ended March 31, 2010, prepared under the cash basis method of accounting, what amount should be reported as capital?
    a. $1,000
    b. $3,000
    c. $6,000
    d. $7,000

51. Compared to the accrual basis of accounting, the cash basis of accounting understates income by the net decrease during the accounting period of

	Accounts receivable	Accrued expenses
a.	Yes	Yes
b.	Yes	No
c.	No	No
d.	No	Yes

52. White Co. wants to convert its 2009 financial statements from the accrual basis of accounting to the cash basis. Both supplies inventory and office salaries payable increased between January 1, 2009, and December 31, 2009. To obtain 2009 cash basis net income, how should these increases be added to or deducted from accrual-basis net income?

	Supplies inventory	Office salaries payable
a.	Deducted	Deducted
b.	Deducted	Added
c.	Added	Deducted
d.	Added	Added

53. Before 2009, Droit Co. used the cash basis of accounting. As of December 31, 2009, Droit changed to the accrual basis. Droit cannot determine the beginning balance of supplies inventory. What is the effect of Droit's inability to determine beginning supplies inventory on its 2009 accrual-basis net income and December 31, 2009 accrual-basis owners' equity?

	2009 net income	12/31/09 owners' equity
a.	No effect	No effect
b.	No effect	Overstated
c.	Overstated	No effect
d.	Overstated	Overstated

54. Gant Co., which began operations on January 1, 2009, appropriately uses the installment method of accounting.

The following information pertains to Gant's operations for the year 2009:

Installment sales	$500,000
Regular sales	300,000
Cost of installment sales	250,000
Cost of regular sales	150,000
General and administrative expenses	50,000
Collections on installment sales	100,000

In its December 31, 2009 balance sheet, what amount should Gant report as deferred gross profit?

a. $250,000
b. $200,000
c. $160,000
d. $ 75,000

55. Since there is no reasonable basis for estimating the degree of collectibility, Astor Co. uses the installment method of revenue recognition for the following sales:

	2009	2008
Sales	$900,000	$600,000
Collections from:		
2008 sales	100,000	200,000
2009 sales	300,000	--
Accounts written off:		
2008 sales	150,000	50,000
2009 sales	50,000	--
Gross profit percentage	40%	30%

What amount should Astor report as deferred gross profit in its December 31, 2009 balance sheet for the 2008 and 2009 sales?

a. $150,000
b. $160,000
c. $225,000
d. $250,000

56. Luge Co., which began operations on January 2, 2010, appropriately uses the installment sales method of accounting. The following information is available for 2010:

Installment accounts receivable, December 31, 2010	$800,000
Deferred gross profit, December 31, 2009 (before recognition of realized gross profit for 2010)	560,000
Gross profit on sales	40%

For the year ended December 31, 2010, cash collections and realized gross profit on sales should be

	Cash collections	Realized gross profit
a.	$400,000	$320,000
b.	$400,000	$240,000
c.	$600,000	$320,000
d.	$600,000	$240,000

57. Dolce Co., which began operations on January 1, 2009, appropriately uses the installment method of accounting to record revenues. The following information is available for the years ended December 31, 2009 and 2010:

	2009	2010
Sales	$1,000,000	$2,000,000
Gross profit realized on sales made in:		
2009	150,000	90,000
2010	--	200,000
Gross profit percentages	30%	40%

What amount of installment accounts receivable should Dolce report in its December 31, 2010 balance sheet?

a. $1,225,000
b. $1,300,000
c. $1,700,000
d. $1,775,000

58. On December 31, 2009, Mill Co. sold construction equipment to Drew, Inc. for $1,800,000. The equipment had a carrying amount of $1,200,000. Drew paid $300,000 cash on December 31, 2009, and signed a $1,500,000 note bearing interest at 10%, payable in five annual installments of $300,000. Mill appropriately accounts for the sale under the installment method. On December 31, 2010, Drew paid $300,000 principal and $150,000 interest. For the year ended December 31, 2010, what total amount of revenue should Mill recognize from the construction equipment sale and financing?

a. $250,000
b. $150,000
c. $120,000
d. $100,000

59. On January 2, 2009, Blake Co. sold a used machine to Cooper, Inc. for $900,000, resulting in a gain of $270,000. On that date, Cooper paid $150,000 cash and signed a $750,000 note bearing interest at 10%. The note was payable in three annual installments of $250,000 beginning January 2, 2010. Blake appropriately accounted for the sale under the installment method. Cooper made a timely payment of the first installment on January 2, 2010, of $325,000, which included accrued interest of $75,000. What amount of deferred gross profit should Blake report at December 31, 2010?

a. $150,000
b. $172,500
c. $180,000
d. $225,000

60. For financial statement purposes, the installment method of accounting may be used if the

a. Collection period extends over more than twelve months.
b. Installments are due in different years.
c. Ultimate amount collectible is indeterminate.
d. Percentage-of-completion method is inappropriate.

61. According to the installment method of accounting, gross profit on an installment sale is recognized in income

a. On the date of sale.
b. On the date the final cash collection is received.
c. In proportion to the cash collection.
d. After cash collections equal to the cost of sales have been received.

62. Income recognized using the installment method of accounting generally equals cash collected multiplied by the

a. Net operating profit percentage.
b. Net operating profit percentage adjusted for expected uncollectible accounts.
c. Gross profit percentage.
d. Gross profit percentage adjusted for expected uncollectible accounts.

63. It is proper to recognize revenue prior to the sale of merchandise when

I. The revenue will be reported as an installment sale.
II. The revenue will be reported under the cost recovery method.

a. I only.
b. II only.
c. Both I and II.
d. Neither I nor II.

64. The following information pertains to a sale of real estate by Ryan Co. to Sud Co. on December 31, 2009:

Carrying amount		$2,000,000
Sales price:		
Cash	$ 300,000	
Purchase money mortgage	2,700,000	3,000,000

The mortgage is payable in nine annual installments of $300,000 beginning December 31, 2010, plus interest of 10%. The December 31, 2010, installment was paid as scheduled, together with interest of $270,000. Ryan uses the cost recovery method to account for the sale. What amount of income should Ryan recognize in 2010 from the real estate sale and its financing?

a. $570,000
b. $370,000
c. $270,000
d. $0

65. Wren Co. sells equipment on installment contracts. Which of the following statements best justifies Wren's use of the cost recovery method of revenue recognition to account for these installment sales?

a. The sales contract provides that title to the equipment only passes to the purchaser when all payments have been made.
b. No cash payments are due until one year from the date of sale.
c. Sales are subject to a high rate of return.
d. There is no reasonable basis for estimating collectibility.

66. According to the cost recovery method of accounting, gross profit on an installment sale is recognized in income

a. After cash collections equal to the cost of sales have been received.
b. In proportion to the cash collections.
c. On the date the final cash collection is received.
d. On the date of sale.

67. On December 31, 2009, Rice, Inc. authorized Graf to operate as a franchisee for an initial franchise fee of $150,000. Of this amount, $60,000 was received upon signing the agreement and the balance, represented by a note, is due in three annual payments of $30,000 each beginning December 31, 2010. The present value on December 31, 2009, of the three annual payments appropriately discounted is $72,000. According to the agreement, the nonrefundable down payment represents a fair measure of the services already performed by Rice; however, substantial future services are required of Rice. Collectibility of the note is reasonably certain. In Rice's December 31, 2009 balance sheet, unearned franchise fees from Graf's franchise should be reported as

a. $132,000
b. $100,000
c. $ 90,000
d. $ 72,000

68. Each of Potter Pie Co.'s twenty-one new franchisees contracted to pay an initial franchise fee of $30,000. By December 31, 2009, each franchisee had paid a nonrefundable $10,000 fee and signed a note to pay $10,000 principal plus the market rate of interest on December 31, 2010, and December 31, 2011. Experience indicates that one franchisee will default on the additional payments. Services for the initial fee will be performed in 2010. What amount of net

unearned franchise fees would Potter report at December 31, 2009?

a. $400,000
b. $600,000
c. $610,000
d. $630,000

69. In which of the following examples of real estate transactions would the seller not transfer the usual risks and rewards of ownership?

I. The buyer can compel the seller to repurchase the property.
II. The seller guarantees the return of the buyer's investment.
III. The seller is required to support operations of the buyer and will be reimbursed on a cost plus 5% basis.

a. I.
b. II.
c. III.
d. I and II.

70. Esker Inc. specializes in real estate transactions other than retail land sales. On January 1, 2010, Esker consummated a sale of property to Kame Ltd. The amount of profit on the sale is determinable and Esker is not obligated to perform any additional activities to earn the profit. Kame's initial and continuing investments were adequate to demonstrate a commitment to pay for the property under SFAS 66. However, Esker's receivable may be subject to future subordination. Esker should account for the sale using the

a. Deposit method.
b. Reduced recovery method.
c. Cost recovery method.
d. Full accrual method.

SIMULATION PROBLEMS

Simulation Problem 1   (50 to 60 minutes)

Situation				
	Account Classifications	**Accrual Basis Worksheet**	**Communication**	**Research**

The following information pertains to Baron Flowers, a calendar-year sole proprietorship, which maintained its books on the cash basis during the year.

Baron Flowers
TRIAL BALANCE
December 31, 2009

	Dr.	Cr.
Cash	$ 25,600	
Accounts receivable, 12/31/08	16,200	
Inventory, 12/31/08	62,000	
Furniture & fixtures	118,200	
Land improvements	45,000	
Accumulated depreciation, 12/31/08		$ 32,400
Accounts payable, 12/31/08		17,000
Baron, Drawings		
Baron, Capital, 12/31/08		124,600
Sales		653,000
Purchases	305,100	
Salaries	174,000	
Payroll taxes	12,400	
Insurance	8,700	
Rent	34,200	
Utilities	12,600	
Living expenses	13,000	
	$827,000	$827,000

Baron has developed plans to expand into the wholesale flower market and is in the process of negotiating a bank loan to finance the expansion. The bank is requesting 2009 financial statements prepared on the accrual basis of accounting from Baron. During the course of a review engagement, Muir, Baron's accountant, obtained the following additional information.

1.   Amounts due from customers totaled $32,000 at December 31, 2009.

2.   An analysis of the above receivables revealed that an allowance for uncollectible accounts of $3,800 should be provided.

3.   Unpaid invoices for flower purchases totaled $30,500 and $17,000, at December 31, 2009, and December 31, 2008, respectively.

4.   The inventory totaled $72,800 based on a physical count of the goods at December 31, 2009. The inventory was priced at cost, which approximates market value.

5.   On May 1, 2009, Baron paid $8,700 to renew its comprehensive insurance coverage for one year. The premium on the previous policy, which expired on April 30, 2009, was $7,800.

6.   On January 2, 2009, Baron entered into a twenty-five-year operating lease for the vacant lot adjacent to Baron's retail store for use as a parking lot. As agreed in the lease, Baron paved and fenced in the lot at a cost of $45,000. The improvements were completed on April 1, 2009, and have an estimated useful life of fifteen years. No provision for depreciation or amortization has been recorded. Depreciation on furniture and fixtures was $12,000 for 2009.

7.   Accrued expenses at December 31, 2008 and 2009, were as follows:

	2008	2009
Utilities	$ 900	$1,500
Payroll taxes	1,100	1,600
	$2,000	$3,100

8.   Baron is being sued for $400,000. The coverage under the comprehensive insurance policy is limited to $250,000. Baron's attorney believes that an unfavorable outcome is probable and that a reasonable estimate of the settlement is $300,000.

9.   The salaries account includes $4,000 per month paid to the proprietor. Baron also receives $250 per week for living expenses.

Situation	Account Classifications	Accrual Basis Worksheet	Communication	Research

Suppose Baron incorporated and had the following accounts. Indicate how each of the following is classified on the financial statements. Below is a list of classifications.

Balance sheet classification
A. Current asset
B. Noncurrent asset
C. Current liability
D. Noncurrent liability
E. Owner's equity
F. Contra asset
G. Contra equity

Income statement classifications
H. Revenue
I. Expense
J. Contra revenue

	Balance sheet classification (A) (B) (C) (D) (E) (F) (G)	Income statement classification (H) (I) (J)
1. Bonds payable, due in 2018	O O O O O O O	O O O
2. Treasury stock	O O O O O O O	O O O
3. Accounts payable	O O O O O O O	O O O
4. Sales discounts	O O O O O O O	O O O
5. Notes payable, due in nine months	O O O O O O O	O O O
6. Inventory	O O O O O O O	O O O
7. Accounts receivable	O O O O O O O	O O O
8. Common stock	O O O O O O O	O O O
9. Cost of goods sold	O O O O O O O	O O O
10. Allowance for uncollectible accounts	O O O O O O O	O O O

Situation	Account Classifications	Accrual Basis Worksheet	Communication	Research

Using the worksheet below, prepare the adjustments necessary to convert the trial balance of Baron Flowers to the accrual basis of accounting for the year ended December 31, 2009. Formal journal entries are not required to support your adjustments. However, use the numbers given with the additional information to cross-reference the postings in the adjustment columns on the worksheet.

Baron Flowers
WORKSHEET TO CONVERT TRIAL BALANCE TO ACCRUAL BASIS
December 31, 2009

Account title	Cash basis Dr.	Cr.	Adjustments Dr.	Cr.	Accrual basis* Dr.*	Cr.*
Cash	25,600					
Accounts receivable	16,200					
Inventory	62,000					
Furniture & fixtures	118,200					
Land improvements	45,000					
Accumulated depreciation & amortization		32,400				
Accounts payable		17,000				
Baron, Drawings						
Baron, Capital		124,600				

Account title	Cash basis		Adjustments		Accrual basis*	
	Dr.	Cr.	Dr.	Cr.	Dr. *	Cr. *
Sales		653,000				
Purchases	305,100					
Salaries	174,000					
Payroll taxes	12,400					
Insurance	8,700					
Rent	34,200					
Utilities	12,600					
Living expenses	13,000					
	827,000	827,000				

Completion of these columns is not required.

Situation	Account Classifications	Accrual Basis Worksheet	Communication	Research

Write a brief memorandum to Baron explaining why the bank would require financial statements prepared on the accrual basis instead of the cash basis.

REMINDER: Your response will be graded for both technical content and writing skills. Technical content will be evaluated for information that is helpful to the intended reader and clearly relevant to the issue. Writing skills will be evaluated for development, organization, and the appropriate expression of ideas in professional correspondence. Use a standard business memo or letter format with a clear beginning, middle, and end. Do not convey information in the form of a table, bullet point list, or other abbreviated presentation.

To: Mr. Baron Flowers
From: CPA Candidate
Re: Accrual-basis financial statements

Situation	Account Classifications	Accrual Basis Worksheet	Communication	Research

Using the FASB Concepts Statements, select and reproduce the following definitions.

1. Revenue
2. Assets
3. Liability

Simulation Problem 2   (45 to 50 minutes)

Situation				
	Concepts	Trial Balance Worksheet	Communication	Research

The accounts listed below appeared in the December 31 trial balance of Jane Alexander Theater.

Equipment	192,000	
Accumulated depreciation equipment		60,000
Notes payable		90,000
Admissions revenue		380,000
Advertising expense	13,680	
Salaries expense	57,600	
Interest expense	1,400	

Additional information follows:

1. The equipment has an estimated life of 16 years and a salvage value of $40,000 at the end of that time. (Use straight-line method.)
2. The note payable is a 90-day note given to the bank October 20 and bearing interest at 10%. (Use 360 days for denominator.)
3. In December, two thousand (2,000) coupon admission books were sold at $25 each. They could be used for admission any time after January 1.

4. Advertising expense paid in advance and included in Advertising Expense, $1,100.

5. Salaries accrued but unpaid, $4,700.

Situation	Concepts	Trial Balance Worksheet	Communication	Research

This question consists of ten items that represent descriptions or definitions of the various elements of the FASB's *Statements of Financial Accounting Concepts*. Select the **best** answer for each item from the terms listed in A – L. A term may be used once, more than once, or not at all.

Terms

A.	Recognition	G.	Gains
B.	Comprehensive Income	H.	Net Income
C.	Representational Faithfulness	I.	Earnings
D.	Revenues	J.	Realization
E.	Predictive Value	K.	Replacement Cost
F.	Consistency	L.	Current Market Value

Concept statement definitions

(A) (B) (C) (D) (E) (F) (G) (H) (I) (J) (K) (L)

1. Component of relevance.   ○ ○ ○ ○ ○ ○ ○ ○ ○ ○ ○ ○

2. Increases in net assets from incidental or peripheral transactions affecting an entity.   ○ ○ ○ ○ ○ ○ ○ ○ ○ ○ ○ ○

3. The process of converting noncash resources and rights into cash or claims to cash.   ○ ○ ○ ○ ○ ○ ○ ○ ○ ○ ○ ○

4. Ingredient of relevance **and** reliability.   ○ ○ ○ ○ ○ ○ ○ ○ ○ ○ ○ ○

5. The process of formally recording an item in the financial statements of an entity after it has met existing criteria and been subject to cost-benefit constraints and materiality thresholds.   ○ ○ ○ ○ ○ ○ ○ ○ ○ ○ ○ ○

6. All changes in net assets of an entity during a period except those resulting from investments by owners and distributions to owners.   ○ ○ ○ ○ ○ ○ ○ ○ ○ ○ ○ ○

7. Inflows or other enhancements of assets of an entity or settlements of its liabilities from delivering or producing goods, rendering services, or other activities that constitute the entity's ongoing operations.   ○ ○ ○ ○ ○ ○ ○ ○ ○ ○ ○ ○

8. The amount of cash, or its equivalent, that could be obtained by selling an asset in orderly liquidation.   ○ ○ ○ ○ ○ ○ ○ ○ ○ ○ ○ ○

9. The quality of information that helps users to increase the likelihood of correctly forecasting the outcome of past or present events.   ○ ○ ○ ○ ○ ○ ○ ○ ○ ○ ○ ○

10. A performance measure concerned primarily with cash-to-cash cycles.   ○ ○ ○ ○ ○ ○ ○ ○ ○ ○ ○ ○

Situation	Concepts	Trial Balance Worksheet	Communication	Research

Using the attached Excel file, complete the adjustments, adjusted trial balance, and the income statement columns of the worksheet. For the # column, insert the number of adjustments. Add accounts as needed.

Jane Alexander Theater
December 31, 200X

a)	Trial balance		#	Adjustments		Adjusted trial balance		Income statement	
	Debit	Credit		Debit	Credit	Debit	Credit	Debit	Credit
Equipment	192,000								
Accumulated depreciation— equipment		60,000							
Notes payable		90,000							
Admissions revenue		380,000							
Advertising expense	13,680								
Salaries expense	57,600								
Interest expense	1,400								
Depreciation expense									

a)	Trial balance		#	Adjustments		Adjusted trial balance		Income statement	
	Debit	Credit		Debit	Credit	Debit	Credit	Debit	Credit
Interest payable									
Unearned adm									
Revenue									
Prepaid advertising									
Salaries payable									

Situation	Concepts	Trial Balance Worksheet	Communication		Research

Write a brief memorandum to the Director of Jane Alexander Theater explaining why adjusting and closing entries are necessary.

REMINDER: Your response will be graded for both technical content and writing skills. Technical content will be evaluated for information that is helpful to the intended reader and clearly relevant to the issue. Writing skills will be evaluated for development, organization, and the appropriate expression of ideas in professional correspondence. Use a standard business memo or letter format with a clear beginning, middle, and end. Do not convey information in the form of a table, bullet point list, or other abbreviated presentation.

To: Ms. Jane Alexander, Theatre Director
From: CPA Candidate
Re: Adjusting and closing entries

Situation	Concepts	Trial Balance Worksheet	Communication	Research	

Using the FASB Concepts Statements, select and reproduce the following definitions.

1. Gain
2. Recognition
3. Reliability

Simulation Problem 3   (30 to 40 minutes)

Situation					
	Concepts	Adjusting Entries	Revenue and Expense Recognition	Communication	Research

Emco is a wholesaler of kitchen appliances to retail dealers. At present, Emco sells to customers on account, with the account receivable due in forty-five days.

	Concepts				
Situation		Adjusting Entries	Revenue and Expense Recognition	Communication	Research

SFAC 5 provides guidance on measuring assets and liabilities. The following measurement methods are available to measure assets and liabilities, as shown in the list below. Identify the appropriate valuation method for each item.

Measurement methods

A.   Historical cost or historical proceeds
B.   Current cost
C.   Current market value
D.   Net realizable value or settlement rate
E.   Present value of future cash flows

Account	(A)	(B)	(C)	(D)	(E)
1. Long-term receivables	○	○	○	○	○
2. Available for sale securities	○	○	○	○	○
3. Equipment	○	○	○	○	○
4. Warranty obligations	○	○	○	○	○
5. Short-term payables	○	○	○	○	○
6. Accounts receivable	○	○	○	○	○
7. Bonds payable, due in ten years	○	○	○	○	○
8. Trading securities	○	○	○	○	○

Situation	Concepts	Adjusting Entries	Revenue and Expense Recognition	Communication	Research

Indicate whether each of the following adjusting entries is an accrual or a deferral type entry.

			Accrual	*Deferral*
1.	Depreciation expense	xx		
	Accumulated deprecation	xx	○	○
2.	Interest receivable	xx		
	Interest revenue	xx	○	○
3.	Rent expense	xx		
	Prepaid rent	xx	○	○
4.	Unearned revenue	xx		
	Rent revenue	xx	○	○
5.	Wage expense	xx		
	Wages payable	xx	○	○

Situation	Concepts	Adjusting Entries	Revenue and Expense Recognition	Communication	Research

Emco has the following transactions in 2009. Indicate the amount of revenue or expense recognized in 2009, 2010, and 2011 for each of these items. You may show expense recognitions in parentheses (xx).

	Amounts to be recognized		
	2009	*2010*	*2011*

1. Emco sells $5,000 of goods to a customer, FOB shipping point on 12/30/09.

2. Emco sells three pieces of equipment on a contract over a three-year period. The sales price of each piece of equipment is $10,000. Delivery of each piece of equipment is on February 10 of each year. In 2009, the customer paid a $20,000 down payment, and paid $5,000 per year in 2010 and 2011. Collectibility is reasonably assured.

3. In 1/1/09, Emco paid $9,000 for a membership to Wholesalers Association for a two-year membership in the trade association.

4. On 6/1/09, Emco signs a contract for $20,000 for goods to be sold on account. Payment is to be made in two installments of $10,000 each on 12/1/10 and 12/1/11. The goods are delivered on 10/1/09. Collection is reasonably assured, and the goods may not be returned.

5. Emco sells goods to a customer on July 1, 2009, for $50,000. If the customer does not sell the goods to retail customers by December 31, 2010, the goods can be returned to Emco. The customer sells the goods to retail customers on October 1, 2010.

				Communication	
Situation	Concepts	Adjusting Entries	Revenue and Expense Recognition		Research

Wyatt, CPA, is meeting with Brown, the controller of Emco, a wholesaler, to discuss the accounting issues regarding two unrelated items.

- Emco is considering offering its customers the right to return its products for a full refund within one year of purchase. Emco expects its sales to increase as a result, but is unable to estimate the amount of future returns.
- Brown is aware that the FASB Codification provides guidance on estimating the value of postretirement benefits. Brown is uncertain about the benefits and beneficiaries covered by the Codification. Also, Brown believes that, regardless of the FASB's authoritative literature, no estimate of postretirement obligation can be reasonable because it would be based on too many assumptions.

Brown has asked Wyatt to write a brief memo to Brown that Brown can use to explain these issues to Emco's president.
Write a brief advisory memorandum from Wyatt to Brown to

1. Explain the general principle of revenue recognition, the method of revenue recognition when right to return exists, and the impact of offering a right to return on Emco's ability to recognize revenue, if any.

2. State the principal benefit covered by the Codification and give an example of other benefits covered by these rules. Explain the reasoning for requiring accruals based on estimates. Indicate the primary recipients of postretirement benefits other than pensions.*

> * This requirement should not be completed until you have done Module 11D, Present Value: Pensions. A cross-reference in the Module 11 problem material will direct you to return to it.

REMINDER: Your response will be graded for both technical content and writing skills. Technical content will be evaluated for information that is helpful to the intended reader and clearly relevant to the issue. Writing skills will be evaluated for development, organization, and the appropriate expression of ideas in professional correspondence. Use a standard business memo or letter format with a clear beginning, middle, and end. Do not convey information in the form of a table, bullet point list, or other abbreviated presentation.

To: Mr. Brown
From: Wyatt, CPA

					Research
Situation	Concepts	Adjusting Entries	Revenue and Expense Recognition	Communication	

Using the FASB Concepts Statements, select and reproduce the following definitions.

1. Relevance
2. Realizable
3. Expense
4. Matching

MULTIPLE-CHOICE ANSWERS*

1. c __ __	16. d __ __	31. b __ __	46. d __ __	61. c __ __
2. d __ __	17. d __ __	32. b __ __	47. d __ __	62. c __ __
3. b __ __	18. c __ __	33. c __ __	48. a __ __	63. d __ __
4. c __ __	19. d __ __	34. d __ __	49. d __ __	64. d __ __
5. b __ __	20. d __ __	35. a __ __	50. c __ __	65. d __ __
6. a __ __	21. b __ __	36. d __ __	51. d __ __	66. a __ __
7. d __ __	22. c __ __	37. c __ __	52. b __ __	67. d __ __
8. a __ __	23. a __ __	38. b __ __	53. c __ __	68. c __ __
9. c __ __	24. c __ __	39. b __ __	54. b __ __	69. d __ __
10. d __ __	25. d __ __	40. b __ __	55. d __ __	70. c __ __
11. b __ __	26. b __ __	41. b __ __	56. d __ __	
12. d __ __	27. c __ __	42. b __ __	57. c __ __	
13. a __ __	28. a __ __	43. a __ __	58. a __ __	
14. c __ __	29. b __ __	44. c __ __	59. a __ __	1st: __/70 = __%
15. d __ __	30. c __ __	45. d __ __	60. c __ __	2nd: __/70 = __%

MULTIPLE-CHOICE ANSWER EXPLANATIONS

A.1. Basic Accounting Theory

1. **(c)** The Statements of Financial Accounting Concepts (SFAC) were issued to establish a framework from which financial accounting and reporting standards could be developed. The SFAC provide the theory behind accounting and reporting and provide guidance when no GAAP exists. The SFAC are not included as GAAP.

2. **(d)** Per SFAC 1, the objectives of financial reporting focus on providing present and potential investors with information useful in making investment decisions. Financial statement users do not have the authority to prescribe the data they desire. Therefore, they must rely on external financial reporting to satisfy their information needs, and the objectives must be based on the needs of those users.

3. **(b)** The FASB conceptual framework has identified two constraints to the usefulness of providing information in financial statements, cost benefit and materiality. Information is **not** disclosed if the costs of disclosure outweigh the benefits or if the information is not material enough to influence users. Consistency is a secondary quality of accounting information; reliability and relevance are the primary qualities of accounting information; and representational faithfulness is a component of reliability.

4. **(c)** Per SFAC 1, the primary focus of financial reporting is to provide information about an enterprise's performance. SFAC 1 states that financial reporting does not directly provide information about the performance of a particular management for the period since actions of past management may also affect the current period earnings. Financial reporting primarily focuses on the enterprise's performance and management performance would only be indirectly illustrated.

5. **(b)** SFAC 2 defines neutrality as the quality of information which requires freedom from bias toward a predetermined result. Since unbiased information would always be more reliable than biased information, this quality contributes to reliability. Other components of reliability include verifiability and representational faithfulness. Neutrality is not an ingredient of relevance because relevance refers to the usefulness of information, characterized by its predictive value, feedback value, and timeliness.

6. **(a)** Per SFAC 2, comparability is a secondary quality which relates to **both** of the primary qualities of relevance and reliability. Both feedback value and timeliness are described by SFAC 2 as ingredients only of relevance. They are not considered ingredients of reliability. Verifiability is described as an ingredient only of reliability.

7. **(d)** Per SFAC 5, recognition is the process of formally recording or incorporating an item into the financial statements as an asset, liability, revenue, expense, or the like. According to SFAC 6, allocation is the process of assigning or distributing an amount according to a plan or formula, matching is the simultaneous recognition of revenues with expenses that are related directly or jointly to the same transactions or events, and realization is the process of converting noncash resources and rights into money.

8. **(a)** Per SFAC 5, earnings and comprehensive income have the same broad components—revenues, expenses, gains, and losses—but are not the same because certain classes of gains and losses are excluded from earnings. Changes in market values of investments in marketable equity securities classified as available-for-sale securities are included in comprehensive income, but are excluded from earnings until realized. Answers (b), (c), and (d) are incorrect because they would be included in both earnings and comprehensive income. Note that unrealized gains and losses on marketable equity securities classified as trading securities are included in earnings. This treatment is in accordance with SFAS 115.

9. **(c)** Per SFAC 6, comprehensive income includes all changes in equity during a period except those resulting from investments by owners and distributions to owners. Dividends paid to stockholders is a change in equity resulting from a distribution to owners, so it is excluded from comprehensive income. Answers (a), (b), and (d) are all included in comprehensive income because they **are** changes in equity, but are **not** investments by, or distributions to, owners.

NOTE: Under SFAS 130, prior period error corrections would also be excluded from comprehensive income. This standard addresses

---

only the display of unrealized gains (losses) on foreign currency items, available-for-sale marketable securities, and the minimum pension liability adjustment. Other changes suggested in SFAC 5 and 6 will be addressed in future SFAS.

10. (d) Reliability has three subcomponents, as defined in SFAC 2: neutrality, representational faithfulness, and verifiability. **Neutrality** means that information should **not** be prepared or reported in such a way as to obtain a predetermined result, and **should** be free from bias. **Representational faithfulness** is defined as the correspondence between a measure and what it purports to represent. **Verifiability** means that two or more individuals who are independent of each other would arrive at a similar conclusion based on an examination of the same evidence. Answer (d) violates verifiability because different individuals would come up with different estimates of market value. Answer (a) is incorrect because reporting data to analysts does not violate reliability. Answers (b) and (c) are incorrect because they are examples of violations of relevance, not reliability. Answer (b) violates the relevance subcomponent of **timeliness,** while answer (c) violates the relevance subcomponent of **feedback value.**

11. (b) According to SFAC 6, realization is the process of converting noncash resources and rights into money through the sale of assets for cash or claims to cash. When equipment is sold for a note receivable, money is realized since a note qualifies as a claim to cash. Answers (a) and (d) relate to cost allocation. Answer (c) is incorrect because accounts receivable represents a claim to cash. Realization occurs at the time of sale rather than when cash is collected.

12. (d) A loss contingency is accrued by a charge to expense if it is reasonably estimable and it is **probable that a liability has been incurred** as of the balance sheet date. The **cause of the liability must have occurred on or before the date of the financial statements** if the liability is to be accrued, because the intention is to recognize the loss in the same period that the underlying cause took place. Therefore, some authorities would say that matching is the underlying concept supporting the immediate recognition of a contingent loss. A larger number, however, would mention conservatism as the more pervasive underlying concept supporting the immediate recognition of these losses.

13. (a) Conservatism means that when in doubt, accountants should choose the procedure that will be least likely to overstate assets and income. This concept underlies the GAAP pertaining to recording gain contingencies. In an effort to not overstate assets or income, gain contingencies are not recorded until they are no longer contingencies, and are disclosed only when probabilities are high that a gain contingency will become reality.

14. (c) Per SFAC 6, the major difference between financial and physical capital maintenance is related to the effects of price changes on assets held and liabilities owed during a period. The financial capital concept is applied in current GAAP. Under this concept, the effects of the price changes described above are considered "holding gains and losses," and are included in computing return on capital. Comprehensive income, which is described in SFAC 5, is "the change in equity of a business enterprise during a period from transactions and other events and circumstances from nonowner sources." It is also a measure of return on **finan-**cial capital. The concept of physical capital maintenance seeks to measure the effects of price changes that are not currently captured under GAAP (e.g., replacement costs of nonmonetary assets). Under this concept, holding gains and losses are considered "capital maintenance adjustments" which would be included directly in equity and excluded from return on capital.

15. (d) Per SFAC 6, revenues are inflows of assets or settlements of liabilities, or both, during a period as a result of an entity's major or primary operations. Two essential characteristics of revenues are that revenues (1) arise from a company's primary earnings activities and (2) are recurring or continuing in nature. Therefore, answer (d) is correct because it meets the above criteria. Answers (b) and (c) are incorrect because they result from incidental transactions. Answer (a) is incorrect because a decrease of an asset is not a revenue.

16. (d) Per SFAC 6, the common quality shared by all assets is "service potential" or "future economic benefit." Per SFAC 6, assets commonly have other distinguishing features, such as being legally enforceable, tangible or acquired at a cost. These features, however, are not essential characteristics of assets.

17. (d) Per SFAC 5, five different attributes are used to measure assets and liabilities in present practice: historical cost, current (replacement) cost, current market value, net realizable value, and present value of future cash flows. Three of these (historical cost, replacement cost, and net realizable value) are used in measuring inventory at lower of cost or market. Present value of future cash flows is not used to measure inventory.

Cash Flow Information and Present Value (SFAC 7)

18. (c) The most relevant measure of a liability always reflects the credit standing of the entity obligated to pay, according to SFAC 7. Those who hold the entity's obligations as assets incorporate the entity's credit standing in determining the prices they are willing to pay.

19. (d) SFAC 7 provides a framework for using future cash flows as the basis for accounting measurements at initial recognition or fresh-start measurements and for the interest method of amortization. **FASB limited SFAC 7 to measurement issues** (how to measure) **and chose not to address recognition questions** (when to measure). SFAC 7 introduces the expected cash flow approach, which differs from the traditional approach by focusing on explicit assumptions about the range of possible estimated cash flows and their respective probabilities.

20. (d) The expected cash flow approach uses all expectations about possible cash flows in developing a measurement, rather than just the single most-likely cash flow. By incorporating a range of possible outcomes (with their respective timing differences), the expected cash flow approach accommodates the use of present value techniques when the timing of cash flows is uncertain. Thus, the expected cash flow is likely to provide a better estimate of fair value than the minimum, most-likely, or maximum taken alone. According to SFAC 7, expected present value refers to the sum of probability-weighted present values in a range of estimated cash flows, all discounted using the same interest rate convention.

21. (b) The computation of expected present value using a single interest rate is as follows:

PV of $200,000 in one year at 5%	$190,476	
Probability	20%	$38,095
PV of $200,000 in two years at 5%	$181,406	
Probability	50%	90,703
PV of $200,000 in three years at 5%	$172,768	
Probability	30%	51,830
		$180,628

According to SFAC 7, expected present value refers to the sum of probability-weighted present values in a range of estimated cash flows, all discounted using the same interest rate convention.

22. (c) Like depreciation and amortization conventions, interest methods are grounded in notions of historical cost, not current cost.

23. (a) According to SFAC 7, the objective of using present value in an accounting measurement is to capture, to the extent possible, the economic difference between sets of future cash flows. The objective of present value, when used in accounting measurements at initial recognition and fresh-start measurements, is to estimate fair value. Stated differently, present value should attempt to capture the elements that taken together would comprise a market price, if one existed, that is fair value. Value-in-use and entity-specific measurements attempt to capture the value of an asset or liability in the context of a particular entity. An entity-specific measurement substitutes the entity's assumptions for those that marketplace participants would make.

24. (c) The Codification provides guidance on the determination of gain or loss on disposal of a component of a business. According to this guidance, such determination should be based on estimates of the net realizable value of the component. Since Brooks Co. plans to discontinue its entire operations, the appropriate measurement basis for its equipment is net realizable value. Historical cost and current reproduction and replacement costs are not appropriate measurement bases for assets once an entity has decided to discontinue its operations because these amounts do not reflect the entity's probable future benefit, which is a characteristic of assets per SFAC 6.

25. (d) The FASB Accounting Standards Codification includes all previous level A–D GAAP. The Codification includes the authoritative literature of the Financial Accounting Standards Board, the Emerging Issues Task Force Abstracts, Accounting Principles Board Opinions, Accounting Research Bulletins, Accounting Interpretations, AICPA Statements of Position, AICPA Audit and Accounting Guides, and Practice Bulletins. The FASB Accounting Standards Codification does not include the AICPA Statements of Auditing Standards. The auditing standards are included in the Professional Standards issued by the AICPA.

A.2. Income Determination

26. (b) Generally, sales revenue is recognized at the date of delivery, because that generally is the time at which a sale has occurred. At that point the two criteria for revenue recognition were met; the revenue is (1) realized or realizable and (2) it is earned (SFAC 6). Therefore, the amount of sales revenue recognized in 2009 is $150,000 (50,000 × $3 = $150,000).

27. (c) Income generally accrues only at the time of sale, and gains may not be anticipated by reflecting assets at their **current** sales prices. Exception to this general rule is granted, however, for agricultural products that are homogenous and have an immediate marketability at quoted prices such as the cotton in this problem (Cod. 905-330-30-1). When these inventories are stated at sales prices, they should be reduced by expenditures to be incurred in disposal. Amar Farms should, therefore, recognize revenue on the entire 300,000 pound crop in 2009 at the guaranteed (and prevailing) market price of $.70 per pound. This amounts to $210,000 (300,000 pounds × $.70 per pound = $210,000). Note that the additional $.02 per pound for the cotton sold in 2010 would be recognized in 2010, since its selling price exceeded the current (2009) market price.

28. (a) Revenue from the sale of a product may be recognized at the time of sale only if **all** of the following conditions are met:

1. The seller's price is fixed or readily determinable.
2. The buyer has paid the seller or is obligated to pay the seller, the obligation not being contingent on resale of the product.
3. The buyer's obligation to the seller remains unchanged in the event of damage or destruction of the product.
4. The buyer is independent from the seller.
5. The seller does not have any significant obligations regarding resale of the product by the buyer.
6. The amount of future returns can be reasonably estimated.

Because the buyer, Zee, has the right to return the machine to the seller, Lin, condition (2) above has not been met. Therefore, the recognition of sales revenue and cost of sales is not allowable for this transaction.

A.3. Accruals and Deferrals

29. (b) Under accrual accounting, events that change an entity's financial position are recorded in the period in which the events occur. This means revenues are recognized when earned rather than when cash is received, and expenses are recognized when incurred rather than when cash is paid. Therefore, when the royalties are paid, Wand should debit an asset account (prepaid royalties) rather than an expense account. The royalties paid should be reported as expense in the period incurred (by debiting royalty expense and crediting prepaid royalties).

30. (c) The balance in the advertising expense account on 12/31/09 before adjustment is $146,000. Since the sales promotional campaign is to be conducted in January, any associated costs are an expense of 2010. Thus, the $15,000 cost of printing catalogs should be removed from the advertising expense account and recorded as a prepaid expense as of 12/31/09. In addition, advertising expense must be increased by the $9,000 cost of December's radio advertisements, which are an expense of 2009 even though they were not billed to Clark or paid until 2010. The $9,000 must be accrued as an expense and a liability at 12/31/09. Therefore, 2009 advertising expense should total $140,000 ($146,000 – $15,000 + $9,000).

31. (b) The opening balance in prepaid expenses ($1,500) results from a one-year insurance premium paid on 7/1/08. Since this policy would have expired by 6/30/09, no part of the $1,500 is included in 12/31/09 prepaid expenses. The insurance premium paid on 7/1/09 ($3,200) would be partially expired (6/12) by 12/31/09. The remainder (6/12 × $3,200 = $1,600) would be a prepaid expense at year-end. The entire advance rental payment ($2,000) is a prepaid expense at 12/31/09 because it applies to 2010. Therefore, total 12/31/09 prepaid expenses are $3,600.

Prepaid insurance ($3,200 × 6/12)	$1,600
Prepaid rent	2,000
Total prepaid expenses	$3,600

32. (b)   Apparently Roro records policy payments as charges to insurance expense and records prepaid insurance at the end of the quarter through an adjusting entry. The unadjusted trial balance amounts at 3/31/09 must represent the final two months of the old policy ($300 of prepaid insurance) and the cost of the new policy ($7,200 of insurance expense). An adjusting entry must be prepared to reflect the correct 3/31/09 balances. Since the new policy has been in force one month (3/1 through 3/31), thirty-five months remain unexpired. Therefore, the balance in prepaid insurance should be $7,000 ($7,200 × 35/36). Insurance expense should include the cost of the last two months of the old policy and the first month of the new policy [$300 + ($7,200 × 1/36) = $500]. Roro's adjusting entry would transfer $6,700 from insurance expense to prepaid insurance to result in the correct balances.

33. (c)   At 12/31/09, the liability account unearned subscription revenue should have a balance which reflects all unexpired subscriptions. Of the 2008 sales, $125,000 expires during 2010 and would still be a liability at 12/31/09. Of the 2009 sales, $340,000 ($200,000 + $140,000) expires during 2010 and 2011, and therefore is a liability at 12/31/09. Therefore, the total liability is $465,000 ($125,000 + $340,000). This amount would have to be removed from the sales account and recorded as a liability in a 12/31/09 adjusting entry.

34. (d)   Regal's unredeemed gift certificates at 12/31/08 are $75,000. During 2009, these certificates are either redeemed ($25,000) or expire by 12/31/09 ($75,000 – $25,000 = $50,000). Therefore, none of the $75,000 affects the 12/31/09 unearned revenue amount. During 2009, additional certificates totaling $250,000 were sold. Of this amount, $225,000 is expected to be redeemed in the future [$250,000 – (10% × $250,000)]. Since $175,000 of 2009 certificates were redeemed in 2009, 12/31/09 unearned revenue is $50,000 ($225,000 – $175,000).

35. (a)   The requirement is to calculate Wren's royalty revenue for 2009. The 3/15/09 royalty receipt ($12,000) would not affect 2009 revenue because this amount pertains to revenues earned for July through December of 2008 and would have been accrued as revenue on 12/31/08. On 9/15/09, Wren received $17,000 in royalties for the first half of 2009. Royalties for the second half of 2009 will not be received until 3/15/10. However, the royalty payment to be received for the second six months (15% × $60,000 = $9,000) has been earned and should be accrued at 12/31/09. Therefore, 2009 royalty revenue is $26,000 ($17,000 + $9,000).

36. (d)   The agreement states that Super is to receive royalties of 20% of revenues associated with the comic strip. Since Fantasy's 2010 revenues from the strip were $1,500,000, Super's royalty revenue is $300,000 ($1,500,000

× 20%). The other information in the problem about the receivable and cash payments is not needed to compute revenues. Super's 2010 summary entries would be

Cash	200,000		
Royalties rec.		75,000	
Royalty revenue		125,000	($200,000 – $75,000)
Royalties rec.	175,000		
Royalty revenue		175,000	($300,000 – $125,000)

37. (c)   Royalty revenues should be recognized when earned, regardless of when the cash is collected. Royalty revenue earned from 12/1/08 to 5/31/09 is $80,000 ($400,000 × 20%). Of this amount, $10,000 ($50,000 × 20%) was earned in December of 2008, so the portion earned in the first five months of 2009 is $70,000 ($80,000 – $10,000). Royalty revenue earned from 6/1/09 to 11/30/09 is $65,000 ($325,000 × 20%). The amount earned from 12/1/09 to 12/31/09, which would be accrued at 12/31, is $14,000 ($70,000 × 20%). Therefore, 2009 royalty revenue is $149,000.

1/1/09 - 5/31/09	$70,000
6/1/09 - 11/30/09	65,000
12/1/09 - 12/31/09	14,000
	$149,000

38. (b)   The requirement is to calculate the amount of royalty income to be recognized in 2009. Cash collected for royalties totaled $200,000 in 2009. However, this amount must be adjusted for changes in the related accounts, as follows:

2009 cash received	$200,000
Royalties receivable 12/31/08	(90,000)
Royalties receivable 12/31/09	85,000
Unearned royalties 12/31/08	60,000
Unearned royalties 12/31/09	(40,000)
Royalty income	$215,000

The beginning receivable balance ($90,000) is subtracted because that portion of the cash collected was recognized as revenue last year. The ending receivable balance ($85,000) is added because that amount is 2009 revenue, even though it has not yet been collected. The beginning balance of unearned royalties ($60,000) is added because that amount is assumed to be earned during the year. Finally, the ending balance of unearned royalties ($40,000) is subtracted since this amount was collected, but not earned as revenue, by 12/31/09.

39. (b)   The requirement is to determine the amount of royalty expense to be recognized in 2009. Cash paid for royalties totaled $300,000 in 2009. However, this amount must be adjusted for changes in the related accounts, as follows:

2009 cash paid	$300,000
Royalties payable 12/31/08	(80,000)
Royalties payable 12/31/09	75,000
Prepaid royalties 12/31/08	55,000
Prepaid royalties 12/31/09	(45,000)
	$305,000

The beginning payable balance ($80,000) is subtracted because that portion of the cash paid was recognized as expense during the previous year. The ending payable balance ($75,000) is added because that amount has been accrued as 2009 expense, even though it has not yet been paid. The beginning balance of prepaid royalties ($55,000) is added because that amount is assumed to have expired during the year. Finally, the ending balance of prepaid royalties

($45,000) is subtracted since this amount was paid, but not incurred as an expense, by 12/31/09.

40. (b) When the insurance policy was initially purchased, the entire balance was debited to a prepaid asset account (i.e., prepaid insurance). The adjusting entry at December 31, 2009, to recognize the expiration of one year of the policy would be

Insurance expense	(1/3 of original pymt.)
Prepaid insurance	(1/3 of original pymt.)

After the adjusting entry, the prepaid asset account would contain 2/3 of the original payment. If the original payment had instead been debited to an expense account (i.e., insurance expense), then the adjusting entry at December 31, 2009 would be

Prepaid insurance	(2/3 of original pymt.)
Insurance expense	(2/3 of original pymt.)

This alternate approach would also result in 1/3 of the original payment being expensed in 2009 and 2/3 of the original payment being carried forward as a prepaid asset. Thus, answer (b) is correct. Answer (a) is incorrect because the premium paid was for a three-year policy, 2/3 of which had not yet expired and would therefore be carried forward in the prepaid asset account. Answer (c) is incorrect because 1/3 of the original payment was already expensed. Answer (d) is incorrect because the amount would be the same as it would have been if the original payment had been debited initially to an expense account (as explained for answer (b) above).

41. (b) Current assets are identified as resources that are reasonably expected to be realized in cash or sold or **consumed** during the normal operating cycle of the business. These resources include prepaid expenses such as royalties. Since the balance remaining in Sip Co.'s royalty prepayment (the payment relating to 2010 royalties) will be consumed within the next year, it should be reported as a current asset. Additionally, the payment relating to 2009 should be reported as an expense.

42. (b) At the time the gift certificates were issued, the following entry was made, reflecting the store's future obligation to honor the certificates:

Cash	xx	
Deferred revenue		xx

Upon redemption of the certificates, the obligation recorded in the deferred revenue account becomes satisfied and the revenue is earned. Similarly, as the certificates expire, the store is no longer under any obligation to honor the certificates and the deferred revenue should be taken into income. In both instances, the deferred revenue account must be reduced (debited) to reflect the earning of revenue. This is done through the following entry:

Deferred revenue	xx	
Revenue		xx

43. (a) The revenues from service contracts should be recognized on a pro rata basis over the term of the contract. This treatment allocates the contract revenues to the period(s) in which they are earned. Since the sale of a service contract does not culminate in the completion of the earnings process (i.e., does not represent the seller's performance of the contract), payments received for such a contract should be recorded initially in a deferred revenue account.

A.4. Cash to Accrual

44. (c) The following formula is used to adjust service revenue from the cash basis to the accrual basis:

Cash fees collected	+	End. AR	−	Beg. AR	+	Beg. unearned fees	−	End. unearned fees	=	Accrual basis service revenue

$200,000 + $60,000 − $40,000 + 0 − $5,000 = $215,000

As an alternative, T-accounts can be used.

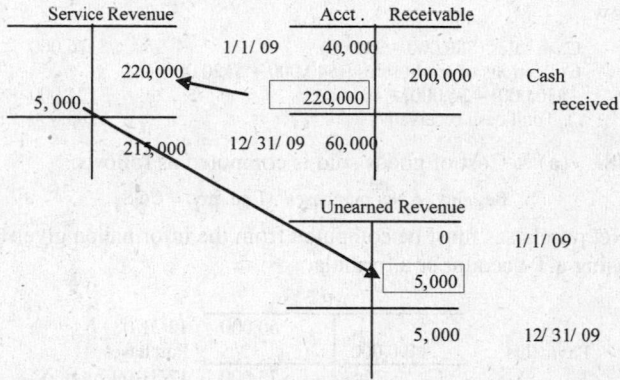

45. (d) To determine cash basis revenue, the solutions approach is to prepare a T-account for accounts receivable.

	Accounts Receivable		
12/31/08	1,000,000		
Sales	4,600,000	20,000	Write-offs
		?	Collections
12/31/09	1,300,000		

The missing amount for cash collections is $4,280,000. Another approach is to use the following formula:

Sales	+ Decrease (− increase) in AR	− Write-offs	= Collections
$4,600,000 −	$300,000	− $20,000	= $4,280,000

The increase in receivables ($300,000) means that cash collected during the period was less than sales during the period and therefore is deducted from sales revenue. The write-offs ($20,000) represent recognized sales that will never be collected in cash and therefore must also be deducted to compute collections.

46. (d) To determine rental revenue, the solutions approach is to prepare a T-account for rents receivable and rent revenues.

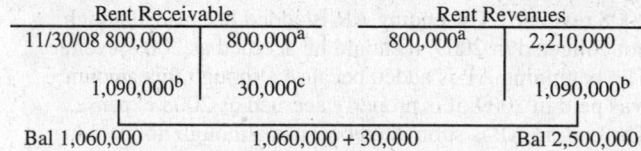

Rent Receivable		Rent Revenues	
11/30/08 800,000	800,000[a]	800,000[a]	2,210,000
1,090,000[b]	30,000[c]		1,090,000[b]
Bal 1,060,000	1,060,000 + 30,000		Bal 2,500,000

[a] To remove 2008 revenue from the $2,210,000 of cash collected and relieve rent receivable of collections from 2008 receivables.
[b] To recognize unrecorded rent earned including write-offs.
[c] To recognize write-offs. Debit would be to the allowance account.

47. (d) Under the cash basis method of accounting, revenue is recognized as it is collected. Cash sales after returns and allowances totaled $76,000 ($80,000 − $4,000). Net credit sales for 2009 were $114,000 ($120,000 credit sales − $6,000 discounts). As made evident by the T-account below, cash collections from credit sales must equal $124,000 ($40,000 + $114,000 − $30,000), since $10,000 in excess of current credit sales was received and reduced Accounts Receivable by this amount.

Accounts Receivable			
Bal. 1/1	40,000		
Net credit sales	114,000	?	Collections
Bal. 12/31	30,000		

A summary journal entry would be

Cash	124,000	
Sales discounts	6,000	
Accounts receivable		130,000

Total cash basis revenue for 2009 is $200,000 as shown below.

Cash sales ($80,000 – $4,000)	$ 76,000
Collections of credit sales [($40,000 + $120,000 – $30,000) – $6,000]	124,000
Total cash received	$200,000

48. (a)   Cost of goods sold is computed as follows:

Beg. inv. + Net purchases – End. inv. = CGS

Net purchases must be computed from the information given using a T-account or a formula.

AP			
		50,000	12/31/08
Payments	490,000	?	Purchases
		75,000	12/31/09

The missing amount for purchases is $515,000. Another approach is to use the following formula:

Payments	+	Ending AP	–	Beginning AP =	Purchases
$490,000	+	$75,000	–	$50,000 =	$515,000

This amount can be used to determine cost of goods sold

Beg. inventory	$290,000
+ Net purchases	515,000
Cost of goods available	805,000
– End. inventory	260,000
Cost of goods sold	$545,000

49. (d)   Cash-basis income of $60,000 must be adjusted for changes in accounts receivable and accounts payable to compute accrual income

Cash-basis income	$ 60,000
12/31/08 AR	(20,000)
12/31/09 AR	40,000
12/31/08 AP	30,000
12/31/09 AP	(15,000)
Accrual income	$ 95,000

The beginning AR ($20,000) is subtracted because although this amount was collected in 2009, it is properly accrued as 2008 revenue. The ending AR is added because although not collected in 2009, it should be accrued as 2009 revenue. The beginning AP is added because although this amount was paid in 2009, it is properly accrued as 2008 expense. The ending AP is subtracted because although not paid in 2009, it should be accrued as 2009 expense.

50. (c)   The ending balance in Tory's capital account on either the accrual or cash basis is computed as follows:

Beginning capital	+	Investments	+	Income	–	Drawings =	Ending capital

Tory's beginning capital is his initial cash investment of $2,000. No other investments were made. Under the cash basis method of accounting, income is the excess of cash revenues ($5,000) over cash expenses ($0, since the expenses were not paid until after March 31). Therefore, cash basis income is $5,000. Drawings are $1,000. Therefore, ending capital is $6,000 ($2,000 + $0 + $5,000 – $1,000).

51. (d)   The requirement of this question is to determine if a decrease in accounts receivable and/or a decrease in accrued expenses would result in **cash-basis income** being **lower** than accrual-basis income.

A decrease in the accounts receivable balance would generally mean that cash was collected. In accordance with the cash basis of accounting when cash is received it is recorded as revenue (Dr. Cash, Cr. Revenue). Whereas under the accrual basis the revenue would have recorded when the receivable was recorded (Dr. AR, Cr. Revenue). Thus, a decreased accounts receivable balance would result in increased revenue/income. Therefore, the answer for this account is No.

A decrease in the accrued expenses account would generally mean cash was paid on some expenses. Under the cash basis, when the cash is paid the expense is recorded (Dr. Expense, Cr. Cash). Whereas under the accrual basis the expense would have been recorded when the accrued expense was recorded (Dr. Expense, Cr. Accrued Expense). Thus, a decreased accrued expenses account would result in increased expenses/lower income for the cash basis. Thus, the answer for this account is Yes.

52. (b)   When a company operates on the accrual basis, supplies are inventoried and expensed as they are used. Under the cash method, however, supplies are expensed as they are paid for. Therefore if White Co. experiences an increase in supplies inventory during the year, this increase must be deducted from accrual income to get to the cash basis, because the cost of the supplies would be expensed at the time of purchase.

Office salaries payable works the opposite way. Under the accrual method, a liability would have been established resulting in additional expense over the amount of cash paid to employees. Under the cash method, no liability is accrued and the unpaid salaries are not expensed. Therefore, the increase must be added to the accrual basis net income.

53. (c)   Prior to 2009, Droit Co. used the cash basis of accounting. Accordingly, Droit would have expensed all purchases of supplies as incurred. In contrast, under the accrual basis of accounting, the cost of unused supplies at each year-end would have been carried as an asset and, therefore, excluded from the current year's supplies expense. In 2009, the year Droit adopted the accrual basis of accounting, Droit would have inventoried unused supplies at December 31 and excluded those costs from 2009 net income. Since the cost of 2009's beginning balance of supplies was expensed during 2008, even though the supplies were not used until 2009, Droit's inability to determine the beginning supplies inventory would result in an understatement of supplies expense and overstatement of 2009 net income. However, since Droit properly inventoried supplies at December 31, 2009, its cumulative (inception-to-date) supplies expense would be properly stated. Therefore, Droit's inability to determine 2009's beginning supplies expense would have no impact on Droit's December 31, 2009 retained earnings.

A.5. Installment Sales

54. (b)   Under the installment method, gross profit is deferred at the time of sale and is recognized by applying the gross profit rate to subsequent cash collections. At the time of sale, gross profit of $250,000 is deferred ($500,000 installment sales less $250,000 cost of installment sales). The gross profit rate is 50% ($250,000 ÷ $500,000). Since 2009 collections on installment sales were $100,000, gross profit of $50,000 (50% × $100,000) is recognized in 2009. This would decrease the deferred gross profit account to a 12/31/09 balance of $200,000 ($250,000 − $50,000). Note that regular sales, cost of regular sales, and general and administrative expenses do not affect the deferred gross profit account.

55. (d) Under the installment sales method, gross profit is deferred to future periods and recognized proportionately to collection of the receivables. Therefore, at each year-end, deferred gross profit can be computed by multiplying the gross profit percentage by the accounts receivable balance, as indicated below.

	2009	2008
Sales	$900,000	$600,000
2008 Collections		(200,000)
2009 Collections	(300,000)	(100,000)
2008 Write-offs		(50,000)
2009 Write-offs	(50,000)	(150,000)
12/31/09 AR	$550,000	$100,000
Gross profit %	x 40%	x 30%
12/31/09 Deferred GP	$220,000	$ 30,000

Thus, total deferred gross profit at 12/31/09 is $250,000 ($220,000 + $30,000).

56. (d) Under the installment sales method, gross profit is deferred to future periods and is recognized proportionately as cash is collected. To determine cash collections in this case, first compute the 2010 installment sales by dividing deferred gross profit by the gross profit percentage ($560,000 ÷ 40% = $1,400,000). Then, the 12/31/10 installment accounts receivable is subtracted to determine cash collections ($1,400,000 − $800,000 = $600,000). Realized gross profit is then computed by multiplying cash collections by the gross profit percentage ($600,000 × 40% = $240,000).

57. (c) When using the installment method, gross profit realized is computed as indicated below.

Cash collections × GP% = GP realized

This equation can be rearranged as follows:

GP realized ÷ GP% = Cash collections

Therefore, cash collected to date on 2009 sales is $800,000 [($150,000 + $90,000) ÷ 30%], and on 2010 sales is $500,000 ($200,000 ÷ 40%). Installment accounts receivable at 12/31/10 is computed by subtracting cash collections from the original sales amount.

Installment AR − 2009 ($1,000,000 − $800,000)	$ 200,000
Installment AR − 2010 ($2,000,000 − $500,000)	1,500,000
Total 12/31/10 installment AR	$1,700,000

58. (a) The equipment sale is accounted for using the installment method. The gross profit percentage on the sale is 33 1/3% ($600,000 profit ÷ $1,800,000 selling price). Since $300,000 of the sales price is collected in 2010, gross profit of $100,000 is recognized (33 1/3% × $300,000). The **total** revenue recognized is $250,000 ($100,000 gross profit + $150,000 interest revenue).

59. (a) The machine sale is accounted for using the installment method, where gross profit is deferred and recognized in proportion to cash collected. Initially, the entire $270,000 gain is deferred. In 2009, $150,000 of the sales price was collected, and the gross profit percentage is 30% ($270,000 ÷ $900,000), so gross profit recognized was $45,000 (30% × $150,000). In 2010, $250,000 of the sales

price was collected, so gross profit recognized was $75,000 (30% × $250,000). Therefore, at 12/31/10, deferred gross profit is $150,000 ($270,000 − $45,000 − $75,000). As a shortcut, you can compute the 12/31/10 note receivable balance ($750,000 − $250,000 = $500,000), and multiply by the 30% gross profit percentage (30% × $500,000 = $150,000). Note that the **interest** collected ($75,000) does not affect the computation because it is not a collection of sales price.

60. (c) The profit on a sale in the ordinary course of business is considered to be realized at the time of sale unless it is uncertain whether the sale price will be collected. The Board concluded that use of the installment method of accounting is not acceptable unless this uncertainty exists. Answers (a), (b), and (d) are incorrect because they do not involve the element of uncertainty regarding the collectibility of the sale price.

61. (c) According to the **installment method** of accounting, gross profit on an installment sale is recognized in income in proportion to the cash collection. The cash collected from a given year's sales is multiplied by that year's gross profit percentage to compute the amount of gross profit to be recognized. Answer (a) describes the **point-of-sale** recognition basis, while answer (d) describes the **cost recovery** method. Answer (b) does not describe any recognition basis currently used.

62. (c) The installment method of accounting is used when there is a high degree of uncertainty regarding the collectibility of the sale price. Under this method, sales revenues and the related cost of goods sold are recognized in the period of the sale. However, the gross profit is deferred to the periods in which cash is collected. Income recognized in the period of collection is generally computed by multiplying the cash collected by the gross margin percentage. The installment method is based upon deferral of the gross profit, not the net operating profit. The installment method is generally only applicable when the reporting company is unable to estimate the amount of uncollectible accounts.

63. (d) Under the installment method (case I) revenue (gross profit) is recognized **after** the sale, in proportion to cash collected. Under the cost recovery method (case II), revenue (gross profit) is again recognized **after** the sale, when cumulative receipts exceed the cost of the asset sold. Therefore, revenue is not recognized prior to the sale of merchandise in either case I or case II.

A.6. Cost Recovery Method

64. (d) Under the cost recovery method **no profit of any type** is recognized until the cumulative receipts (principal and interest) exceed the cost of the asset sold. This means that the entire gross profit ($3,000,000 − $2,000,000 = $1,000,000) and the 2010 interest received ($270,000) will be deferred until cash collections exceed $2,000,000. Therefore, no income is recognized in 2010.

65. (d) The **installment method** is used when collection of the selling price is not reasonably assured. However, when the uncertainty of collection is so great that even the use of the installment method is precluded, then the cost recovery method may be used. Having no reasonable basis for estimating collectibility would provide a great enough uncertainty to use the cost recovery method. It is important to note that anytime the installment method is used, some risk of 100% collection exists, but the risk must be extreme before the cost recovery method is employed.

66. **(a)** Installment methods of recognizing revenue are appropriate only when "collection of the sale price is not reasonably assured." Under the cost recovery method, gross profit is deferred and recognized only when the cumulative receipts exceed the cost of the asset sold.

A.7. Franchise Agreements

67. **(d)** Franchise fee revenue is recognized when all material services have been substantially performed by the franchiser. Substantial performance means the franchiser has performed substantially all of required initial services and has no remaining obligation to refund any cash received. The $60,000 nonrefundable down payment applies to the initial services already performed by Rice. Therefore, the $60,000 may be recognized as revenue in 2009. The three remaining $30,000 installments relate to substantial future services to be performed by Rice. The present value of these payments ($72,000) is recorded as unearned franchise fees and recognized as revenue once substantial performance of the future services has occurred.

Cash	60,000	
Notes receivable	90,000	
Discount on notes receivable		18,000
Franchise revenue		60,000
Unearned franchise fees		72,000

68. **(c)** Initial franchise fees are not recognized as revenue until the franchisor makes substantial performance of the required services, and collection is reasonably assured. Since Potter Pie has not yet performed the required services, the initial franchise fee (21 × $30,000 = $630,000) is reported as **unearned franchise fees** at 12/31/09. The estimated uncollectible amount ($20,000) normally would be recorded as a debit to **bad debt expense** and a credit to **allowance for uncollectible accounts**. However, since no revenue has yet been recognized, it is inappropriate to record bad debt expense. Instead, **unearned franchise fees** is debited, because an unearned revenue should not be recorded when, in effect, no related asset has been received. Therefore, the **net** unearned franchise fees is $610,000 ($630,000 – $20,000).

A.8. Real Estate Transactions

69. **(d)** Items I and II do not transfer the risks and rewards of ownership to the buyer since both scenarios entitle the buyer to a return of his/her initial investment. Thus, the risks of ownership still remain with the seller. The economic substance of such arrangements is that of financing, leasing, or profit-sharing transactions. Item III transfers the risks and rewards of ownership since the seller will be reimbursed for cost plus a 5% profit on the support provided. Therefore, the seller is not required to support operations of the property at its **own** risk.

70. **(c)** The problem states that the sale has been consummated and that Kame's initial and continuing investments are adequate to demonstrate a commitment to pay for the property. However, the fact that Esker's receivable is subject to future subordination precludes recognition of the profit in full. Instead, the cost recovery method must be

used to account for the sale. The deposit method is to be used

1. Until the sale is consummated, when all activities necessary for closing have been performed.
2. If the buyer's initial and continuing investments are not adequate to demonstrate a commitment to pay for the property and the seller is not reasonably assured of recovering the cost of the property if the buyer defaults.

The problem states that the sale has been consummated and that Kame's initial and continuing investments are adequate. Therefore, the deposit method will not be used to account for the sale. The reduced profit method is used only when the initial investment is adequate to demonstrate a commitment to pay for the property but the continuing investments are not. The continuing investments must also meet certain additional requirements for the reduced profit method to be used. Since Kame's continuing investments are adequate, the reduced profit method will not be used to account for the sale. The full accrual method may be used only if profit on the sale is determinable, the earning process is virtually complete, and all of the following:

1. A sale is consummated.
2. The buyer's initial and continuing investments are adequate to demonstrate a commitment to pay for the property.
3. The seller's receivable is not subject to future subordination.
4. The seller has transferred to the buyer the usual risks and rewards of ownership in a transaction that is, in substance, a sale and does not have a substantial continuing involvement in the property.

SOLUTIONS TO SIMULATION PROBLEMS

Simulation Problem 1

Situation	Account Classification	Accrual Basis Worksheet	Communication	Research

Balance sheet classification (A) (B) (C) (D) (E) (F) (G)

Income statement classification (H) (I) (J)

1. Bonds payable, due in 2018 — (D)
2. Treasury stock — (G)
3. Accounts payable — (C)
4. Sales discounts — (J)
5. Notes payable, due in nine months — (C)
6. Inventory — (A)
7. Accounts receivable — (A)
8. Common stock — (E)
9. Cost of goods sold — (I)
10. Allowance for uncollectible accounts — (F)

Situation	Account Classification	Accrual Basis Worksheet	Communication	Research

Baron Flowers
WORKSHEET TO CONVERT TRIAL BALANCE TO ACCRUAL BASIS
December 31, 2009

Account title	Cash basis Dr.	Cash basis Cr.	Adjustments Dr.	Adjustments Cr.	Accrual basis* Dr.*	Accrual basis* Cr.*
Cash	25,600				25,600	
Accounts receivable	16,200		(1) 15,800		32,000	
Inventory	62,000		(4) 10,800		72,800	
Furniture & fixtures	118,200				118,200	
Land improvements	45,000				45,000	
Accumulated depreciation & amortization		32,400		(6) 14,250		46,650
Accounts payable		17,000		(3) 13,500		30,500
Baron, Drawings			(9) 61,000		61,000	
Baron, Capital		124,600	(7) 2,000	(5) 2,600		125,200
Allowance for uncollectible accounts				(2) 3,800		3,800
Prepaid insurance			(5) 2,900		2,900	
Accrued expenses				(7) 3,100		3,100
Estimated liability from lawsuit				(8) 50,000		50,000
Sales		653,000		(1) 15,800		668,800
Purchases	305,100		(3) 13,500		318,600	
Salaries	174,000			(9) 48,000	126,000	
Payroll taxes	12,400		(7) 500		12,900	
Insurance	8,700			(5) 300	8,400	
Rent	34,200				34,200	
Utilities	12,600		(7) 600		13,200	
Living expenses	13,000			(9) 13,000		
Income summary—inventory			(4) 62,000	(4) 72,800		10,800
Uncollectible accounts			(2) 3,800		3,800	
Depreciation & amortization			(6) 14,250		14,250	
Estimated loss from lawsuit			(8) 50,000		50,000	
	827,000	827,000	237,150	237,150	938,850	938,850

* Completion of these columns was not required.

Explanations of Adjustments

[1] To convert 2009 sales to accrual basis.

Accounts receivable balances:	
December 31, 2009	$32,000
December 31, 2008	16,200
Increase in sales	$15,800

[2] To record provision for uncollectible accounts.

[3] To convert 2009 purchases to accrual basis.

Accounts payable balances:	
December 31, 2009	$30,500
December 31, 2008	17,000
Increase in purchases	$13,500

[4] To record increase in inventory from 12/31/08 to 12/31/09.

Inventory balances:	
December 31, 2009	$72,800
December 31, 2008	62,000
Increase in inventory	$10,800

[5] To adjust prepaid insurance.

Prepaid balances:	
December 31, 2009 ($8,700 × 4/12)	$2,900
December 31, 2008 ($7,800 × 4/12)	2,600
Decrease in insurance expense	$ 300

[6] To record 2009 depreciation and amortization expense.

Cost of leasehold improvement	$45,000
Estimated life	15 years
Amortization ($45,000 × 1/15 × 9/12)	2,250
Depreciation expense on fixtures and equipment	12,000
	$14,250

[7] To convert expenses to accrual basis.

	Balances December 31,		Increase
	2009	2008	in expenses
Utilities	$1,500	$ 900	$ 600
Payroll taxes	1,600	1,100	500
	$3,100	$2,000	$1,100

[8] To record lawsuit liability at 12/31/09.

Attorney's estimate of probable loss	$300,000
Amount covered by insurance	250,000
Baron's estimated liability	$ 50,000

[9] To record Baron's drawings for 2009.

Salary ($4,000 × 12)	$48,000
Living expenses	13,000
	$61,000

Situation	Account Classification	Accrual Basis Worksheet	**Communication**	Research

To: Mr. Baron Flowers
From: CPA Candidate
Re: Accrual-basis financial statements

You have asked me to explain why the bank would require financial statements prepared on the accrual basis instead of the cash basis. The bank is concerned about your ability to repay the loan. To assess that ability, bank personnel want information about your earnings for the period, total assets, and all claims on those assets. This information about your enterprise's performance and financial position is provided more completely by accrual-basis financial statements than by cash-basis financial statements.

Under the cash basis, revenues are recognized when received and expenses when paid. Earnings can be manipulated by the timing of cash receipts and disbursements. Accrual basis accounting, while grounded in cash flows, reports transactions and other events with cash consequences at the time the transactions and events occur. Revenues and expenses are reported in the accounting period benefited, not just what the enterprise was able to collect or chose to pay. Therefore, it is understandable why your bank would request accrual-basis financial statements.

If you have any additional questions, please contact me.

Situation	Account Classification	Accrual Basis Worksheet	Communication	**Research**

1. Revenue

Revenues
CON6, Para 78

78. Revenues are inflows or other enhancements of assets of an entity or settlements of its liabilities (or a combination of both) from delivering or producing goods, rendering services, or other activities that constitute the entity's ongoing major or central operations.

2. Assets

Assets
CON6, Para 25

25. Assets are probable future economic benefits obtained or controlled by a particular entity as a result of past transactions or events.

3. Liability

Liabilities
CON6, Para 35

35. Liabilities are probable future sacrifices of economic benefits arising from present obligations of a particular entity to transfer assets or provide services to other entities in the future as a result of past transactions or events.

Simulation Problem 2

Situation	Concepts	Trial Balance Worksheet	Communication	Research

Concept statement definitions	(A)	(B)	(C)	(D)	(E)	(F)	(G)	(H)	(I)	(J)	(K)	(L)
1. Component of relevance.	○	○	○	○	●	○	○	○	○	○	○	○
2. Increases in net assets from incidental or peripheral transactions affecting an entity.	○	○	○	○	○	○	●	○	○	○	○	○
3. The process of converting noncash resources and rights into cash or claims to cash.	○	○	○	○	○	○	○	○	○	●	○	○
4. Ingredient of relevance **and** reliability.	○	○	○	○	○	●	○	○	○	○	○	○
5. The process of formally recording an item in the financial statements of an entity after it has met existing criteria and been subject to cost-benefit constraints and materiality thresholds.	●	○	○	○	○	○	○	○	○	○	○	○
6. All changes in net assets of an entity during a period except those resulting from investments by owners and distributions to owners.	○	●	○	○	○	○	○	○	○	○	○	○
7. Inflows or other enhancements of assets of an entity or settlements of its liabilities from delivering or producing goods, rendering services, or other activities that constitute the entity's ongoing operations.	○	○	○	●	○	○	○	○	○	○	○	○
8. The amount of cash, or its equivalent, that could be obtained by selling an asset in orderly liquidation.	○	○	○	○	○	○	○	○	○	○	○	●
9. The quality of information that helps users to increase the likelihood of correctly forecasting the outcome of past or present events.	○	○	○	○	●	○	○	○	○	○	○	○
10. A performance measure concerned primarily with cash-to-cash cycles.	○	○	○	○	○	○	○	○	●	○	○	○

Explanation of solutions

1. **(E)** SFAC 5 states that "Relevance is a primary qualitative characteristic. To be relevant, information about an item must have feedback value or predictive value (or both) for users and must be timely."

2. **(G)** SFAC 6 states that "Gains are increases in equity (net assets) from peripheral or incidental transactions of an entity and from all other transactions and other events and circumstances affecting the entity except those that result from revenues or investments by owners."

3. **(J)** SFAC 5 states that "Revenues and gains are realized when products (goods or services), merchandise, or other assets are exchanged for cash or claims to cash."

4. **(F)** SFAC 2 states that "Comparability, including consistency, is a secondary quality that interacts with relevance and reliability to contribute to the usefulness of information."

5. **(A)** SFAC 5 states that "Recognition is the process of formally recording or incorporating an item into the financial statements of an entity as an asset, liability, revenue, expense, or the like." SFAC 5 continues the recognition concept by stating, "An item and information about it should meet four fundamental recognition criteria to be recognized and should be recognized when the criteria are met, subject to a cost-benefit constraint and a materiality threshold."

6. **(B)** SFAC 5 states that "Comprehensive income is a broad measure of the effects of transactions and other events on an entity, comprising all recognized changes in equity (net assets) of the entity during a period from transactions and other events and circumstances except those resulting from investments by owners and distributions to owners."

7.   **(D)** SFAC 6 defines revenues as "inflows or other enhancements of assets of an entity or settlements of its liabilities (or a combination of both) from delivering or producing goods, rendering services, or other activities that constitute the entity's ongoing major or central operations."

8.   **(L)** SFAC 5 defines current market value as "the amount of cash, or its equivalent, that could be obtained by selling an asset in orderly liquidation."

9.   **(E)** SFAC 2 defines predictive value as "the quality of information that helps users to increase the likelihood of correctly forecasting the outcome of past or present events."

10.   **(I)** SFAC 5 states that "Earnings is a measure of performance during a period that is concerned primarily with the extent to which asset inflows associated with cash-to-cash cycles substantially completed (or completed) during the period exceed (or are less than) asset outflows associated, directly or indirectly, with the same cycles."

Situation	Concepts	Trial Balance Worksheet	Communication	Research

Jane Alexander Theater
December 31, 200X

a)	Trial balance		#	Adjustments		Adjusted trial balance		Income statement	
	Debit	Credit		Debit	Credit	Debit	Credit	Debit	Credit
Equipment	192,000					192,000			
Accumulated depreciation—equipment		60,000	1		9,500		69,500		
Notes payable		90,000					90,000		
Admissions revenue		380,000	3	50,000			330,000		330,000
Advertising expense	13,680		4		1,100	12,580		12,580	
Salaries expense	57,600		5	4,700		62,300		62,300	
Interest expense	1,400		2	1,800		3,200		3,200	
Depreciation expense			1	9,500		9,500		9,500	
Interest payable			2		1,800		1,800		
Unearned adm revenue			3		50,000		50,000		
Prepaid advertising			4	1,100		1,100			
Salaries payable			5		4,700		4,700		

Situation	Concepts	Trial Balance Worksheet	Communication	Research

To: Ms. Jane Alexander, Theater Director
From: CPA Candidate
Re: Adjusting and closing entries

     This memorandum summarizes the answers to your questions regarding adjusting and closing entries. The purpose of the balance sheet is to fairly represent the financial position of the firm at a specific point in time. The purpose of an income statement is to fairly present the revenues, expenses, and income over a period of time. Adjusting journal entries are necessary at the end of the period in order to properly report assets, liabilities, owner's equity, revenue, and expenses for the period. Adjusting entries are classified as either accrual- or deferral-type entries. An accrual-type entry records a transaction that have not yet been entered into the accounting records. Deferral-type adjusting entries adjust items that were previously recorded on the books, but are not accurately reflected in the records of the company.

     Closing entries are prepared to transfer the effect of nominal accounts to capital (retained earnings) after the adjusting entries have been recorded and the financial statements prepared. Closing entries are necessary to reduce the balances in nominal accounts to zero in order to prepare the accounts for the next period's transactions.

     If you have any additional questions, please contact me.

Situation	Concepts	Trial Balance Worksheet	Communication	Research

1.   Gain

Gains and Losses
CON6, Para 82

82. Gains are increases in equity (net assets) from peripheral or incidental transactions of an entity and from all other transactions and other events and circumstances affecting the entity except those that result from revenues or investments by owners.

2.   Recognition

CON5, Para 6

6. Recognition is the process of formally recording or incorporating an item in the financial statements of an entity as an asset, liability, revenue, expense, or the like. Recognition includes depiction of an item in both words and numbers, with the amount included in the totals of the financial statements. For an asset or liability, recognition involves recording not only acquisition or incurrence of the item but also later changes in it, including changes that result in removal from the financial statements.

3.   Reliability

Reliability
CON5, Para 75

75. Reliability is the other primary qualitative characteristic. To be reliable, information about an item must be representationally faithful, verifiable, and neutral. To be reliable, information must be sufficiently faithful in its representation of the underlying resource, obligation, or effect of events and sufficiently free of error and bias to be useful to investors, creditors, and others in making decisions. To be recognized, information about the existence and amount of an asset, liability, or change therein must be reliable.

Simulation Problem 3

Situation	Concepts	Adjusting Entries	Revenue and Expense Recognition	Communication	Research

Account	(A)	(B)	(C)	(D)	(E)
1. Long-term receivables	○	○	○	○	●
2. Available-for-sale securities	○	○	●	○	○
3. Equipment	●	○	○	○	○
4. Warranty obligations	○	○	○	●	○
5. Short-term payables	●	○	○	○	○
6. Accounts receivable	○	○	○	●	○
7. Bonds payable, due in ten years	○	○	○	○	●
8. Trading securities	○	○	●	○	○

Situation	Concepts	Adjusting Entries	Revenue and Expense Recognition	Communication	Research

			Accrual	Deferral
1. Depreciation expense Accumulated deprecation	xx	xx	○	●
2. Interest receivable Interest revenue	xx	xx	●	○
3. Rent expense Prepaid rent	xx	xx	○	●
4. Unearned revenue Rent revenue	xx	xx	○	●
5. Wage expense Wages payable	xx	xx	●	○

Situation	Concepts	Adjusting Entries	Revenue and Expense Recognition	Communication	Research

		Amounts to be recognized		
		2009	*2010*	*2011*
1.	Emco sells $5,000 of goods to a customer, FOB shipping point on 12/30/09.	5,000	--	--
2.	Emco sells three pieces of equipment on a contract over a three-year period. The sales price of each piece of equipment is $10,000. Delivery of each piece of equipment is on February 10 of each year. In 2009, the customer paid a $20,000 down payment, and paid $5,000 per year in 2010 and 2011. Collectibility is reasonably assured.	10,000	10,000	10,000
3.	In 1/1/09, Emco paid $9,000 for a membership to Wholesalers Association for a two-year membership in the trade association.	(4,500)	(4,500)	--
4.	On 6/1/09, Emco signs a contract for $20,000 for goods to be sold on account. Payment is to be made in two installments of $10,000 each on 12/1/10 and 12/1/11. The goods are delivered on 10/1/09. Collection is reasonably assured, and the goods may not be returned.	20,000	--	--
5.	Emco sells goods to a customer on July 1, 2009, for $50,000. If the customer does not sell the goods to retail customers by December 31, 2010, the goods can be returned to Emco. The customer sells the goods to retail customers on October 1, 2010.	--	50,000	--

Explanation of solutions

   1. When goods are sold FOB shipping point, title passes at the time the goods are shipped. Therefore, Emco may recognize revenue on 12/30/09 at the time the goods are shipped.

   2. Revenue is recognized when earned and realizable. This sale is not complete until each piece of equipment is delivered. Therefore, Emco should recognize $10,000 each year as the equipment is delivered, regardless of payment terms.

   3. Emco should match expenses to the year in which the benefits are received, which is over the two-year period.

   4. Because Emco delivered the goods in 2009, and collectibility is reasonably assured, Emco should recognize all revenue in 2009.

   5. Because there is a sale with a right of return, and the buyer may return the merchandise if it is not sold to a retail customer, recognition should be delayed until the right of return has expired.

Situation	Concepts	Adjusting Entries	Revenue and Expense Recognition	Communication	Research

To: Mr. Brown
From: Wyatt, CPA

   As we discussed, here is a brief overview of the rules for revenue recognition and the accounting for postretirement benefits under the FASB Codification.

   1.   Revenue recognition

   The revenue recognition principle provides that revenue is recognized when it is realized or realizable and it is earned. Accordingly, revenues from the sale of products ordinarily are recognized at the time of sale. Revenue from sales transactions in which the buyer has a right to return the product are recognized at time of sale only if specified conditions are met. If all these conditions are not met, revenue recognition is postponed until the time when all the requirements are met.

   One of the specified conditions for revenue recognition is that the amount of future returns can be reasonably estimated. Since Emco cannot reasonably estimate future returns, Emco should defer recognition of sales revenue and cost of sales until the return privilege has substantially expired or it can reasonably estimate returns, whichever occurs first.

   2.   Employers' accounting for postretirement benefits other than pensions

   The primary recipients of postretirement benefits other than pensions are retired employees, their beneficiaries, and covered dependents. The principal benefit covered by the FASB Codification is postretirement health care benefits. Examples of other benefits include tuition assistance, legal services, life insurance benefits, day care, and housing subsidies.

   The Codification recognizes that estimates of postretirement benefit costs are not precise. However, the statement requires accrual because recording the obligation based on best estimates is superior to implying, by a failure to accrue, that no obligation exists prior to the payment of benefits.

   If you have any additional questions about these matters, please contact me.

Situation	Concepts	Adjusting Entries	Revenue and Expense Recognition	Communication	Research

1. Relevance

Relevance
CON5, Para 73

73. Relevance is a primary qualitative characteristic. To be relevant, information about an item must have feedback value or predictive value (or both) for users and must be timely. 45 Information is relevant if it has the capacity to make a difference in investors', creditors', or other users' decisions. To be recognized, the information conveyed by including an asset, liability, or change therein in the financial statements must be relevant.

2. Realizable

Revenues and Gains
CON5, Para 83

83. Further guidance for recognition of revenues and gains is intended to provide an acceptable level of assurance of the existence and amounts of revenues and gains before they are recognized. Revenues and gains of an enterprise during a period are generally measured by the exchange values of the assets (goods or services) or liabilities involved, and recognition involves consideration of two factors (a) being realized or realizable, and (b) being earned, with sometimes one and sometimes the other being the more important consideration.

    a.   Realized or realizable. Revenues and gains generally are not recognized until realized or realizable. 50 Revenues and gains are realized when products (goods or services), merchandise, or other assets are exchanged for cash or claims to cash. Revenues and gains are realizable when related assets received or held are readily convertible to known amounts of cash or claims to cash. Readily convertible assets have (i) interchangeable (fungible) units and (ii) quoted prices available in an active market that can rapidly absorb the quantity held by the entity without significantly affecting the price.

3. Expense

Expenses
CON6, Para 80

80. Expenses are outflows or other using up of assets or incurrences of liabilities (or a combination of both) from delivering or producing goods, rendering services, or carrying out other activities that constitute the entity's ongoing major or central operations.

4. Matching

CON6, Para 146

146. Matching of costs and revenues is simultaneous or combined recognition of the revenues and expenses that result directly and jointly from the same transactions or other events. In most entities, some transactions or events result simultaneously in both a revenue and one or more expenses. The revenue and expense(s) are directly related to each other and require recognition at the same time. In present practice, for example, a sale of product or merchandise involves both revenue (sales revenue) for receipt of cash or a receivable and expense (cost of goods sold) for sacrifice of the product or merchandise sold to customers. Other examples of expenses that may result from the same transaction and be directly related to sales revenues are transportation to customers, sales commissions, and perhaps certain other selling costs.

MULTIPLE-CHOICE QUESTIONS (1-14)

1. Loeb Corp. frequently borrows from the bank in order to maintain sufficient operating cash. The following loans were at a 12% interest rate, with interest payable maturity. Loeb repaid each loan on its scheduled maturity date.

Date of loan	Amount	Maturity date	Term of loan
11/1/09	$ 5,000	10/31/10	1 year
2/1/10	15,000	7/31/10	6 months
5/1/10	8,000	1/31/11	9 months

Loeb records interest expense when the loans are repaid. As a result, interest expense of $1,500 was recorded in 2010. If no correction is made, by what amount would 2010 interest expense be understated?

- a. $540
- b. $620
- c. $640
- d. $720

2. During 2010, Paul Company discovered that the ending inventories reported on its financial statements were incorrect by the following amounts:

2008	$60,000 understated
2009	75,000 overstated

Paul uses the periodic inventory system to ascertain year-end quantities that are converted to dollar amounts using the FIFO cost method. Prior to any adjustments for these errors and ignoring income taxes, Paul's retained earnings at January 1, 2010, would be

- a. Correct.
- b. $ 15,000 overstated.
- c. $ 75,000 overstated.
- d. $135,000 overstated.

3. Tack, Inc. reported a retained earnings balance of $150,000 at December 31, 2009. In June 2010, Tack discovered that merchandise costing $40,000 had not been included in inventory in its 2009 financial statements. Tack has a 30% tax rate. What amount should Tack report as adjusted beginning retained earnings in its statement of retained earnings at December 31, 2010?

- a. $190,000
- b. $178,000
- c. $150,000
- d. $122,000

4. Conn Co. reported a retained earnings balance of $400,000 at December 31, 2009. In August 2010, Conn determined that insurance premiums of $60,000 for the three-year period beginning January 1, 2009, had been paid and fully expensed in 2009. Conn has a 30% income tax rate. What amount should Conn report as adjusted beginning retained earnings in its 2010 statement of retained earnings?

- a. $420,000
- b. $428,000
- c. $440,000
- d. $442,000

5. Lore Co. changed from the cash basis of accounting to the accrual basis of accounting during 2010. The cumulative effect of this change should be reported in Lore's 2010 financial statements as a

- a. Prior period adjustment resulting from the correction of an error.

- b. Prior period adjustment resulting from the change in accounting principle.
- c. Component of income before extraordinary item.
- d. Component of income after extraordinary item.

6. Bren Co.'s beginning inventory at January 1, 2010, was understated by $26,000, and its ending inventory was overstated by $52,000. As a result, Bren's cost of goods sold for 2010 was

- a. Understated by $26,000.
- b. Overstated by $26,000.
- c. Understated by $78,000.
- d. Overstated by $78,000.

7. On January 2, 2010, Air, Inc. agreed to pay its former president $300,000 under a deferred compensation arrangement. Air should have recorded this expense in 2009 but did not do so. Air's reported income tax expense would have been $70,000 lower in 2009 had it properly accrued this deferred compensation. In its December 31, 2010 financial statements, Air should adjust the beginning balance of its retained earnings by a

- a. $230,000 credit.
- b. $230,000 debit.
- c. $300,000 credit.
- d. $370,000 debit.

8. Net income is understated if, in the first year, estimated salvage value is excluded from the depreciation computation when using the

	Straight-line method	Production or use method
a.	Yes	No
b.	Yes	Yes
c.	No	No
d.	No	Yes

9. At the end of 2009, Ritzcar Co. failed to accrue sales commissions earned during 2009 but paid in 2010. The error was not repeated in 2010. What was the effect of this error on 2009 ending working capital and on the 2010 ending retained earnings balance?

	2009 ending working capital	2010 ending retained earnings
a.	Overstated	Overstated
b.	No effect	Overstated
c.	No effect	No effect
d.	Overstated	No effect

10. On December 31, 2010, special insurance costs were incurred and unpaid, but were not recorded. If these insurance costs were related to a particular job order in work in process that was not completed during the period, what is the effect of the omission on accrued liabilities and retained earnings in the December 31, 2010 balance sheet?

	Accrued liabilities	Retained earnings
a.	No effect	No effect
b.	No effect	Overstated
c.	Understated	No effect
d.	Understated	Overstated

11. Which of the following errors could result in an overstatement of both current assets and stockholders' equity?

- a. An understatement of accrued sales expenses.
- b. Noncurrent note receivable principal is misclassified as a current asset.

    c.   Annual depreciation on manufacturing machinery is understated.

    d.   Holiday pay expense for administrative employees is misclassified as manufacturing overhead.

12. Galaxy Corporation had the following financial statement information:

	2010	2009
Revenue	$135,000	$100,000
Expenses	98,000	65,000
Net income	37,000	35,000

	12/31/10	12/31/09
Total assets	$157,000	$105,000
Total liabilities	50,000	35,000
Total owners' equity	107,000	70,000

Galaxy failed to record $12,000 of accrued wages at the end of 2009. The wages were recorded and paid in January 2010. Assuming that the correct accruals were made on December 31, 2010, what are the corrected balances in the 2009 and 2010 restated financial statements?

	2009 net income	Dec. 31, 2009 total liabilities	Dec. 31, 2010 total owners' equity
a.	$23,000	$23,000	$ 95,000
b.	$47,000	$47,000	$107,000
c.	$23,000	$35,000	$ 95,000
d.	$23,000	$47,000	$107,000

13. Justin Corporation discovered an error in their 2010 financial statements after the statements were issued. This requires that

    a.   The cumulative effect of the error is reported on the 2011 income statement as a cumulative effect of change in accounting principle.

    b.   The cumulative effect of the error is reported in the 2011 beginning balance of each related account.

    c.   The financial statements are restated to reflect the correction of period-specific effects of the error.

    d.   An adjustment to beginning retained earnings in 2011 with a footnote disclosure describing the error.

14. During 2011, Kelly Corporation discovered that ending inventory reported in its 2010 financial statements was understated by $10,000. How should Kelly account for this understatement?

    a.   Adjust the beginning inventory balance in 2011 by $10,000.

    b.   Restate the financial statements with corrected balances for all periods presented.

    c.   Adjust the ending balance in the 2011 retained earnings account.

    d.   Make no entry because the error will self-correct.

SIMULATION PROBLEMS

Simulation Problem 1 (55 to 65 minutes)

Situation					
	Effect of Error	Journal Entries	Corrected Financial Statements	Communication	Research

Cord Corp., a nonpublic enterprise, requires audited financial statements for credit purposes. After making normal adjusting entries, but before closing the accounting records for the year ended December 31, 2010, Cord's controller prepared the following financial statements for 2010:

Cord Corp.
STATEMENT OF FINANCIAL POSITION
December 31, 2010

Assets	
Cash	$1,225,000
Marketable equity securities	125,000
Accounts receivable	460,000
Allowance for doubtful accounts	(55,000)
Inventories	530,000
Property and equipment	620,000
Accumulated depreciation	(280,000)
Total assets	$2,625,000

Liabilities and Stockholders' Equity	
Accounts payable and accrued liabilities	$1,685,000
Income tax payable	110,000
Common stock, $20 par	300,000
Additional paid-in capital	75,000
Retained earnings	455,000
Total liabilities and stockholders' equity	$2,625,000

Cord Corp.
STATEMENT OF INCOME
For the Year Ended December 31, 2010

Net sales		$1,700,000
Operating expenses:		
Cost of sales	570,000	
Selling and administrative	448,000	
Depreciation	42,000	
Total operating expenses		1,060,000
Income before income tax		640,000
Income tax expense		192,000
Net income		$ 448,000

Cord's tax rate for all income items was 30% for all affected years, and it made estimated tax payments when due. Cord has been profitable in the past and expects results in the future to be similar to 2010. During the course of the audit, the following additional information (not considered when the above statements were prepared) was obtained:

1. The investment portfolio consists of short-term investments, classified as available-for-sale, for which total market value equaled cost at December 31, 2009. On February 2, 2010, Cord sold one investment with a carrying value of $100,000 for $130,000. The total of the sale proceeds was credited to the investment account.

2. At December 31, 2010, the market value of the remaining securities in the portfolio was $142,000.

3. The $530,000 inventory total, which was based on a physical count at December 31, 2010, was priced at cost. Subsequently, it was determined that the inventory cost was overstated by $66,000. At December 31, 2010, the inventory's market value approximated the adjusted cost.

4. Pollution control devices costing $48,000, which is high in relation to the cost of the original equipment, were installed on December 29, 2009, and were charged to repairs in 2009.

5. The original equipment referred to in Item 4, which had a remaining useful life of six years on December 29, 2009, is being depreciated by the straight-line method for both financial and tax reporting.

6. A lawsuit was filed against Cord in October 2010 claiming damages of $250,000. Cord's legal counsel believes that an unfavorable outcome is probable, and a reasonable estimate of the court's award to the plaintiff is $60,000, which will be paid in 2011 if the case is settled.

7. Cord determined that its accumulated benefits obligation under the pension plan exceeded the fair value of plan assets by $40,000 at December 31, 2010. Cord has unrecognized prior service cost of $50,000 at December 31, 2010. Cord funds the total pension expense each year.

Situation	Effect of Error	Journal Entries	Corrected Financial Statements	Communication	Research

Indicate the effects of the inventory overstatement in the 2010 and 2011 financial statements by completing the following table. Mark each item overstate, understate, or OK.

	2010 Effects			2011 Effects		
	(Overstate)	(Understate)	(OK)	(Overstate)	(Understate)	(OK)
Inventory on balance sheet	O	O	O	O	O	O
Cost of goods sold	O	O	O	O	O	O
Net income	O	O	O	O	O	O
Retained earnings	O	O	O	O	O	O

Situation	Effect of Error	Journal Entries	Corrected Financial Statements	Communication	Research

Prepare journal entries, without explanations, to record the effects of the foregoing data on Cord's accounting records at December 31, 2010. Do **not** prepare corrected financial statements for 2010. The journal entries should be numbered to correspond with the numbers in the additional information. Include as the last entry any necessary adjustments to the 2010 income tax expense, and support your computations for this entry.

	Dr.	Cr.

Situation	Effect of Error	Journal Entries	Corrected Financial Statements	Communication	Research

Complete the following amounts in the corrected financial statements for Cord Corp.

Cord Corp. STATEMENT OF FINANCIAL POSITION December 31, 2010	
Assets	
Cash	
Marketable equity securities	
Accounts receivable	
Allowance for doubtful accounts	
Inventories	
Deferred tax asset	
Property and equipment	
Accumulated depreciation	
Total assets	
Liabilities and Stockholders' Equity	
Accounts payable and accrued liabilities	
Income tax payable	
Estimated liability from lawsuit	
Pension liability	
Common stock, $20 par	
Additional paid-in capital	
Retained earnings	
Other comprehensive income	
Total liabilities and stockholders' equity	

Cord Corp. STATEMENT OF INCOME For the Year Ended December 31, 2010	
Net sales	
Operating expenses:	
Cost of sales	
Selling and administrative	
Depreciation	
Pension cost	
Total operating expenses	
Other income/loss:	
Gain (loss) on marketable securities	
Estimated loss from lawsuit	
Income before income tax	
Income tax expense	
Net income	

Situation	Effect of Error	Journal Entries	Corrected Financial Statements	Communication	Research

Rex Bowman, controller of Cord Corporation, would like to know why corrections must be made for the items discovered in the audit. Write a brief memo explaining the purpose of financial statements and the necessity for error correction to Mr. Bowman.

REMINDER: Your response will be graded for both technical content and writing skills. Technical content will be evaluated for information that is helpful to the intended reader and clearly relevant to the issue. Writing skills will be evaluated for development, organization, and the appropriate expression of ideas in professional correspondence. Use a standard business memo or letter format with a clear beginning, middle, and end. Do not convey information in the form of a table, bullet point list, or other abbreviated presentation.

To: Mr. Bowman, Controller
From: CPA Candidate
Re: Correction of errors

Situation	Effect of Error	Journal Entries	Corrected Financial Statements	Communication	Research

Use the Financial Accounting Standards to determine how the correction of an accounting error is handled in the financial reporting process. Select the appropriate guidance from the professional standards.

Simulation Problem 2   (50 to 60 minutes)

Situation	Concepts	Analysis of Error	Error Effects	Communication	Research

The auditors of Cardiff Company have found the following errors in the company's accounting records. Cardiff Company uses the guidance in the FASB codification (SFAS 154) in accounting for accounting changes.

Situation	Concepts	Analysis of Error	Error Effects	Communication	Research

Identify whether each of the following statements is True or False.

	(T)	(F)
1. Accounting errors are reported as adjustments to the end of the year retained earnings in the current year's financial statements.	○	○
2. A self-correcting error need not be reported as an error if it has corrected itself in the current year.	○	○
3. A change in depreciation method is treated as an error when adjusting the financial statements for the current year.	○	○

		(T)	(F)

4. An accounting error is treated as a prior period adjustment. ○ ○

5. A change in the useful lives of assets in calculating depreciation is treated as an accounting error and accumulated depreciation is adjusted to reflect this error. ○ ○

Situation	Concepts	**Analysis of Error**		Error Effects	Communication	Research

Indicate how the error will affect the current year's financial statements by choosing an "O" in the column for overstate and "U" in the column for understate.

	Assets (O) (U)	Liabilities (O) (U)	Retained earnings (O) (U)	Net income (O) (U)	Other comprehensive income (O) (U)
1. Cardiff fails to record a sale on account for $8,000.	○ ○	○ ○	○ ○	○ ○	○ ○
2. The inventory was miscounted at year-end and overstated by $5,000.	○ ○	○ ○	○ ○	○ ○	○ ○
3. Cardiff fails to record depreciation expense of $3,500 for the year.	○ ○	○ ○	○ ○	○ ○	○ ○
4. The company receives a utility bill for $400 on December 29, but fails to record the bill.	○ ○	○ ○	○ ○	○ ○	○ ○
5. Available-for-sale securities were not marked to market. Later analysis reveals that the securities increased in value by $4,000 as of the end of the current year. Cardiff does not elect the fair value option for any of its available-for-sale securities.	○ ○	○ ○	○ ○	○ ○	○ ○
6. Cardiff fails to accrue wages of $17,000 at the end of the year.	○ ○	○ ○	○ ○	○ ○	○ ○
7. Trading securities were not marked to market. Later analysis reveals that the securities declined in value by $8,000 as of the end of the current year.	○ ○	○ ○	○ ○	○ ○	○ ○

Situation	Concepts	Analysis of Error	**Error Effects**		Communication	Research

Calculate the total effect of the errors on the following items:

Item	Amount	Overstated	Understated
Net income		○	○
Total assets		○	○
Other comprehensive income		○	○

Situation	Concepts	Analysis of Error	Error Effects	**Communication**		Research

Write a brief memo to the CEO of Cardiff Company explaining accrual basis accounting and the most common errors that must be corrected before issuing financial statements.

REMINDER: Your response will be graded for both technical content and writing skills. Technical content will be evaluated for information that is helpful to the intended reader and clearly relevant to the issue. Writing skills will be evaluated for development, organization, and the appropriate expression of ideas in professional correspondence. Use a standard business memo or letter format with a clear beginning, middle, and end. Do not convey information in the form of a table, bullet point list, or other abbreviated presentation.

To: CEO, Cardiff Company
From: CPA Candidate
Re: Correction of errors

Situation	Concepts	Analysis of Error	Error Effects	Communication	Research

Use the financial accounting standards to answer the following question. Select the appropriate guidance from the literature.

What is the definition of an accounting error?

MULTIPLE-CHOICE ANSWERS

1. a __ __	5. a __ __	8. b __ __	11. d __ __	14. b __ __
2. c __ __	6. c __ __	9. d __ __	12. d __ __	
3. b __ __	7. b __ __	10. c __ __	13. c __ __	1st: __/14 = __%
4. b __ __				2nd: __/14 = __%

MULTIPLE-CHOICE ANSWER EXPLANATIONS

B. Error Correction

1.   (a)   The correct amount of 2010 interest expense is $2,040, as computed below.

11/1/09 note	
Interest from 1/1/10 to 10/31/10	
($5,000 × 12% × 10/12)	$500
2/1/10 note	
Interest from 2/1/10 to 7/31/10	
($15,000 × 12% × 6/12)	900
5/1/10 note	
Interest from 5/1/10 to 12/31/10	
($8,000 × 12% × 8/12)	640
Total 2010 interest	$2,040

Since interest expense of $1,500 was recorded, 2010 interest expense was understated by $540 ($2,040 – $1,500).

2.   (c)   The error in understating the 2008 ending inventory would have self-corrected by 1/1/10 (2008 income understated by $60,000; 2009 income overstated by $60,000). The error in overstating the 2009 ending inventory would **not** have been corrected by 1/1/10. This error overstates both 2009 income and the 1/1/10 retained earnings balance by $75,000.

3.   (b)   A correction of an error is treated as a prior period adjustment, recorded in the year the error is discovered, and is reported in the financial statements as an adjustment to the beginning balance of retained earnings. The adjustment is reported net of the related tax effect. In this case the net-of-tax effect is $28,000 [$40,000 – ($30% × $40,000)]. This should **increase** beginning retained earnings because the understatement of 12/31/09 inventory would have resulted in an overstatement of cost of goods sold and therefore an understatement of retained earnings. Thus, the adjustment 1/1/10 retained earnings is $178,000 ($150,000 + $28,000). Tack's journal entry to record the adjustment is

Inventory	40,000	
Retained earnings		28,000
Taxes payable		12,000

4.   (b)   A correction of an error is treated as a prior period adjustment and is reported in the financial statements as an adjustment to the beginning balance of retained earnings in the year the error is discovered. The adjustment is reported net of the related tax effect. In 2009, insurance expense of $60,000 was recorded. The correct 2009 insurance expense was $20,000 ($60,000 × 1/3). Therefore, before taxes, 1/1/10 retained earnings is understated by $40,000. The net of tax effect is $28,000 [$40,000 – (30% × $40,000)], so the adjusted beginning retained earnings is $428,000 ($400,000 + $28,000).

5.   (a)   A change in accounting principle is a change from one **generally accepted** principle to another **generally accepted** principle. A correction of an error is the correction of a mathematical mistake, a mistake in the application of an accounting principle, an oversight or misuse

of existing facts, or **a change from an unacceptable principle to a generally accepted one**. Therefore, a switch from the cash basis (unacceptable) to the accrual basis (acceptable) is a correction of an error reported as a prior period adjustment.

6.   (c)   The requirement is to determine the effect of inventory errors on cost of goods sold. The effect of the errors on Bren's 2010 cost of goods sold (CGS) is illustrated below.

BI		
+ P	– $26,000	CGS understated $26,000
GAFS		
– EI	(+ $52,000)	CGS understated 52,000
CGS		CGS understated $78,000

Beginning inventory is the starting point for the CGS computation, so BI errors have a direct effect on CGS. The understatement of BI ($26,000) causes an **understatement** of goods available for sale (GAFS) and thus of CGS. Ending inventory is subtracted in the CGS computation, so EI errors have an inverse effect on CGS. The overstatement of EI ($52,000) means that too much was subtracted in the CGS computation, causing another **understatement** of CGS. Therefore, CGS is understated by a total of $78,000.

7.   (b)   The failure to record the $300,000 of deferred compensation expense in 2009 is considered an error. The profession requires that the correction of an error be treated as a prior period adjustment. Thus, the requirement is to determine the retroactive adjustment that should be made to the beginning balance of the retained earnings for 2010 (**including** any income tax effect). The net adjustment to beginning retained earnings would be a debit for $230,000 ($300,000 less the income tax benefit of $70,000).

8.   (b)   The depreciable base used to compute depreciation expense under both the straight-line and production methods is equal to the cost less estimated salvage value of the asset. Depreciation expense is overstated and net income is, therefore, understated when the estimated salvage value is excluded from the depreciation computation under both of these methods.

9.   (d)   The entry Ritzcar should have made to accrue sales commissions earned but unpaid at the end of its 2009 fiscal year is

Commission expense	xxx	
Commissions payable		xxx

Since Commissions payable is a current liability, the 2009 ending working capital is overstated due to Ritzcar's failure to record this entry. Since this error was not repeated at the end of Ritzcar's 2010 fiscal year, the income impact of the 2009 error "self-corrected" during 2010, when Ritzcar recorded both the earned but unpaid 2009 commissions plus the 2010 earned commissions. Therefore, the 2010 ending retained earnings would not be impacted by the error.

10. (c)   A liability is accrued when an obligation to pay or perform services has been incurred. This is the case even if the liability will not be satisfied until a future date. Therefore, accrued liabilities will be understated on the December 31, 2010 balance sheet because the special insurance costs were not recorded. However, there will be no effect on the December 31, 2010 balance of retained earnings because these costs relate to work in process, and work in process does not affect net income currently. Please note that if the special insurance costs related to goods that were sold, cost of goods sold would have been understated that would have caused both net income and retained earnings to be overstated.

11. (d)   The classification of holiday pay expense for administrative employees as manufacturing overhead would result in the capitalization of some or all of these costs as a component of ending inventory, while these costs should be expensed as incurred. This error could overstate ending inventory, a current asset. The overstatement of ending inventory also understates the cost of goods sold (Beginning inventories + Net purchases – Ending inventories = Cost of goods sold), and overstates net income and stockholders' equity. The understatement of accrued sales expenses would not affect current assets. The misclassification of the noncurrent note receivable principal as a current asset would have no impact on stockholders' equity. The understatement of depreciation on **manufacturing** machinery would understate the overhead added to inventories, a current asset.

12. (d)   The entry for the 12/31/09 wage accrual should have been

| Wages expense | 12,000 | |
| Wages payable | | 12,000 |

Failure to accrue wage expense results in an understatement of wage expense and an understatement of wages payable by $12,000 in 2009. As a result, net income and retained earnings are overstated by $12,000 in 2009. The wages were expensed and paid in 2010. Therefore, wage expense for 2010 is overstated, and 2010 net income is understated by $12,000. This is a counterbalancing error, and ending retained earnings in 2010 would be correct. Although this is a self-correcting error, the financial statements must be restated with period-specific effects. The restated financial statements are

Galaxy Corporation
RESTATED FINANCIAL STATEMENTS

	2010	2009
Revenue	$135,000	$100,000
Expenses	86,000	77,000
Net income	49,000	23,000
	12/31/10	12/31/09
Total assets	$157,000	$105,000
Total liabilities	50,000	47,000
Total owners' equity	107,000	58,000

13. (c)   The financial statements of all periods should be restated and corrections made to reflect any period-specific effects of the error. Answer (a) is incorrect because this is an error, not a change in accounting principle. Answer (b) is incorrect because although the

asset accounts may be adjusted to reflect correction of an error, income statement effects must also be disclosed. Answer (d) is incorrect because the financial statements must be restated for all periods presented.

14. (b)   The financial statements must be restated for all periods presented with period-specific effects disclosed. Answer (a) is incorrect because although beginning inventory may be adjusted, prior years' financial statements must also be restated. Answer (c) is incorrect because correcting the balance of ending retained earnings is not sufficient disclosure for error correction. Answer (d) is incorrect because even though it is a self-correcting error, financial statements must be restated with period-specific effects of the error.

SOLUTIONS TO SIMULATION PROBLEMS

Simulation Problem 1

Situation	Effect of Error		Journal Entries	Corrected Financial Statements	Communication	Research

	2010 Effects			2011 Effects		
	(Overstate)	(Understate)	(OK)	(Overstate)	(Understate)	(OK)
Inventory on balance sheet	●	○	○	○	○	●
Cost of goods sold	○	●	○	●	○	○
Net income	●	○	○	○	●	○
Retained earnings	●	○	○	○	○	●

Situation	Effect of Error	Journal Entries	Corrected Financial Statements	Communication	Research

Cord Corp.
ADJUSTING JOURNAL ENTRIES
December 31, 2010
(Explanations not required)

	Dr.	Cr.
(1)		
Marketable equity securities	$ 30,000	
Realized gain on sale of marketable equity securities		$ 30,000 [a]
(2)		
Unrealized loss on marketable equity securities (other comprehensive income)	13,000	
Adjustment to reduce marketable equity securities to market value		13,000 [b]
(3)		
Cost of sales	66,000	
Inventories		66,000
(4)		
Property and equipment	48,000	
Income tax payable		14,400 [c]
Retained earnings		33,600 [c]
(5)		
Depreciation	8,000	
Accumulated depreciation		8,000 [d]
(6)		
Estimated loss from lawsuit	60,000	
Estimated liability from lawsuit		60,000
(7)		
Deferred pension cost	40,000	
Additional pension liability		40,000
(8)		
Deferred tax asset	21,900 [i]	
Income tax payable	13,200 [ii]	
Income tax expense		35,100 [iii]

Supporting Computations for Number 8

Corrected total income tax expense for 2010

Income before income tax, as reported		$640,000
Add adjustment increasing income		
Realized gain on sale of securities		30,000 [1]
		670,000
Deduct adjustments decreasing income		
Increase cost of sales for inventory overstatement	$66,000	
Depreciation on pollution control devices	8,000	74,000
Adjusted taxable income before income tax		$596,000

Corrected current portion income tax expense and income taxes payable ($596,000 × 30%) $178,800

Deferred income tax benefits—based on following temporary differences:

Lawsuit expected to be settled in 2011	$60,000 [6]	
Unrealized loss on short-term marketable equity securities	13,000 [2]	
Total future deductible amounts	$73,000	

[i]   Deferred tax benefit of future deductible amounts ($73,000 × 30%)   21,900
      Corrected total income tax expense $156,900

[ii] Income tax expense as reported (all current, no deferred) $192,000
      Corrected income tax payable and income tax expense   178,800
                                                                                                $ 13,200

[iii] Income tax expense, as reported $192,000
      Corrected total income tax expense   156,900
                                                                                                $ 35,100

Explanations of Amounts
[a]   Gain on sale of marketable equity securities
            Selling price $130,000
            Cost   100,000
            Gain $ 30,000

[b]   Adjustment to reduce marketable equity securities to market value
            Marketable equity securities, at cost
                Balance, 2/2/10 as reported $125,000
                Adjustment for recording error   30,000
                Adjusted balance, 12/31/10   155,000
            Market valuation, 12/31/10   142,000
            Adjustment required, 12/31/10 $ 13,000

[c]   Prior year adjustment for pollution control devices
            Cost of installation, 12/29/09 $ 48,000
            Deduct income tax effect ($48,000 × 30%)   14,400
            Credit adjustment to retained earnings, 1/1/10 $ 33,600

[d]   Depreciation for 2010 on pollution control devices
            Cost of the installation on 12/29/09 $ 48,000
            Depreciation for 2010 ($48,000 ÷ 6 years) $ 8,000

Situation	Effect of Error	Journal Entries	Corrected Financial Statements	Communication	Research

Cord Corp.
STATEMENT OF FINANCIAL POSITION
December 31, 2010

Assets	
Cash	$1,225,000
Marketable equity securities	142,000
Accounts receivable	460,000
Allowance for doubtful accounts	(55,000)
Inventories	464,000
Deferred tax asset	21,900
Deferred pension cost	40,000
Property and equipment	668,000
Accumulated depreciation	(288,000)
Total assets	$2,677,900
Liabilities and Stockholders' Equity	
Accounts payable and accrued liabilities	$1,685,000
Income tax payable	111,200
Estimated liability from lawsuit	60,000
Pension liability	40,000
Common stock, $20 par	300,000
Additional paid-in capital	75,000
Retained earnings	419,700
Other comprehensive income	(13,000)
Total liabilities and stockholders' equity	$2,677,900

Calculation of corrected retained earnings:

Previous retained earnings (incorrect)	455,000
Less: Net income for 2010 (incorrect)	(448,000)
Beginning of year retained earnings (correct)	7,000
Net income (corrected)	379,100
Prior period adjustment for accounting error in expense pollution control devices in 2009	33,600
Corrected retained earnings	419,700

Cord Corp.
STATEMENT OF INCOME
For the Year Ended December 31, 2010

Net sales	$1,700,000
Operating expenses:	
Cost of sales	(636,000)
Selling and administrative	(448,000)
Depreciation	(50,000)
Total operating expenses	(1,134,000)
Other income/loss:	
Gain (loss) on marketable securities	30,000
Estimated loss from lawsuit	(60,000)
Income before income tax	536,000
Income tax expense	(156,900)
Net income	379,100

				Communication	
Situation	Effect of Error	Journal Entries	Corrected Financial Statements		Research

To: Mr. Bowman, Controller of Cord Corporation
From: CPA Candidate
Re: Correction of errors

You have requested that I explain why errors in previously issued financial statements must be corrected. The reliability of the financial reporting process is critical to investors and creditors. They rely on financial statements to make important decisions which often have significant financial consequences. Correction of the errors in previously issued financial statements not only corrects the statements of those periods, it also helps ensure that current and future financial statements are not misstated by the errors. Most accounting errors made in one year automatically correct themselves in future years. Such errors not only misstate results for one year, they also misstate results for two or more years.

In order to maintain the integrity of Cord Corporation's financial statements it is imperative that management correct the prior period financial statements for all material errors.

If you have any further questions or concerns, please contact me.

					Research
Situation	Effect of Error	Journal Entries	Corrected Financial Statements	Communication	

Correction of an Error in Previously Issued Financial Statements
FAS 154, Para 25

25. Any error in the financial statements of a prior period discovered subsequent to their issuance shall be reported as a prior-period adjustment by restating the prior-period financial statements. Restatement requires that

   a. The cumulative effect of the error on periods prior to those presented shall be reflected in the carrying amounts of assets and liabilities as of the beginning of the first period presented.
   b. An offsetting adjustment, if any, shall be made to the opening balance of retained earnings (or other appropriate components of equity or net assets in the statement of financial position) for that period.
   c. Financial statements for each individual prior period presented shall be adjusted to reflect correction of the period-specific effects of the error.

Codification: 250-10-45-23

Simulation Problem 2

	Concepts				
Situation		Analysis of Error	Error Effects	Communication	Research

		(T)	(F)
1.	Accounting errors are reported as adjustments to the end of the year retained earnings in the current year's financial statements.	○	●
2.	A self-correcting error need not be reported as an error if it has corrected itself in the current year.	○	●
3.	A change in depreciation method is treated as an error when adjusting the financial statements for the current year.	○	●

	(T)	(F)
4. An accounting error is treated as a prior period adjustment.	●	○
5. A change in the useful lives of assets in calculating depreciation is treated as an accounting error and accumulated depreciation is adjusted to reflect this error.	○	●

Explanation of solutions

1. False. Accounting errors require an adjustment to the beginning of the year retained earnings in the current year financial statements.

2. False. A self-correcting error would require an adjustment to correct comparative year financial statements. Adjustments to comparative years should be made to reflect retroactive application of the prior period adjustment to the accounts affected.

3. False. A change in depreciation method is treated as accumulative effect of change in accounting principle.

4. True. Correction of errors involve restatements of prior periods.

5. False. A change in the useful lives of an asset is treated on a prospective basis, and depreciation for the current year is calculated based on book value divided by the estimated number of years remaining.

Situation	Concepts	Analysis of Error	Error Effects	Communication	Research

	Assets (O) (U)	Liabilities (O) (U)	Retained earnings (O) (U)	Net income (O) (U)	Other comprehensive income (O) (U)
1. Cardiff fails to record a sale on account for $8,000.	○ ●	○ ○	○ ●	○ ●	○ ○
2. The inventory was miscounted at year-end and overstated by $5,000.	● ○	○ ○	● ○	● ○	○ ○
3. Cardiff fails to record depreciation expense of $3,500 for the year.	● ○	○ ○	● ○	● ○	○ ○
4. The company receives a utility bill for $400 on December 29, but fails to record the bill.	○ ○	○ ●	● ○	● ○	○ ○
5. Available-for-sale securities were not marked to market. Later analysis reveals that the securities increased in value by $4,000 as of the end of the current year. Cardiff does not elect the fair value option for any of its available-for-sale securities.	○ ●	○ ○	○ ○	○ ○	○ ●
6. Cardiff fails to accrue wages of $17,000 at the end of the year.	○ ○	○ ●	● ○	● ○	○ ○
7. Trading securities were not marked to market. Later analysis reveals that the securities declined in value by $8,000 as of the end of the current year.	● ○	○ ○	● ○	● ○	○ ○

Explanation of solutions

1. Cardiff should have debited Accounts Receivable and credited Sales. Therefore, accounts receivable is understated, and retained earnings is understated.

2. Cardiff has overstated ending inventory, which understates cost of goods sold. Understating cost of goods sold results in income being overstated for the period. Net income flows into retained earnings, and thus, retained earnings is also overstated in the current period.

3. Cardiff should have debited Depreciation Expense and credited Accumulated Depreciation. By not making this entry, depreciation expense is too low, overstating net income, and overstating retained earnings. Accumulated depreciation is also too low, which overstates assets.

4. The entry would be to debit Utility Expense and credit Accounts Payable. Failing to make this entry would understate expenses, which results in overstated net income, overstated retained earnings, and understated liabilities.

5.   The unrealized gain on available-for-sale securities is not recognized in net income, but is recognized as an unrealized gain in other comprehensive income. Failing to mark to market when an available-for-sale security has increased in value would result in understating assets and understating other comprehensive income for the period.

6.   The journal entry to accrue wages is to debit Wage Expense and credit Wages Payable. Failure to accrue wages results in expenses being understated, which in turn, overstates net income and overstates retained earnings for the period. Failure to accrue wages also results in liabilities being understated.

7.   The unrealized gains and losses from trading securities should be included in net income for the period. Failure to mark to market and recognize the loss would result in assets being overstated, net income being overstated, and retained earnings being overstated for the period.

			Error Effects		
Situation	**Concepts**	**Analysis of Error**		**Communication**	**Research**

Item	*Amount*	*Overstated*	*Understated*
Net income	25,900	●	○
Total assets	4,500	●	○
Other comprehensive income	4,000	○	●

Explanation of solutions

Net income: Under $8,000 from sale, over $5,000 from inventory error, over $3,500 from depreciation expense, over $400 from utility bill, over $17,000 from failure to accrue wages, over $8,000 from failure to record decline in value of trading security.

Total assets: Under $8,000 from failure to record sale on account, over $5,000 from inventory error, over $3,500 from failure to record accumulated depreciation, under $4,000 for failure to mark to market AFS, over $8,000 for failure to mark trading securities to market.

OCI: Understated $4,000 for failure to mark AFS securities to market.

				Communication	
Situation	**Concepts**	**Analysis of Error**	**Error Effects**		**Research**

To: CEO, Cardiff Company
From: CPA Candidate
Re: Correction of Errors

The purpose of issuing financial statements is to provide users with reliable financial information to make investment and credit decisions. Generally accepted accounting principles require companies to use the accrual basis of accounting. The accrual basis of accounting attempts to measure all economic activity during the period, and record these items as assets, liabilities, owners' equity, revenue, expenses, gains, or losses. Correct measurement and correct classification of these items is essential to provide investors with accurate and reliable information.

The most common errors that must be corrected prior to issuing financial statements are failing to adjust an existing account for items previously recognized, miscounting inventory, failing to accrue liabilities at the end of the period, and failing to properly classify capitalized or expensed items. These errors must be corrected to ensure that the values of the assets and liabilities are accurately stated on the balance sheet. In addition, correcting these errors will also ensure that income and expense for the period is accurately measured and reflected on the income statement.

If I can be of further assistance, please do not hesitate to contact my office.

					Research
Situation	**Concepts**	**Analysis of Error**	**Error Effects**	**Communication**	

FAS 154, Para 2(h)

h.   Error in previously issued financial statements—an error in recognition, measurement, presentation, or disclosure in financial statements resulting from mathematical mistakes, mistakes in the application of GAAP, or oversight or misuse of facts that existed at the time the financial statements were prepared. A change from an accounting principle that is not generally accepted to one that is generally accepted is a correction of an error.

Codification: 250-10-20 Glossary

MULTIPLE-CHOICE QUESTIONS (1-26)

1. On January 1, 2008, Bray Company purchased for $240,000 a machine with a useful life of ten years and no salvage value. The machine was depreciated by the double-declining balance method and the carrying amount of the machine was $153,600 on December 31, 2009. Bray changed to the straight-line method on January 1, 2010. Bray can justify the change. What should be the depreciation expense on this machine for the year ended December 31, 2010?

    a. $15,360
    b. $19,200
    c. $24,000
    d. $30,720

Items 2 and 3 are based on the following:

On January 1, 2008, Warren Co. purchased a $600,000 machine, with a five-year useful life and no salvage value. The machine was depreciated by an accelerated method for book and tax purposes. The machine's carrying amount was $240,000 on December 31, 2009. On January 1, 2010, Warren changed to the straight-line method for financial reporting purposes. Warren can justify the change. Warren's income tax rate is 30%.

2. In its 2010 income statement, what amount should Warren report as the cumulative effect of this change?

    a. $120,000
    b. $ 84,000
    c. $ 36,000
    d. $0

3. On January 1, 2010, what amount should Warren report as deferred income tax liability as a result of the change?

    a. $120,000
    b. $ 72,000
    c. $ 36,000
    d. $0

4. On January 2, 2010, to better reflect the variable use of its only machine, Holly, Inc. elected to change its method of depreciation from the straight-line method to the units of production method. The original cost of the machine on January 2, 2008, was $50,000, and its estimated life was ten years. Holly estimates that the machine's total life is 50,000 machine hours.

Machine hours usage was 8,500 during 2008 and 3,500 during 2009.

Holly's income tax rate is 30%. Holly should report the accounting change in its 2010 financial statements as a(n)

    a.   Cumulative effect of a change in accounting principle of $2,000 in its income statement.
    b.   Entry for current year depreciation expense on the income statement and treated on a prospective basis.
    c.   Cumulative effect of a change in accounting principle of $1,400 in its income statement.
    d.   Adjustment to beginning retained earnings of $1,400.

5. The effects of a change in accounting principle should be recorded on a prospective basis when the change is from the

    a.   Cash basis of accounting for vacation pay to the accrual basis.

    b.   Straight-line method of depreciation for previously recorded assets to the double-declining balance method.
    c.   Presentation of statements of individual companies to their inclusion in consolidated statements.
    d.   Completed-contract method of accounting for long-term construction-type contracts to the percentage-of-completion method.

6. When a company changes from the straight-line method of depreciation for previously recorded assets to the double-declining balance method, which of the following should be used?

	Cumulative effects of change in accounting principle	Retrospective application
a.	No	No
b.	No	Yes
c.	Yes	Yes
d.	Yes	No

Items 7 and 8 are based on the following:

During 2010, Orca Corp. decided to change from the FIFO method of inventory valuation to the weighted-average method. Inventory balances under each method were as follows:

	FIFO	Weighted-average
January 1, 2010	$71,000	$77,000
December 31, 2010	79,000	83,000

Orca's income tax rate is 30%.

7. In its 2010 financial statements, what amount should Orca report as the gain or loss on the cumulative effect of this accounting change?

    a. $2,800
    b. $4,000
    c. $4,200
    d. $0

8. In accordance with the Codification, Orca should report the effect of this accounting change as a(n)

    a.   Prior period adjustment.
    b.   Component of income from continuing operations.
    c.   Retrospective application to previous year's financial statements.
    d.   Component of income after extraordinary items.

9. On January 1, 2010, Roem Corp. changed its inventory method to FIFO from LIFO for both financial and income tax reporting purposes. The change resulted in a $500,000 increase in the January 1, 2010 inventory, which is the only change that could be calculated from the accounting records. Assume that the income tax rate for all years is 30%. Retrospective application would result in

    a.   An increase in ending inventory in the 2009 balance sheet.
    b.   A decrease in ending inventory in the 2010 balance sheet.
    c.   A decrease in net income in 2009.
    d.   A gain from cumulative effect of change on the income statement in 2010.

10. Which of the following would receive treatment as a cumulative effect on an accounting change on the income statement?

	LIFO to weighted-average	*FIFO to weighted-average*
a.	Yes	Yes
b.	Yes	No
c.	No	No
d.	No	Yes

11. On August 31, 2010, Harvey Co. decided to change from the FIFO periodic inventory system to the weighted-average periodic inventory system. Harvey is on a calendar year basis. ASC Topic 250 (SFAS 154) requires the cumulative effect of the change is determined
a. As of January 1, 2010.
b. As of August 31, 2010.
c. During the eight months ending August 31, 2010, by a weighted-average of the purchases.
d. As of the earliest period presented if practicable.

12. In 2010, Brighton Co. changed from the individual item approach to the aggregate approach in applying the lower of FIFO cost or market to inventories. ASC Topic 250 (SFAS 154) requires that the change should be reported in Brighton's financial statements as a
a. Change in estimate on a prospective basis.
b. Cumulative effect of change in accounting principle on the current year income statement.
c. Retrospective application to the earliest period presented if practicable.
d. Prior period adjustment with a separate disclosure.

13. On January 1, 2010, Poe Construction, Inc. changed to the percentage-of-completion method of income recognition for financial statement reporting but not for income tax reporting. Poe can justify this change in accounting principle. As of December 31, 2009, Poe compiled data showing that income under the completed-contract method aggregated $700,000. If the percentage-of-completion method had been used, the accumulated income through December 31, 2009, would have been $880,000. Assuming an income tax rate of 40% for all years, ASC Topic 250 (SFAS 154) requires that the cumulative effect of this accounting change to be reported by Poe as
a. An increase in construction-in-progress for $180,000 in the 2009 balance sheet.
b. A decrease in the beginning balance of retained earnings for $108,000 in 2010.
c. A cumulative effect adjustment of $108,000 on the 2010 income statement.
d. As an increase in ending retained earnings of $180,000 in 2009.

14. The effect of a change in accounting principle that is inseparable from the effect of a change in accounting estimate should be reported
a. By restating the financial statements of all prior periods presented.
b. As a correction of an error.
c. As a component of income from continuing operations, in the period of change and future periods if the change affects both.
d. As a separate disclosure after income from continuing operations, in the period of change and future periods if the change affects both.

15. Which of the following is considered a direct effect of a change in accounting principle?
a. Deferred taxes.
b. Profit sharing.
c. Royalty payments.
d. None of the above.

16. Indirect effects from a change in accounting principle should be reported
a. Retrospectively to the earliest period presented.
b. As a cumulative change in accounting principle in the current period.
c. In the period in which the accounting change occurs.
d. As a prior period adjustment.

17. If it is impracticable to determine the cumulative effect of an accounting change to any of the prior periods, the accounting change should be accounted for
a. As a prior period adjustment.
b. On a prospective basis.
c. As a cumulative effect change on the income statement.
d. As an adjustment to retained earnings in the first period presented.

18. If the cumulative effect of applying an accounting change can be determined but the period-specific effects on all periods cannot be determined, the cumulative effect of the change should be applied to
a. The end balance of retained earnings of the earliest period presented.
b. Net income of the current year.
c. Retained earnings of the current year.
d. The carrying value of the assets and liabilities at the beginning of the earliest period to which it can be applied.

19. On January 1, 2006, Taft Co. purchased a patent for $714,000. The patent is being amortized over its remaining legal life of fifteen years expiring on January 1, 2018. During 2009, Taft determined that the economic benefits of the patent would not last longer than ten years from the date of acquisition. What amount should be reported in the balance sheet for the patent, net of accumulated amortization, at December 31, 2009?
a. $428,400
b. $489,600
c. $504,000
d. $523,600

20. On January 1, 2006, Flax Co. purchased a machine for $528,000 and depreciated it by the straight-line method using an estimated useful life of eight years with no salvage value. On January 1, 2009, Flax determined that the machine had a useful life of six years from the date of acquisition and will have a salvage value of $48,000. An accounting change was made in 2009 to reflect these additional data. The accumulated depreciation for this machine should have a balance at December 31, 2009, of
a. $292,000
b. $308,000
c. $320,000
d. $352,000

21. How should the effect of a change in accounting estimate be accounted for?
- a. By restating amounts reported in financial statements of prior periods.
- b. By reporting pro forma amounts for prior periods.
- c. As a prior period adjustment to beginning retained earnings.
- d. In the period of change and future periods if the change affects both.

22. During 2009, Krey Co. increased the estimated quantity of copper recoverable from its mine. Krey uses the units of production depletion method. As a result of the change, which of the following should be reported in Krey's 2009 financial statements?

	Cumulative effect of a change in accounting principle	Pro forma effects of retroactive application of new depletion base
a.	Yes	Yes
b.	Yes	No
c.	No	No
d.	No	Yes

23. Oak Co. offers a three-year warranty on its products. Oak previously estimated warranty costs to be 2% of sales. Due to a technological advance in production at the beginning of 2009, Oak now believes 1% of sales to be a better estimate of warranty costs. Warranty costs of $80,000 and $96,000 were reported in 2007 and 2008, respectively. Sales for 2009 were $5,000,000. What amount should be presented in Oak's 2009 financial statements as warranty expense?
- a. $ 50,000
- b. $ 88,000
- c. $100,000
- d. $138,000

24. For 2008, Pac Co. estimated its two-year equipment warranty costs based on $100 per unit sold in 2008. Experience during 2009 indicated that the estimate should have been based on $110 per unit. The effect of this $10 difference from the estimate is reported
- a. In 2009 income from continuing operations.
- b. As an accounting change, net of tax, below 2009 income from continuing operations.
- c. As an accounting change requiring 2008 financial statements to be restated.
- d. As a correction of an error requiring 2008 financial statements to be restated.

25. A company has included in its consolidated financial statements this year a subsidiary acquired several years ago that was appropriately excluded from consolidation last year. ASC Topic 250 (SFAS 154) requires this to be reported as
- a. An accounting change that should be reported prospectively.
- b. An accounting change that should be reported retrospectively.
- c. A correction of an error.
- d. Neither an accounting change nor a correction of an error.

26. Which of the following statements is correct regarding accounting changes that result in financial statements that are, in effect, the statements of a different reporting entity?
- a. Cumulative-effect adjustments should be reported as separate items on the financial statements pertaining to the year of change.
- b. No restatements or adjustments are required if the changes involve consolidated methods of accounting for subsidiaries.
- c. No restatements or adjustments are required if the changes involve the cost or equity methods of accounting for investments.
- d. The financial statements of all prior periods presented are adjusted retrospectively.

SIMULATION PROBLEMS

Simulation Problem 1   (50 to 60 minutes)

Situation					
	Accounting Changes	Calculations	Classification/ Disclosure	Communication	Research

On January 2, 2010, Quo, Inc. hired Reed to be its controller. During the year, Reed, working closely with Quo's president and outside accountants, made changes in accounting policies, corrected several errors dating from 2009 and before, and instituted new accounting policies.

Quo's 2010 financial statements will be presented in comparative form with its 2009 financial statements. In 2010, Quo uses the guidance in ASC Topic 250 (SFAS 154) to account for any accounting changes.

	Accounting Changes				
Situation		Calculations	Classification/ Disclosure	Communication	Research

Items 1 through 10 represent Quo's transactions.

List A represents possible classifications of these transactions as: a change in accounting principle, a change in accounting estimate, a correction of an error in previously presented financial statements, or neither an accounting change nor an accounting error.

List B represents the general accounting treatment for these transactions. These treatments are

- Retrospective application approach—Apply the new accounting principle to all prior periods presented showing the cumulative effect of the change in the carrying value of assets and liabilities at the beginning of the first period presented, and adjust financial statements presented to reflect period-specific effects of the change.
- Retroactive restatement approach—Restate the 2009 financial statements and adjust 2009 beginning retained earnings if the error or change affects a period prior to 2009 financial statements.
- Prospective approach—Report 2010 and future financial statements on the new basis, but do **not** restate 2009 financial statements.

For each item, select one from List A and one from List B.

        List A (Select one treatment)   *List B (Select one approach)*

A. Change in accounting principle.   X. Retrospective application approach.

B. Change in accounting estimate.   Y. Retroactive restatement approach.

C. Correction of an error in previously presented financial statements.   Z. Prospective approach.

D. Neither an accounting change nor an accounting error.

Items to be answered

		List A Treatment				List B Approach		
		(A)	(B)	(C)	(D)	(X)	(Y)	(Z)
1.	Quo manufactures heavy equipment to customer specifications on a contract basis. On the basis that it is preferable, accounting for these long-term contracts was switched from the completed-contract method to the percentage-of-completion method.	O	O	O	O	O	O	O
2.	As a result of a production breakthrough, Quo determined that manufacturing equipment previously depreciated over fifteen years should be depreciated over twenty years.	O	O	O	O	O	O	O
3.	The equipment that Quo manufactures is sold with a five-year warranty. Because of a production breakthrough, Quo reduced its computation of warranty costs from 3% of sales to 1% of sales.	O	O	O	O	O	O	O
4.	Quo changed from LIFO to FIFO to account for its finished goods inventory.	O	O	O	O	O	O	O
5.	Quo changed from FIFO to average cost to account for its raw materials and work in process inventories.	O	O	O	O	O	O	O
6.	Quo sells extended service contracts on its products. Because related services are performed over several years, in 2010 Quo changed from the cash method to the accrual method of recognizing income from these service contracts.	O	O	O	O	O	O	O

		List A *Treatment* (A) (B) (C) (D)				List B *Approach* (X) (Y) (Z)		
7.	During 2010, Quo determined that an insurance premium paid and entirely expensed in 2009 was for the period January 1, 2009, through January 1, 2011.	○	○	○	○	○	○	○
8.	Quo changed its method of depreciating office equipment from an accelerated method to the straight-line method to more closely reflect costs in later years.	○	○	○	○	○	○	○
9.	Quo instituted a pension plan for all employees in 2010 and adopted the accounting standards related to pensions. Quo had not previously had a pension plan.	○	○	○	○	○	○	○
10.	During 2010, Quo increased its investment in Worth, Inc. from a 10% interest, purchased in 2009, to 30%, and acquired a seat on Worth's board of directors. As a result of its increased investment, Quo changed its method of accounting for investment in subsidiary from the cost adjusted for fair value method to the equity method. Quo did not elect to use the fair value method to report its 30% investment in Worth.	○	○	○	○	○	○	○

Situation	Accounting Changes	Calculations	Classification/ Disclosure	Communication	Research

Quo has $500,000 in equipment and machinery that was acquired on January 2, 2008. Quo has been using the double-declining balance method to depreciate the equipment over an estimated 10-year economic life with no salvage. On January 1, 2010, Quo decides to change to the straight-line method with no salvage. Quo has a 40% tax rate.

Calculate the following amounts:

1. Accumulated depreciation as of 12/31/09

2. Depreciation expense for 2010

3. Accumulated depreciation as of 12/31/10

4. Indicate the amount of the accounting change shown net of tax if appropriate

Situation	Accounting Changes	Calculations	Classification/ Disclosure	Communication	Research

Quo made the following changes in its accounting policies.

- Quo changed its depreciation method for its production machinery from the double-declining balance method to the straight-line method effective January 1, 2010.
- Quo appropriately changed the salvage values used in computing depreciation for its office equipment.
- Quo appropriately changed the specific subsidiaries constituting the group of companies for which consolidated financial statements are presented.

For each of the items that Quo changed, identify whether Quo should show the following by choosing Yes or No in the appropriate columns.

	Change item	*Cumulative effect of change in principle in net income of the period of change* *Yes* *No*		*Pro forma effects of retroactive application for all prior periods presented currently* *Yes* *No*		*Retrospective application to financial statements of all prior periods presented currently* *Yes* *No*	
1.	Quo changed its depreciation method for its production machinery from the double-declining balance method to the straight-line method effective January 1, 2010.	○	○	○	○	○	○
2.	Quo appropriately changed the salvage values used in computing depreciation for its office equipment.	○	○	○	○	○	○

Change item	Cumulative effect of change in principle in net income of the period of change		Pro forma effects of retroactive application for all prior periods presented currently		Retrospective application to financial statements of all prior periods presented currently	
	Yes	No	Yes	No	Yes	No
3. Quo appropriately changed the specific subsidiaries constituting the group of companies for which consolidated financial statements are presented.	○	○	○	○	○	○

Situation	Accounting Changes	Calculations	Classification/ Disclosure	Communication	Research

Write a brief memorandum to the CEO of Quo, Inc. explaining how to account for each of the three changes.

REMINDER: Your response will be graded for both technical content and writing skills. Technical content will be evaluated for information that is helpful to the intended reader and clearly relevant to the issues. Writing skills will be evaluated for development, organization, and the appropriate expression of ideas in professional correspondence. Use a standard business memo or letter format with a clear beginning, middle, and end. Do not convey information in the form of a table, bullet point list, or other abbreviated presentation.

To: CEO, QUO, Inc.
From: CPA Candidate
Re: Changes in accounting

Situation	Accounting Changes	Calculations	Classification/ Disclosure	Communication	Research

Research each issue as to whether it is considered a change in accounting principle. Select the appropriate citation and place in the table below.

1.	Quo changed its depreciation method for its production machinery from the double-declining balance method to the straight-line method effective January 1, 2010.	
2.	Quo appropriately changed the salvage values used in computing depreciation for its office equipment.	
3.	Quo appropriately changed the specific subsidiaries constituting the group of companies for which consolidated financial statements are presented.	

Simulation Problem 2   (45 to 50 minutes)

Situation	Accounting Treatment	Accounting Change	Communication	Research

Falk Co. began operations in January, 2009. On January 2, 2010, Falk Co. hired a new controller. During the year, the controller, working closely with Falk's president and outside accountants, made changes in existing accounting policies, instituted new accounting policies, and corrected several errors dating from prior to 2010.

Falk's financial statements for the year ended December 31, 2010, will not be presented in comparative form with its 2009 financial statements. Falk uses the guidance in ASC Topic 250 (SFAS 154) to account for accounting changes in 2010.

List A represents possible classifications of these transactions as a change in accounting principle, a change in accounting estimate, correction of an error in previously presented financial statements, or neither an accounting change nor an error correction.

List B represents the general accounting treatment required for these transactions. These treatments are

- Retrospective application approach—Apply the new accounting principle to all prior periods presented showing the cumulative effect of the change in the carrying value of assets and liabilities at the beginning of the first period presented, and adjust financial statements presented to reflect period-specific effects of the change.
- Retroactive restatement approach—Adjust 2010 beginning retained earnings if the error or change affects a period prior to 2010.
- Prospective approach—Report 2010 and future financial statements on the new basis, but do not adjust beginning retained earnings or include the cumulative effect of the change in the 2010 income statements.

List A—Type of change (Select one)	*List B—General accounting treatment (Select one)*
A. Change in accounting principle.	X. Retroactive application approach.
B. Change in accounting estimate.	Y. Retroactive restatement approach.
C. Correction of an error in previously presented financial statements.	Z. Prospective approach.
D. Neither an accounting change nor an error correction.	

Situation	Accounting Treatment	Accounting Change	Communication	Research

For **Items 1 and 2,** select a classification for each transaction from List A and the general accounting treatment required to report the change from List B.

	List A Type of Change (A) (B) (C) (D)	List B Accounting Treatment (X) (Y) (Z)
1. Falk manufactures customized equipment to customer specifications on a contract basis. Falk changed its method of accounting for these long-term contracts from the completed-contract method to the percentage-of-completion method because Falk is now able to make reasonable estimates of future construction costs.	○ ○ ○ ○	○ ○ ○
2. Based on improved collection procedures, Falk changed the percentage of credit sales used to determine the allowance for uncollectible accounts from 2% to 1%.	○ ○ ○ ○	○ ○ ○

Situation	Accounting Treatment	Accounting Change	Communication	Research

On January 1, 2010, Falk changed from the average cost method to the FIFO method to account for its inventory. Ending inventory for each method was as follows:

Year	Average cost	FIFO
2009	$5,000	$ 7,000
2010	$9,000	$14,000

Falk's income statement information calculated by the average cost method was as follows:

Falk Corporation
INCOME STATEMENT

	Before adjustments for the year ending 12-31-10	Before adjustment for the year ending 12-31-09
Sales	$130,000	$100,000
Cost of goods sold	90,000	70,000
Gross profit	40,000	30,000
Operating expense	20,000	17,000
Earnings before taxes	20,000	13,000
Tax expense	8,000	5,200
Net income	12,000	7,800

Assume that Falk has no book/tax differences or deferred taxes. Falk accrues tax expense on December 31 of each year and pays the tax in January of the following year. The income tax rate is 40%.

Prepare an adjusted income statement for 2010 and 2009 after the change to the FIFO inventory method.

Falk Corporation
INCOME STATEMENT

	Adjusted *for the year ending 12-31-10*	*Adjusted* *for the year ending 12-31-09*
Sales		
Cost of goods sold		
Gross profit		
Operating expense		
Earnings before taxes		
Tax expense		
Net income		

Indicate the adjusted balances on the December 31 balance sheet for each year.

	December 31, 2010	*December 31, 2009*
Inventory		
Income tax liability		
Retained earnings		

Situation	Accounting Treatment	Accounting Change	Communication		Research

On January 1, 2010, Falk Co. made the following changes in its accounting policies:

- Changed from the LIFO inventory method to the FIFO inventory method.
- Adopted the straight-line depreciation method for all future machinery acquisitions, but continued to use sum-of-the-years' digits depreciation method for all machinery purchased before 2010.
- Changed from the cash to the accrual basis of accounting for accumulated vacation pay.

Falk prepares two-year comparative financial statements. Write a brief memorandum to the new controller at Falk explaining how these changes should be reported. Specifically, you should address each of the following issues:

1. What type of accounting change is the change from the LIFO to the FIFO inventory costing method? How should Falk report this change in its 2010 comparative financial statements?
2. What type of accounting change is Falk's change from the sum-of-the-years' digits to the straight-line depreciation method for all machinery purchased after 2010? How should Falk report this change?
3. What type of change occurs when recognition of vacation pay expense is changed from the cash basis to the accrual basis? How should Falk report this change?

REMINDER: Your response will be graded for both technical content and writing skills. Technical content will be evaluated for information that is helpful to the intended reader and clearly relevant to the issue. Writing skills will be evaluated for development, organization, and the appropriate expression of ideas in professional correspondence. Use a standard business memo or letter format with a clear beginning, middle, and end. Do not convey information in the form of a table, bullet point list, or other abbreviated presentation.

To: Controller of Falk Co.
From: CPA Candidate
Re: Changes in accounting principle

Situation	Accounting Treatment	Accounting Change	Communication	Research	

Identify the authoritative literature that governs the accounting treatment of a change from the completed-contract method to the percentage-of-completion method.

MULTIPLE-CHOICE ANSWERS

1. b __ __	7. d __ __	13. a __ __	19. b __ __	25. b __ __
2. d __ __	8. c __ __	14. c __ __	20. a __ __	26. d __ __
3. d __ __	9. a __ __	15. a __ __	21. d __ __	
4. b __ __	10. c __ __	16. c __ __	22. c __ __	
5. b __ __	11. d __ __	17. b __ __	23. a __ __	1st: __/26 = __%
6. a __ __	12. c __ __	18. d __ __	24. a __ __	2nd: __/26 = __%

MULTIPLE-CHOICE ANSWER EXPLANATIONS

C.1. Changes in Accounting Principles (SFAS 154)

1. (b) A change in depreciation method is a change in method that is not distinguishable from a change in estimate, and is accounted for as a change in estimate. The change is reported on a prospective basis in the current year and future years. Book value as of 1/1/09 = $153,600/8 years remaining = $19,200 depreciation expense in 2009.

2. (d) Zero. A change in depreciation method is a change in method that is not distinguishable from a change in estimate, and is accounted for as a change in estimate. The change is reported on a prospective basis in the current year and future years. A change in depreciation method is no longer given cumulative effect treatment on the income statement.

3. (d) Zero. A change in depreciation method is a change in method that is not distinguishable from a change in estimate, and is accounted for as a change in estimate. The change is reported on a prospective basis in the current year and future years. Because a change in depreciation method is no longer given cumulative effect treatment on the income statement, there are no deferred income tax liability effects.

4. (b) A change in depreciation method is a change in method that is not distinguishable from a change in estimate, and is accounted for as a change in estimate. The change is reported on a prospective basis in the current year and future years.

5. (b) The requirement is to determine which accounting change should be reported on a prospective basis. A change in depreciation method is a change in principle that is not distinguishable from a change in estimate, and is accounted for as a change in estimate. The change is reported on a prospective basis in the current year and future years. A change from the cash basis to the accrual basis of accounting is a change from non-GAAP to GAAP accounted for as the correction of an error. A change in reporting entity requires retrospective application to the earliest year presented if practicable. A change in the method of accounting for long-term contracts requires retrospective application to the earliest year presented if practicable.

6. (a) The requirement is to determine whether a change in depreciation method from straight-line to double-declining balance should be reported as a cumulative effect of a change in accounting principle and receive retrospective application. A change in depreciation method is a change in method that is not distinguishable from a change in estimate, and is accounted for as a change in estimate. The change is reported on a prospective basis in the current year and future years. Therefore, it does not receive cumulative effect treatment or retrospective treatment.

7. (d) A change in inventory method no longer receives cumulative effect treatment on the income statement. Instead, the accounting change is given retrospective application to the earliest period presented, if practicable. Therefore, the answer is zero.

8. (c) A change in inventory method no longer receives cumulative effect treatment on the income statement. Instead, the accounting change is given retrospective application to the earliest period presented, if practicable.

9. (a) Retrospective application requires applying the new principle to the earliest period presented if practicable. Because 2010 beginning inventory is the previous year's ending inventory, the new principle can be applied to the 2009 financial statements. This would result in an increase in ending inventory in the balance sheet for 2009, a decrease in cost of goods sold in 2009, and an increase in the beginning inventory, which would result in a higher cost of goods sold and a lower net income for 2010.

10. (c) A change in inventory method is given retrospective application to the earliest period presented, if practicable.

11. (d) Retrospective application requires the change to be calculated for the earliest period presented if practicable.

12. (c) A change in inventory method no longer receives cumulative effect treatment on the income statement. The accounting change is given retrospective application to the earliest period presented, if practicable.

13. (a) The requirement is to indicate how a change in accounting principle from the completed-contract method to the percentage-of-completion method should be reported. A change in the method of accounting for long-term contracts requires retrospective application to the earliest year practicable. This results in a $180,000 increase in income for 2009. The assets would be adjusted for the earliest period affected, and construction-in-progress would increase by $180,000. Net income for 2009 would increase by $108,000 ($180,000 less 40% tax effects), and the deferred tax liability account would increase in 2009 by $72,000.

14. (c) The effect of a change in accounting principle which is inseparable from the effect of a change in accounting estimate should be accounted for as a change in accounting estimate. Changes in estimate should be accounted for in the period of change and also in any affected future periods as a component of income from continuing operations. Financial statements are only restated for changes due to an error. Errors include mathematical mistakes, mistakes in applying accounting principles, oversights or misuse of available facts, and changes from unacceptable accounting principles to GAAP. The situation described in this question does not meet the description of an error.

15. **(a)** Deferred taxes is a direct effect from the change in accounting principle, and its effects should be recorded in the earliest period presented, if practicable. Profit sharing and royalty payments are indirect effects and should be reported in the period of the change.

16. **(c)** Indirect effects of a change in accounting principle should be reported in the period in which the accounting change occurs. Direct effects are reported retrospectively to the earliest period presented, if practicable. Answers (b) and (d) are incorrect since accounting changes are no longer treated as cumulative effect changes or prior period adjustments.

17. **(b)** If it is impracticable to determine the cumulative effect of an accounting change to any of the prior periods, the accounting change should be accounted for on a prospective basis. Answer (a) is incorrect because accounting changes are no longer treated as prior period adjustments. Answer (c) is incorrect because accounting changes are no longer treated as cumulative effect changes on the income statement. Answer (d) is incorrect because the change would not be to retained earnings in the first period presented.

18. **(d)** If the cumulative effect of applying an accounting change can be determined, but the period-specific effects on all periods cannot be determined, the cumulative effect of the change should be applied to the carrying value of the assets and liabilities at the beginning of the earliest period to which it can be determined.

C.2. Change in Accounting Estimates

19. **(b)** This situation is a change in accounting estimate and should be accounted for currently and prospectively. From 1/1/06 to 12/31/08, patent amortization was recorded using a fifteen-year life. Yearly amortization was $47,600 ($714,000 ÷ 15), accumulated amortization at 12/31/08 was $142,800 ($47,600 × 3), and the book value of the patent at 12/31/08 was $571,200 ($714,000 – $142,800). Beginning in 2009, this book value must be amortized over its remaining useful life of 7 years (10 years – 3 years). Therefore, 2009 amortization is $81,600 ($571,200 ÷ 7) and the 12/31/09 book value is $489,600 ($571,200 – $81,600).

20. **(a)** From 1/1/06 to 12/31/08, depreciation was recorded using an eight-year life. Yearly depreciation was $66,000 ($528,000 ÷ 8), and accumulated depreciation at 12/31/08 was $198,000 (3 × $66,000). In 2009, the estimated useful life was changed to six years total with a salvage value of $48,000. Therefore, the 12/31/08 book value ($528,000 – $198,000 = $330,000) is depreciated down to the $48,000 salvage value over a remaining useful life of three years (six years total – three years already recorded). Depreciation expense for 2009 is $94,000 [($330,000 – $48,000) ÷ 3], increasing accumulated depreciation to $292,000 ($198,000 + $94,000).

21. **(d)** Changes in accounting estimate are to be accounted for in the period of change and in future periods if the change affects both (i.e., **prospectively**). Pro forma amounts are presented for changes in accounting principle accounted for using the **current** (cumulative effect) approach. Answers (a) and (c) are incorrect because they apply to **retroactive**-type changes in principle and error correction, respectively.

22. **(c)** The effect of a change in accounting estimate should be accounted for in (a) the period of change if the change affects that period only, or (b) the period of change and future periods if the change affects both. The Codification further states that a change in an estimate should not be accounted for by restating amounts reported in financial statements of prior periods or by reporting pro forma amounts for prior periods.

23. **(a)** A change in estimated warranty costs due to technological advances in production qualifies as a change in accounting estimate. Changes in estimate are treated prospectively; there is no retroactive restatement, and the new estimate is used in current and future years. Therefore, in 2009, Oak should use the new estimate of 1% and report warranty expense of $50,000 ($5,000,000 × 1%).

24. **(a)** A change in equipment warranty costs based on additional information obtained through experience qualifies as a change in accounting estimate. Changes in estimate should be accounted for in the period of change as a component of income from continuing operations and in future periods if necessary. No restatement is required for a change in estimate.

C.3. Change in Reporting Entity (ASC Topic 250)

25. **(b)** An accounting change that is a change in reporting entity is given retrospective application to the earliest period presented, if practicable. The term "restatement" refers only to correction of errors in previously issued financial statements.

26. **(d)** An accounting change that is a change in reporting entity is given retrospective application to the earliest period presented, if practicable. The term "restatement" refers only to correction of errors in previously issued financial statements.

SOLUTIONS TO SIMULATION PROBLEMS

Simulation Problem 1

Situation	Accounting Changes	Calculations	Classification/ Disclosure	Communication	Research

	List A Treatment (A) (B) (C) (D)	List B Approach (X) (Y) (Z)

1. Quo manufactures heavy equipment to customer specifications on a contract basis. On the basis that it is preferable, accounting for these long-term contracts was switched from the completed-contract method to the percentage-of-completion method.   ● ○ ○ ○   ● ○ ○

2. As a result of a production breakthrough, Quo determined that manufacturing equipment previously depreciated over fifteen years should be depreciated over twenty years.   ○ ● ○ ○   ○ ○ ●

3. The equipment that Quo manufactures is sold with a five-year warranty. Because of a production breakthrough, Quo reduced its computation of warranty costs from 3% of sales to 1% of sales.   ○ ● ○ ○   ○ ○ ●

4. Quo changed from LIFO to FIFO to account for its finished goods inventory.   ● ○ ○ ○   ● ○ ○

5. Quo changed from FIFO to average cost to account for its raw materials and work in process inventories.   ● ○ ○ ○   ● ○ ○

6. Quo sells extended service contracts on its products. Because related services are performed over several years, in 2010 Quo changed from the cash method to the accrual method of recognizing income from these service contracts.   ○ ○ ● ○   ○ ● ○

7. During 2010, Quo determined that an insurance premium paid and entirely expensed in 2009 was for the period January 1, 2009, through January 1, 2011.   ○ ○ ● ○   ○ ● ○

8. Quo changed its method of depreciating office equipment from an accelerated method to the straight-line method to more closely reflect costs in later years.   ○ ● ○ ○   ○ ○ ●

9. Quo instituted a pension plan for all employees in 2010 and adopted Statement of Financial Accounting Standards 87, *Employers' Accounting for Pensions.* Quo had not previously had a pension plan.   ○ ○ ○ ●   ○ ○ ●

10. During 2010, Quo increased its investment in Worth, Inc. from a 10% interest, purchased in 2009, to 30%, and acquired a seat on Worth's board of directors. As a result of its increased investment, Quo changed its method of accounting for investment in subsidiary from the cost adjusted for fair value method to the equity method.   ○ ○ ○ ●   ○ ● ○

Explanation of solutions

1. (A, X) This situation represents a change in the method of accounting for long-term construction-type contracts and requires retrospective application for all periods presented.

2. (B, Z) This situation is not a change in accounting principle but is a change in an estimate and should be handled prospectively.

3. (B, Z) This situation is a change in an estimate. The change in the percentage of warranty costs is not a change in accounting principle. Changes in estimate are handled prospectively.

4. (A, X) This situation is a change from one acceptable accounting principle to another and requires retrospective application.

5. (A, X) This situation is a change from one acceptable accounting method to another and requires the retrospective application approach.

6. (C, Y) The use of the cash method is considered an error since that method is generally **not** acceptable. The switch to an acceptable method (accrual) is considered the correction of an error and requires the retroactive restatement approach.

7. (C, Y) The write-off of the insurance premium was an error. Since comparative financial statements are prepared, past years must be corrected using the retroactive restatement approach even though this error is self-correcting after two years.

8. (A, Z) This situation is a change in method which is considered a change in estimate effected by a change in principle. Per SFAS 154, a change in depreciation method requires prospective application.

9. (D, Z) Since the company did not previously account for pensions this situation is simply the adoption of an appropriate accounting principle for pensions. No change in principle occurs.

10. (D, Y) Quo's increase in ownership interest (10% to 30%) and its acquisition of a seat on Worth's board of directors has given Quo the ability to exercise significant influence in the operating decisions of Worth. If Quo does not elect to use the fair value option to report its 30% investment in Worth, Quo will use the equity method to account for its investment in Worth. The cost adjusted for fair value method is no longer applicable due to the change in Quo's investment in Worth. However, the change from the cost adjusted for fair value method to the equity method is not a change in accounting principle. A change in accounting principle occurs when an accounting principle different from the one used previously for reporting purposes is adopted. For a change to occur, a choice between two or more accounting principles must exist. In this case, the change in Quo's situation allows the equity method to account for the investment. Quo's current economic situation is clearly different and this necessitates the adoption of a different accounting principle. Consequently, this is not an accounting change. However, the investment account should be retroactively restated to reflect balances as if the equity method had always been used.

Situation	Accounting Changes	Calculations	Classification/ Disclosure	Communication	Research
1. Accumulated depreciation as of 12/31/09				$180,000	
2. Depreciation expense for 2010				$ 40,000	
3. Accumulated depreciation as of 12/31/10				$220,000	
4. Indicate the amount of the accounting change shown net of tax if appropriate				$ 0	

Explanation of solutions

1. Before change, Quo used double-declining balance and 10-year life

2008	1/10 × 2 × $500,000 book value	= $100,000	depreciation expense
2009	1/10 × 2 × $400,000 new book value	= $ 80,000	depreciation expense
	Accumulated depreciation 12/31/09	$180,000	

2. To calculate depreciation expense for 2010:

Historical cost	$500,000
– Accum. depreciation	(180,000)
Book value	$320,000

($320,000 – $0 salvage) ÷ 8 years remaining life = $40,000 depreciation expense

3. To calculate accumulated depreciation as of 12/31/10:

2008	$100,000
2009	80,000
2010	40,000
Accum. depr. 12/31/10	$220,000

4. Accounting change net of tax – zero. Accounting standards treat changes in depreciation method as a change in estimate effected by a change in method. Therefore, a change in depreciation is accounted for on a prospective basis.

Situation	Accounting Changes	Calculations	Classification/ Disclosure	Communication	Research

Change item	Cumulative effect of change in principle in net income of the period of change		Pro forma effects of retroactive application for all prior periods presented currently		Retrospective application to financial statements of all prior periods presented currently	
	Yes	No	Yes	No	Yes	No
1. Quo changed its depreciation method for its production machinery from the double-declining balance method to the straight-line method effective January 1, 2010.	○	●	○	●	○	●

Change item	Cumulative effect of change in principle in net income of the period of change		Pro forma effects of retroactive application for all prior periods presented currently		Retrospective application to financial statements of all prior periods presented currently	
	Yes	*No*	*Yes*	*No*	*Yes*	*No*
2. Quo appropriately changed the salvage values used in computing depreciation for its office equipment.	○	●	○	●	○	●
3. Quo appropriately changed the specific subsidiaries constituting the group of companies for which consolidated financial statements are presented.	○	●	○	●	●	○

Explanation of solutions

1. (N, N, N) Quo's change in depreciation method is a change in accounting estimate effected by a change in accounting principle. This change would be accounted for on a prospective basis in the current year and future periods.

2. (N, N, N) Quo's change in salvage values is a change in accounting estimate. Quo would not report a cumulative effect, nor pro forma effects, nor would prior period financial statements be restated.

3. (N, N, Y) Quo's change in the specific subsidiaries constituting the group of companies for which consolidated financial statements are presented is a change in reporting entity. The change in reporting entity requires the change to be retrospectively applied to the financial statements of all prior periods presented to show financial information for the new reporting entity.

Situation	Accounting Changes	Calculations	Classification/ Disclosure	Communication	Research

To: CEO, Quo, Inc.
From: CPA Candidate
Re: Changes in accounting methods

During 2010, Quo made changes in accounting for certain items. Although these may appear to be similar in nature, for accounting purposes, the changes are handled differently.

First, Quo changed its depreciation method for its production machinery from the double-declining balance method to the straight-line method. This change in depreciation method is considered a change in accounting principle. The change in principle is considered a change in accounting estimate effected by a change in accounting principle. The change in estimate is accounted for on a prospective basis in the current year and future periods. Financial statements of prior periods should not be restated.

The second change made during 2010 was to change the salvage values used in computing depreciation for office equipment. Quo's change in salvage value is a change in estimate and is accounted for on a prospective basis. Quo would not report a cumulative effect, nor pro forma effects, nor would prior period financial statements be restated.

The third change was a change in the specific subsidiaries constituting the group of companies for which Quo prepares consolidated financial statements. This change in subsidiaries constituting the group of companies for which consolidated financial statements are presented is considered a change in reporting entity. The change in reporting entity requires the change to be retrospectively applied to the financial statements of all prior periods presented to show financial information for the new reporting entity.

If you have any additional questions, please contact me.

Situation	Accounting Changes	Calculations	Classification/ Disclosure	Communication	Research

1. Quo changed its depreciation method for its production machinery from the double-declining balance method to the straight-line method effective January 1, 2010.

FAS 154, Para 20

20. Distinguishing between a change in accounting principle and a change in an accounting estimate is sometimes difficult. In some cases, a change in accounting estimate is effected by a change in accounting principle. One example of this type of change is a change in method of depreciation, amortization, or depletion for long-lived, nonfinancial assets (hereinafter referred to as depreciation method). The new depreciation method is adopted in partial or complete recognition of a change in the estimated future benefits inherent in the asset, the pattern of consumption of those benefits, or the information available to the entity about those benefits. The effect of the change in accounting principle, or the method of ap-

plying it, may be inseparable from the effect of the change in accounting estimate. Changes of that type often are related to the continuing process of obtaining additional information and revising estimates and, therefore, are considered changes in estimates for purposes of applying this Statement.

FAS 154, Para 2(e)

2. The following terms are defined as used in this Statement:

e. Change in accounting estimate effected by a change in accounting principle—a change in accounting estimate that is inseparable from the effect of a related change in accounting principle. An example of a change in estimate effected by a change in principle is a change in the method of depreciation, amortization, or depletion for long-lived, nonfinancial assets.

Codification: 250-10-45-18

2. Quo appropriately changed the salvage values used in computing depreciation for its office equipment.

FAS 154, Para 2(d)

2. The following terms are defined as used in this Statement:

d. Change in accounting estimate—a change that has the effect of adjusting the carrying amount of an existing asset or liability or altering the subsequent accounting for existing or future assets or liabilities. A change in accounting estimate is a necessary consequence of the assessment, in conjunction with the periodic presentation of financial statements, of the present status and expected future benefits and obligations associated with assets and liabilities. Changes in accounting estimates result from new information. Examples of items for which estimates are necessary are uncollectible receivables, inventory obsolescence, service lives and salvage values of depreciable assets, and warranty obligations.

Codification: 250-10-20 Glossary

3. Quo appropriately changed the specific subsidiaries constituting the group of companies for which consolidated financial statements are presented.

Change in the Reporting Entity
FAS 154, Para 2(f)

2. The following terms are defined as used in this Statement:

f. Change in the reporting entity—a change that results in financial statements that, in effect, are those of a different reporting entity. A change in the reporting entity is limited mainly to (1) presenting consolidated or combined financial statements in place of financial statements of individual entities, (2) changing specific subsidiaries that make up the group of entities for which consolidated financial statements are presented, and (3) changing the entities included in combined financial statements. Neither a business combination accounted for by the purchase method nor the consolidation of a variable interest entity pursuant to FASB Interpretation No. 46 (revised December 2004), Consolidation of Variable Interest Entities, is a change in reporting entity.

Codification: 250-10-20 Glossary

Simulation Problem 2

Situation	Accounting Treatment	Accounting Change	Communication	Research

	List A Type of Change (A) (B) (C) (D)	List B Accounting Treatment (X) (Y) (Z)

1. Falk manufactures customized equipment to customer specifications on a contract basis. Falk changed its method of accounting for these long-term contracts from the completed-contract method to the percentage-of-completion method because Falk is now able to make reasonable estimates of future construction costs. 　● ○ ○ ○　　● ○ ○

2.   Based on improved collection procedures, Falk changed the per-   ○ ● ○ ○   ○ ○ ●
centage of credit sales used to determine the allowance for un-
collectible accounts from 2% to 1%.

Explanation of solutions

1. (A, X) Changing from using the completed-contract method to the percentage-of-completion method is a change in accounting principle. Therefore, retrospective application to all periods presented is required.

2. (B, Z) The percentage of net credit sales used in determining the amount to be added to the allowance for uncollectible accounts is an estimate made by management. Changing the percentage is a change in accounting estimate, which is treated prospectively.

Situation	Accounting Treatment	Accounting Change	Communication	Research

Falk Corporation
INCOME STATEMENT

	Adjusted for the year ending 12-31-10	Adjusted for the year ending 12-31-09
Sales	$130,000	$100,000
Cost of goods sold	87,000	68,000
Gross profit	43,000	32,000
Operating expenses	20,000	17,000
Earnings before taxes	23,000	15,000
Income tax expense (40%)	9,200	6,000
Net income	13,800	9,000

	December 31, 2010	December 31, 2009
Inventory	$14,000	$7,000
Income tax liability	10,000	6,000
Retained earnings	16,800	9,000

Explanation of solutions

To calculate cost of goods sold using FIFO method, you must first calculate purchases using the average cost method.
Using T-accounts for analysis, the amounts are as shown below.

Inventory
(Weighted-average method)

1-1-09	-0-	70,000	CGS
Purchases	75,000		
12-31-09	5,000	90,000	CGS
Purchases	94,000		
12-31-10	9,000		

Inventory
(FIFO method)

1-1-09	-0-	68,000	CGS
Purchases	75,000		
12-31-09	7,000	87,000	CGS
Purchases	94,000		
12-31-10	14,000		

Income tax liability for December 31, 2010, is calculated as:

2010 earnings before taxes 23,000 × 40% =	$9,200
2009 adjustment to earnings before taxes 2,000 × 40%	+ 800
Total income tax liability at 12-31-10	$10,000

Retained earnings as of December 31, 2010, is calculated as:

Adjusted NI 2009	$ 9,000
Adjusted NI 2010	13,800
Retained earnings 12/31/10	$22,800

			Communication	
Situation	Accounting Treatment	Accounting Change		Research

To: Controller of Falk Co.
From: CPA Candidate
Re: Changes in accounting principle

The appropriate accounting for the accounting changes made by Falk Co. is described in this memorandum.

A change from the LIFO inventory method to the FIFO inventory method is a change in accounting principle. The company should apply this change retrospectively by adjusting the financial statements of the previous periods presented. Retrospective application requires that the cumulative effect of the change to the new accounting principle is reflected by adjusting the carrying amounts of assets and liabilities as of the beginning of the first period presented. An offsetting adjustment, if any, should be made to the opening balance of retained earnings for that period. Financial statements for each period should also be adjusted to reflect the period-specific effects of applying the new accounting principle. However, only the direct effects of the change should be shown. Notes to the financial statements should disclose the nature of the change, the reason for the change, as well as the effects of the change on income from continuing operations, net income, financial statement line item effects, and any per share amounts for the current period and prior periods.

The company's change to the straight-line depreciation method for all future machinery acquisitions is not a change in accounting principle because the previously recorded assets will continue to be depreciated using the sum-of-the-years' digits method. The nature and justification for the change in depreciation methods should be disclosed in the notes to the 2010 comparative financial statements. The 2009 financial statements are unaffected by the change, but the effects of the change on 2010 income components should be disclosed.

A change from the cash basis of vacation pay expense recognition to the accrual basis is a change from an accounting principle that is not generally accepted to one that is generally accepted. Such a change is considered correction of an error. Falk should restate the 2009 financial statements, including adjustment for the effect on January 1, 2009 retained earnings, for prior-period amounts. Falk Co. should disclose the nature and details of the correction in notes to the 2010 financial statements.

If you have any additional questions, please contact me.

				Research
Situation	Accounting Treatment	Accounting Change	Communication	

FAS 154, Para 2(c)

2.   The following terms are defined as used in this Statement:

c.   Change in accounting principle—a change from one generally accepted accounting principle to another generally accepted accounting principle when there are two or more generally accepted accounting principles that apply or when the accounting principle formerly used is no longer generally accepted. A change in the method of applying an accounting principle also is considered a change in accounting principle.

Codification: 250-10-20 Glossary

MULTIPLE-CHOICE QUESTIONS (1-97)

1. In Baer Food Co.'s 2009 single-step income statement, the section titled "Revenues" consisted of the following:

Net sales revenue		$187,000
Results from discontinued operations:		
Loss from discontinued component Z including loss on disposal of $1,200	$ 16,400	
Less tax benefit	4,000	(12,400)
Interest revenue		10,200
Gain on sale of equipment		4,700
Extraordinary gain		1,500
Total revenues		$191,000

In the revenues section of the 2009 income statement, Baer Food should have reported total revenues of

- a. $216,300
- b. $215,400
- c. $203,700
- d. $201,900

Items 2 and 3 are based on the following:

Vane Co.'s trial balance of income statement accounts for the year ended December 31, 2010, included the following:

	Debit	*Credit*
Sales		$575,000
Cost of sales	$240,000	
Administrative expenses	70,000	
Loss on sale of equipment	10,000	
Sales commissions	50,000	
Interest revenue		25,000
Freight out	15,000	
Loss on early retirement of long-term debt	20,000	
Uncollectible accounts expense	15,000	
Totals	$420,000	$600,000

Other information
Finished goods inventory:

January 1, 2010	$400,000
December 31, 2010	360,000

Vane's income tax rate is 30%. In Vane's 2010 multiple-step income statement,

2. What amount should Vane report as the cost of goods manufactured?

- a. $200,000
- b. $215,000
- c. $280,000
- d. $295,000

3. What amount should Vane report as income after income taxes from continuing operations?

- a. $126,000
- b. $129,500
- c. $140,000
- d. $147,000

4. Brock Corp. reports operating expenses in two categories: (1) selling, and (2) general and administrative. The adjusted trial balance at December 31, 2009, included the following expense and loss accounts:

Accounting and legal fees	$120,000
Advertising	150,000
Freight-out	80,000
Interest	70,000
Loss on sale of long-term investment	30,000
Officers' salaries	225,000
Rent for office space	220,000
Sales salaries and commissions	140,000

One-half of the rented premises is occupied by the sales department.

Brock's total selling expenses for 2009 are

- a. $480,000
- b. $400,000
- c. $370,000
- d. $360,000

5. The following costs were incurred by Griff Co., a manufacturer, during 2009:

Accounting and legal fees	$ 25,000
Freight-in	175,000
Freight-out	160,000
Officers salaries	150,000
Insurance	85,000
Sales representatives salaries	215,000

What amount of these costs should be reported as general and administrative expenses for 2009?

- a. $260,000
- b. $550,000
- c. $635,000
- d. $810,000

6. Which of the following should be included in general and administrative expenses?

	Interest	*Advertising*
a.	Yes	Yes
b.	Yes	No
c.	No	Yes
d.	No	No

7. In Yew Co.'s 2009 annual report, Yew described its social awareness expenditures during the year as follows:

The Company contributed $250,000 in cash to youth and educational programs. The Company also gave $140,000 to health and human service organizations, of which $80,000 was contributed by employees through payroll deductions. In addition, consistent with the Company's commitment to the environment, the Company spent $100,000 to redesign product packaging.

What amount of the above should be included in Yew's income statement as charitable contributions expense?

- a. $310,000
- b. $390,000
- c. $410,000
- d. $490,000

8. During 2009 both Raim Co. and Cane Co. suffered losses due to the flooding of the Mississippi River. Raim is located two miles from the river and sustains flood losses every two to three years. Cane, which has been located fifty miles from the river for the past twenty years, has never before had flood losses. How should the flood losses be reported in each company's 2009 income statement?

	Raim	*Cane*
a.	As a component of income from continuing operations	As an extraordinary item
b.	As a component of income from continuing operations	As a component of income from continuing operations
c.	As an extraordinary item	As a component of income from continuing operations
d.	As an extraordinary item	As an extraordinary item

9. Witt Co. incurred the following infrequent losses during 2009:

- $175,000 from a major strike by employees.
- $150,000 from an earthquake (unusual).
- $125,000 from the abandonment of equipment used in the business.

In Witt's 2009 income statement, the total amount of infrequent losses **not** considered extraordinary should be
  a. $275,000
  b. $300,000
  c. $325,000
  d. $450,000

10. Kent Co. incurred the following infrequent losses during 2009:

- A $300,000 loss was incurred on disposal of one of four dissimilar factories.
- A major currency devaluation caused a $120,000 exchange loss on an amount remitted by a foreign customer.
- Inventory valued at $190,000 was made worthless by a competitor's unexpected product innovation.

In its 2009 income statement, what amount should Kent report as losses that are **not** considered extraordinary?
  a. $610,000
  b. $490,000
  c. $420,000
  d. $310,000

11. Midway Co. had the following transactions during 2009:

- $1,200,000 pretax loss on foreign currency exchange due to a major unexpected devaluation by the foreign government.
- $500,000 pretax loss from discontinued operations of a division.
- $800,000 pretax loss on equipment damaged by a hurricane. This was the first hurricane ever to strike in Midway's area. Midway also received $1,000,000 from its insurance company to replace a building, with a carrying value of $300,000, that had been destroyed by the hurricane.

What amount should Midway report in its 2009 income statement as extraordinary loss before income taxes?
  a. $ 100,000
  b. $1,300,000
  c. $1,800,000
  d. $2,500,000

12. Ocean Corp.'s comprehensive insurance policy allows its assets to be replaced at current value. The policy has a $50,000 deductible clause. One of Ocean's waterfront warehouses was destroyed in a winter storm. Such storms occur approximately every four years. Ocean incurred $20,000 of costs in dismantling the warehouse and plans to replace it. The following data relate to the warehouse:

Current carrying amount	$ 300,000
Replacement cost	1,100,000

What amount of gain should Ocean report as a separate component of income before extraordinary items?
  a. $1,030,000
  b. $ 780,000
  c. $ 730,000
  d. $0

13. Purl Corporation's income statement for the year ended December 31, 2009, shows the following:

Income before income tax and extraordinary item	$900,000
Gain on life insurance coverage—included in the above $900,000 income amount	100,000
Extraordinary item—loss due to earthquake damage	300,000

Purl's tax rate for 2009 is 40%. How much should be reported as the provision for income tax in Purl's 2009 income statement?
  a. $200,000
  b. $240,000
  c. $320,000
  d. $360,000

14. Thorpe Co.'s income statement for the year ended December 31, 2010, reported net income of $74,100. The auditor raised questions about the following amounts that had been included in net income:

Unrealized loss on decline in market value of noncurrent in vestments in stock classified as available-for-sale (net of tax)	$(5,400)
Gain on early retirement of bonds payable (net of $11,000 tax effect)	22,000
Adjustment to profits of prior years for errors in depreciation (net of $3,750 tax effect)	(7,500)
Loss from fire (net of $7,000 tax effect)	(14,000)

The loss from the fire was an infrequent but not unusual occurrence in Thorpe's line of business. Thorpe's December 31, 2010 income statement should report net income of
  a. $65,000
  b. $66,100
  c. $81,600
  d. $87,000

15. On January 1, 2009, Brecon Co. installed cabinets to display its merchandise in customers' stores. Brecon expects to use these cabinets for five years. Brecon's 2009 multi-step income statement should include
  a. One-fifth of the cabinet costs in cost of goods sold.
  b. One-fifth of the cabinet costs in selling, general, and administrative expenses.
  c. All of the cabinet costs in cost of good sold.
  d. All of the cabinet costs in selling, general, and administrative expenses.

16. A material loss should be presented separately as a component of income from continuing operations when it is
  a. An extraordinary item.
  b. A discontinued component of the business.
  c. Unusual in nature and infrequent in occurrence.
  d. Not unusual in nature but infrequent in occurrence.

17. During 2009, Peg Construction Co. recognized substantial gains from

- An increase in value of a foreign customer's remittance caused by a major foreign currency revaluation.
- A court-ordered increase in a completed long-term construction contract's price due to design changes.

Should these gains be included in continuing operations or reported as an extraordinary item in Peg's 2009 income statement?

	Gain from major currency revaluation	*Gain from increase in contract's price*
a.	Continuing operations	Continuing operations
b.	Extraordinary item	Continuing operations
c.	Extraordinary item	Extraordinary item
d.	Continuing operations	Extraordinary item

18. An extraordinary item should be reported separately on the income statement as a component of income

	Net of income taxes	Before discontinued operations of a component of a business
a.	Yes	Yes
b.	Yes	No
c.	No	No
d.	No	Yes

19. In 2009, hail damaged several of Toncan Co.'s vans. Hailstorms had frequently inflicted similar damage to Toncan's vans. Over the years, Toncan had saved money by not buying hail insurance and either paying for repairs, or selling damaged vans and then replacing them. In 2009, the damaged vans were sold for less than their carrying amount. How should the hail damage cost be reported in Toncan's 2009 financial statements?
- a. The actual 2009 hail damage loss as an extraordinary loss, net of income taxes.
- b. The actual 2009 hail damage loss in continuing operations, with **no** separate disclosure.
- c. The expected average hail damage loss in continuing operations, with **no** separate disclosure.
- d. The expected average hail damage loss in continuing operations, with separate disclosure.

20. A transaction that is unusual in nature and infrequent in occurrence should be reported separately as a component of income
- a. After cumulative effect of accounting changes and before discontinued operations.
- b. After cumulative effect of accounting changes and after discontinued operations.
- c. Before cumulative effect of accounting changes and before discontinued operations.
- d. Before cumulative effect of accounting changes and after discontinued operations.

21. In 2009, Teller Co. incurred losses arising from its guilty plea in its first antitrust action, and from a substantial increase in production costs caused when a major supplier's workers went on strike. Which of these losses should be reported as an extraordinary item?

	Antitrust action	Production costs
a.	No	No
b.	No	Yes
c.	Yes	No
d.	Yes	Yes

22. In open market transactions, Gold Corp. simultaneously sold its long-term investment in Iron Corp. bonds and purchased its own outstanding bonds. The broker remitted the net cash from the two transactions. Gold's gain on the purchase of its own bonds exceeded its loss on the sale of the Iron bonds. Gold should report the
- a. Net effect of the two transactions as an extraordinary gain.
- b. Net effect of the two transactions in income before extraordinary items.
- c. Effect of its own bond transaction gain in income before extraordinary items, and report the Iron bond transaction as a loss in income before extraordinary items.
- d. Effect of its own bond transaction as an extraordinary gain, and report the Iron bond transaction loss in income before extraordinary items.

23. Under ASC 220, *Comprehensive Income*, corrections of errors are reported in
- a. Other comprehensive income.
- b. Other income/(expense).
- c. Retained earnings.
- d. Stockholders' equity.

24. Service Corp. incurred costs associated with relocating employees in a restructuring of its operations. How should the company account for these costs?
- a. Measured at fair value and recognized over the next two years.
- b. Measured at fair value and recognized when the liability is incurred.
- c. Recognized when the costs are paid.
- d. Measured at fair value and treated as a prior period adjustment.

25. On January 1, 2009, Deer Corp. met the criteria for discontinuance of a business component. For the period January 1 through October 15, 2009, the component had revenues of $500,000 and expenses of $800,000. The assets of the component were sold on October 15, 2009, at a loss for which no tax benefit is available. In its income statement for the year ended December 31, 2009, how should Deer report the component's operations from January 1 to October 15, 2009?
- a. $500,000 and $800,000 should be included with revenues and expenses, respectively, as part of continuing operations.
- b. $300,000 should be reported as part of the loss on operations and disposal of a component.
- c. $300,000 should be reported as an extraordinary loss.
- d. $500,000 should be reported as revenues from operations of a discontinued component.

26. Which of the following criteria is not required for a component's results to be classified as discontinued operations?
- a. Management must have entered into a sales agreement.
- b. The component is available for immediate sale.
- c. The operations and cash flows of the component will be eliminated from the operations of the entity as a result of the disposal.
- d. The entity will not have any significant continuing involvement in the operations of the component after disposal.

27. On November 1, 2009, management of Herron Corporation committed to a plan to dispose of Timms Company, a major subsidiary. The disposal meets the requirements for classification as discontinued operations. The carrying value of Timms Company was $8,000,000 and management estimated the fair value less costs to sell to be $6,500,000. For 2009, Timms Company had a loss of $2,000,000. How much should Herron Corporation present as loss from discontinued operations before the effect of taxes in its income statement for 2009?
- a. $0
- b. $1,500,000
- c. $2,000,000
- d. $3,500,000

28. On December 1, 2009, Greer Co. committed to a plan to dispose of its Hart business component's assets. The disposal meets the requirements to be classified as discontinued operations. On that date, Greer estimated that the loss from the disposition of the assets would be $700,000 and Hart's 2009 operating losses were $200,000. Disregarding income taxes, what net gain (loss) should be reported for discontinued operations in Greer's 2009 income statement?
   a. $0
   b. $(200,000)
   c. $(700,000
   d. $(900,000)

29. A component of Ace, Inc. was discontinued during 2010. Ace's loss on disposal should
   a. Exclude the associated employee relocation costs.
   b. Exclude operating losses for the period.
   c. Include associated employee termination costs.
   d. Exclude associated lease cancellation costs.

30. When a component of a business has been discontinued during the year, this component's operating losses of the current period should be included in the
   a. Income statement as part of revenues and expenses.
   b. Income statement as part of the loss on disposal of the discontinued component.
   c. Income statement as part of the income (loss) from continuing operations.
   d. Retained earnings statement as a direct decrease in retained earnings.

31. When a component of a business has been discontinued during the year, the loss on disposal should
   a. Include operating losses of the current period.
   b. Exclude operating losses during the period.
   c. Be an extraordinary item.
   d. Be an operating item.

32. On January 1, 2010, Shine Co. agreed to sell a business component on March 1, 2010. The gain on the disposal should be
   a. Presented as an extraordinary gain.
   b. Presented as an adjustment to retained earnings.
   c. Netted with the loss from operations of the component as a part of discontinued operations.
   d. None of the above.

33. What is the purpose of reporting comprehensive income?
   a. To report changes in equity due to transactions with owners.
   b. To report a measure of overall enterprise performance.
   c. To replace net income with a better measure.
   d. To combine income from continuing operations with income from discontinued operations and extraordinary items.

34. During 2009, the "other revenues and gains" section of Totman Company's Statement of Earnings and Comprehensive Income contains $5,000 in interest revenue, $15,000 equity in Harpo Co. earnings, and $25,000 gain on sale of available-for-sale securities. Assuming the sale of the securities increased the current portion of income tax expense by $10,000, determine the amount of Totman's reclassification adjustment to other comprehensive income.

   a. $ 5,000
   b. $ 2,500
   c. $35,000
   d. $15,000

35. Which of the following is **not** an acceptable option of reporting other comprehensive income and its components?
   a. In a separate statement of comprehensive income.
   b. In a statement of earnings and comprehensive income.
   c. In the footnotes.
   d. In a statement of changes in stockholders' equity.

36. Accumulated other comprehensive income should be reported on the balance sheet as a component of

	Retained earnings	Additional paid-in capital
a.	No	Yes
b.	Yes	Yes
c.	Yes	No
d.	No	No

37. Which of the following changes during a period is not a component of other comprehensive income?
   a. Unrealized gains or losses as a result of a debt security being transferred from held-to-maturity to available-for-sale.
   b. Stock dividends issued to shareholders.
   c. Foreign currency translation adjustments.
   d. Minimum pension liability adjustments.

38. A company buys ten shares of securities at $2,000 each on December 31, 2007. The securities are classified as available for sale. The company does not elect to use the fair value option for reporting its available-for-sale securities. The fair value of the securities increases to $2,500 on December 31, 2008, and to $2,750 on December 31, 2009. On December 31, 2009, the company sells the securities. Assume no dividends are paid and that the company has a tax rate of 30%. What is the amount of the reclassification adjustment for other comprehensive income on December 31, 2009?
   a. $ 7,500
   b. $ (7,500)
   c. $ 5,250
   d. $ (5,250)

39. A company buys ten shares of securities at $1,000 each on January 15, 2009. The securities are classified as available-for-sale. The fair value of the securities increases to $1,250 per share as of December 31, 2009. The company does not elect to use the fair value option for reporting available-for-sale securities. Assume no dividends are paid and that the company has a 30% tax rate. What is the amount of the holding gain arising during the period that is classified in other comprehensive income for the period ending December 31, 2009?
   a. 0
   b. $7,500
   c. $2,500
   d. $1,750

40. Searles does not elect the fair value option for recording financial assets and liabilities. What amount of comprehensive income should Searles Corporation report on its statement of income and comprehensive income given the following net of tax figures that represent changes during a period?

Pension liability adjustment recognized in OCI	$ (3,000)
Unrealized gain on available-for-sale securities	15,000
Reclassification adjustment, for securities gain	
included in net income	(2,500)
Stock warrants outstanding	4,000
Net income	77,000

    a. $86,500
    b. $89,000
    c. $89,500
    d. $90,500

41. If ($2,450) net of tax is the reclassification adjustment included in other comprehensive income in the year the securities are sold, what is the gain (loss) that is included in income from continuing operations before income taxes? Assume a 30% tax rate.
    a. $(2,450)
    b. $(3,500)
    c. $ 2,450
    d. $ 3,500

42. Which of the following changes during a period is **not** a component of other comprehensive income?
    a. Pension liability adjustment for funded status of plan.
    b. Treasury stock, at cost.
    c. Foreign currency translation adjustment.
    d. Reclassification adjustment, for securities gain included in net income.

43. Which of the following is true?
    a. Separate EPS amounts must be presented for both other comprehensive income and comprehensive income.
    b. Separate EPS amounts must be presented for other comprehensive income but not for comprehensive income.
    c. Separate EPS amounts must be presented for comprehensive income but not for other comprehensive income.
    d. Separate EPS amounts are not required to be presented for either other comprehensive income or comprehensive income.

44. Which of the following options for displaying comprehensive income is(are) preferred by FASB?

  I. A continuation from net income at the bottom of the income statement.
  II. A separate statement that begins with net income.
  III. In the statement of changes in stockholders' equity.

    a. I.
    b. II.
    c. II and III.
    d. I and II.

45. Assume a company does not elect the fair value option for reporting financial assets and liabilities. Which of the following is not classified as other comprehensive income?
    a. An adjustment to pension liability to record the funded status of the plan.
    b. Subsequent decreases of the fair value of available-for-sale securities that have been previously written down as impaired.
    c. Decreases in the fair value of held-to-maturity securities.
    d. None of the above.

46. When a full set of general-purpose financial statements are presented, comprehensive income and its components should
    a. Appear as a part of discontinued operations, extraordinary items, and cumulative effect of a change in accounting principle.
    b. Be reported net of related income tax effect, in total and individually.
    c. Appear in a supplemental schedule in the notes to the financial statements.
    d. Be displayed in a financial statement that has the same prominence as other financial statements.

Items 47 through 49 are based on the following:

The following trial balance of Mint Corp. at December 31, 2009, has been adjusted except for income tax expense.

	Dr.	Cr.
Cash	$ 600,000	
Accounts receivable, net	3,500,000	
Cost in excess of billings on long-term contracts	1,600,000	
Billings in excess of costs on long-term contracts		$ 700,000
Prepaid taxes	450,000	
Property, plant, and equipment, net	1,480,000	
Note payable—noncurrent		1,620,000
Common stock		750,000
Additional paid-in capital		2,000,000
Retained earnings—unappropriated		900,000
Retained earnings—restricted for note payable		160,000
Earnings from long-term contracts		6,680,000
Costs and expenses	5,180,000	
	$12,810,000	$12,810,000

Other financial data for the year ended December 31, 2009, are

- Mint uses the percentage-of-completion method to account for long-term construction contracts for financial statement and income tax purposes. All receivables on these contracts are considered to be collectible within twelve months.
- During 2009, estimated tax payments of $450,000 were charged to prepaid taxes. Mint has not recorded income tax expense. There were no temporary or permanent differences, and Mint's tax rate is 30%.

In Mint's December 31, 2009 balance sheet, what amount should be reported as

47. Total retained earnings?
    a. $1,950,000
    b. $2,110,000
    c. $2,400,000
    d. $2,560,000

48. Total noncurrent liabilities?
    a. $1,620,000
    b. $1,780,000
    c. $2,320,000
    d. $2,480,000

49. Total current assets?
    a. $5,000,000
    b. $5,450,000
    c. $5,700,000
    d. $6,150,000

50. Mirr, Inc. was incorporated on January 1, 2009, with proceeds from the issuance of $750,000 in stock and borrowed funds of $110,000. During the first year of operations, revenues from sales and consulting amounted to $82,000, and operating costs and expenses totaled $64,000. On December 15, Mirr declared a $3,000 cash dividend, payable to stockholders on January 15, 2010. No additional activities affected owners' equity in 2009. Mirr's liabilities increased to $120,000 by December 31, 2009. On Mirr's December 31, 2009 balance sheet, total assets should be reported at

- a. $885,000
- b. $882,000
- c. $878,000
- d. $875,000

51. The following changes in Vel Corp.'s account balances occurred during 2009:

	Increase
Assets	$89,000
Liabilities	27,000
Capital stock	60,000
Additional paid-in capital	6,000

Except for a $13,000 dividend payment and the year's earnings, there were no changes in retained earnings for 2009. What was Vel's net income for 2009?

- a. $ 4,000
- b. $ 9,000
- c. $13,000
- d. $17,000

52. When preparing a draft of its 2009 balance sheet, Mont, Inc. reported net assets totaling $875,000. Included in the asset section of the balance sheet were the following:

Treasury stock of Mont, Inc. at cost, which approximates market value on December 31	$24,000
Idle machinery	11,200
Cash surrender value of life insurance on corporate executives	13,700
Allowance for decline in market value of noncurrent equity investments	8,400

At what amount should Mont's net assets be reported in the December 31, 2009 balance sheet?

- a. $851,000
- b. $850,100
- c. $842,600
- d. $834,500

53. In analyzing a company's financial statements, which financial statement would a potential investor primarily use to assess the company's liquidity and financial flexibility?

- a. Balance sheet.
- b. Income statement.
- c. Statement of retained earnings.
- d. Statement of cash flows.

54. During 2009, Jones Company engaged in the following transactions:

Salary expense to key employees who are also principal owners	$100,000
Sales to affiliated enterprises	250,000

Which of the two transactions would be disclosed as related-party transactions in Jones' 2009 financial statements?

- a. Neither transaction.
- b. The $100,000 transaction only.
- c. The $250,000 transaction only.
- d. Both transactions.

55. Dean Co. acquired 100% of Morey Corp. prior to 2009. During 2009, the individual companies included in their financial statements the following:

	Dean	Morey
Officers' salaries	$ 75,000	$50,000
Officers' expenses	20,000	10,000
Loans to officers	125,000	50,000
Intercompany sales	150,000	--

What amount should be reported as related-party disclosures in the notes to Dean's 2009 consolidated financial statements?

- a. $150,000
- b. $155,000
- c. $175,000
- d. $330,000

56. Which type of material related-party transaction requires disclosure?

- a. Only those not reported in the body of the financial statements.
- b. Only those that receive accounting recognition.
- c. Those that contain possible illegal acts.
- d. All those other than compensation arrangements, expense allowances, and other similar items in the ordinary course of business.

57. Financial statements shall include disclosures of material transactions between related parties except

- a. Nonmonetary exchanges by affiliates.
- b. Sales of inventory by a subsidiary to its parent.
- c. Expense allowance for executives which exceed normal business practice.
- d. A company's agreement to act as surety for a loan to its chief executive officer.

58. Dex Co. has entered into a joint venture with an affiliate to secure access to additional inventory. Under the joint venture agreement, Dex will purchase the output of the venture at prices negotiated on an arm's-length basis. Which of the following is(are) required to be disclosed about the related-party transaction?

I. The amount due to the affiliate at the balance sheet date.
II. The dollar amount of the purchases during the year.

- a. I only.
- b. II only.
- c. Both I and II.
- d. Neither I nor II.

59. What is the purpose of information presented in notes to the financial statements?

- a. To provide disclosures required by generally accepted accounting principles.
- b. To correct improper presentation in the financial statements.
- c. To provide recognition of amounts **not** included in the totals of the financial statements.
- d. To present management's responses to auditor comments.

60. Which of the following information should be included in Melay, Inc.'s 2009 summary of significant accounting policies?

- a. Property, plant, and equipment is recorded at cost with depreciation computed principally by the straight-line method.
- b. During 2009, the Delay component was sold.

c. Business component 2009 sales are Alay $1M, Belay $2M, and Celay $3M.

d. Future common share dividends are expected to approximate 60% of earnings.

61. Which of the following information should be disclosed in the summary of significant accounting policies?

a. Refinancing of debt subsequent to the balance sheet date.

b. Guarantees of indebtedness of others.

c. Criteria for determining which investments are treated as cash equivalents.

d. Adequacy of pension plan assets relative to vested benefits.

62. Swift Corp. prepares its financial statements for its fiscal year ending December 31, 2009. Swift estimates that its product warranty liability is $28,000 at December 31, 2009. On February 12, 2010, before the financial statements were issued, Swift received information about a product defect that will require a recall of all units sold in 2009. It is expected the product recall will cost an additional $40,000 in warranty repairs. What should Swift present in its December 31, 2009 financial statements?

a. A footnote disclosure explaining the product recall.

b. A footnote disclosure listing the estimated amount of $40,000 in warranty repairs and an explanation of the recall.

c. An estimated warranty liability of $68,000.

d. No disclosure is necessary.

63. Colter Corp. has a fiscal year-end of December 31, 2009. On that date, Colter reported total assets of $600,000. On March 1, 2010, before the 2009 financial statements were issued, Colter lost $250,000 of inventory due to a fire. The inventory was a total loss and was uninsured. How should Colter present this information in its December 31, 2009 financial statements?

a. Colter should disclost the loss in a footnote to its 2009 financial statements.

b. Colter should report an extraordinary loss in its 2009 income statement.

c. Colter should report an allowance for lost inventory in its 2009 balance sheet.

d. Colter should not report the loss.

64. Which of the following is a true statement regarding disclosures for subsequent events?

a. Recognize a loss for all recognized and unrecognized subsequent events in the current year financial statements.

b. Recognize a gain or loss for any recognized subsequent event in the current year financial statements.

c. Recognize a loss for a recognized subsequent event in the financial statements in the year when the subsequent event occurs.

d. Recognize a loss for a recognized subsequent event in the current year financial statements.

65. The fair value of an asset should be based upon

a. The replacement cost of an asset.

b. The price that would be received to sell the asset at the measurement date.

c. The original cost of the asset plus an adjustment for obsolescence.

d. The price that would be paid to acquire the asset.

66. Which of the following describes a principal market for establishing fair value of an asset?

a. The market that has the greatest volume and level of activity for the asset.

b. Any broker or dealer market that buys or sells the asset.

c. The most observable market in which the price of the asset is minimized.

d. The market in which the amount received would be maximized.

67. Which of the following is true for valuing an asset to fair value?

a. The price of the asset should be adjusted for transaction costs.

b. The fair value of the asset should be adjusted for costs to sell.

c. The fair value price is based upon an entry price to purchase the asset.

d. The price should be adjusted for transportation costs to transport the asset to its principal market.

68. Which of the following would meet the qualifications as market participants in determining fair value?

a. A liquidation market in which sellers are compelled to sell.

b. A subsidiary of the reporting unit interested in purchasing assets similar to those being valued.

c. An independent entity that is knowledgeable about the asset.

d. A broker or dealer that wishes to establish new market for the asset.

69. Which of the following is an assumption used in fair value measurements?

a. The asset must be in-use.

b. The asset must be considered in-exchange.

c. The most conservative estimate must be used.

d. The asset is in its highest and best use.

70. The fair value of an asset at initial recognition is

a. The price paid to acquire the asset.

b. The price paid to acquire the asset less transaction costs.

c. The price paid to transfer or sell the asset.

d. The book value of the asset acquired.

71. Which of the following is not a valuation technique used in fair value estimates?

a. Income approach.

b. Residual value approach.

c. Market approach.

d. Cost approach.

72. Valuation techniques for fair value that include the Black-Scholes-Merton formula, a binomial model, or discounted cash flows are examples of which valuation technique?

a. Income approach.

b. Market approach.

c. Cost approach.

d. Exit value approach.

73. The market approach valuation technique for measuring fair value requires which of the following?

a. Present value of future cash flows.

b. Prices and other relevant information of transactions from identical or comparable assets.

c. The price to replace the service capacity of the asset.
d. The weighted-average of the present value of future cash flows.

74. A change in valuation techniques used to measure fair value should be reported as
a. A change in accounting principle with retrospective restatement.
b. An error correction with restatement of the financial statements of previous periods.
c. A change in accounting estimate reported on a prospective basis.
d. An extraordinary item on the current year's income statement.

75. When measuring fair value, which level has the highest priority for valuation inputs?
a. Level 1.
b. Level 2.
c. Level 3.
d. Level 4.

76. Which of the following are observable inputs used for fair value measurements?
I. Bank prime rate.
II. Default rates on loans.
III. Financial forecasts.

a. I only.
b. I and II only.
c. I and III only.
d. I, II and III.

77. A company that wishes to disclose information about the effect of changing prices should report this information in
a. The body of the financial statements.
b. The notes to the financial statements.
c. Supplementary information to the financial statements.
d. Management's report to shareholders.

78. Lewis Company was formed on January 1, 2008. Selected balances from the historical cost balance sheet at December 31, 2009, were as follows:

Land (purchased in 2008) $120,000
Investment in nonconvertible bonds (purchased in 2008, and expected to be held to maturity) 60,000
Long-term debt 80,000

The average Consumer Price Index was 100 for 2008, and 110 for 2009. In a supplementary constant dollar balance sheet (adjusted for changing prices) at December 31, 2009, these selected account balances should be shown at

	Land	Investment	Long-term debt
a.	$120,000	$60,000	$88,000
b.	$120,000	$66,000	$88,000
c.	$132,000	$60,000	$80,000
d.	$132,000	$66,000	$80,000

79. The following items were among those that appeared on Rubi Co.'s books at the end of 2009:

Merchandise inventory $600,000
Loans to employees 20,000

What amount should Rubi classify as monetary assets in preparing constant dollar financial statements?

a. $0
b. $ 20,000
c. $600,000
d. $620,000

80. In its financial statements, Hila Co. discloses supplemental information on the effects of changing prices. Hila computed the increase in current cost of inventory as follows:

Increase in current cost (nominal dollars) $15,000
Increase in current cost (constant dollars) $12,000

What amount should Hila disclose as the inflation component of the increase in current cost of inventories?
a. $ 3,000
b. $12,000
c. $15,000
d. $27,000

81. When computing purchasing power gain or loss on net monetary items, which of the following accounts is classified as nonmonetary?
a. Advances to unconsolidated subsidiaries.
b. Allowance for uncollectible accounts.
c. Unamortized premium on bonds payable.
d. Accumulated depreciation of equipment.

82. During a period of inflation in which a liability account balance remains constant, which of the following occurs?
a. A purchasing power gain, if the item is a nonmonetary liability.
b. A purchasing power gain, if the item is a monetary liability.
c. A purchasing power loss, if the item is a nonmonetary liability.
d. A purchasing power loss, if the item is a monetary liability.

83. The following information pertains to each unit of merchandise purchased for resale by Vend Co.:

March 1, 2009
Purchase price $ 8
Selling price $12
Price level index 110

December 31, 2009
Replacement cost $10
Selling price $15
Price level index 121

Under current cost accounting, what is the amount of Vend's holding gain on each unit of this merchandise?
a. $0
b. $0.80
c. $1.20
d. $2.00

84. Kerr Company purchased a machine for $115,000 on January 1, 2009, the company's first day of operations. At the end of the year, the current cost of the machine was $125,000. The machine has no salvage value, a five-year life, and is depreciated by the straight-line method. For the year ended December 31, 2009, the amount of the current cost depreciation expense which would appear in supplementary current cost financial statements is
a. $14,000
b. $23,000
c. $24,000
d. $25,000

85. At December 31, 2009, Jannis Corp. owned two assets as follows:

	Equipment	Inventory
Current cost	$100,000	$80,000
Recoverable amount	$ 95,000	$90,000

Jannis voluntarily disclosed supplementary information about current cost at December 31, 2009. In such a disclosure, at what amount would Jannis report total assets?

- a. $175,000
- b. $180,000
- c. $185,000
- d. $190,000

86. Could current cost financial statements report holding gains for goods sold during the period and holding gains on inventory at the end of the period?

	Goods sold	Inventory
a.	Yes	Yes
b.	Yes	No
c.	No	Yes
d.	No	No

87. Manhof Co. prepares supplementary reports on income from continuing operations on a current cost basis. How should Manhof compute cost of goods sold on a current cost basis?

- a. Number of units sold times average current cost of units during the year.
- b. Number of units sold times current cost of units at year-end.
- c. Number of units sold times current cost of units at the beginning of the year.
- d. Beginning inventory at current cost plus cost of goods purchased less ending inventory at current cost.

88. Which of the following are examples of concentrations that create vulnerabilities and therefore would require disclosure of risks and uncertainties?

I. Market in which an entity conducts its operations.
II. Available sources of supply of materials used in operations of an entity.
III. Volume of business transacted with a certain contributor.

- a. I and II.
- b. II and III.
- c. I and III.
- d. I, II, and III.

89. Which of the following is required to be disclosed regarding the risks and uncertainties that exist?

- a. Factors causing an estimate to be sensitive.
- b. The potential impact of estimates about values of assets and liabilities when it is reasonably possible that the estimate will change in the near future.
- c. The potential impact of estimates about values of assets and liabilities when it is remotely possible that the estimate will change in the near future.
- d. A description of the operations both within and outside of the home country.

90. Which of the following accounting bases may be used to prepare financial statements in conformity with a comprehensive basis of accounting other than generally accepted accounting principles?

I. Basis of accounting used by an entity to file its income tax return.
II. Cash receipts and disbursements basis of accounting.

- a. I only.
- b. II only.
- c. Both I and II.
- d. Neither I nor II.

91. Income tax basis financial statements differ from those prepared under GAAP in that income tax basis financial statements

- a. Do **not** include nontaxable revenues and nondeductible expenses in determining income.
- b. Include detailed information about current and deferred income tax liabilities.
- c. Contain **no** disclosures about capital and operating lease transactions.
- d. Recognize certain revenues and expenses in different reporting periods.

92. In financial statements prepared on the income tax basis, how should the nondeductible portion of expenses such as meals and entertainment be reported?

- a. Included in the expense category in the determination of income.
- b. Included in a separate category in the determination of income.
- c. Excluded from the determination of income but included in the determination of retained earnings.
- d. Excluded from the financial statements.

93. If a company uses the modified cash basis of accounting, the modifications from the pure cash basis should have substantial support. In this context substantial support requires

- a. The financial statements have only minor modifications from GAAP.
- b. The modifications must be the same as those required by tax law.
- c. The modifications must be the same as GAAP and not illogical.
- d. No modifications are allowed.

94. Which of the following is false?

- a. Prospective financial information may be prepared for general or limited users.
- b. The responsible party is the only limited user.
- c. The financial projection may contain assumptions not necessarily expected to occur.
- d. The financial projection may be expressed as a range of dollars.

95. Prospective financial information is defined as

- a. Any financial information about the past, present, or future.
- b. Any financial information about the present or future.
- c. Any financial information about the future related to the day-to-day operations.
- d. Any financial information about the future.

96. To achieve a reasonably objective basis, financial forecasts and projections should be prepared

I. In accordance with GAAP
II. Using information that is in accordance with the plans of the entity.
III. With due professional care.

a. I and III.
b. II and III.
c. I, II, and III.
d. I and II.

97. Which of the following disclosures should prospective
financial statements include?

	Summary of significant accounting policies	*Summary of significant assumptions*
a.	Yes	Yes
b.	Yes	No
c.	No	Yes
d.	No	No

SIMULATION PROBLEMS

Simulation Problem 1   (50 to 60 minutes)

Situation					
	Concepts	Financial Statement Classification	Balance Sheet	Communication	Research

You have been asked to assist the chief accountant of the Stephen King Corporation in the preparation of a balance sheet. Presented below is the balance sheet of Stephen King Corporation for the current year, 2010.

Stephen King Corporation
BALANCE SHEET
December 31, 2010

Current assets		$ 435,000
Investments		640,000
Property, plant, and equipment		1,720,000
Intangible assets		305,000
		$3,100,000
Current liabilities	$ 330,000	
Long-term liabilities	1,000,000	
Stockholders' equity	1,770,000	
	$3,100,000	

Consider the following information:

1. The current assets section includes: cash $100,000, accounts receivable $170,000 less $10,000 for allowance for doubtful accounts, inventories $180,000, and unearned revenue $5,000. The cash balance is composed of $114,000, less a bank overdraft of $14,000. Inventories are stated on the lower of FIFO cost or market.
2. The investments section includes: the cash surrender value of a life insurance contract $40,000; investment in common stock, short-term (trading) $80,000 and long-term (available-for-sale) $270,000; and bond sinking fund $250,000. The cost and fair value of investments in common stock are the same.
3. Property, plant, and equipment includes: buildings $1,040,000 less accumulated depreciation $360,000; equipment $450,000 less accumulated depreciation $180,000; land $500,000; and land held for future use $270,000.
4. Intangible assets include: a franchise $165,000; goodwill $100,000; and discount on bonds payable $40,000.
5. Current liabilities include: accounts payable $90,000; notes payable—short term $80,000 and long-term $120,000; and taxes payable $40,000.
6. Long-term liabilities are compose solely of 10% bonds payable due 2018.
7. Stockholders' equity has: preferred stock, no par value, authorized 200,000 shares, issued 70,000 shares for $450,000; and common stock, $1.00 par value, authorized 400,000 shares, issued 100,000 shares at an average price of $10. In addition, the corporation has retained earnings of $320,000.
8. The company's management does not elect to use the fair value option for any of its financial assets or liabilities.

	Concepts				
Situation		Financial Statement Classification	Balance Sheet	Communication	Research

Identify whether each of the following statements is True or False.

		True	*False*
1.	The gain or loss from discontinued operations is placed in a separate category under other income or loss.	○	○
2.	The gain or loss from infrequent or unusual items is given extraordinary treatment and disclosed on the income statement after discontinued operations.	○	○
3.	Exit and disposal activities are classified as discontinued operations.	○	○
4.	A component of a company can be classified as discontinued in the first period that it meets the criteria as being held for sale.	○	○
5.	A correction of an error is included in the cumulative effect of change in accounting principle on the income statement.	○	○
6.	Other comprehensive income may be presented at the bottom of the income statement.	○	○
7.	Separate earnings per share amounts must be presented for both other comprehensive income and comprehensive income.	○	○
8.	Prospective financial information includes information on the purpose of the statements, assumptions, and significant accounting policies.	○	○

Situation	Concepts	Financial Statement Classification		Balance Sheet	Communication	Research

The outline presented below represents the various classifications suggested by the chief accountant for the balance sheet.

Assets	*Liabilities*	*Owner's equity*	*Other*
A. Current	G. Current	J. Preferred stock	N. Items excluded from the
B. Investments	H. Long-term	K. Common stock	balance sheet.
C. Plant and equipment	I. Other liabilities	L. Paid-in capital excess of par	X. Contra valuation account
D. Intangibles		M. Retained earnings	
E. Deferred charges			
F. Other assets			

Items 1 through 18 represent accounts of the Stephen King Corporation. Determine how each account would be classified from the list above. If the account is a contra or valuation account, mark "X" before the letter. For example: "Allowance for Doubtful Accounts" would be "X–A." An answer may be selected once, more than once, or not at all.

Items to be answered

		Assets (A-F)	*Liabilities* (G, H, I)	*Owner's equity* (J, K, L, M)	*Other* (N or X)

1. Dividend payable (on King's preferred stock).

2. Plant construction in progress by the company.

3. Factory building (retired from use and held for sale).

4. Land (held for possible future building site).

5. Merchandise inventory (held by Stephen King Corporation on consignment).

6. Stock dividend distributable (in common stock to common stockholders and to be issued at par).

7. Office supplies inventory.

8. Sinking fund cash (First National Bank, Trustee).

9. Installment sales accounts receivable (average collection period eighteen months). All sales are installment sales.

10. Temporary decline in inventory value.

11. Advances to officers (indefinite repayment date).

12. Estimated warranty costs. The warranty costs are for a one-year warranty on parts and labor.

13. Inventory of small tools used in the business.

14. Treasury stock under par value method.

15. Common stock subscribed (Stephen King Corporation's stock).

16. Convertible bonds.

17. Securities held as collateral.

18. Bank overdraft (only account with bank).

Situation	Concepts	Financial Statement Classification	Balance Sheet	Communication	Research

Complete the corrected balance sheet. To make it a more realistic exam experience use Excel.

	A	B	C	D	E
1	**Stephen King Corporation**				
2	**Balance Sheet**				
3	**December 31, 2010**				
4					
5	Current assets				
6	Cash				
7	Trading securities				
8	Accounts receivable (net of $xxx allowance for doubtful accounts)				
9	Inventories (lower of FIFO cost or market)				

	A	B	C	D	E
10					
11	Total current assets				
12					
13	Investments				
14	Available-for-sale securities				
15	Bond sinking fund				
16	Land held for future use				
17	Cash surrender value of life insurance contract				
18					
19	Total investments				
20					
21	Property, plant, and equipment				
22	Land				
23	Buildings (net of accumulated depreciation of $xxx)				
24	Equipment (net of accumulated depreciation of $xxx)				
25					
26	Total property, plant, and equipment				
27					
28	Intangible assets				
29	Franchise				
30	Goodwill				
31					
32	Total intangible assets				
33	Total assets				
34					
35	Current liabilities:				
36	Accounts payable				
37	Notes payable				
38	Taxes payable				
39	Bank overdraft				
40	Unearned revenue				
41					
42	Total current liabilities				
43					
44	Long-term liabilities				
45	Notes payable				
46	Bonds payable, 10% due 2018 (less discount of $xxx)				
47					
48	Total long-term liabilities				
49	Total liabilities				
50					
51	Stockholders' equity				
52	Paid-in capital				
53	Preferred stock, no par, authorized xxx shares, issued xxx shares				
54	Common stock, $1.00 par value, authorized xxx shares, issued xxx shares				
55	Paid-in capital in excess of par value common				
56					
57	Total paid-in capital				
58					
59	Retained earnings				
60					
61	Total stockholders' equity				
62	Total liabilities and stockholders' equity				

				Communication		
Situation	Concepts	Financial Statement Classification	Balance Sheet		Research

Entities are required to disclose comprehensive income. Write a memo to the CEO of Stephen King Corporation explaining the following issues related to comprehensive income.

1. Define comprehensive income, **other** comprehensive income, and **accumulated** other comprehensive income. You do not need to list specific items of other comprehensive income.
2. How shall comprehensive income be reported in the financial statements?

3. Explain the purpose of reclassification adjustments in measuring comprehensive income. How should they be reported?

4. What earnings per share disclosures are required for other comprehensive income items and comprehensive income for public companies?

REMINDER: Your response will be graded for both technical content and writing skills. Technical content will be evaluated for information that is helpful to the intended reader and clearly relevant to the issue. Writing skills will be evaluated for development, organization, and the appropriate expression of ideas in professional correspondence. Use a standard business memo or letter format with a clear beginning, middle, and end. Do not convey information in the form of a table, bullet point list, or other abbreviated presentation.

To: CEO, Stephen King Corporation
From: CPA Candidate
Re: Comprehensive income

Situation	Concepts	Financial Statement Classification	Balance Sheet	Communication	**Research**

Research the professional standards for a description of how items in other comprehensive income are classified. Select the appropriate paragraph(s).

Simulation Problem 2   (50 to 60 minutes)

Situation		Journal Entries	Calculations	Classification/Disclosures	Research	Communication

Hillside had the following selected account balances as of December 31, 2009.

Accounts receivable	$250,000
Notes receivable	75,000
Prepaid rent	168,000
Supplies	60,000
Inventory	420,000
Equipment (historical cost)	640,000
Accounts payable	176,000
Salaries payable	15,000
Accumulated depreciation	174,000

The following information was received from Hillside's accountant. Adjusting entries have not yet been made.

1. It is estimated that $16,000 of accounts will not be collectible. A provision for uncollectible accounts has never been made by Hillside.
2. Supplies remaining at the end of the year were $37,000.
3. Equipment is depreciated over 20 years with a $60,000 salvage value.
4. Accrued salaries at 12/31/09 were $37,500.
5. The note receivable was signed by the customer on November 1, 2009. It is a 6-month note with an interest rate of 12%, with the principle and interest paid at maturity.
6. Rent was paid on August 1, 2009, for 24 months and recorded in a prepaid rent account.
7. Hillside does not elect to use the fair value option for any of its financial assets or liabilities.

Situation	Journal Entries		Calculations	Classification/Disclosures	Research	Communication

Prepare the adjusting journal entries necessary for each item. If no entry is necessary, write "no entry."

		Calculations			
Situation	Journal Entries		Classification/Disclosures	Research	Communication

Indicate the adjusted balances in the selected accounts after adjusting entries were made on December 31, 2009.

Accounts receivable (net)	
Notes receivable	
Prepaid rent	
Supplies	
Inventory	
Equipment	
Accounts payable	
Salaries payable	
Accumulated depreciation	

			Classification/Disclosures		
Situation	Journal Entries	Calculations		Research	Communication

Hillside Co. is in the process of preparing its financial statements for the year ended December 31, 2010.

Items 1 through 6 represent various transactions that occurred during 2010. The following **two** responses are required for each item:

Compute the amount of gain, loss, or adjustment to be reported in Hillside's 2010 financial statements. Disregard income taxes. On the CPA exam, a list of numeric answer choices would be provided to select from.

Select from the list below the financial statement category in which the gain, loss, or adjustment should be presented. A category may be used once, more than once, or not at all.

Financial Statement Categories

A. Income from continuing operations.
B. Extraordinary item.
C. Cumulative effect of change in accounting principle.
D. Prior period adjustment to beginning retained earnings.
E. Separate component of other comprehensive income.

	Amount	(A) (B) (C) (D) (E)

1. On June 30, 2010, after paying the semiannual interest due and recording amortization of bond discount, Hillside redeemed its fifteen-year, 8% $1,000,000 par bonds at 102. The bonds, which had a carrying amount of $940,000 on January 1, 2010, had originally been issued to yield 10%. Hillside uses the effective interest method of amortization, and had paid interest and recorded amortization on June 30. Compute the amount of gain or loss on redemption of the bonds and select the proper financial statement category.   _____   O O O O O

2. As of January 1, 2010, Hillside decided to change the method of computing depreciation on its sole piece of equipment from the sum-of-the-years' digits method to the straight-line method. The equipment, acquired in January 2007 for $520,000, had an estimated life of five years and a salvage value of $20,000. Compute the amount of the depreciation expense for 2010 and select the proper financial statement category.   _____   O O O O O

3. In October 2010, Hillside paid $375,000 to a former employee to settle a lawsuit out of court. The lawsuit had been filed in 2009, and at December 31, 2009, Hillside recorded a liability from the lawsuit based on legal counsel's estimate that the loss from the lawsuit would be between $250,000 and $750,000. Compute the amount of gain or loss from settlement of the lawsuit and select the proper financial statement category.   _____   O O O O O

4. In November 2010, Hillside purchased two marketable securities, I and II, which it bought and held principally to sell in the near term by February 28, 2011. Relevant data is as follows:

		Fair value	
	Cost	12/31/10	2/28/11
I	$125,000	$145,000	$155,000
II	235,000	205,000	230,000

Compute the amount of holding gain or loss at December 31, 2010, and select the proper financial statement category, assuming Hillside classifies the securities as trading securities.   _____   O O O O O

	Amount	(A) (B) (C) (D) (E)

5. During 2010, Hillside received $1,000,000 from its insurance company to cover losses suffered during a hurricane. This was the first hurricane ever to strike in Hillside's area. The hurricane destroyed a warehouse with a carrying amount of $470,000, containing equipment with a carrying amount of $250,000, and inventory with a carrying amount of $535,000 and a fair value of $600,000. Compute the amount of gain or loss from the financial statement category.   _____   ○ ○ ○ ○ ○

6. At December 31, 2010, Hillside prepared the following worksheet summarizing the translation of its wholly owned foreign subsidiary's financial statements into dollars. Hillside purchased the foreign subsidiary for $324,000 on January 2, 2010. On that date, the carrying amounts of the subsidiary's assets and liabilities equaled their fair values.   _____   ○ ○ ○ ○ ○

	Foreign currency amounts	Applicable exchange rates	Dollars
Net assets January 2, 2010			
(date of purchase)	720,000	$.45	$324,000
Net income, 2010	250,000	.42	105,000
Net assets at December 31, 2010	970,000		$429,000
Net assets at December 31, 2010	970,000	.40	$388,000

Compute the amount of the foreign currency translation adjustment and select the proper financial statements category.

Situation	Journal Entries	Calculations	Classification/Disclosures	Research	Communication

Hillside Company had a loss during the year ended December 31, 2010, that is properly reported as an extraordinary item. On July 1, 2010, Hillside committed itself to a formal plan for sale of a business component that meets the requirements for treatment as discontinued operations. A loss is expected from the proposed sale. Component operating losses were incurred continuously throughout 2010, and were expected to continue until final disposition in 2011. Costs were incurred in 2010 to relocate component employees.

Hillside is also considering changing its method of accounting for inventory from the last-in, first-out (LIFO) method to the average-cost method.

Using the authoritative literature cut and paste your answer to each of the following questions.

1. How should Hillside report the extraordinary item in its income statement?
2. How should Hillside report the effect of the discontinued operations in its 2010 income statement?
3. How should Hillside report the costs that were incurred to relocate employees of the discontinued component?
4. How should Hillside account for the change in inventory method from LIFO to average-cost?
5. What disclosures are required in the financial statements in the year of the change for a change in inventory method?

Situation	Journal Entries	Calculations	Classification/Disclosures	Research	Communication

Write a memo to the client file answering the following questions:

1. How should Hillside report the extraordinary item in its income statement? Why?
2. How should Hillside report the effect of the discontinued operations in its 2010 income statement?
3. How should Hillside report the costs that were incurred to relocate employees of the discontinued component? Why?

Do not discuss earnings per share requirements.

REMINDER: Your response will be graded for both technical content and writing skills. Technical content will be evaluated for information that is helpful to the intended reader and clearly relevant to the issue. Writing skills will be evaluated for development, organization, and the appropriate expression of ideas in professional correspondence. Use a standard business memo or letter format with a clear beginning, middle, and end. Do not convey information in the form of a table, bullet point list, or other abbreviated presentation.

To: Hillside Company Permanent File
From: CPA Candidate
Re: Accounting issues related to income statement presentation

Simulation Problem 3   (50 to 60 minutes)

Situation					
	Classifications	**Multistep Income Statement**	**Retained Earnings Statement**	**Communication**	**Research**

Presented below is information related to American Horse Company for 2009.

Retained earnings balance, January 1, 2009	$ 980,000
Sales for the year	25,000,000
Cost of goods sold	17,000,000
Interest revenue	70,000
Selling and administrative expenses	4,700,000
Write-off of goodwill (not tax deductible)	820,000
Income taxes for 2009	905,000
Gain on the sale of investments (normal recurring)	110,000
Loss due to flood damage—extraordinary item (net of tax)	390,000
Loss on the disposition of the wholesale division	615,000
Loss on operations of the wholesale division	200,000
Income tax benefit from discontinued wholesale division	285,000
Dividends declared on common stock	250,000
Dividends declared on preferred stock	70,000

American Horse Company decided to discontinue its entire wholesale operations and to retain its manufacturing operations. On September 15, American Horse sold the wholesale operations to Rogers Company. During 2009, there were 300,000 shares of common stock outstanding all year.

	Classifications				
Situation		**Multistep Income Statement**	**Retained Earnings Statement**	**Communication**	**Research**

The illustrations below represent accounting transactions that affect the recognition of income for an accounting period. Their classification is the subject of this objective format matching question.

For each of the ten illustrations below, select the best classification from those listed A–I below. A classification may be used once, more than once, or not at all.

Classification

A. Change in reporting entity
B. Correction of an error
C. Change in accounting principle
D. Change in estimate
E. Extraordinary item

F. Discontinued Operations—Gain or loss from discontinued operations
G. Not an accounting change
H. Part of net income before extraordinary items
I. Discontinued Operations—Gain or loss on disposal

Item	(A)	(B)	(C)	(D)	(E)	(F)	(G)	(H)	(I)
1. Newly acquired assets are depreciated using the sum-of-the-years' digits method; previously recorded assets are depreciated using the straight-line method.	O	O	O	O	O	O	O	O	O
2. Accounting for acquisition of a 100% owned subsidiary.	O	O	O	O	O	O	O	O	O
3. Reported as a restatement of all periods presented.	O	O	O	O	O	O	O	O	O
4. Write-down of inventory due to obsolescence.	O	O	O	O	O	O	O	O	O
5. Gains or losses on the disposal of the net assets of a component are included in this calculation.	O	O	O	O	O	O	O	O	O
6. Changing from the gross profit method for determining year-end inventory balances to dollar value LIFO.	O	O	O	O	O	O	O	O	O
7. Accounting for existing construction contracts is changed from completed contract to percentage-of-completion.	O	O	O	O	O	O	O	O	O
8. The effects of a change in estimate and a change in principle are inseparable for the same event.	O	O	O	O	O	O	O	O	O
9. The excess of cash paid over the carrying value to extinguish bonds.	O	O	O	O	O	O	O	O	O
10. Income or loss of the component for the period of disposal included in this calculation.	O	O	O	O	O	O	O	O	O

Situation	Classifications	Multistep Income Statement	Retained Earnings Statement	Communication	Research

Prepare a multistep income statement.

American Horse Company
INCOME STATEMENT
For the Year Ended December 31, 2009

Sales	.	$25,000,000
Net income		
Earnings per share		
Net income		

Situation	Classifications	Multistep Income Statement	Retained Earnings Statement	Communication	Research

Prepare a retained earnings statement.

American Horse Company
RETAINED EARNINGS STATEMENT
For the Year Ended December 31, 2009

Retained earnings, January 1, 2009		$980,000
Retained earnings, December 31, 2009		

Situation	Classifications	Multistep Income Statement	Retained Earnings Statement	Communication	Research

Write a brief memo to the manager of American Horse explaining the major distinction (1) between revenues and gains, and (2) between expenses and losses.

REMINDER: Your response will be graded for both technical content and writing skills. Technical content will be evaluated for information that is helpful to the intended reader and clearly relevant to the issue. Writing skills will be evaluated for development, organization, and the appropriate expression of ideas in professional correspondence. Use a standard business memo or letter format with a clear beginning, middle, and end. Do not convey information in the form of a table, bullet point list, or other abbreviated presentation.

To: Manager, American Horse Company
From: CPA Candidate
Re: Distinction of income statement items

Situation	Classifications	Multistep Income Statement	Retained Earnings Statement	Communication	Research

Use the Financial Accounting Standards to research the definition of an extraordinary item.

___

Simulation Problem 4   (45 to 55 minutes)

Situation	Financial Statement Classification	Calculate Net Income	Earnings Per Share	Communication	Research

Rap Corp. has 100,000 shares of common stock outstanding. In 2009, the company reports income from continuing operations before taxes of $1,210,000.

Additional transactions not considered in the $1,210,000 are as follows:

1. In 2009, Rap Corp. sold equipment for $40,000. The machine had originally cost $80,000 and had accumulated depreciation of $36,000. The gain or loss is considered ordinary.
2. The company discontinued operations of one of its subsidiaries during the current year at a loss of $190,000 before taxes. Assume that this transaction meets the criteria for discontinued operations. The loss of operations of the discontinued subsidiary was $90,000 before taxes; the loss from disposal of the subsidiary was $100,000 before taxes.
3. In 2009, the company reviewed its accounts receivable and determined that $26,000 of accounts receivable that had been carried for years appeared unlikely to be collected.
4. An internal audit discovered that amortization of intangible assets was understated by $35,000 (net of tax) in a prior period. The amount was charged against retained earnings.
5. The company sold its only investment in common stock during the year at a gain of $145,000. The gain is taxed at a total effective rate of 40%. Assume that the transaction meets the requirements of an extraordinary item.

Situation	Financial Statement Classification	Calculate Net Income	Earnings Per Share	Communication	Research

Select from the list of financial statement categories below the category in which the item should be presented. A financial statement category may be selected once, more than once, or not at all. Assume management does not elect to use the fair value option for any financial assets or liabilities.

Financial Statement Categories

A. Income from continuing operations, with **no** separate disclosure.
B. Income from continuing operations, with separate disclosure (either on the face of statement or in the notes).
C. Other comprehensive income for the period.
D. Extraordinary items.
E. Separate component of stockholders' equity.
F. None of the above categories include this item.

Items to be answered

Item	(A)	(B)	(C)	(D)	(E)	(F)
1. An increase in the unrealized excess of cost over market value of marketable equity securities classified as trading-type securities.	O	O	O	O	O	O
2. The accumulated amount of the unrealized excess of cost over market value of available-for-sale marketable equity securities.	O	O	O	O	O	O
3. Income from operations of a discontinued component in the component's disposal year.	O	O	O	O	O	O
4. A gain on remeasuring a foreign subsidiary's financial statements from the local currency into the functional currency.	O	O	O	O	O	O
5. A loss on translating a foreign subsidiary's financial statements from the functional local currency into the reporting currency during this period.	O	O	O	O	O	O
6. A loss caused by a major earthquake in an area previously considered to be subject to only minor tremors.	O	O	O	O	O	O
7. The probable receipt of $1,000,000 from a pending lawsuit.	O	O	O	O	O	O
8. The purchase of research and development services. There were **no** other research and development activities.	O	O	O	O	O	O

Situation	Financial Statement Classification	Calculate Net Income	Earnings Per Share	Communication	Research

Complete the table below for the calculation of net income. Assume the income tax rate is 38% for income from continuing operations.

Rap Corp. INCOME STATEMENT For the Year Ended December 31, 2009			
Income from continuing operations before income tax			
Income tax			
Income from continuing operations			
Discontinued operations:			
Income before extraordinary item			
Extraordinary item:			
Net income			

Situation	Financial Statement Classification	Calculate Net Income	Earnings Per Share	Communication	Research

Complete the table below for the calculations of earnings per share.

Rap Corp. EARNINGS STATEMENT For the Year Ended December 31, 2009		
Per share of common stock:		
Income from continuing operations		
Discontinued operations, net of tax		
Income before extraordinary item		
Extraordinary item, net of tax		
Net income		

Situation	Financial Statement Classification	Calculate Net Income	Earnings Per Share	Communication	Research

Write a memo to the controller of Rap explaining the various components of earnings per share that must be disclosed on the income statement and in the notes to the financial statements.

REMINDER: Your response will be graded for both technical content and writing skills. Technical content will be evaluated for information that is helpful to the intended reader and clearly relevant to the issue. Writing skills will be evaluated for development, organization, and the appropriate expression of ideas in professional correspondence. Use a standard business memo or letter format with a clear beginning, middle, and end. Do not convey information in the form of a table, bullet point list, or other abbreviated presentation.

To: Controller, Rap Corporation
From: CPA Candidate
Re: Earnings per share

Situation	Financial Statement Classification	Calculate Net Income	Earnings Per Share	Communication	Research

Research in the Financial Accounting Standards for a description of the purpose of reporting comprehensive income. Excerpt your answer below.

MULTIPLE-CHOICE ANSWERS

1. d	__ __	18. b	__ __	35. c	__ __	52. a	__ __	69. d	__ __	86. a	__ __
2. a	__ __	19. b	__ __	36. d	__ __	53. a	__ __	70. a	__ __	87. a	__ __
3. a	__ __	20. d	__ __	37. b	__ __	54. c	__ __	71. b	__ __	88. d	__ __
4. a	__ __	21. c	__ __	38. d	__ __	55. c	__ __	72. a	__ __	89. b	__ __
5. a	__ __	22. c	__ __	39. d	__ __	56. d	__ __	73. b	__ __	90. c	__ __
6. d	__ __	23. c	__ __	40. a	__ __	57. b	__ __	74. c	__ __	91. d	__ __
7. a	__ __	24. b	__ __	41. d	__ __	58. c	__ __	75. a	__ __	92. a	__ __
8. a	__ __	25. b	__ __	42. b	__ __	59. a	__ __	76. b	__ __	93. c	__ __
9. b	__ __	26. a	__ __	43. d	__ __	60. a	__ __	77. c	__ __	94. b	__ __
10. a	__ __	27. d	__ __	44. d	__ __	61. c	__ __	78. c	__ · __	95. d	__ __
11. a	__ __	28. d	__ __	45. c	__ __	62. c	__ __	79. b	__ __	96. c	__ __
12. c	__ __	29. c	__ __	46. d	__ __	63. a	__ __	80. a	__ __	97. a	__ __
13. c	__ __	30. b	__ __	47. b	__ __	64. d	__ __	81. d	__ __		
14. a	__ __	31. a	__ __	48. a	__ __	65. b	__ __	82. b	__ __		
15. b	__ __	32. c	__ __	49. c	__ __	66. a	__ __	83. d	__ __		
16. d	__ __	33. b	__ __	50. a	__ __	67. d	__ __	84. c	__ __	1st: __/97 = __%	
17. a	__ __	34. d	__ __	51. b	__ __	68. c	__ __	85. a	__ __	2nd: __/97 = __%	

MULTIPLE-CHOICE ANSWER EXPLANATIONS

D.1. Income and Retained Earnings Statements

1. **(d)** Baer Food's 2009 revenues should include net sales revenue ($187,000), interest revenue ($10,200), and gain on sale of equipment ($4,700), for a total of $201,900. Discontinued operations (loss of $12,400) and the extraordinary gain ($1,500) are both special items that should be reported as separate components of income, after **income from continuing operations**. Therefore, these items should **not** be included in the revenues section of the income statement (which is placed **before** income from continuing operations).

2. **(a)** To directly compute cost of goods manufactured (CGM), the formula is

          Beginning work in process
        + Direct materials used
        + Direct labor
        + Factory overhead
        – Ending work in process
          Cost of goods manufactured

However, none of these elements are given in this problem, so CGM must be computed indirectly, using the cost of sales formula

	Beginning finished goods	$400,000
+	Cost of goods manufactured	+ CGM
–	Ending finished goods	–360,000
	Cost of sales	$240,000

Solving for the missing amount, CGM is $200,000.

3. **(a)** All of the revenues, gains, expenses, and losses given in this problem are components of income from continuing operations. Income before income taxes is $180,000, as computed below.

Revenues ($575,000 + $25,000)	$600,000
Expenses and losses ($240,000 + $70,000 + $10,000 + $50,000 + $15,000 + $15,000 + $20,000)	420,000
Income before income taxes	$180,000

To compute income from continuing operations (after taxes), income taxes ($180,000 × 30% = $54,000) must also be deducted ($180,000 – $54,000 = $126,000).

4. **(a)** The requirement is to compute the amount of expenses to be included in selling expenses for 2009. Advertising ($150,000) and sales salaries and commissions

($140,000) are clearly selling expenses, as is the rent for the office space occupied by the sales department ($220,000 × 1/2 = $110,000). Additionally, freight-out ($80,000) is a selling expense because shipping the goods **from** the point of sale to the customer is the final effort in the selling process. The total selling expense is, therefore, $480,000 ($150,000 + $140,000 + $110,000 + $80,000). The remaining expenses given are general and administrative expenses, except for interest and the loss on sale of long-term investment, which are nonoperating items (other expenses and losses).

5. **(a)** Operating expenses are usually divided into two categories, **selling expenses** and **general and administrative (G&A) expenses**. Selling expenses are related to the sale of a company's products, while G&A expenses are related to the company's general operations. Therefore, Griff should include the following costs in G&A expense:

Accounting and legal fees	$ 25,000
Officers' salaries	150,000
Insurance	85,000
G&A expense	$260,000

Freight-in ($175,000) is an inventoriable cost which should be reflected in cost of goods sold and ending inventory. Freight-out, the cost of delivering goods to customers ($160,000), is included in selling expenses. Sales representatives salaries ($215,000) is also a selling expense.

6. **(d)** Interest expense is generally considered to be a nonoperating item and is therefore included in **other expenses and losses**. Operating expenses are usually divided into two categories, **selling expenses** and **general and administrative expenses**. Since advertising expense is directly related to the sale of the company's products, it is included in selling expenses. Therefore, neither of the expenses given are general and administrative expenses.

7. **(a)** Charitable contributions expense should include all expenses incurred in 2009 by Yew Co. which involve charitable contributions to other entities. The total charitable contributions expense is $310,000, consisting of the $250,000 donated to youth and educational programs and the $60,000 ($140,000 – $80,000) donated to health and human service organizations. The other $80,000 was given to these organizations **by the employees,** with the company merely acting as an agent collecting that amount through payroll deductions and forwarding it on to the organizations. The expenditure for redesigning product packaging ($100,000) would be properly classified as research and development expense.

8.   (a)   Extraordinary items are material gains or losses which are both **unusual** in nature and **infrequent** in occurrence. For Raim Co., which sustains flood losses every two to three years, the 2009 flood loss is not infrequent, and should be recognized as a component of income from continuing operations. For Cane Co., the 2009 flood loss is both unusual and infrequent, so it should be recognized as an extraordinary item.

9.   (b)   Extraordinary items are material items which are **both unusual** in nature and **infrequent** in occurrence. The effect of a strike ($175,000) and a gain or loss from sale or abandonment of equipment ($125,000) is **not** considered extraordinary. The loss from the earthquake would be considered unusual and infrequent. Therefore the $150,000 loss is extraordinary, and the total amount of infrequent losses **not** considered extraordinary is $300,000 ($175,000 + $125,000).

10.   (a)   Extraordinary items are material items which are **both unusual** in nature and **infrequent** in occurrence. Disposals of plant assets, foreign currency losses, and inventory losses are not considered to be unusual in nature, and thus are not extraordinary. Items that may qualify as extraordinary items include some casualties, expropriations, and prohibitions under a new law. In Kent Co.'s 2009 income statement, losses not considered extraordinary amount to $610,000. The factory disposal ($300,000) is classified as discontinued operations because the operations carried on there are dissimilar from operations carried on at the other factories. The $120,000 foreign currency loss and $190,000 inventory loss are not extraordinary because they are not unusual in nature.

11.   (a)   Extraordinary items are material gains or losses which are both **unusual** in nature and **infrequent** in occurrence. Foreign currency losses ($1,200,000) and losses due to discontinued operations ($500,000) are not considered to be unusual in nature and thus are not extraordinary. Items that may qualify as extraordinary include some casualties, expropriations, prohibitions under a new law, and extinguishment of debt. Midway's casualty loss appears to be extraordinary because the hurricane was the first ever to strike in Midway's area. The net pretax loss was $100,000 [$800,000 equipment loss − $700,000 building gain ($1,000,000 − $300,000)].

12.   (c)   A gain (loss) must be recognized when a nonmonetary asset is involuntarily converted into monetary assets even if the company reinvests the monetary assets in replacement nonmonetary assets. The gain or loss is the difference between the insurance proceeds ($1,100,000 replacement cost − $50,000 deductible = $1,050,000) and the carrying amount of the assets destroyed or used up as a result of the casualty loss. The warehouse (carrying amount of $300,000) was destroyed, and cash of $20,000 was used to cover removal costs. Therefore, the gain is $730,000 [$1,050,000 − ($300,000 + $20,000)]. It is **not** an extraordinary item because storms similar to the one that destroyed the warehouse occur frequently (every four years).

13.   (c)   In this situation, the provision for income tax (income tax expense) will be the amount of the tax liability to the government determined without including the extraordinary loss. This amount is determined by applying the 40% tax rate to pretax accounting income before extraordinary items adjusted for any permanent differences. Accounting income before taxes is $900,000, but that amount includes a gain on life insurance coverage ($100,000). A gain on life insurance coverage is a **permanent** difference because it is included in accounting income but will **never** be included in taxable income. Therefore, the amount of accounting income which will be subject to taxes is $800,000 ($900,000 − $100,000), and the provision for income taxes is $320,000 ($800,000 × 40%). The tax savings from the extraordinary loss ($300,000 × 40% = $120,000) will not affect the provision for income taxes because the extraordinary item must be reported together with its tax effect (extraordinary loss of $180,000; net of tax).

14.   (d)   Net income as reported ($74,100) properly included the gain on early retirement of bonds payable ($22,000) and the loss from fire ($14,000). The fact that the gain and loss were reported net of taxes in the income statement was incorrect, but does not cause the net income amount to be in error. However, the other two items should **not** be reported in the income statement at all. An unrealized loss on **noncurrent** investments in stock ($5,400) is reported in other comprehensive income, not in net income. A correction of an error ($7,500) is treated as a prior period adjustment. It is reported in the financial statements as an adjustment to the beginning balance of retained earnings, rather than in the income statement. Since both of these items were subtracted in the computation of reported net income, they must be added back to compute the correct net income of $87,000 ($74,100 + $5,400 + $7,500).

15.   (b)   In 2009, Brecon Co. would report one fifth of the cabinet costs as depreciation expense in selling, general, and administrative expenses. Four fifths of the cabinet cost would remain capitalized as fixed assets at the end of 2009. The cabinets are considered fixed assets and not a part of cost of goods sold.

16.   (d)   A material gain or loss that is unusual in nature or infrequent in occurrence, but not both, should be presented as a separate component of income or loss from continuing operations. Both discontinued operations and extraordinary items are reported separately **after** income from continuing operations.

17.   (a)   For an item to qualify as an extraordinary item it must be **both** unusual in nature and infrequent in occurrence. The above criteria must take into account the environment in which the entity operates. An entity with sales in different countries will experience foreign currency revaluations on a regular basis, so a currency revaluation would not be infrequent in occurrence and it is not an extraordinary item. Gains from increases in contract prices are neither infrequent nor unusual, so they cannot qualify as extraordinary items.

18.   (b)   Extraordinary items are reported **net of income taxes** as a separate component of income **after** discontinued operations.

19. (b)   Extraordinary items are events and transactions that are distinguished by both their unusual nature and the infrequency of their occurrence. Losses of this type are both common and frequent for Toncan. Estimates of the losses would not be presented in the financial statements. No amount is recorded until a loss actually occurs.

D.2. Unusual or Infrequent Items

20. (d)   A transaction that is unusual in nature and infrequent in occurrence is considered an extraordinary item. An extraordinary item is reported **after** discontinued operations but **before** cumulative effect of accounting changes.

21. (c)   Extraordinary items are events and transactions that are distinguished by both their unusual nature and the infrequency of their occurrence. Teller Co.'s loss arising from its **first** antitrust action meets both of these criteria (particularly since they pleaded guilty) and should therefore be reported as an extraordinary item. The strike against Teller's major supplier, however, should not be reported as an extraordinary item because it is usual in nature but may be expected to recur as a consequence of customary and continuing business activities.

22. (c)   Extraordinary items are material items which are **both unusual** in nature and **infrequent** in occurrence. Therefore, the loss on sale of a bond investment is not extraordinary. Neither item is treated as extraordinary.

23. (c)   Corrections of errors shall continue to be reported net of tax in retained earnings as an adjustment of the beginning balance.

24. (b)   Costs of exit activities (including restructuring charges) should be measured and recognized at fair value when they are incurred.

D.3. Discontinued Operations

25. (b)   The operating loss of $300,000 ($500,000 revenues less $800,000 expenses) relates to a discontinued component, so it is part of discontinued operations, **not** continuing operations. It is combined with the loss from disposal on the income statement. **Discontinued operations** is a category distinct from **extraordinary items**.

26. (a)   Management is not required to have entered into a sales agreement. It is sufficient if management is committed to a disposal plan that is reasonable. The other items are all required for presentation as discontinued operations.

27. (d)   In discontinued operations, presentation of the income or loss from operations of the component and the gain or loss on disposal is required. Since the company met the requirements for "held for sale" status in 2009, the subsidiary should be written down to its fair value less cost to sell. This would result in a loss of $1,500,000 ($8,000,000 carrying amount – $6,500,000 fair value). Therefore, the loss from discontinued operations would be $3,500,000 ($2,000,000 loss from operations + $1,500,000 loss on planned disposal).

28. (d)   The loss from discontinued operations would equal the loss from operations plus the estimated loss from disposal of the component.

29. (c)   Costs of termination benefits, lease termination, and consolidating facilities or relocating employees related to a disposal activity that involves discontinued operations should be included in the results of discontinued operations.

30. (b)   The requirement is to determine how a discontinued component's operating losses for the current period should be classified in the financial statements. The "income (loss) from operations" is combined with the loss on disposal.

31. (a)   Gains or losses from the operation of a discontinued business component realized for the period are combined with the loss of disposal to determine the loss from discontinued operations.

32. (c)   Discontinued operations should include the gain or loss on disposal plus the results of operations during the period.

D.4. Comprehensive Income

33. (b)   The purpose of reporting comprehensive income is to report a measure of overall enterprise performance by displaying all changes in equity of an enterprise that result from recognized transactions and other economic events of the period other than transactions with owners in their capacity as owners. An enterprise should continue to display an amount for net income with equal prominence to the comprehensive income amount displayed.

34. (d)   Once unrealized items recorded and reported in the current or prior period are recognized as realized and reported in net income, it is necessary to reverse them out of other comprehensive income. The reclassification adjustment is to avoid double counting. The reclassification adjustment in this situation is $15,000 ($25,000 gain on AFS securities, net of $10,000 tax).

35. (c)   The FASB allows three presentation formats [answer choices (a), (b), and (d)] with a preference for the first two alternatives.

36. (d)   The accumulated balance of other comprehensive income should be reported as a component of equity, separate from retained earnings and additional paid-in capital.

37. (b)   Comprehensive income is defined as the change in equity of a business during a period from transactions of nonowner sources. Stockholders are owners of the corporation or entity, therefore, transactions between the entity and shareholder are not a component of comprehensive income.

38. (d)   Assuming the fair value option is not elected, the calculation of holding gains recognized in other comprehensive income is as follows:

	Before tax	Income tax	Net of tax
Year ended 12/31/08	$5,000	$1,500	$3,500
Year ended 12/31/09	2,500	750	1,750
Total gain	$7,500	$2,250	$5,250

The reclassification adjustment should be shown net of tax, so ($5,250) is the adjustment amount. $5,250 had been previously added to other comprehensive income when the gains occurred. The $5,250 needs to be taken out in order to avoid counting the gains twice. The securities have been sold so the gains are now realized and will be part of net income.

39. **(d)** The gain for the period is 10 shares times the increase in fair value, which is $250. This gain of $2,500 must be shown net of tax, so the holding gain is $1,750.

40. **(a)** Comprehensive income is computed as follows:

Net income		77,000
Other comprehensive income net of tax:		
Unrealized gain on securities	15,000	
Less: Reclassification adjustment	(2,500)	12,500
Pension liability adjustment	(3,000)	
Other comprehensive income		9,500
Comprehensive income		86,500

Notice that stock warrants outstanding are not included as part of comprehensive income.

41. **(d)** If $2,450 (net of tax) is being deducted from other comprehensive income as a reclassification adjustment, $2,450 must be the amount of unrealized gains (net of tax) that have been recognized in other comprehensive income. The realized gains will then be recognized in income from continuing operations before tax. The gains before tax effects are $3,500 ($2,450 ÷ 70%).

42. **(b)** Comprehensive income disclosures include the changes during a period of the following components of other comprehensive income: unrealized gains and losses on available-for-sale investments and foreign currency items, including any reclassification adjustments, and the pension liability adjustment required to recognize the funded status of the plan. Treasury stock is deducted from stockholders' equity and **not** a component of other comprehensive income.

43. **(d)** Separate EPS calculations are not required for other comprehensive income or comprehensive income.

44. **(d)** The FASB prefers that comprehensive income be shown at the bottom of the income statement as a continuation of net income or in a separate statement beginning with net income. Presenting comprehensive income in the statement of changes in stockholders' equity is not a method that is preferred by the FASB.

45. **(c)** If the fair value option is not elected, held-to-maturity securities are reported at amortized cost. Any decreases or increases in fair value are reported neither in net income nor as part of other comprehensive income. Answers (a) and (b) are incorrect because an adjustment to pension liability to record the funded status of the plan, and subsequent decreases of the fair value of available-for-sale securities that have been previously written down as impaired are included in other comprehensive income. Answer (d) is incorrect because decreases in the fair value of held-to-maturity securities are not part of other comprehensive income.

46. **(d)** Comprehensive income (net income plus other comprehensive income) should be displayed in a financial statement that has the same prominence as other financial statements. Answer (a) is incorrect because the FASB prefers that comprehensive income be displayed either at the bottom of the income statement, continuing from net income to arrive at a comprehensive income figure (equals net income plus other comprehensive income), or in a separate statement of comprehensive income. Answer (b) is incorrect because components of other comprehensive income may be displayed net of related tax effects or before related tax effects with one amount shown for the aggregate income tax effect. Answer (c) is incorrect because comprehensive in-

come can be displayed in the two methods preferred by the FASB (mentioned above) or in the statement of changes in stockholders' equity.

D.5. Balance Sheets

47. **(b)** Total retained earnings includes both unappropriated retained earnings and restricted retained earnings. Therefore, before closing entries, total retained earnings is $1,060,000 ($900,000 + $160,000). Before computing 2009 net income, tax expense must be recorded. Earnings ($6,680,000) less costs and expenses ($5,180,000) result in pretax income of $1,500,000. Since the tax rate is 30%, tax expense is $450,000 (30% × $1,500,000). Therefore, an adjustment is necessary to debit **income tax expense** and credit **prepaid taxes** for $450,000. After the adjustment, net income is $1,050,000 ($6,680,000 – $5,180,000 – $450,000). After closing entries, total retained earnings is $2,110,000 ($1,060,000 + $1,050,000).

48. **(a)** The only liabilities included in the trial balance are billings in excess of costs on long-term contracts ($700,000) and note payable-noncurrent ($1,620,000). Only the note is noncurrent. Billings in excess of costs on long-term contracts is similar to unearned revenue and is always reported as a current liability.

49. **(c)** Current assets listed in the trial balance are cash ($600,000), accounts receivable ($3,500,000), cost in excess of billings on long-term contracts ($1,600,000) and prepaid taxes ($450,000). However, income tax expense has not yet been recorded. Earnings ($6,680,000) less costs and expenses ($5,180,000) result in pretax income of $1,500,000. Since the tax rate is 30%, tax expense is $450,000 (30% × $1,500,000). Therefore, an adjustment is necessary to debit **income tax expense** and credit **prepaid taxes** for $450,000. Total current assets, after this adjustment, are $5,700,000.

Cash	$ 600,000
Accounts receivable	3,500,000
Cost in excess of billings	1,600,000
	$5,700,000

50. **(a)** Mirr began operations on 1/1/09 with the following balance sheet elements:

Assets	=	Liabilities	+	Owners' equity
$860,000	=	$110,000	+	$750,000

During 2009, liabilities increased to $120,000, and owners' equity increased to $765,000 [$750,000 beginning balance + $18,000 net income ($82,000 revenues – $64,000 expenses) – $3,000 dividends declared]. Therefore, 12/31/09 assets must be $885,000.

Assets	=	Liabilities	+	Owners' equity
Assets	=	$120,000	+	$765,000
Assets	=	$885,000		

51. **(b)** The requirement is to determine the net income for 2009 by analyzing changes in the balance sheet. Recall the accounting equation: Assets – Liabilities = Stockholders' equity. By inserting the changes given into this formula, we find an increase of $62,000 exists in the entire stockholders' equity section ($89,000 – $27,000 = $62,000). Stockholders' equity is composed of capital stock, additional paid-in capital and retained earnings. Because increases in the other two balances are given that total $66,000 ($60,000 + $6,000), the retained earnings balance must have decreased by $4,000 ($66,000 – $62,000). When dividends are paid, this reduces retained earnings, while Vel Corp. net income increases the balance of retained earnings. For the equation to balance, the changes in retained earnings account must reduce total stockholders' equity by $4,000. Therefore, if $13,000 in dividends are paid, which reduce retained earnings, and total retained earnings are to be reduced by $4,000, then net income, which increases retained earnings, must be $9,000. This creates the $4,000 difference needed to make the equation balance ($89,000 – $27,000 = $66,000 – $4,000). The following shows the analysis of the retained earnings account:

Retained earnings (beg.)	$ xxx
Net income (plug)	**9,000**
Dividends	(13,000)
Retained earnings (decrease)	($ 4,000)

52. (a)   Idle machinery ($11,200) and cash surrender value of life insurance ($13,700) are both assets. The allowance for decline in market value of noncurrent marketable equity securities ($8,400) is a contra asset that is properly included in the asset section of the balance sheet (as a deduction). The only item listed which should **not** be included in the asset section of the balance sheet is the treasury stock ($24,000). Although the treasury stock account has a debit balance, it is not an asset; instead, it is reported as a contra equity account. Therefore, the $24,000 must be excluded from the asset section, reducing the net asset amount to $851,000 ($875,000 – $24,000).

53. (a)   Although the statement of cash flows provides information about liquidity, solvency, and financial flexibility, a potential investor would **primarily** use the balance sheet to assess liquidity and financial flexibility. The balance sheet helps users analyze the company's ability to use current assets to pay current liabilities (liquidity) and the company's ability to alter the amounts and timing of future cash flows to adapt to unexpected needs or to take advantage of opportunities (flexibility).

D.6.a. Disclosures

54. (c)   Financial statements must include disclosures of material transactions between related parties. Compensation arrangements in the ordinary course of business, however, are specifically excluded from this disclosure requirement. Therefore, only the $250,000 sale to affiliated enterprises must be disclosed.

55. (c)   Disclosure of material transactions between related parties is required except for (1) compensation agreements, expense allowances, and other similar items in the ordinary course of business, and (2) transactions which are eliminated in the preparation of consolidated or combined financial statements. The officers' salaries and officers' expenses fall into category (1), while the intercompany sales fall into category (2). Therefore, only the loans to officers ($125,000 + $50,000 = $175,000) are reported as related-party disclosures.

56. (d)   Disclosure of material transactions between related parties is required except for (1) compensation agreements, expense allowances, and other similar items in the ordinary course of business and (2) transactions eliminated in the preparation of consolidated or combined financial statements.

57. (b)   Disclosure of any material related-party transactions is required except

1.   Compensation agreements, expense allowances, and similar items in the ordinary course of business.
2.   Transactions that are eliminated in the preparation of consolidated or combined financial statements.

Since sales of inventory between subsidiary and parent are eliminated in preparing consolidated financial statements, such sales need not be disclosed as a related-party transaction. Nonmonetary exchanges by affiliates are not specifically exempted from disclosure, and therefore must be disclosed as related-party transactions. Compensation arrangements, expense allowances, and similar items in the ordinary course of business need not be disclosed as related-party transactions. However, in this case the allowances are in excess of normal business practice and therefore must be disclosed. Surety and guaranty agreements between related parties are not specifically exempted from disclosure and therefore must be disclosed as related-party transactions.

58. (c)   Disclosures of material transactions shall include (1) nature of relationship(s), (2) description of transaction(s), including those assigned zero or nominal amounts, (3) dollar amounts of transactions for each income statement period and effect of any change in method of establishing terms, and (4) amounts due to/from related parties, including terms and manner of settlement.

59. (a)   The users of the information are the focus of financial reporting. GAAP requires disclosures in the notes to facilitate the users' understanding of the financial statements. Answer (b) is incorrect because the financial statements should be properly presented in accordance with GAAP; thus no improper presentation should exist. Answer (c) is incorrect because the totals of the financial statements should include all items; thus, no items would be excluded. Answer (d) is incorrect because management's responses to the auditor's comments would be contained in the management letter, which is a separate report typically presented to the audit committee or the board of directors.

D.6.b. Accounting Policies

60. (a)   The requirement is to determine which information should be included in the summary of significant accounting policies. Disclosure of accounting policies should identify and describe the accounting principles followed by the reporting entity and methods of applying those principles. Answer (a) is correct because the method of recording and depreciating assets is an example of such a required disclosure. Answers (b) and (c) are incorrect because both represent detail presented elsewhere in the financial statements. Answer (d) is incorrect because it is an estimate of earnings rather than an accounting policy.

61. (c)   Disclosure of accounting policies should identify and describe the accounting principles followed by the reporting entity and methods of applying those principles. The criteria for determining which investments are treated as cash equivalents is an example of how the entity applies accounting principles. These disclosures should not duplicate details presented elsewhere as part of the financial statements. Answers (a), (b), and (d) are not disclosures of accounting **policies,** and also would be presented elsewhere in the financial statements.

62. (c)   This is a recognized subsequent event in the financial statement because Swift records an estimate for warranty liability. Prior to issuing the financial statements, Swift must make an adjustment for warranty liability for the product recall. Therefore, warranty liability should be $68,000 on the 2009 balance sheet.

63. **(a)** This is an unrecognized subsequent event that did not exist as of the balance sheet date of December 31, 2009. Therefore, there should be no adjustment of the 2009 financial statements. However, since the inventory loss is material in amount and the loss is uninsured, to prevent the financial statements from being misleading, Colter should disclose the loss in a footnote to the 2009 financial statements.

64. **(d)** A loss for a recognized subsequent event should be reported in the current year financial statements. Therefore, answer (d) is correct. Answer (a) is incorrect because a loss would not be recognized in the current year for an unrecognized subsequent event. However, a footnote disclosure would be required for the unrecognized subsequent event if the event is material and the financial statements would be misleading if the event were not disclosed. Answer (b) is incorrect because gains are not recognized until realized. Answer (c) is incorrect because recognized subsequent events result in a loss recognized in the current year and a corresponding adjustment to record the liability.

D.6.d. Fair Value Measurements

65. **(b)** The definition of fair value is the price that would be received to sell an asset in an orderly transaction between market participants at the measurement date. Answer (a) is incorrect because it is an entry price, not an exit price. Answer (c) is incorrect because assets that require to be revalued to fair value should be based on an exit value, not an adjusted historic cost. Answer (d) is incorrect because the price paid to acquire the asset is an entry price, not an exit price.

66. **(a)** The principal market is the market in which the reporting entity would sell the asset or transfer the liability with the greatest volume and level of activity for the asset or liability. Answers (b) and (c) are incorrect because they do not meet the definition of principal market. Answer (d) is incorrect because it describes the most advantageous market.

67. **(d)** If location is an attribute of the asset, the price in the principal market should be adjusted for costs to transport the asset to its principal or most advantageous market. Answers (a) and (b) are incorrect because prices are not adjusted for transaction costs such as selling costs. Answer (c) is incorrect because fair values are not based upon entry prices to the market.

68. **(c)** Market participants are buyers and sellers in the principal market or most advantageous market for the asset or liability. Market participants should be independent, knowledgeable, able to transact for the asset, and willing to transact (i.e., motivated but not compelled to do so). Answer (a) is incorrect because market participants should not be compelled to sell. Answer (b) is incorrect because it is not an independent, unrelated party. Answer (d) is incorrect because the dealer is establishing a new market and is not in the principal market that exists for the asset.

69. **(d)** A fair value measurement assumes the highest and best use of the asset that is physically possible, legally

permissible, and financially feasible. Answers (a) and (b) are incorrect because to determine the valuation premise, the asset can be classified as either in-use or in-exchange. Answer (c) is incorrect because for valuation purposes, the highest and best use would maximize the value of the asset.

70. **(a)** The fair value at initial recognition is the transaction price that represents the price paid to acquire the asset (an entry price). Answer (b) is incorrect because transaction costs are not included. Answer (c) is incorrect because it is an exit price. Answer (d) is incorrect because it is not a fair value measure.

71. **(b)** There are three approaches to valuation techniques for fair value: the market approach, the income approach, and the cost approach. There is no technique called the residual value approach.

72. **(a)** The income approach uses valuation techniques to convert future amounts to a single present value amount. Therefore, Black-Scholes-Merton, binomial models, or discounted cash flow models are examples of the income approach. Answers (b) and (c) are incorrect because these approaches do not use present value techniques. Answer (d) is incorrect because there is no exit value approach.

73. **(b)** The market approach valuation technique uses prices and other relevant information generated by market transactions involving identical or comparable assets or liabilities. Answer (a) is incorrect because it refers to the income approach. Answer (c) is incorrect because it refers to the cost approach. Answer (d) is incorrect because it is not a technique for any of the permissible valuation techniques.

74. **(c)** A change in valuation technique used to measure fair value should be reported as a change in accounting estimate. The change is reported on a prospective basis; however, the disclosures for change in accounting estimate are not required for a change in valuation technique. Answers (a), (b), and (d) are incorrect.

75. **(a)** The fair value hierarchy prioritizes the inputs to valuation techniques into three levels: Level 1, Level 2, and Level 3. The highest priority is given to Level 1 inputs, which are quoted prices in active markets for identical assets and liabilities. Answers (b) and (c) are incorrect, because these levels are lower priority than Level 1. Answer (d) is incorrect because there is no Level 4 input.

76. **(b)** The bank prime rate and the default rates are both observable inputs. A financial forecast is developed by an entity and is an unobservable input or Level 3 input. Therefore, answers (a), (c), and (d) are incorrect.

D.6.f. Constant Dollar Accounting

77. **(c)** The Codification encourages, but does not require, business enterprises to disclose **supplementary information** on the effects of changing prices. The statement presents requirements to be followed by enterprises that voluntarily elect to disclose this information. Answers (a) and (b) are incorrect because the information is not reported in the body of the financial statements or in the notes to the financial statements. Answer (d) is incorrect because management's report to shareholders identifies management's responsibilities, including responsibilities for the internal control system, and would not include information about changing prices.

78.   (c)   The requirement is to determine the amounts to be reported for three balance sheet accounts in a supplementary **constant dollar** balance sheet. In a constant dollar balance sheet, **nonmonetary** items are restated to the current price level, while monetary items are **not** restated because they are already stated in current dollars. The investment in bonds and the long-term debt are monetary items since their amounts are fixed by contract in terms of number of dollars. Therefore, these items are not restated and are reported at $60,000 and $80,000, respectively. The land, however, is a nonmonetary item and its cost ($120,000) must be restated to current dollars by using the TO/FROM ratio (110/100), resulting in an adjusted amount of $132,000 ($120,000 × 110/100).

79.   (b)   The account "loans to employees" is a monetary asset account since its payment amount is fixed at some point in the future. Conversely, merchandise inventory is considered a nonmonetary asset account since its value will change based on relative price levels in the future. The total value of monetary assets is the balance of the loans to employees account, or $20,000.

80.   (a)   The increase in current cost (nominal dollars) of $15,000 is the **total** increase in current cost, including any increase caused by inflation. The effect of changes in the general price level is **not** separated from the effect of changes in specific value. The increase in current cost (constant dollars) of $12,000 is the increase in current cost after eliminating any increase caused by inflation. Therefore, the inflation component of the increase in current cost of inventories is $3,000 ($15,000 – $12,000).

81.   (d)   The requirement is to determine which item is classified as nonmonetary when computing the purchasing power gain or loss on net monetary items. A monetary item is one that is fixed or determinable without reference to future prices. Accumulated depreciation is not a monetary item. Advances to unconsolidated subsidiaries, allowance for doubtful accounts, and unamortized premium on bonds payable are all monetary items.

82.   (b)   A purchasing power gain or loss is the net gain or loss determined by restating in units of constant purchasing power the opening and closing balances of, and transactions in, **monetary** assets and liabilities. During a period of rising prices, monetary liabilities give rise to purchasing power gains because they will be settled with cash which can be used to purchase relatively fewer goods or services at a future time.

D.6.g. Current Cost Accounting

83.   (d)   Current cost accounting is a method of valuing and reporting assets, liabilities, revenues, and expenses at their current cost at the balance sheet date or at the date of their use or sale. A holding gain is recorded as an increase in an item's value. At December 31, 2009, Vend Co. is holding merchandise which is currently valued at $10 per unit (replacement cost), while the original recorded value of the merchandise was $8 per unit (purchase price). Therefore, the holding gain is $2 per unit.

84.   (c)   The requirement is to calculate the amount of current cost depreciation expense which would appear in supplementary current cost financial statements. Depreciation is to be measured based on the **average** current cost of the asset during the period of use. The average

current cost of this machine during 2009 is $120,000 [($115,000 + $125,000) ÷ 2]. Therefore, 2009 depreciation expense is $24,000 ($120,000 ÷ 5-year useful life).

85.   (a)   Current cost for inventories and equipment is measured at the lower of current cost or recoverable amount. For equipment, recoverable amount ($95,000) is lower than current cost; for inventory, current cost ($80,000) is lower than recoverable amount. Therefore, the total amount to be reported for these assets is $175,000 ($95,000 + $80,000).

86.   (a)   Increases or decreases in the current cost of inventory result from the difference between the measures of assets at their entry dates (beginning of year or purchase date) and measures of assets at their exit dates (end of year or date of use/sale). Based on this definition, holding gains would be reported both when inventory is sold during the year (realized gains), and when inventory is held at the end of the year (unrealized gains).

87.   (a)   The current cost of goods sold is computed by multiplying the average cost of units produced or purchased during the year times the number of units sold.

D.6.h.   Risks and Uncertainites

88.   (d)   The market in which an entity conducts its operations, the available sources of supply of materials used in operations of an entity, and the volume of business transacted with a certain contributor are all examples of concentrations that create vulnerabilities that are required to be disclosed.

89.   (b)   The potential impact of estimates about values of assets and liabilities when it is reasonably possible that the estimate will change in the near future is a required disclosure regarding significant risks and uncertainties. Factors causing an estimate to be sensitive is not a required disclosure, only recommended. The potential impact of estimates about values of assets and liabilities when it is remotely possible that the estimate will change in the near future is not a required disclosure. It is only a required disclosure if it is reasonably possible that the estimates will change in the near future. Only a description of operations outside the home country is a required disclosure.

D.8. Other Comprehensive Bases of Accounting

90.   (c)   Other than generally accepted accounting principles, the only other bases which may be used to prepare financial statements in conformity with a comprehensive basis of accounting are the **cash basis** and a **basis of accounting used to file an income tax return**.

91.   (d)   When financial statements are prepared using an income tax basis, two accounting methods can be used: (1) modified cash basis—hybrid method of IRS and (2) accrual basis—IRS. The modified cash basis reflects the use of accrual basis for inventories, cost of goods sold, sales, and depreciation, if these are significant. The accrual basis uses accruals and deferrals with several exceptions (e.g., prepaid income, warranty expense). When financial statements are prepared on an income tax basis, the financial statements should not simply repeat items and amounts reported in the tax return. Thus, items such as nontaxable municipal interest and the nondeductible portion of travel and entertainment expense should be fully reflected in the income statement on the basis used for tax purposes, with footnote disclosure of the differences between the amounts reported in the income statements and tax return.

92.   (a)   In financial statements prepared on the income tax basis, the nondeductible portion of meals and entertainment expense should be included with the deductible portion as a total amount of travel and entertainment expense. Additionally, the nondeductible portion should be footnoted. Answer (a) is the best answer among the alternatives given, although it does not indicate that a footnote is required.

93.   (c)   The requirement is to identify the statement that best describes appropriate modifications in cash basis financial statements. Answer (c) is correct because the modifications should be the same as GAAP and not illogical. Answer (a) is incorrect because modified cash basis financial statements may have substantial modifications from GAAP. Answer (b) is incorrect because the modifications are not required to be the same as those required by tax law. Answer (d) is incorrect because modifications are allowed.

D.9.   Prospective Financial Information

94.   (b)   The responsible party is not the only limited user. Third parties with whom the responsible party is negotiating directly are also limited users. Answer (a) is incorrect because prospective financial information may be prepared for general or limited use. Answer (c) is incorrect because it is true that assumptions not necessarily expected to occur may be included in the financial projection. Answer (d) is incorrect because the financial projection may be expressed as a range of dollars.

95.   (d)   Prospective financial information is defined as any financial information about the future.

96.   (c)   Financial forecasts and projections must be prepared in accordance with GAAP, with the plans of the entity, and with due professional care in order to achieve a reasonably objective basis.

97.   (a)   Prospective financial statements include information on the purpose of the statements, assumptions, and significant accounting policies.

SOLUTIONS TO SIMULATION PROBLEMS

Simulation Problem 1

Situation	Concepts	Financial Statement Classification	Balance Sheet	Communication	Research

	True	*False*
1. The gain or loss from discontinued operations is placed in a separate category under other income or loss.	○	●
2. The gain or loss from infrequent or unusual items is given extraordinary treatment and disclosed on the income statement after discontinued operations.	○	●
3. Exit and disposal activities are classified as discontinued operations.	○	●
4. A component of a company can be classified as discontinued in the first period that it meets the criteria as being held for sale.	●	○
5. A correction of an error is included in the cumulative effect of change in accounting principle on the income statement.	○	●
6. Other comprehensive income may be presented at the bottom of the income statement.	●	○
7. Separate earnings per share amounts must be presented for both other comprehensive income and comprehensive income.	○	●
8. Prospective financial information includes information on the purpose of the statements, assumptions, and significant accounting policies.	●	○

Explanation of solutions

1.   (F) Discontinued operations are placed in a separate category after income from continuing operations and before extraordinary items.

2.   (F) An item must be **both** infrequent and unusual to be treated as an extraordinary item.

3.   (F) Exit and disposal activities that are not in connection with a component of the entity that qualifies for extraordinary treatment should be reported as unusual or infrequent income/loss in income from continuing operations before income taxes.

4.   (T) A component must be classified as discontinued when it meets the criteria.

5.   (F) A correction of an error requires restatement of the financial statements.

6.   (T) Flexibility is allowed for presentation.

7.   (F) Separate EPS amounts are only required for gains/losses from discontinued operations, extraordinary items, and cumulative effect of accounting changes.

8.   (T) The notes to prospective financial statements must include those disclosures.

Situation	Concepts	Financial Statement Classification	Balance Sheet	Communication	Research

	Assets (A-F)	*Liabilities* (G, H, I)	*Owner's equity* (J, K, L, M)	*Other* (N or X)
1. Dividend payable (on King's preferred stock).		G		
2. Plant construction in progress by the company.	C			
3. Factory building (retired from use and held for sale).	F			
4. Land (held for possible future building site).	B			
5. Merchandise inventory (held by Stephen King Corporation on consignment).				N
6. Stock dividend distributable (in common stock to common stockholders and to be issued at par).			K	
7. Office supplies inventory.	A			
8. Sinking fund cash (First National Bank, Trustee).	B			
9. Installment sales accounts receivable (average collection period eighteen months). All sales are installment sales.	A			

	Assets (A-F)	Liabilities (G, H, I)	Owner's equity (J, K, L, M)	Other (N or X)
10. Temporary decline in inventory value.				N
11. Advances to officers (indefinite repayment date).	F			
12. Estimated warranty costs. The warranty costs are for a one-year warranty on parts and labor.		G		
13. Inventory of small tools used in the business.	C			
14. Treasury stock under par value method.				X-K
15. Common stock subscribed (Stephen King Corporation's stock).			K	
16. Convertible bonds.		H		
17. Securities held as collateral.				N
18. Bank overdraft (only account with bank).		G		

Explanation of solutions

1.   **(G)** When a corporation declares a cash or property dividend, the amount to be paid becomes a liability of the corporation. The dividends payable amount would be classified as a current liability on the balance sheet. It is important to note that dividends payable represent the amount distributed to stockholders as a return on their investment. Dividends are not expenses.

2.   **(C)** When an item of property, plant, or equipment is being constructed by the company that intends to use it, all of the relevant costs related to the construction should be included in the asset. The asset would be classified as plant and equipment.

3.   **(F)** A factory building that has been retired from use and held for sale should be classified as an **other asset** rather than as property, plant and equipment. The property, plant and equipment account should include only those tangible assets that are being used in operations.

4.   **(B)** Land that is held for speculative or investment purposes should be classified as an investment rather than as property, plant, and equipment. The property, plant, and equipment account should represent only those assets being used in current operations.

5.   **(N)** Consigned inventory is excluded from the balance sheet because it is not owned by King. Consigned inventory represents an arrangement whereby the owner of the goods transfers physical possession to an agent (King). The agent (consignee) will attempt to sell the goods on the owner's behalf. The inventory remains an asset of its owner.

6.   **(K)** A stock dividend distributable represents a dividend to be distributed to shareholders in the form of additional shares of the corporation's stock. Each shareholder will receive a proportional share of additional stock. The declaration of a stock dividend does not result in a liability, as it does not result in any of the corporation's assets being paid. Thus, a stock dividend distributable would be classified as an addition in the stockholders' equity section in the common stock account.

7.   **(A)** Current assets represent cash or other assets that are expected to be used within the operating cycle. Office supplies inventory represents an asset that could be expected to be used within the operating cycle.

8.   **(B)** Generally, a fund is a group of assets set aside for a future nonoperating purpose. A sinking fund contains assets to be used in the future to retire bonds. These assets are generally invested while waiting to be used and are noncurrent.

9.   **(A)** An installment sales accounts receivable results when the corporation makes a sale to a customer and does not receive payment in full on the date of sale. Since this company normally sells on the installment basis, its operating cycle becomes eighteen months. Its receivables are current assets because their average life falls within the operating cycle.

10.   **(N)** Temporary decline in inventory value is a loss and appears on the income statement.

11.   **(F)** Advances to officers are considered nontrade receivables. These types of receivables should be reported separately on the balance sheet as other assets.

12.   **(G)** A warranty is a guarantee made by the seller to the purchaser against defects in the product's quality. Estimated warranty expense for a given period can be estimated as a percentage of sales. The percentage is based on past warranty experience. The estimated warranty cost represents the warranty expenditures in the future for past sales and is a current liability.

13.   **(C)** Property, plant, and equipment consists of items used in the normal operations of a business. The inventory of small tools represents tools **used** in the business and are not for sale.

14.   **(X-K)** Treasury stock is a corporation's own stock which has been issued and reacquired by the corporation. Treasury stock may be accounted for under the cost or par value method. When the par value method is used, treasury stock would be recorded on the balance sheet as a reduction or contra to the common stock account.

15.   **(K)** Common stock subscribed represents stock subscriptions that have not been fully paid. The stock is not considered to be issued until the full price is paid. This account should be classified as an increase in the common stock and it is offset in stockholders' equity by a contra account for the balance of the subscription due.

16. **(H)** A convertible bond is a bond which may be converted to another form of the corporation's securities during a specified time frame. A bond is typically classified as a long-term liability on the balance sheet.

17. **(N)** Corporations do not own securities they hold as collateral. The corporation will retain the securities only in the event of a default on the receivable the securities are collateralizing. Thus, the securities are excluded from the balance sheet of King and they appear on the balance sheets of their owners.

18. **(G)** A bank overdraft occurs when a check is written for a greater amount than the balance in the bank account. A bank overdraft should be classified as a current liability. It should not be offset against other cash account balances unless the cash account is in the same bank.

Situation	Concepts	Financial Statement Classification	Balance Sheet	Communication	Research

	A	B	C	D	E
1	**Stephen King Corporation**				
2	**Balance Sheet**				
3	**December 31, 2010**				
4					
5	Current assets				
6	Cash				$ 114,000
7	Trading securities				80,000
8	Accounts receivable (net of $10,000 allowance for doubtful accounts)				160,000
9	Inventories (lower of FIFO cost or market)				180,000
10					
11	Total current assets				534,000
12					
13	Investments				
14	Available-for-sale securities				270,000
15	Bond sinking fund				250,000
16	Land held for future use				270,000
17	Cash surrender value of life insurance contract				40,000
18					
19	Total investments				830,000
20					
21	Property, plant, and equipment				
22	Land				500,000
23	Buildings (net of accumulated depreciation of $360,000)				680,000
24	Equipment (net of accumulated depreciation of $180,000)				270,000
25					
26	Total property, plant, and equipment				1,450,000
27					
28	Intangible assets				
29	Franchise				165,000
30	Goodwill				100,000
31					
32	Total intangible assets				265,000
33	Total assets				$3,079,000
34					
35	Current liabilities:				
36	Accounts payable		$90,000		
37	Notes payable		80,000		
38	Taxes payable		40,000		
39	Bank overdraft		14,000		
40	Unearned revenue		5,000		
41					
42	Total current liabilities		229,000		
43					
44	Long-term liabilities				
45	Notes payable		120,000		
46	Bonds payable, 10% due 2018 (less discount of $40,000)		960,000		
47					
48	Total long-term liabilities		1,080,000		
49	Total liabilities		$1,309,000		

	A	B	C	D	E
50					
51	Stockholders' equity				
52	Paid-in capital				
53	Preferred stock, no par, authorized 200,000 shares, issued 70,000 shares		450,000		
54	Common stock, $1.00 par value, authorized 40,000 shares, issued 100,000 shares		100,000		
55	Paid-in capital in excess of par value common		900,000		
56					
57	Total paid-in capital		$1,450,000		
58					
59	Retained earnings		320,000		
60					
61	Total stockholders' equity		1,770,000		
62	Total liabilities and stockholders' equity		$3,079,000		

Situation	Concepts	Financial Statement Classification	Balance Sheet	Communication	Research

To: CEO, Stephen King Corporation
From: CPA Candidate
Re: Comprehensive income

As we discussed, you have requested a description of comprehensive income. Comprehensive income, as defined in ASC Topic 220, includes the total of all items of income of which net income is one part. Additional items are called components of other comprehensive income and include revenues, gains, expenses, and losses that are not included in net income under generally accepted accounting principles. Accumulated other comprehensive income represents cumulative amounts which are included in the stockholders' equity section of the balance sheet, whereas other comprehensive income components are single period amounts.

Comprehensive income may be reported in the financial statements under one of three alternatives.

1.   At the bottom of the income statement, continuing from net income to arrive at a comprehensive income figure,
2.   In a separate comprehensive income statement that starts with net income, or
3.   In the statement of changes in stockholders' equity.

All components should be shown net of tax, or a total tax expense may be shown with the detail for each component in the notes.

Reclassification adjustments are necessary to avoid double counting of items recognized as realized in net income of the current period that were recognized as unrealized in other comprehensive income in the current or prior period. The adjustments are shown as additions or subtractions (net of tax) from each item, except for those relating to the minimum pension liability which is shown net of adjustment for the period.

Disclosure of earnings per share is not required for other comprehensive income items or for comprehensive income.

If you have any other questions, please contact me.

Situation	Concepts	Financial Statement Classification	Balance Sheet	Communication	Research

Classifications within Other Comprehensive Income
FAS 130, Para 17

17. Items included in other comprehensive income shall be classified based on their nature. For example, under existing accounting standards, other comprehensive income shall be classified separately into foreign currency items, minimum pension liability adjustments, and unrealized gains and losses on certain investments in debt and equity securities. Additional classifications or additional items within current classifications may result from future accounting standards.

Codification: 220-10-45-13

Simulation Problem 2

Situation	Journal Entries		Calculations	Classification/Disclosures	Research	Communication

1.	Bad debt expense	16,000
	Allowance for uncollectible account	16,000
2.	Supplies expense	23,000
	Supplies	23,000
	[remaining = 23,000 (60,000 – 37,000)]	
3.	Depreciation expense	29,000
	Accumulated depreciation	29,000
	(640,000 – 60,000) ÷ 20 years = 29,000 per year	
4.	Salary expense	37,500
	Salaries payable	37,500
5.	Interest receivable	1,500
	Interest income	1,500
	75,000 × 12% × 2/12 = 1,500	
6.	Rent expense	35,000
	Prepaid rent	35,000
	168,000 ÷ 24 mo. = 7,000 per month × 5 months = 35,000	

Situation	Journal Entries	Calculations		Classification/Disclosures	Research	Communication

Accounts receivable (net)	234,000	(1)
Notes receivable	75,000	(2)
Prepaid rent	133,000	(3)
Supplies	37,000	(4)
Inventory	420,000	(5)
Equipment (historical cost)	640,000	(6)
Accounts payable	176,000	(7)
Salaries payable	52,500	(8)
Accumulated depreciation	203,000	(9)

Explanation of solutions

1. $250,000 – $16,000 allowance for uncollectible accounts = $234,000

2. No change. Interest receivable is recorded in a separate account.

3. $168,000 – $35,000 = $133,000

4. Given in the problem.

5. No adjustments were made to inventory.

6. Equipment is at historical cost.

7. No change.

8. $15,000 + $37,500 = $52,500

9. $174,000 + $29,000 = $203,000

Situation	Journal Entries	Calculations	Classification/Disclosures		Research	Communication

1. **($73,000, A)** The net carrying amount of the bonds redeemed is determined by adjusting the carrying amount of the bonds at the beginning of the year for any partial year amortization of corresponding premiums or discounts and for any unamortized issue costs. In this example, Hillside would determine its discount amortization by computing the difference between its bond interest expense and its bond interest paid as of June 30, 2010.

Bond interest expense			Bond interest paid			
Carrying amount of bonds at beginning of period	×	Effective interest rate	−	Face value of bonds	×	Stated interest rate	= Amortization amount
$940,000 × 10% × 1/2			−	$1,000,000 × 8% 1/2			= $7,000

This amount is added to the carrying amount of the bonds at the beginning of the year to determine the net carrying amount: $940,000 + $7,000 = $947,000. This amount is subtracted from the reacquisition price to determine the loss on redemption: $1,020,000 ($1,000,000 × 1.02) − $947,000 = $73,000. Gains or losses from early redemption of bonds are treated as gains or losses in determining net income. According to SFAS 145, early extinguishment of debt is no longer routinely considered an extraordinary item.

2. ($50,000, A) The accounting change is accounted for on a prospective basis. Therefore, it is necessary to calculate the book value of the asset as of the beginning of the year of the change.

		SYD	
2007	$500,000 × 5/15 =	$166,667
2008	$500,000 × 4/15 =	$133,333
2009	$500,000 × 3/15 =	$100,000
		$400,000

On January 1, 2010, the book value is calculated as follows:

Historical cost	$520,000
− Accumulated depreciation	(400,000)
Book value 1/1/10	$120,000

Straight-line depreciation for 2010 and future years is calculated as

($120,000 BV − $20,000 salvage value) ÷ 2 years remaining life = $50,000 per year

The depreciation expense would be shown as a part of the calculation of income from continuing operations.

3. ([$125,000], A) Since an accrual was made for Hillside's contingent liability in 2009, one must first determine the amount of the liability recorded. If a range of possible losses exists and no amount within the range is more likely than any other amount, an accrual should be made for the minimum amount of the loss, in this case $250,000. As Hillside accrued a $250,000 liability and loss in 2009, the 2010 loss would be $125,000 ($250,000 − $375,000). Such a loss would be classified under income from continuing operations as it is incurred in conjunction with ordinary operations (amount paid to employee). Such a loss would not be extraordinary as it does not meet the criteria of being both unusual in nature and infrequent in occurrence.

4. ([$10,000], A) Trading securities are securities that are bought and held principally for the purpose of selling them in the near term. As Hillside purchased these securities to sell in the near term, any unrealized holding gain or loss would appear as income from continuing operations on the income statement. The holding gain or loss from marketable equity securities held in the trading portfolio is computed as of December 31, 2010, by comparing the cost of the securities at the purchase date with the fair market value at the end of the year.

	Cost	*FV (12/31/10)*	*Gain (loss)*
I	$125,000	$145,000	$ 20,000
II	235,000	205,000	(30,000)
			$(10,000)

5. ([$255,000], B) The amount of gain or loss from the hurricane would be computed by adding the carrying amounts of the assets destroyed and comparing this amount with the amount of insurance recovery. For Hillside, an extraordinary loss would result as follows:

Insurance recovery	$ 1,000,000
Warehouse	470,000
Equipment	250,000
Inventory	535,000
Total carrying value	$ 1,255,000
Extraordinary loss	$ (255,000)

As this hurricane is unusual in that it is not related to the normal activities of the entity and infrequent in occurrence in that it is not expected to occur again in the foreseeable future (this was the first hurricane ever in Hillside's area), the $255,000 loss would be classified as an extraordinary loss.

6. ($41,000, E) To compute the translation adjustment for 2010, both the net asset figures in dollars must be compared. The $429,000 represents the translation at the date of purchase plus the translation of net income at a weighted-average exchange rate. The $388,000 represents the net assets at the translated rate at the balance sheet date. The $41,000 difference is the translation adjustment necessary to make the balance sheet balance. This translation adjustment should not be included in net income, but shall be reported as a separate component of other comprehensive income.

Situation	Journal Entries	Calculations	Classification/Disclosures	Research	Communication

1. How should Hillside report the extraordinary item in its income statement?

APB30, Para 11

11. In the absence of discontinued operations and changes in accounting principles, the following main captions should appear in an income statement if extraordinary items are reported (paragraphs 17-19 of APB Opinion No. 9).

Income before extraordinary items 4	$xxx
Extraordinary items	
(less applicable income taxes of ($_____) (Note _____)	xxx
Net income	$xxx

The caption extraordinary items should be used to identify separately the effects of events and transactions, other than the disposal of a segment of a business that meet the criteria for classification as extraordinary as discussed in paragraphs 19-24. Descriptive captions and the amounts for individual extraordinary events or transactions should be presented preferably on the face of the income statement, if practicable; otherwise disclosure in related notes is acceptable. The nature of an extraordinary event or transaction and the principal items entering into the determination of an extraordinary gain or loss should be described. The income taxes applicable to extraordinary items should be disclosed on the face of the income statement; alternatively, disclosure in the related notes is acceptable. The caption net income should replace the three captions shown above if the income statement includes no extraordinary items.

Codification: 225-20-45-11

2. How should Hillside report the effect of the discontinued operations in its 2010 income statement?

FAS144, Para 43

43. In a period in which a component of an entity either has been disposed of or is classified as held for sale, the income statement of a business enterprise (or statement of activities of a not-for-profit organization) for current periods shall report the results of operations of the component, including any gain or loss recognized in accordance with paragraph 37, in discontinued operations. The results of operations of a component classified as held for sale shall be reported in discontinued operation in the period(s) in which they occur. The results of discontinued operations, less applicable income taxes (benefit), shall be reported as a separate component of income before extraordinary items and the cumulative effect of accounting changes (if applicable). For example, the results of discontinued operations may be reported in the income statement of a business enterprise as follows:

Income from continuing operations before income taxes	$xxxx
Income taxes	xxxx
Income from continuing operations	$xxxx
Discontinued operations (Note X)	
Loss from operations of discontinued Component x	
(including loss on disposal of $xxx)	xxxx
Income tax benefit	xxxx
Loss on discontinued operations	xxxx
Net income	$xxxx

A gain or loss recognized on the disposal shall be disclosed either on the face of the income statement or in the notes to the financial statements (paragraph 47(b)).

Codification: 205-20-45-3

3. How should Hillside report the costs that were incurred to relocate employees of the discontinued component?

4. How should Hillside account for the change in inventory method from LIFO to average cost?

5. What disclosures are required in the financial statements in the year of the change?

Other Associated Costs
FAS146, Para 17

17. Other costs associated with an exit or disposal activity include, but are not limited to, costs to consolidate or close facilities and relocate employees. A liability for other costs associated with an exit or disposal activity shall be recognized and measured at its fair value in the period in which the liability is incurred (generally, when goods or services associated with the activity are received). The liability shall not be recognized before it is incurred, even if the costs are incremental to other operating costs and will be incurred as a direct result of a plan.

Codification: 420-10-25-14 and 420-10-25-15

Reporting
FAS146, Para 18

18. Costs associated with an exit or disposal activity that does not involve discontinued operation shall be included in income from continuing operations before income taxes in the income statement of a business enterprise and in income from continuing operations in the statement of activities of a not-for-profit organization. If a subtotal such as "income from operations" is presented, it shall include the amounts of those costs. Costs associated with an exit or disposal activity that involves a discontinued operation shall be included in the results of discontinued operations.

Codification: 420-10-45-3

FAS154, Para 7

7. An entity shall report a change in accounting principle through retrospective application of the new accounting principle to all prior periods, unless it is impracticable to do so. Retrospective application requires the following:

a. The cumulative effect of the change to the new accounting prinicple on periods prior to those presented shall be reflected in the carrying amounts of assets and liabilities as of the beginning of the first period presented.
b. An offsetting adjustment, if any, shall be made to the opening balance of retained earnings (or other appropriate components of equity or net assets in the statement of financial position) for that period.
c. Financial statements for each individual prior period presented shall be adjusted to reflect the period-specific effects of applying the new accounting principle.

Codification: 250-10-45-5

FAS154, Para 17

17. An entity shall disclose the following in the fiscal period in which a change in accounting principle is made:

a. The nature of and reason for the change in accounting principle, including an explanation of why the newly adopted accounting principle is preferable.
b. The method of applying the change, and

1. A description of the prior-period information that has been retrospectively adjusted, if any.
2. The effect of the change on income from continuing operations, net income (or other appropriate captions of changes in the applicable net assets or performance indicator), any other affected financial statement line item, and any affected per share amounts for the current period and any prior periods retrospectively adjusted. Presentation of the effect on financial statement subtotals and totals other than income from continuing operations and net income (or other appro-

priate captions of changes in the applicable net assets or performance indicator) is not required.

3. The cumulative effect of the change on retained earnings or other components of equity or net assets in the statement of financial position as of the beginning of the earliest period presented.

4. If retrospective application to all prior periods (paragraph 7) is impracticable, disclosure of the reasons therefor, and a description of the alternative method used to report the change (paragraphs 8 and 9).

c. If indirect effects of a change in accounting principle are recognized

1. A description of the indirect effects of a change in accounting principle, including the amounts that have been recognized in the current period, and the related per-share amounts, if applicable

2. Unless impracticable, the amount of the total recognized indirect effects of the accounting change and the related per share amounts, if applicable, that are attributable to each prior period presented

Financial statements of subsequent periods need not repeat the disclosures required by this paragraph. If a change in accounting principle has no material effect in the period of change but is reasonably certain to have a material effect in later periods, the disclosures required by paragraph 17(a) shall be provided whenever the financial statements of the period of change are presented.

Codification: 250-10-50-1

Situation	Journal Entries	Calculations	Classification/Disclosures	Research	Communication

To: Hillside Company Permanent File
From: CPA Candidate
Re: Accounting issues related to income statement presentation
Date: [*Today's date*]

This memorandum summarizes my research regarding the presentation of certain items in the financial statements of Hillside Company.

Issue 1: How should Hillside report the extraordinary item in its income statement?

Hillside should report the extraordinary item separately, net of applicable income taxes, below the continuing operations section of the income statement. Exclusion of extraordinary items from the results of continuing operations is intended to produce a measure of income from continuing operations that is useful in predicting future operating cash flows.

Issue 2: How should Hillside report the effect of the discontinued operations in its 2010 income statement?

Hillside should report the discontinued operations separately in the 2010 income statement immediately below income from continuing operations. Discontinued operations should be comprised of

• Loss from operations of the discontinued component and the loss on disposal
• Income tax benefit

Issue 3: How should Hillside report the costs that were incurred to relocate employees of the discontinued component?

Hillside should include the costs incurred to relocate employees in the loss on disposal of the discontinued component in its 2010 income statement. These costs are a direct result of the commitment to dispose of the component.

If you have any additional information regarding these matters, please document them.

Simulation Problem 3

Situation	Classifications	Multistep Income Statement	Retained Earnings Statement	Communication	Research

(A) (B) (C) (D) (E) (F) (G) (H) (I)

1. Newly acquired assets are depreciated using the sum-of-the-years' digits method; previously recorded assets are depreciated using the straight-line method. — ○ ○ ○ ○ ○ ○ ● ○ ○

2. Accounting for the acquisition of a 100% owned subsidiary. — ● ○ ○ ○ ○ ○ ○ ○ ○

3. Reported as a restatement of all periods presented. — ○ ● ○ ○ ○ ○ ○ ○ ○

4. Write-down of inventory due to obsolescence. — ○ ○ ○ ○ ○ ○ ○ ● ○

5. Gains or losses on the disposal of the net assets of a component are included in this calculation. — ○ ○ ○ ○ ○ ○ ○ ○ ●

6. Changing from the gross profit method for determining year-end inventory balances to dollar value LIFO. — ○ ● ○ ○ ○ ○ ○ ○ ○

7. Accounting for existing construction contracts is changed from completed contract to percentage-of-completion. — ○ ○ ● ○ ○ ○ ○ ○ ○

8. The effects of a change in estimate and a change in principle are inseparable for the same event. — ○ ○ ○ ● ○ ○ ○ ○ ○

9. The excess of cash paid over the carrying value to extinguish bonds. — ○ ○ ○ ○ ○ ○ ○ ● ○

10. Income or loss of the component for the period of disposal included in this calculation. — ○ ○ ○ ○ ● ○ ○ ○ ○

Explanation of solutions

1.   (G) The acquisition of assets does not necessitate that the same method of depreciation be used for the newly acquired assets as for the existing assets. Therefore, no change in accounting principle has occurred because the previously recorded assets will continue to be depreciated using the straight-line method.

2.   (A) Accounting for the acquisition of a 100% owned subsidiary is properly accounted for as a change in reporting entity.

3.   (B) All corrections of errors should be treated as a restatement of the prior period financial statements. This requires prompt recording of the error in the year in which the error was discovered, and reporting the effects of the error in the financial statements as an adjustment to the carrying value of the assets and liabilities as of the beginning of the first period presented with an offsetting adjustment to the opening balance of retained earnings for that period. Financial statements for each individual period are adjusted to reflect the correction of the period-specific effects of the error.

4.   (H) For an item to qualify as an extraordinary item it must be both unusual in nature and infrequent in occurrence. Clearly, the write-down of inventory due to obsolescence does not qualify for extraordinary treatment; therefore, it should be disclosed separately in the income statement before extraordinary items.

5.   (I) Gains or losses on the disposal of net assets is included in the calculation of gain or loss on disposal of discontinued operations. Therefore, the total gain or loss on disposal should consist of the following two calculations: the net asset gain or loss mentioned above and the income or loss from operations from the measurement date to the disposal date (the phase-out period).

6.   (B) The use of the gross profit method to determine year-end inventory balances is not proper GAAP. Therefore, if a situation such as this existed, it should be treated as a correction of an error.

7.   (C) The change from one generally accepted accounting principle to another is considered a change in accounting principle. Since both the completed contract method and the percentage-of-completion methods are recognized GAAP, the change from one to the other is properly accounted for as a change in accounting principle, and accounted for on a retrospective basis.

8.   (D) When it is impossible to determine whether a change in accounting principle or a change in estimate has occurred, the change should be considered as a change in estimate.

9.   (H) Gains or losses on extinguishment of debt are no longer treated as extraordinary items.

10.   (F) Income or loss from operations is properly included in the calculation of the gain or loss on the discontinued operations. Therefore, this calculation includes both the income or loss from operations and the gain or loss on the disposal of net assets. The gain or loss on the disposal should also be disclosed parenthetically or in the notes to the financial statements.

Situation	Classifications	Multistep Income Statement	Retained Earnings Statement	Communication	Research

American Horse Company
INCOME STATEMENT
For the Year Ended December 31, 2009

Sales		$25,000,000
Less cost of goods sold		(17,000,000)
Gross profit		$ 8,000,000
Less selling and administrative expenses		(4,700,000)
Income from operations		$ 3,300,000
Other revenue and gains		
Interest revenue	$ 70,000	
Gain on the sale of investments	110,000	$180,000
Other expenses and losses		
Write-off of goodwill		(820,000)
Income from continuing operations before income taxes		$2,660,000
Income taxes		(905,000)
Income from continuing operations		$1,755,000
Discontinued operations		
Loss on discontinued wholesale division, including loss on disposal of $200,000	$815,000	
Income tax benefit	(285,000)	
Loss on discontinued operation (net of tax)		(530,000)
Income before extraordinary item		$1,225,000
Extraordinary loss from flood damage, net of tax		(390,000)
Net income		$ 835,000
Earnings per share		
Income from continuing operations		$5.62[a]
Discontinued operations:		(1.77)
Income before extraordinary item		3.85[b]
Extraordinary loss (net of tax)		(1.30)
Net income		$2.55[c]

[a] $\dfrac{\$1,755,000 - \$70,000}{300,000 \text{ shares}} = \$5.62$

[b] $\dfrac{\$1,225,000 - \$70,000}{300,000 \text{ shares}} = \$3.85$

[c] $\dfrac{\$835,000 - \$70,000}{300,000 \text{ shares}} = \$2.55$

Situation	Classifications	Multistep Income Statement	Retained Earnings Statement	Communication	Research

American Horse Company
RETAINED EARNINGS STATEMENT
For the Year Ended December 31, 2009

Retained earnings, January 1, 2009		$980,000
Plus net income		835,000
		1,815,000
Less dividends	$ 70,000	
	250,000	(320,000)
Retained earnings, December 31, 2009		$1,495,000

Situation	Classifications	Multistep Income Statement	Retained Earnings Statement	Communication	Research

To: Manager, American Horse Company
From: CPA Candidate
Re: Distinction between income statement items

This memorandum summarizes the answer to your questions regarding the nature of income statement items. The major distinction between revenues and gains (or expenses and losses) depends on the typical activities of the enterprise. Revenues can occur from a variety of different sources, but these sources constitute the entity's ongoing major or central operations. Gains also can arise from many different sources, but these sources occur from peripheral or incidental transactions of an entity. The same type of distinction is made between an expense and a loss.

If you have any additional questions, please contact me.

Situation	Classifications	Multistep Income Statement	Retained Earnings Statement	Communication	Research

APB30, Para 20

20. Extraordinary items are events and transactions that are distinguished by their unusual nature and by the infrequency of their occurrence. Thus, both of the following criteria should be met to classify an event or transaction as an extraordinary item.

   a. Unusual nature—the underlying event or transactions should possess a high degree of abnormality and be of a type clearly unrelated to, or only incidentally related to, the ordinary and typical activities of the entity, taking into account the environment in which the entity operates. (See discussion in paragraph 21.)
   b. Infrequency of occurrence—the underlying event or transaction should be of a type that would not reasonably be expected to recur in the foreseeable future, taking into account the environment in which the entity operates. (See discussion in paragraph 22.)

Codification: 225-20-45-2

Simulation Problem 4

Situation	Financial Statement Classification	Calculate Net Income	Earnings Per Share	Communication	Research

	(A) (B) (C) (D) (E) (F)
1. An increase in the unrealized excess of cost over market value of marketable equity securities classified as trading-type securities.	○ ● ○ ○ ○ ○
2. The accumulated amount of the unrealized excess of cost over market value of available-for-sale marketable equity securities.	○ ○ ○ ○ ● ○
3. Income from operations of a discontinued component in the component's disposal year.	○ ○ ○ ○ ○ ●
4. A gain on remeasuring a foreign subsidiary's financial statements from the local currency into the functional currency.	○ ● ○ ○ ○ ○
5. A loss on translating a foreign subsidiary's financial statements from the functional local currency into the reporting currency during this period.	○ ○ ● ○ ○ ○
6. A loss caused by a major earthquake in an area previously considered to be subject to only minor tremors.	○ ○ ○ ● ○ ○
7. The probable receipt of $1,000,000 from a pending lawsuit.	○ ○ ○ ○ ○ ●
8. The purchase of research and development services. There were **no** other research and development activities.	○ ● ○ ○ ○ ○

Explanation of solutions

   1.   **(B)** Changes in the market value of (trading type) marketable securities shall be included in the determination of income from continuing operations of the period in which the change in market value occurs.

   2.   **(E)** The accumulated changes in the valuation (unrealized excess of cost over market value) of **available-for-sale** marketable equity securities shall be reported as accumulated other comprehensive income.

3. **(F)** Results of operations of a component that has been or will be discontinued should be reported **separately** as a component of income, after income from continuing operations but before extraordinary items and the cumulative effect of accounting changes.

4. **(B)** A foreign subsidiary must **remeasure** its financial statements when its functional currency (the currency of the primary economic environment in which the entity operates) is different from its local currency (the currency currently used by the entity). The effect of the remeasurement process (gain or loss) should be recognized currently in income. Aggregate gain or loss for the period should also be disclosed either in the financial statements or in the notes.

5. **(C)** When translating a foreign subsidiary's financial statements from functional currency to reporting currency, a translation adjustment will result. The translation adjustment is not included in net income but is reported as a component of comprehensive income and called other comprehensive income.

6. **(D)** Extraordinary items are events and transactions that are **both** unusual and infrequent. The earthquake in this problem occurred in an area previously considered subject to only minor tremors. Therefore, the earthquake would be considered an extraordinary event. Extraordinary items should be shown separately on the income statement, after income from continuing operations.

7. **(F)** The question indicates that it is probable that the company will **receive** $1,000,000 from a pending lawsuit. Thus, the $1,000,000 is a **gain** contingency. Contingencies that may result in **gains** are not reflected in the accounts, as doing so might result in the recognition of revenue before its realization. Adequate disclosure of the gain contingency should be made, but care should be taken to avoid misleading implications as to the likelihood of realization.

8. **(B)** The cost of research and development services performed by others on behalf of the enterprise are included in R&D costs. R&D costs are charged to expense when incurred and thus are included in income from continuing operations of that period. In addition, separate disclosure of the total R&D costs for the period should be made either in the financial statements or in the notes.

Situation	Financial Statement Classification	Calculate Net Income	Earnings Per Share	Communication	Research

Rap Corp.
INCOME STATEMENT
For the Year Ended December 31, 2009

Income from continuing operations before income tax		$1,180,000
Income tax		(448,400)
Income from continuing operations		$ 731,600
Discontinued operations:		
Loss from discontinued operations (including loss from disposal of $100,000)	$(190,000)	
Income tax benefit	72,200	
Loss from discontinued operations (net of tax)		117,800
Income before extraordinary item		$ 613,800
Extraordinary item:		
Gain on sale of investment	145,000	
Less applicable taxes	58,000	87,000
Net income		$ 700,800

Situation	Financial Statement Classification	Calculate Net Income	Earnings Per Share	Communication	Research

Rap Corp.
EARNINGS STATEMENT
For the Year Ended December 31, 2009

Per share of common stock:		
Income from continuing operations		$ 7.32
Discontinued operations, net of tax		(1.18)
Income before extraordinary item		6.14
Extraordinary item, net of tax		0.87
Net income ($700,800/100,000)		$ 7.01

				Communication	
Situation	Financial Statement Classification	Calculate Net Income	Earnings Per Share		Research

To: Controller, Rap Corporation
From: CPA Candidate
Re: Earnings per share

You have requested that I provide a description of the various components of earnings per share that must be disclosed in Rap Corporation's financial statements. The presentation of earnings per share depends on the capital structure of the company and the types of gains and losses the company presents in its income statement. Entities with a simple capital structure, with only common stock outstanding, present basic earnings per share for income from continuing operations and for net income on the face of the income statement. Entities with complex capital structures present both basic and diluted earnings per share amounts for income from continuing operations and for net income on the face of the income statement.

An entity that reports discontinued operations or an extraordinary item should present both basic and diluted per share amounts for those items either on the face of the income statement or in the footnotes to the financial statements.

If you have any further questions, please contact me.

					Research
Situation	Financial Statement Classification	Calculate Net Income	Earnings Per Share	Communication	

FAS130, Para 11

11. The purpose of reporting comprehensive income is to report a measure of all changes in equity of an enterprise that result from recognized transactions and other economic events of the period other than transactions with owners in their capacity as owners. Prior to the issuance of this Statement, some of those changes in equity were displayed in a statement that reports the results of operations, while others were included directly in balances within a separate component of equity in a statement of financial position.

Codification: 220-10-10-1

MULTIPLE-CHOICE QUESTIONS (1-61)

1. The following information applied to Fenn, Inc. for 2010:

Merchandise purchased for resale	$400,000
Freight-in	10,000
Freight-out	5,000
Purchase returns	2,000

Fenn's 2010 inventoriable cost was

   a. $400,000
   b. $404,000
   c. $408,000
   d. $413,000

2. On December 28, 2010, Kerr Manufacturing Co. purchased goods costing $50,000. The terms were FOB destination. Some of the costs incurred in connection with the sale and delivery of the goods were as follows:

Packaging for shipment	$1,000
Shipping	1,500
Special handling charges	2,000

These goods were received on December 31, 2010. In Kerr's December 31, 2010 balance sheet, what amount of cost for these goods should be included in inventory?

   a. $54,500
   b. $53,500
   c. $52,000
   d. $50,000

3. On June 1, 2010, Pitt Corp. sold merchandise with a list price of $5,000 to Burr on account. Pitt allowed trade discounts of 30% and 20%. Credit terms were 2/15, n/40 and the sale was made FOB shipping point. Pitt prepaid $200 of delivery costs for Burr as an accommodation. On June 12, 2010, Pitt received from Burr a remittance in full payment amounting to

   a. $2,744
   b. $2,940
   c. $2,944
   d. $3,140

4. The following information was taken from Cody Co.'s accounting records for the year ended December 31, 2010:

Decrease in raw materials inventory	$ 15,000
Increase in finished goods inventory	35,000
Raw material purchased	430,000
Direct labor payroll	200,000
Factory overhead	300,000
Freight-out	45,000

There was no work in process inventory at the beginning or end of the year. Cody's 2010 cost of goods sold is

   a. $895,000
   b. $910,000
   c. $950,000
   d. $955,000

5. The following information pertains to Deal Corp.'s 2010 cost of goods sold:

Inventory, 12/31/09	$ 90,000
2010 purchases	124,000
2010 write-off of obsolete inventory	34,000
Inventory, 12/31/10	30,000

The inventory written off became obsolete due to an unexpected and unusual technological advance by a competitor. In its 2010 income statement, what amount should Deal report as cost of goods sold?

   a. $218,000
   b. $184,000
   c. $150,000
   d. $124,000

6. How should the following costs affect a retailer's inventory?

	Freight-in	Interest on inventory loan
a.	Increase	No effect
b.	Increase	Increase
c.	No effect	Increase
d.	No effect	No effect

7. According to the net method, which of the following items should be included in the cost of inventory?

	Freight costs	Purchase discounts not taken
a.	Yes	No
b.	Yes	Yes
c.	No	Yes
d.	No	No

8. The following information pertained to Azur Co. for the year:

Purchases	$102,800
Purchase discounts	10,280
Freight in	15,420
Freight out	5,140
Beginning inventory	30,840
Ending inventory	20,560

What amount should Azur report as cost of goods sold for the year?

   a. $102,800
   b. $118,220
   c. $123,360
   d. $128,500

9. When allocating costs to inventory produced for the period, fixed overhead should be based upon

   a. The actual amounts of goods produced during the period.
   b. The normal capacity of production facilities.
   c. The highest production levels in the last three periods.
   d. The lowest production level in the last three periods.

10. Per the Codification, what is considered the normal capacity of production facilities?

   a. The average production over the previous five-year period.
   b. Actual production for the period.
   c. Actual production for the period plus loss of capacity for planned maintenance.
   d. A range that may vary based on business and industry-specific factors.

11. How should unallocated fixed overhead costs be treated?

   a. Allocated to finished goods and cost of goods based on ending balances in the accounts.
   b. Allocated to raw materials, work in process, and finished goods, based on the ending balances in the accounts.
   c. Recognized as an expense in the period in which they are incurred.
   d. Allocated to work in process, finished goods, and cost of goods sold based on ending balances in the accounts.

12. When manufacturing inventory, what is the accounting treatment for abnormal freight-in costs?
   a.   Charge to expense for the period.
   b.   Charge to the finished goods inventory.
   c.   Charge to raw materials inventory.
   d.   Allocate to raw materials, work in process, and finished goods.

13. On December 15, 2010, Flanagan purchased goods costing $100,000. The terms were FOB shipping point. Costs incurred by Flanagan in connection with the purchase and delivery of the goods were as follows:

Normal freight charges	$3,000
Handling costs	2,000
Insurance on shipment	500
Abnormal freight charges for express shipping	1,200

The goods were received on December 17, 2010. What is the amount that Flanagan should charge to inventory and to current period expense?

	Inventory	Current period expense
a.	$3,000	$3,700
b.	$5,000	$1,700
c.	$5,500	$1,200
d.	$6,700	$0

14. Bach Co. adopted the dollar-value LIFO inventory method as of January 1, 2010. A single inventory pool and an internally computed price index are used to compute Bach's LIFO inventory layers. Information about Bach's dollar value inventory follows:

	Inventory	
	at base	at dollar
Date	year cost	value LIFO
1/1/09	$90,000	$90,000
2009 layer	20,000	30,000
2010 layer	40,000	80,000

What was the price index used to compute Bach's 2010 dollar value LIFO inventory layer?
   a.   1.09
   b.   1.25
   c.   1.33
   d.   2.00

15. Nest Co. recorded the following inventory information during the month of January:

	Units	Unit cost	Total cost	Units on hand
Balance on 1/1	2,000	$1	$2,000	2,000
Purchased on 1/8	1,200	3	3,600	3,200
Sold on 1/23	1,800			1,400
Purchased on 1/28	800	5	4,000	2,200

Nest uses the LIFO method to cost inventory. What amount should Nest report as inventory on January 31 under each of the following methods of recording inventory?

	Perpetual	Periodic
a.	$2,600	$5,400
b.	$5,400	$2,600
c.	$2,600	$2,600
d.	$5,400	$5,400

16. The weighted-average for the year inventory cost flow method is applicable to which of the following inventory systems?

	Periodic	Perpetual
a.	Yes	Yes
b.	Yes	No
c.	No	Yes
d.	No	No

17. During January 2010, Metro Co., which maintains a perpetual inventory system, recorded the following information pertaining to its inventory:

	Units	Unit cost	Total cost	Units on hand
Balance on 1/1/10	1,000	$1	$1,000	1,000
Purchased on 1/7/10	600	3	1,800	1,600
Sold on 1/20/10	900			700
Purchased on 1/25/10	400	5	2,000	1,100

Under the moving-average method, what amount should Metro report as inventory at January 31, 2010?
   a. $2,640
   b. $3,225
   c. $3,300
   d. $3,900

18. Based on a physical inventory taken on December 31, 2010, Chewy Co. determined its chocolate inventory on a FIFO basis at $26,000 with a replacement cost of $20,000. Chewy estimated that, after further processing costs of $12,000, the chocolate could be sold as finished candy bars for $40,000. Chewy's normal profit margin is 10% of sales. Under the lower of cost or market rule, what amount should Chewy report as chocolate inventory in its December 31, 2010 balance sheet?
   a. $28,000
   b. $26,000
   c. $24,000
   d. $20,000

19. Reporting inventory at the lower of cost or market is a departure from the accounting principle of
   a.   Historical cost.
   b.   Consistency.
   c.   Conservatism.
   d.   Full disclosure.

20. The original cost of an inventory item is below both replacement cost and net realizable value. The net realizable value less normal profit margin is below the original cost. Under the lower of cost or market method, the inventory item should be valued at
   a.   Replacement cost.
   b.   Net realizable value.
   c.   Net realizable value less normal profit margin.
   d.   Original cost.

21. Which of the following statements are correct when a company applying the lower of cost or market method reports its inventory at replacement cost?

I.   The original cost is less than replacement cost.
II. The net realizable value is greater than replacement cost.

   a.   I only.
   b.   II only.
   c.   Both I and II.
   d.   Neither I nor II.

22. The original cost of an inventory item is above the replacement cost and the net realizable value. The replacement cost is below the net realizable value less the normal profit margin. As a result, under the lower of cost or market method, the inventory item should be reported at the
   a.   Net realizable value.
   b.   Net realizable value less the normal profit margin.

c.   Replacement cost.
d.   Original cost.

23. On January 1, 2010, Card Corp. signed a three-year noncancelable purchase contract, which allows Card to purchase up to 500,000 units of a computer part annually from Hart Supply Co. at $.10 per unit and guarantees a minimum annual purchase of 100,000 units. During 2010, the part unexpectedly became obsolete. Card had 250,000 units of this inventory at December 31, 2010, and believes these parts can be sold as scrap for $.02 per unit. What amount of probable loss from the purchase commitment should Card report in its 2010 income statement?

a. $24,000
b. $20,000
c. $16,000
d. $ 8,000

24. Thread Co. is selecting its inventory system in preparation for its first year of operations. Thread intends to use either the periodic weighted-average method or the perpetual moving-average method, and to apply the lower of cost or market rule either to individual items or to the total inventory. Inventory prices are expected to generally increase throughout 2010, although a few individual prices will decrease. What inventory system should Thread select if it wants to maximize the inventory carrying amount at December 31, 2010?

	Inventory method	*Cost or market application*
a.	Perpetual	Total inventory
b.	Perpetual	Individual item
c.	Periodic	Total inventory
d.	Periodic	Individual item

25. Marsh Company had 150 units of product A on hand at January 1, 2010, costing $21 each. Purchases of product A during the month of January were as follows:

	Units	*Unit cost*
Jan. 10	200	$22
18	250	23
28	100	24

A physical count on January 31, 2010, shows 250 units of product A on hand. The cost of the inventory at January 31, 2010, under the LIFO method is

a. $5,850
b. $5,550
c. $5,350
d. $5,250

26. During January 2010, Metro Co., which maintains a perpetual inventory system, recorded the following information pertaining to its inventory:

	Units	*Unit cost*	*Total cost*	*Units on hand*
Balance on 1/1/10	1,000	$1	$1,000	1,000
Purchased on 1/7/10	600	3	1,800	1,600
Sold on 1/20/10	900			700
Purchased on 1/25/10	400	5	2,000	1,100

Under the LIFO method, what amount should Metro report as inventory at January 31, 2010?

a. $1,300
b. $2,700
c. $3,900
d. $4,100

27. Drew Co. uses the average cost inventory method for internal reporting purposes and LIFO for financial statement and income tax reporting. At December 31, 2010, the inventory was $375,000 using average cost and $320,000 using LIFO. The unadjusted credit balance in the LIFO Reserve account on December 31, 2010, was $35,000. What adjusting entry should Drew record to adjust from average cost to LIFO at December 31, 2010?

		Debit	*Credit*
a.	Cost of goods sold	$55,000	
	Inventory		$55,000
b.	Cost of goods sold	$55,000	
	LIFO reserve		$55,000
c.	Cost of goods sold	$20,000	
	Inventory		$20,000
d.	Cost of goods sold	$20,000	
	LIFO reserve		$20,000

28. A company decided to change its inventory valuation method from FIFO to LIFO in a period of rising prices. What was the result of the change on ending inventory and net income in the year of the change?

	Ending inventory	*Net income*
a.	Increase	Increase
b.	Increase	Decrease
c.	Decrease	Decrease
d.	Decrease	Increase

29. Generally, which inventory costing method approximates most closely the current cost for each of the following?

	Cost of goods sold	*Ending inventory*
a.	LIFO	FIFO
b.	LIFO	LIFO
c.	FIFO	FIFO
d.	FIFO	LIFO

30. During periods of rising prices, a perpetual inventory system would result in the same dollar amount of ending inventory as a periodic inventory system under which of the following inventory cost flow methods?

	FIFO	*LIFO*
a.	Yes	No
b.	Yes	Yes
c.	No	Yes
d.	No	No

31. On January 1, 2009, Poe Company adopted the dollar-value LIFO inventory method. Poe's entire inventory constitutes a single pool. Inventory data for 2009 and 2010 are as follows:

Date	*Inventory at current year cost*	*Inventory at base year cost*	*Relevant price index*
1/1/09	$150,000	$150,000	1.00
12/31/09	220,000	200,000	1.10
12/31/10	276,000	230,000	1.20

Poe's LIFO inventory value at December 31, 2010, is

a. $230,000
b. $236,000
c. $241,000
d. $246,000

32. Brock Co. adopted the dollar-value LIFO inventory method as of January 1, 2009. A single inventory pool and an internally computed price index are used to compute

Brock's LIFO inventory layers. Information about Brock's dollar-value inventory follows:

	Inventory		
Date	At base year cost	At current year cost	At dollar value LIFO
1/1/09	$40,000	$40,000	$40,000
2009 layer	5,000	14,000	6,000
12/31/09	45,000	54,000	46,000
2010 layer	15,000	26,000	?
12/31/10	$60,000	$80,000	?

What was Brock's dollar-value LIFO inventory at December 31, 2010?

- a. $80,000
- b. $74,000
- c. $66,000
- d. $60,000

33. Estimates of price-level changes for specific inventories are required for which of the following inventory methods?

- a. Conventional retail.
- b. Dollar-value LIFO.
- c. Weighted-average cost.
- d. Average cost retail.

34. When the double-extension approach to the dollar-value LIFO inventory method is used, the inventory layer added in the current year is multiplied by an index number. Which of the following correctly states how components are used in the calculation of this index number?

- a. In the numerator, the average of the ending inventory at base year cost and at current year cost.
- b. In the numerator, the ending inventory at current year cost, and, in the denominator, the ending inventory at base year cost.
- c. In the numerator, the ending inventory at base year cost, and, the denominator, the ending inventory at current year cost.
- d. In the denominator, the average of the ending inventory at base year cost and at current year cost.

35. Jones Wholesalers stocks a changing variety of products. Which inventory costing method will be most likely to give Jones the lowest ending inventory when its product lines are subject to specific price increases?

- a. Specific identification.
- b. Weighted-average.
- c. Dollar-value LIFO.
- d. FIFO periodic.

36. Dart Company's accounting records indicated the following information:

Inventory, 1/1/10	$ 500,000
Purchases during 2010	2,500,000
Sales during 2010	3,200,000

A physical inventory taken on December 31, 2010, resulted in an ending inventory of $575,000. Dart's gross profit on sales has remained constant at 25% in recent years. Dart suspects some inventory may have been taken by a new employee. At December 31, 2010, what is the estimated cost of missing inventory?

- a. $ 25,000
- b. $100,000
- c. $175,000
- d. $225,000

37. On July 1, 2010, Casa Development Co. purchased a tract of land for $1,200,000. Casa incurred additional cost of $300,000 during the remainder of 2010 in preparing the land for sale. The tract was subdivided into residential lots as follows:

Lot class	Number of lots	Sales price per lot
A	100	$24,000
B	100	16,000
C	200	10,000

Using the relative sales value method, what amount of costs should be allocated to the Class A lots?

- a. $300,000
- b. $375,000
- c. $600,000
- d. $720,000

38. Herc Co.'s inventory at December 31, 2010, was $1,500,000 based on a physical count priced at cost, and before any necessary adjustment for the following:

- Merchandise costing $90,000, shipped FOB shipping point from a vendor on December 30, 2010, was received and recorded on January 5, 2011.
- Goods in the shipping area were excluded from inventory although shipment was not made until January 4, 2011. The goods, billed to the customer FOB shipping point on December 30, 2010, had a cost of $120,000.

What amount should Herc report as inventory in its December 31, 2010 balance sheet?

- a. $1,500,000
- b. $1,590,000
- c. $1,620,000
- d. $1,710,000

39. Kew Co.'s accounts payable balance at December 31, 2010, was $2,200,000 before considering the following data:

- Goods shipped to Kew FOB shipping point on December 22, 2010 were lost in transit. The invoice cost of $40,000 was not recorded by Kew. On January 7, 2011, Kew filed a $40,000 claim against the common carrier.
- On December 27, 2010, a vendor authorized Kew to return, for full credit, goods shipped and billed at $70,000 on December 3, 2010. The returned goods were shipped by Kew on December 28, 2010. A $70,000 credit memo was received and recorded by Kew on January 5, 2011.
- Goods shipped to Kew FOB destination on December 20, 2010, were received on January 6, 2011. The invoice cost was $50,000.

What amount should Kew report as accounts payable in its December 31, 2010 balance sheet?

- a. $2,170,000
- b. $2,180,000
- c. $2,230,000
- d. $2,280,000

40. Lewis Company's usual sales terms are net sixty days, FOB shipping point. Sales, net of returns and allowances, totaled $2,300,000 for the year ended December 31, 2010, before year-end adjustments. Additional data are as follows:

- On December 27, 2010, Lewis authorized a customer to return, for full credit, goods shipped and billed at $50,000 on December 15, 2010. The returned goods were received by Lewis on January 4, 2011, and a $50,000 credit memo was issued and recorded on the same date.

- Goods with an invoice amount of $80,000 were billed and recorded on January 3, 2011. The goods were shipped on December 30, 2010.
- Goods with an invoice amount of $100,000 were billed and recorded on December 30, 2010. The goods were shipped on January 3, 2011.

Lewis' adjusted net sales for 2010 should be

    a. $2,330,000
    b. $2,280,000
    c. $2,250,000
    d. $2,230,000

41. On January 1, 2010, Dell, Inc. contracted with the city of Little to provide custom built desks for the city schools. The contract made Dell the city's sole supplier and required Dell to supply no less than 4,000 desks and no more than 5,500 desks per year for two years. In turn, Little agreed to pay a fixed price of $110 per desk. During 2010, Dell produced 5,000 desks for Little. At December 31, 2010, 500 of these desks were segregated from the regular inventory and were accepted and awaiting pickup by Little. Little paid Dell $450,000 during 2010. What amount should Dell recognize as contract revenue in 2010?

    a. $450,000
    b. $495,000
    c. $550,000
    d. $605,000

42. On October 20, 2010, Grimm Co. consigned forty freezers to Holden Co. for sale at $1,000 each and paid $800 in transportation costs. On December 30, 2010, Holden reported the sale of ten freezers and remitted $8,500. The remittance was net of the agreed 15% commission. What amount should Grimm recognize as consignment sales revenue for 2010?

    a. $ 7,700
    b. $ 8,500
    c. $ 9,800
    d. $10,000

43. The following items were included in Opal Co.'s inventory account at December 31, 2010:

Merchandise out on consignment, at sales price, including 40% markup on selling price	$40,000
Goods purchased, in transit, shipped FOB shipping point	36,000
Goods held on consignment by Opal	27,000

By what amount should Opal's inventory account at December 31, 2010, be reduced?

    a. $103,000
    b. $ 67,000
    c. $ 51,000
    d. $ 43,000

44. On December 1, 2010, Alt Department Store received 505 sweaters on consignment from Todd. Todd's cost for the sweaters was $80 each, and they were priced to sell at $100. Alt's commission on consigned goods is 10%. At December 31, 2010, five sweaters remained. In its December 31, 2010 balance sheet, what amount should Alt report as payable for consigned goods?

    a. $49,000
    b. $45,400
    c. $45,000
    d. $40,400

45. Southgate Co. paid the in-transit insurance premium for consignment goods shipped to Hendon Co., the consignee. In addition, Southgate advanced part of the commissions that will be due when Hendon sells the goods. Should Southgate include the in-transit insurance premium and the advanced commissions in inventory costs?

	Insurance premium	Advanced commissions
a.	Yes	Yes
b.	No	No
c.	Yes	No
d.	No	Yes

46. Jel Co., a consignee, paid the freight costs for goods shipped from Dale Co., a consignor. These freight costs are to be deducted from Jel's payment to Dale when the consignment goods are sold. Until Jel sells the goods, the freight costs should be included in Jel's

    a. Cost of goods sold.
    b. Freight-out costs.
    c. Selling expenses.
    d. Accounts receivable.

47. Heath Co.'s current ratio is 4:1. Which of the following transactions would normally increase its current ratio?

    a. Purchasing inventory on account.
    b. Selling inventory on account.
    c. Collecting an account receivable.
    d. Purchasing machinery for cash.

48. During 2010, Rand Co. purchased $960,000 of inventory. The cost of goods sold for 2010 was $900,000, and the ending inventory at December 31, 2010, was $180,000. What was the inventory turnover for 2010?

    a. 6.4
    b. 6.0
    c. 5.3
    d. 5.0

49. In a comparison of 2010 to 2009, Neir Co.'s inventory turnover ratio increased substantially although sales and inventory amounts were essentially unchanged. Which of the following statements explains the increased inventory turnover ratio?

    a. Cost of goods sold decreased.
    b. Accounts receivable turnover increased.
    c. Total asset turnover increased.
    d. Gross profit percentage decreased.

50. Selected data pertaining to Lore Co. for the calendar year 2010 is as follows:

Net cash sales	$ 3,000
Cost of goods sold	18,000
Inventory at beginning of year	6,000
Purchases	24,000
Accounts receivable at beginning of year	20,000
Accounts receivable at end of year	22,000

Lore would use which of the following to determine the average days' sales in inventory?

	Numerator	Denominator
a.	365	Average inventory
b.	365	Inventory turnover
c.	Average inventory	Sales divided by 365
d.	Sales divided by 365	Inventory turnover

51. Cord Builders, Inc. has consistently used the percentage-of-completion method of accounting for construction-type contracts. During 2009 Cord started work on a $9,000,000 fixed-price construction contract that was completed in 2011. Cord's accounting records disclosed the following:

	December 31	
	2009	2010
Cumulative contract costs incurred	$3,900,000	$6,300,000
Estimated total cost at completion	7,800,000	8,100,000

How much income would Cord have recognized on this contract for the year ended December 31, 2010?

- a. $100,000
- b. $300,000
- c. $600,000
- d. $700,000

52. State Co. recognizes construction revenue and expenses using the percentage-of-completion method. During 2009, a single long-term project was begun, which continued through 2010. Information on the project follows:

	2009	2010
Accounts receivable from		
construction contract	$100,000	$300,000
Construction expenses	105,000	192,000
Construction in progress	122,000	364,000
Partial billings on contract	100,000	420,000

Profit recognized from the long-term construction contract in 2010 should be

- a. $ 50,000
- b. $108,000
- c. $128,000
- d. $228,000

53. Lake Construction Company has consistently used the percentage-of-completion method of recognizing income. During 2009, Lake entered into a fixed-price contract to construct an office building for $10,000,000. Information relating to the contract is as follows:

	At December 31,	
	2009	2010
Percentage of completion	20%	60%
Estimated total cost at completion	$7,500,000	$8,000,000
Income recognized (cumulative)	500,000	1,200,000

Contract costs incurred during 2010 were

- a. $3,200,000
- b. $3,300,000
- c. $3,500,000
- d. $4,800,000

54. Hansen Construction, Inc. has consistently used the percentage-of-completion method of recognizing income. During 2010, Hansen started work on a $3,000,000 fixed-price construction contract. The accounting records disclosed the following data for the year ended December 31, 2010:

Costs incurred	$ 930,000
Estimated cost to complete	2,170,000
Progress billings	1,100,000
Collections	700,000

How much loss should Hansen have recognized in 2010?

- a. $230,000
- b. $100,000
- c. $ 30,000
- d. $0

Items 55 and 56 are based on the following data pertaining to Pell Co.'s construction jobs, which commenced during 2010:

	Project 1	Project 2
Contract price	$420,000	$300,000
Costs incurred during 2010	240,000	280,000
Estimated costs to complete	120,000	40,000
Billed to customers during 2010	150,000	270,000
Received from customers during 2010	90,000	250,000

55. If Pell used the completed contract method, what amount of gross profit (loss) would Pell report in its 2010 income statement?

- a. $ (20,000)
- b. $ 0
- c. $ 340,000
- d. $ 420,000

56. If Pell used the percentage-of-completion method, what amount of gross profit (loss) would Pell report in its 2010 income statement?

- a. $(20,000)
- b. $ 20,000
- c. $ 22,500
- d. $ 40,000

57. Which of the following is used in calculating the income recognized in the fourth and final year of a contract accounted for by the percentage-of-completion method?

	Actual total costs	Income previously recognized
a.	Yes	Yes
b.	Yes	No
c.	No	Yes
d.	No	No

58. A company used the percentage-of-completion method of accounting for a five-year construction contract. Which of the following items will the company use to calculate the income recognized in the third year?

	Progress billings to date	Income previously recognized
a.	Yes	No
b.	No	Yes
c.	No	No
d.	Yes	Yes

59. The calculation of the income recognized in the third year of a five-year construction contract accounted for using the percentage-of-completion method includes the ratio of

- a. Total costs incurred to date to total estimated costs.
- b. Total costs incurred to date to total billings to date.
- c. Cost incurred in year three to total estimated costs.
- d. Costs incurred in year three to total billings to date.

60. When should an anticipated loss on a long-term contract be recognized under the percentage-of-completion method and the completed-contract method, respectively?

	Percentage-of-completion	Completed-contract
a.	Over life of project	Contract complete
b.	Immediately	Contract complete
c.	Over life of project	Immediately
d.	Immediately	Immediately

61. In accounting for a long-term construction contract using the percentage-of-completion method, the progress billings on contracts account is a

- a. Contra current asset account.
- b. Contra noncurrent asset account.
- c. Noncurrent liability account.
- d. Revenue account

SIMULATION PROBLEMS

Simulation Problem 1   (50 to 60 minutes)

Situation					
	Concepts	Journal Entries	Calculations	Research	Communication

A client, Blaedon Co., sells lawn mowers and garden tillers. The garden tillers are purchased from Bestbuilt Tillers and sold to customers without modification. The lawn mowers, however, are purchased from several contractors. Blaedon then makes ongoing design refinements to the mowers before selling them to customers.

The lawn mowers cost $200. Blaedon then makes the design refinements at a cost of $85 per lawn mower. Blaedon stores the lawn mowers in its own warehouse and sells them directly to retailers at a list price of $500. Blaedon uses the FIFO inventory method. Approximately two-thirds of new lawn mower sales involve trade-ins. For each used lawn mower traded in and returned to Blaedon, retailers receive a $40 allowance regardless of whether the trade-in was associated with a sale of a 2010 or 2011 model. Blaedon's net realizable value on a used lawn mower averages $25.

At December 31, 2010, Blaedon's inventory of new lawn mowers includes both 2010 and 2011 models. When the 2011 model was introduced in September 2010, the list price of the remaining 2010 model lawn mowers was reduced below cost. Blaedon is experiencing rising costs.

Blaedon has contacted your firm for advice on how to report the carrying value of inventory, the impact of the decline in value on the 2010 models, and the effects of using the FIFO method on their December 31, 2010 financial statements.

	Concepts				
Situation		Journal Entries	Calculations	Research	Communication

Indicate whether each of the following is included in the cost of inventory.

	Included	*Not included*
1. Merchandise purchased for resale	O	O
2. Freight out	O	O
3. Direct materials	O	O
4. Sales returns	O	O
5. Packaging for shipment to customer	O	O
6. Factory overhead	O	O
7. Interest on inventory loan	O	O
8. Purchase discounts not taken	O	O
9. Freight in	O	O
10. Direct labor	O	O

		Journal Entries			
Situation	Concepts		Calculations	Research	Communication

Assume that Blaedon uses the periodic inventory method for inventories. Prepare the journal entries for each of the following transactions. Blaedon uses the gross method for recording inventory transactions.

1. On January 5, 2010, purchased $17,000 of garden tillers on account from Bestbuilt Tillers, terms 2/10, n/30, FOB destination. Freight charges were $200.

2. On January 10, 2010, returned garden tillers worth $2,000 to Bestbuilt Tillers due to defects.

3. On January 14, 2010, paid for the remaining tillers purchased in **1**.

4. On January 28, 2010, purchased $30,000 of lawn mowers from Lawn Giant, terms 3/10, n/30, FOB shipping point. The freight charges were $820.

5. On February 6, 2010, paid for the lawn mowers purchased in part **4.** from Lawn Giant.

Situation	Concepts	Journal Entries	Calculations	Research	Communication

Assume that Blaedon had the following information regarding the garden tiller inventory:

Purchases	$210,000
Purchase discounts	38,000
Purchase returns	17,500
Freight in	12,100
Freight out	18,000
Beginning inventory	42,900
Ending inventory	34,250

Calculate the following items:

1. Goods available for sale
2. Costs of goods sold

Situation	Concepts	Journal Entries	Calculations	Research	Communication

Research the following issues in the authoritative literature. Select the appropriate citations to answer each question.

1. What costs should be included in Blaedon's inventory?
2. How should Blaedon report the 2010 inventory that has declined in value below its costs?

Situation	Concepts	Journal Entries	Calculations	Research	Communication

Prepare a memo to your client explaining

- How Blaedon should determine the carrying amounts assigned to its lawn mower inventory for the 2010 and 2011 models.
- Considering only the 2011 model lawn mower, explain in your memo the impact of the FIFO cost flow assumptions in Blaedon's 2010 income statement and balance sheet amounts.

REMINDER: Your response will be graded for both technical content and writing skills. Technical content will be evaluated for information that is helpful to the intended reader and clearly relevant to the issue. Writing skills will be evaluated for development, organization, and the appropriate expression of ideas in professional correspondence. Use a standard business memo or letter format with a clear beginning, middle, and end. Do not convey information in the form of a table, bullet point list, or other abbreviated presentation.

To: CEO, Blaedon Corp.
From: CPA Candidate
Re: Inventory valuation

Simulation Problem 2   (50 to 60 minutes)

Situation					
	Calculation of Gross Profit	Financial Statement Disclosures	Schedule of Income Taxes	Communication	Research

London, Inc. began operation of its construction division on October 1, 2009, and entered into contracts for two separate projects. The Beta project contract price was $600,000 and provided for penalties of $10,000 per week for late completion. Although during 2010 the Beta project had been on schedule for timely completion, it was completed four weeks late in August 2011. The Gamma project's original contract price was $800,000. Change orders during 2011 added $40,000 to the original contract price.

The following data pertains to the separate long-term construction projects in progress:

	Beta	Gamma
As of September 30, 2010:		
Costs incurred to date	$360,000	$410,000
Estimated costs to complete	40,000	410,000
Billings	315,000	440,000
Cash collections	275,000	365,000
As of September 30, 2011:		
Costs incurred to date	450,000	720,000
Estimated costs to complete	--	180,000
Billings	560,000	710,000
Cash collections	560,000	625,000

Additional information

- London accounts for its long-term construction contracts using the percentage-of-completion method for financial reporting purposes and the completed-contract method for income tax purposes.
- Enacted income tax rates are 25% for 2010 and 30% for future years.
- London's income before income taxes from all divisions, before considering revenues from long-term construction projects, was $300,000 for the year ended September 30, 2010. There were no other temporary or permanent differences.

Situation	Calculation of Gross Profit	Financial Statement Disclosures	Schedule of Income Taxes	Communication	Research

Prepare a schedule showing London's gross profit (loss) recognized for the years ended September 30, 2010, and 2011, under the percentage-of-completion method.

London Inc.
SCHEDULE OF GROSS PROFIT (LOSS)

	Beta		Gamma
For the Year Ended September 30, 2010:			
Estimated gross profit (loss):			
Contract price			
Less total costs			
Estimated gross profit (loss)			
Percent complete:			
Costs incurred to date			
Total costs			
Percent complete			
Gross profit (loss) recognized			
For the Year Ended September 30, 2011:			
Estimated gross profit (loss):			
Contract price			
Less total costs			
Estimated gross profit (loss)			
Percent complete:			
Costs incurred to date			
Total costs			
Percent complete			
Gross profit (loss) recognized			
Less gross profit (loss) recognized in prior year			
Gross profit (loss) recognized			

Situation	Calculation of Gross Profit	Financial Statement Disclosures	Schedule of Income Taxes	Communication	Research

Prepare the following schedule showing London's balances in the following accounts at September 30, 2010, under the percentage-of-completion method:

- Accounts receivable
- Costs and estimated earnings in excess of billings
- Billings in excess of costs and estimated earnings

London Inc.
SCHEDULE OF SELECTED BALANCE SHEET ACCOUNTS
September 30, 2010

Accounts receivable		
Costs and estimated earnings in excess of billings:		
Construction in progress		
Less: Billings		
Costs and estimated earnings in excess of billings		
Billings in excess of costs and estimated earnings		
Estimated loss on contract		

Situation	Calculation of Gross Profit	Financial Statement Disclosures	Schedule of Income Taxes	Communication	Research

Prepare the following schedule reconciling London's financial statement income and taxable income for the year ended September 30, 2010, and showing all components of taxes payable and current and deferred income tax expense for the year then ended. Do not consider estimated tax requirements.[1]

London Inc.
SCHEDULE OF INCOME TAXES PAYABLE AND INCOME TAX EXPENSE
September 30, 2010

Financial statement income:		
From other divisions		
From Beta project		
From Gamma project		
Total financial statement income		
Less temporary differences:		
Beta project income		
Gamma project loss		
Total taxable income		
Taxes payable		
Deferred tax liability		
Tax expense:		
Current		
Deferred		

Situation	Calculation of Gross Profit	Financial Statement Disclosures	Schedule of Income Taxes	Communication	Research

London has recently hired Jim Cauley, a new construction supervisor who has not used the percentage-of-completion method for accounting for long-term construction contracts. Write a brief memo to Mr. Cauley on the percentage-of-completion method of accounting for long-term construction contracts, explaining the advantages and disadvantages of this method.

REMINDER: Your response will be graded for both technical content and writing skills. Technical content will be evaluated for information that is helpful to the intended reader and clearly relevant to the issue. Writing skills will be evaluated for development, organization, and the appropriate expression of ideas in professional correspondence. Use a standard business memo or letter format with a clear beginning, middle, and end. Do not convey information in the form of a table, bullet point list, or other abbreviated presentation.

To: Mr. Jim Cauley, Construction Supervisor
From: CPA Candidate
Re: Percentage-of-completion method for construction contracts

---

[1] *This requirement should not be completed until you have done Module 12, Deferred Taxes. A cross-reference in the Module 12 problem material will direct you to return to it.*

Situation	Calculation of Gross Profit	Financial Statement Disclosures	Schedule of Income Taxes	Communication	Research

Using the Accounting Standards Codification, research the following question. Select and insert your answer into the space provided.

A company is using the completed-contract method for long-term construction contracts. The company expects the contract will incur a loss. What disclosures, if any, are necessary if the firm anticipates a loss?

Simulation Problem 3   (50 to 60 minutes)

Situation	Inventory Concepts	Cost Flow Concepts	Schedule of Ending Inventory	Schedule of Cost of Goods Sold	Communication	Research

York Co. sells one product, which it purchases from various suppliers. York's trial balance at December 31, 2010, included the following accounts:

Sales (33,000 units @ $16)	$528,000
Sales discounts	7,500
Purchases	368,900
Purchase discounts	18,000
Freight-in	5,000
Freight-out	11,000

York Co.'s inventory purchases during 2010 were as follows:

	Units	Cost per unit	Total cost
Beginning inventory, January 1	8,000	$8.20	$ 65,600
Purchases, quarter ended March 31	12,000	8.25	99,000
Purchases, quarter ended June 30	15,000	7.90	118,500
Purchases, quarter ended September 30	13,000	7.50	97,500
Purchases, quarter ended December 31	7,000	7.70	53,900
	55,000		$434,500

Additional information

York's accounting policy is to report inventory in its financial statements at the lower of cost or market, applied to total inventory. Cost is determined under the last-in, first-out (LIFO) method.

York has determined that, at December 31, 2010, the replacement cost of its inventory was $8 per unit and the net realizable value was $8.80 per unit. York's normal profit margin is $1.05 per unit.

Situation	Inventory Concepts	Cost Flow Concepts	Schedule of Ending Inventory	Schedule of Cost of Goods Sold	Communication	Research

Items 1 through 13 represent True or False statements concerning inventory accounting methods. Indicate whether each statement is true or false by clicking on the appropriate response.

	True	*False*
1. The gross margin method uses historical sales margins to estimate the cost of inventory.	O	O
2. The dollar-value LIFO method preserves old inventory costs by charging current costs to cost of goods sold.	O	O
3. Inventory should be reported at the lower of cost or market and it may be based on the values of individual items, categories, or the total inventory.	O	O
4. A loss on a purchase commitment should be recorded when the contract price is greater than the market and it is anticipated that a loss will occur when the contract is completed.	O	O
5. Under the dollar-value LIFO method, increases and decreases in a layer would be measured based upon the change in the total dollar value of the layer.	O	O
6. The link-chain method uses a cumulative index to value the base cost of ending inventory.	O	O
7. The price index for dollar-value LIFO is a measure of changes in price levels between the current year and the base year.	O	O
8. Under the LIFO method, an inventory liquidation will result in higher profits in a period of rising prices.	O	O
9. A holding gain results from holding an item while the market value experiences a decline.	O	O

	True	*False*
10. During a period of rising prices, the LIFO cost flow assumption results in a higher net income as compared to FIFO.	○	○
11. In a period of rising prices, when a company changes from FIFO to LIFO the net income will tend to decline as will working capital.	○	○
12. The use of LIFO for book and tax purposes will result in a lower tax payment in a period of rising prices.	○	○
13. Under the LIFO method, the cost of goods sold balance would be the same whether a perpetual or periodic inventory system is used.	○	○

Situation	Inventory Concepts	Cost Flow Concepts	Schedule of Ending Inventory	Schedule of Cost of Goods Sold	Communication	Research

Below are statements describing inventory and cost flow methods. Identify which method matches each description by clicking on the correct term and placing it in the space provided. You may use a term once, more than once, or not at all.

Terms

Specific identification
Weighted-average
Simple average
Moving average
First-in, first-out
Last-in, first-out
Dollar-value LIFO
Gross profit

Method

1. During a period of rising prices, this method results in a higher net income.

2. This method most closely matches the physical flow of inventory.

3. Method that uses historical sales margins to estimate ending inventory.

4. Method that is appropriate when there is a relatively small number of significant dollar value items in inventory.

5. Average cost must be calculated each time additional inventory is purchased.

6. Method that averages the cost of all items on hand and purchased during the period.

7. This method results in the lowest ending inventory in a period of rising prices.

8. Method that uses a price index to measure changes in inventory.

9. If used for tax purposes, this method must also be used for financial reporting purposes.

10. The cost of goods sold balance is the same whether a perpetual or periodic inventory system is used.

Situation	Inventory Concepts	Cost Flow Concepts	Schedule of Ending Inventory	Schedule of Cost of Goods Sold	Communication	Research

York Co.
SUPPORTING SCHEDULE OF ENDING INVENTORY
December 31, 2010

Inventory at cost (LIFO):

	Units	Cost per unit	Total cost
Beginning inventory, January 1			
Purchases, quarter ended March 31			
Purchases, quarter ended June 30			
Totals			

Situation	Inventory Concepts	Cost Flow Concepts	Schedule of Ending Inventory	Schedule of Cost of Goods Sold	Communication	Research

York Co.
SCHEDULE OF COST OF GOODS SOLD
For the Year Ended December 31, 2010

Beginning inventory		
Add: Purchases		
Less: Purchase discounts		
Add: Freight-in		
Goods available for sale		
Less: Ending inventory		
Cost of goods sold		

Situation	Inventory Concepts	Cost Flow Concepts	Schedule of Ending Inventory	Schedule of Cost of Goods Sold	Communication	Research

York Co.'s warehouse supervisor, Mr. Binson, has inquired about the accounting for inventory that has declined in value. Write a brief memo explaining to Mr. Binson the rule of lower of cost or market and its application in this situation.

REMINDER: Your response will be graded for both technical content and writing skills. Technical content will be evaluated for information that is helpful to the intended reader and clearly relevant to the issue. Writing skills will be evaluated for development, organization, and the appropriate expression of ideas in professional correspondence. Use a standard business memo or letter format with a clear beginning, middle, and end. Do not convey information in the form of a table, bullet point list, or other abbreviated presentation.

To: Mr. Binson
From: CPA Candidate
Re: Valuation of inventory

Situation	Inventory Concepts	Cost Flow Concepts	Schedule of Ending Inventory	Schedule of Cost of Goods Sold	Communication	Research

Research the Accounting Standards to answer the following questions:

1. What methods may be used for costing inventories?

2. How is the market value calculated when calculating the lower of cost or market?

MULTIPLE-CHOICE ANSWERS

1.	c	__ __	14.	d	__ __	27.	d	__ __	40.	d	__ __	53.	b __ __
2.	d	__ __	15.	b	__ __	28.	c	__ __	41.	c	__ __	54.	b __ __
3.	c	__ __	16.	b	__ __	29.	a	__ __	42.	d	__ __	55.	a __ __
4.	b	__ __	17.	b	__ __	30.	a	__ __	43.	d	__ __	56.	b __ __
5.	c	__ __	18.	c	__ __	31.	c	__ __	44.	c	__ __	57.	a __ __
6.	a	__ __	19.	a	__ __	32.	c	__ __	45.	c	__ __	58.	b __ __
7.	a	__ __	20.	d	__ __	33.	b	__ __	46.	d	__ __	59.	a __ __
8.	b	__ __	21.	b	__ __	34.	b	__ __	47.	b	__ __	60.	d __ __
9.	b	__ __	22.	b	__ __	35.	c	__ __	48.	b	__ __	61.	a __ __
10.	d	__ __	23.	c	__ __	36.	a	__ __	49.	d	__ __		
11.	c	__ __	24.	a	__ __	37.	c	__ __	50.	b	__ __		
12.	a	__ __	25.	c	__ __	38.	d	__ __	51.	a	__ __	1st:	__/61 = __%
13.	c	__ __	26.	b	__ __	39.	a	__ __	52.	a	__ __	2nd:	__/61 = __%

MULTIPLE-CHOICE ANSWER EXPLANATIONS

A. Determining Inventory and Cost of Goods Sold

1. (c) Inventoriable costs include all costs necessary to prepare goods for sale. For a merchandising concern these costs include the purchase price of the goods, freight-in, insurance, warehousing, and any costs necessary to get the goods to the point of sale (except interest on any loans obtained to purchase the goods). In this problem, inventoriable costs total $408,000.

Purchase price less returns ($400,000 – $2,000)	$398,000
Freight-in	10,000
	$408,000

Note that freight-out is a **selling expense,** not an inventoriable cost, as the diagram below indicates.

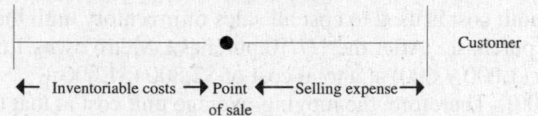

2. (d) When the shipping terms are FOB destination, the seller bears **all** costs of transporting the goods to the buyer. Therefore, the seller is responsible for the payment of packaging costs ($1,000), shipping costs ($1,500), and the special handling charges ($2,000). The only amount to be included as the buyer's cost of the inventory purchased is the purchase price ($50,000).

3. (c) Purchases are always recorded net of trade discounts. When more than one trade discount is applied to a list price, it is called a chain discount. Chain discounts are applied in steps; each discount applies to the previously discounted price. The cost, net of trade discounts, is $2,800 [$5,000 – (30% × $5,000) = $3,500; and $3,500 – (20% × $3,500) = $2,800]. Payment was made within the discount period, so the net purchase price is $2,744 [$2,800 – (2% × $2,800)]. The remittance from Burr would also include reimbursement of the $200 of delivery costs. Since the terms were FOB shipping point, Burr is responsible for paying this amount, and must reimburse Pitt, who prepaid the freight. Thus, the total remittance is $2,944 ($2,744 + $200).

4. (b) Three computations must be performed: raw materials used, cost of goods manufactured, and cost of goods sold.

(1)	Raw materials purchased	$430,000
	Decrease in RM inventory	15,000
	Raw materials used	$445,000

(2)	Beginning WIP	$ --
	RM used (from above)	445,000
	Direct labor	200,000
	Factory overhead	300,000
	Cost to account for	945,000
	Ending WIP	--
	Cost of goods manuf.	$945,000

(3)	Cost of goods manuf.	$945,000
	Increase in FD inventory	35,000

The decrease in RM inventory is added when computing RM used because RM were used in excess of those purchased. The increase in FG inventory is deducted when computing cost of goods sold because it represents the portion of goods manufactured which were not sold. The freight-out is irrelevant for this question because freight-out is a selling expense and therefore does not affect cost of goods sold.

5. (c) To compute cost of goods sold, the solutions approach is to set up a T-account for inventory

	Inventory		
12/31/09	90,000		
Purchases	124,000	34,000	Write-off
		?	Cost of goods sold
12/31/10	30,000		

Purchases increase inventory, while the write-off and cost of goods sold decrease inventory. Cost of goods sold can be computed as $150,000 using the T-account. An alternate solutions approach is to use the CGS computation

BI	$ 90,000	
+ Purchases	124,000	
CGAS	214,000	
– EI	(30,000)	
	$184,000	→ $34,000 recognized as invy loss*
		→ $150,000 recognized as CGS

* *Theoretically correct treatment.*

6. (a) The cost of inventory should include all expenditures (direct and indirect) incurred to bring an item to its existing condition and location. Freight-in charges are thus appropriately included in inventory costs. Interest cost shall not be capitalized for assets that are in use or ready for their intended use in the earnings activities of the enterprise. Thus, interest on an inventory loan should not be included in inventory (it should be expensed as incurred).

7.   (a)   The cost of inventory should include all expenditures (direct and indirect) incurred to bring an item to its existing condition and location. Freight charges are thus appropriately included in inventory costs. Under the net purchase method, purchase discounts not taken are recorded in a Purchase Discounts Lost account. When this method is used, purchase discounts lost are considered a financial (i.e., "other") expense, and are thus excluded from the cost of inventory.

8.   (b)   Azur should report cost of goods sold calculated as

Cost of goods sold (CGS) = Beg. Inventory + Net purchases* + Freight in – Ending Inventory

CGS = $ 30,840 + $92,520** + $15,420 – $20,560

CGS = $118,220

Freight out is a selling expense and does not enter the calculation of cost of goods sold.

* *Net purchase = Purchases – Purchase returns and allowances – Purchase discounts*

** ($102,800 – $10,280)

9.   (b)   Fixed overhead is allocated based on the normal capacity of the production facilities. Normal capacity is the production expected to be achieved over a number of periods or seasons under normal circumstances, taking into account the loss of capacity resulting from planned maintenance. Answer (a) is incorrect, because the actual amount of production may only be used if it approximates normal capacity. Answers (c) and (d) are incorrect because the accounting standards do not specify a formula to calculate normal capacity.

10.   (d)   Normal capacity refers to a range in production levels that will vary based on business and industry-specific factors. Normal capacity is the production expected to be achieved over a number of periods or seasons under normal circumstances, taking into account the loss of capacity resulting from planned maintenance. Answer (a) is incorrect because the Codification does not specify a formula for calculating normal capacity. Answers (b) and (c) are incorrect because actual production may only be used if it approximates normal capacity.

11.   (c)   Unallocated fixed overhead costs are recognized as an expense in the period in which they are incurred. Therefore, answers (a), (b), and (d) are incorrect.

12.   (a)   Any abnormal costs for freight, handling costs, and wasted material are required to be treated as current period charges, and not a part of inventory cost. Therefore, answers (b), (c), and (d) are incorrect.

13.   (c)   Inventoriable costs include all costs necessary to prepare goods for sale. For a merchandising concern, these include the purchase price of the goods, freight-in, insurance, warehousing, and any costs necessary to get the goods to the point of sale. Abnormal freight and handling should be charged to expense of the period. Therefore, the normal costs for inventory are $5,500 ($3,000 + $2,000 + $500) and the abnormal freight of $1,200 is charged to current expense of the period.

B.   Inventory Valuation and Cost-Flow Methods

14.   (d)   Ending inventory at dollar value LIFO is calculated as the base year inventory times the index. Therefore, the index used can be calculated as 2.00 = ($80,000 EI at dollar value LIFO/$40,000 base year cost).

15.   (b)   The inventory valuations are calculated as follows:

Valuations of ending inventory under LIFO perpetual

1,400 units at $1.00	=	$1,400
800 units at $5.00	=	4,000
Total		$5,400

Value of ending inventory under LIFO periodic

2,000 units at $1.00	=	$2,000
200 units at $3.00	=	600
Total		$2,600

B.2.   Weighted-Average

16.   (b)   The requirement is to determine whether the weighted-average inventory method is applicable to a periodic and/or a perpetual inventory system. The weighted-average method computes a weighted-average unit cost of inventory for the entire period and is used with periodic records. The moving-average method requires that a new unit of cost be computed each time new goods are purchased and is used with perpetual records.

B.4.   Moving-Average

17.   (b)   The moving-average method requires that a new unit cost be computed each time goods are purchased. The new unit cost is used to cost all sales of inventory until the next purchase. After the 1/7/10 purchase, Metro owns 1,600 units (1,000 + 600) at a total cost of $2,800 ($1,000 + $1,800). Therefore, the moving-average unit cost at that time is $1.75 ($2,800 ÷ 1,600 units). After the 1/20/10 sale of 900 units (at a unit of cost of $1.75), Metro owns 700 units at a unit cost of $1.75 (700 × $1.75 = $1,225). The 1/25/10 purchase of 400 units at a total cost of $2,000 increases inventory to its 1/31/10 balance of $3,225 ($1,225 + $2,000). The new unit cost (not required) is $2.93 ($3,225 ÷ 1,100).

B.5.   Lower of Cost or Market

18.   (c)   The lower of cost or market (LCM) is used for financial reporting of inventories. The market value of inventory is defined as the replacement cost (RC), as long as it is less than the ceiling (net realizable value, or NRV) and more than the floor (NRV less a normal profit, or NRV – NP). In this case, the amounts are

Ceiling: NRV =	$40,000 est. sell. price	
	– $12,000 disp. cost =	$28,000
Floor: NRV – NP = $28,000 – (10% × $40,000)		$24,000
RC:		$20,000

Since RC falls below the floor, the floor (NRV – NP) is the designated market value. Once market value is designated, LCM can be determined by simply determining the lower of cost ($26,000) or market ($24,000). Therefore, inventory is reported at $24,000.

19.   (a)   SFAC 5 establishes five different attributes on which assets can be measured. The attribute used should be determined by the nature of the item and the relevance and reliability of the attribute measured. The five attributes are historical cost, current cost, current market value, net realizable value, and present value. Historical cost is defined as the amount of cash, or its equivalent, paid to acquire an asset. Reporting inventory at lower of cost or market is a departure from the historical cost principle as the inventory could potentially be carried at the market value if lower. Although, reporting inventory at lower of cost or market does not create a departure from conservatism as this method carries at inventory the lowest or most conservative value. The use of LCM does not violate the principle of consistency either, as it would be reported on this basis continually. Finally the use of LCM would not violate the principle of full disclosure as its use would be discussed in the footnotes.

20.   (d)   Inventory is to be valued at the lower of cost or market. Under this method, market is replacement cost provided that replacement cost is lower than net realizable value (ceiling) and higher than net realizable value less the normal profit margin (floor). The question does not specify whether replacement cost is above or below net realizable value, but since the original cost is below **both** of these values, that information is irrelevant.

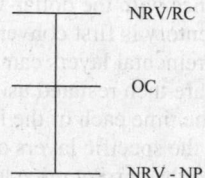

Either NRV or RC will be designated as the market value of the inventory, and since the original cost is below **both** of these values, the inventory will be valued at its original cost. Answer (c) is incorrect because NRV – NP represents the market floor. Answers (a) and (b) are incorrect because they are both **above** the original cost.

21.   (b)   Lower of cost or market (LCM) is used for financial reporting of inventories. The market value of inventory is defined as the replacement cost (RC) as long as it is less than the ceiling (net realizable value, or NRV) and more than the floor (NRV less a normal profit, or NRV – NP). Therefore, if inventory is reported at RC, RC must be less than original cost (meaning statement I is **not** correct), and RC must be less than NRV (meaning statement II **is** correct) and greater than NRV – NP.

22.   (b)   Inventory is priced at market when market value is less than cost. Market value is defined as current replacement cost, subject to a ceiling of net realizable value (NRV) and a floor of net realizable value minus a normal profit margin.

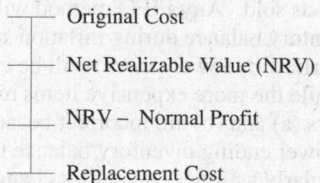

In this situation, replacement cost lies outside of (below) the floor and ceiling limitations. Therefore, NRV less a normal profit margin (the floor), will be used as the market to determine LCM. Since original cost is greater than market, market will be used to price the inventory for the period.

B.6. Losses on Purchase Commitments

23.   (c)   The requirement is to determine the amount of probable loss from the purchase commitment that Card should report in its 2010 income statement. When there is a decline in market value below the contract price at the balance sheet date and the contract is noncancelable, an unrealized loss should be recorded in the period of decline and reported in the income statement. In this case, Card has a contract to purchase a minimum of 100,000 units both in 2011 and 2012 at \$.10 per unit. The \$20,000 loss (200,000 × \$.10) on these obsolete units should be reduced by the amount Card believes is realizable from the sale of these units. Therefore, the loss on **purchase commitment** is \$16,000 [\$20,000 – (200,000 × .02)]. Additionally, Card Corp. would need to record a loss of \$20,000 (\$.08 × 250,000) from **inventory obsolescence**.

24.   (a)   To maximize its inventory carrying amount at December 31, 2010, Thread should use the perpetual moving-average method with the lower of cost or market rule applied to the total inventory. First, when using the perpetual moving-average method, the cost of sales throughout the year are determined using the average cost of purchases up to the time of the sale. On the other hand, under the periodic weighted-average method, the cost of each item is the weighted-average of **all** units purchased during the year. During a period of rising prices, the perpetual moving-average method results in a lower cost of goods sold and a higher ending inventory because the cost of items sold throughout the year is the average of the earlier, lower prices. Second, the application of the lower of cost or market rule to the total inventory will result in a higher ending inventory because market values lower than cost are offset against market values higher than cost.

B.7. & B.8. First-In, First-Out (FIFO), and Last-In, First-Out (LIFO)

25.   (c)   The requirement is to determine the cost of the 1/31/10 inventory, using the LIFO method. LIFO stands for last-in, first-out; this means that the cost of the units purchased most recently are included in cost of goods sold. Therefore, the 1/31/10 inventory consists of the 250 units that were purchased at the earliest date(s). Thus, the 1/31/10 inventory would consist of the 150 units on hand at 1/1/10 (150 × \$21 = \$3,150) plus an additional 100 units purchased at the earliest purchase date in January (January 10; 100 × \$22 = \$2,200). The total value of the inventory at 1/31/10 would be \$5,350 (\$3,150 + \$2,200).

26.   (b)   LIFO stands for last-in, first-out; this means that it is assumed that any units sold are the units most recently purchased. In a perpetual system, LIFO is applied at the time of each sale rather than once a year as in a periodic system. Using LIFO, the 900 units sold on 1/20/10 would consist of the 600 units purchased on 1/7/10 and 300 of the 1,000 units in the 1/1/10 balance. This would leave in inventory 700 units from the 1/1/10 balance. After the 1/25/10 purchase, inventory included those 700 units plus the 400 units purchased on 1/25/10. Therefore, ending inventory is \$2,700 [(700 × \$1) + (400 × \$5)].

27.   (d)   When a company uses LIFO for external reporting purposes and another inventory method for internal purposes, a **LIFO Reserve** account is used to reduce inventory from the internal valuation to the LIFO valuation. LIFO Reserve is a contra account to inventory, and is adjusted up or down at year-end with a corresponding increase or decrease to **Cost of Goods Sold**. In this case, the LIFO Reserve account must be adjusted from a balance of $35,000 to a balance of $55,000 ($375,000 – $320,000). Therefore, LIFO Reserve is credited for $20,000 ($55,000 – $35,000) with a corresponding debit to Cost of Goods Sold.

28.   (c)   In a change **to** LIFO, no recognition is given to any cumulative effect associated with the change because it is usually not determinable. Thus, the effect on ending inventory and net income is the result solely of current year effects. In a period of rising prices, LIFO will result in a **lower ending inventory** amount than FIFO because the earlier lower costs are assumed to remain in ending inventory. LIFO will also result in a **lower net income** because the more recent higher costs are assigned to cost of goods sold.

29.   (a)   The inventory costing method which most closely approximates the current cost for cost of goods sold is LIFO, while the method which more accurately reflects ending inventory is FIFO. Under LIFO, the most recent purchases are assumed to be the first goods sold; thus, cost of goods sold contains relatively current costs. On the other hand, since FIFO assumes that the goods from beginning inventory and the earliest purchases are sold first, the ending inventory is made up of more recent purchases and thus represents a more current value.

30.   (a)   Under the FIFO method, the first goods purchased are considered to be the first goods used or sold. Ending inventory is thus made up of the latest (most recent) purchases. Whenever the FIFO method is used, the ending inventory is the same whether a perpetual or periodic system is used. This is true even during periods of rising or falling prices because the inventory flow is always in chronological order. Under the LIFO method, the latest (most recent) purchases are considered to be the first goods used or sold. Ending inventory is thus made up of the first (oldest) purchases. When a periodic method is used, the first/last purchase determination is made only at the end of the year, based upon the actual chronological order of all purchases. When a perpetual method is used, however, the first/last purchase determination is made continuously throughout the year. When inventory levels get low under the perpetual method, early purchase costs will often be assigned to goods sold, a situation that is much less likely to occur in a periodic system. Therefore, in times of either rising or falling prices, LIFO ending inventory is usually different under a periodic system than under a perpetual system.

B.9.   Dollar-Value LIFO

31.   (c)   When using dollar-value LIFO, the ending inventory at current year cost must first be converted to base year cost. This amount is given at 12/31/10 ($230,000), but it could be computed as follows: $276,000 ÷ 1.20 = $230,000. The next step is to determine the incremental LIFO layers at base year cost. The 1/1/09 (base year) layer is $150,000, the 2009 layer is $50,000 ($200,000 – $150,000), and the 2010 layer is $30,000 ($230,000 – $200,000). Finally, the LIFO layers are restated using the price index in effect at the time each layer was added.

	Base cost		Ending inventory at DV LIFO cost
1/1/09 layer	150,000	× 1.00 =	$150,000
2009 layer	50,000	× 1.10 =	55,000
2010 layer	30,000	× 1.20 =	36,000
	$230,000		$241,000

32.   (c)   When using dollar-value LIFO, the ending inventory at current year cost must first be converted to base year cost. The 12/31/10 inventory at base year cost is given as $60,000. Since the 12/31/09 inventory at base year cost was $45,000 ($40,000 base layer and $5,000 2009 layer), a new layer of $15,000 was added in 2010 ($60,000 – $45,000). This layer must be restated using the 2010 price index. The 2010 price index is computed using the double-extension technique, as illustrated below.

$$\frac{\text{EI at year-end prices}}{\text{EI at base year prices}} = \frac{\$80,000}{\$60,000} = \underline{1.33}$$

Therefore, the 12/31/10 inventory using dollar-value LIFO is $66,000 as computed below.

	Base cost		DV LIFO
Base layer	$40,000		$40,000
2009 layer	5,000		6,000
2010 layer	15,000	× 1.33	20,000
			$66,000

33.   (b)   The requirement is to determine which inventory method requires estimates of price level changes for specific inventories. In accordance with the dollar-value LIFO method, the ending inventory is first converted to the base year cost so that the incremental layers can be determined. The incremental layers are then restated using the price index which was in effect at the time each of the layers were added to the inventory. Thus, the specific layers of the ending inventory are adjusted to the current price level. Therefore, answer (b) is correct. Answers (a), (c), and (d) are incorrect because these methods do not specifically adjust for price level changes.

34.   (b)   The requirement is to determine the appropriate use of ending inventory at current year cost and ending inventory at base year cost in calculating the dollar-value LIFO index. The index number used to convert the current year's inventory layer is calculated as follows:

$$\text{Index} = \frac{\text{Ending inventory at current year cost}}{\text{Ending inventory at base year cost}}$$

This index indicates the relationship between current and base year prices as a percentage, and when multiplied by the new layer (which is the increase in inventory in base year dollars), it will convert the layer to current dollars.

35.   (c)   During periods of rising prices, the inventory costing methods which will give Jones the lowest ending inventory balance are LIFO methods, because inventory items that were purchased at the earliest date (when prices were lower) will remain in inventory and the most recently purchased and more expensive items will be expensed through cost of goods sold. Any FIFO method will produce a higher ending inventory balance during inflation since the items purchased earliest (at lower prices) will be expensed through COGS, while the more expensive items remain in inventory. Answers (a) and (b) are incorrect because neither will give Jones a lower ending inventory balance than dollar-value LIFO, particularly as Jones' inventory changes (because dollar-value LIFO allows the LIFO "layers" to be made up of similar, not necessarily identical, items).

B.10.   Gross Profit

36.   (a)   The gross profit method can be used to estimate the cost of missing inventory. The first step is to compute the cost of goods available for sale.

Beginning inventory	$ 500,000	
Purchases	2,500,000	
Cost of goods available for sale	$3,000,000	

The second step is to estimate cost of goods sold based on the gross profit percentage.

Sales	$3,200,000
Estimated gross profit ($3,200,000 × 25%)	(800,000)
Cost of goods sold ($3,200,000 × 75%)	$2,400,000

Note that a shortcut is to realize that if gross profit is 25% of sales, cost of goods sold must be 75% of sales. The third step is to compute estimated ending inventory.

Cost of goods available for sale	$ 3,000,000
Estimated cost of goods sold	(2,400,000)
Estimated ending inventory	$ 600,000

Since the actual count of ending inventory at December 31 was only $575,000, the estimated shortage in inventory is $25,000 ($600,000 – $575,000).

B.14.   Cost Apportionment by Relative Sales Value

37.   (c)   The total cost of acquiring the land and preparing it for sale ($1,200,000 + $300,000 = $1,500,000) should be allocated to the residential lots based on their relative sales value, as computed below.

Lot class	# of lots		Sales price		Total sales value
A	100	×	$24,000	=	$2,400,000
B	100	×	16,000	=	1,600,000
C	200	×	10,000	=	2,000,000
					$6,000,000

Total cost		Fraction allocated to Class A		Allocated cost
$1,500,000	×	($2,400/$6,000)	=	$600,000

C.   Items to Include in Inventory

38.   (d)   Before adjustment, the inventory based on a physical count was $1,500,000. The $90,000 of merchandise shipped FOB shipping point by a vendor on 12/30/10 should also be included in Herc's 12/31/10 inventory because Herc, the buyer, owns the goods while in transit under these terms. The goods in the shipping area (cost, $120,000) are also owned by Herc because they were not shipped until 2011 and Herc still retains the risks of ownership until that point. Therefore, 12/31/10 inventory is $1,710,000 ($1,500,000 + $90,000 + $120,000).

39.   (a)   Before adjustment, the balance in the Accounts Payable account is $2,200,000. The $40,000 of goods lost in transit from a vendor were shipped FOB **shipping point**. This means the buyer owns the goods while they were in transit; therefore, Kew should record the purchase and accounts payable in 2010. Kew, not the vendor, is ultimately responsible for the lost goods (note that Kew, not the vendor, is suing the common carrier). The $70,000 return that was recorded on 1/5/11 should have been recorded in 2010 when the return was authorized (December 27, 2010). Therefore, Kew should reduce 12/31/10 Accounts Payable by $70,000. The $50,000 of goods received on 1/6/11 were properly recorded in 2011, since the terms were FOB destination (the buyer does not own the goods until they are physically received). Therefore, no adjustment is necessary for this amount. Kew should report 12/31/10 Accounts Payable at $2,170,000 ($2,200,000 + $40,000 – $70,000).

40.   (d)   Net sales is $2,300,000, subject to three possible adjustments. The goods returned ($50,000) should be recorded as a return in 2010, when Lewis authorized the return.

Since this return was not recorded until 2011, 2010 sales must be adjusted downward. The goods shipped on 12/30/10 ($80,000) were recorded as a sale in 2011 Since the terms were FOB shipping point, the sale must be recorded in 2010 when the goods were shipped; therefore, 2010 sales must be adjusted upward. The goods shipped on 1/3/11 ($100,000) should not be recorded as a sale until 2011. Since the sale was recorded in 2010, 2010 sales must be adjusted downward. Therefore, adjusted net sales for 2010 should be $2,230,000 ($2,300,000 – $50,000 + $80,000 – $100,000).

41.   (c)   Generally, goods are considered sold when legal title to the goods passes to the buyer. In certain situations, however, the transfer of title criteria does not reflect the underlying economics of the situation. In this situation, although transfer of legal title may not have occurred for the 500 segregated desks, the economic substance of the transaction is that the seller no longer retains the risks of ownership. Therefore, all 5,000 desks (including the 500 segregated and accepted desks) are considered sold in 2010, and revenue of $550,000 is recognized (5,000 × $110). Note that the amount of cash collected ($450,000) does not affect the amount of revenue recognized in this case.

D.   Consignments

42.   (d)   A consignor recognizes sales revenue from consignments when the consignee sells the consigned goods to the ultimate customer. Sales commissions earned by the consignee ($10,000 × 15% = $1,500) are reported as a selling expense by the consignor and are **not** netted against sales revenue. Therefore, sales revenue is reported at the total selling price of $10,000 (10 × $1,000). Note that the transportation costs ($800) do not affect sales either; one-fourth (10/40) is reflected in cost of goods sold and three-fourths (30/40) is included in ending inventory.

43.   (d)   No adjustment is necessary for the goods in transit ($36,000). The goods were shipped **FOB shipping point,** which means the buyer (Opal) owns the goods while in transit. Therefore, Opal properly included these goods in 12/31/10 inventory. The merchandise **out** on consignment is owned by the consignor (Opal) and should be included in Opal's inventory **at cost** [$40,000 – (40% × $40,000) = $24,000]. Therefore, inventory must be reduced by $16,000 for this item ($40,000 – $24,000). The goods **held** on consignment ($27,000) are owned by the consignor, not Opal; therefore, inventory must be reduced $27,000 for this item. The total reduction in inventory is $43,000 ($16,000 + $27,000).

44.   (c)   Alt sold 500 of the consigned sweaters (505 – 5) at $100 each, resulting in total sales of $50,000 (500 × $100). Alt must report a payable to Todd for this amount, less Alt's commission [$50,000 – (10% × $50,000) = $45,000]. Alt does not owe Todd anything for the unsold sweaters until they are sold.

45.   (c)   Inventoriable costs include all costs necessary to prepare goods for sale. These costs include the purchase price or manufacturing cost of the goods, freight, and any other costs necessary to get the goods to the point of sale. The in-transit insurance premium would therefore be included in inventory costs. Commissions paid to the consignee are selling expenses in the period the consigned goods are sold that are not required to ready the goods for sale. These costs, therefore, are not included in inventory.

46. **(d)** In a consignment, the manufacturer or wholesaler is referred to as the consignor and the dealer or retailer is referred to as the consignee. In such an arrangement, title to the goods remains with the consignor until they are sold to a third party. Jel's payment of reimbursable freight costs results in an account receivable from Dale, which Jel will subtract from the sale proceeds it remits to Dale. Answers (a), (b), and (c) are incorrect because the consignee, Jel, generally does not bear any costs associated with the sale of consigned goods.

E. Ratios

47. **(b)** The formula to compute the current ratio is

$$\text{Current ratio} = \frac{\text{Current assets}}{\text{Current liabilities}}$$

The following entries would be recorded when inventory is sold on account:

Accounts receivable	}	Sales price
Sales		of merchandise
Cost of goods sold	}	Cost of
Inventory		merchandise

Since the selling price (increase to AR) is normally higher than the cost of the merchandise sold (decrease to merchandise inventory) the sale would normally cause a net increase in current assets, and therefore, a net increase in the current ratio. When the existing current ratio is greater than one, increases of equal amounts to the numerator (inventory, a component of current assets) and denominator (accounts payable, a component of current liabilities) will reduce the ratio. When an account receivable is collected, cash (a current asset) is increased by the same amount that accounts receivable (another current asset) is decreased. Thus, the transaction has no impact on the current ratio. When machinery (a noncurrent asset) is purchased for cash (a current asset), there is a **decrease** in the current ratio.

48. **(b)** The formula for inventory turnover is

$$\frac{\text{Cost of goods sold}}{\text{Average inventory}}$$

Average inventory is equal to beginning inventory plus ending inventory, divided by two. Since beginning inventory is not given, it must be computed using the cost of goods sold relationship

	Cost of goods sold	$ 900,000
+	Ending inventory	180,000
	Cost of goods available for sale	$1,080,000
–	Purchases	– 960,000
	Beginning inventory	$ 120,000

Therefore, average inventory is $150,000 [($120,000 + $180,000) ÷ 2], and inventory turnover is 6.0 times ($900,000 ÷ 150,000).

49. **(d)** The solutions approach is to create a numerical example that conforms to the facts given in the question. The inventory turnover ratio is calculated as follows:

$$\frac{\text{Cost of goods sold}}{\text{Average inventory}}$$

If we assume that cost of goods sold has increased from 100 to 150 and average inventory has remained unchanged at 50 then the following ratios result:

$$\frac{\text{Cost of goods sold}}{\text{Average inventory}} \quad \frac{100}{50} = 2 \quad \frac{150}{50} = 3$$

Thus, if cost of goods sold increases while inventory remains unchanged, then the inventory turnover ratio will increase.

In addition, we must examine the effects of the increase in cost of goods sold on the gross profit percentage when sales remain constant. Assuming the same facts as above, and sales of $200, we get the following results:

Sales	200	200
– Cost of goods sales	– 100	– 150
Gross profit	100	50

Thus, as cost of goods sold increases, the gross profit and the gross profit percentage will decrease.

Answer (a) is incorrect because a decrease in cost of goods sold will cause the inventory ratio to increase. Answers (b) and (c) are incorrect because they are not related to inventory turnover.

50. **(b)** Average days' sales in inventory measures the number of days inventory is held before sale; it reflects on efficiency of inventory policies. It is computed using the following formula:

$$\frac{365}{\text{Inventory turnover}}$$

F. Long-Term Construction Contracts

51. **(a)** The total expected income on the contract at 12/31/10 is $900,000 ($9,000,000 – $8,100,000). The formula for recognizing profit under the percentage-of-completion method is

$$\frac{\text{Cost to date}}{\text{Total expected costs}} \times \frac{\text{Expected}}{\text{profit}} = \frac{\text{Profit recog-}}{\text{nized to date}}$$

$$\frac{\$6,300,000}{\$8,100,000} \times \$900,000 = \$700,000$$

This result is the **total** profit on the contract in 2009 and 2010. The 2009 profit recognized must be subtracted from $700,000 to determine the 2010 profit. At 12/31/09, the total expected income on the contract was $1,200,000 ($9,000,000 – $7,800,000). The income recognized in 2009 was $600,000, as computed below.

$$\frac{\$3,900,000}{\$7,800,000} \times \$1,200,000 = \$600,000$$

Therefore, 2010 income is $700,000 less $600,000, or $100,000.

52. **(a)** Profit to be recognized using the percentage-of-completion method is generally computed as follows:

$$\left(\frac{\text{Cost to date}}{\text{Total expected cost}} \times \frac{\text{Expected}}{\text{profit}} \right) - \frac{\text{Profit recognized}}{\text{in previous periods}}$$

Not enough information is given in this problem to perform this computation, so 2010 profit must be computed indirectly. Since only construction expenses and profit are debited to the construction-in-progress (CIP account), 2009 profit must have been $17,000 ($122,000 CIP less $105,000 const. exp.). Cumulative profit recognized by the end of 2010 must be $67,000 [$364,000 CIP less $297,000 cumulative const. exp. ($105,000 + $192,000)]. Therefore, 2010 profit was $50,000 ($67,000 – $17,000).

	CIP	
2009 Exp.	105,000	
2009 Profit	?	2009 Profit = $17,000
2009 End. bal.	122,000	
2010 Exp.	192,000	
2010 Profit	?	2010 Profit = $50,000
2010 End. bal.	364,000	

53. **(b)**   Based on the information given, it must be assumed that costs incurred are used to measure the extent of progress toward project completion. At 12/31/09, the project was 20% complete and total estimated costs were $7,500,000. Therefore, costs incurred as of 12/31/09 were 20% of $7,500,000, or $1,500,000. At 12/31/10, the project was 60% complete and total estimated costs were $8,000,000. Therefore, costs incurred as of 12/31/10 are 60% of $8,000,000 or $4,800,000. The costs incurred during 2010 were $4,800,000 less $1,500,000, or $3,300,000.

54. **(b)**   The requirement is to determine the amount of loss to recognize in 2010 on a long-term, fixed-price construction contract. Under both the percentage-of-completion method and the completed-contract method, an expected **loss** on a contract must be recognized in **full** in the period in which the expected loss is discovered. Therefore, Hanson must recognize a loss of $100,000 in 2010.

Expected contract revenue	$3,000,000
Expected contract costs ($930,000 + $2,170,000)	3,100,000
Expected loss	$ (100,000)

55. **(a)**   The expected income on project 1 [$420,000 – ($240,000 + $120,000) = $60,000] is **not** recognized until the project is completed under the completed contract method. However, under the completed contract method, an expected **loss** on a contract must be recognized in full in the period in which it is discovered. Project two has an expected loss of ($20,000) [$300,000 – ($280,000 + $40,000)] which must be recognized immediately in 2010.

56. **(b)**   Construction companies that use the percentage-of-completion method in accounting for long-term construction contracts usually recognize gross profit according to the cost-to-cost method.

$$\frac{\text{Costs to date}}{\text{Total estimated costs}} \times \text{Estimated profit} = \text{Gross profit to date}$$

Pell would recognize gross profit of $40,000 on project 1

$$\frac{\$240,000}{\$240,000 + \$120,000} \times [\$420,000 - (\$240,000 + \$120,000)] = \$40,000$$

Note that prior years' gross profit need not be subtracted from $40,000 because the project commenced during 2010. Under both the percentage-of-completion method and the completed-contract method, an expected **loss** must be recognized in full in the period in which the expected loss is discovered. Project two has an expected loss of ($20,000) [$300,000 – ($280,000 + $40,000)] which must be recognized in full in 2010. The net gross profit recognized on the two projects is $20,000 ($40,000 profit less ($20,000) loss).

57. **(a)**   In the **final year** of a contract accounted for by the percentage-of-completion method, the percentage of completion is 100%, since costs to date equal total costs. Therefore, the formula to calculate income to be recognized in the final year is simply

$$\underbrace{(\text{Contract price} - \text{Actual costs})}_{\text{Actual income}} - \begin{pmatrix} \text{Income previously} \\ \text{recognized} \end{pmatrix}$$

Therefore both **actual total costs** and **income previously recognized** are used in calculating income.

58. **(b)**   Under the percentage-of-completion method of accounting for long-term contracts, the cost-to-cost formula is used to compute the amount of income to be recognized in a particular year. The formula to calculate current income is as follows:

$$\left(\frac{\text{Cost to date}}{\text{Total expected cost}} \times \begin{matrix} \text{Expected} \\ \text{profit} \end{matrix} \right) - \begin{matrix} \text{Profit recognized} \\ \text{in previous periods} \end{matrix}$$

Progress billings do not impact the amount of income recognized.

59. **(a)**   The requirement is to determine the ratio to be used to calculate income in the third year using the percentage-of-completion method. Income may be recognized on a cost-to-cost basis when the percentage-of-completion method is used.

$$\left(\frac{\text{Cost to date}}{\text{Total expected cost}} \times \begin{matrix} \text{Expected} \\ \text{profit} \end{matrix} \right) - \begin{matrix} \text{Profit recognized} \\ \text{in previous periods} \end{matrix}$$

Answers (b) and (d) are incorrect because billings to date are not used as a basis for recognizing revenues. Answer (c) is incorrect as the cost-to-cost calculation requires a cumulative calculation so changes in expected costs and expected income can be adjusted for; thus, costs incurred in year three would be an incorrect basis for recognition of income.

60. **(d)**   An anticipated loss on a long-term contract should be recognized immediately under **both** the percentage-of-completion and the completed-contract methods.

61. **(a)**   The requirement is to determine the proper classification for the progress billings on contracts account under the percentage-of-completion method. In the construction industry, operating cycles for construction contracts generally exceed one year. Therefore, the predominant practice is to classify all contract-related assets and liabilities as current. On the balance sheet, the Construction in Progress (CIP) account is netted with the contra account, progress billings. If CIP exceeds billings, the excess is reported as a current asset [answer (a)]. If billings exceed CIP, the excess is reported as a current liability. Answers (b) and (c) are incorrect because the accounts related to construction contracts are classified as current. Answer (d) is incorrect because progress billings is not used as a basis for recognizing revenues.

SOLUTIONS TO SIMULATION PROBLEMS

Simulation Problem 1

Situation	Concepts	Journal Entries	Calculations	Research	Communication

	Included	Not included
1. Merchandise purchased for resale	●	○
2. Freight out	○	●
3. Direct materials	●	○
4. Sales returns	○	●
5. Packaging for shipment to customer	○	●
6. Factory overhead	●	○
7. Interest on inventory loan	○	●
8. Purchase discounts not taken	○	●
9. Freight in	●	○
10. Direct labor	●	○

Explanation of solutions

1. Merchandise purchased for resale is a part of inventory.

2. Freight out is part of selling expense.

3. Direct materials are part of work in process, which is an inventory account for manufacturers.

4. Sales returns are a contra account to sales, and are not part of inventory.

5. Packaging for shipment to customer is part of selling expenses.

6. Factory overhead is part of work in process, which is an inventory account for manufacturing firms.

7. Interest on inventory loan is an operating expense. Interest cost should not be capitalized for assets that are in use or ready for their intended use in the earnings activities of the enterprise.

8. Purchase discounts lost are considered a financing expense and are excluded from the cost of inventory.

9. Freight-in is part of getting the goods in place to sell and should be included in inventory.

10. Direct labor is part of work in process, and is an inventory account for manufacturing firms.

Situation	Concepts	Journal Entries	Calculations	Research	Communication

1. On January 5, 2010, purchased $17,000 of garden tillers on account from Bestbuilt Tillers, terms 2/10, n/30, FOB destination. Freight charges were $200.

| Purchases | 17,000 | |
| Accounts payable | | 17,000 |

2. On January 10, 2010, returned garden tillers worth $2,000 to Bestbuilt Tillers due to defects.

| Accounts payable | 2,000 | |
| Purchase returns | | 2,000 |

3. On January 14, 2010, paid for the remaining tillers purchased in **1.**

Accounts payable	15,000	
Purchase discounts		300*
Cash		14,700

  15,000 × .02 = 300

4. On January 28, 2010, purchased $30,000 of lawn mowers from Lawn Giant, terms 3/10, n/30, FOB shipping point. The freight charges were $820.

Purchases	30,000	
Freight-in	820	
Accounts payable		30,820

5. On February 6, 2010, paid for the lawn mowers purchased in part **4.** from Lawn Giant.

Accounts payable	30,000	
Purchase discounts		900
Cash		29,100

(This assumes the freight bill is paid separately to the freight company)

			Calculations		
Situation	**Concepts**	**Journal Entries**		**Research**	**Communication**

Assume that Blaedon had the following information regarding the garden tiller inventory:

Purchases	$210,000
Purchase discounts	38,000
Purchase returns	17,500
Freight in	12,100
Freight out	18,000
Beginning inventory	42,900
Ending inventory	34,250

Calculate the following items:

1. Goods available for sale   209,500
2. Costs of goods sold   175,250

Explanation of solutions

Beginning inventory		42,900
Purchases	210,000	
–Purchase discounts	(38,000)	
–Purchase returns	(17,500)	
Net purchases	154,500	
+Freight in	12,100	
		166,600
Goods available for sale		209,500
–Ending inventory		(34,250)
Cost of goods sold		175,250

				Research	
Situation	**Concepts**	**Journal Entries**	**Calculations**		**Communication**

1. What costs should be included in Blaedon's inventory?

ARB43, Ch. 4, Para 5 (amended by FAS 151, para 2)
Statement 3

The primary basis of accounting for inventories is cost, which has been defined generally as the price paid or consideration given to acquire an asset. As applied to inventories, cost means in principle the sum of the applicable expenditures and charges directly or indirectly incurred in bringing an article to its existing condition and location.

Codification: 330-10-30-1

2. How should Blaedon report the 2010 inventory that has declined in value below its costs?

ARB43, Ch. 4, Para 8
Statement 5

A departure from the cost basis of pricing the inventory is required when the utility of the goods is no longer as great as its cost. Where there is evidence that the utility of goods, in their disposal in the ordinary course of business will be less than cost, whether due to physical deterioration, obsolescence, changes in price levels, or other causes, the difference should be recognized as a loss of the current period. This is generally accomplished by stating such goods at a lower level commonly designated as market.

Codification: 330-10-35-1

ARB43, Ch. 4, Para 9
Statement 6

As used in the phrase lower of cost or market 4 the term market means current replacement cost (by purchase or by reproduction, as the case may be) except that

(1) Market should not exceed the net realizable value (i.e., estimated selling price in the ordinary course of business less reasonably predictable costs of completion and disposal); and

(2) Market should not be less than net realizable value reduced by an allowance for an approximately normal profit margin.

Codification: 330-10-20 Glossary

Situation	Concepts	Journal Entries	Calculations	Research	**Communication**

To: CEO, Blaedon Corp.
From: CPA Candidate
Re: Inventory valuation

In our last meeting, you inquired as to the valuation methods used for Blaedon's lawn mower inventory. Normally, inventory is valued by accumulating all necessary and reasonable costs to get the inventory in place for sale to customers. These costs may include design costs, purchase price from contractors, freight-in, and warehousing costs. For its 2011 models, Blaedon should include all these costs in valuing the lawn mower inventory.

However, when the value of inventory is less than its historical cost, then inventory must be written down to net realizable value. For the 2010 model inventory, net realizable value is the current list price reduced by both disposition costs and two-thirds of the difference between the $40 allowance given and the carrying amount assigned to trade-ins. The trade-ins' carrying amount should equal the $25 average net realizable value less the profit margin, if any, assigned to the trade-in mower.

The FIFO method requires that Blaedon assign the costs of the earliest purchased items to cost of goods sold. With rising costs, this would result in matching old, relatively low inventory costs to current revenues. Therefore, net income will be higher than reported using certain other inventory methods.

Using the FIFO method, Blaedon should assign the costs of items most recently purchased to ending inventory. Normally, the carrying amount of Blaedon's FIFO ending inventory would approximate replacement cost. As a result, retained earnings also will be higher than that reported using certain other inventory methods.

If you have any additional questions, please contact me.

Simulation Problem 2

Situation	Calculation of Gross Profit	Financial Statement Disclosures	Schedule of Income Taxes	Communication	Research

London Inc.
SCHEDULE OF GROSS PROFIT (LOSS)

	Beta	Gamma
For the Year Ended September 30, 2010:		
Estimated gross profit (loss):		
Contract price	$600,000	$800,000
Less total costs	400,000	820,000
Estimated gross profit (loss)	$200,000	$ (20,000)
Percent complete:		
Costs incurred to date	$360,000	$410,000
Total costs	400,000	820,000
Percent complete	90%	50%
Gross profit (loss) recognized	$180,000	$ (20,000)
For the Year Ended September 30, 2011:		
Estimated gross profit (loss):		
Contract price	$560,000	$840,000
Less total costs	450,000	900,000
Estimated gross profit (loss)	$110,000	$ (60,000)

	Beta	_Gamma_
Percent complete:		
Costs incurred to date	$450,000	$720,000
Total costs	450,000	900,000
Percent complete	100%	80%
Gross profit (loss) recognized	110,000	(60,000)
Less gross profit (loss) recognized in prior year	180,000	(20,000)
Gross profit (loss) recognized	$ (70,000)	$ (40,000)

Situation	Calculation of Gross Profit	Financial Statement Disclosures	Schedule of Income Taxes	Communication	Research

London Inc.
SCHEDULE OF SELECTED BALANCE SHEET ACCOUNTS
September 30, 2010

Accounts receivable		$115,000
Costs and estimated earnings in excess of billings:		
Construction in progress	$540,000	
Less: Billings	315,000	
Costs and estimated earnings in excess of billings		225,000
Billings in excess of costs and estimated earnings		30,000
Estimated loss on contract		20,000

Situation	Calculation of Gross Profit	Financial Statement Disclosures	Schedule of Income Taxes	Communication	Research

London Inc.
SCHEDULE OF INCOME TAXES PAYABLE AND INCOME TAX EXPENSE
September 30, 2010

Financial statement income:		
From other divisions		$300,000
From Beta project		180,000
From Gamma project		(20,000)
Total financial statement income		$460,000
Less temporary differences:		
Beta project income		(180,000)
Gamma project loss		20,000
Total taxable income		$300,000
Taxes payable ($300,000 × 25%)		$ 75,000
Deferred tax liability ($160,000 × 30%)		48,000
Tax expense:		
Current	$ 75,000	
Deferred	48,000	$123,000

Explanation of solutions

- This problem consists of three related requirements concerning long-term construction contracts. The candidates must compute gross profit recognized for two years using the percentage-of-completion method, compute balances in various accounts, and reconcile financial statement income and taxable income.
- Using the percentage-of-completion method, gross profit is recognized periodically based on progress toward completion of the project using the following formula.

$$\frac{\text{Costs to date}}{\text{Total estimated costs}} \times \frac{\text{Estimated}}{\text{profit}} = \frac{\text{Gross profit}}{\text{to date}}$$

For the Beta project, London would recognize gross profit of $180,000 the first year.

$$\frac{\$360,000}{(\$360,000 + \$40,000)} \times [\$600,000 - (\$360,000 + \$40,000)] = \$180,000$$

The estimates available at 9/30/10 are used above.

- By the end of the second year, the Beta project is complete and has resulted in actual gross profit of $110,000 ($560,000 revenues less $450,000 costs). Since gross profit of $180,000 was recognized the first year, a loss of $70,000 must be recognized the second year [$110,000 − $180,000 = $(70,000)]. The loss of $70,000 is in effect an adjustment of the excessive gross profit recognized the first year. Instead of restating the prior period, the prior period misstatement is absorbed in the current period, as is appropriate for a change in estimate.
- Under both the percentage-of-completion method and the completed contract method, for financial accounting purposes, an expected **loss** on a contract must be recognized in full in the period in which the expected loss is discovered. At the end of

the first year, London has an expected loss on the Gamma contract [$800,000 – ($410,000 + $410,000) = $(20,000)] that must be recognized immediately.

- By the end of the second year, the expected loss on the Gamma contract has increased to $60,000 [$840,000 – ($720,000 + $180,000)]. Since a loss of $20,000 was recognized the first year, an additional loss of $40,000 must be recognized in the second year to bring the cumulative loss recognized up to the new estimate of $60,000.
- Financial Statement Disclosures require the computation of the 9/30/10 balances of accounts receivable, costs and estimated earnings in excess of billings, and billings in excess of costs and estimated earnings. At 10/1/09, the balances in all three accounts were $0 since the construction division began operations on that date.
- **Accounts receivable** is increased by billings

> Accounts receivable
>   Billings on LT contracts

It is decreased by cash collections

> Cash
>   Accounts receivable

Therefore, 9/30/10 AR is computed by adding the billings on the two projects ($315,000 + $440,000 = $755,000) and subtracting the collections on the two projects ($275,000 + $365,000 = $640,000). The 9/30/10 balance is $115,000 ($755,000 – $640,000).

- **Construction-in-progress** is debited for costs incurred and profit recognized. **Billings on LT contracts** is credited for billings made. In the balance sheet, the two accounts are netted on a project-by-project basis, resulting in a net current asset and/or a net current liability. At 9/30/10, the costs incurred on the Beta project ($360,000) and the estimated earnings ($180,000 from item two of this solution guide) exceed billings ($315,000) by $225,000.
- On the Gamma project billings ($440,000) exceed costs ($410,000) by $30,000. There is no estimated earnings on this project because it is expected, at 9/30/10, to result in a $20,000 loss (see item 2.2 above). This estimated loss does not affect the excess of billings over costs and estimated earnings because it is reported separately as a current liability.
- Financial statement income consists of income before taxes before considering construction projects ($300,000) plus gross profit from construction contracts [$160,000 from part (a) of the solution], less income tax expense. The **pretax** financial income, therefore, is $460,000 ($300,000 + $160,000). The income not from construction projects will be taxed this year, so current income tax expense is $75,000 ($300,000 × 25%). Because the completed contract method is used for tax purposes, the $160,000 gross profit from construction contracts will not be taxed until future years (note that for **tax** purposes no gross profit or gross **loss** is recognized until completion under the completed contract method). Therefore, deferred tax expense is $48,000 (future enacted rate of 30% times $160,000). Financial statement income is $337,000 [$460,000 – ($75,000 + $48,000)].
- Since the $160,000 gross profit will not be recognized for tax purposes until later years, taxable income is $300,000. To reconcile financial statement income ($337,000 from above) to taxable income, the current and deferred income tax must be added back to compute pretax financial income ($337,000 + $75,000 + $48,000 = $460,000). Then the gross profit not recognized for tax purposes is subtracted to reconcile to taxable income ($460,000 – $160,000 = $300,000).

Situation	Calculation of Gross Profit	Financial Statement Disclosures	Schedule of Income Taxes	Communication	Research

To: Mr. Jim Cauley, Construction Supervisor
From: CPA Candidate
Re: Percentage-of-completion method for construction contracts

    You have requested that I explain the percentage-of-completion method of accounting for contracts. The percentage-of-completion method of accounting recognizes income as work is completed on a project. The amount of income recognized is measured by estimating the amount of work completed to date. Two methods can be used to estimate the percent completed: (1) compare the costs to date to the estimated total costs based on the most recent information, or (2) measure the progress toward completion of the work performed to date.

    Income is recognized on the income statement for the percentage of the project that is completed. On the balance sheet a current asset should be recorded for costs and recognized income that has not yet been billed, and a current liability should be recognized for billings in excess of costs. If current estimates indicate that an overall loss on the contract is expected to occur, a provision should be made for the loss on the contract and recognized immediately.

    There are two advantages to the percentage-of-completion method. The first advantage is that income is recognized currently as progress is made on the contract. A second advantage is that the status of uncompleted contracts are provided in the financial statements by providing current estimates of the costs and of the progress toward completion. The disadvantage of the percentage-of-completion method is that it relies upon estimates to measure income and costs, and these estimates are subject to uncertainty.

    If you have any questions, please contact me.

Situation	Calculation of Gross Profit	Financial Statement Disclosures	Schedule of Income Taxes	Communication	Research

ARB45, Para 11

Although the completed-contract method does not permit the recording of any income prior to completion, provision should be made for expected losses in accordance with the well established practice of making provision for foreseeable losses. If there is a close relationship between profitable and unprofitable contracts, such as in the case of contracts which are parts of the same project, the group may be treated as a unit in determining the necessity for a provision for losses.

Codification: 605-35-25-46

Simulation Problem 3

Situation	Inventory Concepts	Cost Flow Concepts	Schedule of Ending Inventory	Schedule of Cost of Goods Sold	Communication	Research

	True	False
1. The gross margin method uses historical sales margins to estimate the cost of inventory.	●	○
2. The dollar value LIFO method preserves old inventory costs by charging current costs to cost of goods sold.	●	○
3. Inventory should be reported at the lower of cost or market and it may be based on the values of individual items, categories, or the total inventory.	●	○
4. A loss on a purchase commitment should be recorded when the contract price is greater than the market and it is anticipated that a loss will occur when the contract is completed.	●	○
5. Under the dollar-value LIFO method, increases and decreases in a layer would be measured based upon the change in the total dollar value of the layer.	●	○
6. The link-chain method uses a cumulative index to value the base cost of ending inventory.	●	○
7. The price index for dollar-value LIFO is a measure of changes in price levels between the current year and the base year.	●	○
8. Under the LIFO method, an inventory liquidation will result in higher profits in a period of rising prices.	●	○
9. A holding gain results from holding an item while the market value experiences a decline.	○	●
10. During a period of rising prices, the LIFO cost flow assumption results in a higher net income as compared to FIFO.	○	●
11. In a period of rising prices, when a company changes from FIFO to LIFO the net income will tend to decline as will working capital.	●	○
12. The use of LIFO for book and tax purposes will result in a lower tax payment in a period of rising prices.	●	○
13. Under the LIFO method, the cost of goods sold balance would be the same whether a perpetual or periodic inventory system is used.	○	●

Explanation of solutions

1. **(T)** The gross margin method uses historical margins on sales to estimate the cost of inventory. This method is typically used for interim reporting only because it may not be precise enough for the year-end financial statements.

2. **(T)** The dollar-value LIFO method groups inventory into layers and charges the most recent items to cost of goods sold before using older layers which have older inventory costs.

3. **(T)** Inventory should be carried at the lower of cost or market. In determining the lower of cost or market it may be based on the values of individual items, item categories, or even total inventory.

4. **(T)** When the market price of a contract to purchase goods falls below the contract price and it is foreseeable that the contract will result in a loss, then a loss on the purchase commitment should be recorded.

5. **(T)** The dollar-value LIFO method measures changes in inventory layers based upon the total dollar value change in the layer.

6. (T) The link-chain method uses a cumulative index to compute the base cost of inventory. The cumulative index is equal to the current year's prices divided by the prior year's prices, multiplied by the prior year's cumulative index. The link-chain method is only used in limited circumstances.

7. (T) A price index provides a measure of the changes in price between base year and the current year. The price index is generally used to compute changes in inventory levels.

8. (T) In a period of rising prices, a liquidation of older inventory, which carries lower costs, will result in a decline in the cost of goods sold and higher profits.

9. (F) A holding gain results from holding an item while the market value **increases**. Thus, the holding gain would be equal to the current market value less the value on the books.

10. (F) During a period of rising prices, the LIFO method will result in higher priced items being charged to cost of goods sold, thus lowering net income. It is the FIFO method which would produce a higher net income because the cost of goods sold would reflect the older or lower cost goods.

11. (T) A change from FIFO to LIFO will tend to result in a decrease in net income and working capital. This is because the LIFO method will put the more recent/higher priced items on the income statement (last in) and the older/less expensive goods will be carried in inventory. Thus, net income will be lower due to higher cost of goods sold, and working capital will be lower due to the lower inventory asset balance.

12. (T) The LIFO method results in the most recently purchased inventory items being expensed first. In a period of rising prices this would result in a lower net income and thus a lower taxes payable. The IRS allows the use of LIFO for tax only if it is also used for external reporting purposes as well.

13. (F) The cost of goods sold would be different because a periodic system will compute the cost of goods sold based on the total goods sold and total purchases for a period, whereas a perpetual one will match each good sold with the most recent purchase on an ongoing basis.

Situation	Inventory Concepts	Cost Flow Concepts	Schedule of Ending Inventory	Schedule of Cost of Goods Sold	Communication	Research

	Method
1. During a period of rising prices, this method results in a higher net income.	FIFO
2. This method most closely matches the physical flow of inventory.	FIFO
3. Method that uses historical sales margins to estimate ending inventory.	Gross profit method
4. Method that is appropriate when there is a relatively small number of significant dollar value items in inventory.	Specific identification
5. Average cost must be calculated each time additional inventory is purchased.	Moving average
6. Method that averages the cost of all items on hand and purchased during the period.	Weighted-average
7. This method results in the lowest ending inventory in a period of rising prices.	LIFO
8. Method that uses a price index to measure changes in inventory.	Dollar value LIFO
9. If used for tax purposes, this method must also be used for financial reporting purposes.	LIFO
10. The cost of goods sold balance is the same whether a perpetual or periodic inventory system is used.	FIFO

Situation	Inventory Concepts	Cost Flow Concepts	Schedule of Ending Inventory	Schedule of Cost of Goods Sold	Communication	Research

York Co.
SUPPORTING SCHEDULE OF ENDING INVENTORY
December 31, 2010

Inventory at cost (LIFO):

	Units	Cost per unit	Total cost
Beginning inventory, January 1	8,000	$8.20	$ 65,600
Purchases, quarter ended March 31	12,000	8.25	99,000
Purchases, quarter ended June 30	2,000	7.90	15,800
	22,000		$180,400

Situation	Inventory Concepts	Cost Flow Concepts	Schedule of Ending Inventory	Schedule of Cost of Goods Sold	Communication	Research

York Co.
SCHEDULE OF COST OF GOODS SOLD
For the Year Ended December 31, 2010

Beginning inventory	$ 65,600
Add: Purchases	368,900
Less: Purchase discounts	(18,000)
Add: Freight-in	5,000
Goods available for sale	421,500
Less: Ending inventory	(176,000) [1]
Cost of Goods Sold	$245,500

[1] Inventory at market:
  22,000 units @ $8 = $176,000

Explanation of solutions

- This problem requires preparation of a cost of goods sold (CGS) schedule with a supporting schedule of ending inventory at lower of cost or market (LCM). York uses the direct method for LCM, which means the LCM amount is used directly in the CGS computation with no separate disclosure of any LCM loss.
- The cost of goods sold schedule can be prepared first, leaving the last two lines (ending inventory and CGS) blank for now. The computation starts with **beginning inventory** plus **cost of goods purchased** equals **cost of goods available for sale** (cost of goods purchased is **purchases** less **purchase discounts** plus **freight-in**). **Freight-out** is a selling expense which does not affect CGS.
- When determining LCM, the market value of inventory is defined as the **replacement cost,** as long as it is less than the ceiling [**net realizable value** (NRV)] and more than the floor (**NRV less a normal profit**).
- There are 22,000 units in ending inventory (55,000 units available less 33,000 units sold). Using LIFO, the earliest units in are assumed to remain in ending inventory. Therefore, ending inventory consists of the 8,000 units from beginning inventory, plus the 12,000 units purchased in the first quarter, plus 2,000 more units from second quarter purchases to get up to the 22,000 unit total. The cost of ending inventory is $180,400 [(8,000 × $8.20) + (12,000 × $8.25) + (2,000 × $7.90)].
- The replacement cost of the inventory is $176,000 (22,000 × $8).
- The ceiling (NRV) is $193,600 (22,000 × $8.80).
- The floor (NRV less a normal profit) is $170,500 [22,000 × ($8.80 – $1.05)].
- Because replacement cost ($176,000) falls between the floor ($170,500) and the ceiling ($193,600), the replacement cost of $176,000 is the designated market value.
- Since the designated market value of $176,000 is less than cost ($180,400), the LCM valuation of ending inventory is $176,000. This amount can be put into the cost of goods sold schedule, resulting in CGS of $245,500.

  - Value inventory at LCM
     Market is replacement with limits
       Market must ≤ NRV and
       Market must ≥ NRV – normal profit
  - Market is replacement cost in this situation
     Replacement cost ($176,000) falls between above limits
  - Inventory reported at market because < cost

Situation	Inventory Concepts	Cost Flow Concepts	Schedule of Ending Inventory	Schedule of Cost of Goods Sold	Communication	Research

To: Mr. Binson
From: CPA Candidate
Re: Valuation of inventory

  This memorandum is designed to provide you with an understanding of the financial accounting standards that apply to inventories. Inventory is normally valued at cost. However, conservatism in accounting provides that assets should not be overstated. If inventory becomes damaged, obsolete, or declines in value, it should be revalued to its market value. In accounting terms, market means current replacement cost. However, the market value used should not exceed the amount that may be realized from the sale of the inventory items. Also, this market value should not be less than what the items can be sold for less a normal profit margin.

  In this particular situation, since replacement cost ($8 per unit) is less than net realizable value, but greater than net realizable value reduced by a normal profit margin, replacement cost is used as market. The inventory valued at market ($176,000) is lower than inventory valued at cost ($180,400). Therefore, inventory should be reported in the financial statements at market value.

  If you have any additional questions, please contact me.

Situation	Inventory Concepts	Cost Flow Concepts	Schedule of Ending Inventory	Schedule of Cost of Goods Sold	Communication	Research

1. What methods may be used for costing inventories?

ARB43, Ch. 4, Para 6
Statement 4

> Cost for inventory purposes may be determined under any one of several assumptions as to the flow of cost factors (such as first-in first-out, average, and last-in first-out); the major objective in selecting a method should be to choose the one which, under the circumstances, most clearly reflects periodic income.

> 6. The cost to be matched against revenue from a sale may not be the identified cost of the specific item which is sold, especially in cases in which similar goods are purchased at different times and at different prices. While in some lines of business specific lots are clearly identified from the time of purchase through the time of sale and are costed on this basis, ordinarily the identity of goods is lost between the time of acquisition and the time of sale. In any event, if the materials purchased in various lots are identical and interchangeable, the use of identified cost of the various lots may not produce the most useful financial statements. This fact has resulted in the development of general acceptance of several assumptions with respect to the flow of cost factors (such as first-in first-out, average, and last-in first-out) to provide practical bases for the measurement of periodic income. In some situations a reversed mark-up procedure of inventory pricing, such as the retail inventory method, may be both practical and appropriate. The business operations in some cases may be such as to make it desirable to apply one of the acceptable methods of determining cost to one portion of the inventory or components thereof and another of the acceptable methods to other portions of the inventory.

> *Codification: 330-10-30-9*

2. How is the market value calculated when calculating the lower of cost or market?

ARB, 43, Ch 4, Para 9
Statement 6

> As used in the phrase lower of cost or market, the term market means current replacement cost (by purchase or by reproduction, as the case may be) except that

> (1) Market should not exceed the net realizable value (i.e., estimated selling price in the ordinary course of business less reasonably predictable costs of completion and disposal); and
> (2) Market should not be less than net realizable value reduced by an allowance for an approximately normal profit margin.

> *Codification: 330-10-20 Glossary*

MULTIPLE-CHOICE QUESTIONS (1-84)

1. Merry Co. purchased a machine costing $125,000 for its manufacturing operations and paid shipping costs of $20,000. Merry spent an additional $10,000 testing and preparing the machine for use. What amount should Merry record as the cost of the machine?

a. $155,000
b. $145,000
c. $135,000
d. $125,000

2. On December 1, 2010, Boyd Co. purchased a $400,000 tract of land for a factory site. Boyd razed an old building on the property and sold the materials it salvaged from the demolition. Boyd incurred additional costs and realized salvage proceeds during December 2010 as follows:

Demolition of old building	$50,000
Legal fees for purchase contract and recording ownership	10,000
Title guarantee insurance	12,000
Proceeds from sale of salvaged materials	8,000

In its December 31, 2010 balance sheet, Boyd should report a balance in the land account of

a. $464,000
b. $460,000
c. $442,000
d. $422,000

3. Cole Co. began constructing a building for its own use in January 2010. During 2010, Cole incurred interest of $50,000 on specific construction debt, and $20,000 on other borrowings. Interest computed on the weighted-average amount of accumulated expenditures for the building during 2010 was $40,000. What amount of interest cost should Cole capitalize?

a. $20,000
b. $40,000
c. $50,000
d. $70,000

4. Clay Company started construction of a new office building on January 1, 2010, and moved into the finished building on July 1, 2011. Of the building's $2,500,000 total cost, $2,000,000 was incurred in 2010 evenly throughout the year. Clay's incremental borrowing rate was 12% throughout 2010, and the total amount of interest incurred by Clay during 2010 was $102,000. What amount should Clay report as capitalized interest at December 31, 2010?

a. $102,000
b. $120,000
c. $150,000
d. $240,000

5. During 2010, Bay Co. constructed machinery for its own use and for sale to customers. Bank loans financed these assets both during construction and after construction was complete. How much of the interest incurred should be reported as interest expense in the 2010 income statement?

	Interest incurred for machinery for own use	Interest incurred for machinery held for sale
a.	All interest incurred	All interest incurred
b.	All interest incurred	Interest incurred after completion
c.	Interest incurred after completion	Interest incurred after completion
d.	Interest incurred after completion	All interest incurred

6. On July 1, 2010, Balt Co. exchanged a truck for twenty-five shares of Ace Corp.'s common stock. On that date, the truck's carrying amount was $2,500, and its fair value was $3,000. Also, the book value of Ace's stock was $60 per share. On December 31, 2010, Ace had 250 shares of common stock outstanding and its book value per share was $50. What amount should Balt report in its December 31, 2010 balance sheet as investment in Ace?

a. $3,000
b. $2,500
c. $1,500
d. $1,250

7. A nonmonetary exchange is recognized at fair value of the assets exchanged unless

a. Exchange has commercial substance.
b. Fair value is not determinable.
c. The assets are similar in nature.
d. The assets are dissimilar.

8. In a nonmonetary exchange, which of the following situations will require the asset to be recognized at the recorded value of the asset relinquished?

a. A delivery truck exchanged for a delivery van that can deliver four times the quantity of goods to customers.
b. The exchanged item is intended to facilitate sales to customers.
c. The cash flows from the new asset will be significantly different from cash flows of the exchanged asset.
d. The assets are both productive assets.

9. For purposes of nonmonetary exchanges, the configuration of cash flows includes which of the following?

a. The implicit rate, maturity date of loan, and amount of loan.
b. The risk, timing, and amount of cash flows of the assets.
c. The entity-specific value of the asset which is equal to the fair value of the asset exchanged.
d. The estimated present value of the assets exchanged.

10. When determining the commercial substance of the exchange, which of the following items is not considered?

a. Cash flow of exchanged asset.
b. Cash flow of new asset.
c. Cash flow from tax effects on the exchange to avoid taxes.
d. Cash flow from potential sale of new equipment at a later date.

11. On March 31, 2010, Winn Company traded in an old machine having a carrying amount of $16,800, and paid a cash difference of $6,000 for a new machine having a total cash price of $20,500. The cash flows from the new machine are expected to be significantly different than the cash flows from the old machine. On March 31, 2010, what amount of loss should Winn recognize on this exchange?

a. $0
b. $2,300

c. $3,700
d. $6,000

12. Amble, Inc. exchanged a truck with a carrying amount of $12,000 and a fair value of $20,000 for a truck and $2,500 cash. The cash flows from the new truck are not expected to be significantly different from the cash flows of the old truck. The fair value of the truck received was $17,500. At what amount should Amble record the truck received in the exchange?

a. $ 7,000
b. $ 9,500
c. $10,500
d. $17,500

13. In an exchange of assets that is deemed to lack commercial substance, Transit Co. received equipment with a fair value equal to the carrying amount of equipment given up. Transit also contributed cash. As a result of the exchange, Transit recognized

a.   A loss equal to the cash given up.
b.   A loss determined by the proportion of cash paid to the total transaction value.
c.   A gain determined by the proportion of cash paid to the total transaction value.
d.   Neither gain **nor** loss.

14. May Co. and Sty Co. exchanged nonmonetary assets. The exchange did not result in the expected cash flows of the assets being significantly different for either May or Sty. May paid cash to Sty in connection with the exchange. To the extent that the amount of cash exceeds a proportionate share of the carrying amount of the asset surrendered, a realized gain on the exchange should be recognized by

	May	_Sty_
a.	Yes	Yes
b.	Yes	No
c.	No	Yes
d.	No	No

15. Vik Auto and King Clothier exchanged goods, held for resale, with equal fair values. Each will use the other's goods to promote their own products. The retail price of the car that Vik gave up is less than the retail price of the clothes received. Assuming the transaction has commercial substance, what profit should Vik recognize for the non-monetary exchange?

a.   A profit is **not** recognized.
b.   A profit equal to the difference between the retail prices of the clothes received and the car.
c.   A profit equal to the difference between the retail price and the cost of the car.
d.   A profit equal to the difference between the fair value and the cost of the car.

16. Yola Co. and Zaro Co. are fuel oil distributors. To facilitate the delivery of oil to their customers, Yola and Zaro exchanged ownership of 1,200 barrels of oil without physically moving the oil. Yola paid Zaro $20,000 to compensate for a difference in the grade of oil. On the date of the exchange, cost and market values of the oil were as follows:

	Yola Co.	_Zaro Co._
Cost	$100,000	$126,000
Market values	130,000	150,000

In Zaro's income statement, what amount of gain should be reported from the exchange of the oil?

a. $0
b. $ 3,200
c. $20,000
d. $24,000

17. An entity disposes of a nonmonetary asset in a non-reciprocal transfer. A gain or loss should be recognized on the disposition of the asset when the fair value of the asset transferred is determinable and the nonreciprocal transfer is to

	Another entity	_A stockholder of the entity_
a.	No	Yes
b.	No	No
c.	Yes	No
d.	Yes	Yes

18. On July 1, 2010, one of Rudd Co.'s delivery vans was destroyed in an accident. On that date, the van's carrying value was $2,500. On July 15, 2010, Rudd received and recorded a $700 invoice for a new engine installed in the van in May 2010, and another $500 invoice for various repairs. In August, Rudd received $3,500 under its insurance policy on the van, which it plans to use to replace the van. What amount should Rudd report as gain (loss) on disposal of the van in its 2010 income statement?

a. $1,000
b. $ 300
c. $0
d. $ (200)

19. Lano Corp.'s forest land was condemned for use as a national park. Compensation for the condemnation exceeded the forest land's carrying amount. Lano purchased similar, but larger, replacement forest land for an amount greater than the condemnation award. As a result of the condemnation and replacement, what is the net effect on the carrying amount of forest land reported in Lano's balance sheet?

a.   The amount is increased by the excess of the replacement forest land's cost over the condemned forest land's carrying amount.
b.   The amount is increased by the excess of the replacement forest land's cost over the condemnation award.
c.   The amount is increased by the excess of the condemnation award over the condemned forest land's carrying amount.
d.   No effect, because the condemned forest land's carrying amount is used as the replacement forest land's carrying amount.

20. On July 1, 2010, Town Company purchased for $540,000 a warehouse building and the land on which it is located. The following data were available concerning the property:

	Current appraised value	_Seller's original cost_
Land	$200,000	$140,000
Warehouse building	300,000	280,000
	$500,000	$420,000

Town should record the land at

a. $140,000
b. $180,000
c. $200,000
d. $216,000

21. During 2010, King Company made the following expenditures relating to its plant building:

Continuing and frequent repairs	$40,000
Repainted the plant building	10,000
Major improvements to the electrical wiring system	32,000
Partial replacement of roof tiles	14,000

How much should be charged to repair and maintenance expense in 2010?

    a. $96,000
    b. $82,000
    c. $64,000
    d. $54,000

22. On June 18, 2010, Dell Printing Co. incurred the following costs for one of its printing presses:

Purchase of collating and stapling attachment	$84,000
Installation of attachment	36,000
Replacement parts for overhaul of press	26,000
Labor and overhead in connection with overhaul	14,000

The overhaul resulted in a significant increase in production. Neither the attachment nor the overhaul increased the estimated useful life of the press. What amount of the above costs should be capitalized?

    a. $0
    b. $84,000
    c. $120,000
    d. $160,000

23. A building suffered uninsured fire damage. The damaged portion of the building was refurbished with higher quality materials. The cost and related accumulated depreciation of the damaged portion are identifiable. To account for these events, the owner should

    a.   Reduce accumulated depreciation equal to the cost of refurbishing.
    b.   Record a loss in the current period equal to the sum of the cost of refurbishing and the carrying amount of the damaged portion of the building.
    c.   Capitalize the cost of refurbishing and record a loss in the current period equal to the carrying amount of the damaged portion of the building.
    d.   Capitalize the cost of refurbishing by adding the cost to the carrying amount of the building.

24. Derby Co. incurred costs to modify its building and to rearrange its production line. As a result, an overall reduction in production costs is expected. However, the modifications did not increase the building's market value, and the rearrangement did not extend the production line's life. Should the building modification costs and the production line rearrangement costs be capitalized?

	Building modification costs	Production line rearrangement costs
a.	Yes	No
b.	Yes	Yes
c.	No	No
d.	No	Yes

25. On January 2, 2010, Lem Corp. bought machinery under a contract that required a down payment of $10,000, plus twenty-four monthly payments of $5,000 each, for total cash payments of $130,000. The cash equivalent price of the machinery was $110,000. The machinery has an estimated useful life of ten years and estimated salvage value of $5,000. Lem uses straight-line depreciation. In its 2010 income statement, what amount should Lem report as depreciation for this machinery?

    a. $10,500
    b. $11,000
    c. $12,500
    d. $13,000

26. Turtle Co. purchased equipment on January 2, 2008, for $50,000. The equipment had an estimated five-year service life. Turtle's policy for five-year assets is to use the 200% double-declining depreciation method for the first two years of the asset's life, and then switch to the straight-line depreciation method. In its December 31, 2010 balance sheet, what amount should Turtle report as accumulated depreciation for equipment?

    a. $30,000
    b. $38,000
    c. $39,200
    d. $42,000

27. Rago Company takes a full year's depreciation expense in the year of an asset's acquisition, and no depreciation expense in the year of disposition. Data relating to one of Rago's depreciable assets at December 31, 2010, are as follows:

Acquisition year	2007
Cost	$110,000
Residual value	20,000
Accumulated depreciation	72,000
Estimated useful life	5 years

Using the same depreciation method as used in 2008, 2009, and 2010, how much depreciation expense should Rago record in 2010 for this asset?

    a. $12,000
    b. $18,000
    c. $22,000
    d. $24,000

28. On January 2, 2007, Union Co. purchased a machine for $264,000 and depreciated it by the straight-line method using an estimated useful life of eight years with no salvage value. On January 2, 2010, Union determined that the machine had a useful life of six years from the date of acquisition and will have a salvage value of $24,000. An accounting change was made in 2010 to reflect the additional data. The accumulated depreciation for this machine should have a balance at December 31, 2010, of

    a. $176,000
    b. $160,000
    c. $154,000
    d. $146,000

29. Weir Co. uses straight-line depreciation for its property, plant, and equipment, which, stated at cost, consisted of the following:

	12/31/10	12/31/09
Land	$ 25,000	$ 25,000
Buildings	195,000	195,000
Machinery and equipment	695,000	650,000
	915,000	870,000
Less accumulated depreciation	400,000	370,000
	$515,000	$500,000

Weir's depreciation expense for 2010 and 2009 was $55,000 and $50,000, respectively. What amount was debited to accumulated depreciation during 2010 because of property, plant, and equipment retirements?

    a. $40,000
    b. $25,000

c. $20,000
d. $10,000

30. On January 1, 2006, Crater, Inc. purchased equipment having an estimated salvage value equal to 20% of its original cost at the end of a ten-year life. The equipment was sold December 31, 2010, for 50% of its original cost. If the equipment's disposition resulted in a reported loss, which of the following depreciation methods did Crater use?
a.   Double-declining balance.
b.   Sum-of-the-years' digits.
c.   Straight-line.
d.   Composite.

31. A depreciable asset has an estimated 15% salvage value. At the end of its estimated useful life, the accumulated depreciation would equal the original cost of the asset under which of the following depreciation methods?

	Straight-line	Productive output
a.	Yes	No
b.	Yes	Yes
c.	No	Yes
d.	No	No

32. In which of the following situations is the units-of-production method of depreciation most appropriate?
a.   An asset's service potential declines with use.
b.   An asset's service potential declines with the passage of time.
c.   An asset is subject to rapid obsolescence.
d.   An asset incurs increasing repairs and maintenance with use.

33. A machine with a five-year estimated useful life and an estimated 10% salvage value was acquired on January 1, 2007. On December 31, 2010, accumulated depreciation, using the sum-of-the-years' digits method, would be
a.   (Original cost less salvage value) multiplied by 1/15.
b.   (Original cost less salvage value) multiplied by 14/15.
c.   Original cost multiplied by 14/15.
d.   Original cost multiplied by 1/15.

34. Spiro Corp. uses the sum-of-the-years' digits method to depreciate equipment purchased in January 2008 for $20,000. The estimated salvage value of the equipment is $2,000 and the estimated useful life is four years. What should Spiro report as the asset's carrying amount as of December 31, 2010?
a. $1,800
b. $2,000
c. $3,800
d. $4,500

35. The graph below depicts three depreciation expense patterns over time.

Which depreciation expense pattern corresponds to the sum-of-the-years' digits method and which corresponds to the double-declining balance method?

	Sum-of-the-years' digits	Double-declining balance
a.	III	II
b.	II	I
c.	I	III
d.	II	III

36. Which of the following uses the straight-line depreciation method?

	Group depreciation	Composite depreciation
a.	No	No
b.	Yes	No
c.	Yes	Yes
d.	No	Yes

37. A company using the composite depreciation method for its fleet of trucks, cars, and campers retired one of its trucks and received cash from a salvage company. The net carrying amount of these composite asset accounts would be decreased by the
a.   Cash proceeds received and original cost of the truck.
b.   Cash proceeds received.
c.   Original cost of the truck less the cash proceeds.
d.   Original cost of the truck.

38. During 2010, the management of West Inc. decided to dispose of some of its older equipment and machinery. By year-end, December 31, 2010, these assets had not been sold, although the company was negotiating their sale to another company. On the December 31, 2010 balance sheet of West Inc., this equipment and machinery should be reported at
a.   Fair value.
b.   Carrying amount.
c.   The lower of carrying amount or fair value.
d.   The lower of carrying amount or fair value less cost to sell.

39. At December 31, 2010, Matson Inc. was holding long-lived assets that it intended to sell. The assets do not constitute a separate component of the company. The company appropriately recognized a loss in 2010 related to these assets. On Matson's income statement for the year ended December 31, 2010, this loss should be reported as a(n)
a.   Extraordinary item.
b.   Component of income from continuing operations before income taxes.
c.   Separate component of selling or general and administrative expenses, disclosed net of tax benefit.
d.   Component of the gain (loss) from sale of discontinued operations, disclosed net of income taxes.

40. Taft Inc. recognized a loss in 2009 related to long-lived assets that it intended to sell. These assets were not sold during 2010, and the company estimated, at December 31, 2010, that the loss recognized in 2009 had been more than recovered. On the December 31, 2010 balance sheet, Taft should report these long-lived assets at their
a.   Fair value on December 31, 2009.
b.   Fair value less cost to sell on December 31, 2009.
c.   Fair value on December 31, 2010.
d.   Carrying amount on December 31, 2009.

41. Cranston Inc. reported an impairment loss of $150,000 on its income statement for the year ended December 31, 2009. This loss was related to long-lived assets which Cranston intended to use in its operations. On the company's December 31, 2009 balance sheet, Cranston reported these long-lived assets at $920,000 and, as of December 31, 2009, Cranston estimated that these long-lived assets would be used for another five years. On December 31, 2010, Cranston determined that the fair values of its impaired long-lived assets had increased by $25,000 over their fair values at December 31, 2009. On the company's December 31, 2010 balance sheet, what amount should be reported as the carrying amount for these long-lived assets? Assume straight-line depreciation and no salvage value for the impaired assets.

    a. $761,000
    b. $736,000
    c. $945,000
    d. $756,000

42. Assets intended to be held and used for productive purposes may suffer from impairment in each of the following circumstances **except**

    a. A change in the way the assets are used or physical change in the assets.
    b. Asset costs incurred exceed the original amounts planned.
    c. Discounted expected future cash flows and interest charges are less than the carrying amount of the assets.
    d. A significant adverse change in legal factors that might affect the assets' fair value.

43. Synthia, Inc., a clothing manufacturer, purchased a sewing machine for $10,000 on July 1, 2008. The machine had a ten-year life, a $500 salvage value, and was depreciated using the straight-line method. On December 31, 2010, a test for impairment indicates that the undiscounted cash flows from the sewing machine are less than its carrying value. The machine's actual fair value on December 31, 2010 is $3,000. What is Synthia's loss on impairment on December 31, 2010?

    a. $6,500
    b. $4,750
    c. $4,625
    d. $4,150

44. With regard to impaired assets, the FASB standards provide for

	Recognition of loss upon impairment	Restoration of previously recognized impairment losses
a.	Yes	Yes
b.	Yes	No
c.	No	Yes
d.	No	No

45. Scarbrough Company had purchased equipment for $280,000 on January 1, 2007. The equipment had an eight-year useful life and a salvage value of $40,000. Scarbrough depreciated the equipment using the straight-line method. In August 2010, Scarbrough questioned the recoverability of the carrying amount of this equipment. At August 31, 2010, the expected net future cash inflows (undiscounted) related to the continued use and eventual disposal of the equipment total $175,000. The equipment's fair value on August 31, 2010, is $150,000. After any loss on impairment has been recognized, what is the carrying value of Scarbrough's equipment as of August 31, 2010?

    a. $175,000
    b. $170,000
    c. $150,000
    d. $130,000

46. Linx Corporation acquired equipment on January 1, 2008, for $100,000. The equipment had a ten-year useful life and no salvage value. On December 31, 2010, the following information was obtained regarding the equipment:

Expected value of undiscounted cash flows	$72,000
Fair value estimated with in-use valuation premise	$74,000
Fair value estimated with in-exchange valuation premise	$70,000

What is the amount of impairment loss that Linx should report in its 2010 income statement?

    a. $ 6,000
    b. $ 8,000
    c. $10,000
    d. $0

47. Conner Corporation has equipment with a carrying value of $160,000 on December 31, 2010, after recording depreciation expense for 2010. The following information was available on December 31, 2010:

Value of similar equipment for sale in market	$140,000
Present value of estimated future cash flows discounted at 10%	$130,000
Estimated undiscounted cash flows of equipment	$135,000

At what amount should the equipment be presented on the December 31, 2010 balance sheet?

    a. $160,000
    b. $140,000
    c. $135,000
    d. $130,000

48. Dahle Corporation has equipment with a carrying value of $450,000 on December 31, 2010. The following information was available on December 31, 2010:

Expected net cash flows (undiscounted)	$420,000
Expected net cash flows discounted at 7%	$400,000
Fair value, using the assets with other assets	$415,000
Fair value, assuming the assets are sold stand-alone	$428,000

What is the impairment loss that Dahle must report in its 2010 income statement for this equipment?

    a. $50,000
    b. $35,000
    c. $30,000
    d. $22,000

49. Under the reporting requirements for impaired assets, impairment losses for assets to be held and used shall be reported

    a. As an extraordinary item.
    b. As a component of discontinued operations.
    c. As a component of income from continuing operations.
    d. As a change in accounting estimate.

50. During December 2010, Bubba Inc. determined that there had been a significant decrease in the market value of its equipment used in its manufacturing process. At December 31, 2010, Bubba compiled the information below.

Original cost of the equipment	$500,000
Accumulated depreciation	300,000
Expected net future cash inflows (undiscounted)	
related to the continued use and eventual disposal of	
the equipment	175,000
Fair value of the equipment	125,000

What is the amount of impairment loss that should be reported on Bubba's income statement prepared for the year ended December 31, 2010?

a. $ 75,000
b. $ 25,000
c. $325,000
d. $375,000

51. Marjorie, Inc. acquired a machine for $320,000 on August 31, 2007. The machine has a five-year life, a $50,000 salvage value, and was depreciated using the straight-line method. On May 31, 2010, a test for recoverability reveals that the expected net future undiscounted cash inflows related to the continued use and eventual disposal of the machine total $150,000. The machine's actual fair value on May 31, 2010, is $135,000, with no salvage value. Assuming a loss on impairment is recognized May 31, 2010, what is Marjorie's depreciation expense for June 2010?

a. $6,352
b. $5,000
c. $4,500
d. $3,148

52. Which of the following statements is(are) correct about the carrying amount of a long-lived asset after an impairment loss has been recognized? Assume the long-lived asset is being held for use in the business and that the asset is depreciable.

I. The reduced carrying amount of the asset may be increased in subsequent years if the impairment loss has been recovered.
II. The reduced carrying amount of the asset represents the amount that should be depreciated over the asset's remaining useful life.

a. I only.
b. II only.
c. Both I and II.
d. Neither I nor II.

53. According to ASC Topic 360, if a long-lived asset is determined to be impaired, how is the loss calculated?

a. Future discounted cash flows less asset's carrying (book) value.
b. Future undiscounted cash flows less asset's carrying (book) value.
c. Fair value less asset's carrying (book) value.
d. Cash outflows needed to obtain cash inflows.

54. In accordance with ASC Topic 360, long-lived assets are required to be reviewed for impairment

a. At the balance sheet date, every three years.
b. When the asset is fully depreciated.
c. When circumstances indicate that the carrying amount of an asset might not be recoverable.
d. At the balance sheet date, every year.

55. During December 2010, Toni Corp. determined that there had been a significant decrease in the market value of its equipment used in its roofing business. At December 31, 2010, Toni compiled the information below.

Original cost of equipment	$800,000
Accumulated depreciation	450,000
Expected net future cash inflows (undiscounted)	
related to the continued use and eventual disposal	
of the equipment	300,000
Fair value of the equipment	250,000

What is the amount of the impairment loss that should be reported on Toni's income statement prepared for the year ended December 31, 2010?

a. $ 50,000
b. $100,000
c. $150,000
d. $200,000

56. Miller Company acquired a machine for $420,000 on June 30, 2008. The machine has a seven-year life, no salvage value, and was depreciated using the straight-line method. On August 31, 2010, a test for recoverability reveals that the expected net future undiscounted cash inflows related to the continued use and eventual disposal of the machine total $275,000. The machine's actual fair value on August 31, 2010, is $261,000. Assuming a loss on impairment is recognized August 31, 2010, what is Miller's depreciation expense for September 2010?

a. $4,000
b. $4,350
c. $4,500
d. $5,000

57. In January 2010, Vorst Co. purchased a mineral mine for $2,640,000 with removable ore estimated at 1,200,000 tons. After it has extracted all the ore, Vorst will be required by law to restore the land to its original condition at an estimated cost of $220,000. The present value of the estimated restoration costs is $180,000. Vorst believes it will be able to sell the property afterwards for $300,000. During 2010, Vorst incurred $360,000 of development costs preparing the mine for production and removed and sold 60,000 tons of ore. In its 2010 income statement, what amount should Vorst report as depletion?

a. $135,000
b. $144,000
c. $150,000
d. $159,000

58. On December 31, 2009, Byte Co. had capitalized software costs of $600,000 with an economic life of four years. Sales for 2010 were 10% of expected total sales of the software. At December 31, 2010, the software had a net realizable value of $480,000. In its December 31, 2010 balance sheet, what amount should Byte report as net capitalized cost of computer software?

a. $432,000
b. $450,000
c. $480,000
d. $540,000

59. On January 2, 2010, Judd Co. bought a trademark from Krug Co. for $500,000. Judd retained an independent consultant, who estimated the trademark's remaining life to be fifty years. Its unamortized cost on Krug's accounting records was $380,000. In Judd's December 31, 2010 balance sheet, what amount should be reported as accumulated amortization?

a. $ 7,600
b. $ 9,500

c. $10,000
d. $12,500

60. On January 2, 2010, Paye Co. purchased Shef Co. at a cost that resulted in recognition of goodwill of $200,000. During the first quarter of 2010, Paye spent an additional $80,000 on expenditures designed to maintain goodwill. In its December 31, 2010 balance sheet, what amount should Paye report as goodwill?
   a. $180,000
   b. $200,000
   c. $252,000
   d. $280,000

61. Northern Airline purchased airline gate rights at Newark International Airport for $2,000,000 with a legal life of five years. However, Northern has the ability and right to extend the rights every ten years for an indefinite period of time. Over what period of time should Northern amortize the gate rights?
   a.   5 years.
   b.   15 years
   c.   40 years.
   d.   The rights should not be amortized.

62. On January 2, 2007, Lava, Inc. purchased a patent for a new consumer product for $90,000. At the time of purchase, the patent was valid for fifteen years; however, the patent's useful life was estimated to be only ten years due to the competitive nature of the product. On December 31, 2010, the product was permanently withdrawn from sale under governmental order because of a potential health hazard in the product. What amount should Lava charge against income during 2010, assuming amortization is recorded at the end of each year?
   a. $ 9,000
   b. $54,000
   c. $63,000
   d. $72,000

63. What does ASC Topic 350 require with respect to accounting for goodwill?
   a.   Goodwill should be amortized over a five-year period.
   b.   Goodwill should be amortized over its expected useful life.
   c.   Goodwill should be recorded and never adjusted.
   d.   Goodwill should be recorded and periodically evaluated for impairment.

64. Which of the following statements concerning patents is correct?
   a.   Legal costs incurred to successfully defend an internally developed patent should be capitalized and amortized over the patent's remaining economic life.
   b.   Legal fees and other direct costs incurred in registering a patent should be capitalized and amortized on a straight-line basis over a five-year period.
   c.   Research and development contract services purchased from others and used to develop a patented manufacturing process should be capitalized and amortized over the patent's economic life.
   d.   Research and development costs incurred to develop a patented item should be capitalized and amortized on a straight-line basis over seventeen years.

65. Under ASC Topic 350, goodwill should be tested periodically for impairment
   a.   For the entity as a whole.
   b.   At the subsidiary level.
   c.   At the industry segment level.
   d.   At the operating segment level or one level below.

66. On July 12, 2010, Carver, Inc. acquired Jones Company in a business combination. As a result of the combination, the following amounts of goodwill were recorded for each of the three reporting units of the acquired company.

Retailing	$30,000
Service	$20,000
Financing	$40,000

Near the end of 2010 a new major competitor entered the company's market and Carver was concerned that this might cause a significant decline in the value of goodwill. Accordingly, Carver computed the implied value of the goodwill for the three major reporting units at December 31, 2010, as follows:

Retailing	$25,000
Service	$10,000
Financing	$60,000

Determine the amount of impairment of goodwill that should be recorded by Carver at December 31, 2010.
   a. $0
   b. $10,000
   c. $15,000
   d. $25,000

67. Sloan Corporation is performing its annual test of the impairment of goodwill for its Financing reporting unit. It has determined that the fair value of the unit exceeds it carrying value. Which of the following is correct concerning this test of impairment?
   a.   Impairment is not indicated and no additional analysis is necessary.
   b.   Goodwill should be written down as impaired.
   c.   The assets and liabilities should be valued to determine if there has been an impairment of goodwill.
   d.   Goodwill should be retested at the entity level.

68. Wilson Corporation is performing the test of impairment of its Technology reporting unit at 9/30/10. In the first step of the process, Wilson has valued the unit using a multiple of earnings approach at $2,000,000. The carrying value of the net assets of the Technology unit is $2,100,000. What should Wilson do with this information?
   a.   Record an impairment loss of $100,000.
   b.   Record no impairment loss.
   c.   Value goodwill individually.
   d.   Perform step two of the test of impairment.

69. Brunson Corp., a major US winery, begins construction of a new facility in Italy. Following are some of the costs incurred in conjunction with the start-up activities of the new facility:

Production equipment	$815,000
Travel costs of salaried employees	40,000
License fees	14,000
Training of local employees for production and maintenance operations	120,000
Advertising costs	85,200

What portion of the organizational costs will be expensed?
   a. $975,000
   b. $160,000

c. $0
d. $139,200

70. On January 1, 2010, Kew Corp. incurred organization costs of $24,000. What portion of the organization costs will Kew defer to years subsequent to 2010?

     a. $23,400
     b. $19,200
     c. $ 4,800
     d. $0

71. Which of the following statements is(are) correct regarding the treatment of start-up activities related to the opening of a new facility?

     I. Costs of raising capital should be expensed as incurred.
     II. Costs of acquiring or constructing long-lived assets and getting them ready for their intended use should be expensed as incurred.
     III. Cost of research and development should be expensed as incurred.

     a. I only.
     b. III only.
     c. Both I and III.
     d. I, II, and III.

72. Cody Corp. incurred the following costs during 2010:

Design of tools, jigs, molds, and dies involving new technology	$125,000
Modification of the formulation of a process	160,000
Troubleshooting in connection with breakdowns during commercial production	100,000
Adaptation of an existing capability to a particular customer's need as part of a continuing commercial activity	110,000

In its 2010 income statement, Cody should report research and development expense of

     a. $125,000
     b. $160,000
     c. $235,000
     d. $285,000

73. In 2010, Ball Labs incurred the following costs:

Direct costs of doing contract research and development work for the government to be reimbursed by governmental unit	$400,000

Research and development costs not included above were

Depreciation	$300,000
Salaries	700,000
Indirect costs appropriately allocated	200,000
Materials	180,000

What was Ball's total research and development expense in 2010?

     a. $1,080,000
     b. $1,380,000
     c. $1,580,000
     d. $1,780,000

74. West, Inc. made the following expenditures relating to Product Y:

- Legal costs to file a patent on Product Y—$10,000. Production of the finished product would not have been undertaken without the patent.
- Special equipment to be used solely for development of Product Y—$60,000. The equipment has no other use and has an estimated useful life of four years.

- Labor and material costs incurred in producing a prototype model—$200,000.
- Cost of testing the prototype—$80,000.

What is the total amount of costs that will be expensed when incurred?

     a. $280,000
     b. $295,000
     c. $340,000
     d. $350,000

75. Brill Co. made the following expenditures during 2010:

Costs to develop computer software for internal use in Brill's general management information system	$100,000
Costs of market research activities	75,000

What amount of these expenditures should Brill report in its 2010 income statement as research and development expenses?

     a. $175,000
     b. $100,000
     c. $ 75,000
     d. $0

76. On January 1, 2010, Jambon purchased equipment for use in developing a new product. Jambon uses the straight-line depreciation method. The equipment could provide benefits over a ten-year period. However, the new product development is expected to take five years, and the equipment can be used only for this project. Jambon's 2010 expense equals

     a. The total cost of the equipment.
     b. One-fifth of the cost of the equipment.
     c. One-tenth of the cost of the equipment.
     d. Zero.

Items 77 and 78 are based on the following:

During 2010, Pitt Corp. incurred costs to develop and produce a routine, low-risk computer software product, as follows:

Completion of detailed program design	$13,000
Costs incurred for coding and testing to establish technological feasibility	10,000
Other coding costs after establishment of technological feasibility	24,000
Other testing costs after establishment of technological feasibility	20,000
Costs of producing product masters for training materials	15,000
Duplication of computer software and training materials from product masters (1,000 units)	25,000
Packaging product (500 units)	9,000

77. In Pitt's December 31, 2010 balance sheet, what amount should be reported in inventory?

     a. $25,000
     b. $34,000
     c. $40,000
     d. $49,000

78. In Pitt's December 31, 2010 balance sheet, what amount should be capitalized as software cost, subject to amortization?

     a. $54,000
     b. $57,000
     c. $59,000
     d. $69,000

79. On December 31, 2009, Bit Co. had capitalized costs for a new computer software product with an economic life of five years. Sales for 2010 were 30% of expected total sales of the software. At December 31, 2010, the software had a net realizable value equal to 90% of the capitalized cost. What percentage of the original capitalized cost should be reported as the net amount on Bit's December 31, 2010 balance sheet?

    a. 70%
    b. 72%
    c. 80%
    d. 90%

80. Which of the following statements is incorrect regarding internal-use software?

    a. The application and development costs of internal-use software should be amortized on a straight-line basis unless another systematic and rational basis is more representative of its costs.
    b. Internal-use software is considered to be software that is marketed as a separate product or as part of a product or process.
    c. The costs of testing and installing computer hardware should be capitalized as incurred.
    d. The costs of training and application maintenance should be expensed as incurred.

81. Which of the following statements is(are) correct regarding the proper accounting treatment for internal-use software costs?

  I. Preliminary costs should be capitalized as incurred.
  II. Application and development costs should be capitalized as incurred.

    a. I only.
    b. II only.
    c. Both I and II.
    d. Neither I nor II.

82. What is the proper accounting treatment for the following stages of internal-use software costs?

	Preliminary stage costs	Post-implementation costs
a.	Capitalized as incurred	Capitalized as incurred
b.	Expensed as incurred	Capitalized as incurred
c.	Capitalized as incurred	Expensed as incurred
d.	Expensed as incurred	Expensed as incurred

83. Financial reporting by a development stage enterprise differs from financial reporting for an established operating enterprise in regard to footnote disclosures

    a. Only.
    b. And expense recognition principles only.
    c. And revenue recognition principles only.
    d. And revenue and expense recognition principles.

84. A development stage enterprise

    a. Issues an income statement that shows only cumulative amounts from the enterprise's inception.
    b. Issues an income statement that is the same as an established operating enterprise, but does **not** show cumulative amounts from the enterprise's inception as additional information.
    c. Issues an income statement that is the same as an established operating enterprise, and shows cumulative amounts from the enterprise's inception as additional information.
    d. Does **not** issue an income statement.

SIMULATION PROBLEMS

Simulation Problem 1   (50 to 60 minutes)

Situation					
	Concepts	Asset Valuation	Depreciation Calculations	Communication	Research

- Link Co. purchased an office building and the land on which it is located by paying $800,000 cash and assuming an existing mortgage of $200,000. The property is assessed at $960,000 for realty tax purposes, of which 60% is allocated to the building.
- Link leased construction equipment under a seven-year capital lease requiring annual year-end payments of $100,000. Link's incremental borrowing rate is 9%, while the lessor's implicit rate, which is not known to Link, is 8%. Present value factors for an ordinary annuity for seven periods are 5.21 at 8% and 5.04 at 9%. Fair value of the equipment is $515,000.
- Link paid $50,000 and gave a plot of undeveloped land with a carrying amount of $320,000 and a fair value of $450,000 to Club Co. in exchange for a plot of undeveloped land with a fair value of $500,000. The land was carried on Club's books at $350,000. This transaction is considered to lack commercial substance; the configuration of cash flows from the land acquired is not expected to be significantly different from the configuration of cash flows of the land exchanged.

	Concepts				
Situation		Asset Valuation	Depreciation Calculations	Communication	Research

For **items 1 through 6,** determine for each item whether the expenditure should be capitalized or expensed as a period cost.

	Capitalize	*Expense*
1. Freight charges paid for goods held for resale.	○	○
2. In-transit insurance on goods held for resale purchased FOB shipping point.	○	○
3. Interest on note payable for goods held for resale.	○	○
4. Installation of equipment.	○	○
5. Testing of newly purchased equipment.	○	○
6. Cost of current year service contract on equipment.	○	○

		Asset Valuation			
Situation	Concepts		Depreciation Calculations	Communication	Research

Calculate the following amounts to be recorded by Link.

Amount

1. Building.
2. Leased equipment.
3. Land received from Club on Link's books.
4. Land received from Link on Club's books.

			Depreciation Calculations		
Situation	Concepts	Asset Valuation		Communication	Research

On January 2, 2009, Link purchased a manufacturing machine for $864,000. The machine has an eight-year estimated life and a $144,000 estimated salvage value. Half expects to manufacture 1,800,000 units over the life of the machine. During 2010, Half manufactured 300,000 units.

Calculate depreciation expense on the manufacturing machine for 2010 for each method listed.

Amount

1. Straight-line.
2. Double-declining balance.
3. Sum-of-years' digits.
4. Units of production.

Situation	Concepts	Asset Valuation	Depreciation Calculations	Communication		Research

Link Co. also rents winter sports equipment to the public. Snowmobiles are depreciated by the double-declining balance method. Before the season began, the estimated lives of several snowmobiles were extended because engines were replaced. Link was given thirty days to pay for the engines. Link gave the old engines to a local mechanic who agreed to provide repairs and maintenance service in the next year equal to the fair value of the engines. Rental skis, poles, and boots are capitalized and depreciated according to the inventory (appraisal) method.

Write a memo to the CEO of Link Co. that explains the following issues:

1. How should Link account for the purchase of the new engines and the transfer of the old engines to the local mechanic if the old engines' costs are

    a. Known?
    b. Unknown?

2. What are two assumptions underlying use of an accelerated depreciation method?
3. How should Link calculate the snowmobiles' depreciation?
4. How should Link calculate and report the costs of the skis, poles, and boots in its balance sheets and income statements?

REMINDER: Your response will be graded for both technical content and writing skills. Technical content will be evaluated for information that is helpful to the intended reader and clearly relevant to the issue. Writing skills will be evaluated for development, organization, and the appropriate expression of ideas in professional correspondence. Use a standard business memo or letter format with a clear beginning, middle, and end. Do not convey information in the form of a table, bullet point list, or other abbreviated presentation.

To: CEO, Link Co.
From: CPA Candidate
Re: Depreciation and sports equipment

Situation	Concepts	Asset Valuation	Depreciation Calculations	Communication	Research

Research the following issues. Select and insert the appropriate sections from the professional standards.

1. What is the definition of an impaired asset?

2. What assumptions are made in determining the price or fair value of an impaired asset?

3. In reporting discontinued operations, how does the accountant determine if the operation qualifies as a component?

4. When there is a gain or loss on an asset that is classified as held-for-sale, where is the gain or loss reported in the financial statements?

Simulation Problem 2   (50 to 55 minutes)

Situation					
	Capitalized Costs	Disposal of Assets	Journal Entry	Balance Sheet Disclosures	Communication	Research

Selected accounts included in the property, plant, and equipment section of Carlton Corporation's balance sheet at December 31, 2009, had the following balances:

Land	$400,000
Land improvements	130,000
Buildings	2,000,000
Machinery and equipment	800,000

During 2010, the following transactions occurred:

1. A tract of land was acquired for $200,000 as a potential future building site from Alison Corp.
2. A plant facility consisting of land and building was acquired from Kaufman Company in exchange for 20,000 shares of Carlton's common stock. On the acquisition date, Carlton's stock had a closing market price of $42 per share on a national stock exchange. The plant facility was carried on Kaufman's books at $178,000 for land and $520,000 for the

building at the exchange date. Current appraised values for the land and the building, respectively, are $200,000 and $800,000. The building has an expected life of forty years with a $20,000 salvage value.

3. Items of machinery and equipment were purchased from Apex Equipment at a total cost of $400,000. Additional costs were incurred as follows: freight and unloading, $13,000; installation, $26,000. The equipment has a useful life of ten years with no salvage value.

4. Expenditures totaling $120,000 were made for new parking lots, street, and sidewalks at the corporation's various plant locations. These expenditures had an estimated useful life of fifteen years.

5. Research and development costs were $110,000 for the year.

6. A machine costing $16,000 on January 1, 2003, was scrapped on June 30, 2010. Straight-line depreciation had been recorded on the basis of a 10-year life with no salvage value.

7. A machine was sold for $48,000 on July 1, 2010. Original cost of the machine was $74,000 on January 1, 2007, and it was depreciated on the straight-line basis over an estimated useful life of eight years and a salvage value of $2,000.

Situation	Capitalized Costs	Disposal of Assets	Journal Entry	Balance Sheet Disclosures	Communication	Research

Indicate the capitalized cost of each asset acquired during 2010, and the depreciation expense recorded for each of the acquired items in 2010.

	Capitalized cost	Depreciation/amortization expense for 2010
Land acquired from Alison Corp.		
Land acquired fro Kaufman		
Building acquired from Kaufman		
Machinery and equipment acquired from Apex Equipment		
Land improvements		
Research and development		

Situation	Capitalized Costs	Disposal of Assets	Journal Entry	Balance Sheet Disclosures	Communication	Research

Calculate the gain or loss on the disposal of each asset. Place your answer in the appropriate column.

Item	Amount of gain	Amount of loss
Scrapped machine on 6/30/10		
Sale of machine on 7/1/10		

Situation	Capitalized Costs	Disposal of Assets	Journal Entry	Balance Sheet Disclosures	Communication	Research

Prepare the journal entries for the sale of the machine on July 1, 2010. Select your account titles from the following list. Assume depreciation is recorded at the date of disposal for any equipment sold.

Cash
Accumulated depreciation
Equipment
Gain on sale of equipment
Loss on sale of equipment
Depreciation expense

	Debit	Credit

Situation	Capitalized Costs	Disposal of Assets	Journal Entry	Balance Sheet Disclosures	Communication	Research

Indicate the balances in each of the following accounts as of December 31, 2010. Assume that all depreciation and amortization entries are recorded separately in contra accounts.

	Balance as of 12/31/10
Land	
Land improvements	
Buildings	
Equipment and machinery	

Situation	Capitalized Costs	Disposal of Assets	Journal Entry	Balance Sheet Disclosures	Communication	Research

Carlton's CEO has contacted you concerning accounting for the impairment of assets. He has presented you with the following list of questions. Prepare a memo to the CEO responding to his questions.

1. Define what is meant by impairment of an operational asset (e.g., equipment).

2. How is the definition of impairment applied in practice? Include in the answer signs or indicators of impairment, loss, determination, and measurement of losses.

3. Describe the accounting and reporting for an impairment loss in current and future periods.

4. How are losses on operational assets that management expects to dispose of measured, accounted for, and reported on the financial statements?

REMINDER: Your response will be graded for both technical content and writing skills. Technical content will be evaluated for information that is helpful to the intended reader and clearly relevant to the issue. Writing skills will be evaluated for development, organization, and the appropriate expression of ideas in professional correspondence. Use a standard business memo or letter format with a clear beginning, middle, and end. Do not convey information in the form of a table, bullet point list, or other abbreviated presentation.

Situation	Capitalized Costs	Disposal of Assets	Journal Entry	Balance Sheet Disclosures	Communication	Research

Research the following accounting issues in the professional literature. You should select and insert your citation in the space provided.

1. What is meant by impairment of an operational asset?

2. When is a long-lived asset tested for recoverability?

3. Describe the accounting and reporting for an impairment loss on the income statement in the current period.

4. Describe the information to be disclosed in the notes to the financial statements regarding asset impairment.

5. Describe the accounting for impairment losses on future financial statements.

6. How are losses of operational assets to be sold measured?

Simulation Problem 3   (45 to 55 minutes)

Situation	Concepts	Intangible Assets	Expenses Resulting from Intangibles	Goodwill Impairment	Communication	Research

During 2010, Broca Co. had the following transactions:

• On January 2, Broca purchased the net assets of Amp Co. for $360,000. The fair value of Amp's identifiable net assets was $172,000. Broca believes that, due to the popularity of Amp's consumer products, the life of the resulting goodwill is unlimited.

- On February 1, Broca purchased a franchise to operate a ferry service from the state government for $60,000 and an annual fee of 1% of ferry revenues. The franchise expires after five years. Broca received $20,000 of ferry revenues in 2009.
- On April 5, Broca was granted a patent that had been applied for by Amp. During 2010, Broca incurred legal costs of $51,000 to register the patent and an additional $85,000 to successfully prosecute a patent infringement suit against a competitor. Broca estimates the patent's economic life to be ten years.

Broca has determined that it is appropriate to amortize these intangibles on the straight-line basis over the maximum period permitted by generally accepted accounting principles, taking a full year's amortization in the year of acquisition.

Situation	Concepts	Intangible Assets	Expenses Resulting from Intangibles	Goodwill Impairment	Communication	Research

Indicate whether each of the following statements is True or False.

		True	*False*
1.	An intangible asset that is determined to have an indefinite life should be amortized over 40 years.	O	O
2.	If the carrying value of the intangible asset exceeds its fair value, an impairment loss must be recognized.	O	O
3.	The impairment test for goodwill must be performed at the end of each fiscal year for each reporting unit.	O	O
4.	When a company borrows funds to finance a construction project and temporarily invests this cash, the interest expense should be offset against the interest expense to be capitalized.	O	O
5.	A company may capitalize interest on inventories it regularly produces for resale to customers.	O	O
6.	Gains are never recognized when similar assets are exchanged.	O	O
7.	In nonmonetary exchanges, losses are only recognized when cash is received in the transactions.	O	O
8.	If the fair value of the asset is unknown in a nonmonetary exchange and no gain can be computed, the asset is recorded at the fair market value of the asset given up.	O	O
9.	A capital expenditure is charged against income over the useful life of the asset.	O	O
10.	Expenditures to improve the efficiency or extend the useful life of an asset should be capitalized.	O	O

Situation	Concepts	Intangible Assets	Expenses Resulting from Intangibles	Goodwill Impairment	Communication	Research

Complete the following schedule for Broca's intangible assets and the related income statement expenses.

Broca Co. SCHEDULE FOR INTANGIBLE ASSETS AND AMORTIZATION EXPENSE December 31, 2010			
Item	*Valuation **before** adjusting entries*	*Amortization expense for the year*	*Valuation on 12/31/10*
Goodwill			
Franchise (net)			
Patent (net)			

Situation	Concepts	Intangible Assets	Expenses Resulting from Intangibles	Goodwill Impairment	Communication	Research

Complete the following schedule for Broca's expenses.

Broca Co. **EXPENSES RESULTING FROM INTANGIBLES** *For the Year Ended December 31, 2010*	
Amortization:	
Franchise	
Patent	
Franchise fee	
Total expenses	

Situation	Concepts	Intangible Assets	Expenses Resulting from Intangibles	Goodwill Impairment	Communication	Research

Broca Corporation is performing its annual test of the impairment of the goodwill related to its Technology reporting unit. The carrying value of goodwill allocated to the unit is $500,000. Using a multiple of revenue, Broca has determined the fair value of the Technology reporting unit to be $1,700,000 at 12/31/10, and the fair value and carrying value of the assets and liabilities were determined as follows:

	(In 000s)	
	Carrying value	*Fair value*
Cash	$ 200	$ 200
Accounts receivable	250	250
Inventory	350	400
Net Equipment	700	700
Patents	400	450
Goodwill	500	?
Accounts payable	(200)	(200)
Long-term debt	(300)	(300)
	1,900	

1. Calculate the following amounts related to the impairment of goodwill.

Implied Goodwill

Impairment of Goodwill

2. Prepare the related journal entry if there is an impairment of goodwill for the Technology reporting unit.

Situation	Concepts	Intangible Assets	Expenses Resulting from Intangibles	Goodwill Impairment	Communication	Research

Write a brief memo to the CEO of Broca Corporation, explaining the following issues with regard to intangible assets.

1. Describe the characteristics of intangible assets. Discuss the accounting for the purchase or internal development of intangible assets with an indeterminable life, such as goodwill.
2. Over what period should intangible assets be amortized? How should this period be determined?
3. Describe the financial statement disclosure requirements relating to Broca's intangible assets and expenses.

REMINDER: Your response will be graded for both technical content and writing skills. Technical content will be evaluated for information that is helpful to the intended reader and clearly relevant to the issue. Writing skills will be evaluated for development, organization, and the appropriate expression of ideas in professional correspondence. Use a standard business memo or letter format with a clear beginning, middle, and end. Do not convey information in the form of a table, bullet point list, or other abbreviated presentation.

To: CEO, Broca Corporation
From: CPA Candidate
Re: Intangible assets

Situation	Concepts	Intangible Assets	Expenses Resulting from Intangibles	Goodwill Impairment	Communication	Research

Research the following issues. Cut and paste your answer from the professional standards.

1. What assets qualify for capitalization of interest?

2. An asset has been acquired in a nonmonetary exchange that lacks commercial substance. At what amount should this asset be capitalized?

3. At what amount should donated assets be recorded?

MULTIPLE-CHOICE ANSWERS

1. a	__ __	19. a	__ __	37. b	__ __	55. b	__ __	73. b	__ __
2. a	__ __	20. d	__ __	38. d	__ __	56. c	__ __	74. c	__ __
3. b	__ __	21. c	__ __	39. b	__ __	57. b	__ __	75. d	__ __
4. a	__ __	22. d	__ __	40. d	__ __	58. b	__ __	76. a	__ __
5. d	__ __	23. c	__ __	41. b	__ __	59. c	__ __	77. b	__ __
6. a	__ __	24. b	__ __	42. c	__ __	60. b	__ __	78. c	__ __
7. b	__ __	25. a	__ __	43. c	__ __	61. d	__ __	79. a	__ __
8. b	__ __	26. b	__ __	44. b	__ __	62. c	__ __	80. b	__ __
9. b	__ __	27. a	__ __	45. b	__ __	63. d	__ __	81. b	__ __
10. c	__ __	28. d	__ __	46. a	__ __	64. a	__ __	82. d	__ __
11. b	__ __	29. b	__ __	47. b	__ __	65. c	__ __	83. a	__ __
12. c	__ __	30. c	__ __	48. d	__ __	66. c	__ __	84. c	__ __
13. a	__ __	31. d	__ __	49. c	__ __	67. a	__ __		
14. c	__ __	32. a	__ __	50. a	__ __	68. d	__ __		
15. d	__ __	33. b	__ __	51. b	__ __	69. b	__ __		
16. b	__ __	34. c	__ __	52. b	__ __	70. d	__ __		
17. d	__ __	35. d	__ __	53. c	__ __	71. b	__ __	1st: __/84 = __%
18. b	__ __	36. c	__ __	54. c	__ __	72. d	__ __	2nd: __/84 = __%

MULTIPLE-CHOICE ANSWER EXPLANATIONS

A. Acquisition Cost

1. **(a)** The cost of machinery includes all expenditures incurred in acquiring the asset and preparing it for use. Cost includes the purchase price, freight and handling charges, insurance on the machine while in transit, cost of special foundations, and costs of assembling, installation, and testing. All of the costs given in this problem are properly recorded as the cost of the machine. Therefore the cost to be recorded is $155,000 ($125,000 + $20,000 + $10,000).

2. **(a)** Any cost involved in preparing land for its ultimate use (such as a factory site) is considered part of the cost of the land. Before the land can be used as a building site, it must be purchased (involving costs such as purchase price, legal fees, and title insurance) and the old building must be razed (cost of demolition less proceeds from sale of scrap). The total balance in the land account should be $464,000.

Purchase price	$400,000
Legal fees	10,000
Title insurance	12,000
Net cost of demolition ($50,000 – $8,000)	42,000
	$464,000

B. Capitalization of Interest

3. **(b)** The amount of interest cost which should be capitalized during building construction is the **lower** of **avoidable interest** or **actual interest**. Avoidable interest equals the interest computed on the weighted-average amount of accumulated expenditures on the building ($40,000). Since actual interest is $70,000 ($50,000 + $20,000), the amount capitalized should be $40,000.

4. **(a)** The requirement is to calculate the amount of capitalized interest at 12/31/10. The requirements for capitalization of interest are met if: (1) expenditures for the asset have been made, (2) activities that are necessary to get the asset ready for its intended use are in progress, and (3) interest cost is being incurred. The amount to be capitalized is the lower of avoidable interest or actual interest. Avoidable interest is the average accumulated expenditures multiplied by the appropriate interest rate or rates. Since

$2,000,000 was spent on the building evenly throughout the year, the average accumulated expenditures were $1,000,000 ($2,000,000 ÷ 2) and the avoidable interest was $120,000 ($1,000,000 × 12%). Since actual interest ($102,000) is less than avoidable interest, the actual interest cost is capitalized.

5. **(d)** Certain assets for which interest costs incurred in their production should be capitalized rather than expensed. Assets which "qualify" for interest capitalization are those constructed or otherwise produced for an enterprise's own use and those intended for sale or lease that are constructed or otherwise produced as **discrete projects**. The capitalization period shall end when the asset is substantially complete and ready for its intended use. Based upon these criteria, the interest costs associated with the machinery for Bay's own use should be capitalized during the construction period and expensed after completion. Additionally, all costs associated with the machinery held for sale should be expensed because the machinery does not meet the "discrete project" criterion.

C. Nonmonetary Exchanges

6. **(a)** When the investment was acquired, it was recorded at cost—the fair market value of the asset surrendered to acquire it. The July 1 entry was

Inv. in Ace stock	3,000	
Truck	2,500	
Gain on disposal	500	($3,000 – $2,500)

The investment would be reported in the 12/31/10 balance sheet at $3,000. The book value of Ace's stock does not affect the amount recorded on Balt's books.

7. **(b)** A nonmonetary exchange is recognized at fair value unless the fair value is not determinable, the exchange transaction is to facilitate sales to customers, or the exchange transactions lacks commercial substance. Answer (a) is incorrect, because the exchange must **lack** commercial substance. Answers (c) and (d) are incorrect because there is no longer the distinction of similar or dissimilar assets in nonmonetary exchanges.

8. **(b)** A nonmonetary exchange is recognized at fair value unless the fair value is not determinable, the exchange transaction is to facilitate sales to customers, or the exchange transactions lacks commercial substance. Answers (a) and (c) are incorrect; these transactions have commercial substance because there is a significant change in the entity's cash flows as a result of the exchange.

9. (b) An entity's cash flows are expected to change significantly if the configuration of the cash flows of the asset received differs significantly from the configuration of the cash flows of the asset transferred. The configuration includes the risk, timing, and amount of the cash flows.

10. (c) In determining cash flows from a transaction, the effect of taxes is not considered unless it serves a legitimate business purpose other than tax avoidance. In assessing the commercial substance of an exchange, tax cash flows arising solely to avoid taxes are not considered. Other cash flows from the nonmonetary exchange are considered.

11. (b) The cash price of the new machine represents its fair market value (FMV). The FMV of the old machine can be determined by subtracting the cash portion of the purchase price ($6,000) from the total cost of the new machine: $20,500 – $6,000 = $14,500. Since the book value of the machine ($16,800) exceeds its FMV on the date of the trade-in ($14,500), the difference of $2,300 must be recognized as a loss.

12. (c) Because the cash flows of the exchanged assets will not be significantly different, the transaction lacks commercial substances. Therefore, book value is used to record the transition. When the assets are exchanged, boot is received, and a gain results, the exchange is treated as part sale and part exchange. The earnings process is assumed to be complete for the portion relating to the boot received. The gain recognized is computed as follows:

$$\frac{\text{Boot received}}{\text{Boot received} + \text{FMV of assets received}} \times \text{Total gain} = \text{Gain recognized}$$

$$\text{Total Gain} = \underbrace{(17,500 + 2,500)}_{\substack{\text{Assets received by} \\ \text{Amble}}} - \underbrace{12,000}_{\substack{\text{Book value of} \\ \text{asset given up} \\ \text{by Beam}}} = 8,000$$

The gain recognized would be calculated as follows:

$$\frac{2,500}{17,500 + 2,500} \times 8,000 = \$1,000 \text{ gain recognized}$$

The asset acquired is recorded at the **book** value of the asset surrendered plus the gain recognized less boot received ($12,000 + $1,000 – $2,500 = $10,500). The journal entry is

Truck (new)	10,500	
Cash	2,500	
Truck (old)		12,000
Gain on sale		1,000

13. (a) If a loss is indicated by the terms of the transaction, the entire loss on the exchange should be recognized. In this case, a loss results because Transit received an asset whose fair value equaled the book value of the asset given up and paid cash. Therefore, Transit gave up more than they received, the difference being the loss.

14. (c) Transactions lacking commercial substance are recorded at book value. When the exchange of nonmonetary assets includes an amount of monetary consideration, the receiver of monetary consideration has realized a partial gain on the exchange. To determine the partial gain to be recognized, first compute the total gain which is the difference

between the fair market value of the nonmonetary asset given up and its book value. Then multiply the ratio of the **monetary** consideration received to the **total** consideration received (i.e., monetary consideration plus the estimated fair market value of the asset received) times the total gain. The result is the realized gain to be recognized. The entity paying the monetary consideration should **not** recognize any gain until the earnings process is culminated. Note, however, that **all losses** on sales or exchanges are recognized immediately.

15. (d) Nonmonetary exchanges of assets that are deemed to have commercial substance are accounted for on the basis of fair values, and both gains and losses recognized. The gain (or loss) for Vik is calculated as the difference between the fair value and cost of the car. Note that the retail/list price of an asset is not always representative of the fair value of the asset. An asset can often be purchased for less than the retail/list price.

16. (b) This transaction qualifies as an exception to fair value measurement and should be measured at book value. However, when these assets are exchanged, and boot is received and a gain results, the exchange is treated as part sale and part exchange. The earnings process is assumed to be complete for the portion relating to the boot received. The gain recognized is computed as follows:

$$\frac{\text{Boot received}}{\text{Boot received} + \text{FMV of assets received}} \times \text{Total gain} = \text{Gain recognized}$$

$$\text{Total gain} = \underbrace{(130,000 + 20,000)}_{\substack{\text{Assets received} \\ \text{by Zaro}}} - \underbrace{126,000}_{\substack{\text{Book value of asset} \\ \text{given up by Zaro}}} = 24,000$$

In this case, it would be calculated as follows:

$$\frac{20,000}{(20,000 + 130,000)} \times 24,000 = \$3,200$$

17. (d) A transfer of a nonmonetary asset in a nonreciprocal transfer should be recorded at the fair value of the asset transferred, with a gain or loss recognized on the disposition, whether the transfer is made to a stockholder or to another entity.

18. (b) A gain (loss) must be recognized when a nonmonetary asset is involuntarily converted into monetary assets even if the company reinvests the monetary assets in replacement nonmonetary assets. The gain or loss is the difference between the insurance proceeds received ($3,500) and the carrying value of the asset destroyed. The unadjusted carrying value ($2,500) must be adjusted for the capital expenditure ($700) which has not yet been recorded. When a major component of an asset like an engine is replaced, the preferred treatment is to take the old component off the books (with a loss recognized) and record the new component. When the book value of the component is unknown (as in this case), the cost of the new component ($700) is simply debited to the accumulated depreciation account. This increases the van's carrying value to $3,200 ($2,500 + $700), which means the gain is $300 ($3,500 – $3,200). Note that the $500 invoice should be recorded as repairs expense, and therefore does not affect the van's carrying value.

19. (a) Involuntary conversions of nonmonetary assets to monetary assets are monetary transactions for which gain or loss shall be recognized even though an enterprise reinvests or is obligated to reinvest the monetary assets in replacement nonmonetary assets. Accordingly, Lano would record the condemnation and replacement of the forest land as two separate transactions. Lano should recognize a gain on the condemnation and subsequently record the replacement land at the total purchase price. The net effect of these events is to increase the amount of forest land on Lano's balance sheet by the excess of the replacement land's cost over the condemned land's carrying amount, as shown below.

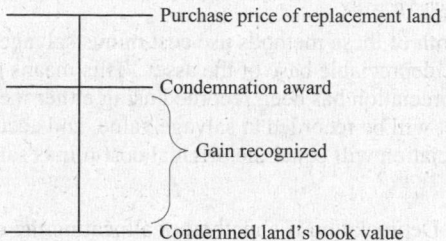

D.   Purchase of Groups of Fixed Assets

20.   (d)   The requirement is to determine the amount at which land acquired in a group purchase of fixed assets should be recorded. The total cost ($540,000) of the land and building should be allocated based on their relative fair value (FV). Current appraised value is a better indicator of FV than the seller's original cost. Therefore, the land should be recorded at $216,000.

$$\frac{\text{FV land}}{\text{Total FV of assets purchased}} \times \text{Purchase price of group assets}$$

$$\frac{200,000}{500,000} \times 540,000 = \$216,000$$

There is no problem in recording the land at more than its appraised value since value is only an estimate of FV.

E. Capital Versus Revenue Expenditures

21.   (c)   The requirement is to calculate the amount to be charged to repair and maintenance expense in 2010. Generally, a cost should be capitalized if it improves the asset and expensed if it merely maintains the asset at its current level. Continuing and frequent repairs ($40,000) should be expensed. Similarly, the cost of repainting the plant building ($10,000) and the cost of partially replacing the roof tiles ($14,000) should be expensed. These are ordinary, regularly occurring expenditures which maintain, rather than improve, the plant building. The work on the electrical wiring system ($32,000) is capitalized instead of expensed since it is a major improvement. Therefore, the total amount expensed is $64,000 ($40,000 + $10,000 + $14,000).

22.   (d)   The cost of the attachment ($84,000) should be capitalized because it is an **addition**. The cost of installing the attachment ($36,000) is also capitalized because this expenditure was required to get the attachment ready for its intended use. The overhaul costs ($26,000 + $14,000 = $40,000) are also capitalized. Even though the overhaul did not increase useful life, it is a capital expenditure because it increased productivity. The total amount capitalized is $160,000 ($84,000 + $36,000 + $40,000).

23.   (c)   When an entity suffers a casualty loss to an asset, the accounting loss is recorded at the net carrying value of the damaged asset, if known. In this case, the cost and

related accumulated depreciation are identifiable. The entity should therefore recognize a loss in the current period equal to the carrying amount of the damaged portion of the building. The refurbishing of the building, which is an economic event separate from the fire damage, should be treated similarly to the purchase of other assets or betterments. The cost of refurbishing the building should therefore be capitalized and depreciated over the shorter of the refurbishment's useful lives or the useful life of the building.

Loss	xxx	(Plug)	
Acc. depr.	xxx		
Building			xxx
Building	xxx		
Cash			xxx

Answer (a) is incorrect because in order to reduce the accumulated depreciation account, the useful life of the asset must be extended. In this case, there is no mention of this fact. Answer (d) is incorrect because it fails to recognize the casualty loss and properly remove the cost and accumulated depreciation on the damaged portion of the building from the accounting records.

NOTE: If the components of the damaged portion are not identifiable, the following entry would be made:

Loss	*xxx*	
Cash		*xxx*

24.   (b)   Generally, a cost should be capitalized if it improves the efficiency of the asset or extends its useful life and expensed if it merely maintains the asset at its current level. Since an overall reduction in production costs is expected, efficiency must have been improved by the steps taken by Derby. In this problem, it appears that both the building modification and the production line rearrangement contributed to the improved efficiency in the production process. Therefore, both costs should be capitalized.

F. Depreciation

25.   (a)   Machinery is recorded at its historical cost, which is measured by the cash or **cash equivalent price** of obtaining the machine and preparing it for use. The journal entry to record this acquisition would be

Machinery	110,000		(cash equiv.)
Discount on N.P.	20,000		($130,000 – $110,000)
Notes payable		120,000	(24 × $5,000)
Cash		10,000	

The $20,000 discount represents future interest expense (the cost associated with paying for the asset over two years instead of immediately) rather than part of the cost of the machine. Straight-line depreciation for 2010 is computed as follows:

(Cost – Salvage value)	×	1/useful life	=	Depr. expense
($110,000 – $5,000)	×	1/10	=	$10,500

26.   (b)   The formula for 200% double-declining balance (DDB) depreciation is

(Beginning-of-year book value) × DDB rate = Depreciation expense

The DDB rate is two times the straight-line rate (in this case, $1/5 \times 2 = 2/5$ or 40%). Therefore, depreciation for the first two years is

2008:	$50,000 × 40%	=	$20,000
2009:	($50,000 – $20,000) × 40%	=	12,000
			$32,000

In 2010, Turtle switches to the straight-line method. The book value ($50,000 – $32,000 = $18,000) would be depreciated over the remaining three years (five years less two gone by). Therefore, 2010 depreciation is $6,000 ($18,000 × 1/3) and 12/31/10 accumulated depreciation is $38,000 ($32,000 + $6,000).

27. **(a)** The requirement is to calculate the amount of depreciation expense to be recorded in 2011. After three years (2008-2010), accumulated depreciation is $72,000. Therefore, the method that was used was the sum-of-the-years' digits (SYD) method. Using this method, after three years the balance in accumulated depreciation would be 12/15 of the depreciable base (5/15 + 4/15 + 3/15). The depreciable base is the cost ($110,000) less the residual value ($20,000), or $90,000. Thus, using the SYD method, accumulated depreciation at 12/31/10 would be $72,000 ($90,000 × 12/15), which matches the amount given in the problem. 2011 depreciation expense, using the SYD method is $12,000 ($90,000 × 2/15).

28. **(d)** From 1/2/07 to 12/31/09, depreciation was recorded using an eight-year life. Yearly depreciation was $33,000 ($264,000 ÷ 8), and accumulated depreciation at 12/31/09 was $99,000 (3 × $33,000). In 2010, the estimated useful life was changed to six years total with a salvage value of $24,000. Therefore, the 12/31/09 book value ($264,000 – $99,000 = $165,000) is depreciated down to the $24,000 salvage value over a remaining useful life of three years (6 years total – 3 years already recorded). The 2010 depreciation expense is $47,000 [($165,000 – $24,000) ÷ 3], increasing accumulated depreciation to $146,000 ($99,000 + $47,000).

29. **(b)** The solutions approach is to set up a T-account for **accumulated depreciation** and solve for the unknown.

	Accumulated Depreciation	
	370,000	12/31/09
2010 retirements ?	55,000	2010 depr. expense
	400,000	12/31/10

The 12/31/09 and 12/31/10 balances were given in the schedule. The 2010 depreciation expense would be recorded by debiting the expense account and crediting accumulated depreciation. The accumulated depreciation would be debited for the property, plant, and equipment retirements. To balance the T-account, the debit must be $25,000. Alternatively, an equation can be used as shown below.

$$\$370,000 + \$55,000 - X = \$400,000$$
$$425,000 - X = 400,000$$
$$X = 25,000$$

$$370,000 = 12/31/09 \text{ balance}$$
$$55,000 = 2010 \text{ depreciation expense}$$
$$400,000 = 12/31/10 \text{ balance}$$
$$X = \text{retirements}$$

30. **(c)** After reviewing the different methods, you might realize that the method with the highest carrying amount would result in a loss or

Gain/loss = Proceeds – Carrying amount
= 50% C – [C – 50% (C – S)]
= 50% C – [C – 50% (C – 20%C)]
= .5C – [1.00C – .5(1.00C – .2C)]
= .5C – [.6C]

Carrying amount > Proceeds

∴ Loss

Straight-line depreciation would result in the highest carrying value.

31. **(d)** The formula to compute straight-line depreciation is

$$\frac{\text{Original cost less salvage value}}{\text{Estimated useful life}}$$

The formula to determine depreciation using the productive output method is

$$\frac{\text{Current activity (output)}}{\text{Total expected activity}} \times \text{Original cost less salvage value}$$

Note that both of these methods use cost minus salvage value as the depreciable base of the asset. This means that after all depreciation has been recorded using either method, the net asset will be recorded at salvage value, and accumulated depreciation will equal the original cost minus salvage value.

32. **(a)** Depreciation is a method of allocating the cost of an asset in a systematic and rational manner. Since the units-of-production method of depreciation is most appropriate when depreciation is a function of activity, answer (a) is correct. Answer (b) is incorrect because this situation warrants the use of a depreciation method based on the passage of time. Answers (c) and (d) are incorrect because both support the use of an accelerated method of depreciation.

33. **(b)** Under the sum-of-the-years' digits (SYD) method, depreciation expense is computed by applying declining fractions to the depreciable cost of the asset. The denominator is the sum of the years in the life of the asset (1 + 2 + 3 + 4 + 5 = 15 in this case). Annual depreciation would be computed as follows:

2007	Original cost less salvage value	×	5/15
2008	Original cost less salvage value	×	4/15
2009	Original cost less salvage value	×	3/15
2010	Original cost less salvage value	×	2/15
Total	Original cost less salvage value	×	14/15

Accumulated depreciation at December 31, 2010, would be (original cost less salvage value) multiplied by 14/15.

34. **(c)** Sum-of-the-years' digits (SYD) depreciation = (Cost less Salvage value) × Applicable fraction.

Where applicable fraction = $\dfrac{\text{Number of years of estimated life remaining as of the beginning of the year}}{\text{SYD}}$

and

$$SYD = \frac{N(n+1)}{2} \text{ Where } n = \text{estimated useful life}$$

Calculated as

$$\text{Year 1 (2008)} = \$18,000^* \times \frac{4}{10} = \$7,200$$

$$\text{Year 2 (2009)} = \$18,000^* \times \frac{3}{10} = \$5,400$$

$$\text{Year 3 (2010)} = \$18,000^* \times \frac{2}{10} = \$3,600$$

* *($20,000 – $2,000)*

On December 31, 2010, the carrying amount of Spiro's asset equals $3,800 (the asset's cost of $20,000 minus accumulated depreciation of $16,200**).

** *($7,200 + $5,400 + $3,600)*

35. (d) Line I represents depreciation expense that stays constant over time (i.e., straight-line). Both sum-of-the-years' digits and double-declining balance are accelerated depreciation methods, and hence the depreciation expense for these two methods does not stay constant over time. Line II represents depreciation expense that decreases at a constant rate (i.e., a linear function) and thus would be the pattern of depreciation for sum-of-the-years' digits. Line III represents depreciation expense that decreases at a decreasing rate (i.e., a nonlinear function) and thus would be the pattern of depreciation for the double-declining balance method.

36. (c) Composite (group) depreciation averages the service life of a number of property units and depreciates the group as if it were a single unit. The term "group" is used when the assets are similar; the term "composite" is used when they are dissimilar. The mechanical application of both of these methods is identical. The depreciation rate is the following ratio:

$$\frac{\text{Sum of annual SL depreciation of individual assets}}{\text{Total asset cost}}$$

Thus, both group and composite depreciation utilize the straight-line depreciation method.

37. (b) The solutions approach is to prepare the journal entry that would be made when an asset is retired under the composite depreciation method.

Cash	(cash proceeds)	
Accumulated depreciation		(plug)
Truck		(original cost)

The net decrease in the carrying amount of the assets is the credit to the asset account less the plug to accumulated depreciation. This amount would be equal to the **cash proceeds received**.

G. Disposals and Impairment of Value

38. (d) When management plans to dispose of long-lived assets and limited-lived intangibles, the assets shall be reported at the lower of carrying amount or fair value less cost to sell.

39. (b) Losses associated with long-lived assets which are to be disposed of are to be reported as a component of income from continuing operations before income taxes for entities preparing income statements. Losses on long-lived assets to be disposed of are neither unusual nor infrequent occurrences. These losses are not part of selling or general and administrative expenses and they are not disclosed net of tax. Discontinued operations result from disposal of a separate business component.

40. (d) In 2009, Taft recognized a loss on the long-lived assets that were to be sold and changed the carrying amount of these assets to fair value less cost to sell. In 2010, the assets have still not been sold. The loss recognized has been more than recovered. Subsequent revisions in estimates of fair value less cost to sell shall be reported as adjustments of the carrying amount of an asset to be disposed of. However, the carrying amount may not be increased above the carrying amount prior to impairment. The same amount recognized as a loss in 2009 would be recognized as a recovery (gain) in the 2010 income statement.

41. (b) The reduced carrying amount of Cranston's assets ($920,000) should be accounted for as their new cost, and this amount should be depreciated over the remaining useful life of five years. Restoration of previously recognized impairment losses is prohibited. Therefore, Cranston should report .80 × $920,000 or $736,000 as the carrying amount of its impaired long-lived assets on its December 31, 2010 balance sheet.

42. (c) The requirement is to determine when an asset is impaired. An asset is impaired when the sum of the expected future cash flows is less than the carrying amount of the asset. The expected future cash flows are **not** discounted and do not consider interest charges. Answer (c) refers to one way to measure a loss once it has been determined that an asset has been impaired.

43. (c) The loss on impairment is calculated by subtracting the machine's actual fair value from its carrying value at the date of impairment.

$10,000	Initial cost of machine	$10,000	Cost on 7/1/08
– 500	Salvage value	– 2,375	Accumulated depreciation
$ 9,500	Depreciable base	$ 7,625	Carrying value on 12/31/10
÷ 10	Year life	– 3,000	Actual fair value on 12/31/10
$950	Depreciation per year	$ 4,625	Loss on impairment
× 2.5	Years (7/1/08–12/31/10)		
$ 2,375	Accumulated depreciation		

44. (b) When an asset has been determined to be impaired, it is written down to fair value and loss on impairment is recognized. Restoration of previously recognized impairment losses is prohibited.

45. (b) A long-lived asset is considered impaired if the future cash flows expected to result from the use of the asset and its eventual disposition are less than the carrying amount of the asset. If deemed impaired, the asset's carrying value is reduced to fair value and a loss on impairment is recognized for the difference (Carrying value – Fair value). In this case, the asset is **not** impaired, as the net cash inflows of $175,000 are greater than the 8/31/10 carrying amount (book value) of $170,000. Therefore, the carrying amount of the asset ($170,000) remains unchanged.

46. (a) The requirement is to determine the amount of impairment loss. The impairment loss recognized is the difference between the asset's fair value and its carrying value. On December 31, 2010, the carrying value of the equipment is $80,000 after recording depreciation expense for the current year. ($100,000/10 years = $10,000 per year × 2 years = $20,000 accumulated depreciation). The fair value is determined by using the principal or most advantageous market assuming the highest and best use of the asset. Since the in-use valuation premise is $74,000, the asset is assumed to be in its highest and best use using an in-use valuation premise. Therefore, the impairment loss recognized in 2010 would be the carrying value of $80,000 less the fair value of $74,000 = $6,000.

47. (b) The requirement is to determine the amount that should be presented for the equipment. An impairment loss is recognized if the carrying value of the asset exceeds the sum of the undiscounted cash flows. Since the carrying value of $160,00 exceeds the sum of the estimated undiscounted cash flows of $135,000, an impairment loss must be measured. The impairment loss is measured by comparing the fair value of the asset to the carrying value. The fair value of the asset is determined by using the lowest level input available. In this situation, a Level 1 input is not available. The value of similar equipment for sale in the market is a Level 2 input because it is a directly or indirectly observable input. The present value of future cash flows is a Level 3 input, and should only be used when Level 1 or Level 2 inputs are not available. Therefore, the asset should be presented at its fair value of $140,000, which uses a Level 2 input to appropriately measure fair value of the equipment.

48. **(d)** The requirement is to determine the impairment loss on the equipment. An impairment loss is recognized when the carrying value of an asset exceeds the expected undiscounted cash flows of the asset. In this case, the undiscounted expected cash flows are $420,000 and are less than the carrying value. Therefore, an impairment loss is measured as the difference between the fair value of the asset and its carrying value. The fair value of the asset should be measured based on the lowest level priority input, and assuming the highest and best use of the asset. The highest and best use of the asset occurs when the asset is sold as standalone for $428,000. Therefore, the impairment loss recognized for 2010 is $428,000 fair value less $450,000 carrying value, or $22,000.

49. **(c)** An impairment loss for assets to be held and used shall be reported as a component of income from continuing operations before income taxes for entities presenting an income statement and in the statement of activities of a not-for-profit organization. Although there is no requirement to report a subtotal such as "income from operations," entities that present such a subtotal must include the impairment loss in that subtotal.

50. **(a)** The undiscounted expected future cash flows ($175,000) are less than the carrying amount of the equipment ($200,000). Therefore, the equipment is deemed impaired. The impairment loss is calculated in the following way:

Carrying amount of the equipment on December 31, 2010	$200,000
Fair value of the equipment on December 31, 2010	125,000
Impairment loss reported on 2010 income statement	$ 75,000

51. **(b)** After an impairment loss is recognized, the reduced carrying amount of the asset shall be accounted for as its new cost. This new cost (the fair value of the asset at the date of impairment, or $135,000) shall be depreciated over the asset's remaining useful life (twenty-seven months). Therefore, the depreciation expense for June is $5,000 ($135,000 ÷ 27 months × 1 month).

52. **(b)** Recoveries of impairment losses shall not be recognized.

53. **(c)** The loss due to impairment of long-lived assets is measured by deducting the asset's fair value from the carrying (book) value.

54. **(c)** Long-lived assets and limited-lived intangibles must be reviewed for impairment whenever circumstances and situations change such that there is an indication that the carrying amount might not be recoverable. A specific time frame for review of asset impairment, every year or every three years, is not required.

55. **(b)** The undiscounted expected future cash flows ($300,000) are less than the carrying amount of the equipment ($350,000). Thus, the equipment is determined to be impaired. The impairment loss is calculated as follows:

Carrying value - 12/31/10	$350,000
Fair value - 12/31/10	250,000
Impairment loss reported on 2010 income statement	$100,000

56. **(c)** After an impairment loss is recognized, the reduced carrying amount of the asset shall be accounted for as its new cost. This new cost (the fair value of the asset at the date of impairment, or $261,000) shall be depreciated over the asset's remaining useful life (58 months). Therefore, the depreciation expense for September is $4,500 ($261,000 ÷ 58 months × 1 month).

H.   Depletion

57. **(b)** The depletion charge per unit is the **depletion base** (net cost of the resource) divided by the **estimated units of the resource**. Vorst's depletion base is $2,880,000, as computed below.

Cost of mine	$2,640,000
Development cost	360,000
Restoration cost	180,000
Residual value	(300,000)
	$2,880,000

Note that the present value of the restoration costs are recorded. The depletion charge is $2.40 per ton ($2,880,000 ÷ 1,200,000 tons). Since 60,000 tons were removed and sold, depletion of $144,000 (60,000 × $2.40) is included in Vorst's 2010 income statement. Note that the amount of depletion included in the income statement depends on the tons **sold**. If more tons were removed than sold, part of the depletion would be included in the cost of ending inventory rather than in the income statement.

J.   Intangible Assets

58. **(b)** The software should be valued at the lower of its unamortized cost or its net realizable value. The software's unamortized cost is $450,000, which is equal to $600,000 – $150,000 ($600,000/4). Answer (c) is incorrect because the software's unamortized cost is less than its net realizable value.

59. **(c)** Judd Company would record the trademark at its cost of $500,000. The unamortized cost on the seller's books ($380,000) is irrelevant to the buyer. The trademark has a remaining useful life of fifty years. Therefore, the 2010 amortization expense and 12/31/10 accumulated amortization is $10,000 ($500,000 ÷ 50 years).

60. **(b)** A company should record as an asset the cost of intangible assets such as goodwill **acquired from other entities**. **Costs of developing** intangible assets such as goodwill "which are not specifically identifiable, have indeterminate lives, or are inherent in a continuing business and related to an entity as a whole" should be expensed when incurred. Therefore, only the $200,000 (and not the additional $80,000) should be capitalized as goodwill. Goodwill should not be amortized.

61. **(d)** In determining the useful life of an intangible, consideration should be given to the legal, regulatory or contractual life, including rights to extension. Since Northern has the ability and intent to renew the rights indefinitely, the intangible should not be amortized.

62. **(c)** Before 2010, Lava would record total amortization of $27,000 [($90,000 × 1/10) × 3 years], resulting in a 12/31/09 carrying amount of $63,000 ($90,000 – $27,000). Since the patent became worthless at 12/31/10 due to government prohibition of the product, the entire carrying amount ($63,000) should be charged against income in 2010 as an impairment loss.

63. **(d)** Goodwill should not be amortized. Instead, goodwill remains at the amount established at the time of the business combination unless it is determined to be impaired. Goodwill should be tested for impairment annually, or more often if events and circumstances indicate that goodwill may be impaired.

64. **(a)** Costs incurred in connection with securing a patent, as well as attorney's fees and other unrecovered costs of a successful legal suit to protect the patent, can be capitalized as part of patent costs. Therefore, answer (a) is correct because legal fees and other costs incurred to successfully defend a patent should be amortized along with the acquisition cost over the remaining economic life of the patent. Answer (b) is incorrect because legal fees and other direct costs incurred in registering a patent should be capitalized and amortized on a straight-line basis over its economic life, not five years. Answers (c) and (d) are incorrect because research and development costs related to the development of the product, process or idea that is subsequently patented must be expensed as incurred, not capitalized and amortized.

65. **(d)** Goodwill is allocated to reporting units which are operating segments of the business or one level below. Goodwill is also tested for impairment at the level of the reporting unit.

66. **(c)** Goodwill impairment is determined at the level of the individual reporting unit. It is the difference between the carrying amount of goodwill and its implied value. The carrying amounts of goodwill of the Retailing and Service reporting units are greater than their implied values. Therefore, an impairment loss should be recognized in the amount of $15,000 ($30,000 + $20,000) – ($25,000 + $10,000).

67. **(a)** There are two steps in the test of impairment of goodwill. The first is to compare the carrying value of the reporting unit to its fair value. If the fair value exceeds the carrying value there is no need to perform the second step of valuing the unit's assets and liabilities. Goodwill is never tested at the entity level.

68. **(d)** Since the fair value of the reporting unit is less than its carrying amount, the second step in the test should be performed. The assets and liabilities of the unit should be valued and compared to value of the total unit. The implied value of goodwill is the difference. The impairment is equal to the difference between the implied value and the carrying amount of the goodwill.

K. Reporting on the Costs of Start-Up Activities

69. **(b)** Start-up activities are defined broadly as those onetime activities related to opening a new facility as well as introducing a new product or service and conducting business in a new territory. Certain costs that may be incurred in conjunction with start-up activities are not subject to these provisions. These costs include the costs of acquiring long-lived assets such as production equipment, costs of advertising, and license fees. Answer (b) which includes the costs of training local employees ($120,000) and travel costs of salaried employees ($40,000) is the correct answer.

70. **(d)** Organization costs are those incurred in the formation of a corporation. These costs should be expensed as incurred. The rationale is that uncertainty exists concerning the future benefit of these costs in future years. Thus, they are properly recorded as an expense in 2010.

71. **(b)** The costs of raising capital and the costs of acquiring or constructing long-lived assets and getting them ready for their intended use are not expensed as incurred. Such costs should be accounted for in accordance with other existing authoritative accounting literature. Research and development (R&D) costs are expensed as incurred.

L. Research and Development Costs (ASC Topic 730)

72. **(d)** Among those items listed as being part of R&D costs are design of tools, jigs, molds, and dies involving new technology ($125,000) and modification of the formulation of a process ($160,000), for a total R&D expense of $285,000. Included in the items **not** being part of R&D costs are troubleshooting breakdowns during production ($100,000), and adaptation of existing capability for a specific customer ($110,000).

73. **(b)** All R&D costs must be expensed when incurred. However, R&D costs incurred when performing R&D work under contract for other entities are specifically excluded from the reporting requirements. Generally such costs are deferred and matched with revenue under the completed-contract or percentage-of-completion method. The other costs listed would all be expensed in 2010. Therefore, Ball's 2010 research and development expense is $1,380,000 ($300,000 + $700,000 + $200,000 + $180,000).

74. **(c)** All R&D costs are to be charged to expense when incurred. Specifically R&D costs include of designing, constructing, and testing preproduction prototypes, and the cost of R&D equipment (unless it has alternative future uses). Therefore, $340,000 ($60,000 + $200,000 + $80,000) is classified as R&D costs and expensed. The legal costs incurred to obtain a patent ($10,000) are capitalized in the patents account.

75. **(d)** The FASB excludes from its definitions of research and development expense the acquisition, development, or improvement of a product or process for use in its **selling or administrative activities**. Both costs given in this problem relate to selling or administrative activities, so the expenditures of $175,000 would not be reported as research and development expense.

76. **(a)** Research and development costs are expensed as incurred except for fixed assets, intangible assets, or materials purchased that have alternative future uses. Jambon purchased equipment to be used for research and development, but the equipment can only be used for that project. Therefore, the cost of the equipment must be expensed in 2010 as it has no alternative future uses.

M.   Computer Software Costs (ASC Topic 985)

77.   (b)   Costs incurred in creating a computer software product should be charged to research and development expense when incurred until **technological feasibility** has been established for the product. Technological feasibility is established upon completion of a detailed program design or working model. In this case, $23,000 would be recorded as expense ($13,000 for completion of detailed program design and $10,000 for coding and testing to establish technological feasibility). Costs incurred from the point of technological feasibility until the time when product costs are incurred are capitalized as software costs. In this situation, $59,000 is capitalized as software cost ($24,000 + $20,000 + $15,000). Product costs that can be easily associated with the inventory items are reported as inventory (in this case, $25,000 for duplication of computer software and training materials and $9,000 of packaging costs, for a total of $34,000).

78.   (c)   Costs incurred in creating a computer software product should be charged to research and development expense when incurred until **technological feasibility** has been established. Technological feasibility is established upon completion of a detailed program design or working model. In this case, $23,000 would be recorded as expense ($13,000 for completion of detailed program design and $10,000 for coding and testing to establish technological feasibility). Costs incurred from the point of technological feasibility until the time when product costs are incurred are capitalized as software costs. In this situation, $59,000 is capitalized as software cost ($24,000 + $20,000 + $15,000). Product costs that can be easily associated with the inventory items are reported as inventory (in this case, $25,000 for duplication of computer software and training materials and $9,000 of packaging costs, for a total of $34,000).

79.   (a)   The annual amortization of capitalized software costs shall be the greater of

1.   The ratio of the software's current sales to its expected total sales, or
2.   The straight-line method over the economic life of the product.

In this case, the ratio of current to expected total sales is 30% (given). The annual straight-line rate is 20% per year (1 ÷ economic life of five years). The 30% amortization should be recorded in 2010, since it is the higher of the two. The unamortized cost on the 12/31/10 balance sheet should, therefore, be 70% (100% – 30% amortization). Note that the unamortized cost of capitalized software products must be compared to the net realizable value of those assets at each balance sheet date. Any excess of the amortized cost over the net realizable value must be written off. In this case, the net realizable value (90%) was **above** the unamortized cost (70%), so no additional write-off was required.

80.   (b)   Internal-use software is software having the following characteristics: (1) The software is acquired, internally developed, or modified solely to meet the entity's internal needs, and (2) during the software's development or modification, no substantive plan exists to market the software externally.

81.   (b)   Application and development costs create probable future benefit. Therefore, they should be capitalized as incurred. However, preliminary costs are similar to research and development costs and are expensed as incurred, not capitalized.

82.   (d)   Preliminary costs are similar to research and development costs; therefore, they are expensed as incurred. Postimplementation costs such as training are not considered software development costs at all and are expensed as incurred.

N.   Development Stage Enterprises (ASC Topic 915)

83.   (a)   A development stage enterprise shall follow the same revenue and expense recognition principles and issue the same basic financial statements as an established operating enterprise, but shall disclose certain additional information. A development stage company shall use the same generally accepted accounting principles that apply to established operating enterprises to govern the recognition of revenue and to determine whether a cost is to be capitalized or expensed as incurred.

84.   (c)   A development stage enterprise shall issue the same basic financial statements as an established operating enterprise, but shall disclose certain additional information. An income statement, in addition to showing amounts of revenues and expenses for each period covered by the income statement, shall include the cumulative amounts from the enterprise's inception.

SOLUTIONS TO SIMULATION PROBLEMS

Simulation Problem 1

Situation	Concepts	Asset Valuation	Depreciation Calculations	Communication	Research

	Capitalize	*Expense*
1. Freight charges paid for goods held for resale.	●	○
2. In-transit insurance on goods held for resale purchased FOB shipping point.	●	○
3. Interest on note payable for goods held for resale.	○	●
4. Installation of equipment.	●	○
5. Testing of newly purchased equipment.	●	○
6. Cost of current year service contract on equipment.	○	●

Explanation of solutions

Items 1 through 6 represent questions concerning expenditures for goods held for resale and equipment and whether these expenditures should be capitalized or expensed as a period cost. The general concept that determines whether expenditures should be product costs and, therefore, capitalized or expensed as period costs is whether or not these expenditures "attach" themselves to the assets of inventory or equipment. Costs that "attach" themselves to assets are those that are directly connected with bringing the goods or equipment to the place of business of the buyer and converting such goods to a salable (inventory) or unusable (equipment) condition.

1. **(C)** Freight charges are directly connected with bringing the goods to the place of business of the buyer.

2. **(C)** Insurance charges are directly connected with bringing the goods to the place of business of the buyer.

3. **(E)** Only interest costs related to continued assets constructed for internal use or assets produced as discrete products for sale or lease should be capitalized. The informational benefit of capitalization does not justify the cost of the accounting for the interest as a product cost.

4. **(C)** Direct cost of bringing the equipment to the buyer.

5. **(C)** Direct cost of converting the equipment to a usable condition.

6. **(E)** Does not relate to bringing the equipment to the buyer or putting it into a usable condition.

Situation	Concepts	Asset Valuation	Depreciation Calculations	Communication	Research

1. **($600,000)** Since the land and building were purchased together, the cost of each must be allocated based on the relative market value. The land and building were purchased together for a total cost of $1,000,000 ($800,000 cash + $200,000 mortgage assumption). For property tax purposes, the building is deemed to be 60% of the value of the land and building. Therefore, the cost of the building should be recorded at $600,000 ($1,000,000 × 60%).

2. **($504,000)** As the lease is classified as a capital lease, Link must record an asset and liability based on the present value of the minimum lease payments. However, the leased assets cannot be recorded at an amount greater than the fair value. To determine the minimum value of the lease payments, Link should discount the future payments using the **lesser** of the lessee's (Link's) incremental borrowing rate (9%) or the lessor's implicit rate if **known** by the lessee. Therefore, since Link does not know the lessor's implicit rate, Link's rate of 9% should be used. The recorded value would be $100,000 × 5.04 = $504,000, which is less than the fair value.

3. **($370,000)** In recording a nonmonetary exchange, if the transaction lacks commercial substance, the asset received is recorded at the book value of the asset given up plus any boot given when gains and losses are not recognized. The following fact pattern exists for Link:

	Boot	*FV*	*BV*	*Gain (Loss)*
Land given	50,000	450,000	320,000	130,000
Land received		500,000		

Link will record the land received from Club at the book value of the land given up plus the boot given ($320,000 + 50,000 = $370,000).

An alternative method to calculate the value to record the land at is to subtract the deferred gain from the fair value of the land received ($500,000 – 130,000 = $370,000).

4. (**$315,000**) On Club's books the following situation exists:

	Boot	FV	BV	Gain (Loss)
Land given		500,000	350,000	150,000
Land received	50,000	450,000		

An exception to the nonrecognition of gain on similar assets exists when boot is received. The earnings process is considered complete for the portion related to the boot received, but not complete for the portion related to the asset received. A gain is recognized only for the portion related to the boot. The gain is computed as follows:

$$\frac{\text{Boot received}}{\text{Boot received} + \text{FMV of assets received}} \times \text{Total gain} = \text{Gain recognized}$$

$$\frac{50,000}{50,000 + 450,000} \times 150,000 = \$15,000$$

The land received will be recorded at its fair value less the gain deferred.

$$\$450,000 - (150,000 - 15,000) = \$315,000.$$

An alternative method is to record the land received at the book value of the land given less the boot received plus the gain recognized, as follows:

$$\$350,000 - 50,000 + 15,000 = \$315,000.$$

Situation	Concepts	Asset Valuation	Depreciation Calculations	Communication	Research

1. (**$90,000**) Under the straight-line method of depreciation, the depreciation expense would be calculated as follows:

$$\frac{\text{Cost salvage value}}{\text{Estimated life}} = \frac{\$864,000 - 144,000}{8} = \$90,000$$

Depreciation expense would be $90,000 for all eight years, 2009-2016.

2. (**$162,000**) The double-declining balance method is calculated by taking two times the straight-line rate times the net book value at the beginning of each year, but not below the salvage value. Furthermore the salvage value is not deducted to arrive at the depreciable base. The calculation would be as follows:

	NBV		Depreciation expense
2009	$864,000 × (1/8 × 2)	=	$216,000
2010	($864,000 − 216,000) × (1/8 × 2)	=	$162,000

3. (**$140,000**) Under the sum-of-the-years' digits method, the depreciation expense is calculated as follows:

$$2009 \quad 8 \div \frac{8(8+1)}{2} \times (\$864,000) - \$144,000 = \$160,000$$

$$2010 \quad (7 \div 36) \times (\$864,000 - \$144,000) = \$140,000$$

4. (**$120,000**) The units of production method is a type of physical usage depreciation that is based on activity. The formula is as follows:

$$\frac{\text{Current activity/output}}{\text{Total expected activity/output}} \times \text{Depreciable base} = \text{Annual depreciation}$$

Depreciation expense for 2010 is calculated as follows:

$$\frac{300,000 \text{ units}}{1,800,000 \text{ units}} \times (\$864,000 - \$144,000) = \$120,000$$

Situation	Concepts	Asset Valuation	Depreciation Calculations	Communication	Research

To: CEO, Link Co.
From: CPA Candidate
Re: Depreciation and sports equipment

Thank you for your inquiry regarding accounting for snowmobiles and other winter sports equipment used in your business.

The proper accounting for the purchase of the new snowmobile engines depends on whether the costs of the old engines are known. When the old engines' costs are known, the snowmobiles account is decreased by the old engines' costs and accumulated depreciation is decreased by the accumulated depreciation on the old engines. The net difference between the old engines' carrying amounts and their fair values is recorded as an operating gain or loss. To record the new engines' acquisition, both the snowmobiles account and accounts payable are increased by the new engines' costs.

If the old engines' costs are unknown, then either the snowmobiles account would be increased or accumulated depreciation would be decreased by the difference between the new engines' costs and the old engines' fair values.

Several assumptions underlie the use of an accelerated depreciation method. The first assumption is that an asset is more productive in the earlier years of its estimated useful life. Therefore, greater depreciation charges in the earlier years would be matched against the greater revenues generated in the earlier years. The second assumption is that repair and maintenance costs are often higher in later periods and an accelerated depreciation method results in a more nearly annual constant total cost over the years of use. Finally, an asset may become obsolete before the end of its originally estimated useful life. The risk associated with estimated long-term cash flows is greater than the risk associated with near-term cash flows. Accelerated depreciation recognizes this condition.

If Link uses double-declining balance depreciation, the accountant should calculate snowmobile depreciation by applying twice the straight-line rate to their carrying amounts. The entry to record depreciation is to debit depreciation expense and credit the accumulated depreciation account. This results in the asset being presented on the statement of financial position at book value.

Under the inventory (appraisal) method, Link should calculate the ending undepreciated cost on the skis, poles, and boots by multiplying the physical quantities of these items on hand by an appraised amount. This ending undepreciated cost is classified as a noncurrent asset. Depreciation included in continuing operations equals the sum of the beginning balance and purchases for the year less ending undepreciated cost.

If you have any questions, please contact my office.

Situation	Concepts	Asset Valuation	Depreciation Calculations	Communication	Research

1. What is the definition of an impaired asset?

FAS144, Para 7

7. For purposes of this Statement, impairment is the condition that exists when the carrying amount of a long-lived asset (asset group) exceeds its fair value. An impairment loss shall be recognized only if the carrying amount of a long-lived asset (asset group) is not recoverable and exceeds its fair value. The carrying amount of a long-lived asset (asset group) is not recoverable if it exceeds the sum of the undiscounted cash flows expected to result from the use and eventual disposition of the asset (asset group). That assessment shall be based on the carrying amount of the asset (asset group) at the date it is tested for recoverability, whether in use (paragraph 19) or under development (paragraph 20). An impairment loss shall be measured as the amount by which the carrying amount of a long-lived asset (asset group) exceeds its fair value.

Codification: 360-10-20 Glossary

2. What assumptions are made in determining the price or fair value of an impaired asset?

FAS157, Para 7

7. A fair value measurement assumes that the asset or liability is exchanged in an orderly transaction between market participants to sell the asset or transfer the liability at the measurement date. An orderly transaction is a transaction that assumes exposure to the market for a period prior to the measurement date to allow for marketing activities that are usual and customary for transactions involving such assets or liabilities; it is not a forced transaction (for example, a forced liquidation or distress sale). The transaction to sell the asset or transfer the liability is a hypothetical transaction at the measurement date, considered from the perspective of a market participant that holds the asset or owes the liability. Therefore, the objective of a fair value measurement is to determine the price that would be received to sell the asset or paid to transfer the liability at the measurement date (an exit price).

Codification: 820-10-35-3

3. In reporting discontinued operations, how does the accountant determine if the operation qualifies as a component?

FAS144, Para 41

41. For purposes of this Statement, a component of an entity comprises operations and cash flows that can be clearly distinguished, operationally and for financial reporting purposes, from the rest of the entity. A component of an entity may be a reportable segment or an operating segment (as those terms are defined in paragraph 10 of Statement 131), a reporting unit (as that term is defined in Statement 142), a subsidiary, or an asset group (as that term is defined in paragraph 4).

Codification: 205-20-20 Glossary

4. When there is a gain or loss on an asset that is classified as held-for-sale, where is the gain or loss reported in the financial statements?

FAS144, Para 45

45. A gain or loss recognized for a long-lived asset (disposal group) classified as held for sale that is not a component of an entity shall be included in income from continuing operations before income taxes in the income statement of a business enterprise and in income from continuing operations in the statement of activities of a not-for-profit organization. If a subtotal such as "income from operations" is presented, it shall include the amounts of those gains or losses.

Codification: 360-10-45-5

Simulation Problem 2

Situation	Capitalized Costs	Disposal of Assets	Journal Entry	Balance Sheet Disclosures	Communication	Research

	Capitalized cost	*Depreciation/amortization expense for 2010*
Land acquired from Alison Corp.	$200,000	0
Land acquired fro Kaufman	168,000	0
Building acquired from Kaufman	672,000	16,300
Machinery and equipment acquired from Apex Equipment	439,000	43,900
Land improvements	120,000	8,000
Research and development	0	0

Explanation of solutions

- Allocation of the land and building for purchase from Kaufman: FMV = 20,000 shares × $42 per share = $840,000.
- Allocate based on relative fair values. Therefore, land is $840,000 × $200,000/$1,000,000 = $168,000; Building is $840,000 × $800,000/$1,000,000 = $672,000. Land is not depreciated. Building is depreciated ($672,000 – $20,000)/40 years = $16,300.
- Items of machinery and equipment should capitalize all costs to get the asset in its intended and useful place.
- Land improvements are depreciated over fifteen years. $120,000/15 years = $8,000 per year.
- Research and development costs should be expensed as incurred. They are not capitalized, and they are not depreciated.

Situation	Capitalized Costs	Disposal of Assets	Journal Entry	Balance Sheet Disclosures	Communication	Research

Item	*Amount of gain*	*Amount of loss*
Scrapped machine on 6/30/10		$4,000
Sale of machine on 7/1/10	$5,500	

Situation	Capitalized Costs	Disposal of Assets	Journal Entry	Balance Sheet Disclosures	Communication	Research

	Debit	*Credit*
Depreciation expense	4,500	
Accumulated depreciation		4,500
Cash	48,000	
Accumulated depreciation	31,500	
Equipment		74,000
Gain on sale of equipment		5,500

Situation	Capitalized Costs	Disposal of Assets	Journal Entry	Balance Sheet Disclosures	Communication	Research

	Balance as of 12/31/10
Land	768,000
Land improvements	250,000
Buildings	2,672,000
Equipment and machinery	1,149,000

Explanation of solutions

- Land $400,000 + $200,000 + $168,000 = $768,000
- Land improvements $130,000 + $120,000 = $250,000.
- Buildings $2,000,000 + $672,000 = $2,672,000
- Equipment and machinery $800,000 + New equipment $439,000 – $16,000 scrapped equipment – $74,000 sold equipment = $1,149,000

Situation	Capitalized Costs	Disposal of Assets	Journal Entry	Balance Sheet Disclosures	Communication	Research

Below are items to include in your memo to the client.

1. An operational asset is impaired if some or all of the carrying amount of that asset will not be recovered.

2. An asset could be impaired if one or more of the following conditions exists:

- Significant decrease in market value
- Change in way the asset is used or physical change in asset
- Legal factors or change in business climate that might affect asset's fair value or adverse action or assessment by regulator
- Asset cost incurred greater than planned
- Operating or cash flow losses from the asset

If at least one of these conditions exists, a recoverability test shall be performed. Under this test, a loss on operational assets shall be recognized if the expected total net future cash flows are less than the carrying amounts of the assets. Assets should be grouped at lowest level for which there are identifiable cash flows independent of other groupings. Expected net future cash flows are future cash inflows to be generated by the assets less the future cash outflows expected to be necessary to obtain those inflows. Expected future cash flows are not discounted. If the ability to recover the asset is not demonstrated (sum of future cash flows < carrying amount) a loss shall be measured and recorded. The loss is measured as the difference between the fair value of the asset(s) and their carrying amounts.

3. A loss is recognized in the current period by a debit to an impairment loss account and a credit to accumulated depreciation. In future periods, if additional impairment is confirmed, an additional loss shall be recognized. However, recoveries of losses recognized in prior periods are not permitted. Impairment losses are reported in income from continuing operations.

4. In situations in which management has made a decision to dispose of an asset, such asset should be recorded at the lower of the asset's carrying amount or net realizable value (NRV). These assets shall no longer be depreciated. In future periods, recoveries are permitted, but are limited to losses previously recognized on these assets. Losses recognized are reported as part of income from continuing operations. The assets to be disposed of shall be reported under other assets on the company's balance sheet.

Situation	Capitalized Costs	Disposal of Assets	Journal Entry	Balance Sheet Disclosures	Communication	Research

1. What is meant by impairment of an operational asset?

Recognition and Measurement of an Impairment Loss FAS144, Para 7

7. For purposes of this Statement, impairment is the condition that exists when the carrying amount of a long-lived asset (asset group) exceeds its fair value. An impairment loss shall be recognized only if the carrying amount of a long-lived asset (asset group) is not recoverable and exceeds its fair value. The carrying amount of a long-lived asset (asset group) is not recoverable if it exceeds the sum of the undiscounted cash flows expected to result from the use and eventual disposition of the asset (asset group). That assessment shall be based on the carrying amount of the asset (asset group) at the date it is tested for recoverability, whether in use (paragraph 19) or under development (paragraph 20). An impairment loss shall be measured as the amount by which the carrying amount of a long-lived asset (asset group) exceeds its fair value.

Codification: 360-10-20 Glossary

2. When is a long-lived asset tested for recoverability?

When to Test a Long-Lived Asset for Recoverability
FAS144, Para 8

8. A long-lived asset (asset group) shall be tested for recoverability whenever events or changes in circumstances indicate that its carrying amount may not be recoverable. The following are examples of such events or changes in circumstances:

   a. A significant decrease in the market price of a long-lived asset (asset group).

   b. A significant adverse change in the extent or manner in which a long-lived asset (asset group) is being used or in its physical condition.

   c. A significant adverse change in legal factors or in the business climate that could affect the value of a long-lived asset (asset group), including an adverse action or assessment by a regulator.

   d. An accumulation of costs significantly in excess of the amount originally expected for the acquisition or construction of a long-lived asset (asset group).

   e. A current period operating or cash flow loss combined with a history of operating or cash flow losses or a projection or forecast that demonstrates continuing losses associated with the use of a long-lived asset (asset group).

   f. A current expectation that more likely than not, 6 a long-lived asset (asset group) will be sold or otherwise disposed of significantly before the end of its previously estimated useful life.

Codification: 360-10-35-21

3. Describe the accounting and reporting for an impairment loss on the income statement in the current period.

Reporting and Disclosure
FAS144, Para 25

25. An impairment loss recognized for a long-lived asset (asset group) to be held and used shall be included in income from continuing operations before income taxes in the income statement of a business enterprise and in income from continuing operations in the statement of activities of a not-for-profit organization. If a subtotal such as "income from operations" is presented, it shall include the amount of that loss.

Codification: 360-10-45-4

4. Describe the information to be disclosed in the notes to the financial statements regarding asset impairment.

FAS144, Para 26

26. The following information shall be disclosed in the notes to the financial statements that include the period in which an impairment loss is recognized:

   a. A description of the impaired long-lived asset (asset group) and the facts and circumstances leading to the impairment.

   b. If not separately presented on the face of the statement, the amount of the impairment loss and the caption in the income statement or the statement of activities that includes that loss.

   c. The method or methods for determining fair value (whether based on a quoted market price, prices for similar assets, or another valuation technique).

   d. If applicable, the segment in which the impaired long-lived asset (asset group) is reported under FASB Statement No. 131, *Disclosures about Segments of an Enterprise and Related Information.*

Codification: 360-10-50-2

5. Describe the accounting for impairment losses **New Cost Basis**
on future financial statements.   **FAS144, Para 15**

> 15. If an impairment loss is recognized, the adjusted carrying amount of a long-lived asset shall be its new cost basis. For a depreciable long-lived asset, the new costs shall be depreciated (amortized) over the remaining useful life of that asset. Restoration of a previously recognized impairment loss is prohibited.

> *Codification: 360-10-35-20*

6. How are losses of operational assets to be sold **Measurement**
measured?   **FAS144, Para 34**

> 34. A long-lived asset (disposal group) classified as held for sale shall be measured at the lower of its carrying amount or fair value less cost to sell. If the asset (disposal group) is newly acquired, the carrying amount of the asset (disposal group) shall be established based on its fair value less cost to sell at the acquisition date. A long-lived asset shall not be depreciated (amortized) while it is classified as held for sale. Interest and other expenses attributable to the liabilities of a disposal group classified as held for sale shall continue to be accrued.

> *Codification: 360-10-35-43*

Simulation Problem 3

Situation	Concepts	Intangible Assets	Expenses Resulting from Intangibles	Goodwill Impairment	Communication	Research

	True	False
1. An intangible asset that is determined to have an indefinite life should be amortized over 40 years.	○	●
2. If the carrying value of the intangible asset exceeds its fair value, an impairment loss must be recognized.	●	○
3. The impairment test for goodwill must be performed at the end of each fiscal year for each reporting unit.	○	●
4. When a company borrows funds to finance a construction project and temporarily invests this cash, the interest expense should be offset against the interest expense to be capitalized.	○	●
5. A company may capitalize interest on inventories it regularly produces for resale to customers.	○	●
6. Gains are never recognized when similar assets are exchanged.	○	●
7. In nonmonetary exchanges, losses are only recognized when cash is received in the transactions.	○	●
8. If the fair value of the asset is unknown in a nonmonetary exchange and no gain can be computed, the asset is recorded at the fair market value of the asset given up.	○	●
9. A capital expenditure is charged against income over the useful life of the asset.	●	○
10. Expenditures to improve the efficiency or extend the useful life of an asset should be capitalized.	●	○

Explanation of solutions

1. **(F)** Intangible assets that have indefinite lives are not amortized.

2. **(T)** The recorded values of intangibles are impaired if they are above fair value.

3. **(F)** The impairment test for goodwill can be performed anytime during the year, but it must be performed at the same time every year.

4. **(F)** Interest earned on temporary investments from borrowed funds used to finance construction projects should be recognized as interest revenue and **not** netted against interest expense during the period.

5. (F) A company may not capitalize interest on funds borrowed to finance routinely produced inventory.

6. (F) Recognition of gain is required unless the transaction lacks commercial substance.

7. (F) Losses on nonmonetary exchanges are recognized.

8. (F) In a nonmonetary exchange, if the fair value is unknown and no gain can be computed, the asset is recorded at the book value of the asset given up.

9. (T) Capital expenditures are amortized over the useful life of the asset.

10. (T) Expenditures to improve capital assets should be capitalized.

Situation	Concepts	Intangible Assets	Expenses Resulting from Intangibles	Goodwill Impairment	Communication	Research

Broca Co.
SCHEDULE FOR INTANGIBLE ASSETS AND AMORTIZATION EXPENSE
December 31, 2010

Item	Valuation *before* adjusting entries		Amortization expense for the year	Valuation on 12/31/10
Goodwill	188,000	[1]	-0-	188,000
Franchise (net)	60,000	[2]	12,000	48,000
Patent (net)	136,000	[3]	13,600	122,400

Explanation of solutions

Broca Co.
SUPPORTING CALCULATIONS FOR INTANGIBLES
December 31, 2010

Goodwill	$188,000	[1]
Franchise, net of accumulated amortization of $12,000	48,000	[2]
Patent, net of accumulated amortization of $13,600	122,400	[3]

[1]	Cash paid	$360,000
	Value of net assets	(172,000)
	Goodwill	188,000
[2]	Franchise	$60,000
	Amortization over 5 years	(12,000)
	Balance	$48,000
[3]	Legal costs ($51,000 + $85,000)	$136,000
	Amortization over 10 years	(13,600)
	Balance	$122,400

[1] Goodwill calculation

In a purchase, the net assets acquired are recorded at their FV. The excess of the cost of the investment ($360,000) over the FV of the net assets acquired ($172,000) is allocated to goodwill ($360,000 – $172,000 = $188,000). Intangible assets with an indeterminate or unlimited life, such as this goodwill, are not amortized. The goodwill is reported in the 12/31/10 balance at its cost.

[2] Franchise fee

The franchise acquired on 2/1/10 is recorded at its cost of $60,000. Since Broca amortizes these intangibles on a straight-line basis, and takes a full year's amortization in the year of acquisition, 2010 amortization is $12,000 ($60,000 × 1/5), and the franchise is reported at cost less accumulated amortization at 12/31/10 ($60,000 – $12,000 = $48,000). In addition to the amortization expense, there is also an annual fee that must be expensed, equal to 1% of ferry revenues.

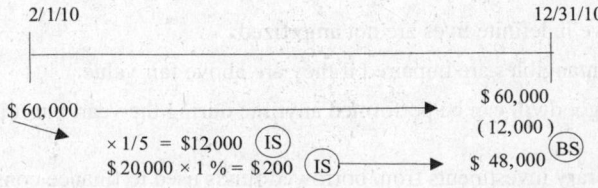

[3] Patents are initially recorded at cost of acquisition, which is purchase price for a purchased patent, or legal and other costs of registration ($51,000) for an internally generated patent. Legal fees incurred in **successfully** defending the patent ($85,000) are also capitalized because such fees help establish the legal right of the holder to any future benefits that will be derived from the patent. Therefore, this patent is capitalized at a total amount of $136,000 ($51,000 + $85,000). Since Broca amortizes these intangibles on a straight-line basis and takes a full-year's amortization in the year of acquisition, amortization is $13,600 ($136,000 x1/10). The patent is reported at cost less accumulated amortization at 12/31/10 ($136,000 – $13,600 = $122,400).

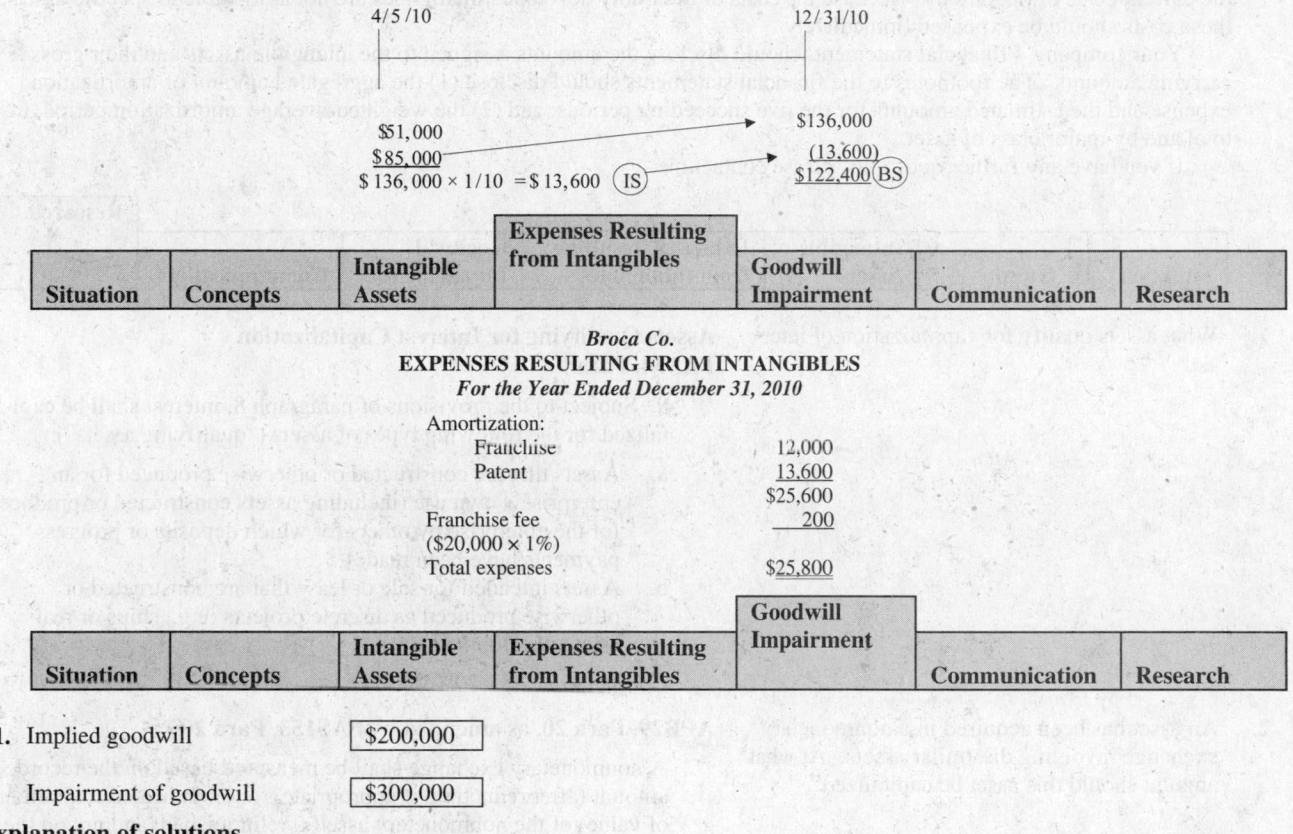

Situation	Concepts	Intangible Assets	**Expenses Resulting from Intangibles**	Goodwill Impairment	Communication	Research

Broca Co.
EXPENSES RESULTING FROM INTANGIBLES
For the Year Ended December 31, 2010

Amortization:

Franchise	12,000	
Patent	13,600	
	$25,600	
Franchise fee	200	
($20,000 × 1%)		
Total expenses	$25,800	

Situation	Concepts	Intangible Assets	Expenses Resulting from Intangibles	**Goodwill Impairment**	Communication	Research

1. Implied goodwill $200,000

   Impairment of goodwill $300,000

Explanation of solutions

1. Goodwill acquired through a business combination is the only type of goodwill that is recognized. Such goodwill is not amortized but is tested periodically for impairment. Internally generated goodwill is not recorded. Expenditures to develop, maintain, or enhance goodwill are expensed as incurred.

   Since the carrying value of the reporting unit ($1,900,000) exceeds the fair value of the unit ($1,700,000), the second step in the test of impairment should be performed.

   The implied value of goodwill is the difference between the fair value of the unit ($1,700,000) and the fair value of its assets and liabilities ($1,500,000). Therefore, the implied value of goodwill is $200,000. Since the carrying value of goodwill is $500,000, there is a $300,000 impairment that must be recognized as shown below.

2. Journal entry required for goodwill impairment

Impairment loss	$300,000	
Goodwill		$300,000

To recognize impairment of goodwill for the Technology reporting unit at 12/31/10.

Situation	Concepts	Intangible Assets	Expenses Resulting from Intangibles	Goodwill Impairment	**Communication**	Research

To: CEO, Broca Corporation
From: CPA Candidate
Re: Intangible assets

This memorandum answers the questions you have regarding intangible assets. The main characteristics of intangible assets are their lack of physical substance, the difficulty of estimating their value, and the high degree of uncertainty regarding their future life. Accounting for intangible assets depends on whether the intangibles have been purchased or developed internally.

Intangible assets purchased from others should be recorded at cost. Then, management should evaluate whether the intangible assets have a finite economic life or an indefinite life. Intangible assets with definite useful lives should be amortized over their estimated useful lives. Estimated useful lives should be determined by consideration of such factors as legal life; provisions for renewal or extensions of contracts; the effects of obsolescence, demand, competition, and other economic factors. Intangible assets with indefinite lives are not amortized. Instead, they are periodically tested for impairment.

The costs of internally developing intangible assets with indeterminable lives are ordinarily not distinguishable from the current costs of operations. Because the costs of internally developed intangibles are not assignable to specific assets, these costs should be expensed immediately.

Your company's financial statements should disclose the amounts assigned to the intangible assets and their gross carrying amounts. The footnotes to the financial statements should disclose (1) the aggregated amount of amortization expense and the estimated amounts for the five succeeding periods; and (2) the weighted-average amortization period, in total and by major class of asset.

If you have any further questions, please contact me.

Situation	Concepts	Intangible Assets	Expenses Resulting from Intangibles	Goodwill Impairment	Communication	Research

1. What assets qualify for capitalization of interest?

Assets Qualifying for Interest Capitalization
FAS34, Para 9

9. Subject to the provisions of paragraph 8, interest shall be capitalized for the following types of assets ("qualifying assets"):

a. Assets that are constructed or otherwise produced for an enterprise's own use (including assets constructed or produced for the enterprise by others for which deposits or progress payments have been made)

b. Assets intended for sale or lease that are constructed or otherwise produced as discrete projects (e.g., ships or real estate developments).

Codification: 835-20-15-5

2. An asset has been acquired in a nonmonetary exchange involving dissimilar assets. At what amount should this asset be capitalized?

APB29, Para 20, as amended by FAS153, Para 2(c)

A nonmonetary exchange shall be measured based on the recorded amount (after reduction, if appropriate, for an indicated impairment of value) of the nonmonetary asset(s) relinquished, and not on the fair values of the exchanged assets, if any of the following conditions apply:

a. *Fair Value Not Determinable.* The fair value of neither the asset(s) received nor the asset(s) relinquished is determinable within reasonable limits (paragraph 25).

b. *Exchange Transaction to Facilitate Sales to Customers.* The transaction is an exchange of a product or property held for sale in the ordinary course of business for a product or property to be sold in the same line of business to facilitate sales to customers other than the parties to the exchange.

c. *Exchange Transaction That Lacks Commercial Substance.* The transaction lacks commercial substance (paragraph 21).

Codification: 845-10-30-3

3. At what amount should donated assets be recorded?

FAS116, Para 8

8. Except as provided in paragraphs 9 and 11, contributions received shall be recognized as revenues or gains in the period received and as assets, decreases of liabilities, or expenses depending on the form of the benefits received. Contributions received shall be measured at their fair values. Contributions received by not-for-profit organizations shall be reported as restricted support or unrestricted support as provided in paragraphs 14-16.

Codification: 958-605-25-2

MULTIPLE-CHOICE QUESTIONS (1-111)

1. Burr Company had the following account balances at December 31, 2010:

Cash in banks	$2,250,000
Cash on hand	125,000
Cash legally restricted for additions to plant (expected to be disbursed in 2011)	1,600,000

Cash in banks includes $600,000 of compensating balances against short-term borrowing arrangements. The compensating balances are not legally restricted as to withdrawal by Burr. In the current assets section of Burr's December 31, 2010 balance sheet, total cash should be reported at

    a. $1,775,000
    b. $2,250,000
    c. $2,375,000
    d. $3,975,000

2. Ral Corp.'s checkbook balance on December 31, 2010, was $5,000. In addition, Ral held the following items in its safe on that date:

Check payable to Ral Corp., dated January 2, 2011, in payment of a sale made in December 2010, not included in December 31 checkbook balance	$2,000
Check payable to Ral Corp., deposited December 15 and included in December 31 checkbook balance, but returned by bank on December 30 stamped "NSF." The check was redeposited on January 2, 2011, and cleared on January 9	500
Check drawn on Ral Corp.'s account, payable to a vendor, dated and recorded in Ral's books on December 31 but not mailed until January 10, 2011	300

The proper amount to be shown as Cash on Ral's balance sheet at December 31, 2010, is

    a. $4,800
    b. $5,300
    c. $6,500
    d. $6,800

3. Trans Co. had the following balances at December 31, 2010:

Cash in checking account	$ 35,000
Cash in money market account	75,000
US Treasury bill, purchased 11/1/2010, maturing 1/31/2011	350,000
US Treasury bill, purchased 12/1/2010, maturing 3/31/2011	400,000

Trans's policy is to treat as cash equivalents all highly liquid investments with a maturity of three months or less when purchased. What amount should Trans report as cash and cash equivalents in its December 31, 2010 balance sheet?

    a. $110,000
    b. $385,000
    c. $460,000
    d. $860,000

4. On October 31, 2010, Dingo, Inc. had cash accounts at three different banks. One account balance is segregated solely for a November 15, 2010 payment into a bond sinking fund. A second account, used for branch operations, is overdrawn. The third account, used for regular corporate operations, has a positive balance. How should these accounts be reported in Dingo's October 31, 2010 classified balance sheet?

    a. The segregated account should be reported as a noncurrent asset, the regular account should be reported as a current asset, and the overdraft should be reported as a current liability.
    b. The segregated and regular accounts should be reported as current assets, and the overdraft should be reported as a current liability.
    c. The segregated account should be reported as a noncurrent asset, and the regular account should be reported as a current asset net of the overdraft.
    d. The segregated and regular accounts should be reported as current assets net of the overdraft.

5. In preparing its August 31, 2010 bank reconciliation, Apex Corp. has available the following information:

Balance per bank statement, 8/31/10	$18,050
Deposit in transit, 8/31/10	3,250
Return of customer's check for insufficient funds, 8/31/10	600
Outstanding checks, 8/31/10	2,750
Bank service charges for August	100

At August 31, 2010, Apex's correct cash balance is

    a. $18,550
    b. $17,950
    c. $17,850
    d. $17,550

6. Poe, Inc. had the following bank reconciliation at March 31, 2010:

Balance per bank statement, 3/31/10	$46,500
Add deposit in transit	10,300
	56,800
Less outstanding checks	12,600
Balance per books, 3/31/10	$44,200

Data per bank for the month of April 2010 follow:

Deposits	$58,400
Disbursements	49,700

All reconciling items at March 31, 2010, cleared the bank in April. Outstanding checks at April 30, 2010, totaled $7,000. There were no deposits in transit at April 30, 2010. What is the cash balance per books at April 30, 2010?

    a. $48,200
    b. $52,900
    c. $55,200
    d. $58,500

7. On the December 31, 2010 balance sheet of Mann Co., the current receivables consisted of the following:

Trade accounts receivable	$ 93,000
Allowance for uncollectible accounts	(2,000)
Claim against shipper for goods lost in transit (November 2010)	3,000
Selling price of unsold goods sent by Mann on consignment at 130% of cost (**not** included in Mann's ending inventory)	26,000
Security deposit on lease of warehouse used for storing some inventories	30,000
Total	$150,000

At December 31, 2010, the correct total of Mann's current net receivables was

    a. $ 94,000
    b. $120,000
    c. $124,000
    d. $150,000

8. The following information relates to Jay Co.'s accounts receivable for 2010:

Accounts receivable, 1/1/10	$ 650,000
Credit sales for 2010	2,700,000
Sales returns for 2010	75,000
Accounts written off during 2010	40,000
Collections from customers during 2010	2,150,000
Estimated future sales returns at 12/31/10	50,000
Estimated uncollectible accounts at 12/31/10	110,000

What amount should Jay report for accounts receivable, before allowances for sales returns and uncollectible accounts, at December 31, 2010?

   a. $1,200,000
   b. $1,125,000
   c. $1,085,000
   d. $ 925,000

9. Frame Co. has an 8% note receivable dated June 30, 2008, in the original amount of $150,000. Payments of $50,000 in principal plus accrued interest are due annually on July 1, 2009, 2010, and 2011. In its June 30, 2010 balance sheet, what amount should Frame report as a current asset for interest on the note receivable?

   a. $0
   b. $ 4,000
   c. $ 8,000
   d. $12,000

10. On December 1, 2010, Tigg Mortgage Co. gave Pod Corp. a $200,000, 12% loan. Pod received proceeds of $194,000 after the deduction of a $6,000 nonrefundable loan origination fee. Principal and interest are due in sixty monthly installments of $4,450, beginning January 1, 2011. The repayments yield an effective interest rate of 12% at a present value of $200,000 and 13.4% at a present value of $194,000. Tigg does not elect the fair value option for recording the note to Pod. What amount of accrued interest receivable should Tigg include in its December 31, 2010 balance sheet?

   a. $4,450
   b. $2,166
   c. $2,000
   d. $0

11. On Merf's April 30, 2010 balance sheet a note receivable was reported as a noncurrent asset and its accrued interest for eight months was reported as a current asset. Which of the following terms would fit Merf's note receivable?

   a. Both principal and interest amounts are payable on August 31, 2010, and August 31, 2011.
   b. Principal and interest are due December 31, 2010.
   c. Both principal and interest amounts are payable on December 31, 2010, and December 31, 2011.
   d. Principal is due August 31, 2011, and interest is due August 31, 2010, and August 31, 2011.

12. On August 15, 2010, Benet Co. sold goods for which it received a note bearing the market rate of interest on that date. The four-month note was dated July 15, 2010. Note principal, together with all interest, is due November 15, 2010. Assume Benet did not elect the fair value option for reporting the note. When the note was recorded on August 15, which of the following accounts increased?

   a. Unearned discount.
   b. Interest receivable.

   c. Prepaid interest.
   d. Interest revenue.

13. Delta, Inc. sells to wholesalers on terms of 2/15, net 30. Delta has no cash sales but 50% of Delta's customers take advantage of the discount. Delta uses the gross method of recording sales and trade receivables. An analysis of Delta's trade receivables balances at December 31, 2010, revealed the following:

Age		Amount	Collectible
0 - 15	days	$100,000	100%
16 - 30	days	60,000	95%
31 - 60	days	5,000	90%
Over 60 days		2,500	$500
		$167,500	

In its December 31, 2010 balance sheet, what amount should Delta report for allowance for discounts?

   a. $1,000
   b. $1,620
   c. $1,675
   d. $2,000

14. Fenn Stores, Inc. had sales of $1,000,000 during December, 2010. Experience has shown that merchandise equaling 7% of sales will be returned within thirty days and an additional 3% will be returned within ninety days. Returned merchandise is readily resalable. In addition, merchandise equaling 15% of sales will be exchanged for merchandise of equal or greater value. What amount should Fenn report for net sales in its income statement for the month of December 2010?

   a. $900,000
   b. $850,000
   c. $780,000
   d. $750,000

15. At January 1, 2010, Jamin Co. had a credit balance of $260,000 in its allowance for uncollectible accounts. Based on past experience, 2% of Jamin's credit sales have been uncollectible. During 2010 Jamin wrote off $325,000 of uncollectible accounts. Credit sales for 2010 were $9,000,000. In its December 31, 2010 balance sheet, what amount should Jamin report as allowance for uncollectible accounts?

   a. $115,000
   b. $180,000
   c. $245,000
   d. $440,000

16. The following accounts were abstracted from Roxy Co.'s unadjusted trial balance at December 31, 2010:

	Debit	Credit
Accounts receivable	$1,000,000	
Allowance for uncollectible accounts	8,000	
Net credit sales		$3,000,000

Roxy estimates that 3% of the gross accounts receivable will become uncollectible. After adjustment at December 31, 2010, the allowance for uncollectible accounts should have a credit balance of

   a. $90,000
   b. $82,000
   c. $38,000
   d. $30,000

17. In its December 31 balance sheet, Butler Co. reported trade accounts receivable of $250,000 and related allowance for uncollectible accounts of $20,000. What is the total

amount of risk of accounting loss related to Butler's trade accounts receivable, and what amount of that risk is off-balance-sheet risk?

	Risk of accounting loss	Off-balance-sheet risk
a.	$0	$0
b.	$230,000	$0
c.	$230,000	$20,000
d.	$250,000	$20,000

18. Inge Co. determined that the net value of its accounts receivable at December 31, 2010, based on an aging of the receivables, was $325,000. Additional information is as follows:

Allowance for uncollectible accounts—1/1/10	$ 30,000
Uncollectible accounts written off during 2010	18,000
Uncollectible accounts recovered during 2010	2,000
Accounts receivable at 12/31/10	350,000

For 2010, what would be Inge's uncollectible accounts expense?

a. $ 5,000
b. $11,000
c. $15,000
d. $21,000

19. The following information pertains to Tara Co.'s accounts receivable at December 31, 2010:

Days outstanding	Amount	Estimated % uncollectible
0 – 60	$120,000	1%
61 – 120	90,000	2%
Over 120	100,000	6%
	$310,000	

During 2010, Tara wrote off $7,000 in receivables and recovered $4,000 that had been written off in prior years. Tara's December 31, 2009 allowance for uncollectible accounts was $22,000. Under the aging method, what amount of allowance for uncollectible accounts should Tara report at December 31, 2010?

a. $ 9,000
b. $10,000
c. $13,000
d. $19,000

20. A method of estimating uncollectible accounts that emphasizes asset valuation rather than income measurement is the allowance method based on

a. Aging the receivables.
b. Direct write-off.
c. Gross sales.
d. Credit sales less returns and allowances.

21. Which method of recording uncollectible accounts expense is consistent with accrual accounting?

	Allowance	Direct write-off
a.	Yes	Yes
b.	Yes	No
c.	No	Yes
d.	No	No

22. When the allowance method of recognizing uncollectible accounts is used, the entry to record the write-off of a specific account

a. Decreases both accounts receivable and the allowance for uncollectible accounts.
b. Decreases accounts receivable and increases the allowance for uncollectible accounts.

c. Increases the allowance for uncollectible accounts and decreases net income.
d. Decreases both accounts receivable and net income.

23. A company uses the allowance method to recognize uncollectible accounts expense. What is the effect at the time of the collection of an account previously written off on each of the following accounts?

	Allowance for uncollectible accounts	Uncollectible accounts expense
a.	No effect	Decrease
b.	Increase	Decrease
c.	Increase	No effect
d.	No effect	No effect

24. Which of the following is a method to generate cash from accounts receivables?

	Assignment	Factoring
a.	Yes	No
b.	Yes	Yes
c.	No	Yes
d.	No	No

25. Gar Co. factored its receivables. Control was surrendered in the transaction which was on a without recourse basis with Ross Bank. Gar received cash as a result of this transaction, which is best described as a

a. Loan from Ross collateralized by Gar's accounts receivable.
b. Loan from Ross to be repaid by the proceeds from Gar's accounts receivable.
c. Sale of Gar's accounts receivable to Ross, with the risk of uncollectible accounts retained by Gar.
d. Sale of Gar's accounts receivable to Ross, with the risk of uncollectible accounts transferred to Ross.

Items 26 through 28 are based on the following:

Taylored Corp. factored $400,000 of accounts receivable to Rich Corp. on July 1, 2010. Control was surrendered by Taylored. Rich accepted the receivables subject to recourse for nonpayment. Rich assessed a fee of 2% and retains a holdback equal to 5% of the accounts receivable. In addition, Rich charged 15% interest computed on a weighted-average time to maturity of the receivables of forty-one days. The fair value of the recourse obligation is $12,000.

26. Taylored will receive and record cash of
a. $385,260
b. $357,260
c. $365,260
d. $377,260

27. Which of the following statements is correct?
a. Rich should record an asset of $8,000 for the recourse obligation.
b. Taylored should record a liability and corresponding loss of $12,000 related to the recourse obligation.
c. Taylored should record a liability of $12,000, but no loss, related to the recourse obligation.
d. No entry for the recourse obligation should be made by Taylored or Rich until the debtor fails to pay.

28. Assuming all receivables are collected, Taylored's cost of factoring the receivables would be

- a. $ 8,000
- b. $34,740
- c. $42,740
- d. $14,740

29. Which of the following is used to account for probable sales discounts, sales returns, and sales allowances?

	Due from factor	*Recourse liability*
a.	Yes	No
b.	Yes	Yes
c.	No	Yes
d.	No	No

30. Scarbrough Corp. factored $600,000 of accounts receivable to Duff Corp. on October 1, 2010. Control was surrendered by Scarbrough. Duff accepted the receivables subject to recourse for nonpayment. Duff assessed a fee of 3% and retains a holdback equal to 5% of the accounts receivable. In addition, Duff charged 15% interest computed on a weighted-average time to maturity of the receivables of fifty-four days. The fair value of the recourse obligation is $9,000. Scarbrough will receive and record cash of

- a. $529,685
- b. $538,685
- c. $547,685
- d. $556,685

31. Synthia Corp. factored $750,000 of accounts receivable to Thomas Company on December 3, 2010. Control was surrendered by Synthia. Thomas accepted the receivables subject to recourse for nonpayment. Thomas assessed a fee of 2% and retains a holdback equal to 4% of the accounts receivable. In addition, Thomas charged 12% interest computed on a weighted-average time to maturity of the receivables of fifty-one days. The fair value of the recourse obligation is $15,000. Assuming all receivables are collected, Synthia's cost of factoring the receivables would be

- a. $12,575
- b. $15,000
- c. $27,575
- d. $42,575

32. Bannon Corp. transferred financial assets to Chapman, Inc. The transfer meets the conditions to be accounted for as a sale. As the transferor, Bannon should do each of the following, **except**

- a. Remove all assets sold from the balance sheet.
- b. Record all assets received and liabilities incurred as proceeds from the sale.
- c. Measure the assets received and liabilities incurred at cost.
- d. Recognize any gain or loss on the sale.

33. If financial assets are exchanged for cash or other consideration, but the transfer does not meet the criteria for a sale, the transferor and the transferee should account for the transaction as a

	Secured borrowing	*Pledge of collateral*
a.	No	Yes
b.	Yes	Yes
c.	Yes	No
d.	No	No

34. All but one of the following are required before a transfer of receivables can be recorded as a sale.

- a. The transferred receivables are beyond the reach of the transferor and its creditors.
- b. The transferor has not kept effective control over the transferred receivables through a repurchase agreement.
- c. The transferor maintains continuing involvement.
- d. The transferee can pledge or sell the transferred receivables.

35. Which of the following is not an objective for each entity accounting for transfers of financial assets?

- a. To derecognize assets when control is gained.
- b. To derecognize liabilities when extinguished.
- c. To recognize liabilities when incurred.
- d. To derecognize assets when control is given up.

36. Which of the following is false?

- a. A servicing asset shall be assessed for impairment based on its fair value.
- b. A servicing liability shall be assessed for increased obligation based on its fair value.
- c. An obligation to service financial assets may result in the recognition of a servicing asset or servicing liability.
- d. A servicing asset or liability should be amortized for a period of five years.

37. Fusion Corporation uses the amortization method to account for its servicing assets. Which of the following statements is true?

- a. Increases in fair value are reported in other comprehensive income.
- b. Increases in fair value are reported in earnings of the period.
- c. The assets are measured at fair value at the end of each reporting period.
- d. The assets are measured for impairment at the end of each reporting period.

38. According to ASC Topic 860, which of the following statements is true regarding servicing assets and servicing liabilities?

  I. Either the amortization method or the fair value method can be used.

  II. Once the fair value method is elected, the election cannot be reversed.

  III. Changes in fair value are reported in other comprehensive income for the period.

- a. I only.
- b. I and II.
- c. II only.
- d. I and III.

39. Binsar Corporation transfers a financial asset but continues to hold an interest in the servicing asset. How should the interest in the servicing asset that continues to be held be measured at the date of the transfer?

- a. At the present value of future cash flows.
- b. At fair value.
- c. By allocating the previous carrying amount between the assets sold and interest that continues to be held based on the relative fair values of the assets.
- d. At net realizable value.

40. Which of the following is true?
   a. A debtor may not grant a security interest in certain assets to a lender to serve as collateral with recourse.
   b. A debtor may not grant a security interest in certain assets to a lender to serve as collateral without recourse.
   c. The arrangement of having collateral transferred to a secured party is known as a pledge.
   d. Secured parties are never permitted to sell collateral held under a pledge.

Items 41 through 43 are based on the following:

Company ABC sells loans with a $2,200 fair value and a carrying amount of $2,000. ABC Company obtains an option to purchase similar loans and assumes a recourse obligation to repurchase loans. ABC Company also agrees to provide a floating rate of interest to the transferee company. The fair values are listed.

Fair values	
Cash proceeds	$2,100
Interest rate swap	140
Call option	80
Recourse obligation	(120)

41. What is the gain (loss) on the sale?
   a. $ 320
   b. $ 200
   c. $(100)
   d. $ 120

42. The journal entry to record the transfer for ABC Company includes
   a. A debit to call option.
   b. A credit to interest rate swap.
   c. A debit to loans.
   d. A credit to cash.

43. Assume for this problem that ABC Company agreed to service the loans without explicitly stating the compensation. The fair value of the service is $50. What are the net proceeds received and the gain (loss) on the sale?

	Net proceeds received	*Gain (loss)*
a.	$2,200	$ 200
b.	$2,250	$ 250
c.	$2,150	$ 150
d.	$2,200	$(250)

44. In accordance with accounting for transfers and servicing, financial assets subject to prepayment should be measured
   a. Like investments in debt securities classified as held-to-maturity.
   b. At cost.
   c. Like investments in debt securities classified as available-for-sale or trading.
   d. At fair value.

45. In accordance with accounting for transfers and servicing, all of the following would be disclosed except
   a. Policy for requiring collateral or other security due to repurchase agreements or securities lending transactions.
   b. Cash flows between the securitization special-purpose entity (SPE) and the transferor.
   c. Accounting policies for measuring retained interest.

   d. Description of assets or liabilities with estimable fair values.

46. Taft Inc. borrowed $1,000,000 from Wilson Company on July 2, 2009. As part of the loan agreement, Taft granted Wilson a security interest in land that originally cost $750,000 when it was acquired by Taft in 2002. The land had a fair value of $900,000 on July 2, 2009. In June 2010, Taft defaulted on its loan to Wilson, and the land was transferred to Wilson in full settlement of the debt on June 30. The land had a fair value of $950,000 on June 30, 2010. What amount should Wilson record for land on June 30, 2010?
   a. $0
   b. $750,000
   c. $900,000
   d. $950,000

47. Lyle, Inc. is preparing its financial statements for the year ended December 31, 2010. Accounts payable amounted to $360,000 before any necessary year-end adjustment related to the following:

   • At December 31, 2010, Lyle has a $50,000 debit balance in its accounts payable to Ross, a supplier, resulting from a $50,000 advance payment for goods to be manufactured to Lyle's specifications.
   • Checks in the amount of $100,000 were written to vendors and recorded on December 29, 2010. The checks were mailed on January 5, 2011.

What amount should Lyle report as accounts payable in its December 31, 2010 balance sheet?
   a. $510,000
   b. $410,000
   c. $310,000
   d. $210,000

48. Rabb Co. records its purchases at gross amounts but wishes to change to recording purchases net of purchase discounts. Discounts available on purchases recorded from October 1, 2009, to September 30, 2010, totaled $2,000. Of this amount, $200 is still available in the accounts payable balance. The balances in Rabb's accounts as of and for the year ended September 30, 2010, before conversion are

Purchases	$100,000
Purchase discounts taken	800
Accounts payable	30,000

What is Rabb's accounts payable balance as of September 30, 2010, after the conversion?
   a. $29,800
   b. $29,200
   c. $28,800
   d. $28,200

49. On March 1, 2009, Fine Co. borrowed $10,000 and signed a two-year note bearing interest at 12% per annum compounded annually. Interest is payable in full at maturity on February 28, 2011. What amount should Fine report as a liability for accrued interest at December 31, 2010?
   a. $0
   b. $1,000
   c. $1,200
   d. $2,320

50. On September 1, 2009, Brak Co. borrowed on a $1,350,000 note payable from Federal Bank. The note bears interest at 12% and is payable in three equal annual principal payments of $450,000. On this date, the bank's prime rate was 11%. The first annual payment for interest and principal was made on September 1, 2010. At December 31, 2010, what amount should Brak report as accrued interest payable?

    a. $54,000
    b. $49,500
    c. $36,000
    d. $33,000

51. In its 2010 financial statements, Cris Co. reported interest expense of $85,000 in its income statement and cash paid for interest of $68,000 in its cash flow statement. There was no prepaid interest or interest capitalization either at the beginning or end of 2010. Accrued interest at December 31, 2009, was $15,000. What amount should Cris report as accrued interest payable in its December 31, 2010 balance sheet?

    a. $ 2,000
    b. $15,000
    c. $17,000
    d. $32,000

52. Ames, Inc. has $500,000 of notes payable due June 15, 2011. Ames signed an agreement on December 1, 2010, to borrow up to $500,000 to refinance the notes payable on a long-term basis with no payments due until 2011. The financing agreement stipulated that borrowings may not exceed 80% of the value of the collateral Ames was providing. At the date of issuance of the December 31, 2010 financial statements, the value of the collateral was $600,000 and is not expected to fall below this amount during 2011. In Ames' December 31, 2010 balance sheet, the obligation for these notes payable should be classified as

	Short-term	Long-term
a.	$500,000	$0
b.	$100,000	$400,000
c.	$ 20,000	$480,000
d.	$0	$500,000

53. A company issued a short-term note payable with a stated 12% rate of interest to a bank. The bank charged a .5% loan origination fee and remitted the balance to the company. The effective interest rate paid by the company in this transaction would be

    a.   Equal to 12.5%.
    b.   More than 12.5%.
    c.   Less than 12.5%.
    d.   Independent of 12.5%.

54. Cali, Inc. had a $4,000,000 note payable due on March 15, 2011. On January 28, 2011, before the issuance of its 2010 financial statements, Cali issued long-term bonds in the amount of $4,500,000. Proceeds from the bonds were used to repay the note when it came due. How should Cali classify the note in its December 31, 2011 financial statements?

    a.   As a current liability, with separate disclosure of the note refinancing.
    b.   As a current liability, with no separate disclosure required.
    c.   As a noncurrent liability, with separate disclosure of the note refinancing.
    d.   As a noncurrent liability, with no separate disclosure required.

55. On December 31, 2010, Largo, Inc. had a $750,000 note payable outstanding, due July 31, 2011. Largo borrowed the money to finance construction of a new plant. Largo planned to refinance the note by issuing long-term bonds. Because Largo temporarily had excess cash, it prepaid $250,000 of the note on January 12, 2011. In February 2011, Largo completed a $1,500,000 bond offering. Largo will use the bond offering proceeds to repay the note payable at its maturity and to pay construction costs during 2011. On March 3, 2011, Largo issued its 2010 financial statements. What amount of the note payable should Largo include in the current liabilities section of its December 31, 2010 balance sheet?

    a. $750,000
    b. $500,000
    c. $250,000
    d. $0

56. Rice Co. salaried employees are paid biweekly. Advances made to employees are paid back by payroll deductions. Information relating to salaries follows:

	12/31/09	12/31/10
Employee advances	$24,000	$ 36,000
Accrued salaries payable	40,000	?
Salaries expense during the year		420,000
Salaries paid during the year (gross)		390,000

In Rice's December 31, 2010 balance sheet, accrued salaries payable was

    a. $94,000
    b. $82,000
    c. $70,000
    d. $30,000

57. Fay Corp. pays its outside salespersons fixed monthly salaries and commissions on net sales. Sales commissions are computed and paid on a monthly basis (in the month following the month of sale), and the fixed salaries are treated as advances against commissions. However, if the fixed salaries for salespersons exceed their sales commissions earned for a month, such excess is not charged back to them. Pertinent data for the month of March 2010 for the three salespersons are as follows:

Salesperson	Fixed salary	Net sales	Commission rate
A	$10,000	$ 200,000	4%
B	14,000	400,000	6%
C	18,000	600,000	6%
Totals	$42,000	$1,200,000	

What amount should Fay accrue for sales commissions payable at March 31, 2010?

    a. $70,000
    b. $68,000
    c. $28,000
    d. $26,000

58. Lime Co.'s payroll for the month ended January 31, 2010, is summarized as follows:

Total wages	$10,000
Federal income tax withheld	1,200

All wages paid were subject to FICA. FICA tax rates were 7% each for employee and employer. Lime remits payroll taxes on the 15th of the following month. In its financial statements for the month ended January 31, 2010, what amounts should Lime report as total payroll tax liability and as payroll tax expense?

	Liability	Expense
a.	$1,200	$1,400
b.	$1,900	$1,400
c.	$1,900	$ 700
d.	$2,600	$ 700

59. Under state law, Acme may pay 3% of eligible gross wages or it may reimburse the state directly for actual unemployment claims. Acme believes that actual unemployment claims will be 2% of eligible gross wages and has chosen to reimburse the state. Eligible gross wages are defined as the first $10,000 of gross wages paid to each employee. Acme had five employees, each of whom earned $20,000 during 2010. In its December 31, 2010 balance sheet, what amount should Acme report as accrued liability for unemployment claims?

a. $1,000
b. $1,500
c. $2,000
d. $3,000

60. Pine Corp. is required to contribute, to an employee stock ownership plan (ESOP), 10% of its income after deduction for this contribution but before income tax. Pine's income before charges for the contribution and income tax was $75,000. The income tax rate is 30%. What amount should be accrued as a contribution to the ESOP?

a. $7,500
b. $6,818
c. $5,250
d. $4,773

61. Able Co. provides an incentive compensation plan under which its president receives a bonus equal to 10% of the corporation's income before income tax but after deduction of the bonus. If the tax rate is 40% and net income after bonus and income tax was $360,000, what was the amount of the bonus?

a. $36,000
b. $60,000
c. $66,000
d. $90,000

62. Ivy Co. operates a retail store. All items are sold subject to a 6% state sales tax, which Ivy collects and records as sales revenue. Ivy files quarterly sales tax returns when due, by the twentieth day following the end of the sales quarter. However, in accordance with state requirements, Ivy remits sales tax collected by the twentieth day of the month following any month such collections exceed $500. Ivy takes these payments as credits on the quarterly sales tax return. The sales taxes paid by Ivy are charged against sales revenue.

Following is a monthly summary appearing in Ivy's first quarter 2010 sales revenue account:

	Debit	Credit
January	$ --	$10,600
February	600	7,420
March	--	8,480
	$600	$26,500

In its March 31, 2010 balance sheet, what amount should Ivy report as sales taxes payable?

a. $ 600
b. $ 900
c. $1,500
d. $1,590

63. Hudson Hotel collects 15% in city sales taxes on room rentals, in addition to a $2 per room, per night, occupancy tax. Sales taxes for each month are due at the end of the following month, and occupancy taxes are due fifteen days after the end of each calendar quarter. On January 3, 2011, Hudson paid its November 2010 sales taxes and its fourth quarter 2010 occupancy taxes. Additional information pertaining to Hudson's operations is

2010	Room rentals	Room nights
October	$100,000	1,100
November	110,000	1,200
December	150,000	1,800

What amounts should Hudson report as sales taxes payable and occupancy taxes payable in its December 31, 2010 balance sheet?

	Sales taxes	Occupancy taxes
a.	$39,000	$6,000
b.	$39,000	$8,200
c.	$54,000	$6,000
d.	$54,000	$8,200

64. On July 1, 2010, Ran County issued realty tax assessments for its fiscal year ended June 30, 2011. On September 1, 2010, Day Co. purchased a warehouse in Ran County. The purchase price was reduced by a credit for accrued realty taxes. Day did not record the entire year's real estate tax obligation, but instead records tax expenses at the end of each month by adjusting prepaid real estate taxes or real estate taxes payable, as appropriate. On November 1, 2010, Day paid the first of two equal installments of $12,000 for realty taxes. What amount of this payment should Day record as a debit to real estate taxes payable?

a. $ 4,000
b. $ 8,000
c. $10,000
d. $12,000

65. Kemp Co. must determine the December 31, 2010 year-end accruals for advertising and rent expenses. A $500 advertising bill was received January 7, 2011, comprising costs of $375 for advertisements in December 2010 issues, and $125 for advertisements in January 2011 issues of the newspaper.

A store lease, effective December 16, 2009, calls for fixed rent of $1,200 per month, payable one month from the effective date and monthly thereafter. In addition, rent equal to 5% of net sales over $300,000 per calendar year is payable on January 31 of the following year. Net sales for 2010 were $550,000.

In its December 31, 2010 balance sheet, Kemp should report accrued liabilities of

a. $12,875
b. $13,000
c. $13,100
d. $13,475

66. On May 1, 2010, Marno County issued property tax assessments for the fiscal year ended June 30, 2011. The first of two equal installments was due on November 1, 2010. On September 1, 2010, Dyur Co. purchased a four-year-old factory in Marno subject to an allowance for accrued taxes. Dyur did not record the entire year's property tax obligation, but instead records tax expenses at the end of each month by adjusting prepaid property taxes or property taxes payable, as appropriate. The recording of the November 1, 2010 payment by Dyur should have been allocated between an increase in prepaid property taxes and a decrease in property taxes payable in which of the following percentages?

	Percentage allocated to	
	Increase in pre-paid property taxes	Decrease in property taxes payable
a.	66 2/3%	33 1/3%
b.	0%	100%
c.	50%	50%
d.	33 1/3%	66 2/3%

67. Black Co. requires advance payments with special orders for machinery constructed to customer specifications. These advances are nonrefundable. Information for 2010 is as follows:

Customer advances—balance 12/31/09	$118,000
Advances received with orders in 2010	184,000
Advances applied to orders shipped in 2010	164,000
Advances applicable to orders cancelled in 2010	50,000

In Black's December 31, 2010 balance sheet, what amount should be reported as a current liability for advances from customer?

a. $0
b. $ 88,000
c. $138,000
d. $148,000

68. Marr Co. sells its products in reusable containers. The customer is charged a deposit for each container delivered and receives a refund for each container returned within two years after the year of delivery. Marr accounts for the containers not returned within the time limit as being retired by sale at the deposit amount. Information for 2010 is as follows:

Container deposits at December 31, 2009, from deliveries in

2008	$150,000	
2009	430,000	$580,000
Deposits for containers delivered in 2010		780,000
Deposits for containers returned in 2010 from deliveries in		
2008	$ 90,000	
2009	250,000	
2010	286,000	626,000

In Marr's December 31, 2010 balance sheet, the liability for deposits on returnable containers should be

a. $494,000
b. $584,000
c. $674,000
d. $734,000

69. Kent Co., a division of National Realty, Inc., maintains escrow accounts and pays real estate taxes for National's mortgage customers. Escrow funds are kept in interest-bearing accounts. Interest, less a 10% service fee, is credited to the mortgagee's account and used to reduce future escrow payments. Additional information follows:

Escrow accounts liability, 1/1/10	$ 700,000
Escrow payments received during 2010	1,580,000
Real estate taxes paid during 2010	1,720,000
Interest on escrow funds during 2010	50,000

What amount should Kent report as escrow accounts liability in its December 31, 2010 balance sheet?

a. $510,000
b. $515,000
c. $605,000
d. $610,000

70. Cobb Company sells appliance service contracts agreeing to repair appliances for a two-year period. Cobb's past experience is that, of the total dollars spent for repairs on service contracts, 40% is incurred evenly during the first contract year and 60% evenly during the second contract year. Receipts from service contract sales for the two years ended December 31, 2010, are as follows:

2009	$500,000
2010	600,000

Receipts from contracts are credited to unearned service contract revenue. Assume that all contract sales are made evenly during the year. What amount should Cobb report as unearned service contract revenue at December 31, 2010?

a. $360,000
b. $470,000
c. $480,000
d. $630,000

71. Toddler Care Co. offers three payment plans on its twelve-month contracts. Information on the three plans and the number of children enrolled in each plan for the September 1, 2010 through August 31, 2011 contract year follows:

Plan	Initial payment per child	Monthly fees per child	Number of children
#1	$500	$ --	15
#2	200	30	12
#3	--	50	9
			36

Toddler received $9,900 of initial payments on September 1, 2010, and $3,240 of monthly fees during the period September 1 through December 31, 2010. In its December 31, 2010 balance sheet, what amount should Toddler report as deferred revenues?

a. $3,300
b. $4,380
c. $6,600
d. $9,900

72. A retail store received cash and issued gift certificates that are redeemable in merchandise. The gift certificates lapse one year after they are issued. How would the deferred revenue account be affected by each of the following transactions?

	Redemption of certificates	Lapse of certificates
a.	Decrease	No effect
b.	Decrease	Decrease
c.	No effect	No effect
d.	No effect	Decrease

73. On March 31, 2010, Dallas Co. received an advance payment of 60% of the sales price for special-order goods to be manufactured and delivered within five months. At the same time, Dallas subcontracted for production of the special-order goods at a price equal to 40% of the main contract price. What liabilities should be reported in Dallas' March 31, 2010 balance sheet?

	Deferred revenues	Payables to subcontractor
a.	None	None
b.	60% of main contract price	40% of main contract price
c.	60% of main contract price	None
d.	None	40% of main contract price

74. In June 2010, Northan Retailers sold refundable merchandise coupons. Northan received $10 for each coupon redeemable from July 1 to December 31, 2010, for merchandise with a retail price of $11. At June 30, 2010, how should Northan report these coupon transactions?
  a. Unearned revenues at the merchandise's retail price.
  b. Unearned revenues at the cash received amount.
  c. Revenues at the merchandise's retail price.
  d. Revenues at the cash received amount.

75. Delect Co. provides repair services for the AZ195 TV set. Customers prepay the fee on the standard one-year service contract. The 2009 and 2010 contracts were identical, and the number of contracts outstanding was substantially the same at the end of each year. However, Delect's December 31, 2010 deferred revenues' balance on unperformed service contracts was significantly less than the balance at December 31, 2009. Which of the following situations might account for this reduction in the deferred revenue balance?
  a. Most 2010 contracts were signed later in the calendar year than were the 2009 contracts.
  b. Most 2010 contracts were signed earlier in the calendar year than were the 2009 contracts.
  c. The 2010 contract contribution margin was greater than the 2009 contract contribution margin.
  d. The 2010 contribution margin was less than the 2009 contract contribution margin.

76. Brad Corp. has unconditional purchase obligations associated with product financing arrangements. These obligations are reported as liabilities on Brad's balance sheet, with the related assets also recognized. In the notes to Brad's financial statements, the aggregate amount of payments for these obligations should be disclosed for each of how many years following the date of the latest balance sheet?
  a. 0
  b. 1
  c. 5
  d. 10

77. On January 17, 2010, an explosion occurred at a Sims Co. plant causing extensive property damage to area buildings. Although no claims had yet been asserted against Sims by March 10, 2010, Sims' management and counsel concluded that it is likely that claims will be asserted and that it is reasonably possible Sims will be responsible for damages. Sims' management believed that $1,250,000 would be a reasonable estimate of its liability. Sims' $5,000,000 comprehensive public liability policy has a $250,000 deductible clause. In Sims' December 31, 2009 financial statements, which were issued on March 25, 2010, how should this item be reported?
  a. As an accrued liability of $250,000.
  b. As a footnote disclosure indicating the possible loss of $250,000.
  c. As a footnote disclosure indicating the possible loss of $1,250,000.
  d. No footnote disclosure or accrual is necessary.

78. Brite Corp. had the following liabilities at December 31, 2010:

Accounts payable	$55,000
Unsecured notes, 8%, due 7/1/11	400,000
Accrued expenses	35,000
Contingent liability	450,000
Deferred income tax liability	25,000
Senior bonds, 7%, due 3/31/11	1,000,000

The contingent liability is an accrual for possible losses on a $1,000,000 lawsuit filed against Brite. Brite's legal counsel expects the suit to be settled in 2012, and has estimated that Brite will be liable for damages in the range of $450,000 to $750,000.

The deferred income tax liability is not related to an asset for financial reporting and is expected to reverse in 2012.

What amount should Brite report in its December 31, 2010 balance sheet for current liabilities?
  a. $ 515,000
  b. $ 940,000
  c. $1,490,000
  d. $1,515,000

79. On February 5, 2011, an employee filed a $2,000,000 lawsuit against Steel Co. for damages suffered when one of Steel's plants exploded on December 29, 2010. Steel's legal counsel expects the company will lose the lawsuit and estimates the loss to be between $500,000 and $1,000,000. The employee has offered to settle the lawsuit out of court for $900,000, but Steel will not agree to the settlement. In its December 31, 2010 balance sheet, what amount should Steel report as liability from lawsuit?
  a. $2,000,000
  b. $1,000,000
  c. $ 900,000
  d. $ 500,000

80. On November 5, 2010, a Dunn Corp. truck was in an accident with an auto driven by Bell. Dunn received notice on January 12, 2011, of a lawsuit for $700,000 damages for personal injuries suffered by Bell. Dunn Corp.'s counsel believes it is probable that Bell will be awarded an estimated amount in the range between $200,000 and $450,000, and that $300,000 is a better estimate of potential liability than any other amount. Dunn's accounting year ends on December 31, and the 2010 financial statements were issued on March 2, 2011. What amount of loss should Dunn accrue at December 31, 2010?
  a. $0
  b. $200,000
  c. $300,000
  d. $450,000

81. During 2010, Haft Co. became involved in a tax dispute with the IRS. At December 31, 2010, Haft's tax advisor believed that an unfavorable outcome was probable. A reasonable estimate of additional taxes was $200,000 but could be as much as $300,000. After the 2010 financial statements were issued, Haft received and accepted an IRS settlement offer of $275,000. What amount of accrued liability should Haft have reported in its December 31, 2010 balance sheet?
  a. $200,000
  b. $250,000
  c. $275,000
  d. $300,000

82. Management can estimate the amount of loss that will occur if a foreign government expropriates some company assets. If expropriation is reasonably possible, a loss contingency should be

a. Disclosed but not accrued as a liability.
b. Disclosed and accrued as a liability.
c. Accrued as a liability but not disclosed.
d. Neither accrued as a liability nor disclosed.

83. Invern, Inc. has a self-insurance plan. Each year, retained earnings is appropriated for contingencies in an amount equal to insurance premiums saved less recognized losses from lawsuits and other claims. As a result of a 2010 accident, Invern is a defendant in a lawsuit in which it will probably have to pay damages of $190,000. What are the effects of this lawsuit's probable outcome on Invern's 2010 financial statements?
a. An increase in expenses and no effect on liabilities.
b. An increase in both expenses and liabilities.
c. No effect on expenses and an increase in liabilities.
d. No effect on either expenses or liabilities.

84. In 2009, a personal injury lawsuit was brought against Halsey Co. Based on counsel's estimate, Halsey reported a $50,000 liability in its December 31, 2009 balance sheet. In November 2010, Halsey received a favorable judgment, requiring the plaintiff to reimburse Halsey for expenses of $30,000. The plaintiff has appealed the decision, and Halsey's counsel is unable to predict the outcome of the appeal. In its December 31, 2010 balance sheet, Halsey should report what amounts of asset and liability related to these legal actions?

	Asset	Liability
a.	$30,000	$50,000
b.	$30,000	$0
c.	$0	$20,000
d.	$0	$0

85. During January 2010, Haze Corp. won a litigation award for $15,000 that was tripled to $45,000 to include punitive damages. The defendant, who is financially stable, has appealed only the $30,000 punitive damages. Haze was awarded $50,000 in an unrelated suit it filed, which is being appealed by the defendant. Counsel is unable to estimate the outcome of these appeals. In its 2010 financial statements, Haze should report what amount of pretax gain?
a. $15,000
b. $45,000
c. $50,000
d. $95,000

86. In May 2006 Caso Co. filed suit against Wayne, Inc. seeking $1,900,000 damages for patent infringement. A court verdict in November 2010 awarded Caso $1,500,000 in damages, but Wayne's appeal is not expected to be decided before 2012. Caso's counsel believes it is probable that Caso will be successful against Wayne for an estimated amount in the range between $800,000 and $1,100,000, with $1,000,000 considered the most likely amount. What amount should Caso record as income from the lawsuit in the year ended December 31, 2010?
a. $0
b. $ 800,000
c. $1,000,000
d. $1,500,000

87. During 2010, Smith Co. filed suit against West, Inc. seeking damages for patent infringement. At December 31, 2010, Smith's legal counsel believed that it was probable that Smith would be successful against West for an esti-

mated amount in the range of $75,000 to $150,000, with all amounts in the range considered equally likely. In March 2011, Smith was awarded $100,000 and received full payment thereof. In its 2010 financial statements, issued in February 2011 how should this award be reported?
a. As a receivable and revenue of $100,000.
b. As a receivable and deferred revenue of $100,000.
c. As a disclosure of a contingent gain of $100,000.
d. As a disclosure of a contingent gain of an undetermined amount in the range of $75,000 to $150,000.

88. In 2010, a contract dispute between Dollis Co. and Brooks Co. was submitted to binding arbitration. In 2010, each party's attorney indicated privately that the probable award in Dollis' favor could be reasonably estimated. In 2011, the arbitrator decided in favor of Dollis. When should Dollis and Brooks recognize their respective gain and loss?

	Dollis' gain	Brooks' loss
a.	2010	2010
b.	2010	2011
c.	2011	2010
d.	2011	2011

89. Eagle Co. has cosigned the mortgage note on the home of its president, guaranteeing the indebtedness in the event that the president should default. Eagle considers the likelihood of default to be remote. How should the guarantee be treated in Eagle's financial statements?
a. Disclosed only.
b. Accrued only.
c. Accrued and disclosed.
d. Neither accrued nor disclosed.

90. North Corp. has an employee benefit plan for compensated absences that gives employees 10 paid vacation days and 10 paid sick days. Both vacation and sick days can be carried over indefinitely. Employees can elect to receive payment in lieu of vacation days; however, no payment is given for sick days not taken. At December 31, 2010, North's unadjusted balance of liability for compensated absences was $21,000. North estimated that there were 150 vacation days and 75 sick days available at December 31, 2010. North's employees earn an average of $100 per day. In its December 31, 2010 balance sheet, what amount of liability for compensated absences is North required to report?
a. $36,000
b. $22,500
c. $21,000
d. $15,000

91. Ross Co. pays all salaried employees on a Monday for the five-day workweek ended the previous Friday. The last payroll recorded for the year ended December 31, 2010, was for the week ended December 25, 2010. The payroll for the week ended January 1, 2011, included regular weekly salaries of $80,000 and vacation pay of $25,000 for vacation time earned in 2010 not taken by December 31, 2010. Ross had accrued a liability of $20,000 for vacation pay at December 31, 2009. In its December 31, 2010 balance sheet, what amount should Ross report as accrued salary and vacation pay?
a. $64,000
b. $68,000
c. $69,000
d. $89,000

92. Gavin Co. grants all employees two weeks of paid vacation for each full year of employment. Unused vacation time can be accumulated and carried forward to succeeding years and will be paid at the salaries in effect when vacations are taken or when employment is terminated. There was no employee turnover in 2010. Additional information relating to the year ended December 31, 2010, is as follows:

Liability for accumulated vacations at 12/31/09	$35,000
Pre-2008 accrued vacations taken from 1/1/10 to 9/30/10 (the authorized period for vacations)	20,000
Vacations earned for work in 2010 (adjusted to current rates)	30,000

Gavin granted a 10% salary increase to all employees on October 1, 2010, its annual salary increase date. For the year ended December 31, 2010, Gavin should report vacation pay expense of
- a. $45,000
- b. $33,500
- c. $31,500
- d. $30,000

93. At December 31, 2010, Taos Co. estimates that its employees have earned vacation pay of $100,000. Employees will receive their vacation pay in 2011. Should Taos accrue a liability at December 31, 2010, if the rights to this compensation accumulated over time or if the rights are vested?

	Accumulated	*Vested*
a.	Yes	No
b.	No	No
c.	Yes	Yes
d.	No	Yes

94. If the payment of employees' compensation for future absences is probable, the amount can be reasonably estimated, and the obligation relates to rights that accumulate, the compensation should be
- a. Accrued if attributable to employees' services not already rendered.
- b. Accrued if attributable to employees' services already rendered.
- c. Accrued if attributable to employees' services whether already rendered or not.
- d. Recognized when paid.

95. During 2009, Gum Co. introduced a new product carrying a two-year warranty against defects. The estimated warranty costs related to dollar sales are 2% within twelve months following the sale and 4% in the second twelve months following the sale. Sales and actual warranty expenditures for the years ended December 31, 2009 and 2010, are as follows:

	Sales	*Actual warranty expenditures*
2009	$150,000	$2,250
2010	250,000	7,500
	$400,000	$9,750

What amount should Gum report as estimated warranty liability in its December 31, 2010 balance sheet?
- a. $ 2,500
- b. $ 4,250
- c. $11,250
- d. $14,250

96. Vadis Co. sells appliances that include a three-year warranty. Service calls under the warranty are performed by an independent mechanic under a contract with Vadis. Based on experience, warranty costs are estimated at $30 for each machine sold. When should Vadis recognize these warranty costs?
- a. Evenly over the life of the warranty.
- b. When the service calls are performed.
- c. When payments are made to the mechanic.
- d. When the machines are sold.

97. Lute Corporation sells furnaces that include a three-year warranty. Lute can contract with a third party to provide these warranty services. Lute elects the fair value option for reporting financial liabilities. At what amount should Lute record the warranty liability on the balance sheet?
- a. The cost of expected warranty services.
- b. The present value of expected warranty costs.
- c. The fair value of the contract to settle the warranty services.
- d. The fair value of the contract to settle less the cost to provide services.

98. Case Cereal Co. frequently distributes coupons to promote new products. On October 1, 2010, Case mailed 1,000,000 coupons for $.45 off each box of cereal purchased. Case expects 120,000 of these coupons to be redeemed before the December 31, 2010, expiration date. It takes thirty days from the redemption date for Case to receive the coupons from the retailers. Case reimburses the retailers an additional $.05 for each coupon redeemed. As of December 31, 2010, Case had paid retailers $25,000 related to these coupons and had 50,000 coupons on hand that had not been processed for payment. What amount should Case report as a liability for coupons in its December 31, 2010 balance sheet?
- a. $35,000
- b. $29,000
- c. $25,000
- d. $22,500

99. Dunn Trading Stamp Co. records stamp service revenue and provides for the cost of redemptions in the year stamps are sold to licensees. Dunn's past experience indicates that only 80% of the stamps sold to licensees will be redeemed. Dunn's liability for stamp redemptions was $6,000,000 at December 31, 2009. Additional information for 2010 is as follows:

Stamp service revenue from stamps sold to licensees	$4,000,000
Cost of redemptions (stamps sold prior to 1/1/10)	2,750,000

If all the stamps sold in 2010 were presented for redemption in 2011, the redemption cost would be $2,250,000. What amount should Dunn report as a liability for stamp redemptions at December 31, 2010?
- a. $7,250,000
- b. $5,500,000
- c. $5,050,000
- d. $3,250,000

Items 100 and 101 are based on the following:

The following trial balance of Trey Co. at December 31, 2010, has been adjusted except for income tax expense.

	Dr.	Cr.
Cash	$ 550,000	
Accounts receivable, net	1,650,000	
Prepaid taxes	300,000	
Accounts payable		$ 120,000
Common stock		500,000
Additional paid-in capital		680,000
Retained earnings		630,000
Foreign currency transla-		
tion adjustment	430,000	
Revenues		3,600,000
Expenses	2,600,000	
	$5,530,000	$5,530,000

Additional information

- During 2010, estimated tax payments of $300,000 were charged to prepaid taxes. Trey has not yet recorded income tax expense. There were no differences between financial statement and income tax income, and Trey's tax rate is 30%.
- Included in accounts receivable is $500,000 due from a customer. Special terms granted to this customer require payment in equal semiannual installments of $125,000 every April 1 and October 1.

100. In Trey's December 31, 2010 balance sheet, what amount should be reported as total current assets?

- a. $1,950,000
- b. $2,200,000
- c. $2,250,000
- d. $2,500,000

101. In Trey's December 31, 2010 balance sheet, what amount should be reported as total retained earnings?

- a. $1,029,000
- b. $1,200,000
- c. $1,330,000
- d. $1,630,000

102. The following is Gold Corp.'s June 30, 2010 trial balance:

Cash overdraft		$ 10,000
Accounts receivable, net	$ 35,000	
Inventory	58,000	
Prepaid expenses	12,000	
Land held for resale	100,000	
Property, plant, and equipment, net	95,000	
Accounts payable and accrued expenses		32,000
Common stock		25,000
Additional paid-in capital		150,000
Retained earnings		83,000
	$300,000	$300,000

Additional information

- Checks amounting to $30,000 were written to vendors and recorded on June 29, 2010, resulting in a cash overdraft of $10,000. The checks were mailed on July 9, 2010.
- Land held for resale was sold for cash on July 15, 2010.
- Gold issued its financial statements on July 31, 2010.

In its June 30, 2010 balance sheet, what amount should Gold report as current assets?

- a. $225,000
- b. $205,000
- c. $195,000
- d. $125,000

103. **Mill** Co.'s trial balance included the following account balances at December 31, 2010:

Accounts payable	$15,000
Bonds payable, due 2011	25,000
Discount on bonds payable, due 2011	3,000
Dividends payable 1/31/11	8,000
Notes payable, due 2012	20,000

What amount should be included in the current liability section of Mill's December 31, 2010 balance sheet?

- a. $45,000
- b. $51,000
- c. $65,000
- d. $78,000

Items 104 and 105 are based on the following:

Rey, Inc.
SELECTED FINANCIAL DATA
December 31,

	2010	2009
Cash	$ 170,000	$ 90,000
Accounts receivable (net)	450,000	400,000
Merchandise inventory	540,000	420,000
Short-term marketable securities	80,000	40,000
Land and building (net)	1,000,000	1,000,000
Mortgage payable—current portion	60,000	50,000
Accounts payable and accrued liabili-		
ties	240,000	220,000
Short-term notes payable	100,000	140,000

Net credit sales totaled $3,000,000 and $2,000,000 for the years ended December 31, 2010 and 2009, respectively.

104. At December 31, 2010, Rey's quick (acid-test) ratio was

- a. 1.50 to 1.
- b. 1.75 to 1.
- c. 2.06 to 1.
- d. 3.10 to 1.

105. For 2010, Rey's accounts receivable turnover was

- a. 1.13
- b. 1.50
- c. 6.67
- d. 7.06

106. Which of the following ratios is(are) useful in assessing a company's ability to meet currently maturing or short-term obligations?

	Acid-test ratio	Debt to equity ratio
a.	No	No
b.	No	Yes
c.	Yes	Yes
d.	Yes	No

107. North Bank is analyzing Belle Corp.'s financial statements for a possible extension of credit. Belle's quick ratio is significantly better than the industry average. Which of the following factors should North consider as a possible limitation of using this ratio when evaluating Belle's creditworthiness?

- a. Fluctuating market prices of short-term investments may adversely affect the ratio.
- b. Increasing market prices for Belle's inventory may adversely affect the ratio.
- c. Belle may need to sell its available-for-sale investments to meet its current obligations.
- d. Belle may need to liquidate its inventory to meet its long-term obligations.

108. On December 30, 2010, Vida Co. had cash of $200,000, a current ratio of 1.5:1 and a quick ratio of .5:1. On December 31, 2010, all cash was used to reduce accounts payable. How did these cash payments affect the ratios?

	Current ratio	Quick ratio
a.	Increased	Decreased
b.	Increased	No effect
c.	Decreased	Increased
d.	Decreased	No effect

109. Tod Corp. wrote off $100,000 of obsolete inventory at December 31, 2010. The effect of this write-off was to decrease

a. Both the current and acid-test ratios.
b. Only the current ratio.
c. Only the acid-test ratio.
d. Neither the current nor the acid-test ratios.

110. The following computations were made from Clay Co.'s 2010 books:

Number of days' sales in inventory	61
Number of days' sales in accounts receivable	33

What was the number of days in Clay's 2010 operating cycle?

a. 33
b. 47
c. 61
d. 94

111. On December 31, 2010, Northpark Co. collected a receivable due from a major customer. Which of the following ratios would be increased by this transaction?

a. Inventory turnover ratio.
b. Receivable turnover ratio.
c. Current ratio.
d. Quick ratio.

SIMULATION PROBLEMS

Simulation Problem 1   (50 to 60 minutes)

Instructions					
	Concepts	Journal Entries	Reporting Requirements	Communication	Research

Chester Company has transactions involving current assets and current liabilities. Complete the various components of the simulation for Chester.

	Concepts				
Instructions		Journal Entries	Reporting Requirements	Communication	Research

Determine whether each statement is True or False.

	True	*False*
1. The balance in "factor's holdback" (due from factor) is reported as an expense of the period.	○	○
2. In a specific assignment of receivables, collections on the assigned accounts are generally remitted to the assignor.	○	○
3. Factors are banks or finance companies that purchase receivables for a fee and then collect the remittances directly from the selling company.	○	○
4. A transfer of receivables with recourse may be accounted for as a sale, provided the transferee can require the transferor to repurchase the receivables.	○	○
5. In a transfer of receivables with recourse accounted for as a borrowing, the difference between the receivables and the total of the factor's holdback plus the proceeds is a financing cost that should be amortized to interest expense over the term of the receivables.	○	○

		Journal Entries			
Instructions	Concepts		Reporting Requirements	Communication	Research

The following items relate to the transfer of accounts and notes receivable. For each item, match the transaction with the appropriate journal entry. Entries may be used once, more than once, or not at all.

Journal entries

A.	Cash	xxx			D.	Cash	xxx	
	Interest expense	xxx				Factor's holdback	xxx	
	Liability on discounted NR		xxx			Loss on sale of AR	xxx	
	Interest revenue		xxx			AR		xxx

B.	Cash	xxx			E.	Parenthetical or note disclosure only.
	Factor's holdback	xxx				
	Interest expense (discount)	xxx				
	Liability on transferred AR		xxx			

C.	Cash	xxx			F.	Cash	xxx	
	Finance charge	xxx				Loss on sale of NR	xxx	
	AR assigned	xxx				NR		xxx
	Note payable		xxx			Interest revenue		xxx
	AR		xxx				

	(A)	(B)	(C)	(D)	(E)	(F)
1. Chester transfers receivables by surrendering control. Collection is to be made by the purchaser (factor), who assumes risk of loss.	○	○	○	○	○	○
2. Chester specifically assigns a portion of its receivables as collateral for a loan. Collections from the assigned receivables will be used to repay the loan and interest.	○	○	○	○	○	○
3. Chester pledges its receivables as collateral to secure a loan and the debtor collects the proceeds.	○	○	○	○	○	○
4. Chester sells accounts receivable to a factor in a transaction considered a borrowing.	○	○	○	○	○	○
5. Chester transfers a note receivable by surrendering control over it. The transfer was on a without recourse basis.	○	○	○	○	○	○
6. Chester pledges its accounts receivable as security for a loan.	○	○	○	○	○	○

Instructions	Concepts	Journal Entries	Reporting Requirements	Communication	Research

Items 1 through 6 are based on the following:

Chester Company is preparing its financial statements for the year ended December 31, 2010.

Items 1 through 6 represent various commitments and contingencies of Chester at December 31, 2010, and events subsequent to December 31, 2010, but prior to the issuance of the 2010 financial statements. For each item, select from the following list the reporting requirement. A reporting requirement may be selected once, more than once, or not at all.

<u>Reporting requirement</u>

D. Disclosure only   B. Both accrual and disclosure
A. Accrual only   N. Neither accrual nor disclosure

	(D)	(A)	(B)	(N)
1. On December 1, 2010, Chester was awarded damages of $75,000 in a patent infringement suit it brought against a competitor. The defendant did not appeal the verdict, and payment was received in January 2011.	○	○	○	○
2. A former employee of Chester has brought a wrongful-dismissal suit against Chester. Chester's lawyers believe the suit to be without merit.	○	○	○	○
3. At December 31, 2010, Chester had outstanding purchase orders in the ordinary course of business for purchase of a raw material to be used in its manufacturing process. The market price is currently higher than the purchase price and is not anticipated to change within the next year.	○	○	○	○
4. A government contract completed during 2010 is subject to renegotiation. Although Chester estimates that it is reasonably possible that a refund of approximately $200,000 – $300,000 may be required by the government, it does not wish to publicize this possibility.	○	○	○	○
5. Chester has been notified by a governmental agency that it will be held responsible for the cleanup of toxic materials at a site where Chester formerly conducted operations. Chester estimates that it is probable that its share of remedial action will be approximately $500,000.	○	○	○	○
6. On January 5, 2011, Chester redeemed its outstanding bonds and issued new bonds with a lower rate of interest. The reacquisition price was in excess of the carrying amount of the bonds.	○	○	○	○

Instructions	Concepts	Journal Entries	Reporting Requirements	Communication	Research

Chester Company has the following contingencies:

- A threat of expropriation exists for one of its manufacturing plants located in a foreign country. Expropriation is deemed to be reasonably possible. Any compensation from the foreign government would be less than the carrying amount of the plant.
- Potential costs exist due to the discovery of a safety hazard related to one of its products. These costs are probable and can be reasonably estimated.
- One of its warehouses located at the base of a mountain could no longer be insured against rock slide losses. No rock slide losses have occurred.

The CEO of Chester would like to know how to account for these items. Write a brief memo to the CEO of Chester explaining the following:

1. How should Chester report the threat of expropriation of assets? Why?
2. How should Chester report the potential costs due to the safety hazard? Why?
3. How should Chester report the noninsurable rock slide risk? Why?

REMINDER: Your response will be graded for both technical content and writing skills. Technical content will be evaluated for information that is helpful to the intended reader and clearly relevant to the issue. Writing skills will be evaluated for development, organization, and the appropriate expression of ideas in professional correspondence. Use a standard business memo or letter format with a clear beginning, middle, and end. Do not convey information in the form of a table, bullet point list, or other abbreviated presentation.

To: CEO, Chester Company
From: CPA Candidate
Re: Contingencies

Instructions	Concepts	Journal Entries	Reporting Requirements	Communication	Research

Research each of the following questions in the authoritative literature. Insert the solution in the space provided.

1. How should short-term obligations be classified on the balance sheet?

2. Next year, Chester intends to refinance some short-term debt with a long-term note due in five years. What are the criteria to reclassify the short-term debt as long-term?

3. When should the company accrue an estimated loss on a contingency?

4. What is a contingency?

5. Define the three terms used to describe the likelihood of a contingent event occurring.

6. What are the conditions required for Chester to accrue vacation pay for its employees?

7. What are the criteria required to determine if a liability should be removed from the balance sheet?

Simulation Problem 2   (50 to 60 minutes)

Situation							
	Concepts	Uncollectible Accounts	Provision for Uncollectible Accounts Expense	Journal Entries	Transfer of Receivables	Communication	Research

Sigma Co. began operations on January 1, 2009. On December 31, 2009, Sigma provided for uncollectible accounts based on 1% of annual credit sales. On January 1, 2010, Sigma changed its method of determining its allowance for uncollectible accounts by applying certain percentages to the accounts receivable aging as follows:

Days past invoice date	Percent deemed to be uncollectible
0–30	1
31–90	5
91–180	20
Over 180	80

In addition, Sigma wrote off all accounts receivable that were over one year old. The following additional information relates to the years ended December 31, 2010, and 2009:

	2010	2009
Credit sales	$3,000,000	$2,800,000
Collections	2,915,000	2,400,000
Accounts written off	27,000	None
Recovery of accounts previously written off	7,000	None
Days past invoice date at 12/31		
0–30	300,000	250,000
31–90	80,000	90,000
91–180	60,000	45,000
Over 180	25,000	15,000

	Concepts						
Situation		Uncollectible Accounts	Provision for Uncollectible Accounts Expense	Journal Entries	Transfer of Receivables	Communication	Research

Identify which of the following items are disclosed as cash or cash equivalents on the balance sheet.

	Cash	Not cash
1. Checking accounts	○	○
2. Treasury stock	○	○
3. Treasury bills	○	○
4. Money market funds	○	○
5. Petty cash	○	○
6. Trading securities	○	○
7. Savings accounts	○	○
8. Sinking fund cash	○	○
9. Compensating balances against long-term borrowings	○	○
10. Cash restricted for new building	○	○
11. Postdated check for customers	○	○
12. Available-for-sale securities	○	○

		Uncollectible Accounts					
Situation	Concepts		Provision for Uncollectible Accounts Expense	Journal Entries	Transfer of Receivables	Communication	Research

Complete the following schedule showing the calculation of the allowance for uncollectible accounts at December 31, 2010.

Schedule to calculate provision and allowance for bad debts

Sigma Company
SCHEDULE OF CALCULATION OF ALLOWANCE FOR UNCOLLECTIBLE ACCOUNTS
December 31, 2010

	Amounts of accounts receivable	*Percentage of uncollectible accounts*	*Estimate of uncollectible accounts*
0 to 30 days			
31 to 90 days			
91 to 180 days			
Over 180 days			
Total accounts receivable			
Total allowance for un-collectible accounts			

Situation	Concepts	Uncollectible Accounts	**Provision for Uncollectible Accounts Expense**	Journal Entries	Transfer of Receivables	Communication	Research

Complete the following table and calculate the provision for uncollectible accounts expense for 2010.
Computation of 2010 provision

Balance December 31, 2009	
Write-offs during 2010	
Recoveries during 2010	
Balance before 2010 provision	
Required allowance at December 31, 2010	
2010 Provision	

Situation	Concepts	Uncollectible Accounts	Provision for Uncollectible Accounts Expense	**Journal Entries**	Transfer of Receivables	Communication	Research

Prepare the journal entries for the write-offs and recoveries for 2010, and for the provision for uncollectible accounts expense at December 31, 2010.

Write-offs

Recoveries

Provision for uncollectible accounts expense at December 31, 2010

Situation	Concepts	Uncollectible Accounts	Provision for Uncollectible Accounts Expense	Journal Entries	**Transfer of Receivables**	Communication	Research

Sigma enters into an agreement with First Finance Corporation to sell a group of receivables without recourse. The total face value of the receivables is $150,000. First Finance Corp. will charge 15% interest on the weighted-average time to maturity of the receivables of 45 days plus a 2% fee.
Prepare the journal entry to record the transfer of the receivables.

Situation	Concepts	Uncollectible Accounts	Provision for Uncollectible Accounts Expense	Journal Entries	Transfer of Receivables	**Communication**	Research

Write a memo to the CEO of Sigma Company explaining the two methods for estimating uncollectible accounts.

REMINDER: Your response will be graded for both technical content and writing skills. Technical content will be evaluated for information that is helpful to the intended reader and clearly relevant to the issue. Writing skills will be evaluated for development, organization, and the appropriate expression of ideas in professional correspondence. Use a standard business memo or letter format with a clear beginning, middle, and end. Do not convey information in the form of a table, bullet point list, or other abbreviated presentation.

To: CEO, Sigma Company
From: CPA Candidate
Re: Estimating uncollectible accounts

Situation	Concepts	Uncollectible Accounts	Provision for Uncollectible Accounts Expense	Journal Entries	Transfer of Receivables	Communication	Research

Sigma is planning to obtain cash by transferring some of its accounts receivable to a factor. Research each of the following questions using the Financial Accounting Research System (FARS) database, and insert your answer in the space provided.

1. With regard to transfers of financial assets, what is the financial components approach?

2. Describe the criteria for determining when control has been surrendered in a transfer of receivables.

3. How are transfers of receivables accounted for if one or more of the criteria for determining whether control has been surrendered are not met?

MULTIPLE-CHOICE ANSWERS

1. c	20. a	39. c	58. d	77. b	96. d
2. a	21. b	40. c	59. a	78. c	97. c
3. c	22. a	41. b	60. b	79. d	98. a
4. a	23. c	42. a	61. b	80. c	99. c
5. a	24. b	43. c	62. b	81. a	100. a
6. a	25. d	44. c	63. b	82. a	101. c
7. a	26. c	45. d	64. b	83. b	102. a
8. c	27. b	46. d	65. d	84. d	103. a
9. c	28. d	47. a	66. d	85. d	104. b
10. c	29. a	48. a	67. b	86. a	105. d
11. d	30. b	49. d	68. c	87. d	106. d
12. b	31. c	50. c	69. c	88. c	107. a
13. a	32. c	51. d	70. d	89. a	108. a
14. a	33. b	52. c	71. c	90. d	109. b
15. a	34. c	53. b	72. b	91. d	110. d
16. d	35. a	54. c	72. c	92. c	111. b
17. b	36. d	55. c	74. b	93. c	
18. b	37. d	56. c	75. b	94. b	1st: __/111 = __%
19. a	38. b	57. c	76. c	95. d	2nd: __/111 = __%

MULTIPLE-CHOICE ANSWER EXPLANATIONS

A. Cash

1. (c) Cash on hand ($125,000) and cash in banks ($2,250,000) are both reported as cash in the current asset section of the balance sheet because they are both unrestricted and readily available for use. Cash legally restricted for additions to plant ($1,600,000) is not available to meet current operating needs, and therefore should be excluded from current assets. Instead, it should be shown in the long-term asset section of the balance sheet as an investment.

2. (a) To be classified as cash, the item must be readily available for current needs with no legal restrictions limiting its use. A postdated check is not acceptable for deposit and therefore is not considered cash. Thus, the $2,000 check was correctly excluded from the 12/31 checkbook balance and no adjustment is necessary. An NSF check should not be included in cash until it has been redeposited and has cleared the bank. At 12/31, the NSF check ($500) had not yet been redeposited, so it was incorrectly included in the 12/31 checkbook balance, and an adjustment must be made. The check which was not mailed until 1/10/10 ($300) should not be subtracted from cash until the company gives up physical control of that amount. Therefore, $300 must be added back to the checkbook balance. As a result of these adjustments, the correct cash balance is $4,800 ($5,000 – $500 + $300).

3. (c) The definition of cash includes both cash (cash on hand and demand deposits) and cash equivalents (short-term, highly liquid investments). Cash equivalents have to be readily convertible into cash and so near maturity that they carry little risk of changing in value due to interest rate changes. This will include only those investments with original maturities of three months or less from the date of purchase by the enterprise. Common examples of cash equivalents include treasury bills, commercial paper, and money market funds. Trans should report a total of $460,000 ($35,000 + $75,000 + $350,000) on its December 31, 2010 balance sheet. The US treasury bill purchased on 12/1/10 is not included in the calculation because its

original maturity is not within three months or less from the date of purchase.

4. (a) Cash which is segregated and deposited into a bond sinking fund is presented in a classified balance sheet as a noncurrent asset because its use is restricted. Bank overdrafts are presented as current liabilities, unless other accounts at the **same bank** contain sufficient cash to offset the overdraft. The operating account that has a positive balance, should be presented as a current asset.

A.1. Bank Reconciliations

5. (a) To determine the correct 8/31/10 cash balance, a partial bank reconciliation should be prepared. The balance per bank statement ($18,050) must be adjusted for any items which the bank has not yet recorded and also for any bank errors (none in this problem).

Balance per bank statement	$18,050
Deposits in transit	3,250
Outstanding checks	(2,750)
Correct balance	$18,550

The deposits in transit and outstanding checks represent transactions that the company has recorded, but the bank has not yet recorded. The insufficient funds check ($600) and bank service charge ($100) are both items which the bank has recorded but the company has not. They would be adjustments to the **book balance**, not the **bank balance**.

6. (a) The balance per books at 3/31/10 is $44,200. The amount would be increased by cash receipts per books and decreased by cash disbursements per books. Cash receipts per the bank in April were $58,400, but this amount includes the $10,300 in transit at 3/31. Therefore, cash receipts per books in April are $48,100 ($58,400 – $10,300). Cash disbursements per the bank in April were $49,700. This amount includes the 3/31 outstanding checks ($12,600) but does **not** include the 4/30 outstanding checks ($7,000). Therefore, April cash disbursements per books is $44,100 ($49,700 – $12,600 + $7,000). The cash balance per books at 4/30/10 is $48,200 ($44,200 at 3/31/10, plus $48,100 receipts, less $44,100 disbursements). An alternative solutions approach is to first compute the 4/30/10 bank balance

($46,500 + $58,400 – $49,700 = $55,200), and then adjust for outstanding checks ($55,200 – $7,000 = $48,200).

B. Receivables

7.   (a)   The 12/31/10 current net receivables would include the trade receivables, net of the allowance account ($93,000 – $2,000 = $91,000). The claim against a shipper for goods lost in transit ($3,000) is also a valid receivable at year-end. Therefore, the total current net receivables are $94,000 ($91,000 + $3,000). The **unsold** goods on consignment do not represent a receivable until sold. Therefore, the $26,000 should be removed from receivables and sales and the cost ($26,000 ÷ 130% = $20,000) should be removed from cost of goods sold and reported as ending inventory. The security deposit ($30,000) should be reported as a **long-term** receivable.

8.   (c)   The solutions approach is to set up a T-account for accounts receivable.

	AR		
1/1/10	650,000		
Credit sales	2,700,000	75,000	Sales returns
		40,000	Write-offs
		2,150,000	Collections
12/31/10	1,085,000		

Credit sales are debited to **AR** and credited to **sales**. Sales returns are debited to **sales returns** and credited to **AR**; write-offs are debited to the **allowance for doubtful accounts** and credited to **AR**; and cash collections are debited to **cash** and credited to **AR**. The estimated future sales returns ($50,000) and estimated uncollectible accounts ($110,000) do not affect the accounts receivable account but are instead recorded in separate allowance accounts. Since the requirement is to determine accounts receivable **before** these allowances, the balance of accounts receivable should include only sales returns and write-offs for 2010.

9.   (c)   Accrued interest receivable at 6/30/10 is interest revenue which has been earned by 6/30/10, but has not yet been received by that date. Interest was last received on 7/1/09; the accrued interest receivable includes interest revenue earned from 7/1/09 through 6/30/10 (a full year). The original balance of the note receivable was $150,000 but the 7/1/09 principal payment of $50,000 reduced this balance to $100,000. Therefore, the 6/30/10 interest receivable is $8,000 ($100,000 × 8%).

10.   (c)   Loan origination fees are recognized over the life of the related loan as an adjustment of yield. These fees are recorded as a discount on the note receivable. Therefore, Tigg's 12/1/10 entry is

Notes receivable	200,000	
Discount on NR		6,000
Cash		194,000

Using the effective interest method, Tigg's 12/31/10 adjusting entry is

Int. receivable	2,000	
Discount on NR	166	
Int. revenue		2,166

The interest receivable is

Face value	×	Stated rate	×	Time		
$200,000	×	12%	×	1/12	=	$2,000

The interest revenue is

Carrying amount	×	Effective rate	×	Time		
$194,000	×	13.4%	×	1/12	=	$2,166

11.   (d)   A current asset is an asset that can be reasonably expected to be converted into cash, sold or consumed in operations, within a single operating cycle or within a year if more than one cycle is completed each year. A noncurrent asset is an asset that can not be expected to be converted to cash, sold or consumed within a single operating cycle or within one year, whichever is longer. Because accrued interest was reported as a current asset on the 2010 balance sheet, it can be assumed interest will be received on August 31, 2010, since current assets are received within one year. Also, because the note receivable was reported as a noncurrent asset it can be assumed that the principal will not be collected within the next twelve months. Principal that is not due until August 31, 2011, coincides with reporting the note as a noncurrent asset.

12.   (b)   Upon receipt of the interest-bearing note for the sale of goods, Benet would record the following entry:

Notes receivable	(face value)
Interest receivable	(interest from 7/15 to 8/15)
Sales	(face + interest)

Note that the interest that accrued on the note from July 15 to August 15 represents part of the sales price of the merchandise (rather than interest income) because Benet did not hold the note during this period. On November 15, Benet will record the following entry:

Cash	(Plug)
Note receivable	(face value)
Interest revenue	(interest from 8/15 to 11/15)
Interest receivable	(interest from 7/15 to 8/15)

B.1. Anticipation of Sales Discounts

13.   (a)   If material, an allowance for discounts must be reported at year-end in order to match the discounts with the related sales and to report receivables at their collectible amount. At 12/31/10, $100,000 of the accounts receivable have the potential to be discounted by 2% because they are less than fifteen days old (terms 2/15, net 30). Since 50% of the customers are expected to take advantage of the 2% discount, the allowance for discounts should be $1,000 [($100,000 × 50%) × 2%]. None of the other categories require a discount allowance because they are older than the maximum age of fifteen days to receive the 2% discount.

14.   (a)   When revenue is recognized from sales and a right of return exists, sales revenue must be reduced to reflect estimated returns. In this case, sales of $1,000,000 must be reduced by estimated returns of $100,000 [(7% + 3%) × $1,000,000], resulting in net sales of $900,000. The estimated exchanges (15%) will not result in a future reduction of sales.

B.2. Bad Debts Expense

15.   (a)   To compute the 12/31/10 allowance for uncollectible accounts, the solutions approach is to set up a T-account for the allowance.

	Allowance for U.A.		
		260,000	1/1/10
		180,000	Expense (2% × 9,000,000)
Write-offs	325,000		
		115,000	12/31/10

The 1/1/10 balance is increased by bad debts expense recorded (2% × credit sales of $9,000,000) and decreased by write-offs of specific uncollectible accounts.

16.   (d)   The balance in the allowance for doubtful accounts should reflect the amount of accounts receivable that are estimated to be uncollectible. Since it is estimated that 3% of the gross accounts receivable will become uncollectible, the allowance account should have a 12/31/10 balance of $30,000 (3% × $1,000,000). Note that **bad debt expense** of $38,000 would be recorded for 2010, as indicated below.

	Allowance		
Bal. before adj.	8,000		
		?	Bad debt expense ($38,000)
		30,000	12/31/10 (3% × $1,000,000)

17.   (b)   The total amount of risk of accounting loss related to Butler's trade accounts receivable is $230,000 ($250,000 trade accounts receivable – $20,000 uncollectible amount). The accounting loss cannot exceed the amount of the account receivable recognized as an asset in the balance sheet ($230,000). Off-balance-sheet risk refers to a potential loss that may exceed the amount recognized as an asset. There is no off-balance-sheet risk in this example.

18.   (b)   The solutions approach is to set up a T-account for the allowance for doubtful accounts.

	Allowance		
		30,000	1/1/10
2010 Write-offs	18,000	2,000	2010 Recoveries
		14,000	12/31/10 Before adj.
		?	Unc. accts. expense
		25,000	12/31/10

In 2010, $18,000 of accounts were written off as uncollectible (debit allowance, credit AR). Also, $2,000 of AR were recovered (debit AR, credit allowance; then, debit cash, credit AR), leaving a balance in the allowance account of $14,000 ($30,000 – $18,000 + $2,000). The desired 12/31/10 balance is $25,000 ($350,000 AR less $325,000 net value per aging schedule). Therefore, to increase the allowance from $14,000 to $25,000, uncollectible accounts expense of $11,000 must be recorded.

19.   (a)   When an aging schedule is used to estimate uncollectibles, the total uncollectibles computed is the amount used for the ending balance in the allowance account. As computed below, the 12/31/10 allowance for uncollectible accounts should be $9,000.

$120,000 × 1%	=	$1,200
90,000 × 2%	=	1,800
100,000 × 6%	=	6,000
		$9,000

The other information given (12/31/09 allowance, write-offs, and recoveries) would be used to determine the bad debt expense adjustment, not the allowance balance. In this case, apparently due to a change in estimate, the bad debt expense adjustment would actually be a credit (to offset the necessary debit to the allowance account).

	Allowance for U.A.		
		22,000	12/31/09
Write-offs	7,000	4,000	Recoveries
		19,000	
Adjustment	10,000		
		9,000	12/31/10

20.   (a)   The aging of receivables method of estimating uncollectible accounts is based on the theory that bad debts are a function of accounts receivable collections during the period. The aging of receivables method emphasizes reporting accounts receivable at their net realizable value. It is a "balance-sheet" approach, which stresses the collectibility (valuation) of the receivable balance. Once the balance of the allowance account required to reduce net accounts receivable to their realizable value has been computed, bad debts expense is merely the amount needed to adjust the allowance account to the computed balance. Answer (b) is incorrect because under the direct write-off method, bad debts are considered expenses in the period in which they are written off; no consideration is given to the valuation of accounts receivable. Answers (c) and (d) are incorrect because both of these methods are based on the theory that bad debts are a function of sales. Thus, these methods emphasize reporting the bad debts expense amount accurately on the income statement.

21.   (b)   A primary objective of accrual accounting is to record the cash consequences of events that change an entity's financial position in the period in which the events occur. This means recognizing revenues when earned rather than when cash is received, and recognizing expenses when incurred rather than when cash is paid. Expenses are incurred when they help the firm earn revenue. Under the allowance method, uncollectible accounts expense is recognized in the same period as the related revenue. The same credit decisions that enabled the entity to earn revenue caused it to incur uncollectible accounts expense. Therefore, under accrual accounting that expense should be recognized in the same period. On the other hand, when the direct write-off method is used, the uncollectible accounts expense is generally recognized after the period in which the revenue is recognized; after the event (credit decision) which changed financial position. Therefore, the direct write-off method is **not** consistent with accrual accounting.

22.   (a)   When the allowance method for recognizing uncollectible accounts is used, the entry to write off a specific account is

Allowance for unc. accts.	xxx	
Accts. receivable		xxx

Answer (a) is correct because this entry decreases both accounts.

23.   (c)   When an account receivable that was previously written off is collected, two entries must be made. The first entry reverses the write-off and reestablishes the receivable.

Accounts receivable	xxx	
Allowance for uncollectible accounts		xxx

The second entry records the cash receipt.

Cash	xxx	
Accounts receivable		xxx

The credit to the allowance account in the first entry increases its balance. Uncollectible accounts expense, however, is not affected by this transaction.

B.3.   Pledging and Selling AR

24.   (b)   An **assignment** of accounts receivable is a financing arrangement whereby the owner of the receivables (assignor) obtains a loan from the lender (assignee) by pledging the accounts receivable as collateral. A **factoring**

of accounts receivable is basically a sale of, or borrowing on, the receivables. "Factors" are intermediaries that buy receivables from companies (for a fee) and then collect payments directly from the customers. Thus, both of these are methods of generating cash from accounts receivable.

25. (d) When receivables are factored and control is surrendered the transaction is treated as a **sale**. A transfer in which control is surrendered will not be treated as a borrowing. The risk of uncollectible accounts is **not** retained by the seller in a sale without recourse.

26. (c) Taylored will receive the value of the receivables ($400,000), reduced by $20,000 for the amount of the holdback ($400,000 × .05), $8,000 withheld as fee income ($400,000 × .02), and $6,740 withheld as interest expense ($400,000 × .15 × 41/365). Answer (c) is therefore correct ($400,000 – $8,000 – $6,740 – $20,000).

27. (b) A sale of receivables with recourse is recorded using a financial components approach because the seller has a continuing involvement. Under this approach the seller would reduce receivables, recognize assets obtained and liabilities incurred, and record gain or loss. The entry would be

Cash	$365,260	
Factor's holdback	20,000	
Loss	26,740*	
Accounts receivable		$400,000
Liability under recourse provision		12,000

* *($6,740 + $8,000 + $12,000)*

28. (d) If all receivables are collected, Taylored would eliminate its recourse liability and the corresponding loss. The costs incurred by Taylored would include a fee of $8,000 ($400,000 × .02) and interest expense of $6,740 ($400,000 × .15 × 41/365) for a total of $14,740.

29. (a) The seller uses a Due from Factor or Factor's Holdback account to account for probable sales discounts, sales returns, and sales allowances. The Recourse liability account is recorded to indicate probable uncollectible accounts.

30. (b) Scarbrough will receive the value of the receivables ($600,000), reduced by $30,000 for the amount of the holdback ($600,000 × .05), $18,000 withheld as fee income ($600,000 × .03), and $13,315 withheld as interest expense ($600,000 × .15 × 54/365). Answer (b) is therefore correct ($600,000 – $30,000 – $18,000 – $13,315).

31. (c) If all receivables are collected, Synthia would eliminate its recourse liability and the corresponding loss. The costs incurred by Synthia would include a fee of $15,000 ($750,000 × .02) and interest expense of $12,575 ($750,000 × .12 × 51/365) for a total of $27,575.

32. (c) The transferor, Bannon, should measure the assets received and liabilities incurred at fair value, not at cost. The transferee, Chapman, should record any assets obtained and liabilities incurred at fair value.

33. (b) If financial assets are exchanged for cash or other consideration, but the transfer does not meet the criteria to be accounted for as a sale, both the transferor and the transferee should account for the transfer as a secured borrowing and a pledge of collateral.

34. (c) A sale occurs if the seller surrenders control of the receivables transferred. Control is deemed to have been surrendered by the seller only if all three conditions listed in (a), (b), and (d) are met. Answer (c) is used to determine whether a recourse liability is recorded as part of the sale, not whether a transaction can be recorded as a sale.

35. (a) To derecognize assets when control is gained is not an objective in accounting for transfers of financial assets. When control is gained, the assets should be recognized. Answer (b) is incorrect because an objective is to derecognize liabilities when extinguished. A liability no longer exists, and it should be removed from the balance sheet. Answer (c) is incorrect because recognizing liabilities when incurred is an objective. Answer (d) is incorrect because derecognizing assets when control is given up is an objective in accounting for transfers of financial assets.

36. (d) A servicing asset or liability should be amortized in proportion to and over the period of estimated net servicing income or net servicing loss. Answer (a) is incorrect because a servicing asset shall be assessed for impairment based on its fair value. Answer (b) is incorrect because a servicing liability shall be assessed for increased obligation based on its fair value. Answer (c) is incorrect because an obligation to service financial assets may result in the recognition of a servicing asset or a servicing liability.

37. (d) The assets must be measured for impairment at the end of each reporting period. Answer (a) is incorrect because increases in fair value are not reported under the amortization method. Answer (a) is also incorrect because when using the fair value method, changes in fair value are reported in earnings, not in other comprehensive income. Answers (b) and (c) are incorrect because these rules refer to the fair value method.

38. (b) Answer (b) is correct. Either the amortization method or the fair value method can be used for servicing assets and servicing liabilities. However, if the fair value method is elected, the election cannot be reversed. Changes in fair value are reported in earnings in the period in which the change occurs.

39. (c) When a company transfers a financial asset but continues to hold an interest in the servicing asset, the transferor should allocate the previous carrying amount between the assets sold and the interest that continues to be held by the transferor based on their relative fair values. Answers (a), (b), and (d) are incorrect because they represent incorrect values.

40. (c) The arrangement of having collateral transferred to a secured party is known as a pledge. Answer (a) is incorrect because a debtor may grant a security interest in certain assets to a lender to serve as collateral with recourse. Answer (b) is incorrect because a debtor may grant a security interest in certain assets to a lender to serve as collateral without recourse. Answer (d) is incorrect because secured parties are sometimes permitted to sell collateral held under a pledge.

41. (b) Net proceeds from the sale are equal to $2,200.

Net proceeds	
Cash received	$2,100
Plus: Interest rate swap	140
Call option	80
Less: Recourse obligation	(120)
Net proceeds	$2,200

The gain is computed as follows:

Net proceeds	$2,200
Carrying amount of loans sold	2,000
Gain on sale	$ 200

42.   (a)   The journal entry to record the transfer for ABC Company is as follows:

Cash	2,100	
Interest rate swap	140	
Call option	80	
Loans		2,000
Recourse obligation		120
Gain on sale		200

Answer (b) is incorrect because is should be a debit to interest rate swap, not a credit. Answer (c) is incorrect because loans should be credited. It was on ABC Company's books as an asset and must be taken off. Answer (d) is incorrect because cash is being received, so it must be debited.

43.   (c)   ABC Company must report a servicing obligation of $50. The calculation of net proceeds is

Cash received		$2,100
Plus: Interest rate swap		140
Call option		80
Less: Recourse obligation		(120)
Servicing obligation		(50)
Net proceeds		$2,150

The gain is

Net proceeds	$2,150
Carrying amount of loans sold	2,000
Gain on sale	$ 150

44.   (c)   Financial assets subject to prepayment should be measured like investments in debt securities classified as available-for-sale or trading.

45.   (d)   Answers (a), (b), and (c) are required disclosures. Answer (d) is the correct answer as disclosure is only required of assets and liabilities with nonestimable fair values.

46.   (d)   If the debtor defaults under the terms of the secured contract and is no longer entitled to redeem the pledged asset, it (Taft) shall derecognize the pledged asset, and the secured party (Wilson) shall recognize the collateral as its asset initially measured at fair value.

C.1.   Examples of Current Liabilities

47.   (a)   Before adjustment, the balance in the Accounts Payable account is $360,000. This amount is net of a $50,000 debit balance in Lyle's account payable to Ross resulting from a $50,000 advance payment for goods to be manufactured to Lyle's specifications. The $50,000 should be reclassified as a current asset, **Advance to Suppliers**. The checks recorded on 12/29/10 incorrectly reduced the accounts payable balance by $100,000. The $100,000 reduction should not have been recorded until the checks were mailed on 1/5/11. The 12/31/10 accounts payable must be increased by $100,000. Therefore, the corrected 12/31/10 accounts payable is $510,000.

Unadjusted AP	$360,000
Reclassification of advance	50,000
Error correction	100,000
	$510,000

48.   (a)   When purchases are recorded using the net method, purchases and accounts payable are recorded at an amount net of the cash discounts, and the failure to take ad-

vantage of a discount is recorded in a Purchase Discounts Lost account. Therefore, when Rabb changes to the net method, gross accounts payable ($30,000) must be adjusted down to the net amount. Since $200 of discounts are still available in the accounts payable balance, the net accounts payable at 9/30/10 is $29,800 ($30,000 − $200). The journal entry is

Purchase discounts lost	1,000	
Purchase discounts	800	
Accts. payable	200	
Purchases		2,000

49.   (d)   Accrued interest payable at 12/31/10 is interest expense which has been incurred by 12/31/10, but has not yet been paid by that date. The note was issued on 3/1/09 and interest is payable in full at maturity on 2/28/11. Therefore, there is one year and ten months of unpaid interest at 12/31/10 (3/1/09 to 12/31/10). Interest for the first year is $1,200 ($10,000 × 12%). Since interest is compounded annually, the new principal amount for the second year includes the original principal ($10,000) plus the first year's interest ($1,200). Therefore, accrued interest for the ten months ended 12/31/10 is $1,120 ($11,200 × 12% × 10/12), and total accrued interest at 12/31/10 is $2,320 ($1,200 + $1,120).

50.   (c)   Accrued interest payable at 12/31/10 is interest expense which has been incurred by 12/31/10, but has not yet been paid by that date. Interest was last paid on 9/1/10; the accrued interest payable includes interest expense incurred from 9/1/10 through 12/31/10 (four months). The original balance of the note payable was $1,350,000 but the 9/1/10 principal payment of $450,000 reduced this balance to $900,000. Therefore, the interest payable at 12/31/10 is $36,000 ($900,000 × 12% × 4/12). The prime rate (11%) does not affect the computation because it is not the stated rate on this note.

51.   (d)   The solutions approach is to analyze the interest payable T-account for 2010, assuming all interest payments flow through interest payable.

	Interest Payable		
		15,000	12/31/09
2010 Int. paid	68,000	85,000	2010 Expense
		?	12/31/10

The beginning interest payable balance ($15,000) is increased by interest expense (debit interest expense, credit interest payable for $85,000) and decreased by interest paid (debit interest payable, credit cash for $68,000), resulting in a 12/31/10 balance of $32,000 ($15,000 + $85,000 − $68,000).

52.   (c)   All of the notes are due 6/15/11, and normally the entire amount would be classified as current. However, a short-term obligation can be reclassified as long-term if the enterprise intends to refinance the obligation on a long-term basis **and** the intent is supported by the ability to refinance. Ames demonstrated its ability by entering into a financing agreement before the statements are issued. The amount to be excluded from current liabilities cannot exceed the amount available for refinancing under the agreement. Ames expects to be able to refinance at least $480,000 (80% × $600,000) of the notes. Therefore, that amount can be classified as long-term, while the remaining $20,000 must be classified as short-term.

53.   (b)   The effective rate of interest paid on a note is computed as follows:

$$\text{Effective interest rate} = \frac{\text{Interest paid}}{\text{Cash received}}$$

In this case, let's assume the short-term note payable was in the amount of $100,000. The effective interest rate would be 12.56%.

$$\frac{(100,000 \times .12) + (\$100,000 \times .005)}{\$99,500} = 12.56$$

This is because the loan origination fee increases the interest paid on the note and reduces the net cash received from the note.

54.   (c)   The $4,000,000 note payable is due March 15, 2011 and normally would be classified as a current liability in the December 31, 2010 financial statements. However, a short-term obligation can be reclassified as long-term if the enterprise intends to refinance the obligation on a long-term basis and the intent is supported by the ability to refinance. Cali demonstrated its ability to refinance by actually issuing bonds and refinancing the note prior to the issuance of the December 31, 2010 financial statements. Since the proceeds from the bonds exceeded the amount needed to retire the note, the entire $4,000,000 notes payable would be classified as a noncurrent liability, with separate disclosure of the note refinancing.

55.   (c)   The notes payable ($750,000) are due 7/31/11, and would normally be included in 12/31/10 current liabilities. However, a short-term obligation can be reclassified as long-term if the enterprise intends to refinance the obligation on a long-term basis and the intent is supported by the ability to refinance. Largo demonstrated its ability to refinance by actually issuing $1,500,000 of bonds in February 2011 before the 12/31/10 financial statements were issued on 3/3/11. The bond proceeds will be used to retire the note at maturity. The amount excluded from current liabilities cannot exceed the amount actually refinanced. Since Largo prepaid $250,000 of the note on 1/12/11 with excess cash, that amount must be included in 12/31/10 current liabilities. Only the remaining $500,000 can be excluded from current liabilities.

56.   (c)   A key to solving this problem is understanding that the employee advances do **not** affect the accrued salaries payable. When advances are made to employees, they are a cash payment separate from the payroll function. The advances made, therefore, are not reflected in salaries expense ($420,000) or **gross** salaries paid ($390,000). Therefore, the solutions approach is to analyze the salaries payable T-account for 2010 (disregarding the employee advances).

	Salaries Payable		
		40,000	12/31/09
2010 sal. paid	390,000	420,000	2010 sal. expense
		?	12/31/10

The beginning salaries payable balance ($40,000) is increased by salaries expense ($420,000) and decreased by salaries paid ($390,000), resulting in a 12/31/10 balance of $70,000.

57.   (c)   No sales commission is due to salesperson A because his commissions earned ($200,000 × 4% = $8,000) are less than his fixed salary ($10,000). Note that the excess of the fixed salary over commissions earned is not charged

back against A. Commissions totaling $28,000 are due to salespersons B and C as computed below.

	Commissions earned		Fixed salary paid	Commissions payable
B	(6% × $400,000)	−	$14,000	$10,000
C	(6% × $600,000)	−	$18,000	18,000
				$28,000

58.   (d)   Lime's payroll tax liability includes amounts withheld from payroll checks [$1,200 of federal income taxes withheld and $700 of the **employees'** share of FICA ($10,000 × 7%)] plus the **employer's** share of FICA (an additional $700). Therefore, the total payroll tax liability is $2,600 ($1,200 + $700 + $700). The amount recorded as payroll tax expense consists only of the employer's share of FICA ($700), since no unemployment taxes are mentioned in the problem.

59.   (a)   The contingent unemployment claims liability is both probable and reasonably estimable, so it must be accrued at 12/31/10. Acme's reasonable estimate of its probable liability is 2% of eligible gross wages. Eligible gross wages are the first $10,000 of gross wages paid to each of the five employees (5 × $10,000 = $50,000), so the accrued liability should be $1,000 (2% × $50,000). Note that the 3% rate is not used because Acme has chosen the option to reimburse the state directly, and its best estimate of this liability is based on 2%, not 3%.

60.   (b)   To compute the amount of the contribution, the requirements described in the problem must be translated into an equation. The contribution must equal 10% of income **after** deduction of the contribution, but **before** income tax. Therefore, the tax rate (30%) does not enter into the computation. The equation is solved below.

$$
\begin{aligned}
C &= .10 \times (\$75,000 - C) \\
C &= \$7,500 - .10C \\
1.1C &= \$7,500 \\
C &= \$7,500 \div 1.1 \\
C &= \$6,818
\end{aligned}
$$

The amount to be accrued as an expense and liability is $6,818.

61.   (b)   If net income **after** bonus and income tax is $360,000, income before taxes can be computed by dividing **$360,000** by **1 minus the tax rate**.

$$\text{Income before taxes} = \frac{\$360,000}{1 - .40} = \underline{\$600,000}$$

The bonus is equal to 10% of income **before** income tax but **after** the bonus. The $600,000 computed above **is** income before tax but after all other expenses including the bonus. Therefore, the bonus must be $60,000 (10% × $600,000). Note that this problem is different from other bonus problems because usually the income before taxes and bonus ($660,000 in this case) is given as the starting point, rather than net income.

62.   (b)   To determine the correct amount for sales revenue, Ivy must divide the total of sales and sales taxes by 100% plus the sales tax percentage (6%) as indicated below.

Month	Total		Percentage		Sales revenue
Jan.	$10,600	÷	106%	=	$10,000
Feb.	$7,420	÷	106%	=	7,000
March	$8,480	÷	106%	=	8,000
Total					$25,000

Sales taxes payable would include all sales taxes collected, less any sales taxes already remitted.

January sales taxes ($10,600 – $10,000)	$600
*February sales taxes ($7,420 – $7,000)	420
March sales taxes ($8,480 – $8,000)	480
Total	$1,500
Less taxes remitted	600
Sales taxes payable	$ 900

Note February sales taxes were not remitted since they did not exceed $500.

63. **(b)** As of 12/31/10 the October sales taxes should have been paid, so there would be no 12/31/10 current liability for those taxes. However, at 12/31/10 sales taxes payable must be reported for the November room rentals as they were not paid until 1/3/11 and the December room rentals [15% × ($110,000 + $150,000) = $39,000]. The fourth quarter occupancy taxes were not paid until 1/3/11, so they would also represent a current liability at 12/31/10 [(1,100 + 1,200 + 1,800) × $2 = $8,200].

64. **(b)** When the warehouse was purchased on 9/1/10, it would be recorded at its total cost before any credit for accrued realty taxes. The offsetting credits would be to **cash** for the net amount paid, and to **real estate taxes payable** for two months' taxes ($12,000 × 2/6 = $4,000). At the end of September and of October, Day would record property tax expense each month as follows:

Real estate tax expense	2,000	
Real estate taxes payable		2,000

Therefore, at October 31, Day has a balance of $8,000 in the payable account ($4,000 + $2,000 + $2,000). On 11/1/10, Day would record the semiannual payment as follows:

Real estate taxes payable	8,000	
Prepaid real estate taxes	4,000	
Cash		12,000

The prepaid real estate taxes would then be expensed $2,000 per month at the end of November and December.

65. **(d)** An accrued liability is an expense which has been incurred, but has not been paid. Of the $500 advertising bill, $375 had been incurred as an expense as of 12/31/10 and should be reported as an accrued liability at that time. For the store lease, the fixed portion ($1,200 per month) is payable on the 16th of each month for the preceding month. Therefore, on 12/16/10, rent was paid for the period 11/16/10 to 12/15/10. An additional one-half month's rent expense (1/2 × $1200 = $600) has been incurred but not paid as of 12/31/10. The variable portion of the rent [5% × ($550,000 – $300,000), or $12,500] was incurred during 2010, but will not be paid until 1/31/11. It, too, is an accrued liability at 12/31/10. Total 12/31/10 accrued liabilities are $13,475.

Advertising	$ 375
Fixed rent (1/2 × $1,200)	600
Variable rent [5% × ($550,000 – $300,000)]	12,500
Total	$13,475

66. **(d)** The solutions approach to this problem is to construct a time line documenting the events in the question.

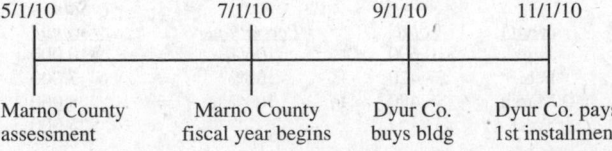

Note that on May 1, 2010, the County has merely determined the amount of property tax owed by each property owner, and no entries would be made by companies subject to property taxes on that date. The fiscal year 2011 taxes are for the period from July 1, 2010, to June 30, 2011. On September 1, 2010, the date on which Dyur purchased the building, two months of the fiscal year had passed, and the property tax expense related to those months was borne by the seller. At October 31, 2010, Dyur would have a liability for four months of property taxes (even though only the months of September and October would have been expensed by Dyur). On November 1, 2010, four months of the fiscal year had passed, and Dyur paid taxes for the first six months of the fiscal year. The entry recorded upon the payment would be

Property taxes payable	(four months)
Prepaid property taxes	(two months)
Cash	(six months)

The payment would therefore be allocated as two-sixths (33 1/3%) to an increase in prepaid property taxes and four-sixths (66 2/3%) to a decrease in property taxes payable.

67. **(b)** To determine the 12/31/10 balance of the liability for customer advances, the solutions approach is to set up a T-account for the liability.

	Customer Advances		
		118,000	12/31/09
		184,000	2010 adv. received
2010 adv. applied	164,000		
2010 cancellations	50,000		
		88,000	12/31/10

When advances are received ($184,000), cash is debited and the liability account is credited. When advances are applied to orders shipped ($164,000), the liability account is debited and sales is credited. When an order is cancelled ($50,000), the liability account is debited and a revenue account is credited, since the advance payments are nonrefundable. Thus, the customer advances balance on 12/31/10 is $88,000.

68. **(c)** The solutions approach is to set up a T-account for the liability.

	Liability for Deposits		
		580,000	12/31/09 balance
		780,000	2010 deliveries
2010 returns	626,000		
2010 sales	60,000		
		674,000	12/31/10 balance

When customers pay the deposit for a container, cash is debited and the liability is credited. Therefore, at 12/31/09 the liability consists of deposits for containers still held by customers from the last two years ($580,000). During 2010, the liability was increased for deposits on containers delivered ($780,000). When containers are returned, the deposits are returned to the customers; in 2010, the liability was debited and cash credited for $626,000. Also, at 12/31/10, some customers still held containers from 2008 ($150,000 – $90,000 = $60,000). The two-year time limit has expired on these, so the company is no longer obligated to return the deposit. The containers are considered sold to the customers, so the liability account is debited and sales credited for $60,000. This results in a 12/31/10 balance of $674,000.

69. **(c)** To compute the escrow liability, the solutions approach is to use a T-account.

	Escrow Liability		
		700,000	1/1/10
Taxes paid	1,720,000	1,580,000	Receipts
		45,000	Net interest
		605,000	12/31/10

Escrow payments received ($1,580,000) would increase the liability because these amounts are payable to taxing authorities. Taxes paid ($1,720,000) decrease the liability. The net interest credited to the escrow accounts [$50,000 − (10% × $50,000) = $45,000] would increase the liability, resulting in a 12/31/10 balance of $605,000.

70.   (d)   All contract sales are made **evenly** during the year. Therefore, the 2009 contracts range from one year expired (if sold on 12/31/09) to two years expired (if sold on 1/1/09), for an average of one and one-half years expired [(2+1)/2]. Similarly, the 2010 contracts range from zero years expired to one year expired, for an average of one-half year expired [(0+1)/2]. The average **unearned** portion of the 2009 contracts is one-half year (two years – one and one-half years), the last half of the second contract year. The amount of unearned revenue related to 2009 contracts is computed as follows:

$$500,000 \times 60\% \times 1/2 = \underline{150,000}$$

The average **unearned** portion of the 2010 contracts is one and one-half years (two years – one-half year), the last half of the first contract year and all of the second contract year. The amount of unearned revenue related to the 2010 contracts is computed as follows:

2010:	$600,000 × 40% × ½	=	$120,000
	$600,000 × 60%	=	360,000
			$480,000

Therefore, the total unearned revenue is $630,000 ($150,000 + $480,000).

71.   (c)   Revenue is earned by Toddler Care Co. as time goes by and care is provided. Therefore, revenue should be recognized on a straight-line basis regardless of the timing of cash receipts. The monthly fees can simply be recognized on a monthly basis, but the initial payment must be deferred and recognized as revenue on a straight-line basis over the twelve-month period. The 12/31/10 deferred revenues are $6,600, as computed below.

Plan	Initial fees	2010 revenue (4/12)	12/31/10 def. rev. (8/12)
1	15 × $500 = $7,500	$2,500	$5,000
2	12 × $200 = $2,400	800	1,600
3	$ 0	0	0
	$9,900	$3,300	$6,600

Since the total initial payments received are given ($9,900), a shortcut is to multiply that amount by 8/12 ($9,900 × 8/12 = $6,600).

72.   (b)   When a company issues gift certificates for cash, the following journal entry is made:

Cash	(amount of certificate)	
Deferred revenue		(amount of certificate)

When the gift certificates are subsequently redeemed, the following journal entry is made:

Deferred revenue	(amount of certificate)	
Revenue		(amount of certificate)

However, if the gift certificates are not redeemed and lapse, the following journal entry is made:

Deferred revenue	(amount of certificate)	
Gain on lapse of certificates		(amount of certificate)

Please note that although different accounts are credited depending on whether the certificates are redeemed or lapse, the Deferred Revenue account is decreased in both cases.

73.   (c)   Revenues are generally recognized when they are both **realized** or **realizable** and **earned**. Therefore, Dallas Co. should report a liability for deferred revenues equal to the advance payment of 60% of the main contract price. One of three essential characteristics of a liability is that the transaction or other event obligating the entity has already happened. Since the subcontractor had not produced the special-order goods as of March 31, Dallas should not record a liability at that time. Therefore, no payable to the subcontractor would be reported for this activity as of March 31.

74.   (b)   At June 30, 2010, Northan Retailers should report the coupon transactions as unearned revenues because the sale of the coupons is not the culmination of the earnings process (i.e., Northan must allow customers to exchange the coupons for merchandise or refund the cost of the coupons at some later date). The unearned revenues should be recorded at the amount of the cash received by debiting cash and crediting an unearned revenue account. The retail price of the merchandise for which coupons may be redeemed does not impact the monetary amount of Northan's liability to its customers, and each coupon redeemed will ultimately result in the recognition of sales of $10, the amount of cash previously received.

75.   (b)   The requirement is to determine the situation that might account for the reduction in the deferred revenue balance. When a service contract is purchased by a customer and the fee prepaid, deferred revenue is recognized at the date of payment. Revenue cannot be recorded because revenue has not yet been earned. Revenue is only recorded when services are performed under the contract. The deferred revenue balance is reduced by the **actual** amount of revenue earned when services are performed under the services contract. If more contracts were signed earlier in one year than another year, there is a greater period of time in which to perform actual services. As previously stated, when actual services are performed, the deferred revenue balance is decreased. Therefore, the more actual services that are performed, the greater the reduction in the deferred revenue balance. If more 2010 contracts were signed later in 2010 than 2009, the deferred revenue balance in 2010 would be larger than 2009. There would be less time to perform actual services, therefore less actual revenue would be recognized, creating a larger deferred revenue balance at year-end. There is no contribution margin recognized on service contracts.

76.   (c)   The aggregate amount of payments for unconditional purchase obligations that have been recognized on the purchaser's balance sheet shall be disclosed for each of the **five** years following the date of the latest balance sheet presented.

C.2.   Current Liabilities—Contingencies

77.   (b)   A loss contingency should be accrued if it is **probable** that a liability has been incurred at the balance sheet date and the amount of the loss is reasonably estimable. With respect to unfiled claims, the enterprise must consider both the probability that a claim will be filed and the probability of an unfavorable outcome. Although it is probable that claims will be asserted against Sims, it is only **reasonably possible** that the claims will be successful. Therefore, this contingent liability should not be accrued, but should be disclosed. The potential loss to be disclosed is $250,000, since the additional amount above the deductible would be covered by the insurance policy, and therefore is not a loss or liability for Sims.

78. (c)   Current liabilities are obligations whose liquidation is reasonably expected to require the use of current assets or the creation of other current liabilities. This means that generally, current liabilities are the liabilities that are due within one year of the balance sheet date. Clearly, accounts payable ($55,000) and accrued expenses ($35,000) are current liabilities. Notes payable ($400,000) and bonds payable ($1,000,000) are usually considered to be long-term, but the maturity dates given (7/1/11 and 3/1/11 respectively) indicate they are current liabilities at 12/31/10. The contingent liability ($450,000) and deferred tax liability ($25,000) will not be settled until 2012 and therefore should be classified as long-term at 12/31/10. Thus, the 12/31/10 current liabilities total is $1,490,000 as follows:

Accounts payable	$ 55,000
Accrued expenses	35,000
Unsecured notes 8%—due 7/1/11	400,000
Senior bonds 7%—due 3/31/11	1,000,000
Total current liabilities	$1,490,000

79. (d)   The lawsuit damages must be accrued as a loss contingency because an unfavorable outcome is **probable** and the amount of the loss is **reasonably estimable**. When a range of possible loss exists, the best estimate within the range is accrued. When no amount within the range is a better estimate than any other amount, the dollar amount at the low end of the range is **accrued** (in this case, $500,000) and the dollar amount of the high end of the range is **disclosed**.

80. (c)   A loss contingency should be accrued if it is **probable** that a liability has been incurred at the balance sheet date and the amount of the loss is **reasonably estimable**. This loss must be accrued because it meets both criteria. Notice that even though the lawsuit was not initiated until 1/12/11, the liability was incurred on 11/5/10 when the accident occurred. When some amount within an estimated range is a better estimate than any other amount in the range, that amount is accrued. Therefore, a loss of $300,000 should be accrued. If no amount within the range is a better estimate than any other amount, the amount at the low end of the range is accrued and the amount at the high end is disclosed.

81. (a)   The additional tax liability must be accrued as a loss contingency because an unfavorable outcome is **probable** and the amount of the loss is **reasonably estimable**. Since $200,000 is the reasonable estimate, that amount should be accrued by debiting Income Tax Expense and crediting Income Tax Payable. The possibility of the liability being as high as $300,000 would be disclosed in the notes. The settlement offer of $275,000 is not accrued at 12/31/10 because prior to financial statement issuance, Haft was unaware of the offer, and $200,000 was the best esti-

mate. In 2011, when the settlement offer was accepted, Haft would record an additional $75,000 of expense and liability.

82. (a)   A loss contingency is accrued if it is **probable** that a liability has been incurred at the balance sheet date and the amount of the loss is reasonably estimable. If no accrual is made for a loss contingency because one or both of the conditions above are not met, disclosure of the contingency shall be made when it is at least **reasonably possible** that a loss was incurred. Therefore, this loss should be disclosed, but not accrued as a liability.

83. (b)   Invern's appropriation of retained earnings for contingencies is merely a reclassification of retained earnings on the balance sheet which tells the readers of the financial statements that such amounts are generally not available to pay dividends. This appropriation has no effect on the income statement. When a loss contingency is probable (as in this instance) **and** reasonably estimable ($190,000 in this instance), accrual of the loss is required. Therefore, Invern must accrue both a liability and an expense of $190,000. Note that Invern will also reclassify $190,000 of appropriated retained earnings into the "general" retained earnings.

84. (d)   At 12/31/10, Halsey's contingent liability of $50,000 is no longer probable due to the favorable judgment and the inability to predict the outcome of the appeal. Therefore, no liability should be reported in the balance sheet. **Gain** contingencies are not reflected in the accounts until realized, so the $30,000 asset is not reported in the 12/31/10 balance sheet, either.

85. (a)   Gain contingencies are not recognized in the income statement until realized. As only $15,000 of the litigation awards has been resolved as of December 31, 2010, Haze should report only $15,000 as a gain in its 2010 financial statements.

86. (a)   **Gain** contingencies are not reflected in the accounts until realized. Since the case is unresolved at 12/31/10, none of this contingent gain should be recorded as income in 2010. Adequate disclosure should be made of the gain contingency, but care should be taken to avoid misleading implications as to the likelihood of realization.

87. (d)   **Gain** contingencies are not reflected in the accounts until realized. Since the case was unresolved at 12/31/10, none of this contingent gain can be recorded as a receivable and/or revenue in 2010. Since the contingency is probable, it should be disclosed along with the 12/31/10 estimate of a range of $75,000 to $150,000. A gain contingency would not be accrued as a receivable. The amount disclosed should be the range because all amounts within the range are considered equally likely.

88. (c)   An estimated loss from a loss contingency shall be accrued by a charge to income if **both** of the following conditions are met:

1.   Information available indicates that it is **probable** that an asset has been impaired or a liability has been incurred.
2.   The amount of the loss can be **reasonably estimated**.

However, gain contingencies are only recognized when a specific event actually occurs, not prior to the event, because to do so would recognize the gain prior to its realization. Therefore, Brooks should recognize the loss in 2010 due to the fact that the event is probable and can be reasonably estimated. Dollis, on the other hand, cannot recognize the gain until 2011, the year they receive the actual award.

89.   (a)   Eagle Co. has a contingent liability where the possibility of loss is **remote**. Loss contingencies are accrued when they are **probable** and **reasonably estimable**. All others are disclosed unless remote. However, some contingencies, such as guarantees of others' debts, standby letters of credit by banks, and agreements to repurchase receivables, are disclosed even if remote. Eagle's contingent liability is **not** accrued, because it is not probable. It **is** disclosed for two reasons: it is a guarantee of other's debt, and it is a related-party transaction.

90.   (d)   An accrual of a liability for future vacation pay is required if all the conditions below are met.

1. Obligation arises from employee services already performed.
2. Obligation arises from rights that vest or accumulate.
3. Payment is probable.
4. Amount can be reasonably estimated.

The criteria are met for the vacation pay ($150 \times \$100 = \$15,000$), so North is required to report a \$15,000 liability. The same criteria apply to accrual of a liability for future sick pay, **except** that if sick pay benefits accumulate but do not vest, accrual is **permitted** but not **required** because its payment is contingent upon future employee sickness. Therefore, no liability is **required** for these sick pay benefits ($75 \times \$100 = \$7500$). Note that the unadjusted balance of the liability account (\$21,000) does not affect the computation of the required 12/31/10 liability.

91.   (d)   The week ended 1/1/11 included four days in 2010 and one day in 2011. The pay due for this week won't be paid until the following Monday (1/4/11). Therefore, Ross has a liability for four days' accrued salaries at 12/31/10 ($4/5 \times \$80,000 = \$64,000$). The entire \$25,000 of vacation pay is an accrued liability at 12/31/10 because it represents vacation time earned by employees in 2010 but not taken by 12/31/10. Therefore, the total accrued salary and vacation pay is \$89,000 (\$64,000 + \$25,000).

92.   (c)   An employer is required to accrue a liability for employees' rights to receive compensation for future absences, such as vacations, when certain conditions are met. The Statement does **not**, however, specify how such liabilities are to be measured. Since vacation time is paid by Gavin Co. at the salaries in effect when vacations are taken or when employment is terminated, Gavin adjusts its vacation liability and expense to current salary levels. Gavin's 2010 vacation pay expense consists of vacations earned for work in 2010 (adjusted to current rates) of \$30,000 plus the amount necessary to adjust its pre-2010 vacation liability for the 10% salary increase. The amount of this adjustment is equal to 10% of the preexisting liability balance at December 31, 2010 [($35,000 − \$20,000) \times 10\% = \$1,500$]. Therefore, total vacation pay expense for the period is equal to \$31,500 (\$30,000 + \$1,500).

93.   (c)   An employer shall accrue a liability for employees' future absences if **all** of the following conditions are met: (1) the employer's obligation relates to employees'

service already rendered, (2) the employees' rights vest **or** accumulate, (3) payment of the compensation is probable, and (4) the amount can be reasonably estimated. All of these conditions are met whether Taos Co.'s employees' rights either accumulate or vest.

94.   (b)   Accrual of a liability for employees' compensation for future absences is required if all of the conditions below are met.

1. Obligation arises from employee services already performed.
2. Obligation arises from rights that vest or accumulate.
3. Payment is probable.
4. Amount can be reasonably estimated.

95.   (d)   The solutions approach is to set up a T-account for warranty liability.

Warranty Liability			
2009 payments	2,250	9,000	2009 exp. (6% × \$150,000)
2010 payments	7,500	15,000	2010 exp. (6% × \$250,000)
		14,250	12/31/10 liability

Each year warranty expense is estimated at 6% of sales and recorded by debiting the expense account and crediting the liability. As warranty expenditures are made, the liability is debited and cash is credited. Note that the total estimated warranty cost for **both** years (2% + 4% = 6%) is recorded in the year of sale in compliance with the matching principle.

96.   (d)   The warranty expense of \$30 for each machine sold, although it will be incurred over the three-year warranty period, is directly related to the sales revenue as an integral and inseparable part of the sale and recognized at the time of the sale. The warranty costs make their contribution to revenue in the year of sale by making the product more attractive to the customer. Therefore, in accordance with the matching principle, the warranty costs should be expensed when the machines are sold with a corresponding credit to accrued liability. Answers (a) and (b) are incorrect; this is a sales warranty approach in which the warranty is sold separately from the product. The revenue is recognized on the straight-line basis and they are expensed as incurred. Answer (c) is incorrect because this describes a cash basis method.

97.   (c)   Warranty services can be recorded at the fair value only if the contract can be settled by a third party. Therefore, the fair value is considered the settlement amount of the contract.

98.   (a)   Case expects 120,000 coupons to be redeemed at a total cost of \$.50 per coupon (\$.45 + \$.05). Therefore, total expected redemptions are \$60,000 (120,000 × \$.50). By 12/31/10, \$25,000 has been paid on coupon redemptions, so a liability of \$35,000 must be established (\$60,000 − \$25,000). Note that this liability would include both payments due for the 50,000 coupons on hand, and payments due on coupons to be received within the first thirty days after the expiration date.

99.   (c)   Dunn records stamp service revenue and provides for the cost of redemptions in the year stamps are sold. Therefore, Dunn's entries are

To record sales of stamps

| Cash | 4,000,000 | |
| Stamp service revenue | | 4,000,000 |

To record cost of redemptions

| Liability for stamp reds. | 2,750,000 | |
| Inventory | | 2,750,000 |

To provide for cost of future redemptions

Cost of redemptions	1,800,000	
Liability for stamp reds.		1,800,000
(80% × $2,250,000)		

The 12/31/10 liability balance is $5,050,000 as shown below.

Liability for Stamp Redemptions

		6,000,000	12/31/09
Redemptions	2,750,000	1,800,000	Provision for reds.
		5,050,000	12/31/10

Miscellaneous

100. (a)   Current assets listed in the trial balance are cash ($550,000), accounts receivable ($1,650,000), and prepaid taxes ($300,000). However, part of the AR must be reclassified, and income tax expense has not yet been recorded. Included in AR is $500,000 due from a customer, for which $250,000 is collectible in 2011 (2 × $125,000) and $250,000 is collectible in 2012. The portion collectible in 2011 should be reclassified as a noncurrent asset. Revenues ($3,600,000) less expenses ($2,600,000) result in pretax income of $1,000,000. Since the tax rate is 30%, tax expense is $300,000 (30% × $1,000,000). Therefore, an adjustment is necessary to debit **income tax expense** and credit **prepaid taxes** for $300,000. Total current assets, after reclassification and adjustment, are $1,950,000 [answer (a)] as calculated below.

Cash	$ 550,000
AR ($1,650,000 − $250,000)	1,400,000
Prepaid taxes ($300,000 − $300,000)	--
	$1,950,000

101. (c)   Before closing entries, retained earnings is $630,000. 2010 net income is revenues ($3,600,000) less expenses ($2,600,000) and income tax expense [30% × ($3,600,000 − $2,600,000) = $300,000]. After adjusting for income tax expense, net income is $700,000 [$3,600,000 − ($2,600,000 + $300,000)]. After closing entries, 12/31/10 retained earnings is $1,330,000 ($630,000 + $700,000). The foreign currency translation adjustment ($430,000) does not affect retained earnings; it is reported as a separate component of stockholders' equity.

102. (a)   Current assets are cash and other assets that are expected to be converted into cash, sold, or consumed either in one year, or in the operating cycle, whichever is longer. Generally included in this category are cash, temporary investments, short-term receivables, inventories, and prepaid expenses. In this situation, there are two special items. Cash must be adjusted because checks that were not mailed until July 9 were recorded June 29. To compute the correct June 30 cash balance, this $30,000 of checks must be added back to the cash balance, turning the $10,000 overdraft into a $20,000 positive balance [(− $10,000) + $30,000 = $20,000]. Also, land held for resale ($100,000) must be included in current assets because, like inventory, at June 30 it is expected to be sold for cash within the next year. Therefore, June 30 current assets total $225,000.

Cash	$20,000
AR, net	35,000
Inventory	58,000
Prepaid expenses	12,000
Land held for resale	100,000
	$225,000

103. (a)   Current liabilities are obligations whose liquidation is reasonably expected to require the use of current assets or the creation of other current liabilities. This means that generally, current liabilities are liabilities due within one year of the balance sheet date. Clearly, accounts payable ($15,000) and dividends payable ($8,000) are current liabilities. Generally, bonds payable are a long-term liability; however, since these bonds are due in 2011, they must be reported as a current liability at 12/31/10 ($25,000 fair value less $3,000 discount, or $22,000). Therefore, total current liabilities are $45,000 ($15,000 + $8,000 + $22,000). The notes payable ($20,000) are classified as long-term because they are not due until 2012.

D.   Ratios

104. (b)   The quick (acid-test) ratio is quick assets (cash, temporary investments in marketable equity securities, and net receivables) divided by current liabilities. The quick ratio measures the ability to pay current liabilities from cash and near-cash items. In this case, quick assets total $700,000 ($170,000 + $450,000 + $80,000) and current liabilities total $400,000 ($60,000 + $240,000 + $100,000), resulting in a quick ratio of 1.75 to 1 ($700,000 ÷ $400,000).

105. (d)   The formula to compute accounts receivable turnover is

$$\frac{\text{Net credit sales}}{\text{Average accounts receivable}}$$

The average receivable is the sum of the beginning and ending net accounts receivable divided by 2. The 2010 beginning accounts receivable equals the 2009 ending balance in accounts receivable. Average accounts receivable is $425,000 [($450,000 + $400,000) ÷ 2]. Applying the formula, the 2010 accounts receivable turnover is 7.06 times ($3,000,000 ÷ $425,000).

106. (d)   Ratios that are useful in assessing a company's ability to meet currently maturing or short-term obligations are referred to as solvency ratios. The acid-test ratio is classified as a solvency ratio, and it measures the ability to pay current liabilities from cash and near-cash items. The acid-test ratio is

$$\frac{\text{Cash + Net receivables + Marketable securities}}{\text{Current liabilities}}$$

The debt to equity ratio is a leverage ratio that measures the relative amount of leverage or debt a company has. The debt to equity ratio is

$$\frac{\text{Total liabilities}}{\text{Common stockholders' equity}}$$

Therefore, answer (d) is correct because the acid-test ratio is useful in assessing a company's ability to meet currently maturing or short-term obligations while the debt to equity ratio is not.

107. (a)   The quick (acid-test) ratio measures the ability to pay current liabilities from cash and near-cash items.

$$\text{Quick ratio} = \frac{\text{Cash, Net receivables, Marketable securities}}{\text{Current liabilities}}$$

Fluctuating market prices of short-term investments may adversely affect Belle's quick ratio and creditworthiness. Inventory and available-for-sale investment items do not affect the quick ratio.

108. (a) The solutions approach is to create a numerical example that conforms to the facts given in the question. Assume the following:

$$\text{Current ratio} = \frac{\$900,000}{\$600,000} = 1.5 \text{ to } 1$$

$$\text{Quick ratio} = \frac{\$300,000}{\$600,000} = .5 \text{ to } 1$$

Payments of accounts payable decrease both cash (a current and quick asset) and accounts payable (a current liability). After payment the following

$$\text{Current ratio} = \frac{900-200}{600-200} = \frac{700}{400} = 1.75 \text{ to } 1$$

$$\text{Quick ratio} = \frac{300-200}{600-200} = \frac{100}{400} = .25 \text{ to } 1$$

Subtracting equal amounts from the numerator and the denominator of a ratio **greater than one** will **increase** the ratio. Subtracting equal amounts from the numerator and the denominator of a ratio **less than one** will **decrease** the ratio. Therefore, the current ratio will increase while the quick ratio decreases.

109. (b) The formula to compute the current ratio is

$$\text{Current ratio} = \frac{\text{Current assets}}{\text{Current liabilities}}$$

The write-off of inventory would decrease current assets and the current ratio. The formula to compute the acid-test (quick) ratio is

$$\text{Acid-test ratio} = \frac{\text{Cash, Net receivables, Marketable securities}}{\text{Current liabilities}}$$

The write-off of inventory has no effect on the acid-test ratio.

110. (d) The number of days in the operating cycle measures the length of time from purchase of inventory to collection of cash. The formula is

$$\left(\begin{array}{c}\text{Number of days'} \\ \text{sales in inventories}\end{array}\right) + \left(\begin{array}{c}\text{Number of days' sales} \\ \text{in accts. receivable}\end{array}\right) = \left(\begin{array}{c}\text{Number of days in} \\ \text{operating cycle}\end{array}\right)$$

$$\text{61 days} \quad + \quad \text{33 days} \quad = \quad \underline{94 \text{ days}}$$

Note that the number of days' sales in inventories measures the number of days from the purchase of inventory to the sale of inventory, while the number of days' sales in accounts receivable measures the number of days from the sale of inventory to the collection of cash.

111. (b) Collection of a receivable results in an increase in cash and a decrease in the accounts receivable balance. The accounts receivable turnover ratio is computed by dividing net credit sales by the average net accounts receivable balance. Collection of a receivable reduces the average net accounts receivable balance. Thus the receivable turnover ratio increases. Since this transaction does not affect cost of goods sold or inventory, the inventory turnover ratio is unaffected. Neither the current ratio nor the quick ratio is affected by the collection; neither current assets nor quick assets would change as a result of the collection.

SOLUTIONS TO SIMULATION PROBLEMS

Simulation Problem 1

Instructions	Concepts		Journal Entries	Reporting Requirements	Communication	Research

	True	False
1. The balance in "factor's holdback" (due from factor) is reported as an expense of the period.	○	●
2. In a specific assignment of receivables, collections on the assigned accounts are generally remitted to the assignor.	●	○
3. Factors are banks or finance companies that purchase receivables for a fee and then collect the remittances directly from the selling company.	○	●
4. A transfer of receivables with recourse may be accounted for as a sale, provided the transferee can require the transferor to repurchase the receivables.	○	●
5. In a transfer of receivables with recourse accounted for as a borrowing, the difference between the receivables and the total of the factor's holdback plus the proceeds is a financing cost that should be amortized to interest expense over the term of the receivables.	●	○

Explanation of solutions

1.   (F) "Factor's holdback" accounts for the proceeds retained by the factor to cover estimated sales discounts, sales returns, and sales allowances. When all amounts have been collected by the factor, the balance in factor's margin is returned to the seller. Therefore, this account is a receivable reported as a current asset on the balance sheet.

2.   (T) A specific assignment of receivables bestows more formal rights upon the assignee (lender) in that the AR do not simply collateralize the loan, but collections on the assigned accounts are actually remitted to the assignor who remits them to the assignee (lender).

3.   (F) Once a company sells receivables to a factor it normally has no further involvement with the receivables. The factor usually collects the remittances directly from the **customer**.

4.   (F) Transfers of receivables in which the transferee can require the transferor to repurchase the receivables may not be considered a sale.

5.   (T) The difference between the amount of receivables sold to a factor in a borrowing transaction and the total of the factor's holdback plus the proceeds is recorded in a "Discount on Transferred AR" or interest expense account (see journal entry (B) in part a.). This account represents interest cost and should be recognized over the term of the receivables. If interest expense is debited, an adjusting entry to defer some of the interest as "Discount" would be required if some of the discount pertains to a later period.

Instructions	Concepts		Journal Entries	Reporting Requirements	Communication	Research

	(A)	(B)	(C)	(D)	(E)	(F)
1. Chester transfers receivables by surrendering control. Collection is to be made by the purchaser (factor), who assumes risk of loss.	○	○	○	●	○	○
2. Chester specifically assigns a portion of its receivables as collateral for a loan. Collections from the assigned receivables will be used to repay the loan and interest.	○	○	●	○	○	○
3. Chester pledges its receivables as collateral to secure a loan and the debtor collects the proceeds.	○	○	○	○	●	○
4. Chester sells accounts receivable to a factor in a transaction considered a borrowing.	○	●	○	○	○	○
5. Chester transfers a note receivable by surrendering control over it. The transfer was on a without recourse basis.	○	○	○	○	○	●
6. Chester pledges its accounts receivable as security for a loan.	○	○	○	○	●	○

Explanation of solutions

1.   (D) In this transaction, receivables are factored by surrendering control and without recourse. This constitutes an outright sale of the receivables in that title, risk of loss, and rights to future benefits are all transferred. Therefore, a loss on the transaction is recognized.

2. **(C)** In a specific assignment of receivables, AR assigned are identified by placing them in an AR assigned account. A finance charge is assessed on assignment transactions that are borrowings.

3. **(E)** When AR are pledged, the receivables serve as collateral for a loan but the proceeds are not remitted to the lender. In this case, the amount of AR pledged is reported at the balance sheet date either parenthetically or in the notes.

4. **(B)** In this transaction, considered a borrowing, receivables are considered to be factored with recourse. Thus, the transaction is viewed as a loan collateralized by AR and the amount of the proceeds plus the factor's holdback and interest charged should be reported as a liability.

5. **(F)** A note discounted on which control is surrendered and the terms include without recourse is considered a sales transaction upon which a loss should be recognized. Notes receivable should be credited.

6. **(E)** A general assignment of receivables is another term for pledging AR, and thus should be disclosed parenthetically or in the notes to the financial statements (no journal entry).

Instructions	Concepts	Journal Entries	Reporting Requirements	Communication	Research

	(D)	(A)	(B)	(N)
1. On December 1, 2010, Chester was awarded damages of $75,000 in a patent infringement suit it brought against a competitor. The defendant did not appeal the verdict, and payment was received in January 2011.	○	○	●	○
2. A former employee of Chester has brought a wrongful-dismissal suit against Chester. Chester's lawyers believe the suit to be without merit.	○	○	○	●
3. At December 31, 2010, Chester had outstanding purchase orders in the ordinary course of business for purchase of a raw material to be used in its manufacturing process. The market price is currently higher than the purchase price and is not anticipated to change within the next year.	○	○	○	●
4. A government contract completed during 2010 is subject to renegotiation. Although Chester estimates that it is reasonably possible that a refund of approximately $200,000 – $300,000 may be required by the government, it does not wish to publicize this possibility.	●	○	○	○
5. Chester has been notified by a governmental agency that it will be held responsible for the cleanup of toxic materials at a site where Chester formerly conducted operations. Chester estimates that it is probable that its share of remedial action will be approximately $500,000.	○	○	●	○
6. On January 5, 2011, Chester redeemed its outstanding bonds and issued new bonds with a lower rate of interest. The reacquisition price was in excess of the carrying amount of the bonds.	●	○	○	○

Explanation of solutions

1. **(B)** Contingencies that might result in gains usually are not reflected in the accounts since to do so might be to recognize revenue prior to its realization. Since this gain contingency was resolved before the issuance of the financial statements, it is handled similar to an ordinary transaction that occurred prior to the year-end and is accrued in the year of its occurrence.

However, disclosure of the contingencies that might result in gains is made in the notes to financial statements

2. **(N)** To accrue an estimated loss from a loss contingency it is necessary that it is probable that an asset has been impaired or a liability has been incurred and that the amount of loss can be reasonably estimated. Since Chester's lawyers believe the suit to be without merit, neither condition has been met.

Disclosure is also required of some loss contingencies that do not meet the accrual requirements if there is a **reasonable possibility** that a loss may be incurred. Again, this condition has not been met.

3. **(N)** The conditions described in this question would be considered general or unspecified business risks that do not meet the conditions for accrual or disclosure.

4. **(D)** The words "reasonably possible" require the disclosure of this item. No accrual need be made since the question does not state it is **probable** that an asset has been impaired or a liability incurred and that the amount of loss can be reasonably estimated.

5. **(B)** The word "probable" and the inclusion of the estimated amount of $500,000 mean that this situation meets the criteria of (1) a probable incurrence of a liability and (2) a reasonable estimate of an amount.

6. **(D)** Disclosure is made for commitments such as an obligation to reduce debts. Since the entire transaction took place in the next accounting period it does not meet the conditions for an accrual in the current period even though it would be disclosed in a footnote.

Instructions	Concepts	Journal Entries	Reporting Requirements	Communication	Research

To: CEO, Chester Company
From: CPA Candidate
Re: Contingencies

As we discussed, you have requested an explanation of the accounting for certain contingencies. A contingency is a situation with an outcome that depends on the occurrence of a future event. In order to account for a contingency, you must assess the likelihood of the event occurring, and estimate the potential loss. For accounting purposes, a contingency is classified as probable, reasonably possible, or remote.

Chester Company has a threat of expropriation of one of its manufacturing plants located in a foreign country. Because this is only reasonably possible, accrual of a loss is inappropriate. However, the company should disclose the threat in a note to the financial statements. This note should include an estimate of the possible loss or an estimate of the range of the loss.

Chester Company has a potential loss due to the discovery of a safety hazard related to one of its products. Because these costs are probable and can be reasonably estimated, the company should accrue a loss in the income statement and record a liability in the balance sheet. Accrual is required in this situation because (1) it is probable that a liability has been incurred; and (2) the amount of the loss can be reasonably estimated. In addition, the company should separately disclose in a note to the financial statements the nature of this safety hazard.

The third situation, wherein Chester Company cannot insure one of its warehouses against rockslide losses, does not require disclosure. An asset has not been impaired, nor has a liability been incurred. Therefore, disclosure of the uninsured rockslide risk is not required.

If you have any additional questions, please contact me.

Instructions	Concepts	Journal Entries	Reporting Requirements	Communication	Research

1. How should short-term obligations be classified on the balance sheet?

FAS6, Para 8

8. Short-term obligations arising from transactions in the normal course of business that are due in customary terms shall be classified as current liabilities. Those obligations (as described in the second sentence of paragraph 7 of Chapter 3A of ARB No. 43) are "obligations for items which have entered into the operating cycle, such as payables incurred in the acquisition of materials and supplies to be used in the production of goods or in providing services to be offered for sale; collections received in advance of the delivery of goods or performance of services; . . . and debts which arise from operations directly related to the operating cycle, such as accruals for wages, salaries, commissions, rentals, royalties, and income and other taxes."

Codification: 470-10-45-13

2. Next year, Chester intends to refinance some short-term debt with a long-term note due in five years. What are the criteria to reclassify the short-term debt as long-term?

FAS6, Para 11

11. The enterprise's intent to refinance the short-term obligation on a long-term basis is supported by an ability to consummate the refinancing demonstrated in either of the following ways:

a. Post-balance-sheet-date issuance of a long-term obligation or equity securities. After the date of an enterprise's balance sheet, but before that balance sheet is issued, a long-term obligation or equity securities have been issued for the purpose of refinancing the short-term obligation on a long-term basis; or

b. Financing agreement. Before the balance sheet is issued, the enterprise has entered into a financing agreement that clearly permits the enterprise to refinance the short-term obligation on a long-term basis on terms that are readily determinable, and all of the following conditions are met:

(i) The agreement does not expire within one year (or operating cycle—see paragraph 2) from the date of the enterprise's balance sheet and during that period the agreement is not cancelable by the lender or the prospective lender or investor (and obligations incurred under the agreement are not callable during that period) except for violation of a provision with which compliance is objectively determinable or measurable.

(ii) No violation of any provision in the financing agreement exists at the balance-sheet date and no available information indicates that a violation has occurred thereafter but prior to the issuance of the balance sheet, or, if one exists at the balance-sheet date or has occurred thereafter, a waiver has been obtained.

(iii) The lender or the prospective lender or investor with which the enterprise has entered into the financing agreement is expected to be financially capable of honoring the agreement.

Codification: 470-10-45-14

3. When should the company accrue an estimated loss on a contingency?

FAS5, Para 8

8.   An estimated loss from a loss contingency (as defined in paragraph 1) shall be accrued by a charge to income if both of the following conditions are met:

   a.   Information available prior to issuance of the financial statements indicates that it is probable that an asset had been impaired or a liability has been incurred at the date of the financial statements. It is implicit in this condition that it must be probable that one or more future events will occur confirming the fact of the loss.

   b.   The amount of loss can be reasonably estimated.

Codification: 450-20-25-2

4. What is a contingency?

FAS5, Para 1

1.   For the purpose of this Statement, a contingency is defined as an existing condition, situation, or set of circumstances involving uncertainty as to possible gain (hereinafter a "gain contingency") or loss (hereinafter a "loss contingency") to an enterprise that will ultimately be resolved when one or more future events occur or fail to occur. Resolution of the uncertainty may confirm the acquisition of an asset or the reduction of a liability or the loss or impairment of an asset or the incurrence of a liability.

Codification: 450-10-05-4

5. Define the three terms used to describe the likelihood of a contingent event occurring.

FAS5, Para 3

3.   When a loss contingency exists, the likelihood that the future event or events will confirm the loss or impairment of an asset or the incurrence of a liability can range from probably to remote. This Statement uses the terms probable, reasonably possible, and remote to identify three areas within that range, as follows:

   a.   Probable. The future event or events are likely to occur.

   b.   Reasonably possible. The chance of the future event or events occurring is more than remote, but less than likely.

   c.   Remote. The change of the future event or events occurring is slight.

Codification: 450-20-25-1

6. What are the conditions required for Chester to accrue vacation pay for its employees?

FAS43, Para 6

6. An employer shall accrue a liability for employees' compensation for future absences if all of the following conditions are met:

   a. The employer's obligation relating to employees' rights to receive compensation for future absences is attributable to employees' services already rendered,

   b. The obligation relates to rights that vest or accumulate,

   c. Payment of the compensation is probable, and

   d. The amount can be reasonably estimated.

Codification: 710-10-25-1

7. What are the criteria required to determine if a liability should be removed from the balance sheet?

FAS140, Para 16

16. A debtor shall derecognize a liability if and only if it has been extinguished. A liability has been extinguished if either of the following conditions is met:

   a. The debtor pays the creditor and is relieved of its obligation for the liability. Paying the creditor includes delivery of cash, other financial assets, goods, or services, or reacquisition by the debtor of its outstanding debt securities whether the securities are canceled or held as so-called treasury bonds.

   b. The debtor is legally released from being the primary obligor under the liability, either judicially or by the creditor.

Codification: 405-20-40-1

Simulation Problem 2

Situation	Concepts	Uncollectible Accounts	Provision for Uncollectible Accounts Expense	Journal Entries	Transfer of Receivables	Communication	Research

	Cash	Not Cash
1. Checking accounts	●	○
2. Treasury stock	○	●
3. Treasury bills	●	○
4. Money market funds	●	○
5. Petty cash	●	○
6. Trading securities	○	●
7. Savings accounts	●	○
8. Sinking fund cash	○	●
9. Compensating balances against long-term borrowings	○	●
10. Cash restricted for new building	○	●
11. Postdated check for customers	○	●
12. Available-for-sale securities	○	●

Situation	Concepts	Uncollectible Accounts	Provision for Uncollectible Accounts Expense	Journal Entries	Transfer of Receivables	Communication	Research

Schedule to calculate provision and allowance for bad debts

Sigma Company
SCHEDULE OF CALCULATION OF ALLOWANCE FOR UNCOLLECTIBLE ACCOUNTS
December 31, 2010

	Amounts of accounts receivable	*Percentage of uncollectible accounts*	*Estimate of uncollectible accounts*
0 to 30 days	$300,000	x 1%	$3,000
31 to 90 days	80,000	x 5%	4,000
91 to 180 days	60,000	x 20%	12,000
Over 180 days	25,000	x 80%	20,000
Total accounts receivable	$465,000		
Total allowance for un-collectible accounts			$39,000

Explanation of solutions

1. This problem consists of two related parts: part a. requires a calculation of the allowance for uncollectible accounts at 12/31/10 using an aging approach, and part b. requires a computation of the 2010 provision for uncollectible accounts (uncollectible accounts expense). The solutions approach is to quickly review the basics of accounting for uncollectible accounts, visualize the solution format, and begin. Some candidates may benefit from preparation of T-accounts (see item 4. below).

2. When using the aging approach, the **total** uncollectible accounts (in other words, the required ending balance in the allowance account) is estimated by applying a different percentage to the various age categories. The percentage increases as the age of the receivables increases because the older a receivable is, the less likely is its ultimate collection.

2.1 In this case, Sigma estimates that 1% of its receivables in the zero-thirty days age category will prove to be uncollectible. Therefore, of that $300,000 of accounts receivable, it is estimated that $3,000 (1% × $300,000) will be uncollectible. Similar computations are performed for the other age categories, resulting in an estimate that $39,000 of the $465,000 accounts receivable will prove to be uncollectible. This is the required 12/31/10 balance in the allowance account.

3. When using the aging approach, the first step is to compute the required ending balance in the allowance account (as discussed in items 2. and 2.1 above). The second step is to compute the uncollectible accounts expense necessary to bring the **unadjusted** allowance balance up to the **required** allowance balance.

3.1 The only item affecting the allowance account in 2009 was the recording of uncollectible accounts expense of $28,000 (1% × $2,800,000 credit sales). Therefore, the 1/1/10 balance in this account is $28,000. No adjustment is necessary for the change in the method of estimating this expense (from percent of sales to aging schedule) because any such change is handled prospectively.

  NOTE: Using the aging percents given also results in a $28,000 balance at 1/1/10. Even if the result was different, though, no adjustment is necessary.

3.2 During 2010, this $28,000 credit balance was decreased by write-offs of $27,000 (debit allowance, credit AR) and increased by $7,000 of recoveries (debit AR, credit allowance; and debit cash, credit AR). Therefore, the 12/31/10 balance in the allowance account, **before adjustment,** is $8,000 ($28,000 − $27,000 + $7,000).

3.3 To increase the allowance account from $8,000 (see 3.2 above) to $39,000 (see 2.1 above), a provision for uncollectible accounts (uncollectible accounts expense) of $31,000 must be recorded for 2010.

4. Some candidates may benefit from the preparation of T-accounts for the allowance account and accounts receivable. These T-accounts are provided below.

T-accounts for 2009

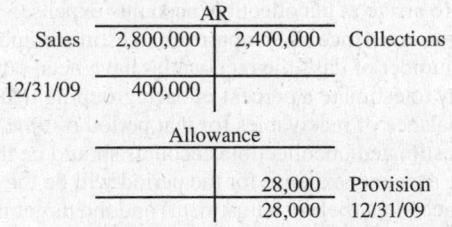

Situation	Concepts	Uncollectible Accounts	Provision for Uncollectible Accounts Expense	Journal Entries	Transfer of Receivables	Communication	Research

Computation of 2010 provision

Balance December 31, 2009	$28,000
Write-offs during 2010	(27,000)
Recoveries during 2010	7,000
Balance before 2010 provision	8,000
Required allowance at December 31, 2010	39,000
2010 Provision	$31,000

Situation	Concepts	Uncollectible Accounts	Provision for Uncollectible Accounts Expense	Journal Entries	Transfer of Receivables	Communication	Research

Write-offs

Allowance for uncollectible accounts		27,000	
Accounts receivable			27,000

Recoveries

Accounts receivable		7,000	
Allowance for uncollectible accounts			7,000
To reinstate the account receivable			
Cash		7,000	
Accounts receivable			7,000
To show payment on the account			

Provision for uncollectible accounts expense at December 31, 2010

Uncollectible accounts expense		31,000	
Allowance for uncollectible accounts			31,000

Situation	Concepts	Uncollectible Accounts	Provision for Uncollectible Accounts Expense	Journal Entries	Transfer of Receivables	Communication	Research

Cash		144,226	
Interest expense (150,000 × .15 × 45/365)		2,774	
Factoring fee (2% × 150,000)		3,000	
Accounts receivable			150,000

Situation	Concepts	Uncollectible Accounts	Provision for Uncollectible Accounts Expense	Journal Entries	Transfer of Receivables	Communication	Research

To: CEO, Sigma Company
From: CPA Candidate
Re: Estimating uncollectible accounts

This memorandum is designed to answer your questions about the accounting for uncollectible accounts. Under generally accepted accounting principles there are two acceptable methods for estimating uncollectible accounts. One method uses an income statement approach, and the other method uses a balance sheet approach. Either method is acceptable; however, a company should select a method and continue to use the same method.

The income statement (percent-of-credit-sales) approach estimates uncollectible accounts based on credit sales. This approach focuses on income determination by attempting to match uncollectible accounts expense with the revenues generated during the period. A company may use a historical analysis to estimate the percent of credit sales that will not be collected. This percent is multiplied by the credit sales for the period to arrive at uncollectible accounts expense.

The second approach, the aging of accounts receivable method, uses a balance sheet approach to estimate uncollectible accounts. The aging approach groups the accounts receivable by the number of days the receivables have been outstanding. Management then uses historical data or loss experience in the industry to estimate a percent of each grouping that may not be collected. The estimated percent is multiplied by the outstanding balance of receivables for that period of time, and the sum of these estimated uncollectible accounts is totaled. The total of estimated uncollectible accounts should be the ending balance in the allowance for uncollectible accounts. The uncollectible accounts expense for the period will be the difference between the year-end balance in the allowance for uncollectible accounts (before adjustment) and the target number for the allowance account based on the most recent aging schedule.

If you would like assistance in preparing the aging schedule, please contact my office.

Situation	Concepts	Uncollectible Accounts	Provision for Uncollectible Accounts Expense	Journal Entries	Transfer of Receivables	Communication	Research

1. With regard to transfers of financial assets, what is the financial components approach?

FAS140, Para 7

7.   Before FASB Statement No. 125, *Accounting for Transfers and Servicing of Financial Assets and Extinguishments of Liabilities*, accounting standards generally required that a transferor account for financial assets transferred as an inseparable unit that had been either entirely sold or entirely retained. Those standards were difficult to apply and produced inconsistent and arbitrary results. For example, whether a transfer "purported to be a sale" was sufficient to determine whether the transfer was accounted for and reported as a sale of receivables under one accounting standard or as a secured borrowing under another. After studying many of the complex developments that have occurred in financial markets during recent years, the Board concluded that previous approaches that viewed each financial asset as an indivisible unit do not provide an appropriate basis for developing consistent and operational standards for dealing with transfers and servicing of financial assets and extinguishments of liabilities. To address those issues adequately and consistently, the Board decided to adopt as the basis for the Statement a financial-components approach that focuses on control and recognizes that financial assets and liabilities can be divided into a variety of components.

Codification: 860-10-10-2

2. Describe the criteria for determining when control has been surrendered in a transfer of receivables.

FAS140, Para 9

9.   A transfer of financial assets (or all or a portion of a financial asset) in which the transferor surrenders control over those financial assets shall be accounted for as a sale to the extent that consideration other than beneficial interests in the transferred assets is received in exchange. The transferor has surrendered control over transferred assets if and only if all of the following conditions are met:

a.   The transferred assets have been isolated from the transferor—put presumptively beyond the reach of the transferor and its creditors, even in bankruptcy or other receivership (paragraphs 27 and 28).

b.   Each transferee (or, if the transferee is a qualifying SPE (paragraph 35), each holder of its beneficial interests) has the right to pledge or exchange the assets (or beneficial interests) it received, and no condition both constrains the transferee (or holder) from taking advantage of its right to pledge or exchange and provides more than a trivial benefit to the transferor (paragraphs 29-34).

c.   The transferor does not maintain effective control over the transferred assets through either (1) an agreement that both entitles and obligates the transferor to repurchase or redeem them before their maturity (paragraphs 47-49) or (2) the ability to unilaterally cause the holder to return specific assets, other than through a cleanup call (paragraphs 50-54).

Codification: 860-10-40-5

3. How are transfers of receivables accounted for if one or more of the criteria for determining whether control has been surrendered are not met?

FAS140, Para 12

12. If a transfer of financial assets in exchange for cash or other consideration (other than beneficial interests in the transferred assets) does not meet the criteria for a sale in paragraph 9, the transferor and transferee shall account for the transfer as a secured borrowing with pledge of collateral (paragraph 15).

Codification: 860-30-25-2

MULTIPLE-CHOICE QUESTIONS (1-25)

1. On March 15, 2009, Ashe Corp. adopted a plan to accumulate $1,000,000 by September 1, 2013. Ashe plans to make four equal annual deposits to a fund that will earn interest at 10% compounded annually. Ashe made the first deposit on September 1, 2009. Future value and future amount factors are as follows:

Future value of $1 at 10% for 4 periods	1.46
Future amount of ordinary annuity of $1 at 10% for four periods	4.64
Future amount of annuity in advance of $1 at 10% for four periods	5.11

Ashe should make four annual deposits (rounded) of
- a. $250,000
- b. $215,500
- c. $195,700
- d. $146,000

2. On July 1, 2009, James Rago signed an agreement to operate as a franchisee of Fast Foods, Inc. for an initial franchise fee of $60,000. Of this amount, $20,000 was paid when the agreement was signed and the balance is payable in four equal annual payments of $10,000 beginning July 1, 2010. The agreement provides that the down payment is not refundable and no future services are required of the franchisor. Rago's credit rating indicates that he can borrow money at 14% for a loan of this type. Information on present and future value factors is as follows:

Present value of $1 at 14% for four periods	0.59
Future amount of $1 at 14% for four periods	1.69
Present value of an ordinary annuity of $1 at 14% for four periods	2.91

Rago should record the acquisition cost of the franchise on July 1, 2009 at
- a. $43,600
- b. $49,100
- c. $60,000
- d. $67,600

3. On November 1, 2009, a company purchased a new machine that it does not have to pay for until November 1, 2011. The total payment on November 1, 2011, will include both principal and interest. Assuming interest at a 10% rate, the cost of the machine would be the total payment multiplied by what time value of money concept?
- a. Present value of annuity of $1.
- b. Present value of $1.
- c. Future amount of annuity of $1.
- d. Future amount of $1.

4. For which of the following transactions would the use of the present value of an annuity due concept be appropriate in calculating the present value of the asset obtained or liability owed at the date of incurrence?
- a. A capital lease is entered into with the initial lease payment due one month subsequent to the signing of the lease agreement.
- b. A capital lease is entered into with the initial lease payment due upon the signing of the lease agreement.
- c. A ten-year 8% bond is issued on January 2 with interest payable semiannually on July 1 and January 1 yielding 7%.
- d. A ten-year 8% bond is issued on January 2 with interest payable semiannually on July 1 and January 1 yielding 9%.

5. Jole Co. lent $10,000 to a major supplier in exchange for a noninterest-bearing note due in three years and a contract to purchase a fixed amount of merchandise from the supplier at a 10% discount from prevailing market prices over the next three years. The market rate for a note of this type is 10%. On issuing the note, Jole should record

	Discount on note receivable	Deferred charge
a.	Yes	Yes
b.	Yes	No
c.	No	Yes
d.	No	No

6. On December 30, 2009, Chang Co. sold a machine to Door Co. in exchange for a noninterest-bearing note requiring ten annual payments of $10,000. Door made the first payment on December 30, 2009. The market interest rate for similar notes at date of issuance was 8%. Information on present value factors is as follows:

Period	Present value of $1 at 8%	Present value of ordinary annuity of $1 at 8%
9	0.50	6.25
10	0.46	6.71

In its December 31, 2009 balance sheet, what amount should Chang report as note receivable?
- a. $45,000
- b. $46,000
- c. $62,500
- d. $67,100

Items 7 and 8 are based on the following:

On January 2, 2009, Emme Co. sold equipment with a carrying amount of $480,000 in exchange for a $600,000 noninterest-bearing note due January 2, 2012. There was no established exchange price for the equipment. The prevailing rate of interest for a note of this type at January 2, 2009, was 10%. The present value of $1 at 10% for three periods is 0.75.

7. In Emme's 2009 income statement, what amount should be reported as interest income?
- a. $ 9,000
- b. $45,000
- c. $50,000
- d. $60,000

8. In Emme's 2009 income statement, what amount should be reported as gain (loss) on sale of machinery?
- a. $(30,000) loss.
- b. $ 30,000 gain.
- c. $120,000 gain.
- d. $270,000 gain.

9. On December 31, 2009, Jet Co. received two $10,000 notes receivable from customers in exchange for services rendered. On both notes, interest is calculated on the outstanding balance at the interest rate of 3% compounded annually and payable at maturity. The note from Hart Corp., made under customary trade terms, is due in nine months and the note from Maxx, Inc. is due in five years. The market interest rate for similar notes on December 31, 2009, was 8%. The compound interest factors are as follows:

Future value of $1 due in nine months at 3%	1.0225	
Future value of $1 due in five years at 3%	1.1593	
Present value of $1 due in nine months at 8%	.944	
Present value of $1 due in five years at 8%	.680	

Jet does not elect the fair value option for reporting its financial assets. At what amounts should these two notes receivable be reported in Jet's December 31, 2009 balance sheet?

	Hart	Maxx
a.	$ 9,440	$6,800
b.	$ 9,652	$7,820
c.	$10,000	$6,800
d.	$10,000	$7,883

10. Leaf Co. purchased from Oak Co. a $20,000, 8%, five-year note that required five equal annual year-end payments of $5,009. The note was discounted to yield a 9% rate to Leaf. At the date of purchase, Leaf recorded the note at its present value of $19,485. Leaf does not elect the fair value option for reporting its financial liabilities. What should be the total interest revenue earned by Leaf over the life of this note?

a. $5,045
b. $5,560
c. $8,000
d. $9,000

Items 11 and 12 are based on the following:

House Publishers offered a contest in which the winner would receive $1,000,000, payable over twenty years. On December 31, 2009, House announced the winner of the contest and signed a note payable to the winner for $1,000,000, payable in $50,000 installments every January 2. Also on December 31, 2009, House purchased an annuity for $418,250 to provide the $950,000 prize monies remaining after the first $50,000 installment, which was paid on January 2, 2010.

11. In its December 31, 2009 balance sheet, what amount should House report as note payable—contest winner, net of current portion?

a. $368,250
b. $418,250
c. $900,000
d. $950,000

12. In its 2009 income statement, what should House report as contest prize expense?

a. $0
b. $ 418,250
c. $ 468,250
d. $1,000,000

13. On December 31, 2009, Roth Co. issued a $10,000 face value note payable to Wake Co. in exchange for services rendered to Roth. The note, made at usual trade terms, is due in nine months and bears interest, payable at maturity, at the annual rate of 3%. The market interest rate is 8%. The compound interest factor of $1 due in nine months at 8% is .944. At what amount should the note payable be reported in Roth's December 31, 2009 balance sheet?

a. $10,300
b. $10,000
c. $ 9,652
d. $ 9,440

14. On January 1, 2009, Parke Company borrowed $360,000 from a major customer evidenced by a noninterest-bearing note due in three years. Parke agreed to supply the customer's inventory needs for the loan period at lower than market price. At the 12% imputed interest rate for this type of loan, the present value of the note is $255,000 at January 1, 2009. What amount of interest expense should be included in Parke's 2009 income statement?

a. $43,200
b. $35,000
c. $30,600
d. $0

15. Pie Co. uses the installment sales method to recognize revenue. Customers pay the installment notes in twenty-four equal monthly amounts, which include 12% interest. What is an installment note's receivable balance six months after the sale?

a. 75% of the original sales price.
b. Less than 75% of the original sales price.
c. The present value of the remaining monthly payments discounted at 12%.
d. Less than the present value of the remaining monthly payments discounted at 12%.

16. On July 1, 2009, a company obtained a two-year 8% note receivable for services rendered. At that time the market rate of interest was 10%. The face amount of the note and the entire amount of the interest are due on June 30, 2011. Interest receivable at December 31, 2009, was

a. 5% of the face value of the note.
b. 4% of the face value of the note.
c. 5% of the July 1, 2009, present value of the amount due June 30, 2011.
d. 4% of the July 1, 2009, present value of the amount due June 30, 2011.

17. Which of the following is reported as interest expense?
a. Pension cost interest.
b. Postretirement health-care benefits interest.
c. Imputed interest on noninterest-bearing note.
d. Interest incurred to finance construction of machinery for own use.

18. Norton Corp. does not elect the fair value option for recording its financial liabilities. The discount resulting from the determination of a note payable's present value should be reported on its balance sheet as a(n)
a. Addition to the face amount of the note.
b. Deferred charge separate from the note.
c. Deferred credit separate from the note.
d. Direct reduction from the face amount of the note.

19. In calculating the carrying amount of a loan, the lender adds to the principal

	Direct loan origination costs incurred by the lender	Loan origination fees charged to the borrower
a.	Yes	Yes
b.	Yes	No
c.	No	Yes
d.	No	No

20. Duff, Inc. borrowed from Martin Bank under a ten-year loan in the amount of $150,000 with a stated interest rate of 6%. Payments are due monthly, and are computed to be $1,665. Martin Bank incurs $4,000 of direct loan origination costs and $2,000 of indirect loan origination costs. In addition, Martin Bank charges Duff, Inc. a four-point nonrefundable loan origination fee.

Martin Bank, the lender, has a carrying amount of
- a. $144,000
- b. $148,000
- c. $150,000
- d. $152,000

21. Martin Bank grants a ten-year loan to Duff, Inc. in the amount of $150,000 with a stated interest rate of 6%. Payments are due monthly, and are computed to be $1,665. Martin Bank incurs $4,000 of direct loan origination costs and $2,000 of indirect loan origination costs. In addition, Martin Bank charges Duff, Inc. a four-point nonrefundable loan origination fee.

Duff, the borrower, has a carrying amount of
- a. $144,000
- b. $148,000
- c. $150,000
- d. $152,000

22. On December 1, 2009, Money Co. gave Home Co. a $200,000, 11% loan. Money paid proceeds of $194,000 after the deduction of a $6,000 nonrefundable loan origination fee. Principal and interest are due in sixty monthly installments of $4,310, beginning January 1, 2010. The repayments yield an effective interest rate of 11% at a present value of $200,000 and 12.4% at a present value of $194,000. What amount of income from this loan should Money report in its 2009 income statement?
- a. $0
- b. $1,833
- c. $2,005
- d. $7,833

23. On July 1, 2010, Marseto Corporation borrows $100,000 on a 10%, five-year interest-bearing note. At December 31, 2010, the fair value of the note is determined to be $97,500. Marseto elects the fair value option for reporting its financial liabilities. On its December 31, 2010 financial statements, what amounts should be presented for this note?

	Interest Expense	Note Payable	Gain (Loss)
a.	$10,000	$100,000	$0
b.	$10,000	$ 97,500	$ 2,500
c.	$ 5,000	$ 97,500	$ 2,500
d.	$0	$ 97,500	$(7,500)

24. On January 1, 2010, Connor Corporation signed a $100,000 noninterest-bearing note due in three years at a discount rate of 10%. Connor elects to use the fair value option for reporting its financial liabilities. On December 31, 2010, Connor's credit rating and risk factors indicated that the rate of interest applicable to its borrowings was 9%. The present value factors at 10% and 9% are presented below.

PV factor 10%, 3 periods	.751
PV factor 10%, 2 periods	.826
PV factor 10%, 1 period	.909
PV factor 9%, 3 periods	.772
PV factor 9%, 2 periods	.842
PV factor 9%, 1 period	.917

At what amount should Connor present the note on the December 31, 2010 balance sheet?
- a. $75,100
- b. $77,200

- c. $82,610
- d. $84,200

25. On January 1, 2010, London Corporation borrowed $500,000 on a 8%, noninterest-bearing note due in four years. The present value of the note on January 1, 2010, was $367,500. London Corporation elects the fair value method for reporting its financial liabilities. On December 31, 2010, it is determined the fair value of the note is $408,150. At what amount should the discount on notes payable be presented on the balance sheet on December 31, 2010?
- a. $132,500
- b. $103,100
- c. $ 91,850
- d. $0

SIMULATION PROBLEMS

Simulation Problem 1   (60 to 75 minutes)

Situation						
	Present Value Concepts	Long-Term Receivables Disclosure	Balance Sheet Disclosure	Income Statement Disclosure	Research	Communication

Kern, Inc. had the following long-term receivable account balances at December 31, 2008:

Note receivable from the sale of an idle building	$750,000
Note receivable from an officer	200,000

Transactions during 2009 and other information relating to Kern's long-term receivables follow:

- The $750,000 note receivable is dated May 1, 2008, bears interest at 9%, and represents the balance of the consideration Kern received from the sale of its idle building to Able Co. Principal payments of $250,000 plus interest are due annually beginning May 1, 2009. Able made its first principal and interest payment on May 1, 2009. Collection of the remaining note installments is reasonably assured.
- The $200,000 note receivable is dated December 31, 2006, bears interest at 8%, and is due on December 31, 2011. The note is due from Frank Black, president of Kern, Inc., and is collateralized by 5,000 shares of Kern's common stock. Interest is payable annually on December 31, and all interest payments were made through December 31, 2009. The quoted market price of Kern's common stock was $45 per share on December 31, 2009.
- On April 1, 2009, Kern sold a patent to Frey Corp. in exchange for a $100,000 noninterest-bearing note due on April 1, 2011. There was no established exchange price for the patent, and the note had no ready market. The prevailing interest rate for this type of note was 10% at April 1, 2009. The present value of $1 for two periods at 10% is 0.826. The patent had a carrying amount of $40,000 at January 1, 2009, and the amortization for the year ended December 31, 2009, would have been $8,000. Kern is reasonably assured of collecting the note receivable from Frey.
- On July 1, 2009, Kern sold a parcel of land to Barr Co. for $400,000 under an installment sale contract. Barr made a $120,000 cash down payment on July 1, 2009, and signed a four-year 10% note for the $280,000 balance. The equal annual payments of principal and interest on the note will be $88,332, payable on July 1 of each year from 2010 through 2013. The fair value of the land at the date of sale was $400,000. The cost of the land to Kern was $300,000. Collection of the remaining note installments is reasonably assured.

	Present Value Concepts					
Situation		Long-Term Receivables Disclosure	Balance Sheet Disclosure	Income Statement Disclosure	Research	Communication

Assume that you are the accountant for Kern Corporation and are working on various debt accounting issues. Use the following responses to define the terms in the table that follows.

Responses to be selected
A.   Effective interest rate × Net receivable or payable balance at the beginning of the period
B.   Periodic interest is computed on principal balance and interest earned to date
C.   Represents the debtor's incremental borrowing rate
D.   Series of payments/receipts which occur at beginning of the period
E.   The difference between the present value of the note and the cash exchanged when the market rate of interest < rate on note
F.   Periodic interest is computed based on the principal balance only
G.   Maturity value of note and interest payments discounted to the present value
H.   This will result when face rate of the note < yield rate
I.   The amount which will be available in the future as a result of consecutive payments/receipts at the end of each period—compounded at a specified interest rate
J.   Series of payments/receipts which are made at the end of the period
K.   No premium or discount exists

	(A)	(B)	(C)	(D)	(E)	(F)	(G)	(H)	(I)	(J)	(K)
1. Annuity due	O	O	O	O	O	O	O	O	O	O	O
2. Imputed interest rate	O	O	O	O	O	O	O	O	O	O	O
3. Market value of note	O	O	O	O	O	O	O	O	O	O	O
4. Note issued at a discount	O	O	O	O	O	O	O	O	O	O	O
5. Premium on a note	O	O	O	O	O	O	O	O	O	O	O
6. Simple interest method	O	O	O	O	O	O	O	O	O	O	O
7. Interest revenue/expense	O	O	O	O	O	O	O	O	O	O	O
8. Future value of annuity	O	O	O	O	O	O	O	O	O	O	O
9. Face of note equals present value of the note	O	O	O	O	O	O	O	O	O	O	O

Situation	Present Value Concepts	Long-Term Receivables Disclosure	Balance Sheet Disclosure	Income Statement Disclosure	Research	Communication

Complete the following section of the long-term receivables on the balance sheet.

Kern, Inc.
LONG-TERM RECEIVABLES SECTION
OF BALANCE SHEET
December 31, 2009

9% note receivable from sale of idle building, due in annual installments of $250,000 to May 1, 2011, less current installment		
8% note receivable from officer, due December 31, 2011 collateralized by 5,000 shares of Kern, Inc. common stock with a fair value of $225,000		
Noninterest-bearing note from sale of patent, net of 10% imputed interest due April 1, 2011		
Installment contract receivable, due in annual installments of $88,332 to July 1, 2013, less current installment		
Total long-term receivables		

Situation	Present Value Concepts	Long-Term Receivables Disclosure	Balance Sheet Disclosure	Income Statement Disclosure	Research	Communication

Complete the following amounts for balance sheet disclosures.

Kern, Inc.
SELECTED BALANCE SHEET ACCOUNTS
December 31, 2009

Current portion of long-term receivables:		
Note receivable from sale of idle building		
Installment contract receivable		
Total		
Accrued interest receivable:		
Note receivable from sale of idle building		
Installment contract receivable		
Total		

Situation	Present Value Concepts	Long-Term Receivables Disclosure	Balance Sheet Disclosure	Income Statement Disclosure	Research	Communication

Complete the following schedule showing interest revenue from long-term receivables and gains recognized on the sale of assets to be reported in Kern's 2009 income statement.

Kern, Inc.
INTEREST REVENUE FROM LONG-TERM RECEIVABLES
AND GAINS RECOGNIZED ON SALE OF ASSETS
For the Year Ended December 31, 2009

Interest revenue:		
Note receivable from sale of idle building		
Note receivable from sale of patent		
Note receivable from officer		
Installment contract receivable from sale of land		
Total interest revenue		
Gains recognized on sale of assets:		
Patent		
Land		
Total gains recognized		

Situation	Present Value Concepts	Long-Term Receivables Disclosure	Balance Sheet Disclosure	Income Statement Disclosure	Research	Communication

For each of the following, find the appropriate paragraph in FARS to answer each question. Cut and paste the appropriate guidance from the accounting standards.

1. On July 1, 2009, Kern borrows $100,000 on a noninterest-bearing three-year note and received $85,000 in proceeds. How should Kern value the note in its July 1, 2009 financial statements?

2. Where is a discount or premium disclosed on the financial statements?

3. How is a discount or premium on a note amortized?

4. What information must a company disclose regarding long-term debt on its financial statements?

5. How does a lender account for loan origination fees?

Situation	Present Value Concepts	Long-Term Receivables Disclosure	Balance Sheet Disclosure	Income Statement Disclosure	Research	Communication

Certain of Kern's notes receivable have a zero interest rate. Write a memorandum to the audit staff explaining why it is necessary to record zero interest rate notes receivable at their present value.

REMINDER: Your response will be graded for both technical content and writing skills. Technical content will be evaluated for information that is helpful to the intended reader and clearly relevant to the issue. Writing skills will be evaluated for development, organization, and the appropriate expression of ideas in professional correspondence. Use a standard business memo or letter format with a clear beginning, middle, and end. Do not convey information in the form of a table, bullet point list, or other abbreviated presentation.

To: Audit Staff
From: CPA Candidate
Re: Notes receivable

Simulation Problem 2   (50 to 60 minutes)

Situation	Sales Price	Carrying Value	Amortization Table	Gain or Loss	Research	Communication

Assume that you are the CPA for Dawson Corporation. On January 1, 2009, Catrina Corporation sold to Dawson Corporation equipment that originally cost $320,000, with accumulated depreciation of $75,000 for a noninterest-bearing note with a face value of $300,000 due January 1, 2013. The fair market value of the equipment is readily determinable and the market rate for a note of this type is 6%. Dawson depreciates equipment over a five-year life with no residual value.

Situation	Sales Price	Carrying Value	Amortization Table	Gain or Loss	Research	Communication

The sales price of the equipment would be calculated as (select the answer from the following list)

    Book value on Catrina's books.
    Cost on Catrina's records.
    Maturity value of the note signed by Dawson.
    Present value of the note at 6% for four periods.
    Future value of the book value at 6% for four periods.

Situation	Sales Price	Carrying Value	Amortization Table	Gain or Loss	Research	Communication

Calculate the carrying value of the note on 1/1/09 on Catrina's books.

<u>Time value of money factors</u>

FV of $1 for 3 periods	1.191
FV of $1 for 4 periods	1.262
FVA of $1 for 3 periods	3.184
FVA of $1 for 4 periods	4.375
PV of $1 for 3 periods	.8396
PV of $1 for 4 periods	.7921
PVA of $1 for 3 periods	2.673
PVA of $1 for 4 periods	3.465
PVA of $1 due for 3 periods	2.833
PVA of $1 due for 4 periods	3.673

Situation	Sales Price	Carrying Value	**Amortization Table**	Gain or Loss	Research	Communication

Prepare an amortization table and calculate the interest income and carrying value of the note for Catrina for the years 2009 and 2010. Indicate whether the note has a premium or discount by completing the correct columns in the schedule. (For a more realistic exam experience, complete the problem using a spreadsheet program, such as Excel.)

Year	Interest income	Premium on note	Discount on note	Carrying value

Situation	Sales Price	Carrying Value	Amortization Table	**Gain or Loss**	Research	Communication

Prepare a schedule calculating the gain or loss on Catrina's books for the sale of the fixed asset on 1/1/09. (For a more realistic exam experience, complete the problem using a spreadsheet program, such as Excel.)

Original cost	$320,000	Proceeds of note	???
Maturity value note	$300,000	Premium on note	???
Accumulated depreciation	$ 75,000	Discount on note	???
Interest rate	6%		

Situation	Sales Price	Carrying Value	Amortization Table	Gain or Loss	**Research**	Communication

Research the accounting standards and select the appropriate sections that explain how the equipment should be valued on Dawson's financial statements at date of acquisition.

Situation	Sales Price	Carrying Value	Amortization Table	Gain or Loss	Research	**Communication**

Write a memo to your client with your recommendations and your rationale for the method of valuing the equipment on the date of acquisition, and any accounting entries that will be necessary for Dawson after the acquisition of the equipment.

REMINDER: Your response will be graded for both technical content and writing skills. Technical content will be evaluated for information that is helpful to the intended reader and clearly relevant to the issue. Writing skills will be evaluated for development, organization, and the appropriate expression of ideas in professional correspondence. Use a standard business memo or letter format with a clear beginning, middle, and end. Do not convey information in the form of a table, bullet point list, or other abbreviated presentation.

To: CFO, Dawson Corporation
From: CPA Candidate
Re: Acquisition of equipment on January 1, 2009

MULTIPLE-CHOICE ANSWERS

1. c	__ __	7. b	__ __	13. b	__ __	19. b	__ __	25. d	__ __
2. b	__ __	8. a	__ __	14. c	__ __	20. b	__ __		
3. b	__ __	9. d	__ __	15. c	__ __	21. a	__ __		
4. b	__ __	10. b	__ __	16. b	__ __	22. c	__ __		
5. a	__ __	11. b	__ __	17. c	__ __	23. c	__ __	1st: __/25 = __%	
6. c	__ __	12. c	__ __	18. d	__ __	24. d	__ __	2nd: __/25 = __%	

MULTIPLE-CHOICE ANSWER EXPLANATIONS

A. Fundamentals

1.   (c)   The desired fund balance on September 1, 2013, ($1,000,000) is a **future amount**. The series of four equal annual deposits is an **annuity in advance,** as illustrated in the diagram below.

D	D	D	D	$1,000,000
9/1/09	9/1/10	9/1/11	9/1/12	9/1/13

This is an annuity in advance, rather than an ordinary annuity, because the last deposit (9/1/12) is made one year prior to the date the future amount is needed. Therefore, these are beginning-of-year payments. The deposit amount is computed by dividing the future amount by the factor for the future amount of an annuity in advance.

$$\$1,000,000 \div 5.11 = \$195,700$$

2.   (b)   The requirement is to determine the acquisition cost of a franchise. The cost of this franchise is the down payment of $20,000 plus the present value of the four equal annual payments of $10,000. The annual payments represent an annuity, so the $10,000 annual payment is multiplied by the present value factor of 2.91. Therefore, the franchise cost is $49,100 ($20,000 + $29,100). The journal entry is

Franchise	49,100	
Discount on notes payable	10,900	
Notes payable		40,000
Cash		20,000

3.   (b)   The requirement is to determine what time value of money concept would be used to determine the cost of a machine when a payment (principal plus interest) is to be made in two years. Answer (b) is correct because the cost of the machine is to be recorded immediately; therefore, the cost of the present value of a lump-sum payment would be used. Answer (c) is incorrect because a future amount would be used in computing the payment and not the cost of the machine. Also, a lump-sum payment is involved and not an annuity. Answer (d) is incorrect because a future amount would be used in computing the payment and not the cost. Answer (a) is incorrect because a lump-sum payment is involved, not an annuity.

4.   (b)   The requirement is the situation which illustrates an annuity due. An annuity due (annuity in advance) is a series of payments where the first payment is made at the beginning of the first period, in contrast to an ordinary annuity (annuity in arrears), in which the first payment is made at the end of the first period. Answer (b) is correct because the initial lease payment is due immediately (at the beginning of the first period). Answers (a), (c), and (d) all illustrate situations in which the first lease or interest payment occurs at the end of the first period. Note that in answers (c) and (d), the stated rate and yield rate of the bonds differ; while this would affect the present value of the bonds, it has

no effect on the classification as an annuity due or an ordinary annuity.

5.   (a)   In recording the transaction recognition should be given to both the imputed interest rate and the deferred charge related to the merchandise discount. Answer (b) is incorrect because the deferred charge should also be recognized. Answer (c) is incorrect because a discount on the noninterest-bearing note should also be recognized. Answer (d) is incorrect because both the discount and the deferred charge should be recognized.

A.9. Notes Receivable and Payable

6.   (c)   If the FMV of the machine and the FMV of the note are not known, the transaction should be recorded at the PV of the note by imputing interest at the prevailing rate (8%) for similar notes. This series of ten payments is an **annuity in advance,** because the first payment is due immediately on 12/30/09. However, the problem requires the amount to be reported for the note receivable on **12/31/09,** after the first payment is received. The remaining nine payments are an ordinary annuity, as illustrated in the diagram below.

PV = ?

	R1	R2	R8	R9
12/30/09	12/30/10	12/30/11	12/30/17	12/30/18

In a PV computation, one must look at the first rent to see if it is an ordinary annuity or annuity in advance. If the first rent occurs one period after the computation date, it is an ordinary annuity. Therefore, the PV to be reported for the note receivable at 12/31/09 is $62,500 (10,000 × 6.25).

7.   (b)   The $600,000 noninterest-bearing note should be recorded at its present value of $450,000 ($600,000 × .75). The journal entry is

Loss on sale of equip.	30,000		
Note receivable	600,000		
Discount on NR		150,000 }	450,000
Equipment (net)		480,000	

At 12/31/09, interest income would be recognized using the effective interest method. Using this method, interest is computing by multiplying the book value of the note ($600,000 – $150,000 = $450,000) by the effective interest rate ($450,000 × 10% = $45,000).

8.   (a)   The $600,000 noninterest-bearing note should be recorded at its present value of $450,000 ($600,000 × .75). The journal entry is

Loss on sale of equip.	30,000		
Note receivable	600,000		
Discount on NR		150,000 }	450,000
Equipment (net)		480,000	

The loss is recognized because the fair value of the note received ($450,000) is $30,000 less than the carrying amount of the equipment sold ($480,000).

9. (d) Receivables bearing an unreasonably low stated interest rate should be recorded at their present value. However, this rule does **not** apply to receivables arising through the normal course of business that mature in less than one year. Therefore, the Hart receivable would be recorded at face value ($10,000), since it matures in nine months. The Maxx receivable would be recorded at its present value, since it matures in five years. The Maxx receivable will result in a lump-sum collection of $11,593 ($10,000 × 1.1593), so its present value is $7,883 ($11,593 × .680).

10. (b) The total interest revenue earned over the life of the note equals the excess of the cash received over the cash paid to acquire the note. The cash received over the five years is $25,045 (5 receipts of $5,009 each). The cash paid to acquire the $20,000 note was $19,485. Therefore, the total interest revenue is $5,560 ($25,045 – $19,485).

11. (b) The $1,000,000 note is payable $50,000 in 2009 (current portion) and $950,000 after 2009 (long-term portion). This noninterest-bearing long-term note should be recorded at its present value, which can be measured as the amount required to purchase an annuity sufficient to provide the funds to satisfy the obligation. Therefore, the note payable, net of current portion, should be reported at $418,250.

12. (c) The contest prize expense must be recognized at the present value of the obligation incurred as a result of the contest. The obligation consists of $50,000 payable in two days, and $950,000 payable over the next nineteen years. The $950,000 long-term portion has a present value of $418,250, as evidenced by the cost of an annuity contract sufficient to satisfy it. Therefore, the total PV of the obligation is $468,250 ($50,000 + $418,250). The journal entry to record the expense is

Contest prize expense	$468,250	
Discount on NP	$531,750	
Notes payable		$1,000,000

13. (b) All receivables and payables are subject to present value measurement techniques and interest imputation, if necessary, with certain exceptions. One exception is normal course of business receivables and payables maturing in less than one year. Therefore this note payable, due in nine months at usual trade terms, would be reported at face value ($10,000) rather than at present value ($10,225 × .944 = $9,652).

14. (c) The requirement is to determine the amount of interest expense to be recognized in 2009 from a noninterest-bearing note. Parke Company is able to borrow on a noninterest basis because they agree to sell their product at less than the market price. In this type of situation, the note payable is recorded at present value, and the difference between the present value and the cash received is recorded as **unearned sales revenue** (to be recognized when the product is sold at less than market value). The initial journal entry is

Cash	360,000		
Discount on NP	105,000		
Note payable		360,000	} 255,000
Unearned sales revenue		105,000	

When interest expense is recognized at the end of 2009, the effective interest method must be used. Using this method, interest expense is computed by multiplying the book value of the liability ($360,000 – $105,000 = $255,000) by the effective interest rate (12%), resulting in interest expense of $30,600.

15. (c) The entry made to record an installment sale (ignoring the cost of sale and inventory) is as follows:

Note receivable	(Sale price)
Installment sales	(PV of note @ 12%)
Discount on notes receivable	(Plug)

Although the customer would have paid 25% (six out of twenty-four months) of the total payments due under the terms of the installment sale, the **net** carrying value of the note (equal to the principal balance of the note less the unamortized discount) is equal to the present value of the remaining monthly payments discounted at 12%. Under the effective interest method, the carrying value of the note will at all times be equal to the present value of the remaining installment payments, regardless of whether the note is recorded gross or net in Pie Co.'s accounts.

16. (b) When a note is issued with a stated rate (8% in this case) below the market rate (10% in this case), the note will be issued at a discount. The entry for the recipient of the note on July 1 would be as follows:

Notes receivable	xxx
Disc. on notes rec.	xxx
Service revenue	xxx

On December 31, the company must accrue interest on the note. The following entry would be made:

Interest receivable	(6 months at stated rate)
Disc. on notes rec.	(6 months amortization)
Interest revenue	(6 months interest at market rate)

Note that interest receivable is debited for an amount based upon the **stated** (face) rate of the note. This is because the stated rate will determine the amount of cash interest that will be received upon maturity of the note. Since the bond was held for six months (7/1/09 to 12/31/09) as of 12/31/09, the amount of the receivable would be determined as follows:

$$\text{Interest receivable} = \text{Face value of note} \times \text{Stated rate} \times \text{Period held}$$
$$= \text{Face value} \times 8\% \times (6/12 \text{ months})$$
$$= 4\% \times \text{Face value}$$

17. (c) When a noninterest-bearing note is issued, interest must be imputed on the note and amortized to interest expense over the life of the note using the effective interest rate. Answers (a) and (b) are incorrect because interest on pension cost and postretirement health-care benefits is included as a component of future benefit obligation. Answer (d) is incorrect because interest incurred to finance construction of machinery for a company's own use may be capitalized and amortized.

18. (d) **Discount on notes payable** is a liability valuation account. It should be reported as a direct reduction from the face amount of the note (contra account). A **premium on notes payable** would be reported as an addition to the face amount of the note. A discount is not recorded as a separate asset because it does not provide any future economic benefit. It is not a deferred credit separate from the note because it is a debit, not a credit, and because it is inseparable from the note. Thus, a discount on notes payable should be reported on the balance sheet as a direct reduction from the face amount of the note.

A.10. Lending Activities

19. (b)   In calculating the carrying amount of a loan, loan origination costs are added to the principal by the lender. Any fee charged to the borrower is **deducted** from the principal by both parties (the lender and the borrower) in calculating the carrying amount.

20. (b)   The lender's carrying amount of the loan is calculated by adding the direct loan origination costs to the principal and deducting the loan origination fee charged to the borrower. Indirect loan origination costs are charged to expense as incurred, and are not considered when calculating the carrying amount of the loan. Therefore, Martin Bank has a carrying amount of $148,000 [$150,000 principal plus $4,000 direct loan origination costs minus $6,000 ($150,000 × 0.04) nonrefundable loan origination fee]. The $2,000 indirect loan origination costs are expensed in the period incurred.

21. (a)   Duff, Inc., the borrower, receives 4% less than the face amount of $150,000. Duff's carrying amount is, therefore, $150,000 – $6,000, or $144,000. Loan origination fees charged to the borrower are deducted from the principal in calculating the carrying amount.

NOTE: Loan origination fees are frequently assessed in the form of points, where a point is 1% of the face amount of the loan.

22. (c)   Money Co. made a cash outflow of $194,000 for the $200,000 loan Money gave to Home Co. The book value of the loan is $194,000 on Money's books. Money will receive an effective interest rate of 12.4% on its cash outflow. Income from the loan would be calculated by multiplying the book value, times the effective interest rate, and the number of months of the year (in this case just one— December). $194,000 × .124 × 1/12 = $2,004.67. The stated rate is 11% and is not used in the calculation. Money Co. will receive equal monthly installments over the sixty-month life of the loan. Money Co. will effectively earn 12.4% on its initial cash outflow of $194,000, because Home Co. will repay principal for the total loan amount of $200,000.

23. (c)   The requirement is to determine the amounts presented in the financial statements. If the fair value option is elected for reporting financial liabilities, the liability would be reported on the balance sheet at its fair value of $97,500, with a resulting gain of $2,500 ($100,000 – $97,500) on the income statement. The interest expense for the period would be calculated as $100,000 × 10% × 6/12 = $5,000. Answers (a) and (b) are incorrect because interest is calculated for the amount of time the loan is outstanding. In this case, the loan was outstanding for six months. Answer (d) is incorrect because if interest expense were netted against the gain of $2,500 the total expense or loss would be $2,500 for the period ($5,000 interest expense less $2,500 gain on note payable).

24. (d)   The requirement is to determine the amount at which the note should be presented on the balance sheet. On January 1, 2010, the note payable would be recorded at its present value of $75,100 (PV factor of 10% for 3 periods

(.751 × $100,000 = $75,100). At December 31, 2010, the note would be revalued to fair value using the appropriate interest rate of 9%. At December 31, 2010, the note is valued at the PV factor of 9% for 2 periods. Therefore, the note would be valued at $84,200 (.842 × $100,000).

25. (d)   The requirement is to determine the amount to be presented on the balance sheet. When the fair value option is elected, any effects of discounts or premiums are removed from the financial statements, and the accounting rules for reporting discounts and premiums no longer apply.

SOLUTIONS TO SIMULATION PROBLEMS

Simulation Problem 1

Situation	Present Value Concepts	Long-Term Receivables Disclosure	Balance Sheet Disclosure	Income Statement Disclosure	Research	Communication

(A) (B) (C) (D) (E) (F) (G) (H) (I) (J) (K)

		A	B	C	D	E	F	G	H	I	J	K
1.	Annuity due	○	○	○	●	○	○	○	○	○	○	○
2.	Imputed interest rate	○	○	●	○	○	○	○	○	○	○	○
3.	Market value of note	○	○	○	○	○	○	●	○	○	○	○
4.	Note issued at a discount	○	○	○	○	○	○	○	●	○	○	○
5.	Premium on a note	○	○	○	○	●	○	○	○	○	○	○
6.	Simple interest method	○	○	○	○	○	●	○	○	○	○	○
7.	Interest revenue/expense	●	○	○	○	○	○	○	○	○	○	○
8.	Future value of annuity	○	○	○	○	○	○	○	○	●	○	○
9.	Face of note equals present value of the note	○	○	○	○	○	○	○	○	○	○	●

Explanation of solutions

1. **(D)** An annuity due (annuity in advance) represents a series of payments made or received at the beginning of the period.

2. **(C)** An imputed interest rate is used when the rate on a note is not fair and the market value of the items being exchanged is not readily determinable. An imputed interest rate represents the rate at which the debtor could obtain financing from a different source; this is known as the debtor's incremental borrowing rate.

3. **(G)** The market value of a note is equal to the maturity value and the interest payments discounted to the present value. The present value represents the amount you would pay now for an amount to be received in the future. Thus, answer G is the correct response, as the present value equals the current market value of the principal and interest amounts.

4. **(H)** When a note is exchanged for cash and no other rights or privileges exist, the present value of the note will equal the cash received if the stated rate on the note equals the market yield rate. However, if the stated rate is less than the market rate, then the note will be issued at a discount to compensate.

5. **(E)** A premium on a note occurs when the interest rate on a note is greater than the market yield rate. The market bids up the price of the bond above par until the effective interest rate on the note equals the market yield rate.

6. **(F)** The simple interest method computes interest based upon the amount of principal only. Interest is computed as Principal × Interest × Time. The compound interest method computes interest on principal and any interest earned and not withdrawn.

7. **(A)** The interest revenue or expense on a note is computed by taking the effective interest rate times the net receivable or payable balance.

8. **(I)** An annuity is a periodic payment or receipt made in consecutive intervals over time compounded at a stated interest rate. The future value of an annuity represents the total of the periodic payments and accumulated interest at some point in the future.

9. **(K)** When a note is exchanged for cash and no other rights or privileges exist, the present value of the note will be equal to the cash exchanged if the stated rate of interest equals the market yield rate. No premium or discount exists if the stated rate on the note equals the market yield rate.

Situation	Present Value Concepts	Long-Term Receivables Disclosure	Balance Sheet Disclosure	Income Statement Disclosure	Research	Communication

Kern, Inc.
LONG-TERM RECEIVABLES SECTION
OF BALANCE SHEET
December 31, 2009

9% note receivable from sale of idle building, due in annual installments of $250,000 to May 1, 2011, less current installment	$250,000	[1]
8% note receivable from officer, due December 31, 2011 collateralized by 5,000 shares of Kern, Inc. common stock with a fair value of $225,000	200,000	
Noninterest-bearing note from sale of patent, net of 10% imputed interest, due April 1, 2011	88,795	[2]
Installment contract receivable, due in annual installments of $88,332 to July 1, 2013, less current installment	219,668	[3]
Total long-term receivables	$758,463	

Explanation of Amounts
See explanations under Income Statement Disclosure

Situation	Present Value Concepts	Long-Term Receivables Disclosure	Balance Sheet Disclosure	Income Statement Disclosure	Research	Communication

Kern, Inc.
SELECTED BALANCE SHEET ACCOUNTS
December 31, 2009

Current portion of long-term receivables:		
Note receivable from sale of idle building	$250,000	[1]
Installment contract receivable	60,332	[3]
Total	$310,332	
Accrued interest receivable:		
Note receivable from sale of idle building	$30,000	[4]
Installment contract receivable	14,000	[5]
Total	$44,000	

Explanation of Amounts
See explanations under Income Statement Disclosure

Situation	Present Value Concepts	Long-Term Receivables Disclosure	Balance Sheet Disclosure	Income Statement Disclosure	Research	Communication

Kern, Inc.
INTEREST REVENUE FROM LONG-TERM RECEIVABLES
AND GAINS RECOGNIZED ON SALE OF ASSETS
For the Year Ended December 31, 2009

Interest revenue:		
Note receivable from sale of idle building	$52,500	[6]
Note receivable from sale of patent	6,195	[2]
Note receivable from officer	16,000	[7]
Installment contract receivable from sale of land	14,000	[5]
Total interest revenue	$88,695	
Gains recognized on sale of assets:		
Patent	$ 44,600	[8]
Land	100,000	[9]
Total gains recognized	$144,600	

Explanation of Amounts

[1] Long-term portion of 9% note receivable at 12/31/09

Face amount, 5/1/08	$750,000
Less installment received 5/1/09	250,000
Balance, 12/31/09	500,000
Less installment due 5/1/10	250,000
Long-term portion, 12/31/09	$250,000

[2] Noninterest-bearing note, net of imputed interest at 12/31/09

Face amount, 4/1/09	$100,000
Less imputed interest [$100,000 – $82,600 ($100,000 × 0.826)]	17,400
Balance, 4/1/09	82,600
Add interest earned to 12/31/09 [$82,600 × 10% × 9/12]	6,195
Balance, 12/31/09	$ 88,795

[3] Long-term portion of installment contract receivable at 12/31/09
        Contract selling price, 7/1/09 $400,000
        Less cash down payment   120,000
        Balance, 12/31/09   280,000
        Less installment due 7/1/10 [$88,332 – $28,000 ($280,000 × 10%)]   60,332
        Long-term portion, 12/31/09 $219,668

[4] Accrued interest—note receivable, sale of idle building at 12/31/09
        Interest accrued from 5/1 to 12/31/09 [$500,000 × 9% × 8/12] $ 30,000

[5] Accrued interest—installment contract at 12/31/09
        Interest accrued from 7/1 to 12/31/09 [$280,000 × 10% × 1/2] $ 14,000

[6] Interest revenue—note receivable, sale of idle building, for 2009
        Interest earned from 1/1/ to 5/1/09 [$750,000 × 9% × 4/12] $ 22,500
        Interest earned from 5/1 to 12/31/09 [$500,000 × 9% × 8/12]   30,000
        Interest revenue $ 52,500

[7] Interest revenue—note receivable, officer, for 2009
        Interest earned 1/1 to 12/31/09 [$200,000 × 8%] $ 16,000

[8] Gain recognized on sale of patent
        Stated selling price $100,000
        Less imputed interest   17,400   [2]
        Actual selling price   82,600
        Less cost of patent (net)
            Carrying value 1/1/09 $40,000   38,000
            Less amortization 1/1 to 4/1/09 [$8,000 × 1/4]   2,000   2,000
        Gain recognized $ 44,600

[9] Gain recognized on sale of land
        Selling price $400,000
        Less cost   300,000
        Gain recognized $100,000

Situation	Present Value Concepts	Long-Term Receivables Disclosure	Balance Sheet Disclosure	Income Statement Disclosure	Research	Communication

1. On July 1, 2009, Kern borrows $100,000 on a noninterest-bearing three-year note and received $85,000 in proceeds. How should Kern value the note in its July 1, 2009 financial statements?

APB21, Para 11

11. Note exchanged for cash. When a note is received solely for cash and no other right or privilege is exchanged, it is presumed to have a present value at issuance measured by the cash proceeds exchanged. If cash and some other rights or privileges are exchanged for a note, the value of the rights or privileges should be given accounting recognition as described in paragraph 7.

Codification: 835-30-25-4

2. Where is a discount or premium disclosed on the financial statements?

APB21, Para 16

16. Statement presentation of discount and premium. The discount or premium resulting from the determination of present value in cash or noncash transactions is not an asset or liability separable from the note which gives rise to it. Therefore, the discount or premium should be reported in the balance sheet as a direct deduction from or addition to the face amount of the note. It should not be classified as a deferred charge or deferred credit. The description of the note should include the effective interest rate; the face amount should also be disclosed in the financial statements or in the notes to the statements. Amortization of discount or premium should be reported as interest in the statement of income. Issue costs should be reported in the balance sheet as deferred charges.

Codification: 835-30-45-1A

3. How is a discount or premium on a note amortized?

APB21, Para 15

15. Amortization of discount and premium. With respect to a note which by the provisions of this Opinion requires the imputation of interest, the difference between the present value and the face amount should be treated as discount or premium and amortized as interest expense or income over the life of the note in such a way as to result in a constant rate of interest when applied to the amount outstanding at the beginning of any given period. This is the "interest" method described in and supported by paragraphs 16 and 17 of APB Opinion No. 12, Omnibus Opinion—1967. However, other methods of amortization may be used if the results obtained are not materially different from those which would result from the "interest" method.

Codification: 835-30-35-2 and 835-30-35-3

4. What information must a company disclose regarding long-term debt on its financial statements?

FAS47, Para 10

10. The following information shall be disclosed for each of the five years following the date of the latest balance sheet presented:

a. The aggregate amount of payments for unconditional purchase obligations that meet the criteria of paragraph 6 and that have been recognized on the purchaser's balance sheet.

b. The combined aggregate amount of maturities and sinking fund requirements for all long-term borrowings.

Codification: 470-10-50-1

5. How does a lender account for loan origination fees?

FAS91, Para 5

5. Loan origination fees shall be deferred and recognized over the life of the loan as an adjustment of yield (interest income). Likewise, direct loan origination costs defined in paragraph 6 shall be deferred and recognized as a reduction in the yield of the loan except as set forth in paragraph 14 (for a troubled debt restructuring). Loan origination fees and related direct loan origination costs for a given loan shall be offset and only the net amount shall be deferred and amortized. The practice of recognizing a portion of loan origination fees as revenue in a period to offset all or part of the costs of origination shall no longer be acceptable.

Codification: 310-20-35-2

Situation	Present Value Concepts	Long-Term Receivables Disclosure	Balance Sheet Disclosure	Income Statement Disclosure	Research	Communication

To: Audit Staff
From: CPA Candidate
Re: Notes receivable

   In performing the audit of Kern, Inc., a staff member noted that certain of Kern's notes receivable bear no interest. Such notes should be recorded at their discounted present value at the time they are acquired. The discount rate used should be the market rate for notes receivable with a similar level of risk. If management does not discount the notes receivable, the notes will be overvalued.

   Please indicate your concurrence with this memorandum.

Simulation Problem 2

Situation	Sales Price	Carrying Value	Amortization Table	Gain or Loss	Research	Communication

PV of $300,000 at 6% for four periods.

When a note is exchanged for property, goods, and services, the note, the sales price, and the cost of the property should be recorded at the fair value of the property goods, or services at an amount that approximates the market value of the note, whichever is more clearly determinable. Since the value of the property is known, it is assumed that 6% is the appropriate market rate of interest that will equal the value of the property.

Situation	Sales Price	Carrying Value	Amortization Table	Gain or Loss	Research	Communication

PV ($300,000) at 6% for four periods = .792 × $300,000 = $237,630

Situation	Sales Price	Carrying Value	Amortization Table	Gain or Loss	Research	Communication

Amortization Table (Off in Year 5 due to rounding).

Year	Interest income	Premium on note	Discount on note	Carrying value
1/1/2009			$62,370	$237,630
12/31/2009	$14,258		48,112	251,888
12/31/2010	15,113		32,999	267,001
12/31/2011	16,020		16,979	283,021
			rounding	
12/31/2012	16,981		(2)	300,002

Situation	Sales Price	Carrying Value	Amortization Table	Gain or Loss	Research	Communication

Catrina—Sale of Equipment

Original cost	$320,000
Less: Accumulated depreciation	(75,000)
Book value	$245,000
Fair market value received	$237,630
Less: Book value	(245,000)
Loss on sale of equipment	$ 7,370

Since the problem states that the fair market value of the equipment is determinable, it is assumed that the interest rate is fair. Therefore, the 6% market rate is used to calculate the present value of the note and value the equipment. The fair value of equipment is $237,630. Because the fair market value received is less than the book value given up, there is a loss on the sale of the equipment. The Discount on Note represents interest income that Catrina will earn over the life of the note.

Situation	Sales Price	Carrying Value	Amortization Table	Gain or Loss	Research	Communication

Authoritative Literature
APB21, Para 12

12. Note exchanged for property, goods, or service. When a note is exchanged for property, goods, or service in a bargained transaction entered into at arm's length, there should be a general presumption that the rate of interest stipulated by the parties to the transaction represents fair and adequate compensation to the supplier for the use of the related funds. That presumption, however, must not permit the form of the transaction to prevail over its economic substance and thus would not apply if (1) interest is not stated, or (2) the stated interest rate is unreasonable (paragraphs 13 and 14), or (3) the stated face amount of the note is materially different from the current cash sales price for the same or similar items or from the market value of the note at the date of the transaction. In these circumstances, the note, the sales price, and the cost of the property, goods, or service exchanged for the note should be recorded at the fair value of the property, goods, or services or at an amount that reasonably approximates the market value of the note, whichever is the more clearly determinable. That amount may or may not be the same as its face amount, and any resulting discount or premium should be accounted for as an element of interest over the life of the note (paragraph 15). In the absence of established exchange prices for the related property, goods, or service or evidence of the market value of the note (paragraph 9), the present value

of a note that stipulates either no interest or a rate of interest that is clearly unreasonable should be determined by discounting all future payments on the notes using an imputed rate of interest as described in paragraphs 13 and 14. This determination should be made at the time the note is issued, assumed, or acquired; any subsequent changes in prevailing interest rates should be ignored.

Codification: 310-10-30-3

Situation	Sales Price	Carrying Value	Amortization Table	Gain or Loss	Research	Communication

A sample memo follows.

> To: CFO, Dawson Corporation
> From: CPA Candidate
> Re: Acquisition of equipment on January 1, 2009
> Date: [*Today's date*]

On January 1, 2009, Dawson Corporation signed a four-year, noninterest-bearing note payable for $300,000 at 6% interest to purchase equipment. We have reviewed this transaction, and we recommend the following accounting treatment.

The Accounting Principles Board Opinion No. 21, paragraph 12, specifies that on the date of acquisition, the equipment should be valued at the fair market value of the equipment or the present value of the note, whichever is more clearly determinable. Using a 6% interest rate, the present value of the note payable was calculated to be $237,600. As 6% reflects the current market rate of interest, and it is a reasonable rate, we can infer that the fair value of the equipment is accurately reflected in this rate. Therefore, Dawson should record the equipment on its balance sheet at $237,630.

The note payable should be recorded at its "face" or maturity value, and a discount on note payable account should be created as a valuation account to correctly record the note at its present value. The amount in the discount account will be amortized using the effective interest method, and a portion will be recognized as interest expense each year during the life of the four-year note. Dawson should calculate interest expense each year by multiplying the carrying value of the note payable times 6%, and the discount on notes payable should be reduced by the amount of interest expense recognized each year. This will, in effect, increase the carrying value of the note each year, until the note reaches its maturity value on January 1, 2013.

Below is an amortization table indicating the amount of interest expense Dawson should record each year on its income statement.

Year	Interest expense	Discount on note	Carrying value
1/1/2009		$62,370	$237,630
12/31/2009	$14,258	48,112	251,888
12/31/2010	15,113	32,999	267,001
12/31/2011	16,020	16,979	283,021
		rounding	
12/31/2012	16,981	(2)	300,002

Each year the carrying value of the note must be recalculated as indicated in the above table. As no part of the note payable will be due until January 1, 2013, Dawson should report the note at its carrying value in the long-term liabilities section of the balance sheet until December 31, 2011. On January 1, 2012, Dawson should reclassify the note payable as a current liability because the note will be repaid within twelve months.

Dawson's normal depreciation method for equipment is straight-line method with a five-year life and no residual value. Therefore, each year Dawson should also record depreciation expense on the equipment at the straight-line rate of $47,526 ($237,630 / 5 years). A contra account "accumulated depreciation" should be established for this equipment, and the related accumulated depreciation should be recorded each year. The book value of the equipment (Cost less accumulated depreciation) should be disclosed on the balance sheet under noncurrent assets each year.

If we can be of further assistance or clarify any other issues for you, please contact me at 555-1234.

MULTIPLE-CHOICE QUESTIONS (1-42)

1. Hancock Co.'s December 31, 2009 balance sheet contained the following items in the long-term liabilities section:

Unsecured

9.375% registered bonds ($25,000 maturing annually beginning in 2013)	$275,000
11.5% convertible bonds, callable beginning in 2017, due 2029	125,000

Secured

9.875% guaranty security bonds, due 2029	$275,000
10.0% commodity backed bonds ($50,000 maturing annually beginning in 2014)	200,000

What are the total amounts of serial bonds and debenture bonds?

	Serial bonds	*Debenture bonds*
a.	$475,000	$400,000
b.	$475,000	$125,000
c.	$450,000	$400,000
d.	$200,000	$650,000

2. Blue Corp.'s December 31, 2009 balance sheet contained the following items in the long-term liabilities section:

9 3/4% registered debentures, callable in 2020, due in 2025	$700,000
9 1/2% collateral trust bonds, convertible into common stock beginning in 2018, due in 2028	600,000
10% subordinated debentures ($30,000 maturing annually beginning in 2015)	300,000

What is the total amount of Blue's term bonds?
- a. $ 600,000
- b. $ 700,000
- c. $1,000,000
- d. $1,300,000

3. Bonds payable issued with scheduled maturities at various dates are called

	Serial bonds	*Term bonds*
a.	No	Yes
b.	No	No
c.	Yes	No
d.	Yes	Yes

4. The following information pertains to Camp Corp.'s issuance of bonds on July 1, 2009:

Face amount	$800,000
Term	Ten years
Stated interest rate	6%
Interest payment dates	Annually on July 1
Yield	9%

	At 6%	*At 9%*
Present value of one for ten periods	0.558	0.422
Future value of one for ten periods	1.791	2.367
Present value of ordinary annuity of one for ten periods	7.360	6.418

What should be the issue price for each $1,000 bond?
- a. $1,000
- b. $ 864
- c. $ 807
- d. $ 700

5. Perk, Inc. issued $500,000, 10% bonds to yield 8%. Bond issuance costs were $10,000. How should Perk calculate the net proceeds to be received from the issuance?
- a. Discount the bonds at the stated rate of interest.

- b. Discount the bonds at the market rate of interest.
- c. Discount the bonds at the stated rate of interest and deduct bond issuance costs.
- d. Discount the bonds at the market rate of interest and deduct bond issuance costs.

6. The market price of a bond issued at a discount is the present value of its principal amount at the market (effective) rate of interest
- a. Less the present value of all future interest payments at the market (effective) rate of interest.
- b. Less the present value of all future interest payments at the rate of interest stated on the bond.
- c. Plus the present value of all future interest payments at the market (effective) rate of interest.
- d. Plus the present value of all future interest payments at the rate of interest stated on the bond.

7. On July 1, 2009, Eagle Corp. issued 600 of its 10%, $1,000 bonds at 99 plus accrued interest. The bonds are dated April 1, 2009, and mature on April 1, 2019. Interest is payable semiannually on April 1 and October 1. What amount did Eagle receive from the bond issuance?
- a. $579,000
- b. $594,000
- c. $600,000
- d. $609,000

8. During 2009, Lake Co. issued 3,000 of its 9%, $1,000 face value bonds at 101 1/2. In connection with the sale of these bonds, Lake paid the following expenses:

Promotion costs	$ 20,000
Engraving and printing	25,000
Underwriters' commissions	200,000

What amount should Lake record as bond issue costs to be amortized over the term of the bonds?
- a. $0
- b. $220,000
- c. $225,000
- d. $245,000

9. Dixon Co. incurred costs of $3,300 when it issued, on August 31, 2009, five-year debenture bonds dated April 1, 2009. What amount of bond issue expense should Dixon report in its income statement for the year ended December 31, 2009?
- a. $ 220
- b. $ 240
- c. $ 495
- d. $3,300

10. On November 1, 2009, Mason Corp. issued $800,000 of its ten-year, 8% term bonds dated October 1, 2009. The bonds were sold to yield 10%, with total proceeds of $700,000 plus accrued interest. Interest is paid every April 1 and October 1. Mason does not elect the fair value option for reporting financial liabilities. What amount should Mason report for interest payable in its December 31, 2009 balance sheet?
- a. $17,500
- b. $16,000
- c. $11,667
- d. $10,667

11. Which one of the following is a true statement for a firm electing the fair value option for valuing its bonds payable?

a. The effective interest method of amortization must be used to calculate interest expense.
b. Discount or premium is disclosed in the notes to the financial statements.
c. The fair value of the bond and the principal obligation value must be disclosed.
d. If the fair value option is elected, it must be applied to all bonds.

12. On January 1, 2010, Southern Corporation received $107,720 for a $100,000 face amount, 12% bond, a price that yields 10%. The bonds pay interest semiannually. Southern elects the fair value option for valuing its financial liabilities. On December 31, 2010, the fair value of the bond is determined to be $106,460. Southern recognized interest expense of $12,000 in its 2010 income statement. What was the gain or loss recognized on the 2010 income statement to report this bond at fair value?
   a. $1,260 gain
   b. $6,460 gain
   c. $12,000 loss
   d. $13,260 loss

13. On July 1, 2009, Day Co. received $103,288 for $100,000 face amount, 12% bonds, a price that yields 10%. Assuming management does not elect the fair value option, interest expense for the six months ended December 31, 2009, should be
   a. $6,197
   b. $6,000
   c. $5,164
   d. $5,000

14. On January 2, 2009, West Co. issued 9% bonds in the amount of $500,000, which mature on January 2, 2019. The bonds were issued for $469,500 to yield 10%. Interest is payable annually on December 31. West uses the interest method of amortizing bond discount and does not elect the fair value option for reporting financial liabilities. In its June 30, 2009 balance sheet, what amount should West report as bonds payable?
   a. $469,500
   b. $470,475
   c. $471,025
   d. $500,000

15. Webb Co. has outstanding a 7%, ten-year $100,000 face-value bond. The bond was originally sold to yield 6% annual interest. Webb uses the effective interest rate method to amortize bond premium, and does not elect the fair value option for reporting financial liabilities. On June 30, 2009, the carrying amount of the outstanding bond was $105,000. What amount of unamortized premium on bond should Webb report in its June 30, 2010 balance sheet?
   a. $1,050
   b. $3,950
   c. $4,300
   d. $4,500

16. For the issuer of a ten-year term bond, the amount of amortization using the interest method would increase each year if the bond was sold at a

	Discount	Premium
a.	No	No
b.	Yes	Yes
c.	No	Yes
d.	Yes	No

17. On January 2, 2009, Nast Co. issued 8% bonds with a face amount of $1,000,000 that mature on January 2, 2015. The bonds were issued to yield 12%, resulting in a discount of $150,000. Nast incorrectly used the straight-line method instead of the effective interest method to amortize the discount. Nast does not elect the fair value option for reporting financial liabilities. How is the carrying amount of the bonds affected by the error?

	At December 31, 2009	At January 2, 2015
a.	Overstated	Understated
b.	Overstated	No effect
c.	Understated	Overstated
d.	Understated	No effect

18. The following information relates to noncurrent investments that Fall Corp. placed in trust as required by the underwriter of its bonds:

Bond sinking fund balance, 12/31/09	$ 450,000
2010 additional investment	90,000
Dividends on investments	15,000
Interest revenue	30,000
Administration costs	5,000
Carrying amount of bonds payable	1,025,000

What amount should Fall report in its December 31, 2010 balance sheet related to its noncurrent investment for bond sinking fund requirements?
   a. $585,000
   b. $580,000
   c. $575,000
   d. $540,000

19. Witt Corp. has outstanding at December 31, 2009, two long-term borrowings with annual sinking fund requirements and maturities as follows:

	Sinking fund requirements	Maturities
2009	$1,000,000	$ --
2010	1,500,000	2,000,000
2011	1,500,000	2,000,000
2012	2,000,000	2,500,000
2013	2,000,000	3,000,000
	$8,000,000	$9,500,000

In the notes to its December 31, 2009 balance sheet, how should Witt report the above data?
   a. No disclosure is required.
   b. Only sinking fund payments totaling $8,000,000 for the next five years detailed by year need be disclosed.
   c. Only maturities totaling $9,500,000 for the next five years detailed by year need to be disclosed.
   d. The combined aggregate of $17,500,000 of maturities and sinking fund requirements detailed by year should be disclosed.

20. On March 1, 2007, a company established a sinking fund in connection with an issue of bonds due in 2019. At December 31, 2009, the independent trustee held cash in the sinking fund account representing the annual deposits to the fund and the interest earned on those deposits. How should the sinking fund be reported in the company's balance sheet at December 31, 2009?
   a. The cash in the sinking fund should appear as a current asset.
   b. Only the accumulated deposits should appear as a noncurrent asset.

c. The entire balance in the sinking fund account should appear as a current asset.

d. The entire balance in the sinking fund account should appear as a noncurrent asset.

21. An issuer of bonds uses a sinking fund for the retirement of the bonds. Cash was transferred to the sinking fund and subsequently used to purchase investments. The sinking fund

I. Increases by revenue earned on the investments.
II. Is **not** affected by revenue earned on the investments.
III. Decreases when the investments are purchased.

a. I only.
b. I and III.
c. II and III.
d. III only.

22. On July 2, 2009, Wynn, Inc., purchased as a short-term investment a $1,000,000 face value Kean Co. 8% bond for $910,000 plus accrued interest to yield 10%. The bonds mature on January 1, 2016, pay interest annually on January 1, and are classified as trading securities. On December 31, 2009, the bonds had a market value of $945,000. On February 13, 2010, Wynn sold the bonds for $920,000. In its December 31, 2009 balance sheet, what amount should Wynn report for short-term investments in trading debt securities?

a. $910,000
b. $920,000
c. $945,000
d. $950,000

23. On July 1, 2009, East Co. purchased as a long-term investment $500,000 face amount, 8% bonds of Rand Corp. for $461,500 to yield 10% per year. The bonds pay interest semiannually on January 1 and July 1. East does not elect the fair value option for reporting these securities. In its December 31, 2009 balance sheet, East should report interest receivable of

a. $18,460
b. $20,000
c. $23,075
d. $25,000

24. On October 1, 2008, Park Co. purchased 200 of the $1,000 face value, 10% bonds of Ott, Inc., for $220,000, including accrued interest of $5,000. The bonds, which mature on January 1, 2015, pay interest semiannually on January 1 and July 1. Park used the straight-line method of amortization and appropriately classified the bonds as held-to-maturity. On Park's December 31, 2009 balance sheet, the bonds should be reported at

a. $215,000
b. $214,400
c. $214,200
d. $212,000

25. On July 1, 2009, York Co. purchased as a held-to-maturity investment $1,000,000 of Park, Inc.'s 8% bonds for $946,000, including accrued interest of $40,000. The bonds were purchased to yield 10% interest. The bonds mature on January 1, 2016, and pay interest annually on January 1. York uses the effective interest method of amortization. In its December 31, 2009 balance sheet, what amount should York report as investment in bonds?

a. $911,300
b. $916,600

c. $953,300
d. $960,600

26. In 2008, Lee Co. acquired, at a premium, Enfield, Inc. ten-year bonds as a long-term investment. At December 31, 2009, Enfield's bonds were quoted at a small discount. Which of the following situations is the most likely cause of the decline in the bonds' market value?

a. Enfield issued a stock dividend.
b. Enfield is expected to call the bonds at a premium, which is less than Lee's carrying amount.
c. Interest rates have declined since Lee purchased the bonds.
d. Interest rates have increased since Lee purchased the bonds.

27. An investor purchased a bond as a held-to-maturity investment on January 2. Assume the fair value option is not elected for these securities. The investor's carrying value at the end of the first year would be highest if the bond was purchased at a

a. Discount and amortized by the straight-line method.
b. Discount and amortized by the effective interest method.
c. Premium and amortized by the straight-line method.
d. Premium and amortized by the effective interest method.

28. An investor purchased a bond as a long-term investment on January 1. Annual interest was received on December 31. The investor's interest income for the year would be highest if the bond was purchased at

a. Par.
b. Face value.
c. A discount.
d. A premium.

29. On March 1, 2009, Clark Co. issued bonds at a discount. Clark incorrectly used the straight-line method instead of the effective interest method to amortize the discount. Clark does not elect the fair value option to report these securities. How were the following amounts, as of December 31, 2009, affected by the error?

	Bond carrying amount	*Retained earnings*
a.	Overstated	Overstated
b.	Understated	Understated
c.	Overstated	Understated
d.	Understated	Overstated

30. Jent Corp. purchased bonds at a discount of $10,000. Subsequently, Jent sold these bonds at a premium of $14,000. During the period that Jent held this investment, amortization of the discount amounted to $2,000. Jent did not elect the fair value option to report these bonds. What amount should Jent report as gain on the sale of bonds?

a. $12,000
b. $22,000
c. $24,000
d. $26,000

31. On July 1, 2009, after recording interest and amortization, York Co. converted $1,000,000 of its 12% convertible bonds into 50,000 shares of $1 par value common stock. On the conversion date the carrying amount of the bonds was $1,300,000, the market value of the bonds was $1,400,000, and York's common stock was publicly trading at $30 per share. Using the book value method, what amount of additional paid-in capital should York record as a result of the conversion?

- a. $ 950,000
- b. $1,250,000
- c. $1,350,000
- d. $1,500,000

32. On March 31, 2009, Ashley, Inc.'s bondholders exchanged their convertible bonds for common stock. The carrying amount of these bonds on Ashley's books was less than the market value but greater than the par value of the common stock issued. If Ashley used the book value method of accounting for the conversion, which of the following statements correctly states an effect of this conversion?

- a. Stockholders' equity is increased.
- b. Additional paid-in capital is decreased.
- c. Retained earnings is increased.
- d. An extraordinary loss is recognized.

Items 33 and 34 are based on the following:

On January 2, 2006, Chard Co. issued ten-year convertible bonds at 105. During 2009, these bonds were converted into common stock having an aggregate par value equal to the total face amount of the bonds. At conversion, the market price of Chard's common stock was 50% above its par value.

33. On January 2, 2006, cash proceeds from the issuance of the convertible bonds should be reported as

- a. Contributed capital for the entire proceeds.
- b. Contributed capital for the portion of the proceeds attributable to the conversion feature and as a liability for the balance.
- c. A liability for the face amount of the bonds and contributed capital for the premium over the face amount.
- d. A liability for the entire proceeds.

34. Depending on whether the book value method or the market value method was used, Chard would recognize gains or losses on conversion when using the

	Book value method	Market value method
a.	Either gain or loss	Gain
b.	Either gain or loss	Loss
c.	Neither gain **nor** loss	Loss
d.	Neither gain **nor** loss	Gain

35. On December 30, 2009, Fort, Inc. issued 1,000 of its 8%, ten-year, $1,000 face value bonds with detachable stock warrants at par. Each bond carried a detachable warrant for one share of Fort's common stock at a specified option price of $25 per share. Immediately after issuance, the market value of the bonds without the warrants was $1,080,000 and the market value of the warrants was $120,000. In its December 31, 2009 balance sheet, what amount should Fort report as bonds payable?

- a. $1,000,000
- b. $ 975,000
- c. $ 900,000
- d. $ 880,000

36. On December 31, 2009, Moss Co. issued $1,000,000 of 11% bonds at 109. Each $1,000 bond was issued with fifty detachable stock warrants, each of which entitled the bond-

holder to purchase one share of $5 par common stock for $25. Immediately after issuance, the market value of each warrant was $4. On December 31, 2009, what amount should Moss record as discount or premium on issuance of bonds?

- a. $ 40,000 premium.
- b. $ 90,000 premium.
- c. $110,000 discount.
- d. $200,000 discount.

37. On March 1, 2009, Evan Corp. issued $500,000 of 10% nonconvertible bonds at 103, due on February 28, 2019. Each $1,000 bond was issued with thirty detachable stock warrants, each of which entitled the holder to purchase, for $50, one share of Evan's $25 par common stock. On March 1, 2009, the market price of each warrant was $4. By what amount should the bond issue proceeds increase stockholders' equity?

- a. $0
- b. $15,000
- c. $45,000
- d. $60,000

38. Main Co. issued bonds with detachable common stock warrants. Only the warrants had a known market value. The sum of the fair value of the warrants and the face amount of the bonds exceeds the cash proceeds. This excess is reported as

- a. Discount on bonds payable.
- b. Premium on bonds payable.
- c. Common stock subscribed.
- d. Contributed capital in excess of par—stock warrants.

39. When bonds are issued with stock purchase warrants, a portion of the proceeds should be allocated to paid-in capital for bonds issued with

	Detachable stock purchase warrants	Nondetachable stock purchase warrants
a.	No	Yes
b.	No	No
c.	Yes	No
d.	Yes	Yes

40. On June 30, 2009, King Co. had outstanding 9%, $5,000,000 face value bonds maturing on June 30, 2014. Interest was payable semiannually every June 30 and December 31. King did not elect the fair value option for reporting its financial liabilities. On June 30, 2009, after amortization was recorded for the period, the unamortized bond premium and bond issue costs were $30,000 and $50,000, respectively. On that date, King acquired all its outstanding bonds on the open market at 98 and retired them. At June 30, 2009, what amount should King recognize as gain before income taxes on redemption of bonds?

- a. $ 20,000
- b. $ 80,000
- c. $120,000
- d. $180,000

41. On January 1, 2004, Fox Corp. issued 1,000 of its 10%, $1,000 bonds for $1,040,000. These bonds were to mature on January 1, 2014 but were callable at 101 any time after December 31, 2007. Interest was payable semiannually on July 1 and January 1. Fox did not elect the fair value option for reporting its financial liabilities. On July 1, 2009, Fox called all of the bonds and retired them. Bond premium was amortized on a straight-line basis. Before income taxes, Fox's gain or loss in 2009 on this early extinguishment of debt was

    a. $30,000 gain.
    b. $12,000 gain.
    c. $10,000 loss.
    d. $ 8,000 gain.

42. On January 1, 2010, Hart, Inc. redeemed its fifteen-year bonds of $500,000 par value for 102. They were originally issued on January 1, 1998, at 98 with a maturity date of January 1, 2013. The bond issue costs relating to this trans-action were $20,000. Hart did not elect the fair value option for reporting its financial liabilities. Hart amortizes discounts, premiums, and bond issue costs using the straight-line method. What amount of loss should Hart recognize on the redemption of these bonds?

    a. $16,000
    b. $12,000
    c. $10,000
    d. $0

SIMULATION PROBLEMS

Simulation Problem 1   (50 to 60 minutes)

Situation						
	Concepts	Bond Valuation	Amortization Schedule	Journal Entries	Communication	Research

On January 2, 2009, Parker Co. issued 6% bonds with a face value of $400,000 when the market interest rate was 8%. The bonds are due in ten years, and interest is payable every June 30 and December 31. Parker does not elect the fair value option for reporting its financial liabilities.

	Concepts					
Situation		Bond Valuation	Amortization Schedule	Journal Entries	Communication	Research

Parker Co. $50 par value common stock has always traded above par. During 2009, Parker had several transactions that affected the following balance sheet accounts:

I. Bond discounts
II. Bond premium
III. Bond payable
IV. Common stock
V. Additional paid-in capital
VI. Retained earnings

For each of the following items, determine whether the transaction Increased, Decreased, or had No effect for each of the items in the chart.

	Bond discounts	Bond premium	Bond payable	Common stock	Additional paid-in capital	Retained earnings
1. Parker issued bonds payable with a nominal interest rate that was less than the market rate of interest.						
2. Parker issued convertible bonds, which are common stock equivalents, for an amount in excess of the bonds' face amount.						
3. Parker issued common stock when the convertible bonds described in item **2.** were submitted for conversion. Each $1,000 bond was converted into twenty common shares. The book value method was used for the early conversion.						
4. Parker issued bonds with nondetachable warrants for an amount equal to the face amount of the bonds. The stock warrants do not have a determinable value.						
5. Parker issued bonds, with detachable stock warrants, for an amount equal to the face amount of the bonds. The stock warrants have a determinable value.						
6. Parker redeemed a bond issued at 8% at a discount for an amount that was 102% of face value.						
7. Parker issued bonds payable with a nominal rate of interest that is higher than the market rate.						
8. Parker called a bond that was issued at 105 at a time when the market value of the bond was less than its carrying value.						

Situation	Concepts	Bond Valuation	Amortization Schedule	Journal Entries	Communication	Research

Use the following present value and present value annuity tables to calculate the selling price of the bond on January 2, 2009. Round your final answer to the nearest dollar.

Present Value Ordinary Annuity of $1

Periods	3%	4%	6%	8%	12%	16%
5 periods	4.5797	4.4518	4.2124	3.9927	3.6048	3.2743
10 periods	8.5302	8.1109	7.3601	6.7101	5.6502	4.8337
20 periods	14.8775	13.5903	11.4699	9.8181	7.4694	5.9288

Present Value of $1

Periods	3%	4%	6%	8%	12%	16%
5 periods	.8626	.8219	.7473	.6806	.5674	.4761
10 periods	.7441	.6756	.5584	.4632	.3220	.2267
20 periods	.5537	.4564	.3118	.2145	.1037	.0514

Selling price of the bond [   ]

Situation	Concepts	Bond Valuation	Amortization Schedule	Journal Entries	Communication	Research

Prepare the amortization schedule for the bond through December 31, 2009. Round all numbers to the nearest dollar.

Date	Interest paid	Interest expense	Amortization of discount	Discount on bond payable	Carrying value of bond payable
1/2/09					
6/30/09					
12/31/09					

Situation	Concepts	Bond Valuation	Amortization Schedule	Journal Entries	Communication	Research

1. Prepare the journal entries for the bond issue on January 2, 2009.

2. Prepare the journal entry for the interest payment on June 30, 2009.

Situation	Concepts	Bond Valuation	Amortization Schedule	Journal Entries	Communication	Research

On June 30, 2006, Parker Co. issued fifteen-year 12% bonds at a premium (effective yield 10%). On November 30, 2009, Parker transferred both cash and property to the bondholders to extinguish the entire debt. The fair value of the transferred property equaled its carrying amount. The fair value of the cash and property transferred exceeded the bonds' carrying amount. Write a memorandum to the finance manager of Parker that

1. Explains the purpose of the effective interest method and the effect of applying the method in 2006 on Parker's bond premium.

2. States the effect on 2006 interest expense, net income, and the carrying amount of the bonds if Parker had incorrectly adopted the straight-line interest method instead of the effective interest method.

3. Describes how Parker should calculate and report the effects of the November 30, 2009 transaction in its 2009 income statement. Why is this presentation appropriate? (Ignore income taxes.)

To: Finance Manager, Parker Co.
From: CPA Candidate
Re: Accounting for bonds

						Research
Situation	Concepts	Bond Valuation	Amortization Schedule	Journal Entries	Communication	

Research the accounting standards regarding guidance on the appropriate interest rate to use to discount a note payable with an unrealistic rate. Indicate the appropriate source in the box below.

Simulation Problem 2   (50 to 60 minutes)

Situation				
	Concepts	Journal Entries	Communication	Research

On January 1, 2009, Castle issued $400,000 of 6% bonds. The bonds were issued at 98 and pay interest semiannually on July 1 and December 31 each year.

On September 1, 2009, Castle issued for $530,000 cash, 500 7% five-year nonconvertible bonds dated September 1, 2009. Each $1,000 bond had a detachable stock purchase warrant to purchase 20 shares of $3 par value stock for $10 per share. Immediately after issuance, the warrants had a market value of $45,000, and the bonds were selling at 102 without the warrant.

On January 1, 2005, Castle issued 100 ten-year convertible bonds. Each $1,000 bond is convertible into 20 shares of Castle's $10 par value common stock. The bonds were issued at 105 when the common stock traded for $40 per share. The bonds pay interest annually. The conversation features of the bond are not beneficial. On October 1, 2009, half of the bonds were tendered for conversion when the common stock was trading at $62 per share. Castle uses the book value method to account for the conversion. At the time of conversion, the bonds had a carrying value of $104,300. Castle does not elect the fair value option for reporting these financial liabilities.

	Concepts			
Situation		Journal Entries	Communication	Research

Indicate whether each item is True or False.

	True	*False*
1. Bond issue costs should be treated as deferred charges and amortized over the life of the bond.	O	O
2. Early extinguishment of debt is treated as an extraordinary item.	O	O
3. Losses from extinguishment of debt should be amortized over the remaining life of the debt.	O	O
4. The straight-line method of amortization should be used for bonds due in less than five years.	O	O
5. Bonds that mature on a single date are called serial bonds.	O	O
6. The effective interest is calculated by multiplying the maturity value of the bond by the coupon rate.	O	O
7. A bond premium represents a reduction of interest expense on the books of the issuer.	O	O
8. When the contract or coupon rate is greater than the effective rate, the bonds will sell at a premium.	O	O

		Journal Entries		
Situation	Concepts		Communication	Research

Prepare the journal entries for the bond transactions during 2009.

1.   January 1, 2009 Issue bonds

2.   September 1, 2009 Issue bonds with detachable warrants

3.   October 1, 2009 Conversion of bonds

			Communication	
Situation	Concepts	Journal Entries		Research

Castle Co. also had 12-year convertible bonds that were issued and dated April 1, 2005. Each $1,000 bond is convertible at the holder's option into twenty shares of Castle's $25 par value common stock. The bonds were issued at a premium when the common stock traded at $45 per share. After payment of interest on April 1, 2009, 30% of the bonds were tendered for conversion when the common stock was trading at $57 per share. Castle used the book value method to account for the conversion.

Write a brief memo to the controller of Castle Co. answering the following questions relating to the bonds.

1.   How would the issue price of Castle's convertible bonds be determined?

2.   How should Castle account for the issuance of the convertible bonds? Give the rationale for this accounting practice.

3.   How should Castle account for the conversion of the bonds into common stock?

REMINDER: Your response will be graded for both technical content and writing skills. Technical content will be evaluated for information that is helpful to the intended reader and clearly relevant to the issue. Writing skills will be evaluated for development, organization, and the appropriate expression of ideas in professional correspondence. Use a standard business memo or letter format with a clear beginning, middle, and end. Do not convey information in the form of a table, bullet point list, or other abbreviated presentation.

To: Controller, Castle Co.
From: CPA Candidate
Re: Bonds

Situation	Concepts	Journal Entries	Communication	Research

Identify the authoritative literature that explains how to account for the three bond issues in the **Journal Entries** section. Select the appropriate paragraph from the accounting literature into the chart below.

1. March 1, 2009 issue of bonds   _____
                                           _____
                                           _____

2. September 1, 2009 issue of bonds   _____
     with warrants   _____
                                           _____

3. October 1, 2009 conversion of   _____
     bonds   _____
                                           _____

MULTIPLE-CHOICE ANSWERS

1. a __ __	10. b __ __	19. d __ __	28. c __ __	37. d __ __
2. d __ __	11. c __ __	20. d __ __	29. c __ __	38. a __ __
3. c __ __	12. a __ __	21. a __ __	30. b __ __	39. c __ __
4. c __ __	13. c __ __	22. c __ __	31. b __ __	40. b __ __
5. d __ __	14. b __ __	23. b __ __	32. a __ __	41. d __ __
6. c __ __	15. c __ __	24. d __ __	33. d __ __	42. a __ __
7. d __ __	16. b __ __	25. a __ __	34. c __ __	
8. d __ __	17. b __ __	26. d __ __	35. c __ __	1st: __/42 = __%
9. b __ __	18. b __ __	27. d __ __	36. c __ __	2nd: __/42 = __%

MULTIPLE-CHOICE ANSWER EXPLANATIONS

B.1.-4. Bonds

1. (a) **Serial** bonds are bond issues that mature in installments (usually on the same date each year over a period of years). In this case, serial bonds total $475,000 ($275,000 + $200,000). **Debenture** bonds are bonds that are **not** secured by specifically designated collateral, but rather by the general assets of the corporation. The unsecured bonds total $400,000 ($275,000 + $125,000).

2. (d) **Term bonds** are bond issues that mature on a single date, as opposed to **serial bonds,** which mature in installments. In this case, the 9 3/4% bonds and the 9 1/2% bonds are term bonds ($700,000 + $600,000 = $1,300,000), while the 10% bonds are serial bonds ($300,000).

3. (c) Serial bonds are bond issues that mature in installments (i.e., on the same date each year over a period of years). Term bonds, on the other hand, are bond issues that mature on a single date.

4. (c) The issue price of each bond is equal to the present value (PV) of the maturity value plus the PV of the interest annuity. The PV must be computed using the yield rate (9%). The computation is

Amount		PV factor		PV
$1,000	×	.422	=	$422
60	×	6.418	=	385
				$807

The annuity interest amount above ($60) is the principal ($1,000) times the stated cash rate (6%).

5. (d) The question asks for net proceeds to be received from the issuance. The market value of a bond is equal to the maturity value and the interest payments discounted at the market rate of interest. The net proceeds will be the market value of the bond less the bond issuance costs.

6. (c) The market price of a bond issued at any amount (par, premium, or discount) is equal to the present value of all of its future cash flows, discounted at the current market (effective) interest rate. The market price of a bond issued at a discount is equal to the present value of both its principal and periodic future cash interest payments at the stated (cash) rate of interest, discounted at the current market (effective) rate.

7. (d) To determine the net cash received from the bond issuance, the solutions approach is to prepare the journal entry for the issuance

Cash	?	
Discount on BP	6,000	
Bonds payable		600,000
Interest expense		15,000

The bonds were issued at 99 ($600,000 × 99% = $594,000), so the discount is $6,000 ($600,000 – $594,000). The accrued interest covers the three months from 4/1 to 7/1 ($600,000 × 10% × 3/12 = $15,000). The cash received includes the $594,000 for the bonds and the $15,000 for the accrued interest, for a total of $609,000.

8. (d) Engraving and printing costs, legal and accounting fees, commissions, promotion costs, and other similar costs should be recorded as bond issue costs and amortized over the term of the bonds. All the costs given are bond issue costs, so the amount reported as bond issue costs is $245,000 ($20,000 + $25,000 + $200,000).

9. (b) Bond issue costs are treated as deferred charges and amortized on a straight-line basis over the life of the bond. These five-year bonds were issued five months late (4/1/09 to 8/31/09), so they will be outstanding only fifty-five months (60 – 5). During 2009, the bonds were outstanding for four months (8/31/09 to 12/31/09). Therefore, the bond issue costs must be amortized for four months out of fifty-five months total, resulting in bond issue expense of $240 ($3,300 × 4/55).

10. (b) Interest payable reported in the 12/31/09 balance sheet would consist of interest due from the bond date (10/1/09) to the year-end (12/31/09); in other words, three months' interest. The formula for interest payable is

Face value	×	Stated rate	×	Time period	=	Interest payable
$800,000	×	8%	×	3/12	=	$16,000

This amount would result from two entries.

Issuance

Cash	705,333	
Discount on BP	100,000	
Bonds payable		800,000
Int. payable		5,333
		($800,000 × 8% × 1/12)

Adjusting entry

Interest expense	11,667	($700,000 × 10% × 2/12)
Int. payable		10,667
		($800,000 × 8% × 2/12)
Discount on BP		1,000

11. (c) Answer (a) is incorrect because various methods may be used to measure interest expense. Answer (b) is incorrect because when the fair value option is elected, the effects of discount or premiums are removed from the balance sheet. Answer (d) is incorrect because the fair value option may be applied on an instrument-by-instrument basis.

12. (a) Interest expense can be measured using various methods. In this situation, Southern recognized interest expense by debiting interest expense for $12,000 and crediting cash for $12,000, which represents the coupon interest paid on the bond. Therefore, interest expense was recognized on the income statement as a separate line item. The change in fair value from January 1, 2010, to December 31, 2010, would, therefore, be recognized as a gain or loss to revalue the bond's carrying value to fair value. The change in value is calculated as beginning of year carrying value of $107,720 less end of year carrying value of 106,460, or $1,260. Since the value of the liability decreased, this indicates a gain of $1,260 that would be recognized on the 2010 income statement.

13.   (c)   A bond premium must be amortized using the interest method or the straight-line method if the results are not materially different. To use the straight-line method, the amount of time the bonds will be outstanding must be known. Since this time period is not given, the interest method must be used. Under the interest method, interest expense is computed as follows:

$$\begin{array}{ccccccc} \text{BV of} \\ \text{bonds} & \times & \text{Yield} \\ \text{rate} & \times & \text{Time} \\ \text{period} & = & \text{Interest} \\ \text{expense} \end{array}$$

$$\$103,288 \ \times \ 10\% \ \times \ 6/12 \ = \ \$5,164$$

The interest payable at 12/31/09 is $6,000 ($100,000 × 12% × 6/12), so the 12/31/09 journal entry is

Interest expense	5,164	
Premium on BP	836	
Interest payable		6,000

14.   (b)   Under the effective interest method, interest expense is computed as follows:

$$\begin{array}{ccccccc} \text{BV of} \\ \text{bonds} & \times & \text{Yield} \\ \text{rate} & \times & \text{Time} \\ \text{period} & = & \text{Interest} \\ \text{expense} \end{array}$$

$$\$469,500 \ \times \ 10\% \ \times \ 6/12 \ = \ \$23,475$$

The cash interest payable is computed below.

$$\begin{array}{ccccccc} \text{FV of} \\ \text{bonds} & \times & \text{Stated} \\ \text{rate} & \times & \text{Time} \\ \text{period} & = & \text{Interest} \\ \text{payable} \end{array}$$

$$\$500,000 \ \times \ 9\% \ \times \ 6/12 \ = \ \$22,500$$

The bond discount amortization is the difference between these two amounts computed above ($23,475 – $22,500 = $975). This amortization would increase the carrying amount of the bonds to $470,475 ($469,500 original carrying amount + $975 amortization).

15.   (c)   Under the effective interest method, interest expense is computed as follows:

$$\begin{array}{ccccccc} \text{CA of} \\ \text{bonds} & \times & \text{Yield} \\ \text{rate} & \times & \text{Time} \\ \text{period} & = & \text{Interest} \\ \text{payable} \end{array}$$

$$\$105,000 \ \times \ 6\% \ \times \ 12/12 \ = \ \$6,300$$

The cash interest payable is computed as follows:

$$\begin{array}{ccccccc} \text{FV of} \\ \text{bonds} & \times & \text{Stated} \\ \text{rate} & \times & \text{Time} \\ \text{period} & = & \text{Cash} \\ \text{interest} \end{array}$$

$$\$100,000 \ \times \ 7\% \ \times \ 12/12 \ = \ \$7,000$$

The bond premium amortization is the difference between these two amounts ($7,000 – $6,300 = $700). Therefore, the unamortized premium at 6/30/10 is $4,300 ($5,000 – $700).

16.   (b)   The requirement is to determine whether the amount of amortization increases each year using the interest method when a bond is sold either at a discount or premium or both. Using the interest method, interest expense for the period is based on the carrying value of the bond multiplied

by the effective rate of interest. Cash interest paid for the period equals the face value of the bond multiplied by the stated rate of interest. The difference between these two resulting figures is the amortization of the discount or premium each period. The solutions approach is to prepare a table for a bond issued at a discount and at a premium and examine the direction of the successive amortization amounts. Consider $100,000 of 8% bonds issued on January 1, 2009, due on January 1, 2016, with interest payable each July 1 and January 1. Investors wish to obtain a yield of 10% on the issue. The amortization for the first two periods is as follows:

Dates	Credit cash	Debit interest expense	Credit bond discount	Carrying value of bonds
1/1/09				$92,278
7/1/09	$4,000	$4,614	$614	92,892
1/1/10	4,000	4,645	645	93,537

Assume the same facts, except the investors wish to obtain a yield of only 6% on the issue.

Dates	Credit cash	Debit interest expense	Debit bond premium	Carrying value of bonds
1/1/09				$108,530
7/1/09	$4,000	$3,256	$744	107,786
1/1/10	4,000	3,234	766	107,020

The above tables show that when bonds are sold at either a discount or a premium, the amount of amortization using the interest method will increase each year.

17.   (b)   Using the effective interest method, interest expense is computed as the **carrying amount** of the bonds multiplied by the **effective rate** of interest. Cash interest paid equals the **face value** of the bonds multiplied by the **stated rate** of interest. The difference between interest expense and cash interest paid is discount amortization. When bonds are issued at a discount, the carrying amount increases each year, so interest expense increases each year, which causes a larger difference between interest expense and interest paid. Therefore, under the effective interest method, the discount amortization amount increases yearly. Under the straight-line method, discount amortization is constant each period. After one year, the incorrect use of the straight-line method would overstate the carrying amount of the bonds since more discount would have been amortized than under the effective interest method. By the time the bonds mature at 1/2/15, the entire discount would have been amortized under both methods, so the carrying amount would be the same for both methods.

18.   (b)   The 12/31/09 bond sinking fund balance ($450,000) was increased by the additional investment ($90,000), dividends ($15,000), and interest ($30,000). It was decreased by administration costs ($5,000), resulting in a 12/31/10 balance of $580,000 ($450,000 + $90,000 + $15,000 + $30,000 – $5,000).

19.   (d)   Disclosure is required at the balance sheet date of future payments for sinking fund requirements and maturity amounts of long-term debt during each of the next five years. Therefore, the combined aggregate of $17,500,000 of maturities and sinking fund requirements detailed by year should be disclosed.

20.   (d)   Companies sometimes place assets in segregated funds for special needs. These funds may become unavailable for normal operations due to debt covenants or other contractual requirements. Funds segregated for long-term needs, such as the bond sinking fund established in this problem, are reported as investments in the noncurrent section of the balance sheet. When interest is earned on investments held in a bond sinking fund, the following journal entry would be made:

Bond sinking fund cash	(revenue earned)
Bond sinking fund revenue	(revenue earned)

The debit to the bond sinking fund increases the balance of the fund. The amount credited to bond sinking fund revenue is reported in the "Other Income (Expense)" section of the income statement.

21. **(a)** Businesses occasionally accumulate a fund of cash and/or investments for a specific purpose, such as the retirement of bonds in this problem. These funds are referred to as "sinking funds." The sinking fund is increased when periodic additions are made to the fund and when revenue is earned on the investments held in the fund. When cash is used to purchase investments, the components of the fund change (i.e., cash is invested and replaced by bonds or other securities), but the total fund balance is not affected.

22. **(c)** Debt and equity securities that are classified as **trading securities** are reported at fair market value, with unrealized gains and losses included in earnings. Therefore, at 12/31/09 Wynn would recognize an unrealized holding gain of $35,000 ($945,000 – $910,000) on the income statement, and report the securities at their fair market value of $945,000. Securities classified as trading securities are reported at fair market value on the balance sheet.

23. **(b)** Interest **receivable** on an investment in bonds is computed using the basic interest formula

Face value		Stated rate		Time period		Interest receivable
$500,000	×	8%	×	6/12	=	$20,000

Note that interest **revenue** is $23,075 ($461,500 × 10% × 6/12) using the interest method.

24. **(d)** The bonds should be recorded at an original cost of $215,000 ($220,000 less accrued interest of $5,000). The premium of $15,000 is amortized using the straight-line method over the period from the 10/1/08 date of purchase to the 1/1/15 maturity date (seventy-five months). By 12/31/09, amortization has been recorded for fifteen months (10/1/08 to 12/31/09), so total amortization is $3,000 ($15,000 × 15/75). Therefore, the bonds should be reported on the 12/31/09 balance sheet at $212,000 ($215,000 – $3,000).

25. **(a)** When using the interest method of amortization, interest revenue is computed as follows:

BV of bonds		Yield rate		Time period		Interest expense
$906,000	×	10%	×	6/12	=	$45,300

The initial BV is the total amount paid less the accrued interest ($946,000 – $40,000 = $906,000). The amount of interest receivable for the six months is computed below.

FV of bonds		Stated rate		Time period		Interest receivable
$1,000,000	×	8%	×	6/12	=	$40,000

The discount amortized at 12/31/09 is the difference in these two amounts ($45,300 – $40,000 = $5,300). This increases

the book value of the investment to $911,300 ($906,000 + $5,300).

26. **(d)** The requirement is to determine the most likely cause of the decline in the bonds' market value. When the bonds were acquired at a premium, they sold above their face value. This meant that the stated rate of the bonds was greater than the market rate of interest on an alternative investment of equal risk. Thus, the investors paid more than the face value to acquire the bonds. However, when bonds are quoted at a discount, the stated rate of the bonds is less than the market rate. Therefore, the market rate of interest has increased since Lee purchased the bonds.

27. **(d)** At any point in time, an investor's carrying value of a bond held as a long-term investment is equal to the par value of the bond, plus the amount of the unamortized premium, or less the amount of the unamortized discount. A bond purchased at a premium, thus, has a higher carrying value at any point in time than if it had been purchased at a discount. This is logical since its initial cost is also higher when purchased at a premium.

Having determined that the bond purchased at a premium will result in the highest carrying value, we must now determine which amortization method will result in the higher carrying value at the end of the first year. Under the straight-line method, the periodic amortization is constant; it is computed by dividing the total premium by the number of periods involved. Under the effective interest method, the periodic amortization changes over the term of the bond. A review of amortization tables for bonds issued at a premium will demonstrate that the periodic amortization of the premium is lowest in the first period, but increases over subsequent periods. Therefore, the straight-line method would result in higher amortization of the premium at the end of the first year than under the effective interest method. The higher amortization would result in a smaller unamortized premium and lower, overall carrying value at the end of the first year under the straight-line method than under the effective interest method.

28. **(c)** The requirement is to determine the purchase price of a bond which will yield the highest interest income for the investor. If the bond's market rate of interest on the date of acquisition is different than the stated rate, the bonds will sell at a premium or discount. If the market rate of interest is higher than the bond's stated rate, the purchase price will be lower than the face value (i.e., discounted). The discount will be recognized over the life of the investment as an addition to interest income. Annual interest income will equal the cash interest received plus the discount amortization for the year. If the bonds are purchased at par (face value), the interest income will equal the cash interest received. The interest income for a bond purchased at a premium would equal the cash interest received less the premium amortization for the year.

29. **(c)** When a company uses the effective interest method to amortize a discount on bonds payable, interest expense (which is based on the carrying value of the bonds) is lower in earlier years when compared to interest expense under the straight-line method. Therefore, the straight-line method results in higher interest expense, lower net income, and **understated** retained earnings. Since more interest expense is recorded under the straight-line method, amortization of the discount on bonds payable will be greater under the straight-line method when compared to the effective-interest method. Therefore, the carrying amount of the bonds under the straight-line method is **overstated**.

30. (b)   The gain on sale of the bond investment is the excess of the selling price over the carrying amount. The selling price was $14,000 **above** face value. The bonds were purchased at a discount of $10,000, but after amortization of $2,000 the carrying amount at the time of sale was $8,000 **below** face value. Therefore, the selling price exceeded the carrying amount by $22,000 ($14,000 premium + $8,000 remaining discount).

B.5. Convertible Bonds

31. (b)   Using the book value method, the common stock is recorded at the carrying amount of the converted bonds, less any conversion expenses. Since there are no conversion expenses in this case, the common stock is recorded at the $1,300,000 carrying amount of the converted bonds. The par value of the stock issued is $50,000 (50,000 × $1), so additional paid-in capital (APIC) of $1,250,000 ($1,300,000 – $50,000) is recorded. The entry is

Bonds payable	1,000,000	
Premium on B.P.	300,000	
Common stock		50,000
APIC		1,250,000

Note that when the book value method is used, the fair value is not considered, and no gain or loss is recognized.

32. (a)   Under the book value method, the common stock will be recorded at the book value of the bonds at the date of conversion. Thus, no gain or loss is recognized on the conversion. The conversion entry credits common stock and APIC, which increases stockholders' equity. The amount of additional paid-in capital is the difference between the book value of the bonds and the par value of the stock. The effect of the conversion would be to increase the APIC. The conversion has no effect on retained earnings. No gain or loss is recognized.

33. (d)   Convertible debt securities which may be converted into common stock at the option of the holder, and whose issue price is not significantly greater than face value, should be reported as debt upon issuance for the entire proceeds of the bonds. This reasoning is based on the inseparability of the debt and the conversion option, and the mutually exclusive options of the holder (i.e., holding either bonds or stock). Contributed capital would be recorded only upon conversion of the bonds to common stock.

34. (c)   When the **book value method** of accounting for the conversion of bonds into common stock is used, the common stock will be recorded at the book value of the bonds at the date of conversion. Thus, no gain or loss is recognized on the conversion. When the **market value method** of accounting for the conversion is used, the following journal entry would be made on the books of the issuer (assuming market value > book value):

Loss on redemption	(plug)	
Bonds payable	(book value)	
Common stock		(par)
APIC-common stock		(mkt.-par)

The debit to the loss account would be for the difference between the market value of the stock and the book value of the bonds. The market value method assumes a culmination

of the earnings process, and a gain or loss on the conversion may be recognized. In this case, the market value of the stock exceeds the book value of the bonds, and a loss is recognized.

B.6. Debt Issued with Detachable Purchase Warrants

35. (c)   The proceeds of bonds issued with **detachable** warrants are allocated between the bonds and the warrants based upon their relative fair value at the time of issuance. In this case, the portion allocated to the bonds is $900,000, calculated as follows:

$$\frac{\$1,080,000}{\$1,080,000 + \$120,000} = 90\%; \ 90\% \times \$1,000,000 = \$900,000$$

Therefore, the bonds payable are reported at $900,000 (face value $1,000,000 less discount $100,000).

36. (c)   The proceeds from the issuance of debt with **detachable** stock warrants should be allocated between the debt and equity elements. 1,000 bonds ($1,000,000 ÷ $1,000) were issued with fifty detachable stock warrants each, for a total of 50,000 warrants. Paid-in capital from stock warrants is $200,000 (50,000 × $4). Since the bonds and warrants were issued for $1,090,000 ($1,000,000 × 109%), the portion of the proceeds allocated to the bonds is $890,000 ($1,090,000 – $200,000) and the discount is $110,000 ($1,000,000 – $890,000). Note that if a fair value is given for the **bonds without warrants,** ASC Subtopic 470-20 states that the proceeds should be allocated between the bonds and warrants based on their relative fair value at the time of issuance.

37. (d)   The proceeds from the issuance of debt with **detachable** stock warrants should be allocated between the debt and equity elements. 500 bonds ($500,000 ÷ $1,000) were issued with thirty detachable stock warrants each, for a total of 15,000 warrants. Paid-in capital from stock warrants is $60,000 (15,000 × $4). Note that if a fair value was given for the **bonds without warrants,** ASC Subtopic 470-20 states that the proceeds should be allocated between the bonds and warrants based on their relative fair value at the time of issuance.

38. (a)   The solutions approach is to set up the original journal entry on the books of the issuer. The entry would be made as follows:

Cash	(proceeds)	
Discount on bonds payable	(plug)	
Bonds payable		(face)
APIC—Stock warrants		(fair value)

Since the APIC—Stock warrants account is already stated at market value, any remaining difference must be allocated to the **bonds**. Bonds payable would be credited only at their face (par) value. Therefore, Discount on bonds payable is debited for the excess of the fair value of the warrants and the face amount of the bonds over cash proceeds.

39. (c)   Bonds issued with stock purchase warrants are, in substance, composed of two elements: a debt element, and a stockholders' equity element. Proceeds from bonds issued with **detachable** stock purchase warrants should be allocated between the bonds and the warrants on the basis of their relative fair market values. Detachable warrants trade separately from the debt; thus, a market value is available. The amount allocated to the warrants should be accounted for as paid-in capital. Bonds issued with **nondetachable**

stock purchase warrants must be surrendered in order to exercise the warrants. Since this inseparability prevents the determination of individual market values, no allocation is permitted.

B.7. Extinguishment of Debt

40. (b)   A gain or loss on redemption of bonds is the difference between the **cash paid** ($5,000,000 × 98% = $4,900,000) and the **net book value of the bonds**. To compute the net book value, premium or discount and bond issue costs must be considered. Book value is $4,980,000 ($5,000,000 face value, less $50,000 bond issue costs, plus $30,000 premium). Therefore the gain or redemption is $80,000 ($4,980,000 book value less $4,900,000 cash paid).

41.   (d)   The gain on early extinguishment of debt is the excess of the book value of the bonds at the time of retirement over the cash paid ($1,000,000 × 101% = $1,010,000). On 1/1/04, the original balance in the premium account was $40,000 ($1,040,000 – $1,000,000). At 7/1/09, the premium had been amortized for five and one-half years, or eleven six-month periods (1/1/04 to 7/1/09). Since the bond term was ten years, or twenty six-month periods, the total premium amortized was $22,000 ($40,000 × 11/20). Therefore, the unamortized premium was $18,000 ($40,000 – $22,000) and the book value of the bonds was $1,018,000 ($1,000,000 + $18,000). A shortcut approach is to take the 1/1/04 book value ($1,040,000) and subtract the amortization ($22,000) to determine the 7/1/09 book value of $1,018,000. The gain is $8,000 ($1,018,000 book value less $1,010,000 cash paid).

42.   (a)   The total bond discount and bond issue costs were $30,000 at the time of issuance [(.02 × $500,000) + $20,000]. By 1/1/10, twelve years have passed since the bonds were issued on 1/1/98. Since the bonds have a fifteen-year life, 12/15 of the discount and issue costs have been amortized, leaving 3/15 unamortized (3/15 × $30,000 = $6,000). When bonds are retired, the bonds and unamortized premium or discount, and/or issue costs must be removed from the books. In this situation, the difference between the net book value of the bonds ($500,000 – $6,000 = $494,000) and the cash paid ($500,000 × 1.02 = $510,000) is recognized as a loss ($510,000 – $494,000 = $16,000).

SOLUTIONS TO SIMULATION PROBLEMS

Simulation Problem 1

Situation	Concepts	Bond Valuation	Amortization Schedule	Journal Entries	Communication	Research
		Bond discounts	*Bond premium*	*Bond payable*	*Common stock*	*Additional paid-in capital*	*Retained earnings*

	Situation	Bond discounts	Bond premium	Bond payable	Common stock	Additional paid-in capital	Retained earnings
1.	Parker issued bonds payable with a nominal interest rate that was less than the market rate of interest.	Increase	No effect	Increase	No effect	No effect	No effect
2.	Parker issued convertible bonds, which are common stock equivalents, for an amount in excess of the bonds' face amount.	No effect	Increase	Increase	No effect	No effect	No effect
3.	Parker issued common stock when the convertible bonds described in item 2 were submitted for conversion. Each $1,000 bond was converted into twenty common shares. The book value method was used for the early conversion.	No effect	Decrease	Decrease	Increase	Increase	No effect
4.	Parker issued bonds, with nondetachable warrants for an amount equal to the face amount of the bonds. The stock warrants do not have a determinable value.	No effect	No effect	Increase	No effect	No effect	No effect
5.	Parker issued bonds, with detachable stock warrants, for an amount equal to the face amount of the bonds. The stock warrants have a determinable value.	Increase	No effect	Increase	No effect	Increase	No effect
6.	Parker redeemed a bond issued at 8% at a discount for an amount that was 102% of face value.	Decrease	No effect	Decrease	No effect	No effect	Decrease
7.	Parker issued bonds payable with a nominal rate of interest that is higher than the market rate.	No effect	Increase	Increase	No effect	No effect	No effect
8.	Parker called a bond that was issued at 105 at a time when the market value of the bond was less than its carrying value.	No effect	Decrease	Decrease	No effect	No effect	Increase

Explanation of solutions

1.   Since the nominal rate of interest was less than the market rate of interest, the bonds sold at a discount. In other words, the investors paid less than the face value to acquire the bonds. The journal entry to record the transaction is

Cash	xx	
Discount on bonds payable	xx	
Bonds payable		xx

Therefore, the issuance of the bonds would increase both bonds payable and discount on bonds payable.

2.   Convertible debt securities which may be converted into common stock at the option of the holder, and whose issue price is not significantly greater than face value, should be reported as debt upon issuance for the entire proceeds of the bonds. This reasoning is based on the inseparability of the debt and the conversion option, and the mutually exclusive options of the holder (i.e., holding either bonds or stock). The journal entry to record the transaction is

Cash	xx	
Premium on bonds payable		xx
Bonds payable		xx

Therefore, the issuance of the convertible bonds would increase both bonds payable and premium on bonds payable.

3.   When the book value method of accounting for the conversion of bonds into common stock is used, the common stock will be recorded at the book value of the bonds at the date of conversion. Thus, no gain or loss is recognized on the conversion. The journal entry to record the transaction is

Bonds payable	xx	
Premium on bonds payable	xx	
Common stock		xx
Additional paid-in capital		xx

Therefore, the conversion of the bonds would decrease bonds payable and premium on bonds payable while increasing common stock and additional paid-in capital.

4.   Nondetachable warrants are not valued separately from the bond. Therefore, the entry to record the bond is

Cash	xx	
Bonds payable		xx

5.   The proceeds of bonds issued with detachable warrants are allocated between the bonds and the warrants based upon their relative fair market values at the time of issuance. In this case, the bonds, with detachable stock warrants, were issued for an amount equal to the face amount of the bonds. Since part of the proceeds is allocated to the stock warrants, the bonds were issued at a discount. The journal entry to record the transaction is

Cash	xx	
Discount on bonds payable	xx	
Bonds payable		xx
Additional paid-in capital—Stock warrants		xx

Therefore, the issuance of the bonds, with detachable stock warrants, would increase bonds payable, discount on bonds payable, and additional paid-in capital.

6.   The bond was sold at a discount. Therefore, when the bond is redeemed, the bonds payable and the discount account must be removed from the records. The net carrying amount is less than the reacquisition price. Therefore, there is a loss on the extinguishment of debt. It will be an ordinary loss on the income statement. The journal entry for the transaction is

Bonds payable	xx	
Loss on bond	xx	
Discount on bond		xx
Cash		xx

7.   Since the nominal rate of interest is greater than the market rate, the bonds sold at a premium. In other words, the investors paid more than face value for the bond. The journal entry to record the transaction is

Cash	xx	
Bonds payable		xx
Premium on bond		xx

8.   The net carrying value is greater than the market value of the bond (reacquisition price). Therefore, there is a gain on the redemption of the bond. The journal entry for this transaction is

Premium on bonds payable	xx	
Bonds payable	xx	
Cash		xx
Gain on extinguishment of debt		xx

Situation	Concepts	**Bond Valuation**	Amortization Schedule	Journal Entries	Communication	Research

PVA of $12,000 at 4% for 20 periods   +   PV of $400,000 at 4% after 20 periods

    (13.5903 × 12,000)   +   (.4564 × $400,000)

      163,083.60   +   183,560

                  =   345,643.60

                     Rounds to 345,644

Situation	Concepts	Bond Valuation	**Amortization Schedule**	Journal Entries	Communication	Research

Date	Interest paid	Interest expense	Amortization of discount	Discount on bond payable	Carrying value of bond payable
1/2/09	0	0	0	54,356	345,644
6/30/09	12,000	13,826	1,826	52,530	347,470
12/31/09	12,000	13,899	1,899	50,631	349,369

1. The discount on bonds is (face – carrying value). The carrying value is $345,644, the issue price. Therefore, the discount account is $54,356 ($400,000 – $345,644).

2. The carrying amount at date of issue is the issue price, $345,644.

3. The cash interest payment is $12,000 and is given in the problem. This represents a semiannual interest rate of 3% ($400,000 × 3% = $12,000).

4. The interest expense is $13,826 ($345,644 × 4%) and is given in the problem.

5. Amortization of discount is interest expense minus cash interest payment ($12,000 – $13,826) = $1,826.

6. The discount is amortized by $1,826. The discount account approaches zero as the bond approaches maturity date. Therefore, the discount on 6/30/09 is $52,530 ($54,356 – $1,826).

7. The new carrying amount on 6/30/09 is $347,470 ($345,644 + $1,826).

8. The cash interest payment is the same as the previous period. It is always coupon interest rate times the face of the bond (3% × $400,000) = $12,000.

9. Interest expense is the carrying value times the effective rate. $13,899 = ($347,470 × 4%).

10. Amortization is the difference between the cash payment and the interest expense. $1,899 ($12,000 – $13,899).

11. Discount on bonds is $50,631 ($52,530 – $1,899).

12. Carrying amount is $349,369 ($347,470 + $1,899).

Situation	Concepts	Bond Valuation	Amortization Schedule	**Journal Entries**	Communication	Research

1. January 2, 2009	Cash		345,644			
	Discount on bonds payable		54,356			
	Bonds payable			400,000		
2. June 30, 2009	Interest expense		13,826			
	Cash			12,000		
	Discount on bonds payable			1,826		

Situation	Concepts	Bond Valuation	Amortization Schedule	Journal Entries	**Communication**	Research

To: Finance Manager, Parker Co.
From: CPA Candidate
Re: Accounting for bonds

   I have researched your issues regarding accounting for bonds. This memorandum provides explanations to your questions relating to the amortization and financial statement disclosures for bonds.
   The purpose of the effective interest method is to provide periodic interest expense based on a constant rate over the life of the bonds. The impact of applying the effective interest method on Parker's bond premium in 2006 is to decrease the premium by a lesser amount as compared to using the straight-line method of amortization.
   Under the straight-line interest method, the premium is amortized at a constant periodic amount, and in 2006 the premium amortization would have been greater than amortization under the effective interest method. Consequently, for 2006, interest expense would have been understated, net income would have been overstated, and the carrying amount of the bonds would have been understated.
   The November 30, 2009 transaction results in an ordinary loss. The loss is equal to the excess of the fair value of the cash and property transferred over the bonds' carrying amount on November 30, 2009. This accounting is appropriate because the transaction involves the early extinguishment of debt.
   If you have any additional questions, please contact me.

Situation	Concepts	Bond Valuation	Amortization Schedule	Journal Entries	Communication	**Research**

APB 21, Para 13–14

13. Determining an appropriate interest rate. The variety of transactions encountered precludes any specific interest rate from being applicable in all circumstances. However, some general guides may be stated. The choice of a rate may be affected by the credit standing of the issuer, restrictive covenants, the collateral, payment and other terms pertaining to the debt, and, if appropriate, the tax consequences to the buyer and seller. The prevailing rates for similar instruments of issuers with similar credit ratings will normally help determine the appropriate interest rate for determining the present value of a specific note at its date of issuance. In any event, the rate used for valuation purposes will normally be at least equal to

the rate at which the debtor can obtain financing of a similar nature from other sources at the date of the transaction. The objective is to approximate the rate which would have resulted if an independent borrower and an independent lender had negotiated a similar transaction under comparable terms and conditions with the option to pay the cash price upon purchase or to give a note for the amount of the purchase which bears the prevailing rate of interest to maturity.

Codification: 835-30-25-12

APB21, Para 14

14. The selection of a rate may be affected by many considerations. For instance, where applicable, the choice of a rate may be influenced by (a) an approximation of the prevailing market rates for the source of credit that would provide a market for sale or assignment of the note; (b) the prime or higher rate for notes which are discounted with banks, giving due weight to the credit standing of the maker; (c) published risks that are traded in open markets; and (e) the current rate charged by investors for first or second mortgage loans on similar property.

Codification: 835-30-25-13

Simulation Problem 2

	Concepts			
Situation		Journal Entries	Communication	Research

Indicate whether each item is True or False.

		True	False
1.	Bond issue costs should be treated as deferred charges and amortized over the life of the bond.	●	○
2.	Early extinguishment of debt is treated as an extraordinary item.	○	●
3.	Losses from extinguishment of debt should be amortized over the remaining life of the debt.	○	●
4.	The straight-line method of amortization should be used for bonds due in less than five years.	○	●
5.	Bonds that mature on a single date are called serial bonds.	○	●
6.	The effective interest is calculated by multiplying the maturity value of the bond by the coupon rate.	○	●
7.	A bond premium represents a reduction of interest expense on the books of the issuer.	●	○
8.	When the contract or coupon rate is greater than the effective rate, the bonds will sell at a premium.	●	○

Explanation of solutions

1. **(T)** Bond issue costs are amortized over the bond life.

2. **(F)** Early extinguishment of debt does not receive routine treatment as an extraordinary item. It must meet the test for an extraordinary item (infrequent **and** usual) in order to receive extraordinary treatment.

3. **(F)** Losses shall be recognized in the period of extinguishment.

4. **(F)** The effective amortization method should be used.

5. **(F)** Bonds that mature on a single date are called term bonds.

6. **(F)** The effective interest in calculated by the carrying value times the effective rate.

7. **(T)** As the premium is amortized, interest expense is decreased.

8. **(T)** When a bond pays a higher rate than the market, it will sell for a premium.

Situation	Concepts	Journal Entries		Communication	Research

1. January 1, 2009 Issue bonds

Cash		392,000	
Discount on bonds		8,000	
Bonds payable			400,000

2. September 1, 2009 Issue bonds with detachable warrants

Cash		530,000	
Discount on bonds		12,973	
Bonds payable			500,000
Additional paid-in capital—warrants			42,973

3. October 1, 2009 Conversion of bonds

Bonds payable		50,000	
Premium on bonds payable		2,150	
Common stock			10,000
Additional paid-in capital			42,150

Situation	Concepts	Journal Entries	Communication		Research

To: Controller, Castle Co.
From: CPA Candidate
Re: Accounting for bonds

I have received your note inquiring about the proper accounting for bonds. Below are answers to your specific questions.

The bond issue price would be determined by the expected future cash flows of principal and interest, discounted at the market rate of interest, plus the value of the conversion option at the date of issuance.

Castle should account for the issuance of the convertible bonds by increasing cash for the issue price, increasing bonds payable by the face amount, and increasing premium on bonds payable for the balance. The convertible debt is accounted for solely as debt. The conversion option is not recognized primarily because it is inseparable from the debt, and secondarily because of the practical difficulty of assigning it a value.

Castle should account for the conversion of the bonds into common stock by decreasing both bonds payable and unamortized bond premium by 30%, increasing common stock by $25 for each share issued, and increasing additional paid-in capital by the difference between the three previous amounts.

If we can be of further assistance, please do not hesitate to contact my office.

Situation	Concepts	Journal Entries	Communication	Research	

The authoritative literature for each of the following transactions is shown below.

1.   March 1, 2009 issue of bonds   **APB21, Para 16**

16. Statement presentation of discount and premium. The discount or premium resulting from the determination of present value in cash or noncash transactions is not an asset or liability separable from the note which gives rise to it. Therefore, the discount or premium should be reported in the balance sheet as a direct deduction from or addition to the face amount of the note. It should not be classified as a deferred charge or deferred credit. The description of the note should include the effective interest rate; the face amount should also be disclosed in the financial statements or in the notes to the statements. Amortization of discount or premium should be reported as interest in the statement of income. Issue costs should be reported in the balance sheet as deferred charges.

Codification: 835-30-45-1A

2.   September 1, 2009 issue of bonds with warrants

APB14, Para 16

16. The Board is of the opinion that the portion of the proceeds of debt securities issued with detachable stock purchase warrants which is allocable to the warrants should be accounted for as paid-in capital. The allocation should be based on the relative fair values of the two securities at time of issuance. Any resulting discount or premium on the debt securities should be accounted for as such. The same accounting treatment applies to issues of debt securities (issued with detachable warrants) which may be surrendered in settlement of the exercise price of the warrant. However, when stock purchase warrants are not detachable from the debt and the debt security must be surrendered in order to exercise the warrant, the two securities taken together are substantially equivalent to convertible debt and the accounting specified in paragraph 12 should apply.

Codification: 470-20-25-2

3.   October 1, 2009 conversion of bonds

AIN-APB 26, #1

In practice, the carrying amount, including any unamortized premium or discount, is credited to the capital accounts upon conversion to reflect the stock issued and no gain or loss is recognized.

Codification: 470-20-40-4

MULTIPLE-CHOICE QUESTIONS (1-8)

1. For a troubled debt restructuring involving only a modification of terms, which of the following items specified by the new terms would be compared to the carrying amount of the debt to determine if the debtor should report a gain on restructuring?

   a. The total future cash payments.
   b. The present value of the debt at the original interest rate.
   c. The present value of the debt at the modified interest rate.
   d. The amount of future cash payments designated as principal repayments.

Items 2 and 3 are based on the following:

The following information pertains to the transfer of real estate pursuant to a troubled debt restructuring by Knob Co. to Mene Corp. in full liquidation of Knob's liability to Mene:

Carrying amount of liability liquidated	$150,000
Carrying amount of real estate transferred	100,000
Fair value of real estate transferred	90,000

2. What amount should Knob report as a gain (loss) on restructuring of payables?

   a. $(10,000)
   b. $0
   c. $50,000
   d. $60,000

3. What amount should Knob report as a gain (loss) on transfer of real estate?

   a. $(10,000)
   b. $0
   c. $50,000
   d. $60,000

4. On October 15, 2010, Kam Corp. informed Finn Co. that Kam would be unable to repay its $100,000 note due on October 31 to Finn. Finn agreed to accept title to Kam's computer equipment in full settlement of the note. The equipment's carrying value was $80,000 and its fair value was $75,000. Kam's tax rate is 30%. What amounts should Kam report as the gain (loss) on the transfer of assets, and the gain on restructuring of debt?

	Transfer gain (loss)	*Restructuring gain*
a.	$(5,000)	$25,000
b.	$0	$30,000
c.	$0	$20,000
d.	$20,000	$0

5. Colt, Inc. is indebted to Kent under an $800,000, 10%, four-year note dated December 31, 2007. Annual interest of $80,000 was paid on December 31, 2008 and 2009. During 2010, Colt experienced financial difficulties and is likely to default unless concessions are made. On December 31, 2010, Kent agreed to restructure the debt as follows:

   • Interest of $80,000 for 2010, due December 31, 2010, was made payable December 31, 2011.
   • Interest for 2011 was waived.
   • The principal amount was reduced to $700,000.

Assume Colt does not elect the fair value option for reporting the debt modification. How much should Colt report as a gain in its income statement for the year ended December 31, 2010?

   a. $0
   b. $100,000
   c. $ 60,000
   d. $120,000

6. Grey Company holds an overdue note receivable of $800,000 plus recorded accrued interest of $64,000. The effective interest rate is 8%. As the result of a court-imposed settlement on December 31, 2010, Grey agreed to the following restructuring arrangement:

   • Reduced the principal obligation to $600,000.
   • Forgave the $64,000 accrued interest.
   • Extended the maturity date to December 31, 2012.
   • Annual interest of $40,000 is to be paid to Grey on December 31, 2011 and 2012.

The present value of the interest and principal payments to be received by Grey Company discounted for two years at 8% is $585,734. Grey does not elect the fair value option for reporting the debt modification. On December 31, 2010, Grey would recognize a valuation allowance for impaired loans of

   a. $ 14,266
   b. $184,000
   c. $278,266
   d. $0

7. On December 31, 2008, Marsh Company entered into a debt restructuring agreement with Saxe Company, which was experiencing financial difficulties. Marsh restructured a $100,000 note receivable as follows:

   • Reduced the principal obligation to $70,000.
   • Forgave $12,000 of accrued interest.
   • Extended the maturity date from December 31, 2008 to December 31, 2010.
   • Reduced the interest rate from 12% to 8%. Interest is payable annually on December 31, 2009 and 2010.

Present value factors:

Single sum, two years @ 8%	.85734
Single sum, two years @ 12%	.79719
Ordinary annuity, two years @ 8%	1.78326
Ordinary annuity, two years @ 12%	1.69006

In accordance with the agreement, Saxe made payments to Marsh on December 31, 2009 and 2010. Marsh does not elect the fair value option for reporting the modification of debt. How much interest income should Marsh report for the year ended December 31, 2010?

   a. $0
   b. $ 5,600
   c. $ 8,100
   d. $11,200

8. Casey Corp. entered into a troubled debt restructuring agreement with First State Bank. First State agreed to accept land with a carrying amount of $85,000 and a fair value of $120,000 in exchange for a note with a carrying amount of $185,000. What amount should Casey report as a gain from extinguishment of debt in its income statement?

   a. $0
   b. $ 35,000
   c. $ 65,000
   d. $100,000

SIMULATION PROBLEM

Simulation Problem 1   (40 to 50 minutes)

Situation				
	Present Value	Analysis	Journal Entries	Communication	Research

Jayson Company has an overdue note receivable from Simpson Corporation for $300,000. The note was dated January 1, 2008. It has an annual interest rate of 9%, and interest is paid December 31 of each year. Simpson paid the interest on the note on December 31, 2008, but Simpson did not pay the interest due in December of 2009. The current effective rate of interest is 6%.

On January 1, 2010, Jayson agrees to the following restructuring arrangement:

- Reduce the principal to $250,000.
- Forgive the accrued interest.
- Reduce the interest rate to 6%.
- Extend the maturity date of the note to December 31, 2012.

Assume that Jayson does not elect to use the fair value option for reporting the debt modification.

	Present Value			
Situation		Analysis	Journal Entries	Communication	Research

Calculate the present value of the future cash flows of the restructured note.

		Analysis		
Situation	Present Value		Journal Entries	Communication	Research

Calculate the net carrying amount of the prestructured loan. (For a more realistic exam experience complete this requirement using a spreadsheet program such as Excel.)

			Journal Entries	
Situation	Present Value	Analysis		Communication	Research

Prepare the journal entries needed by Jayson for the restructuring of the loan and the interest payment received on December 31, 2010.

January 1, 2010

December 31, 2010

Situation	Present Value	Analysis	Journal Entries	Communication		Research

Write a memo to the CEO of Jayson Company, advising her on the necessary accounting disclosures and the financial statement impact of restructuring the loan from Simpson Corp.

REMINDER: Your response will be graded for both technical content and writing skills. Technical content will be evaluated for information that is helpful to the intended reader and clearly relevant to the issue. Writing skills will be evaluated for development, organization, and the appropriate expression of ideas in professional correspondence. Use a standard business memo or letter format with a clear beginning, middle, and end. Do not convey information in the form of a table, bullet point list, or other abbreviated presentation.

Situation	Present Value	Analysis	Journal Entries	Communication	Research	

Using the authoritative literature, determine the interest rate that should be used to calculate the carrying value of the loan after restructuring. Copy or reference the appropriate literature in the space provided.

| 1. a __ __ | 3. a __ __ | 5. b __ __ | 7. c __ __ | 1st: __/8 = __% |
| 2. d __ __ | 4. a __ __ | 6. a __ __ | 8. c __ __ | 2nd: __/8 = __% |

MULTIPLE-CHOICE ANSWER EXPLANATIONS

C. Debt Restructure

1. (a)   In a restructuring involving only a change in terms, the total future cash payments should be compared to the carrying amount to determine if a gain should be recognized. Answers (b) and (c) are incorrect because the undiscounted future cash flows are compared to the carrying amount. Answer (d) is incorrect because the total amount of future cash flows are compared to the carrying amount.

2. (d)   In this restructure, the debt is retired by the transfer of real estate to the creditor. A gain or loss is recognized on the transfer of real estate, and a gain or loss is recognized on the restructuring. The loss on the transfer of assets is the excess of the real estate's carrying amount over its FV ($100,000 – $90,000 = $10,000). The restructuring gain is the excess of the carrying amount of the liability over the FV of the real estate transferred. The restructuring gain is $60,000 ($150,000 – $90,000). The journal entry is

Liability	150,000	
Loss on transfer	10,000	
Real estate		100,000
Gain on restructuring		60,000

3. (a)   In this restructure, the debt is retired by the transfer of real estate to the creditor. A gain or loss is recognized on the transfer of real estate, and a gain or loss is recognized on the restructuring. The loss on the transfer of assets is the excess of the real estate's carrying amount over its FV ($100,000 – $90,000 = $10,000). The restructuring gain is the excess of the carrying amount of the liability over the FV of the real estate transferred, net of the related tax effect. The restructuring gain is $60,000 ($150,000 – $90,000). The journal entry is

Liability	150,000	
Loss on transfer	10,000	
Real estate		100,000
Gain on restructuring		60,000

4. (a)   In this restructure, the debt is retired by the transfer of equipment to the creditor. A gain or loss is recognized on the transfer of the equipment, and a gain or loss is recognized on the retirement of the debt. The loss on the transfer of equipment is the excess of the equipment's carrying amount over its fair value ($80,000 – $75,000 = $5,000). The gain on retirement of debt is the excess of the carrying amount of the debt over the fair value of the equipment transferred ($100,000 – $75,000 = $25,000).

5. (b)   The requirement is to determine the amount of gain to be recognized from a troubled debt restructure. If the debt is continued with a modification of terms, a gain is recognized by the debtor if the future cash payments on the debt are less than the carrying value of the debt. For troubled debt restructures, carrying value is defined as the principal amount ($800,000) plus accrued interest ($80,000), or $880,000. The future payments total $780,000 ($700,000 reduced principal and $80,000 interest). The $100,000 difference ($880,000 – $780,000) is recognized as a restructuring gain.

6. (a)   If the present value of future cash flows is less than the carrying amount of the loan (Principal + Accrued interest) then bad debt expense should be recorded for the total impairment, the accrued interest account should be written off, and the principal balance in the loan receivable account should be reduced to reflect any amounts forgiven. Any remaining balance should be recorded in an allowance account, as follows:

Present value of interest and principal payments to be received by Grey Company (as stated in the problem)	585,734
Recorded investment by Grey Company ($800,000 principal + $64,000 interest)	864,000
Less present value of future cash flows	(585,734)
	278,266
Bad debt expense 278,266	
Loan receivable	200,000
Accrued interest receivable	64,000
Valuation allowance for impaired loans	14,266

Thus, the valuation allowance Grey must recognize is $14,266.

7. (c)   The requirement is to determine the amount of interest revenue to be recorded by Marsh, after a modification of terms type of troubled debt restructure on December 31, 2008.

When a modification of terms results in the present value of future cash flows being less than the carrying amount, then the interest revenue is calculated by using the effective interest method. In this problem the expected future cash flows is determined by discounting the principal and interest at the original effective rate of 12%.

70,000	×	.79719	=	55,803
5,600	×	1.69005	=	9,464
Present value of future cash flows				65,267

The interest revenue to be recognized can then be determined using the effective interest method.

PV at 12/31/08		$65,267
Interest income at 12/31/08 ($65,267 × 12%)	$7,832	
Interest receivable at 12/31/09 (70,000 × 8%)	5,600	
Increase in carrying value of loan		2,232
PV at 12/31/09		67,499
Interest revenue at 12/31/10 (67,499 × 12%)	$8,100	

8. (c)   If a debt is settled by the exchange of assets, a restructuring gain is recognized for the difference between the carrying amount of the debt and the fair value of the consideration given to extinguish the debt. If a noncash asset is given, a separate gain or loss is recorded to revalue the nonasset to fair market value as the basis of the noncash asset given. Therefore, a gain of $35,000 ($120,000 – $85,000) will be recorded to revalue the land to fair market value, and a gain of $65,000 ($185,000 – $120,000) will be recorded for the extinguishment of the debt in Casey's income statement.

SOLUTIONS TO SIMULATION PROBLEM

Simulation Problem 1

Situation	Present Value	Analysis	Journal Entries	Communication	Research

PVA ($15,000) at 9%, 3 periods + PV ($250,000) at 9%, 3 periods
2.53130 ($15,000) + .77218 ($250,000)
$37,969 + $193,046 = $231,015.

Situation	Present Value	Analysis	Journal Entries	Communication	Research

Prestructure amount	$300,000
+ Accrued interest (9% × 300,000)	27,000
Prestructured loan carrying amount	327,000
Less PV future cash flows	(231,015)
Loss on impairment (Bad debt expense)	$ 95,985

Situation	Present Value	Analysis	Journal Entries	Communication	Research

Journal entries for Jayson Company to record the loan restructure and the interest payment on 12-31-10

Bad debt expense	95,985	
Loan receivable		50,000
Interest receivable		27,000
Valuation allowance for loan impairment		18,985

Cash	15,000	
Valuation allowance for loan impairment (plug)	5,791	
Interest income		20,791
($250,000 – $18,985) × 9% = $20,791 interest income		

Situation	Present Value	Analysis	Journal Entries	Communication	Research

Memo to client should contain the following information:

1. This information is based on requirements by ASC Topics 310 and 470, which require creditors to account for impaired loans.
2. Because Simpson cannot repay on a timely basis, the loan is considered impaired. Since there is a modification in the terms of the agreement, the loan must be written down to present value of the future cash flows that will be collected based on the new loan payment.
3. The interest rate used for discounting is the rate of interest on the original contract.
4. Jayson will need to calculate the prestructure investment in the loan (the carrying amount), which is the face of the loan, accrued interest on the loan, net deferred loan costs, and unamortized premium or discount.
5. This net carrying amount is then compared to the present value of the future cash flows after the restructure, and the difference is considered a loss on the impairment of the loan. The loss on impairment is expensed through the bad debt expense account if a provision has not already been made for the bad debt.
6. An entry should be made to record bad debt expense, reduce the loan receivable to the new restructured amount, and reduce the interest receivable that was accrued and not paid. Any difference will be credited to a valuation allowance for impaired loans, and this amount will be amortized over the life of the loan. Interest revenue will be calculated based on the carrying value of the loan (present value of future cash flows less the valuation allowance) multiplied by the original contract rate before restructure.

Situation	Present Value	Analysis	Journal Entries	Communication	Research

SFAS 114, Para 14

14. If a creditor measures an impaired loan using a present value amount, the creditor shall calculate that present value amount based on an estimate of the expected future cash flows of the impaired loan, discounted at the loan's effective interest rate. The effective interest rate of a loan is the rate of return implicit in the loan (i.e., the contractual interest rate adjusted for any net deferred loan fees or costs, premium, or discount existing at the origination or acquisition of the loan.

3. The effective interest rate for a loan restructured in a troubled debt restructuring is based on the original contractual rate, not the rate specified in the restructuring agreement. If the loan's contractual interest rate varies on subsequent changes in an independent factor, such as an index rate (for example, the prime rate, the London offered rate, or the US Treasury bill weekly average), that loan's effective interest rate may be calculated based on the factor as it changes over the life of the loan or may be fixed at the rate in effect at the date the loan meets the impairment criterion in paragraph 9. The creditor's choice shall be applied consistently for all loans whose contractual interest rate varies based on subsequent changes in an independent factor. Projection of changes in the factor should not be made for purposes of determining the effective interest rate or estimating expected future cash flows.

Codification: 310-40-35-12

MULTIPLE-CHOICE QUESTIONS (1-41)

1. The following information pertains to Lee Corp.'s defined benefit pension plan for 2009:

Service cost	$160,000
Actual and expected gain on plan assets	35,000
Unexpected loss on plan assets related to a 2009 disposal of a subsidiary	40,000
Amortization of unrecognized prior service cost	5,000
Annual interest on pension obligation	50,000

What amount should Lee report as pension cost in its 2009 income statement?
- a. $250,000
- b. $220,000
- c. $210,000
- d. $180,000

2. Jordon Corporation obtains the following information from its actuary. All amounts given are **as of** 1/1/09 (beginning of the year).

	1/1/09
Projected benefit obligation	$1,530,000
Market-related asset value	1,650,000
Unrecognized net loss	235,000
Average remaining service period	5.5 years

What amount of unrecognized net loss should be recognized as part of pension cost in 2009?
- a. $70,000
- b. $42,727
- c. $14,909
- d. $12,727

3. Which of the following disclosures is not required of companies with a defined benefit pension plan?
- a. A description of the plan.
- b. The amount of pension expense by component.
- c. The weighted-average discount rate.
- d. The estimates of future contributions for the next five years.

4. Bulls Corporation amends its pension plan on 1/1/09. The following information is available:

	1/1/09 *amendment*	*1/1/09 after* *amendment*
Accumulated benefit obligation	$ 950,000	$1,425,000
Projected benefit obligation	1,300,000	1,900,000

The total amount of unrecognized prior service cost to be amortized over future periods as a result of this amendment is
- a. $950,000
- b. $600,000
- c. $475,000
- d. $125,000

5. On January 2, 2009, Loch Co. established a noncontributory defined benefit plan covering all employees and contributed $1,000,000 to the plan. At December 31, 2009, Loch determined that the 2009 service and interest costs on the plan were $620,000. The expected and the actual rate of return on plan assets for 2009 was 10%. There are no other components of Loch's pension expense. What amount should Loch report in its December 31, 2009 balance sheet as prepaid pension cost?
- a. $280,000
- b. $380,000
- c. $480,000
- d. $620,000

6. Webb Co., a publicly traded company, implemented a defined benefit pension plan for its employees on January 1, 2006. During 2006 and 2007, Webb's contributions fully funded the plan. The following data are provided for 2009 and 2008:

	2009 *Estimated*	*2008* *Actual*
Projected benefit obligation, December 31	$750,000	$700,000
Accumulated benefit obligation, December 31	520,000	500,000
Plan assets at fair value, December 31	675,000	600,000
Projected benefit obligation in excess of plan assets	75,000	100,000
Pension expense	90,000	75,000
Employer's contribution	90,000	50,000

What amount should Webb report as a pension liability in its December 31, 2009 balance sheet?
- a. $ 50,000
- b. $ 60,000
- c. $ 75,000
- d. $100,000

7. Visor Co. maintains a defined benefit pension plan for its employees. The service cost component of Visor's net periodic pension cost is measured using the
- a. Unfunded accumulated benefit obligation.
- b. Unfunded vested benefit obligation.
- c. Projected benefit obligation.
- d. Expected return on plan assets.

8. Which of the following components should be included in the calculation of net pension cost recognized for a period by an employer sponsoring a defined benefit pension plan?

	Actual return on *plan assets, if any*	*Amortization of unrecognized* *prior service cost, if any*
a.	No	Yes
b.	No	No
c.	Yes	No
d.	Yes	Yes

9. Interest cost included in the net pension cost recognized by an employer sponsoring a defined benefit pension plan represents the
- a. Amortization of the discount on unrecognized prior service costs.
- b. Increase in the fair value of plan assets due to the passage of time.
- c. Increase in the projected benefit obligation due to the passage of time.
- d. Shortage between the expected and actual returns on plan assets.

10. On July 31, 2009, Tern Co. amended its single employee defined benefit pension plan by granting increased benefits for services provided prior to 2009. This prior service cost will be reflected in the financial statement(s) for
- a. Years before 2009 only.
- b. Year 2009 only.
- c. Year 2009, and years before and following 2009.
- d. Year 2009, and following years only.

11. Effective January 1, 2009, Flood Co. established a defined benefit pension plan with no retroactive benefits. The first of the required equal annual contributions was paid on December 31, 2009. A 10% discount rate was used to calculate service cost and a 10% rate of return was assumed for plan assets. All information on covered employees for 2009 and 2010 is the same. How should the service cost for 2010 compare with 2009, and should the 2009 balance sheet report an accrued or a prepaid pension cost?

	Service cost for 2010 compared to 2009	Pension cost reported on the 2009 balance sheet
a.	Equal to	Accrued
b.	Equal to	Prepaid
c.	Greater than	Accrued
d.	Greater than	Prepaid

12. A company that maintains a defined benefit pension plan for its employees reports an unfunded accrued pension cost. This cost represents the amount that the
a. Cumulative net pension cost accrued exceeds contributions to the plan.
b. Cumulative net pension cost accrued exceeds the vested benefit obligation.
c. Vested benefit obligation exceeds plan assets.
d. Vested benefit obligation exceeds contributions to the plan.

13. The following information pertains to Seda Co.'s pension plan:

Actuarial estimate of projected benefit obligation at 1/1/09	$72,000
Assumed discount rate	10%
Service costs for 2009	18,000
Pension benefits paid during 2009	15,000

If **no** change in actuarial estimates occurred during 2009, Seda's projected benefit obligation at December 31, 2009 was
a. $64,200
b. $75,000
c. $79,200
d. $82,200

14. Which of the following terms includes assumptions concerning projected changes in future compensation when the pension benefit formula is based on future compensation levels (e.g., pay-related and final pay plans)?

	Service cost component	Projected benefit obligation	Accumulated benefit obligation
a.	Yes	Yes	Yes
b.	Yes	Yes	No
c.	No	Yes	No
d.	Yes	No	Yes

15. For a defined benefit pension plan, the discount rate used to calculate the projected benefit obligation is determined by the

	Expected return on plan assets	Actual return on plan assets
a.	Yes	Yes
b.	No	No
c.	Yes	No

16. At December 31, 2009, the following information was provided by the Kerr Corp. pension plan administrator:

Fair value of plan assets	$3,450,000
Accumulated benefit obligation	4,300,000
Projected benefit obligation	5,700,000

Assume Kerr is a publicly traded company. What is the amount of the pension liability that should be shown on Kerr's December 31, 2009 balance sheet?
a. $5,700,000
b. $2,250,000
c. $1,400,000
d. $ 850,000

17. Nome Co. sponsors a defined benefit plan covering all employees. Benefits are based on years of service and compensation levels at the time of retirement. Nome determined that, as of September 30, 2009, its accumulated benefit obligation was $380,000, and its plan assets had a $290,000 fair value. The projected benefit obligation on September 30, 2009, was $400,000. In its September 30, 2009 balance sheet, what amount should Nome report as pension liability?
a. $110,000
b. $ 90,000
c. $380,000
d. $400,000

18. Payne, Inc., a nonpublicly traded company, implemented a defined benefit pension plan for its employees on January 2, 2009. The following data are provided for 2009, as of December 31, 2009:

Projected benefit obligation	$103,000
Plan assets at fair value	78,000
Net periodic pension cost	90,000
Employer's contribution	70,000

What amount should Payne record as pension liability at December 31, 2009?
a. $0
b. $25,000
c. $20,000
d. $45,000

Items 19 and 20 are based on the following:

The following data pertains to Hall Co.'s defined-benefit pension plan at December 31, 2009:

Unfunded projected benefit obligation	$25,000
Unrecognized prior service cost	12,000
Net periodic pension cost	8,000

Hall made no contributions to the pension plan during 2009.

19. At December 31, 2009, what amount should Hall record as pension liability on the balance sheet?
a. $ 5,000
b. $13,000
c. $17,000
d. $25,000

20. In its December 31, 2009 statement of stockholders' equity, what amount should Hall report as accumulated other comprehensive income for pension liabilities before tax effects?
a. $ 5,000
b. $13,000
c. $17,000
d. $25,000

21. An employer sponsoring a defined benefit pension plan must report a liability on the balance sheet equal to
a. The current year pension cost that was not funded.
b. The difference between the fair value of plan assets less the accumulated benefit obligation.

c. The difference between the accumulated benefit obligation and the projected benefit obligation.

d. The difference between the fair value of plan assets less the projected benefit obligation.

22. Claire, a publicly traded company, has the following defined benefit pension plans with the following information as of December 31, 2009:

	Plan A	Plan B	Plan C
Projected benefit obligation	100,000	150,000	180,000
Accumulated benefit obligation	80,000	140,000	150,000
Fair value of plan assets	110,000	125,000	160,000

Assume Claire will make no payments within the next 24 months to any pension plan. How should Claire report the pension plans on the December 31, 2009 balance sheet?

a. A noncurrent liability of $35,000.

b. A noncurrent asset of $10,000 and a noncurrent liability of $45,000.

c. A noncurrent liability of $25,000.

d. A noncurrent asset of $30,000 and a noncurrent liability of $25,000.

23. Dawson Corporation, a publicly traded company, implemented a defined benefit pension plan for its employees on January 2, 2007. The following data are provided for 2009 and as of December 31, 2009:

Projected benefit obligation	$350,000
Accumulated benefit obligation	320,000
Plan assets at fair value	362,000
Pension cost for 2009	100,000
Employer's contribution for 2009	95,000

What amount should Dawson report for the pension plan on its December 31, 2009 balance sheet?

a. A current liability of $5,000.

b. No asset or liability.

c. A noncurrent asset of $12,000.

d. A noncurrent asset of $42,000.

24. Rose Corporation, a publicly traded company, implemented a defined benefit pension plan for its employees on January 2, 2008. The following data are provided for 2009 and as of December 31, 2009:

Projected benefit obligation	$400,000
Accumulated benefit obligation	360,000
Plan assets at fair value	362,000
Pension cost for 2009	150,000
Pension contribution for 2009	150,000

Assume that as of January 1, 2009, Rose's pension plan was fully funded, and there were no recorded pension assets or liabilities on the balance sheet. Ignoring tax effects, which of the following entries would be needed to properly record the funding status of Rose's pension plan at December 31, 2009?

a. A debit to noncurrent pension asset of $2,000.

b. A debit to prepaid pension for $150,000.

c. A credit to noncurrent pension liability for $40,000.

d. A debit to other comprehensive income for $38,000.

25. Tulip Corporation, a publicly traded company, implemented a defined benefit pension plan for its employees on January 2, 2007. The following data are provided for 2009 and as of December 31, 2009:

Projected benefit obligation	$700,000
Accumulated benefit obligation	550,000
Plan assets at fair value	520,000
Pension cost for 2009	180,000
Pension contribution for 2009	150,000

Assume that as of January 1, 2009, Tulip's pension plan was fully funded, and there were no recorded pension assets or liabilities on the balance sheet. Assuming a tax rate of 40%, what is the net effect of the required adjustment on accumulated other comprehensive income on December 31, 2009?

a. $90,000 decrease.

b. $108,000 decrease.

c. $36,000 decrease.

d. $0

26. On September 1, 2009, Howe Corp. offered special termination benefits to employees who had reached the early retirement age specified in the company's pension plan. The termination benefits consisted of lump-sum and periodic future payments. Additionally, the employees accepting the company offer receive the usual early retirement pension benefits. The offer expired on November 30, 2009. Actual or reasonably estimated amounts at December 31, 2009, relating to the employees accepting the offer are as follows:

- Lump-sum payments totaling $475,000 were made on January 1, 2010.
- Periodic payments of $60,000 annually for three years will begin January 1, 2011. The present value at December 31, 2009, of these payments was $155,000.
- Reduction of accrued pension costs at December 31, 2009, for the terminating employees was $45,000.

In its December 31, 2009 balance sheet, Howe should report a total liability for special termination benefits of

a. $475,000

b. $585,000

c. $630,000

d. $655,000

27. The Codification requires a reconciliation of the beginning and ending balances of the benefit obligation for both defined benefit pension plans and defined postretirement plans. Which of the following items would appear in the schedule related to defined benefit pension plans?

	Service cost	Benefits paid
a.	Yes	No
b.	Yes	Yes
c.	No	Yes
d.	No	No

28. A company with a defined benefit pension plan must disclose in the notes to its financial statements

a. A reconciliation of the vested and nonvested benefit obligation of its pension plan with the accumulated benefit obligation.

b. A reconciliation of the accrued or prepaid pension cost reported in its balance sheet with the pension expense reported in its income statement.

c. A reconciliation of the accumulated benefit obligation of its pension plan with its projected benefit obligation.

d. The funded status of its pension plan and the amounts recognized in the balance sheet showing separately the noncurrent assets, current liabilities, and noncurrent liabilities reported.

29. Which of the following items would appear in the reconciliation schedule related to defined pension plans?

	Benefit payments	Actual return on plan assets
a.	No	Yes
b.	No	No
c.	Yes	No
d.	Yes	Yes

30. Which of the following defined benefit pension plan disclosures should be made in a company's financial statements?

I. The amount of net periodic pension cost for the period.
II. The fair value of plan assets.

    a. Both I and II.
    b. I only.
    c. II only.
    d. Neither I nor II.

31. Which of the following is not a required disclosure for defined benefit pension plans?
    a. An explanation of a significant change in plan assets if not apparent from other disclosures.
    b. The amount of any unamortized prior service cost or credit not recognized in the statement of financial position (balance sheet).
    c. The effect of a two-percentage-point increase in the assumed health care cost trend rate(s).
    d. Reconciliation of beginning and ending balance of the projected benefit obligation.

32. Which of the following rates must be disclosed for defined benefit pension plans?

I. Assumed discount rate.
II. Expected long-term rate of return on all of the employer's assets.
III. Rate of compensation increase.

    a. I and III.
    b. II and III.
    c. I, II, and III.
    d. III only.

33. Jan Corp. amended its defined benefit pension plan, granting a total credit of $100,000 to four employees for services rendered prior to the plan's adoption. The employees, A, B, C, and D, are expected to retire from the company as follows:

A will retire after three years.
B and C will retire after five years.
D will retire after seven years.

What is the amount of prior service cost amortization in the first year?
    a. $0
    b. $ 5,000
    c. $20,000
    d. $25,000

34. The effects of a one-percentage-point increase or decrease in the trend rates for health care costs must be disclosed for which of the following relating to defined benefit postretirement plans?

I. The aggregate of the service and interest cost components.
II. The accumulated postretirement benefit obligation.

    a. Both I and II.
    b. I only.
    c. II only.
    d. Neither I nor II.

35. A company with a defined benefit pension plan must disclose in the notes to its financial statements all of the following **except**
    a. The funded status of its pension plan with the amounts recognized in the balance sheet showing separately the assets, current liabilities, and noncurrent liabilities recognized.
    b. Rates for assumed discount rate, rate of compensation increase, and expected long-term rate of return on plan assets.
    c. A reconciliation of the accrued or prepaid pension cost reported in its balance sheet with the pension expense reported in its income statement.
    d. The recognized amount of the net periodic benefit cost with the components shown separately.

36. The following information pertains to Foster Co.'s defined benefit postretirement plan for the year 2009.

Service cost	$120,000
Benefit payment	55,000
Interest on the accumulated postretirement benefit obligation	20,000
Unrecognized transition obligation (to be amortized over twenty years)	200,000

Foster Co.'s 2009 net periodic postretirement benefit cost was
    a. $205,000
    b. $150,000
    c. $ 95,000
    d. $285,000

37. Kemp Company provides a defined benefit postretirement plan for its employees. Kemp adopted the plan on January 1, 2008. Data relating to the pension plan for 2009 are as follows:

Service cost for 2009	28,000
Interest on the accumulated postretirement benefit obligation	5,000
Amortization of the unrecognized transition obligation	8,000

At the end of 2009, Kemp makes a benefit payment of $10,000 to employees. In its December 31, 2009 balance sheet, Kemp should record accrued postretirement benefit cost of
    a. $35,000
    b. $31,000
    c. $51,000
    d. $15,000

38. Bounty Co. provides postretirement health care benefits to employees who have completed at least ten years service and are aged fifty-five years or older when retiring. Employees retiring from Bounty have a median age of sixty-two, and no one has worked beyond age sixty-five. Fletcher is hired at forty-eight years old. The attribution period for accruing Bounty's expected postretirement health care benefit obligation to Fletcher is during the period when Fletcher is aged

    a. 48 to 65.
    b. 48 to 58.
    c. 55 to 65.
    d. 55 to 62.

39. An employer's obligation for postretirement health benefits that are expected to be provided to or for an employee must be fully accrued by the date the

    a. Employee is fully eligible for benefits.
    b. Employee retires.
    c. Benefits are utilized.
    d. Benefits are paid.

40. Which of the following are correct regarding a transition obligation resulting from the adoption of a defined benefit postretirement plan?

  I. A transition obligation may be recognized immediately.
 II. The transition obligation represents the difference between the accumulated postretirement benefit obligation and the fair value of plan assets at the beginning of the year the plan is adopted.
III. A transition obligation may be amortized on a straight-line basis over a maximum period of twenty years.

    a. I and II.
    b. II only.
    c. I, II, and III.
    d. II and III.

41. Which of the following information should be disclosed by a company providing health care benefits to its retirees?

  I. The assumed health care cost trend rate used to measure the expected cost of benefits covered by the plan.
 II. The accumulated postretirement benefit obligation.

    a. Both I and II.
    b. I only.
    c. II only.
    d. Neither I nor II.

SIMULATION PROBLEMS

Simulation Problem 1   (25 to 35 minutes)

Situation						
	Concepts	Pension Calculations	Journal Entry	Balance Sheet	Communication	Research

The following information pertains to Winger Co.'s defined benefit pension plan. The common stock of Winger is publicly traded.

Discount rate	6%
At January 1, 2009:	
Projected benefit obligation	$600,000
Fair value of pension plan assets	420,000
Accumulated benefit obligation	380,000
Unrecognized prior service cost	240,000
At December 31, 2009:	
Projected benefit obligation	?
Fair value of pension plan assets	470,200

Service cost for 2009 was $80,000. The actual and expected return on assets was 6%. A contribution for pension of $40,000 was made during the year, and $15,000 of benefits were paid. Winger had no prepaid pension or accrued pension liability at December 31, 2008. Winger amortizes the unrecognized service costs at $20,000 per year. Assume no pension benefits are expected to be paid in the next 12 months.

	Concepts					
Situation		Pension Calculations	Journal Entry	Balance Sheet	Communication	Research

Identify whether each of the following statements is True or False.

		True	*False*
1.	A defined contribution plan is a plan where an employer agrees to provide a benefit at retirement defined by a formula.	○	○
2.	The present value of the projected benefit obligation is calculated using the benefits years of service method.	○	○
3.	Pension liability is calculated by comparing the accumulated benefit obligation with the fair value of plan assets.	○	○
4.	A company is required to net overfunded pension plans with underfunded pension plans and report the net amount as either noncurrent asset or noncurrent liability on the balance sheet.	○	○
5.	Prior service costs are caused by new individuals entering the plan after the vesting date.	○	○
6.	In a defined benefit plan, interest cost represents the increase in the fair value of the plan assets due to the passage of time.	○	○
7.	Companies must disclose in the notes to the financial statements the effect that a two percentage point increase in interest costs would have on the aggregate service and interest costs of the accumulated postretirement benefit obligation on health care benefits.	○	○
8.	The actual return on plan assets is defined as the difference in the fair value of plan assets at the beginning and the end of the year.	○	○

		Pension Calculations				
Situation	Concepts		Journal Entry	Balance Sheet	Communication	Research

Part I.

Calculate the following amounts for Winger's pension cost for 2009.

1. _____ Interest cost
2. _____ Actual return on plan assets
3. _____ Amortization of prior service costs or credits
4. _____ Gain or (Loss)
5. _____ Pension cost for 2009
6. _____ Projected benefit obligation at December 31, 2009

Part II.

For the following items determine whether the component Increases or Decreases Winger's unfunded accrued pension liability.

		Increase	*Decrease*	*No effect*
1.	Service cost	O	O	O
2.	Interest cost	O	O	O
3.	Actual return on plan assets	O	O	O
4.	Amortization of prior service costs or credits	O	O	O
5.	Gain or loss in 2009	O	O	O

Situation	Concepts	Pension Calculations	Journal Entry	Balance Sheet	Communication	Research

Prepare the journal entry to record Winger's pension cost for the period.

Situation	Concepts	Pension Calculations	Journal Entry	Balance Sheet	Communication	Research

What is the amount of pension assets or liabilities that will be disclosed in each of the following categories on the balance sheet?

1.   Current asset   _____

2.   Noncurrent asset   _____

3.   Current liability   _____

4.   Noncurrent liability   _____

Winger has no other items that have affected other comprehensive income for the current period or in previous periods. Assuming the tax rate is 30%, what is the amount shown in accumulated other comprehensive income for the period ending December 31, 2009? Indicate whether this amount is a debit or credit.

5.   Amount in AOCI   _____   Debit   Credit

Situation	Concepts	Pension Calculations	Journal Entry	Balance Sheet	Communication	Research

Winger Co. has just hired a new president, Palmer, and is reviewing its employee benefit plans with the new employee. For current employees, Winger offers a compensation plan for future vacations. Winger also provides postemployment benefits to former or inactive employees.

On the date of Palmer's hire, Palmer entered into a deferred compensation contract with Winger. Palmer is expected to retire in ten years. The contract calls for a payment of $150,000 upon termination of employment following a minimum three-year service period. The contract also provides that interest of 10%, compounded annually, be credited on the amount due each year after the third year.

Mr. Palmer would like to know more about the accounting for postemployment benefits. Write a memo explaining the following issues regarding postemployment benefits:

1. Give an example of postemployment benefits. State the conditions under which Winger is required to accrue liabilities for compensated absences and postemployment benefits. State Winger's disclosure requirements if these conditions, in full or in part, are not met.

2. Describe the general accrual period for amounts to be paid under a deferred compensation contract. State the theoretical rationale for requiring accrual of these liabilities and related expenses.

3. Prepare a schedule of the expense and accrued liability related to Palmer's deferred compensation agreement to be reported in Winger's financial statements for the first four years of the contract.

REMINDER: Your response will be graded for both technical content and writing skills. Technical content will be evaluated for information that is helpful to the intended reader and clearly relevant to the issue. Writing skills will be evaluated for development, organization, and the appropriate expression of ideas in professional correspondence. Use a standard business memo or letter format with a clear beginning, middle, and end. Do not convey information in the form of a table, bullet point list, or other abbreviated presentation.

To: Mr. Palmer, Winger Company
From: CPA Candidate
Re: Postemployment benefits

Situation	Concepts	Pension Calculations	Journal Entry	Balance Sheet	Communication	Research

Winger Company has a single-employer defined benefit pension plan, and a compensation plan for future vacations for its employees.

You have been asked to research the following items and write a memorandum explaining your results.

1. Define the interest cost component of net pension cost for a period.

2. How should Winger determine its interest cost component of net pension cost for a period?

3. Define prior service cost or credits.

4. How should Winger account for prior service cost or credits?

5. What conditions must be met for Winger to accrue compensation for future vacations?

MULTIPLE-CHOICE ANSWERS

1. d __ __	10. d __ __	19. d __ __	28. d __ __	37. b __ __
2. d __ __	11. d __ __	20. c __ __	29. d __ __	38. b __ __
3. d __ __	12. a __ __	21. d __ __	30. a __ __	39. a __ __
4. b __ __	13. d __ __	22. b __ __	31. c __ __	40. c __ __
5. c __ __	14. b __ __	23. c __ __	32. a __ __	41. a __ __
6. c __ __	15. b __ __	24. d __ __	33. c __ __	
7. c __ __	16. b __ __	25. a __ __	34. a __ __	
8. d __ __	17. a __ __	26. c __ __	35. c __ __	1st: __/41 = __%
9. c __ __	18. b __ __	27. b __ __	36. b __ __	2nd: __/41 = __%

MULTIPLE-CHOICE ANSWER EXPLANATIONS

D.1.-5. Pensions

1. **(d)** The six elements which an employer sponsoring a defined benefit pension plan must include in its net pension cost are service cost, interest cost, actual return on plan assets, amortization of unrecognized prior service cost, deferral of unexpected gain or loss, and amortization of the unrecognized net obligation or unrecognized net asset existing at the date of initial application. Lee Corp's pension expense is calculated as follows:

Service cost	$160,000
Gain (actual and expected) on plan assets	(35,000)
Amortization	5,000
Interest	50,000
	180,000

Gains and losses that arise from a single occurrence which is not directly related to the operation of the plan should be reported as part of that occurrence and not as part of the plan's activity. Therefore, the $40,000 unexpected loss on plan assets related to a 2009 disposal of a subsidiary should be reported as part of the "loss on disposal" and not as part of the 2009 pension cost.

2. **(d)** The requirement is to determine the amount of unrecognized net loss to be recognized as a part of pension expense in 2009. The **corridor approach** is to be used to determine gain or loss amortization. Under this approach, only the unrecognized net gain or loss in excess of 10% of the **greater** of the projected benefit obligation (PBO) or the market-related asset value (M-RAV) is amortized. In this case, the M-RAV ($1,650,000) is larger than the PBO ($1,530,000). The corridor is $165,000 (10% × $1,650,000). The unrecognized net loss ($235,000) exceeds the corridor by $70,000 ($235,000 – $165,000). This excess is amortized over the average remaining service period of active employees expected to participate in the plan ($70,000 ÷ 5.5 = $12,727).

3. **(d)** Estimates of future contributions to a defined benefit pension plan are required to be disclosed only for the next fiscal year. Answer (a) is incorrect because a description of the plan is a required disclosure. Answer (b) is incorrect because the amount of pension expense by component is a required disclosure. Answer (c) is incorrect because the weighted-average discount rate is a required disclosure.

4. **(b)** The requirement is to calculate the total amount of unrecognized prior service cost to be amortized over future periods as a result of a pension plan amendment. Prior service cost is the present value of retroactive benefits given to employees for years of service provided before the date of an amendment to the plan. The cost of these retroactive benefits is measured by the increase in the projected benefit

obligation at the date of amendment ($1,900,000 – $1,300,000 = $600,000). This amount will be recognized as expense (amortized) during the service periods of those employees who are expected to receive benefits under the plan.

5. **(c)** Prepaid pension cost is the cumulative excess of the amount funded over the amount recorded as pension expense. In 2009, pension expense is $520,000.

Service cost and interest on PBO	$620,000
Actual return on plan assets ($1,000,000 × 10%)	(100,000)
Pension expense	$520,000

Since 2009 funding was $1,000,000, 12/31/09 prepaid pension cost is $480,000 ($1,000,000 – $520,000).

6. **(c)** As of December 31, 2008, the pension liability for the current year underfunding was $25,000. As of December 31, 2008, there was a pension liability only for the current year's portion of the pension cost that was not funded. The PBO is compared with the fair value of plan assets, and a liability must be recorded in the balance sheet for the underfunded plan. Therefore, the difference between the PBO and the fair value of the plan assets as of December 31, 2009 ($75,000 minus $675,000) of $75,000 must be reported as a liability on the balance sheet.

7. **(c)** The requirement is to determine how the service cost component of the net periodic pension cost is measured in a defined benefit pension plan. The service cost component recognized shall be determined as "the actuarial present value of benefits attributed by the pension benefit formula to employee service during the period" that is known as the **projected benefit obligation**.

8. **(d)** Among the components which should be included in the net pension cost recognized for a period by an employer sponsoring a defined benefit pension plan are **both** actual return on plan assets, if any, and amortization of unrecognized prior service cost, if any.

9. **(c)** Net pension cost (expense) is comprised of six elements. One of these elements is interest on the projected benefit obligation, which is defined as the increase in the amount of the projected benefit obligation due to the passage of time. Candidates must be careful so as not to confuse "interest cost" with the "actual return" component of net pension cost which is the earnings on the plan assets. If the latter component is positive, it reduces the net pension cost for the period.

10. **(d)** Plan amendments are granted with the expectation that the employer will realize economic benefits in future periods. Therefore, the prior service cost will be reflected in the financial statements for 2009 and future years only.

11. **(d)** This question addresses the behavior of the components of pension expense over a period of time. Service cost is the actuarial present value of benefits attributed by the pension benefit formula to services rendered by employees during that period. This problem states that "all information on covered employees for 2009 and 2010 is the same," which indicates that there has been no change in Flood's work force during this two-year period. The only difference in the service cost for these two years would, therefore, be attributable to differences in the discounting of the benefits. Each year a group of employees works, the group becomes one year closer to retirement age and to collecting their retirement benefits. The present value of the benefits earned by employees each year grows as their retirement date grows nearer, because the benefits are discounted over a shorter period of time. If, for instance, the "average" retirement date for Flood's employees is January 1, 2019, the present value of the benefits for 2010's service will be greater than the present value of 2009 service, because it is discounted eleven years for 2009 versus ten years for 2010. (This is because every additional year of discounting reduces the present value of the benefits.) Therefore, the service cost for 2010 will be greater than for 2009. The problem also states that Flood intends to fund the plan in equal annual installments, and that the discount rate which was used to calculate the service cost is equal to the assumed rate of return on plan assets. Under these circumstances, to fully fund the pension obligation in equal payments, Flood will contribute an amount which exceeds the pension cost in the first years of the plan and which is less than the pension cost in later years. Prepaid pension cost is the cumulative employer contributions in excess of accrued pension cost. Since 2009's funding would exceed its pension cost, Flood would report a prepaid pension cost on its 2009 balance sheet. The journal entry to record the funding would be

Pension expense	xxx	
Prepaid pension cost	xxx	
Cash		xxx

12. **(a)** The requirement is to determine what the "unfunded accrued pension cost" represents. The unfunded accrued pension cost is a liability recognized when the net periodic pension cost exceeds the amount the employer has contributed to the plan.

13. **(d)** The projected benefit obligation is the actuarial present value of the pension obligation at the end of the period. Since there were no changes in actuarial estimates during the year, the end of period projected benefit obligation is computed as follows:

Projected benefit obligation, 1/1/09	$72,000
Service cost	18,000
Interest on projected benefit obligation	
(10% × $72,000)	7,200
Benefit payments	(15,000)
Pension benefit obligation, 12/31/09	$82,200

Service cost and interest on the projected benefit obligation increase the projected benefit obligation; benefit payments decrease the projected benefit obligation.

14. **(b)** The requirement is to determine which of the listed pension terms includes assumptions concerning pro-

jected changes in future compensation levels if the pension benefit formula is based on future compensation levels. The service cost component and the projected benefit obligation reflect projected future compensation levels while the accumulated benefit obligation is measured based on employees' history of service and compensation without an estimate of projected future compensation levels.

15. **(b)** The assumed discount rate should reflect the rates at which pension benefits could be effectively settled. This rate is sometimes referred to as the "settlement rate." To determine the settlement rate, it is appropriate to look at rates implicit in current prices of annuity contracts that could be used to settle the obligation under the defined benefit plan. The expected return on plan assets is **not** used to calculate the projected benefit obligation. The actual return on plan assets is also **not** used to calculate the projected benefit obligation.

16. **(b)** The funding status of the plan is recognized as an asset or liability on the balance sheet. The difference between Kerr's fair value of plan assets and the projected benefit obligation ($3,450,000 – $5,700,000 = $02,250,000) is the amount of the plan that is underfunded and must be reported as a liability on Kerr's December 31, 2009 balance sheet.

17. **(a)** The recognition of a **pension liability** is required if the projected benefit obligation (PBO) exceeds the FV of the plan assets. In this case, the excess of the PBO over the FV of plan assets is $110,000 ($400,000 – $290,000).

18. **(b)** The reporting of a **pension liability** is required if the projected benefit obligation (PBO) exceeds the FV of the plan assets. In this case, the excess of the PBO over the FV of plan assets is $25,000 ($103,000 – $78,000).

19. **(d)** A **pension liability** must be reported for the excess of the projected benefit obligation (PBO) over the fair value of the plan assets. The unfunded projected benefit obligation is this excess. Therefore, the required liability amount is $25,000.

20. **(c)** At December 31, 2009, Hall will record a pension expense of $8,000 and a pension liability of $8,000 for the current year's pension journal entry. The overfunded or underfunded status of the plan must be recognized on the balance sheet. Therefore, the unfunded PBO of $25,000 must be recognized as a liability. An entry must be made to record the adjustment to pension liability for $17,000 (25,000 – 8,000 liability already recorded). Ignoring the tax effect, the journal entry will include a debit to OCI for $17,000 and a credit to pension liability for $17,000.

21. **(d)** An employer must recognize the overfunded or underfunded status of the pension plan. A liability is reported when the fair value of the plan assets is less than the projected benefit obligation.

22. **(b)** The funded status of the plan is recognized on the balance sheet. The fair value of plan assets is compared with the projected benefit obligation. Overfunded plans are aggregated and recognized as noncurrent assets on the balance sheet. Underfunded plans are aggregated and recognized as current, noncurrent liabilities, or both. Claire must aggregate Plans B and C, because they are both underfunded. Plan B is underfunded by $25,000 ($125,000 –

$150,000), and Plan C is underfunded by $20,000 ($160,000 – $180,000). Because Claire expects to make no payments within the next 12 months, the aggregated underfunded plans are recorded as noncurrent liabilities on the balance sheet. The overfunded amount (Plan A: $110,000 – 100,000) of $10,000 is recognized as a noncurrent asset on the balance sheet. Answer (a) is incorrect because all plans cannot be aggregated. Answers (c) and (d) are incorrect because according to ASC Topic 715, the accumulated benefit obligation is no longer used to measure the funding status of the plan.

23. (c) The funding status of the pension plan is recorded on the balance sheet. The funding status is determined by comparing the fair value of plan assets to the projected benefit obligation. Dawson's plan assets are $12,000 higher than the projected benefit obligation ($362,000 – 350,000). Therefore, Dawson would be required to report a noncurrent asset of $12,000 on their balance sheet at December 31, 2009. Answer (a) is incorrect because the current liability of $5,000 is part of the journal entry required to record pension cost for the period, and does not reflect the overall funding status of the plan. Answer (b) is incorrect because overfunded or underfunded plans must be recognized on the balance sheet. Answer (d) is incorrect because according to ASC Topic 715, the accumulated benefit obligation is not used to measure the funding status of the plan.

24. (d) The funding status of the pension plan is recorded on the balance sheet. The funding status is determined by comparing the fair value of plan assets to the projected benefit obligation. Because Rose was completely funded as of December 31, 2008, no pension assets or liabilities existed on its balance sheet. The journal entry for 2009 would include a debit to pension cost and a credit to cash for the 2009 pension contribution, which was fully funded for the current year. However, in comparing the PBO and the fair value of plan assets at the end of the year, Rose's pension plan is underfunded by $38,000 ($362,000 – 400,000). Ignoring income tax effects, the entry to record the underfunded plan is to debit other comprehensive income for $38,000 and credit pension liability for $38,000.

25. (a) The funded status of the plan is recognized in the balance sheet. The funding status is determined by comparing the fair value of plan assets to the projected benefit obligation. The pension plan for Rose is underfunded by a total of $180,000 ($520,000 – 700,000). As of December 31, 2009, Rose has recognized a pension liability of $30,000, which is the difference between pension cost for the period and the pension contribution for the period. This $30,000 liability has been recognized as an expense and reduces net income for the period. Because Rose must recognize a $180,000 liability in the balance sheet, an entry must be recorded for the $150,000 needed to increase the pension liability account to the underfunded amount of $180,000. Therefore, the entry to recognize the underfunded portion of the plan would be

OCI ($150,000 × 60%)	90,000	(net of tax)
Deferred tax asset	60,000	
Pension liability		150,000

Answer (b) is incorrect because it is necessary to adjust for any existing pension or liability that may exist at year-end. Answers (c) and (d) are incorrect because the accumulated benefit obligation is not used to determine the funded status of the plan.

26. (c) When special termination benefits are offered to employees, a loss and liability must be recognized when the employee accepts the offer and the amount can be reasonably estimated. The amount to be recognized shall include any lump-sum payments ($475,000) and the present value of any expected future payments ($155,000). Therefore, the total liability for special termination benefits is $630,000 ($475,000 + $155,000). Note that the reduction of accrued pension costs ($45,000) would reduce the amount of the loss, but would **not** affect the liability. Instead it would be recorded as a reduction of accrued pension costs. The journal entry would be

Loss from termination benefits	585,000	
Accrued pension costs	45,000	
Liability from termination benefits		630,000

27. (b) The reconciliation schedule for the benefit obligation related to defined benefit pension plans would disclose both the amounts for service cost and benefits paid. Other items that would be disclosed in this reconciliation schedule include (1) interest cost, (2) contributions by plan participants, (3) actuarial gains and losses, (4) plan amendments, (5) divestitures, curtailments, and settlements, and (6) special termination benefits.

28. (d) The funded status of the pension plans and the amounts are recognized in the balance sheet showing separately the assets, current liabilities, and noncurrent liabilities.

29. (d) The reconciliation schedule for the plan assets related to defined benefit pension plans would disclose both the benefit payments and the actual return on plan assets. Other items that would be disclosed in this reconciliation schedule include (1) contributions by the employer, (2) contributions by plan participants, and (3) settlements and divestitures.

30. (a) An employer sponsoring a defined benefit pension plan must disclose a great deal of information related to the plan. These disclosures include the amount of net periodic pension cost for the period and the fair value of plan assets.

31. (c) The effect of a one-percentage-point increase in the assumed health care cost trend rate(s) is required, not a two-percentage-point increase. An explanation of a significant change in plan assets, if not apparent from other disclosures, is required according to ASC Topic 715. The amount of any unamortized prior service cost or credit not recognized in the statement of financial position (balance sheet) is a required disclosure. Another required disclosure per ASC Topic 715 is a reconciliation of beginning and ending balances of the projected benefit obligation.

32. (a) The assumed discount rate and the rate of compensation increase are both required disclosures. The expected long-term rate of return on all of the employer's assets is not required. The expected long-term rate of return on plan assets is required, however.

33. (c) There are two methods approved for use in determining the assignment of prior service cost: the expected years of service method, and the straight-line basis over the average remaining service period of active employees method. Under the expected future years of service method, the total number of employee service years is calculated by grouping employees according to the time remaining to their retirement and multiplying the number in each group by the number of periods remaining to retirement. [(1 person × 3) + (2 people × 5) + (1 person × 7) = 20]. To calculate the amortization of prior service costs for a given year, the number of employee service years applicable to that period is used as the numerator of the fraction, and the denominator is the total employee service years based on all the identified groups. (4/20 × $100,000 = $20,000) For the straight-line basis over the average remaining service period method, the total number of service years (calculated above) is divided by the number of employees to find the weighted-average service life of each employee. (20/4 = 5 yrs.) The $100,000 of prior service cost will be amortized over the five years, or at $20,000 ($100,000 ÷ 5 = $20,000) a year.

34.   (a)   A disclosure is made of the effects of a one-percentage-point increase or decrease of the trend rates for health care costs on: the aggregate of the service and interest cost components and the accumulated postretirement obligation.

35.   (c)   A reconciliation of the accrued or prepaid pension cost reported in its balance sheet with the pension expense reported in its income statement is not required. Answer (a) is incorrect because the funded status of the pension plan must be reported in the balance sheet as non-current assets, current liabilities, and noncurrent liabilities. Answer (b) is also incorrect because rates for assumed discount rate, rate of compensation increase, and expected long-term rate of return on plan assets are also required. Another required disclosure is the recognized amount of the net periodic benefit cost with the components shown separately.

D.6. Postretirement Benefits other than Pensions (OPEB)

36.   (b)   Net periodic postretirement benefit cost is a net amount calculated by adding or subtracting six components. Three components present in this problem are combined as follows:

Service cost	$120,000
Interest on the accumulated postretirement benefit obligation	20,000
Amortization of transition obligation ($200,000 ÷ 20 years)	10,000
Postretirement benefit cost	$150,000

Service cost and interest on the accumulated postretirement benefit obligation always increase postretirement benefit cost. Foster Co. has elected to amortize the unrecognized transition obligation over a twenty-year period. Amortization of the $200,000 obligation on the straight-line basis increases postretirement benefit cost by $10,000 per year. The benefit payment represents a cash payment made for benefits by the employer; however, this is not a component of net periodic postretirement benefit cost.

37.   (b)   To determine the accrued postretirement benefit cost, the net periodic postretirement benefit cost must first be calculated as follows:

Service cost	$28,000
Interest on the accumulated postretirement benefit obligation	5,000
Amortization of the unrecognized transition obligation	8,000
Net periodic postretirement benefit cost	$41,000

An adjusting entry is required at year-end to record net periodic postretirement benefit cost and the cash benefit payments made to employees. An accrued postretirement benefit cost will be recorded if the net postretirement benefit cost exceeds the cash payments to employees. The journal entry would be

Postretirement benefit cost	41,000	
Cash		10,000
Accrued postretirement benefit cost		31,000

The balance in the accrued postretirement benefit cost account would be $31,000.

38.   (b)   The requirement is to determine the attribution period for accruing the expected postretirement health care benefit obligation. The beginning of the attribution period is generally the date of hire, and the end shall be the date of full eligibility. Fletcher's age at the date of hire is forty-eight and the period of eligibility is ten years. Thus, the attribution period is forty-eight to fifty-eight.

39.   (a)   An employer's obligation for postretirement benefits expected to be provided to an employee must be fully accrued by the full eligibility date of the employee, even if the employee is to render additional service beyond that date.

40.   (c)   A transition obligation is measured as the difference between the accumulated postretirement benefit obligation and the fair value of plan assets at the beginning of the fiscal year for which ASC Topic 715 is adopted. A transition obligation may be recognized immediately in net income of the period of the change, or recognized on a delayed basis as a component of net periodic postretirement benefit cost. If delayed recognition is elected, the transition obligation should be amortized on a straight-line basis over the average remaining service period of plan participants. If the average remaining service period is less than twenty years, the employer may elect to use a twenty-year amortization period.

41.   (a)   The employer must disclose the amount of the accumulated postretirement benefit obligation. The employer must also disclose the assumed health care cost trend rate used to measure the expected cost of benefits covered by the plan.

SOLUTIONS TO SIMULATION PROBLEMS

Simulation Problem 1

	Concepts					
Situation		Pension Calculations	Journal Entry	Balance Sheet	Communication	Research

		True	False
1.	A defined contribution plan is a plan where an employer agrees to provide a benefit at retirement defined by a formula.	○	●
2.	The present value of the projected benefit obligation is calculated using the benefits years of service method.	●	○
3.	Pension liability is calculated by comparing the accumulated benefit obligation with the fair value of plan assets.	○	●
4.	A company is required to net overfunded pension plans with underfunded pension plans and report the net amount as either noncurrent asset or noncurrent liability on the balance sheet.	○	●
5.	Prior service costs are caused by new individuals entering the plan after the vesting date.	○	●
6.	In a defined benefit plan, interest cost represents the increase in the fair value of the plan assets due to the passage of time.	○	●
7.	Companies must disclose in the notes to the financial statements the effects that a two-percentage-point increase in interest costs would have on the aggregate service and interest costs of the accumulated postretirement benefit obligation on health care benefits.	○	●
8.	The actual return on plan assets is defined as the difference in the fair value of plan assets at the beginning and the end of the year.	○	●

Explanation of solutions

1. (F) A defined contribution plan is a plan where the employer defines the contribution. No benefit is promised. The benefit is provided by a trust that is funded by the defined contribution of the employer.

2. (T) The projected benefit obligation is calculated using the benefits years of service method.

3. (F) The funded status of the pension plan is calculated by subtracting the projected benefit obligation and the fair value of plan assets at year-end.

4. (F) A company may not net the overfunded and underfunded plans. Overfunded plans must be shown as noncurrent assets on the balance sheet. Underfunded plans should be shown as current liabilities, noncurrent liabilities, or both.

5. (F) Prior service costs are caused by amendments to the plan or initiation of a new plan with a retroactive allowance.

6. (F) In a defined benefit plan, the interest cost represents the increase in the projected benefit obligation due to the passage of time.

7. (F) Companies must disclose the effect that a one percentage point increase would have on the aggregate service and interest costs of the accumulated postretirement benefit obligation on health-care benefits.

8. (F) The actual return on plan assets is defined as the difference in the fair value adjusted for contributions made to the plan and benefits paid.

		Pension Calculations				
Situation	Concepts		Journal Entry	Balance Sheet	Communication	Research

Part I.

1. $ 36,000   Interest cost (PBO at BOY $600,000 × 6% = $36,000)

2. $ 25,200   Actual return on plan assets (FV of plan assets BOY $420,000 × 6% = $25,200)

3. $ 20,000   Amortization of prior service costs or credits ($240,000/12 years = $20,000 per year)

4. $ 0   Gain or (Loss) (Actual returns = expected returns)

5. $110,800   Pension cost for 2009 ($80,000 service cost + $36,000 interest cost – $25,200 ROA + $20,000 amortization of prior service cost = $110,800)

6. $701,000   Projected benefit obligation at December 31, 2009 (PBO at BOY $600,000 + Service Costs $80,000 + Interest Cost $36,000 – Benefits Paid $15,000 = $701,000 PBO at EOY)

Part II.

		Increase	Decrease	No effect
1.	Service cost	●	○	○
2.	Interest cost	●	○	○
3.	Actual return on plan assets	○	●	○
4.	Amortization of prior service costs or credits	●	○	○
5.	Gain or loss in 2009	○	○	●

Explanation of solutions

1. **(I)** Service cost increases pension cost for the period.

2. **(I)** Interest cost increases pension cost for the period.

3. **(D)** Actual return on assets decreases pension costs for the period.

4. **(I)** Amortization of prior service cost increases pension cost for the period.

5. **(N)** Winger had no gain or loss because actual and expected return on assets were the same for 2009.

Situation	Concepts	Pension Calculations	Journal Entry	Balance Sheet	Communication	Research

Debit pension cost		110,800		
Credit cash			40,000	
Credit pension liability			70,800	

Situation	Concepts	Pension Calculations	Journal Entry	Balance Sheet	Communication	Research

What is the amount of pension assets or liabilities that will be disclosed in each of the following categories on the balance sheet?

1.	Current asset	0
2.	Noncurrent asset	0
3.	Current liability	0
4.	Noncurrent liability	$230,800

Explanation

The funded status of the plan is determined by comparing the Projected Benefit Obligation at year-end to the fair value of plan assets on December 31, 2009. The PBO of $701,000 – FV of plan assets of $470,200 = $230,800, which is the amount of the pension plan that is underfunded. A liability of $230,800 must be recognized on the balance sheet. A liability of $70,800 exists for the portion of the current year pension cost that was unfunded. Therefore, the increase in pension liability due to items not recognized in pension costs is $160,000 ($230,800 – $70,800). This is recognized as a noncurrent liability because Winger does not expect to pay any pension benefits within the next 12 months.

5.	Amount in AOCI	$112,000	**Debit**

Explanation

The journal entry to record this would be as follows:

Other comprehensive income	112,000*	
Deferred tax asset	48,000	
Pension liability		160,000

* *$160,000 × 70% = $112,000 (net of tax)*

Situation	Concepts	Pension Calculations	Journal Entry	Balance Sheet	Communication	Research

To: Mr. Palmer, Winger Company
From: CPA Candidate
Re: Postemployment benefits

   Thank you for your inquiry regarding accounting for postemployment benefits. I have analyzed the company's employment agreements, and I have identified the following postemployment benefits that required financial statement presentation.

   One postemployment benefit offered by Winger Company is continuation of health care benefits. The company is required to accrue liabilities for this benefit if all of the following conditions are met:

   • The obligation is attributable to employees' services already rendered,
   • The employees' rights accumulate or vest,
   • Payment is probable, and
   • The amount of the benefits can be reasonably estimated.

If an obligation cannot be accrued solely because the amount cannot be reasonably estimated, the financial statements should disclose that fact.

   Winger Company also has several deferred compensation contracts. Estimated amounts to be paid under a deferred compensation contract should be accrued over the period of an employee's active employment from the time the contract is signed to the employee's full eligibility date. The theoretical rationale for accrual of these obligations is that accrual matches the cost of the benefits to the period in which services are rendered.

   Based on the information given to me by your accounting manager, I have prepared the following schedule detailing the company's deferred compensation amounts.

Winger Co.
SCHEDULE OF DEFERRED COMPENSATION AMOUNTS
For the Years 2009 through 2012

For the year ended	Accrued liability	Deferred compensation expense
12/31/09	$ 50,000	$50,000 [a]
12/31/10	$100,000	$50,000
12/31/11	$150,000	$50,000
12/31/12	$165,000	$15,000 [b]

   [a] $150,000 ÷ 3 (straight-line method)
   [b] $150,000 × 10%

   If I can be of further assistance, please do not hesitate to contact me.

Situation	Concepts	Pension Calculations	Journal Entry	Balance Sheet	Communication	Research

1.   Define the interest cost component of net pension cost for a period.

FAS87, Para 22
Interest cost

22. The interest cost component recognized in a period shall be determined as the increase in the projected benefit obligation due to the passage of time. Measuring the projected benefit obligation as a present value requires accrual of an interest cost at rates equal to the assumed discount rates.

Codification: 715-30-20 Glossary

2.   How should Winger determine its interest cost component of net pension cost for a period?

FAS87, Para 22
Interest cost

22. The interest cost component recognized in a period shall be determined as the increase in the projected benefit obligation due to the passage of time. Measuring the projected benefit obligation as a present value requires accrual of an interest cost at rates equal to the assumed discount rates.

Codification: 715-30-35-8

3.   Define prior service cost.

FAS87, Para 24
Prior service cost

24. Plan amendments (including initiation of a plan) often include provisions that grant increased benefits based on services rendered in prior periods. Because plan amendments are granted with the expectation that the employer will realize economic benefits in future periods, this Statement does not require the cost of providing such retroactive benefits (that is, prior service cost) to be included in net periodic pension cost entirely in the year of the amendment but provides for recognition during the future service period of those employees active at the date of the amendment who are expected to received benefits under the plan.

FAS87, Para 264 (Glossary)
Prior service cost

The cost of retroactive benefits granted in a plan amendment. See also Unrecognized prior service cost.

Codification: 715-30-20 Glossary

4.   How should Winger account for prior service cost?

FAS87, Para 25 (As amended by SFAS 158)

25. A plan amendment that retroactively increases benefits (including benefits that are granted to retirees) increases the projected benefit obligation. Except as specified in paragraphs 26 and 27, that prior service cost shall be amortized as a component of net periodic pension cost by assigning an equal amount to each future period of service of each employee active at the date of the amendment who is expected to receive benefits under the plan If all or almost all of a plan's participants are inactive, the cost of retroactive plan amendments affecting benefits of inactive participants shall be amortized based on the remaining life expectancy of those participants instead of based on the remaining service period. Other comprehensive income is adjusted each period as prior service cost is amortized.

Codification: 715-30-35-11

5.   What conditions must be met for Winger to accrue compensation for future vacations?

FAS43, Para 6

6.   An employer shall accrue a liability for employees' compensation for future absences if all of the following conditions are met:

a. The employer's obligation relating to employees' rights to receive compensation for future absences is attributable to employees' services already rendered,

b. The obligation relates to rights that vest or accumulate,

c. Payment of the compensation is probable, and

d. The amount can be reasonably estimated.

If an employer meets conditions (a), (b), and (c) and does not accrue a liability because condition (d) is not met, that fact shall be disclosed.

Codification: 710-10-25-1

MULTIPLE-CHOICE QUESTIONS (1-56)

1. Rapp Co. leased a new machine to Lake Co. on January 1, 2010. The lease is an operating lease and expires on January 1, 2015. The annual rental is $90,000. Additionally, on January 1, 2010, Lake paid $50,000 to Rapp as a lease bonus and $25,000 as a security deposit to be refunded upon expiration of the lease. In Rapp's 2010 income statement, the amount of rental revenue should be

   a. $140,000
   b. $125,000
   c. $100,000
   d. $ 90,000

2. Wall Co. leased office premises to Fox, Inc. for a five-year term beginning January 2, 2010. Under the terms of the operating lease, rent for the first year is $8,000 and rent for years two through five is $12,500 per annum. However, as an inducement to enter the lease, Wall granted Fox the first six months of the lease rent-free. In its December 31, 2010 income statement, what amount should Wall report as rental income?

   a. $12,000
   b. $11,600
   c. $10,800
   d. $ 8,000

3. On January 1, 2010, Wren Co. leased a building to Brill under an operating lease for ten years at $50,000 per year, payable the first day of each lease year. Wren paid $15,000 to a real estate broker as a finder's fee. The building is depreciated $12,000 per year. For 2010, Wren incurred insurance and property tax expense totaling $9,000. Wren's net rental income for 2010 should be

   a. $27,500
   b. $29,000
   c. $35,000
   d. $36,500

4. On July 1, 2008, Gee, Inc. leased a delivery truck from Marr Corp. under a three-year operating lease. Total rent for the term of the lease will be $36,000, payable as follows:

   12 months at $ 500 = $ 6,000
   12 months at $ 750 = 9,000
   12 months at $1,750 = 21,000

All payments were made when due. In Marr's June 30, 2010 balance sheet, the accrued rent receivable should be reported as

   a. $0
   b. $ 9,000
   c. $12,000
   d. $21,000

5. On January 1, 2010, Glen Co. leased a building to Dix Corp. under an operating lease for a ten-year term at an annual rental of $50,000. At inception of the lease, Glen received $200,000 covering the first two years' rent of $100,000 and a security deposit of $100,000. This deposit will not be returned to Dix upon expiration of the lease but will be applied to payment of rent for the last two years of the lease. What portion of the $200,000 should be shown as a current and long-term liability, respectively, in Glen's December 31, 2010 balance sheet?

	Current liability	Long-term liability
a.	$0	$200,000
b.	$ 50,000	$100,000
c.	$100,000	$100,000
d.	$100,000	$ 50,000

6. As an inducement to enter a lease, Graf Co., a lessor, granted Zep, Inc., a lessee, twelve months of free rent under a five-year operating lease. The lease was effective on January 1, 2010, and provides for monthly rental payments to begin January 1, 2011. Zep made the first rental payment on December 30, 2010. In its 2010 income statement, Graf should report rental revenue in an amount equal to

   a. Zero.
   b. Cash received during 2010.
   c. One-fourth of the total cash to be received over the life of the lease.
   d. One-fifth of the total cash to be received over the life of the lease.

7. Quo Co. rented a building to Hava Fast Food. Each month Quo receives a fixed rental amount plus a variable rental amount based on Hava's sales for that month. As sales increase so does the variable rental amount, but at a reduced rate. Which of the following curves reflects the monthly rentals under the agreement?

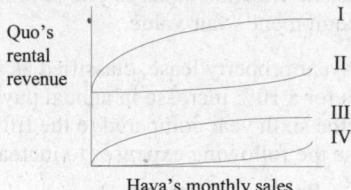

   a. I
   b. II
   c. III
   d. IV

8. As an inducement to enter a lease, Arts, Inc., a lessor, grants Hompson Corp., a lessee, nine months of free rent under a five-year operating lease. The lease is effective on July 1, 2010 and provides for monthly rental of $1,000 to begin April 1, 2011. In Hompson's income statement for the year ended June 30, 2011, rent expense should be reported as

   a. $10,200
   b. $ 9,000
   c. $ 3,000
   d. $ 2,550

9. On January 1, 2010, Park Co. signed a ten-year operating lease for office space at $96,000 per year. The lease included a provision for additional rent of 5% of annual company sales in excess of $500,000. Park's sales for the year ended December 31, 2010, were $600,000. Upon execution of the lease, Park paid $24,000 as a bonus for the lease. Park's rent expense for the year ended December 31, 2010, is

   a. $ 98,400
   b. $101,000
   c. $103,400
   d. $125,000

10. On July 1, 2010, South Co. entered into a ten-year operating lease for a warehouse facility. The annual minimum lease payments are $100,000. In addition to the base rent,

South pays a monthly allocation of the building's operating expenses, which amounted to $20,000 for the year ended June 30, 2011. In the notes to South's June 30, 2011 financial statements, what amounts of subsequent years' lease payments should be disclosed?

   a. $100,000 per annum for each of the next five years and $500,000 in the aggregate.
   b. $120,000 per annum for each of the next five years and $600,000 in the aggregate.
   c. $100,000 per annum for each of the next five years and $900,000 in the aggregate.
   d. $120,000 per annum for each of the next five years and $1,080,000 in the aggregate.

11. On January 1, 2010, Mollat Co. signed a seven-year lease for equipment having a ten-year economic life. The present value of the monthly lease payments equaled 80% of the equipment's fair value. The lease agreement provides for neither a transfer of title to Mollat nor a bargain purchase option. In its 2010 income statement Mollat should report

   a. Rent expense equal to the 2010 lease payments.
   b. Rent expense equal to the 2010 lease payments less interest expense.
   c. Lease amortization equal to one-tenth of the equipment's fair value.
   d. Lease amortization equal to one-seventh of 80% of the equipment's fair value.

12. A twenty-year property lease, classified as an operating lease, provides for a 10% increase in annual payments every five years. In the sixth year compared to the fifth year, the lease will cause the following expenses to increase

	Rent	Interest
a.	No	Yes
b.	Yes	No
c.	Yes	Yes
d.	No	No

13. On December 1, 2010, Clark Co. leased office space for five years at a monthly rental of $60,000. On the same date, Clark paid the lessor the following amounts:

First month's rent	$ 60,000
Last month's rent	60,000
Security deposit (refundable at lease expiration)	80,000
Installation of new walls and offices	360,000

What should be Clark's 2010 expense relating to utilization of the office space?

   a. $ 60,000
   b. $ 66,000
   c. $120,000
   d. $140,000

14. Star Co. leases a building for its product showroom. The ten-year nonrenewable lease will expire on December 31, 2015. In January 2010, Star redecorated its showroom and made leasehold improvements of $48,000. The estimated useful life of the improvements is eight years. Star uses the straight-line method of amortization. What amount of leasehold improvements, net of amortization, should Star report in its June 30, 2010 balance sheet?

   a. $45,600
   b. $45,000
   c. $44,000
   d. $43,200

15. On January 2, 2010, Ral Co. leased land and building from an unrelated lessor for a ten-year term. The lease has a renewal option for an additional ten years, but Ral has not reached a decision with regard to the renewal option. In early January of 2010, Ral completed the following improvements to the property:

Description	Estimated life	Cost
Sales office	10 years	$47,000
Warehouse	25 years	75,000
Parking lot	15 years	18,000

Amortization of leasehold improvements for 2010 should be

   a. $ 7,000
   b. $ 8,900
   c. $12,200
   d. $14,000

16. On January 1, 2008, Nobb Corp. signed a twelve-year lease for warehouse space. Nobb has an option to renew the lease for an additional eight-year period on or before January 1, 2012. During January 2010, Nobb made substantial improvements to the warehouse. The cost of these improvements was $540,000, with an estimated useful life of fifteen years. At December 31, 2010, Nobb intended to exercise the renewal option. Nobb has taken a full year's amortization on this leasehold. In Nobb's December 31, 2010 balance sheet, the carrying amount of this leasehold improvement should be

   a. $486,000
   b. $504,000
   c. $510,000
   d. $513,000

17. During January 2010, Vail Co. made long-term improvements to a recently leased building. The lease agreement provides for neither a transfer of title to Vail nor a bargain purchase option. The present value of the minimum lease payments equals 85% of the building's market value, and the lease term equals 70% of the building's economic life. Should assets be recognized for the building and the leasehold improvements?

	Building	Leasehold improvements
a.	Yes	Yes
b.	No	Yes
c.	Yes	No
d.	No	No

18. A lessee incurred costs to construct office space in a leased warehouse. The estimated useful life of the office is ten years. The remaining term of the nonrenewable lease is fifteen years. The costs should be

   a. Capitalized as leasehold improvements and depreciated over fifteen years.
   b. Capitalized as leasehold improvements and depreciated over ten years.
   c. Capitalized as leasehold improvements and expensed in the year in which the lease expires.
   d. Expensed as incurred.

19. Glade Co. leases computer equipment to customers under direct-financing leases. The equipment has no residual value at the end of the lease and the leases do not contain bargain purchase options. Glade wishes to earn 8% interest on a five-year lease of equipment with a fair value of $323,400. The present value of an annuity due of $1 at 8% for five years is 4.312. What is the total amount of interest revenue that Glade will earn over the life of the lease?

MODULE 11   PRESENT VALUE: E. LEASES

a. $ 51,600
b. $ 75,000
c. $129,360
d. $139,450

20. On January 1, 2009, JCK Co. signed a contract for an eight-year lease of its equipment with a ten-year life. The present value of the sixteen equal semiannual payments in advance equaled 85% of the equipment's fair value. The contract had no provision for JCK, the lessor, to give up legal ownership of the equipment. Should JCK recognize rent or interest revenue in 2010, and should the revenue recognized in 2010 be the same or smaller than the revenue recognized in 2009?

	2010 revenues recognized	2010 amount recognized compared to 2009
a.	Rent	The same
b.	Rent	Smaller
c.	Interest	The same
d.	Interest	Smaller

21. Peg Co. leased equipment from Howe Corp. on July 1, 2010 for an eight-year period expiring June 30, 2018. Equal payments under the lease are $600,000 and are due on July 1 of each year. The first payment was made on July 1, 2010. The rate of interest contemplated by Peg and Howe is 10%. The cash selling price of the equipment is $3,520,000, and the cost of the equipment on Howe's accounting records is $2,800,000. The lease is appropriately recorded as a sales-type lease. What is the amount of profit on the sale and interest revenue that Howe should record for the year ended December 31, 2010?

	Profit on sale	Interest revenue
a.	$720,000	$176,000
b.	$720,000	$146,000
c.	$ 45,000	$176,000
d.	$ 45,000	$146,000

22. Howe Co. leased equipment to Kew Corp. on January 2, 2010, for an eight-year period expiring December 31, 2017. Equal payments under the lease are $600,000 and are due on January 2 of each year. The first payment was made on January 2, 2010. The list selling price of the equipment is $3,520,000 and its carrying cost on Howe's books is $2,800,000. The lease is appropriately accounted for as a sales-type lease. The present value of the lease payments is $3,300,000. What amount of profit on the sale should Howe report for the year ended December 31, 2010?

a. $720,000
b. $500,000
c. $ 90,000
d. $0

23. The excess of the fair value of leased property at the inception of the lease over its cost or carrying amount should be classified by the lessor as
a.   Unearned income from a sales-type lease.
b.   Unearned income from a direct-financing lease.
c.   Manufacturer's or dealer's profit from a sales-type lease.
d.   Manufacturer's or dealer's profit from a direct-financing lease.

24. In a lease that is recorded as a sales-type lease by the lessor, interest revenue

a.   Should be recognized in full as revenue at the lease's inception.
b.   Should be recognized over the period of the lease using the straight-line method.
c.   Should be recognized over the period of the lease using the interest method.
d.   Does **not** arise.

25. Lease M does not contain a bargain purchase option, but the lease term is equal to 90% of the estimated economic life of the leased property. Lease P does not transfer ownership of the property to the lessee at the end of the lease term, but the lease term is equal to 75% of the estimated economic life of the leased property. How should the lessee classify these leases?

	Lease M	Lease P
a.	Capital lease	Operating lease
b.	Capital lease	Capital lease
c.	Operating lease	Capital lease
d.	Operating lease	Operating lease

26. On December 31, 2010, Day Co. leased a new machine from Parr with the following pertinent information:

Lease term	6 years
Annual rental payable at beginning of each year	$50,000
Useful life of machine	8 years
Day's incremental borrowing rate	15%
Implicit interest rate in lease (known by Day)	12%
Present value of annuity of 1 in advance for 6 periods at	
12%	4.61
15%	4.35

The lease is not renewable, and the machine reverts to Parr at the termination of the lease. The cost of the machine on Parr's accounting records is $375,500. At the beginning of the lease term, Day should record a lease liability of
a. $375,500
b. $230,500
c. $217,500
d. $0

27. On January 1, 2010, Day Corp. entered into a ten-year lease agreement with Ward, Inc. for industrial equipment. Annual lease payments of $10,000 are payable at the end of each year. Day knows that the lessor expects a 10% return on the lease. Day has a 12% incremental borrowing rate. The equipment is expected to have an estimated useful life of ten years. In addition, a third party has guaranteed to pay Ward a residual value of $5,000 at the end of the lease.

The present value of an ordinary annuity of $1 at
  12% for ten years is 5.6502
  10% for ten years is 6.1446

The present value of $1 at
  12% for ten years is .3220
  10% for ten years is .3855

In Day's October 31, 2010 balance sheet, the principal amount of the lease obligation was
a. $63,374
b. $61,446
c. $58,112
d. $56,502

28. Robbins, Inc. leased a machine from Ready Leasing Co. The lease qualifies as a capital lease and requires ten annual payments of $10,000 beginning immediately. The lease specifies an interest rate of 12% and a purchase option of $10,000 at the end of the tenth year, even though the machine's estimated value on that date is $20,000. Robbins' incremental borrowing rate is 14%.

The present value of an annuity due of one at
    12% for ten years is 6.328
    14% for ten years is 5.946

The present value of one at
    12% for ten years is .322
    14% for ten years is .270

What amount should Robbins record as lease liability at the beginning of the lease term?

    a. $62,160
    b. $64,860
    c. $66,500
    d. $69,720

29. Neal Corp. entered into a nine-year capital lease on a warehouse on December 31, 2010. Lease payments of $52,000, which includes real estate taxes of $2,000, are due annually, beginning on December 31, 2011, and every December 31 thereafter. Neal does not know the interest rate implicit in the lease; Neal's incremental borrowing rate is 9%. The rounded present value of an ordinary annuity for nine years at 9% is 5.6. What amount should Neal report as capitalized lease liability at December 31, 2010?

    a. $280,000
    b. $291,200
    c. $450,000
    d. $468,000

30. East Company leased a new machine from North Company on May 1, 2010, under a lease with the following information:

Lease term	10 years
Annual rental payable at beginning of each lease year	$40,000
Useful life of machine	12 years
Implicit interest rate	14%
Present value of an annuity of one in advance for ten	
periods at 14%	5.95
Present value of one for ten periods at 14%	0.27

East has the option to purchase the machine on May 1, 2020 by paying $50,000, which approximates the expected fair value of the machine on the option exercise date. On May 1, 2010, East should record a capitalized lease asset of

    a. $251,500
    b. $238,000
    c. $224,500
    d. $198,000

31. On January 1, 2010, Babson, Inc. leased two automobiles for executive use. The lease requires Babson to make five annual payments of $13,000 beginning January 1, 2010. At the end of the lease term, December 31, 2014, Babson guarantees the residual value of the automobiles will total $10,000. The lease qualifies as a capital lease. The interest rate implicit in the lease is 9%. Present value factors for the 9% rate implicit in the lease are as follows:

For an annuity due with five payments	4.240
For an ordinary annuity with five payments	3.890
Present value of $1 for five periods	0.650

Babson's recorded capital lease liability immediately after the first required payment should be

    a. $48,620
    b. $44,070
    c. $35,620
    d. $31,070

32. On December 30, 2010, Rafferty Corp. leased equipment under a capital lease. Annual lease payments of $20,000 are due December 31 for ten years. The equipment's useful life is ten years, and the interest rate implicit in the lease is 10%. The capital lease obligation was recorded on December 30, 2010, at $135,000, and the first lease payment was made on that date. What amount should Rafferty include in current liabilities for this capital lease in its December 31, 2010 balance sheet?

    a. $ 6,500
    b. $ 8,500
    c. $11,500
    d. $20,000

33. Oak Co. leased equipment for its entire nine-year useful life, agreeing to pay $50,000 at the start of the lease term on December 31, 2010, and $50,000 annually on each December 31 for the next eight years. The present value on December 31, 2010, of the nine lease payments over the lease term, using the rate implicit in the lease which Oak knows to be 10%, was $316,500. The December 31, 2010 present value of the lease payments using Oak's incremental borrowing rate of 12% was $298,500. Oak made a timely second lease payment. What amount should Oak report as capital lease liability in its December 31, 2011 balance sheet?

    a. $350,000
    b. $243,150
    c. $228,320
    d. $0

34. On December 31, 2010, Roe Co. leased a machine from Colt for a five-year period. Equal annual payments under the lease are $105,000 (including $5,000 annual executory costs) and are due on December 31 of each year. The first payment was made on December 31, 2010, and the second payment was made on December 31, 2011. The five lease payments are discounted at 10% over the lease term. The present value of minimum lease payments at the inception of the lease and before the first annual payment was $417,000. The lease is appropriately accounted for as a capital lease by Roe. In its December 31, 2011 balance sheet, Roe should report a lease liability of

    a. $317,000
    b. $315,000
    c. $285,300
    d. $248,700

35. In the long-term liabilities section of its balance sheet at December 31, 2010, Mene Co. reported a capital lease obligation of $75,000, net of current portion of $1,364. Payments of $9,000 were made on both January 2, 2011, and January 2, 2012. Mene's incremental borrowing rate on the date of the lease was 11% and the lessor's implicit rate, which was known to Mene, was 10%. In its December 31, 2011 balance sheet, what amount should Mene report as capital lease obligation, net of current portion?

    a. $66,000
    b. $73,500
    c. $73,636
    d. $74,250

36. For a capital lease, the amount recorded initially by the lessee as a liability should normally

    a. Exceed the total of the minimum lease payments.

b. Exceed the present value of the minimum lease payments at the beginning of the lease.
c. Equal the total of the minimum lease payments.
d. Equal the present value of the minimum lease payments at the beginning of the lease.

37. At the inception of a capital lease, the guaranteed residual value should be
a. Included as part of minimum lease payments at present value.
b. Included as part of minimum lease payments at future value.
c. Included as part of minimum lease payments only to the extent that guaranteed residual value is expected to exceed estimated residual value.
d. Excluded from minimum lease payments.

38. A six-year capital lease entered into on December 31, 2010, specified equal minimum annual lease payments due on December 31 of each year. The first minimum annual lease payment, paid on December 31, 2010, consists of which of the following?

	Interest expense	Lease liability
a.	Yes	Yes
b.	Yes	No
c.	No	Yes
d.	No	No

39. A six-year capital lease expiring on December 31 specifies equal minimum annual lease payments. Part of this payment represents interest and part represents a reduction in the net lease liability. The portion of the minimum lease payment in the fifth year applicable to the reduction of the net lease liability should be
a. Less than in the fourth year.
b. More than in the fourth year.
c. The same as in the sixth year.
d. More than in the sixth year.

40. A lessee had a ten-year capital lease requiring equal annual payments. The reduction of the lease liability in year two should equal
a. The current liability shown for the lease at the end of year one.
b. The current liability shown for the lease at the end of year two.
c. The reduction of the lease obligation in year one.
d. One-tenth of the original lease liability.

41. On January 2, 2010, Cole Co. signed an eight-year noncancelable lease for a new machine, requiring $15,000 annual payments at the beginning of each year. The machine has a useful life of twelve years, with no salvage value. Title passes to Cole at the lease expiration date. Cole uses straight-line depreciation for all of its plant assets. Aggregate lease payments have a present value on January 2, 2010, of $108,000 based on an appropriate rate of interest. For 2010, Cole should record depreciation (amortization) expense for the leased machine at
a. $0
b. $ 9,000
c. $13,500
d. $15,000

42. On January 2, 2010, Nori Mining Co. (lessee) entered into a five-year lease for drilling equipment. Nori accounted for the acquisition as a capital lease for $240,000, which

includes a $10,000 bargain purchase option. At the end of the lease, Nori expects to exercise the bargain purchase option. Nori estimates that the equipment's fair value will be $20,000 at the end of its eight-year life. Nori regularly uses straight-line depreciation on similar equipment. For the year ended December 31, 2010, what amount should Nori recognize as depreciation expense on the leased asset?
a. $48,000
b. $46,000
c. $30,000
d. $27,500

43. The lessee should amortize the capitalizable cost of the leased asset in a manner consistent with the lessee's normal depreciation policy for owned assets for leases that

	Contain a bargain purchase option	Transfer ownership of the property to the lessee by the end of the lease term
a.	No	No
b.	No	Yes
c.	Yes	Yes
d.	Yes	No

44. On January 1, 2010, Harrow Co. as lessee signed a five-year noncancelable equipment lease with annual payments of $100,000 beginning December 31, 2010. Harrow treated this transaction as a capital lease. The five lease payments have a present value of $379,000 at January 1, 2010, based on interest of 10%. What amount should Harrow report as interest expense for the year ended December 31, 2010?
a. $37,900
b. $27,900
c. $24,200
d. $0

45. On January 1, 2010, West Co. entered into a ten-year lease for a manufacturing plant. The annual minimum lease payments are $100,000. In the notes to the December 31, 2011 financial statements, what amounts of subsequent years' lease payments should be disclosed?

	Amount for appropriate required period	Aggregate amount for the lease term
a.	$100,000	$0
b.	$300,000	$500,000
c.	$500,000	$800,000
d.	$500,000	$0

46. Cott, Inc. prepared an interest amortization table for a five-year lease payable with a bargain purchase option of $2,000, exercisable at the end of the lease. At the end of the five years, the balance in the leases payable column of the spreadsheet was zero. Cott has asked Grant, CPA, to review the spreadsheet to determine the error. Only one error was made on the spreadsheet. Which of the following statements represents the best explanation for this error?
a. The beginning present value of the lease did **not** include the present value of the bargain purchase option.
b. Cott subtracted the annual interest amount from the lease payable balance instead of adding it.
c. The present value of the bargain purchase option was subtracted from the present value of the annual payments.
d. Cott discounted the annual payments as an ordinary annuity, when the payments actually occurred at the beginning of each period.

47. On December 31, 2010, Lane, Inc. sold equipment to Noll, and simultaneously leased it back for twelve years. Pertinent information at this date is as follows:

Sales price	$480,000
Carrying amount	360,000
Estimated remaining economic life	15 years

At December 31, 2010, how much should Lane report as deferred gain from the sale of the equipment?

    a. $0
    b. $110,000
    c. $112,000
    d. $120,000

48. The following information pertains to a sale and lease-back of equipment by Mega Co. on December 31, 2010:

Sales price	$400,000
Carrying amount	$300,000
Monthly lease payment	$3,250
Present value of lease payments	$36,900
Estimated remaining life	25 years
Lease term	1 year
Implicit rate	12%

What amount of deferred gain on the sale should Mega report at December 31, 2010?

    a. $0
    b. $ 36,900
    c. $ 63,100
    d. $100,000

49. On December 31, 2010, Parke Corp. sold Edlow Corp. an airplane with an estimated remaining useful life of ten years. At the same time, Parke leased back the airplane for three years. Additional information is as follows:

Sales price	$600,000
Carrying amount of airplane at date of sale	$100,000
Monthly rental under lease	$ 6,330
Interest rate implicit in the lease as computed by	
Edlow and known by Parke (this rate is lower	
than the lessee's incremental borrowing rate)	12%
Present value of operating lease rentals ($6,330	
for 36 months @ 12%)	$190,581

The leaseback is considered an operating lease. In Parke's December 31, 2010 balance sheet, what amount should be included as deferred revenue on this transaction?

    a. $0
    b. $190,581
    c. $309,419
    d. $500,000

50. On June 30, 2010, Lang Co. sold equipment with an estimated useful life of eleven years and immediately leased it back for ten years. The equipment's carrying amount was $450,000; the sale price was $430,000; and the present value of the lease payments, which is equal to the fair value of the equipment, was $465,000. In its June 30, 2010 balance sheet, what amount should Lang report as deferred loss?

    a. $35,000
    b. $20,000
    c. $15,000
    d. $0

51. On January 1, 2010, Hooks Oil Co. sold equipment with a carrying amount of $100,000, and a remaining useful life of ten years, to Maco Drilling for $150,000. Hooks immediately leased the equipment back under a ten-year capital lease with a present value of $150,000 and will depreciate

the equipment using the straight-line method. Hooks made the first annual lease payment of $24,412 in December 2010. In Hooks' December 31, 2010 balance sheet, the unearned gain on equipment sale should be

    a. $50,000
    b. $45,000
    c. $25,588
    d. $0

52. In a sale-leaseback transaction, the seller-lessee has retained the property. The gain on the sale should be recognized at the time of the sale-leaseback when the lease is classified as a(n)

	Capital lease	*Operating lease*
a.	Yes	Yes
b.	No	No
c.	No	Yes
d.	Yes	No

53. Able sold its headquarters building at a gain, and simultaneously leased back the building. The lease was reported as a capital lease. At the time of sale, the gain should be reported as

    a.   Operating income.
    b.   An extraordinary item, net of income tax.
    c.   A separate component of stockholders' equity.
    d.   An asset valuation allowance.

54. On January 1, 2008, Goliath entered into a five-year operating lease for equipment. In January 2010, Goliath decided that it no longer needs the equipment and terminates the contract by paying a penalty of $3,000. How should Goliath account for the lease termination costs?

    a.   Recognize $3,000 termination cost in 2010 as a loss from continuing operations.
    b.   Recognize $1,000 termination cost each year for the remaining three years of the lease term.
    c.   Recognize the $3,000 termination cost as an extraordinary item in 2010.
    d.   Recognize the $3,000 termination cost as a discontinued operation in 2010.

55. In January 2008, Hopper Corp. signed a capital lease for equipment with a term of twenty years. In 2010, Hopper negotiated a modification to a capital lease that resulted in the lease being reclassified as an operating lease. Hopper calculated the company had a gain of $8,000 on the lease modification. Hopper retains all rights to use the property during the remainder of the lease term. How should Hopper account for the lease modification?

    a.   Recognize an $8,000 gain from lease modification during 2010.
    b.   Defer the gain and recognize it over the life of the operating lease.
    c.   Recognize the $8,000 gain as an extraordinary item in 2010.
    d.   Recognize the $8,000 gain as a discontinued operation in 2010.

56. On January 1, 2007, Belkor entered into a 10-year capital lease for equipment. On December 1, 2010, Belkor terminates the capital lease and incurs a $20,000 loss. How should Belkor recognize the lease termination on their financial statements?

    a.   Recognize a $20,000 loss in 2010 as a discontinued operation.

    b.   Recognize a $20,000 loss in 2010 as an extraordinary item.

    c.   Recognize a $20,000 loss from continuing operations in 2010.

    d.   Defer recognition of the loss and recognize pro rata over the life of the lease term.

SIMULATION PROBLEMS

Simulation Problem 1   (50 to 60 minutes)

Situation					
	Journal Entries	Concepts	Classification	Communication	Research

On January 2, 2010, Nesbitt Co. leased equipment from Grant, Inc. Lease payments are $100,000, payable annually every December 31 for twenty years. Title to the equipment passes to Nesbitt at the end of the lease term. The lease is noncancelable.

- The equipment has a $750,000 carrying amount on Grant's books. Its estimated economic life was twenty-five years on January 2, 2010.
- The rate implicit in the lease, which is known to Nesbitt, is 10%. Nesbitt's incremental borrowing rate is 12%.
- Nesbitt uses the straight-line method of depreciation.

The rounded present value factors of an ordinary annuity for twenty years are as follows:

$$\begin{array}{ll} 12\% & 7.5 \\ 10\% & 8.5 \end{array}$$

	Journal Entries				
Situation		Concepts	Classification	Communication	Research

Prepare the necessary journal entries, without explanations, to be recorded by Nesbitt for

1. Entering into the lease on January 2, 2010.
2. Making the lease payment on December 31, 2010.
3. Expenses related to the lease for the year ended December 31, 2010.

		Concepts			
Situation	Journal Entries		Classification	Communication	Research

The terms listed below refer to lessee and lessor accounting for operating, capital, direct financing, and sales-type leases. For each term, select the **best** phrase or description from the answers listed A–Q below. An answer may be used once, more than once, or not at all.

Answer list

A. The substance of this transaction is that it consists of two separate and distinct transactions.
B. Rental payments are recognized on a straight-line basis, even though the lease calls for payments that increase over the term of the lease.
C. Depreciation expense related to the leased asset is reported on the lessee's income statement over the lease term.
D. Sales revenue (the present value of the minimum lease payments) less the carrying amount of the leased asset is reported on the lessor's income statement at the inception of the lease.
E. The rate used by the lessee to determine the present value of the minimum lease payments if the lessee's incremental borrowing rate is less than the lessor's implicit rate.
F. Initial direct costs should be treated as an asset and amortized over the life of the lease on a straight-line basis.
G. The difference between the fair value of the asset leased and the total payments to be received over the lease term.
H. Included in the lessor's gross investment, whether guaranteed or unguaranteed.
I. Interest revenue is the only item reported on the income statement over the lease term.
J. The excess of the sales price over the carrying amount of the leased equipment is considered profit and is included in income over the duration of the lease term.
K. Should be recorded as both an asset and a liability by the lessee when the lease contains a bargain purchase option.
L. Produces a constant periodic rate of return on the net investment.
M. The principal portion of the lease liability which must be paid within the next operating cycle.
N. Produces a desired rate of return which causes the aggregate present value of the minimum lease payments to be equal to the fair value of the leased property.
O. Lessee's right to purchase leased property for an amount substantially lower than the expected FV at exercise date.
P. Costs, such as appraisal fees, incurred by the lessor in setting up the lease agreement.
Q. A lease agreement which requires the annual payments to be made at the beginning of each period.

	(A)	(B)	(C)	(D)	(E)	(F)	(G)	(H)	(I)	(J)	(K)	(L)	(M)	(N)	(O)	(P)	(Q)
1. Sales-type lease	O	O	O	O	O	O	O	O	O	O	O	O	O	O	O	O	O
2. Direct financing lease	O	O	O	O	O	O	O	O	O	O	O	O	O	O	O	O	O
3. Operating lease—lessee	O	O	O	O	O	O	O	O	O	O	O	O	O	O	O	O	O
4. Operating lease—lessor	O	O	O	O	O	O	O	O	O	O	O	O	O	O	O	O	O
5. Unearned interest revenue	O	O	O	O	O	O	O	O	O	O	O	O	O	O	O	O	O
6. Residual value	O	O	O	O	O	O	O	O	O	O	O	O	O	O	O	O	O
7. Capital lease	O	O	O	O	O	O	O	O	O	O	O	O	O	O	O	O	O
8. Implicit rate	O	O	O	O	O	O	O	O	O	O	O	O	O	O	O	O	O
9. Interest method	O	O	O	O	O	O	O	O	O	O	O	O	O	O	O	O	O
10. Present value of the minimum lease payments	O	O	O	O	O	O	O	O	O	O	O	O	O	O	O	O	O
11. Bargain purchase option	O	O	O	O	O	O	O	O	O	O	O	O	O	O	O	O	O
12. Sale-leaseback	O	O	O	O	O	O	O	O	O	O	O	O	O	O	O	O	O
13. Annuity due	O	O	O	O	O	O	O	O	O	O	O	O	O	O	O	O	O
14. Initial direct costs	O	O	O	O	O	O	O	O	O	O	O	O	O	O	O	O	O
15. Current lease obligation	O	O	O	O	O	O	O	O	O	O	O	O	O	O	O	O	O

Situation	Journal Entries	Concepts	**Classification**		Communication	Research

Nesbitt Co. has the following rental agreements. You have been asked to advise the accounting treatment for each of these items.

In the space provided, indicate whether each of these agreements is an operating lease or a capital lease.

	Operating lease	*Capital lease*
1. Nesbitt rents equipment for three years for $20,000 per year. The equipment is valued at $200,000. At the end of the rental term the equipment must be returned to the dealer.	O	O
2. Nesbitt rents equipment for five years for $80,000 per year. At the end of the rental term Nesbitt can purchase the equipment for $500. At the date the contract was signed the equipment had a value of $300,000. At the end of five years, it is expected the equipment will have a value of $42,000.	O	O
3. Nesbitt received six months of free rent on an office building it was leasing for two years. Rent is normally $1,500 per month.	O	O
4. Nesbitt rents equipment for eight years. The present value of the lease payments are $80,000. The market value of the equipment is $90,000 and the useful life of the equipment is ten years.	O	O
5. Nesbitt rents equipment for ten years. At the end of the lease Nesbitt receives title to the equipment.	O	O
6. Nesbitt rents equipment for seven years. The life of the equipment is ten years. The fair value of the equipment is $100,000. The present value of the minimum lease payments is $85,000.	O	O

Situation	Journal Entries	Concepts	Classification	**Communication**	Research

On December 31, 2010, Nesbitt Co. sold a building for its fair value and leased it back. The building was sold for more than its carrying amount and a gain was recorded. Lease payments are due at the end of each month. Nesbitt accounted for the transaction as a capital lease. The lease's interest rate was equal to Nesbitt's incremental borrowing rate.

Write a brief memorandum to the CEO of Nesbitt Co. explaining the following:

1. How should Nesbitt account for the sale portion of the sale-leaseback transaction at December 31, 2010? Why is this an appropriate method of accounting for this portion of the contract?

2.   How should Nesbitt report the leaseback portion of the sale-leaseback transaction on its December 31, 2011 balance sheet? How are these reported amounts determined?

REMINDER: Your response will be graded for both technical content and writing skills. Technical content will be evaluated for information that is helpful to the intended reader and clearly relevant to the issue. Writing skills will be evaluated for development, organization, and the appropriate expression of ideas in professional correspondence. Use a standard business memo or letter format with a clear beginning, middle, and end. Do not convey information in the form of a table, bullet point list, or other abbreviated presentation.

To: CEO, Nesbitt Co.
From: CPA Candidate
Re: Sales-Leaseback Transaction

					Research
Situation	Journal Entries	Concepts	Classification	Communication	

Research the following issues. Select your answer from the professional standards.

1. How is a liability related to a capital lease disclosed in the balance sheet of the lessee?

2. How does the lessee value the liability for termination costs to cancel an operating lease?

3. What items are included in calculating the minimum lease payment for the lessee?

Simulation Problem 2   (50 to 60 minutes)

Situation						
	Valuation of Lease	Journal Entries	Amortization Schedule	Financial Statement Disclosures	Communication	Research

On December 30, 2010, Kelty Corporation signed an agreement to lease equipment for ten years. The lease payments of $70,000 are due each year on December 30. Kelty paid its first lease payment immediately after the lease was signed. The interest rate was 6%. The fair market value of the leased equipment on December 30, 2010, was $600,000. At the end of the lease term, Kelty may exercise a bargain purchase option to purchase the equipment for $10,000. The asset has a useful life of twelve years. Kelty uses the net method for recording lease obligations.

	Valuation of Lease					
Situation		Journal Entries	Amortization Schedule	Financial Statement Disclosures	Communication	Research

Calculate the lease liability and the value of the leased asset at the time the lease is signed. (For a more realistic exam experience, complete the problem using a spreadsheet program, such as Excel.)

		Journal Entries				
Situation	Valuation of Lease		Amortization Schedule	Financial Statement Disclosures	Communication	Research

Prepare the journal entry or journal entries to record the lease transactions on December 30, 2010.

			Amortization Schedule			
Situation	Valuation of Lease	Journal Entries		Financial Statement Disclosures	Communication	Research

Prepare an amortization table for the lease through December 30, 2013.

Year ending	Interest expense	Lease payment	Amounts applied to carrying value	Carrying value of lease
At signing of note	Not applicable	Not applicable	Not applicable	
December 30, 2010				
December 30, 2011				
December 30, 2012				
December 30, 2013				

Situation	Valuation of Lease	Journal Entries	Amortization Schedule	Financial Statement Disclosures	Communication	Research

Determine the following amounts to be recognized in the financial statements.

Interest expense for 2011	
Interest expense for 2012	
Carrying value of lease on 12/31/12	
Depreciation expense for 2011	

Situation	Valuation of Lease	Journal Entries	Amortization Schedule	Financial Statement Disclosures	Communication	Research

The Chief Executive Officer of Kelty is unsure if the company should sign the ten-year lease. Upon discussion of his concerns with the equipment company, the sales agent presented him with two more alternatives to leasing.

1.   Purchase the equipment for the retail value of $600,000.

2.   Sign a five-year lease and pay rent of $90,000 per year with no option to purchase the equipment later.

Prepare a memo to the CEO of Kelty Corporation discussing the advantages and disadvantages of each of the three alternatives for the equipment, along with your recommendation for the best alternative.

REMINDER: Your response will be graded for both technical content and writing skills. Technical content will be evaluated for information that is helpful to the intended reader and clearly relevant to the issue. Writing skills will be evaluated for development, organization, and the appropriate expression of ideas in professional correspondence. Use a standard business memo or letter format with a clear beginning, middle, and end. Do not convey information in the form of a table, bullet point list, or other abbreviated presentation.

To: Mr. George Timms
          Chief Executive Officer
          Kelty Corporation
From: CPA Candidate
Re: Options for acquisition of equipment

Situation	Valuation of Lease	Journal Entries	Amortization Schedule	Financial Statement Disclosures	Communication	Research

Identify the answers to the following issues by selecting the appropriate citation to the authoritative literature into the space provided.

1. How should Kelty calculate the   _____
    amount to record the lease liability   _____
    on December 30, 2010?   _____
    _____
    _____

2. How should Kelty calculate amorti-   _____
    zation expense on the leased   _____
    equipment?   _____
    _____
    _____

Simulation Problem 3   (50 to 60 minutes)

Situation						
	Leasing Concepts	**Journal Entries**	**Interest Expense**	**Liability Section of Balance Sheet**	**Communication**	**Research**

The following information relates to the obligations of Villa Watch Co. as of December 31, 2010:

- Accounts payable for goods and services purchased on open account amounted to $35,000 at December 31, 2010.
- On December 15, 2010, Villa declared a cash dividend of $.05 per common share, payable on January 12, 2011, to shareholders of record as of December 31, 2010. Villa had 1,000,000 shares of common stock issued and outstanding throughout 2010.
- On December 31, 2010, Villa entered into a six-year capital lease on a warehouse and made the first annual lease payment of $100,000. Villa's incremental borrowing rate was 12%, and the interest rate implicit in the lease, which was known to Villa, was 10%. The rounded present value factors for an annuity due for six years are 4.6 at 12% and 4.8 at 10%.
- On July 1, 2010, Villa issued $500,000, 8% bonds for $440,000 to yield 10%. The bonds mature on June 30, 2016, and pay interest annually every June 30. At December 31, 2010, the bonds were trading on the open market at 86 to yield 12%. Villa uses the effective interest method.
- Villa's 2010 pretax financial income was $850,000 and its taxable income was $600,000. The difference is due to $100,000 of permanent differences and $150,000 of temporary differences related to noncurrent assets. At December 31, 2010, Villa had cumulative taxable differences of $300,000 related to noncurrent assets. Villa's effective tax rate is 30%. Villa made no estimated tax payments during the year.

	Leasing Concepts					
Situation		**Journal Entries**	**Interest Expense**	**Liability Section of Balance Sheet**	**Communication**	**Research**

Identify whether each statement is True or False.

		True	*False*
1.	Free or uneven lease payments should be recognized by the lessor when the lease payment is received.	○	○
2.	Initial direct costs are expensed by the lessor when the lease is signed.	○	○
3.	A refundable security deposit is treated as an asset by the lessor.	○	○
4.	Leasehold improvements should be amortized over the longer of the remaining lease term or the useful life of the asset.	○	○
5.	The minimum lease payment includes any penalty for failure to renew.	○	○
6.	The unguaranteed residual value is considered part of the minimum lease payment for the lessee's liability.	○	○
7.	If a seller-lessee retains substantially all rights to use the property in a sales-leaseback transaction, the gain on sale is deferred by the seller-lessee.	○	○
8.	If a capital lease is modified in such a way that it qualifies as an operating lease, it should be treated as a sales-leaseback transaction.	○	○

		Journal Entries				
Situation	**Leasing Concepts**		**Interest Expense**	**Liability Section of Balance Sheet**	**Communication**	**Research**

Prepare the journal entries necessary in 2010 for each of the following transactions.

1. Dividend declaration on December 15, 2010

2. Capital lease agreement and first lease payment on December 31, 2010

3. Bond issue on July 1, 2010

4. Interest accrual(s) on December 31, 2010

Situation	Leasing Concepts	Journal Entries	Interest Expense	Liability Section of Balance Sheet	Communication	Research

Calculate the total interest expense for 2010.

Interest expense for 2010:	Amount
Interest on capital lease	
Interest on bonds	
Total interest expense	

Situation	Leasing Concepts	Journal Entries	Interest Expense	Liability Section of Balance Sheet	Communication	Research

Complete the following schedule for the liability section of the balance sheet for Villa Watch Company as of December 31, 2010.

Villa Co.
BALANCE SHEET—LIABILITIES SECTION
December 31, 2010

Accounts payable	
Accrued interest payable	
Income taxes payable	
Dividends payable	
Current portion, long-term debt	
Total current liabilities	
Capital lease payable, less $xxx current portion	
Bonds payable	
Deferred tax liability	
Total liabilities	

Situation	Leasing Concepts	Journal Entries	Interest Expense	Liability Section of Balance Sheet	Communication	Research

Villa has the following information regarding contingencies for 2010.

• Contingency information

- Villa has been named a liable party for toxic waste cleanup on its land, and must pay an as-yet-undetermined amount for environmental remediation activities.
- An adjoining landowner, Clear Toothpaste Co., sold its property because of possible toxic contamination of the water supply and resulting potential adverse public reaction toward its product. Clear sued Villa for damages. There is a reasonable possibility that Clear will prevail and be awarded between $250,000 and $600,000.
- As a result of comprehensive risk assessment, Villa has discontinued rockslide insurance for its warehouse, which is located at the base of a mountain. The warehouse has never sustained rockslide damage, and the probability of sustaining future damage is only slight.

Write a brief memo to the CEO of Villa Watch Corporation, explaining how the company should account for each contingency.

REMINDER: Your response will be graded for both technical content and writing skills. Technical content will be evaluated for information that is helpful to the intended reader and clearly relevant to the issue. Writing skills will be evaluated for development, organization, and the appropriate expression of ideas in professional correspondence. Use a standard business memo or letter format with a clear beginning, middle, and end. Do not convey information in the form of a table, bullet point list, or other abbreviated presentation.

To: CEO, Villa Watch Corp.
From: CPA Candidate
Re: Accounting for contingencies

Situation	Leasing Concepts	Journal Entries	Interest Expense	Liability Section of Balance Sheet	Communication	Research

Answer each of the following questions by selecting the authoritative literature from the accounting standards.

1. For how many years must Villa disclose future minimum lease payments?

2. What interest rate is used in calculating the present value of minimum lease payments for the lessee?

3. What are the criteria to determine if a lease is an operating or a capital lease?

MULTIPLE-CHOICE ANSWERS

1. c __ __	13. b __ __	25. b __ __	37. a __ __	49. b __ __
2. c __ __	14. c __ __	26. b __ __	38. c __ __	50. b __ __
3. a __ __	15. d __ __	27. b __ __	39. b __ __	51. b __ __
4. b __ __	16. b __ __	28. c __ __	40. a __ __	52. b __ __
5. b __ __	17. b __ __	29. a __ __	41. b __ __	53. d __ __
6. d __ __	18. b __ __	30. b __ __	42. d __ __	54. a __ __
7. a __ __	19. a __ __	31. a __ __	43. c __ __	55. b __ __
8. a __ __	20. d __ __	32. b __ __	44. a __ __	56. c __ __
9. c __ __	21. b __ __	33. b __ __	45. c __ __	
10. c __ __	22. b __ __	34. d __ __	46. a __ __	1st: __/56 = __%
11. a __ __	23. c __ __	35. b __ __	47. d __ __	2nd: __/56 = __%
12. d __ __	24. c __ __	36. d __ __	48. a __ __	

MULTIPLE-CHOICE ANSWER EXPLANATIONS

E.1.d.(1) Operating Leases: Lessor/Lessee

1. **(c)** In an operating lease, the lessor should recognize rental revenue on a straight-line basis. This means that the lease bonus ($50,000) should be recorded as unearned revenue on 1/1/10, and recognized as rental revenue over the five-year lease term. Therefore, 2010 rental revenue should be $100,000 [$90,000 + ($50,000 ÷ 5)]. The security deposit ($25,000) does not affect rental revenue. Since it is to be refunded to the lessee upon expiration of the lease, it is recorded as a deposit, a long-term liability when received.

2. **(c)** Rental revenue on operating leases should be recognized on a straight-line basis unless another method more reasonably reflects the pattern of use given by the lessor. When the pattern of cash flows under the lease agreement is other than straight-line, this will result in the recording of rent receivable or unearned rent. Wall's total rent revenue [(1/2 × $8,000) + (4 × $12,500) = $54,000] should be recognized on a straight-line basis over the five-year lease term ($54,000 × 1/5 = $10,800). Since cash collected in 2010 is only $4,000 (one-half of $8,000, since the first six months are rent-free), Wall would accrue rent receivable and rental revenue of $6,800 ($10,800 – $4,000) at year-end to bring the rental revenue up to $10,800.

3. **(a)** Net rental income on an operating lease is equal to rental revenue less related expenses, as computed below.

Rental revenue	$50,000
Depreciation expense	(12,000)
Executory costs	(9,000)
Finder's fee ($15,000 ÷ 10)	(1,500)
Net rental income	$27,500

The finder's fee ($15,000) is capitalized as a deferred charge at the inception of the lease and amortized over ten years to match the expense to the revenues it enabled the lessor to earn.

4. **(b)** For an operating lease, rental revenue should be recognized on a straight-line basis unless another method more reasonably reflects the pattern of use given by the lessor. When the pattern of cash flows under the lease agreement is other than straight-line, this will result in the recording of rent receivable or unearned rent. Gee's total rent revenue ($36,000) should be recognized on a straight-line basis over the thirty-six-month lease, resulting in monthly entries debiting **rent receivable** and crediting **rent revenue** for $1,000. Cash collections will result in entries debiting **cash** and crediting **rent receivable** for $500 per month for the first twelve months and $750 per month for the second

twelve months. Therefore, rent receivable at 6/30/10 is $9,000, as indicated by the T-account below.

Rent Receivable			
Accruals (24 × $1,000)	24,000	6,000	Collections (12 × $500)
		9,000	Collections (12 × $750)
6/30/10 Balance	9,000		

An alternative way to analyze this problem if Gee records the entry as the customer pays at the beginning of the month. During Year 1, the entry each month will be

Cash	500	
Rent receivable	500	
Rent revenue		1,000

During Year 2, the entry each month will be

Cash	750	
Rent receivable	250	
Rent revenue		1,000

The Rent receivable account will accrue as follows:

Rent Receivable		
Accruals Year 1	6,000	(500 × 12 mo.)
Accruals Year 2	3,000	(250 × 12 mo.)
6/30/10 Balance	9,000	

5. **(b)** At 1/1/10, Glen would record as a current liability unearned rent of $50,000, and as a long-term liability unearned rent of $150,000. During 2010, the current portion of unearned rent was earned and would be recognized as revenue. At 12/31/10, the portion of the long-term liability representing the second year's rent ($50,000) would be reclassified as current, leaving as a long-term liability the $100,000 representing the last two years' rent.

6. **(d)** Rental revenue on operating leases should be recognized on a straight-line basis unless another method more reasonably reflects the pattern of use given by the lessor. When the pattern of cash flows under the lease agreement is other than straight-line, this will result in the recording of rent receivable or unearned rent. Therefore, even though Graf received only one monthly payment in 2010 (1/48 of the total rent to received over the life of the lease), they would accrue as rent receivable and rent revenue an amount sufficient to increase the rent revenue account to a balance equal to one-fifth of the total cash to be received over the five-year life of the lease.

7. **(a)** The graph presented in the problem can be interpreted as follows:

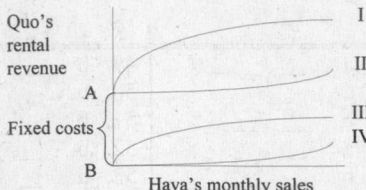

Line AB is considered to be fixed rental costs per month. Therefore, answers (c) and (d) are incorrect because lines III and IV do not include the fixed portion of the rental payment, in its graphical representation. The problem states that as the variable rental amount increases, it does so at a decreasing rate. Answer (b) is incorrect because line II is increasing, but at an increasing rate, not a decreasing rate, as line I represents. Therefore, answer (a) is the correct answer because line I is increasing, at a decreasing rate.

8. (a)   Rent on operating leases should be expensed on a straight-line basis unless another method is better suited to the particular benefits and costs associated with the lease. In this lease, the lessee must pay rent of $1,000 monthly for five years excluding the first nine months, or fifty-one months (60 – 9). Therefore, total rent expense for the five years is $51,000 (51 × $1,000). Recognizing rent expense on a straight-line basis, rent expense for the first year is $10,200 ($51,000 ÷ 5 years).

9. (c)   In an operating lease, the lessee should recognize rent expense on a straight-line basis unless another method is better suited to the particular lease. Therefore, the lease bonus should be recognized as rent expense on a straight-line basis over the ten-year lease term ($24,000 ÷ 10 = $2,400). However, the contingent rentals, which are based on company sales, shall be expensed in the period to which they relate. Therefore, in 2010, contingent rentals of $5,000 [5% × ($600,000 – $500,000)] should be included in rent expense. Total rent expense is $103,400, as computed below.

Base rental	$ 96,000
Lease bonus ($24,000 ÷ 10)	2,400
Cont. rental [5% × ($600,000 – $500,000)]	5,000
	$103,400

10. (c)   For operating leases having noncancelable remaining lease terms of more than one year, the lessee must disclose future minimum lease payments in the aggregate and for each of the five succeeding fiscal years. Since the annual **minimum** lease payments are $100,000, South must disclose subsequent years' lease payments of $100,000 per annum for each of the next five years and $900,000 (nine remaining payments × $100,000) in the aggregate.

11. (a)   To qualify for treatment as a capital lease, a lease must meet one or more of the following criteria:

1. Transfers ownership to lessee.
2. Contains bargain purchase option.
3. Lease term is ≥ 75% of the economic life of the leased asset.
4. Present value of minimum lease payments is ≥ 90% of the FV of the leased asset.

Since the lease signed by Mollat Company does not meet any of these criteria, it must be classified as an operating lease. For operating leases, the lessee's lease payments are recorded as debits to rent expense. Mollat would report rent

expense equal to the 2010 lease payments in its 2010 income statement.

12. (d)   When a leasing agreement is accounted for as an operating lease, the lessor and the lessee recognize rental revenue and rental expense respectively on a straight-line basis unless another systematic and rational basis more clearly reflects the time pattern in which use benefit is given (received) by the respective parties. The straight-lining of uneven lease payments includes scheduled rent increases. Even though the amount of the annual lease payment increases in year six, rental expense would not change. Interest is not an element of revenue (expense) in operating leases.

E.1.d.(1)(e)   Leasehold Improvements

13. (b)   The first month's rent ($60,000) should be expensed in 2010. The prepayment of the last month's rent (also $60,000) should be deferred and recognized as an expense in November 2015. The security deposit ($80,000) should be recorded as a long-term receivable, since Clark can expect to receive the deposit back at lease end. The installation of new walls and offices ($360,000) is recorded as a leasehold improvement at 12/1/10. At 12/31/10, amortization must be recorded for one month ($360,000 × 1/60 = $6,000). Therefore, 2010 expense is $66,000 ($60,000 + $6,000). The journal entries are

Rent expense	60,000	
Prepaid rent	60,000	
Sec. deposit receivable	80,000	
Leasehold improvements	360,000	
Cash		560,000
Amortization expense	6,000	
Leasehold improvements		6,000

14. (c)   Leasehold improvements are capitalized and amortized over the shorter of the remaining life of the lease (six years from 1/1/10 to 12/31/15) or the useful life of the improvements (eight years). Therefore, the $48,000 cost is amortized over six years, resulting in annual amortization of $8,000 ($48,000 ÷ 6). For the period 1/1/10 to 6/30/10, amortization is $4,000 ($8,000 × 6/12), so the 6/30/10 net amount for leasehold improvements is $44,000 ($48,000 – $4,000).

15. (d)   Leasehold improvements are properly capitalized and amortized over the shorter of the remaining life of the lease or the useful life of the improvement. If the lease contains an option to renew and the likelihood of renewal is uncertain (as it is in this case), then the remaining life of the lease is based on the initial lease term. In this case, the remaining life of the lease is therefore ten years. Since the estimated lives of all improvements in this case are greater than or equal to ten years, the appropriate amortization period is ten years. The 2010 amortization is thus computed as the total cost of $140,000 ($47,000 + $75,000 + $18,000 = $140,000), divided by ten years, or $14,000. There is no salvage value for leasehold improvements, because the assets revert to the lessor at the end of the lease term. Note that if the renewal of the lease for an additional ten years were considered a certainty, the amortization periods would be as follows: ten years for the sales office (estimated life); twenty years for the warehouse (lease term); and fifteen years for the parking lot (estimated life).

16. **(b)** The cost of the leasehold improvements ($540,000) should be amortized over the remaining life of the lease, or over the useful life of the improvements, whichever is **shorter**. The remaining life of the lease should include periods covered by a renewal option **if** it is probable that the option will be exercised. In this case, the remaining life of the lease is eighteen years (12 years of original lease + 8 years in option period – 2 years gone by), and the useful life of the improvements is fifteen years. Therefore, amortization is based on a fifteen-year life ($540,000 ÷ 15 = $36,000). The 12/31/10 carrying amount is $504,000 ($540,000 – $36,000).

17. **(b)** A lease should be classified as a capital lease by the lessee if the lease terms meet any one of the following four criteria: (1) the lease transfers ownership of the property to the lessee by the end of the lease term, (2) the lease contains a bargain purchase option, (3) the lease term is greater than or equal to 75% of the economic life of the leased property, or (4) the present value of the minimum lease payments is greater than or equal to 90% of the fair market value of the leased property. In this question, the terms of Vail's lease do not meet any of the four criteria for treatment as a capital lease, so the lease should be accounted for as an operating lease. Vail should therefore **not** recognize the building as an asset. In an operating lease, the lessee should capitalize the cost of the leasehold improvements, recognizing them as assets, and amortize their cost over the shorter of their useful lives or the term of the lease.

18. **(b)** Leasehold improvements are properly capitalized and amortized over the remaining life of the lease, or the useful life of the improvements, whichever is shorter. Since the useful life of the office is only ten years and the remaining term of the lease is fifteen years, the cost should be depreciated over the ten-year period.

E.1.d.(2)   Direct Financing Leases: Lessor

19. **(a)** The annual lease payment is $75,000 ($323,400 ÷ 4.312). After five years, total lease payments will be $375,000 (5 × $75,000). The total interest revenue over the life of the lease is the excess of total lease payments over the fair value of the leased asset ($375,000 – $323,400 = $51,600).

20. **(d)** This lease qualifies as a direct financing lease; therefore interest revenue will be recognized rather than rent revenue. Had the lease qualified as an operating lease, rent revenue would have been recognized. The lessor's criteria for direct financing classification is as follows:

(1) The lease transfers ownership to the lessee, at the end of the lease
(2) The lease contains a bargain purchase option
(3) The lease term is ≥ 75% of an asset's economic life
(4) The present value of the minimum lease payments is ≥ 90% of the fair market value of the leased asset.

Note that the question is silent concerning the two additional criteria that apply to lessors: (1) collectibility of minimum lease payments is predictable, and (2) no important uncertainties exist concerning costs yet to be incurred by the lessee. Recall that if one of the four criteria are met, the lease is treated as a capital lease. In this case, since the lease term is for 80% of the asset's economic life, test (3) is met, and the lease is properly treated as a capital lease. In addition,

the amount of interest revenue will be smaller in 2010 than the revenue in 2009. This result occurs because the present value of the minimum lease payments or carrying value of the obligation decreases each year as lease payments are received. As this occurs, the amount of interest revenue on the outstanding amount of the investment will decrease as well. Over the course of time, the investment reduction portion of each level payment increases and the amount of interest declines.

E.1.d.(3)   Sales-Type Leases: Lessor

21. **(b)** This is a sales-type lease, so at the inception of the lease, the lessor would recognize sales of $3,520,000 and cost of goods sold of $2,800,000, resulting in a **profit on sale of $720,000**. In addition, interest revenue is recognized for the period July 1, 2010, to December 31, 2010. The initial net lease payments receivable on 7/1/10 is $3,520,000. The first rental payment received on 7/1/10 consists entirely of principal, reducing the net receivable to $2,920,000 ($3,520,000 – $600,000). Therefore, 2010 **interest revenue for the six months from 7/1/10 to 12/31/10 is $146,000** ($2,920,000 × 10% × 6/12).

22. **(b)** This is a sales-type lease, so at the inception of the lease, the lessor would recognize sales of $3,300,000 (the PV of the lease payments), and cost of goods sold of $2,800,000, resulting in profit on the sale of $500,000 ($3,300,000 – $2,800,000). Note that the list selling price of an asset ($3,520,000 in this case) is not always representative of its FV. An asset can often be purchased for less than its list price.

23. **(c)** The excess of the fair value of leased property at the inception of the lease over the lessor's cost is defined as the manufacturer's or dealer's profit. Answer (a) is incorrect because the unearned income from a sales-type lease is defined as the difference between the gross investment in the lease and the sum of the present values of the components of the gross investment. Answer (b) is incorrect because the unearned income from a direct-financing lease is defined as the excess of the gross investment over the cost (also the PV of lease payments) of the leased property. Answer (d) is incorrect because a sales-type lease involves a manufacturer's or dealer's profit while a direct financing lease does not.

24. **(c)** Revenue is to be recognized for a sales-type lease over the lease term so as to produce a **constant rate** of return on the net investment in the lease. This requires the use of the **interest method**. Interest revenue **does** arise in a sales-type lease. Answer (a) is incorrect because the interest is to be earned over the life of the lease, not in full at the lease's inception.

E.1.d.(4)   Capital Leases: Lessee

25. **(b)** If **any** of the criteria for classification as a capital lease are met, the lease is classified as such. One of the capital lease criterion is that the lease term is equal to 75% or more of the estimated economic life of the leased property. Thus, both leases M and P should be classified as capital leases.

26. **(b)** This is a capital lease for the lessee because the lease term is 75% of the useful life of the machine [6 years = (75% × 8 years)]. For a capital lease, the lessee records as a

leased asset and a **lease obligation** the lower of the PV of the minimum lease payments or the FV of the leased asset (not given in this problem). The PV of the minimum lease payments is computed using the lower of the lessee's incremental borrowing rate (15%) or the implicit rate used by the lessor if known by the lessee (12%). Since the implicit rate is lower, and known by the lessee, it is used to compute the PV ($50,000 × 4.61 = $230,500). The cost of the asset on the lessor's books ($375,500) is irrelevant.

27. **(b)** This is a capital lease since the lease term (ten years) is the same as the useful life of the leased asset. In a capital lease, the lessee records an asset and a liability based on the PV of the minimum lease payments. The minimum lease payments includes rentals and a guaranteed residual value, **if guaranteed by the lessee**. In this case the minimum lease payments include only the rentals, since the residual value is guaranteed by a third party. The minimum lease payments are discounted using the **lower** of the lessee's incremental borrowing rate or the implicit rate used by the lessor, if known. In this case, the lessee knows the implicit rate is 10%, which is lower than the incremental borrowing rate of 12%. Thus, the present value or principal amount of the lease obligation is $61,446 ($10,000 × 6.1446) through the first year. Although accrued interest would be recognized at 10/31/10, the principal amount does not change until 1/1/11.

28. **(c)** The lessee records a capital lease at the present value of the minimum lease payments. The minimum lease payments includes rental payments and bargain purchase options (among other items). The $10,000 purchase option is a **bargain** purchase option because it allows the lessor to purchase the leased asset at an amount **less** than its expected fair value. The lessee computes the present value using its incremental borrowing rate (14%), unless the lessor's implicit rate (12%) is lower and is known by the lessee. This question indicates that the implicit rate is stated in the lease; therefore it would be known to the lessee. At the beginning of the lease term, Robbins should record a leased asset and lease liability at $66,500.

PV of rentals	($10,000 × 6.328)	=	$63,280
PV of BPO	($10,000 × .322)	=	3,220
PV at 12%			$66,500

29. **(a)** The annual executory costs (real estate taxes of $2,000) are **not** an expense or liability until incurred; therefore they are excluded from the minimum lease payments and are **not** reflected in the initial lease liability. The 12/31/10 capital lease liability is recorded at the PV of the minimum lease payments [5.6 × ($52,000 − $2,000) = $280,000].

30. **(b)** The requirement is to determine the amount to be recorded as a capitalized leased asset. This is a capital lease for the lessee because the lease term exceeds 75% of the economic life of the leased asset (10/12 > 75%). In a capital lease, the lessee records as an asset and liability the present value (PV) of the minimum lease payments (unless the PV exceeds the asset's FV, in which case the FV is recorded). The minimum lease payments include rentals, and a lessee-guaranteed residual value or a bargain purchase option. Only rentals apply in this case. Note that the $50,000 purchase option is not a **bargain** purchase option that the lessee would be compelled to exercise. A bargain purchase option is an option to purchase the leased asset at

an amount **less** than its expected fair value. Therefore, the present value of the minimum lease payments is $238,000 ($40,000 × 5.95).

31. **(a)** The initial lease liability at 1/1/10, before the 1/1/10 payment, is the present value of the five rental payments (an **annuity due** since the first payment is made on 1/1/10) plus the present value of the guaranteed residual value. The computation is below.

PV of rentals ($13,000 × 4.240)	$55,120
PV of residual ($10,000 × 0.650)	6,500
Initial liability	$61,620

The 1/1/10 payment consists entirely of principal, bringing the 1/1/10 liability down to $48,620 ($61,620 − $13,000).

32. **(b)** The initial lease obligation at 12/30/10 was $135,000. The first lease payment was made the same day, and therefore consisted entirely of principal reduction. After the payment, the lease obligation was $115,000 ($135,000 − $20,000). This balance will be reported as current (for the portion to be paid in 2011) and long-term (for the portion to be paid beyond 2011). The next lease payment of $20,000 will be paid 12/31/11, and will consist of both interest ($115,000 × 10% = $11,500) and principal reduction ($20,000 − $11,500 = $8,500). Thus, the portion of the $115,000 lease obligation to be paid in the next year (and therefore reported as a current liability) is $8,500. Note that the interest to be paid next year ($11,500) is not a liability at 12/31/10 because it has not yet been incurred.

33. **(b)** This is a capital lease for the lessee because the lease term (nine years) exceeds 75% of the useful life of the machine (also nine years). For a capital lease, the lessee records as a **leased asset** and a **lease obligation** at the lower of the PV of the minimum lease payments or the FV of the leased asset (not given in this problem). The PV of the minimum lease payments is computed using the lower of the lessee's incremental borrowing rate (12%) or the implicit rate used by the lessor if known by the lessee (10%). Since the implicit rate is lower, and known by the lessee, it is used to compute the PV ($316,500). The initial lease payment ($50,000) is entirely principal because it was made at the inception of the lease. Therefore, after the 12/31/10 payment, the lease liability is $266,500 ($316,500 − $50,000). The 12/31/11 payment consists of interest incurred during 2011 ($266,500 × 10% = $26,650) and principal reduction ($50,000 − $26,650 = $23,350). Therefore, the 12/31/11 capital lease liability is $243,150 ($266,500 − $23,350).

34. **(d)** The initial lease liability at 12/31/10 is $417,000 (the PV of the minimum lease payments). The annual executory costs ($5,000) are **not** an expense or liability until incurred; therefore, they are excluded from the minimum lease payments and are **not** reflected in the initial lease liability. The 12/31/10 payment of $105,000 includes $5,000 of executory costs; the remainder ($100,000) is entirely principal since the payment was made at the inception of the lease. Therefore, after the 12/31/10 payment, the lease liability is $317,000 ($417,000 − $100,000). The 12/31/11 payment consists of executory costs ($5,000), interest incurred during 2010 ($317,000 × 10% = $31,700), and reduction of principal ($105,000 − $5,000 − $31,700 = $68,300). Therefore, the 12/31/11 balance sheet should include a lease liability of $248,700 ($317,000 − $68,300).

35.   (b)   On 1/2/11, Mene made a lease payment of $9,000, which included payment of the current portion of the lease obligation ($1,364) and interest ($9,000 – $1,364 = $7,636). After this payment, the total lease obligation was $75,000. The 1/2/12 payment would include interest of $7,500 ($75,000 × 10%), and principal of $1,500 ($9,000 – $7,500). This $1,500 amount would represent the current portion of the lease obligation at 12/31/11, so the long-term lease obligation net of the current portion at 12/31/11 is $73,500 ($75,000 – $1,500).

36.   (d)   If a lease is classified as a capital lease, the lessee must record an asset and a liability, each for an amount equal to the present value of the minimum lease payments at the beginning of the lease.

37.   (a)   At the inception of a capital lease, the lessee must record an asset and a liability based on the PV of the minimum lease payments. The minimum lease payments are the payments that lessee is required to make in connection with the leased property, including rent payments, bargain purchase option, and guaranteed residual value. Minimum lease payments (MLP) are recorded at present value. The whole guaranteed residual value is included in MLP.

38.   (c)   In a capital lease where the first annual lease payment is made immediately upon signing the lease (annuity due), the first payment consists solely of lease liability reduction, since no time has transpired during which interest expense could be incurred. Subsequent payments include both interest expense and reduction of the liability.

39.   (b)   Each minimum lease payment shall be allocated between a reduction of the obligation and interest expense so as to produce a constant periodic rate of interest on the remaining balance of the obligation. Since the interest will be computed based upon a **declining** obligation balance, the interest component of each payment will also be declining. The result will be a relatively larger portion of the minimum lease payment allocated to the reduction of the lease obligation in the latter portion of the lease term.

40.   (a)   When a leasing agreement is accounted for as capital lease, the lessee recognizes a liability on its books equal to the present value of the minimum lease payments. The liability should be divided between current and noncurrent based upon when each lease payment is due. At the end of year one, the current lease liability should equal the principal portion of the lease payment due in year two. Therefore, when the lease payment is made in year two, the reduction of the lease liability will equal the current liability shown at the end of year one.

41.   (b)   This is a capital lease since title passes to Cole, the lessee, at the end of the lease. At the inception of the lease on 1/2/10, the lessee records the PV of the lease payments ($108,000) as an asset and a liability. The asset is depreciated on a straight-line basis over its useful life of twelve years, resulting in a yearly depreciation charge of $9,000 ($108,000 ÷ 12). The asset is depreciated over its useful life rather than over the lease term (eight years) because title transfers to the lessee, allowing the lessee to use the asset for twelve years.

42.   (d)   A leased asset acquired in a capital lease should be depreciated over the period of time the lessee expects to use the asset (either the lease term or the useful life, de-

pending on the situation). In this case, Nori expects to use the leased asset for its entire eight-year useful life, due to the expected exercise of the bargain purchase option at the end of the five-year lease term. Therefore, Nori's 2010 depreciation expense is $27,500

$$\frac{(\$240,000 \text{ cost}) - (\$20,000 \text{ salvage})}{8 \text{ years}} = \$27,500$$

43.   (c)   The requirement is to determine whether a lessee should amortize the capitalizable cost of a leased asset in a manner consistent with the lessee's normal depreciation policy for owned assets for leases that contained a bargain purchase option and/or transferred ownership at the end of the lease term. Transfer of ownership of the property to the lessee by the end of the lease term and a lease that contains a bargain purchase option are properly classified as capital leases. If the lease meets either of the above criteria, the asset shall be amortized in a manner consistent with the lessee's normal depreciation policy for owned assets.

44.   (a)   At the inception of the lease on 1/1/10, the capitalized liability is $379,000 (the present value of the lease payments). Since the first payment is not due until the **end** of the first year, 2010 interest expense is based on the full initial liability ($379,000 × 10% = $37,900).

45.   (c)   The future minimum lease payments (MLP) for each of the next five years and the aggregate amount of MLP for the lease term must be disclosed. At 12/31/11, eight annual payments of $100,000 each have not yet been paid. Therefore, future MLP are $800,000 (8 × $100,000). The amount for the appropriate required period (five years) is $500,000 ($100,000 per year for 5 years).

46.   (a)   At the end of the lease, the balance in the lease payable column should equal the bargain purchase option price. Failure to include the present value of the bargain purchase option price in the beginning present value of the lease would result in an ending balance in the lease payable column of zero. Both answers (b) and (c) would have resulted in an ending balance of less than zero, while answer (d) would have resulted in an ending balance greater than zero.

E.2.b.   Sale-Leaseback

47.   (d)   Sale-leaseback arrangements are treated as though two transactions were a single financing transaction, if the lease qualifies as a capital lease. Any gain or loss on the sale is deferred and amortized over the lease term (if possession reverts to the lessor) or the economic life (if ownership transfers to the lessee). In this case, the lease qualifies as a capital lease because the lease term (twelve years) is 80% of the remaining economic life of the leased property (fifteen years). Therefore, at 12/31/10, all of gain ($480,000 – $360,000 = $120,000) would be deferred and amortized over twelve years. Since the sale took place on 12/31/10, there is no amortization for 2010.

48.   (a)   A sale-leaseback is generally treated as a single financing transaction in which any profit on the sale is deferred and amortized by the seller. However, there is an exception to this general rule when either **only a minor part** of the remaining use of the leased asset is retained (case one) or when **more than a minor part but less than substantially all** of the remaining use of the leased asset is retained (case two). Case one occurs when the PV of the lease payments is 10% or less of the FV of the sale-leaseback property. Case two occurs when the leaseback is more than minor but does **not** meet the criteria of a capital lease. This problem is an example of case one, because the PV of the lease payments ($36,900) is less than 10% of the FV of the asset (10% × $400,000 = $40,000). Under these circumstances, the full gain ($400,000 – $300,000 = $100,000) is recognized, and **none is deferred**.

49.   (b)   A sale-leaseback is generally treated as a single financing transaction in which any profit on the sale is deferred and amortized by the seller. However, there is an exception to this general rule when either **only a minor part** of the remaining use of the leased asset is retained (case one) or when **more than a minor part but less than substantially all** of the remaining use of the leased asset is retained (case two). Case one occurs when the PV of the lease payments is 10% or less of the FV of the sale-leaseback property. Case two occurs when the leaseback is more than minor but does **not** meet the criteria of a capital lease. This is an example of case two because while the PV of the lease payments ($190,581) is more than 10% of the FV of the asset ($600,000), the lease falls into the operating lease category. Under these circumstances, the gain on sale ($600,000 – $100,000 = $500,000) is recognized to the extent that it exceeds the PV of the lease payments ($190,581). The gain reported would be $309,419 ($500,000 – $190,581). The portion of the gain represented by the $190,581 PV of the lease payments is deferred and amortized on a straight-line basis over the life of the lease.

50.   (b)   On a sale-leaseback, generally **losses** are recognized immediately. However, there can be two types of losses in sale-leasebacks. The type that is **recognized immediately** is a **real economic loss,** where the carrying amount of the asset is higher than its FV. The type that is **deferred** is an **artificial loss** where the sale price ($430,000) is below the carrying amount ($450,000), but the FV ($465,000) is above the carrying amount ($450,000). The loss in this problem ($450,000 – $430,000 = $20,000) is an artificial loss that must be deferred.

51.   (b)   Sale-leaseback transactions are treated as though two transactions were a single financing transaction, if the lease qualifies as a capital lease. Any gain on the sale is deferred and amortized over the lease term (if possession reverts to the lessor) or the economic life (if ownership transfers to the lessee); both are ten years in this case. Since this is a capital lease, the entire gain ($150,000 – $100,000 = $50,000) is deferred at 1/1/10. At 12/31/10, an adjusting entry must be prepared to amortize 1/10 of the unearned gain (1/10 × $50,000 = $5,000), because the lease covers ten years. Therefore, the unearned gain at 12/31/10 is $45,000 ($50,000 – $5,000).

52.   (b)   Any profit related to a sale-leaseback transaction in which the seller-lessee retains the property leased (i.e., the seller-lessee retains substantially all of the benefits and risks of the ownership of the property sold), shall be deferred and amortized in proportion to the amortization of the leased asset, if a capital lease. If it is an operating lease, the profit will be deferred in proportion to the related gross rental charged to expense over the lease term. It is important to note that **losses,** however, are recognized immediately for either a capital or operating lease. Since the gain on the sale

should be deferred in either case, no gain is recognized at the time of the sale.

NOTE: An example of an operating lease in which substantially all of the remaining use of the leased asset is retained by the lessee occurs when the lease term begins within the last 25% of the asset's original useful life.

53.   (d)   In a sale-leaseback transaction, if the leaseback is recorded as a capital lease and the lessee has retained **substantially all** of the rights to use the property, then any gain on the sale must be deferred and amortized over the life of the property in proportion to the amortization of the leased asset. This deferred gain acts as an asset valuation allowance resulting in the net amount shown for the leased asset being equal to the same carrying value as if the sale and leaseback transaction had not occurred.

54.   (a)   A termination of an operating lease requires that the fair value of the termination costs be recognized as an expense or loss in calculating income from continuing operations in the year the lease was terminated.

55.   (b)   A modification to a capital lease that changes the classification of the lease to an operating lease requires the transaction be accounted for as a sales-leaseback transaction. Since Hopper retains substantially all rights to use the property (and the property is not within the last 25% of its useful life), the gain will be deferred and recognized over the remaining lease term.

56.   (c)   A loss on a capital lease termination is recognized immediately as a loss from continuing operations.

SOLUTIONS TO SIMULATION PROBLEMS

Simulation Problem 1

Situation	Journal Entries	Concepts	Classification	Communication	Research

	Debits	Credits
1. January 2, 2010—to record lease:		
Equipment	850,000	
Capital lease liability		850,000
2. December 31, 2010—to record payment:		
Capital lease liability	100,000	
Cash		100,000
3. December 31, 2010—to record depreciation:		
Depreciation expense	34,000	
Accumulated depreciation		34,000
Interest expense	85,000	
Capital lease liability		85,000

Explanation of solutions

1. This problem requires preparation of the lessee's journal entries for the first year of a lease. The lease is a capital lease because title passes to the lessee at the end of the lease and the lease term (twenty years) is greater than 75% of the useful life (twenty-five years).

2. In a capital lease, the lessee records a **leased asset** and a **lease obligation** at the present value of the minimum lease payments. The lessee's incremental borrowing rate (12%) should be used to determine the present value unless the lessor's implicit rate is lower and is known by the lessee. The lessor's 10% rate is lower and is known by the lessee, so it is used to compute the PV of $850,000 ($100,000 × 8.5).

3. The first lease payment on 12/31/10 consists of interest expense incurred during 2010 ($850,000 × 10% = $85,000) and reduction of lease obligation ($100,000 payment – $85,000 interest = $15,000). The $100,000 credit to cash is offset by debits to interest expense ($85,000) and lease obligation ($15,000).

The only other expense related to this lease is depreciation of the leased asset. Leased assets are depreciated over the lease term (twenty years) unless the lease transfers ownership (as this one does) or contains a bargain purchase option. If either of these is present, then the asset is depreciated over the estimated useful life of the asset (twenty-five years). Depreciation expense is cost ($850,000) divided by useful life ($850,000 ÷ 25 years = $34,000). If a salvage value had been given, it would be subtracted from cost before dividing by useful life.

Situation	Journal Entries	Concepts	Classification	Communication	Research

	(A)	(B)	(C)	(D)	(E)	(F)	(G)	(H)	(I)	(J)	(K)	(L)	(M)	(N)	(O)	(P)	(Q)
1. Sales-type lease	○	○	○	●	○	○	○	○	○	○	○	○	○	○	○	○	○
2. Direct financing lease	○	○	○	○	○	○	○	○	●	○	○	○	○	○	○	○	○
3. Operating lease—lessee	○	●	○	○	○	○	○	○	○	○	○	○	○	○	○	○	○
4. Operating lease—lessor	○	○	○	○	●	○	○	○	○	○	○	○	○	○	○	○	○
5. Unearned interest revenue	○	○	○	○	○	○	●	○	○	○	○	○	○	○	○	○	○
6. Residual value	○	○	○	○	○	○	○	●	○	○	○	○	○	○	○	○	○
7. Capital lease	○	○	●	○	○	○	○	○	○	○	○	○	○	○	○	○	○
8. Implicit rate	○	○	○	○	○	○	○	○	○	○	○	○	○	●	○	○	○
9. Interest method	○	○	○	○	○	○	○	○	○	○	○	●	○	○	○	○	○
10. Present value of the minimum lease payments	○	○	○	○	○	○	○	○	○	○	○	●	○	○	○	○	○
11. Bargain purchase option	○	○	○	○	○	○	○	○	○	○	○	○	○	○	●	○	○
12. Sale-leaseback	●	○	○	○	○	○	○	○	○	○	○	○	○	○	○	○	○
13. Annuity due	○	○	○	○	○	○	○	○	○	○	○	○	○	○	○	○	●
14. Initial direct costs	○	○	○	○	○	○	○	○	○	○	○	○	○	○	○	●	○
15. Current lease obligation	○	○	○	○	○	○	○	○	○	○	○	○	●	○	○	○	○

Situation	Journal Entries	Concepts	Classification	Communication	Research

1. Nesbitt rents equipment for three years for $20,000 per year. The equipment is valued at $200,000. At the end of the rental term the equipment must be returned to the dealer.

   Operating lease. Does not meet any of the four criteria.

2. Nesbitt rents equipment for five years for $80,000 per year. At the end of the rental term Nesbitt can purchase the equipment for $500. At the date the contract was signed the equipment had a value of $300,000. At the end of five years, it is expected the equipment will have a value of $42,000.

   Capital lease. The lease has a bargain purchase option.

3. Nesbitt received six months of free rent on an office building it was leasing for two years. Rent is normally $1,500 per month.

   Operating lease. The building is only leased for two years, and it is doubtful that it is greater than 75% of the building's economic life.

4. Nesbitt rents equipment for eight years. The present value of the lease payments are $80,000. The market value of the equipment is $90,000 and the useful life of the equipment is ten years.

   Capital lease. The present value of the lease payments is not greater than 90% of the fair market value of the leased asset; however, the rental term is 80%, which is greater than 75% of the economic life of the asset.

5. Nesbitt rents equipment for ten years. At the end of the lease Nesbitt receives title to the equipment.

   Capital lease. Transfer of title.

6. Nesbitt rents equipment for seven years. The life of the equipment is ten years. The fair value of the equipment is $100,000. The present value of the minimum lease payments is $85,000.

   Operating lease. The lease is not greater than 75% of the economic life of the asset, and the present value of the minimum lease payments is not greater than 90% of the fair market value of the asset.

Situation	Journal Entries	Concepts	Classification	Communication	Research

To: CEO, Nesbitt Co.
From: CPA Candidate
Re: Sales-Leaseback Transaction

This letter is in response to your questions regarding sales-leaseback transactions. A sales-leaseback transaction is a transaction wherein a company sells an asset and immediately leases it back. Nesbitt should account for the sale portion of the sale-leaseback transaction by increasing cash for the sale price, decreasing property, plant, and equipment for the building's carrying amount, and recording a deferred gain for the excess of the sale price over the building's carrying amount. This accounting is appropriate because Nesbitt still retains substantial ownership rights and obligations pertaining to the building. Since no earning process occurred, this sale-leaseback is not in substance a sale but a financing transaction. Therefore, the gain should be deferred.

The leased building is included on Nesbitt's December 31, 2010 balance sheet as leased property at its discounted present value on December 31, 2010, less accumulated depreciation, and less unamortized deferred gain on the sale. Its discounted present value at December 31, 2010, represents the future lease payments, discounted at Nesbitt's current borrowing rate.

The lease obligation on Nesbitt's December 31, 2011 balance sheet equals the building's December 31, 2010 present value less principal repaid in 2011. An amount equal to the principal to be repaid in 2012 should be reported as a current liability. The balance of the obligation should be reported as a noncurrent liability.

If you have any additional questions, please contact me.

Situation	Journal Entries	Concepts	Classification	Communication	Research

1. How is a liability related to a capital lease disclosed in the balance sheet of the lessee?

FAS13, Para 13

13. Assets recorded under capital leases and the accumulated amortization thereon shall be separately identified in the lessee's balance sheet or in footnotes thereto. Likewise, the related obligations shall be separately identified in the balance sheet as obligations under capital leases and shall be subject to the same considerations as other obligations in classifying them with current and noncurrent liabilities in classified balance sheets. Unless the charge to income resulting from amortization of assets recorded under capital leases is included with depreciation expense and the fact that it is so included is disclosed, the amortization charge shall be separately disclosed in the financial statements or footnotes thereto.

Codification: 840-30-45-2

2. How does the lessee value the liability for termination costs to cancel an operating lease?

FAS146, Para 16

16. A liability for costs that will continue to be incurred under a contract for its remaining term without economic benefit to the entity shall be recognized and measured at its fair value when the entity ceases using the right conveyed by the contract, for example, the right to use a leased property or to receive future goods or services (hereinafter referred to as the cease-use date). If the contract is an operating lease, the fair value of the liability at the cease-use date shall be determined based on the remaining lease rentals, reduced by estimated sublease rentals that could be reasonably obtained for the property, even if the entity does not intend to enter into a sublease. Remaining lease rentals shall not be reduced to an amount less than zero. The provisions of paragraph 6 shall apply in periods subsequent to the cease-use date. (Example 4 of Appendix A illustrates that situation.).

Codification: 420-10-30-8

3. What items are included in calculating the minimum lease payment for the lessee?

FAS13, Para 5(j)

j.   *Minimum lease payments.*

   i.   From the standpoint of the lessee: The payments that the lessee is obligated to make or can be required to make in connection with the lease property. However, a guarantee by the lessee of the lessor's debt and the lessee's obligation to pay (apart from the rental payments) executory costs such as insurance, maintenance, and taxes in connection with the lease property shall be excluded. If the lease contains a bargain purchase option, only the minimum rental payments over the lease term [as defined in paragraph 5(f)] and the payment called for by the bargain purchase option shall be included in the minimum lease payments. Otherwise, minimum lease payments include the following:

   (a)   The minimum rental payments called for by the lease over the lease term.

   (b)   Any guarantee by the lessee of the residual value at the expiration of the lease term, whether or not payment of the guarantee constitutes a purchase of the leased property. When the lessor has the right to require the lessee to purchase the property at termination of the lease for a certain or determinable amount, that amount shall be considered a lessee guarantee. When the lessee agrees to make up any deficiency below a stated amount in the lessor's realization of the residual value, the guarantee to be included in the minimum lease payments shall be the stated amount, rather than an estimate of the deficiency to be made up.

(c) Any payment that the lessee must make or can be required to make upon failure to renew or extend the lease at the expiration of the lease term, whether or not the payment would constitute a purchase of the lease property. In this connection, it should be noted that the definition of lease term in paragraph 5(f) includes "all periods, if any, for which failure to renew the lease imposes a penalty on the lessee in an amount such that renewal appears, at the inception of the lease, to be reasonably assured." If the lease term has been extended because of that provision, the related penalty shall not be included in minimum lease payments.

ii. From the standpoint of the lessor: The payments described in (i) above plus any guarantee of the residual value or of rental payments beyond the lease term by a third party unrelated to either the lessee or the lessor, provided the third party is financially capable of discharging the obligations that may arise from the guarantee.

Codification: 840-10-25-6

Simulation Problem 2

Situation	Valuation of Lease	Journal Entries	Amortization Schedule	Financial Statement Disclosures	Communication	Research

Calculate the lease liability and the value of the leased asset at the time the lease is signed.

PVA due ($70,000) at 6% for 10 periods + PV ($10,000) at 6% for 10 periods
7.80169 ($70,000) + .55839 ($10,000)
$551,702

Situation	Valuation of Lease	Journal Entries	Amortization Schedule	Financial Statement Disclosures	Communication	Research

Prepare the journal entry or journal entries to record the lease transactions on December 30, 2010.

Leased asset	551,702	
Obligation under capital lease		551,702
Obligation under capital lease	70,000	
Cash		70,000

Situation	Valuation of Lease	Journal Entries	Amortization Schedule	Financial Statement Disclosures	Communication	Research

Prepare an amortization table for the lease through December 30, 2013.

Year ending	Interest expense	Lease payment	Amounts applied to carrying value	Carrying value of lease
At signing of note	Not applicable	Not applicable	Not applicable	$551,702
December 30, 2010	$ 0	$70,000	$ 0	481,702
December 30, 2011	28,902	70,000	41,098	440,604
December 30, 2012	26,436	70,000	43,564	397,040
December 30, 2013	23,822	70,000	46,178	350,863

Situation	Valuation of Lease	Journal Entries	Amortization Schedule	Financial Statement Disclosures	Communication	Research

Interest expense for 2011	28,902
Interest expense for 2012	26,436
Carrying value of lease on 12/31/12	397,040
Depreciation expense for 2011	45,975

Explanation of solutions

Interest expense recognized in 2011

$28,902 (6% × $481,702)

Interest expense recognized in 2012

$26,436 (6% × $440,604)

Carrying value of the lease on December 31, 2012

$397,040 (See table)

Depreciation expense for 2011

$551,702 / 12 years = $45,975

The leased asset is depreciated over the asset's life because there is a bargain purchase option.

Situation	Valuation of Lease	Journal Entries	Amortization Schedule	Financial Statement Disclosures	Communication		Research

To: Mr. George Timms
          Chief Executive Officer
          Kelty Corporation
From: CPA Candidate
Re: Options for acquisition of equipment
Date: [*today's date*]

This memorandum summarizes our views regarding the financial implications of the alternative methods of acquiring the equipment. As we discussed, you are considering the following three options.

Capital Lease

The total cash payments under the capital lease option ($70,000 annual payments for ten years plus a $10,000 bargain purchase option) is $710,000. In absolute dollars, this appears to be a greater amount than the $600,000 for outright purchase of the equipment. However, after taking into consideration the time value of money at 6%, the present value of the lease payments and the bargain purchase option is only $551,720. At the end of the lease term, Kelty will own the equipment. Since this is a capital lease, the obligation must be recorded. Increasing the level of debt will increase the firm's debt ratio.

Purchase

Although Kelty would receive title to the equipment immediately, Kelty must spend $600,000 cash today to purchase the equipment. If Kelty uses existing cash, this option would decrease the firm's liquidity. If the funds are borrowed, it will increase the firm's debt ratio.

Five-Year Rental Contract

The five-year rental contract would qualify for operating lease treatment, meaning that Kelty would not record a liability on the balance sheet. Kelty would recognize rent expense of $100,000 per year. However, the rental payments are significantly higher than the annual lease payments. Ignoring present value considerations, the total cash outflow would be $500,000 over five years. This cash overflow is a significant payment for equipment that the company would not own, as there is no option to purchase the equipment at the end of the rental period.

Conclusions and Recommendations

The operating lease is the most costly alternative. Due to the high rental payments, the company should avoid the operating lease, unless there are extenuating circumstances that preclude the company from acquiring the equipment outright or entering into the ten-year lease agreement.

If Kelty purchases the equipment, it will have a significant cash outflow immediately or an increase in long-term debt to finance the acquisition. While the lease will also result in a liability, the liability is only $551,702, the present value of the future lease payments.

Considering the time value of money, leasing the equipment for ten years with the option to buy appears to be the most economical alternative.

If you have any questions regarding my recommendations, please contact me.

Situation	Valuation of Lease	Journal Entries	Amortization Schedule	Financial Statement Disclosures	Communication	Research

1. How should Kelty calculate the amount to record the lease liability on December 30, 2010?

FAS13, Para 10

10. The lessee shall record a capital lease as an asset and an obligation at an amount equal to the present value at the beginning of the lease term of minimum lease payments during the lease term, excluding that portion of the payments representing executory costs such as insurance, maintenance, and taxes to be paid by the lessor, together with any profit thereon. However, if the amount so determined exceeds the fair value of the leased property at the inception of the lease, the amount recorded as the asset and obligation shall be the fair value. If the portion of the minimum lease payments representing executory costs, including profit thereon, is not determinable from the provisions of the lease, an estimate of the amount shall be made. The discount rate to be used in determining present value of the minimum lease payments shall be that prescribed for the lessee in paragraph 7(d). (See Appendix C for illustrations.)

Codification: 840-30-30-1 and *840-30-30-2*

2. How should Kelty calculate amortization expense on the leased equipment?

FAS13, Para 11

11. Except as provided in paragraphs 25 and 26 with respect to leases involving land, the asset recorded under a capital lease shall be amortized as follows:

     a.   If the lease meets the criterion of either paragraph 7(a) or 7(b), the asset shall be amortized in a manner consistent with the lessee's normal depreciation policy for owned assets.

     b.   If the lease does not meet either criterion 7(a) or 7(b), the asset shall be amortized in a manner consistent with the lessee's normal depreciation policy except that the period of amortization shall be the lease term. The asset shall be amortized to its expected value, if any, to the lessee at the end of the lease term. As an example, if the lessee guarantees a residual value at the end of the lease term and has no interest in any excess which might be realized, the expected value of the leased property to him is the amount that can be realized from it up to the amount of the guarantee.

Codification: 840-30-35-1

FAS13, Para 7

7. The criteria for classifying leases set forth in this paragraph and in paragraph 8 derive from the concept set forth in paragraph 60. If at its inception [as defined in paragraph 5(b)] a lease meets one or more of the following four criteria, the lease shall be classified as a capital lease by the lessee. Otherwise, it shall be classified as an operating lease. (See Appendix C for an illustration of the application of these criteria.)

     a.   The lease transfers ownership of the property to the lessee by the end of the lease term [as defined in paragraph 5(f)].

     b.   The lease contains a bargain purchase option [as defined in paragraph 5(d)].

     c.   The lease term [as defined in paragraph 5(f)] is equal to 75% or more of the estimated economic life of the leased property [as defined in paragraph 5(g)]. However, if the beginning of the lease term falls within the last 25% of the total estimated economic life of the leased property, including earlier years of use, this criterion shall not be used for purposes of classifying the lease.

d. The present value at the beginning of the lease term of the minimum lease payments [as defined in paragraph 5(j)], excluding that portion of the payments representing executory costs such as insurance, maintenance, and taxes to be paid by the lessor, including any profit thereon, equals or exceeds 90% of the excess of the fair value of the leased property [as defined in paragraph 5(c)] to the lessor at the inception of the lease over any related investment tax credit retained by the lessor and expected to be realized by him. However, if the beginning of the lease term falls within the last 25% of the total estimated economic life of the leased property, including earlier years of use, this criterion shall not be used for purposes of classifying the lease. A lessor shall compute the present value of the minimum lease payments using the interest rate implicit in the lease [as defined in paragraph 5(k)]. A lessee shall compute the present value of the minimum lease payments using his incremental borrowing rate [as defined in paragraph 5(l)], unless (i) it is practicable for him to learn the implicit rate computed by the lessor and (ii) the implicit rate computed by the lessor is less than the lessee's incremental borrowing rate. If both of those conditions are met, the lessee shall use the implicit rate.

Codification: 840-10-25-1

Simulation Problem 3

Situation	Leasing Concepts	Journal Entries	Interest Expense	Liability Section of Balance Sheet	Communication	Research

		True	*False*
1.	Free or uneven lease payments should be recognized by the lessor when the lease payment is received.	○	●
2.	Initial direct costs are expensed by the lessor when the lease is signed.	○	●
3.	A refundable security deposit is treated as an asset by the lessor.	○	●
4.	Leasehold improvements should be amortized over the longer of the remaining lease term or the useful life of the asset.	○	●
5.	The minimum lease payment includes any penalty for failure to renew.	●	○
6.	The unguaranteed residual value is considered part of the minimum lease payment for the lessee's liability.	○	●
7.	If a seller-lessee retains substantially all rights to use the property in a sales-leaseback transaction, the gain on sale is deferred by the seller-lessee.	●	○
8.	If a capital lease is modified in such a way that it qualifies as an operating lease, it should be treated as a sales-leaseback transaction.	●	○

Explanation of solutions

1. (F) Free or uneven lease payments received by the lessor should be recognized as revenue on a straight-line basis and prorated over the life of the lease.

2. (F) Initial direct costs should be capitalized and amortized straight-line over the life of the lease.

3. (F) A refundable security deposit is a liability to the lessor and a receivable to the lessee.

4. (F) Leasehold improvements should be amortized over the longer of the remaining lease term or the useful life of the asset.

5. (T) The minimum lease payment includes any penalty.

6. (F) The unguaranteed residual is considered part of the lessor's net investment in lease unless there is a transfer of title or a bargain purchase option. The unguaranteed residual is not part of the minimum lease payment for the lessee; it is ignored.

7. **(T)** Gain is deferred in these situations.

8. **(T)** Sales-leaseback treatment is appropriate.

Situation	Leasing Concepts	Journal Entries	Interest Expense	Liability Section of Balance Sheet	Communication	Research

1. December 15, 2010

Dividends or retained earnings		50,000		
Dividend payable				50,000

2. December 31, 2010

Leased asset		480,000		
Obligation under capital lease				480,000
Lease obligation		100,000		
Cash				100,000

3. July 1, 2010

Cash		440,000		
Discounts on bonds payable		60,000		
Bonds payable				500,000

4. Interest expense

Interest expense (440,000 × 10% × 6/12)		22,000		
Discount on bonds payable				2,000
Interest payable (4% × $500,000)				20,000

(Interest expense is only needed for the bond because the capital lease was signed on December 31, 2010, and no interest has accrued on the lease for 2010.)

Situation	Leasing Concepts	Journal Entries	Interest Expense	Liability Section of Balance Sheet	Communication	Research

	Amount
Interest expense for 2010:	
Interest on capital lease	0
Interest on bonds	22,000
Total interest expense	22,000

Note there is no interest on the capital lease for 2010 because the lease was signed on December 31, 2010.

Situation	Leasing Concepts	Journal Entries	Interest Expense	Liability Section of Balance Sheet	Communication	Research

Villa Co.
BALANCE SHEET—LIABILITIES SECTION
December 31, 2010

Accounts payable	$ 35,000	
Accrued interest payable	20,000	[2]
Income taxes payable	180,000	[3]
Dividends payable	50,000	
Current portion, long-term debt	62,000	[1]
Total current liabilities	347,000	
Capital lease payable, less $62,000 current portion	318,000	[1]
Bonds payable	442,000	[2]
Deferred tax liability	90,000	[3]
Total liabilities	$1,197,000	

[1]	$100,000 × 4.8	=	$480,000
	$480,000 – $100,000	=	$380,000
	$380,000 × 10%	=	$ 38,000
	$100,000 – $38,000	=	$ 62,000
	$380,000 – $62,000	=	$318,000
[2]	500K × 8% × 1/2	=	20K
	440K × 10% × 1/2	=	22K
	440 K + (22K – 20K)	=	442K
[3]	600K × 30%	=	180K
	300K × 30%	=	90K

Explanation of solutions

1. The accounts payable are current because these amounts are typically due in less than one year.

2. The cash dividends payable are current because they will be paid in the following January. The cash dividends payable is computed as follows:

Dividend per share		# Outstanding shares		Dividends payable
$.05	×	1,000,000	=	$50,000

3. The lease obligation must be separated into a current and noncurrent portion. The current portion is the amount by which the lease obligation's principal will be reduced in the next year. The carrying value of the lease obligation at 12/31/10 is $380,000 and is computed as follows:

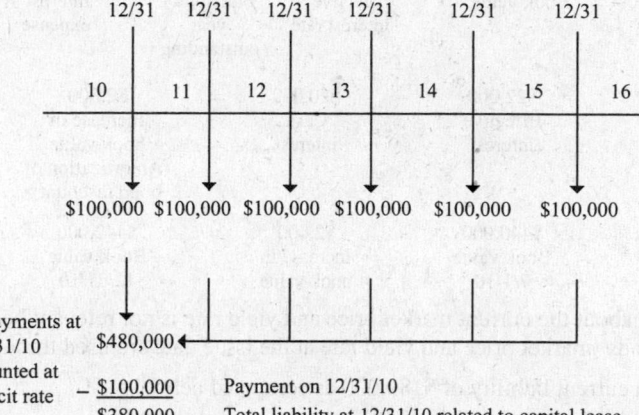

The amount of principal reduction (current liability) for 2011 is $62,000 and is computed as follows:

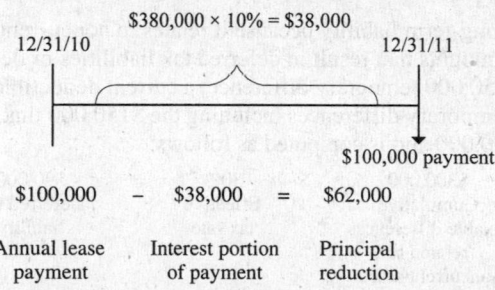

$100,000	− $38,000 =	$62,000
Annual lease payment	Interest portion of payment	Principal reduction

The noncurrent liability is $318,000 as computed below.

$380,000	−	$62,000	=	$318,000
Capital lease liability		Current portion of liability		Noncurrent liability

Note that because the lessor's implicit rate of 10% is lower than Villa's incremental borrowing rate and Villa is aware of the lessor's implicit rate, it shall be used.

4. Accrued interest on the bonds is a current liability. The amount is $20,000 for the six months they are outstanding in 2010 and is computed as follows:

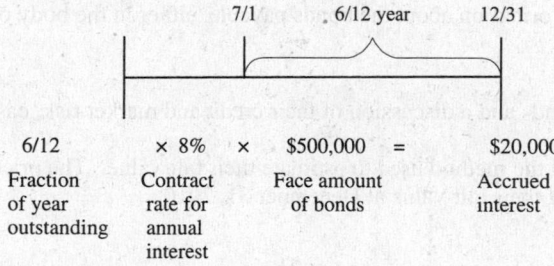

6/12	× 8% ×	$500,000	=	$20,000
Fraction of year outstanding	Contract rate for annual interest	Face amount of bonds		Accrued interest

5. The bonds payable are all noncurrent because they do not mature until 2016. The carrying amount of the bonds payable is the issue amount of the bonds plus the amortization of the bond discount for six months, or $442,000 and is computed below.

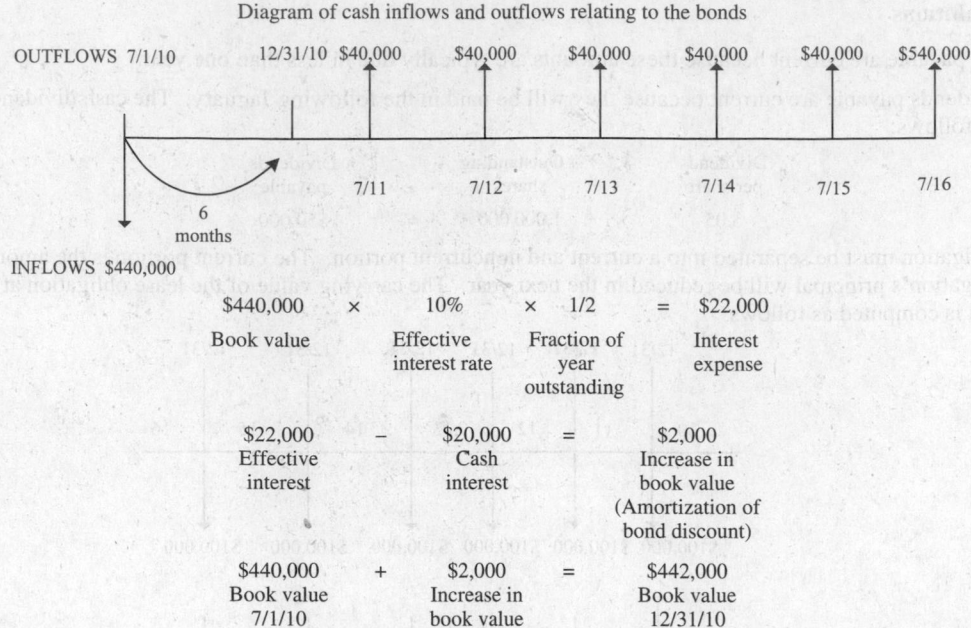

Diagram of cash inflows and outflows relating to the bonds

	$440,000	×	10%	×	1/2	=	$22,000
	Book value		Effective interest rate		Fraction of year outstanding		Interest expense

	$22,000	–	$20,000	=	$2,000
	Effective interest		Cash interest		Increase in book value (Amortization of bond discount)

	$440,000	+	$2,000	=	$442,000
	Book value 7/1/10		Increase in book value		Book value 12/31/10

Note that the information about the current market price and yield rate is not relevant because under the historical cost model per GAAP, the bonds' market price and yield rate at the issue date are used throughout the life of the bond issue.

6. Income taxes payable is a current liability of $180,000 as computed below.

	$600,000	×	30%	=	$180,000
	Taxable income		Effective tax rate		Income taxes payable

7. Deferred income tax liability is a long-term liability because it relates to noncurrent assets. Only temporary differences have future taxable or deductible amounts that result in deferred tax liabilities or deferred tax assets. Current pretax financial income was reduced by the $150,000 temporary difference, a current deductible amount that will result in future taxable amount(s). The cumulative temporary differences including the $150,000 that arose this period are $300,000. Therefore, the deferred tax liability is $90,000 and is computed as follows:

	$300,000	×	30%	=	$90,000
	Cumulative taxable differences related to noncurrent assets		Effective tax rate		Deferred tax liability

Other disclosures and information

Villa should disclose the following information about the capital leases, either in the body of the financial statements or in the notes thereto:

- The gross amount of assets recorded under the capital leases, presented by major classes. This information may be combined with owned assets.
- Future minimum lease payments as of the balance sheet date, in the aggregate and for each of the five succeeding years.
- A general description of the leasing arrangement, including the existence and terms of renewal, escalation clauses, and restrictions imposed by the lease agreements.

Villa should disclose the following information about the bonds payable, either in the body of the financial statements or in the notes thereto:

- The face amount.
- The nature and terms of the bonds and a discussion of their credit and market risk, cash requirements, and related accounting policies.
- The fair value of the bonds and the method used to estimate their fair value. The price at which the bonds are trading is the most reasonable estimate of their fair value at December 31, 2010.

Situation	Leasing Concepts	Journal Entries	Interest Expense	Liability Section of Balance Sheet	Communication	Research

To: CEO, Villa Watch Corp.
From: CPA Candidate
Re: Accounting for contingencies

This memorandum is in response to your questions about accounting for contingencies. An accounting contingency is an existing condition, situation, or set of circumstances that possibly could result in a gain or loss to the company. The contingency is resolved at some time in the future when one or more events occur or fail to occur. If a contingency is both probable and reasonably estimable, a loss should be recorded in the current period. However, if a contingency is only reasonably possible or not estimable, only an explanation of the situation is required in the footnotes to the financial statements. If the likelihood of the contingency is remote, then it need not be disclosed. Villa should account for each of its contingencies in a slightly different way because the likelihood of Villa incurring a loss differs in each situation.

For the toxic waste cleanup, a loss has been incurred. In the notes to its financial statements, Villa should disclose the nature of the loss on cleanup and indicate that an estimate of the loss, or range of the loss, cannot be made. No accrual should be made because the loss cannot be reasonably estimated and accrual of an uncertain amount would impair the integrity of the financial statements.

With regard to Clear's claim, it is only reasonably possible, and not probable, that Villa will have to pay. Accordingly, Villa should not accrue the loss. Villa should disclose the existence and nature of Clear's claim in the notes to its financial statements. Disclosure should include an estimate of the potential range of loss.

Regarding the lack of rockslide insurance, no asset has been impaired, and no liability has been incurred. Accordingly, Villa should not accrue a loss. Since the likelihood of a rockslide is remote, disclosure of the uninsured risk, while permitted, is not required.

If further clarification of these contingencies is needed, please contact my office.

Situation	Leasing Concepts	Journal Entries	Interest Expense	Liability Section of Balance Sheet	Communication	Research

1.   For how many years must Villa disclose future minimum lease payments?

FAS13, Para 16

16. The following information with respect to leases shall be disclosed in the lessee's financial statements or the footnotes thereto (see Appendix D for illustrations).

a. For capital leases

i.   The gross amount of assets recorded under capital leases as of the date of each balance sheet presented by major classes according to nature or function. This information may be combined with the comparable information for owned assets.

ii. Future minimum lease payments as of the date of the latest balance sheet presented, in the aggregate and for each of the five succeeding fiscal years, with separate deductions from the total for the amount representing executory costs, including any profit thereon, included in the minimum lease payments and for the amount of the imputed interest necessary to reduce the net minimum lease payments to present value (see paragraph 10).

iii. The total of minimum sublease rentals to be received in the future under noncancelable subleases as of the date of the latest balance sheet presented.

iv. Total contingent rentals (rentals on which the amounts are dependent on some factor other than the passage of time) actually incurred for each period for which an income statement is presented.

b. For operating leases having initial or remaining noncancelable lease terms in excess of one year:

i.   Future minimum rental payments required as of the date of the latest balance sheet presented, in the aggregate and for each of the five succeeding fiscal years.

      ii.   The total of minimum rentals to be received in the future under noncancelable subleases as of the date of the latest balance sheet presented.

c.   For all operating leases, rental expenses for each period for which an income statement is presented, with separate amounts for minimum rentals, contingent rentals, and sublease rentals. Rental payments under leases with terms of a month or less that were not renewed need not be included.

d.   A general description of the lessee's leasing arrangements including, but not limited to, the following:

      i.   The basis on which contingent rental payments are determined.

      ii.   The existence and terms of renewal or purchase options and escalation clauses.

      iii.   Restrictions imposed by lease agreements, such as those concerning dividends, additional debt, and further leasing.

Codification: 840-30-50-1

2.   What interest rate is used in calculating the present value of minimum lease payments for the lessee?

FAS13, Para 7

d.   The present value at the beginning of the lease term of the minimum lease payments [as defined in paragraph 5(j)], excluding that portion of the payments representing executory costs such as insurance, maintenance, and taxes to be paid by the lessor, including any profit thereon, equals or exceeds 90% of the excess of the fair value of the leased property [as defined in paragraph 5(c)] to the lessor at the inception of the lease over any related investment tax credit retained by the lessor and expected to be realized by him. However, if the beginning of the lease term falls within the last 25% of the total estimated economic life of the leased property, including earlier years of use, this criterion shall not be used for purposes of classifying the lease. A lessor shall compute the present value of the minimum lease payments using the interest rate implicit in the lease [as defined in paragraph 5(k)]. A lessee shall compute the present value of the minimum lease payments using his incremental borrowing rate [as defined in paragraph 5(1)], unless (i) it is practicable for him to learn the implicit rate computed by the lessor and (ii) the implicit rate computed by the lessor is less than the lessee's incremental borrowing rate. If both of those conditions are met, the lessee shall use the implicit rate.

FAS13, Para 5

k.   Interest rate implicit in the lease. The discount rate that, when applied to (i) the minimum lease payments [as defined in paragraph 5(j)], excluding that portion of the payments representing executory costs to be paid by the lessor, together with any profit thereon, and (ii) the unguaranteed residual value [as defined in paragraph 5(i)] accruing to the benefit of the lessor, causes the aggregate present value at the beginning of the lease term to be equal to the fair value of the leased property [as defined in paragraph 5(c)] to the lessor at the inception of the lease, minus any investment tax credit retained by the lessor and expected to be realized by him. (This definition does not necessarily purport to include all factors that a lessor might recognize in determining his rate of return, e.g., see paragraph 44.)

1.   Lessee's incremental borrowing rate. The rate that, at the inception of the lease, the lessee would have incurred to borrow over a similar term the funds necessary to purchase the leased asset.

Codification: 840-10-25-31

3.   What are the criteria to determine if a lease is an operating or a capital lease?

FAS13, Para 7

7.   The criteria for classifying leases set forth in this paragraph and in paragraph 8 derive from the concept as set forth in paragraph 60. If at its inception [as defined in paragraph 5(b)] a lease meets one or more of the following four criteria, the lease shall be classified as a capital lease by the lessee. Otherwise, it shall be classified as an operating lease. (See Appendix C for an illustration of the application of these criteria.)

a.   The lease transfers ownership of the property to the lessee by the end of the lease term [as defined in paragraph 5(f)].

b.   The lease contains a bargain purchase option [as defined in paragraph 5(d)].

c.   The lease term [as defined in paragraph 5(f)] is equal to 75% or more of the estimated economic life of the leased property [as defined in paragraph 5(g)]. However, if the beginning of the lease term falls within the last 25% of the total estimated economic life of the leased property, including earlier years of use, this criterion shall not be used for purposes of classifying the lease.

d.   The present value at the beginning of the lease term of the minimum lease payments [as defined in paragraph 5(j)], excluding that portion of the payments representing executory costs such as insurance, maintenance, and taxes to be paid by the lessor, including any profit thereon, equals or exceeds 90% of the excess of the fair value of the leased property [as defined in paragraph 5(c)] to the lessor at the inception of the lease over any related investment tax credit retained by the lessor and expected to be realized by him. However, if the beginning of the lease term falls within the last 25% of the total estimated economic life of the leased property, including earlier years of use, this criterion shall not be used for purposes of classifying the lease. A lessor shall compute the present value of the minimum lease payments using the interest rate implicit in the lease [as defined in paragraph 5(k)]. A lessee shall compute the present value of the minimum lease payments using his incremental borrowing rate [as defined in paragraph 5(1)], unless (i) it is practicable for him to learn the implicit rate computed by the lessor and (ii) the implicit rate computed by the lessor is less than the lessee's incremental borrowing rate. If both of those conditions are met, the lessee shall use the implicit rate.

Codification: 840-10-25-1

MULTIPLE-CHOICE QUESTIONS (1-41)

1. Justification for the method of determining periodic deferred tax expense is based on the concept of
   a. Matching of periodic expense to periodic revenue.
   b. Objectivity in the calculation of periodic expense.
   c. Recognition of assets and liabilities.
   d. Consistency of tax expense measurements with actual tax planning strategies.

2. Among the items reported on Cord, Inc.'s income statement for the year ended December 31, 2009, were the following:

Payment of penalty	$ 5,000
Insurance premium on life of an officer with Cord as owner and beneficiary	10,000

Temporary differences amount to
   a. $0
   b. $ 5,000
   c. $10,000
   d. $15,000

3. Caleb Corporation has three financial statement elements for which the December 31, 2009 book value is different than the December 31, 2009 tax basis

	Book value	Tax basis	Difference
Equipment	$200,000	$120,000	$80,000
Prepaid officers insurance policy	75,000	0	75,000
Warranty liability	50,000	0	50,000

As a result of these differences, future taxable amounts are
   a. $ 50,000
   b. $ 80,000
   c. $155,000
   d. $205,000

4. Temporary differences arise when revenues are taxable

	After they are recognized in financial income	Before they are recognized in financial income
a.	Yes	Yes
b.	Yes	No
c.	No	No
d.	No	Yes

5. Which of the following differences would result in future taxable amounts?
   a. Expenses or losses that are deductible after they are recognized in financial income.
   b. Revenues or gains that are taxable before they are recognized in financial income.
   c. Expenses or losses that are deductible before they are recognized in financial income.
   d. Revenues or gains that are recognized in financial income but are never included in taxable income.

6. Dunn Co.'s 2009 income statement reported $90,000 income before provision for income taxes. To compute the provision for federal income taxes, the following 2009 data are provided:

Rent received in advance	$16,000
Income from exempt municipal bonds	20,000
Depreciation deducted for income tax purposes in excess of depreciation reported for financial statements purposes	10,000
Enacted corporate income tax rate	30%

If the alternative minimum tax provisions are ignored, what amount of current federal income tax liability should be reported in Dunn's December 31, 2009 balance sheet?
   a. $18,000
   b. $22,800
   c. $25,800
   d. $28,800

7. Pine Corp.'s books showed pretax income of $800,000 for the year ended December 31, 2009. In the computation of federal income taxes, the following data were considered:

Gain on an involuntary conversion	$350,000
(Pine has elected to replace the property within the statutory period using total proceeds.)	
Depreciation deducted for the tax purposes in excess of depreciation deducted for book purposes	50,000
Federal estimated tax payments, 2009	70,000
Enacted federal tax rates, 2009	30%

What amount should Pine report as its current federal income tax liability on its December 31, 2009 balance sheet?
   a. $ 50,000
   b. $ 65,000
   c. $120,000
   d. $135,000

8. For the year ended December 31, 2009, Tyre Co. reported pretax financial statement income of $750,000. Its taxable income was $650,000. The difference is due to accelerated depreciation for income tax purposes. Tyre's effective income tax rate is 30%, and Tyre made estimated tax payments during 2009 of $90,000. What amount should Tyre report as current income tax expense for 2009?
   a. $105,000
   b. $135,000
   c. $195,000
   d. $225,000

9. Tower Corp. began operations on January 1, 2008. For financial reporting, Tower recognizes revenues from all sales under the accrual method. However, in its income tax returns, Tower reports qualifying sales under the installment method. Tower's gross profit on these installment sales under each method was as follows:

Year	Accrual method	Installment method
2008	$1,600,000	$ 600,000
2009	2,600,000	1,400,000

The income tax rate is 30% for 2008 and future years. There are no other temporary or permanent differences. In its December 31, 2009 balance sheet, what amount should Tower report as a liability for deferred income taxes?
   a. $840,000
   b. $660,000
   c. $600,000
   d. $360,000

10. On June 30, 2009, Ank Corp. prepaid a $19,000 premium on an annual insurance policy. The premium payment was a tax deductible expense in Ank's 2009 cash basis tax return. The accrual basis income statement will report a $9,500 insurance expense in 2009 and 2010.
   Ank's income tax rate is 30% in 2009 and 25% thereafter. In Ank's December 31, 2009 balance sheet, what amount related to the insurance should be reported as a deferred income tax liability?
   a. $5,700

b. $4,750
c. $2,850
d. $2,375

11. Mill, which began operations on January 1, 2007, recognizes income from long-term construction contracts under the percentage-of-completion method in its financial statements and under the completed-contract method for income tax reporting. Income under each method follows:

Year	Completed-contract	Percentage-of-completion
2007	$ --	$300,000
2008	400,000	600,000
2009	700,000	850,000

The income tax rate was 30% for 2007 through 2009. For years after 2009, the enacted tax rate is 25%. There are no other temporary differences. Mill should report in its December 31, 2009 balance sheet a deferred income tax liability of

a. $ 87,500
b. $105,000
c. $162,500
d. $195,000

Items 12 and 13 are based on the following:

Zeff Co. prepared the following reconciliation of its pretax financial statement income to taxable income for the year ended December 31, 2009, its first year of operations:

Pretax financial income	$160,000
Nontaxable interest received on municipal securities	(5,000)
Long-term loss accrual in excess of deductible amount	10,000
Depreciation in excess of financial statement amount	(25,000)
Taxable income	$140,000

Zeff's tax rate for 2009 is 40%. .

12. In its 2009 income statement, what amount should Zeff report as income tax expense—current portion?
a. $52,000
b. $56,000
c. $62,000
d. $64,000

13. In its December 31, 2009 balance sheet, what should Zeff report as deferred income tax liability?
a. $2,000
b. $4,000
c. $6,000
d. $8,000

14. West Corp. leased a building and received the $36,000 annual rental payment on June 15, 2009. The beginning of the lease was July 1, 2009. Rental income is taxable when received. West's tax rates are 30% for 2009 and 40% thereafter. West had no other permanent or temporary differences. West determined that no valuation allowance was needed. What amount of deferred tax asset should West report in its December 31, 2009 balance sheet?
a. $ 5,400
b. $ 7,200
c. $10,800
d. $14,400

15. Black Co., organized on January 2, 2009, had pretax accounting income of $500,000 and taxable income of $800,000 for the year ended December 31, 2009. The only

temporary difference is accrued product warranty costs that are expected to be paid as follows:

2010	$100,000
2011	50,000
2012	50,000
2013	100,000

Black has never had any net operating losses (book or tax) and does not expect any in the future. There were no temporary differences in prior years. The enacted income tax rates are 35% for 2009, 30% for 2010 through 2012, and 25% for 2013. In Black's December 31, 2009 balance sheet, the deferred income tax asset should be
a. $ 60,000
b. $ 70,000
c. $ 85,000
d. $105,000

16. A temporary difference that would result in a deferred tax liability is
a. Interest revenue on municipal bonds.
b. Accrual of warranty expense.
c. Excess of tax depreciation over financial accounting depreciation.
d. Subscriptions received in advance.

17. Orleans Co., a cash-basis taxpayer, prepares accrual basis financial statements. In its 2010 balance sheet, Orleans' deferred income tax liabilities increased compared to 2009. Which of the following changes would cause this increase in deferred income tax liabilities?

I. An increase in prepaid insurance.
II. An increase in rent receivable.
III. An increase in warranty obligations.

a. I only.
b. I and II.
c. II and III.
d. III only.

18. At the end of year one, Cody Co. reported a profit on a partially completed construction contract by applying the percentage-of-completion method. By the end of year two, the total estimated profit on the contract at completion in year three had been drastically reduced from the amount estimated at the end of year one. Consequently, in year two, a loss equal to one-half of the year one profit was recognized. Cody used the completed-contract method for income tax purposes and had no other contracts. The year two balance sheet should include a deferred tax

	Asset	Liability
a.	Yes	Yes
b.	No	Yes
c.	Yes	No
d.	No	No

19. A deferred tax liability is computed using
a. The current tax laws, regardless of expected or enacted future tax laws.
b. Expected future tax laws, regardless of whether those expected laws have been enacted.
c. Current tax laws, unless enacted future tax laws are different.
d. Either current or expected future tax laws, regardless of whether those expected laws have been enacted.

20. For the year ended December 31, 2009, Grim Co.'s pretax financial statement income was $200,000 and its taxable income was $150,000. The difference is due to the following:

Interest on municipal bonds	$70,000
Premium expense on keyman life insurance	(20,000)
Total	$50,000

Grim's enacted income tax rate is 30%. In its 2009 income statement, what amount should Grim report as current provision for income tax expense?

- a. $45,000
- b. $51,000
- c. $60,000
- d. $66,000

Items 21 and 22 are based on the following:

Venus Corp.'s worksheet for calculating current and deferred income taxes for 2009 follows:

	2009	2010	2011
Pretax income	$1,400		
Temporary differences:			
Depreciation	(800)	$(1,200)	$2,000
Warranty costs	400	(100)	(300)
Taxable income	$1,000		
Enacted rate	30%	30%	25%

Deferred tax accounts	Asset	Liability
Current	$ (30)ᵃ	
Noncurrent (before netting)	$ (75)ᵇ	$ 140ᶜ

ᵃ *[($100) × 30%]*
ᵇ *[($300) × 25%]*
ᶜ *[($1,200) × 30%] + [$2,000 × 25%]*

Venus had no prior deferred tax balances. In its 2009 income statement, what amount should Venus report as

21. Current income tax expense?

- a. $420
- b. $350
- c. $300
- d. $0

22. Deferred income tax expense?

- a. $350
- b. $300
- c. $120
- d. $ 35

23. Shear, Inc. began operations in 2009. Included in Shear's 2009 financial statements were bad debt expenses of $1,400 and profit from an installment sale of $2,600. For tax purposes, the bad debts will be deducted and the profit from the installment sale will be recognized in 2010. The enacted tax rates are 30% in 2009 and 25% in 2010. In its 2009 income statement, what amount should Shear report as deferred income tax expense?

- a. $300
- b. $360
- c. $650
- d. $780

24. Quinn Co. reported a net deferred tax asset of $9,000 in its December 31, 2008 balance sheet. For 2009, Quinn reported pretax financial statement income of $300,000. Temporary differences of $100,000 resulted in taxable income of $200,000 for 2009. At December 31, 2009, Quinn had cumulative taxable differences of $70,000. Quinn's

effective income tax rate is 30%. In its December 31, 2009, income statement, what should Quinn report as deferred income tax expense?

- a. $12,000
- b. $21,000
- c. $30,000
- d. $60,000

25. Rein Inc. reported deferred tax assets and deferred tax liabilities at the end of 2008 and at the end of 2009. For the year ended 2009, Rein should report deferred income tax expense or benefit equal to the

- a. Decrease in the deferred tax assets.
- b. Increase in the deferred tax liabilities.
- c. Amount of the current tax liability plus the sum of the net changes in deferred tax assets and deferred tax liabilities.
- d. Sum of the net changes in deferred tax assets and deferred tax liabilities.

26. On its December 31, 2009 balance sheet, Shin Co. had income taxes payable of $13,000 and a current deferred tax asset of $20,000 before determining the need for a valuation account. Shin had reported a current deferred tax asset of $15,000 at December 31, 2008. No estimated tax payments were made during 2009. At December 31, 2009, Shin determined that it was more likely than not that 10% of the deferred tax asset would not be realized. In its 2009 income statement, what amount should Shin report as total income tax expense?

- a. $ 8,000
- b. $ 8,500
- c. $10,000
- d. $13,000

27. Under current generally accepted accounting principles, which approach is used to determine income tax expense?

- a. Asset and liability approach.
- b. A "with and without" approach.
- c. Net of tax approach.
- d. Periodic expense approach.

28. Bart, Inc., a newly organized corporation, uses the equity method of accounting for its 30% investment in Rex Co.'s common stock. During 2009, Rex paid dividends of $300,000 and reported earnings of $900,000. In addition

- The dividends received from Rex are eligible for the 80% dividends received deductions.
- All the undistributed earnings of Rex will be distributed in future years.
- There are no other temporary differences.
- Bart's 2009 income tax rate is 30%.
- The enacted income tax rate after 2009 is 25%.

In Bart's December 31, 2009 balance sheet, the deferred income tax liability should be

- a. $10,800
- b. $ 9,000
- c. $ 5,400
- d. $ 4,500

29. Leer Corp.'s pretax income in 2009 was $100,000. The temporary differences between amounts reported in the financial statements and the tax return are as follows:

- Depreciation in the financial statements was $8,000 more than tax depreciation.

- The equity method of accounting resulted in financial statement income of $35,000. A $25,000 dividend was received during the year, which is eligible for the 80% dividends received deduction.

Leer's effective income tax rate was 30% in 2009. In its 2009 income statement, Leer should report a current provision for income taxes of

a. $26,400
b. $23,400
c. $21,900
d. $18,600

30. Dix, Inc., a calendar-year corporation, reported the following operating income (loss) before income tax for its first three years of operations:

2007	$100,000
2008	(200,000)
2009	400,000

There are no permanent or temporary differences between operating income (loss) for financial and income tax reporting purposes. When filing its 2008 tax return, Dix did not elect to forego the carryback of its loss for 2008. Assume a 40% tax rate for all years. What amount should Dix report as its income tax liability at December 31, 2009?

a. $160,000
b. $120,000
c. $ 80,000
d. $ 60,000

31. Town, a calendar-year corporation incorporated in January 2007, experienced a $600,000 net operating loss (NOL) in 2009 due to a prolonged strike. Town never had a strike in the past that significantly affected its income and does not expect such a strike in the future. Additionally, there is no other negative evidence concerning future operating income. For the years 2007-2009, Town reported a taxable income in each year, and a total of $450,000 for the two years. Assume that: (1) there is no difference between pretax accounting income and taxable income for all years, (2) the income tax rate is 40% for all years, (3) the NOL will be carried back to the profit years 2007-2009 to the extent of $450,000, and $150,000 will be carried forward to future periods. In its 2009 income statement, what amount should Town report as the reduction of loss due to NOL carryback and carryforward?

a. $240,000
b. $180,000
c. $270,000
d. $360,000

32. Bishop Corporation began operations in 2007 and had operating losses of $200,000 in 2007 and $150,000 in 2008. For the year ended December 31, 2009, Bishop had pretax book income of $300,000. For the three-year period 2007 to 2009, assume an income tax rate of 40% and no permanent or temporary differences between book and taxable income. Because Bishop began operations in 2007, the entire amount of deferred tax assets recognized in 2007 and 2008 were offset with amounts added to the allowance account. In Bishop's 2009 income statement, how much should be reported as current income tax expense?

a. $0
b. $ 40,000
c. $ 60,000
d. $120,000

33. Mobe Co. reported the following operating income (loss) for its first three years of operations:

2007	$ 300,000
2008	(700,000)
2009	1,200,000

For each year, there were no deferred income taxes, and Mobe's effective income tax rate was 30%. In its 2008 income tax return, Mobe elected to carry back the maximum amount of loss possible. Additionally, there was more negative evidence than positive evidence concerning profitability for Mobe in 2009. In its 2009 income statement, what amount should Mobe report as total income tax expense?

a. $120,000
b. $150,000
c. $240,000
d. $360,000

34. In 2008, Rand, Inc. reported for financial statement purposes the following items, which were not included in taxable income:

Installment gain to be collected equally in 2010 through 2012	$1,500,000
Estimated future warranty costs to be paid equally in 2010 through 2012	2,100,000

There were no temporary differences in prior years. Rand's enacted tax rates are 30% for 2009 and 25% for 2010 through 2012.

In Rand's December 31, 2009 balance sheet, what amounts of the deferred tax asset should be classified as current and noncurrent?

	Current	Noncurrent
a.	$60,000	$100,000
b.	$60,000	$120,000
c.	$50,000	$100,000
d.	$50,000	$120,000

35. Thorn Co. applies ASC Topic 740, *Income Taxes*. At the end of 2009, the tax effects of temporary differences were as follows:

	Deferred tax assets (liabilities)	Related asset classification
Accelerated tax depreciation	$(75,000)	Noncurrent asset
Additional costs in inventory for tax purposes	25,000	Current asset
	$(50,000)	

A valuation allowance was not considered necessary. Thorn anticipates that $10,000 of the deferred tax liability will reverse in 2010. In Thorn's December 31, 2009 balance sheet, what amount should Thorn report as noncurrent deferred tax liability?

a. $40,000
b. $50,000
c. $65,000
d. $75,000

36. Because Jab Co. uses different methods to depreciate equipment for financial statement and income tax purposes, Jab has temporary differences that will reverse during the next year and add to taxable income. Deferred income taxes that are based on these temporary differences should be classified in Jab's balance sheet as a

a. Contra account to current assets.

b.   Contra account to noncurrent assets.
c.   Current liability.
d.   Noncurrent liability.

37. At the most recent year-end, a company had a deferred income tax liability arising from accelerated depreciation that exceeded a deferred income tax asset relating to rent received in advance which is expected to reverse in the next year. Which of the following should be reported in the company's most recent year-end balance sheet?
a.   The excess of the deferred income tax liability over the deferred income tax asset as a noncurrent liability.
b.   The excess of the deferred income tax liability over the deferred income tax asset as a current liability.
c.   The deferred income tax liability as a noncurrent liability.
d.   The deferred income tax liability as a current liability.

38. On December 31, 2009, Oak Co. recognized a receivable for taxes paid in prior years and refundable through the carryback of all of its 2009 operating loss. Also, Oak had a 2009 deferred tax liability derived from the temporary difference between tax and financial statement depreciation, which reverses over the period 2010–2014. The amount of this tax liability is less than the amount of the tax asset. Which of the following 2009 balance sheet sections should report tax-related items?

 I.   Current assets.
 II. Current liabilities.
 III. Noncurrent liabilities.

a.   I only.
b.   I and III.
c.   I, II, and III.
d.   II and III.

39. The amount of income tax applicable to transactions that are not reported in the continuing operations section of the income statement is computed
a.   By multiplying the item by the effective income tax rate.
b.   As the difference between the tax computed based on taxable income without including the item and the tax computed based on taxable income including the item.
c.   As the difference between the tax computed on the item based on the amount used for financial reporting and the amount used in computing taxable income.
d.   By multiplying the item by the difference between the effective income tax rate and the statutory income tax rate.

40. No net deferred tax asset (i.e., deferred tax asset net of related valuation allowance) was recognized in the 2008 financial statements by the Chaise Company when a loss from discontinued operations was carried forward for tax purposes because it was more likely than not that none of this deferred tax asset would be realized. Chaise had no temporary differences. The tax benefit of the loss carried forward reduced current taxes payable on 2009 continuing operations. The 2009 income statement would include the tax benefit from the loss brought forward in
a.   Income from continuing operations.

b.   Gain or loss from discontinued operations.
c.   Extraordinary gains.
d.   Cumulative effect of accounting changes.

41. Which of the following statements is correct regarding the provision for income taxes in the financial statements of a sole proprietorship?
a.   The provision for income taxes should be based on business income using individual tax rates.
b.   The provision for income taxes should be based on business income using corporate tax rates.
c.   The provision for income taxes should be based on the proprietor's total taxable income, allocated to the proprietorship at the percentage that business income bears to the proprietor's total income.
d.   No provision for income taxes is required.

SIMULATION PROBLEMS

Simulation Problem 1 (40 to 50 minutes)

Directions					
	Situation	Tax Calculations	Tax Differences	Deferred Tax Classification	Research

In the following simulation you are asked to complete several tasks related to deferred taxes. The tasks are identified by the tabs shown above.

	Situation				
Directions		Tax Calculations	Tax Differences	Deferred Tax Classification	Research

The following partially completed worksheet contain Lane Co.'s reconciliation between financial statement income and taxable income for the three years ended April 30, 2009, and additional information.

Lane Co.
INCOME TAX WORKSHEET
For the Three Years Ended April 30, 2009

	April 30, 2007	*April 30, 2008*	*April 30, 2009*
Pretax financial income	$900,000	$1,000,000	$1,200,000
Permanent differences	100,000	100,000	100,000
Temporary differences	200,000	100,000	150,000
Taxable income	$600,000	$ 800,000	$ 950,000
Cumulative temporary differences (future taxable amounts)	$200,000	$ (2)	$ 450,000
Tax rate	20%	25%	30%
Deferred tax liability	$ 40,000	$ 75,000	$ (4)
Deferred tax expense	--	$ (3)	--
Current tax expense	$ (1)	--	--

The tax rate changes were enacted at the beginning of each tax year and were not known to Lane at the end of the prior year.

		Tax Calculations			
Directions	Situation		Tax Differences	Deferred Tax Classification	Research

Items 1 through 4 represent amounts omitted from the worksheet. For each item, determine the amount omitted from the worksheet. Select the amount from the following list. An answer may be used once, more than once, or not at all.

Amount

A.	$ 25,000	H.	$135,000
B.	$ 35,000	I.	$140,000
C.	$ 45,000	J.	$160,000
D.	$ 75,000	K.	$180,000
E.	$100,000	L.	$200,000
F.	$112,500	M.	$300,000
G.	$120,000	N.	$400,000

Specific audit objective	(A) (B) (C) (D) (E) (F) (G) (H) (I) (J) (K) (L) (M) (N)
1. Current tax expense for the year ended April 30, 2007.	O O O O O O O O O O O O O O
2. Cumulative temporary differences at April 30, 2008.	O O O O O O O O O O O O O O
3. Deferred tax expense for the year ended April 30, 2008.	O O O O O O O O O O O O O O
4. Deferred tax liability at April 30, 2009.	O O O O O O O O O O O O O O

			Tax Differences		
Directions	Situation	Tax Calculations		Deferred Tax Classification	Research

Items 1 through 7 describe circumstances resulting in differences between financial statement income and taxable income. For each numbered item, determine whether the difference is

<u>*List*</u>
A. A temporary difference resulting in a deferred tax asset.
B. A temporary difference resulting in a deferred tax liability.
C. A permanent difference.

Indicate the classification of each item. An answer may be selected once, more than once, or not at all.

		A *Temporary difference* DTA	B *Temporary difference* DTL	C *Permanent difference*
1.	For plant assets, the depreciation expense deducted for tax purposes is in excess of the depreciation expense used for financial reporting purposes.	O	O	O
2.	A landlord collects some rents in advance. Rents received are taxable in the period in which they are received.	O	O	O
3.	Interest is received on an investment in tax-exempt municipal obligations.	O	O	O
4.	Costs of guarantees and warranties are estimated and accrued for financial reporting purposes.	O	O	O
5.	Life insurance proceeds are collected on the death of a key officer.	O	O	O
6.	Bad debts are estimated and expensed on the income statement. No bad debts were charged to the allowance account and written off during the year.	O	O	O
7.	Goodwill is deducted on the tax return.	O	O	O

Directions	Situation	Tax Calculations	Tax Differences	Deferred Tax Classification	Research

Identify whether each item would create a deferred tax asset or a deferred tax liability, and whether each item would be classified as current or noncurrent.

		Deferred tax asset	*Deferred tax liability*	*Current*	*Noncurrent*
1.	Tax depreciation in excess of book depreciation	O	O	O	O
2.	Bad debts expense in excess of actual write-offs	O	O	O	O
3.	Rent collected in advance for next 12 months	O	O	O	O

Directions	Situation	Tax Calculations	Tax Differences	Deferred Tax Classification	Research

The CEO of Lane Corporation has contacted you regarding questions she has about deferred taxes. She has requested that you research a list of questions in the authoritative literature, copy the relevant paragraphs, and fax her a copy of the results for her review. Below is her list of questions.

1. What are the primary objectives of accounting for income taxes?

2. What is a temporary difference?

3. How are deferred taxes presented in the financial statements?

4. What tax rate is used to calculate deferred taxes?

5. What components of income tax expense that relate to continuing operations must be included in the notes to the financial statements?

Simulation Problem 2   (50 to 60 minutes)

Directions								
	Situation	Temporary and Permanent Differences	Deferred Tax Schedule	Calculate Taxable Income	Journal Entries	Disclosures	Communication	Research

In the following simulation you are asked to complete several tasks related to deferred taxes. The tasks are identified by the tabs shown above.

	Situation							
Directions		Temporary and Permanent Differences	Deferred Tax Schedule	Calculate Taxable Income	Journal Entries	Disclosures	Communication	Research

Jasco Corporation is in its first year of operations. The company has pretax income of $400,000. The company has the following items recorded in its records. No estimated tax payments were made during 2009.

Premiums on life insurance of key officer	$10,000
Depreciation on tax return in excess of book depreciation	12,000
Interest on municipal bonds	5,300
Warranty expense	4,000
Actual warranty repairs	3,250
Bad debt expense	1,400
Beginning balance in allowance for uncollectible accounts	0
End balance for allowance for uncollectible accounts	800
Rent received in advance from clients that will be recognized evenly over the next three years	24,000
Tax rate for 2009 and future years	40%

		Temporary and Permanent Differences						
Directions	Situation		Deferred Tax Schedule	Calculate Taxable Income	Journal Entries	Disclosures	Communication	Research

Identify for Jasco which of the following items create temporary differences and which create permanent differences.

	Temporary	*Permanent*
Premiums on life insurance of key officer	O	O
Depreciation	O	O
Interest on municipal bonds	O	O
Warranties	O	O
Bad debts	O	O
Rent received in advance from clients	O	O

			Deferred Tax Schedule					
Directions	Situation	Temporary and Permanent Differences		Calculate Taxable Income	Journal Entries	Disclosures	Communication	Research

Prepare the following schedule for the deferred tax amounts for the year. Choose items from the following list:

Items

Premium on life insurance	Warranties
Depreciation	Bad debts
Interest on municipal bonds	Rent received

Item	Difference between taxable amount and income statement amount	Classification: Deferred tax asset Deferred tax liability	Current or noncurrent	Deferred tax amount

Directions	Situation	Temporary and Permanent Differences	Deferred Tax Schedule	Calculate Taxable Income	Journal Entries	Disclosures	Communication	Research

Complete the following table to calculate taxable income. If no adjustment is needed for a particular item enter 0 as your calculation.

Pretax financial income	
Premiums on life insurance of key officer	
Interest on municipal bonds	
Depreciation for tax in excess of book depreciation	
Adjustment for warranties	
Adjustment for bad debts	
Adjustment for rent received in advance	
Taxable income	

Directions	Situation	Temporary and Permanent Differences	Deferred Tax Schedule	Calculate Taxable Income	Journal Entries	Disclosures	Communication	Research

Prepare the journal entries to record tax expense for 2009. Select your account titles from the following list:

Deferred tax asset—Current
Deferred tax asset—Noncurrent
Deferred tax liability—Current
Deferred tax liability—Noncurrent
Income tax expense
Income taxes payable
Prepaid income taxes

Account title	Debit	Credit

Directions	Situation	Temporary and Permanent Differences	Deferred Tax Schedule	Calculate Taxable Income	Journal Entries	Disclosures	Communication	Research

Using the appropriate netting procedures, indicate the amounts that will be shown in which of the following classifications on the balance sheet.

Deferred tax asset—Current	
Deferred tax asset—Noncurrent	
Deferred tax liability—Current	
Deferred tax liability—Noncurrent	

Directions	Situation	Temporary and Permanent Differences	Deferred Tax Schedule	Calculate Taxable Income	Journal Entries	Disclosures	Communication	Research

Chris Green, CPA, is auditing Jasco Co.'s 2009 financial statements. The controller, Dunn, has provided Green with the following information relating to income taxes:

- Dunn has prepared a schedule of all differences between financial statement and income tax return income. Dunn believes that as a result of pending legislation, the enacted tax rate at December 31, 2009, will be increased for 2009. Dunn is uncertain which differences to include and which rates to apply in computing deferred taxes under ASC Topic 740. Dunn has requested an overview of ASC Topic 740, *Income Taxes,* from Green.

Required:

Prepare a brief memo to Dunn from Green

- Identifying the objectives of accounting for income taxes,
- Defining temporary differences,
- Explaining how to measure deferred tax assets and liabilities, and
- Explaining how to measure deferred income tax expense or benefit.

REMINDER: Your response will be graded for both technical content and writing skills. Technical content will be evaluated for information that is helpful to the intended reader and clearly relevant to the issue. Writing skills will be evaluated for development, organization, and the appropriate expression of ideas in professional correspondence. Use a standard business memo or letter format with a clear beginning, middle, and end. Do not convey information in the form of a table, bullet point list, or other abbreviated presentation.

To: Mr. Dunn
From: Mr. Green, CPA
Re: Accounting for income taxes

Directions	Situation	Temporary and Permanent Differences	Deferred Tax Schedule	Calculate Taxable Income	Journal Entries	Disclosures	Communication	Research

Using the authoritative literature from the accounting standards, select the appropriate paragraph that provides the definition for deferred tax expense.

MULTIPLE-CHOICE ANSWERS

1. c __ __	10. d __ __	19. c __ __	28. b __ __	37. c __ __
2. a __ __	11. c __ __	20. a __ __	29. b __ __	38. b __ __
3. b __ __	12. b __ __	21. c __ __	30. b __ __	39. b __ __
4. a __ __	13. c __ __	22. d __ __	31. a __ __	40. a __ __
5. c __ __	14. b __ __	23. a __ __	32. a __ __	41. d __ __
6. b __ __	15. c __ __	24. c __ __	33. c __ __	
7. a __ __	16. c __ __	25. d __ __	34. c __ __	1st: __/41 = __%
8. c __ __	17. b __ __	26. c __ __	35. d __ __	2nd: __/41 = __%
9. b __ __	18. b __ __	27. a __ __	36. d __ __	

MULTIPLE-CHOICE ANSWER EXPLANATIONS

A. Overview of Deferred Tax Theory

1. (c) The objective of accounting for income taxes is to recognize the amount of current and deferred taxes payable or refundable at the date of the financial statements. The standard further states that this objective is implemented through recognition of deferred tax liabilities or assets. Deferred tax expense results from changes in deferred tax assets and liabilities.

B. Permanent and Temporary Differences Defined

2. (a) **Temporary** differences are differences between taxable income and accounting income which originate in one period and reverse in one or more subsequent periods. The payment of a penalty ($5,000) and insurance premiums where the corporation is the beneficiary ($10,000) are **not** temporary differences because they never reverse. These are examples of **permanent** differences, which are items that either enter into accounting income but never into taxable income (such as these two items), or enter into taxable income but never into accounting income.

3. (b) The officer insurance policy difference ($75,000) is a permanent difference which does not result in future taxable or deductible amounts. The warranty difference ($50,000) is a temporary difference, but it results in future **deductible** amounts in future years when tax warranty expense exceeds book warranty expense. However, the equipment difference ($80,000) is a temporary difference that results in future taxable amounts in future years when tax depreciation is less than book depreciation.

4. (a) Examples of temporary differences are revenues which are taxable both before and after they are recognized in financial income. Note that emphasis is placed on the difference between book and tax, not the chronological order of the reporting.

5. (c) Expenses or losses that are deductible before they are recognized in financial income would result in future taxable amounts. For example, the cost of an asset may have been deducted for tax purposes faster than it was depreciated for financial reporting. In future years, tax depreciation will be less than financial accounting depreciation, meaning future taxable income will exceed future financial accounting income. Answers (a) and (b) are temporary differences that would result in future deductible amounts. Answer (d) is a permanent difference that does not result in either future taxable or future deductible amounts.

C. Deferred Tax Assets and Liabilities

6. (b) To determine the current federal tax liability, **book** income ($90,000) must be adjusted for any temporary or permanent differences to determine **taxable** income.

Book income	$90,000
Rent received in advance	16,000
Municipal interest	(20,000)
Excess tax depreciation	(10,000)
Taxable income	$76,000

Rent received in advance (temporary difference) is added to book income because rent is taxable when received, but is not recognized as book revenue until earned. Municipal interest (permanent difference) is subtracted from book income because it is excluded from taxable income. The excess tax depreciation (temporary difference) is subtracted because this excess amount is an additional tax deduction beyond accounting depreciation. The current tax liability is computed by multiplying taxable income by the tax rate ($76,000 × 30% = $22,800).

7. (a) The **current** federal income tax liability is based on **taxable** income, which is computed in the "book to tax reconciliation" below.

Accounting income	$ 800,000
Nontaxable gain	(350,000)
Excess tax depreciation	(50,000)
Taxable income	$ 400,000

The gain on involuntary conversion was included in accounting income but is deferred for tax purposes. Depreciation deducted for tax purposes in excess of book depreciation also causes taxable income to be less than accounting income. Taxes payable before considering estimated tax payments is $120,000 ($400,000 × 30%). Since tax payments of $70,000 have already been made, the 12/31/09 current federal income tax liability is $50,000 ($120,000 – $70,000).

8. (c) Income tax expense must be reported in two components: the amount currently payable (current portion) and the tax effects of temporary differences (deferred portion). The current portion is computed by multiplying taxable income by the current enacted tax rate ($650,000 × 30% = $195,000). The deferred portion is $30,000 ($100,000 temporary difference × 30%). The estimated tax payments ($90,000) do not affect the amount of tax expense, although the payments would decrease taxes payable.

9. (b) Over the two years, accounting income on the accrual basis is $4,200,000 ($1,600,000 + $2,600,000) and taxable income using the installment method is $2,000,000 ($600,000 + $1,400,000). This results in future taxable amounts at 12/31/09 of $2,200,000 ($4,200,000 – $2,000,000). Therefore, at 12/31/09, Tower should report a deferred tax liability of $660,000 ($2,200,000 × 30%).

10. (d) For accounting purposes, prepaid insurance is $9,500 at 12/31/09. For tax purposes, there was no prepaid insurance at 12/31/09, since the entire amount was deducted on the 2009 tax return. Therefore, the temporary difference is $9,500. This temporary difference will result in a future taxable amount in 2010, when the tax rate is 25%. Therefore, at 12/31/09, a deferred tax liability of $2,375 (25% × $9,500) must be reported.

11. (c) Mill's total accounting income using percentage-of-completion ($300,000 + $600,000 + $850,000 = $1,750,000) will eventually be subject to federal income taxes. However, by 12/31/09, only $1,100,000 of income ($400,000 + $700,000) has been reported as taxable income using the completed-contract method. The amount of accounting income which has not yet been taxed ($1,750,000 – $1,100,000 = $650,000 temporary difference) will be taxed eventually when the related contracts are completed. The resulting future taxable amounts will all be taxed after 2009 when the enacted tax rate is 25%. Therefore, the 12/31/09 deferred tax liability is $162,500 ($650,000 × 25%). To record the liability, the following entries would be made each year:

2007

Income tax expense—deferred	90,000	
Deferred tax liability		90,000

2008

Income tax expense—deferred	60,000	
Deferred tax liability		60,000

2009

Income tax expense—deferred	12,500	
Deferred tax liability		12,500

The total in the deferred tax liability account on 12/31/09 should be $162,500. Therefore, the entry in 2009 is the amount needed to correctly state the deferred tax liability account. Since $150,000 was already accrued in the deferred tax liability account in 2007 and 2008, the entry for 2009 is $162,500 – $150,000.

12. (b) Income tax expense must be reported in two components: the amount currently payable (current portion) and the tax effects of temporary differences (deferred portion). The amount currently payable, or current income tax expense, is computed by multiplying taxable income by the current enacted tax rate ($140,000 × 40% = $56,000).

13. (c) The deferred tax liability reported at 12/31/08 results from future taxable (and possibly deductible) amounts which exist as a result of past transactions, multiplied by the appropriate tax rate. The nontaxable interest received on municipal securities ($5,000) is a **permanent** difference that does **not** result in future taxable or deductible amounts. The Codification requires the netting of current deferred tax assets and liabilities, and noncurrent deferred tax assets and liabilities. The future deductible amount ($10,000) resulting from a loss accrual results in a **long-term** deferred tax asset of $4,000 ($10,000 × 40%) because it is related to a **long-term** loss accrual. The future taxable amount ($25,000) caused by depreciation results in a **long-term** deferred tax liability of $10,000 ($25,000 × 40%) because it is related to a **long-term** asset (property, plant, and equipment). Since these are both long-term, they are netted and a long-term deferred tax liability of $6,000 is reported in the balance sheet ($10,000 liability less $4,000 asset).

14. (b) At 12/31/09, unearned rent for financial accounting purposes is $18,000 ($36,000 × 6/12). The amount of rent revenue recognized on the income statement is six of twelve months (36,000 × 6/12) = 18,000. Rental income on the tax return is $36,000 because rental income is taxed when received. Therefore, the timing difference is $18,000 ($36,000 – $18,000 = $18,000) giving rise to a deferred tax asset on the balance sheet of $18,000 × 40% = $7,200. The deferred tax asset to be recorded is measured using the future enacted tax rate of 40%.

15. (c) A deferred tax asset is recognized for all deductible temporary differences. The computation of the deferred tax asset for Black Co. arising from the accrued product warranty costs of $300,000 is shown below.

	2010	*2011*	*2012*	*2013*	*Total*
Future deductible amounts	$100,000	$50,000	$50,000	$100,000	$300,000
Tax rate	30%	30%	30%	25%	
Deferred tax asset	$30,000	$15,000	$15,000	$25,000	$85,000

Thus, the total deferred tax asset at the end of 2009 is $85,000.

16. (c) An excess of tax depreciation over financial accounting depreciation results in future taxable amounts and, therefore, a deferred tax liability. Answer (a) is an example of a permanent difference that does not result in future taxable or deductible amounts. Answers (b) and (d) are examples of temporary differences that result in future deductible amounts and a possible deferred tax asset.

17. (b) The increase in prepaid insurance in 2010 creates a deductible amount for income tax reporting purposes for the insurance paid; however, for financial reporting purposes the expense is not recognized until years subsequent to 2010. As a result, net taxable income for future years is increased, thus, the deferred income tax liability increases. The increase in rent receivable in 2010 also increases the deferred tax liability. For income tax purposes, rents are not included in income until received (i.e., years subsequent to 2010). However, the amount of the receivable is earned and recognized in the income statement in 2010. The increase in warranty obligations results in warranty expense for 2010 and will provide future deductible amounts, because under the IRC, a deduction for warranty cost is not permitted until such cost is incurred. Future deductible amounts lead to deferred tax assets.

18. (b) A deferred tax liability is recognized for temporary differences that will result in **net** taxable amounts (taxable income exceeds book income) in future years. Although Cody Co. has recognized a loss (per books) in year two of the construction contract, the contract is still profitable over the three years. Therefore, in year three when the contract is completed, Cody will recognize the total profit on its tax return, and only a portion of the profit will be recorded in its income statement. Thus, the contract will result in a taxable amount in year three and a deferred tax liability exists. Note that this liability was recorded at the end of year 1 and reduced by one-half at the end of year two due to the change in estimated profit. Answers (a) and (c) are incorrect because no deferred tax asset is created. Answer (d) is incorrect because Cody will include a deferred tax liability on its balance sheet.

19.   (c)   A deferred tax liability is recognized for the amount of taxes payable in **future** years as a result of the deferred tax consequences (as measured by the provisions of **enacted** tax laws) of events recognized in the financial statements in the current or preceding years.

20.   (a)   Income tax provision (expense) must be reported in two components: the amount currently payable (current portion) and the tax effects of temporary differences (deferred portion). The current portion is computed by multiplying taxable income by the current enacted tax rate ($150,000 × 30% = $45,000). Note that in this case, the deferred portion is $0, because both differences are permanent differences, which do not result in a deferred tax liability. Therefore, the current provision for income taxes should be reported at $45,000. It is important to note that if temporary differences did exist the tax effects would have been included in the tax expense for the current period.

21.   (c)   Income tax expense must be reported in two components: the amount currently payable (current portion) and the tax effects of temporary differences (deferred portion). The amount currently payable, or current income tax expense, is computed by multiplying taxable income by the current enacted tax rate ($1,000 × 30% = $300).

22.   (d)   Income tax expense must be reported on the IS in two components: the amount currently payable (current portion) and the tax effects of temporary differences (deferred portion). Note that scheduling is required in this question because the tax rates are not the same in all future years. The worksheet indicates two temporary differences: depreciation and warranty costs. The scheduling contained in the worksheet shows that these two temporary differences will result in a deferred tax asset of $105 ($30 + $75) and deferred tax liability of $140. The liability has the effect of increasing 2009 tax expense while the asset has the effect of decreasing 2009 tax expense. The net effect is deferred income tax expense of $35 for 2009 [$140 – ($30 + $75)].

Not required:

The balance sheet presentation would show a current deferred tax asset of $30 and a noncurrent deferred tax liability of $65 ($140 – $75).

23.   (a)   The deferred portion of income tax expense can be computed by determining the tax effect of the two temporary differences. The installment sale profit results in a future taxable amount in 2010 of $2,600, and the bad debt expense results in a future deductible amount of $1,400. The deferred tax consequences of these temporary differences will be measured by Shear in 2009 using the enacted tax rate expected to apply to taxable income in the year the deferred amounts are expected to be settled. The following journal entry is necessary to record the deferred tax liability related to the installment sale:

Deferred tax expense	650	
Deferred tax liability		650
[$2,600 × .25]		

To record the deferred tax asset related to the bad debt expense, the following journal entry is required:

Deferred tax asset	350	
Deferred tax expense		350
[$1,400 × .25]		

The amount of deferred tax expense to be reported by Shear in its 2009 income statement is $300 ($650 – $350). Note that one journal entry could have been used. Using two entries more clearly shows the opposite effect of an asset versus a liability on deferred tax expense.

24.   (c)   Income tax expense must be reported in two components: the amount currently payable (current portion) and the tax effects of temporary differences (deferred portion). The current portion is computed by multiplying taxable income by the current enacted tax rate ($200,000 × 30% = $60,000). The deferred portion is $30,000 ($100,000 temporary difference × 30%). An alternative computation for the deferred portion is shown below.

DT asset at 12/31/09	$ 0	
DT asset at 12/31/08	9,000	
Decrease in DT asset		$ 9,000
DT liability at 12/31/09 ($70,000 × 30%)	$21,000	
DT liability at 12/31/08	0	
Increase in DT liability		21,000
Deferred portion of tax expense		$30,000

25.   (d)   The deferred income tax expense or benefit is the net change during the year in an enterprise's deferred tax liabilities or assets. The deferred income tax expense or benefit must consider the net effect of changes (both increases and decreases) in both deferred tax assets and deferred tax liabilities. The decrease in deferred tax assets alone or the increase in deferred tax liabilities alone will not be equal to the deferred income tax expense. The amount of income tax liability (current portion which comes off the tax return) plus the sum of the net changes in deferred tax assets and deferred tax liabilities is the total amount of income tax expense or benefit for the year. The question asks only for the deferred portion.

26.   (c)   From 12/31/08 to 12/31/09, the deferred tax asset increased by $5,000 (from $15,000 to $20,000). Income taxes payable at 12/31/09 are $13,000. Based on this information, the following journal entries can be recreated.

Income tax expense—current	13,000	
Income tax payable		13,000
Deferred tax asset	5,000	
Income tax expense—deferred		5,000

An additional entry would be prepared by Shin to record an allowance to reduce the deferred tax asset to its realizable value (10% × $20,000 = $2,000).

Income tax expense—deferred	2,000	
Allowance to reduce deferred		
tax asset to realizable value		2,000

Based on these three entries, total 2009 income tax expense is $10,000 ($13,000 – $5,000 + $2,000).

27.   (a)   Income tax expense is the sum of income taxes currently payable or refundable and the deferred tax expense or benefit which is the change during the year in an enterprise's deferred tax liabilities and assets. This method is more commonly called the asset and liability approach.

D. Deferred Tax Related to Business Investments

28.   (b)   The deferred income tax liability is the result of the undistributed earnings of an equity investee, which are expected to be distributed as dividends in future periods. For accounting purposes, investment revenue is $270,000 ($900,000 × 30%). For tax purposes, dividend revenue is

$90,000 ($300,000 × 30%), which will be partially offset by the 80% dividends received deduction. Because of this 80% deduction, the difference ($270,000 – $90,000 = $180,000) is partially a permanent difference (80% × $180,000 = $144,000 which will never be subject to taxes) and partially a temporary difference (20% × $180,000 = $36,000 which will be taxable in future years). This future taxable amount of $36,000 will become taxable after 2009, when the expected tax rate is 25%. Therefore, the deferred tax liability is $9,000 (25% × $36,000). The entry to record the liability is as follows:

Income tax expense—deferred	9,000	
Deferred tax liability		9,000

29. (b) The **current** provision for income taxes is computed by multiplying taxable income on the Form 1120 by the current tax rate. Since taxable income is not given, pretax book income must be adjusted to compute taxable income.

Pretax book income	$100,000
Excess book depreciation	8,000
Excess book investment revenue	
[$35,000 – (20% × $25,000)]	(30,000)
Taxable income	$78,000

Excess book depreciation is added because it causes book income to be lower than taxable income. For book purposes, investment revenue of $35,000 was recognized using the equity method; for tax purposes, net dividend revenue of $5,000 was recognized [$25,000 – (80% × $25,000)]. The excess book revenue ($35,000 – $5,000 = $30,000) is deducted to compute taxable income. Therefore, the **current** provision for income taxes is $23,400 ($78,000 × 30%).

E. Loss Carryforwards and Carrybacks

30. (b) Dix did **not** elect to forego the loss carryback, so $100,000 of the $200,000 loss will be carried back to offset 2007 income, resulting in a tax refund of $40,000 (40% × $100,000). The remaining $100,000 of the 2008 loss will be carried forward to offset part of 2009 income. Thus, the income tax **liability** at 12/31/09 will be $120,000 [40% × ($400,000 – $100,000)].

31. (a) The requirement is to determine the amount to be reported in 2009 as the reduction of loss due to NOL carryback and carryforward (i.e., benefit [negative tax expense] on the face of the IS). A deferred tax liability or asset is recognized for all temporary differences, operating losses, and tax credit carryforwards.

Income Tax Return Analysis

	2007-2008	2009
Inc (loss)	450,000	$(600,000)
Carryback	(450,000)	450,000
Unused NOL		$150,000

Town can thus recognize tax benefits from both the NOL carryback and carryforward. Town may carryback $450,000 of the NOL which will provide a tax benefit of $180,000 ($450,000 × .40). The journal entry to recognize the loss carryback would be as follows:

Tax refund receivable	180,000	
Benefit due to loss carryback		180,000

The additional $150,000 NOL can be carried forward to future periods to provide a benefit of $60,000 ($150,000 × .40). The following journal entry reflects the loss carryforward:

Deferred tax asset	60,000	
Benefit due to loss carryforward		60,000

Therefore, the reduction of the loss due to NOL carryback and carryforward is $240,000. Note that an allowance for nonrealization of the deferred tax asset is not necessary because the information given about the strike indicates that it is not more likely than not that part of the deferred tax asset may not be recognized.

The carryback and carryforward would be shown in the income statement as follows:

Loss before income taxes		$(600,000)
Less:		
Benefit from operating loss carryback	$180,000	
Benefit from operating loss carryforward	60,000	240,000
Net loss		$(360,000)

32. (a) The requirement is to determine the amount of 2009 current income tax expense (or income taxes payable from tax return) to be reported in the income statement. For tax purposes, loss carryforwards should not be recognized until they are actually realized.

Income Tax Return Analysis

	2007	2008	2009
Income or loss	$(200,000)	$(150,000)	$300,000
Carryforward	200,000	100,000	(300,000)
Unused Carryforward	0	$50,000	0

Bishop would recognize, in the income statement, income tax expense of $0 as the loss carryforward fully offsets the 2009 income.

Not required:

The deferred tax component for 2009 would be as follows:

Balance in the deferred tax asset and allowance accounts at 1/1/09

	Deferred Tax Asset		Allow for Reduction, etc.	
12/31/07	80,000		80,000	12/31/07
12/31/08	60,000		60,000	12/31/08
12/31/08 balance	140,000		140,000	12/31/08 balance

The deferred tax entry for 2009 would be

Allow for reduction, etc.	140,000	
Deferred tax asset		120,000
Income tax expense—deferred		20,000

The bottom of the income statement would be

Income before taxes		$300,000
Income tax expense or benefit		
Current		0
Deferred **benefit**		20,000
Net income		$320,000

33. (c) A deferred tax liability or asset is recognized for all temporary differences and operating loss carryforwards. In 2008, Mobe would prepare the following entries:

Tax refund receivable ($300,000 × 30%)	90,000	
Deferred tax asset ($400,000 × 30%)	120,000	
Tax loss benefit (income tax expense)		210,000
Tax loss benefit (income tax expense)	120,000	
Allowance to reduce deferred tax asset to realizable value		120,000

The tax refund receivable results from carrying $300,000 of the 2008 loss **back** to offset 2007 taxable income. The deferred tax asset results from the potential **carryforward** of the remaining $400,000 loss ($700,000 − $300,000). However, the inconsistent performance of the company (profitable operations in the first year, loss in the second year) coupled with the lack of positive evidence concerning future operations indicate that at the end of 2008 it is more likely than not that none of the deferred tax asset will be realized. Therefore, Mobe must establish a valuation allowance to reduce this asset to its expected realizable value. In 2009, the entries are

Income tax expense ($1,200,000 × 30%)	360,000	
Deferred tax asset		120,000
Income taxes payable		
[($1,200,000 − $400,000) × 30%]		240,000
Allowance to reduce deferred tax asset		
to realizable value	120,000	
Benefit due to loss carryforward		
(income tax expense)		120,000

Income taxes payable is 2009 income of $1,200,000 less the $400,000 loss carryforward, times 30%. Total income tax expense for 2009 is $240,000 ($360,000 − $120,000). Note that if the facts had indicated positive evidence following 2008 for 2009 operations, the allowance account would not have been recognized and 2009 expense would have been $360,000.

F. Financial Statement Presentation of Income Tax

34. (c) The warranty temporary difference results in future deductible amounts of $700,000 per year in 2010 through 2012 ($2,100,000 ÷ 3). The installment temporary difference results in future taxable amounts of $500,000 per year in 2010 through 2012 ($1,500,000 ÷ 3). The portions of the resulting deferred tax asset and deferred tax liability that will be netted to find the amount of the current asset/current liability to be presented on the BS are shown below.

Deferred tax asset:	
$(700,000) × 25% =	$(175,000)
Deferred tax liability:	
$500,000 × 25% =	125,000
Current deferred tax asset (CDTA) shown on BS	$ (50,000)

The noncurrent deferred tax asset is $100,000 [25% × ($2,100,000 − $1,500,000)] − $50,000 CDTA.

35. (d) Deferred tax liabilities and assets are classified as current or noncurrent based on the classification of the related asset or liability for financial reporting. The deferred tax liability resulting from accelerated tax depreciation should be considered noncurrent because the related asset is classified as noncurrent. The deferred tax asset resulting from additional costs in inventory for tax purposes is classified as current because the related asset is classified as current. Therefore, Thorn would report a **noncurrent deferred tax liability** of **$75,000**.

36. (d) Deferred tax liabilities and assets are classified as current or noncurrent based on the related asset or liability. A deferred tax liability or asset is considered to be related to an asset or liability if reduction of the asset or liability will cause the temporary difference to reverse. If the deferred tax liability or asset is **not** related to any asset or liability, then it is classified based on the timing of its expected reversal or utilization date. This deferred tax liability is related to equipment, which is noncurrent, so the deferred

tax liability should also be classified as a noncurrent liability. Deferred taxes are always classified as assets or liabilities, rather than as contra accounts.

37. (c) Deferred tax assets and liabilities are classified as current or noncurrent based on the classification of the related asset or liability for financial reporting. Therefore, a deferred tax liability relating to depreciation of a fixed asset would be noncurrent in nature. The deferred tax asset relating to rent received in advance that is expected to reverse in the following year would be classified as current. No netting of net current amounts and net noncurrent amounts can occur.

38. (b) A **deferred** tax liability or asset should be classified in two categories (the current amount and the noncurrent amount) on the balance sheet based on the classification of the related asset or liability for financial reporting. The receivable for taxes paid in prior years and refundable through the carryback of the 2009 operating loss is **not** considered a **deferred** tax asset. A current asset should be reported on the balance sheet for the amount of the refund due to Oak Co. Note that if there was a current deferred tax liability it would not be netted with the refund receivable. However, a current deferred tax asset would be so netted. A noncurrent deferred tax liability should be reported on the balance sheet for temporary differences related to depreciation of fixed assets.

39. (b) Income tax expense must be associated with (i.e., allocated among) income from continuing operations, discontinued operations, extraordinary items, cumulative effect of an accounting change, and prior period adjustments. The tax effect to be associated with any of the special items (other than income from continuing operations) is computed by determining the income tax on overall taxable income and comparing it with the income tax on continuing operations. If more than one special item exists, the difference between tax on ordinary operations and tax on overall taxable income must be allocated proportionately among the special items.

40. (a) The tax benefit of an operating loss carryforward or carryback shall be reported in the same manner as the **source of income (loss) in the current year**. Thus, in 2009, the tax benefit shall be reported under income from continuing operations.

41. (d) Sole proprietorships do not pay any income taxes as the tax items related to a sole proprietorship flow through to the owner's tax return. Because the sole proprietorship is not a taxable entity, no provision for income taxes would be included in the financial statements of the sole proprietorship. Although answer (a) illustrates the correct formula for calculating the taxes payable related to a sole proprietorship's operations, it is an incorrect response because the tax provision would not be shown on the sole proprietorship's financial statements since it flows through to the owner and is a liability of the owner. The income tax expense would be calculated using the owner's tax rates, as it is the owner's personal liability, not the entity's. The proprietorship would have **no** provision for income taxes on its books. The entire income tax liability is the personal responsibility of the owner.

SOLUTIONS TO SIMULATION PROBLEMS

Simulation Problem 1

Directions	Situation	Tax Calculations		Tax Differences	Deferred Tax Classification	Research

	Specific audit objective	(A) (B) (C) (D) (E) (F) (G) (H) (I) (J) (K) (L) (M) (N)
1.	Current tax expense for the year ended April 30, 2007.	○ ○ ○ ○ ○ ○ ● ○ ○ ○ ○ ○ ○ ○
2.	Cumulative temporary differences at April 30, 2008.	○ ○ ○ ○ ○ ○ ○ ○ ○ ○ ○ ○ ● ○
3.	Deferred tax expense for the year ended April 30, 2008.	○ ● ○ ○ ○ ○ ○ ○ ○ ○ ○ ○ ○ ○
4.	Deferred tax liability at April 30, 2009.	○ ○ ○ ○ ○ ○ ○ ● ○ ○ ○ ○ ○ ○

Explanation of solutions

1. **(G)** Current tax expense for FY 2007 is equal to taxable income (Form 1120) of $600,000 times 20% or $120,000.

2. **(M)** The $100,000 temporary difference for FY 2008 is deducted from pretax financial income to arrive at taxable income. Therefore, cumulative temporary differences or future taxable amounts are increased. Thus, $300,000 ($200,000 + $100,000) will be added to pretax financial income in future reversal years.

3. **(B)** Deferred tax expense is equal to the increased rate on future taxable amounts outstanding at the beginning of FY 2008 plus the amount related to the $100,000 of temporary differences that originated in FY 2008. Thus, deferred tax expense is equal to $35,000 [$200,000 × (.25 − .20) + $100,000 × .25]. The entry is

Deferred tax expense	35,000	
Deferred tax liability		35,000

4. **(H)** In FY 2009 cumulative temporary differences (future taxable amounts) increased by $150,000. The deferred tax liability account for three years is shown below.

Deferred Tax Liability		
	40,000	*2007* (200,000 × .20)
	10,000	*2008* [200,000 × (.25 − .20)]
	25,000	(100,000 × .25)
	15,000	*2009* [300,000 × (.30 − .25)]
	45,000	(150,000 × .30)
	Bal. 135,000	

The $135,000 is equal to the cumulative temporary differences of $450,000 ×.30.

Directions	Situation	Tax Calculations	Tax Differences		Deferred Tax Classification	Research

		A *Temporary difference DTA*	B *Temporary difference DTL*	C *Permanent difference*
1.	For plant assets, the depreciation expense deducted for tax purposes is in excess of the depreciation expense used for financial reporting purposes.	○	●	○
2.	A landlord collects some rents in advance. Rents received are taxable in the period in which they are received.	●	○	○
3.	Interest is received on an investment in tax-exempt municipal obligations.	○	○	●
4.	Costs of guarantees and warranties are estimated and accrued for financial reporting purposes.	●	○	○
5.	Life insurance proceeds are collected on the death of a key officer.	○	○	●

		A Temporary difference DTA	B Temporary difference DTL	C Permanent difference
6.	Bad debts are estimated and expensed on the income statement. No bad debts were charged to the allowance account and written off during the year.	●	○	○
7.	Goodwill is deducted on the tax return.	○	●	○

Explanation of solutions

1.   **(B)** In cases in which tax depreciation is greater than accounting (book) depreciation, taxable income will be less than accounting income and a deferred tax liability results. The reason is that in future years tax depreciation will be less than book depreciation and taxable income will be greater than book income. This will result in future cash flows for the income tax liability shown on the Form 1120 exceeding those that would occur based on pretax accounting income. Thus a deferred tax liability will result. The entry is

> Deferred income tax expense   xx
>   Deferred tax liability   xx

In the reversal year, the entry would be

> Deferred tax liability   xx
>   Deferred tax expense   xx

2.   **(A)** Taxable income will exceed pretax accounting (book) income in the year in which the rents are received. In effect, income taxes on the portion of the rent that is unearned for financial reporting under GAAP must be prepaid under the Internal Revenue Code. Thus, a deferred tax asset would result because in future years when the rent received in advance is earned, no taxes will be payable on the amount earned, because the taxes were paid in the year rent was received. The entry is

> Deferred tax asset   xx
>   Deferred tax expense   xx

3.   **(C)** Interest earned on a tax-exempt municipal obligation is a permanent difference. The interest is deducted in the year received from pretax accounting income to arrive at taxable income. However, it will never be reported as income on the firm's Form 1120. Therefore, such a difference does not result in deferred income taxes.

4.   **(A)** Costs of guarantees and warranties are not deductible under the Internal Revenue Code until incurred. Under ASC Topic 450, however they are estimated and recorded as an expense (loss) and a liability in the period of sale. In effect, income taxes are prepaid because in later years a benefit is received when these costs are incurred and deducted on the tax return. The entry in the origination year is

> Deferred tax asset   xx
>   Deferred tax expense   xx

The entry when the warranty costs are deducted is

> Deferred tax expense   xx
>   Deferred tax asset   xx

5.   **(C)** life insurance proceeds are not taxable under the Internal Revenue Code. This gives rise to a permanent difference.

6.   **(A)** The Internal Revenue Code requires the direct write-off method for bad debts. Therefore, bad debts cannot be deducted until the debt becomes uncollectible and is written off. Since no deduction is allowed in the current year, this leads to a future deductible amount and is a deferred tax asset.

7.   **(B)** Goodwill is amortized for tax purposes and tested for impairment for GAAP purposes. Therefore, it results in a temporary difference.

Directions	Situation	Tax Calculations	Tax Differences	Deferred Tax Classification		Research

			Deferred tax asset	Deferred tax liability	Current	Noncurrent
1.	Tax depreciation in excess of book depreciation		○	●	○	●
2.	Bad debts expense in excess of actual write-offs		●	○	●	○
3.	Rent collected in advance for next 12 months		●	○	●	○

		Tax		Deferred Tax	Research
Directions	Situation	Calculations	Tax Differences	Classification	

1. What are the primary objectives of accounting for income taxes?

Objectives and Basic Principles
FAS109, Para 6

> 6. One objective of accounting for income taxes is to recognize the amount of taxes payable or refundable for the current year. A second objective is to recognize deferred tax liabilities and assets for the future tax consequences of events that have been recognized in an enterprise's financial statements or tax returns.

FAS109, Para 7

> 7. Ideally, the second objective might be stated more specifically to recognize the expected future tax consequences of events that have been recognized in the financial statements or tax returns. However, that objective is realistically constrained because (a) the tax payment or refund that results from a particular tax return is a joint result of all the items included in that return, (b) taxes that will be paid or refunded in future years are the result of events of the current or prior years and events of future years, and (c) information available about the future is limited. As a result, attribution of taxes to individual items and events is arbitrary and except in the simplest situations, requires estimates and approximations.

Codification: 740-10-10-1

2. What is a temporary difference?

Temporary Differences
FAS109, Para 10

> 10. Income taxes currently payable for a particular year usually include the tax consequences of most events that are recognized in the financial statements for that year. However, because tax laws and financial accounting standards differ in their recognition and measurement of assets, liabilities, equity, revenues, expenses, gains, and losses, differences arise between
>
> > a. The amount of taxable income and pretax financial income for a year
> > b. The tax bases of assets or liabilities and their reported amounts in financial statements

FAS109, Para 13

> 13. This Statement refers collectively to the types of differences illustrated by those eight examples and to the ones described in paragraph 15 as temporary differences. Temporary differences that will result in taxable amounts in future years when the related asset or liability is recovered or settled are often referred to in this Statement as taxable temporary differences (examples a., b., and c., in paragraph 11 are taxable temporary differences). Likewise, temporary differences that will result in deductible amounts in future years are often referred to as deductible temporary differences (examples b., c., f., and g., in paragraph 11 are deductible temporary differences). Business combinations accounted for by the purchase method (example h.) may give rise to both taxable and deductible temporary differences.

FAS109, Appendix A., Para 289
Temporary difference

> A difference between the tax basis of an asset or liability and its reported amount in the financial statements that will result in taxable or deductible amounts in future years when the reported amount of the asset or liability is recovered or settled, respectively. Paragraph 11 cites 8 examples of temporary differences. Some temporary differences cannot be identified with a particular asset or liability for financial reporting (paragraph 15), but those temporary differences (a) result from events that have been recognized in the

financial statements and (b) will result in taxable or deductible amounts in future years based on provisions of the tax law. Some events recognized in financial statements do not have tax consequences. Certain revenues are exempt from taxation and certain expenses are not deductible. Events that do not have tax consequences do not give rise to temporary differences.

Codification: 740-10-05-7

3. How are deferred taxes presented in the financial statements?

Financial Statement Presentation
FAS109, Para 41

41. In a classified statement of financial position, an enterprise shall separate deferred tax liabilities and assets into a current amount and a noncurrent amount. Deferred tax liabilities and assets shall be classified as current or noncurrent based on the classification of the related asset or liability for financial reporting. A deferred tax liability or asset that is not related to an asset or liability for financial reporting (paragraph 15), including deferred tax assets related to carryforwards, shall be classified according to the expected reversal date of the temporary difference pursuant to FASB Statement No. 37, *Balance Sheet Classification of Deferred Income Taxes*. The valuation allowance for a particular tax jurisdiction shall be allocated between current and noncurrent deferred tax assets for that tax jurisdiction on a pro rata basis.

FAS109, Para 42

42. For a particular tax-paying component of an enterprise and within a particular tax jurisdiction, (a) all current deferred tax liabilities and assets shall be offset and presented as a single amount and (b) all noncurrent deferred tax liabilities and assets shall be offset and presented as a single amount. However, an enterprise shall not offset deferred tax liabilities and assets attributable to different tax paying components of the enterprise or to different tax jurisdictions.

Codification: 740-10-45-4

4. What tax rate is used to calculate deferred taxes?

FAS109, Para 18

18. The objective is to measure a deferred tax liability or asset using the enacted tax rate(s) expected to apply to taxable income in the periods in which the deferred tax liability or asset is expected to be settled or realized. Under current US federal tax law, if taxable income exceeds a specified amount, all taxable income is taxed, in substance, at a single flat tax rate. That tax rate shall be used for measurement of a deferred tax liability or asset by enterprises for which graduated tax rates are not a significant factor. Enterprises for which graduated tax rates are a significant factor shall measure a deferred tax liability or asset using the average graduated tax rate applicable to the amount of estimated annual taxable income in the periods in which the deferred tax liability or asset is estimated to be settled or realized (paragraph 236). Other provisions of enacted tax laws should be considered when determining the tax rate to apply to certain types of temporary differences and carryforwards (for example, the tax law may provide for different tax rates on ordinary income and capital gains). If there is a phased-in change in tax rates, determination of the applicable tax rate requires knowledge about when deferred tax liabilities and assets will be settled and realized.

An Enacted Change in Tax Laws or Rates
FAS109, Para 27

27. Deferred tax liabilities and assets shall be adjusted for the effect of a change in tax laws or rates. The effects shall be included in income from continuing operations for the period that includes the enactment date.

Codification: 740-10-30-8

5. What components of income tax expense that relate to continuing operations must be included in the notes to the financial statements?

FAS109, Para 45

45. The significant components of income tax expense attributable to continuing operations for each year presented shall be disclosed in the financial statements or notes thereto. Those components would include, for example

a. Current tax expense or benefit
b. Deferred tax expense or benefit (exclusive of the effects of other components listed below)
c. Investment tax credits
d. Government grants (to the extent recognized as a reduction of income tax expense)
e. The benefits of operating loss carryforwards
f. Tax expense that results from allocating certain tax benefits either directly to contributed capital or to reduce goodwill to other noncurrent intangible assets of an acquired entity
g. Adjustments of a deferred tax liability or asset for enacted changes in tax laws or rates or a change in the tax status of the enterprise
h. Adjustments of the beginning-of-the-year balance of a valuation allowance because of a change in circumstances that causes a change in judgment about the realizability of the related deferred tax asset in future years

Codification: 740-10-50-9

Simulation Problem 2

Directions	Situation	Temporary and Permanent Differences	Deferred Tax Schedule	Calculate Taxable Income	Journal Entries	Disclosures	Communication	Research

	Temporary	*Permanent*
Premiums on life insurance of key officer	O	●
Depreciation	●	O
Interest on municipal bonds	O	●
Warranties	●	O
Bad debts	●	O
Rent received in advance from clients	●	O

Directions	Situation	Temporary and Permanent Differences	Deferred Tax Schedule	Calculate Taxable Income	Journal Entries	Disclosures	Communication	Research

Item	Difference between taxable amount and income statement amount	Classification: Deferred tax asset Deferred tax liability	Current or noncurrent	Deferred tax amount
Depreciation	12,000	Deferred tax liability	Noncurrent	4,800
Warranties	750	Deferred tax asset	Current	300
Bad debts	800	Deferred tax asset	Current	320
Rent received	8,000	Deferred tax asset	Current	3,200
Rent received	16,000	Deferred tax asset	Noncurrent	6,400

Explanation of solutions

The adjustment to warranties is the difference between warranty expense deducted on the income statement and the actual warranty work performed during the period ($4,000 – $3,250 = $750). The adjustment to bad debt is the difference between bad debt expense subtracted on the balance sheet, and the actual bad debts written off during the period ($1,400 – $600 = $800). Note that rent received is taxable in the period received, and for deferred tax purposes, it must be fragmented into two components, current and noncurrent.

Directions	Situation	Temporary and Permanent Differences	Deferred Tax Schedule	Calculate Taxable Income	Journal Entries	Disclosures	Communication	Research

Pretax financial income	$400,000
Premiums on life insurance of key officer	10,000
Interest on municipal bonds	(5,300)
Depreciation for tax in excess of book depreciation	(12,000)
Adjustment for warranties	750
Adjustment for bad debts	800
Adjustment for rent received in advance	24,000
Taxable income	418,250

Directions	Situation	Temporary and Permanent Differences	Deferred Tax Schedule	Calculate Taxable Income	Journal Entries	Disclosures	Communication	Research

Account title	Debit	Credit
Deferred tax asset—Current	3,820	
Deferred tax asset—Noncurrent	6,400	
Tax expense	161,880	
Deferred tax liability—Noncurrent		4,800
Income taxes payable		167,300

Explanation of solutions

The total for deferred tax asset—current can be found by adding the current items in the deferred tax schedule in one of the previous simulation tasks.

Directions	Situation	Temporary and Permanent Differences	Deferred Tax Schedule	Calculate Taxable Income	Journal Entries	Disclosures	Communication	Research

Deferred tax asset—Current	3,820
Deferred tax asset—Noncurrent	1,600
Deferred tax liability—Current	0
Deferred tax liability—Noncurrent	0

Explanation of solutions

The netting rules for deferred taxes require that current assets be netted against current deferred tax liabilities. Noncurrent deferred tax assets are netted against noncurrent deferred tax liabilities. Using the journal entries from the previous task, we find that total current deferred tax assets are $3,820. There are no current deferred tax liabilities. Netting noncurrent deferred tax assets and liabilities ($6,400 – $4,800) = $1,600 disclosed on the balance sheet as a noncurrent deferred tax asset.

Directions	Situation	Temporary and Permanent Differences	Deferred Tax Schedule	Calculate Taxable Income	Journal Entries	Disclosures	Communication	Research

To: Mr. Dunn
From: Mr. Green, CPA
Re: Accounting for income taxes

You have requested that I provide a brief overview of accounting for income taxes in accordance with SFAS 109. The objectives of accounting for income taxes are to recognize (1) the amount of taxes payable or refundable for the current year, and (2) deferred tax liabilities and assets for the estimated future tax consequences of temporary differences and carryforwards. Temporary differences are differences between the tax basis of assets or liabilities and their reported amounts in the financial statements that will result in taxable or deductible amounts in future years.

Deferred tax assets and liabilities are measured based on the provisions of enacted tax law; the effects of future changes in the tax laws or rates are not anticipated. The measurement of deferred tax assets is reduced, if necessary, by a valuation allowance to reflect the net asset amount that is more likely than not to be realized. Deferred income tax expense or benefit is measured as the change during the year in an enterprise's deferred tax liabilities and assets.

If you have any other questions, please contact me.

Directions	Situation	Temporary and Permanent Differences	Deferred Tax Schedule	Calculate Taxable Income	Journal Entries	Disclosures	Communication	Research

FAS109, Para 16

16. An enterprise shall recognize a deferred tax liability or asset for all temporary differences and operating loss and tax credit carryforwards in accordance with the provisions of paragraph 17. Deferred tax expense or benefit is the change during the year in an enterprise's deferred tax liabilities and assets. For deferred tax liabilities and assets acquired in a purchase business combination during the year, it is the change since the combination date. Total income tax expense or benefit for the year is the sum of deferred tax expense or benefit and income taxes currently payable or refundable.

Codification: 740-10-30-4

MULTIPLE-CHOICE QUESTIONS (1-91)

1. East Co. issued 1,000 shares of its $5 par common stock to Howe as compensation for 1,000 hours of legal services performed. Howe usually bills $160 per hour for legal services. On the date of issuance, the stock was trading on a public exchange at $140 per share. By what amount should the additional paid-in capital account increase as a result of this transaction?

    a. $135,000
    b. $140,000
    c. $155,000
    d. $160,000

2. On July 1, 2010, Cove Corp., a closely held corporation, issued 6% bonds with a maturity value of $60,000, together with 1,000 shares of its $5 par value common stock, for a combined cash amount of $110,000. The market value of Cove's stock cannot be ascertained. If the bonds were issued separately, they would have sold for $40,000 on an 8% yield to maturity basis. What amount should Cove report for additional paid-in capital on the issuance of the stock?

    a. $75,000
    b. $65,000
    c. $55,000
    d. $45,000

3. Beck Corp. issued 200,000 shares of common stock when it began operations in 2008 and issued an additional 100,000 shares in 2009. Beck also issued preferred stock convertible to 100,000 shares of common stock. In 2010, Beck purchased 75,000 shares of its common stock and held it in Treasury. At December 31, 2010, how many shares of Beck's common stock were outstanding?

    a. 400,000
    b. 325,000
    c. 300,000
    d. 225,000

4. A corporation was organized in January 2010 with authorized capital of $10 par value common stock. On February 1, 2010, shares were issued at par for cash. On March 1, 2010, the corporation's attorney accepted 5,000 shares of the common stock in settlement for legal services with a fair value of $60,000. Additional paid-in capital would increase on

	February 1, 2010	March 1, 2010
a.	Yes	No
b.	Yes	Yes
c.	No	No
d.	No	Yes

5. On April 1, 2010, Hyde Corp., a newly formed company, had the following stock issued and outstanding:

- Common stock, no par, $1 stated value, 20,000 shares originally issued for $30 per share.
- Preferred stock, $10 par value, 6,000 shares originally issued for $50 per share.

Hyde's April 1, 2010 statement of stockholders' equity should report

	Common stock	Preferred stock	Additional paid-in capital
a.	$ 20,000	$ 60,000	$820,000
b.	$ 20,000	$300,000	$580,000

c.	$600,000	$300,000	$0
d.	$600,000	$ 60,000	$240,000

6. On March 1, 2010, Rya Corp. issued 1,000 shares of its $20 par value common stock and 2,000 shares of its $20 par value convertible preferred stock for a total of $80,000. At this date, Rya's common stock was selling for $36 per share, and the convertible preferred stock was selling for $27 per share. What amount of the proceeds should be allocated to Rya's convertible preferred stock?

    a. $60,000
    b. $54,000
    c. $48,000
    d. $44,000

7. During 2008, Brad Co. issued 5,000 shares of $100 par convertible preferred stock for $110 per share. One share of preferred stock can be converted into three shares of Brad's $25 par common stock at the option of the preferred shareholder. On December 31, 2010, when the market value of the common stock was $40 per share, all of the preferred stock was converted. What amount should Brad credit to Common Stock and to Additional Paid-in Capital— Common Stock as a result of the conversion?

	Common stock	Additional paid-in capital
a.	$375,000	$175,000
b.	$375,000	$225,000
c.	$500,000	$ 50,000
d.	$600,000	$0

8. Quoit, Inc. issued preferred stock with detachable common stock warrants. The issue price exceeded the sum of the warrants' fair value and the preferred stock's par value. The preferred stock's fair value was not determinable. What amount should be assigned to the warrants outstanding?

    a. Total proceeds.
    b. Excess of proceeds over the par value of the preferred stock.
    c. The proportion of the proceeds that the warrants' fair value bears to the preferred stock's par value.
    d. The fair value of the warrants.

9. Blue Co. issued preferred stock with detachable common stock warrants at a price that exceeded both the par value and the market value of the preferred stock. At the time the warrants are exercised, Blue's total stockholders' equity is increased by the

	Cash received upon exercise of the warrants	Carrying amount of warrants
a.	Yes	No
b.	Yes	Yes
c.	No	No
d.	No	Yes

10. When collectibility is reasonably assured, the excess of the subscription price over the stated value of the no par common stock subscribed should be recorded as

    a. No par common stock.
    b. Additional paid-in capital when the subscription is recorded.
    c. Additional paid-in capital when the subscription is collected.
    d. Additional paid-in capital when the common stock is issued.

11. On December 1, 2010, shares of authorized common stock were issued on a subscription basis at a price in excess of par value. A total of 20% of the subscription price of each share was collected as a down payment on December 1, 2010, with the remaining 80% of the subscription price of each share due in 2011. Collectibility was reasonably assured. At December 31, 2010, the stockholders' equity section of the balance sheet would report additional paid-in capital for the excess of the subscription price over the par value of the shares of common stock subscribed and

    a. Common stock issued for 20% of the par value of the shares of common stock subscribed.
    b. Common stock issued for the par value of the shares of common stock subscribed.
    c. Common stock subscribed for 80% of the par value of the shares of common stock subscribed.
    d. Common stock subscribed for the par value of the shares of common stock subscribed.

12. In 2009, Seda Corp. acquired 6,000 shares of its $1 par value common stock at $36 per share. During 2010, Seda issued 3,000 of these shares at $50 per share. Seda uses the cost method to account for its treasury stock transactions. What accounts and amounts should Seda credit in 2010 to record the issuance of the 3,000 shares?

	Treasury stock	Additional paid-in capital	Retained earnings	Common stock
a.		$102,000	$42,000	$6,000
b.		$144,000		$6,000
c.	$108,000	$ 42,000		
d.	$108,000		$42,000	

13. At December 31, 2009, Rama Corp. had 20,000 shares of $1 par value treasury stock that had been acquired in 2009 at $12 per share. In May 2010, Rama issued 15,000 of these treasury shares at $10 per share. The cost method is used to record treasury stock transactions. Rama is located in a state where laws relating to acquisition of treasury stock restrict the availability of retained earnings for declaration of dividends. At December 31, 2010, what amount should Rama show in notes to financial statements as a restriction of retained earnings as a result of its treasury stock transactions?

    a. $ 5,000
    b. $10,000
    c. $60,000
    d. $90,000

14. United, Inc.'s unadjusted current assets section and stockholders' equity section of its December 31, 2010 balance sheet are as follows:

Current assets	
Cash	$ 60,000
Investments in trading securities (including $300,000 of United, Inc. common stock)	400,000
Trade accounts receivable	340,000
Inventories	148,000
Total	$ 948,000

Stockholders' equity	
Common stock	$2,224,000
Retained earnings (deficit)	(224,000)
Total	$2,000,000

The investments and inventories are reported at their costs, which approximate market values. In its 2010 statement of stockholders' equity, United's total amount of equity at December 31, 2010, is

    a. $2,224,000

    b. $2,000,000
    c. $1,924,000
    d. $1,700,000

15. Cyan Corp. issued 20,000 shares of $5 par common stock at $10 per share. On December 31, 2009, Cyan's retained earnings were $300,000. In March 2010, Cyan reacquired 5,000 shares of its common stock at $20 per share. In June 2010, Cyan sold 1,000 of these shares to its corporate officers for $25 per share. Cyan uses the cost method to record treasury stock. Net income for the year ended December 31, 2010, was $60,000. At December 31, 2010, what amount should Cyan report as retained earnings?

    a. $360,000
    b. $365,000
    c. $375,000
    d. $380,000

16. Victor Corporation was organized on January 2, 2010, with 100,000 authorized shares of $10 par value common stock. During 2010 Victor had the following capital transactions:

January 5—issued 75,000 shares at $14 per share.
December 27—purchased 5,000 shares at $11 per share.

Victor used the par value method to record the purchase of the treasury shares. What would be the balance in the paid-in capital from treasury stock account at December 31, 2010?

    a. $0
    b. $ 5,000
    c. $15,000
    d. $20,000

17. On incorporation, Dee Inc. issued common stock at a price in excess of its par value. No other stock transactions occurred except treasury stock was acquired for an amount exceeding this issue price. If Dee uses the par value method of accounting for treasury stock appropriate for retired stock, what is the effect of the acquisition on the following?

	Net common stock	Additional paid-in capital	Retained earnings
a.	No effect	Decrease	No effect
b.	Decrease	Decrease	Decrease
c.	Decrease	No effect	Decrease
d.	No effect	Decrease	Decrease

18. Posy Corp. acquired treasury shares at an amount greater than their par value, but less than their original issue price. Compared to the cost method of accounting for treasury stock, does the par value method report a greater amount for additional paid-in capital and a greater amount for retained earnings?

	Additional paid-in capital	Retained earnings
a.	Yes	Yes
b.	Yes	No
c.	No	No
d.	No	Yes

19. In 2008, Rona Corp. issued 5,000 shares of $10 par value common stock for $100 per share. In 2010, Rona reacquired 2,000 of its shares at $150 per share from the estate of one of its deceased officers and immediately canceled these 2,000 shares. Rona uses the cost method in accounting for its treasury stock transactions. In connection with the retirement of these 2,000 shares, Rona should debit

	Additional paid-in capital	Retained earnings
a.	$ 20,000	$280,000
b.	$100,000	$180,000
c.	$180,000	$100,000
d.	$280,000	$0

20. The following accounts were among those reported on Luna Corp.'s balance sheet at December 31, 2009:

Available-for-sale securities (market value $140,000)	$ 80,000
Preferred stock, $20 par value, 20,000 shares issued and outstanding	400,000
Additional paid-in capital on preferred stock	30,000
Retained earnings	900,000

On January 20, 2010, Luna exchanged all of the available-for-sale securities for 5,000 shares of Luna's preferred stock. Market values at the date of the exchange were $150,000 for the available-for-sale securities and $30 per share for the preferred stock. The 5,000 shares of preferred stock were retired immediately after the exchange. Which of the following journal entries should Luna record in connection with this transaction?

		Debit	Credit
a.	Preferred stock	100,000	
	Additional paid-in capital on preferred stock	7,500	
	Retained earnings	42,500	
	Available-for-sale securities		80,000
	Gain on exchange of securities		70,000
b.	Preferred stock	100,000	
	Additional paid-in capital on preferred stock	30,000	
	Available-for-sale securities		80,000
	Additional paid-in capital from retirement of preferred stock		50,000
c.	Preferred stock	150,000	
	Available-for-sale securities		80,000
	Additional paid-in capital on preferred stock		70,000
d.	Preferred stock	150,000	
	Available-for-sale securities		80,000
	Gain on exchange of securities		70,000

21. On December 31, 2010, Pack Corp.'s board of directors canceled 50,000 shares of $2.50 par value common stock held in treasury at an average cost of $13 per share. Before recording the cancellation of the treasury stock, Pack had the following balances in its stockholders' equity accounts:

Common stock	$540,000
Additional paid-in capital	750,000
Retained earnings	900,000
Treasury stock, at cost	650,000

In its balance sheet at December 31, 2010, Pack should report a common stock balance of

a. $0
b. $250,000

c. $415,000
d. $540,000

22. In 2009, Fogg, Inc. issued $10 par value common stock for $25 per share. No other common stock transactions occurred until March 31, 2011, when Fogg acquired some of the issued shares for $20 per share and retired them. Which of the following statements correctly states an effect of this acquisition and retirement?

a.   2011 net income is decreased.
b.   2011 net income is increased.
c.   Additional paid-in capital is decreased.
d.   Retained earnings is increased.

23. Plack Co. purchased 10,000 shares (2% ownership) of Ty Corp. on February 14, 2010. Plack received a stock dividend of 2,000 shares on April 30, 2010, when the market value per share was $35. Ty paid a cash dividend of $2 per share on December 15, 2010. In its 2010 income statement, what amount should Plack report as dividend income?

a. $20,000
b. $24,000
c. $90,000
d. $94,000

24. Arp Corp.'s outstanding capital stock at December 15, 2010, consisted of the following:

- 30,000 shares of 5% cumulative preferred stock, par value $10 per share, fully participating as to dividends. No dividends were in arrears.
- 200,000 shares of common stock, par value $1 per share.

On December 15, 2010, Arp declared dividends of $100,000. What was the amount of dividends payable to Arp's common stockholders?

a. $10,000
b. $34,000
c. $40,000
d. $47,500

25. At December 31, 2009 and 2010, Apex Co. had 3,000 shares of $100 par, 5% cumulative preferred stock outstanding. No dividends were in arrears as of December 31, 2008. Apex did not declare a dividend during 2009. During 2010, Apex paid a cash dividend of $10,000 on its preferred stock. Apex should report dividends in arrears in its 2010 financial statements as a(n)

a.   Accrued liability of $15,000.
b.   Disclosure of $15,000.
c.   Accrued liability of $20,000.
d.   Disclosure of $20,000.

26. East Corp., a calendar-year company, had sufficient retained earnings in 2010 as a basis for dividends, but was temporarily short of cash. East declared a dividend of $100,000 on April 1, 2010, and issued promissory notes to its stockholders in lieu of cash. The notes, which were dated April 1, 2010, had a maturity date of March 31, 2011, and a 10% interest rate. How should East account for the scrip dividend and related interest?

a.   Debit retained earnings for $110,000 on April 1, 2010.
b.   Debit retained earnings for $110,000 on March 31, 2011.

c. Debit retained earnings for $100,000 on April 1, 2010, and debit interest expense for $10,000 on March 31, 2011.

d. Debit retained earnings for $100,000 on April 1, 2010, and debit interest expense for $7,500 on December 31, 2010.

27. On January 2, 2010, Lake Mining Co.'s board of directors declared a cash dividend of $400,000 to stockholders of record on January 18, 2010, payable on February 10, 2010. The dividend is permissible under law in Lake's state of incorporation. Selected data from Lake's December 31, 2009 balance sheet are as follows:

Accumulated depletion	$100,000
Capital stock	500,000
Additional paid-in capital	150,000
Retained earnings	300,000

The $400,000 dividend includes a liquidating dividend of
a. $0
b. $100,000
c. $150,000
d. $300,000

28. On June 27, 2010, Brite Co. distributed to its common stockholders 100,000 outstanding common shares of its investment in Quik, Inc., an unrelated party. The carrying amount on Brite's books of Quik's $1 par common stock was $2 per share. Immediately after the distribution, the market price of Quik's stock was $2.50 per share. In its income statement for the year ended June 30, 2010, what amount should Brite report as gain before income taxes on disposal of the stock?
a. $250,000
b. $200,000
c. $ 50,000
d. $0

29. On December 1, 2010, Nilo Corp. declared a property dividend of marketable securities to be distributed on December 31, 2010, to stockholders of record on December 15, 2010. On December 1, 2010, the trading securities had a carrying amount of $60,000 and a fair value of $78,000. What is the effect of this property dividend on Nilo's 2010 retained earnings, after all nominal accounts are closed?
a. $0.
b. $18,000 increase.
c. $60,000 decrease.
d. $78,000 decrease.

30. Long Co. had 100,000 shares of common stock issued and outstanding at January 1, 2010. During 2010, Long took the following actions:

March 15	—	Declared a 2-for-1 stock split, when the fair value of the stock was $80 per share.
December 15	—	Declared a $.50 per share cash dividend.

In Long's statement of stockholders' equity for 2010, what amount should Long report as dividends?
a. $ 50,000
b. $100,000
c. $850,000
d. $950,000

31. A company declared a cash dividend on its common stock on December 15, 2010, payable on January 12, 2011.

How would this dividend affect stockholders' equity on the following dates?

	December 15, 2010	December 31, 2010	January 12, 2011
a.	Decrease	No effect	Decrease
b.	Decrease	No effect	No effect
c.	No effect	Decrease	No effect
d.	No effect	No effect	Decrease

32. Ole Corp. declared and paid a liquidating dividend of $100,000. This distribution resulted in a decrease in Ole's

	Paid-in capital	Retained earnings
a.	No	No
b.	Yes	Yes
c.	No	Yes
d.	Yes	No

33. Instead of the usual cash dividend, Evie Corp. declared and distributed a property dividend from its overstocked merchandise. The excess of the merchandise's carrying amount over its market value should be
a. Ignored.
b. Reported as a separately disclosed reduction of retained earnings.
c. Reported as an extraordinary loss, net of income taxes.
d. Reported as a reduction in income before extraordinary items.

34. The following stock dividends were declared and distributed by Sol Corp.:

Percentage of common share outstanding at declaration date	Fair value	Par value
10	$15,000	$10,000
28	40,000	30,800

What aggregate amount should be debited to retained earnings for these stock dividends?
a. $40,800
b. $45,800
c. $50,000
d. $55,000

35. Ray Corp. declared a 5% stock dividend on its 10,000 issued and outstanding shares of $2 par value common stock, which had a fair value of $5 per share before the stock dividend was declared. This stock dividend was distributed sixty days after the declaration date. By what amount did Ray's current liabilities increase as a result of the stock dividend declaration?
a. $0
b. $ 500
c. $1,000
d. $2,500

36. How would total stockholders' equity be affected by the declaration of each of the following?

	Stock dividend	Stock split
a.	No effect	Increase
b.	Decrease	Decrease
c.	Decrease	No effect
d.	No effect	No effect

37. On July 1, 2010, Bart Corporation has 200,000 shares of $10 par common stock outstanding and the market price of the stock is $12 per share. On the same date, Bart declared a 1-for-2 reverse stock split. The par of the stock was increased from $10 to $20 and one new $20 par share was issued for each two $10 par shares outstanding. Immediately before the 1-for-2 reverse stock split, Bart's additional paid-in capital was $450,000. What should be the balance in Bart's additional paid-in capital account immediately after the reverse stock split is effected?

- a. $0
- b. $450,000
- c. $650,000
- d. $850,000

38. How would a stock split in which the par value per share decreases in proportion to the number of additional shares issued affect each of the following?

	Additional paid-in capital	Retained earnings
a.	Increase	No effect
b.	No effect	No effect
c.	No effect	Decrease
d.	Increase	Decrease

39. At December 31, 2009, Eagle Corp. reported $1,750,000 of appropriated retained earnings for the construction of a new office building, which was completed in 2010 at a total cost of $1,500,000. In 2010, Eagle appropriated $1,200,000 of retained earnings for the construction of a new plant. Also, $2,000,000 of cash was restricted for the retirement of bonds due in 2011. In its 2010 balance sheet, Eagle should report what amount of appropriated retained earnings?

- a. $1,200,000
- b. $1,450,000
- c. $2,950,000
- d. $3,200,000

40. The following information pertains to Meg Corp.:

- Dividends on its 1,000 shares of 6%, $10 par value cumulative preferred stock have not been declared or paid for three years.
- Treasury stock that cost $15,000 was reissued for $8,000.

What amount of retained earnings should be appropriated as a result of these items?

- a. $0
- b. $1,800
- c. $7,000
- d. $8,800

41. A retained earnings appropriation can be used to

- a. Absorb a fire loss when a company is self-insured.
- b. Provide for a contingent loss that is probable and reasonably estimable.
- c. Smooth periodic income.
- d. Restrict earnings available for dividends.

42. On January 1, 2010, Doro Corp. granted an employee an option to purchase 3,000 shares of Doro's $5 par value common stock at $20 per share. The option became exercisable on December 31, 2011, after the employee completed two years of service. The option was exercised on January 10, 2012. The market prices of Doro's stock and stock options were as follows:

Date	Market price of stock	Market price of similar stock option
January 1, 2010	$30	$8
December 31, 2011	50	9
January 10, 2012	45	11

For 2010, Doro should recognize compensation expense of

- a. $45,000
- b. $30,000
- c. $15,000
- d. $12,000

43. In connection with a stock option plan for the benefit of key employees, Ward Corp. intends to distribute treasury shares when the options are exercised. These shares were bought in 2009 at $42 per share. On January 1, 2010, Ward granted stock options for 10,000 shares at $38 per share as additional compensation for services to be rendered over the next three years. The options are exercisable during a four-year period beginning January 1, 2013, by grantees still employed by Ward. Market price of Ward's stock was $47 per share at the grant date. The fair value of a similar stock option with the same terms was $12 at the grant date. No stock options were terminated during 2010. In Ward's December 31, 2010 income statement, what amount should be reported as compensation expense pertaining to the options?

- a. $90,000
- b. $40,000
- c. $30,000
- d. $0

Items 44 and 45 are based on the following:

On January 2, 2010, Kine Co. granted Morgan, its president, compensatory stock options to buy 1,000 shares of Kine's $10 par common stock. The options call for a price of $20 per share and are exercisable for three years following the grant date. Morgan exercised the options on December 31, 2010. The market price of the stock was $50 on January 2, 2010, and $70 on December 31, 2010. The fair value of a similar stock option with the same terms was $28 on the grant date.

44. What is compensation expense for 2010 for the share-based payments?

- a. $ 9,333
- b. $10,000
- c. $20,000
- d. $28,000

45. By what net amount should stockholders' equity increase as a result of the grant and exercise of the options?

- a. $20,000
- b. $30,000
- c. $50,000
- d. $70,000

46. On January 2, 2010, Morey Corp. granted Dean, its president, 20,000 stock appreciation rights for past services. Those rights are exercisable immediately and expire on January 1, 2013. On exercise, Dean is entitled to receive cash for the excess of the stock's market price on the exercise date over the market price on the grant date. Dean did not exercise any of the rights during 2010. The market price of Morey's stock was $30 on January 2, 2010, and $45 on December 31, 2010. As a result of the stock appreciation rights, Morey should recognize compensation expense for 2010 of

- a. $0
- b. $100,000
- c. $300,000
- d. $600,000

47. Wall Corp.'s employee stock purchase plan specifies the following:

- For every $1 withheld from employees' wages for the purchase of Wall's common stock, Wall contributes $2.
- The stock is purchased from Wall's treasury stock at market price on the date of purchase.

The following information pertains to the plan's 2010 transactions:

Employee withholdings for the year	$ 350,000
Market value of 150,000 shares issued	1,050,000
Carrying amount of treasury stock issued (cost)	900,000

Before payroll taxes, what amount should Wall recognize as expense in 2010 for the stock purchase plan?

a. $1,050,000
b. $ 900,000
c. $ 700,000
d. $ 550,000

48. In accounting for stock-based compensation, what interest rate is used to discount both the exercise price of the option and the future dividend stream?

a. The firm's known incremental borrowing rate.
b. The current market rate that firms in that particular industry use to discount cash flows.
c. The risk-free interest rate.
d. Any rate that firms can justify as being reasonable.

49. In what circumstances is compensation expense immediately recognized?

a. In all circumstances.
b. In circumstances when the options are exercisable within two years for services rendered over the next two years.
c. In circumstances when options are granted for prior service, and the options are immediately exercisable.
d. In no circumstances is compensation expense immediately recognized.

50. Compensation cost for a share-based payment to employees that is classified as a liability is measured as

a. The change in fair value of the instrument for each reporting period.
b. The total fair value at grant date.
c. The present value of cash payments due over the life of the grant.
d. The actual cash outlay for the period.

51. What is the measurement date for a share-based payment to employees that is classified as a liability?

a. The service inception date.
b. The grant date.
c. The settlement date.
d. The end of the reporting period.

52. Shafer Corporation (a nonpublic company) established an employee stock option plan on January 1, 2010. The plan allows its employees to acquire 20,000 shares of its $5 par value common stock at $70 per share, when the market price is $75. The options may not be exercised until five years from the grant date. The risk-free interest rate is 6%, and the stock is expected to pay dividends of $3 annually. The fair value of a similar option at the grant date is $6.40. What is the amount of deferred compensation expense that should be recorded in year one?

a. $ 20,000
b. $ 25,000
c. $100,000
d. $128,000

53. Galaxy has a tax benefit and cash retained of $20,000 as a result of share-based payments to employees. How is this tax benefit disclosed in the financial statements?

a. As a component of other comprehensive income.
b. As a prior period adjustment.
c. As a current liability on the balance sheet.
d. As a cash inflow from financing activities on the statement of cash flows.

54. On July 1, 2010, Jordan Corp. granted employees share-based payments in the form of compensatory stock options. How should Jordan account for the outstanding options in calculating earnings per share for 2010 if the options are not antidilutive?

a. Include the options in the denominator of basic and diluted earnings per share for the entire year.
b. Include the options in the denominator of diluted earnings per share for the entire year.
c. Include the options in the denominator of diluted earnings per share weighted by number of months outstanding.
d. Ignore the options in the calculation of diluted earnings per share.

55. At December 31, 2010 and 2009, Gow Corp. had 100,000 shares of common stock and 10,000 shares of 5%, $100 par value cumulative preferred stock outstanding. No dividends were declared on either the preferred or common stock in 2010 or 2009. Net income for 2010 was $1,000,000. For 2010, basic earnings per share amounted to

a. $10.00
b. $ 9.50
c. $ 9.00
d. $ 5.00

56. Ute Co. had the following capital structure during 2009 and 2010:

Preferred stock, $10 par, 4% cumulative, 25,000 shares issued and outstanding	$ 250,000
Common stock, $5 par, 200,000 shares issued and outstanding	1,000,000

Ute reported net income of $500,000 for the year ended December 31, 2010. Ute paid no preferred dividends during 2009 and paid $16,000 in preferred dividends during 2010. In its December 31, 2010 income statement, what amount should Ute report as basic earnings per share?

a. $2.42
b. $2.45
c. $2.48
d. $2.50

57. The following information pertains to Jet Corp.'s outstanding stock for 2010:

Common stock, $5 par value	
Shares outstanding, 1/1/10	20,000
2-for-1 stock split, 4/1/10	20,000
Shares issued, 7/1/10	10,000

Preferred stock, $10 par value, 5% cumulative	
Shares outstanding, 1/1/10	4,000

What are the number of shares Jet should use to calculate 2010 basic earnings per share?

a. 40,000
b. 45,000
c. 50,000
d. 54,000

58. Timp, Inc. had the following common stock balances and transactions during 2010

1/1/10	Common stock outstanding	30,000
2/1/10	Issued a 10% common stock dividend	3,000
7/1/10	Issued common stock for cash	8,000
12/31/10	Common stock outstanding	41,000

What were Timp's 2010 weighted-average shares outstanding?

a. 30,000
b. 34,000
c. 36,750
d. 37,000

59. Strauch Co. has one class of common stock outstanding and no other securities that are potentially convertible into common stock. During 2009, 100,000 shares of common stock were outstanding. In 2010, two distributions of additional common shares occurred: On April 1, 20,000 shares of treasury stock were sold, and on July 1, a 2-for-1 stock split was issued. Net income was $410,000 in 2010 and $350,000 in 2009. What amounts should Strauch report as basic earnings per share in its 2010 and 2009 comparative income statements?

	2010	2009
a.	$1.78	$3.50
b.	$1.78	$1.75
c.	$2.34	$1.75
d.	$2.34	$3.50

60. Earnings per share data must be reported on the income statement for

	Cumulative effect of a change in accounting principle	Extraordinary items
a.	Yes	No
b.	No	No
c.	No	Yes
d.	Yes	Yes

61. On January 31, 2010, Pack, Inc. split its common stock 2 for 1, and Young, Inc. issued a 5% stock dividend. Both companies issued their December 31, 2009 financial statements on March 1, 2010. Should Pack's 2009, basic earnings per share (BEPS) take into consideration the stock split, and should Young's 2009 BEPS take into consideration the stock dividend?

	Pack's 2009 BEPS	Young's 2009 BEPS
a.	Yes	No
b.	No	No
c.	Yes	Yes
d.	No	Yes

62. Mann, Inc. had 300,000 shares of common stock issued and outstanding at December 31, 2009. On July 1, 2010, an additional 50,000 shares of common stock were issued for cash. Mann also had unexercised stock options to purchase 40,000 shares of common stock at $15 per share outstanding at the beginning and end of 2010. The average market price of Mann's common stock was $20 during 2010. What is the number of shares that should be used in computing diluted earnings per share for the year ended December 31, 2010?

a. 325,000
b. 335,000
c. 360,000
d. 365,000

63. Peters Corp.'s capital structure was as follows:

	December 31	
	2009	2010
Outstanding shares of stock:		
Common	110,000	110,000
Convertible preferred	10,000	10,000

During 2010, Peters paid dividends of $3.00 per share on its preferred stock. The preferred shares are convertible into 20,000 shares of common stock and are considered common stock equivalents. Net income for 2010 was $850,000. Assume that the income tax rate is 30%. The diluted earnings per share for 2010 is

a. $6.31
b. $6.54
c. $7.08
d. $7.45

64. Cox Corporation had 1,200,000 shares of common stock outstanding on January 1 and December 31, 2010. In connection with the acquisition of a subsidiary company in June 2009, Cox is required to issue 50,000 additional shares of its common stock on July 1, 2011, to the former owners of the subsidiary. Cox paid $200,000 in preferred stock dividends in 2010, and reported net income of $3,400,000 for the year. Cox's diluted earnings per share for 2010 should be

a. $2.83
b. $2.72
c. $2.67
d. $2.56

65. On June 30, 2009, Lomond, Inc. issued twenty $10,000, 7% bonds at par. Each bond was convertible into 200 shares of common stock. On January 1, 2010, 10,000 shares of common stock were outstanding. The bondholders converted all the bonds on July 1, 2010. The following amounts were reported in Lomond's income statement for the year ended December 31, 2010:

Revenues	$977,000
Operating expenses	920,000
Interest on bonds	7,000
Income before income tax	50,000
Income tax at 30%	15,000
Net income	$ 35,000

What is Lomond's 2010 diluted earnings per share?

a. $2.50
b. $2.85
c. $2.92
d. $3.50

66. West Co. had earnings per share of $15.00 for 2010 before considering the effects of any convertible securities. No conversion or exercise of convertible securities occurred during 2010. However, possible conversion of convertible bonds, not considered common stock equivalents, would have reduced earnings per share by $0.75. The effect of possible exercise of common stock options would have increased earnings per share by $0.10. What amount should West report as diluted earnings per share for 2010?

a. $14.25
b. $14.35

c. $15.00
d. $15.10

67. In determining diluted earnings per share, dividends on nonconvertible cumulative preferred stock should be
a. Disregarded.
b. Added back to net income whether declared or not.
c. Deducted from net income only if declared.
d. Deducted from net income whether declared or not.

68. The if-converted method of computing earnings per share data assumes conversion of convertible securities as of the
a. Beginning of the earliest period reported (or at time of issuance, if later).
b. Beginning of the earliest period reported (regardless of time of issuance).
c. Middle of the earliest period reported (regardless of time of issuance).
d. Ending of the earliest period reported (regardless of time of issuance).

69. In determining earnings per share, interest expense, net of applicable income taxes, on convertible debt that is dilutive should be
a. Added back to weighted-average common shares outstanding for diluted earnings per share.
b. Added back to net income for diluted earnings per share.
c. Deducted from net income for diluted earnings per share.
d. Deducted from weighted-average common shares outstanding for diluted earnings per share.

70. For contingent issue agreements requiring passage of time or earnings threshold that is met, before issuing stock, these should be

	Included in basic earnings per share	*Included in computing diluted earnings per share*
a.	No	No
b.	No	Yes
c.	Yes	No
d.	Yes	Yes

71. Kent Co. filed a voluntary bankruptcy petition on August 15, 2010, and the statement of affairs reflects the following amounts:

	Book value	Estimated current value
Assets		
Assets pledged with fully secured creditors	$ 300,000	$370,000
Assets pledged with partially secured creditors	180,000	120,000
Free assets	420,000	320,000
	$ 900,000	$810,000
Liabilities		
Liabilities with priority	$ 70,000	
Fully secured creditors	260,000	
Partially secured creditors	200,000	
Unsecured creditors	540,000	
	$1,070,000	

Assume that the assets are converted to cash at the estimated current values and the business is liquidated. What amount of cash will be available to pay unsecured nonpriority claims?
a. $240,000
b. $280,000
c. $320,000
d. $360,000

72. Seco Corp. was forced into bankruptcy and is in the process of liquidating assets and paying claims. Unsecured claims will be paid at the rate of 40 cents on the dollar. Hale holds a $30,000 noninterest-bearing note receivable from Seco collateralized by an asset with a book value of $35,000 and a liquidation value of $5,000. The amount to be realized by Hale on this note is
a. $ 5,000
b. $12,000
c. $15,000
d. $17,000

73. Kamy Corp. is in liquidation under of the Federal Bankruptcy Code. The bankruptcy trustee has established a new set of books for the bankruptcy estate. After assuming custody of the estate, the trustee discovered an unrecorded invoice of $1,000 for machinery repairs performed before the bankruptcy filing. In addition, a truck with a carrying amount of $20,000 was sold for $12,000 cash. This truck was bought and paid for in the year before the bankruptcy. What amount should be debited to estate equity as a result of these transactions?
a. $0
b. $1,000
c. $8,000
d. $9,000

74. On December 30, 2010, Hale Corp. paid $400,000 cash and issued 80,000 shares of its $1 par value common stock to its unsecured creditors on a pro rata basis pursuant to a reorganization plan under Chapter 11 of the bankruptcy statutes. Hale owed these unsecured creditors a total of $1,200,000. Hale's common stock was trading at $1.25 per share on December 30, 2010. As a result of this transaction, Hale's total stockholders' equity had a net increase of
a. $1,200,000
b. $ 800,000
c. $ 100,000
d. $ 80,000

75. The primary purpose of a quasi reorganization is to give a corporation the opportunity to
a. Obtain relief from its creditors.
b. Revalue understated assets to their fair values.
c. Eliminate a deficit in retained earnings.
d. Distribute the stock of a newly created subsidiary to its stockholders in exchange for part of their stock in the corporation.

76. When a company goes through a quasi reorganization, its balance sheet carrying amounts are stated at
a. Original cost.
b. Original book value.
c. Replacement value.
d. Fair value.

77. The stockholders' equity section of Brown Co.'s December 31, 2010 balance sheet consisted of the following:

Common stock, $30 par, 10,000 shares au-	
thorized and outstanding	$300,000
Additional paid-in capital	150,000
Retained earnings (deficit)	(210,000)

On January 2, 2011, Brown put into effect a stockholder-approved quasi reorganization by reducing the par value of the stock to $5 and eliminating the deficit against additional paid-in capital. Immediately after the quasi reorganization, what amount should Brown report as additional paid-in capital?

    a. $ (60,000)
    b. $150,000
    c. $190,000
    d. $400,000

78. On July 1, 2010, Vail Corp. issued rights to stockholders to subscribe to additional shares of its common stock. One right was issued for each share owned. A stockholder could purchase one additional share for 10 rights plus $15 cash. The rights expired on September 30, 2010. On July 1, 2010, the market price of a share with the right attached was $40, while the market price of one right alone was $2. Vail's stockholders' equity on June 30, 2010, comprised the following:

Common stock, $25 par value, 4,000 shares	
issued and outstanding	$100,000
Additional paid-in capital	60,000
Retained earnings	80,000

By what amount should Vail's retained earnings decrease as a result of issuance of the stock rights on July 1, 2010?

    a. $0
    b. $ 5,000
    c. $ 8,000
    d. $10,000

79. In September 2008, West Corp. made a dividend distribution of one right for each of its 120,000 shares of outstanding common stock. Each right was exercisable for the purchase of 1/100 of a share of West's $50 variable rate preferred stock at an exercise price of $80 per share. On March 20, 2010, none of the rights had been exercised, and West redeemed them by paying each stockholder $0.10 per right. As a result of this redemption, West's stockholders' equity was reduced by

    a. $ 120
    b. $ 2,400
    c. $12,000
    d. $36,000

80. On November 2, 2010, Finsbury, Inc. issued warrants to its stockholders giving them the right to purchase additional $20 par value common shares at a price of $30. The stockholders exercised all warrants on March 1, 2011. The shares had market prices of $33, $35, and $40 on November 2, 2010; December 31, 2010; and March 1, 2011, respectively. What were the effects of the warrants on Finsbury's additional paid-in capital and net income?

	Additional paid-in capital	Net income
a.	Increased in 2011	No effect
b.	Increased in 2010	No effect
c.	Increased in 2011	Decreased in 2010 and 2011
d.	Increased in 2010	Decreased in 2010 and 2011

81. A company issued rights to its existing shareholders to purchase, for $30 per share, unissued shares of $15 par value

common stock. Additional paid-in capital will be credited when the

	Rights are issued	Rights lapse
a.	Yes	No
b.	No	No
c.	No	Yes
d.	Yes	Yes

Items 82 and 83 are based on the following:

On January 1, 2010, Fay Corporation established an employee stock ownership plan (ESOP). Selected transactions relating to the ESOP during 2010 were as follows:

- On April 1, 2010, Fay contributed $30,000 cash and 3,000 shares of its $10 par common stock to the ESOP. On this date the market price of the stock was $18 a share.
- On October 1, 2010, the ESOP borrowed $100,000 from Union National Bank and acquired 5,000 shares of Fay's common stock in the open market at $17 a share. The note is for one year, bears interest at 10%, and is guaranteed by Fay.
- On December 15, 2010, the ESOP distributed 6,000 shares of Fay common stock to employees of Fay in accordance with the plan formula.

82. In its 2010 income statement, how much should Fay report as compensation expense relating to the ESOP?

    a. $184,000
    b. $120,000
    c. $ 84,000
    d. $ 60,000

83. In Fay's December 31, 2010 balance sheet, how much should be reported as a reduction of shareholders' equity and as an endorsed note payable in respect of the ESOP?

	Reduction of shareholders' equity	Endorsed note payable
a.	$0	$0
b.	$0	$100,000
c.	$100,000	$0
d.	$100,000	$100,000

84. Zinc Co.'s adjusted trial balance at December 31, 2010, includes the following account balances:

Common stock, $3 par	$600,000
Additional paid-in capital	800,000
Treasury stock, at cost	50,000
Net unrealized loss on available-for-sale securities	20,000
Retained earnings: appropriated for uninsured	
earthquake losses	150,000
Retained earnings: unappropriated	200,000

What amount should Zinc report as total stockholders' equity in its December 31, 2010 balance sheet?

    a. $1,680,000
    b. $1,720,000
    c. $1,780,000
    d. $1,820,000

85. Rudd Corp. had 700,000 shares of common stock authorized and 300,000 shares outstanding at December 31, 2009. The following events occurred during 2010:

January 31	Declared 10% stock dividend
June 30	Purchased 100,000 shares
August 1	Reissued 50,000 shares
November 30	Declared 2-for-1 stock split

At December 31, 2010, how many shares of common stock did Rudd have outstanding?

- a. 560,000
- b. 600,000
- c. 630,000
- d. 660,000

86. Nest Co. issued 100,000 shares of common stock. Of these, 5,000 were held as treasury stock at December 31, 2009. During 2010, transactions involving Nest's common stock were as follows:

May 3	1,000 shares of treasury stock were sold.
August 6	10,000 shares of previously unissued stock were sold.
November 18	A 2-for-1 stock split took effect.

Laws in Nest's state of incorporation protect treasury stock from dilution. At December 31, 2010, how many shares of Nest's common stock were issued and outstanding?

	Shares	
	Issued	*Outstanding*
a.	220,000	212,000
b.	220,000	216,000
c.	222,000	214,000
d.	222,000	218,000

87. The following information pertains to Ali Corp. as of and for the year ended December 31, 2010:

Liabilities	$ 60,000
Stockholders' equity	$500,000
Shares of common stock issued and outstanding	10,000
Net income	$ 30,000

During 2010, Ali's officers exercised stock options for 1,000 shares of stock at an option price of $8 per share. What was the effect of exercising the stock options?

- a. Debt to equity ratio decreased to 12%.
- b. Earnings per share increased by $0.33.
- c. Asset turnover increased to 5.4%.
- d. No ratios were affected.

88. Selected information for Irvington Company is as follows:

	December 31	
	2009	2010
Preferred stock, 8%, par $100, non-convertible, noncumulative	$125,000	$125,000
Common stock	300,000	400,000
Retained earnings	75,000	185,000
Dividends paid on preferred stock for year ended	10,000	10,000
Net income for year ended	60,000	120,000

Irvington's return on common stockholders' equity, rounded to the nearest percentage point, for 2010 is

- a. 17%
- b. 19%
- c. 23%
- d. 25%

89. Hoyt Corp.'s current balance sheet reports the following stockholders' equity:

5% cumulative preferred stock, par value $100 per share; 2,500 shares issued and outstanding	$250,000
Common stock, par value $3.50 per share; 100,000 shares issued and outstanding	350,000
Additional paid-in capital in excess of par value of common stock	125,000
Retained earnings	300,000

Dividends in arrears on the preferred stock amount to $25,000. If Hoyt were to be liquidated, the preferred stockholders would receive par value plus a premium of $50,000. The book value per share of common stock is

- a. $7.75
- b. $7.50
- c. $7.25
- d. $7.00

90. Grid Corp. acquired some of its own common shares at a price greater than both their par value and original issue price but less than their book value. Grid uses the cost method of accounting for treasury stock. What is the impact of this acquisition on total stockholders' equity and the book value per common share?

	Total stockholders' equity	*Book value per share*
a.	Increase	Increase
b.	Increase	Decrease
c.	Decrease	Increase
d.	Decrease	Decrease

91. How are dividends per share for common stock used in the calculation of the following?

	Dividend per share payout ratio	*Earnings per share*
a.	Numerator	Numerator
b.	Numerator	Not used
c.	Denominator	Not used
d.	Denominator	Denominator

SIMULATION PROBLEMS

Simulation Problem 1   (40 to 50 minutes)

Situation					
	Concepts	Statement of Retained Earnings	Financial Statement Disclosures	Research	Communication

Min Co. is a publicly held company whose shares are traded in the over-the-counter market. The stockholders' equity accounts at December 31, 2009, had the following balances:

Preferred stock, $100 par value, 6% cumulative; 5,000 shares authorized; 2,000 issued and outstanding	$200,000
Common stock, $1 par value, 150,000 shares authorized; 100,000 issued and outstanding	100,000
Additional paid-in capital	800,000
Retained earnings	1,586,000
Total stockholders' equity	$2,686,000

Transactions during 2010 and other information relating to the stockholders' equity accounts were as follows:

- February 1, 2010—Issued 13,000 shares of common stock to Ram Co. in exchange for land. On the date issued, the stock had a market price of $11 per share. The land had a carrying value on Ram's books of $135,000, and an assessed value for property taxes of $90,000.

- March 1, 2010—Purchased 5,000 shares of its own common stock to be held as treasury stock for $14 per share. Min uses the cost method to account for treasury stock. Transactions in treasury stock are legal in Min's state of incorporation.

- May 10, 2010—Declared a property dividend of marketable securities held by Min to common shareholders. The securities had a carrying value of $600,000; fair value on relevant dates were

Date of declaration (May 10, 2010)	$720,000
Date of record (May 25, 2010)	758,000
Date of distribution (June 1, 2010)	736,000

- October 1, 2010—Reissued 2,000 shares of treasury stock for $16 per share.

- November 4, 2010—Declared a cash dividend of $1.50 per share to all common shareholders of record November 15, 2010. The dividend was paid on November 25, 2010.

- December 20, 2010—Declared the required annual cash dividend on preferred stock for 2010. The dividend was paid on January 5, 2011.

- January 16, 2011—Before closing the accounting records for 2010, Min became aware that no amortization had been recorded for 2009 for a patent purchased on July 1, 2009. Amortization expense was properly recorded in 2010. The patent was properly capitalized at $320,000 and had an estimated useful life of eight years when purchased. Min's income tax rate is 30%. The appropriate correcting entry was recorded on the same day.

- Adjusted net income for 2010 was $838,000.

	Concepts				
Situation		Statement of Retained Earnings	Financial Statement Disclosures	Research	Communication

Items 1 through 10 require the candidate to select the best response from the responses to be selected.

Responses to be selected

A. Contains no potentially dilutive securities
B. A form of compensation which allows employees to receive stock or cash for the difference between the stated value and the market value
C. Legal or contractual restrictions on the number of shares an employee may own
D. Issuance of additional shares in order to reduce the market value
E. Purchase by the corporation of its own stock
F. The value of treasury shares are recorded at cost of acquisition
G. A dividend paid which is considered a return of the shareholders' investment
H. Actions by the board of directors to disclose amounts not available for dividends
I. The balance of the treasury stock account reflects the par value
J. A form of compensation which allows employees to purchase shares at a specified price
K. A dividend issued in the form of a note payable
L. A stock transaction resulting in a reduced number of shares outstanding and a higher market value
M. Assumes convertible securities were converted at the beginning of the period

	(A)	(B)	(C)	(D)	(E)	(F)	(G)	(H)	(I)	(J)	(K)	(L)	(M)
1. Par value method	O	O	O	O	O	O	O	O	O	O	O	O	O
2. Appropriations of retained earnings	O	O	O	O	O	O	O	O	O	O	O	O	O
3. Stock split	O	O	O	O	O	O	O	O	O	O	O	O	O
4. Simple capital structure	O	O	O	O	O	O	O	O	O	O	O	O	O
5. If-converted method	O	O	O	O	O	O	O	O	O	O	O	O	O
6. Scrip dividend	O	O	O	O	O	O	O	O	O	O	O	O	O
7. Stock appreciation rights	O	O	O	O	O	O	O	O	O	O	O	O	O
8. Stock option	O	O	O	O	O	O	O	O	O	O	O	O	O
9. Liquidating dividend	O	O	O	O	O	O	O	O	O	O	O	O	O
10. Treasury stock	O	O	O	O	O	O	O	O	O	O	O	O	O

Situation	Concepts	Statement of Retained Earnings	Financial Statement Disclosures	Research	Communication

Calculate the amounts to be reported on Min's 2010 statement of retained earnings.

	Amount
1. Prior period adjustment	_____
2. Preferred dividends	_____
3. Common dividends—cash	_____
4. Common dividends—property	_____

Situation	Concepts	Statement of Retained Earnings	Financial Statement Disclosures	Research	Communication

Calculate the following amounts to be reported on Min's statement of stockholders' equity at December 31, 2010.

	Amount
1. Number of common shares issued at December 31, 2010	_____
2. Amount of common stock issued	_____
3. Additional paid-in capital, including treasury stock transactions	_____
4. Treasury stock	_____

Items 5 and 6 represent other financial information for 2009 and 2010.

	Amount
5. Book value per share at December 31, 2009, before prior period adjustment	_____
6. Numerator used in calculation of 2010 earnings per share for the year	_____

Situation	Concepts	Statement of Retained Earnings	Financial Statement Disclosures	Research	Communication

You have been asked to find the appropriate authoritative literature on the following questions. Insert the appropriate citation from the authoritative accounting literature.

1. A company issues a small stock dividend. At what amount should the stock dividend be recorded?

2. A company issues a property dividend. How should the property dividend be valued?

3. A company appropriates retained earnings for a loss contingency. How should this be disclosed in the financial statements?

Situation	Concepts	Statement of Retained Earnings	Financial Statement Disclosures	Research	Communication

Kay Smith, the CEO of Min Co., has asked you to explain the difference between common stock and cumulative preferred stock. Write a memorandum to Kay describing the difference between these two types of financial instruments.

REMINDER: Your response will be graded for both technical content and writing skills. Technical content will be evaluated for information that is helpful to the intended reader and clearly relevant to the issue. Writing skills will be evaluated for development, organization, and the appropriate expression of ideas in professional correspondence. Use a standard business memo or letter format with a clear beginning, middle, and end. Do not convey information in the form of a table, bullet point list, or other abbreviated presentation.

To: Ms. Kay Smith, CEO, Min Co.
From: CPA Candidate
Re: Preferred and Common Stock

Simulation Problem 2   (50 to 60 minutes)

Situation	Analysis of Transactions	Balance Sheet Disclosures	Calculation Basic EPS	Calculation Diluted EPS	Communication	Research

M Corporation was incorporated in 2009. During 2009, the company issued 100,000 shares of $1 par value common stock for $27 per share. During 2010, the company had the following transactions.

1/2/10	Issued 10,000 shares of $100 par value cumulative preferred stock at par. The preferred stock was convertible into five shares of common stock and had a dividend rate of 6%.
3/1/10	Issued 3,000 shares of common stock for legal service performed. The value of the legal services was $100,000. The stock was actively traded on a stock exchange and valued on 3/1/10 at $32 per share.
7/1/10	Issued 40,000 shares of common stock for $42 per share.
10/1/10	Repurchased 16,000 shares of treasury stock for $34 per share. M Corp. uses the cost method to account for treasury shares.
12/1/10	Sold 3,000 shares of treasury stock for $29 per share.
12/30/10	Declared and paid a dividend of $0.20 per share on common stock and a 6% dividend on the preferred stock.

During 2009, M Corporation had net income of $250,000 and paid dividends of $28,000. During 2010 M Corporation had net income of $380,000.

Situation	Analysis of Transactions	Balance Sheet Disclosures	Calculation Basic EPS	Calculation Diluted EPS	Communication	Research

Indicate the impact that the transactions for M Company have on its owner equity accounts. Place the appropriate amounts in the table below. If an amount is negative, show the amount in parentheses.

Date	Transaction	Preferred stock	APIC – Preferred stock	Common stock	APIC – Common stock	Retained earnings	Treasury stock	APIC – Treasury stock
1/2/10	Issue preferred stock at par							
3/1/10	Issue common stock for services							
7/1/10	Issue common stock for cash							
10/1/10	Repurchase treasury stock							
12/1/10	Sell treasury stock							
12/30/10	Declare and pay dividends							

Situation	Analysis of Transactions	Balance Sheet Disclosures	Calculation Basic EPS	Calculation Diluted EPS	Communication	Research

Prepare the stockholders' equity section of the balance sheet by completing the following schedule.

Owners' equity:	
Preferred stock	
Common stock	
Additional paid-in capital preferred stock	
Additional paid-in capital common stock	
Additional paid-in capital treasury stock	
Retained earnings	
Treasury stock	
Other comprehensive income	
Total owners' equity	

Situation	Analysis of Transactions	Balance Sheet Disclosures	Calculation Basic EPS	Calculation Diluted EPS	Communication	Research

Calculate basic earnings per share. Show the components of your solution in the following table:

Numerator	
Denominator	
Basic earnings per share	

Situation	Analysis of Transactions	Balance Sheet Disclosures	Calculation Basic EPS	Calculation Diluted EPS	Communication	Research

Calculate diluted earnings per share. Show the components of your solution in the following table:

Numerator	
Denominator	
Diluted earnings per share	

Situation	Analysis of Transactions	Balance Sheet Disclosures	Calculation Basic EPS	Calculation Diluted EPS	Communication	Research

Mr. Fenton, the CEO of M Corporation, does not understand the purpose of earnings per share. He has contacted you for information regarding the reasons for calculating earnings per share and why there are two forms of earnings per share. Write a brief memo to Mr. Fenton explaining the purpose of earnings per share and the difference between basic earnings per share and diluted earnings per share.

REMINDER: Your response will be graded for both technical content and writing skills. Technical content will be evaluated for information that is helpful to the intended reader and clearly relevant to the issue. Writing skills will be evaluated for development, organization, and the appropriate expression of ideas in professional correspondence. Use a standard business memo or letter format with a clear beginning, middle, and end. Do not convey information in the form of a table, bullet point list, or other abbreviated presentation.

To: Mr. Fenton, CEO, M Corporation
From: CPA Candidate
Re: Earnings per share

Situation	Analysis of Transactions	Balance Sheet Disclosures	Calculation Basic EPS	Calculation Diluted EPS	Communication	Research

Research the professional standards to obtain the appropriate section to answer the following question:

When treasury shares are sold for more than purchased, how is it recorded on the financial statements?

Simulation Problem 3   (50 to 60 minutes)

Situation						
	Concepts	Journal Entries	Retained Earnings	Stockholders' Equity Section of Balance Sheet	Communication	Research

Field Co.'s stockholders' equity account balances at December 31, 2009, were as follows:

Common stock	$ 800,000
Additional paid-in capital	1,600,000
Retained earnings	1,845,000

The following 2010 transactions and other information relate to the stockholders' equity accounts:

- Field had 400,000 authorized shares of $5 par common stock, of which 160,000 shares were issued and outstanding.
- On March 5, 2010, Field acquired 5,000 shares of its common stock for $10 per share to hold as treasury stock. The shares were originally issued at $15 per share. Field uses the cost method to account for treasury stock. Treasury stock is permitted in Field's state of incorporation.
- On July 15, 2010, Field declared and distributed a property dividend of inventory. The inventory had a $75,000 carrying value and a $60,000 fair market value.
- On January 2, 2006, Field granted stock options to employees to purchase 20,000 shares of Field's common stock at $18 per share, which was the market price on that date. The options may be exercised within a three-year period beginning January 2, 2010. The measurement date is the same as the grant date. On October 1, 2010, employees exercised all 20,000 options when the market value of the stock was $25 per share. Field issued new shares to settle the transaction. The stock options were accounted for in accordance with the intrinsic value method, which was in effect at the time.
- Field's net income for 2010 was $240,000.

	Concepts					
Situation		Journal Entries	Retained Earnings	Stockholders' Equity Section of Balance Sheet	Communication	Research

Identify whether each of the following statements is True or False.

		True	*False*
1.	Mandatorily redeemable preferred stock is classified as owners' equity and is disclosed after common stock.	○	○
2.	Property dividends are valued at the book value of the property.	○	○
3.	When a company makes a liquidating dividend, it debits the common stock account.	○	○
4.	Scrip dividends are a liability on the date of declaration.	○	○
5.	Stock dividends of 40% of the outstanding shares of stock are valued at fair market value on the date of declaration.	○	○
6.	If a company has cumulative preferred stock, all dividends in arrears must be subtracted from net income in the numerator of basic earnings per share.	○	○
7.	Cash dividends become a liability to the corporation when declared.	○	○
8.	Stock issued for services should be recorded at the fair market value of the services rendered if that value is greater than the fair market value of the stock traded on the exchange.	○	○

		Journal Entries				
Situation	Concepts		Retained Earnings	Stockholders' Equity Section of Balance Sheet	Communication	Research

Prepare journal entries for the following transactions in 2010.

1. Treasury stock purchased on March 5, 2010

2. Declaration and distribution of a property dividend on July 15, 2010

3. Issue of common stock on October 1, 2010

Situation	Concepts	Journal Entries	Retained Earnings	Stockholders' Equity Section of Balance Sheet	Communication	Research

Complete the following schedule for retained earnings for Field Company.

Field Company
STATEMENT OF RETAINED EARNINGS
for the Year ending December 31, 2010

Beginning retained earnings, 1-1-10	
Net income	
Dividends	
End retained earnings, 12-31-10	

Situation	Concepts	Journal Entries	Retained Earnings	Stockholders' Equity Section of Balance Sheet	Communication	Research

Field Company
STOCKHOLDERS' EQUITY SECTION OF BALANCE SHEET
December 31, 2010

Common stock	
Additional paid-in capital	
Retained earnings	
Treasury stock	
Accumulated other comprehensive income	
Total stockholders' equity	

Situation	Concepts	Journal Entries	Retained Earnings	Stockholders' Equity Section of Balance Sheet	Communication	Research

The CEO of Field Company has inquired about calculating earnings per share. Write a brief memo explaining basic and diluted earnings per share.

REMINDER: Your response will be graded for both technical content and writing skills. Technical content will be evaluated for information that is helpful to the intended reader and clearly relevant to the issue. Writing skills will be evaluated for development, organization, and the appropriate expression of ideas in professional correspondence. Use a standard business memo or letter format with a clear beginning, middle, and end. Do not convey information in the form of a table, bullet point list, or other abbreviated presentation.

To: CEO, Field Company
From: CPA Candidate
Re: Earnings per share

Situation	Concepts	Journal Entries	Retained Earnings	Stockholders' Equity Section of Balance Sheet	Communication	Research

Answer the following questions using the Financial Accounting Research System (FARS) database. Select and insert your answer from the authoritative literature.

1. How is diluted earnings per share calculated?

2. What is the purpose of reporting comprehensive income?

3. A company has available-for-sale securities and recognizes an unrealized holding gain in year 1. In year 2, the company sells these securities. How should this affect other comprehensive income on the financial statements?

MULTIPLE-CHOICE ANSWERS

1. a	__ __	20. a	__ __	39. a	__ __	58. d	__ __	77. c	__ __
2. b	__ __	21. c	__ __	40. a	__ __	59. b	__ __	78. a	__ __
3. d	__ ·	22. c	__ __	41. d	__ __	60. b	__ __	79. c	__ __
4. d	__ __	23. b	__ __	42. d	__ __	61. c	· __	80. a	__ __
5. a	__ __	24. c	__ __	43. b	__ __	62. b	__ __	81. b	__ __
6. c	__ __	25. d	__ __	44. d	__ __	63. b	__ __	82. c	__ __
7. a	__ __	26. d	__ __	45. a	__ __	64. d	__ __	83. d	__ __
8. d	__ __	27. b	__ __	46. c	__ ·	65. b	__ __	84. a	__ __
9. a	__ __	28. c	__ __	47. c	__ __	66. a	__ __	85. a	__ __
10. b	__ __	29. c	__ __	48. c	__ __	67. d	__ __	86. a	__ __
11. d	__ __	30. b	__ __	49. c	__ __	68. a	__ __	87. a	__ __
12. c	__ __	31. b	__ __	50. a	__ __	69. b	__ __	88. c	__ __
13. c	__ __	32. d	__ __	51. c	__ __	70. b	__ __	89. d	__ __
14. d	__ __	33. d	__ __	52. d	__ __	71. d	__ __	90. c	__ __
15. a	__ __	34. b	__ __	53. d	__ __	72. c	__ __	91. b	__ __
16. c	__ __	35. a	__ __	54. c	__ __	73. d	__ __		
17. b	__ __	36. d	__ __	55. b	__ __	74. b	__ __		
18. c	__ __	37. b	__ __	56. b	· __	75. c	__ __	1st: __/91 = __%
19. c	__ __	38. b	__ __	57. b	__ __	76. d	__ __	2nd: __/91 = __%

MULTIPLE-CHOICE ANSWER EXPLANATIONS

A. Common Stock

1. (a) When stock is issued for services, the transaction should be recorded at either the FV of the stock issued or the FV of the services received, whichever is more clearly determinable. The FV of stock traded on a public exchange is a more objective, reliable measure than a normal billing rate for legal services, which is likely to be negotiable. If the transaction is valued at $140 per share, legal expense would be debited for $140,000 (1,000 × $140), common stock would be credited for the par value of $5,000 (1,000 × $5), and additional paid-in capital would be credited for the difference ($140,000 − $5,000 = $135,000).

2. (b) When stock is issued in combination with other securities (lump sum sales), the proceeds can be allocated by the **proportional method** or by the **incremental method**. If the FV of each class of securities is determinable, the proceeds should be allocated to each class of securities based on their relative FV. In the instances where the FV of all classes of securities is not determinable, the incremental method should be used. The market value of the securities is used as a basis for those classes that are known, and the remainder of the lump sum is allocated to the class for which the market value is not known. In this problem, the FV of the stock is unknown. As such, the incremental method must be used as follows:

Lump sum receipt	$110,000
FV of bonds	40,000
Balance allocated to common stock	$ 70,000

As the par value of the common stock is $5,000 (1,000 shares × $5), $65,000 ($70,000 − $5,000) should be reported as additional paid-in capital on the issuance of the stock.

3. (d) The number of common shares outstanding is equal to the issued shares less treasury shares. Beck Corp. had 300,000 shares outstanding at 1/1/10. The purchase of treasury shares in 2010 reduced the number of shares outstanding to 225,000 (300,000 − 75,000). The preferred stock convertible into 100,000 shares of common stock is recorded as preferred stock until it is **converted** by the stockholder.

4. (d) On February 1, 2010, when shares were issued at par for cash, the following journal entry would have been made:

Cash	(cash received)	
Common stock		(par)

On March 1, 2010, however, the issuance of 5,000 shares in settlement for legal services rendered would have been recorded as follows:

Legal fees	60,000	
Common stock ($10 × 5,000		
shares)		50,000
Addl. paid-in capital		10,000

Stock issued for services (i.e., in a nonmonetary transaction) should be recorded at the fair market value of those services (in this case $60,000).

B. Preferred Stock

5. (a) When the common stock was issued, it was recorded at stated value with the excess recorded as additional paid-in capital.

Cash	600,000	
Common stock		20,000
Addl. paid-in capital		580,000

The preferred stock was recorded at par value with the excess credited to additional paid-in capital.

Cash	300,000	
Preferred stock		60,000
Addl. paid-in capital		240,000

Therefore, at 4/1/10, the balances are common stock ($20,000), preferred stock ($60,000), and additional paid-in capital ($580,000 + $240,000 = $820,000).

6. (c) In a lump-sum issuance of common and preferred stock, the proceeds ($80,000) are generally allocated based on the relative fair market values of the securities issued. The FV of the convertible preferred stock is $54,000 ($27 × 2,000) and the FV of the common stock is $36,000 ($36 × 1,000). The proceeds are allocated as follows:

Convertible preferred	$\dfrac{\$54,000}{\$90,000}$	×	$80,000	=	$48,000
Common	$\dfrac{\$36,000}{\$90,000}$	×	$80,000	=	$32,000

7. **(a)** All 5,000 shares of convertible preferred stock were converted to common stock at a rate of 3 shares of common for every share of preferred. Therefore, 15,000 shares of common stock were issued (5,000 × 3). The common stock account is credited for the par value of these shares (15,000 × $25 = $375,000). APIC – CS ($550,000 – $375,000 = $175,000) is credited for the difference between the carrying amount of the preferred stock (5,000 × $110 = $550,000) and the par value of the common stock. The journal entry is

Preferred stock	500,000	
APIC-PS	50,000	
Common stock		375,000
APIC-CS		175,000

Note that the $40 market value of the common stock is ignored. The book value method must be used for conversion of preferred stock, so no gains or losses can be recognized.

8. **(d)** When an issuance of debt, or in this case preferred stock, contains detachable common stock warrants the total proceeds from the sale should be allocated to both the preferred stock and the detachable stock warrants. This treatment arises due to the separability of the stock and the detachable warrants. The allocation of the proceeds is based on the relative fair values of both the stock and the warrants at the time of the issuance. However, in instances where only one of the fair values is known, the known fair value will be used to allocate proceeds to the security in which the fair value is determinable. The remainder is then allocated to the security for which the fair value is unknown. Therefore, because only the fair value of the warrants is known, answer (d) is correct. Answers (a) and (b) are incorrect because fair market value is used to allocate proceeds to the warrants, not the total proceeds or excess proceeds over par value. Answer (c) is incorrect because proceeds are allocated in proportion to both fair values, if determinable, not the fair market value and par value.

9. **(a)** When the preferred stock and detachable warrants are issued, the following journal entry is made:

Cash	(cash received)
Preferred stock	(par value)
APIC—preferred stock	(FV of preferred stock – par value)
APIC—stock warrants	(plug)

When the stock warrants are exercised, the following journal entry is made:

Cash	(cash received)
APIC—stock warrants	(original amount credited)
Common stock	(par value)
APIC—common stock	(plug)

Therefore, stockholders' equity is increased by the cash received upon the exercise of the common stock warrants. The carrying amount of the warrants increased total stockholders' equity when the preferred stock was issued, not when the warrants were issued.

C. Stock Subscriptions

10. **(b)** When no par common stock is sold on a subscription basis at a price above the stock's stated value, the stock is not issued until the full subscription price is received. The journal entry on the subscription contract date would be

Cash	(amount received—if any)
Subscription receivable	(balance due)
Common stock subscribed	(stated value)
Additional paid-in capital	(plug)

The journal entry on the date the balance of the subscription is collected and the common stock issued would be

Cash	(balance due)
Common stock subscribed	(stated value)
Common stock	(stated value)
Subscription receivable	(balance due)

Additional paid-in capital increases on the date that the stock is subscribed, not paid for or issued.

11. **(d)** When stock is sold on a subscription basis, the full price of the stock is not received initially, and the stock is not issued until the full subscription price is received. On the subscription contract date of December 1, 2010, the journal entry would be

Cash	(amount received)
Subscriptions receivable	(balance due)
Common stock subscribed	(par)
Additional paid-in capital	(plug)

D. Treasury Stock Transactions

12. **(c)** Under the cost method, the treasury stock account is debited for the cost of the shares acquired. If the treasury shares are reissued at a price in excess of the acquisition cost, the excess is credited to an account titled Paid-in Capital from Treasury Stock. This question refers to it as Additional Paid-in Capital because typically companies do not segregate the two accounts on the balance sheet for reporting purposes. If the treasury shares are reissued at less than the acquisition cost, the deficiency is treated first as a reduction to any paid-in capital related to previous reissuances or retirements of treasury stock of the same class. If the balance in Paid-in Capital from Treasury Stock is not sufficient to absorb the deficiency, the remainder is recorded as a reduction of retained earnings. As the shares in this question were reissued at a price in excess of the acquisition price, the following journal entry would be made at the time of reissue:

Cash (3,000 × $50)	150,000	
Treasury stock (3,000 × $36)		108,000
Additional paid-in capital ($150,000 – $108,000)		42,000

13. **(c)** The entry that Rama made on acquisition of treasury stock was as follows using the **cost method:**

Treasury stock (20,000 × $12)	240,000	
Cash		240,000

When some of the shares are later reissued, the entry is

Cash (15,000 × $10)	150,000	
Retained earnings	30,000	
Treasury stock (15,000 × $12)		180,000

It is assumed there was no balance in APIC—Treasury stock prior to this entry. If the problem had stated there was a credit balance, APIC—Treasury stock would be debited before retained earnings to the extent a credit balance existed in APIC—Treasury stock. When retained earnings are legally restricted the restriction must be disclosed. In this case, the net treasury stock account balance is $60,000 ($240,000 – $180,000), and this is the amount of retained earnings that must be disclosed as legally restricted.

14.   (d)   The unadjusted stockholders' equity section shows a total of $2,000,000. However, analysis of the current asset section reveals that United has incorrectly classified $300,000 of treasury stock as a current asset. Although this account has a debit balance, it is **not an asset**. Treasury stock should be reported as a reduction of stockholders' equity. Therefore, total equity at 12/31/10 should be $1,700,000 ($2,000,000 – $300,000).

15.   (a)   Under the cost method, when treasury stock is acquired, **treasury stock** is debited and **cash** is credited for the cost.

Treasury stock	100,000	
Cash		100,000

When the treasury stock is resold at an amount above cost, **cash** is debited for the proceeds, **treasury stock** is credited at cost, and the difference is credited to **additional paid-in capital—treasury stock**.

Cash	25,000	
Treasury stock		20,000
APIC—TS		5,000

Neither of these two transactions affect **retained earnings**. Therefore, 12/31/10 retained earnings consists of the 12/31/09 balance ($300,000) plus 2010 net income ($60,000), or $360,000.

16.   (c)   The requirement is to determine the balance in the paid-in capital from treasury stock account at 12/31/10. Using the par value method, treasury stock is debited for par value (5,000 × $10, or $50,000) when purchased. Any excess over par from the original issuance (5,000 × $4, or $20,000) is removed from the appropriate paid-in capital account. In effect, the total original issuance price (5,000 × $14, or $70,000) is charged to the two accounts. Any difference between the original issue price ($70,000) and the cost of the treasury stock (5,000 × $11, or $55,000) is credited to paid-in capital from treasury stock, as illustrated below.

Treasury stock	50,000		(5,000 × $10)
APIC	20,000		(5,000 × $ 4)
Cash		55,000	(5,000 × $11)
PIC—Treasury stock		15,000	($70,000 – $55,000)

17.   (b)   When Dee Inc. issued common stock at a price in excess of its par value, the following journal entry was made:

Cash	(Cash received)
Common stock	(Par)
Additional paid-in capital	(Excess of cash capital received over par)

When Dee Inc. acquires treasury stock using the par method for an amount exceeding the issue price the following journal entry is made:

Treasury stock	(Par)
Additional paid-in capital	(Excess of original issue price over par)
Retained earnings	(Excess of acquisition price over issue price)
Cash	(Cash paid)

Net common stock decreases by the par value of treasury stock acquired. Additional paid-in capital decreases by the excess of the original issue price over the par value. Retained earnings decreases by the excess of the acquisition price over the original issue price.

18.   (c)   In this case, the par value method does not report a greater amount for additional paid-in capital or retained earnings than the cost method. The entries for an acquisition of treasury shares at greater than par but less than the original issue price are as follows:

Cost method		*Par value method*	
Treasury stock xxx		Treasury stock	xxx
Cash	xxx	PIC in excess of par	xxx
		Cash	xxx
		PIC from treasury stock	xxx

Since under the par value method the original paid-in capital in excess of par must be removed from the accounts upon reacquisition, the par value method actually reports a decrease in additional paid-in capital. On the other hand, under the cost method no change in additional paid-in capital is recorded. There is no change in retained earnings under either method.

E.   Retirement of Stock

19.   (c)   When accounting for the retirement of stock, common stock and additional paid-in capital are removed from the books based on the original issuance of the stock. Cash is credited for the cost of the shares. Any difference is debited to **retained earnings** or credited to **paid-in capital from retirement**. The entry in this case is

Common stock	20,000 (2,000 × $10)	
APIC	180,000 (2,000 × $90)	
Retained earnings	100,000 (2,000 × $50)	
Cash		300,000

Therefore, APIC should be debited for $180,000 and retained earnings should be debited for $100,000.

20.   (a)   In this problem, Luna Corp. is exchanging its available-for-sale securities (AFS) for its preferred stock (i.e., they are retiring some of their preferred stock by exchanging AFS). Upon disposition of the AFS, a gain of $70,000, which is the difference between the carrying amount ($80,000) and the FV ($150,000), must be recognized. Upon retirement of the stock, the preferred stock is debited for the $100,000 par amount (5,000 shares × $20 par). The additional paid-in capital (APIC) is debited for $7,500, which is 1/4 of the original APIC (i.e., 5,000 of the 20,000 shares were retired). The remainder of the FV of the preferred stock ($42,500 = $150,000 – $100,000 – $7,500) is debited to retained earnings.

21.   (c)   When accounting for the retirement of treasury stock that was initially recorded using the cost method, common stock and additional paid-in capital are removed from the books based on the original issuance of the stock. Treasury stock is credited for the cost of the shares acquired. Any difference is debited to retained earnings or credited to paid-in capital from retirement. In this problem, common stock should be debited for $125,000 (50,000 shares × $2.50), and the common stock balance at December 31, 2010, is $415,000 ($540,000 – $125,000).

22. (c) The requirement is to determine which of the statements correctly identifies an effect of the acquisition and retirement of common stock. The entry to record the retirement of common stock appears as follows:

Common stock (par)	xxx	
Additional paid-in capital	xxx	
Retained earnings	xxx	
Cash		xxx

Additional paid-in capital is debited to the extent it exists. In this case, based on the original issuance, the additional paid-in capital (APIC) balance was $15 per share on the shares retired. When stock is repurchased, if the APIC balance is depleted to zero, retained earnings must also be debited. In this case, retained earnings would not be needed, however. Common stock would be debited for $10 per share and additional paid-in capital would be debited for $10 a share. Excess APIC remains, so retained earnings are not needed to retire the stock. When common stock is repurchased and retired, additional paid-in capital decreases. When common stock is retired, net income is never affected; only stockholders' equity balances are affected. If retained earnings are needed to retire stock, the account decreases, not increases.

F. Dividends

23. (b) Since this is an investment accounted for on the cost basis, the dividend income should be the amount of cash dividends received. Since Plack Co. had 12,000 shares at the time the cash dividend was paid, the total amount of cash dividends received is $24,000 (12,000 × $2.00).

24. (c) When preferred stock is participating, there may be different agreements as to how the participation feature is to be executed. However, in the absence of any specific agreement, the following procedure should be used:

After the preferred stock is allocated its current year dividend, the common stock will receive a "like" percentage of par value outstanding. If there are remaining declared dividends, this amount should be shared by both the preferred and common stock in proportion to the par value dollars outstanding of each stock as follows:

Current year's dividend:		
Preferred, 5% of $300,000		
(30,000 shares × $10 Par)	$15,000	
Common, 5% of $200,000		
(200,000 shares × $1 Par)	10,000	$ 25,000
Amount available for participation		
($100,000 – $25,000)		$ 75,000
Par value of stock that is to participate		
($300,000 + $200,000)		$500,000
Proportional share of participating dividend:		
Preferred $\dfrac{\$300,000}{\$500,000}$ × 75,000 = $ 45,000		
Common $\dfrac{\$200,000}{\$500,000}$ × 75,000 = $ 30,000		

Thus, the dividends payable to common shareholders is $40,000 ($10,000 + $30,000).

25. (d) For **cumulative** preferred stock, dividends not paid in **any** year will accumulate and must be paid in a later year before any dividends can be paid to common stockholders. The unpaid prior year dividends are called "dividends in arrears." The balance of dividends in arrears should be disclosed in the financial statements rather than accrued, as they are not considered a liability until they are declared. Dividends in arrears at 12/31/10 total $20,000, as computed below.

2009 $300,000 × 5%	=	$15,000
2010 $300,000 × 5%	=	15,000
Total cumulative preferred dividends		$30,000
Less 2010 dividend payment		(10,000)
Balance of dividends in arrears		$20,000

Answer (c) is incorrect because dividends in arrears are not considered to be a liability until they are declared. They should be disclosed parenthetically or in the notes to the financial statements. Answer (b) is incorrect because the total dividends amount needs to reflect both the 2009 and 2010 unpaid dividends since it is cumulative preferred stock. Answer (a) is incorrect because the dividends in arrears would not be considered a liability until they are declared and the $15,000 amount is the incorrect balance as discussed above.

26. (d) The interest is not an expense or liability until incurred, thus, none of it is recorded on April 1. The April 1 entry would be

Retained earnings	100,000	
Scrip dividends payable		100,000

By December 31 (the year-end for this calendar-year company), nine months' interest had been incurred, which would not be paid until the maturity date of 3/31/11. The $7,500 of interest expense ($100,000 × 10% × 9/12) must be accrued at 12/31/10 with the following entry:

Interest expense	7,500	
Interest payable		7,500

27. (b) Dividends that are based on funds other than retained earnings are considered to be liquidating dividends. The cash dividend declared of $400,000 is first assumed to be a return **on** capital for the distribution of the retained earnings balance of $300,000. The excess $400,000 dividend – $300,000 RE = $100,000 is considered to be a return **of** capital or a liquidating dividend rather than a return **on** capital. Note that the amount of liquidating dividend also equals the balance in accumulated depletion. Companies in the extractive industries may pay dividends equal to the accumulated income **and** depletion.

28. (c) A transfer of a nonmonetary asset to a stockholder or to another entity in a nonreciprocal transfer should be recorded at the fair value of the asset transferred, and a gain or loss should be recognized on the disposition of the asset. The fair value of the nonmonetary asset distributed is measured by the amount that would be realized in an outright sale at or near the time of distribution. In this case, a gain should be recognized for the difference between the fair value of $2.50 per share and the carrying amount of $2 per share, or a total gain of $50,000 [100,000 × ($2.50 – $2.00)].

29. (c) A transfer of a nonmonetary asset to a stockholder or to another entity in a nonreciprocal transfer should be recorded at the fair market value of the asset transferred, and a gain or loss should be recognized on the disposition of the asset. At the date of declaration, Nilo records

Trading securities	18,000	
Gain on disposition of securities		18,000
Retained earnings (dividends)	78,000	
Property dividends payable		78,000

At the date of distribution, Nilo records

Property dividends payable	78,000	
Trading securities		78,000

After all nominal accounts are closed, the effect on retained earnings from the above entries would be $60,000 ($78,000 debit to retained earnings less $18,000 credit to retained earnings when the "gain on disposition" account is closed out).

30. **(b)** A stock split is **not** a dividend. Stock splits change the number of shares outstanding and the par value per share. Par value per share is reduced in proportion to the increase in the number of shares. Therefore, the total par value outstanding does not change, and no journal entry is required. The only dividend to be reported in Long's 2010 statement of stockholders' equity is the 12/15 cash dividend. The stock split increased the number of shares outstanding to 200,000 (100,000 × 2), so the amount of the cash dividend is $100,000 (200,000 × $.50).

31. **(b)** The requirement is to determine the effect of a cash dividend on stockholders' equity at the three dates listed. On the date of declaration, December 15, 2010, the following entry should be made:

Retained earnings	xxx	
Dividends payable		xxx

Thus, at December 15, 2010, stockholders' equity is reduced due to the debit to retained earnings. On December 31, 2010, there is no effect on stockholders' equity because an entry would not be recorded. On January 12, 2011, the following entry would be made:

Dividends payable	xxx	
Cash		xxx

The net effect of this entry is to decrease assets and liabilities by an equal amount. Thus, stockholders' equity (or net assets) would be unaffected.

32. **(d)** Any dividend not based on earnings must be a reduction of corporate paid-in capital and, to that extent, it is a liquidating dividend. The following journal entries would be made for this situation:

At date of declaration:

Additional paid-in capital	100,000	
Dividends payable		100,000

At date of payment:

Dividends payable	100,000	
Cash		100,000

Thus, a liquidating dividend would decrease Ole's paid-in capital, not its retained earnings.

33. **(d)** A property dividend is a nonreciprocal transfer of nonmonetary assets between an enterprise and its owners. A nonreciprocal transfer of nonmonetary assets to a stockholder or another entity shall be recorded at the fair value of the asset transferred. Additionally, a gain or loss shall be recognized on the disposition of the asset. Accordingly, Evie Corp. should record the following journal entries to reflect the property dividend:

At the date of declaration:

Loss on decline in inventory value (Carrying amount – Market value)	xxx	
Merchandise inventory		xxx

Retained earnings (market value)	xxx	
Property dividends payable		xxx

At the date of distribution:

Property dividends payable	xxx	
Merchandise inventory		xxx

The loss recorded in the above journal entry does not qualify as unusual and infrequent, thus it is not an extraordinary item. The loss should be reported as a reduction in income before extraordinary items.

34. **(b)** The requirement is to determine the amount to be debited to retained earnings for these stock dividends. The issuance of a stock dividend less than **20-25%** (a "small" stock dividend) requires that the **market value** of the stock be transferred from retained earnings, and a dividend greater than **20-25%** (a "large" stock dividend) requires the **par value** of the stock to be transferred from retained earnings. Thus, a 10% stock dividend is considered to be "small" and should be transferred from retained earnings at the FV of $15,000. A 28% stock dividend is considered to be "large" and should be transferred at the par value of $30,800. The aggregate amount to be transferred from retained earnings is $45,800.

35. **(a)** When the stock dividend is less than 20-25% of the common shares outstanding at the time of the declaration, generally accepted accounting principles require that the FV of the stock issued be transferred from retained earnings. At the date of declaration, the following entry would be made:

Retained earnings (Stock dividends declared) (.05 × 10,000 shares × $5)	2,500	
Common stock dividend distributable (.05 × 10,000 × $2)		1,000
Additional paid-in capital (plug)		1,500

Note from the entry above that no asset or liability has been affected. The entry merely reflects a reclassification within the equity accounts. When a balance sheet is prepared between the dates of declaration and distribution, the common stock dividend distributable should be shown in the stockholders' equity section as an addition to capital stock.

G. Stock Splits

36. **(d)** A stock dividend is an issuance by a corporation of its own common shares to its common shareholders without consideration to give the recipient shareholders evidence of a part of their respective interests in accumulated corporate earnings without distribution of cash or other property. A stock split is defined as an issuance by a corporation of common shares to its common shareholders without consideration...prompted mainly by a desire to increase the number of outstanding shares for the purpose of effecting a reduction in their unit market price and, thereby, of obtaining wider distribution and improved marketability of the shares. Thus, neither of these transactions results in a transfer of assets among the shareholders and the corporation. While the allocation of stockholders' equity among the various accounts (retained earnings, common stock, and additional paid-in capital) will change, the **total** stockholders' equity is **not** affected.

37. **(b)** The requirement is to determine the balance of additional paid-in capital immediately after a reverse stock split. Stock splits change the number of shares outstanding and the par value per share, but the total par value outstanding does not change. Stock splits do not affect any account balances, including additional paid-in capital. Therefore, the balance of additional paid-in capital remains at $450,000.

38. (b) A stock split does not affect either the balance of the additional paid-in capital or the retained earnings accounts. The number of shares outstanding and the par value per share merely change in proportion to each other. When this occurs, only a memorandum entry is made.

H. Appropriations of Retained Earnings (Reserves)

39. (a) The requirement is to determine the amount of appropriated retained earnings Eagle should report in its 2010 balance sheet. The entry to record the appropriation of retained earnings in 2010 for the construction of a new plant is as follows:

RE (or Unappropriated RE)	$1,200,000	
RE Appropriated for plant expansion		$1,200,000

The cash restricted for the retirement of bonds due in 2010 should **not** be reported as an appropriation of retained earnings because the facts in the question do not indicate that appropriation was made by management. When an appropriation is no longer needed, it must be returned directly to unappropriated retained earnings by reversing the entry that created it. Therefore, when the office building was completed in 2010, the following entry was made:

RE Appropriated for plant expansion	$1,750,000	
RE (or Unappropriated RE)		$1,750,000

The total cost to complete the building has no effect on appropriated retained earnings.

40. (a) Retained earnings are typically appropriated due to legal requirements, contractual requirements, or through the discretion of the board of directors. Dividends in arrears are not considered a liability to the company, and retained earnings would not be appropriated for this amount. In many cases, retained earnings must be appropriated for an amount equal to the cost of treasury stock acquired. However, this appropriation would be removed upon reissuance of the treasury stock.

41. (d) Appropriations of retained earnings are not prohibited provided that the appropriation is clearly identified as such in the stockholders' equity section of the balance sheet. Costs or losses cannot be charged to an appropriation of retained earnings. A contingent loss that is probable and reasonably estimable should be accrued as a loss and liability.

I.1. Stock Options

42. (d) Employee compensation expense as the result of a stock option plan is calculated as the fair value of the equity instrument **at the date of grant** times the number of option shares.

3,000 shares × $8 fair value of option = $24,000

The total compensation expense must be recognized over the requisite service period for which the option plan represents compensation. If not otherwise specified, the required service period (two years) is assumed to be the period benefited. Therefore, 2010 compensation expense is $12,000 ($24,000 ÷ 2). Note that compensation expense is

not affected by changes in the market value of the stock after the measurement date.

43. (b) Total compensation expense as a result of a stock option plan is calculated as the fair value of the equity instruments at the date of grant times the number of options.

10,000 options × $12 fair value of option = $120,000

The total compensation expense must be recognized over the requisite service period for which the option plan represents compensation. Therefore, 2010 compensation expense is $40,000 ($120,000 ÷ 3 years). Note that the cost of treasury stock distributed in an option plan does not determine compensation expense.

44. (d) The fair value of the stock option at date of grant was $28 ($28 × 1,000 shares = $28,000). The entire amount is recognized because the options are exercisable immediately for three years after the grant date.

45. (a) The net increase in stockholders' equity (SE) as a result of the grant and exercise of the options is equal to the increase in cash (1,000 shares × $20 option price = $20,000). The journal entry to record the options has no effect on SE because a SE account will be credited while a contra SE account will be debited as follows:

Deferred compensation	28,000	
Paid-in capital stock options		28,000
(1000 shares × $28 per option)		

The entry to recognize compensation expense has no effect on SE because the debit decreases SE while the credit increases SE by reducing the contra account as follows:

Compensation expense	28,000	
Deferred compensation		28,000

The only entry which does affect SE is the entry for the exercise of the options, which decreases SE by $28,000 while increasing it by $48,000 (a net increase of $20,000).

Cash (1,000 × $20)	20,000	
Paid-in capital stock options (1,000 × $28)	28,000	
Common stock (1,000 × $10)		10,000
Paid-in capital in × of PV (plug)		38,000

Thus, the net increase in stockholders' equity is $20,000.

I.2. Stock Appreciation Rights

46. (c) The 20,000 stock appreciation rights (SAR) each entitle the holder to receive cash equal to the excess of the market price of the stock on the exercise date over the market price on the grant date ($30). Since these SAR are payment for past services and are exercisable immediately, there is no required service period. Therefore, the expense computed at 12/31/10 does **not** have to be allocated to more than one period. At 12/31/10, compensation expense is measured based on the excess of the 12/31/10 market price ($45) over the predetermined price ($30), resulting in compensation expense of $300,000 [20,000 ($45 − $30)]. Note that **if** Dean were **required** to work three years **before** the SAR could be exercised, the expense would be allocated over the three years of required service ($300,000 × 1/3 = $100,000).

J. Stock Compensation

47. (c) When accounting for stock compensation plans, total compensation expense is computed as the excess of the fair value of the equity instrument over the amount contributed by employees. In this case, the fair value of the

150,000 shares issued in 2011 is $1,050,000, and the employees' contributions for these shares is $350,000. Therefore, Wall should recognize $700,000 ($1,050,000 – $350,000) as expense in 2011 for the stock compensation plan.

48. (c) The rate of interest used to discount both the exercise price and dividends is the risk-free interest rate.

49. (c) If the stock options are for past services, as indicated when the options are immediately exercisable by the holders, compensation cost must be fully expensed at the grant date. Answer (a) is incorrect because usually deferred compensation expense is recognized. Answer (b) is incorrect because deferred compensation expense is recognized when service has not yet been provided. Answer (d) is incorrect because when options are provided for prior service compensation expense must immediately be recognized.

50. (a) Compensation cost for a share-based payment to employees that is classified as a liability is measured by the change in fair value of the instrument for each reporting period.

51. (c) The final measurement date is the settlement date for share-based payments to employees classified as liabilities.

52. (d) Accounting for stock-based compensation using the fair value method is as follows:

Fair value of option at grant date	6.40
Times # of options	× 20,000
Deferred compensation expense	$128,000

53. (d) Cash retained as a result of excess tax benefits in connection with share-based payments to employees should be recognized as a cash inflow from financing activities in the statement of cash flows.

54. (c) The options should be included in the denominator of diluted earnings per share unless the shares are antidilutive. If the equity share options are outstanding for only a part of a period, the shares are weighted to reflect the period of time outstanding.

K. Basic Earnings Per Share

55. (b) The formula for basic earnings per share (BEPS) is

$$\frac{\underset{\text{net income}}{\$1,000,000} - \underset{\text{preferred dividends}}{\$50,000}}{200,000 \text{ common shares outstanding}} = \$9.50$$

In calculating the numerator, the claims of preferred shareholders against 2010 earnings should be deducted to arrive at the 2010 earnings attributable to common shareholders. This amount is 50,000 (5% × $100 × 10,000 shares). The $50,000 preferred dividends in arrears is not deducted to compute the numerator in determining 2010 BEPS. This is because the $50,000 dividends in arrears is a claim of preferred shareholders against 2009 earnings and would reduce 2009 BEPS.

56. (b) The formula for basic earnings per share (BEPS) is

$$\frac{\underset{\text{net income}}{\$500,000} - \underset{\text{dividends}}{10,000 \text{ preferred}}}{200,000 \text{ common shares outstanding}} = \$2.45$$

In calculating the numerator, the claims of preferred shareholders against 2010 earnings should be deducted to arrive at the 2010 earnings attributable to common shareholders. This amount is $10,000 ($250,000 × 4%). During 2009, the BEPS numerator would have been reduced by $10,000 even though no preferred dividends were declared, because the cumulative feature means that $10,000 of 2009 earnings are reserved for, and will ultimately be paid to, preferred stockholders. In 2010, the 2009 dividends in arrears are paid, as well as $6,000 of the $10,000 2010 preferred dividend. Even though only $6,000 is paid, the entire $10,000 is subtracted for reasons explained above.

57. (b) For EPS purposes, shares of stock issued as a result of stock dividends or splits should be considered outstanding for the entire period in which they were issued. Therefore, both the original 20,000 shares and the additional 20,000 issued in the 4/1 stock split are treated as outstanding for the entire year (20,000 × 2 = 40,000). The 7/1 issuance of 10,000 shares results in a weighted-average of 5,000 shares (10,000 × 6/12) because the shares were outstanding for only six months during the year. Therefore, Jet should use 45,000 shares (40,000 + 5,000) to calculate EPS.

58. (d) The computation of weighted-average shares outstanding is

Date	# of shares		Fraction		WA
1/1	30,000	×	12/12	=	30,000
2/1	3,000	×	12/12	=	3,000
7/1	8,000	×	6/12	=	4,000
					37,000

The 3,000 shares issued as a result of a stock dividend are weighted at 12/12 instead of 11/12 because for EPS purposes stock dividends are treated as if they occurred at the beginning of the year.

59. (b) The formula for computing BEPS for a simple capital structure is

$$\frac{\text{Net income} - \text{Applicable pref. stock dividends}}{\text{Weighted-average \# of common shares outstanding}}$$

Net income is $410,000 and $350,000 in 2010 and 2009, respectively, and there are no preferred dividends. The weighted-average number of common shares outstanding must be computed for 2010. Stock dividends and stock splits are handled retroactively for comparability. The 2010 computation is

Dates	Number of Shares	Fraction	WA
1/1 to 3/31	100,000 × 2 = 200,000	3/12	50,000
4/1 to 6/30	(100,000 + 20,000) × 2 = 240,000	3/12	60,000
7/1 to 12/31	120,000 × 2 = 240,000	6/12	120,000
			230,000

The 2009 weighted-average of 100,000 is retroactively restated to 200,000 for comparability. Therefore, the BEPS amounts are

2010		*2009*	
$\dfrac{\$410,000}{230,000}$	= $1.78	$\dfrac{\$350,000}{200,000}$	= $1.75

60. (b) Earnings per share must be shown on the face of the income statement for income from continuing operations and net income. Discontinued operations, extraordinary items, and cumulative effect of change in accounting principle may be shown on the income statement or in the notes.

61. **(c)**   If the number of common shares outstanding increases as a result of a stock dividend or stock split or decreases as a result of a reverse split, the computations of EPS should give retroactive recognition for all periods presented. If these events take place after the close of the period but before completion of the financial report, the per share computations should be based on the new number of shares. Note that when per share computations reflect such changes in the number of shares after the close of the period, this fact should be disclosed.

L. Diluted Earnings Per Share

62. **(b)**   The requirement is to determine the number of shares that should be used in computing 2010 diluted earnings per share. The first step is to compute the weighted-average number of common shares outstanding. 300,000 shares were outstanding the entire year, and 50,000 more shares were outstanding for six months, resulting in a weighted-average of 325,000 [300,000 + (50,000 × 6/12)]. Second, the stock options increase the number of shares used in the computation **only** if they are dilutive. The stock options are dilutive because the exercise price is less than the market value. Thus, the denominator effect of the options must be computed. This is done using the **treasury stock method,** as illustrated below.

Assumed proceeds (40,000 × $15)	$600,000
Shares issued	40,000
Shares reacquired ($600,000 ÷ $20)	(30,000)
Shares issued, not reacquired	10,000

Therefore, the number of shares used for computing diluted earnings per share is 335,000 (325,000 + 10,000).

63. **(b)**   Diluted earnings per share is based on common stock and all dilutive potential common shares. To determine if a security is dilutive, EPS, including the effect of the dilutive security, must be compared to the basic EPS. In this case, basic EPS is $7.45.

$$\frac{850,000 \text{ (NI)} - 30,000 \text{ (pref. div.)}}{110,000 \text{ shares}} = \$7.45$$

The effect of the convertible preferred stock is to increase the numerator by $30,000 ($3.00 dividend per share × 10,000 shares) for the amount of the preferred dividends that would not be paid (assuming conversion) and increase the denominator by 20,000 shares. This security is dilutive because it decreases the EPS from $7.45 to $6.54.

$$\frac{850,000 - 30,000 + 30,000}{110,000 + 20,000} = \$6.54$$

If the EPS increases due to the inclusion of a security, that security is antidilutive and should not be included.

64. **(d)**   The requirement is to compute the diluted earnings per share for 2010. Therefore, **all** potential common shares that **reduce** current EPS must be included in the computation. The formula for diluted EPS is

$$\frac{\text{Net income available to common shareholders}}{\text{Weighted-average common shares outstanding}}$$

The net income available to common shareholders is $3,200,000. This is the net income of $3,400,000 less the preferred stock dividend of $200,000. The weighted-average common shares outstanding is 1,250,000. This is computed as the actual common shares outstanding for the full year of 1,200,000 plus the contingent common shares of

50,000 that were outstanding for the full year because the contingency was incurred in 2009. Thus,

$$\text{Diluted EPS} = \frac{\$3,200,000}{1,250,000} = \$2.56$$

65. **(b)**   The effect of convertible bonds is included in diluted EPS under the if converted method, if they are dilutive. The bonds are dilutive as shown below.

$$\text{Basic EPS} = \frac{\$35,000}{(1/2)\ 10,000 + (1/2)\ 14,000} = \$2.92$$

$$\text{Incremental per share effect} = \frac{(7\% \times \$10,000) - 30\% \ (7\% \times \$10,000)}{200 \text{ shares per bond}} = \frac{\$490}{200} = \$2.45$$

Since $2.45 < $2.92, the bonds are dilutive. Under the if converted method, the assumption is made that the bonds were converted at the beginning of the current year (1/1) or later in the current year if the bonds were issued during the current year. In this case, conversion is assumed for the first six months of 2010 only because the bonds were actually converted on July 1. Under their assumed conversion, the numerator would increase because bond interest expense would not have been incurred for the first six months of the year [1/2 ($14,000 − 30% × $14,000) = $4,900]. The denominator would increase because the 4,000 shares (20 × 200) would have been outstanding for the first six months of the year (4,000 × 6/12 = 2,000). Therefore, diluted EPS is $2.85.

$$\frac{\$35,000 + \$4,900}{12,000 + 2,000} = \frac{\$39,900}{14,000} = \$2.85$$

66. **(a)**   Diluted EPS takes into account the effect of all dilutive potential common shares that were outstanding during the period. Thus, the possible conversion of convertible bonds would be included because they are dilutive (i.e., EPS would be reduced), but the possible exercise of common stock options would not be included because they are antidilutive (i.e., EPS would be increased). Diluted EPS = $15.00 − $.75 = $14.25.

67. **(d)**   The requirement is to determine the treatment of nonconvertible cumulative preferred dividends in determining diluted EPS. Dividends on nonconvertible cumulative preferred shares should be deducted from net income whether an actual liability exists or not. This is because cumulative preferred stock owners must receive any dividends in arrears before future dividend distributions can be made to common stockholders.

68. **(a)**   The if-converted method of computing earnings per share assumes that convertible securities are converted at the beginning of the earliest period reported or, if later, at the time of issuance.

69. **(b)**   If convertible securities are deemed to be dilutive, then interest expense should be added back to net income when computing diluted earnings per share.

70. **(b)**   The effect of contingent issue agreements are not included in basic earnings per share. They are included in diluted earnings per share if the contingency is met.

M. Corporate Bankruptcy

71. **(d)**   The total cash available to pay **all** unsecured claims, including priority claims, is the cash obtained from free assets ($320,000) and any excess cash available from assets pledged with fully secured creditors after they are used to satisfy those claims ($370,000 – $260,000 = $110,000). Therefore, total cash available is $430,000 ($320,000 + $110,000). After paying priority claims, $360,000 will remain to pay all unsecured nonpriority claims ($430,000 – $70,000).

72. (c) Bankruptcy law requires that the claims of secured creditors be satisfied before any unsecured claims are paid. Hale is a secured creditor in the amount of $5,000 (the liquidation value of the collateral). The remainder of Hale's claim ($30,000 – $5,000 = $25,000) is an unsecured claim, because it is not secured by any collateral. Therefore, Hale will receive a total of $15,000 on this note: $5,000 received in full as a secured creditor, and $10,000 received as an unsecured creditor ($25,000 × $.40).

73. (d) A bankruptcy trustee may establish a new set of accounting records to maintain accountability for the bankruptcy estate. Once the trustee assumes custody of the estate, the trustee will enter any unrecorded assets or liabilities in the estate equity account. Any gains or losses and liquidation expenses incurred will also be recorded. In the Kamy Corp. bankruptcy, both the $8,000 loss on sale of the truck ($20,000 carrying value – $12,000 cash selling price) and the $1,000 unrecorded liability would be debited to the estate equity account as follows:

Estate equity	1,000	
Accounts payable		1,000
Cash	12,000	
Estate equity	8,000	
Truck		20,000

N. Reorganizations

74. (b) The requirement is to determine the net increase in total stockholders' equity as a result of the payments to unsecured creditors pursuant to a reorganization plan under Chapter 11. The net increase in stockholders' equity can be determined as follows:

Fair value of liabilities owed to unsecured creditors	$1,200,000
Cash paid	(400,000)
Common stock issued (80,000 × $1.25)	(100,000)
Gain on settlement of debt	$ 700,000

The gain on the settlement of debt would be included in the income statement and closed to retained earnings. The net increase in stockholders' equity would equal $800,000 ($700,000 gain + $100,000 FV of stock issued).

O. Quasi Reorganization

75. (c) Although assets are often revalued to fair value during a quasi reorganization, the **primary** purpose of a quasi reorganization is to eliminate a deficit in retained earnings so that dividends may be paid without waiting years to eliminate the deficit through future earnings. A quasi reorganization does not directly allow a corporation to obtain relief from creditors or result in a distribution of stock.

76. (d) In certain instances an entity may elect to restate its assets, capital stock, and surplus through a readjustment (or "quasi reorganization") and thus avail itself of permission to relieve its future income account or earned surplus account of charges which would otherwise be made there against. In such instances, the entity should present a **fair (value)** balance sheet as of the date of the reorganization.

77. (c) A quasi reorganization generally involves (1) revaluing assets, (2) reducing par, and (3) writing the deficit off against additional paid-in capital. In this case, no mention is made of the first step, revaluing assets. The second step, reducing par, results in a decrease to **common stock** and an increase to **additional paid-in capital** of $250,000 [10,000 × ($30 – $5)]. The third step, writing off the deficit, increases **retained earnings** by $210,000 (creating a $0 balance) and decrease **additional paid-in capital** by the same amount. Immediately after the quasi reorganization, Brown should report additional paid-in capital of $190,000 ($150,000 + $250,000 – $210,000).

P. Stock Rights

78. (a) When a corporation issues rights to its stockholders, it only makes a memorandum entry. If rights are later exercised, the corporation would make the following entry:

Cash	xxx	
Common stock		xxx
Additional paid-in capital		xxx

79. (c) The only time a journal entry is recorded for the issuance and exercise of stock rights is on the date of exercise. At the date of issuance, only a memorandum entry is recorded. The redemption of the rights issued to the shareholders should be treated like a dividend. Accordingly, retained earnings will be decreased by the amount paid to the shareholders (120,000 × $0.10 = $12,000).

80. (a) The requirement is to determine the effects of the stock warrants on the additional paid-in capital account and on net income. When a corporation issues stock warrants to its stockholders it only makes a memorandum entry. Then, when the warrants are exercised, the following entry is made:

Cash	xxx	
Common stock		xxx
Additional paid-in capital		xxx

Net income is not affected by the exercise of stock warrants because the transaction represents a process of raising capital and is not related to the earnings process. Additional paid-in capital is not affected until the exercise date in 2010.

81. (b) Note that the only time an entry related to the issuance and exercise of stock rights, which affects the equity accounts of a corporation, is recorded is on the date of exercise. At the date of issuance, only a memorandum entry is recorded, and on the date of the rights lapsing, no entry is recorded which would affect the company's equity accounts. Thus, the correct answer is (b): the additional paid-in capital account would not be credited at the time the rights are issued or at the date on which the rights lapse.

Q. Employee Stock Ownership Plan (ESOP)

82. (c) The amount contributed or committed to be contributed to an employee stock ownership plan (ESOP) in a given year should be the measure of the amount to be charged to expense by the employer. Therefore, Fay should record 2010 compensation expense of $84,000 [contribution of $30,000 cash and common stock with a FV of $54,000 (3,000 × $18)].

83. (d) An obligation of an Employee Stock Ownership Plan (ESOP) should be recorded as a liability in the financial statements of the employer when the obligation is covered by either a guarantee of the employer or a commitment by the employer to make future contributions to the ESOP sufficient to meet the debt service requirements. Therefore, the note payable of $100,000 (which is guaranteed by Fay) should be reported in Fay's 12/31/10 balance sheet. The offsetting debit to the employer's liability should be reported as a reduction of stockholders' equity. Therefore, Fay should also report $100,000 as a reduction of stockholders' equity.

Stockholders' Equity: Comprehensive

84. **(a)** All of the accounts given are stockholders' equity accounts. Total stockholders' equity is computed below.

Paid-in capital		$ 600,000
Common stock		800,000
Addl. paid-in capital		1,400,000
Retained earinings		
Appropriated	$150,000	
Unappropriated	200,000	350,000
		1,750,000
Accumulated other comprehensive income		
Unrealized loss on available-for-sale securities		(20,000)
Less: Treasury stock		(50,000)
		$1,680,000

Both **treasury stock** and **net unrealized loss on available-for-sale securities** are contra stockholders' equity accounts.

85. **(a)** The number of shares outstanding is equal to the issued shares less treasury shares. The table below shows the effects of each of the stock transactions on the common shares outstanding.

	Outstanding shares
1/1/10	300,000
1/31/10 declaration of 10% stock dividend	30,000
6/30/10 purchase of TS	(100,000)
8/1/10 sale of TS	50,000
Subtotal	280,000
11/30/10 stock split	× 2
12/31/10	560,000

86. **(a)** Shares issued and outstanding are computed below.

	Issued	*Outstanding*
12/31/09	100,000	95,000
5/3/10		1,000
8/6/10	10,000	10,000
Subtotal	110,000	106,000
11/18/10	110,000	106,000
12/31/10	220,000	212,000

At 12/31/09, shares issued were 100,000 and outstanding 95,000 (100,000 issued less 5,000 treasury). The reissuance of treasury stock does not increase shares issued, but does increase shares outstanding by 1,000 to 96,000 (100,000 issued less 4,000 treasury). The issuance of previously unissued stock on 8/6/10 increases both issued and outstanding shares by 10,000, bringing the totals to 110,000 issued and 106,000 outstanding prior to the stock split. Since treasury stock is protected from dilution, shares issued, treasury shares, and outstanding shares are all doubled by the stock split.

R. Ratios

87. **(a)** The requirement is to determine the effect on Ali Corp. of exercising the stock options. First, the debt to equity ratio is calculated as follows:

$$\text{Debt to equity} = \frac{\text{Total liabilities}}{\text{Common stockholders' equity}}$$

The figures given in the problem reflect the account balances **after** the exercise of the stock options. Thus, Ali's debt to equity ratio after the exercise is

$$\frac{\$60,000}{\$500,000} = 12\%$$

When the options were exercised, total stockholders' equity would have increased by the amount of the option price as follows:

Common stock	↑	by par value × 1,000 shares
Paid-in capital	↑	by (option price-par) × 1,000 shares

Note that the information given is incomplete as to whether compensation was recorded under the stock option plan. However, even if compensation were recorded, the entries are made only to accounts that impact stockholders' equity, and the net effect is no change. Thus, the only change is an increase resulting from the exercise of the options. Since common stockholders' equity increased, the denominator of the debt to equity ratio also increased. As the denominator becomes larger and the numerator remains constant, the quotient becomes smaller. Therefore, the debt to equity ratio must have **decreased** to its current level of 12%. Answer (b) is incorrect because earnings per share decreased by $0.33. Answer (c) is incorrect because not enough information is given to calculate the asset turnover. Answer (d) is incorrect because the debt to equity ratio, rate of return on common stock, earnings per share, price earnings ratio, and book value per share were all affected by exercising the stock options.

88. **(c)** The requirement is to determine Irvington's return on common stockholders' equity for 2010, which is computed by dividing net income available to common stockholders (net income less preferred dividends) by average common stockholders' equity.

$$\frac{\$120,000 - \$10,000}{(\$375,000 + \$585,000)/2} = 23\%$$

89. **(d)** The requirement is to determine the book value per common share. The book value per common share is the amount each share would receive if the company were liquidated. The book value per common share is calculated as follows:

	Preferred	*Common*
Preferred stock, 5%	$250,000	
Common stock		$350,000
APIC in excess of par value of common stock		125,000
Retained earnings:		
Dividends in arrears	25,000	
Liquidation premium	50,000	
Remainder to common (Plug)		225,000
Totals	$325,000	$700,000
Shares outstanding		100,000
Book value per share		$ 7.00

Note that when calculating the remainder to common, total stockholders' equity before the liquidation must be equal to the amount after the assumed liquidation.

90. **(c)** Under the cost method, treasury stock is debited for the cost of the treasury stock, thus decreasing total stockholders' equity. However, the book value per share will increase due to the acquisition of the treasury stock. Book value per share is calculated by dividing common stockholders' equity by the shares outstanding. An example will help illustrate.

$$\frac{\text{Stockholders' equity}}{\text{Common stock (30,000 shares)}}$$

$5 par	$150,000
Additional paid-in capital	550,000
Retained earnings	250,000
	$950,000

$$\text{Book value per share} = \frac{\$950,000}{30,000} = \$31.67$$

Per the facts in the question, treasury stock was acquired at more than par and original issue price, but less than book value per share. Therefore, the acquisition price must be greater than $23.33 per share (700,000 ÷ 30,000) and less than $31.67 per share.

Let's say 1,000 shares of treasury stock were acquired at $27.00 per share.

$$\text{Book value per share} = \frac{\$950,000 - (1,000 \times \$27)}{30,000 - 1,000}$$
$$= \frac{923,000}{29,000}$$
$$= \$31.83$$

The book value per share increased after the acquisition of the treasury stock.

91. **(b)** Dividends per share is used in the numerator of the dividend payout ratio as shown below.

$$\frac{\text{Dividend}}{\text{payout ratio}} = \frac{\text{Dividends per share}}{\text{Earnings per share}}$$

However, dividends per share are not used in the calculation of earnings per share.

$$\frac{\text{Earnings}}{\text{per share}} = \frac{\text{Net income} - \text{Preferred dividends}}{\text{Weighted-average number of shares outstanding}}$$

SOLUTIONS TO SIMULATION PROBLEMS

Simulation Problem 1

Situation	Concepts	Statement of Retained Earnings	Financial Statement Disclosures		Research	Communication
			(A) (B) (C) (D) (E) (F) (G) (H) (I) (J) (K) (L) (M)			

	(A)	(B)	(C)	(D)	(E)	(F)	(G)	(H)	(I)	(J)	(K)	(L)	(M)
1. Par value method	○	○	○	○	○	○	○	○	●	○	○	○	○
2. Appropriations of retained earnings	○	○	○	○	○	○	○	●	○	○	○	○	○
3. Stock split	○	○	○	●	○	○	○	○	○	○	○	○	○
4. Simple capital structure	●	○	○	○	○	○	○	○	○	○	○	○	○
5. If-converted method	○	○	○	○	○	○	○	○	○	○	○	○	●
6. Scrip dividend	○	○	○	○	○	○	○	○	○	○	●	○	○
7. Stock appreciation rights	○	●	○	○	○	○	○	○	○	○	○	○	○
8. Stock option	○	○	○	○	○	○	○	○	○	●	○	○	○
9. Liquidating dividend	○	○	○	○	○	○	●	○	○	○	○	○	○
10. Treasury stock	○	○	○	○	●	○	○	○	○	○	○	○	○

Explanation of solutions

1. **(I)** In accordance with the par value method, treasury shares are recorded at par value by debiting treasury stock when acquired. Any additional paid-in capital from the original issue of the acquired shares is also debited, cash is credited, and either additional paid-in capital—treasury stock is credited or retained earnings are debited for the difference between cash and the other two debits previously mentioned.

2. **(H)** Appropriations of retained earnings are actions by the board of directors to disclose amounts not available for dividends.

3. **(D)** A stock split changes the number of shares outstanding and the par value per share. The purpose of a stock split is to reduce the market price per share.

4. **(A)** A simple capital structure for a corporation exists if there are no potentially dilutive securities.

5. **(M)** The if-converted method for convertible securities assumes that the securities were converted at the later of the beginning of the period or the date of issue. The method thus increases the weighted-average number of shares in the denominator of the EPS equation. Since the method assumes conversion at the beginning of the period, no preferred dividends or interest would be considered to have been paid.

6. **(K)** A scrip dividend is a dividend issued by the corporation in the form of a note payable.

7. **(B)** A stock appreciation right allows an employee to receive the excess of the market value of the stock over a preestablished value in the form of cash, shares of stock, or both on the exercise date.

8. **(J)** A stock option is a form of compensation given to employees which allows them to purchase shares of stock at a specified price.

9. **(G)** A dividend paid to shareholders in excess of the retained earnings balance which is considered to be a return of capital and a liquidating dividend.

10. **(E)** When a corporation purchases its own stock in the market, the stock is termed treasury stock. Treasury stock is not an asset as a corporation cannot invest in itself. Treasury stock is recorded in a contra equity account.

Situation	Concepts	Statement of Retained Earnings	Financial Statement Disclosures		Research	Communication

This problem is a collection of miscellaneous stockholders' equity problems. The candidate should start the problem by scanning the required information to determine the amounts to be calculated. While scanning, the candidate should recognize that some of the required items are related, such as number 2 (preferred dividends) in the Statement of Retained Earnings, and numbers 1,2,4 and 6 in the Financial Statement Disclosures. These relationships require that the candidate label each answer, so that it will be possible to quickly find that answer when it is used in a subsequent problem.

Unlike many previous exam problems, the order of the information concerning the transactions does not coincide with the order of the required answers. This arrangement makes it necessary to read the required amount and then hunt for the transaction information needed to calculate that required amount.

1. **($14,000)** Prior period adjustment is the term generally applied to corrections of errors of prior periods. In this problem no amortization had been recorded in a prior year—an error. Since this is not a self-correcting error, it still existed in 2011. The calculation is cost ($320,000) ÷ useful life (eight years) for 1/2 year (purchased July 1). Prior period adjustments are disclosed net of tax (30%). $320,000/8 × 1/2 × (1 − .3) = $14,000.

2. **($12,000)** Preferred dividends are 6% and cumulative. They were declared during 2010 and paid in 2011. The declaration is sufficient to record and recognize the dividends legally; they do not have to be paid in the current year to be recognized during that time period. These dividends will be used in the numerator in question 20 when calculating the 2010 EPS. Since these dividends are cumulative, they would be used in the calculation of EPS even if they had not been declared. The amount of preferred dividends is derived by multiplying the par value of the stock by its rate. 6% × $200,000 par = $12,000 dividends.

3. **($165,000)** Common dividends—cash is calculated by the formula: Common shares outstanding × Dividend per share. In this problem the number of shares outstanding is affected by the beginning shares (100,000), shares issued (13,000), and treasury shares purchased and sold (5,000 purchased, 2,000 sold) prior to the dividend date of November 4. 100,000 + 13,000 − 5,000 + 2,000 = 110,000 shares outstanding × dividend rate $1.50 = $165,000.

4. **($720,000)** Common dividends—property differs from cash dividends because the property may be carried in the accounts at an amount which does not equal its fair value (cash is always at its fair value). Management intends to distribute the property at its fair value, therefore it is necessary to bring the property to fair value on the date management is legally forced to distribute it (the declaration date). Value fluctuations beyond that date are irrelevant.

Situation	Concepts	Statement of Retained Earnings	Financial Statement Disclosures	Research	Communication

1. **(113,000)** The number of shares issued differs from the number of shares outstanding which was used in question 3 under Calculations. Shares issued include those outstanding as well as those held in the treasury. Shares outstanding from question 3 above, 110,000 plus 3,000 treasury shares = 113,000 shares.

2. **($113,000)** Amount of common stock issued—This question takes the answer from question 1 above (113,000 shares) and multiplies that figure by the par value of each share, $1.

3. **($934,000)** The additional paid-in capital, including treasury stock transactions, is derived by adding the beginning balance ($800,000) to the excess ($10) of issue price ($11) over par value ($1) for the shares issued (13,000) to acquire land on February 1, 2010. In addition, the sale of the treasury stock (2,000 shares) at an amount ($16) greater than cost ($14) gives rise to a nonoperating gain that cannot be included in net income since it was both not related to operations and is a transaction in the company's own stock. $800,000 + (13,000 × $10) + [2,000 × (16-14)] = $934,000.

4. **($42,000)** Treasury stock—Since Min Co. follows the cost method of accounting for treasury stock, this answer is derived by multiplying the shares of treasury stock (3,000) by their cost ($14). 3,000 × $14 = $42,000.

5. **($24.86)** Book value per share is a concept that relates common stockholders' equity to shares of common stock. The "per share" referred to is always the **common** shares unless the problem states some other type of shares. In this case it is to be calculated before the prior period adjustment. It is necessary to subtract preferred stock's total liquidating value ($100 × 2,000 sh = $200,000) from total stockholders' equity ($2,686,000) to obtain common stockholders' equity. In this problem no liquidating value is given, so par value is used. The resulting amount ($2,686,000 − $200,000 = $2,486,000) is divided by the common shares outstanding (100,000) to obtain book value per share ($24.86). ($2,686,000 − $200,000) ÷ 100,000 = $24.86.

6. **($826,000)** The formula for calculating earnings per share is (NI − Preferred dividends) ÷ Wtd.-avg. shares outstanding. The numerator is income available to common stockholders. The problem states that adjusted net income for 2010 was $838,000. The word "adjusted" tells the candidate that net income includes all information concerning transactions in the problem and need not be changed in any way. Preferred dividends ($12,000) were calculated in question 2 under Calculations. $838,000 − $12,000 = $826,000.

Situation	Concepts	Statement of Retained Earnings	Financial Statement Disclosures	Research	Communication

1. A company issues a small stock dividend. At what amount should the stock dividend be recorded?

As to the Issuer
ARB43, Ch. 7B, Para 10
Stock dividends

10. As has been previously stated, a stock dividend does not, in fact, give rise to any change whatsoever in either the corporation's assets or its respective shareholders' proportionate interests therein. However, it cannot fail to be recognized that, merely as a consequence of the expressed purpose of the transaction and its characterization as a dividend in related notices to shareholders and the public at large, many recipients of stock dividends look upon them as distributions of corporate earnings and usually in an amount equivalent to the fair value of the additional shares received. Furthermore, it is to be presumed that such views of recipients are ma-

terially strengthened in those instances, which are by far the most numerous, where the issuances are so small in comparison with the shares previously outstanding that they do not have any apparent effect upon the share market price and, consequently, the market value of the shares previously held remains substantially unchanged. The committee therefore believes that where theses circumstances exist the corporation should in the public interest account for the transaction by transferring from earned surplus to the category of permanent capitalization (represented by the capital stock and capital surplus accounts) an amount equal to the fair value of the additional shares issued. Unless this is done, the amount of earnings which the shareholder may believe to have been distributed to him will be left except to the extent otherwise dictated by legal requirements, in earned surplus subject to possible further similar stock issuance or cash distributions.

Codification 505-20-30-3

2. A company issues a property dividend. How should the property dividend be valued?

APB29, Para 18

18. The Board concludes that in general accounting for nonmonetary transactions should be based on the fair values of the assets (or services) involved which is the same basis as that used in monetary transactions. Thus, the cost of a nonmonetary asset acquired in exchange for another nonmonetary asset is the fair value of the asset surrendered to obtain it, and a gain or loss should be recognized on the exchange. The fair value of the asset received should be used to measure the cost if it is more clearly evident than the fair value of the asset surrendered. Similarly, a nonmonetary asset received in a nonreciprocal transfer should be recorded at the fair value of the asset received. A transfer of a nonmonetary asset to a stockholder or to another entity in a nonreciprocal transfer should be recorded at the fair value of the asset transferred, and a gain or loss should be recognized on the disposition of the asset. The fair value of an entity's own stock reacquired may be a more clearly evident measure of the fair value of the asset distributed in a nonreciprocal transfer if the transaction involves distribution of a nonmonetary asset to eliminate a disproportionate part of owners' interests (that is, to acquire stock for the treasury or for retirement).

Codification: 845-10-30-1

3. A company appropriates retained earnings for a loss contingency. How should this be disclosed in the financial statements?

Appropriation of Retained Earnings
FAS5, Para 15

15. Some enterprises have classified a portion of retained earnings as "appropriated" for loss contingencies. In some cases, the appropriation has been shown outside the stockholders' equity section of the balance sheet. Appropriation of retained earnings is not prohibited by this Statement provided that it is shown within the stockholders' equity section of the balance sheet and is clearly identified as an appropriation of retained earnings. Costs or losses shall not be charged to an appropriation of retained earnings, and no part of the appropriation shall be transferred to income.

Codification: 505-10-45-3

Situation	Concepts	Statement of Retained Earnings	Financial Statement Disclosures	Research	Communication

To: Ms. Kay Smith, CEO, Min Co.
From: CPA Candidate
Re: Preferred and common stock

You have requested that I provide a description of the differences between common stock and cumulative preferred stock. While both of these types of financial instruments reflect an ownership interest in the company, preferred stock is closer to a debt instrument in that the holders are entitled to their stated dividend before any distributions are made to common stockholders. This is true with respect to the current dividend as well as any dividends unpaid from prior years. In addition, preferred stockholders have preference over common stockholders when the company is liquidated. While preferred stockholders are limited to their stated dividend rate, common stockholder's dividends are limited only by the earnings of the company.

If you have any other questions, please contact me.

Simulation Problem 2

Situation	Analysis of Transactions	Balance Sheet Disclosures	Calculation Basic EPS	Calculation Diluted EPS	Communication	Research

Date	Transaction	Preferred stock	APIC—preferred stock	Common stock	APIC—common stock	Retained earnings	Treasury stock	APIC—treasury stock
1/2/10	Issue preferred stock at par	1,000,000						
3/1/10	Issue common stock for services			3,000	93,000			
7/1/10	Issue common stock for cash			40,000	1,640,000			
10/1/10	Repurchase treasury stock						544,000	
12/1/10	Sell treasury stock					(15,000)	(102,000)	
12/30/10	Declare and pay dividends					(86,000)		

Explanation of solutions

- Preferred stock 10,000 × $100 = $1,000,000
- Value of services = Fair value of stock which is more reliable since stock is traded on the open market. 3,000 shares × $32 per share = $96,000
- Common stock: 40,000 shares of common stock × $1 par = $40,000 to common stock account; $40,000 × 41 = $1,640,000 to APIC
- Treasury stock is recorded at cost. 16,000 shares × $34 per share = $544,000
- Treasury stock is reduced by the cost paid 3,000 × $34 per share = $102,000. There is a $5 per share loss on the treasury shares which is debited to retained earnings 3,000 shares × $5 = $15,000
- Dividends to preferred shareholders = 10,000 × $100 par = $1,000,000 × 6% = $60,000 preferred dividends
- Dividends to common shareholders. Number of common shares outstanding equals 100,000 shares + 3,000 shares issued + 40,000 shares issued – 16,000 treasury shares purchased + 3,000 treasury shares reissued = 130,000 outstanding shares × $0.20 = $26,000. Therefore, total dividend is $86,000

Situation	Analysis of Transactions	Balance Sheet Disclosures	Calculation Basic EPS	Calculation Diluted EPS	Communication	Research

Owners' equity:	
Preferred stock	1,000,000
Common stock	143,000
Additional paid-in capital preferred stock	0
Additional paid-in capital common stock	4,333,000
Additional paid-in capital treasury stock	0
Retained earnings	501,000
Treasury stock	(442,000)
Other comprehensive income	0
Total owners' equity	5,535,000

Explanation of solutions

- Preferred stock: Issued at par. 10,000 shares × $100 = $1,000,000
- Common stock: $100,000 + $3,000 + $40,000 = $143,000
- Additional paid-in capital—Common stock: $2,600,000 + $93,000 + $1,640,000 = $4,333,000
- Retained earnings: $250,000 – $28,000 = $222,000 at end of 2006
- Retained earnings for 2007: $222,000 – $15,000 – $86,000 + $380,000 = $501,000
- Treasury stock: $544,000 – $102,000 = $442,000

Situation	Analysis of Transactions	Balance Sheet Disclosures	Calculation Basic EPS	Calculation Diluted EPS	Communication	Research

Numerator	320,000
Denominator	118,750
Basic earnings per share	2.6947

Explanation of solutions

Numerator: $380,000 net income – $60,000 in preferred dividends = $320,000. Denominator – Weighted-average common shares.

Date	*# shares*	*Time outstanding*	*WACS*
1/1	100,000	12/12	100,000
3/1	3,000	10/12	2,500
7/1	40,000	6/12	20,000
10/1	(16,000) treasury shares	3/12	(4,000)
12/1	3,000 treasury shares sold	1/12	250
	Total WACS outstanding		118,750

Situation	Analysis of Transactions	Balance Sheet Disclosures	Calculation Basic EPS	Calculation Diluted EPS	Communication	Research

Numerator	380,000
Denominator	168,750
Diluted earnings per share	2.2519

WACS outstanding: Basic EPS 118,750 + Convertible preferred (10,000 shares preferred × 5 shares common) 50,000 = 168,750

Situation	Analysis of Transactions	Balance Sheet Disclosures	Calculation Basic EPS	Calculation Diluted EPS	Communication	Research

To: Mr. Fenton, CEO, M Corporation
From: CPA Candidate
Re: Earnings per share

As you requested, I have prepared this memorandum to answer your questions about earnings per share. The objective of earnings per share is to measure the performance of an entity over a reporting period. There are two computations for earnings per share: basic and diluted. Basic earnings per share is computed by dividing the income available to common stockholders by the weighted-average number of common shares outstanding for the period. Shares issued and reacquired during the period are weighted for the period of time they were outstanding. Diluted earnings per share is another measure of performance; however, diluted earnings per share gives the effect of all potentially dilutive common shares that were outstanding during the period. Hence, diluted earnings per share will be less than basic earnings per share.

If you have any other questions, please contact me.

Situation	Analysis of Transactions	Balance Sheet Disclosures	Calculation Basic EPS	Calculation Diluted EPS	Communication	Research

APB6, Para 12

12. The Board considers that the following accounting practices, in addition to the accounting practices indicated in Chapter 1B, are acceptable, and that they appear to be more in accord with current developments in practice:

a. When a corporation's stock is retired, or purchased for constructive retirement (with or without an intention to retire the stock formally in accordance with applicable laws)

i. An excess of purchase price over par or stated value may be allowed between capital surplus and retained earnings. The portion of the excess allocated to capital surplus should be limited to the sum of (a) all capital surplus arising from previous retirements and net "gains" on sales of treasury stock of the same issue, and (b) the pro rata portion of capital surplus paid in, voluntary transfers of retained earnings, capitalization of stock dividends, etc., on the same issue. For this purpose, any remaining capital surplus applicable to issues fully retired (formal or constructive) is deemed to be applicable pro rata to shares of common stock. Alternatively, the excess may be charged entirely to retained earnings in recognition of the fact that a corporation can always capitalize or allocate retained earnings for such purposes.

ii. An excess of par or stated value over purchase price should be credited to capital surplus.

b.　When a corporation's stock is acquired for purposes other than retirement (formal or constructive), or when ultimate disposition has not yet been decided, the cost of acquired stock may be shown separately as a deduction from the total of capital stock, capital surplus, and retained earnings, or may be accorded the accounting treatment appropriate for retired stock, or in some circumstances may be shown as an asset in accordance with paragraph 4 of Chapter 1A of ARB43. "Gains" on sales of treasury stock not previously accounted for as constructively retired should be credited to capital surplus; "losses" may be charged to capital surplus to the extent that previous net "gains" from sales or retirements of the same class of stock are included therein, otherwise to retained earnings.

Codification: 505-30-30-10

Simulation Problem 3

Situation	Concepts	Journal Entries	Retained Earnings	Stockholders' Equity Section of Balance Sheet	Communication	Research

		True	*False*
1.	Mandatorily redeemable preferred stock is classified as owners' equity and is disclosed after common stock.	○	●
2.	Property dividends are valued at the book value of the property.	○	●
3.	When a company makes a liquidating dividend, it debits the common stock account.	○	●
4.	Scrip dividends are a liability on the date of declaration.	●	○
5.	Stock dividends of 40% of the outstanding shares of stock are valued at fair market value on the date of declaration.	○	●
6.	If a company has cumulative preferred stock, all dividends in arrears must be subtracted from net income in the numerator of basic earnings per share.	○	●
7.	Cash dividends become a liability to the corporation when declared.	●	○
8.	Stock issued for services should be recorded at the fair market value of the services rendered if that value is greater than the fair market value of the stock traded on the exchange.	○	●

Explanation of solutions

1.　(F) Mandatorily redeemable preferred is classified as a liability on the balance sheet.

2.　(F) Property dividends are valued at fair market value of the property at the date of declaration.

3.　(F) When a company makes a liquidating dividend, a company usually debits additional paid-in capital rather than retained earnings. Common stock cannot be debited because it is considered legal capital which is only eliminated upon the dissolution of the corporation.

4.　(T) All dividends are liabilities on the dates declared.

5.　(F) Large stock dividends are recorded at par. A stock dividend of 40% of the shares outstanding is considered a large stock dividend.

6.　(F) If a company has cumulative preferred stock, only the current year dividends in arrears are subtracted from net income in the numerator of basic earnings per share.

7.　(T) All dividends are liabilities on the dates declared.

8.　(F) The more objective measurement of the value of the goods or services exchanged for stock is the fair market value of the stock if the stock is traded on a stock exchange.

Situation	Concepts	Journal Entries	Retained Earnings	Stockholders' Equity Section of Balance Sheet	Communication	Research

1.　Treasury stock purchased on March 5, 2010

Treasury stock	50,000	
Cash		50,000

(5,000 shares at $10 per share)

2. Declaration and distribution of a property dividend on July 15, 2010

Loss on inventory	15,000	
Inventory		15,000
Retained earnings	60,000	
Inventory		60,000

3. Issue of common stock on October 1, 2010

Cash	360,000	
Common stock (20,000 × $5)		100,000 (par)
Additional paid-in capital		260,000 (plug)

(20,000 shares × $18 exercise price)

Situation	Concepts	Journal Entries	Retained Earnings	Stockholders' Equity Section of Balance Sheet	Communications	Research

Field Company
STATEMENT OF RETAINED EARNINGS
For the Year ending December 31, 2010

Beginning retained earnings, 1-1-10	1,845,000
Net income	240,000
Dividends	(60,000)
End retained earnings, 12-31-10	2,025,000

Situation	Concepts	Journal Entries	Retained Earnings	Stockholders' Equity Section of Balance Sheet	Communication	Research

Field Company
STOCKHOLDERS' EQUITY SECTION OF BALANCE SHEET
December 31, 2010

Common Stock [1]	900,000
Additional paid-in capital [2]	1,860,000
Retained earnings	2,025,000
Treasury stock	(50,000)
Accumulated other comprehensive income	0
Total stockholders' equity	4,735,000

[1] Shares issued: 160,000 + 20,000 = 180,000 × $5 = $900,000
[2] Additional paid-in capital $1,600,000 + [20,000 × ($18 − 5)] = $1,860,000 (1,600,000 + 260,000)

Explanation of solutions

To prepare the stockholders' equity section of Field's December 31, 2010 balance sheet, certain computations need to be made first.

1. The common stock authorized does not change throughout the problem; it is 400,000 shares. The number of shares outstanding increases by the 20,000 shares issued when the stock options were exercised. The balance in the common stock account is the number of shares issued times the par value of the common stock (180,000 × $5 = $900,000).

2. The treasury stock is accounted for by the cost method, which means the treasury stock is recorded at cost (5,000 shares × $10 = $50,000). The journal entry for the treasury stock is

| Treasury stock | 50,000 | |
| Cash | | 50,000 |

3. The information given indicates that the intrinsic value method is used. Because the intrinsic value method is used, compensation cost is zero and no entry is made until the options are recognized. Additional paid-in capital is the amount of money received for stock above the par value. The exercise or option price of the stock options exercised was $18 per share. The $13 per share paid above the par value of the stock needs to be added to the additional paid-in capital account, so $260,000 ($13 × 20,000 shares) should be added to the beginning balance of $1,600,000 for a total of $1,860,000 in the additional paid-in capital account.

4. The formula for retained earnings is

Beginning balance
Add: Net income
Less: Dividends
Ending balance

The amount of the dividends is the fair market value of the property distributed, which is $60,000 in this case. A $15,000 loss is recognized from the property dividend for the difference between the $75,000 carrying value and market value of the inventory. However, this loss would already be included in 2010 net income. Retained earnings is calculated as follows:

Beginning balance	$1,845,000
Add: Net income	240,000
Less: Dividend	(60,000)
Ending balance	$2,025,000

					Communication	
Situation	Concepts	Journal Entries	Retained Earnings	Stockholders' Equity Section of Balance Sheet		Research

To: CEO, Field Company
From: CPA Candidate
Re: Earnings per share

This memorandum explains the presentation of basic and diluted earnings per share. A company is required to calculate earnings per share and disclose this information on the bottom of the income statement for each year presented. If a company has a simple capital structure with no convertible securities or common stock equivalents, the company presents only basic earnings per share. However, if a company has a complex capital structure with convertible securities or common stock equivalents, a second calculation for diluted earnings per share must be made. In the case of companies with complex capital structures, both basic and diluted earnings per share must be disclosed on the face of the income statement.

Basic earnings per share is based on income available for common stockholders divided by the weighted-average number of outstanding shares. Income available to common stockholders is net income less preferred dividends declared. Preferred dividends on cumulative preferred stock are deducted from net income. However, preferred dividends on noncumulative preferred stock are deducted for the current year only if declared.

Diluted earnings per share is basic earnings per share adjusted for the effects of dilutive securities. Dilutive securities include options, warrants, convertible bonds, and preferred stock. The adjustments include positive numerator adjustments for bond interest (net of tax), and preferred dividends. The positive denominator adjustments are for dilutive shares that would be issued upon conversion of convertible securities and from applying the treasury stock method for dilutive options and warrants.

If you need assistance with calculating earnings per share, please contact my office.

						Research
Situation	Concepts	Journal Entries	Retained Earnings	Stockholders' Equity Section of Balance Sheet	Communication	

1. How is diluted earnings per share calculated?

FAS128, Para 11

11. The objective of diluted EPS is consistent with that of basic EPS—to measure the performance of an entity over the reporting period—while giving effect to all dilutive potential common shares that were outstanding during the period. The computation of diluted EPS is similar to the computation of basic EPS except that the denominator is increased to include the number of additional common shares that would have been outstanding if the dilutive potential common shares had been issued. In addition, in computing the dilutive effect of convertible securities, the numerator is adjusted to add back (a) any convertible preferred dividends, and (b) the after-tax amount of interest recognized in the period associated with any convertible debt. The numerator also is adjusted for any other changes in income or loss that would result from the assumed conversion of those potential common shares, such as profit-sharing expenses. Similar adjustments also may be necessary for certain contracts that provide issuer or holder with a choice between settlement methods.

FAS128, Para 12

12. Diluted EPS shall be based on the most advantageous conversion rate or exercise price from the standpoint of the security holder. Previously reported diluted EPS data shall not be retroactively adjusted for subsequent conversions or subsequent changes in the market price of the common stock.

Codification: 260-10-45-16

2. What is the purpose of reporting comprehensive income?

3. A company has available-for-sale securities and recognizes an unrealized holding gain in year 1. In year 2, the company sells these securities. How should this affect other comprehensive income on the financial statements?

Purpose of Reporting Comprehensive Income
FAS130, Para 11

11. The purpose of reporting comprehensive income is to report a measure of all changes in equity of an enterprise that result from recognized transactions and other economic events of the period other than transactions with owners in their capacity as owners. Prior to the issuance of this Statement, some of those changes in equity were displayed in a statement that reports the results of operations, while others were included directly in balances within a separate component of equity in a statement of financial position.

FAS130, Para 12

12. If used with related disclosures and other information in the financial statements, the information provided by reporting comprehensive income should assist investors, creditors, and others in assessing an enterprise's activities and the timing and magnitude of an enterprise's future cash flows.

Codification: 220-10-10-1

Reclassification adjustments
FAS130, Para 18

18. Adjustments shall be made to avoid double counting in comprehensive income items that are displayed as part of net income for a period that also had been displayed as part of other comprehensive income in that period or earlier periods. For example, gains on investment securities that were realized and included in net income of the current period that also had been included in other comprehensive income as unrealized holding gains in the period in which they arose must be deducted through other comprehensive income of the period in which they are included in net income to avoid including them in comprehensive income twice. Those adjustments are referred to in this Statement as reclassification adjustments.

Codification: 220-10-45-15

MULTIPLE-CHOICE QUESTIONS (1-59)

1. Puff Co. acquired 40% of Straw, Inc.'s voting common stock on January 2, 2010, for $400,000. The carrying amount of Straw's net assets at the purchase date totaled $900,000. Fair values equaled carrying amounts for all items except equipment, for which fair values exceeded carrying amounts by $100.000. The equipment has a five-year life. During 2010, Straw reported net income of $150,000. What amount of income from this investment should Puff report in its 2010 income statement if Puff uses the equity method to account for the investment?

  a. $40,000
  b. $52,000
  c. $56,000
  d. $60,000

2. On April 1, 2009, Saxe, Inc. purchased $200,000 face value, 9% US Treasury Notes for $198,500, including accrued interest of $4,500. The notes mature July 1, 2010, and pay interest semiannually on January 1 and July 1. Saxe uses the straight-line method of amortization and intends to hold the notes to maturity. Saxe does not elect the fair value option for recording the securities. In its October 31, 2009 balance sheet, the carrying amount of this investment should be

  a. $194,000
  b. $196,800
  c. $197,200
  d. $199,000

3. Kale Co. purchased bonds at a discount on the open market as an investment and intends to hold these bonds to maturity. Kale does not elect the fair value option for the bonds. Kale should account for these bonds at

  a. Cost.
  b. Amortized cost.
  c. Fair value.
  d. Lower of cost or market.

4. For a marketable debt securities portfolio classified as held-to-maturity, which of the following amounts should be included in the period's net income, assuming the fair value option is not elected.

  I. Unrealized temporary losses during the period.
  II. Realized gains during the period.
  III. Changes in the valuation allowance during the period.

  a. III only.
  b. II only.
  c. I and II.
  d. I, II, and III.

5. Bing Corporation purchased bonds at a discount on the open market as an investment and intends to hold these bonds to maturity. Assume that Bing elects the fair value option. Bing should account for these bonds at

  a. Cost.
  b. Amortized cost.
  c. Fair value.
  d. Lower of cost or market.

6. For a marketable debt securities portfolio classified as held-to-maturity, which of the following amounts should be included in the period's net income, assuming the company elects the fair value option of reporting all of its financial instruments in the portfolio?

  I. Unrealized temporary losses during the period.
  II. Realized gains during the period.
  III. Changes in the valuation allowance during the period.
  IV. Unrealized gains during the period.

  a. I only
  b. I and II
  c. I and III.
  d. I, II, and IV.

Items 7 and 8 are based on the following:

The following data pertains to Tyne Co.'s investments in marketable equity securities:

| | | Market value | |
	Cost	12/31/09	12/31/08
Trading	$150,000	$155,000	$100,000
Available-for-sale	150,000	130,000	120,000

7. What amount should Tyne report as unrealized holding gain in its 2009 income statement, assuming Tyne does not elect to use the fair value option to report its investments?

  a. $50,000
  b. $55,000
  c. $60,000
  d. $65,000

8. Assume Tyne does not elect the fair value option to report investments. What amount should Tyne report as net unrealized loss on marketable equity securities at December 31, 2009, in accumulated other comprehensive income in stockholders' equity?

  a. $0
  b. $10,000
  c. $15,000
  d. $20,000

9. Reed Insurance Co. began operations on January 1, 2008. The following information pertains to Reed's December 31, 2009 portfolio of marketable equity securities:

	Trading securities	Available-for-sale securities
Aggregate cost	$360,000	$550,000
Aggregate market value	320,000	450,000
Aggregate lower of cost or market value applied to each security in the portfolio	304,000	420,000

Reed does not elect the fair value option. If the market declines are judged to be temporary, what amounts should Reed report as a loss on these securities in its December 31, 2009 income statement?

	Trading securities	Available-for-sale securities
a.	$40,000	$0
b.	$0	$100,000
c.	$40,000	$100,000
d.	$56,000	$130,000

10. Stone does not use the fair value option to account for available-for-sale securities. Information regarding Stone Co.'s portfolio of available-for-sale securities is as follows:

Aggregate cost as of 12/31/09	$170,000
Unrealized gains as of 12/31/09	4,000
Unrealized losses as of 12/31/09	26,000
Net realized gains during 2009	30,000

At December 31, 2008, Stone reported an unrealized loss of $1,500 in other comprehensive income to reduce these securities to market. Under the accumulated other comprehensive income in stockholders' equity section of its December 31, 2009 balance sheet, what amount should Stone report?

a. $26,000
b. $22,000
c. $20,500
d. $0

11. Data regarding Ball Corp.'s available-for-sale securities follow:

	Cost	Market value
December 31, 2008	$150,000	$130,000
December 31, 2009	150,000	160,000

Differences between cost and market values are considered temporary. Ball does not elect the fair value option to account for available-for-sale securities. The effect on Ball's 2009 other comprehensive income would be

a. $30,000
b. $20,000
c. $10,000
d. $0

12. Alton Co. began operations on January 1, 2010. The following information pertains to Alton's December 31, 2010 portfolio of marketable equity securities:

	Trading securities	Available-for-sale securities
Aggregate cost	$360,000	$550,000
Aggregate market value	320,000	450,000
Aggregate lower of cost or market value applied to each security in the portfolio	304,000	420,000

Alton elects the fair value option for all financial instruments. If the market declines are judged to be temporary, what amounts should Alton report as a loss on these securities in its December 31, 2010 income statement?

	Trading securities	Available-for-sale securities
a.	$40,000	$0
b.	$0	$100,000
c.	$40,000	$100,000
d.	$56,000	$130,000

13. Information regarding Shelton Co.'s portfolio of available-for-sale securities is as follows:

Aggregate cost as of 12/31/10	$150,000
Unrealized gains as of 12/31/10	14,000
Unrealized losses as of 12/31/10	26,000
Net realized gains during 2010	30,000

Shelton elects to use the fair value option for reporting all available-for-sale securities. At December 31, 2010, what total amount should Shelton report on its income statement?

a. $ 4,000 gain
b. $18,000 gain
c. $30,000 gain
d. $44,000 gain

14. Data regarding Shannon Corp.'s available-for-sale securities follow:

	Cost	Market value
December 31, 2010	$150,000	$130,000
December 31, 2011	150,000	160,000

Differences between cost and market values are considered temporary. Shannon elects to use the fair value option for reporting all available-for-sale securities. The effect of accounting for available-for-sale securities on other comprehensive income in 2011 would be

a. $30,000
b. $20,000
c. $10,000
d. $0

15. Antonio Corp. acquired a portfolio of marketable equity securities that it does not intend to sell in the near term. Antonio elects the fair value option for reporting its financial assets. How should Antonio classify these securities, and how should it report unrealized gains and losses?

	Classify as	Report as a
a.	Trading securities	Component of income from continuing operations
b.	Available-for-sale securities	Separate component of other comprehensive income
c.	Trading securities	Separate component of other comprehensive income
d.	Available-for-sale securities	Component of income from continuing operations

16. During 2009, Rex Company purchased marketable equity securities as a short-term investment. These securities are classified as available-for-sale. Rex does not elect the fair value option to account for available-for-sale securities. The cost and market value at December 31, 2009, were as follows:

Security	Cost	Market value
A—100 shares	$ 2,800	$ 3,400
B—1,000 shares	17,000	15,300
C—2,000 shares	31,500	29,500
	$51,300	$48,200

Rex sold 1,000 shares of Company B stock on January 31, 2010, for $15 per share, incurring $1,500 in brokerage commission and taxes. On the sale, Rex should report a realized loss of

a. $ 300
b. $1,800
c. $2,000
d. $3,500

17. Cap Corp. reported accrued investment interest receivable of $38,000 and $46,500 at January 1 and December 31, 2009, respectively. During 2009, cash collections from the investments included the following:

Capital gains distributions	$145,000
Interest	152,000

What amount should Cap report as interest revenue from investments for 2009?

a. $160,500
b. $153,500
c. $152,000
d. $143,500

18. Nola has a portfolio of marketable equity securities that it does not intend to sell in the near term. Assume that Nola does not elect the fair value option to report these securities. How should Nola classify these securities, and how should it report unrealized gains and losses from these securities?

	Classify as	Report as a
a.	Trading securities	Component of income from continuing operations
b.	Available-for-sale securities	Separate component of other comprehensive income
c.	Trading securities	Separate component of other comprehensive income

(top of right column)

a. $30,000
b. $20,000
c. $10,000
d. $0

d.   Available-for-   Component of income from
      sale securities   continuing operations

19. On December 29, 2009, BJ Co. sold a marketable equity security that had been purchased on January 4, 2008. BJ owned no other marketable equity security. An unrealized loss was reported in 2008 as other comprehensive income. A realized gain was reported in the 2009 income statement. Was the marketable equity security classified as available-for-sale and did its 2008 market price decline exceed its 2009 market price recovery?

	Available-for-sale	_2008 market price decline exceeded 2009 market recovery_
a.	Yes	Yes
b.	Yes	No
c.	No	Yes
d.	No	No

20. On January 10, 2009, Box, Inc. purchased marketable equity securities of Knox, Inc. and Scot, Inc., neither of which Box could significantly influence. Box classified both securities as available-for-sale. At December 31, 2009, the cost of each investment was greater than its fair market value. The loss on the Knox investment was considered other-than-temporary and that on Scot was considered temporary. How should Box report the effects of these investing activities in its 2009 income statement, assuming Box does not elect the fair value option to account for these securities?

I.   Excess of cost of Knox stock over its market value.
II.   Excess of cost of Scot stock over its market value.

   a.   An unrealized loss equal to I plus II.
   b.   An unrealized loss equal to I only.
   c.   A realized loss equal to I only.
   d.   No income statement effect.

21. On both December 31, 2008, and December 31, 2009, Kopp Co.'s only marketable equity security had the same market value, which was below cost. Kopp considered the decline in value to be temporary in 2008 but other than temporary in 2009. At the end of both years the security was classified as a noncurrent asset. Kopp considers the investment to be available-for-sale. Assume that Kipp does not elect the fair value option to account for its available-for-sale securities. What should be the effects of the determination that the decline was other than temporary on Kopp's 2009 net noncurrent assets and net income?

   a.   No effect on both net noncurrent assets and net income.
   b.   No effect on net noncurrent assets and decrease in net income.
   c.   Decrease in net noncurrent assets and **no** effect on net income.
   d.   Decrease in both net noncurrent assets and net income.

22. For the last ten years, Woody Co. has owned cumulative preferred stock issued by Hadley, Inc. During 2009, Hadley declared and paid both the 2009 dividend and the 2008 dividend in arrears. How should Woody report the 2008 dividend in arrears that was received in 2009?

   a.   As a reduction in cumulative preferred dividends receivable.
   b.   As a retroactive change of the prior period financial statements.

c.   Include, net of income taxes, after 2009 income from continuing operations.
d.   Include in 2009 income from continuing operations.

Items 23 and 24 are based on the following:

Deed Co. owns 2% of Beck Cosmetic Retailers. A property dividend by Beck consisted of merchandise with a fair value lower than the listed retail price. Deed in turn gave the merchandise to its employees as a holiday bonus.

23. How should Deed report the receipt and distribution of the merchandise in its income statement?
   a.   At fair value for both dividend revenue and employee compensation expense.
   b.   At listed retail price for both dividend revenue and employee compensation expense.
   c.   At fair value for dividend revenue and listed retail price for employee compensation expense.
   d.   By disclosure only.

24. How should Deed report the receipt and distribution of the merchandise in its statement of cash flows?
   a.   As both an inflow and outflow for operating activities.
   b.   As both an inflow and outflow for investing activities.
   c.   As an inflow for investing activities and outflow for operating activities.
   d.   As a noncash activity.

25. Pal Corp.'s 2009 dividend revenue included only part of the dividends received from its Ima Corp. investment. Pal Corp. has an investment in Ima Corp. that it intends to hold indefinitely. The balance of the dividend reduced Pal's carrying amount for its Ima investment. This reflects the fact that Pal accounts for its Ima investment
   a.   As an available-for-sale investment, and only a portion of Ima's 2009 dividends represent earnings after Pal's acquisition.
   b.   As an available-for-sale investment and its carrying amount exceeded the proportionate share of Ima's market value.
   c.   As an equity investment, and Ima incurred a loss in 2009.
   d.   As an equity investment, and its carrying amount exceeded the proportionate share of Ima's market value.

26. In its financial statements, Pare, Inc. uses the cost method of accounting for its 15% ownership of Sabe Co. At December 31, 2009, Pare has a receivable from Sabe. How should the receivable be reported in Pare's December 31, 2009 balance sheet?
   a.   The total receivable should be reported separately.
   b.   The total receivable should be included as part of the investment in Sabe, without separate disclosure.
   c.   85% of the receivable should be reported separately, with the balance offset against Sabe's payable to Pare.
   d.   The total receivable should be offset against Sabe's payable to Pare, without separate disclosure.

Items 27 and 28 are based on the following:

Sun Corp. had investments in marketable debt securities costing $650,000 that were classified as available-for-sale. On June 30, 2009, Sun decided to hold the investments to maturity and accordingly reclassified them to the held-to-maturity category on that date. The investments' market value was $575,000 at December 31, 2008, $530,000 at June 30, 2009, and $490,000 at December 31, 2009. Sun does not elect the fair value option to account for these investments.

27. What amount of loss from investments should Sun report in its 2009 income statement?
   a. $ 45,000
   b. $ 85,000
   c. $120,000
   d. $0

28. What amount should Sun report as net unrealized loss on marketable debt securities in its 2009 statement of stockholders' equity?
   a. $ 40,000
   b. $ 45,000
   c. $160,000
   d. $120,000

29. A marketable debt security is transferred from available-for-sale to held-to-maturity securities. At the transfer date, the security's carrying amount exceeds its market value. Assume the fair value option is not elected to report this security. What amount is used at the transfer date to record the security in the held-to-maturity portfolio?
   a.   Market value, regardless of whether the decline in market value below cost is considered permanent or temporary.
   b.   Market value, only if the decline in market value below cost is considered permanent.
   c.   Cost, if the decline in market value below cost is considered temporary.
   d.   Cost, regardless of whether the decline in market value below cost is considered permanent or temporary.

Items 30 and 31 are based on the following:

Jill Corp. had investments in marketable debt securities purchased on January 1, 2009, for $650,000 that were classified as trading securities and accounted for using the cost adjusted to fair value method. On June 30, 2010, Jill decided to hold the investments to maturity and accordingly reclassified them to the held-to-maturity category on that date. The investments' market value was $575,000 at December 31, 2009, $530,000 at June 30, 2010, and $490,000 at December 31, 2010. Jill elects the fair value option for reporting these held-to-maturity securities.

30. What amount of loss from investments should Jill report in its 2010 income statement?
   a. $ 40,000
   b. $ 85,000
   c. $160,000
   d. $0

31. What amount should Jill report as net unrealized loss on marketable debt securities in other comprehensive income in its 2010 statement of stockholders' equity?
   a. $0
   b. $ 40,000

   c. $ 45,000
   d. $120,000

Items 32 through 34 are based on the following:

Grant, Inc. acquired 30% of South Co.'s voting stock for $200,000 on January 2, 2008. Grant's 30% interest in South gave Grant the ability to exercise significant influence over South's operating and financial policies. During 2008, South earned $80,000 and paid dividends of $50,000. South reported earnings of $100,000 for the six months ended June 30, 2009, and $200,000 for the year ended December 31, 2009. On July 1, 2009, Grant sold half of its stock in South for $150,000 cash. South paid dividends of $60,000 on October 1, 2009. Grant does not elect the fair value option to report this investment.

32. Before income taxes, what amount should Grant include in its 2008 income statement as a result of the investment?
   a. $15,000
   b. $24,000
   c. $50,000
   d. $80,000

33. In Grant's December 31, 2008 balance sheet, what should be the carrying amount of this investment?
   a. $200,000
   b. $209,000
   c. $224,000
   d. $230,000

34. In its 2009 income statement, what amount should Grant report as gain from the sale of half of its investment?
   a. $24,500
   b. $30,500
   c. $35,000
   d. $45,500

35. Moss Corp. owns 20% of Dubro Corp.'s preferred stock and 80% of its common stock. Dubro's stock outstanding at December 31, 2009, is as follows:

10% cumulative preferred stock	$100,000
Common stock	700,000

Dubro reported net income of $60,000 for the year ended December 31, 2009. Assume that Moss does not elect the fair value option to report the investment in Dubro. What amount should Moss record as equity in earnings of Dubro for the year ended December 31, 2009?
   a. $42,000
   b. $48,000
   c. $48,400
   d. $50,000

36. Sage, Inc. bought 40% of Adams Corp.'s outstanding common stock on January 2, 2009, for $400,000. The carrying amount of Adams' net assets at the purchase date totaled $900,000. Fair values and carrying amounts were the same for all items except for plant and inventory, for which fair values exceeded their carrying amounts by $90,000 and $10,000, respectively. The plant has an eighteen-year life. All inventory was sold during 2009. During 2009, Adams reported net income of $120,000 and paid a $20,000 cash dividend. Assume that Sage uses the equity method to account for this investment. What amount should Sage report in its income statement from its investment in Adams for the year ended December 31, 2009?

a. $48,000
b. $42,000
c. $36,000
d. $32,000

37. Pear Co.'s income statement for the year ended December 31, 2009, as prepared by Pear's controller, reported income before taxes of $125,000. The auditor questioned the following amounts that had been included in income before taxes:

Unrealized gain on available-for-sale investment	$40,000
Equity in earnings of Cinn Co.	20,000
Dividends received from Cinn	8,000
Adjustments to profits of prior years for arithmetical errors in depreciation	(35,000)

Pear owns 40% of Cinn's common stock. Pear accounts for its investment in Cinn in accordance with the requirements of the equity method. Pear's December 31, 2009 income statement should report income before taxes of

a. $ 85,000
b. $117,000
c. $112,000
d. $152,000

38. On January 2, 2009, Saxe Company purchased 20% of Lex Corporation's common stock for $150,000. Saxe Corporation intends to hold the stock indefinitely. This investment did not give Saxe the ability to exercise significant influence over Lex. During 2009 Lex reported net income of $175,000 and paid cash dividends of $100,000 on its common stock. There was no change in the market value of the common stock during the year. The balance in Saxe's investment in Lex Corporation account at December 31, 2009 should be

a. $130,000
b. $150,000
c. $165,000
d. $185,000

39. On January 2, 2009, Well Co. purchased 10% of Rea, Inc.'s outstanding common shares for $400,000. Well is the largest single shareholder in Rea, and Well's officers are a majority on Rea's board of directors. Rea reported net income of $500,000 for 2009, and paid dividends of $150,000. Well does not elect the fair value option to report its investment in Rea. In its December 31, 2009 balance sheet, what amount should Well report as investment in Rea?

a. $450,000
b. $435,000
c. $400,000
d. $385,000

40. On January 2, 2009, Kean Co. purchased a 30% interest in Pod Co. for $250,000. On this date, Pod's stockholders' equity was $500,000. The carrying amounts of Pod's identifiable net assets approximated their fair values, except for land whose fair value exceeded its carrying amount by $200,000. Pod reported net income of $100,000 for 2009, and paid no dividends. Kean accounts for this investment using the equity method. In its December 31, 2009 balance sheet, what amount should Kean report as investment in subsidiary?

a. $210,000
b. $220,000
c. $270,000
d. $280,000

41. On January 1, 2009, Mega Corp. acquired 10% of the outstanding voting stock of Penny, Inc. On January 2, 2010, Mega gained the ability to exercise significant influence over financial and operating control of Penny by acquiring an additional 20% of Penny's outstanding stock. The two purchases were made at prices proportionate to the value assigned to Penny's net assets, which equaled their carrying amounts. Mega does not elect the fair value option to report its investment in Penny. For the years ended December 31, 2009 and 2010, Penny reported the following:

	2009	2010
Dividends paid	$200,000	$300,000
Net income	600,000	650,000

In 2010, what amounts should Mega report as current year investment income and as an adjustment, before income taxes, to 2009 investment income?

	2010 investment income	Adjustment to 2009 investment income
a.	$195,000	$160,000
b.	$195,000	$100,000
c.	$195,000	$ 40,000
d.	$105,000	$ 40,000

42. Pare, Inc. purchased 10% of Tot Co.'s 100,000 outstanding shares of common stock on January 2, 2009, for $50,000. On December 31, 2009, Pare purchased an additional 20,000 shares of Tot for $150,000. There was no goodwill as a result of either acquisition, and Tot had not issued any additional stock during 2009. Tot reported earnings of $300,000 for 2009. Pare does not elect the fair value option to report its investment in Tot. What amount should Pare report in its December 31, 2009 balance sheet as investment in Tot?

a. $170,000
b. $200,000
c. $230,000
d. $290,000

43. When the equity method is used to account for investments in common stock, which of the following affects the investor's reported investment income?

	Equipment amortization related to purchase	Cash dividends from investee
a.	Yes	Yes
b.	No	Yes
c.	No	No
d.	Yes	No

44. Park Co. uses the equity method to account for its January 1, 2009 purchase of Tun Inc.'s common stock. On January 1, 2009, the fair values of Tun's FIFO inventory and land exceeded their carrying amounts. How do these excesses of fair values over carrying amounts affect Park's reported equity in Tun's 2009 earnings?

	Inventory excess	Land excess
a.	Decrease	Decrease
b.	Decrease	No effect
c.	Increase	Increase
d.	Increase	No effect

45. An investor in common stock received dividends in excess of the investor's share of investee's earnings subsequent to the date of the investment. How will the investor's investment account be affected by those dividends for each of the following investments?

	Available-for-sale securities	Equity method investment
a.	No effect	No effect
b.	Decrease	No effect
c.	No effect	Decrease
d.	Decrease	Decrease

46. Peel Co. received a cash dividend from a common stock investment. Should Peel report an increase in the investment account if it has classified the stock as available-for-sale or uses the equity method of accounting?

	Available-for-sale	Equity
a.	No	No
b.	Yes	Yes
c.	Yes	No
d.	No	Yes

47. On January 1, 2009, Point, Inc. purchased 10% of Iona Co.'s common stock. Point purchased additional shares bringing its ownership up to 40% of Iona's common stock outstanding on August 1, 2009. During October 2009, Iona declared and paid a cash dividend on all of its outstanding common stock. Point uses the equity method to account for its investment in Iona. How much income from the Iona investment should Point's 2009 income statement report?

- a.   10% of Iona's income for January 1 to July 31, 2009, plus 40% of Iona's income for August 1 to December 31, 2009.
- b.   40% of Iona's income for August 1 to December 31, 2009 only.
- c.   40% of Iona's 2009 income.
- d.   Amount equal to dividends received from Iona.

48. In its financial statements, Pulham Corp. uses the equity method of accounting for its 30% ownership of Angles Corp. At December 31, 2009, Pulham has a receivable from Angles. How should the receivable be reported in Pulham's 2009 financial statements?

- a.   None of the receivable should be reported, but the entire receivable should be offset against Angles' payable to Pulham.
- b.   70% of the receivable should be separately reported, with the balance offset against 30% of Angles' payable to Pulham.
- c.   The total receivable should be disclosed separately.
- d.   The total receivable should be included as part of the investment in Angles, without separate disclosure.

49. Wood Co. owns 2,000 shares of Arlo, Inc.'s 20,000 shares of $100 par, 6% cumulative, nonparticipating preferred stock and 1,000 shares (2%) of Arlo's common stock. During 2009, Arlo declared and paid dividends of $240,000 on preferred stock. No dividends had been declared or paid during 2008. In addition, Wood received a 5% common stock dividend from Arlo when the quoted market price of Arlo's common stock was $10 per share. What amount should Wood report as dividend income in its 2009 income statement?

- a. $12,000
- b. $12,500
- c. $24,000
- d. $24,500

50. Stock dividends on common stock should be recorded at their fair market value by the investor when the related

investment is accounted for under which of the following methods?

	Cost	Equity	Fair value
a.	Yes	Yes	Yes
b.	Yes	No	No
c.	No	Yes	Yes
d.	No	No	No

51. On March 4, 2009, Evan Co. purchased 1,000 shares of LVC common stock at $80 per share. On September 26, 2009, Evan received 1,000 stock rights to purchase an additional 1,000 shares at $90 per share. The stock rights had an expiration date of February 1, 2010. On September 30, 2009, LVC's common stock had a market value, ex-rights, of $95 per share and the stock rights had a market value of $5 each. What amount should Evan report on its September 30, 2009 balance sheet as the cost of its investment in stock rights?

- a. $ 4,000
- b. $ 5,000
- c. $10,000
- d. $15,000

52. On January 3, 2007, Falk Co. purchased 500 shares of Milo Corp. common stock for $36,000. On December 2, 2009, Falk received 500 stock rights from Milo. Each right entitles the holder to acquire one share of stock for $85. The market price of Milo's stock was $100 a share immediately before the rights were issued, and $90 a share immediately after the rights were issued. Falk sold its rights on December 3, 2009, for $10 a right. Falk's gain from the sale of the rights is

- a. $0
- b. $1,000
- c. $1,400
- d. $5,000

53. In 2006, Chain, Inc. purchased a $1,000,000 life insurance policy on its president, of which Chain is the beneficiary. Information regarding the policy for the year ended December 31, 2009, follows:

Cash surrender value, 1/1/09	$ 87,000
Cash surrender value, 12/31/09	108,000
Annual advance premium paid 1/1/09	40,000

During 2009, dividends of $6,000 were applied to increase the cash surrender value of the policy. What amount should Chain report as life insurance expense for 2009?

- a. $40,000
- b. $25,000
- c. $19,000
- d. $13,000

54. An increase in the cash surrender value of a life insurance policy owned by a company would be recorded by

- a.   Decreasing annual insurance expense.
- b.   Increasing investment income.
- c.   Recording a memorandum entry only.
- d.   Decreasing a deferred charge.

55. Upon the death of an officer, Jung Co. received the proceeds of a life insurance policy held by Jung on the officer. The proceeds were not taxable. The policy's cash surrender value had been recorded on Jung's books at the time of payment. What amount of revenue should Jung report in its statements?

a. Proceeds received.
b. Proceeds received less cash surrender value.
c. Proceeds received plus cash surrender value.
d. None.

Items 56 through 58 are based on the following data:

Lake Corporation's accounting records showed the following investments at January 1, 2009:

Common stock:	
Kar Corp. (1,000 shares)	$ 10,000
Aub Corp. (5,000 shares)	100,000
Real estate:	
Parking lot (leased to Day Co.)	300,000
Other:	
Trademark (at cost, less accumulated amortization)	25,000
Total investments	$435,000

Lake owns 1% of Kar and 30% of Aub. Lake's directors constitute a majority of Aub's directors. The Day lease, which commenced on January 1, 2007, is for ten years, at an annual rental of $48,000. In addition, on January 1, 2007, Day paid a nonrefundable deposit of $50,000, as well as a security deposit of $8,000 to be refunded upon expiration of the lease. The trademark was licensed to Barr Co. for royalties of 10% of sales of the trademarked items. Royalties are payable semiannually on March 1 (for sales in July through December of the prior year), and on September 1 (for sales in January through June of the same year).

During the year ended December 31, 2009, Lake received cash dividends of $1,000 from Kar, and $15,000 from Aub, whose 2009 net incomes were $75,000 and $150,000, respectively. Lake also received $48,000 rent from Day in 2009 and the following royalties from Barr:

	March 1	September 1
2008	$3,000	$5,000
2009	4,000	7,000

Barr estimated that sales of the trademarked items would total $20,000 for the last half of 2009.

56. In Lake's 2009 income statement, how much should be reported for dividend revenue?
     a. $16,000
     b. $ 2,400
     c. $ 1,000
     d. $ 150

57. In Lake's 2009 income statement, how much should be reported for royalty revenue?
     a. $14,000
     b. $13,000
     c. $11,000
     d. $ 9,000

58. In Lake's 2009 income statement, how much should be reported for rental revenue?
     a. $43,000
     b. $48,000
     c. $53,000
     d. $53,800

59. Band Co. uses the equity method to account for its investment in Guard, Inc. common stock. How should Band record a 2% stock dividend received from Guard?
     a. As dividend revenue at Guard's carrying value of the stock.

b. As dividend revenue at the market value of the stock.
c. As a reduction in the total cost of Guard stock owned.
d. As a memorandum entry reducing the unit cost of all Guard stock owned.

SIMULATION PROBLEMS

Simulation Problem 1   (50 to 60 minutes)

Situation					
	Concepts	Accounting Treatment	Financial Statement Disclosures	Research	Communication

The following information pertains to Dayle, Inc.'s portfolio of marketable investments for the year ended December 31, 2009:

	Cost	Fair value 12/31/08	2009 activity Purchases	Sales	Fair value 12/31/09
Held-to-maturity securities					
Security ABC			$100,000		$95,000
Trading securities					
Security DEF	$150,000	$160,000			155,000
Available-for-sale securities					
Security GHI	190,000	165,000			
Security JKL	170,000	175,000		$175,000	160,000

Security ABC was purchased at par. All declines in fair value are considered to be temporary. Dayle does not elect the fair value option for any of its financial assets.

	Concepts				
Situation		Accounting Treatment	Financial Statement Disclosures	Research	Communication

The following questions relate to investments in debt securities and in equity securities that do not involve significant influence. For each item, match the accounting treatment with the appropriate concept. Concepts may be used once, more than once, or not at all. Assume the fair value option is not elected.

Concept

A. Available-for-sale securities
B. Valuation allowance
C. Transfer from trading to available-for-sale
D. Held-to-maturity securities
E. Permanent impairment

F. Other-than-temporary securities
G. Amortization of differential
H. Trading securities
I. Transfer from available-for-sale to held-to-maturity

	Accounting treatment								
	(A)	(B)	(C)	(D)	(E)	(F)	(G)	(H)	(I)
1. Cash flows from purchases and sales of these securities are reported as an operating activity on the statement of cash flows.	O	O	O	O	O	O	O	O	O
2. Include unrealized holding gains/losses in earnings of current period.	O	O	O	O	O	O	O	O	O
3. Amortize unrealized holding gain/loss over life of security.	O	O	O	O	O	O	O	O	O
4. Report at amortized cost.	O	O	O	O	O	O	O	O	O
5. Report unrealized holding gains/losses as other comprehensive income and close to accumulated other comprehensive income, a separate component of stockholders' equity.	O	O	O	O	O	O	O	O	O
6. Classify as a current asset.	O	O	O	O	O	O	O	O	O
7. Subsequent recovery not recognized unless realized.	O	O	O	O	O	O	O	O	O

		Accounting Treatment			
Situation	Concepts		Financial Statement Disclosures	Research	Communication

Determine whether each statement is True or False.

	True	False
1. Held-to-maturity securities are classified as current or noncurrent on an individual basis.	O	O
2. For trading securities, some realized gains/losses are excluded from earnings.	O	O
3. A premature sale of held-to-maturity securities may be considered maturity if at least 80% of the principal has already been collected.	O	O
4. Dividends received on available-for-sale securities decrease the investment account.	O	O
5. A company that owns more than 50% of the outstanding shares of stock of another company must use the fair value method.	O	O

Situation	Concepts	Accounting Treatment	Financial Statement Disclosures	Research	Communication

For the following questions, choose from the answer list below.

Answer List

A. $0	D. $ 15,000	G. $100,000	J. $160,000
B. $ 5,000	E. $ 25,000	H. $150,000	K. $170,000
C. $ 10,000	F. $ 95,000	I. $155,000	

Items 1 through 6 describe amounts to be reported in Dayle's 2009 financial statements. For each item, select from the following list the correct numerical response. An amount may be selected once, more than once, or not at all. Ignore income tax considerations.

Amount

	(A)	(B)	(C)	(D)	(E)	(F)	(G)	(H)	(I)	(J)	(K)
1. Carrying amount of security ABC at December 31, 2009.	○	○	○	○	○	○	○	○	○	○	○
2. Carrying amount of security DEF at December 31, 2009.	○	○	○	○	○	○	○	○	○	○	○
3. Carrying amount of security JKL at December 31, 2009.	○	○	○	○	○	○	○	○	○	○	○

Items 4 through 6 require a second response. For each item, indicate whether a gain or a loss is to be reported.

	Amount											*Gain*	*Loss*
	(A)	(B)	(C)	(D)	(E)	(F)	(G)	(H)	(I)	(J)	(K)		
4. Recognized gain or loss on sale of security GHI.	○	○	○	○	○	○	○	○	○	○	○	○	○
5. Unrealized gain or loss to be reported in 2009 net income.	○	○	○	○	○	○	○	○	○	○	○	○	○
6. Unrealized gain or loss to be reported at December 31, 2009, as a separate component of stockholders' equity entitled "accumulated other comprehensive income."	○	○	○	○	○	○	○	○	○	○	○	○	○

Situation	Concepts	Accounting Treatment	Financial Statement Disclosures	Research	Communication

Suppose that Dayle has two portfolios of marketable equity securities. One is classified as available-for-sale and the other is classified as trading securities. Dayle does not have the ability to exercise significant influence over any of the companies in either portfolio. Some securities from each portfolio were sold during the year. One of the securities in the trading securities portfolio was reclassified to the available-for-sale securities portfolio when its market value was less than cost. At the beginning and end of the year, the aggregate cost of each portfolio exceeded its aggregate market value by different amounts. Assume that Dayle does not elect the fair value option for reporting its financial assets.

Research the following issues. Cut and paste the appropriate authoritative literature.

1. How should Dayle report the effects of unrealized gains and losses during the year from each portfolio?

2. How should Dayle account for the security that was reclassified from the trading securities portfolio to the available-for-sale securities portfolio?

3. How should Dayle report the investments in each portfolio in its balance sheet as of the end of the period?

Situation	Concepts	Accounting Treatment	Financial Statement Disclosures	Research	Communication

Prepare a memo for the client file answering the questions that you researched.

1. How should Dayle report the effects of unrealized gains and losses during the year from each portfolio?

2. How should Dayle account for the security that was reclassified from the trading securities portfolio to the available-for-sale securities portfolio?

3. How should Dayle report the investments in each portfolio in its balance sheet as of the end of the period? Why?

REMINDER: Your response will be graded for both technical content and writing skills. Technical content will be evaluated for information that is helpful to the intended reader and clearly relevant to the issue. Writing skills will be evaluated for development, organization, and the appropriate expression of ideas in professional correspondence. Use a standard business memo or letter format with a clear beginning, middle, and end. Do not convey information in the form of a table, bullet point list, or other abbreviated presentation.

To: Dayle Inc. Permanent File
From: CPA Candidate
Re: Accounting issues related to marketable securities

Simulation Problem 2   (50 to 60 minutes)

Situation	Classification of Securities	Journal Entries	Financial Statement Disclosures	Communication	Research

Harold Johnson, an investor in Acme Co., asked you for advice on the propriety of Acme's financial reporting for two of its investments. Assume that Acme does not elect the fair value option for reporting its financial assets and liabilities. You obtained the following information related to the investments from Acme's December 31, 2009 financial statements:

- 20% ownership interest in Kern Co., represented by 200,000 shares of outstanding common stock purchased on January 2, 2009, for $600,000.
- 20% ownership interest in Wand Co., represented by 20,000 shares of outstanding common stock purchased on January 2, 2009, for $300,000.
- On January 2, 2009, the carrying values of the acquired shares of both investments equaled their purchase price.
- Kern reported earnings of $400,000 for the year ended December 31, 2009, and declared and paid dividends of $100,000 during 2009.
- Wand reported earnings of $350,000 for the year ended December 31, 2009, and declared and paid dividends of $60,000 during 2009.
- On December 31, 2009, Kern's and Wand's common stock were trading over-the-counter at $18 and $20 per share, respectively.
- The investment in Kern is accounted for using the equity method.
- The investment in Wand is accounted for as available-for-sale securities.

You recalculated the amounts reported in Acme's December 31, 2009 financial statements, and determined that they were correct. Stressing that the information available in the financial statements was limited, you advised Johnson that, assuming Acme properly applied generally accepted accounting principles, Acme may have appropriately used two different methods to account for its investments in Kern and Wand, even though the investments represent equal ownership interests.

Situation	Classification of Securities	Journal Entries	Financial Statement Disclosures	Communication	Research

Items 1 through 4 are based on the following:

Acme Co. purchased various securities during 2009 to be classified as held-to-maturity securities, trading securities, or available-for-sale securities.

Items 1 through 4 describe various securities purchased by Acme. For each item, select from the following list the appropriate category for each security. A category may be used once, more than once, or not at all.

<u>Categories</u>
H. Held-to-maturity
T. Trading
A. Available-for-sale

	Category (H)	(T)	(A)
1. Debt securities bought and held for the purpose of selling in the near term.	O	O	O
2. US Treasury bonds that Acme has both the positive intent and the ability to hold to maturity.	O	O	O
3. $3 million debt security bought and held for the purpose of selling in three years to finance payment of Acme's $2 million long-term note payable when it matures.	O	O	O
4. Convertible preferred stock that Acme does not intend to sell in the near term.	O	O	O

		Journal Entries			
Situation	Classification of Securities		Financial Statement Disclosures	Communication	Research

1. Prepare the journal entry for Acme's investment in Kern Co. on January 2, 2009.

2. Prepare the journal entry for the dividends received from Kern in 2009.

3. Prepare the journal entry required for Kern's reported income for the year ending on December 31, 2009.

			Financial Statement Disclosures		
Situation	Classification of Securities	Journal Entries		Communication	Research

Identify the following amounts on Acme's financial statements.

Carrying value of Kern investment	
Carrying value of Wand investment	
Income on Income Statement	
Kern investment	
Wand investment	
Other comprehensive income	
Kern investment	
Wand investment	

				Communication	
Situation	Classification of Securities	Journal Entries	Financial Statement Disclosures		Research

Prepare a detailed memorandum to Mr. Johnson supporting your conclusion that, under generally accepted accounting principles, Acme may have appropriately used two different methods to account for its investments representing equal ownership interests.

REMINDER: Your response will be graded for both technical content and writing skills. Technical content will be evaluated for information that is helpful to the intended reader and clearly relevant to the issue. Writing skills will be evaluated for development, organization, and the appropriate expression of ideas in professional correspondence. Use a standard business memo or letter format with a clear beginning, middle, and end. Do not convey information in the form of a table, bullet point list, or other abbreviated presentation.

To: Mr. Harold Johnson
From: CPA Candidate
Re: Acme Co. Investments in Kern Co. and Wand Co.

					Research
Situation	Classification of Securities	Journal Entries	Financial Statement Disclosures	Communication	

Research the following accounting issues. Excerpt the appropriate guidance from the professional standards.

1. What is a trading security?

2. A company sells available-for-sale securities. Where is this transaction found on the statement of cash flows?

3. A company has dividend income from available-for-sale securities. Where is this dividend income found on the financial statements?

Simulation Problem 3   (50 to 60 minutes)

Situation						
	Concepts	Available for Sale Securities	Long-Term Marketable Equity Securities	Investment Income	Communication	Research

At December 31, 2008, Poe Corp. properly reported as available-for-sale securities the following marketable equity securities:

	Cost	Fair value
Axe Corp., 1,000 shares, $2.40 convertible preferred stock	$ 40,000	$ 42,000
Purl, Inc., 6,000 shares of common stock	60,000	66,000
Day Co., 2,000 shares of common stock	55,000	40,000
Total available-for-sale securities	$155,000	$148,000

On January 2, 2009, Poe purchased 100,000 shares of Scott Corp. common stock for $1,700,000, representing 30% of Scott's outstanding common stock and an underlying equity of $1,400,000 in Scott's net assets on January 2. Poe had no other financial transactions with Scott during 2009. As a result of Poe's 30% ownership of Scott, Poe has the ability to exercise significant influence over Scott's financial and operating policies.

During 2009, Poe disposed of the following securities:

• January 18—sold 2,500 shares of Purl for $13 per share.
• June 1—sold 500 shares of Day, after a 10% stock dividend was received, for $21 per share.
• October 1—converted 500 shares of Axe's preferred stock into 1,500 shares of Axe's common stock, when the market price was $60 per share for the preferred stock and $21 per share for the common stock.

The following 2009 dividend information pertains to stock owned by Poe:

• February 14—Day issued a 10% stock dividend, when the market price of Day's common stock was $22 per share.
• April 5 and October 5—Axe paid dividends of $1.20 per share on its $2.40 preferred stock, to stockholders of record on March 9 and September 9, respectively. Axe did not pay dividends on its common stock during 2009.
• June 30—Purl paid a $1.00 per share dividend on its common stock.
• March 1, June 1, September 1, and December 1—Scott paid quarterly dividends of $0.50 per share on each of these dates. Scott's net income for the year ended December 31, 2009, was $1,200,000.

At December 31, 2009, Poe's management intended to hold Scott's stock on a long-term basis. The remaining investments were considered temporary. Market prices per share of the marketable equity securities were as follows:

	At December 31	
	2009	2008
Axe Corp.—preferred	$56	$42
Axe Corp.—common	20	18
Purl, Inc.—common	11	11
Day Co.—common	22	20
Scott Corp.—common	16	18

All of the foregoing stocks are listed on major stock exchanges. Declines in market value from cost would not be considered permanent. Poe does not elect the fair value option for reporting its financial assets and liabilities.

	Concepts					
Situation		Available-for-Sale Securities	Long-Term Marketable Equity Securities	Investment Income	Communication	Research

Identify whether each of the following statements is True or False. Assume the fair value option is not elected.

	True	False
1. Unrealized gains from trading securities are reported in other comprehensive income.	O	O
2. Investments in stocks and bonds may be classified as trading securities, available-for-sale securities, and held-to-maturity securities.	O	O
3. X Company has significant influence over Y Company and owns 35% of the voting stock of Y Company. X Company must use the equity method of accounting for the investment in Y Company.	O	O
4. Unrealized gains and losses from available-for-sale securities that result from the change in fair value during the period should be reported as other comprehensive income.	O	O
5. The temporary unrealized gain or loss from held-to-maturity securities must be reported in income for the current period.	O	O
6. If a security is transferred from available-for-sale to trading securities classification, unrealized holding gains and losses are recognized immediately in the income statement.	O	O

	True	False
7. The equity method of accounting requires a company to include the percent of income of the investee in the investor company's net income for the period.	○	○
8. The equity method of accounting requires that a company adjust the cost of the investee to fair value at the end of each period.	○	○
9. A company that receives stock dividends records income equal to the fair value of the stock on the date the dividend is declared.	○	○
10. Held-to-maturity securities are carried at amortized cost using the effective interest method.	○	○

Situation	Concepts	Available-for-Sale Securities	Long-Term Marketable Equity Securities	Investment Income	Communication	Research

Complete the following schedule for the available-for-sale securities of Poe Corp. as of December 31, 2009.

Poe Corp.
SCHEDULE OF AVAILABLE-FOR-SALE
SECURITIES
December 31, 2009

	Number of shares	Cost	Beginning carrying amount at market	Ending market price per share	Market value	Cumulative gain or (loss)	Unrealized gain or (loss) in 2009
Axe—preferred							
Axe—common							
Purl—common							
Day—common							

Situation	Concepts	Available-for-Sale Securities	Long-Term Marketable Equity Securities	Investment Income	Communication	Research

Prepare the following schedule for the long-term marketable equity securities for Poe Corp. as of December 31, 2009.

Poe Corp.
SCHEDULE OF LONG-TERM MARKETABLE
EQUITY SECURITIES
December 31, 2009

Scott Corp.—100,000 shares of common stock:	
Cost:	
Acquisition price	
Increase in equity during 2009:	
Poe's interest in Scott's income	
Less:	
Dividends received	
Net increase in equity	
Carrying amount of Poe Corp.'s investment in Scott	

Situation	Concepts	Available-for-Sale Securities	Long-Term Marketable Equity Securities	Investment Income	Communication	Research

Complete the following schedule outlining the income for Poe Corp. for the year ended December 31, 2009.

Poe Corp.
SCHEDULE OF INVESTMENT INCOME
For the Year Ended December 31, 2009

Dividends:	
Axe Corp.—preferred	
Purl, Inc.—common	
Total dividend revenue	
Gains on marketable equity securities:	
Realized gain/(loss) on sale of securities:	
Purl, Inc.—common	
Day Co.—common	
Net realized gain on sale of securities	
Equity in income of Scott Corp.:	
Total investment income	

Situation	Concepts	Available-for-Sale Securities	Long-Term Marketable Equity Securities	Investment Income	Communication	Research

Write a brief memo to the CEO of Poe Corp. explaining the equity method of accounting for investments in other companies.

REMINDER: Your response will be graded for both technical content and writing skills. Technical content will be evaluated for information that is helpful to the intended reader and clearly relevant to the issue. Writing skills will be evaluated for development, organization, and the appropriate expression of ideas in professional correspondence. Use a standard business memo or letter format with a clear beginning, middle, and end. Do not convey information in the form of a table, bullet point list, or other abbreviated presentation.

To: CEO, Poe Corp.
From: CPA Candidate
Re: Equity method of accounting

Situation	Concepts	Available-for-Sale Securities	Long-Term Marketable Equity Securities	Investment Income	Communication	Research

Use the FARS research database to answer the following questions. Insert the appropriate paragraphs.

1. When a company owns between 20% and 50% of the outstanding stock of another company and uses the equity method of accounting, how is income from the investee disclosed?

2. What are the three classifications for investment in debt and equity securities?

3. When a security is removed from the trading category, should the earnings previously recorded be reversed? (Assume the fair value option is not elected.)

MULTIPLE-CHOICE ANSWERS

1. b	14. d	27. d	40. d	53. c
2. b	15. d	28. d	41. c	54. a
3. b	16. d	29. a	42. c	55. b
4. b	17. a	30. b	43. d	56. c
5. c	18. b	31. a	44. b	57. d
6. d	19. b	32. b	45. d	58. c
7. b	20. c	33. b	46. a	59. d
8. d	21. b	34. b	47. a	
9. a	22. d	35. a	48. c	
10. b	23. a	36. b	49. c	
11. a	24. d	37. c	50. d	
12. c	25. a	38. b	51. a	1st: ___/59= ___%
13. b	26. a	39. b	52. c	2nd: ___/59= ___%

MULTIPLE-CHOICE ANSWER EXPLANATIONS

A. Concepts of Accounting and Investment Percentage

1. (b) The investment should be accounted for on the equity basis and the calculation of Puff's income from the investment is shown below.

Straw's net income	$150,000
	× 40%
Puff's share of Straw's net income	$ 60,000
Less: Puff's depreciation of excess value of equipment	
Excess cost	$100,000
	× 40%
Puff's share	$ 40,000
Remaining useful life	÷ 5
Puff's share of excess depreciation for 2009	(8,000)
Income from investment on the equity basis	$ 52,000

B.1. No Significant Influence: Held-to-Maturity

2. (b) Held-to-maturity securities are to be carried at amortized cost. Therefore, the investment is recorded on 4/1/09 at its cost of $194,000 ($198,500 less accrued interest of $4,500). The carrying amount is calculated as cost plus amortized discount, which at 10/31/09 is $196,800 [$194,000 + ($6,000 × 7/15)].

3. (b) **Held-to-maturity** securities, which include only debt securities, are reported on the balance sheet at **amortized cost** without adjustment to fair value. If the investment in bonds had been classified as trading or available-for-sale, answer (c) would be correct. **Trading** securities are reported at **fair value** with holding gains or losses flowing through the income statements. **Available-for-sale** securities are reported at **fair value** with holding gains or losses reported as a component of other comprehensive income. Cost and lower of cost or market are not used as reporting bases for bond investments.

4. (b) Held-to-maturity securities are carried at cost, so unrealized holding gains and losses are not reported. However, realized gains and losses on held-to-maturity securities should always be included in the income statement of the appropriate period. No valuation allowance exists for any marketable debt or equity securities. Realized gains for the period are the only item listed that is included in that period's net income.

5. (c) A company may elect to value held-to-maturity securities at fair value. Any increase or decrease in value is reported as a gain or loss and included in earnings for the period. Answer (a) is incorrect because bonds are recorded at cost, but reported at amortized cost at year-end. Answer (b) is incorrect because Bing elected the fair value option. Answer (d) is incorrect because investments are not recorded at lower of cost or market.

6. (d) A company may elect to value held-to-maturity securities at fair value. Any increase or decrease in value, whether realized or unrealized, is reported in earnings for the period. Therefore, I, II, and IV should be reported in earnings if the fair value option of reporting is elected. Changes in the valuation allowance are not relevant because when an election is made to use the fair value option, any related allowance accounts are removed from the balance sheet.

B.2. No Significant Influence: Trading

7. (b) Debt and equity securities that are classified as **trading securities** are reported at fair value with unrealized gains and losses included in earnings. During 2009, Tyne had an unrealized holding gain of $55,000 ($155,000 − $100,000) on its trading securities. The unrealized holding gain on **available-for-sale** securities ($130,000 − $120,000 = $10,000) is excluded from earnings and reported as other comprehensive income.

8. (d) The requirement is to determine the accumulated other comprehensive income to be reported in the December 31, 2009 statement of stockholders' equity. Unrealized gains and losses on **trading securities** are included in earnings. Unrealized gains and losses on **available-for-sale** securities are excluded from earnings and reported as accumulated other comprehensive income in a separate component of shareholders' equity. This amount is the net unrealized loss on available-for-sale securities at 12/31/09 is $20,000 ($150,000 − $130,000).

9. (a) Unrealized holding gains and losses for trading securities are to be reported in earnings. On the other hand, this statement also states that unrealized gains or losses on available-for-sale securities should be excluded from earnings and reported as other comprehensive income. Therefore, only the $40,000 ($360,000 − $320,000) unrealized loss on trading securities is included in income.

B.3.   No Significant Influence: Available-for-Sale

10.   (b)   Available-for-sale securities are reported at market value on the balance sheet. At 12/31/09, Stone has incurred gross unrealized gains of $4,000 and gross unrealized losses of $26,000 on its available-for-sale securities. Therefore, at 12/31/09, the net unrealized loss is $22,000 ($26,000 – $4,000). Stone would have to increase the balance in accumulated other comprehensive income from $1,500 to $22,000 at 12/31/09.

11.   (a)   Unrealized holding gains and losses on available-for-sale securities be reported as other comprehensive income. At 12/31/08, available-for-sale securities would have been reported in the balance sheet at their fair value of $130,000, with a corresponding unrealized loss of $20,000. At 12/31/09, the fair value of these securities is $160,000. Therefore, an unrealized gain of $30,000 ($160,000 – $130,000) would result in other comprehensive income of $30,000 as **accumulated** other comprehensive income.

12.   (c)   A $40,000 loss is recorded on the income statement for the loss on trading securities. An election can be made to value available-for-sale securities at fair value. Therefore, the available-for-sale securities are valued at fair value, and the loss is reported on the income statement.

13.   (b)   A company may elect the fair value option for reporting available-for-sale securities. If the fair value option is elected, realized and unrealized gains and losses from available-for-sale securities are included in earnings of the period. Therefore, the net gain of $18,000 ($14,000 unrealized gains + $30,000 realized gains – $26,000 unrealized losses) is reported on the income statement for the period.

14.   (d)   If Shannon elects the fair value option for reporting available-for-sale securities, any unrealized gains or losses are recorded in earnings for the period. In 2010, Shannon would report a loss on the income statement of $20,000, and the available-for-sale securities would be carried on the balance sheet at the market value of $130,000. On December 31, 2011, the securities would be valued at $160,000 and an unrealized gain of $30,000 ($160,000 – $130,000) would be recognized on the 2011 income statement. Therefore, under the provisions of ASC Topic 825 (SFAS 159), there would be no entry to other comprehensive income for available-for-sale securities.

15.   (d)   Marketable equity securities that are not intended to be sold in the near future are classified as available-for-sale securities. A company may elect to record an available-for-sale security at its fair value, and any unrealized gains or losses may be recognized as a component of income from continuing operations on the income statement. Answer (a) is incorrect because Antonio does not intend to sell the asset in the near future; therefore, it cannot be classified as a trading security. Answer (b) is incorrect because when the fair value option is elected, the unrealized gain or loss is reported in earnings, not in other comprehensive income. Answer (c) is incorrect because the securities are not classified as trading and the gain is not recognized in OCI.

16.   (d)   The securities purchased by Rex are classified as available-for-sale securities and accounted for at fair value. At 12/31/09, the fair value of security B was $15,300; an unrealized loss of $1,700 resulted in other comprehensive income in that amount. At 1/31/10, the stock was sold when its fair value was $15,000 and the following entry would have been made:

Cash (net)	13,500	
Loss on sale of stock	3,500	
Investment in Security B		15,300
Unrealized loss on Sec. B.		1,700

The unrealized loss of $1,700 on Security B is a credit. It would be netted with unrealized gains and/or losses recognized in 2010. The effect is to offset the $1,700 loss recognized in 2009 that was closed to other comprehensive income, net retained earnings, thus avoiding double counting.

17.   (a)   The capital gains distribution ($145,000) would not be reported as interest revenue. The solutions approach is to set up a T-account for interest receivable.

Interest Receivable			
Beg. bal.	38,000		
Int. rev.	?	152,000	Int. collected
End. bal.	46,500		

Beginning and ending balances are given in the question. Interest receivable would be credited for cash collections to reduce the receivable.

Cash	152,000	
Interest receivable		152,000

Interest receivable would be debited for interest revenue.

Interest receivable	xxx	
Interest revenue		xxx

Solve for interest revenue ($46,500 + $152,000 – $38,000 = $160,500).

18.   (b)   Marketable equity securities (MES) are classified as either trading (held for current resale) or available-for-sale (if not categorized as trading). Since Nola does not intend to sell these securities in the near term, they should be classified as available-for-sale. MES are carried at market value. The unrealized gains or losses of available-for-sale MES are reported as a separate component of other comprehensive income. It is important to note that unrealized gains or losses on **trading** securities would be reported as a component of income from continuing operations on the income statement. Thus, answer (b) is correct because the securities would be classified as available-for-sale and unrealized gains and losses from these securities would be reported as other comprehensive income.

19.   (b)   Unrealized losses on available-for-sale securities are reported as a separate component of other comprehensive income, while unrealized gains and losses on trading securities are recognized in income and unrealized gains and losses on held-to-maturity securities are ignored. Thus, this security is classified as available-for-sale. A realized gain will be reported only if the security was sold for a price in excess of its cost. Therefore, the 2008 price decline was **less than** the 2009 price recovery. For example, assume that the investment was purchased for $1,000 on 1/07/08. At 12/31/08, its market value was $800, and on 12/29/09 its market value was $1,200. The following entries would have been made:

1/07/08	Investment	1,000	
	Cash		1,000
12/31/08	Unrealized loss	200	
	Investment		200
12/29/09	Cash	1,200	
	Investment		800
	Unrealized loss		200
	Gain on sale of securities		**200**

20. (c) The requirement is to determine how the losses on the securities classified as available-for-sale should be reported. A decline in market value of a security, which is considered to be **other-than-temporary,** should be reported on the income statement in the current period. A decline in market value, which is considered to be **temporary,** would be recorded as an unrealized loss, and recognized as other comprehensive income. Therefore, answer (c) is correct as the loss on the Knox stock is considered to be other-than-temporary and it would be reported on the income statement. Answer (a) is incorrect because the unrealized loss on the Scot stock would be reported as other comprehensive income. Answer (b) is incorrect because the loss on the Knox stock is considered to be a realized loss as it is other-than-temporary. Answer (d) is incorrect because the other-than-temporary decline in Knox stock results in a realized loss that is reported on the income statement.

21. (b) The carrying amount of a marketable equity security classified as available-for-sale shall be the fair market value and the unrealized holding gain or loss should be reported as other comprehensive income. In 2008 when the value declined, the portfolio was reported at market with an unrealized holding loss recorded as other comprehensive income. In 2009, the decline is considered to be other than temporary. Thus, the security must be written down to market and a realized loss recognized. However, since there is no actual change in value, in 2009 the security will be reported at the same amount (Cost – Write-down of asset) as in 2008. Therefore, there is no effect on **net** noncurrent assets in 2009. However, net income will be affected because a realized loss is recorded on the income statement. Note that the unrealized loss account charged to other comprehensive income in 2008 would be credited and the realized loss account would be debited for the same amount. The allowance accounts will be closed against each other because the new basis after the write-down will equal the lower FV amount. Answer (a) is incorrect because net income is affected. Note that if the decline was merely temporary, there would be no net income effect because temporary declines in value of noncurrent portfolios are reported as other comprehensive income, rather than net income. Answer (c) is incorrect because there is no net decrease in noncurrent assets, but there is a net income effect. Answer (d) is incorrect because only net income decreases.

22. (d) Dividends in arrears are not a receivable to the cumulative preferred stockholder until the issuing corporation's board of directors formally declares the dividend. In this case, Hadley, Inc. did not declare the 2008 dividends in arrears until 2009. At the 2009 dividend declaration date, Woody Co. records dividends receivable and dividend income. Dividend income is included in income from continuing operations.

23. (a) A nonmonetary asset (the merchandise in this case) received in a nonreciprocal transfer should be recorded at the fair value of the asset received. Additionally, the transfer of a nonmonetary asset to a stockholder or other entity (Deed's employees in this case) should be recorded at the fair value of the asset received.

24. (d) Noncash transactions should be excluded from the statement of cash flows to better achieve the statement's objectives. However, information about noncash investing and financing transactions be must reported in related disclosures.

25. (a) An investor carries an investment in the stock of an investee at market, and recognizes as income dividends received that are distributed from the net accumulated earnings of the investee **since the date of acquisition** by the investor. Dividends received in excess of earnings subsequent to the date of investment are considered to be return of investment or a liquidating dividend and are recorded as reductions of the cost of the investment. Therefore, Pal Corp.'s accounting treatment of the dividend it received from Ima Corp. indicates that Pal is accounting for the securities as an available-for-sale investment in Ima. Answer (b) is incorrect because Ima's market value does not impact Pal's treatment of dividends received. Answers (c) and (d) are incorrect because all dividends received are treated as reductions in an investee's carrying value under the equity method.

26. (a) Intercompany receivables and payables are not eliminated unless consolidated financial statements are prepared. Since Pare only has a 15% interest in Sabe, consolidated financial statements would not be prepared. Thus, on the 12/31/09 balance sheet, Pare should separately report the total amount of the receivable.

B.4. No Significant Influence: Transfers

27. (d) The requirement is to determine the amount of loss on investments to be reported in Sun's 2009 income statement. This transfer is accounted for at fair market value and any holding gains or losses on securities that are transferred to held-to-maturity from available-for-sale be reported as accumulated other comprehensive income. This amount is then amortized over the remaining life of the security as an adjustment to yield. Since cost is greater than market value by $75,000 at 12/31/08 ($650,000 cost – $575,000 fair market value), the following entry would be recorded:

Unrealized loss	75,000	
Marketable debt securities		75,000

Then on June 30, 2009, when Sun decides to hold the investments to maturity, an additional $45,000 will be recorded in the valuation account ($575,000 value on books – $530,000 FMV) to reflect the change in FMV. The following entry would be recorded:

Unrealized loss	45,000	
Marketable debt securities		45,000

Each year the unrealized loss would be reported as other comprehensive income that would be closed to "accumulated other comprehensive income."

28. (d) When a security is transferred to held-to-maturity from available-for-sale the unrealized holding gain or loss continues to be reported as a separate component of stockholders' equity. Held-to-maturity securities are carried at amortized cost, and any unrealized holding gains or losses are not reported. Thus, the balance in the "accumulated other comprehensive income" in stockholders' equity on the 2009 statement of stockholders' equity would be $120,000 ($75,000 amount reported at 12/31/08 plus the $45,000 amount reported at June 30, 2009). The $120,000 will be amortized over the remaining life of the security as an adjustment to yield. The additional decline in value from 6/30/09 to 12/31/09 would not be reported, as held-to-maturity securities do not report unrealized losses.

29. (a) The transfer of a security between categories of investments shall be accounted for at fair value." If fair value is less than the security's carrying amount at the date of transfer, it is irrelevant whether the decline is temporary or permanent.

30. (b) An election can be made to use the fair value option when financial assets cease to qualify for fair value treatment due to specialized accounting rules. On June 30, 2010, the trading securities were reclassified to the held-to-maturity category, and an election was made to report them at fair value. On June 30, 2010, the held-to-maturity securities were valued at $530,000, and Jill would recognize a loss of $45,000 ($575,000 – $530,000). At December 31, 2010, the securities declined in value an additional $40,000. Therefore, the total loss recognized in 2010 was $85,000 ($45,000 + $40,000). Answer (a) is incorrect because the entire amount of loss in fair value should be recognized in 2010. Answer (c) is incorrect because the loss from January 1, 2009 to December 31, 2009, would have been recognized in 2009 because it was classified as a trading security. Answer (d) is incorrect because if the fair value option is elected, unrealized gains and losses are recognized in the current year's earnings.

31. (a) Jill would recognize the unrealized loss on trading securities in the income statement. On June 30, 2010, when the securities were classified as held-to-maturity, Jill elected the fair value option for reporting the investment. Therefore, any unrealized gain or loss on the held-to-maturity securities would be reported in earnings for the period. An unrealized gain or a temporary loss on available-for-sale securities would be reported in other comprehensive income only if the fair value option were not elected. Held-to-maturity securities would be valued at amortized cost if the fair value option of reporting were not elected. Therefore, answers (b), (c), and (d) are incorrect because Jill elects the fair value option on the held-to-maturity securities.

C. Investment Where Significant Influence Does Exist

32. (b) This investment should be accounted for using the equity method since Grant owns a 30% interest and can exercise significant influence over South. Grant's share of South's 2008 earnings (30% × $80,000 = $24,000) would be recognized as investment revenue under the equity method. If there was any excess of cost over book value of assets with finite useful lives, resulting from the purchase of the investment, it would be amortized, reducing investment revenue. However, not enough information was given to determine if there was an excess. The dividends received by Grant (30% × $50,000 = $15,000) do not affect investment revenue using the equity method; they are recorded as a reduction of the investment account.

33. (b) The equity method is used because Grant owns a 30% interest and can exercise significant influence. Under this method, the investment account is increased by Grant's equity in South's earnings (30% × $80,000 = $24,000) and is decreased by Grant's dividends received from South (30% × $50,000 = $15,000). This results in a 12/31/08 carrying amount for the investment of $209,000, as indicated in the T-account below.

	Investment in South		
1/2/08	200,000		
Equity in earnings	24,000	15,000	Dividends
12/31/08	209,000		

34. (b) The equity method is used because Grant owns a 30% interest and can exercise significant influence. Under this method, the investment account is increased by Grant's equity in South's earnings (30% × $80,000 = $24,000 in 2008; 30% × $100,000 = $30,000 for first six months of 2009) and is decreased by Grant's dividends received from South (30% × $50,000 = $15,000 in 2009; none in first six months of 2008). This results in a 7/1/09 carrying amount of $239,000, as indicated in the T-account below.

	Investment in South		
1/2/08	200,000		
Equity in earnings	24,000	15,000	Dividends
Equity in earnings	30,000		
7/1/09	239,000		

The gain on sale is the excess of the proceeds ($150,000) over the carrying amount of the shares sold (1/2 × $239,000 = $119,500), or $30,500 ($150,000 – $119,500).

35. (a) An investor's share of the income of a company in which it holds a 20% or greater investment is referred to as the investor's equity in earnings of the investee. The investor's share of the investee's earnings should be computed after deducting the investee's cumulative preferred dividends (whether declared or not). In this case, the income available to common stockholders is $50,000 [$60,000 income – (10% × $100,000 total pref. div.)], so Moss Corp.'s equity in earnings is $40,000 (80% ownership × $50,000). Since $40,000 is not one of the answer choices, apparently the candidate is expected to include the preferred dividend revenue of $2,000 [20% ownership × ($100,000 × 10% total pref. div.)] on the income statement in the equity in earnings line item. Although preferred dividends are usually classified separately, answer (a) is the best answer given. The answer, therefore, is $42,000.

Equity in earnings	$40,000
Dividend revenue	2,000
	$42,000

36. (b) Sage paid $400,000 for its 40% investment in Adams when Adams' net assets had a carrying amount of $900,000. Therefore, the book value Sage purchased is $360,000 (40% × $900,000), resulting in an excess of cost over book value of $40,000 ($400,000 – $360,000). This excess must be attributed to specific assets of Adams; any amount not attributed to specific assets is attributed to goodwill. In this case, the excess is attributed to plant assets (40% × $90,000 = $36,000) and inventory (40% × $10,000 = $4,000). The portion attributed to plant assets is amortized over eighteen years, while the portion attributed to inventory is expensed immediately (since all inventory was sold during 2009). Therefore, Sage's investment income is $42,000, as computed below.

Share of income (40% × $120,000)	$48,000
Excess amortization [($36,000/18) + $4,000]	(6,000)
	$42,000

37. (c) The unrealized gain on the available-for-sale securities is improperly included in Pear's $125,000 income before taxes. Unrealized holding gains and losses on available-for-sale securities are reported as a separate component of stockholders' equity. The equity in Cinn's earnings is properly included in Pear Co.'s pretax income.

However, the dividends from Cinn are also improperly included in income because under the equity method, dividends received are a reduction of the investment account rather than dividend revenue. The adjustments to profits of prior years for arithmetic errors in depreciation ($35,000) should be recorded as a retroactive adjustment to beginning retained earnings and should **not** have been deducted when computing 2009 income before taxes. Therefore, 2009 income before taxes should be $112,000 as computed below.

Tentative income	$125,000
Unrealized holding gain	(40,000)
Dividends received	(8,000)
Prior period adjustment	35,000
Correct income	$112,000

38.   (b)   The equity method is to be used when the investor owns 20% or more of the investee's voting stock, unless there is evidence that the investor does **not** have the ability to exercise significant influence over the investee. Since this is the case, Saxe must carry the stock at market in the available-for-sale category. Under this method, dividends received are to be recognized as income to the investor, and the investment account is unaffected. Also, under this method, the investor's share of the investee's net income is not recognized. Any changes in the market value of the stock would be reflected in the book value of the stock with a corresponding amount in a separate account in stockholders' equity. As there has been no change in the market value, the investment account would still have a balance of $150,000 at 12/31/09. Note that the dividends received by Saxe were distributed from Lex's net accumulated earnings since the date of acquisition by Saxe. However, if dividends received had been in excess of earnings subsequent to the investment date, they are considered a return of capital and would be recorded as a reduction in the investment account.

39.   (b)   Ownership of less than 20% leads to the presumption of **no substantial influence** unless evidence to the contrary exists. Well's position as Rea's largest single shareholder and the presence of Well's officers as a **majority** of Rea's board of directors constitute evidence that Well **does have significant influence** despite less than 20% ownership. Therefore, the equity method is used. The investment account had a beginning balance of $400,000 (purchase price). This amount is increased by Well's equity in Rea's earnings (10% ownership × $500,000 income = $50,000) and decreased by Well's dividends received from Rea (10% share × $150,000 total div. = $15,000), resulting in a balance of $435,000 (see T-account below).

	Investment in Rea		
1/2/09	400,000		
Equity in earnings	50,000	15,000	Dividends
12/31/09	435,000		

40.   (d)   The investment should have been originally recorded at the $250,000 purchase price. This amount would be increased by Kean's share of Pod's earnings (30% × $100,000 = $30,000), decreased by the amortization of excess of cost over book value, and decreased by dividends received by Kean (none in this case). The book value Kean purchased is $150,000 (30% × $500,000), resulting in an excess of cost over book value of $100,000 ($250,000 − $150,000). This excess must be attributed to the specific assets of Pod that have a fair value greater than their book value; any amount not attributed to specific assets is attributed to goodwill. In this case, the excess would be attributed first to land (30% × $200,000 = $60,000) and the remainder to goodwill ($100,000 − $60,000 = $40,000). The portion attributed to land and goodwill should not be amortized. Therefore, Kean's 12/31/09 balance of the investment in subsidiary is $280,000 as computed below.

Original cost	$250,000
Share of income (30% × $100,000)	30,000
	$280,000

41.   (c)   When an investment that has been accounted for using another method qualifies for the use of the equity method due to a change in ownership level (such as from 10% to 30%), the change to the equity method should be reported **retroactively**. At the date of the change (1/2/10), the **investment** account and **retained earnings** are adjusted as if the equity method had been used all along, and the results of operations in prior years are restated to reflect the equity method. In 2010, use of the equity method results in recognition of investment income of $195,000 (30% × $650,000 investee income). 2009 investment income must be restated from the previously reported dividend income (10% × $200,000 = $20,000) to equity method income (10% × $600,000 = $60,000), an adjustment of $40,000 ($60,000 − $20,000 = $40,000).

42.   (c)   The requirement is to determine the balance in the December 31, 2009 investment account. When an investment that has been accounted for using another method qualifies for the use of the equity method due to a change in ownership level (in this case, from 10% to 30%), the change to the equity method should be applied retroactively. At the date of the change (12/31/09), the accounts are adjusted as if the equity method had been used all along. If the equity method had been used beginning at 1/2/09, Pare would have recorded its share of Tot's earnings (10% × $300,000 = $30,000) as investment revenue and as an increase in the investment account. Therefore, at 12/31/09, Pare's investment in Tot would be reported at $230,000.

	Investment in Tot	
1/2/09 purchase	50,000	
12/31/09 purchase	150,000	
Equity in earnings	30,000	
	230,000	

43.   (d)   Under the equity method, a reciprocal relationship is formed between the investment account on the investor's books and the book values of the net assets on the investee's books. As changes in the investee's net assets occur (earnings, dividends, etc.), the investor will recognize the percentage of ownership share of that change in the investment account. Therefore, cash dividends from the investee will be recorded in the investment account, not the investment income account. The entry includes a debit to cash and a credit to the investment account. Another aspect of the equity method is the amortization of the equipment related to the purchase. The investment income account and the investment in stock account should include all the income recognitions and amortizations resulting from the investment. The entry to record the equipment amortization is a debit to Investment income and a credit to Investment in stock.

44.   (b)   When the equity method is used, the investor should amortize any portion of the excess of fair values over carrying amounts (differential) that relates to depreciable or amortizable assets held by the investee. Amortization of the differential results in a reduction of the investment account and a reduction in the equity of the investee's earnings. For inventory, an excess of FV over cost, FIFO cost in this case, has the same effect on the investment account and equity in investee earnings in the period in which the goods are sold. Therefore, the portion of the differential that relates to inventory would decrease Park's reported equity in Tun's earnings, and answers (c) and (d) are incorrect. Land is not a depreciable asset, so there would be no amortization of the differential related to land, and answer (a) is incorrect.

45. (d) Dividends received in excess of earnings subsequent to the date of investment are considered a return of investment and are recorded as reductions of cost of the investment. Additionally, under the equity method, "dividends received from an investee reduce the carrying amount of the investment."

46. (a) The requirement is to determine the effects of a cash dividend on an investors investment account, accounted for both as an available-for-sale security, and under the equity method. Dividends received on available-for-sale securities are to be recognized as income to the investor and the investment account is unaffected. If the dividends received are in excess of earnings to date, then they would be considered a return of the investment and would result in a reduction of the investment account. Under the equity method, the receipt of cash dividends reduces the carrying value of the investment. Therefore, answer (a) is correct as the receipt of a cash dividend would not result in an increase in the investment account under either method.

47. (a) The requirement is to determine the amount of investment income to be reported in the 2009 income statement. When an investment which has been accounted for using a different method qualifies for the use of the equity method, due to a change in ownership level (such as 10% to 40%), then the change to the equity method should be reported **retroactively**. At the date of the change, the investment account and the retained earnings account are adjusted as if the equity method had been used all along. Therefore answer (a) is correct as Point owned 10% of Iona's stock from January 1 to July 31, 2009, and 40% of Iona's stock from August 1 to December 31, 2009. Answers (b) and (c) are incorrect because income should be recognized under the equity method according to the percentage of ownership existing during each of the periods. Answer (d) is incorrect because when Iona reports its earnings to Point, Point will record its share of the revenue. When Point receives the dividends, (which may be in a different period than Point recognized its share of Iona's income), the carrying amount of the investment will be reduced by the amount received. Therefore, the income recognized does not usually equal the dividends received.

48. (c) The equity method is used when accounting for investments in which the investor has the ability to exercise significant influence over the operating and financial policies of the investee. Ownership of 20% or more of the outstanding common stock demonstrates this ability. In this case, Pulham Corp. owns 30% of Angles and properly uses the equity method. Under the equity method intercompany profits and losses are eliminated. However, receivables and payables are not eliminated as they are in the case of consolidated financial statements. On the December 31, 2009 balance sheet, Pulham should separately disclose the total

amount of the receivable. Additionally, this receivable should be shown separately from other receivables.

E. Stock Dividends and Splits

49. (c) Arlo's annual preferred stock dividend is $120,000 ($2,000,000 × 6%). The $240,000 dividend paid includes $120,000 dividends in arrears from 2008 and $120,000 for 2009. Therefore, Wood would receive **$24,000 of cash dividends** ($200,000 × 6% × 2) which would be reported as **dividend income** in 2009 (preferred dividends in arrears are not recognized as income until declared). No dividend income is recognized when an investor receives a proportional **stock** dividend, because the investor continues to own the same proportion of the investee as before the stock dividend, and the investee has not distributed any assets to the investor.

50. (d) Regardless of the accounting method used, no dividend revenue is recognized when an investor receives a proportional **stock** dividend, because the investor continues to own the same proportion of the investee as before the stock dividend. In addition, the investee has not distributed any assets to the investor. Therefore, **no entry** is prepared to record the receipt of a stock dividend. The investor simply makes a memo entry to record the additional number of shares owned, while leaving the balance in the investment account unchanged. The balance is then spread over the total number of shares (previous holdings + stock dividend) to determine the new per share cost of the stock.

F. Stock Rights

51. (a) When stock rights are received, the cost of the investment (1,000 × $80 = $80,000) is allocated between the stock and the rights based on the relative fair market value of each, as calculated below.

FMV of stock	1,000 × $95	=	$ 95,000
FMV of rights	1,000 × $ 5	=	5,000
Total FMV			$100,000

The cost allocated to the stock is $76,000 ($80,000 × 95/100) and the cost allocated to the rights is $4,000 ($80,000 × 5/100).

52. (c) When the rights are received, the cost of the investment ($36,000) is allocated between the stock and the rights based on their relative fair market values, calculated below.

FMV of stock	500 × $90	=	$45,000
FMV of rights	500 × $10	=	5,000
Total FMV			$50,000

The cost allocated to the stock is $32,400 ($45,000/$50,000, or 90%, of $36,000) and to the rights is $3,600 ($5,000/$50,000, or 10%, of $36,000). The net proceeds from the sale of the rights is $5,000 (500 × $10), so the gain on the sale of the rights is $1,400 ($5,000 – $3,600).

G. Cash Surrender Value of Life Insurance

53. (c) The cash surrender value (CSV) of the life insurance policy increased by $21,000 during 2009 ($108,000 – $87,000). Therefore, part of the premium paid is not expense but a payment to increase the CSV. The formula to compute insurance expense is

Cash paid	–	(Ending CSV – Beginning CSV)	–	Cash divs. received	
$40,000	–	($108,000 – $87,000)	–	$0	= $19,000

The dividends in this problem are **not** cash dividends received. They are dividends that the insurance company applied to increase the CSV. They are not separately considered in the formula above because the effect of the dividends is reflected in the increase in CSV, which **is** included in the formula. 2009 journal entries are presented below.

Cash surr. value	$15,000		($21,000 – $6,000)
Ins. expense	25,000		
Cash		$40,000	
Cash surr. value	$ 6,000		
Ins. expense		$ 6,000	

54. (a) When a company insures the lives of employees and names itself the beneficiary, the cash surrender value of the policies is considered an asset. During the first few years of a policy, no cash surrender value may accrue. If no increase in cash surrender value (CSV) occurs, the journal entry to record a premium paid would be

Insurance expense	xxx	
Cash		xxx

However, if cash surrender value increases, part of the cash paid is recorded as an increase in the CSV. The entry is

Insurance expense	xx	
Cash surrender value	xx	
Cash		xxx

Therefore, the increase in CSV decreases insurance expense because the same amount of cash paid must be allocated between the two accounts. The increase in CSV does **not** affect investment income or deferred charges.

55. (b) When a company insures the lives of employees and names itself as the beneficiary, the cash surrender value (CSV) of the policy is considered an asset. Premiums paid are debited to CSV for the increase in CSV that year and to insurance expense for the excess of cash paid over increase in CSV. Upon the death of the insured employee, the company recognizes a gain for the excess of proceeds received over CSV.

Miscellaneous

56. (c) In determining the amount which should be reported in Lake's 2009 income statement as dividend revenue, the first step is to determine what method should be used in accounting for Lake's investments. The equity method of accounting for an investment in common stock should be followed by an investor whose investment in common stock gives it the ability to exercise significant influence over the operating and financial policies of an investee even though the investor may hold 50% or less of the voting stock. Ability to exercise that influence may be indicated in several ways, such as representation on the board of directors. Another important consideration is the extent of ownership by an investor. The Board concluded that an investment of 20% or more of the voting stock of an investee should lead to a presumption, in the absence of evidence to the contrary, that an investor has the ability to exercise significant influence over an investee. Conversely, an investment of less than 20% of the voting stock of an investee should lead to a presumption that an investor does **not** have the ability to exercise significant influence unless such ability can be demonstrated. Lake's 30% ownership of Aub and its representation on Aub's board of directors clearly indicate that the investment in Aub should be accounted for using the equity method. Lake's 1% ownership in Kar and

lack of evidence in this problem that Lake has "significant influence" over Kar indicate that this investment should be accounted for using the cost adjusted for fair value method. When the **equity** method is used, dividends received from an investee reduce the carrying amount of the investment (i.e., are **not** reported as dividend revenue). However, the investor recognizes dividends received from investees as **income** under the **cost adjusted for fair value** method. Therefore, the $1,000 of cash dividends from Kar would be reported as dividend revenue by Lake, while the $15,000 of cash dividends from Aub would reduce the carrying amount of Lake's investment in Aub.

57. (d) Lake's royalty revenue results from the licensing of their trademark to Barr Co. Lake receives royalties of 10% of Barr's sales of trademarked items. To determine royalty revenue for 2009, it must first be realized that the royalty payment on September 1, 2009, is for sales in January through June of 2009. This royalty payment of $7,000 is the first portion of royalty revenue for 2009. The second portion of royalty revenue is for Barr's sales of trademarked items for July through December of 2009. This second portion consists of 10% of Barr's estimated sales of trademarked items for the last half of 2009. Royalty revenue for the second half of 2009 is then $2,000 (10% × $20,000). Therefore, answer (d) is correct because royalty revenue would be $9,000 for 2009 and is comprised of the $7,000 royalty payment received on September 1, 2009, plus 10% of estimated sales for months July through December.

58. (c) Lake receives rental revenue from leasing a parking lot to Day Co. The annual rental payment made by Day Co. to Lake is $48,000. However, Day Co. also paid a nonrefundable deposit of $50,000 on January 1, 2007. This $50,000 deposit, since it is nonrefundable, is considered unearned revenue that must be recognized over the life of the lease on a straight-line basis. Therefore, in addition to the $48,000 annual rental payment, $5,000 ($50,000 ÷ 10 years) of the nonrefundable deposit will be recognized as rental revenue in 2009. Thus, answer (c) is correct because $53,000 will be recognized as rental revenue in 2009. Note that the $8,000 security deposit will not be revenue because it is to be refunded at the end of the lease period. It is deferred in its entirety and recorded as a long-term liability. Only a nonrefundable deposit would be recognized as rental revenue over the life of the lease.

59. (d) Stock dividends are not income to the recipient, but rather, are an adjustment of the per share basis of the investment. Answer (c) is incorrect because no change in the total investment cost is made when an investor receives stock dividends. Answer (d) is correct because some companies make a memorandum journal entry to note the receipt of the stock dividend and the adjustment of the per share basis of the investment.

SOLUTIONS TO SIMULATION PROBLEMS

Simulation Problem 1

Situation	Concepts	Accounting Treatment	Financial Statement Disclosures	Research	Communication

Accounting treatment

	(A)	(B)	(C)	(D)	(E)	(F)	(G)	(H)	(I)
1. Cash flows from purchases and sales of these securities are reported as an operating activity on the statement of cash flows.	○	○	○	○	○	○	○	●	○
2. Include unrealized holding gains/losses in earnings of current period.	○	○	○	○	○	○	○	●	○
3. Amortize unrealized holding gain/loss over life of security.	○	○	○	○	○	○	○	○	●
4. Report at amortized cost.	○	○	○	●	○	○	○	○	○
5. Report unrealized holding gains/losses as other comprehensive income and close to accumulated other comprehensive income, a separate component of stockholders' equity.	●	○	○	○	○	○	○	○	○
6. Classify as a current asset.	○	○	○	○	○	○	○	●	○
7. Subsequent recovery not recognized unless realized.	○	○	○	○	●	○	○	○	○

Explanation of solutions

1.   (H) Purchases and sales of trading portfolio securities be classified as operating activities on the statement of cash flows due to the short-term, profit-seeking nature of the investment. In contrast, available-for-sale and held-to-maturity securities are classified as investing activities.

2.   (H) Unrealized holding gains and losses on trading securities are included in income of the period.

3.   (I) Unrealized holding gains and losses on securities transferred to held-to-maturity from available-for-sale are reported as a separate component of stockholders' equity (accumulated other comprehensive income) and amortized over the remaining life of the security.

4.   (D) Held-to-maturity securities are carried at amortized cost.

5.   (A) Unrealized holding gains and losses on available-for-sale securities are reported as other comprehensive income, whereas those on trading securities are included in income and those on held-to-maturity securities are not reported.

6.   (H) Trading securities appear on the balance sheet as current assets.

7.   (E) When a decline in value of a security is deemed to be other than temporary, the impaired security is written down to fair value. Any subsequent recovery may not be recognized in earnings unless realized through sale of the security.

Situation	Concepts	Accounting Treatment	Financial Statement Disclosures	Research	Communication

	True	False
1 Held-to-maturity securities are classified as current or noncurrent on an individual basis.	●	○
2. For trading securities, some realized gains/losses are excluded from earnings.	●	○
3. A premature sale of held-to-maturity securities may be considered maturity if at least 80% of the principal has already been collected.	○	●
4. Dividends received on available-for-sale securities decrease the investment account.	○	●
5. A company that owns more than 50% of the outstanding shares of stock of another company must use the fair value method.	○	●

Explanation of solutions

1.   (T) Held-to-maturity securities are classified as current or noncurrent according to how soon they will mature, (i.e., a security maturing within one year is classified as current, while one with a more distant maturity date is considered noncurrent).

2.   (T) Some unrealized holding gains and losses on trading securities could have already been included in income as unrealized components. Thus, to recognize them again upon realization would result in an erroneous doubling of the actual gain/loss.

3.   (F) Premature sale of held-to-maturity securities are considered at maturity if either (1) the sale occurs so close to maturity that interest rate risk is virtually eliminated, or (2) the sale occurs after at least 85% of the principal has been collected.

4.   **(F)** Dividends received on available-for-sale securities are treated as dividend income on the income statement.

5.   **(F)** A company that owns more than 50% of the outstanding shares of stock should use the equity method and prepare consolidated financial statements (assuming the company exercises control).

Situation	Concepts	Accounting Treatment	Financial Statement Disclosures		Research	Communication

Amount

	(A)	(B)	(C)	(D)	(E)	(F)	(G)	(H)	(I)	(J)	(K)
1. Carrying amount of security ABC at December 31, 2009.	○	○	○	○	○	○	●	○	○	○	○
2. Carrying amount of security DEF at December 31, 2009.	○	○	○	○	○	○	○	○	●	○	○
3. Carrying amount of security JKL at December 31, 2009.	○	○	○	○	○	○	○	○	○	●	○

	Amount											*Gain*	*Loss*
	(A)	(B)	(C)	(D)	(E)	(F)	(G)	(H)	(I)	(J)	(K)		
4. Recognized gain or loss on sale of security GHI.	○	○	○	●	○	○	○	○	○	○	○	○	●
5. Unrealized gain or loss to be reported in 2009 net income.	○	●	○	○	○	○	○	○	○	○	○	○	●
6. Unrealized gain or loss to be reported at December 31, 2009, as a separate component of stockholders' equity entitled "accumulated other comprehensive income."	○	○	●	○	○	○	○	○	○	○	○	○	●

Explanation of solutions

1.   **(G; $100,000)** Held-to-maturity securities shall be measured at amortized cost. Since this debt security was purchased at par, there is neither a discount nor a premium to amortize, therefore amortized cost equals par or $100,000. Ignore fair value.

2.   **(I; $155,000)** Investments in securities that are not classified as held-to-maturity and that have readily determinable fair values shall be measured at fair value. $155,000 is fair value.

3.   **(J; $160,000)** Same answer as question 6. Since security JKL is not a debt security classified as held-to-maturity and since it has a readily determinable fair value it shall be . . .measured at fair value.

4.   **(D, L)** Recognized gains and losses on the sale of available-for-sale securities are measured as the difference between original cost ($190,000) and the selling price of the securities ($175,000). The unrealized loss that existed in accumulated other comprehensive income in the equity section prior to the sale ($25,000) will be reversed as a credit to unrealized loss and that reversal will be reported as other comprehensive income and closed to accumulated other comprehensive income that is reported in the equity section of the balance sheet (see question 10 below). The journal entry to record the sale would be

Cash	175,000	
Realized loss on sale of A-F-S securities	15,000	
A-F-S securities		165,000
Unrealized loss on A-F-S securities		25,000

5.   **(B, L)** The only unrealized gains or losses on securities reported in the net income relate to value changes in trading securities. In this case the value of the JKL securities has decreased from $160,000 to $155,000.

6.   **(C, L)** The 1/1/09 balance of the unrealized gain or loss on A-F-S securities reported in the equity section was $20,000, the difference between the 1/1/09 $25,000 unrealized loss of GHI ($190,000 – $165,000) and the 1/1/09 $5,000 unrealized gain of JKL ($175,000 – $170,000). The changes during the year were (1) the $25,000 reversal (credit) of the unrealized loss of GHI when it was sold and (2) the $15,000 loss ($175,000 – $160,000) in value during the year of JKL. The Other Comprehensive Income account would appear as follows:

Other Comprehensive Income			
Beg. bal.	--		
12/31/09 JKL	15,000	12/31/09 Reverse GHI 25,000	
Close to Accumulated Other Comprehensive Income	10,000		

The Accumulated Other Comprehensive Income account would appear as follows:

Accumulated Other Comprehensive Income		
	1/1/09	20,000
	12/31/09 Close from Other Comprehensive Income	
	12/31/09 Balance	10,000

Situation	Concepts	Accounting Treatment	Financial Statement Disclosures	Research	Communication

1. How should Dayle report the effects of unrealized losses and gains during the year from each portfolio?

FAS115, Para 13 (as amended)

13. Unrealized **holding gains and losses** for trading securities shall be included in earnings. Unrealized holding gains and losses for available-for-sale securities (including those classified as current assets) shall be excluded from earnings and reported [FAS115, ¶13] in other comprehensive income [as required in Section C49, "Comprehensive Income: Financial Statement Presentation,"] [FAS130, ¶33(a)] until realized except as indicated in the following sentence. All or a portion of the unrealized holding gain or loss of an available-for-sale security that is designated as being hedged in a fair value hedge shall be recognized in earnings during the period of the hedge, pursuant to paragraph .119 of Section D50. [FAS133, ¶534(b)] Paragraph .135 of Section 127, "Income Taxes," provides guidance on reporting the tax effects of unrealized holding gains and losses reported in [FAS115, ¶13] other comprehensive income. [FAS130, ¶33(a)] [Refer to paragraph .1001 for an EITF Issue that provides interpretive guidance on this paragraph.]

Codification: 320-10-35-1

2. How should Dayle account for the security that was reclassified from the trading securities portfolio to the available-for-sale securities portfolio?

FAS115, Para 15

15. The transfer of a security between categories of investments shall be accounted for at fair value. At the date of the transfer, the security's unrealized holding gain or loss shall be accounted for as follows:

    a. For a security transferred from the trading category, the unrealized holding gain or loss at the date of the transfer will have already been recognized in earnings and shall not be reversed.

Codification: 320-10-35-10

3. How should Dayle report investments in each portfolio in its balance sheet as of the end of the period?

Financial Statement Presentation
FAS115, Para 17, as amended by FAS159

17. An enterprise shall report its investments in available-for-sale securities and trading securities separately from similar assets that are subsequently measured using another measurement attribute on the face of the statement of financial position. To accomplish that, an entity shall either (a) present the aggregate of those fair value and non-fair-value amounts in the same line item and parenthetically disclose the amount of fair value included in the aggregate amount or (b) present two separate line items to display the fair value and non-fair-value carrying amounts. An enterprise that presents a classified statement of financial position shall report individual held-to-maturity securities, individual available-for-sale securities, and individual trading securities as either current or noncurrent, as appropriate, under the provisions of ARB No. 43, Chapter 3A, *Working Capital—Current Assets and Current Liabilities.*

Codification: 320-10-45-1

Situation	Concepts	Accounting Treatment	Financial Statement Disclosures	Research	Communication

To: Dayle Inc. Permanent File
From: CPA Candidate
Re: Accounting issues related to marketable securities
Date: [*Today's date*]

This memorandum summarizes my research regarding the accounting for marketable securities by Dayle, Inc.

Issue 1:   How should Dayle report the effects of unrealized gains and losses during the year for each portfolio?

For investments classified as trading securities, the unrealized holding gains and losses should be included in earnings. The unrealized gains and losses of investments classified as available-for-sale securities should be excluded from earnings and reported in other comprehensive income.

Issue 2:   How should Dayle account for the security that was reclassified from the trading securities portfolio to the available-for-sale securities portfolio?

The transfer of a security between portfolios should be effected at the fair value of the security on the date of transfer. Because the transfer in question was from the trading portfolio to the available-for-sale portfolio, the loss has already been taken to earnings and should not be reversed.

Issue 3:   How should Dayle present the investments in each portfolio in its balance sheet at the end of the period?

The firm should report individual available-for-sale and trading securities as current or noncurrent under the provisions of ASC Topic 210.

The term current assets is used to designate cash and other assets or resources commonly identified as those which are reasonably expected to be realized in cash or sold or consumed during the normal operating cycle of the business or one year whichever is longer. Therefore, securities that are available to meet current cash needs should be classified as current; other investments should be classified as noncurrent.

If you have any additional questions, please contact me.

Simulation Problem 2

Situation	Classification of Securities	Journal Entries	Financial Statement Disclosures	Communication	Research

Category

(H) (T) (A)

1.   Debt securities bought and held for the purpose of selling in the near term.   ○ ● ○

2.   US Treasury bonds that Acme has both the positive intent and the ability to hold to maturity.   ● ○ ○

3. $3 million debt security bought and held for the purpose of selling in three years to finance payment of Acme's $2 million long-term note payable when it matures.   ○ ○ ●

4.   Convertible preferred stock that Acme does not intend to sell in the near term.   ○ ○ ●

Explanation of solutions

1.   **(T)** Trading. Securities that are bought and held principally for the purpose of selling them in the near term (thus held for only a short period of time) shall be classified as **trading securities**.

2.   **(H)** Held-to-maturity. Investments in debt securities shall be classified as **held-to-maturity** and measured at amortized cost only if the reporting enterprise has the positive intent and ability to hold those securities to maturity. Both conditions are met in this case.

3.   **(A)** Available-for-sale. The company does not have the positive intent to hold this debt security to maturity, therefore the security cannot be classified as held-to-maturity. Also, since it will be sold beyond the "near term," it cannot be classified as "trading." Investments not classified as trading (nor as held-to-maturity securities) shall be classified as **available-for-sale securities**.

4.   **(A)** Available-for-sale. Since this security is neither a debt security nor a security that will be sold in the near term, it is classified as available-for-sale.

Situation	Classification of Securities	Journal Entries	Financial Statement Disclosures	Communication	Research

1.   Prepare the journal entry for the investment in Kern Co. on January 2, 2009.

Investment in Kern	600,000	
Cash		600,000

2.   Prepare the journal entry for the dividends received from Kern in 2009.

Cash	20,000	
Investment in Kern		20,000
[100,000 × 20% = 20,000]		

3. Prepare the journal entry required for Kern's reported income for the year ending December 31, 2009.

Investment in Kern	80,000	
Income from Kern		80,000
[400,000 × 20% = 80,000]		

Situation	Classification of Securities	Journal Entries	Financial Statement Disclosures	Communication	Research

Identify the following amounts on Acme's financial statements.

Carrying value of Kern investment	$660,000
Carrying value of Wand investment	$400,000
Income on Income Statement	
Kern investment	$ 80,000
Wand investment	$ 12,000
Other comprehensive income	
Kern investment	$ --
Wand investment	$100,000

Explanation of solutions

Carrying value of Kern.

Kern

Balance sheet–Acme reported its investment in Kern at a carrying amount of $660,000

Calculations:

Equity in earnings = $80,000 ($400,000 × 20%)

Dividend rec'd = $20,000 ($100,000 × 20%)

Carrying amount = $600,000 + $80,000 – $20,000 = $660,000

Carrying value of Wand.

Wand

Balance sheet–Acme reported its investment in Wand at a fair value of $400,000

Calculation:

20,000 shares × $20 per share = $400,000

Income Statement Amounts

Income from Kern	$400,000 × 20% = $80,000
Income from Wand	$12,000 dividend income
	Dividend income $12,000
	Calculation:
	$60,000 × 20% = $12,000

Other Comprehensive Income

Kern Investment	$0
Wand investment	Unrealized gain $100,000
	Calculation:
	$400,000 – $300,000 = $100,000

Situation	Classification of Securities	Journal Entries	Financial Statement Disclosures	Communication	Research

To: Mr. Harold Johnson
From: CPA Candidate
Re: Acme Co. Investments in Kern Co. and Wand Co.

The purpose of this memorandum is to explain to you the reasoning behind our belief that although Acme's investment in Wand and Kern represents equal ownership interests of 20%, the use of different accounting methods may be appropriate under generally accepted accounting principles.

Under generally accepted accounting principles, Acme must use the equity method to account for an investment if Acme's ownership interest allows it to exercise significant influence over the investee company. Generally, an investor is presumed to be able to exercise significant influence when it has an ownership interest of 20% or more, and is presumed to be unable to exercise significant influence when it has an ownership interest of less than 20%. However, either presumption may be overcome by predominant evidence to the contrary. The determination of whether an investor can exercise significant influence is not always clear and often requires judgment in light of such factors as an investor's representation on the investee's board of directors, participation in policymaking activities, and/or the extent of ownership as compared to that investee's other shareholders.

Acme used the equity method to account for its investment in Kern which indicates that its 20% ownership interest allowed it to exercise significant influence over Kern's operating and financial policies.

Acme accounted for its investment in Wand as available-for-sale securities. Despite its 20% ownership interest, there was evidence that Acme could not exercise significant influence over Wand's operating and financial policies. Hence, Acme did not use the equity method to account for its investment in Wand.

If you have any other questions, please contact me.

Situation	Classification of Securities	Journal Entries	Financial Statement Disclosures	Communication	Research

1. What is a trading security?

FAS115, Para 12a

12. Investments in debt securities that are not classified as held-to-maturity and equity securities that have readily determinable fair values shall be classified in one of the following categories and measured at fair value in the statement of financial position:

a.   Trading securities. Securities that are bought and held principally for the purpose of selling them in the near term (thus held for only a short period of time) shall be classified as trading securities. Trading generally reflects active and frequent buying and selling, and trading securities are generally used with the objective of generating profits on short-term differences in price. Mortgage-backed securities that are held-for-sale in conjunction with mortgage banking activities, as described in FASB Statement No. 65, *Accounting for Certain Mortgage Banking Activities*, shall be classified as trading securities. (Other mortgage-backed securities not held-for-sale in conjunction with mortgage banking activities shall be classified based on the criteria in this paragraph and paragraph 7.)

b.   Available-for-sale securities. Investments not classified as trading securities (nor as held-to-maturity securities) shall be classified as available-for-sale securities.

Codification: 320-10-20 Glossary

2. A company sells available-for-sale securities. Where is this transaction found on the statement of cash flows?

FAS115, Para 18, as amended by FAS 159

18. Cash flows from purchases, sales, and maturities of available-for-sale securities and held-to-maturity securities shall be classified as cash flows from investing activities and reported gross for each security classification in the statement of cash flows. Cash flows from purchases, sales, and maturities of trading securities shall be classified based on the nature and purpose for which the securities were acquired.

Codification: 320-10-45-11

3. A company has dividend income from available-for-sale securities. Where is this dividend income found on the financial statements?

FAS115, Para 14

14. Dividend and interest income, including amortization of the premium and discount arising at acquisition, for all three categories of investments in securities shall continue to be included in earnings. This Statement does not affect the methods used for recognizing and measuring the amount of dividend and interest income. Realized gains and losses for securities classified as either available-for-sale or held-to-maturity also shall continue to be reported in earnings.

Codification: 320-10-35-4

Simulation Problem 3

Situation	Concepts	Available-for-Sale Securities	Long-Term Marketable Equity Securities	Investment Income	Communication	Research

Identify whether each of the following statements is True or False.

	True	*False*
1. Unrealized gains from trading securities are reported in other comprehensive income.	○	●
2. Investments in stocks and bonds may be classified as trading securities, available-for-sale securities, and held-to-maturity securities.	○	●
3. X Company has significant influence over Y Company and owns 35% of the voting stock of Y Company. X Company must use the equity method of accounting for the investment in Y Company.	●	○
4. Unrealized gains and losses from available-for-sale securities that result from the change in fair value during the period should be reported as other comprehensive income.	●	○
5. The temporary unrealized gain or loss from held-to-maturity securities must be reported in income for the current period.	○	●
6. If a security is transferred from available-for-sale to trading securities classification, unrealized holding gains and losses are recognized immediately in the income statement.	●	○
7. The equity method of accounting requires a company to include the percent of income of the investee in the investor company's net income for the period.	●	○
8. The equity method of accounting requires that a company adjust the cost of the investee to fair value at the end of each period.	○	●
9. A company that receives stock dividends records income equal to the fair value of the stock on the date the dividend is declared.	○	●
10. Held-to-maturity securities are carried at amortized cost using the effective interest method.	●	○

Explanation of solutions

1. **(F)** Unrealized gains from trading securities are reported in income for the period.

2. **(F)** Stocks cannot be classified as held-to-maturity because they have no maturity date.

3. **(T)** The equity method is required when an investor exercises significant influence over the investee.

4. **(T)** Unrealized gains and losses are reported as other comprehensive income.

5. **(F)** The temporary unrealized gain from held-to-maturity securities is excluded from earnings; instead, the held-to-maturities are reported at amortized cost.

6. **(T)** Unrealized gains or losses are recognized when transferred.

7. **(T)** The investor recognizes its share of income as earned.

8. **(F)** In the equity method, the investor does not revalue the stock to fair value. The equity method requires that the investor record the percentage share of net income and percentage share of dividends of the investee.

9. **(F)** Stock dividends require a memo entry to show receipt of additional shares of stock. The company then recomputes the cost per share based upon the new number of shares.

10. **(T)** Held-to-maturity securities are carried at amortized cost.

Situation	Concepts	Available-for-Sale Securities	Long-Term Marketable Equity Securities	Investment Income	Communication	Research

Complete the following schedule for the available-for-sale securities of Poe Corp. as of December 31, 2009.

Poe Corp.
SCHEDULE OF AVAILABLE-FOR-SALE
SECURITIES
December 31, 2009

	Number of shares	*Cost*	*Beginning carrying amount at market*	*Ending market price per share*	*Market value*	*Cumulative gain or (loss)*	*Unrealized gain or (loss) in 2009*
Axe—preferred	500	$ 20,000	$ 21,000	$56	$ 28,000	$ 8,000	$ 7,000
Axe—common	1,500	20,000	21,000	20	30,000	10,000	9,000
Purl—common	3,500	35,000	38,500	11	38,500	3,500	--
Day—common	1,700	42,500	30,900	22	37,400	(5,100)	6,500
		$117,500	$111,400		$133,900	$16,400	$22,500

Situation	Concepts	Available-for-Sale Securities	Long-Term Marketable Equity Securities	Investment Income	Communication	Research

Prepare the following schedule for the long-term marketable equity securities for Poe Corp. as of December 31, 2009.

Poe Corp.
SCHEDULE OF LONG-TERM MARKETABLE
EQUITY SECURITIES
December 31, 2009

Scott Corp.—100,000 shares of common stock:	
Cost:	
Acquisition price	$1,700,000
Increase in equity during 2009:	
Poe's interest in Scott's income	$ 360,000
Less:	
Dividends received	200,000
Net increase in equity	160,000
Carrying amount of Poe Corp.'s investment in Scott	$1,860,000

Situation	Concepts	Available-for-Sale Securities	Long-Term Marketable Equity Securities	Investment Income	Communication	Research

Complete the following schedule outlining the income for Poe Corp. for the year ended December 31, 2009.

Poe Corp.
SCHEDULE OF INVESTMENT INCOME
For the Year Ended December 31, 2009

Dividends:	
Axe Corp.—preferred (1,000 shares × $2.40 per share)	$2,400
Purl, Inc.—common (3,500 shares × $1.00 per share)	3,500
Total dividend revenue	$5,900
Gains on marketable equity securities: [1]	
Realized gain/(loss) on sale of securities:	
Purl, Inc.—common ($13 – $10 = $3 × 2,500 shares	$7,500
Day Co.—common ($55,000/2,000 shares × 110%, or cost per share of $25 – $21 selling price per share = $4 loss per share × 500 shares sold)	(2,000)
Net realized gain on sale of securities	5,500
Equity in income of Scott Corp.:	
Poe's 30% interest in Scott's net income of $1,200,000	360,000
Total investment income	$371,400

Explanation of amount

[1]   Unrealized gains (losses) on available-for-sale securities are excluded from investment income and thus are excluded from Poe's schedule of investment income. They are reported as other comprehensive income.

Explanation of calculations and problem solving

1.   This problem consists of three related requirements concerning a company's investments in marketable equity securities.

1.1   A schedule of Poe's available-for-sale securities at 12/31/09 must be prepared. This schedule should include columns for cost, market, and unrealized gain or loss.

1.2   A schedule to show the carrying amount of Poe's long-term investments accounted for by the equity method at 12/31/09 is required.

1.3   Finally, a schedule showing all revenues, gains, and losses for 2009 relating to Poe's investments must be prepared.

1.4   The solutions approach for problems of this type in which the requirements are interrelated is to prepare time lines for each security and proceed through the given information making computations and notations on the appropriate time line. Labeling of computations by requirement helps to organize your data. For example, if a computation or number relates to requirement c., it can be labeled "c." Using this approach, the candidate will be solving a part of two to three requirements as each security is covered, but not necessarily in the same order as given on the exam. After working through all the information given, the formal required schedules can be prepared.

2.   At 12/31/08, Poe owned 1,000 shares of Axe preferred with a fair value of $42,000 ($42/share). At 10/1/09, Poe converted 500 shares of Axe preferred into 1,500 shares of Axe common. The preferred fair value is allocated to the common since half of the preferred $21,000 was surrendered to acquire it. The remaining preferred is still carried at $21,000

($42 × 500 shares). At year-end, the preferred is reported at $28,000 ($56 FV/sh × 500 sh) and the common stock is reported at $30,000 ($20 FV/sh × 1,500 sh). See time line after 2.1.

2.1   Dividend revenue received on the Axe preferred stock should be included in Poe's income statement. The Axe preferred stock paid a $1.20 dividend on 1,000 shares twice during the year, for a total of $2,400. Note that the second dividend was received on October 5, after 500 shares of preferred were converted. However, the dividend was received for all 1,000 shares, since the date of record was September 9.

Preferred: Div. Record   Div. Record
Date   Date

1/1   3/9   4/5   9/9   10/1   10/5   12/31

(a) Cost $20,000 (500 shares)
(a) Mkt. $28,000 (500 × $56)

$40,000
(1,000 shares) $42,000 FV (1,000 shares)
Preferred Dividend   −21,000 FV (500 shares)
                            $21,000 FV (500 shares)
2 × 1,000 shares × $1.20 =
$2,900 (c)

Converted
10/1   12/31

Common: $28,000   (a)   Cost $20,000 (1,500 shares)
          (1,500 shares) (a)   Mkt. $30,000 (1,500 × $20)

3.   Poe owned 6,000 shares of Purl common that originally cost $60,000 ($10/sh) and had a fair value of $66,000 ($11/sh) at 12/31/09. 2,500 of these shares were sold. The 3,500 still held have a carrying value of $38,500 (3,500 sh × $11). See time line after 3.2.

3.1   On 1/18/09, Poe sold 2,500 shares of Purl common for $32,500 (2,500 sh × $13) when the carrying value (fair value) was $27,500 (2,500 sh × $11). Since unrealized gains/losses on available-for-sale securities are not recognized in income the gain on the sale is $7,500 ($32,500 – $25,000).

3.2   Dividend income received on the Purl common stock should also be included in Poe's income statement. A $1.00 per share dividend was received on the Purl common stock (3,500 shares × $1.00 per share or $3,500).

1/18   6/30   12/31

$60,000 $60,000 (6,000 shares)   (a) Cost $35,000 (2,500
shares)
(6,000   - $25,000 (2,500 shares)   (a) Mkt. $38,500 (3,500 × $11)
shares) $35,000 (3,500 shares)   Dividend:
                                        3,500 shares × $1 =
                                        $3,500 (c)
Received (2,500 × $13) = $32,500
Cost   (2,500 × $10) = 25,000
Realized Loss $ 7,500 (c)

4.   At 1/1/09, Poe owned 2,000 shares of Day common that cost $55,000 and had a fair value of $40,000. Day issued a 10% stock dividend on February 14 when the stock's fair value was $44,000 (2,000 × $22), which gave Poe an additional 200 shares (2,000 × 10%) at no additional cost. Therefore, the 2,200 shares had an adjusted cost of $25 per share ($55,000 ÷ 2,200). The adjusted carrying value per share was $18.18 ($40,000 ÷ 2,200 shs). The stock dividend is not reflected in income. Poe sold 500 shares on June 1. The 1,700 still held have a cost of $42,500 (1,700 × $25), a carrying value of $30,900 (1,700 × $18.18) and a fair value of $37,400 (1,700 × $22). See time line after 4.1.

4.1   The Day stock sold for $10,500 (500 × $21) and had a cost of $12,500 (500 × $25). Thus, a $2,000 loss was realized on the sale of Day common and should be included in Poe's income statement.

1/1   2/4   6/1   12/31

$55,000   10% $55,000 (2,200 shares) (a) Cost $35,000 (2,500 shares)
(2,000   Stock   - $12,500 (500 shares) (a) Mkt. $38,500 (3,500 × $11)
shares)   Dividend: $42,500 (1,700 shares)
           $55,000
           (2,200 shares)
                           Received (500 × $21) = $10,500
                           Cost   (500 × $25) = 12,500
                           Realized Loss $ 2,000 (c)

5.   Poe intends to hold the Scott stock as a long-term investment. Since Poe owns 30% of the voting stock and can exercise significant influence over Scott, the use of the equity method is appropriate.

5.1   The original cost of the investment was $1,700,000. The excess of investment cost ($1,700,000) over the book value of the net assets purchased ($1,400,000) is $300,000. This amount is not amortized, in accordance with ASC Topic 350 (SFAS 142).

5.2   The investment account is also reduced by dividends received when the equity method is used. Scott paid quarterly dividends of $.50 a share, or a total of $50,000 each quarter to Poe (100,000 × $.50). Therefore, Poe received a total of $200,000 in dividends (4 × $50,000) from Scott. See time line after 5.3.

Cash	200,000	
Investment in Scott		200,000

Note that the dividend received from Scott is not recognized as income under the equity method.

5.3   Using the equity method, the investment account is increased by the investor's share of investee earnings 30% × $1,200,000 = $360,000).

Investment in Scott	360,000	
Investment revenue		360,000

Situation	Concepts	Available-for-Sale Securities	Long-Term Marketable Equity Securities	Investment Income	Communication	Research

To: CEO, Poe Corp.
From: CPA Candidate
Re: Equity method of accounting

    This memorandum is designed to explain the equity method of accounting for an investment. When a company owns stock in another company and can exercise significant influence over the operating and financial policies of that company, the equity method of accounting should be used. Generally, ownership between 20 and 50% of the outstanding stock of another company will result in the investor having significant influence over the investee.

    The equity method requires that the investor recognize its percentage share of income or loss and dividends received for a period. The full equity method may also require that a company amortize the difference between the investment cost and book value of the investment. In addition, the full equity method requires that the effects of intercompany transactions be eliminated. If you have an investment that you believe qualifies for treatment under the equity method, please contact my office. We will be glad to assist you with the accounting for your investments.

Situation	Concepts	Available-for-Sale Securities	Long-Term Marketable Equity Securities	Investment Income	Communication	Research

1.   When a company owns between 20% and 50% of the outstanding stock of another company and uses the equity method of accounting, how is income from the investee disclosed?

APB18, Para 19

c. The investment(s) in common stock should be shown in the balance sheet of an investor as a single amount, and the investor's share of earnings or losses of an investee(s) should ordinarily be shown in the income statement as a single amount except for the extraordinary items as specified in (d) below.

Codification: 323-10-35-4

2.   What are the three classifications for investment in debt and equity securities?

FAS115, Para 6

6. At acquisition, an enterprise shall classify debt and equity securities into one of three categories: held-to-maturity, available-for-sale, or trading. At each reporting date, the appropriateness of the classification shall be reassessed.

Codification: 320-10-25-1

3.   When a security is removed from the trading category, should the earnings previously recorded be reversed?

FAS115, Para 15

a. For a security transferred from the trading category, the unrealized holding gain or loss at the date of the transfer will have already been recognized in earnings and shall not be reversed.

Codification: 320-10-35-10

MULTIPLE-CHOICE QUESTIONS (1-37)

1. At December 31, 2009, Kale Co. had the following balances in the accounts it maintains at First State Bank:

Checking account #101	$175,000
Checking account #201	(10,000)
Money market account	25,000
90-day certificate of deposit, due 2/28/10	50,000
180-day certificate of deposit, due 3/15/10	80,000

Kale classifies investments with original maturities of three months or less as cash equivalents. In its December 31, 2009 balance sheet, what amount should Kale report as cash and cash equivalents?

    a. $190,000
    b. $200,000
    c. $240,000
    d. $320,000

2. The primary purpose of a statement of cash flows is to provide relevant information about

    a. Differences between net income and associated cash receipts and disbursements.
    b. An enterprise's ability to generate future positive net cash flows.
    c. The cash receipts and cash disbursements of an enterprise during a period.
    d. An enterprise's ability to meet cash operating needs.

3. Mend Co. purchased a three-month US Treasury bill. Mend's policy is to treat as cash equivalents all highly liquid investments with an original maturity of three months or less when purchased. How should this purchase be reported in Mend's statement of cash flows?

    a. As an outflow from operating activities.
    b. As an outflow from investing activities.
    c. As an outflow from financing activities.
    d. Not reported.

4. Alp, Inc. had the following activities during 2009:

- Acquired 2,000 shares of stock in Maybel, Inc. for $26,000. Alp intends to hold the stock as a long-term investment.
- Sold an investment in Rate Motors for $35,000 when the carrying value was $33,000.
- Acquired a $50,000, four-year certificate of deposit from a bank. (During the year, interest of $3,750 was paid to Alp.)
- Collected dividends of $1,200 on stock investments.

In Alp's 2009 statement of cash flows, net cash used in investing activities should be

    a. $37,250
    b. $38,050
    c. $39,800
    d. $41,000

5. In 2009, a tornado completely destroyed a building belonging to Holland Corp. The building cost $100,000 and had accumulated depreciation of $48,000 at the time of the loss. Holland received a cash settlement from the insurance company and reported an extraordinary loss of $21,000. In Holland's 2009 cash flow statement, the net change reported in the cash flows from investing activities section should be a

    a. $10,000 increase.
    b. $21,000 decrease.

    c. $31,000 increase.
    d. $52,000 decrease.

6. In a statement of cash flows, if used equipment is sold at a gain, the amount shown as a cash inflow from investing activities equals the carrying amount of the equipment

    a. Plus the gain.
    b. Plus the gain and less the amount of tax attributable to the gain.
    c. Plus both the gain and the amount of tax attributable to the gain.
    d. With **no** addition or subtraction.

7. On September 1, 2009, Canary Co. sold used equipment for a cash amount equaling its carrying amount for both book and tax purposes. On September 15, 2009, Canary replaced the equipment by paying cash and signing a note payable for new equipment. The cash paid for the new equipment exceeded the cash received for the old equipment. How should these equipment transactions be reported in Canary's 2009 statement of cash flows?

    a. Cash outflow equal to the cash paid less the cash received.
    b. Cash outflow equal to the cash paid and note payable less the cash received.
    c. Cash inflow equal to the cash received and a cash outflow equal to the cash paid and note payable.
    d. Cash inflow equal to the cash received and a cash outflow equal to the cash paid.

Items 8 and 9 are based on the following:

A company acquired a building, paying a portion of the purchase price in cash and issuing a mortgage note payable to the seller for the balance.

8. In a statement of cash flows, what amount is included in investing activities for the above transaction?

    a. Cash payment.
    b. Acquisition price.
    c. Zero.
    d. Mortgage amount.

9. In a statement of cash flows, what amount is included in financing activities for the above transaction?

    a. Cash payment.
    b. Acquisition price.
    c. Zero.
    d. Mortgage amount.

10. Fara Co. reported bonds payable of $47,000 at December 31, 2008, and $50,000 at December 31, 2009. During 2009, Fara issued $20,000 of bonds payable in exchange for equipment. There was no amortization of bond premium or discount during the year. What amount should Fara report in its 2009 statement of cash flows for redemption of bonds payable?

    a. $ 3,000
    b. $17,000
    c. $20,000
    d. $23,000

Items 11 and 12 are based on the following:

In preparing its cash flow statement for the year ended December 31, 2009, Reve Co. collected the following data:

Gain on sale of equipment	$ (6,000)
Proceeds from sale of equipment	10,000
Purchase of A.S., Inc. bonds (par value $200,000)	(180,000)
Amortization of bond discount	2,000
Dividends declared	(45,000)
Dividends paid	(38,000)
Proceeds from sale of treasury stock (carrying amount $65,000)	75,000

In its December 31, 2009 statement of cash flows,

11. What amount should Reve report as net cash used in investing activities?
   a. $170,000
   b. $176,000
   c. $188,000
   d. $194,000

12. What amount should Reve report as net cash provided by financing activities?
   a. $20,000
   b. $27,000
   c. $30,000
   d. $37,000

13. On July 1, 2009, Dewey Co. signed a twenty-year building lease that it reported as a capital lease. Dewey paid the monthly lease payments when due. How should Dewey report the effect of the lease payments in the financing activities section of its 2009 statement of cash flows?
   a. An inflow equal to the present value of future lease payments at July 1, 2009, less 2009 principal and interest payments.
   b. An outflow equal to the 2009 principal and interest payments on the lease.
   c. An outflow equal to the 2009 principal payments only.
   d. The lease payments should **not** be reported in the financing activities section.

14. Which of the following should be reported when preparing a statement of cash flows?

	Conversion of long-term debt to common stock	Conversion of preferred stock
a.	No	No
b.	No	Yes
c.	Yes	Yes
d.	Yes	No

15. Which of the following information should be disclosed as supplemental information in the statement of cash flows?

	Cash flow per share	Conversion of debt to equity
a.	Yes	Yes
b.	Yes	No
c.	No	Yes
d.	No	No

16. Which of the following is **not** disclosed on the statement of cash flows when prepared under the direct method, either on the face of the statement or in a separate schedule?
   a. The major classes of gross cash receipts and gross cash payments.
   b. The amount of income taxes paid.
   c. A reconciliation of net income to net cash flow from operations.
   d. A reconciliation of ending retained earnings to net cash flow from operations.

Items 17 through 21 are based on the following:

Flax Corp. uses the direct method to prepare its statement of cash flows. Flax's trial balances at December 31, 2009 and 2008 are as follows:

	December 31	
	2009	2008
Debits		
Cash	$ 35,000	$ 32,000
Accounts receivable	33,000	30,000
Inventory	31,000	47,000
Property, plant, & equipment	100,000	95,000
Unamortized bond discount	4,500	5,000
Cost of goods sold	250,000	380,000
Selling expenses	141,500	172,000
General and administrative expenses	137,000	151,300
Interest expense	4,300	2,600
Income tax expense	20,400	61,200
	$756,700	$976,100
Credits		
Allowance for uncollectible accounts	$ 1,300	$ 1,100
Accumulated depreciation	16,500	15,000
Trade accounts payable	25,000	17,500
Income taxes payable	21,000	27,100
Deferred income taxes	5,300	4,600
8% callable bonds payable	45,000	20,000
Common stock	50,000	40,000
Additional paid-in capital	9,100	7,500
Retained earnings	44,700	64,600
Sales	538,800	778,700
	$756,700	$976,100

• Flax purchased $5,000 in equipment during 2009.
• Flax allocated one third of its depreciation expense to selling expenses and the remainder to general and administrative expenses. There were no write-offs of accounts receivable during 2009.

What amounts should Flax report in its statement of cash flows for the year ended December 31, 2009, for the following:

17. Cash collected from customers?
   a. $541,800
   b. $541,600
   c. $536,000
   d. $535,800

18. Cash paid for goods to be sold?
   a. $258,500
   b. $257,500
   c. $242,500
   d. $226,500

19. Cash paid for interest?
   a. $4,800
   b. $4,300
   c. $3,800
   d. $1,700

20. Cash paid for income taxes?
   a. $25,800
   b. $20,400
   c. $19,700
   d. $15,000

21. Cash paid for selling expenses?
   a. $142,000
   b. $141,500
   c. $141,000
   d. $140,000

22. In a statement of cash flows, which of the following would increase reported cash flows from operating activities using the direct method? (Ignore income tax considerations.)

   a. Dividends received from investments.
   b. Gain on sale of equipment.
   c. Gain on early retirement of bonds.
   d. Change from straight-line to accelerated depreciation.

23. A company's wages payable increased from the beginning to the end of the year. In the company's statement of cash flows in which the operating activities section is prepared under the direct method, the cash paid for wages would be

   a. Salary expense plus wages payable at the beginning of the year.
   b. Salary expense plus the increase in wages payable from the beginning to the end of the year.
   c. Salary expense less the increase in wages payable from the beginning to the end of the year.
   d. The same as salary expense.

24. Metro, Inc. reported net income of $150,000 for 2009. Changes occurred in several balance sheet accounts during 2009 as follows:

Investment in Videogold, Inc. stock, carried on the equity basis	$5,500 increase
Accumulated depreciation, caused by major repair to projection equipment	2,100 decrease
Premium on bonds payable	1,400 decrease
Deferred income tax liability (long-term)	1,800 increase

In Metro's 2009 cash flow statement, the reported net cash provided by operating activities should be

   a. $150,400
   b. $148,300
   c. $144,900
   d. $142,800

25. Lino Co.'s worksheet for the preparation of its 2009 statement of cash flows included the following:

	December 31	January 1
Accounts receivable	$29,000	$23,000
Allowance for uncollectible accounts	1,000	800
Prepaid rent expense	8,200	12,400
Accounts payable	22,400	19,400

Lino's 2009 net income is $150,000. What amount should Lino include as net cash provided by operating activities in the statement of cash flows?

   a. $151,400
   b. $151,000
   c. $148,600
   d. $145,400

26. In a statement of cash flows (using indirect approach for operating activities) an increase in inventories should be presented as a(n)

   a. Outflow of cash.
   b. Inflow and outflow of cash.
   c. Addition to net income.
   d. Deduction from net income.

27. How should a gain from the sale of used equipment for cash be reported in a statement of cash flows using the indirect method?

   a. In investment activities as a reduction of the cash inflow from the sale.
   b. In investment activities as a cash outflow.
   c. In operating activities as a deduction from income.
   d. In operating activities as an addition to income.

28. Would the following be added back to net income when reporting operating activities' cash flows by the indirect method?

	Excess of treasury stock acquisition cost over sales proceeds (cost method)	Bond discount amortization
a.	Yes	Yes
b.	No	No
c.	No	Yes
d.	Yes	No

29. Which of the following should **not** be disclosed in an enterprise's statement of cash flows prepared using the indirect method?

   a. Interest paid, net of amounts capitalized.
   b. Income taxes paid.
   c. Cash flow per share.
   d. Dividends paid on preferred stock.

Items 30 through 32 are based on the following:

The differences in Beal Inc.'s balance sheet accounts at December 31, 2009 and 2008, are presented below.

	Increase (Decrease)
Assets	
Cash and cash equivalents	$ 120,000
Available-for-sale securities	300,000
Accounts receivable, net	--
Inventory	80,000
Long-term investments	(100,000)
Plant assets	700,000
Accumulated depreciation	--
	$1,100,000
Liabilities and Stockholders' Equity	
Accounts payable and accrued liabilities	$ (5,000)
Dividends payable	160,000
Short-term bank debt	325,000
Long-term debt	110,000
Common stock, $10 par	100,000
Additional paid-in capital	120,000
Retained earnings	290,000
	$1,100,000

The following additional information relates to 2009:

- Net income was $790,000.
- Cash dividends of $500,000 were declared.
- Building costing $600,000 and having a carrying amount of $350,000 was sold for $350,000.
- Equipment costing $110,000 was acquired through issuance of long-term debt.
- A long-term investment was sold for $135,000. There were no other transactions affecting long-term investments.
- 10,000 shares of common stock were issued for $22 a share.

In Beal's 2009 statement of cash flows,

30. Net cash provided by operating activities was

   a. $1,160,000
   b. $1,040,000
   c. $ 920,000
   d. $ 705,000

31. Net cash used in investing activities was
- a. $1,005,000
- b. $1,190,000
- c. $1,275,000
- d. $1,600,000

32. Net cash provided by financing activities was
- a. $ 20,000
- b. $ 45,000
- c. $150,000
- d. $205,000

Items 33 through 36 relate to data to be reported in the statement of cash flows of Debbie Dress Shops, Inc. based on the following information:

Debbie Dress Shops, Inc.
BALANCE SHEETS

	December 31	
	2009	2008
Assets		
Current assets:		
Cash	$ 300,000	$ 200,000
Accounts receivable—net	840,000	580,000
Merchandise inventory	660,000	420,000
Prepaid expenses	100,000	50,000
Total current assets	1,900,000	1,250,000
Long-term investments	80,000	--
Land, buildings, and fixtures	1,130,000	600,000
Less accumulated depreciation	110,000	50,000
	1,020,000	550,000
Total assets	$3,000,000	$1,800,000
Equities		
Current liabilities:		
Accounts payable	$ 530,000	$ 440,000
Accrued expenses	140,000	130,000
Dividends payable	70,000	--
Total current liabilities	740,000	570,000
Note payable—due 2011	500,000	--
Stockholders' equity:		
Common stock	1,200,000	900,000
Retained earnings	560,000	330,000
	1,760,000	1,230,000
Total liabilities and stock-holders' equity	$3,000,000	$1,800,000

Debbie Dress Shops, Inc.
INCOME STATEMENTS

	Year ended December 31	
	2009	2008
Net credit sales	$6,400,000	$4,000,000
Cost of goods sold	5,000,000	3,200,000
Gross profit	1,400,000	800,000
Expenses (including income taxes)	1,000,000	520,000
Net income	$ 400,000	$ 280,000

Additional information available included the following:

- All accounts receivable and accounts payable related to trade merchandise. Accounts payable are recorded net and always are paid to take all of the discount allowed. The allowance for doubtful accounts at the end of 2009 was the same as at the end of 2008; no receivables were charged against the allowance during 2009.
- The proceeds from the note payable were used to finance a new store building. Capital stock was sold to provide additional working capital.

33. Cash collected during 2009 from accounts receivable amounted to
- a. $5,560,000

- b. $5,840,000
- c. $6,140,000
- d. $6,400,000

34. Cash payments during 2009 on accounts payable to suppliers amounted to
- a. $4,670,000
- b. $4,910,000
- c. $5,000,000
- d. $5,150,000

35. Net cash provided by financing activities for 2009 totaled
- a. $140,000
- b. $300,000
- c. $500,000
- d. $700,000

36. Net cash used in investing activities during 2009 was
- a. $ 80,000
- b. $530,000
- c. $610,000
- d. $660,000

37. Bee Co. uses the direct write-off method to account for uncollectible accounts receivable. During an accounting period, Bee's cash collections from customers equal sales adjusted for the addition or deduction of the following amounts:

	Accounts written off	Increase in accounts receivable balance
a.	Deduction	Deduction
b.	Addition	Deduction
c.	Deduction	Addition
d.	Addition	Addition

SIMULATION PROBLEMS

Simulation Problem 1   (50 to 60 minutes)

Situation				
	Concepts— Direct Method	Statement of Cash Flows— Indirect Method	Communication	Research

The following is a condensed trial balance of Probe Co., a publicly held company, after adjustments for income tax expense.

Probe Co.
CONDENSED TRIAL BALANCE

	12/31/09 Balances Dr. (Cr.)	12/31/08 Balances Dr. (Cr.)	Net change Dr. (Cr.)
Cash	$ 484,000	$ 817,000	$(333,000)
Accounts receivable, net	670,000	610,000	60,000
Property, plant, and equipment	1,070,000	995,000	75,000
Accumulated depreciation	(345,000)	(280,000)	(65,000)
Dividends payable	(25,000)	(10,000)	(15,000)
Income taxes payable	(60,000)	(150,000)	90,000
Deferred income tax liability	(63,000)	(42,000)	(21,000)
Bonds payable	(500,000)	(1,000,000)	500,000
Unamortized premium on bonds	(71,000)	(150,000)	79,000
Common stock	(350,000)	(150,000)	(200,000)
Additional paid-in capital	(430,000)	(375,000)	(55,000)
Retained earnings	(185,000)	(265,000)	80,000
Sales	(2,420,000)		
Cost of sales	1,863,000		
Selling and administrative expenses	220,000		
Interest income	(14,000)		
Interest expense	46,000		
Depreciation	88,000		
Loss on sale of equipment	7,000		
Gain on extinguishment of bonds	(90,000)		
Income tax expense	105,000		
	$ 0	$ 0	$300,000

Additional information

- During 2009 equipment with an original cost of $50,000 was sold for cash, and equipment costing $125,000 was purchased.
- On January 1, 2009, bonds with a par value of $500,000 and related premium of $75,000 were redeemed. The $1,000 face value, 10% par bonds had been issued on January 1, 2000, to yield 8%. Interest is payable annually every December 31 through 2019.
- Probe's tax payments during 2009 were debited to Income Taxes Payable. Probe recorded a deferred income tax liability of $42,000 based on temporary differences of $120,000 and an enacted tax rate of 35% at December 31, 2008; prior to 2008 there were no temporary differences. Probe's 2009 financial statement income before income taxes was greater than its 2009 taxable income, due entirely to temporary differences, by $60,000. Probe's cumulative net taxable temporary differences at December 31, 2009, were $180,000. Probe's enacted tax rate for the current and future years is 35%.
- 60,000 shares of common stock, $2.50 par, were outstanding on December 31, 2008. Probe issued an additional 80,000 shares on April 1, 2009.
- There were no changes to retained earnings other than dividends declared.

	Concepts— Direct Method			
Situation		Statement of Cash Flows— Indirect Method	Communication	Research

Below is a list of accounts and transactions. Prepare the outline of a statement of cash flows using the **direct method** by placing the appropriate items in the correct location on the statement of cash flows. Indicate whether each item selected for use in the statement of cash flows would be a cash inflow or a cash outflow.

Amortization of patents	Dividends received on trading securities	Issue of common stock
Borrow on long-term note payable	Gain on sale of land	Loss on sale of equipment
Cash collected on account	Increase in accounts receivable	Net income
Cash paid for inventory	Increase in dividends payable	Payment of dividend
Cash paid for supplies	Increase in inventories	Purchase of held-to-maturity securities
Cash sales	Increase in taxes payable	Purchase of treasury stock
Decrease in accounts payable	Interest accrued at December 31	Redemption of bonds
Decrease in prepaid expenses	Interest expense	Sale of land
Depreciation expense	Interest paid on note	Taxes paid

Probe Co. **STATEMENT OF CASH FLOWS** *For the Year Ending 12/31/09*	
	Cash Inflow or Cash Outflow
From Operating Activities	
From Investing Activities	
From Financing Activities	

		Statement of Cash Flows—			
	Concepts—	**Indirect Method**			
Situation	**Direct Method**			**Communication**	**Research**

Prepare a statement of cash flows using the **indirect method**. Select the titles and the numbers from the lists provided. You may use a number more than once, if necessary. You should also enter the following amounts:

- Subtotals for each class of activity.
- Net Change in cash for the year.
- Reconciliation to cash amounts

Complete the following statement of cash flows using the **indirect method**. (Select from titles and amounts from the tables that follow.)

	Cash Source (Use)
Probe Co. **STATEMENT OF CASH FLOWS** *For the Year Ending 12/31/09*	
From Operating Activities	
From Investing Activities	
From Financing Activities	

Titles

Increase in accounts receivable	Decrease in bonds payable	Net income
Decrease in accounts receivable	Issue bonds	Net loss
Increase in property, plant, equipment	Redeem bonds	Taxes paid
Decrease in property, plant, equipment	Increase in unamortized premium on bonds	Interest paid
Purchase of equipment	Decrease in unamortized premium on bonds	Cash collections from customers
Sale of equipment	Gain on sale of bonds	Cash paid for expenses
Loss on sale of equipment	Increase in common stock	Net cash flows from operating activities
Increase in accumulated depreciation	Decrease in common stock	Net cash flows from investing activities
Decrease in accumulated depreciation	Issue common stock	Net cash flows from financing activities
Increase in income taxes payable	Repurchase common stock	Other significant noncash transactions
Decrease in income taxes payable	Increase in additional paid-in capital	Net increase in cash
Increase in deferred income tax liability	Decrease in additional paid-in capital	Net decrease in cash
Decrease in deferred income tax liability	Increase in retained earnings	Cash at beginning of year
Increase in bonds payable	Decrease in retained earnings	Cash at end of year

Amounts

4,000	46,000	88,000	255,000	610,000
7,000	50,000	90,000	300,000	670,000
10,000	55,000	95,000	333,000	780,000
13,000	60,000	120,000	350,000	817,000
14,000	63,000	125,000	410,000	1,000,000
15,000	65,000	150,000	484,000	2,360,000
20,000	74,000	174,000	485,000	2,420,000
21,000	75,000	185,000	500,000	2,480,000
23,000	79,000	195,000	515,000	3,030,000
25,000	80,000	200,000	575,000	
42,000	85,000	240,000	590,000	

Situation	Concepts— Direct Method	Statement of Cash Flows— Indirect Method	Communication		Research

The CEO of Probe would like to know what effect, if any, each of the following seven items have upon the preparation of a cash flow statement, assuming **direct** presentation is used to present cash flows from operations.

1. Accounts receivable—trade

2. Inventory

3. Depreciation

4. Deferred tax liability from interperiod allocation

5. Issuance of long-term debt in payment for a building

6. Payoff of current portion of debt

7. Sale of fixed asset resulting in a loss

Write a brief memorandum explaining how these items would be disclosed on the statement of cash flows.

REMINDER: Your response will be graded for both technical content and writing skills. Technical content will be evaluated for information that is helpful to the intended reader and clearly relevant to the issue. Writing skills will be evaluated for development, organization, and the appropriate expression of ideas in professional correspondence. Use a standard business memo or letter format with a clear beginning, middle, and end. Do not convey information in the form of a table, bullet point list, or other abbreviated presentation.

To: CEO, Probe Co.
From: CPA Candidate
Re: Statement of Cash Flows

Situation	Concepts— Direct Method	Statement of Cash Flows— Indirect Method	Communication	Research

Suppose Probe had the following transactions. Research each item and select the appropriate paragraph from the authoritative literature that indicates how the item is disclosed on the statement of cash flows. Assume Probe uses the indirect method.

1. On February 2, 2009, Probe purchased 10,000 shares of stock of Stone Corporation. Stone Corporation paid a dividend of $2 per share to Probe on November 5, 2009. Probe's management believes it will hold the stock of Stone for at least 2 years.

2. Probe purchased new equipment for $100,000.

3. On June 1, 2009, Probe repurchased 4,000 shares of its own stock for $20 per share and immediately retired the shares.

Simulation Problem 2   (50 to 60 minutes)

Situation				
	Concepts	Calculations	Communication	Research

The following is a condensed trial balance of Probe Co., a publicly held company, after adjustments for income tax expense.

Probe Co.
CONDENSED TRIAL BALANCE

	12/31/09 Balances Dr. (Cr.)	12/31/08 Balances Dr. (Cr.)	Net change Dr. (Cr.)
Cash	$ 484,000	$ 817,000	$(333,000)
Accounts receivable, net	670,000	610,000	60,000
Property, plant, and equipment	1,070,000	995,000	75,000
Accumulated depreciation	(345,000)	(280,000)	(65,000)
Dividends payable	(25,000)	(10,000)	(15,000)
Income taxes payable	(60,000)	(150,000)	90,000
Deferred income tax liability	(63,000)	(42,000)	(21,000)
Bonds payable	(500,000)	(1,000,000)	500,000

	12/31/09 Balances Dr. (Cr.)	12/31/08 Balances Dr. (Cr.)	Net change Dr. (Cr.)
Unamortized premium on bonds	(71,000)	(150,000)	79,000
Common stock	(350,000)	(150,000)	(200,000)
Additional paid-in capital	(430,000)	(375,000)	(55,000)
Retained earnings	(185,000)	(265,000)	80,000
Sales	(2,420,000)		
Cost of sales	1,863,000		
Selling and administrative expenses	220,000		
Interest income	(14,000)		
Interest expense	46,000		
Depreciation	88,000		
Loss on sale of equipment	7,000		
Gain on extinguishment of bonds	(90,000)		
Income tax expense	105,000		
	$ 0	$ 0	$300,000

Additional information

- During 2009 equipment with an original cost of $50,000 was sold for cash, and equipment costing $125,000 was purchased.
- On January 1, 2009, bonds with a par value of $500,000 and related premium of $75,000 were redeemed. The $1,000 face value, 10% par bonds had been issued on January 1, 2000, to yield 8%. Interest is payable annually every December 31 through 2018.
- Probe's tax payments during 2009 were debited to Income Taxes Payable. Probe recorded a deferred income tax liability of $42,000 based on temporary differences of $120,000 and an enacted tax rate of 35% at December 31, 2008; prior to 2008 there were no temporary differences. Probe's 2009 financial statement income before income taxes was greater than its 2009 taxable income, due entirely to temporary differences, by $60,000. Probe's cumulative net taxable temporary differences at December 31, 2009, were $180,000. Probe's enacted tax rate for the current and future years is 35%.
- 60,000 shares of common stock, $2.50 par, were outstanding on December 31, 2008. Probe issued an additional 80,000 shares on April 1, 2009.
- There were no changes to retained earnings other than dividends declared.

	Concepts			
Situation		**Calculations**	**Communication**	**Research**

Indicate whether each of the following should be classified as an operating, investing, or financing activity on the statement of cash flows.

		Operating	*Investing*	*Financing*
1.	Payment for inventory	O	O	O
2.	Payment of dividend	O	O	O
3.	Cash received from sale of equipment	O	O	O
4.	Cash sales	O	O	O
5.	Issuance of stock to investors	O	O	O
6.	Payment of utility bill	O	O	O
7.	Payment of interest on long-term note payable	O	O	O
8.	Purchase of treasury stock	O	O	O

		Calculations		
Situation	**Concepts**		**Communication**	**Research**

For each transaction in **items 1 through 7**

- Determine the amount to be reported in Probe's 2009 statement of cash flows prepared using the **direct method**.
- Select from the list the appropriate classification of the item on the statement of cash flows.
- Indicate whether the item is a cash inflow or cash outflow.

Calculate the amount, and select the classification and direction from the items shown below.

Classification of Activity

Operating
Investing
Financing
Supplementary information
Not reported on Probe's statement of cash flows

Direction of Cash Flow

Inflow
Outflow

	Amount	*Classification of Activity*	*Direction of Cash Flow*

1. Cash paid for income taxes
2. Cash paid for interest
3. Redemption of bonds payable
4. Issuance of common stock
5. Cash dividends paid
6. Proceeds from sale of equipment
7. Cash collections from customers

Situation	Concepts	Calculations	Communication	Research

The CEO of Probe has several questions related to the statement of cash flows. Write a brief memorandum to her, answering her two questions as shown below.

1. What are the objectives of the statement of cash flows?

2. What are the two types of transactions that would be disclosed in a separate schedule in the statement of cash flows although they do not affect cash during the report period?

REMINDER: Your response will be graded for both technical content and writing skills. Technical content will be evaluated for information that is helpful to the intended reader and clearly relevant to the issue. Writing skills will be evaluated for development, organization, and the appropriate expression of ideas in professional correspondence. Use a standard business memo or letter format with a clear beginning, middle, and end. Do not convey information in the form of a table, bullet point list, or other abbreviated presentation.

To: CEO, Probe Co.
From: CPA Candidate
Re: Statement of Cash Flows

Situation	Concepts	Calculations	Communication	Research

Suppose Probe had the following transactions. Research each item and select the appropriate paragraph from the authoritative literature that indicates how the item is disclosed on the statement of cash flows. Assume Probe uses the indirect method.

1. Probe exchanged a delivery vehicle with a historical cost of $70,000 and a book value of $40,000 for a new forklift.

2. Probe pays $10,000 interest on long-term note payable.

3. Probe has 1,000 convertible bonds with a $100 par value that can be converted to 200 shares of $1 par common stock. During the year, the bondholders converted the bonds to shares of common stock.

MULTIPLE-CHOICE ANSWERS

1. c __ __	9. c __ __	17. d __ __	25. a __ __	33. c __ __
2. c __ __	10. b __ __	18. d __ __	26. d __ __	34. d __ __
3. d __ __	11. a __ __	19. c __ __	27. c __ __	35. d __ __
4. d __ __	12. d __ __	20. a __ __	28. c __ __	36. c __ __
5. c __ __	13. c __ __	21. c __ __	29. c __ __	37. a __ __
6. a __ __	14. c __ __	22. a __ __	30. c __ __	
7. d __ __	15. c __ __	23. c __ __	31. a __ __	1st: __/37 = __%
8. a __ __	16. d __ __	24. c __ __	32. d __ __	2nd: __/37 = __%

MULTIPLE-CHOICE ANSWER EXPLANATIONS

A. Objectives of the Statement of Cash Flows

1. (c) The 12/31/09 cash and cash equivalents balance is $240,000, as computed below.

Checking account #101	$175,000
Checking account #201	(10,000)
Money market account	25,000
90-day CD	50,000
Total cash and cash equivalents	$240,000

Bank overdrafts (like account #201) are normally reported as a current liability. However, when available cash is present in another account **in the same bank,** as in this case, offsetting is required. The money market account of $25,000 and the 90-day CD of $50,000 are considered cash equivalents because they had original maturities of three months or less. The 180-day CD of $80,000 is excluded because its original maturity was more than three months.

2. (c) The **primary** purpose of a statement of cash flows is to provide relevant information about the enterprise's cash receipts and cash payments during a period. Answers (a), (b), and (d) are incorrect because, although they represent uses of the statement of cash flows, they are not the primary use.

3. (d) The statement of cash flows is required to be prepared based on inflows and outflows of cash and cash equivalents during the period. The purchase of a cash equivalent using cash is **not** an outflow of cash and cash equivalents; it is merely a change in the composition of cash and cash equivalents. Cash has decreased and cash equivalents have increased, but total cash and cash equivalents is unchanged. Therefore this purchase is **not** reported in the statement of cash flows.

B. Statement of Cash Flows Classification

4. (d) Investing activities include all cash flows involving **assets,** other than operating items. The investing activities are

Purchase of inv. in stock	$(26,000)
Sale of inv. in stock	35,000
Acquisition of CD	(50,000)
Net cash used	(41,000)

The gain on sale of investment in Rate Motors ($35,000 – $33,000 = $2,000), the interest earned ($3,750), and dividends earned ($1,200) are all operating items. Note that the sale of investment is reported in the investing section at the cash inflow amount ($35,000), not at the carrying value of the investment ($33,000). If the CD had been for three months instead of four years, it would be part of "Cash and Cash equivalents" and would not be shown under investing activities.

5. (c) The building which was destroyed had a book value of $52,000 ($100,000 – $48,000). The cash settlement from the insurance company resulted in a loss of $21,000. Therefore, the cash inflow from this investing activity must be $31,000 as shown below.

Proceeds	–	Book value	=	Loss
?	–	$52,000	=	($21,000)
$31,000	–	$52,000	=	($21,000)

Note that the $21,000 extraordinary loss must be before any income tax effect because ASC Topic 230 requires that any tax effect be left in operating activities.

6. (a) The cash inflow from the sale of equipment is the carrying amount plus the gain. Answers (b) and (c) are incorrect because the tax attributable to the gain is a cash outflow in the operating activities section of the statement of cash flows. Note that when using the indirect method, the gain is deducted from operating activities, as to not double count the gain.

7. (d) The requirement is to determine how the equipment transactions should be reported in the statement of cash flows. Companies are required to report the gross amounts of cash receipts and cash payments, rather than net amounts. Therefore, the gross cash inflow from the sale of equipment and the gross outflow for the payment of new equipment should be reported. Answer (a) is incorrect because both gross inflow and outflow should be reported, rather than reporting the net cash flow from the transaction. Answer (b) is incorrect because gross cash flows, not net, are reported and because a note payable is not reported since the transaction results in no actual inflow or outflow in the period in which the payable occurs. This noncash activity would be reported in a separate schedule or in the footnotes. Noncash transactions commonly recognized in a separate schedule in the financial statements include: conversion of debt to equity and acquisition of assets by assuming liabilities, including lease obligations. Answer (c) is incorrect because the note payable is not reported on the statement of cash flows; rather it is shown in a separate schedule.

8. (a) Payments at the time of purchase or soon before or after purchase to acquire property, plant, and equipment and other productive assets are categorized as cash outflows for investing activities. Generally, these payments only include advance payments, down payments, or payments made at the time of purchase or soon before or after purchase. Therefore, only the cash payment is considered a cash outflow for investing activities.

9. (c) Noncash investing and financing activities include acquiring assets by assuming directly related liabilities, such as purchasing a building by incurring a mortgage to the seller. This type of transaction does not involve the flow of cash. Therefore, cash flows for financing activities related to this transaction would be zero. Note that the cash down payment would be reported as a cash outflow for **investing** activities. The amount of the mortgage payment would be included in the noncash activities at the bottom of the statement of cash flows.

10. (b) To determine the cash paid for redemption of bonds payable, the solutions approach is to set up a T-account for bonds payable.

Bonds Payable			
		47,000	12/31/08
Bonds redeemed	?	20,000	Bonds issued
		50,000	12/31/09

The amount of bonds redeemed can be computed as $17,000. ($47,000 + $20,000 − $50,000 = $17,000)

11. (a) Investing activities include all cash flows involving **assets** other than operating items. The investing activities are

Proceeds from sale of equipment	$ 10,000
Purchase of A.S., Inc. bonds	(180,000)
Net cash used in investing activities	$(170,000)

The gain on sale of equipment ($6,000) and amortization of bond discount ($2,000) are net income adjustments in the operating section, while dividends paid ($38,000) and proceeds from sale of treasury stock ($75,000) are financing items. The excess of dividends declared over dividends paid is a noncash financing activity.

12. (d) Financing activities include all cash flows involving **liabilities and owners' equity** other than operating items. The financing activities are

Dividends paid	$(38,000)
Proceeds from sale of treasury stock	75,000
Net cash provided by financing activities	$ 37,000

The excess of dividends declared over dividends paid is a **noncash** financing activity. The gain on sale of equipment ($6,000) and amortization of bond discount ($2,000) are net income adjustments in the operating section, while the proceeds from sale of equipment ($10,000) and purchase of A.S., Inc. bonds ($180,000) are investing items.

13. (c) Financing activities include the repayment of debt principal or, as in this case, the payment of the capital lease obligation. Thus, the cash outflow is equal to the 2009 principal payments only. The interest on the capital lease is classified as an operating cash outflow.

14. (c) Information about all investing and financing activities of an enterprise during a period that affect recognized assets and liabilities but that do not affect cash receipts or cash payments in the period should be reported in a supplemental schedule to the financial statements. This schedule includes all noncash investing and financing activities for the period. The conversion of long-term debt into common stock does not have any effect on cash flow, and it also results in a reduction of liabilities and an increase in stockholders' equity. Therefore, the conversion of long-term debt into common stock should be reported as a noncash financing activity in the supplemental schedule. Mandatorily redeemable preferred stock should be classified as a liability. On the date the preferred stock is redeemable, it is considered liability. Therefore, when the preferred stock is

converted into common stock, the conversion should be reported as a noncash financing activity in the supplemental schedule.

15. (c) Noncash investing and financing activities are reported as supplemental information to the statement of cash flows because while they do not affect cash in the current year, they may have a significant effect on the prospective cash flows of the company. Therefore, conversion of debt to equity is disclosed as supplemental information to the statement of cash flows. However, cash flow per share should **not** be reported on the statement of cash flows because it may be misleading and may be incorrectly used as a measure of profitability.

C. Direct or Indirect Presentation in Reporting Operating Activities

16. (d) Under either the direct method or indirect method, the major classes of gross cash receipts and gross cash payments must be reported in the statement of cash flows. Under the direct method, the amount of income taxes paid is one of the components of net cash flows from operating activities; under the indirect method, it is a required supplemental disclosure. A reconciliation of net income to net cash flow from operations is a required supplemental disclosure under the direct method, and is included in the body of the statement under the indirect method. Only a reconciliation of ending retained earnings to net cash flow from operations is **not** required under either method.

17. (d) Cash collected from customers can be computed using either a formula or a T-account. The formula is

Sales	[End AR	−	(Beg AR	−	Write-offs)]	=	Collections
$538,800	[$33,000	−	($30,000	−	$0)]	=	$535,800

In the formula above, sales is adjusted for the **change in AR, exclusive of write-offs,** because write-offs represent sales (and AR) which will never be collected in cash. In this problem, there were no write-offs, so it must be assumed that the change in the allowance account results solely from bad debt expense (no write-offs). Since there are no write-offs, the increase in AR ($33,000 − $30,000 = $3,000) is subtracted from sales because those sales increased AR instead of cash. The T-account solution is below.

Accounts Receivable			
12/31/08	30,000		
Sales	538,800	0	Write-offs
		?	Collections = 535,800
12/31/09	33,000		

18. (d) Cash paid for goods to be sold can be computed using either a formula or T-accounts. The formula is

CGS	+	(End. inv. − Beg. inv.)	−	(End. AP − Beg. AP)	−	Cash paid
$250,000	+	($31,000 − $47,000)	−	($25,000 − $17,500)	−	Cash paid
$250,000	−	$16,000	−	$75,000	−	$226,500

The decrease in inventory ($16,000) is subtracted from CGS because that portion of CGS resulted from a use of inventory purchased in prior years, rather than from a cash payment. The increase in AP is subtracted because that portion of CGS was not paid this year. Using T-accounts, first purchases are computed using the inventory account, then payments are computed using the accounts payable account.

Inventory			
12/31/08	47,000		
Purchases	?	250,000	CGS
12/31/09	31,000		

1. Purchases = $234,000

Accounts Payable		
	17,500	12/31/08
Payments ?	234,000	Purchases
	25,000	12/31/09

2. Payments = $226,500

19. (c) The trial balance does **not** include prepaid interest or interest payable, both of which would affect the computation of cash paid for interest. In the absence of those accounts, cash paid for interest is equal to interest expense plus (minus) bond premium (discount) amortization.

Interest expense	–	Discount amortization	=	Cash paid
$4,300	–	($5,000 – $4,500)	=	$3,800

Flax's 2009 entry to record interest expense was

Interest expense	4,300	
Cash		3,800
Discount on bonds payable		500

20. (a) Cash paid for income taxes can be computed using the following formula:

Inc. tax expense	–	(End. inc. tax payable – Beg. inc. tax payable)	–	(End. def. tax liability – Beg. def. tax liability)	=	Cash paid for inc. tax
$20,400	–	($21,000 – $27,000)	–	($5,300 – $4,600)	=	Cash paid
$20,400	+	$6,100	–	$700	=	$25,800

The decrease in income taxes payable is added to income tax expense because cash was used to decrease the liability as well as to pay tax expense. The increase in the deferred tax liability is deducted from income tax expense because that portion of tax expense was deferred (not paid in cash). Flax's summary journal entry to record income taxes for 2010 is

Inc. tax expense	20,400	
Inc. tax payable	6,100	
Cash		25,800
Deferred taxes		700

21. (c) In general, cash paid for selling expenses is affected by prepaid selling expenses, accrued selling expenses, depreciation and/or amortization expense, and possibly bad debts expense. In this case, there are no prepaid or accrued selling expenses in the trial balances, and bad debts expense is apparently included in general and administrative expenses (see discussion below). Therefore, cash paid for selling expenses is $141,000 ($141,500 selling expenses less $500 depreciation expense). Total depreciation expense can be determined from the change in the accumulated depreciation account ($16,500 – $15,000 = $1,500), and 1/3 of that amount is selling expense (1/3 × $1,500 = $500). Note that bad debt expense ($1,300 – $1,100 = $200) must be included in general and administrative expenses, because the answer obtained by assuming it is part of selling expenses ($141,000 – $200 = $140,800) is not given as one of the four choices.

22. (a) Businesses are encouraged to use the direct method of reporting operating activities under which major classes of cash receipts and cash payments are shown. The minimum cash flows to be disclosed under this method are cash collected from customers, interest and dividends received, cash paid to employees and suppliers, income taxes paid, and interest paid.

23. (c) In a statement of cash flows in which the operating activities section is prepared using the direct method, the cash paid for wages would be equal to the accrual-basis sal-ary expense, plus/minus any decrease/increase in the wages payable account. (The logic is essentially the same as an accrual-basis to cash-basis adjustment.)

24. (c) Net income was $150,000. Three of the four items given are net income adjustments (the major repair to projection equipment [$2,100] is a cash outflow under investing activities), resulting in net cash provided by operating activities of $144,900.

Net income	$150,000
Equity method income	(5,500)
Premium amortization	(1,400)
Increase in def. tax liability	1,800
Cash provided by operating activities	$144,900

When equity method income is recorded, the offsetting debit is to the investment account, not cash; when premium on bonds payable is amortized, the credit to interest expense is offset by a debit to the premium account, not cash. Therefore, both of these items **increase** income without increasing cash, and must be **deducted** as a net income adjustment. For the deferred tax items, when income tax expense is debited, the offsetting credit is to deferred tax liability, not cash. Therefore, this item **decreases** net income without decreasing cash, and it must be **added back** as a net income adjustment. Note that there should normally be depreciation expense as a net income adjustment, but it is not given.

25. (a) Based only on the items given, net cash provided by operating activities is $151,400, as computed below.

Net income	$150,000
Increase in net AR	
[($29,000 – 1,000) – ($23,000 – 800)]	(5,800)
Decrease in prepaid rent ($12,400 – $8,200)	4,200
Increase in AP ($22,400 – $19,400)	3,000
Cash provided by ops.	$151,400

The increase in net AR is deducted from net income because it indicates that cash collected is less than sales revenue. The decrease in prepaid rent is added because it reflects rent expense that was **not** a cash payment, but an allocation of previously recorded prepaid rent. Finally, the increase in AP is added because it also represents an expense (cost of goods sold) that was not yet paid.

26. (d) The objective of a statement of cash flows is to explain what caused the change in the cash balance. The first step in this process is to determine cash provided by operations. When presenting cash from operating activities under the indirect approach, net income must be adjusted for changes in current assets other than cash and in current liabilities. These adjustments are required because items that resulted from noncash events must be removed from accrual-based income. For example, when inventory increases during the period, inventory sold is less than inventory purchased. Considering only the increase in the inventory account, cost of goods sold on an accrual basis is less than it would have been if cash basis were being used. In converting to the cash basis, the increase in inventory must be subtracted from net income to arrive at cash from operations. Answer (a) is incorrect because even though an increase in inventories requires an outflow of cash, inventories are shown as adjustments to net income under the indirect method. Answer (b) is incorrect because changes in inventories are shown as adjustments to net income under the indirect method. Answer (c) is incorrect because an increase in an inventory would be a deduction from net income, not an addition.

27. **(c)** When using the indirect method for reporting net cash flows from operations, you start with net income from continuing operations and adjust for changes in operating related accounts (i.e., inventory, accounts payable) and noncash expenses, revenues, gains and losses. The proceeds from the sale of equipment is reported as an inflow in the investing section of the statement of cash flows, at its gross amount. This gross amount includes the gain. Therefore, to avoid double counting and to properly classify cash inflows, the gain is subtracted from net income to show the proper cash balance from operating activities.

28. **(c)** Under the indirect method of reporting cash flows from operations, income from continuing operations is adjusted for changes in operating related accounts and noncash expenses, revenues, losses, and gains. Noncash items that were subtracted in determining income must be added back in. This would include amortization of bond discount, as it is a charge against income but does not decrease cash. The excess of treasury stock acquisition cost over sales proceeds would not be added back to net income. Under the cost method, this loss would not be included in net income but would be charged back to a paid-in capital account or retained earnings. The acquisition and sale of treasury stock, furthermore, would be financing activities.

29. **(c)** Cash flow per share should **not** be reported on the statement of cash flows because it may be misleading and may be incorrectly used as a measure of profitability. Answers (a) and (b) are incorrect because, when the indirect method is used, separate disclosure is required for **interest paid** (net of amounts capitalized) and **income taxes paid**. Answer (d) is incorrect because, regardless of the method used, **dividends paid** on preferred stock are reported as a **financing activity**.

D. Example of Statement of Cash Flows

30. **(c)** Net cash provided by operating activities can be computed by using either the **direct** or **indirect** approach. In this case, there is not enough information to use the direct approach. In the indirect approach, net income is adjusted for noncash items, as shown below.

Net income	$790,000
Gain on sale of LT investment	(35,000)
Increase in inventory	(80,000)
Depreciation expense	250,000
Decrease in AP and accrued liabs.	(5,000)
	$920,000

The additional information indicates that a LT investment was sold for $135,000. The listing of accounts shows a decrease in LT investments of $100,000. The gain on sale ($135,000 − $100,000 = $35,000) is deducted because the total cash effect of this transaction ($135,000) will be reported as an investing activity. Two of the working capital accounts that changed are related to net income. The increase in inventory ($80,000) is deducted because cash was used to increase inventory. The decrease in accounts payable and accrued liabilities is deducted because cash was used to pay these liabilities. The increase of $300,000 for Available-for-Sale Securities is an investing activity. The only other information or account given which affects net income is accumulated depreciation. Although this account did not show any net decrease or increase during 2009, we know it was decreased by $250,000 when the building was sold ($600,000 cost less $350,000 carrying amount equals

$250,000 accumulated depreciation). Therefore, depreciation expense of $250,000 must have increased the accumulated depreciation account to result in a net effect for the year of $0. Depreciation expense is added because it is a noncash expense.

An alternative method of computing net cash provided by operating activities is to back into the answer after determining cash used in investing activities and cash provided by financing activities.

Cash provided by Operating Activities	$?
Cash used in Investing Activities	(1,005,000)
Cash provided by Financing Activities	205,000
Net increase in Cash	$ 120,000

The problem tells us that cash and cash equivalents increased by $120,000. Therefore, cash provided by operating activities is $920,000 ($920,000 − $1,005,000 + $205,000 = $120,000).

31. **(a)** **Investing** activities include all cash flows involving **assets**, other than operating items. **Financing** activities include all cash flows involving **liabilities and equity**, other than operating items. The common stock issued is a financing activity. In this case, the changes in the inventory and accumulated depreciation accounts are operating items. The cash flows involving the other assets, listed below, are investing activities

Purchase of AFS Securities	$ (300,000)
Sale of LT investments	135,000
Sale of plant assets	350,000
Purchase of plant assets	(1,190,000)
	$(1,005,000)

The amounts above were given, except for the purchase of plant assets, the amount of which can be determined from the following T-account:

	Plant Assets		
Cost of equip. acquired	110,000	600,000	Cost of
Cost of plant assets purchased	?		bldg. sold
Net increase	700,000		

The equipment acquired through issuance of LT debt is a **noncash** investing and financing activity so it does not affect net **cash** used in investing activities.

32. **(d)** **Financing** activities include all cash flows involving **liabilities and equity**, other than operating items. **Investing** activities include all cash flows involving **assets**, other than operating items. In this case, the change in the **accounts payable and accrued liabilities** account is an operating item. The part of the change in **retained earnings** caused by net income ($790,000) is also an operating item. The cash flows involving the other liability and equity accounts, listed below, are financing activities.

Payment of dividends ($500,000 − $160,000)	$(340,000)
Issuance of ST debt	325,000
Issuance of common stock (10,000 × $22)	220,000
	$205,000

The problem states that $500,000 of dividends were **declared**, and this is confirmed by the change in the retained earnings account ($790,000 net income − $500,000 dividends declared = $290,000 net increase). However, since dividends payable increased by $160,000, only $340,000 of dividends were **paid** ($500,000 − $160,000). The issuance of common stock (10,000 shares × $22 per share = $220,000) is confirmed by the increases in the **common stock** and **additional paid-in capital** accounts ($100,000 +

$120,000 = $220,000). The issuance of LT debt for equipment ($110,000) is a **noncash** financing and investing activity, so it does not affect net **cash** provided by financing activities. Note that the answers to the three related questions can be verified by comparing them to the increase in cash and cash equivalents ($120,000) given in the problem.

Cash provided by oper. acts.	$ 920,000
Cash used in inv. acts.	(1,005,000)
Cash provided by fin. acts.	205,000
Increase in cash and cash equivalents	$ 120,000

33. (c) The requirement is to calculate the amount of cash collected during 2009 from accounts receivable. The solutions approach is to prepare a T-account for accounts receivable. The allowance account has no effect on this analysis, because the problem states that the balance in this account has not changed and no accounts receivable were written off. Net credit sales are the only debit to accounts receivable because all accounts receivable relate to trade merchandise. In the T-account below, you must solve for the missing credit to determine that $6,140,000 was collected on account during 2009.

AR—Net			
12/31/08 balance	580,000	?	2009 Collections
2009 net credit sales	6,400,000		
12/31/09 balance	840,000		

NOTE: Based on the information given in this problem, no bad debt expense was recorded during 2009. However unrealistic this assumption might be, it is important to simply work with the information as given.

34. (d) The requirement is to calculate the amount of cash payments during 2009 on accounts payable. The solutions approach is to visualize the accounts payable T-account.

Accounts Payable			
		440,000	12/31/08
Payments	?	?	Purchases
		530,000	12/31/09

It is apparent that to determine payments to suppliers, purchases of trade merchandise must first be computed. The cost of goods sold statement can be used to compute purchases.

Beginning inventory	$ 420,000
+ Purchases	+ ?
− Ending inventory	− 660,000
Cost of goods sold	$5,000,000

Purchases = $5,000,000 − ($420,000 − $660,000)

= $5,240,000

Finally, the purchases are entered into the accounts payable T-account, and payments to suppliers of $5,150,000 can be plugged in.

Accounts Payable			
		440,000	12/31/08
Payments	5,150,000	5,240,000	Purchases
		530,000	12/31/09

35. (d) The requirement is to determine net cash flows provided by financing activities in 2009. The solutions approach is to work through the comparative balance sheets noting increases and decreases in liability accounts other than those related to operations and increases or decreases in stockholders' equity accounts. The additional information given must be considered in connection with these changes.

Notice the note payable was issued for cash and the proceeds were used to purchase a building. Cash inflows from financing activities include proceeds from long-term borrowing, and issuance of capital stock.

Proceeds from long-term note	$500,000
Proceeds from issuance of common stock	300,000
	$800,000

To determine the amount of dividends paid, it is necessary to analyze both the retained earnings and the dividends payable accounts.

Dividends Payable					Retained Earnings		
		--	12/31/08			330,000	12/31/08
Dividends			Dividends				
paid	?	?	declared		?	400,000	Net income
		70,000	12/31/09			560,000	12/31/09

Dividends declared = $330,000 + 400,000 − 560,000 = $170,000
Dividends paid   = $0 + 170,000 − 70,000 = $100,000

Net cash flows provided by financing activities is $700,000 ($800,000 − $100,000).

36. (c) The requirement is to compute the cash used in investing activities during 2009. The two assets other than those related to operations shown on the balance sheet (long-term investments and land, building, and fixtures) have increased from 12/31/08 to 12/31/09, indicating cash purchases since the additional information does not suggest any other means of acquisition. Therefore, cash outflows from investing activities include $80,000 for long-term investments and $530,000 ($1,130,000 − $600,000) for land, building, and fixtures. Notice that the building was purchased for $500,000, so fixtures or land must have been acquired for $30,000.

37. (a) The solutions approach is to set up T-accounts for the related accounts.

Sales			AR		
	Sales		Beg. Bal.	Collections	
			Sales	Write-offs	
			End. Bal.		

Sales are debited to AR and credited to sales; collections are debited to cash and credited to AR. Under the direct write-off method, write-offs of customer accounts are debited to bad debts expense, and credited to AR. To adjust sales to cash collections from customers, Bee must subtract the increase in accounts receivable (because Bee has not yet received cash for the sales remaining in AR). Bee must also subtract the accounts written off, because these sales have not resulted in cash receipts (and probably never will).

SOLUTIONS TO SIMULATION PROBLEMS

Simulation Problem 1

Situation	Concepts—Direct Method	Statement of Cash Flows–Indirect Method	Communication	Research

Probe Co.
STATEMENT OF CASH FLOWS
For the Year Ending 12/31/09

	Cash Inflow or Cash Outflow
From Operating Activities	
Cash paid for inventory	Outflow
Cash paid for supplies	Outflow
Cash collected on account	Inflow
Cash sales	Inflow
Dividends received on trading securities	Inflow
Interest paid on note	Outflow
Taxes paid	Outflow
From Investing Activities	
Purchase of held-to-maturity securities	Outflow
Sale of land	Inflow
From Financing Activities	
Borrow on long-term note payable	Inflow
Issue of common stock	Inflow
Payment of dividend	Outflow
Purchase of treasury stock	Outflow
Redemption of bonds	Outflow

Situation	Concepts—Direct Method	Statement of Cash Flows–Indirect Method	Communication	Research

Probe Co.
STATEMENT OF CASH FLOWS
For the Year Ending 12/31/09

	Cash Source (Use)
From Operating Activities	
Net income	195,000
Loss on sale of equipment	7,000
Gain on extinguishments of bonds	(90,000)
Depreciation Expense	88,000
Increase in Account Receivable	(60,000)
Decrease in Income Tax Payable	(90,000)
Increase in Deferred Tax Liability	21,000
Amortization of Premium on Bond	(4,000)
Net cash flows from operating activities	67,000
From Investing Activities	
Sale of equipment	20,000
Purchase of equipment	(125,000)
Net cash flow from investing activities	(105,000)
From Financing Activities	
Redeem bonds	(485,000)
Issue common stock	255,000
Pay dividends	(65,000)
Net cash flows from financing activities	(295,000)
Net decrease in cash	(333,000)
Cash at beginning of year	817,000
Cash at end of year	484,000

Situation	Concepts—Direct Method	Statement of Cash Flows—Indirect Method	Communication	Research

To: CEO, Probe Co.
From: CPA Candidate
Re: Statement of Cash Flows

This memorandum is in response to your questions regarding the statement of cash flows. The effects and procedural considerations of the seven account balances (transactions) that you had questions about are summarized below.

1. Accounts receivable—trade are generated as a result of credit sales. A balance in accounts receivable—trade represents sales (a part of operating earnings) not represented by cash. An increase in the accounts receivable—trade balance indicates that the actual cash generated is equal to sales as reported on the earnings statement less the increase in accounts receivable—trade balance. Conversely, a net decrease in the accounts receivable—trade balance would have to be added to sales as reported on the earnings statement to arrive at cash generated from sales. In the preparation of a statement of cash flows the increase (decrease) in this account balance between two periods is subtracted from (or added to) net sales to arrive at cash received from customers for sales.

2. Inventory is a component part of cost of goods sold. The net change in inventory balances affects the cash used to purchase inventory. An increase in ending inventory over beginning inventory increases the cash used to purchase inventory because cash was presumed to be used to increase the inventory balance. Therefore, when there is an increase in inventory balances, the cash to purchase inventory is the cost of goods sold as shown in the current earnings statement plus the increase in inventory balance.

A similar analysis leads to the conclusion that a decrease in inventory gives rise to a reduction in the cash used to purchase inventory.

3. Depreciation represents a systematic allocation of the cost of a fixed asset to the accounting periods benefited by the asset. The process of recognizing depreciation does not affect cash. Accordingly, cash paid for operating expenses is determined by deducting depreciation expense from total operating expenses and adjusting the operating expenses for prepaid expenses.

4. Deferred income taxes are the difference between income taxes matched against earnings and the actual amount paid or payable for the period. If the balance of the deferred tax liability account, for example, increases between two periods, the amount of income taxes paid was less than the indicated income tax expense. Conversely, if deferred liability tax account decreases, the amount paid was greater than the amount of income tax expense. Although the change in the deferred tax liability account is included in the indirect approach, the direct approach is not affected by the change. To determine the cash paid for taxes under the direct presentation, the **current** portion of income tax expense is adjusted for the increase or decrease in the income tax payable account.

5. The purchase of a building by issuing long-term debt obviously does not require a cash outlay. However, this noncash activity should be reported in a separate schedule as a noncash financing and investing activity.

6. The payment of the current portion of debt represents a cash outflow from financing activities.

7. The total proceeds from the sale of the fixed asset should be shown as an inflow from investing activities. This transaction would not be reflected under operating activities when the **direct** presentation is used.

If you have any further questions, please contact my office.

Situation	Concepts—Direct Method	Statement of Cash Flows—Indirect Method	Communication	Research

1. On February 2, 2009, Probe purchased 10,000 shares of stock of Stone Corporation. Stone **Corporation** paid a dividend of $2 per share to Probe on November 5, 2009. Probe's management believes it will hold the stock of Stone for at least 2 years.

Definition

FAS115, Para 18, as amended by FAS 159

18. Cash flows from purchases, sales, and maturities of available-for-sale securities and held-to-maturity securities shall be classified as cash flows from investing activities and reported gross for each security classification in the statement of cash flows. Cash flows from purchases, sales, and maturities of trading securities shall be classified based on the nature and purpose for which the securities were acquired.

Codification: 230-10-45-13

FAS95, Para 17

22. Cash inflows from operating activities are

    a. Cash receipts from sales of goods or services, including receipts from collection or sale of accounts and both short- and long-term notes receivable from customers arising from those sales

b.   Cash receipts from returns on loans, other debt instruments of other entities, and equity securities—interest and dividends

c.   All other cash receipts that do not stem from transactions defined as investing or financing activities, such as amounts received to settle lawsuits; proceeds of insurance settlements except for those that are directly related to investing or financing activities, such as from destruction of a building, and refunds from suppliers.

Codification: 230-10-45-13

2.   Probe purchased new equipment for $100,000.

FAS95, Para 17

17.   Cash outflows for investing activities are

a.   Disbursements for loans made by the enterprise and payments to acquire debt instruments of other entities (other than cash equivalents and certain debt instruments that are acquired specifically for resale as discussed in Statement 102)

b.   Payments to acquire equity instruments of other enterprises (other than certain equity instruments carried in a trading account as described in Statement 102)

c.   Payments at the time of purchase or soon before or after purchase to acquire property, plant, and equipment and other productive assets.

Codification: 230-10-45-13

3.   On June 1, 2009, Probe repurchased 4,000 shares of its own stock for $20 per share and immediately retired the shares.

FAS95, Para 20

20.   Cash outflows for financing activities are

a.   Payment of dividends or other distributions to owners, including outlays to reacquire the enterprise's equity instruments

b.   Repayments of amounts borrowed

c.   Other principal payments to creditors who have extended long-term credit.

Codification: 230-10-45-15

Simulation Problem 2

	Concepts			
Situation		Calculations	Communication	Research

Indicate whether each of the following should be classified as an operating, investing, or financing activity on the statement of cash flows.

		Operating	*Investing*	*Financing*
1.	Payment for inventory	●	○	○
2.	Payment of dividend	○	○	●
3.	Cash received from sale of equipment	○	●	○
4.	Cash sales	●	○	
5.	Issuance of stock to investors	○	○	●
6.	Payment of utility bill	●	○	○
7.	Payment of interest on long-term note payable	●	○	○
8.	Purchase of treasury stock	○	○	●

		Calculations			
Situation	Concepts			Communication	Research

Item	Amount	Classification on Statement of Cash Flows	Cash Inflow/Cash Outflow
1. Cash paid for income taxes	174,000	Operating Activity	Outflow
2. Cash paid for interest	50,000	Operating Activity	Outflow
3. Redemption of bonds payable	485,000	Financing Activity	Outflow
4. Issuance of common stock	255,000	Financing Activity	Inflow
5. Cash dividends paid	65,000	Financing Activity	Outflow
6. Proceeds from sale of equipment	20,000	Investing	Inflow
7. Cash collections from customers	2,360,000	Operating Activity	Inflow

Explanation of solutions

1. (**$174,000, O**) The payments for income taxes during the year were debited to the income taxes payable account. To arrive at the amount of payments, a T-account can be used as follows:

```
                   Income Taxes Payable
                        |   150,000   12/31/08
          Payments  174,000 |   84,000   Income Tax Accrual
                        |   60,000   12/31/09
```

Note that the deferred tax liability account increased by 21,000 (120,000 × 35%). Therefore, the entry for tax expense for 2009 would have been

```
Tax Expense                      105,000
    Deferred Tax Liability                    21,000
    Taxes Payable                             84,000
```

Using the direct method, the payment of taxes would appear in the operating section of the cash flow statement.

2. (**$50,000, O**) Interest paid on the bonds in 2009 would be $50,000 ($500,000 × 10%). Alternatively, the $46,000 plus the $4,000 premium amortization (see explanation for the next item below) also results in $50,000 as the amount paid for interest. The amount paid for interest would be included in the operating activities section of the cash flow statements if the direct method is used. (Note: The amount of cash paid for interest would be reported separately as supplementary information for a statement of cash flows using the indirect method.)

3. (**$485,000, F**) Through the following T-account analyses, a journal entry for the redemption of the bonds payable can be determined:

```
              Bonds Payable                            Unamortized Premium on Bonds
                    |  1,000,000  12/31/08       Amortization  4,000  |  150,000   12/31/08
Redemption  500,000 |                            Redemption   75,000  |
                    |    500,000  12/31/09                             |   71,000   12/31/09

      Gain on Extinguishment of Bonds                          Cash
                    |    90,000  12/31/09                         ?    |
```

Journal entry for redemption

```
Bonds payable                        500,000
Unamortized premium on bonds          75,000
    Gain on extinguishment of bonds              90,000
    Cash                                        485,000
```

This amount paid for the redemption of the bonds would be separately reported in the financing section on the statement of cash flows prepared using the indirect method. Financing activities include obtaining resources from owners and returning the investment, as well as obtaining resources from creditors and **repaying the amounts borrowed**.

4. (**$255,000, F**) An additional 80,000 shares of $2.50 par value common stock were issued during 2009. The following T-accounts depict the changes in the common stock and additional paid-in capital accounts:

```
              Common Stock
                    |  150,000  12/31/08
                    |  200,000  Issuance        (80,000 × $2.50)
                    |  350,000  12/31/09
```

Additional Paid-in Capital

	375,000 12/31/08
	55,000 Issuance
	430,000 12/31/09

The journal entry for the issuance of the stock would have been

Cash	255,000	
Common stock		200,000
Additional paid-in capital		55,000

This amount received for the issuance of the common stock would be reported separately in the financing section of the statement of cash flows prepared using the indirect method. Financing activities include **obtaining resources from owners** and returning the investment, as well as obtaining resources from creditors and repaying the amounts borrowed.

5. **($65,000, F)** The problem states that there were no changes to retained earnings during the year other than dividends declared. Therefore, the following T-account analyses depict the dividend activity during the year:

Retained Earnings

		265,000 12/31/08
Dividends declared	80,000	
		185,000 12/31/09

Dividends Payable

		10,000 12/31/08
Dividends paid ?		80,000 Accrual during 2009
		25,000 12/31/09

Cash

	?

The following journal entry would have been made:

Retained earnings	80,000	
Dividends payable		80,000
Dividends payable	65,000	
Cash		65,000

This amount paid for the dividends would be reported separately in the financing section of the statement of cash flows prepared using the indirect method. Financing activities include obtaining resources from owners and **returning the investment,** as well as obtaining resources from creditors and repaying the amounts borrowed.

6. **($20,000, I)** The following T-account analyses depict the sale of the equipment during 2009:

Property, Plant and Equipment

12/31/08	995,000	
		50,000 Sale
Purchase	125,000	
12/31/09	1,070,000	

Accumulated Depreciation

		280,000 12/31/08
Depreciation on sold asset	23,000	88,000 Depreciation expense
		345,000 12/31/09

Loss on Sale of Equipment

12/31/09	7,000

Cash

	?

The following journal entry would have been made for the sale of the equipment:

Cash	20,000	
Accumulated depreciation	23,000	
Loss on sale of equipment	7,000	
Property, plant and equipment		50,000

The proceeds from the sale of equipment would be reported separately in the investing section of the statement of cash flows. Included in the investing section are the acquisition and disposition of long-term productive assets or securities (not considered cash equivalents), as well as the lending of money and collection of loans.

7. The following T-account analysis depicts the cash received from customers. Assume all sales are made on account.

Accounts Receivable

12/31/08	610,000	
Sale on Account	2,420,000	
		2,360,000 Collections on account
12/31/09	670,000	

Therefore, the cash collections on account were 610,000 + 2,420,000 – 670,000 = 2,360,000.

			Communication	
Situation	Concepts	Calculations		Research

To: CEO, Probe Co.
From: CPA Candidate
Re: Statement of Cash Flows

This memorandum is in response to your questions regarding the statement of cash flows. The objective of the statement of cash flows is to provide information about cash receipts and payments from operating, investing, and financing activities. This information helps users assess the company's ability to generate future net cash flows, to meet obligations, and to pay dividends. The statement also helps users assess the differences between income and associated cash receipts and payments.

Companies sometimes make significant noncash transactions. Investing and financing activities that do not involve cash receipts and payments during the period should be excluded from the cash flow statement and reported in a separate schedule. Transactions that would be classified as significant noncash financing and investing activities would include the following:

1. Purchase of assets by the issuance of capital stock or debt
2. Purchase of assets by a trade or a reduction in another asset
3. Reduction of a liability by the issuance of capital stock
4. Reduction of a liability by incurrence of another liability (refinancing)
5. Reduction in a liability by repayment with an asset, resulting in a reduction in an asset

If you have any transactions that you cannot classify, please contact my office for further assistance.

				Research
Situation	Concepts	Calculations	Communication	

1. Probe exchanged a delivery vehicle with an historical cost of $70,000 and a book value of $40,000 for a new forklift.

FAS95, Para 32

32. Information about all investing and financing activities of an enterprise during a period that affect recognized assets or liabilities but that do not result in cash receipts or cash payments in the period shall be reported in related disclosures. Those disclosures may be either narrative or summarized in a schedule, and they shall clearly relate the cash and noncash aspects of transactions involving similar items. Examples of noncash investing and financing transactions are converting debt to equity; acquiring assets by assuming directly related liabilities, such as purchasing a building by incurring a mortgage to the seller; obtaining an asset by entering into a capital lease; and exchanging noncash assets or liabilities for other noncash assets or liabilities. Some transactions are part cash and part noncash; only the cash portion shall be reported in the statement of cash flows.

Codification: 230-10-50-3 and *230-10-50-4*

2. Probe pays $10,000 interest on long-term note payable.

FAS95, Para 23 (d)

23. Cash outflows for operating activities are

a. Cash payments to acquire materials for manufacture or goods for resale, including principal payments on accounts and both short- and long-term notes payable to suppliers for those materials or goods
b. Cash payments to other suppliers and employees for other goods and services
c. Cash payments to governments for taxes, duties, fines, and other fees or penalties
d. Cash payments to lenders and other creditors for interest
e. All other cash payments that do not stem from transactions defined as investing or financing activities, such as payments to settle lawsuits, cash contributions to charities, and cash refunds to customers.

Codification: 230-10-45-17

3. Probe has 1,000 convertible bonds with a
    $100 par value that can be converted to 200
    shares of $1 par common stock. During the
    year, the bondholders converted the bonds to
    shares of common stock.

FAS95, Para 32

32. Information about all investing and financing activities of an
enterprise during a period that affect recognized assets or liabilities
but that do not result in cash receipts or cash payments in the period shall be reported in related disclosures. Those disclosures may
be either narrative or summarized in a schedule, and they shall
clearly relate the cash and noncash aspects of transactions involving similar items. Examples of noncash investing and financing
transactions are converting debt to equity; acquiring assets by assuming directly related liabilities, such as purchasing a building by
incurring a mortgage to the seller; obtaining an asset by entering
into a capital lease; and exchanging noncash assets or liabilities for
other noncash assets or liabilities. Some transactions are part cash
and part noncash; only the cash portion shall be reported in the
statement of cash flows.

Codification: 230-10-50-3 and 230-10-50-4

MULTIPLE-CHOICE QUESTIONS (1-77)

1. On April 1, 2010, Dart Co. paid $620,000 for all the issued and outstanding common stock of Wall Corp. The recorded assets and liabilities of Wall Corp. on April 1, 2010, follow:

Cash	$ 60,000
Inventory	180,000
Property and equipment (net of accumulated depreciation of $220,000)	320,000
Goodwill	100,000
Liabilities	(120,000)
Net assets	$ 540,000

On April 1, 2010, Wall's inventory had a fair value of $150,000, and the property and equipment (net) had a fair value of $380,000. What is the amount of goodwill resulting from the business combination?
a. $150,000
b. $120,000
c. $ 50,000
d. $ 20,000

2. Which of the following expenses related to the business acquisition should be included, in total, in the determination of net income of the combined corporation for the period in which the expenses are incurred?

	Fees of finders and consultants	Registration fees for equity securities issued
a.	Yes	Yes
b.	Yes	No
c.	No	Yes
d.	No	No

3. On August 31, 2010, Wood Corp. issued 100,000 shares of its $20 par value common stock for the net assets of Pine, Inc., in a business combination accounted for by the acquisiton method. The market value of Wood's common stock on August 31 was $36 per share. Wood paid a fee of $160,000 to the consultant who arranged this acquisition. Costs of registering and issuing the equity securities amounted to $80,000. No goodwill was involved in the purchase. What amount should Wood capitalize as the cost of acquiring Pine's net assets?
a. $3,600,000
b. $3,680,000
c. $3,760,000
d. $3,840,000

Items 4 and 5 are based on the following:

On December 31, 2010, Saxe Corporation was acquired by Poe Corporation. In the business combination, Poe issued 200,000 shares of its $10 par common stock, with a market price of $18 a share, for all of Saxe's common stock. The stockholders' equity section of each company's balance sheet immediately before the combination was

	Poe	Saxe
Common stock	3,000,000	$1,500,000
Additional paid-in capital	1,300,000	150,000
Retained earnings	2,500,000	850,000
	$6,800,000	$2,500,000

4. In the December 31, 2010 consolidated balance sheet, additional paid-in capital should be reported at
a. $ 950,000
b. $1,300,000
c. $1,450,000
d. $2,900,000

5. In the December 31, 2010 consolidated balance sheet, common stock should be reported at
a. $3,000,000
b. $3,500,000
c. $4,000,000
d. $5,000,000

6. On December 31, 2010, Neal Co. issued 100,000 shares of its $10 par value common stock in exchange for all of Frey Inc.'s outstanding stock. The fair value of Neal's common stock on December 31, 2010, was $19 per share. The carrying amounts and fair values of Frey's assets and liabilities on December 31, 2010, were as follows:

	Carrying amount	Fair value
Cash	$ 240,000	$ 240,000
Receivables	270,000	270,000
Inventory	435,000	405,000
Property, plant, and equipment	1,305,000	1,440,000
Liabilities	(525,000)	(525,000)
Net assets	$1,725,000	$1,830,000

What is the amount of goodwill resulting from the business combination?
a. $175,000
b. $105,000
c. $ 70,000
d. $0

7. Consolidated financial statements are typically prepared when one company has a controlling financial interest in another **unless**
a. The subsidiary is a finance company.
b. The fiscal year-ends of the two companies are more than three months apart.
c. Such control is likely to be temporary.
d. The two companies are in unrelated industries, such as manufacturing and real estate.

8. On January 1, 2010, Lake Corporation acquired 100% of the outstanding common stock of Shore Corporation for $800,000. On the date of acquisition, the fair value of Shore's net identifiable assets is $820,000. The book value of Shore Corporation's net assets is $760,000. In Lake's 2010 financial statements, Lake should recognize
a. Goodwill on the balance sheet.
b. A gain from bargain purchase.
c. A reduction in certain noncurrent assets on the balance sheet.
d. An extraordinary gain.

9. A business combination is accounted for appropriately as an acquisition. Which of the following should be deducted in determining the combined corporation's net income for the current period?

	Direct costs of acquisition	General expenses related to acquisition
a.	Yes	No
b.	Yes	Yes
c.	No	Yes
d.	No	No

10. Which of the following situations would require the use of the acquisition method in a business combination?
a. The acquisition of a group of assets.
b. The formation of a joint venture.
c. The purchase of more than 50% of a business.
d. All of the above would require the use of the acquisition method.

11. ASC Topic 805 (SFAS 141[R]) sets forth certain steps in accounting for an acquisition. Which of the following is not one of those steps?
    a. Prepare pro forma financial statements prior to acquisition.
    b. Determine the acquisition date.
    c. Identify the acquirer.
    d. Expense the costs and general expenses of the acquisition in the period of acquisition.

12. Kennedy Company is acquiring Ross Company in an acquisition. What date should be used as the acquisition date for the transaction?
    a. The date Kennedy signs the contract to purchase the business.
    b. The date Kennedy obtains control of Ross.
    c. The date that all contingencies related to the transaction are resolved.
    d. The date Kennedy purchased more than 20% of the stock of Ross.

13. Lebow Corp. acquired control of Wilson Corp. by purchasing stock in steps. Which of the following regarding this type of acquisition is true?
    a. The cost of acquisition equals the amount paid for the previously held shares plus the fair value of shares issued at the date of acquisition.
    b. The previously held shares should be remeasured at fair value on the acquisition date, and any gain on previously held shares should be included in other comprehensive income for the period.
    c. The previously held shares should be remeasured at fair value on the acquisition date and the gain recognized in earnings of the period.
    d. The acquisition cost includes only the newly issued shares measured at fair value on the date of acquisition.

14. In accounting for a business combination, which of the following intangibles should not be recognized as an asset apart from goodwill?
    a. Trademarks.
    b. Lease agreements.
    c. Employee quality.
    d. Patents.

15. With respect to the allocation of the cost of a business acquisition, ASC Topic 805 (SFAS 141[R]) requires
    a. Cost to be allocated to the assets based on their carrying values.
    b. Cost to be allocated based on relative fair values.
    c. Cost to be allocated based on original costs.
    d. None of the above.

Items 16 through 20 are based on the following:

On January 1, 2010, Polk Corp. and Strass Corp. had condensed balance sheets as follows:

	Polk	Strass
Current assets	$ 70,000	$20,000
Noncurrent assets	90,000	40,000
Total assets	$160,000	$60,000
Current liabilities	$ 30,000	$10,000
Long-term debt	50,000	--
Stockholders' equity	80,000	50,000
Total liabilities and stockholders' equity	$160,000	$60,000

On January 2, 2010, Polk borrowed $60,000 and used the proceeds to purchase 90% of the outstanding common shares of Strass. This debt is payable in ten equal annual principal payments, plus interest, beginning December 30, 2010. The excess cost of the investment over Strass' book value of acquired net assets should be allocated 60% to inventory and 40% to goodwill. On January 1, 2010, the fair value of Polk shares held by noncontrolling parties was $10,000.

On Polk's January 2, 2010 consolidated balance sheet,

16. Current assets should be
    a. $ 90,000
    b. $ 99,000
    c. $100,000
    d. $102,000

17. Noncurrent assets should be
    a. $130,000
    b. $136,000
    c. $138,000
    d. $140,000

18. Current liabilities should be
    a. $50,000
    b. $46,000
    c. $40,000
    d. $30,000

19. Noncurrent liabilities should be
    a. $115,000
    b. $109,000
    c. $104,000
    d. $ 55,000

20. Stockholders' equity including noncontrolling interests should be
    a. $ 80,000
    b. $ 85,000
    c. $ 90,000
    d. $130,000

21. On November 30, 2010, Parlor, Inc. purchased for cash at $15 per share all 250,000 shares of the outstanding common stock of Shaw Co. At November 30, 2010, Shaw's balance sheet showed a carrying amount of net assets of $3,000,000. At that date, the fair value of Shaw's property, plant and equipment exceeded its carrying amount by $400,000. In its November 30, 2010 consolidated balance sheet, what amount should Parlor report as goodwill?
    a. $750,000
    b. $400,000
    c. $350,000
    d. $0

22. On April 1, 2010, Parson Corp. purchased 80% of the outstanding stock of Sloan Corp. for $700,000 cash. Parson determined that the fair value of the net identifiable assets was $800,000 on the date of acquisition. The fair value of Sloan's stock at date of acquisition was $18 per share. Sloan had a total of 50,000 shares of stock issued and outstanding prior to the acquisition. What is the amount of goodwill that should be recorded by Parson at date of acquisition?
    a. $0
    b. $ 60,000
    c. $ 80,000
    d. $120,000

23. A subsidiary, acquired for cash in a business combination, owned inventories with a market value greater than the book value as of the date of combination. A consolidated balance sheet prepared immediately after the acquisition would include this difference as part of
- a. Deferred credits.
- b. Goodwill.
- c. Inventories.
- d. Retained earnings.

24. Company J acquired all of the outstanding common stock of Company K in exchange for cash. The acquisition price exceeds the fair value of net assets acquired. How should Company J determine the amounts to be reported for the plant and equipment and long-term debt acquired from Company K?

	Plant and equipment	Long-term debt
a.	K's carrying amount	K's carrying amount
b.	K's carrying amount	Fair value
c.	Fair value	K's carrying amount
d.	Fair value	Fair value

25. In a business combination accounted for as an acquisition the appraised values of the identifiable assets acquired exceeded the acquisition price. How should the excess appraised value be reported?
- a. As negative goodwill.
- b. As additional paid-in capital.
- c. As a reduction of the values assigned to certain assets and an extraordinary gain for any unallocated portion.
- d. As a gain in net income for the period.

26. Wright Corp. has several subsidiaries that are included in its consolidated financial statements. In its December 31, 2010 trial balance, Wright had the following intercompany balances before eliminations:

	Debit	Credit
Current receivable due from Main Co.	$ 32,000	
Noncurrent receivable from Main	114,000	
Cash advance to Corn Corp.	6,000	
Cash advance from King Co.		$ 15,000
Intercompany payable to King		101,000

In its December 31, 2010 consolidated balance sheet, what amount should Wright report as intercompany receivables?
- a. $152,000
- b. $146,000
- c. $ 36,000
- d. $0

27. Shep Co. has a receivable from its parent, Pep Co. Should this receivable be separately reported in Shep's balance sheet and in Pep's consolidated balance sheet?

	Shep's balance sheet	Pep's consolidated balance sheet
a.	Yes	No
b.	Yes	Yes
c.	No	No
d.	No	Yes

Items 28 through 30 are based on the following:

Selected information from the separate and consolidated balance sheets and income statements of Pard, Inc. and its subsidiary, Spin Co., as of December 31, 2010, and for the year then ended is as follows:

	Pard	Spin	Consolidated
Balance sheet accounts			
Accounts receivable	$ 26,000	$ 19,000	$ 39,000
Inventory	30,000	25,000	52,000
Investment in Spin	67,000	--	--
Goodwill	--	--	30,000
Noncontrolling interest	--	--	10,000
Stockholders' equity	154,000	50,000	154,000
Income statement accounts			
Revenues	$200,000	$140,000	$308,000
Cost of goods sold	150,000	110,000	231,000
Gross profit	50,000	30,000	77,000
Equity in earnings of Spin	20,000	--	--
Net income	36,000	20,000	40,000

Additional information

- During 2010, Pard sold goods to Spin at the same mark-up on cost that Pard uses for all sales. At December 31, 2010, Spin had not paid for all of these goods and still held 37.5% of them in inventory.
- Pard acquired its interest in Spin on January 2, 2010.

28. What was the amount of intercompany sales from Pard to Spin during 2010?
- a. $ 3,000
- b. $ 6,000
- c. $29,000
- d. $32,000

29. At December 31, 2010, what was the amount of Spin's payable to Pard for intercompany sales?
- a. $ 3,000
- b. $ 6,000
- c. $29,000
- d. $32,000

30. In Pard's consolidated balance sheet, what was the carrying amount of the inventory that Spin purchased from Pard?
- a. $ 3,000
- b. $ 6,000
- c. $ 9,000
- d. $12,000

31. On January 1, 2010, Palm, Inc. purchased 80% of the stock of Stone Corp. for $4,000,000 cash. Prior to the acquisition, Stone had 100,000 shares of stock outstanding. On the date of acquisition, Stone's stock had a fair value of $52 per share. During the year Stone reported $280,000 in net income and paid dividends of $50,000. What is the balance in the noncontrolling interest account on Palm's balance sheet on December 31, 2010?
- a. $1,000,000
- b. $1,040,000
- c. $1,086,000
- d. $1,096,000

32. On January 1, 2010, Owen Corp. purchased all of Sharp Corp.'s common stock for $1,200,000. On that date, the fair values of Sharp's assets and liabilities equaled their carrying amounts of $1,320,000 and $320,000, respectively. During 2010, Sharp paid cash dividends of $20,000.

Selected information from the separate balance sheets and income statements of Owen and Sharp as of December 31, 2010, and for the year then ended follows:

	Owen	Sharp
Balance sheet accounts		
Investment in subsidiary	$1,320,000	--
Retained earnings	1,240,000	560,000
Total stockholders' equity	2,620,000	1,120,000

Income statement accounts	Owen	Sharp
Operating income	420,000	200,000
Equity in earnings of Sharp	140,000	--
Net income	400,000	140,000

In Owen's December 31, 2010 consolidated balance sheet, what amount should be reported as total retained earnings?

    a. $1,240,000
    b. $1,360,000
    c. $1,380,000
    d. $1,800,000

33. When a parent-subsidiary relationship exists, consolidated financial statements are prepared in recognition of the accounting concept of

    a.   Reliability.
    b.   Materiality.
    c.   Legal entity.
    d.   Economic entity.

34. A subsidiary was acquired for cash in a business combination on January 1, 2010. The consideration given exceeded the fair value of identifiable net assets. The acquired company owned equipment with a market value in excess of the carrying amount as of the date of combination. A consolidated balance sheet prepared on December 31, 2010, would

    a.   Report the unamortized portion of the excess of the market value over the carrying amount of the equipment as part of goodwill.
    b.   Report the unamortized portion of the excess of the market value over the carrying amount of the equipment as part of plant and equipment.
    c.   Report the excess of the market value over the carrying amount of the equipment as part of plant and equipment.
    d.   Not report the excess of the market value over the carrying amount of the equipment because it would be expensed in the year of the acquisition.

35. Pride, Inc. owns 80% of Simba, Inc.'s outstanding common stock. Simba, in turn, owns 10% of Pride's outstanding common stock. What percentage of the common stock cash dividends declared by the individual companies should be reported as dividends declared in the consolidated financial statements?

	Dividends declared by Pride	Dividends declared by Simba
a.	90%	0%
b.	90%	20%
c.	100%	0%
d.	100%	20%

36. It is generally presumed that an entity is a variable interest entity subject to consolidation if its equity is

    a.   Less than 50% of total assets.
    b.   Less than 25% of total assets.
    c.   Less than 10% of total assets.
    d.   Less than 10% of total liabilities.

37. Morton Inc., Gilman Co., and Willis Corporation established a special-purpose entity (SPE) to perform leasing activities for the three corporations. If at the time of formation the SPE is determined to be a variable interest entity subject to consolidation, which of the corporations should consolidate the SPE?

    a.   The corporation with the largest interest in the entity.
    b.   The corporation that will absorb a majority of the expected losses if they occur.
    c.   The corporation that has the most voting equity interest.
    d.   Each corporation should consolidate one-third of the SPE.

38. The determination of whether an interest holder must consolidate a variable interest entity is made

    a.   Each reporting period.
    b.   When the interest holder initially gets involved with the variable interest entity.
    c.   Every time the cash flows of the variable interest entity change.
    d.   Interests in variable interest entities are never consolidated.

39. Matt Co. included a foreign subsidiary in its 2010 consolidated financial statements. The subsidiary was acquired in 2006 and was excluded from previous consolidations. The change was caused by the elimination of foreign exchange controls. Including the subsidiary in the 2010 consolidated financial statements results in an accounting change that should be reported

    a.   By footnote disclosure only.
    b.   Currently and prospectively.
    c.   Currently with footnote disclosure of pro forma effects of retroactive application.
    d.   By restating the financial statements of all prior periods presented.

40. On June 30, 2010, Purl Corp. issued 150,000 shares of its $20 par common stock for which it received all of Scott Corp.'s common stock. The fair value of the common stock issued is equal to the book value of Scott Corp.'s net assets. Both corporations continued to operate as separate businesses, maintaining accounting records with years ending December 31. Net income from separate company operations and dividends paid were

	Purl	Scott
Net income		
Six months ended 6/30/10	$750,000	$225,000
Six months ended 12/31/10	825,000	375,000
Dividends paid		
March 25, 2010	950,000	--
November 15, 2010	--	300,000

On December 31, 2010, Scott held in its inventory merchandise acquired from Purl on December 1, 2010, for $150,000, which included a $45,000 markup. In the 2010 consolidated income statement, net income should be reported at

    a. $1,650,000
    b. $1,905,000
    c. $1,950,000
    d. $2,130,000

41. On January 1, 2010, Pane Corp. exchanged 150,000 shares of its $20 par value common stock for all of Sky Corp.'s common stock. At that date, the fair value of Pane's common stock issued was equal to the book value of Sky's net assets. Both corporations continued to operate as separate businesses, maintaining accounting records with years ending December 31. Pane uses the equity method to account for its investment in Sky. Information from separate company operations follows:

	Pane	Sky
Retained earnings— 12/31/09	$3,200,000	$925,000
Net income—six months ended 6/30/10	800,000	275,000
Dividends paid—3/25/10	750,000	--

What amount of retained earnings would Pane report in its June 30, 2010 consolidated balance sheet?

a. $5,200,000
b. $4,450,000
c. $3,525,000
d. $3,250,000

Items 42 and 43 are based on the following:

Scroll, Inc., a wholly owned subsidiary of Pirn, Inc., began operations on January 1, 2010. The following information is from the condensed 2010 income statements of Pirn and Scroll:

	Pirn	Scroll
Sales to Scroll	$100,000	$ --
Sales to others	400,000	300,000
	500,000	300,000
Cost of goods sold:		
Acquired from Pirn	--	80,000
Acquired from others	350,000	190,000
Gross profit	150,000	30,000
Depreciation	40,000	10,000
Other expenses	60,000	15,000
Income from operations	50,000	5,000
Gain on sale of equipment to Scroll	12,000	--
Income before income taxes	$ 62,000	$ 5,000

Additional information

- Sales by Pirn to Scroll are made on the same terms as those made to third parties.
- Equipment purchased by Scroll from Pirn for $36,000 on January 1, 2010, is depreciated using the straight-line method over four years.

42. In Pirn's December 31, 2010, consolidating worksheet, how much intercompany profit should be eliminated from Scroll's inventory?

a. $30,000
b. $20,000
c. $10,000
d. $ 6,000

43. What amount should be reported as depreciation expense in Pirn's 2010 consolidated income statement?

a. $50,000
b. $47,000
c. $44,000
d. $41,000

44. Clark Co. had the following transactions with affiliated parties during 2010:

- Sales of $60,000 to Dean, Inc., with $20,000 gross profit. Dean had $15,000 of this inventory on hand at year-end. Clark owns a 15% interest in Dean and does not exert significant influence.
- Purchases of raw materials totaling $240,000 from Kent Corp., a wholly owned subsidiary. Kent's gross profit on the sale was $48,000. Clark had $60,000 of this inventory remaining on December 31, 2010.

Before eliminating entries, Clark had consolidated current assets of $320,000. What amount should Clark report in its

December 31, 2010 consolidated balance sheet for current assets?

a. $320,000
b. $317,000
c. $308,000
d. $303,000

45. Parker Corp. owns 80% of Smith Inc.'s common stock. During 2010, Parker sold Smith $250,000 of inventory on the same terms as sales made to third parties. Smith sold all of the inventory purchased from Parker in 2010. The following information pertains to Smith and Parker's sales for 2010:

	Parker	Smith
Sales	$1,000,000	$700,000
Cost of sales	400,000	350,000
	$ 600,000	$350,000

What amount should Parker report as cost of sales in its 2010 consolidated income statement?

a. $750,000
b. $680,000
c. $500,000
d. $430,000

46. Selected information from the separate and consolidated balance sheets and income statements of Pare, Inc. and its subsidiary, Shel Co., as of December 31, 2010, and for the year then ended is as follows:

	Pare	Shel	Consolidated
Balance sheet accounts			
Accounts receivable	$ 52,000	$ 38,000	$ 78,000
Inventory	60,000	50,000	104,000
Income statement accounts			
Revenues	$400,000	$280,000	$616,000
Cost of goods sold	300,000	220,000	462,000
Gross profit	$100,000	$ 60,000	$154,000

Additional information:

During 2010, Pare sold goods to Shel at the same markup on cost that Pare uses for all sales.

In Pare's consolidating worksheet, what amount of unrealized intercompany profit was eliminated?

a. $ 6,000
b. $12,000
c. $58,000
d. $64,000

47. During 2010, Pard Corp. sold goods to its 80%-owned subsidiary, Seed Corp. At December 31, 2010, one-half of these goods were included in Seed's ending inventory. Reported 2010 selling expenses were $1,100,000 and $400,000 for Pard and Seed, respectively. Pard's selling expenses included $50,000 in freight-out costs for goods sold to Seed. What amount of selling expenses should be reported in Pard's 2010 consolidated income statement?

a. $1,500,000
b. $1,480,000
c. $1,475,000
d. $1,450,000

48. On January 1, 2010, Poe Corp. sold a machine for $900,000 to Saxe Corp., its wholly owned subsidiary. Poe paid $1,100,000 for this machine, which had accumulated depreciation of $250,000. Poe estimated a $100,000 salvage value and depreciated the machine on the straight-line method over twenty years, a policy which Saxe continued. In

Poe's December 31, 2010 consolidated balance sheet, this machine should be included in cost and accumulated depreciation as

	Cost	Accumulated depreciation
a.	$1,100,000	$300,000
b.	$1,100,000	$290,000
c.	$ 900,000	$ 40,000
d.	$ 850,000	$ 42,500

49. Wagner, a holder of a $1,000,000 Palmer, Inc. bonds, collected the interest due on March 31, 2010, and then sold the bonds to Seal, Inc. for $975,000. On that date, Palmer, a 75% owner of Seal, had a $1,075,000 carrying amount for the bonds. What was the effect of Seal's purchase of Palmer's bond on the retained earnings and noncontrolling interest amounts reported in Palmer's March 31, 2010 consolidated balance sheet?

	Retained earnings	Noncontrolling interest
a.	$100,000 increase	$0
b.	$ 75,000 increase	$ 25,000 increase
c.	$0	$ 25,000 increase
d.	$0	$100,000 increase

50. Sun, Inc. is a wholly owned subsidiary of Patton, Inc. On June 1, 2010, Patton declared and paid a $1 per share cash dividend to stockholders of record on May 15, 2010. On May 1, 2010, Sun bought 10,000 shares of Patton's common stock for $700,000 on the open market, when the book value per share was $30. What amount of gain should Patton report from this transaction in its consolidated income statement for the year ended December 31, 2010?

a. $0
b. $390,000
c. $400,000
d. $410,000

51. Perez, Inc. owns 80% of Senior, Inc. During 2010, Perez sold goods with a 40% gross profit to Senior. Senior sold all of these goods in 2010. For 2010 consolidated financial statements, how should the summation of Perez and Senior income statement items be adjusted?

a. Sales and cost of goods sold should be reduced by the intercompany sales.
b. Sales and cost of goods sold should be reduced by 80% of the intercompany sales.
c. Net income should be reduced by 80% of the gross profit on intercompany sales.
d. No adjustment is necessary.

52. Winston Co. owns 80% of the outstanding common stock of Foster Co. On December 31, 2009, Winston sold equipment to Foster at a price in excess of Winston's carrying amount, but less than its original cost. On a consolidated balance sheet at December 31, 2009, the carrying amount of the equipment should be reported at

a. Foster's original cost.
b. Winston's original cost.
c. Foster's original cost less Winston's recorded gain.
d. Foster's original cost less 80% of Winston's recorded gain.

53. Port, Inc. owns 100% of Salem, Inc. On January 1, 2010, Port sold Salem delivery equipment at a gain. Port had owned the equipment for two years and used a five-year straight-line depreciation rate with no residual value. Salem is using a three-year straight-line depreciation rate with no

residual value for the equipment. In the consolidated income statement, Salem's recorded depreciation expense on the equipment for 2010 will be decreased by

a. 20% of the gain on sale.
b. 33 1/3% of the gain on sale.
c. 50% of the gain on sale.
d. 100% of the gain on sale.

54. P Co. purchased term bonds at a premium on the open market. These bonds represented 20% of the outstanding class of bonds issued at a discount by S Co., P's wholly owned subsidiary. P intends to hold the bonds until maturity. In a consolidated balance sheet, the difference between the bond carrying amounts in the two companies would

a. Decrease retained earnings.
b. Increase retained earnings.
c. Be reported as a deferred debit to be amortized over the remaining life of the bonds.
d. Be reported as a deferred credit to be amortized over the remaining life of the bonds.

55. Planet Company acquired a 70% interest in the Star Company in 2009. For the year ended December 31, 2010, Star reported net income of $80,000. During 2010, Planet sold merchandise to Star for $10,000 at a profit of $2,000. The merchandise remained in Star's inventory at the end of 2010. For consolidation purposes what is the noncontrolling interest's share of Star's net income for 2010?

a. $23,400
b. $24,000
c. $24,600
d. $26,000

Items 56 and 57 are based on the following:

On January 1, 2010, Ritt Corp. purchased 80% of Shaw Corp.'s $10 par common stock for $975,000. On this date, the carrying amount of Shaw's net assets was $1,000,000. The fair values of Shaw's identifiable assets and liabilities were the same as their carrying amounts except for plant assets (net) with fair values of $100,000 in excess of their carrying amount. The fair value of the noncontrolling interest in Shaw on January 1, 2010, was $250,000. For the year ended December 31, 2010, Shaw had net income of $190,000 and paid cash dividends totaling $125,000.

56. In the January 1, 2010 consolidated balance sheet, goodwill should be reported at

a. $0
b. $ 75,000
c. $ 95,000
d. $125,000

57. In the December 31, 2010 consolidated balance sheet, noncontrolling interest should be reported at

a. $200,000
b. $213,000
c. $233,000
d. $263,000

Items 58 through 60 are based on the following:

On January 2, 2010, Pare Co. purchased 75% of Kidd Co.'s outstanding common stock. On that date, the fair value of the 25% noncontrolling interest was $35,000. During 2010, Kidd had net income of $20,000. Selected balance sheet data at December 31, 2010, is as follows:

	Pare	*Kidd*
Total assets	$420,000	$180,000
Liabilities	$120,000	$ 60,000
Common stock	100,000	50,000
Retained earnings	200,000	70,000
	$420,000	$180,000

During 2010 Pare and Kidd paid cash dividends of $25,000 and $5,000, respectively, to their shareholders. There were no other intercompany transactions.

58. In its December 31, 2010 consolidated statement of retained earnings, what amount should Pare report as dividends paid?
- a. $ 5,000
- b. $25,000
- c. $26,250
- d. $30,000

59. In Pare's December 31, 2010 consolidated balance sheet, what amount should be reported as noncontrolling interest in net assets?
- a. $30,000
- b. $35,000
- c. $38,750
- d. $40,000

60. In its December 31, 2010 consolidated balance sheet, what amount should Pare report as common stock?
- a. $ 50,000
- b. $100,000
- c. $137,500
- d. $150,000

61. In a business acquisition, consideration transferred includes which of the following?

I.   The fair value of assets transferred by the acquirer.
II. The fair value of the liabilities incurred by the acquirer.
III. The fair value of contingent consideration transferred by the acquirer.
IV. The fair value of the equity interests issued by the acquirer as a part of the acquisition.
V.   The fair value of share-based payments voluntarily exchanged for outstanding share-based payment awards of the acquiree.

- a. I and II.
- b. I, II, and IV.
- c. I, II, IV, and V.
- d. I, II, III, and IV.

62. On June 30, 2010, Wyler Corporation acquires Boston Corporation in a transaction properly accounted for as a business acquisition. At the time of the acquisition, some of the information for valuing assets was incomplete. How should Corporation Wyler, account for the incomplete information in preparing its financial statements immediately after the acquisition?
- a. Do not record the uncertain items until complete information is available.
- b. Record a contra account to the investment account for the amounts involved.
- c. Record the uncertain items at the book value of the acquiree.
- d. Record the uncertain items at a provisional amount measured at the date of acquisition.

63. When does the measurement period end for a business combination in which there was incomplete accounting information on the date of acquisition?
- a. When the acquirer receives the information or one year from the acquisition date, whichever occurs earlier.
- b. On the final date when all contingencies are resolved.
- c. Thirty days from the date of acquisition.
- d. At the end of the reporting period in the year of acquisition.

64. Ross Corporation recorded a provisional amount for an identifiable asset at the date of its acquisition of Layton Inc. because the asset's fair value was uncertain. Before the measurement period ends, Ross obtains new information that indicates that the asset was overvalued by $20,000. How should Ross report the effects of this new information?
- a. As an expense in the current period income statement.
- b. As an extraordinary loss on the current period income statement.
- c. As a reduction in recorded goodwill.
- d. As a gain from bargain purchase.

65. Able Corp. acquires Bailey Company in a transaction that is properly accounted for as a business acquisition. The acquisition contract and Bailey's share-based compensation agreement require Able stock to be exchanged for Bailey common stock issued to Bailey's employees as share-based payments. No further service is required by the employees of Bailey to qualify for the replacement awards. How should Able account for the shares of stock issued as replacement awards to employees of Bailey?
- a. As a cost of acquisition.
- b. As an expense in the current period.
- c. As a loss in the current period.
- d. As an extraordinary loss in the period.

66. On January 1, 2010, Post Inc. acquires Sam Company in a transaction properly accounted for as a business combination. Sam's employees have share-based payments that will expire as a consequence of the business combination. In order to maintain employee morale, Post voluntarily replaces the awards to employees 30 days after the date of acquisition. How should Post account for the replacement awards given to Sam's employees?
- a. Post should include the fair value of the awards as consideration paid in the cost of acquisition.
- b. Post should recognize compensation expense for the value of the awards in the postcombination financial statements.
- c. Post should recognize an extraordinary loss for the fair value of the replacement awards in its financial statements.
- d. Post should capitalize the cost of the awards and amortize the cost over the remaining service years of the employees.

67. When should an acquirer derecognize a contingent liability recognized as the result of an acquisition?
- a. When it becomes more likely than not that the firm will not be liable.
- b. When the contingency is resolved.
- c. At the end of the year of acquisition.
- d. When it is reasonably possible that the liability will not require payment.

68. On September 1, 2009 Phillips, Inc. issued common stock in exchange for 20% of Sago, Inc.'s outstanding common stock. On July 1, 2010, Phillips issued common stock for an additional 75% of Sago's outstanding common stock. Sago continues in existence as Phillips' subsidiary. How much of Sago's 2010 net income should be reported as attributable to Phillips?

    a. 20% of Sago's net income to June 30 and all of Sago's net income from July 1 to December 31.
    b. 20% of Sago's net income to June 30 and 95% of Sago's net income from July 1 to December 31.
    c. 95% of Sago's net income.
    d. All of Sago's net income.

69. Mr. & Mrs. Dart own a majority of the outstanding capital stock of Wall Corp., Black Co., and West, Inc. During 2010, Wall advanced cash to Black and West in the amount of $50,000 and $80,000, respectively. West advanced $70,000 in cash to Black. At December 31, 2010, none of the advances was repaid. In the combined December 31, 2010 balance sheet of these companies, what amount would be reported as receivables from affiliates?

    a. $200,000
    b. $130,000
    c. $ 60,000
    d. $0

70. Selected data for two subsidiaries of Dunn Corp. taken from December 31, 2010 preclosing trial balances are as follows:

	Banks Co. debit	Lamm Co. credit
Shipments to Banks	$ --	$150,000
Shipments from Lamm	200,000	--
Intercompany inventory profit on total shipments	--	50,000

Additional data relating to the December 31, 2010 inventory are as follows:

Inventory acquired from outside parties	$175,000	$250,000
Inventory acquired from Lamm	60,000	--

At December 31, 2010, the inventory reported on the combined balance sheet of the two subsidiaries should be

    a. $425,000
    b. $435,000
    c. $470,000
    d. $485,000

71. Ahm Corp. owns 90% of Bee Corp.'s common stock and 80% of Cee Corp.'s common stock. The remaining common shares of Bee and Cee are owned by their respective employees. Bee sells exclusively to Cee, Cee buys exclusively from Bee, and Cee sells exclusively to unrelated companies. Selected 2010 information for Bee and Cee follows:

	Bee Corp.	Cee Corp.
Sales	$130,000	$91,000
Cost of sales	100,000	65,000
Beginning inventory	None	None
Ending inventory	None	65,000

What amount should be reported as gross profit in Bee and Cee's combined income statement for the year ended December 31, 2010?

    a. $26,000
    b. $41,000

    c. $47,800
    d. $56,000

72. The following information pertains to shipments of merchandise from Home Office to Branch during 2010:

Home Office's cost of merchandise	$160,000
Intracompany billing	200,000
Sales by Branch	250,000
Unsold merchandise at Branch on December 31, 2010	20,000

In the combined income statement of Home Office and Branch for the year ended December 31, 2010, what amount of the above transactions should be included in sales?

    a. $250,000
    b. $230,000
    c. $200,000
    d. $180,000

73. Mr. and Mrs. Gasson own 100% of the common stock of Able Corp. and 90% of the common stock of Baker Corp. Able previously paid $4,000 for the remaining 10% interest in Baker. The condensed December 31, 2010 balance sheets of Able and Baker are as follows:

	Able	Baker
Assets	$600,000	$60,000
Liabilities	$200,000	$30,000
Common stock	100,000	20,000
Retained earnings	300,000	10,000
	$600,000	$60,000

In a combined balance sheet of the two corporations at December 31, 2010, what amount should be reported as total stockholders' equity?

    a. $430,000
    b. $426,000
    c. $403,000
    d. $400,000

74. Mr. Cord owns four corporations. Combined financial statements are being prepared for these corporations, which have intercompany loans of $200,000 and intercompany profits of $500,000. What amount of these intercompany loans and profits should be included in the combined financial statements?

	Intercompany	
	Loans	Profits
a.	$200,000	$0
b.	$200,000	$500,000
c.	$0	$0
d.	$0	$500,000

75. Combined statements may be used to present the results of operations of

	Companies under common management	Commonly controlled companies
a.	No	Yes
b.	Yes	No
c.	No	No
d.	Yes	Yes

76. Which of the following items should be treated in the same manner in both combined financial statements and consolidated statements?

	Income taxes	Noncontrolling interest
a.	No	No
b.	No	Yes

c.	Yes	Yes
d.	Yes	No

77. Which of the following items should be treated in the same manner in both combined financial statements and consolidated statements?

	Different fiscal periods	*Foreign operations*
a.	No	No
b.	No	Yes
c.	Yes	Yes
d.	Yes	No

SIMULATION PROBLEMS

Simulation Problem 1   (50 to 60 minutes)

Situation					
	Concepts	**Journal Entries**	**Financial Statement Amounts**	**Communication**	**Research**

Presented below are selected amounts from the separate unconsolidated financial statements of Poe Corp. and its 90%-owned subsidiary, Shaw Co., at December 31, 2010. Additional information follows:

	Poe	Shaw
Selected income statement amounts		
Sales	$710,000	$530,000
Cost of goods sold	490,000	370,000
Gain on sale of equipment	--	21,000
Earnings from investment in subsidiary	63,000	--
Interest expense	--	16,000
Depreciation	25,000	20,000
Selected balance sheet amounts		
Cash	$ 50,000	$ 15,000
Inventories	229,000	150,000
Equipment	440,000	360,000
Accumulated depreciation	(200,000)	(120,000)
Investment in Shaw	191,000	--
Investment in Shaw bonds	100,000	--
Discount on bonds	(9,000)	--
Bonds payable	--	(200,000)
Common stock	(100,000)	(10,000)
Additional paid-in capital	(250,000)	(40,000)
Retained earnings	(404,000)	(140,000)
Selected statement of retained earnings amounts		
Beginning balance, December 31, 2009	$272,000	$100,000
Net income	212,000	70,000
Dividends paid	80,000	30,000

Additional information

- On January 2, 2010, Poe, Inc. purchased 90% of Shaw Co.'s 100,000 outstanding common stock for cash of $155,000. On that date the fair value of the noncontrolling interest was $1.70 per share. On that date, Shaw's stockholders' equity equaled $150,000 and the fair values of Shaw's identifiable assets and liabilities equaled their carrying amounts. Poe has accounted for the purchase as an acquisition.
- On January 3, 2010, Poe sold equipment with an original cost of $30,000 and a carrying value of $15,000 to Shaw for $36,000. The equipment had a remaining life of three years and was depreciated using the straight-line method by both companies.
- During 2010, Poe sold merchandise to Shaw for $60,000, which included a profit of $20,000. At December 31, 2010, half of this merchandise remained in Shaw's inventory.
- On December 31, 2010, Poe paid $91,000 to purchase 50% of the outstanding bonds issued by Shaw. The bonds mature on December 31, 2014, and were originally issued at par. The bonds pay interest annually on December 31 of each year, and the interest was paid to the prior investor immediately before Poe's purchase of the bonds.
- On September 4, 2010, Shaw paid cash dividends of $30,000.
- On December 31, 2010, Poe recorded its equity in Shaw's earnings.

	Concepts				
Situation		**Journal Entries**	**Financial Statement Amounts**	**Communication**	**Research**

Items 1 through 12 below refer to accounts that may or may not be included in Poe and Shaw's consolidated financial statements. The list below refers to the various possibilities of those amounts to be reported in Poe's consolidated financial statements for the year ended December 31, 2010. Consider all transactions stated in items 1 through 4 in determining your answer. Ignore income tax considerations.

Responses to be selected

A. Sum of amounts on Poe and Shaw's separate unconsolidated financial statements
B. Less than the sum of amounts on Poe and Shaw's separate unconsolidated financial statements but not the same as the amount on either
C. Same as amount for Poe only
D. Same as amount for Shaw only
E. Eliminated entirely in consolidation
F. Shown in consolidated financial statements but not in separate unconsolidated financial statements
G. Neither in consolidated nor in separate unconsolidated financial statements

		(A)	(B)	(C)	(D)	(E)	(F)	(G)
1.	Cash	O	O	O	O	O	O	O
2.	Equipment	O	O	O	O	O	O	O
3.	Investment in subsidiary	O	O	O	O	O	O	O
4.	Bonds payable	O	O	O	O	O	O	O
5.	Noncontrolling interest	O	O	O	O	O	O	O
6.	Common stock	O	O	O	O	O	O	O
7.	Beginning retained earnings	O	O	O	O	O	O	O
8.	Dividends paid	O	O	O	O	O	O	O
9.	Gain on retirement of bonds	O	O	O	O	O	O	O
10.	Cost of goods sold	O	O	O	O	O	O	O
11.	Interest expense	O	O	O	O	O	O	O
12.	Depreciation expense	O	O	O	O	O	O	O

Situation	Concepts	Journal Entries	Financial Statement Amounts	Communication	Research

Items 1 through 3 below represent transactions between Poe and Shaw during 2010. Prepare the eliminating entries in general journal format for each of these transactions.

1. On January 3, 2010, Poe sold equipment with an original cost of $30,000 and a carrying value of $15,000 to Shaw for $36,000. The equipment had a remaining life of three years and was depreciated using the straight-line method by both companies.

2. During 2010, Poe sold merchandise to Shaw for $60,000, which included a profit of $20,000. At December 31, 2010, half of this merchandise remained in Shaw's inventory.

3. On December 31, 2010, Poe paid $91,000 to purchase 50% of the outstanding bonds issued by Shaw. The bonds mature on December 31, 2014, and were originally issued at par. The bonds pay interest annually on December 31 of each year, and the interest was paid to the prior investor immediately before Poe's purchase of the bonds.

Situation	Concepts	Journal Entries	Financial Statement Amounts	Communication	Research

Calculate the amounts that will appear on Poe's consolidated financial statement on December 31, 2010.

1. Cash
2. Goodwill
3. Equipment
4. Common stock
5. Investment in Shaw
6. Dividends
7. Bonds payable
8. Noncontrolling interest

Situation	Concepts	Journal Entries	Financial Statement Amounts	Communication	Research

Write a brief memo to the CEO of Poe Corporation explaining the various accounting methods for investments in other company's stock and the rationale for consolidated financial statements.

REMINDER: Your response will be graded for both technical content and writing skills. Technical content will be evaluated for information that is helpful to the intended reader and clearly relevant to the issue. Writing skills will be evaluated for development, organization, and the appropriate expression of ideas in professional correspondence. Use a standard business memo or letter format with a clear beginning, middle, and end. Do not convey information in the form of a table, bullet point list, or other abbreviated presentation.

To: CEO, Poe Corporation
From: CPA Candidate
Re: Consolidated Financial Statements

Situation	Concepts	Journal Entries	Financial Statement Amounts	Communication	Research

Research the following issues. Cut and paste the appropriate sections of professional standards.

1. What method of accounting is used to record a business combination?

2. In a business combination, what is the definition of goodwill?

3. At what amount should the assets, liabilities, and noncontrolling interest of the acquiree be recorded?

Simulation Problem 2   (45 to 55 minutes)

Situation	Concepts	Consolidation at Date of Acquisition	Intercompany Transactions & Eliminations	Consolidation at Year-End	Communication	Research

On January 1, 2010, Arcelia Corporation acquired Gavino corporation by purchasing 100% of the stock of Gavino in exchange for 20,000 shares of Arcelia stock. On the date of acquisition Arcelia stock traded for $18 per share on the stock exchange.

The book values of each company on January 1, 2010, are shown below.

	Arcelia Corp.	Gavino Corp.
Current assets	$320,000	70,000
Noncurrent assets	640,000	380,000
Current liabilities	210,000	50,000
Noncurrent liabilities	150,000	90,000
Owners' equity	600,000	310,000

Additional information

- The fair market value of Gavino's inventory is $10,000 higher than the book value.
- During 2010, the following transactions occurred:

1. Arcelia sold inventory to Gavino for $50,000 on account. The normal profit on sales for Arcelia is 40%. At December 31, 2010, Gavino had 20% of the goods remaining in ending inventory. At December 31, 2010, Gavino had not paid Arcelia for $8,000 of the inventory.
2. On October 1, 2010, Gavino Corp. sold equipment to Arcelia for $24,000. The equipment was purchased by Gavino on 1/1/07 for $60,000 and was depreciated straight-line over five years with no salvage value. Arcelia depreciated the new equipment over three years with no salvage value.

- During 2010, Arcelia did not make entries to record the income of Gavino.
- At December 31, 2010, totals from the preclosing trial balances of both firms are as follows:

Arcelia Corporation & Subsidiaries
UNADJUSTED TRIAL BALANCE
December 31, 2010

	Arcelia Corp.	Gavino Corp.
Revenues	1,000,000	400,000
Expenses	780,000	335,000
Current assets	400,000	110,000
Noncurrent assets	1,260,000	420,000
Current liabilities	300,000	70,000
Noncurrent liabilities	180,000	85,000
Owners' equity	960,000	310,000

Situation	Concepts	Consolidation at Date of Acquisition	Intercompany Transactions & Eliminations	Consolidation at Year-End	Communication	Research

Answer True or False to each of the following questions by checking the correct box.

		True	*False*
1.	A company can use either the purchase or the pooling method for business combinations.	○	○
2.	Total revenues for a consolidated entity are calculated by adding the total revenue of the parent for the year and the total revenue of the subsidiary from the date of acquisition.	○	○
3.	Goodwill is amortized over a period of forty years.	○	○
4.	Goodwill is classified and included with other intangible assets for purposes of measuring impairment.	○	○
5.	Intangible assets with indefinite lives are not amortized.	○	○
6.	The stockholder equity accounts in the consolidated balance sheet are those of the parent company.	○	○
7.	The effect of unrealized profits and sales between the acquirer and acquiree is subsidiaries is classified as an intercompany transaction and must be eliminated.	○	○
8.	A newly identified intangible asset must meet the contractual legal or the separability criterion to be recognized as an intangible asset at the time of consolidation.	○	○

Situation	Concepts	Consolidation at Date of Acquisition	Intercompany Transactions & Eliminations	Consolidation at Year-End	Communication	Research

Calculate each of the following balance sheet amounts for Arcelia Corporation immediately following the acquisition of Gavino.

Total current assets	
Total noncurrent assets	
Total current liabilities	
Total noncurrent liabilities	
Total owners' equity	

Situation	Concepts	Consolidation at Date of Acquisition	Intercompany Transactions & Eliminations	Consolidation at Year-End	Communication	Research

Below is a consolidation worksheet dated December 31, 2010 (before closing the books of Arcelia and Gavino). Prepare the following worksheet with working paper eliminations and entries.

Arcelia Corporation
CONSOLIDATION WORKSHEET
December 31, 2010

	Arcelia Corp.	Gavino Corp.	Elimination entries Debit	Elimination entries Credit	End balance
Revenues	1,000,000	400,000			
Expenses	780,000	335,000			
Current assets	400,000	110,000			
Noncurrent assets	1,260,000	420,000			
Current liabilities	300,000	70,000			
Noncurrent liabilities	180,000	85,000			
Owners' equity	960,000	310,000			

Situation	Concepts	Consolidation at Date of Acquisition	Intercompany Transactions & Eliminations	Consolidation at Year-End	Communication	Research

Indicate the balances of each of the following that will be found on the 2010 financial statements after all consolidation entries have been made and the books have been closed.

Arcelia Corporation & Subsidiaries
CONSOLIDATED BALANCES
December 31, 2010

Total revenues	
Total expenses	
Total current assets	
Total noncurrent assets	
Total current liabilities	
Total noncurrent liabilities	
Total owners' equity	

Situation	Concepts	Consolidation at Date of Acquisition	Intercompany Transactions & Eliminations	Consolidation at Year-End	Communication	Research

The CEO of Arcelia has inquired as to why the acquisition cost of Gavino could exceed the book value of the assets. Explain the valuation methods for acquiring the firm, the concept of goodwill, and how assets of the newly acquired subsidiary are recorded on the financial statements. Explain the calculation of goodwill and whether subsequent entries are necessary in accounting for goodwill.

REMINDER: Your response will be graded for both technical content and writing skills. Technical content will be evaluated for information that is helpful to the intended reader and clearly relevant to the issue. Writing skills will be evaluated for development, organization, and the appropriate expression of ideas in professional correspondence. Use a standard business memo or letter format with a clear beginning, middle, and end. Do not convey information in the form of a table, bullet point list, or other abbreviated presentation.

To: CEO, Arcelia Corporation
From: CPA Candidate
Re: Valuation of acquired firm

Situation	Concepts	Consolidation at Date of Acquisition	Intercompany Transactions & Eliminations	Consolidation at Year-End	Communication	Research

What is an intercompany transaction and how should it be treated for financial reporting purposes?

Simulation Problem 3   (10 to 20 minutes)

On January 2, 2010, Purl Co. purchased 90% of Strand Co.'s outstanding common stock at a purchase price that was in excess of Strand's stockholders' equity. On that date, the fair value of Strand's assets and liabilities equaled their carrying amounts. Purl has accounted for the purchase as a business acquisition. Transactions during 2010 were as follows:

- On February 15, 2010, Purl sold equipment to Strand at a price higher than the equipment's carrying amount. The equipment has a remaining life of three years and was depreciated using the straight-line method by both companies.
- During 2010, Purl sold merchandise to Strand under the same terms it offered to third parties. At December 31, 2010, one-third of this merchandise remained in Strand's inventory.
- On November 15, 2010, both Purl and Strand paid cash dividends to their respective stockholders.
- On December 31, 2010, Purl recorded its equity in Strand's earnings.

Situation	Financial Statement Amounts

Items 1 through 10 relate to accounts that may or may not be included in Purl and Strand's consolidated financial statements. The list below refers to the possible ways those accounts may be reported in Purl's consolidated financial statements for the year ended December 31, 2010. An answer may be selected once, more than once, or not at all.

Responses to be selected

A. Sum of the amounts on Purl and Strand's separate unconsolidated financial statements
B. Less than the sum of the amounts on Purl and Strand's separate unconsolidated financial statements, but not the same as the amount on either separate unconsolidated financial statement
C. Same as the amount for Purl only
D. Same as the amount for Strand only
E. Eliminated entirely in consolidation
F. Shown in the consolidated financial statements but not in the separate unconsolidated financial statements

	(A)	(B)	(C)	(D)	(E)	(F)
1. Cash	○	○	○	○	○	○
2. Equipment	○	○	○	○	○	○
3. Investment in subsidiary	○	○	○	○	○	○
4. Noncontrolling interest	○	○	○	○	○	○
5. Common stock	○	○	○	○	○	○
6. Beginning retained earnings	○	○	○	○	○	○
7. Dividends paid	○	○	○	○	○	○
8. Cost of goods sold	○	○	○	○	○	○
9. Interest expense	○	○	○	○	○	○
10. Depreciation expense	○	○	○	○	○	○

MULTIPLE-CHOICE ANSWERS

1. a	17. c	33. d	49. a	65. a
2. b	18. b	34. b	50. a	66. b
3. a	19. c	35. a	51. a	67. b
4. d	20. c	36. c	52. c	68. b
5. d	21. c	37. b	53. b	69. d
6. c	22. c	38. b	54. c	70. c
7. c	23. c	39. d	55. b	71. b
8. b	24. d	40. b	56. d	72. a
9. b	25. d	41. d	57. d	73. b
10. c	26. d	42. d	58. b	74. c
11. a	27. a	43. b	59. c	75. d
12. b	28. d	44. c	60. b	76. c
13. c	29. b	45. c	61. d	77. c
14. c	30. c	46. a	62. d	
15. b	31. c	47. d	63. a	1st: __/77 = __%
16. d	32. a	48. a	64. c	2nd: __/77 = __%

MULTIPLE-CHOICE ANSWER EXPLANATIONS

A. Accounting for the Combination, and Sections A. – C.

1. (a) In an acquisition, the net assets of the acquired firm are recorded at their FV. The excess of the cost of the investment over the FV of the net assets acquired is allocated to goodwill. The cost of the investment is $620,000, and the FV of the net assets acquired, **excluding goodwill**, is $470,000, as computed below.

	FMV
Cash	$ 60,000
Inventory (BV = $180,000)	150,000
Prop. and equip. (BV = $320,000)	380,000
Liabilities	(120,000)
Total FV	$470,000

Therefore, the amount allocated to goodwill is $150,000 ($620,000 – $470,000).

2. (b) Acquisition costs such as finder's fees are expensed in the period incurred. Registration fees for equity securities are a reduction in the issue price of the securities. Therefore, answer (b) is correct.

3. (a) In a business combination accounted for as an acquisition, the fair market value of the net assets is used as the valuation basis for the combination. In this case, the net assets of the subsidiary have an implied fair market value of $3,600,000 which is the value of the common stock issued to Pine's shareholders (100,000 shares × $36). The direct cost of acquisition should not be included as part of the cost of a company acquired, and the cost of registering equity securities should be a reduction of the issue price of the securities (i.e., additional paid-in capital). Thus, the $160,000 paid for a consultant who arranged the acquisition should be expensed, and the $80,000 cost for registering and issuing the equity securities should be treated as a reduction of additional paid-in capital. Answer (a) is correct because the total amount to be capitalized is $3,600,000.

4. (d) In a business combination accounted for as an acquisition, the fair market value of the net assets is used as the valuation basis for the combination. In this case, the net assets of the subsidiary have an implied fair market value of $3,600,000 which is the value of the common stock issued to Saxe's shareholders (200,000 × $18). Since $3,600,000 is the basis for recording this purchase, the common stock is-

sued is recorded at $2,000,000 (200,000 shares × $10 par value per share) and additional paid-in capital is recorded at $1,600,000 ($3,600,000 – $2,000,000). Therefore, answer (d) is correct because additional paid-in capital should be reported at $2,900,000 ($1,300,000 + $1,600,000).

5. (d) In a business combination, the common stock account of the combined entity is the number of shares outstanding multiplied by the par value of the stock. The total common stock account of the combined entity is equal to $5,000,000, the $3,000,000 originally outstanding plus the total par value of the stock issued in the acquisition, $2,000,000 (200,000 × $10).

6. (c) In a business combination accounted for as an acquisition, the fair market value of the net assets is used as the valuation basis for the combination. In this case, Frey's assets have an implied fair market value of $1,900,000 which is the market value of the common stock issue (100,000 shares × $19). The value assigned to goodwill is $70,000, which is the value of the stock minus the fair value of Frey's identifiable assets ($1,900,000 – $1,830,000).

7. (c) A subsidiary should not be consolidated when control is likely to be temporary. Consolidation of all majority-owned subsidiaries is required regardless of the industry or business of the subsidiary. A difference in fiscal periods of a parent and a subsidiary does not of itself justify the exclusion of the subsidiary from consolidation.

8. (b) The consideration paid plus the fair value of the noncontrolling interest plus the fair value of any previous purchases of common stock is less than the fair value of the net identifiable assets acquired, the acquirer should recognize a gain from bargain purchase on the income statement. The gain would be equal to $20,000 ($820,000 – 800,000). Answer (a) is incorrect because goodwill is only recognized when the purchase price is greater than the fair value of the recorded assets. Answer (c) is incorrect because it describes an inappropriate method. Answer (d) is incorrect because the gain is not treated as extraordinary.

9. (b) The direct costs of acquisition should be an expense of the period in a business combination accounted for by the acquisition method. General expenses related to the acquisition are also deducted as incurred in determining the combined corporation's net income for the current period.

10. **(c)**   Answer (c) is correct because the acquisition method applies only to acquisitions of a business. Answers (a), (b), and (d) are incorrect because none of these situations would constitute an acquisition,

11. **(a)**   Preparing pro forma financial statements prior to acquisition is not required in the application of the acquisition method. Answers (b) and (c) are incorrect because identifying the acquirer and determining the acquisition date are both steps in applying the acquisition method. Answer (d) is incorrect because direct costs of acquisitions and general expenses related to an acquisition should be expensed in the period of acquisition.

12. **(b)**   The acquisition date is the date the acquirer obtains control of the acquiree. Answer (a) is incorrect because the date a contract is signed usually does not correspond with the date control is acquired. Answer (c) is incorrect because the acquisition may occur before all contingencies are resolved. Answer (d) is incorrect because control constitutes owning more than 50% of the shares of stock outstanding.

13. **(c)**   Any previously held shares should be remeasured at fair value as of the date control is acquired, and the gain is recognized in earnings of the period. If an unrealized gain was previously recognized in other comprehensive income, the amount recognized in other comprehensive income should also be recognized as a gain in the current period. Answer (a) is incorrect because previously held shares are remeasured to fair value on the acquisition date. Answer (b) is incorrect because any gain is recognized in earnings of the period. Answer (d) is incorrect because the previously issued shares must be revalued at the acquisition date and included as part of the cost of the acquisition.

14. **(c)**   Intangibles are recognized as assets apart from goodwill if they arise from contractual or legal rights, regardless of whether those rights are transferable or separable from the acquired entity or from other rights and obligations. If an intangible asset does not arise from contractual or other legal rights, it is recognized as an asset apart from goodwill only if it is separable (i.e., capable of being sold, transferred, or licensed). Trademarks, lease agreements, and patents all arise from contractual or legal rights. Employee quality does not and is not separable.

15. **(b)**   The acquisition method is required for all business combinations. In applying the acquisition method, the acquisition cost is allocated to acquired assets and liabilities based on their relative fair values. Any excess of cost over the fair value of net identifiable assets is allocated to goodwill.

D. and E.   Date of Combination Consolidated Balance Sheet—Acquisition Accounting

16. **(d)**   The cost of the investment is $60,000. The fair value of the noncontrolling interest, $10,000, is added to the cost of the investment of $60,000, to get the fair value of the net assets of the business, $70,000. Next, the book value ($50,000) is subtracted from the fair value to arrive at the differential of $20,000 ($70,000 – $50,000), which represents the amount used to write up undervalued assets and recognize goodwill. Inventory is increased by 60% of the $20,000, or $12,000. Therefore, current assets should be reported at $102,000, as calculated below.

Current assets—Polk	$70,000
Current assets—Strass	20,000
Excess allocated to inventory	12,000
Total current assets	$102,000

17. **(c)**   The acquisition method requires the assets of the acquired firm to be recorded at their fair values. The fair value of the net assets of the acquiree is determined by adding the acquirer's cost to the fair value of noncontrolling interest. In this case the fair value would be equal to $70,000 ($60,000 + $10,000). The excess of the fair value over book value is allocated 60% to inventory and 40% to goodwill. Goodwill would be recorded at $8,000 ($20,000 × 40%). Therefore, noncurrent assets should be reported at $138,000 as calculated below.

Noncurrent assets—Polk	$90,000
Noncurrent assets—Strass	40,000
Excess allocated to goodwill	8,000
Total noncurrent assets	$138,000

18. **(b)**   In the consolidated balance sheet, the parent company's "investment in subsidiary" account should be eliminated and replaced by the assets and liabilities of the subsidiary. Therefore, the consolidated balance sheet should include the current liabilities of both companies, plus the current portion of the debt incurred on 1/2/10 ($60,000 ÷ 10 = $6,000). Thus, current liabilities should be reported at $46,000 as computed below.

Current liabilities—Polk	$30,000
Current liabilities—Strass	10,000
Current portion of new debt	6,000
Total	$46,000

19. **(c)**   In the consolidated balance sheet, the parent company's "investment in subsidiary" account should be eliminated and replaced by the assets and liabilities of the subsidiary. Therefore, the consolidated balance sheet should include the noncurrent liabilities of both companies, plus the noncurrent portion of the debt incurred on 1/2/10 ($60,000 – $6,000 = $54,000).

Noncurrent liabilities—Polk	$ 50,000
Noncurrent liabilities—Strass	0
Noncurrent portion of new debt	54,000
Total	$104,000

20. **(c)**   In the consolidated balance sheet, neither the parent company's investment account nor the subsidiary's stockholders' equity is reported. These amounts are eliminated in the same journal entry that records the excess of cost over book value. The portion of the subsidiary's stockholders' equity that is **not** eliminated is reported as noncontrolling interest in the equity section of the consolidated balance sheet. Therefore, the parent's stockholders' equity ($90,000) equals the consolidated stockholders' equity. Note that once the candidate has completed items 16 through 20, the answers can be checked using the balance sheet equation.

Current assets	+	Non-current assets	=	Current liabilities	+	Non-current liabilities	+	Stock-holders' equity
$102,000	+	$138,000	=	$46,000	+	$104,000	+	$90,000

21. **(c)**   In an acquisition, the net assets of the acquired firm are recorded at their FV. The excess of the cost of the investment over the FV of the net assets acquired is allocated to goodwill. The cost of this investment is $3,750,000 (250,000 shares × $15), and the FV of the net assets acquired, **excluding goodwill** is $3,400,000 ($3,000,000 +

$400,000). Therefore, the amount allocated to goodwill is $350,000 ($3,750,000 – $3,400,000).

22. (c) The correct answer is calculated as illustrated below.

Assets transferred	$700,000
Plus: Noncontrolling interest in Sloan	
10,000 shares × $18	180,000
Less: Fair value of net identifiable assets of	
Sloan	(800,000)
Goodwill recognized	$ 80,000

23. (c) The assets acquired would be revalued to their fair market value. Answer (c) is correct because the inventory account would then include the difference between the market value and book value. Answer (a) is incorrect because a deferred credit is never recorded. Answer (b) is incorrect because goodwill represents the excess of cost plus the fair value of previously held interests plus the fair value of noncontrolling interest less the fair value of net identifiable assets. Answer (d) is incorrect because the retained earnings account is not affected by this transaction when acquisition accounting is used.

24. (d) Answer (d) is correct because all assets and liabilities (including plant and equipment and long-term debt) should be reported at fair value.

25. (d) When the fair value of identifiable assets acquired in a business acquisition exceeds the sum of the consideration given and the fair value of previously held interest plus the fair value of noncontrolling interests, the difference is recorded as a bargain purchase. Answer (d) is correct because a gain is recognized on the income statement in the current period. Answer (a) is incorrect because negative goodwill is not recorded. Answer (b) is incorrect because the difference is not treated as a part of additional paid-in capital. Answer (c) is incorrect because it describes the accounting treatment no longer allowed.

F. Consolidated Financial Statements subsequent to Acquisition

26. (d) Consolidated statements are prepared as if the parent and subsidiaries were one economic entity. From the point of view of the consolidated entity, any intercompany receivables or payables from parent to subsidiary or vice versa are **not** payable to or receivable from any **outside** company. In other words, the consolidated entity does not have a receivable or payable. Therefore, all of Wright's intercompany receivables, payables and advances are eliminated. None are reported as intercompany receivables.

27. (a) When a subsidiary prepares separate financial statements, intercompany receivables (and payables) should be reported in the balance sheet as a separate line item. When consolidated financial statements are prepared by the parent company, all intercompany receivables (and payables) should be eliminated to avoid overstating assets and liabilities.

28. (d) Pard's separate revenues are $200,000, and Spin's separate revenues are $140,000, resulting in a total of $340,000 ($200,000 + $140,000). Since the consolidated income statement shows sales of only $308,000, intercompany sales of $32,000 ($340,000 – $308,000) from Pard to Spin must have been eliminated during consolidation.

29. (b) Pard's separate accounts receivable is $26,000, and Spin's separate accounts receivable is $19,000, resulting in a total of $45,000 ($26,000 + $19,000). Since the consolidated balance sheet shows accounts receivable of only $39,000, intercompany receivables of $6,000 ($45,000 – $39,000) must have been eliminated during consolidation. Since Pard sold goods to Spin that Spin had not fully paid for by 12/31/10, the eliminated receivable must be Pard's receivable from Spin. Therefore, Spin's 12/31/10 payable to Pard is also $6,000.

30. (c) Pard's intercompany sales to Spin totaled $32,000 during 2010. Therefore, Spin recorded a purchase of inventory of $32,000. At 12/31/10, Spin still held 37.5% of these goods in inventory; in Spin's books, this inventory was carried at $12,000 (37.5% × $32,000). In the consolidated balance sheet, the intercompany profit would be eliminated, and this inventory would be carried at Pard's original cost. Pard's sales to Spin were at the same markup on cost that Pard uses for all sales. In Pard's income statement, cost of sales is 75% of sales ($150,000 ÷ $200,000). Therefore, Pard's original cost for the $12,000 of goods in Spin's inventory is $9,000 (75% × $12,000).

31. (c) The fair value of the 20,000 (100,000 × 20%) shares of noncontrolling interest in Stone on the date of acquisition is $1,040,000 (20,000 shares × $52 per share). This amount is adjusted for the noncontrolling interest's share of net income and dividends received as calculated below.

Fair value of noncontrolling	
interest, acquisition date	$1,040,000
Plus: Share of net income	
(20% × $280,000)	56,000
Less: Share of dividends	
(20% × 50,000)	(10,000)
Noncontrolling interest	
12/31/10	$1,086,000

32. (a) When the equity method of accounting is used the parent company's retained earnings will be equal to the consolidated retained earnings balance. It can be determined that the equity method is being followed because the account "Equity in earnings of Sharp" appears in the parent's income statement. In addition it is important to note that the balance sheet accounts presented are dated as of the end of the year; therefore, the parent company's retained earnings of $1,240,000, should already include **all** income statement balance account adjustments. Thus, no additional income amounts will need to be added to the $1,240,000 retained earnings balance, in order to determine the total retained earnings balance.

33. (d) The requirement is to determine which accounting concept relates to the preparation of consolidated financial statements. Answer (d) is correct because when a parent-subsidiary relationship exists, the financial statements of each separate entity are brought together, or consolidated. When financial statements represent a consolidated entity, the concept of economic entity applies. Answer (a) is incorrect because reliability is a concept that applies to all financial statements, not just consolidated financial statements. Reliability is a primary quality that makes accounting information useful for decision making. This quality should be found in all statements. Answer (b) is incorrect because the concept of materiality applies to all financial statements, not just consolidated financial statements. The concept of materiality, as applied to financial statements, deals with the impact an item in the financial statements will have on a user's decision-making process. Answer (c) is incorrect because the concept of legal entity refers to the form or type of combination that takes place between entities (i.e., mergers, consolidations or acquisitions), not the basis on which financial statements are prepared.

34.   (b)   In general, all assets and liabilities (including equipment) should be reported at market value. The excess of the equipment's market value over its carrying amount is allocated to the equipment and amortized over the equipment's useful life. The unamortized portion of the excess of the market value over the carrying amount of the equipment is then reported as part of plant and equipment. Only the excess of the acquisition cost over the market value of the net identifiable assets acquired is reported as goodwill. The excess of the market value over the carrying amount of the equipment is capitalized and subsequently amortized over the equipment's useful life, **not** expensed on the date of the acquisition.

35.   (a)   When two companies own stock in each other, a reciprocal ownership relationship exists. In this case, Pride (the parent) owns 80% of Simba (the sub), and Simba owns 10% of Pride. When Pride declares a cash dividend, 90% of it is distributed to outside parties and 10% goes to Simba. Because Simba is part of the consolidated entity, its 10% share of Pride's dividend is eliminated when determining consolidated dividends declared. Thus, only 90% of dividends declared by Pride will be reported in the consolidated financial statements. When Simba declares a dividend, 80% of the dividend is distributed to Pride (the parent), and 20% is distributed to outside parties (the noncontrolling interest of Simba stock). The 80% share to Pride is eliminated when determining consolidated dividends declared because it represents an intercompany transaction. The remaining 20% to the noncontrolling interest is likewise not included in consolidated dividends declared because, from the parent company's point of view, subsidiary dividends do not represent dividends of the consolidated entity and must be eliminated.

36.   (c)   It is presumed that an entity with equity of less than 10% of total assets does not have sufficient funding to finance its activities unless there is definitive evidence to the contrary (e.g., a source of outside financing).

37.   (b)   A variable interest entity should be consolidated by the enterprise that will absorb the majority of the entity's expected losses if they occur, or receive the majority of the residual returns if they occur, or both.

38.   (b)   The determination of whether an entity is a variable interest entity and which enterprise should consolidate that entity is made at the time the enterprise initially gets involved with the variable interest entity. The determination does not change unless there is a fundamental change in the nature of the entity or the relationship between the interest holders.

39.   (d)   Accounting changes that result in financial statements that are, in effect, financial statements of a different reporting entity (such as presenting consolidated statements in place of statements of individual companies) should be reported by restating the financial statements of all prior periods presented so that the resulting restated prior periods'

statements on a consolidated basis are the same as if the subsidiary had been consolidated since it was acquired.

40.   (b)   In an acquisition, the consolidated financial statements reflect the combined operations of the parent and subsidiary **from the date of combination**. Earnings of the subsidiary prior to the combination are **not** included with the parent's income. The parent's 2010 income is $1,575,000 ($750,000 + $825,000), while the subsidiary's income after the combination is $375,000 for a total of $1,950,000 ($1,575,000 + $375,000). The unrealized inventory profit of $45,000 must be eliminated, because from a consolidated viewpoint, revenue cannot be recognized until these goods are sold to a third party (i.e., a sale has not yet occurred). Therefore, 2010 consolidated net income is $1,905,000 ($1,950,000 – $45,000). Note that the net income amounts given are from **separate company operations,** so no elimination of equity earnings or dividend income is necessary.

41.   (d)   In combined financial statements, the statements include only the adjusted retained earnings of the parent. The subsidiary's retained earnings are **not** included. Since Pane uses the equity method to account for its investment in Sky, Pane's net income will include its share of the net earnings of Sky. Therefore, 6/30/10 consolidated retained earnings is equal to $3,250,000 ($3,200,000 + $800,000 – $750,000).

G. and H.   Intercompany Transactions and Profit Confirmation

42.   (d)   Unrealized profit in ending inventory arises when intercompany sales are made at prices above cost and the merchandise is not resold to third parties prior to year-end. The profit is unrealized because the inventory has not yet been sold outside of the consolidated entity. In this case, Pirn sold goods to Scroll for $100,000, which would become Scroll's cost. However, Scroll's cost of goods sold includes only $80,000 of goods acquired from Pirn. Therefore, $20,000 of original $100,000 remains in Scroll's ending inventory. Since Pirn's gross profit rate is 30% ($150,000 ÷ $500,000), the gross profit Pirn recognized on the original $20,000 amount in Scroll's inventory was $6,000 (30% × $20,000). This intercompany profit must be eliminated on the consolidating worksheet.

43.   (b)   When computing consolidated income, the objective is to restate the accounts as if the intercompany transactions had not occurred. When Scroll recorded depreciation, it included depreciation on the asset purchased from Pirn for $36,000. Since Pirn recorded a $12,000 gain when it sold the asset to Scroll, Pirn's book value at the time of sale must have been $24,000. Therefore, consolidated depreciation expense should be based on $24,000 rather than on $36,000. Depreciation expense for 2010 must be decreased by $3,000 ($12,000 excess ÷ 4 years). Depreciation expense in Pirn's 2010 consolidated income statement should therefore be $47,000, as computed below.

Pirn's recorded depr.	$40,000
Scroll's recorded depr.	10,000
Less adjustment ($12,000 ÷ 4)	(3,000)
	$47,000

44.   (c)   Unrealized profit in ending inventory arises when intercompany sales are made at prices above cost and the merchandise is not resold to third parties prior to year-end. The profit is unrealized because the inventory has not yet been sold outside of the consolidated entity. In this case, there is no unrealized profit on the sales to Dean because the consolidated statements would not include Dean, and the equity method is not applicable. (Clark owns only 15% of Dean). However, there is unrealized profit on the materials sold by Kent, a wholly owned subsidiary, to Clark. Sixty thousand dollars of the $240,000 of materials sold by Kent to Clark remains in ending inventory. The gross profit Kent recognized on this $60,000 of materials at the time of sale was $12,000 ($48,000 ÷ $240,000 = 20% gross profit rate; 20% × $60,000 = $12,000). For the consolidated entity, this $12,000 gross profit has not been earned and must be eliminated. Therefore, consolidated current assets should be $308,000 ($320,000 – $12,000).

45. (c) When preparing the consolidated income statement, the objective is to restate the accounts as if the intercompany transactions had not occurred. As a result of the intercompany sale, Parker has recorded $250,000 of sales and Smith has recorded $250,000 cost of sales which should be eliminated (note that Parker's **cost of sales** on the original sale is the amount left in consolidated cost of sales, and Smith's **sales** when the goods were sold to outside parties is the amount left in consolidated sales). Therefore, Parker should report $500,000 as cost of sales in the 2010 consolidated income statement ($400,000 + $350,000 – $250,000).

46. (a) Pare's separate gross profit is $100,000, and Shel's separate gross profit is $60,000, resulting in a total of $160,000. Since the consolidated income statement shows gross profit of only $154,000, unrealized intercompany profit of $6,000 ($160,000 – $154,000) must have been eliminated.

47. (d) The requirement is to determine the amount of **selling** expenses to be reported in Pard's 2010 consolidated income statement. Pard's selling expenses for 2010 include $50,000 in freight-out costs for goods sold to Seed, its subsidiary. This $50,000 becomes part of Seed's inventory because it is a cost directly associated with bringing the goods to a salable condition. None of the $50,000 represents a selling expense for the consolidated entity, and $1,450,000 ($1,100,000 + $400,000 – $50,000) should be reported as selling expenses in the consolidated income statement.

48. (a) When preparing consolidated financial statements, the objective is to restate the accounts as if the intercompany transactions had not occurred. Therefore, the 2010 gain on sale of machine of $50,000 [$900,000 – ($1,100,000 – $250,000)] must be eliminated, since the consolidated entity has not realized a gain. In effect, the machine must be reflected on the consolidated balance sheet at 1/1/10 at Poe's cost of $1,100,000, and accumulated depreciation of $250,000, instead of at a new "cost" of $900,000. For consolidated statement purposes, 2010 depreciation is based on the original amounts [($1,100,000 – $100,000) × 1/20 = $50,000]. Therefore, in the 12/31/10 **consolidated** balance sheet, the machine is shown at a cost of $1,100,000 less accumulated depreciation of $300,000 ($250,000 + $50,000).

49. (a) When Seal purchased the bonds from Wagner, the bonds were viewed as retired from a consolidated viewpoint since there is no longer any obligation to an outside party. Therefore, the consolidated entity would recognize a $100,000 gain ($1,075,000 carrying amount – $975,000 cash paid), which would increase consolidated retained earnings.

This transaction has no effect on noncontrolling interest, since the subsidiary (Seal) has merely exchanged one asset for another (cash for investment in bonds).

50. (a) The requirement is to determine the amount of gain to be reported on the consolidated income statement when a wholly owned subsidiary purchases parent company stock. A parent company reports no gain or loss when a wholly owned subsidiary purchases its common stock. In effect, the consolidated entity is purchasing treasury stock when the purchase is made, and gains are not recognized on treasury stock transactions. The dividends paid by the parent to the subsidiary also do not affect income because such intercompany transactions are eliminated when consolidated financial statements are prepared. Therefore, $0 gain should be reported by the consolidated entity.

51. (a) When computing consolidated income, the objective is to restate the accounts as if the intercompany transactions had not occurred. As a result of the intercompany sales, sales and cost of goods sold are overstated and an eliminating entry is needed to reduce these accounts by the entire amount of the intercompany sales. Therefore, answer (a) is correct. Answer (b) is incorrect because sales and cost of goods sold need to be reduced by the entire amount of the intercompany sales in order to arrive at their proper consolidated amounts. Answer (c) is incorrect because net income is not affected by the intercompany sale. Sales and cost of goods sold are overstated by the same amount; thus, net income is correct for consolidated purposes. Answer (d) is incorrect because an adjustment is necessary.

52. (c) The key to this problem is that the equipment must be revalued at Winston's carrying amount (Winston's original cost less accumulated depreciation) in the consolidation process. Assume the following potential scenario:

Winston buys a piece of equipment on 12/31/09 for $1,000. At 12/31/09, the equipment was depreciated $200, and Winston's carrying value is $800 ($1,000 – $200). On 12/31/09, Winston sells the equipment to Foster for $900. Foster's original cost is therefore $900, and Winston will record a $100 gain that must be eliminated. After consolidation, the equipment is reported at $800, Winston's carrying value. Winston's carrying value is also equal to Foster's original cost ($900) less Winston's recorded gain ($100). Answer (a) is incorrect because Foster's original cost includes an unrealized gain that must be eliminated. Answer (b) is incorrect because revaluing the equipment at Winston's original cost would not take into consideration the depreciation already recorded by Winston. Answer (d) is incorrect because the entire gain, not 80% of the gain, must be eliminated because this is a downstream sale from the parent to the subsidiary.

53. (b) The requirement is to determine by how much depreciation will be reduced. Use the solutions approach and set up a simple numerical example.

Port's original cost = $1,000
Depreciation per yr = $200
Selling price = $810

If Port sells equipment for $810, it recognizes a $210 gain on the sale (selling price of $810 – carrying value of the equipment $600). Salem, Inc. will now depreciate the equipment on their books at $810, the price that they paid.

Because the gain was not realized with an entity outside of the consolidated entity, it must be eliminated. In the consolidated financial statements, equipment will be reported at its original carrying value, the gain on the sale will be removed and depreciation expense must be recorded at Port, Inc. original amount ($200), not the amount of depreciation that Salem, Inc. records. Salem would record depreciation of $270 ($810/3). Therefore, depreciation must be reduced by $70 on the consolidated financial statements to reflect the original depreciation recorded by Port. Depreciation is reduced by $70, which as shown by the example, is 33 1/3% of the gain ($70/$210).

54. (a) This question is silent as to which year consolidated financial statements are being prepared. However, answer (a) is correct for either the year of acquisition or a subsequent year. If financial statements were being prepared for the current year the loss would be reported as an ordinary loss on the income statement. P Co. acquired the 20% interest in S Company bonds and incurred a loss on them. This loss would be carried through to the consolidated balance sheet as a decrease in retained earnings. In subsequent years, the unamortized portion of the loss would also decrease retained earnings.

I. Noncontrolling Interest

55. (b) Because Planet owns 70% interest in Star, the noncontrolling interest in star is 30%. Therefore, the noncontrolling interest's share in Star's net income of $80,000 is 30% × $80,000 = $24,000. Planet's sale of merchandise to Star for $10,000 will be eliminated on the consolidated worksheet, and Planet's income will be reduced by the intercompany profit of $2,000. This will not affect the noncontrolling interest's share of income because it was a downstream sale from the parent to the subsidiary and is eliminated by the parent.

56. (d) The cost of acquisition is $975,000. The fair value of Shaw's assets is equal to their book values plus the amount of the write-up, or $1,100,000 ($1,000,000 + 100,000). Goodwill is calculated as follows:

Consideration transferred	$975,000
Plus: Fair value of noncontrolling interest	250,000
Less: Fair value of net identifiable assets	(1,100,000)
Amount of goodwill	$125,000

57. (d) The percentage of the subsidiary's stockholders' equity not owned by the parent represents the noncontrolling interest's share of the fair value of net assets of the subsidiary. The fair value of the noncontrolling interest is measured at the acquisition date, and adjusted in future periods for the portion of the acquiree's income and dividends attributable to the noncontrolling interest. Therefore, the noncontrolling interest at 12/31/10 is calculated as follows:

Fair value of noncontrolling interests	$250,000
Plus: Share of net income ($190,000 × 20%)	38,000
Less: Share of dividends ($125,000 × 20%)	(25,000)
Noncontrolling interest 12/31/10	$263,000

58. (b) Pare paid cash dividends of $25,000 and Kidd, the 75%-owned subsidiary, paid cash dividends of $5,000. The dividends paid by Pare are all payments to owners of the consolidated company and are reported as dividends paid in the consolidated statement of retained earnings. The $5,000 dividend paid by Kidd is paid 75% to Pare, and 25% to outside parties (the noncontrolling interest in Kidd's stock). The 75% share to Pare is eliminated when deter-

mining consolidated dividends declared because it is an intracompany transaction. The remaining 25% to the noncontrolling interest is likewise not included in consolidated dividends declared because, from the parent company's point of view, subsidiary dividends do not represent dividends of the consolidated entity.

59. (c) The percentage of the subsidiary's stockholders' equity not owned by the parent represents the noncontrolling interest's share of the fair value of net assets of the subsidiary. The fair value of the noncontrolling interest is measured at the acquisition date, and adjusted in future periods for the portion of the acquiree's income and dividends attributable to the noncontrolling interest. Therefore, the noncontrolling interest at 12/31/10 is calculated as follows:

Fair value of noncontrolling interest	$35,000
Plus: Share of net income (25% × 20,000)	5,000
Less: Share of dividends (25% × $5,000)	(1,250)
Noncontrolling interest 12/31/10	$38,750

60. (b) In the consolidated balance sheet, neither the parent company's investment account nor the subsidiary's stockholders' equity is reported. These amounts are eliminated in the same journal entry that records the excess of cost over book value. The portion of the subsidiary's stockholders' equity that is **not** eliminated is reported as noncontrolling interest. Therefore, the amount reported as common stock in the 12/31/10 consolidated balance sheet consists solely of Pare's common stock ($100,000). Kidd's common stock ($50,000) is eliminated along with the rest of its stockholders' equity.

61. (d) Consideration includes the fair value of the assets transferred, the fair value of the liabilities incurred by the acquirer, the fair value of any contingent consideration, and any equity interest issued by the acquirer. Consideration does not include share-based payments exchanged voluntarily by the acquirer.

62. (d) If information is incomplete at the acquisition date, the items should be recorded at a provisional amount measured at the date of acquisition. Answers (a), (b), and (c) are incorrect because they do not describe appropriate ways to account for situations in which there is incomplete information.

63. (a) If the acquirer has incomplete accounting information on the date of acquisition, the measurement period ends when the acquirer receives the information or one year from the date of acquisition, whichever occurs first. Answer (b) is incorrect because contingent consideration is recorded at a provisional amount during the measurement period, and is remeasured each reporting period until the contingency is resolved. Remeasuring the contingency does not affect the measurement period. Answers (c) and (d) are incorrect because they do not describe the end of the measurement period.

64. (c) If it is determined during the measurement period that a provisional amount is not accurate, the change is recognized by retrospectively adjusting the provisional amount and making a corresponding adjustment to goodwill. Answers (a), (b), and (d) are incorrect because they describe inappropriate ways of handling the new information.

65. (a) If the acquirer is required to replace share-based payments, and no further service is required of the employees, the share-based payments are treated as part of the consideration transferred in the acquisition. The amount should be capitalized as a cost of acquisition of the acquiree. Answers (b), (c), and (d) are incorrect because the amount should not affect the income statement.

66. (b) If no further service is required to be provided and Post voluntarily replaces the awards, compensation expense is recognized in the postcombination financial statements when the awards are made. Answers (a), (c), and (d) are incorrect because they describe inappropriate ways to account for the awards.

67. (b) A liability for a contingency should be derecognized only after the contingency has been resolved. Answers (a), (c), and (d) are incorrect because they represent inappropriate points in time to derecognize a contingent liability.

J. Additional Issues Regarding Business Combinations

68. (b) The requirement is to determine how much of Sago's 2010 net income should be reported as accruing to Phillips. In an acquisition, consolidated net income reflects the parent's net income to the date of combination and both entities' income after the combination. Phillips, Inc. can only recognize the net income of Sago, based on their 20% interest, up to the date of combination. However, after the date of combination they will recognize 95% of Sago's net income, their new ownership interest.

L. Combined Financial Statements

69. (d) **Combined financial statements** are financial statements prepared for companies that are owned by the same parent company or individual. Combined financial statements are prepared by combining all the companies' financial statement classifications. Intercompany transactions and profits should be eliminated in the same way as for consolidated statements. Therefore, **none** of the intercompany receivables should be included in the combined financial statements.

70. (c) The inventory reported on the 12/31/10 combined balance sheet should reflect the **original cost** to the companies of any inventory on hand. The inventory on hand that was acquired from outside parties should be reported at its cost ($175,000 + $250,000 = $425,000). The Banks inventory on hand that was acquired from Lamm must be restated back to the cost Lamm originally paid when it was purchased from outside parties. This must be done to eliminate intercompany profits. During 2010, Lamm shipped inventory that originally cost $150,000 to Banks at a billing price of $200,000. Therefore, the original cost is 75% of Banks' carrying amount. Therefore, the correct inventory amount is $470,000 [$175,000 + $250,000 + ($60,000 × 75%)].

71. (b) Combined financial statements are prepared for companies that are owned by the same parent company or individual but are not consolidated. These statements are prepared by combining the separate companies' financial statement classifications. Intercompany transactions, balances, and profit (loss) should be eliminated. Therefore, to determine the gross profit in Bee and Cee's combined income statement, the intercompany profit resulting from Bee's sales to Cee should be eliminated. Cee sold to outsiders 50% ($65,000/$130,000) of the inventory purchased from Bee. The cost of sales to the combined entity is thus 50% of the $100,000 cost of sales reported by Bee. Gross profit of the combined entity amounts to $41,000, which is $91,000 of sales to unrelated companies less $50,000 cost of sales.

72. (a) When computing sales to be reported in the combined income statement, the objective is to restate the accounts as if the intercompany transaction had not occurred. Assuming that there were no sales between Home Office and Branch, the correct amount of sales to be included in the combined income statement is the $250,000 sold by Branch to unrelated customers.

73. (b) Combined financial statements is the term used to describe financial statements prepared for companies that are owned by the same parent company or individual. Combined financial statements are prepared by combining all of the subsidiaries' financial statement classifications. Intercompany transactions should be eliminated in the same way as for consolidated statements. Combining the stockholders' equity accounts of Able and Baker results in a total of $430,000 ($100,000 + $20,000 + $300,000 + $10,000). The intercompany balances (Investment in Baker, $4,000; and Common Stock, $4,000) must be eliminated, which reduces combined stockholders' equity to $426,000 ($430,000 – $4,000).

74. (c) **Combined financial statements** are financial statements prepared for companies that are owned by the same parent company or individual. Combined financial statements are prepared by combining all the companies' financial statement classifications. Intercompany transactions and profits should be eliminated in the same way as for consolidated statements. Therefore, **none** of the intercompany loans or profits should be included in the combined financial statements.

75. (d) Combined statements may be used to present the financial position and results of operations of commonly controlled companies, companies under common management, and of a group of unconsolidated subsidiaries.

76. (c) Where combined statements are prepared for a group of related companies, intercompany transactions and profit and losses should be eliminated. Matters such as noncontrolling interests, income taxes, foreign operations, or different fiscal periods should be treated in the same manner for both combined financial statements and consolidated statements.

77. (c) When combined statements are prepared for a group of related companies, and there are issues in connection with such matters as noncontrolling interests, foreign operations, different fiscal periods, or income taxes, they should be treated in the same manner as in consolidated statements.

SOLUTIONS TO SIMULATION PROBLEMS

Simulation Problem 1

Situation	Concepts	Journal Entries	Financial Statement Amounts	Communication	Research

	(A)	(B)	(C)	(D)	(E)	(F)	(G)
1. Cash	●	○	○	○	○	○	○
2. Equipment	○	●	○	○	○	○	○
3. Investment in subsidiary	○	○	○	○	●	○	○
4. Bonds payable	○	●	○	○	○	○	○
5. Noncontrolling interest	○	○	○	○	○	●	○
6. Common stock	○	○	●	○	○	○	○
7. Beginning retained earnings	○	○	●	○	○	○	○
8. Dividends paid	○	○	●	○	○	○	○
9. Gain on retirement of bonds	○	○	○	○	○	●	○
10. Cost of goods sold	○	●	○	○	○	○	○
11. Interest expense	○	○	○	●	○	○	○
12. Depreciation expense	○	●	○	○	○	○	○

Explanation of solutions

1. **(A)** Consolidated statements are prepared as if the parent and subsidiaries are one economic entity. Therefore, cash is included in the consolidated balance sheet at their full amounts regardless of the percentage ownership held by the parent.

2. **(B)** When preparing consolidated financial statements, the objective is to restate the accounts as if the intercompany transaction had not occurred. Therefore, on the consolidated balance sheet the equipment needs to be stated at its historical cost less accumulated deprecation.

3. **(E)** In the consolidated balance sheet, the parent company's "Investment in subsidiary" should be eliminated completely and replaced by the net assets of the subsidiary.

4. **(B)** When Poe purchased the bonds from an investor outside the consolidated entity, the bonds are viewed as retired from a consolidated viewpoint since there is no longer any obligation to an outside party. Therefore, the consolidated balance sheet will show the bonds payable at $100,000.

5. **(F)** The percentage of the subsidiary's stockholders' equity not owned by the parent company represents the noncontrolling interest's share of the net assets of the subsidiary. This amount is only reported in the consolidated balance sheet in the equity section.

6. **(C)** In the consolidated balance sheet the subsidiary's common stock is not reported. Therefore, the parent's common stock equals the consolidated common stock.

7. **(C)** In the consolidated balance sheet, the subsidiary's beginning retained earnings is not reported. Therefore, the parent's beginning retained earnings equals the consolidated beginning retained earnings.

8. **(C)** The dividends paid by the subsidiary are eliminated in the consolidated financial statements. Ninety percent of the dividends paid are eliminated along with the "Investment in subsidiary" elimination. The remaining 10% is reflected in "Noncontrolling Interest." Therefore, only the parent's dividends paid are included on the consolidated financial statements.

9. **(F)** When Poe purchased the bonds from an investor outside the consolidated entity, the bonds are viewed as retired from a consolidated viewpoint since there is no longer any obligation to an outside party. Therefore, the consolidated entity would recognize a gain of $9,000 ($100,000 carrying value of the bonds – $91,000 purchase price) on the retirement of the debt. Since the bonds are still outstanding in relation to Shaw, no gain would be recognized on Shaw's unconsolidated income statement.

10. **(B)** When preparing the consolidated income statement, the objective is to restate the accounts as if the intercompany transactions had not occurred. As a result of the intercompany sale, Shaw has recorded cost of sales of $30,000 and Poe has recorded cost of sales of $40,000. The actual cost of sales to third parties outside the consolidated entity is $20,000 (1/2 of the merchandise Shaw sold to third parties at the original cost of the merchandise purchased by Poe).

11. **(D)** The requirement is to determine how the interest expense is to be reported in Poe's consolidated financial statements for December 31, 2010. As the Shaw bonds were held by an unaffiliated party for the entire period, the entire interest expense amount recorded by Shaw relates to payments outside the consolidated entity. Thus, the entire portion on Shaw's books should be included in the 12/31/10 consolidated financial statements. Therefore, answer D is correct.

12. **(B)** When preparing consolidated financial statements, the objective is to restate the accounts as if the intercompany transactions had not occurred. As a result of the sale of the equipment, Shaw recorded depreciation expense of $12,000 ($36,000 ÷ 3 years). For consolidated purposes, depreciation must be computed based on the cost of the asset to the consolidated entity, which is the cost ($30,000) of the asset to Poe. Therefore, depreciation expense should be $5,000 ($30,000 ÷ 6 yrs.) on the consolidated income statement.

Situation	Concepts	Journal Entries	Financial Statement Amounts	Communication	Research

1.

Gain on equipment	21,000		
Accumulated depreciation		15,000	
Equipment		6,000	
Accumulated depreciation	7,000		
Depreciation expense		7,000	

2.

Sales	60,000		
Cost of goods sold		50,000	
Ending inventory		10,000	

3.

Bonds payable	100,000		
Discount on bonds	9,000		
Gain on retirement of bonds		9,000	
Investment in bonds		100,000	

Explanation of solutions

1. **($14,000)** When preparing consolidated financial statements, the objective is to restate the accounts as if the intercompany transactions had not occurred. Therefore, the 2010 gain on sale of equipment of $21,000 ($36,000 – $15,000) must be eliminated, since the consolidated entity has not realized any gain. In addition, for consolidated statement purposes, 2010 depreciation is based on the original cost of the equipment to Poe. This elimination entry can be made in two separate entries. The first entry eliminated the gain, and restores the accumulated depreciation and equipment accounts as if the intercompany sale were never made. The second entry adjusts the current year depreciation expense to the amount that would have been recorded if the sale were never made. New depreciation is $36,000 ÷ 3 years = $12,000 for Shaw. Poe's depreciation was book value $15,000 ÷ 3 years = $5,000 per year. Therefore, depreciation expense must be adjusted by $12,000 – $5,000 = $7,000.

2. **($10,000)** Unrealized profit in ending inventory arises when intercompany sales are made at prices above cost and the merchandise is not resold to third parties prior to year-end. The profit is unrealized because the inventory has not yet been sold outside the consolidated entity. In this case, one half of the merchandise was left in Shaw's inventory at year-end. For the consolidated entity, one half of the $20,000 profit has not been earned and must be eliminated.

3. **($9,000)** When Poe purchased the bonds from an investor outside the consolidated entity, the bonds are viewed as retired from a consolidated viewpoint since there is no longer any obligation to an outside party. Therefore, the consolidated entity would recognize an ordinary gain of $9,000 ($100,000 carrying value of the bonds – $91,000 purchase price) on the retirement of the debt.

Situation	Concepts	Journal Entries	Financial Statement Amounts	Communication	Research

Calculate the amounts that will appear on Poe's consolidated financial statement in December 31, 2010.

1. Cash $ 65,000
2. Goodwill $ 22,000
3. Equipment $794,000
4. Common stock $100,000
5. Investment in Shaw $0
6. Dividends $ 80,000
7. Bonds payable $100,000
8. Noncontrolling interest $ 21,000

Explanation of solution

1. $50,000 + $15,000 = $65,000

2. The goodwill from Poe's 90% purchase of Shaw can be determined as follows:

Acquisition cost	$155,000
+ Fair value of noncontrolling interest	17,000
(10,000 shares × $1.70)	
Fair value of interests	172,000
– Fair value of net identifiable assets	(150,000)
Goodwill	$ 22,000

3. $440,000 + $360,000 – $6,000 = $794,000

4. $100,000, common stock of parent

5. The investment in Shaw account is eliminated.

6. Dividends paid of the subsidiary are eliminated.

7. $100,000. $200,000 bonds payable – $100,000 bonds payable eliminated

8. Noncontrolling interest

Fair value at acquisition date	$17,000
+ 10% net income	7,000
– 10% dividend	(3,000)
End of year noncontrolling interest	$21,000

Situation	Concepts	Journal Entries	Financial Statement Amounts	Communication	Research

To: CEO, Poe Corporation
From: CPA Candidate
Re: Consolidated Financial Statements

   This memorandum was prepared to answer your questions about investments in other companies. A company may invest in another corporation by purchasing stock of that corporation. If the investment is less than 20% of the outstanding shares of stock, the fair value method of accounting is used. Under this method, the investment is recorded at the price paid for the stock, and value of the investment is adjusted to fair value at the end of each accounting period.

   If a company purchases between 20 and 50% of the stock of another corporation, the acquiring company is assumed to have significant influence over the other company. In these instances, the equity method of accounting is used. The company includes its proportionate share of net income of the acquired company by increasing the investment account. Similarly, the company decreases its investment account by the amount of dividends paid by the investee. However, the acquirer may also elect to account for the investment at fair value.

   If a company purchases greater than 50% of the voting shares of stock of another corporation and can exercise control, then consolidated financial statements must be prepared. These consolidated statements reflect the consolidated operating results, cash flows, and financial position as if a parent company and its subsidiaries are a single entity.

   Consolidated financial statements are required because they better reflect the operating results, financial status, and central management ties that bind the company into a single economic and financial unit. These consolidated financial statements are representationally more faithful and fair because they are not biased and do not exclude or net data. Consolidated financial statements are also more comparable with information about other economic entities regardless of the company's legal framework. Finally, consolidated financial statements are more complete and relevant for investors and other parties basing decisions on the data.

   If you have any further questions on consolidated financial statements, please do not hesitate to call me.

Situation	Concepts	Journal Entries	Financial Statement Amounts	Communication	Research

1. What method of accounting is used to record a business combination?

FAS141(R), Para 6

6. An entity shall account for each business combination by applying the acquisition method.

Codification: 805-10-05-4 and *805-10-25-1*

2. In a business combination, what is the definition of goodwill?

FAS141(R), Para 3.j.

j. *Goodwill* is an asset representing the future economic benefits arising from other assets acquired in a business combination that are not individually identified and separately recognized.

Codification: 805-10-20 Glossary

3. At what amount should the assets, liabilities, and noncontrolling interest of the acquiree be recorded?

FAS141(R), Para 20

20. The acquirer shall measure the identifiable assets acquired, the liabilities assumed, and any noncontrolling interest in the acquiree at their acquisition-date fair values.

Codification: 805-20-30-1

Simulation Problem 2

Situation	Concepts	Consolidation at Date of Acquisition	Intercompany Transactions & Eliminations	Consolidation at Year-End	Communication	Research

				True	*False*
1.	A company can use either the acquisition method or the pooling method for business combinations.			○	●
2.	Total revenues for a consolidated entity are calculated by adding the total revenue of the parent for the year and the total revenue of the subsidiary from the date of acquisition.			●	○
3.	Goodwill is amortized over a period of forty years.			○	●
4.	Goodwill is classified and included with other intangible assets for purposes of measuring impairment.			○	●
5.	Intangible assets with indefinite lives are not amortized.			●	○
6.	The stockholder equity accounts in the consolidated balance sheet are those of the parent company.			●	○
7.	The effect of unrealized profits and sales between the acquirer and the acquiree is classified as an intercompany transaction and must be eliminated.			●	○
8.	A newly identified intangible asset must meet the contractual legal or the separability criterion to be recognized as an intangible asset at the time of consolidation.			○	●

Situation	Concepts	Consolidation at Date of Acquisition	Intercompany Transactions & Eliminations	Consolidation at Year-End	Communication	Research

Total current assets	$400,000
Total noncurrent assets	1,060,000
Total current liabilities	260,000
Total noncurrent liabilities	240,000
Total owners' equity	960,000

Explanation of solutions

Current assets: $320,000 parent + $70,000 book value subsidiary + $10,000 inventory write-up = $400,000

Noncurrent assets: $640,000 parent + $380,000 book value subsidiary + $40,000 goodwill = $1,060,000

Total current liabilities: $210,000 parent + $50,000 subsidiary = $260,000

Noncurrent liabilities: $150,000 + $90,000 = $240,000

Total owners' equity: $600,000 parent + $360,000 new stock of parent issued in acquisition = $960,000

Situation	Concepts	Consolidation at Date of Acquisition	Intercompany Transactions & Eliminations	Consolidation at Year-End	Communication	Research

Arcelia Corporation
CONSOLIDATION WORKSHEET
December 31, 2010

	Arcelia Corp.	Gavino Corp.		Debt	Credit		End balance
				Elimination entries			
Revenues & gains	1,000,000	400,000	(c)	50,000			1,341,000
			(e)	9,000			
Expenses	780,000	335,000	(f)	1,000	46,000	(c)	1,070,000
Current assets	400,000	110,000	(b)	10,000	4,000	(c)	508,000
					8,000	(d)	
Noncurrent assets	1,260,000	420,000	(b)	40,000	360,000	(a)	1,350,000
			(e)	36,000	45,000	(e)	
					1,000	(f)	
Differential			(a)	50,000	50,000	(b)	
Current liabilities	300,000	70,000	(d)	8,000			362,000
Noncurrent liabilities	180,000	85,000					265,000
Owners' equity	960,000	310,000	(a)	310,000			960,000

Elimination entries in journal entry form

a.   Eliminate subsidiary equity accounts

Common stock & APIC	310,000	
Differential	50,000	
Investment in Gavino		360,000

b.   To record asset write-up and goodwill. Goodwill = Acquisition cost $360,000 – FMV of net identifiable assets $320,000 ($460,000 – $140,000) = $40,000 goodwill.

Inventory	10,000	
Goodwill	40,000	
Differential		50,000

c.   Eliminate the excess sales and costs of sales and profits in inventory not sold. The intercompany sales of $50,000 must be eliminated, along with the $50,000 in cost of sales reduced by the amount by which ending inventory is overstated. Ending inventory is carried on Gavino's books at $10,000. Ending inventory should be 20% × $30,000 cost to manufacture = $6,000. Therefore, inventory is overstated by $4,000 and cost of sales is overstated by $46,000 ($50,000 – $4,000).

Sales	50,000	
Cost of goods sold		46,000
Ending inventory		4,000

d.   Eliminate intercompany receivable and payable

Accounts payable	8,000	
Accounts receivable		8,000

e.   Eliminate sale of equipment

Gain on sale of equipment	9,000	
Equipment	36,000	
Accumulated depreciation		45,000

f.   Restore depreciation expense as if equipment had not been sold. Normally Gavino depreciates equipment $60,000/5 years = $12,000 per year. Equipment sold on 10/1/10; therefore, Gavino recorded depreciation of 3/4 × $12,000 = $9,000. Arcelia's cost is $24,000 and depreciation is recorded straight-line over 3 years = $8,000 per year. However, Arcelia depreciated equipment 3/12 months = $2,000 per year. Total depreciation by both firms = $11,000. Total depreciation if the asset was not sold = $12,000. Therefore, an additional $1,000 depreciation must be recorded.

Depreciation expense	1,000	
Accumulated depreciation		1,000

Situation	Concepts	Consolidation at Date of Acquisition	Intercompany Transactions & Eliminations	Consolidation at Year-End	Communication	Research

Ending balances on financial statements, 2010

Arcelia Corporation & Subsidiaries
CONSOLIDATED BALANCES
December 31, 2010

Total revenues	$1,341,000
Total expenses	1,070,000
Total current assets	508,000
Total noncurrent assets	1,350,000
Total current liabilities	362,000
Total noncurrent liabilities	265,000
Total owners' equity	1,231,000

Situation	Concepts	Consolidation at Date of Acquisition	Intercompany Transactions & Eliminations	Consolidation at Year-End	Communication	Research

To: CEO, Arcelia Corporation
From: CPA Candidate
Re: Valuation of acquired firm

This memorandum was prepared to answer your questions about business combinations. When a company acquires another firm, the assets are appraised and revalued to fair value. Any new assets which meet the legal contractual criterion or the separability criterion are also valued at fair value and recorded as assets on the acquiring firm's financial statements. If the sum of the consideration transferred, the fair value of previously held shares, and the fair value of noncontrolling interest for the acquired firm exceeds the fair market value of net identifiable assets (assets minus liabilities), the amount in excess of the fair value is allocated to goodwill.

Goodwill is assigned to reporting units of the firm and it is not amortized. However, goodwill must be tested each year for impairment. If it is deemed that goodwill is impaired, an entry should be recorded to recognize a loss and write goodwill down to its new value. There are two steps to the impairment test. The first step compares the fair value of a reporting unit with its carrying amount including goodwill. If the carrying amount of the reporting unit exceeds its fair value, the second step of the goodwill impairment test is performed to measure the impairment loss. The second step involves a comparison of the implied fair value of reporting unit goodwill with the carrying amount of the goodwill. If the carrying amount of the reporting unit goodwill exceeds the implied fair value of that goodwill, an impairment loss is recognized. After a goodwill impairment loss is recognized, the carrying amount of the goodwill is adjusted for the loss. Once a loss is recognized, subsequent reversal of the impairment loss is not allowed. If you have any additional questions regarding this issue, please contact me.

						Research
Situation	Concepts	Consolidation at Date of Acquisition	Intercompany Transactions & Eliminations	Consolidation at Year-End	Communication	

What is an intercompany transaction and how should it be treated for financial reporting purposes?

ARB51, Para 6

6. In the preparation of consolidated statements, intercompany balances and transactions should be eliminated. This includes intercompany open account balances, security holdings, sales and purchases, interest, dividends, etc. As consolidated statements are based on the assumption that they represent the financial position and operating results of a single business enterprise, such statements should not include gain or loss on transactions among the companies in the group. Accordingly, any intercompany profit or loss on assets remaining within the group should be eliminated; the concept usually applied for this purpose is gross profit or loss. (See also paragraph 17.)

Codification: 810-10-45-1

Simulation Problem 3

Situation	Financial Statement Amounts	

		(A)	(B)	(C)	(D)	(E)	(F)
1.	Cash	●	○	○	○	○	○
2.	Equipment	○	●	○	○	○	○
3.	Investment in subsidiary	○	○	○	○	●	○
4.	Noncontrolling interest	○	○	○	○	○	●
5.	Common stock	○	○	●	○	○	○
6.	Beginning retained earnings	○	○	●	○	○	○
7.	Dividends paid	○	○	●	○	○	○
8.	Cost of goods sold	○	●	○	○	○	○
9.	Interest expense	●	○	○	○	○	○
10.	Depreciation expense	○	●	○	○	○	○

Explanation of solutions

1.   **(A)** The total of cash on each entity's books equals the total for the consolidated entity.

2.   **(B)** The amount shown for equipment on the consolidated balance sheet is less than the sum of the amounts on Purl's and Strand's unconsolidated balance sheets because on an upstream intercompany transaction the parent's share (90%) of the gain would be eliminated. The equipment now on the parent's books would be reduced on the worksheet by subtracting 90% of the gain not realized through depreciation from equipment.

3.   **(E)** The investment in subsidiary would be eliminated in the process of consolidation in the same entry in which the subsidiary's equity accounts are eliminated.

4.   **(F)** Noncontrolling interest is presented only in the consolidated balance sheet.

5.   **(C)** Only Purl's common stock would be included in the consolidated balance sheet. All of Strand's common stock would be eliminated. Ten percent would be included in noncontrolling interest.

6.   (C) Beginning retained earnings would be the same as Purl's. Under the purchase method none of the acquiree's (Strand's) retained earnings is carried forward in recording the business combination.

7.   (C) Dividends paid would include only the parent's. The dividends of the subsidiary are all eliminated in consolidation.

8.   (B) Cost of goods would be less than the sum of that of Purl and Strand because intercompany profit would be eliminated from cost of goods sold. The amount eliminated would be 100% of the intercompany profit on two-thirds of the downstream sale from Purl to Strand.

9.   (A) No information is given to indicate that there is any intercompany interest-bearing debt. Thus, the amount included for interest expense in the consolidated financial statements would be the sum of the two entities.

10.   (B) Depreciation expense would be less on the consolidated financial statements than the sum of depreciation in each firm's unconsolidated financial statements because the part relating to the intercompany profit on equipment sold upstream would be eliminated in consolidation.

MULTIPLE-CHOICE QUESTIONS (1-50)

1. On September 1, 2009, Bain Corp. received an order for equipment from a foreign customer for 300,000 local currency units (LCU) when the US dollar equivalent was $96,000. Bain shipped the equipment on October 15, 2009, and billed the customer for 300,000 LCU when the US dollar equivalent was $100,000. Bain received the customer's remittance in full on November 16, 2009, and sold the 300,000 LCU for $105,000. In its income statement for the year ended December 31, 2009, Bain should report as part of net income a foreign exchange transaction gain of
   a. $0
   b. $4,000
   c. $5,000
   d. $9,000

2. On September 1, 2009, Cano & Co., a US corporation, sold merchandise to a foreign firm for 250,000 Botswana pula. Terms of the sale require payment in pula on February 1, 2010. On September 1, 2009, the spot exchange rate was $.20 per pula. At December 31, 2009, Cano's year-end, the spot rate was $.19, but the rate increased to $.22 by February 1, 2010, when payment was received. How much should Cano report as foreign exchange transaction gain or loss as part of 2010 income?
   a. $0.
   b. $2,500 loss.
   c. $5,000 gain.
   d. $7,500 gain.

3. Lindy, a US corporation, bought inventory items from a supplier in Argentina on November 5, 2008, for 100,000 Argentine pesos, when the spot rate was $.4295. At Lindy's December 31, 2008 year-end, the spot rate was $.4245. On January 15, 2009, Lindy bought 100,000 pesos at the spot rate of $.4345 and paid the invoice. How much should Lindy report as part of net income for 2008 and 2009 as foreign exchange transaction gain or loss?

	2008	2009
a.	$ 500	$(1,000)
b.	$0	$ (500)
c.	$ (500)	$0
d.	$(1,000)	$ 500

4. Hunt Co. purchased merchandise for £300,000 from a vendor in London on November 30, 2009. Payment in British pounds was due on January 30, 2010. The exchange rates to purchase one pound were as follows:

	November 30, 2009	December 31, 2009
Spot-rate	$1.65	$1.62
30-day rate	1.64	1.59
60-day rate	1.63	1.56

In its December 31, 2009, income statement, what amount should Hunt report as foreign exchange transaction gain as part of net income?
   a. $12,000
   b. $ 9,000
   c. $ 6,000
   d. $0

5. Ball Corp. had the following foreign currency transactions during 2009:

• Merchandise was purchased from a foreign supplier on January 20, 2009, for the US dollar equivalent of $90,000. The invoice was paid on March 20, 2009, at the US dollar equivalent of $96,000.
• On July 1, 2009, Ball borrowed the US dollar equivalent of $500,000 evidenced by a note that was payable in the lender's local currency on July 1, 2011. On December 31, 2009, the US dollar equivalents of the principal amount and accrued interest were $520,000 and $26,000, respectively. Interest on the note is 10% per annum.

In Ball's 2009 income statement, what amount should be included as foreign exchange transaction loss as part of net income?
   a. $0
   b. $ 6,000
   c. $21,000
   d. $27,000

6. On November 30, 2009, Tyrola Publishing Company, located in Colorado, executed a contract with Ernest Blyton, an author from Canada, providing for payment of 10% royalties on Canadian sales of Blyton's book. Payment is to be made in Canadian dollars each January 10 for the previous year's sales. Canadian sales of the book for the year ended December 31, 2009, totaled $50,000 Canadian. Tyrola paid Blyton his 2009 royalties on January 10, 2009. Tyrola's 2009 financial statements were issued on February 1, 2010. Spot rates for Canadian dollars were as follows:

November 30, 2008	$.87
January 1, 2009	$.88
December 31, 2009	$.89
January 10, 2010	$.90

How much should Tyrola accrue for royalties payable at December 31, 2009?
   a. $4,350
   b. $4,425
   c. $4,450
   d. $4,500

7. Shore Co. records its transactions in US dollars. A sale of goods resulted in a receivable denominated in Japanese yen, and a purchase of goods resulted in a payable denominated in euros. Shore recorded a foreign exchange transaction gain on collection of the receivable and an exchange transaction loss on settlement of the payable. The exchange rates are expressed as so many units of foreign currency to one dollar. Did the number of foreign currency units exchangeable for a dollar increase or decrease between the contract and settlement dates?

	Yen exchangeable for $1	Euros exchangeable for $1
a.	Increase	Increase
b.	Decrease	Decrease
c.	Decrease	Increase
d.	Increase	Decrease

8. On October 1, 2009, Mild Co., a US company, purchased machinery from Grund, a German company, with payment due on April 1, 2010. If Mild's 2009 operating income included no foreign exchange transaction gain or loss, then the transaction could have
   a.   Resulted in an extraordinary gain.
   b.   Been denominated in US dollars.

c. Caused a foreign currency gain to be reported as a contra account against machinery.

d. Caused a foreign currency translation gain to be reported as other comprehensive income.

9. On October 1, 2009, Velec Co., a US company, contracted to purchase foreign goods requiring payment in Qatari riyals, one month after their receipt at Velec's factory. Title to the goods passed on December 15, 2009. The goods were still in transit on December 31, 2009. Exchange rates were one dollar to twenty-two riyals, twenty riyals, and twenty-one riyals on October 1, December 15, and December 31, 2009, respectively. Velec should account for the exchange rate fluctuation in 2009 as

a. A loss included in net income before extraordinary items.

b. A gain included in net income before extraordinary items.

c. An extraordinary gain.

d. An extraordinary loss.

10. Derivatives are financial instruments that derive their value from changes in a benchmark based on any of the following except

a. Stock prices.

b. Mortgage and currency rates.

c. Commodity prices.

d. Discounts on accounts receivable.

11. Derivative instruments are financial instruments or other contracts that must contain

a. One or more underlyings, **or** one or more notional amounts.

b. No initial net investment or smaller net investment than required for similar response contacts.

c. Terms that do not require or permit net settlement or delivery of an asset.

d. All of the above.

12. The basic purpose of derivative financial instruments is to manage some kind of risk such as all of the following except

a. Stock price movements.

b. Interest rate variations.

c. Currency fluctuations.

d. Uncollectibility of accounts receivables.

13. Which of the following statements is(are) true regarding derivative financial instruments?

I. Derivative financial instruments should be measured at fair value and reported in the balance sheet as assets or liabilities.

II. Gains and losses on derivative instruments not designated as hedging activities should be reported and recognized in earnings in the period of the change in fair value.

a. I only.

b. II only.

c. Both I and II.

d. Neither I nor II.

14. Which of the following is an underlying, according to ASC Topic 815 (SFAS 133)?

a. A credit rating.

b. A security price.

c. An average daily temperature.

d. All of the above could be underlyings.

15. If the price of the underlying is greater than the strike or exercise price of the underlying, the call option is

a. At the money.

b. In the money.

c. On the money.

d. Out of the money.

16. Which of the following is **not** a distinguishing characteristic of a derivative instrument?

a. Terms that require or permit net settlement.

b. Must be "highly effective" throughout its life.

c. No initial net investment.

d. One or more underlyings and notional amounts.

17. An example of a notional amount is

a. Number of barrels of oil.

b. Interest rates.

c. Currency swaps.

d. Stock prices.

18. Disclosures related to financial instruments, both derivative and nonderivative, used as hedging instruments must include

a A list of hedged instruments.

b. Maximum potential accounting loss.

c. Objectives and strategies for achieving them.

d. Only a. and c.

19. Which of the following financial instruments or other contracts is not specifically excluded from the definition of derivative instruments in ASC Topic 815 (SFAS 133)?

a. Leases.

b. Call (put) option.

c. Adjustable rate loans.

d. Equity securities.

20. Which of the following is **not** a derivative instrument?

a. Futures contracts.

b. Credit indexed contracts.

c. Interest rate swaps.

d. Variable annuity contracts.

21. Which of the following criteria must be met for bifurcation to occur?

a. The embedded derivative meets the definition of a derivative instrument.

b. The hybrid instrument is regularly recorded at fair value.

c. Economic characteristics and risks of the embedded instrument are "clearly and closely" related to those of the host contract.

d. All of the above.

22. Financial instruments sometimes contain features that separately meet the definition of a derivative instrument. These features are classified as

a. Swaptions.

b. Notional amounts.

c. Embedded derivative instruments.

d. Underlyings.

23. The process of bifurcation

a. Protects an entity from loss by entering into a transaction.

b. Includes entering into agreements between two counterparties to exchange cash flows over specified period of time in the future.

c. Is the interaction of the price or rate with an associated asset or liability.
d. Separates an embedded derivative from its host contract.

24. Alvarez Corporation has two hybrid financial instruments. According to ASC Topic 815, how can Alvarez account for these instruments?
a. Alvarez must bifurcate all hybrid financial instruments and record the components separately.
b. Alvarez can elect to not disclose the financial instruments on the balance sheet.
c. Alvarez can elect not to bifurcate the hybrid instruments on an instrument by instrument basis.
d. Alvarez can make an election that requires all hybrid financial instruments not to be bifurcated.

25. According to ASC Topic 815, when a company elects not to bifurcate a hybrid financial instrument, the entire hybrid instrument should be valued at
a. Fair value.
b. Net present value.
c. Net realizable value.
d. Book value.

26. When an election is made not to bifurcate a hybrid financial instrument, how should this be disclosed on the financial statements?

I. As separate line items for the fair value and non–fair value instruments on the balance sheet.
II. As an aggregate amount of all hybrid instruments with the amount of the hybrid instruments at fair value shown in parentheses.
III. As a footnote disclosure.

a. I only.
b. II and III only.
c. III only.
d. I and II only.

27. If a company elects not to bifurcate a hybrid financial instrument and records the entire instrument at fair value, which of the following is true?
a. No changes in value are recorded until the hybrid instrument is sold.
b. Changes in fair value of the hybrid instrument are recognized each year in other comprehensive income.
c. Changes in fair value of the hybrid instrument are recognized each year in earnings.
d. Changes in fair value of the hybrid instrument are recognized each year by recognizing a cumulative effect adjustment to the beginning balance of retained earnings for the period.

28. Hedge accounting is permitted for all of the following types of hedges except
a. Trading securities.
b. Unrecognized firm commitments.
c. Available-for-sale securities.
d. Net investments in foreign operations.

29. Which of the following is a general criterion for a hedging instrument?
a. Sufficient documentation must be provided at the beginning of the process.
b. Must be "highly effective" only in the first year of the hedge's life.

c. Must contain a nonperformance clause that makes performance probable.
d. Must contain one or more underlyings.

30. For an unrecognized firm commitment to qualify as a hedged item it must
a. Be binding on both parties.
b. Be specific with respect to all significant terms.
c. Contain a nonperformance clause that makes performance probable.
d. All of the above.

31. A hedge of the exposure to changes in the fair value of a recognized asset or liability, or an unrecognized firm commitment, is classified as a
a. Fair value hedge.
b. Cash flow hedge.
c. Foreign currency hedge.
d. Underlying.

32. Gains and losses on the hedged asset/liability and the hedged instrument for a fair value hedge will be recognized
a. In current earnings.
b. In other comprehensive income.
c. On a cumulative basis from the change in expected cash flows from the hedged instrument.
d. On the balance sheet either as an asset or a liability.

33. Gains and losses of the effective portion of a hedging instrument will be recognized in current earnings in each reporting period for which of the following?

	Fair value hedge	Cash flow hedge
a.	Yes	No
b.	Yes	Yes
c.	No	No
d.	No	Yes

34. Which of the following risks are inherent in an interest rate swap agreement?

I. The risk of exchanging a lower interest rate for a higher interest rate.
II. The risk of nonperformance by the counterparty to the agreement.

a. I only.
b. II only.
c. Both I and II.
d. Neither I nor II.

35. Which of the following meet the definition of assets and/or liabilities?

	Derivative instruments	G/L on the fair value of derivatives
a.	Yes	No
b.	No	Yes
c.	Yes	Yes
d.	No	No

36. Which of the following is **not** a type of foreign currency hedge?
a. A forecasted transaction.
b. An available-for-sale security.
c. A recognized asset or liability.
d. An unrecognized firm commitment.

37. Which of the following foreign currency transactions is not accounted for using hedge accounting?
   a. Available-for-sale securities.
   b. Unrecognized firm commitments.
   c. Net investments in foreign operations.
   d. Foreign currency denominated forecasted transactions.

Items 38 through 41 are based on the following:

On December 12, 2009, Imp Co. entered into three forward exchange contracts, each to purchase 100,000 euros in ninety days. The relevant exchange rates are as follows:

	Spot rate	Forward rate (for March 12, 2010)
November 30, 2009	$.87	$.89
December 12, 2009	.88	.90
December 31, 2009	.92	.93

38. Imp entered into the first forward contract to hedge a purchase of inventory in November 2009, payable in March 2010. At December 31, 2009, what amount of foreign currency transaction gain from this forward contract should Imp include in net income?
   a. $0
   b. $ 3,000
   c. $ 5,000
   d. $10,000

39. At December 31, 2009, what amount of foreign currency transaction loss should Imp include in income from the revaluation of the Accounts Payable of 100,000 euros incurred as a result of the purchase of inventory at November 30, 2009, payable in March 2010?
   a. $0
   b. $3,000
   c. $4,000
   d. $5,000

40. Imp entered into the second forward contract to hedge a commitment to purchase equipment being manufactured to Imp's specifications. The expected delivery date is March 2010 at which time settlement is due to the manufacturer. The hedge qualifies as a fair value hedge. At December 31, 2009, what amount of foreign currency transaction gain from this forward contract should Imp include in net income?
   a. $0
   b. $ 3,000
   c. $ 5,000
   d. $10,000

41. Imp entered into the third forward contract for speculation. At December 31, 2009, what amount of foreign currency transaction gain from this forward contract should Imp include in net income?
   a. $0
   b. $ 3,000
   c. $ 5,000
   d. $10,000

42. The risk of an accounting loss from a financial instrument due to possible failure of another party to perform according to terms of the contract is known as
   a. Off-balance-sheet risk.
   b. Market risk.
   c. Credit risk.
   d. Investment risk.

43. Examples of financial instruments with off-balance-sheet risk include all of the following except
   a. Outstanding loan commitments written.
   b. Recourse obligations on receivables.
   c. Warranty obligations
   d. Futures contracts.

44. Off-balance-sheet risk of accounting loss does not result from
   a. Financial instruments recognized as assets entailing conditional rights that result in a loss greater than the amount recognized in the balance sheet.
   b. Financial instruments not recognized as either assets or liabilities yet still expose the entity to risk of accounting loss.
   c. Financial instruments recognized as assets or liabilities where the amount recognized reflects the risk of accounting loss to the entity.
   d. Financial instruments recognized as liabilities that result in an ultimate obligation that is greater than the amount recognized in the balance sheet.

45. If it is **not** practicable for an entity to estimate the fair value of a financial instrument, which of the following should be disclosed?
   I. Information pertinent to estimating the fair value of the financial instrument.
   II. The reasons it is not practicable to estimate fair value.
   a. I only.
   b. II only.
   c. Both I and II.
   d. Neither I nor II.

46. Disclosure requirements for financial instruments include
   a. Method(s) and significant assumptions used in estimating fair value.
   b. Distinction between financial instruments held or issued for trading purposes and purposes other than trading.
   c. A note containing a summary table cross-referencing the location of other financial instruments disclosed in another area of the financial statements.
   d. All of the above should be disclosed.

47. Disclosure of credit risk of financial instruments with off-balance-sheet risk does **not** have to include
   a. The amount of accounting loss the entity would incur should any party to the financial instrument fail to perform.
   b. The entity's policy of requiring collateral or security.
   c. The class of financial instruments held.
   d. The specific names of the parties associated with the financial instrument.

48. Disclosure of information about significant concentrations of credit risk is required for
   a. All financial instruments.
   b. Financial instruments with off-balance-sheet credit risk only.
   c. Financial instruments with off-balance-sheet market risk only.
   d. Financial instruments with off-balance-sheet risk of accounting loss only.

49. Kline Bank has large amounts of notes receivable from companies with high debt-to-equity ratios as a result of buy-out transactions. Kline is contemplating the following disclosures for the notes receivable in its year-end financial statements:

I. Information about shared activity, region, or economic characteristic.
II. A brief description of collateral supporting these financial instruments.

Which of the above disclosures are required under GAAP?

    a.   I only.
    b.   II only.
    c.   Neither I nor II.
    d.   Both I and II.

50. Whether recognized or unrecognized in an entity's financial statements, disclosure of the fair values of the entity's financial instruments is required when

    a.   It is practicable to estimate those values.
    b.   The entity maintains accurate cost records.
    c.   Aggregated fair values are material to the entity.
    d.   Individual fair values are material to the entity.

SIMULATION PROBLEMS

Simulation Problem 1   (50 to 60 minutes)

Situation					
	Terminology	**Concepts**	**Applicability of SFAS 133**	**Communication**	**Research**

Riley Corp. has entered into several derivative contracts in order to manage its risk exposure.

	Terminology				
Situation		**Concepts**	**Applicability of SFAS 133**	**Communication**	**Research**

Select the **best** answer for each item from the terms listed in A-L. No term should be used more than once.

Answer List

A. A hedge of the exposure to changes in the fair value of a recognized asset or liability or an unrecognized firm commitment.

B. A hedge of the exposure to variability in the cash flows of a forecasted transaction or a recognized asset or liability.

C. A hedge of the foreign currency exposure of an unrecognized firm commitment, an available-for-sale security, a forecasted transaction, or a net investment in a foreign operation.

D. Financial instruments that contain features which, if they stood alone, would meet the definition of a derivative instrument.

E. Two or more separate derivatives traded as a set.

F. Commonly a specified price or rate such as a stock price, interest rate, currency rate, commodity price, or a related index.

G. A legally enforceable, binding agreement with an unrelated party, specifying all significant terms and including a disincentive for nonperformance sufficient to make performance likely.

H. The referenced associated asset or liability, commonly a number of units.

I. The difference between an option's price and its intrinsic value.

J. A transaction expected to occur for which there is no firm commitment, which gives the entity no present rights or obligations.

K. With regard to put options, it is the larger of zero or the spread between the exercise price and the stock price.

L. Agreement between two parties to buy and sell a specific quantity of a commodity, foreign currency, or financial instrument at an agreed-upon price, with delivery and/or settlement at a designated future date.

		(A)	(B)	(C)	(D)	(E)	(F)	(G)	(H)	(I)	(J)	(K)	(L)
1.	Forward contract	O	O	O	O	O	O	O	O	O	O	O	O
2.	Forecasted transaction	O	O	O	O	O	O	O	O	O	O	O	O
3.	Firm commitment	O	O	O	O	O	O	O	O	O	O	O	O
4.	Embedded derivative	O	O	O	O	O	O	O	O	O	O	O	O
5.	Intrinsic value	O	O	O	O	O	O	O	O	O	O	O	O
6.	Underlying	O	O	O	O	O	O	O	O	O	O	O	O
7.	Notional amount	O	O	O	O	O	O	O	O	O	O	O	O
8.	Cash flow hedge	O	O	O	O	O	O	O	O	O	O	O	O
9.	Fair value hedge	O	O	O	O	O	O	O	O	O	O	O	O
10.	Foreign currency hedge	O	O	O	O	O	O	O	O	O	O	O	O

		Concepts			
Situation	**Terminology**		**Applicability of SFAS 133**	**Communication**	**Research**

Select the **best** answer for each item from the terms listed in A-E. All terms should be used once.

Answer List

A. Granted special hedge accounting treatment.

B. Resulting gains or losses are taken into current earnings in the period in which they arise.

C. Two currencies other than a functional currency expected to move relative to an entity's functional currency.

D. A hedge against an exposed asset position created by having an account in a denomination other than the functional currency.

E. The difference between the futures rate and the spot rate at the date of a forward contract.

	(A) (B) (C) (D) (E)
1. Tandem currencies	○ ○ ○ ○ ○
2. Discount or premium	○ ○ ○ ○ ○
3. Ineffective portion of a hedge	○ ○ ○ ○ ○
4. Effective portion of a hedge	○ ○ ○ ○ ○
5. Forward contract	○ ○ ○ ○ ○

Situation	Terminology	Concepts	Applicability of SFAS 133	Communication	Research

This question consists of 14 items that represent financial instruments and other contracts that may be included in or excluded from the requirements of ASC Topic 815, *Derivatives and Hedging*.

For the following items, determine if they are (I) included under the requirement of ASC Topic 815, or (E) excluded from ASC Topic 815 treatment.

I.   Item meets the definition of a derivative instrument and must be accounted for using ASC Topic 815.

E.   Item is not required to be accounted for under ASC Topic 815, either because it does not meet the definition of derivative instrument or because the item is specifically excluded from ASC Topic 815 treatment.

	(I) (E)
1. Leases	○ ○
2. Guaranteed investment contracts	○ ○
3. Futures contracts	○ ○
4. Equity securities	○ ○
5. Credit indexed contracts	○ ○
6. Mortgage-backed securities	○ ○
7. Debt securities	○ ○
8. Interest rate caps	○ ○
9. Swaptions	○ ○
10. Employee stock options	○ ○
11. Options to purchase or sell exchange-traded securities	○ ○
12. Variable annuity contracts	○ ○
13. Adjustable rate loans	○ ○
14. Interest rate swaps	○ ○

Situation	Terminology	Concepts	Applicability of SFAS 133	Communication	
					Research

Write a brief memorandum to the CEO of Riley Corp. explaining the required disclosures related to the company's financial instruments (SFAS 133).

REMINDER: Your response will be graded for both technical content and writing skills. Technical content will be evaluated for information that is helpful to the intended reader and clearly relevant to the issue. Writing skills will be evaluated for development, organization, and the appropriate expression of ideas in professional correspondence. Use a standard business memo or letter format with a clear beginning, middle, and end. Do not convey information in the form of a table, bullet point list, or other abbreviated presentation.

To: CEO, Riley Corporation
From: CPA Candidate
Re: Financial Instrument Disclosures

Situation	Terminology	Concepts	Applicability of SFAS 133	Communication	Research

Research the following issues. Select the appropriate sections from the professional standards.

1.   What is a derivative instrument?

2.   A company has a foreign currency fair value hedge. Where is the gain or loss reported in the financial statements?

3.   Where is the effective portion of a gain or loss on a cash flow hedge reported on the financial statements?

Simulation Problem 2   (50 to 60 minutes)

Situation	Terminology	Journal Entries	Foreign Currency Transaction Gains/Losses	Financial Statement Disclosures	Communication	Research

Logan Corporation markets their products internationally. The company buys and sells goods in Great Britain, France, and Germany. Although Logan's functional currency is the US dollar, the transactions are denominated in the currencies for each country as shown in the table below.

Country	Currency
Great Britain	£
France	€
Germany	€

The spot rates for various dates throughout the year are shown below.

Date	US $ per £1	US $ per €1
January 1, 2009	1.786	1.258
March 1, 2009	1.869	1.249
April 15, 2009	1.791	1.197
November 10, 2009	1.857	1.290
December 1, 2009	1.911	1.329
December 20, 2009	1.945	1.333
December 31, 2009	1.927	1.364
January 15, 2010	1.869	1.311
Average daily rate, 2009	1.886	1.279

Situation	Terminology	Journal Entries	Foreign Currency Transaction Gains/Losses	Financial Statement Disclosures	Communication	Research

Select the **best** answer for each item from the terms listed in A-O. No answer should be used more than once.

Answer List

A.   An agreement with an unrelated party, binding on both, usually legally enforceable, specifying all significant terms and including a disincentive for nonperformance sufficient to make performance likely.

B.   A call option where the price of the underlying is greater than the strike or exercise price of the underlying.

C.   A feature on a financial instrument or other contract, which if the feature stood alone, would meet the definition of a derivative.

D.   A forward-based contract or agreement generally between two counterparties to exchange streams of cash flows over a specified period in the future.

E.   With regard to call options, it is the larger of zero or the spread between the stock price and the exercise price.

F.   Provides the holder the right to acquire an underlying at an exercise or stock price, anytime during the option term.

G.   An agreement between the two parties to buy and sell a specific quantity of a commodity, foreign currency, or financial instrument at an agreed-upon price, with delivery and/or settlement at a designated future date.

H.   A call option where the strike or exercise price is greater than the price of the underlying.

I.   The process of separating an embedded derivative from its host contract.

J.   The referenced associated asset or liability, commonly a number of units.

K.   A specified price or rate such as a stock price, interest rate, or commodity price.

L.   An option where the price of the underlying is equal to the strike or exercise price.

M.   The difference between an option's price and its intrinsic value.

N.   Provides the holder the right to sell the underlying at an exercise or strike price, anytime during the option term.

O.   A forward-based contract to make or take delivery of a designated financial instrument, foreign currency, or commodity during a designated period, at a specified price or yield.

	(A)	(B)	(C)	(D)	(E)	(F)	(G)	(H)	(I)	(J)	(K)	(L)	(M)	(N)	(O)
1. At the money	O	O	O	O	O	O	O	O	O	O	O	O	O	O	O
2. Bifurcation	O	O	O	O	O	O	O	O	O	O	O	O	O	O	O
3. Call option	O	O	O	O	O	O	O	O	O	O	O	O	O	O	O
4. Embedded derivative	O	O	O	O	O	O	O	O	O	O	O	O	O	O	O
5. Forward contract	O	O	O	O	O	O	O	O	O	O	O	O	O	O	O
6. Futures contract	O	O	O	O	O	O	O	O	O	O	O	O	O	O	O
7. In the money	O	O	O	O	O	O	O	O	O	O	O	O	O	O	O
8. Notional amount	O	O	O	O	O	O	O	O	O	O	O	O	O	O	O
9. Out of the money	O	O	O	O	O	O	O	O	O	O	O	O	O	O	O
10. Put option	O	O	O	O	O	O	O	O	O	O	O	O	O	O	O
11. Swap	O	O	O	O	O	O	O	O	O	O	O	O	O	O	O
12. Underlying	O	O	O	O	O	O	O	O	O	O	O	O	O	O	O

Situation	Terminology	Journal Entries	Foreign Currency Transaction Gains/Losses	Financial Statement Disclosures	Communication	Research

The following transactions are denominated in each country's local currency.

On March 1, 2009, Logan sells goods on account to Lexington Corporation, located in London, for £370,000. The account is due in 60 days. Lexington pays the full balance due on April 15, 2009.

On November 10, 2009, Logan purchases supplies from Dietmar Corporation in Germany for €190,000. On December 1, 2009, Logan pays Dietmar for the supplies.

On December 20, 2009, Logan sells goods on account to Cordier Corporation in France for €250,000. Cordier pays for the goods on January 15, 2010.

1. Prepare the journal entry for the sale of goods to Lexington on March 1.

2. Prepare the journal entry on April 15, 2009, when Lexington pays for the goods.

3. Prepare the journal entry for the purchase of supplies from Dietmar Corporation on November 10, 2009.

4. Prepare the journal entry for the payment to Dietmar on December 1, 2009.

5. Prepare the journal entry for the sale of goods to Cordier Corporation.

6. Prepare any entries necessary on December 31, 2009, with regard to the foreign currency transactions with Lexington, Dietmar, and Cordier Corporation.

7. Prepare the journal entry for Cordier's payment of goods on January 15, 2010.

Situation	Terminology	Journal Entries	Foreign Currency Transaction Gains/Losses		Financial Statement Disclosures	Communication	Research

Prepare the following schedule outlining the foreign currency transaction gains and losses for 2009 and 2010 for Logan Corporation.

Logan Corporation
SCHEDULE OF FOREIGN CURRENCY TRANSACTION GAIN/LOSSES
For the years 2009 and 2010

	2009 gain/(loss)	2010 gain/(loss)
Lexington Corporation		
Dietmar Corporation		
Cordier Corporation		
Total FC gain/(loss)		

Situation	Terminology	Journal Entries	Foreign Currency Transaction Gains/Losses	Financial Statement Disclosures		Communication	Research

Indicate from the list below where the foreign currency transaction gain or loss in 2009 will be disclosed on the financial statements.

A. Extraordinary gain/loss
B. Other gain/loss
C. Other comprehensive income
D. Revenue
E. Expense

(A) (B) (C) (D) (E)

1. Foreign currency transaction gain/loss for 2009 will be disclosed where on the financial statement? ○ ○ ○ ○ ○

Situation	Terminology	Journal Entries	Foreign Currency Transaction Gains/Losses	Financial Statement Disclosures	Communication		Research

Logan Corporation is the holder of several hybrid instruments. Write a brief memo to the CEO of Logan Corporation answering the following questions:

1. What is a hybrid instrument?
2. What is bifurcation?
3. Identify the three criteria used to determine if bifurcation must occur.
4. List three examples of hybrid instruments that would require bifurcation under ASC Topic 815.

REMINDER: Your response will be graded for both technical content and writing skills. Technical content will be evaluated for information that is helpful to the intended reader and clearly relevant to the issue. Writing skills will be evaluated for development, organization, and the appropriate expression of ideas in professional correspondence. Use a standard business memo or letter format with a clear beginning, middle, and end. Do not convey information in the form of a table, bullet point list, or other abbreviated presentation.

To: CEO, Logan Corporation
From: CPA Candidate
Re: Hybrid Financial Instruments

Situation	Terminology	Journal Entries	Foreign Currency Transaction Gains/Losses	Financial Statement Disclosures	Communication	Research	

Research the professional standards and select the paragraphs that answer the following questions.

1. What is the definition of functional currency?
2. Sometimes foreign currency receivables or payables have not been settled by year-end. At what amount should these transactions be disclosed in the balance sheet?
3. At what exchange rate should a foreign currency transaction be recorded?

MULTIPLE-CHOICE ANSWERS

1. c	__ __	12. d	__ __	23. d	__ __	34. c	__ __	45. c	__ __
2. d	__ __	13. c	__ __	24. c	__ __	35. a	__ __	46. d	__ __
3. a	__ __	14. a	__ __	25. a	__ __	36. c	__ __	47. d	__ __
4. b	__ __	15. b	__ __	26. d	__ __	37. c	__ __	48. a	__ __
5. d	__ __	16. b	__ __	27. c	__ __	38. b	__ __	49. d	__ __
6. c	__ __	17. a	__ __	28. a	__ __	39. d	__ __	50. a	__ __
7. b	__ __	18. d	__ __	29. a	__ __	40. b	__ __		
8. b	__ __	19. b	__ __	30. d	__ __	41. b	__ __		
9. b	__ __	20. d	__ __	31. a	__ __	42. c	__ __		
10. d	__ __	21. a	__ __	32. a	__ __	43. c	__ __	1st: __/50 = __%
11. b	__ __	22. c	__ __	33. a	__ __	44. c	__ __	2nd: __/50 = __%

MULTIPLE-CHOICE ANSWER EXPLANATIONS

A.   Foreign Currency Transactions

1.   (c)   When the **sale is made** on 10/15/09, Bain would record a receivable and sales at $100,000, the US dollar equivalent on that date.

Accounts receivable	100,000	
Sales		100,000

On 11/16/09, Bain receives foreign currency worth $105,000. Since the receivable was recorded at $100,000, a $5,000 gain must be recorded.

Foreign currency	105,000	
Accounts receivable		100,000
Foreign exchange transaction gain		5,000

The US dollar equivalent when the order was received on 9/1/09 ($96,000) is not used to compute the gain because no entry is recorded on this date. The receipt and acceptance of a purchase order from a customer is an executory commitment which is not generally recorded.

2.   (d)   On 9/1/09, Cano obtained a receivable which will be collected in a foreign currency. A gain (loss) will result if the exchange rate on the settlement date is different from the rate existing on the transaction date. A gain (loss) must be recognized at any intervening balance sheet dates, if necessary. Therefore, Cano would recognize a $2,500 foreign exchange transaction loss in its **2009** income statement since a change in the exchange rate reduced the receivable (in US dollars) from $50,000 on 9/1/09 (250,000 × $.20) to $47,500 on 12/31/09 (250,000 × $.19). In 2010, a foreign exchange transaction gain of $7,500 is recognized because the receivable (in US dollars) increased from $47,500 on 12/31/09 to $55,000 when received (250,000 × $.22) on February 1, 2010.

3.   (a)   A transaction has occurred in which settlement will be made in Argentine pesos. Since Lindy's functional currency is the US dollar, a foreign exchange transaction gain (loss) will result if the spot rate on the settlement date is different than the rate on the transaction date. A provision must be made at any intervening year-end date if there has been a rate change. Thus, in 2008, a $500 foreign exchange transaction gain [100,000 × ($.4295 – $.4245)] would be recognized, while in 2009 a $1,000 foreign exchange transaction loss [100,000 × ($.4245 – $.4345)] would be recognized.

4.   (b)   A purchase has been made for which payment will be made in British pounds. A foreign exchange transaction gain or loss will result if the spot rate on the settle-ment date is different from the rate used on the transaction date. A gain or loss must also be recorded at any interven-ing balance sheet date if there has been a rate change. Thus, at 12/31/09 a foreign exchange transaction gain of $9,000 is recognized [300,000 × ($1.65 – $1.62)] as the foreign cur-rency payable is reduced from $495,000 (300,000 × $1.65) to $486,000 (300,000 × $1.62). The thirty-day and sixty-day rates would affect Hunt only if the company had entered into forward contracts.

5.   (d)   On 1/20/09, Ball would record purchases and accounts payable at $90,000. When the account was paid, the equivalent of $96,000 was required to liquidate the $90,000 liability, resulting in a foreign exchange transaction loss of $6,000. Foreign exchange transaction gains (losses) are recognized at intervening balance sheet dates. The note payable originally recorded at $500,000 was equivalent to a liability of $520,000 at the balance sheet date, resulting in a 2009 loss of $20,000. The interest payable of $25,000 ($500,000 × 10% × 6/12) was equivalent to a liability of $26,000 at year-end, resulting in an additional 2009 loss of $1,000. Therefore, the total 2009 foreign exchange transac-tion loss is $27,000 ($6,000 + $20,000 + $1,000).

6.   (c)   The requirement is to determine the amount that Tyrola should accrue for royalties payable, 12/31/09. This situation is a foreign currency transaction in which settle-ment is denominated in other than a company's functional currency. In this case the functional currency is the US dollar because it is the currency of the primary economic environment in which the Colorado firm operates. Note that in this royalty agreement, 12/31/09 is the point at which the amount due to the author (50,000 Canadian dollars × 10% = 5,000 Canadian dollars) is determined. Royalty expense is measured and the related liability is denominated at 12/31/09. The year-end accrual would be

$$.89 \ (10\% \times 50,000 \text{ Canadian dollars}) = \$4,450.$$

On January 10, 2010, Tyrola will have to purchase 5,000 Canadian dollars for payment to the Canadian author. The amount of US dollars required to accomplish this will de-pend on the spot rate on January 10 ($.90 in this case). The number of US dollars required to satisfy the obligation will be $50 greater [($.90 – .89) × 5,000 Canadian dollars]. This will result in a $50 foreign exchange transaction loss which would be included in 2010 net income.

7.   (b)   In the case of the receivable denominated in Japanese yen, a foreign exchange transaction gain was re-corded on the collection of the receivable. This means that more yen was received than was recorded in the receivable account. For that to happen the rate of yen exchangeable for a dollar would have had to decrease, requiring more yen to be paid at the settlement date for the same amount of dollars at the contract date. On the other hand, there was a foreign exchange transaction loss on the payable denominated in euros. This means that at the settlement date Shore Co. had to pay more euros than were recorded in the payable account. For this to occur the rate of euros exchangeable for a dollar would have had to decrease, requiring more euros to be paid at the settlement date for the same amount of dollars at the contract date.

8.   (b)   A transaction that is denominated in a currency other than the entity's functional currency, which is payable at a fixed amount at a later date, may result in an increased or decreased amount payable because of a change in the exchange rate. This increase/decrease would be classified as a foreign exchange transaction gain/loss, and would be included as a component of income. The gain/loss would not be considered extraordinary.

9.   (b)   The requirement is to determine how Velec should account for the exchange rate fluctuation in 2009. A foreign currency transaction is a transaction denominated in a currency other than the entity's functional currency. Denominated means that the balance is fixed in terms of the number of units of a foreign currency, regardless of changes in the exchange rate. When a US company buys or sells to an unrelated foreign company, and the US company agrees either to pay for goods or receive payment for the goods in foreign currency units, this is a foreign currency transaction from the point of view of the US company (the functional currency is the US dollar). In these situations, the US company has "crossed currencies" and directly assumes the risk of fluctuating foreign exchange rates of the foreign currency units. As exchange rates fluctuate, a company will record an ordinary gain or loss on their income statement, **not** an extraordinary gain or loss. Velec has an accounts payable denominated in a foreign currency (Qatari riyals) as of December 15, the date the title to the goods passes to Velec. As the value of the riyal per dollar rises above twenty riyals per dollar, Velec Co. will have to come up with less dollars to pay off the payable, as of December 31, 2009, than they would have on December 15, 2009. This creates a foreign exchange transaction gain. As shown numerically, if 4000 riyals are assumed as being payable, on December 15 you would need $200 (4000/20) to pay off the payable. However, on December 31, $190 would be needed (4000/21). The difference between $200 and $190 represents the gain. A foreign exchange transaction gain should be included in net income, not a loss.

B.1.-2.   Derivative Instruments and Hedging Activities

10.   (d)   Derivatives are financial instruments that derive their value from changes in a benchmark based on stock prices, interest rates, mortgage rates, currency rates, commodity prices, or some other agreed-upon base. Discounts on accounts receivable are not the basis of a benchmark for a derivative financial instrument.

11.   (b)   Derivative instruments must contain one or more underlyings **and** one or more notional amounts. Derivative instruments do contain terms that require or permit net settlement or delivery of an asset.

12.   (d)   Derivative financial instruments are contracts that are supposed to protect or hedge one or more of the parties from adverse movement in the underlying base. Answer (d) is correct because it does not fit the definition of a financial instrument. Risk of uncollectable accounts can be managed by effective credit policies.

13.   (c)   Derivative instruments meet the definition of assets and liabilities. As such they should be reported on the entity's financial statements. The most relevant measure for reporting financial instruments is fair value. Thus, statement I is true. If a derivative instrument does not qualify as a hedging instrument, then its gains or losses must be reported and recognized in current earnings. Thus, statement II is also true.

14.   (d)   All of the above meet the basic definition of an underlying, which is any financial or physical variable that has either observable changes or objectively verifiable changes.

15.   (b)   A call option is in the money if the price of the underlying is greater than the strike or exercise price of the underlying. An at-the-money option is one in which the price of the underlying is equal to the strike or exercise price. A call option is out of the money if the strike or exercise price is greater than the price of the underlying.

16.   (b)   Derivative instruments contain

1.   One or more underlyings and one or more notional amounts
2.   No initial net investment or smaller net investment than required for contracts with an expected similar response to market changes, and
3.   Terms that require or permit net settlement, net settlement by means outside the contract, and delivery of an asset that is substantially the same as net settlement.

17.   (a)   Notional amounts are the referenced associated asset or liability that are commonly a number of units such as barrels of oil. Answers (b) and (d) are incorrect because they are examples of underlyings. Answer (c) is incorrect because it is an example of a derivative instrument.

18.   (d)   Disclosures related to financial instruments that are used as hedging instruments must include the following information:

1.   Objectives and strategies for achieving them.
2.   Context to understand the instrument.
3.   Risk management policies.
4.   A list of hedged instruments.

Disclosure of the maximum potential accounting loss is only required for financial instruments with concentrations of credit risk.

B.3.   Inclusions in and Exclusions from Derivative Instruments

19.   (b)   Only call (put) options are included in the definition of derivative financial instruments. Leases are excluded because they require a payment equal to the value of the right to use the property. Equity securities and adjustable rate loans are excluded because they require an initial net investment equivalent to the fair value.

20. (d) Futures contracts, credit indexed contracts, and interest rate swaps are all included in derivative instruments.

B.4. Embedded Derivative Instruments and Bifurcation

21. (a) The hybrid instrument is **not** recorded at fair value. Economic characteristics and risks of the embedded instrument are **not** "clearly and closely" related to those of the host contract. The embedded derivative must meet the definition of a derivative instrument.

22. (c) An embedded derivative is a feature of a financial instrument or other contract, which if the feature stood alone, would meet the definition of a derivative.

23. (d) Bifurcation is the process of separating an embedded derivative from its host contract. This process is necessary so that hybrid instruments can be separated into their component parts, each being accounted for using the appropriate valuation techniques.

24. (c) Alvarez can elect not to bifurcate the hybrid instrument, and this election can be made on an instrument by instrument basis. Answer (a) is incorrect because an election can be made not to bifurcate an instrument. Answer (b) is incorrect because hybrid financial instruments must be disclosed. Answer (d) is incorrect because the hybrid financial instruments can be selected on an instrument by instrument basis.

25. (a) If a company elects not to bifurcate a hybrid financial instrument, the entire instrument is valued at fair value. Answers (b), (c), and (d) are incorrect because these valuation models are incorrect.

26. (d) The balance sheet disclosure may be presented in one of two ways: as a separate line item for the fair value and non–fair value instruments on the balance sheet, or as an aggregate amount of all hybrid instruments with the amount of the hybrid instruments at fair value shown in parentheses. Answers (a), (b), and (c) are incorrect because two disclosures are permissible on the balance sheet.

27. (c) If a company elects not to bifurcate a hybrid financial instrument, the entire instrument is recorded at fair value. Changes in fair value each year are recognized in earnings for the period. Answer (a) is incorrect because changes in fair value must be recognized. Answer (b) is incorrect because the changes are not recognized in other comprehensive income. Answer (d) is incorrect, because an adjustment is only made to beginning retained earnings in the year that a company initially adopts the new accounting pronouncement.

B.5.-8 Hedging Instruments

28. (a) Hedge accounting is permitted for four types of hedges.

1. Unrecognized firm commitments.
2. Available-for-sale securities.
3. Foreign currency denominated hedge forecasted transactions.
4. Net investments in foreign operations.

Trading securities is not one of the four types.

29. (a) The general criteria for a hedging instrument are that sufficient documentation must be provided at the beginning of the process and the hedge must be "highly effective" throughout its life.

30. (d) For an unrecognized firm commitment to qualify as a hedged item it must

1. Be binding on both parties.
2. Be specific with respect to all significant items including quantity to be exchanged, the fixed price, and the timing of the transaction.
3. Contain a nonperformance clause that makes performance probable.

31. (a) A fair value hedge is a hedge of the exposure to changes in the fair value of a recognized asset or liability or firm commitment. Two other types of hedges are cash flow and foreign currency hedges. An underlying is commonly a specified price or rate.

32. (a) Gains and losses of a fair value hedge will be recognized in current earnings. The effective portion of a cash flow hedge is reported in other comprehensive income and the ineffective portion is reported on a cumulative basis to reflect the lessor of the cumulative gain/loss on the derivative or the cumulative gain/loss from the change in expected cash flows from the hedged instrument. Gains and losses from a change in the fair value of derivative instruments are not assets and liabilities and should not be reported on the balance sheet.

33. (a) Fair value hedges will recognize gains and losses for the effective portion of the hedging instrument in each reporting period. Cash flow hedges will recognize gains and losses for the effect portion of the hedging instrument in other comprehensive income.

34. (c) An interest rate swap agreement involves the exchange of cash flows determined by various interest rates. Fluctuations in interest rates after the agreement is entered into may result in the risk of exchanging a lower interest rate for a higher interest rate. Financial instruments, including swaps, also bear credit risk or the risk that a counterparty to the agreement will not perform as expected.

35. (a) Derivatives do meet the definition of assets/liabilities and, therefore, should be recognized and reported as such on the financial statements. In contrast, gains and losses that result from the change in the fair value of derivatives are not assets/liabilities and should either appear in other comprehensive income or be reported in current earnings.

36. (c) The four foreign currency hedges are an unrecognized firm commitment, an available-for-sale security, a foreign currency denominated forecasted transaction, and a net investment in foreign operations. A hedge of a recognized asset or liability is a fair value hedge or cash flow hedge, not a foreign currency hedge.

37. (c) The hedged net investment is viewed as a single asset. The provisions for recognizing the gain or loss on the hedged asset/liability and the hedging instrument rules do not apply to the hedges of net investments in foreign operations.

B.9. Forward Exchange Contracts

38. (b) Forward exchange contracts are measured at fair value. Each period this is accomplished by marking the forward exchange contract to market using the forward rate at the FS date. At 12/31/09 the forward rate is $.93. The difference between $.93 and $.90, the forward rate on the date the contracts were entered into, times 100,000 euros is $3,000, the forward exchange gain. The entry would be as follows:

Forward contract receivable	3,000	
Forward contract gain		3,000

The $3,000 forward exchange contract gain would be included in 2009 net income.

39. (d) The accounting for gains and losses from foreign currency transactions requires a revaluation of exposed net assets and liabilities denominated in foreign currency units at the current spot rate. At 12/31/09 there is a foreign exchange transaction loss of $5,000 [($.92 − .87) × 100,000 euros]. Note that accounts payable was created on 11/30/09. The entry to record the loss is as follows:

Foreign exchange loss	5,000	
Accounts payable		5,000

The loss would be reported in 2009 net income.

40. (b) Hedges involving firm purchase commitments are treated in the same manner as a forward exchange contract that was entered into to hedge an exposure of a liability.

Forward contract receivable	3,000	
Forward contract gain		3,000
To revalue forward contract using forward rates		
Foreign exchange loss	3,000	
Firm purchase commitment		3,000
To recognize loss on firm commitment		

Note that this hedge is 100% effective because the gain on the forward contract and the loss on the firm purchase commitment offset each other, net.

41. (b) Using a forward exchange contract to speculate would result in a gain or loss each period FS are prepared. The contract would be revalued each reporting period using the forward rate. The gain or loss calculated would be reported in net income. The journal entry would be as follows:

Forward contract receivable	3,000	
Forward contract gain		3,000

B.11. Fair Value and Credit Risk Disclosures

42. (c) Credit risk is the risk of accounting loss from a financial instrument due to possible failure of another party to perform according to the terms of the contract. Off-balance-sheet risk is the possible amount of loss from an instrument that is not reflected on the balance sheet. Market risk is the risk that future changes in market prices may make a financial instrument less valuable.

43. (c) The value of derivative financial instruments is typically derived from the value of an underlying asset or is tied to an index. As the price of the underlying asset changes, the price of the derivative changes. Outstanding loan commitments written, recourse obligations on receivables, and futures contracts are all tied to an asset account. Warranty obligations are the result of the sale of goods.

44. (c) Off-balance-sheet risk is the possible amount of loss from an instrument that is not reflected on the balance sheet because a loss has not yet occurred or because the item is not recognized as an asset or liability. If the amount recognized on the balance sheet reflects the accounting loss to the entity, then there is no off-balance-sheet risk to consider.

45. (c) If it is not practicable for an entity to estimate the fair value of a financial instrument, (1) information pertinent to estimating fair value **and** (2) the reasons why it is not practicable to estimate fair value should be disclosed.

46. (d) The following disclosures are required:

- Method(s) and significant assumptions used in estimating fair value.
- A distinction between financial instruments held or issued for trading purposes and purposes other than trading.
- Information pertinent to estimating the fair value of a financial instrument if it is not practicable for the entity to estimate and the reason why estimation is not practicable.
- Derivative financial instruments may not be combined, aggregated, or netted with nonderivative or other derivative financial instruments.
- If financial instruments are disclosed in more than one area in the financial statements, one note must contain a summary table cross-referencing the location of the other instruments.

47. (d) The following disclosures are required about credit risk for financial instruments with off-balance-sheet credit risk:

- The amount of accounting loss the entity would incur should any party to the financial instrument fail to perform according to the terms of the contract and the collateral, if any, is of no value.
- The class of financial instruments held.
- Categorization between instruments held for trading purposes and purposes other than trading.

48. (a) Concentrations of credit risk exist when an entity has a business activity, economic characteristic, or location that is common to most of its financial instruments. Disclosure of information about significant concentrations of credit risk for **all** financial instruments is required.

49. (d) Since many of Kline Bank's debtors have high debt-to-equity ratios, this group of debtors has a similar economic characteristic, and thus, would be considered a concentration of credit risk to Kline Bank. The entity must disclose the following information regarding concentrations of credit risk:

1. Information about the shared activity, region, or economic characteristic of the group.
2. Amount of accounting loss that the entity would incur as a result of the concentrated parties' failure to perform according to the terms of the contracts.
3. Information regarding entity's policy of requiring collateral.

50. (a) Entities must disclose the fair market value of financial instruments, both assets and liabilities whether recognized or not recognized in the statement of financial position, for which it is practicable to estimate fair value. Pertinent descriptive information as to the fair value of the instrument is to be disclosed if an estimate of fair value cannot be made without incurring excessive costs.

SOLUTIONS TO SIMULATION PROBLEMS

Simulation Problem 1

		Terminology			Concepts			Applicability of SFAS 133		Communication	Research

		(A)	(B)	(C)	(D)	(E)	(F)	(G)	(H)	(I)	(J)	(K)	(L)
1.	Forward contract	○	○	○	○	○	○	○	○	○	○	○	●
2.	Forecasted transaction	○	○	○	○	○	○	○	○	○	●	○	○
3.	Firm commitment	○	○	○	○	○	○	●	○	○	○	○	○
4.	Embedded derivative	○	○	○	●	○	○	○	○	○	○	○	○
5.	Intrinsic value	○	○	○	○	○	○	○	○	○	○	●	○
6.	Underlying	○	○	○	○	○	●	○	○	○	○	○	○
7.	Notional amount	○	○	○	○	○	○	○	●	○	○	○	○
8.	Cash flow hedge	○	●	○	○	○	○	○	○	○	○	○	○
9.	Fair value hedge	●	○	○	○	○	○	○	○	○	○	○	○
10.	Foreign currency hedge	○	○	●	○	○	○	○	○	○	○	○	○

Explanation of solutions

1. **(L)** Agreement for purchase and sale of a specified quantity of a commodity, foreign currency, or financial instrument at an agreed-upon price, with future delivery and/or settlement at a designated future date.

2. **(J)** A transaction expected to occur for which there is no firm commitment, which gives the entity no present rights or obligations.

3. **(G)** A legally enforceable, binding agreement with an unrelated party, specifying all significant terms and including a disincentive for nonperformance sufficient to make performance likely.

4. **(D)** Financial instruments that contain features which, if they stood alone, would meet the definition of a derivative instrument.

5. **(K)** With regard to put options, it is the larger of zero or the spread between the exercise price and the stock price.

6. **(F)** Commonly a specified price or rate such as a stock price, interest rate, currency rate, commodity price, or a related index.

7. **(H)** The referenced associated asset or liability, commonly a number of units.

8. **(B)** A hedge of the exposure to variability in the cash flows of a forecasted transaction or a recognized asset or liability.

9. **(A)** A hedge of the exposure to changes in the fair value of a recognized asset or liability or an unrecognized firm commitment.

10. **(C)** A hedge of the foreign currency exposure of an unrecognized firm commitment, an available-for-sale security, a forecasted transaction, or a net investment in a foreign operation.

Situation	Terminology	Concepts		Applicability of SFAS 133	Communication	Research

		(A)	(B)	(C)	(D)	(E)
1.	Tandem currencies	○	○	●	○	○
2.	Discount or premium	○	○	○	○	●
3.	Ineffective portion of a hedge	○	●	○	○	○
4.	Effective portion of a hedge	●	○	○	○	○
5.	Forward contract	○	○	○	●	○

Explanation of solutions

1. **(C)** Tandem currencies are two currencies other than a functional currency expected to move in tandem with each other relative to an entity's functional currency.

2. **(E)** A discount or premium is the difference between the futures rate and the spot rate at the date of a forward contract.

3. **(B)** The ineffective portion of a hedge has resulting gains or losses taken into income in the period in which they arise.

4. (A) The effective portion of a hedge is given special hedge accounting treatment. The evaluation of effectiveness is done no less than every three months. A highly effective hedge will have a value change ranging from roughly .8 to 1.2 times the variability of the cash flows being hedged.

5. (D) A forward contract is a hedge against an exposed asset position created by having an account in a denomination other than the functional currency.

Situation	Terminology	Concepts	Applicability of SFAS 133		Communication	Research
			(I)	(E)		
1. Leases			○	●		
2. Guaranteed investment contracts			○	●		
3. Futures contracts			●	○		
4. Equity securities			○	●		
5. Credit indexed contracts			●	○		
6. Mortgage-backed securities			○	●		
7. Debt securities			○	●		
8. Interest rate caps			●	○		
9. Swaptions			●	○		
10. Employee stock options			○	●		
11. Options to purchase or sell exchange-traded securities			●	○		
12. Variable annuity contracts			○	●		
13. Adjustable rate loans			○	●		
14. Interest rate swaps			●	○		

Explanation of solutions

1. (E) Leases are excluded from accounting for derivatives treatment.

2. (E) Guaranteed investment contracts are not required to be accounted for under derivative rules.

3. (I) Futures contracts must be accounted for using the rules for derivatives.

4. (E) Equity securities do not fall under the requirements of accounting for derivatives.

5. (I) Credit indexed contracts are required to be accounted for under the rules for derivatives.

6. (E) Mortgage-backed securities are excluded from derivatives treatment.

7. (E) Debt securities are not required to be accounted for using the rules for derivatives.

8. (I) Interest rate caps must be accounted for using the rules for derivatives.

9. (I) Swaptions meet the definition of a derivative instrument.

10. (E) Employee stock options are excluded from derivatives treatment.

11. (I) Options to purchase (call) or sell (put) exchange-traded securities are included under derivatives.

12. (E) Variable annuity contracts do not fall under the requirements of accounting for derivatives.

13. (E) Adjustable rate loans are not required to be accounted for under the rules for derivatives.

14. (I) Interest rate swaps must be accounted for using the rules for edrivatives.

Situation	Terminology	Concepts	Applicability of SFAS 133	Communication	Research

To: CEO, Riley Corporation
From: CPA Candidate
Re: Financial Instrument Disclosures

Thank you for your inquiry regarding financial statement disclosures for derivatives and hedging. An entity that holds or issues derivative or nonderivative financial instruments that are used as hedging instruments is required to disclose its objectives for holding or issuing those instruments as well as its strategies for achieving those objectives. The context needed to understand the instruments must also be disclosed. In addition, the entity must disclose its risk management policies and a list of hedged instruments. These disclosures must be separated by type of hedge. Finally, entities must make these financial instrument disclosures for every reporting period for which a complete set of financial statements is issued.

　　If you have further questions, please contact my office.

Situation	Terminology	Concepts	Applicability of SFAS 133	Communication	Research

1. What is a derivative instrument?

FAS133, Para 6

6. A derivative instrument is a financial instrument or other contract with all three of the following characteristics:

　　a.　It has (1) one or more underlyings and (2) one or more notional amounts or payment provisions or both. Those terms determine the amount of the settlement or settlements, and, in some cases, whether or not a settlement is required.

　　b.　It requires no initial net investment or an initial net investment that is smaller than would be required for other types of contracts that would be expected to have a similar response to changes in market factors.

　　c.　Its terms require or permit net settlement, it can readily be settled net by a means outside the contract, or it provides for delivery of an asset that puts the recipient in a position not substantially different from net settlement.

Codification: 815-10-15-83

2. A company has a foreign currency fair value hedge. Where is the gain or loss reported in the financial statements?

FAS133, Para 39

39. Gains and losses on a qualifying foreign currency fair value hedge shall be accounted for as specified in paragraphs 22-27. The gain or loss on a nonderivative hedging instrument attributable to foreign currency risk is the foreign currency transaction gain or loss as determined under Statement 52. That foreign currency transaction gain or loss shall be recognized currently in earnings along with the change in the carrying amount of the hedged firm commitment.

Codification: 815-25-35-15 and 815-25-35-16

3. Where is the effective portion of a gain or loss on a cash flow hedge reported on the financial statements?

FAS133, Para 30

30. The effective portion of the gain or loss on a derivative designated as a cash flow hedge is reported in other comprehensive income, and the ineffective portion is reported in earnings. More specifically, a qualifying cash flow hedge shall be accounted for as follows:

　　a.　If an entity's defined risk management strategy for a particular hedging relationship excludes a specific component of the gain or loss, or related cash flows, on the hedging derivative from the assessment of hedge effectiveness (as discussed in paragraph 63 in Section 2 of Appendix A), that excluded component of the gain or loss shall be recognized currently in earnings. For example, if the effectiveness of a hedge with an option contract is assessed based on changes in the option's intrinsic value, the changes in the option's time value would be recognized in earnings. Time value is equal to the fair value of the option less its intrinsic value.

　　b.　Accumulated other comprehensive income associated with the hedged transaction shall be adjusted to a balance that reflects the lesser of the following (in absolute amounts):

　　　　(1)　The cumulative gain or loss on the derivative from inception of the hedge less (a) the excluded component discussed in paragraph 30(a) above and (b) the derivative's gains or losses previously reclassified from accumulated other comprehensive income into earnings pursuant to paragraph 31.

(2) The portion of the cumulative gain or loss on the derivative necessary to offset the cumulative change in expected future cash flows on the hedged transaction from inception of the hedge less the derivative's gains or losses previously reclassified from accumulated other comprehensive income into earnings pursuant to paragraph 31.

That adjustment of accumulated other comprehensive income shall incorporate recognition in other comprehensive income of part or all of the gain or loss on the hedging derivative, as necessary.

c.   A gain or loss shall be recognized in earnings, as necessary, for any remaining gain or loss on the hedging derivative or to adjust other comprehensive income to the balance specified in paragraph 30(b) above.

Codification: 815-30-35-3

Simulation Problem 2

Situation	Terminology	Journal Entries	Foreign Currency Transaction Gains/Losses	Financial Statement Disclosures	Communication	Research

	(A)	(B)	(C)	(D)	(E)	(F)	(G)	(H)	(I)	(J)	(K)	(L)	(M)	(N)	(O)
1. At the money	○	○	○	○	○	○	○	○	○	○	○	●	○	○	○
2. Bifurcation	○	○	○	○	○	○	○	○	●	○	○	○	○	○	○
3. Call option	○	○	○	○	○	●	○	○	○	○	○	○	○	○	○
4. Embedded derivative	○	○	●	○	○	○	○	○	○	○	○	○	○	○	○
5. Forward contract	○	○	○	○	○	○	●	○	○	○	○	○	○	○	○
6. Futures contract	○	○	○	○	○	○	○	○	○	○	○	○	○	○	●
7. In the money	○	●	○	○	○	○	○	○	○	○	○	○	○	○	○
8. Notional amount	○	○	○	○	○	○	○	○	○	●	○	○	○	○	○
9. Out of the money	○	○	○	○	○	○	○	●	○	○	○	○	○	○	○
10. Put option	○	○	○	○	○	○	○	○	○	○	○	○	●	○	○
11. Swap	○	○	○	●	○	○	○	○	○	○	○	○	○	○	○
12. Underlying	○	○	○	○	○	○	○	○	○	○	●	○	○	○	○

Explanation of solutions

1.   **(L)** An at-the-money option is one in which the price of the underlying is equal to the strike or exercise price.

2.   **(I)** Bifurcation is the process of separating an embedded derivative from its host contract. This process is necessary so that hybrid instruments (a financial instrument or other contract that contains an embedded derivative) can be separated into their component parts, each being accounted for using the appropriate valuation techniques.

3.   **(F)** An American call option provides the holder the right to acquire an underlying at an exercise or strike price anytime during the option term. A premium is paid by the holder for the right to benefit from the appreciation in the underlying.

4.   **(C)** An embedded derivative is a feature on a financial instrument or other contract which, if the feature stood alone, would meet the definition of a derivative.

5.   **(G)** A forward contract is an agreement between two parties to buy and sell a specific quantity of a commodity, foreign currency, or financial instrument at an agreed-upon price, with delivery and/or settlement at a designated future date. Because a forward contract is not formally regulated by an organized exchange, each party to the contract is subject to the default of the other party.

6.   **(O)** A futures contract is a forward-based contract to make or take delivery of a designated financial instrument, foreign currency, or commodity during a designated period, at a specified price or yield. The contract frequently has provisions for cash settlement. A future contract is traded on a regulated exchange and, therefore, involves less credit risk than a forward contract.

7.   **(B)** A call option is in the money if the price of the underlying is greater than the strike or exercise price of the underlying.

8.   **(J)** The notional amount (or payment provision) is the referenced associated asset or liability. A notional amount is commonly a number of units such as shares of stock, principal amount, face value, stated value, basis points, barrels of oil, etc. It may be that amount plus a premium or minus a discount. The interaction of the price or rate (underlying) with the referenced associated asset or liability (notional amount) determines whether settlement is required and, if so, the amount.

9.   **(H)** A call option is out of the money if the strike or exercise price is greater than the price of the underlying. A put option is out of the money if the price of the underlying is greater than the strike or exercise option.

10.   **(N)** An American put option provides the holder the right to sell the underlying at an exercise or strike price, anytime during the option term. A gain accrues to the holder as the market price of the underlying falls below the strike price.

11.   **(D)** A swap is a forward-based contract or agreement generally between two counterparties to exchange streams of cash flows over a specified period in the future.

12.   **(K)** An underlying is commonly a specified price or rate such as a stock price, interest rate, currency rate, commodity price, or a related index. However, any variable (financial or physical) with (1) observable changes or (2) objectively verifiable changes such as a credit rating, insurance index, climatic or geological condition (temperature, rainfall) qualifies. Unless it is specifically excluded, a contract based on any qualifying variable is accounted for under the rules for derivatives if it has the distinguishing characteristics stated above.

Situation	Terminology	Journal Entries		Foreign Currency Transaction Gains/Losses	Financial Statement Disclosures	Communication	Research
1.	Accounts receivable (£)	691,530					
	Sales		691,530				

£370,000 × 1.869 = $691,530

2.	Cash	662,670					
	Loss on FC transaction	28,860					
	Accounts receivable (£)		691,530				

£370,000 × 1.791 = $662,670

3.	Supplies	245,100					
	Accounts payable (€)		245,100				

€190,000 × 1.290 = $245,100

4.	Accounts payable (€)	245,100					
	Loss on FC transaction	7,410					
	Cash		252,510				

€190,000 × 1.329 = $252,510

5.	Accounts receivable (€)	333,250					
	Sales		333,250				

€250,000 × 1.333 = $333,250

6.	Accounts receivable (€)	7,750					
	Gain on FC transaction		7,750				

Adjust to spot rate on balance sheet date
€250,000 × (1.364 − 1.333) = $7,750 gain

7.	Cash	327,750					
	Loss on FC transaction	13,250					
	Accounts receivable (€)		341,000				

€250,000 × 1.311 = $327,750
Original A/R of $333,250 + $7,750 gain = $341,000 balance in A/R as of 12/31/09
Loss is $341,000 − $327,750 = $13,250

Explanation of solutions

Foreign currency transactions are recorded at the spot rate on the date of the transaction. When the account is settled in the foreign currency, the currency is exchanged at the spot rate on the date of settlement, and any gain or loss is recognized as a transaction gain/loss.

If the account is outstanding at the balance sheet date, the account receivable or payable is adjusted to the spot rate on the balance sheet date and the gain/loss from foreign currency transaction is recognized as other income for the period.

Situation	Terminology	Journal Entries	**Foreign Currency Transaction Gains/Losses**	Financial Statement Disclosures	Communication	Research

Prepare the following schedule outlining the foreign currency transaction gains and losses for 2009 and 2010 for Logan Corporation.

Logan Corporation
SCHEDULE OF FOREIGN CURRENCY TRANSACTION GAIN/LOSSES
For the years 2009 and 2010

	2009 gain/(loss)	2010 gain/(loss)
Lexington Corporation	(28,860)	0
Dietmar Corporation	(7410)	0
Cordier Corporation	7,750	(13,250)
Total FC gain/(loss)	(28,520)	(13,250)

Situation	Terminology	Journal Entries	Foreign Currency Transaction Gains/Losses	**Financial Statement Disclosures**	Communication	Research

Indicate from the list below where the foreign currency transaction gain or loss in 2009 will be disclosed on the financial statements.

A. Extraordinary gain/loss
B. Other gain/loss
C. Other comprehensive income
D. Revenue
E. Expense

(A) (B) (C) (D) (E)

1. Foreign currency transaction gain/loss for 2009 will be disclosed where on the financial statement? ○ ● ○ ○ ○

Situation	Terminology	Journal Entries	Foreign Currency Transaction Gains/Losses	Financial Statement Disclosures	**Communication**	Research

To: CEO, Logan Corporation
From: CPA Candidate
Re: Hybrid Financial Instruments

This memorandum provides a definition of a number of terms related to derivatives, which will help you understand the accounting for financial instruments.

A hybrid instrument is a financial instrument or other contract containing a feature that, if it stood alone, would meet the definition of a derivative instrument. This feature is known as an embedded derivative instrument. There is a basic contract in a hybrid instrument that is called the host contract that has the embedded derivative instrument.

Bifurcation is the process of separating the embedded derivative instrument from its host contract. The embedded derivative instrument should then be treated as if it were a stand-alone instrument. The host contract (excluding the embedded derivative) should be accounted for in the normal manner, as if it had never contained the embedded derivative.

Bifurcation must occur if, and only if, all of the following three criteria are met. First, the embedded derivative instrument must meet the definition of a derivative instrument. Second, the hybrid instrument must not be regularly reported at fair value, with changes in its fair value being reported in current earnings. Finally, the economic characteristics and risks of the embedded derivative must not be clearly and closely related to the economic characteristics and risks of the host contract.

Examples of hybrid instruments that would require bifurcation include the following: (1) a bond payable with an interest rate based on the S&P 500 Index; (2) equity instrument with a call option, allowing the issuing company to buy back the stock; and (3) loans with term-extending options whose values are based on the prime rate at the time of the extension.

If you have further questions or need additional assistance with hybrid instruments, please contact my office.

Situation	Terminology	Journal Entries	Foreign Currency Transaction Gains/Losses	Financial Statement Disclosures	Communication	Research

1. What is the definition of functional currency?

FAS52, Para 57

5. The assets, liabilities, and operations of a foreign entity shall be measured using the functional currency of that entity. An entity's functional currency is the currency of the primary economic environment in which the entity operates; normally, that is the currency of the environment in which an entity primarily generates and expends cash. Appendix A provides guidance for determination of the functional currency. The economic factors cited in Appendix A, and possibly others, should be considered both individually and collectively when determining the functional currency.

Codification: 830-10-20 Glossary

2. Sometimes foreign currency receivables or payables have not been settled by year-end. At what amount should these transactions be disclosed in the balance sheet?

FAS52, Para 16

16. For other than forward exchange contracts (paragraphs 17-19), the following shall apply to all foreign currency transactions of an enterprise and its investees:

a. At the date the transaction is recognized, each asset, liability, revenue, expense, gain, or loss arising from the transaction shall be measured and recorded in the functional currency of the recording entity by use of the exchange rate in effect at that date (paragraphs 26-28).

b. At each balance sheet date, recorded balances that are denominated in a currency other than the functional currency of the recording entity shall be adjusted to reflect the current exchange rate.

Codification: 830-20-35-2

3. At what exchange rate should a foreign currency transaction be recorded?

FAS52, Para 27

27. The exchange rates to be used for translation of foreign currency transactions and foreign currency statements are as follows:

a. Foreign Currency Transactions—The applicable rate at which a particular transaction could be settled at the transaction date shall be used to translate and record the transaction. At a subsequent balance sheet date, the current rate is that rate at which the related receivable or payable could be settled at that date.

Codification: 830-20-30-3

MULTIPLE-CHOICE QUESTIONS (1-17)

1. Green, a calendar-year taxpayer, is preparing a personal statement of financial condition as of April 30, 2009. Green's 2008 income tax liability was paid in full on April 15, 2009. Green's tax on income earned between January and April 2009 is estimated at $20,000. In addition, $40,000 is estimated for income tax on the differences between the estimated current values and current amounts of Green's assets and liabilities and their tax bases at April 30, 2009. No withholdings or payments have been made towards the 2009 income tax liability. In Green's April 30, 2009 statement of financial condition, what amount should be reported, between liabilities and net worth, as estimated income taxes?

    a. $0
    b. $20,000
    c. $40,000
    d. $60,000

2. On December 31, 2009, Shane is a fully vested participant in a company-sponsored pension plan. According to the plan's administrator, Shane has at that date the nonforfeitable right to receive a lump sum of $100,000 on December 28, 2010. The discounted amount of $100,000 is $90,000 at December 31, 2009. The right is not contingent on Shane's life expectancy and requires no future performance on Shane's part. In Shane's December 31, 2009, personal statement of financial condition, the vested interest in the pension plan should be reported at

    a. $0
    b. $ 90,000
    c. $ 95,000
    d. $100,000

3. The following information pertains to marketable equity securities owned by Kent:

	Fair value at December 31,		Cost in
Stock	2010	2009	2008
City Mfg., Inc.	$95,500	$93,000	$89,900
Tri Corp.	3,400	5,600	3,600
Zee, Inc.		10,300	15,000

The Zee stock was sold in January 2010 for $10,200. In Kent's personal statement of financial condition at December 31, 2010, what amount should be reported for marketable equity securities?

    a. $93,300
    b. $93,500
    c. $94,100
    d. $98,900

4. Clint owns 50% of Vohl Corp.'s common stock. Clint paid $20,000 for this stock in 2006. At December 31, 2009, Clint's 50% stock ownership in Vohl had a fair value of $180,000. Vohl's cumulative net income and cash dividends declared for the five years ended December 31, 2009, were $300,000 and $40,000, respectively. In Clint's personal statement of financial condition at December 31, 2009, what amount should be shown as the investment in Vohl?

    a. $ 20,000
    b. $150,000
    c. $170,000
    d. $180,000

5. Jen has been employed by Komp, Inc. since February 1, 2007. Jen is covered by Komp's Section 401(k) deferred compensation plan. Jen's contributions have been 10% of salaries. Komp has made matching contributions of 5%. Jen's salaries were $21,000 in 2007, $23,000 in 2008, and $26,000 in 2009. Employer contributions vest after an employee completes three years of continuous employment. The balance in Jen's 401(k) account was $11,900 at December 31, 2009, which included earnings of $1,200 on Jen's contributions. What amount should be reported for Jen's vested interest in the 401(k) plan in Jen's December 31, 2009 personal statement of financial condition?

    a. $11,900
    b. $ 8,200
    c. $ 7,000
    d. $ 1,200

6. The following information pertains to an insurance policy that Barton owns on his life:

Face amount	$100,000
Accumulated premiums paid up to December 31, 2010	8,000
Cash value at December 31, 2010	12,000
Policy loan	3,000

In Barton's personal statement of financial condition at December 31, 2010, what amount should be reported for the investment in life insurance?

    a. $97,000
    b. $12,000
    c. $ 9,000
    d. $ 8,000

7. Ely had the following personal investments at December 31, 2009:

- Realty held as a limited business activity not conducted in a separate business entity. Mortgage payments were made with funds from sources unrelated to the realty. The cost of this realty was $500,000, and the related mortgage payable was $100,000 at December 31, 2009.
- Sole proprietorship marketable as a going concern. Its cost was $900,000, and it had related accounts payable of $80,000 at December 31, 2009.

The costs of both investments equal estimated current values. The balances of liabilities equal their estimated current amounts.

How should the foregoing information be reported in Ely's statement of financial condition at December 31, 2009?

		Assets	Liabilities
a.	Investment in real estate	$ 400,000	
	Investment in sole proprietorship	820,000	
b.	Investment in real estate	$ 500,000	
	Investment in sole proprietorship	820,000	
	Mortgage payable		$100,000
c.	Investment in real estate	$ 500,000	
	Investment in sole proprietorship	900,000	
	Mortgage payable		$100,000
	Accounts payable		80,000
d.	Investments	$1,400,000	
	Accounts and mortgage payable		$180,000

8. At December 31, 2009, Ryan had the following non-cancelable personal commitments:

Pledge to be paid to County Welfare Home
thirty days after volunteers paint the walls and
ceiling of the Home's recreation room $ 5,000
Pledge to be paid to City Hospital on the recovery of
Ryan's comatose sister $25,000

What amount should be included in liabilities in Ryan's personal statement of financial condition at December 31, 2009?

    a. $0
    b. $ 5,000
    c. $25,000
    d. $30,000

9. The estimated current values of Lane's personal assets at December 31, 2009, totaled $1,000,000, with tax bases aggregating $600,000. Included in these assets was a vested interest in a deferred profit-sharing plan with a current value of $80,000 and a tax basis of $70,000. The estimated current amounts of Lane's personal liabilities equaled their tax bases at December 31, 2009. Lane's 2009 effective income tax rate was 30%. In Lane's personal statement of financial condition at December 31, 2009, what amount should be provided for estimated income taxes relating to the excess of current values over tax bases?

    a. $120,000
    b. $117,000
    c. $ 3,000
    d. $0

10. Shea, a calendar-year taxpayer, is preparing a personal statement of financial condition as of April 30, 2009. Shea's 2008 income tax liability was paid in full on April 15, 2009. Shea's tax on income earned from January through April 2009 is estimated at $30,000. In addition, $25,000 is estimated for income tax on the differences between the estimated current values of Shea's assets and the current amounts of liabilities and their tax bases at April 30, 2009. No withholdings or payments have been made towards the 2009 income tax liability. In Shea's statement of financial condition at April 30, 2009, what is the total of the amount or amounts that should be reported for income taxes?

    a. $0
    b. $25,000
    c. $30,000
    d. $55,000

11. The following information pertains to Smith's personal assets and liabilities at December 31, 2009:

	Historical cost	Estimated current values	Estimated current amounts
Assets	$500,000	$900,000	
Liabilities	100,000		$80,000

Smith's 2009 income tax rate was 30%. In Smith's personal statement of financial condition at December 31, 2009, what amount should be reported as Smith's net worth?

    a. $294,000
    b. $420,000
    c. $694,000
    d. $820,000

12. Personal financial statements usually consist of

    a.   A statement of net worth and a statement of changes in net worth.
    b.   A statement of net worth, an income statement, and a statement of changes in net worth.
    c.   A statement of financial condition and a statement of changes in net worth.
    d.   A statement of financial condition, a statement of changes in net worth, and a statement of cash flows.

13. Personal financial statements should report assets and liabilities at

    a.   Estimated current values at the date of the financial statements and, as additional information, at historical cost.
    b.   Estimated current values at the date of the financial statements.
    c.   Historical cost and, as additional information, at estimated current values at the date of the financial statements.
    d.   Historical cost.

14. A business interest that constitutes a large part of an individual's total assets should be presented in a personal statement of financial condition as

    a.   A separate listing of the individual assets and liabilities at cost.
    b.   Separate line items of both total assets and total liabilities at cost.
    c.   A single amount equal to the proprietorship equity.
    d.   A single amount equal to the estimated current value of the business interest.

15. Smith owns several works of art. At what amount should these artworks be reported in Smith's personal financial statements?

    a.   Original cost.
    b.   Insured amount.
    c.   Smith's estimate.
    d.   Appraised value.

16. For the purpose of estimating income taxes to be reported in personal financial statements, assets and liabilities measured at their tax bases should be compared to assets and liabilities measured at their

	Assets	_Liabilities_
a.	Estimated current value	Estimated current amount
b.	Historical cost	Historical cost
c.	Estimated current value	Historical cost
d.	Historical cost	Estimated current amount

17. In personal financial statements, how should estimated income taxes on the excess of the estimated current values of assets over their tax bases be reported in the statement of financial condition?

    a.   As liabilities.
    b.   As deductions from the related assets.
    c.   Between liabilities and net worth.
    d.   In a footnote disclosure only.

MULTIPLE-CHOICE ANSWERS

1. c __ __	5. b __ __	9. a __ __	13. b __ __	17. c __ __
2. b __ __	6. c __ __	10. d __ __	14. d __ __	
3. d __ __	7. b __ __	11. c __ __	15. d __ __	1st: __/17 = __%
4. d __ __	8. a __ __	12. c __ __	16. a __ __	2nd: __/17 = __%

MULTIPLE-CHOICE ANSWER EXPLANATIONS

A. Personal Financial Statements

1. **(c)** Only the estimated amount of income taxes on the differences between the estimated current values and current amounts of assets and liabilities is presented between liabilities and net worth. Answer (a) is incorrect because the $40,000 estimated income taxes on the differences between the estimated current values and current amounts of assets and liabilities is presented between liabilities and net worth. Answer (b) is incorrect because the $20,000 current tax liability would be presented as a liability. Answer (d) is incorrect because the $20,000 current tax liability would be presented as a liability while the $40,000 amount would be presented between liabilities and net worth.

2. **(b)** In a personal statement of financial condition, assets are generally presented at estimated current values. Depending on the nature of the asset, current value can be estimated using fair market value, net realizable value, discounted cash flow, or appraised value. A future interest that is nonforfeitable should be valued using discounted cash flow. Therefore, the interest in the pension plan should be valued at $90,000.

3. **(d)** Assets are generally presented at their estimated current values on personal financial statements. For Kent's December 31, 2010 personal statement of financial condition, the current values of the marketable equity securities held as of that date should be used. Thus, Kent should report $98,900 ($95,500 + $3,400) for marketable equity securities.

4. **(d)** Assets are generally presented at their estimated current values. Depending on the nature of the asset, current value can be estimated using fair value (FV), net realizable value, discounted cash flow, or appraised value. In this problem, the fair value of the stock ($180,000) is known and should be shown as the investment in Vohl. Note that the net income and dividends have nothing to do with the amount shown as the investment in Vohl, and this information is irrelevant.

5. **(b)** This problem requires that we determine Jen's vested interest in the 401(k) plan to be reported in her December 31, 2009 personal statement of financial condition. The problem states that employer contributions vest after an employee completes three years of service. As Jen has not completed three years of service as of December 31, 2009, none of the employer's contributions have vested. Thus, the problem is to determine Jen's contributions and the earnings on **her** contributions as follows:

2007 contributions	2,100
2008 contributions	2,300
2009 contributions	2,600
	7,000
Earnings on above contributions	1,200
Jen's vested interest	8,200

6. **(c)** Assets are generally presented at their estimated current values in personal financial statements. Specifically, investments in life insurance are to be valued at their cash surrender value less outstanding loans on the policy. Therefore, the investment should be reported at $9,000 ($12,000 cash value – $3,000 outstanding loan).

7. **(b)** When investments in a limited business activity are not conducted in a separate business entity, separate asset and liability amounts of the investment should be shown on the statement of financial condition. Thus, the realty (asset) and the mortgage (liability) should be reported separately at $500,000 and $100,000, respectively (their estimated current values). An investment in a separate entity that is marketable as a going concern (e.g., closely held corporation) should be presented as one amount. Thus, the $80,000 in accounts payable should be netted against the current value of $900,000 to report a net investment of $820,000.

8. **(a)** Noncancelable personal commitments should be reported at their discounted cash flow. A commitment must have all of the following attributes: (1) are for fixed or determinable amounts; (2) are not contingent on others' life expectancies or occurrence of a particular event (e.g., disability/death); and (3) do not require future performance of service by others. As the pledge to County Welfare Home is contingent upon the volunteers painting the walls and ceiling and the pledge to City Hospital is contingent upon the recovery of Ryan's comatose sister, both liabilities should be excluded from Ryan's personal statement of financial condition at December 31, 2009.

9. **(a)** Estimated taxes that would be paid if all the assets were converted to cash and all the liabilities were paid should be included with the liabilities. Thus, $120,000 [($1,000,000 – $600,000) × .30] should be provided for estimated income taxes relating to the excess of current values over tax bases.

10. **(d)** A personal statement of financial condition presents estimated current values of assets and liabilities, estimated income taxes, and estimated net worth at a specified date. Income taxes payable should include unpaid income taxes for completed tax years, the estimated tax for the elapsed portion of the current year, and the estimated income tax on the difference between the current value of assets and the current amounts of liabilities and their respective tax bases. Thus, the amount to be reported on Shea's statement of financial condition for income taxes is $55,000, equal to the sum of $30,000 tax on income earned from January through April and $25,000 estimated income tax on the difference between the current value and tax bases of assets and liabilities.

11. **(c)** Assets are generally presented at their estimated current values on personal financial statements. Therefore, the assets should be reported at their fair value of $900,000, rather than at their cost of $500,000. ASC Topic 274 also states that liabilities are presented at the lesser of the discounted amount of cash to be paid, or the current cash settlement amount. Therefore, the liabilities should be reported at $80,000. Estimated taxes that would be paid if all the assets were converted to cash and all the liabilities were paid should be included with the liabilities. Thus, 126,000 [(820,000 – 400,000) × .30] should be provided for estimated income taxes relating to the excess of current values over tax bases. Smith's net worth should be reported as $694,000 ($900,000 – $80,000 – $126,000).

12. **(c)** Personal financial statements consist of (1) a statement of financial condition and (2) a statement of changes in net worth.

13. **(b)** A personal financial statement presents the estimated current values of assets and liabilities. Additional information at historical cost is not required.

14. **(d)** Business interests that constitute a large part of a person's total assets should be shown separately from other investments. The estimated **current value** of an investment in a separate entity, such as a closely held corporation, a partnership, or a sole proprietorship, should be shown in **one amount** as an investment if the entity is marketable as a going concern.

15. **(d)** Assets are generally presented at their estimated current values in a personal statement of financial condition. Depending on the nature of the asset, current value can be estimated using fair market value, net realizable value, discounted cash flow, or appraised value. The best estimate of the fair value of art is the appraised value.

16. **(a)** In personal financial statements assets should be stated at their estimated current values and liabilities should be stated at the lower of the discounted value of their future cash payments or their current cash settlement amounts. These current amounts will differ from their tax bases and will give rise to **unrealized** tax gains and losses. A provision for estimated income taxes on these unrealized amounts should be incorporated into personal financial statements because when the unrealized gains and losses are realized, the related income taxes will have to be either paid or received.

17. **(c)** The estimated income taxes should be presented between liabilities and net worth in the statement of financial condition.

MULTIPLE-CHOICE QUESTIONS (1-16)

1. On January 1, 2009, Builder Associates entered into a $1,000,000 long-term, fixed-price contract to construct a factory building for Manufacturing Company. Builder accounts for this contract under the percentage-of-completion, and estimated costs at completion at the end of each quarter for 2009 were as follows:

Quarter	Estimated percentage-of-completion	Estimated costs at completion
1	10%	$750,000
2*	10%	$750,000
3	25%	$960,000
4*	25%	$960,000

*No work performed in the 2nd and 4th quarters.

What amounts should be reported by Builder as "Income on Construction Contract" in its quarterly income statements based on the above information?

	Gain (loss) for the three months ended			
	3/31/09	6/30/09	9/30/09	12/31/09
a.	$0	$0	$0	$10,000
b.	$25,000	$0	$(15,000)	$0
c.	$25,000	$0	$0	$0
d.	$25,000	$0	$ 6,000	$0

2. Kell Corp.'s $95,000 net income for the quarter ended September 30, 2009, included the following after-tax items:

- A $60,000 extraordinary gain, realized on April 30, 2009, was allocated equally to the second, third, and fourth quarters of 2009.
- A $16,000 cumulative-effect loss resulting from a change in inventory valuation method was recognized on August 2, 2009.

In addition, Kell paid $48,000 on February 1, 2009, for 2009 calendar-year property taxes. Of this amount, $12,000 was allocated to the third quarter of 2009.

For the quarter ended September 30, 2009, Kell should report net income of
- a. $ 91,000
- b. $103,000
- c. $111,000
- d. $115,000

3. Vilo Corp. has estimated that total depreciation expense for the year ending December 31, 2009, will amount to $60,000, and that 2009 year-end bonuses to employees will total $120,000. In Vilo's interim income statement for the six months ended June 30, 2009, what is the total amount of expense relating to these two items that should be reported?
- a. $0
- b. $ 30,000
- c. $ 90,000
- d. $180,000

4. On June 30, 2009, Mill Corp. incurred a $100,000 net loss from disposal of a business segment. Also, on June 30, 2009, Mill paid $40,000 for property taxes assessed for the calendar year 2009. What amount of the foregoing items should be included in the determination of Mill's net income or loss for the six-month interim period ended June 30, 2009?
- a. $140,000
- b. $120,000
- c. $ 90,000
- d. $ 70,000

5. During the first quarter of 2009, Tech Co. had income before taxes of $200,000, and its effective income tax rate was 15%. Tech's 2008 effective annual income tax rate was 30%, but Tech expects its 2009 effective annual income tax rate to be 25%. In its first quarter interim income statement, what amount of income tax expense should Tech report?
- a. $0
- b. $30,000
- c. $50,000
- d. $60,000

6. Bailey Company, a calendar-year corporation, has the following income before income tax provision and estimated effective annual income tax rates for the first three quarters of 2009:

Quarter	Income before income tax provision	Estimated effective annual tax rate at end of quarter
First	$60,000	40%
Second	70,000	40%
Third	40,000	45%

Bailey's income tax provision in its interim income statement for the third quarter should be
- a. $18,000
- b. $24,500
- c. $25,500
- d. $76,500

7. Advertising costs may be accrued or deferred to provide an appropriate expense in each period for

	Interim financial reporting	Year-end financial reporting
a.	Yes	No
b.	Yes	Yes
c.	No	No
d.	No	Yes

8. A planned volume variance in the first quarter, which is expected to be absorbed by the end of the fiscal period, ordinarily should be deferred at the end of the first quarter if it is

	Favorable	Unfavorable
a.	Yes	No
b.	No	Yes
c.	No	No
d.	Yes	Yes

9. Due to a decline in market price in the second quarter, Petal Co. incurred an inventory loss. The market price is expected to return to previous levels by the end of the year. At the end of the year the decline had not reversed. When should the loss be reported in Petal's interim income statements?
- a. Ratably over the second, third, and fourth quarters.
- b. Ratably over the third and fourth quarters.
- c. In the second quarter only.
- d. In the fourth quarter only.

10. An inventory loss from a market price decline occurred in the first quarter. The loss was not expected to be restored in the fiscal year. However, in the third quarter the inventory had a market price recovery that exceeded the market decline that occurred in the first quarter. For interim financial reporting, the dollar amount of net inventory should
- a. Decrease in the first quarter by the amount of the market price decline and increase in the third quarter by the amount of the market price recovery.

b. Decrease in the first quarter by the amount of the market price decline and increase in the third quarter by the amount of decrease in the first quarter.

c. Not be affected in the first quarter and increase in the third quarter by the amount of the market price recovery that exceeded the amount of the market price decline.

d. Not be affected in either the first quarter or the third quarter.

11. For external reporting purposes, it is appropriate to use estimated gross profit rates to determine the cost of goods sold for

	Interim financial reporting	Year-end financial reporting
a.	Yes	Yes
b.	Yes	No
c.	No	Yes
d.	No	No

12. For interim financial reporting, the computation of a company's second quarter provision for income taxes uses an effective tax rate expected to be applicable for the full fiscal year. The effective tax rate should reflect anticipated

	Foreign tax rates	Available tax planning alternatives
a.	No	Yes
b.	No	No
c.	Yes	No
d.	Yes	Yes

13. For interim financial reporting, a company's income tax provision for the second quarter of 2009 should be determined using the

a. Effective tax rate expected to be applicable for the full year of 2009 as estimated at the end of the first quarter of 2009.

b. Effective tax rate expected to be applicable for the full year of 2009 as estimated at the end of the second quarter of 2009.

c. Effective tax rate expected to be applicable for second quarter of 2009.

d. Statutory tax rate for 2009.

14. ASC Topic 270, *Interim Reporting*, states that interim financial reporting should be viewed primarily in which of the following ways?

a. As useful only if activity is spread evenly throughout the year.

b. As if the interim period were an annual accounting period.

c. As reporting for an integral part of an annual period.

d. As reporting under a comprehensive basis of accounting other than GAAP.

15. Conceptually, interim financial statements can be described as emphasizing

a. Timeliness over reliability.

b. Reliability over relevance.

c. Relevance over comparability.

d. Comparability over neutrality.

16. Wilson Corp. experienced a $50,000 decline in the market value of its inventory in the first quarter of its fiscal year. Wilson had expected this decline to reverse in the third quarter, and in fact, the third quarter recovery exceeded the previous decline by $10,000. Wilson's inventory did not experience any other declines in market value during the fiscal year. What amounts of loss and/or gain should Wilson report in its interim financial statements for the first and third quarters?

	First quarter	Third quarter
a.	$0	$0
b.	$0	$10,000 gain
c.	$50,000 loss	$50,000 gain
d.	$50,000 loss	$60,000 gain

MULTIPLE-CHOICE ANSWERS

1. b	__ __	5. c	__ __	9. d	__ __	13. b	__ __	16. a	__ __				
2. a	__ __	6. b	__ __	10. b	__ __	14. c	__ __						
3. c	__ __	7. b	__ __	11. b	__ __	15. a	__ __	1st: __/16 = __%					
4. b	__ __	8. d	__ __	12. d	__ __			2nd: __/16 = __%					

MULTIPLE-CHOICE ANSWER EXPLANATIONS

B. Interim Reporting

1. (b) The requirement is to compute the income to be recognized in quarterly (interim) financial statements on a construction contract using the percentage-of-completion method. The solutions approach is to compute the income on the contract at the end of each quarter by (1) applying the estimated percentage-of-completion to the total estimated income to be recognized on the contract, and (2) subtracting the income recognized in preceding quarters to arrive at the income for the latest quarter. In the second and fourth quarters there was no work done on the contract and no change in the total estimated cost of completion. In quarter three the estimated costs of completion are revised upward. Since the cumulative income to date is less than income recognized in the first quarter, it is necessary to recognize a loss in the third quarter. The loss is handled as a change in accounting estimate rather than restating the first quarter.

Quarter 1:
  10% ($1,000,000 – $750,000) = $25,000 income recognized

Quarter 2:
  -0-

Quarter 3:
  25% ($1,000,000 – $960,000) = $10,000 income earned to date

  $10,000 income to date – $25,000 income recognized in previous periods = $(15,000) loss for quarter

Quarter 4:
  -0-

2. (a) Extraordinary items, gains or losses from disposal of a segment of a business, and unusual or infrequently occurring items should not be prorated over the balance of the fiscal year. Thus, the $20,000 ($60,000 ÷ 3) extraordinary gain that was allocated to the third quarter should be subtracted from net income as it actually occurred in the second quarter. Consistent with the view that all accounting changes should be made effective as of the beginning of the fiscal period, the cumulative effect of the accounting change on retained earnings is computed at the beginning of the fiscal year and reported in the first interim period's income statement. If a cumulative-effect type change is made during an interim period subsequent to the first one, the prior interim reports must be restated as if the changes had been effective as of the first day of the fiscal year. Thus, the $16,000 cumulative-effect loss should not be recognized in the third quarter. The prior interim reports should be restated and the $16,000 loss should be added back to income of the third quarter to correct the income to be reported for the quarter. Property taxes should be allocated among the applicable quarters. As Kell Corp. properly allocated their property taxes, no adjustment to income is needed. Kell should report $91,000 ($95,000 – $20,000 + $16,000) as net income for the quarter ended September 30, 2009.

3. (c) A cost charged to expense in an annual period should be allocated among the interim periods which clearly benefit from the expense through the use of accruals and/or deferrals. Both yearly bonuses and the use of an asset (depreciation expense) benefit the entire year. The expense for the **six month** interim statement should be ($60,000 + $120,000) ÷ 2 = $90,000.

4. (b) Revenues and gains should be recognized in interim reports on the same basis as used in annual reports. At June 30, 2009, Mill Corp. would report the entire $100,000 loss on the disposal of its business segment since the loss was incurred during the interim period. ASC Topic 270 also states that a cost charged to an expense in an annual period should be allocated among the interim periods that clearly benefit from the expense through the use of accruals and/or deferrals. Since the $40,000 property tax payment relates to the entire 2009 calendar year, $20,000 of the payment would be reported as an expense at June 30, 2009, while the remaining $20,000 would be reported as a prepaid expense.

5. (c) The tax provision for an interim period is the tax for the year to date (estimated effective rate for the year times year-to-date income) less the total tax provisions reported for previous interim periods. In this case, the requirement is to calculate the tax provision for the first quarter interim income statement. The tax expense is $50,000 ($200,000 × 25%).

6. (b) The requirement is to calculate Bailey's income tax provision (expense) in its interim income statement for the third quarter. The tax provision for an interim period is the tax for the year-to-date (estimated effective rate for the year times year-to-date income) less the total tax provisions reported for previous interim periods.

Year-to-date tax (45%)($170,000)	$76,500
Previously reported tax (40% × $130,000)	52,000
Third quarter tax provision	$24,500

7. (b) Advertising costs may be deferred within a fiscal year if the benefits clearly extend beyond the interim period that the expense was paid. Also, advertising costs may be accrued and assigned to interim periods in relation to sales. Year-end accruals and deferrals of costs are also considered appropriate accounting treatment. Note, however, that deferral in year-end reporting is permitted only if the advertising has not been run in the media.

8. (d) A planned volume variance that is expected to be absorbed by the end of the fiscal year should be deferred at interim reporting dates.

9. (d) The requirement is to determine when the inventory loss should be reported. Inventory losses from market declines should not be deferred beyond the interim period in which the loss occurs. However, if the market decline is considered to be **temporary** and will be recovered by year-end, no loss needs to be recognized. A loss will be recognized in the fourth quarter only. In the second quarter the loss is considered temporary, therefore no loss is recognized.

However, in the fourth quarter, when the decline does not reverse, it is deemed permanent and recognized in the fourth quarter. Losses are recognized in the period in which they occur, not ratably over several periods. Only expenses that benefit several periods (i.e., repairs and maintenance) are recognized ratably. The loss is not recorded in a period of temporary decline, only when the decline is considered to be permanent.

10. (b) A decline in inventory market price, expected to be other than temporary, should be recognized in the period of decline. A subsequent recovery of market value should be recognized as a cost recovery in the period of increase, but **never** above original cost. The decline should be recognized when it occurs in the first quarter. The subsequent recovery should be recognized when it occurs in the third quarter. The subsequent recovery cannot exceed the amount .of decline. A nontemporary decline should be shown in the quarter of price decrease.

11. (b) The requirement is to determine the appropriateness of estimated gross profit rates in determining cost of goods sold for interim and year-end external financial reporting purposes. The use of estimated gross profit rates to determine the cost of goods sold for an interim period is appropriate. The method of estimation used and any significant adjustments that result from reconciliations with the annual physical inventory should be disclosed. An estimation of cost of goods sold is not allowable for year-end financial reporting. (The actual cost of the goods sold must be determined by the use of a cost flow assumption that most clearly reflects periodic income.) Thus, an estimated cost of goods sold figure may be used for interim but not year-end statements.

12. (d) The effective tax rate should reflect anticipated investment tax credits, foreign tax rates, percentage depletion, capital gains rates, and other available tax planning alternatives.

13. (b) The requirement is to determine what tax rate should be used to calculate the income tax provision for interim reporting. Each interim period is considered to be an integral part of the annual period. Therefore, expectations for the annual period must be reflected in the interim report. The income tax expense should be calculated using the estimated annual effective tax rate. The estimated tax rate should be updated as of the end of each interim period (here, as of the second quarter). The statutory tax rate is only a part of the effective tax. The effective tax rate includes the statutory tax rate and a variety of other items.

14. (c) The **integral view,** used for interim reporting, holds that each interim period is an integral part of an annual period, must reflect expectations for the annual period, and must utilize special accruals, deferrals, and allocations.

15. (a) The primary purposes of interim reporting are to provide information which is more **timely** than is available in annual reports and to highlight business turning points which could be "buried" in annual reports. This emphasis on timeliness comes at the expense of **reliability**. Accounting information pertaining to shorter periods may require more arbitrary allocations, and may not be as verifiable or representationally faithful as information contained in annual reports. Interim reports are generally more relevant and less reliable. Interim financial statements should not be any more or less comparable than annual reports.

16. (a) Temporary declines in inventory market values are not recognized. Only declines that are apparently permanent or other than temporary need to be recognized. In this case, Wilson expected the decline to reverse in the third quarter; therefore, the decline is temporary and no loss would be recorded in the first quarter. Because no loss was recorded for the decline, no gain will be recognized in the third quarter for the recovery of the $50,000 decline. Also, assuming that the inventory was valued at cost at the beginning of the fiscal year, no gain will be recorded for the recovery excess of $10,000 since inventory may not be valued at an amount in excess of cost.

MULTIPLE-CHOICE QUESTIONS (1-11)

1. Correy Corp. and its divisions (each is an operating segment) are engaged solely in manufacturing operations. The following data (consistent with prior years' data) pertain to the operations conducted for the year ended December 31, 2009:

(Industry operating segment)	Total revenue	Operating profit	Identifiable assets at 12/31/09
A	$10,000,000	$1,750,000	$20,000,000
B	8,000,000	1,400,000	17,500,000
C	6,000,000	1,200,000	12,500,000
D	3,000,000	550,000	7,500,000
E	4,250,000	675,000	7,000,000
F	1,500,000	225,000	3,000,000
	$32,750,000	$5,800,000	$67,500,000

In its segment information for 2009, how many reportable segments does Correy have?
- a. Three.
- b. Four.
- c. Five.
- d. Six.

2. The following information pertains to Aria Corp. and its operating segments for the year ended December 31, 2009:

Sales to unaffiliated customers	$2,000,000
Intersegment sales of products similar to those sold to unaffiliated customers	600,000
Interest earned on loans to other industry segments	40,000

Aria and all of its divisions are engaged solely in manufacturing operations and evaluates divisional performance based on controllable contribution. Aria has a reportable segment if that segment's revenue exceeds
- a. $264,000
- b. $260,000
- c. $204,000
- d. $200,000

Items 3 and 4 are based on the following:

Grum Corp., a publicly owned corporation, is subject to the requirements for segment reporting. In its income statement for the year ended December 31, 2009, Grum reported revenues of $50,000,000, operating expenses of $47,000,000, and net income of $3,000,000. Operating expenses include payroll costs of $15,000,000. Grum's combined identifiable assets of all industry segments at December 31, 2009, were $40,000,000. Reported revenues include $30,000,000 of sales to external customers.

3. In its 2009 financial statements, Grum should disclose major customer data if sales to any single customer amount to at least
- a. $ 300,000
- b. $1,500,000
- c. $4,000,000
- d. $5,000,000

4. External revenue reported by operating segments must be at least
- a. $22,500,000
- b. $15,000,000
- c. $12,500,000
- d. $37,500,000

5. Enterprise-wide disclosures include disclosures about

	Geographic areas	Allocated costs
a.	Yes	Yes
b.	Yes	No
c.	No	Yes
d.	No	No

6. Enterprise-wide disclosures are required by publicly held companies with

	Only one reportable segment	More than one reportable segment
a.	Yes	Yes
b.	Yes	No
c.	No	Yes
d.	No	No

7. An enterprise must disclose all of the following about each reportable segment if the amounts are used by the chief operating decision maker, except
- a. Depreciation expense.
- b. Allocated expenses.
- c. Interest expense.
- d. Income tax expense.

8. In financial reporting for segments of a business, an enterprise shall disclose all of the following except
- a. Types of products and services from which each reportable segment derives its revenues.
- b. The title of the chief operating decision maker of each reportable segment.
- c. Factors used to identify the enterprises reportable segments.
- d. The basis of measurement of segment profit or loss and segment assets.

9. In financial reporting for segments of a business enterprise, segment data may be aggregated
- a. Before performing the 10% tests if a majority of the aggregation criteria are met.
- b. If the segments do not meet the 10% tests but meet all of the aggregation criteria.
- c. Before performing the 10% tests if all of the aggregation criteria are met.
- d. If any one of the aggregation criteria are met.

10. The method used to determine what information to report for business segments is referred to as the
- a. Segment approach.
- b. Operating approach.
- c. Enterprise approach.
- d. Management approach.

11. Taylor Corp., a publicly owned corporation, assesses performance and makes operating decisions using the following information for its reportable segments:

Total revenues	$768,000
Total profit and loss	40,600

Included in the total profit and loss are intersegment profits of $6,100. In addition, Taylor has $500 of common costs for its reportable segments that are not allocated in reports used internally. For purposes of segment reporting, Taylor should report segment profit of
- a. $35,000
- b. $34,500
- c. $41,100
- d. $40,600

SIMULATION PROBLEMS

Simulation Problem 1   (50 to 60 minutes)

Situation						
	Income Test	Revenue Test	Asset Test	Reportable Segments	Segment Reporting Test	Research	Communication

Caslow Co. is a new manufacturing company located in the United States, with divisions that operate in Spain, Turkey, and Thailand.

Each division has several reporting units that report its activities and financial information to the chief operating decision maker. Below is a list of the units and information for each unit of the three divisions. All amounts are in thousands.

Division	Reporting unit	Total revenue	Total income	Total assets	External revenue	Affiliated revenue
Spain	A	$100,000	$20,000	$260,000	$60,000	$40,000
	B	45,000	6,000	110,000	20,000	25,000
Turkey	C	85,000	19,000	120,000	50,000	35,000
	D	65,000	11,000	150,000	50,000	15,000
	E	25,000	5,000	60,000	25,000	0
Thailand	F	38,000	7,000	90,000	30,000	8,000
	G	120,000	39,000	290,000	50,000	70,000

	Income Test						
Situation		Revenue Test	Asset Test	Reportable Segments	Segment Reporting Test	Research	Communication

Identify which reporting units meet the income threshold to be a reportable segment.

	Division	Reporting unit	Income threshold
1.	Spain	A	○
2.		B	○
3.	Turkey	C	○
4.		D	○
5.		E	○
6.	Thailand	F	○
7.		G	○

		Revenue Test					
Situation	Income Test		Asset Test	Reportable Segments	Segment Reporting Test	Research	Communication

Identify which reporting units meet the revenue threshold to be a reportable segment.

	Division	Reporting unit	Revenue threshold
1.	Spain	A	○
2.		B	○
3.	Turkey	C	○
4.		D	○
5.		E	○
6.	Thailand	F	○
7.		G	○

			Asset Test				
Situation	Income Test	Revenue Test		Reportable Segments	Segment Reporting Test	Research	Communication

Identify which reporting units meet the asset threshold to be a reportable segment.

	Division	*Reporting unit*	*Asset threshold*
1.	Spain	A	○
2.		B	○
3.	Turkey	C	○
4.		D	○
5.		E	○
6.	Thailand	F	○
7.		G	○

Situation	Income Test	Revenue Test	Asset Test	Reportable Segments	Segment Reporting Test	Research	Communication

Which segments are reportable?

	Division	*Reporting unit*	*Reportable segment*
1.	Spain	A	○
2.		B	○
3.	Turkey	C	○
4.		D	○
5.		E	○
6.	Thailand	F	○
7.		G	○

Situation	Income Test	Revenue Test	Asset Test	Reportable Segments	Segment Reporting Test	Research	Communication

Complete the following schedule to determine if enough segments have been reported.

Total external revenues	
× percent	
Amount of unaffiliated revenue that must be reported	
Amount of unaffiliated revenue reported	

1. Indicate whether enough segments have been reported.   *Yes* ○   *No* ○

Situation	Income Test	Revenue Test	Asset Test	Reportable Segments	Segment Reporting Test	Research	Communication

Using the authoritative literature, answer each of the following questions by cutting and pasting the appropriate citation from FARS in the space provided.

1. What is the definition of an operating segment?

2. What are the three tests that determine if a company must report information about an operating segment?

3. What types of geographic information should a company report if practical?

Situation	Income Test	Revenue Test	Asset Test	Reportable Segments	Segment Reporting Test	Research	Communication

Using the results of your research, prepare a memo to the client explaining the requirements of segment reporting.

REMINDER: Your response will be graded for both technical content and writing skills. Technical content will be evaluated for information that is helpful to the intended reader and clearly relevant to the issue. Writing skills will be evaluated for development, organization, and the appropriate expression of ideas in professional correspondence. Use a standard business memo or letter format with a clear beginning, middle, and end. Do not convey information in the form of a table, bullet point list, or other abbreviated presentation.

Simulation Problem 2   (40 to 50 minutes)

Situation		Concepts	Segment Tests	Reportable Segments	Disclosures	Communication	Research

Barnet Co. has distinct operating units in its operations. Each of these components of the business reports its activities and its financial information to the chief operating decision maker. The company has no foreign operations, sales, or major individual customers. Below is information provided by Barnet's operating units (in millions).

Reporting unit	Total revenue	External revenue	Affiliated revenue	Income	Assets
A	4,200	3,000	1,200	1,200	15,900
B	500	200	300	(300)	6,700
C	800	650	150	250	4,420
D	1,400	800	600	510	7,800
E	2,300	1,200	1,100	(900)	6,500
F	5,000	4,000	1,000	2,600	28,600

Situation	Concepts		Segment Tests	Reportable Segments	Disclosures	Communication	Research

Indicate whether each of the following statements is True or False.

Statement	True	False
1. The method used for reporting segment information is the asset-liability approach.	○	○
2. If management judges that an operating segment is reportable in 2008 and is of continuing significance, information about that segment should be reported in 2009 even if it does not meet the requirements for reportability in 2009.	○	○
3. An enterprise must report separate information about an operating segment if its assets are 10% or more of the combined assets of all operating segments.	○	○
4. An enterprise must report separately the costs and expenses incurred by each segment.	○	○
5. One of the requirements of segment reporting is to report cash flows for each reportable segment.	○	○
6. An enterprise must report the interest revenue for each reportable segment if this information is normally reviewed by the chief operating decision maker.	○	○

Situation	Concepts	Segment Tests		Reportable Segments	Disclosures	Communication	Research

Identify which of the segments meets the quantitative threshold for revenues, profits/losses, and assets.

	Reporting unit	Revenue threshold	Profits/losses threshold	Asset threshold
1.	A	○	○	○
2.	B	○	○	○
3.	C	○	○	○
4.	D	○	○	○
5.	E	○	○	○
6.	F	○	○	○

Situation	Concepts	Segment Tests	Reportable Segments	Disclosures	Communication	Research

Which segments are reportable?

	Reporting unit	Reportable segment
1.	A	○
2.	B	○
3.	C	○
4.	D	○
5.	E	○
6.	F	○

Situation	Concepts	Segment Tests	Reportable Segments	Disclosures	Communication	Research

Answer each of the following questions related to disclosure of segment information.

1. What is the amount of external revenue that must be included from all reportable segments in order to meet the segment reporting requirements?

Amount
_____

2. Based on your evaluation of reportable segments, have enough segments been reported? (Yes or No)

Yes	*No*
○	○

Situation	Concepts	Segment Tests	Reportable Segments	Disclosures	Communication	Research

Barnet Company's CEO has contacted you and would like information on segment reporting. He has asked the following questions:

1. What is the purpose of segment disclosure?

2. Define operating segments and describe the approach used to identify operating segments.

3. What tests should Barnet apply in determining its reportable segments?

Write a memo to Barnet's CEO responding to each of his questions.

REMINDER: Your response will be graded for both technical content and writing skills. Technical content will be evaluated for information that is helpful to the intended reader and clearly relevant to the issue. Writing skills will be evaluated for development, organization, and the appropriate expression of ideas in professional correspondence. Use a standard business memo or letter format with a clear beginning, middle, and end. Do not convey information in the form of a table, bullet point list, or other abbreviated presentation.

To: CEO, Barnet Co.
From: CPA Candidate
Re: Segment reporting

Situation	Concepts	Segment Tests	Reportable Segments	Disclosures	Communication	Research

Identify the types of information that an enterprise should report in its segment reporting.

MULTIPLE-CHOICE ANSWERS

1. c __ __	4. a __ __	7. b __ __	9. c __ __	11. d __ __
2. b __ __	5. b __ __	8. b __ __	10. d __ __	1st: __/11 = __%
3. d __ __	6. a __ __			2nd: __/11 = __%

MULTIPLE-CHOICE ANSWER EXPLANATIONS

C. Segment Reporting

1.   (c)   A division is a reportable segment if it is significant. A division is significant if it satisfies at least **one** of
the three 10% tests:

1.   **Revenue** is 10% or more of the combined segment
     revenue (including intersegment revenue).
2.   **Operating profit** (loss) is 10% or more of the
     greater of the **absolute** combined segment profit or
     loss.
3.   **Identifiable assets** are 10% or more of the com-
     bined segment identifiable assets.

Industry A, B, C, and E pass the revenue and operating
profit tests, but A, B, C, D, and E all pass the identifiable
assets test. Since a division only has to pass one of the three
10% tests to be considered a reportable segment, Corey
Corp. has five reportable segments.

2.   (b)   Selected data for a segment is reported separately if one of three criteria is met. One of these criteria is
met when a segment's revenue is greater than or equal to
10% of the combined revenues of all industry segments.
Combined revenue includes sales to unaffiliated customers
and intersegment sales or transfers. Thus, Aria has a reportable segment if that segment's revenues exceed $260,000
[($2,000,000 + $600,000) × 10%]. The $40,000 interest
would not be included in combined revenue because it is not
controllable at the division level.

3.   (d)   If 10% or more of the revenue of an enterprise is
derived from sales to any single customer, that fact and the
amount of revenue from each customer shall be disclosed.
In this problem, Grum reported revenues of $50,000,000 and
thus should disclose major customer data if sales to any single customer amount to $5,000,000 ($50,000,000 × 10%).

4.   (a)   There must be enough segments reported so that
at least 75% of unaffiliated revenues is shown by reportable
segments (75% test). Sales to external customers total
$30,000,000 so external revenues reported by operating
segments must be at least $22,500,000 ($30,000,000 ×
75%).

5.   (b)   Enterprise-wide disclosures about products and
services, geographic areas, and major customers are required
for all enterprises.

6.   (a)   Enterprise-wide disclosures are to be reported by
all public business enterprises, including those with a single
reportable segment because the criteria for splitting the enterprise into reportable segments are not met.

7.   (b)   The enterprise shall disclose the following about
each reportable segment if the specified amounts are reviewed by the chief operating decision maker:

a.   Revenues from external customers
b.   Intrasegment revenues
c.   Interest revenue and expense (reported separately
     unless majority of segment's revenues are from

interest and management relies primarily on net
interest revenue to assess performance)
d.   Depreciation, depletion, and amortization expense
e.   Unusual items, extraordinary items
f.   Equity in the net income of investees accounted for
     by the equity method
g.   Income tax expense or benefit
h.   Significant noncash items

Allocated expenses are not specifically included as a required disclosure.

8.   (b)   An enterprise shall disclose general information,
including factors used to identify reportable segments and
the types of products and services from which each reportable segment derives its revenues. An enterprise shall disclose certain information about reported segment profit and
loss, assets, and basis of measurement. The accounting
standards do not require disclosures about the term chief
operating decision maker and specifically states that this
term identifies a function, not necessarily a manager with a
specific title.

9.   (c)   Two or more operating segments may be aggregated into a single operating segment if all of the aggregation criteria are met or if after performing the 10% test a
majority of the aggregation criteria are met.

10.   (d)   The method chosen for determining what information to report is referred to as the management approach.

11.   (d)   An enterprise shall report a measure of profit
and loss based on the measure reported to the chief operating
decision maker for purposes of making decisions. The information used by management includes intersegment profits and should be included, but common costs are not allocated to the segments when assessing performance and
should not be included.

SOLUTIONS TO SIMULATION PROBLEMS

Simulation Problem 1

Situation	Income Test	Revenue Test	Asset Test	Reportable Segments	Segment Reporting Test	Research	Communication

Total income = $107,000

$107,000 × 10% = $10,700

Identify which reporting units meet the income threshold to be a reportable segment.

	Division	*Reporting unit*	*Income threshold*
1.	Spain	A	●
2.		B	○
3.	Turkey	C	●
4.		D	●
5.		E	○
6.	Thailand	F	○
7.		G	●

Situation	Income Test	Revenue Test	Asset Test	Reportable Segments	Segment Reporting Test	Research	Communication

Total revenue = $478,000

$478,000 × 10% = $47,800

Identify which reporting units meet the revenue threshold to be a reportable segment.

	Division	*Reporting unit*	*Revenue threshold*
1.	Spain	A	●
2.		B	○
3.	Turkey	C	●
4.		D	●
5.		E	○
6.	Thailand	F	○
7.		G	●

Situation	Income Test	Revenue Test	Asset Test	Reportable Segments	Segment Reporting Test	Research	Communication

Total assets = $1,060,000

$1,060,000 × 10% = $106,000

Identify which reporting units meet the asset threshold to be a reportable segment.

	Division	*Reporting unit*	*Asset threshold*
1.	Spain	A	●
2.		B	●
3.	Turkey	C	●
4.		D	●
5.		E	○
6.	Thailand	F	○
7.		G	●

Situation	Income Test	Revenue Test	Asset Test	Reportable Segments	Segment Reporting Test	Research	Communication

Which segments are reportable?

	Division	Reporting unit	Reportable segment
1.	Spain	A	●
2.		B	●
3.	Turkey	C	●
4.		D	●
5.		E	○
6.	Thailand	F	○
7.		G	●

Situation	Income Test	Revenue Test	Asset Test	Reportable Segments	Segment Reporting Test	Research	Communication

Complete the following schedule to determine if enough segments have been reported.

Total external revenues	$285,000
× percent	75%
Amount of unaffiliated revenue that must be reported	$213,750
Amount of unaffiliated revenue reported	$230,000

	Yes	No
1. Indicate whether enough segments have been reported.	●	○

Explanation of solution

1. Yes, because we have reported $230,000 of unaffiliated (external) revenue from A, B, C, D, and G, and the reported unaffiliated revenue is greater than $213,750.

Situation	Income Test	Revenue Test	Asset Test	Reportable Segments	Segment Reporting Test	Research	Communication

1. What is the definition of an operating segment?

Definition
FAS131, Para 10

10. An operating segment is a component of an enterprise

    a. That engages in business activities from which it may earn revenues and incur expenses (including revenues and expenses relating to transactions with other components of the same enterprise),

    b. Whose operating results are regularly reviewed by the enterprise's chief operating decision maker to make decisions about resources to be allocated to the segment and assess its performance, and

    c. For which discrete financial information is available.

An operating segment may engage in business activities for which is has yet to earn revenues, for example, start-up operations may be operating segments before earning revenues.

Codification: 280-10-50-1

2. What are the three tests that determine if a company must report information about an operating segment?

Quantitative Thresholds
FAS131, Para 18

18. An enterprise shall report separately information about an operating segment that meets any of the following quantitative thresholds:

    a. Its reported revenue, including both sales to external customers and intersegment sales or transfers, is 10% or more of the combined revenue, internal and external, of all reported operating segments.

b. The absolute amount of its reported profit or loss is 10% or more of the greater, in absolute amount, of (1) the combined reported profit of all operating segments that did not report a loss, or (2) the combined reported loss of all operating segments that did report a loss.

c. Its assets are 10% or more of the combined assets of all operating segments.

Information about operating segments that do not meet any of the quantitative thresholds may be disclosed separately.

Codification: 280-10-50-12

3. What types of geographic information should a company report if practical?

Information about Geographic Areas
FAS131, Para 38

38. An enterprise shall report the following geographic information unless it is impracticable to do so:

a. Revenues from external customers (1) attributed to the enterprise's country of domicile, and (2) attributed to all foreign countries in total from which the enterprise derives revenues. If revenues from external customers attributed to an individual foreign country are material, those revenues shall be disclosed separately. An enterprise shall disclose the basis for attributing revenues from external customers to individual countries.

b. Long-lived assets other than financial instruments, long-term customer relationships of a financial institution, mortgage and other servicing rights, deferred policy acquisition costs, and deferred tax assets (1) located in the enterprise's country of domicile, and (2) located in all foreign countries in total in which the enterprise holds assets. If assets in an individual foreign country are material, those assets shall be disclosed separately.

The amounts reported shall be based on the financial information that is used to produce the general-purpose financial statements. If providing the geographic information is impracticable, that fact shall be disclosed. An enterprise may wish to provide, in addition to the information required by this paragraph, subtotals of geographic information about groups of countries.

Codification: 280-10-50-41

Situation	Income Test	Revenue Test	Asset Test	Reportable Segments	Segment Reporting Test	Research	Communication

Key points in the memo to the client

1. Segment disclosures assist in analyzing and understanding financial statements by permitting better assessment of past performance and future prospects. Disaggregated information provides more precise details of the uncertainties surrounding the timing and the amount of expected cash flows, because the various segments may have different rates of profitability, degrees and types of risk, opportunities for growth, and future capital demands.

2. An operating segment is a component of an enterprise engaged in business activity for which it may earn revenues and incur expenses about which separate financial information is prepared and evaluated by the chief operating decision makers to assess performance and allocate resources.

The approach used to identify segments is referred to as the management approach, meaning it is based on the way management organizes segments internally to make operating decisions and assess performance. The management approach will provide that external descriptions of an enterprise are consistent with internal descriptions and that external reporting will more closely conform to internal reporting used by management.

3. Caslow should have reported a segment that satisfies one or more of the following tests:

• The segment's revenue, including both sales to unaffiliated customers and intersegment sales or transfers, is 10% or more of the combined revenue of all Caslow's segments.

• The segment's absolute amount of operating profit or loss is 10% or more of the greater in absolute amount of

- The combined operating profits of all segments with operating profits, or
- The combined operating losses of all segments with operating losses.

- The segment's identifiable assets are 10% or more of the combined identifiable assts of all segments.

4. If the company operates in an environment where they collect discrete information on separate divisions or units, Caslow needs to organize their accounting system to collect information on revenues based on whether items are sold to outside parties (unaffiliated revenue) or to other units within the company (affiliated revenues or intersegment revenues). If the company already prepares operating profit/loss statements for each division or unit, they should aggregate that information in order to perform the required test to determine which units qualify as an operating segment. They should also identify how many assets are assigned or utilized by each unit in order to comply with the asset threshold test.

5. Caslow should provide enterprise-wide disclosures regarding products and services, as well as information about geographic areas. If practical, Caslow should report revenues from external customers attributed to the United States and attributed to the other three foreign countries. Caslow should also disclose long-lived assets, deferred policy acquisition costs, and deferred tax assets in the United States and in foreign countries, as well as total assets in each foreign country, if material.

6. Caslow should also report information regarding reliance on major customers if sales to a single customer amount to 10% or more of Caslow's revenues.

Simulation Problem 2

Situation	Concepts	Segment Tests	Reportable Segments	Disclosures	Communication	Research

	Statement	*True*	*False*
1.	The method used for reporting segment information is the asset-liability approach.	○	●
2.	If management judges that an operating segment is reportable in 2008 and is of continuing significance, information about that segment should be reported in 2009 even if it does not meet the requirements for reportability in 2009.	●	○
3.	An enterprise must report separate information about an operating segment if its assets are 10% or more of the combined assets of all operating segments.	●	○
4.	An enterprise must report separately the costs and expenses incurred by each segment.	○	●
5.	One of the requirements of segment reporting is to report cash flows for each reportable segment.	○	●
6.	An enterprise must report the interest revenue for each reportable segment if this information is normally reviewed by the chief operating decision maker.	●	○

Situation	Concepts	Segment Tests	Reportable Segments	Disclosures	Communication	Research

	Reporting unit	*Revenue threshold*	*Profits/losses threshold*	*Asset threshold*
1.	A	●	●	●
2.	B	○	○	○
3.	C	○	○	○
4.	D	○	●	●
5.	E	●	●	○
6.	F	●	●	●

Explanation of solutions

Revenue threshold: Total revenues $14,200 \times 10\% = \$1,420$. Segment should be reported if it exceeds this revenue amount.

Income threshold: Total profit = $4,560. Total loss = $1,200. Segment should be reported if the profit/loss in absolute value is greater than 10% of $4,560 (the larger amount of profit or loss), $456.

Asset threshold: Total assets $69,920 \times 10\% = \$6,992$. Segment should be reported if it exceeds this asset amount.

Situation	Concepts	Segment Tests	Reportable Segments	Disclosures	Communication	Research

	Reporting unit	Reportable segment
1.	A	●
2.	B	○
3.	C	○
4.	D	●
5.	E	●
6.	F	●

Explanation of solutions

Segment is reportable if it meets any **one** of the three threshold tests in previous question.

A meets all tests.

B and C do not meet any of the tests.

D meets income and asset test.

E meets revenue and income/loss test.

F meets all three tests.

Situation	Concepts	Segment Tests	Reportable Segments	Disclosures	Communication	Research

		Amount
1.	What is the amount of external revenue that must be included from all reportable segments in order to meet the segment reporting requirements?	$7,387.50

		Yes	No
2.	Based on your evaluation of reportable segments, have enough segments been reported? (Yes or No)	●	○

Explanation of solutions

Threshold for reporting revenue: Total external revenue reported must be at least 75% total external revenues. 75% × Total external revenue of $9,850 = $7,387.50. Based on reporting only segments A, D, E, and F, there is $9,000 of external revenue reported. Therefore, there are enough segments reported for Barnet.

Situation	Concepts	Segment Tests	Reportable Segments	Disclosures	Communication	Research

To: CEO, Barnet Co.
From: CPA Candidate
Re: Segment reporting

I am pleased to respond to your questions about segment reporting. Segment disclosures assist in analyzing and understanding financial statements by permitting better assessment of past performance and future prospects. Disaggregated information provides more precise details of the uncertainties surrounding the timing and the amount of expected cash flows, because various segments may have different rates of profitability, degrees and types of risk, opportunities for growth, and future capital demands.

An operating segment is a component of an enterprise engaged in business activity for which it may earn revenues and incur expenses, and for which separate financial information is prepared and evaluated by the chief operating decision makers to assess performance and allocate resources.

The approach used to identify segments is referred to as the management approach, meaning it is based on the way management organizes segments internally to make operating decisions and assess performance. The management approach will help ensure that external descriptions of an enterprise are consistent with internal descriptions, and that external reporting will more closely conform to internal reporting used by management.

Barnet should report information about segments that satisfy one or more of the following tests: (1) the segment's revenue, including both sales to unaffiliated customers and intersegment sales or transfers, is 10% or more of the combined revenue of all Barnet's segments; (2) the segment's absolute amount of operating profit or loss is 10% or more of the greater in absolute amount of (a) the combined operating profits of all segments with operating profits, or (b) the combined operating losses of all segments with operating losses; (3) the segment's identifiable assets are 10% or more of the combined identifiable assets of all segments.

If you have any other questions, please contact me.

Situation	Concepts	Segment Tests	Reportable Segments	Disclosures	Communication	Research

1. Identify the types of information that an enterprise should report in its segment reporting.

Information about Profit or Loss and Assets
FAS131, Para 27

27. An enterprise shall report a measure of profit or loss and total assets for each reportable segment. An enterprise also shall disclose the following about each reportable segment if the specified amounts are included in the measure of segment profit or loss reviewed by the chief operating decision maker:

   a. Revenues from external customers
   b. Revenues from transactions with other operating segments of the same enterprise
   c. Interest revenue
   d. Interest expense
   e. Depreciation, depletion, and amortization expense
   f. Unusual items as described in paragraph 26 of APB Opinion No. 30, *Reporting the Results of Operations—Reporting the Effects of Disposal of a Segment of a Business, and Extraordinary, Unusual and Infrequently Occurring Events and Transactions*
   g. Equity in the net income of investees accounted for by the equity method
   h. Income tax expense or benefit
   i. Extraordinary items
   j. Significant noncash items other than depreciation, depletion, and amortization expense

An enterprise shall report interest revenue separately from interest expense for each reportable segment unless a majority of the segment's revenues are from interest and the chief operating decision maker relies primarily on net interest revenue to assess the performance of the segment and make decisions about resources to be allocated to the segment. In that situation, an enterprise may report that segment's interest revenue net of its interest expense and disclose that it has done so.

Codification: 280-10-50-22

MULTIPLE-CHOICE QUESTIONS (1-23)

1. Roberts and Smith drafted a partnership agreement that lists the following assets contributed at the partnership's formation:

	Contributed by	
	Roberts	Smith
Cash	$20,000	$30,000
Inventory	--	15,000
Building	--	40,000
Furniture & equipment	15,000	--

The building is subject to a mortgage of $10,000, which the partnership has assumed. The partnership agreement also specifies that profits and losses are to be distributed evenly. What amounts should be recorded as capital for Roberts and Smith at the formation of the partnership?

	Roberts	Smith
a.	$35,000	$85,000
b.	$35,000	$75,000
c.	$55,000	$55,000
d.	$60,000	$60,000

2. On April 30, 2009, Algee, Belger, and Ceda formed a partnership by combining their separate business proprietorships. Algee contributed cash of $50,000. Belger contributed property with a $36,000 carrying amount, a $40,000 original cost, and $80,000 fair value. The partnership accepted responsibility for the $35,000 mortgage attached to the property. Ceda contributed equipment with a $30,000 carrying amount, a $75,000 original cost, and $55,000 fair value. The partnership agreement specifies that profits and losses are to be shared equally but is silent regarding capital contributions. Which partner has the largest April 30, 2009 capital account balance?

    a. Algee.
    b. Belger.
    c. Ceda.
    d. All capital account balances are equal.

3. Abel and Carr formed a partnership and agreed to divide initial capital equally, even though Abel contributed $100,000 and Carr contributed $84,000 in identifiable assets. Under the bonus approach to adjust the capital accounts, Carr's unidentifiable asset should be debited for

    a. $46,000
    b. $16,000
    c. $ 8,000
    d. $0

4. When property other than cash is invested in a partnership, at what amount should the noncash property be credited to the contributing partner's capital account?

    a. Fair value at the date of contribution.
    b. Contributing partner's original cost.
    c. Assessed valuation for property tax purposes.
    d. Contributing partner's tax basis.

5. Red and White formed a partnership in 2009. The partnership agreement provides for annual salary allowances of $55,000 for Red and $45,000 for White. The partners share profits equally and losses in a 60/40 ratio. The partnership had earnings of $80,000 for 2009 before any allowance to partners. What amount of these earnings should be credited to each partner's capital account?

	Red	White
a.	$40,000	$40,000
b.	$43,000	$37,000
c.	$44,000	$36,000
d.	$45,000	$35,000

6. Fox, Greg, and Howe are partners with average capital balances during 2008 of $120,000, $60,000, and $40,000, respectively. Partners receive 10% interest on their average capital balances. After deducting salaries of $30,000 to Fox and $20,000 to Howe, the residual profit or loss is divided equally. In 2009 the partnership sustained a $33,000 loss before interest and salaries to partners. By what amount should Fox's capital account change?

    a. $ 7,000 increase.
    b. $11,000 decrease.
    c. $35,000 decrease.
    d. $42,000 increase.

7. The partnership agreement of Axel, Berg & Cobb provides for the year-end allocation of net income in the following order:

- First, Axel is to receive 10% of net income up to $100,000 and 20% over $100,000.
- Second, Berg and Cobb each are to receive 5% of the remaining income over $150,000.
- The balance of income is to be allocated equally among the three partners.

The partnership's 2009 net income was $250,000 before any allocations to partners. What amount should be allocated to Axel?

    a. $101,000
    b. $103,000
    c. $108,000
    d. $110,000

8. The partnership agreement of Reid and Simm provides that interest at 10% per year is to be credited to each partner on the basis of weighted-average capital balances. A summary of Simm's capital account for the year ended December 31, 2009, is as follows:

Balance, January 1	$140,000
Additional investment, July 1	40,000
Withdrawal, August 1	(15,000)
Balance, December 31	165,000

What amount of interest should be credited to Simm's capital account for 2009?

    a. $15,250
    b. $15,375
    c. $16,500
    d. $17,250

9. The Flat and Iron partnership agreement provides for Flat to receive a 20% bonus on profits before the bonus. Remaining profits and losses are divided between Flat and Iron in the ratio of 2:3, respectively. Which partner has a greater advantage when the partnership has a profit or when it has a loss?

	Profit	Loss
a.	Flat	Iron
b.	Flat	Flat
c.	Iron	Flat
d.	Iron	Iron

10. Blau and Rubi are partners who share profits and losses in the ratio of 6:4, respectively. On May 1, 2009, their respective capital accounts were as follows:

Blau	$60,000
Rubi	50,000

On that date, Lind was admitted as a partner with a one-third interest in capital and profits for an investment of $40,000. The new partnership began with total capital of $150,000. Immediately after Lind's admission, Blau's capital should be

- a. $50,000
- b. $54,000
- c. $56,667
- d. $60,000

11. Kern and Pate are partners with capital balances of $60,000 and $20,000, respectively. Profits and losses are divided in the ratio of 60:40. Kern and Pate decided to form a new partnership with Grant, who invested land valued at $15,000 for a 20% capital interest in the new partnership. Grant's cost of the land was $12,000. The partnership elected to use the bonus method to record the admission of Grant into the partnership. Grant's capital account should be credited for

- a. $12,000
- b. $15,000
- c. $16,000
- d. $19,000

12. Dunn and Grey are partners with capital account balances of $60,000 and $90,000, respectively. They agree to admit Zorn as a partner with a one-third interest in capital and profits, for an investment of $100,000, after revaluing the assets of Dunn and Grey. Goodwill to the original partners should be

- a. $0
- b. $33,333
- c. $50,000
- d. $66,667

Items 13 and 14 are based on the following:

The following condensed balance sheet is presented for the partnership of Alfa and Beda, who share profits and losses in the ratio of 60:40, respectively:

Cash	$ 45,000
Other assets	625,000
Beda, loan	30,000
	$700,000
Accounts payable	$120,000
Alfa, capital	348,000
Beda, capital	232,000
	$700,000

13. The assets and liabilities are fairly valued on the balance sheet. Alfa and Beda decide to admit Capp as a new partner with 20% interest. No goodwill or bonus is to be recorded. What amount should Capp contribute in cash or other assets?

- a. $110,000
- b. $116,000
- c. $140,000
- d. $145,000

14. Instead of admitting a new partner, Alfa and Beda decide to liquidate the partnership. If the other assets are sold for $500,000, what amount of the available cash should be distributed to Alfa?

- a. $255,000
- b. $273,000
- c. $327,000
- d. $348,000

15. In the Adel-Brick partnership, Adel and Brick had a capital ratio of 3:1 and a profit and loss ratio of 2:1, respectively. The bonus method was used to record Colter's admittance as a new partner. What ratio would be used to allocate, to Adel and Brick, the excess of Colter's contribution over the amount credited to Colter's capital account?

- a.   Adel and Brick's new relative capital ratio.
- b.   Adel and Brick's new relative profit and loss ratio.
- c.   Adel and Brick's old capital ratio.
- d.   Adel and Brick's old profit and loss ratio.

Items 16 and 17 are based on the following:

On June 30, 2009, the condensed balance sheet for the partnership of Eddy, Fox, and Grimm, together with their respective profit and loss sharing percentages were as follows:

Assets, net of liabilities	$320,000
Eddy, capital (50%)	$160,000
Fox, capital (30%)	96,000
Grimm, capital (20%)	64,000
	$320,000

16. Eddy decided to retire from the partnership and by mutual agreement is to be paid $180,000 out of partnership funds for his interest. Total goodwill implicit in the agreement is to be recorded. After Eddy's retirement, what are the capital balances of the other partners?

	Fox	Grimm
a.	$ 84,000	$56,000
b.	$102,000	$68,000
c.	$108,000	$72,000
d.	$120,000	$80,000

17. Assume instead that Eddy remains in the partnership and that Hamm is admitted as a new partner with a 25% interest in the capital of the new partnership for a cash payment of $140,000. Total goodwill implicit in the transaction is to be recorded. Immediately after admission of Hamm, Eddy's capital account balance should be

- a. $280,000
- b. $210,000
- c. $160,000
- d. $140,000

18. On June 30, 2009, the balance sheet for the partnership of Coll, Maduro, and Prieto, together with their respective profit and loss ratios, were as follows:

Assets, at cost	$180,000
Coll, loan	$ 9,000
Coll, capital (20%)	42,000
Maduro, capital (20%)	39,000
Prieto, capital (60%)	90,000
Total	$180,000

Coll has decided to retire from the partnership. By mutual agreement, the assets are to be adjusted to their fair value of $216,000 at June 30, 2009. It was agreed that the partnership would pay Coll $61,200 cash for Coll's partnership interest, including Coll's loan which is to be repaid in full. No goodwill is to be recorded. After Coll's retirement, what is the balance of Maduro's capital account?

- a. $36,450
- b. $39,000

c. $45,450
d. $46,200

19. Allen retired from the partnership of Allen, Beck, and Chale. Allen's cash settlement from the partnership was based on new goodwill determined at the date of retirement plus the carrying amount of the other net assets. As a consequence of the settlement, the capital accounts of Beck and Chale were decreased. In accounting for Allen's withdrawal, the partnership could have used the

	Bonus method	Goodwill method
a.	No	Yes
b.	No	No
c.	Yes	Yes
d.	Yes	No

20. When Mill retired from the partnership of Mill, Yale, and Lear, the final settlement of Mill's interest exceeded Mill's capital balance. Under the bonus method, the excess
  a. Was recorded as goodwill.
  b. Was recorded as an expense.
  c. Reduced the capital balances of Yale and Lear.
  d. Had **no** effect on the capital balances of Yale and Lear.

21. The following condensed balance sheet is presented for the partnership of Smith and Jones, who share profits and losses in the ratio of 60:40, respectively:

Other assets	$450,000
Smith, loan	20,000
	$470,000
Accounts payable	$120,000
Smith, capital	195,000
Jones, capital	155,000
	$470,000

The partners have decided to liquidate the partnership. If the other assets are sold for $385,000, what amount of the available cash should be distributed to Smith?
  a. $136,000
  b. $156,000
  c. $159,000
  d. $195,000

22. On January 1, 2009, the partners of Cobb, Davis, and Eddy, who share profits and losses in the ratio of 5:3:2, respectively, decided to liquidate their partnership. On this date the partnership condensed balance sheet was as follows:

Assets	
Cash	$ 50,000
Other assets	250,000
	$300,000
Liabilities and Capital	
Liabilities	$ 60,000
Cobb, capital	80,000
Davis, capital	90,000
Eddy, capital	70,000
	$300,000

On January 15, 2009, the first cash sale of other assets with a carrying amount of $150,000 realized $120,000. Safe installment payments to the partners were made the same date. How much cash should be distributed to each partner?

	Cobb	Davis	Eddy
a.	$15,000	$51,000	$44,000
b.	$40,000	$45,000	$35,000
c.	$55,000	$33,000	$22,000
d.	$60,000	$36,000	$24,000

23. Jay & Kay partnership's balance sheet at December 31, 2009, reported the following:

Total assets	$100,000
Total liabilities	20,000
Jay, capital	40,000
Kay, capital	40,000

On January 2, 2010, Jay and Kay dissolved their partnership and transferred all assets and liabilities to a newly formed corporation. At the date of incorporation, the fair value of the net assets was $12,000 more than the carrying amount on the partnership's books, of which $7,000 was assigned to tangible assets and $5,000 was assigned to goodwill. Jay and Kay were each issued 5,000 shares of the corporation's $1 par value common stock. Immediately following incorporation, additional paid-in capital in excess of par should be credited for
  a. $68,000
  b. $70,000
  c. $77,000
  d. $82,000

SIMULATION PROBLEMS

Simulation Problem 1   (45 to 55 minutes)

Situation				
	Liquidation Schedule	**Schedule of Safe Payments**	**Incorporation of Partnership**	**Communication**

On January 1, 2010, the partners of Dove, Eagle, and Falcon who share profits and losses in the ratio of 5:3:2, respectively decided to liquidate their partnership. On this date, the partnership's condensed balance sheet was as follows:

Assets	
Cash	$80,000
Note receivable—(loan to Eagle)	20,000
Plant, property, and equipment	300,000
	400,000
Liabilities and Capital	
Liabilities	120,000
Dove, capital	150,000
Eagle, capital	70,000
Falcon, capital	60,000

On January 30, 2010, the first cash sale of other assets with a carrying amount of $120,000 was sold for $150,000. On February 5, 2010, the remaining assets were sold for $100,000.

	Liquidation Schedule			
Situation		**Schedule of Safe Payments**	**Incorporation of Partnership**	**Communication**

Prepare a Schedule of Partnership Liquidation for the partnership. Indicate the cash distribution to each partner. (For a more realistic exam experience, prepare the schedule using a spreadsheet program such as Excel.)

Partnership of Dove, Eagle, and Falcon
SCHEDULE OF PARTNERSHIP LIQUIDATION
February 5, 2010

	Cash	Notes receivable	Plant, property, and equip.	Liabilities	Dove	Eagle	Falcon
Balances							
Partner loans							
Sale of assets, Jan. 30							
Sale of assets, Feb. 5							
Payment of liabilities							
Amount distributed to each partner							

		Schedule of Safe Payments		
Situation	**Liquidation Schedule**		**Incorporation of Partnership**	**Communication**

Suppose that on January 30, 2010, the first cash sale of other assets was sold for $180,000. The carrying value of the assets sold was $160,000.

Prepare a schedule of safe payments for the partnership after the sale on January 30, 2010.

Partnership of Dove, Eagle, and Falcon
SCHEDULE OF SAFE PAYMENTS
January 30, 2010

	Cash	Notes receivable	Plant, property, and equip.	Liabilities	Dove	Eagle	Falcon
Balances							
Partner loans							
Sale of assets, Jan. 30							
Subtotal							
Payment of liabilities							
Subtotal							
Assume total loss on other assets							
Amount distributed to each partner							

Situation	Liquidation Schedule	Schedule of Safe Payments	Incorporation of Partnership	Communication

Suppose that rather than liquidate the partnership, the partners choose to incorporate the partnership on January 30, 2010. After adjusting the partnership's books to fair value, the capital balances of the partners are as follows:

Dove	$175,000
Eagle	$ 65,000
Falcon	$ 70,000

The new company, Canary Corp., is incorporated in the state of Delaware with 300,000 authorized shares of $2 par value common stock. The corporation retains the partnership's books and closes the partners' capital accounts. Dove receives 50,000 shares of stock, Eagle receives 30,000 shares of stock, and Falcon receives 20,000 shares of stock.

Prepare the journal entry to record the incorporation of the partnership.

				Communication
Situation	Liquidation Schedule	Schedule of Safe Payments	Incorporation of Partnership	

Write a memo to the partners explaining the difference between a liquidation schedule and a schedule of safe payments.

To: Mr. Dove, Mr. Eagle, and Mr. Falcon
From: CPA Candidate
Re: Liquidation and safe payment schedules

Simulation Problem 2   (45 to 55 minutes)

Situation					
	Journal Entries	Allocation of Income	Admission of New Partner	Partnership Liquidation	Communication

On January 2, 2009, Alkire and Higdon drafted a partnership agreement to create a new partnership. The following items were contributed by each of the partners:

	Alkire	Higdon
Cash	$40,000	$60,000
Inventory		10,000
Building		180,000
Equipment	60,000	

The building is subject to a mortgage of $50,000 which the partnership has assumed. The partnership agreement specifies that each partner receives 10% interest on his beginning capital balance. Alkire receives an annual salary of $15,000; Higdon receives an annual salary of $20,000. The residual profit or loss is divided using a 2:3 ratio with 2 parts assigned to Alkire and 3 parts assigned to Higdon.

During 2009 the partnership had income of $185,000. Assume there were no drawings during 2009.

	Journal Entries				
Situation		Allocation of Income	Admission of New Partner	Partnership Liquidation	Communication

Record the journal entry for each partner's contribution to the partnership.

- Journal entry for Alkire's contribution
- Journal entry for Higdon's contribution

		Allocation of Income			
Situation	Journal Entries		Admission of New Partner	Partnership Liquidation	Communication

Complete the following schedule showing the allocation of partnership income for each partner.

	Alkire	Higdon
Beginning capital balance		
Interest on capital balance		
Annual salary		
Remainder		
Ending capital balance		

Situation	Journal Entries	Allocation of Income	Admission of New Partner	Partnership Liquidation	Communication

On January 1, 2010, Alkire and Higdon decide to admit a new partner, Zukoski, for a 1/6 interest in the firm for $175,000. The bonus method is used to record the admission of the new partner. After admitting the new partner, the partnership agreement is amended as follows:

Each partner receives 10% interest on his beginning capital balance. Each partner receives an annual salary of $20,000. The residual profit or loss is divided in a ratio of 30% to Alkire, 50% to Higdon, and 20% to Zukoski.

Record the entry for admission of Zukoski to the partnership.

Situation	Journal Entries	Allocation of Income	Admission of New Partner	Partnership Liquidation	Communication

Assume that on 12/31/11, the partnership is dissolved. On that date, after closing the books, the following information is available:

Cash	$160,000
Loan to Higdon	50,000
Other assets	700,000
Liabilities	110,000
Capital, Alkire	200,000
Capital, Higdon	400,000
Capital, Zukoski	200,000

Other information necessary for the liquidation is as follows:

During the month of January 2012, assets with a book value of $180,000 were sold for $210,000.

Prepare a schedule of safe payments as of January 31, 2012.

Partnership of Alkire, Higdon, and Zukoski
SCHEDULE OF SAFE PAYMENTS
January 31, 2012

	Cash	Notes receivable	Plant, property, and equip.	Liabilities	Alkire	Higdon	Zukoski
Balances	$160,000	$50,000	$700,000	$110,000	$200,000	$400,000	$200,000
Partner loans							
Sale of assets, Jan.							
Payment of liabilities							
Loss on other assets							
Safe payment to partners							

Situation	Journal Entries	Allocation of Income	Admission of New Partner	Partnership Liquidation	Communication

When the partnership was admitting Zukoski, the existing partners Alkire and Higdon did not understand the accounting methods used to admit a new partner. Write a brief memo explaining to Mr. Alkire and Mr. Higdon the bonus method for accounting for the admission of Zukoski to the partnership.

To: Mr. Alkire
         Mr. Higdon
From: CPA Candidate
Re: Admission of new partner

MULTIPLE-CHOICE ANSWERS

1. b __ __	6. a __ __	11. d __ __	16. c __ __	21. a __ __
2. c __ __	7. c __ __	12. c __ __	17. b __ __	22. a __ __
3. d __ __	8. b __ __	13. d __ __	18. c __ __	23. d __ __
4. a __ __	9. b __ __	14. b __ __	19. d __ __	1st: __/23 = __%
5. b __ __	10. b __ __	15. d __ __	20. c __ __	2nd: __/23 = __%

MULTIPLE-CHOICE ANSWER EXPLANATIONS

D.1. Partnership Formation

1. (b) The requirement is to determine the amounts to be recorded as capital for Roberts and Smith at the formation of the partnership. Unless otherwise agreed upon by the partners, individual capital accounts should be credited for the fair market value (on the date of contribution) of the net assets contributed by that partner. It is necessary to assume that the amounts listed are fair market values. The amount of net assets that Roberts contributed is $35,000 ($20,000 + $15,000). The fair market value of the net assets Smith contributed is $75,000 ($30,000 + $15,000 + $40,000 − $10,000). The partners' profit and loss sharing ratio does not affect the initial recording of the capital accounts.

2. (c) The requirement is to determine which partner has the largest capital account balance. Use the solutions approach to solve the problem.

	Algee	Belger	Ceda
Partner contribution	50,000	80,000	55,000
Less: Liabilities as-sumed by the partner-ship	0	(35,000)	0
Ending capital balance	$50,000	$45,000	$55,000

Each partner values his contribution to the partnership at its fair market value. The fair market value becomes the partner's balance in his capital account and is basis to the partnership under generally accepted accounting principles. Any liabilities assumed by the partnership, reduces the partners' capital balance by the amount assumed.

3. (d) Under the bonus method, unidentifiable assets (i.e., goodwill) are not recognized. The total resulting capital is the FV of the tangible investments of the partners. Thus, there would be no unidentifiable assets recognized by the creation of this new partnership.

4. (a) Noncash assets contributed to an entity should be recorded at fair market value at the date of contribution. The creation of a new entity creates a new accountability for these assets. The partner's original cost relates to a previous accountability. The assessed valuation and the tax basis may differ from fair market value.

D.2. Allocation of Partnership Income (Loss)

5. (b) Credits to partners' capital accounts are based upon earnings after allowance for interest, salary and bonus. The earnings before any allowance of $80,000 is reduced by the salary allowances of $100,000 and results in a loss of $20,000. The $20,000 loss is then distributed to the partners in relation to their profit and loss ratios as follows:

	Red	White	Total
Profit before allowance			$ 80,000
Salary allowances	$55,000	$45,000	(100,000)
Loss after allowances 60/40	(12,000)	(8,000)	(20,000)
Earnings credited to partners	$43,000	$37,000	$ 80,000

It is important to note that the losses are distributed 60/40 while profits are shared equally.

6. (a) When dividing the partnership loss of $33,000, first interest and salaries are allocated to the partners, **increasing** their capital balances. This allocation of interest and salaries will also increase the amount of loss. This increased loss amount would then be allocated to the partners, **decreasing** their capital accounts. The computations are shown below.

	Fox	Greg	Howe
Interest allowance (10% of avg. cap. balances)	$12,000	$ 6,000	$ 4,000
Salaries	30,000		20,000
Residual* ($105,000 ÷ 3)	(35,000)	(35,000)	(35,000)
Increase (decrease) in cap. account	$ 7,000	$(29,000)	$(11,000)

Thus, Fox's account increases by $7,000.

The residual loss of $105,000 is the loss resulting after the interest and salary allowances are deducted [$33,000 loss − ($12,000 + $6,000 + $4,000) − ($30,000 + $20,000)].

7. (c) The distribution of the partnership net income of $250,000 occurs in three steps as follows:

Step	Axel	Berg	Cobb
1. Axel: 10% of first $100,000, 20% over $100,000	$ 10,000 30,000		
2. Berg & Cobb: 5% of remaining income over $150,000 [($250,000 − $10,000 − $30,000 − $150,000) × .05]		$ 3,000	$ 3,000
3. Remaining allocated equally: [($250,000 − $10,000 − $30,000 − $3,000 − $3,000) × 1/3]	68,000	68,000	68,000
Totals	$108,000	$71,000	$71,000

Thus, $108,000 would be distributed to Axel.

8. (b) We must first determine Simm's weighted-average capital balance for 2009 as follows:

Capital bal.	×	# of months/12	=	Weighted-avg.
140,000	×	6/12	=	$ 70,000
180,000	×	1/12	=	15,000
165,000	×	5/12	=	68,750
				$153,750

The problem states that interest of 10% per year is to be credited to each partner's capital account, and 10% of Simm's weighted-average capital balance of $153,750 is $15,375.

9.   (b)   In both the case of a profit or a loss, Flat will have a greater advantage. When there is a profit, Flat will obtain a 20% bonus on profits before the bonus, and also take 40% of the profit after the bonus. Iron on the other hand, will only receive 60% of the profit after the bonus. The following example illustrates this:

	Flat	*Iron*	*Profit*
P & L ratio	40%	60%	1,000
20% Bonus	200	0	(200)
			800
Share in profit	320	480	
Total distribution	520	480	

In the case of a loss, it can easily be seen that since Flat has a smaller percentage share in the loss that he has a greater advantage.

D.3.a.(1) Admission of a New Partner

10.   (b)   The requirement is to calculate the balances in the capital accounts of a partnership after the admission of a new partner. In this case, the new partner is investing $40,000 for a 1/3 interest in the new total capital of $150,000. No goodwill is recorded because the new capital ($150,000) equals the total of the old capital ($110,000) and Carter's investment ($40,000). However, a bonus of $10,000 is being credited to the new partner's capital account because his interest (1/3 of $150,000, or $50,000) exceeds his investment ($40,000). The bonus to the new partner is charged to the old partners in their profit and loss ratios as shown below.

Blau [60,000 – 3/5 (10,000)]	$54,000
Rubi [50,000 – 2/5 (10,000)]	46,000
Lind (150,000 ÷ 3)	50,000
	$150,000

11.   (d)   The requirement is to determine the balance in the new partner's capital account after admission using the bonus method. In this case, Grant is investing land with a FV of $15,000 for a 1/5 interest in the new total capital of $95,000. Using the bonus method, the new capital $95,000 equals the total of the old capital plus Grant's investment ($60,000 + $20,000 + $15,000). Thus, a bonus of $4,000 is being credited to Grant's capital account because his interest (1/5 of $95,000, or $19,000) exceeds his investment ($15,000). The bonus to the new partner is charged to the old partners' capital accounts in their profit and loss ratios.

12.   (c)   The requirement is to determine the amount of goodwill implied by Zorn's investment. Zorn is investing $100,000 for a 1/3 interest in the partnership. Therefore, $100,000 represents 1/3 of the value of the equity of the new partnership ($100,000 ÷ 1/3 = $300,000). The tangible portion of the equity is $250,000 ($60,000 + $90,000 + $100,000). Thus, the total implied goodwill is $50,000 ($300,000 – $250,000).

13.   (d)   If no goodwill or bonus is to be recorded, the formula to determine the necessary contribution is

Partnership interest of new partner	×	$\left(\begin{array}{c}\text{Capital bal.}\\\text{of existing}\\\text{partners}\end{array}\right.$ + $\left.\begin{array}{c}\text{Amount}\\\text{to be}\\\text{contributed}\end{array}\right)$	=	Amount to be contributed

$$\begin{aligned} 20\% \times (\$580,000 + x) &= x \\ \$116,000 + .2x &= x \\ \$116,000 &= .8x \\ \$145,000 &= x \end{aligned}$$

An alternative computation is to divide the old partner's capital ($580,000) by their interest after the new partner's admission. The result is the total capital after admission ($580,000 ÷ 80% = $725,000). To compute the new partner's contribution, the old partners' capital can be subtracted from total capital ($725,000 – $580,000 = $145,000), or total capital can be multiplied by 20% (20% × $725,000 = $145,000).

14.   (b)   To determine the amount of cash distributed during liquidation, the solutions approach is to prepare an abbreviated statement of partnership liquidation. In a partnership liquidation, cash is distributed based on the capital balances of the partners **after** adjusting them for any income (loss) to the date of liquidation and any loans or advances between the partners and the partnership. The abbreviated statement follows:

	Alfa	*Beda*	*Total*
Beg. capital balance	$348,000	$232,000	$580,000
Adj. for loans		(30,000)	(30,000)
Adj. for loss on sale of assets* (60-40)	(75,000)	(50,000)	(125,000)
Adj. capital balance	$273,000	152,000	$425,000

*($500,000 – $625,000)

Note that the total cash available also equals $425,000.

Beginning cash	$ 45,000
Proceeds from sale	500,000
Payment of AP	(120,000)
	$425,000

Therefore, Alfa can receive $273,000 in cash in full liquidation of his capital balance.

15.   (d)   The bonus method implies that the old partners either received a bonus from the new partner, or they paid a bonus to the new partner. In this case, Colter, the new partner, contributed an amount in excess of the amount credited to Colter's capital account. Accordingly, the excess should be treated as a bonus to Adel and Brick. This bonus should be treated as an adjustment to the old partners' capital accounts and should be allocated by using Adel and Brick's old profit and loss ratio.

D.3.a.(2) Partner Death or Withdrawal

16.   (c)   Eddy is to be paid $180,000 for his 50% interest in the partnership. This implies that the net assets of the partnership are worth $360,000 ($180,000 ÷ 50%). Since the net assets are currently reported at $320,000, implied goodwill is $40,000 ($360,000 – $320,000). When goodwill is recorded, the goodwill account is debited and the partners' capital accounts are credited for their share of the goodwill. Therefore, the capital balances of Fox and Grimm are $108,000 and $72,000, as computed below.

	Fox	*Grimm*
Previous capital balance	$96,000	$64,000
Share of goodwill		
Fox (30% × $40,000)	12,000	
Grimm (20% × $40,000)	--	8,000
New capital balance	$108,000	$72,000

17.   (b)   Hamm will pay $140,000 for a 25% interest in the partnership. This implies that the net assets of the partnership, including the new investment, are worth $560,000

($140,000 ÷ 25%). Net assets are currently reported at $320,000, and Hamm's cash payment of $140,000 brings that total up to $460,000. Therefore, implied goodwill is $100,000 [$560,000 – ($320,000 + $140,000)]. When goodwill is recorded, the goodwill account is debited and the partners' capital accounts are credited for their share of goodwill. Therefore, Eddy's capital balance ($160,000) is increased by his share of the goodwill (50% × $100,000 = $50,000), to result in a balance of $210,000 ($160,000 + $50,000).

18.   (c)   The requirement is to determine the balance in Maduro's capital account after Coll's retirement. When a partner withdraws from a partnership a determination of the fair value of the entity must be made. Since it is stated in the problem that the withdrawing partner is selling his interest to the partnership and that no goodwill is to be recorded, the bonus method must be employed after restatement of assets to FV. The capital accounts after restatement to FV would be

Coll
   [$42,000 + 20%($216,000 – $180,000)] = $ 49,200

Maduro
   [$39,000 + 20%($216,000 – $180,000)] = $ 46,200

Prieto
   [$90,000 + 60%($216,000 – $180,000)] = $111,600

The bonus paid to Coll is the difference between the cash paid to him for his partnership interest and the balance of that interest plus his loan balance.

   Bonus = [$61,200 – ($49,200 + $9,000)] = $3,000

Maduro's capital account would be reduced by his proportionate share of the bonus, based on the profit and loss ratio of the remaining partners [20%/(20% + 60%) = 25%].

   Maduro's capital [$46,200 – 25% ($3,000)] = $45,450.

19.   (d)   Under both the bonus and goodwill methods, the assets of the partnership must first be restated to their fair market value. Then, the withdrawing partner's capital account must be adjusted to the amount that the withdrawing partner is expected to receive. When the bonus method is used, no new goodwill is recorded. Instead, the existing partners' capital accounts are reduced by the amount necessary to increase the withdrawing partner's capital to the amount s/he is to be paid. When the goodwill method is used, new goodwill is recorded, and each partner's capital account is increased accordingly. Therefore, the bonus method results in a **decrease** of existing partners' capital accounts, while the goodwill method results in an **increase** of existing partners' capital accounts.

20.   (c)   Under the bonus method, adjustments are made only among partner's capital accounts (no goodwill is recorded on the partnership books). Since Mill's partnership interest exceeded the amount of Mill's capital balance, the excess interest would reduce the capital balances of Yale and Lear. Only under the goodwill method can the excess interest be recorded as goodwill. Under no circumstances should the excess partnership interest be recorded as an expense.

D.4. Partnership Liquidation

21.   (a)   This situation represents a simple liquidation since all assets are distributed at one point in time rather than in installments. In a simple liquidation all of the non-

cash assets are sold and the proceeds from their sale are compared to their book value to compute the gain or loss. The gain or loss on the assets is then distributed to the partners' accounts before any of the cash is distributed. The partner loan should not be considered a noncash asset for the purpose of determining gain or loss, thus, Smith is responsible to the partnership for the repayment of the entire amount of the loan. The repayment of the loan reduces that partner's (Smith) distribution as follows:

Partner balances before liquidation	Smith	Jones	Total
Loan (debit)	$ (20,000)		$ (20,000)
Capital (credit)	195,000	$155,000	350,000
Net balances	$175,000	$155,000	$330,000
Loss on sale of other assets (450 – 385)	39,000	26,000	(65,000)
Cash available for partners	$136,000	$129,000	$265,000
Cash available for credits			120,000
Total cash from sale of noncash assets			$385,000

22.   (a)   A schedule of safe payments must be prepared to determine the amount of cash to be distributed to each partner at January 15, 2009. The first cash sale of other assets with a total book value of $150,000 realized $120,000 in cash, resulting in a $30,000 loss. This loss is allocated among the partners based upon their profit and loss ratios. The schedule is completed based upon the assumption that the remaining other assets are totally worthless, and their book values are distributed to the partners as losses, based upon the partners' profit and loss ratios. The cash payments to each partner can be found at the bottom of the schedule.

	Cash	O/A	Liab.
Beginning	$ 50	$ 250	$ 60
Sale of assets	+120	–150	--
	170	100	60
Dist. to creditors	–60	--	–60
	110	100	0
Disposal of other assets	--	–100	--
Dist. to partners	–110	--	--
	0	0	0

	Capital		
	C	D	E
Beginning	$80,000	$90,000	$70,000
Sale of assets	–15,000	– 9,000	– 6,000
	65,000	81,000	64,000
Disposal of other assets	–50,000	–30,000	–20,000
	15,000	51,000	44,000
Dist. to partners	–15,000	–51,000	–44,000
	0	0	0

Thus, the cash should be distributed as follows: $15,000 to Cobb, $51,000 to Davis, and $44,000 to Eddy.

D.5. Incorporation of a Partnership

23.   (d)   When a partnership incorporates, assets and liabilities must be revalued to their fair market values on the date of incorporation. In this case, the net assets have a fair market value of $92,000 ($80,000 + $12,000) and the amount to be credited to Additional Paid-in Capital is $82,000 ($92,000 – $10,000 par value).

SOLUTIONS TO SIMULATION PROBLEMS

Simulation Problem 1

Situation	Liquidation Schedule	Schedule of Safe Payments	Incorporation of Partnership	Communication

Steps in Preparing Partnership Liquidation Schedule

1. Net out loans to partners.
2. Sale of assets on January 30: FV received minus book value given up = Gain/Loss on sale of assets $150,000 – $120,000 = $30,000 gain. Allocate gain as follows: Dove 50% × $30,000 = $15,000; Eagle $30,000 × 30% = $9,000; Falcon $30,000 × 20% = $6,000.
3. Sale of assets on February 5: $100,000 received – $180,000 carrying value = $80,000 loss. Allocate as follows: Dove $80,000 × 50% = $40,000 loss; Eagle $80,000 × 30% = $24,000 loss; Falcon $80,000 × 20% = $16,000 loss.
4. Pay liabilities $120,000.
5. Amount to distribute to partners: Dove = $125,000; Eagle = $35,000; Falcon = $50,000.

Partnership of Dove, Eagle, and Falcon
SCHEDULE OF PARTNERSHIP LIQUIDATION
February 5, 2010

	Cash	Notes receivable	Plant, property, and equip.	Liabilities	Dove	Eagle	Falcon
Balances	$80,000	$20,000	$300,000	$120,000	$150,000	$70,000	$60,000
Partner loans		(20,000)				(20,000)	
Sale of assets, Jan. 30	150,000		(120,000)		15,000	9,000	6,000
Sale of assets, Feb. 5	100,000		(180,000)		(40,000)	(24,000)	(16,000)
Payment of liabilities	(120,000)			(120,000)			
Amount distributed to each partner	$210,000	$ --	$ --	$ --	$125,000	$35,000	$50,000

Situation	Liquidation Schedule	Schedule of Safe Payments	Incorporation of Partnership	Communication

Partnership of Dove, Eagle, and Falcon
SCHEDULE OF SAFE PAYMENTS
January 30, 2010

	Cash	Notes receivable	Plant, property, and equip.	Liabilities	Dove	Eagle	Falcon
Balances	80,000	20,000	300,000	120,000	150,000	70,000	60,000
Partner loans		(20,000)				(20,000)	
Sale of assets, Jan. 30	180,000		(160,000)		10,000	6,000	4,000
Subtotal	260,000	0	140,000	120,000	160,000	56,000	64,000
Payment of liabilities	(120,000)			(120,000)	0	0	0
Subtotal	140,000		(140,000)	0	160,000	56,000	64,000
Assume total loss on other assets			140,000		(70,000)	(42,000)	(28,000)
Amount distributed to each partner	140,000				90,000	14,000	36,000

Explanation of solutions

Steps in the schedule of safe payments

1. Net out loans to partners.
2. Sale of assets results in a $20,000 gain which is allocated on a 5:3:2 basis.

   - Dove receives 50% × $20,000 = $10,000
   - Eagle receives 30% × $20,000 = $6,000
   - Falcon receives 20% × $20,000 = $4,000

3. Pay liabilities with cash.
4. Assume a total loss on other assets of $140,000.

   - Dove receives 50% × $140,000 of loss = $70,000 loss
   - Eagle receives 30% × $140,000 = $42,000 loss
   - Falcon receives 20% × $140,000 = $28,000 loss

5. Safe payment is made based on balances in the capital accounts.

Situation	Liquidation Schedule	Schedule of Safe Payments	Incorporation of Partnership	Communication

Dove, capital	175,000		
Eagle, capital	65,000		
Falcon, capital	70,000		
Common stock		200,000	
Additional paid-in capital		110,000	

Situation	Liquidation Schedule	Schedule of Safe Payments	Incorporation of Partnership	Communication

To: Mr. Dove, Mr. Eagle, and Mr. Falcon
From: CPA Candidate
Re: Liquidation and safe payment schedules

This memorandum is designed to describe the difference between a liquidation schedule and a schedule of safe payment. A liquidation schedule is prepared to calculate the amount of cash to be distributed to each partner upon complete liquidation of the partnership. First, the assets are sold, and any gain or loss is recognized on the sale of assets. Each partner's account is adjusted for the gain or loss based on his/her profit/loss sharing ratio. Then, the liabilities are paid with cash, and the remaining cash is distributed to the partners.

A schedule of safe payment is prepared when partners desire a distribution before all of the partnership assets are sold, and the partnership is completely liquidated. First, some of the assets are sold, and the resulting gain or loss is recorded in each partner's capital account based on the profit/loss sharing ratio of each partner. The existing cash and cash proceeds from the sale of assets are used to pay all liabilities. Then, it is assumed that the remaining assets will be a total loss. This assumed loss is recorded in each partner's capital account, based on the profit/loss sharing ratio of each partner. The remaining cash is then distributed to the partners based on the ending capital balance in each account.

In either situation, if the partners have loans to or from the partnership, these loans are netted against the partner's capital account as the first step in the liquidation or safe payment schedule. For example, if a partner has a loan from the partnership for $10,000, the note receivable of the partnership is reduced by $10,000 and the partner's capital account is reduced by $10,000. Similarly, if a partner has loaned money to the partnership, the note payable account is reduced, and the partner's capital account is increased.

If you need assistance with preparing one of these schedules, please contact my office.

Simulation Problem 2

Situation	Journal Entries	Allocation of Income	Admission of New Partner	Partnership Liquidation	Communication

Journal entry for Alkire's contribution

Cash	40,000	
Equipment	60,000	
Capital, Alkire		100,000

Journal entry for Higdon's contribution

Cash	60,000	
Inventory	10,000	
Building	180,000	
Note payable		50,000
Capital, Higdon		200,000

Situation	Journal Entries	Allocation of Income	Admission of New Partner	Partnership Liquidation	Communication

	Alkire	Higdon
Beginning capital balance	$100,000	$200,000
Interest on capital balance	10,000	20,000
Annual salary	15,000	20,000
Remainder	48,000	72,000
Ending capital balance	$173,000	$312,000

Explanation of solution

Each partner receives 10% on beginning capital balance. Each partner receives his respective income ($15,000 to Alkire and $20,000 to Higdon). The amount distributed thus far is $65,000. The remainder to be distributed is $120,000 (185,000 – 30,000 – 35,000). Two-fifths of this remainder 2/5 × 120,000 = 48,000 is allocated to Alkire; 3/5 × $120,000 = 72,000 is allocated to Higdon. The total income allocated to Alkire is $73,000; total income allocated to Higdon is $112,000.

Situation	Journal Entries	Allocation of Income	Admission of New Partner	Partnership Liquidation	Communication

Entry for admission of Zukoski to the partnership

Cash	175,000	
Capital, Zukoski		110,000
Capital, Alkire		26,000
Capital, Higdon		39,000

Explanation of solution

The book value of the partnership after the income distribution in 2009 was $485,000 (A = $173,000 and B = $312,000). After Zukoski's contribution, the value of the partnership is $485,000 + $175,000 = $660,000. A one-sixth interest in the partnership is $660,000 × 1/6 = $110,000. Using the bonus method, we calculate a bonus of $175,000 – $110,000 = $65,000. Using the 2:3 profit sharing ratio, the amount allocated to Alkire is 2/5 × $65,000 = $26,000; the amount allocated to Higdon is 3/5 × $65,000 = $39,000.

Situation	Journal Entries	Allocation of Income	Admission of New Partner	Partnership Liquidation	Communication

Partnership of Alkire, Higdon, and Zukoski
SCHEDULE OF SAFE PAYMENTS
January 31, 2012

	Cash	Notes receivable	Plant, property, and equip.	Liabilities	Alkire	Higdon	Zukoski
Balances	$160,000	$50,000	$700,000	$110,000	$200,000	$400,000	$200,000
Partner loans		(50,000)				(50,000)	
Sale of assets, Jan. (1)	210,000		(180,000)		9,000	15,000	(6,000)
Payment of liabilities	(110,000)			(110,000)			
Loss on other assets			(520,000)		(156,000)	(260,000)	(104,000)
Safe payment to partners	$260,000				53,000	105,000	102,000

Explanation of solution

(1) The sale of assets produced a $30,000 dividend gain, which is distributed to the partners based on the new profit sharing ratio: 30% to Alkire (9,000), 50% to Higdon (15,000), and 20% to Zukoski (6,000). Liabilities are paid. A total loss is assumed on other assets and the assumed loss of $520,000 is distributed 30% to Alkire (156,000), 50% to Higdon (260,000), and 20% to Zukoski (104,000).

Situation	Journal Entries	Allocation of Income	Admission of New Partner	Partnership Liquidation	Communication

To: Mr. Alkire
         Mr. Higdon
From: CPA Candidate
Re: Admission of new partner

This memorandum is designed to answer your questions regarding the admission of a new partner. When a partnership admits a new partner to the partnership, two situations can occur. If the new partner invests assets equal to the capital balance received, the new partner's capital account will be credited for that amount. However, if the amount invested is not equal to the capital balance received, the partnership must select an accounting method to calculate the new capital balances. The partnership may choose either the bonus method or the goodwill method.

The bonus method records the new partnership's capital by first calculating the new partnership's book value. The new book value is calculated by adding the old partnership capital plus the new partner's asset contribution. The new partner is then allocated his percentage of the share of purchased capital by taking his ownership percentage times the new book value of the firm. The old partner accounts are adjusted as if they had been paid a bonus (or in some cases, as if they had given a bonus to the new partner). The old partner accounts are adjusted based on their profit-loss sharing ratio.

In your case, Mr. Zukoski paid more than the partnership share allocated to him. This implies that the old partners received a bonus from the new partner, Mr. Zukoski. Prior to Zukoski's admission, the book value of the partnership was $485,000. After admitting Zukoski, the book value increased by $175,000 (the amount invested by Zukoski) to $660,000.

Mr. Zukoski would receive a 1/6 interest in the new capital balance of $660,000, and his capital account would be credited for $110,000. The bonus of $65,000 ($175,000 – $110,000) would be allocated to the existing partners based on their 2:3 profit/loss sharing ratio. Therefore, Alkire's capital balance would increase by $26,000, and Higdon's capital balance would increase by $39,000.

If you have any questions concerning these issues, please contact me.

MULTIPLE-CHOICE QUESTIONS (1-9)

1. Certain balance sheet accounts of a foreign subsidiary of Rowan, Inc., at December 31, 2009, have been translated into US dollars as follows:

	Translated at	
	Current rates	Historical rates
Note receivable, long-term	$240,000	$200,000
Prepaid rent	85,000	80,000
Patent	150,000	170,000
	$475,000	$450,000

The subsidiary's functional currency is the currency of the country in which it is located. What total amount should be included in Rowan's December 31, 2009 consolidated balance sheet for the above accounts?

- a. $450,000
- b. $455,000
- c. $475,000
- d. $495,000

2. A wholly owned subsidiary of Ward, Inc. has certain expense accounts for the year ended December 31, 2009, stated in local currency units (LCU) as follows:

	LCU
Depreciation of equipment (related assets were purchased January 1, 2007)	120,000
Provision for doubtful accounts	80,000
Rent	200,000

The exchange rates at various dates are as follows:

	Dollar equivalent of 1 LCU
December 31, 2009	$.40
Average for year ended 12/31/09	.44
January 1, 2007	.50

Assume that the LCU is the subsidiary's functional currency and that the charges to the expense accounts occurred approximately evenly during the year. What total dollar amount should be included in Ward's 2009 consolidated income statement to reflect these expenses?

- a. $160,000
- b. $168,000
- c. $176,000
- d. $183,200

3. Which of the following should be reported as a stockholders' equity account?

- a. Discount on convertible bonds.
- b. Premium on convertible bonds.
- c. Cumulative foreign exchange translation loss.
- d. Organization costs.

4. A foreign subsidiary's functional currency is its local currency, which has not experienced significant inflation. The weighted-average exchange rate for the current year would be the appropriate exchange rate for translating

	Sales to customers	Wages expense
a.	No	No
b.	Yes	Yes
c.	No	Yes
d.	Yes	No

5. The functional currency of Nash, Inc.'s subsidiary is the French franc. Nash borrowed French francs as a partial hedge of its investment in the subsidiary. In preparing consolidated financial statements, Nash's translation loss on its investment in the subsidiary exceeded its exchange gain on the borrowing. How should the effects of the loss and gain be reported in Nash's consolidated financial statements?

- a. The translation loss less the exchange gain is reported as other comprehensive income.
- b. The translation loss less the exchange gain is reported in net income.
- c. The translation loss is reported as other comprehensive income and the exchange gain is reported in net income.
- d. The translation loss is reported in net income and the exchange gain is reported as other comprehensive income.

6. A balance arising from the translation or remeasurement of a subsidiary's foreign currency financial statements is reported in the consolidated income statement when the subsidiary's functional currency is the

	Foreign currency	US dollar
a.	No	No
b.	No	Yes
c.	Yes	No
d.	Yes	Yes

7. When remeasuring foreign currency financial statements into the functional currency, which of the following items would be remeasured using historical exchange rate?

- a. Inventories carried at cost.
- b. Marketable equity securities reported at market values.
- c. Bonds payable.
- d. Accrued liabilities.

8. Park Co.'s wholly owned subsidiary, Schnell Corp., maintains its accounting records in German marks. Because all of Schnell's branch offices are in Switzerland, its functional currency is the Swiss franc. Remeasurement of Schnell's 2009 financial statements resulted in a $7,600 gain, and translation of its financial statements resulted in an $8,100 gain. What amount should Park report as a foreign exchange gain as net income in its income statement for the year ended December 31, 2009?

- a. $0
- b. $ 7,600
- c. $ 8,100
- d. $15,700

9. In preparing consolidated financial statements of a US parent company with a foreign subsidiary, the foreign subsidiary's functional currency is the currency

- a. In which the subsidiary maintains its accounting records.
- b. Of the country in which the subsidiary is located.
- c. Of the country in which the parent is located.
- d. Of the environment in which the subsidiary primarily generates and expends cash.

SIMULATION PROBLEMS

Simulation Problem 1   (45 to 55 minutes)

Situation						
	Concepts	**Translation of Income Statement**	**Translation of Retained Earnings Statement**	**Translation of Balance Sheet**	**Communication**	**Research**

Your client, Jay, Inc., prepares consolidated financial statements, which include two subsidiaries, Jay Co. of Australia (Jay A), and Jay Co. of France (Jay F). Jay A operates with US dollars, but maintains its financial statements in Australian dollars. Jay F operates primarily with euros and maintains its financial statements in euros.

Your client has asked for assistance with translating the financial statements of Jay F into US dollars. Below are the financial statements of Jay F in euros.

Jay F
INCOME STATEMENT
For the year ended December 31, 2009

	In euros
Revenue	650,000
Cost of goods sold	(390,000)
Gross profit	260,000
Sales expense	(50,000)
General and administrative expense	(110,000)
Depreciation expense	(15,000)
Net income	85,000

Jay F
STATEMENT OF RETAINED EARNINGS
For the year ended December 31, 2009

	In euros
Beginning retained earnings, 1/1/09	140,000
Add: Net income	85,000
Less: Dividends	0
End retained earnings, 12/3/09	225,000

Jay F
BALANCE SHEET
December 31, 2009

	In euros
Assets:	
Cash	18,000
Accounts receivable	42,000
Inventory	137,000
Land	120,000
Building	250,000
Less: Accumulated depreciation	(30,000)
Total assets	537,000
Liabilities:	
Accounts payable	49,000
Note payable, due 12-5-2015	100,000
Common stock	50,000
Additional paid-in capital	113,000
Retained earnings	225,000
Total liabilities and owners' equity	537,000

Additional information

Jay F began operations on January 2, 2007. All outstanding stock was issued on January 2, 2007. Jay F earned the following income since the company began operations. No dividends have been paid to date.

Year	Income
2007	60,000
2008	80,000

The exchange rates are as follows:

Date	Dollars per euro
January 2, 2007	1.10
January 1, 2009	1.24
December 31, 2009	1.36
Weighted-average rate 2007	1.15
Weighted-average rate for 2008	1.18
Weighted-average rate for 2009	1.31

Situation	Concepts	Translation of Income Statement	Translation of Retained Earnings Statement	Translation of Balance Sheet	Communication	Research

Items 1 through 9 are based on the following:

A foreign subsidiary's trial balance is translated from its functional currency to the functional currency of the parent.

For each item determine which date the exchange rate from Table A should be used for the translation. The subsidiary's functional currency is its **local** currency.

TABLE A

	Event	Date
A.	Company begins	12/31/07
B.	Beginning of current year	1/1/09
C.	1st quarter	4/1/09
D.	2nd quarter	7/1/09
E.	3rd quarter	10/1/09
F.	Year-end	12/31/09
G.	1st quarter	4/1/10
H.	Year average	
I.	Average since acquisition	
J.	No translation rate used	

Indicate the correct exchange rate by placing an x in the table in the appropriate box.

	A 12/31/07	B 1/1/09	C 4/1/09	D 7/1/09	E 10/1/09	F 12/31/09	G 4/1/10	H Year average	I Average since acquisition	J No translation rate used
1. Cash										
2. Inventory that had been purchased evenly throughout the year										
3. Account payable for equipment purchased on 4/1/09										
4. Cost of goods sold										
5. Sales										
6. Dividends declared on 10/1/09										
7. Dividends declared in (6) were paid 1/2/10										
8. Retained earnings										
9. Common stock										

Situation	Concepts	Translation of Income Statement	Translation of Retained Earnings Statement	Translation of Balance Sheet	Communication	Research

Complete the following table for the foreign currency translation into US dollars for Jay F.

Jay F
INCOME STATEMENT
For the year ended December 31, 2009

	In euros	Exchange rate	US dollars
Revenue	650,000		
Cost of goods sold	(390,000)		
Gross profit	260,000		
Sales expense	(50,000)		
General and administrative expense	(110,000)		
Depreciation expense	(15,000)		
Net income	85,000		

Situation	Concepts	Translation of Income Statement	Translation of Retained Earnings Statement	Translation of Balance Sheet	Communication	Research

Complete the following table to translate the retained earnings of Jay F into US dollars.

Jay F
STATEMENT OF RETAINED EARNINGS
For the year ended December 31, 2009

	In euros	Exchange rate	US dollars
Beginning retained earnings, 1/1/09			
2007 net income	60,000		
2008 net income	80,000		
Net income for 2009	85,000		
Less: Dividends	0		
End retained earnings, 12/31/09	225,000		

Situation	Concepts	Translation of Income Statement	Translation of Retained Earnings Statement	Translation of Balance Sheet	Communication	Research

Complete the following table to translate the balance sheet accounts of Jay F into US dollars.

Jay F
BALANCE SHEET
December 31, 2009

	In euros	Exchange rate	Translation into US dollars
Assets:			
Cash	18,000		
Accounts receivable	42,000		
Inventory	137,000		
Land	120,000		
Building	250,000		
Less: Accumulated depreciation	(30,000)		
Total assets	537,000		
Liabilities:			
Accounts payable	49,000		
Note payable, due 12-5-2015	100,000		
Common stock	50,000		
Additional paid in capital	113,000		
Retained earnings	225,000		
Other comprehensive income (foreign currency translation adjustment)	-0-		
Total liabilities and owners' equity	537,000		

Situation	Concepts	Translation of Income Statement	Translation of Retained Earnings Statement	Translation of Balance Sheet	Communication	Research

Write a memorandum to the CEO of Jay F Co. Explain the objectives of translating the company's subsidiary financial statements.

To: CEO, Jay F Co.
From: CPA Candidate
Re: Translating foreign subsidiary financial statements

Situation	Concepts	Translation of Income Statement	Translation of Retained Earnings Statement	Translation of Balance Sheet	Communication	Research

Research each of the following issues using the authoritative literature, and select paragraph(s) that address the issue.

1. What are the objectives of translating a foreign subsidiary's financial statements?

2. How are gains and losses arising from remeasuring Jay A subsidiary's financial statements reported on Jay Inc.'s consolidated financial statements?

3. How are gains and losses arising from translating Jay F subsidiary's financial statements measured in Jay Inc. consolidated financial statements?

4. The financial accounting standards identify several economic indicators that are to be considered both individually and collectively in determining the functional currency for a consolidated subsidiary. List three of those indicators.

5. What exchange rate is used to incorporate Jay F's assets, liabilities, revenues, and expenses in Jay Inc.'s consolidated financial statements on 12/31/09?

MULTIPLE-CHOICE ANSWERS

1. c	_ _	4. b	_ _	6. b	_ _	8. b	_ _	1st:	_/9 = _%
2. c	_ _	5. a	_ _	7. a	_ _	9. d	_ _	2nd:	_/9 = _%
3. c	_ _								

MULTIPLE-CHOICE ANSWER EXPLANATIONS

E.2. Translation of Foreign Currency Statements

1. (c) When the **functional currency** of a foreign subsidiary is the **foreign currency,** asset and liability accounts are **translated** using the **current** exchange rate (the rate of translation in effect at the balance sheet date). Therefore, these accounts should be included in the balance sheet at $475,000. Note that if the **functional currency** was the **US dollar,** balance sheet accounts would be **remeasured** using a combination of **historical and current rates**.

2. (c) The requirement is to determine the total amount of various expenses incurred by a foreign subsidiary which should be reported in the 2009 consolidated income statement. If the foreign currency is the functional currency of the subsidiary, the **current rate** method should be used to translate the financial statements. In this method, revenues and expenses are translated at the rates in effect at the time these items were recognized during the period. Because translation at the date the revenues and expenses were recognized is generally deemed impractical, An appropriate weighted-average rate may be used to translate these items. This results in a translated expense of $176,000 [($120,000 + $80,000 + $200,000) × .44].

3. (c) The requirement is to determine which item is reported in the stockholders' equity section. Accumulated gains and losses on certain foreign currency transactions should be reported as a component of stockholders' equity entitled other comprehensive income. Answers (a), (b), and (d) are incorrect because these items are reported on the balance sheet in the assets and liabilities sections and are amortized over their respective lives.

4. (b) The current rate method for the translation of foreign currency financial statements is used when a foreign subsidiary's functional currency is its local currency. Using the current rate method, revenue and expenses should be translated into US dollars at the weighted-average rate for the current year. Thus, both sales to customers and wages expense should be translated at the weighted-average rate.

5. (a) Translation adjustments resulting from the translation of foreign currency statements should be reported separately as components of other comprehensive income, accumulated other comprehensive income, and stockholders' equity. Additionally, gains and losses on certain foreign currency transactions should also be reported similarly. Those gains and losses which should be excluded from net income and instead reported as components of other comprehensive income and of accumulated other comprehensive income in stockholders' equity include foreign currency transactions designated as economic hedges of a net investment in a foreign entity. Thus, both the translation loss and the exchange gain are to be reported as other comprehensive income and accumulated other comprehensive income in the stockholders' equity section of the balance sheet. Because the translation loss on the investment exceeds the exchange gain on the borrowing, the translation loss less the exchange

gain is the amount to be reported as separate components of other comprehensive income and accumulated other comprehensive income equity in the consolidated financial statements.

6. (b) **Translation** adjustments result from translating an entity's financial statements into the reporting currency. Such adjustments, which result when the entity's functional currency is the **foreign currency,** should not be included in net income. Instead, such adjustments should be reported as other comprehensive income and accumulated other comprehensive income in the stockholders' equity section of the balance sheet. If the functional currency is the **reporting currency** (US dollar), a **remeasurement** process takes place, with the resulting gain or loss included in net income.

7. (a) The requirement is to determine which item would be remeasured using historical exchange rates when foreign currency financial statements are being remeasured into the functional currency. When an entity's books are not maintained in the functional currency, it is necessary to use historical exchange rates in the remeasurement process of certain accounts. Among the accounts listed is inventories carried at cost. Only marketable equity securities reported at **cost** would be remeasured using historical exchange rates. Bonds payable and accrued liabilities would be remeasured at the current rate.

8. (b) Schnell's accounting records are kept in German marks, and its functional currency is the Swiss franc. Before Schnell's financial statements can be consolidated with Park's financial statements, they must be remeasured from German marks to Swiss francs, and then translated from Swiss francs to US dollars. As a result of these restatements, there is a remeasurement gain of $7,600, and a credit translation adjustment of $8,100. A remeasurement gain or loss is included in net income, but a translation adjustment is **not.** Therefore, Park would report a foreign exchange gain of $7,600 in its 2009 income statement.

9. (d) An entity's functional currency is the currency of the primary economic environment in which the entity operates; normally, that is the currency of the environment in which an entity primarily generates and expends cash.

SOLUTIONS TO SIMULATION PROBLEMS

Simulation Problem 1

Situation	Concepts	Translation of Income Statement	Translation of Retained Earnings Statement	Translation of Balance Sheet	Communication	Research

		A	B	C	D	E	F	G	H	I	J
		12/31/07	1/1/09	4/1/09	7/1/09	10/1/09	12/31/09	4/1/10	Year average	Average since acquisition	No translation rate used
1.	Cash						x				
2.	Inventory that had been purchased evenly throughout the year						x				
3.	Account payable for equipment purchased on 4/1/09						x				
4.	Cost of goods sold								x		
5.	Sales								x		
6.	Dividends declared on 10/1/09					x					
7.	Dividends declared in (6) were paid 1/2/10						x				
8.	Retained earnings										x
9.	Common stock		x								

Explanation of solutions

1. **(F)** Assets are valued at the current rate at year-end.

2. **(F)** Assets are valued at the current rate at year-end.

3. **(F)** Liabilities are valued at the current rate at year-end.

4. **(H)** Expense accounts are valued at the average rate for the current year of business.

5. **(H)** Revenue accounts are valued at the average rate for the current year of business.

6. **(E)** Dividends are valued at the rate of the date of declaration.

7. **(F)** Liabilities (dividends payable) are valued at the current rate at year-end.

8. **(J)** The retained earnings are carried over from 1/1/09 with the translated net income added and translated dividends subtracted.

9. **(A)** Common stock is valued at the historical rate when it was issued.

Situation	Concepts	Translation of Income Statement	Translation of Retained Earnings Statement	Translation of Balance Sheet	Communication	Research

Complete the following table for the foreign currency translation into US dollars for Jay F.

Jay F
INCOME STATEMENT
For the year ended December 31, 2009

	In euros	Exchange rate	US dollars
Revenue	650,000	1.31	$ 851,500
Cost of goods sold	(390,000)	1.31	(510,000)
Gross profit	260,000	1.31	340,600
Sales expense	(50,000)	1.31	(65,500)
General and administrative expense	(110,000)	1.31	(144,100)
Depreciation expense	(15,000)	1.31	(19,650)
Net income	85,000	1.31	$ 111,350

Situation	Concepts	Translation of Income Statement	Translation of Retained Earnings Statement	Translation of Balance Sheet	Communication	Research

Complete the following table to translate the retained earnings of Jay F into US dollars.

Jay F
STATEMENT OF RETAINED EARNINGS
For the year ended December 31, 2009

	In euros	Exchange rate	US dollars
Beginning retained earnings, 1/1/09			
2007 net income	60,000	1.15	$ 69,000
2008 net income	80,000	1.18	94,400
Net income for 2009	85,000	1.31	111,350
Less: Dividends	0		
End retained earnings, 12/31/09	225,000		$274,750

Situation	Concepts	Translation of Income Statement	Translation of Retained Earnings Statement	Translation of Balance Sheet	Communication	Research

Complete the following table to translate the balance sheet accounts of Jay F into US dollars.

Jay F
BALANCE SHEET
December 31, 2009

	In euros	Exchange rate	Translation into US dollars
Assets:			
Cash	18,000	1.36	$24,480
Accounts receivable	42,000	1.36	57,120
Inventory	137,000	1.36	186,320
Land	120,000	1.36	163,200
Building	250,000	1.36	340,000
Less: Accumulated depreciation	(30,000)	1.36	(40,800)
Total assets	537,000		$730,320
Liabilities:			
Accounts payable	49,000	1.36	$66,640
Note payable, due 12-5-2015	100,000	1.36	136,000
Common stock	50,000	1.10	55,000
Additional paid in capital	113,000	1.10	124,300
Retained earnings	225,000		274,750
Other comprehensive income (foreign currency translation adjustment)	-0-		73,630
Total liabilities and owners' equity	537,000		$730,320

Explanation of solutions

For Jay F, the functional currency is the foreign currency (euros).

Therefore, the current rate method is used.

The following rules apply to the current rate method:

- Assets and liabilities—use current rate at balance sheet date
- Revenues and expenses—use weighted-average rate (or rate at time of exchange if known)
- Owners' equity—use historical rates
- Dividends—use historical rates

Because Jay F's retained earnings is from three years, each year must be translated at the appropriate rate. The weighted-average rate is used for each year.

The translation gain is the plug figure to bring the balance sheet into balance, and is reported as "other comprehensive income" in the owners' equity section of the balance sheet.

Total assets = $730,320
Total liabilities + Owners' equity **before** translation adjustment = $656,690
Translation adjustment = $730,320 – 656,690 = $73,630.

Situation	Concepts	Translation of Income Statement	Translation of Retained Earnings Statement	Translation of Balance Sheet	Communication	Research

To: CEO, Jay Co.
From: CPA Candidate
Re: Translating foreign subsidiary financial statements

You have asked us to explain the objectives of translating your company's foreign subsidiary's financial statements. The primary reason for translation is to allow the consolidation of the financial statements of Jay Co. with its foreign subsidiary. In addition, translation provides users information about the effects of currency rate changes on the consolidated company's financial statements.

If you have additional questions, please contact us.

Situation	Concepts	Translation of Income Statement	Translation of Retained Earnings Statement	Translation of Balance Sheet	Communication	Research

1. What are the objectives of translating a foreign subsidiary's financial statements?

Objectives of Translation
FAS52, Para 4

4. Financial statements are intended to present information in financial terms about the performance, financial position, and cash flows of an enterprise. For this purpose, the financial statements of separate entities within an enterprise, which may exist and operate in different economic and currency environments, are consolidated and presented as though they were the financial statements of a single enterprise. Because it is not possible to combine, add, or subtract measurements expressed in different currencies, it is necessary to translate into a single reporting currency those assets, liabilities, revenues, expenses, gains, and losses that are measured or denominated in a foreign currency. However, the unity presented by such translation does not alter the underlying significance of the results and relationships of the constituent parts of the enterprise. It is only through the effective operation of its constituent parts that the enterprise as a whole is able to achieve its purpose. Accordingly, the translation of the financial statements of each component entity of an enterprise should accomplish the following objectives:

a. Provide information that is generally compatible with the expected economic effects of a rate change on an enterprise's cash flows and equity.

b. Reflect in consolidated statements the financial results and relationships of the individual consolidated entities as measured in their functional currencies in conformity with US generally accepted accounting principles.

Codification: 830-10-10-1

2. How are gains and losses arising from remeasuring Jay A subsidiary's financial statements reported on Jay Inc.'s consolidated financial statements?

FAS52, Para 10

10. If an entity's books of record are not maintained in its functional currency, remeasurement into the functional currency is required. That remeasurement is required before translation into the reporting currency. If a foreign entity's functional currency is the reporting currency, remeasurement into the reporting currency obviates translation. The remeasurement process is intended to produce the same results as if the entity's books of record had been maintained in the functional currency. The remeasurement of and subsequent accounting for transactions denominated in a currency other than the functional currency shall be in accordance with the requirements of this Statement (paragraphs 15 and 16). Appendix B provides guidance for remeasurement into the functional currency.

FAS52, Para 15

15. Foreign currency transactions are transactions denominated in a currency other than the entity's functional currency. Foreign currency transactions may produce receivables or payables that are fixed in terms of the amount of foreign currency that will be received or paid. A change in exchange rates between the functional currency and the currency in which a transaction is denominated increases or decreases the expected amount of functional currency cash flows upon settlement of the transaction. That increase or decrease in expected functional currency cash flows is a foreign currency transaction gain or loss that generally shall be included in determining net income for the period in which the exchange rate changes. Likewise, a transaction gain or loss (measured from the transaction date or the most recent intervening balance sheet date, whichever is later) realized upon settlement of a foreign currency transaction generally shall be included in determining net income for the period in which the transaction is settled. The exceptions to this requirement for inclusion in net income of transaction gains and losses are set forth in paragraphs 20 and 21 and pertain to certain intercompany transactions and to transactions that are designated as, and effective as, economic hedges of net investments and foreign currency commitments.

Codification: 830-30-45-12

3. How are gains and losses arising from translating Jay F subsidiary's financial statements measured in Jay Inc. consolidated financial statements?

Translation of Foreign Currency Statements
FAS52, Para 12

12. All elements of financial statements shall be translated by using a current exchange rate. For assets and liabilities, the exchange rate at the balance sheet date shall be used. For revenues, expenses, gains, and losses, the exchange rate at the dates on which those elements are recognized shall be used. Because translation at the exchange rates at the dates the numerous revenues, expenses, gains, and losses are recognized is generally impractical, an appropriately weighted-average exchange rate for the period may be used to translate those elements.

FAS135, Para 4(1)

1. FASB Statement 52, *Foreign Currency Translation.*

(1) In paragraph 24, a separate component of equity in the second sentence and that separate component of equity in the last sentence are replaced by other comprehensive income (effectively amended by FASB Statement 130, *Reporting Comprehensive Income*).

Codification: 830-30-45-3

4. The financial accounting standards identify several economic indicators that are to be considered both individually and collectively in determining the functional currency for a consolidated subsidiary. List three of those indicators.

FAS52, Para 41

41. The Board has developed, with significant input from its task force and other advisors, the following general guidance on indicators of facts to be considered in identifying the functional currency. In those instances in which the indicators are mixed and the functional currency is not obvious, management's judgment will be required in order to determine the functional currency that most faithfully portrays the economic results of the entity's operations and thereby best achieves the objectives of foreign currency translation set forth in paragraph 4. Management is in the best position to obtain the pertinent facts and weigh their relative importance in determining the functional currency for each operation. It is important to recognize that management's judgment is essential and paramount in this determination, provided only that it is not contradicted by the facts.

FAS52, Para 42

42. The salient economic factors set forth below, and possibly others, should be considered both individually and collectively when determining the functional currency.

a.   Cash flow indicators

 (1) Foreign currency—Cash flows related to the foreign entity's individual assets and liabilities are primarily in the foreign currency and do not directly impact the parent company's cash flows.

 (2) Parent's currency—Cash flows related to the foreign entity's individual assets and liabilities directly impact the parent's cash flows on a current basis and are readily available for remittance to the parent company.

b.   Sales price indicators

 (1) Foreign currency—Sales prices for the foreign entity's products are not primarily responsive in a short-term basis to changes in exchange rates but are determined more by local competition or local government regulation.

 (2) Parent's currency—Sales prices for the foreign entity's products are primarily responsive on a short-term basis to changes in exchange rates; for example, sales prices are determined more by worldwide competition or by international prices.

c.   Sales market indicators

 (1) Foreign currency—There is an active local sales market for the foreign entity's products, although there also might be significant amounts of exports.

 (2) Parent's currency—The sales market is mostly in the parent's country or sales contracts are denominated in the parent's currency.

d.   Expense indicators

 (1) Foreign currency—Labor, materials, and other costs for the foreign entity's products or services are primarily local costs, even though there also might be imports from other countries.

 (2) Parent's currency—Labor, materials, and other costs for the foreign entity's products or services, on a continuing basis, are primarily costs for components obtained from the country in which the parent company is located.

e.   Financing indicators

 (1) Foreign currency—Financing is primarily denominated in foreign currency, and funds generated by the foreign entity's operations are sufficient to service existing and normally expected debt obligations.

 (2) Parent's currency—Financing is primarily from the parent or other dollar-denominated obligations, or funds generated by the foreign entity's operations are not sufficient to service existing and normally expected debt obligations without the infusion of additional funds from the parent company. Infusion of additional funds from the parent company for expansion is not a factor, provided funds generated by the foreign entity's expanded operations are expected to be sufficient to service that additional financing.

f.   Intercompany transactions and arrangements indicators

(1) Foreign currency—There is a low volume of intercompany transactions and there is not an extensive interrelationship between the operations of the foreign entity and the parent company. However, the foreign entity's operations may rely on the parent's or affiliates' competitive advantages, such as patents and trademarks.

(2) Parent's currency—There is a high volume of intercompany transactions and there is an extensive interrelationship between the operations of the foreign entity and the parent company. Additionally, the parent's currency generally would be the functional currency if the foreign entity is a device or shell corporation for holding investments, obligations, intangible assets, etc., that could readily be carried on the parent's or an affiliate's books.

Codification: 830-10-55-5

5.   What exchange rate is used to incorporate Jay F's assets, liabilities, revenues, and expenses in Jay Inc.'s consolidated financial statements on 12/31/09?

Translation of Foreign Currency Statements
FAS52, Para 12

12. All elements of financial statements shall be translated by using a current exchange rate. For assets and liabilities, the exchange rate at the balance sheet date shall be used. For revenues, expenses, gains, and losses, the exchange rate at the dates on which those elements are recognized shall be used.   Because translation at the exchange rates at the dates the numerous revenues, expenses, gains, and losses are recognized is generally impractical, an appropriately weighted-average exchange rate for the period may be used to translate those elements.

Codification: 830-30-45-3

MULTIPLE-CHOICE QUESTIONS (1-117)

1. Which of the following statements about the statistical section of the Comprehensive Annual Financial Report (CAFR) of a governmental unit is true?
   a. Statistical tables may **not** cover more than two fiscal years.
   b. Statistical tables may **not** include nonaccounting information.
   c. The statistical section is **not** part of the basic financial statements.
   d. The statistical section is an integral part of the basic financial statements.

2. What is the basic criterion used to determine the reporting entity for a governmental unit?
   a. Special financing arrangement.
   b. Geographic boundaries.
   c. Scope of public services.
   d. Financial accountability.

3. South City School District has a separately elected governing body that administers the public school system. The district's budget is subject to the approval of the city council. The district's financial activity should be reported in the City's financial statements by
   a. Blending only.
   b. Discrete presentation.
   c. Inclusion as a footnote only.
   d. Either blending or inclusion as a footnote.

4. Marta City's school district is a legally separate entity, but two of its seven board members are also city council members and the district is financially dependent on the city. The school district should be reported as a
   a. Blended unit.
   b. Discrete presentation.
   c. Note disclosure.
   d. Primary government.

5. Darien Village adopted the provision of GASB 34, *Basic Financial Statements—and Management's Discussion and Analysis—for State and Local Governments*, for its financial statements issued for 2005. As of December 31, 2005, Darien determined that it had spent $5,000,000 on infrastructure assets since the village was incorporated in 1980, and that infrastructure had an expected life of fifty years. These infrastructure assets consist primarily of roads and bridges that were financed with general long-term debt. Darien decided to use the modified approach for reporting its infrastructure assets on its government-wide financial statements for 2005. During 2005, Darien spent $250,000 maintaining and preserving its roads and bridges, and $500,000 to extend the life of existing infrastructure. On the statement of net assets at December 31, 2005, what amount should Darien report for infrastructure under the governmental activities column?
   a. $5,000,000
   b. $0
   c. $4,900,000
   d. $5,500,000

6. Hunt Community Development Agency (HCDA), a financially independent authority, provides loans to commercial businesses operating in Hunt County. This year, HCDA made loans totaling $500,000. How should HCDA

classify the disbursements of loans on the cash flow statement?
   a. Operating activities.
   b. Noncapital financing activities.
   c. Capital and related financing activities.
   d. Investing activities.

7. The statement of activities of the government-wide financial statements is designed primarily to provide information to assess which of the following?
   a. Operational accountability.
   b. Financial accountability.
   c. Fiscal accountability.
   d. Functional accountability.

Items 8 and 9 are based on the following:

As of December 31, 2009, Fullerton City compiled the information below for its capital assets, exclusive of infrastructure assets.

Cost of capital assets financed with general obligation debt and tax revenues	$3,500,000
Accumulated depreciation on the capital assets	750,000
Outstanding debt related to the capital assets	1,250,000

8. On the government-wide statement of net assets at December 31, 2009, under the governmental activities column, what amount should be reported for capital assets?
   a. $3,500,000
   b. $1,500,000
   c. $2,250,000
   d. $2,750,000

9. On the government-wide statement of net assets at December 31, 2009, under the governmental activities column, the information related to capital assets should be reported in the net assets section at which of the following amounts?
   a. $3,500,000
   b. $1,500,000
   c. $2,250,000
   d. $2,750,000

10. Which of the following statements is correct about the accounting for infrastructure assets using the modified approach?
   I. Depreciation expense on the infrastructure assets should be reported on the government-wide statement of activities, under the governmental activities column.
   II. Certain information about infrastructure assets reported using the modified approach is required supplementary information in the annual report.

   a. I only.
   b. II only.
   c. Both I and II.
   d. Neither I nor II.

11. Depreciation expense would be reported on which of the following financial statements?
   I. The government-wide statement of activities.
   II. The statement of revenues, expenses, and changes in fund net assets prepared for proprietary funds.

   a. I only.
   b. II only.
   c. Both I and II.
   d. Neither I nor II.

12. In accordance with GASB 34, *Basic Financial Statements—and Management's Discussion and Analysis—for State and Local Governments*, governments should prepare

    a. Combined financial statements, using the modified accrual basis of accounting and the flow of economic resources.

    b. Combined financial statements, using the accrual basis of accounting and the flow of financial resources.

    c. Government-wide financial statements, using the accrual basis of accounting and the flow of financial resources.

    d. Government-wide financial statements, using the accrual basis of accounting and the flow of economic resources.

13. In accordance with GASB 34, *Basic Financial Statements—and Management's Discussion and Analysis—for State and Local Governments*, which of the following statements is true?

  I. Infrastructure assets do not need to be reported on the government-wide statement of net assets if the government decides to use the modified approach in its accounting for infrastructure.

  II. Component units are reported on the financial statements for governmental funds.

    a. I only.

    b. II only.

    c. Both I and II.

    d. Neither I nor II.

14. Fund accounting is used by governmental units with resources that must be

    a. Composed of cash or cash equivalents.

    b. Incorporated into combined or combining financial statements.

    c. Segregated for the purpose of carrying on specific activities or attaining certain objectives.

    d. Segregated physically according to various objectives.

15. Dogwood City's water enterprise fund received interest of $10,000 on long-term investments. How should this amount be reported on the Statement of Cash Flows?

    a. Operating activities.

    b. Noncapital financing activities.

    c. Capital and related financing activities.

    d. Investing activities.

16. The primary authoritative body for determining the measurement focus and basis of accounting standards for governmental fund operating statements is the

    a. Governmental Accounting Standards Board (GASB).

    b. National Council on Governmental Accounting (NCGA).

    c. Governmental Accounting and Auditing Committee of the AICPA (GAAC).

    d. Financial Accounting Standards Board (FASB).

17. Which event(s) should be included in a statement of cash flows for a governmental entity?

  I. Cash inflow from issuing bonds to finance city hall construction.

  II. Cash outflow from a city utility representing payments in lieu of property taxes.

    a. I only.

    b. II only.

    c. Both I and II.

    d. Neither I nor II.

18. The following transactions were among those reported by Corfe City's electric utility enterprise fund for 2009:

Capital contributed by subdividers	$ 900,000
Cash received from customer households	2,700,000
Proceeds from sale of revenue bonds	4,500,000

In the electric utility enterprise fund's statement of cash flows for the year ended December 31, 2009, what amount should be reported as cash flows from capital and related financing activities?

    a. $4,500,000

    b. $5,400,000

    c. $7,200,000

    d. $8,100,000

19. For which of the following governmental entities that use proprietary fund accounting should a statement of cash flows be presented?

	Tollway authorities	*Governmental utilities*
a.	No	No
b.	No	Yes
c.	Yes	Yes
d.	Yes	No

20. In accordance with GASB 34, *Basic Financial Statements—and Management's Discussion and Analysis—for State and Local Governments*, which of the following financial statements should be prepared for proprietary funds?

    a. Statement of revenues, expenditures, and changes in fund balances.

    b. Statement of activities.

    c. Statement of changes in proprietary net assets.

    d. Statement of cash flows.

21. In accordance with GASB 34, *Basic Financial Statements—and Management's Discussion and Analysis—for State and Local Governments*, which of the following statements is correct about the information reported on the balance sheet prepared for the governmental funds?

  I. The focus is on reporting major funds, with all nonmajor funds aggregated and reported in a single column.

  II. Fund balances are reported in two amounts—restricted and unrestricted.

    a. I only.

    b. II only.

    c. Both I and II.

    d. Neither I nor II.

22. In accordance with GASB 34, *Basic Financial Statements—and Management's Discussion and Analysis—for State and Local Governments*, which of the following statements is correct about the information reported on the statement of net assets for the proprietary funds?

  I. Assets and liabilities are classified into current and noncurrent classifications.

  II. All activities of internal service funds are aggregated and reported in a single column.

    a. I only.

b. II only.
c. Both I and II.
d. Neither I nor II.

23. Which of the following financial statements is prepared using the accrual basis of accounting and the economic resources measurement focus?

I. The statement of net assets for proprietary funds.
II. The statement of revenues, expenditures, and changes in fund balances for the governmental funds.

a. I only.
b. II only.
c. Both I and II.
d. Neither I nor II.

24. In accordance with GASB 34, *Basic Financial Statements—and Management's Discussion and Analysis—for State and Local Governments*, agency funds are reported on which of the following financial statements?

I. Statement of fiduciary net assets.
II. Statement of changes in fiduciary net assets.

a. I only.
b. II only.
c. Both I and II.
d. Neither I nor II.

25. Private-purpose trust funds are reported on which of the following financial statements?

I. Government-wide statement of net assets.
II. Statement of changes in fiduciary net assets.

a. I only.
b. II only.
c. Both I and II.
d. Neither I nor II.

26. In accordance with GASB 34, *Basic Financial Statements—and Management's Discussion and Analysis—for State and Local Governments*, which fund type(s) is(are) reported on the statement of cash flows?
a. Governmental and fiduciary fund types.
b. Governmental and proprietary fund types.
c. Fiduciary and proprietary fund types.
d. Proprietary fund type only.

27. In accordance with GASB 34, *Basic Financial Statements—and Management's Discussion and Analysis—for State and Local Governments*, which of the following statements is(are) true regarding the statement of cash flows?

I. The statement of cash flows is a government-wide financial statement.
II. The statement of cash flows reports cash flows from three activities—operating, investing, and financing.

a. I only.
b. II only.
c. Both I and II.
d. Neither I nor II.

28. A reconciliation must be shown of the items that cause the difference between (1) the total of the fund balances that appears on the balance sheet for the governmental funds and (2) the total net assets that are disclosed for governmental activities on the government-wide statement of net assets.

Which of the following items would be disclosed in this reconciliation?

I. Capital assets used in governmental activities.
II. The assets and liabilities of internal service funds included in governmental activities.

a. I only.
b. II only.
c. Both I and II.
d. Neither I nor II.

29. In accordance with GASB 34, *Basic Financial Statements—and Management's Discussion and Analysis—for State and Local Governments*, a reconciliation must be shown of the items that cause the difference between (1) the net change in fund balances for the governmental funds on the statement of revenues, expenditures, and changes in fund balances, and (2) the change in net assets of governmental activities on the statement of activities. Which of the following items would be disclosed in this reconciliation?

I. Revenues and expenses of internal service funds that were reported in proprietary funds.
II. The amount by which capital outlays exceeded depreciation expense for the period.

a. I only.
b. II only.
c. Both I and II.
d. Neither I nor II.

30. What measurement focus should be used for the preparation of the following financial statements?

	Statement of changes in fiduciary net assets	Government-wide statement of net assets
a.	Financial resources	Economic resources
b.	Economic resources	Financial resources
c.	Economic resources	Economic resources
d.	Financial resources	Financial resources

31. Which of the following statements is(are) true?

I. Pension trust funds are reported on the statement of changes in fiduciary net assets.
II. Retained earnings is reported in the net assets section of the statement of net assets for proprietary funds.

a. I only.
b. II only.
c. Both I and II.
d. Neither I nor II.

32. In accordance with GASB 34, *Basic Financial Statements—and Management's Discussion and Analysis—for State and Local Governments*, which of the following statements is correct concerning the statement of cash flows prepared for proprietary funds?
a. The statement format is the same as that of a business enterprise's statement of cash flows.
b. Cash flows from capital financing activities are reported separately from cash flows from noncapital financing activities.
c. Cash flows from operating activities may not be reported using the direct method.
d. Cash received from interest revenue and cash paid for interest expense are both reported as operating activities.

33. For governmental fund reporting, which item is considered the primary measurement focus?

a. Income determination.
b. Flows and balances of current financial resources.
c. Capital maintenance.
d. Cash flows and balances.

34. Which of the following funds of a governmental unit recognizes revenues in the accounting period in which they become available and measurable?

	General fund	Enterprise fund
a.	Yes	No
b.	No	Yes
c.	Yes	Yes
d.	No	No

35. Property taxes and fines represent which of the following classes of nonexchange transactions for governmental units?
a. Derived tax revenues.
b. Imposed nonexchange revenues.
c. Government-mandated nonexchange transactions.
d. Voluntary nonexchange transactions.

36. In accordance with GASB 33, *Accounting and Financial Reporting for Nonexchange Transactions*, which of the following transactions would qualify as a nonexchange transaction in the City of Geneva?
a. The water utility (enterprise) fund billed the general fund for water usage.
b. Property taxes were levied by the general fund.
c. The motor pool (internal service) fund billed other departments for services rendered.
d. The general fund sold police cars for their estimated residual value.

Items 37 and 38 are based on the following:

The general fund of Elizabeth City received a $100,000 grant from the state to be used for retraining its police force in modern crime-fighting methods. The state recently passed legislation that requires retraining for all police departments in the state. The grant was received in cash on June 15, 2009, and was used for retraining seminars during July 2009. The state mandated that the grant be spent in the fiscal year ending June 30, 2010. Elizabeth's fiscal year ends on June 30. Answer each of the questions below based upon the guidance provided by GASB 33, *Accounting and Financial Reporting for Nonexchange Transactions*.

37. What account should be credited in the general fund on the date the grant was received?
a. Restricted revenue.
b. Deferred revenue.
c. Revenue.
d. Unreserved fund balance.

38. The grant from the state is an example of what type of nonexchange transaction?
a. Government-mandated.
b. Imposed.
c. Voluntary.
d. Derived.

Items 39 and 40 are based on the following:

The merchants of Eldorado City collect a sales tax of 5% on retail sales. The sales taxes are remitted by retailers to the state and distributed by the state to the various governmental units that are within the boundaries of Eldorado City. During the month of June 2009, the state received

$50,000 of sales taxes from merchants in Eldorado. As of June 30, 2009, none of the sales taxes had been remitted to Eldorado or to any of the other governments that were within the boundaries of Eldorado. However, Eldorado estimated that its share of the sales taxes would be received in early July 2009, and would be used to pay for expenditures incurred during the year ended June 30, 2009. Eldorado's fiscal year ends on June 30. Answer both of the questions below using the guidance provided in GASB 33, *Accounting and Financial Reporting for Nonexchange Transactions*.

39. From the perspective of Eldorado City, the sales taxes are an example of what type of nonexchange transaction?
a. Imposed.
b. Voluntary.
c. Derived.
d. Government-mandated

40. On the statement of revenues, expenditures, and changes in fund balance for the year ended June 30, 2009, how should the general fund of Eldorado report its share of the sales taxes that will be received in July 2009?
a. Deferred revenue.
b. Restricted revenue.
c. Revenue.
d. Unreserved fund balance.

41. On July 1, 2009, the general fund of Sun City levied property taxes for the fiscal year ending June 30, 2010. According to GASB 33, *Accounting and Financial Reporting for Nonexchange Transactions*, property taxes are an example of what type of nonexchange transaction?
a. Voluntary.
b. Government-mandated.
c. Imposed.
d. Derived.

42. For the year ended December 31, 2009, the general fund of Karsten City levied property taxes of $1,000,000. The city estimated that $10,000 of the levy would not be collectible. By December 31, 2009, the city had collected $850,0000 of property taxes and expected to collect the remainder of the taxes as follows:

• $100,000 by March 1, 2010
• $40,000 during the remainder of 2010

In accordance with GASB 33, *Accounting and Reporting for Nonexchange Transactions*, how much property tax revenue should be reported by the general fund on the statement of revenues, expenditures, and changes in fund balances prepared for the year ended December 31, 2009?
a. $ 850,000
b. $ 950,000
c. $ 990,000
d. $1,000,000

43. For the year ended December 31, 2009, the general fund of Ward Village reported revenues from the following sources on the statement of revenues, expenditures, and changes in fund balances:

Sales taxes	$ 25,000
Property taxes	125,000
Income taxes	15,000
Fines	10,000

In accordance with GASB 33, *Accounting and Reporting for Nonexchange Transactions*, what is the amount of revenues that came from imposed nonexchange transactions?

a. $175,000
b. $150,000
c. $140,000
d. $135,000

44. In December 2009, the general fund of Millard City received $25,000 from the state as an advance on the city's portion of sales tax revenues, and it received $20,000 from property owners for property taxes to be levied in 2010. The advance payment of sales taxes represented the amount that the state collected in 2009 that would have been distributed to Millard in the early part of 2010. Millard used the advance to pay for expenditures incurred by the general fund in 2009. The cash received from property owners for property taxes to be levied in 2010 will be used to pay for expenditures incurred in 2010. In accordance with GASB 33, *Accounting and Reporting for Nonexchange Transactions*, what amount of revenue from these transactions should be reported by Millard's general fund on the statement of revenues, expenditures, and changes in fund balances for the year ended December 31, 2009?

    a. $25,000
    b. $20,000
    c. $0
    d. $45,000

45. In accordance with GASB 33, *Accounting and Reporting for Nonexchange Transactions*, which of the following revenues results from taxes assessed by a government on exchange transactions (a derived tax revenue)?

    a. Property tax revenues.
    b. Fines and forfeits.
    c. Motor fuel taxes.
    d. Unrestricted government grants.

46. In accordance with GASB 33, *Accounting and Reporting for Nonexchange Transactions*, which of the following revenues results from taxes and other assessments imposed by governments that are not derived from underlying transactions?

    a. Income taxes.
    b. Sales taxes.
    c. Motor fuel taxes.
    d. Fines and forfeits.

47. Devon County is developing its own software system to maintain property tax records. Which of the following is not required for Devon to begin capitalizing the software costs?

    a. Devon has established the objective for the project and the proposed scope of the software system.
    b. Devon has established the feasibility of creating the software system.
    c. Devon has established an accurate budget for the software system.
    d. Devon has established its intention to complete or continue developing the system.

48. The State of Texas is scheduled to receive a substantial amount of revenues as a part of a tobacco settlement. The revenues for the next five years have been sold to a commercial business for $5,000,000. Assuming that Texas has no involvement with the future revenues, how should it account for this transaction?

    a. Recognize $5,000,000 of revenue at the date of the transaction.

    b. Recognize $5,000,000 in liability to the commercial business.
    c. Recognize $5,000,000 in deferred revenue and recognize the revenue over a five-year period.
    d. Recognize the difference between the cash received and the amount of future revenues sold as an expense.

Items 49 and 50 are based on the following:

Ridge Township's governing body adopted its general fund budget for the year ended July 31, 2009, comprised of Estimated Revenues of $100,000 and Appropriations of $80,000. Ridge formally integrates its budget into the accounting records.

49. To record the appropriations of $80,000, Ridge should
    a. Credit Appropriations Control.
    b. Debit Appropriations Control.
    c. Credit Estimated Expenditures Control.
    d. Debit Estimated Expenditures Control.

50. To record the $20,000 budgeted excess of estimated revenues over appropriations, Ridge should
    a. Credit Estimated Excess Revenues Control.
    b. Debit Estimated Excess Revenues Control.
    c. Credit Budgetary Fund Balance.
    d. Debit Budgetary Fund Balance.

51. For the budgetary year ending December 31, 2009, Maple City's general fund expects the following inflows of resources:

Property Taxes, Licenses, and Fines	$9,000,000
Proceeds of Debt Issue	5,000,000
Interfund Transfers for Debt Service	1,000,000

In the budgetary entry, what amount should Maple record for estimated revenues?
    a. $ 9,000,000
    b. $10,000,000
    c. $14,000,000
    d. $15,000,000

52. In 2009, New City issued purchase orders and contracts of $850,000 that were chargeable against 2009 budgeted appropriations of $1,000,000. The journal entry to record the issuance of the purchase orders and contracts should include a
    a. Credit to Vouchers Payable of $1,000,000.
    b. Credit to Budgetary Fund Balance—Reserved for Encumbrances of $850,000.
    c. Debit to Expenditures of $1,000,000.
    d. Debit to Appropriations of $850,000.

53. During its fiscal year ended June 30, 2009, Cliff City issued purchase orders totaling $5,000,000, which were properly charged to Encumbrances at that time. Cliff received goods and related invoices at the encumbered amounts totaling $4,500,000 before year-end. The remaining goods of $500,000 were not received until after year-end. Cliff paid $4,200,000 of the invoices received during the year. What amount of Cliff's encumbrances were outstanding at June 30, 2009?
    a. $0
    b. $300,000
    c. $500,000
    d. $800,000

54. Elm City issued a purchase order for supplies with an estimated cost of $5,000. When the supplies were received, the accompanying invoice indicated an actual price of $4,950. What amount should Elm debit (credit) to Budgetary Fund Balance—Reserved for Encumbrances after the supplies and invoice were received?
a. $ (50)
b. $ 50
c. $4,950
d. $5,000

55. A budgetary fund balance reserved for encumbrances in excess of a balance of encumbrances indicates
a. An excess of vouchers payable over encumbrances.
b. An excess of purchase orders over invoices received.
c. An excess of appropriations over encumbrances.
d. A recording error.

56. Encumbrances outstanding at year-end in a state's general fund should be reported as a
a. Liability in the general fund.
b. Fund balance reserve in the general fund.
c. Liability in the General Long-Term Debt Account Group.
d. Fund balance designation in the general fund.

57. When Rolan County adopted its budget for the year ending June 30, 2009, $20,000,000 was recorded for Estimated Revenues Control. Actual revenues for the year ended June 30, 2009, amounted to $17,000,000. In closing the budgetary accounts at June 30, 2009,
a. Revenues Control should be debited for $3,000,000.
b. Estimated Revenues Control should be debited for $3,000,000.
c. Revenues Control should be credited for $20,000,000.
d. Estimated Revenues Control should be credited for $20,000,000.

58. The budget of a governmental unit, for which the appropriations exceed the estimated revenues, was adopted and recorded in the general ledger at the beginning of the year. During the year, expenditures and encumbrances were less than appropriations, whereas revenues equaled estimated revenues. The Budgetary Fund Balance account is
a. Credited at the beginning of the year and debited at the end of the year.
b. Credited at the beginning of the year and **not** changed at the end of the year.
c. Debited at the beginning of the year and credited at the end of the year.
d. Debited at the beginning of the year and **not** changed at the end of the year.

59. The following information pertains to Park Township's general fund at December 31, 2009:

Total assets, including $200,000 of cash	$1,000,000
Total liabilities	600,000
Fund balance—Reserved for encumbrances	100,000

Appropriations do not lapse at year-end. At December 31, 2009, what amount should Park report as unreserved fund balance in its general fund balance sheet?
a. $200,000
b. $300,000

c. $400,000
d. $500,000

60. The following information pertains to Pine City's general fund for 2009:

Appropriations Control	$6,500,000
Expenditures Control	5,000,000
Other Financing Sources Control	1,500,000
Other Financing Uses Control	2,000,000
Revenues Control	8,000,000

After Pine's general fund accounts were closed at the end of 2009, the fund balance increased by
a. $3,000,000
b. $2,500,000
c. $1,500,000
d. $1,000,000

61. Cedar City issues $1,000,000, 6% revenue bonds at par on April 1 to build a new water line for the water enterprise fund. Interest is payable every six months. What amount of interest expense should be reported for the year ended December 31?
a. $0
b. $30,000
c. $45,000
d. $60,000

62. The expenditure element "salaries and wages" is an example of which type of classification?
a. Object.
b. Program.
c. Function.
d. Activity.

Items 63 and 64 are based on the following information for Oak City for the calendar year 2009:

Collections during 2009	$500,000
Expected collections during the first sixty days of 2010	100,000
Expected collections during the balance of 2010	60,000
Expected collections during January 2011	30,000
Estimated to be uncollectible	10,000
Total levy	$700,000

63. What amount should Oak City report for 2009 property tax revenues in the Statement of Revenues, Expenditures, and Changes in Fund Balances prepared for governmental funds?
a. $700,000
b. $690,000
c. $600,000
d. $500,000

64. What amount should Oak City report for 2009 property tax revenues in the government-wide Statement of Activities?
a. $700,000
b. $690,000
c. $600,000
d. $500,000

65. Which of the following transactions is an expenditure of a governmental unit's general fund?
a. Contribution of enterprise fund capital by the general fund.
b. Transfer from the general fund to a capital projects fund.

    c.   Operating subsidy transfer from the general fund to an enterprise fund.

    d.   Routine employer contributions from the general fund to a pension trust fund.

66. During the year, a city's electric utility, which is operated as an enterprise fund, rendered billings for electricity supplied to the general fund. Which of the following accounts should be debited by the general fund?

    a.   Appropriations.

    b.   Expenditures

    c.   Due to Electric Utility Enterprise Fund.

    d.   Transfers.

67. Which of the following fund types used by a government most likely would have a Fund Balance—Reserved for Inventory of Supplies?

    a.   General.

    b.   Internal service.

    c.   Enterprise.

    d.   Debt service.

68. The following revenues were among those reported by Ariba Township in 2009:

Net rental revenue (after depreciation) from a parking garage owned by Ariba	$ 40,000
Interest earned on investments held for employees' retirement benefits	100,000
Property taxes	6,000,000

What amount of the foregoing revenues should be accounted for in Ariba's governmental-type funds?

    a. $6,140,000

    b. $6,100,000

    c. $6,040,000

    d. $6,000,000

Items 69 through 70 are based on the following:

The general fund of Cliff Township acquired two police cars at the beginning of January 2009, at a total cost of $40,000. The cars are expected to last for four years and have a $10,000 residual value. Straight-line depreciation is used. Cliff adopted the provisions of GASB 34, *Basic Financial Statements—and Management's Discussion and Analysis—for State and Local Governments,* for its financial statements issued for 2009.

69. On the balance sheet for the governmental funds at December 31, 2009, the police cars will be reported under assets in the general fund column at which of the following amounts?

    a. $40,000

    b. $32,500

    c. $0

    d. $22,500

70. On the government-wide statement of net assets at December 31, 2009, the police cars will be reported under assets in the governmental activities column at which of the following amounts?

    a. $40,000

    b. $32,500

    c. $0

    d. $22,500

71. On the statement of revenues, expenditures, and changes in fund balances prepared for the governmental

funds for the year ended December 31, 2009, the police cars will be reported as

    a.   Expenditures of $40,000.

    b.   Expense of $7,500.

    c.   Expenditures of $7,500.

    d.   Expense of $40,000.

Items 72 through 75 are based on the following:

The City of Vicksburg adopted the provisions of GASB 34, *Basic Financial Statements—and Management's Discussion and Analysis—for State and Local Governments,* for its financial statements issued for the year ended December 31, 2009. During the year ended December 31, 2009, the general fund of Vicksburg has the following selected transactions:

- Acquired police cars for $75,000 in January 2009. The cars have an estimated five-year useful life and a $15,000 salvage value. The City uses the straight-line method to depreciate all of its capital assets.

- Transferred $30,000 to the pension trust fund. The amount represented the employer's contribution.

- Levied property taxes in the amount of $800,000. Two percent of the levy was not expected to be collected. At December 31, 2009, $750,000 of the property taxes were collected, but the remainder was not expected to be collected within sixty days after the end of 2009.

- Received $100,000 of sales tax revenues from the state and was owed another $25,000 by the state for sales taxes collected in 2009 that will not be remitted to Vicksburg until mid-March 2010. The sales taxes expected to be received in March will be used to pay for expenditures incurred in 2010.

72. On the statement of revenues, expenditures, and changes in fund balances prepared for the governmental funds for the year ended December 31, 2009, what amount should be reported for expenditures in Vicksburg's general fund related to the acquisition of police cars and to the pension transfer?

    a. $ 42,000

    b. $105,000

    c. $ 75,000

    d. $ 30,000

73. On the statement of revenues, expenditures, and changes in fund balances prepared for the governmental funds for the year ended December 31, 2009, what amount should be reported for revenues in Vicksburg's general fund related to property taxes and sales taxes?

    a. $884,000

    b. $909,000

    c. $850,000

    d. $875,000

74. On the government-wide statement of activities prepared for the year ended December 31, 2009, what amount should be reported for expenses for governmental activities related to the acquisition of the police cars and to the pension transfer?

    a. $ 42,000

    b. $105,000

    c. $ 75,000

    d. $ 30,000

75. On the government-wide statement of activities prepared for the year ended December 31, 2009, what amount

should be reported for revenues from governmental activities related to the property taxes and the sales taxes?
- a. $884,000
- b. $909,000
- c. $850,000
- d. $875,000

76. In November 2008, Maple Township received an unexpected state grant of $100,000 to finance the purchase of
school buses, and an additional grant of $5,000 was received
for bus maintenance and operations. According to the terms
of the grant, the State reimbursed Maple Township for
$60,000 for the purchase of school buses and an additional
$5,000 for bus maintenance during the year ended June 30,
2009. The remaining $40,000 of the capital grant is ex-
pected to be spent during the next fiscal year June 30, 2010.
Maple's school bus system is appropriately accounted for in
a special revenue fund. In connection with the grants for the
purchase of school buses and bus maintenance, what amount
should be reported as grant revenues for the year ending
June 30, 2009, when using modified accrual accounting?
- a. $ 5,000
- b. $ 60,000
- c. $ 65,000
- d. $100,000

77. Lake County received the following proceeds that are
legally restricted to expenditure for specified purposes:

Levies on affected property owners to install sidewalks	$500,000
Gasoline taxes to finance road repairs	900,000

What amount should be accounted for in Lake's special
revenue funds?
- a. $1,400,000
- b. $ 900,000
- c. $ 500,000
- d. $0

78. Should a major special revenue fund with a legally
adopted budget maintain its accounts on an accrual basis and
integrate budgetary accounts into its accounting system?

	Maintain on accrual basis	Integrate budgetary accounts
a.	Yes	Yes
b.	Yes	No
c.	No	Yes
d.	No	No

79. In 2009, Menton City received $5,000,000 of bond
proceeds to be used for capital projects. Of this amount,
$1,000,000 was expended in 2009. Expenditures for the
$4,000,000 balance were expected to be incurred in 2010.
These bond proceeds should be recorded in capital projects
funds for
- a. $5,000,000 in 2009.
- b. $5,000,000 in 2010.
- c. $1,000,000 in 2009 and $4,000,000 in 2010.
- d. $1,000,000 in 2009 and in the general fund for $4,000,000 in 2009.

80. Financing for the renovation of Fir City's municipal
park, begun and completed during 2009, came from the following sources:

Grant from state government	$400,000
Proceeds from general obligation bond issue	500,000
Transfer from Fir's general fund	100,000

In its 2009 capital projects fund operating statement, Fir
should report these amounts as

	Revenues	Other financing sources
a.	$1,000,000	$0
b.	$ 900,000	$ 100,000
c.	$ 400,000	$ 600,000
d.	$0	$1,000,000

81. An impaired capital asset that is no longer used by a
government should be reported in the financial statements at
- a. Historical cost.
- b. Historical cost adjusted for depreciation.
- c. The lower of carrying value or fair value.
- d. Fair value.

82. A government should recognized the impairment of a
capital asset when events or circumstances indicate that
there is a significant decline in service utility and
- a. The asset is not in service.
- b. The event or circumstance is outside the normal life cycle of the asset.
- c. The asset is not covered by insurance.
- d. The asset is not fully depreciated.

83. In which of the following fund types of a city government are revenues and expenditures recognized on the same
basis of accounting as the general fund?
- a. Pension trust.
- b. Internal service.
- c. Enterprise.
- d. Debt service.

84. Japes City issued $1,000,000 general obligation bonds
at 101 to build a new city hall. As part of the bond issue, the
city also paid a $500 underwriter fee and $2,000 in debt
issue costs. What amount should Japes City report as other
financing sources?
- a. $1,010,000
- b. $1,008,000
- c. $1,007,500
- d. $1,000,000

85. Dale City is accumulating financial resources that are
legally restricted to payments of general long-term debt
principal and interest maturing in future years. At December 31, 2009, $5,000,000 has been accumulated for principal
payments and $300,000 has been accumulated for interest
payments. These restricted funds should be accounted for in
the

	Debt service fund	General fund
a.	$0	$5,300,000
b.	$ 300,000	$5,000,000
c.	$5,000,000	$ 300,000
d.	$5,300,000	$0

86. On April 1, 2009, Oak County incurred the following
expenditures in issuing long-term bonds:

Issue costs	$400,000
Debt insurance	90,000

Oak County has established a debt service fund for the payment of interest and principal of its long-term bonds. Assuming Oak County's fiscal year ends of June 30, what
amount of issue costs and debt insurance costs should be
reported as an asset on the governmental funds' balance
sheet at June 30, 2009?

a. $0
b. $ 90,000
c. $400,000
d. $490,000

87. Receipts from a special tax levy to retire and pay interest on general obligation bonds should be recorded in which fund?

a.   General.
b.   Capital projects.
c.   Debt service.
d.   Special revenue.

88. Wood City, which is legally obligated to maintain a debt service fund, issued the following general obligation bonds on July 1, 2009:

Term of bonds	10 years
Face amount	$1,000,000
Issue price	101
Stated interest rate	6%

Interest is payable January 1 and July 1. What amount of bond premium should be amortized in Wood's debt service fund for the year ended December 31, 2009?

a. $1,000
b. $ 500
c. $ 250
d. $0

89. The debt service fund of a governmental unit is used to account for the accumulation of resources for, and the payment of, principal and interest in connection with a

	Trust fund	Proprietary fund
a.	No	No
b.	No	Yes
c.	Yes	Yes
d.	Yes	No

90. Tott City's serial bonds are serviced through a debt service fund with cash provided by the general fund. In a debt service fund's statements, how are cash receipts and cash payments reported?

	Cash receipts	Cash payments
a.	Revenues	Expenditures
b.	Revenues	Other Financing Use
c.	Other Financing Source	Expenditures
d.	Other Financing Source	Other Financing Use

91. On March 2, 2009, Finch City issued ten-year general obligation bonds at face amount, with interest payable March 1 and September 1. The proceeds were to be used to finance the construction of a civic center over the period April 1, 2009, to March 31, 2010. During the fiscal year ended June 30, 2009, no resources had been provided to the debt service fund for the payment of principal and interest.

On June 30, 2009, Finch's debt service fund should include interest payable on the general obligation bonds for

a.   0 months.
b.   Three months.
c.   Four months.
d.   Six months.

92. According to GASB 52, real estate held as an investment by a government endowment should be reported at

a.   Fair value.
b.   Historical cost.
c.   Historical cost less accumulated depreciation.

d.   A nominal value.

93. Fish Road property owners in Sea County are responsible for special assessment debt that arose from a storm sewer project. If the property owners default, Sea has no obligation regarding debt service, although it does bill property owners for assessments and uses the monies it collects to pay debt holders. What fund type should Sea use to account for these collection and servicing activities?

a.   Agency.
b.   Debt service.
c.   Investment trust funds.
d.   Capital projects.

94. Cy City's Municipal Solid Waste Landfill Enterprise Fund was established when a new landfill was opened January 3, 2009. The landfill is expected to reach capacity and close December 31, 2027. Cy's 2009 expenses would include a portion of which of the year 2028 expected disbursements?

I. Cost of a final cover to be applied to the landfill.
II. Cost of equipment to be installed to monitor methane gas buildup.

a.   I only.
b.   II only.
c.   Both I and II.
d.   Neither I nor II.

95. Chase City uses an internal service fund for its central motor pool. The assets and liabilities account balances for this fund that are not eliminated normally should be reported in the government-wide statement of net assets as

a.   Governmental activities.
b.   Business-type activities.
c.   Fiduciary activities.
d.   Note disclosures only.

96. The billings for transportation services provided to other governmental units are recorded by an internal service fund as

a.   Transportation appropriations.
b.   Operating revenues.
c.   Interfund exchanges.
d.   Intergovernmental transfers.

97. The following information for the year ended June 30, 2009, pertains to a proprietary fund established by Burwood Village in connection with Burwood's public parking facilities:

Receipts from users of parking facilities	$400,000
Expenditures	
Parking meters	210,000
Salaries and other cash expenses	90,000
Depreciation of parking meters	70,000

For the year ended June 30, 2009, this proprietary fund should report net income of

a. $0
b. $ 30,000
c. $100,000
d. $240,000

98. A state government had the following activities:

I.	State-operated lottery	$10,000,000
II.	State-operated hospital	3,000,000

Which of the above activities should be accounted for in an enterprise fund?

a. Neither I nor II.
b. I only.
c. II only.
d. Both I and II.

99. For governmental units, depreciation expense on assets acquired with capital grants externally restricted for capital acquisitions should be reported in which type of fund?

	Governmental fund	Proprietary fund
a.	Yes	No
b.	Yes	Yes
c.	No	No
d.	No	Yes

100. An enterprise fund would be used when the governing body requires that

I. Accounting for the financing of an agency's services to other government departments be on a cost-reimbursement basis.
II. User charges cover the costs of general public services.
III. Net income information be reported for an activity.

a. I only.
b. I and II.
c. I and III.
d. II and III.

101. The following transactions were among those reported by Cliff County's water and sewer enterprise fund for 2009:

Proceeds from sale of revenue bonds	$5,000,000
Cash received from customer households	3,000,000
Capital contributed by subdividers	1,000,000

In the water and sewer enterprise fund's statement of cash flows for the year ended December 31, 2009, what amount should be reported as cash flows from capital and related financing activities?

a. $9,000,000
b. $8,000,000
c. $6,000,000
d. $5,000,000

102. The orientation of accounting and reporting for all proprietary funds of governmental units is

a. Income determination.
b. Project.
c. Flow of funds.
d. Program.

Items 103 through 105 are based on the following:

Rock County has acquired equipment through a noncancelable lease-purchase agreement dated December 31, 2009. This agreement requires no down payment and the following minimum lease payments:

December 31	Principal	Interest	Total
2010	$50,000	$15,000	$65,000
2011	50,000	10,000	60,000
2011	50,000	5,000	55,000

103. What account should be debited for $150,000 in the general fund at inception of the lease if the equipment is a general fixed asset and Rock does **not** use a capital projects fund?

a. Other Financing Uses Control.
b. Equipment.
c. Expenditures Control.
d. Memorandum entry only.

104. If the equipment is used in enterprise fund operations and the lease payments are to be financed with enterprise fund revenues, what account should be debited for $150,000 in the enterprise fund at the inception of the lease?

a. Expenses Control.
b. Expenditures Control.
c. Other Financing Sources Control.
d. Equipment.

105. If the equipment is used in internal service fund operations and the lease payments are financed with internal service fund revenues, what account or accounts should be debited in the internal service fund for the December 31, 2009 lease payment of $65,000?

a.	Expenditures Control	$65,000
b.	Expenses Control	$65,000
c.	Capital Lease Payable	$50,000
	Expenses Control	15,000
d.	Expenditures Control	$50,000
	Expenses Control	15,000

106. Hill City's water utility fund held the following investments in US Treasury securities at June 30, 2009:

Investment	Date purchased	Maturity date	Carrying amount
Three-month T-bill	5/31/09	7/31/09	$30,000
Three-year T-note	6/15/09	8/31/09	50,000
Five-year T-note	10/1/05	9/30/10	100,000

In the fund's balance sheet, what amount of these investments should be reported as cash and cash equivalents at June 30, 2009?

a. $0
b. $ 30,000
c. $ 80,000
d. $180,000

107. The following fund types used by Green Township had total assets at June 30, 2009, as follows:

Agency funds	$ 300,000
Debt service funds	1,000,000

Total fiduciary fund assets amount to

a. $0
b. $ 300,000
c. $1,000,000
d. $1,300,000

108. Grove County collects property taxes levied within its boundaries and receives a 1% fee for administering these collections on behalf of the municipalities located in the county. In 2009, Grove collected $1,000,000 for its municipalities and remitted $990,000 to them after deducting fees of $10,000. In the initial recording of the 1% fee, Grove's agency fund should credit

a. Net Assets—Agency Fund, $10,000.
b. Fees Earned—Agency Fund, $10,000.
c. Due to Grove County General Fund, $10,000.
d. Revenues Control, $10,000.

Items 109 and 110 are based on the following:

Elm City contributes to and administers a single-employer defined benefit pension plan on behalf of its covered employees. The plan is accounted for in a pension trust fund. For the year ended December 31, 2009, employer contributions to the pension trust fund amounted to $11,000.

109. What account should be credited in the pension trust fund to record the 2009 employer contribution of $11,000?

    a.   Additions.

    b.   Other Financing Sources Control.

    c.   Due from Special Revenue Fund.

    d.   Pension Benefit Obligation.

110. To record the 2009 pension contribution of $11,000, what debit is required in the governmental-type fund used in connection with employer pension contributions?

    a.   Other Financing Uses Control.

    b.   Expenditures Control.

    c.   Expenses Control.

    d.   Due to Pension Trust Fund.

111. In accordance with GASB 34, *Basic Financial Statements—and Management's Discussion and Analysis— for State and Local Governments*, what types of interfund transactions are included in the amount reported for transfers on the government-wide statement of activities?

   I.   Yearly operating subsidies from the general fund to an enterprise fund.

  II.   Billings from an enterprise fund to an internal service fund for services rendered.

    a.   I only.

    b.   II only.

    c.   Both I and II.

    d.   Neither I nor II.

112. Jamestown adopted the provisions of GASB 34, *Basic Financial Statements—and Management's Discussion and Analysis—for State and Local Governments*, for its financial statements issued for the year ended December 31, 2009. During the year ended December 31, 2009, Jamestown had the following selected transactions:

- The general fund made a $100,000 advance to an internal service fund. The internal service fund will repay the advance in 2010.
- The water utility enterprise fund billed the general fund $25,000 for water usage.
- The general fund transferred $30,000 to a debt service fund to pay interest on general obligation bonds.

On Jamestown's government-wide statement of activities for the year ended December 31, 2009, what amount should be reported for transfers?

    a. $125,000

    b. $ 55,000

    c. $0

    d. $130,000

113. The town of Harrisville adopted the provisions of GASB 34, *Basic Financial Statements—and Management's Discussion and Analysis—for State and Local Governments*, for its financial statements issued for the year ended December 31, 2009. During the year ended December 31, 2009, Harrisville had the following selected transactions:

- The general fund made a permanent transfer of $100,000 to an enterprise fund. The enterprise fund used the amount transferred to acquire capital assets.
- The general fund transferred $1,000,000 to a capital projects fund for the town's portion of the cost for the renovation of the town hall.
- The general fund was reimbursed $5,000 by an enterprise fund for expenses paid by the general fund that were properly charged as operating expenses of the enterprise fund.

On Harrisville's government-wide statement of activities for the year ended December 31, 2009, what amount should be reported as transfers?

    a. $ 100,000

    b. $1,100,000

    c. $1,005,000

    d. $ 105,000

114. In accordance with GASB 35, a public college or university that chooses to report only business-type activities should present only the financial statements required for

    a.   Enterprise funds.

    b.   Government funds.

    c.   Internal service funds.

    d.   Enterprise and internal service funds.

115. In accordance with GASB 35, a public college or university that chooses to report both governmental and business-type activities should report

	Fund financial statements	Government-wide financial statements
a.	No	Yes
b.	Yes	No
c.	Yes	Yes
d.	No	No

116. A public college had tuition and fees of $20,000,000. Scholarships, for which no services were required, amounted to $1,000,000. Employee discounts, which were provided in exchange for services, amounted to $2,000,000. The amount to be reported as net tuition and fees by the public college would be

    a. $20,000,000.

    b. $19,000,000.

    c. $18,000,000.

    d. $17,000,000.

117. Which of the following is true regarding the Statement of Revenues, Expenses, and Changes in Net Assets for a public college choosing to report as a special-purpose entity engaged in business-type activities only?

    a.   State appropriations should be reported as nonoperating income.

    b.   An operating income figure must be displayed.

    c.   Both contributions for plant and for endowment purposes must be reported separately after both operating and nonoperating revenues and expenses.

    d.   All of the above.

MULTIPLE-CHOICE ANSWERS

1.	c	__	__	27.	d	__	__	53.	c	__	__	79.	a	__	__	105.	c	__	__
2.	d	__	__	28.	c	__	__	54.	d	__	__	80.	c	__	__	106.	c	__	__
3.	b	__	__	29.	c	__	__	55.	d	__	__	81.	c	__	__	107.	b	__	__
4.	b	__	__	30.	c	__	__	56.	b	__	__	82.	b	__	__	108.	c	__	__
5.	a	__	__	31.	a	__	__	57.	d	__	__	83.	d	__	__	109.	a	__	__
6.	a	__	__	32.	b	__	__	58.	c	__	__	84.	a	__	__	110.	b	__	__
7.	a	__	__	33.	b	__	__	59.	b	__	__	85.	d	__	__	111.	a	__	__
8.	d	__	__	34.	a	__	__	60.	b	__	__	86.	a	__	__	112.	c	__	__
9.	b	__	__	35.	b	__	__	61.	c	__	__	87.	c	__	__	113.	a	__	__
10.	b	__	__	36.	b	__	__	62.	a	__	__	88.	d	__	__	114.	a	__	__
11.	c	__	__	37.	b	__	__	63.	c	__	__	89.	a	__	__	115.	c	__	__
12.	d	__	__	38.	a	__	__	64.	b	__	__	90.	c	__	__	116.	b	__	__
13.	d	__	__	39.	c	__	__	65.	d	__	__	91.	a	__	__	117.	d	__	__
14.	c	__	__	40.	c	__	__	66.	b	__	__	92.	a	__	__				
15.	d	__	__	41.	c	__	__	67.	a	__	__	93.	a	__	__				
16.	a	__	__	42.	b	__	__	68.	d	__	__	94.	c	__	__				
17.	b	__	__	43.	d	__	__	69.	c	__	__	95.	a	__	__				
18.	b	__	__	44.	a	__	__	70.	b	__	__	96.	b	__	__				
19.	c	__	__	45.	c	__	__	71.	a	__	__	97.	d	__	__				
20.	d	__	__	46.	d	__	__	72.	b	__	__	98.	d	__	__				
21.	a	__	__	47.	c	__	__	73.	c	__	__	99.	d	__	__				
22.	c	__	__	48.	c	__	__	74.	a	__	__	100.	d	__	__				
23.	a	__	__	49.	a	__	__	75.	b	__	__	101.	c	__	__				
24.	a	__	__	50.	c	__	__	76.	c	__	__	102.	a	__	__				
25.	b	__	__	51.	a	__	__	77.	b	__	__	103.	c	__	__	1st:	__/117 = __%
26.	d	__	__	52.	b	__	__	78.	c	__	__	104.	d	__	__	2nd:	__/117 = __%

MULTIPLE-CHOICE ANSWER EXPLANATIONS

B. The Reporting Entity

1. (**c**) GASB 34 indicates that the basic financial statements include only the government-wide statements, the fund statements, and the notes to the financial statements.

2. (**d**) The concept underlying the definition of the financial reporting entity is that elected officials are accountable to their constituents for their actions. Accordingly, the financial reporting entity consists of (1) the primary government, (2) organizations for which the primary government is **financially accountable,** and (3) other organizations for which the nature and significance of their relationship with the primary government is such that exclusion would cause the reporting entity's financial statements to be misleading or incomplete. Thus, the basic criterion used to determine the reporting entity is financial accountability.

3. (**b**) The requirement is to determine how the school district's financial activity should be reported. The school district is a component unit, which means it is a legally separate organization for which the elected officials of a primary government are financially accountable. Component units can be presented either discretely or blended. If the component unit is so closely tied to the primary government that the activities seem to be indistinguishable, the presentation should be blended. The school district's budget requires separate approval of the city council, so it is not indistinguishable. In addition, the school board members are independently elected. The activities of the component unit are distinguishable from the primary government, and therefore should be shown discretely.

4. (**b**) The requirement is to determine how the school district should be reported. A component unit is a legally

separate organization for which the elected officials of a primary government are financially accountable. The school district is a component unit, which can be presented either discretely or blended. The unit is blended if the activities of the unit are so closely tied to the primary government as to be indistinguishable. Even though two of the district's members are city council members, the activities of the school district are distinct from the primary government and should be presented discretely.

D. Government-Wide Financial Statements

5. (**a**) In accordance with GASB 34, state and local governments are required to report infrastructure assets on the government-wide statement of net assets. However, GASB 34 does not require infrastructure assets to be depreciated. GASB 34 permits governments to use a modified approach in its accounting for infrastructure assets. The modified approach results in the government reporting expense for the maintenance costs related to infrastructure assets (on the government-wide statement of activities) and in its reporting no depreciation expense, if certain conditions are met by the government as specified in GASB 34. Therefore, on the statement of net assets for Darien Village at December 31, 2005, infrastructure assets would be reported at $5,000,000 without any reduction for accumulated depreciation.

6. (**a**) GASB 9, para 19, indicates that "cash flows from operating activities include transactions of certain loan programs." These include "program loan" programs that are undertaken to fulfill a governmental responsibility, such as the loan program mentioned in this problem.

7. (**a**) GASB 34, para 296, (part of the basis of conclusions) indicates that "The Board concluded that a government's basic financial statements should provide operational accountability information for the government as a whole, including information about the cost of services, operating results, and financial position."

8. **(d)** In accordance with GASB 34, capital assets, exclusive of infrastructure assets, are reported on the government-wide statement of net assets at cost less accumulated depreciation. In the case involving Fullerton City, the amount reported under assets is $2,750,000, computed by subtracting $750,000 of accumulated depreciation from the $3,500,000 cost of the capital assets.

9. **(b)** In the net assets section of the government-wide statement of net assets, GASB 34 requires that the amount invested in capital assets be reported net of related debt. In the case of Fullerton City, the amount reported would be $1,500,000, computed by subtracting $1,250,000 from $2,750,000, the amount reported for capital assets in the asset section of the statement of net assets.

10. **(b)** In accordance with GASB 34, depreciation expense on infrastructure assets is not required if the government chooses the modified approach. Under the modified approach, infrastructure assets are reported on the government-wide statement of net assets at their cost without reduction for accumulated depreciation. On the government-wide statement of activities, the cost to extend the life of the infrastructure assets is reported as an expense, and certain information about infrastructure assets is disclosed as required supplementary information.

11. **(c)** According to GASB 34, the government-wide statement of activities should be prepared using the accrual basis of accounting and the flow of economic resources measurement focus. As a result, capital assets are reported as assets and depreciated over their useful lives, and depreciation expense should be reported on the statement of activities. The statement of revenues, expenses, and changes in fund net assets prepared for the proprietary funds is also prepared using the accrual basis of accounting and the flow of economic resources measurement focus. Therefore, capital assets are depreciated over their useful lives, and depreciation expense is reported on the statement of revenues, expenses, and changes in fund net assets.

12. **(d)** According to GASB 34, governments should prepare government-wide financial statements based upon the accrual basis of accounting and the economic resources measurement focus. In addition to the government-wide financial statements, governments are also required to report financial statements for governmental funds, proprietary funds, and fiduciary funds. The financial statements for governmental funds are based upon the modified accrual basis and the financial resources measurement focus, while the financial statements for proprietary and fiduciary funds are based upon the accrual basis of accounting and the flow of economic resources measurement focus.

13. **(d)** According to GASB 34, infrastructure assets are required to be reported on the government-wide statement of net assets. The use of the modified approach for infrastructure assets means that these assets are not depreciated if certain conditions are satisfied. However, infrastructure assets are reported on the statement of net assets, even if they are not depreciated. According to GASB 34, component units are reported on the entity-wide financial state-

ments. They are not reported on the financial statements of the governmental funds.

E. Fund Financial Statements

14. **(c)** A fund is defined as a fiscal and accounting entity with a self balancing set of accounts. These funds record cash and other financial resources, together with all related liabilities and residual equities or balances, and changes therein, **and are segregated for the purpose of carrying on specific activities or attaining certain objectives** in accordance with special regulations, restrictions, or limitations.

15. **(d)** GASB 9, para 27, indicates that cash flows from investing activities includes interest received as returns on investments. The candidate should note that this is different from SFAS 95, which classifies interest on investments as cash flows from operating activities.

16. **(a)** The Governmental Accounting Standards Board (GASB) has the authority to establish standards of financial reporting for all units of state and local government. Upon its formation in 1984, GASB adopted the past pronouncements of its predecessor organization, the National Council on Governmental Accounting (NCGA), and guidelines in the AICPA *Audits of State and Local Governmental Units*, which the GASB later modified. The FASB sets standards for profit-seeking businesses, and not governmental units.

17. **(b)** The requirement is to determine which event(s) should be included in a statement of cash flows for a government entity. Governmental funds do not have a statement of cash flows because they are accounted for on the modified accrual basis. A statement of cash flows is included for proprietary funds because they are accounted for on the accrual basis. The cash inflow from issuing bonds to finance city hall construction is accounted for in the governmental funds. The cash outflow from a city utility representing payments in lieu of property taxes is accounted for in the proprietary funds.

18. **(b)** Cash flows from sale of revenue bonds and capital contributed by subdividers are classified as cash flows from capital and related financing activities. Both the $4,500,000 proceeds from sale of revenue bonds and $900,000 capital contributed by subdividers would be reported as cash flows from capital and related financing activities. Cash flows from customer households are operating cash flows.

19. **(c)** The statement of cash flows is applicable to proprietary funds and governmental entities that use proprietary fund accounting, including public benefit corporations and authorities, governmental utilities, and governmental hospitals. PERS (Public Employee Retirement Systems) and pension trust funds are exempt from this requirement.

20. **(d)** In accordance with GASB 34, there are three financial statements that should be prepared for proprietary funds. The financial statements for proprietary funds include

1. The statement of net assets
2. The statement of revenues, expenses, and changes in fund net assets
3. The statement of cash flows

21. **(a)** In accordance with GASB 34, the focus of fund financial statements is on major and nonmajor funds, not on fund types. On the balance sheet for the governmental funds, the general fund is always reported as a major fund, while other funds are evaluated as major or nonmajor based upon criteria specified in GASB 34. A separate column is required for each major fund, while all nonmajor funds are aggregated in a single column. On the balance sheet for the governmental funds, fund balances are reported in two categories—reserved and unreserved. The terms restricted and unrestricted are not used on the balance sheet for the governmental funds.

22. **(c)** In accordance with GASB 34, the statement of net assets for proprietary funds should (1) report assets and liabilities in current and noncurrent classifications, and (2) report all the activities of internal service funds in a single column.

23. **(a)** According to GASB 34, the financial statements of proprietary funds should be based upon the accrual basis of accounting and the economic resources measurement focus. Therefore, the statement of net assets for proprietary funds is prepared on the accrual basis and the economic resources measurement focus. On the other hand, the financial statements prepared for governmental funds should be based upon the modified accrual basis of accounting and the financial resources measurement focus. Therefore, the statement of revenues, expenditures, and changes in fund balances prepared for governmental funds is not prepared on the accrual basis and the economic resources measurement focus.

24. **(a)** According to GASB 34, two financial statements should be prepared for fiduciary funds—the statement of fiduciary net assets and the statement of changes in fiduciary net assets. Fiduciary funds include pension trust, investment trust, private-purpose trust, and agency funds. Agency funds should be reported on the statement of fiduciary net assets, but not on the statement of changes in fiduciary net assets. Since agency funds report only assets and liabilities, they are reported on the statement of fiduciary net assets, but they are not reported on the statement of changes in fiduciary net assets.

25. **(b)** According to GASB 34, private-purpose trust funds are fiduciary funds that should be reported on two fiduciary fund financial statements: (1) the statement of fiduciary net assets and (2) the statement of changes in fiduciary net assets. Therefore, private-purpose trust funds are reported on the statement of changes in fiduciary net assets. According to GASB 34, the government-wide statement of net assets discloses information about governmental activities, business-type activities, and component units. Fiduciary activities are not disclosed on the government-wide financial statements. This means that private-purpose trust funds would not be reported on the statement of net assets for governmental and business-type activities.

26. **(d)** According to GASB 34, the statement of cash flows is prepared only for the proprietary funds. The statement of cash flows is not a government-wide financial statement. Therefore, governmental and fiduciary fund types are not reported on the statement of cash flows.

27. **(d)** According to GASB 34, the statement of cash flows is prepared only for the proprietary funds. The state-

ment of cash flows is not a government-wide financial statement. The format of the statement of cash flows consists of four sections. The sections include cash flows from (1) operating activities, (2) noncapital financing activities, (3) capital and related financing activities, and (4) investing activities. This format for the statement of cash flows is different from the format used by business enterprises that discloses operating, investing, and financing activities.

28. **(c)** According to GASB 34, the balance sheet prepared for the governmental funds is based on the modified accrual basis of accounting and financial resources measurement focus. However, the government-wide statement of net assets is prepared based on the accrual basis of accounting and the economic resources measurement focus. The differences between these two financial statements result in a difference between the amount reported for net assets for governmental activities on the statement of net assets and the amount reported for fund balances on the balance sheet for the governmental funds. GASB 34 requires that the reasons for this difference be reported in a reconciliation schedule. One of the reasons for the difference is the acquisition of capital assets by governmental funds during the year. These capital assets do not appear under assets on the balance sheet of the governmental funds because they are recorded as expenditures using the modified accrual basis of accounting and the financial resources measurement focus. Therefore, the acquisition of capital assets has the effect of reducing the fund balances of governmental funds on the balance sheet. However, capital assets are reported as assets on the government-wide statement of net assets. Capital assets acquired by governmental funds are reported on this statement as assets under governmental activities. Therefore, total net assets related to governmental activities are not affected on the statement of net assets when capital assets are acquired. Accordingly, capital assets used in governmental activities are items that are reported in the schedule that reconciles the net assets of governmental activities with the fund balances of the governmental funds. The assets and liabilities of internal service funds are additional items that cause a difference between the fund balances of the government funds and the net assets of governmental activities. The reason that the assets and liabilities of internal service funds cause a difference is that they are included with governmental activities on the statement of net assets, thereby causing net assets of governmental activities to increase. However, internal service fund assets and liabilities are not reported in the governmental fund financial statements; rather, they are included in the proprietary fund financial statements. Therefore, the fund balances of the governmental funds do not include these items. Accordingly, the assets and liabilities of internal service funds are reported in the schedule that reconciles the net assets of governmental activities with the fund balances of the governmental funds.

29. **(c)** According to GASB 34, the statement of revenues, expenditures, and changes in fund balances prepared for the governmental funds is prepared using the modified accrual basis of accounting and the financial resources measurement focus. However, the government-wide statement of activities is prepared using the accrual basis of accounting and the economic resources measurement focus. The differences between these two financial statements result in a difference between the amount reported for the change in net assets for governmental activities on the statement of activities, and the amount reported for the net change in fund balances on the statement of revenues, expenditures, and changes in fund balances for the governmental funds. GASB 34 requires that the reasons for this difference be reported in a reconciliation schedule. One of the reasons for the difference is capital assets that were acquired by governmental funds during the year. On the statement of revenues, expenditures, and changes in fund balances, capital assets are reported as expenditures, using the modified accrual basis of accounting and the financial resources measurement focus. However, capital assets acquired by governmental funds are reported as assets and are depreciated on the government-wide statement of activities. Therefore, the difference between capital expenditures and depreciation expense is reported as a reconciling item. On the other hand, the revenues and expenses of internal service funds are additional items that cause a difference between the net change in the fund balances reported on the statement of revenues, expenditures, and changes in fund balances of the governmental funds and the change in the net assets of governmental activities reported on the statement of activities. The reason that the revenues and expenses of internal service funds cause a difference is that they are included with governmental activities on the statement of activities, thereby causing the net change in fund balances of governmental activities to increase. However, internal service fund revenues and expenses are not reported in the governmental fund financial statements; rather, they are included in the proprietary fund financial statements. Therefore, the net change in fund balances of the governmental funds do not include internal service fund revenues and expenses. Accordingly, the revenues and expenses of internal service funds should be reported in the schedule that reconciles the change in net assets of governmental activities with the net change in the fund balances of the governmental funds.

30. **(c)** According to GASB 34, the accrual basis of accounting and the economic resources measurement focus are concepts that go together. This means that financial statements prepared using the accrual basis also are based upon the economic resources measurement focus. Both the government-wide statement of net assets and the statement of changes in fiduciary net assets are prepared using the accrual basis of accounting and the economic resources measurement focus. The only financial statements that use the financial resources measurement focus are those prepared for governmental funds—the balance sheet and the statement of revenues, expenditures, and changes in fund balances.

31. **(a)** According to GASB 34, pension trust funds are fiduciary funds that are reported on the statement of changes in fiduciary net assets. On the statement of net assets for proprietary funds, net assets are disclosed in three classifications: (1) invested in capital assets, net of related debt, (2) restricted, and (3) unrestricted. Retained earnings is not disclosed on the statement of net assets for proprietary funds; the term "net assets" is used as the equity account.

32. **(b)** According to GASB 34, the statement of cash flows is prepared for proprietary funds. The statement format is not the same as that for business enterprises. The format for the statement of cash flows for proprietary funds contains four sections: (1) cash flows from operating activities, (2) cash flows from noncapital financing activities, (3)

cash flows from capital and related financing activities, and (4) cash flows from investing activities. The cash flows from operating activities must be presented using the direct method. Cash paid for interest is not reported in the operating activities section. It would be disclosed either in the noncapital financing activities' section or the capital and related financing activities' section, depending upon where the debt that caused the interest payments was reported. Interest revenue received in cash is not reported in the operating activities' section. It is reported in the investing activities' section because this is where the investments were reported that resulted in the interest revenue.

H. Measurement Focus and Basis of Accounting

33. **(b)** The governmental fund measurement focus is on determination of current financial position (sources, uses, and balances of financial resources), rather than upon income determination.

34. **(a)** Governmental fund revenues should be recognized in the accounting period in which they become available and measurable. Governmental funds include the general fund, special revenue funds, capital projects funds, debt service funds, and permanent funds. Proprietary fund revenues should be recognized in the accounting period in which they are earned and become measurable. Proprietary funds include the enterprise and internal service funds. As the question requires the funds in which revenue is recognized in the period it becomes available and measurable, this would include the general fund but not the enterprise fund.

I. Accounting by Governments for Certain Events and Transactions

35. **(b)** GASB 33, para 7, indicates that "imposed nonexchange revenues result from assessments by governments on nongovernmental entities, including individuals, other than assessments on nonexchange transactions. Examples include property (ad valorem) taxes; fines and penalties...."

36. **(b)** The levy of property taxes is a nonexchange transaction. GASB 33 defines nonexchange transactions as transactions "in which a government gives (or receives) value without directly receiving (or giving) equal value in exchange." Exchange transactions are transactions "in which each party receives and gives up essentially equal values." In the case of a property tax levy, the government is receiving value, the right to receive payments from property owners, without directly giving equal value in return. The government services that are financed from a property tax levy are not provided to individual taxpayers in proportion to the amount of property taxes that are paid. The other answers are incorrect because they are examples of exchange transactions.

37. **(b)** Deferred revenue should be credited upon receipt of the grant. According to the guidance provided in GASB 33, cash received from government-mandated grants should be reported as deferred revenue when cash is received prior to all eligibility requirements being met. A time restriction is one example of eligibility requirements not being met before the end of the fiscal period. Note that, if there was no time restriction placed on the government-mandated grant by the state, Elizabeth City would have reported revenue for the year ended June 30, 2009.

38. **(a)** According to the guidance provided in GASB 33, the grant from the state is an example of a government-mandated type of nonexchange transaction. Government-mandated nonexchange transactions exists when the providing government, such as a state government, requires the receiving government to expend the funds for a specific purpose.

39. **(c)** According to the guidance provided by GASB 33, sales tax revenues are an example of a derived tax revenue. Derived tax revenues result from taxes assessed by government on exchange transactions. In the case of sales taxes, exchange transactions between merchants and consumers provide the basis for the collection of the sales tax revenues.

40. **(c)** The general fund of Eldorado should report the sales taxes to be received in July 2009 as revenue for the year ended June 30, 2009. Under the modified accrual measurement focus, the sales taxes should be reported as revenue for the year ended June 30, 2009, because the sales taxes are available to finance expenditures made in the year ended June 30, 2009.

41. **(c)** According to the guidance provided by GASB 33, property tax revenues are an example of an imposed tax revenue. Imposed revenues result from taxes and other assessments imposed by governments that are not derived from underlying transactions.

42. **(b)** In accordance with GASB 33, the modified accrual basis of accounting should be used for recording and reporting property tax revenues for the general fund on the statement of revenues, expenditures, and changes in fund balances. Under the modified accrual basis of accounting, revenues are recognized in the period when they are both measurable and available to pay for expenditures incurred during the current fiscal period. With respect to property tax revenues, "available" means collected during the year and within the first sixty days after the end of the year. For the general fund of Karsten City, the property taxes collected in 2009 of $850,000 as well as the $100,000 expected to be collected by March 1 of 2010 would be added to get the property tax revenues recognized in 2009. The sum of $950,000 of property tax revenues would be reported by the general fund on the statement of revenues, expenditures, and changes in fund balances for the year ended December 31, 2009. The journal entries to record the property tax levy and collections for 2009 appear below.

Property taxes receivable—Current	1,000,000	
Property tax revenues ($850,000 + 100,000)		950,000
Deferred revenues (report as a liability on the balance sheet)		40,000
Allowance for estimated uncollectible property taxes—Current		10,000
Cash	850,000	
Property taxes receivable—Current		850,000

The deferred revenue account of $40,000 represents the property taxes expected to be collected after March 1, 2010. Because the taxes are expected to be collected after sixty days from the end of 2009, the taxes are not considered available to pay for expenditures incurred in 2009. This is the reason for crediting deferred revenue in 2009.

43. **(d)** In accordance with GASB 33, imposed nonexchange transactions include taxes and other assessments derived from underlying transactions. Examples include property taxes, special assessments, and fines and forfeits. For the general fund of Ward Village, imposed nonexchange transactions would include property tax revenues of $125,000 and fines of $10,000. Sales taxes and income taxes would be classified as derived tax revenues.

44. **(a)** In accordance with GASB 33, the modified accrual basis of accounting should be used for recording and reporting revenues reported by the general fund on the Statement of Revenues, Expenditures, and Changes in Fund Balances. The modified accrual basis of accounting for revenues results in revenues being recognized in the period in which they are both measurable and available to pay for expenditures incurred during the current fiscal period. The sales tax advance of $25,000 should be reported as revenue in 2009 because it was available to pay for expenditures incurred by the general fund in 2009. On the other hand, the cash received from property owners of $20,000 should not be reported as revenue in 2009 because the money cannot be used to pay for expenditures incurred by the general fund in 2009. The property taxes received in December 2009 should be reported as deferred revenue on the December 31, 2009 balance sheet for the general fund. Deferred revenue would appear under the liabilities classification. The entry to record both of the cash receipts in the general fund in December 2009 appears below.

Cash	45,000	
Sales tax revenues		25,000
Deferred revenue		20,000

45. **(c)** According to GASB 33, revenues that result from taxes assessed by government on exchange transactions are classified as derived tax revenues. Examples of derived tax revenue include sales taxes, income taxes, and motor fuel taxes. Property tax revenues and fines and forfeits are examples of revenues that come from imposed nonexchange transactions. Imposed nonexchange transactions are taxes and other assessments imposed by governments that are not derived from underlying transactions. Unrestricted government grants are an example of voluntary nonexchange transactions. This category includes grants and entitlements from one government to another where the providing government does not impose certain requirements on the receiving government.

46. **(d)** According to GASB 33, revenues that result from taxes and other assessments imposed by governments that are not derived from underlying transactions are categorized as imposed nonexchange transactions. Examples include property taxes, special assessments, and fines and forfeits. Income taxes, sales taxes, and motor fuel taxes are examples of derived tax revenues. Derived tax revenues result from taxes assessed by government on exchange transactions.

47. **(c)** The requirement is to identify the item that is not a requirement for a government to start capitalizing software costs. GASB 51 establishes three requirements to begin capitalizing the cost of an internally generated intangible asset: (1) the government must determine the objective and the service capacity of the project, (2) the government must establish the feasibility of the project, and (3) the government must establish its intention to complete or continue the project. There is no specific requirement in GASB 51 to have developed an accurate budget for the project. Therefore, answer (c) is correct.

48.   (c)   The requirement is to identify the item that correctly describes the proper accounting for the transfer of future revenue. Answer (c) is correct because GASB 48 states that a sale of future revenue should be recorded as deferred revenue and recognized over the life of the agreement.

J. Budgetary Accounting for the General and Special Revenue Funds

49.   (a)   To record the budget, Ridge would make the following journal entry:

Estimated Revenues Control	100,000	
Appropriations Control		80,000
Budgetary Fund Balance		20,000

Therefore, as the Appropriations account is credited for the anticipated expenditures.

50.   (c)   To record the budget, Ridge would make the following journal entry:

Estimated Revenues Control	100,000	
Appropriations Control		80,000
Budgetary Fund Balance		20,000

Therefore, the Budgetary Fund Balance account is credited for the anticipated surplus of revenues over expenditures.

51.   (a)   Revenues to the general fund are defined as "increases in fund financial resources other than from interfund transfers and debt issue proceeds." Transfers to a fund and debt issue proceeds received by a fund are classified as other financing sources of the fund. Therefore, in Maple's budgetary entry, estimated revenues would be debited for the $9,000,000 expected from property taxes, licenses, and fines. The Estimated Other Financing Sources account would be debited for the $6,000,000, consisting of the debt issue proceeds and the interfund transfers.

52.   (b)   Assuming that encumbrance accounting is utilized by the city, the journal entry to record the issuance of purchase orders and contracts is a debit to Encumbrances Control and a credit to Budgetary Fund Balance—Reserved for Encumbrances for the amount of the purchase order or estimated cost of the contracts.

53.   (c)   As Cliff approves and issues its purchase orders, the purchase order amount ($5,000,000) is recorded in the Encumbrances Control account. As the goods are received, the related purchase order amount of these goods (i.e., the amount that was originally recorded, $4,500,000) is removed from the Encumbrances Control account. Therefore, at year-end, the amount of outstanding encumbrances is $500,000. Keep in mind that the actual invoice amount is not the amount removed from the Encumbrances Control account. The invoice amount will be vouchered and charged to Expenditures Control.

54.   (d)   When Elm issued its purchase order, the following journal entry would have been made to encumber the amount:

Encumbrances Control	5,000	
Budgetary Fund Balance—Reserved for Encumbrances		5,000

When the supplies were received the following journal entries would have been made:

Budgetary Fund Balance—Reserved for Encumbrances	5,000	
Encumbrances Control		5,000
Expenditures Control	4,950	
Vouchers Payable		4,950

55.   (d)   When purchase orders for goods or services are approved and issued, the Encumbrances Control account is debited and the Budgetary Fund Balance—Reserved for Encumbrances is credited for the amount of the purchase orders. As goods are received or services are rendered the above encumbrance entry is reversed. Thus, the amount left in each would be zero. Note that the same amount is initially recorded in each of the accounts (i.e., the debit equals the credit). The same amount is also relieved from both accounts. A Budgetary Fund Balance—Reserved for Encumbrances in excess of a balance in the Encumbrances Control account indicates there has been a recording error.

56.   (b)   Encumbrances outstanding at year-end represent the estimated amount of the expenditures that could result if unperformed contracts in process at year-end are computed. Encumbrances outstanding at year-end are not expenditures or liabilities. Where appropriations do not lapse at year-end, encumbrances outstanding at year-end should be reported as reservations of fund balance for the subsequent year expenditures. Where appropriations lapse at year-end, the governmental unit may honor the contracts in progress at year-end or cancel them. If the governmental unit intends to honor them, the encumbrances outstanding at year-end should be disclosed by reservation of fund balance.

57.   (d)   When closing entries are made for a governmental unit, Estimated Revenues Control is credited for the same amount that it was debited for in the beginning of the period budget/entry. Also, Revenues Control is debited in the amount of recorded revenue for the year. In this case, Estimated Revenues Control would be credited for $20,000,000 and Revenues Control would be debited for $17,000,000 to close the books. Revenues Control and Estimated Revenues Control are not netted in the closing entry.

58.   (c)   The Budgetary Fund Balance account is debited upon budget adoption when the appropriations exceed the estimated revenues. The following entry is made when the budget is adopted:

Estimated Revenues Control	xx	
Budgetary Fund Balance	xx	
Appropriations Control		xx

At the end of the year, the budgetary accounts must be closed out. The budgetary closing entry is simply a reverse of the adoption entry.

Appropriations Control	xx	
Estimated Revenues Control		xx
Budgetary Fund Balance		xx

The Budgetary Fund Balance is debited at the beginning of the year when appropriations exceed the estimated revenues. An entry must be made to close the Budgetary Fund Balance account at the end of the year. Note that any differences between the budgetary revenues and appropriations and the actual revenues and expenditures and encumbrances do not affect the **Budgetary** Fund Balance account. They would, however, affect the Unreserved Fund Balance account when the operations accounts are closed out.

59. (b) The $100,000 balance in the Fund Balance— Reserved for Encumbrances account indicates that there were open purchase orders at year-end. Since the appropriations do not lapse at year-end, the Fund Balance— Reserved for Encumbrances account will not be closed but will be reported as a separate line item in the fund balance section of the balance sheet. The term "reserve" indicates that the funds are not available for expenditure. Therefore, the $100,000 cannot be included in the unreserved fund balance amount. Therefore, the amount of the Unreserved Fund Balance in the 2009 balance sheet would be $300,000 ($1,000,000 – $600,000 – $100,000).

60. (b) The closing of the general fund accounts is done by closing the budgetary accounts against each other and the actual revenue, expenditure and other accounts to the Unreserved Fund Balance. This is done most easily by reversing the beginning of the year budget entry in one entry and then using a separate entry to close the actual accounts to fund balance. The following entry would therefore be made to close the actual accounts to obtain the amount of increase in the fund balance:

General Fund

Other Financing Sources Control	1,500,000	
Revenues Control	8,000,000	
Expenditures Control		5,000,000
Other Financing Uses Control		2,000,000
Fund Balance—Unreserved		2,500,000

The Appropriations account would be closed in the reversal of the budget entry and has no effect on fund balance.

61. (c) GASB 34, para 92, indicates that proprietary funds (including enterprise funds) are to use accrual accounting. Paragraph 93 indicates that FASB pronouncements issued on or before November 30, 1989, are to be followed unless superceded by a GASB pronouncement. Accrual accounting recognizes interest expense over time; in this case, interest expense would be $1,000,000 × .06 × 9/12 = $45,000.

K. Expenditure Classification for Governmental Funds

62. (a) Expenditure classification by object is based upon the type of items purchased or services obtained. Examples of "Current Operations" object of expenditure classifications are personal services, supplies, and other services and charges. Salaries are an example of classification by object. Function or program classifications provide information regarding the overall purpose or objectives of expenditures (i.e., police protection, sanitation, highways and streets, etc.). Activity classification provides data for calculating expenditures per unit of activity (i.e., street resurfacing).

L. Accounting for the General Fund

63. (c) "When a property tax assessment is made, it is to finance the budget of a particular period, and the revenue produced from any property tax assessment should be recognized in the fiscal period for which it was levied, provided the 'available' criteria are met. 'Available' means then due, or past due and receivable within the current period, and collected within the current period or expected to be collected soon enough thereafter to pay liabilities of the current period. Such time thereafter shall not exceed sixty days." This is how property tax revenues are reported on the Statement of Revenues, Expenditures, and Changes in Fund Balances for governmental funds. Therefore, both the collections during 2009 of $500,000 and the expected collections during the first sixty days of 2010 of $100,000 would be reported as property tax revenues for 2009. Remember that the estimated uncollectible amounts are not reported on the operating statement as an offset to revenues, but rather are reported as a contra asset account. The governmental unit, in calculating the amount of the levy, factors in what has historically been uncollectible, so that the revenues in effect have already been adjusted.

64. (b) Under GASB Statement 33, imposed nonexchange revenues, including property taxes, should be recorded in the year for which budgeted. In this case, the amount would be $690,000, the total levy less the estimated uncollectible amount.

65. (d) Interfund services provided and used are transactions that would be treated as revenues or expenditures/ expenses if they involved organizations external to the government (i.e., **routine employer contributions from a general fund to a pension trust fund,** internal service fund billings to departments, enterprise funds billing for services provided to the general fund). The proper accounting for interfund services provided and used is to treat them as revenues in the fund providing the goods or services and **as expenditures/ expenses in the fund receiving the goods or services,** exactly as if the transactions involved parties external to the government. Thus, answer (d) is correct because the general fund should record an expenditure for routine employer contributions to the pension trust fund. Answer (a) is incorrect because the contribution of enterprise fund capital by the general fund should be recorded in the general fund as a transfer. Answers (b) and (c) are incorrect because routine transfers between funds should also be recorded as transfers.

66. (b) Interfund services provided and used are treated as revenues or expenditures/expenses if they involved organizations external to the government (i.e., a city's electric utility providing electricity to the general fund, internal service fund billings to departments, routine employer contributions from a general fund to a pension trust fund). The proper accounting for interfund services provided and used transactions is to treat them as revenues in the fund providing the goods or services and as expenditures/expenses in the fund receiving the goods or services, exactly as if the transactions involved parties external to the government. The general fund should recognize an expenditure for the amount billed by the city's electric utility.

67. (a) The internal service fund and the enterprise fund use the accrual basis of accounting and both report net assets, not fund balances. Net assets are reported in the following manner: (1) invested in capital assets, net of related debt, (2) restricted, and (3) unrestricted. The capital projects fund does not keep an inventory of supplies and therefore would not have a Fund Balance—Reserved for Inventory of Supplies. The general fund does maintain an inventory of supplies and would therefore have a Fund Balance— Reserved for Inventory of Supplies.

68.   (d)   The $6,000,000 in property taxes would be accounted for in Ariba's general fund, which is a governmental fund. The $40,000 of net rental revenue (after depreciation) from a parking garage would be accounted for in an enterprise fund, which is a proprietary fund. An enterprise fund provides products or services to the public, such as the use of the parking garage. The $100,000 interest earned on investments held for employees' retirement benefits would be included in a trust fund (more than likely a pension trust fund).

69.   (c)   In accordance with GASB 34, the balance sheet prepared for the governmental funds should be based on the current financial resources measurement focus and the modified accrual basis of accounting. This means that capital assets, such as police cars, are not reported on the balance sheet for governmental funds. Instead, the police cars are reported as expenditures on the statement of revenues, expenditures, and changes in fund balances for the year ended December 31, 2009.

70.   (b)   In accordance with GASB 34, the government-wide statement of net assets is prepared using the economic resources measurement focus and the full accrual basis of accounting. In the column for governmental activities, the police cars would be reported at $32,500. This amount is the original cost of $40,000 less accumulated depreciation of $7,500. The use of full accrual accounting means that the police cars are depreciated. The depreciation expense is reported on the government-wide statement of activities. Depreciation expense would be $7,500, computed by taking $40,000 less the salvage value of $10,000, and dividing by the useful life of four years.

71.   (a)   GASB 34 requires use of the current financial resources measurement focus and the modified accrual basis of accounting for governmental funds. On the statement of revenues, expenditures, and changes in fund balances prepared for 2009 for the governmental funds, the acquisition of the police cars is reported as expenditures of $40,000.

72.   (b)   According to GASB 34, the statement of revenues, expenditures, and changes in fund balances prepared for governmental funds is based upon the modified accrual basis of accounting and the financial resources measurement focus. On the statement of revenues, expenditures, and changes in fund balances, the acquisition of police cars is reported as expenditures of $75,000. The $30,000 payment by the general fund to the pension trust fund is reported as an interfund services provided and used transaction. On the statement of revenues, expenditures, and changes in fund balances, the $30,000 should be reported as expenditures. Therefore, the acquisition of the police cars and the pension transfer result in $105,000 of expenditures being reported on the statement of revenues, expenditures, and changes in fund balances for the governmental funds.

73.   (c)   According to GASB 34, the statement of revenues, expenditures, and changes in fund balances prepared for governmental funds is based upon the modified accrual basis of accounting and the financial resources measurement focus. On the statement of revenues, expenditures, and changes in fund balances, the revenue from property taxes should be reported at $750,000. The levy of $800,000 less the 2% that was not expected to be collected results in $784,000, of which $750,000 was collected in 2009. Be-

cause the remaining $34,000 was not expected to be collected within sixty days of the end of 2009, the $34,000 is not considered available in 2009, and, therefore, it is not reported as revenue in 2009. At December 31, 2009, the $34,000 should be reported as deferred revenue on the balance sheet prepared for the governmental funds. Deferred revenues are reported as liabilities on this balance sheet. On the other hand, sales tax revenues for 2009 would be $100,000. The amount of sales taxes that are expected to be received in mid-March of 2010 is not considered available in 2009, and should not be included in revenues on the statement of revenues, expenditures, and changes in fund balances prepared for the governmental funds for the year ended December 31, 2009. Therefore, property tax revenues and sales tax revenues for 2009 would be reported at $850,000.

74.   (a)   According to GASB 34, the government-wide statement of activities should be prepared based upon the accrual basis of accounting and the economic resources measurement focus. The statement of activities reports governmental activities, business-type activities, and component units. For the police cars that were purchased in 2009, this means that depreciation expense of $12,000 would be reported under governmental activities. The police cars would be reported as assets on the government-wide statement of net assets, and the depreciation expense for 2009 would be computed by dividing five years into $75,000 less the salvage value of $15,000. The transfer to the pension trust fund would be reported under governmental activities as an expense of $30,000. The transfer is accounted for as an interfund services provided and used transaction in 2009. This means that the transfer would be reported in expenses under governmental activities for the year ended December 31, 2009. Therefore, $42,000 of expenses result from the acquisition of the police cars and the pension transfer in 2009. These expenses would be reported on the government-wide statement of activities for 2009.

75.   (b)   According to GASB 34, the government-wide statement of activities should be prepared based upon the accrual basis of accounting and the economic resources measurement focus. The statement of activities reports governmental activities, business-type activities, and component units. For 2009, property tax revenues should be reported at the full amount of the levy of $800,000 less the 2% that was not expected to be collected. This means that $784,000 would be reported for property tax revenues in 2009. The $34,000 of property taxes that were not collected in 2009 are reported as revenues in 2009 because the statement of activities is based upon accrual accounting. For 2009, sales tax revenues should be reported at $125,000. Sales tax revenues reported for 2008 include the $100,000 collected during 2009 as well as the $25,000 that will be collected in mid-March of 2010. The $25,000 of sales taxes that will be collected in mid-March 2010 are reported as revenues in 2009 on the statement of activities because the sales taxes were collected by the state in 2009. Therefore, the accrual basis of accounting mandates that the $25,000 be reported as revenue under governmental activities in 2009. Therefore, for the year ended December 31, 2009, a total of $909,000 of revenues are reported for property taxes ($784,000) and sales taxes ($125,000) on the government-wide statement of activities.

M. Accounting for Special Revenue Funds

76. (c) According to GASB 33, the grant received by Maple Township is an example of a voluntary nonexchange transaction in which the providing State government imposes purpose restrictions on the grant to Maple Township. Under modified accrual accounting, grant revenue should be recognized when it is both measurable and available. Applying these criteria to the grant, revenues should be recognized in the period that Maple received reimbursement from the state for the purchase of buses ($60,000) and for bus maintenance ($5,000). It is at the point of reimbursement that the grant becomes available.

77. (b) Special revenue funds are used to account for the proceeds of specific revenue sources (other than expendable trusts or for major capital projects) that are legally restricted to expenditures for specified purposes. Thus, the gasoline taxes to finance road repairs should be accounted for in a special revenue fund. The levies to property owners to install sidewalks would be recorded either in an agency fund (if special assessment debt is not backed by the government) or by a debt service fund (if the debt is backed by the government).

78. (c) A major special revenue fund is a governmental fund and therefore uses the modified accrual basis of accounting, not the accrual basis. Budgetary accounts should be used in the general fund and special revenue fund.

N. Accounting for Capital Projects Funds

79. (a) The objective of a capital projects fund is to account for the financial resources to be used for the acquisition or construction of major capital facilities. The inflow of bond proceeds should be accounted for in the year received, regardless of when the bond proceeds are expended. Therefore, the $5,000,000 of bond proceeds should be recorded in the capital projects fund in 2009, the year received. They should be treated as an "other financing source" in the operating statement of the fund. Note that the servicing of the debt will be accounted for in the debt service fund.

80. (c) Grants received by the capital projects fund from another governmental unit are considered revenues of the capital projects fund. Also, taxes or other revenues raised specifically for the capital projects fund are recorded as revenues of the fund. However, proceeds of debt issues should be recorded as proceeds of bonds/long-term debt and should be reported as an other financing source in the operating statement. Similarly, resources transferred to the capital projects fund generally from the general or special revenue fund are recorded as transfers in and reported in the other financing sources section of the operating statement. Thus, Fir should report only the $400,000 from the grant as a revenue. The $600,000 consisting of the bond issue proceeds and general fund transfer should be reported as other financing sources.

81. (c) The requirement is to identify how an impaired capital asset that is no longer used by a government should be reported in the financial statements. The correct answer is (c). GASB 42 indicates that the asset should be reported at the lower of carrying value or fair value. Answers (a) and (b) are incorrect because they are often elements of the carrying value of the asset. Answer (d) is incorrect because the required valuation is the lower of carrying value or fair value.

82. (b) The requirement is to identify when impairment of a capital asset should be recognized. The correct answer is (b). GASB 42 states that impairment of a capital asset should be recognized when an event or change in circumstance causes a decline in service utility of the asset, and (1) the decline is large in magnitude and (2) the event or change in circumstance is outside the normal life cycle of the capital asset.

O. Debt Service Funds

83. (d) Governmental fund revenues and expenditures should be recognized on the modified accrual basis. Governmental funds include the general fund, special revenue funds, capital projects funds, debt service funds, and permanent funds. Proprietary fund revenues and expenses should be recognized on the accrual basis. Proprietary funds include enterprise funds and internal service funds. Fiduciary fund additions and deductions should be recognized on the accrual basis. Pension trust funds should be accounted for on the accrual basis.

84. (a) GASB 37, para 16, indicates that proceeds of long-term issues not recorded as fund liabilities should be reported as other financing sources in governmental funds. In addition, general long-term debt issue premiums should also be reported as other financing sources. Paragraph 87 of GASB 34 indicates that debt issue costs, including underwriter fees, should be reported as expenditures.

85. (d) Debt service funds are to account for the accumulation of resources for and payment of, general long-term debt principal and interest. The general fund does not account for resources restricted for payment of general long-term debt principal and interest.

86. (a) According to GASB 34, the balance sheet prepared for governmental funds is prepared using the modified accrual basis of accounting and the flow of financial resources measurement focus. Under the modified accrual basis of accounting and the financial resources measurement focus, the bond issue costs of $400,000 and the debt insurance costs of $90,000 should be charged to expenditures in the debt service fund on June 30, 2009. This means that none of the costs will be reported as an asset on the governmental funds' balance sheet prepared at June 30, 2009.

87. (c) The requirement is to determine which fund should record receipts from a special tax levy to retire and pay interest on general obligation bonds. The correct answer is (c) because the debt service fund usually handles the repayment of general obligation long-term debt interest. A levy allocable to the debt service fund is recorded in the fund. Answer (a) is incorrect because levies for the purpose of paying interest do not get recorded in the general fund. The general fund records levies that do not have a specific purpose. Answer (b) is incorrect because capital projects funds are for construction or the purchase of fixed assets. Answer (d) is incorrect because special revenue funds are for earmarked revenue that is not to pay interest on general obligation debt.

88. (d) The bond premium amount is usually deemed to be another financing source in a governmental fund and is recorded as such when the bonds are sold. The premium is not capitalized and amortized.

89. **(a)** The GASB classifies three types of funds used in governmental accounting: governmental, proprietary, and fiduciary. Debt service funds are used to accumulate resources to pay general long-term debt of governmental funds. The debt service fund is not used in connection with either a trust fund or a proprietary fund.

90. **(c)** Cash received in the debt service fund from the general fund for debt service is recorded as a transfer. Cash payments of principal and interest on the debt are then recorded as expenditures in the debt service fund. The following entries would be made in the debt service fund:

Cash	xx	
Transfers In—General Fund		xx
Expenditures—Principal	xx	
Expenditures—Interest	xx	
Cash (Payable)		xx

91. **(a)** Interest on the general obligation bonds is payable on March 1 and September 1. The debt service fund accounts for the accumulation of cash to pay the interest and principal on general obligation bonds. However, interest on the bonds is not recorded until it is legally payable. On June 30, 2009, no interest is legally payable, so there would be no accrual of interest to be paid as of that date.

P. Permanent Funds

92. **(a)** According to GASB 52, land and other real estate held by an endowment as an investment should be reported at fair value at each reporting date. Therefore, answer (a) is correct. Answers (b), (c) and (d) are incorrect because GASB 52 requires the use of fair value.

Q. Accounting for Special Assessments

93. **(a)** The debt service transactions of a special assessment issue for which the government is not obligated in any manner should be reported in an agency fund, rather than a debt service fund. The government's duties are limited to acting as an agent for the assessed property owners and the bondholders.

R. Accounting for Proprietary Funds

94. **(c)** Municipal solid waste landfills that use proprietary accounting (i.e., enterprise fund) should recognize as expense (and liability) a portion of the estimated total cost of closure and post closure in each period that the landfill accepts solid waste. Estimated total costs should be assigned to periods based on use rather than on the passage of time, using a formula based on the percentage of capacity used each period. Because Cy City's landfill operates as an enterprise fund, the city's 2009 expenses should include a portion of the year 2028 expected disbursements for both the final cover (I) and cost of equipment to monitor methane gas buildup (II).

95. **(a)** GASB 34, para 13, clearly states that, in the government-wide statements, governmental activities normally include transactions that are reported in governmental and internal service funds.

96. **(b)** Internal service funds account for activities that produce goods or services to be provided to other departments or governmental units on a cost reimbursement basis.

Internal service funds also use the full accrual method of accounting. When the governmental units are billed, the internal service fund would record the following entry:

Billings to Departments	xx	
Operating Revenues		xx

97. **(d)** A proprietary fund is created to account for goods or services the governmental unit provides to benefit the general public. It uses the accrual basis of accounting and the flow of economic resources measurement focus (i.e., capital maintenance is an objective). Fixed assets and depreciation expense on them are recorded in such funds. Therefore, the $210,000 expenditure for the parking meters would be capitalized and shown net of accumulated depreciation on Burwood's June 30, 2009 balance sheet. Burwood's net income for the year ending June 30, 2009, would be $240,000 calculated as

Receipts from users	$400,000
Expenses	
Depreciation—Parking meters	(70,000)
Salaries and other	(90,000)
Net income	$240,000

98. **(d)** Enterprise funds are used to account for operations that are financed and operated in a manner similar to private business enterprises—where the intent of the government is that costs of providing goods or services to the general public on a continuing basis be financed or recovered primarily through user charges; or where the government has decided that periodic determination of net income is appropriate for accountability purposes. Accordingly, revenues from lotteries need to be matched with related expenses for prizes. Thus, lotteries should be accounted for in a fund type that uses full accrual accounting, most commonly an enterprise fund. In addition, the GASB *Codification*, Section H05, requires that hospitals be reported as a single enterprise fund when they are included as part of another government's reporting entity.

99. **(d)** Depreciation of general fixed assets should **not** be recorded in the accounts of governmental funds. Depreciation of fixed assets accounted for in a proprietary fund should be recorded in the accounts of that fund. The determination of recording depreciation expense in a governmental unit's fund does not change as a result of the funding source used to acquire the asset.

100. **(d)** An enterprise fund is used to account for operations where the intent of the governing body is to finance the cost of the operations through user charges or where the governing body has decided revenue, expenses, and net income information is necessary. A fund that accounts for the financing of an agency's services to other government departments on a cost-reimbursement basis is an internal service fund.

101. **(c)** Cash flows from sale of revenue bonds and capital contributed by subdividers are classified as cash flows from capital and related financing activities. Both the $5,000,000 proceeds from sale of revenue bonds and $1,000,000 capital contributed by subdividers would be reported as cash flows from capital and related financing activities. Cash flows from customer households are operating cash flows.

102. **(a)** Proprietary funds are used to account for a government's ongoing organizations and activities that are similar to those often found in the private sector. The generally accepted accounting principles here are those applicable to similar businesses in the private sector; and the measurement focus is on **determination of net income,** financial position, and cash flows.

103. (c) As described in the GASB *Codification*, the aggregate lease liability is recorded as an expenditure and an "Other Financing Source" in the general fund. Therefore, Expenditures Control is debited. Answer (b) is incorrect because capital assets are not reported in the general fund. Answer (d) is incorrect because an entry needs to be recorded and posted on the books when equipment is acquired through noncancelable lease-purchase agreement. A memorandum entry is not sufficient. Answer (a) is incorrect because "Other Financing Uses" account is used for transfers out of a fund.

104. (d) The enterprise fund is a proprietary fund and all assets and liabilities of proprietary funds are accounted for and reported in their respective funds. Therefore, transactions for enterprise fund capital leases are accounted for and reported entirely within the enterprise fund. Equipment would be debited for $150,000 in the enterprise fund.

105. (c) All assets and liabilities of proprietary funds are accounted for and reported in their respective funds. The entry to establish the capital lease in the internal service fund would include a debit to Equipment for $150,000 and a credit to Capital Lease Payable for $150,000. Using general business accounting, the entry to make the December 31, 2009 payment of $65,000 would debit Capital Lease Payable for the principal of $50,000 and Expenses Control for the interest of $15,000, and credit Cash for $65,000. The internal service fund is nonexpendable and **expenses (not** expenditures) are recognized on the full accrual basis. Expenses should only be debited for the interest of $15,000, not for the principal of $50,000.

106. (c) Per the GASB *Codification*, cash includes both cash and cash equivalents. Cash equivalents are highly liquid investments readily convertible into cash, usually maturing within three months (ninety days) or less from the date the entity **purchased** the security. Maturity is not measured from the original issuance date. Therefore, in this question, the three-month treasury bill would be included in cash and cash equivalents as well as the three-year treasury note. The three-year treasury note was purchased on 6/15/09 and matures 8/31/09. Therefore, it will be held less than ninety days. The correct answer is (c), $80,000 ($30,000 + $50,000).

S. Accounting for Fiduciary Funds

107. (b) Fiduciary funds are used to account for assets held by a governmental unit in a trustee capacity or as an agent for individuals, private organizations, other governmental units, and/or other funds. They include investment trust, private-purpose trust, pension trust, and agency funds. Therefore, the total fiduciary fund assets of Green Township at June 30, 2009, is $300,000. The debt service fund is a governmental-type fund.

108. (c) Fiduciary funds (i.e., agency funds and trust funds) are used to account for assets held by a governmental unit in a trustee capacity or as an agent for individuals, private organizations, other governmental units, and/or other

funds. The entry to record the 1% fee and the disbursement to the municipalities would be as follows:

Due to Various Municipalities	1,000,000	
Due to Grove County		10,000
General Fund Cash		990,000

Note that the general fund would make the following entry:

| Due from Agency Fund | xxx | |
| Revenue from Tax Collec. Serv. | | xxx |

Agency funds have only assets and liabilities as accounts and do not record revenues, expenditures, or transfers. In addition, agency funds do not have net assets.

109. (a) The entry to record the 2009 employer contribution in the Pension Trust Fund consists of a debit to Cash (or a "Due From" account) and a credit to Additions—Employer Contributions, both for $11,000. The GASB *Codification* classifies this contribution as an interfund services provided and used transaction that would be treated as an addition if it involved organizations external to the governmental unit. Therefore, the GASB states that it should be accounted for as an addition for the pension trust fund. Answer (b) is incorrect because Other Financing Sources include transfers to a fund which are recurring, routine transfers from one fund to another. The employer contribution is not a transfer. Answer (c) is incorrect because "Due From" is a debit account and the question asks for the credit account. Answer (d) is incorrect because Pension Benefit Obligation is the actuarial present value of credited projected benefits. It measures the present value of pension benefits adjusted for the effects of projected salary increases and any step-rate benefits estimated to be payable in the future as a result of employer service to date. The employer contribution is not included in this definition.

110. (b) The employer pension contribution is an interfund services provided and used transaction, one that would be treated as an addition, revenue, expense, or expenditure if it involved organizations external to the governmental unit. In this case, the entry for the governmental-type fund would include a debit to Expenditures Control for $11,000 and a credit to Cash (or a "Due To" account) for $11,000. Answer (a) is incorrect because Other Financing Uses include transfers out of a fund, which are routine recurring transfers of resources from one fund to another. Consequently, the employer contribution does not fall under the category of an Other Financing Use. Answer (c) is incorrect because governmental funds use modified accrual accounting and report expenditures, not expenses. Answer (d) is incorrect because Due To Pension Trust Fund could be the credit entry, and not the debit entry asked for in the question.

T. Reporting Interfund Activity

111. (a) On the government-wide statement of activities, transfers are reported between government activities and business-type activities. The business-type activities include the activities of enterprise funds, while the governmental activities include those of governmental funds and internal service funds. Transfers that are made to establish enterprise funds as well as yearly transfers to help subsidize enterprise funds are both reported as transfers, according to the guidance provided by GASB 34. On the other hand, billings by an enterprise fund to an internal service fund for services rendered are not reported as transfers on the statement of activities. This transition is a quasi-external transaction that should be reported on the statement of activities as an expense of governmental activities and as an operating revenue for business-type activities. The revenues and expenses of internal service funds are reported as governmental activities on the government-wide statement of activities.

112. (c) According to GASB 34, the amount reported for transfers on the government-wide statement of activities represents transfers between governmental activities and business-type activities. Examples of transfers would be permanent transfers from governmental activities to business-type activities in order to establish enterprise funds and annual transfers from governmental activities to help subsidize enterprise fund activities. The activities of internal service funds are included with governmental activities, while the activities of enterprise funds are reported under business-type activities. The $100,000 advance to an internal service fund constitutes a loan, and the general fund asset and internal service fund liability that result would be eliminated in preparing the government-wide statement of net assets. Therefore, the advance would not be reported in transfers on the statement of activities. The $25,000 billing by the enterprise fund to the general fund is recorded as a quasi-external transaction. Under governmental activities, $25,000 would be included in expenses, while, under business-type activities, the $25,000 would be reported as revenues. Therefore, the quasi-external transaction would not be reported in transfers. Finally, the $30,000 transferred by the general fund to a debt service fund is recorded as a transfer in by the debt service fund and as a transfer out by the general fund. However, because both of these funds are reported in governmental activities, the transfer in and transfer out are eliminated in preparing the statement of activities and are not reported in the governmental activities column on the statement of activities. Therefore, the general fund transfer to the debt service fund would not be reported as a transfer on the statement of activities.

113. (a) According to GASB 34, transfers are reported on the government-wide statement of activities. For transfers to be reported, they must be between governmental activities and business-type activities. Governmental activities include the activities of internal service funds, while business-type activities include the activities of enterprise funds. Two kinds of transfers that are reported on the statement of activities include (1) permanent transfers either from governmental activities to business-type activities or from business-type activities to governmental activities and (2) recurring transfers from governmental activities to business-type activities or from business-type activities to governmental activities. Permanent transfers are typically made once, while the recurring transfers are typically made annually. The $100,000 transfer from the general fund to an enterprise fund would be reported as a transfer on the statement of activities because it is an example of a permanent transfer. The $1,000,000 transfer from the general fund to a capital project fund is a transfer made within governmental activities and, therefore, would not be disclosed as a transfer on the statement of activities. The $5,000 reimbursement from the enterprise fund to the general fund is not reported as a transfer on the statement of activities. The effect of this transaction is to increase expenses under business-type activities and to decrease expenses under governmental activities.

W. College and University Accounting—Public (Governmental)—GASB 35

114. (a) According to GASB 35, public colleges and universities that choose to report only business-type activities should present only the financial statements required for enterprise funds.

115. (c) According to GASB 35, public colleges and universities that choose to report both governmental and business-type activities should report both government-wide and fund financial statements.

116. (b) Both public and private colleges report tuition and fee income net of the amount provided for scholarships, for which no services are provided. On the other hand, scholarships provided in exchange for services are reported as an expense and are not deducted from revenues. As a result, the net tuition and fees would be the $20,000,000 less the $1,000,000 scholarships provided, not in exchange for services, or $19,000,000.

117. (d) GASB Statement 35 provides that public colleges may choose to report as special-purpose entities engaged in business-type activities. GASB Statement 34 requires that special-purpose entities engaged only in business-type activities should prepare the statements required for enterprises funds, including a Statement of Revenues, Expenses, and Changes in Net Assets. One requirement for that statement is that an operating income figure must be displayed (answer b). GASB Statement 34 also indicates that contributions for plant and endowment purposes are not recorded as revenues but in separate categories; GASB Statement 35 illustrations show those items listed after revenues and expenses (answer c). GASB Statement 35 specifically requires that state appropriations must be reported as nonoperating income (answer a). Since answers (a), (b), and (c) are correct, answer (d) is the choice.

MULTIPLE-CHOICE QUESTIONS (1-83)

1. A statement of functional expenses is required for which one of the following private nonprofit organizations?
    a. Colleges.
    b. Hospitals.
    c. Voluntary health and welfare organizations.
    d. Performing arts organizations.

2. The statement of financial position (balance sheet) for Founders Library, a private nonprofit organization, should report separate dollar amounts for the library's net assets according to which of the following classifications?
    a. Unrestricted and permanently restricted.
    b. Temporarily restricted and permanently restricted.
    c. Unrestricted and temporarily restricted.
    d. Unrestricted, temporarily restricted, and perma-
       nently restricted.

3. Chicago Museum, a private nonprofit organization, has both regular and term endowments. On the museum's statement of financial position (balance sheet), how should the net assets of each type of endowment be reported?

	Term endowments	Regular endowments
a.	Temporarily restricted	Permanently restricted
b.	Permanently restricted	Permanently restricted
c.	Unrestricted	Temporarily restricted
d.	Temporarily restricted	Temporarily restricted

4. Kerry College, a private not-for-profit college, received $25,000 from Ms. Mary Smith on April 30, 2009. Ms. Smith stipulated that her contribution be used to support faculty research during the fiscal year beginning on July 1, 2009. On July 15, 2009, administrators of Kerry awarded research grants totaling $25,000 to several faculty in accordance with the wishes of Ms. Smith. For the year ended June 30, 2009, Kerry College should report the $25,000 contribution as
    a. Temporarily restricted revenues on the statement
       of activities.
    b. Unrestricted revenue on the statement of activities.
    c. Temporarily restricted deferred revenue on the
       statement of activities.
    d. An increase in fund balance on the statement of fi-
       nancial position.

5. Good Hope, a private not-for-profit voluntary health and welfare organization, received a cash donation of $500,000 from Mr. Charles Peobody on November 15, 2009. Mr. Peobody directed that his donation be used to acquire equipment for the organization. Good Hope used the donation to acquire equipment costing $500,000 in January of 2010. For the year ended December 31, 2009, Good Hope should report the $500,000 contribution on its
    a. Statement of activities as unrestricted revenue.
    b. Statement of financial position as temporarily re-
       stricted deferred revenue.
    c. Statement of financial position as unrestricted de-
       ferred revenue.
    d. Statement of activities as temporarily restricted
       revenue.

6. On the statement of activities for a private not-for-profit performing arts center, expenses should be deducted from

 I. Unrestricted revenues.
 II. Temporarily restricted revenues.
 III. Permanently restricted revenues.

    a. I, II, and III.
    b. Both I and II.
    c. I only.
    d. II only.

7. Albert University, a private not-for-profit university, had the following cash inflows during the year ended June 30, 2009:

 I. $500,000 from students for tuition.
 II. $300,000 from a donor who stipulated that the money be
    invested indefinitely.
 III. $100,000 from a donor who stipulated that the money be
    spent in accordance with the wishes of Albert's governing
    board.

On Albert University's statement of cash flows for the year ended June 30, 2009, what amount of these cash flows should be reported as operating activities?
    a. $900,000
    b. $400,000
    c. $800,000
    d. $600,000

8. Gamma Pi, a private nonprofit fraternal organization, should prepare a statement of financial position and which of the following financial statements?

 I. Statement of activities.
 II. Statement of changes in fund balances.
 III. Statement of cash flows.

    a. I, II, and III.
    b. III only.
    c. II and III.
    d. I and III.

9. Save the Planet, a private nonprofit research organization, received a $500,000 contribution from Ms. Susan Clark. Ms. Clark stipulated that her donation be used to purchase new computer equipment for Save the Planet's research staff. The contribution was received in August of 2009, and the computers were acquired in January of 2010. For the year ended December 31, 2009, the $500,000 contribution should be reported by Save the Planet on its
    a. Statement of activities as unrestricted revenue.
    b. Statement of activities as deferred revenue.
    c. Statement of activities as temporarily restricted
       revenue.
    d. Statement of financial position as deferred revenue.

10. United Ways, a private not-for-profit voluntary health and welfare organization, received a contribution of $10,000 from a donor in 2009. The donor did not specify any use restrictions on the contribution; however, the donor specified that the donation should not be used until 2010. The governing board of United Ways spent the contribution in 2010 for fund-raising expenses. For the year ended December 31, 2009, United Ways should report the contribution on its
    a. Statement of financial position as deferred revenue.
    b. Statement of activities as unrestricted revenue.
    c. Statement of financial position as an increase in
       fund balance.
    d. Statement of activities as temporarily restricted
       revenue.

11. The statement of cash flows for a private not-for-profit hospital should report cash flows according to which of the following classifications?

   I. Operating activities.
  II. Investing activities.
 III. Financing activities.

    a. I, II, and III.
    b. II and III.
    c. I only.
    d. I and III.

12. Pharm, a nongovernmental not-for-profit organization, is preparing its year-end financial statements. Which of the following statements is required?
    a. Statement of changes in financial position.
    b. Statement of cash flows.
    c. Statement of changes in fund balance.
    d. Statement of revenue, expenses and changes in fund balance.

13. Stanton College, a not-for-profit organization, received a building with no donor stipulations as to its use. Stanton does not have an accounting policy implying a time restriction on donated fixed assets. What type of net assets should be increased when the building is received?

   I. Unrestricted.
  II. Temporarily restricted.
 III. Permanently restricted.

    a. I only.
    b. II only.
    c. III only.
    d. II or III.

14. Sea Lion Park, a private not-for-profit zoological society, received contributions restricted for research totaling $50,000 in 2008. None of the contributions were spent on research in 2008. In 2009, $35,000 of the contributions were used to support the research activities of the society. The net effect on the statement of activities for the year ended December 31, 2009, for Sea Lion Park would be a
    a. $15,000 increase in temporarily restricted net assets.
    b. $35,000 decrease in temporarily restricted net assets.
    c. $35,000 increase in unrestricted net assets.
    d. $35,000 decrease in unrestricted net assets.

15. Clara Hospital, a private not-for-profit hospital, earned $250,000 of gift shop revenues and spent $50,000 on research during the year ended December 31, 2009. The $50,000 spent on research was part of a $75,000 contribution received during December of 2008 from a donor who stipulated that the donation be used for medical research. Assume none of the gift shop revenues were spent in 2009. For the year ended December 31, 2009, what was the increase in unrestricted net assets from the events occurring during 2009?
    a. $300,000
    b. $200,000
    c. $250,000
    d. $275,000

16. Which of the following transactions of a private not-for-profit voluntary health and welfare organization would increase temporarily restricted net assets on the statement of activities for the year ended June 30, 2009?

   I. Received a contribution of $10,000 from a donor on May 15, 2009, who stipulated that the donation not be spent until August of 2009.
  II. Spent $25,000 for fund-raising on June 20, 2009. The amount expended came from a $25,000 contribution on March 12, 2009. The donor stipulated that the contribution be used for fund-raising activities.

    a. Both I and II.
    b. Neither I nor II.
    c. I only.
    d. II only.

17. Catherine College, a private not-for-profit college, received the following contributions during 2009:

   I. $5,000,000 from alumni for construction of a new wing on the science building to be constructed in 2009.
  II. $1,000,000 from a donor who stipulated that the contribution be invested indefinitely and that the earnings be used for scholarships. As of December 31, 2009, earnings from investments amounted to $50,000.

For the year ended December 31, 2009, what amount of these contributions should be reported as temporarily restricted revenues on the statement of activities?
    a. $ 50,000
    b. $5,050,000
    c. $5,000,000
    d. $6,050,000

18. On December 31, 2009, Hope Haven, a private not-for-profit voluntary health and welfare organization, received a pledge from a donor who stipulated that $1,000 would be given to the organization each year for the next five years, starting on December 31, 2010. Present value factors at 6% for five periods are presented below.

Present value of an ordinary annuity for 5 periods at 6%	4.21236
Present value of an annuity due for 5 periods at 6%	4.46511

For the year ended December 31, 2009, Hope Haven should report, on its statement of activities,
    a. Unrestricted revenues of $5,000.
    b. Temporarily restricted revenues of $4,465.
    c. Unrestricted revenues of $4,465.
    d. Temporarily restricted revenues of $4,212.

19. For Guiding Light, a nongovernmental nonprofit religious organization, net assets that can be expended in accordance with the wishes of the governing board of the organization should be reported as

   I. Unrestricted.
  II. Temporarily restricted.
 III. Permanently restricted.

    a. I only.
    b. Both I and II.
    c. I, II, and III.
    d. Either I or II.

20. The Jackson Foundation, a private not-for-profit organization, had the following cash contributions and expenditures in 2009:

Unrestricted cash contributions of $500,000.
Cash contributions of $200,000 restricted by the donor to the acquisition of property.

Cash expenditures of $200,000 to acquire property with the donation in the above item.

Jackson's statement of cash flows should include which of the following amounts?

	Operating activities	Investing activities	Financing activities
a.	$700,000	$(200,000)	$0
b.	$500,000	$0	$0
c.	$500,000	$(200,000)	$200,000
d.	$0	$500,000	$200,000

21. United Hope, a private not-for-profit voluntary health and welfare organization, received the following contributions in 2009:

I. $500 from donors who stipulated that the money not be spent until 2010.
II. $1,000 from donors who stipulated that the contributions be used for the acquisition of equipment, none of which was acquired in 2009.

Which of the above events increased temporarily restricted net assets for the year ending December 31, 2009?

    a.   I only.
    b.   Both I and II.
    c.   II only.
    d.   Neither I nor II.

22. A statement of financial position (balance sheet), which reports unrestricted, temporarily restricted, and permanently restricted net assets, is required for which one of the following organizations?

I. A public university.
II. A private, not-for-profit hospital.

    a.   Both I and II.
    b.   I only.
    c.   Neither I nor II.
    d.   II only.

23. A storm broke glass windows in the building of Lea Meditators, a not-for-profit religious organization. A member of Lea's congregation, a professional glazier, replaced the windows at no charge. In Lea's statement of activities, the breakage and replacement of the windows should

    a.   Not be reported.
    b.   Be reported by note disclosure only.
    c.   Be reported as an increase in both expenses and contributions.
    d.   Be reported as an increase in both net assets and contributions.

24. SFAS 117, *Financial Statements of Not-for-Profit Organizations,* focuses on

    a.   Basic information for the organization as a whole.
    b.   Standardization of funds nomenclature.
    c.   Inherent differences of not-for-profit organizations that impact reporting presentations.
    d.   Distinctions between current fund and noncurrent fund presentations.

25. On December 30, 2009, Leigh Museum, a not-for-profit organization, received a $7,000,000 donation of Day Co. shares with donor-stipulated requirements as follows:

Shares valued at $5,000,000 are to be sold, with the proceeds used to erect a public viewing building.
Shares valued at $2,000,000 are to be retained, with the dividends used to support current operations.

As a consequence of the receipt of the Day shares, how much should Leigh report as temporarily restricted net assets on its 2009 statement of financial position (balance sheet)?

    a. $0
    b. $2,000,000
    c. $5,000,000
    d. $7,000,000

26. The Jones family lost its home in a fire. On December 25, 2009, a philanthropist sent money to the Amer Benevolent Society, a not-for-profit organization, to purchase furniture for the Jones family. During January 2010, Amer purchased this furniture for the Jones family. How should Amer report the receipt of the money in its 2009 financial statements?

    a.   As an unrestricted contribution.
    b.   As a temporarily restricted contribution.
    c.   As a permanently restricted contribution.
    d.   As a liability.

27. If the Pel Museum, a not-for-profit organization, received a contribution of historical artifacts, it need **not** recognize the contribution if the artifacts are to be sold and the proceeds used to

    a.   Support general museum activities.
    b.   Acquire other items for collections.
    c.   Repair existing collections.
    d.   Purchase buildings to house collections.

28. A large not-for-profit organization's statement of activities should report the net change for net assets that are

	Unrestricted	Permanently restricted
a.	Yes	Yes
b.	Yes	No
c.	No	No
d.	No	Yes

29. Which of the following classifications is required for reporting of expenses by all not-for-profit organizations?

    a.   Natural classification in the statement of activities or notes to the financial statements.
    b.   Functional classification in the statement of activities or notes to the financial statements.
    c.   Functional classification in the statement of activities and natural classification in a matrix format in a separate statement.
    d.   Functional classification in the statement of activities and natural classification in the notes to the financial statements.

30. Rosary Botanical Gardens, a private not-for-profit organization, established a $500,000 quasi endowment on September 1, 2009. On the garden's statement of financial position at December 31, 2009, the assets in this quasi endowment should be included in which of the following classifications?

    a.   Temporarily restricted net assets.
    b.   Unrestricted net assets.
    c.   Permanently restricted net assets.
    d.   Either temporarily or permanently restricted net assets, depending on the expected term of the quasi endowment.

31. During 2009, an alumnus of Smith College, a private not-for-profit college, transferred $100,000 to the college with the stipulation that it be spent for library acquisitions. However, the alumnus specified that none of the cash transferred could be spent until the college had matched the entire amount transferred with donations from other alumni by December 31, 2010. As of December 31, 2009, the college had received matching cash donations of only $5,000 from other alumni, and the college estimated that it was reasonably possible that it would not reach the goal of $100,000 by December 31, 2010. If the funds are not matched by December 31, 2010, the cash will be returned to the alumnus. On the college's statement of financial position at December 31, 2009, the cash transfer of $100,000 would be included in the amount reported for

    a.   Liabilities.
    b.   Unrestricted net assets.
    c.   Temporarily restricted net assets.
    d.   Permanently restricted net assets.

32. During the year ended December 31, 2009, a not-for-profit performing arts entity received the following donor-restricted contribution and investment income:

    Cash contribution of $100,000 to be permanently invested.
    Cash dividends and interest of $6,000 to be used for the acquisition of theater equipment.

As a result of these cash receipts, the statement of cash flows for the year ended December 31, 2009, would report an increase of

    a. $106,000 from operating activities.
    b. $106,000 from financing activities.
    c. $6,000 from operating activities and an increase of $100,000 from financing activities.
    d. $100,000 from operating activities and an increase of $6,000 from financing activities.

33. Which of the following private, nonprofit entities is required to report expenses both by function and by natural classification?

    a.   Hospitals.
    b.   Colleges and universities.
    c.   Voluntary health and welfare organizations.
    d.   Performing arts organizations.

34. On December 5, 2009, Jones Heating and Air Conditioning Service repaired the heating system in the building occupied by Good Hope, a private not-for-profit voluntary health and welfare organization. An invoice for $1,500 was received by Good Hope for the repairs on December 15, 2009. On December 30, 2009, Jones notified Good Hope that the invoice was canceled and that the repairs were being donated without charge. For the year ended December 31, 2009, how should Good Hope report these contributed services?

    a.   Only in the notes to the financial statements.
    b.   No disclosure is required either in the financial statements or in the notes.
    c.   As an increase in unrestricted revenues and as an increase in expenses on the statements of activities.
    d.   As an increase in temporarily restricted net assets on the statement of activities.

35. During the year ended December 31, 2009, the James Community Foundation, a private not-for-profit organization, received the following contributed services:

I.   Anderson & Anderson, attorneys-at-law, contributed their services which involved advice related to the foundation's regular endowments.

II.   Senior citizens participated in a telethon to raise money for a new music building.

Which of these contributed services should be included in unrestricted revenues, gains, and other support on James Community Foundation's statement of activities for the year ended December 31, 2009?

    a.   Both I and II.
    b.   Neither I nor II.
    c.   II only.
    d.   I only.

36. Child Care Centers, Inc., a not-for-profit organization, receives revenue from various sources during the year to support its day care centers. The following cash amounts were received during 2009:

    $2,000 restricted by the donor to be used for meals for the children.
    $1,500 received for subscriptions to a monthly child-care magazine with a fair market value to subscribers of $1,000.
    $10,000 to be used only upon completion of a new playroom that was only 50% complete at December 31, 2009.

What amount should Child Care Centers record as contribution revenue in its 2009 Statement of Activities?

    a. $ 2,000
    b. $ 2,500
    c. $10,000
    d. $11,000

37. On December 20, 2009, United Appeal, a private not-for-profit voluntary health and welfare organization, received a donation of computer equipment valued at $25,000 from a local computer retailer. The equipment is expected to have a useful life of three years. The donor placed no restrictions on how long the computer equipment was to be used, and United has an accounting policy that does not imply a time restriction on gifts of long-lived assets. On United's statement of activities prepared for the year ended December 31, 2009, the donation of computer equipment should be reported

    a.   As an increase in temporarily restricted net assets.
    b.   Only in the notes to the financial statements.
    c.   As an increase in unrestricted net assets.
    d.   As either an increase in temporarily restricted net assets or as an increase in unrestricted net assets.

38. On December 30, 2009, the Board of Trustees of Henry Museum, a private not-for-profit organization, designated $4,000,000 of unrestricted net assets for the construction of an addition to its building. What effect does this designation have on the museum's unrestricted and temporarily restricted net assets which are reported on the statement of financial position (balance sheet) at December 31, 2009?

	Unrestricted net assets	*Temporarily restricted net assets*
a.	No effect	Increase
b.	Decrease	Increase
c.	Decrease	No effect
d.	No effect	No effect

39. Darlin Hospital, a private not-for-profit hospital, had the following cash receipts for the year ended December 31, 2009:

Patient service revenue	$300,000
Gift shop revenue	25,000
Interest revenue restricted by donor stipula-	
tion for acquisition of equipment	50,000

As a result of these cash receipts, the hospital's statement of cash flows for the year ended December 31, 2009 would report an increase in operating activities of

- a. $325,000
- b. $375,000
- c. $350,000
- d. $300,000

40. For a private, not-for-profit organization, when is a donor's conditional promise to give considered to be unconditional?

- a. When the condition is partially met.
- b. When the possibility that the condition will not be met is remote.
- c. When the conditional promise is made.
- d. When cash or other assets promised are received.

41. A not-for-profit organization receives $150 from a donor. The donor receives two tickets to a theater show and an acknowledgment in the theater program. The tickets have a fair market value of $100. What amount is recorded as contribution revenue?

- a. $0
- b. $ 50
- c. $100
- d. $150

42. On November 30, 2008, Justin Barlow, an alumnus of Murry School, a private, not-for-profit high school, contributed $15,000, with the stipulation that the donation be used for faculty travel expenses during 2009. During 2009, Murry spent all of the donation in accordance with Mr. Barlow's wishes. For the year ended December 31, 2009, what was the effect of the donation on unrestricted and temporarily restricted net assets?

	Unrestricted net assets	Temporarily restricted net assets
a.	Increase	Decrease
b.	No effect	Decrease
c.	Increase	No effect
d.	No effect	No effect

43. A private not-for-profit voluntary health and welfare organization received a cash donation in 2008 that contained a donor-imposed restriction that stipulated that the donation could not be spent until 2009. The voluntary health and welfare organization spent the donation in 2009 on fundraising activities. On the statement of activities prepared for the year ended December 31, 2009, the expiration of the time restriction would result in reporting a(n)

- a. Increase in temporarily restricted net assets.
- b. Reclassification that decreased temporarily restricted net assets.
- c. Increase in unrestricted net assets.
- d. Expense that decreased temporarily restricted net assets.

44. According to SFAS 117, which prescribes the financial statements of not-for-profit organizations, reporting reclassifications is caused by which of the following?

I. Expiration of donor-imposed conditions.
II. Expiration of donor-imposed restrictions.

- a. I only.
- b. Both I and II.
- c. II only.
- d. Neither I nor II.

45. Which of the following transactions would result in an increase in unrestricted net assets for the year ended December 31, 2009?

I. A private, not-for-profit hospital earned interest on investments that were board-designated.
II. A private, not-for-profit voluntary health and welfare organization received unconditional promises to give (pledges) which will not be received until the beginning of 2010. The donors placed no restrictions on their donations.

- a. Both I and II.
- b. I only.
- c. II only.
- d. Neither I nor II.

46. Benevolent Society, a private not-for-profit organization, should recognize contributed services on its statement of activities if which of the following conditions is(are) met?

I. The contributed services create or enhance nonfinancial assets.
II. The contributed services require specialized skills, are provided by individuals possessing those skills, and would typically need to be purchased if not provided by donation.

- a. Both I and II.
- b. Neither I nor II.
- c. I only.
- d. Either I or II.

47. During 2009, Margaret Billingsley, a prominent art collector, donated several items in her collection to the Darrwin Museum, a private, not-for-profit organization. Ms. Billingsley stipulated that her contribution be shown to the public, that it should be preserved, and not be sold. Darrwin's accounting policy is to capitalize all donations of art, historical treasures, and similar items. On the date of donation, what was the effect of Ms. Billingsley's donation on Darrwin's financial statements?

- a. Temporarily restricted net assets increased.
- b. Reclassifications caused a simultaneous increase in permanently restricted net assets and a decrease in temporarily restricted net assets.
- c. There was no effect on any class of Darrwin's net assets.
- d. Permanently restricted net assets increased.

48. Which of the following transactions or events would cause an increase in unrestricted net assets for the year ended December 31, 2009?

I. A private not-for-profit voluntary health and welfare organization spent a restricted donation that was received in 2008. In accordance with the donor's wishes, the donation was spent on public health education during 2009.
II. During 2009, a private, not-for-profit college earned dividends and interest on term endowments. Donors placed no restrictions on the earnings of term endowments. The governing board of the college intends to use this investment income to fund undergraduate scholarships for 2010.

a. II only.
b. I only.
c. Neither I nor II.
d. Both I and II.

49. Mary Egbart promised Columbus College, a private, not-for-profit college, that she would provide 80% of the funds needed to construct a new performing arts center, if the college could get the remaining 20% of the funds needed from other donors by July 1, 2010. The promise was made in 2009. At December 31, 2009, the governing board of the college had received donations from other donors for approximately 15% of the cost of the new center and believed that the probability of not getting the remaining 5% of the necessary funds was remote. For the year ended December 31, 2009, Ms. Egbart's promise would

a. Be reported as an increase in permanently restricted net assets on the statement of activities.
b. Not be reported on the statement of activities.
c. Be reported as an increase in deferred support on the statement of financial position.
d. Be reported as an increase in temporarily restricted net assets on the statement of activities.

50. A private, not-for-profit hospital adopted SFAS 124, *Accounting for Certain Investments Held by Not-for-Profit Organizations*. For the year ended December 31, 2009, how should the hospital report its investments in debt securities that are classified as current assets and noncurrent assets on its statement of financial position (balance sheet)?

	Debt securities in current assets	Debt securities in noncurrent assets
a.	Fair value	Amortized cost
b.	Amortized cost	Fair value
c.	Fair value	Fair value
d.	Amortized cost	Amortized cost

51. The governing board of Crestfallen, a private not-for-profit voluntary health and welfare organization, acquired equity securities of BMZ Company at a cost of $35,000 on May 1, 2009. The governing board used unrestricted net assets to acquire this investment, and it intends to use the income from its investment in BMZ, as well as other investments, to acquire much needed computer equipment for the organization. The investment in the equity securities of BMZ Company, which is listed on a national stock exchange, represents less than a 1% interest in the company. On November 15, 2009, Crestfallen received $1,000 of dividends from BMZ, and the fair value of the BMZ equity securities was $42,000 on December 31, 2009. Assume Crestfallen adopted SFAS 124, *Accounting for Certain Investments Held by Not-for-Profit Organizations*. As a result of Crestfallen's investment in BMZ Company, the statement of activities for the year ended December 31, 2009, would report an increase of

a. $8,000 in unrestricted net assets.
b. $8,000 in temporarily restricted net assets.
c. $1,000 in unrestricted net assets.
d. $7,000 in unrestricted net assets.

52. Jazz Planners, a private not-for-profit performing arts organization, has donor-restricted permanent endowment funds which include investments in equity securities. These equity securities all have readily determinable fair values because they are all traded on national security exchanges. Most of the equity investments represent between 1% and

3% of the common stock of the investee companies; however, a few of Jazz Planners' investments permit the organization significant influence over the operating and financing policies of the investee companies. Jazz Planners adopted SFAS 124, *Accounting for Certain Investments Held by Not-for-Profit Organizations*. How should the organization report these equity securities on its statement of financial position (balance sheet)?

	Equity securities: 1% to 3% ownership	Equity securities: significant influence
a.	Fair value	Fair value
b.	Fair value	Use equity method
c.	Lower of cost or market	Fair value
d.	Fair value	Lower of cost or market

53. Rose Smith made a cash donation for a specific purpose in December 2009, to United Ways, a nongovernmental, nonprofit organization that raises contributions for others. Assume United Ways was (1) not granted variance power by Rose Smith over her donation and (2) the beneficiaries of the donation are not financially related to United Ways. According to SFAS 136, *Transfer of Assets to a Not-for-Profit Organization or Charitable Trust That Raises or Holds Contributions for Others*, how should United Ways account for Rose's cash donation?

a. As an increase in contribution revenue.
b. As an increase in liabilities.
c. As either an increase in contribution revenue or liabilities.
d. As neither an increase in contribution revenue nor liabilities.

54. World-Wide Helpers Foundation, a nonprofit entity, received a cash donation in 2009 from Herold Smith. World-Wide Helpers Foundation is controlled by World-Wide Helpers, a nonprofit entity that raises resources for others. The resources of World-Wide Helpers Foundation are used for the benefit of World-Wide Helpers. World-Wide Helpers and its foundation have adopted SFAS 136, *Transfer of Assets to a Not-for-Profit Organization or Charitable Trust That Raises or Holds Contributions for Others,* for its 2009 financial statements. How should World-Wide Helpers Foundation account for the cash donation?

a. As an increase in contribution revenues.
b. As an increase in liabilities.
c. As either an increase in contribution revenue or liabilities.
d. As neither an increase in contribution revenue or liabilities.

55. In accordance with SFAS 136, *Transfer of Assets to a Not-for-Profit Organization or Charitable Trust That Raises or Holds Contributions for Others*, a cash donation from a resource provider should be reported as contribution revenue by a recipient organization when which of the following exists?

a. The recipient organization and beneficiary are **not** financially interrelated.
b. The resource provider does **not** allow the recipient organization to use the donation for beneficiaries other than those specified by the resource provider.
c. The resource provider does **not** grant variance power to the recipient organization to redirect the donation to other beneficiaries.

d. The resource provider grants variance power to the recipient organization to redirect the donation to other beneficiaries.

56. Peter Smith made a cash donation in January 2009, to World-Wide Helpers, a nongovernmental, nonprofit organization that raises contributions for others. Peter specified the beneficiaries for his contribution, but provided variance power to World-Wide Helpers to use the donation for beneficiaries not specified by Peter. According to SFAS 136, *Transfer of Assets to a Not-for-Profit Organization or Charitable Trust That Raises or Holds Contributions for Others*, how should World-Wide Helpers account for Peter's cash donation?

a. As an increase in contribution revenue.
b. As an increase in liabilities.
c. As either an increase in contribution revenue or liabilities.
d. As neither an increase in contribution revenue nor liabilities.

57. The Taft family lost its home in a flood in October 2009. In November of 2009, Mary Wilson donated cash to Goodbody Benevolent Society to purchase furniture for the Taft family. In December 2009, Goodbody purchased this furniture for the Taft family. Goodbody has adopted SFAS 136, *Transfer of Assets to a Not-for-Profit Organization or Charitable Trust That Raises or Holds Contributions for Others*. How should Goodbody report the receipt of the cash donation in its 2009 financial statements?

a. As an unrestricted contribution.
b. As a temporarily restricted contribution.
c. As a liability.
d. As either a liability or as a temporarily restricted contribution.

58. An arrangement where a donor makes an initial gift to a trust or directly to the not-for-profit organization, in which the not-for-profit organization has a beneficial interest but is not the sole beneficiary is known as a

a. Donor-imposed condition.
b. Donor-imposed restriction.
c. Share-the-wealth agreement.
d. Split-interest agreement.

59. Under which of the following cases should joint costs be allocated between fund-raising and the appropriate program or management and general function?

a. An appeal for funds accompanied by a statement of the mission of the not-for-profit entity.
b. An appeal for funds accompanied by a brochure explaining why funds are needed and how they will be used.
c. An organization seeks the involvement of the public in the attainment of their missions by telling people what they should do about particular issues in addition to fund-raising appeals.
d. An appeal for funds and education materials sent to a person based on his/her presumed ability to provide financial support.

60. Which of the following are considered to be capital additions in the statement of activity of a not-for-profit organization?

I. Nonexpendable gifts, grants, and bequests restricted by donors to endowment funds.

II. Legally restricted investment income on investments held in endowment funds that must be added to the principal.
III. Donor-restricted gifts for program or supporting services.

a. I, II, and III.
b. I and III only.
c. I and II only.
d. III only.

61. Depending on the extent of discretion that the not-for-profit recipient has over the use or subsequent disposition of the assets, gifts in kind may be treated as

	Agency transactions	Contributions
a.	No	No
b.	No	Yes
c.	Yes	Yes
d.	Yes	No

62. A not-for-profit organization receives an asset for which they have little or no discretion over the use of the asset. The organization should report the asset as a(n)

a. Contribution.
b. Agency transaction.
c. Exchange.
d. Conditional transfer.

63. Elizabeth Hospital, a nonprofit hospital affiliated with a religious group, should prepare which of the following financial statements?

	Statement of changes in net assets	Statement of operations
a.	Yes	No
b.	No	Yes
c.	Yes	Yes
d.	No	No

64. Williams Hospital, a nonprofit hospital affiliated with a religious group, reported the following information for the year ended December 31, 2009:

Gross patient service revenue at the hospital's full established rates	$980,000
Bad debts expense	10,000
Contractual adjustments with third-party payors	100,000
Allowance for discounts to hospital employees	15,000

On the hospital's statement of operations for the year ended December 31, 2009, what amount should be reported as net patient service revenue?

a. $865,000
b. $880,000
c. $855,000
d. $955,000

65. For private sector health care organizations, which of the following is included in patient service revenue?

a. Contractual adjustments.
b. Charity care.
c. Significant revenue under capitation agreements (premium revenue).
d. Unrestricted contributions.

66. Which of the following is **not** covered by the AICPA Audit and Accounting Guide, *Health Care Organizations*?

a. Nursing homes.
b. Home health agencies.
c. Hospitals.
d. Voluntary health and welfare organizations.

67. Which of the following can be included in the performance indicator on the statement of operations for private sector health care organizations?
- a. Extraordinary items.
- b. Premium revenue from capitation agreements.
- c. Equity transfers.
- d. Contributions of long-lived assets.

68. If private not-for-profit health care entities do not use this expense classification on the operating statement, they must provide it in the notes.
- a. Natural.
- b. Character.
- c. Functional.
- d. Object.

69. When functional classifications are used by private sector health care organizations, they should be based on
- a. Net present value.
- b. Full cost allocations.
- c. Percentage allocations.
- d. Resale value.

70. Which of the following would be acceptable as a performance indicator on a private sector health care entity's statement of operations?
- a. Increase in unrestricted net assets.
- b. Net income.
- c. Increase in net assets.
- d. Excess of revenues over expenses.

71. How is charity care accounted for on the financial statements of a not-for-profit private sector health care organization?
- a. As patient service revenue.
- b. As bad debt expense.
- c. As a separate component of revenue.
- d. Not included on the financial statements.

72. How are nonrefundable advance fees representing payments for future services to be accounted for by nonprofit continuing care retirement communities?
- a. As revenue.
- b. As a liability.
- c. As other financing sources.
- d. In a trust fund.

73. Kash Hospital, a private sector, not-for-profit organization, has gross patient service revenues of $750,000, charity care of $75,000, amounts disallowed by third-party payors of $63,000, and donor-unrestricted contributions of $110,000. What is the amount of net patient service revenue?
- a. $687,000
- b. $722,000
- c. $785,000
- d. $797,000

74. James Hospital, a nonprofit hospital affiliated with a private university, provided $200,000 of charity care for patients during the year ended December 31, 2009. The hospital should report this charity care
- a. As net patient service revenue of $200,000 on the statement of operations.
- b. As net patient service revenue of $200,000 and as an operating expense of $200,000 on the statement of operations.

- c. As accounts receivable of $200,000 on the balance sheet at December 31, 2009.
- d. Only in the notes to the financial statements for 2009.

75. Michael Hospital, a nonprofit hospital affiliated with a private university, reported the following information for the year ended December 31, 2009:

Cash contributions received from donors for capital additions to be acquired in 2010	$150,000
Proceeds from sales at hospital gift shop and snack bar	75,000
Dividend revenue not restricted by donors or by law	25,000

Using the information provided, what amount should be reported as "other revenue and gains" on the hospital's statement of operations for the year ended December 31, 2009?
- a. $ 25,000
- b. $ 75,000
- c. $100,000
- d. $250,000

76. Swathmore Hospital, a nonprofit hospital affiliated with Swathmore University, received the following cash contributions from donors during the year ended December 31, 2008:

Contributions restricted by donors for research	$ 50,000
Contributions restricted by donors for capital acquisitions	250,000

Neither of the contributions was spent during 2008; however, during 2009, the hospital spent the entire $50,000 contribution on research and the entire $250,000 contribution on a capital asset that was placed into service during the year. The hospital has adopted an accounting policy that does not imply a time restriction on gifts of long-lived assets. On the hospital's statement of operations for the year ended December 31, 2009, what total amount should be reported for "net assets released from restrictions"?
- a. $ 50,000
- b. $300,000
- c. $250,000
- d. $0

77. The governing board of Smithson Hospital, a nonprofit hospital affiliated with a religious organization, acquired 100 BMI Company bonds for $103,000 on June 30, 2009. The bonds pay interest on June 30 and December 30. On December 31, 2009, interest of $3,000 was received from BMI, and the fair value of the BMI bonds was $105,000. The governing board acquired the BMI bonds with cash which was unrestricted, and it classified the bonds as trading securities at December 31, 2009, since it intends to sell all of the bonds in January 2010. As a result of the investment in BMI bonds, what amount should be included in revenue, gains, and other support on the statement of operations for the year ended December 31, 2009?
- a. $0
- b. $3,000
- c. $2,000
- d. $5,000

78. On the statement of operations for a nonprofit, nongovernmental hospital, which of the items below is included in the amount reported for "revenue and gains over expenses and losses" (the performance indicator)?

I. Unrealized loss on other than trading securities. The securities are included in unrestricted net assets.

II. Contribution received from a donor that cannot be used until next year.

    a. I only.
    b. II only.
    c. Both I and II.
    d. Neither I nor II.

79. Tucker Hospital, a nonprofit hospital affiliated with Tucker University, received a donation of medical supplies during the year ended December 31, 2009. The supplies cost the vendor $10,000 and had a selling price of $15,000 on the date they were donated. The vendor did not place any restrictions on how the supplies were to be used. During 2009, all of the donated medical supplies were used. On the hospital's statement of operations for the year ended December 31, 2009, how should the donation be reported?

    a. The donation should be included in both revenue and operating expenses in the amount of $10,000.
    b. The donation should be excluded from the statement of operations.
    c. The donation should be included in both revenue and operating expenses in the amount of $15,000.
    d. The donation should be included in revenue in the amount of $15,000 and in operating expenses in the amount of $10,000.

80. Wilson Hospital, a nonprofit hospital affiliated with Wilson College, had the following cash receipts for the year ended December 31, 2009:

Collections of health care receivables	$750,000
Contribution from donor to establish a term endowment	250,000
Tuition from nursing school	50,000
Dividends received from investments in permanent endowment	80,000

The dividends received are restricted by the donor for hospital building improvements. No improvements were made during 2009. On the hospital's statement of cash flows for the year ended December 31, 2009, what amount of these cash receipts would be included in the amount reported for net cash provided (used) by operating activities?

    a. $ 880,000
    b. $ 800,000
    c. $1,050,000
    d. $ 750,000

81. Which of the following financial statements of a private, nonprofit hospital reports the changes in unrestricted, temporarily restricted, and permanently restricted net assets for a time period?

	Balance sheet	*Statement of operations*
a.	Yes	Yes
b.	Yes	No
c.	No	Yes
d.	No	No

82. Unrealized gains on investments which are permanently restricted as to use by donors are reported by a private, nonprofit hospital on the

    a. Statement of operations.
    b. Statement of cash flows.
    c. Statement of changes in net assets.

    d. Statement of operations and statement of cash flows.

83. The statement of operations for a private, nonprofit hospital should include a performance indicator that indicates the results of operations for a period. Which of the following items would be included in a hospital's performance indicator reported on the statement of operations?

I. Proceeds from sales of cafeteria meals and guest trays to employees, medical staff, and visitors.

II. Net assets released from restrictions used for operating expenses.

    a. I only.
    b. Both I and II.
    c. II only.
    d. Neither I nor II.

MULTIPLE-CHOICE ANSWERS

1. c __ __	19. a __ __	37. c __ __	55. d __ __	73. a __ __
2. d __ __	20. c __ __	38. d __ __	56. a __ __	74. d __ __
3. a __ __	21. b __ __	39. a __ __	57. c __ __	75. c __ __
4. a __ __	22. d __ __	40. b __ __	58. d __ __	76. b __ __
5. d __ __	23. c __ __	41. b __ __	59. c __ __	77. d __ __
6. c __ __	24. a __ __	42. b __ __	60. c __ __	78. d __ __
7. d __ __	25. c __ __	43. b __ __	61. c __ __	79. c __ __
8. d __ __	26. d __ __	44. c __ __	62. b __ __	80. b __ __
9. c __ __	27. b __ __	45. b __ __	63. c __ __	81. d __ __
10. d __ __	28. a __ __	46. d __ __	64. a __ __	82. c __ __
11. a __ __	29. b __ __	47. c __ __	65. a __ __	83. b __ __
12. b __ __	30. b __ __	48. a __ __	66. d __ __	
13. a __ __	31. a __ __	49. d __ __	67. b __ __	
14. b __ __	32. b __ __	50. c __ __	68. c __ __	
15. c __ __	33. c __ __	51. a __ __	69. b __ __	
16. c __ __	34. c __ __	52. b __ __	70. d __ __	
17. b __ __	35. d __ __	53. b __ __	71. d __ __	1st: __/83 = __%
18. d __ __	36. b __ __	54. a __ __	72. b __ __	2nd: __/83 = __%

MULTIPLE-CHOICE ANSWER EXPLANATIONS

A. FASB and AICPA Standards for Private Sector Nonprofits

1. **(c)** According to SFAS 117, a statement of functional expenses is required for voluntary health and welfare organizations. Other private nonprofit organizations are encouraged to disclose this information, but they are not required to.

2. **(d)** According to SFAS 117, a statement of financial position for a nongovernmental nonprofit entity, like a library, should report net assets according to whether the net assets are unrestricted, temporarily restricted, or permanently restricted.

3. **(a)** According to SFAS 117, the net assets of term endowments should be reported as temporarily restricted, while the net assets of regular endowments should be reported as permanently restricted. The net assets of term endowments are temporarily restricted because the donor of a term endowment stipulates that the endowment last only a specific number of years. Donors of regular endowments intend that these endowments last indefinitely; hence, the net assets are permanently restricted.

4. **(a)** According to SFAS 116, contributions are reported as revenue in the year received even though there are donor-imposed use or time restrictions on the donation. Since Ms. Smith's donation was use and time restricted, the donation should be reported as a temporarily restricted revenue on the statement of activities for the year ended June 30, 2009. This reporting is in accordance with SFAS 117.

5. **(d)** According to SFAS 116, contributions are reported as revenue in the year received even though there are donor-imposed use or time restrictions on the contribution. Since Mr. Peobody's contribution was use restricted, the contribution would be reported as temporarily restricted revenue on the statement of activities for the year ended December 31, 2009. This reporting is in accordance with SFAS 117.

6. **(c)** According to SFAS 117, all expenses are reported as unrestricted on the statement of activities. This means that expenses are deducted only from unrestricted revenues.

7. **(d)** In accordance with SFAS 117, nongovernmental not-for-profit organizations are required to report a statement of cash flows. On this statement, cash flows are reported using the classifications of operating, investing, and financing activities. Cash flows related to revenues and expenses that are unrestricted should be reported in the operating activities section. The cash inflows from both tuition ($500,000) and the unrestricted contribution ($100,000) are both unrestricted and should be reported as operating activities. Restricted contributions for long-term purposes, like the $300,000 endowment, are reported as financing activities on the statement of cash flows.

8. **(d)** According to SFAS 117, nongovernmental, not-for-profit entities should prepare the following financial statements:

1. Statement of financial position
2. Statement of activities
3. Statement of cash flows

In addition, a voluntary health and welfare organization should also prepare a statement of functional expenses.

9. **(c)** According to SFAS 116, donor restricted contributions should be reported as revenue in the period received. According to SFAS 117, donor restricted contributions which are restricted according to use should be reported as either temporarily restricted revenues or as permanently restricted revenues, depending on the restriction. In the case of Save the Planet, the restriction is temporary, not permanent. Therefore, Ms. Clark's contribution should be reported as temporarily restricted revenue on the statement of activities for the year ended December 31, 2009.

10. **(d)** According to SFAS 116, donor restricted contributions are revenues in the year the contribution is made, not in the year the contribution is spent. According to SFAS 117, contributions that are restricted temporarily should be reported on the statement of activities as temporarily restricted revenues.

11. (a) According to SFAS 117, the statement of cash flows for a nongovernmental not-for-profit entity should report its cash flows from operating, investing, and financing activities.

12. (b) SFAS 117, para 6, indicates that "a complete set of financial statements of not-for-profit organization shall include a statement of financial position as of the end of the reporting period, a statement of activities and a statement of cash flows for the reporting period, and accompanying notes to financial statements."

13. (a) SFAS 116, para 16, states

Gifts of long-lived assets received without stipulations about how long the donated asset must be used shall be reported as restricted support if it is an organization's accounting policy to imply a time restriction that expires over the useful life of the donated assets...In the absence of that policy and other donor-imposed restrictions on use of the asset, gifts of long-lived assets shall be reported as unrestricted support.

14. (b) For the year ended December 31, 2008, the contributions received for research would be reported on the statement of activities as an increase of $50,000 in temporarily restricted net assets. According to SFAS 116, contributions received from outside donors for use in research are reported as temporarily restricted net assets. For the year ended December 21, 2009, a reclassification of net assets would be reported on the statement of activities. A reclassification of $35,000 would be reported as both a decrease in temporarily restricted net assets and an increase in unrestricted net assets. In addition, research expense of $35,000 would be reported as a decrease in unrestricted net assets on the statement of activities for the year ended December 31, 2009. Therefore, as a result of the transactions in 2009, there was a decrease of $35,000 in temporarily restricted net assets and no effect on unrestricted net assets (the $35,000 reclassification to unrestricted net assets is offset by a $35,000 increase in research expense).

15. (c) Unrestricted net assets increased $250,000 for the year ended December 31, 2009. According to SFAS 117, the $50,000 spent on research during 2009 would be reclassified (added) to unrestricted net assets when the money was spent for research. The $50,000 addition to unrestricted revenues, gains, and other support would be accompanied by a $50,000 reclassification (deduction) from temporarily restricted revenues. The expenses of $50,000 for research are deducted from unrestricted revenues, etc., which include the $50,000 reclassification. Therefore, the net effect on unrestricted net assets of spending $50,000 on research is zero. The $250,000 of gift shop revenue is unrestricted revenue because the governing board has control of this revenue.

16. (c) According to SFAS 116, contributions should be reported as revenue in the period of contribution, even though a donor has placed a time or use restriction on the contribution. According to SFAS 117, the $10,000 and the $25,000 contributions should be reported as temporarily restricted revenues on the statement of activities for the year ended June 30, 2009. When the $25,000 is spent on fund-raising, a reclassification of $25,000 should be reported as a deduction from temporarily restricted revenues. This $25,000 deduction results in a net increase in temporarily restricted net assets of $10,000 on the statement of activities for the year ended June 30, 2009. The deduction of $25,000

from temporarily restricted revenues also results in an increase in unrestricted revenues, gains, and other support of $25,000. According to SFAS 117, expenses can only be deducted from unrestricted revenues on the statement of activities. Therefore, the fund-raising expenses of $25,000 will be deducted from unrestricted revenues, gains, and other support that includes the $25,000 reclassification from temporarily restricted revenues. Alternatively, SFAS 117 also permits temporarily restricted revenues to be reported as unrestricted revenues in the year the resources are received. This alternative is allowed only for the amount of temporarily restricted revenues that are spent during the year. In the situation presented, $25,000 would be disclosed as both an unrestricted revenue and expense for 2009. There would be no need for a reclassification; however, the answer would not change because temporarily restricted net assets increase $10,000 as a result of the contribution that was not spent in 2009.

17. (b) According to SFAS 116, contributions should be reported as revenues in the period received, even though donors have placed time or use restrictions on the contributions. According to SFAS 117, the $5,000,000 contribution from alumni for a new wing for the science building should be reported as a temporarily restricted revenue on the statement of activities for the year ended December 31, 2009. Also, the $50,000 of earnings related to the investments should also be reported as temporarily restricted revenues on the statement of activities for the year ended December 31, 2009. The $1,000,000 contribution from the donor, who stipulated that the contribution be invested indefinitely, should be reported as a permanently restricted revenue on the statement of activities for the year ended December 31, 2009.

18. (d) According to SFAS 116, a multiyear pledge should be reported at its present value. According to SFAS 117, if there is a time restriction on the pledge, the pledge should be reported as a temporarily restricted revenue in the year the pledge is given. In Hope Haven's situation, the pledge should be reported as temporarily restricted revenue in 2009. The pledge should be reported at its present value. This amount is calculated by using the present value of an ordinary annuity factor for five periods at 6% ($1,000 × 4.21236 = $4,212 rounded).

19. (a) According to SFAS 117, net assets under the control of the governing board are reported as unrestricted net assets.

20. (c) The requirement is to determine how to report three cash flows on the statement of cash flows for a nongovernmental, nonprofit entity, the Jackson Foundation. According to the guidance provided in SFAS 117, the $500,000 cash inflow from unrestricted contributions should be reported as an increase in the operating activities section. The $200,000 cash inflow restricted for the acquisition of property should be reported as an increase in the financing activities section, while the use of the $200,000 to acquire property should be shown as a decrease in the investing activities section.

21. (b) According to SFAS 116, contributions are reported as revenue in the year received, whether the donors place time or use restrictions on the resources. According to SFAS 117, net assets should be disclosed according to whether they are unrestricted, temporarily restricted, and permanently restricted. Both of the events listed would increase temporarily restricted net assets for the year ending December 31, 2009.

22.   (d)   SFAS 117 requires a statement of financial position which reports unrestricted, temporarily restricted, and permanently restricted net assets for nongovernmental, not-for-profit organizations. Therefore, the statement of financial position is required for a private, not-for-profit hospital, but not for a public university, which is supported by government.

23.   (c)   Per SFAS 116, contributed services which would be purchased if not donated, and which require performance by a specialist, shall be recorded as an increase in both expenses and contributions. In this case, the requirements of SFAS 116 are met since the window needs to be replaced and the work is performed by a professional glazier (specialist).

24.   (a)   SFAS 117 establishes standards for general-purpose external financial statements. This statement focuses on the basic information of the organization as a whole so as to enhance the relevance, understandability, and comparability of the financial statements by the external users. Thus, answer (a) is correct since the overall objective is the enhancement of the basic information, while answers (b), (c), and (d) address factors that are taken into consideration to achieve the objective.

25.   (c)   SFAS 117 requires classification of an organization's net assets and its revenues, expenses, gains, and losses based on the existence or absence of donor-imposed restrictions. It requires that the amount for **each** of three classes of net assets—permanently restricted, temporarily restricted, and unrestricted—be displayed in a statement of financial position and that the amounts of change in each of those classes of net assets be displayed in a statement of activities.

A temporary restriction is a donor-imposed restriction that permits the donee organization to use up or expend the donated assets as specified; it is satisfied either by the passage of time or by actions of the organizations involved. Accordingly, the $5,000,000 contribution of Day Co. shares represents temporarily restricted net assets until the shares are sold and the proceeds used to erect a public viewing building. The $2,000,000 contribution of Day Co. shares represents permanently restricted net assets because the shares are to be retained permanently.

26.   (d)   A liability (not revenue) is recorded when the reporting entity acts as an agent or trustee. A recipient of assets who is an agent or trustee has little or no discretion in determining how the assets transferred will be used. The receipt of cash to purchase furniture specifically for the Jones family would constitute a "transfer" of assets. Upon receipt of the asset (cash), the Amer Benevolent society must expend (i.e., purchase furniture) the contribution to comply with the restrictions of the donor. Answer (a) is incorrect because the donee restricted the use of the contribution. Answer (c) is incorrect because a permanent restriction stipulates that the resources be maintained permanently (but permits the donee organization to expend part or all of the income or other economic benefits derived from the donated assets).

27.   (b)   Per SFAS 116, an entity need not recognize the contributions of works of art and historical artifacts if the collection is held for public exhibition rather than financial profit, cared for and preserved, and, if sold, the proceeds are used to acquire other items for collections.

28.   (a)   A Statement of Activities reports revenues, expenses, gains, losses, and reclassifications. Resources are divided into three classes: unrestricted, temporarily restricted, and permanently restricted. Separate revenues, expenses, gains, losses, and reclassifications for each class may or may not be reported, but the change in net assets for each class **must** be reported.

29.   (b)   The requirement is to determine what classification is required to report expenses of all not-for-profit organizations. All not-for-profit organizations must classify expenses according to their function in either the financial statement or in the notes to the financial statements.

30.   (b)   Quasi endowment funds are established by the governing board of an organization using unrestricted net assets. Therefore, the assets in the quasi endowment would be included in the unrestricted net assets category.

31.   (a)   According to SFAS 116, a transfer of assets with a conditional promise to contribute them shall be accounted for as a refundable advance until the conditions have been substantially met. The conditions have been substantially met when the possibility that they will not be met is remote. In this question, the chance that the condition will not be met is reasonably possible, which is a higher level of doubt than remote and thus results in reporting the cash transfer as a liability at December 31, 2009.

32.   (b)   According to SFAS 117, the receipt of cash from a donor to establish a permanent endowment should be reported as a financing activity on the statement of cash flows. This same paragraph also states that receipts from investment income that by donor stipulation are restricted for the purposes of acquiring plant, equipment, and other long-lived assets should also be reported as a financing activity.

33.   (c)   According to SFAS 117, voluntary health and welfare organizations should provide a statement of functional expenses. This statement reports expenses by both function (program and supporting) and by their natural classification (salaries expense, depreciation expense, etc.).

34.   (c)   According to SFAS 116, donations of services are recognized on the statement of activities if either of the following two conditions are met: (1) the services create or enhance a nonfinancial asset, or (2) the services require specialized skills, are provided by individuals possessing those skills, and would typically need to be purchased if not provided by donation. The services provided by Jones Heating and Air Conditioning would clearly meet the second criterion. Good Hope would record the invoice in the following manner:

Supporting Expenses	1,500	
Accounts Payable		1,500

Upon notification that the invoice was canceled, Good Hope would make the following journal entry:

Accounts Payable	1,500	
Unrestricted Revenues		1,500

Therefore, the net effect of the contributed services is an increase in expenses and an increase in unrestricted revenues.

35. (d) According to SFAS 116, donations of services are recognized on the statement of activities if either of the following conditions are met: (1) the services create or enhance a nonfinancial asset, or (2) the services require specialized skills, are provided by individuals possessing those skills, and would typically need to be purchased if not provided by donation. The services of Anderson and Anderson, attorneys-at-law, clearly meet criterion 2 and should be reported as unrestricted revenues on James' statement of activities. However, the services provided by the senior citizens do not meet either criterion, and should not be reported on the foundation's statement of activities.

36. (b) The requirement is to determine what amount should be reported as contribution revenue in the 2009 statement of activities. The $2,000 restricted for meals is considered contribution revenue even though it is restricted. The amount received over the fair market value of the subscriptions is considered to be contribution revenue, which is $500 ($1,500 – $1,000). The $10,000 to be used upon completion of a new playroom is not part of 2009 revenue contribution because a condition, completion of a new playroom, has not been fulfilled. The money is only available upon completion, and the building is not complete in 2009. What is included in contribution revenue is $2,500 ($2,000 + $500).

37. (c) According to SFAS 116, gifts of long-lived assets should be reported as unrestricted support if the organization has an accounting policy which does not imply a time restriction on such gifts.

38. (d) The designation of unrestricted net assets by the board of Henry Museum for the building addition does not change the classification of the net assets which were designated. The assets designated were unrestricted before the designation, and they remain unrestricted after the designation.

39. (a) Cash flows from operating activities would include both the cash received from patient service revenue of $300,000 and the cash received from gift shop sales of $25,000. According to SFAS 117, cash received from investment income that is restricted by donors for the acquisition of long-lived fixed assets should be reported as financing activities.

40. (b) According to SFAS 116, a conditional promise to give is considered unconditional if the possibility that the condition will not be met is remote.

41. (b) The requirement is to determine how much of the $150 from a donor in exchange for theater tickets and an acknowledgment is considered contribution revenue. Contribution revenue is the amount given above the fair market value. The amount given, $150, is $50 more than fair market value of the tickets, which is $100.

42. (b) The use of the cash donation for faculty travel in 2009 is reported as a reclassification on the high school's statement of activities for 2009. Reclassifications are reported on the statement of activities as "net assets released from restrictions." Net assets released from restrictions of $15,000 are reported as a negative amount for temporarily restricted

net assets in 2009, while net assets released from restrictions of $15,000 are reported as a positive amount for unrestricted net assets for 2009. However, the $15,000 of travel expense is reported on the statement of activities as an expense for 2009. According to SFAS 117, all expenses are reported on the statement of activities as decreases in unrestricted net assets. This means that the use of the donation for faculty travel had no effect on unrestricted net assets in 2009. Note that, when the donation was received in 2008, temporarily restricted net assets increased by $15,000 on the statement of activities prepared for 2008.

43. (b) According to SFAS 117, expiration of donor-imposed restrictions that simultaneously increase one class of net assets and decrease another should be reported as reclassifications on the statement of activities. Reclassifications are reported as "net assets released from restrictions." When the time restriction on the donation expired in 2009, unrestricted net assets increased while temporarily restricted net assets decreased. The spending of the donation on fund-raising should be reported as an expense, which, according to SFAS 117, is a deduction from unrestricted net assets. Therefore, the net effect of the reclassification and the use of the donation is zero on unrestricted net assets. However, the reclassification decreased temporarily restricted net assets for 2009.

44. (c) According to SFAS 117, reclassifications result from expirations of donor-imposed restrictions. The donor-imposed restrictions may be either time or purpose related. When a donor-imposed condition is satisfied, the conditional promise to give assets becomes unconditional, and there is an increase in the appropriate classification of net assets, depending on the restrictions placed upon the assets by the donors. However, this increase is reported as either revenue or support at the time the promise becomes unconditional.

45. (b) Interest earned on board-designated investments is reported as unrestricted revenue. When the governing board of a not-for-profit organization places limitations on assets, they are designating the use of unrestricted net assets. Therefore, income earned on board-designated investments represents an increase in unrestricted net assets. Unconditional promises to give are reported in the period the pledges are made, not in the period of cash collection. However, since the contributions will not be received until 2010, the contributions should be reported as an increase in temporarily restricted net assets on the statement of activities for 2009 because of this time restriction.

46. (d) According to SFAS 116, contributed services should be recognized if either of the following conditions is met: (1) the services create or enhance nonfinancial assets, or (2) the services require specialized skills, are provided by individuals possessing those skills, and would typically need to be purchased if not provided by donation.

47. (d) According to SFAS 117, donations of works of art for which the donor stipulated a specified purpose and which are to be preserved and not be sold, represent permanently restricted net assets. Since the museum's policy is to capitalize all donations of art, Ms. Billingsley's donation would be reported as an increase in permanently restricted net assets on the statement of activities.

48. (a) The restricted donation of the voluntary health and welfare organization is reported as a reclassification on the statement of activities for 2009. The net effect of the reclassification and the recognition of the expense is zero. The reclassification resulting from the expiration of the donor-imposed restriction increases unrestricted net assets; however, the expense resulting from using the funds for public health education is subtracted from this increase, causing no effect on unrestricted net assets. The interest and dividends earned on the term endowments are unrestricted, and should be reported as an increase in unrestricted revenue for 2009. Since no expenses have been incurred from the use of the investment income for 2009, the net effect is an increase in unrestricted net assets for 2009.

49. (**d**)   According to SFAS 116, a conditional promise to give is considered unconditional if the possibility that the condition will not be met is remote. At December 31, 2009, Ms. Egbart's promise would be considered unconditional. This means that the college should report the funds that Ms. Egbart promised as an increase in temporarily restricted net assets on its statement of activities prepared for the year ended December 31, 2009.

50. (**c**)   According to SFAS 124, all investments in debt securities should be measured at fair value in the statement of financial position.

51. (**a**)   According to SFAS 124, the investment in BMZ is covered by the standard, since the standard does not apply to investments in equity securities which are accounted for under the equity method or are consolidated. Since Crestfallen owns less than 1% of BMZ Company, the equity method cannot be used to account for the investment. Therefore, the provisions of paragraph 7 apply to the investment in BMZ.

According to SFAS 124, investments in equity securities with readily determinable market values should be reported at fair value in the statement of financial position. In order to report BMZ's equity securities at their market value of $42,000, a gain of $7,000 should be recognized on the statement of activities. This gain represents an increase in unrestricted net assets, since the gain is related to an investment made by the governing board with unrestricted net assets. In addition, the dividends of $1,000 would also be reported as an increase in unrestricted net assets, since the dividends were earned on unrestricted net assets. Therefore, the investment in BMZ would result in an $8,000 increase in unrestricted net assets on the statement of activities prepared for the year ended December 31, 2009.

52. (**b**)   According to SFAS 124, investments in equity securities that are accounted for under the equity method are not covered by the standard. Therefore, Jazz Planners' investments that permit it to have significant influence over the operating and financing policies of the investee companies should be reported on the statement of financial position using the equity method. On the other hand, the investments that represent 1% to 3% ownership interests would be covered by SFAS 124. According to of SFAS 124, these investments in equity securities should be reported on the statement of financial position at fair value.

53. (**b**)   According to SFAS 136, when a resource provider transfers assets to a nonprofit entity and (1) does not grant the recipient organization variance power and (2) the recipient organization and the beneficiaries are not financially interrelated, the recipient entity should record an increase in assets and liabilities as a result of the donation. In the case at hand, United Ways is the recipient entity that should record the cash donation by increasing both assets and liabilities.

54. (**a**)   According to SFAS 136, when the recipient organization and the beneficiary are financially interrelated organizations, and the resources held by the recipient organization must be used for the benefit of the beneficiary, the recipient entity should account for the asset transfer as an increase in assets and as an increase in contribution revenue. In the case at hand, World-Wide Helpers Foundation is the recipient entity that should record the asset transfer by increasing cash and increasing contribution revenue.

55. (**d**)   According to SFAS 136, a contribution from a resource provider is reported as contribution revenue if (1) the recipient organization is granted variance power by the resource provider or (2) the recipient organization and the beneficiary are financially interrelated organizations. In the case at hand, answer (d) is correct because the resource provider granted variance power to the recipient organization. Answers (b) and (c) are incorrect because the resource provider designates the beneficiaries and does not grant the recipient organization the ability to redirect the donation to other than the specified beneficiaries. For both situations (b) and (c), the recipient organization should record the donation by increasing both assets and liabilities. Answer (a) is incorrect because contribution revenue is reported by a recipient organization if the recipient organization and the beneficiary are financially interrelated. If they are not financially interrelated, the recipient organization should report the donation as an increase in assets and an increase in liabilities.

56. (**a**)   According to SFAS 136, when the resource provider provides variance power over transferred assets, the recipient entity should account for the assets donated as an increase in assets and an increase in contribution revenue. Variance power means the ability of the recipient organization to redirect the resources transferred to it by a resource provider. In case at hand, World-Wide Helpers is the recipient entity that should record the cash donation by increasing both assets and contribution revenue.

57. (**c**)   According to SFAS 136, a recipient organization that receives a contribution from a resource provider is required to report the contribution as an asset and a liability unless one of two condition exist (1) the recipient organization is granted variance power to redirect the resources, or (2) the recipient organization and the beneficiary are financially interrelated organizations. Since Mary Wilson did not grant variance power to Goodbody to redirect her donation to other flood victims, and the Taft family and Goodbody are not financially interrelated organizations, the cash donation should be reported as a liability in Goodbody's 2009 financial statements.

58. (**d**)   According to the AICPA Audit and Accounting Guide, *Not-for-Profit Organizations,*

> *Under a split-interest agreement, a donor makes an initial gift to a trust or directly to the not-for-profit organization, in which the not-for-profit organization has a beneficial interest but is not the sole beneficiary....The assets are invested and administered by the organization, a trustee, or a fiscal agent, and distributions are made to a beneficiary or beneficiaries during the term of the agreement. At the end of the*

agreement's term, the remaining assets covered by the agreement are distributed to or retained by either the not-for-profit organization or another beneficiary or beneficiaries.

59. (c)   According to the Not-for-Profit Guide, all joint costs of informational materials or activities that include a fund-raising appeal should be reported as fund-raising expense unless an appeal is designed to motivate its audience to action other than providing financial support. Answer (c) is the only alternative that requires both other action and financial support.

60. (c)   According to the Not-for-Profit Guide, capital additions include nonexpendable gifts restricted to endowment, plant, or loan funds and the legally restricted investment income on investments in such funds. Donor-restricted gifts for programs or supporting services are not capital additions.

61. (c)   According to the Not-for-Profit Guide, gifts in kind are noncash assets received by not-for-profit organizations from resource providers. These gifts in kind are reported as agency transactions or as contributions depending on the extent of discretion that the not-for-profit recipient has over the use or subsequent disposition of the assets.

62. (b)   According to the Not-for-Profit Guide, when a not-for-profit organization has little or no discretion over the use of the asset, the transaction is an agency transaction.

C. Health Care Organization Accounting—Private Sector

63. (c)   According to the AICPA Audit and Accounting Guide, *Health Care Organizations*, the basic financial statements for a hospital include a balance sheet, a statement of operations, a statement of changes in net assets, and a statement of cash flows. Accordingly, Elizabeth Hospital should prepare both a statement of changes in net assets as well as a statement of operations.

64. (a)   According to the AICPA Audit and Accounting Guide, *Health Care Organizations*, the provision for contractual adjustments and discounts is recognized on the accrual basis and deducted from gross patient service revenue to determine net patient revenue. Bad debts expense is reported as an operating expense, not as a contra to gross patient service revenue. Accordingly, net patient service revenue for 2009 is $865,000. This amount is determined by subtracting the contractual adjustments of $100,000 and the discounts of $15,000 from gross patient service revenue of $980,000.

65. (a)   Patient service revenue is to be reported net of adjustments for contractual and other adjustments in the operating statement. Provisions recognizing contractual adjustments and other adjustments are recorded on an accrual basis and deducted from gross service revenue to determine net service revenue.

66. (d)   Voluntary health and welfare organizations are categorized as not-for-profit, nonbusiness-oriented organizations that are covered by the AICPA Audit and Accounting Guide, *Not-for-Profit Organizations*. Nursing home, home health agencies, and hospitals are all considered health care entities and are covered in the AICPA Audit and Accounting Guide, *Health Care Organizations*.

67. (b)   The AICPA Audit and Accounting Guide, *Health Care Organizations* lists the items that must be reported separately from the performance indicator. Among these are extraordinary items (and other items required by GAAP to be reported separately), equity transfers, receipt of restricted contributions, contributions of long-lived assets, restricted investment returns, and unrealized gains/losses of unrestricted investments (except trading securities). Premium revenue is included in the performance indicator.

68. (c)   The AICPA Audit and Accounting Guide, *Health Care Organizations* states that expenses may be reported on the face of the financial statements using either a natural classification or functional presentation. Not-for-profit organizations that report using a natural classification of expenses are required to disclose expenses by functional classification in the notes.

69. (b)   Functional classifications should be based on full cost allocations. Health care organizations may report depreciation, interest, and bad debts along with functions.

70. (d)   The performance indicator should report the results of operations. However, it should not include such items as extraordinary items, unrealized gains and losses on nontrading securities, and contributions of long-lived assets. Increase in unrestricted net assets and increase in net assets include these items and so cannot be performance indicators. Net income is a term associated with for-profit enterprises and so is not used by health care entities.

71. (d)   According to the AICPA Audit and Accounting Guide, *Health Care Organizations*,

Charity care represents health care services that are provided but are never expected to result in cash flows. As a result, charity care does not qualify for recognition as receivables or revenue in the financial statements. Distinguishing charity care from bad-debt expense requires the exercise of judgment. Charity care is provided to a patient with demonstrated inability to pay. Each organization establishes its own criteria for charity care consistent with its mission statement and financial ability. Only the portion of a patient's account that meets the organization's charity care criteria is recognized as charity. Although it is not necessary for the entity to make this determination upon admission or registration of an individual, at some point the entity must determine that the individual meets the established criteria for charity care.

Therefore, charity care is not included on the financial statements.

72. (b)   According to the AICPA Audit and Accounting Guide, *Health Care Organizations*, "Under provisions of continuing-care contracts entered into by a CCRC and residents, nonrefundable advance fees represent payment for future services and should be accounted for as deferred revenue." Deferred revenue is classified as a liability.

73. (a)   Patient service revenue is to be reported net of contractual adjustments. Contractual adjustments are the difference between revenue at established rates and the amounts realizable from third-party payors under contractual agreements. Charity care is not part of patient service revenue, and donor contributions are reported separately. Therefore,

	Gross patient service revenue	$750,000
−	Contractual adjustments	− 63,000
=	Net patient service revenue	$687,000

74.   (d)   According to the AICPA Audit and Accounting Guide, *Health Care Organizations*, charity care does not qualify for recognition as receivables or revenue in the financial statements. According to the AICPA Audit and Accounting Guide, *Health Care Organizations,* management's policy for providing charity care, as well as the level of charity care provided, should be disclosed in the financial statements. Such disclosure generally is made in the notes to the financial statement and is measured based on the providers' rates, costs, units of service, or other statistical measure.

75.   (c)   According to the AICPA Audit and Accounting Guide, *Health Care Organizations*, a hospital's other revenue, gains, and losses are derived from services other than providing health care services or coverage to patients. Other revenue, gains, and losses typically include interest and dividends that are unrestricted as well as proceeds from sales at gift shops and snack bars. Cash contributions from donors that are restricted to the acquisition of capital assets during 2010 are not reported on the statement of operations for 2009. The capital contribution should be reported on the statement of changes in net assets for the year ended December 31, 2009, as an increase in temporarily restricted net assets. Therefore, the amount that Michael should report as other revenue and gains on its statement of operations for 2009 is $100,000.

76.   (b)   According to the AICPA Audit and Accounting Guide, *Health Care Organizations*, expirations of donor restrictions on temporarily restricted net assets should be reported on the statement of operations as net assets released from restrictions. On Swathmore's statement of operations for 2009, the use of the $50,000 contribution for research in 2009 should be reported as "net assets released from restrictions." This amount should be included in revenues, gains, and other support on the statement of operations, and it is also included in the "performance indicator" reported on the statement of operations. The use of the $250,000 contribution to acquire a capital asset placed into service during 2009 is also reported as "net assets released from restrictions" on the 2009 statement of operations. This results because the hospital adopted an accounting policy that did not imply a time restriction on gifts of long-lived assets. However, this amount is reported after the performance indicator on the statement of operations. Accordingly, the total amount reported as net assets released from restrictions on the 2009 statement of operations is $300,000.

77.   (d)   According to the AICPA Audit and Accounting Guide, *Health Care Organizations*, unrealized gains on trading securities should be included as part of the amount reported for revenue, gains, and other support on the statement of operations. These unrealized gains are included in the performance indicator. Likewise, unrestricted revenues from interest and dividends are included as part of the amount reported for revenue, gains, and other support on the statement of operations. Therefore, Smithson Hospital should report both the $3,000 of interest revenue and the $2,000 unrealized holding gain ($105,000 less $103,000) in the amount reported for revenue, gains, and other support on its statement of operations for the year ended December 31, 2009.

78.   (d)   According to the AICPA Audit and Accounting Guide, *Health Care Organizations*, unrealized gains and losses from other than trading securities, which are not restricted by donors, are reported after the performance indicator on the statement of operations. Therefore, the unrealized loss in item I is reported on the statement of operations, but it is not included in the amount reported for revenue and gains over expenses and losses, the performance indicator. The donor contribution that cannot be used until next year is not reported on the statement of operations. The contribution represents an increase in temporarily restricted net assets and is reported on the statement of changes in net assets.

79.   (c)   According to the AICPA Audit and Accounting Guide, *Health Care Organizations*, a donation of noncash assets should be reported at fair value and reported as an increase in the appropriate net asset class. If there are no donor-imposed restrictions on the donation, the donation increases unrestricted net assets on the statement of operations. More specifically, the donation is included in the amount reported for revenue, gains, and other support if the donation is used for the operations of the hospital. The use of the donation in the operations of the hospital is reported as part of the operations expenses for the period. The donation of medical supplies to Tucker Hospital should be reported as both a revenue and as an operating expense in the amount of $15,000 on the statement of operations for the year ended December 31, 2009.

80.   (b)   The cash flows from revenues, gains, and other support, which are reported on the hospital's statement of operations, would be included in the net cash provided (used) by operating activities on the statement of cash flows. Both net patient service revenue and tuition revenue are included in the amount reported for revenue, gains, and other support on the hospital's statement of operations. Accordingly, cash received from patient service revenue and from tuition revenue are both included in the amount reported for cash flows from operating activities. The cash received for the term endowment as well as the cash received from dividends would not be included in the amount reported for net cash provided (used) by operating activities. Both of these cash receipts would be reported as increases in cash flows provided by financing activities. According to SFAS 117, cash contributions that are donor-restricted for long-term purposes are reported as financing activities on the statement of cash flows. In addition, the AICPA Audit and Accounting Guide, *Health Care Organizations*, states that cash received for long-term purposes, for example, the cash received for the term endowment and the building improvements, is not reported as a current asset. So that the statement of cash flows will reconcile with the change in cash and cash equivalents reported as current assets on the balance sheet, an amount equal to the cash received for the two financing activities is included in the amount reported for cash flows from investing activities. For Wilson Hospital, this would mean that $330,000, the sum of the $250,000 for the term endowment and the $80,000 of restricted dividends, is reported as a negative amount in the investing activities' section of the statement of cash flows. Note that both of these amounts are reported as investing activities whether the cash was spent this period or in subsequent period(s).

81.   (d)   The statement of changes in net assets reports the changes in the hospital's unrestricted, temporarily restricted, and permanently restricted net assets for a time period. The statement of operations discloses only the changes in unrestricted net assets for a time period, while the balance sheet discloses the amounts of unrestricted, temporarily restricted, and permanently restricted net assets as of a specific date. Therefore, neither the balance sheet nor the statement of operations discloses the changes in unrestricted, temporarily restricted, and permanently restricted net assets for a time period.

82. **(c)** According to the AICPA Audit and Accounting Guide, *Health Care Organizations*, investment returns not restricted by donors are reported on the statement of operations. The statement of operations explains the change in the hospital's unrestricted net assets for a period. Consequently, investment returns that are permanently restricted would not be reported on the statement of operations. Investment returns that are realized in cash are reported on the statement of cash flows. However, investment returns that are not realized in cash are not reported on the statement of cash flows. Investment returns, whether realized or unrealized, that are restricted by donors are reported on the statement of changes in net assets. Unrealized gains on investments that are permanently restricted represent investment returns which would be reported as an increase in permanently restricted net assets on the statement of changes in net assets.

83. **(b)** The AICPA Audit and Accounting Guide, *Health Care Organizations,* lists proceeds from sales of cafeteria meals and guest trays to employees, medical staff, and visitors as one of the items reported as other revenue on the statement of operations. Other revenue is included in the performance indicator on the statement of operations. Net assets released from restrictions are also reported in the performance indicator if the net assets are used for operating expenses.

4 REGULATION PROBLEMS AND SOLUTIONS

The Regulation Exam is scheduled for three hours. Based on information released by the AICPA, candidates should expect three multiple-choice testlets of approximately thirty questions each, and two simulations.

The Uniform CPA Examination Content Specifications appear in *Volume 1, Outlines and Study Guides*.

5 PROFESSIONAL RESPONSIBILITIES AND BUSINESS LAW

MULTIPLE-CHOICE QUESTIONS (1-66)

1. Which of the following best describes what is meant by the term generally accepted auditing standards?
   a. Rules acknowledged by the accounting profession because of their universal application.
   b. Pronouncements issued by the Auditing Standards Board.
   c. Measures of the quality of the auditor's performance.
   d. Procedures to be used to gather evidence to support financial statements.

2. For which of the following can a member of the AICPA receive an automatic expulsion from the AICPA?

  I. Member is convicted of a felony.
 II. Member files his own fraudulent tax return.
III. Member files fraudulent tax return for a client knowing that it is fraudulent.

   a. I only.
   b. I and II only.
   c. I and III only.
   d. I, II, and III.

3. Which of the following is an example of a safeguard implemented by the client that might mitigate a threat to independence?
   a. Required continuing education for all attest engagement team members.
   b. An effective corporate governance structure.
   c. Required second partner review of an attest engagement.
   d. Management selection of the CPA firm.

4. Which of the following is a "self review" threat to member independence?
   a. An engagement team member has a spouse that serves as CFO of the attest client.
   b. A second partner review is required on all attest engagements.
   c. An engagement team member prepares invoices for the attest client.
   d. An engagement team member has a direct financial interest in the attest client.

5. According to the standards of the profession, which of the following circumstances will prevent a CPA performing audit engagements from being independent?
   a. Obtaining a collateralized automobile loan from a financial institution client.
   b. Litigation with a client relating to billing for consulting services for which the amount is immaterial.
   c. Employment of the CPA's spouse as a client's director of internal audit.
   d. Acting as an honorary trustee for a not-for-profit organization client.

6. The profession's ethical standards most likely would be considered to have been violated when a CPA represents that specific consulting services will be performed for a stated fee and it is apparent at the time of the representation that the
   a. Actual fee would be substantially higher.
   b. Actual fee would be substantially lower than the fees charged by other CPAs for comparable services.

   c. CPA would **not** be independent.
   d. Fee was a competitive bid.

7. According to the ethical standards of the profession, which of the following acts is generally prohibited?
   a. Issuing a modified report explaining a failure to follow a governmental regulatory agency's standards when conducting an attest service for a client.
   b. Revealing confidential client information during a quality review of a professional practice by a team from the state CPA society.
   c. Accepting a contingent fee for representing a client in an examination of the client's federal tax return by an IRS agent.
   d. Retaining client records after an engagement is terminated prior to completion and the client has demanded their return.

8. According to the profession's ethical standards, which of the following events may justify a departure from a Statement of the Governmental Accounting Standards Board?

	New legislation	*Evolution of a new form of business transaction*
a.	No	Yes
b.	Yes	No
c.	Yes	Yes
d.	No	No

9. May a CPA hire for the CPA's public accounting firm a non-CPA systems analyst who specializes in developing computer systems?
   a. Yes, provided the CPA is qualified to perform each of the specialist's tasks.
   b. Yes, provided the CPA is able to supervise the specialist and evaluate the specialist's end product.
   c. No, because non-CPA professionals are **not** permitted to be associated with CPA firms in public practice.
   d. No, because developing computer systems is **not** recognized as a service performed by public accountants.

10. Stephanie Seals is a CPA who is working as a controller for Brentwood Corporation. She is not in public practice. Which statement is true?
   a. She may use the CPA designation on her business cards if she also puts her employment title on them.
   b. She may use the CPA designation on her business cards as long as she does not mention Brentwood Corporation or her title as controller.
   c. She may use the CPA designation on company transmittals but not on her business cards.
   d. She may not use the CPA designation because she is not in public practice.

11. According to the standards of the profession, which of the following activities would most likely **not** impair a CPA's independence?
   a. Providing advisory services for a client.
   b. Contracting with a client to supervise the client's office personnel.
   c. Signing a client's checks in emergency situations.
   d. Accepting a luxurious gift from a client.

12. Which of the following reports may be issued only by an accountant who is independent of a client?

    a.   Standard report on an examination of a financial forecast.

    b.   Report on consulting services.

    c.   Compilation report on historical financial statements.

    d.   Compilation report on a financial projection.

13. According to the standards of the profession, which of the following activities may be required in exercising due care?

	Consulting with experts	Obtaining specialty accreditation
a.	Yes	Yes
b.	Yes	No
c.	No	Yes
d.	No	No

14. Larry Sampson is a CPA and is serving as an expert witness in a trial concerning a corporation's financial statements. Which of the following is(are) true?

  I. Sampson's status as an expert witness is based upon his specialized knowledge, experience, and training.

  II. Sampson is required by AICPA ruling to present his position objectively.

  III. Sampson may regard himself as acting as an advocate.

    a.   I only.

    b.   I and II only.

    c.   I and III only.

    d.   III only.

15. According to the ethical standards of the profession, which of the following acts is generally prohibited?

    a.   Purchasing a product from a third party and reselling it to a client.

    b.   Writing a financial management newsletter promoted and sold by a publishing company.

    c.   Accepting a commission for recommending a product to an audit client.

    d.   Accepting engagements obtained through the efforts of third parties.

16. To exercise due professional care an auditor should

    a.   Critically review the judgment exercised by those assisting in the audit.

    b.   Examine all available corroborating evidence supporting managements assertions.

    c.   Design the audit to detect all instances of illegal acts.

    d.   Attain the proper balance of professional experience and formal education.

17. Kar, CPA, is a staff auditor participating in the audit engagement of Fort, Inc. Which of the following circumstances impairs Kar's independence?

    a.   During the period of the professional engagement, Fort gives Kar tickets to a football game worth $75.

    b.   Kar owns stock in a corporation that Fort's 401(k) plan also invests in.

    c.   Kar's friend, an employee of another local accounting firm, prepares Fort's tax returns.

    d.   Kar's sibling is director of internal audit at Fort.

18. On June 1, 2008, a CPA obtained a $100,000 personal loan from a financial institution client for whom the CPA provided compilation services. The loan was fully secured and considered material to the CPA's net worth. The CPA paid the loan in full on December 31, 2009. On April 3, 2009, the client asked the CPA to audit the client's financial statements for the year ended December 31, 2009. Is the CPA considered independent with respect to the audit of the client's December 31, 2009 financial statements?

    a.   Yes, because the loan was fully secured.

    b.   Yes, because the CPA was **not** required to be independent at the time the loan was granted.

    c.   No, because the CPA had a loan with the client during the period of a professional engagement.

    d.   No, because the CPA had a loan with the client during the period covered by the financial statements.

19. Which of the following statements is(are) correct regarding a CPA employee of a CPA firm taking copies of information contained in client files when the CPA leaves the firm?

  I. A CPA leaving a firm may take copies of information contained in client files to assist another firm in serving that client.

  II. A CPA leaving a firm may take copies of information contained in client files as a method of gaining technical expertise.

    a.   I only.

    b.   II only.

    c.   Both I and II.

    d.   Neither I nor II.

20. Which of the following statements is correct regarding an accountant's working papers?

    a.   The accountant owns the working papers and generally may disclose them as the accountant sees fit.

    b.   The client owns the working papers but the accountant has custody of them until the accountant's bill is paid in full.

    c.   The accountant owns the working papers but generally may **not** disclose them without the client's consent or a court order.

    d.   The client owns the working papers but, in the absence of the accountant's consent, may **not** disclose them without a court order.

21. According to the profession's standards, which of the following would be considered consulting services?

	Advisory services	Implementation services	Product services
a.	Yes	Yes	Yes
b.	Yes	Yes	No
c.	Yes	No	Yes
d.	No	Yes	Yes

22. According to the standards of the profession, which of the following events would require a CPA performing a consulting services engagement for a nonaudit client to withdraw from the engagement?

  I. The CPA has a conflict of interest that is disclosed to the client and the client consents to the CPA continuing the engagement.

  II. The CPA fails to obtain a written understanding from the client concerning the scope of the engagement.

a.   I only.
b.   II only.
c.   Both I and II.
d.   Neither I nor II.

23. Which of the following services may a CPA perform in carrying out a consulting service for a client?

I.   Analysis of the client's accounting system.
II. Review of the client's prepared business plan.
III. Preparation of information for obtaining financing.

a.   I and II only.
b.   I and III only.
c.   II and III only.
d.   I, II, and III.

24. Under the Statements on Standards for Consulting Services, which of the following statements best reflects a CPA's responsibility when undertaking a consulting services engagement? The CPA must

a.   Not seek to modify any agreement made with the client.
b.   Not perform any attest services for the client.
c.   Inform the client of significant reservations concerning the benefits of the engagement.
d.   Obtain a written understanding with the client concerning the time for completion of the engagement.

25. Which of the following services is a CPA generally required to perform when conducting a personal financial planning engagement?

a.   Assisting the client to identify tasks that are essential in order to act on planning decisions.
b.   Assisting the client to take action on planning decisions.
c.   Monitoring progress in achieving goals.
d.   Updating recommendations and revising planning decisions.

26. Cable Corp. orally engaged Drake & Co., CPAs, to audit its financial statements. Cable's management informed Drake that it suspected the accounts receivable were materially overstated. Though the financial statements Drake audited included a materially overstated accounts receivable balance, Drake issued an unqualified opinion. Cable used the financial statements to obtain a loan to expand its operations. Cable defaulted on the loan and incurred a substantial loss.

If Cable sues Drake for negligence in failing to discover the overstatement, Drake's best defense would be that Drake did **not**

a.   Have privity of contract with Cable.
b.   Sign an engagement letter.
c.   Perform the audit recklessly or with an intent to deceive.
d.   Violate generally accepted auditing standards in performing the audit.

27. Which of the following statements best describes whether a CPA has met the required standard of care in conducting an audit of a client's financial statements?

a.   The client's expectations with regard to the accuracy of audited financial statements.
b.   The accuracy of the financial statements and whether the statements conform to generally accepted accounting principles.

c.   Whether the CPA conducted the audit with the same skill and care expected of an ordinarily prudent CPA under the circumstances.
d.   Whether the audit was conducted to investigate and discover all acts of fraud.

28. Ford & Co., CPAs, issued an unqualified opinion on Owens Corp.'s financial statements. Relying on these financial statements, Century Bank lent Owens $750,000. Ford was unaware that Century would receive a copy of the financial statements or that Owens would use them to obtain a loan. Owens defaulted on the loan.

To succeed in a common law fraud action against Ford, Century must prove, in addition to other elements, that Century was

a.   Free from contributory negligence.
b.   In privity of contract with Ford.
c.   Justified in relying on the financial statements.
d.   In privity of contract with Owens.

29. When performing an audit, a CPA

a.   Must exercise the level of care, skill, and judgment expected of a reasonably prudent CPA under the circumstances.
b.   Must strictly adhere to generally accepted accounting principles.
c.   Is strictly liable for failing to discover client fraud.
d.   Is **not** liable unless the CPA commits gross negligence or intentionally disregards generally accepted auditing standards.

30. When performing an audit, a CPA will most likely be considered negligent when the CPA fails to

a.   Detect all of a client's fraudulent activities.
b.   Include a negligence disclaimer in the client engagement letter.
c.   Warn a client of known internal control weaknesses.
d.   Warn a client's customers of embezzlement by the client's employees.

31. A CPA's duty of due care to a client most likely will be breached when a CPA

a.   Gives a client an oral instead of written report.
b.   Gives a client incorrect advice based on an honest error of judgment.
c.   Fails to give tax advice that saves the client money.
d.   Fails to follow generally accepted auditing standards.

32. Which of the following elements, if present, would support a finding of constructive fraud on the part of a CPA?

a.   Gross negligence in applying generally accepted auditing standards.
b.   Ordinary negligence in applying generally accepted accounting principles.
c.   Identified third-party users.
d.   Scienter.

33. If a CPA recklessly departs from the standards of due care when conducting an audit, the CPA will be liable to third parties who are unknown to the CPA based on

a.   Negligence.
b.   Gross negligence.
c.   Strict liability.
d.   Criminal deceit.

34. In a common law action against an accountant, lack of privity is a viable defense if the plaintiff

    a. Is the client's creditor who sues the accountant for negligence.

    b. Can prove the presence of gross negligence that amounts to a reckless disregard for the truth.

    c. Is the accountant's client.

    d. Bases the action upon fraud.

35. A CPA audited the financial statements of Shelly Company. The CPA was negligent in the audit. Sanco, a supplier of Shelly, is upset because Sanco had extended Shelly a high credit limit based on the financial statements which were incorrect. Which of the following statements is the most correct?

    a. In most states, both Shelly and Sanco can recover from the CPA for damages due to the negligence.

    b. States that use the Ultramares decision will allow both Shelly and Sanco to recover.

    c. In most states, Sanco cannot recover as a mere foreseeable third party.

    d. Generally, Sanco can recover but Shelly cannot.

36. Under the Ultramares rule, to which of the following parties will an accountant be liable for negligence?

	Parties in privity	Foreseen parties
a.	Yes	Yes
b.	Yes	No
c.	No	Yes
d.	No	No

Items 37 and 38 are based on the following:

While conducting an audit, Larson Associates, CPAs, failed to detect material misstatements included in its client's financial statements. Larson's unqualified opinion was included with the financial statements in a registration statement and prospectus for a public offering of securities made by the client. Larson knew that its opinion and the financial statements would be used for this purpose.

37. In a suit by a purchaser against Larson for common law negligence, Larson's best defense would be that the

    a. Audit was conducted in accordance with generally accepted auditing standards.

    b. Client was aware of the misstatements.

    c. Purchaser was **not** in privity of contract with Larson.

    d. Identity of the purchaser was **not** known to Larson at the time of the audit.

38. In a suit by a purchaser against Larson for common law fraud, Larson's best defense would be that

    a. Larson did **not** have actual or constructive knowledge of the misstatements.

    b. Larson's client knew or should have known of the misstatements.

    c. Larson did **not** have actual knowledge that the purchaser was an intended beneficiary of the audit.

    d. Larson was **not** in privity of contract with its client.

39. Quincy bought Teal Corp. common stock in an offering registered under the Securities Act of 1933. Worth & Co., CPAs, gave an unqualified opinion on Teal's financial statements that were included in the registration statement filed with the SEC. Quincy sued Worth under the provisions of the 1933 Act that deal with omission of facts required to be in the registration statement. Quincy must prove that

    a. There was fraudulent activity by Worth.

    b. There was a material misstatement in the financial statements.

    c. Quincy relied on Worth's opinion.

    d. Quincy was in privity with Worth.

40. Beckler & Associates, CPAs, audited and gave an unqualified opinion on the financial statements of Queen Co. The financial statements contained misstatements that resulted in a material overstatement of Queen's net worth. Queen provided the audited financial statements to Mac Bank in connection with a loan made by Mac to Queen. Beckler knew that the financial statements would be provided to Mac. Queen defaulted on the loan. Mac sued Beckler to recover for its losses associated with Queen's default. Which of the following must Mac prove in order to recover?

    I. Beckler was negligent in conducting the audit.

    II. Mac relied on the financial statements.

    a. I only.

    b. II only.

    c. Both I and II.

    d. Neither I nor II.

Items 41 and 42 are based on the following:

Dart Corp. engaged Jay Associates, CPAs, to assist in a public stock offering. Jay audited Dart's financial statements and gave an unqualified opinion, despite knowing that the financial statements contained misstatements. Jay's opinion was included in Dart's registration statement. Larson purchased shares in the offering and suffered a loss when the stock declined in value after the misstatements became known.

41. In a suit against Jay and Dart under the Section 11 liability provisions of the Securities Act of 1933, Larson must prove that

    a. Jay knew of the misstatements.

    b. Jay was negligent.

    c. The misstatements contained in Dart's financial statements were material.

    d. The unqualified opinion contained in the registration statement was relied on by Larson.

42. If Larson succeeds in the Section 11 suit against Dart, Larson would be entitled to

    a. Damages of three times the original public offering price.

    b. Rescind the transaction.

    c. Monetary damages only.

    d. Damages, but only if the shares were resold before the suit was started.

Items 43 and 44 are based on the following:

Under the liability provisions of Section 11 of the Securities Act of 1933, a CPA may be liable to any purchaser of a security for certifying materially misstated financial statements that are included in the security's registration statement.

43. Under Section 11, a CPA usually will **not** be liable to the purchaser

    a. If the purchaser is contributorily negligent.

    b. If the CPA can prove due diligence.

c. Unless the purchaser can prove privity with the CPA.

d. Unless the purchaser can prove scienter on the part of the CPA.

44. Under Section 11, which of the following must be proven by a purchaser of the security?

	Reliance on the financial statements	Fraud by the CPA
a.	Yes	Yes
b.	Yes	No
c.	No	Yes
d.	No	No

45. Ocean and Associates, CPAs, audited the financial statements of Drain Corporation. As a result of Ocean's negligence in conducting the audit, the financial statements included material misstatements. Ocean was unaware of this fact. The financial statements and Ocean's unqualified opinion were included in a registration statement and prospectus for an original public offering of stock by Drain. Sharp purchased shares in the offering. Sharp received a copy of the prospectus prior to the purchase but did not read it. The shares declined in value as a result of the misstatements in Drain's financial statements becoming known. Under which of the following Acts is Sharp most likely to prevail in a lawsuit against Ocean?

	Securities Exchange Act of 1934, Section 10(b), Rule 10b-5	Securities Act of 1933, Section 11
a.	Yes	Yes
b.	Yes	No
c.	No	Yes
d.	No	No

46. Danvy, a CPA, performed an audit for Lank Corporation. Danvy also performed an S-1 review to review events subsequent to the balance sheet date. If Danvy fails to further investigate suspicious facts, under which of these can he be found negligent?

a. The audit but not the review.

b. The review but not the audit.

c. Neither the audit nor the review.

d. Both the audit and the review.

47. Dart Corp. engaged Jay Associates, CPAs, to assist in a public stock offering. Jay audited Dart's financial statements and gave an unqualified opinion, despite knowing that the financial statements contained misstatements. Jay's opinion was included in Dart's registration statement. Larson purchased shares in the offering and suffered a loss when the stock declined in value after the misstatements became known.

In a suit against Jay under the antifraud provisions of Section 10(b) and Rule 10b-5 of the Securities Exchange Act of 1934, Larson must prove all of the following **except**

a. Larson was an intended user of the false registration statement.

b. Larson relied on the false registration statement.

c. The transaction involved some form of interstate commerce.

d. Jay acted with intentional disregard of the truth.

48. Under the antifraud provisions of Section 10(b) of the Securities Exchange Act of 1934, a CPA may be liable if the CPA acted

a. Negligently.

b. With independence.

c. Without due diligence.

d. Without good faith.

49. Under Section 11 of the Securities Act of 1933, which of the following standards may a CPA use as a defense?

	Generally accepted accounting principles	Generally accepted fraud detection standards
a.	Yes	Yes
b.	Yes	No
c.	No	Yes
d.	No	No

50. Dart Corp. engaged Jay Associates, CPAs, to assist in a public stock offering. Jay audited Dart's financial statements and gave an unqualified opinion, despite knowing that the financial statements contained misstatements. Jay's opinion was included in Dart's registration statement. Larson purchased shares in the offering and suffered a loss when the stock declined in value after the misstatements became known.

If Larson succeeds in the Section 10(b) and Rule 10b-5 suit, Larson would be entitled to

a. Only recover the original public offering price.

b. Only rescind the transaction.

c. The amount of any loss caused by the fraud.

d. Punitive damages.

51. Which of the following statements is correct with respect to ownership, possession, or access to a CPA firm's audit working papers?

a. Working papers may **never** be obtained by third parties unless the client consents.

b. Working papers are **not** transferable to a purchaser of a CPA practice unless the client consents.

c. Working papers are subject to the privileged communication rule which, in most jurisdictions, prevents any third-party access to the working papers.

d. Working papers are the client's exclusive property.

52. Which of the following statements is correct regarding a CPA's working papers? The working papers must be

a. Transferred to another accountant purchasing the CPA's practice even if the client hasn't given permission.

b. Transferred permanently to the client if demanded.

c. Turned over to any government agency that requests them.

d. Turned over pursuant to a valid federal court subpoena.

53. To which of the following parties may a CPA partnership provide its working papers, without being lawfully subpoenaed or without the client's consent?

a. The IRS.

b. The FASB.

c. Any surviving partner(s) on the death of a partner.

d. A CPA before purchasing a partnership interest in the firm.

54. To which of the following parties may a CPA partnership provide its working papers without either the client's consent or a lawful subpoena?

	The IRS	The FASB
a.	Yes	Yes
b.	Yes	No

c.   No   Yes
d.   No   No

55. A CPA is permitted to disclose confidential client information without the consent of the client to

I. Another CPA who has purchased the CPA's tax practice.
II. Another CPA firm if the information concerns suspected tax return irregularities.
III. A state CPA society voluntary quality control review board.

    a. I and III only.
    b. II and III only.
    c. II only.
    d. III only.

56. Thorp, CPA, was engaged to audit Ivor Co.'s financial statements. During the audit, Thorp discovered that Ivor's inventory contained stolen goods. Ivor was indicted and Thorp was subpoenaed to testify at the criminal trial. Ivor claimed accountant-client privilege to prevent Thorp from testifying. Which of the following statements is correct regarding Ivor's claim?

    a. Ivor can claim an accountant-client privilege only in states that have enacted a statute creating such a privilege.
    b. Ivor can claim an accountant-client privilege only in federal courts.
    c. The accountant-client privilege can be claimed only in civil suits.
    d. The accountant-client privilege can be claimed only to limit testimony to audit subject matter.

57. A violation of the profession's ethical standards most likely would have occurred when a CPA

    a. Issued an unqualified opinion on the 2002 financial statements when fees for the 2001 audit were unpaid.
    b. Recommended a controller's position description with candidate specifications to an audit client.
    c. Purchased a CPA firm's practice of monthly write-ups for a percentage of fees to be received over a three-year period.
    d. Made arrangements with a financial institution to collect notes issued by a client in payment of fees due for the current year's audit.

58. Which of the following statements concerning an accountant's disclosure of confidential client data is generally correct?

    a. Disclosure may be made to any state agency without subpoena.
    b. Disclosure may be made to any party on consent of the client.
    c. Disclosure may be made to comply with an IRS audit request.
    d. Disclosure may be made to comply with generally accepted accounting principles.

59. McGee is auditing Nevus Corporation and detects probable criminal activity by one of the employees. McGee believes this will have a material impact on the financial statements. The financial statements of Nevus Corporation are under the Securities Exchange Act of 1934. Which of the following is correct?

    a. McGee should report this to the Securities Exchange Commission.
    b. McGee should report this to the Justice Department.
    c. McGee should report this to Nevus Corporation's audit committee or board of directors.
    d. McGee will discharge his duty by requiring that a note of this be included in the financial statements.

60. Which of the following is an auditor not required to establish procedures for under the Private Securities Litigation Reform Act?

    a. To develop a comprehensive internal control system.
    b. To evaluate the ability of the firm to continue as a going concern.
    c. To detect material illegal acts.
    d. To identify material related-party transactions.

61. Which of the following is an auditor required to do under the Private Securities Litigation Reform Act concerning audits under the Federal Securities Exchange Act of 1934?

I. Establish procedures to detect material illegal acts of the client being audited.
II. Evaluate the ability of the firm being audited to continue as a going concern.

    a. Neither I nor II.
    b. I only.
    c. II only.
    d. Both I and II.

62. Lin, CPA, is auditing the financial statements of Exchange Corporation under the Federal Securities Exchange Act of 1934. He detects what he believes are probable material illegal acts. What is his duty under the Private Securities Litigation Reform Act?

    a. He must inform the principal shareholders within ten days.
    b. He must inform the audit committee or the board of directors.
    c. He need not inform anyone, beyond requiring that the financial statements are presented fairly.
    d. He should not inform anyone since he owes a duty of confidentiality to the client.

63. The Private Securities Litigation Reform Act

    a. Applies only to securities not purchased from a stock exchange.
    b. Does not apply to common stock of a publicly held corporation.
    c. Amends the Federal Securities Act of 1933 and the Federal Securities Exchange Act of 1934.
    d. Does not apply to preferred stock of a publicly held corporation.

64. Bran, CPA, audited Frank Corporation. The shareholders sued both Frank and Bran for securities fraud under the Federal Securities Exchange Act of 1934. The court determined that there was securities fraud and that Frank was 80% at fault and Bran was 20% at fault due to her negligence in the audit. Both Frank and Bran are solvent and the damages were determined to be $1 million. What is the maximum liability of Bran?

    a. $0
    b. $ 200,000
    c. $ 500,000
    d. $1,000,000

65. Which of the following nonattest services are auditors allowed to perform for a public company?

    a.   Bookkeeping services.
    b.   Appraisal services.
    c.   Tax services.
    d.   Internal audit services.

66. Which of the following Boards has the responsibility to regulate CPA firms that audit public companies?

    a.   Auditing Standards Board.
    b.   Public Oversight Board.
    c.   Public Company Accounting Oversight Board.
    d.   Accounting Standards Board.

SIMULATION PROBLEMS

Simulation Problem 1   (10 to 15 minutes)

Situation	
	Analysis

Under Section 11 of the Securities Act of 1933 and Section 10(b), Rule 10b-5, of the Securities Exchange Act of 1934, a CPA may be sued by a purchaser of registered securities.

	Analysis
Situation	

Items 1 through 6 relate to what a plaintiff who purchased securities must prove in a civil liability suit against a CPA. For each item determine whether the statement must be proven under Section 11 of the Securities Act of 1933, under Section 10(b), Rule 10b-5, of the Securities Exchange Act of 1934, both Acts, or neither Act.

		Only *Section 11* (A)	*Only* *Section 10(b)* (B)	*Both* (C)	*Neither* (D)
The plaintiff security purchaser must allege or prove					
1.	Material misstatements were included in a filed document.	○	○	○	○
2.	A monetary loss occurred.	○	○	○	○
3.	Lack of due diligence by the CPA.	○	○	○	○
4.	Privity with the CPA.	○	○	○	○
5.	Reliance on the document.	○	○	○	○
6.	The CPA had scienter.	○	○	○	○

Simulation Problem 2   (10 to 15 minutes)

Situation	
	Analysis

Assume that you are analyzing relationships for your firm to identify independence problems.

	Analysis
Situation	

Determine for each of the following numbered situations whether or not the auditor (a covered member of the firm) is considered to be independent. If the auditor's independence would **not** be impaired select No. If the auditor's independence would be impaired select Yes.

		Yes	*No*
1.	The auditor is a cosigner of a client's checks.	○	○
2.	The auditor is a member of a country club which is a client.	○	○
3.	The auditor owns a large block of stock in a client but has placed it in a blind trust.	○	○
4.	The auditor placed her checking account in a bank which is her client. The account is fully insured by a federal agency.	○	○
5.	The client has not paid the auditor for services for the past two years.	○	○
6.	The auditor is leasing part of his building to a client.	○	○
7.	The auditor joins, as an ordinary member, a trade association which is also a client.	○	○
8.	The auditor has an immaterial, indirect financial interest in the client.	○	○

MULTIPLE-CHOICE ANSWERS*

1. c	__ __	16. a	__ __	31. d	__ __	46. d	__ __	61. d	__ __
2. d	__ __	17. d	__ __	32. a	__ __	47. a	__ __	62. b	__ __
3. b	__ __	18. b	__ __	33. b	__ __	48. d	__ __	63. c	__ __
4. c	__ __	19. d	__ __	34. a	__ __	49. b	__ __	64. b	__ __
5. c	__ __	20. c	__ __	35. c	__ __	50. c	__ __	65. c	__ __
6. a	__ __	21. a	__ __	36. b	__ __	51. b	__ __	66. c	__ __
7. d	__ __	22. d	__ __	37. a	__ __	52. d	__ __		
8. c	__ __	23. d	__ __	38. a	__ __	53. c	__ __		
9. b	__ __	24. c	__ __	39. b	__ __	54. d	__ __		
10. a	__ __	25. a	__ __	40. c	__ __	55. d	__ __		
11. a	__ __	26. d	__ __	41. c	__ __	56. a	__ __		
12. a	__ __	27. c	__ __	42. c	__ __	57. a	__ __		
13. b	__ __	28. c	__ __	43. b	__ __	58. b	__ __		
14. b	__ __	29. a	__ __	44. d	__ __	59. c	__ __	1st: __/66 = __%
15. c	__ __	30. c	__ __	45. c	__ __	60. a	__ __	2nd: __/66 = __%

MULTIPLE-CHOICE ANSWER EXPLANATIONS

A.2. Code of Professional Conduct—Principles

1.   (c)   The requirement is to identify the statement that best describes the meaning of generally accepted auditing standards. Answer (c) is correct because generally accepted auditing standards deal with measures of the quality of the performance of audit procedures (AU 150). Answer (d) is incorrect because procedures relate to acts to be performed, not directly to the standards. Answer (b) is incorrect because generally accepted auditing standards have been issued by predecessor groups, as well as by the Auditing Standards Board. Answer (a) is incorrect because there may or may not be **universal** compliance with the standards.

2.   (d)   All of these can result in the automatic expulsion of the member from the AICPA. Answer (a) is incorrect because although the conviction of a felony can result in automatic expulsion, likewise can the other two. Answers (b) and (c) are incorrect because all three can result in automatic expulsion from the AICPA.

A.3. Code of Professional Conduct—Rules, Interpretations, and Rulings

3.   (b)   Answer (b) is correct because an effective corporate governance structure is a control that can be implemented by a client that increases independence of the attest team. Answer (a) is incorrect because it is a safeguard that is implemented by regulation or the CPA firm. Answer (c) is incorrect because it is a safeguard that is required by regulation or the CPA firm. Answer (d) is incorrect because it represents a threat rather than a safeguard.

4.   (c)   Answer (c) is correct because the team member would be reviewing his or her own work. Answer (a) is incorrect because this is an example of a familiarity threat. Answer (b) is incorrect because this is an example of a safeguard to threats to independence. Answer (d) is incorrect because this represents a financial self-interest threat to independence.

5.   (c)   According to the Code of Professional Conduct, Rule 101 regarding independence, a spouse may be employed by a client if s/he does not exert significant influence over the contents of the client's financial statements. This is a key position as defined by the Interpretation of Rule 101.

6.   (a)   According to Rule 102 of the Code of Professional Conduct, in performing any professional service, a member shall maintain objectivity and integrity, avoid conflicts of interest, and not knowingly misrepresent facts. Answer (a) is correct as this would be knowingly misrepresenting the facts. Answers (b) and (d) are incorrect as these are not intentional misstatements. Answer (c) is incorrect because while one must remain objective while performing consulting services, independence is not required unless the CPA also performs attest services for that client.

7.   (d)   The requirement is to determine which act is generally prohibited. Answer (d) is correct because "If an engagement is terminated prior to completion, the member is required to return only client records" (ET 501). Answer (a) is incorrect because issuing a modified report explaining a failure to follow a governmental regulatory agency's standards when conducting an attest service is not prohibited. Answer (c) is incorrect because accepting a contingent fee is allowable when representing a client in an examination by a revenue agent of the client's federal or state income tax return (ET 302). Answer (b) is incorrect because revealing confidential client information during a quality review of a professional practice by a team from the state CPA society is not prohibited (ET 301).

8.   (c)   According to Rule 203 of the Code of Professional Conduct, CPAs are allowed to depart from a GASB Statement only when results of the Standard would be misleading. Examples of possible circumstances justifying departure are new legislation and a new form of business transaction.

9.   (b)   The requirement is to determine whether a CPA may hire a non-CPA systems analyst and, if so, under what conditions. Answer (b) is correct because ET 291 allows such a situation when the CPA is qualified to supervise and evaluate the work of the specialist. Answer (a) is incorrect because the CPA need not be qualified to perform the specialist's tasks. Answer (c) is incorrect because non-CPA professionals are permitted to be associated with CPA firms

---

* *Explanation of how to use this performance record appears on page 1.*

in public practice. Answer (d) is incorrect because nonprofessionals may be hired, and because developing computer systems is recognized as a service performed by public accountants.

10.   (a)   She may use the CPA designation on her business cards when she does not imply independence but shows her title and her employer. Therefore, answer (b) is incorrect. Answer (c) is incorrect because she may use the CPA designation on her business cards or company transmittals if she does not imply independence. Answer (d) is incorrect because under the above situations, she can use the CPA designation.

11.   (a)   The requirement is to determine the activity that would most likely **not** impair a CPA's independence. Accounting and consulting services do not normally impair independence because the member's role is advisory in nature (ET 191). Answers (b) and (c) are incorrect because management functions are being performed (ET 191). Answer (d) is incorrect because accepting a luxurious gift impairs a CPA's independence (ET 191).

12.   (a)   The requirement is to identify the type of report that may be issued only by an independent accountant. Answer (a) is correct because AT 101 requires an accountant be independent for all attestation engagements. An attestation engagement is one in which the accountant expresses a conclusion about the reliability of assertions which are the responsibility of another party. A standard report on an examination of a financial forecast requires the auditor to express an opinion, which requires an accountant to be independent. Answer (b) is incorrect because CS 100 indicates that consulting services are fundamentally different from the attestation function, and therefore do not require independence of the accountant. Answers (c) and (d) are incorrect because AR 100 indicates that an accountant who is not independent is not precluded from issuing a report on a compilation of financial statements.

13.   (b)   Per ET 56, due care requires a member to discharge professional responsibilities with competence and diligence. Competence represents the attainment and maintenance of a level of understanding and knowledge that enables a member to render services with facility and acumen. It also establishes the limitations of a member's capabilities by dictating that consultation or referral may be required when a professional engagement exceeds the personal competence of a member or a member's firm. Accordingly, answer (b) is correct as it may be required to consult with experts in exercising due care. Due care does not require obtaining specialty accreditation.

14.   (b)   Under ruling 101 under Rule of Conduct 102, when a CPA is acting as an expert witness, s/he should **not** act as an advocate but should give his/her position based on objectivity. The expert witness does this based on specialized knowledge, training, and experience.

15.   (c)   The requirement is to determine which act is generally prohibited. Answer (c) is correct because "a member in public practice shall not for a commission recommend or refer to a client any product or service, or for a commission recommend or refer any product or service to be supplied by a client, or receive a commission when the member or the member's firm perform for that client: (1) an audit of a financial statement; or (2) a compilation of a fi-

nancial statement when the member expects that a third party will use the financial statement and the member's compilation report does not disclose a lack of independence; or (3) an examination of prospective financial information." Answer (a) is incorrect because a member may purchase a product and resell it to a client. Any profit on sale would not constitute a commission (ET 591).

16.   (a)   The principle of due care requires the member to observe the profession's technical and ethical standards, strive continually to improve competence and the quality of services, and discharge responsibility to the best of the member's ability. Answer (b) is incorrect as the auditor is not required to examine **all** corroborating evidence supporting management's assertions, but rather to examine evidence on a scope basis based on his/her consideration of materiality and level of risk assessed. Answer (c) is incorrect as the auditor should be aware of the possibility of illegal acts, but an audit provides no assurance that all or any illegal acts will be detected. Answer (d) is not the best answer because competence is derived from both education and experience. The principle of due care requires the member to strive to improve competence, however, attaining the proper balance of professional experience and formal education is not a criterion for exercising due care.

17.   (d)   The fact that a close relative of Kar works for Fort impairs Kar's independence. Answer (a) is incorrect because the gift is of a token amount which does not impair Kar's independence. Answer (b) is incorrect because a joint financial investment must be material to impair independence, and this would generally not occur with respect to a retirement plan. Answer (c) is incorrect because preparation of the client's tax return is not a service that impairs independence.

18.   (b)   Independence was not required at the time the loan was obtained, and because it is fully secured it is grandfathered by 101-5. Answer (a) is incorrect because if the CPA is required to be independent, a mortgage loan would not be permitted even if it was fully secured. Answer (c) is incorrect because the CPA was not required to be independent of the client. Answer (d) is incorrect because the CPA was not required to be independent of the client.

19.   (d)   Both of the statements are incorrect; either would violate Rule 301 on confidential client information. Answer (a) is incorrect because statement I also is incorrect. Answer (b) is incorrect because statement II also is incorrect. Answer (c) is incorrect because statements I and II are both incorrect.

20.   (c)   Information in the CPA's working papers is confidential and may not be disclosed except with the client's consent or by court order. Answer (a) is incorrect because disclosure of the information would generally violate Rule 301 on confidential client information. Answers (b) and (d) are incorrect because the CPA owns the working papers.

A.4. Responsibilities in Consulting Services

21.   (a)   Types of consulting services include consultations, advisory services, implementation services, transaction services, staff and other support services, and product services.

22.   (d)   According to the Statements on Standards for Consulting Services, independence is not required for performance of consulting services unless the CPA also performs attest services for that client. However, the CPA must remain objective in performing the consulting services. Furthermore, the understanding with the client for performing the services can be established either in writing or orally.

23.   (d)   CS 100 indicates that the nature and scope of consulting services is determined solely by the practitioner and the client, typically in which the practitioner develops findings, conclusions, and recommendations for the client. All three services listed would fall under the definition of consulting services.

24.   (c)   The AICPA Statement on Standards for Consulting Services, Section 100, describes general standards for all consulting services, in addition to those established under the AICPA Code of Professional Conduct. Section 100 addresses the areas of client interest, understanding with the client, and communication with the client. Specifically, this section states that the accountant should inform the client of significant reservations concerning the scope or benefits of the engagement.

25.   (a)   Personal financial planning engagements are only those that involve developing strategies and making recommendations to assist a client in defining and achieving personal financial goals. Personal financial engagements involve all of the following:

1.   Defining engagement objectives
2.   Planning specific procedures appropriate to engagement
3.   Developing basis for recommendations
4.   Communicating recommendations to client
5.   Identifying tasks for taking action on planning decisions.

Other engagements may also include, but generally are not **required** to perform, the following:

1.   Assisting client to take action on planning decisions
2.   Monitoring client's progress in achieving goals
3.   Updating recommendations and helping client revise planning decisions.

B.1.   Common Law Liability to Clients

26.   (d)   A CPA is not automatically liable for failure to discover a materially overstated account. The CPA can be liable if the failure to discover was due to the CPA's own negligence. Although performing an audit in accordance with GAAS does not guarantee that there is no negligence, it is normally a good defense against negligence. Answer (a) is incorrect because there was privity of contract with Cable. There was an oral agreement constituting a contractual relationship, therefore this would not be a good defense. Answer (b) is incorrect because an oral contract for an audit is still enforceable without a signed engagement letter. Answer (c) is incorrect because a CPA does not have to perform an audit recklessly or with an intent to deceive to be liable for negligence. Negligence simply means that a CPA failed to exercise due care owed of the average reasonable accountant in performing an audit.

27.   (c)   In order to meet the required standard of due care in conducting an audit of a client's financial statements, a CPA has the duty to perform with the same degree of skill and judgment expected of an ordinarily prudent CPA under the circumstances. Answer (a) is incorrect because the client's expectations do not guide the standard of due care. Rather, the standard of due care is guided by state and federal statute, court decisions, the contract with the client, GAAS and GAAP, and customs of the profession. Answer (b) is incorrect because it is generally the client's responsibility to prepare its financial statements in accordance with generally accepted accounting principles. Answer (d) is incorrect because a CPA is not normally liable for failure to detect fraud or irregularities unless (1) a "normal" audit would have detected it, (2) the accountant by agreement has undertaken greater responsibility, or (3) the wording of the audit report indicates greater responsibility.

28.   (c)   The following elements are needed to establish fraud against an accountant: (1) misrepresentation of the accountant's expert opinion, (2) scienter shown by either the accountant's knowledge of falsity or reckless disregard of the truth, (3) reasonable reliance by injured party, and (4) actual damages. Answer (a) is incorrect because contributory negligence of a third party is not a defense available for the accountant in cases of fraud. Answers (b) and (d) are incorrect because privity of contract is not a requirement for an accountant to be held liable for fraud.

29.   (a)   In the performance of an audit, a CPA has the duty to exercise the level of care, skill, and judgment expected of a reasonably prudent CPA under the circumstances. Answer (b) is incorrect because a CPA performing an audit must adhere to generally accepted **auditing** standards. It is the client's responsibility to prepare its financial statements in accordance with generally accepted accounting principles. Answer (c) is incorrect because an accountant is not liable for failure to detect fraud unless (1) a "normal" audit would have detected it, (2) the accountant by agreement has undertaken greater responsibility such as a defalcation audit, or (3) the wording of the audit report indicates greater responsibility for detecting fraud. Answer (d) is incorrect because a CPA **can** be liable for negligence, which is simply a failure to exercise due care in performing an audit. The CPA does not have to be grossly negligent or intentionally disregard generally accepted auditing standards to be held liable for negligence.

30.   (c)   A CPA will be liable for negligence when s/he fails to exercise due care. The standard for due care is guided by state and federal statutes, court decisions, contracts with clients, conformity with GAAS and GAAP, and the customs of the profession. Per the AICPA Professional Standards, AU 325, requires that if the auditor becomes aware of weaknesses in the design or operation of the internal control structure, these weaknesses, termed reportable conditions, be communicated to the audit committee of the client. Answer (a) is incorrect because a CPA is not normally liable for failure to detect fraud. Answer (b) is incorrect because including a negligence disclaimer in an engagement letter has no bearing on whether the CPA is negligent. Answer (d) is incorrect because generally a CPA is not required to inform a client's customers of embezzlements although knowledge of the embezzlements may adversely affect the CPA's audit opinion.

31.   (d)   A CPA's duty of due care is guided by the following standards: (1) state and federal statutes, (2) court decisions, (3) contract with the client, (4) GAAS and GAAP, and (5) customs of the profession. Therefore, failure to follow GAAS constitutes a breach of a CPA's duty of due care. Answer (a) is incorrect because issuance of an oral rather than written report does not necessarily constitute a failure to exercise due care. Answers (b) and (c) are incorrect because the standard of due care requires the CPA to exercise the skill and judgment of an ordinary, prudent accountant. An honest error of judgment or failure to provide money saving tax advice would not breach the duty of due care if the CPA acted in a reasonable manner.

32. **(a)** A CPA's liability for constructive fraud is established by the following elements: (1) misrepresentation of a material fact, (2) reckless disregard for the truth, (3) reasonable reliance by the injured party, and (4) actual damages. Gross negligence constitutes a reckless disregard for the truth. Answer (b) is incorrect because ordinary negligence is not sufficient to support a finding of constructive fraud. Answer (c) is incorrect because the liability for constructive fraud does not depend upon the identification of third-party users. Answer (d) is incorrect because the presence of the intent to deceive is needed to satisfy the scienter requirement for fraud. However, even in the absence of the intent to deceive, the CPA can be liable for constructive fraud based on reckless disregard of the truth.

B.2.   Common Law Liability to Third Parties (Nonclients)

33. **(b)** A foreseeable third party is someone not identified to the CPA, but who may be expected to receive the accountant's audit report and rely upon it. Even though this party is unknown to the CPA, the CPA is liable for gross negligence or fraud.

34. **(a)** Lack of privity can be a viable defense against third parties in a common law case of negligence or breach of contract. A client's creditor is not in privity of contract with the accountant. Answers (b) and (d) are incorrect because plaintiffs who are suing for fraud, constructive fraud, or gross negligence, which involves a reckless disregard for the truth, need not show privity of contract. Answer (c) is incorrect because the accountant's client is in privity of contract with the accountant due to their contractual agreement.

35. **(c)** Since Sanco was a foreseeable third party instead of an actually foreseen third party by the CPA, Sanco in most states cannot recover. Answer (a) is incorrect because most states do not extend liability to mere foreseeable third parties for simple negligence. Answer (b) is incorrect because the Ultramares decision limited liability to parties in privity of contract with the CPA. Answer (d) is incorrect because the client can recover for damages caused to it when negligence is established.

36. **(b)** Under the Ultramares rule, the accountant is held liable only to parties whose primary benefit the financial statements are intended. This generally means only the client or third-party beneficiaries who are in privity of contract with the accountant. Many courts have more recently departed from the Ultramares decision to allow foreseen third parties to recover from the accountant. However, those courts that adhere to the Ultramares rule do not expand liability to foreseen parties.

37. **(a)** In order to establish common law liability against an accountant based upon negligence, it must be proven that (1) the accountant had the duty to exercise due care, (2) the accountant breached the duty of due care, (3) damage or loss resulted, and (4) a causal relationship exists between the fault of the accountant and the resulting damages. The accountant may escape liability if due care can be established. The standard for due care is guided by state and federal statute, court decisions, contract with client, GAAS and GAAP, and customs of the profession. Although following GAAS does not automatically preclude negligence, it is strong evidence for the presence of due care. Answer (b) is incorrect because although the client may be aware of the misstatement, the auditor has the responsibility to detect the material misstatement if it is such that an average, reasonable accountant should have detected it. Answer (c) is incorrect because the client and Larson intended for the opinion and the financial statements to be used by purchasers. Therefore, a purchaser is considered a third-party beneficiary and is in privity of contract. Answer (d) is incorrect because the accountant need not know the specific identity of a third-party beneficiary to be held liable for negligence.

38. **(a)** To establish a CPA's liability for common law fraud, the following elements must be present: (1) misrepresentation of a material fact or the accountant's expert opinion, (2) scienter, shown by either an intent to mislead or reckless disregard for the truth, (3) reasonable or justifiable reliance by injured party, and (4) actual damages resulted. If Larson did not have actual or constructive knowledge of the misstatements, the scienter element would not be present and thus Larson would not be liable. Answers (b) and (d) are incorrect because neither contributory negligence of the client nor lack of privity of contract are defenses available to the accountant in cases of fraud. Answer (c) is incorrect because an accountant is generally liable to all parties defrauded. Therefore, the accountant need not have actual knowledge that the purchaser was an intended beneficiary.

B.3.   Statutory Liability to Third Parties—Securities Act of 1933

39. **(b)** The Securities Act of 1933 requires that a plaintiff need only prove that damages were incurred and that there was a material misstatement or omission in order to establish a prima facie case against a CPA. The Act does not require that the plaintiff prove that s/he relied on the financial information or that there was negligence or fraud present. The Securities Act of 1933 eliminates the necessity for privity of contract.

40. **(c)** Mac is a third party that the accountant knew would rely on the financial statements. Queen's financial statements contained material misstatements. Mac can recover by showing that the accountant was negligent in the audit. Mac also needs to establish that it did rely on the financial statements in order to recover from the accountant for the losses on Queen.

41. **(c)** Under the Securities Act of 1933, a CPA is liable to any third-party purchaser of registered securities for losses resulting from misstatements in the financial statements included in the registration statement. The plaintiff (purchaser) must establish that damages were incurred, and that the misstatements were material misstatements of facts.

Answer (a) is incorrect because under the 1933 Act it is not necessary for the purchaser of securities to prove "scienter," or knowledge of material misstatement, on the part of the CPA. Answers (b) and (d) are incorrect because under the 1933 Act, the plaintiff need not prove negligence on the part of the CPA or that there was reliance by the plaintiff on the financial statements included in the registration statement.

42. (c) In a Section 11 suit under the 1933 Act, the plaintiff may recover damages equal to the difference between the amount paid and the market value of the stock at the time of the suit. If the stock has been sold, then the damages are the difference between the amount paid and the sale price. Answer (a) is incorrect because damages of triple the original price are not provided for under this act. Answer (b) is incorrect because rescission is not a remedy under this act. Answer (d) is incorrect because if the shares have not been sold before the suit, then the court uses the difference between the amount paid and the market value at the time of the suit.

43. (b) Under Section 11 of the 1933 Act, if the plaintiff proves damages and the existence of a material misstatement or omission in the financial statements included in the registration statement, these are sufficient to win against the CPA unless the CPA can prove one of the applicable defenses. Due diligence is one of the defenses. Answer (a) is incorrect because contributory negligence is not a defense under Section 11. Answer (c) is incorrect because the purchaser need not prove privity with the CPA. Answer (d) is not correct because the purchaser needs to prove the above two elements but not scienter.

44. (d) To impose liability under Section 11 of the Securities Act of 1933 for a misleading registration statement, the plaintiff must prove the following: (1) damages were incurred, and (2) a material misstatement or omission was present in financial statements included in the registration statement. The plaintiff generally is not required to prove the defendant's intent to deceive nor must the plaintiff prove reliance on the registration statement.

45. (c) The proof requirements necessary to establish an accountant's liability under the Securities Act of 1933, Section 11 are as follows: (1) the plaintiff must prove damages were incurred, and (2) the plaintiff must prove there was a material misstatement or omission in financial statements included in the registration statement. To establish an accountant's liability under the Securities Exchange Act of 1934, Section 10(b), Rule 10b-5, the following elements must be proven: (1) damages resulted to the plaintiff in connection with the purchase or sale of a security in interstate commerce, (2) a material misstatement or omission existed in information released by the firm, (3) the plaintiff justifiably relied on the financial information, and (4) the existence of scienter. Because Sharp can prove that damages were incurred and that the statements contained material misstatements, Sharp is likely to prevail in a lawsuit under the Securities Act of 1933, Section 11. However, Sharp would be unable to prove justifiable reliance on the misstated information or the existence of scienter; thus, recovery under the Securities Exchange Act of 1934, Section 10(b), Rule 10b-5, is unlikely.

46. (d) If an accountant is negligent, s/he may have liability not only for a negligently performed audit but also for a negligently performed review when there were facts that should require the accountant to investigate further because of their suspicious nature. This is true even though a review is not a full audit.

B.4. Statutory Liability to Third Parties—Securities Exchange Act of 1934

47. (a) In order to establish a case under the antifraud provisions of Section 10(b) and Rule 10b-5 of the 1934 Act, the plaintiff has to prove that the defendant either had knowledge of the falsity in the registration statement or acted with reckless disregard for the truth. In addition, the plaintiff must show that the transaction involved interstate commerce so that there is a constitutional basis for using this federal law. S/he also must prove justifiable reliance. The plaintiff need not prove that s/he was an intended user of the false registration statement.

48. (d) Under Rule 10b-5 of Section 10(b) of the Securities Exchange Act of 1934, a CPA may be liable if s/he makes a false statement of a material fact or an omission of a material fact in connection with the purchase or sale of a security. Scienter is required which is shown by either knowledge of falsity or reckless disregard for the truth. Of the four answers given, lack of good faith best describes this scienter requirement. Answer (a) is incorrect because negligence is not enough under this rule. Answer (b) is incorrect because independence is not the issue under scienter. Answer (c) is incorrect because although due diligence can be a defense under Section 11 of the Securities Act of 1933, it is not the standard used under Section 10(b) of the Securities Exchange Act of 1934.

49. (b) Under Section 11 of the Securities Act of 1933, the CPA may be liable for material misstatements or omissions in certified financial statements. The CPA may escape liability by showing due diligence. This can often be proven by the CPA showing that s/he followed Generally Accepted Accounting Principles. There are not generally accepted fraud detection standards that the CPA can use as a defense.

50. (c) In a civil suit under Section 10(b) and Rule 10b-5, the damages are generally the difference between the amount paid and the market value at the time of suit, or the difference between the amount paid and the sales price if sold. Answer (a) is incorrect because recovery of the full original public offering price is not used as the damages. Answer (b) is incorrect because the above described monetary damages are used. Answer (d) is incorrect because punitive damages are not given under this rule.

C.1. Accountant's Working Papers

51. (b) In general, the accountant's workpapers are owned by the accountant. However, the CPA's ownership of the working papers is custodial in nature and the CPA is required to preserve confidentiality of the client's affairs. Normally, the CPA firm cannot allow transmission of information included in the working papers to third parties without the client's consent. This prevents a CPA firm from transferring workpapers to a purchaser of a CPA practice unless the client consents. Answer (c) is incorrect because the privileged communication rule does not exist at common law and has only been enacted by a few states. Additionally, the privileged communications rule only applies to communications which were intended to be privileged at the time of communication. Answer (a) is incorrect because working papers may be obtained by third parties without the client's consent when they appear to be relevant to issues raised in litigation (through a subpoena).

52. **(d)** The working papers are owned by the CPA, but the CPA must preserve confidentiality. They cannot be transmitted to another party unless the client consents or unless the CPA is required to under a valid court or governmental agency subpoena. Answers (a) and (c) are incorrect because these do not preserve the confidentiality. Answer (b) is incorrect because the CPA retains the working papers as evidence of the work done.

53. **(c)** Any of the partners of a CPA partnership can have access to the partnership's working papers. Third parties outside the firm need to have the client's consent or a legal subpoena.

C.2. Privileged Communications between Accountant and Client

54. **(d)** To preserve confidentiality, a CPA (including a CPA partnership) may not allow transmission of information in the working papers to other parties. Exceptions are consent of the client or the production of an enforceable subpoena. There are no exceptions for the IRS or the FASB, thus making answers (a), (b), and (c) incorrect.

55. **(d)** In a jurisdiction having an accountant-client privilege statute, the CPA generally may not turn over workpapers without the client's permission. It is allowable to do so, however, for use in a quality review under AICPA authorization or to be given to the state CPA society quality control panel. Answers (a), (b), and (c) are incorrect because the client would have to give permission for the CPA to turn over the confidential workpapers to the purchaser of the CPA practice, as well as to another CPA firm in regard to suspected tax return irregularities.

56. **(a)** Privileged communications between the accountant and client are recognized only in a few states. Therefore, if a state statute has been enacted creating such a privilege, Ivor will be able to prevent Thorp from testifying. Answer (b) is incorrect because federal law does not recognize accountant-client privileged communication. Answer (d) is incorrect because Ivor will not be able to prevent Thorp from testifying about the nature of the work performed in the audit unless a privileged communication statute has been enacted in that state. Answer (c) is incorrect because privileged communication does not exist at common law but must be created by state statute. Criminal law is based on common law and varies by state. However, as a general rule, in states that recognize accountant-client privilege, it can be claimed in both civil and criminal suits.

57. **(a)** The requirement is to identify the situation in which it is most likely that a violation of the profession's ethical standards would have occurred. Answer (a) is correct because independence is impaired if fees remain unpaid for professional services of the preceding year when the report on the client's current year is issued. Accordingly, no report should have been issued on the 2002 financial statements when fees for the 2001 audit were unpaid. Answer (b) is incorrect because CPAs may recommend a position description (ET 191) without violating the profession's ethical standards. Answer (c) is incorrect because a practice

may be purchased for a percentage of fees to be received. Answer (d) is incorrect because the Code of Professional Conduct does not prohibit arrangements with financial institutions to collect notes issued by a client in payment of professional fees.

58. **(b)** A CPA must not disclose confidential information of a client unless the client gives consent to disclose it to that third party. Answer (a) is incorrect because state agencies need a subpoena before the CPA must comply. Answer (c) is incorrect because the IRS does not have the right to force a CPA to turn over confidential information of a client without either the client's consent or an enforceable subpoena. Answer (d) is incorrect because although the CPA can use the client information to defend a lawsuit, the CPA is not normally requested to disclose confidential information to comply with generally accepted accounting principles.

E. Responsibilities of Auditors under Private Securities Litigation Reform Act

59. **(c)** Under the Private Securities Litigation Reform Act, the auditor should inform first the audit committee or the board of directors. Answer (a) is incorrect because the Securities Litigation Reform Act does not require that the SEC be informed unless after the audit committee or board of directors is informed, no remedial action is taken. Answer (b) is incorrect because the Justice Department need not be informed of this under the Private Securities Litigation Reform Act. Answer (d) is incorrect because inclusion of the problem in a note of the financial statements is not enough; the audit committee or the board of directors should be informed.

60. **(a)** The Private Securities Litigation Reform Act requires that auditors of firms covered under the Securities Exchange Act of 1934 establish procedures to do the items in (b), (c), and (d). Developing a comprehensive internal control system is not specifically mentioned, although part of this would be helpful in accomplishing the three stated items.

61. **(d)** Under the Private Securities Litigation Reform Act, an auditor who audits financial statements under the Federal Securities Exchange Act of 1934 is required to establish procedures to (1) detect illegal acts, (2) identify material related-party transactions, and (3) evaluate the ability of the firm to continue as a going concern.

62. **(b)** Under the Private Securities Litigation Reform Act, he is required to report this to the audit committee of the firm or the board of directors. Answer (a) is incorrect because he need not report this to the shareholders but to the audit committee or the board of directors. Answers (c) and (d) are incorrect because he is required under the Reform Act to inform the audit committee or the board of directors.

63. **(c)** The Private Securities Litigation Reform Act amends both the 1933 and 1934 Acts. Answer (a) is incorrect because it applies to the 1933 and 1934 Acts which apply to stocks sold on a stock exchange. Answers (b) and (d) are incorrect because this Reform Act applies to securities covered under the 1933 and 1934 Acts which may include both common and preferred stock of a publicly held corporation.

64.   (b)   Bran is liable under the Private Securities Litigation Reform Act for her proportionate fault of the liability since she acted unknowingly. Answer (a) is incorrect because Bran was determined to be 20% at fault. Answers (c) and (d) are incorrect because the Reform Act changes the joint and several liability for unknowing conduct and substitutes proportionate liability.

65.   (c)   The Sarbanes-Oxley Act of 2002 established a number of nonattest services that may not be performed by the auditor for a public company. Tax services may be performed but must be approved by the company's audit committee.

66.   (c)   The Sarbanes-Oxley Act established the Public Accounting Oversight Board to regulate CPA firms that audit public companies.

SOLUTIONS TO SIMULATION PROBLEMS

Simulation Problem 1

		Only Section 11 (A)	Only Section 10(b) (B)	Both (C)	Neither (D)
	The plaintiff security purchaser must allege or prove				
1.	Material misstatements were included in a filed document.	○	○	●	○
2.	A monetary loss occurred.	○	○	●	○
3.	Lack of due diligence by the CPA.	○	○	○	●
4.	Privity with the CPA.	○	○	○	●
5.	Reliance on the document.	○	●	○	○
6.	The CPA had scienter.	○	●	○	○

Explanation of solutions

1. **(C)** Section 11 of the Securities Act of 1933 imposes liability on auditors for misstatements or omissions of a material fact in certified financial statements or other information provided in registration statements. Similarly, under Section 10(b), Rule 10b-5 of the Securities Exchange Act of 1934, the plaintiff must prove there was a material misstatement or omission in information released by the firm such as audited financial statements. Actually, if the examiners wish to emphasize the phrase "filed document" in the question, then the answer would be (A). Under Section 10(b), the material misstatement may occur in information released by the firm rather than filed. Since the requirements state "...**must** allege or prove," technically the answer would be (D), since the plaintiff could allege or prove **omission** of material facts instead of material **misstatements** stated in the question. Therefore, this question depends upon how technical one decides to get on these points.

2. **(C)** Under both Section 11 of the 1933 Act and Section 10(b) of the 1934 Act, the plaintiff must allege or prove that s/he incurred monetary damages.

3. **(D)** Under Section 11 of the 1933 Act, the burden of proof is shifted to the defendant, accountant. The accountant may then defend him- or herself by establishing due diligence. The plaintiff does not have to show lack of due diligence by the CPA. Under Section 10(b), the plaintiff must prove scienter.

4. **(D)** The plaintiff does not have to prove that s/he was in privity with the CPA under either section.

5. **(B)** Under Section 10(b), the plaintiff must prove justifiable reliance on the financial information. This is not true under Section 11 in which the plaintiff need prove only the items in item **1.** and item **2.** discussed above.

6. **(B)** The plaintiff does have to prove that the CPA had scienter under Section 10(b) of the 1934 Act. Scienter is not needed under the 1933 Act, however.

Simulation Problem 2

		Yes	No
1.	The auditor is a cosigner of a client's checks.	●	○
2.	The auditor is a member of a country club which is a client.	○	●
3.	The auditor owns a large block of stock in a client but has placed it in a blind trust.	●	○
4.	The auditor placed her checking account in a bank which is her client. The account is fully insured by a federal agency.	○	●
5.	The client has not paid the auditor for services for the past two years.	●	○
6.	The auditor is leasing part of his building to a client.	●	○
7.	The auditor joins, as an ordinary member, a trade association which is also a client.	○	●
8.	The auditor has an immaterial, indirect financial interest in the client.	○	●

Explanation of solutions

1.   **(Y)** Since the auditor is a cosigner on a client's check, the auditor could become liable if the client defaults. This relationship impairs the auditor's independence.

2.   **(N)** Independence is not impaired because membership in the country club is essentially a social matter.

3.   **(Y)** An auditor may not hold a direct financial interest in a client. Putting it in a blind trust does not solve the impairment of independence.

4.   **(N)** If the auditor places his/her account in a client bank, this does not impair independence if the accounts are state or federally insured. If the accounts are not insured, independence is not impaired if the amounts are immaterial.

5.   **(Y)** The auditor's independence is impaired when prior years' fees for professional services remain unpaid for more than one year.

6.   **(Y)** The auditor's independence is impaired when s/he leases space out of a building s/he owns to a client.

7.   **(N)** When the auditor does not serve in management, s/he may join a trade association who is a client.

8.   **(N)** Independence is impaired for direct financial interests and material, indirect financial interests but not for immaterial, indirect financial interests.

MULTIPLE-CHOICE QUESTIONS (1-44)

1. A preliminary prospectus, permitted under SEC Regulations, is known as the
   a. Unaudited prospectus.
   b. Qualified prospectus.
   c. "Blue-sky" prospectus.
   d. "Red-herring" prospectus.

2. Under the Securities Exchange Act of 1934, which of the following types of instruments is excluded from the definition of "securities"?
   a. Investment contracts.
   b. Convertible debentures.
   c. Nonconvertible debentures.
   d. Certificates of deposit.

3. A tombstone advertisement
   a. May be substituted for the prospectus under certain circumstances.
   b. May contain an offer to sell securities.
   c. Notifies prospective investors that a previously-offered security has been withdrawn from the market and is therefore effectively "dead."
   d. Makes known the availability of a prospectus.

4. Under the Securities Act of 1933, which of the following statements most accurately reflects how securities registration affects an investor?
   a. The investor is provided with information on the stockholders of the offering corporation.
   b. The investor is provided with information on the principal purposes for which the offering's proceeds will be used.
   c. The investor is guaranteed by the SEC that the facts contained in the registration statement are accurate.
   d. The investor is assured by the SEC against loss resulting from purchasing the security.

5. Which of the following statements concerning the prospectus required by the Securities Act of 1933 is correct?
   a. The prospectus is a part of the registration statement.
   b. The prospectus should enable the SEC to pass on the merits of the securities.
   c. The prospectus must be filed after an offer to sell.
   d. The prospectus is prohibited from being distributed to the public until the SEC approves the accuracy of the facts embodied therein.

Items 6 and 7 are based on the following facts:

Sandy Corporation is considering the following issuances:

I. Notes with maturities of three months to be used for commercial purposes and having a total aggregate value of $500,000.
II. Notes with maturities of two years to be used for investment purposes and having a total aggregate value of $300,000.
III. Notes with maturities of two years to be used for commercial purposes and having a total aggregate value of $200,000.

6. Which of the above notes is(are) exempt securities and need not be registered under the Securities Act of 1933?
   a. I only.
   b. II only.

   c. I and III only.
   d. I, II, and III.

7. Which of the above notes is(are) subject to the antifraud provisions of the Securities Act of 1933?
   a. I only.
   b. II only.
   c. I and III only.
   d. I, II, and III.

8. Which of the following is **not** a security under the definition for the Securities Act of 1933?
   a. Any note.
   b. Bond certificate of interest.
   c. Debenture.
   d. All of the above are securities under the Act.

9. Which of the following requirements must be met by an issuer of securities who wants to make an offering by using shelf registration?

	Original registration statement must be kept updated	The offer must be a first-time issuer of securities
a.	Yes	Yes
b.	Yes	No
c.	No	Yes
d.	No	No

10. Which of the following securities would be regulated by the provisions of the Securities Act of 1933?
   a. Securities issued by not-for-profit, charitable organizations.
   b. Securities guaranteed by domestic governmental organizations.
   c. Securities issued by savings and loan associations.
   d. Securities issued by insurance companies.

11. Which of the following securities is exempt from registration under the Securities Act of 1933?
   a. Shares of nonvoting common stock, provided their par value is less than $1.00.
   b. A class of stock given in exchange for another class by the issuer to its existing stockholders without the issuer paying a commission.
   c. Limited partnership interests sold for the purpose of acquiring funds to invest in bonds issued by the United States.
   d. Corporate debentures that were previously subject to an effective registration statement, provided they are convertible into shares of common stock.

12. Universal Corp. intends to sell its common stock to the public in an interstate offering that will be registered under the Securities Act of 1933. Under the Act,
   a. Universal can make offers to sell its stock before filing a registration statement, provided that it does **not** actually issue stock certificates until after the registration is effective.
   b. Universal's registration statement becomes effective at the time it is filed, assuming the SEC does **not** object within twenty days thereafter.
   c. A prospectus must be delivered to each purchaser of Universal's common stock unless the purchaser qualifies as an accredited investor.

d. Universal's filing of a registration statement with the SEC does **not** automatically result in compliance with the "blue-sky" laws of the states in which the offering will be made.

13. If securities are exempt from the registration provisions of the Securities Act of 1933, any fraud committed in the course of selling such securities can be challenged by

	SEC	Person defrauded
a.	Yes	Yes
b.	Yes	No
c.	No	Yes
d.	No	No

14. Issuers of securities are normally required under the Securities Act of 1933 to file a registration statement with the Securities Exchange Commission before these securities are either offered or sold to the general public. Which of the following is a reason why the SEC adopted the registration statement forms called Form S-2 and Form S-3?
a. To require more extensive reporting.
b. To be filed along with Form S-1.
c. To reduce the burden that issuers have under the securities laws.
d. To reduce the burden of disclosure that issuers have for intrastate issues of securities.

15. Regulation D provides for important exemptions to registration of securities under the Securities Act of 1933. Which of the following would be exempt?

I. Issuance of $500,000 of securities sold in a twelve-month period to forty investors.
II. Issuance of $2,000,000 of securities sold in a twelve-month period to ten investors. The issuer restricts the right of the purchasers to resell for two years.

a. I only.
b. II only.
c. Both I and II.
d. Neither I nor II.

16. Pix Corp. is making a $6,000,000 stock offering. Pix wants the offering exempt from registration under the Securities Act of 1933. Which of the following provisions of the Act would Pix have to comply with for the offering to be exempt?
a. Regulation A.
b. Regulation D, Rule 504.
c. Regulation D, Rule 505.
d. Regulation D, Rule 506.

17. Eldridge Corporation is seeking to offer $7,000,000 of securities under Regulation D of the Securities Act of 1933. Which of the following is(are) true if Eldridge wants an exemption from registration under the Securities Act of 1933?

I. Eldridge must comply with Rule 506 of Regulation D.
II. These securities could be debentures.
III. These securities could be investment contracts.

a. I only.
b. I and II only.
c. II and III only.
d. I, II, and III.

18. An offering made under the provisions of Regulation A of the Securities Act of 1933 requires that the issuer
a. File an offering circular with the SEC.

b. Sell only to accredited investors.
c. Provide investors with the prior four years' audited financial statements.
d. Provide investors with a proxy registration statement.

19. Which of the following facts will result in an offering of securities being exempt from registration under the Securities Act of 1933?
a. The securities are nonvoting preferred stock.
b. The issuing corporation was closely held prior to the offering.
c. The sale or offer to sell the securities is made by a person other than an issuer, underwriter, or dealer.
d. The securities are AAA-rated debentures that are collateralized by first mortgages on property that has a market value of 200% of the offering price.

20. Regulation D of the Securities Act of 1933
a. Restricts the number of purchasers of an offering to thirty-five.
b. Permits an exempt offering to be sold to both accredited and nonaccredited investors.
c. Is limited to offers and sales of common stock that do not exceed $1.5 million.
d. Is exclusively available to small business corporations as defined by Regulation D.

21. Frey, Inc. intends to make a $2,000,000 common stock offering under Rule 505 of Regulation D of the Securities Act of 1933. Frey
a. May sell the stock to an unlimited number of investors.
b. May make the offering through a general advertising.
c. Must notify the SEC within fifteen days after the first sale of the offering.
d. Must provide all investors with a prospectus.

22. Under Regulation D of the Securities Act of 1933, which of the following conditions apply to private placement offerings? The securities
a. Cannot be sold for longer than a six-month period.
b. Cannot be the subject of an immediate unregistered reoffering to the public.
c. Must be sold to accredited institutional investors.
d. Must be sold to fewer than twenty nonaccredited investors.

23. Which of the following statements concerning an initial intrastate securities offering made by an issuer residing in and doing business in that state is correct?
a. The offering would be exempt from the registration requirements of the Securities Act of 1933.
b. The offering would be subject to the registration requirements of the Securities Exchange Act of 1934.
c. The offering would be regulated by the SEC.
d. The shares of the offering could **not** be resold to investors outside the state for at least one year.

24. Pix Corp. is making a $6,000,000 stock offering. Pix wants the offering exempt from registration under the Securities Act of 1933. Which of the following requirements would Pix have to comply with when selling the securities?
a. No more than thirty-five investors.

b. No more than thirty-five nonaccredited investors.
c. Accredited investors only.
d. Nonaccredited investors only.

25. Which of the following transactions will be exempt from the full registration requirements of the Securities Act of 1933?
a. All intrastate offerings.
b. All offerings made under Regulation A.
c. Any resale of a security purchased under a Regulation D offering.
d. Any stockbroker transaction.

26. Under Rule 504 of Regulation D of the Securities Act of 1933, which of the following is(are) required?

I. No general offering or solicitation is permitted.
II. The issuer must restrict the purchasers' right to resell the securities.

a. I only.
b. II only.
c. Both I and II.
d. Neither I nor II.

27. Dean, Inc., a publicly traded corporation, paid a $10,000 bribe to a local zoning official. The bribe was recorded in Dean's financial statements as a consulting fee. Dean's unaudited financial statements were submitted to the SEC as part of a quarterly filing. Which of the following federal statutes did Dean violate?
a. Federal Trade Commission Act.
b. Securities Act of 1933.
c. Securities Exchange Act of 1934.
d. North American Free Trade Act.

28. The Securities Exchange Commission promulgated Rule 10b-5 under Section 10(b) of the Securities Exchange Act of 1934. Which of the following is(are) purpose(s) of the Act?

	To rate securities so investors can choose more wisely	To encourage disclosure of information relevant to investors	To deter fraud involving securities
a.	No	No	Yes
b.	No	Yes	Yes
c.	Yes	Yes	Yes
d.	Yes	Yes	No

29. Integral Corp. has assets in excess of $4 million, has 350 stockholders, and has issued common and preferred stock. Integral is subject to the reporting provisions of the Securities Exchange Act of 1934. For its 2008 fiscal year, Integral filed the following with the SEC: quarterly reports, an annual report, and a periodic report listing newly appointed officers of the corporation. Integral did not notify the SEC of stockholder "short swing" profits; did not report that a competitor made a tender offer to Integral's stockholders; and did not report changes in the price of its stock as sold on the New York Stock Exchange. Under SEC reporting requirements, which of the following was Integral required to do?
a. Report the tender offer to the SEC.
b. Notify the SEC of stockholder "short swing" profits.
c. File the periodic report listing newly appointed officers.
d. Report the changes in the market price of its stock.

30. Which of the following factors, by itself, requires a corporation to comply with the reporting requirements of the Securities Exchange Act of 1934?
a. Six hundred employees.
b. Shares listed on a national securities exchange.
c. Total assets of $2 million.
d. Four hundred holders of equity securities.

31. The registration provisions of the Securities Exchange Act of 1934 require disclosure of all of the following information **except** the
a. Names of owners of at least 5% of any class of nonexempt equity security.
b. Bonus and profit-sharing arrangements.
c. Financial structure and nature of the business.
d. Names of officers and directors.

32. Under the Securities Act of 1933, which of the following statements is correct concerning a public issuer of securities who has made a registered offering?
a. The issuer is required to distribute an annual report to its stockholders.
b. The issuer is subject to the proxy rules of the SEC.
c. The issuer must file an annual report (Form 10-K) with the SEC.
d. The issuer is **not** required to file a quarterly report (Form 10-Q) with the SEC, unless a material event occurs.

33. Which of the following persons is **not** an insider of a corporation subject to the Securities Exchange Act of 1934 registration and reporting requirements?
a. An attorney for the corporation.
b. An owner of 5% of the corporation's outstanding debentures.
c. A member of the board of directors.
d. A stockholder who owns 10% of the outstanding common stock.

34. The Securities Exchange Commission promulgated Rule 10b-5 from power it was given the Securities Exchange Act of 1934. Under this rule, it is unlawful for any person to use a scheme to defraud another in connection with the

	Purchase of any security	Sale of any security
a.	Yes	Yes
b.	Yes	No
c.	No	Yes
d.	No	No

35. The antifraud provisions of Rule 10b-5 of the Securities Exchange Act of 1934
a. Apply only if the securities involved were registered under either the Securities Act of 1933 or the Securities Exchange Act of 1934.
b. Require that the plaintiff show negligence on the part of the defendant in misstating facts.
c. Require that the wrongful act must be accomplished through the mail, any other use of interstate commerce, or through a national securities exchange.
d. Apply only if the defendant acted with intent to defraud.

Items 36 through 38 are based on the following:

Link Corp. is subject to the reporting provisions of the Securities Exchange Act of 1934.

36. Which of the following situations would require Link to be subject to the reporting provisions of the 1934 Act?

	Shares listed on a national securities exchange	More than one class of stock
a.	Yes	Yes
b.	Yes	No
c.	No	Yes
d.	No	No

37. Which of the following documents must Link file with the SEC?

	Quarterly reports (Form 10-Q)	Proxy Statements
a.	Yes	Yes
b.	Yes	No
c.	No	Yes
d.	No	No

38. Which of the following reports must also be submitted to the SEC?

	Report by any party making a tender offer to purchase Link's stock	Report of proxy solicitations by Link stockholders
a.	Yes	Yes
b.	Yes	No
c.	No	Yes
d.	No	No

39. Which of the following events must be reported to the SEC under the reporting provisions of the Securities Exchange Act of 1934?

	Tender offers	Insider trading	Soliciting proxies
a.	Yes	Yes	Yes
b.	Yes	Yes	No
c.	Yes	No	Yes
d.	No	Yes	Yes

40. Adler, Inc. is a reporting company under the Securities Exchange Act of 1934. The only security it has issued is voting common stock. Which of the following statements is correct?

    a. Because Adler is a reporting company, it is **not** required to file a registration statement under the Securities Act of 1933 for any future offerings of its common stock.

    b. Adler need **not** file its proxy statements with the SEC because it has only one class of stock outstanding.

    c. Any person who owns more than 10% of Adler's common stock must file a report with the SEC.

    d. It is unnecessary for the required annual report (Form 10-K) to include audited financial statements.

41. Which of the following is correct concerning financial statements in annual reports (Form 10-K) and quarterly reports (Form 10-Q)?

    a. Both Form 10-K and Form 10-Q must be audited by independent public accountants and both must be filed with the SEC.

    b. Both Form 10-K and Form 10-Q must be audited by independent public accountants but neither need be filed with the SEC.

    c. Although both Form 10-K and Form 10-Q must be filed with the SEC, only Form 10-K need be audited by independent public accountants.

    d. Form 10-K must be audited by independent public accountants and must also be filed with the SEC; however, Form 10-Q need not be audited by independent public accountants nor filed with the SEC.

42. Burk Corporation has issued securities that must be registered with the Securities Exchange Commission under the Securities Exchange Act of 1934. A material event took place yesterday, that is, there was a change in the control of Burk Corporation. Which of the following statements is correct?

    a. Because of this material event, Burk Corporation is required to file with the SEC, Forms 10-K and 10-Q.

    b. Because of this material event, Burk Corporation is required to file Form 8-K.

    c. Burk Corporation need not file any forms with the SEC concerning this material event if the relevant facts are fully disclosed in the audited financial statements.

    d. Burk Corporation need not file any form concerning the material event if Burk Corporation has an exemption under Rules 504, 505, or 506 of Regulation D.

43. Loop Corp. has made a major breakthrough in the development of a micropencil. Loop has patented the product and is seeking to maximize the profit potential. In this effort, Loop can legally

    a. Require its retailers to sell only Loop's products, including the micropencils, and **not** sell similar competing products.

    b. Require its retailers to take stipulated quantities of its other products in addition to the micropencils.

    c. Sell the product at whatever price the traffic will bear even though Loop has a monopoly.

    d. Sell the product to its retailers upon condition that they do not sell the micropencils to the public for less than a stated price.

44. Robinson's pricing policies have come under attack by several of its retailers. In fact, one of those retailers, Patman, has instigated legal action against Robinson alleging that Robinson charges other favored retailers prices for its products which are lower than those charged to it. Patman's legal action against Robinson

    a. Will fail unless Patman can show that there has been an injury to competition.

    b. Will be sufficient if the complaint alleges that Robinson charged different prices to different customers and there is a reasonable possibility that competition may be adversely affected.

    c. Is groundless since one has the legal right to sell at whatever price one wishes as long as the price is determined unilaterally.

    d. Is to be tested under the Rule of Reason and if the different prices charged are found to be reasonable, the complaint will be dismissed.

SIMULATION PROBLEMS

Simulation Problem 1   (10 to 15 minutes)

Situation			
	Rule 504	Rule 506	Rule 505

You will have 15 questions based on the following information:

Butler Manufacturing Corp. planned to raise capital for a plant expansion by borrowing from banks and making several stock offerings. Butler engaged Weaver, CPA, to audit its December 31, 2007 financial statements. Butler told Weaver that the financial statements would be given to certain named banks and included in the prospectuses for the stock offerings.

In performing the audit, Weaver did not confirm accounts receivable and, as a result, failed to discover a material overstatement of accounts receivable. Also, Weaver was aware of a pending class action product liability lawsuit that was not disclosed in Butler's financial statements. Despite being advised by Butler's legal counsel that Butler's potential liability under the lawsuit would result in material losses, Weaver issued an unqualified opinion on Butler's financial statements.

In May 2008, Union Bank, one of the named banks, relied on the financial statements and Weaver's opinion in giving Butler a $500,000 loan.

Butler raised an additional $16,450,000 through the following stock offerings, which were sold completely:

- June 2008—Butler made a $450,000 unregistered offering of Class B nonvoting common stock under Rule 504 of Regulation D of the Securities Act of 1933. This offering was sold over one year to twenty accredited investors by general solicitation. The SEC was notified eight days after the first sale of this offering.
- September 2008—Butler made a $10,000,000 unregistered offering of Class A voting common stock under Rule 506 of Regulation D of the Securities Act of 1933. This offering was sold over one year to 200 accredited investors and thirty nonaccredited investors through a private placement. The SEC was notified fourteen days after the first sale of this offering.
- November 2008—Butler made a $6,000,000 unregistered offering of preferred stock under Rule 505 of Regulation D of the Securities Act of 1933. This offering was sold during a one-year period to forty nonaccredited investors by private placement. The SEC was notified eighteen days after the first sale of this offering.

Shortly after obtaining the Union loan, Butler began experiencing financial problems but was able to stay in business because of the money raised by the offerings. Butler was found liable in the product liability suit. This resulted in a judgment Butler could not pay. Butler also defaulted on the Union loan and was involuntarily petitioned into bankruptcy. This caused Union to sustain a loss and Butler's stockholders to lose their investments. As a result

- The SEC claimed that all three of Butler's offerings were made improperly and were not exempt from registration.
- Union sued Weaver for

  - Negligence
  - Common Law Fraud

- The stockholders who purchased Butler's stock through the offerings sued Weaver, alleging fraud under Section 10(b) and Rule 10b-5 of the Securities Exchange Act of 1934.

These transactions took place in a jurisdiction providing for accountant's liability for negligence to known and intended users of financial statements.

	Rule 504		
Situation		Rule 506	Rule 505

Items 1 through 5 are questions related to the June 2008 offering made under Rule 504 of Regulation D of the Securities Act of 1933. For each item, indicate your answer by choosing either Yes or No.

	Yes	*No*
1. Did the offering comply with the dollar limitation of Rule 504?	O	O
2. Did the offering comply with the method of sale restrictions?	O	O
3. Was the offering sold during the applicable time limit?	O	O
4. Was the SEC notified timely of the first sale of the securities?	O	O
5. Was the SEC correct in claiming that this offering was not exempt from registration?	O	O

		Rule 506	
Situation	Rule 504		Rule 505

Items 1 through 5 are questions related to the September 2008 offering made under Rule 506 of Regulation D of the Securities Act of 1933. For each item, indicate your answer by choosing either Yes or No.

	Yes	*No*
1. Did the offering comply with the dollar limitation of Rule 506?	○	○
2. Did the offering comply with the method of sale restrictions?	○	○
3. Was the offering sold to the correct number of investors?	○	○
4. Was the SEC notified timely of the first sale of the securities?	○	○
5. Was the SEC correct in claiming that this offering was not exempt from registration?	○	○

			Rule 505
Situation	Rule 504	Rule 506	

Items 1 through 5 are questions related to the November 2008 offering made under Rule 505 of Regulation D of the Securities Act of 1933. For each item, indicate your answer by choosing either Yes or No.

	Yes	*No*
1. Did the offering comply with the dollar limitation of Rule 505?	○	○
2. Was the offering sold during the applicable time limit?	○	○
3. Was the offering sold to the correct number of investors?	○	○
4. Was the SEC notified timely of the first sale of the securities?	○	○
5. Was the SEC correct in claiming that this offering was not exempt from registration?	○	○

Simulation Problem 2   (10 to 15 minutes)

Coffee Corp., a publicly held corporation, wants to make an $8,000,000 exempt offering of its shares as a private placement offering under Regulation D, Rule 506, of the Securities Act of 1933. Coffee has more than 500 shareholders and assets in excess of $1 billion, and has its shares listed on a national securities exchange.

Items 1 through 5 relate to the application of the provisions of the Securities Act of 1933 and the Securities Exchange Act of 1934 to Coffee Corp. and the offering. For each item, select from List II whether only statement I is correct, whether only statement II is correct, whether both statements I and II are correct, or whether neither statement I nor II is correct.

List II
A. I only
B. II only
C. Both I and II
D. Neither I nor II

		(A)	(B)	(C)	(D)
1.	I. Coffee Corp. may make the Regulation D, Rule 506, exempt offering.	○	○	○	○
	II. Coffee Corp., because it is required to report under the Securities Exchange Act of 1934, may **not** make an exempt offering.				
2.	I. Shares sold under a Regulation D, Rule 506, exempt offering may only be purchased by accredited investors.	○	○	○	○
	II. Shares sold under a Regulation D, Rule 506, exempt offering may be purchased by any number of investors provided there are **no** more than thirty-five nonaccredited investors.				

		(A)	(B)	(C)	(D)

3. I.   An exempt offering under Regulation D, Rule 506, must **not** be for more than $10,000,000.

II.   An exempt offering under Regulation D, Rule 506, has **no** dollar limit.

      (A) ○   (B) ○   (C) ○   (D) ○

4. I.   Regulation D, Rule 506, requires that all investors in the exempt offering be notified that for nine months after the last sale **no** resale may be made to a nonresident.

II.   Regulation D, Rule 506, requires that the issuer exercise reasonable care to assure that purchasers of the exempt offering are buying for investment and are **not** underwriters.

      (A) ○   (B) ○   (C) ○   (D) ○

5. I.   The SEC must be notified by Coffee Corp. within five days of the first sale of the exempt offering securities.

II.   Coffee Corp. must include an SEC notification of the first sale of the exempt offering securities in Coffee's next filed Quarterly Report (Form 10-Q).

      (A) ○   (B) ○   (C) ○   (D) ○

MULTIPLE-CHOICE ANSWERS

1. d ___ ___	11. b ___ ___	21. c ___ ___	31. a ___ ___	41. c ___ ___
2. d ___ ___	12. d ___ ___	22. b ___ ___	32. c ___ ___	42. b ___ ___
3. d ___ ___	13. a ___ ___	23. a ___ ___	33. b ___ ___	43. c ___ ___
4. b ___ ___	14. c ___ ___	24. b ___ ___	34. a ___ ___	44. b ___ ___
5. a ___ ___	15. c ___ ___	25. b ___ ___	35. c ___ ___	
6. a ___ ___	16. d ___ ___	26. d ___ ___	36. b ___ ___	
7. d ___ ___	17. d ___ ___	27. c ___ ___	37. a ___ ___	
8. d ___ ___	18. a ___ ___	28. c ___ ___	38. a ___ ___	
9. b ___ ___	19. c ___ ___	29. c ___ ___	39. a ___ ___	1st: ___/44= ___%
10. d ___ ___	20. b ___ ___	30. b ___ ___	40. c ___ ___	2nd: ___/44= ___%

MULTIPLE-CHOICE ANSWER EXPLANATIONS

A. Securities Act of 1933

1. **(d)** A preliminary prospectus is usually called a "red-herring" prospectus. The preliminary prospectus indicates that a registration statement has been filed but has not become effective.

2. **(d)** Securities include debentures, stocks, bonds, some notes, and investment contracts. The main idea is that the investor intends to make a profit on the investment through the efforts of others. A certificate of deposit is a type of commercial paper, not a security.

3. **(d)** A tombstone advertisement is allowed to inform potential investors that a prospectus for the given company is available. It is not an offer to sell or the solicitation of an offer to buy the securities. Answer (a) is incorrect because the tombstone ad informs potential purchasers of the prospectus and cannot be used as a substitute for the prospectus. Answer (b) is incorrect because it informs of the availability of the prospectus and cannot be construed as an offer to sell securities. Answer (c) is incorrect because the tombstone ad notifies potential purchasers of the prospectus. It does not notify that the securities have been withdrawn from the market.

4. **(b)** The registration of securities under the Securities Act of 1933 has as its purpose to provide potential investors with full and fair disclosure of all material information relating to the issuance of securities, including such information as the principal purposes for which the offering's proceeds will be used. Answer (a) is incorrect because information on the stockholders of the offering corporation is not required to be reported. Answer (c) is incorrect because the SEC does not guarantee the accuracy of the registration statements. Answer (d) is incorrect because although the SEC does seek to compel full and fair disclosure, it does not evaluate the securities on merit or value, or give any assurances against loss.

5. **(a)** If no exemption is applicable under the Securities Act of 1933, public offerings must be registered with the SEC accompanied by a prospectus. Answer (b) is incorrect because the SEC does not pass on nor rate the securities. Answer (c) is incorrect because the prospectus is given to prospective purchasers of the securities. Answer (d) is incorrect because the SEC does not pass on the merits or accuracy of the prospectus.

6. **(a)** Notes are exempt securities under the Securities Act of 1933 if they have a maturity of nine months or less and if they are also used for commercial purposes rather than investments. The actual dollar amounts in the question

are not a factor. The notes described in II are not exempt for two reasons; they have a maturity of two years and are used for investment purposes. The notes in III are not exempt because the maturity is two years even though they are for commercial purposes.

7. **(d)** Whether the securities are exempt from registration or not, they are still subject to the antifraud provisions of the Securities Act of 1933.

8. **(d)** The definition of a security is very broad under the Securities Act of 1933. The basic idea is that the investor intends to make a profit through the efforts of others rather than through his/her own efforts. Notes, bond certificates of interest, and debentures are all considered securities.

9. **(b)** If an issuer of securities wants to make an offering by using shelf registration, the actual issuance takes place over potentially a long period of time. Therefore, s/he must keep the original registration statement updated. There is no requirement that the offeror must be a first-time issuer of securities.

10. **(d)** Under the 1933 Act, certain securities are exempt. Although insurance and annuity contracts are exempt, securities issued by the insurance companies are not. Answer (a) is incorrect because securities of nonprofit organizations are exempt. Answer (b) is incorrect because securities issued by or guaranteed by domestic government organizations are exempt. Answer (c) is incorrect because securities issued by savings and loan associations are exempt.

11. **(b)** Securities exchanged for other securities by the issuer exclusively with its existing shareholders are exempt from registration under the 1933 Act as long as no commission is paid and both sets of securities are issued by the same issuer. Answer (a) is incorrect because nonvoting common stock is not exempted under the Act. The amount of the par value is irrelevant. Answer (c) is incorrect because although the securities of governments are themselves exempt, the limited partnership interests are not. Answer (d) is incorrect because no such exemption is allowed.

12. **(d)** Even though the issuer may comply with the Federal Securities Act of 1933, it must also comply with any applicable state "blue-sky" laws that regulate the securities at the state level. Answer (a) is incorrect because it is unlawful for the company to offer or sell the securities prior to the effective registration date. Answer (b) is incorrect because registration becomes effective on the twentieth day after filing unless the SEC issues a stop order. Answer (c) is incorrect because a prospectus is any notice, circular, advertisement, letter, or communication offering the security for sale. No general offering or solicitation is allowed under Rules 505 or 506 of Regulation D whether the purchaser is accredited or not.

13. **(a)** Even if the securities are exempt under the Securities Act of 1933, they are still subject to the antifraud provisions. Both the person defrauded and the SEC can challenge the fraud committed in the course of selling the securities.

14. **(c)** The SEC adopted the Forms S-2 and S-3 to decrease the work that issuers have in preparing registration statements by permitting them to give less detailed disclosure under certain conditions than Form S-1 which is the basic long form. Answer (a) is incorrect because these forms decrease, not increase, reporting required. Answer (b) is incorrect because when permitted, these forms are used instead of Form S-1 which is the standard long-form registration statement. Answer (d) is incorrect because the purpose of the forms was not directed at intrastate issues.

A.5.   Exempt Transactions or Offerings

15. **(c)** The issuance described in I is exempt because Rule 504 exempts an issuance of securities up to $1,000,000 sold in a twelve-month period to any number of investors. The issuer is not required to restrict the purchasers' resale. The issuance described in II is also exempt because Rule 505 exempts an issuance up to $5,000,000 sold in a twelve-month period. It permits sales to thirty-five unaccredited investors and to any number of accredited investors. Since there were only ten investors, this is met. The issuer also restricted the purchasers' right to resell for two years as required.

16. **(d)** Under Regulation D, Rule 504 exempts an issuance of securities up to $1,000,000 sold in a twelve-month period. Rule 505 exempts an issuance of up to $5,000,000 in a twelve-month period. So Rule 506 has to be resorted to for amounts over $5,000,000. Regulation A can be used only for issuances up to $1,500,000.

17. **(d)** When more than $5,000,000 in securities are being offered, an exemption from the registration requirements of the Securities Act of 1933 is available under Rule 506 of Regulation D. Securities under the Act include debentures and investment contracts.

18. **(a)** Under Regulation A of the 1933 Act, the issuer must file an offering circular with the SEC. Answer (b) is incorrect because the rules involving sales to unaccredited and accredited investors are in Regulation D, not Regulation A. Answer (c) is incorrect because although financial information about the corporation must be provided to offerees, the financial statements in the offering circular need not be audited. Answer (d) is incorrect because the issuer is not required to provide investors with a proxy registration statement under Regulation A.

19. **(c)** Sales or offers to sell by any person **other than** an issuer, underwriter, or dealer are exempt under the 1933 Act. Answer (a) is incorrect because the Act covers all types of securities including preferred stock. Answer (b) is incorrect because closely held corporations are not automatically exempt. Answer (d) is incorrect because debentures, as debt

securities, are covered under the Act even if they are highly rated or backed by collateral.

20. **(b)** Regulation D of the Securities Act of 1933 establishes three important exemptions in Rules 504, 505, and 506. Although Rules 505 and 506 have some restrictions on sales to nonaccredited investors, all three rules under Regulation D allow sales to both nonaccredited and accredited investors with varying restrictions. Answer (a) is incorrect because although Rules 505 and 506 allow sales to up to thirty-five nonaccredited investors, all three rules allow sales to an unlimited number of accredited investors. Answer (c) is incorrect because Rule 506 has no dollar limitation. Rule 505 has a $5,000,000 limitation in a twelve-month period and Rule 504 has a $1,000,000 limitation in a twelve-month period. Answer (d) is incorrect because Regulation D is not restricted to only small corporations.

21. **(c)** Under Rule 505 of Regulation D, the issuer must notify the SEC of the offering within fifteen days after the first sale of the securities. Answer (a) is incorrect because under Rule 505, the issuer may sell to an unlimited number of **accredited** investors and to thirty-five unaccredited investors. Answer (b) is incorrect because no general offering or solicitation is permitted. Answer (d) is incorrect because the accredited investors need not receive any formal information. The unaccredited investors, however, must receive a formal registration statement that gives a description of the offering.

22. **(b)** The private placement exemption permits sales of an unlimited number of securities for any dollar amount when sold to accredited investors. This exemption also allows sales to up to thirty-five nonaccredited investors if they are also sophisticated investors under the Act. Resales of these securities are restricted for two years after the date that the issuer sells the last of the securities. Answer (a) is incorrect because there is no such restriction of sale. Answer (c) is incorrect because sales may be made to an unlimited number of accredited investors and up to thirty-five nonaccredited investors. Answer (d) is incorrect because sales can be made to up to thirty-five nonaccredited investors.

23. **(a)** When the issuer is a resident of that state, doing 80% of its business in that state, and only sells or offers the securities to residents of the same state, the offering qualifies for an exemption under the 1933 Act as an intrastate issue. Answer (b) is incorrect as the offering also qualifies for an exemption under the 1934 Act. Therefore, as the offering is exempted from both the 1933 and 1934 Acts, it would not be regulated by the SEC. Answer (d) is incorrect because resales can only be made to residents of that state nine months after the issuer's last sale.

24. **(b)** Rule 506 permits sales to thirty-five unaccredited investors and to an unlimited number of accredited investors. The unaccredited investors must also be sophisticated investors (i.e., individuals with knowledge and experience in financial matters).

25. **(b)** Under Regulation A, an offering statement is required instead of the more costly disclosure requirements of full registration under the Securities Act of 1933. Answer (a) is incorrect because not all intrastate offerings are exempt. They must meet specified requirements to be exempt. Answer (c) is incorrect because many securities sold under Regulation D cannot be resold for two years. Answer (d) is incorrect because there is no such exemption for stockbroker transactions.

26. **(d)** Under Rule 504 of Regulation D, general offerings and solicitations are permitted. Also, the issuer need not restrict the purchasers' right to resell. Note that both I and II are requirements of Rules 505 and 506 of Regulation D.

B. Securities Exchange Act of 1934

27. **(c)** Under the Securities Exchange Act of 1934, issuers of securities registered under this Act must file quarterly reports (Form 10-Q) for the first three quarters of each fiscal year. The financial data in these may be unaudited; however, material misinformation is a violation of the 1934 Act. Answer (a) is incorrect—the Federal Trade Commission Act does not apply to this action. Answer (b) is incorrect because the Securities Act of 1933 applies to the initial issuance of securities and not to the secondary market of publicly traded securities. Answer (d) is incorrect because NAFTA is an agreement designed to promote free trade between the US, Mexico, and Canada.

28. **(b)** Purposes of Section 10(b) of the Securities Exchange Act of 1934 include deterring fraud in the securities industry and encouraging disclosure of relevant information so investors can make better decisions. The SEC does not rate the securities.

29. **(c)** Under the Securities Exchange Act of 1934, issuers of securities registered under this Act must file annual and quarterly reports with the SEC. The company must also file current reports covering certain material events such as a change in the amount of issued securities, a change in corporate control, or a change in newly appointed officers. Answer (a) is incorrect because a competitor's making a tender offer need not be reported to the SEC. Answer (b) is incorrect because Integral Corp. need not notify the SEC of stockholder "short swing profits." Answer (d) is incorrect because the company need not report information on the market price of its stock to the SEC. This market price information is already public information because the stock is traded on the New York Stock Exchange.

30. **(b)** Securities must be registered with the SEC if they are traded on any national securities exchange. Securities must also be registered if they are traded in interstate commerce where the corporation has more than $10 million in assets **and** 500 or more shareholders.

31. **(a)** The Securities Exchange Act of 1934 has registration provisions that require specified disclosures including bonus and profit-sharing arrangements, the financial structure and nature of this business, and names of officers and directors.

32. **(c)** Under the Federal Securities Act of 1933, which incorporates the filing requirements of the Federal Securities Exchange Act of 1934, the issuer must file with the SEC an annual report on Form 10-K. Answer (a) is incorrect because the issuer must file the annual report with the SEC but is not required to distribute it to its stockholders. Answer (b) is incorrect because the solicitation of proxies triggers certain proxy solicitation rules. Answer (d) is incorrect because it is the current report on Form 8-K that is filed when material events occur. The Form 10-Q is filed each of the first three quarters of each year and is known as the quarterly report.

33. **(b)** Under the 1934 Act, insiders include officers and directors of the corporation as well as owners of 10% or more of the stock of the corporation. Accountants, attorneys, and consultants can also be insiders subject to further regulation under the 1934 Act. Creditors, that is, owners of debentures are not considered to be insiders.

34. **(a)** Under Rule 10b-5, it is unlawful to use schemes to defraud in connection with the purchase **or** sale of any security. Note that this rule was made from powers given the SEC under the Securities Exchange Act of 1934, which applies to purchases in addition to sales of securities.

35. **(c)** For the Securities Exchange Act of 1934 to apply, including the antifraud provisions of Rule 10b-5, there must be shown a federal constitutional basis such as use of the mail, interstate commerce, or a national securities exchange. Answer (a) is incorrect because the antifraud provisions apply whether or not the securities had to be registered under either the 1933 Act or the 1934 Act. Answer (b) is incorrect because under Rule 10b-5, the plaintiff must prove more than negligence (i.e., either knowledge of falsity or reckless disregard for the truth in misstating facts). Answer (d) is incorrect because the plaintiff could recover if the defendant acted with reckless disregard for the truth.

36. **(b)** If the shares are listed on a national securities exchange, they are subject to the reporting provisions of the 1934 Act. There is no provision concerning a corporation owning more than one class of stock that by itself requires that it be subject to the reporting provisions of the 1934 Act.

37. **(a)** Under the 1934 Act, Link must file with the SEC annual reports (Form 10-K), quarterly reports (form 10-Q), current reports (Form 8-K) of certain material events, and proxy statements when proxy solicitations exist.

38. **(a)** When there is a proxy solicitation, Link must make a report of this to the SEC. Also, reports of tender offers to purchase securities need to be submitted to the SEC.

39. **(a)** A tender offer is a request to the shareholders of a given company to tender their shares for a stated price. If the tender offer was unsolicited, the corporation must report this to the SEC under the reporting provisions of the Securities Exchange Act of 1934. Also, trading by insiders such as officers, directors, or shareholders owning at least 10% of the stock of a corporation registered with the SEC must also be reported to the SEC under the 1934 Act. Likewise, solicitation of proxies must be reported to the SEC.

40. **(c)** Under the Securities Exchange Act of 1934 which applies if interstate commerce or the mail is used, any purchaser of more than 5% of a class of equity securities must file a report with the SEC. Answer (d) is incorrect because the required annual report (Form 10-K) must be certified by independent public accountants. Answer (a) is incorrect because each company must also comply with the filing requirements under the Securities Act of 1933. Answer (b) is incorrect because there is no exemption from filing proxy statements simply because the company has only one class of stock.

41. (**c**)   Forms 10-K (annual reports) and 10-Q (quarterly reports) must be filed with the SEC. Forms 10-K containing financial statements must be audited by independent public accountants. However, this is not true of Forms 10-Q which cover the first three fiscal quarters of each fiscal year of the issuer. The financial statements in 10-Qs must be reviewed by public accountants.

42. (**b**)   When certain material events take place, such as a change in corporate control, the corporation covered under the 1934 Act must file Form 8-K, a current report, with the SEC within four days after the material event occurs. Answer (a) is incorrect because Burk Corporation must file Forms 10-K, annual reports, and Forms 10-Q, quarterly reports, whether or not a material event has taken place. Answer (c) is incorrect because there is no such exception provided. Answer (d) is incorrect because Rules 504, 505, and 506 under Regulation D apply to the initial issuance of securities under the Securities Act of 1933 and do not relieve Burk Corporation from the filing requirements with the SEC under the 1934 Act.

43. (**c**)   Government creation of monopoly status through a patent is permissible under the antitrust law as long as no other anticompetitive conduct is involved. Loop Corporation is, therefore, entitled to sell the micropencil at a price determined by the normal competitive forces of supply and demand. A patent grants the holder a twenty-year exclusive right to market the product. The twenty years starts at the application date. For design patents, the period is fourteen years. Answer (a) is incorrect because prohibiting the retailers from selling competing products is an exclusive dealing agreement which is illegal where the effect is to substantially lessen competition in that market. Answer (b) is incorrect because tying agreements involving patented products are illegal per se if a substantial amount of business is involved. Answer (d) is incorrect because imposing a minimum resale price on the retailers is a vertical price fixing agreement which is also illegal per se.

44. (**b**)   The Robinson-Patman Act prohibits price discrimination in interstate commerce of commodities of like grade and quality. A violation of the act exists if the effect of the price discrimination may be to substantially lessen competition or tend to create a monopoly. Therefore, all that Patman must do to maintain a sufficient legal action is to allege that due to Robinson's pricing activities there is a reasonable possibility that competition may be adversely affected. Answer (a) is incorrect because Patman does not have to show actual injury to competition; Patman must show that such discrimination may substantially lessen competition. Answer (c) is incorrect because Congress purposely adopted the Robinson-Patman Act to prevent unilateral price determination which has the resultant effect of lessening competition or tending to create a monopoly. Answer (d) is incorrect because the reasonableness of the prices charged is irrelevant. The issue is whether the price discrimination may substantially lessen competition or tend to create a monopoly.

SOLUTIONS TO SIMULATION PROBLEMS

Simulation Problem 1

	Rule 504		
Situation		Rule 506	Rule 505

	Yes	No
1. Did the offering comply with the dollar limitation of Rule 504?	●	○
2. Did the offering comply with the method of sale restrictions?	●	○
3. Was the offering sold during the applicable time limit?	●	○
4. Was the SEC notified timely of the first sale of the securities?	●	○
5. Was the SEC correct in claiming that this offering was not exempt from registration?	○	●

Explanation of solutions

1. **(Y)** Rule 504 exempts an issuance of securities up to $1,000,000 sold in a twelve-month period to any number of investors. Butler made the offering for $450,000.

2. **(Y)** This offering involved a general solicitation which is now allowed under Rule 504 providing the solicitation is to only accredited investors.

3. **(Y)** This offering was sold over the applicable twelve-month period in Rule 504.

4. **(Y)** The SEC was sent notice of this offering eight days after the first sale. Under Rule 504, the SEC must be notified within fifteen days of the first sale of the securities.

5. **(N)** Even though this stock was sold by general solicitation, this is allowed under Rule 504.

		Rule 506	
Situation	Rule 504		Rule 505

	Yes	No
1. Did the offering comply with the dollar limitation of Rule 506?	●	○
2. Did the offering comply with the method of sale restrictions?	●	○
3. Was the offering sold to the correct number of investors?	●	○
4. Was the SEC notified timely of the first sale of the securities?	●	○
5. Was the SEC correct in claiming that this offering was not exempt from registration?	○	●

Explanation of solutions

1. **(Y)** Rule 506 allows private placement of an unlimited dollar amount of securities.

2. **(Y)** These securities were sold through private placement which is appropriate under Rule 506.

3. **(Y)** Rule 506 allows sales to up to thirty-five nonaccredited investors who are sophisticated investors with knowledge and experience in financial matters. It allows sales to an unlimited number of accredited investors.

4. **(Y)** The SEC was notified fourteen days after the first sale of the offering which is within the fifteen-day rule.

5. **(N)** Since this offering met the requirements discussed in 6. through 9. above, the SEC was incorrect.

			Rule 505
Situation	Rule 504	Rule 506	

	Yes	No
1. Did the offering comply with the dollar limitation of Rule 505?	○	●
2. Was the offering sold during the applicable time limit?	●	○
3. Was the offering sold to the correct number of investors?	○	●
4. Was the SEC notified timely of the first sale of the securities?	○	●
5. Was the SEC correct in claiming that this offering was not exempt from registration?	●	○

Explanation of solutions

1. (N) Rule 505 exempts an issuance of securities up to $5,000,000. Butler made a $6,000,000 unregistered offering of preferred stock.

2. (Y) The offering was sold during the applicable twelve-month period.

3. (N) Rule 505 permits sales to thirty-five nonaccredited investors. Butler went over this limit by selling to forty nonaccredited investors.

4. (N) The SEC was notified eighteen days after the first sale of this offering which is over the fifteen-day requirement.

5. (Y) This offering was not exempt from registration because it went over the $5,000,000 limit and the stock was sold to more than thirty-five nonaccredited investors.

Simulation Problem 2

Analysis

Situation

		(A)	(B)	(C)	(D)
1.	I. Coffee Corp. may make the Regulation D, Rule 506, exempt offering.	●	○	○	○
	II. Coffee Corp., because it is required to report under the Securities Exchange Act of 1934, may **not** make an exempt offering.				
2.	I. Shares sold under a Regulation D, Rule 506, exempt offering may only be purchased by accredited investors.	○	●	○	○
	II. Shares sold under a Regulation D, Rule 506, exempt offering may be purchased by any number of investors provided there are **no** more than thirty-five nonaccredited investors.				
3.	I. An exempt offering under Regulation D, Rule 506, must **not** be for more than $10,000,000.	○	●	○	○
	II. An exempt offering under Regulation D, Rule 506, has **no** dollar limit.				
4.	I. Regulation D, Rule 506, requires that all investors in the exempt offering be notified that for nine months after the last sale **no** resale may be made to a nonresident.	○	●	○	○
	II. Regulation D, Rule 506, requires that the issuer exercise reasonable care to assure that purchasers of the exempt offering are buying for investment and are **not** underwriters.				
5.	I. The SEC must be notified by Coffee Corp. within five days of the first sale of the exempt offering securities.	○	○	○	●
	II. Coffee Corp. must include an SEC notification of the first sale of the exempt offering securities in Coffee's next filed Quarterly Report (Form 10-Q).				

Explanation of solutions

1. (A) Statement I is correct because under Regulation D, Rule 506, the corporation may make a private placement of an unlimited amount of securities if it meets certain requirements. Statement II is incorrect. Coffee Corp. may still make an exempt offering under the Securities Act of 1933 even if it will be subject to the requirements of the Securities Exchange Act of 1934.

2. (B) Statement I is incorrect because up to thirty-five non-accredited investors may purchase shares under Regulation D, Rule 506, if they are sophisticated investors. Statement II is correct because Rule 506 does allow sales to up to thirty-five nonaccredited investors **assuming they are also** sophisticated investors, that is, individuals with knowledge and experience in financial matters, or individuals represented by people with such knowledge and experience.

3. (B) Statement I is incorrect and Statement II is correct for the same reason. Regulation D, Rule 506, has no dollar limit on the placement of securities as long as other requirements are met.

4. (B) Statement I is incorrect because Regulation D has no requirements putting restrictions on resales to nonresidents. Statement II is correct because Regulation D requires that the issuer take reasonable steps to see that purchasers of the exempt offering are not underwriters and are buying for investment.

5. (D) Statement I is incorrect. Under Regulation D, the SEC must be notified within fifteen days of the first sale of the securities. Statement II is incorrect because the Quarterly Reports do not require SEC notification of the first sale of exempt securities.

MULTIPLE-CHOICE QUESTIONS (1-57)

1. Carson Corp., a retail chain, asked Alto Construction to fix a broken window at one of Carson's stores. Alto offered to make the repairs within three days at a price to be agreed on after the work was completed. A contract based on Alto's offer would fail because of indefiniteness as to the
   a. Price involved.
   b. Nature of the subject matter.
   c. Parties to the contract.
   d. Time for performance.

2. On September 10, Harris, Inc., a new car dealer, placed a newspaper advertisement stating that Harris would sell ten cars at its showroom for a special discount only on September 12, 13, and 14. On September 12, King called Harris and expressed an interest in buying one of the advertised cars. King was told that five of the cars had been sold and to come to the showroom as soon as possible. On September 13, Harris made a televised announcement that the sale would end at 10:00 PM that night. King went to Harris' showroom on September 14 and demanded the right to buy a car at the special discount. Harris had sold the ten cars and refused King's demand. King sued Harris for breach of contract. Harris' best defense to King's suit would be that Harris'
   a. Offer was unenforceable.
   b. Advertisement was **not** an offer.
   c. Television announcement revoked the offer.
   d. Offer had **not** been accepted.

3. On June 15, Peters orally offered to sell a used lawn mower to Mason for $125. Peters specified that Mason had until June 20 to accept the offer. On June 16, Peters received an offer to purchase the lawn mower for $150 from Bronson, Mason's neighbor. Peters accepted Bronson's offer. On June 17, Mason saw Bronson using the lawn mower and was told the mower had been sold to Bronson. Mason immediately wrote to Peters to accept the June 15 offer. Which of the following statements is correct?
   a. Mason's acceptance would be effective when received by Peters.
   b. Mason's acceptance would be effective when mailed.
   c. Peters' offer had been revoked and Mason's acceptance was ineffective.
   d. Peters was obligated to keep the June 15 offer open until June 20.

4. Calistoga offers to sell her home to Drake for $300,000. Drake asks her if she would accept $250,000. Which of the following is true?
   a. Drake's response is mere inquiry; therefore, the $300,000 offer by Calistoga is still in force.
   b. Drake's response is a counteroffer effectively terminating the $300,000 offer and instigating an offer for $250,000.
   c. Drake's response is a rejection of the $300,000 offer, and there is no offer for $250,000 because it is too indefinite to be an offer.
   d. Because of ambiguity, both offers are terminated by operation of law.

5. Opal offered, in writing, to sell Larkin a parcel of land for $300,000. If Opal dies, the offer will

   a. Terminate prior to Larkin's acceptance only if Larkin received notice of Opal's death.
   b. Remain open for a reasonable period of time after Opal's death.
   c. Automatically terminate despite Larkin's prior acceptance.
   d. Automatically terminate prior to Larkin's acceptance.

6. On April 1, Fine Corp. faxed Moss an offer to purchase Moss' warehouse for $500,000. The offer stated that it would remain open only until April 4 and that acceptance must be received to be effective. Moss sent an acceptance on April 4 by overnight mail and Fine received it on April 5. Which of the following statements is correct?
   a. No contract was formed because Moss sent the acceptance by an unauthorized method.
   b. No contract was formed because Fine received Moss' acceptance after April 4.
   c. A contract was formed when Moss sent the acceptance.
   d. A contract was formed when Fine received Moss' acceptance.

7. On February 12, Harris sent Fresno a written offer to purchase Fresno's land. The offer included the following provision: "Acceptance of this offer must be by registered or certified mail, received by Harris no later than February 18 by 5:00 p.m. CST." On February 18, Fresno sent Harris a letter accepting the offer by private overnight delivery service. Harris received the letter on February 19. Which of the following statements is correct?
   a. A contract was formed on February 19.
   b. Fresno's letter constituted a counteroffer.
   c. Fresno's use of the overnight delivery service was an effective form of acceptance.
   d. A contract was formed on February 18 regardless of when Harris actually received Fresno's letter.

8. Kay, an art collector, promised Hammer, an art student, that if Hammer could obtain certain rare artifacts within two weeks, Kay would pay for Hammer's postgraduate education. At considerable effort and expense, Hammer obtained the specified artifacts within the two-week period. When Hammer requested payment, Kay refused. Kay claimed that there was no consideration for the promise. Hammer would prevail against Kay based on
   a. Unilateral contract.
   b. Unjust enrichment.
   c. Public policy.
   d. Quasi contract.

9. On September 27, Summers sent Fox a letter offering to sell Fox a vacation home for $150,000. On October 2, Fox replied by mail agreeing to buy the home for $145,000. Summers did not reply to Fox. Do Fox and Summers have a binding contract?
   a. No, because Fox failed to sign and return Summers' letter.
   b. No, because Fox's letter was a counteroffer.
   c. Yes, because Summers' offer was validly accepted.
   d. Yes, because Summers' silence is an implied acceptance of Fox's letter.

10. Wick Company made a contract in writing to hire Zake for five years for $150,000 per year. After two years, Zake asked Wick for a raise of $20,000 per year. Wick at first refused but agreed after Zake put on some pressure. After the fifth year, Zake left and Wick sued to get back the extra $20,000 per year for the last three years. Who wins?

    a. Zake, because Wick agreed to the raise.
    b. Zake, if the raise was agreed to in writing.
    c. Wick, even though Wick agreed to the raise.
    d. Wick, because Zake had applied some pressure to get the raise.

11. Grove is seeking to avoid performing a promise to pay Brook $1,500. Grove is relying on lack of consideration on Brook's part. Grove will prevail if he can establish that

    a. Prior to Grove's promise, Brook had already performed the requested act.
    b. Brooks' only claim of consideration was the relinquishment of a legal right.
    c. Brook's asserted consideration is only worth $400.
    d. The consideration to be performed by Brook will be performed by a third party.

12. Dunne and Cook signed a contract requiring Cook to rebind 500 of Dunne's books at $0.80 per book. Later, Dunne requested, in good faith, that the price be reduced to $.70 per book. Cook agreed orally to reduce the price to $.70. Under the circumstances, the oral agreement is

    a. Enforceable, but proof of it is inadmissible into evidence.
    b. Enforceable, and proof of it is admissible into evidence.
    c. Unenforceable, because Dunne failed to give consideration, but proof of it is otherwise admissible into evidence.
    d. Unenforceable, due to the statute of frauds, and proof of it is inadmissible into evidence.

13. In which of the following situations does the first promise serve as valid consideration for the second promise?

    a. A police officer's promise to catch a thief for a victim's promise to pay a reward.
    b. A builder's promise to complete a contract for a purchaser's promise to extend the time for completion.
    c. A debtor's promise to pay $500 for a creditor's promise to forgive the balance of a $600 liquidated debt.
    d. A debtor's promise to pay $500 for a creditor's promise to forgive the balance of a $600 disputed debt.

14. Which of the following will be legally binding despite lack of consideration?

    a. An employer's promise to make a cash payment to a deceased employee's family in recognition of the employee's many years of service.
    b. A promise to donate money to a charity on which the charity relied in incurring large expenditures.
    c. A modification of a signed contract to purchase a parcel of land.
    d. A merchant's oral promise to keep an offer open for sixty days.

15. Rail, who was sixteen years old, purchased an $800 computer from Elco Electronics. Rail and Elco are located in a state where the age of majority is eighteen. On several occasions Rail returned the computer to Elco for repairs.

Rail was very unhappy with the computer. Two days after reaching the age of eighteen, Rail was still frustrated with the computer's reliability, and returned it to Elco, demanding an $800 refund. Elco refused, claiming that Rail no longer had a right to disaffirm the contract. Elco's refusal is

    a. Correct, because Rail's multiple requests for service acted as a ratification of the contract.
    b. Correct, because Rail could have transferred good title to a good-faith purchaser for value.
    c. Incorrect, because Rail disaffirmed the contract within a reasonable period of time after reaching the age of eighteen.
    d. Incorrect, because Rail could disaffirm the contract at any time.

16. Green was adjudicated incompetent by a court having proper jurisdiction. Which of the following statements is correct regarding contracts subsequently entered into by Green?

    a. All contracts are voidable.
    b. All contracts are valid.
    c. All contracts are void.
    d. All contracts are enforceable.

17. All of the following are effective methods of ratifying a contract entered into by a minor **except**

    a. Expressly ratifying the contract after reaching the age of majority.
    b. Failing to disaffirm the contract within a reasonable time after reaching the age of majority.
    c. Ratifying the contract before reaching the age of majority.
    d. Ratifying the contract by implication after reaching the age of majority.

18. Under a personal services contract, which of the following circumstances will cause the discharge of a party's duties?

    a. Death of the party who is to receive the services.
    b. Cost of performing the services has doubled.
    c. Bankruptcy of the party who is to receive the services.
    d. Illegality of the services to be performed.

19. Which of the following would be unenforceable because the subject matter is illegal?

    a. A contingent fee charged by an attorney to represent a plaintiff in a negligence action.
    b. An arbitration clause in a supply contract.
    c. A restrictive covenant in an employment contract prohibiting a former employee from using the employer's trade secrets.
    d. An employer's promise **not** to press embezzlement charges against an employee who agrees to make restitution.

20. Which of the following, if intentionally misstated by a seller to a buyer, would be considered a fraudulent inducement to make a contract?

    a. Nonexpert opinion.
    b. Appraised value.
    c. Prediction.
    d. Immaterial fact.

21. If a buyer accepts an offer containing an immaterial unilateral mistake, the resulting contract will be

    a. Void as a matter of law.

b.   Void at the election of the buyer.
c.   Valid as to both parties.
d.   Voidable at the election of the seller.

22. If a person is induced to enter into a contract by another person because of the close relationship between the parties, the contract may be voidable under which of the following defenses?
a.   Fraud in the inducement.
b.   Unconscionability.
c.   Undue influence.
d.   Duress.

23. Long purchased a life insurance policy with Tempo Life Insurance Co. The policy named Long's daughter as beneficiary. Six months after the policy was issued, Long died of a heart attack. Long had failed to disclose on the insurance application a known preexisting heart condition that caused the heart attack. Tempo refused to pay the death benefit to Long's daughter. If Long's daughter sues, Tempo will
a.   Win, because Long's daughter is an incidental beneficiary.
b.   Win, because of Long's failure to disclose the pre-existing heart condition.
c.   Lose, because Long's death was from natural causes.
d.   Lose, because Long's daughter is a third-party donee beneficiary.

24. Petersen went to Jackson's home to buy a used car advertised in the newspaper. Jackson told Petersen that "it is a great car" and that "the engine had been overhauled a year ago." Shortly after he bought the car, Petersen began experiencing problems with the engine. When Jackson refused to refund his money, Petersen sued for fraud based on it was not a "great car" and also based on the fact, as learned later, the overhaul was done thirteen months ago, not a year. Will Petersen win his case?
a.   Yes, Jackson's statement that "it is a great car" is actionable fraud.
b.   Yes, Jackson's statement about the overhaul is actionable fraud.
c.   Yes, both the statement that "it is a great car" and the statement about the overhaul are actionable fraud.
d.   No.

25. A building subcontractor submitted a bid for construction of a portion of a high-rise office building. The bid contained material computational errors. The general contractor accepted the bid with knowledge of the errors. Which of the following statements best represents the subcontractor's liability?
a.   Not liable because the contractor knew of the errors.
b.   Not liable because the errors were a result of gross negligence.
c.   Liable because the errors were unilateral.
d.   Liable because the errors were material.

26. Maco, Inc. and Kent contracted for Kent to provide Maco certain consulting services at an hourly rate of $20. Kent's normal hourly rate was $90 per hour, the fair market value of the services. Kent agreed to the $20 rate because Kent was having serious financial problems. At the time the

agreement was negotiated, Maco was aware of Kent's financial condition and refused to pay more than $20 per hour for Kent's services. Kent has now sued to rescind the contract with Maco, claiming duress by Maco during the negotiations. Under the circumstances, Kent will
a.   Win, because Maco refused to pay the fair market value of Kent's services.
b.   Win, because Maco was aware of Kent's serious financial problems.
c.   Lose, because Maco's actions did **not** constitute duress.
d.   Lose, because Maco **cannot** prove that Kent, at the time, had **no** other offers to provide consulting services.

27. To prevail in a common law action for fraud in the inducement, a plaintiff must prove that the
a.   Defendant was an expert with regard to the misrepresentations.
b.   Defendant made the misrepresentations with knowledge of their falsity and with an intention to deceive.
c.   Misrepresentations were in writing.
d.   Plaintiff was in a fiduciary relationship with the defendant.

28. Under the UCC Sales Article, a plaintiff who proves fraud in the formation of a contract may
a.   Elect to rescind the contract and need **not** return the consideration received from the other party.
b.   Be entitled to rescind the contract and sue for damages resulting from the fraud.
c.   Be entitled to punitive damages provided physical injuries resulted from the fraud.
d.   Rescind the contract even if there was **no** reliance on the fraudulent statement.

29. On June 1, 2001, Decker orally guaranteed the payment of a $5,000 note Decker's cousin owed Baker. Decker's agreement with Baker provided that Decker's guaranty would terminate in eighteen months. On June 3, 2001, Baker wrote Decker confirming Decker's guaranty. Decker did not object to the confirmation. On August 23, 2001, Decker's cousin defaulted on the note and Baker demanded that Decker honor the guaranty. Decker refused. Which of the following statements is correct?
a.   Decker is liable under the oral guaranty because Decker did **not** object to Baker's June 3 letter.
b.   Decker is **not** liable under the oral guaranty because it expired more than one year after June 1.
c.   Decker is liable under the oral guaranty because Baker demanded payment within one year of the date the guaranty was given.
d.   Decker is **not** liable under the oral guaranty because Decker's promise was **not** in writing.

30. Nolan agreed orally with Train to sell Train a house for $100,000. Train sent Nolan a signed agreement and a downpayment of $10,000. Nolan did not sign the agreement, but allowed Train to move into the house. Before closing, Nolan refused to go through with the sale. Train sued Nolan to compel specific performance. Under the provisions of the Statute of Frauds
a.   Train will win because Train signed the agreement and Nolan did **not** object.

b.   Train will win because Train made a downpayment and took possession.

c.   Nolan will win because Nolan did **not** sign the agreement.

d.   Nolan will win because the house was worth more than $500.

31.   Cherry contracted orally to purchase Picks Company for $1,500,000 if it is profitable for one full year after the making of the oral contract. An auditor would be brought in at the end of the year to verify this. Even though the company turns out to be profitable during the upcoming year, Cherry refuses to go through with the contract, claiming that it was unenforceable because it was not in writing. Is Cherry correct?

a.   Yes, because the contract could not be completed within one year.

b.   Yes, because the contract was for $500 or more.

c.   No, because the company was profitable as agreed for one year.

d.   No, because Picks Company relied on Cherry's promise.

32.   Which of the following statements is true with regard to the Statute of Frauds?

a.   All contracts involving consideration of more than $500 must be in writing.

b.   The written contract must be signed by all parties.

c.   The Statute of Frauds applies to contracts that can be fully performed within one year from the date they are made.

d.   The contract terms may be stated in more than 1 document.

33.   Carson agreed orally to repair Ives' rare book for $450. Before the work was started, Ives asked Carson to perform additional repairs to the book and agreed to increase the contract price to $650. After Carson completed the work, Ives refused to pay and Carson sued. Ives' defense was based on the Statute of Frauds. What total amount will Carson recover?

a. $0

b. $200

c. $450

d. $650

34.   Landry Company contracted orally with Newell to pay her $50,000 for the completion of an ethics audit of Landry Company. The report is to span a period of time of at least ten months and is due in fourteen months from now. Newell has agreed orally to perform the ethics audit and says that she will begin within three months, noting that even if she delays the full three months, she will have the report ready within the fourteen-month deadline. Does this contract fall under the Statute of Frauds?

a.   Yes, because the contract is for $500 or more.

b.   Yes, because the deadline for the contract is over one year.

c.   No, despite the due date of fourteen months.

d.   No, because both parties waived the Statute of Frauds by their oral agreement.

35.   Rogers and Lennon entered into a written computer consulting agreement that required Lennon to provide certain weekly reports to Rogers. The agreement also stated that Lennon would provide the computer equipment necessary to perform the services, and that Rogers' computer would not be used. As the parties were executing the agreement, they orally agreed that Lennon could use Rogers' computer. After executing the agreement, Rogers and Lennon orally agreed that Lennon would report on a monthly, rather than weekly, basis. The parties now disagree on Lennon's right to use Rogers' computer and how often Lennon must report to Rogers. In the event of a lawsuit between the parties, the parol evidence rule will

a.   Not apply to any of the parties' agreements because the consulting agreement did **not** have to be in writing.

b.   Not prevent Lennon from proving the parties' oral agreement that Lennon could use Rogers' computer.

c.   Not prevent the admission into evidence of testimony regarding Lennon's right to report on a monthly basis.

d.   Not apply to the parties' agreement to allow Lennon to use Rogers' computer because it was contemporaneous with the written agreement.

36.   Where the parties have entered into a written contract intended as the final expression of their agreement, which of the following agreements will be admitted into evidence because they are **not** prohibited by the parol evidence rule?

	Subsequent oral agreements	Prior written agreements
a.	Yes	Yes
b.	Yes	No
c.	No	Yes
d.	No	No

37.   In negotiations with Andrews for the lease of Kemp's warehouse, Kemp orally agreed to pay one-half of the cost of the utilities. The written lease, later prepared by Kemp's attorney, provided that Andrews pay all of the utilities. Andrews failed to carefully read the lease and signed it. When Kemp demanded that Andrews pay all of the utilities, Andrews refused, claiming that the lease did not accurately reflect the oral agreement. Andrews also learned that Kemp intentionally misrepresented the condition of the structure of the warehouse during the negotiations between the parties. Andrews sued to rescind the lease and intends to introduce evidence of the parties' oral agreement about sharing the utilities and the fraudulent statements made by Kemp. The parol evidence rule will prevent the admission of evidence concerning

	Oral agreement regarding who pays the utilities	Fraudulent statements by Kemp
a.	Yes	Yes
b.	No	Yes
c.	Yes	No
d.	No	No

38.   Joan Silver had viewed some land that she wished to purchase. It was offered for sale by Daniel Tweney over the Internet for $200,000. Silver believes this to be a good deal for her and thus wishes to purchase it. Silver and Tweney have communicated online and wish to make a contract for the land over the Internet. Which of the following statements is(are) correct?

I.   Because this contract is covered by the Statute of Frauds, this contract cannot be accomplished over the Internet.

II. Because of the parol evidence rule, this contract cannot be completed over the Internet.
III. Because this contract is covered by the Uniform Commerical Code, it may not be accomplished over the Internet.

  a. Only I is correct.
  b. I and II only are correct.
  c. I and III only are correct.
  d. Neither I, II, nor III is correct.

39. Generally, which of the following contract rights are assignable?

	Option contract rights	*Malpractice insurance policy rights*
a.	Yes	Yes
b.	Yes	No
c.	No	Yes
d.	No	No

40. One of the criteria for a valid assignment of a sales contract to a third party is that the assignment must
  a. Be supported by adequate consideration from the assignee.
  b. Be in writing and signed by the assignor.
  c. Not materially increase the other party's risk or duty.
  d. Not be revocable by the assignor.

Items 41 and 42 are based on the following:
  Egan contracted with Barton to buy Barton's business. The contract provided that Egan would pay the business debts Barton owed Ness and that the balance of the purchase price would be paid to Barton over a ten-year period. The contract also required Egan to take out a decreasing term life insurance policy naming Barton and Ness as beneficiaries to ensure that the amounts owed Barton and Ness would be paid if Egan died.

41. Barton's contract rights were assigned to Vim, and Egan was notified of the assignment. Despite the assignment, Egan continued making payments to Barton. Egan died before completing payment and Vim sued Barton for the insurance proceeds and the other payments on the purchase price received by Barton after the assignment. To which of the following is Vim entitled?

	Payments on purchase price	*Insurance proceeds*
a.	No	Yes
b.	No	No
c.	Yes	Yes
d.	Yes	No

42. Which of the following would describe Ness' status under the contract and insurance policy?

	Contract	*Insurance policy*
a.	Donee beneficiary	Donee beneficiary
b.	Donee beneficiary	Creditor beneficiary
c.	Creditor beneficiary	Donee beneficiary
d.	Creditor beneficiary	Creditor beneficiary

43. Your client, Bugle, owns a parking lot near downtown San Francisco. One day Bugle is excited because he learns that Fargo, who owns a parking lot next door, has made a contract with ABC Company to sell her land. ABC Company can then construct a building that will contain several nice professional offices. Bugle figures that he will charge more for his parking. He later discovers that the contract fell

through. He says that when he finds out who breached the contract, he will sue that party for lost profits that he would have earned. Which of the following is correct?
  a. If Fargo was the one who breached the contract, Bugle may sue her if ABC had already made some payments on the contract.
  b. If ABC was the party who breached, ABC is liable to Bugle.
  c. Bugle may sue either party, and the nonbreaching party may then recover from the breaching party.
  d. Bugle has no legal rights against either party.

44. Baxter, Inc. and Globe entered into a contract. After receiving valuable consideration from Clay, Baxter assigned its rights under the contract to Clay. In which of the following circumstances would Baxter **not** be liable to Clay?
  a. Clay released Globe.
  b. Globe paid Baxter.
  c. Baxter released Globe.
  d. Baxter breached the contract.

45. Mackay paid Manus $1,000 to deliver a painting to Mackay's friend Mann. When they met and signed the contract, Mackay said she wanted the painting delivered as soon as possible because it was a gift for Mann's birthday. Several months have passed without the delivery. Mann can maintain lawsuits against which parties to get the painting?
  a. Manus only.
  b. Mackay only.
  c. Manus, but only if he also brings suit against Mackay.
  d. Manus or Mackay at Mann's option.

46. Ferco, Inc. claims to be a creditor beneficiary of a contract between Bell and Allied Industries, Inc. Allied is indebted to Ferco. The contract between Bell and Allied provides that Bell is to purchase certain goods from Allied and pay the purchase price directly to Ferco until Allied's obligation is satisfied. Without justification, Bell failed to pay Ferco and Ferco sued Bell. Ferco will
  a. Not prevail, because Ferco lacked privity of contract with either Bell or Allied.
  b. Not prevail, because Ferco did **not** give any consideration to Bell.
  c. Prevail, because Ferco was an intended beneficiary of the contract between Allied and Bell.
  d. Prevail, provided Ferco was aware of the contract between Bell and Allied at the time the contract was entered into.

47. Parc hired Glaze to remodel and furnish an office suite. Glaze submitted plans that Parc approved. After completing all the necessary construction and painting, Glaze purchased minor accessories that Parc rejected because they did not conform to the plans. Parc refused to allow Glaze to complete the project and refused to pay Glaze any part of the contract price. Glaze sued for the value of the work performed. Which of the following statements is correct?
  a. Glaze will lose because Glaze breached the contract by **not** completing performance.
  b. Glaze will win because Glaze substantially performed and Parc prevented complete performance.
  c. Glaze will lose because Glaze materially breached the contract by buying the accessories.
  d. Glaze will win because Parc committed anticipatory breach.

48. Which of the following types of conditions affecting performance may validly be present in contracts?

	Conditions precedent	Conditions subsequent	Current conditions
a.	Yes	Yes	Yes
b.	Yes	Yes	No
c.	Yes	No	Yes
d.	No	Yes	Yes

49. Which of the following actions if taken by one party to a contract generally will discharge the performance required of the other party to the contract?
a. Material breach of the contract.
b. Delay in performance.
c. Tender.
d. Assignment of rights.

50. Which of the following actions will result in the discharge of a party to a contract?

	Prevention of performance	Accord and satisfaction
a.	Yes	Yes
b.	Yes	No
c.	No	Yes
d.	No	No

51. To cancel a contract and to restore the parties to their original positions before the contract, the parties should execute a
a. Novation.
b. Release.
c. Rescission.
d. Revocation.

52. Kaye contracted to sell Hodges a building for $310,000. The contract required Hodges to pay the entire amount at closing. Kaye refused to close the sale of the building. Hodges sued Kaye. To what relief is Hodges entitled?
a. Punitive damages and compensatory damages.
b. Specific performance and compensatory damages.
c. Consequential damages or punitive damages.
d. Compensatory damages or specific performance.

53. Ames Construction Co. contracted to build a warehouse for White Corp. The construction specifications required Ames to use Ace lighting fixtures. Inadvertently, Ames installed Perfection lighting fixtures which are of slightly lesser quality than Ace fixtures, but in all other respects meet White's needs. Which of the following statements is correct?
a. White's recovery will be limited to monetary damages because Ames' breach of the construction contract was **not** material.
b. White will **not** be able to recover any damages from Ames because the breach was inadvertent.
c. Ames did not breach the construction contract because the Perfection fixtures were substantially as good as the Ace fixtures.
d. Ames must install Ace fixtures or White will **not** be obligated to accept the warehouse.

54. Master Mfg., Inc. contracted with Accur Computer Repair Corp. to maintain Master's computer system. Master's manufacturing process depends on its computer system operating properly at all times. A liquidated damages clause in the contract provided that Accur pay $1,000 to Master for each day that Accur was late responding to a service request.

On January 12, Accur was notified that Master's computer system failed. Accur did not respond to Master's service request until January 15. If Master sues Accur under the liquidated damage provision of the contract, Master will
a. Win, unless the liquidated damage provision is determined to be a penalty.
b. Win, because under all circumstances liquidated damage provisions are enforceable.
c. Lose, because Accur's breach was **not** material.
d. Lose, because liquidated damage provisions violate public policy.

55. Nagel and Fields entered into a contract in which Nagel was obligated to deliver certain goods to Fields by September 10. On September 3, Nagel told Fields that Nagel had no intention of delivering the goods required by the contract. Prior to September 10, Fields may successfully sue Nagel under the doctrine of
a. Promissory estoppel.
b. Accord and satisfaction.
c. Anticipatory repudiation.
d. Substantial performance.

56. Maco Corp. contracted to sell 1,500 bushels of potatoes to LBC Chips. The contract did not refer to any specific supply source for the potatoes. Maco intended to deliver potatoes grown on its farms. An insect infestation ruined Maco's crop but not the crops of other growers in the area. Maco failed to deliver the potatoes to LBC. LBC sued Maco for breach of contract. Under the circumstances, Maco will
a. Lose, because it could have purchased potatoes from other growers to deliver to LBC.
b. Lose, unless it can show that the purchase of substitute potatoes for delivery to LBC would make the contract unprofitable.
c. Win, because the infestation was an act of nature that could **not** have been anticipated by Maco.
d. Win, because both Maco and LBC are assumed to accept the risk of a crop failure.

57. Ordinarily, in an action for breach of a construction contract, the statute of limitations time period would be computed from the date the
a. Contract is negotiated.
b. Contract is breached.
c. Construction is begun.
d. Contract is signed.

SIMULATION PROBLEMS

Simulation Problem 1   (5 to 10 minutes)

Consideration

For each of the numbered statements or groups of statements select either A, B, or C.

List

A.   Both parties have given consideration legally sufficient to support a contract.

B.   One of the parties has **not** given consideration legally sufficient to support a contract.
     The promise, agreement, or transaction is generally **not** enforceable.

C.   One of the parties has **not** given consideration legally sufficient to support a contract.
     However, the promise, agreement, or transaction **is** generally enforceable.

	(A)	(B)	(C)
1. Party S feels a moral obligation because Party F let S stay in his place for free when S attended college. S now promises to pay F for the past kindness.	O	O	O
2. F agrees to deliver all of the sugar that Company S will need in her business for the following year. S agrees to purchase it at the market price.	O	O	O
3. F does not smoke for one year pursuant to S's agreement to pay F $200 if she does not smoke for one year.	O	O	O
4. F dies leaving a valid will which gives S $100,000.	O	O	O
5. F is an auditor of XYZ Company. S is a potential investor of XYZ and offers to pay F $1,000 if F performs a professional, quality audit of XYZ Company. The $1,000 is in addition to the fee F will get from XYZ. F does perform a professional, quality audit.	O	O	O
6. F had agreed, in writing, to work for S for five years for $100,000 per year. After two years, F asks for a 20% raise. S first agrees then later changes his mind. F, while not agreeing to additional duties or changing his position, wants to enforce the raise in salary.	O	O	O
7. S promised to pay F $1,000 if he crosses the Golden Gate Bridge on his hands and knees. F does so.	O	O	O
8. F promised to pay S $200 for a computer worth $2,000. S agreed to the deal.	O	O	O
9. F agreed to purchase all of the parts from S that S can produce in her business for the next six months. S also agreed.	O	O	O
10. S agreed to accept $1,000 from F for a $1,500 debt that is not disputed. S now wants the additional $500. Focus on the agreement to accept the lesser amount.	O	O	O
11. S agreed to accept $1,000 from F for a debt that S claims is $1,500 but F in good faith claims is $800. F agreed to the $1,000 initially, then decides he will pay only $800. Focus on the enforceability of the agreement for $1,000.	O	O	O
12. S agreed to donate $100 to F, a public charity.	O	O	O

Simulation Problem 2   (10 to 15 minutes)

Situation			
	Contractual Relationship	Assignment	Memo

On December 15, Blake Corp. telephoned Reach Consultants, Inc. and offered to hire Reach to design a security system for Blake's research department. The work would require two years to complete. Blake offered to pay a fee of $100,000 but stated that the offer must be accepted in writing, and the acceptance received by Blake no later than December 20.

On December 20, Reach faxed a written acceptance to Blake. Blake's offices were closed on December 20 and Reach's fax was not seen until December 21.

Reach's acceptance contained the following language:

"We accept your $1,000,000 offer. Weaver has been assigned $5,000 of the fee as payment for sums owed Weaver by Reach. Payment of this amount should be made directly to Weaver."

On December 22, Blake sent a signed memo to Reach rejecting Reach's December 20 fax but offering to hire Reach for a $75,000 fee. Reach telephoned Blake on December 23 and orally accepted Blake's December 22 offer.

Situation	Contractual Relationship	Assignment	Memo

Items 1 through 7 relate to whether a contractual relationship exists between Blake and Reach. For each item, determine whether the statement is True or False.

		True	*False*
1.	Blake's December 15 offer had to be in writing to be a legitimate offer.	○	○
2.	Reach's December 20 fax was an improper method of acceptance.	○	○
3.	Reach's December 20 fax was effective when sent.	○	○
4.	Reach's acceptance was invalid because it was received after December 20.	○	○
5.	Blake's receipt of Reach's acceptance created a voidable contract.	○	○
6.	If Reach had rejected the original offer by telephone on December 17, he could not validly accept the offer later.	○	○
7.	Reach's December 20 fax was a counteroffer.	○	○

Situation	Contractual Relationship	Assignment	Memo

Items 1 through 5 relate to the attempted assignment of part of the fee to Weaver. Assume that a valid contract exists between Blake and Reach. For each item, determine whether the statement is True or False.

		True	*False*
1.	Reach is prohibited from making an assignment of any contract right or duty.	○	○
2.	Reach may validly assign part of the fee to Weaver.	○	○
3.	Under the terms of Reach's acceptance, Weaver would be considered a third-party creditor beneficiary.	○	○
4.	In a breach of contract suit by Weaver, against Blake, Weaver would not collect any punitive damages.	○	○
5.	In a breach of contract suit by Weaver, against Reach, Weaver would be able to collect punitive damages.	○	○

Situation	Contractual Relationship	Assignment	Memo

Items 1 through 3 relate to Blake's December 22 signed memo. For each item, determine whether the statement is True or False.

		True	*False*
1.	Reach's oral acceptance of Blake's December 22 memo may be enforced by Blake against Reach.	○	○
2.	Blake's memo is a valid offer even though it contains no date for acceptance.	○	○
3.	Blake's memo may be enforced against Blake by Reach.	○	○

MULTIPLE-CHOICE ANSWERS

1. a __ __	13. d __ __	25. a __ __	37. c __ __	49. a __ __
2. b __ __	14. b __ __	26. c __ __	38. d __ __	50. a __ __
3. c __ __	15. c __ __	27. b __ __	39. b __ __	51. c __ __
4. a __ __	16. c __ __	28. b __ __	40. c __ __	52. d __ __
5. d __ __	17. c __ __	29. d __ __	41. c __ __	53. a __ __
6. b __ __	18. d __ __	30. b __ __	42. d __ __	54. a __ __
7. b __ __	19. d __ __	31. a __ __	43. d __ __	55. c __ __
8. a __ __	20. b __ __	32. d __ __	44. a __ __	56. a __ __
9. b __ __	21. c __ __	33. d __ __	45. a __ __	57. b __ __
10. c __ __	22. c __ __	34. c __ __	46. c __ __	
11. a __ __	23. b __ __	35. c __ __	47. b __ __	1st: __/57 = __%
12. c __ __	24. d __ __	36. b __ __	48. a __ __	2nd: __/57 = __%

MULTIPLE-CHOICE ANSWER EXPLANATIONS

C.1. Offer

1. **(a)** Under common law, an offer must be definite and certain as to what will be agreed upon in the contract. Essential terms are the parties involved, the price, the time for performance, and the subject matter (quantity and type). The price element of the contract was not present.

2. **(b)** Advertisements in almost all cases are merely invitations for interested parties to make an offer. Thus, Harris has not made an offer, but is seeking offers through the use of the advertisement.

3. **(c)** Generally an offeror may revoke an offer at any time prior to acceptance by the offeree. Revocation is effective when it is received by the offeree. Revocation also occurs if the offeree learns by a reliable means that the offeror has already sold the subject of the offer. In this situation, Peters' offer was effectively revoked when Mason learned that the lawn mower had been sold to Bronson. Therefore, Mason's acceptance was ineffective. Answers (a) and (b) are incorrect because the offer had been revoked prior to Mason's acceptance. Answer (d) is incorrect because Peters was not obligated to keep the offer open. Note that if consideration had been paid by Mason to keep the offer open, an option contract would exist and the offer could not be revoked before the stated time.

4. **(a)** Drake did not intend to reject the $300,000 offer but is simply seeing if Calistoga might consider selling the home for less. Answer (b) is incorrect because a counteroffer takes place when the original offer is rejected and a new offer takes its place. Answer (c) is incorrect because Drake showed no intention of rejecting the offer by his mere inquiry. Answer (d) is incorrect because ambiguity is not one of the grounds to have an offer terminated by operation of law.

5. **(d)** An offer automatically terminates upon the occurrence of any of the following events: (1) the death or insanity of either the offeror or offeree, (2) bankruptcy or insolvency of either the offeror or offeree, or (3) the destruction of the specific, identified subject matter. Thus the offer automatically terminates at the date of Opal's death. It does not matter whether Larkin received notice of the death. If Larkin had accepted the offer prior to Opal's death, a valid contract would have been formed.

C.2. Acceptance

6. **(b)** Under the mailbox rule, an acceptance is ordinarily effective when sent if transmitted by the means authorized by the offeror, or by the same means used to transmit the offer if no means was authorized. However, the offeror may stipulate that acceptance is effective only when received by the offeror. In this situation, no contract was formed because Moss' acceptance was not received by the date specified in Fine's offer. Under common law, a method of acceptance other than the means specified in the offer or the method used to communicate the offer, is considered effective when received by the offeror.

7. **(b)** Fresno's acceptance by overnight delivery was made by a method other than the methods specified by Harris in the written offer. When acceptance is sent by a method other than the method specified in the offer or different than the method used to transmit the offer, acceptance is considered valid only when actually received by the offeror. Late acceptance is not valid, but instead constitutes a counteroffer. A valid contract would be formed only if the original offeror (Harris) then accepts.

8. **(a)** A unilateral offer exists when the offeror expects acceptance of an offer by action of the offeree. A unilateral contract is then formed when the offeree accepts the contract through performance of the offeror's required action. In this case, a valid contract is formed when Hammer accepts Kay's unilateral offer by obtaining the artifacts within a two-week period. Answers (b) and (d) are incorrect because a quasi contract is an implied-in-law rather than express agreement which results when one of the parties has been unjustly enriched at the expense of the other. The law creates such a contract when there is no binding agreement present to keep the unjust enrichment from occurring. Answer (c) is incorrect because public policy causes enforcement of promises despite lack of any other legal enforcement of the contract. For example, public policy would normally allow enforcement of a promise by a debtor to pay a debt barred by the statute of limitations.

9. **(b)** Common law applies to this contract because it involves real estate. In this situation, Fox's reply on October 2 is a counteroffer and terminates Summers' original offer made on September 27. The acceptance of an offer must conform exactly to the terms of the offer under common law. By agreeing to purchase the vacation home at a price different from the original offer, Fox is rejecting Summers' offer and is making a counteroffer. Answer (a) is incorrect because the fact that Fox failed to return Summers' letter is irrelevant to the formation of a binding contract. Fox's reply constitutes a counteroffer as Fox did not intend to accept Summers' original offer. Answer (c) is incorrect because Summers' offer was rejected by Fox's counteroffer. Answer (d) is incorrect because with rare exceptions, silence does not constitute acceptance.

C.3. Consideration

10. **(c)** Both Zake and Wick had a contract that was binding for five years. For them to modify this contract, both of them must give new consideration under common law rules which apply to employment contracts such as this one. When Wick agreed to the raise, only Wick gave new consideration in the form of $20,000 additional each year. Zake did not give new consideration because he would perform in the last three years as originally agreed. Answers (a) and (b) are incorrect because Zake did not give new consideration whether or not the raise was in writing. Answer (d) is incorrect because duress needed to make a contract voidable or void requires more than "some pressure."

11. **(a)** Consideration is an act, promise, or forbearance which is offered by one party and accepted by another as inducement to enter into an agreement. A party must bind him/herself to do something s/he is not legally obligated to do. Furthermore, the consideration must be bargained for. Past consideration is not sufficient to serve as consideration for a new contract because it is not bargained for. Answer (b) is incorrect because relinquishment of a legal right constitutes consideration. Answer (c) is incorrect because even though the consideration must be adequate, courts generally do not look into the amount of exchange, as long as it is legal consideration and is bargained for. Answer (d) is incorrect as this performance by a third party is still deemed consideration.

12. **(c)** The rebinding of Dunne's books is considered a service and not a sale of goods, therefore, common law applies. Under common law, modification of an existing contract needs new consideration by both parties to be legally binding. Since Dunne has not given any new consideration for Cook's reduction in price, the contract is unenforceable. Additionally, the parol evidence rule prohibits the presentation of evidence of any prior or contemporaneous oral or written statements for the purpose of modifying or changing a written agreement intended by the payor to be the final and complete expression of their contract. However, it does not bar from evidence any oral or written agreements entered into by the parties subsequent to the written contract. Therefore, the agreement between Dunne and Cook is unenforceable, but evidence of the modification is admissible into evidence. Note that if the contract had been for the sale of goods (UCC), modification of the contract terms would have been enforceable. Under the UCC, a contract for the sale of goods may be modified orally or in writing without new consideration if such modification is done in good faith.

13. **(d)** A preexisting legal duty is not sufficient as consideration because no new legal detriment is suffered by performing the prior obligation. For example, when a creditor agrees to accept as full payment an amount less than the full amount of the undisputed (liquidated) debt, the agreement lacks valid consideration to be enforceable. However, when the amount of an obligation is disputed, the creditor's promise to accept a lesser amount as full payment of the debt is enforceable. Preexisting legal duties are not valid as consideration.

14. **(b)** A promise to donate money to a charity which the charity relied upon in incurring large expenditures is a situation involving promissory estoppel. Promissory estoppel acts as a substitute for consideration and renders the promise enforceable. The elements necessary for promissory estoppel are (1) detrimental reliance on a promise, (2) reliance on the promise is reasonable and foreseeable, and (3) damage results (injustice) if the promise is not enforced. Answer (a) is incorrect because the failure to enforce an employer's promise to make a cash payment to a deceased employee's family will not result in damages, and therefore, promissory estoppel will not apply. Answer (c) is incorrect because the modification of a contract requires consideration, unless the contract involves the sale of goods under the UCC. Answer (d) is incorrect because an irrevocable oral promise by a merchant to keep an offer open for sixty days is an option contract that must be supported by consideration. A firm offer under the UCC requires an offer signed by the merchant.

C.4. Legal Capacity

15. **(c)** A minor may disaffirm a contract at any time during his minority and within a reasonable time after reaching the age of majority. When Rail disaffirmed the contract two days after reaching the age of eighteen, he did so within a reasonable time after reaching majority age. Answer (a) is incorrect because Rail could ratify the contract only after reaching the age of majority. Answer (b) is incorrect because although Rail could have transferred good title to a good-faith purchaser for value, Rail's title was still voidable and subject to disaffirmance. Answer (d) is incorrect because Rail could disaffirm the contract only for a reasonable time after reaching the age of majority. Failure to disaffirm within a reasonable time serves to act as ratification.

16. **(c)** When a person has previously been adjudicated by a court of law to be incompetent, all of the contracts that s/he makes are void. Answer (a) is incorrect because the contracts are only voidable at the option of Green if there was no formal, previous court determination of incompetence for Green. Answer (b) is incorrect because once the court determines that Green is incompetent, all of the contracts that s/he makes are not valid but are void. Answer (d) is incorrect because the contracts cannot be enforced by either Green or the other contracting party.

17. **(c)** Ratification of a contract prior to reaching majority age is not effective. A minor **may** ratify a contract expressly or by actions indicating ratification after reaching the age of majority. Failure to disaffirm within a reasonable time after reaching majority age **does** act as ratification.

C.5. Legality

18. **(d)** An agreement is unenforceable if it is illegal or violates public policy. Therefore, if the personal services of the contract are illegal, the party will not have to perform them. Answer (a) is incorrect because the death of the party who is to **receive** the benefits does not terminate the duties under the contract. His/her heirs can still receive and pay for the personal services. Answer (b) is incorrect because making less profit or losing money are not grounds for getting out of a contract. Answer (c) is incorrect because bankruptcy of the receiver does not discharge the performer from the contract, although it can allow for forgiveness of all or part of the payment.

19. (d) An employer's promise not to press criminal charges against an employee-embezzler who agrees to return the embezzled money is not legally binding. The promise not to press charges is an illegal bargain, and, even if the employee returns the money, the employer is free to cooperate in prosecution of the criminal.

C.6. Reality of Consent

20. (b) Fraud is the intentional misrepresentation of a material fact upon which a third party reasonably relies to his or her detriment. An intentionally misstated appraised value would be an example of a fraudulent inducement to make a contract. Answers (a) and (c) are incorrect because a third party cannot reasonably rely on a nonexpert opinion or a prediction. Answer (d) is incorrect because by definition, fraud applies to material facts.

21. (c) An immaterial unilateral mistake generally does not allow either party to void the contract.

22. (c) Undue influence is a defense that makes a contract voidable. Classic situations of this concept involve close relationships in which a dominant person has extreme influence over a weaker person. Answer (a) is incorrect because although fraud in the inducement can make a contract voidable, it typically does not occur between parties that have a close relationship. Answer (b) is incorrect because unconscionability involves an oppressive contract in which one party has taken severe, unfair advantage of another which is often based on the latter's absence of choice or poor education rather than the parties' close relationship. Answer (d) is incorrect because duress involves acts or threats of violence or pressure, which need not result from close relationships.

23. (b) An insurance policy is voidable at the option of the insurer if the insured failed to inform the insurer at the time of application of a fact material to the insurer's risk (e.g., failure to disclose a preexisting heart condition on a life insurance application). The insured's concealment causes the policy to be voidable regardless of the type of beneficiary designated or the nature of the insured's death.

24. (d) One of the elements needed to prove fraud is a misrepresentation of a material fact. That statement that "it is a great car" is sales talk or puffing and does not establish this element. The fact that the overhaul was done thirteen months earlier instead of the stated one year is not a misrepresentation of a **material** fact.

25. (a) A mistake is an understanding that is not in agreement with a fact. A unilateral mistake (made by one party) generally does not allow the party to void the contract. However, a mistake unknown to the party making it becomes voidable if the other party recognizes it as a mistake. Particularly, this is the case in bid contract computations. The contract is voidable by the party making the mistake if the other party knew of the mistake or if the calculation was far enough off that the other party should have known that a mistake was made.

26. (c) Duress is any wrongful threat or act of violence made toward a person (or his family) which forces a person to enter into a contract against his will. For duress to be present, a threat must be made and the threatened party must believe that the other party has the ability to carry out the threat. In this situation, Maco's actions did not constitute duress. Kent's safety and property were in no way threatened by Maco and Kent was able to validly consent to the contract. Answers (a) and (b) are incorrect because regardless of Kent's financial problems and the FMV of Kent's services, duress was not present in that Kent was able to enter into the contract at will. Answer (d) is incorrect because Maco does not need to prove that Kent had no other offers to provide financial services.

27. (b) To establish a common law action for fraud, the following elements must be present: (1) misrepresentation of a material fact, (2) either knowledge of the falsity with intent to mislead or reckless disregard for the truth (scienter), (3) reasonable reliance by third party, and (4) injury resulted from misrepresentation. If the misrepresentation occurs during contract negotiations, fraud in the inducement is present resulting in a contract voidable at the option of the injured party. Answer (a) is incorrect because the defendant need not be an expert with regard to the misrepresentation to establish fraud in the inducement. Answer (c) is incorrect because the misrepresentation may be written or oral. Answer (d) is incorrect because the presence of fraud in the inducement does not require a fiduciary relationship between the parties.

28. (b) There are two remedies for fraud under the UCC Sales Article: (1) the plaintiff may affirm the agreement and sue for damages under the tort of deceit, or (2) the plaintiff may rescind the contract and sue for damages resulting from the fraud. Answer (a) is incorrect because the plaintiff must return any consideration received from the other party when the contract is rescinded. Answer (c) is incorrect because although punitive damages are allowed in fraud actions because they are intentional torts, they do not require physical injuries. Answer (d) is incorrect because without reliance by the plaintiff on the misrepresentation, there is no fraud, and therefore, the plaintiff may not rescind the contract.

C.7. Conformity with the Statute of Frauds

29. (d) The Statute of Frauds requires that a contract to answer the debt or default of another be in writing and signed by the party to be charged. The guarantee that Decker made was only oral. Answer (b) is incorrect, as the reason Decker is not liable for the oral guaranty is not because it expires more than one year after June 1, but because a contract of guaranty must be in writing. Decker is not liable regardless of Baker's confirmation letter; thus answer (a) is incorrect. Answer (c) is incorrect because Decker's oral guaranty is not enforceable. The time period between the date of the oral guaranty and the date payment is demanded has no bearing in this situation.

30. (b) Any agreement to sell land or any interest in land falls under the requirements of the Statute of Frauds. Agreements within the Statute of Frauds require contracts to be in writing and signed by the party to be charged (the party being sued). An exception to the above rule is "part performance" by the purchaser. Part performance exists when the purchaser of property takes possession of the property with the landowner's consent. Some states also require either partial payment for the property or permanent improvement of the property by the purchaser. Answer (b) is correct because even though Nolan failed to sign a written agreement, the part performance exception has been satisfied. Answer (a) is incorrect because the fact that Nolan simply failed to object to the agreement does not make the contract valid under the Statute of Frauds. Answer (c) is incorrect because the part performance exception has been met and Train will therefore prevail. Answer (d) is incorrect because no such requirement exists to alleviate Nolan's liability. The part performance rule allows Train to prevail. Note that **all** sales of land are covered under the Statute of Frauds, and not just those greater than $500.

31. **(a)** Contracts that cannot be performed within one year must be in writing. In this case Cherry agreed to purchase Picks Company if an audit after one year shows that the company has been profitable. This would take longer than a year to perform. Answer (b) is incorrect because the $500 provision is in the Uniform Commercial Code for a sale of goods. Answer (c) is incorrect because despite the actual profitability, the contract could not be completed within one year of the making of the contract. Answer (d) is incorrect because although promissory estoppel may be used in the absence of a writing, there are not the facts sufficient to show promissory estoppel.

32. **(d)** Contracts which fall within the requirements of the Statute of Frauds are required to be in writing and signed by the party to be charged. It is not required that the contract terms be formalized in a single writing. Two or more documents may be combined to create a writing which satisfies the Statute of Frauds as long as one of the documents refers to the others. Answer (a) is incorrect because the Statute of Frauds requires that agreements for the sale of goods for $500 or more be in writing; however, contracts that come under common law are not included in this requirement. Answer (b) is incorrect because the Statute of Frauds requires that the written contract be signed by the party to be charged, not by all parties to the contract. Answer (c) is incorrect because the Statute of Frauds applies to contracts that **cannot** be performed within one year from the making of the agreement.

33. **(d)** The Statute of Frauds applies to the following types of contracts: (1) an agreement to sell land or any interest in land, (2) an agreement that cannot be performed within one year from the making of the agreement, (3) an agreement to answer for the debt or default of another, and (4) an agreement for the sale of goods for $500 or more. Since the agreement between Carson and Ives meets none of the above requirements, it is an enforceable oral contract under common law. Furthermore, under common law, modification of an existing contract needs new consideration by both parties to be legally binding. Since Ives received the benefit of additional repairs to his book, Carson's increase in the contract price is enforceable. Therefore, Carson will recover $650.

34. **(c)** Under The Statute of Frauds, agreements that can be performed within one year of their making can be oral. In this case the ethics audit need only span ten months and the completion of the report will take less than one additional month for a total of less than one year. We know that the report can be done in less than a month because

Newell points out that even if she delays start for three months, she will still complete the ten-month audit before the fourteen-month deadline. The fact that it might take longer than a year does not require it to be in writing since it **possibly could** be completed within one year. Answer (a) is incorrect because the $500 provision is for sales of goods not services. Answer (b) is incorrect because the contract can be completed within one year. Answer (d) is incorrect because there is no such provision involved here for the Statute of Frauds.

C.7.d.(1) Parol Evidence Rule

35. **(c)** The parol evidence rule provides that a written agreement intended by contracting parties to be a final and complete contract may not be contradicted by previous or contemporaneous oral evidence. The parol evidence rule does not apply to any subsequent oral promises made after the original agreement. Thus, the subsequent oral agreement between Rogers and Lennon regarding Lennon's right to report on a monthly basis will be allowed as evidence in a lawsuit between the parties. Answer (a) is incorrect because the parol evidence rule applies to all written contracts regardless of the applicability of the Statute of Frauds. Answer (b) is incorrect because the parol evidence rule will prevent the admission into evidence of the contemporaneous oral agreement that Lennon could use Rogers' computer. Answer (d) is incorrect because the parol evidence rule does apply to the contemporaneous oral agreement.

36. **(b)** The parol evidence rule provides that any written agreement intended by parties to be final and complete contract may not be contradicted by previous or contemporaneous evidence, written or oral. Thus, previous written agreements are prohibited by the rule. Exceptions to the parol evidence rule include proof to invalidate the contract between the parties, to show terms not inconsistent with writing that parties would not be expected to have included, to explain the intended meaning of an ambiguity, or to show a condition precedent. The parol evidence rule does not apply to subsequent transactions, such as oral promises made after the original agreement.

37. **(c)** The parol evidence rule prohibits the presentation as evidence of any prior or contemporaneous oral statements concerning a written agreement intended by the parties to be the final and complete expression of their contract. Therefore, the evidence related to the oral agreement regarding the payment of utilities would not be allowed. However, the parol evidence rule does **not** bar the admission of evidence which is presented to establish fraud.

C.9. Contracting Online

38. **(d)** Even though this contract falls under the Statute of Frauds and, therefore, generally must be written and signed, most states have passed laws allowing contracts to be made over the Internet to facilitate commerce. The statutes encourage technology to overcome concerns over authenticity of such contracts. Therefore, answer (a) is incorrect. Answer (b) is incorrect because the parol evidence rule does not specify when a contract must be written and signed. Answer (c) is incorrect because a sale of land is governed by common law rules and not the UCC.

D. Assignment and Delegation

39. (b) Assignment is the transfer of a right under a contract by one person to another. Almost all contract rights are assignable as long as the parties agree to it, but there are some exceptions. Contracts involving personal services, trust or confidence are not assignable. If assignment would materially change the risk or burden of the obligor, it is not allowed. For example, a contract for insurance against certain risks are not assignable because they were made upon the character of the contracting party (the insured). Assigning the rights to another party would alter the risk. Therefore, malpractice insurance policy rights are not assignable. A further exception is that future rights are not assignable, with the exception under the UCC that future rights for the sale of goods are assignable, whether based on an existing or nonexisting contract. As the assignment of option contract rights does not fall under any exception, they would be assignable.

40. (c) Assignment is the transfer of a right under a contract by one person to another. No consideration is needed for valid assignment. Normally an assignment is done in writing, but any act, oral or written, is sufficient if it gives clear intent of the assignment. Only situations included under the Statute of Frauds are required to be in writing. When consideration is given in exchange for an assignment, it is irrevocable. Also, as a general rule a gratuitous assignment is revocable unless it is evidenced by a writing signed by the assignor, effected by a delivery of a writing used as evidence of the right (i.e., bill of lading), and the assignment is executed. A contract right cannot be assigned if it would materially change the risk or burden of the obligor.

41. (c) Assignment is the transfer of a right under a contract by one person to another. If the obligor has notice of the assignment, s/he must pay the assignee, not the assignor. The contract between Barton and Egan provided for both payments on the purchase price and the insurance policy in case of Egan's death. Because Barton assigned his contract rights to Vim, Vim was then entitled to payments on the purchase price and the insurance proceeds. Since Barton received payments on the purchase price and insurance proceeds after the assignment, Vim is entitled to sue Barton for these amounts.

E. Third-Party Beneficiary Contracts

42. (d) When a debtor contracts with a second party to pay the debt owed to a creditor, the creditor becomes a creditor beneficiary. Barton contracted with Egan for Egan to pay Ness the business' debts. The contract also required Egan to provide a life insurance policy to pay Ness if Egan died. In both the contract and the insurance policy, Ness was a creditor beneficiary. Neither the contract nor the insurance policy were entered into to confer a gift to Ness, and therefore he was not a donee beneficiary.

43. (d) Bugle would have received an unintended benefit under the contract between Fargo and ABC Company. Therefore, Bugle is an incidental beneficiary, not an intended beneficiary and, thus, has no legal rights against either Fargo or ABC. No matter who breached the contract, Bugle has no rights against either party.

44. (a) In an assignment, the assignee (Clay) acquires the assignor's (Baxter) rights against the obligor (Globe) and has the right to performance. Baxter is still liable to the assignee if Globe does not perform. However, if Clay released Globe from the contract, Baxter would also be released and no longer liable to Clay. Answer (b) is incorrect because if the obligor has notice of the assignment, s/he may pay the assignor, and the assignee must recover from the assignor. Thus, if Globe was unaware of the assignment and paid Baxter, Clay would have to collect from Baxter. Answers (c) and (d) are incorrect because even if Baxter released Globe or breached the contract, Baxter would still be liable to Clay.

45. (a) Mann is a donee beneficiary and, thus, can bring suit against the promissor, Manus, only. He cannot maintain a suit against Mackay, who was just giving a gift. Mann cannot maintain any action against Mackay either alone or in combination with Manus.

46. (c) When a debtor contracts with a second party to pay the debt owed to a creditor, the creditor becomes a creditor beneficiary. A creditor beneficiary has the right to enforce the contract which gives him the intended benefits and may commence an action for nonperformance against either of the contracting parties. For this reason, Ferco (creditor beneficiary) will prevail in a lawsuit against Bell because Ferco has an enforceable right to receive payment. Answer (a) is incorrect because Ferco, as a creditor beneficiary, has the right to recover from either Bell or Allied. Answer (b) is incorrect because the creditor beneficiary is not required to give consideration to have an enforceable right. Answer (d) is incorrect because having knowledge of the contract between Bell and Allied at the time the contract was made is not necessary to later enforce this legal action. Ferco must establish that he is a creditor beneficiary to maintain an action for nonperformance.

F. Performance of Contract

47. (b) Under the doctrine of substantial performance, a contract obligation may be discharged even though the performance tendered was not in complete conformity with the terms of the agreement. Under this doctrine, if it can be shown that the defect in performance was only minor in nature, that a good-faith effort was made to conform completely with the terms of the agreement, and if the performing party is willing to accept a decrease in compensation equivalent to the amount of the minor defect in performance, the contractual obligation will be discharged. Since the defect in Glaze's performance was only minor in nature, and since Parc refused to allow Glaze to complete the project, Glaze will prevail in its action against Parc. Anticipatory breach applies only to executory bilateral contracts. An executory contract is a contract wherein both parties have yet to perform. In this instance, Glaze has substantially performed its part of the agreement.

48. (a) The duty to perform a contract may depend upon a condition. Conditions that could be present include: condition precedent, which is one that must occur before there is duty to perform; condition subsequent, which is one that removes a preexisting duty to perform; or condition concurrent, which is mutually dependent upon performance at nearly the same time.

G. Discharge of Contracts

49. **(a)** Once one party materially breaches the contract, the other party is discharged from performing his or her obligations under the contract. Answer (b) is incorrect because a reasonable delay in the performance of the contract is not a breach unless time was of the essence. Answer (c) is incorrect because tender or offer to pay or perform obligates the other party to do what s/he promised. Answer (d) is incorrect because assignment of rights typically is allowed under contract law.

50. **(a)** The discharge of a contract can come about in several ways. The first is by agreement. Accord and satisfaction involves an agreed substitute for performance under the contract (accord) and the actual performance of that substitute (satisfaction). An agreement can also be entered into by three parties whereby the previous agreement is discharged by the creation of a new agreement (a novation). The second method of discharge is by release of the contract or parties from performance. Another method of discharging a contract is by performance of the specified action becoming impossible, such as destruction of the subject matter, or death of a party where personal service is necessary. Lastly, breach of the contract discharges the injured party.

51. **(c)** Rescission entails canceling a contract and placing the parties in the position they were in before the contract was formed. Answer (a) is incorrect as a novation is an agreement between three parties whereby a previous agreement is discharged by the creation of a new agreement. Answer (b) is incorrect because release is a means of discharging (abandoning) a contract but it does not place the parties in the same position as before the contract. Answer (d) is incorrect because revocation is used by an offeror to terminate an offer.

H. Remedies

52. **(d)** The remedy of specific performance is used when money damages will not sufficiently compensate the afflicted party due to the unique nature of the subject matter of the contract. In a contract for the sale of land, the buyer has the right to enforce the agreement by seeking the remedy of specific performance because real property is considered unique. Another remedy for this breach of contract would be for the buyer to seek compensatory damages. If the buyer desires, s/he may seek this remedy instead of specific performance. However, in this situation, Hodges could only sue for either specific performance or compensatory damages but would not be entitled to both remedies. An injured party is generally not allowed to seek punitive damages. Punitive damages are awarded only when the court is seeking to punish a party for their improper actions and are not usually granted in breach of contract actions.

53. **(a)** Under the doctrine of substantial performance, a contract obligation may be discharged even though the performance tendered was not in complete conformity with the terms of the agreement. If it can be shown that the defect in performance was only minor in nature, that a good-faith effort was made to conform completely with the terms of the agreement, and if the performing party is willing to accept a decrease in compensation equivalent to the amount of the minor defect in performance, the contractual obligation will be discharged. Because Ames' breach of contract was both inadvertent and not material, the doctrine of substantial per-

formance applies and recovery will be limited to monetary damages. The installation of fixtures other than those specified in the contract constitutes a breach, although the breach is considered immaterial. The doctrine of substantial performance applies in this situation and the contractual obligation will be discharged.

54. **(a)** A liquidated damage clause is a contractual provision which states the amount of damages that will occur if a party breaches the contract. The liquidated damage clause is enforceable if the amount is reasonable in light of the anticipated or actual harm caused by the breach. Excessive liquidated damages will not be enforceable in court even if both parties have agreed in writing. A clause providing for excessive damages is a penalty and the courts will not enforce a penalty. Materiality does not impact the enforceability of liquidated damage provisions.

55. **(c)** The doctrine of anticipatory repudiation allows a party to either sue at once or wait until after performance is due when the other party indicates s/he will not perform. This doctrine is in effect because Nagel told Fields that Nagel had no intention of delivering the goods (i.e., repudiation of the contract) prior to the date of performance. Answer (a) is incorrect because promissory estoppel acts as a substitute for consideration which is an element in the forming of a contract but is not relevant in this fact situation. Answer (b) is incorrect because accord and satisfaction is an agreement wherein a party with an existing duty or performance under a contract promises to do something other than perform the duty originally promised in the contract. Answer (d) is incorrect because the doctrine of substantial performance would allow for a contract obligation to be discharged even though the performance tendered was not in complete conformity with the terms of the agreement. In this case, Fields is suing Nagel for breach of contract.

56. **(a)** Events occurring after a contract is entered into usually do not affect performance. Some exceptions to this rule include subsequent illegality of the performance, death of a party, or destruction of the subject matter, all of which constitute impossibility of performance. In this case, even though Maco's own potatoes were destroyed, it wasn't specified that Maco's own potato crop be used to fulfill the contract. It was not impossible, therefore, for Maco to perform, because he could have purchased potatoes from another grower to deliver to LBC. If there had been a worldwide infestation of the potato crop, Maco would have reason to not perform on the basis of impossibility.

I. Statute of Limitations

57. **(b)** The statute of limitations bars suit if it is not brought within the statutory period. The period varies for different types of cases and from state to state. The statute begins to run from the time the cause of action accrues (e.g., breach).

SOLUTIONS TO SIMULATION PROBLEMS

Simulation Problem 1

> **Consideration**

		(A)	(B)	(C)
1.	Party S feels a moral obligation because Party F let S stay in his place for free when S attended college. S now promises to pay F for the past kindness.	○	●	○
2.	F agrees to deliver all of the sugar that Company S will need in her business for the following year. S agrees to purchase it at the market price.	●	○	○
3.	F does not smoke for one year pursuant to S's agreement to pay F $200 if she does not smoke for one year.	●	○	○
4.	F dies leaving a valid will which gives S $100,000.	○	○	●
5.	F is an auditor of XYZ Company. S is a potential investor of XYZ and offers to pay F $1,000 if F performs a professional, quality audit of XYZ Company. The $1,000 is in addition to the fee F will get from XYZ. F does perform a professional, quality audit.	○	●	○
6.	F had agreed, in writing, to work for S for five years for $100,000 per year. After two years, F asks for a 20% raise. S first agrees then later changes his mind. F, while not agreeing to additional duties or changing his position, wants to enforce the raise in salary.	○	●	○
7.	S promised to pay F $1,000 if he crosses the Golden Gate Bridge on his hands and knees. F does so.	●	○	○
8.	F promised to pay S $200 for a computer worth $2,000. S agreed to the deal.	●	○	○
9.	F agreed to purchase all of the parts from S that S can produce in her business for the next six months. S also agreed.	●	○	○
10.	S agreed to accept $1,000 from F for a $1,500 debt that is not disputed. S now wants the additional $500. Focus on the agreement to accept the lesser amount.	○	●	○
11.	S agreed to accept $1,000 from F for a debt that S claims is $1,500 but F in good faith claims is $800. F agreed to the $1,000 initially, then decides he will pay only $800. Focus on the enforceability of the agreement for $1,000.	●	○	○
12.	S agreed to donate $100 to F, a public charity.	○	○	●

Explanation of solutions

1.   (**B**) Party F gave S a gift in the past. S's promise to now pay for the usage is not enforceable because F's action is past consideration, and the contract needs consideration on both sides. Furthermore, S's feeling of a moral obligation does not create consideration.

2.   (**A**) This is an example of a requirements contract. F has given consideration because s/he gave up the right to sell that sugar to someone else.

3.   (**A**) F refrained from doing something which she had a right to do. This constitutes consideration.

4.   (**C**) This is not enforceable under contract law because S does not give any consideration in return. It is enforceable, however, as a will which does not require the elements of a contract such as consideration, but does require other formalities.

5.   (**B**) F already had a preexisting legal duty to do a professional, quality audit of XYZ Company.

6.   (**B**) F had a contract to work for S for five years for $100,000 per year. F is not giving any new consideration for the raise since during that five years, he already is obligated to complete the contract.

7.   (**A**) F did something which he did not have to do in exchange for the agreed $1,000. This is a unilateral contract.

8.   (**A**) F agreed to pay $200 and in exchange S agreed to sell the computer. Both have given consideration that is **legally** sufficient. Legally sufficient refers to the validity of the consideration, not the amount. Consideration does not have to be of equal value as long as it is legal consideration and bargained for.

9.   (**A**) Both parties have given consideration for this output contract. F gave up the right to buy these parts elsewhere and S gave up the right to sell her output to someone else.

10.   (**B**) F has a preexisting legal duty to pay the full $1,500. When S agreed to accept less, F gave up nothing. F still owes the remaining $500.

11.   (**A**) In this case, both parties gave consideration. S, in agreeing to accept the $1,000, gave up the right to collect more of the disputed amount. F gave up the right to pay less of the disputed amount.

12.   (**C**) Although the charity gave no consideration in exchange for the promised donation, the promise to donate to a charity is generally enforceable based on public policy reasons.

Simulation Problem 2

Situation	Contractual Relationship	Assignment	Memo

		True	False
1.	Blake's December 15 offer had to be in writing to be a legitimate offer.	○	●
2.	Reach's December 20 fax was an improper method of acceptance.	○	●
3.	Reach's December 20 fax was effective when sent.	○	●
4.	Reach's acceptance was invalid because it was received after December 20.	○	●
5.	Blake's receipt of Reach's acceptance created a voidable contract.	○	●
6.	If Reach had rejected the original offer by telephone on December 17, he could not validly accept the offer later.	●	○
7.	Reach's December 20 fax was a counteroffer.	●	○

Explanation of solutions

1. (F) Although the final contract has to be in writing to be enforceable since performance of contract would take longer than a year, the offer itself can be oral.

2. (F) The offer specified that the acceptance must be in writing. Since Reach put the acceptance in writing and faxed it to Blake, this was a proper method of acceptance.

3. (F) Common law applies to this fact pattern since the contract does not involve a sale of goods. Reach's attempted acceptance stated $1,000,000 instead of $100,000 as contained in the offer. Reach's attempted acceptance thus was instead a counteroffer. Under both common law and the Uniform Commercial Code, offers, revocations, rejections and counteroffers are valid when received.

4. (F) Blake's offer specified that the acceptance must be received no later than December 20. Reach's faxed acceptance was received in Blake's office on December 20 on the fax machine. Therefore, Blake did receive the fax on time even though it was not seen until the following day.

5. (F) Reach's attempted acceptance stated $1,000,000 instead of $100,000 as contained in the offer. Since the terms did not match, no contract was formed, voidable or otherwise.

6. (T) Since there is no firm offer or option contract, the rejection terminates the offer.

7. (T) Since the December 20 fax terms did not match the original offer's terms, it serves as a counteroffer which rejects the original offer and creates a new offer.

Situation	Contractual Relationship	Assignment	Memo

		True	False
1.	Reach is prohibited from making an assignment of any contract right or duty.	○	●
2.	Reach may validly assign part of the fee to Weaver.	●	○
3.	Under the **terms** of Reach's acceptance, Weaver would be considered a third-party creditor beneficiary.	●	○
4.	In a breach of **contract** suit by Weaver, against Blake, Weaver would not collect any punitive damages.	●	○
5.	In a breach of **contract** suit by Weaver, against Reach, Weaver would be able to collect punitive damages.	○	●

Explanation of solutions

1. (F) Parties may typically assign the contract right to receive money to another party.

2. (T) When parties have a right to receive money, they may validly assign all or a portion of this right to a third party.

3. (T) The terms of Reach's acceptance names Weaver as a third-party beneficiary to receive $5,000. Since the intent was to pay a debt owed by Reach to Weaver, this makes Weaver a creditor beneficiary.

4. (T) Punitive damages are not awarded for mere breach of contract cases such as this suit by Weaver against Blake.

5. (F) In a suit by Weaver against Reach, no punitive damages will be awarded since this would be only a breach of contract case.

			Memo
Situation	Contractual Relationship	Assignment	

	True	*False*
1. Reach's oral acceptance of Blake's December 22 memo may be enforced by Blake against Reach.	○	●
2. Blake's memo is a valid offer even though it contains no date for acceptance.	●	○
3. Blake's memo may be enforced against Blake by Reach.	●	○

Explanation of solutions

1. **(F)** Since the work would require two years to complete, the contract cannot be performed within one year and, therefore, must be in writing to be enforceable. The party to be charged must have signed the contract and Reach did not do this.

2. **(T)** An offer does not need to have a date for acceptance, in which case, the offer remains open for a reasonable time.

3. **(T)** Blake's signed memo sets forth an offer which was later accepted orally by Reach. This can be construed as enough written evidence to satisfy the Statute of Frauds. Because Blake, the party to be charged, signed the memo, it is enforceable against Blake by Reach.

MULTIPLE-CHOICE QUESTIONS (1-47)

1. Under the Sales Article of the UCC, when a written offer has been made without specifying a means of acceptance but providing that the offer will only remain open for ten days, which of the following statements represent(s) a valid acceptance of the offer?

I. An acceptance sent by regular mail the day before the ten-day period expires that reaches the offeror on the eleventh day.

II. An acceptance faxed the day before the ten-day period expires that reaches the offeror on the eleventh day, due to a malfunction of the offeror's printer.

   a. I only.
   b. II only.
   c. Both I and II.
   d. Neither I nor II.

2. Under the Sales Article of the UCC, a firm offer will be created only if the

   a. Offer states the time period during which it will remain open.
   b. Offer is made by a merchant in a signed writing.
   c. Offeree gives some form of consideration.
   d. Offeree is a merchant.

3. On May 2, Mason orally contracted with Acme Appliances to buy for $480 a washer and dryer for household use. Mason and the Acme salesperson agreed that delivery would be made on July 2. On May 5, Mason telephoned Acme and requested that the delivery date be moved to June 2. The Acme salesperson agreed with this request. On June 2, Acme failed to deliver the washer and dryer to Mason because of an inventory shortage. Acme advised Mason that it would deliver the appliances on July 2 as originally agreed. Mason believes that Acme has breached its agreement with Mason. Acme contends that its agreement to deliver on June 2 was not binding. Acme's contention is

   a. Correct, because Mason is not a merchant and was buying the appliances for household use.
   b. Correct, because the agreement to change the delivery date was not in writing.
   c. Incorrect, because the agreement to change the delivery date was binding.
   d. Incorrect, because Acme's agreement to change the delivery date is a firm offer that cannot be withdrawn by Acme.

4. Under the Sales Article of the UCC, which of the following statements is correct?

   a. The obligations of the parties to the contract must be performed in good faith.
   b. Merchants and nonmerchants are treated alike.
   c. The contract must involve the sale of goods for a price of more than $500.
   d. None of the provisions of the UCC may be disclaimed by agreement.

5. Which of the following contracts is handled under common law rules rather than under Article 2 of the Uniform Commercial Code?

   a. Oral contract to have hair styled in which expensive products will be used on the hair.
   b. Oral contract to purchase a textbook for $100.
   c. Written contract to purchase an old handcrafted chair for $600 from a private party.

   d. Written contract to purchase a heater from a dealer to be installed by the buyer in her home.

6. Cookie Co. offered to sell Distrib Markets 20,000 pounds of cookies at $1.00 per pound, subject to certain specified terms for delivery. Distrib replied in writing as follows:

We accept your offer for 20,000 pounds of cookies at $1.00 per pound, weighing scale to have valid city certificate.

Under the UCC

   a. A contract was formed between the parties.
   b. A contract will be formed only if Cookie agrees to the weighing scale requirement.
   c. No contract was formed because Distrib included the weighing scale requirement in its reply.
   d. No contract was formed because Distrib's reply was a counteroffer.

7. EG Door Co., a manufacturer of custom exterior doors, verbally contracted with Art Contractors to design and build a $2,000 custom door for a house that Art was restoring. After EG had completed substantial work on the door, Art advised EG that the house had been destroyed by fire and Art was canceling the contract. EG finished the door and shipped it to Art. Art refused to accept delivery. Art contends that the contract cannot be enforced because it violated the Statute of Frauds by not being in writing. Under the Sales Article of the UCC, is Art's contention correct?

   a. Yes, because the contract was not in writing.
   b. Yes, because the contract cannot be fully performed due to the fire.
   c. No, because the goods were specially manufactured for Art and cannot be resold in EG's regular course of business.
   d. No, because the cancellation of the contract was not made in writing.

8. On May 2, Handy Hardware sent Ram Industries a signed purchase order that stated, in part, as follows:

Ship for May 8 delivery 300 Model A-X socket sets at current dealer price. Terms 2/10/net 30.

Ram received Handy's purchase order on May 4. On May 5, Ram discovered that it had only 200 Model A-X socket sets and 100 Model W-Z socket sets in stock. Ram shipped the Model A-X and Model W-Z sets to Handy without any explanation concerning the shipment. The socket sets were received by Handy on May 8.

Which of the following statements concerning the shipment is correct?

   a. Ram's shipment is an acceptance of Handy's offer.
   b. Ram's shipment is a counteroffer.
   c. Handy's order must be accepted by Ram in writing before Ram ships the socket sets.
   d. Handy's order can only be accepted by Ram shipping conforming goods.

9. Under the UCC Sales Article, which of the following conditions will prevent the formation of an enforceable sale of goods contract?

   a. Open price.
   b. Open delivery.
   c. Open quantity.
   d. Open acceptance.

10. Webstar Corp. orally agreed to sell Northco, Inc. a computer for $20,000. Northco sent a signed purchase order to Webstar confirming the agreement. Webstar received the purchase order and did not respond. Webstar refused to deliver the computer to Northco, claiming that the purchase order did not satisfy the UCC Statute of Frauds because it was not signed by Webstar. Northco sells computers to the general public and Webstar is a computer wholesaler. Under the UCC Sales Article, Webstar's position is

- a. Incorrect because it failed to object to Northco's purchase order.
- b. Incorrect because only the buyer in a sale-of-goods transaction must sign the contract.
- c. Correct because it was the party against whom enforcement of the contract is being sought.
- d. Correct because the purchase price of the computer exceeded $500.

11. Patch, a frequent shopper at Soon-Shop Stores, received a rain check for an advertised sale item after Soon-Shop's supply of the product ran out. The rain check was in writing and stated that the item would be offered to the customer at the advertised sale price for an unspecified period of time. A Soon-Shop employee signed the rain check. When Patch returned to the store one month later to purchase the item, the store refused to honor the rain check. Under the Sales Article of the UCC, will Patch win a suit to enforce the rain check?

- a. No, because one month is too long a period of time for a rain check to be effective.
- b. No, because the rain check did not state the effective time period necessary to keep the offer open.
- c. Yes, because Soon-Shop is required to have sufficient supplies of the sale item to satisfy all customers.
- d. Yes, because the rain check met the requirements of a merchant's firm offer even though no effective time period was stated.

12. A sheep rancher agreed in writing to sell all the wool shorn during the shearing season to a weaver. The contract failed to establish the price and a minimum quantity of wool. After the shearing season, the rancher refused to deliver the wool. The weaver sued the rancher for breach of contract. Under the Sales Article of the UCC, will the weaver win?

- a. Yes, because this was an output contract.
- b. Yes, because both price and quantity terms were omitted.
- c. No, because quantity cannot be omitted for a contract to be enforceable.
- d. No, because the omission of price and quantity terms prevents the formation of a contract.

13. Under the Sales Article of the UCC, the warranty of title

- a. Provides that the seller cannot disclaim the warranty if the sale is made to a bona fide purchaser for value.
- b. Provides that the seller deliver the goods free from any lien of which the buyer lacked knowledge when the contract was made.
- c. Applies only if it is in writing and assigned by the seller.
- d. Applies only if the seller is a merchant.

14. Under the Sales Article of the UCC, most goods sold by merchants are covered by certain warranties. An example of an express warranty would be a warranty of

- a. Usage of trade.
- b. Fitness for a particular purpose.
- c. Merchantability.
- d. Conformity of goods to sample.

15. Under the Sales Article of the UCC, which of the following statements is correct regarding the warranty of merchantability arising when there has been a sale of goods by a merchant seller?

- a. The warranty must be in writing.
- b. The warranty arises when the buyer relies on the seller's skill in selecting the goods purchased.
- c. The warranty cannot be disclaimed.
- d. The warranty arises as a matter of law when the seller ordinarily sells the goods purchased.

16. On May 2, Handy Hardware sent Ram Industries a signed purchase order that stated, in part, as follows:

Ship for May 8 delivery 300 Model A-X socket sets at current dealer price. Terms 2/10/net 30.

Ram received Handy's purchase order on May 4. On May 5, Ram discovered that it had only 200 Model A-X socket sets and 100 Model W-Z socket sets in stock. Ram shipped the Model A-X and Model W-Z sets to Handy without any explanation concerning the shipment. The socket sets were received by Handy on May 8.

Assuming a contract exists between Handy and Ram, which of the following implied warranties would result?

I. Implied warranty of merchantability.
II. Implied warranty of fitness for a particular purpose.
III. Implied warranty of title.

- a. I only.
- b. III only.
- c. I and III only.
- d. I, II, and III.

17. Under the UCC Sales Article, an action for breach of the implied warranty of merchantability by a party who sustains personal injuries may be successful against the seller of the product only when

- a. The seller is a merchant of the product involved.
- b. An action based on negligence can also be successfully maintained.
- c. The injured party is in privity of contract with the seller.
- d. An action based on strict liability in tort can also be successfully maintained.

18. Which of the following conditions must be met for an implied warranty of fitness for a particular purpose to arise in connection with a sale of goods?

I. The warranty must be in writing.
II. The seller must know that the buyer was relying on the seller in selecting the goods.

- a. I only.
- b. II only.
- c. Both I and II.
- d. Neither I nor II.

19. Under the UCC Sales Article, the implied warranty of merchantability

a. May be disclaimed by a seller's oral statement that mentions merchantability.
b. Arises only in contracts involving a merchant seller and a merchant buyer.
c. Is breached if the goods are **not** fit for all purposes for which the buyer intends to use the goods.
d. Must be part of the basis of the bargain to be binding on the seller.

20. Cook Company, a common carrier trucking company, made a contract to transport some video equipment for Jackson Company. Cook is trying to limit its liability in the contract. In which of the following situations can Cook **not avoid** liability?

 I. In transit, the driver of Cook's truck damages the video equipment when the driver causes an accident.
 II. An unknown thief steals the video equipment while in transit. Cook committed no negligence in this theft.
 III. The video equipment is destroyed when a bridge under the truck collapses because of an earthquake.

a. I only.
b. I and II only.
c. I, II, and III.
d. I and III only.

21. High sues the manufacturer, wholesaler, and retailer for bodily injuries caused by a power saw High purchased. Which of the following statements is correct under strict liability theory?
a. Contributory negligence on High's part will always be a bar to recovery.
b. The manufacturer will avoid liability if it can show it followed the custom of the industry.
c. Privity will be a bar to recovery insofar as the wholesaler is concerned if the wholesaler did **not** have a reasonable opportunity to inspect.
d. High may recover even if he **cannot** show any negligence was involved.

22. To establish a cause of action based on strict liability in tort for personal injuries that result from the use of a defective product, one of the elements the injured party must prove is that the seller
a. Was aware of the defect in the product.
b. Sold the product to the injured party.
c. Failed to exercise due care.
d. Sold the product in a defective condition.

23. A common carrier bailee generally would avoid liability for loss of goods entrusted to its care if the goods are
a. Stolen by an unknown person.
b. Negligently destroyed by an employee.
c. Destroyed by the derailment of the train carrying them due to railroad employee negligence.
d. Improperly packed by the party shipping them.

24. McGraw purchased an antique rocking chair from Tillis by check. The check was dishonored by the bank due to insufficient funds. In the meantime, McGraw sold the rocking chair to Rio who had no knowledge that McGraw's check had been dishonored. Which of the following is correct?
a. Tillis may repossess the rocking chair from Rio.
b. Tillis may recover money damages from Rio.

c. Tillis may recover money damages from McGraw.
d. Tillis may recover damages from McGraw based on fraud.

25. Yancie took her bike in to Pete's Bike Sales and Repair to have it repaired. Pete said he would need to have her leave it for two days. The next day, one of Pete's employees sold Yancie's bike to Jake. Jake paid for the bike with a credit card, unaware that Pete did not own the bike. Which of the following is correct?
a. Yancie can repossess the bike from Jake if she pays Jake. Yancie then recovers the price from Pete.
b. Pete can repossess the bike from Jake and then return it to Yancie.
c. Yancie can sue Jake for monetary damages only.
d. Jake has title to the bike.

26. Under the Sales Article of the UCC, unless a contract provides otherwise, before title to goods can pass from a seller to a buyer, the goods must be
a. Tendered to the buyer.
b. Identified to the contract.
c. Accepted by the buyer.
d. Paid for.

27. Under the Sales Article of the UCC, in an FOB place of shipment contract, the risk of loss passes to the buyer when the goods
a. Are identified to the contract.
b. Are placed on the seller's loading dock.
c. Are delivered to the carrier.
d. Reach the buyer's loading dock.

28. On May 2, Lace Corp., an appliance wholesaler, offered to sell appliances worth $3,000 to Parco, Inc., a household appliances retailer. The offer was signed by Lace's president, and provided that it would not be withdrawn before June 1. It also included the shipping terms: "FOB Parco's warehouse." On May 29, Parco mailed an acceptance of Lace's offer. Lace received the acceptance June 2.

If Lace inadvertently ships the wrong appliances to Parco and Parco rejects them two days after receipt, title to the goods will
a. Pass to Parco when they are identified to the contract.
b. Pass to Parco when they are shipped.
c. Remain with Parco until the goods are returned to Lace.
d. Revert to Lace when they are rejected by Parco.

29. Under the Sales Article of the UCC and the United Nations Convention for the International Sale of Goods (CISG), absent specific terms in an international sales shipment contract, when will risk of loss pass to the buyer?
a. When the goods are delivered to the first carrier for transmission to the buyer.
b. When the goods are tendered to the buyer.
c. At the conclusion of the execution of the contract.
d. At the time the goods are identified to the contract.

30. Which of the following statements applies to a sale on approval under the UCC Sales Article?
a. Both the buyer and seller must be merchants.
b. The buyer must be purchasing the goods for resale.
c. Risk of loss for the goods passes to the buyer when the goods are accepted after the trial period.

d.   Title to the goods passes to the buyer on delivery of the goods to the buyer.

31. Under the Sales Article of UCC, which of the following events will result in the risk of loss passing from a merchant seller to a buyer?

	Tender of the goods at the seller's place of business	Use of the seller's truck to deliver the goods
a.	Yes	Yes
b.	Yes	No
c.	No	Yes
d.	No	No

32. Cey Corp. entered into a contract to sell parts to Deck, Ltd. The contract provided that the goods would be shipped "FOB Cey's warehouse." Cey shipped parts different from those specified in the contract. Deck rejected the parts. A few hours after Deck informed Cey that the parts were rejected, they were destroyed by fire in Deck's warehouse. Cey believed that the parts were conforming to the contract. Which of the following statements is correct?

a.   Regardless of whether the parts were conforming, Deck will bear the loss because the contract was a shipment contract.

b.   If the parts were nonconforming, Deck had the right to reject them, but the risk of loss remains with Deck until Cey takes possession of the parts.

c.   If the parts were conforming, risk of loss does **not** pass to Deck until a reasonable period of time after they are delivered to Deck.

d.   If the parts were nonconforming, Cey will bear the risk of loss, even though the contract was a shipment contract.

33. Under the Sales Article of the UCC, which of the following factors is most important in determining who bears the risk of loss in a sale of goods contract?

a.   The method of shipping the goods.

b.   The contract's shipping terms.

c.   Title to the goods.

d.   How the goods were lost.

34. Bond purchased a painting from Wool, who is not in the business of selling art. Wool tendered delivery of the painting after receiving payment in full from Bond. Bond informed Wool that Bond would be unable to take possession of the painting until later that day. Thieves stole the painting before Bond returned. The risk of loss

a.   Passed to Bond at Wool's tender of delivery.

b.   Passed to Bond at the time the contract was formed and payment was made.

c.   Remained with Wool, because the parties agreed on a later time of delivery.

d.   Remained with Wool, because Bond had **not** yet received the painting.

35. Funston, a retailer, shipped goods worth $600 to a customer by using a common carrier. The contract used by the common carrier, and agreed to by Funston, limited liability to $100 unless a higher fee is paid. Funston did not pay the higher fee. The goods were shipped FOB destination point and were destroyed in transit due to a flash flood. Which of the following is correct?

a.   Funston will suffer a loss of $500.

b.   Funston will suffer a loss of $600.

c.   Funston's customer will suffer a loss of $500.

d.   Funston's customer will suffer a loss of $600.

36. Under the Sales Article of the UCC, which of the following statements regarding liquidated damages is(are) correct?

I.   The injured party may collect any amount of liquidated damages provided for in the contract.

II.   The seller may retain a deposit of up to $500 when a buyer defaults even if there is no liquidated damages provision in the contract.

a.   I only.

b.   II only.

c.   Both I and II.

d.   Neither I nor II.

37. Under the Sales Article of the UCC, and unless otherwise agreed to, the seller's obligation to the buyer is to

a.   Deliver the goods to the buyer's place of business.

b.   Hold conforming goods and give the buyer whatever notification is reasonably necessary to enable the buyer to take delivery.

c.   Deliver all goods called for in the contract to a common carrier.

d.   Set aside conforming goods for inspection by the buyer before delivery.

38. Under the Sales Article of the UCC, which of the following rights is(are) available to a seller when a buyer materially breaches a sales contract?

	Right to cancel the contract	Right to recover damages
a.	Yes	Yes
b.	Yes	No
c.	No	Yes
d.	No	No

39. Under the Sales Article of the UCC, the remedies available to a seller when a buyer breaches a contract for the sale of goods may include

	The right to resell goods identified to the contract	The right to stop a carrier from delivering the goods
a.	Yes	Yes
b.	Yes	No
c.	No	Yes
d.	No	No

40. Lazur Corp. entered into a contract with Baker Suppliers, Inc. to purchase a used word processor from Baker. Lazur is engaged in the business of selling new and used word processors to the general public. The contract required Baker to ship the goods to Lazur by common carrier pursuant to the following provision in the contract: "FOB Baker Suppliers, Inc. loading dock." Baker also represented in the contract that the word processor had been used for only ten hours by its previous owner. The contract included the provision that the word processor was being sold "as is" and this provision was in a larger and different type style than the remainder of the contract.

Assume that Lazur refused to accept the word processor even though it was in all respects conforming to the contract and that the contract is otherwise silent. Under the UCC Sales Article,

a. Baker can successfully sue for specific performance and make Lazur accept and pay for the word processor.

b. Baker may resell the word processor to another buyer.

c. Baker must sue for the difference between the market value of the word processor and the contract price plus its incidental damages.

d. Baker cannot successfully sue for consequential damages unless it attempts to resell the word processor.

41. On February 15, Mazur Corp. contracted to sell 1,000 bushels of wheat to Good Bread, Inc. at $6.00 per bushel with delivery to be made on June 23. On June 1, Good advised Mazur that it would not accept or pay for the wheat. On June 2, Mazur sold the wheat to another customer at the market price of $5.00 per bushel. Mazur had advised Good that it intended to resell the wheat. Which of the following statements is correct?

a. Mazur can successfully sue Good for the difference between the resale price and the contract price.

b. Mazur can resell the wheat only after June 23.

c. Good can retract its anticipatory breach at any time before June 23.

d. Good can successfully sue Mazur for specific performance.

42. Pickens agreed to sell Crocket 100 cases of napkins with the name of Crocket's restaurant on the napkins. In the enforceable contract, it was specified that delivery will take place on April 15, 2001, which is one month after Pickens and Crocket signed the contract. Crocket wanted the napkins by April 15 because the grand opening of the restaurant was scheduled for April 17. On April 11, Pickens tells Crocket that he has too many orders and will not be able to deliver the napkins. What options does Crocket have?

I. Treat it as a present breach of contract and cancel the contract.

II. Wait for a reasonable time to see if Pickens will deliver.

a. I only.

b. II only.

c. Either I or II.

d. Neither I nor II.

43. Under the Sales Article of the UCC, which of the following rights is(are) available to the buyer when a seller commits an anticipatory breach of contract?

	Demand assurance of performance	Cancel the contract	Collect punitive damages
a.	Yes	Yes	Yes
b	Yes	Yes	No
c.	Yes	No	Yes
d.	No	Yes	Yes

44. Larch Corp. manufactured and sold Oak a stove. The sale documents included a disclaimer of warranty for personal injury. The stove was defective. It exploded causing serious injuries to Oak's spouse. Larch was notified one week after the explosion. Under the UCC Sales Article, which of the following statements concerning Larch's liability for personal injury to Oak's spouse would be correct?

a. Larch **cannot** be liable because of a lack of privity with Oak's spouse.

b. Larch will **not** be liable because of a failure to give proper notice.

c. Larch will be liable because the disclaimer was **not** a disclaimer of all liability.

d. Larch will be liable because liability for personal injury **cannot** be disclaimed.

45. Under the Sales Article of the UCC, which of the following events will release the buyer from all its obligations under a sales contract?

a. Destruction of the goods after risk of loss passed to the buyer.

b. Impracticability of delivery under the terms of the contract.

c. Anticipatory repudiation by the buyer that is retracted before the seller cancels the contract.

d. Refusal of the seller to give written assurance of performance when reasonably demanded by the buyer.

46. Rowe Corp. purchased goods from Stair Co. that were shipped COD. Under the Sales Article of the UCC, which of the following rights does Rowe have?

a. The right to inspect the goods before paying.

b. The right to possession of the goods before paying.

c. The right to reject nonconforming goods.

d. The right to delay payment for a reasonable period of time.

47. Sklar, CPA, purchased from Wiz Corp. two computers. Sklar discovered material defects in the computers ten months after taking delivery. Three years after discovering the defects, Sklar commenced an action for breach of warranty against Wiz. Wiz has raised the statute of limitations as a defense. The original contract between Wiz and Sklar contained a conspicuous clause providing that the statute of limitations for breach of warranty actions would be limited to eighteen months. Under the circumstances, Sklar will

a. Win because the action was commenced within the four-year period as measured from the date of delivery.

b. Win because the action was commenced within the four-year period as measured from the time he discovered the breach or should have discovered the breach.

c. Lose because the clause providing that the statute of limitations would be limited to eighteen months is enforceable.

d. Lose because the statute of limitations is three years from the date of delivery with respect to written contracts.

SIMULATION PROBLEMS

Simulation Problem 1   (10 to 15 minutes)

Situation
Analysis

Angler Corp., a food distributor, is involved in the following disputes:

- On September 8, Angler shipped the wrong grade of tuna to Mason Restaurants, Inc. under a contract that stated as follows: "FOB Angler's loading dock." During shipment, the tuna was destroyed in an accident involving the common carrier's truck. Mason has refused to pay for the tuna, claiming the risk of loss belonged to Angler at the time of the accident.
- On October 3, Angler shipped 100 bushels of peaches to Classic Foods, Inc., a retail grocer. Because of a delay in shipping, the peaches rotted. Classic elected to reject the peaches and notified Angler of this decision. Angler asked Classic to return the peaches at Angler's expense. Classic refused the request, claiming it had no obligation to do so.
- On October 23, Angler orally contracted to sell Regal Fast-Food 1,500 pounds of hamburger meat for $1,500. Delivery was to be made on October 31. On October 29, after Angler had shipped the hamburger meat to Regal, Regal sent Angler the following signed correspondence:

    "We are not going to need the 1,500 pounds of meat we ordered on October 23. Don't ship."

Regal rejected the shipment and claimed it is not obligated to purchase the hamburger meat because there is no written contract between Angler and Regal.

Analysis
Situation

Determine whether each of the numbered legal conclusions is Correct or Incorrect.

		Correct	Incorrect
1.	When the accident happened, the risk of loss belonged to Angler.	O	O
2.	If Angler had shipped the correct grade of tuna to Mason, the risk of loss would have been Angler's at time of the accident.	O	O
3.	The contract between Angler and Mason was an FOB destination point contract.	O	O
4.	Angler had title to the tuna at time of the accident since Angler shipped nonconforming goods.	O	O
5.	Classic is required to return the peaches at Angler's expense per Angler's instructions.	O	O
6.	Classic may throw the peaches away because they were rotted.	O	O
7.	Since Classic elected to reject the rotted peaches, Classic may not also sue for damages.	O	O
8.	Regal is not obligated to purchase the hamburger meat because there was no written contract between Angler and Regal.	O	O
9.	The Uniform Commercial Code applies to the contract between Angler and Regal.	O	O
10.	Regal's correspondence to Angler, dated October 29, satisfies the appropriate Statute of Frauds.	O	O
11.	Angler should keep the hamburger until Regal finally accepts it and sue Regal for $1,500.	O	O
12.	Assuming that all of the original facts are the same except that Regal never sent Angler the correspondence dated October 29, then Angler may hold Regal in breach of contract.	O	O
13.	Assuming that all of the original facts are the same except that the contract was for $450, then Angler may hold Regal in breach of contract.	O	O
14.	Assume that all of the original facts are the same except that Regal never sent Angler the correspondence and Angler shipped to Regal 800 pounds of the hamburger on October 29. Regal accepted the 800 pounds. Regal, then, on October 31 orally rejected the shipment for the remaining 700 pounds. Under these facts, the contract is enforceable against Regal for the 800 pounds but not the full 1,500 pounds.	O	O
15.	Under the same facts found in 14. above, the contract is enforceable against Regal for the full 1,500 pounds.	O	O

Simulation Problem 2   (5 to 10 minutes)

Situation	
	Analysis

On February 1, Grand Corp., a manufacturer of custom cabinets, contracted in writing with Axle Co., a kitchen contractor, to sell Axle 100 unique, custom-designed, kitchen cabinets for $250,000. Axle had contracted to install the cabinets in a luxury condominium complex. The contract provided that the cabinets were to be ready for delivery by April 15 and were to be shipped FOB seller's loading dock. On April 15, Grand had eighty-five cabinets complete and delivered them, together with fifteen standard cabinets, to the trucking company for delivery to Axle. Grand faxed Axle a copy of the shipping invoice, listing the fifteen standard cabinets. On May 1, before reaching Axle, the truck was involved in a collision and all the cabinets were damaged beyond repair.

	Analysis
Situation	

Items 1 through 5 refer to the above fact pattern. For each item, determine whether (A), (B), or (C) is correct.

	(A)	**(B)**	**(C)**
1. A. The contract between Grand and Axle was a shipment contract. B. The contract between Grand and Axle was a destination contract. C. The contract between Grand and Axle was a consignment contract.	○	○	○
2. A. The risk of loss for the eighty-five custom cabinets passed to Axle on April 15. B. The risk of loss for the 100 cabinets passed to Axle on April 15. C. The risk of loss for the 100 cabinets remained with Grand.	○	○	○
3. A. The contract between Grand and Axle was invalid because **no** delivery date was stated. B. The contract between Grand and Axle was voidable because Grand shipped only eighty-five custom cabinets. C. The contract between Grand and Axle was void because the goods were destroyed.	○	○	○
4. A. Grand's shipment of the standard cabinets was a breach of the contract with Axle. B. Grand would **not** be considered to have breached the contract until Axle rejected the standard cabinets. C. Grand made a counteroffer by shipping the standard cabinets.	○	○	○
5. A. Axle is entitled to specific performance from Grand because of the unique nature of the goods. B. Axle is required to purchase substitute goods (cover) and is entitled to the difference in cost from Grand. C. Axle is entitled to punitive damages because of Grand's intentional shipment of nonconforming goods.	○	○	○

MULTIPLE-CHOICE ANSWERS

1. c	__ __	11. d	__ __	21. d	__ __	31. d	__ __	41. a	__ __
2. b	__ __	12. a	__ __	22. d	__ __	32. d	__ __	42. c	__ __
3. c	__ __	13. b	__ __	23. d	__ __	33. b	__ __	43. b	__ __
4. a	__ __	14. d	__ __	24. c	__ __	34. a	__ __	44. d	__ __
5. a	__ __	15. d	__ __	25. d	__ __	35. b	__ __	45. d	__ __
6. a	__ __	16. c	__ __	26. b	__ __	36. b	__ __	46. c	__ __
7. c	__ __	17. a	__ __	27. c	__ __	37. b	__ __	47. c	__ __
8. a	__ __	18. b	__ __	28. d	__ __	38. a	__ __		
9. d	__ __	19. a	__ __	29. a	__ __	39. a	__ __	1st: __/47 = __%
10. a	__ __	20. b	__ __	30. c	__ __	40. b	__ __	2nd: __/47 = __%

MULTIPLE-CHOICE ANSWER EXPLANATIONS

A. Contracts for Sale of Goods

1. (c)   Under the Sales Article of the UCC, acceptance is valid when sent if a reasonable method is used; therefore answer (c) is correct as both acceptances were sent prior to the end of the ten-day period.

2. (b)   A firm offer is a written, signed offer concerning the sale of goods, by a merchant, giving assurance that it will be held open for a specified time and is irrevocable for that period, not to exceed three months. Answer (a) is incorrect because if the firm offer does not state a period of time, it will remain open for a reasonable period of time, not to exceed three months. Answer (c) is incorrect as consideration is not required for a firm offer, but for an option contract. Answer (d) is incorrect because under the firm offer rule, only the offeror need be a merchant.

3. (c)   Under the UCC, an oral modification of an existing contract for the sale of goods for a price less than $500 is considered binding. Since the washer and dryer Mason contracted to buy cost less than $500, Acme's oral agreement to change the date of delivery would be enforceable. The fact that Mason is not a merchant won't affect whether or not the oral modification is binding. In order to have a firm offer, the offer must be made by a merchant in a signed writing which gives assurance that the offer will be held open. In this situation, the modification of an offer already accepted is being discussed rather than a firm offer.

4. (a)   Under the Sales Article of the UCC, both the seller and buyer are obligated to perform a contract in good faith. Answer (b) is incorrect because certain provisions, such as the battle of forms provision, only apply to merchants. Answer (c) is incorrect because the Sales Article of the UCC applies to the sale of goods without regard to the price of goods. Answer (d) is incorrect because certain provisions of the UCC may be disclaimed by written or oral agreement, such as warranty liability.

5. (a)   Article 2 of the UCC applies to sales of goods. Common law generally applies to contracts for services and real estate. Even though goods are used in this service contract, the predominate feature of this contract is the service. Article 2 of the UCC governs this contract even though it is oral and for a small sum. Even though the chair at one time involved a lot of labor, it is still a sale of goods. Also, whether the parties are merchants or not is not an issue on whether Article 2 applies. The heater which is not yet installed in the home is a sale of goods. Once it is installed in the home, it becomes part of the real estate for any future

sale of the home. Common law rules would apply to any such future sale.

6. (a)   Under common law, an acceptance must be unequivocal and unqualified in agreeing to the precise terms specified by the offer. However, the Uniform Commercial Code alters this general rule as far as the sales of goods is concerned. Under the UCC, an acceptance containing additional terms is a valid acceptance unless the acceptance is expressly conditional upon the offeror's agreement to the additional terms. In this situation, a valid contract has been formed between Cookie Co. and Distrib Markets. Distrib Markets' acceptance was not conditional upon Cookie's agreement to the additional term and, thus, a contract is formed regardless of Cookie's agreement or objection to the additional term. This contract was for the sale of goods and is governed by the UCC rather than by common law. Under common law, Distrib Markets' reply would have been a rejection and counteroffer; but under the UCC, a contract was formed.

7. (c)   This exception for specially manufactured goods, even if the contract is for over $500, is one of the important exceptions found in the Statute of Fraud provisions of the Uniform Commercial Code. Answer (a) is incorrect because the exception for specially manufactured goods applies to this fact pattern and thus this contract need not be in writing. Answer (b) is incorrect because the fire did not prevent the custom door contract from being performed. Answer (d) is incorrect because the contract was fully enforceable and Art had no legal right to cancel the contract.

8. (a)   Ram may accept the offer by shipping the goods. Under the UCC, shipping nonconforming goods constitutes an acceptance, also unless the seller notifies the buyer that the shipment is given only as an accommodation to the buyer. Answer (b) is incorrect because this shipment counts as an acceptance, not as a counteroffer. Answer (c) is incorrect because an order to buy goods for prompt shipment allows the seller to accept by either a prompt promise to ship or by the actual prompt shipment itself.

9. (d)   In order to have a contract, there must be both an offer and an acceptance. Even though an acceptance can occur in different ways, by speech, by writing, or by action, the actual acceptance is a required element of a contract. Under the UCC Sales Article, a binding contract may be present if the parties had intended to form a contract even though certain elements of the contract are missing. These open terms will be filled by specific provisions of the UCC, including provisions for open price, open delivery, or open quantity. Note that in the case of quantity, output contracts, requirements contracts, and exclusive dealing's contracts are enforceable though the actual quantity may not be known in advance.

10. **(a)** The UCC provides that a confirmation satisfies the UCC Statute of Frauds, if an oral contract between merchants is confirmed in writing within a reasonable period of time, and the confirmation is signed by the party sending it and received by the other party. Both parties are bound unless the party receiving the confirmation submits a written objection within ten days of receipt. In this situation, a valid contract has been formed since Webstar did not object to Northco's purchase order. In a sale-of-goods transaction, the contract must be signed by the party to be charged to be enforceable. However, in the case of a written confirmation of an oral agreement between merchants, the confirmation need only be signed by the party sending the confirmation. The use of a signed purchase order satisfies the UCC Statute of Frauds.

11. **(d)** A firm offer is an offer for the sale of goods that is written and signed by a merchant (or employee of the merchant) that agrees to keep the offer open. This offer is valid without consideration for three months since no time was specified in the fact pattern. Patch will win in a suit to enforce the rain check because Patch tried to use it one month later. Answer (a) is incorrect because the UCC specifies a three-month period when no time is detailed in the firm offer. Answer (b) is incorrect because when no time is specified, the UCC gives Patch three months to accept the offer. Answer (c) is incorrect because there was no offer and acceptance when Patch first tried to purchase the advertised item.

12. **(a)** An output contract is enforceable under the UCC even though an actual quantity is not mentioned in the contract. The output contract is supported by consideration because the seller has agreed not to sell that output to any other party. Answer (b) is incorrect because when the price is omitted, the UCC construes it as the reasonable price at the time of delivery. The quantity is construed as the output of the sheep rancher. Answer (c) is incorrect because although quantity is an important term in the contract, the UCC allows the quantity term to be defined by output. Answer (d) is incorrect because the UCC allows price terms to be based on the reasonable price and quantity terms to be defined by output.

B.1.a. Warranty of Title

13. **(b)** Under the warranty of title, the seller warrants good title, rightful transfer and freedom from any security interest or lien of which the buyer has no knowledge at the time of sale. Answer (a) is incorrect because the warranty of title can be disclaimed by specific language or circumstances which give the buyer reason to know s/he is receiving less than full title. Answer (c) is incorrect because the warranty does not have to be in writing. Answer (d) is incorrect because the seller does not have to be a merchant for the seller to give the warranty of title.

B.1.b. Express Warranties

14. **(d)** In the Sales Article of the UCC, express warranties include warranties that the goods will conform to any description used or any sample or model shown. Answer (a)

is incorrect because although usage of trade can help interpret terms used in contracts, it is not a warranty. Answers (b) and (c) are incorrect because the warranty of fitness for a particular purpose and the warranty of merchantability are both implied warranties.

B.1.c. Implied Warranties

15. **(d)** The implied warranty of merchantability, which guarantees that goods are fit for ordinary purposes, arises as a matter of law when the seller is a merchant who ordinarily sells the goods purchased. Answer (a) is incorrect because the warranty is implied, and therefore need not be in writing. Answer (c) is incorrect because the warranty applies unless specifically disclaimed by the merchant.

16. **(c)** The implied warranty of merchantability is always implied if the seller is a merchant with respect to the type of goods being sold. Since Ram is a merchant, this warranty would apply. Also, under the UCC, the seller warrants good title, rightful transfer, and freedom from any security interest or lien of which the buyer has no knowledge when the contract was made. This warranty of title applies unless the merchant specifically disclaims it. In this situation, both the implied warranty of merchantability and the implied warranty of title apply. The implied warranty of fitness for a particular purpose is created only when a seller has reason to know the buyer's particular purpose and knows the buyer is relying on the skill and judgment of the seller selecting the goods.

17. **(a)** The implied warranty of merchantability applies only when the seller is a merchant with respect to the type of goods being sold. The seller must be a merchant in order for the buyer to successfully sue under this warranty. Answer (b) is incorrect because the buyer does not have to prove negligence to be able to recover under this implied warranty. Answer (c) is incorrect because the implied warranty of merchantability extends to parties other than the purchaser even without privity of contract. Answer (d) is incorrect because an action for a breach based on the warranty of merchantability would not depend on the outcome of an action based on strict liability.

18. **(b)** The implied warranty of fitness for a particular purpose is created when a seller (merchant or nonmerchant) has reason to know the buyer's particular purpose and knows the buyer is relying on the skill and judgment of the seller selecting the goods. Since the warranty of fitness for a particular purpose is an implied warranty, there is no requirement that it be made in writing.

19. **(a)** The implied warranty of merchantability may be disclaimed by a seller's oral or written statement. This statement normally must contain some form of the word "merchantability" to be effective. However, goods sold "as is" or "with all faults" are an exception to that rule. Answer (b) is incorrect because the implied warranty of merchantability arises whenever the seller is a merchant with respect to the goods being sold. The status of the buyer is irrelevant. Answer (c) is incorrect because the implied warranty of merchantability guarantees that the goods are of an average fair quality and are fit for ordinary purposes. Under this warranty, the seller does not guarantee that the goods are fit for all purposes for which the buyer intends to use the goods. Answer (d) is incorrect because this warranty is always implied if the seller is a merchant. It does not have to be a part of the basis of the bargain to be binding on the seller.

B.3. Strict Liability

20. (b)   Common carriers' liability is based on strict liability. As such, the common carrier is liable for losses to property whether or not the common carrier was negligent. Common law exceptions to strict liability include natural disasters which are responsible for damages.

21. (d)   Under the theory of strict liability, the plaintiff must establish the following: (1) the seller was engaged in the business of selling the product, (2) the product was defective, (3) the defect was unreasonably dangerous to the plaintiff, and (4) the defect caused injury to the plaintiff. If the plaintiff can prove these elements, then the seller will be liable regardless of whether the seller was negligent or at fault for the defect. Thus, High can recover even if he cannot show any negligence was involved. Answer (a) is incorrect because contributory negligence is not an available defense in a strict liability case. Answer (b) is incorrect because the manufacturer's only defenses are misuse and assumption of risk by the buyer. The fact that the manufacturer followed the custom of the industry is irrelevant under strict liability. Answer (c) is incorrect because privity of contract is not a defense under strict liability since the suit is not based on contract law.

22. (d)   Under the theory of strict liability, the plaintiff must establish the following: (1) the seller was engaged in the business of selling the product, (2) the product was defective when sold, (3) the defect was unreasonably dangerous to the plaintiff, and (4) the defect caused injury to the plaintiff. If the plaintiff can prove these elements, then the seller will be liable regardless of whether the seller was negligent or at fault for the defect.

23. (d)   The standard of care required for a common carrier bailee is based on strict liability rather than reasonable care. Common carrier bailees, however, are not liable for acts of God, acts of the shipper, or acts of a public enemy. In this case, the improper packing was done by the party doing the shipping. Answer (a) is incorrect because acts or theft by other parties make the common carrier liable. Answer (b) is incorrect because acts such as negligence, by others, still leave the common carrier liable. Answer (c) is incorrect because acts of a railroad employee cause the common carrier to be liable.

C. Transfer of Property Rights

24. (c)   Since Rio was a good-faith purchaser, Rio obtains good title to the rocking chair. Therefore, the remedy that Tillis has left is to sue McGraw for money damages. There are insufficient facts to show fraud.

25. (d)   If a person entrusts possession of goods to a merchant who normally deals in that type of goods, a good-faith purchaser obtains title to those goods. Jake purchased the bike as he was unaware that Pete did not own the bike. As a good-faith purchaser, he obtains title to the bike. Answer (a) is incorrect because Yancie cannot repossess the bike from Jake because Jake obtained good title to the bike. Yancie can, however, get the value of the bike from Pete. Answer (b) is incorrect because Jake obtains title to the bike and, thus, Pete cannot repossess it from him. Answer (c) is

incorrect because Yancie can recover the value of the bike from Pete, not Jake.

26. (b)   A requirement needed for the title of goods to pass to the buyer is that the goods must have been identified to the contract. Answers (a) and (c) are incorrect because the seller can keep possession of goods and identify them to the contract and still have title pass to the buyer. Answer (d) is incorrect because title passes to the buyer based upon the terms of the agreement. Payment can take place before or after.

D. Risk of Loss and Title

27. (c)   In an FOB place of shipment contract, the buyer obtains the risk of loss once the goods are delivered to the carrier.

28. (d)   The title of goods generally passes to the buyer when the seller completes performance with respect to the physical delivery of the goods. Because the shipping terms of the contract are FOB Parco's warehouse, the title of goods passes to Parco on tender at the destination. This is true even if the goods are nonconforming. However, Parco's rejection of the appliances will revert the title of the goods back to Lace at the time of the rejection.

29. (a)   Under the Sales Article of the Uniform Commercial Code and the United Nations Convention for the International Sale of Goods, generally the risk of loss of the goods sold will pass to the buyer when the seller delivers goods to the first carrier for transmission to the buyer. Answers (b), (c), and (d) are incorrect because these would result in risk of loss to the buyer only if the contract specifically stated so, thus changing the general rule.

30. (c)   The purchase of goods on a sale on approval allows the buyer to return the goods even if they conform to the contract. Therefore, the seller retains the title and the risk of loss until the buyer accepts the goods.

31. (d)   Risk of loss transfers from a merchant seller to a buyer upon the buyer's physical receipt of goods. Therefore, neither tender of the goods at the seller's place of business, nor use of the seller's truck to deliver the goods are events which transfer risk of loss to the buyer as the merchant seller still retains possession of the goods.

32. (d)   The UCC places risk of loss on the breaching party. Since Cey shipped nonconforming goods, it breached the contract and would have risk of loss until the nonconforming goods were accepted by the buyer or until the goods were cured by Cey. Since Deck rejected the goods and Cey did not cure the goods, risk of loss remained with Cey. Shipping terms have no bearing on risk of loss in this situation because the goods did not conform to the contract. Answer (a) is incorrect because Deck would only bear risk of loss if the goods conformed to the contract. Answer (b) is incorrect because the risk of loss was never transferred to Deck since the goods were nonconforming. Answer (c) is incorrect because if the goods were conforming, risk of loss would pass to Deck at Cey's warehouse based on the shipping terms "FOB Cey's warehouse."

33. (b)   The parties to the contract may agree as to which party bears risk of loss. In the absence of this, under the UCC, the shipping terms determine who bears risk of loss.

34. **(a)**   In this situation, since Wool is not a merchant seller, the risk of loss passed to Bond on Wool's tender of delivery. If Wool had been a merchant seller, then the risk of loss would not have passed until the buyer received the goods. Answers (c) and (d) are incorrect because the risk of loss passed when the nonmerchant seller (Wool) tendered delivery of the painting. Answer (b) is incorrect because the risk of loss would not pass at the time the contract was formed since the seller still had possession of the painting and had not attempted to deliver it to the buyer.

35. **(b)**   Common carriers are not liable for losses due to causes deemed acts of God. Although a common carrier may limit its damages to a dollar amount specified in the contract, it is not liable at all in this case. Funston, not the customer, had the risk of loss due to the FOB terms.

E.5. Seller's Remedies

36. **(b)**   Statement I is incorrect because a liquidated damages provision is enforced if it is not punitive but amounts to a reasonable estimate of what the loss will be in the event of a breach of contract. If a reasonable estimate of the loss from a breach of contract cannot be estimated with a reasonable degree of certainty, the parties can agree on an amount, but still the amount cannot be punitive. Statement II is correct because a seller is allowed to retain a deposit of up to $500 when a buyer defaults even if the parties had not agreed to a liquidated damages clause.

37. **(b)**   The seller generally discharges his obligation to the buyer by placing conforming goods at the buyer's disposition and giving the buyer reasonable notice to enable the buyer to take delivery.

38. **(a)**   Under the Sales Article of the UCC, the seller has the following remedies against the buyer upon breach: withhold delivery of the goods; stop delivery of the carrier of the goods; resell the goods; recover compensatory and incidental damages; recover the goods from the buyer upon the buyer's insolvency; cancel the contract. Therefore, answer (a) is correct as the seller has the rights of contract cancellation and damage recovery available to him/her.

39. **(a)**   The UCC gives the seller a choice of many remedies when the buyer breaches the contract involving a sale of goods. These remedies include allowing the seller to resell the goods identified to the contract and to recover the amount that the seller receives that is less than the contract price. Also, once the buyer breaches, the seller may suspend his/her performance and may prevent the carrier from making the delivery of the goods.

40. **(b)**   A seller has the right to resell goods to another if the buyer refuses to accept the goods upon delivery. Answer (a) is incorrect because specific performance is not a remedy available to the seller. Baker cannot force Lazur to accept the word processor. Answer (c) is incorrect because Baker has a couple of additional remedies available. Baker can recover the full contract price plus incidental damages if he is unable to resell the identified goods. Alternatively, if the difference between the market value and contract price is inadequate to place Baker in as good a position as performance would have, then Baker can sue for lost profits plus incidental damages. Answer (d) is incorrect because Baker could sue for consequential damages that Lazur had reason to know Baker would incur as a result of Lazur's breach.

41. **(a)**   By advising Mazur on June 1 that it would not accept or pay for the wheat, Good has engaged in anticipatory repudiation. Anticipatory repudiation occurs when a party renounces the duty to perform the contract before the party's obligation to perform arises. Anticipatory repudiation discharges the nonrepudiating party (Mazur) from the contract and allows this party to sue for breach immediately. In this situation, Mazur could successfully sue Good for the difference between the resale price and the contract price on June 2. Answer (b) is incorrect because Mazur was discharged from the contract on June 1 and would not have to wait until after June 23 to resell the wheat. Answer (c) is incorrect because Good would only be allowed to retract its anticipatory breach if Mazur had ignored this breach and awaited performance at the appointed date. Answer (d) is incorrect because specific performance is only allowed for unique goods or for other situations in which monetary damages are not appropriate.

E.6. Buyer's Remedies

42. **(c)**   Pickens has committed an anticipatory breach of contract. Thus, Crocket, as the aggrieved party, has different options. Crocket may treat it as a present breach of contract with the remedies available for breach of contract. One of these remedies is that the aggrieved party (Crocket) may cancel the contract. Another option is that Crocket may wait for a reasonable time to see if Pickens will change his/her mind and still deliver.

43. **(b)**   The buyer has the following remedies against the seller: upon receipt of nonconforming goods, the buyer may reject the goods, accept the goods, or accept any unit and reject the remainder; the buyer has the right to cover (purchase goods elsewhere upon the seller's breach); the buyer may recover damages (not punitive) for nondelivery of goods or repudiation of the sales contract by the seller; the buyer may recover damages (not punitive) for breach in regard to accepted goods; the buyer may recover goods identified in the contract in possession of the seller upon the seller's insolvency; the buyer may sue for specific performance when the goods are unique; the buyer has the right of replevin (form of legal action to recover specific goods from the seller which are being withheld from the buyer wrongfully); the buyer can cancel the contract; the buyer has a security interest in the goods after the seller's breach; the buyer can recover liquidated damages.

44. **(d)**   UCC Section 2-719(3) states that a limitation of damages for personal injury **in the case of consumer goods** is considered to be unconscionable and thus not allowed. Although limitations of damages for personal injury in the case of nonconsumer goods can be allowed, answer (d) is correct since one limits "personal injury" to the stove which was apparently being used for consumer use in this fact pattern. Answer (a) is incorrect because under the UCC, the spouse, being a member of the household expecting to use the stove, may recover for damages. Answer (b) is incorrect because Larch was notified shortly after the explosion. This notice, however, was not required. Answer (c) is incorrect because even though the disclaimer did not disclaim all liability, it did attempt to disclaim personal injury. This disclaimer for personal injuries, however, is not allowed for the reasons mentioned above. Answer (d) is chosen as being more specific than answer (c).

45.   (d)   Either party in a sales contract under the Sales Article of the UCC may demand adequate assurance of performance when reasonable grounds for insecurity exist with respect to the performance of the other party. Refusal to give written assurance will release the other party from all obligations from the sales contract. Answer (a) is incorrect because the buyer has assumed the risk of loss. Answer (b) is incorrect because a seller may substitute another reasonable delivery method if the method of delivery specified in the contract has been made impracticable. A seller may recover damages based on a buyer's repudiation of the agreement, but here the repudiation has been retracted and the obligations of buyer and seller remain intact.

46.   (c)   The Sales Article of the UCC provides that a buyer has the right to reject goods which are not in conformity with the terms of contract between seller and buyer. The buyer also has the option to accept nonconforming goods and recover damages resulting from the nonconformity. The UCC allows the buyer to inspect the goods before payment except when they are shipped COD. When goods are shipped COD, the buyer's payment for the goods is required for delivery.

E.7. Statute of Limitations

47.   (c)   The statute of limitations for the sale of goods is generally four years; however, the parties may agree to reduce the statute to a period of not less than one year. Therefore, Sklar will lose because the clause providing that the statute of limitations would be limited to eighteen months is enforceable, and the action was not brought within the required time period. Answer (b) is incorrect because a breach of warranty occurs upon the tender of delivery, not upon the discovery of the defect, and the statute begins running at the time the breach occurs. Answer (d) is incorrect because the statute is eighteen months as outlined in the contract.

SOLUTIONS TO SIMULATION PROBLEMS

Simulation Problem 1

		Analysis	
	Situation		

		Correct	*Incorrect*
1.	When the accident happened, the risk of loss belonged to Angler.	●	○
2.	If Angler had shipped the correct grade of tuna to Mason, the risk of loss would have been Angler's at time of the accident.	○	●
3.	The contract between Angler and Mason was an FOB destination point contract.	○	●
4.	Angler had title to the tuna at time of the accident since Angler shipped nonconforming goods.	○	●
5.	Classic is required to return the peaches at Angler's expense per Angler's instructions.	●	○
6.	Classic may throw the peaches away because they were rotted.	○	●
7.	Since Classic elected to reject the rotted peaches, Classic may not also sue for damages.	○	●
8.	Regal is not obligated to purchase the hamburger meat because there was no written contract between Angler and Regal.	○	●
9.	The Uniform Commercial Code applies to the contract between Angler and Regal.	●	○
10.	Regal's correspondence to Angler, dated October 29, satisfies the appropriate Statute of Frauds.	●	○
11.	Angler should keep the hamburger until Regal finally accepts it and sue Regal for $1,500.	○	●
12.	Assuming that all of the original facts are the same except that Regal never sent Angler the correspondence dated October 29, then Angler may hold Regal in breach of contract.	○	●
13.	Assuming that all of the original facts are the same except that the contract was for $450, then Angler may hold Regal in breach of contract.	●	○
14.	Assume that all of the original facts are the same except that Regal never sent Angler the correspondence and Angler shipped to Regal 800 pounds of the hamburger on October 29. Regal accepted the 800 pounds. Regal, then, on October 31 orally rejected the shipment for the remaining 700 pounds. Under these facts, the contract is enforceable against Regal for the 800 pounds but not the full 1,500 pounds.	●	○
15.	Under the same facts found in **14.** above, the contract is enforceable against Regal for the full 1,500 pounds.	○	●

Explanation of solutions

   1.   (C) Angler breached the contract by shipping nonconforming goods to Mason. Therefore, Angler retains the risk of loss until it cures or until Mason accepts the goods despite the nonconformity.

   2.   (I) This was an FOB shipping point contract so that the risk of loss would have passed over to the buyer upon delivery to the carrier.

   3.   (I) Because the terms were FOB the seller's loading dock, it was an FOB shipping point contract.

   4.   (I) Title and risk of loss do not necessarily pass to a buyer at the same time. In this case, risk of loss remained with the seller because of the shipment of nonconforming goods. However, title passed under the original terms despite the breach of contract.

   5.   (C) Classic is obligated to follow any reasonable instructions of the seller as a merchant who rejects goods, even nonconforming, under a contract.

   6.   (I) Classic must follow the reasonable instructions given by Angler to return the peaches at Angler's expense.

   7.   (I) Classic may also sue for any damages that were caused by the delay in shipping.

   8.   (I) Although the contract must be evidenced by a writing because it involved a sale of goods for more than $500, the correspondence that Regal sent to Angler on October 29 satisfies the writing requirement under the UCC Statute of Frauds. It indicated that a contract had been made. It was signed by Regal, the party to be charged, and it stated the quantity. The price was not needed in the correspondence.

   9.   (C) The Uniform Commercial Code applies because the contract was for a sale of goods (i.e., hamburger meat).

   10.   (C) The correspondence satisfies the UCC Statute of Frauds which does not require that all terms be in writing.

11.   (**I**) Angler should resort to an appropriate remedy such as reselling the hamburger to someone else in a commercially reasonable fashion. If Angler gets less than the original contract price, it may recover the difference from Regal.

12.   (**I**) Since there was no writing to evidence the contract for $1,500, it is not enforceable.

13.   (**C**) The contract need not be in writing because it was for less than $500.

14.   (**C**) Since Angler shipped and Regal accepted a portion of the goods, the oral contract is enforceable up to the amount shipped and accepted. This is one of the exceptions in the UCC Statute of Frauds.

15.   (**I**) The exception in the UCC Statute of Frauds allows the oral contract to be enforced up to the amount delivered and accepted or paid for.

Simulation Problem 2

	(A)	(B)	(C)
1. A. The contract between Grand and Axle was a shipment contract.	●	○	○
B. The contract between Grand and Axle was a destination contract.			
C. The contract between Grand and Axle was a consignment contract.			
2. A. The risk of loss for the eighty-five custom cabinets passed to Axle on April 15.	○	○	●
B. The risk of loss for the 100 cabinets passed to Axle on April 15.			
C. The risk of loss for the 100 cabinets remained with Grand.			
3. A. The contract between Grand and Axle was invalid because **no** delivery date was stated.	○	●	○
B. The contract between Grand and Axle was voidable because Grand shipped only eighty-five custom cabinets.			
C. The contract between Grand and Axle was void because the goods were destroyed.			
4. A. Grand's shipment of the standard cabinets was a breach of the contract with Axle.	●	○	○
B. Grand would **not** be considered to have breached the contract until Axle rejected the standard cabinets.			
C. Grand made a counteroffer by shipping the standard cabinets.			
5. A. Axle is entitled to specific performance from Grand because of the unique nature of the goods.	●	○	○
B. Axle is required to purchase substitute goods (cover) and is entitled to the difference in cost from Grand.			
C. Axle is entitled to punitive damages because of Grand's intentional shipment of nonconforming goods.			

Explanation of solutions

1.   (**A**) The terms of the contract were "FOB seller's loading dock" which is a shipment contract. Answer (B) is incorrect because a destination contract would state terms meaning FOB buyer's location. Answer (C) is incorrect because a consignment is treated as a sale or return. That is, the owner of the goods delivers them to another party to attempt to sell them. If this other party, known as the consignee, does not sell the goods, they are returned. Such is not the case in this fact pattern.

2.   (**C**) Risk of loss would normally pass to the buyer, Axle Co., under this shipment contract. However, since the seller, Grand, breached the contract, risk of loss remains with Grand. Since the cabinets are "custom designed, kitchen cabinets" for a luxury condominium complex, they would need to match. Therefore, the 100 units could be construed as a commercial unit and the risk of loss for the entire 100 cabinets remained with Grand. Answer (A) is incorrect because the 100 cabinets were a commercial unit and thus the risk of loss of the entire commercial unit remained with Grand. Answer (B) is incorrect because even though the terms were "FOB seller's loading dock," the risk of loss remained with the seller, Grand, because of Grand's breach of contract.

3.   (**B**) The contract between Grand and Axle was voidable because Axle may at its option choose to accept or reject all or part of the cabinets. Answer (C) is incorrect because if the contract were void, neither party would have the option of remaining in the contract. Answer (A) is incorrect because under the UCC, if the delivery date is not stated, the time becomes within a reasonable time.

4.   (**A**) Once Grand ships nonconforming goods, a breach of contract has occurred. Answer (B) is incorrect because the breach has occurred even without Axle needing to reject the shipment. Axle then has the right to accept all, part, or none of the shipment. Answer (C) is incorrect because the shipment of nonconforming goods acts as a breach rather than a counteroffer.

5.   (**A**) Since the cabinets are unique and custom-designed, specific performance is allowed if Axle so chooses. Answer (B) is incorrect because Axle is not required to cover, especially because the cabinets are unique. Answer (C) is incorrect because punitive damages are generally not allowed for a breach of contract even if the breach is intentional.

MULTIPLE-CHOICE QUESTIONS (1-50)

1. Under the Negotiable Instruments Article of the UCC, an endorsement of an instrument "for deposit only" is an example of what type of endorsement?
   a.   Blank.
   b.   Qualified.
   c.   Restrictive.
   d.   Special.

2.

To: Middlesex National Bank	
Nassau, N.Y.	
	September 15, 2001
Pay to the order of Robert Silver	$4,000.00
Four Thousand and xx/100	Dollars
On October 1, 2001	
	Lynn Dexter
	Lynn Dexter

The above instrument is a
   a.   Draft.
   b.   Postdated check.
   c.   Trade acceptance.
   d.   Promissory note.

3. Which of the following statements regarding negotiable instruments is **not** correct?
   a.   A certificate of deposit is a type of note.
   b.   A check is a type of draft.
   c.   A promissory note is a type of draft.
   d.   A certificate of deposit is issued by a bank.

4. Based on the following instrument:

May 19, 2001
I promise to pay to the order of A. B. Shark $1,000 (one thousand and one hundred dollars) with interest thereon at the rate of 12% per annum.
T. T. Tile
T. T. Tile
Guaranty
I personally guaranty payment by T. T. Tile.
N. A. Abner
N. A. Abner

The instrument is a
   a.   Promissory demand note.
   b.   Sight draft.
   c.   Check.
   d.   Trade acceptance.

5. Under the Commercial Paper Article of the UCC, which of the following documents would be considered an order to pay?
   I. Draft
   II. Certificate of deposit
   a.   I only.
   b.   II only.
   c.   Both I and II.
   d.   Neither I nor II.

6. An instrument that is otherwise negotiable on its face states "Pay to Jenny Larson." Which of the following statements is(are) correct?

   I. It is negotiable if it is a check.
   II. It is negotiable if it is a draft drawn on a corporation.
   III. It is negotiable if it is a promissory note.
   a.   I only.
   b.   I and II only.
   c.   II and III only.
   d.   I, II, and III.

7. Under the Commercial Paper Article of the UCC, for a note to be negotiable it must
   a.   Be payable to order or to bearer.
   b.   Be signed by the payee.
   c.   Contain references to all agreements between the parties.
   d.   Contain necessary conditions of payment.

8. On February 15, 2001, P.D. Stone obtained the following instrument from Astor Co. for $1,000. Stone was aware that Helco, Inc. disputed liability under the instrument because of an alleged breach by Astor of the referenced computer purchase agreement. On March 1, 2001, Willard Bank obtained the instrument from Stone for $3,900. Willard had no knowledge that Helco disputed liability under the instrument.

February 12, 2001
Helco, Inc. promises to pay to Astor Co. or bearer the sum of $4,900 (four thousand four hundred and 00/100 dollars) on March 12, 2001 (maker may elect to extend due date to March 31, 2001) with interest thereon at the rate of 12% per annum.
HELCO, INC.
By: *A. J. Help*
A. J. Help, President
Reference: Computer purchase agreement dated February 12, 2001

The reverse side of the instrument is endorsed as follows:

Pay to the order of Willard Bank, without recourse
P.D. Stone
P.D. Stone

The instrument is
   a.   Nonnegotiable, because of the reference to the computer purchase agreement.
   b.   Nonnegotiable, because the numerical amount differs from the written amount.
   c.   Negotiable, even though the maker has the right to extend the time for payment.
   d.   Negotiable, when held by Astor, but nonnegotiable when held by Willard Bank.

9. A draft made in the United States calls for payment in Canadian dollars.
   a.   The draft is nonnegotiable because it calls for payment in money of another country.
   b.   The draft is nonnegotiable because the rate of exchange may fluctuate thus violating the sum certain rule.
   c.   The instrument is negotiable if it satisfies all of the other elements of negotiability.
   d.   The instrument is negotiable only if it has the exchange rate written on the draft.

10. An instrument reads as follows:

> $10,000   Ludlow, Vermont   February 1, 2001
>
> I promise to pay to the order of Custer Corp. $10,000 within ten days after the sale of my two-carat diamond ring. I pledge the sale proceeds to secure my obligation hereunder.
>
> *R. Harris*
> _____
> R. Harris

Which of the following statements correctly describes the above instrument?

    a.   The instrument is nonnegotiable because it is **not** payable at a definite time.

    b.   The instrument is nonnegotiable because it is secured by the proceeds of the sale of the ring.

    c.   The instrument is a negotiable promissory note.

    d.   The instrument is a negotiable sight draft payable on demand.

11. Kline is holding a promissory note in which he is the payer and Breck is the promissor. One of the terms of the note states that payment is subject to the terms of the contract dated March 1 of the current year between Breck and Kline. Does this term destroy negotiability?

    a.   No, if the contract is readily available.

    b.   No, since the note can be enforced without regard to the mentioned contract.

    c.   No, as long as the terms in the mentioned contract are commercially reasonable.

    d.   Yes, since this term causes the note to have a conditional promise.

12. Based on the following instrument:

> May 19, 2001
>
> I promise to pay to the order of A. B. Shark $1,000 (one thousand and one hundred dollars) with interest thereon at the rate of 12% per annum.
>
> *T. T. Tile*
> _____
> T. T. Tile
>
> **Guaranty**
>
> I personally guaranty payment by T. T. Tile.
>
> *N. A. Abner*
> _____
> N. A. Abner

The instrument is

    a.   Nonnegotiable even though it is payable on demand.

    b.   Nonnegotiable because the numeric amount differs from the written amount.

    c.   Negotiable even though a payment date is **not** specified.

    d.   Negotiable because of Abner's guaranty.

13. A note has an interest rate that varies based on the stated rate of 2% above the prime rate as determined by XYZ Bank in New York City. Under the Revised Article 3 of the Uniform Commercial Code, which of the following is true?

    a.   This interest rate provision destroys negotiability since it does not constitute a sum certain.

    b.   This note is not negotiable because the holder has to look outside the instrument to determine what the prime rate is.

    c.   The interest rate provision destroys negotiability because the prime rate can vary before the time the note comes due.

    d.   The interest rate provision is allowed in negotiable notes and does not destroy negotiability.

14. While auditing your client, Corbin Company, you see a check that is postdated and states "Pay to Corbin Company." You also see a note that is due in forty days and also says "Pay to Corbin Company." You note that both instruments contain all of the elements of negotiability except for possibly the ones raised by this fact pattern. Which of the following is(are) negotiable instruments?

    a.   The check.

    b.   The note.

    c.   Both the check and the note.

    d.   Neither the check nor the note.

15. Under the Revised Article 3 of the Uniform Code, which of the following is true if the maker of a note provides that payment must come out of a designated fund?

    a.   This is allowed even though the maker is not personally obligated to pay.

    b.   Since the instrument is not based on the general credit of the maker, the instrument is not negotiable.

    c.   The promise to pay is conditional; therefore, the note is not negotiable.

    d.   The instrument is not negotiable if the designated fund has insufficient funds.

16. Wyden holds a check that is written out to him. The check has the amount in words as five hundred dollars. The amount in figures on this check states $200. Which of the following is correct?

    a.   The check is cashable for $500.

    b.   The check is cashable for $200.

    c.   The check is not cashable because the amounts differ.

    d.   The check is not cashable because the amounts differ by more than 10%.

17. Under the Commercial Paper Article of the UCC, which of the following requirements must be met for a transferee of order paper to become a holder?

    I. Possession
   II. Endorsement of transferor

    a.   I only.

    b.   II only.

    c.   Both I and II.

    d.   Neither I nor II.

18. The following endorsements appear on the back of a negotiable promissory note payable to Lake Corp.

> Pay to John Smith only
> *Frank Parker*, President of Lake Corp.
>
> *John Smith*
>
> Pay to the order of Sharp, Inc. without recourse, but only if Sharp delivers computers purchased by Mary Harris by March 15, 2001.
> *Mary Harris*
>
> *Sarah Sharp*, President of Sharp, Inc.

Which of the following statements is correct?

a. The note became nonnegotiable as a result of Parker's endorsement.

b. Harris' endorsement was a conditional promise to pay and caused the note to be nonnegotiable.

c. Smith's endorsement effectively prevented further negotiation of the note.

d. Harris' signature was **not** required to effectively negotiate the note to Sharp.

19. A note is made payable to the order of Ann Jackson on the front. On the back, Ann Jackson signs it in blank and delivers it to Jerry Lin. Lin puts "Pay to Jerry Lin" above Jackson's endorsement. Which of the following statements is **false** concerning this note?

a. After Lin wrote "Pay to Jerry Lin," the note became order paper.

b. After Jackson endorsed the note but before Lin wrote on it, the note was bearer paper.

c. Lin needs to endorse this note to negotiate it further, even though he personally wrote "Pay to Jerry Lin" on the back.

d. The note is not negotiable because Lin wrote "Pay to Jerry Lin" instead of "Pay to the order of Jerry Lin."

20. You are examining some negotiable instruments for a client. Which of the following endorsements can be classified as a special restrictive endorsement?

a. Pay to Alex Ericson if he completes the contracted work within ten days, (signed) Stephanie Sene.

b. Pay to Alex Ericson without recourse (signed) Stephanie Sene.

c. For deposit only, (signed) Stephanie Sene.

d. Pay to Alex Ericson, (signed) Stephanie Sene.

21. On February 15, 2001, P.D. Stone obtained the following instrument from Astor Co. for $1,000. Stone was aware that Helco, Inc. disputed liability under the instrument because of an alleged breach by Astor of the referenced computer purchase agreement. On March 1, 2001, Willard Bank obtained the instrument from Stone for $3,900. Willard had no knowledge that Helco disputed liability under the instrument.

February 12, 2001

Helco, Inc. promises to pay to Astor Co. or bearer the sum of $4,900 (four thousand four hundred and 00/100 dollars) on March 12, 2001 (maker may elect to extend due date to March 31, 2001) with interest thereon at the rate of 12% per annum.

HELCO, INC.

By: *A. J. Help*

A. J. Help, President

Reference: Computer purchase agreement dated February 12, 2001

The reverse side of the instrument is endorsed as follows:

Pay to the order of Willard Bank, without recourse

P.D. Stone

P.D. Stone

Which of the following statements is correct?

a. Willard Bank **cannot** be a holder in due course because Stone's endorsement was without recourse.

b. Willard Bank must endorse the instrument to negotiate it.

c. Neither Willard Bank **nor** Stone are holders in due course.

d. Stone's endorsement was required for Willard Bank to be a holder in due course.

22. Under the Commercial Paper Article of the UCC, which of the following circumstances would prevent a person from becoming a holder in due course of an instrument?

a. The person was notified that payment was refused.

b. The person was notified that one of the prior endorsers was discharged.

c. The note was collateral for a loan.

d. The note was purchased at a discount.

23. One of the requirements needed for a holder of a negotiable instrument to be a holder in due course is the value requirement. Ruper is a holder of a $1,000 check written out to her. Which of the following would not satisfy the value requirement?

a. Ruper received the check from a tax client to pay off a four-month-old debt.

b. Ruper took the check in exchange for a negotiable note for $1,200 which was due on that day.

c. Ruper received the check in exchange for a promise to do certain specified services three months later.

d. Ruper received the check for a tax service debt for a close relative.

24. Larson is claiming to be a holder in due course of two instruments. One is a draft that is drawn on Picket Company and says "Pay to Brunt." The other is a check that says "Pay to Brunt." Both are endorsed by Brunt on the back and made payable to Larson. Larson gave value for and acted in good faith concerning both the draft and the check. Larson also claims to be ignorant of any adverse claims on either instrument which are not overdue or have not been dishonored. Which of the following is(are) true?

I. Larson is a holder in due course of the draft.
II. Larson is a holder in due course of the check.

a. I only.
b. II only.
c. Both I and II.
d. Neither I nor II.

25. In order to be a holder in due course, the holder, among other requirements, must give value. Which of the following will satisfy this value requirement?

I. An antecedent debt.
II. A promise to perform services at a future date.

a. I only.
b. II only.
c. Both I and II.
d. Neither I nor II.

26. Bond fraudulently induced Teal to make a note payable to Wilk, to whom Bond was indebted. Bond delivered the note to Wilk. Wilk negotiated the instrument to Monk, who purchased it with knowledge of the fraud and after it was overdue. If Wilk qualifies as a holder in due course, which of the following statements is correct?

a. Monk has the standing of a holder in due course through Wilk.

b. Teal can successfully assert the defense of fraud in the inducement against Monk.

    c.   Monk personally qualifies as a holder in due course.

    d.   Teal can successfully assert the defense of fraud in the inducement against Wilk.

27. To the extent that a holder of a negotiable promissory note is a holder in due course, the holder takes the note free of which of the following defenses?

    a.   Minority of the maker where it is a defense to enforcement of a contract.

    b.   Forgery of the maker's signature.

    ç.   Discharge of the maker in bankruptcy.

    d.   Nonperformance of a condition precedent.

28. Under the Commercial Paper Article of the UCC, in a nonconsumer transaction, which of the following are real defenses available against a holder in due course?

	Material alteration	Discharge of bankruptcy	Breach of contract
a.	No	Yes	Yes
b.	Yes	Yes	No
c.	No	No	Yes
d.	Yes	No	No

29. On February 15, 2001, P.D. Stone obtained the following instrument from Astor Co. for $1,000. Stone was aware that Helco, Inc. disputed liability under the instrument because of an alleged breach by Astor of the referenced computer purchase agreement. On March 1, 2001, Willard Bank obtained the instrument from Stone for $3,900. Willard had no knowledge that Helco disputed liability under the instrument.

February 12, 2001

Helco, Inc. promises to pay to Astor Co. or bearer the sum of $4,900 (four thousand four hundred and 00/100 dollars) on March 12, 2001 (maker may elect to extend due date to March 31, 2001) with interest thereon at the rate of 12% per annum.

HELCO, INC.

By: *A. J. Help*
      A. J. Help, President

Reference: Computer purchase agreement dated February 12, 2001

The reverse side of the instrument is endorsed as follows:

Pay to the order of Willard Bank, without recourse

      P.D. Stone
      P.D. Stone

If Willard Bank demands payment from Helco and Helco refuses to pay the instrument because of Astor's breach of the computer purchase agreement, which of the following statements would be correct?

    a.   Willard Bank is **not** a holder in due course because Stone was **not** a holder in due course.

    b.   Helco will **not** be liable to Willard Bank because of Astor's breach.

    c.   Stone will be the only party liable to Willard Bank because he was aware of the dispute between Helco and Astor.

    d.   Helco will be liable to Willard Bank because Willard Bank is a holder in due course.

30. Northup made out a negotiable promissory note that was payable to the order of Port. This promissory note was meant to purchase some furniture that Port used to own, but he lied to Northup when he claimed he still owned it. Port immediately negotiated the note to Johnson who knew about Port's lie. Johnson negotiated the note to Kenner who was a holder in due course. Kenner then negotiated the note back to Johnson. When Johnson sought to enforce the promissory note against Northup, she refused claiming fraud. Which of the following is correct?

    a.   Johnson, as a holder through a holder in due course, can enforce the promissory note.

    b.   Northup wins because Johnson does not have the rights of a holder in due course.

    c.   Northup wins because she has a real defense on this note.

    d.   Johnson's knowledge of the lie does not affect his rights on this note.

31. Goran wrote out a check to Ruz to pay for a television set he purchased at a flea market from Ruz. When Goran got home, he found out the box did not have the television set but some weights. Goran immediately gave his bank a stop payment order over the phone. He followed this up with a written stop payment order. In the meantime, Ruz negotiated the check to Schmidt who qualified as a holder in due course. Schmidt gave the check as a gift to Buck. When Buck tried to cash the check, the bank and Goran both refused to pay. Which of the following is correct?

    a.   Buck cannot collect on the check from the bank because Goran has a real defense.

    b.   Buck cannot collect on the check from Goran because Goran has a personal defense.

    c.   Buck can require the bank to pay because Buck is a holder through a holder in due course.

    d.   Buck can require Goran to pay on the check even though the check was a gift.

32. Under the Negotiable Instruments Article of the UCC, which of the following parties will be a holder but **not** be entitled to the rights of a holder in due course?

    a.   A party who, knowing of a real defense to payment, received an instrument from a holder in due course.

    b.   A party who found an instrument payable to bearer.

    c.   A party who received, as a gift, an instrument from a holder in due course.

    d.   A party who, in good faith and without notice of any defect, gave value for an instrument.

33. A holder in due course will take free of which of the following defenses?

    a.   Infancy, to the extent that it is a defense to a simple contract.

    b.   Discharge of the maker in bankruptcy.

    c.   A wrongful filling-in of the amount payable that was omitted from the instrument.

    d.   Duress of a nature that renders the obligation of the party a nullity.

34. Cobb gave Garson a signed check with the amount payable left blank. Garson was to fill in, as the amount, the price of fuel oil Garson was to deliver to Cobb at a later date. Garson estimated the amount at $700, but told Cobb it would be no more than $900. Garson did not deliver the fuel oil, but filled in the amount of $1,000 on the check. Garson then negotiated the check to Josephs in satisfaction of a $500 debt with the $500 balance paid to Garson in cash.

Cobb stopped payment and Josephs is seeking to collect $1,000 from Cobb. Cobb's maximum liability to Josephs will be

    a. $0
    b. $ 500
    c. $ 900
    d. $1,000

35. A maker of a note will have a real defense against a holder in due course as a result of any of the following conditions **except**

    a. Discharge in bankruptcy.
    b. Forgery.
    c. Fraud in the execution.
    d. Lack of consideration.

36. Which of the following parties has(have) primary liability on a negotiable instrument?

  I. Drawer of a check.
  II. Drawee of a time draft before acceptance.
 III. Maker of a promissory note.

    a. I and II only.
    b. II and III only.
    c. I and III only.
    d. III only.

37. Which of the following actions does **not** discharge a prior party to a commercial instrument?

    a. Good faith payment or satisfaction of the instrument.
    b. Cancellation of that prior party's endorsement.
    c. The holder's oral renunciation of that prior party's liability.
    d. The holder's intentional destruction of the instrument.

38. Under the Negotiable Instruments Article of the UCC, when an instrument is indorsed "Pay to John Doe" and signed "Faye Smith," which of the following statements is(are) correct?

	Payment of the instrument is guaranteed	*The instrument can be further negotiated*
a.	Yes	Yes
b.	Yes	No
c.	No	Yes
d.	No	No

39.

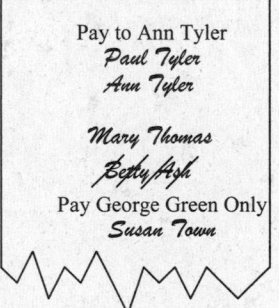

Pay to Ann Tyler
Paul Tyler
Ann Tyler

Mary Thomas
Betty Ash
Pay George Green Only
Susan Town

Susan Town, on receiving the above instrument, struck Betty Ash's endorsement. Under the Commercial Paper Article of the UCC, which of the endorsers of the above instrument will be completely discharged from secondary liability to later endorsers of the instrument?

    a. Ann Tyler.
    b. Mary Thomas.

    c. Betty Ash.
    d. Susan Town.

40. A subsequent holder of a negotiable instrument may cause the discharge of a prior holder of the instrument by any of the following actions **except**

    a. Unexcused delay in presentment of a time draft.
    b. Procuring certification of a check.
    c. Giving notice of dishonor the day after dishonor.
    d. Material alteration of a note.

41. A check has the following endorsements on the back:

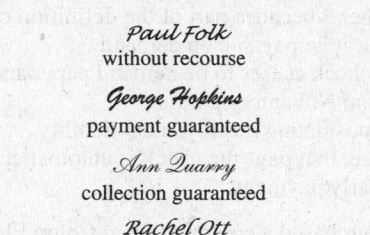

Paul Folk
without recourse

George Hopkins
payment guaranteed

Ann Quarry
collection guaranteed

Rachel Ott

Which of the following conditions occurring subsequent to the endorsements would discharge all of the endorsers?

    a. Lack of notice of dishonor.
    b. Late presentment.
    c. Insolvency of the maker.
    d. Certification of the check.

42. Robb, a minor, executed a promissory note payable to bearer and delivered it to Dodsen in payment for a stereo system. Dodsen negotiated the note for value to Mellon by delivery alone and without endorsement. Mellon endorsed the note in blank and negotiated it to Bloom for value. Bloom's demand for payment was refused by Robb because the note was executed when Robb was a minor. Bloom gave prompt notice of Robb's default to Dodsen and Mellon. None of the holders of the note were aware of Robb's minority. Which of the following parties will be liable to Bloom?

	Dodsen	*Mellon*
a.	Yes	Yes
b.	Yes	No
c.	No	No
d.	No	Yes

43. Vex Corp. executed a negotiable promissory note payable to Tamp, Inc. The note was collateralized by some of Vex's business assets. Tamp negotiated the note to Miller for value. Miller endorsed the note in blank and negotiated it to Bilco for value. Before the note became due, Bilco agreed to release Vex's collateral. Vex refused to pay Bilco when the note became due. Bilco promptly notified Miller and Tamp of Vex's default. Which of the following statements is correct?

    a. Bilco will be unable to collect from Miller because Miller's endorsement was in blank.
    b. Bilco will be able to collect from either Tamp or Miller because Bilco was a holder in due course.
    c. Bilco will be unable to collect from either Tamp or Miller because of Bilco's release of the collateral.
    d. Bilco will be able to collect from Tamp because Tamp was the original payee.

44. Under the Commercial Paper Article of the UCC, which of the following statements best describes the effect of a person endorsing a check "without recourse"?

a. The person has **no** liability to prior endorsers.
b. The person makes **no** promise or guarantee of payment on dishonor.
c. The person gives **no** warranty protection to later transferees.
d. The person converts the check into order paper.

45. A check is postdated to November 20 even though the check was written out on November 3 of the same year. Which of the following is correct under the Revised Article 3 of the Uniform Commercial Code?

a. The check is payable on demand on or after November 3 because part of the definition of a check is that it be payable on demand.
b. The check ceases to be demand paper and is payable on November 20.
c. The postdating destroys negotiability.
d. A bank that pays the check is automatically liable for early payment.

46. Stanley purchased a computer from Comp Electronics with a personal check. Later that day, Stanley saw a better deal on the computer so he orally stopped payment on the check with his bank. The bank, however, still paid Comp Electronics when the check was presented three days later. Which of the following is correct?

a. The bank is liable to Stanley for failure to follow the oral stop payment order.
b. The bank is not liable to Stanley because the stop payment order was not in writing.
c. The bank is not liable to Stanley if Comp Electronics qualifies as a holder in due course.
d. Comp Electronics is liable to Stanley to return the amount of the check.

47. A trade acceptance is an instrument drawn by a

a. Seller obligating the seller or designee to make payment.
b. Buyer obligating the buyer or designee to make payment.
c. Seller ordering the buyer or designee to make payment.
d. Buyer ordering the seller or designee to make payment.

48. Under the Documents of Title Article of the UCC, which of the following statements is(are) correct regarding a common carrier's duty to deliver goods subject to a negotiable bearer bill of lading?

I. The carrier may deliver the goods to any party designated by the holder of the bill of lading.
II. A carrier who, without court order, delivers goods to a party claiming the goods under a missing negotiable bill of lading is liable to any person injured by the misdelivery.

a. I only.
b. II only.
c. Both I and II.
d. Neither I nor II.

49. Which of the following is **not** a warranty made by the seller of a negotiable warehouse receipt to the purchaser of the document?

a. The document transfer is fully effective with respect to the goods it represents.
b. The warehouseman will honor the document.

c. The seller has **no** knowledge of any facts that would impair the document's validity.
d. The document is genuine.

50. Under the UCC, a warehouse receipt

a. Will **not** be negotiable if it contains a contractual limitation on the warehouseman's liability.
b. May qualify as both a negotiable warehouse receipt and negotiable commercial paper if the instrument is payable either in cash or by the delivery of goods.
c. May be issued only by a bonded and licensed warehouseman.
d. Is negotiable if by its terms the goods are to be delivered to bearer or the order of a named person.

SIMULATION PROBLEMS

Simulation Problem 1   (10 to 15 minutes)

Instructions				
	Fact Pattern I	**Fact Pattern II**	**Fact Pattern III**	**Fact Pattern IV**

This simulation has four separate fact patterns, each followed by five legal conclusions relating to the fact pattern preceding those five numbered legal conclusions. Determine whether each conclusion is Correct or Incorrect.

	Fact Pattern I			
Instructions		**Fact Pattern II**	**Fact Pattern III**	**Fact Pattern IV**

An instrument purports to be a negotiable instrument. It otherwise fulfills all the elements of negotiability and it states "Pay to Rich Crane."

		Correct	*Incorrect*
1.	It is negotiable if it is a check and Rich Crane has possession of the check.	○	○
2.	It is negotiable if it is a draft drawn on a corporation.	○	○
3.	It is negotiable if it is a promissory note due one year later with 5% interest stated on its face.	○	○
4.	It is negotiable if it is a certificate of deposit.	○	○
5.	It is negotiable even if it is a cashier's check.	○	○

		Fact Pattern II		
Instructions	**Fact Pattern I**		**Fact Pattern III**	**Fact Pattern IV**

Another instrument fulfills all of the elements of negotiability except possibly one, that is, the instrument does not identify any payee.

		Correct	*Incorrect*
1.	The instrument is **not** negotiable if it is a draft.	○	○
2.	The instrument is bearer paper if it is a check.	○	○
3.	The instrument is negotiable if it is a promissory note.	○	○
4.	The instrument is bearer paper if it is a promissory note.	○	○
5.	The instrument is negotiable only if it also states the word "negotiable" on its face.	○	○

			Fact Pattern III	
Instructions	**Fact Pattern I**	**Fact Pattern II**		**Fact Pattern IV**

A promissory note states that the maker promises to pay to the order of ABC Company $10,000 plus interest at 2% above the prime rate of XYZ Bank in New York City one year from the date on the promissory note.

		Correct	*Incorrect*
1.	The interest rate provision destroys negotiability because the prime rate can fluctuate during the year.	○	○
2.	The interest rate provision destroys negotiability because one has to look outside the note to see what the prime rate of XYZ Bank is.	○	○
3.	The maker is obligated to pay only the $10,000 because the amount of interest is not a sum certain.	○	○
4.	The maker must pay $10,000 plus the judgment rate of interest because the amount of interest cannot be determined without referring to facts outside the instrument.	○	○
5.	Any holder of this note could not qualify as a holder in due course because of the interest provision.	○	○

Instructions	Fact Pattern I	Fact Pattern II	Fact Pattern III	Fact Pattern IV

An individual fills out his personal check. He postdates the check for ten days later and notes on the face of the check that it is for "Payment for textbooks."

		Correct	*Incorrect*
1.	The instrument is demand paper because it is a check and is thus payable immediately.	○	○
2.	The check is not payable before the date on its face.	○	○
3.	If a bank pays on this check before its stated date, the bank is liable to the drawer.	○	○
4.	The notation "Payment for textbooks" destroys negotiability because it makes payment conditional.	○	○
5.	The notation "Payment for textbooks" does **not** destroy negotiability but only if the check was actually used to pay for textbooks.	○	○

Simulation Problem 2   (10 to 15 minutes)

During an audit of Trent Realty Corp.'s financial statements, Clark, CPA, reviewed two instruments.

Instrument 1

$300,000	Belle, MD
	April 1, 2004

For value received, ten years after date, I promise to pay to the order of Dart Finance Co. Three Hundred Thousand and 00/100 dollars with interest at 9% per annum compounded annually until fully paid.

This instrument arises out of the sale of land located in MD.

It is further agreed that:

1. Maker will pay all costs of collection including reasonable attorney fees.
2. Maker may prepay the amount outstanding on any anniversary date of this instrument.

> *G. Evans*
> _____
> G. Evans

The following transactions relate to Instrument 1.

- On March 15, 2005, Dart endorsed the instrument in blank and sold it to Morton for $275,000.
- On July 10, 2005, Evans informed Morton that Dart had fraudulently induced Evans into signing the instrument.
- On August 15, 2005, Trent, which knew of Evans' claim against Dart, purchased the instrument from Morton for $50,000.

Items 1 through 5 relate to Instrument 1. For each item, select from List I the correct answer. An answer may be selected once, more than once, or not at all.

List I

A. Draft	E. Holder in due course	H. Nonnegotiable
B. Promissory Note	F. Holder with rights of a holder in due	I. Evans, Morton, and Dart
C. Security Agreement	course under the shelter provision	J. Morton and Dart
D. Holder	G. Negotiable	K. Only Dart

		(A)	(B)	(C)	(D)	(E)	(F)	(G)	(H)	(I)	(J)	(K)
1.	Instrument 1 is a (type of instrument)	○	○	○	○	○	○	○	○	○	○	○
2.	Instrument 1 is (negotiability)	○	○	○	○	○	○	○	○	○	○	○
3.	Morton is considered a (type of ownership)	○	○	○	○	○	○	○	○	○	○	○
4.	Trent is considered a (type of ownership)	○	○	○	○	○	○	○	○	○	○	○
5.	Trent could recover on the instrument from [liable party(s)]	○	○	○	○	○	○	○	○	○	○	○

Instrument 2

Front	Back

To: Pure Bank
       Upton, VT
 	
                        April 5, 2004
 	
Pay to the order of M. West $1,500.00
One Thousand Five Hundred and 00/100 Dollars
on May 1, 2004
 	
                W. Fields
                W. Fields
	M. West
	
	Pay to C. Larr
	T. Keetin
	
	C. Larr
	without recourse

Items 1 through 8 relate to Instrument 2. For each item, select from List II the correct answer. An answer may be selected once, more than once, or not at all.

List II

A.	Bearer paper	F.	Nonnegotiable
B.	Blank	G.	Note
C.	Check	H.	Order paper
D.	Draft	I.	Qualified
E.	Negotiable	J.	Special

(A) (B) (C) (D) (E) (F) (G) (H) (I) (J)

1. Instrument 2 is a (type of instrument)   ○ ○ ○ ○ ○ ○ ○ ○ ○ ○

2. Instrument 2 is (negotiability)   ○ ○ ○ ○ ○ ○ ○ ○ ○ ○

3. West's endorsement makes the instrument (type of instrument)   ○ ○ ○ ○ ○ ○ ○ ○ ○ ○

4. Keetin's endorsement makes the instrument (type of instrument)   ○ ○ ○ ○ ○ ○ ○ ○ ○ ○

5. Larr's endorsement makes the instrument (type of instrument)   ○ ○ ○ ○ ○ ○ ○ ○ ○ ○

6. West's endorsement would be considered (type of endorsement)   ○ ○ ○ ○ ○ ○ ○ ○ ○ ○

7. Keetin's endorsement would be considered (type of endorsement)   ○ ○ ○ ○ ○ ○ ○ ○ ○ ○

8. Larr's endorsement would be considered (type of endorsement)   ○ ○ ○ ○ ○ ○ ○ ○ ○ ○

MULTIPLE-CHOICE ANSWERS

1. c	12. c	22. c	34. d	45. b
2. a	13. d	24. b	35. d	46. c
3. c	14. a	25. a	36. d	47. c
4. a	15. a	26. a	37. c	48. c
5. a	16. a	27. d	38. a	49. b
6. a	17. c	28. b	39. c	50. d
7. a	18. d	29. d	40. c	
8. c	19. d	30. b	41. d	
9. c	20. a	31. d	42. d	
10. a	21. b	32. b	43. c	1st: __/50 = __%
11. d	22. a	33. c	44. b	2nd: __/50 = __%

MULTIPLE-CHOICE ANSWER EXPLANATIONS

B. Types of Commercial Paper

1.   (c)   This is a very common type of restrictive endorsement. Answer (a) is incorrect because a blank endorsement is one that does not specify any endorsee. Answer (b) is incorrect because a qualified endorsement is one in which the endorser disclaims liability to pay the holder or any subsequent endorser for the instrument if it is later dishonored. An example of this is the endorser putting in the words "without recourse" on the back of the instrument. Answer (d) is incorrect because a special endorsement refers to when the endorser indicates a specific person who needs to subsequently endorse it.

2.   (a)   This instrument is a draft because it is a three-party instrument where a drawer (Dexter) orders a drawee (Middlesex National Bank) to pay a fixed amount in money to the payee (Silver). Answer (b) is incorrect because in order for the instrument to qualify as a check, the instrument must be payable on demand. In this situation, the instrument held by Silver is a time draft which specifies the payment date as October 1, 2001. Answer (d) is incorrect because a promissory note is a two-party instrument in which one party promises to pay a fixed amount in money to the payee. Answer (c) is incorrect because a trade acceptance is a special type of draft in which a seller of goods extends credit to the buyer by drawing a draft on that buyer directing the buyer to pay a fixed amount in money to the seller on a specified date. The seller is therefore both the drawer and payee in a trade acceptance.

3.   (c)   Under the Revised Article 3 of the UCC, there are two basic categories of negotiable instruments (i.e., promissory notes and drafts). A certificate of deposit is a promissory note issued by a bank. A check is a draft drawn on a bank and payable on demand unless it is postdated.

4.   (a)   A promissory demand note is a two-party instrument in which the maker (T. T. Tile) promises to pay to the order of the payee (A. B. Shark) and the payment is made upon demand with no time period stated. N. A. Abner made a guaranty but it is still a two-party note. Answers (b), (c), and (d) are all incorrect because sight drafts, checks, and trade acceptances are all three-party instruments requiring a drawee.

5.   (a)   Drafts and checks are three-party instruments in which the drawer orders the drawee to pay the payee. Notes and certificates of deposit are two-party instruments in which the maker promises to pay the payee.

C. Requirements of Negotiability

6.   (a)   All negotiable instruments are required to be payable to order or bearer with the exception of checks. This instrument says "Pay to Jenny Larson"; therefore, it can only be negotiable if it is a check. All of these instruments in the question would be negotiable if they said "Pay to the order of Jenny Larson," including a check.

7.   (a)   One of the elements of negotiability is that the note be payable to order or to bearer. Under the revised UCC, this is true for all negotiable instruments except checks that do not need the words "to the order of" or "bearer." Answer (b) is incorrect because signing by the payee is a method of negotiation but is not a requirement to make the instrument negotiable. Answer (c) is incorrect because such references are not required. Answer (d) is incorrect because the elements of negotiability do not require the stating of any conditions of payment. In fact, such conditions can destroy negotiability.

8.   (c)   This promissory note is negotiable because it meets all of the requirements of negotiability. It is written and signed. It contains an unconditional promise to pay a fixed amount in money. It is payable at a definite time under the UCC even though the maker may extend the due date to March 31, 2001, because this option of the maker to extend the time is limited to a definite date. And finally, the instrument is payable to bearer because it states "Pay to Astor Co. or bearer." Answer (a) is incorrect because the reference to the computer purchase agreement does not condition payment on this agreement, it simply refers to it. Answer (b) is incorrect because when the words and numbers are contradictory, the written words control and thus, the instrument still contains a fixed amount. Answer (d) is incorrect because once an instrument is negotiable and remains unaltered, it is negotiable for all parties.

9.   (c)   The Revised Article 3 of the UCC allows a negotiable instrument to be payable in any medium of exchange of the US or a foreign government. Therefore, answer (a) is incorrect. Answer (b) is incorrect because negotiability is maintained despite the fact that rate of exchange can fluctuate. This is a fact of doing business internationally. Answer (d) is incorrect because the exchange rate can be determined readily.

10.   (a)   This instrument satisfies all of the requirements for negotiability except for the requirement that it be payable on demand or at a definite time. Since it is payable ten days after the sale of the maker's diamond ring, the time of payment is not certain as to the time of occurrence. Answer (b) is incorrect because a negotiable instrument may contain a promise to provide collateral. Answer (c) is incorrect because although it is a two-party note, it is not negotiable because it is not payable at a definite time. Answer (d) is incorrect because it is not negotiable and is not a draft. A draft requires a drawer ordering a drawee to pay the payee.

11.   (d)   Since this note is subject to the terms of another document, the promise in the note is conditional, causing negotiability to be destroyed. Answer (a) is incorrect because since one must look to a document outside of the note, this destroys negotiability. Answer (b) is incorrect because the note itself makes its promise conditioned on the contract. Thus, the contract cannot be ignored. Answer (c) is incorrect because the contract, which is outside of the note, must be examined. This destroys the note's negotiability.

12.   (c)   For a note to be negotiable, it must be written and signed by the maker, contain an unconditional promise to pay a fixed amount in money, be payable at a definite time or on demand, and be payable to order or to bearer. This note fulfills all of these requirements. It is therefore negotiable and does not require that the payment date be specified because it is payable on demand. Answer (a) is incorrect because the note fulfills all the requirements of negotiability. Answer (b) is incorrect because in cases of inconsistencies between words and figures, the words control. Answer (d) is incorrect because although the guaranty may make the note more desirable, it was already negotiable.

13.   (d)   Under the Revised Article 3 of the UCC, interest rates are allowed to be variable or fluctuate. Negotiability is not destroyed. Answer (a) is incorrect because the sum certain rule allows the interest rate to vary based on such things as the prime rate of interest of a given bank. Answer (b) is incorrect because negotiability is not destroyed by needing to resort to information outside of the negotiable instrument. Answer (c) is incorrect because it is allowed for the interest to vary while the negotiable instrument is still outstanding.

14.   (a)   Under the Revised Article 3 of the UCC, a check may be postdated and need not be payable to order. The words "Pay to Corbin Company" are allowed for checks. However, all negotiable instruments other than checks need to be payable to order or to bearer.

15.   (a)   Under the Revised Article 3 of the UCC, unlike under earlier versions, payment on a negotiable instrument may be designated to come from a particular source or fund. The maker or drawer does not have to be personally obligated. Therefore, answer (b) is incorrect. Answer (c) is incorrect because this provision is not deemed to make the instrument not negotiable for reason of a conditional promise. Answer (d) is incorrect because lack of payment due to insufficient funds does not destroy negotiability.

D.   Interpretation of Ambiguities in Negotiable Instruments

16.   (a)   When the amount in words differs from the amount in figures on a negotiable instrument, the words control over the figures. Answer (b) is incorrect because the law has settled this ambiguity in favor of the words on negotiable instruments. Answer (c) is incorrect because the

instrument is still negotiable and can be cashed. Answer (d) is incorrect because there is no such rule involving 10%.

E.   Negotiation

17.   (c)   Although negotiating bearer paper only requires delivery, negotiating order paper requires both delivery and endorsement by the transferor. Delivery requires that the holder get possession of the instrument.

18.   (d)   Since John Smith endorsed the instrument in blank (i.e., did not specify any endorsee) it became bearer paper. Since it was bearer paper in Harris's hands, she did not need to endorse it to negotiate it to the next party, Sharp. Answer (a) is incorrect because when Parker endorsed "Pay to John Smith only" he made the instrument require John Smith's signature to negotiate it further. Parker's endorsement will not restrict negotiations beyond John Smith's and it does not destroy negotiability. Answer (b) is incorrect as although conditions on the front generally destroy the negotiability of an instrument, conditions put into an endorsement do not. Answer (c) is incorrect because the wording "Pay to John Smith only" will not restrict further negotiation after John Smith. When John Smith endorsed it in blank, it became bearer paper.

19.   (d)   The words "Pay to the order of Jerry Lin" are not necessary because the note is already negotiable on its face where it was payable to the order of Ann Jackson. Answer (a) is not chosen because although when Jackson endorsed the note in blank, it became bearer paper, it was converted back to order paper when Lin put "Pay to Jerry Lin" above Jackson's endorsement. Answer (b) should not be chosen because when Jackson endorsed it without specifying any payee, the note became bearer paper. Answer (c) should not be chosen because it became order paper once "Pay to Jerry Lin" was written, whether he personally did it or not.

20.   (a)   This endorsement is special because it indicates "Pay to Alex Ericson" and it is restrictive because of the phrase "if he completes…." Answer (b) is incorrect because this endorsement is special and qualified. Answer (c) is incorrect because although it is restrictive, it is also a blank endorsement. Answer (d) is incorrect because although it is a special endorsement stating "Pay to Alex Ericson," it is not restrictive.

21.   (b)   Although the note was originally a bearer instrument, Stone endorsed it with a special endorsement when s/he indicated "Pay to the order of Willard Bank, without recourse" above the endorsement. This means that Willard Bank must endorse the note to negotiate it further. Answer (a) is incorrect because qualified endorsements such as "without recourse" disclaim some liability but do not prevent subsequent parties from becoming a holder in due course. Answer (c) is incorrect because although Stone is not a holder in due course because s/he had notice that the maker disputed liability under the note, Willard Bank is a holder in due course because Willard was unaware that Helco disputed liability on the note. Additionally, Willard meets the other requirements to be a holder in due course, because he was a holder of a negotiable note, gave value ($3,900) for it, took in good faith, and had no notice, not only of the alleged breach by Astor, but of any other relevant problems such as being overdue or having been dishonored. Answer (d) is incorrect because the note was bearer paper when Stone received it and thus did not require an endorsement.

F. Holder in Due Course

22.   (a)   To be a holder in due course, the holder must, among other things, take without notice that the instrument is overdue, has been dishonored, or that any person has a defense or claim to it. In this case, the person was notified that payment was refused. Answer (b) is incorrect because a prior endorser being discharged does not mean that person necessarily had a defense to the instrument. Answer (c) is incorrect because the use of a note as collateral does not prevent a holder from becoming a holder in due course. Answer (d) is incorrect because reasonable discounts are allowed and do not indicate bad faith or that a person has a defense or claim to the instrument.

23.   (c)   An executory promise does not satisfy the value requirement to be a holder in due course until the promise is actually performed. Answer (a) is incorrect because Ruper received the check to pay off a previous debt owed to her. Taking in satisfaction of a previous debt constitutes value to be a holder in due course. Answer (b) is incorrect because she took the check in exchange for another negotiable instrument. The fact that the check was for less than the face value of the negotiable note does not violate the value requirements. Answer (d) is incorrect because taking the check to pay off an antecedent debt constitutes value whether the debtor was a relative or not.

24.   (b)   In order to be a holder in due course, the individual must be a holder of a negotiable instrument as well as fulfilling the additional requirements referred to in the question. In this case, the draft is not negotiable because it is not payable to order or to bearer. However, the check is negotiable because checks do not have to be payable to order or to bearer to be negotiable.

25.   (a)   Even though an antecedent debt would not be valid for the consideration requirement under contract law, it is valid for the value requirement under negotiable instruments law. A promise to perform services at a future date is an executory promise and is not value until actually performed.

G. Rights of a Holder in Due Course

26.   (a)   Monk is not personally a HDC because although he was a holder of the negotiable note for which he gave value, he did not take in good faith because he had knowledge of the fraud before he purchased the note. Furthermore, he had notice that the note was overdue. Therefore, answer (c) can be ruled out. Answer (a) however, is correct because even though Monk was not a HDC, he obtained the instrument from Wilk who was a HDC. Therefore, Monk qualifies as a holder through a HDC and thus obtains all of the rights of a HDC. Answers (b) and (d) are incorrect because fraud in the inducement is a personal defense. Wilk, as a HDC, and Monk, as a holder through a HDC, both take the note free of personal defenses.

27.   (d)   A holder in due course takes an instrument free of personal defenses but is subject to real defenses. Answer (d) is correct because it involves a breach of contract or nonperformance of a condition precedent which describes a personal defense. Answer (c) is incorrect because bankruptcy is a real defense. Answer (a) is incorrect because

when a minor may disaffirm a contract, it is treated as a real defense. Answer (b) is incorrect because a forgery of a maker's or drawer's signature is a real defense.

28.   (b)   Real defenses include bankruptcy and material alterations of the instrument. Material alterations include a change of any monetary amount. They also include changes in the interest rate, if any, on the instrument or changes in the date if the date affects when it is paid or the amount of interest to be paid. Personal defenses include the more typical defenses such as breach of contract, breach of warranty, and fraud in the inducement.

29.   (d)   Helco is claiming breach of contract which is a personal defense. The general rule is that transfer of a negotiable instrument to a holder in due course cuts off all personal defenses against the holder in due course. Since Willard Bank is a holder in due course, Helco is liable to Willard Bank. Answer (a) is incorrect because Willard Bank meets all of the requirements to be a holder in due course. That is, Willard is a holder of a negotiable instrument, gave value, took in good faith, and took without notice of certain problems such as Helco's disputed liability. The fact that Stone was not a holder in due course does not change this. Answer (b) is incorrect because Willard Bank as a holder in due course wins against Helco's claim of Astor's breach. The breach of contract would only constitute a personal defense. Answer (c) is incorrect because Helco is liable to Willard Bank.

30.   (b)   When a negotiable instrument is negotiated from a holder in due course to another holder, this other holder normally obtains the rights of a holder in due course. However, an important exception applies to this case. Since Johnson knew of the lie when he first acquired the note, he was not a HDC and cannot improve his status by reacquiring from a HDC. Answer (a) is incorrect because he did not qualify as a HDC due to his knowledge of the defense. Answer (c) is incorrect because fraud in the inducement is a personal, not real, defense. Answer (d) is incorrect because his knowledge of the lie prevents his becoming a HDC at first and prevents his later becoming a holder through a holder in due course.

31.   (d)   Even though Buck did not personally qualify as a HDC, he was a holder through a holder in due course and can collect from the drawer despite the drawer's personal defense. Answer (a) is incorrect because Goran's defense is a personal defense. Also, the bank is permitted to follow the customer's stop payment order. Answer (b) is incorrect because Buck as a holder through a holder in due course can collect despite the personal defense. Answer (c) is incorrect because the bank is permitted to refuse payment and then Buck collects from the drawer.

32.   (b)   A party who found an instrument payable to bearer is a holder but not a holder through a holder in due course. To be the latter, s/he must obtain a negotiable instrument from a holder in due course. If this had been the case, s/he would have obtained the rights of a holder in due course. However, since s/he found the instrument, it cannot be established that the previous holder was a holder in due course. Answer (a) is incorrect because s/he did receive the instrument from a holder in due course. S/he, therefore, does obtain the rights of a holder in due course even though s/he cannot be a holder in due course him/herself because of having notice of the defense on the instrument. Answer (c) is incorrect because the party received the instrument from a holder in due course and thus becomes a holder through a holder in due course. Answer (d) is incorrect because this party personally qualifies as a holder in due course, thereby obtaining those rights.

33. (c) An unauthorized completion of an incomplete instrument is a personal defense, and, as such, will not be valid against a HDC. Infancy (unless the instrument is exchanged for necessaries), bankruptcy of the maker, and extreme duress are all real defenses which are good against a HDC.

34. (d) Since Cobb left the amount blank on the signed check and Garson filled it in contrary to Cobb's instructions, this is a case of unauthorized completion which is a personal defense. Garson then negotiated the check to Josephs who is a holder in due course because he gave value for the negotiable instrument and took in good faith without notice of any problems. He gave value for the full $1,000 since cash and taking the check for a previous debt are both value under negotiable instrument law. Therefore, Josephs may collect the full $1,000 and win over the personal defense that Cobb has.

35. (d) A maker of a note may use real defenses against a holder in due course but not personal defenses. Lack of consideration is a personal defense. Discharge in bankruptcy, forgery, and fraud in the execution are all real defenses, which create a valid defense against a holder in due course.

H. Liability of Parties

36. (d) The maker of a note has primary liability on that note. No one has primary liability on a draft or check unless the drawee accepts it. This is true because although the drawee has been ordered by the drawer to pay, the drawee has not agreed to pay unless it accepts the draft or check.

37. (c) When there are multiple endorsers on a negotiable instrument, each is liable to subsequent endorsers or holders. Oral renunciation of a prior party's liability does not discharge that party's liability. Answer (a) is incorrect because once the primary party pays on the instrument, all endorsers are discharged from liability. Answer (b) is incorrect because cancellation of a prior party's endorsement does discharge that party's liability. Answer (d) is incorrect because when a holder intentionally destroys a negotiable instrument, the prior endorsers are discharged.

38. (a) When a negotiable instrument is indorsed and a specific person is indicated, the instrument is order paper and can be further negotiated by that person. Note also that payment of the instrument is guaranteed. If the primary party to the negotiable instrument does not pay, the indorser(s) are obligated to pay on the instrument when the holder demands payment or acceptance in a timely manner.

39. (c) Striking out the endorsement of a person discharges that person's secondary liability and discharges subsequent endorsers who have already endorsed. This does not, however, discharge any of the prior parties. Therefore, in this case, Betty Ash is discharged from secondary liability to the later endorsers.

40. (c) Various acts or failures of a holder can cause a discharge of prior holders of an instrument. Among these are an unexcused delay in presenting an instrument, cancellation or renunciation of the instrument, fraudulent or material alteration, and certification of a check. Notice of dishonor generally should be given by midnight of the third business day after the dishonor or notice of the dishonor. Banks must give notice by midnight of the next banking day. In either case, answer (c) is correct. Answers (a), (b), and (d) are all incorrect because they are all acts that cause the discharge of prior holders.

41. (d) When a holder procures certification of a check, all prior endorsers are discharged. This is true because when a bank certifies a check, it has accepted the check and agreed to honor it as presented. Answers (a) and (b) are incorrect because although lack of notice of dishonor to other endorsers and late presentment of the instrument will normally discharge all endorsers, this is not true if the lack of notice of dishonor or the late presentment is excused. They can be excused in such cases as the delay is beyond the party's control or the presentment is waived. Furthermore in this fact pattern, Hopkins endorsed the check "payment guaranteed" and Quarry endorsed it "collection guaranteed." When words of guaranty are used, presentment or notice of dishonor are not required to hold the users liable. Answer (c) is incorrect because when the maker is insolvent the endorsers will likely be sought after for payment.

42. (d) Since Dodsen did not endorse the note, s/he gave transfer warranties and presentment warranties only to the immediate transferee (i.e., Mellon). Mellon gave these warranties to Bloom. Therefore although Mellon will be liable to Bloom, Dodsen will not be.

43. (c) Normally, Bilco could seek collection on the defaulted note from the previous endorsers, Tamp and Miller. However, in this case, Bilco agreed to release the collateral underlying this note. Since this materially affects the rights of Tamp and Miller to use this collateral, this act releases them. Answer (a) is incorrect because except for the release of the collateral, Bilco could have collected from his/her immediate transferor even without the endorsement. Answers (b) and (d) are incorrect because the release of the collateral releases Tamp and Miller.

44. (b) When a person endorses a negotiable instrument, s/he is normally secondarily liable to later endorsers. This liability means that the endorser can be required to make good on the instrument. If s/he endorses without recourse, the endorser can avoid this liability. Answer (a) is incorrect because the endorser is not liable to prior endorsers anyway whether or not s/he endorses without recourse. Answer (c) is incorrect because the endorser still gives the transferor's warranties with some modification. Answer (d) is incorrect because a check is converted into order paper only if the endorser also specifies a payee.

J. Banks

45. (b) Under the Revised Article 3, postdating a check does not destroy negotiability but makes the check properly payable on or after the date written on the check. Although the postdated check is not properly payable before the date on the instrument, if a bank pays it earlier, it is not liable unless the drawer had notified the bank that the check was postdated.

46. **(c)** If the bank fails to follow a stop payment order, it is liable to the customer only if the customer had a valid defense on the check and therefore suffers a loss. Comp Electronics, the payee, can qualify as a HDC and Stanley would have to pay anyway despite the stop payment order. Answer (a) is incorrect because the bank did not cause Stanley a loss. Answer (b) is incorrect because oral stop payment orders are valid for fourteen days. Answer (d) is incorrect because from the facts given, there is no evidence that Comp Electronics breached the contract.

M. Transfer of Negotiable Documents of Title

47. **(c)** A trade acceptance is a special type of draft in which a seller of goods extends credit to the buyer by drawing the draft on the buyer ordering the buyer to make payment to the seller on a specified date.

48. **(c)** A negotiable bearer bill of lading is a document of title that under the UCC allows the bearer the rights to the goods mentioned including the right to designate who will receive delivery of the goods. The carrier is required to deliver the goods to the holder of negotiable bearer bill of lading or to that holder's designee. The carrier is liable for any misdelivery for any damages caused.

49. **(b)** A person who negotiates a negotiable document of title for value extends the following warranties to the immediate purchaser: (1) negotiation by the transferor is rightful and fully effective with respect to the goods it represents, (2) the transferor has no knowledge of any facts that would impair the document's validity or worth, and (3) the document is genuine. However, the transferor of a negotiable warehouse receipt does not necessarily warrant that the warehouseman will honor the document.

50. **(d)** A negotiable warehouse receipt is a document issued as evidence of receipt of goods by a person engaged in the business of storing goods for hire. The warehouse receipt is negotiable if the face of the document contains the words of negotiability (order or bearer). Answer (a) is incorrect because the negotiability of the warehouse receipt is not destroyed by the inclusion of a contractual limitation on the warehouseman's liability. Answer (b) is incorrect because to qualify as commercial paper, the instrument must be payable only in money. If an instrument is payable in money or by the delivery of goods, it is a nonnegotiable instrument. Answer (c) is incorrect because the UCC does not state that only a bonded and licensed warehouseman can issue a warehouse receipt.

SOLUTIONS TO SIMULATION PROBLEMS

Simulation Problem 1

Instructions	**Fact Pattern I**	**Fact Pattern II**	**Fact Pattern III**	**Fact Pattern IV**

		Correct	*Incorrect*
1.	It is negotiable if it is a check and Rich Crane has possession of the check.	●	○
2.	It is negotiable if it is a draft drawn on a corporation.	○	●
3.	It is negotiable if it is a promissory note due one year later with 5% interest stated on its face.	○	●
4.	It is negotiable if it is a certificate of deposit.	○	●
5.	It is negotiable even if it is a cashier's check.	●	○

Explanation of solutions

1.   **(C)** Even though the instrument states "Pay to Rich Crane," it is negotiable because a check does **not** have to be payable to order or bearer.

2.   **(I)** A draft to be negotiable must be payable to order or to bearer. "Pay to the order of Rich Crane" would have made it negotiable.

3.   **(I)** Promissory notes to be negotiable must be payable to order or to bearer.

4.   **(I)** Certificates of deposit, unlike checks, must be payable to order or to bearer.

5.   **(C)** A cashier's check is an actual check and thus does **not** have to be payable to order or to bearer.

Instructions	**Fact Pattern I**	**Fact Pattern II**	**Fact Pattern III**	**Fact Pattern IV**

		Correct	*Incorrect*
1.	The instrument is **not** negotiable if it is a draft.	○	●
2.	The instrument is bearer paper if it is a check.	●	○
3.	The instrument is negotiable if it is a promissory note.	●	○
4.	The instrument is bearer paper if it is a promissory note.	●	○
5.	The instrument is negotiable only if it also states the word "negotiable" on its face.	○	●

Explanation of solutions

1.   **(I)** If an instrument does not name any payee, it is considered to be payable to bearer. Thus, negotiability is not destroyed.

2.   **(C)** If no payee is named, it is bearer paper.

3.   **(C)** Since no payee was named, it is bearer paper and thus negotiability is maintained.

4.   **(C)** Like the cases of drafts, checks, and certificates of deposit, it is bearer paper.

5.   **(I)** There is no such requirement to state "negotiable" on its face.

Instructions	**Fact Pattern I**	**Fact Pattern II**	**Fact Pattern III**	**Fact Pattern IV**

		Correct	*Incorrect*
1.	The interest rate provision destroys negotiability because the prime rate can fluctuate during the year.	○	●
2.	The interest rate provision destroys negotiability because one has to look outside the note to see what the prime rate of XYZ Bank is.	○	●
3.	The maker is obligated to pay only the $10,000 because the amount of interest is not a sum certain.	○	●
4.	The maker must pay $10,000 plus the judgment rate of interest because the amount of interest cannot be determined without referring to facts outside the instrument.	○	●

		Correct	Incorrect
5.	Any holder of this note could not qualify as a holder in due course because of the interest provision.	○	●

Explanation of solutions

1. (**I**) The negotiability of an instrument is not destroyed simply because the interest rate used may fluctuate.

2. (**I**) Negotiability is not destroyed even if one has to look outside of the document to determine what the actual rate is.

3. (**I**) Even though the interest rate may fluctuate, the maker is still obligated to pay the $10,000 plus the interest.

4. (**I**) The maker must pay the $10,000 plus the interest described on the promissory note.

5. (**I**) Since this note is negotiable despite the possible fluctuation of the interest rate, a holder could qualify to be a holder in due course under those applicable rules.

Instructions	Fact Pattern I	Fact Pattern II	Fact Pattern III	Fact Pattern IV

		Correct	Incorrect
1.	The instrument is demand paper because it is a check and is thus payable immediately.	○	●
2.	The check is not payable before the date on its face.	●	○
3.	If a bank pays on this check before its stated date, the bank is liable to the drawer.	○	●
4.	The notation "Payment for textbooks" destroys negotiability because it makes payment conditional.	○	●
5.	The notation "Payment for textbooks" does **not** destroy negotiability but only if the check was actually used to pay for textbooks.	○	●

Explanation of solutions

1. (**I**) Normally a check is demand paper. However, when it is postdated, it is not payable until that date.

2. (**C**) The postdating overrides the normal characteristic that it is payable on demand.

3. (**I**) The bank is not liable unless the drawer has given the bank prior notice of the postdating.

4. (**I**) Notations on negotiable instruments that note what it is for do not put conditions on the payment and thus do not destroy negotiability.

5. (**I**) These notations can be ignored because they are not conditions of payment.

Simulation Problem 2

Situation	Instrument 1	Instrument 2

		(A)	(B)	(C)	(D)	(E)	(F)	(G)	(H)	(I)	(J)	(K)
1.	Instrument 1 is a (type of instrument)	○	●	○	○	○	○	○	○	○	○	○
2.	Instrument 1 is (negotiability)	○	○	○	○	○	○	●	○	○	○	○
3.	Morton is considered a (type of ownership)	○	○	○	○	●	○	○	○	○	○	○
4.	Trent is considered a (type of ownership)	○	○	○	○	○	●	○	○	○	○	○
5.	Trent could recover on the instrument from [liable party(s)]	○	○	○	○	○	○	○	○	●	○	○

Explanation of solutions

1. (**B**) Instrument 1 is a two-party instrument in which Evans promises to pay a fixed amount in money to Dart; therefore it qualifies as a promissory note. A promissory note may be payable on demand or at a specific point in time.

2. (**G**) Instrument 1 meets the requirements of negotiability. It is written and signed by the maker. It contains an unconditional promise or order to pay a fixed amount in money, at a definite time or on demand. The document is also payable to order. The fact that it is payable on a certain date subject to acceleration does not destroy its negotiability.

3. (**E**) To qualify as a holder in due course, an individual must be a holder of a properly negotiated negotiable instrument, give value for the instrument, and take the instrument in good faith and without notice that it is overdue, has been dishonored, or that any person has a defense or claim to it.

4.   **(F)** When a negotiable instrument is negotiated from a holder in due course to a second holder, the second holder usually acquires the rights of a holder in due course through the shelter provision. The shelter provision applies to holders who have not previously held the instrument with knowledge of any defenses.

5.   **(I)** A holder with rights of a holder in due course under the shelter provision obtains all the rights of a holder in due course. A holder in due course takes an instrument free of personal defenses, including fraud in the inducement. Therefore, Evans' claim that Dart had fraudulently induced Evans into signing the instrument would not prevent Trent from recovering from Evans. Trent would also be able to recover from Morton and Dart based on his holder in due course status.

Situation	Instrument 1	Instrument 2

	(A) (B) (C) (D) (E) (F) (G) (H) (I) (J)
1. Instrument 2 is a (type of instrument)	○ ○ ○ ● ○ ○ ○ ○ ○ ○
2. Instrument 2 is (negotiability)	○ ○ ○ ○ ● ○ ○ ○ ○ ○
3. West's endorsement makes the instrument (type of instrument)	● ○ ○ ○ ○ ○ ○ ○ ○ ○
4. Keetin's endorsement makes the instrument (type of instrument)	○ ○ ○ ○ ○ ○ ○ ● ○ ○
5. Larr's endorsement makes the instrument (type of instrument)	● ○ ○ ○ ○ ○ ○ ○ ○ ○
6. West's endorsement would be considered (type of endorsement)	○ ● ○ ○ ○ ○ ○ ○ ○ ○
7. Keetin's endorsement would be considered (type of endorsement)	○ ○ ○ ○ ○ ○ ○ ○ ○ ●
8. Larr's endorsement would be considered (type of endorsement)	○ ○ ○ ○ ○ ○ ○ ○ ● ○

Explanation of solutions

1.   **(D)** Instrument 2 is a draft because it is a three-party instrument where a drawer (Fields) orders a drawee (Pure Bank) to pay a fixed amount in money to the payee (West). It is not a check because it is not payable on demand.

2.   **(E)** The draft qualifies as a negotiable instrument as it meets all of the required elements of negotiability. The draft is written and signed by the drawer. It contains an unconditional order to pay a fixed amount in money. It is made payable to order and is payable at a definite time.

3.   **(A)** A blank endorsement which does not specify any endorsee converts order paper to bearer paper.

4.   **(H)** An endorsement which indicates the specific person to whom the endorsee wishes to negotiate the instrument is a special endorsement. The use of a special endorsement converts bearer paper into order paper.

5.   **(A)** Because Larr's endorsement does not specify any endorsee, the endorsement converts the order paper into bearer paper.

6.   **(B)** West's endorsement is a blank endorsement because it does not specify any endorsee.

7.   **(J)** Because Keetin's endorsement indicates a specific person to whom the instrument is being negotiated, the endorsement is a special endorsement.

8.   **(I)** Larr's endorsement is a qualified endorsement because Larr disclaimed liability by signing without recourse.

MULTIPLE-CHOICE QUESTIONS (1-30)

1.　Under the Revised UCC Secured Transaction Article, when collateral is in a secured party's possession, which of the following conditions must also be satisfied to have attachment?
 a.　There must be a written security agreement.
 b.　The public must be notified.
 c.　The secured party must receive consideration.
 d.　The debtor must have rights to the collateral.

2.　Under the Revised UCC Secured Transaction Article, which of the following after-acquired property may be attached to a security agreement given to a secured lender?

	Inventory	Equipment
a.	Yes	Yes
b.	Yes	No
c.	No	Yes
d.	No	No

3.　Gardner Bank loaned Holland Company $20,000 to purchase some inventory to resell in its store. Gardner had Holland sign a security agreement that listed as collateral all present and future inventory of Holland as well as the proceeds of any sales of the inventory. Later, Boldon Company, who was aware of Gardner's security interest, extended credit to Holland but Holland failed to pay back either Gardner or Boldon. Boldon has sought to defeat the security interest pointing out that Gardner never filled out a financing statement. Which of the following is correct?
 a.　Gardner has an enforceable security interest that is valid against Holland and has priority over Boldon's interests.
 b.　Gardner does not have an enforceable security interest valid against Holland or against Boldon.
 c.　Gardner does have an enforceable security interest valid against Holland but not valid against Boldon.
 d.　Gardner does not have an enforceable security interest valid against Holland but does have one valid against Boldon.

4.　Article 9 of the UCC which governs security interests has added some items that now are covered by security interests law. Which of the following is true?
 a.　Security interests in tort claims already assessed by a court of law are covered.
 b.　After-acquired commercial tort claims are covered.
 c.　Both a. and b.
 d.　Neither a. nor b.

5.　Under the Revised Secured Transactions Article of the UCC, which of the following requirements is necessary to have a security interest attach?

	Debtor had rights in the collateral	Proper filing of a security agreement	Value given by the creditor
a.	Yes	Yes	Yes
b.	Yes	Yes	No
c.	Yes	No	Yes
d.	No	Yes	Yes

6.　Under the Revised UCC Secured Transaction Article, which of the following events will always prevent a security interest from attaching?
 a.　Failure to have a written security agreement.
 b.　Failure of the creditor to have possession of the collateral.
 c.　Failure of the debtor to have rights in the collateral.
 d.　Failure of the creditor to give present consideration for the security interest.

7.　Perfection of a security interest permits the secured party to protect its interest by
 a.　Avoiding the need to file a financing statement.
 b.　Preventing another creditor from obtaining a security interest in the same collateral.
 c.　Establishing priority over the claims of most subsequent secured creditors.
 d.　Denying the debtor the right to possess the collateral.

8.　Under the Revised UCC Secured Transaction Article, what is the effect of perfecting a security interest by filing a financing statement?
 a.　The secured party can enforce its security interest against the debtor.
 b.　The secured party has permanent priority in the collateral even if the collateral is removed to another state.
 c.　The debtor is protected against all other parties who acquire an interest in the collateral after the filing.
 d.　The secured party has priority in the collateral over most creditors who acquire a security interest in the same collateral after the filing.

9.　A secured creditor wants to file a financing statement to perfect its security interest. Under the Revised UCC Secured Transaction Article, which of the following must be included in the financing statement?
 a.　A listing or description of the collateral.
 b.　An after-acquired property provision.
 c.　The creditor's signature.
 d.　The collateral's location.

10.　Which of the following transactions would illustrate a secured party perfecting its security interest by taking possession of the collateral?
 a.　A bank receiving a mortgage on real property.
 b.　A wholesaler borrowing to purchase inventory.
 c.　A consumer borrowing to buy a car.
 d.　A pawnbroker lending money.

11.　Under the Revised UCC Secured Transaction Article, which of the following actions will best perfect a security interest in a negotiable instrument against any other party?
 a.　Filing a security agreement.
 b.　Taking possession of the instrument.
 c.　Perfecting by attachment.
 d.　Obtaining a duly executed financing statement.

12.　Grey Corp. sells computers to the public. Grey sold and delivered a computer to West on credit. West executed and delivered to Grey a promissory note for the purchase price and a security agreement covering the computer. West purchased the computer for personal use. Grey did not file a financing statement. Is Grey's security interest perfected?
 a.　Yes, because Grey retained ownership of the computer.
 b.　Yes, because it was perfected at the time of attachment.
 c.　No, because the computer was a consumer good.

d. No, because Grey failed to file a financing statement.

13. In which of the following cases does a seller have automatic perfection of a security interest as soon as attachment takes place?

  I. Purchase money security interest in consumer goods.
  II. Purchase money security interest in inventory.
  III. Purchase money security interest in equipment.

    a. I only.
    b. I and II only.
    c. II and III only.
    d. I, II and III.

14. Mars, Inc. manufactures and sells VCRs on credit directly to wholesalers, retailers, and consumers. Mars can perfect its security interest in the VCRs it sells without having to file a financing statement or take possession of the VCRs if the sale is made to

    a. Retailers.
    b. Wholesalers that sell to distributors for resale.
    c. Consumers.
    d. Wholesalers that sell to buyers in the ordinary course of business.

15. Under the Revised Secured Transaction Article of the UCC, which of the following purchasers will own consumer goods free of a perfected security interest in the goods?

    a. A merchant who purchases the goods for resale.
    b. A merchant who purchases the goods for use in its business.
    c. A consumer who purchases the goods from a consumer purchaser who gave the security interest.
    d. A consumer who purchases the goods in the ordinary course of business.

16. Under the Revised UCC Secured Transaction Article, what is the order of priority for the following security interests in store equipment?

  I. Security interest perfected by filing on April 15, 2001.
  II. Security interest attached on April 1, 2001.
  III. Purchase money security interest attached April 11, 2001 and perfected by filing on April 20, 2001.

    a. I, III, II.
    b. II, I, III.
    c. III, I, II.
    d. III, II, I.

17. Noninventory goods were purchased and delivered on June 15, 2001. Several security interests exist in these goods. Which of the following security interests has priority over the others?

    a. Security interest in future goods attached June 10, 2001.
    b. Security interest attached June 15, 2001.
    c. Security interest perfected June 20, 2001.
    d. Purchase money security interest perfected June 24, 2001.

18. Under the Revised Secured Transaction Article of the UCC, what would be the order of priority for the following security interests in consumer goods?

  I. Financing agreement filed on April 1.
  II. Possession of the collateral by a creditor on April 10.
  III. Financing agreement perfected on April 15.

    a. I, II, III.
    b. II, I, III.
    c. II, III, I.
    d. III, II, I.

19. A party who filed a security interest in inventory on April 1, 2001, would have a superior interest to which of the following parties?

    a. A holder of a mechanic's lien whose lien was filed on March 15, 2001.
    b. A holder of a purchase money security interest in after-acquired property filed on March 20, 2001.
    c. A purchaser in the ordinary course of business who purchased on April 10, 2001.
    d. A judgment lien creditor who filed its judgment on April 15, 2001.

20. W & B, a wholesaler, sold on credit some furniture to Broadmore Company, a retailer. W & B perfected its security interest by filing a financing statement. Lean purchased some furniture from Broadmore for his home. He was unaware of W & B's perfected security interest. McCoy purchased some furniture from Broadmore for her home. She was aware that Broadmore's inventory was subject to security interests since Broadmore was having financial problems and had to buy the furniture on credit. Norsome purchased some furniture from Broadmore for use in his business. Broadmore defaults on its loans from W & B, who wants to repossess the furniture purchased and delivered to Lean, McCoy, and Norsome. From which parties can W & B legally repossess the furniture?

    a. McCoy.
    b. Lean and McCoy.
    c. Norsome.
    d. None of these parties.

21. Rand purchased a sofa from Abby Department Store for use in her home. Abby had her sign a security agreement for the balance Rand owed. Rand did not pay the balance and sold the sofa to her neighbor, Gram, for use in his home. Gram did not realize that Rand had not paid off the balance. Abby filed a financing statement after Rand defaulted. This filing was also after Gram purchased the sofa from Rand. Which of the following is correct?

    a. Abby can repossess the sofa from Gram since it has a written security agreement covering the sofa.
    b. Abby can repossess the sofa from Gram since it perfected its security agreement by filing.
    c. Abby can repossess the sofa from Gram since it obtained automatic perfection.
    d. Abby has no right to repossess the sofa from Gram.

22. Wine purchased a computer using the proceeds of a loan from MJC Finance Company. Wine gave MJC a security interest in the computer. Wine executed a security agreement and financing statement, which was filed by MJC. Wine used the computer to monitor Wine's personal investments. Later, Wine sold the computer to Jacobs, for Jacobs' family use. Jacobs was unaware of MJC's security interest. Wine now is in default under the MJC loan. May MJC repossess the computer from Jacobs?

    a. No, because Jacobs was unaware of the MJC security interest.
    b. No, because Jacobs intended to use the computer for family or household purposes.

c. Yes, because MJC's security interest was perfected before Jacobs' purchase.

d. Yes, because Jacobs' purchase of the computer made Jacobs personally liable to MJC.

23. Rally Co. has purchased some inventory from Kantar Corporation to sell to customers who will use the inventory primarily for consumer use. Which of the following is **not** correct?

a. If Kantar sells the inventory to Rally on credit and takes out a security interest using the inventory as collateral, this a purchase money security interest.

b. If Kantar sells the inventory to Rally on credit and takes out a security interest using the inventory as collateral, this is a purchase money security interest in consumer goods.

c. If Kantar sells the inventory to Rally but Rally pays for it by getting a loan from a bank who takes out a security interest using the inventory as collateral, this is a purchase money security interest.

d. If a customer purchases some inventory on credit from Rally for home use and signs a written security agreement presented by Rally that lists the inventory as collateral for the credit, this is a purchase money security interest in consumer goods.

24. On June 15, Harper purchased equipment for $100,000 from Imperial Corp. for use in its manufacturing process. Harper paid for the equipment with funds borrowed from Eastern Bank. Harper gave Eastern a security agreement and financing statement covering Harper's existing and after-acquired equipment. On June 21, Harper was petitioned involuntarily into bankruptcy under Chapter 7 of the Federal Bankruptcy Code. A bankruptcy trustee was appointed. On June 23, Eastern filed the financing statement. Which of the parties will have a superior security interest in the equipment?

a. The trustee in bankruptcy, because the filing of the financing statement after the commencement of the bankruptcy case would be deemed a preferential transfer.

b. The trustee in bankruptcy, because the trustee became a lien creditor before Eastern perfected its security interest.

c. Eastern, because it had a perfected purchase money security interest without having to file a financing statement.

d. Eastern, because it perfected its security interest within the permissible time limits.

Items 25 and 26 are based on the following:

Drew bought a computer for personal use from Hale Corp. for $3,000. Drew paid $2,000 in cash and signed a security agreement for the balance. Hale properly filed the security agreement. Drew defaulted in paying the balance of the purchase price. Hale asked Drew to pay the balance. When Drew refused, Hale peacefully repossessed the computer.

25. Under the Revised UCC Secured Transaction Article, which of the following remedies will Hale have?

a. Obtain a deficiency judgment against Drew for the amount owed.

b. Sell the computer and retain any surplus over the amount owed.

c. Retain the computer over Drew's objection.

d. Sell the computer without notifying Drew.

26. Under the Revised UCC Secured Transaction Article, which of the following rights will Drew have?

a. Redeem the computer after Hale sells it.

b. Recover the sale price from Hale after Hale sells the computer.

c. Force Hale to sell the computer.

d. Prevent Hale from selling the computer.

27. Under the Revised UCC Secured Transaction Article, which of the following statements is correct concerning the disposition of collateral by a secured creditor after a debtor's default?

a. A good-faith purchaser for value and without knowledge of any defects in the sale takes free of any subordinate liens or security interests.

b. The debtor may not redeem the collateral after the default.

c. Secured creditors with subordinate claims retain the right to redeem the collateral after the collateral is sold to a third party.

d. The collateral may only be disposed of at a public sale.

28. Bean defaulted on a promissory note payable to Gray Co. The note was secured by a piece of equipment owned by Bean. Gray perfected its security interest on May 29, 2001 Bean had also pledged the same equipment as collateral for another loan from Smith Co. after he had given the security interest to Gray. Smith's security interest was perfected on June 30, 2001. Bean is current in his payments to Smith. Subsequently, Gray took possession of the equipment and sold it at a private sale to Walsh, a good-faith purchaser for value. Walsh will take the equipment

a. Free of Smith's security interest because Bean is current in his payments to Smith.

b. Free of Smith's security interest because Walsh acted in good faith and gave value.

c. Subject to Smith's security interest because the equipment was sold at a private sale.

d. Subject to Smith's security interest because Smith is a purchase money secured creditor.

29. Under the Revised Secured Transactions Article of the UCC, which of the following remedies is available to a secured creditor when a debtor fails to make a payment when due?

	Proceed against the collateral	Obtain a general judgment against the debtor
a.	Yes	Yes
b.	Yes	No
c.	No	Yes
d.	No	No

30. In what order are the following obligations paid after a secured creditor rightfully sells the debtor's collateral after repossession?

I. Debt owed to any junior security holder.
II. Secured party's reasonable sale expenses.
III. Debt owed to the secured party.

a. I, II, III.
b. II, I, III.
c. II, III, I.
d. III, II, I.

SIMULATION PROBLEM

Simulation Problem 1   (10 to 15 minutes)

Situation
Analysis

On January 2, 2004, Gray Interiors Corp., a retailer of sofas, contracted with Shore Furniture Co. to purchase 150 sofas for its inventory. The purchase price was $250,000. Gray paid $50,000 cash and gave Shore a note and security agreement for the balance. On March 1, 2004, the sofas were delivered. On March 10, 2004, Shore filed a financing statement.

On February 1, 2004, Gray negotiated a $1,000,000 line of credit with Float Bank, pledged its present and future inventory as security, and gave Float a security agreement. On February 20, 2004, Gray borrowed $100,000 from the line of credit. On March 5, 2004, Float filed a financing statement.

On April 1, 2004, Dove, a consumer purchaser in the ordinary course of business, purchased a sofa from Gray. Dove was aware of both security interests.

Analysis
Situation

Items 1 through 6 refer to the fact pattern. For each item, determine whether (A), (B), or (C) is correct.

	(A)	(B)	(C)

1. Shore's security interest in the sofas attached on   ○   ○   ○
    A. January 2, 2004.
    B. March 1, 2004.
    C. March 10, 2004.

2. Shore's security interest in the sofas was perfected on   ○   ○   ○
    A. January 2, 2004.
    B. March 1, 2004.
    C. March 10, 2004.

3. Float's security interest in Gray's inventory attached on   ○   ○   ○
    A. February 1, 2004.
    B. March 1, 2004.
    C. March 5, 2004.

4. Float's security interest in Gray's inventory was perfected on ○   ○   ○
    A. February 1, 2004.
    B. February 20, 2004.
    C. March 5, 2004.

5. A. Shore's security interest has priority because it was a purchase money security interest.   ○   ○   ○
    B. Float's security interest has priority because Float's financing statement was filed before
       Shore's.
    C. Float's security interest has priority because Float's interest attached before Shore's.

6. A. Dove purchased the sofa subject to Shore's security interest.   ○   ○   ○
    B. Dove purchased the sofa subject to both the Shore and Float security interests.
    C. Dove purchased the sofa free of either the Shore or Float security interests.

MULTIPLE-CHOICE ANSWERS

1. d __ __	8. d __ __	15. d __ __	22. c __ __	29. a __ __
2. a __ __	9. a __ __	16. c __ __	23. b __ __	30. c __ __
3. a __ __	10. d __ __	17. d __ __	24. d __ __	
4. a __ __	11. b __ __	18. a __ __	25. a __ __	
5. c __ __	12. b __ __	19. d __ __	26. c __ __	
6. c __ __	13. a __ __	20. d __ __	27. a __ __	1st: __/30 = __%
7. c __ __	14. c __ __	21. d __ __	28. b __ __	2nd: __/30 = __%

MULTIPLE-CHOICE ANSWER EXPLANATIONS

B. Attachment of Security Interests

1. **(d)** Under the Revised Article 9 on Secured Transactions, attachment of a security interest takes place when the secured party gives value, the debtor has rights in the collateral, and one of the following three is true:

    a. The secured party must possess the collateral if the debtor agrees to it

    b. The secured party must have control of certain types of collateral, or

    c. The secured party must have a signed security agreement (or an authenticated electronic transmission).

2. **(a)** An after-acquired property clause in a security agreement allows the secured party's interest in such property to attach once the debtor acquires the property, without the need to make a new security agreement. These clauses are typically used for inventory and accounts receivable, and can also be used for equipment.

3. **(a)** The security interest did attach because there was a signed security agreement, Gardner gave value, and Holland had rights in the collateral. Upon attachment, Gardner's security interest is fully enforceable against Holland. Even though Gardner never perfected the security interest, it still has priority over Boldon's interests because Boldon was aware of the security interest.

4. **(a)** Security interests in tort claims are covered under the Revised UCC Secured Transactions Article; this is not true of after-acquired commercial tort claims.

5. **(c)** In order for attachment of a security interest to occur, three elements must take place. First, the secured party must give value, second, the debtor must have rights in the collateral, and third, there must be a security agreement. This security agreement may be oral if the secured party has possession or control of the collateral. Otherwise, it must be in writing and signed by the debtor. An exception to the signature requirement is made if it is an authenticated electronic transmission.

6. **(c)** In order for a security interest to attach, there must be a valid security agreement, the secured party must have given value, and the debtor must have rights in the collateral. If any one of these items is missing, attachment cannot take place. Answer (a) is incorrect because the security interest may be oral if the secured party has possession or control of the collateral. Answer (b) is incorrect because if the security agreement is in writing, the secured party does not need possession of the collateral to achieve attachment. Answer (d) is incorrect because the secured party must give value, not necessarily consideration. A preexisting claim, although not consideration, does count as value.

C.4. Filing a Financing Statement

7. **(c)** Perfection of a security interest is important in that it establishes for a secured party priority over the claims that may be made by most subsequent secured creditors. Answer (a) is incorrect because there are three methods of obtaining perfection and one of them is filing a financing statement. Answer (b) is incorrect because subsequent creditors may still obtain security interests in the same collateral although they will normally obtain a lower priority. Answer (d) is incorrect because of times the debtor retains possession of the collateral.

8. **(d)** Perfection by filing a financing statement will not defeat all other parties who acquire an interest in the same collateral; rather, perfection by filing gives the secured party most possible rights in the collateral. Note, purchasers from a merchant in the ordinary course of business take the collateral free from any prior perfected security interest. The only time a purchaser would take the collateral subject to a prior perfected security interest would be when the purchaser knew that the merchant was selling the goods in violation of a financing statement. A creditor need not perfect the security interest in order to enforce it against the debtor. The filing of a financing statement does not protect the debtor's rights but rather the creditor's rights.

9. **(a)** Filing a financing statement is one method of perfecting a security interest in personal property. Under the Revised UCC Secured Transaction Article, a financing statement must include the following: the names of the debtor and creditor, and a listing or description of the collateral. An after-acquired property provision, the creditor's signature, and the collateral's location are not required to be included in the financing statement.

C.5. Perfection by Possession

10. **(d)** One way to perfect a security interest is for the secured party to take possession of the collateral in addition to attaining attachment. A pawnbroker lending money is such a case. There is a security agreement which may be oral since the secured party has possession of the collateral. The secured party gives value by lending the money. The third step in attachment is that the debtor has rights in the collateral such as ownership. Since these steps constitute attachment, perfection is accomplished by the pawnbroker, the secured party, taking possession of the collateral. The secured transactions laws apply to security interests in personal property, not real property. The wholesaler (car buyer), not the secured party, will have possession of the collateral.

11. **(b)** In general, the best way to perfect a security interest in a negotiable instrument is to take possession of the instrument. This is true because negotiable instruments are easily negotiated to other holders who can become holders in due course. Answer (a) is incorrect because a holder can become a holder in due course even if a security agreement is filed. Answer (c) is incorrect because perfecting by attachment requires a purchase money security interest in consumer goods. Answer (d) is incorrect because this cannot even accomplish perfection until it is filed.

C.6. Automatic Perfection

12. (b) Since West purchased the computer for personal use and the computer itself was the collateral for the security agreement, the fact pattern involves a purchase money security interest in consumer goods. Therefore, once attachment took place, perfection was automatic. Answer (c) is incorrect because since the computer was a consumer good, perfection was automatic upon attachment. Answer (d) is incorrect because filing a financing statement is not required for perfecting a purchase money security interest in consumer goods. Answer (a) is incorrect because retaining or obtaining possession, not ownership, by the secured party is a way to perfect. In any event, Grey Corp. did not retain either ownership or possession since they sold and delivered the computer to West.

13. (a) Automatic perfection (perfection by attachment) takes place in the case of a purchase money security interest (PMSI) in consumer goods only. Answers (b), (c), and (d) are incorrect because they include PMSI in inventory or equipment which do not qualify for automatic perfection.

14. (c) Mars holds a purchase money security interest in the goods sold, which allowed the buyers of these goods to secure the credit for their purchase. When a purchase money security interest is in consumer goods, the secured party (Mars) obtains perfection when attachment takes place without the need to file a financing statement or take possession or control of the collateral. Answers (a), (b), and (d) are incorrect because in those cases the goods comprise inventory, not consumer goods.

E. Priorities

15. (d) Buyers in the ordinary course of business take goods free of any security interest whether perfected or not. The buyer can be, but need not be, a consumer. Answer (a) is incorrect because a merchant who purchases consumer goods for resale may not be buying in the ordinary course of business. Answer (b) is incorrect because the merchant who buys the consumer goods for use in his/her business may not be buying in the ordinary course of business. Answer (c) is incorrect because although a consumer can take goods free of a security interest when buying from another consumer, this requires certain facts along with a purchase money security interest in consumer goods. There are no facts in the question to show this.

16. (c) In general, a purchase money security interest in noninventory has priority over nonpurchase money security interests if it was perfected within 20 days after the debtor received the collateral. Item III, therefore, has the first priority because the purchase money security interest was perfected on April 20, 2001, which was within twenty days of the attachment. Item I has priority over Item II because the security interest in Item I was perfected, while the security interest in Item II was not.

17. (d) A purchase money security interest in noninventory goods has a special rule. Since it was perfected within twenty days after the debtor got possession of the collateral, it has priority over all of the others. Answers (a) and (b) are incorrect because unperfected security interests have a lower priority than perfected security interests. Answer (c) is incorrect because although this security interest was perfected before the purchase money security interest, the latter has priority if perfected within twenty days of the debtor taking possession of the collateral.

18. (a) Since security interest I was perfected first when the financing agreement was filed on April 1, it has the first priority. Security interest II was perfected on April 10 when the creditor took possession of the collateral. It has the second priority. Security interest III has the third priority since it was perfected last on April 15.

19. (d) The party perfected by filing a security interest in inventory on April 1, 2001. S/he would therefore have priority over a judgment lien creditor who filed later on April 15, 2001. Answer (a) is incorrect because the mechanic's lien was filed on March 15 before the perfection of the security interest. Therefore, the mechanic's lien has priority over the perfected security interest. Answer (b) is incorrect because the holder of the purchase money security interest in after-acquired property filed and perfected before April 1. Answer (c) is incorrect because a purchaser in the ordinary course of business is free of other security interests even if they are perfected before s/he purchases the inventory.

20. (d) Lean, McCoy, and Norsome all purchased the furniture in the ordinary course of business. As such, all three parties take free of the security interest even if it was perfected. This is true whether they purchased the furniture for consumer or business use and whether they knew of the security agreement or not.

21. (d) Abby had a perfected security agreement because of the purchase money security interest in consumer goods. This, however, is not effective against a good-faith purchaser for value who buys from a consumer for consumer use as in the case of Gram. Perfection by filing is, however, effective in such a case but only if the filing is done before Gram purchases the sofa. Answer (a) is incorrect because the attachment of the written security interest makes it enforceable against Rand, not Gram. Answer (b) is incorrect because the filing of the financing statement took place after Gram bought the sofa. Answer (c) is incorrect because, although Abby did accomplish automatic perfection by way of the PMSI in consumer goods, this type of perfection was not effective against Gram because he was a good-faith purchaser for value who bought it from a consumer (Rand) for consumer use.

22. (c) MJC obtained a security interest in the computer purchased by Wine and perfected it by filing. Even though when Jacobs later purchased it for consumer use he was unaware of MJC's security interest, MJC still has priority. This is true because the filing is constructive notice to all subsequent parties. MJC has priority and may repossess the computer even if Jacobs was unaware of the filed security interest. The filing gives MJC priority over Jacob despite his intended use for family. Jacobs is not personally liable to MJC because he made no contract and did not agree to take on liability with MJC.

23. (b) Because Kantar has a security interest in the inventory it sold and is also using the same inventory as collateral for the credit, this is a purchase money security interest. However, because the items Rally purchased are inventory, not consumer goods, in **Rally's** hands, this is not a PMSI in consumer goods. Answer (a) is not chosen because this does describe a PMSI since Kantar retained a security interest in the same items sold on credit to secure payment. Answer (c) is not chosen because a PMSI includes a third party giving a loan who retains a security interest in the same items purchased by the loan. Answer (d) is not chosen because this is a PMSI in consumer goods since the customer purchased the items for his/her home use.

24. (d) When a purchase money security interest uses noninventory as collateral, it has priority over prior competing interests as long as it is perfected within twenty days of the debtor obtaining possession of the collateral. Since the collateral in this fact pattern was equipment, and Eastern filed within twenty days, Eastern has priority over the trustee in bankruptcy. Perfection was not automatic since it was a purchase money security interest in equipment, not in consumer goods. Furthermore, since the secured party did not have possession of the collateral, the way to perfect this security interest is by filing a financing statement.

F. Rights of Parties upon Default

25. (a) After Hale repossesses the computer and sells it in a commercially reasonable fashion, Hale may obtain a deficiency judgment for the amount still owed after the proceeds from the sale pay the expenses of repossession and sale and the debt owed to Hale. Any remaining proceeds go to the debtor after repossession and sale expenses and secured parties are paid. For consumer goods, such as the personal computer in this fact pattern, the goods must be sold if the debtor has paid more than 60% of the debt secured by the consumer goods. In this fact pattern, Drew paid two-thirds of the debt. Hale must notify Drew in writing of the impending sale unless Drew had agreed otherwise in writing.

26. (c) Since Drew has paid two-thirds of the price, which is over 60% payment on the secured debt for consumer goods, Hale is obligated to sell the computer rather than keep it in satisfaction of the debt. The debtor may redeem before, not after, the sale. Hale may keep the proceeds needed to pay off repossession and sale expenses and the debt owed to Hale. Any excess would go to Drew. Hale has the right to sell the repossessed computer to pay off the secured debt unless Drew properly redeems the interest s/he has in the computer.

27. (a) Upon the debtor's default, the secured party may take possession of the collateral and sell it. A good-faith purchaser for value buys the collateral free of any liens or security interests. Answer (b) is incorrect because the debtor has the right to redeem the collateral before the secured party disposes of it. The debtor does this by paying the debt in full as well as the secured party's reasonable expenses. Answer (c) is incorrect as a good-faith purchaser of the collateral takes it free of the debtor's rights and any secured interest or lien subordinate to it. Answer (d) is incorrect because although the collateral may be disposed of by a public sale, it also may be disposed of by a private sale if the sale uses commercially reasonable practices.

28. (b) A good-faith purchaser for value at a private sale will take the property free from any security interest or subordinate liens in the property, but remains subject to security interests which are senior to that being discharged at the sale. In this case, Smith perfected his security interest later than Gray and has a subordinate interest in the property. Thus, Walsh takes the equipment free from this subordinate security interest. The fact that Bean is current in his payments to Smith would not affect Smith's interest in the property. As long as Walsh is a good-faith purchaser for value, it doesn't matter if the equipment is sold at a public or private sale. Smith is not a purchase money secured creditor since the proceeds of Smith's loan to Bean were not used to purchase the equipment acting as collateral.

29. (a) If the debtor defaults on the debt, the secured party may proceed against the collateral. This extra protection is one of the main reasons for having secured transactions. If the creditor chooses, s/he may obtain a general judgment against the debtor.

30. (c) Under the UCC, after a secured creditor rightfully sells the debtor's collateral after repossession, the secured party's reasonable sale expenses are paid first. Next, the debt owed to the secured party is paid. Any junior security holders then get paid to the extent of any money remaining.

SOLUTION TO SIMULATION PROBLEM

Simulation Problem 1

Analysis

Situation

                                                                    (A)   (B)   (C)
1. Shore's security interest in the sofas attached on   ○   ●   ○
    A. January 2, 2004.
    B. March 1, 2004.
    C. March 10, 2004.

2. Shore's security interest in the sofas was perfected on   ○   ○   ●
    A. January 2, 2004.
    B. March 1, 2004.
    C. March 10, 2004.

3. Float's security interest in Gray's inventory attached on   ●   ○   ○
    A. February 1, 2004.
    B. March 1, 2004.
    C. March 5, 2004.

4. Float's security interest in Gray's inventory was perfected on   ○   ○   ●
    A. February 1, 2004.
    B. February 20, 2004.
    C. March 5, 2004.

5. A. Shore's security interest has priority because it was a purchase money security interest.   ○   ●   ○
    B. Float's security interest has priority because Float's financing statement was filed before
       Shore's.
    C. Float's security interest has priority because Float's interest attached before Shore's.

6. A. Dove purchased the sofa subject to Shore's security interest.   ○   ○   ●
    B. Dove purchased the sofa subject to both the Shore and Float security interests.
    C. Dove purchased the sofa free of either the Shore or Float security interests.

Explanation of solutions

1. **(B)** Gray gave Shore a security agreement on January 2. Shore also gave value but Gray did not receive the goods or have rights in them until March 1. Therefore, it was not until March 1 that attachment occurred.

2. **(C)** Perfection took place on March 10, when Shore filed the financing statement, since attachment had already been accomplished. Note that the filing was needed for perfection since this was not a purchase money security interest in consumer goods but in inventory.

3. **(A)** Float gave value by giving the $1,000,000 line of credit on February 1. On this same date, Gray gave Float a security agreement. Since Gray had rights in the collateral it already possessed, attachment took place on February 1 for that inventory possessed.

4. **(C)** Perfection occurred on March 5, when Float filed the financing statement, since attachment had already taken place previously.

5. **(B)** Generally, when two parties have perfected security interests in the same collateral, the first to either file or perfect has priority. When a purchase money security interest exists in the collateral, however, the general rule may vary, depending on whether the collateral is inventory or noninventory. In this case the collateral is inventory. A purchase money security interest in inventory may obtain priority over previously perfected conflicting security interests if (1) the purchase money security holder perfects his interest in the inventory at the time the debtor receives the inventory, and (2) the purchase money security holder provides written notice of his purchase money security interest and a description of the inventory to all holders of conflicting security interests who have filed financing statements covering the same type of inventory. If the purchase money security holder does not take these steps, the general rule applies. Answer (A) is incorrect because Shore did not take the necessary steps for its purchase money security interest to obtain priority. Answer (B) is correct because the general rule applies, and Float filed first. Answer (C) is incorrect because when both security interests are perfected, priority is not based on the order of attachment.

6. **(C)** A buyer in the ordinary course of business takes free of any security interests even if perfected and even if the buyer is aware of the security interests. Therefore, answers (A) and (B) are incorrect because Dove purchased the goods in the ordinary course of business.

MULTIPLE-CHOICE QUESTIONS (1-31)

1.   Which of the following statements is correct concerning the voluntary filing of a petition in bankruptcy?
    a.   If the debtor has twelve or more creditors, the unsecured claims must total at least $13,475.
    b.   The debtor must be insolvent.
    c.   If the debtor has less than twelve creditors, the unsecured claims must total at least $13,475.
    d.   The petition may be filed jointly by spouses.

2.   A voluntary petition filed under the liquidation provisions of Chapter 7 of the Federal Bankruptcy Code
    a.   Is **not** available to a corporation unless it has previously filed a petition under the reorganization provisions of Chapter 11 of the Federal Bankruptcy Code.
    b.   Automatically stays collection actions against the debtor **except** by secured creditors.
    c.   Will be dismissed unless the debtor has twelve or more unsecured creditors whose claims total at least $13,475.
    d.   Does **not** require the debtor to show that the debtor's liabilities exceed the fair market value of assets.

3.   On February 28, 2008, Master, Inc. had total assets with a fair market value of $1,200,000 and total liabilities of $990,000. On January 15, 2008, Master made a monthly installment note payment to Acme Distributors Corp., a creditor holding a properly perfected security interest in equipment having a fair market value greater than the balance due on the note. On March 15, 2008, Master voluntarily filed a petition in bankruptcy under the liquidation provisions of Chapter 7 of the Federal Bankruptcy Code. One year later, the equipment was sold for less than the balance due on the note to Acme.

If a creditor challenged Master's right to file, the petition would be dismissed
    a.   If Master had less than twelve creditors at the time of filing.
    b.   Unless Master can show that a reorganization under Chapter 11 of the Federal Bankruptcy Code would have been unsuccessful.
    c.   Unless Master can show that it is unable to pay its debts in the ordinary course of business or as they come due.
    d.   If Master is an insurance company.

4.   Which of the following conditions, if any, must a debtor meet to file a voluntary bankruptcy petition under Chapter 7 of the Federal Bankruptcy Code?

	Insolvency	Three or more creditors
a.	Yes	Yes
b.	Yes	No
c.	No	Yes
d.	No	No

5.   Brenner Corporation is trying to avoid bankruptcy but its four creditors are trying to force Brenner into bankruptcy. The four creditors are owed the following amounts:

Anteed Corporation	-	$6,000 of unsecured debt
Bounty Corporation	-	$5,000 of unsecured debt and $8,500 of secured debt
Courtney Corporation	-	$2,000 of unsecured debt
Dauntless Corporation	-	$1,000 of unsecured debt

Which of the creditors must sign the petition to force Brenner into bankruptcy?
    a.   Bounty is sufficient.
    b.   At least Anteed and Bounty are needed.
    c.   At least Bounty, Courtney, and Dauntless are needed.
    d.   All of these four creditors are needed.

Items 6 through 10 are based on the following:

Dart Inc., a closely held corporation, was petitioned involuntarily into bankruptcy under the liquidation provisions of Chapter 7 of the Federal Bankruptcy Code. Dart contested the petition.

Dart has not been paying its business debts as they became due, has defaulted on its mortgage loan payments, and owes back taxes to the IRS. The total cash value of Dart's bankruptcy estate after the sale of all assets and payment of administration expenses is $100,000.

Dart has the following creditors:

-   Fracon Bank is owed $75,000 principal and accrued interest on a mortgage loan secured by Dart's real property. The property was valued at and sold, in bankruptcy, for $70,000.
-   The IRS has a $12,000 recorded judgment for unpaid corporate income tax.
-   JOG Office Supplies has an unsecured claim of $3,000 that was timely filed.
-   Nanstar Electric Co. has an unsecured claim of $1,200 that was not timely filed.
-   Decoy Publications has a claim of $16,000, of which $2,000 is secured by Dart's inventory that was valued and sold, in bankruptcy, for $2,000. The claim was timely filed.

6.   Which of the following statements would correctly describe the result of Dart's opposing the petition?
    a.   Dart will win because the petition should have been filed under Chapter 11.
    b.   Dart will win because there are **not** more than 12 creditors.
    c.   Dart will lose because it is **not** paying its debts as they become due.
    d.   Dart will lose because of its debt to the IRS.

7.   Which of the following events will follow the filing of the Chapter 7 involuntary petition?

	A trustee will be appointed	A stay against creditor collection proceedings will go into effect
a.	Yes	Yes
b.	Yes	No
c.	No	Yes
d.	No	No

For **items 8 through 10** assume that the bankruptcy estate was distributed.

8.   What dollar amount would Nanstar Electric Co. receive?
    a. $0
    b. $ 800
    c. $1,000
    d. $1,200

9.   What total dollar amount would Fracon Bank receive on its secured and unsecured claims?
    a. $70,000

b. $72,000
c. $74,000
d.   None of the above.

10.   What dollar amount would the IRS receive?
a. $0
b. $ 8,000
c. $10,000
d. $12,000

11.   Which of the following is **not** allowed as a federal exemption under the Federal Bankruptcy Code?
a.   Some specified amount of equity in one motor vehicle.
b.   Unemployment compensation.
c.   Some specified amount of value in books and tools of one's trade.
d.   All of the above are allowed.

12.   Flax, a sole proprietor, has been petitioned involuntarily into bankruptcy under the Federal Bankruptcy Code's liquidation provisions. Simon & Co., CPAs, has been appointed trustee of the bankruptcy estate. If Simon also wishes to act as the tax return preparer for the estate, which of the following statements is correct?
a.   Simon is prohibited from serving as both trustee and preparer under any circumstances because serving in that dual capacity would be a conflict of interest.
b.   Although Simon may serve as both trustee and preparer, it is entitled to receive a fee only for the services rendered as a preparer.
c.   Simon may employ itself to prepare tax returns if authorized by the court and may receive a separate fee for services rendered in each capacity.
d.   Although Simon may serve as both trustee and preparer, its fees for services rendered in each capacity will be determined solely by the size of the estate.

13.   Which of the following transfers by a debtor, within 90 days of filing for bankruptcy, could be set aside as a preferential payment?
a.   Making a gift to charity.
b.   Paying a business utility bill.
c.   Borrowing money from a bank secured by giving a mortgage on business property.
d.   Prepaying an installment loan on inventory.

Items 14 and 15 are based on the following:

On August 1, 2008, Hall filed a voluntary petition under Chapter 7 of the Federal Bankruptcy Code. Hall's assets are sufficient to pay general creditors 40% of their claims.
The following transactions occurred before the filing:

- On May 15, 2008, Hall gave a mortgage on Hall's home to National Bank to secure payment of a loan National had given Hall two years earlier. When the loan was made, Hall's twin was a National employee.
- On June 1, 2008, Hall purchased a boat from Olsen for $10,000 cash.
- On July 1, 2008, Hall paid off an outstanding credit card balance of $500. The original debt had been $2,500.

14.   The National mortgage was
a.   Preferential, because National would be considered an insider.

b.   Preferential, because the mortgage was given to secure an antecedent debt.
c.   Not preferential, because Hall is presumed insolvent when the mortgage was given.
d.   Not preferential, because the mortgage was a security interest.

15.   The payment to Olsen was
a.   Preferential, because the payment was made within ninety days of the filing of the petition.
b.   Preferential, because the payment enabled Olsen to receive more than the other general creditors.
c.   Not preferential, because Hall is presumed insolvent when the payment was made.
d.   Not preferential, because the payment was a contemporaneous exchange for new value.

16.   Under the liquidation provisions of Chapter 7 of the Federal Bankruptcy Code, a debtor will be denied a discharge in bankruptcy if the debtor
a.   Fails to list a creditor.
b.   Owes alimony and support payments.
c.   Cannot pay administration expenses.
d.   Refuses to satisfactorily explain a loss of assets.

17.   On May 1, 2008, two months after becoming insolvent, Quick Corp., an appliance wholesaler, filed a voluntary petition for bankruptcy under the provisions of Chapter 7 of the Federal Bankruptcy Code. On October 15, 2007, Quick's board of directors had authorized and paid Erly $50,000 to repay Erly's April 1, 2007, loan to the corporation. Erly is a sibling of Quick's president. On March 15, 2008, Quick paid Kray $100,000 for inventory delivered that day.

Which of the following is **not** relevant in determining whether the repayment of Erly's loan is a voidable preferential transfer?
a.   Erly is an insider.
b.   Quick's payment to Erly was made on account of an antecedent debt.
c.   Quick's solvency when the loan was made by Erly.
d.   Quick's payment to Erly was made within one year of the filing of the bankruptcy petition.

18.   Brook Corporation has filed for bankruptcy. Of the following debts Brook owes, indicate their priorities from the highest to the lowest.

I.   Federal taxes unpaid for the previous year.
II.   Wages of $3,000 owed to employees.
III.   Balance of $5,000 owed to a creditor that had a security interest. This creditor got paid fully by selling off the collateral except for this $5,000 deficiency.

a.   I, II, III.
b.   I, III, II.
c.   II, I, III.
d.   III, I, II.

19.   Kessler Company has filed a voluntary bankruptcy petition. Kessler's debts include administration costs owed to accountants, attorneys, and appraisers. It also owes federal and state taxes. Kessler still owes various employees for the previous month's wages accrued before the petition was filed. None of these wages are owed to the officers and at most total $4,000 per employee. The company also owes several creditors for claims arising in the ordinary course of business. All of these latter claims arose before Kessler

filed the bankruptcy petition. What are the priorities from highest to lowest of these listed debts and claims?

a. The claims arising in the ordinary course of business; the administration costs; the employees' wages; the federal and state taxes.

b. The administration costs; the employees' wages; the federal and state taxes; the claims arising in the ordinary course of business.

c. The federal and state taxes; the administration costs; the claims arising in the ordinary course of business; the employees' wages.

d. The claims arising in the ordinary course of business; the federal and state taxes; the administration costs; the employees' wages.

20. Which of the following acts will not bar a general discharge in bankruptcy?

a. The debtor tried to hide some property to prevent the estate from getting it.

b. The debtor intentionally injured a creditor during an argument about the bankruptcy proceedings.

c. The debtor is unwilling to explain satisfactorily why some assets are missing.

d. The debtor intentionally destroyed records of his assets.

21. Chapter 7 of the Federal Bankruptcy Code will deny a debtor a discharge when the debtor

a. Made a preferential transfer to a creditor.

b. Accidentally destroyed information relevant to the bankruptcy proceeding.

c. Obtained a Chapter 7 discharge ten years previously.

d. Is a corporation or a partnership.

22. Eckson was granted an order for relief after having filed a petition in bankruptcy. Which of the following actions would bar a general discharge in bankruptcy?

I. Ten months before the bankruptcy proceedings, Eckson had obtained credit from Cardinal Corporation by using false information on the credit application.

II. Six months before he filed the petition, Eckson removed a vehicle from his land with the intent to defraud a creditor.

III. During the bankruptcy proceedings, Eckson made a false entry on some records pertaining to his assets.

a. I only.

b. I and II only.

c. II and III only.

d. I, II, and III.

23. Which of the following acts by a debtor could result in a bankruptcy court revoking the debtor's discharge?

I. Failure to list one creditor.

II. Failure to answer correctly material questions on the bankruptcy petition.

a. I only.

b. II only.

c. Both I and II.

d. Neither I nor II.

24. Which of the following debts will **not** be discharged by bankruptcy even though a general discharge is allowed?

I. Debt owed to a corporation because the debtor was caught embezzling from it.

II. Money owed to a bank because the debtor was found to have committed fraud about her financial condition to get a loan.

III. Damages owed to a major customer because the debtor intentionally breached an important contract.

a. I only.

b. II only.

c. I and II only.

d. I, II, and III.

25. Which of the following claims will **not** be discharged in bankruptcy?

a. A claim that arises from alimony or maintenance.

b. A claim that arises out of the debtor's breach of contract.

c. A claim brought by a secured creditor that remains unsatisfied after the sale of the collateral.

d. A claim brought by a judgment creditor whose judgment resulted from the debtor's negligent operation of a motor vehicle.

26. By signing a reaffirmation agreement on April 15, 2008, a debtor agreed to pay certain debts that would be discharged in bankruptcy. On June 20, 2008, the debtor's attorney filed the reaffirmation agreement and an affidavit with the court indicating that the debtor understood the consequences of the reaffirmation agreement. The debtor obtained a discharge on August 25, 2008. The reaffirmation agreement would be enforceable only if it was

a. Made after discharge.

b. For debts aggregating less than $5,000.

c. Not for a household purpose debt.

d. Not rescinded before discharge.

27. Strong Corp. filed a voluntary petition in bankruptcy under the reorganization provisions of Chapter 11 of the Federal Bankruptcy Code. A reorganization plan was filed and agreed to by all necessary parties. The court confirmed the plan and a final decree was entered.

Which of the following statements best describes the effect of the entry of the court's final decree?

a. Strong Corp. will be discharged from all its debts and liabilities.

b. Strong Corp. will be discharged only from the debts owed creditors who agreed to the reorganization plan.

c. Strong Corp. will be discharged from all its debts and liabilities that arose before the date of confirmation of the plan.

d. Strong Corp. will be discharged from all its debts and liabilities that arose before the confirmation of the plan, except as otherwise provided in the plan, the order of confirmation, or the Bankruptcy Code.

28. Which of the following statements is correct with respect to the reorganization provisions of Chapter 11 of the Federal Bankruptcy Code?

a. A trustee must always be appointed.

b. The debtor must be insolvent if the bankruptcy petition was filed voluntarily.

c. A reorganization plan may be filed by a creditor anytime after the petition date.

d. The commencement of a bankruptcy case may be voluntary or involuntary.

29. Under Chapter 11 of the Federal Bankruptcy Code, which of the following would **not** be eligible for reorganization?

    a.   Retail sole proprietorship.
    b.   Advertising partnership.
    c.   CPA professional corporation.
    d.   Savings and loan corporation.

30. Which of the following is false regarding a Chapter 13 bankruptcy?

    a.   Individuals in general need not have regular income.
    b.   Creditors may not file involuntary petitions under this chapter.
    c.   It is initiated when the debtor files a voluntary petition in a bankruptcy court.
    d.   All of the above are true.

31. Under the Bankruptcy Abuse Prevention and Consumer Protection Act of 2005, which of the following type(s) of debts is(are) nondischargeable in bankruptcy?

  I. Death caused while intoxicated when operating an aircraft.
  II. Injury caused while intoxicated when driving any motor vehicle.
 III. Debts for Homeowner Association fees.

    a.   Only I.
    b.   I and II but not III.
    c.   I and III but not II.
    d.   I, II, and III.

SIMULATION PROBLEMS

Simulation Problem 1   (10 to 15 minutes)

Situation		
	Analysis	Transactions

On May 1, 2008, Able Corp. was petitioned involuntarily into bankruptcy under the provisions of Chapter 7 of the Federal Bankruptcy Code.

When the petition was filed, Able had the following unsecured creditors:

Creditor	Amount owed
Cole	$14,000
Lake	2,000
Young	1,500
Thorn	1,000

The following transactions occurred before the bankruptcy petition was filed:

- On February 15, 2008, Able paid Vista Bank the $1,000 balance due on an unsecured business loan.
- On February 28, 2008, Able paid $1,000 to Owen, an officer of Able, who had lent Able money.
- On March 1, 2008, Able bought a computer for use in its business from Core Computer Co. for $2,000 cash.

	Analysis	
Situation		Transactions

Items 1 through 3 refer to the bankruptcy filing. For each item, determine whether the statement is True or False.

	True	*False*
1. Able can file a voluntary petition for bankruptcy if it is solvent.	○	○
2. Lake, Young, and Thorn can file a valid involuntary petition.	○	○
3. Cole alone can file a valid involuntary petition.	○	○

		Transactions
Situation	Analysis	

Items 1 through 3 refer to the transactions that occurred before the filing of the involuntary bankruptcy petition. Assuming the bankruptcy petition was validly filed, for each item determine whether the statement is True or False.

	True	*False*
1. The payment to Vista Bank would be set aside as a preferential transfer.	○	○
2. The payment to Owen would be set aside as a preferential transfer.	○	○
3. The purchase from Core Computer Co. would be set aside as a preferential transfer.	○	○

Simulation Problem 2   (10 to 15 minutes)

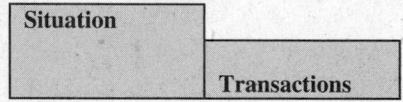

Situation	
	Transactions

On March 15, 2008, Rusk Corporation was petitioned involuntarily into bankruptcy. At the time of the filing, Rusk had the following creditors:

- Safe Bank, for the balance due on the secured note and mortgage on Rusk's warehouse.
- Employee salary claims.
- 2005 federal income taxes due.
- Accountant's fees outstanding.
- Utility bills outstanding.

Prior to the bankruptcy filing, but while insolvent, Rusk engaged in the following transactions:

- On January 15, 2008, Rusk repaid all corporate directors' loans made to the corporation.
- On February 1, 2008, Rusk purchased raw materials for use in its manufacturing business and paid cash to the supplier.

| Transactions |
| Situation |

Items 1 through 4 relate to Rusk's creditors and the January 15 and February 1 transactions. For each item, select from List I whether only statement I is correct, whether only statement II is correct, whether both statements I and II are correct, or whether neither statement I nor II is correct.

List I

A. I only.
B. II only.
C. Both I and II.
D. Neither I nor II.

                                     (A) (B) (C) (D)

1. I. Safe Bank's claim will be the first paid of the listed claims because Safe is a secured creditor.
    II. Safe Bank will receive the entire amount of the balance of the mortgage due as a secured creditor   O O O O
        regardless of the amount received from the sale of the warehouse.

2. I. The claim for 2008 federal income taxes due will be paid as a secured creditor claim.
    II. The claim for 2008 federal income taxes due will be paid prior to the general creditor claims.   O O O O

3. I. The January 15 repayments of the directors' loans were preferential transfers even though the
        payments were made more than ten days before the filing of the petition.
    II. The January 15 repayments of the directors' loans were preferential transfers because the   O O O O
        payments were made to insiders.

4. I. The February 1 purchase and payment was **not** a preferential transfer because it was a transaction
        in the ordinary course of business.
    II. The February 1 purchase and payment was a preferential transfer because it occurred within   O O O O
        ninety days of the filing of the petition.

MULTIPLE-CHOICE ANSWERS

1. d	__ __	8. a	__ __	15. d	__ __	22. c	__ __	29. d	__ __
2. d	__ __	9. c	__ __	16. d	__ __	23. b	__ __	30. a	__ __
3. d	__ __	10. d	__ __	17. c	__ __	24. c	__ __	31. d	__ __
4. d	__ __	11. d	__ __	18. c	__ __	25. a	__ __		
5. d	__ __	12. c	__ __	19. b	__ __	26. d	__ __		
6. c	__ __	13. d	__ __	20. b	__ __	27. d	__ __	1st: __/31 = __%
7. a	__ __	14. b	__ __	21. d	__ __	28. d	__ __	2nd: __/31 = __%

MULTIPLE-CHOICE ANSWER EXPLANATIONS

C. Chapter 7 Voluntary Bankruptcy Petitions

1.   (d)   Voluntary bankruptcy petition is a formal request by the debtor for an order of relief. This voluntary bankruptcy petition may be filed jointly by a husband and a wife. Answer (b) is incorrect because the debtor in a voluntary bankruptcy petition need not be insolvent but needs to state that s/he has debts. Answers (a) and (c) are incorrect because there is no requirement as to the minimum amount of the debtor's liabilities in a voluntary proceeding.

2.   (d)   Under Chapter 7 of the Federal Bankruptcy Code, a debtor may file a voluntary petition without showing that s/he is insolvent. S/he merely has to state the existence of debts. Therefore, the debtor is not required to show that liabilities exceed the fair market value of assets. Answer (a) is incorrect because a corporation may generally file a voluntary bankruptcy petition and there is not a requirement that it has previously filed under Chapter 11. Answer (b) is incorrect because when the debtor is automatically given an order for relief upon filing the petition, the actions to collect money by creditors are stayed. Secured creditors will resort to the collateral, however. Answer (c) is incorrect because the debtor is voluntarily going into bankruptcy and there is no requirement that twelve or more unsecured creditors be owed at least $13,475. Note that this requirement, as written, does not exist for an involuntary bankruptcy petition either.

3.   (d)   Most debtors may file a voluntary bankruptcy petition. Among those that may not are insurance companies, banks, and saving and loan associations. Answer (a) is incorrect because the number of creditors is not relevant for a voluntary bankruptcy petition. Answer (b) is incorrect because there is no need to show that a Chapter 11 bankruptcy would have been unsuccessful. Answer (c) is incorrect because the inability of the debtor to pay its debts as they become due is not relevant to a voluntary bankruptcy.

4.   (d)   A debtor may file a voluntary bankruptcy petition without showing that s/he is insolvent. The debtor may merely state that s/he has debts. There is also no requirement as to the number of creditors needed.

D. Chapter 7 Involuntary Bankruptcy Petitions

5.   (d)   Since there are fewer than twelve creditors, it is true that only one creditor is needed to file the petition. However, no one creditor is owed at least $13,475 of unsecured debt. Therefore, the claims can be aggregated to total at least $13,475 of unsecured debt. The only way this can be accomplished is by aggregating the claims of all four creditors. Note that Bounty Corporation is not enough because the secured debt is not counted in the total.

6.   (c)   When the debtor contests the petition s/he can still be forced into bankruptcy if the debtor is generally not paying his/her debts as they become due. Answer (a) is incorrect because the petition may be filed under either Chapter 7 (straight bankruptcy) or Chapter 11 (business reorganization). When the bankruptcy is involuntary, Chapter 7 and Chapter 11 are alternatives and have the same requirements for filing against business debtors. Answer (b) is incorrect because although the rules are different when there are fewer than twelve creditors versus when there are twelve or more creditors, Dart can be forced into bankruptcy when Decoy Publications files the petition because Decoy is owed over $13,475 of unsecured debt. Answer (d) is incorrect because there is no exception for the IRS.

7.   (a)   Once a valid petition in bankruptcy is filed, this automatically stays other legal proceedings against the debtor's estate. Also, the court appoints an interim trustee.

8.   (a)   The bankruptcy estate contains $100,000 after the sale of all assets and payment of administration expenses. The secured debt of $70,000 to Fracon Bank and the secured debt of $2,000 to Decoy Publications are satisfied first. (This actually takes place as a higher priority over the administrative expenses.) Therefore, after paying this $72,000 there is $28,000 left. The $12,000 of unpaid income tax has the next highest priority of those listed. This leaves $16,000 for the general creditors who filed on time. There are three of these, that is, Fracon who is owed $5,000 in excess of what the sale of the property brought, JOG who is owed $3,000, and Decoy who is still owed $14,000 in excess of the security interest. These three creditors together are owed $22,000 ($5,000 + $3,000 + $14,000). Since this is more than the $16,000 left, these 3 general creditors' debts are prorated. The last priority of unsecured claimants who filed late get nothing. Therefore, Nanstar Electric gets $0.

9.   (c)   The bankruptcy estate contains $100,000 after the sale of all assets and payment of administration expenses. The secured debt of $70,000 to Fracon Bank and the secured debt of $2,000 to Decoy Publications are satisfied first. (This actually takes place as a higher priority over the administrative expenses.) Therefore, after paying this $72,000 there is $28,000 left. The $12,000 of unpaid income tax has the next highest priority of those listed. This leaves $16,000 for the general creditors who filed on time. There are three of these, that is, Fracon who is owed $5,000 in excess of what the sale of the property brought, JOG who is owed $3,000, and Decoy who is still owed $14,000 in excess of the security interest. These three creditors together are owed $22,000 ($5,000 + $3,000 + $14,000). Since this is more than the $16,000 left, these three general creditors' debts are prorated. Fracon Bank gets money from both the unsecured and secured claims. From the unsecured claim, Fracon receives a prorated share or

$$\frac{\$5,000}{\$5,000 + \$3,000 + \$14,000} \times \$16,000 = \$3,636$$

Add this prorated share of $3,636 to the $70,000 Fracon received from the sold property to arrive at $73,636.

10. **(d)** The bankruptcy estate contains $100,000 after the sale of all assets and payment of administration expenses. The secured debt of $70,000 to Fracon Bank and the secured debt of $2,000 to Decoy Publications are satisfied first. (This actually takes place as a higher priority over the administrative expenses.) Therefore, after paying this $72,000 there is $28,000 left. The $12,000 of unpaid income tax has the next highest priority of those listed.

E. Chapter 7 Bankruptcy Proceedings

11. **(d)** Federal exemptions allowed under the Federal Bankruptcy Code include some equity in one motor vehicle and $2,025 in books and tools of one's trade. They also include, among others, unemployment compensation.

12. **(c)** A trustee in bankruptcy has the power to employ court approved professionals, such as accountants and attorneys, to handle estate matters which require professional expertise. These professionals have the right to reimbursement for services rendered. A trustee is not deemed to have the appropriate expertise required to prepare tax returns; thus, a trustee may employ a CPA to perform this function. Simon, as trustee, has the power to employ himself to prepare tax returns if authorized by the court and may receive a separate fee for services rendered. Simon may serve as both trustee and preparer if authorized to do so by the court. Simon has the right to receive fees for services rendered as both a trustee and a preparer. The fee for services rendered in each capacity is determined on the basis of the value of the services rendered, not solely the size of the estate.

E.6.f.(3) Exceptions to Trustee's Power to Avoid Preferential Transfers

13. **(d)** Preferential transfers are payments made for antecedent debts which enable the creditor to receive more than s/he would under a Chapter 7 liquidation proceeding. A gift is not payment for an antecedent debt. Transfers made in the ordinary course of business are exceptions to the trustee's power to avoid a preferential transfer. A contemporaneous exchange between a creditor and the debtor whereby the debtor receives new value is not a preferential transfer. Prepaying an existing installment loan on inventory is making a payment on an antecedent debt which enables the creditor to receive more than s/he would in a liquidation proceeding.

14. **(b)** Under Chapter 7 of the Federal Bankruptcy Code, the trustee may set aside preferential transfers made to a creditor within ninety days prior to the filing of the petition for bankruptcy. Preferential transfers are those made for antecedent debts that allow the creditor to receive more than s/he would have under the bankruptcy law. All of these conditions were met for the National mortgage. Answer (a) is incorrect because National would not be considered an insider. Even though Hall's twin was a National employee, he was not an officer, director, or controlling stockholder of National. Furthermore, the preferential transfer was not made to him personally but to National Bank. Answer (c) is incorrect because to set aside a preferential transfer, the debtor must have made the transfer while he was insolvent in the bankruptcy sense. Therefore, if Hall was presumed insolvent when the mortgage was given, the trustee is able to

set aside the preferential transfer. Note that insolvency is irrelevant to whether a transfer is preferential or non-preferential. Answer (d) is incorrect because when Hall gave National Bank the mortgage to secure payment of the two-year-old loan, this was a preferential transfer because it attempted to give National Bank more priority than it would have had as a general unsecured creditor.

15. **(d)** An exception to the trustee's powers to avoid preferential transfers is a contemporaneous exchange between the debtor and creditor for new values. When Hall paid the $10,000 cash, he received the boat he had purchased from Olsen. Therefore, this $10,000 payment was a contemporaneous exchange for new value. Answer (a) is incorrect because this fact pattern fits the contemporaneous exchange exception. It does not matter that the exchange occurred within ninety days of the filing. Answer (b) is incorrect because Olsen received the $10,000 cash in exchange for the boat. Olsen therefore has not been put in a better position than other general creditors, as Hall received new value for the cash. Answer (c) is incorrect because the issue of presumption of insolvency is not relevant when determining whether a transfer is preferential or nonpreferential.

16. **(d)** Improper actions during a bankruptcy that bar a discharge of all of the debts include concealing property and refusing to explain a loss of assets. Answer (a) is incorrect because this action means that this particular creditor's claim will not be discharged but does not bar a general discharge of the other debts. Answer (b) is incorrect because although alimony and support payments are not discharged themselves, their existence does not bar a general discharge. Answer (c) is incorrect because the inability to pay does not bar a general discharge.

17. **(c)** The trustee in bankruptcy may set aside preferential transfers made within ninety days before the filing of the bankruptcy petition while the debtor is insolvent. The time is extended to the previous twelve months if the preferential transfer was made to an insider. In this question, Quick's solvency when the loan was made by Erly is not relevant because this loan was made thirteen months before the filing of the petition for bankruptcy. Answer (a) is incorrect because since payment to Erly was made more than three months but less than twelve months before the filing, it is important that Erly is an insider. Answer (b) is incorrect because the definition of a preferential transfer incorporates transfers made for an antecedent debt. Answer (d) is incorrect because since Erly is an insider, it is relevant that the payment to Erly was made within one year of the filing of the bankruptcy petition.

F. Claims

18. **(c)** Of those listed, wages of the bankrupt's employees receive the highest priority for up to a specified formula. Federal taxes have a low priority but are ahead of general creditors. Any deficiency for secured creditors after the collateral is sold is paid along with the general creditors.

19. **(b)** The highest priority includes the administration costs. Of those listed, the wages to employees up to a specified formula each accrued within 180 days before the petition was filed have the next priority. Federal and state taxes have the second lowest priority but are next because the claims in the ordinary course of business arose **before** the petition was filed and therefore get the lowest priority as general creditors.

G. Discharge of a Bankrupt

20. (b)   This is an intentional tort and the liability for these injuries would not be discharged in bankruptcy; however, this does not bar a general discharge of the debts. Answer (a) is incorrect because this is one of the prime acts that the law attempts to prevent. Answer (c) is incorrect because failing to satisfactorily explain a loss of assets can bar a general discharge. Answer (d) is incorrect because this is an act that can bar a general discharge.

21. (d)   Corporations and partnerships cannot receive a discharge under Chapter 7 of the Federal Bankruptcy Code. Answer (a) is incorrect because although preferential transfers can be set aside, this would not prevent the discharge in bankruptcy. Answer (b) is incorrect because the rule is that destroying information relevant to the bankruptcy proceeding can bar a general discharge unless the act was justified under the circumstances. The accidental nature of the act in answer (b) is not a good case to bar the discharge. Answer (c) is incorrect because the rule states that the discharge is not allowed if the debtor has been discharged in bankruptcy within the past six years rather than ten years.

22. (c)   Actions that bar a general discharge in bankruptcy include removing or destroying property within twelve months prior to filing the petition with an intent to hinder, delay, or defraud a creditor. Also included is making a false entry in a document related to the bankrupt's affairs. Obtaining credit by fraud involving the debtor's financial condition causes that debt to be nondischargeable. It, however, does not prevent a general discharge of all debts.

23. (b)   The bankruptcy court can revoke the debtor's discharge if the debtor committed fraud during the bankruptcy proceedings, refused to obey lawful court orders, or failed to answer correctly material questions on the bankruptcy petition. Failure to list a creditor causes that creditor's debt not to be discharged but does not cause a revocation of the discharge.

H. Debts Not Discharged by Bankruptcy

24. (c)   There is a list of various types of debts that will not be discharged in bankruptcy, even though a general discharge is allowed. Among these are liabilities from theft, embezzlement, and committing fraud about one's financial condition. Note that liabilities from ordinary negligence or from breaches of contract, whether intentional or not, are dischargeable in bankruptcy.

25. (a)   Debts that are not discharged in bankruptcy include alimony, separate maintenance, and child support. A claim from a breach of contract is a typical type of claim discharged. Any amount unsatisfied after sale of the collateral is paid along with the rest of the general creditors if sufficient funds remain after all of the other creditors are paid. These are discharged in bankruptcy. Although intentional torts are not dischargable in bankruptcy, claims based on mere negligence are.

J. Reaffirmation

26. (d)   To get debtors to reaffirm debts that have been discharged in bankruptcy, creditors must comply with certain procedures. In general, the reaffirmation must take place before the discharge is granted and it must be approved by the bankruptcy court. The debtor is given sixty days to rescind the reaffirmation after s/he agrees to it. Answer (a) is incorrect because it must be agreed to before discharge. Answer (b) is incorrect because there is no such limitation on the dollar amounts. Answer (c) is incorrect because the reaffirmation agreement is valid for almost all debt including household purpose debt.

K. Business Reorganization—Chapter 11

27. (d)   Under the reorganization provisions of Chapter 11 of the Federal Bankruptcy Code, a court supervised rehabilitation plan is adopted. It typically allows for the continued operation of the business and provides for the payment of all or part of the debts over an extended period of time. The payments to the creditors often come largely from future earnings. Answer (a) is incorrect because the court typically does not discharge the debtor from all of its debts under a Chapter 11 bankruptcy but provides for payments of debts out of future earnings. Answer (b) is incorrect because the plans can apply to any creditors whether they were in the portion that agreed to the plan or not. Answer (c) is incorrect because the debtor under Chapter 11 is often required to pay all or part of the debts out of future earnings.

28. (d)   The Chapter 11 bankruptcy petition may either be filed voluntarily by the debtor or filed by the creditors to force the debtor into bankruptcy. Answer (a) is incorrect because a trustee need not be appointed. Answer (b) is incorrect because the debtor need not be insolvent to file a voluntary bankruptcy petition. Answer (c) is incorrect because only the debtor has the right to file the reorganization plan during the first 120 days the order for relief occurs.

29. (d)   Under Chapter 11 of the Federal Bankruptcy Code, individuals, partnerships, and corporations are eligible for reorganization. Savings and loan companies, banks, and insurance companies are not eligible.

L. Debts Adjustment Plans—Chapter 13

30. (a)   It is a false statement and therefore the correct answer to be chosen because under a Chapter 13 bankruptcy—Debts Adjustment Plan—in general individuals need to have regular income along with other specified requirements. Answers (b) and (c) are not correct because they are both accurate statements for a Chapter 13 bankruptcy. Answer (d) is incorrect because response (a) is an accurate statement.

M. The Bankruptcy Abuse Prevention and Consumer Protection Act of 2005

31. (d)   Under the Bankruptcy Abuse Prevention and Consumer Protection Act of 2005, all three of the listed types of debts are nondischargeable in bankruptcy. Note that this act causes bankruptcy law to be much less friendly to debtors over previous law. Also note that Statement I is still true even if the situation caused injury rather than death.

SOLUTIONS TO SIMULATION PROBLEMS

Simulation Problem 1

	Analysis	
Situation		Transactions

	True	*False*
1. Able can file a voluntary petition for bankruptcy if it is solvent.	●	○
2. Lake, Young, and Thorn can file a valid involuntary petition.	○	●
3. Cole alone can file a valid involuntary petition.	●	○

Explanation of solutions

1. (T) A debtor need not be insolvent to file a voluntary petition for bankruptcy. S/he merely needs to state that s/he has debts. Thus, Able could file even if solvent.

2. (F) In order to file a valid involuntary petition when there are fewer than twelve creditors, a single creditor may file the petition as long as s/he is owed at least $13,475 of unsecured debt. More than one creditor may be used to reach the $13,475 requirement. However, Lake, Young, and Thorn may not file a valid involuntary petition because they are collectively owed only $4,500.

3. (T) In order to file a valid involuntary petition when there are fewer than twelve creditors, a single creditor can file the petition as long as s/he is owed at least $13,475 of unsecured debt. Cole may file alone as s/he is owed $14,000.

		Transactions
Situation	Analysis	

	True	*False*
1. The payment to Vista Bank would be set aside as a preferential transfer.	●	○
2. The payment to Owen would be set aside as a preferential transfer.	●	○
3. The purchase from Core Computer Co. would be set aside as a preferential transfer.	○	●

Explanation of solutions

1. (T) The trustee may set aside preferential transfers of nonexempt property to a creditor made within the previous ninety days while insolvent. The payment made to Vista Bank is a preferential transfer because it was made less than ninety days before May 1, 2008, the date the involuntary petition was filed.

2. (T) The trustee may set aside preferential transfers of nonexempt property to a creditor made within the previous ninety days while insolvent. If the creditor was an insider, the time period is extended to within one year prior to the filing of the bankruptcy petition. The payment to Owen is a preferential transfer because Owen, an officer of Able Corp., is an insider, and the payment was made within one year prior to the filing of the petition.

3. (F) The payment to Core is not a preferential transfer because contemporaneously, Able received new value; that is, the computer. A contemporaneous exchange between creditor and debtor whereby the debtor receives new value is an exception to the trustee's power to set aside as a preferential transfer.

Simulation Problem 2

	Transactions
Situation	

	(A) (B) (C) (D)
1. I. Safe Bank's claim will be the first paid of the listed claims because Safe is a secured creditor. II. Safe Bank will receive the entire amount of the balance of the mortgage due as a secured creditor regardless of the amount received from the sale of the warehouse.	● ○ ○ ○
2. I. The claim for 2008 federal income taxes due will be paid as a secured creditor claim. II. The claim for 2008 federal income taxes due will be paid prior to the general creditor claims.	○ ● ○ ○
3. I. The January 15 repayments of the directors' loans were preferential transfers even though the payments were made more than ten days before the filing of the petition. II. The January 15 repayments of the directors' loans were preferential transfers because the payments were made to insiders.	○ ○ ● ○

(A) (B) (C) (D)

4. I. The February 1 purchase and payment was **not** a preferential transfer because it was a transaction
in the ordinary course of business.
II. The February 1 purchase and payment was a preferential transfer because it occurred within
ninety days of the filing of the petition.   ● ○ ○ ○

Explanation of solutions

1. **(A)** Statement I is correct since secured creditors receive payments before unsecured creditors (up to the value of the collateral) or receive the collateral itself. Statement II is incorrect because a secured creditor gets paid first only up to the value of the security. Any debt above the value of the security is given the lowest priority along with the general creditors.

2. **(B)** Statement I is incorrect because there is no collateral backing the 2008 federal income tax claim. It will thus not be paid as a secured creditor. Statement II is correct because taxes (federal, state, or local) have a higher priority than the general creditors.

3. **(C)** Statement I is correct because preferential transfers to insiders may be set aside when made within the previous **twelve** months. Thus, the January 15 repayment of corporate directors' loans are preferential transfers. Statement II is correct because the preferential transfer rule of ninety days is extended to twelve months in the case of insiders.

4. **(A)** Both transfers in the ordinary course of business and contemporaneous exchanges between creditors and debtors (whereby the debtors receive new value) are exceptions to the trustee's power to avoid preferential transfers. In this case, Rusk had purchased raw materials for use in its manufacturing business and paid cash to the supplier. These facts constitute an exception to the trustee's power to avoid a preferential transfer. Statement II is incorrect because the purchase and payment constitute an exception to the preferential transfer avoiding powers.

MULTIPLE-CHOICE QUESTIONS (1-27)

1. A debtor may attempt to conceal or transfer property to prevent a creditor from satisfying a judgment. Which of the following actions will be considered an indication of fraudulent conveyance?

	Debtor remaining in possession after conveyance	Secret conveyance	Debtor retains an equitable benefit in the property conveyed
a.	Yes	Yes	Yes
b.	No	Yes	Yes
c.	Yes	Yes	No
d.	Yes	No	Yes

2. A homestead exemption ordinarily could exempt a debtor's equity in certain property from postjudgment collection by a creditor. To which of the following creditors will this exemption apply?

	Valid home mortgage lien	Valid IRS tax lien
a.	Yes	Yes
b.	Yes	No
c.	No	Yes
d.	No	No

3. Which of the following statements is(are) correct regarding debtors' rights?

I. State exemption statutes prevent all of a debtor's personal property from being sold to pay a federal tax lien.
II. Federal social security benefits received by a debtor are exempt from garnishment by creditors.

a. I only.
b. II only.
c. Both I and II.
d. Neither I nor II.

4. Under the Federal Fair Debt Collection Practices Act, which of the following would a collection service using improper debt collection practices be subject to?
a. Abolishment of the debt.
b. Reduction of the debt.
c. Civil lawsuit for damages for violating the Act.
d. Criminal prosecution for violating the Act.

5. Which of the following liens generally require(s) the lienholder to give notice of legal action before selling the debtor's property to satisfy the debt?

	Mechanic's lien	Artisan's lien
a.	Yes	Yes
b.	Yes	No
c.	No	Yes
d.	No	No

6. Which of the following prejudgment remedies would be available to a creditor when a debtor owns **no** real property?

	Writ of attachment	Garnishment
a.	Yes	Yes
b.	Yes	No
c.	No	Yes
d.	No	No

7. Which of the following events will release a noncompensated surety from liability to the creditor?
a. The principal debtor was involuntarily petitioned into bankruptcy.

b. The creditor failed to notify the surety of a partial surrender of the principal debtor's collateral.
c. The creditor was adjudicated incompetent after the debt arose.
d. The principal debtor exerted duress to obtain the surety agreement.

8. Which of the following involve(s) a suretyship relationship?

I. Transferee of a note requires transferor to obtain an accommodation endorser to guarantee payment.
II. The purchaser of goods agrees to pay for the goods but to have them shipped to another party.
III. The shareholders of a small, new corporation agree in writing to be personally liable on a corporate loan if the corporation defaults.

a. I only.
b. II only.
c. I and II only.
d. I and III only.

9. Reuter Bank loaned Sabean Corporation $500,000 in writing. As part of the agreement, Reuter required that the three owners of Sabean act as sureties on the loan. The corporation also required that some real estate owned by Sabean Corporation be used as collateral for 40% of the loan. The collateral and suretyship agreements were put in writing and signed by all relevant parties. When the $500,000 loan became due, which of the following rights does Reuter Bank have?

I. May demand payment of the full amount immediately from the sureties whether or not the corporation defaults on the loan.
II. May demand payment of the full amount immediately from the sureties even if Reuter does not attempt to recover any amount from the collateral.
III. May attempt to recover up to $200,000 from the collateral and the remainder from the sureties, even if the remainder is more than $300,000.
IV. Must first attempt to collect the debt from Sabean Corporation before it can resort to the sureties or the collateral.

a. I and III only.
b. II only.
c. I, II, and III only.
d. IV only.

10. Belmont acts as a surety for a loan to Diablo from Chaffin. In which of the following cases would Belmont be released from liability?

I. Diablo dies.
II. Diablo files bankruptcy.
III. Chaffin modifies Diablo's contract, increasing Diablo's risk of nonpayment.

a. I only.
b. III only.
c. I and III only.
d. I, II, and III.

11. A party contracts to guaranty the collection of the debts of another. As a result of the guaranty, which of the following statements is correct?
a. The creditor may proceed against the guarantor without attempting to collect from the debtor.

b.   The guaranty must be in writing.
c.   The guarantor may use any defenses available to the debtor.
d.   The creditor must be notified of the debtor's default by the guarantor.

12. Sorus and Ace have agreed, in writing, to act as guarantors of collection on a debt owed by Pepper to Towns, Inc. The debt is evidenced by a promissory note. If Pepper defaults, Towns will be entitled to recover from Sorus and Ace unless

a.   Sorus and Ace are in the process of exercising their rights against Pepper.
b.   Sorus and Ace prove that Pepper was insolvent at the time the note was signed.
c.   Pepper dies before the note is due.
d.   Towns has **not** attempted to enforce the promissory note against Pepper.

13. Which of the following rights does a surety have?

	Right to compel the creditor to collect from the principal debtor	Right to compel the creditor to proceed against the principal debtor's collateral
a.	Yes	Yes
b.	Yes	No
c.	No	Yes
d.	No	No

14. Under the law of suretyship, which are generally among the rights that the surety may use?

I. Subrogation.
II. Exoneration.
III. Reimbursement from debtor.

a.   I only.
b.   III only.
c.   I and II only.
d.   I, II, and III.

15. Which of the following defenses would a surety be able to assert successfully to limit the surety's liability to a creditor?

a.   A discharge in bankruptcy of the principal debtor.
b.   A personal defense the principal debtor has against the creditor.
c.   The incapacity of the surety.
d.   The incapacity of the principal debtor.

16. Which of the following events will release a noncompensated surety from liability?

a.   Release of the principal debtor's obligation by the creditor but with the reservation of the creditor's rights against the surety.
b.   Modification by the principal debtor and creditor of their contract that materially increases the surety's risk of loss.
c.   Filing of an involuntary petition in bankruptcy against the principal debtor.
d.   Insanity of the principal debtor at the time the contract was entered into with the creditor.

17. Which of the following is **not** a defense that a surety may use to avoid payment of a debtor's obligation to a creditor?

a.   The creditor had committed fraud against the debtor to induce the debtor to take on the debt with this creditor.
b.   The creditor had committed fraud against the surety to induce the surety to guarantee the debtor's payment of a loan.
c.   The statute of limitations has run on the debtor's obligation.
d.   The debtor took out bankruptcy.

18. Which of the following acts always will result in the total release of a compensated surety?

a.   The creditor changes the manner of the principal debtor's payment.
b.   The creditor extends the principal debtor's time to pay.
c.   The principal debtor's obligation is partially released.
d.   The principal debtor's performance is tendered.

19. Green was unable to repay a loan from State Bank when due. State refused to renew the loan unless Green provided an acceptable surety. Green asked Royal, a friend, to act as surety on the loan. To induce Royal to agree to become a surety, Green fraudulently represented Green's financial condition and promised Royal discounts on merchandise sold at Green's store. Royal agreed to act as surety and the loan was renewed. Later, Green's obligation to State was discharged in Green's bankruptcy. State wants to hold Royal liable. Royal may avoid liability

a.   If Royal can show that State was aware of the fraudulent representations.
b.   If Royal was an uncompensated surety.
c.   Because the discharge in bankruptcy will prevent Royal from having a right of reimbursement.
d.   Because the arrangement was void at the inception.

20. Wright cosigned King's loan from Ace Bank. Which of the following events would release Wright from the obligation to pay the loan?

a.   Ace seeking payment of the loan only from Wright.
b.   King is granted a discharge in bankruptcy.
c.   Ace is paid in full by King's spouse.
d.   King is adjudicated mentally incompetent.

21. A distinction between a surety and a cosurety is that only a cosurety is entitled to

a.   Reimbursement (Indemnification).
b.   Subrogation.
c.   Contribution.
d.   Exoneration.

22. Ivor borrowed $420,000 from Lear Bank. At Lear's request, Ivor entered into an agreement with Ash, Kane, and Queen for them to act as cosureties on the loan. The agreement between Ivor and the cosureties provided that the maximum liability of each cosurety was: Ash, $84,000; Kane, $126,000; and Queen, $210,000. After making several payments, Ivor defaulted on the loan. The balance was $280,000. If Queen pays $210,000 and Ivor subsequently pays $70,000, what amounts may Queen recover from Ash and Kane?

a. $0 from Ash and $0 from Kane.
b. $42,000 from Ash and $63,000 from Kane.
c. $70,000 from Ash and $70,000 from Kane.

d. $56,000 from Ash and $84,000 from Kane.

23. Nash, Owen, and Polk are cosureties with maximum liabilities of $40,000, $60,000 and $80,000, respectively. The amount of the loan on which they have agreed to act as cosureties is $180,000. The debtor defaulted at a time when the loan balance was $180,000. Nash paid the lender $36,000 in full settlement of all claims against Nash, Owen, and Polk. The total amount that Nash may recover from Owen and Polk is

   a. $0
   b. $ 24,000
   c. $ 28,000
   d. $140,000

24. Ingot Corp. lent Flange $50,000. At Ingot's request, Flange entered into an agreement with Quill and West for them to act as compensated cosureties on the loan in the amount of $100,000 each. Ingot released West without Quill's or Flange's consent, and Flange later defaulted on the loan. Which of the following statements is correct?

   a.   Quill will be liable for 50% of the loan balance.
   b.   Quill will be liable for the entire loan balance.
   c.   Ingot's release of West will have **no** effect on Flange's and Quill's liability to Ingot.
   d.   Flange will be released for 50% of the loan balance.

25. Mane Bank lent Eller $120,000 and received securities valued at $30,000 as collateral. At Mane's request, Salem and Rey agreed to act as uncompensated cosureties on the loan. The agreement provided that Salem's and Rey's maximum liability would be $120,000 each.

Mane released Rey without Salem's consent. Eller later defaulted when the collateral held by Mane was worthless and the loan balance was $90,000. Salem's maximum liability is

   a. $30,000
   b. $45,000
   c. $60,000
   d. $90,000

26. Lane promised to lend Turner $240,000 if Turner obtained sureties to secure the loan. Turner agreed with Rivers, Clark, and Zane for them to act as cosureties on the loan from Lane. The agreement between Turner and the cosureties provided that compensation be paid to each of the cosureties. It further indicated that the maximum liability of each cosurety would be as follows: Rivers $240,000, Clark $80,000, and Zane $160,000. Lane accepted the commitments of the sureties and made the loan to Turner. After paying ten installments totaling $100,000, Turner defaulted. Clark's debts, including the surety obligation to Lane on the Turner loan, were discharged in bankruptcy. Later, Rivers properly paid the entire outstanding debt of $140,000. What amount may Rivers recover from Zane?

   a. $0
   b. $56,000
   c. $70,000
   d. $84,000

27. Which of the following rights does one cosurety generally have against another cosurety?

   a.   Exoneration.
   b.   Subrogation.
   c.   Reimbursement.
   d.   Contribution.

SIMULATION PROBLEM

Simulation Problem 1   (10 to 15 minutes)

> **Consideration**

For each of the numbered words or phrases, select the one best phrase or sentence from the list A through J. Each response may be used only once.

A. Relationship whereby one person agrees to answer for the debt or default of another.
B. Requires certain contracts to be in writing to be enforceable.
C. Jointly and severally liable to creditor.
D. Promises to pay debt on default of principal debtor.
E. One party promises to reimburse debtor for payment of debt or loss if it arises.
F. Receives intended benefits of a contract.
G. Right of surety to require the debtor to pay before surety pays.
H. Upon payment of more than his/her proportionate share, each cosurety may compel other cosureties to pay their shares.
I. Upon payment of debt, surety may recover payment from debtor.
J. Upon payment, surety obtains same rights against debtor that creditor had.

	(A)	(B)	(C)	(D)	(E)	(F)	(G)	(H)	(I)	(J)
1. Indemnity contract	O	O	O	O	O	O	O	O	O	O
2. Suretyship contract	O	O	O	O	O	O	O	O	O	O
3. Surety	O	O	O	O	O	O	O	O	O	O
4. Third-party beneficiary	O	O	O	O	O	O	O	O	O	O
5. Cosurety	O	O	O	O	O	O	O	O	O	O
6. Statute of Frauds	O	O	O	O	O	O	O	O	O	O
7. Right of contribution	O	O	O	O	O	O	O	O	O	O
8. Reimbursement	O	O	O	O	O	O	O	O	O	O
9. Subrogation	O	O	O	O	O	O	O	O	O	O
10. Exoneration	O	O	O	O	O	O	O	O	O	O

1.	a	__ __	7.	b	__ __	13.	d	__ __	19.	a	__ __	25.	b	__ __
2.	d	__ __	8.	d	__ __	14.	d	__ __	20.	c	__ __	26.	b	__ __
3.	b	__ __	9.	c	__ __	15.	c	__ __	21.	c	__ __	27.	d	__ __
4.	c	__ __	10.	b	__ __	16.	b	__ __	22.	b	__ __			
5.	a	__ __	11.	b	__ __	17.	d	__ __	23.	c	__ __	1st:	__/27 = __%
6.	a	__ __	12.	d	__ __	18.	d	__ __	24.	a	__ __	2nd:	__/27 = __%

MULTIPLE-CHOICE ANSWER EXPLANATIONS

A. Rights and Duties of Debtors and Creditors

1. **(a)** Fraudulent conveyance of property is done with the intent to defraud a creditor, hinder or delay him/her, or put the property out of his/her reach. If the debtor maintains possession of the property, secretly transfers or hides the property, or retains an equitable interest in the property, then a fraudulent conveyance has occurred as all of the three actions prevent the creditor from receiving the full property.

2. **(d)** Although a homestead exemption can exempt a debtor's equity in certain property from postjudgment collection by a creditor, the collections to which it applies vary among the states. The best answer is that it does not apply to valid home mortgage liens or valid IRS tax liens.

3. **(b)** Under garnishment procedures, creditors may attach a portion of the debtor's wages to pay off a debt. There are legal limits as to how much of the wages can be garnished. Likewise, federal social security benefits are protected from garnishment by creditors. Therefore, statement II is correct. Statement I, however, is incorrect because federal tax liens can be used to sell a debtor's personal property to pay taxes.

4. **(c)** The Federal Fair Debt Collection Practices Act was passed to prevent debt collectors from using unfair or abusive collection methods. The Federal Trade Commission is charged with enforcement of this Act but aggrieved parties may also use a civil lawsuit against the debt collector who violates this Act. Answers (a) and (b) are incorrect because the remedy is a suit for damages or a suit for up to $1,000 for violation of the Act if damages are not proven. The remedy is not a reduction or abolishment of the debt. Answer (d) is incorrect because this Act does not provide for criminal prosecution.

5. **(a)** Liens are used by creditors to secure payment for services or materials, in the case of a mechanic's lien, or for repairs, in the case of an artisan's lien. They require that notice be given to the debtor before the creditor can sell the property to satisfy the debt.

6. **(a)** When a creditor wishes to collect a past-due debt from the debtor, s/he may use a writ of attachment. This is a prejudgment remedy in which the creditor is allowed to take into possession some personal property of the debtor prior to getting a judgment in a lawsuit for the past-due debt. The debtor may also wish to collect the debt by use of garnishment. This allows the creditor to obtain property of the debtor that is held by a third party. Typical examples include garnishing wages owed by the employer to the employee-debtor or garnishing the debtor's bank account. To avoid abuses, there are limitations on both of these remedies.

B. Nature of Suretyship and Guaranty

7. **(b)** Any acts of the creditor that materially affect the surety's obligation will release the surety. In this case, the surety was not notified that the creditor partially surrendered the principal debtor's collateral. The surety will not have this collateral as a possible partial protection and the law allows the noncompensated surety to be released. Answer (a) is incorrect—bankruptcy is a personal defense of the debtor and is not a defense for the surety. Answer (c) is incorrect because this is a debt that is voidable at the option of the creditor. Answer (d) is incorrect because there is a possible wrong against the debtor but this does not release the surety.

8. **(d)** Statement I illustrates a suretyship relationship in which the endorser of the note is the surety. Statement II illustrates a third-party beneficiary contract, not a suretyship relationship. The purchaser has agreed to pay for the goods as his/her own debt. The party to receive the goods is the third-party beneficiary. Statement III illustrates a suretyship relationship in which the shareholders are sureties.

C. Creditor's Rights and Remedies

9. **(c)** The creditor, Reuter Bank, has a lot of flexibility in remedies. Although Reuter may attempt to collect from Sabean when the loan is due, it is not required to but instead may resort to the sureties or to the collateral up to the 40% agreed upon, or both.

10. **(b)** When the creditor modifies the debtor's contract, increasing the surety's risk, the surety is released. Note that death of the principal debtor or the debtor's filing bankruptcy are personal defenses of the debtor that the surety cannot use. Such risks are some of the reasons creditors prefer sureties.

11. **(b)** Under the Statute of Frauds under contract law, a surety's (guarantor's) agreement to answer for the debt or default of another must be in writing. Answer (a) is incorrect, as a guarantor of collection's liability is conditioned on the creditor notifying the guarantor of the debtor's default and the creditor first attempting to collect from the debtor. Answer (c) is incorrect as the guarantor may not use the debtor's personal defenses, such as death or insolvency. Answer (d) is incorrect because it is the creditor that must notify the guarantor of the debtor's default, not vice versa.

12. **(d)** A guarantor's liability is conditioned on the creditor notifying the guarantor of the debtor's default and the creditor first attempting to collect from the debtor. In this case, if Towns has not attempted to collect against Pepper, then Towns would not yet be able to collect against Sorus and Ace. Answer (a) is incorrect because Sorus' and Ace's performance of the right of reimbursement from Pepper does not preclude Towns' recovery from Sorus and Ace.

Answers (b) and (c) are incorrect because insolvency of the debtor and death of the debtor are not valid defenses of the guarantor against the creditor.

D.   Surety's and Guarantor's Rights and Remedies

13.   (d)   The surety is primarily liable on the debt of the principal debtor. Therefore, the creditor can seek payment directly from the surety as soon as the debt is due. For this reason, the surety cannot require the creditor to collect from the debtor nor can s/he compel the creditor to proceed against any collateral the principal debtor may have.

14.   (d)   Upon payment, the surety obtains the right of subrogation which is the ability to use the same rights the creditor had. Also, the surety may resort to the right of exoneration by requiring the debtor to pay when s/he is able if the creditor has not demanded immediate payment directly from the surety. If the surety has paid the debtor's obligation, the surety may attempt reimbursement from the debtor.

E.   Surety's and Guarantor's Defenses

15.   (c)   The surety may use his/her own defenses of incapacity of the **surety** or bankruptcy of the **surety** to limit his/her own liability. Although the surety may use most defenses that the **debtor** has to limit his/her (surety's) liability, the surety may not use the **personal** defenses of the debtor. These include the debtor's bankruptcy and the debtor's incapacity.

16.   (b)   A modification by the principal debtor and creditor in the terms and conditions of their original contract without the surety's consent will automatically release the surety if the surety's risk of loss is thereby materially increased. Note that a noncompensated surety is discharged even if the creditor does not change the surety's risk. However, a compensated surety is discharged only if the modification causes a material increase in risk. Answers (c) and (d) are incorrect because a surety may not exercise the principal debtor's personal defenses (i.e., insolvency and insanity). Answer (a) is incorrect because although a release of the principal debtor without the surety's consent will usually discharge the surety, there is no discharge if the creditor expressly reserves rights against the surety.

17.   (d)   Personal defenses that the debtor has such as bankruptcy or death of the debtor cannot be used by the surety to avoid payment of the debtor's obligation to the creditor. Answer (a) is incorrect because the surety may generally exercise the defenses on the contract that the debtor has against the creditor. Answer (b) is incorrect because the surety may take advantage of his/her own personal defenses such as fraud by the creditor against the surety. Answer (c) is incorrect because the surety generally may exercise the defenses on the contract that would be available to the debtor such as the running of the statute of limitations.

18.   (d)   A compensated surety will be released from an obligation to the creditor upon tender of performance by either the principal debtor or the surety. A compensated surety will also be completely released if modifications are made to the principal debtor's contract which materially increase risk to the surety. However, if the risk is not materially increased, the surety is not completely released but rather his/her obligation is reduced by the amount of loss due to modification. The surety also is not released if the modifications are beneficial to the surety. Answers (a)

and (b) are incorrect because these modifications will not necessarily result in a material increase in the surety's risk or could even be beneficial to the surety. Answer (c) is incorrect because partial release of the principal debtor's obligation will result in partial release of the surety.

19.   (a)   Normally, fraud by the debtor on the surety to induce him/her to act as a surety will not release the surety. However, when the creditor is aware of the debtor's fraudulent misrepresentation, then the surety can avoid liability. Answer (b) is incorrect because the above principle is true whether the surety is compensated or not. Answer (c) is incorrect because the risk of bankruptcy is one of the reasons that the creditor desires a surety. Answer (d) is incorrect because fraudulent misrepresentations do not make a contract void but can make it voidable.

20.   (c)   Once the debt is paid by someone, both the principal debtor and the cosigner are released from obligations to pay the loan. Answer (a) is incorrect because the creditor may proceed against the cosigner without needing to proceed against the principal debtor. Answer (b) is incorrect because the possibility that the principal debtor may qualify for bankruptcy is one of the reasons that the creditor may desire a cosigner. Answer (d) is incorrect because even if the main debtor is adjudicated mentally incompetent, this can allow the main debtor to escape liability but not the cosigner.

F.   Cosureties

21.   (c)   A suretyship relationship exists when one party agrees to answer for the obligations of another. Cosureties exist when there is more than one surety guaranteeing the same obligation of the principal debtor. Both sureties and cosureties are entitled to reimbursement from the debtor if the surety pays the obligation. Sureties and cosureties both have the right of subrogation in that upon making payment, the surety has the same rights against the principal debtor that the creditor had. Both are also entitled to exoneration. Sureties and cosureties both may require the debtor to pay the obligation for which they have given promise if the debtor is able to do so. The right of contribution, however, exists only among cosureties. If a cosurety pays more than his/her proportionate share of the total liability, he/she is entitled to be compensated by the other cosureties for the excess amount paid.

22.   (b)   The right of contribution arises when one cosurety, in performance of the principal debtor's obligation, pays more than his/her proportionate share of the total liability. The right of contribution allows the performing cosurety to receive reimbursement from the other cosureties for their pro rata shares of the liability. The pro rata shares of the cosureties are determined as follows:

	Surety's pro rata share		Remaining liability		Surety's liability
Queen	(210,000/420,000)	×	210,000	=	105,000
Ash	(84,000/420,000)	×	210,000	=	42,000
Kane	(126,000/420,000)	×	210,000	=	63,000

Thus, Queen is entitled to receive $42,000 from Ash and $63,000 from Kane.

23.   (c)   A surety relationship is present when one party agrees to answer for the obligation of another. When there is more than one surety guaranteeing the same obligation of the principal debtor, the sureties become cosureties jointly

and severally liable to the claims of the creditor. A right of contribution arises when one cosurety, in performance of the debtor's obligation, pays more than his proportionate share of the total liability. The right of contribution entitles the performing cosurety to reimbursement from the other cosureties for their pro rata shares of the liability. The pro rata shares of the cosureties are determined as follows:

	Surety's pro rata share		Remaining liability		Surety's liability
Nash	(40,000/180,000)	×	36,000	=	8,000
Owen	(60,000/180,000)	×	36,000	=	12,000
Polk	(80,000/180,000)	×	36,000	=	16,000

Thus, Nash is entitled to recover $12,000 from Owen and $16,000 from Polk for a total of $28,000.

24.   (a)   A discharge or release of one cosurety by a creditor results in a reduction of liability of the remaining cosurety. The remaining cosurety is released to the extent of the released cosurety's pro rata share of debt liability, unless there is a reservation of rights by the creditor against the remaining cosurety. Quill and West each had maximum liability of $100,000. Thus, Ingot's release of West will result in Quill's liability being reduced by West's pro rata share of the total debt liability, which was one-half. Therefore, Quill's liability has been reduced to $25,000 (i.e., 50% of the loan balance) due to the release of West as a cosurety. Answer (c) is therefore incorrect. Answer (d) is incorrect because the release of the cosurety does not release the principal debtor since the debtor's obligation is not affected in any way by Ingot's release of West. Answer (b) is incorrect because as discussed above, Quill's liability has been reduced due to Ingot's release of West.

25.   (b)   The discharge or release of one cosurety by the creditor results in a reduction of liability of the remaining cosurety. This reduction of liability is limited to the released cosurety's pro rata share of debt liability (unless there is a reservation of rights by the creditor against the remaining cosurety). Since Mane released Rey without reserving rights against Salem, Salem is released to the extent of Rey's pro rata share of the $90,000 liability. Salem's maximum liability can be calculated as follows:

Rey's %	$\dfrac{\$120,000}{\$240,000} = .50$
Loan balance	$ 90,000
× Rey's %	× .50
	$ 45,000
Loan balance	$ 90,000
Rey's pro rata share	(45,000)
Salem's maximum liability	$ 45,000

26.   (b)   The right of contribution arises when one cosurety, in performance of debtor's obligation, pays more than his proportionate share of the total liability. The right of contribution entitles the performing cosurety to reimbursement from the other cosureties for their pro rata shares of the liability. Since Clark's debts have been discharged in bankruptcy, River may only exercise his right of contribution against Zane, and may recover nothing from Clark. Zane's pro rata share of the remaining $140,000 would be determined as follows:

$$\frac{\text{Dollar amount guaranteed by Zane}}{\substack{\text{Total amount of risk assumed by} \\ \text{remaining cosureties}}} \times \text{Remaining obligation}$$

$$\frac{160,000}{160,000 + 240,000} \times 140,000 = 56,000$$

27.   (d)   Cosureties are jointly and severally liable to the creditor up to the amount of liability each agreed to. If a cosurety pays more than his/her proportionate share of the debt, s/he may seek contribution from the other cosureties for the excess. Answer (a) is incorrect because the right of exoneration refers to the surety requiring the debtor to pay the debt when able. Answer (b) is incorrect because subrogation refers to the right of the surety to obtain the same rights against the debtor that the creditor had, once the surety pays the creditor. Answer (c) is incorrect because the right of reimbursement allows the surety to recover payments from the debtor that the surety has made to the creditor.

SOLUTION TO SIMULATION PROBLEM

Simulation Problem 1

> **Consideration**

	(A)	(B)	(C)	(D)	(E)	(F)	(G)	(H)	(I)	(J)
1. Indemnity contract	○	○	○	○	●	○	○	○	○	○
2. Suretyship contract	●	○	○	○	○	○	○	○	○	○
3. Surety	○	○	○	●	○	○	○	○	○	○
4. Third-party beneficiary	○	○	○	○	○	●	○	○	○	○
5. Cosurety	○	○	●	○	○	○	○	○	○	○
6. Statute of Frauds	○	●	○	○	○	○	○	○	○	○
7. Right of contribution	○	○	○	○	○	○	○	●	○	○
8. Reimbursement	○	○	○	○	○	○	○	○	●	○
9. Subrogation	○	○	○	○	○	○	○	○	○	●
10. Exoneration	○	○	○	○	○	○	●	○	○	○

Explanation of solutions

1. **(E)** An indemnity contract is not a suretyship contract. Instead it is a contract involving two parties in which the first party agrees to indemnify and reimburse the second party for covered debts or losses should they take place.

2. **(A)** The suretyship contract involves three parties. The surety agrees with the creditor to pay for the debt or default if the debtor does not.

3. **(D)** The surety is the party that agrees to pay the creditor if the debtor defaults.

4. **(F)** When two parties make a contract that intends to benefit a third party, that party is a third-party beneficiary.

5. **(C)** When two or more sureties agree to be sureties for the same obligation to the same creditor, they are known as cosureties. They have joint and several liability.

6. **(B)** The Statute of Frauds sets out rules that require certain contracts to be in writing, such as those in which a surety agrees to answer for the debt or default of another.

7. **(H)** Cosureties are liable in contribution for their proportionate shares of the debt. If a cosurety pays more than this amount, s/he may seek contribution for the excess from the other cosureties.

8. **(I)** The right of reimbursement is against the debtor to collect any amounts paid by the surety.

9. **(J)** When the surety pays the creditor, it "steps into the shoes of the creditor" and obtains the same rights against the debtor that the creditor had.

10. **(G)** If the debtor is able to pay, the surety may require the debtor to pay before the surety pays. This is called exoneration.

MULTIPLE-CHOICE QUESTIONS (1-25)

1. Noll gives Carr a written power of attorney. Which of the following statements is correct regarding this power of attorney?

    a. It must be signed by both Noll and Carr.
    b. It must be for a definite period of time.
    c. It may continue in existence after Noll's death.
    d. It may limit Carr's authority to specific transactions.

2. A principal and agent relationship requires a

    a. Written agreement.
    b. Power of attorney.
    c. Meeting of the minds and consent to act.
    d. Specified consideration.

3. Lee repairs high-speed looms for Sew Corp., a clothing manufacturer. Which of the following circumstances best indicates that Lee is an employee of Sew and **not** an independent contractor?

    a. Lee's work is not supervised by Sew personnel.
    b. Lee's tools are owned by Lee.
    c. Lee is paid weekly by Sew.
    d. Lee's work requires a high degree of technical skill.

4. Harris, while delivering parts to a customer for his employer, negligently ran into and injured Wolfe. Harris had been asked by his employer to make these deliveries even though Harris was using his personal pickup truck. Neither Harris nor the employer had insurance to cover this injury. Which of the following is correct?

    a. Wolfe can hold Harris liable but not the employer because Harris was driving his own vehicle.
    b. Wolfe can hold the employer liable but not Harris because the employer had asked Harris to make the deliveries.
    c. Wolfe can hold either Harris or the employer or both liable.
    d. Wolfe can hold either Harris or the employer liable but not both.

5. Chiron employed Sherwin as a mechanic. Chiron has various rules that all employed mechanics must follow. One day a customer was injured severely when her car's brakes failed. It was shown that her car's brakes failed because Sherwin did not follow one of the specific rules of Chiron. Which of the following is correct?

    a. Sherwin is liable to the customer but Chiron is not because the accident was caused by Sherwin breaking one of Chiron's specific rules.
    b. The customer should sue Sherwin for fraud, not negligence, because Sherwin broke a rule of the employer.
    c. The customer can hold Chiron liable but not Sherwin, because her contract to get the car repaired was with Chiron.
    d. The customer may choose to recover damages from both Chiron and Sherwin.

6. Pine, an employee of Global Messenger Co., was hired to deliver highly secret corporate documents for Global's clients throughout the world. Unknown to Global, Pine carried a concealed pistol. While Pine was making a delivery, he suspected an attempt was being made to steal the pack-

age, drew his gun and shot Kent, an innocent passerby. Kent will **not** recover damages from Global if

    a. Global discovered that Pine carried a weapon and did nothing about it.
    b. Global instructed its messengers **not** to carry weapons.
    c. Pine was correct and an attempt was being made to steal the package.
    d. Pine's weapon was unlicensed and illegal.

7. When an agent acts for an undisclosed principal, the principal will **not** be liable to third parties if the

    a. Principal ratifies a contract entered into by the agent.
    b. Agent acts within an implied grant of authority.
    c. Agent acts outside the grant of actual authority.
    d. Principal seeks to conceal the agency relationship.

8. Trent was retained, in writing, to act as Post's agent for the sale of Post's memorabilia collection. Which of the following statements is correct?

    I. To be an agent, Trent must be at least twenty-one years of age.
    II. Post would be liable to Trent if the collection was destroyed before Trent found a purchaser.

    a. I only.
    b. II only.
    c. Both I and II.
    d. Neither I nor II.

9. Blue, a used car dealer, appointed Gage as an agent to sell Blue's cars. Gage was authorized by Blue to appoint subagents to assist in the sale of the cars. Vond was appointed as a subagent. To whom does Vond owe a fiduciary duty?

    a. Gage only.
    b. Blue only.
    c. Both Blue and Gage.
    d. Neither Blue nor Gage.

10. Which of the following under agency law is **not** a type of authority that an agent might have?

    a. Actual express.
    b. Actual implied.
    c. Resulting.
    d. Apparent.

11. Which of the following actions requires an agent for a corporation to have a written agency agreement?

    a. Purchasing office supplies for the principal's business.
    b. Purchasing an interest in undeveloped land for the principal.
    c. Hiring an independent general contractor to renovate the principal's office building.
    d. Retaining an attorney to collect a business debt owed the principal.

12. Frost's accountant and business manager has the authority to

    a. Mortgage Frost's business property.
    b. Obtain bank loans for Frost.
    c. Insure Frost's property against fire loss.
    d. Sell Frost's business.

13. Ames, claiming to be an agent of Clar Corporation, makes a contract with Trimon in the name of Clar Corporation. Later, Clar Corporation, for the first time, learns what Ames has done and notifies Trimon of the truth that Ames was not an agent of Clar Corporation. Which of the following statements is incorrect?

a. Clar Corporation may ratify this contract if it does so with the entire contract.
b. Trimon may withdraw from the contract before Clar attempts to ratify it.
c. Clar Corporation may ratify this contract by performing under the contract without stating that it is ratifying.
d. Trimon may enforce this contract even if Clar Corporation does not wish to be bound.

14. Which of the following generally may ratify a contract that was agreed to by his/her agent without authority from the principal?

	Fully disclosed principal	Partially disclosed principal	Undisclosed principal
a.	Yes	Yes	Yes
b.	Yes	Yes	No
c.	Yes	No	No
d.	No	No	Yes

15. Beele authorized McDonald to be his agent to go to Denver and purchase some real estate that would be suitable to open up a branch office for Beele's business. He tells McDonald not to pay more than $125,000 for the real estate. McDonald contacts York to buy some real estate she owns. York calls Beele and Beele tells York that McDonald is his agent to buy the real estate. Nothing is mentioned about the $125,000 limitation. After negotiations between McDonald and York, McDonald signs a contract purchasing the real estate for $140,000. McDonald signed it indicating on the contract that he was signing as agent for Beele.

Further facts show that the real estate is worth $140,000. Which of the following is correct?

a. There is a fully enforceable contract between Beele and York for $140,000.
b. Beele may enforce the contract with York for $125,000.
c. There is no contract between Beele and York because McDonald did not have authority to purchase the real estate for $140,000.
d. York may require that Beele pay $140,000 because the real estate was worth $140,000 not $125,000.

16. Young Corp. hired Wilson as a sales representative for six months at a salary of $5,000 per month plus 6% of sales. Which of the following statements is correct?

a. Young does **not** have the power to dismiss Wilson during the six-month period without cause.
b. Wilson is obligated to act solely in Young's interest in matters concerning Young's business.
c. The agreement between Young and Wilson is **not** enforceable unless it is in writing and signed by Wilson.
d. The agreement between Young and Wilson formed an agency coupled with an interest.

17. Which of the following statement(s) concerning agency law is(are) true?

I. A contract is needed to have an agency relationship.
II. The agent owes a fiduciary duty to the principal.
III. The principal owes a fiduciary duty to the agent.

a. I and II only.
b. I and III only.
c. II only.
d. I, II, and III.

18. Easy Corp. is a real estate developer and regularly engages real estate brokers to act on its behalf in acquiring parcels of land. The brokers are authorized to enter into such contracts, but are instructed to do so in their own names without disclosing Easy's identity or relationship to the transaction. If a broker enters into a contract with a seller on Easy's behalf,

a. The broker will have the same actual authority as if Easy's identity has been disclosed.
b. Easy will be bound by the contract because of the broker's apparent authority.
c. Easy will **not** be liable for any negligent acts committed by the broker while acting on Easy's behalf.
d. The broker will **not** be personally bound by the contract because the broker has express authority to act.

19. An agent will usually be liable under a contract made with a third party when the agent is acting on behalf of a(n)

	Disclosed principal	Undisclosed principal
a.	Yes	Yes
b.	Yes	No
c.	No	Yes
d.	No	No

20. When a valid contract is entered into by an agent on the principal's behalf, in a nondisclosed principal situation, which of the following statements concerning the principal's liability is correct?

	The principal may be held liable once disclosed	The principal must ratify the contract to be held liable
a.	Yes	Yes
b.	Yes	No
c.	No	Yes
d.	No	No

21. Which of the following rights will a third party be entitled to after validly contracting with an agent representing an undisclosed principal?

a. Disclosure of the principal by the agent.
b. Ratification of the contract by the principal.
c. Performance of the contract by the agent.
d. Election to void the contract after disclosure of the principal.

22. Able, as agent for Baker, an undisclosed principal, contracted with Safe to purchase an antique car. In payment, Able issued his personal check to Safe. Able could not cover the check but expected Baker to give him cash to deposit before the check was presented for payment. Baker did not do so and the check was dishonored. Baker's identity became known to Safe. Safe may **not** recover from

a. Baker individually on the contract.
b. Able individually on the contract.
c. Baker individually on the check.
d. Able individually on the check.

23. Thorp was a purchasing agent for Ogden, a sole proprietor, and had the express authority to place purchase orders with Ogden's suppliers. Thorp placed an order with Datz, Inc. on Ogden's behalf after Ogden was declared incompetent in a judicial proceeding. Thorp was aware of Ogden's incapacity. Which of the following statements is correct concerning Ogden's liability to Datz?

   a.   Ogden will be liable because Datz was **not** informed of Ogden's incapacity.
   b.   Ogden will be liable because Thorp acted with express authority.
   c.   Ogden will **not** be liable because Thorp's agency ended when Ogden was declared incompetent.
   d.   Ogden will **not** be liable because Ogden was a nondisclosed principal.

24. Generally, an agency relationship is terminated by operation of law in all of the following situations **except** the

   a.   Principal's death.
   b.   Principal's incapacity.
   c.   Agent's renunciation of the agency.
   d.   Agent's failure to acquire a necessary business license.

25. Bolt Corp. dismissed Ace as its general sales agent and notified all of Ace's known customers by letter. Young Corp., a retail outlet located outside of Ace's previously assigned sales territory, had never dealt with Ace. Young knew of Ace as a result of various business contacts. After his dismissal, Ace sold Young goods, to be delivered by Bolt, and received from Young a cash deposit for 20% of the purchase price. It was not unusual for an agent in Ace's previous position to receive cash deposits. In an action by Young against Bolt on the sales contract, Young will

   a.   Lose, because Ace lacked any implied authority to make the contract.
   b.   Lose, because Ace lacked any express authority to make the contract.
   c.   Win, because Bolt's notice was inadequate to terminate Ace's apparent authority.
   d.   Win, because a principal is an insurer of an agent's acts.

SIMULATION PROBLEM

Simulation Problem 1   (10 to 15 minutes)

Situation

Relationships

Lace Computer Sales Corp. orally contracted with Banks, an independent consultant, for Banks to work part time as Lace's agent to perform Lace's customers' service calls. Banks, a computer programmer and software designer, was authorized to customize Lace's software to the customers' needs, on a commission basis, but was specifically told not to sell Lace's computers.

On March 15, Banks made a service call on Clear Co. to repair Clear's computer. Banks had previously called on Clear, customized Lace's software for Clear, and collected cash payments for the work performed. During the call, Banks convinced Clear to buy an upgraded Lace computer for a price much lower than Lace would normally charge. Clear had previously purchased computers from other Lace agents and had made substantial cash down payments to the agents. Clear had no knowledge that the price was lower than normal. Banks received a $1,000 cash down payment and promised to deliver the computer the next week. Banks never turned in the down payment and left town. When Clear called the following week to have the computer delivered, Lace refused to honor Clear's order.

Relationships

Situation

Items 1 through 5 relate to the relationships between the parties. For each item, select from List I whether only statement I is correct, whether only statement II is correct, whether both statements I and II are correct, or whether neither statement I nor II is correct.

List I
A. I only
B. II only
C. Both I and II
D. Neither I nor II

			(A)	(B)	(C)	(D)
1.	I.	Lace's agreement with Banks had to be in writing for it to be a valid agency agreement.	○	○	○	○
	II.	Lace's agreement with Banks empowered Banks to act as Lace's agent.				
2.	I.	Clear was entitled to rely on Banks' implied authority to customize Lace's software.	○	○	○	○
	II.	Clear was entitled to rely on Banks' express authority when buying the computer.				
3.	I.	Lace's agreement with Banks was automatically terminated by Banks' sale of the computer.	○	○	○	○
	II.	Lace must notify Clear before Banks' apparent authority to bind Lace will cease.				
4.	I.	Lace is **not** bound by the agreement made by Banks with Clear.	○	○	○	○
	II.	Lace may unilaterally amend the agreement made by Banks to prevent a loss on the sale of the computer to Clear.				
5.	I.	Lace, as a disclosed principal, is solely contractually liable to Clear.	○	○	○	○
	II.	Both Lace and Banks are contractually liable to Clear.				

MULTIPLE-CHOICE ANSWERS

1. d __ __	7. c __ __	13. d __ __	19. c __ __	25. c __ · __
2. c __ __	8. d __ __	14. b __ __	20. b __ __	
3. c __ __	9. c __ __	15. a __ __	21. c __ __	
4. c __ __	10. c __ __	16. b __ __	22. c __ __	
5. d __ __	11. b __ __	17. c __ __	23. c __ __	1st: __/25 = __%
6. d __ __	12. c __ __	18. a __ __	24. c __ __	2nd: __/25 = __%

MULTIPLE-CHOICE ANSWER EXPLANATIONS

A. Characteristics

1. **(d)** A power of attorney is written authority conferred to an agent. It is conferred in a formal writing. A power of attorney can be general or it can grant the agent only restricted authority. Answer (a) is incorrect because the power of attorney must be signed only by the person granting such authority. Answer (b) is incorrect because the power of attorney does not have to be for a definite, specified time period. Answer (c) is incorrect because the death of the principal constitutes the termination of an agency relationship by operation of law.

2. **(c)** The relationship between a principal and agent is based upon the consent of both parties, also involving a meeting of the minds. Answer (d) is incorrect because specified consideration is not needed to create an agency relationship; the relationship between the principal and the agent need not be contractual. Answer (a) is incorrect because although the principal and agent relationship may be written, a written agreement is not required. Answer (b) is incorrect because power of attorney is not needed to create an agency relationship.

3. **(c)** An employee is generally subject to control as to the methods used to complete the work. An independent contractor is typically paid for the completion of the project rather than on an hourly, weekly, or monthly basis. Answer (a) is incorrect because supervision by Sew Corp. personnel shows an employment relationship. Answer (b) is incorrect because independent contractors typically provide their own tools. Answer (d) is incorrect because the work of both employees and independent contractors can require a high degree of skill.

A.2. Employee (Servant)

4. **(c)** Since Harris was acting within the scope of his employment when he negligently injured Wolfe, both Harris and his employer are liable. Wolfe can recover from either one or both. Answer (a) is incorrect because both are liable since Harris was acting within the scope of the employment. The ownership of the vehicle does not change this. Answer (b) is incorrect because Harris is liable for his own tort even though the employer can also be held liable. Answer (d) is incorrect because Wolfe may recover the full damages from either or may recover a portion of the damages from both.

5. **(d)** Because the repairs Sherwin did were within the scope of the employment, the employer is also liable. This is true even if the employer was diligent in creating excellent rules that were not followed by an employee. Answer (a) is incorrect because the repairs were within the scope of the employment. Answer (b) is incorrect because the customer can sue for negligence and hold both parties liable. Answer (c) is incorrect because the customer may recover from both under tort law.

6. **(d)** In general, the employer is not responsible for the crimes of the employee unless the employer aided or permitted the illegal activity, even if the activity was within the scope of the employment. Answer (a) is incorrect because if the employer did nothing to instruct the employee about the use of the weapon, this could help establish negligence on the part of the employer and would not prevent the use of the doctrine of respondeat superior, which makes employers liable for the tortious acts of their employees within the scope of the employment. Answer (b) is incorrect because the employer is liable for torts of the employee committed within the course and scope of the employment even if the employee was violating the employer's instructions. Answer (c) is incorrect because even if the employee's suspicions were correct, the shooting of an innocent passerby should establish at least negligence for which the employer and the employee are liable.

A.5. Types of Principals

7. **(c)** A principal, whether disclosed, partially disclosed, or undisclosed is liable on contracts where the agent has actual or apparent authority, or where the principal ratifies an agent's contract. Actual authority includes express or implied authority projected by the principal to the agent. Apparent authority of an agent is authority perceived by a third party based on the principal's representations. Therefore, apparent authority can exist only where there is a disclosed or a partially disclosed principal. It follows, then, that an undisclosed principal will **not** be liable to third parties if the agent acts outside the grant of **actual** authority.

B. Methods of Creation

8. **(d)** An agent must merely have sufficient mental and physical ability to carry out instructions of his/her principal. An agent can bind the principal even if the agent is a minor. If the memorabilia collection was destroyed before Trent found a purchaser, Post would not be liable to Trent. Upon the loss or destruction of the subject matter on which the agency relationship is based, the agency relationship is terminated.

9. **(c)** The fiduciary duty is an important duty owed by agents to their principals. Gage as Blue's agent was authorized by Blue to appoint subagents to assist in the sales transactions. Since Gage did appoint Vond as a subagent, legally Bond is an agent both of Blue and Gage. Therefore, Vond owes a fiduciary duty to both Blue and Gage making (a), (b), and (d) all incorrect.

10. **(c)** Resulting authority is not one of the types of authority that an agent might have. Answer (a) is not chosen because actual express authority is a common type of authority and consists of all authority expressly given by the principal to his/her agent. Answer (b) includes the authority that can be reasonably implied from the express authority and the conduct of the principal. Answer (d) is not chosen because even though a party was never authorized by a principal to be an agent, if the principal leads a third party to believe that the party did have authority, this is apparent agency.

11.   (b)   An agency agreement normally does not need to be in writing. Exceptions to this general rule include agency contracts that cannot be completed within one year and agreements whereby the agent is to buy specific real estate for the principal. This question incorporates the latter. Typical agency agreements need not be in writing; these would include purchasing office supplies, retaining an independent contractor to do renovation work, or hiring an attorney to collect a business debt.

12.   (c)   An agent has implied authority to do what is customary for agents of that type to do under the circumstances. It would be customary for one who is a principal's accountant and business manager to have authority to insure the principal's property against fire loss. Answers (a), (b), and (d) are incorrect because they involve authority that is beyond customary, ordinary authority.

B.5.   Ratification

13.   (d)   Since Ames had no express, implied, or actual authority, Trimon cannot enforce the contract. Answer (a) is not chosen because ratifications under agency law require that the contract be ratified in its entirety or not at all. Answer (b) is not chosen because until Clar ratifies the contract in its entirety, Trimon may withdraw from the contract since Ames had no authority to make the contract. Answer (c) is not chosen because ratification can be accomplished by actions as well as words.

14.   (b)   When the third party is aware that there is a principal, that principal, fully disclosed or partially disclosed, may generally ratify the contract when he or she is aware of all material facts and if ratification of the entire contract takes place.

C.   Authority

15.   (a)   Since Beele authorized McDonald to be his agent, the secret limitation has no effect on York. York may enforce the contract for the full $140,000. Answer (b) is incorrect because Beele authorized McDonald to be his agent. Even though his agent was instructed to pay at most $125,000 in the contract, this was a secret limitation that did not limit York who was unaware of it. Answer (c) is incorrect because McDonald was given authority to purchase real estate on Beele's behalf. The limitation on the dollar amount was not known by York and therefore does not limit her. Answer (d) is incorrect because although York can enforce the contract against Beele, it is because Beele gave authority to McDonald rather than how much the real estate is worth.

E.   Obligations and Rights

16.   (b)   As a fiduciary to the principal, an agent must act in the best interest of the principal. Therefore, the agent has an obligation to refrain from competing with or acting adversely to the principal, unless the principal knows and approves of such activity. Answer (c) is incorrect because the Statute of Frauds would not require that the described agency relationship be contained in a signed writing since it is possible for the contract to be performed within one year. Answer (d) is incorrect because the mere right of the agent to receive a percentage of proceeds is not sufficient to constitute an agency coupled with an interest. In order to have an agency coupled with an interest, the agent must have either a property interest or a security interest in the subject matter of the agency relationship. Answer (a) is incorrect because in all agency relationships, except agencies coupled with an interest, the principal always has the power to dismiss the agent. However, the principal does not necessarily have the right to terminate the relationship. In certain situations the dismissed agent could sue for breach of contract.

17.   (c)   In an agency relationship, the agent owes a fiduciary duty to the principal but the principal does not owe a fiduciary duty to the agent. Also, even though there is often a contract between the principal and agent, this is not a requirement, for example, when the agent consents to act for the principal as a friend.

E.3.   Principal's Liability to Third Parties

18.   (a)   When the principal is undisclosed in an agency relationship, the agent generally has the same authority as if the principal were disclosed. The main difference is in the liability of the agent to third parties. Answer (b) is incorrect because the principal is liable on the contract because of the express authority given to the agent to make the contract on behalf of the principal. Apparent authority exists when the principal represents the agent to third parties to be his/her agent. In this case, the principal wished to be undisclosed. Answer (c) is incorrect because principal can be held liable for negligence committed by the agent within the course and scope of the agency. Answer (d) is incorrect because the agent can be held liable on the contract by third parties when the principal is undisclosed.

19.   (c)   An agent is liable to a third party on a contract when the principal is undisclosed or partially disclosed. If the principal is fully disclosed, the agent is not liable.

E.4.   Agent's Liability to Third Parties

20.   (b)   When an agent enters into a contract with a third person on behalf of an undisclosed principal, the agent is personally liable, unless the third person discovers the existence and identity of the principal and chooses to hold the principal to the contract instead of the agent. Ratification is the approval after the fact of an unauthorized act done by an agent or of an act done by someone who is not yet an agent. Undisclosed principals cannot ratify unauthorized acts of the agent.

21.   (c)   When a third party contracts with an agent representing an undisclosed principal, the agent is liable for performance of the contract. The third party is not entitled to disclosure of the principal. Answer (b) is incorrect because ratification of a contract by the principal is the approval required after the fact related to an unauthorized act by the agent or one not yet an agent. Answer (d) is incorrect because the third party generally is not allowed the option of voiding the contract after disclosure of the principal.

22.   (c)   One who issues a personal check is liable on it; however, any party or principal who is not disclosed on the check is not liable on the negotiable instrument. Answers (a) and (b) are incorrect because the third party can elect to hold either the agent or the principal liable when the agent makes a contract for an undisclosed principal. Answer (d) is incorrect because the party who signs a check is liable on it.

F.   Termination of Principal-Agent Relationship

23.   (c)   The declaration of Ogden's incapacity constitutes the termination of the agency relationship by operation of law. When an agency relationship is terminated by operation of law, the agent's authority to enter into a binding agreement on behalf of the principal ceases. There is no requirement that notice be given to third parties when the agency relationship is terminated by operation of law. In this case, Ogden will not be liable to Datz because Thorp was without authority to enter into the contract. Answer (a) is incorrect because insanity of the principal terminates the agency relationship even though the third parties are unaware of the principal's insanity. Answer (b) is incorrect because Thorp's authority terminated upon the declaration of Ogden's incapacity. Answer (d) is incorrect because an undisclosed principal is liable unless the third party holds the agent responsible, the agent has fully performed the contract, the undisclosed principal is expressly excluded by contract or the contract is a negotiable instrument. However, Ogden will not be liable as Thorp was without authority to enter into the agreement.

24.   (c)   An agency relationship is terminated by operation of law if the subject of the agreement becomes illegal or impossible, the principal or the agent dies or becomes insane, or the principal becomes bankrupt. Answers (a), (b), and (d) are incorrect because they will cause the termination of an agency relationship by operation of law. Answer (c), agent's renunciation of the agency, will not cause the termination of an agency relationship.

25.   (c)   When the agency relationship is terminated by an act of the principal and/or agent, third parties are entitled to notice of the termination from the principal. Failure of the principal to give the required notice gives the agent apparent authority to act on behalf of the principal. Specifically, the principal must give actual notice to all parties who had prior dealings with the agent or principal. Constructive or public notice must be given to parties who knew of the existence of the agency relationship, but did not actually have business dealings with the agent or principal. Since Bolt Corp. did not give proper constructive notice to Young Corp., Ace had apparent authority to bind the principal and, therefore, Young Corp. will win. Accordingly, answer (a) is incorrect. Answer (b) is incorrect because although Ace lacked express authority, apparent authority was present due to the inadequacy of Bolt's notice. Answer (d) is incorrect because a principal is not an absolute insurer of his agent's acts. A principal is liable for his agent's torts only if the principal expressly authorizes the conduct or the tort is committed within the scope of the agent's employment.

SOLUTION TO SIMULATION PROBLEM

Simulation Problem 1

	Relationships
Situation	

	(A)	(B)	(C)	(D)
1. I. Lace's agreement with Banks had to be in writing for it to be a valid agency agreement.	○	●	○	○
II. Lace's agreement with Banks empowered Banks to act as Lace's agent.				
2. I. Clear was entitled to rely on Banks' implied authority to customize Lace's software.	●	○	○	○
II. Clear was entitled to rely on Banks' express authority when buying the computer.				
3. I. Lace's agreement with Banks was automatically terminated by Banks' sale of the computer.	○	●	○	○
II. Lace must notify Clear before Banks' apparent authority to bind Lace will cease.				
4. I. Lace is **not** bound by the agreement made by Banks with Clear.	○	○	○	●
II. Lace may unilaterally amend the agreement made by Banks to prevent a loss on the sale of the computer to Clear.				
5. I. Lace, as a disclosed principal, is solely contractually liable to Clear.	●	○	○	○
II. Both Lace and Banks are contractually liable to Clear.				

Explanation of solutions

1. **(B)** Statement I is incorrect because normally an agency agreement need not be in writing unless the agency contract cannot be completed in one year. Statement II is correct because Lace authorized Banks to be Lace's agent.

2. **(A)** Statement I is correct because Banks was given actual, express authority by Lace to perform Lace's customers' service calls and to customize Lace's software to the customer's needs. As an extension to this actual, express authority, Clear can also rely on what is customary and ordinary for such an agent to be able to do under implied authority. Statement II is incorrect because Banks did not have express authority to sell the computer. In fact, Banks was told **not** to sell Lace's computers.

3. **(B)** Banks breached his/her fiduciary duty to Lace and breached his/her duty to follow instructions when s/he sold the computer. This, however, does not automatically terminate their agreement. Statement II is correct because Banks had dealt with Clear before as Lace's agent. Therefore, Clear must receive actual notice to terminate the apparent authority.

4. **(D)** Statement I is incorrect because Banks had apparent authority to sell the computer even though Banks did not have actual authority to do so. Statement II is incorrect because Lace is bound by the contract with Clear. Any modification of the contract must be made by both parties to the contract, not just one.

5. **(A)** Statement I is correct because since Lace was a disclosed principal, only Lace, the principal, is liable under the contract to Clear, the third party. Banks, the agent, is not. For the same reason, statement II is incorrect.

MULTIPLE-CHOICE QUESTIONS (1-44)

1.   Taxes payable under the Federal Unemployment Tax Act (FUTA) are
   a.   Calculated as a fixed percentage of all compensation paid to an employee.
   b.   Deductible by the employer as a business expense for federal income tax purposes.
   c.   Payable by employers for all employees.
   d.   Withheld from the wages of all covered employees.

2.   An unemployed CPA generally would receive unemployment compensation benefits if the CPA
   a.   Was fired as a result of the employer's business reversals.
   b.   Refused to accept a job as an accountant while receiving extended benefits.
   c.   Was fired for embezzling from a client.
   d.   Left work voluntarily without good cause.

3.   After serving as an active director of Lee Corp. for twenty years, Ryan was appointed an honorary director with the obligation to attend directors' meetings with no voting power. In 2001, Ryan received an honorary director's fee of $5,000. This fee is
   a.   Reportable by Lee as employee compensation subject to social security tax.
   b.   Reportable by Ryan as self-employment income subject to social security self-employment tax.
   c.   Taxable as "other income" by Ryan, **not** subject to any social security tax.
   d.   Considered to be a gift **not** subject to social security self-employment or income tax.

4.   Syl Corp. does **not** withhold FICA taxes from its employees' compensation. Syl voluntarily pays the entire FICA tax for its share and the amounts that it could have withheld from the employees. The employees' share of FICA taxes paid by Syl to the IRS is
   a.   Deductible by Syl as additional compensation that is includible in the employees' taxable income.
   b.   Not deductible by Syl because it does **not** meet the deductibility requirement as an ordinary and necessary business expense.
   c.   A nontaxable gift to each employee, provided that the amount is less than $1,000 annually to each employee.
   d.   Subject to prescribed penalties imposed on Syl for its failure to withhold required payroll taxes.

5.   Social security benefits may include all of the following **except**
   a.   Payments to divorced spouses.
   b.   Payments to disabled children.
   c.   Medicare payments.
   d.   Medicaid payments.

6.   Which of the following forms of income, if in excess of the annual exempt amount, will cause a reduction in a retired person's social security benefits?
   a.   Annual proceeds from an annuity.
   b.   Director's fees.
   c.   Pension payments.
   d.   Closely held corporation stock dividends.

7.   Which of the following payments are deducted from an employee's salary?

	Unemployment compensation insurance	Worker's compensation insurance
a.	Yes	Yes
b.	Yes	No
c.	No	Yes
d.	No	No

8.   Which of the following types of income is subject to taxation under the provisions of the Federal Insurance Contributions Act (FICA)?
   a.   Interest earned on municipal bonds.
   b.   Capital gains of $3,000.
   c.   Car received as a productivity award.
   d.   Dividends of $2,500.

9.   Under the Federal Insurance Contributions Act (FICA), which of the following acts will cause an employer to be liable for penalties?

	Failure to supply taxpayer identification numbers	Failure to make timely FICA deposits
a.	Yes	Yes
b.	Yes	No
c.	No	Yes
d.	No	No

10.   Which of the following parties generally is ineligible to collect workers' compensation benefits?
   a.   Minors.
   b.   Truck drivers.
   c.   Union employees.
   d.   Temporary office workers.

11.   Kroll, an employee of Acorn, Inc., was injured in the course of employment while operating a forklift manufactured and sold to Acorn by Trell Corp. The forklift was defectively designed by Trell. Under the state's mandatory workers' compensation statute, Kroll will be successful in

	Obtaining workers' compensation benefits	A negligence action against Acorn
a.	Yes	Yes
b.	Yes	No
c.	No	Yes
d.	No	No

12.   Which of the following provisions is basic to all workers' compensation systems?
   a.   The injured employee must prove the employer's negligence.
   b.   The employer may invoke the traditional defense of contributory negligence.
   c.   The employer's liability may be ameliorated by a coemployee's negligence under the fellow-servant rule.
   d.   The injured employee is allowed to recover on strict liability theory.

13.   Workers' Compensation Acts require an employer to
   a.   Provide coverage for all eligible employees.
   b.   Withhold employee contributions from the wages of eligible employees.
   c.   Pay an employee the difference between disability payments and full salary.
   d.   Contribute to a federal insurance fund.

14. Generally, which of the following statements concerning workers' compensation laws is correct?
    a. The amount of damages recoverable is based on comparative negligence.
    b. Employers are strictly liable without regard to whether or **not** they are at fault.
    c. Workers' compensation benefits are **not** available if the employee is negligent.
    d. Workers' compensation awards are payable for life.

15. Workers' compensation laws provide for all of the following benefits **except**
    a. Burial expenses.
    b. Full pay during disability.
    c. The cost of prosthetic devices.
    d. Monthly payments to surviving dependent children.

16. Which of the following claims is(are) generally covered under workers' compensation statutes?

	Occupational disease	*Employment aggravated preexisting disease*
a.	Yes	Yes
b.	Yes	No
c.	No	Yes
d.	No	No

17. Under which of the following conditions is an on-site inspection of a workplace by an investigator from the Occupational Safety and Health Administration (OSHA) permissible?
    a. Only if OSHA obtains a search warrant after showing probable cause.
    b. Only if the inspection is conducted after working hours.
    c. At the request of employees.
    d. After OSHA provides the employer with at least twenty-four hours notice of the prospective inspection.

18. Which of the following Acts prohibit(s) an employer from discriminating among employees based on sex?

	Equal Pay Act	*Title VII of the Civil Rights Act*
a.	Yes	Yes
b.	Yes	No
c.	No	Yes
d.	No	No

19. Under the Age Discrimination in Employment Act, which of the following remedies is(are) available to a covered employee?

	Early Retirement	*Back pay*
a.	Yes	Yes
b.	Yes	No
c.	No	Yes
d.	No	No

20. Which of the following company policies would violate the Age Discrimination in Employment Act?
    a. The company will not hire any accountant below twenty-five years of age.
    b. The office staff must retire at age sixty-five or younger.
    c. Both of the above.
    d. None of the above.

21. Under the provisions of the Americans With Disabilities Act of 1990, in which of the following areas is a disabled person protected from discrimination?

	Public transportation	*Privately operated public accommodations*
a.	Yes	Yes
b.	Yes	No
c.	No	Yes
d.	No	No

22. Under the Americans with Disabilities Act, which is(are) true?
    I. The Act requires that companies with at least ten employees set up a specified plan to hire people with disabilities.
    II. The Act requires companies to make reasonable accommodations for disabled persons unless this results in undue hardship on the operations of the company.
    a. I only.
    b. II only.
    c. Both I and II.
    d. Neither I nor II.

23. The Americans With Disabilities Act has as a purpose to give remedies for discrimination to individuals with disabilities. Which of the following is(are) true of this Act?
    I. It protects most individuals with disabilities working for companies but only if the companies do not need to incur any expenses to modify the work environment to accommodate the disability.
    II. It may require a company to modify work schedules to accommodate persons with disabilities.
    III. It may require a company to purchase equipment at company expense to accommodate persons with disabilities.
    a. I only.
    b. I and II only.
    c. II and III only.
    d. III only.

24. Which of the following is **not** true under the Family and Medical Leave Act?
    a. An employee has a right to take a leave from work for the birth and care of her child for one month at half of her regular pay.
    b. An employee has a right to take a leave from work for twelve workweeks to care for his/her seriously ill parent.
    c. An employee, upon returning under the provisions of the Act, must get back the same or equivalent position in the company.
    d. This Act does not cover all employees.

25. The Family Medical Leave Act provides for
    I. Unpaid leave for the employee to care for a newborn baby.
    II. Unpaid leave for the employee to care for the serious health problem of his or her parent.
    III. Paid leave for the employee to care for a serious health problem of his or her spouse.
    a. I only.
    b. II only.
    c. I and II but not III.
    d. III but not I or II.

26. Under the Fair Labor Standards Act, which of the following pay bases may be used to pay covered, nonexempt employees who earn, on average, the minimum hourly wage?

	Hourly	Weekly	Monthly
a.	Yes	Yes	Yes
b.	Yes	Yes	No
c.	Yes	No	Yes
d.	No	Yes	Yes

27. Under the Fair Labor Standards Act, if a covered, non-exempt employee works consecutive weeks of forty-five, forty-two, thirty-eight, and thirty-three hours, how many hours of overtime must be paid to the employee?
- a. 0
- b. 7
- c. 18
- d. 20

28. Which of the following employee benefits is(are) exempt from the provisions of the National Labor Relations Act?

	Sick pay	Vacation pay
a.	Yes	Yes
b.	Yes	No
c.	No	Yes
d.	No	No

29. Under the Federal Consolidated Budget Reconciliation Act of 1985 (COBRA), when an employee voluntarily resigns from a job, the former employee's group health insurance coverage that was in effect during the period of employment with the company
- a. Automatically ceases for the former employee and spouse, if the resignation occurred before normal retirement age.
- b. Automatically ceases for the former employee's spouse, but continues for the former employee for an eighteen-month period at the former employer's expense.
- c. May be retained by the former employee at the former employee's expense for at least eighteen months after leaving the company, but must be terminated for the former employee's spouse.
- d. May be retained for the former employee and spouse at the former employee's expense for at least eighteen months after leaving the company.

30. Under the Employee Retirement Income Security Act of 1974 (ERISA), which of the following areas of private employer pension plans is(are) regulated?

	Employee vesting	Plan funding
a.	Yes	Yes
b.	Yes	No
c.	No	Yes
d.	No	No

31. Under the provisions of the Employee Retirement Income Security Act of 1974 (ERISA), which of the following statements is correct?
- a. Employees are entitled to have an employer established pension plan.
- b. Employers are prevented from unduly delaying an employee's participation in a pension plan.
- c. Employers are prevented from managing retirement plans.

- d. Employees are entitled to make investment decisions.

32. Under the Comprehensive Environmental Response, Compensation, and Liability Act (CERCLA), commonly known as Superfund, which of the following parties would be liable to the Environmental Protection Agency (EPA) for the expense of cleaning up a hazardous waste disposal site?

I. The current owner or operator of the site.
II. The person who transported the wastes to the site.
III. The person who owned or operated the site at the time of the disposal.
- a. I and II.
- b. I and III.
- c. II and III.
- d. I, II, and III.

33. Which of the following activities is(are) regulated under the Federal Water Pollution Control Act (Clean Water Act)?

	Discharge of heated water by nuclear power plants	Dredging of wetlands
a.	Yes	Yes
b.	Yes	No
c.	No	Yes
d.	No	No

34. Environmental Compliance Audits are used for which of the following purpose(s)?

I. To voluntarily discover violations to avoid criminal sanctions.
II. To discover violations to avoid civil litigation.
III. To meet disclosure requirements to the SEC under the securities laws.
- a. I only.
- b. I and II only.
- c. II only.
- d. I, II and III.

35. Which of the following is(are) true under the Federal Insecticide, Fungicide, and Rodenticide Act?

I. Herbicides and pesticides must be certified and can be used only for applications that are approved.
II. Herbicides and pesticides must be registered under the Act before companies can sell them.
III. Pesticides, when used on food crops, can only be used in quantities that are limited under the Act.
- a. I only.
- b. I and II only.
- c. II and III only.
- d. I, II, and III.

36. Under the Comprehensive Environmental Response, Compensation and Liability Act as amended by the Superfund Amendments, which of the following is(are) true?

I. The present owner of land can be held liable for cleanup of hazardous chemicals placed on the land by a previous owner.
II. An employee of a company that had control over the disposal of hazardous substances on the company's land can be held personally liable for cleanup costs.
- a. I only.
- b. II only.
- c. Both I and II.
- d. Neither I nor II.

37. The National Environmental Policy Act was passed to enhance and preserve the environment. Which of the following is **not** true?

    a.   The Act applies to all federal agencies.

    b.   The Act requires that an environmental impact statement be provided if any proposed federal legislation may significantly affect the environment.

    c.   Enforcement of the Act is primarily accomplished by litigation of persons who decide to challenge federal government decisions.

    d.   The Act provides generous tax breaks to those companies that help accomplish national environmental policy.

38. Under the federal statutes governing water pollution, which of the following areas is(are) regulated?

	Dredging of coastal or freshwater wetlands	Drinking water standards
a.	Yes	Yes
b.	Yes	No
c.	No	Yes
d.	No	No

39. The Clean Air Act provides for the enforcement of standards for

  I. The emissions of radioactive particles from private nuclear power plants.

  II. The emissions of pollution from privately owned automobiles.

  III. The emissions of air pollution from factories.

    a.   I and II only.

    b.   I and III only.

    c.   II and III only.

    d.   I, II and III.

40. Under the Clean Air Act, which of the following statements is(are) correct regarding actions that may be taken against parties who violate emission standards?

  I. The federal government may require an automobile manufacturer to recall vehicles that violate emission standards.

  II. A citizens' group may sue to force a coal burning power plant to comply with emission standards.

    a.   I only.

    b.   II only.

    c.   Both I and II.

    d.   Neither I nor II.

41. The Environmental Protection Agency is an administrative agency in the federal government that aids in the protection of the environment. Which of the following is **not** a purpose or function of this agency?

    a.   It adopts regulations to protect the quality of water.

    b.   It aids private citizens to make cases for private civil litigation.

    c.   It may refer criminal matters to the Department of Justice.

    d.   It may refer civil cases to the Department of Justice.

42. Whenever a federal agency recommends actions or legislation that may affect the environment, the agency must prepare an environmental impact statement. Which of the following is **not** required in the environmental impact statement?

    a.   A description of the source of funds to accomplish the action without harming the environment.

    b.   An examination of alternate methods of achieving the goals of the proposed actions or legislation.

    c.   A description in detail of the proposed actions or legislation on the environment.

    d.   A description of any unavoidable adverse consequences.

43. Which of the following is(are) possible when a company violates the Clean Air Act?

  I. The company can be assessed a criminal fine.

  II. Officers of the company can be imprisoned.

  III. The Environmental Protection Agency may assess a civil penalty equal to the savings of costs by the company for noncompliance.

    a.   I only.

    b.   I or II only.

    c.   III only.

    d.   I, II or III.

44. Green, a former owner of Circle Plant, caused hazardous waste pollution at the Circle Plant site two years ago. Sason purchased the plant and caused more hazardous waste pollution. It can be shown that 20% of the problem was caused by Green and that 80% of the problem was caused by Sason. Sason went bankrupt recently. The government wishes to clean up the site and hold Green liable. Which of the following is true?

    a.   The most Green can be held liable for is 20%.

    b.   Green is not liable for any of the cleanup costs since the site was sold.

    c.   Green is not liable for any of the cleanup costs because Green was responsible for less than half of the problem.

    d.   Green can be held liable for all the cleanup costs even if Sason has some funds.

SIMULATION PROBLEM

Simulation Problem 1   (5 to 10 minutes)

Consideration

  For each of the numbered items, indicate: Yes, this item is considered to be wages under the Social Security Act, or No, this item is **not** considered to be wages under the Social Security Act.

		Yes	*No*
1.	Wages, paid in money, to a construction worker.	○	○
2.	Reimbursed normal travel expenses of a salesperson.	○	○
3.	Compensation not paid in cash.	○	○
4.	Commissions of a salesperson.	○	○
5.	Bonuses paid to employees.	○	○
6.	Employee insurance premiums paid by the employer.	○	○
7.	Wages paid to a secretary who is working part time.	○	○
8.	Vacation allowance pay given to employees who are working full time.	○	○
9.	Wages paid to a full-time secretary who wishes to elect not to be covered under the Social Security Act.	○	○
10.	Tips of a waitress.	○	○

MULTIPLE-CHOICE ANSWERS

1. b __ __	11. b __ __	21. a __ __	31. b __ __	41. b __ __
2. a __ __	12. d __ __	22. b __ __	32. d __ __	42. a __ __
3. b __ __	13. a __ __	23. c __ __	33. a __ __	43. d __ __
4. a __ __	14. b __ __	24. a __ __	34. d __ __	44. d __ __
5. d __ __	15. b __ __	25. c __ __	35. d __ __	
6. b __ __	16. a __ __	26. a __ __	36. c __ __	
7. d __ __	17. c __ __	27. b __ __	37. d __ __	
8. c __ __	18. a __ __	28. d __ __	38. a __ __	
9. a __ __	19. c __ __	29. d __ __	39. d __ __	1st: __/44 = __%
10. d __ __	20. b __ __	30. a __ __	40. c __ __	2nd: __/44 = __%

MULTIPLE-CHOICE ANSWER EXPLANATIONS

A. Federal Social Security Act

1. (b) Taxes payable under the Federal Unemployment Tax Act (FUTA) are used to provide unemployment compensation benefits to workers who lose jobs and cannot find replacement work. These taxes paid are deductible by the employer as a business expense for federal income tax purposes. Therefore, answer (b) is correct. Answer (c) is incorrect because only those employers who paid wages of $1,500 or more during any calendar quarter or who employed at least one employee for at least one day a week for twenty weeks must pay FUTA taxes. Answer (d) is incorrect because it is the employer, not the employee, who pays the taxes. Answer (a) is incorrect because the taxes payable under the FUTA are calculated as a fixed percentage of only the first $6,000 of wages of each employee.

2. (a) Unemployment compensation is intended for workers who lose jobs through no fault of their own and cannot find replacement work. Answer (a) is correct because a CPA fired as a result of the employer's business reversals is entitled to receive unemployment compensation. Answer (b) is incorrect because an accountant who refuses to accept replacement work offered him/her would not receive unemployment compensation. Answers (c) and (d) are incorrect because unemployment compensation is not intended for an employee whose actions led to his/her loss of a job.

3. (b) Directors' fees are generally treated as self-employment income and thus are subject to social security self-employment tax.

4. (a) Answer (a) is best since the nondeduction of the FICA tax **and** the payment of it by the employer effectively raises the income of the employee. Answer (d) is not correct because although the employer is required to withhold tax on wages and is liable for payment of such tax whether or not it is collected, the employer's liability can be relieved after showing the employee's related income tax liability has been paid. Therefore, since the employer has paid the taxes, the employer is not subject to penalty. Answer (c) is not correct since no mention is made of a gift. Answer (b) is not correct since no reference is made to wages not being an ordinary and necessary business expense.

5. (d) Social security benefits may include payments to spouses, including divorced spouses in some cases, and to children. It may also include medicare payments but not medicaid payments.

6. (b) **Earned** income in excess of the annual limitation will cause a reduction in a retired person's social security benefits. Answer (b) is therefore correct, since "director's fees" are considered earned income. Answers (a), (c), and (d) are incorrect because proceeds from an annuity, pension payments, and stock dividends are not considered earned income.

7. (d) Unemployment insurance tax must be paid by the employer if the employer employs one or more persons covered by the act. Payments for unemployment insurance are not deducted from employees' salaries. Workers' compensation is a form of strict liability whereby the employer is liable to the employee for injuries or diseases sustained by the employee which arise out of and in the course of employment. The insurance is paid by the employer and the cost is passed on as an expense of doing business. Thus, worker's compensation insurance also is not paid by the employee.

8. (c) Social security tax applies to wages, defined as all compensation for employment. Employment compensation does not have to be in the form of cash to be included in wages taxed under the Federal Insurance Contributions Act (FICA). Therefore, a car received as a productivity award is considered employment compensation subject to the social security tax and answers (a), (b), and (d) are incorrect, because these are not wages.

9. (a) Both a failure to supply taxpayer identification numbers and a failure to make timely FICA deposits would be violations of the Act. As all employees are required to participate in Social Security, their identification numbers must be supplied in order to track employment and cumulative FICA tax paid to the government. The Act also explicitly states that an employer's failure to collect and deposit taxes in a timely manner subjects him/her to penalties and interest.

B. Workers' Compensation Act

10. (d) Workers' compensation benefits arise out of a type of strict liability whereby employers are liable for injuries or diseases sustained by employees which arise from the scope of the employment. Temporary office workers are usually either independent contractors or are employees of a separate employment agency. Answer (a) is incorrect because the employment laws are especially meant to protect minors. Answer (b) is incorrect because truck drivers are not exempted. Answer (c) is incorrect because union affiliation does not create an exemption.

11. (b) Under workers' compensation laws, any employee injured during the course of employment is entitled to workers' compensation benefits regardless of fault, as long as the injury is not self-inflicted, and not the result of a fight or intoxication. However, acceptance of benefits under workers' compensation laws precludes an employee from suing the employer for damages in a civil court.

12. (d) Workers' compensation is a form of strict liability in which an employer is liable to employees for injuries or diseases sustained in the course of employment, without regard to fault. Answer (a) is incorrect because the injured employee is not required to establish employer negligence to recover a workers' compensation action. Answer (b) is incorrect because contributory negligence of the employee is not a valid defense in workers' compensation cases. The workers' compensation act removes the employer's common law defense of negligence of a fellow employee, therefore answer (c) is incorrect.

13. (a) Workers' Compensation Acts require an employer to provide coverage for all eligible employees. Furthermore, the employer is required to cover the cost of injuries to employees, and no amount is deducted from the employees' wages. Therefore, answer (b) is incorrect. Answer (c) is incorrect because under workers' compensation, the disability benefit payments are usually a percentage of weekly earnings. The employer does not have to make up the difference between the benefit payments and the employee's salary. Answer (d) is incorrect because a business covered under workers' compensation laws may be self-insured but it must show proof of financial responsibility to carry this risk.

14. (b) Most workers' compensation laws provide that the employer is strictly liable to an employee without regard to negligence of the employer or employee. Therefore, answers (a) and (c) are incorrect. Answer (d) is incorrect because worker's compensation awards may or may not be payable for life.

15. (b) The following are some examples of workers' compensation benefits: burial expenses, the cost of prosthetic devices, monthly payments to surviving dependent children, and **partial** wage continuation during disability.

16. (a) Both occupational disease and employment aggravated preexisting disease are covered by the statutes in that all consequences of an injury on the job, regardless of whether such injury was actually caused by an accident, are deemed to be "accidental" injuries resulting from employment. If any conditions in the workplace could have possibly contributed to or aggravated consequences, the doctrine of strict employer liability applies.

D. Employee Safety

17. (c) OSHA investigates complaints and makes inspections of the workplace. Employers can require that OSHA obtain a search warrant in most cases to conduct the search. Probable cause is needed to obtain a search warrant and complaints by employees can provide the needed probable cause. Answer (a) is incorrect because the employer can allow the search or give permission, in which cases, search warrants are not needed. Answer (b) is incorrect because inspections can be made during working hours. In fact, this may be the only or most effective time to conduct the inspection. Answer (d) is incorrect because there is no requirement that OSHA give the employers advance notice of the inspections. Such a requirement would make many inspections less effective.

E. Employment Discrimination

18. (a) Under the Equal Pay Act, employers cannot pay some employees less money than that paid to employees of the opposite sex when equal work is performed. Under Title VII of the Civil Rights Act, employers cannot discriminate against a prospective employee on the basis of race, color, national origin, religion, or sex.

19. (c) The Age Discrimination in Employment Act does not specifically use the term "back pay" but the Act provides equitable relief as deemed appropriate and otherwise authorizes back pay. The Act does provide for employment reinstatement or promotion, but does not provide for early retirement.

20. (b) The Age Discrimination in Employment Act generally prohibits mandatory retirement under age seventy. Answers (a) and (c) are incorrect because the Act generally applies to individuals over forty years old. Answer (d) is incorrect because forced retirement under the age of seventy is generally prohibited under the Act.

21. (a) The Americans With Disabilities Act of 1990 prohibits all businesses with fifteen employees or more from considering a person's handicap when making a hiring decision. Also, the act requires businesses to make special accommodations available to handicapped employees and customers, unless the cost is too burdensome. Therefore, answer (a) is correct as the act covers both public transportation and privately operated public accommodations.

22. (b) The Americans with Disabilities Act provides the disabled with better access to employment, public accommodations, and transportation. The Act requires companies to make reasonable accommodations for the disabled unless this would cause undue hardship for the business. The Act does not require companies to set up a hiring plan.

23. (c) The Americans With Disabilities Act requires most companies and entities to not discriminate against qualified individuals with disabilities who can perform the essential functions of the job either with or without reasonable accommodation, unless the company can show undue hardship. Reasonable accommodation may include purchasing new equipment, modifying facilities, or modifying work schedules.

E.10. Family and Medical Leave Act

24. (a) A covered employee has the right to a leave from work for specified reasons for twelve workweeks in a twelve-month period but typically receives leave without pay. Answer (b) is incorrect because it mentions one of the specified reasons allowed for a leave. Answer (c) is incorrect because an important right under the Act is to get back the same or similar position upon returning. Answer (d) is an incorrect response because not all employees are covered. To be covered employees must have worked for twelve months, for at least 1,250 hours in those twelve months, and be one of at least fifty employees.

25. (c) The Act provides for up to twelve workweeks of unpaid leave for the employee to care for serious health problems of his or her parent, spouse, or child. It also provides the same right to care for his or her newborn baby. Note that (d) is incorrect because it provides for paid leave to care for his or her spouse who is seriously ill.

F. Federal Fair Labor Standards Act

26.   (a)   The Fair Labor Standards Act allows employees to be paid on a piecework basis or salary. Workers must receive at least the equivalent of the minimum hourly rate, but the basis on which the workers are paid can be hourly, weekly, or monthly.

27.   (b)   The Fair Labor Standards Act requires overtime pay to be paid when hours worked in any given week exceed forty hours. Therefore, the additional five hours and two hours worked in the first two weeks constitute overtime.

G. National Labor Relations Act (Wagner Act)

28.   (d)   Among other fringe benefits, sick pay and vacation pay are subjects for collective bargaining. Therefore, sick pay and vacation pay are not exempt from the provisions of the National Labor Relations Act.

J. Federal Consolidated Budget Reconciliation Act

29.   (d)   Under the Federal Consolidated Budget Reconciliation Act of 1985 (COBRA), a former employee may retain group health coverage under the employer for him/herself and his/her spouse at the former employee's expense for at least eighteen months after leaving the company. Answer (a) is incorrect because the former employee and spouse may retain the coverage for at least eighteen months. Answers (b) and (c) are incorrect because not only the former employee but also the spouse may retain the coverage for eighteen months at the former employee's expense.

K. Pensions

30.   (a)   If a pension plan is established, employee contributions to the pension plan vest immediately. In addition, standards on investment of funds are set up to avoid mismanagement.

31.   (b)   The Employee Retirement Income Security Act of 1974 (ERISA) does not require an employer to establish a pension plan. Therefore, answer (a) is incorrect. If the employer does set up a plan, it must meet certain standards. These standards prevent employers from unduly delaying an employee's participation in a pension plan. Therefore, answer (b) is correct. Standards are also set up for the investment of funds to avoid mismanagement. However, employers are able to manage the retirement plans. Therefore, answer (c) is incorrect. Answer (d) is incorrect because ERISA provisions do not require that the employees make the investment decisions. This is a function of the particular company's plan.

N. Environmental Regulation

32.   (d)   CERCLA imposes environmental liability on a broad group of potentially responsible parties. The courts have included the following classes: (1) current owners and operators, (2) owners and operators at the time of waste disposal, (3) generators of hazardous waste, (4) transporters of hazardous waste, and (5) lenders who finance borrowers' hazardous waste sites.

33.   (a)   The Clean Water Act regulates the dredging or filling of wetlands. Without a permit, these are generally prohibited. The discharging of heated water by nuclear power plants is also regulated.

34.   (d)   All of the purposes listed are reasons to have an Environmental Compliance Audit. Since the environmental laws and regulations can be complex and may result in both criminal violations and civil liability, both statements I and II are correct. Statement III is also correct because problems with the environmental laws can be significant under the federal securities laws.

35.   (d)   The Federal Insecticide, Fungicide, and Rodenticide Act does have all three of the provisions. Herbicides and pesticides are required to be registered before they can be sold. Furthermore, they need to be used only for the purposes certified. Also, when used on food crops, the amount that can be used is limited.

36.   (c)   The provisions of the Comprehensive Environmental Response, Compensation, and Liability Act (CERCLA) as amended is very broad in scope. If the EPA cleans up the hazardous chemicals, it can recover the costs from any responsible party including present owners of the facility and any person who arranged for the disposal of the hazardous substance.

37.   (d)   The National Environmental Policy Act is centered around requiring the federal government and its agencies to consider the effects of its actions on the environment. It does not provide tax breaks to companies to accomplish environmental goals. Answer (a) is not chosen because it correctly states that the Act applies to all federal agencies. Answer (b) is not chosen because it is also correct. The Act does require an environmental impact statement if the environment may be significantly hurt. Answer (c) is not chosen because private litigation is the main way this Act is enforced.

38.   (a)   The Clean Water Act regulates the dredging of both coastal and freshwater wetlands. The Safe Drinking Water act regulates the safety of water supplied by public water systems to homes.

39.   (d)   The Clean Air Act regulates emissions into the air from automobiles, factories, and nuclear power plants. Note that emissions from the nuclear power plant are handled by the Clean Air Act rather than the Nuclear Waste Policy Act. The latter creates a national plan to dispose of highly radioactive nuclear waste.

40.   (c)   The Clean Air Act sets air quality standards for mobile sources such as autos, and for stationary sources such as power plants. The federal government has ways to encourage and require compliance, such as requiring manufacturers to recall vehicles that violate emission standards. The Act also allows private citizens to sue violators to enforce compliance.

41.   (b)   The Environmental Protection Agency (EPA) is an administrative agency designed to aid the federal government in national environmental policy. When citizens have private lawsuits about the environment, they would typically seek remedies by resorting to common law or statutory remedies. The Environmental Protection Agency was not set up to help in this manner. This agency does, however, adopt regulations on the environment. Therefore answer (a) is not chosen. Answers (c) and (d) are not chosen because the EPA does refer both criminal and civil cases over to the Department of Justice.

42.   (a)   The environmental impact statement is not designed to show the cost or source of the funds for the actions or legislation being proposed. Answers (b), (c), and (d) are all not chosen because these are all required as part of the environmental impact statement.

43.   (d)   The Clean Air Act provides for both criminal and civil penalties against violators. For criminal violations, both fines and prison are possible. Civil penalties can also be assessed by the EPA including an amount equal to any benefits in costs for not complying.

44.   (d)   Green as a part owner is one of the parties that has joint and several liability for the cleanup costs. Even though Sason also has joint and several liability, Green can be held liable for any portion or all of the cleanup costs without regard to percent of responsibility. Answer (a) is incorrect because Green, having joint and several liability, can be held liable for all of the cleanup costs. Answer (b) is incorrect because past as well as present owners have potential liability. Answer (c) is incorrect because there is no such defense as having less than half of the responsibility.

SOLUTION TO SIMULATION PROBLEM

Simulation Problem 1

> **Consideration**

		Yes	No
1.	Wages, paid in money, to a construction worker.	●	○
2.	Reimbursed normal travel expenses of a salesperson.	○	●
3.	Compensation not paid in cash.	●	○
4.	Commissions of a salesperson.	●	○
5.	Bonuses paid to employees.	●	○
6.	Employee insurance premiums paid by the employer.	○	●
7.	Wages paid to a secretary who is working part time.	●	○
8.	Vacation allowance pay given to employees who are working full time.	●	○
9.	Wages paid to a full-time secretary who wishes to elect not to be covered under the Social Security Act.	●	○
10.	Tips of a waitress.	●	○

Explanation of solutions

1. **(Y)** Under the Social Security Act, money wages are considered wages.
2. **(N)** Reimbursed travel expenses are generally excluded from wages.
3. **(Y)** Compensation whether in cash or not is generally considered to be wages.
4. **(Y)** Commissions are a method of compensation.
5. **(Y)** Bonuses are a method of compensation.
6. **(N)** Insurance premiums paid by employers for employees generally are excluded from wages.
7. **(Y)** Part-time employees are covered under this law.
8. **(Y)** Vacation allowance pay is another form of compensation.
9. **(Y)** Qualifying employees may not elect to avoid the Social Security Act.
10. **(Y)** Tips are another form of wages.

MULTIPLE-CHOICE QUESTIONS (1-43)

1. Which of the following items is tangible personal property?
   a.   Share of stock.
   b.   Trademark.
   c.   Promissory note.
   d.   Oil painting.

2. What is an example of property that can be considered either personal property or real property?
   a.   Air rights.
   b.   Mineral rights.
   c.   Harvested crops.
   d.   Growing crops.

3. Which of the following factors help determine whether an item of personal property is a fixture?
   I.   Degree of the item's attachment to the property.
   II. Intent of the person who had the item installed.

   a.   I only.
   b.   II only.
   c.   Both I and II.
   d.   Neither I nor II.

4. Getty owned some personal property which was later found by Morris. Both Getty and Morris are claiming title to this personal property. In which of the following cases will Getty win over Morris?

   I.   Getty had mislaid the property and had forgotten to take it with him.
   II. Getty had lost the property out of his van while driving down a road.
   III. Getty had abandoned the property but later changed his mind after Morris found it.

   a.   I only.
   b.   II only.
   c.   I and II only.
   d.   I, II, and III.

5. Rand discarded an old rocking chair. Stone found the rocking chair and, realizing that it was valuable, took it home. Later, Rand learned that Stone had the rocking chair and wanted it back. Rand subsequently put a provision in his will that his married daughter Walters will get the rocking chair. Who has the actual title to the rocking chair?

	Stone has title	Rand, while living, has title	Walters obtains title upon Rand's death
a.	No	Yes	Yes
b.	No	Yes	No
c.	Yes	Yes	Yes
d.	Yes	No	No

6. Which of the following standards of liability best characterizes the obligation of a common carrier in a bailment relationship?
   a.   Reasonable care.
   b.   Gross negligence.
   c.   Shared liability.
   d.   Strict liability.

7. Multicomp Company wishes to protect software it has developed. It is concerned about others copying this software and taking away some of its profits. Which of the following is true concerning the current state of the law?
   a.   Computer software is generally copyrightable.

   b.   To receive protection, the software must have a conspicuous copyright notice.
   c.   Software in human readable source code is copyrightable but in machine language object code is not.
   d.   Software can be copyrighted for a period not to exceed twenty years.

8. Which of the following is **not** correct concerning computer software purchased by Gultch Company from Softtouch Company? Softtouch originally created this software.
   a.   Gultch can make backup copies in case of machine failure.
   b.   Softtouch can typically copyright its software for at least seventy-five years.
   c.   If the software consists of compiled computer databases it cannot be copyrighted.
   d.   Computer programs are generally copyrightable.

9. Which of the following statements is correct?
   a.   Patent law is largely based on state law.
   b.   Accessing a digital work is protected by the fair use doctrine.
   c.   Financial and business models used over the internet can be patented.
   d.   All of the above statements are incorrect.

10. Professor Bell runs off fifteen copies to distribute to his accounting class using his computer from a database in some software he had purchased for his personal research. The creator of this software is claiming a copyright. Which of the following is correct?
   a.   This is an infringement of a copyright since he bought the software for personal use.
   b.   This is not an infringement of a copyright since databases cannot be copyrighted.
   c.   This is not an infringement of a copyright because the copies were made using a computer.
   d.   This is not an infringement of a copyright because of the fair use doctrine.

11. Intellectual property rights included in software may be protected under which of the following?
   a.   Patent law.
   b.   Copyright law.
   c.   Both of the above.
   d.   None of the above.

12. Which of the following statements is **not** true of the law of trademarks in the United States?
   a.   Trademark law may protect distinctive shapes as well as distinctive packaging.
   b.   Trademark protection can be lost if the trademark becomes so popular that its use becomes commonplace.
   c.   Trademarks to receive protection need not be registered.
   d.   Trademarks are valid for twenty years after their formation.

13. Diane Trucco recently wrote a novel which is an excellent work of art. She wishes to copyright and publish this novel. Which of the following is correct?
   a.   Her copyright is valid for her life plus seventy years.
   b.   She must register her copyright to receive protection under the law.

c.   She is required to put on a copyright notice to obtain a copyright.

d.   All of the above are correct.

14. Long, Fall, and Pear own a building as joint tenants with the right of survivorship. Long gave Long's interest in the building to Green by executing and delivering a deed to Green. Neither Fall nor Pear consented to this transfer. Fall and Pear subsequently died. After their deaths, Green's interest in the building would consist of

a.   A 1/3 interest as a joint tenant.

b.   A 1/3 interest as a tenant in common.

c.   No interest because Fall and Pear did **not** consent to the transfer.

d.   Total ownership due to the deaths of Fall and Pear.

15. What interest in real property generally gives the holder of that interest the right to sell the property?

a.   Easement.

b.   Leasehold.

c.   License.

d.   Fee simple.

16. Which of the following unities (elements) are required to establish a joint tenancy?

	Time	Title	Interest	Possession
a.	Yes	Yes	Yes	Yes
b.	Yes	Yes	No	No
c.	No	No	Yes	Yes
d.	Yes	No	Yes	No

17. Which of the following is not an interest that a person can have in real property?

a.   Fee simple absolute.

b.   Tenancy by default.

c.   Life interest.

d.   Remainder.

18. On July 1, 2001, Quick, Onyx, and Nash were deeded a piece of land as tenants in common. The deed provided that Quick owned 1/2 the property and Onyx and Nash owned 1/4 each. If Nash dies, the property will be owned as follows:

a.   Quick 1/2, Onyx 1/2.

b.   Quick 5/8, Onyx 3/8.

c.   Quick 1/3, Onyx 1/3, Nash's heirs 1/3.

d.   Quick 1/2, Onyx 1/4, Nash's heirs 1/4.

19. Brett conveys his real property by deed to his sister, Jan, for life with the remainder to go to his friend, Randy, for his life. Brett is still living. Randy died first and Jan died second. Who has title to this real property?

a.   Brett.

b.   Brett's heirs.

c.   Jan's heirs.

d.   Randy's heirs.

20. Court, Fell, and Miles own a parcel of land as joint tenants with right of survivorship. Court's interest was sold to Plank. As a result of the sale from Court to Plank

a.   Fell, Miles, and Plank each own one-third of the land as joint tenants.

b.   Fell and Miles each own one-third of the land as tenants in common.

c.   Plank owns one third of the land as a tenant in common.

d.   Plank owns one-third of the land as a joint tenant.

21. The following contains three fact patterns involving land. In which of the following is an easement involved?

I.   O sells land to B in which O retains in the deed the right to use a roadway on B's newly purchased property.

II. O sells land to B in which O in the deed has the right to cut and keep ten specified trees on the land sold.

III. O sells land to B. O continues that year to use a roadway on B's newly purchased property when B is not looking.

a.   I only.

b.   I and II only.

c.   II and III only.

d.   I, II, and III.

22. A method of transferring ownership of real property that most likely would be considered an arm's-length transaction is transfer by

a.   Inheritance.

b.   Eminent domain.

c.   Adverse possession.

d.   Sale.

23. Which of the following elements must be contained in a valid deed?

	Purchase price	Description of the land
a.	Yes	Yes
b.	Yes	No
c.	No	Yes
d.	No	No

24. Which of the following warranties is(are) contained in a general warranty deed?

I.   The grantor has the right to convey the property.

II. The grantee will **not** be disturbed in possession of the property by the grantor or some third party's lawful claim of ownership.

a.   I only.

b.   II only.

c.   Both I and II.

d.   Neither I nor II.

25. For a deed to be effective between the purchaser and seller of real estate, one of the conditions is that the deed must

a.   Contain the signatures of the seller and purchaser.

b.   Contain the actual sales price.

c.   Be delivered by the seller with an intent to transfer title.

d.   Be recorded within the permissible statutory time limits.

Items 26 and 27 are based on the following:

On February 1, Frost bought a building from Elgin, Inc. for $250,000. To complete the purchase, Frost borrowed $200,000 from Independent Bank and gave Independent a mortgage for that amount; gave Elgin a second mortgage for $25,000; and paid $25,000 in cash. Independent recorded its mortgage on February 2 and Elgin recorded its mortgage on March 12.

The following transactions also took place:

• On March 1, Frost gave Scott a $20,000 mortgage on the building to secure a personal loan Scott had previously made to Frost.

• On March 10, Scott recorded this mortgage.

• On March 15, Scott learned about both prior mortgages.

- On June 1, Frost stopped making payments on all the mortgages.
- On August 1, the mortgages were foreclosed. Frost, on that date, owed Independent, $195,000; Elgin, $24,000; and Scott, $19,000.

A judicial sale of the building resulted in proceeds of $220,000 after expenses were deducted. The above transactions took place in a notice-race jurisdiction.

26. What amount of the proceeds will Scott receive?
a. $0
b. $ 1,000
c. $12,500
d. $19,000

27. Why would Scott receive this amount?
a. Scott knew of the Elgin mortgage.
b. Scott's mortgage was recorded before Elgin's and before Scott knew of Elgin's mortgage.
c. Elgin's mortgage was first in time.
d. After Independent is fully paid, Elgin and Scott share the remaining proceeds equally.

28. A purchaser who obtains real estate title insurance will
a. Have coverage for the title exceptions listed in the policy.
b. Be insured against all defects of record other than those excepted in the policy.
c. Have coverage for title defects that result from events that happen after the effective date of the policy.
d. Be entitled to transfer the policy to subsequent owners.

29. Which of the following is a defect in marketable title to real property?
a. Recorded zoning restrictions.
b. Recorded easements referred to in the contract of sale.
c. Unrecorded lawsuit for negligence against the seller.
d. Unrecorded easement.

30. Which of the following is not a necessary element for an individual to obtain title of a piece of real estate by adverse possession?
a. Continuous possession.
b. Possession that is to the exclusion of others.
c. Possession permitted by the actual owner.
d. Open and notorious possession.

31. Rake, twenty-five years ago, put a fence around a piece of land. At the time, Rake knew that fence not only surrounded his land but also a sizable piece of Howe's land. Every summer Rake planted a garden on this land surrounded by the fence. Howe recently sold all of his land to Cross. Cross has found out about the fence line and has asked Rake to either move the fence or pay Cross for the land in question. What is the result?
a. Rake does not have to move the fence but must pay Cross for the land in question.
b. Rake does not have to move the fence but must pay Howe for the land in question.
c. Rake must move the fence.
d. Rake must neither move the fence nor pay either party for the land in question.

32. Generally, which of the following federal acts regulate mortgage lenders?

	Real Estate Settlement Procedures Act (RESPA)	Federal Trade Commission Act
a.	Yes	Yes
b.	Yes	No
c.	No	Yes
d.	No	No

33. Gilmore borrowed $60,000 from Dix Bank. The loan was used to remodel a building owned by Gilmore as investment property and was secured by a second mortgage that Dix did not record. FCA Loan Company has a recorded first mortgage on the building. If Gilmore defaults on both mortgages, Dix
a. Will **not** be entitled to any mortgage foreclosure sale proceeds, even if such proceeds are in excess of the amount owed to FCA.
b. Will be unable to successfully claim any security interest in the building.
c. Will be entitled to share in any foreclosure sale proceeds pro rata with FCA.
d. Will be able to successfully claim a security interest that is subordinate to FCA's security interest.

34. Wilk bought an apartment building from Dix Corp. There was a mortgage on the building securing Dix's promissory note to Xeon Finance Co. Wilk took title subject to Xeon's mortgage. Wilk did not make the payments on the note due Xeon and the building was sold at a foreclosure sale. If the proceeds of the foreclosure sale are less than the balance due on the note, which of the following statements is correct regarding the deficiency?
a. Xeon must attempt to collect the deficiency from Wilk before suing Dix.
b. Dix will **not** be liable for any of the deficiency because Wilk assumed the note and mortgage.
c. Xeon may collect the deficiency from either Dix or Wilk.
d. Dix alone would be liable for the entire deficiency.

35. On April 6, Ford purchased a warehouse from Atwood for $150,000. Atwood had executed two mortgages on the property: a purchase money mortgage given to Lang on March 2, which was not recorded; and a mortgage given to Young on March 9, which was recorded the same day. Ford was unaware of the mortgage to Lang. Under the circumstances
a. Ford will take title to the warehouse subject only to Lang's mortgage.
b. Ford will take title to the warehouse free of Lang's mortgage.
c. Lang's mortgage is superior to Young's mortgage because Lang's mortgage is a purchase money mortgage.
d. Lang's mortgage is superior to Young's mortgage because Lang's mortgage was given first in time.

36. Which of the following conditions must be met to have an enforceable mortgage?
a. An accurate description of the property must be included in the mortgage.
b. A negotiable promissory note must accompany the mortgage.
c. Present consideration must be given in exchange for the mortgage.

d.   The amount of the debt and the interest rate must be stated in the mortgage.

37. On February 1, Frost bought a building from Elgin, Inc. for $250,000. To complete the purchase, Frost borrowed $200,000 from Independent Bank and gave Independent a mortgage for that amount; gave Elgin a second mortgage for $25,000; and paid $25,000 in cash. Independent recorded its mortgage on February 2 and Elgin recorded its mortgage on March 12.

The following transactions also took place:

- On March 1, Frost gave Scott a $20,000 mortgage on the building to secure a personal loan Scott had previously made to Frost.
- On March 10, Scott recorded this mortgage.
- On March 15, Scott learned about both prior mortgages.
- On June 1, Frost stopped making payments on all the mortgages.
- On August 1, the mortgages were foreclosed. Frost, on that date, owed Independent, $195,000; Elgin, $24,000; and Scott, $19,000.

A judicial sale of the building resulted in proceeds of $220,000 after expenses were deducted. The above transactions took place in a notice-race jurisdiction.

Frost may redeem the property before the judicial sale only if

a.   There is a statutory right of redemption.
b.   It is probable that the sale price will result in a deficiency.
c.   All mortgages are paid in full.
d.   All mortgagees are paid a penalty fee.

38. A mortgagor's right of redemption will be terminated by a judicial foreclosure sale unless

a.   The proceeds from the sale are not sufficient to fully satisfy the mortgage debt.
b.   The mortgage instrument does not provide for a default sale.
c.   The mortgagee purchases the property for market value.
d.   The jurisdiction has enacted a statutory right of redemption.

39. Rich purchased property from Sklar for $200,000. Rich obtained a $150,000 loan from Marsh Bank to finance the purchase, executing a promissory note and a mortgage. By recording the mortgage, Marsh protects its

a.   Rights against Rich under the promissory note.
b.   Rights against the claims of subsequent bona fide purchasers for value.
c.   Priority against a previously filed real estate tax lien on the property.
d.   Priority against all parties having earlier claims to the property.

40. Which of the following provisions must be included to have an enforceable written residential lease?

	A description of the leased premises	A due date for the payment of rent
a.	Yes	Yes
b.	Yes	No
c.	No	Yes
d.	No	No

41. Which of the following rights is(are) generally given to a lessee of residual property?

I. A covenant of quiet enjoyment.
II. An implied warranty of habitability.

a.   I only.
b.   II only.
c.   Both I and II.
d.   Neither I nor II.

42. Which of the following methods of obtaining personal property will give the recipient ownership of the property?

	Lease	Finding abandoned property
a.	Yes	Yes
b.	Yes	No
c.	No	Yes
d.	No	No

43. Which of the following forms of tenancy will be created if a tenant stays in possession of the leased premises without the landlord's consent, after the tenant's one-year written lease expires?

a.   Tenancy at will.
b.   Tenancy for years.
c.   Tenancy from period to period.
d.   Tenancy at sufferance.

SIMULATION PROBLEM

Simulation Problem 1   (10 to 15 minutes)

Situation						
	Priority	Rationale	Sales Proceeds	Deficiency Fair	Deficiency Heath Finance	Deficiency Knox

On June 10, 1998, Bond sold real property to Edwards for $100,000. Edwards assumed the $80,000 recorded mortgage Bond had previously given to Fair Bank and gave a $20,000 purchase money mortgage to Heath Finance. Heath did not record this mortgage. On December 15, 1999, Edwards sold the property to Ivor for $115,000. Ivor bought the property subject to the Fair mortgage but did not know about the Heath mortgage. Ivor borrowed $50,000 from Knox Bank and gave Knox a mortgage on the property. Knox knew of the unrecorded Heath mortgage when its mortgage was recorded. Ivor, Edwards, and Bond defaulted on the mortgages. Fair, Heath, and Knox foreclosed and the property was sold at a judicial foreclosure sale for $60,000. At the time of the sale, the outstanding balance of principal and accrued interest on the Fair mortgage was $75,000. The Heath mortgage balance was $18,000 and the Knox mortgage was $47,500.

Fair, Heath, and Knox all claim that their mortgages have priority and should be satisfied first from the sale proceeds. Bond, Edwards, and Ivor all claim that they are not liable for any deficiency resulting from the sale.

The above transactions took place in a jurisdiction that has a notice-race recording statute and allows foreclosure deficiency judgments.

	Priority					
Situation		Rationale	Sales Proceeds	Deficiency Fair	Deficiency Heath Finance	Deficiency Knox

Items 1 through 3. For each mortgage, select from List A the priority of that mortgage. A priority should be selected only once.

List A

A. First Priority.
B. Second Priority.
C. Third Priority.

	(A)	(B)	(C)
1. Knox Bank.	○	○	○
2. Heath Finance.	○	○	○
3. Fair Bank.	○	○	○

		Rationale				
Situation	Priority		Sales Proceeds	Deficiency Fair	Deficiency Heath Finance	Deficiency Knox

Items 1 through 3. For each mortgage, select from List B the reason for its priority. A reason may be selected once, more than once, or not at all.

List B

A. An unrecorded mortgage has priority over any subsequently recorded mortgage.
B. A recorded mortgage has priority over any unrecorded mortgage.
C. The first recorded mortgage has priority over all subsequent mortgages.
D. An unrecorded mortgage has priority over a subsequently recorded mortgage if the subsequent mortgagee knew of the unrecorded mortgage.
E. A purchase money mortgage has priority over a previously recorded mortgage.

	(A)	(B)	(C)	(D)	(E)
1. Knox Bank.	○	○	○	○	○
2. Heath Finance.	○	○	○	○	○
3. Fair Bank.	○	○	○	○	○

			Sales Proceeds			
Situation	Priority	Rationale		Deficiency Fair	Deficiency Heath Finance	Deficiency Knox

Items 1 through 3. For each mortgage, select from List C the amount of the sale proceeds that each mortgagee would be entitled to receive. An amount may be selected once, more than once, or not at all.

List C

A.	$0	E.	$42,000
B.	$12,500	F.	$47,500
C.	$18,000	G.	$60,000
D.	$20,000		

	(A)	(B)	(C)	(D)	(E)	(F)	(G)
1. Knox Bank.	○	○	○	○	○	○	○
2. Heath Finance.	○	○	○	○	○	○	○
3. Fair Bank.	○	○	○	○	○	○	○

Situation	Priority	Rationale	Sales Proceeds	Deficiency Fair	Deficiency Heath Finance	Deficiency Knox

Items 1 through 3. Determine whether each party would be liable to pay a mortgage foreclosure deficiency judgment on the Fair Bank mortgage. If the party would be held liable, select from List D the reason for that party's liability. A reason may be selected once, more than once, or not at all.

List D

A.	Original mortgagor.	C.	Took subject to the mortgage.
B.	Assumed the mortgage.	D.	Not liable.

	(A)	(B)	(C)	(D)
1. Edwards.	○	○	○	○
2. Bond.	○	○	○	○
3. Ivor.	○	○	○	○

Situation	Priority	Rationale	Sales Proceeds	Deficiency Fair	Deficiency Heath Finance	Deficiency Knox

For **items 1 through 3,** determine whether each party would be liable to pay a mortgage foreclosure deficiency judgment on the Heath Finance mortgage. If the party would be held liable, select from List E the reason for that party's liability. A reason may be selected once, more than once, or not at all.

List E

A.	Original mortgagor.	C.	Took subject to the mortgage.
B.	Assumed the mortgage.	D.	Not liable.

	(A)	(B)	(C)	(D)
1. Edwards.	○	○	○	○
2. Bond.	○	○	○	○
3. Ivor.	○	○	○	○

Situation	Priority	Rationale	Sales Proceeds	Deficiency Fair	Deficiency Heath Finance	Deficiency Knox

For **items 1 through 3,** determine whether each party would be liable to pay a mortgage foreclosure deficiency judgment on the Knox Bank mortgage. If the party would be held liable, select from List F the reason for that party's liability. A reason may be selected once, more than once, or not at all.

List F

A.	Original mortgagor.	C.	Took subject to the mortgage.
B.	Assumed the mortgage.	D.	Not liable.

	(A)	(B)	(C)	(D)
1. Edwards.	○	○	○	○
2. Bond.	○	○	○	○
3. Ivor.	○	○	○	○

MULTIPLE-CHOICE ANSWERS

1.	d	__ __	10.	d	__ __	19.	a	__ __	28.	b	__ __
2.	d	__ __	11.	c	__ __	20.	c	__ __	29.	d	__ __
3.	c	__ __	12.	d	__ __	21.	a	__ __	30.	c	__ __
4.	c	__ __	13.	a	__ __	22.	d	__ __	31.	d	__ __
5.	d	__ __	14.	b	__ __	23.	c	__ __	32.	b	__ __
6.	d	__ __	15.	d	__ __	24.	c	__ __	33.	d	__ __
7.	a	__ __	16.	a	__ __	25.	c	__ __	34.	d	__ __
8.	c	__ __	17.	b	__ __	26.	d	__ __	35.	b	__ __
9.	c	__ __	18.	d	__ __	27.	b	__ __	36.	a	__ __

37.	c	__ __
38.	d	__ __
39.	b	__ __
40.	b	__ __
41.	c	__ __
42.	c	__ __
43.	d	__ __
1st:	__/43=	__%
2nd:	__/43=	__%

MULTIPLE-CHOICE ANSWER EXPLANATIONS

A. Distinctions between Real and Personal Property

1. **(d)** Real property is land and objects attached to land in a relatively permanent manner; personal property is property not classified as real. Tangible property is subject to physical possession; intangible property cannot be physically possessed, but can be legally owned. Ownership of intangible property is often represented by a piece of paper, but the property itself is intangible. A share of stock is part ownership of a company; a trademark is ownership of the use of a particular mark, design, word, or picture, and a promissory note is ownership of the right to receive payment of a debt at a future date. These are all usually represented by a piece of paper, but are intangible. An oil painting is personal property subject to physical possession.

2. **(d)** Growing crops generally are part of the land and therefore considered real property. However, the crops can be sold separately from the land, in which case they are considered personal property under the UCC, whether the buyer or the seller will sever the growing crops later from the land. Answer (a) is incorrect because air rights are not discussed in the UCC as one of those that can be either. Answer (b) is incorrect because mineral rights are associated with land or realty. Answer (c) is incorrect because unlike growing crops that may be realty until sold in a contract, harvested crops are personal property separate from the realty.

B. Personal Property

3. **(c)** The factors used to determine whether an item of personal property is considered a fixture are (1) the affixer's intent, (2) the method and permanence of attachment, and (3) whether the personal property is customarily necessary to use the real property.

4. **(c)** When the owner mislays personal property and forgets to take it with him or her, the finder does not obtain title but the owner of the premise acts as caretaker in case the true owner comes back. In the case of lost property (involuntarily left), the finder obtains title; however, the true owner, Getty, wins over this title. In the case of abandoned property, the finder gets valid title that is even valid against Getty.

5. **(d)** When property is discarded with no intention of keeping ownership over it, it is considered abandoned property. In such cases, the one who finds and keeps the abandoned property becomes the owner with title that is good against all other parties, even the owner who abandoned it. Note that Walters cannot obtain title from Rand because Rand no longer owns the rocking chair.

C. Bailments

6. **(d)** The general rule for a bailee is to exercise reasonable care in light of the particular facts and circumstances. However, a common carrier holds itself out as a public delivery service, and is held to a very high standard for property placed in its care. Therefore, answer (d) is correct.

D. Intellectual Property and Computer Technology Rights

7. **(a)** Computer software is covered under the general copyright laws and is therefore usually copyrightable as an expression of ideas. Answer (b) is incorrect because copyrights in general do not need a copyright notice for works published after March 1, 1989. Answer (c) is incorrect because a recent court ruled that programs in both source codes, which are human readable, and in machine readable object code can be copyrighted. Answer (d) is incorrect because copyrights taken out by corporations or businesses are valid for 100 years from creation of the copyrighted item or seventy-five years from its publication, whichever is shorter.

8. **(c)** Computer databases are generally copyrightable as compilations. Answer (a) is not chosen because copies for archival purposes are allowed. Answer (b) is not chosen because in the case of corporations or businesses, the copyright is valid for the shorter of 100 years after the creation of the work or seventy-five years from its date of publication. Answer (d) is not chosen because computer programs are now generally recognized as copyrightable.

9. **(c)** Even though earlier views of financial and business models that were used over the internet often categorized them as based on ideas and thus not patentable, more recent authority says they can be patented. Answer (a) is incorrect because patent law is exclusively federal law. Answer (b) is incorrect because accessing a digital work is not protected by the fair use doctrine. Answer (d) is incorrect because answer (c) is correct.

10. **(d)** Under the fair use doctrine, copyrighted items can be used for teaching, including distributing multiple copies for class use. Answer (a) is incorrect because although he originally purchased this software for personal use, he may still use it for his class, in which case, the fair use doctrine applies. Answer (b) is incorrect because databases can be copyrighted as derivative works. Answer (c) is incorrect because the use of the computer is not the issue but the fair use doctrine is.

11.　(c)　Both patent and copyright law are used under modern law to protect computer technology rights. Answer (a) is incorrect because copyright law now also protects software. Answer (b) is incorrect because modern law also protects software as patentable. Answer (d) is incorrect because modern law generally protects intellectual property rights in software under both patent law and copyright law.

12.　(d)　Trademarks are valid indefinitely until they are actually abandoned or the company allows the trademark to lose its distinctiveness. Answer (a) is not chosen because trademarks can protect many distinctive things such as shapes, packaging, or graphic designs. Answer (b) is not chosen because a company must take steps to keep the trademark distinctive or it can lose it through others' common usage. For example, elevator was once a trademark which has since been lost. Answer (c) is not chosen because although a company may register a trademark to better protect its legal rights, it may still receive protection without registering it by proving the facts.

13.　(a)　Since January 1, 1978, this is the life of a copyright. Answer (b) is incorrect because the copyright is valid when the author puts the work of art in tangible form. Answer (c) is incorrect because works published after March 1, 1989 no longer require a copyright notice placed on them. Answer (d) is incorrect because under current copyright law, (b) and (c) are no longer required.

E.　Interests in Real Property

14.　(b)　In a joint tenancy, each joint tenant has an equal and undivided interest in the property. Each joint tenant can transfer his/her interest in the property without the prior consent of the other joint tenants. When this occurs, the conveyance destroys the joint tenancy and creates a tenancy in common between the remaining joint tenants and the third party. When Long gave his/her interest in the building to Green, Green became a tenant in common with a 1/3 interest in the property. Therefore, answer (a) is incorrect. Answer (d) is incorrect because Green would have total interest in the building after the deaths of Fall and Pear only if Green had been a joint tenant rather than a tenant in common. Answer (c) is incorrect because a joint tenant may convey rights in property without the consent of other joint tenants.

15.　(d)　A fee simple is generally the most comprehensive interest that a person may have in property under the law of the United States. It allows the owner to sell it or to pass it on to heirs. Answer (a) is incorrect because an easement is not ownership of the land but the right to use it in a way such as using a roadway along with the owner. Answer (b) is incorrect because a leasehold gives the lessee the right to possess the premises under the lease but not the ownership of the premises. Answer (c) is incorrect because a license is permission given by the owner to use or occupy the real estate but not to own it.

16.　(a)　In a joint tenancy, each joint tenant has an equal and undivided interest in the property. Joint tenancy ownership consists of the unities of time, title, interest, and possession and carries with it the right of survivorship. Thus, all the elements listed in the question are required to establish a joint tenancy and answers (b), (c), and (d) are incorrect.

17.　(b)　A tenancy by default is not one of the recognized interests in real estate. Answer (a) is incorrect be-cause a fee simple absolute is the highest estate recognized in American law. Answer (c) is incorrect because a life interest is an interest measured by the life of the holder or some other person. Answer (d) is incorrect because a remainder is the future interest that a third party acquires after the interest of a transferee terminates.

18.　(d)　In a tenancy in common, each tenant essentially owns an undivided fractional share of the property. Each tenant has the right to convey his/her interest in the property and if one of the tenants dies, that tenant's interest passes to his/her heirs. Therefore, if Nash dies, Nash's interest would pass to Nash's heirs and the ownership of the property would be as follows: Quick 1/2, Onyx 1/4, and Nash's heirs 1/4.

19.　(a)　Jan had title to the property when Brett granted it to her for her life. Randy never got title to it because he died before Jan's life estate terminated. When Jan died, her life estate terminated and the property reverted back to Brett, who was still living. Answer (b) is incorrect because Brett was still living. Answers (c) and (d) are incorrect because Jan and Randy had been granted life estates which automatically terminate upon their deaths.

20.　(c)　When rights in property held in joint tenancy are conveyed without the consent of the other joint tenants, the new owner becomes a tenant in common rather than a joint tenant. The remaining cotenants are still joint tenants. Thus, after the sale of land from Court to Plank without the consent of the others, Plank owns one third of the land as a tenant in common. Both Fell and Miles will continue to each own one third of the land as joint tenants.

21.　(a)　Fact pattern I involves an easement in which O reserves the right to use B's land in the deed to B. O does not any longer own the roadway but retains the right to use it. Fact pattern II is a profit rather than an easement in which O has the right to enter B's land to cut and keep the ten trees. Fact pattern III is not an easement because O has not retained nor has s/he been given the right to use the roadway. Note that this is not an easement by prescription in that the use is not open and notorious nor has it occurred for several years.

G.　Types of Deeds

22.　(d)　An arm's-length transaction is a negotiation between unrelated parties acting in his/her interest. A way to test an arm's-length transaction is to consider what a disinterested third party would pay for the property. Answer (d) is correct because a sale involves the transfer of property for consideration in which a third party would generally negotiate and act in his/her interest. Answer (a) is incorrect because the property passes to a party as the decedent directs, subject to certain state limitations. Answer (b) is incorrect because eminent domain is the power of the government to take, with just compensation, private property for public use. Answer (c) is incorrect because adverse possession allows a person to gain title to real property if the person has continuously and openly occupied the land of another for a statutory period of time.

23.　(c)　In order for a deed to be valid, a description of the land must be included. The purchase price of the land need not be present to form a valid deed.

24. **(c)** A general warranty deed warrants that (1) the seller has title and the power to convey the property described in the deed, (2) the property is free from any encumbrances, except as disclosed in the deed, and (3) the grantee (purchaser) will not be disturbed in his/her possession of the property by the grantor (seller) or some third party's lawful claim of ownership. Thus, a general warranty deed would contain both of the warranties listed and answers (a), (b), and (d) are incorrect.

I. Recording a Deed

25. **(c)** In order for a deed to be effective between the purchaser and seller of real estate, the deed must be delivered by the seller with an intent to transfer title. Even though a deed may be executed it does not become effective until delivery is made with the proper intent. Answer (d) is incorrect because a deed need not be recorded in order for it to be valid between the seller and purchaser. Recordation of a deed is important because it gives constructive notice to all third parties of the grantee's ownership; however, it does not affect the resolution of any disputes between the grantor and the grantee. Answer (a) is incorrect since a deed need be signed by only the seller in order for it to be effective; it does not have to be signed by the purchaser. Answer (b) is incorrect since the form of a deed is very different from a contract for the sale of real property. There is no requirement that the deed must contain the actual sales price.

26. **(d)** Under a notice-race statute, if a mortgagee fails to record its mortgage, a subsequent mortgagee who records will have a superior security interest if s/he did not have notice of the prior mortgage. In this situation, Independent Bank was the first to record its mortgage and would receive the $195,000 owed it. Scott would then receive $19,000 because Scott recorded his/her mortgage before Elgin. Since Scott did not have knowledge of Elgin's mortgage until after Scott had recorded his/her mortgage, Scott would have priority over Elgin.

27. **(b)** Under a notice-race statute, a subsequent mortgagee (lender) who loans money without notice of a previous mortgage and records the mortgage first has priority over that previous mortgage. Thus, since Scott recorded his/her mortgage before Elgin and without knowledge of Elgin's mortgage, Scott would have priority in a notice-race jurisdiction. Answer (a) is incorrect because Scott did not know of Elgin's mortgage at the time Scott recorded his/her mortgage. Although Scott later learned about both prior mortgages, this would not affect Scott's priority over Elgin's mortgage. Answer (c) is incorrect because Elgin's mortgage would have priority only if it had been recorded before Scott's. Answer (d) is incorrect because Scott's mortgage had priority over Elgin's. Therefore, Scott would be entitled to receive the full $19,000 before Elgin received any of the proceeds from the judicial sale.

J. Title Insurance

28. **(b)** Title insurance insures against all defects of record and defects the grantee may be aware of. Any exceptions not insured by the title policy must be shown on the face of the policy. Answer (a) is incorrect because title exceptions are not insured by the title policy. Answer (c) is incorrect because title insurance covers only defects of record. Answer (d) is incorrect because title insurance does not pass to subsequent purchasers.

29. **(d)** Marketable title means that the title to real property is free from encumbrances, such as mortgages, easements, and liens and defects in the chain of title. However, there is an exception. Most courts hold that the seller's obligation to convey marketable title does not require the seller to convey the title free from recorded zoning restrictions, visible public rights-of-way or recorded easements. An unrecorded easement, however, would be a defect in marketable title. Therefore, answer (d) is correct. An unrecorded lawsuit for negligence against the seller would not cause a defect in marketable title.

K. Adverse Possession

30. **(c)** One of the elements to obtain title to property by adverse possession is that the possession be hostile to the ownership interests of the actual owner. This does not occur when possession is permitted by the actual owner. All of the others are necessary elements to obtain ownership by adverse possession.

31. **(d)** Rake has fulfilled the elements necessary to gain title to this land in question by adverse possession. These are: (1) open and notorious possession, (2) hostile possession shown by the fence, (3) actual possession, (4) continuous possession, and (5) exclusive possession for twenty-five years. Note that it is considered continuous possession even though the gardening is only during the summer, because the fence is constantly there. Answers (a), (b), and (c) are incorrect because since Rake obtained title to the land in question, he does not have to move the fence or pay for the land.

M. Mortgages

32. **(b)** Congress enacted the Real Estate Settlement Procedures Act (RESPA) in 1974 to provide home buyers with more extensive information about the settlement process and to protect them from unnecessarily high settlement fees. The act applies to all federally related mortgage loans, and nearly all first mortgage loans. Therefore, the general purpose of this act is to regulate mortgage lenders.

The purpose of the Federal Trade Commission Act is to prevent unfair methods of competition and unfair or deceptive practices in commerce. It is a general consumer protection act, and regulates compliance with antitrust laws. Although it may apply to mortgage lenders, its general purpose is not to regulate mortgage lenders.

33. **(d)** Dix's second mortgage on Gilmore's property will allow Dix to claim a security interest subordinate to FCA's first mortgage security interest. Dix's failure to record the second mortgage will not affect their right to successfully enforce the mortgage against Gilmore. Therefore, answer (b) is incorrect. Answer (a) is incorrect because Dix would be entitled to receive mortgage foreclosure sale proceeds if such proceeds were in excess of the amount owed to FCA. Answer (c) is incorrect because FCA's first mortgage must be fully satisfied before any payments can be made to Dix.

34. **(d)** If a buyer takes a mortgage "subject to," then the buyer accepts no liability for the mortgage and the seller is still primarily liable. The mortgagor does not have to attempt to collect from the buyer first; he can go directly against the seller. Therefore, answer (d) is correct, and answers (a) and (c) are incorrect. Answer (b) is incorrect because Wilk did not **assume** the mortgage but bought the building **subject to** the mortgage.

35.   (b)   A purchaser of real estate takes title subject to any mortgage he was aware of or any mortgage that was recorded before the purchase. Ford, therefore, takes title to the warehouse subject to Young's mortgage, but free of Lang's mortgage. Therefore, answer (b) is correct and answer (a) is incorrect. Answer (c) is incorrect because there is no such provision. Answer (d) is incorrect because the recording statutes change the first in time concept to encourage the recording of mortgages.

36.   (a)   To have an enforceable mortgage it must be in writing and must include a description of the property and debt to be incurred. Therefore, answer (a) is correct. Answer (b) is incorrect, because although debt is usually evidenced by a promissory note, this is not required to be. Answer (c) is incorrect because the promise to pay is adequate consideration. Answer (d) is incorrect because the amount of the debt and the interest rate are not required to be stated in the mortgage.

37.   (c)   A mortgagor has the right to redeem the mortgaged property after default and before a judicial sale by payment of all principal and interest due on the mortgage note. Thus, Frost may redeem the property only if all mortgages are paid in full prior to the judicial sale. Answer (a) is incorrect because the right of redemption is a right that occurs **after** the judicial sale. Most states allow a mortgagor a period of time, usually one year after the foreclosure sale, to reinstate the debt and mortgage by paying to the purchaser at the judicial sale the amount of the purchase price plus the statutory interest rate. Answer (b) is incorrect because Frost may redeem the property prior to the judicial sale by paying all mortgages in full without regard to the probable sale price of the property. Answer (d) is incorrect because Frost would not have to pay penalty fees to the mortgagees.

38.   (d)   After foreclosure of the mortgage, the mortgagor may redeem the property by payment of all principal and interest due on the mortgage note. However, the right of redemption will terminate at the time of the judicial foreclosure sale unless the jurisdiction has enacted a statutory right of redemption. Answers (a), (b), and (c) are incorrect because they do not affect when the mortgagor's right of redemption terminates.

39.   (b)   Recording a mortgage protects the mortgagee against **subsequent** mortgagees, purchasers, or other takers. Therefore, answers (a), (c), and (d) are incorrect because those answers involve parties with existing claims on the property.

N. Lessor-Lessee

40.   (b)   A residential lease agreement must contain the following essential elements: the parties involved, lease payment amount, lease term, and a description of the leased property. The omission of any of these terms will cause the agreement to fail for indefiniteness. The other terms of payment due date, liability insurance requirements, and responsibility for repairs are optional, but not required. They will not cause the contract to fail for indefiniteness.

41.   (c)   The lessee of residential property, although not the owner, generally has the right to possession of the prop-

erty and the right to quiet enjoyment of the property. The right to quiet enjoyment means that neither the lessor nor a third party with a valid claim will evict the lessee unless the lessee has breached the lease contract. The lessee also has the implied warranty of habitability which means that s/he has the right to inhabit premises that are fit for human occupation.

42.   (c)   A lease is not a sale and does not involve a transfer of title. A lessee may have possession and control of the property but will not have ownership. When property is abandoned, the owner relinquishes possession and title of the property. Subsequent parties who acquire abandoned property with the intent to own it acquire title.

43.   (d)   A tenancy at sufferance is created when a tenant stays in possession of the leased property after the expiration of the lease without the landlord's consent. A tenant at sufferance is a trespasser and the landlord may evict the tenant by instituting legal proceedings. Answer (a) is incorrect because a tenancy at will is an agreement that is not for a fixed period but is terminable at the will of the landlord or tenant. In this situation, the tenant does not have the consent of the landlord to stay in possession of the property and a tenancy at will is not created. Answer (b) is incorrect because a tenancy for years is a tenancy that has a fixed beginning and end at the time of creation of the tenancy. Answer (c) is incorrect because a tenancy from period to period would only be created if the landlord allowed the tenant to remain in possession of the property.

SOLUTION TO SIMULATION PROBLEM

Simulation Problem 1

Situation	Priority			Rationale	Sales Proceeds	Deficiency Fair	Deficiency Heath Finance	Deficiency Knox

	(A)	(B)	(C)
1. Knox Bank.	○	○	●
2. Heath Finance.	○	●	○
3. Fair Bank.	●	○	○

Explanation of solutions

1. (C) 2. (B) 3. (A) Under a notice-race recording statute, a subsequent mortgagee (lender) who loans money without notice of the previous mortgagee and records the mortgage first has priority over that previous mortgagee. Once a mortgagee records, this gives constructive notice to any subsequent parties who then cannot obtain priority over the one who recorded. In this fact pattern, Fair Bank was the first mortgagee. Since Fair Bank also recorded this mortgage first, Fair Bank has the first priority over the subsequent mortgagees. Therefore, the answer to number 3 is (A). Of the two remaining mortgagees, Heath Finance was next in time but did not record the mortgage. Knox Bank was third in time and did record. However, Knox is unable to gain priority over Heath because Knox, when it recorded, knew of the Heath mortgage. Therefore, Knox does not meet all of the rules necessary to have priority over Heath. Thus Heath has the second priority after Fair Bank and Knox has the third priority. Therefore, the answer to number 2 is (B) and number 1 is (C).

Situation	Priority	Rationale		Sales Proceeds	Deficiency Fair	Deficiency Heath Finance	Deficiency Knox

	(A)	(B)	(C)	(D)	(E)
1. Knox Bank.	○	○	○	●	○
2. Heath Finance.	○	○	○	●	○
3. Fair Bank.	○	○	●	○	○

Explanation of solutions

1. (D) 2. (D) 3. (C) This part covers the reason for the priority that applies to each of the mortgagees. Reason (A) states that "an unrecorded mortgage has priority over any subsequently recorded mortgage." This is incorrect for all mortgagees and goes against the policy behind the recording statutes to encourage recording to warn subsequent parties of the previous mortgages. Reason (B) is not a correct statement. It states that "A recorded mortgage has priority over any unrecorded mortgage." In this fact pattern, Knox recorded but Heath did not; however, Knox still has a lower priority because Knox knew of the Heath mortgage when its mortgage was recorded. Reason (C) is the correct answer for Fair Bank. It states that "The first recorded mortgage has priority over all subsequent mortgages." This is true because once Fair Bank recorded, subsequent mortgagees had constructive notice of the Fair Bank mortgage and thus could not obtain priority. The correct answer to number 3 is therefore (C). Reason (D) states that "An unrecorded mortgage has priority over a subsequently recorded mortgage if the subsequent mortgagee knew of the unrecorded mortgage." In this fact pattern, the Heath mortgage was the unrecorded mortgage that still had a higher priority than the recorded Knox mortgage because Knox Bank knew of the Heath mortgage when its mortgage was recorded. Thus Knox never fulfilled the rule which would allow it as the subsequent mortgagee, to gain a higher priority. Therefore, reason (D) is the correct answer for both Knox Bank, number 1, and Heath Finance, number 2, because the same rule determines the relative priority of these two parties. Note that reason (E) is not a correct statement for any of the mortgagees because there is no rule that gives purchase money mortgages priority over previously recorded mortgages.

Situation	Priority	Rationale	Sales Proceeds		Deficiency Fair	Deficiency Heath Finance	Deficiency Knox

	(A)	(B)	(C)	(D)	(E)	(F)	(G)
1. Knox Bank.	●	○	○	○	○	○	○
2. Heath Finance.	●	○	○	○	○	○	○
3. Fair Bank.	○	○	○	○	○	○	●

Explanation of solutions

1. (A) **2.** (A) **3.** (G) Since Fair Bank has the highest priority, its mortgage will be satisfied first. Since the outstanding balance of the Fair Bank mortgage was greater than the $60,000 received at the judicial foreclosure, Fair Bank receives all of the $60,000 and Knox Bank and Heath Finance each receive nothing.

Situation	Priority	Rationale	Sales Proceeds	Deficiency Fair	Deficiency Heath Finance	Deficiency Knox

	(A)	(B)	(C)	(D)
1. Edwards.	○	●	○	○
2. Bond.	●	○	○	○
3. Ivor.	○	○	○	●

Explanation of solutions

1. (B) **2.** (A) **3.** (D) When a foreclosure sale does not provide enough money to pay off the mortgages, the mortgagee, in states that allow foreclosure deficiency judgments, will attempt to collect any deficiency from the parties involved. In this fact pattern, Bond is liable because s/he was the original mortgagor on the property and as such agreed to pay the mortgage. Thus, (A) is the correct answer for number 2. When Edwards later bought the property from Bond, s/he assumed the Fair Bank mortgage. Edwards, thus, became personally liable on the mortgage even though the seller, Bond, also remained liable. Therefore, (B) is the correct answer for number 1. When Ivor subsequently purchased the property from Edwards, Ivor purchased the property subject to the Fair Bank mortgage. In so doing, s/he did not accept any liability on the mortgage. Note that although reason (C) states "Took subject to the mortgage," the correct answer for number 3 is (D) "Not liable." This is true because the directions to part d. indicate that reasons (A), (B), or (C) are to be chosen as reasons **for liability** and (D) is to be chosen if the party is **not** liable.

Situation	Priority	Rationale	Sales Proceeds	Deficiency Fair	Deficiency Heath Finance	Deficiency Knox

	(A)	(B)	(C)	(D)
1. Edwards.	●	○	○	○
2. Bond.	○	○	○	●
3. Ivor.	○	○	○	●

Explanation of solutions

1. (A) **2.** (D) **3.** (D) When Edwards purchased the property, s/he gave a mortgage to Heath Finance. Therefore, (A) is the correct answer for number 1 because as the original mortgagor on the Heath mortgage, s/he agreed to be liable on it. Bond is not liable on the Heath mortgage because s/he having owned the property earlier, never agreed to be liable on this mortgage. Therefore, the correct answer to number 2 is (D). Ivor is not liable on the Heath mortgage because s/he never had actual notice or constructive notice of the unrecorded mortgage, and never agreed to be liable on it. Therefore, the correct answer to number 3 is (D).

Situation	Priority	Rationale	Sales Proceeds	Deficiency Fair	Deficiency Heath Finance	Deficiency Knox

	(A)	(B)	(C)	(D)
1. Edwards.	○	○	○	●
2. Bond.	○	○	○	●
3. Ivor.	●	○	○	○

Explanation of solutions

1. (D) **2.** (D) **3.** (A) Since Ivor borrowed from Knox Bank and gave Knox a mortgage on the property, Ivor is liable as the original mortgagor, making (A) the correct reason for number 1. Both Edwards and Bond owned the property prior to the Knox mortgage and never agreed to be liable on it. Therefore, the correct answer to numbers 1 and 2 is (D).

MULTIPLE-CHOICE QUESTIONS (1-8)

1.   Which of the following statements correctly describes the requirement of insurable interest relating to property insurance? An insurable interest

    a.   Must exist when any loss occurs.

    b.   Must exist when the policy is issued and when any loss occurs.

    c.   Is created only when the property is owned in fee simple.

    d.   Is created only when the property is owned by an individual.

2.   In which of the following cases would Brown not have an insurable interest?

    a.   Brown is a general creditor of Winfield Corporation which is having financial problems.

    b.   Brown is a mortgagee on some real property purchased by Wilson.

    c.   Brown, as an owner of Winfield Company, wishes to insure the life of an officer critical to Winfield.

    d.   Brown wishes to take out a life insurance policy on his partner of a partnership in which both Brown and his partner have important skills for that partnership.

3.   Which of the following parties has an insurable interest?

  I.   A corporate retailer in its inventory.

  II.   A partner in the partnership property.

    a.   I only.

    b.   II only.

    c.   Both I and II.

    d.   Neither I nor II.

4.   Massaro is hit by Lux in a two-car accident that is later determined to be completely Lux's fault. Massaro's auto insurance policy paid her for the complete damages to her car and her person. Can Massaro's insurance company collect the amount it paid from another party?

    a.   No, because Massaro's insurance company had been paid for the risk it took.

    b.   Yes, it can recover from Lux or Lux's insurance company based on the right of subrogation.

    c.   Yes, it can recover from Lux's insurance company, if insured, based on the right of contribution.

    d.   Yes, it can recover from Lux or Lux's insurance company, if insured, based on the right of contribution.

5.   On February 1, Papco Corp. entered into a contract to purchase an office building from Merit Company for $500,000 with closing scheduled for March 20. On February 2, Papco obtained a $400,000 standard fire insurance policy from Abex Insurance Company. On March 15, the office building sustained a $90,000 fire loss. On March 15, which of the following is correct?

  I.   Papco has an insurable interest in the building.

  II.   Merit has an insurable interest in the building.

    a.   I only.

    b.   II only.

    c.   Both I and II.

    d.   Neither I nor II.

6.   Clark Corp. owns a warehouse purchased for $150,000 in 1995. The current market value is $200,000. Clark has the warehouse insured for fire loss with Fair Insurance Corp. and Zone Insurance Co. Fair's policy is for $150,000 and Zone's policy is for $75,000. Both policies contain the standard 80% coinsurance clause. If a fire totally destroyed the warehouse, what total dollar amount would Clark receive from Fair and Zone?

    a. $225,000

    b. $200,000

    c. $160,000

    d. $150,000

Items 7 and 8 are based on the following:

In 1997, Pod bought a building for $220,000. At that time, Pod purchased a $150,000 fire insurance policy with Owners Insurance Co. and a $50,000 fire insurance policy with Group Insurance Corp. Each policy contained a standard 80% coinsurance clause. In 2001, when the building had a fair market value of $250,000, it was damaged in a fire.

7.   How much would Pod recover from Owners if the fire caused $180,000 in damage?

    a. $ 90,000

    b. $120,000

    c. $135,000

    d. $150,000

8.   How much would Pod recover from Owners and Group if the fire totally destroyed the building?

    a. $160,000

    b. $200,000

    c. $220,000

    d. $250,000

SIMULATION PROBLEMS

Simulation Problem 1   (10 to 15 minutes)

Situation				
	Anderson vs. Harvest	Anderson vs. Beach	Anderson vs. Edge	Foreclosure Proceeds

On June 1, 2002, Anderson bought a one-family house from Beach for $240,000. At the time of the purchase, the house had a market value of $200,000 and the land was valued at $40,000. Anderson assumed the recorded $150,000 mortgage Beach owed Long Bank, gave a $70,000 mortgage to Rogers Loan Co., and paid $20,000 cash. Rogers did not record its mortgage. Rogers did not know about the Long mortgage.

Beach gave Anderson a quitclaim deed that failed to mention a recorded easement on the property held by Dalton, the owner of the adjacent piece of property. Anderson purchased a title insurance policy from Edge Title Insurance Co. Edge's policy neither disclosed nor excepted Dalton's easement.

On August 1, 2003, Anderson borrowed $30,000 from Forrest Finance to have a swimming pool dug. Anderson gave Forrest a $30,000 mortgage on the property. Forrest, knowing about the Long mortgage but not the Rogers mortgage, recorded its mortgage on August 10, 2003. After the digging began, Dalton sued to stop the work claiming violation of the easement. The court decided in Dalton's favor.

At the time of the purchase, Anderson had taken out two fire insurance policies; a $120,000 face value policy with Harvest Fire Insurance Co., and a $60,000 face value policy with Grant Fire Insurance Corp. Both policies contained a standard 80% coinsurance clause.

On December 1, 2003, a fire caused $180,000 damage to the house. At that time, the house had a market value of $250,000. Harvest and Grant refused to honor the policies, claiming that the house was underinsured.

Anderson made no mortgage payments after the fire and on April 4, 2004, after the house had been rebuilt, the mortgages were foreclosed. The balances due for principal and accrued interest were as follows: Long, $140,000; Rogers, $65,000; and Forrest, $28,000. At a foreclosure sale, the house and land were sold. After payment of all expenses, $200,000 of the proceeds remained for distribution. As a result of the above events, the following actions took place:

• Anderson sued Harvest and Grant for the face values of the fire insurance policies.
• Anderson sued Beach for failing to mention Dalton's easement in the quitclaim deed.
• Anderson sued Edge for failing to disclose Dalton's easement.
• Long, Rogers, and Forrest all demanded full payment of their mortgages from the proceeds of the foreclosure sale.

The preceding took place in a notice-race jurisdiction.

	Anderson vs. Harvest			
Situation		Anderson vs. Beach	Anderson vs. Edge	Foreclosure Proceeds

Items 1 through 3 relate to Anderson's suit against Harvest and Grant. For each item, select from List I the dollar amount Anderson will receive.

List I

A.	$0	G.	$ 96,000
B.	$ 20,000	H.	$108,000
C.	$ 48,000	I.	$120,000
D.	$ 54,000	J.	$144,000
E.	$ 60,000	K.	$162,000
F.	$ 80,000	L.	$180,000

(A) (B) (C) (D) (E) (F) (G) (H) (I) (J) (K) (L)

1. What will be the dollar amount of Anderson's total fire insurance recovery?   ○ ○ ○ ○ ○ ○ ○ ○ ○ ○ ○ ○

2. What dollar amount will be payable by Harvest?   ○ ○ ○ ○ ○ ○ ○ ○ ○ ○ ○ ○

3. What dollar amount will be payable by Grant?   ○ ○ ○ ○ ○ ○ ○ ○ ○ ○ ○ ○

		Anderson vs. Beach		
Situation	Anderson vs. Harvest		Anderson vs. Edge	Foreclosure Proceeds

Items 1 through 3 relate to Anderson's suit against Beach. For each item, determine whether that statement is True or False.

					True	False
1. Anderson will win the suit against Beach.					○	○
2. A quitclaim deed conveys only the grantor's interest in the property.					○	○
3. A warranty deed protects the purchaser against any adverse title claim against the property.					○	○

Situation	Anderson vs. Harvest	Anderson vs. Beach	Anderson vs. Edge	Foreclosure Proceeds

Items 1 through 3 relate to Anderson's suit against Edge. For each item, determine whether that statement is True or False.

	True	False
1. Anderson will win the suit against Edge.	○	○
2. Edge's policy should insure against all title defects of record.	○	○
3. Edge's failure to disclose Dalton's easement voids Anderson's contract with Beach.	○	○

Situation	Anderson vs. Harvest	Anderson vs. Beach	Anderson vs. Edge	Foreclosure Proceeds

Items 1 through 3 relate to the demands Long, Rogers, and Forrest have made to have their mortgages satisfied out of the foreclosure proceeds. For each item, select from List II the dollar amount to be paid.

List II
A. $0
B. $ 28,000
C. $ 32,000
D. $ 65,000
E. $107,000
F. $135,000
G. $140,000

	(A)	(B)	(C)	(D)	(E)	(F)	(G)
1. What dollar amount of the foreclosure proceeds will Long receive?	○	○	○	○	○	○	○
2. What dollar amount of the foreclosure proceeds will Rogers receive?	○	○	○	○	○	○	○
3. What dollar amount of the foreclosure proceeds will Forrest receive?	○	○	○	○	○	○	○

Simulation Problem 2   (10 to 15 minutes)

Situation	
	Analysis

On January 12, 2004, Frank, Inc. contracted in writing to purchase a factory building from Henderson for $250,000 cash. Closing took place on March 15, 2004. Henderson had purchased the building in 1997 for $225,000 and had, at that time, taken out a $180,000 fire insurance policy with Summit Insurance Co.

On January 15, 2004, Frank took out a $140,000 fire insurance policy with Unity Insurance Co. and a $70,000 fire insurance policy with Imperial Insurance, Inc.

On March 16, 2004, a fire caused $150,000 damage to the building. At that time the building had a market value of $250,000. All fire insurance policies contain a standard 80% coinsurance clause. The insurance carriers have refused any payment to Frank or Henderson alleging lack of insurable interest and insufficient coverage. Frank and Henderson have sued to collect on the policies.

Analysis
Situation

Items 1 through 6 relate to the suits by Frank and Henderson. For each item, determine whether the statement is True or False.

	True	*False*
1. Frank had an insurable interest at the time the Unity and Imperial policies were taken out.	○	○
2. Henderson had an insurable interest at the time of the fire.	○	○
3. Assuming Frank had an insurable interest, Frank's coverage would be insufficient under the Unity and Imperial coinsurance clauses.	○	○
4. Assuming Henderson had an insurable interest, Henderson's coverage would be insufficient under the Summit coinsurance clause.	○	○
5. Assuming only Frank had an insurable interest, Frank will recover $100,000 from Unity and $50,000 from Imperial.	○	○
6. Assuming only Henderson had an insurable interest, Henderson will recover $135,000 from Summit.	○	○

1.	a	__ __	3.	c	__ __	5.	c	__ __	7.	c	__ __	1st: __/8 = __%
2.	a	__ __	4.	b	__ __	6.	b	__ __	8.	b	__ __	2nd: __/8 = __%

MULTIPLE-CHOICE ANSWER EXPLANATIONS

B.6. Insurable Interest

1. (a)   In the case of property insurance, the insurable interest must exist when the loss occurs. It need not exist when the policy is issued. Therefore, answer (b) is incorrect. Answers (c) and (d) are incorrect because there are no such requirements that the property be owned in fee simple or by individuals.

2. (a)   To have an insurable interest in property, there must be both a legal interest and a possibility of pecuniary loss. Although a legal interest may involve ownership or a security interest, general creditors do not have the requisite interest to have an insurable interest. Answer (b) is incorrect because a mortgagee has an insurable interest for the mortgage balance still owed. Answer (c) is incorrect because Brown has an insurable interest in key company personnel whose death could result in pecuniary loss for Brown. Answer (d) is incorrect because Brown has an insurable interest in his partner whose death could cause him great monetary loss.

3. (c)   An insurable interest in property exists if the insured has both a legal interest in the property and the possibility of incurring a pecuniary loss. The legal interest may be ownership or a security interest. A corporate retailer has an ownership interest in its inventory, and the possibility of incurring a monetary loss. A partner also has an ownership interest in partnership property, with the possibility of incurring a monetary loss.

C. Subrogation

4. (b)   Once the insurance company pays its insured, Massaro, it steps into Massaro's shoes and obtains the same rights against third parties that Massaro had. Since Lux was at fault in this accident, the insurance company has rights against Lux as well as any insurance company that has insured Lux. Answer (a) is incorrect because the insurance company can nevertheless recover from third parties based on the right of subrogation. Answer (c) is incorrect because the insurance company has the right to collect from Lux as well as an insurer. Answer (d) is incorrect because the relevant concept is the right of subrogation, not contribution.

E. Fire Insurance

5. (c)   An important element of a property insurance contract is the existence of an insurable interest. The insurable interest requirement is met when an entity has both a legal interest in the property and a possibility of monetary loss if the property is damaged. Since Merit still owns the office building at the time of the fire, they fulfill both these requirements. Papco also has an insurable interest which began on February 1 when they entered into the contract to purchase the building. Papco's legal interest results from their contract to purchase the building. Papco's monetary interest results from their potential loss of future use of the building. Thus, in this situation, both Papco and Merit have an insurable interest.

E.6. Coinsurance Clause

6. (b)   Although Clark has insurance coverage exceeding the fair value of the warehouse, he may only recover the actual amount of his loss. The coinsurance clause does not apply when the insured property is totally destroyed. Fair Insurance will pay 150/225 of the $200,000 loss, or $133,333, while Zone Insurance will pay 75/225 of the $200,000 loss, or $66,667. Thus, Clark will receive a total of $200,000 from Fair and Zone.

7. (c)   The recoverable loss is calculated using the coinsurance formula.

$$\text{Actual loss} \times \frac{\text{Amount of insurance}}{\text{Coinsurance \%} \times \text{FMV of property at time of loss}}$$

The amount recoverable from Owners is calculated as follows:

$$\$180,000 \times \frac{\$150,000}{80\% \times \$250,000} = \$135,000$$

8. (b)   When property is covered by a coinsurance clause, the insured party agrees to maintain insurance equal to a given percentage of the value of the property, usually 80%. If the percentage of coverage is less than the specified percentage and partial destruction of the property occurs, then the insured will be liable for a portion of the loss. However, a coinsurance clause applies only when there has been partial destruction of property. If the insured property is totally destroyed, the coinsurance clause does not apply and the insured party will recover the face value of the insurance policy. Thus, Pod will recover $150,000 from Owners Insurance Co. and $50,000 from Group Insurance Co. for a total of $200,000.

SOLUTIONS TO SIMULATION PROBLEMS

Simulation Problem 1

Situation	Anderson vs. Harvest	Anderson vs. Beach	Anderson vs. Edge	Foreclosure Proceeds

	(A)	(B)	(C)	(D)	(E)	(F)	(G)	(H)	(I)	(J)	(K)	(L)
1. What will be the dollar amount of Anderson's total fire insurance recovery?	○	○	○	○	○	○	○	○	○	○	●	○
2. What dollar amount will be payable by Harvest?	○	○	○	○	○	○	○	●	○	○	○	○
3. What dollar amount will be payable by Grant?	○	○	○	●	○	○	○	○	○	○	○	○

Explanation of solutions

1.   (K) In order to calculate the dollar amount of Anderson's total fire insurance recovery, use the coinsurance clause formula, adding together the amount of insurance for both Harvest and Grant, as follows:

$$\text{Recovery} = \text{Actual loss} \times \frac{\text{Amount of insurance}}{\text{Coinsurance \%} \times \text{FMV of property at time of loss}}$$

$$\text{Recovery} = \$180,000 \times \frac{\$120,000 + \$60,000}{80\% \times \$250,000}$$

$$\text{Recovery} = \$162,000$$

2.   (H) In order to calculate the dollar amount that will be payable to Harvest only, use the coinsurance clause formula.

$$\text{Recovery} = \$180,000 \times \frac{\$120,000}{80\% \times \$250,000}$$

$$\text{Recovery} = \$108,000$$

3.   (D) In order to calculate the dollar amount payable to Grant only, use the same coinsurance clause formula.

$$\$180,000 \times \frac{\$60,000}{80\% \times \$250,000} = \$54,000$$

Situation	Anderson vs. Harvest	Anderson vs. Beach	Anderson vs. Edge	Foreclosure Proceeds

	True	False
1. Anderson will win the suit against Beach.	○	●
2. A quitclaim deed conveys only the grantor's interest in the property.	●	○
3. A warranty deed protects the purchaser against any adverse title claim against the property.	●	○

Explanation of solutions

1.   (F) Since Beach had given Anderson a quitclaim deed, Anderson loses in the suit against Beach for failing to mention Dalton's easement in the quitclaim deed.

2.   (T) Unlike a warranty deed, a quitclaim deed conveys only whatever interest in land the grantor has. No warranty concerning title or easements is given.

3.   (T) A warranty deed contains covenants that generally protect the grantee against any adverse title claim against the property.

Situation	Anderson vs. Harvest	Anderson vs. Beach	Anderson vs. Edge	Foreclosure Proceeds

	True	False
1. Anderson will win the suit against Edge.	●	○
2. Edge's policy should insure against all title defects of record.	●	○
3. Edge's failure to disclose Dalton's easement voids Anderson's contract with Beach.	○	●

Explanation of solutions

1. (T) This statement is true because Edge failed to mention a recorded easement on the property. Note that when Edge failed to disclose the recorded easement, this allows Anderson to recover from Edge but does not void the contract between Anderson and the seller of the property.

2. (T) Standard title insurance policies generally insure against all title defects of record. This would be true of the title insurance policy that Anderson purchased from Edge.

3. (F) Since Edge failed to disclose the recorded easement, this allows Anderson to recover from Edge. However, it does not void the contract between Anderson and Beach.

Situation	Anderson vs. Harvest	Anderson vs. Beach	Anderson vs. Edge	Foreclosure Proceeds

	(A)	(B)	(C)	(D)	(E)	(F)	(G)
1. What dollar amount of the foreclosure proceeds will Long receive?	○	○	○	○	○	○	●
2. What dollar amount of the foreclosure proceeds will Rogers receive?	○	○	●	○	○	○	○
3. What dollar amount of the foreclosure proceeds will Forrest receive?	○	●	○	○	○	○	○

Explanation of solutions

1. (G) Under a notice-race statute, the subsequent good-faith mortgagee wins over a previous mortgagee only if s/he also records first. In this fact pattern, Long has the first priority because its mortgage was recorded before mortgages were given to Forrest or Rogers. Since $200,000 remained to be distributed, Long gets all of its $140,000.

2. (C) Forrest has the second priority because although its mortgage was granted after Rogers, Rogers did not record its mortgage and Forrest was unaware of it when its mortgage was given. Therefore, Rogers has the third priority. After Long received his $140,000, there is $60,000 left. Forrest has second priority and will receive his full $28,000. Since there is not enough left to pay Rodgers the full $65,000, Rogers only gets the balance remaining of $32,000.

3. (B) Forrest has the second priority because although its mortgage was granted after Rogers, Rogers did not record its mortgage and Forrest was unaware of it when its mortgage was given. Therefore, Rogers has the third priority. After Long received his $140,000, there is $60,000 left. Forrest has second priority and will receive his full $28,000.

Simulation Problem 2

Situation	Analysis

	True	False
1. Frank had an insurable interest at the time the Unity and Imperial policies were taken out.	●	○
2. Henderson had an insurable interest at the time of the fire.	○	●
3. Assuming Frank had an insurable interest, Frank's coverage would be insufficient under the Unity and Imperial coinsurance clauses.	○	●
4. Assuming Henderson had an insurable interest, Henderson's coverage would be insufficient under the Summit coinsurance clause.	●	○
5. Assuming only Frank had an insurable interest, Frank will recover $100,000 from Unity and $50,000 from Imperial.	●	○
6. Assuming only Henderson had an insurable interest, Henderson will recover $135,000 from Summit.	●	○

Explanation of solutions

1. **(T)** In property, there must be both a legal interest and a possibility of pecuniary loss. This insurable interest need not be present at the inception of the policy so long as it is present at the time of loss. A contract to purchase or the possession of property can give an insurable interest. Frank had an insurable interest at the time the Unity and Imperial policies were taken out as Frank contracted to purchase the property prior to taking out the insurance policies.

2. **(F)** A contract to purchase or possession of the property can give an insurable interest. The closing of the sale of the property to Frank took place on March 15, 2004. At this point Henderson no longer had an insurable interest as he no longer had possession nor had he contracted to repurchase the property. Therefore, when the fire occurred on March 16, 2004, Henderson did not have an insurable interest.

3. **(F)** The recoverable loss is calculated using the coinsurance formula.

$$\text{Actual loss} \times \frac{\text{Amount of insurance}}{\text{Coinsurance \%} \times \text{FMV of property at time of loss}}$$

The amount recoverable from Unity is calculated as follows:

$$\$150,000 \times \frac{\$140,000}{80\% \times \$250,000} = \$105,000$$

The amount recoverable from Imperial is calculated as follows:

$$\$150,000 \times \frac{\$70,000}{80\% \times \$250,000} = \$52,500$$

The total amount recoverable from the combined insurance policies is therefore sufficient to cover the loss.

4. **(T)** The recoverable loss is calculated using the coinsurance formula.

$$\text{Actual loss} \times \frac{\text{Amount of insurance}}{\text{Coinsurance \%} \times \text{FMV of property at time of loss}}$$

The amount recoverable from Summit is calculated as follows:

$$\$150,000 \times \frac{\$180,000}{80\% \times \$250,000} = \$135,000$$

Thus, Henderson's coverage would be insufficient.

5. **(T)** The recoverable loss is calculated using the coinsurance formula.

$$\text{Actual loss} \times \frac{\text{Amount of insurance}}{\text{Coinsurance \%} \times \text{FMV of property at time of loss}}$$

The amount recoverable from Unity is calculated as follows:

$$\$150,000 \times \frac{\$140,000}{80\% \times \$250,000} = \$105,000$$

The amount recoverable from Imperial is calculated as follows:

$$\$150,000 \times \frac{\$70,000}{80\% \times \$250,000} = \$52,500$$

Combined insurance policies are sufficient but only $150,000 can be recovered. Therefore, Frank can only recover proportionately from Unity and Imperial as follows:

$$\text{Unity} - \frac{\$140,000}{\$140,000 + \$70,000} = 67\%$$

$$\text{Unity} - \frac{\$70,000}{\$140,000 + \$70,000} = 33\%$$

Therefore, Frank will receive $100,000 (67% × $150,000 loss) from Unity and $50,000 (33% × $150,000 loss) from Imperial.

6. **(T)** The recoverable loss is calculated using the coinsurance formula.

$$\text{Actual loss} \times \frac{\text{Amount of insurance}}{\text{Coinsurance \%} \times \text{FMV of property at time of loss}}$$

The amount recoverable from Summit is calculated as follows:

$$\$150,000 \times \frac{\$180,000}{80\% \times \$250,000} = \$135,000$$

6 FEDERAL TAXATION

MULTIPLE-CHOICE QUESTIONS (1-219)

1. Richard Brown, who retired on May 31, 2009, receives a monthly pension benefit of $700 payable for life. His life expectancy at the date of retirement is ten years. The first pension check was received on June 15, 2009. During his years of employment, Brown contributed $12,000 to the cost of his company's pension plan. How much of the pension amounts received may Brown exclude from taxable income for the years 2009, 2010, and 2011?

	2009	2010	2011
a.	$0	$0	$0
b.	$4,900	$4,900	$4,900
c.	$ 700	$1,200	$1,200
d.	$4,900	$8,400	$8,400

2. Fuller was the owner and beneficiary of a $200,000 life insurance policy on a parent. Fuller sold the policy to Decker, for $25,000. Decker paid a total of $40,000 in premiums. Upon the death of the parent, what amount must Decker include in gross income?
- a. $0
- b. $135,000
- c. $160,000
- d. $200,000

3. Seymour Thomas named his wife, Penelope, the beneficiary of a $100,000 (face amount) insurance policy on his life. The policy provided that upon his death, the proceeds would be paid to Penelope with interest over her present life expectancy, which was calculated at twenty-five years. Seymour died during 2010, and Penelope received a payment of $5,200 from the insurance company. What amount should she include in her gross income for 2010?
- a. $ 200
- b. $1,200
- c. $4,200
- d. $5,200

4. Under a "cafeteria plan" maintained by an employer,
- a. Participation must be restricted to employees, and their spouses and minor children.
- b. At least three years of service are required before an employee can participate in the plan.
- c. Participants may select their own menu of benefits.
- d. Provision may be made for deferred compensation other than 401(k) plans.

5. David Autrey was covered by an $80,000 group-term life insurance policy of which his wife was the beneficiary. Autrey's employer paid the entire cost of the policy, for which the uniform annual premium was $8 per $1,000 of coverage. Autrey died during 2010, and his wife was paid the $80,000 proceeds of the insurance policy. What amount of group-term life insurance proceeds must be included in gross income by Autrey's widow?
- a. $0
- b. $30,000
- c. $50,000
- d. $80,000

6. Howard O'Brien, an employee of Ogden Corporation, died on June 30, 2010. During July, Ogden made employee death payments (which do not represent the proceeds of life insurance) of $10,000 to his widow, and $10,000 to his fifteen-year-old son. What amounts should be included in gross income by the widow and son in their respective tax returns for 2010?

	Widow	Son
a.	$ 5,000	$ 5,000
b.	$ 5,000	$10,000
c.	$ 7,500	$ 7,500
d.	$10,000	$10,000

7. John Budd files a joint return with his wife. Budd's employer pays 100% of the cost of all employees' group-term life insurance under a qualified plan. Under this plan, the maximum amount of tax-free coverage that may be provided for Budd by his employer is
- a. $100,000
- b. $ 50,000
- c. $ 10,000
- d. $ 5,000

8. During the current year Hal Leff sustained a serious injury in the course of his employment. As a result of this injury, Hal received the following payments during the year:

Workers' compensation	$2,400
Reimbursement from his employer's accident and health plan for medical expenses paid by Hal and not deducted by him	1,800
Damages for physical injuries	8,000

The amount to be included in Hal's gross income for the current year should be
- a. $12,200
- b. $ 8,000
- c. $ 1,800
- d. $0

9. James Martin received the following compensation and fringe benefits from his employer during 2009:

Salary	$50,000
Year-end bonus	10,000
Medical insurance premiums paid by employer	1,000
Reimbursement of qualified moving expenses	5,000

What amount of the preceding payments should be included in Martin's 2009 gross income?
- a. $60,000
- b. $61,000
- c. $65,000
- d. $66,000

10. On February 1, 2009, Hall learned that he was bequeathed 500 shares of common stock under his father's will. Hall's father had paid $2,500 for the stock in 2005. Fair market value of the stock on February 1, 2009, the date of his father's death, was $4,000 and had increased to $5,500 six months later. The executor of the estate elected the alternate valuation date for estate tax purposes. Hall sold the stock for $4,500 on June 1, 2009, the date that the executor distributed the stock to him. How much income should Hall include in his 2009 individual income tax return for the inheritance of the 500 shares of stock that he received from his father's estate?
- a. $5,500
- b. $4,000
- c. $2,500
- d. $0

11. In 2010, Gail Judd received the following dividends from

Benefit Life Insurance Co., on Gail's life insurance policy (Total dividends received have not yet exceeded accumulated premiums paid) $100
Safe National Bank, on bank's common stock 300
Roe Mfg. Corp., a Delaware corporation, on preferred stock 500

What amount of dividend income should Gail report in her 2010 income tax return?

a. $900
b. $800
c. $500
d. $300

12. Amy Finch had the following cash receipts during 2010:

Dividend from a mutual insurance company on a life insurance policy $500
Dividend on listed corporation stock; payment date by corporation was 12/30/09, but Amy received the dividend in the mail on 1/2/10 875

Total dividends received to date on the life insurance policy do not exceed the aggregated premiums paid by Amy. How much should Amy report for dividend income for 2010?

a. $1,375
b. $ 875
c. $ 500
d. $0

13. Jack and Joan Mitchell, married taxpayers and residents of a separate property state, elect to file a joint return for 2010 during which they received the following dividends:

| | Received by | |
	Jack	Joan
Alert Corporation (a qualified, domestic corporation)	$400	$ 50
Canadian Mines, Inc. (a Canadian company)		300
Eternal Life Mutual Insurance Company (dividends on life insurance policy)		200

Total dividends received to date on the life insurance policy do not exceed cumulative premiums paid. For 2010, what amount should the Mitchells report on their joint return as dividend income?

a. $550
b. $600
c. $750
d. $800

14. During 2008, Karen purchased 100 shares of preferred stock of Boling Corp. for $5,500. During 2010, Karen received a stock dividend of ten additional shares of Boling Corp. preferred stock. On the date the preferred stock was distributed, it had a fair market value of $60 per share. What is Karen's basis in the ten shares of preferred stock that she received as a dividend?

a. $0
b. $500
c. $550
d. $600

15. Micro Corp., a calendar-year accrual-basis corporation, purchased a five-year, 8%, $100,000 taxable corporate bond for $108,530 on July 1, 2010, the date the bond was issued. The bond paid interest semiannually. Micro elected to amortize the bond premium. For Micro's 2010 tax return, the bond premium amortization for 2010 should be

I. Computed under the constant yield to maturity method.
II. Treated as an offset to the interest income on the bond.

a. I only.
b. II only.
c. Both I and II.
d. Neither I nor II.

16. In a tax year where the taxpayer pays qualified education expenses, interest income on the redemption of qualified US Series EE Bonds may be excluded from gross income. The exclusion is subject to a modified gross income limitation and a limit of aggregate bond proceeds in excess of qualified higher education expenses. Which of the following is(are) true?

I. The exclusion applies for education expenses incurred by the taxpayer, the taxpayer's spouse, or any person whom the taxpayer may claim as a dependent for the year.
II. "Otherwise qualified higher education expenses" must be reduced by qualified scholarships not includible in gross income.

a. I only.
b. II only.
c. Both I and II.
d. Neither I nor II.

17. During 2010 Kay received interest income as follows:

On US Treasury certificates $4,000
On refund of 2008 federal income tax 500

The total amount of interest subject to tax in Kay's 2010 tax return is

a. $4,500
b. $4,000
c. $ 500
d. $0

18. Charles and Marcia are married cash-basis taxpayers. In 2010, they had interest income as follows:

- $500 interest on federal income tax refund.
- $600 interest on state income tax refund.
- $800 interest on federal government obligations.
- $1,000 interest on state government obligations.

What amount of interest income is taxable on Charles and Marcia's 2010 joint income tax return?

a. $ 500
b. $1,100
c. $1,900
d. $2,900

19. Clark bought Series EE US Savings Bonds in 2010. Redemption proceeds will be used for payment of college tuition for Clark's dependent child. One of the conditions that must be met for tax exemption of accumulated interest on these bonds is that the

a. Purchaser of the bonds must be the sole owner of the bonds (or joint owner with his or her spouse).
b. Bonds must be bought by a parent (or both parents) and put in the name of the dependent child.
c. Bonds must be bought by the owner of the bonds before the owner reaches the age of twenty-four.
d. Bonds must be transferred to the college for redemption by the college rather than by the owner of the bonds.

20. Daniel Kelly received interest income from the following sources in 2010:

New York Port Authority bonds	$1,000
Puerto Rico Commonwealth bonds	1,800

What portion of such interest is tax exempt?
- a. $0
- b. $1,000
- c. $1,800
- d. $2,800

21. In 2010 Uriah Stone received the following interest payments:

- Interest of $400 on refund of federal income tax for 2008.
- Interest of $300 on award for personal injuries sustained in an automobile accident during 2007.
- Interest of $1,500 on municipal bonds.
- Interest of $1,000 on United States savings bonds (Series HH).

What amount, if any, should Stone report as interest income on his 2010 tax return?
- a. $0
- b. $ 700
- c. $1,700
- d. $3,200

22. For the year ended December 31, 2009, Don Raff earned $1,000 interest at Ridge Savings Bank on a certificate of deposit scheduled to mature in 2010. In January 2010, before filing his 2009 income tax return, Raff incurred a forfeiture penalty of $500 for premature withdrawal of the funds. Raff should treat this $500 forfeiture penalty as a
- a. Reduction of interest earned in 2009, so that only $500 of such interest is taxable on Raff's 2009 return.
- b. Deduction from 2010 adjusted gross income, deductible only if Raff itemizes his deductions for 2010.
- c. Penalty **not** deductible for tax purposes.
- d. Deduction from gross income in arriving at 2010 adjusted gross income.

23. Which payment(s) is(are) included in a recipient's gross income?

I. Payment to a graduate assistant for a part-time teaching assignment at a university. Teaching is not a requirement toward obtaining the degree.
II. A grant to a Ph.D. candidate for his participation in a university-sponsored research project for the benefit of the university.

- a. I only.
- b. II only.
- c. Both I and II.
- d. Neither I nor II.

24. Majors, a candidate for a graduate degree, received the following scholarship awards from the university in 2010:

- $10,000 for tuition, fees, books, and supplies required for courses.
- $2,000 stipend for research services required by the scholarship.

What amount of the scholarship awards should Majors include as taxable income in 2010?
- a. $12,000
- b. $10,000

- c. $ 2,000
- d. $0

25. In July 1995, Dan Farley leased a building to Robert Shelter for a period of fifteen years at a monthly rental of $1,000 with no option to renew. At that time the building had a remaining estimated useful life of twenty years.

Prior to taking possession of the building, Shelter made improvements at a cost of $18,000. These improvements had an estimated useful life of twenty years at the commencement of the lease period. The lease expired on June 30, 2010, at which point the improvements had a fair market value of $2,000. The amount that Farley, the landlord, should include in his gross income for 2010 is
- a. $ 6,000
- b. $ 8,000
- c. $10,000
- d. $18,500

26. Bob and Sue Stewart were divorced in 2008. Under the terms of their divorce decree, Bob paid alimony to Sue at the rate of $50,000 in 2008, $20,000 in 2009, and nothing in 2010. What amount of alimony recapture must be included in Bob's gross income for 2010?
- a. $0
- b. $23,283
- c. $30,000
- d. $32,500

27. Which of the following conditions must be present in a post-1984 divorce agreement for a payment to qualify as deductible alimony?

I. Payments must be in cash.
II. The payment must end at the recipient's death

- a. I only.
- b. II only.
- c. Both I and II.
- d. Neither I nor II.

28. Darr, an employee of Sorce C corporation, is not a shareholder. Which of the following would be included in a taxpayer's gross income?
- a. Employer-provided medical insurance coverage under a health plan.
- b. A $10,000 gift from the taxpayer's grandparents.
- c. The fair market value of land that the taxpayer inherited from an uncle.
- d. The dividend income on shares of stock that the taxpayer received for services rendered.

29. With regard to the inclusion of social security benefits in gross income for the 2010 tax year, which of the following statements is correct?
- a. The social security benefits in excess of modified adjusted gross income are included in gross income.
- b. The social security benefits in excess of one half the modified adjusted gross income are included in gross income.
- c. Eighty-five percent of the social security benefits is the maximum amount of benefits to be included in gross income.
- d. The social security benefits in excess of the modified adjusted gross income over $32,000 are included in gross income.

30. Perle, a dentist, billed Wood $600 for dental services. Wood paid Perle $200 cash and built a bookcase for Perle's office in full settlement of the bill. Wood sells comparable bookcases for $350. What amount should Perle include in taxable income as a result of this transaction?

- a. $0
- b. $200
- c. $550
- d. $600

31. John and Mary were divorced in 2009. The divorce decree provides that John pay alimony of $10,000 per year, to be reduced by 20% on their child's 18th birthday. During 2010, John paid $7,000 directly to Mary and $3,000 to Spring College for Mary's tuition. What amount of these payments should be reported as income in Mary's 2010 income tax return?

- a. $ 5,600
- b. $ 8,000
- c. $ 8,600
- d. $10,000

32. Clark filed Form 1040EZ for the 2009 taxable year. In July 2010, Clark received a state income tax refund of $900, plus interest of $10, for overpayment of 2009 state income tax. What amount of the state tax refund and interest is taxable in Clark's 2010 federal income tax return?

- a. $0
- b. $ 10
- c. $900
- d. $910

33. Hall, a divorced person and custodian of her twelve-year-old child, submitted the following information to the CPA who prepared her 2009 return:

The divorce agreement, executed in 2006, provides for Hall to receive $3,000 per month, of which $600 is designated as child support. After the child reaches age eighteen, the monthly payments are to be reduced to $2,400 and are to continue until remarriage or death. However, for the year 2009, Hall received a total of only $5,000 from her former husband. Hall paid an attorney $2,000 in 2009 in a suit to collect the alimony owed.

What amount should be reported in Hall's 2009 return as alimony income?

- a. $28,800
- b. $ 5,000
- c. $ 3,000
- d. $0

34. Lee, an attorney, uses the cash receipts and disbursements method of reporting. In 2009, a client gave Lee 500 shares of a listed corporation's stock in full satisfaction of a $10,000 legal fee the client owed to Lee. This stock had a fair market value of $8,000 on the date it was given to Lee. The client's basis for this stock was $6,000. Lee sold the stock for cash in January 2010. In Lee's 2009 income tax return, what amount of income should be reported in connection with the receipt of the stock?

- a. $10,000
- b. $ 8,000
- c. $ 6,000
- d. $0

35. In 2005, Ross was granted an incentive stock option (ISO) by her employer as part of an executive compensation package. Ross exercised the ISO in 2008 and sold the stock in 2010 at a gain. Ross was subject to regular tax for the year in which the

- a. ISO was granted.
- b. ISO was exercised.
- c. Stock was sold.
- d. Employer claimed a compensation deduction for the ISO.

36. Ed and Ann Ross were divorced in January 2010. In accordance with the divorce decree, Ed transferred the title in their home to Ann in 2010. The home, which had a fair market value of $150,000, was subject to a $50,000 mortgage that had twenty more years to run. Monthly mortgage payments amount to $1,000. Under the terms of settlement, Ed is obligated to make the mortgage payments on the home for the full remaining twenty-year term of the indebtedness, regardless of how long Ann lives. Ed made twelve mortgage payments in 2010. What amount is taxable as alimony in Ann's 2010 return?

- a. $0
- b. $ 12,000
- c. $100,000
- d. $112,000

37. Income in respect of a cash-basis decedent

- a. Covers income earned and collected after a decedent's death.
- b. Receives a stepped-up basis in the decedent's estate.
- c. Includes a bonus earned before the taxpayer's death but not collected until after death.
- d. Must be included in the decedent's final income tax return.

38. The following information is available for Ann Drury for 2010:

Salary	$36,000
Premiums paid by employer on group-term life insurance in excess of $50,000	500
Proceeds from state lottery	5,000

How much should Drury report as gross income on her 2010 tax return?

- a. $36,000
- b. $36,500
- c. $41,000
- d. $41,500

39. Mr. and Mrs. Alvin Charak took a foster child, Robert, into their home in 2010. A state welfare agency paid the Charaks $3,900 during the year for related expenses. Actual expenses incurred by the Charaks during 2010 in caring for Robert amounted to $3,000. The remaining $900 was spent by the Charaks in 2010 towards their own personal expenses. How much of the foster child payments is taxable income to the Charaks in 2010?

- a. $0
- b. $ 900
- c. $2,900
- d. $3,900

40. Pierre, a headwaiter, received tips totaling $2,000 in December 2009. On January 5, 2010, Pierre reported this tip income to his employer in the required written statement. At what amount, and in which year, should this tip income be included in Pierre's gross income?

a. $2,000 in 2009.
b. $2,000 in 2009.
c. $1,000 in 2009, and $1,000 in 2010.
d. $ 167 in 2009, and $1,833 in 2010.

41. With regard to the alimony deduction in connection with a 2010 divorce, which one of the following statements is correct?

a.   Alimony is deductible by the payor spouse, and includible by the payee spouse, to the extent that payment is contingent on the status of the divorced couple's children.
b.   The divorced couple may be members of the same household at the time alimony is paid, provided that the persons do not live as husband and wife.
c.   Alimony payments must terminate on the death of the payee spouse.
d.   Alimony may be paid either in cash or in property.

42. In 2010, Joan accepted and received a $10,000 award for outstanding civic achievement. Joan was selected without any action on her part, and no future services are expected of her as a condition of receiving the award. What amount should Joan include in her 2010 adjusted gross income in connection with this award?

a. $0
b. $ 4,000
c. $ 5,000
d. $10,000

43. In 2009, Emil Gow won $5,000 in a state lottery. Also in 2009, Emil spent $400 for the purchase of lottery tickets. Emil elected the standard deduction on his 2009 income tax return. The amount of lottery winnings that should be included in Emil's 2009 taxable income is

a. $0
b. $2,000
c. $4,600
d. $5,000

44. Lake Corp., an accrual-basis calendar-year corporation, had the following 2010 receipts:

Advanced rental payments where the lease ends in 2012	$125,000
Lease cancellation payment from a five-year lease tenant	50,000

Lake had no restrictions on the use of the advanced rental payments and renders no services. What amount of income should Lake report on its 2010 tax return?

a. $0
b. $ 50,000
c. $125,000
d. $175,000

45. Paul Bristol, a cash-basis taxpayer, owns an apartment building. The following information was available for 2009:

- An analysis of the 2009 bank deposit slips showed recurring monthly rents received totaling $50,000.
- On March 1, 2009, the tenant in apartment 2B paid Bristol $2,000 to cancel the lease expiring on December 31, 2009.
- The lease of the tenant in apartment 3A expired on December 31, 2009, and the tenant left improvements valued at $1,000. The improvements were not in lieu of any rent required to have been paid.

In computing net income from that apartment building for 2009, Bristol should report gross income of

a. $50,000
b. $51,000
c. $52,000
d. $53,000

46. Emil Gow owns a two-family house that has two identical apartments. Gow lives in one apartment and rents out the other. In 2009, the rental apartment was fully occupied and Gow received $7,200 in rent. During the year ended December 31, 2009, Gow paid the following:

Real estate taxes	$6,400
Painting of rental apartment	800
Annual fire insurance premium	600

In 2009, depreciation for the entire house was determined to be $5,000. What amount should Gow include in his adjusted gross income for 2009?

a. $2,900
b. $ 800
c. $ 400
d. $ 100

47. Amy Finch had the following cash receipts during 2010:

Net rent on vacant lot used by a car dealer (lessee pays all taxes, insurance, and other expenses on the lot)	$6,000
Advance rent from lessee of above vacant lot, such advance to be applied against rent for the last two months of the five-year lease in 2014	1,000

How much should Amy include in her 2010 taxable income for rent?

a. $7,000
b. $6,800
c. $6,200
d. $6,000

48. Royce Rentals, Inc., an accrual-basis taxpayer, reported rent receivable of $25,000 and $35,000 in its 2010 and 2009 balance sheets, respectively. During 2010, Royce received $50,000 in rent payments and $5,000 in nonrefundable rent deposits. In Royce's 2010 corporate income tax return, what amount should Royce include as rent revenue?

a. $45,000
b. $50,000
c. $55,000
d. $65,000

49. John Budd is single, with no dependents. During 2009, John received wages of $11,000 and state unemployment compensation benefits of $2,000. He had no other source of income. The amount of state unemployment compensation benefits that should be included in John's 2009 adjusted gross income is

a. $2,000
b. $1,000
c. $ 500
d. $0

50. A cash-basis taxpayer should report gross income

a.   Only for the year in which income is actually received in cash.
b.   Only for the year in which income is actually received whether in cash or in property.

c. For the year in which income is either actually or constructively received in cash only.

d. For the year in which income is either actually or constructively received, whether in cash or in property.

51. Which of the following taxpayers may use the cash method of accounting?

a. A tax shelter.

b. A qualified personal service corporation.

c. A C corporation with annual gross receipts of $50,000,000.

d. A manufacturer with annual gross receipts of $3,000,000.

52. In 2009, Stewart Corp. properly accrued $5,000 for an income item on the basis of a reasonable estimate. In 2010, after filing its 2009 federal income tax return, Stewart determined that the exact amount was $6,000. Which of the following statements is correct?

a. No further inclusion of income is required as the difference is less than 25% of the original amount reported and the estimate had been made in good faith.

b. The $1,000 difference is includible in Stewart's 2010 income tax return.

c. Stewart is required to notify the IRS within 30 days of the determination of the exact amount of the item.

d. Stewart is required to file an amended return to report the additional $1,000 of income.

53. Axis Corp. is an accrual-basis calendar-year corporation. On December 13, 2009, the Board of Directors declared a 2% of profits bonus to all employees for services rendered during 2009 and notified them in writing. None of the employees own stock in Axis. The amount represents reasonable compensation for services rendered and was paid on March 13, 2010. Axis' bonus expense may

a. Not be deducted on Axis' 2009 tax return because the per share employee amount **cannot** be determined with reasonable accuracy at the time of the declaration of the bonus.

b. Be deducted on Axis' 2009 tax return.

c. Be deducted on Axis' 2010 tax return.

d. Not be deducted on Axis' tax return because payment is a disguised dividend.

54. On December 1, 2009, Michaels, a self-employed cash-basis taxpayer, borrowed $100,000 to use in her business. The loan was to be repaid on November 30, 2010. Michaels paid the entire interest of $12,000 on December 1, 2009. What amount of interest is deductible on Michaels' 2010 income tax return?

a. $12,000

b. $11,000

c. $ 1,000

d. $0

55. Blair, CPA, uses the cash receipts and disbursements method of reporting. In 2009, a client gave Blair 100 shares of a listed corporation's stock in full satisfaction of a $5,000 accounting fee the client owed Blair. This stock had a fair market value of $4,000 on the date it was given to Blair. The client's basis for this stock was $3,000. Blair sold the stock for cash in January 2010. In Blair's 2009 return, what amount of income should be reported in connection with the receipt of the stock?

a. $0

b. $3,000

c. $4,000

d. $5,000

56. Unless the Internal Revenue Service consents to a change of method, the accrual method of tax reporting is generally mandatory for a sole proprietor when there are

	Accounts receivable for services rendered	Year-end merchandise inventories
a.	Yes	Yes
b.	Yes	No
c.	No	No
d.	No	Yes

57. Alex Burg, a cash-basis taxpayer, earned an annual salary of $80,000 at Ace Corp. in 2009, but elected to take only $50,000. Ace, which was financially able to pay Burg's full salary, credited the unpaid balance of $30,000 to Burg's account on the corporate books in 2009, and actually paid this $30,000 to Burg on January 30, 2010. How much of the salary is taxable to Burg in 2009?

a. $50,000

b. $60,000

c. $65,000

d. $80,000

58. Dr. Berger, a physician, reports on the cash basis. The following items pertain to Dr. Berger's medical practice in 2009:

Cash received from patients in 2009	$200,000
Cash received in 2009 from third-party reimbursers for services provided by Dr. Berger in 2008	30,000
Salaries paid to employees in 2009	20,000
Year-end 2009 bonuses paid to employees in 2010	1,000
Other expenses paid in 2009	24,000

What is Dr. Berger's net income for 2009 from his medical practice?

a. $155,000

b. $156,000

c. $185,000

d. $186,000

59. Which of the following taxpayers may use the cash method of accounting for tax purposes?

a. Partnership that is designated as a tax shelter.

b. Retail store with $2 million inventory, and $9 million average annual gross receipts.

c. An international accounting firm.

d. C corporation manufacturing exercise equipment with average annual gross receipts of $8 million.

60. The uniform capitalization method must be used by

I. Manufacturers of tangible personal property.

II. Retailers of personal property with $2 million dollars in average annual gross receipts for the three preceding years.

a. I only.

b. II only.

c. Both I and II.

d. Neither I nor II.

61. Mock operates a retail business selling illegal narcotic substances. Which of the following item(s) may Mock deduct in calculating business income?

I. Cost of merchandise.
II. Business expenses other than the cost of merchandise.

   a. I only.
   b. II only.
   c. Both I and II.
   d. Neither I nor II.

62. Banks Corp., a calendar-year corporation, reimburses employees for properly substantiated qualifying business meal expenses. The employees are present at the meals, which are neither lavish nor extravagant, and the reimbursement is not treated as wages subject to withholdings. For 2010, what percentage of the meal expense may Banks deduct?

   a. 0%
   b. 50%
   c. 80%
   d. 100%

63. Which of the following costs is not included in inventory under the Uniform Capitalization rules for goods manufactured by the taxpayer?

   a. Research.
   b. Warehousing costs.
   c. Quality control.
   d. Taxes excluding income taxes.

64. Under the uniform capitalization rules applicable to property acquired for resale, which of the following costs should be capitalized with respect to inventory if **no** exceptions are met?

	Marketing costs	Off-site storage costs
a.	Yes	Yes
b.	Yes	No
c.	No	No
d.	No	Yes

65. In the case of a corporation that is **not** a financial institution, which of the following statements is correct with regard to the deduction for bad debts?

   a. Either the reserve method or the direct charge-off method may be used, if the election is made in the corporation's first taxable year.
   b. On approval from the IRS, a corporation may change its method from direct charge-off to reserve.
   c. If the reserve method was consistently used in prior years, the corporation may take a deduction for a reasonable addition to the reserve for bad debts.
   d. A corporation is required to use the direct charge-off method rather than the reserve method.

66. Ram Corp.'s operating income for the year ended December 31, 2009, amounted to $100,000. Included in Ram's 2009 operating expenses is a $6,000 insurance premium on a policy insuring the life of Ram's president. Ram is beneficiary of this policy. In Ram's 2009 tax return, what amount should be deducted for the $6,000 life insurance premium?

   a. $6,000
   b. $5,000
   c. $1,000
   d. $0

67. Jason Budd, CPA, reports on the cash basis. In April 2009, Budd billed a client $3,500 for the following professional services:

Personal estate planning	$2,000
Personal tax return preparation	1,000
Compilation of business financial statements	500

No part of the $3,500 was ever paid. In April 2010, the client declared bankruptcy, and the $3,500 obligation became totally uncollectible. What loss can Budd deduct on his 2010 tax return for this bad debt?

   a. $0
   b. $ 500
   c. $1,500
   d. $3,500

68. Earl Cook, who worked as a machinist for Precision Corp., loaned Precision $1,000 in 2007. Cook did not own any of Precision's stock, and the loan was not a condition of Cook's employment by Precision. In 2010, Precision declared bankruptcy, and Cook's note receivable from Precision became worthless. What loss can Cook claim on his 2010 income tax return?

   a. $0
   b. $ 500 long-term capital loss.
   c. $1,000 short-term capital loss.
   d. $1,000 business bad debt.

69. During the 2009 holiday season, Palo Corp. gave business gifts to seventeen customers. These gifts, which were not of an advertising nature, had the following fair market values:

4	at	$ 10
4	at	25
4	at	50
5	at	100

How much of these gifts was deductible as a business expense for 2009?

   a. $840
   b. $365
   c. $140
   d. $0

70. Jennifer, who is single, has the following items of income and deduction for 2009:

Salary	$30,000
Itemized deductions (all attributable to a personal casualty loss when a hurricane destroyed her residence	45,000
Personal exemption	3,650

What is the amount of Jennifer's net operating loss for 2009?

   a. $0
   b. $15,000
   c. $18,650
   d. $45,000

71. Robin Moore, a self-employed taxpayer, reported the following information for 2009:

Income:	Dividends from investments	$ 500
	Net short-term capital gain on sale of investment	1,000
Deductions:	Net loss from business	(6,000)
	Personal exemption	(3,650)
	Standard deduction	(5,700)

What is the amount of Moore's net operating loss for 2009?

   a. $ 4,500
   b. $ 5,000

c. $ 6,000
d. $10,200

72. Destry, a single taxpayer, reported the following on his US Individual Income Tax Return Form 1040:

Income	
Wages	$ 5,000
Interest on savings account	1,000
Net rental income	4,000
Deductions	
Personal exemption	$ 3,650
Standard deduction	5,700
Net business loss	16,000
Net short-term capital loss	2,000

What is Destry's net operating loss that is available for carryback or carryforward?

    a. $ 7,000
    b. $ 9,000
    c. $13,000
    d. $16,000

73. Cobb, an unmarried individual, had an adjusted gross income of $200,000 in 2010 before any IRA deduction, taxable social security benefits, or passive activity losses. Cobb incurred a loss of $30,000 in 2010 from rental real estate in which he actively participated. What amount of loss attributable to this rental real estate can be used in 2010 as an offset against income from nonpassive sources?

    a. $0
    b. $12,500
    c. $25,000
    d. $30,000

74. The rule limiting the allowability of passive activity losses and credits applies to

    a. Partnerships.
    b. S corporations.
    c. Personal service corporations.
    d. Widely held C corporations.

75. Don Wolf became a general partner in Gata Associates on January 1, 2009, with a 5% interest in Gata's profits, losses, and capital. Gata is a distributor of auto parts. Wolf does not materially participate in the partnership business. For the year ended December 31, 2009, Gata had an operating loss of $100,000. In addition, Gata earned interest of $20,000 on a temporary investment. Gata has kept the principal temporarily invested while awaiting delivery of equipment that is presently on order. The principal will be used to pay for this equipment. Wolf's passive loss for 2009 is

    a. $0
    b. $4,000
    c. $5,000
    d. $6,000

76. With regard to the passive loss rules involving rental real estate activities, which one of the following statements is correct?

    a. The term "passive activity" includes any rental activity without regard as to whether or not the taxpayer materially participates in the activity.
    b. Gross investment income from interest and dividends **not** derived in the ordinary course of a trade or business is treated as passive activity income that can be offset by passive rental activity losses

when the "active participation" requirement is **not** met.

    c. Passive rental activity losses may be deducted only against passive income, but passive rental activity credits may be used against tax attributable to nonpassive activities.
    d. The passive activity rules do **not** apply to taxpayers whose adjusted gross income is $300,000 or less.

77. If an individual taxpayer's passive losses relating to rental real estate activities cannot be used in the current year, then they may be carried

    a. Back two years, but they cannot be carried forward.
    b. Forward up to a maximum period of twenty years, but they cannot be carried back.
    c. Back two years or forward up to twenty years, at the taxpayer's election.
    d. Forward indefinitely or until the property is disposed of in a taxable transaction.

78. Aviation Corp. manufactures model airplanes for children. During 2009, Aviation purchased $820,000 of production machinery to be used in its business. For 2009, Aviation's taxable income before any Sec. 179 expense deduction was $195,000. What is the maximum amount of Sec. 179 expense election Aviation will be allowed to deduct for 2009 and the maximum amount of Sec. 179 expense election that can carryover to 2010?

	Expense	*Carryover*
a.	$ 195,000	$35,000
b.	$ 195,000	$55,000
c.	$230,000	$0
d.	$250,000	$0

79. Which of the following conditions must be satisfied for a taxpayer to expense, in the year of purchase, under Internal Revenue Code Section 179, the cost of new or used tangible depreciable personal property?

  I. The property must be purchased for use in the taxpayer's active trade or business.
  II. The property must be purchased from an unrelated party.

    a. I only.
    b. II only.
    c. Both I and II.
    d. Neither I nor II.

80. Krol Corp., a calendar-year taxpayer, purchased furniture and fixtures for use in its business and placed the property in service on November 1, 2009. The furniture and fixtures cost $56,000 and represented Krol's only acquisition of depreciable property during the year. Krol did **not** elect to expense any part of the cost of the property under Sec. 179, and elected not to take bonus depreciation. What is the amount of Krol Corp.'s depreciation deduction for the furniture and fixtures under the Modified Accelerated Cost Recovery System (MACRS) for 2009?

    a. $ 2,000
    b. $ 2,667
    c. $ 8,000
    d. $16,000

81. On June 29, 2010, Sullivan purchased and placed into service an apartment building costing $360,000 including

$30,000 for the land. What was Sullivan's MACRS deduction for the apartment building in 2010?

- a. $7,091
- b. $6,500
- c. $6,000
- d. $4,583

82. Data Corp., a calendar-year corporation, purchased and placed into service office equipment during October 2010. No other equipment was placed into service during 2010. Under the general MACRS depreciation system, what convention must Data use?

- a.   Full-year.
- b.   Half-year.
- c.   Midquarter.
- d.   Midmonth.

83. Under the modified accelerated cost recovery system (MACRS) of depreciation for property placed in service after 1986,

- a.   Used tangible depreciable property is excluded from the computation.
- b.   Salvage value is ignored for purposes of computing the MACRS deduction.
- c.   No type of straight-line depreciation is allowable.
- d.   The recovery period for depreciable realty must be at least 27.5 years.

84. With regard to depreciation computations made under the general MACRS method, the half-year convention provides that

- a.   One-half of the first year's depreciation is allowed in the year in which the property is placed in service, regardless of when the property is placed in service during the year, and a half-year's depreciation is allowed for the year in which the property is disposed of.
- b.   The deduction will be based on the number of months the property was in service, so that one-half month's depreciation is allowed for the month in which the property is placed in service and for the month in which it is disposed of.
- c.   Depreciation will be allowed in the first year of acquisition of the property only if the property is placed in service **no** later than June 30 for calendar-year corporations.
- d.   Depreciation will be allowed in the last year of the property's economic life only if the property is disposed of after June 30 of the year of disposition for calendar-year corporations.

85. In 2010, Roe Corp. purchased and placed in service a machine to be used in its manufacturing operations. This machine cost $814,000. What portion of the cost may Roe elect to treat as an expense rather than as a capital expenditure?

- a. $100,000
- b. $114,000
- c. $236,000
- d. $250,000

86. Easel Co. has elected to reimburse employees for business expenses under a nonaccountable plan. Easel does not require employees to provide proof of expenses and allows employees to keep any amount not spent. Under the plan, Mel, an Easel employee for a full year, gets $400 per month for business automobile expenses. At the end of the year

Mel informs Easel that the only business expense incurred was for business mileage of 9,000 at a rate of 50.5 cents per mile, the IRS standard mileage rate at the time. Mel encloses a check for $255 to refund the overpayment to Easel. What amount should be reported in Mel's gross income for the year?

- a. $0
- b. $ 255
- c. $4,545
- d. $4,800

87. Adams owns a second residence that is used for both personal and rental purposes. During 2010, Adams used the second residence for 50 days and rented the residence for 200 days. Which of the following statements is correct?

- a.   Depreciation may not be deducted on the property under any circumstances.
- b.   A rental loss may be deducted if rental-related expenses exceed rental income.
- c.   Utilities and maintenance on the property must be divided between personal and rental use.
- d.   All mortgage interest and taxes on the property will be deducted to determine the property's net income or loss

88. Charles Gilbert, a corporate executive, incurred business-related unreimbursed expenses in 2009 as follows:

Entertainment	$900
Travel	700
Education	400

Assuming that Gilbert does not itemize deductions, how much of these expenses should he deduct on his 2009 tax return?

- a. $0
- b. $ 700
- c. $1,300
- d. $1,600

89. James, a calendar-year taxpayer, was employed and resided in Boston. On February 4, 2010, James was permanently transferred to Florida by his employer. James worked full-time for the entire year. In 2010, James incurred and paid the following unreimbursed expenses in relocating.

Lodging and travel expenses while moving	$1,000
Meals while in route to Florida	300
Cost of insuring household goods and personal effects during move	200
Cost of shipping household pets to new home	100
Costs of moving household furnishings and personal effects	3,000

What amount was deductible as moving expenses on James' 2010 tax return?

- a. $4,600
- b. $4,500
- c. $4,300
- d. $4,000

90. Martin Dawson, who resided in Detroit, was unemployed for the last six months of 2009. In January 2010, he moved to Houston to seek employment, and obtained a full-time job there in February. He kept this job for the balance of the year. Martin paid the following expenses in 2010 in connection with his move:

Rental of truck to move his personal belongings to Houston	$ 800
Penalty for breaking the lease on his Detroit apartment	300
Total	$1,100

How much can Martin deduct in 2010 for moving expenses?
- a. $0
- b. $ 300
- c. $ 800
- d. $1,100

91. Richard Putney, who lived in Idaho for five years, moved to Texas in 2010 to accept a new position. His employer reimbursed him in full for all direct moving costs, but did not pay for any part of the following indirect moving expenses incurred by Putney:

Househunting trips to Texas	$800
Temporary housing in Texas	900

How much of the indirect expenses can be deducted by Putney as moving expenses?
- a. $0
- b. $ 900
- c. $1,500
- d. $1,700

92. Which one of the following statements concerning Roth IRAs is **not** correct?
- a. The maximum annual contribution to a Roth IRA is reduced if adjusted gross income exceeds certain thresholds.
- b. Contributions to a Roth IRA are not deductible.
- c. An individual is allowed to make contributions to a Roth IRA even after age 70½.
- d. A contribution to a Roth IRA must be made by the due date for filing the individual's tax return for the year (including extensions).

93. What is the maximum amount of adjusted gross income that a taxpayer may have for 2009 and still qualify to roll over the balance from a traditional individual retirement account (IRA) into a Roth IRA?
- a. $ 50,000
- b. $ 80,000
- c. $100,000
- d. $150,000

94. Which one of the following statements concerning an education IRA (Coverdell Education Savings Account) is **not** correct?
- a. Contributions to an education IRA are not deductible.
- b. A taxpayer may contribute up to $2,000 in 2009 to an education IRA to pay the costs of the designated beneficiary's higher education.
- c. Eligibility for an education IRA is phased out if adjusted gross income exceeds certain threshold levels.
- d. Contributions can be made to an education IRA on behalf of a beneficiary until the beneficiary reaches age twenty-one.

95. For 2009, Val and Pat White (both age 40) filed a joint return. Val earned $35,000 in wages and was covered by his employer's qualified pension plan. Pat was unemployed and received $4,000 in alimony payments for the first four months of the year before remarrying. The couple had no other income. Each contributed $5,000 to an IRA account. The allowable IRA deduction on their 2009 joint tax return is
- a. $10,000
- b. $ 9,000

- c. $ 8,000
- d. $ 5,000

96. Davis, a sole proprietor with no employees, has a Keogh profit-sharing plan to which he may contribute 15% of his annual earned income. For this purpose, "earned income" is defined as net self-employment earnings reduced by the
- a. Deductible Keogh contribution.
- b. Self-employment tax.
- c. Self-employment tax and one-half of the deductible Keogh contribution.
- d. Deductible Keogh contribution and one-half of the self-employment tax.

97. Ronald Birch, who is single and age 28, earned a salary of $65,000 in 2009 as a plumber employed by Lupo Company. Birch was covered for the entire year 2009 under Lupo's qualified pension plan for employees. In addition, Birch had a net income of $15,000 from self-employment in 2009. What is the maximum amount that Birch can deduct in 2009 for contributions to an individual retirement account (IRA)?
- a. $5,000
- b. $4,000
- c. $3,000
- d. $0

98. Sol and Julia Crane (both age 43) are married and filed a joint return for 2009. Sol earned a salary of $110,000 in 2009 from his job at Troy Corp., where Sol is covered by his employer's pension plan. In addition, Sol and Julia earned interest of $3,000 in 2009 on their joint savings account. Julia is not employed, and the couple had no other income. On July 15, 2009, Sol contributed $5,000 to an IRA for himself, and $5,000 to an IRA for his spouse. The allowable IRA deduction in the Cranes' 2009 joint return is
- a. $0
- b. $ 4,000
- c. $ 5,000
- d. $10,000

99. Paul and Lois Lee, both age fifty, are married and filed a joint return for 2009. Their 2009 adjusted gross income was $85,000, including Paul's $75,000 salary. Lois had no income of her own. Neither spouse was covered by an employer-sponsored pension plan. What amount could the Lees contribute to IRAs for 2009 to take advantage of their maximum allowable IRA deduction in their 2009 return?
- a. $ 5,000
- b. $ 8,000
- c. $10,000
- d. $12,000

100. In 2009, contributions to a defined contribution qualified retirement plan on behalf of a self-employed individual whose income from self-employment is $50,000 are limited to
- a. $ 4,000
- b. $40,000
- c. $49,000
- d. $50,000

101. Which allowable deduction can be claimed in arriving at an individual's 2009 adjusted gross income?
- a. Charitable contribution.
- b. Foreign income taxes.

c.   Tax return preparation fees.

d.   Self-employed health insurance deduction.

102. Which one of the following statements concerning the deduction for interest on qualified education loans is **not** correct?

a.   The deduction is available even if the taxpayer does not itemize deductions.

b.   The deduction only applies to the first sixty months of interest payments.

c.   Qualified education expenses include tuition fees, room, and board.

d.   The educational expenses must relate to a period when the student was enrolled on at least a half-time basis.

103. Dale received $1,000 in 2010 for jury duty. In exchange for regular compensation from her employer during the period of jury service, Dale was required to remit the entire $1,000 to her employer in 2010. In Dale's 2010 income tax return, the $1,000 jury duty fee should be

a.   Claimed in full as an itemized deduction.

b.   Claimed as an itemized deduction to the extent exceeding 2% of adjusted gross income.

c.   Deducted from gross income in arriving at adjusted gross income.

d.   Included in taxable income without a corresponding offset against other income.

104. During 2009, George (age ten and claimed as a dependency exemption by his parents) received dividend income of $3,700, and had wages from an after-school job of $1,700. What is the amount that will be reported as George's taxable income for 2009?

a. $ 250

b. $3,400

c. $3,450

d. $5,400

105. Which of the following requirements must be met in order for a single individual to qualify for the additional standard deduction?

	Must be age 65 or older or blind	Must support dependent child or aged parent
a.	Yes	Yes
b.	No	No
c.	Yes	No
d.	No	Yes

106. Carroll, an unmarried taxpayer with an adjusted gross income of $100,000, incurred and paid the following unreimbursed medical expenses for the year:

Doctor bills resulting from a serious fall	$5,000
Cosmetic surgery that was necessary to correct a congenital deformity	$15,000

Carroll had no medical insurance. For regular income tax purposes, what was Carroll's maximum allowable medical expense deduction, after the applicable threshold limitation, for the year?

a. $0

b. $12,500

c. $15,000

d. $20,000

107. Charlene and Gene Blair are married and filed a joint return for 2009. Their medical related expenditures for 2009 included the following:

Medical insurance premiums	$ 800
Medicines prescribed by doctors	450
Aspirin and over-the-counter cold capsules	80
Unreimbursed doctor fees	1,000
Transportation to and from doctors	150
Emergency room fee	500

The emergency room fee related to an injury incurred by the Blair's son, Eric, during a visit to their home. The Blairs graciously paid the bill; however, they provided no other support for Eric during the year. For 2009, Eric earned $12,000 as a self-employed house painter. Assuming the Blairs' adjusted gross income was $30,000, what amount of medical expenses can the Blairs deduct as an itemized deduction for 2009?

a. $0

b. $ 150

c. $ 650

d. $1,750

108. Tom and Sally White, married and filing joint income tax returns, derive their entire income from the operation of their retail stationery shop. Their 2009 adjusted gross income was $100,000. The Whites itemized their deductions on Schedule A for 2009. The following unreimbursed cash expenditures were among those made by the Whites during 2009:

Repair and maintenance of motorized wheelchair for physically handicapped dependent child	$ 600
Tuition, meals, lodging at special school for physically handicapped dependent child in an institution primarily for the availability of medical care, with meals and lodging furnished as necessary incidents to that care	8,000

Without regard to the adjusted gross income percentage threshold, what amount may the Whites claim in their 2009 return as qualifying medical expenses?

a. $8,600

b. $8,000

c. $ 600

d. $0

109. In 2009, Wells paid the following expenses:

Premiums on an insurance policy against loss of earnings due to sickness or accident	$3,000
Physical therapy after spinal surgery	2,000
Premium on an insurance policy that covers reimbursement for the cost of prescription drugs	500

In 2009, Wells recovered $1,500 of the $2,000 that she paid for physical therapy through insurance reimbursement from a group medical policy paid for by her employer. Disregarding the adjusted gross income percentage threshold, what amount could be claimed on Wells' 2009 income tax return for medical expenses?

a. $4,000

b. $3,500

c. $1,000

d. $ 500

110. Mr. and Mrs. Sloan incurred the following expenses on December 15, 2009, when they adopted a child:

Child's medical expenses	$5,000
Legal expenses	9,000
Agency fee	4,000

Before consideration of any "floor" or other limitation on deductibility, what amount of the above expenses may the Sloans deduct on their 2009 joint income tax return?

a. $18,000
b. $14,000
c. $13,000
d. $ 5,000

111. Ruth and Mark Cline are married and will file a joint 2010 income tax return. Among their expenditures during 2010 were the following discretionary costs that they incurred for the sole purpose of improving their physical appearance and self-esteem:

Face-lift for Ruth, performed by a licensed
  surgeon $5,000
Hair transplant for Mark, performed by a licensed surgeon   3,600

Disregarding the adjusted gross income percentage threshold, what total amount of the aforementioned doctors' bills may be claimed by the Clines in their 2010 return as qualifying medical expenses?

a. $0
b. $3,600
c. $5,000
d. $8,600

112. During 2009, Scott charged $4,000 on his credit card for his dependent son's medical expenses. Payment to the credit card company had not been made by the time Scott filed his income tax return in 2010. However, in 2009, Scott paid a physician $2,800 for the medical expenses of his wife, who died in 2008. Disregarding the adjusted gross income percentage threshold, what amount could Scott claim in his 2009 income tax return for medical expenses?

a. $0
b. $2,800
c. $4,000
d. $6,800

113. Which one of the following expenditures qualifies as a deductible medical expense for tax purposes?

a. Diaper service.
b. Funeral expenses.
c. Nursing care for a healthy baby.
d. Premiums paid for Medicare B supplemental medical insurance.

114. Jon Stenger, a cash-basis taxpayer, had adjusted gross income of $35,000 in 2009. During the year he incurred and paid the following medical expenses:

Drugs and medicines prescribed by doctors $ 300
Health insurance premiums   750
Doctors' fees   2,550
Eyeglasses   75
                            $3,675

Stenger received $900 in 2009 as reimbursement for a portion of the doctors' fees. If Stenger were to itemize his deductions, what would be his allowable net medical expense deduction?

a. $0
b. $ 150
c. $1,050
d. $2,475

115. During 2009, Mr. and Mrs. Benson provided substantially all the support, in their own home, for their son John, age twenty-six, and for Mrs. Benson's cousin Nancy, age seventeen. John had $3,900 of income for 2009, and Nancy's income was $2,500. The Bensons paid the following medical expenses during the year:

Medicines and drugs:	
For themselves	$400
For John	500
For Nancy	100
Doctors:	
For themselves	600
For John	900
For Nancy	200

What is the total amount of medical expenses (before application of any limitation rules), that would enter into the calculation of itemized deductions on the Bensons' 2009 tax return?

a. $1,000
b. $1,300
c. $2,400
d. $2,700

116. All of the following taxes are deductible as itemized deductions by a self-employed taxpayer **except:**

a. Foreign real estate taxes.
b. Foreign income taxes.
c. Personal property taxes.
d. One-half of self-employment taxes.

117. Matthews was a cash-basis taxpayer whose records showed the following:

2009 state and local income taxes withheld	$1,500
2009 state estimated income taxes paid December 30, 2009	400
2009 federal income taxes withheld	2,500
2009 state and local income taxes paid April 17, 2010	300

What total amount was Matthews entitled to claim for taxes on her 2009 Schedule A of Form 1040?

a. $4,700
b. $2,200
c. $1,900
d. $1,500

118. In 2009, Farb, a cash-basis individual taxpayer, received an $8,000 invoice for personal property taxes. Believing the amount to be overstated by $5,000, Farb paid the invoiced amount under protest and immediately started legal action to recover the overstatement. In June 2010, the matter was resolved in Farb's favor, and he received a $5,000 refund. Farb itemizes his deductions on his tax returns. Which of the following statements is correct regarding the deductibility of the property taxes?

a. Farb should deduct $8,000 in his 2009 income tax return and should report the $5,000 refund as income in his 2010 income tax return.
b. Farb should **not** deduct any amount in his 2009 income tax return and should deduct $3,000 in his 2010 income tax return.
c. Farb should deduct $3,000 in his 2009 income tax return.
d. Farb should **not** deduct any amount in his 2009 income tax return when originally filed, and should file an amended 2009 income tax return in 2010.

119. In 2010, Burg paid $8,000 to the tax collector of Sun City for realty taxes on a two-family house owned in joint tenancy between Burg and his mother. Of this amount, $3,800 covered back taxes for 2009, and $4,200 covered 2010 taxes. Burg resides on the second floor of the house, and his mother resides on the first floor. In Burg's itemized deductions on his 2010 return, what amount was Burg entitled to claim for realty taxes?

a. $0
b. $4,000
c. $4,200
d. $8,000

120. Sara Harding is a cash-basis taxpayer who itemized her deductions. The following information pertains to Sara's state income taxes for the taxable year 2009:

Withheld by employer in 2009		$2,000
Payments on 2009 estimate:		
4/15/09	$300	
6/15/09	300	
9/15/09	300	
1/15/10	300	1,200
Total paid and withheld		$3,200
Actual tax, per state return		3,000
Overpayment		$ 200

There was no balance of tax or refund due on Sara's 2008 state tax return. How much is deductible for state income taxes on Sara's 2009 federal income tax return?
a. $2,800
b. $2,900
c. $3,000
d. $3,200

121. During 2010, Jack and Mary Bronson paid the following taxes:

Taxes on residence (for period January 1 to December 31, 2010)	$2,700
State motor vehicle tax on value of the car	360

The Bronsons sold their house on June 30, 2010, under an agreement in which the real estate taxes were not prorated between the buyer and sellers. What amount should the Bronsons deduct as taxes in calculating itemized deductions for 2010?
a. $1,350
b. $1,692
c. $2,160
d. $3,060

122. George Granger sold a plot of land to Albert King on July 1, 2010. Granger had not paid any realty taxes on the land since 2008. Delinquent 2009 taxes amounted to $600, and 2010 taxes amounted to $700. King paid the 2009 and 2010 taxes in full in 2010, when he bought the land. What portion of the $1,300 is deductible by King in 2010?
a. $ 353
b. $ 700
c. $ 952
d. $1,300

123. During 2010 Mr. and Mrs. West paid the following taxes:

Property taxes on residence	$1,800
Special assessment for installation of a sewer system in their town	1,000
State personal property tax on their automobile	600
Property taxes on land held for long-term appreciation	300

What amount can the Wests deduct as property taxes in calculating itemized deductions for 2010?
a. $2,100
b. $2,700
c. $3,100
d. $3,700

124. Alex and Myra Burg, married and filing joint income tax returns, derive their entire income from the operation of their retail candy shop. Their 2009 adjusted gross income was $50,000. The Burgs itemized their deductions on Schedule A for 2009. The following unreimbursed cash expenditures were among those made by the Burgs during 2009:

State income tax	$1,200
Self-employment tax	7,650

What amount should the Burgs deduct for taxes in their itemized deductions on Schedule A for 2009?
a. $1,200
b. $3,825
c. $5,025
d. $7,650

125. The 2010 deduction by an individual taxpayer for interest on investment indebtedness is
a. Limited to the investment interest paid in 2010.
b. Limited to the taxpayer's 2010 interest income.
c. Limited to the taxpayer's 2010 net investment income.
d. Not limited.

126. The Browns borrowed $20,000, secured by their home, to purchase a new automobile. At the time of the loan, the fair market value of their home was $400,000, and it was unencumbered by other debt. The interest on the loan qualifies as
a. Deductible personal interest.
b. Deductible qualified residence interest.
c. Nondeductible interest.
d. Investment interest expense.

127. On January 2, 2007, the Philips paid $50,000 cash and obtained a $200,000 mortgage to purchase a home. In 2010 they borrowed $15,000 secured by their home, and used the cash to add a new room to their residence. That same year they took out a $5,000 auto loan.

The following information pertains to interest paid in 2010:

Mortgage interest	$17,000
Interest on room construction loan	1,500
Auto loan interest	500

For 2010, how much interest is deductible, prior to any itemized deduction limitations?
a. $17,000
b. $17,500
c. $18,500
d. $19,000

128. Jackson owns two residences. The second residence, which has never been used for rental purposes, is the only residence that is subject to a mortgage. The following expenses were incurred for the second residence in 2010:

Mortgage interest	$5,000
Utilities	1,200
Insurance	6,000

For regular income tax purposes, what is the maximum amount allowable as a deduction for Jackson's second residence in 2010?
a. $6,200 in determining adjusted gross income.
b. $11,000 in determining adjusted gross income.
c. $5,000 as an itemized deduction.
d. $12,200 as an itemized deduction.

129. Robert and Judy Parker made the following payments during 2009:

Interest on a life insurance policy loan (the loan proceeds were used for personal use)	$1,200
Interest on home mortgage for period January 1 to October 4, 2009	3,600
Penalty payment for prepayment of home mortgage on October 4, 2009	900

How much can the Parkers utilize as interest expense in calculating itemized deductions for 2009?
- a. $5,700
- b. $4,620
- c. $4,500
- d. $3,600

130. Charles Wolfe purchased the following long-term investments at par during 2009:

$20,000 general obligation bonds of Burlington County (wholly tax-exempt)
$10,000 debentures of Arrow Corporation

Wolfe financed these purchases by obtaining a $30,000 loan from the Union National Bank. For the year 2009, Wolfe made the following interest payments:

Union National Bank	$3,600
Interest on home mortgage	3,000
Interest on credit card charges (items purchased for personal use)	500

What amount can Wolfe utilize as interest expense in calculating itemized deductions for 2009?
- a. $3,000
- b. $4,200
- c. $5,400
- d. $7,100

131. During 2010, William Clark was assessed a deficiency on his 2008 federal income tax return. As a result of this assessment he was required to pay $1,120 determined as follows:

Additional tax	$900
Late filing penalty	60
Negligence penalty	90
Interest	70

What portion of the $1,120 would qualify as itemized deductions for 2010?
- a. $0
- b. $ 14
- c. $150
- d. $220

132. Smith, a single individual, made the following charitable contributions during the current year. Smith's adjusted gross income is $60,000.

Donation to Smith's church	$5,000
Artwork donated to the local art museum. Smith purchased it for $2,000 four months ago. A local art dealer appraised it for	3,000
Contribution to a needy family	1,000

What amount should Smith deduct as a charitable contribution?
- a. $5,000
- b. $7,000
- c. $8,000
- d. $9,000

133. Stein, an unmarried taxpayer, had adjusted gross income of $80,000 for the year and qualified to itemize deductions. Stein had no charitable contribution carryovers and only made one contribution during the year. Stein donated stock, purchased seven years earlier for $17,000, to a tax-exempt educational organization. The stock was valued at $25,000 when it was contributed. What is the amount of charitable contributions deductible on Stein's current year income tax return?
- a. $17,000
- b. $21,000
- c. $24,000
- d. $25,000

134. Moore, a single taxpayer, had $50,000 in adjusted gross income for 2009. During 2009 she contributed $18,000 to her church. She had a $10,000 charitable contribution carryover from her 2008 church contributions. What was the maximum amount of properly substantiated charitable contributions that Moore could claim as an itemized deduction for 2009?
- a. $10,000
- b. $18,000
- c. $25,000
- d. $28,000

135. Spencer, who itemizes deductions, had adjusted gross income of $60,000 in 2009. The following additional information is available for 2009:

Cash contribution to church	$4,000
Purchase of art object at church bazaar (with a fair market value of $800 on the date of purchase)	1,200
Donation of used clothing to Salvation Army (fair value evidenced by receipt received)	600

What is the maximum amount Spencer can claim as a deduction for charitable contributions in 2009?
- a. $5,400
- b. $5,200
- c. $5,000
- d. $4,400

136. Ruth Lewis has adjusted gross income of $100,000 for 2009 and itemizes her deductions. On September 1, 2009, she made a contribution to her church of stock held for investment for two years that cost $10,000 and had a fair market value of $70,000. The church sold the stock for $70,000 on the same date. Assume that Lewis made no other contributions during 2009 and made no special election in regard to this contribution on her 2009 tax return. How much should Lewis claim as a charitable contribution deduction for 2009?
- a. $50,000
- b. $30,000
- c. $20,000
- d. $10,000

137. On December 15, 2009, Donald Calder made a contribution of $500 to a qualified charitable organization, by charging the contribution on his bank credit card. Calder paid the $500 on January 20, 2010, upon receipt of the bill from the bank. In addition, Calder issued and delivered a promissory note for $1,000 to another qualified charitable organization on November 1, 2009, which he paid upon maturity six months later. If Calder itemizes his deductions, what portion of these contributions is deductible in 2009?
- a. $0
- b. $ 500
- c. $1,000
- d. $1,500

138. Under a written agreement between Mrs. Norma Lowe and an approved religious exempt organization, a ten-year-old girl from Vietnam came to live in Mrs. Lowe's home on August 1, 2009, in order to be able to start school in the US on September 3, 2009. Mrs. Lowe actually spent $500 for food, clothing, and school supplies for the student during 2009, without receiving any compensation or reimbursement of costs. What portion of the $500 may Mrs. Lowe deduct on her 2009 income tax return as a charitable contribution?

    a. $0
    b. $200
    c. $250
    d. $500

139. During 2009, Vincent Tally gave to the municipal art museum title to his private collection of rare books that was assessed and valued at $60,000. However, he reserved the right to the collection's use and possession during his lifetime. For 2009, he reported an adjusted gross income of $100,000. Assuming that this was his only contribution during the year, and that there were no carryovers from prior years, what amount can he deduct as contributions for 2009?

    a. $0
    b. $30,000
    c. $50,000
    d. $60,000

140. Jimet, an unmarried taxpayer, qualified to itemize 2009 deductions. Jimet's 2009 adjusted gross income was $30,000 and he made a $2,000 cash donation directly to a needy family. In 2009, Jimet also donated stock, valued at $3,000, to his church. Jimet had purchased the stock four months earlier for $1,500. What was the maximum amount of the charitable contribution allowable as an itemized deduction on Jimet's 2009 income tax return?

    a. $0
    b. $1,500
    c. $2,000
    d. $5,000

141. Taylor, an unmarried taxpayer, had $90,000 in adjusted gross income for 2009. During 2009, Taylor donated land to a church and made no other contributions. Taylor purchased the land in 1997 as an investment for $14,000. The land's fair market value was $25,000 on the day of the donation. What is the maximum amount of charitable contribution that Taylor may deduct as an itemized deduction for the land donation for 2009?

    a. $25,000
    b. $14,000
    c. $11,000
    d. $0

142. In 2010, Joan Frazer's residence was totally destroyed by fire. The property had an adjusted basis and a fair market value of $130,000 before the fire. During 2010, Frazer received insurance reimbursement of $120,000 for the destruction of her home. Frazer's 2010 adjusted gross income was $70,000. Frazer had no casualty gains during the year. What amount of the fire loss was Frazer entitled to claim as an itemized deduction on her 2010 tax return?

    a. $ 2,500
    b. $ 8,500
    c. $ 8,600
    d. $10,000

143. Alex and Myra Burg, married and filing joint income tax returns, derive their entire income from the operation of their retail candy shop. Their 2010 adjusted gross income was $50,000. The Burgs itemized their deductions on Schedule A for 2010. The following unreimbursed cash expenditures were among those made by the Burgs during 2010:

> Repair of glass vase accidentally broken in home by
>   dog; vase cost $500 in 2007; fair value $600 before
>   accident and $200 after accident $90

Without regard to the $100 "floor" and the adjusted gross income percentage threshold, what amount should the Burgs deduct for the casualty loss in their itemized deductions on Schedule A for 2010?

    a. $0
    b. $ 90
    c. $300
    d. $400

144. Hall, a divorced person and custodian of her twelve-year-old child, filed her 2009 federal income tax return as head of a household. During 2009 Hall paid a $490 casualty insurance premium on her personal residence. Hall does not rent out any portion of the home, nor use it for business.

    The casualty insurance premium of $490 is

    a.   Allowed as an itemized deduction subject to the $100 floor and the 10% of adjusted gross income floor.
    b.   Allowed as an itemized deduction subject to the 2% of adjusted gross income floor.
    c.   Deductible in arriving at adjusted gross income.
    d.   Not deductible in 2009.

Items 145 and 146 are based on the following selected 2010 information pertaining to Sam and Ann Hoyt, who filed a joint federal income tax return for the calendar year 2010. The Hoyts had adjusted gross income of $34,000 and itemized their deductions for 2010. Among the Hoyts' cash expenditures during 2010 were the following:

> $2,500 repairs in connection with 2010 fire damage to the Hoyt
>   residence. This property has a basis of $50,000. Fair market
>   value was $60,000 before the fire and $55,000 after the fire.
>   Insurance on the property had lapsed in 2009 for nonpayment
>   of premium.
> $800 appraisal fee to determine amount of fire loss.

145. What amount of fire loss were the Hoyts entitled to deduct as an itemized deduction on their 2010 return?

    a. $5,000
    b. $2,500
    c. $1,600
    d. $1,100

146. The appraisal fee to determine the amount of the Hoyts' fire loss was

    a.   Deductible from gross income in arriving at adjusted gross income.
    b.   Subject to the 2% of adjusted gross income floor for miscellaneous itemized deductions.
    c.   Deductible after reducing the amount by $100.
    d.   Not deductible.

147. Which of the following is **not** a miscellaneous itemized deduction?

    a.   Legal fee for tax advice related to a divorce.
    b.   IRA trustee's fees that are separately billed and paid.

c. Appraisal fee for a charitable contribution.
d. Check-writing fees for a personal checking account.

148. Hall, a divorced person and custodian of her twelve-year-old child, submitted the following information to the CPA who prepared her 2009 return:

> The divorce agreement, executed in 2006, provides for Hall to receive $3,000 per month, of which $600 is designated as child support. After the child reaches eighteen, the monthly payments are to be reduced to $2,400 and are to continue until remarriage or death. However, for the year 2009, Hall received a total of only $5,000 from her former husband. Hall paid an attorney $2,000 in 2009 in a suit to collect the alimony owed.

The $2,000 legal fee that Hall paid to collect alimony should be treated as

a. A deduction in arriving at adjusted gross income.
b. An itemized deduction subject to the 2% of adjusted gross income floor.
c. An itemized deduction **not** subject to the 2% of adjusted gross income floor.
d. A nondeductible personal expense.

149. Hall, a divorced person and custodian of her twelve-year-old child, submitted the following information to the CPA who prepared her 2009 return:

> During 2009, Hall spent a total of $1,000 for state lottery tickets. Her lottery winnings in 2009 totaled $200.

Hall's lottery transactions should be reported as follows:

	Other income on page 1	*Schedule A—itemized deductions* *Other miscellaneous deductions*	
		Subject to 2% *AGI floor*	*Not subject to* *2% AGI floor*
a.	$0	$0	$0
b.	$200	$0	$200
c.	$200	$200	$0
d.	$200	$0	$0

150. Joel Rich is an outside salesman, deriving his income solely from commissions, and personally bearing all expenses without reimbursement of any kind. During 2010, Joel paid the following expenses pertaining directly to his activities as an outside salesman:

Travel	$10,000
Secretarial	7,000
Telephone	1,000

How should these expenses be deducted in Joel's 2010 return?

	From gross income, in arriving *at adjusted gross income*	*As itemized* *deductions*
a.	$18,000	$0
b.	$11,000	$ 7,000
c.	$10,000	$ 8,000
d.	$0	$18,000

151. Magda Micale, a public school teacher with adjusted gross income of $10,000, paid the following items in 2009 for which she received no reimbursement:

Initiation fee for membership in teachers' union	$100
Dues to teachers' union	180
Voluntary unemployment benefit fund contributions to union-established fund	72

How much can Magda claim in 2009 as allowable miscellaneous deductions on Schedule A of Form 1040?

a. $ 80
b. $280

c. $252
d. $352

152. Harold Brodsky is an electrician employed by a contracting firm. His adjusted gross income is $25,000. During the current year he incurred and paid the following expenses:

Use of personal auto for company business (reimbursed under an accountable plan by employer for $200)	$300
Specialized work clothes	550
Union dues	600
Cost of income tax preparation	150
Preparation of will	100

If Brodsky were to itemize his personal deductions, what amount should he claim as miscellaneous deductible expenses?

a. $ 800
b. $ 900
c. $1,500
d. $1,700

153. Which items are **not** subject to the phaseout of the amount of certain itemized deductions that may be claimed by high-income individuals for 2009?

a. Qualified residence interest.
b. Charitable contributions.
c. Investment interest expenses.
d. Real estate taxes.

154. For 2009, Dole's adjusted gross income exceeds $500,000. After the application of any other limitation, itemized deductions are reduced by

a. The **lesser** of 3% of the excess of adjusted gross income over the applicable amount or 80% of **certain** itemized deductions.
b. The **lesser** of 3% of the excess of adjusted gross income over the applicable amount or 80% of **all** itemized deductions.
c. The **greater** of 3% of the excess of adjusted gross income over the applicable amount or 80% of **certain** itemized deductions.
d. The **greater** of 3% of the excess of adjusted gross income over the applicable amount or 80% of **all** itemized deductions.

155. Which one of the following is **not** included in determining the total support of a dependent?

a. Fair rental value of dependent's lodging.
b. Medical insurance premiums paid on behalf of the dependent.
c. Birthday presents given to the dependent.
d. Nontaxable scholarship received by the dependent.

156. In 2009, Smith, a divorced person, provided over one-half the support for his widowed mother, Ruth, and his son, Clay, both of whom are US citizens. During 2009, Ruth did not live with Smith. She received $9,000 in social security benefits. Clay, a full-time graduate student, and his wife lived with Smith. Clay had no income but filed a joint return for 2009, owing an additional $500 in taxes on his wife's income. How many exemptions was Smith entitled to claim on his 2009 tax return?

a. 4
b. 3
c. 2
d. 1

157. Jim and Kay Ross contributed to the support of their two children, Dale and Kim, and Jim's widowed parent, Grant. For 2009, Dale, a twenty-year-old full-time college student, earned $4,500 from a part-time job. Kim, a twenty-three-year-old bank teller, earned $18,000. Grant received $5,000 in dividend income and $4,000 in nontaxable social security benefits. Grant, Dale, and Kim are US citizens and were over one-half supported by Jim and Kay. How many exemptions can Jim and Kay claim on their 2009 joint income tax return?

    a.   Two
    b.   Three
    c.   Four
    d.   Five

158. Joe and Barb are married, but Barb refuses to sign a 2009 joint return. On Joe's separate 2009 return, an exemption may be claimed for Barb if

    a.   Barb was a full-time student for the entire 2009 school year.
    b.   Barb attaches a written statement to Joe's income tax return, agreeing to be claimed as an exemption by Joe for 2009.
    c.   Barb was under the age of nineteen.
    d.   Barb had **no** gross income and was **not** claimed as another person's dependent in 2009.

159. Al and Mary Lew are married and filed a joint 2009 income tax return in which they validly claimed the $3,650 personal exemption for their dependent seventeen-year-old daughter, Doris. Since Doris earned $5,400 in 2009 from a part-time job at the college she attended full-time, Doris was also required to file a 2009 income tax return. What amount was Doris entitled to claim as a personal exemption in her 2009 individual income tax return?

    a. $0
    b. $ 950
    c. $3,650
    d. $5,700

160. During 2009 Robert Moore, who is fifty years old and unmarried, maintained his home in which he and his widower father, age seventy-five, resided. His father had $3,700 interest income from a savings account and also received $2,400 from social security during 2009. Robert provided 60% of his father's total support for 2009. What is Robert's filing status for 2009, and how many exemptions should he claim on his tax return?

    a.   Head of household and two exemptions.
    b.   Single and two exemptions.
    c.   Head of household and one exemption.
    d.   Single and one exemption.

161. John and Mary Arnold are a childless married couple who lived apart (alone in homes maintained by each) the entire year 2009. On December 31, 2009, they were legally separated under a decree of separate maintenance. Which of the following is the only filing status choice available to them when filing for 2009?

    a.   Single.
    b.   Head of household.
    c.   Married filing separate return.
    d.   Married filing joint return.

162. Albert and Lois Stoner, age sixty-six and sixty-four, respectively, filed a joint tax return for 2009. They provided all of the support for their blind nineteen-year-old son, who has no gross income. Their twenty-three-year-old daughter, a full-time student until her graduation on June 14, 2009, earned $4,900, which was 40% of her total support during 2009. Her parents provided the remaining support. The Stoners also provided the total support of Lois' father, who is a citizen and lifelong resident of Peru. How many exemptions can the Stoners claim on their 2009 income tax return?

    a.   4
    b.   5
    c.   6
    d.   7

163. Jim Planter, who reached age sixty-five on January 1, 2009, filed a joint return for 2009 with his wife Rita, age fifty. Mary, their twenty-one-year-old daughter, was a full-time student at a college until her graduation on June 2, 2009. The daughter had $6,500 of income and provided 25% of her own support during 2009. In addition, during 2009 the Planters were the sole support for Rita's niece, age 27, who had no income. How many exemptions should the Planters claim on their 2009 tax return?

    a.   2
    b.   3
    c.   4
    d.   5

164. In 2009, Sam Dunn provided more than half the support for his wife, his father's brother, and his cousin. Sam's wife was the only relative who was a member of Sam's household. None of the relatives had any income, nor did any of them file an individual or a joint return. All of these relatives are US citizens. Which of these relatives should be claimed as a dependent or dependents on Sam's 2009 return?

    a.   Only his wife.
    b.   Only his father's brother.
    c.   Only his cousin.
    d.   His wife, his father's brother, and his cousin.

165. In 2009, Alan Kott provided more than half the support for his following relatives, none of whom qualified as a member of Alan's household:

        Cousin
        Niece
        Foster parent

None of these relatives had any income, nor did any of these relatives file an individual or joint return. All of these relatives are US citizens. Which of these relatives could be claimed as a dependent on Alan's 2009 return?

    a.   No one.
    b.   Niece.
    c.   Cousin.
    d.   Foster parent.

166. Sara Hance, who is single and lives alone in Idaho, has no income of her own and is supported in full by the following persons:

	Amount of support	Percent of total
Alma (an unrelated friend)	$2,400	48
Ben (Sara's brother)	2,150	43
Carl (Sara's son)	450	9
	$5,000	100

Under a multiple support agreement, Sara's dependency exemption can be claimed by

    a. No one.
    b. Alma.
    c. Ben.
    d. Carl.

167. Mr. and Mrs. Vonce, both age sixty-two, filed a joint return for 2009. They provided all the support for their daughter, who is nineteen, legally blind, and who has no income. Their son, age twenty-one and a full-time student at a university, had $6,200 of income and provided 70% of his own support during 2009. How many exemptions should Mr. and Mrs. Vonce have claimed on their 2009 joint income tax return?

    a. 2
    b. 3
    c. 4
    d. 5

168. Which of the following is(are) among the requirements to enable a taxpayer to be classified as a "qualifying widow(er)"?

I. A dependent has lived with the taxpayer for six months.
II. The taxpayer has maintained the cost of the principal residence for six months.

    a. I only.
    b. II only.
    c. Both I and II.
    d. Neither I nor II.

169. For head of household filing status, which of the following costs are considered in determining whether the taxpayer has contributed more than one-half the cost of maintaining the household?

	Insurance on the home	Rental value of home
a.	Yes	Yes
b.	No	No
c.	Yes	No
d.	No	Yes

170. A husband and wife can file a joint return even if

    a. The spouses have different tax years, provided that both spouses are alive at the end of the year.
    b. The spouses have different accounting methods.
    c. Either spouse was a nonresident alien at any time during the tax year, provided that at least one spouse makes the proper election.
    d. They were divorced before the end of the tax year.

171. Emil Gow's wife died in 2007. Emil did not remarry, and he continued to maintain a home for himself and his dependent infant child during 2008 and 2009, providing full support for himself and his child during these years. For 2007, Emil properly filed a joint return. For 2009, Emil's filing status is

    a. Single.
    b. Head of household.
    c. Qualifying widower with dependent child.
    d. Married filing joint return.

172. Nell Brown's husband died in 2006. Nell did not remarry, and continued to maintain a home for herself and her dependent infant child during 2007, 2008, and 2009, providing full support for herself and her child during these

three years. For 2006, Nell properly filed a joint return. For 2009, Nell's filing status is

    a. Single.
    b. Married filing joint return.
    c. Head of household.
    d. Qualifying widow with dependent child.

173. Mrs. Irma Felton, by herself, maintains her home in which she and her unmarried twenty-six-year-old son reside. Her son, however, does not qualify as her dependent. Mrs. Felton's husband died in 2009. What is Mrs. Felton's filing status for 2010?

    a. Single.
    b. Qualifying widow with dependent child.
    c. Head of household.
    d. Married filing jointly.

174. Poole, forty-five years old and unmarried, is in the 15% tax bracket. He had 2009 adjusted gross income of $20,000. The following information applies to Poole:

Medical expenses	$7,500
Standard deduction	5,700
Personal exemption	3,650

Poole wishes to minimize his income tax. What is Poole's 2009 total income tax?

    a. $3,000
    b. $1,733
    c. $1,553
    d. $1,455

175. Which of the following itemized deductions are deductible when computing the alternative minimum tax for individuals?

    a. State income taxes.
    b. Home equity mortgage interest when the loan proceeds were used to purchase an auto.
    c. Unreimbursed employee expenses in excess of 2% of adjusted gross income.
    d. Gambling losses.

176. Randy Lowe reported the following items in computing his regular federal income tax for 2009:

Personal exemption	$3,650
Itemized deduction for state taxes	1,500
Cash charitable contributions	1,250
Net long-term capital gain	700
Excess of accelerated depreciation over straight-line depreciation on real property placed in service prior to 1987	600
Tax-exempt interest from private activity bonds	400

What are the amounts of tax preference items and adjustments that must be added to or subtracted from regular taxable income in order to compute Lowe's alternative minimum taxable income for 2009?

	Preferences	Adjustments
a.	$1,000	$5,150
b.	$1,000	$5,850
c.	$1,700	$6,150
d.	$2,250	$5,400

177. In 2008, Karen Miller had an alternative minimum tax liability of $20,000. This was the first year that she paid an alternative minimum tax. When she recomputed her 2008 alternative minimum tax using only exclusion preferences and adjustments, her alternative minimum tax was $9,000. For 2009, Karen had a regular tax liability of $50,000 and a tentative minimum tax of $45,000. What is the amount of

Karen's unused minimum tax credit from 2009 that will carry over to 2010?

   a. $0
   b. $4,000
   c. $5,000
   d. $6,000

178. In 2009, Don Mills, a single taxpayer, had $70,000 in taxable income before personal exemptions. Mills had no tax preferences. His itemized deductions were as follows:

State and local income taxes	$5,000
Home mortgage interest on loan to acquire residence	6,000
Miscellaneous deductions that exceed 2% of adjusted gross income	2,000

What amount did Mills report as alternative minimum taxable income before the AMT exemption?

   a. $72,000
   b. $75,000
   c. $77,000
   d. $83,000

179. An individual's alternative minimum tax adjustments include

	Net long-term capital gain in excess of net short-term capital loss	Home equity interest expense where loan proceeds not used to buy, build, or improve home
a.	Yes	Yes
b.	Yes	No
c.	No	Yes
d.	No	No

180. The credit for prior year alternative minimum tax liability may be carried

   a. Forward for a maximum of five years.
   b. Back to the three preceding years or carried forward for a maximum of five years.
   c. Back to the three preceding years.
   d. Forward indefinitely.

181. The alternative minimum tax (AMT) is computed as the

   a. Excess of the regular tax over the tentative AMT.
   b. Excess of the tentative AMT over the regular tax.
   c. The tentative AMT plus the regular tax.
   d. Lesser of the tentative AMT or the regular tax.

182. The following information pertains to Joe Diamond, a cash-method sole proprietor for 2009:

Gross receipts from business	$150,000
Interest income from personal investments	10,000
Cost of goods sold	80,000
Other business operating expenses	40,000

What amount of net earnings from self-employment would be multiplied by the applicable self-employment tax rate to compute Diamond's self-employment tax for 2009?

   a. $25,410
   b. $27,705
   c. $30,000
   d. $40,000

183. Freeman, a single individual, reported the following income in the current year:

Guaranteed payment from services rendered to a partnership	$50,000
Ordinary income from an S corporation	20,000

What amount of Freeman's income is subject to self-employment tax?

   a. $0
   b. $20,000
   c. $50,000
   d. $70,000

184. Rich is a cash-basis self-employed air-conditioning repairman with 2009 gross business receipts of $20,000. Rich's cash disbursements were as follows:

Air conditioning parts	$2,500
Yellow Pages listing	2,000
Estimated federal income taxes on self-employment income	1,000
Business long-distance telephone calls	400
Charitable contributions	200

What amount should Rich report as net self-employment income?

   a. $15,100
   b. $14,900
   c. $14,100
   d. $13,900

185. The self-employment tax is

   a. Fully deductible as an itemized deduction.
   b. Fully deductible in determining net income from self-employment.
   c. One-half deductible from gross income in arriving at adjusted gross income.
   d. Not deductible.

186. An employee who has had social security tax withheld in an amount greater than the maximum for a particular year, may claim

   a. Such excess as either a credit or an itemized deduction, at the election of the employee, if that excess resulted from correct withholding by two or more employers.
   b. Reimbursement of such excess from his employers, if that excess resulted from correct withholding by two or more employers.
   c. The excess as a credit against income tax, if that excess resulted from correct withholding by two or more employers.
   d. The excess as a credit against income tax, if that excess was withheld by one employer.

187. Alex Berger, a retired building contractor, earned the following income during 2010:

Director's fee received from Keith Realty Corp.	$ 600
Executor's fee received from the estate of his deceased sister	7,000

Berger's gross income from self-employment for 2010 is

   a. $0
   b. $ 600
   c. $7,000
   d. $7,600

188. Smith, a retired corporate executive, earned consulting fees of $8,000 and director's fees of $2,000 in 2010. Smith's gross income from self-employment for 2010 is

   a. $0
   b. $ 2,000
   c. $ 8,000
   d. $10,000

189. Which one of the following credits is not a component of the general business credit?
a. Disabled access credit.
b. Employer social security credit.
c. Foreign tax credit.
d. Work opportunity credit.

190. Which of the following credits is a combination of several tax credits to provide uniform rules for the current and carryback-carryover years?
a. General business credit.
b. Foreign tax credit.
c. Minimum tax credit.
d. Enhanced oil recovery credit.

191. Melvin Crane is sixty-six years old, and his wife, Matilda, is sixty-five. They filed a joint income tax return for 2009, reporting an adjusted gross income of $20,200, on which they owed a tax of $60. They received $3,000 from social security benefits in 2009. How much can they claim on Form 1040 in 2009, as a credit for the elderly?
a. $0
b. $ 60
c. $255
d. $675

192. Nora Hayes, a widow, maintains a home for herself and her two dependent preschool children. In 2009, Nora's earned income and adjusted gross income was $44,000. During 2009, Nora paid work-related expenses of $6,000 for a housekeeper to care for her children. How much can Nora claim for child care credit in 2009?
a. $0
b. $ 960
c. $1,200
d. $2,100

193. Robert and Mary Jason, filing a joint tax return for 2009, had a tax liability of $9,000 based on their tax table income and three exemptions. Robert and Mary had earned income of $30,000 and $22,000, respectively, during 2009. In order for Mary to be gainfully employed, the Jasons incurred the following employment-related expenses for their four-year-old son John in 2009:

Payee	Amount
Union Day Care Center	$2,500
Acme Home Cleaning Service	500
Wilma Jason, babysitter (Robert Jason's mother)	1,000

Assuming that the Jasons do not claim any other credits against their tax, what is the amount of the child care tax credit they should report on their tax return for 2009?
a. $ 500
b. $ 600
c. $ 700
d. $1,050

194. To qualify for the child care credit on a joint return, at least one spouse must

	Have an adjusted gross income of $10,000 or less	Be gainfully employed when related expenses are incurred
a.	Yes	Yes
b.	No	No
c.	Yes	No
d.	No	Yes

195. Sunex Co., an accrual-basis, calendar-year domestic C corporation, is taxed on its worldwide income. In the current year, Sunex's US tax liability on its domestic and foreign-source income is $60,000 and no prior year foreign income taxes have been carried forward. Which factor(s) may affect the amount of Sunex's foreign tax credit available in its current year corporate income tax return?

	Income source	The foreign tax rate
a.	Yes	Yes
b.	Yes	No
c.	No	Yes
d.	No	No

196. The following information pertains to Wald Corp.'s operations for the year ended December 31, 2009:

Worldwide taxable income	$300,000
US source taxable income	180,000
US income tax before foreign tax credit	96,000
Foreign nonbusiness-related interest earned	30,000
Foreign income taxes paid on nonbusiness-related interest earned	12,000
Other foreign source taxable income	90,000
Foreign income taxes paid on other foreign source taxable income	27,000

What amount of foreign tax credit may Wald claim for 2009?
a. $28,800
b. $36,600
c. $38,400
d. $39,000

197. Foreign income taxes paid by a corporation
a. May be claimed either as a deduction or as a credit, at the option of the corporation.
b. May be claimed only as a deduction.
c. May be claimed only as a credit.
d. Do **not** qualify either as a deduction or as a credit.

198. Which of the following credits can result in a refund even if the individual had **no** income tax liability?
a. Credit for prior year minimum tax.
b. Credit for the elderly or the disabled.
c. Earned income credit.
d. Child and dependent care credit.

199. Kent qualified for the earned income credit in 2009. This credit could result in a
a. Refund even if Kent had no tax withheld from wages.
b. Refund only if Kent had tax withheld from wages.
c. Carryback or carryforward for any unused portion.
d. Subtraction from adjusted gross income to arrive at taxable income.

200. Which one of the following statements is correct with regard to the earned income credit?
a. The credit is available only to those individuals whose earned income is equal to adjusted gross income.
b. For purposes of the earned income test, "earned income" includes workers' compensation benefits.
c. The credit can result in a refund even if the individual had **no** tax withheld from wages.
d. The credit is available on a tax return that covers less than twelve months.

201. Which of the following tax credits **cannot** be claimed by a corporation?
- a.   Foreign tax credit.
- b.   Earned income credit.
- c.   Alternative fuel production credit.
- d.   General business credit.

202. Which one of the following statements is correct regarding the credit for adoption expenses?
- a.   The credit for adoption expenses is a refundable credit.
- b.   The maximum credit is $5,000 for the adoption of a child with special needs.
- c.   Qualified adoption expenses are taken into account in the year that the adoption becomes final.
- d.   An eligible child is an individual who has not attained the age of twenty-one as of the time of adoption.

203. Which one of the following statements is **not** correct with regard to the child tax credit?
- a.   The credit is $1,000 per qualifying child for tax years beginning in 2009.
- b.   The amount of credit is reduced if modified adjusted gross income exceeds certain thresholds.
- c.   To qualify for the credit, a dependent child must be less than sixteen years old.
- d.   A qualifying child must be a US citizen or resident.

204. Which one of the following statements concerning the 2009 Hope scholarship credit is **not** correct?
- a.   The credit is available for the first four years of postsecondary education program.
- b.   The credit is available on a per student basis.
- c.   To be eligible for the credit, the student must be enrolled full-time for at least one academic period during the year.
- d.   If a parent claims a child as a dependent, any qualified expenses paid by the child are deemed to be paid by the parent.

205. Which one of the following statements concerning the lifetime learning credit is **not** correct?
- a.   The credit is 20% of the first $10,000 of qualified tuition and related expenses for 2009.
- b.   Qualifying expenses include the cost of tuition for graduate courses at an eligible educational institution.
- c.   The credit may be claimed for an unlimited number of years.
- d.   The credit is available on a per student basis.

206. Chris Baker's adjusted gross income on her 2009 tax return was $160,000. The amount covered a twelve-month period. For the 2010 tax year, Baker may avoid the penalty for the underpayment of estimated tax if the timely estimated tax payments equal the required annual amount of

- I.   90% of the tax on the return for the current year, paid in four equal installments.
- II. 100% of prior year's tax liability, paid in four equal installments.

- a.   I only.
- b.   II only.
- c.   Both I and II.
- d.   Neither I nor II.

207. Krete, an unmarried taxpayer, had income exclusively from wages. By December 31, 2009, Krete's employer had withheld $16,000 in federal income taxes and Krete had made no estimated tax payments. On April 15, 2010, Krete timely filed an extension request to file her individual tax return and paid $300 of additional taxes. Krete's 2009 income tax liability was $16,500 when she timely filed her return on April 30, 2010, and paid the remaining income tax liability balance. What amount would be subject to the penalty for the underpayment of estimated taxes?
- a. $0
- b. $ 200
- c. $ 500
- d. $16,500

208. John Smith is the executor of his father's estate. His father, a calendar-year taxpayer, died on July 15, 2009. As executor of his father's estate, John is required to file a final income tax return Form 1040 for his father's 2009 tax year. What is the due date of his father's 2009 federal income tax return assuming John does not file for an extension?
- a.   November 1, 2009.
- b.   November 15, 2009.
- c.   March 15, 2010.
- d.   April 15, 2010.

209. Ray Birch, age sixty, is single with no dependents. Birch's only income is from his occupation as a self-employed plumber. Birch must file a return for 2009 if his net earnings from self-employment are at least
- a. $ 400
- b. $ 950
- c. $3,650
- d. $5,700

210. Jackson Corp., a calendar-year corporation, mailed its 2009 tax return to the Internal Revenue Service by certified mail on Thursday, March 12, 2009. The return, postmarked March 12, 2009, was delivered to the Internal Revenue Service on March 17, 2009. The statute of limitations on Jackson's corporate tax return begins on
- a.   December 31, 2008.
- b.   March 12, 2009.
- c.   March 16, 2009.
- d.   March 17, 2009.

211. A calendar-year taxpayer files an individual tax return for 2009 on March 20, 2010. The taxpayer neither committed fraud nor omitted amounts in excess of 25% of gross income on the tax return. What is the latest date that the Internal Revenue Service can assess tax and assert a notice of deficiency?
- a.   March 20, 2013.
- b.   March 20, 2012.
- c.   April 15, 2013.
- d.   April 15, 2012.

212. Harold Thompson, a self-employed individual, had income transactions for 2009 (duly reported on his return filed in April 2010) as follows:

Gross receipts	$400,000
Less cost of goods sold and deductions	320,000
Net business income	$ 80,000
Capital gains	36,000
Gross income	$116,000

In November 2010, Thompson discovers that he had inadvertently omitted some income on his 2009 return and retains Mann, CPA, to determine his position under the statute of limitations. Mann should advise Thompson that the six-year statute of limitations would apply to his 2009 return only if he omitted from gross income an amount in excess of

a. $ 20,000
b. $ 29,000
c. $100,000
d. $109,000

213. If a taxpayer omits from his or her income tax return an amount that exceeds 25% of the gross income reported on the return, the Internal Revenue Service can issue a notice of deficiency within a maximum period of

a. Three years from the date the return was filed, if filed before the due date.
b. Three years from the date the return was due, if filed by the due date.
c. Six years from the date the return was filed, if filed before the due date.
d. Six years from the date the return was due, if filed by the due date.

214. A claim for refund of erroneously paid income taxes, filed by an individual before the statute of limitations expires, must be submitted on Form

a. 1139
b. 1045
c. 1040X
d. 843

215. If an individual paid income tax in 2009 but did **not** file a 2009 return because his income was insufficient to require the filing of a return, the deadline for filing a refund claim is

a. Two years from the date the tax was paid.
b. Two years from the date a return would have been due.
c. Three years from the date the tax was paid.
d. Three years from the date a return would have been due.

216. A married couple filed their joint 2008 calendar-year return on March 15, 2009, and attached a check for the balance of tax due as shown on the return. On June 15, 2010, the couple discovered that they had failed to include $2,000 of home mortgage interest in their itemized deductions. In order for the couple to recover the tax that they would have saved by using the $2,000 deduction, they must file an amended return no later than

a. December 31, 2011.
b. March 15, 2012.
c. April 15, 2012.
d. June 15, 2012.

217. Richard Baker filed his 2008 individual income tax return on April 15, 2009. On December 31, 2009, he learned that 100 shares of stock that he owned had become worthless in 2008. Since he did not deduct this loss on his 2008 return, Baker intends to file a claim for refund. This refund claim must be filed not later than April 15,

a. 2009
b. 2011
c. 2014
d. 2015

218. A taxpayer filed his income tax return after the due date but neglected to file an extension form. The return

indicated a tax liability of $50,000 and taxes withheld of $45,000. On what amount would the penalties for late filing and late payment be computed?

a. $0
b. $ 5,000
c. $45,000
d. $50,000

219. An accuracy-related penalty applies to the portion of tax underpayment attributable to

I. Any substantial gift or estate tax valuation understatement
II. Any substantial income tax valuation overstatement.

a. I only.
b. II only.
c. Both I and II.
d. Neither I nor II.

SIMULATION PROBLEMS

Simulation Problem 1   (35 to 45 minutes)

Situation			
	Tax Treatment	Research	Communication

Cole, a newly licensed CPA, opened an office in 2009 as a sole practitioner engaged in the practice of public accountancy. Cole reports on the cash basis for income tax purposes.

	Tax Treatment		
Situation		Research	Communication

Listed below are Cole's 2009 business and nonbusiness transactions, as well as possible tax treatments. For each of Cole's transactions (**Items 1 through 20**), select the appropriate tax treatment. A tax treatment may be selected once, more than once, or not at all.

Tax treatments

A. Taxable as interest income in Schedule B—Interest and Dividend Income.
B. Taxable as other income on page 1 of Form 1040.
C. Not taxable.
D. Deductible on page 1 of Form 1040 to arrive at adjusted gross income.
E. Deductible in Schedule A—Itemized Deductions, subject to threshold of 7.5% of adjusted gross income.
F. Deductible in Schedule A—Itemized Deductions, subject to threshold of 10% of adjusted gross income and additional threshold of $500.
G. Deductible in full in Schedule A—Itemized Deductions (cannot be claimed as a credit).

H. Deductible in Schedule B—Interest and Dividend Income.
I. Deductible in Schedule C—Profit or Loss from Business.
J. Deductible in Schedule D—Capital Gains or Losses.
K. Deductible in Schedule E—Supplemental Income and Loss.
L. Deductible in Form 4797—Sales of Business Property.
M. Claimed in Form 1116—Foreign Tax Credit, or in Schedule A—Itemized Deductions, at taxpayer's option.
N. Based on gross self-employment income.
O. Based on net earnings from self-employment.
P. Not deductible.

Transactions	(A)	(B)	(C)	(D)	(E)	(F)	(G)	(H)	(I)	(J)	(K)	(L)	(M)	(N)	(O)	(P)
1. Fees received for jury duty.	○	○	○	○	○	○	○	○	○	○	○	○	○	○	○	○
2. Interest income on mortgage loan receivable.	○	○	○	○	○	○	○	○	○	○	○	○	○	○	○	○
3. Penalty paid to bank on early withdrawal of savings.	○	○	○	○	○	○	○	○	○	○	○	○	○	○	○	○
4. Write-offs of uncollectible accounts receivable from accounting practice.	○	○	○	○	○	○	○	○	○	○	○	○	○	○	○	○
5. Cost of attending review course in preparation for the Uniform CPA Examination.	○	○	○	○	○	○	○	○	○	○	○	○	○	○	○	○
6. Fee for the biennial permit to practice as a CPA.	○	○	○	○	○	○	○	○	○	○	○	○	○	○	○	○
7. Costs of attending CPE courses in fulfillment of state board requirements.	○	○	○	○	○	○	○	○	○	○	○	○	○	○	○	○
8. Contribution to a qualified Keogh retirement plan.	○	○	○	○	○	○	○	○	○	○	○	○	○	○	○	○
9. Loss sustained from nonbusiness bad debt.	○	○	○	○	○	○	○	○	○	○	○	○	○	○	○	○
10. Loss sustained on sale of "Small Business Corporation" (Section 1244) stock.	○	○	○	○	○	○	○	○	○	○	○	○	○	○	○	○
11. Taxes paid on land owned by Cole and rented out as a parking lot.	○	○	○	○	○	○	○	○	○	○	○	○	○	○	○	○
12. Interest paid on installment purchases of household furniture.	○	○	○	○	○	○	○	○	○	○	○	○	○	○	○	○
13. Alimony paid to former spouse who reports the alimony as taxable income.	○	○	○	○	○	○	○	○	○	○	○	○	○	○	○	○

Transactions	(A)	(B)	(C)	(D)	(E)	(F)	(G)	(H)	(I)	(J)	(K)	(L)	(M)	(N)	(O)	(P)
14. Personal medical expenses charged on credit card in December 2009 but not paid until January 2010.	○	○	○	○	○	○	○	○	○	○	○	○	○	○	○	○
15. Personal casualty loss sustained.	○	○	○	○	○	○	○	○	○	○	○	○	○	○	○	○
16. State inheritance tax paid on bequest received.	○	○	○	○	○	○	○	○	○	○	○	○	○	○	○	○
17. Foreign income tax withheld at source on dividend received.	○	○	○	○	○	○	○	○	○	○	○	○	○	○	○	○
18. Computation of self-employment tax.	○	○	○	○	○	○	○	○	○	○	○	○	○	○	○	○
19. One-half of self-employment tax paid with 2009 return filed in April 2010.	○	○	○	○	○	○	○	○	○	○	○	○	○	○	○	○
20. Insurance premiums paid on Cole's life.	○	○	○	○	○	○	○	○	○	○	○	○	○	○	○	○

Mr. Cole is considering purchasing a new principal residence for $1,500,000, and intends to finance the purchase with a mortgage in the amount of $1,150,000. Which code section and subsection provide the maximum amount of acquisition indebtedness mortgage on which the interest expense will be deductible? Indicate the reference to that citation in the shaded boxes below.

Section	Subsection
§ ▭	(▭)

Write a memorandum to Mr. Cole describing the results of your research above.

REMINDER: Your response will be graded for both technical content and writing skills. Technical content will be evaluated for information that is helpful to the intended reader and clearly relevant to the issues. Writing skills will be evaluated for development, organization, and the appropriate expression of ideas in professional correspondence. Use a standard business memo or letter format with a clear beginning, middle, and end. Do not convey information in the form of a table, bullet point list, or other abbreviated presentation.

To: Mr. Cole
From: CPA Candidate
Re: Deductibility of interest on mortgage

Simulation Problem 2   (50 to 60 minutes)

Situation				
	Tax Treatment I	Tax Treatment II	Research	Communication

Green is self-employed as a human resources consultant and reports on the cash basis for income tax purposes. Green is an unmarried custodial parent with one dependent child.

	Tax Treatment I			
Situation		Tax Treatment II	Research	Communication

Listed below are Green's 2009 business and nonbusiness transactions, as well as possible tax treatments. For each of Green's transactions (**Items 1 through 25**), select the appropriate tax treatment. A tax treatment may be selected once, more than once, or not at all.

Tax treatments

A. Taxable as other income on Form 1040.
B. Reported in Schedule B—Interest and Dividend Income.
C. Reported in Schedule C as trade or business income.
D. Reported in Schedule E—Supplemental Income and Loss.
E. Not taxable.
F. Fully deductible on Form 1040 to arrive at adjusted gross income.
G. Fifty percent deductible on Form 1040 to arrive at adjusted gross income.
H. Reported in Schedule A—Itemized Deductions (deductibility subject to threshold of 7.5% of adjusted gross income).
I. Reported in Schedule A—Itemized Deductions (deductibility subject to threshold of 2% of adjusted gross income).

J. Reported in Form 4562—Depreciation and Amortization and deductible in Schedule A—Itemized Deductions (deductibility subject to threshold of 2% of adjusted gross income).
K. Reported in Form 4562—Depreciation and Amortization, and deductible in Schedule C—Profit or Loss from Business.
L. Fully deductible in Schedule C—Profit or Loss from Business.
M. Partially deductible in Schedule C—Profit or Loss from Business.
N. Reported in Form 2119—Sale of Your Home, and deductible in Schedule D—Capital Gains and Losses.
O. Not deductible.

Transactions

1. Retainer fees received from clients.
2. Oil royalties received.
3. Interest income on general obligation state and local government bonds.
4. Interest on refund of federal taxes.
5. Death benefits from term life insurance policy on parent.
6. Interest income on US Treasury bonds.
7. Share of ordinary income from an investment in a limited partnership reported in Form 1065, Schedule K-1.
8. Taxable income from rental of a townhouse owned by Green.
9. Prize won as a contestant on a TV quiz show.
10. Payment received for jury service.
11. Dividends received from mutual funds that invest in tax-free government obligations.
12. Qualifying medical expenses not reimbursed by insurance.
13. Personal life insurance premiums paid by Green.
14. Expenses for business-related meals where clients were present.
15. Depreciation on personal computer purchased in 2009 used for business.
16. Business lodging expenses, while out of town.
17. Subscriptions to professional journals used for business.
18. Self-employment taxes paid.
19. Qualifying contributions to a simplified employee pension plan.
20. Election to expense business equipment purchased in 2009.
21. Qualifying alimony payments made by Green.

Transactions	(A) (B) (C) (D) (E) (F) (G) (H) (I) (J) (K) (L) (M) (N) (O)
22. Subscriptions for investment-related publications.	O O O O O O O O O O O O O O O
23. Interest expense on a home-equity line of credit for an amount borrowed to finance Green's business.	O O O O O O O O O O O O O O O
24. Interest expense on a loan for an auto used 75% for business.	O O O O O O O O O O O O O O O
25. Loss on sale of residence.	O O O O O O O O O O O O O O O

Situation	Tax Treatment I	Tax Treatment II	Research	Communication

For 2009, Green, who had adjusted gross income of $40,000, qualified to itemize deductions and was subject to federal income tax liability. For **items 1 through 9,** select from the following list of tax treatments the appropriate tax treatment. A tax treatment may be selected once, more than once, or not at all.

Selections

A. Not deductible on Form 1040.
B. Deductible in full on Schedule A—Itemized Deductions.
C. Deductible in Schedule A—Itemized Deductions subject to a limitation of 50% of adjusted gross income.
D. Deductible in Schedule A—Itemized Deductions as miscellaneous deductions subject to a threshold of 2% of adjusted gross income.

E. Deductible in Schedule A—Itemized Deductions as miscellaneous deductions not subject to a threshold of 2% adjusted gross income.
F. Deductible on Schedule E—Supplemental Income and Loss.
G. A credit is allowable.

	(A) (B) (C) (D) (E) (F) (G)
1. In 2009, Green paid $2,000 interest on the $25,000 home equity mortgage on his vacation home, which he used exclusively for personal use. The mortgage is secured by Green's vacation home, and the loan proceeds were used to purchase an automobile.	O O O O O O O
2. For 2009, Green had a $30,000 cash charitable contribution carryover from his 2008 cash donation to the American Red Cross. Green made no additional charitable contributions in 2009.	O O O O O O O
3. During 2009, Green had investment interest expense that did not exceed his net investment income.	O O O O O O O
4. Green's 2009 lottery ticket losses were $450. He had no gambling winnings.	O O O O O O O
5. During 2009, Green paid $2,500 in real property taxes on his vacation home, which he used exclusively for personal use.	O O O O O O O
6. In 2009, Green paid a $500 premium for a homeowner's insurance policy on his principal residence.	O O O O O O O
7. For 2009, Green paid $2,000 to an unrelated babysitter to care for his child while he worked.	O O O O O O O
8. In 2009, Green paid $4,000 interest on the $60,000 acquisition mortgage of his principal residence. The mortgage is secured by Green's home.	O O O O O O O
9. During 2009, Green paid $3,600 real property taxes on residential rental property in which he actively participates. There was no personal use of the rental property.	O O O O O O O

Situation	Tax Treatment I	Tax Treatment II	Research	Communication

Mr. Green paid $5,000 to an unrelated babysitter for the care of his child while he worked. Which code section and subsection provide the maximum amount of employment-related child care expenses that qualify for a tax credit? Indicate the reference to that citation in the shaded boxes below.

Section	Subsection
§ [ ]	([ ])

Situation	Tax Treatment I	Tax Treatment II	Research	Communication

Assuming that Mr. Green has adjusted gross income for 2009 in the amount of $70,000, write a memorandum to Mr. Green explaining how the babysitter payments will affect his tax liability.

REMINDER: Your response will be graded for both technical content and writing skills. Technical content will be evaluated for information that is helpful to the intended reader and clearly relevant to the issues. Writing skills will be evaluated for development, organization, and the appropriate expression of ideas in professional correspondence. Use a standard business memo or letter format with a clear beginning, middle, and end. Do not convey information in the form of a table, bullet point list, or other abbreviated presentation.

To: Mr. Green
From: CPA Candidate
Re: Dependent care payments

Simulation Problem 3   (30 to 40 minutes)

Situation			
	Deductibility	Research	Communication

Mark Smith is an employee of Patton Corporation. Additionally, Smith operates a consulting business as a sole proprietor and owns an apartment building. Smith made the expenditures listed below during 2009.

	Deductibility		
Situation		Research	Communication

For each of the following items, indicate whether each expenditure is deductible for AGI, from AGI (not subject to 2% limitation), from AGI (subject to 2% limitation), or not deductible. Assume Smith plans to itemize deductions for 2009.

	For AGI (A)	From AGI (No 2%) (B)	From AGI (2% Floor) (C)	Not ded. (D)
1. Smith paid the medical expenses of his mother-in-law. Although Smith provided more than half of her support, she does not qualify as Smith's dependent because she had gross income of $5,000.	O	O	O	O
2. Smith paid the real estate taxes on his rental apartment building.	O	O	O	O
3. Smith paid state sales taxes of $1,500 on a used automobile that he purchased for personal use.	O	O	O	O
4. Smith paid the real estate taxes on his mother-in-law's home. She is the owner of the home.	O	O	O	O
5. Smith paid $1,500 of interest on credit card charges. The charges were for items purchased for personal use.	O	O	O	O
6. Smith paid an attorney $500 to prepare Smith's will.	O	O	O	O
7. Smith incurred $750 of expenses for business meals and entertainment in his position as an employee of Patton Corporation. Smith's expenses were not reimbursed.	O	O	O	O
8. Smith paid self-employment taxes of $3,000 as a result of earnings from the consulting business that he conducts as a sole proprietor.	O	O	O	O
9. Smith made a contribution to his self-employed retirement plan (Keogh Plan).	O	O	O	O
10. Smith had gambling losses totaling $2,500 for the year. He is including a lottery prize of $5,000 in his gross income this year.	O	O	O	O

In January of 2010, Mark Smith had to have heart surgery. The total cost of the surgery was $100,000, and his insurance covered a total of $82,000. Smith paid the remaining $18,000 in February of 2010. Which code section and subsection determine the extent to which Smith's unreimbursed medical expenses will be deductible? Indicate the reference to that citation in the shaded boxes below.

Section	Subsection
§ [ ]	([ ])

			Communication
Situation	Deductibility	Research	

Write a memorandum to Mr. Smith describing the results of your research above.

REMINDER: Your response will be graded for both technical content and writing skills. Technical content will be evaluated for information that is helpful to the intended reader and clearly relevant to the issues. Writing skills will be evaluated for development, organization, and the appropriate expression of ideas in professional correspondence. Use a standard business memo or letter format with a clear beginning, middle, and end. Do not convey information in the form of a table, bullet point list, or other abbreviated presentation.

To: Mr. Mark Smith
From: CPA Candidate
Re: Deductibility of surgery costs

Simulation Problem 4   (35 to 45 minutes)

Situation				
	Adjusted Gross Income	Exemptions	Research	Communication

Frank and Dale Cumack are married and filing a joint 2009 income tax return. During 2009, Frank, sixty-five, was retired from government service and Dale, fifty-five, was employed as a university instructor. In 2009, the Cumacks contributed all of the support to Dale's father, Jacques, an unmarried French citizen and French resident who had no gross income.

	Adjusted Gross Income			
Situation		Exemptions	Research	Communication

For **items 1 through 10,** select the correct amount of income, loss, or adjustment to income that should be reported on page 1 of the Cumacks' 2009 Form 1040—Individual Income Tax Return to arrive at the adjusted gross income for each separate transaction. A tax treatment may be selected once, more than once, or not at all.

Any information contained in an item is unique to that item and is not to be incorporated in your calculations when answering other items.

Selections

A. $0	D. $3,000	F. $4,000	I. $10,000	K. $ 30,000
B. $1,000	E. $3,500	G. $5,000	J. $25,000	L. $125,000
C. $2,000		H. $9,000		M. $150,000

(A) (B) (C) (D) (E) (F) (G) (H) (I) (J) (K) (L) (M)

1. During 2009, Dale received a $30,000 cash gift from her aunt.   ○ ○ ○ ○ ○ ○ ○ ○ ○ ○ ○ ○ ○

2. Dale contributed $3,500 to her traditional Individual Retirement Account (IRA) on January 15, 2009. In 2009, she earned $60,000 as a university instructor. During 2009 the Cumacks were not active participants in an employer's qualified pension or annuity plan.   ○ ○ ○ ○ ○ ○ ○ ○ ○ ○ ○ ○ ○

(A) (B) (C) (D) (E) (F) (G) (H) (I) (J) (K) (L) (M)

3. In 2009, the Cumacks received a $1,000 federal income tax refund.

    ○ ○ ○ ○ ○ ○ ○ ○ ○ ○ ○ ○ ○

4. During 2009, Frank, a 50% partner in Diske General Partnership, received a $4,000 guaranteed payment from Diske for services that he rendered to the partnership that year.

    ○ ○ ○ ○ ○ ○ ○ ○ ○ ○ ○ ○ ○

5. In 2009, Frank received $10,000 as beneficiary of his deceased brother's life insurance policy.

    ○ ○ ○ ○ ○ ○ ○ ○ ○ ○ ○ ○ ○

6. Dale's employer pays 100% of the cost of all employees' group-term life insurance under a qualified plan. Policy cost is $5 per $1,000 of coverage. Dale's group-term life insurance coverage equals $450,000.

    ○ ○ ○ ○ ○ ○ ○ ○ ○ ○ ○ ○ ○

7. In 2009, Frank won $5,000 at a casino and had $2,000 in gambling losses.

    ○ ○ ○ ○ ○ ○ ○ ○ ○ ○ ○ ○ ○

8. During 2009, the Cumacks received $1,000 interest income associated with a refund of their prior years' federal income tax.

    ○ ○ ○ ○ ○ ○ ○ ○ ○ ○ ○ ○ ○

9. In 2009, the Cumacks sold their first and only residence for $400,000. They purchased their home in 1992 for $50,000 and have lived there since then. There were no other capital gains, losses, or capital loss carryovers. The Cumacks do not intend to buy another residence.

    ○ ○ ○ ○ ○ ○ ○ ○ ○ ○ ○ ○ ○

10. In 2009, Zeno Corp. declared a stock dividend and Dale received one additional share of Zeno common stock for three shares of Zeno common stock that she held. The stock that Dale received had a fair market value of $9,000. There was no provision to receive cash instead of stock.

    ○ ○ ○ ○ ○ ○ ○ ○ ○ ○ ○ ○ ○

		Exemptions		
Situation	Adjusted Gross Income		Research	Communication

Frank and Dale Cumack are married and filing a joint 2009 income tax return. During 2009, Frank, sixty-five, was retired from government service and Dale, fifty-five, was employed as a university instructor. In 2009, the Cumacks contributed all of the support to Dale's father, Jacques, an unmarried French citizen and French resident who had no gross income.

Determine whether the Cumacks overstated, understated, or correctly determined the number of both personal and dependency exemptions.

Selections

    O. Overstated the number of both personal and dependency exemptions.
    U. Understated the number of both personal and dependency exemptions.
    C. Correctly determined the number of both personal and dependency exemptions.

                                           (O) (U) (C)
The Cumacks claimed three exemptions on their 2009 joint income tax return.   ○ ○ ○

			Research	
Situation	Adjusted Gross Income	Exemptions		Communication

Assume that the Cumacks' automobile was stolen in 2010. The automobile was uninsured for theft and had a fair market value of $7,000, and an adjusted basis of $10,000. Which code section and subsection provide the limitations that apply to the deductibility of the Cumacks' uninsured theft loss? Indicate the reference to that citation in the shaded boxes below.

Section	Subsection
§ [ ]	([ ])

Situation	Adjusted Gross Income	Exemptions	Research	Communication

Write a memorandum to Dale Cumack describing your research relevant to the above issue.

REMINDER: Your response will be graded for both technical content and writing skills. Technical content will be evaluated for information that is helpful to the intended reader and clearly relevant to the issues. Writing skills will be evaluated for development, organization, and the appropriate expression of ideas in professional correspondence. Use a standard business memo or letter format with a clear beginning, middle, and end. Do not convey information in the form of a table, bullet point list, or other abbreviated presentation.

To: Dale Cumack
From: CPA Candidate
Re: Theft loss

Simulation Problem 5   (40 to 45 minutes)

Situation	Filing Status	Adjusted Gross Income	Tax Treatment	Research	Communication

Mrs. Vick, a forty-year-old cash-basis taxpayer, earned $45,000 as a teacher and $5,000 as a part-time real estate agent in 2009. Mr. Vick, who died on July 1, 2009, had been permanently disabled on his job and collected state disability benefits until his death. For all of 2009 and 2010, the Vicks' residence was the principal home of both their eleven-year-old daughter Joan and Mrs. Vick's unmarried cousin, Fran Phillips, who had no income in either year. During 2009 Joan received $200 a month in survivor social security benefits that began on August 1, 2009, and will continue at least until her eighteenth birthday. In 2009 and 2010, Mrs. Vick provided over one-half the support for Joan and Fran, both of whom were US citizens. Mrs. Vick did not remarry. Mr. and Mrs. Vick received the following in 2009:

Earned income	$50,000
State disability benefits	1,500
Interest on:	
Refund from amended tax return	50
Savings account and certificates of deposit	350
Municipal bonds	100
Gift	3,000
Pension benefits	900
Jury duty pay	200
Gambling winnings	450
Life insurance proceeds	5,000

Additional information:

- Mrs. Vick received the $3,000 cash gift from her uncle.
- Mrs. Vick received the pension distributions from a qualified pension plan, paid for exclusively by her husband's employer.
- Mrs. Vick had $100 in gambling losses in 2009.
- Mrs. Vick was the beneficiary of the life insurance policy on her husband's life. She received a lump-sum distribution. The Vicks had paid $500 in premiums.
- Mrs. Vick received Mr. Vick's accrued vacation pay of $500 in 2010.

Situation	Filing Status	Adjusted Gross Income	Tax Treatment	Research	Communication

For **items 1 and 2,** determine and select from the choices below, **BOTH** the filing status and the number of exemptions for each item.

	Filing Status	Exemptions
S.	Single	1
M.	Married filing joint	2
H.	Head of household	3
Q.	Qualifying widow with dependent child	4

		Filing Status				Exemptions			
		(S)	(M)	(H)	(Q)	(1)	(2)	(3)	(4)
1. Determine the filing status and the number of exemptions that Mrs. Vick can claim on the 2009 federal income tax return, to get the most favorable tax results.		○	○	○	○	○	○	○	○
2. Determine the filing status and the number of exemptions that Mrs. Vick can claim on the 2010 federal income tax return to get the most favorable tax results, if she solely maintains the costs of her home.		○	○	○	○	○	○	○	○

Situation	Filing Status	**Adjusted Gross Income**	Tax Treatment	Research	Communication

For **items 1 through 7,** determine the amount, if any, that is taxable and should be included in Adjusted Gross Income (AGI) on the 2009 federal income tax return filed by Mrs. Vick.

1. State disability benefits
2. Interest income
3. Pension benefits
4. Gift
5. Life insurance proceeds
6. Jury duty pay
7. Gambling winnings

Situation	Filing Status	Adjusted Gross Income	**Tax Treatment**	Research	Communication

During 2009 the following payments were made or losses were incurred. For **items 1 through 14,** select the appropriate tax treatment. A tax treatment may be selected once, more than once, or not at all.

Tax treatment

A. Not deductible.
B. Deductible in Schedule A—Itemized Deductions, subject to threshold of 7.5% of adjusted gross income.
C. Deductible in Schedule A—Itemized Deductions, subject to threshold of 2% of adjusted gross income.
D. Deductible on page 1 of Form 1040 to arrive at adjusted gross income.
E. Deductible in full in Schedule A—Itemized Deductions.
F. Deductible in Schedule A—Itemized Deductions, subject to maximum of 50% of adjusted gross income.

	(A)	(B)	(C)	(D)	(E)	(F)
1. Premiums on Mr. Vick's personal life insurance policy.	○	○	○	○	○	○
2. Penalty on Mrs. Vick's early withdrawal of funds from a certificate of deposit.	○	○	○	○	○	○
3. Mrs. Vick's substantiated cash donation to the American Red Cross.	○	○	○	○	○	○
4. Payment of estimated state income taxes.	○	○	○	○	○	○
5. Payment of real estate taxes on the Vick home.	○	○	○	○	○	○
6. Loss on the sale of the family car.	○	○	○	○	○	○
7. Cost in excess of the increase in value of residence, for the installation of a stairlift in January 2009, related directly to the medical care of Mr. Vick.	○	○	○	○	○	○
8. The Vicks' health insurance premiums for hospitalization coverage.	○	○	○	○	○	○
9. CPA fees to prepare the 2008 tax return.	○	○	○	○	○	○
10. Amortization over the life of the loan of points paid to refinance the mortgage at a lower rate on the Vick home.	○	○	○	○	○	○
11. One-half the self-employment tax paid by Mrs. Vick.	○	○	○	○	○	○
12. Mrs. Vick's $100 in gambling losses.	○	○	○	○	○	○

	(A)	(B)	(C)	(D)	(E)	(F)
13. Mrs. Vick's union dues.	○	○	○	○	○	○
14. 2008 federal income tax paid with the Vicks' tax return on April 15, 2009.	○	○	○	○	○	○

				Research	
Situation	Filing Status	Adjusted Gross Income	Tax Treatment		Communication

Mrs. Vick is considering making contributions to a qualified tuition program to provide savings for her daughter's college education. However, Mrs. Vick is concerned that the contributions will be considered a gift of a future interest and result in a taxable gift. Which code section and subsection provide the gift tax treatment for contributions to a qualified tuition program? Indicate the reference to that citation in the shaded boxes below.

Section	Subsection
§ [ ]	([ ])

					Communication
Situation	Filing Status	Adjusted Gross Income	Tax Treatment	Research	

Describe the results of your research in a memorandum to Mrs. Vick.

REMINDER: Your response will be graded for both technical content and writing skills. Technical content will be evaluated for information that is helpful to the intended reader and clearly relevant to the issues. Writing skills will be evaluated for development, organization, and the appropriate expression of ideas in professional correspondence. Use a standard business memo or letter format with a clear beginning, middle, and end. Do not convey information in the form of a table, bullet point list, or other abbreviated presentation.

To: Mrs. Vick
From: CPA Candidate
Re: College savings plan

Simulation Problem 6   (40 to 45 minutes)

Situation					
	Income and Loss	Adjustments	Tax Treatments	Communication	Research

Tom and Joan Moore, both CPAs, filed a joint 2009 federal income tax return showing $70,000 in taxable income. During 2009, Tom's daughter Laura, age sixteen, resided with Tom's former spouse. Laura had no income of her own and was not Tom's dependent.

	Income and Loss				
Situation		Adjustments	Tax Treatments	Communication	Research

For **items 1 through 10,** determine the amount of income or loss, if any, that should be included on page one of the Moores' 2009 Form 1040.

1. The Moores had no capital loss carryovers from prior years. During 2009 the Moores had the following stock transactions that resulted in a net capital loss:

	Date acquired	Date sold	Sales price	Cost
Revco	2/1/09	3/17/09	$15,000	$25,000
Abbco	2/18/08	4/1/09	8,000	4,000

2. In 2006, Joan received an acre of land as an inter vivos gift from her grandfather. At the time of the gift, the land had a fair market value of $50,000. The grandfather's adjusted basis was $60,000. Joan sold the land in 2009 to an unrelated third party for $56,000.

3. The Moores received a $500 security deposit on their rental property in 2009. They are required to return the amount to the tenant.

4. Tom's 2009 wages were $53,000. In addition, Tom's employer provided group-term life insurance on Tom's life in excess of $50,000. The value of such excess coverage was $2,000.

5. During 2009, the Moores received a $2,500 federal tax refund and a $1,250 state tax refund for 2008 overpayments. In 2008, the Moores were not subject to the alternative minimum tax and were not entitled to any credit against income tax. The Moores' 2008 adjusted gross income was $80,000 and itemized deductions were $1,450 in excess of the standard deduction. The state tax deduction for 2008 was $2,000.

6. In 2009, Joan received $1,300 in unemployment compensation benefits. Her employer made a $100 contribution to the unemployment insurance fund on her behalf.

7. The Moores received $8,400 in gross receipts from their rental property during 2009. The expenses for the residential rental property were

Bank mortgage interest	$1,200
Real estate taxes	700
Insurance	500
MACRS depreciation	3,500

8. The Moores received a stock dividend in 2009 from Ace Corp. They had the option to receive either cash or Ace stock with a fair market value of $900 as of the date of distribution. The par value of the stock was $500.

9. In 2009, Joan received $3,500 as beneficiary of the death benefit that was provided by her brother's employer. Joan's brother did not have a nonforfeitable right to receive the money while living, and the death benefit does not represent the proceeds of life insurance.

10. Tom received $10,000, consisting of $5,000 each of principal and interest, when he redeemed a Series EE savings bond in 2009. The bond was issued in his name in 2000 and the proceeds were used to pay for Laura's college tuition. Tom had not elected to report the yearly increases in the value of the bond.

		Adjustments			
Situation	**Income and Loss**		**Tax Treatments**	**Communication**	**Research**

Determine the amount of the adjustment, if any, to arrive at adjusted gross income.

As required by a 2004 divorce agreement, Tom paid an annual amount of $8,000 in alimony and $10,000 in child support during 2009.

			Tax Treatments		
Situation	**Income and Loss**	**Adjustments**		**Communication**	**Research**

During 2009, the following events took place. For **items 1 through 12,** select the appropriate tax treatment. A tax treatment may be selected once, more than once, or not at all.

Tax treatment

A. Not deductible on Form 1040.
B. Deductible in full in Schedule A—Itemized Deductions.
C. Deductible in Schedule A—Itemized Deductions, subject to a threshold of 7.5% of adjusted gross income.
D. Deductible in Schedule A—Itemized Deductions, subject to a limitation of 50% of adjusted gross income.

E. Deductible in Schedule A—Itemized Deductions, subject to a $500 floor and a threshold of 10% of adjusted gross income.
F. Deductible in Schedule A—Itemized Deductions, subject to a threshold of 2% of adjusted gross income.

	(A)	(B)	(C)	(D)	(E)	(F)
1. On March 23, 2009, Tom sold fifty shares of Zip stock at a $1,200 loss. He repurchased fifty shares of Zip on April 15, 2009.	○	○	○	○	○	○
2. Payment of a personal property tax based on the value of the Moores' car.	○	○	○	○	○	○
3. Used clothes were donated to church organizations.	○	○	○	○	○	○
4. Premiums were paid covering insurance against Tom's loss of earnings.	○	○	○	○	○	○
5. Tom paid for subscriptions to accounting journals.	○	○	○	○	○	○
6. Interest was paid on a $10,000 home-equity line of credit secured by the Moores' residence. The fair market value of the home exceeded the mortgage by $50,000. Tom used the proceeds to purchase a sailboat.	○	○	○	○	○	○
7. Amounts were paid in excess of insurance reimbursement for prescription drugs.	○	○	○	○	○	○
8. Funeral expenses were paid by the Moores for Joan's brother.	○	○	○	○	○	○
9. Theft loss was incurred on Joan's jewelry in excess of insurance reimbursement. There were no 2009 personal casualty gains.	○	○	○	○	○	○

	(A)	(B)	(C)	(D)	(E)	(F)
10. Loss on the sale of the family's sailboat.	○	○	○	○	○	○
11. Interest was paid on the $300,000 acquisition mortgage on the Moores' home. The mortgage is secured by their home.	○	○	○	○	○	○
12. Joan performed free accounting services for the Red Cross. The estimated value of the services was $500.	○	○	○	○	○	○

The Moores contact you and indicate that they are considering buying a more expensive home, as well as using a home equity loan to purchase an automobile. They want to know what possible limitations might apply to their deduction for the interest expense that will result from these purchases. Write a letter to the Moores explaining the limitations that would apply to their deduction for the interest expense they might incur.

REMINDER: Your response will be graded for both technical content and writing skills. Technical content will be evaluated for information that is helpful to the intended reader and clearly relevant to the issues. Writing skills will be evaluated for development, organization, and the appropriate expression of ideas in professional correspondence. Use a standard business memo or letter format with a clear beginning, middle, and end. Do not convey information in the form of a table, bullet point list, or other abbreviated presentation.

To: Tom and Joan Moore
From: CPA Candidate
Re: Interest expense deduction limitations

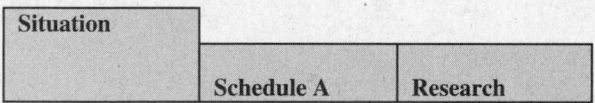

Adjustments must be made to regular taxable income in order to compute an individual's alternative minimum taxable income (AMTI). Which code section and subsection provide the adjustments that only apply to individuals when computing the alternative minimum tax? Indicate the reference to that citation in the shaded boxes below.

Section	Subsection
§ ▢	(▢)

Simulation Problem 7   (30 to 35 minutes)

Situation		
	Schedule A	Research

Fred (social security number 123-67-5489) and Laura Shaw provided you with the following tax return data. The amount from Form 1040, line 38 is $80,000.

Medical and dental expenses	
Medical insurance premiums	$3,600
Disability income insurance premiums	800
Prescription drugs	825
Nonprescription medicine	280
Dr. Jones – neurologist	2,250
Dentist	750
Dr. Smith – LASIK surgery	900
Insurance reimbursement for medical bills	2,000
Transportation to and from doctors	80

Taxes	
Balance of state income taxes due for 2008 paid on April 15, 2009	$ 225
State income taxes withheld for 2009	975
Real estate taxes on principal residence	7,000
Real estate taxes on summer residence	3,000
County personal property tax	410
Registration fee for automobiles	160

Interest
    Mortgage interest on principal residence $5,500
    Mortgage interest on summer residence   2,200
    Interest paid on automobile loan   800
    Interest paid on personal use credit cards   500

Contributions
    Cash donated to church $2,500
    Stock donated to church. (The Shaws purchased it for $3,000 18 months ago)   4,000

Miscellaneous payments
    Legal fee for preparation of a will $ 350
    Rent for safety-deposit box containing stocks and bonds   120
    Union dues   600
    Subscriptions to investment publications   300
    Life insurance premiums   2,800
    Transportation to and from work   2,400
    Fee paid for tax return preparation   400
    Unreimbursed business travel away from home overnight   900
    Contribution to a national political party   200
    Repairs to principal residence   2,000

Schedule A		
Situation		Research

Complete the following 2009 Form 1040 Schedule A-Itemized Deductions for Fred and Laura Shaw.

		Research
Situation	Schedule A	

    The Shaws are considering donating a painting to a state university for display in the university's library. The Shaws acquired the painting six months ago for $90,000 and believe that the painting is now worth $105,000. Which code section and subsection determine the amount of charitable contribution to which the Shaws will be entitled if they donate the painting at the present time? Indicate the reference to that citation in the shaded boxes below.

Section	Subsection
§	( )

SCHEDULE A
(Form 1040)

Department of the Treasury
Internal Revenue Service (99)

Itemized Deductions

► Attach to Form 1040.   ► See Instructions for Schedule A (Form 1040).

OMB No. 1545-0074

2009

Attachment
Sequence No. **07**

Name(s) shown on Form 1040

Your social security number

Medical and Dental Expenses

Caution. Do not include expenses reimbursed or paid by others.

1 Medical and dental expenses (see page A-1) . . . . . . | 1 |
2 Enter amount from Form 1040, line 38 | 2 |
3 Multiply line 2 by 7.5% (.075) | 3 |
4 Subtract line 3 from line 1. If line 3 is more than line 1, enter -0- . . . . | 4 |

Taxes You Paid

(See page A-2.)

5 State and local **(check only one box):**
a ☐ Income taxes, **or**
b ☐ General sales taxes | 5 |
6 Real estate taxes (see page A-5) . . . . | 6 |
7 New motor vehicle taxes from line 11 of the worksheet on back. Skip this line if you checked box 5b . . . . . | 7 |
8 Other taxes. List type and amount ► _____ | 8 |
9 Add lines 5 through 8 . . . . | 9 |

Interest You Paid

(See page A-6.)

Note. Personal interest is not deductible.

10 Home mortgage interest and points reported to you on Form 1098 | 10 |
11 Home mortgage interest not reported to you on Form 1098. If paid to the person from whom you bought the home, see page A-7 and show that person's name, identifying no., and address ►
_____
_____ | 11 |
12 Points not reported to you on Form 1098. See page A-7 for special rules . . . . . . | 12 |
13 Qualified mortgage insurance premiums (see page A-7) | 13 |
14 Investment interest. Attach Form 4952 if required. (See page A-8.) | 14 |
15 Add lines 10 through 14 . . . . | 15 |

Gifts to Charity

If you made a gift and got a benefit for it, see page A-8.

16 Gifts by cash or check. If you made any gift of $250 or more, see page A-8 . . . . . | 16 |
17 Other than by cash or check. If any gift of $250 or more, see page A-8. You **must** attach Form 8283 if over $500 . . . | 17 |
18 Carryover from prior year | 18 |
19 Add lines 16 through 18 . . . . | 19 |

Casualty and Theft Losses

20 Casualty or theft loss(es). Attach Form 4684. (See page A-10.) | 20 |

Job Expenses and Certain Miscellaneous Deductions

(See page A-10.)

21 Unreimbursed employee expenses—job travel, union dues, job education, etc. Attach Form 2106 or 2106-EZ if required. (See page A-10.) ► _____ | 21 |
22 Tax preparation fees . . . . | 22 |
23 Other expenses—investment, safe deposit box, etc. List type and amount ► _____ | 23 |
24 Add lines 21 through 23 . . . . . | 24 |
25 Enter amount from Form 1040, line 38 | 25 |
26 Multiply line 25 by 2% (.02) . . . . . . | 26 |
27 Subtract line 26 from line 24. If line 26 is more than line 24, enter -0- . . . . . . | 27 |

Other Miscellaneous Deductions

28 Other—from list on page A-11. List type and amount ► _____
_____ | 28 |

Total Itemized Deductions

29 Is Form 1040, line 38, over $166,800 (over $83,400 if married filing separately)?
☐ **No.** Your deduction is not limited. Add the amounts in the far right column for lines 4 through 28. Also, enter this amount on Form 1040, line 40a.
☐ **Yes.** Your deduction may be limited. See page A-11 for the amount to enter. | 29 |
30 If you elect to itemize deductions even though they are less than your standard deduction, check here ► ☐

For Paperwork Reduction Act Notice, see Form 1040 instructions.   Cat. No. 17145C   Schedule A (Form 1040) 2009

MULTIPLE-CHOICE ANSWERS*

1. c __ __	46. c __ __	91. a __ __	136. b __ __	181. b __ __
2. b __ __	47. a __ __	92. d __ __	137. b __ __	182. b __ __
3. b __ __	48. a __ __	93. c __ __	138. b __ __	183. c __ __
4. c __ __	49. d __ __	94. d __ __	139. a __ __	184. a __ __
5. a __ __	50. d __ __	95. a __ __	140. b __ __	185. c __ __
6. d __ __	51. b __ __	96. d __ __	141. a __ __	186. c __ __
7. b __ __	52. b __ __	97. d __ __	142. a __ __	187. b __ __
8. d __ __	53. b __ __	98. c __ __	143. a __ __	188. d __ __
9. a __ __	54. b __ __	99. d __ __	144. d __ __	189. c __ __
10. d __ __	55. c __ __	100. c __ __	145. d __ __	190. a __ __
11. b __ __	56. d __ __	101. d __ __	146. b __ __	191. a __ __
12. b __ __	57. d __ __	102. b __ __	147. d __ __	192. c __ __
13. c __ __	58. d __ __	103. c __ __	148. b __ __	193. b __ __
14. d __ __	59. c __ __	104. b __ __	149. b __ __	194. b __ __
15. c __ __	60. a __ __	105. c __ __	150. d __ __	195. a __ __
16. c __ __	61. a __ __	106. b __ __	151. a __ __	196. b __ __
17. a __ __	62. b __ __	107. b __ __	152. b __ __	197. a __ __
18. c __ __	63. a __ __	108. a __ __	153. c __ __	198. c __ __
19. a __ __	64. d __ __	109. c __ __	154. a __ __	199. a __ __
20. d __ __	65. d __ __	110. d __ __	155. d __ __	200. c __ __
21. c __ __	66. d __ __	111. a __ __	156. c __ __	201. b __ __
22. d __ __	67. a __ __	112. d __ __	157. b __ __	202. c __ __
23. c __ __	68. c __ __	113. d __ __	158. d __ __	203. c __ __
24. c __ __	69. b __ __	114. b __ __	159. a __ __	204. c __ __
25. a __ __	70. b __ __	115. d __ __	160. d __ __	205. d __ __
26. d __ __	71. c __ __	116. d __ __	161. a __ __	206. a __ __
27. c __ __	72. a __ __	117. c __ __	162. a __ __	207. a __ __
28. d __ __	73. a __ __	118. a __ __	163. c __ __	208. d __ __
29. c __ __	74. c __ __	119. d __ __	164. b __ __	209. a __ __
30. c __ __	75. c __ __	120. b __ __	165. b __ __	210. c __ __
31. b __ __	76. c __ __	121. b __ __	166. c __ __	211. c __ __
32. b __ __	77. d __ __	122. a __ __	167. b __ __	212. d __ __
33. d __ __	78. a __ __	123. b __ __	168. d __ __	213. d __ __
34. b __ __	79. c __ __	124. a __ __	169. c __ __	214. c __ __
35. c __ __	80. a __ __	125. c __ __	170. b __ __	215. a __ __
36. a __ __	81. b __ __	126. b __ __	171. c __ __	216. c __ __
37. c __ __	82. c __ __	127. c __ __	172. c __ __	217. d __ __
38. d __ __	83. b __ __	128. c __ __	173. a __ __	218. b __ __
39. b __ __	84. a __ __	129. c __ __	174. c __ __	219. c __ __
40. b __ __	85. c __ __	130. a __ __	175. d __ __	
41. c __ __	86. d __ __	131. a __ __	176. a __ __	
42. d __ __	87. c __ __	132. b __ __	177. d __ __	
43. d __ __	88. a __ __	133. c __ __	178. c __ __	
44. d __ __	89. c __ __	134. c __ __	179. c __ __	1st: __/219 = __%
45. c __ __	90. c __ __	135. c __ __	180. d __ __	2nd: __/219 = __%

MULTIPLE-CHOICE ANSWER EXPLANATIONS

I.B.3. Annuities

1. (c) The requirement is to determine the pension (annuity) amounts excluded from income for 2009, 2010, and 2011. Brown's contribution of $12,000 will be recovered pro rata over the life of the annuity. Under this rule, $100 per month (12,000 ÷ 120 months) is excluded from income.

	Received	Excluded	Included
2009	$4,900	$ 700	$4,200
2010	8,400	1,200	7,200
2011	8,400	1,200	7,200

I.B.4. Life Insurance Proceeds

2. (b) The requirement is to determine the amount of life insurance proceeds that must be included in gross income by Decker, on the death of Fuller's parent. Life insurance proceeds paid because of the insured person's death are generally excluded from gross income. However, the exclusion generally does not apply if the insurance policy was obtained by the beneficiary in exchange for valuable consideration from a person other than the insurance company. Here, Decker purchased the policy from Fuller for $25,000 and paid an additional $40,000 in premiums, so Decker must include in gross income the excess of insurance proceeds

---

Explanation of how to use this performance record appears on page 1.

over his investment in the policy [$200,000 – ($25,000 + $40,000) = $135,000.

3. (b) The requirement is to determine the amount of life insurance payments to be included in a widow's gross income. Life insurance proceeds paid by reason of death are excluded from income if paid in a lump sum or in installments. If the payments are received in installments, the principal amount of the policy divided by the number of annual payments is excluded each year. Therefore, $1,200 of the $5,200 insurance payment is included in Penelope's gross income.

Annual installment	$ 5,200
Principal amount ($100,000 ÷ 25)	– 4,000
Gross income	$ 1,200

I.B.5. Employee Benefits

4. (c) The requirement is to determine the correct statement regarding a "cafeteria plan" maintained by an employer. Cafeteria plans are employer-sponsored benefit packages that offer employees a choice between taking cash and receiving qualified benefits (e.g., accident and health insurance, group-term life insurance, coverage under a dependent care or group legal services program). Thus, employees "may select their own menu of benefits." If an employee chooses qualified benefits, they are excluded from the employee's gross income to the extent allowed by law. If an employee chooses cash, it is includible in the employee's gross income as compensation. Answer (a) is incorrect because participation is restricted to employees only. Answer (b) is incorrect because there is no minimum service requirement that must be met before an employee can participate in a plan. Answer (d) is incorrect because deferred compensation plans other than 401(k) plans are not included in the definition of a cafeteria plan.

5. (a) The requirement is to determine the amount of group-term life insurance proceeds that must be included in gross income by Autrey's widow. Life insurance proceeds paid by reason of death are generally excluded from gross income. Note that although only the cost of the first $50,000 of group-term insurance coverage can be excluded from gross income during the employee's life, the entire amount of insurance proceeds paid by reason of death will be excluded from the beneficiary's income.

6. (d) The requirement is to determine the amount of employee death payments to be included in gross income by the widow and the son. The $5,000 employee death benefit exclusion was repealed for decedents dying after August 20, 1996.

7. (b) The requirement is to determine the maximum amount of tax-free group-term life insurance coverage that can be provided to an employee by an employer. The cost of the first $50,000 of group-term life insurance coverage provided by an employer will be excluded from an employee's income.

8. (d) The requirement is to determine the amount to be included in Hal's gross income for the current year. All three amounts that Hal received as a result of his injury are excluded from gross income. Benefits received as workers' compensation and compensation for damages for physical injuries are always excluded from gross income. Amounts received from an employer's accident and health plan as reimbursement for medical expenses are excluded so long as the medical expenses are not deducted as itemized deductions.

9. (a) James Martin's gross income consists of

Salary	$50,000
Bonus	10,000
	$60,000

Medical insurance premiums paid by an employer are excluded from an employee's gross income. Additionally, qualified moving expense reimbursements are an employee fringe benefit and can be excluded from gross income. This means that an employee can exclude an amount paid by an employer as payment for (or reimbursement of) expenses that would be deductible as moving expenses if directly paid or incurred by the employee.

I.B.8. Gifts and Inheritances

10. (d) The requirement is to determine how much income Hall should include in his 2009 tax return for the inheritance of stock which he received from his father's estate. Since the definition of gross income excludes property received as a gift, bequest, devise, or inheritance, Hall recognizes no income upon receipt of the stock. Since the executor of his father's estate elected the alternate valuation date (August 1), and the stock was distributed to Hall before that date (June 1), Hall's basis for the stock would be its $4,500 FMV on June 1. Since Hall also sold the stock on June 1 for $4,500, Hall would have no gain or loss resulting from the sale.

I.B.9. Stock Dividends

11. (b) The requirement is to determine the amount of dividend income that should be reported by Gail Judd. The $100 dividend on Gail's life insurance policy is treated as a reduction of the cost of insurance (because total dividends have not yet exceeded accumulated premiums paid) and is excluded from gross income. Thus, Gail will report the $300 dividend on common stock and the $500 dividend on preferred stock, a total of $800 as dividend income for 2010.

12. (b) The requirement is to determine the amount of dividend income to be reported on Amy's 2010 return. Dividends are included in income at earlier of actual or constructive receipt. When corporate dividends are paid by mail, they are included in income for the year in which received. Thus, the $875 dividend received 1/2/10 is included in income for 2010. The $500 dividend on a life insurance policy from a mutual insurance company is treated as a reduction of the cost of insurance and is excluded from gross income.

13. (c) The requirement is to determine the amount of dividends to be reported by the Mitchells on a joint return. The amount of dividends would be ($400 + $50 + $300) = $750. The $200 dividend on the life insurance policy is not gross income, but is considered a reduction of the cost of the policy.

14. (d) The requirement is to determine Karen's basis in the 10 shares of preferred stock received as a stock dividend. Generally, stock dividends are nontaxable, and a taxpayer's basis for original stock is allocated to the dividend stock in proportion to fair market values. However, any stock that is distributed **on** preferred stock results in a taxable stock dividend. The amount to be included in the shareholder's income is the stock's fair market value on date of distribution. Similarly, the shareholder's basis for the dividend shares will be equal to their fair market value on date of distribution (10 × $60 = $600).

I.B.10. Interest Income

15.   (c)   The requirement is to determine the correct statement(s) regarding the amortization of bond premium on a taxable bond. The amount of premium amortization on taxable bonds acquired by the taxpayer after 1987 is treated as an offset to the amount of interest income reported on the bond. The method of calculating the annual amortization is determined by the date the bond was issued, as opposed to the acquisition date. If the bond was issued after September 27, 1985, the amortization must be calculated under the constant yield to maturity method. Otherwise, the amortization must be made ratably over the life of the bond. Under the constant yield to maturity method, the amortizable bond premium is computed on the basis of the taxpayer's yield to maturity, using the taxpayer's basis for the bond, and compounding at the close of each accrual period.

16.   (c)   The requirement is to determine whether two statements are true concerning the exclusion of interest income on US Series EE Bonds that are redeemed to pay for higher education. The accrued interest on US Series EE savings bonds that are redeemed by a taxpayer is excluded from gross income to the extent that the aggregate redemption proceeds (principal plus interest) are used to finance the higher education of the taxpayer, taxpayer's spouse, or dependents. Qualified higher educational expenses include tuition and fees, but not room and board or the cost of courses involving sports, games, or hobbies that are not part of a degree program. In determining the amount of available exclusion, qualified educational expenses must be reduced by qualified scholarships that are exempt from tax, and any other nontaxable payments such as veteran's educational assistance and employer-provided educational assistance.

17.   (a)   The requirement is to determine the amount of interest subject to tax in Kay's 2010 tax return. Interest must generally be included in gross income, unless a specific statutory provision provides for its exclusion (e.g., interest on municipal bonds). Interest on US Treasury certificates and on a refund of federal income tax would be subject to tax on Kay's 2010 tax return.

18.   (c)   The requirement is to determine the amount of interest income taxable on Charles and Marcia's joint income tax return. A taxpayer's income includes interest on state and federal income tax refunds and interest on federal obligations, but excludes interest on state obligations. Here, their joint taxable income must include the $500 interest on federal income tax refund, $600 interest on state income tax refund, and $800 interest on federal government obligations, but will exclude the $1,000 tax-exempt interest on state government obligations. Although a refund of federal income tax would be excluded from gross income, any interest on a refund must be included in gross income.

19.   (a)   The requirement is to determine the condition that must be met for tax exemption of accumulated interest on Series EE US Savings Bonds. An individual may be able to exclude from income all or a part of the interest received on the redemption of Series EE US Savings Bonds. To

qualify, the bonds must be issued after December 31, 1989, the purchaser of the bonds must be the sole owner of the bonds (or joint owner with his or her spouse), and the owner(s) must be at least twenty-four years old before the bond's issue date. To exclude the interest the redemption proceeds must be used to pay the tuition and fees incurred by the taxpayer, spouse, or dependents to attend a college or university or certain vocational schools.

20.   (d)   The requirement is to determine the amount of tax-exempt interest. Interest on obligations of a state or one of its political subdivisions (e.g., New York Port Authority bonds), or a possession of the US (e.g., Puerto Rico Commonwealth bonds) is tax-exempt.

21.   (c)   Stone will report $1,700 of interest income. Interest on FIT refunds, personal injury awards, US savings bonds, and most other sources is fully taxable. However, interest on state or municipal bonds is generally not taxable.

22.   (d)   The requirement is to determine how Don Raff's $500 interest forfeiture penalty should be reported. An interest forfeiture penalty for making a premature withdrawal from a certificate of deposit should be deducted from gross income in arriving at adjusted gross income in the year in which the penalty is incurred, which in this case is 2010.

I.B.12. Scholarships and Fellowships

23.   (c)   The requirement is to determine which payment(s) must be included in a recipient's gross income. A candidate for a degree can exclude amounts received as a scholarship or fellowship if, according to the conditions of the grant, the amounts are used for the payment of tuition and fees, books, supplies, and equipment required for courses at an educational institution. All payments received for services must be included in income, even if the services are a condition of receiving the grant or are required of all candidates for the degree. Here, the payment to a graduate assistant for a part-time teaching assignment and the grant to a Ph.D. candidate for participation in research are payments for services and must be included in income.

24.   (c)   The requirement is to determine the amount of scholarship awards that Majors should include as taxable income in 2010. Only a candidate for a degree can exclude amounts received as a scholarship award. The exclusion available to degree candidates is limited to amounts received for the payment of tuition and fees, books, supplies, and equipment required for courses at the educational institution. Since Majors is a candidate for a graduate degree, Majors can exclude the $10,000 received for tuition, fees, books, and supplies required for courses. However, the $2,000 stipend for research services required by the scholarship must be included in taxable income for 2010.

I.B.16. Lease Improvements

25.   (a)   The requirement is to determine a lessor's 2010 gross income. A lessor excludes from income any increase in the value of property caused by improvements made by the lessee, unless the improvements were made in lieu of rent. In this case, there is no indication that the improvements were made in lieu of rent. Therefore, for 2010, Farley should only include the six rent payments in income: 6 × $1,000 = $6,000.

I.C. Items to Be Included in Gross Income

26. (d) The requirement is to determine the amount of alimony recapture that must be included in Bob's gross income for 2010. Alimony recapture may occur if alimony payments sharply decline in the second and third years that payments are made. The payor must report the recaptured alimony as gross income in the third year, and the payee is allowed a deduction for the same amount. Recapture for the second year (2009) occurs to the extent that the alimony paid in the second year ($20,000) exceeds the alimony paid in the third year ($0) by more than $15,000 [i.e., $20,000 – ($0 + $15,000) = $5,000 of recapture].

Recapture for the first year (2008) occurs to the extent that the alimony paid in the first year ($50,000) exceeds the *average alimony* paid in the second and third years by more than $15,000. For this purpose, the alimony paid in the second year ($20,000) must be reduced by the amount of recapture for that year ($5,000).

First year (2008) payment		$50,000
Second year (2009) payment		
($20,000 – $5,000)	$15,000	
Third year (2010) payment	+ 0	
Total	$15,000	
	÷ 2	(7,500)
		(15,000)
Recapture for first year (2008)		$ 27,500

Thus, the total recapture to be included in Bob's gross income for 2010 is $5,000 + $27,500 = $32,500.

27. (c) The requirement is to determine which conditions must be present in a post-1984 divorce agreement for a payment to qualify as deductible alimony. In order for a payment to be deductible by the payor as alimony, the payment must be made in cash or its equivalent, the payment must be received by or on behalf of a spouse under a divorce or separation instrument, the payments must terminate at the recipient's death, and must not be designated as other than alimony (e.g., child support).

28. (d) The requirement is to determine which of the following would be included in gross income by Darr who is an employee of Sorce C corporation. The definition of gross income includes income from whatever source derived and would include the dividend income on shares of stock that Darr received for services rendered. However, items specifically excluded from gross income include amounts received as a gift or inheritance, as well as employer-provided medical insurance coverage under a health plan.

29. (c) The requirement is to determine the correct statement regarding the inclusion of social security benefits in gross income for 2010. A maximum of 85% of social security benefits may be included in gross income for high-income taxpayers. Thus, no matter how high a taxpayer's income, 85% of the social security benefits is the maximum amount of benefits to be included in gross income.

30. (c) The requirement is to determine the amount that Perle should include in taxable income as a result of performing dental services for Wood. An exchange of services for property or services is sometimes called bartering. A taxpayer must include in income the amount of cash and the fair market value of property or services received in exchange for the performance of services. Here, Perle's taxable income should include the $200 cash and the bookcase with a comparable value of $350, a total of $550.

31. (b) The requirement is to determine the amount of payments to be included in Mary's income tax return for 2010. Alimony must be included in gross income by the payee and is deductible by the payor. In order to be treated as alimony, a payment must be made in cash and be received by or paid on behalf of the former spouse. Amounts treated as child support are not alimony; they are neither deductible by the payor, nor taxable to the payee. Payments will be treated as child support to the extent that payments will be reduced upon the happening of a contingency relating to a child (e.g., the child attaining a specified age, marrying, becoming employed). Here, since future payments will be reduced by 20% on their child's 18th birthday, the total cash payments of $10,000 ($7,000 paid directly to Mary plus the $3,000 of tuition paid on Mary's behalf) must be reduced by 20% and result in $8,000 of alimony income for Mary. The remaining $2,000 is treated as child support and is not taxable.

32. (b) The requirement is to determine the amount of interest for overpayment of 2009 state income tax and state income tax refund that is taxable in Clark's 2010 federal income tax return. The $10 of interest income on the tax refund is taxable and must be included in gross income. On the other hand, a state income tax refund is included in gross income under the "tax benefit rule" only if the refunded amount was deducted in a prior year and the deduction provided a benefit because it reduced the taxpayer's federal income tax. The payment of state income taxes will not result in a "benefit" if an individual does not itemize deductions, or is subject to the alternative minimum tax for the year the taxes are paid. Individuals who file Form 1040EZ are not allowed to itemize deductions and must use the standard deduction. Since state income taxes are only allowed as an itemized deduction and Clark did not itemize for 2009 (he used Form 1040EZ), his $900 state income tax refund is nontaxable and is excluded from gross income.

33. (d) The requirement is to determine the amount to be reported in Hall's 2009 return as alimony income. If a divorce agreement specifies both alimony and child support, but less is paid than required, then payments are first allocated to child support, with only the remainder in excess of required child support to be treated as alimony. Pursuant to Hall's divorce agreement, $3,000 was to be paid each month, of which $600 was designated as child support, leaving a balance of $2,400 per month to be treated as alimony. However, during 2009, only $5,000 was paid to Hall by her former husband which was less than the $36,000 required by the divorce agreement. Since required child support payments totaled $600 × 12 = $7,200 for 2009, all $5,000 of the payments actually received by Hall during 2009 is treated as child support, with nothing remaining to be reported as alimony.

34. (b) The requirement is to determine the amount of income to be reported by Lee in connection with the receipt of stock for services rendered. Compensation for services rendered that is received by a cash method taxpayer must be included in income at its fair market value on the date of receipt.

35. (c) The requirement is to determine when Ross was subject to "regular tax" with regard to stock that was acquired through the exercise of an incentive stock option. There are no tax consequences when an incentive stock option is granted to an employee. When the option is exercised, any excess of the stock's FMV over the option price is a tax preference item for purposes of the employee's alternative minimum tax. However, an employee is not subject to regular tax until the stock acquired through exercise of the option is sold.

If the employee holds the stock acquired through exercise of the option at least two years from the date the option was granted (and holds the stock itself at least one year), the employee's realized gain is treated as long-term capital gain in the year of sale, and the employer receives no compensation deduction. If the preceding holding period rules are not met at the time the stock is sold, the employee must report ordinary income to the extent that the stock's FMV at date of exercise exceeded the option price, with any remaining gain reported as long-term or short-term capital gain. As a result, the employer receives a compensation deduction equal to the amount of ordinary income reported by the employee.

36. (a) The requirement is to determine the amount that is taxable as alimony in Ann's return. In order to be treated as alimony, a payment must be made in cash and be received by or on behalf of the payee spouse. Furthermore, cash payments must be required to terminate upon the death of the payee spouse to be treated as alimony. In this case, the transfer of title in the home to Ann is not a cash payment and cannot be treated as alimony. Although the mortgage payments are cash payments made on behalf of Ann, the payments are not treated as alimony because they will be made throughout the full twenty-year mortgage period and will not terminate in the event of Ann's death.

37. (c) The requirement is to determine the correct statement with regard to income in respect of a cash basis decedent. Income in respect of a decedent is income earned by a decedent before death that was not includible in the decedent's final income tax return because of the decedent's method of accounting (e.g., receivables of a cash basis decedent). Such income must be included in gross income by the person who receives it and has the same character (e.g., ordinary or capital) as it would have had if the decedent had lived.

38. (d) The requirement is to determine the amount of gross income. Drury's gross income includes the $36,000 salary, the $500 of premiums paid by her employer for group-term life insurance coverage in excess of $50,000, and the $5,000 proceeds received from a state lottery.

39. (b) The requirement is to determine the amount of foster child payments to be included in income by the Charaks. Foster child payments are excluded from income to the extent they represent reimbursement for expenses incurred for care of the foster child. Since the payments ($3,900) exceeded the expenses ($3,000), the $900 excess used for the Charaks' personal expenses must be included in their gross income.

40. (b) The requirement is to determine the amount and the year in which the tip income should be included in Pierre's gross income. If an individual receives less than $20 in tips during one month while working for one employer, the tips do not have to be reported to the employer and the tips are included in the individual's gross income when received. However, if an individual receives $20 or more in

tips during one month while working for one employer, the individual must report the total amount of tips to that employer by the tenth day of the next month. Then the tips are included in gross income for the month in which they are reported to the employer. Here, Pierre received $2,000 in tips during December 2009 that he reported to his employer in January 2010. Thus, the $2,000 of tips will be included in Pierre's gross income for 2010.

41. (c) The requirement is to determine the correct statement regarding the alimony deduction in connection with a 2010 divorce. To be considered alimony, cash payments must terminate on the death of the payee spouse. Answer (a) is incorrect because alimony payments cannot be contingent on the status of the divorced couple's children. Answer (b) is incorrect because the divorced couple cannot be members of the same household at the time the alimony is paid. Answer (d) is incorrect because only cash payments can be considered alimony.

42. (d) The requirement is to determine the amount of a $10,000 award for outstanding civic achievement that Joan should include in her 2010 adjusted gross income. An award for civic achievement can be excluded from gross income only if the recipient was selected without any action on his/her part, is not required to render substantial future services as a condition of receiving the award, and designates that the award is to be directly transferred by the payor to a governmental unit or a tax-exempt charitable, educational, or religious organization. Here, since Joan accepted and actually received the award, the $10,000 must be included in her adjusted gross income.

43. (d) The requirement is to determine the amount of lottery winnings that should be included in Gow's taxable income. Lottery winnings are gambling winnings and must be included in gross income. Gambling losses are deductible from AGI as a miscellaneous deduction (to the extent of winnings) not subject to the 2% of AGI floor if a taxpayer itemizes deductions. Since Gow elected the standard deduction for 2009, the $400 spent on lottery tickets is not deductible. Thus, all $5,000 of Gow's lottery winnings are included in his taxable income.

I.C.5. Rents and Royalties

44. (d) The requirement is to determine the amount of advance rents and lease cancellation payments that should be reported on Lake Corp.'s 2010 tax return. Advance rental payments must be included in gross income when received, regardless of the period covered or whether the taxpayer uses the cash or accrual method. Similarly, lease cancellation payments are treated as rent and must be included in income when received, regardless of the taxpayer's method of accounting.

45. (c) The requirement is to determine the amount to be reported as gross income. Gross income includes the $50,000 of recurring rents plus the $2,000 lease cancellation payment. The $1,000 of lease improvements are excluded from income since they were **not** required in lieu of rent.

46. (c) The requirement is to determine the amount of net rental income that Gow should include in his adjusted gross income. Since Gow lives in one of two identical apartments, only 50% of the expenses relating to both apartments can be allocated to the rental unit.

Rent	$7,200
Less:	
Real estate taxes (50% × $6,400)	(3,200)
Painting of rental apartment	(800)
Fire insurance (50% × $600)	(300)
Depreciation (50% × $5,000)	(2,500)
Net rental income	$ 400

47. (a) The requirement is to determine the amount of rent income to be reported on Amy's 2010 return. Both the $6,000 of rent received for 2010, as well as the $1,000 of advance rent received in 2010 for the last two months of the lease must be included in income for 2010. Advance rent must be included in income in the year received regardless of the period covered or the accounting method used.

48. (a) The requirement is to determine the amount to be reported as rent revenue in an accrual-basis taxpayer's tax return for 2010. An accrual-basis taxpayer's rent revenue would consist of the amount of rent earned during the taxable year plus any advance rent received. Advance rents must be included in gross income when received under both the cash and accrual methods, even though they have not yet been earned. In this case, Royce's rent revenue would be determined as follows:

Rent receivable 12/31/09	$35,000
Rent receivable 12/31/10	25,000
Decrease in receivables	(10,000)
Rent collections during 2010	50,000
Rent deposits	5,000
Rent revenue for 2010	$45,000

The rent deposits must be included in gross income for 2010 because they are nonrefundable deposits.

I.C.19. Unemployment Compensation

49. (d) The requirement is to determine the amount of state unemployment benefits that should be included in adjusted gross income for 2009. Although unemployment compensation benefits received must generally be included in gross income, up to $2,400 of unemployment compensation can be excluded from gross income for tax years beginning in 2009.

I.D. Tax Accounting Methods

50. (d) The requirement is to determine the correct statement regarding the reporting of income by a cash-basis taxpayer. A cash-basis taxpayer should report gross income for the year in which income is either actually or constructively received, whether in cash or in property. Constructive receipt means that an item of income is unqualifiedly available to the taxpayer without restriction (e.g., interest on bank deposit is income when credited to account).

51. (b) The requirement is to determine which taxpayer may use the cash method of accounting. The cash method cannot generally be used if inventories are necessary to clearly reflect income, and cannot generally be used by C corporations, partnerships that have a C corporation as a partner, tax shelters, and certain tax-exempt trusts. Taxpayers permitted to use the cash method include a qualified personal service corporation, an entity (other than a tax shelter) if for every year it has average gross receipts of $5 million or less for any prior three-year period (and provided it does not have inventories), and a small taxpayer with average annual gross receipts of $1 million or less for any prior three-year period may use the cash method and is excepted from the requirement to account for inventories

52. (b) The requirement is to select the correct statement regarding the $1,000 of additional income determined by Stewart, an accrual method corporation. Under the accrual method, income generally is reported in the year earned. If an amount is included in gross income on the basis of a reasonable estimate, and it is later determined that the exact amount is more, then the additional amount is included in income in the tax year in which the determination of the exact amount is made. Here, Stewart properly accrued $5,000 of income for 2009, and discovered that the exact amount was $6,000 in 2010. Therefore, the additional $1,000 of income is properly includible in Stewart's 2010 income tax return.

53. (b) The requirement is to determine the correct statement regarding Axis Corp.'s deduction for its employees bonus expense. An accrual-method taxpayer can deduct compensation (including a bonus) when there is an obligation to make payment, the services have been performed, and the amount can be determined with reasonable accuracy. It is not required that the exact amount of compensation be determined during the taxable year. As long as the computation is known and the liability is fixed, accrual is proper even though the profits upon which the compensation are based are not determined until after the end of the year.

Although compensation is generally deductible only for the year in which the compensation is paid, an exception is made for accrual method taxpayers so long as payment is made within 2 1/2 months after the end of the year. Here, since the services were performed, the method of computation was known, the amount was reasonable, and payment was made by March 15, 2010, the bonus expense may be deducted on Axis Corp.'s 2009 tax return. Note that the bonus could not be a disguised dividend because none of the employees were shareholders.

54. (b) The requirement is to determine the amount of the 2009 interest payment of $12,000 that was deductible on Michaels' 2010 income tax return. Generally, there is no deduction for prepaid interest. When a taxpayer pays interest for a period that extends beyond the end of the tax year, the interest paid in advance must be spread over the period to which it applies. Michaels paid $12,000 of interest during 2009 that relates to the period beginning December 1, 2009, and ending November 30, 2010. Therefore, 1/12 × $12,000 = $1,000 of interest was deductible for 2009, and 11/12 × $12,000 = $11,000 is deductible for 2010.

55. (c) The requirement is to determine the amount of income to be reported in Blair's 2009 return for the stock received in satisfaction of a client fee owed to Blair. Since Blair is a cash method taxpayer, the amount of income to be recognized equals the $4,000 fair market value of the stock on date of receipt. Note that the $4,000 of income is reported by Blair in 2009 when the stock is received; not in 2010 when the stock is sold.

56. (d) The requirement is to determine whether the accrual method of tax reporting is mandatory for a sole proprietor when there are accounts receivable for services rendered, or year-end merchandise inventories. A taxpayer's taxable income should be computed using the method of accounting by which the taxpayer regularly computes income in keeping the taxpayer's books. Either the cash or the accrual method generally can be used so long as the method is consistently applied and clearly reflects income. However, when the production, purchase, or sale of merchandise is an income producing factor, inventories must be maintained to clearly reflect income. If merchandise inventories are necessary to clearly determine income, only the accrual method of tax reporting can be used for purchases and sales.

57. (d)   The requirement is to determine the amount of salary taxable to Burg in 2009. Since Burg is a cash-basis taxpayer, salary is taxable to Burg when actually or constructively received, whichever is earlier. Since the $30,000 of unpaid salary was unqualifiedly available to Burg during 2009, Burg is considered to have constructively received it. Thus, Burg must report a total of $80,000 of salary for 2009; the $50,000 actually received plus $30,000 constructively received.

58. (d)   The requirement is to determine the 2009 medical practice net income for a cash basis physician. Dr. Berger's income consists of the $200,000 received from patients and the $30,000 received from third-party reimbursers during 2009. His 2009 deductions include the $20,000 of salaries and $24,000 of other expenses paid in 2009. The year-end bonuses will be deductible for 2010.

59. (c)   The requirement is to determine which taxpayer may use the cash method of accounting for tax purposes. The cash method generally cannot be used (and the accrual method must be used to measure sales and cost of goods sold) if inventories are necessary to clearly determine income. Additionally, the cash method generally cannot generally be used by (1) a corporation (other than an S corporation), (2) a partnership with a corporation as a partner, and (3) a tax shelter. However, this prohibition against the use of the cash method in the preceding sentence does not apply to a farming business, a qualified personal service corporation (e.g., a corporation performing services in health, law, engineering, architecture, accounting, actuarial science, performing arts, or consulting), and a corporation or partnership (that is not a tax shelter) that does not have inventories and whose average annual gross receipts for the most recent three-year period do not exceed $5 million.

I.E. Business Income and Deductions

60. (a)   Uniform capitalization rules generally require that all costs incurred (both direct and indirect) in manufacturing or constructing real or personal property, or in purchasing or holding property for sale, must be capitalized as part of the cost of the property. However, these rules do not apply to a "small retailer or wholesaler" who acquires personal property for resale if the retailer's or wholesaler's average annual gross receipts for the three preceding taxable years do not exceed $10 million.

61. (a)   The requirement is to determine whether the cost of merchandise, and business expenses other than the cost of merchandise, can be deducted in calculating Mock's business income from a retail business selling illegal narcotic substances. Generally, business expenses that are incurred in an illegal activity are deductible if they are ordinary and necessary, and reasonable in amount. Under a special exception, no deduction or credit is allowed for any amount that is paid or incurred in carrying on a trade or business which consists of trafficking in controlled substances. However, this limitation that applies to expenditures in connection with the illegal sale of drugs does not alter the normal definition of gross income (i.e., sales minus cost of goods sold). As a result, in arriving at gross income from the busi-

ness, Mock may reduce total sales by the cost of goods sold, and thus is allowed to deduct the cost of merchandise in calculating business income.

62. (b)   The requirement is to determine the percentage of business meals expense that Banks Corp. can deduct for 2010. Generally, only 50% of business meals and entertainment is deductible. When an employer reimburses its employees' substantiated qualifying business meal expenses, the 50% limitation on deductibility applies to the employer.

63. (a)   The requirement is to determine which of the costs is **not** included in inventory under the Uniform Capitalization (UNICAP) rules for goods manufactured by a taxpayer. UNICAP rules require that specified overhead items must be included in inventory including factory repairs and maintenance, factory administration and officers' salaries related to production, taxes (other than income taxes), the costs of quality control and inspection, current and past service costs of pension and profit-sharing plans, and service support such as purchasing, payroll, and warehousing costs. Nonmanufacturing costs such as selling, advertising, and research and experimental costs are not required to be included in inventory.

64. (d)   If no exceptions are met, the uniform capitalization rules generally require that all costs incurred in purchasing or holding inventory for resale must be capitalized as part of the cost of the inventory. Costs that must be capitalized with respect to inventory include the costs of purchasing, handling, processing, repackaging and assembly, and off-site storage. An off-site storage facility is one that is not physically attached to, and an integral part of, a retail sales facility. Service costs such as marketing, selling, advertising, and general management are immediately deductible and need not be capitalized as part of the cost of inventory.

65. (d)   The requirement is to determine the correct statement regarding the deduction for bad debts in the case of a corporation that is not a financial institution. Except for certain small banks that can use the experience method of accounting for bad debts, all taxpayers (including those that previously used the reserve method) are required to use the direct charge-off method of accounting for bad debts.

66. (d)   The requirement is to determine the amount of life insurance premium that can be deducted in Ram Corp.'s income tax return. Generally, no deduction is allowed for expenditures that produce tax-exempt income. Here, no deduction is allowed for the $6,000 life insurance premium because Ram is the beneficiary of the policy, and the proceeds of the policy will be excluded from Ram's income when the officer dies.

67. (a)   The requirement is to determine the amount of bad debt deduction for a cash-basis taxpayer. Accounts receivable resulting from services rendered by a cash-basis taxpayer have a zero tax basis, because the income has not yet been reported. Thus, failure to collect the receivable results in a nondeductible loss.

68. (c)   The requirement is to determine the loss that Cook can claim as a result of the worthless note receivable in 2010. Cook's $1,000 loss will be treated as a nonbusiness bad debt, deductible as a short-term capital loss. The loss is **not** a business bad debt because Cook was not in the business of lending money, nor was the loan required as a condition of Cook's employment. Since Cook owned no stock in Precision, the loss could **not** be deemed to be a loss from worthless stock, deductible as a long-term capital loss.

69. **(b)** The requirement is to determine the amount of gifts deductible as a business expense. The deduction for business gifts is limited to $25 per recipient each year. Thus, Palo Corporation's deduction for business gifts would be [(4 × $10) + (13 × $25)] = $365.

I.E.3   Net Operating Loss (NOL)

70. **(b)** The requirement is to determine Jennifer's net operating loss (NOL) for 2009. Jennifer's personal casualty loss of $45,000 incurred as a result of the destruction of her personal residence is allowed as a deduction in the computation of her NOL and is subtracted from her salary income of $30,000, to arrive at a NOL of $15,000. No deduction is allowed for personal and dependency exemptions in the computation of a NOL.

71. **(c)** The requirement is to determine the amount of net operating loss (NOL) for a self-employed taxpayer for 2009. A NOL generally represents a loss from the conduct of a trade or business and can generally be carried back two years and forward twenty years to offset income in the carryback and carryforward years. Since a NOL generally represents a business loss, an individual taxpayer's personal exemptions and an excess of nonbusiness deductions over nonbusiness income cannot be subtracted in computing the NOL. Nonbusiness deductions generally include itemized deductions as well as the standard deduction if the taxpayer does not itemize. In this case, the $5,700 standard deduction offsets the $1,500 of nonbusiness income received in the form of dividends and short-term capital gain, but the excess ($4,200) cannot be included in the NOL computation. Thus, the taxpayer's NOL simply consists of the $6,000 business loss.

72. **(a)** The requirement is to determine Destry's net operating loss (NOL). A net operating loss generally represents a loss from the conduct of a trade or business and can generally be carried back two years and forward twenty years to offset income in the carryback and carryforward years. Since a NOL generally represents a business loss, an individual taxpayer's personal exemption and an excess of nonbusiness deductions (e.g., standard deduction) over nonbusiness income (e.g., interest from savings account) cannot be subtracted in computing the NOL. Similarly, no deduction is allowed for a net capital loss. As a result, Destry's NOL consists of his net business loss of $16,000 reduced by his business income of $5,000 from wages and $4,000 of net rental income, resulting in a NOL of $7,000.

I.E.6.   Losses and Credits from Passive Activities

73. **(a)** The requirement is to determine the amount of Cobb's rental real estate loss that can be used as an offset against income from nonpassive sources. Losses from passive activities may generally only be used to offset income from other passive activities. Although a rental activity is defined as a passive activity regardless of the owner's participation in the operation of the rental property, a special rule permits an individual to offset up to $25,000 of income that is not from passive activities by losses from a rental real estate activity if the individual actively participates in the

rental real estate activity. However, this special $25,000 allowance is reduced by 50% of the taxpayer's AGI in excess of $100,000, and is fully phased out when AGI exceeds $150,000. Since Cobb's AGI is $200,000, the special $25,000 allowance is fully phased out and no rental loss can be offset against income from nonpassive sources.

74. **(c)** The requirement is to determine the entity to which the rules limiting the allowability of passive activity losses and credits applies. The passive activity limitations apply to individuals, estates, trusts, closely held C corporations, and personal service corporations. Application of the passive activity loss limitations to personal service corporations is intended to prevent taxpayers from sheltering personal service income by creating personal service corporations and acquiring passive activity losses at the corporate level. A personal service corporation is a corporation (1) whose principal activity is the performance of personal services, and (2) such services are substantially performed by owner-employees. Since passive activity income, losses, and credits from partnerships and S corporations flow through to be reported on the tax returns of the owners of such entities, the passive activity limitations are applied at the partner and shareholder level, rather than to partnerships and S corporations themselves.

75. **(c)** The requirement is to determine Wolf's passive loss resulting from his 5% general partnership interest in Gata Associates. A partnership is a pass-through entity and its items of income and loss pass through to partners to be included on their tax returns. Since Wolf does not materially participate in the partnership's auto parts business, Wolf's distributable share of the loss from the partnership's auto parts business is classified as a passive activity loss. Portfolio income or loss must be excluded from the computation of the income or loss resulting from a passive activity, and must be separately passed through to partners.

Portfolio income includes all interest income, other than interest income derived in the ordinary course of a trade or business. Interest income derived in the ordinary course of a trade or business includes only interest income on loans and investments made in the ordinary course of a trade or business of lending money, and interest income on accounts receivable arising in the ordinary course of a trade or business. Since the $20,000 of interest income derived by the partnership resulted from a temporary investment, the interest income must be classified as portfolio income and cannot be netted against the $100,000 operating loss from the auto parts business. Thus, Wolf will report a passive activity loss of $100,000 × 5% = $5,000; and will report portfolio income of $20,000 × 5% = $1,000.

76. **(a)** The requirement is to determine the correct statement regarding the passive loss rules involving rental real estate activities. By definition, any rental activity is a passive activity without regard as to whether or not the taxpayer materially participates in the activity. Answer (b) is incorrect because interest and dividend income not derived in the ordinary course of business is treated as **portfolio** income, and **cannot** be offset by passive rental activity losses when the "active participation" requirement is **not** met. Answer (c) is incorrect because passive rental activity credits **cannot** be used to offset the tax attributable to **nonpassive** activities. Answer (d) is incorrect because the passive activity rules contain no provision that excludes taxpayers below a certain income level from the limitations imposed by the passive activity rules.

77. (d) The requirement is to determine the correct statement regarding an individual taxpayer's passive losses relating to rental real estate activities that cannot be currently deducted. Generally, losses from passive activities can only be used to offset income from passive activities. If there is insufficient passive activity income to absorb passive activity losses, the unused losses are carried forward indefinitely or until the property is disposed of in a taxable transaction. Answers (a) and (c) are incorrect because unused passive losses are never carried back to prior taxable years. Answer (b) is incorrect because there is no maximum carryforward period.

I.F. Depreciation, Depletion, and Amortization

78. (a) The requirement is to determine the maximum amount of Sec. 179 expense election that Aviation Corp. will be allowed to deduct for 2009, and the maximum amount of expense election that it can carry over to 2010. Sec. 179 permits a taxpayer to elect to treat up to $250,000 (for 2009) of the cost of qualifying depreciable personal property as an expense rather than as a capital expenditure. However, the $250,000 maximum is reduced dollar-for-dollar by the cost of qualifying property placed in service during the taxable year that exceeds $800,000. Here, the maximum amount that can be expensed is $250,000 − ($820,000 − $800,000) = $230,000 for 2009. However, this amount is further limited as a deduction for 2009 to Aviation's taxable income of $195,000 before the Sec. 179 expense deduction. The remainder ($230,000 − $195,000 = $35,000) that is not currently deductible because of the taxable income limitation can be carried over and will be deductible subject to the taxable income limitation in 2010.

79. (c) The requirement is to determine which conditions must be satisfied to enable a taxpayer to expense the cost of new or used tangible depreciable personal property under Sec. 179. Taxpayers may elect to expense up to $250,000 of the cost of new or used tangible depreciable personal property placed in service during the taxable year. To qualify, the property must be acquired by purchase from an unrelated party for use in the taxpayer's active trade or business. The maximum cost that can be expensed of $250,000 is reduced dollar-for-dollar by the cost of qualifying property that is placed in service during the year that exceeds $800,000. Additionally, the amount that can be expensed is further limited to the aggregate taxable income derived from the active conduct of any trade or business of the taxpayer.

80. (a) The requirement is to determine the MACRS deduction for the furniture and fixtures placed in service during 2009. The furniture and fixtures qualify as seven-year property and under MACRS will be depreciated using the 200% declining balance method. Normally, a half-year convention applies to the year of acquisition. However, the midquarter convention must be used if more than 40% of all personal property is placed in service during the last quarter of the taxpayer's taxable year. Since this was Krol's only acquisition of personal property and the property was placed in service during the last quarter of Krol's calendar year, the midquarter convention must be used. Under this convention, property is treated as placed in service during the middle of

the quarter in which placed in service. Since the furniture and fixtures were placed in service in November, the amount of allowable MACRS depreciation is limited to $56,000 × 2/7 × 1/8 = $2,000.

81. (b) The requirement is to determine Sullivan's MACRS deduction for the apartment building in 2010. The MACRS deduction for residential real property placed in service during 2010 must be determined using the mid-month convention (i.e., property is treated as placed in service at the midpoint of the month placed in service) and the straight-line method of depreciation over a 27.5-year recovery period. Here, the $360,000 cost must first be reduced by the $30,000 allocated to the land, to arrive at a basis for depreciation of $330,000. Since the building was placed in service on June 29, the mid-month convention results in 6.5 months of depreciation for 2010. The MACRS deduction for 2010 is [$330,000 × (6.5 months)/(27.5 × 12 months)] = $6,500.

82. (c) The requirement is to determine the depreciation convention that must be used when a calendar-year taxpayer's only acquisition of equipment during the year occurs during November. Generally, a half-year convention applies to depreciable personal property, and a mid-month convention applies to depreciable real property. Under the half-year convention, a half-year of depreciation is allowed for the year in which property is placed in service, regardless of when the property is placed in service during the year, and a half-year of depreciation is allowed for the year in which the property is disposed of. However, a taxpayer must instead use a midquarter convention if more than 40% of all depreciable personal property acquired during the year is placed in service during the last quarter of the taxable year. Under this convention, property is treated as placed in service (or disposed of) in the middle of the quarter in which placed in service (or disposed of). Since Data Corp. is a calendar-year taxpayer and its only acquisition of depreciable personal property was placed in service during October (i.e., the last quarter of its taxable year), it must use the midquarter convention, and will only be allowed a half-quarter of depreciation of its office equipment for 2010.

83. (b) The requirement is to determine the correct statement regarding the modified accelerated cost recovery system (MACRS) of depreciation for property placed in service after 1986. Under MACRS, salvage value is completely ignored for purposes of computing the depreciation deduction, which results in the recovery of the entire cost of depreciable property. Answer (a) is incorrect because used tangible depreciable property is depreciated under MACRS. Answer (c) is incorrect because the cost of some depreciable realty must be depreciated using the straight-line method. Answer (d) is incorrect because the cost of some depreciable realty is included in the ten-year (e.g., single purpose agricultural and horticultural structures) and twenty-year (e.g., farm buildings) classes.

84. (a) The requirement is to determine the correct statement regarding the half-year convention under the general MACRS method. Under the half-year convention that generally applies to depreciable personal property, one-half of the first year's depreciation is allowed in the year in which the property is placed in service, regardless of when the property is placed in service during the year, and a half-year's depreciation is allowed for the year in which the property is disposed of, regardless of when the property is disposed of during the year. Answer (b) is incorrect because allowing one-half month's depreciation for the month that property is placed in service or disposed of is known as the "midmonth convention."

85. **(c)** The requirement is to determine the portion of the $814,000 cost of the machine that can be treated as an expense for 2010. Sec. 179 permits a taxpayer to elect to treat up to $250,000 (for 2010) of the cost of qualifying depreciable personal property as an expense rather than as a capital expenditure. However, the $250,000 maximum is reduced dollar-for-dollar by the cost of qualifying property placed in service during the taxable year that exceeds $800,000. Here, the maximum amount that can be expensed is [$250,000 – ($814,000 – $800,000)] = $236,000.

II. "Above the Line" Deductions

86. **(d)** The requirement is to determine the amount to be reported in Mel's gross income for the $400 per month received for business automobile expenses under a nonaccountable plan from Easel Co. Reimbursements and expense allowances paid to an employee under a nonaccountable plan must be included in the employee's gross income and are reported on the employee's W-2. The employee must then complete Form 2106 and itemize to deduct business-related expenses such as the use of an automobile.

87. **(c)** The requirement is to determine the correct statement regarding a second residence that is rented for 200 days and used 50 days for personal use. Deductions for expenses related to a dwelling that is also used as a residence by the taxpayer may be limited. If the taxpayer's personal use exceeds the greater of 14 days, or 10% of the number of days rented, deductions allocable to rental use are limited to rental income. Here, since Adams used the second residence for 50 days and rented the residence for 200 days, no rental loss can be deducted. All expenses related to the property, including utilities and maintenance, must be allocated between personal use and rental use. Answer (d) is incorrect because only the mortgage interest and taxes allocable to rental use would be deducted in determining the property's net rental income or loss. Answer (a) is incorrect, since depreciation on the property could be deducted if Adams' gross rental income exceeds allocable out-of-pocket rental expenses.

88. **(a)** The requirement is to determine the amount of unreimbursed employee expenses that can be deducted by Gilbert if he does not itemize deductions. Gilbert cannot deduct any of the expenses listed if he does not itemize deductions. The unreimbursed employee business expenses are deductible only as itemized deductions, subsequent to the 2% of AGI floor.

II.E. Moving Expenses

89. **(c)** The requirement is to determine the amount of moving expense that James can deduct for 2010. Direct moving expenses are deductible if closely related to the start of work at a new location and a distance test (i.e., distance from new job to former residence is at least fifty miles further than distance from old job to former residence) and a time test (i.e., employed at least thirty-nine weeks out of twelve months following move) are met. Since both tests are met, James' unreimbursed lodging and travel expenses

($1,000), cost of insuring household goods and personal effects during move ($200), cost of shipping household pets ($100), and cost of moving household furnishings and personal effects ($3,000) are deductible. Indirect moving expenses such as premove househunting, temporary living expenses, and meals while moving are not deductible.

90. **(c)** The requirement is to determine Martin's deductible moving expenses. Moving expenses are deductible if closely related to the start of work at a new location and a distance (i.e., new job must be at least fifty miles from former residence) and time (i.e., employed at least thirty-nine weeks out of twelve months following move) tests are met. Here, both tests are met and Martin's $800 cost of moving his personal belongings is deductible. However, the $300 penalty for breaking his lease is not deductible.

91. **(a)** Only the direct costs incurred for transporting a taxpayer, his or her family, and their household goods and personal effects from their former residence to their new residence can qualify as deductible moving expenses. The indirect moving expense costs incurred for meals while in transit, house hunting, temporary lodging, to sell or purchase a home, and to break or acquire a lease are not deductible.

II.F. Contributions to Certain Retirement Plans

92. **(d)** The requirement is to determine the incorrect statement concerning a Roth IRA. The maximum annual contribution to a Roth IRA is subject to reduction if the taxpayer's adjusted gross income exceeds certain thresholds. Unlike a traditional IRA, contributions are not deductible and can be made even after the taxpayer reaches age 70½. The contribution must be made by the due date of the taxpayer's tax return (**not** including extensions).

93. **(c)** The requirement is to determine the maximum amount of adjusted gross income that a taxpayer may have and still qualify to roll over a traditional IRA into a Roth IRA for 2009. A conversion or rollover of a traditional IRA to a Roth IRA can occur if the taxpayer's AGI does not exceed $100,000, the taxpayer is not married filing a separate return, and the rollover occurs within sixty days of the IRA distribution. For purposes of the determining eligibility, the $100,000 AGI ceiling is determined by including taxable social security and is determined before the exclusions for interest on Series EE bonds used for higher education, employer provided adoption assistance, and foreign earned income. The IRA conversion or rollover amount is not taken into account in determining the $100,000 AGI ceiling. Finally, note that the AGI limit and the joint filing requirement have been eliminated for tax years beginning after 2009.

94. **(d)** The requirement is to determine which statement concerning an education IRA is not correct. Contributions to an education IRA are not deductible, but withdrawals of earnings will be tax-free if used to pay the qualified higher education expenses of the designated beneficiary. The maximum amount that can be contributed to an education IRA for 2009 is limited to $2,000, but the annual contribution is phased out by adjusted gross income in excess of certain thresholds. Contributions generally cannot be made to an education IRA after the date on which the designated beneficiary reaches age eighteen.

95. **(a)** The requirement is to determine the Whites' allowable IRA deduction on their 2009 joint return. For married taxpayers filing a joint return for 2009, up to $5,000 can be deducted for contributions to the IRA of each spouse (even if one spouse is not working), provided that the combined earned income of both spouses is at least equal to the amounts contributed to the IRAs. Even though Val is covered by his employer's qualified pension plan, the Whites are eligible for the maximum deduction because their gross income of $35,000 + $4,000 = $39,000 does not exceed the base amount ($85,000) at which the maximum $5,000 deduction would be reduced. Also note that Pat's $4,000 of taxable alimony payments is treated as compensation for purposes of qualifying for an IRA deduction. Since they each contributed $5,000 to an IRA account, the allowable deduction on their joint return is $10,000.

96. **(d)** The requirement is to determine the definition of "earned income" for purposes of computing the annual contribution to a Keogh profit-sharing plan by Davis, a sole proprietor. A self-employed individual may contribute to a qualified retirement plan called a Keogh plan. For 2009, the maximum contribution to a Keogh profit-sharing plan is the lesser of $49,000 or 25% of earned income. For this purpose, "earned income" is defined as net earnings from self-employment (i.e., business gross income minus allowable business deductions) reduced by the deduction for one-half of the self-employment tax, and the deductible Keogh contribution itself.

97. **(d)** A single individual with AGI over $65,000 for 2009 would only be entitled to an IRA deduction if the taxpayer is not covered by a qualified employee pension plan.

98. **(c)** The requirement is to determine the allowable IRA deduction on the Cranes' 2009 joint return. Since Sol is covered by his employer's pension plan, Sol's contribution of $5,000 is proportionately phased out as a deduction by AGI between $89,000 and $109,000. Since the Cranes' AGI exceeded $109,000, no deduction is allowed for Sol's contribution. Although Julia is not employed, $5,000 can be contributed to her IRA because the combined earned income on the Cranes' return is at least $10,000. The maximum IRA deduction for an individual who is not covered by an employer plan, but whose spouse is, is proportionately phased out for AGI between $166,000 and $176,000. Since Julia is not covered by an employer plan and the Cranes' AGI is below $166,000, the $5,000 contribution to Julia's IRA is fully deductible for 2009.

99. **(d)** The requirement is to determine the Lees' maximum IRA contribution and deduction on a joint return for 2009. Since neither taxpayer was covered by an employer-sponsored pension plan, there is no phaseout of the maximum deduction due to the level of their adjusted gross income. For married taxpayers filing a joint return, up to $5,000 can be deducted for contributions to the IRA of each spouse (even if one spouse is not working), provided that the combined earned income of both spouses is at least equal to the amounts contributed to the IRAs. Additionally, an individual at least age 50 can make a special catch-up contribution of $1,000 for 2009, resulting in an increased maximum contribution and deduction of $6,000 for 2009. Thus, the Lees may contribute and deduct a maximum of $12,000 to their individual retirement accounts for 2009, with a maximum of $6,000 placed into each account.

100. **(c)** The maximum amount of contributions to a defined contribution self-employed retirement plan is limited to the lesser of $49,000, or 100% of self-employment income for 2009.

101. **(d)** The requirement is to determine which allowable deduction can be claimed in arriving at an individual's adjusted gross income. One hundred percent of a self-employed individual's health insurance premiums are deductible in arriving at an individual's adjusted gross income for 2009. Charitable contributions, foreign income taxes (if not used as a credit), and tax return preparation fees can be deducted only from adjusted gross income if an individual itemizes deductions.

II.G. Deduction for Interest on Education Loan

102. **(b)** The requirement is to determine the incorrect statement concerning the deduction for interest on qualified education loans. For a tax year beginning in 2009, an individual is allowed to deduct up to $2,500 for interest on qualified education loans in arriving at AGI. The deduction is subject to an income phase-out and the loan proceeds must have been used to pay for the qualified higher education expenses (e.g., tuition, fees, room, board) of the taxpayer, spouse, or a dependent (at the time the debt was incurred). The education expenses must relate to a period when the student was enrolled on at least a half-time basis. The sixty-month limitation was repealed for tax years beginning after 2002.

103. **(c)** The requirement is to determine how Dale should treat her $1,000 jury duty fee that she remitted to her employer. Fees received for serving on a jury must be included in gross income. If the recipient is required to remit the jury duty fees to an employer in exchange for regular compensation, the remitted jury duty fees are allowed as a deduction from gross income in arriving at adjusted gross income.

III.   Itemized Deductions from Adjusted Gross Income

104. **(b)** The requirement is to determine George's taxable income. George's adjusted gross income consists of $3,700 of dividends and $1,700 of wages. Since George is eligible to be claimed as a dependency exemption by his parents, there will be no personal exemption on George's return and his basic standard deduction is limited to the greater of $950, or George's earned income of $1,700, plus $300. Thus, George's taxable income would be computed as follows:

Dividends	$ 3,700
Wages	1,700
AGI	$ 5,400
Exemption	0
Std. deduction	(2,000)
Taxable income	$ 3,400

105. **(c)** The item asks you to determine the requirements that must be met in order for a single individual to qualify for the additional standard deduction. A single individual who is age sixty-five or older or blind is eligible for an additional standard deduction ($1,400 for 2009 and 2010). Two additional standard deductions are allowed for an individual who is age sixty-five or older **and** blind. It is not required that an individual support a dependent child or aged parent in order to qualify for an additional standard deduction.

III.A. Medical and Dental Expenses

106. (b) The requirement is to determine Carroll's maximum medical expense deduction after the applicable threshold limitation for the year. An individual taxpayer's unreimbursed medical expenses are deductible to the extent in excess of 7.5% of the taxpayer's adjusted gross income. Although the cost of cosmetic surgery is generally not deductible, the cost is deductible if the cosmetic surgery or procedure is necessary to ameliorate a deformity related to a congenital abnormality or personal injury resulting from an accident, trauma, or disfiguring disease. Here, Carroll's deduction is ($5,000 + $15,000) − ($100,000 × 7.5%) = $12,500.

107. (b) The requirement is to determine the Blairs' itemized deduction for medical expenses for 2009. A taxpayer can deduct the amounts paid for the medical care of himself, spouse, or dependents. The Blairs' qualifying medical expenses include the $800 of medical insurance premiums, $450 of prescribed medicines, $1,000 of unreimbursed doctor's fees, and $150 of transportation related to medical care. These expenses, which total $2,400, are deductible to the extent they exceed 7.5% of adjusted gross income, and result in a deduction of $150. Note that nonprescription medicines, including aspirin and over-the-counter cold capsules, are not deductible. Additionally, the Blairs cannot deduct the emergency room fee they paid for their son because they did not provide more than half of his support and he therefore does not qualify as their dependent.

108. (a) The requirement is to determine the amount the Whites may deduct as qualifying medical expenses without regard to the adjusted gross income percentage threshold. The Whites' deductible medical expenses include the $600 spent on repair and maintenance of the motorized wheelchair and the $8,000 spent for tuition, meals, and lodging at the special school for their physically handicapped dependent child. Payment for meals and lodging provided by an institution as a necessary part of medical care is deductible as a medical expense if the main reason for being in the institution is to receive medical care. Here, the item indicates that the Whites' physically handicapped dependent child was in the institution primarily for the availability of medical care, and that meals and lodging were furnished as necessary incidents to that care.

109. (c) The requirement is to determine the amount Wells can deduct as qualifying medical expenses without regard to the adjusted gross income percentage threshold. Wells' deductible medical expenses include the $500 premium on the prescription drug insurance policy and the $500 unreimbursed payment for physical therapy. The earnings protection policy is not considered medical insurance because payments are not based on the amount of medical expenses incurred. As a result, the $3,000 premium is a nondeductible personal expense.

110. (d) The requirement is to determine the amount of expenses incurred in connection with the adoption of a child that can be deducted by the Sloans on their 2009 joint return. A taxpayer can deduct the medical expenses paid for a child at the time of adoption if the child qualifies as the taxpayer's dependent when the medical expenses are paid. Additionally, if a taxpayer pays an adoption agency for medical expenses the adoption agency already paid, the tax-

payer is treated as having paid those expenses. Here, the Sloans can deduct the child's medical expenses of $5,000 that they paid. On the other hand, the legal expenses of $9,000 and agency fee of $4,000 incurred in connection with the adoption are treated as nondeductible personal expenses. However, the Sloans will qualify to claim a nonrefundable tax credit of up to $12,150 (for 2009) for these qualified adoption expenses.

111. (a) The requirement is to determine the amount that can be claimed by the Clines in their 2010 return as qualifying medical expenses. No medical expense deduction is allowed for cosmetic surgery or similar procedures, unless the surgery or procedure is necessary to ameliorate a deformity related to a congenital abnormality or personal injury resulting from an accident, trauma, or disfiguring disease. Cosmetic surgery is defined as any procedure that is directed at improving a patient's appearance and does not meaningfully promote the proper function of the body or prevent or treat illness or disease. Thus, Ruth's face-lift and Mark's hair transplant do not qualify as deductible medical expenses in 2010.

112. (d) The requirement is to determine the amount that Scott can claim as deductible medical expenses. The medical expenses incurred by a taxpayer for himself, spouse, or a dependent are deductible when paid or charged to a credit card. The $4,000 of medical expenses for his dependent son are deductible by Scott in 2009 when charged on Scott's credit card. It does not matter that payment to the credit card issuer had not been made when Scott filed his return. Expenses paid for the medical care of a decedent by the decedent's spouse are deductible as medical expenses in the year they are paid, whether the expenses are paid before or after the decedent's death. Thus, the $2,800 of medical expenses for his deceased spouse are deductible by Scott when paid in 2009, even though his spouse died in 2008.

113. (d) The requirement is to determine which expenditure qualifies as a deductible medical expense. Premiums paid for Medicare B supplemental medical insurance qualify as a deductible expense. Diaper service, funeral expenses, and nursing care for a healthy baby are not deductible as medical expenses.

114. (b) The requirement is to determine Stenger's net medical expense deduction for 2009. It would be computed as follows:

Prescription drugs	$ 300
Medical insurance premiums	750
Doctors ($2,550 − $900)	1,650
Eyeglasses	75
	$2,775
Less 7.5% of AGI ($35,000)	2,625
Medical expense deduction for 2009	$ 150

115. (d) The requirement is to determine the total amount of deductible medical expenses for the Bensons before the application of any limitation rules. Deductible medical expenses include those incurred by a taxpayer, taxpayer's spouse, dependents of the taxpayer, or any person for whom the taxpayer could claim a dependency exemption except that the person had gross income of $3,650 or more, or filed a joint return. Thus, the Bensons may deduct medical expenses incurred for themselves, for John (i.e., no dependency exemption only because his gross income is $3,650 or more), and for Nancy (i.e., a dependent of the Bensons).

III.B. Taxes

116. (d) The requirement is to determine the tax that is not deductible as an itemized deduction. One-half of a self-employed taxpayer's self-employment tax is deductible from gross income in arriving at adjusted gross income. Foreign real estate taxes, foreign income taxes, and personal property taxes can be deducted as itemized deductions from adjusted gross income.

117. (c) The requirement is to determine the amount that Matthews can deduct as taxes on her 2009 Schedule A of Form 1040. An individual's state and local income taxes are deductible as an itemized deduction, while federal income taxes are not deductible. For a cash-basis taxpayer, state and local taxes are deductible for the year in which paid or withheld. As a result, Matthew's deduction for 2009 consists of her state and local taxes withheld of $1,500 and the December 30 estimated payment of $400. The state and local income taxes that Matthews paid in April 2010 will be deductible for 2010.

118. (a) The requirement is to determine the correct statement regarding Farb, a cash-basis individual taxpayer who paid an $8,000 invoice for personal property taxes under protest in 2009, and received a $5,000 refund of the taxes in 2010. If a taxpayer receives a refund or rebate of taxes deducted in an earlier year, the taxpayer must generally include the refund or rebate in income for the year in which received. Here, Farb should deduct $8,000 in his 2009 income tax return and should report the $5,000 refund as income in his 2010 income tax return.

119. (d) The requirement is to determine the amount of itemized deduction for realty taxes that can be deducted by Burg. Generally, an individual's payment of state, local, or foreign real estate taxes is deductible as an itemized deduction if the individual is the owner of the property on which the taxes are imposed. Because the property is jointly owned by Burg, he is individually liable for the entire amount of realty taxes and may deduct the entire payment on his return. Even back taxes can be deducted by Burg as long as he was the owner of the property during the period of time to which the back taxes are related.

120. (b) The requirement is to determine Sara's deduction for state income taxes in 2009. Sara's deduction would consist of the $2,000 withheld by her employer in 2009, plus the three estimated payments (3 × $300 = $900) actually paid during 2009, a total of $2,900. Note that the 1/15/10 estimated payment would be deductible for 2010.

121. (b) The requirement is to determine the amount of **taxes** deductible as an itemized deduction. The $360 vehicle tax based on value is deductible as a personal property tax. The real property tax of $2,700 must be apportioned between the Bronsons and the buyer for tax purposes according to the number of days in the real property tax year that each owns the property even though they did not actually make an apportionment. Taxes are apportioned to the seller up to, but not including, the date of the sale, and apportioned to the buyer beginning with the date of sale. Since the house was sold June 30, the Bronson's deduction for real estate taxes would be $2,700 × 180/365 = $1,332. The buyer would deduct the remaining $1,368.

122. (a) The requirement is to determine what portion of the $1,300 of realty taxes is deductible by King in 2010. The $600 of delinquent taxes charged to the seller and paid by King are not deductible, but are added to the cost of the property. The $700 of taxes for 2010 are apportioned between the seller and King according to the number of days that each held the property during the year. King's deduction would be

$$\frac{184}{365} \times \$700 = \$353$$

123. (b) The requirement is to determine the amount of property taxes deductible as itemized deductions. The property taxes on the residence and the land held for appreciation, together with the personal property taxes on the auto are deductible. The special assessment is not deductible, but would be added to the basis of the residence.

124. (a) The requirement is to determine the amount the Burgs should deduct for taxes in their itemized deductions. The $1,200 of state income tax paid by the Burgs is deductible as an itemized deduction. However, the $7,650 of self-employment tax is not deductible as an itemized deduction. Instead, 50% × $7,650 = $3,825 of self-employment tax is deductible from gross income in arriving at the Burgs' adjusted gross income.

III.C. Interest Expense

125. (c) The requirement is to determine the correct statement regarding an individual taxpayer's deduction for interest on investment indebtedness. The deduction for interest expense on investment indebtedness is limited to the taxpayer's net investment income. Net investment income includes such income as interest, dividends, and short-term capital gains, less any related expenses.

126. (b) The requirement is to determine the correct statement regarding the interest on the Browns' $20,000 loan that was secured by their home and used to purchase an automobile. Qualified residence interest consists of interest on acquisition indebtedness and home equity indebtedness. Interest on home equity indebtedness loans of up to $100,000 is deductible as qualified residence interest if the loans are secured by a taxpayer's principal or second residence regardless of how the loan proceeds are used. The amount of home equity indebtedness cannot exceed the fair market value of a home as reduced by any acquisition indebtedness. Since the Browns' home had a FMV of $400,000 and was unencumbered by other debt, the interest on the $20,000 home equity loan is deductible as qualified residence interest.

127. (c) The requirement is to determine how much interest is deductible by the Philips for 2010. Qualified residence interest includes the interest on acquisition indebtedness. Such interest is deductible on up to $1 million of loans secured by a principal or second residence if the loans were used to purchase, construct, or substantially improve a home. Here, the Philips' original mortgage of $200,000 as well as the additional loan of $15,000 qualify as acquisition indebtedness, and the resulting $17,000 + $1,500 = $18,500 of interest is deductible. On the other hand, the $500 of interest on the auto loan is considered personal interest and not deductible.

128. (c) The requirement is to determine the maximum amount allowable as a deduction for Jackson's second residence. Qualified residence interest includes acquisition indebtedness and home equity indebtedness on the taxpayer's principal residence and a second residence. Here, the $5,000 of mortgage interest on the second residence is qualified residence interest and is deductible as an itemized deduction. In contrast, the $1,200 of utilities expense and $6,000 of insurance expense are nondeductible personal expenses.

129. (c) The requirement is to determine the amount of interest expense deductible as an itemized deduction. The $3,600 of home mortgage interest, and the $900 mortgage prepayment penalty are fully deductible as interest expense in computing itemized deductions. The $1,200 interest on the life insurance policy is not deductible since it is classified as personal interest.

130. (a) The requirement is to determine the amount of interest deductible as an itemized deduction. Since 2/3 of the loan proceeds were used to purchase tax-exempt bonds, 2/3 of the bank interest is nondeductible. The remaining 1/3 of the bank interest ($1,200) is related to the purchase of the Arrow debentures and is classified as investment interest deductible to the extent of net investment income ($0). The $3,000 of home mortgage interest is fully deductible as qualified residence interest. The interest on credit card charges is personal interest and is not deductible.

131. (a) None of the items listed relating to the tax deficiency for 2008 are deductible. The interest on the tax deficiency is considered personal interest and is not deductible. The additional federal income tax, the late filing penalty, and the negligence penalty are also not deductible.

III.D.   Charitable Contributions

132. (b) The requirement is to determine the amount that Smith should deduct as a charitable contribution. If appreciated property is contributed, the amount of contribution is generally the property's FMV if a sale of the property would result in a long-term capital gain. Here, the art object worth $3,000 was purchased for $2,000 just four months earlier. Since its holding period did not exceed twelve months, a sale of the art object would result in only a short-term capital gain, and the amount of allowable contribution deduction is limited to its $2,000 cost basis. Additionally, the donation of $5,000 cash to Smith's church is deductible but no deduction is available for the $1,000 contribution to a needy family. To be deductible, a contribution must be made to a qualifying organization.

133. (c) The requirement is to determine the amount of charitable contributions deductible on Stein's current year income tax return. The donation of appreciated stock held more than twelve months is a contribution of intangible, long-term capital gain appreciated property. The amount of contribution is the stock's FMV of $25,000, but is limited in deductibility for the current year to 30% of AGI. Thus, the current year deduction is limited to 30% × $80,000 = $24,000. The remaining $1,000 of contributions can be carried forward for up to five years, subject to the 30% limitation in the carryforward years.

134. (c) The requirement is to determine the maximum amount of properly substantiated charitable contributions

that Moore could claim as an itemized deduction for 2009. Moore gave $18,000 to her church during 2009 and had a $10,000 charitable contribution carryover from 2008, resulting in a total of $28,000 of contributions. Since an individual's deduction for charitable contributions cannot exceed an overall limitation of 50% of adjusted gross income, Moore's charitable contribution deduction for 2009 is limited to ($50,000 AGI × 50%) = $25,000. Since Moore's 2009 contributions will be deducted before her carryforward from 2008, Moore will carry over $3,000 of her 2008 contributions to 2010.

135. (c) The requirement is to determine the maximum amount that Spencer can claim as a deduction for charitable contributions in 2009. The cash contribution of $4,000 to church and the $600 fair market value of the used clothing donated to Salvation Army are fully deductible. However, the deduction for the art object is limited to the $400 excess of its cost ($1,200) over its fair market value ($800).

136. (b) The requirement is to determine Lewis' charitable contribution deduction. The donation of appreciated stock held more than twelve months is a contribution of intangible, long-term capital gain appreciated property. The amount of contribution is the stock's FMV of $70,000, but is limited in deductibility for 2009 to 30% of AGI. Thus, the 2009 deduction is $100,000 × 30% = $30,000. The amount of contribution in excess of the 30% limitation ($70,000 − $30,000 = $40,000) can be carried forward for up to five years, subject to the 30% limitation in the carryforward years.

137. (b) The requirement is to determine the amount of contributions deductible in 2009. Charitable contributions are generally deductible in the year actually paid. The $500 charge to his bank credit card made on December 15, 2009, is considered a payment, and is deductible for 2009. The $1,000 promissory note delivered on November 1, 2009, is not considered a contribution until payment of the note upon maturity in 2010.

138. (b) The requirement is to determine the amount of student expenses deductible as a charitable contribution. A taxpayer may deduct as a charitable contribution up to $50 per **school month** of unreimbursed expenses incurred to maintain a student (in the 12th or lower grade) in the taxpayer's home pursuant to a written agreement with a qualified organization. Since the student started school in September, the amount deductible as a charitable contribution is $50 × 4 = $200.

139. (a) Vincent Tally is not entitled to a deduction for contributions in 2009 because he did not give up his entire interest in the book collection. By reserving the right to use and possess the book collection for his lifetime, Vincent Tally has not made a completed gift. Therefore, no deduction is available. The contribution will be deductible when his entire interest in the books is transferred to the art museum.

140. (b) The requirement is to determine the maximum amount of charitable contribution allowable as an itemized deduction on Jimet's 2009 income tax return. If appreciated property is contributed, the amount of contribution is generally the property's FMV if the property would result in a long-term capital gain if sold. If not, the amount of contribution for appreciated property is generally limited to the property's basis. Here, the stock worth $3,000 was purchased for $1,500 just four months earlier. Since its holding period did not exceed twelve months, a sale of the stock would result in a short-term capital gain, and the amount of allowable contribution deduction is limited to the stock's basis of $1,500. Additionally, to be deductible, a contribution must be made to a qualifying **organization**. As a result, the $2,000 cash given directly to a needy family is not deductible.

141. (a) The requirement is to determine the maximum amount of charitable contribution deductible as an itemized deduction on Taylor's tax return for 2009. The donation of appreciated land purchased for investment and held for more than twelve months is a contribution of real capital gain property (property that would result in long-term capital gain if sold). The amount of contribution is the land's FMV of $25,000, limited in deductibility for the current year to 30% of AGI. In this case, since 30% of AGI would be 30% × $90,000 = $27,000, the full amount of the land contribution ($25,000) is deductible for 2009.

III.E.   Personal Casualty and Theft Gains and Losses

142. (a) The requirement is to determine the amount of the fire loss to her personal residence that Frazer can claim as an itemized deduction. The amount of a personal casualty loss is computed as the lesser of (1) the adjusted basis of the property ($130,000), or (2) the decline in the property's fair market value resulting from the casualty ($130,000 – $0 = $130,000); reduced by any insurance recovery ($120,000), and a $500 floor. Since Frazer had no casualty gains during the year, the net casualty loss is then deductible as an itemized deduction to the extent that it exceeds 10% of adjusted gross income.

Fire loss	$ 130,000
Insurance proceeds	(120,000)
$500 floor	(500)
10% of $70,000 AGI	(7,000)
Casualty loss itemized deduction	$ 2,500

143. (a) The requirement is to determine the amount the Burgs should deduct for the casualty loss (repair of glass vase accidentally broken by their dog) in their itemized deductions. A casualty is the damage, destruction, or loss of property resulting from an identifiable event that is sudden, unexpected, or unusual. Deductible casualty losses may result from earthquakes, tornadoes, floods, fires, vandalism, auto accidents, etc. However, a loss due to the accidental breakage of household articles such as glassware or china under normal conditions is not a casualty loss. Neither is a loss due to damage caused by a family pet.

144. (d) The requirement is to determine the proper treatment of the $490 casualty insurance premium. Casualty insurance premiums on an individual's personal residence are considered nondeductible personal expenses. Even though a casualty is actually incurred during the year, no deduction is available for personal casualty insurance premiums.

145. (d) The requirement is to determine the amount of the fire loss damage to their personal residence that the Hoyts can deduct as an itemized deduction. The amount of a nonbusiness casualty loss is computed as the lesser of (1) the adjusted basis of the property, or (2) the property's decline in FMV; reduced by any insurance recovery, and a

$500 floor. If an individual has a net casualty loss for the year, it is then deductible as an itemized deduction to the extent that it exceeds 10% of adjusted gross income.

Lesser of:			
Adjusted basis	=	$50,000	
Decline in FMV			
($60,000 – $55,000)	=	$ 5,000	$ 5,000
Reduce by:			
Insurance recovery			(0)
$500 floor			(500)
10% of $34,000 AGI			(3,400)
Casualty loss itemized deduction			$ 1,100

Note that the $2,500 spent for repairs is not included in the computation of the loss.

146. (b) The requirement is to determine the proper treatment for the $800 appraisal fee that was incurred to determine the amount of the Hoyts' fire loss. The appraisal fee is considered an expense of determining the Hoyts' tax liability; it is not a part of the casualty loss itself. Thus, the appraisal fee is deductible as a miscellaneous itemized deduction subject to a 2% of adjusted gross income floor.

III.F.   Miscellaneous Deductions

147. (d) The requirement is to determine which item is **not** a miscellaneous itemized deduction. A legal fee for tax advice related to a divorce, IRA trustee's fees that are separately billed and paid, and an appraisal fee for valuing a charitable contribution qualify as miscellaneous itemized deductions subject to the 2% of AGI floor. On the other hand, the check writing fees for a personal checking account are a personal expense and not deductible.

148. (b) The requirement is to determine the proper treatment of the $2,000 legal fee that was incurred by Hall in a suit to collect the alimony owed her. The $2,000 legal fee is considered an expenditure incurred in the production of income. Expenses incurred in the production of income are deductible as miscellaneous itemized deductions subject to the 2% of adjusted gross income floor.

149. (b) The requirement is to determine the proper reporting of Hall's lottery transactions. Hall's lottery winnings of $200 must be reported as other income on page 1 of Hall's Form 1040. Hall's $1,000 expenditure for state lottery tickets is deductible as a miscellaneous itemized deduction not subject to the 2% of AGI floor, but is limited in amount to the $200 of lottery winnings included in Hall's gross income.

150. (d) The requirement is to determine how expenses pertaining to business activities should be deducted by an outside salesman. An outside salesman is an employee who principally solicits business for his employer while away from the employer's place of business. All unreimbursed business expenses of an outside salesman are deducted as miscellaneous itemized deductions, subject to a 2% of AGI floor. Deductible expenses include business travel, secretarial help, and telephone expenses.

151. (a) The requirement is to determine the amount that can be claimed as miscellaneous itemized deductions. Both the initiation fee and the union dues are fully deductible. The voluntary benefit fund contribution is not deductible. Miscellaneous itemized deductions are generally deductible only to the extent they exceed 2% of AGI. In this case the deductible amount is $80 [$280 – (.02 × $10,000)].

152. (b) The requirement is to compute the amount of miscellaneous itemized deductions. The cost of uniforms not adaptable to general use (specialized work clothes), union dues, unreimbursed auto expenses, and the cost of income tax preparation are all miscellaneous itemized deductions. The preparation of a will is personal in nature, and is not deductible. Thus, the computation of Brodsky's miscellaneous itemized deductions in excess of the 2% of AGI floor is as follows:

Unreimbursed auto expenses	$ 100
Specialized work clothes	550
Union dues	600
Cost of income tax preparation	150
	$1,400
Less (2% × $25,000)	(500)
Deduction allowed	$ 900

III.G. Reduction of Itemized Deductions

153. (c) The requirement is to determine the item that is not subject to the phaseout of itemized deductions for high-income individuals for 2009. An individual whose adjusted gross income exceeds a threshold amount ($166,800 for 2009) is required to reduce the amount of allowable itemized deductions by 3% of the excess of adjusted gross income over the threshold amount. All itemized deductions are subject to this reduction **except** medical expenses, nonbusiness casualty losses, investment interest expense, and gambling losses.

154. (a) The requirement is to determine the correct statement regarding the reduction in itemized deductions for 2009. For an individual whose AGI exceeds a threshold amount, the amount of otherwise allowable itemized deductions is reduced by the lesser of (1) 3% of the excess of AGI over the threshold amount, or (2) 80% of certain itemized deductions. The itemized deductions that are subject to reduction include taxes, qualified residence interest, charitable contributions, and miscellaneous itemized deductions (other than gambling losses). The reduction of these itemized deductions can not exceed 80% of the amount that is otherwise allowable.

IV. Exemptions

155. (d) The requirement is to determine which item is not included in determining the total support of a dependent. Support includes food, clothing, FMV of lodging, medical, recreational, educational, and certain capital expenditures made on behalf of a dependent. Excluded from support is life insurance premiums, funeral expenses, nontaxable scholarships, and income and social security taxes paid from a dependent's own income.

156. (c) The requirement is to determine the number of exemptions that Smith was entitled to claim on his 2009 tax return. Smith will be allowed one exemption for himself and one exemption for his dependent mother. Smith is entitled to an exemption for his mother because he provided over half of her support, and her gross income ($0) was less than $3,650. Note that her $9,000 of social security benefits is excluded from her gross income, and that she did not have to live with Smith because she is related to him. No exemption is available to Smith for his son, Clay, because his son filed a joint return on which there was a tax liability.

157. (b) The requirement is to determine how many exemptions Jim and Kay can claim on their 2009 joint income tax return. Jim and Kay are entitled to one personal exemption each on their joint return. They also are entitled to one exemption for their son, Dale, since he is a *qualifying child* (i.e., Dale did not provide more than half of his own support, and Dale is a full-time student under age twenty-four). However, no dependency exemptions are available for Kim and Grant. Kim is not a qualifying child because she is at least age 19 and not a full-time student, and she is not a qualifying relative because her gross income was at least $3,650. Similarly, Grant is not a qualifying relative because his gross income was at least $3,650.

158. (d) The requirement is to determine the requirements which must be satisfied in order for Joe to claim an exemption for his spouse on Joe's separate return for 2009. An exemption can be claimed for Joe's spouse on Joe's separate 2009 return only if the spouse had **no** gross income and was **not** claimed as another person's dependent in 2009.

159. (a) The requirement is to determine the amount of personal exemption on a dependent's tax return. No personal exemption is allowed on an individual's tax return if the individual can be claimed as a dependency exemption by another taxpayer.

160. (d) The requirement is to determine Robert's filing status and the number of exemptions that he should claim. Robert's father does not qualify as Robert's dependent because his father's gross income (interest income of $3,700) was not less than $3,650. Social security is not included in the gross income test. Since his father does not qualify as his dependent, Robert does not qualify for head-of-household filing status. Thus, Robert will file as single with one exemption.

161. (a) The requirement is to determine the filing status of the Arnolds. Since they were legally separated under a decree of separate maintenance on the last day of the taxable year and do not qualify for head-of-household status, they must each file as single.

162. (a) Mr. and Mrs. Stoner are entitled to one exemption each. They are entitled to one exemption for their daughter since she is a qualifying child (i.e., she did not provide more than half of her own support, and she is a full-time student under age twenty-four). An exemption can be claimed for their son because he is a qualifying relative (i.e., they provided more than half of his support, and his gross income was less than $3,650). No exemption is allowable for Mrs. Stoner's father since he was neither a US citizen nor resident of the US, Canada, or Mexico. There is no additional exemption for being age sixty-five or older.

163. (c) The requirement is to determine the number of exemptions the Planters may claim on their joint tax return. There is one exemption for Mr. Planter, and one exemption for his spouse. In addition there is one dependency exemption for their daughter who is a qualifying child (i.e., she did not provide more than half of her own support, and she is a full-time student under age twenty-four). There is also one dependency exemption for their niece who is a qualifying relative (i.e., they provided more than half of her support, and her gross income was less than $3,650). However, there is no additional exemption for being age sixty-five or older.

164. (b) The requirement is to determine which of the relatives can be claimed as a dependent (or dependents) on Sam's 2009 return. A taxpayer's own spouse is never a dependent of the taxpayer. Although a personal exemption is generally available for a taxpayer's spouse on the taxpayer's return, it is not a "dependency exemption." Generally, a dependency exemption is available for a qualifying relative if (1) the taxpayer furnishes more than 50% of the dependent's support, (2) the dependent's gross income is less than $3,650, (3) the dependent is of specified relationship to the taxpayer or lives in the taxpayer's household for the entire year, (4) the dependent is a US citizen or resident of the US, Canada, or Mexico, and (5) the dependent does not file a joint return. Here, the support, gross income, US citizen, and joint return tests are met with respect to both Sam's cousin and his father's brother (i.e., Sam's uncle). However, Sam's cousin is not of specified relationship to Sam as defined in the IRC, and could only be claimed as a dependent if the cousin lived in Sam's household for the entire year. Since Sam's cousin did not live in Sam's household, Sam cannot claim a dependency exemption for his cousin. On the other hand, Sam's uncle is of specified relationship to Sam as defined in the IRC and can be claimed as a dependency exemption by Sam.

165. (b) The requirement is to determine which relative could be claimed as a dependent. One of the requirements that must be satisfied to claim a dependency exemption for a person as a qualifying relative is that the person must be (1) of specified relationship to the taxpayer, or (2) a member of the taxpayer's household. Cousins and foster parents are not of specified relationship and only qualify if a member of the taxpayer's household. Since Alan's cousin and foster parent do not qualify as members of Alan's household, only Alan's niece can be claimed as a dependent.

166. (c) The requirement is to determine who can claim Sara's dependency exemption under a multiple support agreement. A multiple support agreement can be used if (1) no single taxpayer furnishes more than 50% of a dependent's support, and (2) two or more persons, each of whom would be able to take the exemption but for the support test, together provide more than 50% of the dependent's support. Then, any taxpayer who provides more than 10% of the dependent's support can claim the dependent if (1) the other persons furnishing more than 10% agree not to claim the dependent as an exemption, and (2) the other requirements for a dependency exemption are met. One of the other requirements that must be met is that the dependent be related to the taxpayer or live in the taxpayer's household. Alma is not eligible for the exemption because Sara is unrelated to Alma and did not live in Alma's household. Carl is not eligible for the exemption because he provided only 9% of Sara's support. Ben is eligible to claim the exemption for Sara under a multiple support agreement because Ben is related to Sara and has provided more than 10% of her support.

167. (b) The requirement is to determine the number of exemptions allowable in 2009. Mr. and Mrs. Vonce are entitled to one exemption each. They are also entitled to one exemption for their dependent daughter since they provided over one half of her support and she had less than $3,650 of gross income. An exemption is not available for their son because he provided over one-half of his own support.

V.C. Filing Status

168. (d) The requirement is to determine which statements (if any) are among the requirements to enable a taxpayer to be classified as a "qualifying widow(er)." Qualifying widow(er) filing status is available for the two years following the year of a spouse's death if (1) the surviving spouse was eligible to file a joint return in the year of the spouse's death, (2) does not remarry before the end of the current year, and (3) the surviving spouse pays **over 50%** of the cost of maintaining a household that is the principal home for the **entire year** of the surviving spouse's dependent child.

169. (c) The requirement is to determine which items are considered in determining whether an individual has contributed more than one half the cost of maintaining the household for purposes of head of household filing status. The cost of maintaining a household includes such costs as rent, mortgage interest, taxes, insurance on the home, repairs, utilities, and food eaten in the home. The cost of maintaining a household does **not** include the cost of clothing, education, medical treatment, vacations, life insurance, transportation, the rental value of a home an individual owns, or the value of an individual's services or those of any member of the household.

170. (b) The requirement is to determine the correct statement regarding the filing of a joint tax return. A husband and wife can file a joint return even if they have different accounting methods. Answer (a) is incorrect because spouses must have the same tax year to file a joint return. Answer (c) is incorrect because if either spouse was a nonresident alien at any time during the tax year, **both** spouses must elect to be taxed as US citizens or residents for the entire tax year. Answer (d) is incorrect because taxpayers cannot file a joint return if divorced before the end of the year.

171. (c) The requirement is to determine Emil Gow's filing status for 2009. Emil should file as a "Qualifying widower with dependent child" (i.e., surviving spouse) which will entitle him to use the joint return tax rates. This filing status is available for the two taxable years following the year of a spouse's death if (1) the surviving spouse was eligible to file a joint return in the year of the spouse's death, (2) does not remarry before the end of the current tax year, and (3) the surviving spouse pays over 50% of the cost of maintaining a household that is the principal home for the entire year of the surviving spouse's dependent child.

172. (c) The requirement is to determine Nell's filing status for 2009. Nell qualifies as a head of household because she is unmarried and maintains a household for her infant child. Answer (a) is incorrect because although Nell is single, head of household filing status provides for lower tax rates. Answer (b) is incorrect because Nell is unmarried at the end of 2009. Since Nell's spouse died in 2006, answer (d) is incorrect because the filing status of a "qualifying widow" is only available for the two years following the year of the spouse's death.

173. (a) Mrs. Felton must file as a single taxpayer. Even though she is unmarried, Mrs. Felton does not qualify as a head of household because her son is neither a qualifying child (because of his age) nor a qualifying relative (because he is not her dependent). Answer (b) is incorrect because in order for Mrs. Felton to qualify, her son must qualify as a dependent, which he does not. Although Mrs. Felton would have qualified as married filing jointly, answer (d), in 2009 (the year of her husband's death), the problem requirement is her 2010 filing status.

174. (c)   The requirement is to determine the 2009 income tax for Poole, an unmarried taxpayer in the 15% bracket with $20,000 of adjusted gross income. To determine Poole's taxable income, his adjusted gross income must be reduced by the greater of his itemized deductions or a standard deduction, and a personal exemption. Since Poole's medical expenses of $7,000 are deductible to the extent in excess of 7.5% of his AGI of $20,000, his itemized deductions of $5,500 exceed his available standard deduction of $5,450. Poole's tax computation is as follows:

Adjusted gross income		$20,000
Less:		
Itemized deductions	$6,000	
Personal exemption	3,650	9,650
Taxable income		$10,350
Tax rate		× 15%
Income tax		$ 1,553

V.D.   Alternative Minimum Tax (AMT)

175. (d)   The requirement is to determine the itemized deduction that is deductible when computing an individual's alternative minimum tax (AMT). For purposes of computing an individual's AMT, no deduction is allowed for personal, state, and local income taxes, and miscellaneous itemized deductions subject to the 2% of adjusted gross income threshold. Similarly, no deduction is allowed for home mortgage interest if the loan proceeds were not used to buy, build, or substantially improve the home.

176. (a)   The requirement is to determine the amount of tax preferences and adjustments that must be included in the computation of Randy's 2009 alternative minimum tax. The tax preferences include the $600 of excess depreciation on real property placed in service prior to 1987, and the $400 of tax-exempt interest on private activity bonds. These must be added to regular taxable income in arriving at alternative minimum taxable income (AMTI). The adjustments include the $3,650 personal exemption and $1,500 of state income taxes that are deductible in computing regular taxable income but are not deductible in computing AMTI.

177. (d)   The requirement is to determine the amount of Karen's unused alternative minimum tax credit that will carry over to 2010. The amount of alternative minimum tax paid by an individual that is attributable to timing preferences and adjustments is allowed as a tax credit (i.e., minimum tax credit) that can be applied against regular tax liability in future years. The minimum tax credit is computed as the excess of the AMT actually paid over the AMT that would have been paid if AMTI included only exclusion preferences and adjustments (e.g., disallowed itemized deductions, excess percentage depletion, tax-exempt private activity bond interest). Since the minimum tax credit can only be used to reduce future regular tax liability, the credit can only reduce regular tax liability to the point at which it equals the taxpayer's tentative minimum tax. In this case, Karen's payment of $20,000 of alternative minimum tax in 2008 generates a minimum tax credit of $20,000 – $9,000 = $11,000 which is carried forward to 2009. Since Karen's 2009 regular tax liability of $50,000 exceeded her tentative

minimum tax of $45,000, $5,000 of Karen's minimum tax credit would be used to reduce her 2009 tax liability to $45,000. Therefore, $11,000 – $5,000 = $6,000 of unused minimum tax credit would carry over to 2010.

178. (c)   The requirement is to determine the amount that Mills should report as alternative minimum taxable income (AMTI) before the AMT exemption. Certain itemized deductions, although allowed for regular tax purposes, are not deductible in computing an individual's AMTI. As a result, no AMT deduction is allowed for state, local, and foreign income taxes, real and personal property taxes, and miscellaneous itemized deductions subject to the 2% of AGI floor. Also, the deduction for medical expenses is computed using a 10% floor (instead of the 7.5% floor used for regular tax), and no deduction is allowed for qualified residence interest if the mortgage proceeds were **not** used to buy, build, or substantially improve the taxpayer's principal residence or a second home. Additionally, no AMT deduction is allowed for personal exemptions and the standard deduction.

Here, Mills' $5,000 of state and local income taxes and $2,000 of miscellaneous itemized deductions that were deducted for regular tax purposes must be added back to his $70,000 of regular taxable income before personal exemption to arrive at Mills' AMTI before AMT exemption of ($70,000 + $5,000 + $2,000)= $77,000. Note that no adjustment was necessary for the mortgage interest because the mortgage loan was used to acquire his residence.

179. (c)   The requirement is to determine whether a net capital gain and home equity interest expense are adjustments for purposes of computing the alternative minimum tax. Although an excess of net long-term capital gain over net short-term capital loss may be subject to a reduced maximum tax rate, the excess is neither a tax preference nor an adjustment in computing the alternative minimum tax. On the other hand, home equity interest expense where the home equity loan proceeds were not used to buy, build, or improve the home is an adjustment because the interest expense, although deductible for regular tax purposes, is not deductible for purposes of computing an individual's alternative minimum tax.

180. (d)   The requirement is to determine the proper treatment for the credit for prior year alternative minimum tax (AMT). The amount of AMT paid by an individual taxpayer that is attributable to timing differences can be carried forward indefinitely as a minimum tax credit to offset the individual's future regular tax liability (not future AMT liability). The amount of AMT credit to be carried forward is the excess of the AMT actually paid over the AMT that would have been paid if AMTI included only exclusion preferences (e.g., disallowed itemized deductions, preferences for excess percentage depletion, and tax-exempt private activity bond interest).

181. (b)   The requirement is to determine the correct statement regarding the computation of the alternative minimum tax (AMT). A taxpayer is subject to the AMT only if the taxpayer's tentative AMT exceeds the taxpayer's regular tax. Thus, the alternative minimum tax is computed as the excess of the tentative AMT over the regular tax.

V.E.   Other Taxes

182. (b)   The requirement is to determine the amount of net earnings from self-employment that would be multiplied by the self-employment tax rate to compute Diamond's self-employment tax for 2009. Since self-employment earnings generally represent earnings derived from a trade or business carried on as a sole proprietor, the $10,000 of interest income from personal investments would be excluded from the computation. On the other hand, a self-employed taxpayer is allowed a deemed deduction equal to 7.65% of self-employment earnings in computing the amount of net earnings upon which the tax is based. The purpose of this deemed deduction is to reflect the fact that employees do not pay FICA tax on the corresponding 7.65% FICA tax paid by their employers.

Gross receipts from business	$150,000
Cost of goods sold	(80,000)
Operating expenses	(40,000)
Self-employment earnings	$ 30,000
Less deemed deduction (100%- 7.65%)	× 92.35%
Net earnings to be multiplied by self-employment tax rate	$ 27,705

183. (c) The requirement is to determine the amount of Freeman's income that is subject to self-employment tax. The self-employment tax is imposed on self-employment income to provide Social Security and Medicare benefits for self-employed individuals. Self-employment income includes an individual's net earnings from a trade or business carried on as sole proprietor or as an independent contractor. The term also includes a partner's distributive share of partnership ordinary income or loss from trade or business activities, as well as guaranteed payments received by a partner for services rendered to a partnership. Self-employment income excludes gains and losses from the disposition of property used in a trade or business, as well as a shareholder's share of ordinary income from an S corporation.

184. (a) The requirement is to determine the amount of Rich's net self-employment income. Income from self-employment generally includes all items of business income less business deductions. Excluded from the computation would be estimated income taxes on self-employment income, charitable contributions, investment income, and gains and losses on the disposition of property used in a trade or business. An individual's charitable contributions can only be deducted as an itemized deduction. Rich's net self-employment income would be

Business receipts	$20,000
Air conditioning parts	(2,500)
Yellow Pages listing	(2,000)
Business telephone calls	(400)
	$15,100

185. (c) The requirement is to determine the correct statement regarding the self-employment tax. The self-employment tax is imposed at a rate of 15.3% on individuals who work for themselves (e.g., sole proprietor, independent contractor, partner). One-half of an individual's self-employment tax is deductible from gross income in arriving at adjusted gross income.

186. (c) The requirement is to determine the correct statement with regard to social security tax (FICA) withheld in an amount greater than the maximum for a particular year. If an individual works for more than one employer, and combined wages exceed the maximum used for FICA purposes, too much FICA tax will be withheld. In such case, since the excess results from correct withholding by two or more employers, the excess should be claimed as a

credit against income tax. Answer (a) is incorrect because the excess cannot be used as an itemized deduction. Answer (b) is incorrect because if employers withhold correctly, no reimbursement can be obtained from the employers. Answer (d) is incorrect because if the excess FICA tax withheld results from incorrect withholding by any one employer, the employer must reimburse the excess and it cannot be claimed as a credit against tax.

187. (b) The requirement is to determine Berger's gross income from self-employment for 2010. Self-employment income represents the net earnings of an individual from a trade or business carried on as a proprietor or partner, or from rendering services as an independent contractor. The director's fee is self-employment income since it is related to a trade or business, and Berger is not an employee. Fees received by a fiduciary (e.g., executor) are generally not related to a trade or business and not self-employment income. However, executor's fees may constitute self-employment income if the executor is a professional fiduciary or carries on a trade or business in the administration of an estate.

188. (d) The requirement is to determine Smith's gross income from self-employment. Self-employment income represents the net earnings of an individual from a trade or business carried on as a sole proprietor or partner, or from rendering services as an independent contractor (i.e., not an employee). The $8,000 consulting fee and the $2,000 of director's fees are self-employment income because they are related to a trade or business and Smith is not an employee.

VI.A. General Business Credit

189. (c) The requirement is to determine which credit is not a component of the general business credit. The general business credit is a combination of several credits that provide uniform rules for current and carryback-carryover years. The general business credit is composed of the investment credit, work opportunity credit, alcohol fuels credit, research credit, low-income housing credit, enhanced oil recovery credit, disabled access credit, renewable electricity production credit, empowerment zone employment credit, Indian employment credit, employer social security credit, orphan drug credit, the new markets credit, the small employer pension plan start-up costs credit, and the employer-provided child care facilities credit. A general business credit in excess of the limitation amount is carried back one year and forward twenty years to offset tax liability in those years.

190. (a) The requirement is to determine which tax credit is a combination of credits to provide for uniform rules for the current and carryback-carryover years. The general business credit is composed of the investment credit, work opportunity credit, welfare-to-work credit, alcohol fuels credit, research credit, low-income housing credit, enhanced oil recovery credit, disabled access credit, renewable electricity production credit, empowerment zone employment credit, Indian employment credit, employer social security credit, orphan drug credit, the new markets credit, the small employer pension plan start-up costs credit, and the employer-provided child care facilities credit. A general business credit in excess of the limitation amount is carried back one year and forward twenty years to offset tax liability in those years.

VI.K. Credit for the Elderly and the Disabled

191. (a) The requirement is to determine the amount that can be claimed as a credit for the elderly. The amount of credit (limited to tax liability) is 15% of an initial amount reduced by social security and 50% of AGI in excess of $10,000. Here, the credit is the lesser of (1) the taxpayers' tax liability of $60, or (2) 15% [$7,500 – $3,000 – (.50)($20,200 – $10,000)] = $0.

VI.L. Child and Dependent Care Credit

192. (c) The requirement is to compute Nora's child care credit for 2009. Since she has two dependent preschool children, all $6,000 paid for child care qualifies for the credit. The credit is 35% of qualified expenses, but is reduced by one percentage point for each $2,000 (or fraction thereof) of AGI over $15,000 down to a minimum of 20%. Since Nora's AGI is $44,000, her credit is 20% × $6,000 = $1,200.

193. (b) The requirement is to determine the amount of the child care credit allowable to the Jasons. The credit is from 20% to 35% of certain dependent care expenses limited to the lesser of (1) $3,000 for one qualifying individual, $6,000 for two or more; (2) taxpayer's earned income, or spouse's if smaller; or (3) actual expenses. The $2,500 paid to the Union Day Care Center qualifies, as does the $1,000 paid to Wilma Jason. Payments to relatives qualify if the relative is not a dependent of the taxpayer. Since Robert and Mary Jason only claimed three exemptions, Wilma was not their dependent. The $500 paid to Acme Home Cleaning Service does not qualify since it is *completely* unrelated to the care of their child. To qualify, expenses must be at least partly for the care of a qualifying individual. Since qualifying expenses exceed $3,000, the Jasons' credit is 20% × $3,000 = $600.

194. (b) The requirement is to determine the qualifications for the child care credit that at least one spouse must satisfy on a joint return. The child care credit is a percentage of the amount paid for qualifying household and dependent care expenses incurred to enable an individual to be gainfully employed or look for work. To qualify for the child care credit on a joint return, at least one spouse must be gainfully employed or be looking for work when the related expenses are incurred. Note that it is not required that at least one spouse be gainfully employed, but only needs to be looking for work when the expenses are incurred. Additionally, at least one spouse must have earned income during the year. However, there is no limit as to the maximum amount of earned income or adjusted gross income reported on the joint return.

VI.M. Foreign Tax Credit

195. (a) The requirement is to determine which factor(s) may affect the amount of Sunex's foreign tax credit available in its current year corporate income tax return. Since US taxpayers are subject to US income tax on their worldwide income, they are allowed a credit for the income taxes paid to foreign countries. The applicable foreign tax rate will affect the amount of foreign taxes paid, and thereby affect the amount available as a foreign tax credit. Additionally, since the amount of credit that can be currently used cannot exceed the amount of US tax attributable to the foreign-source income, the income source will affect the

amount of available foreign tax credit for the current year if the limitation based on the amount of US tax is applicable.

196. (b) The requirement is to determine the amount of foreign tax credit that Wald Corp. may claim for 2009. Since US taxpayers are subject to US income tax on their worldwide income, they are allowed a credit for the income taxes paid to foreign countries. However, the amount of credit that can be currently used cannot exceed the amount of US tax that is attributable to the foreign income. This foreign tax credit limitation can be expressed as follows:

$$\frac{\text{Foreign TI}}{\text{Worldwide TI}} \times \text{(US tax)} = \text{Foreign tax credit limitation}$$

One limitation must be computed for foreign source passive income (e.g., interest, dividends, royalties, rents, annuities), with a separate limitation computed for all other foreign source taxable income.

In this case, the foreign income taxes paid on other foreign source taxable income of $27,000 is fully usable as a credit in 2009 because it is less than the applicable limitation amount (i.e., the amount of US tax attributable to the income).

$$\frac{\$90,000}{\$300,000} \times (\$96,000) = \$28,000$$

On the other hand, the credit for the $12,000 of foreign income taxes paid on non-business-related interest is limited to the amount of US tax attributable to the foreign interest income, $9,600.

$$\frac{\$30,000}{\$300,000} \times (\$96,000) = \$9,600$$

Thus, Wald Corp.'s foreign tax credit for 2009 totals $27,000 + $9,600 = $36,600. The $12,000 – $9,600 = $2,400 of unused foreign tax credit resulting from the application of the limitation on foreign taxes attributable to foreign source interest income can be carried back one year and forward ten years to offset US income tax in those years.

197. (a) The requirement is to determine the correct statement regarding a corporation's foreign income taxes. Foreign income taxes paid by a corporation may be claimed either as a credit or as a deduction, at the option of the corporation.

VI.N. Earned Income Credit

198. (c) The requirement is to determine the credit that can result in a refund even if an individual had no income tax liability. The earned income credit is a refundable credit and can result in a refund even if the individual had no tax withheld from wages.

199. (a) The requirement is to choose the correct statement regarding Kent's earned income credit. The earned income credit could result in a refund even if Kent had no tax withheld from wages. Since the credit is refundable, answer (c) is incorrect because there will never be any unused credit to carry back or forward. Answer (d) is incorrect because the credit is a direct subtraction from the computed tax.

200. (c) The requirement is to determine the correct statement regarding the earned income credit. The earned income credit is a refundable credit and can result in a refund even if the individual had no tax withheld from wages. To qualify, an individual must have earned income, but the amount of earned income does not have to equal adjusted gross income. For purposes of the credit, earned income excludes workers' compensation benefits. Additionally, the credit is available only if the tax return covers a full twelve-month period.

201. (b)   The requirement is to determine the tax credit that cannot be claimed by a corporation. The foreign tax credit, alternative fuel production credit, and general business credit may be claimed by a corporation. The earned income credit cannot be claimed by a corporation; it is available only to individuals.

VI.O.   Credit for Adoption Expenses

202. (c)   The requirement is to determine the correct statement regarding the credit for adoption expenses. The adoption expenses credit is a nonrefundable credit for up to $12,150 (for 2009) of expenses (including special needs children) incurred to adopt an eligible child. An eligible child is one who is under eighteen years of age at time of adoption, or physically or mentally incapable of self-care. Qualified adoption expenses are taken as a credit in the year the adoption becomes final.

VI.P.   Child Tax Credit

203. (c)   The requirement is to determine the incorrect statement concerning the child tax credit. Individual taxpayers are permitted to take a tax credit based solely on the number of their dependent children under age seventeen. The amount of the credit is $1,000 per qualifying child, but is subject to reduction if adjusted gross income exceeds certain income levels. A qualifying child must be a US citizen or resident.

VI.Q.   Modified Hope Scholarship Credit

204. (c)   The requirement is to determine the incorrect statement concerning the 2009 Hope scholarship credit. The Hope scholarship credit provides for a maximum credit of $2,500 per year (100% of the first $2,000, plus 25% of the next $2,000 of tuition fees, and course materials) for the first four years of postsecondary education. The credit is available on a per student basis and covers tuition paid for the taxpayer, spouse, and dependents. To be eligible, the student must be enrolled on at least a part-time basis for one academic period during the year. If a parent claims a child as a dependent, only the parent can claim the credit and any qualified expenses paid by the child are deemed paid by the parent.

VI.R.   Lifetime Learning Credit

205. (d)   The requirement is to determine the incorrect statement concerning the lifetime learning credit. The lifetime learning credit provides a credit of 20% of up to $10,000 of tuition and fees paid by a taxpayer for one or more students for graduate and undergraduate courses at an eligible educational institution. The credit may be claimed for an unlimited number of years, is available on a per taxpayer basis, and covers tuition paid for the taxpayer, spouse, and dependents.

VI.S.   Estimated Tax Payments

206. (a)   The requirement is to determine which statement(s) describe how Baker may avoid the penalty for the underpayment of estimated tax for the 2010 tax year. An individual whose regular and alternative minimum tax liability is not sufficiently covered by withholding from wages must pay estimated tax in quarterly installments or be subject to penalty. Individuals will incur no underpayment penalty for 2010 if the amount of tax withheld plus estimated payments are at least equal to the lesser of (1) 90% of the current year's tax; (2) 100% of the prior year's tax; or (3) 90% of the tax determined by annualizing current year taxable income through each quarter. However, note that for 2010, high-income individuals (i.e., individuals whose adjusted gross income for the preceding year exceeds $150,000) must use 110% (instead of 100%) if they wish to base their estimated tax payments on their prior year's tax liability.

207. (a)   The requirement is to determine what amount would be subject to penalty for the underpayment of estimated taxes. A taxpayer will be subject to an underpayment of estimated tax penalty if the taxpayer did not pay enough tax either through withholding or by estimated tax payments. For 2009, there will be no penalty if the total tax shown on the return less the amount paid through withholding (including excess social security tax withholding) is less than $1,000. Additionally, for 2009, individuals will incur no penalty if the amount of tax withheld plus estimated payments are at least equal to the lesser of (1) 90% of the current year's tax (determined on the basis of actual income or annualized income), or (2) 100% of the prior year's tax. In this case, since the tax shown on Krete's return ($16,500) less the tax paid through withholding ($16,000) was less than $1,000, there will be no penalty for the underpayment of estimated taxes.

VII.   Filing Requirements

208. (d)   The requirement is to determine the original due date for a decedent's federal income tax return. The final return of a decedent is due on the same date the decedent's return would have been due had death not occurred. An individual's federal income tax return is due on the 15th day of the fourth calendar month following the close of the tax year (e.g., April 15 for a calendar-year taxpayer).

209. (a)   The requirement is to determine Birch's filing requirement. A self-employed individual must file an income tax return if net earnings from self-employment are $400 or more.

VIII.B.   Assessments

210. (c)   The requirement is to determine the date on which the statute of limitations begins for Jackson Corp.'s 2008 tax return. Generally, any tax that is imposed must be assessed within three years of the filing of the return, or if later, the due date of the return. Since Jackson Corp.'s 2008 return was filed on March 12, 2009, and the return was due on March 15, 2009, the statute of limitations expires on March 15, 2012. This means that the statute of limitations begins on March 16, 2009.

211. (c)   The requirement is to determine the latest date that the IRS can assert a notice of deficiency for a 2009 calendar-year return if the taxpayer neither committed fraud nor omitted amounts in excess of 25% of gross income. The normal period for assessment is the later of three years after a return is filed, or three years after the due date of the return. Since the 2009 calendar-year return was filed on March 20, 2010, and was due on April 15, 2010, the IRS must assert a deficiency no later than April 15, 2013.

212. (**d**)   A six-year statute of limitations applies if gross income omitted from the return exceeds 25% of the gross income reported on the return. For this purpose, gross income of a business includes total gross receipts before subtracting cost of goods sold and deductions. Thus, a six-year statute of limitations will apply to Thompson if he omitted from gross income an amount in excess of ($400,000 + $36,000) × 25% = $109,000.

213. (**d**)   The requirement is to determine the maximum period during which the IRS can issue a notice of deficiency if the gross income omitted from a taxpayer's return exceeds 25% of the gross income reported on the return. A **six-year** statute of limitations applies if gross income omitted from the return exceeds 25% of the gross income reported on the return. Additionally, a tax return filed **before** its due date is treated as filed **on** its due date. Thus, if a return is filed before its due date, and the gross income omitted from the return exceeds 25% of the gross income reported on the return, the IRS has **six** years from the due date of the return to issue a notice of deficiency.

VIII.E.   Claims for Refund

214. (**c**)   The requirement is to determine the form that must be filed by an individual to claim a refund of erroneously paid income taxes. Form 1040X, Amended US Individual Income Tax Return, should be used to claim a refund of erroneously paid income taxes. Form 843 should be used to file a refund claim for taxes other than income taxes. Form 1139 may be used by a corporation to file for a tentative adjustment or refund of taxes when an overpayment of taxes for a prior year results from the carryback of a current year's net operating loss or net capital loss. Form 1045 may be used by taxpayers other than corporations to apply for similar adjustments.

215. (**a**)   The requirement is to determine the date by which a refund claim must be filed if an individual paid income tax during 2009 but did not file a tax return. An individual must file a claim for refund within three years from the date a return was filed, or two years from the date of payment of tax, whichever is later. If no return was filed, the claim for refund must be filed within two years from the date that the tax was paid.

216. (**c**)   The requirement is to determine the date by which a taxpayer must file an amended return to claim a refund of tax paid on a calendar-year 2008 return. A taxpayer must file an amended return to claim a refund within three years from the date a return was filed, or two years from the date of payment of tax, whichever is later. If a return is filed before its due date, it is treated as filed on its due date. Thus, the taxpayer's 2008 calendar-year return that was filed on March 15, 2009, is treated as filed on April 15, 2009. Therefore, an amended return to claim a refund must be filed not later than April 15, 2012.

217. (**d**)   The requirement is to determine the date by which a refund claim due to worthless security must be filed. The normal three-year statute of limitations is extended to seven years for refund claims resulting from bad debts or worthless securities. Since the securities became worthless during 2008, and Baker's 2008 return was filed on April 15, 2009, Baker's refund claim must be filed no later than April 15, 2016.

VIII.G.   Taxpayer Penalties

218. (**b**)   The requirement is to determine the amount on which the penalties for late filing and late payment would be computed. The late filing and late payment penalties are based on the amount of net tax due. If a taxpayer's tax return indicated a tax liability of $50,000, and $45,000 of taxes were withheld, the late filing and late payment penalties would be based on the $5,000 of tax that is owed.

219. (**c**)   An accuracy-related penalty equal to 20% of the underpayment of tax may be imposed if the underpayment of tax is attributable to one or more of the following: (1) negligence or disregard of the tax rules and regulations; (2) any substantial understatement of income tax; (3) any substantial valuation overstatement; (4) any substantial overstatement of pension liabilities; or (5) any substantial gift or estate tax valuation understatement. The penalty for gift or estate tax valuation understatement may apply if the value of property on a gift or estate tax return is 50% or less of the amount determined to be correct. The penalty for a substantial income tax valuation overstatement may apply if the value (or adjusted basis) of property is 200% or more of the amount determined to be correct.

SOLUTIONS TO SIMULATION PROBLEMS

Simulation Problem 1

Tax Treatment			
Situation		Research	Communication

Transactions	(A)	(B)	(C)	(D)	(E)	(F)	(G)	(H)	(I)	(J)	(K)	(L)	(M)	(N)	(O)	(P)
1. Fees received for jury duty.	○	●	○	○	○	○	○	○	○	○	○	○	○	○	○	○
2. Interest income on mortgage loan receivable.	●	○	○	○	○	○	○	○	○	○	○	○	○	○	○	○
3. Penalty paid to bank on early withdrawal of savings.	○	○	○	●	○	○	○	○	○	○	○	○	○	○	○	○
4. Write-offs of uncollectible accounts receivable from accounting practice.	○	○	○	○	○	○	○	○	○	○	○	○	○	○	○	●
5. Cost of attending review course in preparation for the Uniform CPA Examination.	○	○	○	○	○	○	○	○	○	○	○	○	○	○	○	●
6. Fee for the biennial permit to practice as a CPA.	○	○	○	○	○	○	○	●	○	○	○	○	○	○	○	○
7. Costs of attending CPE courses in fulfillment of state board requirements.	○	○	○	○	○	○	○	●	○	○	○	○	○	○	○	○
8. Contribution to a qualified Keogh retirement plan.	○	○	○	●	○	○	○	○	○	○	○	○	○	○	○	○
9. Loss sustained from nonbusiness bad debt.	○	○	○	○	○	○	○	○	○	●	○	○	○	○	○	○
10. Loss sustained on sale of "Small Business Corporation" (Section 1244) stock.	○	○	○	○	○	○	○	○	○	○	○	●	○	○	○	○
11. Taxes paid on land owned by Cole and rented out as a parking lot.	○	○	○	○	○	○	○	○	○	○	●	○	○	○	○	○
12. Interest paid on installment purchases of household furniture.	○	○	○	○	○	○	○	○	○	○	○	○	○	○	○	●
13. Alimony paid to former spouse who reports the alimony as taxable income.	○	○	○	●	○	○	○	○	○	○	○	○	○	○	○	○
14. Personal medical expenses charged on credit card in December 2009 but not paid until January 2010.	○	○	○	○	●	○	○	○	○	○	○	○	○	○	○	○
15. Personal casualty loss sustained.	○	○	○	●	○	○	○	○	○	○	○	○	○	○	○	○
16. State inheritance tax paid on bequest received.	○	○	○	○	○	○	○	○	○	○	○	○	○	○	○	●
17. Foreign income tax withheld at source on dividend received.	○	○	○	○	○	○	○	○	○	○	○	○	●	○	○	○
18. Computation of self-employment tax.	○	○	○	○	○	○	○	○	○	○	○	○	○	○	●	○
19. One-half of self-employment tax paid with 2009 return filed in April 2010.	○	○	○	●	○	○	○	○	○	○	○	○	○	○	○	○
20. Insurance premiums paid on Cole's life.	○	○	○	○	○	○	○	○	○	○	○	○	○	○	○	●

Explanation of solutions

1. (B) Fees received for jury duty represent compensation for services and must be included in gross income. Since there is no separate line for jury duty fees, they are taxable as other income on page 1 of Form 1040.

2. (A) Interest income on a mortgage loan receivable must be included in gross income and is taxable as interest income in Schedule B—Interest and Dividend Income.

3. (D) An interest forfeiture penalty for making an early withdrawal from a certificate of deposit is deductible on page 1 of Form 1040 to arrive at adjusted gross income.

4. (P) The problem indicates that Cole is a CPA reporting on the cash basis. Accounts receivable resulting from services rendered by a cash-basis taxpayer have a zero tax basis, because the income has not yet been reported. Therefore, the write-offs of zero basis uncollectible accounts receivable from Cole's accounting practice are not deductible.

5. (P) An educational expense that is part of a program of study that can qualify an individual for a new trade or business is not deductible. This is true even if the individual is not seeking a new job. In this case, the cost of attending a review course in preparation for the CPA examination is a nondeductible personal expense since it qualifies Cole for a new profession.

6. (I) Licensing and regulatory fees paid to state or local governments are an ordinary and necessary trade or business expense and are deductible by a sole proprietor on Schedule C—Profit or Loss from Business. Since Cole is a cash method tax payor, he can deduct the fee for the biennial permit to practice when paid in 2009.

7. (I) All trade or business expenses of a self-employed individual are deductible on Schedule C—Profit or Loss from Business. Education must meet certain requirements before the related expenses can be deducted. Generally, deductible education expenses must not be a part of a program that will qualify the individual for a new trade or business and must (1) be required by an employer or by law to keep the individual's present position, or (2) maintain or improve skills required in the individual's present work. In this case, Cole already is a CPA and is fulfilling state CPE requirements, so his education costs of attending CPE courses are deductible in Schedule C—Profit or Loss from Business.

8. (D) Contributions to a self-employed individual's qualified Keogh retirement plan are deductible on page 1 of Form 1040 to arrive at adjusted gross income. The maximum deduction for contributions to a defined contribution Keogh retirement plan is limited to the lesser of $49,000 (for 2009), or 100% of self-employment income.

9. (J) A loss sustained from a nonbusiness bad debt is always classified as a short-term capital loss. Therefore, Cole's nonbusiness bad debt is deductible in Schedule D—Capital Gains or Losses.

10. (L) A loss sustained on the sale of Sec. 1244 stock is generally deductible as an ordinary loss, with the amount of ordinary loss deduction limited to $50,000. On a joint return, the limit is increased to $100,000, even if the stock was owned by only one spouse. The ordinary loss resulting from the sale of Sec. 1244 stock is deductible in Form 4797—Sales of Business Property. To the extent that a loss on Sec. 1244 stock exceeds the applicable $50,000 or $100,000 limit, the loss is deductible as a capital loss in Schedule D—Capital Gains or Losses. Similarly, if Sec. 1244 stock is sold at a gain, the gain would be reported as a capital gain in Schedule D if the stock is a capital asset.

11. (K) Rental income and expenses related to rental property are generally reported in Schedule E. Here, the taxes paid on land owned by Cole and rented out as a parking lot are deductible in Schedule E—Supplemental Income and Loss. Schedule E also is used to report the income or loss from royalties, partnerships, S corporations, estates, and trusts.

12. (P) The interest paid on installment purchases of household furniture is considered personal interest and is not deductible. Personal interest is any interest that is not qualified residence interest, investment interest, passive activity interest, or business interest. Personal interest generally includes interest on car loans, interest on income tax, underpayments, installment plan interest, credit card finance charges, and late payment charges by a utility.

13. (D) Alimony paid to a former spouse who reports the alimony as taxable income is deductible on page 1 of Form 1040 to arrive at adjusted gross income.

14. (E) Personal medical expenses are generally deductible as an itemized deduction subject to a 7.5% of AGI threshold for the year in which they are paid. Additionally, an individual can deduct medical expenses charged to a credit card in the year the charge is made. It makes no difference when the amount charged is actually paid. Here, Cole's personal medical expenses charged on a credit card in December 2009 but not paid until January 2010 are deductible for 2009 in Schedule A—Itemized Deductions, subject to a threshold of 7.5% of adjusted gross income.

15. (F) If an individual sustains a personal casualty loss, it is deductible in Schedule A—Itemized Deductions subject to a threshold of $500 and an additional threshold of 10% of adjusted gross income.

16. (P) State inheritance taxes paid on a bequest that was received are not deductible. Other taxes not deductible in computing an individual's federal income tax include federal estate and gift taxes, federal income taxes, and social security and other employment taxes paid by an employee.

17. (M) An individual can deduct foreign income taxes as an itemized deduction or can deduct foreign income taxes as a tax credit. Cole's foreign income tax withheld at source on foreign dividends received can be claimed in Form 1116—Foreign Tax Credit, or in Schedule A—Itemized Deductions, at Cole's option.

18. (O) A self-employed individual is subject to a self-employment tax if the individual's net earnings from self-employment are at least $400.

19. (D) An individual's self-employment tax is computed in Schedule SE and is added as an additional tax in arriving at the individual's total tax. One-half of the computed self-employment tax is allowed as a deduction in arriving at adjusted gross income. Here, one-half of Cole's self-employment tax for 2009 is deductible for 2009 on page 1 of Form 1040 to arrive at adjusted gross income, even though the tax was not paid until the return was filed in April 2010.

20. (P) Insurance premiums paid on Cole's life are classified as a personal expense and are not deductible.

Situation	Tax Treatment	Research	Communication

Internal Revenue Code Section 163, subsection (h) provides that interest is deductible on up to $1,000,000 of qualified residence acquisition indebtedness.

Section	Subsection
§ 163	(h)

		Communication	
Situation	Tax Treatment	Research	

To: Mr. Cole
From: CPA Candidate
Re: Deductibility of interest on mortgage

As you requested, I researched the issue of limitations on the deductibility of home mortgage interest. I understand that you plan to purchase a residence for $1,500,000 and finance the purchase with a mortgage totaling $1,150,000.

Internal Revenue Code section 163(h)(3)(B) limits the interest deduction on a primary residence to the interest on $1,000,000 of qualified acquisition indebtedness. However, section 163(h)(3)(C) allows an additional deduction of interest on up to $100,000 of home equity indebtedness. On your proposed transaction, this means that you would be entitled to deduct the interest on all but $50,000 of the mortgage loan.

If you have any additional questions please contact me.

Simulation Problem 2

	Tax Treatment I					
Situation			Tax Treatment II	Research	Communication	

Transactions	(A)	(B)	(C)	(D)	(E)	(F)	(G)	(H)	(I)	(J)	(K)	(L)	(M)	(N)	(O)
1. Retainer fees received from clients.	○	○	●	○	○	○	○	○	○	○	○	○	○	○	○
2. Oil royalties received.	○	○	○	●	○	○	○	○	○	○	○	○	○	○	○
3. Interest income on general obligation state and local government bonds.	○	○	○	○	●	○	○	○	○	○	○	○	○	○	○
4. Interest on refund of federal taxes.	○	●	○	○	○	○	○	○	○	○	○	○	○	○	○
5. Death benefits from term life insurance policy on parent.	○	○	○	○	●	○	○	○	○	○	○	○	○	○	○
6. Interest income on US Treasury bonds.	○	●	○	○	○	○	○	○	○	○	○	○	○	○	○
7. Share of ordinary income from an investment in a limited partnership reported in Form 1065, Schedule K-1.	○	○	○	●	○	○	○	○	○	○	○	○	○	○	○
8. Taxable income from rental of a townhouse owned by Green.	○	○	○	●	○	○	○	○	○	○	○	○	○	○	○
9. Prize won as a contestant on a TV quiz show.	●	○	○	○	○	○	○	○	○	○	○	○	○	○	○
10. Payment received for jury service.	●	○	○	○	○	○	○	○	○	○	○	○	○	○	○
11. Dividends received from mutual funds that invest in tax-free government obligations.	○	○	○	○	●	○	○	○	○	○	○	○	○	○	○
12. Qualifying medical expenses not reimbursed by insurance.	○	○	○	○	○	○	○	●	○	○	○	○	○	○	○
13. Personal life insurance premiums paid by Green.	○	○	○	○	○	○	○	○	○	○	○	○	○	○	●
14. Expenses for business-related meals where clients were present.	○	○	○	○	○	○	○	○	○	○	○	○	●	○	○
15. Depreciation on personal computer purchased in 2009 used for business.	○	○	○	○	○	○	○	○	○	○	○	●	○	○	○
16. Business lodging expenses, while out of town.	○	○	○	○	○	○	○	○	○	○	○	●	○	○	○
17. Subscriptions to professional journals used for business.	○	○	○	○	○	○	○	○	○	○	○	●	○	○	○
18. Self-employment taxes paid.	○	○	○	○	○	●	○	○	○	○	○	○	○	○	○
19. Qualifying contributions to a simplified employee pension plan.	○	○	○	○	●	○	○	○	○	○	○	○	○	○	○

Transactions	(A)	(B)	(C)	(D)	(E)	(F)	(G)	(H)	(I)	(J)	(K)	(L)	(M)	(N)	(O)
20. Election to expense business equipment purchased in 2009.	○	○	○	○	○	○	○	○	○	○	●	○	○	○	○
21. Qualifying alimony payments made by Green.	○	○	○	○	○	●	○	○	○	○	○	○	○	○	○
22. Subscriptions for investment-related publications.	○	○	○	○	○	○	○	●	○	○	○	○	○	○	○
23. Interest expense on a home-equity line of credit for an amount borrowed to finance Green's business.	○	○	○	○	○	○	○	○	○	○	●	○	○	○	○
24. Interest expense on a loan for an auto used 75% for business.	○	○	○	○	○	○	○	○	○	○	○	○	●	○	○
25. Loss on sale of residence.	○	○	○	○	○	○	○	○	○	○	○	○	○	○	●

Explanation of solutions

1. (C) All trade or business income and deductions of a self-employed individual are reported on Schedule C—Profit or Loss from Business. Retainer fees received from clients is reported in Schedule C as trade or business income.

2. (D) Income derived from royalties is reported in Schedule E—Supplemental Income and Loss. Schedule E also is used to report the income or loss from rental real estate, partnerships, S corporations, estates, and trusts.

3. (E) Interest from general obligation state and local government bonds is tax-exempt and is excluded from gross income.

4. (B) The interest income on a refund of federal income taxes must be included in gross income and is reported in Schedule B—Interest and Dividend Income. The actual refund of federal income taxes itself is excluded from gross income.

5. (E) Life insurance proceeds paid by reason of death are generally excluded from gross income. Here, the death benefits received by Green from a term life insurance policy on the life of Green's parent are not taxable.

6. (B) Interest income from US Treasury bonds and treasury bills must be included in gross income and is reported in Schedule B—Interest and Dividend Income.

7. (D) A partner's share of a partnership's ordinary income that is reported to the partner on Form 1065, Schedule K-1 must be included in the partner's gross income and is reported in Schedule E—Supplemental Income and Loss.

8. (D) The taxable income from the rental of a townhouse owned by Green must be included in gross income and is reported in Schedule E—Supplemental Income and Loss.

9. (A) A prize won as a contestant on a TV quiz show must be included in gross income. Since there is no separate line on Form 1040 for prizes, they are taxable as other income on Form 1040.

10. (A) Fees received for jury duty represent compensation for services and must be included in gross income. Since there is no separate line for jury duty fees, they are taxable as other income on Form 1040.

11. (E) An investor in a mutual fund may receive several different kinds of distributions including ordinary dividends, capital gain distributions, tax-exempt interest dividends, and return of capital distributions. A mutual fund may pay tax-exempt interest dividends to its shareholders if it meets certain requirements. These dividends are paid from the tax-exempt state and local obligation interest earned by the fund and retain their tax-exempt character when reported by the shareholder. Thus, Green's dividends received from mutual funds that invest in tax-free government obligations are not taxable.

12. (H) Qualifying medical expenses not reimbursed by insurance are deductible in Schedule A as an itemized deduction to the extent in excess of 7.5% of adjusted gross income.

13. (O) Personal life insurance premiums paid on Green's life are classified as a personal expense and not deductible.

14. (M) All trade or business expenses of a self-employed individual are deductible on Schedule C—Profit or Loss from Business. However, only 50% of the cost of business meals and entertainment is deductible. Therefore, Green's expenses for business-related meals where clients were present are partially deductible in Schedule C.

15. (K) The deduction for depreciation on listed property (e.g., automobiles, cellular telephones, computers, and property used for entertainment etc.) is computed on Form 4562—Depreciation and Amortization. Since Green's personal computer was used in his business as a self-employed consultant, the amount of depreciation computed on Form 4562 is then deductible in Schedule C—Profit or Loss from Business.

16. (L) Lodging expenses while out of town on business are an ordinary and necessary business expense and are fully deductible by a self-employed individual in Schedule C—Profit or Loss from Business.

17. (L) The cost of subscriptions to professional journals used for business are an ordinary and necessary business expense and are fully deductible by a self-employed individual in Schedule C—Profit or Loss from Business.

18. (G) An individual's self-employment tax is computed in Schedule SE and is added as an additional tax in arriving at the individual's total tax liability. One-half of the computed self-employment tax is then allowed as a deduction on Form 1040 in arriving at adjusted gross income.

19. (**F**) Qualifying contributions to a self-employed individual's simplified employee pension plan are deductible on page 1 of Form 1040 to arrive at adjusted gross income.

20. (**K**) For 2009, Sec. 179 permits a taxpayer to elect to treat up to $250,000 of the cost of qualifying depreciable personal business property as an expense rather than as a capital expenditure. In this case, Green's election to expense business equipment would be computed on Form 4562—Depreciation and Amortization, and then would be deductible in Schedule C—Profit or Loss from Business.

21. (**F**) Qualifying alimony payments made by Green to a former spouse are fully deductible on Form 1040 to arrive at adjusted gross income.

22. (**I**) The costs of subscriptions for investment publications are not related to Green's trade or business, but instead are considered expenses incurred in the production of portfolio income and are reported as miscellaneous itemized deductions in Schedule A—Itemized Deductions. These investment expenses are deductible to the extent that the aggregate of expenses in this category exceed 2% of adjusted gross income.

23. (**L**) The nature of interest expense is determined by using a tracing approach (i.e., the nature depends upon how the loan proceeds were used). Since the interest expense on Green's home-equity line of credit was for a loan to finance Green's business, the best answer is to treat the interest as a business expense fully deductible in Schedule C—Profit or Loss from Business.

24. (**M**) The interest expense on a loan for an auto used by a self-employed individual in a trade or business is deductible as a business expense. Since Green's auto was used 75% for business, only 75% of the interest expense is deductible in Schedule C—Profit or Loss from Business. The remaining 25% is considered personal interest expense and is not deductible.

25. (**O**) The loss resulting from the sale of Green's personal residence is not deductible because the property was held for personal use. Only losses due to casualty or theft are deductible for personal use property.

		Tax Treatment II		
Situation	**Tax Treatment I**		**Research**	**Communication**

	(A)	(B)	(C)	(D)	(E)	(F)	(G)
1. In 2009, Green paid $2,000 interest on the $25,000 home equity mortgage on his vacation home, which he used exclusively for personal use. The mortgage is secured by Green's vacation home, and the loan proceeds were used to purchase an automobile.	○	●	○	○	○	○	○
2. For 2009, Green had a $30,000 cash charitable contribution carryover from his 2008 cash donation to the American Red Cross. Green made no additional charitable contributions in 2009.	○	○	●	○	○	○	○
3. During 2009, Green had investment interest expense that did not exceed his net investment income.	○	●	○	○	○	○	○
4. Green's 2009 lottery ticket losses were $450. He had no gambling winnings.	●	○	○	○	○	○	○
5. During 2009, Green paid $2,500 in real property taxes on his vacation home, which he used exclusively for personal use.	○	●	○	○	○	○	○
6. In 2009, Green paid a $500 premium for a homeowner's insurance policy on his principal residence.	●	○	○	○	○	○	○
7. For 2009, Green paid $1,500 to an unrelated babysitter to care for his child while he worked.	○	○	○	○	○	●	○
8. In 2009, Green paid $4,000 interest on the $60,000 acquisition mortgage of his principal residence. The mortgage is secured by Green's home.	○	●	○	○	○	○	○
9. During 2009, Green paid $3,600 real property taxes on residential rental property in which he actively participates. There was no personal use of the rental property.	○	○	○	○	○	●	○

Explanation of solutions

1. (**B**) Interest expense on home equity indebtedness is deductible on up to $100,000 of home equity loans secured by a first or second residence regardless of how the loan proceeds were used.

2. (**C**) Contributions in excess of applicable percentage limitations can be carried forward for up to five tax years. Here, the $30,000 of charitable contribution carryover from 2008 is deductible as an itemized deduction for 2009 subject to a limitation of 50% of AGI.

3. (**B**) Investment interest expense is deductible as an itemized deduction to the extent of net investment income. Since Green's investment interest expense did not exceed his net investment income, it is deductible in full.

4. (**A**) Gambling losses (including lottery ticket losses) are deductible as an itemized deduction to the extent of the gambling winnings included in gross income. Since Green had no gambling winnings, the losses are not deductible.

5. (B) State, local, or foreign real estate taxes imposed on the taxpayer for property held for personal use are fully deductible as an itemized deduction.

6. (A) A premium for a homeowner's insurance policy on a principal residence is a nondeductible personal expense.

7. (G) Payments to an unrelated babysitter to care for his child while Green worked would qualify for the child and dependent care credit. For 2009, the credit may vary from 20% to 35% of up to $3,000 ($6,000 for two or more qualifying individuals) of qualifying household and dependent care expenses incurred to enable the taxpayer to be gainfully employed or look for work.

8. (B) Interest expense on acquisition indebtedness is deductible on up to $1 million of loans secured by the residence if such loans were used to acquire, construct, or substantially improve a principal residence or a second residence.

9. (F) Expenses incurred in the production of rental income (e.g., interest, taxes, depreciation, insurance, utilities) are deductible on Schedule E and are included in the computation of net rental income or loss.

Situation	Tax Treatment I	Tax Treatment II	Research	Communication

Internal Revenue Code Section 21, subsection (c) provides that the maximum amount of employment-related expenses that qualify for a credit is limited to $3,000 for one qualifying individual.

Section	Subsection
§ 21	(c)

Situation	Tax Treatment I	Tax Treatment II	Research	Communication

To: Mr. Green
From: CPA Candidate
Re: Dependent care payments

   You have requested that I research the effects of the payments to a babysitter for care of your child on your tax liability. The payments will entitle you to a dependent child credit. For 2009, the credit varies from 20% to 35% of qualified employment-related expenses, limited to $3,000 for one qualifying child. Because your adjusted gross income is greater than $45,000, your credit is limited to 20% of $3,000, or $600. Your tax liability will be reduced by that amount.
   If you have any other questions, please contact me.

Simulation Problem 3

Situation	Deductibility	Research	Communication

	For AGI (A)	*From AGI (No 2%)* (B)	*From AGI (2% Floor)* (C)	*Not ded.* (D)
1. Smith paid the medical expenses of his mother-in-law. Although Smith provided more than half of her support, she does not qualify as Smith's dependent because she had gross income of $5,000.	○	●	○	○
2. Smith paid the real estate taxes on his rental apartment building.	●	○	○	○
3. Smith paid state sales taxes of $1,500 on a used automobile that he purchased for personal use.	○	●	○	○
4. Smith paid the real estate taxes on his mother-in-law's home. She is the owner of the home.	○	○	○	●
5. Smith paid $1,500 of interest on credit card charges. The charges were for items purchased for personal use.	○	○	○	●
6. Smith paid an attorney $500 to prepare Smith's will.	○	○	○	●
7. Smith incurred $750 of expenses for business meals and entertainment in his position as an employee of Patton Corporation. Smith's expenses were not reimbursed.	○	○	●	○

	For AGI (A)	From AGI (No 2%) (B)	From AGI (2% Floor) (C)	Not ded. (D)
8. Smith paid self-employment taxes of $3,000 as a result of earnings from the consulting business that he conducts as a sole proprietor.	●	○	○	○
9. Smith made a contribution to his self-employed retirement plan (Keogh Plan).	●	○	○	○
10. Smith had gambling losses totaling $2,500 for the year. He is including a lottery prize of $5,000 in his gross income this year.	○	●	○	○

Explanation of solutions

1. (B) Deductible medical expenses include amounts paid for the diagnosis, cure, relief, treatment or prevention of disease of the taxpayer, spouse, and dependents. The term **dependent** includes any person who qualifies as a dependency exemption, or would otherwise qualify as a dependency exemption except that the gross income and joint return tests are not met. Therefore, the medical expenses of Smith's mother-in-law are properly deductible from Smith's AGI and are not subject to the 2% limitation.

2. (A) Expenses attributable to property held for the production of rents or royalties are properly deductible "above the line." "Above the line" deductions are subtracted from gross income to determine adjusted gross income. Therefore, expenses incurred from a passive activity such as Smith's rental apartment building are deductible for AGI.

3. (B) For tax years beginning after December 31, 2003, and before January 1, 2010, an individual may elect to deduct state and local general sales taxes in lieu of state and local income taxes. The amount that can be deducted is either the total of actual general sales taxes paid as substantiated by receipts, or an amount from IRS-provided tables, plus the amount of general sales taxes paid with regard to the purchase of a motor vehicle, boat, and specified other items. The deduction for sales taxes is not subject to the 2% of AGI floor.

4. (D) Real estate (real property) taxes are deductible only if imposed on property owned by the taxpayer. Since Smith's mother-in-law is the legal owner of the house, Smith cannot deduct his payment of those real estate taxes.

5. (D) No deduction is allowed for personal interest.

6. (D) Personal legal expenses are not a deductible expense. Only legal counsel obtained for advice concerning tax matters or incurred in the production of income are deductible. Therefore, Smith cannot deduct the $500 incurred to prepare his will.

7. (C) Unreimbursed employee expenses including business meals and entertainment (subject to the 50% rule) are deductible to the extent they exceed 2% of AGI. Therefore, $375 ($750 × 50%) is deductible from AGI, subject to the 2% floor.

8. (A) An individual is allowed to deduct one half of the self-employment tax paid for the taxable year in the computation of AGI. Therefore, $1,500 is deductible for AGI.

9. (A) Contributions by self-employed individuals to a qualified retirement plan (Keogh Plan) are a deduction for AGI.

10. (B) Gambling losses to the extent of gambling winnings are categorized as miscellaneous deductions not subject to the 2% floor. Therefore, the $2,500 of Smith's gambling losses would be deductible in full since he properly included his $5,000 winnings in his gross income for 2009.

Situation	Deductibility	Research	Communication

Internal Revenue Code Section 213, subsection (a) provides that the unreimbursed medical expenses of a taxpayer, spouse, and dependents are deductible to the extent in excess of 7.5% of adjusted gross income.

Section	Subsection
§ 213	(a)

Situation	Deductibility	Research	Communication

To: Mr. Mark Smith
From: CPA Candidate
Re: Deductibility of surgery costs

    You requested that I research the deductibility of the cost of your heart surgery. As you indicated, the total cost of the surgery was $100,000 of which $82,000 was covered by insurance. The Internal Revenue Code provides that such expenses are deductible to the extent they are not reimbursed by insurance. However, deductibility of medical expenses is limited to the amount in excess of 7.5% of adjusted gross income. As a result, you can only deduct the excess of your total medical expenses (including the $18,000 cost of surgery) above 7.5% of your adjusted gross income for 2010.

If you have any additional questions, please contact me.

Simulation Problem 4

Situation	Adjusted Gross Income	Exemptions	Research	Communication

	(A)	(B)	(C)	(D)	(E)	(F)	(G)	(H)	(I)	(J)	(K)	(L)	(M)
1.	●	○	○	○	○	○	○	○	○	○	○	○	○
2.	○	○	○	○	●	○	○	○	○	○	○	○	○
3.	●	○	○	○	○	○	○	○	○	○	○	○	○
4.	○	○	○	○	○	●	○	○	○	○	○	○	○
5.	●	○	○	○	○	○	○	○	○	○	○	○	○
6.	○	○	●	○	○	○	○	○	○	○	○	○	○
7.	○	○	○	○	○	○	●	○	○	○	○	○	○
8.	○	●	○	○	○	○	○	○	○	○	○	○	○
9.	●	○	○	○	○	○	○	○	○	○	○	○	○
10.	●	○	○	○	○	○	○	○	○	○	○	○	○

1. During 2009, Dale received a $30,000 cash gift from her aunt.

2. Dale contributed $3,500 to her traditional Individual Retirement Account (IRA) on January 15, 2009. In 2009, she earned $60,000 as a university instructor. During 2009 the Cumacks were not active participants in an employer's qualified pension or annuity plan.

3. In 2009, the Cumacks received a $1,000 federal income tax refund.

4. During 2009, Frank, a 50% partner in Diske General Partnership, received a $4,000 guaranteed payment from Diske for services that he rendered to the partnership that year.

5. In 2009, Frank received $10,000 as beneficiary of his deceased brother's life insurance policy.

6. Dale's employer pays 100% of the cost of all employees' group-term life insurance under a qualified plan. Policy cost is $5 per $1,000 of coverage. Dale's group-term life insurance coverage equals $450,000.

7. In 2009, Frank won $5,000 at a casino and had $2,000 in gambling losses.

8. During 2009, the Cumacks received $1,000 interest income associated with a refund of their prior years' federal income tax.

9. In 2009, the Cumacks sold their first and only residence for $400,000. They purchased their home in 1992 for $50,000 and have lived there since then. There were no other capital gains, losses, or capital loss carryovers. The Cumacks do not intend to buy another residence.

10. In 2009, Zeno Corp. declared a stock dividend and Dale received one additional share of Zeno common stock for three shares of Zeno common stock that she held. The stock that Dale received had a fair market value of $9,000. There was no provision to receive cash instead of stock.

Explanation of solutions

1. **($0)** Amounts received as a gift are fully excluded from gross income.

2. **($3,500)** The maximum deduction for contributions to a traditional IRA by an individual at least age 50 is the lesser of $6,000, or 100% of compensation for 2009. Since the Cumacks were not active participants in an employer's qualified pension or annuity plan, there is no phaseout of the deduction based on AGI.

3. **($0)** Since federal income taxes are not deductible in computing a taxpayer's federal income tax liability, a refund of federal income taxes is excluded from gross income.

4. **($4,000)** Guaranteed payments are partnership payments to partners for services rendered or for the use of capital without regard to partnership income. A guaranteed payment is deductible by the partnership, and the receipt of a guaranteed payment must be included in the partner's gross income, and is reported as self-employment income in the computation of the partner's self-employment tax.

5. **($0)** The proceeds of life insurance policies paid by reason of death of the insured are generally excluded from the beneficiary's gross income.

6. ($2,000) An employer's payment of the cost of the first $50,000 of coverage for group-term life insurance can be excluded from an employee's gross income. Since Dale's employer provided group-term insurance of $450,000, and the cost of coverage was $5 per $1,000 of coverage, $5 × 400 = $2,000, must be included in Dale's gross income.

7. ($5,000) Gambling winnings must be included in gross income. Gambling losses cannot be offset against gambling winnings, but instead are deducted from AGI as a miscellaneous itemized deduction limited in amount to the gambling winnings included in gross income.

8. ($1,000) Although a federal income tax refund can be excluded from gross income, interest on the refund must be included in gross income.

9. ($0) Up to $250,000 of gain can be excluded from gross income if an individual owned and occupied a residence as a principal residence for an aggregate of at least two of the five years preceding sale. The excludable gain is increased to $500,000 for married individuals filing jointly if either spouse meets the ownership requirement, and both spouses meet the use requirement.

10. ($0) Stock dividends are generally excluded from gross income because a shareholder's relative interest in earnings and assets is unaffected.

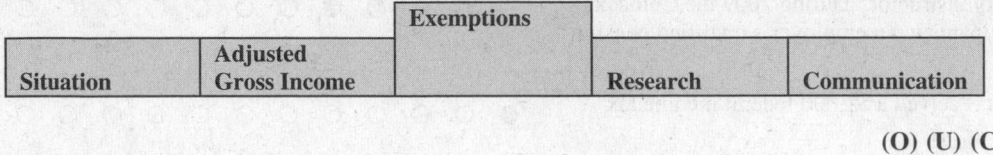

The Cumacks claimed three exemptions on their 2009 joint income tax return.

(O) (U) (C)
● ○ ○

Explanation of solution

(O) To qualify as a dependency exemption, a dependent must be a US citizen or resident of the US, Canada, or Mexico. Since Dale's father, Jacques, is both a French citizen and French resident, he does not qualify as a dependency exemption even though the Cumacks provided all of his support.

Internal Revenue Code Section 165, subsection (h) provides that an individual's personal casualty loss is allowable to the extent that it exceeds $500, and that a net personal casualty loss is deductible to the extent that it exceeds 10% of adjusted gross income.

Section	Subsection
§ 165	(h)

Situation	Adjusted Gross Income	Exemptions	Research	Communication

To: Ms. Dale Cumack
From: CPA Candidate
Re: Theft loss

You have requested that I research the tax implications of your theft loss that occurred during 2010. In this situation, the amount of your theft loss is $7,000, which is the lesser of the fair market value or the adjusted basis of the automobile. Theft losses are deductible as itemized deductions subject to two limitations. First the loss is reduced by a $500 floor amount. Second, the remaining $6,500 loss is deductible only to the extent that it exceeds 10% of your adjusted gross income.

If you have any additional questions, please contact me.

Simulation Problem 5

Situation	Filing Status	Adjusted Gross Income	Tax Treatment	Research	Communication

For **items 1 and 2,** candidates were asked to determine the filing status and number of exemptions for Mrs. Vick.

1. (M, 4) Since Mr. Vick died during the year, Mrs. Vick is considered married for the entire year for filing status purposes. There would be four exemptions on the Vicks' joint return—one each for Mr. and Mrs. Vick, one for their 11-year-old daughter Joan, and one for Mrs. Vick's unmarried cousin Fran Phillips. Although Fran is treated as unrelated to the Vicks for dependency exemption purposes, Fran qualifies as a dependency exemption because the Vicks' residence was Fran's principal home for 2009.

2. (Q, 3) Mrs. Vick will file as a "qualifying widow with dependent child" which will entitle her to use the joint return rates for 2010. This filing status is available for the two years following the year of the spouse's death if (1) the surviving spouse was eligible to file a joint return in the year of the spouse's death, (2) does not remarry before the end of the taxable year, and (3) the surviving spouse pays over 50% of the cost of maintaining a household that is the principal home for the entire year of the surviving spouse's dependent child. There will be three exemptions on the return—one for Mrs. Vick, a dependency exemption for her daughter Joan, and a dependency exemption for her cousin Fran.

Situation	Filing Status	Adjusted Gross Income	Tax Treatment	Research	Communication

For **items 1 through 7,** candidates were asked to determine the amount that is taxable and should be included in Adjusted Gross Income (AGI) on the 2009 federal income tax return filed by Mrs. Vick.

1. ($0) State disability benefits are excluded from gross income.

2. ($400) The $50 interest on the tax refund and $350 interest from a savings account and certificates of deposit are taxable; the $100 interest on municipal bonds is excluded from gross income.

3. ($900) The pension benefits are fully taxable because they were paid for exclusively by Mr. Vick's employer.

4. ($0) Property received as a gift is always excluded from gross income.

5. ($0) The proceeds of life insurance paid because of Mr. Vick's death are excluded from gross income, without regard to the amount of premiums paid.

6. ($200) Jury duty pay represents compensation for services and must be included in gross income.

7. ($450) The $450 of gambling winnings must be included in gross income. Mrs. Vick's $100 of gambling losses are deductible only from AGI as a miscellaneous itemized deduction.

Situation	Filing Status	Adjusted Gross Income	Tax Treatment	Research	Communication

For **items 1 through 14,** candidates were asked to select the appropriate tax treatment for the payments made or losses incurred by Mrs. Vick for 2008.

1. (A) Life insurance premiums are considered a personal expense and are not deductible.

2. (D) An interest forfeiture penalty for making an early withdrawal from a certificate of deposit is deductible on page 1 of Form 1040 to arrive at adjusted gross income.

3. (F) Charitable contributions are generally deductible as an itemized deduction up to a **maximum of 50% of AGI**.

4. (E) Estimated state income tax payments are deductible in full as an itemized deduction on Schedule A.

5. (E) Real estate taxes on a principal residence are deductible in full as an itemized deduction on Schedule A.

6. (A) A family car is a personal use asset and a loss from its sale is not deductible. The only type of loss that can be deducted on a personal use asset is a casualty or theft loss.

7. (B) A capital expenditure made for medical reasons that improves a residence is deductible as a medical expense to the extent that the expenditure exceeds the increase in value of the residence. As a medical expense, the excess expenditure is deductible as an itemized deduction on Schedule A subject to a 7.5% of AGI threshold.

8. (B) Health insurance premiums qualify as a medical expense and are deductible as an itemized deduction on Schedule A subject to a 7.5% of AGI threshold.

9. (C) Tax return preparation fees are deductible as an itemized deduction on Schedule A subject to a 2% of AGI threshold.

10. (E) Points paid to refinance a mortgage are deductible as interest expense over the term of the loan. Interest expense on a personal residence is deductible as an itemized deduction on Schedule A.

11. (D) One-half of a self-employed taxpayer's self-employment tax is deductible on page 1 of Form 1040 to arrive at AGI.

12. (E) Gambling losses are deductible as a miscellaneous itemized deduction on Schedule A to the extent that the taxpayer's gambling winnings are included in gross income. Since Mrs. Vick reported $450 of gambling winnings, her $100 of gambling losses are deductible.

13. (C) Unreimbursed employee expenses (including union dues) are generally deductible as miscellaneous itemized deductions on Schedule A subject to a 2% of AGI threshold.

14. (A) A payment of federal income tax is not deductible in computing a taxpayer's taxable income.

Situation	Filing Status	Adjusted Gross Income	Tax Treatment	Research	Communication

Internal Revenue Code Section 529, subsection (c) provides that any contribution to a qualified tuition program on behalf of a beneficiary shall be treated as a completed gift and not a gift of a future interest in property.

Section	Subsection
§ 529	(c)

Situation	Filing Status	Adjusted Gross Income	Tax Treatment	Research	Communication

To: Mrs. Vick
From: CPA Candidate
Re: College savings plan

    As you requested, I have researched the gift tax implications of contributions that you are considering making to a qualified tuition program on behalf of your daughter. Contributions to these programs (often referred to as Sec. 529 plans) on behalf of a beneficiary are treated as a completed gift to such beneficiary and not a gift of a future interest. This means that the contributions are eligible for the annual gift tax exclusion which is $13,000 for 2009. Furthermore, if the amount of contribution exceeds $13,000, an election can be made to treat the contribution as a gift made ratably over a five-year period which would permit you to make a contribution of $13,000 × 5 = $65,000 to your daughter's program without making a taxable gift.

    In summary, your contributions to your daughter's 529 plan should result in minimal gift tax consequences. Please contact me if you have any additional questions.

Simulation Problem 6

Situation	Income and Loss	Adjustments	Tax Treatments	Communication	Research

1. ($3,000) The Moores have a net capital loss of $6,000, of which $3,000 can be currently deducted, with the remaining $3,000 carried forward as a LTCL.

2. ($0) Joan received the land as a gift, and her basis for gain is the land's adjusted basis of $60,000, while her basis for loss is the land's $50,000 fair market value on date of gift. Joan recognizes no gain or loss on the sale because she sold the land for $56,000 and the use of her basis for gain ($60,000) does not result in a gain, and the use of her basis for loss ($50,000) does not result in a loss.

3. ($0) The security deposit is not treated as rent and only will be included in gross income when not returned to the tenant.

4. ($55,000) Tom's compensation consists of the wages of $53,000 plus the $2,000 value of group-term life insurance coverage in excess of $50,000.

5. ($1,250) Since the Moores' itemized deductions exceeded their available standard deduction by $1,450, all $1,250 of the state income tax refund must be included in gross income for 2009 because its deduction in 2008 reduced the Moores' federal income tax.

6. ($0) Although unemployment compensation if generally taxable, up to $2,400 of unemployment compensation benefits can be excluded from gross income for 2009.

7. ($2,500) The net rental income is computed on Schedule E and reported on page 1 of Form 1040.

8. ($900) Although generally nontaxable, a stock dividend will be taxable if any shareholder can elect to receive the distribution in either stock or in property. The amount of dividend is equal to the stock's $900 fair market value on date of distribution.

9. ($3,500) The $5,000 employee death benefit exclusion was repealed for decedents dying after August 20, 1996.

10. ($5,000) The accrued interest on redeemed Series EE US savings bonds can be excluded from gross income to the extent that the aggregate redemption proceeds (principal plus interest) are used to finance the higher education expenses (tuition and fees) of the taxpayer, taxpayer's spouse, or dependents. Here, there is no interest exclusion available for Tom because the proceeds were used to pay for Laura's tuition, and Laura does not qualify as Tom's dependent.

Situation	Income and Loss	Adjustments		Tax Treatments	Communication	Research

($8,000) The alimony is deductible in arriving at AGI, but child support is not deductible.

Situation	Income and Loss	Adjustments	Tax Treatments		Communication	Research

	(A)	(B)	(C)	(D)	(E)	(F)
1. On March 23, 2009, Tom sold fifty shares of Zip stock at a $1,200 loss. He repurchased fifty shares of Zip on April 15, 2009.	●	○	○	○	○	○
2. Payment of a personal property tax based on the value of the Moores' car.	○	●	○	○	○	○
3. Used clothes were donated to church organizations.	○	○	○	●	○	○
4. Premiums were paid covering insurance against Tom's loss of earnings.	●	○	○	○	○	○
5. Tom paid for subscriptions to accounting journals.	○	○	○	○	○	●
6. Interest was paid on a $10,000 home-equity line of credit secured by the Moores' residence. The fair market value of the home exceeded the mortgage by $50,000. Tom used the proceeds to purchase a sailboat.	○	●	○	○	○	○
7. Amounts were paid in excess of insurance reimbursement for prescription drugs.	○	○	●	○	○	○
8. Funeral expenses were paid by the Moores for Joan's brother.	●	○	○	○	○	○
9. Theft loss was incurred on Joan's jewelry in excess of insurance reimbursement. There were no 2009 personal casualty gains.	○	○	○	○	●	○
10. Loss on the sale of the family's sailboat.	●	○	○	○	○	○
11. Interest was paid on the $300,000 acquisition mortgage on the Moores' home. The mortgage is secured by their home.	○	●	○	○	○	○
12. Joan performed free accounting services for the Red Cross. The estimated value of the services was $500.	●	○	○	○	○	○

Explanation of solutions

1. (A) No loss is deductible if stock is sold at a loss and within thirty days before or after the sale, substantially identical stock in the same corporation is purchased. Here, the loss on the March 23 sale of 50 shares of Zip stock cannot be recognized because Tom repurchased fifty shares of Zip stock on April 15. The $1,200 loss not recognized is added to the basis of the newly acquired stock.

2. (B) Personal property taxes based on value are fully deductible as an itemized deduction.

3. (D) The fair market value of used clothing donated to a qualified charitable organization is deductible as an itemized deduction subject to a 50% of AGI limitation.

4. (A) Premiums on insurance against the loss of earnings in the event of disability are a nondeductible personal expense.

5. (F) Since Tom is a CPA working as an employee, the unreimbursed cost of subscriptions to accounting journals is deductible as an itemized deduction subject to a threshold of 2% of AGI.

6. (B) Interest on home-equity indebtedness of up to $100,000 is fully deductible as an itemized deduction regardless of how the proceeds of the loan were used.

7. (C) The unreimbursed cost of prescriptions qualify as a medical expense deductible as an itemized deduction subject to a threshold of 7.5% of AGI.

8. (A) Funeral expenses are a nondeductible personal expense.

9. (E) A theft loss on personal use property is deductible as an itemized deduction subject to a $500 floor and a threshold of 10% of AGI.

10. (A) A loss resulting from the sale of personal use property is not deductible.

11. (B) Interest on acquisition indebtedness of up to $1 million is fully deductible as an itemized deduction if the mortgage is secured by the taxpayer's principal or second residence.

12. (A) No charitable deduction is allowable for the value of a taxpayer's services performed for a charitable organization.

Situation	Income and Loss	Adjustments	Tax Treatments	Communication	Research

The technical points to be covered in this response should include

The interest on acquisition indebtedness and home equity indebtedness secured by a taxpayer's principal or second residence is deductible subject to limitations. Acquisition indebtedness interest is deductible on up to $1 million of loans ($500,000 if married filing separately) used to acquire, build, or substantially improve a principal or second residence. Home equity indebtedness interest is deductible on up to $100,000 of loans ($50,000 if married filing separately) regardless of how the loan proceeds are used. Home equity indebtedness is all nonacquisition indebtedness that is secured by a principal or second residence to the extent that it does not exceed the fair market value of the residence reduced by any acquisition indebtedness.

Situation	Income and Loss	Adjustments	Tax Treatments	Communication	Research

Internal Revenue Code Section 56, subsection (b) provides the adjustments to regular taxable income that are applicable only to individuals when computing the alternative minimum tax.

Section	Subsection
§ 56	(b)

Simulation Problem 7

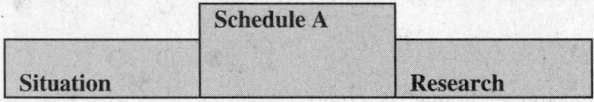

Situation	Schedule A	Research

(See Schedule A on the next page)

Medical and Dental Expenses

The disability income insurance premiums do not represent medical insurance and are not deductible. Similarly, although prescription drugs are deductible, nonprescription medicine is not deductible.

Taxes

The automobile registration fee is not deductible.

Interest

Only home mortgage interest and investment interest expense can be deducted as an itemized deduction. The interest on the automobile loan and the credit card interest are considered personal interest and are not deductible.

Contributions

The stock was appreciated and held for more than one year so it qualifies as capital gain property. As a result, the amount of contribution is the stock's fair market value of $4,000.

Miscellaneous

The legal fee for preparation of a will and life insurance premiums are nondeductible personal expenses. Similarly, no deduction is available for transportation to and from work (commuting), political contributions, and repairs to a principal residence.

Situation	Schedule A	Research

Internal Revenue Code Section 170, subsection (e) provides that the amount of the Shaws' charitable contribution will be limited to the painting's cost of $90,000, since the painting would not result in long-term capital gain if sold (i.e., it has not been held for more than 12 months).

Section	Subsection
§ 170	(e)

SCHEDULE A (Form 1040)	**Itemized Deductions**	OMB No. 1545-0074

Department of the Treasury
Internal Revenue Service (99)

► **Attach to Form 1040.**   ► **See Instructions for Schedule A (Form 1040).**

20 09

Attachment
Sequence No. **07**

Name(s) shown on Form 1040

Fred & Laura Shaw

Your social security number

123-67-5489

Medical and Dental Expenses		**Caution.** Do not include expenses reimbursed or paid by others.			
	1	Medical and dental expenses (see page A-1)	1	6,405	
	2	Enter amount from Form 1040, line 38 ▕ 2 ▏ 80,000			
	3	Multiply line 2 by 7.5% (.075)	3	6,000	
	4	Subtract line 3 from line 1. If line 3 is more than line 1, enter -0-	4		405
Taxes You Paid (See page A-2.)	5	State and local **(check only one box):** a ☑ Income taxes, **or** ⎱ b ☐ General sales taxes ⎰	5	1,200	
	6	Real estate taxes (see page A-5)	6	10,000	
	7	New motor vehicle taxes from line 11 of the worksheet on back. Skip this line if you checked box 5b	7		
	8	Other taxes. List type and amount ► _____ **Personal property taxes** _____	8	410	
	9	Add lines 5 through 8	9		11,610
Interest You Paid (See page A-6.) **Note.** Personal interest is not deductible.	10	Home mortgage interest and points reported to you on Form 1098	10	7,700	
	11	Home mortgage interest not reported to you on Form 1098. If paid to the person from whom you bought the home, see page A-7 and show that person's name, identifying no., and address ► _____ _____	11		
	12	Points not reported to you on Form 1098. See page A-7 for special rules	12		
	13	Qualified mortgage insurance premiums (see page A-7) .	13		
	14	Investment interest. Attach Form 4952 if required. (See page A-8.)	14		
	15	Add lines 10 through 14	15		7,700
Gifts to Charity If you made a gift and got a benefit for it, see page A-8.	16	Gifts by cash or check. If you made any gift of $250 or more, see page A-8	16	2,500	
	17	Other than by cash or check. If any gift of $250 or more, see page A-8. You **must** attach Form 8283 if over $500 . .	17	4,000	
	18	Carryover from prior year	18		
	19	Add lines 16 through 18	19		6,500
Casualty and Theft Losses	20	Casualty or theft loss(es). Attach Form 4684. (See page A-10.)	20		
Job Expenses and Certain Miscellaneous Deductions (See page A-10.)	21	Unreimbursed employee expenses—job travel, union dues, job education, etc. Attach Form 2106 or 2106-EZ if required. (See page A-10.) ► **Dues $600; Travel $900**	21	1,500	
	22	Tax preparation fees	22	400	
	23	Other expenses—investment, safe deposit box, etc. List type and amount ► **Subscriptions $300; Safe deposit box $120**	23	420	
	24	Add lines 21 through 23	24	2,320	
	25	Enter amount from Form 1040, line 38 ▕ 25 ▏ 80,000			
	26	Multiply line 25 by 2% (.02)	26	1,600	
	27	Subtract line 26 from line 24. If line 26 is more than line 24, enter -0-	27		720
Other Miscellaneous Deductions	28	Other—from list on page A-11. List type and amount ► _____ _____	28		
Total Itemized Deductions	29	Is Form 1040, line 38, over $166,800 (over $83,400 if married filing separately)? ☑ **No.** Your deduction is not limited. Add the amounts in the far right column for lines 4 through 28. Also, enter this amount on Form 1040, line 40a. ⎱ ► ☐ **Yes.** Your deduction may be limited. See page A-11 for the amount to enter. ⎰	29		26,935
	30	If you elect to itemize deductions even though they are less than your standard deduction, check here . . . . ► ☐			

For Paperwork Reduction Act Notice, see Form 1040 instructions.   Cat. No. 17145C   Schedule A (Form 1040) 2009

MULTIPLE-CHOICE QUESTIONS (1-62)

1. Ralph Birch purchased land and a building which will be used in connection with Birch's business. The costs associated with this purchase are as follows:

Cash down payment	$ 40,000
Mortgage on property	350,000
Survey costs	2,000
Title and transfer taxes	2,500
Charges for hookup of gas, water, and sewer lines	3,000
Back property taxes owed by the seller that were paid by Birch	5,000

What is Birch's tax basis for the land and building?

- a. $ 44,500
- b. $394,500
- c. $397,500
- d. $402,500

2. Fred Berk bought a plot of land with a cash payment of $40,000 and a purchase money mortgage of $50,000. In addition, Berk paid $200 for a title insurance policy. Berk's basis in this land is

- a. $40,000
- b. $40,200
- c. $90,000
- d. $90,200

3. Smith made a gift of property to Thompson. Smith's basis in the property was $1,200. The fair market value at the time of the gift was $1,400. Thompson sold the property for $2,500. What was the amount of Thompson's gain on the disposition?

- a. $0
- b. $1,100
- c. $1,300
- d. $2,500

4. Julie received a parcel of land as a gift from her Aunt Agnes. At the time of the gift, the land had a fair market value of $83,000 and an adjusted basis of $23,000. This was the only gift that Julie received from Agnes during 2009. If Agnes paid a gift tax of $14,000 on the transfer of the gift to Julie, what tax basis will Julie have for the land?

- a. $23,000
- b. $35,000
- c. $36,000
- d. $82,000

Items 5 and 6 are based on the following data:

In 2007 Iris King bought shares of stock as an investment, at a cost of $10,000. During 2009, when the fair market value was $8,000, Iris gave the stock to her daughter, Ruth.

5. If Ruth sells the shares of stock in 2010 for $7,000, Ruth's recognized loss would be

- a. $3,000
- b. $2,000
- c. $1,000
- d. $0

6. Ruth's holding period of the stock for purposes of determining her loss

- a. Started in 2007.
- b. Started in 2009.
- c. Started in 2010.
- d. Is irrelevant because Ruth received the stock for no consideration of money or money's worth.

Items 7 through 9 are based on the following data:

Laura's father, Albert, gave Laura a gift of 500 shares of Liba Corporation common stock in 2010. Albert's basis for the Liba stock was $4,000. At the date of this gift, the fair market value of the Liba stock was $3,000.

7. If Laura sells the 500 shares of Liba stock in 2010 for $5,000, her basis is

- a. $5,000
- b. $4,000
- c. $3,000
- d. $0

8. If Laura sells the 500 shares of Liba stock in 2010 for $2,000, her basis is

- a. $4,000
- b. $3,000
- c. $2,000
- d. $0

9. If Laura sells the 500 shares of Liba stock in 2010 for $3,500, what is the reportable gain or loss in 2010?

- a. $3,500 gain.
- b. $ 500 gain.
- c. $ 500 loss.
- d. $0.

10. On June 1, 2009, Ben Rork sold 500 shares of Kul Corp. stock. Rork had received this stock on May 1, 2009, as a bequest from the estate of his uncle, who died on March 1, 2009. Rork's basis was determined by reference to the stock's fair market value on March 1, 2009. Rork's holding period for this stock was

- a. Short-term.
- b. Long-term.
- c. Short-term if sold at a gain; long-term if sold at a loss.
- d. Long-term if sold at a gain; short-term if sold at a loss.

11. Fred Zorn died on January 5, 2009, bequeathing his entire $4,000,000 estate to his sister, Ida. The alternate valuation date was validly elected by the executor of Fred's estate. Fred's estate included 2,000 shares of listed stock for which Fred's basis was $380,000. This stock was distributed to Ida nine months after Fred's death. Fair market values of this stock were

At the date of Fred's death	$400,000
Six months after Fred's death	450,000
Nine months after Fred's death	480,000

Ida's basis for this stock is

- a. $380,000
- b. $400,000
- c. $450,000
- d. $480,000

Items 12 and 13 are based on the following data:

On March 1, 2009, Lois Rice learned that she was bequeathed 1,000 shares of Elin Corp. common stock under the will of her uncle, Pat Prevor. Pat had paid $5,000 for the Elin stock in 2004. Fair market value of the Elin stock on March 1, 2009, the date of Pat's death, was $8,000 and had increased to $11,000 six months later. The executor of Pat's estate elected the alternative valuation for estate tax purposes. Lois sold the Elin stock for $9,000 on May 1, 2009, the date that the executor distributed the stock to her.

12. Lois' basis for gain or loss on sale of the 1,000 shares of Elin stock is
- a. $ 5,000
- b. $ 8,000
- c. $ 9,000
- d. $11,000

13. Lois should treat the 1,000 shares of Elin stock as a
- a. Short-term Section 1231 asset.
- b. Long-term Section 1231 asset.
- c. Short-term capital asset.
- d. Long-term capital asset.

Items 14 and 15 are based on the following data:

In January 2010, Joan Hill bought one share of Orban Corp. stock for $300. On March 1, 2010, Orban distributed one share of preferred stock for each share of common stock held. This distribution was nontaxable. On March 1, 2010, Joan's one share of common stock had a fair market value of $450, while the preferred stock had a fair market value of $150.

14. After the distribution of the preferred stock, Joan's bases for her Orban stocks are

	Common	Preferred
a.	$300	$0
b.	$225	$ 75
c.	$200	$100
d.	$150	$150

15. The holding period for the preferred stock starts in
- a. January 2010.
- b. March 2010.
- c. September 2010.
- d. December 2010.

16. On July 1, 2005, Lila Perl paid $90,000 for 450 shares of Janis Corp. common stock. Lila received a nontaxable stock dividend of 50 new common shares in August 2009. On December 20, 2009, Lila sold the 50 new shares for $11,000. How much should Lila report in her 2009 return as long-term capital gain?
- a. $0
- b. $ 1,000
- c. $ 2,000
- d. $11,000

17. Tom Gow owned a parcel of investment real estate that had an adjusted basis of $25,000 and a fair market value of $40,000. During 2010, Gow exchanged his investment real estate for the items of property listed below.

Land to be held for investment (fair market value)	$35,000
A small sailboat to be held for personal use (fair market value)	3,000
Cash	2,000

What is Tom Gow's recognized gain and basis in his new investment real estate?

	Gain recognized	Basis for real estate
a.	$2,000	$22,000
b.	$2,000	$25,000
c.	$5,000	$25,000
d.	$5,000	$35,000

18. In a "like-kind" exchange of an investment asset for a similar asset that will also be held as an investment, no taxable gain or loss will be recognized on the transaction if both assets consist of

- a. Convertible debentures.
- b. Convertible preferred stock.
- c. Partnership interests.
- d. Rental real estate located in different states.

19. Pat Leif owned an apartment house that he bought in 1997. Depreciation was taken on a straight-line basis. In 2010, when Pat's adjusted basis for this property was $200,000, he traded it for an office building having a fair market value of $600,000. The apartment house has 100 dwelling units, while the office building has 40 units rented to business enterprises. The properties are **not** located in the same city. What is Pat's reportable gain on this exchange?
- a. $400,000 Section 1250 gain.
- b. $400,000 Section 1231 gain.
- c. $400,000 long-term capital gain.
- d. $0.

20. On July 1, 2010, Riley exchanged investment real property, with an adjusted basis of $160,000 and subject to a mortgage of $70,000, and received from Wilson $30,000 cash and other investment real property having a fair market value of $250,000. Wilson assumed the mortgage. What is Riley's recognized gain in 2010 on the exchange?
- a. $ 30,000
- b. $ 70,000
- c. $ 90,000
- d. $100,000

21. On October 1, 2010, Donald Anderson exchanged an apartment building having an adjusted basis of $375,000 and subject to a mortgage of $100,000 for $25,000 cash and another apartment building with a fair market value of $550,000 and subject to a mortgage of $125,000. The property transfers were made subject to the outstanding mortgages. What amount of gain should Anderson recognize in his tax return for 2010?
- a. $0
- b. $ 25,000
- c. $125,000
- d. $175,000

22. The following information pertains to the acquisition of a six-wheel truck by Sol Barr, a self-employed contractor:

Cost of original truck traded in	$20,000
Book value of original truck at trade-in date	4,000
List price of new truck	25,000
Trade-in allowance for old truck	6,000
Business use of both trucks	100%

The basis of the new truck is
- a. $27,000
- b. $25,000
- c. $23,000
- d. $19,000

23. An office building owned by Elmer Bass was condemned by the state on January 2, 2009. Bass received the condemnation award on March 1, 2010. In order to qualify for nonrecognition of gain on this involuntary conversion, what is the last date for Bass to acquire qualified replacement property?
- a. August 1, 2011.
- b. January 2, 2012.
- c. March 1, 2013.
- d. December 31, 2013.

24. In March 2010, Davis, who is single, purchased a new residence for $200,000. During that same month he sold his former residence for $380,000 and paid the realtor a $20,000 commission. The former residence, his first home, had cost $65,000 in 1991. Davis added a bathroom for $5,000 in 2006. What amount of gain is recognized from the sale of the former residence on Davis' 2010 tax return?

    a. $160,000
    b. $ 90,000
    c. $ 40,000
    d. $0

25. The following information pertains to the sale of Al and Beth Oran's principal residence:

Date of sale	February 2010
Date of purchase	October 1993
Net sales price	$760,000
Adjusted basis	$170,000

Al and Beth owned their home jointly and had occupied it as their principal residence since acquiring the home in 1993. In June 2010, the Orans bought a condo for $190,000 to be used as their principal residence. What amount of gain must the Orans recognize on their 2010 joint return from the sale of their residence?

    a. $ 90,000
    b. $150,000
    c. $340,000
    d. $400,000

26. Ryan, age fifty-seven, is single with no dependents. In January 2010, Ryan's principal residence was sold for the net amount of $400,000 after all selling expenses. Ryan bought the house in 1997 and occupied it until sold. On the date of sale, the house had a basis of $180,000. Ryan does not intend to buy another residence. What is the maximum exclusion of gain on sale of the residence that may be claimed in Ryan's 2010 income tax return?

    a. $250,000
    b. $220,000
    c. $125,000
    d. $0

27. Miller, an individual calendar-year taxpayer, purchased 100 shares of Maples Inc. common stock for $10,000 on July 10, 2009, and an additional fifty shares of Maples Inc. common stock for $4,000 on December 24, 2009. On January 8, 2010, Miller sold the 100 shares purchased on July 10, 2009, for $7,000. What is the amount of Miller's recognized loss for 2010 and what is the basis for her remaining fifty shares of Maples Inc. stock?

    a. $3,000 recognized loss; $4,000 basis for her remaining stock.
    b. $1,500 recognized loss; $5,500 basis for her remaining stock.
    c. $1,500 recognized loss; $4,000 basis for her remaining stock.
    d. $0 recognized loss; $7,000 basis for her remaining stock.

28. Smith, an individual calendar-year taxpayer, purchased 100 shares of Core Co. common stock for $15,000 on December 15, 2009, and an additional 100 shares for $13,000 on December 30, 2009. On January 3, 2010, Smith sold the shares purchased on December 15, 2009, for $13,000. What amount of loss from the sale of Core stock is deductible on Smith's 2009 and 2010 income tax returns?

	2009	2010
a.	$0	$0
b.	$0	$2,000
c.	$1,000	$1,000
d.	$2,000	$0

29. On March 10, 2010, James Rogers sold 300 shares of Red Company common stock for $4,200. Rogers acquired the stock in 2007 at a cost of $5,000.

On April 4, 2010, he repurchased 300 shares of Red Company common stock for $3,600 and held them until July 18, 2010, when he sold them for $6,000.

How should Rogers report the above transactions for 2010?

    a. A long-term capital loss of $800.
    b. A long-term capital gain of $1,000.
    c. A long-term capital gain of $1,600.
    d. A long-term capital loss of $800 and a short-term capital gain of $2,400.

30. Murd Corporation, a domestic corporation, acquired a 90% interest in the Drum Company in 2006 for $30,000. During 2010, the stock of Drum was declared worthless. What type and amount of deduction should Murd take for 2010?

    a. Long-term capital loss of $1,000.
    b. Long-term capital loss of $15,000.
    c. Ordinary loss of $30,000.
    d. Long-term capital loss of $30,000.

31. If an individual incurs a loss on a nonbusiness deposit as the result of the insolvency of a bank, credit union, or other financial institution, the individual's loss on the nonbusiness deposit may be deducted in any one of the following ways **except:**

    a. Miscellaneous itemized deduction.
    b. Casualty loss.
    c. Short-term capital loss.
    d. Long-term capital loss.

Items 32 and 33 are based on the following:

Conner purchased 300 shares of Zinco stock for $30,000 in 2005. On May 23, 2009, Conner sold all the stock to his daughter Alice for $20,000, its then fair market value. Conner realized no other gain or loss during 2009. On July 26, 2009, Alice sold the 300 shares of Zinco for $25,000.

32. What amount of the loss from the sale of Zinco stock can Conner deduct in 2009?

    a. $0
    b. $ 3,000
    c. $ 5,000
    d. $10,000

33. What was Alice's recognized gain or loss on her sale?

    a. $0.
    b. $5,000 long-term gain.
    c. $5,000 short-term loss.
    d. $5,000 long-term loss.

34. In 2010, Fay sold 100 shares of Gym Co. stock to her son, Martin, for $11,000. Fay had paid $15,000 for the stock in 2007. Subsequently in 2010, Martin sold the stock to an unrelated third party for $16,000. What amount of gain from the sale of the stock to the third party should Martin report on his 2010 income tax return?

a. $0
b. $1,000
c. $4,000
d. $5,000

35. Among which of the following related parties are losses from sales and exchanges not recognized for tax purposes?
a. Mother-in-law and daughter-in-law.
b. Uncle and nephew.
c. Brother and sister.
d. Ancestors, lineal descendants, and all in-laws.

36. On May 1, 2010, Daniel Wright owned stock (held for investment) purchased two years earlier at a cost of $10,000 and having a fair market value of $7,000. On this date he sold the stock to his son, William, for $7,000. William sold the stock for $6,000 to an unrelated person on July 1, 2010. How should William report the stock sale on his 2010 tax return?
a. As a short-term capital loss of $1,000.
b. As a long-term capital loss of $1,000.
c. As a short-term capital loss of $4,000.
d. As a long-term capital loss of $4,000.

37. Al Eng owns 50% of the outstanding stock of Rego Corp. During 2010, Rego sold a trailer to Eng for $10,000, the trailer's fair value. The trailer had an adjusted tax basis of $12,000, and had been owned by Rego and used in its business for three years. In its 2010 income tax return, what is the allowable loss that Rego can claim on the sale of this trailer?
a. $0
b. $2,000 capital loss.
c. $2,000 Section 1231 loss.
d. $2,000 Section 1245 loss.

38. For a cash basis taxpayer, gain or loss on a year-end sale of listed stock arises on the
a. Trade date.
b. Settlement date.
c. Date of receipt of cash proceeds.
d. Date of delivery of stock certificate.

39. Lee qualified as head of a household for 2009 tax purposes. Lee's 2009 taxable income was $100,000, exclusive of capital gains and losses. Lee had a net long-term capital loss of $8,000 in 2009. What amount of this capital loss can Lee offset against 2009 ordinary income?
a. $0
b. $3,000
c. $4,000
d. $8,000

40. For the year ended December 31, 2009, Sol Corp. had an operating income of $20,000. In addition, Sol had capital gains and losses resulting in a net short-term capital gain of $2,000 and a net long-term capital loss of $7,000. How much of the excess of net long-term capital loss over net short-term capital gain could Sol offset against ordinary income for 2009?
a. $5,000
b. $3,000
c. $1,500
d. $0

41. In 2009, Nam Corp., which is not a dealer in securities, realized taxable income of $160,000 from its business op-

erations. Also, in 2009, Nam sustained a long-term capital loss of $24,000 from the sale of marketable securities. Nam did not realize any other capital gains or losses since it began operations. In Nam's income tax returns, what is the proper treatment for the $24,000 long-term capital loss?
a. Use $3,000 of the loss to reduce 2009 taxable income, and carry $21,000 of the long-term capital loss forward for five years.
b. Use $6,000 of the loss to reduce 2009 taxable income by $3,000, and carry $18,000 of the long-term capital loss forward for five years.
c. Use $24,000 of the long-term capital loss to reduce 2009 taxable income by $12,000.
d. Carry the $24,000 long-term capital loss forward for five years, treating it as a short-term capital loss.

42. For assets acquired in 2010, the holding period for determining long-term capital gains and losses is more than
a. 18 months.
b. 12 months.
c. 9 months.
d. 6 months.

43. On July 1, 2010, Kim Wald sold an antique for $12,000 that she had bought for her personal use in 2008 at a cost of $15,000. In her 2010 return, Kim should treat the sale of the antique as a transaction resulting in
a. A nondeductible loss.
b. Ordinary loss.
c. Short-term capital loss.
d. Long-term capital loss.

44. Paul Beyer, who is unmarried, has taxable income of $30,000 exclusive of capital gains and losses and his personal exemption. In 2009, Paul incurred a $1,000 net short-term capital loss and a $5,000 net long-term capital loss. His capital loss carryover to 2010 is
a. $0
b. $1,000
c. $3,000
d. $5,000

45. Capital assets include
a. A corporation's accounts receivable from the sale of its inventory.
b. Seven-year MACRS property used in a corporation's trade or business.
c. A manufacturing company's investment in US Treasury bonds.
d. A corporate real estate developer's unimproved land that is to be subdivided to build homes, which will be sold to customers.

46. Joe Hall owns a limousine for use in his personal service business of transporting passengers to airports. The limousine's adjusted basis is $40,000. In addition, Hall owns his personal residence and furnishings, that together cost him $280,000. Hall's capital assets amount to
a. $320,000
b. $280,000
c. $ 40,000
d. $0

47. In 2010, Ruth Lee sold a painting for $25,000 that she had bought for her personal use in 2004 at a cost of $10,000.

In her 2010 return, Lee should treat the sale of the painting as a transaction resulting in
- a. Ordinary income.
- b. Long-term capital gain.
- c. Section 1231 gain.
- d. No taxable gain.

48. In 2009, a capital loss incurred by a married couple filing a joint return
- a. Will be allowed only to the extent of capital gains.
- b. Will be allowed to the extent of capital gains, plus up to $3,000 of ordinary income.
- c. Will be allowed to the extent of capital gains, plus up to $6,000 of ordinary income.
- d. Is **not** an allowable loss.

49. Platt owns land that is operated as a parking lot. A shed was erected on the lot for the related transactions with customers. With regard to capital assets and Section 1231 assets, how should these assets be classified?

	Land	Shed
a.	Capital	Capital
b.	Section 1231	Capital
c.	Capital	Section 1231
d.	Section 1231	Section 1231

50. In 2006, Iris King bought a diamond necklace for her own use, at a cost of $10,000. In 2010, when the fair market value was $12,000, Iris gave this necklace to her daughter, Ruth. No gift tax was due. This diamond necklace is a
- a. Capital asset.
- b. Section 1231 asset.
- c. Section 1245 asset.
- d. Section 1250 asset.

51. Which of the following is a capital asset?
- a. Delivery truck.
- b. Personal-use recreation equipment.
- c. Land used as a parking lot for customers.
- d. Treasury stock, at cost.

52. Don Mott was the sole proprietor of a high-volume drug store which he owned for fifteen years before he sold it to Dale Drug Stores, Inc. in 2010. Besides the $900,000 selling price for the store's tangible assets and goodwill, Mott received a lump sum of $30,000 in 2010 for his agreement not to operate a competing enterprise within ten miles of the store's location for a period of six years. The $30,000 will be taxed to Mott as
- a. $30,000 ordinary income in 2010.
- b. $30,000 short-term capital gain in 2010.
- c. $30,000 long-term capital gain in 2010.
- d. Ordinary income of $5,000 a year for six years.

53. In June 2010, Olive Bell bought a house for use partially as a residence and partially for operation of a retail gift shop. In addition, Olive bought the following furniture:

Kitchen set and living room pieces for the residential portion	$ 8,000
Showcases and tables for the business portion	12,000

How much of this furniture comprises capital assets?
- a. $0
- b. $ 8,000
- c. $12,000
- d. $20,000

54. An individual's losses on transactions entered into for personal purposes are deductible only if
- a. The losses qualify as casualty or theft losses.
- b. The losses can be characterized as hobby losses.
- c. The losses do not exceed $3,000 ($6,000 on a joint return).
- d. No part of the transactions was entered into for profit.

55. Evon Corporation, which was formed in 2006, had $50,000 of net Sec. 1231 gain for its 2009 calendar year. Its net Sec. 1231 gains and losses for its three preceding tax years were as follows:

Year	Sec. 1231 results
2006	Gain of $10,000
2007	Loss of $15,000
2008	Loss of $20,000

As a result, Evon Corporation's 2009 net Sec. 1231 gain would be characterized as
- a. A net long-term capital gain of $50,000.
- b. A net long-term capital gain of $35,000 and ordinary income of $15,000.
- c. A net long-term capital gain of $25,000 and ordinary income of $25,000.
- d. A net long-term capital gain of $15,000 and ordinary income of $35,000.

56. Which one of the following would **not** be Sec. 1231 property even though held for more than twelve months?
- a. Business inventory.
- b. Unimproved land used for business.
- c. Depreciable equipment used in a business.
- d. Depreciable real property used in a business.

57. Vermont Corporation distributed packaging equipment that it no longer needed to Michael Jason who owns 20% of Vermont's stock. The equipment, which was acquired in 2006, had an adjusted basis of $2,000 and a fair market value of $9,000 at the date of distribution. Vermont had properly deducted $6,000 of straight-line depreciation on the equipment while it was used in Vermont's manufacturing activities. What amount of ordinary income must Vermont recognize as a result of the distribution of the equipment?
- a. $0
- b. $3,000
- c. $6,000
- d. $7,000

58. Tally Corporation sold machinery that had been used in its business for a loss of $22,000 during 2010. The machinery had been purchased and placed in service sixteen months earlier. For 2010, the $22,000 loss will be treated as a
- a Capital loss.
- b. Sec. 1245 loss.
- c. Sec. 1231 loss.
- d. Casualty loss because the machinery was held less than two years.

59. On January 2, 2008, Bates Corp. purchased and placed into service seven-year MACRS tangible property costing $100,000. On July 31, 2010, Bates sold the property for $102,000, after having taken $47,525 in MACRS depreciation deductions. What amount of the gain should Bates recapture as ordinary income?
- a. $0
- b. $ 2,000

c. $47,525
d. $49,525

60. Thayer Corporation purchased an apartment building on January 1, 2006, for $200,000. The building was depreci-ated using the straight-line method. On December 31, 2009, the building was sold for $220,000, when the asset balance net of accumulated depreciation was $170,000. On its 2009 tax return, Thayer should report

    a. Section 1231 gain of $42,500 and ordinary income of $7,500.
    b. Section 1231 gain of $44,000 and ordinary income of $6,000.
    c. Ordinary income of $50,000.
    d. Section 1231 gain of $50,000.

61. For the year ended December 31, 2009, McEwing Cor-poration, a calendar-year corporation, reported book income before income taxes of $120,000. Included in the determi-nation of this amount were the following gain and losses from property that had been held for more than one year:

Loss on sale of building depreciated on the straight-line method	$(7,000)
Gain on sale of land used in McEwing's business	16,000
Loss on sale of investments in marketable securities	(8,000)

For the year ended December 31, 2009, McEwing's taxable income was

    a. $113,000
    b. $120,000
    c. $125,000
    d. $128,000

62. David Price owned machinery which he had acquired in 2009 at a cost of $100,000. During 2010, the machinery was destroyed by fire. At that time it had an adjusted basis of $86,000. The insurance proceeds awarded to Price am-ounted to $125,000, and he immediately acquired a similar machine for $110,000.

    What should Price report as ordinary income resulting from the involuntary conversion for 2010?

    a. $14,000
    b. $15,000
    c. $25,000
    d. $39,000

SIMULATION PROBLEMS

Simulation Problem 1   (30 to 35 minutes)

Situation			
	Schedule D	Communication	Research

Lou Tomsik (social security #324-65-7037) reported the following transactions for calendar-year 2009:

- Lou sold 100 shares of Copperleaf Industries on October 20, 2009, for $4,200. Lou had acquired the stock for $2,500 on March 1, 2008.
- Lou sold 200 shares of King Corporation stock for $5,000 on November 15, 2009. He had purchased the stock on February 24, 2009, for $4,000.
- Tomsik had a net short-term capital loss carryforward from 2008 of $7,300, and during December 2009 received a $1,500 capital gain distribution from the Brooks Mutual fund.
- Tomsik did not receive any qualified dividends during this year.

	Schedule D		
Situation		Communication	Research

Use the above information to complete the following 2009 Form 1040 Schedule D for Tomsik.

		Communication	
Situation	Schedule D		Research

Tomsik contacts you and indicates that he expects to incur a substantial net capital loss for calendar-year 2010 and wonders what the treatment of the carryforwards will be in future years. Write a letter to Tomsik explaining the treatment of an individual's capital loss carryforwards.

REMINDER: Your response will be graded for both technical content and writing skills. Technical content will be evaluated for information that is helpful to the intended reader and clearly relevant to the issue. Writing skills will be evaluated for development, organization, and the appropriate expression of ideas in professional correspondence. Use a standard business memo or letter format with a clear beginning, middle, and end. Do not convey information in the form of a table, bullet point list, or other abbreviated presentation.

Dear Mr. Tomsik:

			Research
Situation	Schedule D	Communication	

Special rules apply to the gains and losses from capital assets. What Internal Revenue Code section defines "capital assets"?

SCHEDULE D
(Form 1040)

Department of the Treasury
Internal Revenue Service (99)

Capital Gains and Losses

▶ **Attach to Form 1040 or Form 1040NR.**   ▶ **See Instructions for Schedule D (Form 1040).**
▶ **Use Schedule D-1 to list additional transactions for lines 1 and 8.**

OMB No. 1545-0074

2009

Attachment
Sequence No. **12**

Name(s) shown on return | Your social security number

Part I Short-Term Capital Gains and Losses—Assets Held One Year or Less

	(a) Description of property (Example: 100 sh. XYZ Co.)	(b) Date acquired (Mo., day, yr.)	(c) Date sold (Mo., day, yr.)	(d) Sales price (see page D-7 of the instructions)	(e) Cost or other basis (see page D-7 of the instructions)	(f) Gain or (loss) Subtract (e) from (d)
1						

2	Enter your short-term totals, if any, from Schedule D-1, line 2	**2**		
3	**Total short-term sales price amounts.** Add lines 1 and 2 in column (d)	**3**		

4	Short-term gain from Form 6252 and short-term gain or (loss) from Forms 4684, 6781, and 8824	**4**	
5	Net short-term gain or (loss) from partnerships, S corporations, estates, and trusts from Schedule(s) K-1	**5**	
6	Short-term capital loss carryover. Enter the amount, if any, from line 10 of your **Capital Loss Carryover Worksheet** on page D-7 of the instructions	**6**	( )
7	**Net short-term capital gain or (loss).** Combine lines 1 through 6 in column (f)	**7**	

Part II Long-Term Capital Gains and Losses—Assets Held More Than One Year

	(a) Description of property (Example: 100 sh. XYZ Co.)	(b) Date acquired (Mo., day, yr.)	(c) Date sold (Mo., day, yr.)	(d) Sales price (see page D-7 of the instructions)	(e) Cost or other basis (see page D-7 of the instructions)	(f) Gain or (loss) Subtract (e) from (d)
8						

9	Enter your long-term totals, if any, from Schedule D-1, line 9	**9**		
10	**Total long-term sales price amounts.** Add lines 8 and 9 in column (d)	**10**		

11	Gain from Form 4797, Part I; long-term gain from Forms 2439 and 6252; and long-term gain or (loss) from Forms 4684, 6781, and 8824	**11**	
12	Net long-term gain or (loss) from partnerships, S corporations, estates, and trusts from Schedule(s) K-1	**12**	
13	Capital gain distributions. See page D-2 of the instructions	**13**	
14	Long-term capital loss carryover. Enter the amount, if any, from line 15 of your **Capital Loss Carryover Worksheet** on page D-7 of the instructions	**14**	( )
15	**Net long-term capital gain or (loss).** Combine lines 8 through 14 in column (f). Then go to Part III on the back	**15**	

For Paperwork Reduction Act Notice, see Form 1040 or Form 1040NR instructions.   Cat. No. 11338H   **Schedule D (Form 1040) 2009**

Part III   Summary

16 Combine lines 7 and 15 and enter the result **16**

   If line 16 is:
   - A **gain**, enter the amount from line 16 on Form 1040, line 13, or Form 1040NR, line 14. Then go to line 17 below.
   - A **loss**, skip lines 17 through 20 below. Then go to line 21. Also be sure to complete line 22.
   - **Zero**, skip lines 17 through 21 below and enter -0- on Form 1040, line 13, or Form 1040NR, line 14. Then go to line 22.

17 Are lines 15 and 16 **both** gains?
   ☐ **Yes.** Go to line 18.
   ☐ **No.** Skip lines 18 through 21, and go to line 22.

18 Enter the amount, if any, from line 7 of the **28% Rate Gain Worksheet** on page D-8 of the instructions . . . . ▶   **18**

19 Enter the amount, if any, from line 18 of the **Unrecaptured Section 1250 Gain Worksheet** on page D-9 of the instructions . . . . ▶   **19**

20 Are lines 18 and 19 **both** zero or blank?
   ☐ **Yes.** Complete Form 1040 through line 43, or Form 1040NR through line 40. Then complete the **Qualified Dividends and Capital Gain Tax Worksheet** on page 39 of the Instructions for Form 1040 (or in the Instructions for Form 1040NR). **Do not** complete lines 21 and 22 below.
   ☐ **No.** Complete Form 1040 through line 43, or Form 1040NR through line 40. Then complete the **Schedule D Tax Worksheet** on page D-10 of the instructions. **Do not** complete lines 21 and 22 below.

21 If line 16 is a loss, enter here and on Form 1040, line 13, or Form 1040NR, line 14, the **smaller** of:

   - The loss on line 16 or ⎫
   - ($3,000), or if married filing separately, ($1,500) ⎭   . . . .   **21** (   )

   Note. When figuring which amount is smaller, treat both amounts as positive numbers.

22 Do you have qualified dividends on Form 1040, line 9b, or Form 1040NR, line 10b?

   ☐ **Yes.** Complete Form 1040 through line 43, or Form 1040NR through line 40. Then complete the **Qualified Dividends and Capital Gain Tax Worksheet** on page 39 of the Instructions for Form 1040 (or in the Instructions for Form 1040NR).
   ☐ **No.** Complete the rest of Form 1040 or Form 1040NR.

MULTIPLE-CHOICE ANSWERS

1. d		15. a		29. c		43. a		57. c	
2. d		16. c		30. c		44. c		58. c	
3. c		17. c		31. d		45. c		59. c	
4. b		18. d		32. a		46. b		60. b	
5. c		19. d		33. a		47. b		61. b	
6. b		20. d		34. b		48. b		62. a	
7. b		21. b		35. c		49. d			
8. b		22. c		36. a		50. a			
9. d		23. c		37. c		51. b			
10. b		24. c		38. a		52. a			
11. c		25. a		39. b		53. b			
12. c		26. b		40. d		54. a			
13. d		27. b		41. d		55. d		1st: __/62 = __%	
14. b		28. a		42. b		56. a		2nd: __/62 = __%	

MULTIPLE-CHOICE ANSWER EXPLANATIONS

A.1. Basis of Property

1. (d) The requirement is to determine Birch's tax basis for the purchased land and building. The basis of property acquired by purchase is a cost basis and includes not only the cash paid and liabilities incurred, but also includes certain settlement fees and closing costs such as abstract of title fees, installation of utility services, legal fees (including title search, contract, and deed fees), recording fees, surveys, transfer taxes, owner's title insurance, and any amounts the seller owes that the buyer agrees to pay, such as back taxes and interest, recording or mortgage fees, charges for improvements or repairs, and sales commissions.

2. (d) The requirement is to determine the basis for the purchased land. The basis of the land consists of the cash paid ($40,000), the purchase money mortgage ($50,000), and the cost of the title insurance policy ($200), a total of $90,200.

A.1.c. Acquired by Gift

3. (c) The requirement is to determine the amount of gain recognized by Thompson resulting from the sale of appreciated property received as a gift. A donee's basis for appreciated property received as a gift is generally the same as the donor's basis. Since Smith had a basis for the property of $1,200 and Thompson sold the property for $2,500, Thompson must recognize a gain of $1,300.

4. (b) The requirement is to determine Julie's basis for the land received as a gift. A donee's basis for gift property is generally the same as the donor's basis, increased by any gift tax paid that is attributable to the property's net appreciation in value. That is, the amount of gift tax that can be added is limited to the amount that bears the same ratio as the property's net appreciation bears to the amount of taxable gift. For this purpose, the amount of gift is reduced by any portion of the $13,000 annual exclusion that is allowable with respect to the gift. Thus, Julie's basis is $23,000 + [$14,000 ($83,000 – 23,000) / ($83,000 – $13,000)] = $35,000.

5. (c) The requirement is to determine Ruth's recognized loss if she sells the stock received as a gift for $7,000. Since the stock's FMV ($8,000) was less than its basis ($10,000) at date of gift, Ruth's basis for computing a loss is the stock's FMV of $8,000 at date of gift. As a result, Ruth's recognized loss is $8,000 – $7,000 = $1,000.

6. (b) The requirement is to determine Ruth's holding period for stock received as a gift. If property is received as a gift, and the property's FMV on date of gift is used to determine a loss, the donee's holding period begins when the gift was received. Thus, Ruth's holding period starts in 2009.

7. (b) The requirement is to determine the basis of the Liba stock if it is sold for $5,000. If property acquired by gift is sold at a gain, its basis is the donor's basis ($4,000), increased by any gift tax paid attributable to the net appreciation in value of the gift ($0).

8. (b) The requirement is to determine the basis of the Liba stock if it is sold for $2,000. If property acquired by gift is sold at a loss, its basis is the lesser of (1) its gain basis ($4,000 above), or (2) its FMV at date of gift ($3,000).

9. (d) The requirement is to determine the amount of reportable gain or loss if the Liba stock is sold for $3,500. No gain or loss is recognized on the sale of property acquired by gift if the basis for loss ($3,000) results in a gain and the basis for gain ($4,000) results in a loss.

A.1.d. Acquired from Decedent

10. (b) The requirement is to determine the holding period for stock received as a bequest from the estate of a deceased uncle. Property received from a decedent is deemed to be held long-term regardless of the actual period of time that the decedent or beneficiary actually held the property and is treated as held for more than twelve months.

11. (c) The requirement is to determine Ida's basis for stock inherited from a decedent. The basis of property received from a decedent is generally the property's FMV at date of the decedent's death, or FMV on the alternate valuation date (six months after death). Since the executor of Zorn's estate elected to use the alternate valuation for estate tax purposes, the stock's basis to Ida is its $450,000 FMV six months after Zorn's death.

NOTE: If the stock had been distributed to Ida within six months of Zorn's death, the stock's basis would be its FMV on date of distribution.

12. (c) The requirement is to determine Lois' basis for gain or loss on the sale of Elin stock acquired from a decedent. Since the alternate valuation was elected for Prevor's estate, but the stock was distributed to Lois within six months of date of death, Lois' basis is the $9,000 FMV of the stock on date of distribution (5/1/09).

13. (d) The requirement is to determine how Lois should treat the shares of Elin stock. The stock should be treated as a capital asset held long-term since (1) property acquired from a decedent is considered to be held for more than twelve months regardless of its actual holding period, and (2) the stock is an investment asset in Lois' hands. The stock is not a Sec. 1231 asset because it was not held for use in Lois' trade or business.

A.1.e. Stock Received as a Dividend

14. (b) The requirement is to determine the basis for the common stock and the preferred stock after the receipt of a nontaxable preferred stock dividend. Joan's original common stock basis must be allocated between the common stock and the preferred stock according to their relative fair market value.

Common stock (FMV)	$450
Preferred stock (FMV)	150
Total value	$600

The ratio of the common stock to total value is $450/$600 or 3/4. This ratio multiplied by the original common stock basis of $300 results in a basis for the common stock of $225. The basis of the preferred stock would be ($150/$600 × $300) = $75.

15. (a) The requirement is to determine the holding period for preferred stock that was received in a nontaxable distribution on common stock. Since the tax basis of the preferred stock is determined in part by the basis of the common stock, the holding period of the preferred stock includes the holding period of the common stock (i.e., the holding period of the common stock tacks on to the preferred stock). Thus, the holding period of the preferred stock starts when the common stock was acquired, January 2010.

16. (c) The requirement is to determine the amount of long-term capital gain to be reported on the sale of fifty shares of stock received as a nontaxable stock dividend. After the stock dividend, the basis of each share would be determined as follows:

$$\frac{\$90,000}{450 + 50} = \$180 \text{ per share}$$

Since the holding period of the new shares includes the holding period of the old shares, the sale of the fifty new shares for $11,000 results in a LTCG of $2,000 [$11,000 – (50 shares × $180)].

A.4.a. Like-Kind Exchange

17. (c) The requirement is to determine Gow's recognized gain and basis for the investment real estate acquired in a like-kind exchange. In a like-kind exchange of property held for investment, a realized gain ($15,000 in this case) will be recognized only to the extent of unlike property (i.e., boot) received. Here the unlike property consists of the $2,000 cash and $3,000 FMV of the sailboat received, resulting in the recognition of $5,000 of gain. The basis of the acquired like-kind property reflects the deferred gain resulting from the like-kind exchange, and is equal to the basis of the property transferred ($25,000), increased by the amount of gain recognized ($5,000), and decreased by the amount of boot received ($2,000 +$3,000), or $25,000.

18. (d) The requirement is to determine which exchange qualifies for nonrecognition of gain or loss as a like-kind exchange. The exchange of business or investment property solely for like-kind business or investment property is treated as a nontaxable exchange. Like-kind means "the same class of property." Real property must be exchanged for real property, and personal property must be exchanged for personal property. Here, the exchange of rental real estate is an exchange of like-kind property, even though the real estate is located in different states. The like-kind exchange provisions do not apply to exchanges of stocks, bonds, notes, convertible securities, the exchange of partnership interests, and property held for personal use.

19. (d) The requirement is to determine the reportable gain resulting from the exchange of an apartment building for an office building. No gain or loss is recognized on the exchange of business or investment property for property of a like-kind. The term "like-kind" means the same class of property (i.e., real estate must be exchanged for real estate, personal property exchanged for personal property). Thus, the exchange of an apartment building for an office building qualifies as a like-kind exchange. Since no boot (money or unlike property) was received, the realized gain of $600,000 – $200,000 = $400,000 is not recognized.

20. (d) The requirement is to determine the amount of recognized gain resulting from a like-kind exchange of investment property. In a like-kind exchange, gain is recognized to the extent of the lesser of (1) "boot" received, or (2) gain realized.

FMV of property received	$ 250,000
Cash received	30,000
Mortgage assumed	70,000
Amount realized	$ 350,000
Basis of property exchanged	(160,000)
Gain realized	$ 190,000

Since the "boot" received includes both the cash and the assumption of the mortgage, gain is recognized to the extent of the $100,000 of "boot" received.

21. (b) The requirement is to determine the amount of gain recognized to Anderson on the like-kind exchange of apartment buildings. Anderson's realized gain is computed as follows:

FMV of building received		$550,000
Mortgage on old building		100,000
Cash received		25,000
Amount realized		$675,000
Less:		
Basis of old building	$375,000	
Mortgage on new building	125,000	500,000
Realized gain		$175,000

Since the boot received in the form of cash cannot be offset against boot given in the form of an assumption of a mortgage, the realized gain is recognized to the extent of the $25,000 cash received.

22. (c) The requirement is to determine the basis of a new truck acquired in a like-kind exchange. The basis of the new truck is the book value (i.e., adjusted basis) of the old truck of $4,000 plus the additional cash paid of $19,000 (i.e., the list price of the new truck of $25,000 less the trade-in allowance of $6,000).

A.4.b.   Involuntary Conversions

23.   (d)   The requirement is to determine the end of the replacement period for nonrecognition of gain following the condemnation of real property. For a condemnation of real property held for productive use in a trade or business or for investment, the replacement period ends three years after the close of the taxable year in which the gain is first realized. Since the gain was realized in 2010, the replacement period ends December 31, 2013.

A.4.c.   Sale or Exchange of Residence

24.   (c)   The requirement is to determine the amount of gain from the sale of the former residence that is recognized on Davis' 2010 return. An individual may exclude from income up to $250,000 of gain that is realized on the sale or exchange of a residence, if the individual owned and occupied the residence as a principal residence for an aggregate of at least two of the five years preceding the sale or exchange. Davis' former residence cost $65,000 and he had made improvements costing $5,000, resulting in a basis of $70,000. Since Davis sold his former residence for $380,000 and paid a realtor commission of $20,000, the net amount realized from the sale was $360,000. Thus, Davis realized a gain of $360,000 – $70,000 = $290,000. Since Davis qualifies to exclude $250,000 of the gain from income, the remaining $40,000 of gain is recognized and included in Davis' income for 2010.

25.   (a)   The requirement is to determine the amount of gain to be recognized on the Orans' 2010 joint return from the sale of their residence. An individual may exclude from income up to $250,000 of gain that is realized on the sale or exchange of a residence, if the individual owned and occupied the residence as a principal residence for an aggregate of at least two of the five years preceding the sale or exchange. The amount of excludable gain is increased to $500,000 for married individuals filing jointly if either spouse meets the ownership requirement, and both spouses meet the use requirement. Here, the Orans realized a gain of $760,000 – $170,000 = $590,000, and qualify to exclude $500,000 of the gain from income. The remaining $90,000 of gain is recognized and taxed to the Orans for 2010.

26.   (b)   The requirement is to determine the maximum exclusion of gain on the sale of Ryan's principal residence. An individual may exclude from income up to $250,000 of gain that is realized on the sale or exchange of a residence, if the individual owned and occupied the residence as a principal residence for an aggregate of at least two of the five years preceding the sale or exchange. Since Ryan meets the ownership and use requirements, and realized a gain of $400,000 – $180,000 = $220,000, all of Ryan's gain will be excluded from his gross income.

A.5.   Sales and Exchanges of Securities

27.   (b)   The requirement is to determine Miller's recognized loss and the basis for her remaining fifty shares of Maples Inc. stock. No loss can be deducted on the sale of stock if substantially identical stock is purchased within thirty days before or after the sale. Any loss that is not deductible because of this rule is added to the basis of the new stock. If the taxpayer acquires less than the number of shares sold, the amount of loss that cannot be recognized is determined by the ratio of the number of shares acquired to

the number of shares sold. Miller purchased 100 shares of Maples stock for $10,000 and sold the stock on January 8, 2010, for $7,000, resulting in a loss of $3,000. However, only half of the loss can be deducted by Miller because on December 24, 2009 (within thirty days before the January 8, 2010 sale), Miller purchased an additional 50 shares of Maples stock. Since only $1,500 of the loss can be recognized, the $1,500 of loss not recognized is added to the basis of Miller's remaining 50 shares resulting in a basis of $4,000 + $1,500 = $5,500.

28.   (a)   The requirement is to determine the amount of loss from the sale of Core stock that is deductible on Smith's 2009 and 2010 income tax returns. No loss can be deducted on the sale of stock if substantially identical stock is purchased within thirty days before or after the sale. Any loss that is not deductible because of this rule is added to the basis of the new stock. In this case, Smith purchased 100 shares of Core stock for $15,000 and sold the stock on January 3, 2010, for $13,000, resulting in a loss of $2,000. However, the loss cannot be deducted by Smith because on December 30, 2009 (within thirty days prior to the January 3, 2009 sale), Smith purchased an additional 100 shares of Core stock. Smith's disallowed loss of $2,000 is added to the $13,000 cost of the 100 Core shares acquired on December 30 resulting in a tax basis of $15,000 for those shares.

29.   (c)   The purchase of substantially identical stock within thirty days of the sale of stock at a loss is known as a wash sale. The $800 loss incurred in the wash sale ($5,000 basis less $4,200 amount realized) is disallowed. The basis of the replacement (substantially identical) stock is its cost ($3,600) plus the disallowed wash sale loss ($800). The holding period of the replacement stock includes the holding period of the wash sale stock. The amount realized ($6,000) less the basis ($4,400) results in a long-term gain of $1,600.

30.   (c)   Worthless securities generally receive capital loss treatment. However, if the loss is incurred by a corporation on its investment in an affiliated corporation (80% or more ownership), the loss is generally treated as an ordinary loss.

A.6.   Losses on Deposits in Insolvent Financial Institutions

31.   (d)   A loss resulting from a nonbusiness deposit in an insolvent financial institution is generally treated as a nonbusiness bad debt deductible as a short-term capital loss. However, subject to certain limitations, an individual may elect to treat the loss as a casualty loss or as a miscellaneous itemized deduction.

A.7.   Losses, Expenses, and Interest between Related Taxpayers

32.   (a)   The requirement is to determine the amount of the $10,000 loss that Conner can deduct from the sale of stock to his daughter, Alice. Losses are disallowed on sales or exchanges of property between related taxpayers, including members of a family. For this purpose, the term *family* includes an individual's spouse, brothers, sisters, ancestors, and lineal descendants (e.g., children, grandchildren, etc.). Since Conner sold the stock to his daughter, no loss can be deducted.

33.   (a)   The requirement is to determine the recognized gain or loss on Alice's sale of the stock that she had purchased from her father. Losses are disallowed on sales or exchanges of property between related taxpayers, including family members. Any gain later realized by the related transferee on the subsequent disposition of the property is not recognized to the extent of the transferor's disallowed loss. Here, her father's realized loss of $30,000 − $20,000 = $10,000 was disallowed because he sold the stock to his daughter, Alice. Her basis for the stock is her cost of $20,000. On the subsequent sale of the stock, Alice realizes a gain of $25,000 − $20,000 = $5,000. However, this realized gain of $5,000 is not recognized because of her father's disallowed loss of $10,000.

34. (b) The requirement is to determine the amount of gain from the sale of stock to a third party that Martin should report on his 2010 income tax return. Losses are disallowed on sales of property between related taxpayers, including family members. Any gain later realized by the transferee on the disposition of the property is not recognized to the extent of the transferor's disallowed loss. Here, Fay's realized loss of $15,000 − $11,000 = $4,000 is disallowed because she sold the stock to her son, Martin. Martin's basis for the stock is his cost of $11,000. On the subsequent sale of the stock to an unrelated third party, Martin realizes a gain of $16,000 − $11,000 = $5,000. However, this realized gain of $5,000 is recognized only to the extent that it exceeds Fay's $4,000 disallowed loss, or $1,000.

35. (c) The requirement is to determine among which of the related individuals are losses from sales and exchanges not recognized for tax purposes. No loss deduction is allowed on the sale or exchange of property between members of a family. For this purpose, an individual's *family* includes only brothers, sisters, half-brothers and half-sisters, spouse, ancestors (parents, grandparents, etc.) and lineal descendants (children, grandchildren, etc.) Since in-laws and uncles are excluded from this definition of a family, a loss resulting from a sale or exchange with an uncle or between in-laws would be recognized.

36. (a) Losses are disallowed on sales between related taxpayers, including family members. Thus, Daniel's loss of $3,000 is disallowed on the sale of stock to his son, William. William's basis for the stock is his $7,000 cost. Since William's stock basis is determined by his cost (not by reference to Daniel's cost), there is no "tack-on" of Daniel's holding period. Thus, a later sale of the stock for $6,000 on July 1 generates a $1,000 STCL for William.

37. (c) The requirement is to determine the amount of loss that Rego Corp. can deduct on a sale of its trailer to a 50% shareholder. Losses are disallowed on transactions between related taxpayers, including a corporation and a shareholder owning more than 50% of its stock. Since Al Eng owns only 50% (not more than 50%), the loss is recognized by Rego. Since the trailer was held for more than one year and used in Rego's business, the $2,000 loss is a Sec. 1231 loss. Answer (d) is incorrect because Sec. 1245 only applies to gains.

B. Capital Gains and Losses

38. (a) The requirement is to determine when gain or loss on a year-end sale of listed stock arises for a cash basis taxpayer. If stock or securities that are traded on an established securities market are sold, any resulting gain or loss is recognized on the trade date (i.e., the date on which the trade is executed) by both cash and accrual method taxpayers.

39. (b) The requirement is to determine the amount of an $8,000 net long-term capital loss that can be offset against Lee's taxable income of $100,000. An individual's net capital loss can be offset against ordinary income up to a maximum of $3,000 ($1,500 if married filing separately). Since a net capital loss offsets ordinary income dollar for dollar, Lee has a $3,000 net capital loss deduction for 2009 and a long-term capital loss carryover of $5,000 to 2010.

40. (d) The requirement is to determine the amount of excess of net long-term capital loss over net short-term capital gain that Sol Corp. can offset against ordinary income. A corporation's net capital loss cannot be offset against ordinary income. Instead, a net capital loss is generally carried back three years and forward five years as a STCL to offset capital gains in those years.

41. (d) The requirement is to determine the proper treatment for a $24,000 NLTCL for Nam Corp. A corporation's capital losses can only be used to offset capital gains. If a corporation has a net capital loss, the net capital loss cannot be currently deducted, but must be carried back three years and forward five years as a STCL to offset capital gains in those years. Since Nam had not realized any capital gains since it began operations, the $24,000 LTCL can only be carried forward for five years as a STCL.

42. (b) The requirement is to determine the holding period for determining long-term capital gains and losses. Long-term capital gains and losses result if capital assets are held more than twelve months.

43. (a) The requirement is to determine the treatment for the sale of the antique by Wald. Since the antique was held for personal use, the sale of the antique at a loss is not deductible.

44. (c) The requirement is to determine the capital loss carryover to 2010. The NSTCL and the NLTCL result in a net capital loss of $6,000. LTCLs are deductible dollar for dollar, the same as STCLs. Since an individual can deduct a net capital loss up to a maximum of $3,000, the net capital loss of $6,000 results in a capital loss deduction of $3,000 for 2009, and a long-term capital loss carryover to 2010 of $3,000.

B.1. Capital Assets

45. (c) The requirement is to determine the item that is included in the definition of capital assets. The definition of capital assets includes property held as an investment and would include a manufacturing company's investment in US Treasury bonds. In contrast, the definition specifically excludes accounts receivable arising from the sale of inventory, depreciable property used in a trade or business, and property held primarily for sale to customers in the ordinary course of a trade or business.

46. (b) The requirement is to determine the amount of Hall's capital assets. The definition of capital assets includes investment property and property held for personal use (e.g., personal residence and furnishings), but excludes property used in a trade or business (e.g., limousine).

47.   (b)   The requirement is to determine the proper treatment for the gain recognized on the sale of a painting that was purchased in 2003 and held for personal use. The definition of "capital assets" includes investment property and property held for personal use (if sold at a gain). Because the painting was held for more than one year, the gain from the sale of the painting must be reported as a long-term capital gain. Note that if personal-use property is sold at a loss, the loss is not deductible.

48.   (b)   The requirement is to determine the correct treatment for a capital loss incurred by a married couple filing a joint return for 2009. Capital losses first offset capital gains, and then are allowed as a deduction of up to $3,000 against ordinary income, with any unused capital loss carried forward indefinitely. Note that a married taxpayer filing separately can only offset up to $1,500 of net capital loss against ordinary income.

49.   (d)   The requirement is to determine the proper classification of land used as a parking lot and a shed erected on the lot for customer transactions. The definition of capital assets includes investment property and property held for personal use, but excludes any property used in a trade or business. The definition of Sec. 1231 assets generally includes business assets held more than one year. Since the land and shed were used in conjunction with a parking lot business, they are properly classified as Sec. 1231 assets.

50.   (a)   The requirement is to determine the classification of Ruth's diamond necklace. The diamond necklace is classified as a capital asset because the definition of "capital asset" includes investment property and *property held for personal use*. Answers (b), (c), and (d) are incorrect because Sec. 1231 generally includes only assets used in a trade or business, while Sections 1245 and 1250 only include depreciable assets.

51.   (b)   The requirement is to determine which asset is a capital asset. The definition of capital assets includes personal-use property, but excludes property used in a trade or business (e.g., delivery truck, land used as a parking lot). Treasury stock is not considered an asset, but instead is treated as a reduction of stockholders' equity.

52.   (a)   The requirement is to determine how a lump sum of $30,000 received in 2010, for an agreement not to operate a competing enterprise, should be treated. A covenant not to compete is not a capital asset. Thus, the $30,000 received as consideration for such an agreement must be reported as ordinary income in the year received.

53.   (b)   The requirement is to determine the amount of furniture classified as capital assets. The definition of capital assets includes investment property and property held for personal use (e.g., kitchen and living room pieces), but excludes property used in a trade or business (e.g., showcases and tables).

C.   Personal Casualty and Theft Gains and Losses

54.   (a)   The requirement is to determine the correct statement regarding the deductibility of an individual's losses on transactions entered into for personal purposes. An individual's losses on transactions entered into for personal purposes are deductible only if the losses qualify as casualty or theft losses. Answer (b) is incorrect because hobby losses are not deductible. Answers (c) and (d) are

incorrect because losses (other than by casualty or theft) on transactions entered into for personal purposes are not deductible.

D.   Gains and Losses on Business Property

55.   (d)   The requirement is to determine the characterization of Evon Corporation's $50,000 of net Sec. 1231 gain for its 2009 tax year. Although a net Sec. 1231 gain is generally treated as a long-term capital gain, it instead must be treated as ordinary income to the extent of the taxpayer's nonrecaptured net Sec. 1231 losses for its five preceding taxable years. Here, since the nonrecaptured net Sec. 1231 losses for 2007 and 2008 total $35,000, only $15,000 of the $50,000 net Sec. 1231 gain will be treated as a long-term capital gain.

56.   (a)   The requirement is to determine which item would not be characterized as Sec. 1231 property. Sec. 1231 property generally includes both depreciable and nondepreciable property used in a trade or business or held for the production of income if held for more than twelve months. Specifically excluded from Sec. 1231 is inventory and property held for sale to customers, as well as accounts and notes receivable arising in the ordinary course of a trade or business.

57.   (c)   The requirement is to determine the amount of ordinary income that must be recognized by Vermont Corporation from the distribution of the equipment to a shareholder. When a corporation distributes appreciated property, it must recognize gain just as if it had sold the property for its fair market value. As a result Vermont must recognize a gain of $9,000 – $2,000 = $7,000 on the distribution of the equipment. Since the distributed property is depreciable personal property, the gain is subject to Sec. 1245 recapture as ordinary income to the extent of the $6,000 of straight-line depreciation deducted by Vermont. The remaining $1,000 of gain would be treated as Sec. 1231 gain.

58.   (c)   The requirement is to determine the nature of a loss resulting from the sale of business machinery that had been held sixteen months. Property held for use in a trade or business is specifically excluded from the definition of capital assets, and if held for more than one year is considered Sec. 1231 property. Answer (b) is incorrect because Sec. 1245 only applies to gains.

59.   (c)   The requirement is to determine the amount of gain from the sale of property that must be recaptured as ordinary income. A gain from the disposition of seven-year tangible property is subject to recapture under Sec. 1245 which recaptures gain to the extent of all depreciation previously deducted. Here, Bates' gain from the sale of the property is determined as follows:

Selling price		$102,000
Cost	$100,000	
Depreciation	– 47,525	
Adjusted basis		– 52,475
Gain		$ 49,525

Under Sec. 1245, Bates Corp's gain is recaptured as ordinary income to the extent of the $47,525 deducted as depreciation. The remaining $2,000 of gain would be classified as Sec. 1231 gain.

60.   (b)   The requirement is to determine the proper treatment of the $50,000 gain on the sale of the building, which is Sec. 1250 property. Sec. 1250 recaptures gain as ordinary income to the extent of "excess" depreciation (i.e., depreciation deducted in excess of straight-line). The total gain less any depreciation recapture is Sec. 1231 gain. Since straight-line depreciation was used, there is no recapture under Sec. 1250. However, Sec. 291 requires that the amount of ordinary income on the disposition of Sec. 1250 property by corporations be increased by 20% of the additional amount that would have been ordinary income if the property had instead been Sec. 1245 property. If the building had been Sec. 1245 property the amount of recapture would have been $30,000 ($200,000 − $170,000). Thus, the Sec. 291 ordinary income is $30,000 × 20% = $6,000. The remaining $44,000 is Sec. 1231 gain.

61. **(b)** The requirement is to determine McEwing Corporation's taxable income given book income plus additional information regarding items that were included in book income. The loss on sale of the building ($7,000) and gain on sale of the land ($16,000) are Sec. 1231 gains and losses. The resulting Sec. 1231 net gain of $9,000 is then treated as LTCG and will be offset against the LTCL of $8,000 resulting from the sale of investments. Since these items have already been included in book income, McEwing's taxable income is the same as its book income, $120,000.

62. **(a)** The realized gain resulting from the involuntary conversion ($125,000 insurance proceeds − $86,000 adjusted basis = $39,000) is recognized only to the extent that the insurance proceeds are not reinvested in similar property ($125,000 − $110,000 = $15,000). Since the machinery was Sec. 1245 property, the recognized gain of $15,000 is recaptured as ordinary income to the extent of the $14,000 of depreciation previously deducted. The remaining $1,000 is Sec. 1231 gain.

SOLUTIONS TO SIMULATION PROBLEMS

Simulation Problem 1

Situation	Schedule D	Communication	Research

SCHEDULE D
(Form 1040)

Department of the Treasury
Internal Revenue Service (99)

Capital Gains and Losses

▶ Attach to Form 1040 or Form 1040NR.   ▶ See Instructions for Schedule D (Form 1040).
▶ Use Schedule D-1 to list additional transactions for lines 1 and 8.

OMB No. 1545-0074

2009

Attachment
Sequence No. **12**

Name(s) shown on return	Your social security number
Lou Tomsik	324-65-7037

Part I Short-Term Capital Gains and Losses—Assets Held One Year or Less

(a) Description of property (Example: 100 sh. XYZ Co.)	(b) Date acquired (Mo., day, yr.)	(c) Date sold (Mo., day, yr.)	(d) Sales price (see page D-7 of the instructions)	(e) Cost or other basis (see page D-7 of the instructions)	(f) Gain or (loss) Subtract (e) from (d)
1 200 shs King Corporation	2-24-09	11-15-09	5,000	4,000	1,000

2 Enter your short-term totals, if any, from Schedule D-1, line 2	**2**		
3 Total short-term sales price amounts. Add lines 1 and 2 in column (d)	**3**	5,000	

4 Short-term gain from Form 6252 and short-term gain or (loss) from Forms 4684, 6781, and 8824	**4**	
5 Net short-term gain or (loss) from partnerships, S corporations, estates, and trusts from Schedule(s) K-1	**5**	
6 Short-term capital loss carryover. Enter the amount, if any, from line 10 of your **Capital Loss Carryover Worksheet** on page D-7 of the instructions	**6**	(7,300)
7 Net short-term capital gain or (loss). Combine lines 1 through 6 in column (f)	**7**	6,300

Part II Long-Term Capital Gains and Losses—Assets Held More Than One Year

(a) Description of property (Example: 100 sh. XYZ Co.)	(b) Date acquired (Mo., day, yr.)	(c) Date sold (Mo., day, yr.)	(d) Sales price (see page D-7 of the instructions)	(e) Cost or other basis (see page D-7 of the instructions)	(f) Gain or (loss) Subtract (e) from (d)
8 100 shs Copperleaf Industries	3-1-08	10-20-09	4,200	2,500	1,700

9 Enter your long-term totals, if any, from Schedule D-1, line 9	**9**		
10 Total long-term sales price amounts. Add lines 8 and 9 in column (d)	**10**	4,200	

11 Gain from Form 4797, Part I; long-term gain from Forms 2439 and 6252; and long-term gain or (loss) from Forms 4684, 6781, and 8824	**11**	
12 Net long-term gain or (loss) from partnerships, S corporations, estates, and trusts from Schedule(s) K-1	**12**	
13 Capital gain distributions. See page D-2 of the instructions	**13**	1,500
14 Long-term capital loss carryover. Enter the amount, if any, from line 15 of your **Capital Loss Carryover Worksheet** on page D-7 of the instructions	**14**	( )
15 Net long-term capital gain or (loss). Combine lines 8 through 14 in column (f). Then go to Part III on the back	**15**	3,200

For Paperwork Reduction Act Notice, see Form 1040 or Form 1040NR instructions.   Cat. No. 11338H   Schedule D (Form 1040) 2009

Schedule D (Form 1040) 2009   Page **2**

Part III   Summary

16 Combine lines 7 and 15 and enter the result . . . . | **16** | 3,100

     If line 16 is:

       ● A **gain**, enter the amount from line 16 on Form 1040, line 13, or Form 1040NR, line 14. Then go to line 17 below.

       ● A **loss**, skip lines 17 through 20 below. Then go to line 21. Also be sure to complete line 22.

       ● **Zero**, skip lines 17 through 21 below and enter -0- on Form 1040, line 13, or Form 1040NR, line 14. Then go to line 22.

17 Are lines 15 and 16 **both** gains?

     ☐ **Yes.** Go to line 18.

     ☐ **No.** Skip lines 18 through 21, and go to line 22.

18 Enter the amount, if any, from line 7 of the **28% Rate Gain Worksheet** on page D-8 of the instructions . . . . ▶ | **18** |

19 Enter the amount, if any, from line 18 of the **Unrecaptured Section 1250 Gain Worksheet** on page D-9 of the instructions . . . . ▶ | **19** |

20 Are lines 18 and 19 **both** zero or blank?

     ☐ **Yes.** Complete Form 1040 through line 43, or Form 1040NR through line 40. Then complete the **Qualified Dividends and Capital Gain Tax Worksheet** on page 39 of the Instructions for Form 1040 (or in the Instructions for Form 1040NR). **Do not** complete lines 21 and 22 below.

     ☐ **No.** Complete Form 1040 through line 43, or Form 1040NR through line 40. Then complete the **Schedule D Tax Worksheet** on page D-10 of the instructions. **Do not** complete lines 21 and 22 below.

21 If line 16 is a loss, enter here and on Form 1040, line 13, or Form 1040NR, line 14, the **smaller** of:

       ● The loss on line 16 or

       ● ($3,000), or if married filing separately, ($1,500)   } . . . . | **21** | (3,000   )

     Note. When figuring which amount is smaller, treat both amounts as positive numbers.

22 Do you have qualified dividends on Form 1040, line 9b, or Form 1040NR, line 10b?

     ☐ **Yes.** Complete Form 1040 through line 43, or Form 1040NR through line 40. Then complete the **Qualified Dividends and Capital Gain Tax Worksheet** on page 39 of the Instructions for Form 1040 (or in the Instructions for Form 1040NR).

     ☑ **No.** Complete the rest of Form 1040 or Form 1040NR.

Schedule D (Form 1040) 2009

Situation	Schedule D	**Communication**	
			Research

Dear Mr. Tomsik:

     You have asked me to research the tax treatment of your anticipated capital loss carryforwards. Individuals may carry over a net capital loss to future tax years until the loss is used. A capital loss that is carried over to a later tax year retains its short-term or long-term character for the year to which it is carried. A short-term capital loss carryover first offsets short-term gain in the carryover year. If a net short-term capital loss results, this loss first offsets net long-term capital gain and then up to $3,000 of ordinary income. A long-term capital loss carryover first reduces long-term capital gain in the carryover year, then net short-term capital gain, and finally up to $3,000 of ordinary income.

     If you have any additional questions about this tax issue, please contact me.

Situation	Schedule D	Communication	**Research**

Internal Revenue Code Section 1221 provides a definition of capital assets.

MULTIPLE-CHOICE QUESTIONS (1-69)

1. At partnership inception, Black acquires a 50% interest in Decorators Partnership by contributing property with an adjusted basis of $250,000. Black recognizes a gain if

I. The fair market value of the contributed property exceeds its adjusted basis.

II. The property is encumbered by a mortgage with a balance of $100,000.

    a.   I only.
    b.   II only.
    c.   Both I and II.
    d.   Neither I nor II.

2. On June 1, 2010, Kelly received a 10% interest in Rock Co., a partnership, for services contributed to the partnership. Rock's net assets at that date had a basis of $70,000 and a fair market value of $100,000. In Kelly's 2010 income tax return, what amount must Kelly include as income from transfer of the partnership interest?

    a. $ 7,000 ordinary income.
    b. $ 7,000 capital gain.
    c. $10,000 ordinary income.
    d. $10,000 capital gain.

3. Ola Associates is a limited partnership engaged in real estate development. Hoff, a civil engineer, billed Ola $40,000 in 2010 for consulting services rendered. In full settlement of this invoice, Hoff accepted a $15,000 cash payment plus the following:

	Fair market value	Carrying amount on Ola's books
3% limited partnership interest in Ola	$10,000	N/A
Surveying equipment	7,000	$3,000

What amount should Hoff, a cash-basis taxpayer, report in his 2010 return as income for the services rendered to Ola?

    a. $15,000
    b. $28,000
    c. $32,000
    d. $40,000

4. The following information pertains to property contributed by Gray on July 1, 2010, for a 40% interest in the capital and profits of Kag & Gray, a partnership:

As of June 30, 2010

Adjusted basis	Fair market value
$24,000	$30,000

After Gray's contribution, Kag & Gray's capital totaled $150,000. What amount of gain was reportable in Gray's 2010 return on the contribution of property to the partnership?

    a. $0
    b. $ 6,000
    c. $30,000
    d. $36,000

5. The holding period of a partnership interest acquired in exchange for a contributed capital asset begins on the date

    a.   The partner is admitted to the partnership.
    b.   The partner transfers the asset to the partnership.
    c.   The partner's holding period of the capital asset began.
    d.   The partner is first credited with the proportionate share of partnership capital.

6. The following information pertains to Carr's admission to the Smith & Jones partnership on July 1, 2010:

> Carr's contribution of capital: 800 shares of Ed Corp. stock bought in 1997 for $30,000; fair market value $150,000 on July 1, 2010.
> Carr's interest in capital and profits of Smith & Jones: 25%.
> Fair market value of net assets of Smith & Jones on July 1, 2010, after Carr's admission: $600,000.

Carr's gain in 2010 on the exchange of the Ed Corp. stock for Carr's partnership interest was

    a. $120,000 ordinary income.
    b. $120,000 long-term capital gain.
    c. $120,000 Section 1231 gain.
    d. $0.

7. The holding period of property acquired by a partnership as a contribution to the contributing partner's capital account

    a.   Begins with the date of contribution to the partnership.
    b.   Includes the period during which the property was held by the contributing partner.
    c.   Is equal to the contributing partner's holding period prior to contribution to the partnership.
    d.   Depends on the character of the property transferred.

8. On September 1, 2010, James Elton received a 25% capital interest in Bredbo Associates, a partnership, in return for services rendered plus a contribution of assets with a basis to Elton of $25,000 and a fair market value of $40,000. The fair market value of Elton's 25% interest was $50,000. How much is Elton's basis for his interest in Bredbo?

    a. $25,000
    b. $35,000
    c. $40,000
    d. $50,000

9. Basic Partnership, a cash-basis calendar-year entity, began business on February 1, 2010. Basic incurred and paid the following during 2010:

Filing fees incident to the creation of the partnership	$ 3,600
Accounting fees to prepare the representations in offering materials	12,000

If Basic elects to deduct organizational costs, what is the maximum amount that Basic can deduct on the 2010 partnership return?

    a. $15,600
    b. $ 3,600
    c. $ 660
    d. $ 220

10. Thompson's basis in Starlight Partnership was $60,000 at the beginning of the year. Thompson materially participates in the partnership's business. Thompson received $20,000 in cash distributions during the year. Thompson's share of Starlight's current operations was a $65,000 ordinary loss and a $15,000 net long-term capital gain. What is the amount of Thompson's deductible loss for the period?

    a. $15,000
    b. $40,000
    c. $55,000
    d. $65,000

11. In computing the ordinary income of a partnership, a deduction is allowed for

- a. Contributions to recognized charities.
- b. The first $100 of dividends received from qualifying domestic corporations.
- c. Short-term capital losses.
- d. Guaranteed payments to partners.

12. Which of the following limitations will apply in determining a partner's deduction for that partner's share of partnership losses?

	At-risk	_Passive loss_
a.	Yes	No
b.	No	Yes
c.	Yes	Yes
d.	No	No

13. Dunn and Shaw are partners who share profits and losses equally. In the computation of the partnership's 2010 book income of $100,000, guaranteed payments to partners totaling $60,000 and charitable contributions totaling $1,000 were treated as expenses. What amount should be reported as ordinary income on the partnership's 2010 return?

- a. $100,000
- b. $101,000
- c. $160,000
- d. $161,000

14. The partnership of Martin & Clark sustained an ordinary loss of $84,000 in 2010. The partnership, as well as the two partners, are on a calendar-year basis. The partners share profits and losses equally. At December 31, 2010, Clark, who materially participates in the partnership's business, had an adjusted basis of $36,000 for his partnership interest, before consideration of the 2010 loss. On his individual income tax return for 2010, Clark should deduct a(n)

- a. Ordinary loss of $36,000.
- b. Ordinary loss of $42,000.
- c. Ordinary loss of $36,000 and a capital loss of $6,000.
- d. Capital loss of $42,000.

15. The partnership of Felix and Oscar had the following items of income during the taxable year ended December 31, 2010.

Income from operations	$156,000
Tax-exempt interest income	8,000
Dividends from foreign corporations	6,000
Net rental income	12,000

What is the total ordinary income of the partnership for 2010?

- a. $156,000
- b. $174,000
- c. $176,000
- d. $182,000

16. A guaranteed payment by a partnership to a partner for services rendered, may include an agreement to pay

I. A salary of $5,000 monthly without regard to partnership income.
II. A 25% interest in partnership profits.

- a. I only.
- b. II only.
- c. Both I and II.
- d. Neither I nor II.

17. Chris, a 25% partner in Vista partnership, received a $20,000 guaranteed payment in 2010 for deductible services rendered to the partnership. Guaranteed payments were not made to any other partner. Vista's 2010 partnership income consisted of

Net business income before guaranteed payments	$80,000
Net long-term capital gains	10,000

What amount of income should Chris report from Vista Partnership on her 2010 tax return?

- a. $37,500
- b. $27,500
- c. $22,500
- d. $20,000

18. On January 2, 2010, Arch and Bean contribute cash equally to form the JK Partnership. Arch and Bean share profits and losses in a ratio of 75% to 25%, respectively. For 2010, the partnership's ordinary income was $40,000. A distribution of $5,000 was made to Arch during 2010. What amount of ordinary income should Arch report from the JK Partnership for 2010?

- a. $ 5,000
- b. $10,000
- c. $20,000
- d. $30,000

19. Guaranteed payments made by a partnership to partners for services rendered to the partnership, that are deductible business expenses under the Internal Revenue Code, are

I. Deductible expenses on the US Partnership Return of Income, Form 1065, in order to arrive at partnership income (loss).
II. Included on Schedule K-1 to be taxed as ordinary income to the partners.

- a. I only.
- b. II only.
- c. Both I and II.
- d. Neither I nor II.

20. The method used to depreciate partnership property is an election made by

- a. The partnership and must be the same method used by the "principal partner."
- b. The partnership and may be any method approved by the IRS.
- c. The "principal partner."
- d. Each individual partner.

21. Under the Internal Revenue Code sections pertaining to partnerships, guaranteed payments are payments to partners for

- a. Payments of principal on secured notes honored at maturity.
- b. Timely payments of periodic interest on bona fide loans that are **not** treated as partners' capital.
- c. Services or the use of capital without regard to partnership income.
- d. Sales of partners' assets to the partnership at guaranteed amounts regardless of market values.

22. Dale's distributive share of income from the calendar-year partnership of Dale & Eck was $50,000 in 2009. On December 15, 2009, Dale, who is a cash-basis taxpayer, received a $27,000 distribution of the partnership's 2009 income, with the $23,000 balance paid to Dale in February

2010. In addition, Dale received a $10,000 interest-free loan from the partnership in 2009. This $10,000 is to be offset against Dale's share of 2010 partnership income. What total amount of partnership income is taxable to Dale in 2009?

a. $27,000
b. $37,000
c. $50,000
d. $60,000

23. At December 31, 2009, Alan and Baker were equal partners in a partnership with net assets having a tax basis and fair market value of $100,000. On January 1, 2010, Carr contributed securities with a fair market value of $50,000 (purchased in 2008 at a cost of $35,000) to become an equal partner in the new firm of Alan, Baker, and Carr. The securities were sold on December 15, 2010, for $47,000. How much of the partnership's capital gain from the sale of these securities should be allocated to Carr?

a. $0
b. $ 3,000
c. $ 6,000
d. $12,000

24. Gilroy, a calendar-year taxpayer, is a partner in the firm of Adams and Company which has a fiscal year ending June 30. The partnership agreement provides for Gilroy to receive 25% of the ordinary income of the partnership. Gilroy also receives a guaranteed payment of $1,000 monthly which is deductible by the partnership. The partnership reported ordinary income of $88,000 for the year ended June 30, 2009, and $132,000 for the year ended June 30, 2010. How much should Gilroy report on his 2009 return as total income from the partnership?

a. $25,000
b. $30,500
c. $34,000
d. $39,000

25. On December 31, 2009, Edward Baker gave his son, Allan, a gift of a 50% interest in a partnership in which capital is a material income-producing factor. For the year ended December 31, 2010, the partnership's ordinary income was $100,000. Edward and Allan were the only partners in 2010. There were no guaranteed payments to partners. Edward's services performed for the partnership were worth a reasonable compensation of $40,000 for 2010. Allan has never performed any services for the partnership. What is Allan's distributive share of partnership income for 2010?

a. $20,000
b. $30,000
c. $40,000
d. $50,000

Items 26 and 27 are based on the following:

Jones and Curry formed Major Partnership as equal partners by contributing the assets below.

	Asset	Adjusted basis	Fair market value
Jones	Cash	$45,000	$45,000
Curry	Land	30,000	57,000

The land was held by Curry as a capital asset, subject to a $12,000 mortgage, that was assumed by Major.

26. What was Curry's initial basis in the partnership interest?

a. $45,000
b. $30,000
c. $24,000
d. $18,000

27. What was Jones' initial basis in the partnership interest?

a. $51,000
b. $45,000
c. $39,000
d. $33,000

Items 28 and 29 are based on the following:

Flagg and Miles are each 50% partners in Decor Partnership. Each partner had a $200,000 tax basis in the partnership on January 1, 2010. Decor's 2010 net business income before guaranteed payments was $45,000. During 2010, Decor made a $7,500 guaranteed payment to Miles for deductible services rendered.

28. What total amount from Decor is includible in Flagg's 2010 tax return?

a. $15,000
b. $18,750
c. $22,500
d. $37,500

29. What is Miles's tax basis in Decor on December 31, 2010?

a. $211,250
b. $215,000
c. $218,750
d. $222,500

30. Peters has a one-third interest in the Spano Partnership. During 2010, Peters received a $16,000 guaranteed payment, which was deductible by the partnership, for services rendered to Spano. Spano reported a 2010 operating loss of $70,000 before the guaranteed payment. What is(are) the net effect(s) of the guaranteed payment?

I. The guaranteed payment decreases Peters' tax basis in Spano by $16,000.
II. The guaranteed payment increases Peters' ordinary income by $16,000.

a. I only.
b. II only.
c. Both I and II.
d. Neither I nor II.

31. Dean is a 25% partner in Target Partnership. Dean's tax basis in Target on January 1, 2010, was $20,000. At the end of 2010, Dean received a nonliquidating cash distribution of $8,000 from Target. Target's 2010 accounts recorded the following items:

Municipal bond interest income	$12,000
Ordinary income	40,000

What was Dean's tax basis in Target on December 31, 2010?

a. $15,000
b. $23,000
c. $25,000
d. $30,000

32. On January 4, 2010, Smith and White contributed $4,000 and $6,000 in cash, respectively, and formed the Macro General Partnership. The partnership agreement allocated profits and losses 40% to Smith and 60% to White. In 2010, Macro purchased property from an unrelated seller for $10,000 cash and a $40,000 mortgage note that was the general liability of the partnership. Macro's liability
   a.   Increases Smith's partnership basis by $16,000.
   b.   Increases Smith's partnership basis by $20,000.
   c.   Increases Smith's partnership basis by $24,000.
   d.   Has **no** effect on Smith's partnership basis.

33. Gray is a 50% partner in Fabco Partnership. Gray's tax basis in Fabco on January 1, 2010, was $5,000. Fabco made no distributions to the partners during 2010, and recorded the following:

Ordinary income	$20,000
Tax exempt income	8,000
Portfolio income	4,000

What is Gray's tax basis in Fabco on December 31, 2010?
   a. $21,000
   b. $16,000
   c. $12,000
   d. $10,000

34. On January 1, 2010, Kane was a 25% equal partner in Maze General Partnership, which had partnership liabilities of $300,000. On January 2, 2010, a new partner was admitted and Kane's interest was reduced to 20%. On April 1, 2010, Maze repaid a $100,000 general partnership loan. Ignoring any income, loss, or distributions for 2010, what was the **net** effect of the two transactions for Kane's tax basis in Maze partnership interest?
   a.   Has **no** effect.
   b.   Decrease of $35,000.
   c.   Increase of $15,000.
   d.   Decrease of $75,000.

35. Lee inherited a partnership interest from Dale. The adjusted basis of Dale's partnership interest was $50,000, and its fair market value on the date of Dale's death (the estate valuation date) was $70,000. What was Lee's original basis for the partnership interest?
   a. $70,000
   b. $50,000
   c. $20,000
   d. $0

36. Which of the following should be used in computing the basis of a partner's interest acquired from another partner?

	Cash paid by transferee to transferor	Transferee's share of partnership liabilities
a.	No	Yes
b.	Yes	No
c.	No	No
d.	Yes	Yes

37. Hall and Haig are equal partners in the firm of Arosa Associates. On January 1, 2010, each partner's adjusted basis in Arosa was $40,000. During 2010 Arosa borrowed $60,000, for which Hall and Haig are personally liable. Arosa sustained an operating loss of $10,000 for the year ended December 31, 2010. The basis of each partner's interest in Arosa at December 31, 2010, was
   a. $35,000
   b. $40,000

   c. $65,000
   d. $70,000

38. Doris and Lydia are sisters and also are equal partners in the capital and profits of Agee & Nolan. The following information pertains to 300 shares of Mast Corp. stock sold by Lydia to Agee & Nolan.

Year of purchase	2003
Year of sale	2010
Basis (cost)	$9,000
Sales price (equal to fair market value)	$4,000

The amount of long-term capital loss that Lydia recognized in 2010 on the sale of this stock was
   a. $5,000
   b. $3,000
   c. $2,500
   d. $0

39. In March 2010, Lou Cole bought 100 shares of a listed stock for $10,000. In May 2010, Cole sold this stock for its fair market value of $16,000 to the partnership of Rook, Cole & Clive. Cole owned a one-third interest in this partnership. In Cole's 2010 tax return, what amount should be reported as short-term capital gain as a result of this transaction?
   a. $6,000
   b. $4,000
   c. $2,000
   d. $0

40. Kay Shea owns a 55% interest in the capital and profits of Dexter Communications, a partnership. In 2010, Kay sold an oriental lamp to Dexter for $5,000. Kay bought this lamp in 2004 for her personal use at a cost of $1,000 and had used the lamp continuously in her home until the lamp was sold to Dexter. Dexter purchased the lamp as an investment. What is Kay's reportable gain in 2010 on the sale of the lamp to Dexter?
   a. $4,000 ordinary income.
   b. $4,000 long-term capital gain.
   c. $2,200 ordinary income.
   d. $1,800 long-term capital gain.

41. Gladys Peel owns a 50% interest in the capital and profits of the partnership of Peel and Poe. On July 1, 2010, Peel bought land the partnership had used in its business for its fair market value of $10,000. The partnership had acquired the land five years ago for $16,000. For the year ended December 31, 2010, the partnership's net income was $94,000 after recording the $6,000 loss on the sale of land. Peel's distributive share of ordinary income from the partnership for 2010 was
   a. $47,000
   b. $48,500
   c. $49,000
   d. $50,000

42. Under Section 444 of the Internal Revenue Code, certain partnerships can elect to use a tax year different from their required tax year. One of the conditions for eligibility to make a Section 444 election is that the partnership must
   a.   Be a limited partnership.
   b.   Be a member of a tiered structure.
   c.   Choose a tax year where the deferral period is **not** longer than three months.
   d.   Have less than seventy-five partners.

43. Which one of the following statements regarding a partnership's tax year is correct?

    a. A partnership formed on July 1 is required to adopt a tax year ending on June 30.

    b. A partnership may elect to have a tax year other than the generally required tax year if the deferral period for the tax year elected does **not** exceed three months.

    c. A "valid business purpose" can **no** longer be claimed as a reason for adoption of a tax year other than the generally required tax year.

    d. Within thirty days after a partnership has established a tax year, a form must be filed with the IRS as notification of the tax year adopted.

44. Without obtaining prior approval from the IRS, a newly formed partnership may adopt

    a. A taxable year which is the same as that used by one or more of its partners owning an aggregate interest of more than 50% in profits and capital.

    b. A calendar year, only if it comprises a twelve-month period.

    c. A January 31 year-end if it is a retail enterprise, and all of its principal partners are on a calendar year.

    d. Any taxable year that it deems advisable to select.

45. Irving Aster, Dennis Brill, and Robert Clark were partners who shared profits and losses equally. On February 28, 2010, Aster sold his interest to Phil Dexter. On March 31, 2010, Brill died, and his estate held his interest for the remainder of the year. The partnership continued to operate and for the fiscal year ending June 30, 2010, it had a profit of $45,000. Assuming that partnership income was earned on a pro rata monthly basis and that all partners were calendar-year taxpayers, the distributive shares to be included in 2010 gross income should be

    a. Aster $10,000, Brill $0, Estate of Brill $15,000, Clark $15,000, and Dexter $5,000.

    b. Aster $10,000, Brill $11,250, Estate of Brill $3,750, Clark $15,000, and Dexter $5,000.

    c. Aster $0, Brill $11,250, Estate of Brill $3,750, Clark $15,000, and Dexter $15,000.

    d. Aster $0, Brill $0, Estate of Brill $15,000, Clark $15,000, and Dexter $15,000.

46. On January 3, 2010, the partners' interests in the capital, profits, and losses of Able Partnership were

	% of capital profits and losses
Dean	25%
Poe	30%
Ritt	45%

On February 4, 2010, Poe sold her entire interest to an unrelated person. Dean sold his 25% interest in Able to another unrelated person on December 20, 2010. No other transactions took place in 2010. For tax purposes, which of the following statements is correct with respect to Able?

    a. Able terminated as of February 4, 2010.

    b. Able terminated as of December 20, 2010.

    c. Able terminated as of December 31, 2010.

    d. Able did **not** terminate.

47. Curry's sale of her partnership interest causes a partnership termination. The partnership's business and financial operations are continued by the other members. What is(are) the effect(s) of the termination?

  I. There is a deemed distribution of assets to the remaining partners and the purchaser.

  II. There is a hypothetical recontribution of assets to a new partnership.

    a. I only.

    b. II only.

    c. Both I and II.

    d. Neither I nor II.

48. Cobb, Danver, and Evans each owned a one-third interest in the capital and profits of their calendar-year partnership. On September 18, 2009, Cobb and Danver sold their partnership interests to Frank, and immediately withdrew from all participation in the partnership. On March 15, 2010, Cobb and Danver received full payment from Frank for the sale of their partnership interests. For tax purposes, the partnership

    a. Terminated on September 18, 2009.

    b. Terminated on December 31, 2009.

    c. Terminated on March 15, 2010.

    d. Did **not** terminate.

49. Partnership Abel, Benz, Clark & Day is in the real estate and insurance business. Abel owns a 40% interest in the capital and profits of the partnership, while Benz, Clark, and Day each owns a 20% interest. All use a calendar year. At November 1, 2010, the real estate and insurance business is separated, and two partnerships are formed: Partnership Abel & Benz takes over the real estate business, and Partnership Clark & Day takes over the insurance business. Which one of the following statements is correct for tax purposes?

    a. Partnership Abel & Benz is considered to be a continuation of Partnership Abel, Benz, Clark & Day.

    b. In forming Partnership Clark & Day, partners Clark and Day are subject to a penalty surtax if they contribute their entire distributions from Partnership Abel, Benz, Clark & Day.

    c. Before separating the two businesses into two distinct entities, the partners must obtain approval from the IRS.

    d. Before separating the two businesses into two distinct entities, Partnership Abel, Benz, Clark & Day must file a formal dissolution with the IRS on the prescribed form.

50. Under which of the following circumstances is a partnership that is not an electing large partnership considered terminated for income tax purposes?

  I. Fifty-five percent of the total interest in partnership capital and profits is sold within a twelve-month period.

  II. The partnership's business and financial operations are discontinued.

    a. I only.

    b. II only.

    c. Both I and II.

    d. Neither I nor II.

51. David Beck and Walter Crocker were equal partners in the calendar-year partnership of Beck & Crocker. On July 1, 2009, Beck died. Beck's estate became the successor in interest and continued to share in Beck & Crocker's profits until Beck's entire partnership interest was liquidated on April 30, 2010. At what date was the partnership considered terminated for tax purposes?

    a. April 30, 2010.
    b. December 31, 2010.
    c. July 31, 2009.
    d. July 1, 2009.

52. On December 31, 2010, after receipt of his share of partnership income, Clark sold his interest in a limited partnership for $30,000 cash and relief of all liabilities. On that date, the adjusted basis of Clark's partnership interest was $40,000, consisting of his capital account of $15,000 and his share of the partnership liabilities of $25,000. The partnership has no unrealized receivables or appreciated inventory. What is Clark's gain or loss on the sale of his partnership interest?

    a. Ordinary loss of $10,000.
    b. Ordinary gain of $15,000.
    c. Capital loss of $10,000.
    d. Capital gain of $15,000.

Items 53 and 54 are based on the following:

The personal service partnership of Allen, Baker & Carr had the following cash basis balance sheet at December 31, 2009:

Assets	Adjusted basis per books	Market value
Cash	$102,000	$102,000
Unrealized accounts receivable	--	420,000
Totals	$102,000	$522,000
Liability and Capital		
Note payable	$ 60,000	$ 60,000
Capital accounts:		
Allen	14,000	154,000
Baker	14,000	154,000
Carr	14,000	154,000
Totals	$102,000	$522,000

Carr, an equal partner, sold his partnership interest to Dole, an outsider, for $154,000 cash on January 1, 2010. In addition, Dole assumed Carr's share of the partnership's liability.

53. What was the total amount realized by Carr on the sale of his partnership interest?

    a. $174,000
    b. $154,000
    c. $140,000
    d. $134,000

54. What amount of ordinary income should Carr report in his 2010 income tax return on the sale of his partnership interest?

    a. $0
    b. $ 20,000
    c. $ 34,000
    d. $140,000

55. On April 1, 2010, George Hart, Jr. acquired a 25% interest in the Wilson, Hart and Company partnership by gift from his father. The partnership interest had been acquired by a $50,000 cash investment by Hart, Sr. on July 1, 2004. The tax basis of Hart, Sr.'s partnership interest was $60,000 at the time of the gift. Hart, Jr. sold the 25% partnership interest for $85,000 on December 17, 2010. What type and amount of capital gain should Hart, Jr. report on his 2010 tax return?

    a. A long-term capital gain of $25,000.
    b. A short-term capital gain of $25,000.
    c. A long-term capital gain of $35,000.
    d. A short-term capital gain of $35,000.

56. On June 30, 2010, James Roe sold his interest in the calendar-year partnership of Roe & Doe for $30,000. Roe's adjusted basis in Roe & Doe at June 30, 2010, was $7,500 before apportionment of any 2010 partnership income. Roe's distributive share of partnership income up to June 30, 2010, was $22,500. Roe acquired his interest in the partnership in 2004. How much long-term capital gain should Roe report in 2010 on the sale of his partnership interest?

    a. $0
    b. $15,000
    c. $22,500
    d. $30,000

57. Stone and Frazier decided to terminate the Woodwest Partnership as of December 31. On that date, Woodwest's balance sheet was as follows:

Cash	$2,000
Land (adjusted basis)	2,000
Capital—Stone	3,000
Capital—Frazier	1,000

The fair market value of the land was $3,000. Frazier's outside basis in the partnership was $1,200. Upon liquidation, Frazier received $1,500 in cash. What gain should Frazier recognize?

    a. $0
    b. $250
    c. $300
    d. $500

58. Curry's adjusted basis in Vantage Partnership was $5,000 at the time he received a nonliquidating distribution of land. The land had an adjusted basis of $6,000 and a fair market value of $9,000 to Vantage. What was the amount of Curry's basis in the land?

    a. $9,000
    b. $6,000
    c. $5,000
    d. $1,000

59. Hart's adjusted basis in Best Partnership was $9,000 at the time he received the following nonliquidating distribution of partnership property:

Cash	$ 5,000
Land	
Adjusted basis	7,000
Fair market value	10,000

What was the amount of Hart's basis in the land?

    a. $0
    b. $ 4,000
    c. $ 7,000
    d. $10,000

60. Day's adjusted basis in LMN Partnership interest is $50,000. During the year Day received a nonliquidating distribution of $25,000 cash plus land with an adjusted basis of $15,000 to LMN, and a fair market value of $20,000. How much is Day's basis in the land?

a. $10,000
b. $15,000
c. $20,000
d. $25,000

Items 61 and 62 are based on the following:

The adjusted basis of Jody's partnership interest was $50,000 immediately before Jody received a current distribution of $20,000 cash and property with an adjusted basis to the partnership of $40,000 and a fair market value of $35,000.

61. What amount of taxable gain must Jody report as a result of this distribution?
a. $0
b. $ 5,000
c. $10,000
d. $20,000

62. What is Jody's basis in the distributed property?
a. $0
b. $30,000
c. $35,000
d. $40,000

63. On June 30, 2009, Berk, a calendar-year taxpayer, retired from his partnership. At that time, his capital account was $50,000 and his share of the partnership's liabilities was $30,000. Berk's retirement payments consisted of being relieved of his share of the partnership liabilities and receipt of cash payments of $5,000 per month for eighteen months, commencing July 1, 2009. Assuming Berk makes no election with regard to the recognition of gain from the retirement payments, he should report income of

	2009	2010
a.	$13,333	$26,667
b.	20,000	20,000
c.	40,000	--
d.	--	40,000

64. The basis to a partner of property distributed "in kind" in complete liquidation of the partner's interest is the
a. Adjusted basis of the partner's interest increased by any cash distributed to the partner in the same transaction.
b. Adjusted basis of the partner's interest reduced by any cash distributed to the partner in the same transaction.
c. Adjusted basis of the property to the partnership.
d. Fair market value of the property.

Items 65 and 66 are based on the following data:

Mike Reed, a partner in Post Co., received the following distribution from Post:

	Post's basis	Fair market value
Cash	$11,000	$11,000
Inventory	5,000	12,500

Before this distribution, Reed's basis in Post was $25,000.

65. If this distribution were nonliquidating, Reed's basis for the inventory would be
a. $14,000
b. $12,500
c. $ 5,000
d. $ 1,500

66. If this distribution were in complete liquidation of Reed's interest in Post, Reed's recognized gain or loss resulting from the distribution would be
a. $7,500 gain.
b. $9,000 loss
c. $1,500 loss.
d. $0

67. In 2005, Lisa Bara acquired a one-third interest in Dee Associates, a partnership. In 2010, when Lisa's entire interest in the partnership was liquidated, Dee's assets consisted of the following: cash, $20,000 and tangible property with a basis of $46,000 and a fair market value of $40,000. Dee has no liabilities. Lisa's adjusted basis for her one-third interest was $22,000. Lisa received cash of $20,000 in liquidation of her entire interest. What was Lisa's recognized loss in 2010 on the liquidation of her interest in Dee?
a. $0.
b. $2,000 short-term capital loss.
c. $2,000 long-term capital loss.
d. $2,000 ordinary loss.

68. For tax purposes, a retiring partner who receives retirement payments ceases to be regarded as a partner
a. On the last day of the taxable year in which the partner retires.
b. On the last day of the particular month in which the partner retires.
c. The day on which the partner retires.
d. Only after the partner's entire interest in the partnership is liquidated.

69. John Albin is a retired partner of Brill & Crum, a personal service partnership. Albin has not rendered any services to Brill & Crum since his retirement in 2008. Under the provisions of Albin's retirement agreement, Brill & Crum is obligated to pay Albin 10% of the partnership's net income each year. In compliance with this agreement, Brill & Crum paid Albin $25,000 in 2010. How should Albin treat this $25,000?
a. Not taxable.
b. Ordinary income.
c. Short-term capital gain.
d. Long-term capital gain.

SIMULATION PROBLEM

Simulation Problem 1   (30 to 35 minutes)

Situation				
	Partner's Basis	Concepts	Research	Communication

During 2010, Adams, a general contractor, Brinks, an architect, and Carson, an interior decorator, formed the Dex Home Improvement General Partnership by contributing the assets below.

	Asset	Adjusted basis	Fair market value	% of partner share in capital, profits & losses
Adams	Cash	$40,000	$40,000	50%
Brinks	Land	$12,000	$21,000	20%
Carson	Inventory	$24,000	$24,000	30%

The land was a capital asset to Brinks, subject to a $5,000 mortgage, which was assumed by the partnership.

	Partner's Basis			
Situation		Concepts	Research	Communication

For items 1 and 2, determine and select the initial basis of the partner's interest in Dex.

                                                      (A) (B) (C)
                                                       ○   ○   ○
1. Brinks' initial basis in Dex is
   A. $21,000
   B. $12,000
   C. $ 8,000

                                                      (A) (B) (C)
                                                       ○   ○   ○
2. Carson's initial basis in Dex is
   A. $25,500
   B. $24,000
   C. $19,000

During 2010, the Dex Partnership breaks even but decides to make distributions to each partner.

		Concepts		
Situation	Partner's Basis		Research	Communication

For items 1 through 6, determine whether the statement is True or False.

		True	*False*
1.	A nonliquidating cash distribution may reduce the recipient partner's basis in his partnership interest below zero.	○	○
2.	A nonliquidating distribution of unappreciated inventory reduces the recipient partner's basis in his partnership interest.	○	○
3.	In a liquidating distribution of property other than money, where the partnership's basis of the distributed property exceeds the basis of the partner's interest, the partner's basis in the distributed property is limited to his predistribution basis in the partnership interest.	○	○
4.	Gain is recognized by the partner who receives a nonliquidating distribution of property, where the adjusted basis of the property exceeds his basis in the partnership interest before the distribution.	○	○
5.	In a nonliquidating distribution of inventory, where the partnership has no unrealized receivables or appreciated inventory, the basis of inventory that is distributed to a partner cannot exceed the inventory's adjusted basis to the partnership.	○	○
6.	The partnership's nonliquidating distribution of encumbered property to a partner who assumes the mortgage, does not affect the other partners' bases in their partnership interests.	○	○

			Research	
Situation	Partner's Basis	Concepts		Communication

The Dex Home Improvement General Partnership is planning to adopt a fiscal year ending September 30, while Brinks (a 20% partner) uses the calendar year as his taxable year. Research the Internal Revenue Code to determine how Brinks should determine the amount of income and other partnership items from the fiscal-year partnership that must be reported on Brinks' calendar-year tax return. Indicate the section and subsection from the IRC in the boxes below.

Section	Subsection
§ ☐	(☐)

				Communication
Situation	Partner's Basis	Concepts	Research	

Write a memorandum to Mr. Brinks describing the results of your research above.

REMINDER: Your response will be graded for both technical content and writing skills. Technical content will be evaluated for information that is helpful to the intended reader and clearly relevant to the issue. Writing skills will be evaluated for development, organization, and the appropriate expression of ideas in professional correspondence. Use a standard business memo or letter format with a clear beginning, middle, and end. Do not convey information in the form of a table, bullet point list, or other abbreviated presentation.

To: Mr. Brinks
From: CPA Candidate
Re: Partnership accounting

Simulation Problem 2   (40 to 45 minutes)

Topic—Partnership Taxation

Situation					
	Form 1065	Schedule K	Schedule K-1	Research	Communication

The Madison Restaurant (identification number 86-0806200) was formed as a cash method general partnership to operate the Madison Restaurant, which is located at 6001 Palm Trace Landing in Davie, Florida 33314. Bob Buran (social security number 347-54-1212) manages the restaurant and has a 60% capital and profits interest. His address is 1104 North 8th Court, Plantation, Florida 33324. Ray Hughes owns the remaining 40% partnership interest but is not active in the restaurant business. The partnership made cash distributions of $66,000 and $44,000 to Buran and Hughes respectively, on December 31, 2009, but made no other property distributions. Madison's income statement for the year, ended December 31, 2009, is presented below.

Sales		$980,000
Cost of sales		460,000
Gross profit		520,000
Operating expenses		
Salaries and wages (excluding partners)	$190,000	
Guaranteed payment to Bob Buran	70,000	
Repairs and maintenance	10,000	
Rent expense	24,000	
Amortization of permanent liquor license	2,000	
Annual liquor license fee	1,000	
Depreciation	49,000	
Advertising	20,000	
Charitable contributions (cash)	8,000	
Total expenses		$374,000
Operating profit		$146,000
Other income and losses		
Gain on sale of ABE stock held 13 months	$12,000	
Loss on sale of TED stock held 7 months	(7,000)	
Sec. 1231 gain on sale of land	8,500	
Interest from US Treasury bills	3,000	
Dividends from ABE stock	1,500	
Interest from City of Ft. Lauderdale general obligation bonds	1,000	
Net other income		19,000
Net income		$165,000

Additional information

- Madison Restaurant began business on July 14, 2001, and its applicable business code number is 722110. It files its tax return with the Ogden, Utah IRS Service Center. The partnership had recourse liabilities at the end of the year of $25,000, and total assets of $282,000.
- The guaranteed payment to Bob Buran was for services rendered and was determined without regard to partnership profits. Buran's capital account at the beginning of 2009 totaled $135,000.
- The permanent liquor license was purchased for $10,000 from a café that had gone out of business. This license, which is renewable for an indefinite period, is being amortized per books over the five-year term of Madison's lease.
- The cost of depreciable personal property used in the restaurant operations was $200,000. Madison elected to expense $24,000 of the cost for these Sec. 179 assets. The $49,000 depreciation includes the Sec. 179 expense deduction.
- The gain on the sale of land resulted from the sale of a parking lot that the restaurant no longer needed.

Situation	Form 1065	Schedule K	Schedule K-1	Research	Communication

Prepare Madison Restaurant's income and deductions on page 1 of Form 1065, Partnership Return.

Form **1065**	**U.S. Return of Partnership Income**	OMB No. 1545-0099
Department of the Treasury Internal Revenue Service	For calendar year 2009, or tax year beginning _____ , 2009, ending _____ , 20 ___ . ▶ See separate instructions.	20**09**

A Principal business activity	Use the IRS label. Other-wise, print or type.	Name of partnership	**D** Employer identification number
B Principal product or service		Number, street, and room or suite no. If a P.O. box, see the instructions.	**E** Date business started
C Business code number		City or town, state, and ZIP code	**F** Total assets (see the instructions) $

G Check applicable boxes: **(1)** ☐ Initial return   **(2)** ☐ Final return   **(3)** ☐ Name change   **(4)** ☐ Address change   **(5)** ☐ Amended return
     (6) ☐ Technical termination - also check (1) or (2)

H Check accounting method: **(1)** ☐ Cash   **(2)** ☐ Accrual   **(3)** ☐ Other (specify) ▶ _____

I Number of Schedules K-1. Attach one for each person who was a partner at any time during the tax year ▶ _____

J Check if Schedules C and M-3 are attached . . . . ☐

Caution. *Include **only** trade or business income and expenses on lines 1a through 22 below. See the instructions for more information.*

Income	**1a** Gross receipts or sales	**1a**		
	b Less returns and allowances	**1b**	**1c**	
	2 Cost of goods sold (Schedule A, line 8)		**2**	
	3 Gross profit. Subtract line 2 from line 1c		**3**	
	4 Ordinary income (loss) from other partnerships, estates, and trusts *(attach statement)* . .		**4**	
	5 Net farm profit (loss) *(attach Schedule F (Form 1040))*		**5**	
	6 Net gain (loss) from Form 4797, Part II, line 17 *(attach Form 4797)*		**6**	
	7 Other income (loss) *(attach statement)*		**7**	
	8 **Total income (loss).** Combine lines 3 through 7		**8**	
Deductions (see the instructions for limitations)	**9** Salaries and wages (other than to partners) (less employment credits)		**9**	
	10 Guaranteed payments to partners		**10**	
	11 Repairs and maintenance		**11**	
	12 Bad debts		**12**	
	13 Rent		**13**	
	14 Taxes and licenses		**14**	
	15 Interest		**15**	
	16a Depreciation *(if required, attach Form 4562)* . . .	**16a**		
	b Less depreciation reported on Schedule A and elsewhere on return	**16b**	**16c**	
	17 Depletion **(Do not deduct oil and gas depletion.)** . . .		**17**	
	18 Retirement plans, etc.		**18**	
	19 Employee benefit programs		**19**	
	20 Other deductions *(attach statement)*		**20**	
	21 **Total deductions.** Add the amounts shown in the far right column for lines 9 through 20 .		**21**	
	22 **Ordinary business income (loss).** Subtract line 21 from line 8		**22**	

Sign Here	Under penalties of perjury, I declare that I have examined this return, including accompanying schedules and statements, and to the best of my knowledge and belief, it is true, correct, and complete. Declaration of preparer (other than general partner or limited liability company member manager) is based on all information of which preparer has any knowledge.	May the IRS discuss this return with the preparer shown below (see instructions)? ☐ Yes ☐ No
	▶ _____ ▶ _____ Signature of general partner or limited liability company member manager Date	

Paid Preparer's Use Only	Preparer's signature	Date	Check if self- employed ▶ ☐	Preparer's SSN or PTIN
	Firm's name (or yours if self-employed), address, and ZIP code		EIN ▶ Phone no.	

For Privacy Act and Paperwork Reduction Act Notice, see separate instructions.   Cat. No. 11390Z   Form **1065** (2009)

| Situation | Form 1065 | Schedule K | Schedule K-1 | Research | Communication |

Prepare Madison Restaurant's Schedule K, Partners' Shares of Income, Credits, Deductions, etc.

Form 1065 (2009)   Page **4**

Schedule K		Partners' Distributive Share Items		Total amount
Income (Loss)	1	Ordinary business income (loss) (page 1, line 22)	1	
	2	Net rental real estate income (loss) (*attach Form 8825*)	2	
	3a	Other gross rental income (loss) 3a		
	b	Expenses from other rental activities (*attach statement*) . 3b		
	c	Other net rental income (loss). Subtract line 3b from line 3a	3c	
	4	Guaranteed payments	4	
	5	Interest income	5	
	6	Dividends: a Ordinary dividends	6a	
		b Qualified dividends 6b		
	7	Royalties	7	
	8	Net short-term capital gain (loss) (*attach Schedule D (Form 1065)*)	8	
	9a	Net long-term capital gain (loss) (*attach Schedule D (Form 1065)*)	9a	
	b	Collectibles (28%) gain (loss) 9b		
	c	Unrecaptured section 1250 gain (*attach statement*) . . 9c		
	10	Net section 1231 gain (loss) (*attach Form 4797*)	10	
	11	Other income (loss) (*see instructions*) Type ▶ _____	11	
Deductions	12	Section 179 deduction (*attach Form 4562*)	12	
	13a	Contributions	13a	
	b	Investment interest expense	13b	
	c	Section 59(e)(2) expenditures: **(1)** Type ▶ _____ **(2)** Amount ▶	13c(2)	
	d	Other deductions (*see instructions*) Type ▶ _____	13d	
Self-Employ-ment	14a	Net earnings (loss) from self-employment	14a	
	b	Gross farming or fishing income	14b	
	c	Gross nonfarm income	14c	
Credits	15a	Low-income housing credit (section 42(j)(5))	15a	
	b	Low-income housing credit (other)	15b	
	c	Qualified rehabilitation expenditures (rental real estate) (*attach Form 3468*)	15c	
	d	Other rental real estate credits (*see instructions*) Type ▶ _____	15d	
	e	Other rental credits (*see instructions*) Type ▶ _____	15e	
	f	Other credits (*see instructions*) Type ▶ _____	15f	
Foreign Transactions	16a	Name of country or U.S. possession ▶ _____		
	b	Gross income from all sources	16b	
	c	Gross income sourced at partner level	16c	
		Foreign gross income sourced at partnership level		
	d	Passive category ▶ _____ **e** General category ▶ _____ **f** Other ▶	16f	
		Deductions allocated and apportioned at partner level		
	g	Interest expense ▶ _____ **h** Other . . . . ▶	16h	
		Deductions allocated and apportioned at partnership level to foreign source income		
	i	Passive category ▶ _____ **j** General category ▶ _____ **k** Other ▶	16k	
	l	Total foreign taxes (check one): ▶ Paid ☐ Accrued ☐	16l	
	m	Reduction in taxes available for credit (*attach statement*)	16m	
	n	Other foreign tax information (*attach statement*)		
Alternative Minimum Tax (AMT) Items	17a	Post-1986 depreciation adjustment	17a	
	b	Adjusted gain or loss	17b	
	c	Depletion (other than oil and gas)	17c	
	d	Oil, gas, and geothermal properties—gross income	17d	
	e	Oil, gas, and geothermal properties—deductions	17e	
	f	Other AMT items (*attach statement*)	17f	
Other Information	18a	Tax-exempt interest income	18a	
	b	Other tax-exempt income	18b	
	c	Nondeductible expenses	18c	
	19a	Distributions of cash and marketable securities	19a	
	b	Distributions of other property	19b	
	20a	Investment income	20a	
	b	Investment expenses	20b	
	c	Other items and amounts (*attach statement*)		

Form **1065** (2009)

Situation	Form 1065	Schedule K	**Schedule K-1**	Research	Communication

Prepare Bob Buran's Schedule K-1, Partner's Share of Income, Credits, Deductions, etc. (Do **not** prepare a Schedule K-1 for Ray Hughes.)

651109

Schedule K-1
(Form 1065)

Department of the Treasury
Internal Revenue Service

2009

For calendar year 2009, or tax
year beginning _____, 2009
ending _____, 20 _____

Partner's Share of Income, Deductions, Credits, etc. ▶ See back of form and separate instructions.

☐ Final K-1   ☐ Amended K-1   OMB No. 1545-0099

Part III	**Partner's Share of Current Year Income, Deductions, Credits, and Other Items**

Part I	Information About the Partnership

A   Partnership's employer identification number

B   Partnership's name, address, city, state, and ZIP code

C   IRS Center where partnership filed return

D   ☐ Check if this is a publicly traded partnership (PTP)

Part II	Information About the Partner

E   Partner's identifying number

F   Partner's name, address, city, state, and ZIP code

G   ☐ General partner or LLC member-manager   ☐ Limited partner or other LLC member

H   ☐ Domestic partner   ☐ Foreign partner

I   What type of entity is this partner? _____

J   Partner's share of profit, loss, and capital (see instructions):

	Beginning	Ending
Profit	_____ %	_____ %
Loss	_____ %	_____ %
Capital	_____ %	_____ %

K   Partner's share of liabilities at year end:

Nonrecourse	. . . . . .	$ _____
Qualified nonrecourse financing	.	$ _____
Recourse	. . . . . .	$ _____

L   Partner's capital account analysis:

Beginning capital account	. . .	$ _____
Capital contributed during the year	.	$ _____
Current year increase (decrease)	.	$ _____
Withdrawals & distributions	. .	$ (_____)
Ending capital account	. . . .	$ _____

☐ Tax basis   ☐ GAAP   ☐ Section 704(b) book
☐ Other (explain)

M   Did the partner contribute property with a built-in gain or loss?
☐ Yes   ☐ No
If "Yes", attach statement (see instructions)

1	Ordinary business income (loss)	15	Credits
2	Net rental real estate income (loss)		
3	Other net rental income (loss)	16	Foreign transactions
4	Guaranteed payments		
5	Interest income		
6a	Ordinary dividends		
6b	Qualified dividends		
7	Royalties		
8	Net short-term capital gain (loss)		
9a	Net long-term capital gain (loss)	17	Alternative minimum tax (AMT) items
9b	Collectibles (28%) gain (loss)		
9c	Unrecaptured section 1250 gain		
10	Net section 1231 gain (loss)	18	Tax-exempt income and nondeductible expenses
11	Other income (loss)		
		19	Distributions
12	Section 179 deduction		
13	Other deductions		
		20	Other information
14	Self-employment earnings (loss)		

*See attached statement for additional information.

For IRS Use Only

For Paperwork Reduction Act Notice, see Instructions for Form 1065.   Cat. No. 11394R   Schedule K-1 (Form 1065) 2009

Situation	Form 1065	Schedule K	Schedule K-1	Research		Communication

In 2010, Madison is considering making a proportionate nonliquidating distribution of shares of stock that it owns in CDE Corporation to its partners. Research the Internal Revenue Code to determine the basis that the partners will have for the CDE stock that they receive. Indicate the section and subsection from the IRC in the boxes below.

Section	Subsection
§ [ ]	([ ])

Situation	Form 1065	Schedule K	Schedule K-1	Research	Communication

Buran and Hughes are concerned that the Madison Restaurant will have to recognize gain if it distributes shares of stock in CDE Corporation since the stock has appreciated in value. Write a memo to Buran and Hughes indicating whether the Madison Restaurant will have to recognize gain on the stock distribution to partners.

REMINDER: Your response will be graded for both technical content and writing skills. Technical content will be evaluated for information that is helpful to the intended reader and clearly relevant to the issue. Writing skills will be evaluated for development, organization, and the appropriate expression of ideas in professional correspondence. Use a standard business memo or letter format with a clear beginning, middle, and end. Do not convey information in the form of a table, bullet point list, or other abbreviated presentation.

To: Mr. Buran and Mr. Hughes
From: CPA Candidate

MULTIPLE-CHOICE ANSWERS

1. d	__ __	16. a	__ __	31. c	__ __	46. b	__ __	61. a	__ __
2. c	__ __	17. a	__ __	32. a	__ __	47. c	__ __	62. b	__ __
3. c	__ __	18. d	__ __	33. a	__ __	48. a	__ __	63. d	__ __
4. a	__ __	19. c	__ __	34. b	__ __	49. a	__ __	64. b	__ __
5. c	__ __	20. b	__ __	35. a	__ __	50. c	__ __	65. c	__ __
6. d	__ __	21. c	__ __	36. d	__ __	51. a	__ __	66. b	__ __
7. b	__ __	22. c	__ __	37. c	__ __	52. d	__ __	67. c	__ __
8. b	__ __	23. d	__ __	38. d	__ __	53. a	__ __	68. d	__ __
9. b	__ __	24. c	__ __	39. a	__ __	54. d	__ __	69. b	__ __
10. c	__ __	25. b	__ __	40. b	__ __	55. a	__ __		
11. d	__ __	26. c	__ __	41. d	__ __	56. a	__ __		
12. c	__ __	27. a	__ __	42. c	__ __	57. c	__ __		
13. b	__ __	28. b	__ __	43. b	__ __	58. c	__ __		
14. a	__ __	29. c	__ __	44. a	__ __	59. b	__ __	1st: __/69= __%
15. a	__ __	30. b	__ __	45. b	__ __	60. b	__ __	2nd: __/69= __%

MULTIPLE-CHOICE ANSWER EXPLANATIONS

B. Partnership Formation

1.   (d) The requirement is to determine which statements are correct regarding Black's recognition of gain on transferring property with an adjusted basis of $250,000 in exchange for a 50% partnership interest. Generally, no gain is recognized when appreciated property is transferred to a partnership in exchange for a partnership interest. However, gain will be recognized if the transferred property is encumbered by a mortgage, and the partnership's assumption of the mortgage results in a decrease in the transferor's individual liabilities that exceeds the basis of the property transferred. Here, the basis of the property transferred is $250,000, and the net decrease in Black's individual liabilities is $50,000 (i.e., $100,000 × 50%), so no gain is recognized.

2.   (c) The requirement is to determine the amount that must be included on Kelly's 2010 income tax return as the result of the receipt of a 10% partnership interest in exchange for services. A taxpayer must recognize ordinary income when a capital interest in a partnership is received as compensation for services rendered. The amount of ordinary income to be included on Kelly's 2010 return is the fair market value of the partnership interest received ($100,000 × 10% = $10,000).

3.   (c) The requirement is to determine the amount that Hoff, a cash-basis taxpayer, should report as income for the services rendered to Ola Associates. A cash-basis taxpayer generally reports income when received, unless constructively received at an earlier date. The amount of income to be reported is the amount of money, plus the fair market value of other property received. In this case, Hoff must report a total of $32,000, which includes the $15,000 cash, the $10,000 FV of the limited partnership interest, and the $7,000 FV of the surveying equipment received. Note that since Hoff is a cash-basis taxpayer, he would not report income at the time that he billed Ola $40,000, nor would he be entitled to a bad debt deduction when he accepts $32,000 of consideration in full settlement of his $40,000 invoice.

4.   (a) The requirement is to determine the amount of gain reportable in Gray's return as a result of Gray's contribution of property in exchange for a 40% partnership interest. Generally, no gain or loss is recognized on the contribution of property in exchange for a partnership interest. Note that this nonrecognition rule applies even though the

value of the partnership capital interest received (40% × $150,000 = $60,000) exceeds the fair market value of the property contributed ($30,000).

5.   (c) The requirement is to determine the correct statement regarding the holding period for a partnership interest acquired in exchange for a contributed capital asset. The holding period for a partnership interest that is acquired through a contribution of property depends upon the nature of the contributed property. If the contributed property was a capital asset or Sec. 1231 asset to the contributing partner, the holding period of the acquired partnership interest includes the period of time that the capital asset or Sec. 1231 asset was held by the partner. For all other contributed property, a partner's holding period for a partnership interest begins when the partnership interest is acquired.

6.   (d) The requirement is to determine the amount of gain recognized on the exchange of stock for a partnership interest. Generally no gain or loss is recognized on the transfer of property to a partnership in exchange for a partnership interest. Since Carr's gain is not recognized, there will be a carryover basis of $30,000 for the stock to the partnership, and Carr will have a $30,000 basis for the 25% partnership interest received.

7.   (b) The requirement is to determine the holding period for property acquired by a partnership as a contribution to the contributing partner's capital account. Generally no gain or loss is recognized on the contribution of property to a partnership in exchange for a capital interest. Since the partnership's basis for the contributed property is determined by reference to the contributing partner's former basis for the property (i.e., a transferred basis), the partnership's holding period includes the period during which the property was held by the contributing partner.

8.   (b) The requirement is to determine Elton's basis for his 25% interest in the Bredbo partnership. Since Elton received a capital interest with a FV of $50,000 in exchange for property worth $40,000 and services, Elton must recognize compensation income of $10,000 ($50,000 – $40,000) on the transfer of services for a capital interest. Thus, Elton's basis for his partnership interest consists of the $25,000 basis of assets transferred plus the $10,000 of income recognized on the transfer of services, a total of $35,000.

9. **(b)** The requirement is to determine the maximum amount of filing fees and accounting fees that Basic could deduct on the 2010 partnership return. The filing fees incident to the creation of the partnership are organizational expenditures. A partnership may deduct up to $5,000 of organizational expenditures for the tax year in which the partnership begins business, with any remaining expenditures deducted ratably over the 180-month period beginning with the month in which the partnership begins business. Here, since the organizational expenditures total only $3,600, they can be fully deducted for 2010.

The accounting fees to prepare the representations in offering materials are considered syndication fees. *Syndication fees* include the costs connected with the issuing and marketing of partnership interests such as commissions, professional fees, and printing costs. These costs must be capitalized and can neither be amortized nor depreciated.

C. Partnership Income and Loss

10. **(c)** The requirement is to determine the amount of loss that Thompson can deduct as a result of his interest in the Starlight Partnership. A partner's distributive share of partnership losses is generally deductible to the extent of the tax basis for the partner's partnership interest at the end of the year. All positive basis adjustments and all reductions for distributions must be taken into account before determining the amount of deductible loss. Here, Thompson's basis of $60,000 at the beginning of the year would be increased by the $15,000 of net long-term capital gain, reduced by the $20,000 cash distribution, to $55,000. As a result, Thompson's deduction of the ordinary loss for the current year is limited to $55,000 which reduces the basis for his partnership interest to zero. He cannot deduct the remaining $10,000 of ordinary loss currently, but will carry it forward and deduct it when he has sufficient basis for his partnership interest.

11. **(d)** The requirement is to determine the item that is deductible in the computation of the ordinary income of a partnership. Guaranteed payments to partners are always deductible in computing a partnership's ordinary income. Contributions to recognized charities and short-term capital losses cannot be deducted in computing a partnership's ordinary income because they are subject to special limitations and must be separately passed through so that any applicable limitations can be applied at the partner level. Similarly, dividends are an item of portfolio income and must be separately passed through to partners in order to retain its character as portfolio income when reported on partners' returns.

12. **(c)** The requirement is to determine whether the at-risk and passive activity loss limitations apply in determining a partner's deduction for that partner's share of partnership losses. A partner's distributive share of partnership losses is generally deductible by the partner to the extent of the partner's basis in the partnership at the end of the taxable year. Additionally, the deductibility of partnership losses is limited to the amount of the partner's at-risk basis, and will also be subject to the passive activity loss limitations if they are applicable. Note that the at-risk and passive activity loss limitations apply at the partner level, rather than at the partnership level.

13. **(b)** The requirement is to determine the amount to be reported as ordinary income on the partnership's return given partnership book income of $100,000. The $60,000 of guaranteed payments to partners were deducted in computing partnership book income and are also deductible in computing partnership ordinary income. However, the $1,000 charitable contribution deducted in arriving at partnership book income must be separately passed through to partners on Schedule K-1 and cannot be deducted in computing partnership ordinary income. Thus, the partnership's ordinary income is $100,000 + $1,000 = $101,000.

14. **(a)** The requirement is to determine the amount and type of partnership loss to be deducted on Clark's individual return. Since a partnership functions as a pass-through entity, the nature of a loss as an ordinary loss is maintained when passed through to partners. However, the amount of partnership loss that can be deducted by a partner is limited to a partner's tax basis in the partnership at the end of the partnership taxable year. Thus, Clark's distributive share of the ordinary loss ($42,000) is only deductible to the extent of $36,000. The remaining $6,000 of loss would be carried forward by Clark and could be deducted after his partnership basis has been increased.

15. **(a)** The requirement is to determine the ordinary income of the partnership. Income from operations is considered ordinary income. The net rental income and the dividends from foreign corporations are separately allocated to partners and must be excluded from the computation of the partnership's ordinary income. Tax-exempt income remains tax-exempt and must also be excluded from the computation of ordinary income. Thus, ordinary income only consists of the income from operations of $156,000.

D. Partnership Agreements

16. **(a)** The requirement is to determine the correct statement(s) concerning agreements for guaranteed payments. Guaranteed payments are payments made to a partner for services or for the use of capital if the payments are determined *without regard to the amount of partnership income*. Guaranteed payments are deductible by a partnership in computing its ordinary income or loss from trade or business activities, and must be reported as self-employment income by the partner receiving payment. A payment that represents a 25% interest in partnership profits could not be classified as a guaranteed payment because the payment is conditioned on the partnership having profits.

17. **(a)** The requirement is to determine the amount of income that Chris should report as a result of her 25% partnership interest. A partnership is a pass-through entity and its items of income and deduction pass through to be reported on partners' returns even though not distributed. The amount to be reported by Chris consists of her guaranteed payment, plus her 25% share of the partnership's business income and capital gains. Since Chris's $20,000 guaranteed payment is for deductible services rendered to the partnership, it must be subtracted from the partnership's net business income before guaranteed payments of $80,000 to determine the amount of net business income to be allocated among partners. Chris's reportable income from the partnership includes

Guaranteed payment	$20,000
Business income [($80,000 − $20,000) × 25%]	15,000
Net long-term capital gain ($10,000 × 25%)	2,500
	$37,500

18. (d) The requirement is to determine Arch's share of the JK Partnership's ordinary income for 2010. A partnership functions as a pass-through entity and its items of income and deduction are passed through to partners according to their profit and loss sharing ratios, which may differ from the ratios used to divide capital. Here, Arch's distributive share of the partnership's ordinary income is $40,000 × 75% = $30,000. Note that Arch will be taxed on his $30,000 distributive share of ordinary income even though only $5,000 was distributed to him.

19. (c) The requirement is to determine whether the statements regarding partners' guaranteed payments are correct. Guaranteed payments made by a partnership to partners for services rendered are an ordinary deduction in computing a partnership's ordinary income or loss from trade or business activities on page 1 of Form 1065. Partners must report the receipt of guaranteed payments as ordinary income (self-employment income) and that is why the payments also must be separately listed on Schedule K and Schedule K-1.

20. (b) The requirement is to determine the correct statement regarding a partnership's election of a depreciation method. The method used to depreciate partnership property is an election made by the partnership and may be any method approved by the IRS. The partnership is not restricted to using the same method as used by its "principal partner." Since the election is made at the partnership level, and not by each individual partner, partners are bound by whatever depreciation method that the partnership elects to use.

21. (c) The requirement is to determine the correct statement regarding guaranteed payments to partners. Guaranteed payments are payments made to partners for their services or for the use of capital without regard to the amount of the partnership's income. Guaranteed payments are deductible by the partnership in computing its ordinary income or loss from trade of business activities, and must be reported as self-employment income by the partners receiving payment.

22. (c) The requirement is to determine the total amount of partnership income that is taxable to Dale in 2009. A partnership functions as a pass-through entity and its items of income and deduction are passed through to partners on the last day of the partnership's taxable year. Income and deduction items pass through to be reported by partners even though not actually distributed during the year. Here, Dale is taxed on his $50,000 distributive share of partnership income for 2009, even though $23,000 was not received until 2010. The $10,000 interest-free loan does not effect the pass-through of income for 2009, and the $10,000 offset against Dale's distributive share of partnership income for 2010 will not effect the pass-through of that income in 2010.

23. (d) The requirement is to determine the amount of the partnership's capital gain from the sale of securities to be allocated to Carr. Normally, the entire amount of precontribution gain would be allocated to Carr. However, in this case the allocation to Carr is limited to the partnership's recognized gain resulting from the sale, $47,000 selling price – $35,000 basis = $12,000.

24. (c) The requirement is to determine the amount that Gilroy should report for 2009 as total income from the part-

nership. Gilroy's income will consist of his share of the partnership's ordinary income for the fiscal year ending June 30, 2009 (the partnership year that ends within his year), plus the twelve monthly guaranteed payments that he received for that period of time.

25% × $88,000	=	$22,000
12 × $ 1,000	=	12,000
Total income	=	$34,000

25. (b) The requirement is to determine Allan's distributive share of the partnership income. In a family partnership, services performed by family members must first be reasonably compensated before income is allocated according to the capital interests of the partners. Since Edward's services were worth $40,000, Allan's distributive share of partnership income is ($100,000 – $40,000) × 50% = $30,000.

26. (c) The requirement is to determine Curry's initial basis for the 50% partnership interest received in exchange for a contribution of property subject to a $12,000 mortgage that was assumed by the partnership. Generally, no gain or loss is recognized on the contribution of property in exchange for a partnership interest. As a result, Curry's initial basis for the partnership interest received consists of the $30,000 adjusted basis of the land contributed to the partnership, less the net reduction in Curry's individual liability resulting from the partnership's assumption of the $12,000 mortgage. Since Curry received a 50% partnership interest, the net reduction in Curry's individual liability is $12,000 × 50% = $6,000. As a result, Curry's basis for the partnership interest is $30,000 – $6,000 = $24,000.

27. (a) The requirement is to determine Jones' initial basis for the 50% partnership interest received in exchange for a contribution of cash of $45,000. Since partners are individually liable for their share of partnership liabilities, an increase in partnership liabilities increases a partner's basis in the partnership by the partner's share of the increase. Jones' initial basis consists of the $45,000 of cash contributed, increased by the increase in Jones' individual liability resulting from the partnership's assumption of Curry's mortgage ($12,000 × 50% = $6,000). Thus, Jones' initial basis for the partnership interest is $45,000 + $6,000 = $51,000.

28. (b) The requirement is to determine the total amount includible in Flagg's 2010 tax return as a result of Flagg's 50% interest in the Decor Partnership. Decor's net business income of $45,000 would be reduced by the guaranteed payment of $7,500, resulting in $37,500 of ordinary income that would pass through to be reported on partners' returns. Here, Flagg's share of the includible income would be $37,500 × 50% = $18,750.

29. (c) The requirement is to determine Miles's tax basis for his 50% interest in the Decor Partnership on December 31, 2010. The basis for a partner's partnership interest is increased by the partner's distributive share of partnership income that is taxed to the partner. Here, Decor's net business income of $45,000 would be reduced by the guaranteed payment of $7,500, resulting in $37,500 of ordinary income that would pass through to be reported on partners' returns and increase the basis of their partnership interests. Here, Miles's beginning tax basis for the partnership interest of $200,000 would be increased by Miles's distributive share of ordinary income ($37,500 × 50% = $18,750), to $218,750.

30. **(b)** The requirement is to determine the net effect(s) of the $16,000 guaranteed payment made to Peters by the Spano Partnership who reported an operating loss of $70,000 before deducting the guaranteed payment. A guaranteed payment is a partnership payment made to a partner for services or for the use of capital if the payment is determined without regard to the amount of partnership income. A guaranteed payment is deductible by a partnership in computing its ordinary income or loss from trade or business activities and must be reported as self-employment income by the partner receiving the payment, thereby increasing Peters' ordinary income by $16,000. However, since Peters has only a one-third interest in the Spano Partnership, the $16,000 of guaranteed payment deducted by Spano would have the effect of reducing Peters' tax basis in Spano by only one-third of $16,000.

E. Partner's Basis in Partnership

31. **(c)** The requirement is to determine the basis for Dean's 25% partnership interest at December 31, 2010. A partner's basis for a partnership interest is increased or decreased by the partner's distributive share of all partnership items. Basis is increased by the partner's distributive share of all income items (including tax-exempt income) and is decreased by all loss and deduction items (including nondeductible items) and distributions received from the partnership. In this case, Dean's beginning basis of $20,000 would be increased by the pass-through of his distributive share of the partnership's ordinary income ($40,000 × 25% = $10,000) and municipal bond interest income ($12,000 × 25% = $3,000), and would be decreased by the $8,000 cash nonliquidating distribution that he received.

32. **(a)** The requirement is to determine the effect of a $40,000 increase in partnership liabilities on the basis for Smith's 40% partnership interest. Since partners are individually liable for their share of partnership liabilities, a change in the amount of partnership liabilities affects a partner's basis for a partnership interest. When partnership liabilities increase, it is effectively treated as if each partner individually borrowed money and then made a capital contribution of the borrowed amount. As a result, an increase in partnership liabilities increases each partner's basis in the partnership by each partner's share of the increase. Here, Smith's basis is increased by his 40% share of the mortgage ($40% × $40,000 = $16,000).

33. **(a)** The requirement is to determine Gray's tax basis for a 50% interest in the Fabco Partnership. The basis for a partner's partnership interest is increased by the partner's distributive share of all partnership items of income and is decreased by the partner's distributive share of all loss and deduction items. Here, Gray's beginning basis of $5,000 would be increased by Gray's 50% distributive share of ordinary income ($10,000), tax-exempt income ($4,000), and portfolio income ($2,000), resulting in an ending basis of $21,000 for Gray's Fabco partnership interest.

34. **(b)** The requirement is to determine the net effect of the two transactions on Kane's tax basis for his Maze partnership interest. A partner's basis for a partnership interest consists of the partner's capital account plus the partner's share of partnership liabilities. A decrease in a partner's share of partnership liabilities is considered to be a deemed distribution of money and reduces a partner's basis for the partnership interest. Here, Kane's partnership interest was reduced from 25% to 20% on January 2, resulting in a reduction in Kane's share of liabilities of 5% × $300,000 = $15,000. Subsequently, on April 1, when there was a $100,000 repayment of partnership loans, there was a further reduction in Kane's share of partnership liabilities of 20% × $100,000 = $20,000. Thus, the net effect of the reduction of Kane's partnership interest to 20% from 25%, and the repayment of $100,000 of partnership liabilities would be to reduce Kane's basis for the partnership interest by $15,000 + $20,000 = $35,000.

35. **(a)** The requirement is to determine the original basis of Lee's partnership interest that was received as an inheritance from Dale. The basis of property received from a decedent is generally its fair market value as of date of death. Since fair market value on the date of Dale's death was used for estate tax purposes, Lee's original basis is $70,000.

36. **(d)** The requirement is to determine whether cash paid by a transferee, and the transferee's share of partnership liabilities are to be included in computing the basis of a partner's interest acquired from another partner. When an existing partner sells a partnership interest, the consideration received by the transferor partner, and the basis of the transferee's partnership interest includes both the cash actually paid by the transferee to the transferor, as well as the transferee's assumption of the transferor's share of partnership liabilities.

37. **(c)** The requirement is to determine the basis of each partner's interest in Arosa at December 31, 2010. Since there are two equal partners, each partner's adjusted basis in Arosa of $40,000 on January 1, 2010, would be increased by 50% of the $60,000 loan and would be decreased by 50% of the $10,000 operating loss. Thus, each partner's basis in Arosa at December 31, 2010, would be $40,000 + $30,000 liability – $5,000 loss = $65,000.

F. Transactions with Controlled Partnerships

38. **(d)** The requirement is to determine the amount of long-term capital loss recognized by Lydia from the sale of stock to Agee & Nolan. A loss is disallowed if incurred in a transaction between a partnership and a person owning (directly or constructively) more than a 50% capital or profits interest. Although Lydia directly owns only a 50% partnership interest, she constructively owns her sister's 50% partnership interest. Since Lydia directly and constructively has a 100% partnership interest, her $5,000 loss is disallowed.

39. **(a)** The requirement is to determine the amount to be reported as short-term capital gain on Cole's sale of stock to the partnership. If a person engages in a transaction with a partnership other than as a partner of such partnership, any resulting gain is generally recognized just as if the transaction had occurred with a nonpartner. Here, Cole's gain of $16,000 – $10,000 = $6,000 is fully recognized. Since the stock was not held for more than twelve months, Cole's $6,000 gain is treated as a short-term capital gain.

40. **(b)** The requirement is to determine the amount and nature of Kay's gain from the sale of the lamp to Admor. A gain that is recognized on a sale of property between a partnership and a person owning a more than 50% partnership interest will be treated as ordinary income if the property is not a capital asset in the hands of the transferee. Although Kay has a 55% partnership interest, the partnership purchased the lamp as an investment (i.e., a capital asset), and Kay's gain will solely depend on how she held the lamp. Since she used the lamp for personal use, Kay has a $5,000 – $1,000 = $4,000 long-term capital gain.

41. (d) The requirement is to determine Peel's distributive share of ordinary income from the partnership. Although the $6,000 loss that was deducted in arriving at the partnership's net income would also be deductible for tax purposes, it must be separately passed through to partners because it is a Sec. 1231 loss. Thus, the $6,000 loss must be added back to the $94,000 of partnership net income and results in partnership ordinary income of $100,000. Peel's share is $100,000 × 50% = $50,000.

G. Taxable Year of Partnership

42. (c) The requirement is to determine the correct statement regarding a partnership's eligibility to make a Sec. 444 election. A partnership must generally adopt the same taxable year as used by its one or more partners owning an aggregate interest of more than 50% in partnership profits and capital. However, under Sec. 444, a partnership can instead elect to adopt a fiscal year that does not result in a deferral period of longer than three months. The deferral period is the number of months between the end of its selected year and the year that it generally would be required to adopt. For example, a partnership that otherwise would be required to adopt a taxable year ending December 31, could elect to adopt a fiscal year ending September 30. The deferral period would be the months of October, November, and December. The partnership is not required to be a limited partnership, be a member of tiered structure, or have less than seventy-five partners.

43. (b) The requirement is to determine the correct statement regarding a partnership's tax year. A partnership must generally determine its taxable year in the following order: (1) it must adopt the taxable year used by its one or more partners owning an aggregate interest of more than 50% in profits and capital; (2) if partners owning a more than 50% interest in profits and capital do not have the same year-end, the partnership must adopt the same taxable year as used by all of its principal partners; and (3) if principal partners have different taxable years, the partnership must adopt the taxable year that results in the least aggregate deferral of income to partners.

A different taxable year other than the year determined above can be used by a partnership if a valid business purpose can be established and IRS permission is received. Alternatively, a partnership can elect to use a tax year (other than one required under the general rules in the first paragraph), if the election does not result in a deferral of income of more than three months. The deferral period is the number of months between the close of the elected tax year and the close of the year that would otherwise be required under the general rules. Thus, a partnership that would otherwise be required to adopt a tax year ending December 31 could elect to adopt a fiscal year ending September 30 (three-month deferral), October 31 (two-month deferral), or November 30 (one-month deferral). Note that a partnership that makes this election must make "required payments" which are in the nature of refundable, noninterest-bearing deposits that are intended to compensate the Treasury for the revenue lost as a result of the deferral period.

44. (a) A newly formed partnership must adopt the same taxab year as is used by its partners owning a more than 50% erest in profits and capital. If partners owning more than)% do not have the same taxable year, a partnership must opt the same taxable year as used by all of its principal p tners (i.e., partners with a 5% or more interest in capital d profits). If its principal partners have different taxable ye s, a partnership must adopt the tax year that results in th east aggregate deferral of income to partners.

45. (b) The requirement is to determine the distributive shares of rtnership income for the partnership fiscal year ended Ju 30, 2010, to be included in gross income by Aster, Brill, tate of Brill, Clark, and Dexter. Clark was a partner fo he entire year and is taxed on his distributive 1/3 share ($4 000 × 1/3 = $15,000). Since Aster sold his entire partnersh interest to Dexter, the partnership tax year closes with resp t to Aster on February 28. As a result, Aster's distributi share is $45,000 × 1/3 × 8/12 = $10,000. Dexter's dist butive share is $45,000 × 1/3 / 4/12 = $5,000.

Ad onally, a partnership tax year closes with respect to a dec ed partner as of date of death. Since Brill died on March 3 he distributive share to be included in Brill's 2010 Fo 1040 would be $45,000 × 1/3 × 9/12 = $11,250. Since B s estate held his partnership interest for the remainde the year, the estate's distributive share of income is $45,0 0 × 1/3 × 3/12 = $3,750.

I. Te ination or Continuation of Partnership

46. ( ) The requirement is to determine the correct statem regarding the termination of the Able Partnership. A part ship is terminated for tax purposes when there is a sale o change of 50% or more of the total interests in partne p capital and profits within any twelve-month period. ce Poe sold her 30% interest on February 4, 2010, and D sold his 25% partnership interest on December 20, 201 re has been a sale of 55% of the total interests with twelve-month period and the Able Partnership is term ed on December 20, 2010.

47.) The requirement is to determine which statements re correct concerning the termination of a partnership. partnership will terminate when there is a sale of 50 more of the total interests in partnership capital and pr within any twelve-month period. When this occurs, th s a deemed distribution of assets to the remaining p rs and the purchaser, and a hypothetical recontribution o se same assets to a new partnership.

. (a) The requirement is to determine the date on ch the partnership terminated for tax purposes. The nership was terminated on September 18, 2009, the date which Cobb and Danver sold their partnership interests to ank, since on that date there was a sale of 50% or more of e total interests in partnership capital and profit.

9. (a) The requirement is to determine the correct tatement concerning the division of Partnership Abel, Benz, Clark, & Day into two partnerships. Following the division of a partnership, a resulting partnership is deemed to be a continuation of the prior partnership if the resulting partnership's partners had a more than 50% interest in the prior partnership. Here, as a result of the division, Partnership Abel & Benz is considered to be a continuation of the prior partnership because its partners (Abel and Benz) owned more than 50% of the interests in the prior partnership (i.e., Abel 40% and Benz 20%).

50. (c) The requirement is to determine under which circumstances a partnership, other than an electing large partnership, is considered terminated for income tax purposes. A partnership will be terminated when (1) there are no longer at least two partners, (2) no part of any business, financial operation, or venture of the partnership continues to be carried on by any of its partners in a partnership, or (3) within a twelve-month period there is a sale or exchange of 50% or more of the total interest in partnership capital and profits.

51. (a) The requirement is to determine the date on which the partnership was terminated. A partnership generally does not terminate for tax purposes upon the death of a partner, since the deceased partner's estate or successor in interest continues to share in partnership profits and losses. However, the Beck and Crocker Partnership was terminated when Beck's entire partnership interest was liquidated on April 30, 2009, since there no longer were at least two partners and the business ceased to exist as a partnership.

J. Sale of a Partnership Interest

52. (d) The requirement is to determine the amount and character of gain or loss recognized on the sale of Clark's partnership interest. A partnership interest is a capital asset and a sale generally results in capital gain or loss, except that ordinary income must be reported to the extent of the selling partner's share of unrealized receivables and appreciated inventory. Here, Clark realized $55,000 from the sale of his partnership interest ($30,000 cash + relief from his $25,000 share of partnership liabilities). Since the partnership had no unrealized receivables or appreciated inventory and the basis of Clark's interest was $40,000, Clark realized a capital gain of $55,000 – $40,000 = $15,000 from the sale.

53. (a) The requirement is to determine the total amount realized by Carr on the sale of his partnership interest. The total amount realized consists of the amount of cash received plus the buyer's assumption of Carr's share of partnership liabilities. Thus, the total amount realized is $154,000 + ($60,000 × 1/3) = $174,000.

54. (d) The requirement is to determine the amount of ordinary income that Carr should report on the sale of his partnership interest. Although the sale of a partnership interest generally results in capital gain or loss, ordinary income must be recognized to the extent of the selling partner's share of unrealized receivables and appreciated inventory. Here, Carr must report ordinary income to the extent of his 1/3 share of the unrealized accounts receivable of $420,000, or $140,000.

55. (a) The requirement is to determine the amount and type of capital gain to be reported by Hart, Jr. from the sale of his partnership interest. Since the partnership interest was acquired by gift from Hart, Sr., Jr.'s basis would be the same as Sr.'s basis at date of gift, $60,000. Since Jr.'s basis is determined from Sr.'s basis, Jr.'s holding period includes the period the partnership interest was held by Sr. Thus, Hart, Jr. will report a LTCG of $85,000 – $60,000 = $25,000.

56. (a) The requirement is to determine the amount of LTCG to be reported by Roe on the sale of his partnership interest. Roe's basis for his partnership interest of $7,500 must first be increased by his $22,500 distributive share of partnership income, to $30,000. Since the selling price also

was $30,000, Roe will report no gain or loss on the sale of his partnership interest.

K. Pro Rata Distributions from Partnership

57. (c) The requirement is to determine Frazier's recognized gain resulting from the cash received in liquidation of his partnership interest. A distributee partner will recognize any realized gain or loss resulting from the complete liquidation of the partner's interest if only cash is received. Since Frazier's basis for his partnership interest was $1,200 and he received $1,500 cash, Frazier must recognize a $300 capital gain.

58. (c) The requirement is to determine the basis for land acquired in a nonliquidating partnership distribution. Generally, no gain or loss is recognized on the distribution of partnership property to a partner. As a result, the partner's basis for distributed property is generally the same as the partnership's former basis for the property (a transferred basis). However, since the distribution cannot reduce the basis for the partner's partnership interest below zero, the distributed property's basis to the partner is limited to the partner's basis for the partnership interest before the distribution. In this case, Curry's basis for the land will be limited to the $5,000 basis for his partnership interest before the distribution.

59. (b) The requirement is to determine Hart's basis for the land received in a nonliquidating partnership distribution. If both cash and noncash property are received in a single distribution, the basis for the partner's partnership interest is first reduced by the cash, before being reduced by noncash property. Although a partner's basis for noncash property is generally the same as the partnership's basis for the property ($7,000 in this case), the partner's basis for distributed property will be limited to the partner's basis for the partnership interest reduced by any cash received in the same distribution. Here, the $9,000 basis of Hart's partnership interest is first reduced by the $5,000 cash received, with the remaining basis of $4,000 allocated as basis for the land received.

60. (b) The requirement is to determine Day's basis in the land received in a nonliquidating distribution. If both cash and noncash property are received in a single distribution, the basis for the partner's partnership interest is first reduced by the cash, before the noncash property. Since partnership distributions are generally nontaxable, a distributee partner's basis for distributed property is generally the same as the partnership's former basis for the property (a transferred basis). Here, the basis of Day's partnership interest of $50,000 is first reduced by the $25,000 of cash received, and then reduced by the $15,000 adjusted basis of the land, to $10,000. Day's basis for the land received is $15,000.

61. (a) The requirement is to determine the amount of taxable gain that Jody must report as the result of a current distribution of cash and property from her partnership. No loss can be recognized as a result of a proportionate current (nonliquidating) distribution, and gain will be recognized only if the amount of cash received exceeds the basis for the partner's partnership interest. If both cash and noncash property are received in a single distribution, the basis for the partner's interest is first reduced by the cash, before noncash property. Since the $20,000 cash received does not exceed the $50,000 basis of Jody's partnership interest immediately before the distribution, no gain is recognized.

62. **(b)** The requirement is to determine the basis of property received in a current distribution. If both cash and noncash property are received in a single distribution, the basis for the partner's partnership interest is first reduced by the cash, before being reduced by noncash property. Although a partner's basis for distributed property is generally the same as the partnership's basis for the property ($40,000 in this case), the partner's basis for distributed property will be limited to the partner's basis for the partnership interest reduced by any money received in the same distribution. Here, the $50,000 basis of Jody's partnership interest is first reduced by the $20,000 of cash received, with the remaining basis of $30,000 allocated as the basis for the property received.

63. **(d)** The requirement is to determine the amount of income from the receipt of retirement payments to be reported by Berk in 2009 and 2010. Payments to a retiring partner are generally treated as received in exchange for the partner's interest in partnership property. As such, they are generally treated under the rules that apply to liquidating distributions. Retirement payments are not deductible by the partnership as guaranteed payments and are not treated as distributive shares of income. Under the rules for liquidating distributions, the $5,000 per month cash payments are treated as a reduction of the basis for Berk's partnership interest, and result in gain to the extent in excess of basis. Berk's $80,000 basis for his partnership interest ($50,000 capital + $30,000 share of liabilities) would first be reduced by the relief from $30,000 of liabilities to $50,000. Next, the $30,000 of cash payments received during 2009 (6 × $5,000) would reduce Berk's basis to $20,000 and result in no gain to be reported for 2009. Finally, the $60,000 of payments for 2010 (12 × $5,000) would exceed his remaining basis and result in Berk's reporting of $40,000 of capital gain for 2010.

64. **(b)** The requirement is to determine the correct statement regarding the basis of property to a partner that is distributed "in-kind" in complete liquidation of the partner's interest. In a complete liquidation of a partner's interest in a partnership, the in-kind property distributed will have a basis equal to the adjusted basis of the partner's partnership interest reduced by any money received in the same distribution. Generally, in a liquidating distribution, the basis for a partnership interest is (1) first reduced by the amount of money received, (2) then reduced by the partnership's basis for any unrealized receivables and inventory received, (3) with any remaining basis for the partnership interest allocated to other property received in proportion to their adjusted bases (not FV) to the partnership.

65. **(c)** The requirement is to determine the basis of the inventory received in a nonliquidating partnership distribution of cash and inventory. Here, the $25,000 basis of Reed's partnership interest would first be reduced by the $11,000 of cash received, and then reduced by the $5,000 basis of the inventory to $9,000. Reed's basis for the inventory received is $5,000.

66. **(b)** The requirement is to determine Reed's recognized gain or loss resulting from the cash and inventory received in complete liquidation of Reed's partnership interest.

A distributee partner can recognize loss only upon the complete liquidation of the partner's interest through the receipt of only money, unrealized receivables, or inventory. Since Reed received only money and inventory, the amount of recognized loss is the $9,000 difference between the $25,000 basis of his partnership interest and the $11,000 of cash and $5,000 basis for the inventory received.

67. **(c)** The requirement is to determine the amount of loss recognized by Lisa on the complete liquidation of her one-third partnership interest. A distributee partner can recognize loss only upon the complete liquidation of the partner's interest through receipt of only money, unrealized receivables, or inventory. Since Lisa only received cash, the amount of recognized loss is the $2,000 difference between the $22,000 adjusted basis of her partnership interest and the $20,000 of cash received. Since a partnership interest is a capital asset and Lisa acquired her one-third interest in 2005, Lisa has a $2,000 long-term capital loss.

68. **(d)** The requirement is to determine when a retiring partner who receives retirement payments ceases to be regarded as a partner. A retiring partner continues to be a partner for income tax purposes until the partner's entire interest has been completely liquidated through distributions or payments.

69. **(b)** The requirement is to determine the treatment for the payments received by Albin. Payments made by a personal service partnership to a retired partner that are determined by partnership income are distributive shares of partnership income, regardless of the period over which they are paid. Thus, they are taxable to Albin as ordinary income.

SOLUTIONS TO SIMULATION PROBLEMS

Simulation Problem 1

	Partner's Basis			
Situation		Concepts	Research	Communication

1. Brinks' initial basis in Dex is   (A) (B) (C)
   A. $21,000   ○   ○   ●
   B. $12,000
   C. $ 8,000

2. Carson's initial basis in Dex is   (A) (B) (C)
   A. $25,500   ●   ○   ○
   B. $24,000
   C. $19,000

Explanation of solutions

1. (C) The requirement is to determine Brinks' initial basis for his 20% partnership interest received in exchange for a contribution of property subject to a $5,000 mortgage. Generally, no gain or loss is recognized on the contribution of property in exchange for a partnership interest. As a result, Brinks' initial basis for the partnership interest received consists of the $12,000 basis of the land contributed to the partnership, less the net reduction in Brinks' individual liability resulting from the partnership's assumption of the mortgage. Since Brinks received a 20% partnership interest, the net reduction in Brinks' individual liability equals $5,000 × 80% = $4,000. As a result, Brinks' basis for the partnership interest is $12,000 – $4,000 = $8,000.

2. (A) The requirement is to determine Carson's initial basis for his 30% partnership interest received in exchange for a contribution of inventory. Since partners are individually liable for their share of partnership liabilities, an increase in partnership liabilities increases a partner's basis in the partnership by the partner's share of the increase. Carson's initial basis is the $24,000 adjusted basis of the inventory contributed, increased by the increase in his individual liability resulting from the partnership's assumption of Brinks' mortgage ($5,000 × 30% = $1,500). Thus, Carson's initial basis for the partnership interest is $24,000 + $1,500 = $25,500.

		Concepts		
Situation	Partner's Basis		Research	Communication

	True	False
1. A nonliquidating cash distribution may reduce the recipient partner's basis in his partnership interest below zero.	○	●
2. A nonliquidating distribution of unappreciated inventory reduces the recipient partner's basis in his partnership interest.	●	○
3. In a liquidating distribution of property other than money, where the partnership's basis of the distributed property exceeds the basis of the partner's interest, the partner's basis in the distributed property is limited to his predistribution basis in the partnership interest.	●	○
4. Gain is recognized by the partner who receives a nonliquidating distribution of property, where the adjusted basis of the property exceeds his basis in the partnership interest before the distribution.	○	●
5. In a nonliquidating distribution of inventory, where the partnership has no unrealized receivables or appreciated inventory, the basis of inventory that is distributed to a partner cannot exceed the inventory's adjusted basis to the partnership.	●	○
6. The partnership's nonliquidating distribution of encumbered property to a partner who assumes the mortgage, does not affect the other partners' bases in their partnership interests.	○	●

Explanation of solutions

1. (F) A partner can never have a negative basis for a partnership interest. Partnership distributions can only reduce a partner's basis to zero.

2. (T) Partnership distributions are generally nontaxable and reduce the recipient partner's basis by the adjusted basis of the property distributed.

3. (T) A liquidating distribution of property other than money generally does not cause the distributee partner to recognize gain. As a result, the distributee partner's basis in the distributed property is limited to the partner's predistribution basis for the partnership interest.

4. (F) Gain is recognized by a distributee partner only if the amount of money distributed exceeds the partner's predistribution basis for the partnership interest. Distributions of property other than money never result in the recognition of gain by the distributee partner.

5. (T) Generally, a nonliquidating distribution of inventory is not taxable, and the adjusted basis for the inventory carries over to the distributee partner. As a result, the distributee partner's basis for the inventory cannot exceed the inventory's adjusted basis to the partnership.

6. (F) Since partners are individually liable for partnership liabilities, a decrease in partnership liabilities will decrease the basis for a partner's partnership interest by the partner's share of the decrease. Thus, if a distributee partner assumes a mortgage on encumbered property, the other partners' bases in their partnership interests will be decreased by their share of the decrease in partnership liabilities.

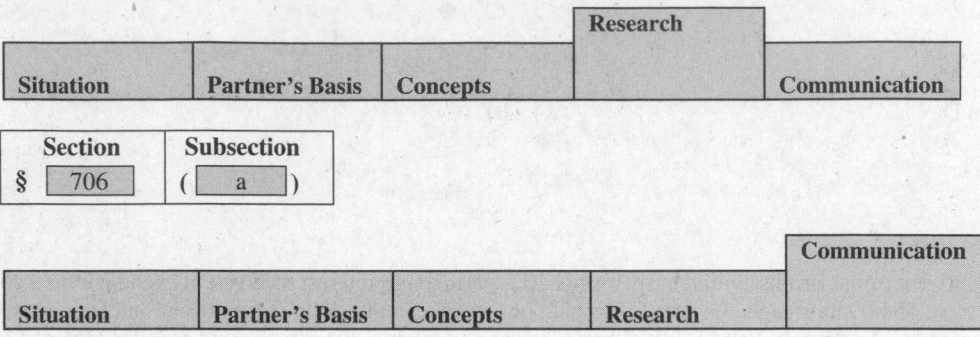

To: Mr. Brinks
From: CPA Candidate
Re: Partnership accounting

    I have researched the issue of reporting of income and other partnership items from the Dex fiscal-year partnership on your calendar-year tax return. Code Sec. 706(a) provides that in computing the taxable income of a partner for a taxable year, the partnership items of income, gain, loss, deduction, or credit that should be included should be based on the taxable year of the partnership that ends with or within the taxable year of the partner. Therefore, your calendar year 2010 tax return ending December 31 should reflect only your distributive share of partnership items for the Dex Partnership fiscal year ended September 30, 2010.

    Please contact me if you should have any additional questions.

Simulation Problem 2

Situation	Form 1065	Schedule K	Schedule K-1	Research	Communication

    A partnership is a pass-through entity acting as a conduit to pass through items of income, deduction, and credit to be reported on the tax returns of its partners. Partnership items having special tax characteristics (e.g., passive activity losses, deductions subject to dollar or percentage limitations, etc.) must be separately listed and shown on Schedules K and K-1 so that their special characteristics are preserved when reported on partners' tax returns. In contrast, partnership ordinary income and deduction items having no special tax characteristics can be netted together in the computation of a partnership's ordinary income and deductions from trade or business activities on page 1 of Form 1065.

    The solutions approach is to determine whether each item listed in the problem should be included in the computation of Madison's ordinary income and deductions on page 1 of Form 1065, or should be separately shown on Madison's Schedule K and Bob Buran's Schedule K-1 to retain any special tax characteristics that the item may have.

    Schedule K is a summary schedule, listing the total of all partners' shares of income, deductions, and credits, including the net amount of a partnership's ordinary income (loss) from trade or business activities that is computed on page 1 of Form 1065. A Schedule K-1 is prepared for each partner listing only that particular partner's share of partnership income, deductions, credits, etc. Since Bob Buran has a 60% partnership interest, Buran's Schedule K-1 will generally reflect a 60% share of the amounts reported on Madison's Schedule K.

Specific Items

- Guaranteed payments made to a partner for services or for the use of capital are determined without regard to the income of the partnership. The $70,000 of guaranteed payments made to Bob Buran are deductible by the partnership in computing its ordinary income on page 1 of Form 1065, and must also be separately reported on line 4 of Schedules K and K-1 since the receipt of the guaranteed payments by Buran must be reported as ordinary income.
- No amortization of the permanent liquor license is allowed for tax purposes because the license is renewable for an indefinite period.
- The cost of qualifying property did not exceed $800,000 for 2009, so the Sec. 179 expense deduction of $24,000 is available on Madison's return. Since the Sec. 179 expense deduction is subject to a dollar limitation at both the partnership and partner levels, the Sec. 179 expense deduction must be separately reported on Schedules K and K-1. Since the depreciation deducted in the income statement includes the $24,000 of expense deduction, the income statement deprecia-

tion of $49,000 must be reduced by $24,000, which results in the $25,000 of depreciation that is deductible in computing Madison's ordinary income. The $24,000 Sec. 179 expense deduction must be separately shown on line 12 of Madison's Schedule K. $24,000 × 60% = $14,400 of Sec. 179 expense deduction reported on Bob Buran's Schedule K-1.

- The $8,000 of charitable contributions are not deductible in computing the partnership's ordinary income. Instead, charitable contributions are separately reported on line 13a of Madison's Schedule K and each partner's Schedule K-1 so the appropriate percentage limitation can be applied on partners' returns.

- The $12,000 of long-term capital gain, $7,000 of short-term capital loss, $3,000 of interest income from Treasury bills, and $1,500 of dividends are items of portfolio income and must be separately reported on Madison's Schedule K, with 60% of each item reported on Buran's Schedule K-1. Similarly, the $8,500 of Sec. 1231 gain must be separately reported on Madison's Schedule K and partners' Schedules K-1 so that the Sec. 1231 netting process can take place at the partner level.

- The $1,000 of interest from City of Ft. Lauderdale bonds is tax-exempt and is reported on line 18a of Schedules K and K-1, while the $110,000 of cash distributions to partners is reported on line 19a of Schedules K and K-1.

- Partners are not employees but instead are treated as self-employed individuals. A partner's share of a partnership's ordinary income plus any guaranteed payments received by the partner must be reported as self-employment income and is subject to self-employment tax. On Schedule K, the ordinary income from trade or business activities of $180,000 (line 1) is added to the $70,000 of guaranteed payments (line 5), with the total of $250,000 reported on lines 14a and 14c as net earnings from self-employment. On Schedule K-1, Buran's 60% share of the ordinary income ($180,000 × 60% = $108,000) is added to the $70,000 of guaranteed payments received by Buran with the total of $178,000 reported as Buran's net earnings from self-employment in box 14.

Form 1065				
Situation		**Schedule K**	**Schedule K-1**	**Research**	**Communication**

Form 1065
Department of the Treasury
Internal Revenue Service

U.S. Return of Partnership Income

For calendar year 2009, or tax year beginning _____, 2009, ending _____, 20_____

► See separate instructions.

OMB No. 1545-0099

2009

A Principal business activity		Name of partnership	D Employer identification number
Food Service	Use the IRS label. Other- wise, print or type.	**Madison Restaurant**	86-0806200
B Principal product or service		Number, street, and room or suite no. If a P.O. box, see the instructions.	E Date business started
Food & Drinks		**6001 Palm Trace Landing**	**7-14-01**
C Business code number		City or town, state, and ZIP code	F Total assets (see the instructions)
722110		**Davie, FL 33314**	$ 282,000

G Check applicable boxes: **(1)** ☐ Initial return   **(2)** ☐ Final return   **(3)** ☐ Name change   **(4)** ☐ Address change   **(5)** ☐ Amended return
      (6) ☐ Technical termination - also check (1) or (2)

H Check accounting method: **(1)** ☑ Cash   **(2)** ☐ Accrual   **(3)** ☐ Other (specify) ► _____

I   Number of Schedules K-1. Attach one for each person who was a partner at any time during the tax year ► **2** _____

J   Check if Schedules C and M-3 are attached . . . . ☐

Caution. *Include only trade or business income and expenses on lines 1a through 22 below. See the instructions for more information.*

Income	**1a**	Gross receipts or sales	**1a**	980,000	
	b	Less returns and allowances	**1b**		**1c**	980,000
	2	Cost of goods sold (Schedule A, line 8)	**2**	460,000
	3	Gross profit. Subtract line 2 from line 1c	**3**	520,000
	4	Ordinary income (loss) from other partnerships, estates, and trusts *(attach statement)* . .	**4**	
	5	Net farm profit (loss) *(attach Schedule F (Form 1040))*	**5**	
	6	Net gain (loss) from Form 4797, Part II, line 17 *(attach Form 4797)*	**6**	
	7	Other income (loss) *(attach statement)*	**7**	
	8	**Total income (loss).** Combine lines 3 through 7	**8**	520,000

Deductions *(see the instructions for limitations)*	**9**	Salaries and wages (other than to partners) (less employment credits) . . .	**9**	190,000
	10	Guaranteed payments to partners	**10**	70,000
	11	Repairs and maintenance	**11**	10,000
	12	Bad debts	**12**	
	13	Rent	**13**	24,000
	14	Taxes and licenses	**14**	1,000
	15	Interest	**15**	
	16a	Depreciation *(if required, attach Form 4562)*	**16a**	25,000	
	b	Less depreciation reported on Schedule A and elsewhere on return	**16b**		**16c**	25,000
	17	Depletion **(Do not deduct oil and gas depletion.)**	**17**	
	18	Retirement plans, etc.	**18**	
	19	Employee benefit programs	**19**	
	20	Other deductions *(attach statement)*	**20**	20,000
	21	**Total deductions.** Add the amounts shown in the far right column for lines 9 through 20 .	**21**	340,000
	22	**Ordinary business income (loss).** Subtract line 21 from line 8	**22**	180,000

Sign Here

Under penalties of perjury, I declare that I have examined this return, including accompanying schedules and statements, and to the best of my knowledge and belief, it is true, correct, and complete. Declaration of preparer (other than general partner or limited liability company member manager) is based on all information of which preparer has any knowledge.

May the IRS discuss this return with the preparer shown below (see instructions)? ☐ Yes ☐ No

► _____   ► _____
Signature of general partner or limited liability company member manager   Date

Paid Preparer's Use Only	Preparer's signature		Date	Check if self-employed ► ☐	Preparer's SSN or PTIN
	Firm's name (or yours if self-employed), address, and ZIP code			EIN ►	
				Phone no.	

For Privacy Act and Paperwork Reduction Act Notice, see separate instructions.   Cat. No. 11390Z   Form **1065** (2009)

| Situation | Form 1065 | Schedule K | Schedule K-1 | Research | Communication |

Form 1065 (2009) Page **4**

Schedule K		Partners' Distributive Share Items		Total amount
Income (Loss)	1	Ordinary business income (loss) (page 1, line 22)	**1**	180,000
	2	Net rental real estate income (loss) (attach Form 8825) . . .	**2**	
	3a	Other gross rental income (loss)	**3a**	
	b	Expenses from other rental activities (attach statement) .	**3b**	
	c	Other net rental income (loss). Subtract line 3b from line 3a	**3c**	
	4	Guaranteed payments	**4**	70,000
	5	Interest income	**5**	3,000
	6	Dividends: **a** Ordinary dividends	**6a**	1,500
		b Qualified dividends	**6b** 1,500	
	7	Royalties	**7**	
	8	Net short-term capital gain (loss) (attach Schedule D (Form 1065))	**8**	(7,000)
	9a	Net long-term capital gain (loss) (attach Schedule D (Form 1065))	**9a**	12,000
	b	Collectibles (28%) gain (loss)	**9b**	
	c	Unrecaptured section 1250 gain (attach statement) . .	**9c**	
	10	Net section 1231 gain (loss) (attach Form 4797)	**10**	8,500
	11	Other income (loss) (see instructions) Type ▶	**11**	
Deductions	12	Section 179 deduction (attach Form 4562)	**12**	24,000
	13a	Contributions	**13a**	8,000
	b	Investment interest expense	**13b**	
	c	Section 59(e)(2) expenditures: **(1)** Type ▶ **(2)** Amount ▶	**13c(2)**	
	d	Other deductions (see instructions) Type ▶	**13d**	
Self-Employ-ment	14a	Net earnings (loss) from self-employment	**14a**	250,000
	b	Gross farming or fishing income	**14b**	
	c	Gross nonfarm income	**14c**	250,000
Credits	15a	Low-income housing credit (section 42(j)(5))	**15a**	
	b	Low-income housing credit (other)	**15b**	
	c	Qualified rehabilitation expenditures (rental real estate) (attach Form 3468)	**15c**	
	d	Other rental real estate credits (see instructions) Type ▶	**15d**	
	e	Other rental credits (see instructions) Type ▶	**15e**	
	f	Other credits (see instructions) Type ▶	**15f**	
Foreign Transactions	16a	Name of country or U.S. possession ▶		
	b	Gross income from all sources	**16b**	
	c	Gross income sourced at partner level	**16c**	
		Foreign gross income sourced at partnership level		
	d	Passive category ▶ **e** General category ▶ **f** Other ▶	**16f**	
		Deductions allocated and apportioned at partner level		
	g	Interest expense ▶ **h** Other ▶	**16h**	
		Deductions allocated and apportioned at partnership level to foreign source income		
	i	Passive category ▶ **j** General category ▶ **k** Other ▶	**16k**	
	l	Total foreign taxes (check one): ▶ Paid ☐ Accrued ☐	**16l**	
	m	Reduction in taxes available for credit (attach statement)	**16m**	
	n	Other foreign tax information (attach statement)		
Alternative Minimum Tax (AMT) Items	17a	Post-1986 depreciation adjustment	**17a**	
	b	Adjusted gain or loss	**17b**	
	c	Depletion (other than oil and gas)	**17c**	
	d	Oil, gas, and geothermal properties—gross income	**17d**	
	e	Oil, gas, and geothermal properties—deductions	**17e**	
	f	Other AMT items (attach statement)	**17f**	
Other Information	18a	Tax-exempt interest income	**18a**	1,000
	b	Other tax-exempt income	**18b**	
	c	Nondeductible expenses	**18c**	
	19a	Distributions of cash and marketable securities	**19a**	110,000
	b	Distributions of other property	**19b**	
	20a	Investment income	**20a**	
	b	Investment expenses	**20b**	
	c	Other items and amounts (attach statement)		

Form **1065** (2009)

Situation	Form 1065	Schedule K	Schedule K-1	Research	Communication

651109

☐ Final K-1   ☐ Amended K-1   OMB No. 1545-0099

Schedule K-1
(Form 1065)   20**09**

Department of the Treasury
Internal Revenue Service

For calendar year 2009, or tax
year beginning _____, 2009
ending _____, 20 _____

Partner's Share of Income, Deductions,
Credits, etc. ▶ See back of form and separate instructions.

Part I   Information About the Partnership

A   Partnership's employer identification number
    86-0806200

B   Partnership's name, address, city, state, and ZIP code

Madison Restaurant
6001 Palm Trace Landing
Davie, FL 33314

C   IRS Center where partnership filed return
Ogden, Utah

D   ☐ Check if this is a publicly traded partnership (PTP)

Part II   Information About the Partner

E   Partner's identifying number
    347-54-1212

F   Partner's name, address, city, state, and ZIP code

Bob Buran
1104 North 8th Court
Plantation, FL 33324

G   ☑ General partner or LLC   ☐ Limited partner or other LLC
    member-manager   member

H   ☐ Domestic partner   ☐ Foreign partner

I   What type of entity is this partner?   **Individual**

J   Partner's share of profit, loss, and capital (see instructions):

	Beginning	Ending
Profit	%	60 %
Loss	%	60 %
Capital	%	60 %

K   Partner's share of liabilities at year end:

Nonrecourse	$	
Qualified nonrecourse financing	$	
Recourse	$	15,000

L   Partner's capital account analysis:

Beginning capital account	$	135,000
Capital contributed during the year	$	
Current year increase (decrease)	$	100,200
Withdrawals & distributions	$ (	66,000)
Ending capital account	$	169,200

☑ Tax basis   ☐ GAAP   ☐ Section 704(b) book
☐ Other (explain)

M   Did the partner contribute property with a built-in gain or loss?
    ☐ Yes   ☑ No
    If "Yes", attach statement (see instructions)

Part III   Partner's Share of Current Year Income, Deductions, Credits, and Other Items

1	Ordinary business income (loss) 108,000	15	Credits
2	Net rental real estate income (loss)		
3	Other net rental income (loss)	16	Foreign transactions
4	Guaranteed payments 70,000		
5	Interest income 1,800		
6a	Ordinary dividends 900		
6b	Qualified dividends 900		
7	Royalties		
8	Net short-term capital gain (loss) (4,200)		
9a	Net long-term capital gain (loss) 7,200	17	Alternative minimum tax (AMT) items
9b	Collectibles (28%) gain (loss)		
9c	Unrecaptured section 1250 gain		
10	Net section 1231 gain (loss) 5,100	18	Tax-exempt income and nondeductible expenses
11	Other income (loss)	A	600
12	Section 179 deduction 14,400	19	Distributions
		A	66,000
13	Other deductions	20	Other information
A	4,800		
14	Self-employment earnings (loss)		
A	178,000		

*See attached statement for additional information.

For IRS Use Only

For Paperwork Reduction Act Notice, see Instructions for Form 1065.   Cat. No. 11394R   Schedule K-1 (Form 1065) 2009

Explanation of Schedule K-1, Line L current year increase:

The tax basis for the partner's capital account is increased by all income items and reduced by all loss and deduction items.

The basis for the capital account is increased by the ordinary income of $108,000, interest of $1,800, dividends of $900, net long-term capital gain of $7,200, net Sec. 1231 gain of $5,100, and tax-exempt income of $600.

The basis for the capital account is decreased by the net short-term capital loss of $4,200, Sec. 179 deduction of $14,400, and other deductions of $4,800. The resulting net change is an increase of $100,200.

Note that the guaranteed payments of $70,000 were already deducted in the computation of ordinary income and are not separately taken into account. Also note that there is only $900 of dividends even though that amount is reported on two lines.

Situation	Form 1065	Schedule K	Schedule K-1	Research	Communication

Sec. 732 (a) provides the basis of distributed property to partners.

Section	Subsection
§ 732	(a)

Situation	Form 1065	Schedule K	Schedule K-1	Research	Communication

To: Mr. Buran and Mr. Hughes
From: CPA Candidate

This memorandum describes the results of my research regarding the recognition of gain if the appreciated CDE stock is distributed by the Madison Restaurant to its partners. A partnership generally recognizes no gain or loss when making a nonliquidating distribution of property to its partners so long as the distribution is proportionate among partners. There is an exception which treats a disproportionate distribution as a sale of property, but that exception will not apply in your situation.

If you require any additional information about this potential distribution, please contact me.

MULTIPLE-CHOICE QUESTIONS (1-162)

1. Alan, Baker, and Carr formed Dexter Corporation during 2010. Pursuant to the incorporation agreement, Alan transferred property with an adjusted basis of $30,000 and a fair market value of $45,000 for 450 shares of stock, Baker transferred cash of $35,000 in exchange for 350 shares of stock, and Carr performed services valued at $25,000 in exchange for 250 shares of stock. Assuming the fair market value of Dexter Corporation stock is $100 per share, what is Dexter Corporation's tax basis for the property received from Alan?

    a. $0
    b. $30,000
    c. $45,000
    d. $65,000

2. Clark and Hunt organized Jet Corp. with authorized voting common stock of $400,000. Clark contributed $60,000 cash. Both Clark and Hunt transferred other property in exchange for Jet stock as follows:

| | Other property | | |
	Adjusted basis	Fair market value	Percentage of Jet stock acquired
Clark	$ 50,000	$100,000	40%
Hunt	120,000	240,000	60%

What was Clark's basis in Jet stock?

    a. $0
    b. $100,000
    c. $110,000
    d. $160,000

3. Adams, Beck, and Carr organized Flexo Corp. with authorized voting common stock of $100,000. Adams received 10% of the capital stock in payment for the organizational services that he rendered for the benefit of the newly formed corporation. Adams did not contribute property to Flexo and was under no obligation to be paid by Beck or Carr. Beck and Carr transferred property in exchange for stock as follows:

	Adjusted basis	Fair market value	Percentage of Flexo stock acquired
Beck	5,000	20,000	20%
Carr	60,000	70,000	70%

What amount of gain did Carr recognize from this transaction?

    a. $40,000
    b. $15,000
    c. $10,000
    d. $0

4. Jones incorporated a sole proprietorship by exchanging all the proprietorship's assets for the stock of Nu Co., a new corporation. To qualify for tax-free incorporation, Jones must be in control of Nu immediately after the exchange. What percentage of Nu's stock must Jones own to qualify as "control" for this purpose?

    a.   50.00%
    b.   51.00%
    c.   66.67%
    d.   80.00%

5. Feld, the sole stockholder of Maki Corp., paid $50,000 for Maki's stock in 2004. In 2010, Feld contributed a parcel of land to Maki but was not given any additional stock for this contribution. Feld's basis for the land was $10,000, and its fair market value was $18,000 on the date of the transfer of title. What is Feld's adjusted basis for the Maki stock?

    a. $50,000
    b. $52,000
    c. $60,000
    d. $68,000

6. Rela Associates, a partnership, transferred all of its assets, with a basis of $300,000, along with liabilities of $50,000, to a newly formed corporation in return for all of the corporation's stock. The corporation assumed the liabilities. Rela then distributed the corporation's stock to its partners in liquidation. In connection with this incorporation of the partnership, Rela recognizes

    a.   No gain or loss on the transfer of its assets nor on the assumption of Rela's liabilities by the corporation.
    b.   Gain on the assumption of Rela's liabilities by the corporation.
    c.   Gain or loss on the transfer of its assets to the corporation.
    d.   Gain, but **not** loss, on the transfer of its assets to the corporation.

7. Roberta Warner and Sally Rogers formed the Acme Corporation on October 1, 2009. On the same date Warner paid $75,000 cash to Acme for 750 shares of its common stock. Simultaneously, Rogers received 100 shares of Acme's common stock for services rendered. How much should Rogers include as taxable income for 2009 and what will be the basis of her stock?

	Taxable income	Basis of stock
a.	$0	$0
b.	$0	$10,000
c.	$10,000	$0
d.	$10,000	$10,000

8. Jackson, a single individual, inherited Bean Corp. common stock from Jackson's parents. Bean is a qualified small business corporation under Code Sec. 1244. The stock cost Jackson's parents $20,000 and had a fair market value of $25,000 at the parents' date of death. During the year, Bean declared bankruptcy and Jackson was informed that the stock was worthless. What amount may Jackson deduct as an ordinary loss in the current year?

    a. $0
    b. $ 3,000
    c. $20,000
    d. $25,000

9. Which of the following is **not** a requirement for stock to qualify as Sec. 1244 small business corporation stock?

    a.   The stock must be issued to an individual or to a partnership.
    b.   The stock was issued for money or property (other than stock and securities).
    c.   The stock must be common stock.
    d.   The issuer must be a domestic corporation.

10. During the current year, Dinah sold Sec. 1244 small business corporation stock that she owned for a loss of $125,000. Assuming Dinah is married and files a joint income tax return for 2010, what is the character of Dinah's recognized loss from the sale of the stock?

    a. $125,000 capital loss.
    b. $25,000 capital loss; $100,000 ordinary loss.

c. $75,000 capital loss; $50,000 ordinary loss.
d. $0 capital loss; $125,000 ordinary loss.

11. Nancy, who is single, formed a corporation during 2005 using a tax-free asset transfer that qualified under Sec. 351. She transferred property having an adjusted basis of $80,000 and a fair market value of $60,000, and in exchange received Sec. 1244 small business corporation stock. During February 2010, Nancy sold all of her stock for $35,000. What is the amount and character of Nancy's recognized loss resulting from the sale of the stock in 2010?
a. $0 ordinary loss; $45,000 capital loss.
b. $25,000 ordinary loss; $10,000 capital loss.
c. $25,000 ordinary loss; $20,000 capital loss.
d. $45,000 ordinary loss; $0 capital loss.

12. A civil fraud penalty can be imposed on a corporation that underpays tax by
a. Omitting income as a result of inadequate record-keeping.
b. Failing to report income it erroneously considered **not** to be part of corporate profits.
c. Filing an incomplete return with an appended statement, making clear that the return is incomplete.
d. Maintaining false records and reporting fictitious transactions to minimize corporate tax liability.

13. Bass Corp., a calendar-year C corporation, made qualifying 2009 estimated tax deposits based on its actual 2008 tax liability. On March 15, 2010, Bass filed a timely automatic extension request for its 2009 corporate income tax return. Estimated tax deposits and the extension payment totaled $7,600. This amount was 95% of the total tax shown on Bass' final 2009 corporate income tax return. Bass paid $400 additional tax on the final 2009 corporate income tax return filed before the extended due date. For the 2009 calendar year, Bass was subject to pay

I. Interest on the $400 tax payment made in 2010.
II. A tax delinquency penalty.

a. I only.
b. II only.
c. Both I and II.
d. Neither I nor II.

14. Edge Corp., a calendar-year C corporation, had a net operating loss and zero tax liability for its 2009 tax year. To avoid the penalty for underpayment of estimated taxes, Edge could compute its first quarter 2010 estimated income tax payment using the

	Annualized income method	Preceding year method
a.	Yes	Yes
b.	Yes	No
c.	No	Yes
d.	No	No

15. A corporation's tax year can be reopened after all statutes of limitations have expired if

I. The tax return has a 50% nonfraudulent omission from gross income.
II. The corporation prevails in a determination allowing a deduction in an open tax year that was taken erroneously in a closed tax year.

a. I only.
b. II only.

c. Both I and II.
d. Neither I nor II.

16. A corporation's penalty for underpaying federal estimated taxes is
a. Not deductible.
b. Fully deductible in the year paid.
c. Fully deductible if reasonable cause can be established for the underpayment.
d. Partially deductible.

17. Blink Corp., an accrual-basis calendar-year corporation, carried back a net operating loss for the tax year ended December 31, 2009. Blink's gross revenues have been under $500,000 since inception. Blink expects to have profits for the tax year ending December 31, 2010. Which method(s) of estimated tax payment can Blink use for its quarterly payments during the 2010 tax year to avoid underpayment of federal estimated taxes?

I. 100% of the preceding tax year method
II. Annualized income method

a. I only.
b. Both I and II.
c. II only.
d. Neither I nor II.

18. When computing a corporation's income tax expense for estimated income tax purposes, which of the following should be taken into account?

	Corporate tax credits	Alternative minimum tax
a.	No	No
b.	No	Yes
c.	Yes	No
d.	Yes	Yes

19. Finbury Corporation's taxable income for the year ended December 31, 2009, was $2,000,000 on which its tax liability was $680,000. In order for Finbury to escape the estimated tax underpayment penalty for the year ending December 31, 2010, Finbury's 2010 estimated tax payments must equal at least
a. 90% of the 2010 tax liability.
b. 93% of the 2010 tax liability.
c. 100% of the 2010 tax liability.
d. The 2009 tax liability of $680,000.

20. Kisco Corp.'s taxable income for 2010 before taking the dividends received deduction was $70,000. This includes $10,000 in dividends from a 15%-owned taxable domestic corporation. Given the following tax rates, what would Kisco's income tax be before any credits?

Taxable income partial rate table	Tax rate
Up to $50,000	15%
Over $50,000 but not over $75,000	25%

a. $10,000
b. $10,750
c. $12,500
d. $15,750

21. Green Corp. was incorporated and began business in 2007. In computing its alternative minimum tax for 2008, it determined that it had adjusted current earnings (ACE) of $400,000 and alternative minimum taxable income (prior to the ACE adjustment) of $300,000. For 2009, it had adjusted current earnings of $100,000 and alternative minimum taxable income (prior to the ACE adjustment) of $300,000. What is the amount of Green Corp.'s adjustment for adjusted current earnings that will be used in calculating its alternative minimum tax for 2009?

     a. $ 75,000
     b. $ (75,000)
     c. $(100,000)
     d. $(150,000)

22. Eastern Corp., a calendar-year corporation, was formed during 2008. On January 3, 2009, Eastern placed five-year property in service. The property was depreciated under the general MACRS system. Eastern did not elect to use the straight-line method, and elected not to use bonus depreciation. The following information pertains to Eastern:

Eastern's 2009 taxable income	$300,000
Adjustment for the accelerated depreciation taken on 2009 5-year property	1,000
2009 tax-exempt interest from private activity bonds	5,000

What was Eastern's 2009 alternative minimum taxable income before the adjusted current earnings (ACE) adjustment?

     a. $306,000
     b. $305,000
     c. $304,000
     d. $301,000

23. If a corporation's tentative minimum tax exceeds the regular tax, the excess amount is

     a.   Carried back to the first preceding taxable year.
     b.   Carried back to the third preceding taxable year.
     c.   Payable in addition to the regular tax.
     d.   Subtracted from the regular tax.

24. Rona Corp.'s 2009 alternative minimum taxable income was $200,000. The exempt portion of Rona's 2009 alternative minimum taxable income was

     a. $0
     b. $12,500
     c. $27,500
     d. $52,500

25. A corporation's tax preference items that must be taken into account for 2010 alternative minimum tax purposes include

     a.   Use of the percentage-of-completion method of accounting for long-term contracts.
     b.   Casualty losses.
     c.   Tax-exempt interest on private activity bonds issued in 2009.
     d.   Capital gains.

26. In computing its 2010 alternative minimum tax, a corporation must include as an adjustment

     a.   The dividends received deduction.
     b.   The difference between regular tax depreciation and straight-line depreciation over forty years for real property placed in service in 1998.
     c.   Charitable contributions.
     d.   Interest expense on investment property.

27. A corporation will not be subject to the alternative minimum tax for calendar year 2010 if

     a.   The corporation's net assets do not exceed $7.5 million.
     b.   The corporation's average annual gross receipts do not exceed $10 million.

     c.   The corporation has less than ten shareholders.
     d.   2010 is the corporation's first tax year.

28. Bradbury Corp., a calendar-year corporation, was formed on January 2, 2006, and had gross receipts for its first four taxable years as follows:

Year	Gross receipts
2006	$4,500,000
2007	9,000,000
2008	9,500,000
2009	6,500,000

What is the first taxable year that Bradbury Corp. is **not exempt** from the alternative minimum tax (AMT)?

     a.   2007
     b.   2008
     c.   2009
     d.   Bradbury is exempt from AMT for its first four taxable years.

29. Which of the following entities must include in gross income 100% of dividends received from unrelated taxable domestic corporations in computing regular taxable income?

	Personal service corporations	Personal holding companies
a.	Yes	Yes
b.	No	No
c.	Yes	No
d.	No	Yes

30. Andi Corp. issued $1,000,000 face amount of bonds in 2001 and established a sinking fund to pay the debt at maturity. The bondholders appointed an independent trustee to invest the sinking fund contributions and to administer the trust. In 2009, the sinking fund earned $60,000 in interest on bank deposits and $8,000 in net long-term capital gains. All of the trust income is accumulated with Andi's periodic contributions so that the aggregate amount will be sufficient to pay the bonds when they mature. What amount of trust income was taxable to Andi in 2009?

     a. $0
     b. $ 8,000
     c. $60,000
     d. $68,000

31. The following information pertains to treasury stock sold by Lee Corp. to an unrelated broker in 2010:

Proceeds received	$50,000
Cost	30,000
Par value	9,000

What amount of capital gain should Lee recognize in 2010 on the sale of this treasury stock?

     a. $0
     b. $ 8,000
     c. $20,000
     d. $30,500

32. During 2010, Ral Corp. exchanged 5,000 shares of its own $10 par common stock for land with a fair market value of $75,000. As a result of this exchange, Ral should report in its 2010 tax return

     a. $25,000 Section 1245 gain.
     b. $25,000 Section 1231 gain.
     c. $25,000 ordinary income.
     d.   No gain.

33. Pym, Inc., which had earnings and profits of $100,000, distributed land to Kile Corporation, a stockholder. Pym's adjusted basis for this land was $3,000. The land had a fair market value of $12,000 and was subject to a mortgage liability of $5,000, which was assumed by Kile Corporation. The dividend was declared and paid during March 2010.

How much of the distribution would be reportable by Kile as a dividend, before the dividends received deduction?

- a. $0
- b. $ 3,000
- c. $ 7,000
- d. $12,000

34. Which of the following costs are deductible organizational expenditures?

- a. Professional fees to issue the corporation's stock.
- b. Commissions paid by the corporation to underwriters for stock issue.
- c. Printing costs to issue the corporation's stock.
- d. Expenses of temporary directors meetings.

35. Brown Corp., a calendar-year taxpayer, was organized and actively began operations on July 1, 2010, and incurred the following costs:

Legal fees to obtain corporate charter	$40,000
Commission paid to underwriter	25,000
Temporary directors' meetings	15,000
State incorporation fees	4,400

For 2010, what amount should Brown Corp. deduct for organizational expenses?

- a. $1,980
- b. $2,814
- c. $5,940
- d. $6,812

36. The costs of organizing a corporation during 2010

- a. May be deducted in full in the year in which these costs are incurred if they do not exceed $5,000.
- b. May be deducted only in the year in which these costs are paid.
- c. May be amortized over a period of not less than sixty months even if these costs are capitalized on the company's books.
- d. Are nondeductible capital expenditures.

37. Silo Corp. was organized on March 1, 2010, began doing business on September 1, 2010, and elected to file its income tax return on a calendar-year basis. The following qualifying organizational expenditures were incurred in organizing the corporation:

July 1, 2010	$3,000
September 3, 2010	5,600

The maximum allowable deduction for organizational expenditures for 2010 is

- a. $ 600
- b. $3,000
- c. $5,000
- d. $5,080

38. During 2009, Jackson Corp. had the following income and expenses:

Gross income from operations	$100,000
Dividend income from taxable domestic 20%-owned corporations	10,000
Operating expenses	35,000
Officers' salaries	20,000
Contributions to qualified charitable organizations	8,000
Net operating loss carryforward from 2008	30,000

What is the amount of Jackson Corp.'s charitable contribution carryover to 2010?

- a. $0
- b. $2,500
- c. $5,500
- d. $6,300

39. In 2010, Cable Corp., a calendar-year C corporation, contributed $80,000 to a qualified charitable organization. Cable's 2010 taxable income before the deduction for charitable contributions was $820,000 after a $40,000 dividends received deduction. Cable also had carryover contributions of $10,000 from the prior year. In 2010, what amount can Cable deduct as charitable contributions?

- a. $90,000
- b. $86,000
- c. $82,000
- d. $80,000

40. Tapper Corp., an accrual-basis calendar-year corporation, was organized on January 2, 2009. During 2009, revenue was exclusively from sales proceeds and interest income. The following information pertains to Tapper:

Taxable income before charitable contributions for the year ended December 31, 2009	$500,000
Tapper's matching contribution to employee-designated qualified universities made during 2009	10,000
Board of Directors' authorized contribution to a qualified charity (authorized December 1, 2009, made February 1, 2010)	30,000

What is the maximum allowable deduction that Tapper may take as a charitable contribution on its tax return for the year ended December 31, 2009?

- a. $0
- b. $10,000
- c. $30,000
- d. $40,000

41. Lyle Corp. is a distributor of pharmaceuticals and sells only to retail drug stores. During 2010, Lyle received unsolicited samples of nonprescription drugs from a manufacturer. Lyle donated these drugs in 2010 to a qualified exempt organization and deducted their fair market value as a charitable contribution. What should be included as gross income in Lyle's 2010 return for receipt of these samples?

- a. Fair market value.
- b. Net discounted wholesale price.
- c. $25 nominal value assigned to gifts.
- d. $0.

42. During 2010, Nale Corp. received dividends of $1,000 from a 10%-owned taxable domestic corporation. When Nale computes the maximum allowable deduction for contributions in its 2010 return, the amount of dividends to be included in the computation of taxable income is

- a. $0
- b. $ 200
- c. $ 300
- d. $1,000

43. Gero Corp. had operating income of $160,000, after deducting $10,000 for contributions to State University, but not including dividends of $2,000 received from nonaffiliated taxable domestic corporations.

In computing the maximum allowable deduction for contributions, Gero should apply the percentage limitation to a base amount of

    a. $172,000
    b. $170,400
    c. $170,000
    d. $162,000

44. Norwood Corporation is an accrual-basis taxpayer. For the year ended December 31, 2009, it had book income before tax of $500,000 after deducting a charitable contribution of $100,000. The contribution was authorized by the Board of Directors in December 2009, but was not actually paid until March 1, 2010. How should Norwood treat this charitable contribution for tax purposes to minimize its 2009 taxable income?

    a.   It cannot claim a deduction in 2009, but must apply the payment against 2010 income.
    b.   Make an election claiming a deduction for 2009 of $50,000 and carry the remainder over a maximum of five succeeding tax years.
    c.   Make an election claiming a deduction for 2009 of $60,000 and carry the remainder over a maximum of five succeeding tax years.
    d.   Make an election claiming a 2009 deduction of $100,000.

45. In 2009, Best Corp., an accrual-basis calendar-year C corporation, received $100,000 in dividend income from the common stock that it held in a 15%-owned domestic corporation. The stock was not debt-financed, and was held for over a year. Best recorded the following information for 2009:

Loss from Best's operations	$ (10,000)
Dividends received	100,000
Taxable income (before dividends received deduction)	$ 90,000

Best's dividends received deduction on its 2009 tax return was

    a. $100,000
    b. $ 80,000
    c. $ 70,000
    d. $ 63,000

46. In 2010, Acorn, Inc. had the following items of income and expense:

Sales	$500,000
Cost of sales	250,000
Dividends received	25,000

The dividends were received from a corporation of which Acorn owns 30%. In Acorn's 2010 corporate income tax return, what amount should be reported as income before special deductions?

    a. $525,000
    b. $505,000
    c. $275,000
    d. $250,000

47. The corporate dividends received deduction

    a.   Must exceed the applicable percentage of the recipient shareholder's taxable income.

    b.   Is affected by a requirement that the investor corporation must own the investee's stock for a specified minimum holding period.
    c.   Is unaffected by the percentage of the investee's stock owned by the investor corporation.
    d.   May be claimed by S corporations.

48. In 2010, Ryan Corp. had the following income:

Income from operations	$300,000
Dividends from unrelated taxable domestic corporations less than 20% owned	2,000

Ryan had no portfolio indebtedness. In Ryan's 2010 taxable income, what amount should be included for the dividends received?

    a. $ 400
    b. $ 600
    c. $1,400
    d. $1,600

49. In 2010, Daly Corp. had the following income:

Profit from operations	$100,000
Dividends from 20%-owned taxable domestic corporation	1,000

In Daly's 2010 taxable income, how much should be included for the dividends received?

    a. $0
    b. $ 200
    c. $ 800
    d. $1,000

50. Cava Corp., which has **no** portfolio indebtedness, received the following dividends in 2010:

From a mutual savings bank	$1,500
From a 20%-owned unaffiliated domestic taxable corporation	7,500

How much of these dividends qualifies for the 80% dividends received deduction?

    a. $9,000
    b. $7,500
    c. $1,500
    d. $0

51. During 2009, Stark Corp. reported gross income from operations of $350,000 and operating expenses of $400,000. Stark also received dividend income of $100,000 (not included in gross income from operations) from an investment in a taxable domestic corporation in which it owns 10% of the stock. Additionally, Stark had a net operating loss carryover from 2008 of $30,000. What is the amount of Stark Corp.'s net operating loss for 2009?

    a. $0
    b. $(20,000)
    c. $(30,000)
    d. $(50,000)

52. A C corporation's net capital losses are

    a.   Carried forward indefinitely until fully utilized.
    b.   Carried back three years and forward five years.
    c.   Deductible in full from the corporation's ordinary income.
    d.   Deductible from the corporation's ordinary income only to the extent of $3,000.

53. For the year ended December 31, 2009, Taylor Corp. had a net operating loss of $200,000. Taxable income for the earlier years of corporate existence, computed without reference to the net operating loss, was as follows:

	Taxable income
2004	$ 5,000
2005	$10,000
2006	$20,000
2007	$30,000
2008	$40,000

If Taylor makes **no** special election to waive a net operating loss carryback period, what amount of net operating loss will be available to Taylor for the year ended December 31, 2010?

- a. $200,000
- b. $130,000
- c. $110,000
- d. $ 95,000

54. When a corporation has an unused net capital loss that is carried back or carried forward to another tax year,

- a. It retains its original identity as short-term or long-term.
- b. It is treated as a short-term capital loss whether or not it was short-term when sustained.
- c. It is treated as a long-term capital loss whether or not it was long-term when sustained.
- d. It can be used to offset ordinary income up to the amount of the carryback or carryover.

55. For the year ended December 31, 2009, Haya Corp. had gross business income of $600,000 and expenses of $800,000. Contributions of $5,000 to qualified charities were included in expenses. In addition to the expenses, Haya had a net operating loss carryover of $9,000. What was Haya's net operating loss for 2009?

- a. $209,000
- b. $204,000
- c. $200,000
- d. $195,000

56. Dorsett Corporation's income tax return for 2010 shows deductions exceeding gross income by $56,800. Included in the tax return are the following items:

Net operating loss deduction (carryover from 2009)	$15,000
Dividends received deduction	6,800

What is Dorsett's net operating loss for 2010?

- a. $56,800
- b. $50,000
- c. $41,800
- d. $35,000

57. Ram Corp.'s operating income for the year ended December 31, 2009, amounted to $100,000. Also in 2009, a machine owned by Ram was completely destroyed in an accident. This machine's adjusted basis immediately before the casualty was $15,000. The machine was not insured and had no salvage value.

In Ram's 2009 tax return, what amount should be deducted for the casualty loss?

- a. $ 5,000
- b. $ 5,400
- c. $14,900
- d. $15,000

58. For the first taxable year in which a corporation has qualifying research and experimental expenditures, the corporation

- a. Has a choice of either deducting such expenditures as current business expenses, or capitalizing these expenditures.

- b. Has to treat such expenditures in the same manner as they are accounted for in the corporation's financial statements.
- c. Is required to deduct such expenditures currently as business expenses or lose the deductions.
- d. Is required to capitalize such expenditures and amortize them ratably over a period of not less than sixty months.

59. For the year ended December 31, 2010, Kelly Corp. had net income per books of $300,000 before the provision for federal income taxes. Included in the net income were the following items:

Dividend income from a 5%-owned domestic taxable corporation (taxable income limitation does not apply and there is no portfolio indebtedness)	$50,000
Bad debt expense (represents the increase in the allowance for doubtful accounts)	80,000

Assuming no bad debt was written off, what is Kelly's taxable income for the year ended December 31, 2010?

- a. $250,000
- b. $330,000
- c. $345,000
- d. $380,000

60. For the year ended December 31, 2009, Maple Corp.'s book income, before federal income tax, was $100,000. Included in this $100,000 were the following:

Provision for state income tax	$1,000
Interest earned on US Treasury Bonds	6,000
Interest expense on bank loan to purchase US Treasury Bonds	2,000

Maple's taxable income for 2009 was

- a. $ 96,000
- b. $ 97,000
- c. $100,000
- d. $101,000

61. For the year ended December 31, 2009, Dodd Corp. had net income per books of $100,000. Included in the computation of net income were the following items:

Provision for federal income tax	$27,000
Net long-term capital loss	5,000
Keyman life insurance premiums (corporation is beneficiary)	3,000

Dodd's 2009 taxable income was

- a. $127,000
- b. $130,000
- c. $132,000
- d. $135,000

62. For the year ended December 31, 2009, Bard Corp.'s income per accounting records, before federal income taxes, was $450,000 and included the following:

State corporate income tax refunds	$ 4,000
Life insurance proceeds on officer's death	15,000
Net loss on sale of securities bought for investment in 2007	20,000

Bard's 2009 taxable income was

- a. $435,000
- b. $451,000
- c. $455,000
- d. $470,000

63. Dewey Corporation's book income before federal income taxes was $520,000 for the year ended December 31,

2009. Dewey was incorporated during 2009 and began business in June. Organization costs of $257,400 were expensed for financial statement purposes during 2009. For tax purposes these costs are being written off over the minimum allowable period. For the year ended December 31, 2009, Dewey's taxable income was

a. $520,000
b. $747,900
c. $767,390
d. $778,000

64. Bishop Corporation reported taxable income of $700,000 on its federal income tax return for calendar year 2009. Selected information for 2009 is available from Bishop's records as follows:

Provision for federal income tax per books	$280,000
Depreciation claimed on the tax return	130,000
Depreciation recorded in the books	75,000
Life insurance proceeds on death of corporate officer	100,000

Bishop reported net income per books for 2009 of

a. $855,000
b. $595,000
c. $575,000
d. $475,000

65. For the year ended December 31, 2009, Ajax Corporation had net income per books of $1,200,000. Included in the determination of net income were the following items:

Interest income on municipal bonds	$ 40,000
Damages received from settlement of patent infringement lawsuit	200,000
Interest paid on loan to purchase municipal bonds	8,000
Provision for federal income tax	524,000

What should Ajax report as its taxable income for 2009?

a. $1,492,000
b. $1,524,000
c. $1,684,000
d. $1,692,000

66. For its taxable year 2009, Farve Corp. had net income per books of $80,000, which included municipal bond interest of $5,000, dividend income of $10,000, a deduction for a net capital loss of $6,000, a deduction for business meals of $4,000, and a deduction for federal income taxes of $18,000. What is the amount of income that would be shown on the last line of Schedule M-1 (Reconciliation of Income [Loss] Per Books with Income [Loss] Per Return) of Farve Corp.'s corporate income tax return for 2009?

a. $ 90,000
b. $ 93,000
c. $ 99,000
d. $101,000

67. In 2009, Starke Corp., an accrual-basis calendar-year corporation, reported book income of $380,000. Included in that amount was $50,000 municipal bond interest income, $170,000 for federal income tax expense, and $2,000 interest expense on the debt incurred to carry the municipal bonds. What amount should Starke's taxable income be as reconciled on Starke's Schedule M-1 of Form 1120, US Corporation Income Tax Return?

a. $330,000
b. $500,000
c. $502,000
d. $550,000

68. Would the following expense items be reported on Schedule M-1 of the corporation income tax return (Form 1120) showing the reconciliation of income per books with income per return?

	Lodging expenses for executive out-of-town travel	Deduction for a net capital loss
a.	Yes	Yes
b.	No	No
c.	Yes	No
d.	No	Yes

69. In the reconciliation of income per books with income per return

a. Only temporary differences are considered.
b. Only permanent differences are considered.
c. Both temporary and permanent differences are considered.
d. Neither temporary nor permanent differences are considered.

70. Media Corp. is an accrual-basis, calendar-year C corporation. Its 2009 reported book income included $6,000 in municipal bond interest income. Its expenses included $1,500 of interest incurred on indebtedness used to carry municipal bonds and $8,000 in advertising expense. What is Media's net M-1 adjustment on its 2009 Form 1120, US Corporation Income Tax Return, to reconcile to its 2009 taxable income?

a. $(4,500)
b. $ 1,500
c. $ 3,500
d. $ 9,500

71. Barbaro Corporation's retained earnings at January 1, 2009, was $600,000. During 2009 Barbaro paid cash dividends of $150,000 and received a federal income tax refund of $26,000 as a result of an IRS audit of Barbaro's 2006 tax return. Barbaro's net income per books for the year ended December 31, 2009, was $274,900 after deducting federal income tax of $183,300. How much should be shown in the reconciliation Schedule M-2, of Form 1120, as Barbaro's retained earnings at December 31, 2009?

a. $443,600
b. $600,900
c. $626,900
d. $750,900

72. Olex Corporation's books disclosed the following data for the calendar year 2009:

Retained earnings at beginning of year	$50,000
Net income for year	70,000
Contingency reserve established at end of year	10,000
Cash dividends paid during year	8,000

What amount should appear on the last line of reconciliation Schedule M-2 of Form 1120?

a. $102,000
b. $120,000
c. $128,000
d. $138,000

73. Bank Corp. owns 80% of Shore Corp.'s outstanding capital stock. Shore's capital stock consists of 50,000 shares of common stock issued and outstanding. Shore's 2009 net income was $140,000. During 2009, Shore declared and paid dividends of $60,000. In conformity with generally accepted accounting principles, Bank recorded the following entries in 2009:

	Debit	Credit
Investment in Shore Corp. common stock	$112,000	
Equity in earnings of subsidiary		$112,000
Cash	48,000	
Investment in Shore Corp. common stock		48,000

In its 2009 consolidated tax return, Bank should report dividend revenue of

  a. $48,000
  b. $14,400
  c. $ 9,600
  d. $0

74. In 2010, Portal Corp. received $100,000 in dividends from Sal Corp., its 80%-owned subsidiary. What net amount of dividend income should Portal include in its 2010 consolidated tax return?

  a. $100,000
  b. $ 80,000
  c. $ 70,000
  d. $0

75. Potter Corp. and Sly Corp. file consolidated tax returns. In January 2009, Potter sold land, with a basis of $60,000 and a fair value of $100,000, to Sly for $100,000. Sly sold the land in June 2010 for $125,000. In its 2010 and 2009 tax returns, what amount of gain should be reported for these transactions in the consolidated return?

	2010	2009
a.	$25,000	$40,000
b.	$25,000	$0
c.	$40,000	$25,000
d.	$65,000	$0

76. When a consolidated return is filed by an affiliated group of includible corporations connected from inception through the requisite stock ownership with a common parent

  a. Intercompany dividends are excludable to the extent of 80%.
  b. Operating losses of one member of the group offset operating profits of other members of the group.
  c. Each of the subsidiaries is entitled to an alternative minimum tax exemption.
  d. Each of the subsidiaries is entitled to an accumulated earnings tax credit.

77. Dana Corp. owns stock in Seco Corp. For Dana and Seco to qualify for the filing of consolidated returns, at least what percentage of Seco's total voting power and total value of stock must be directly owned by Dana?

	Total voting power	Total value of stock
a.	51%	51%
b.	51%	80%
c.	80%	51%
d.	80%	80%

78. Consolidated returns may be filed

  a. Either by parent-subsidiary corporations or by brother-sister corporations.
  b. Only by corporations that formally request advance permission from the IRS.
  c. Only by parent-subsidiary affiliated groups.
  d. Only by corporations that issue their financial statements on a consolidated basis.

79. Parent Corporation and Subsidiary Corporation file consolidated returns on a calendar-year basis. In January 2009, Subsidiary sold land, which it had used in its business, to Parent for $50,000. Immediately before this sale, Subsidiary's basis for the land was $30,000. Parent held the land primarily for sale to customers in the ordinary course of business. In July 2010, Parent sold the land to Adams, an unrelated individual. In determining consolidated taxable income for 2010, how much should Subsidiary take into account as a result of the 2009 sale of the land from Subsidiary to Parent?

  a. $0
  b. $20,000
  c. $30,000
  d. $50,000

80. At the beginning of the year, Westwind, a C corporation, had a deficit of $45,000 in accumulated earnings and profits. For the current year, Westwind reported earnings and profits of $15,000. Westwind distributed $12,000 during the year. What was the amount of Westwind's accumulated earnings and profits deficit at year-end?

  a. $(30,000)
  b. $(42,000)
  c. $(45,000)
  d. $(57,000)

81. At the beginning of the year, Cable, a C corporation, had accumulated earnings and profits of $100,000. Cable reported the following items on its current year tax return:

Taxable income	$50,000
Federal income taxes paid	5,000
Current year charitable contributions in excess of 10% limitation	1,000
Net capital loss for current year	2,000

What is Cable's accumulated earnings and profits at the end of the year?

  a. $142,000
  b. $145,000
  c. $147,000
  d. $150,000

82. On January 1, 2009, Locke Corp., an accrual-basis, calendar-year C corporation, had $30,000 in accumulated earnings and profits. For 2009, Locke had current earnings and profits of $20,000 and made two $40,000 cash distributions to its shareholders, one in April and one in September of 2009. What amount of the 2009 distributions is classified as dividend income to Locke's shareholders?

  a. $0
  b. $20,000
  c. $50,000
  d. $80,000

83. Chicago Corp., a calendar-year C corporation, had accumulated earnings and profits of $100,000 as of January 1, 2009 and had a **deficit** in its current earnings and profits for the entire 2009 tax year in the amount of $140,000. Chicago Corp. distributed $30,000 cash to its shareholders on December 31, 2009. What would be the balance of Chicago Corp.'s accumulated earnings and profits as of January 1, 2010?

  a. $0
  b. $(30,000)
  c. $(40,000)
  d. $(70,000)

84. Salon, Inc. distributed cash and personal property to its sole shareholder. Using the following facts, determine the amount of gain that would be recognized by Salon, Inc. as the result of making the distribution to its shareholder?

Item	Amount
Cash	$20,000
Personal property:	
Fair market value	6,000
Adjusted basis	3,000
Liability on property assumed by	
shareholder	10,000

    a. $ 3,000
    b. $ 4,000
    c. $ 7,000
    d. $23,000

85. Kent Corp. is a calendar-year, accrual-basis C corporation. In 2009, Kent made a nonliquidating distribution of property with an adjusted basis of $150,000 and a fair market value of $200,000 to Reed, its sole shareholder. The following information pertains to Kent:

Reed's basis in Kent stock at January 1, 2009	$500,000
Accumulated earnings and profits at January 1, 2009	125,000
Current earnings and profits for 2009	60,000

What was taxable as dividend income to Reed for 2009?
    a. $ 60,000
    b. $150,000
    c. $185,000
    d. $200,000

86. Ridge Corp., a calendar-year C corporation, made a nonliquidating cash distribution to its shareholders of $1,000,000 with respect to its stock. At that time, Ridge's current and accumulated earnings and profits totaled $750,000 and its total paid-in capital for tax purposes was $10,000,000. Ridge had no corporate shareholders. Ridge's cash distribution

    I. Was taxable as $750,000 of dividend income to its shareholders.
    II. Reduced its shareholders' adjusted bases in Ridge stock by $250,000.

    a.   I only.
    b.   II only.
    c.   Both I and II.
    d.   Neither I nor II.

87. Tour Corp., which had earnings and profits of $400,000, made a nonliquidating distribution of property to its shareholders in 2010. This property, which had an adjusted basis of $30,000 and a fair market value of $20,000 at date of distribution, did not constitute assets used in the active conduct of Tour's business. How much loss did Tour recognize on this distribution?
    a. $30,000
    b. $20,000
    c. $10,000
    d. $0

88. On January 1, 2009, Kee Corp., a C corporation, had a $50,000 deficit in earnings and profits. For 2009 Kee had current earnings and profits of $10,000 and made a $30,000 cash distribution to its stockholders. What amount of the distribution is taxable as dividend income to Kee's stockholders?
    a. $30,000
    b. $20,000

    c. $10,000
    d. $0

89. Dahl Corp. was organized and commenced operations in 1999. At December 31, 2009, Dahl had accumulated earnings and profits of $9,000 before dividend declaration and distribution. On December 31, 2009, Dahl distributed cash of $9,000 and a vacant parcel of land to Green, Dahl's only stockholder. At the date of distribution, the land had a basis of $5,000 and a fair market value of $40,000. What was Green's taxable dividend income in 2009 from these distributions?
    a. $ 9,000
    b. $14,000
    c. $44,000
    d. $49,000

90. On June 30, 2010, Ral Corporation had retained earnings of $100,000. On that date, it sold a plot of land to a noncorporate stockholder for $50,000. Ral had paid $40,000 for the land in 2002, and it had a fair market value of $80,000 when the stockholder bought it. The amount of dividend income taxable to the stockholder in 2010 is
    a. $0
    b. $10,000
    c. $20,000
    d. $30,000

91. On December 1, 2009, Gelt Corporation declared a dividend and distributed to its sole shareholder a parcel of land that was not an inventory asset. On the date of the distribution, the following data were available:

Adjusted basis of land	$ 6,500
Fair market value of land	14,000
Mortgage on land	5,000

For the year ended December 31, 2009, Gelt had earnings and profits of $30,000 without regard to the dividend distribution. By how much should the dividend distribution reduce the earnings and profits for 2009?
    a. $ 1,500
    b. $ 6,500
    c. $ 9,000
    d. $14,000

92. Two unrelated individuals, Mark and David, each own 50% of the stock of Pike Corporation, which has accumulated earnings and profits of $250,000. Because of his inactivity in the business in recent years, Mark has decided to retire from the business and wishes to sell his stock. Accordingly, Pike will distribute cash of $500,000 in redemption of all of the stock owned by Mark. If Mark's adjusted basis for his stock at date of redemption is $300,000, what will be the tax effect of the redemption to Mark?
    a. $125,000 dividend.
    b. $200,000 dividend.
    c. $200,000 capital gain.
    d. $250,000 dividend.

93. How does a noncorporate shareholder treat the gain on a redemption of stock that qualifies as a partial liquidation of the distributing corporation?
    a.   Entirely as capital gain.
    b.   Entirely as a dividend.
    c.   Partly as capital gain and partly as a dividend.
    d.   As a tax-free transaction.

94. In 2010, Kara Corp. incurred the following expenditures in connection with the repurchase of its stock from shareholders to avert a hostile takeover:

Interest on borrowings used to repurchase stock	$100,000
Legal and accounting fees in connection with the repurchase	400,000

The total of the above expenditures deductible in 2010 is
a. $0
b. $100,000
c. $400,000
d. $500,000

95. A corporation was completely liquidated and dissolved during 2010. The filing fees, professional fees, and other expenditures incurred in connection with the liquidation and dissolution are
a. Deductible in full by the dissolved corporation.
b. Deductible by the shareholders and not by the corporation.
c. Treated as capital losses by the corporation.
d. Not deductible either by the corporation or shareholders.

96. What is the usual result to the shareholders of a distribution in complete liquidation of a corporation?
a. No taxable effect.
b. Ordinary gain to the extent of cash received.
c. Ordinary gain or loss.
d. Capital gain or loss.

97. Par Corp. acquired the assets of its wholly owned subsidiary, Sub Corp., under a plan that qualified as a tax-free complete liquidation of Sub. Which of the following of Sub's unused carryovers may be transferred to Par?

	Excess charitable contributions	Net operating loss
a.	No	Yes
b.	Yes	No
c.	No	No
d.	Yes	Yes

98. Kappes Corp. distributed marketable securities in a pro rata redemption of its stock in a complete liquidation. These securities, which had been purchased in 2004 for $150,000, had a fair market value of $100,000 when distributed. What loss does Kappes recognize as a result of the distribution?
a. $0.
b. $50,000 long-term capital loss.
c. $50,000 Section 1231 loss.
d. $50,000 ordinary loss.

99. When a parent corporation completely liquidates its 80%-owned subsidiary, the parent (as stockholder) will ordinarily
a. Be subject to capital gains tax on 80% of the long-term gain.
b. Be subject to capital gains tax on 100% of the long-term gain.
c. Have to report any gain on liquidation as ordinary income.
d. Not recognize gain or loss on the liquidating distributions.

100. Lark Corp. and its wholly owned subsidiary, Day Corp., both operated on a calendar year. In January 2010, Day adopted a plan of complete liquidation. Two months later, Day paid all of its liabilities and distributed its remaining assets to Lark. These assets consisted of the following:

Cash	$50,000
Land (at cost)	10,000

Fair market value of the land was $30,000. Upon distribution of Day's assets to Lark, all of Day's capital stock was canceled. Lark's basis for the Day stock was $7,000. Lark's recognized gain in 2010 on receipt of Day's assets in liquidation was
a. $0
b. $50,000
c. $53,000
d. $73,000

101. On June 1, 2010, Green Corp. adopted a plan of complete liquidation. The liquidation was completed within a twelve-month period. On August 1, 2010, Green distributed to its stockholders installment notes receivable that Green had acquired in connection with the sale of land in 2009. The following information pertains to these notes:

Green's basis	$ 90,000
Fair market value	162,000
Face amount	185,000

How much gain must Green recognize in 2010 as a result of this distribution?
a. $0
b. $23,000
c. $72,000
d. $95,000

102. Carmela Corporation had the following assets on January 2, 2009, the date on which it adopted a plan of complete liquidation:

	Adjusted basis	Fair market value
Land	$ 75,000	$150,000
Inventory	43,500	66,000
Totals	$118,500	$216,000

The land was sold on June 30, 2009, to an unrelated party at a gain of $75,000. The inventory was sold to various customers during 2009 at an aggregate gain of $22,500. On December 10, 2009, the remaining asset (cash) was distributed to Carmela's stockholders, and the corporation was liquidated. What is Carmela's recognized gain in 2009?
a. $0
b. $22,500
c. $75,000
d. $97,500

103. Mintee Corp., an accrual-basis calendar-year C corporation, had no corporate shareholders when it liquidated in 2010. In cancellation of all their Mintee stock, each Mintee shareholder received in 2010 a liquidation distribution of $2,000 cash and land with a tax basis of $5,000 and a fair market value of $10,500. Before the distribution, each shareholder's tax basis in Mintee stock was $6,500. What amount of gain should each Mintee shareholder recognize on the liquidating distribution?
a. $0
b. $ 500
c. $4,000
d. $6,000

104. Edge Corp. met the stock ownership requirements of a personal holding company. What sources of income must

Edge consider to determine if the income requirements for a personal holding company have been met?

I. Interest earned on tax-exempt obligations.
II. Dividends received from an unrelated domestic corporation.

    a. I only.
    b. II only.
    c. Both I and II.
    d. Neither I nor II.

105. Kane Corp. is a calendar-year domestic personal holding company. Which deduction(s) must Kane make from 2010 taxable income to determine undistributed personal holding company income prior to the dividend-paid deduction?

	Federal income taxes	Net long-term capital gain less related federal income taxes
a.	Yes	Yes
b.	Yes	No
c.	No	Yes
d.	No	No

106. Dart Corp., a calendar-year domestic C corporation, is not a personal holding company. For purposes of the accumulated earnings tax, Dart has accumulated taxable income for 2009. Which step(s) can Dart take to eliminate or reduce any 2009 accumulated earnings tax?

I. Demonstrate that the "reasonable needs" of its business require the retention of all or part of the 2009 accumulated taxable income.
II. Pay dividends by March 15, 2010.

    a. I only.
    b. II only.
    c. Both I and II.
    d. Neither I nor II.

107. The accumulated earnings tax can be imposed
    a. On both partnerships and corporations.
    b. On companies that make distributions in excess of accumulated earnings.
    c. On personal holding companies.
    d. Regardless of the number of stockholders in a corporation.

108. Zero Corp. is an investment company authorized to issue only common stock. During the last half of 2009, Edwards owned 240 of the 1,000 outstanding shares of stock in Zero. Another 560 shares of stock outstanding were owned, twenty shares each, by twenty-eight shareholders who are neither related to each other nor to Edwards. Zero could be a personal holding company if the remaining 200 shares of common stock were owned by
    a. An estate where Edwards is the beneficiary.
    b. Edwards' brother-in-law.
    c. A partnership where Edwards is not a partner.
    d. Edwards' cousin.

109. Arbor Corp. has nine common stockholders. Arbor derives all of its income from investments in stocks and securities, and regularly distributes 51% of its taxable income as dividends to its stockholders. Arbor is a
    a. Regulated investment company.
    b. Personal holding company.

    c. Corporation subject to the accumulated earnings tax.
    d. Corporation subject to tax on income not distributed to stockholders.

110. Kari Corp., a manufacturing company, was organized on January 2, 2009. Its 2009 federal taxable income was $400,000 and its federal income tax was $100,000. What is the maximum amount of accumulated taxable income that may be subject to the accumulated earnings tax for 2009 if Kari takes only the minimum accumulated earnings credit?
    a. $300,000
    b. $150,000
    c. $ 50,000
    d. $0

111. The following information pertains to Hull, Inc., a personal holding company, for the year ended December 31, 2009:

Undistributed personal holding company income	$100,000
Dividends paid during 2009	20,000
Consent dividends reported in the 2009 individual income tax returns of the holders of Hull's common stock, but **not** paid by Hull to its stockholders	10,000

In computing its 2009 personal holding company tax, what amount should Hull deduct for dividends paid?
    a. $0
    b. $10,000
    c. $20,000
    d. $30,000

112. Benson, a singer, owns 100% of the outstanding capital stock of Lund Corp. Lund contracted with Benson, specifying that Benson was to perform personal services for Magda Productions, Inc., in consideration of which Benson was to receive $50,000 a year from Lund. Lund contracted with Magda, specifying that Benson was to perform personal services for Magda, in consideration of which Magda was to pay Lund $1,000,000 a year. Personal holding company income will be attributable to
    a. Benson only.
    b. Lund only.
    c. Magda only.
    d. All three contracting parties.

113. The personal holding company tax
    a. Qualifies as a tax credit that may be used by partners or stockholders to reduce their individual income taxes.
    b. May be imposed on both corporations and partnerships.
    c. Should be self-assessed by filing a separate schedule with the regular tax return.
    d. May be imposed regardless of the number of equal stockholders in a corporation.

114. The accumulated earnings tax does **not** apply to
    a. Corporations that have more than 100 stockholders.
    b. Personal holding companies.
    c. Corporations filing consolidated returns.
    d. Corporations that have more than one class of stock.

115. The personal holding company tax may be imposed
    a. As an alternative tax in place of the corporation's regularly computed tax.

b. If more than 50% of the corporation's stock is owned, directly or indirectly, by more than ten stockholders.

c. If at least 60% of the corporation's adjusted ordinary gross income for the taxable year is personal holding company income, and the stock ownership test is satisfied.

d. In conjunction with the accumulated earnings tax.

116. The accumulated earnings tax

a. Should be self-assessed by filing a separate schedule along with the regular tax return.

b. Applies only to closely held corporations.

c. Can be imposed on S corporations that do not regularly distribute their earnings.

d. Cannot be imposed on a corporation that has undistributed earnings and profits of less than $150,000.

117. Kee Holding Corp. has eighty unrelated equal stockholders. For the year ended December 31, 2009, Kee's income comprised the following:

Net rental income	$ 1,000
Commissions earned on sales of franchises	3,000
Dividends from taxable domestic corporations	90,000

Deductible expenses for 2009 totaled $10,000. Kee paid no dividends for the past three years. Kee's liability for personal holding company tax for 2009 will be based on

a. $12,000

b. $11,000

c. $ 9,000

d. $0

118. The accumulated earnings tax

a. Depends on a stock ownership test based on the number of stockholders.

b. Can be avoided by sufficient dividend distributions.

c. Is computed by the filing of a separate schedule along with the corporation's regular tax return.

d. Is imposed when the entity is classified as a personal holding company.

119. Where passive investment income is involved, the personal holding company tax may be imposed

a. On both partnerships and corporations.

b. On companies whose gross income arises solely from rentals, if the lessors render no services to the lessees.

c. If more than 50% of the company is owned by five or fewer individuals.

d. On small business investment companies licensed by the Small Business Administration.

120. In determining accumulated taxable income for the purpose of the accumulated earnings tax, which one of the following is allowed as a deduction?

a. Capital loss carryover from prior year.

b. Dividends received deduction.

c. Net operating loss deduction.

d. Net capital loss for current year.

121. The minimum accumulated earnings credit is

a. $150,000 for all corporations.

b. $150,000 for nonservice corporations only.

c. $250,000 for all corporations.

d. $250,000 for nonservice corporations only.

122. Daystar Corp. which is not a mere holding or investment company, derives its income from consulting services. Daystar had accumulated earnings and profits of $45,000 at December 31, 2008. For the year ended December 31, 2009, it had earnings and profits of $115,000 and a dividends-paid deduction of $15,000. It has been determined that $20,000 of the accumulated earnings and profits for 2009 is required for the reasonable needs of the business. How much is the allowable accumulated earnings credit at December 31, 2009?

a. $105,000

b. $205,000

c. $150,000

d. $250,000

123. Stahl, an individual, owns 100% of Talon, an S corporation. At the beginning of the year, Stahl's basis in Talon was $65,000. Talon reported the following items from operations during the current year:

Ordinary loss	$10,000
Municipal interest income	6,000
Long-term capital gain	4,000
Short-term capital loss	9,000

What was Stahl's basis in Talon at year-end?

a. $50,000

b. $55,000

c. $56,000

d. $61,000

124. Baker, an individual, owned 100% of Alpha, an S corporation. At the beginning of the year, Baker's basis in Alpha Corp. was $25,000. Alpha realized ordinary income during the year in the amount of $1,000 and a long-term capital loss in the amount of $3,000 for this year. Alpha distributed $30,000 in cash to Baker during the year. What amount of the $30,000 cash distribution is taxable to Baker?

a. $0

b. $ 4,000

c. $ 7,000

d. $30,000

125. Lane Inc., an S corporation, pays single coverage health insurance premiums of $4,800 per year and family coverage premiums of $7,200 per year. Mill is a 10% shareholder-employee in Lane. On Mill's behalf, Lane pays Mill's family coverage under the health insurance plan. What amount of insurance premiums is includible in Mill's gross income?

a. $0

b. $ 720

c. $4,800

d. $7,200

126. Beck Corp. has been a calendar-year S corporation since its inception on January 2, 2005. On January 1, 2009, Lazur and Lyle each owned 50% of the Beck stock, in which their respective tax bases were $12,000 and $9,000. For the year ended December 31, 2009, Beck had $81,000 in ordinary business income and $10,000 in tax-exempt income. Beck made a $51,000 cash distribution to each shareholder on December 31, 2009. What was Lazur's tax basis in Beck after the distribution?

a. $ 1,500

b. $ 6,500

c. $52,500

d. $57,500

127. Graphite Corp. has been a calendar-year S corporation since its inception on January 2, 2005. On January 1, 2009, Smith and Tyler each owned 50% of the Graphite stock, in which their respective bases were $12,000 and $9,000. For the year ended December 31, 2009, Graphite had $80,000 in ordinary business income and $6,000 in tax-exempt income. Graphite made a $53,000 cash distribution to each shareholder on December 31, 2009. What total amount of income from Graphite is includible in Smith's 2009 adjusted gross income?

    a. $96,000
    b. $93,000
    c. $43,000
    d. $40,000

128. Dart Corp., a calendar-year S corporation, had 60,000 shares of voting common stock and 40,000 shares of nonvoting common stock issued and outstanding. On February 23, 2009, Dart filed a revocation statement with the consent of shareholders holding 30,000 shares of its voting common stock and 10,000 shares of its nonvoting common stock. Dart's S corporation election

    a.   Did not terminate.
    b.   Terminated as of January 1, 2009.
    c.   Terminated on February 24, 2009.
    d.   Terminated as of January 1, 2010.

129. Which one of the following statements concerning the eligibility requirements for S corporations is **not** correct?

    a.   An S corporation is permitted to own 90% of the stock of a C corporation.
    b.   An S corporation is permitted to own 100% of the stock of another S corporation.
    c.   An S corporation is permitted to be a partner in a partnership.
    d.   A partnership is permitted to be a shareholder of an S corporation.

130. Dart Corp., a calendar-year corporation, was formed in 1999 and made an S corporation election in 2001 that is still in effect. Its books and records for 2009 reflect the following information:

Accumulated earnings and profits at 1/1/09	$90,000
Accumulated adjustments account at 1/1/09	50,000
Ordinary income for 2009	200,000

Dart Corp. is solely owned by Robert, whose basis in Dart's stock was $100,000 on January 1, 2009. During 2009, Dart distributed $310,000 to Robert. What is the amount of the $310,000 distribution that Robert must report as dividend income for 2009 assuming no special elections were made with regard to the distribution?

    a. $0
    b. $ 60,000
    c. $ 90,000
    d. $140,000

131. Village Corp., a calendar-year corporation, began business in 2003. Village made a valid S Corporation election on September 5, 2009, with the unanimous consent of its shareholders. The eligibility requirements for S status continued to be met throughout 2009. On what date did Village's S status become effective?

    a.   January 1, 2009.
    b.   January 1, 2010.
    c.   September 5, 2009.
    d.   September 5, 2010.

132. A shareholder's basis in the stock of an S corporation is increased by the shareholder's pro rata share of income from

	Tax-exempt interest	*Taxable interest*
a.	No	No
b.	No	Yes
c.	Yes	No
d.	Yes	Yes

133. Zinco Corp. was a calendar-year S corporation. Zinco's S status terminated on April 1, 2010, when Case Corp. became a shareholder. During 2010 (365-day calendar year), Zinco had nonseparately computed income of $310,250. If no election is made by Zinco, what amount of the income, if any, should be allocated to the S short year for 2010?

    a. $78,200
    b. $77,350
    c. $76,500
    d. $0

134. Bristol Corp. was formed as a C corporation on January 1, 1999, and elected S corporation status on January 1, 2007. At the time of the election, Bristol had accumulated C corporation earnings and profits that have not been distributed. Bristol has had the same twenty-five shareholders throughout its existence. In 2010 Bristol's S election will terminate if it

    a.   Increases the number of shareholders to one hundred.
    b.   Adds a decedent's estate as a shareholder to the existing shareholders.
    c.   Takes a charitable contribution deduction.
    d.   Has passive investment income exceeding 90% of gross receipts in each of the three consecutive years ending December 31, 2009.

135. As of January 1, 2010, Kane owned all the 100 issued shares of Manning Corp., a calendar-year S corporation. On the 40th day of 2010, Kane sold twenty-five of the Manning shares to Rodgers. For the year ended December 31, 2010 (a 365-day calendar year), Manning had $73,000 in nonseparately stated income and made no distributions to its shareholders. What amount of nonseparately stated income from Manning should be reported on Kane's 2010 tax return?

    a. $56,900
    b. $56,750
    c. $54,750
    d. $48,750

136. On February 10, 2009, Ace Corp., a calendar-year corporation, elected S corporation status and all shareholders consented to the election. There was no change in shareholders in 2009. Ace met all eligibility requirements for S status during the preelection portion of the year. What is the earliest date on which Ace can be recognized as an S corporation?

    a.   February 10, 2008.
    b.   February 10, 2009.
    c.   January 1, 2009.
    d.   January 1, 2010.

137. An S corporation has 30,000 shares of voting common stock and 20,000 shares of nonvoting common stock issued and outstanding. The S election can be revoked voluntarily with the consent of the shareholders holding, on the day of the revocation,

	Shares of voting stock	Shares of nonvoting stock
a.	0	20,000
b.	7,500	5,000
c.	10,000	16,000
d.	20,000	0

138. The Haas Corp., a calendar-year S corporation, has two equal shareholders. For the year ended December 31, 2010, Haas had income of $60,000, which included $50,000 from operations and $10,000 from investment interest income. There were no other transactions that year. Each shareholder's basis in the stock of Haas will increase by

     a. $50,000
     b. $30,000
     c. $25,000
     d. $0

139. Which of the following conditions will prevent a corporation from qualifying as an S Corporation?

     a. The corporation owns 100% of the stock of a C corporation.
     b. The corporation is a partner in a partnership.
     c. 30% of the corporation's stock is held by a voting trust.
     d. The corporation has common voting stock and preferred nonvoting stock outstanding.

140. If an S corporation has **no** accumulated earnings and profits, the amount distributed to a shareholder

     a. Must be returned to the S corporation.
     b. Increases the shareholder's basis for the stock.
     c. Decreases the shareholder's basis for the stock.
     d. Has no effect on the shareholder's basis for the stock.

141. A corporation that has been an S corporation from its inception may

	Have both passive and nonpassive income	Be owned by a bankruptcy estate
a.	No	Yes
b.	Yes	No
c.	No	No
d.	Yes	Yes

142. Bern Corp., an S corporation, had an ordinary loss of $36,500 for the year ended December 31, 2009. At January 1, 2009, Meyer owned 50% of Bern's stock. Meyer held the stock for forty days in 2009 before selling the entire 50% interest to an unrelated third party. Meyer's basis for the stock was $10,000. Meyer was a full-time employee of Bern until the stock was sold. Meyer's share of Bern's 2009 loss was

     a. $0
     b. $ 2,000
     c. $ 4,000
     d. $18,300

143. A calendar-year corporation whose status as an S corporation was terminated during 2010 must wait how many years before making a new S election, in the absence of IRS consent to an earlier election?

     a. Can make a new S election for calendar year 2010.
     b. Must wait three years.
     c. Must wait five years.
     d. Must wait six years.

144. Which one of the following will render a corporation ineligible for S corporation status?

     a. One of the stockholders is a decedent's estate.
     b. One of the stockholders is a bankruptcy estate.
     c. The corporation has both voting and nonvoting common stock issued and outstanding.
     d. The corporation has 110 stockholders.

145. With regard to S corporations and their stockholders, the "at risk" rules applicable to losses

     a. Depend on the type of income reported by the S corporation.
     b. Are subject to the elections made by the S corporation's stockholders.
     c. Take into consideration the S corporation's ratio of debt to equity.
     d. Apply at the shareholder level rather than at the corporate level.

146. An S corporation may deduct

     a. Foreign income taxes.
     b. A net Section 1231 loss.
     c. Investment interest expense.
     d. The amortization of organizational expenditures.

147. An S corporation's accumulated adjustments account, which measures the amount of earnings that may be distributed tax-free

     a. Must be adjusted downward for the full amount of federal income taxes attributable to any taxable year in which the corporation was a C corporation.
     b. Must be adjusted upward for the full amount of federal income taxes attributable to any taxable year in which the corporation was a C corporation.
     c. Must be adjusted upward or downward for only the federal income taxes affected by capital gains or losses, respectively, for any taxable year in which the corporation was a C corporation.
     d. Is not adjusted for federal income taxes attributable to a taxable year in which the corporation was a C corporation.

148. If a calendar-year S corporation does **not** request an automatic six-month extension of time to file its income tax return, the return is due by

     a. January 31.
     b. March 15.
     c. April 15.
     d. June 30.

149. An S corporation is **not** permitted to take a deduction for

     a. Compensation of officers.
     b. Interest paid to individuals who are not stockholders of the S corporation.
     c. Charitable contributions.
     d. Employee benefit programs established for individuals who are not stockholders of the S corporation.

150. An S corporation may

     a. Have both common and preferred stock outstanding.
     b. Have a partnership as a shareholder.

   c.   Have a nonresident alien as a shareholder.
   d.   Have as many as 100 shareholders.

151. Which of the following is **not** a requirement for a corporation to elect S corporation status (Subchapter S)?
   a.   Must be a member of a controlled group.
   b.   Must confine stockholders to individuals, estates, and certain qualifying trusts.
   c.   Must be a domestic corporation.
   d.   Must have only one class of stock.

152. Brooke, Inc., an S corporation, was organized on January 2, 2009, with two equal stockholders who materially participate in the S corporation's business. Each stockholder invested $5,000 in Brooke's capital stock, and each loaned $15,000 to the corporation. Brooke then borrowed $60,000 from a bank for working capital. Brooke sustained an operating loss of $90,000 for the year ended December 31, 2009. How much of this loss can each stockholder claim on his 2009 income tax return?
   a. $ 5,000
   b. $20,000
   c. $45,000
   d. $50,000

153. Jaxson Corp. has 200,000 shares of voting common stock issued and outstanding. King Corp. has decided to acquire 90% of Jaxson's voting common stock solely in exchange for 50% of its voting common stock and retain Jaxson as a subsidiary after the transaction. Which of the following statements is true?
   a.   King must acquire 100% of Jaxson stock for the transaction to be a tax-free reorganization.
   b.   The transaction will qualify as a tax-free reorganization.
   c.   King must issue at least 60% of its voting common stock for the transaction to qualify as a tax-free reorganization.
   d.   Jaxson must surrender assets for the transaction to qualify as a tax-free reorganization.

154. Ace Corp. and Bate Corp. combine in a qualifying reorganization and form Carr Corp., the only surviving corporation. This reorganization is tax-free to the

	Shareholders	*Corporations*
a.	Yes	Yes
b.	Yes	No
c.	No	Yes
d.	No	No

155. In a type B reorganization, as defined by the Internal Revenue Code, the

I.   Stock of the target corporation is acquired solely for the voting stock of either the acquiring corporation or its parent.
II.   Acquiring corporation must have control of the target corporation immediately after the acquisition.

   a.   I only.
   b.   II only.
   c.   Both I and II.
   d.   Neither I nor II.

156. Pursuant to a plan of corporate reorganization adopted in July 2010, Gow exchanged 500 shares of Lad Corp. common stock that he had bought in January 2007 at a cost of $5,000 for 100 shares of Rook Corp. common stock hav-ing a fair market value of $6,000. Gow's recognized gain on this exchange was
   a. $1,000 long-term capital gain.
   b. $1,000 short-term capital gain.
   c. $1,000 ordinary income.
   d. $0

157. Which one of the following is a corporate reorganization as defined in the Internal Revenue Code?
   a.   Mere change in place of organization of one corporation.
   b.   Stock redemption.
   c.   Change in depreciation method from accelerated to straight-line.
   d.   Change in inventory costing method from FIFO to LIFO.

158. With regard to corporate reorganizations, which one of the following statements is correct?
   a.   A mere change in identity, form, or place of organization of one corporation does **not** qualify as a reorganization.
   b.   The reorganization provisions **cannot** be used to provide tax-free treatment for corporate transactions.
   c.   Securities in corporations **not** parties to a reorganization are always "boot."
   d.   A "party to the reorganization" does **not** include the consolidated company.

159. Which one of the following is **not** a corporate reorganization as defined in the Internal Revenue Code?
   a.   Stock redemption.
   b.   Recapitalization.
   c.   Mere change in identity.
   d.   Statutory merger.

160. Claudio Corporation and Stellar Corporation both report on a calendar-year basis. Claudio merged into Stellar on June 30, 2009. Claudio had an allowable net operating loss carryover of $270,000. Stellar's taxable income for the year ended December 31, 2009, was $360,000 before consideration of Claudio's net operating loss carryover. Claudio's fair market value before the merger was $1,500,000. The federal long-term tax-exempt rate is 3%. As a result of the merger, Claudio's former shareholders own 10% of Stellar's outstanding stock. How much of Claudio's net operating loss carryover can be used to offset Stellar's 2009 taxable income?
   a. $ 22,685
   b. $ 45,000
   c. $180,000
   d. $180,984

161. In 2007, Celia Mueller bought a $1,000 bond issued by Disco Corporation for $1,100. Instead of paying off the bondholders in cash, Disco issued 100 shares of preferred stock in 2010 for each bond outstanding. The preferred stock had a fair market value of $15 per share. What is the recognized gain to be reported by Mueller in 2010?
   a. $0.
   b. $400 dividend.
   c. $400 long-term capital gain.
   d. $500 long-term capital gain.

162. On April 1, 2010, in connection with a recapitalization
of Oakbrook Corporation, Mary Roberts exchanged 500
shares that cost her $95,000 for 1,000 shares of new stock
worth $91,000 and bonds in the principal amount of $10,000
with a fair market value of $10,500. What is the amount of
Roberts' recognized gain during 2010?

    a. $0
    b. $ 6,500
    c. $10,000
    d. $10,500

SIMULATION PROBLEMS

Simulation Problem 1   (10 to 15 minutes)

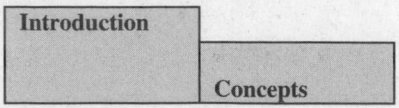

Given below are terms appearing in the federal income tax code, regulations and explanations.

A. Accumulated earnings tax
B. Capital assets
C. Capital contribution
D. Claim of right
E. Consent divided
F. Constructive dividend
G. Constructive receipt
H. Deficiency dividend
I. Dividends paid deduction

J. Dividends received deduction
K. Earned income
L. Exchanged basis
M. Excise tax
N. Fair market value
O. Head of household
P. Nontaxable exchange
Q. Passive income
R. Personal holding company

S. Personal holding company tax
T. Personal service corporation
U. Portfolio income
V. Regulated investment company
W. Sec. 1231 assets
X. Surviving spouse
Y. Taxable exchange
Z. Transferred basis

Indicate your choice of the best term applying to each of the statements below. Each term may be selected once, more than once, or not at all.

1. A corporation whose income was derived solely from dividends, interest, and royalties, and during the last six months of its year more than 50% of the value of its outstanding stock is owned by five or fewer individuals.

2. The basis used to determine gain on sale of property that was received as a gift.

3. The trade-in of production machinery for new production machinery by a corporation, when the corporation pays additional cash.

4. An unmarried individual whose filing status enables the taxpayer to use a set of income tax rates that are lower than those applicable to other unmarried individuals, but are higher than those applicable to married persons filing a joint return.

5. If income is unqualifiedly available, it will be subject to the income tax even though it is not physically in the taxpayer's possession.

6. A special tax imposed on corporations that accumulate their earnings beyond the reasonable needs of the business.

7. The classification of income from interest, dividends, annuities, and certain royalties.

8. The classification of depreciable assets and real estate used in a trade or business and held for more than one year.

9. This deduction attempts to mitigate the triple taxation that would occur if one corporation paid dividends to a corporate shareholder who, in turn, distributed such amounts to its individual shareholders.

10. Sale of property to a corporation by a shareholder for a selling price that is in excess of the property's fair market value.

	(A)	(B)	(C)	(D)	(E)	(F)	(G)	(H)	(I)	(J)	(K)	(L)	(M)	(N)	(O)	(P)	(Q)	(R)	(S)	(T)	(U)	(V)	(W)	(X)	(Y)	(Z)
1.	○	○	○	○	○	○	○	○	○	○	○	○	○	○	○	○	○	○	○	○	○	○	○	○	○	○
2.	○	○	○	○	○	○	○	○	○	○	○	○	○	○	○	○	○	○	○	○	○	○	○	○	○	○
3.	○	○	○	○	○	○	○	○	○	○	○	○	○	○	○	○	○	○	○	○	○	○	○	○	○	○
4.	○	○	○	○	○	○	○	○	○	○	○	○	○	○	○	○	○	○	○	○	○	○	○	○	○	○
5.	○	○	○	○	○	○	○	○	○	○	○	○	○	○	○	○	○	○	○	○	○	○	○	○	○	○
6.	○	○	○	○	○	○	○	○	○	○	○	○	○	○	○	○	○	○	○	○	○	○	○	○	○	○
7.	○	○	○	○	○	○	○	○	○	○	○	○	○	○	○	○	○	○	○	○	○	○	○	○	○	○
8.	○	○	○	○	○	○	○	○	○	○	○	○	○	○	○	○	○	○	○	○	○	○	○	○	○	○
9.	○	○	○	○	○	○	○	○	○	○	○	○	○	○	○	○	○	○	○	○	○	○	○	○	○	○
10.	○	○	○	○	○	○	○	○	○	○	○	○	○	○	○	○	○	○	○	○	○	○	○	○	○	○

Simulation Problem 2 (45 to 55 minutes)

Situation				
	Tax Return Amount	**Schedule M-1**	**Research**	**Communication**

The following adjusted revenue and expense accounts appeared in the accounting records of Aviator, Inc., an accrual-basis taxpayer, for the year ended December 31, 2009:

Revenues	
Net sales	$2,000,000
Dividends	50,000
Interest	22,000
Gains on the sale of stock	20,000
Total	$2,092,000
Expenses	
Cost of goods sold	$1,000,000
Salaries and wages	400,000
Interest	25,000
Contributions	40,000
Depreciation (see note)	260,000
Losses on the sale of stock	30,000
Total	$1,755,000
Net Income	$ 337,000

NOTE: *There is no Sec. 1245, Sec. 1250, or Sec. 291 recapture.*

Additional information for 2009

(1) The dividends were received from a taxable domestic corporation, whose stock is traded on a major stock exchange.

(2) Interest expense consists of: $20,000 interest on funds borrowed for working capital and $5,000 interest on funds borrowed to purchase municipal bonds.

(3) Interest revenue consists of interest earned on

Corporate bonds purchased in 2008	$20,000
Municipal bonds purchased in 2009	2,000

(4) Contributions of $40,000 were made to qualified charitable organizations.

(5) On January 2, 2009, Aviator, Inc. commenced active operations. In connection with creating the business, Aviator incurred the following organizational expenditures:

Legal fees	$30,000
State incorporation fees	20,000
Brokers commission on the sale of stock	15,000

Aviator is amortizing the deductible expenses over the minimum allowable period. The expenditures were erroneously excluded from the accounts shown above.

(6) Gains from the sale of stock arose from the following sales of stock of unrelated corporations:

Tech. Corp (bought February 2009; sold April 2009)	$15,000
Major Corp (bought June 2009; sold September 2009)	5,000

(7) All losses from the sale of stock are classified as long-term capital losses.

Aviator provides the following information for 2010:

Net income per books (after tax)	$310,000
Federal income tax liability deducted per books	104,150
Retained earnings at January 1, 2010	425,000
Interest income from municipal general obligation bonds	20,000
Cash dividends paid to shareholders	60,000
Life insurance proceeds received on death of Aviator's president (Aviator was the owner and beneficiary of the policy)	100,000
Premiums paid on policy insuring Aviator's president	5,000
Excess of capital losses over capital gains for 2010	7,000
Employee entertainment expenses reimbursed by Aviator	6,000
Dividend income received from 5%-owned taxable domestic corporation	10,000
MACRS depreciation for 2010 in excess of straight-time depreciation deducted per books	9,000
Retained earnings at December 31, 2010	645,000

Situation	Tax Return Amount	Schedule M-1	Research	Communication

For **items 1 through 7** record the appropriate amount as it would appear on the Aviator, Inc. corporate tax return. On the exam, a list of numeric answers would be presented for the candidate to select from.

1. What is the amount of interest expense that Aviator, Inc. can deduct on its tax return?
2. What is the amount of interest income that must be included in Aviator's gross income?
3. What is the allowable amount of organizational expenditures that is deductible on Aviator's tax return?
4. How much of the capital gains must be included in Aviator's gross income?
5. How much of the capital losses can be deducted on Aviator's tax return?
6. What is the amount of Aviator's dividends received deduction?
7. What is Aviator's maximum charitable contributions deduction?

Situation	Tax Return Amount	Schedule M-1	Research	Communication

Prepare Schedule M-1, which will reconcile Aviator's income reported per books for 2010 with its income reported on its 2010 tax return Form 1120.

Schedule M-1   Reconciliation of Income (Loss) per Books With Income per Return

Note: Schedule M-3 required instead of Schedule M-1 if total assets are $10 million or more—see instructions

1 Net income (loss) per books
2 Federal income tax per books
3 Excess of capital losses over capital gains
4 Income subject to tax not recorded on books this year (itemize):
5 Expenses recorded on books this year not deducted on this return (itemize):
  a Depreciation $
  b Charitable contributions $
  c Travel and entertainment $
6 Add lines 1 through 5

7 Income recorded on books this year not included on this return (itemize):
  Tax-exempt interest $
8 Deductions on this return not charged against book income this year (itemize):
  a Depreciation $
  b Charitable contributions $
9 Add lines 7 and 8
10 Income (page 1, line 28)—line 6 less line 9

Situation	Tax Return Amount	Schedule M-1	Research	Communication

Aviator's gains from the sale of stock investments totaled $20,000, while its losses from the sale of other stock investments totaled $30,000. What Internal Revenue Code section and subsection limits the deduction of a corporation's capital losses?

Section § [ ]   **Subsection** ([ ])

Situation	Tax Return Amount	Schedule M-1	Research	Communication

Mr. Tyler, the majority owner of Aviator, Inc., contacts you and indicates that he is determined to never again let Aviator invest in the stock of other corporations since he believes that the losses from Aviator's stock sales cannot be deducted. Write a letter to Mr. Tyler explaining the appropriate tax treatment of Aviator's stock losses and any possible tax benefits that can be derived.

REMINDER: Your response will be graded for both technical content and writing skills. Technical content will be evaluated for information that is helpful to the intended reader and clearly relevant to the issue. Writing skills will be evaluated for development, organization, and the appropriate expression of ideas in professional correspondence. Use a standard business memo or letter format with a clear beginning, middle, and end. Do not convey information in the form of a table, bullet point list, or other abbreviated presentation.

Dear Mr. Tyler:

Simulation Problem 3   (50 to 60 minutes)

Situation			
	Tax Return Amounts	Research	Communication

Following is Ral Corp.'s condensed income statement, before federal income tax, for the year ended December 31, 2009:

Sales		$1,000,000
Cost of sales		700,000
Gross profit		300,000
Operating expenses		220,000
Operating income		80,000
Other income (loss):		
Interest	$ 5,200	
Dividends	19,200	
Net long-term capital loss	(6,400)	18,000
Income before federal income tax		$ 98,000

Additional information

Interest arose from the following sources:

US Treasury notes	$3,000
Municipal arbitrage bonds	2,000
Other municipal bonds	200
Total interest	$5,200

Dividends arose from the following sources:

Taxable domestic corporation	Date stock acquired	Percent owned by Ral	
Clove Corp.	7/1/02	30.0	$ 7,000
Ramo Corp.	9/1/04	10.0	6,000
Sol Corp. (stock sold 1/10/10)	12/1/09	5.0	1,000
Real Estate Investment Trust	6/1/07	1.0	2,700
Mutual Fund Corp. (capital gains dividends only)	4/1/06	0.1	400
Money Market Fund (invests only in interest/paying securities)	3/1/05	0.1	2,100
Total dividends			$19,200

Operating expenses include the following:

Bonus of $5,000 paid to Ral's sales manager on January 31, 2010. This bonus was based on a percentage of Ral's 2009 sales and was computed on January 25, 2010, under a formula in effect in 2009.

Estimate of $10,000 for bad debts. Actual bad debts for the year amounted to $8,000.

Keyman life insurance premiums of $4,000. Ral is the beneficiary of the policies.

State income taxes of $12,000.

During 2009, Ral made estimated federal income tax payments of $25,000. These payments were debited to prepaid tax expense on Ral's books.

Ral does not exercise significant influence over Clove and accordingly did **not** use the equity method of accounting for this investment.

Ral declared and paid dividends of $11,000 during 2009.

Corporate income tax rates are as follows:

Taxable income				% on	Of the amount
over	but not over	Pay	+	excess	over/
$ 0 /	$ 50,000	$ 0		15%	$ 0
50,000 /	75,000	7,500		25	50,000
75,000 /	100,000	13,750		34	75,000
100,000 /	335,000	22,250		39	100,000

Ral was not subject to the alternative minimum tax in 2009.

	Tax Return Amounts		
Situation		Research	Communication

Items 1 through 14 below pertain to the computation of Ral Corp.'s 2009 federal income tax. For each item, select the appropriate amount. An amount may be selected once, more than once, or not at all.

Amount

A.	$0	J.	$ 3,000	S.	$ 6,400
B.	$ 280	K.	$ 3,200	T.	$ 7,000
C.	$ 320	L.	$ 4,000	U.	$ 8,000
D.	$ 1,000	M.	$ 4,200	V.	$10,000
E.	$ 1,470	N.	$ 4,800	W.	$11,000
F.	$ 1,680	O.	$ 4,900	X.	$12,000
G.	$ 1,890	P.	$ 5,000	Y.	$13,750
H.	$ 2,000	Q.	$ 5,200	Z.	$22,250
I.	$ 2,200	R.	$ 5,600		

Item for Ral's 2009 federal income tax

1. Amount of deduction for manager's $5,000 bonus for 2009.

2. Deduction for bad debts for 2009.

3. Deduction for keyman life insurance premiums for 2009.

4. Deduction for state income taxes for 2009.

5. Amount of interest to be included in gross income for 2009.

6. Dividends received deduction for dividends received from Clove Corp.

7. Dividends received deduction for dividends received from Ramo Corp.

8. Dividends received deduction for dividends received from Sol Corp.

9. Dividends received deduction for dividends received from Real Estate Investment Trust.

10. Dividends received deduction for dividends received from Mutual Fund Corp.

11. Dividends received deduction for dividends received from Money Market Fund.

12. Deduction for the $11,000 of dividends paid by Ral to its shareholders.

13. Deduction for net capital loss for 2009.

14. Ral's federal income tax for 2009 if taxable income were $100,000.

	(A)	(B)	(C)	(D)	(E)	(F)	(G)	(H)	(I)	(J)	(K)	(L)	(M)	(N)	(O)	(P)	(Q)	(R)	(S)	(T)	(U)	(V)	(W)	(X)	(Y)	(Z)
1.	O	O	O	O	O	O	O	O	O	O	O	O	O	O	O	O	O	O	O	O	O	O	O	O	O	O
2.	O	O	O	O	O	O	O	O	O	O	O	O	O	O	O	O	O	O	O	O	O	O	O	O	O	O
3.	O	O	O	O	O	O	O	O	O	O	O	O	O	O	O	O	O	O	O	O	O	O	O	O	O	O
4.	O	O	O	O	O	O	O	O	O	O	O	O	O	O	O	O	O	O	O	O	O	O	O	O	O	O
5.	O	O	O	O	O	O	O	O	O	O	O	O	O	O	O	O	O	O	O	O	O	O	O	O	O	O
6.	O	O	O	O	O	O	O	O	O	O	O	O	O	O	O	O	O	O	O	O	O	O	O	O	O	O
7.	O	O	O	O	O	O	O	O	O	O	O	O	O	O	O	O	O	O	O	O	O	O	O	O	O	O
8.	O	O	O	O	O	O	O	O	O	O	O	O	O	O	O	O	O	O	O	O	O	O	O	O	O	O
9.	O	O	O	O	O	O	O	O	O	O	O	O	O	O	O	O	O	O	O	O	O	O	O	O	O	O
10.	O	O	O	O	O	O	O	O	O	O	O	O	O	O	O	O	O	O	O	O	O	O	O	O	O	O
11.	O	O	O	O	O	O	O	O	O	O	O	O	O	O	O	O	O	O	O	O	O	O	O	O	O	O
12.	O	O	O	O	O	O	O	O	O	O	O	O	O	O	O	O	O	O	O	O	O	O	O	O	O	O
13.	O	O	O	O	O	O	O	O	O	O	O	O	O	O	O	O	O	O	O	O	O	O	O	O	O	O
14.	O	O	O	O	O	O	O	O	O	O	O	O	O	O	O	O	O	O	O	O	O	O	O	O	O	O

Situation	Tax Return Amounts	Research	Communication

Dividends received from taxable domestic corporations are generally eligible for a dividends received deduction. What Internal Revenue Code section provides a special restriction on the dividends received deduction if the stock investment is financed with debt?

Section

§ [   ]

Situation	Tax Return Amounts	Research	Communication

Ray Lathan, the CEO of Ral Corp., has indicated that Ral is considering purchasing 8% of the outstanding stock of Diamond Corporation, one of its suppliers. However, because of a cash shortage, Ral would have to borrow $320,000 of the projected $400,000 cost of the Diamond stock. Ral projects that it will receive dividends totaling $20,000 from its stock investment in Diamond during 2010, and will have to pay $23,000 of interest expense on the funds borrowed to purchase the Diamond stock during that period. Write a letter to Lathan explaining the tax effect that the proposed investment will have on Ral's income and deductions for its 2010 tax year.

REMINDER: Your response will be graded for both technical content and writing skills. Technical content will be evaluated for information that is helpful to the intended reader and clearly relevant to the issue. Writing skills will be evaluated for development, organization, and the appropriate expression of ideas in professional correspondence. Use a standard business memo or letter format with a clear beginning, middle, and end. Do not convey information in the form of a table, bullet point list, or other abbreviated presentation.

Dear Mr. Lathan:

Simulation Problem 4   (35 to 40 minutes)

Situation			
	Tax Return Amounts	Research	Communication

Lan Corp., an accrual-basis calendar-year repair service corporation, was formed and began business on January 6, 2009. Lan's valid S corporation election took effect retroactively on January 6, 2009. Since the question requires a numeric answer, a list of numeric amounts would be provided for the candidate to select from.

	Tax Return Amounts		
Situation		Research	Communication

For **items 1 through 4,** determine the amount, if any, using the fact pattern for each item.

1. Assume the following facts:

Lan's 2009 books recorded the following items:

Gross receipts	$7,260
Interest income on investments	50
Charitable contributions	1,000
Supplies	1,120

What amount of net business income should Lan report on its 2009 Form 1120S, US Income Tax Return for an S Corporation, Schedule K?

2. Assume the following facts:

As of January 6, 2009, Taylor and Barr each owned 100 shares of the 200 issued shares of Lan stock. On January 31, 2009, Taylor and Barr each sold twenty shares to Pike. No election was made to terminate the tax year. Lan had net business income of $14,400 for the year ended December 31, 2009, and made no distributions to its shareholders. Lan's 2009 calendar year had 360 days.

What amount of net business income should have been reported on Pike's 2009 Schedule K-1 from Lan? (2009 is a 360-day tax year.) Round the answer to the nearest hundred.

3. Assume the following facts:

Pike purchased forty Lan shares on January 31, 2009, for $4,000. Lan made no distributions to shareholders, and Pike's 2009 Schedule K-1 from Lan reported

Ordinary business loss	$(1,000)
Municipal bond interest income	150

What was Pike's basis in his Lan stock at December 31, 2009?

4. Assume the following facts:

On January 6, 2009, Taylor and Barr each owned 100 shares of the 200 issued shares of Lan stock. Taylor's basis in Lan shares on that date was $10,000. Taylor sold all of his Lan shares to Pike on January 31, 2009, and Lan made a valid election to terminate its tax year. Taylor's share of ordinary income from Lan prior to the sale was $2,000. Lan made a cash distribution of $3,000 to Taylor on January 30, 2009.

What was Taylor's basis in Lan shares for determining gain or loss from the sale to Pike?

Situation	Tax Return Amounts	Research		Communication

Mr. Perry is the sole shareholder of Arrow, Inc., a calendar-year S corporation. Due to the pass-through of losses in previous years, Perry's aggregate basis for the Arrow stock and debt that he owns has been reduced to zero. For its calendar year 2009, Arrow expects to incur another large loss which Perrry wishes to deduct on his 2009 Form 1040 tax return. What Internal Revenue Code section and subsection limits a shareholder's deduction of an S corporation's losses to the shareholder's basis for stock and debt?

Section	Subsection
§ [ ]	([ ])

Situation	Tax Return Amounts	Research	Communication

Perry contacts you and asks what he can do to enable him to deduct the pass-through of Arrow's projected loss for 2009. Specifically, Perry wants to know whether contributing his own note to Arrow, or guaranteeing Arrow's loan from the Fifth-First Bank will allow him to deduct Arrow's loss for 2009. Write a letter to Perry explaining what options are available to him that will allow him to deduct Arrow's loss on his 2009 Form 1040.

REMINDER: Your response will be graded for both technical content and writing skills. Technical content will be evaluated for information that is helpful to the intended reader and clearly relevant to the issue. Writing skills will be evaluated for development, organization, and the appropriate expression of ideas in professional correspondence. Use a standard business memo or letter format with a clear beginning, middle, and end. Do not convey information in the form of a table, bullet point list, or other abbreviated presentation.

Dear Mr. Perry:

Simulation Problem 5   (40 to 45 minutes)

Introduction	Schedule M-1 Adjustments	Deductibility	Taxability	Alternative Minimum Tax	Communication	Research

Reliant Corp., an accrual-basis calendar-year C corporation, filed its 2009 federal income tax return on March 15, 2010.

Introduction	Schedule M-1 Adjustments	Deductibility	Taxability	Alternative Minimum Tax	Communication	Research

The following **two** responses are required for each of the **items 1 through 6**.

• Determine the amount of Reliant's 2009 Schedule M-1 adjustment.
• Indicate if the adjustment increases, decreases, or has no effect, on Reliant's 2009 taxable income.

Selections

I.   Increases Reliant's 2009 taxable income.
D.   Decreases Reliant's 2009 taxable income.
N.   Has no effect on Reliant's 2009 taxable income.

	Schedule M-1 Adjustment	(I)	(D)	(N)
1. Reliant's disbursements included reimbursed employees' expenses in 2009 for travel of $100,000, and business meals of $30,000. The reimbursed expenses met the conditions of deductibility and were properly substantiated under an accountable plan. The reimbursement was not treated as employee compensation.	_____	○	○	○
2. Reliant's books expensed $7,000 in 2009 for the term life insurance premiums on the corporate officers. Reliant was the policy owner and beneficiary.	_____	○	○	○
3. Reliant's books indicated an $18,000 state franchise tax expense for 2009. Estimated state tax payments for 2009 were $15,000.	_____	○	○	○
4. Book depreciation on computers for 2009 was $10,000. These computers, which cost $50,000, were placed in service on January 2, 2008. Tax depreciation used MACRS with the half-year convention. No election was made to expense part of the computer cost and Reliant elected not to use bonus depreciation.	_____	○	○	○
5. For 2009, Reliant's books showed a $4,000 short-term capital gain distribution from a mutual fund corporation and a $5,000 loss on the sale of Retro stock that was purchased in 2007. The stock was an investment in an unrelated corporation. There were no other 2009 gains or losses and no loss carryovers from prior years.	_____	○	○	○
6. Reliant's 2009 taxable income before the charitable contribution and the dividends received deductions was $500,000. Reliant's books expensed $15,000 in board of director authorized charitable contributions that were paid on January 5, 2010. Charitable contributions paid and expensed during 2009 were $35,000. All charitable contributions were properly substantiated. There were no net operating losses or charitable contributions that were carried forward.	_____	○	○	○

		Deductibility					
Introduction	**Schedule M-1 Adjustments**			**Taxability**	**Alternative Minimum Tax**	**Communication**	**Research**

For the following, indicate if the expenses are fully deductible, partially deductible, or nondeductible for regular tax purposes on Reliant's 2009 federal income tax return.

Selections

F. Fully deductible for regular tax purposes on Reliant's 2009 federal income tax return.
P. Partially deductible for regular tax purposes on Reliant's 2009 federal income tax return.
N. Nondeductible for regular tax purposes on Reliant's 2009 federal income tax return.

	(F)	(P)	(N)
1. Reliant purchased theater tickets for its out of town clients. The performances took place after Reliant's substantial and bona fide business negotiations with its clients.	○	○	○
2. Reliant accrued advertising expenses to promote a new product line. Ten percent of the new product line remained in ending inventory.	○	○	○
3. Reliant incurred interest expense on a loan to purchase municipal bonds.	○	○	○
4. Reliant paid a penalty for the underpayment of 2008 estimated taxes.	○	○	○
5. On December 9, 2009, Reliant's board of directors voted to pay a $500 bonus to each nonstockholder employee for 2009. The bonuses were paid on February 3, 2010.	○	○	○

			Taxability			
Introduction	**Schedule M-1 Adjustments**	**Deductibility**		**Alternative Minimum Tax**	**Communication**	**Research**

For the following, indicate if the items are fully taxable, partially taxable, or nontaxable for regular tax purposes on Reliant's 2009 federal income tax return. All transactions occurred during 2009.

Selections

F. Fully taxable for regular tax purposes on Reliant's 2009 federal income tax return.
P. Partially taxable for regular tax purposes on Reliant's 2009 federal income tax return.
N. Nontaxable for regular tax purposes on Reliant's 2009 federal income tax return.

Items are based on the following:

Reliant filed an amended federal income tax return for 2007 and received a refund that included both the overpayment of the federal taxes and interest.

	(F)	(P)	(N)
1. The portion of Reliant's refund that represented the overpayment of the 2007 federal taxes.	○	○	○
2. The portion of Reliant's refund that is attributable to the interest on the overpayment of federal taxes.	○	○	○
3. Reliant received dividend income from a mutual fund that solely invests in municipal bonds.	○	○	○
4. Reliant, the lessor, benefited from the capital improvements made to its property by the lessee in 2009. The lease agreement is for one year ending December 31, 2009, and provides for a reduction in rental payments by the lessee in exchange for the improvements.	○	○	○
5. Reliant collected the proceeds on the term life insurance policy on the life of a debtor who was not a shareholder. The policy was assigned to Reliant as collateral security for the debt. The proceeds exceeded the amount of the debt.	○	○	○

Introduction	Schedule M-1 Adjustments	Deductibility	Taxability	Alternative Minimum Tax	Communication	Research

Indicate if the following items increase, decrease, or have no effect on Reliant's 2009 alternative minimum taxable income (AMTI) **prior to** the adjusted current earnings adjustment (ACE).

Selections

I. Increases Reliant's 2009 AMTI.
D. Decreases Reliant's 2009 AMTI.
N. Has no effect on Reliant's 2009 AMTI.

	(I)	(D)	(N)
1. Reliant used the 70% dividends received deduction for regular tax purposes.	○	○	○
2. Reliant received interest from a state's general obligation bonds.	○	○	○
3. Reliant used MACRS depreciation on seven-year personal property placed into service January 3, 2009, for regular tax purposes. No expense election was made, and Reliant elected not to use bonus depreciation.	○	○	○
4. Depreciation on nonresidential real property placed into service on January 3, 2009, was under the general MACRS depreciation system for regular tax purposes.	○	○	○
5. Reliant had only cash charitable contributions for 2009.	○	○	○

Introduction	Schedule M-1 Adjustments	Deductibility	Taxability	Alternative Minimum Tax	Communication	Research

The owner of Reliant Corporation, Mary Evans, contacts you and indicates that Reliant expects to form a wholly owned subsidiary, Surety Corporation, to conduct business unrelated to Reliant's current operations. Mary wants to have Surety expense the costs of formation, including the amounts paid for legal fees and the cost of issuing stock. Write a letter to Mary Evans explaining the appropriate tax treatment of the costs of forming Surety Corporation.

REMINDER: Your response will be graded for both technical content and writing skills. Technical content will be evaluated for information that is helpful to the intended reader and clearly relevant to the issue. Writing skills will be evaluated for development, organization, and the appropriate expression of ideas in professional correspondence. Use a standard business memo or letter format with a clear beginning, middle, and end. Do not convey information in the form of a table, bullet point list, or other abbreviated presentation.

Dear Ms. Evans:

Introduction	Schedule M-1 Adjustments	Deductibility	Taxability	Alternative Minimum Tax	Communication	Research

What Internal Revenue Code section, subsection, and paragraph limits a corporation's deduction for charitable contributions to a percentage of its taxable income before specified deductions?

Section	Subsection	Paragraph
§ [ ]	([ ])	[ ]

Simulation Problem 6   (40 to 45 minutes)

Situation	Schedule M-1 Adjustments	Taxability	Deductibility	Alternative Minimum Tax	Communication	Research

Capital Corp., an accrual-basis calendar-year C corporation, began operations on January 2, 2007. Capital timely filed its 2009 federal income tax return on March 15, 2010.

	Schedule M-1 Adjustments					
Situation		Taxability	Deductibility	Alternative Minimum Tax	Communication	Research

The following items each require **two** responses:

- For each item below, determine the amount of Capital's 2009 Schedule M-1 adjustment necessary to reconcile book income to taxable income. On the CPA exam, a list of numeric answers would be presented for the candidate to select from.
- In addition, determine if the Schedule M-1 adjustment necessary to reconcile book income to taxable income increases, decreases, or has no effect on Capital's 2009 taxable income. An answer may be selected once, more than once, or not at all.

Selections

I.   Increases Capital's 2009 taxable income.
D.   Decreases Capital's 2009 taxable income.
N.   Has no effect on Capital's 2009 taxable income.

	Amount of Adjustment	(I)	(D)	(N)
1. At its corporate inception in 2007, Capital incurred and paid $40,100 in organizational costs for legal fees to draft the corporate charter. In 2007, Capital correctly elected, for book purposes, to expense the organizational costs and to amortize the organizational expenditures over the minimum allowable period on its federal income tax return. For 2009, no organizational costs were deducted on its books.	_____	O	O	O
2. Capital's 2009 disbursements included $10,000 for reimbursed employees' expenses for business meals and entertainment. The reimbursed expenses met the conditions of deductibility and were properly substantiated under an accountable plan. The reimbursement was not treated as employee compensation.	_____	O	O	O
3. Capital's 2009 disbursements included $15,000 for life insurance premium expense paid for its executives as part of their taxable compensation. Capital is neither the direct nor the indirect beneficiary of the policy, and the amount of the compensation is reasonable.	_____	O	O	O
4. In 2009, Capital increased its allowance for uncollectible accounts by $10,000. No bad debt was written off in 2009.	_____	O	O	O

		Taxability				
Situation	Schedule M-1 Adjustments		Deductibility	Alternative Minimum Tax	Communication	Research

Sunco Corp., an accrual-basis calendar-year C corporation, timely filed its 2009 federal income tax return on March 15, 2010. Determine if the following items are fully taxable, partially taxable, or nontaxable for regular income tax purposes on Sunco's 2009 federal income tax return. An answer may be selected once, more than once, or not at all.

Selections

F.   Fully taxable for regular income tax purposes on Sunco's 2009 federal income tax return.
P.   Partially taxable for regular income tax purposes on Sunco's 2009 federal income tax return.
N.   Nontaxable for regular income tax purposes on Sunco's 2009 federal income tax return.

			(F)	(P)	(N)
1. In 2009, Sunco received dividend income from a 35%-owned domestic corporation. The dividends were not from debt-financed portfolio stock, and the taxable income limitation did not apply.			○	○	○
2. In 2009, Sunco received a $2,800 lease cancellation payment from a three-year lease tenant.			○	○	○

Situation	Schedule M-1 Adjustments	Taxability	Deductibility	Alternative Minimum Tax	Communication	Research

Quest Corp., an accrual-basis calendar-year C corporation, timely filed its 2009 federal income tax return on March 15, 2010. Determine if the following items are fully deductible, partially deductible, or nondeductible for regular income tax purposes on Quest's 2009 federal income tax return. An answer may be selected once, more than once, or not at all.

Selections

F.   Fully deductible for regular income tax purposes on Quest's 2009 federal income tax return.
P.   Partially deductible for regular income tax purposes on Quest's 2009 federal income tax return.
N.   Nondeductible for regular income tax purposes on Quest's 2009 federal income tax return.

	(F)	(P)	(N)
1. Quest's 2009 taxable income before charitable contributions and dividends received deduction was $200,000. Quest's Board of Directors authorized a $38,000 contribution to a qualified charity on December 1, 2009. The payment was made on February 1, 2010. All charitable contributions were properly substantiated.	○	○	○
2. During 2009 Quest was assessed and paid a $300 uncontested penalty for failure to pay its 2008 federal income taxes on time.	○	○	○

Situation	Schedule M-1 Adjustments	Taxability	Deductibility	Alternative Minimum Tax	Communication	Research

On its 2009 federal income tax return, Gelco Corp., an accrual-basis calendar-year C corporation, reported the same amounts for regular income tax and alternative minimum tax purposes. Determine if each item, taken separately, contributes to overstating, understating, or correctly stating Gelco's 2009 alternative minimum taxable income (AMTI) prior to the adjusted current earnings adjustment (ACE). An answer may be selected once, more than once, or not at all.

Selections

O.   Overstating Gelco's 2009 AMTI prior to the ACE.
U.   Understating Gelco's 2009 AMTI prior to the ACE.
C.   Correctly stating Gelco's 2009 AMTI prior to the ACE.

	(O)	(U)	(C)
1. For regular tax purposes, Gelco deducted the maximum MACRS depreciation on seven-year personal property placed in service on January 2, 2009. Gelco did not elect to expense any part of the cost of the property under Sec. 179, and elected not to take bonus depreciation.	○	○	○
2. For regular income tax purposes, Gelco depreciated nonresidential real property placed in service on January 2, 1998, under the general MACRS depreciation system for a thirty-nine-year depreciable life.	○	○	○
3. Gelco excluded state highway construction general obligation bond interest income earned in 2009 for regular income tax and alternative minimum tax (AMT) purposes.	○	○	○

Situation	Schedule M-1 Adjustments	Taxability	Deductibility	Alternative Minimum Tax	Communication	Research

Dan King contacts you and indicates that he is considering incorporating a business by transferring investment property with a fair market value of $500,000 and an adjusted basis of $150,000. In the exchange, King would receive all of the corporation's stock and the corporation would assume a $180,000 recourse liability on the transferred property that was incurred when the property was acquired. King is concerned that the assumption of the liability by the corporation may cause him to recognize gain and wants to know what can be done in the incorporation process to avoid recognition of gain. Write a letter to King addressing his concerns regarding the transfer of the liability.

REMINDER: Your response will be graded for both technical content and writing skills. Technical content will be evaluated for information that is helpful to the intended reader and clearly relevant to the issue. Writing skills will be evaluated for development, organization, and the appropriate expression of ideas in professional correspondence. Use a standard business memo or letter format with a clear beginning, middle, and end. Do not convey information in the form of a table, bullet point list, or other abbreviated presentation.

Dear Mr. King:

Situation	Schedule M-1 Adjustments	Taxability	Deductibility	Alternative Minimum Tax	Communication	Research

Assuming King's transfer in the Communication section qualifies under Sec. 351 as a transfer to a corporation controlled by the transferor, what Internal Revenue Code section and paragraph determines whether King's holding period for the stock received will include his holding period for the property transferred?

Section	Paragraph
§	( )

Simulation Problem 7 (40 to 45 minutes)

Situation				
	Tax Return Amounts	Deductibility	Research	Communication

Kimberly Corp. is a calendar-year accrual-basis corporation that commenced operations on January 1, 2007. The following adjusted accounts appear on Kimberly's records for the year ended December 31, 2009. Kimberly is not subject to the uniform capitalization rules.

Revenues and gains	
Gross sales	$2,000,000
Dividends:	
30%-owned domestic corporation	10,000
XYZ Corp.	10,000
Interest:	
US treasury bonds	26,000
Municipal bonds	25,000
Insurance proceeds	40,000
Gain on sale:	
Unimproved lot (1)	20,000
XYZ stock (2)	5,000
State franchise tax refund	14,000
Total	2,150,000
Costs and expenses	
Cost of goods sold	350,000
Salaries and wages	470,000
Depreciation:	
Real property	50,000
Personal property (3)	100,000
Bad debt (4)	10,000
State franchise tax	25,000
Vacation expense	10,000
Interest expense (5)	16,000
Life insurance premiums	20,000
Federal income taxes	200,000
Entertainment expense	20,000
Other expenses	29,000
Total	1,300,000
Net income	$ 850,000

Additional information

(1) Gain on the sale of unimproved lot: Purchased in 2007 for use in business for $50,000. Sold in 2009 for $70,000. Kimberly has never had any Sec. 1231 losses.

(2) Gain on sale of XYZ Stock: Purchased in 2007.

(3) Personal Property: The book depreciation is the same as tax depreciation for all the property that was placed in service before January 1, 2009. The book depreciation is straight-line over the useful life, which is the same as class life. Com-

pany policy is to use the half-year convention per books for personal property. Furniture and fixtures costing $56,000 were placed in service on January 2, 2009.

(4) Bad Debt: Represents the increase in the allowance for doubtful accounts based on an aging of accounts receivable. Actual bad debts written off were $7,000.

(5) Interest expense on

Mortgage loan	$10,000
Loan obtained to purchase municipal bonds	4,000
Line of credit loan	2,000

Situation	Tax Return Amounts	Deductibility	Research	Communication

For **items 1 through 5,** determine the amount that should be reported on Kimberly Corporation's 2009 Federal income tax return.

Items to be answered

1. What amount of interest income is taxable from the US Treasury bonds?

2. Determine the tax depreciation expense under the Modified Accelerated Cost Recovery System (MACRS), for the furniture and fixtures that were placed in service on January 2, 2009. Round the answer to the nearest thousand. Kimberly did not use the alternative depreciation system (ADS) or a straight-line method of depreciation. No election was made to expense part of the cost of the property, and Kimberly elected not to use bonus depreciation.

3. Determine the amount of bad debt to be included as an expense item.

4. Determine Kimberly's net long-term capital gain.

5. What amount of interest expense is deductible?

Situation	Tax Return Amounts	Deductibility	Research	Communication

For **items 1 through 5,** select whether the following expenses are fully deductible, partially deductible, or nondeductible, for regular tax purposes, on Kimberly's 2009 federal income tax return.

Selections

F.   Fully deductible for regular tax purposes on Kimberly Corp's 2009 federal income tax return.
P.   Partially deductible for regular tax purposes on Kimberly Corp's 2009 federal income tax return.
N.   Nondeductible for regular tax purposes on Kimberly Corp's 2009 federal income tax return.

	(F)	(P)	(N)
1. Organization expense incurred at corporate inception in 2007 to draft the corporate charter. No deduction was taken for the organization expense in 2007.	○	○	○
2. Life insurance premiums paid by the corporation for its executives as part of their compensation for services rendered. The corporation is neither the direct nor the indirect beneficiary of the policy and the amount of compensation is reasonable.	○	○	○
3. Vacation pay earned by employees which vested under a plan by December 31, 2009, and was paid February 1, 2010.	○	○	○
4. State franchise tax liability that has accrued during the year and was paid on March 15, 2010.	○	○	○
5. Entertainment expense to lease a luxury skybox during football season to entertain clients. A bona fide business discussion precedes each game. The cost of regular seats would have been one-half the amount paid.	○	○	○

Situation	Tax Return Amounts	Deductibility	Research	Communication

Research the allowable deduction for the dividend received from the 30%-owned domestic corporation. Cut and paste the applicable Internal Revenue Code sections.

Situation	Tax Return Amounts	Deductibility	Research	Communication

Write a memo to files indicating the dividends received deduction percentage that Kimberly Corp. is entitled to deduct for the dividends received from the 30%-owned corporation.

REMINDER: Your response will be graded for both technical content and writing skills. Technical content will be evaluated for information that is helpful to the intended reader and clearly relevant to the issue. Writing skills will be evaluated for development, organization, and the appropriate expression of ideas in professional correspondence. Use a standard business memo or letter format with a clear beginning, middle, and end. Do not convey information in the form of a table, bullet point list, or other abbreviated presentation.

To: The files
From: CPA Candidate

MULTIPLE-CHOICE ANSWERS

1. c	29. a	57. d	85. c	113. c	141. d
2. c	30. d	58. a	86. c	114. b	142. b
3. d	31. a	59. c	87. d	115. c	143. c
4. d	32. a	60. c	88. c	116. d	144. d
5. c	33. c	61. d	89. c	117. d	145. d
6. a	34. a	62. c	90. d	118. b	146. d
7. d	35. a	63. c	91. a	119. c	147. d
8. a	36. a	64. c	92. c	120. d	148. b
9. c	37. d	65. c	93. a	121. d	149. c
10. b	38. c	66. d	94. b	122. a	150. d
11. c	39. b	67. c	95. a	123. c	151. a
12. d	40. d	68. d	96. a	124. b	152. b
13. a	41. a	69. c	97. a	125. d	153. b
14. b	42. d	70. a	98. b	126. b	154. a
15. b	43. a	71. d	99. d	127. d	155. c
16. a	44. c	72. a	100. a	128. a	156. d
17. c	45. d	73. d	101. c	129. d	157. a
18. d	46. c	74. d	102. a	130. b	158. c
19. c	47. b	75. d	103. d	131. b	159. a
20. b	48. b	76. b	104. b	132. d	160. a
21. b	49. b	77. d	105. a	133. c	161. a
22. a	50. b	78. c	106. c	134. d	162. b
23. c	51. b	79. b	107. d	135. b	
24. c	52. b	80. b	108. a	136. c	
25. c	53. b	81. a	109. b	137. c	
26. b	54. b	82. c	110. c	138. b	
27. d	55. d	83. c	111. d	139. d	1st: __/162 = __%
28. c	56. c	84. c	112. b	140. c	2nd: __/162 = __%

MULTIPLE-CHOICE ANSWER EXPLANATIONS

A. Transfers to a Controlled Corporation

1. (c) The requirement is to determine Dexter Corporation's tax basis for the property received in the incorporation from Alan. Since Alan and Baker are the only transferors of property and they, in the aggregate, own only 800 of the 1,050 shares outstanding immediately after the incorporation, Sec. 351 does not apply to provide nonrecognition treatment for Alan's transfer of property. As a result, Alan is taxed on his realized gain of $15,000, and Dexter Corporation has a cost (i.e., FMV) basis of $45,000 for the transferred property.

2. (c) The requirement is to determine Clark's basis for the Jet Corp. stock received in exchange for a contribution of cash and other property. Generally, no gain or loss is recognized if property is transferred to a corporation solely in exchange for stock, if immediately after the transfer, the transferors of property are in control of the corporation. Since Clark and Hunt both transferred property solely in exchange for stock, and together own all of the corporation's stock, their realized gains on the "other property" transferred are not recognized. As a result, Clark's basis for his Jet stock is equal to the $60,000 of cash plus the $50,000 adjusted basis of other property transferred, or $110,000. Hunt's basis for his Jet stock is equal to the $120,000 adjusted basis of the other property that he transferred.

3. (d) The requirement is to determine Carr's recognized gain on the transfer of appreciated property in connection with the organization of Flexo Corp. No gain or loss is recognized if property is transferred to a corporation solely in exchange for stock, if the transferors of property are in

control of the corporation immediately after the exchange. "Control" means that the transferors of property must, in the aggregate, own at least 80% of the corporation's stock immediately after the exchange. Since both Beck and Carr transferred property in exchange for stock, and in the aggregate they own 90% of Flexo's stock immediately after the exchange, the requirements for nonrecognition are met.

4. (d) The requirement is to determine the percentage of Nu's stock that Jones must own to qualify for a tax-free incorporation. No gain or loss is recognized if property is transferred to a corporation solely in exchange for stock and the transferor(s) are in control of the corporation immediately after the exchange. For this purpose, the term "control" means the ownership of at least 80% of the combined voting power of stock entitled to vote, and at least 80% of each class of nonvoting stock.

5. (c) The requirement is to determine Feld's stock basis following the contribution of a parcel of land to his solely owned corporation. When a shareholder makes a contribution to the capital of a corporation, no gain or loss is recognized to the shareholder, the corporation has a transferred (carryover) basis for the property, and the shareholder's original stock basis is increased by the adjusted basis of the additional property contributed. Here, Feld's beginning stock basis of $50,000 is increased by the $10,000 basis for the contributed land, resulting in a stock basis of $60,000.

6. (a) The requirement is to determine whether gain or loss is recognized on the incorporation of Rela Associates (a partnership). No gain or loss is recognized if property is transferred to a corporation solely in exchange for stock, if immediately after the transfer, the transferor is in control of the corporation. For purposes of determining whether consideration other than stock (boot) has been received, the assumption of liabilities by the transferee corporation is not to be treated as the receipt of money or other property by the transferor. Thus, Rela Associates recognizes no gain or loss on the transfer of its assets and liabilities to a newly formed corporation in return for all of the corporation's stock.

Also note that no gain or loss will be recognized by Rela Associates on the distribution of the corporation's stock to its partners in liquidation, and no gain or loss will be recognized by the partners when they receive the corporation's stock in liquidation of their partnership interests.

7.   (d)   The requirement is to determine the taxable income to Rogers and the basis of her stock. Since services are excluded from the definition of "property," Rogers' transfer does not fall under the nonrecognition provision of Sec. 351. Rogers must report $10,000 of compensation income and the basis for the stock is $10,000, the amount reported as income.

B.   Sec. 1244 Stock

8.   (a)   The requirement is to determine the amount of ordinary loss that Jackson can deduct as a result of the worthlessness of the Bean Corp. stock that he inherited from his parents. Sec. 1244 permits a shareholder to deduct an ordinary loss of up to $50,000 per year ($100,000 if married filing jointly) if qualifying stock is sold, exchanged, or becomes worthless. The qualifying stock must have been issued in exchange for money or other property and must have been issued to the individual or partnership sustaining the loss. Ordinary loss treatment is not available if the shareholder sustaining the loss was **not** the original holder of the stock. As a result, an individual who acquires stock by purchase, gift, or inheritance from another shareholder is not entitled to ordinary loss treatment. Since Jackson inherited the Bean stock from his parents, Jackson does not qualify for ordinary loss treatment and his $25,000 loss will be recognized as a long-term capital loss.

9.   (c)   The requirement is to determine which statement is **not** a requirement for stock to qualify as Sec. 1244 small business corporation stock. To qualify as Sec. 1244 small business corporation stock, the stock must be issued by a domestic corporation to an individual or partnership in exchange for money or property (other than stock or securities). Any type of stock can qualify, whether common or preferred, voting or nonvoting.

10.   (b)   The requirement is to determine the character of Dinah's recognized loss from the sale of Sec. 1244 stock to be reported on her joint income tax return for 2010. Sec. 1244 permits an individual to deduct an ordinary loss on the sale or worthlessness of stock. The amount of ordinary loss deduction is annually limited to $50,000 ($100,000 for a married taxpayer filing a joint return), with any excess loss treated as a capital loss. Since Dinah is married filing a joint return, her ordinary loss is limited to $100,000, with the remaining $25,000 recognized as a capital loss.

11.   (c)   The requirement is to determine the amount and character of Nancy's recognized loss resulting from the sale of Sec. 1244 stock for $35,000 in 2010. Sec. 1244 permits a single individual to annually deduct up to $50,000 of ordi-

nary loss from the sale or exchange of small business corporation stock. Since Nancy acquired her stock in a tax-free asset transfer under Sec. 351, her stock's basis is $80,000 and the sale of the stock for $35,000 results in a loss of $45,000. However, because the property that Nancy transferred in exchange for the stock had an adjusted basis ($80,000) in excess of its fair market value ($60,000), the stock's basis must be reduced by the excess ($20,000) for purposes of determining the amount that can be treated as an ordinary loss. Thus, the amount of ordinary loss is limited to $60,000 – $35,000 = $25,000, with the remaining loss ($45,000 – $25,000 = $20,000) treated as a capital loss.

C.1.   Filing and Payment of Tax

12.   (d)   The requirement is to determine the correct statement concerning the imposition of a civil fraud penalty on a corporation. If part of a tax underpayment is the result of fraud, a fraud penalty equal to 75% of the portion of the underpayment attributable to fraud will be assessed. Fraud differs from simple, honest mistakes and negligence. Fraud involves a taxpayer's actual, deliberate, or intentional wrongdoing with the specific purpose to evade a tax believed to be owing. Examples of conduct from which fraud may be inferred include keeping a double set of books; making false entries or alterations, false invoices or documents; destroying books or records; and, concealing assets or covering up sources of income. Answers (a), (b), and (c) are incorrect because omitting income as a result of inadequate recordkeeping, erroneously failing to report income, and filing an incomplete return with a statement attached making clear that the return is incomplete, do not constitute deliberate actions with the specific intent of evading tax.

13.   (a)   The requirement is to determine whether Bass Corp. has to pay interest on the $400 tax payment made in 2010 and/or a tax delinquency penalty. A corporation is generally required to make estimated tax payments and to pay all of its remaining tax liability on or before the original due date of its tax return. Filing for an extension of time to file the tax return does not extend the time to pay the tax liability. If any amount of tax is not paid by the original due date, interest must be paid from the due date until the tax is paid. Additionally, a failure-to-pay tax delinquency penalty will be owed if the amount of tax paid by the original due date of the return is less than 90% of the tax shown on the return. The failure-to-pay penalty is imposed at a rate of 0.5% per month (or fraction thereof), with a maximum penalty of 25%. The penalty is imposed on the amount of unpaid tax at the beginning of the month for which the penalty is being computed. Bass Corp. is not subject to the failure-to-pay delinquency penalty because it paid in 95% of the total tax shown on its return by the original due date of the return.

14.   (b)   The requirement is to determine whether Edge Corp. could compute its first quarter 2010 estimated income tax payment using the annualized income method and/or the preceding year method. A corporation generally must pay four installments of estimated tax, each equal to 25% of its required annual payment. A penalty for the underpayment of estimated taxes can be avoided if a corporation's quarterly estimated payments are at least equal to the least of (1) 100% of the tax shown on the current year's tax return, (2) 100% of the tax that would be due by placing the current year's income for specified monthly periods on an annualized basis, or (3) 100% of the tax shown on the corporation's return for the preceding year. However, the preceding year's tax liability cannot be used to determine estimated payments if no tax liability existed in the preceding year or a short-period tax return was filed for the preceding year.

15. (b) The requirement is to determine which statements are correct in regard to the reopening of a tax year after the statute of limitations have expired. The statute of limitations stipulate a time limit for the government's assessment of tax or a taxpayer's claim for refund. The normal period for the statute of limitations is the later of three years after a return is filed, or three years after the due date of the return. A six-year statute of limitations will apply if the gross income omitted from the return exceeds 25% of the gross income reported on the return. If a taxpayer's return was false or fraudulent with the intent to evade tax, or the taxpayer engaged in a willful attempt to evade tax, there is no statute of limitations. If a tax return has a 50% non-fraudulent omission from gross income, there would be a six-year statute of limitations. However, once the six-year period expired, the year could not be reopened. In contrast, a closed year can be reopened if a corporation prevails in a determination allowing a deduction in an open year that the taxpayer erroneously had taken in a closed tax year. This special rule for the reopening of a tax year is intended to prevent the double inclusion of an item of income, or the double allowance of a deduction or credit that would otherwise occur.

16. (a) Even though a corporation's penalty for underpaying federal estimated taxes is in the nature of interest, it is treated as an addition to tax, and as such, the penalty is not deductible.

17. (c) The requirement is to determine which methods of estimated tax payment can be used by Blink Corp. to avoid the penalty for underpayment of federal estimated taxes. Generally, to avoid a penalty for the underpayment of estimated taxes a corporation's quarterly estimated payments must be at least equal to the least of (1) 100% of the tax shown on the current year's tax return, (2) 100% of the tax that would be due by placing income for specified monthly periods on an annualized basis, or (3) 100% of the tax shown on the corporation's return for the preceding year, provided the preceding year showed a positive tax liability and consisted of twelve months. In this case, Blink cannot base its estimated payments on its preceding year because Blink had a net operating loss for 2009.

18. (d) The requirement is to indicate whether corporate tax credits and the alternative minimum tax must be taken into account for purposes of computing a corporation's estimated income tax payments. A corporation must make estimated tax payments unless its tax liability can reasonably be expected to be less than $500. A corporation's estimated tax is its expected tax liability (including the alternative minimum tax) less its allowable tax credits.

19. (c) The requirement is to determine the minimum estimated tax payments that must be made by Finbury Corporation to avoid the estimated tax underpayment penalty for 2010. Since Finbury is a large corporation (i.e., a corporation with taxable income of $1,000,000 or more in any of its three preceding tax years), its estimated tax payments must be at least equal to 100% of its 2010 tax liability.

C.2.a. Corporate Tax Rates

20. (b) The requirement is to determine Kisco's income tax before credits given $70,000 of taxable income before a dividends received deduction that included a $10,000 dividend from a 15%-owned taxable domestic corporation. Since the $10,000 dividend would be eligible for a 70% dividends received deduction, Kisco's taxable income would be reduced by $7,000, resulting in taxable income of $63,000. The computation of tax would be

$50,000	×	15%	=	$ 7,500
$13,000	×	25%	=	3,250
		Tax	=	$10,750

C.2.c. Alternative Minimum Tax (AMT)

21. (b) The requirement is to determine the adjustment for adjusted current earnings (ACE) that will be used in the computation of Green Corp.'s alternative minimum tax for 2009. The ACE adjustment is equal to 75% of the difference between ACE and pre-ACE alternative minimum taxable income (AMTI). The ACE adjustment can be positive or negative, but a negative ACE adjustment is limited in amount to prior years' net positive ACE adjustments. For 2008, Green had a positive ACE adjustment of ($400,000 – $300,000) × 75% = $75,000. For 2009, Green's ACE is less than its pre-ACE AMTI leading to a negative ACE adjustment of ($100,000 – $300,000) × 75% = $150,000. However, this negative ACE adjustment is allowed only to the extent of $75,000, the amount of Green's net positive adjustment for prior years.

22. (a) The requirement is to determine Eastern's alternative minimum taxable income before the adjusted current earnings (ACE) adjustment. The starting point for computing a corporation's alternative minimum taxable income (AMTI) is its regular taxable income, which is then increased by tax preferences, and increased or decreased by specified adjustments. One tax preference that must be added to a corporation's regular taxable income is the amount of tax-exempt interest from private activity bonds. One adjustment that must be made to convert regular taxable income to AMTI is the adjustment for depreciation on personal business property placed in service after 1986. For regular tax purposes, Eastern utilized the general MACRS depreciation system and would have used the 200% declining balance method for computing regular tax depreciation on the five-year property placed in service during 2009. However, for AMT purposes, depreciation on five-year property must be computed using the 150% declining balance method. In this case, it means that Eastern's regular tax depreciation exceeded its allowable AMT depreciation by $1,000, and this amount must be added back to regular taxable income to arrive at AMTI. Thus, Eastern's AMTI (before ACE adjustment) is its regular taxable income of $300,000, plus its $5,000 of tax-exempt interest from private activity bonds and $1,000 of depreciation adjustment, or $306,000.

23. (c) The requirement is to determine the correct statement regarding the amount of excess of a corporation's tentative minimum tax over its regular tax. If a corporation's tentative minimum tax exceeds its regular tax, the excess represents the corporation's alternative minimum tax and is payable in addition to its regular tax.

24.   (c)   The requirement is to determine the exempt portion of Rona Corp.'s alternative minimum taxable income (AMTI). A corporation is allowed an exemption of $40,000 in computing its AMTI. However, the $40,000 exemption is reduced by 25% of the corporation's AMTI in excess of $150,000. Here, the amount of exemption is $40,000 – [($200,000 – $150,000) × 25%] = $27,500.

25.   (c)   The requirement is to determine which item is a tax preference that must be included in the computation of a corporation's alternative minimum tax (AMT) for 2010. Tax-exempt interest on private activity bonds issued in 2009 is a tax preference item. Answer (a) is incorrect because it is the excess of income under the percentage-of-completion method over the amount reported using the completed-contract method that is a positive adjustment in computing the AMT. Answer (b) is incorrect because a deduction for casualty losses is allowed in the computation of AMT. Answer (d) is incorrect because capital gains are not a preference item in computing the AMT.

26.   (b)   For real property that was placed in service before January 1, 1999, an AMT adjustment is necessary because for AMT purposes, real property must be depreciated using the straight-line method over a forty-year recovery period, rather than the thirty-nine year or twenty-seven and one-half year recovery period used for regular tax purposes. However, note that this adjustment has been eliminated for real property first placed in service after December 31, 1998. The dividends received deduction, charitable contributions, and investment interest expense are neither adjustments nor tax preference items.

27.   (d)   The requirement is to determine when a corporation will not be subject to the alternative minimum tax (AMT) for 2010. A corporation is exempt from AMT for its first tax year. After the first year, a corporation is exempt from AMT for each year that it passes a gross receipts test. A corporation is exempt for its second year if its gross receipts for the first year did not exceed $5 million. For all subsequent years, a corporation is exempt if its average annual gross receipts for the testing period do not exceed $7.5 million. Exemption from the AMT is not based on asset size nor number of shareholders.

28.   (c)   A corporation is exempt from the corporate AMT for its first tax year. It is exempt for its second year if its first year's gross receipts were $5 million or less. To be exempt for its third year, the corporation's average gross receipts for the first two years must be $7.5 million or less. To be exempt for the fourth year (and subsequent years), the corporation's average gross receipts for all prior three-year periods also must be $7.5 million or less. Here, Bradbury is exempt for 2008 because its average gross receipts for 2006-2007 were $6.75 million. However, Bradbury loses its exemption for 2009 and all subsequent years because its average gross receipts for 2006-2008 exceed $7.5 million ($7.67 million).

C.3.   Gross Income

29.   (a)   The requirement is to indicate whether personal service corporations and personal holding companies must include 100% of dividends received from unrelated taxable domestic corporations in gross income in computing regular taxable income. Since the question concerns **gross income,** not taxable income, no part of the dividend income would be

offset by a dividends received deduction. Therefore, both personal service corporations and personal holding companies must include 100% of dividends received from unrelated taxable domestic corporations in gross income.

30.   (d)   The requirement is to determine the amount of bond sinking fund trust income taxable to Andi Corp. in 2009. Since the trust income will be accumulated and benefit Andi Corp. by reducing the amount of future contributions that Andi must make to the bond sinking fund, all of the trust income, consisting of $60,000 of interest and $8,000 of long-term capital gain, is taxable to Andi Corp.

31.   (a)   The requirement is to determine the amount of capital gain recognized by Lee Corp. on the sale of its treasury stock. A corporation will never recognize gain or loss on the receipt of money or other property in exchange for its stock, including treasury stock.

32.   (d)   The requirement is to determine the amount of gain to be recognized by Ral Corp. when it issues its stock in exchange for land. No gain or loss is ever recognized by a corporation on the receipt of money or other property in exchange for its own stock (including treasury stock).

33.   (c)   The requirement is to determine the amount of dividend reportable by a corporate distributee on a property distribution. The amount of dividend to be reported by a corporate distributee is the FMV of the property less any liability assumed. Kile's dividend would be $12,000, reduced by the liability of $5,000 = $7,000.

C.4.b.   Organizational Expenditures

34.   (d)   The requirement is to determine which costs are deductible organizational expenditures. Organizational expenditures include fees for accounting and legal services incident to incorporation (e.g., fees for drafting corporate charter, bylaws, terms of stock certificates), expenses of organizational meetings and of temporary directors meetings, and fees paid to the state of incorporation. However, the costs incurred in issuing and selling stock and securities (e.g., professional fees to issue stock, printing costs, underwriting commissions) do not qualify as organizational expenditures and are not tax deductible.

35.   (a)   The requirement is to determine the amount that Brown should deduct for organizational expenditures for 2010. For organizational expenditures incurred or paid after October 22, 2004, a corporation may elect to deduct up to $5,000 for the tax year in which the corporation begins business. The $5,000 amount must be reduced by the amount by which organizational expenditures exceed $50,000. Remaining expenditures are deducted ratably over the 180-month period beginning with the month in which the corporation begins business. Brown's qualifying organizational expenditures include the $40,000 of legal fees, $15,000 for temporary directors' meetings, and $4,400 of state incorporation fees, a total of $59,400. The $25,000 of underwriting commissions and other costs of issuing stock are not deductible, and merely reduce paid-in capital. Since Brown began business in July, Brown's deduction for 2010 is $59,400 × 6/180 = $1,980.

36.   (a)   The requirement is to determine the correct statement regarding the costs of organizing a corporation during 2010. A corporation's organizational expenditures (e.g., legal fees for drafting the corporate charter, bylaws, and terms of original stock certificates, necessary accounting services, expenses of temporary directors, fees paid to the state of incorporation) are incidental to the creation of the corporation. For organizational expenditures incurred or paid after October 22, 2004, a corporation may elect to deduct up to $5,000 for the tax year in which the corporation begins business. The $5,000 amount must be reduced by the amount by which organizational expenditures exceed $50,000. Remaining expenditures are deducted ratably over the 180-month period beginning with the month in which the corporation begins business.

37. (d) The requirement is to determine the maximum allowable deduction for organizational expenditures for 2010. For organizational expenditures incurred or paid after October 22, 2004, a corporation may elect to deduct up to $5,000 for the tax year in which the corporation begins business. The $5,000 amount must be reduced by the amount by which organizational expenditures exceed $50,000. Remaining expenditures are deducted ratably over the 180-month period beginning with the month in which the corporation begins business. Here, since organizational expenditures total $8,600, $5,000 can be deducted for 2010, with the remaining $3,600 deducted ratably over the 180-month period beginning with September (the month in which the corporation began business). Thus, the maximum deduction for 2010 would be $5,000 + ($3,600 × 4/180) = $5,080.

C.4.c.   Charitable Contributions

38. (c) The requirement is to determine the amount of Jackson Corp.'s charitable contributions carryover to 2010. A corporation's charitable contributions deduction is limited to 10% of its taxable income computed before the deduction for charitable contributions, the dividends received deduction, and before deductions for a NOL carryback and capital loss carryback. Although the limitation is computed before deducting NOL and capital loss carrybacks, NOL and capital loss carryforwards are deducted in arriving at the contribution base amount. Thus, of the $8,000 given to charitable organizations during 2009, $2,500 can be currently deducted, leaving $5,500 to be carried over to 2010.

Gross income from operations	$100,000
Dividend income	10,000
Operating expenses	(35,000)
Officers' salaries	(20,000)
NOL carryover from 2008	(30,000)
TI before contributions and DRD	$ 25,000
	× 10%
Contributions deduction for 2009	$ 2,500

39. (b) The requirement is to determine the amount that Cable Corp. can deduct for charitable contributions for 2010. A corporation's charitable contribution deduction is limited to 10% of its taxable income computed before the charitable contribution and dividends received deductions. Since Cable's taxable income of $820,000 already included a $40,000 dividends received deduction, $40,000 must be added back to arrive at Cable's contribution base of $860,000. Thus, Cable's maximum contribution deduction for 2010 would be limited to $860,000 × 10% = $86,000. Cable would deduct the $80,000 contributed during 2010, plus $6,000 of its $10,000 carryover from 2009. This means that Cable will have a $4,000 contributions carryover from 2009 to 2011.

40. (d) The requirement is to determine the **maximum** charitable contribution deduction that Tapper Corp. may take on its 2009 return. Since Tapper is an accrual method calendar-year corporation, it can deduct contributions actually made during 2009, plus Tapper can elect to deduct any contribution authorized by its board of directors during 2009, so long as the contribution is subsequently made no later than 2 1/2 months after the end of the tax year. Thus, to maximize its deduction for 2009, Tapper can deduct both the $10,000 contribution made during 2009 as well as the $30,000 contribution authorized during 2009 and paid on February 1, 2010. The total ($40,000) is deductible for 2009 since it is less than the limitation amount ($500,000 × 10% = $50,000).

41. (a) The requirement is to determine the amount to be included as gross income in Lyle Corp.'s 2010 return for the receipt of nonprescription drug samples that were later donated to an exempt organization. When unsolicited samples of items that are normally inventoried and sold in the ordinary course of business are received from a supplier, and later donated as a charitable contribution, the fair market value of the items received must be included in gross income. The taxpayer is then allowed a charitable contribution deduction equal to the fair market value of the items donated.

42. (d) The requirement is to determine the portion of the dividends received of $1,000 that is to be included in taxable income when Nale Corp. computes its maximum allowable deduction for contributions. A corporation's maximum allowable deduction for charitable contributions is limited to 10% of its taxable income before the charitable contributions and dividends received deductions. Thus, Nale must include all $1,000 of dividends in its taxable income for purposes of computing its maximum allowable deduction for contributions.

43. (a) The requirement is to determine the contribution base for purposes of computing Gero Corp.'s charitable contributions deduction. A corporation's contribution base is its taxable income before the charitable contributions deduction, the dividends received deduction, and before deductions for NOL and capital loss carrybacks. Since Gero had operating income of $160,000 after deducting $10,000 of contributions, its contribution base would be $160,000 + $10,000 + $2,000 dividends = $172,000.

44. (c) The requirement is to determine the maximum charitable contribution deduction for 2009. Since Norwood is an accrual-basis calendar-year corporation, it can elect to deduct a contribution authorized by its board of directors during 2009, so long as the contribution is subsequently paid no later than two and one-half months after year-end (i.e., by March 15th). Thus, to maximize its deduction for 2009, Norwood can elect to deduct the $10,000 contribution authorized during 2009 and paid on March 1, 2010, but its deduction is limited to 10% of taxable income before the charitable contribution deduction. The maximum amount deductible for 2009 is

Book income	$500,000
+ Charitable contribution	100,000
TI before CC deduction	$600,000
	× 10%
Maximum CC deduction	$ 60,000

The remaining $40,000 can be carried over a maximum of five years.

C.4.e.   Dividends Received Deduction (DRD)

45. (d)   The requirement is to determine Best Corp.'s dividends received deduction for the $100,000 of dividends received from an unrelated domestic corporation. Dividends received from less than 20%-owned corporations are generally eligible for a 70% DRD (i.e., 70% × dividend). However, if the corporation's taxable income before the DRD is less than the amount of dividend, the DRD will be limited to 70% of taxable income, unless the full DRD (70% × dividend) creates or increases a net operating loss. Here, since taxable income before the DRD ($90,000) is less than the amount of dividends ($100,000), and the full DRD (70% × $100,000 = $70,000) would not create a NOL, the DRD is limited to 70% × $90,000 = $63,000.

46. (c)   The requirement is to determine the amount to be reported as income before special deductions on Acorn's tax return. A corporation's taxable income before special deductions generally includes all income and all deductions except for the dividends received deduction. Thus, Acorn's income before special deductions would include the sales of $500,000 and dividend income of $25,000, less the cost of sales of $250,000, a total of $275,000.

47. (b)   The requirement is to determine the correct statement regarding the corporate dividends received deduction (DRD). To qualify for a DRD, the investor corporation must own the investee's stock for more than forty-five days (ninety days for preferred stock if the dividends received are in arrears for more than one year). Answer (a) is incorrect because the DRD may be limited to the applicable percentage of the investor corporation's taxable income. Answer (c) is incorrect because a 70% DRD applies to dividends from less-than-20%-owned corporations, an 80% DRD applies to dividends from unaffiliated corporations that are at least 20%-owned, while a 100% DRD applies to dividends from corporations that are at least 80%-owned when a consolidated tax return is not filed.

48. (b)   The requirement is to determine the amount of dividends to be included in Ryan Corp.'s taxable income. Since the dividends were received from less than 20%-owned taxable domestic corporations, they are eligible for a 70% dividends received deduction. Thus, the amount of dividends to be included in taxable income is $2,000 – (70% × $2,000) = $600.

49. (b)   The requirement is to determine the amount of dividends to be included in Daly Corp.'s **taxable income** for 2010. Since the dividends were received from 20%-owned taxable domestic corporations, they are eligible for an 80% dividends received deduction. Thus, the amount of dividends to be included in taxable income is $1,000 – (80% × $1,000) = $200.

50. (b)   The requirement is to determine the amount of dividends that qualifies for the 80% dividends received deduction. Only dividends received from taxable domestic unaffiliated corporations that are at least 20%-owned qualify for the 80% dividends received deduction ($7,500). So-called "dividends" paid by mutual savings banks are reported as interest, and are not eligible for the dividends received deduction.

C.4.j.   Losses

51. (b)   The requirement is to determine Stark Corp.'s net operating loss (NOL) for 2009. A NOL carryover from 2008 would not be allowed in computing the 2009 NOL. In contrast, a dividends received deduction (DRD) is allowed in computing a NOL since a corporation's DRD is not subject to limitation if it creates or increases a NOL. Stark Corp.'s NOL would be computed as follows:

Gross income from operations	$ 350,000
Dividend income	100,000
Less operating expenses	(400,000)
TI before DRD	$ 50,000
DRD (70% × $100,000)	(70,000)
Net operating loss for 2009	$ (20,000)

52. (b)   The requirement is to determine the proper treatment of a C corporation's net capital losses. A corporation's capital losses can only be used to offset capital gains. If a corporation has a net capital loss, it cannot be currently deducted, but instead must be carried back three years and forward five years as a STCL to offset capital gains in those years.

53. (b)   The requirement is to determine the amount of Taylor Corp.'s 2009 net operating loss (NOL) that is available for use in its 2010 return. A net operating loss is generally carried back two years and forward twenty years to offset taxable income in the carryback and carryforward years. Since Taylor Corp. made no election to waive a carryback period, the 2009 NOL would be used to offset Taylor's 2007 and 2008 taxable income in the two carryback years (a total of $70,000) leaving $200,000 – $70,000 = $130,000 to be carried forward as an NOL deduction in its 2010 return.

54. (b)   The requirement is to determine the correct statement regarding the carryback or carryforward of an unused net capital loss. A corporation's unused net capital loss is carried back three years and forward for up to five years to offset capital gains in the carryback and carryforward years. An unused net capital loss is always carried back and forward as a short-term capital loss whether or not it was short-term when sustained.

55. (d)   The requirement is to determine Haya Corporation's net operating loss (NOL) for 2009. A deduction for a net operating loss carryover is not allowed in computing a NOL. Furthermore, a deduction for charitable contributions is generally not allowed, since the charitable contributions deduction is limited to 10% of taxable income before the charitable contributions and dividends received deductions. Thus, Haya's NOL for 2009 would be computed as follows:

Gross income	$ 600,000
Less expenses	(800,000)
	$(200,000)
Add back contributions included in expenses	5,000
NOL for 2009	$(195,000)

56. (c)   The requirement is to determine the NOL for 2010 given that deductions in the tax return exceed gross income by $56,800. In computing the NOL for 2010, the DRD of $6,800 would be fully allowed, but the $15,000 NOL deduction (carryover from 2009) would not be allowed. $56,800 – $15,000 = $41,800.

57. (d)   The requirement is to determine the amount of casualty loss deduction available to Ram Corp. due to the complete destruction of its machine. If business property is completely destroyed, the amount of casualty loss deduction is the property's adjusted basis immediately before the casualty. Note that the "$100 floor" and "10% of adjusted gross income" limitations that apply to personal casualty losses, do not apply to business casualty losses.

C.4.l.   R&D Expenditures

58.   (a)   The requirement is to determine the proper treatment for qualifying research and experimentation expenditures. A taxpayer can elect to deduct qualifying research and experimentation expenditures as a current expense if the taxpayer so elects for the first taxable year in which the expenditures are incurred. Otherwise, the taxpayer must capitalize the expenditures. Then, if the capitalized costs are not subject to depreciation (because there is no determinable life), the taxpayer can amortize them over a period of sixty months or longer.

C.6.   Reconcile Book and Taxable Income

59.   (c)   The requirement is to determine Kelly Corp.'s taxable income given net income per books of $300,000, that included $50,000 of dividend income and an $80,000 deduction for bad debt expense. Since the dividends were received from a 5%-owned taxable domestic corporation, they are eligible for a 70% dividends received deduction ($50,000 × 70% = $35,000). Since no bad debts were actually written off and the reserve method cannot be used for tax purposes, the $80,000 of bad debt expense per books is not deductible for tax purposes and must be added back to book income to arrive at taxable income. Kelly's taxable income is $300,000 − $35,000 + $80,000 = $345,000.

60.   (c)   The requirement is to determine Maple Corp.'s taxable income given book income before federal income taxes of $100,000. The provision for state income taxes of $1,000 that was deducted per books is also an allowable deduction in computing taxable income. The interest earned on US Treasury Bonds of $6,000 that was included in book income must also be included in computing taxable income. The $2,000 of interest expense on the bank loan to purchase the US Treasury Bonds was deducted per books and is also an allowable deduction in computing taxable income, because the interest income from the obligations is taxable. Since there are no differences between the book and tax treatment of these items, taxable income is the same as book income before federal income taxes, $100,000.

61.   (d)   The requirement is to determine Dodd Corp.'s taxable income given net income per books of $100,000. The $27,000 provision for federal income tax deducted per books is not deductible in computing taxable income. The $5,000 net capital loss deducted per books is not deductible in computing taxable income because a corporation can only use capital losses to offset capital gains. The life insurance premiums of $3,000 deducted per books are not deductible in computing taxable income because life insurance proceeds are excluded from gross income. Thus, Dodd Corp.'s taxable income is $100,000 + $27,000 + $5,000 + $3,000 = $135,000.

62.   (c)   The requirement is to determine Bard Corp.'s taxable income given book income of $450,000. No adjustment is necessary for the $4,000 of state corporate income tax refunds since they were included in book income

and would also be included in taxable income due to the "tax benefit rule" (i.e., an item of deduction that reduces a taxpayer's income tax for a prior year must be included in gross income if later recovered). The life insurance proceeds of $15,000 must be subtracted from book income because they were included in book income, but would be excluded from taxable income. The net capital loss of $20,000 that was subtracted in computing book income must be added back to book income because a net capital loss is not deductible in computing taxable income. Thus, Bard Corp.'s taxable income would be $450,000 − $15,000 + $20,000 = $455,000.

63.   (c)   The requirement is to determine Dewey Corporation's taxable income, given that organization costs of $257,400 were deducted as an expense in arriving at book income of $520,000. For organizatinal expenditures incurred or paid after October 22, 2004, a corporation may elect to deduct up to $5,000 for the tax year in which the corporation begins business. The $5,000 amount must be reduced by the amount by which organizational expenditures exceed $50,000. Remaining expenditures are deducted ratably over the 180-month period beginning with the month in which the corporation begins business. Since Dewey began business in June, the allowable amortization for 2009 would be $257,400 × 7/180 = $10,010. Thus, adding back the $257,400 deduction for organization expense to book income, and subtracting the $10,010 of allowable amortization for tax purposes results in taxable income of $520,000 + $257,400 − $10,010 = $767,390.

64.   (c)   The requirement is to determine net income per books given TI of $700,000.

Taxable income	$700,000
Provision for federal income tax	− 280,000
Depreciation on tax return	+ 130,000
Depreciation per books	− 75,000
Life insurance proceeds	+ 100,000
Net income per books	$575,000

The provision for federal income tax is not deductible in computing TI but must be deducted per books. The life insurance proceeds are tax exempt, but must be included per books.

65.   (d)   The requirement is to compute Ajax's taxable income given book income of $1,200,000 and items included in the computation of book income. Book income must be adjusted for the tax-exempt interest (net of related expenses) and the provision for federal income tax:

Book income	$1,200,000
Municipal bond interest	(40,000)
Nondeductible interest expense (to produce tax-exempt interest income)	8,000
Provision for federal income tax	524,000
Taxable income	$1,692,000

The damages received for patent infringement that were included in book income are similarly included in taxable income, so no adjustment is necessary.

C.6.c.   Schedule M-1

66.   (d)   The requirement is to determine the amount of income to be shown on the last line of Farve Corp.'s Schedule M-1 for 2009. Schedule M-1 provides a reconciliation of income reported per books with income reported on the tax return. Generally, items of income and deduction whose book and tax treatment differ, result in Schedule M-1 items. However, since Schedule M-1 reconciles to taxable income before the dividends received and net operating loss deductions, the dividends received deduction will not be a reconciling item on Schedule M-1. In this case, Farve Corp.'s $80,000 of book income would be increased by the $18,000 of federal income tax, $6,000 of net capital loss, and 50% of the $4,000 of business meals which were deducted per books, but are not deductible for tax purposes. Book income would be reduced by the $5,000 of municipal bond interest that is tax-exempt.

67. (c) The requirement is to determine Starke Corp.'s taxable income as reconciled on Schedule M-1 of Form 1120. Schedule M-1 provides a reconciliation of a corporation's book income with its taxable income before the dividends received and net operating loss deductions. Starke reported book income of $380,000 that included $50,000 of municipal bond interest income, and deductions for $170,000 of federal income tax expense and $2,000 of interest expense incurred to carry the municipal bonds. Since municipal bond interest is tax-exempt, the $50,000 of interest income must be subtracted from book income, and the $2,000 of interest expense incurred to carry the municipal bonds is not deductible and must be added back to book income. Similarly, the $170,000 of federal income tax expense is not deductible and must be added back to book income. Thus, Starke's taxable income is $380,000 − $50,000 + $2,000 + $170,000 = $502,000.

68. (d) The requirement is to determine whether lodging expenses for out-of-town travel and the deduction of a net capital loss would be reported on Schedule M-1 of the US corporate income tax return (Form 1120). Schedule M-1 generally provides a reconciliation of a corporation's income per books with the corporation's taxable income before the NOL and dividends received deductions. Since a net capital loss deducted per books would not be deductible for tax purposes, the net capital loss would be added back to book income on Schedule M-1. However, since out-of-town lodging expenses are deductible for both book and tax purposes, the expenses would not appear on Schedule M-1.

69. (c) The reconciliation of income per books with income per return is accomplished on Schedule M-1 of Form 1120. Both temporary differences (e.g., accelerated depreciation on tax return and straight-line on books) and permanent differences (e.g., tax-exempt interest) must be considered to convert book income to taxable income.

70. (a) The requirement is to determine Media Corporation's net M-1 adjustment on its 2009 Form 1120. Generally, items of income and deduction whose book and tax treatment differ result in Schedule M-1 adjustments that reconcile income reported per books with taxable income. Media reported book income that included $6,000 in municipal bond interest income, and deductions that included $1,500 of interest expense incurred on debt to carry the municipal bonds, and $8,000 in advertising expense. Since municipal bond interest is tax-exempt, the $6,000 of interest income must be subtracted from book income. Additionally, since the $1,500 of interest expense to carry the municipal bonds is an expense incurred in the production of exempt income, it is not tax deductible and must be added back to book income. On the other hand, the $8,000 of advertising expense is deductible for book as well as taxable income purposes, and no Schedule M-1 adjustment is necessary. Thus, Media's net Schedule M-1 adjustment to reconcile

book income to taxable income is $1,500 − $6,000 = ($4,500).

C.6.d. Schedule M-2

71. (d) The requirement is to determine the amount to be shown on Schedule M-2 of Form 1120 as Barbaro's retained earnings at December 31, 2009. Beginning with the balance at January 1, 2009, the end of year balance would be computed as follows:

Balance, 1/1/09	$600,000
Net income for year	+ 274,900
Federal income tax refund	+ 26,000
Cash dividends	− 150,000
Balance, 12/31/09	$750,900

72. (a) The requirement is to determine the amount that should appear on the last line of Schedule M-2 of Form 1120. Schedule M-2 is an "Analysis of Unappropriated Retained Earnings Per Books." Its first line is the balance at the beginning of the year and its last line is the balance at the end of the year. The end-of-year balance would be computed as follows:

Retained earnings, beginning	$ 50,000
Net income for year	+ 70,000
Contingency reserve	− 10,000
Cash dividends	− 8,000
Retained earnings, end of year	$102,000

D. Affiliated and Controlled Corporations

73. (d) The requirement is to determine the amount of dividend revenue to be reported on Bank Corp.'s consolidated tax return for the $48,000 of dividends received from Bank Corp.'s 80%-owned subsidiary, Shore Corp. Instead of filing separate tax returns, an affiliated group of corporations (i.e., corporations connected through 80% or more stock ownership) can elect to file a consolidated tax return. If a consolidated return is filed, dividends received from affiliated group members are eliminated in the consolidation process, and are not reported on the consolidated tax return.

74. (d) The requirement is to determine the amount of net dividend income received from an affiliated corporation that should be included in Portal Corporation's 2010 consolidated tax return. When dividends are received from an affiliated corporation (i.e., at least 80%-owned subsidiary) during a consolidated return year, the intercompany dividends are eliminated in the consolidation process and are not included in gross income.

75. (d) The requirement is to determine the amount of gain to be reported in the 2010 and 2009 consolidated tax returns. Generally, gains and losses on intercompany transactions during consolidated return years are deferred and reported in subsequent years when a restoration event occurs. Since Potter and Sly filed a consolidated tax return for 2009, Potter's gain on the sale of land to Sly in 2009 is deferred and will be reported when Sly sells the land outside of the affiliated group in 2010. Thus, the 2009 consolidated return will report no gain with regard to the land, while the 2010 consolidated return will report the aggregate amount of gain, $125,000 − $60,000 = $65,000.

76. (b) The requirement is to determine the correct statement regarding an affiliated group of includible corporations filing a consolidated return. One of the advantages of filing a consolidated return is that operating losses of one member of the group offset operating profits of other members of the group. Answer (a) is incorrect because inter-company dividends are eliminated in the consolidation process and are excluded from the return. Answers (c) and (d) are incorrect because an affiliated group of includible corporations is also a controlled group and is therefore limited to one alternative minimum tax exemption and one accumulated earnings credit.

77. (d) The requirement is to determine the stock ownership requirement that must be satisfied to enable Dana Corp. to elect to file a consolidated tax return that includes Seco Corp. For Dana and Seco to qualify for filing a consolidated tax return, Dana must directly own stock possessing at least 80% of the total voting power, and at least 80% of the total value of Seco stock.

78. (c) The requirement is to determine the correct statement regarding the filing of consolidated returns. The election to file consolidated returns is limited to affiliated corporations. Affiliated corporations are parent-subsidiary corporations that are connected through stock ownership wherein at least 80% of the combined voting power and value of all stock (except the common parent's) is directly owned by other includible corporations. Answer (a) is incorrect because brother-sister corporations are not affiliated corporations. Answer (b) is incorrect because no advance permission is required. Answer (d) is incorrect because an affiliated group's election to file consolidated returns is independent of its issuing financial statements on a consolidated basis.

79. (b) The requirement is to determine the amount of gain for 2010 that Subsidiary should take into account as a result of the 2009 sale of land to Parent. Since Parent and Subsidiary are filing consolidated tax returns, the $20,000 of gain to Subsidiary in 2009 is not recognized, but instead is deferred and recognized when the land is sold outside the affiliated group in 2010.

E. Dividends and Distributions

80. (b) The requirement is to determine Westwind's accumulated earnings and profits at year-end. Here, Westwind had a beginning deficit of $45,000, had current earnings and profits of $15,000, and distributed $12,000 cash during the year. As a result, Westwind's beginning deficit of $45,000 would be reduced by the $3,000 of current earnings and profits that were not distributed, resulting in a deficit of $42,000 at the end of the year.

81. (a) The requirement is to determine Cable's accumulated earnings and profits (AEP) at the end of the year. Cable's beginning AEP of $100,000 would be increased by its earnings and profits for the current tax year (CEP). The starting point for computing Cable's CEP would be its taxable income of $50,000. Taxable income would be reduced by the $5,000 of federal income taxes paid, and would also be reduced by the $1,000 of current year charitable contributions which would not be allowed as a deduction in computing taxable income because of the 10% of taxable income limitation. Additionally, CEP would be reduced by the current year net capital loss of $2,000 which would not be allowed as a deduction in computing current year taxable income because a corporation cannot deduct a net capital loss. As a result, Cable's CEP is $50,000 – ($5,000 + $1,000 + $2,000) = $42,000, and its AEP at the end of the current year is $100,000 + $42,000 = $142,000.

82. (c) The requirement is to determine the amount of the 2009 distributions classified as dividend income to Locke's shareholders. A corporation's distributions to shareholders on their stock are treated as a dividend to the extent of a corporation's current earnings and profits and/or accumulated earnings and profits. Here, the $80,000 distributed to shareholders would be treated as a dividend to the extent of Locke's current ($20,000) and accumulated ($30,000) earnings and profits, or $50,000.

83. (c) The requirement is to determine the balance of Chicago Corp.'s accumulated earnings and profits (AEP) at January 1, 2010. The AEP beginning balance of $100,000 would be reduced by the 2009 deficit of ($140,000), resulting in a deficit of ($40,000). Since distributions only pay out a corporation's positive AEP, and neither create nor increase a deficit in AEP, the AEP deficit of ($40,000) is not affected by the $30,000 distributed to shareholders.

84. (c) The requirement is to determine the amount of gain recognized by Salon, Inc. as a result of the distribution of property and liability to its sole shareholder. Generally, a corporation must recognize gain when it distributes appreciated property to a shareholder. The gain is measured by treating the corporation as if it had sold the property to the shareholder for its fair market value. However, if there is a liability on the property that is assumed by the shareholder and the amount of liability exceeds the property's fair market value, then the amount of liability is used to measure the gain. Here, Salon's recognized gain would total $10,000 liability – $3,000 basis = $7,000.

85. (c) The requirement is to determine the amount received from Kent Corp. that is taxable as dividend income to Reed for 2009. The term "dividend" means any distribution of property made by a corporation to its shareholders out of its current earnings and profits and/or accumulated earnings and profits. For distributions of property other than cash, the amount of distribution is the property's fair market value reduced by any liabilities that are assumed or liabilities to which the property is subject. In this case, the amount of distribution made by Kent Corp. to Reed is the property's fair market value of $200,000. This $200,000 of distribution is taxable as dividend income to Reed to the extent of Kent Corp.'s current earnings and profits ($60,000) and accumulated earnings and profits ($125,000), a total of $185,000. Note that this answer assumes that the gain that was recognized by Kent Corp. on the distribution ($200,000 FMV – $150,000 adjusted basis = $50,000) has already been included in the amount provided as Kent's current earnings and profits for 2009. This assumption can be made because the item indicates "Current earnings and profits for 2009," not "Current earnings and profits before the distribution." Also, note that the portion of the distribution that is not a dividend ($200,000 – $185,000 = $15,000) is a nontaxable return of Reed's stock basis, and reduces stock basis from $500,000 to $485,000.

86. (c) The requirement is to determine which statements are correct concerning Ridge Corp.'s cash distribution of $1,000,000 to its shareholders with respect to its stock. A corporation's distributions to shareholders on their stock will be taxed as dividend income to the extent of the corporation's current and accumulated earnings and profits. Any distributions in excess of earnings and profits are treated as a nontaxable return of stock basis, with any distributions in excess of a shareholder's stock basis treated as capital gain. Therefore, $750,000 of the distribution to Ridge's shareholders was taxable as a dividend, with the remaining $250,000 treated as a nontaxable return of stock basis.

87. (d) The requirement is to determine the amount of loss recognized by Tour Corporation on the nonliquidating distribution of property to shareholders. Although a gain would be recognized, no loss can be recognized on nonliquidating corporate distributions to shareholders.

88. (c) The requirement is to determine the amount taxable as a dividend to Kee's shareholders for 2009. Corporate distributions of property to shareholders on their stock are taxed as dividends to the extent of accumulated and/or current earnings and profits. Even though a corporation has an accumulated deficit in earnings and profits for prior years ($50,000 in this case), a distribution will nevertheless be taxed as a dividend to the extent of the corporation's earnings and profits for the current taxable year when measured at the end of the year. Thus, the $30,000 distribution will be taxed as a dividend to the extent of the current earnings and profits for 2009 of $10,000.

89. (c) The requirement is to determine the amount of taxable dividend income resulting from Dahl Corp.'s distribution of cash and land to Green. The amount of distribution received by Green equals the amount of cash ($9,000) plus the FMV of the land ($40,000), a total of $49,000. This $49,000 will be taxable as dividend income to Green to the extent that it is paid out of Dahl Corp.'s current and accumulated earnings and profits. Dahl had accumulated earnings and profits of $9,000 before consideration of the dividend declaration and distribution. Since a distributing corporation recognizes gain on the distribution of appreciated property, Dahl must recognize a gain of $40,000 – $5,000 = $35,000 on the distribution of the land. This $35,000 of gain increases Dahl Corp.'s available earnings and profits from $9,000 to $44,000. Thus, Green's $49,000 distribution will be taxed as a dividend to the extent of $44,000.

90. (d) The requirement is to determine the amount of dividend income taxable to the shareholder. If a corporation sells property to a shareholder for less than fair market value, the shareholder is considered to have received a constructive dividend to the extent of the difference between the fair market value of the property and the price paid. Thus, the shareholder's dividend income is $80,000 – $50,000 = $30,000.

91. (a) Distributions of property to shareholders reduce earnings and profits (E&P) by the greater of the property's adjusted basis, or its FMV at date of distribution. E&P must be adjusted by any gain recognized to the distributing corporation, and any liabilities to which the property being distributed is subject. Gelt Corporation would recognize a gain of $7,500 on the distribution (i.e., $14,000 FMV – $6,500 basis). The adjustments to E&P (before tax) would be

	E&P
Gain recognized	$ 7,500
Distribution of property (FMV)	(14,000)
Distribution of liability	5,000
Net decrease in E&P (before tax)	$ (1,500)

E.3. Stock Redemptions

92. (c) The requirement is to determine the tax effect of Mark's stock redemption. Since the redemption is a complete redemption of all of Mark's stock ownership, the redemption proceeds of $500,000 qualify for exchange treatment. Thus, Mark will report a capital gain of $500,000 – $300,000 = $200,000.

93. (a) The requirement is to determine how the gain resulting from a stock redemption should be treated by a noncorporate shareholder if the redemption qualifies as a partial liquidation of the distributing corporation. A corporate stock redemption is treated as an exchange, generally resulting in capital gain or loss treatment to a shareholder if the redemption meets any one of five tests. Redemptions qualifying for exchange treatment include (1) a redemption that is not essentially equivalent to a dividend, (2) a redemption that is substantially disproportionate, (3) a redemption that completely terminates a shareholder's interest, (4) a redemption of a noncorporate shareholder in a partial liquidation, and (5) a redemption to pay death taxes. If none of the above five tests are met, the redemption proceeds are generally treated as a dividend.

94. (b) The requirement is to determine the amount of interest and legal and accounting fees that were incurred in connection with Kara Corp.'s stock repurchase that is deductible for 2009. No deduction is allowed for any amount paid or incurred by a corporation in connection with the redemption of its stock, except for interest expense on loans to repurchase stock. Thus, the $100,000 of interest expense on loans used to repurchase stock is deductible, while the $400,000 of legal and accounting fees incurred in connection with the repurchase of stock is not deductible.

E.4. Complete Liquidations

95. (a) The requirement is to determine the correct statement regarding the expenses incurred in completely liquidating and dissolving a corporation. The general expenses incurred in the complete liquidation and dissolution of a corporation are deductible by the corporation as ordinary and necessary business expenses. These expenses include filing fees, professional fees, and other expenditures incurred in connection with the liquidation and dissolution.

96. (d) The requirement is to determine the usual result to the shareholders of a distribution in complete liquidation of a corporation. Amounts received by shareholders in complete liquidation of a corporation are treated as received in exchange for stock, generally resulting in capital gain or loss because the stock was held as an investment. Because liquidating distributions are generally treated as received in a taxable exchange, any property received by shareholders will have a basis equal to fair market value.

97. (d) The requirement is to determine whether the unused carryovers for excess charitable contributions and net operating loss of a wholly owned subsidiary carryover to a parent corporation as a result of a tax-free complete liquidation of the subsidiary. When a parent corporation completely liquidates its 80% or more owned subsidiary under Sec. 332, the liquidation is treated as a mere change in form and the parent corporation will not recognize any gain or loss on the receipt of liquidating distributions from its subsidiary. Similarly, the subsidiary corporation will not recognize any gain or loss on distributions to its parent corporation. As a result, there will be a carryover basis for all of the subsidiary's assets that are received by the parent corporation, as well as a carryover of all of the subsidiary's tax attributes to the parent corporation. The subsidiary's tax attributes that carryover to the parent include such items as earnings and profits, capital loss carryovers, accounting methods, and tax credit carryovers, as well as unused excess charitable contributions, and net operating losses.

98. (b) The requirement is to determine the amount of Kappes Corp.'s recognized loss resulting from the distribution of marketable securities in complete liquidation. Generally, a corporation will recognize gain or loss on the distribution of its property in complete liquidation just as if the property were sold to the distributee for its fair market value. Since the marketable securities were a capital asset and held for more than one year, the distribution results in a long-term capital loss of $150,000 – $100,000 = $50,000.

99. (d) When a parent corporation liquidates its 80% or more owned subsidiary, the parent corporation (as stockholder) will ordinarily not recognize any gain or loss on the receipt of liquidating distributions from its subsidiary.

100. (a) The requirement is to determine the recognized gain to Lark Corp. on the complete liquidation of its wholly owned subsidiary, Day Corp. No gain or loss will be recognized by a parent corporation (Lark Corp.) on the receipt of property in complete liquidation of an 80% or more owned subsidiary (Day Corp.).

101. (c) The requirement is to determine the amount of gain to be recognized by Green Corp. as a result of the distribution of installment notes in the process of liquidation. A corporation generally recognizes gain on the distribution of appreciated property in the process of liquidation. Thus, Green Corp. must recognize gain on the distribution of the notes to the extent that the FMV of the notes ($162,000) exceeds the basis of the notes ($90,000), or $72,000.

102. (d) The requirement is to determine Carmela's recognized gain from the sale of assets during a complete liquidation. Gain or loss is generally recognized by a corporation on the sale of property following the adoption of a plan of complete liquidation even if the corporation then distributes all of its assets within twelve months after the plan of liquidation is adopted. Carmela would recognize gain on the land of $75,000 ($150,000 – $75,000) and on the inventory of $22,500 ($66,000 – $43,500).

103. (d) The requirement is to determine the amount of gain that each Mintee Corp. shareholder should recognize as a result of a liquidating distribution from Mintee. Amounts received by noncorporate shareholders in complete liquidation of a corporation are treated as received in exchange for stock, generally resulting in capital gain or loss because the stock was held as an investment. Here the amount realized by each shareholder consists of $2,000 cash plus the $10,500 FMV of the land, for a total of $12,500. Since each shareholder's stock basis was $6,500, each shareholder has a gain of $12,500 – $6,500 = $6,000.

G. Personal Holding Company and Accumulated Earnings Taxes

104. (b) The requirement is to determine what sources of income that Edge Corp. must consider to determine whether the income requirements for a personal holding company have been met. A corporation is a personal holding company if (1) five or fewer individuals own more than 50% of its stock at any time during the last half of its taxable year, and (2) at least 60% of its adjusted gross income is personal holding company income (e.g., dividends, interest, rent). The computation of the personal holding company income requirement includes only items that are included in gross income. Since interest on tax-exempt obligations would be excluded from gross income, tax-exempt interest would not be considered in determining whether the income requirement is met.

105. (a) The requirement is to determine which deduction(s) can be subtracted from taxable income in arriving at a corporation's undistributed personal holding company income (UPHCI). A series of adjustments must be made to a corporation's taxable income in order to arrive at UPHCI. These adjustments include the deduction of federal income taxes (including AMT and foreign income taxes), and the deduction for a net capital gain (i.e., the excess of NLTCG over NSTCL) less the amount of federal income taxes attributable to the net capital gain. This deduction prevents a personal holding company from paying the PHC tax on its net long-term capital gains.

106. (c) The requirement is to determine which step(s) Dart Corp. can take to eliminate or reduce any 2009 accumulated earnings tax (AET). The AET is a penalty tax that can be imposed (in addition to regular income tax) on a corporation if it accumulates earnings in excess of reasonable business needs. To avoid the AET, Dart can demonstrate that the reasonable needs of its business require the retention of all or part of the 2009 accumulated taxable income. Additionally, Dart can reduce its accumulated taxable income by paying a dividend to its shareholders. For this purpose, any dividends paid within the first 2 1/2 months of the tax year are treated as if paid on the last day of the preceding tax year. Thus, Dart's payment of dividends by March 15, 2010, would reduce its exposure to the AET for 2009.

107. (d) The requirement is to determine the correct statement regarding the accumulated earnings tax (AET). The AET is a penalty tax that can be imposed on a corporation if it accumulates earnings in excess of reasonable business needs, regardless of the number of shareholders that the corporation has. Answer (a) is incorrect because the AET cannot be imposed on partnerships. Answer (b) is incorrect because a corporation that distributes all of its accumulated earnings would not be subject to the AET. Answer (c) is incorrect because the AET cannot be imposed on personal holding companies.

108. (a) The requirement is to determine whose ownership of the remaining 200 shares of common stock could make Zero Corp. (with 1,000 outstanding shares) a personal holding company. A corporation is a personal holding company if (1) at least 60% of its adjusted ordinary gross income is derived from investment sources (e.g., interest, dividends, royalties), and (2) five or fewer individuals own more than 50% of the value of its stock at any time during the last half of its taxable year. In determining whether the more than 50% stock ownership requirement is met, the constructive ownership rules of Sec. 544 apply. Under these rules, an individual is considered as owning the stock owned by his family including only brothers and sisters, spouse, ancestors, and lineal descendants. Additionally, stock owned by a corporation, partnership, estate, or trust is considered as being owned proportionately by its shareholders, partners, or beneficiaries. Here, Edwards directly owns 240 shares and if he were the beneficiary of an estate that owned 200 shares, Edwards would directly and constructively own 440 shares. Then with four other unrelated shareholders, each owning twenty shares, there would be five shareholders who directly or constructively own 520 shares, more than 50% of the corporation's outstanding stock.

109. (b) The requirement is to determine the status of Arbor Corp. A corporation is a personal holding company (PHC) if (1) five or fewer individuals own more than 50% of its stock during the last half of its taxable year, and (2) at least 60% of its adjusted gross income is derived from investment sources (e.g., dividends, interest, rents). Although the amount of dividends paid to its shareholders may affect the computation of the PHC tax, the amount of dividends paid has no effect on the determination of PHC status. Answer (a) is incorrect because a regulated investment company is a status obtained by registering under the Investment Company Act of 1940, and is not determined by the facts and circumstances present for any given year. Answer (c) is incorrect because the accumulated earnings tax does not apply to personal holding companies. Answer (d) is incorrect because all of Arbor's taxable income is subject to regular federal income tax.

110. (c) The requirement is to determine the maximum amount of accumulated taxable income that may be subject to the accumulated earnings tax for 2009 if Kari Corp. takes only the minimum accumulated earnings credit. Since Kari is a manufacturing company that was first organized in 2009, it is entitled to a minimum accumulated earnings credit of $250,000. To determine its potential exposure to the accumulated earnings tax, its 2009 taxable income of $400,000 must be reduced by its federal income taxes of $100,000 and its minimum accumulated earnings credit of $250,000, to arrive at its maximum exposure of $50,000.

111. (d) The requirement is to determine the amount that Hull, Inc. can deduct for dividends paid in the computation of its personal holding company (PHC) tax. The PHC tax is a penalty tax imposed at a 15% tax rate on a corporation's undistributed personal holding company income. A PHC is allowed a dividends paid deduction that is subtracted from its adjusted taxable income in arriving at its undistributed personal holding company income. Hull's dividends paid deduction consists of the $20,000 of dividends actually paid to its shareholders during 2009, plus the $10,000 of consent dividends reported in its shareholders' individual income tax returns for 2009.

Consent dividends are hypothetical dividends that are treated as if they were paid on the last day of the corporation's tax year. Since consent dividends are taxable to shareholders but not actually distributed, shareholders increase their stock basis by the amount of consent dividends included in their gross income. The consent dividend procedure has the same result as an actual dividend distribution, followed by the shareholders making a capital contribution of the dividend back to the corporation.

112. (b) The requirement is to determine the taxpayer to whom the personal holding company (PHC) income will be attributed. A corporation will be classified as a personal

holding company if (1) it is more than 50% owned by five or fewer individuals, and (2) at least 60% of the corporation's adjusted ordinary gross income is PHC income. PHC income is generally passive income and includes dividends, interest, adjusted rents, adjusted royalties, compensation for the use of corporate property by a 25% or more shareholder, and certain personal service contracts involving a 25% or more shareholder. An amount received from a personal service contract is classified as PHC income if (1) some person other than the corporation has the right to designate, by name or by description, the individual who is to perform the services, and (2) the person so designated is (directly or constructively) a 25% or more shareholder. Here, since Benson owns 100% of Lund Corp. and Lund Corp. contracted with Magda specifying that Benson is to perform personal services for Magda, the income from the personal service contract will be personal holding company income to Lund Corp.

113. (c) The requirement is to determine the correct statement regarding the personal holding company (PHC) tax. The PHC tax should be self-assessed by filing a separate schedule 1120-PH along with the regular tax return Form 1120. Answer (a) is incorrect because the PHC tax is a penalty tax imposed in addition to regular federal income taxes. Answer (b) is incorrect because the PHC tax can only be imposed on corporations. Answer (d) is incorrect because the PHC tax can only be imposed if five or fewer individuals own more than 50% of the value of a corporation's stock. Thus, if a corporation's stock is owned by ten or more equal unrelated shareholders, the corporation cannot be a PHC.

114. (b) The requirement is to determine the correct statement regarding the accumulated earnings tax (AET). The AET does not apply to corporations that are personal holding companies. Answer (a) is incorrect because the AET can apply regardless of the number of shareholders that a corporation has. Answers (c) and (d) are incorrect because the AET applies to corporations that accumulate earnings in excess of their reasonable business needs and is not dependent upon whether a corporation files a consolidated return or the number of classes of stock that a corporation has.

115. (c) The requirement is to determine the correct statement concerning the personal holding company (PHC) tax. The personal holding company tax may be imposed if at least 60% of the corporation's adjusted ordinary gross income for the taxable year is personal holding company income, and the stock ownership test is satisfied. Answer (b) is incorrect because the stock ownership test is met if more than 50% of the corporation's stock is owned, directly or indirectly, by **five or fewer** stockholders. Answer (a) is incorrect because the PHC tax is a penalty tax imposed in addition to the regular corporate income tax. Answer (d) is incorrect because the PHC tax takes precedent over the accumulated earnings tax. The accumulated earnings tax does not apply to a personal holding company.

116. (d) The requirement is to determine the correct statement concerning the accumulated earnings tax (AET). Answer (d), "The accumulated earnings tax can **not** be imposed on a corporation that has undistributed earnings and profits of less than $150,000," is correct because every corporation (even a personal service corporation) is eligible for an accumulated earnings credit of at least $150,000. Answer (a) is incorrect because the AET is not self-assessing, but instead is assessed by the IRS after finding a tax avoidance intent on the part of the taxpayer. Answer (b) is incorrect because the AET may be imposed regardless of the number of shareholders that a corporation has. Answer (c) is incorrect because the AET cannot be imposed on a corporation for any year in which an S corporation election is in effect because an S corporation's earnings pass through and are taxed to shareholders regardless of whether the earnings are actually distributed.

117. (d)   The requirement is to determine the amount on which Kee Holding Corp.'s liability for personal holding company (PHC) tax will be based. To be classified as a personal holding company, a corporation must meet both a "stock ownership test" and an "income test." The "stock ownership test" requires that more than 50% of the stock must be owned (directly or indirectly) by five or fewer individuals. Since Kee has eighty unrelated equal shareholders, the stock ownership test is not met. Thus, Kee is not a personal holding company and has no liability for the PHC tax.

118. (b)   The accumulated earnings tax (AET) can be avoided by sufficient dividend distributions. The imposition of the AET does not depend on a stock ownership test, nor is it self-assessing requiring the filing of a separate schedule attached to the regular tax return. The AET cannot be imposed on personal holding companies.

119. (c)   The personal holding company (PHC) tax may be imposed if more than 50% of a corporation's stock is owned by five or fewer individuals. The PHC tax cannot be imposed on partnerships. Additionally, small business investment companies licensed by the Small Business Administration are excluded from the tax. If a corporation's gross income arises solely from rents, the rents will not be PHC income (even though no services are rendered to lessees) and thus, the PHC tax cannot be imposed.

120. (d)   A net capital loss for the current year is allowed as a deduction in determining accumulated taxable income for purposes of the accumulated earnings tax. A capital loss carryover from a prior year, a dividends received deduction, and a net operating loss deduction would all be added back to taxable income in arriving at accumulated taxable income.

121. (d)   The minimum accumulated earnings credit is $250,000 for nonservice corporations; $150,000 for service corporations.

122. (a)   The requirement is to determine Daystar's allowable accumulated earnings credit for 2009. The credit is the greater of (1) the earnings and profits of the tax year retained for reasonable business needs of $20,000; or (2) $150,000 less the accumulated earnings and profits at the end of the preceding year of $45,000. Thus, the credit is $150,000 – $45,000 = $105,000.

H. S Corporations

123. (c)   The requirement is to determine Stahl's basis for his S corporation stock at the end of the year. A shareholder's basis for S corporation stock is increased by the pass-through of all income items (including tax-exempt income) and is decreased by distributions that are excluded from the shareholder's gross income, as well as the pass-through of all loss and deduction items (including non-deductible items). Here, Stahl's beginning stock basis of

$65,000 is increased by the $6,000 of municipal interest income and $4,000 of long-term capital gain, and is decreased by the ordinary loss of $10,000 and short-term capital loss of $9,000, resulting in a stock basis of $56,000 at the end of the year.

124. (b)   The requirement is to determine the amount of the $30,000 distribution from an S corporation that is taxable to Baker. If an S corporation has no accumulated earnings and profits from C years, distributions to shareholders are generally nontaxable and reduce a shareholder's stock basis. To the extent that distributions exceed stock basis, they result in capital gain. A shareholder's basis for S corporation stock is first increased by the pass through of income, then reduced by distributions that are excluded from gross income, and finally reduced by the pass through of losses and deductions. Here, Baker's beginning stock basis of $25,000 would first be increased by the pass through of the $1,000 of ordinary income, to $26,000. Then the $30,000 cash distribution would be a nontaxable return of stock basis to the extent of $26,000, with the remaining $4,000 in excess of stock basis taxable to Baker as capital gain. Baker will not be able to deduct the long-term capital loss of $3,000 this year because the cash distribution reduced his stock basis to zero. Instead, the $3,000 loss will be carried forward and will be available as a deduction when Baker has sufficient basis to absorb the loss.

125. (d)   The requirement is to determine the amount of the $7,200 of health insurance premiums paid by Lane, Inc. (an S corporation) to be included in gross income by Mill. Compensation paid by an S corporation includes fringe benefit expenditures made on behalf of officers and employees owning more than 2% of the S corporation' stock. Since Mill is a 10% shareholder-employee, Mill's compensation income reported on his W-2 from Lane must include the $7,200 of health insurance premiums paid by Lane for health insurance covering Mill, his spouse, and dependents. Note that Mill may qualify to deduct 100% of the $7,200 for AGI as a self-employed health insurance deduction.

126. (b)   The requirement is to determine Lazur's tax basis for the Beck Corp. stock after the distribution. A shareholder's basis for stock of an S corporation is increased by the pass-through of all income items (including tax-exempt income) and is decreased by distributions that are excluded from the shareholder's gross income. Here, Lazur's beginning basis of $12,000 is increased by his 50% share of Beck's ordinary business income ($40,500) and tax-exempt income ($5,000) and is decreased by the $51,000 cash distribution excluded from his gross income, resulting in a stock basis of $6,500.

127. (d)   The requirement is to determine the amount of income from Graphite Corp. (an S corporation) that should be included in Smith's 2009 adjusted gross income. An S corporation is a pass-through entity and its items of income and deduction flow through to be reported on shareholders' returns. Since Smith is a 50% shareholder, half of the ordinary business income ($80,000 × 50% = $40,000) and half of the tax-exempt interest ($6,000 × 50% = $3,000) would pass through to Smith. Since the income passed through to Smith would retain its character, Smith must include the $40,000 of ordinary income in gross income, while the $3,000 of tax-exempt interest retains its exempt characteristic and would be excluded from Smith's gross income.

Smith's $12,000 of stock basis at the beginning of the year would be increased by the pass-through of the $40,000 of ordinary income as well as the $3,000 of tax-exempt income, to $55,000. As a result, the $53,000 cash distribution received by Smith would be treated as a nontaxable return of stock basis and would reduce the basis of Smith's stock to $2,000.

128.   (a)   The requirement is to determine the effect of the revocation statement on Dart Corp.'s S corporation election. A revocation of an S election will be effective if it is signed by shareholders owning more than 50% of the S corporation's outstanding stock. For this purpose, both voting and nonvoting shares are counted. Here Dart Corp. has a total of 100,000 shares outstanding. As a result, the revocation statement consented to by shareholders holding a total of 40,000 shares, would not be effective and would not terminate Dart Corp.'s S corporation election.

129.   (d)   The requirement is to determine the incorrect statement regarding S corporation eligibility requirements. The eligibility requirements restrict S corporation shareholders to individuals (other than nonresident aliens), estates, and certain trusts. Partnerships and C corporations are not permitted to own stock in an S corporation. However, an S corporation is permitted to be a partner in a partnership, and may own any percentage of stock of a C corporation, as well as own 100% of the stock of a qualified subchapter S subsidiary.

130.   (b)   The requirement is to determine the portion of the $310,000 distribution that must be reported as dividend income by Robert. Distributions from an S corporation are generally treated as first coming from its accumulated adjustment account (AAA), and then are treated as coming from its accumulated earnings and profits (AEP). A positive balance in an S corporation's AAA is generally nontaxable when distributed because it represents amounts that have already been taxed to shareholders during S years. In contrast, an S corporation's AEP represents earnings accumulated during C years that have never been taxed to shareholders, and must be reported as dividend income when received. In this case, the beginning balance in the AAA and shareholder stock basis must first be increased by the pass through of the $200,000 of ordinary income that is taxed to Robert for 2009. This permits the first $250,000 of the distribution to be nontaxable and will reduce the balance in the AAA to zero and Robert's stock basis to $50,000. The remaining $60,000 of distribution is a distribution of the corporation's AEP and must be reported as dividend income by Robert.

131.   (b)   The requirement is to determine the date on which Village Corp.'s S status became effective. A subchapter S election that is filed on or before the 15th day of the third month of a corporation's taxable year is generally effective as of the beginning of the taxable year in which filed. If the S election is filed after the 15th day of the third month, the election is generally effective as of the first day of the corporation's next taxable year. Here, Village Corp. uses a calendar year and its S election was filed on September 5, 2009, which is beyond the 15th day of the third month of the taxable year (March 15). As a result, Village's subchapter S status becomes effective as of the first day of its next taxable year, January 1, 2010.

132.   (d)   The requirement is to determine whether a shareholder's basis in the stock of an S corporation is increased by the shareholder's pro rata share of tax-exempt interest and taxable interest. An S corporation is a pass through entity and its items of income and deduction pass through to be reported on shareholder returns. As a result, a shareholder's S corporation stock basis is increased by the pass through of all items of income, including both taxable as well as tax-exempt interest. An S shareholder's stock basis must be increased by tax-exempt interest in order to permit a later distribution of that interest to be nontaxable.

133.   (c)   The requirement is to determine the amount of income that should be allocated to Zinco Corp.'s short S year when its S election is terminated on April 1, 2010. When a corporation's subchapter S election is terminated during a taxable year, its income for the entire year must be allocated between the resulting S short year and C short year. If no special election is made, the income must be allocated on a daily basis between the S and C short years. In this case, the daily income equals $318,250/365 days = $850 per day. Since the election was terminated on April 1, there would be ninety days in the S short year, and $850 × 90 = $76,500 of income would be allocated to the tax return for the S short year to be passed through and taxed to shareholders.

134.   (d)   The requirement is to determine the correct statement regarding the termination of an S election. Answer (d) is correct because an S election will be terminated if an S corporation has passive investment income in excess of 25% of gross receipts for three consecutive taxable years, if the corporation also has subchapter C accumulated earnings and profits at the end of each of those three years. Answer (a) is incorrect because an S corporation is permitted to have a maximum of one hundred shareholders. Answer (b) is incorrect because a decedent's estate may be a shareholder of an S corporation. Answer (c) is incorrect because S corporations are allowed to make charitable contributions. Contributions separately pass through to shareholders and can be deducted as charitable contributions on shareholder returns.

135.   (b)   The requirement is to determine the amount of income from Manning (an S corporation) that should be reported on Kane's 2010 tax return. An S corporation's tax items are allocated to shareholders on a per share, per day basis. Since Manning had income of $73,000 for its entire year, its per day income is $73,000/365 = $200. Since there are 100 shares outstanding, Manning's daily income per share is $200/100 = $2. Since Kane sold twenty-five of his shares on the 40th day of 2010 and held his remaining seventy-five shares throughout the year, the amount of income to be reported on Kane's 2010 return would be determined as follows:

75 shares	×	$2	×	365 days	=	$54,750
25 shares	×	$2	×	40 days	=	2,000
						$56,750

136.   (c)   The requirement is to determine the earliest date on which Ace Corp. (a calendar-year corporation) can be recognized as an S corporation. Generally, an S election will be effective as of the first day of a taxable year if the election is made on or before the 15th day of the third month of the taxable year. Since there was no change in shareholders during the year, all of Ace's shareholders consented to the election, and Ace met all eligibility requirements during the preelection portion of the year, its election filed on February 10, 2009, is effective as of January 1, 2009. Note that if either a shareholder who held stock during the taxable year and before the date of election did not consent to the election, or the corporation did not meet the eligibility requirements before the date of election, then an otherwise valid election would be treated as made for the following taxable year.

137. (c) The requirement is to determine the number of shares of voting and nonvoting stock that must be owned by shareholders making a revocation of an S election. A revocation of an S election may be filed by shareholders owning more than 50% of an S corporation's outstanding stock. For this purpose, both voting and nonvoting shares are counted. In this case, since the S corporation has a total of 50,000 voting and nonvoting shares outstanding, the shareholders consenting to the revocation must own more than 25,000 shares.

138. (b) The requirement is to determine the amount of increase for each shareholder's basis in the stock of Haas Corp., a calendar-year S corporation, for the year ended December 31, 2010. An S corporation shareholder's basis for stock is increased by the pass through of all S corporation income items (including tax-exempt income), and is decreased by all loss and deduction items, as well as nondeductible expenses not charged to capital. Since Haas has two equal shareholders, each shareholder's stock basis will be increased by 50% of the operating income of $50,000, and 50% of the interest income of $10,000, resulting in an increase for each shareholder of $30,000.

139. (d) The requirement is to determine the condition that will prevent a corporation from qualifying as an S corporation. Certain eligibility requirements must be satisfied before a corporation can make a subchapter S election. Generally, in order to be an S corporation, a corporation must have only one class of stock outstanding and have no more than one hundred shareholders, who are either individuals, estates, or certain trusts. An S corporation may own any percentage of the stock of a C corporation, and 100% of the stock of a qualified subchapter S subsidiary.

140. (c) The requirement is to determine the correct statement regarding distributions to shareholders by an S corporation that has no accumulated earnings and profits. S corporations do not generate any earnings and profits, but may have accumulated earnings and profits from prior years as a C corporation. If accumulated earnings and profits are distributed to shareholders, the distributions will be taxed as dividend income to the shareholders. However, if an S corporation has no accumulated earnings and profits, distributions are generally nontaxable and reduce a shareholder's basis for stock. To the extent distributions exceed stock basis, they result in capital gain.

141. (d) The requirement is to determine whether a corporation that has been an S corporation from its inception may have both passive and nonpassive income, and be owned by a bankruptcy estate. To qualify as an S corporation, a corporation must have one hundred or fewer shareholders who are individuals (other than nonresident aliens), certain trusts, or estates (including bankruptcy estates). If a corporation has been an S corporation since its inception,

there is no limitation on the amount or type of income that it generates, and it can have both passive and nonpassive income.

142. (b) The requirement is to determine Meyer's share of an S corporation's $36,500 ordinary loss. An S corporation's items of income and deduction are allocated on a daily basis to anyone who was a shareholder during the taxable year. Here, the $36,500 ordinary loss would be divided by 365 days to arrive at a loss of $100 per day. Since Meyer held 50% of the S corporation's stock for forty days, Meyer's share of the loss would be ($100 × 50%) × 40 days = $2,000.

143. (c) The requirement is to determine the period that a calendar-year corporation must wait before making a new S election following the termination of its S status during 2010. Generally, following the revocation or termination of an S election, a corporation must wait five years before reelecting subchapter S status unless the IRS consents to an earlier election.

144. (d) The requirement is to determine which will render a corporation ineligible for S corporation status. Answer (d) is correct because an S corporation is limited to 100 shareholders for tax years beginning after December 31, 2004. Answers (a) and (b) are incorrect because a decedent's estate and a bankruptcy estate are allowed as S corporation shareholders. Although an S corporation may only have one class of stock issued and outstanding, answer (c) is incorrect because a difference in voting rights among outstanding common shares is not treated as having more than one class of stock outstanding.

145. (d) The requirement is to determine the correct statement with regard to the application of the "at-risk" rules to S corporations and their shareholders. The at-risk rules limit a taxpayer's deduction of losses to the amount that the taxpayer can actually lose (i.e., generally the amount of cash and the adjusted basis of property invested by the taxpayer, plus any liabilities for which the taxpayer is personally liable). The at-risk rules apply to S corporation shareholders rather than at the corporate level, with the result that the deduction of S corporation losses is limited to the amount of a shareholder's at-risk investment. The application of the at-risk rules does not depend on the type of income reported by the S corporation, are not subject to any elections made by S corporation shareholders, and are applied without regard to the S corporation's ratio of debt to equity.

146. (d) The requirement is to determine the item that may be deducted by an S corporation. Items having no special tax characteristics can be netted together in the computation of the S corporation's ordinary income or loss, with only the net amount passed through to shareholders. Thus, only ordinary items (e.g., amortization of organizational expenditures) can be deducted by an S corporation. Answer (a) is incorrect because foreign income taxes must be separately passed through to shareholders so that the shareholders can individually elect to treat the payment of foreign income taxes as a deduction or as a credit. Answer (b) is incorrect because a net Sec. 1231 loss must be separately passed through to shareholders so that the Sec. 1231 netting process can take place at the shareholder level. Answer (c) is incorrect because investment interest expense must be separately passed through to shareholders so the deduction limitation (i.e., limited to net investment income) can be applied at the shareholder level.

147. (d) The requirement is to determine the correct statement regarding an S corporation's Accumulated Adjustments Account (AAA). An S corporation that has accumulated earnings and profits must maintain an AAA. The AAA represents the cumulative balance of all items of the undistributed net income and deductions for S corporation years beginning after 1982. The AAA is generally increased by all income items and is decreased by distributions and all loss and deduction items except no adjustment is made for tax-exempt income and related expenses, and no adjustment is made for federal income taxes attributable to a taxable year in which the corporation was a C corporation. The payment of federal income taxes attributable to a C corporation year would decrease an S corporation's accumulated earnings and profits (AEP). Note that the amounts represented in the AAA differ from AEP. A positive AEP balance represents earnings and profits accumulated in C corporation years that have never been taxed to shareholders. A positive AAA balance represents income from S corporation years that has already been taxed to shareholders but not yet distributed. An S corporation will not generate any earnings and profits for taxable years beginning after 1982.

148. (b) The requirement is to determine the due date of a calendar-year S corporation's tax return. An S corporation must file its federal income tax return (Form 1120-S) by the 15th day of the third month following the close of its taxable year. Thus, a calendar-year S corporation must file its tax return by March 15, if an automatic six-month extension of time is not requested.

149. (c) The requirement is to determine the item for which an S corporation is not permitted a deduction. Compensation of officers, interest paid to nonshareholders, and employee benefits for nonshareholders are deductible by an S corporation in computing its ordinary income or loss. However, charitable contributions, since they are subject to percentage limitations at the shareholder level, must be separately stated and are not deductible in computing an S corporation's ordinary income or loss.

150. (d) For tax years beginning after December 31, 2004, an S corporation may have as many as 100 shareholders. However, an S corporation cannot have both common and preferred stock outstanding because an S corporation is limited to a single class of stock. Similarly, a partnership is not permitted to be a shareholder in an S corporation because all S corporation shareholders must be individuals, estates, or certain trusts. Additionally, an S corporation cannot have a nonresident alien as a shareholder.

151. (a) The requirement is to determine which is **not** a requirement for a corporation to elect S corporation status. An S corporation must generally have only one class of stock, be a domestic corporation, and confine shareholders to individuals, estates, and certain trusts. An S corporation need **not** be a member of a controlled group.

152. (b) The requirement is to determine the amount of loss from an S corporation that can be deducted by each of two equal shareholders. An S corporation loss is passed through to shareholders and is deductible to the extent of a shareholder's basis for stock plus the basis for any debt owed the shareholder by the corporation. Here, each share-

holder's allocated loss of $45,000 ($90,000 ÷ 2) is deductible to the extent of stock basis of $5,000 plus debt basis of $15,000, or $20,000. The remainder of the loss ($25,000 for each shareholder) can be carried forward indefinitely by each shareholder and deducted when there is basis to absorb it.

I.   Corporate Reorganizations

153. (b) The requirement is to determine the correct statement regarding King Corp.'s acquisition of 90% of Jaxson Corp.'s voting common stock solely in exchange for 50% of King Corp.'s voting common stock. The acquisition by one corporation, in exchange **solely** for part of its voting stock, of stock of another corporation qualifies as a tax-free type B reorganization if immediately after the acquisition, the acquiring corporation is in control of the acquired corporation. The term **control** means the ownership of at least 80% of the acquired corporation's stock. Since King Corp. will use solely its voting stock to acquire 90% of Jaxson Corp. the acquisition will qualify as a tax-free type B reorganization. Answer (c) is incorrect because there is no requirement concerning the minimum percentage of King Corp. stock that must be used. Answer (d) is incorrect because a type B reorganization involves the acquisition of stock, not assets.

154. (a) The requirement is to determine whether a qualifying reorganization is tax-free to the corporations and their shareholders. Corporate reorganizations are generally nontaxable. As a result, a corporation will not recognize gain or loss on the transfer of its assets, and shareholders do not recognize gain or loss when they exchange stock and securities in parties to the reorganization. Here, Ace and Bate combine and form Carr, the only surviving corporation. This qualifies as a consolidation (Type A reorganization) and is tax-free to Ace and Bate on the transfer of their assets to Carr, and also is tax-free to the shareholders when they exchange their Ace and Bate stock for Carr stock. Similarly, the reorganization is tax-free to Carr when it issues its shares to acquire the Ace and Bate assets.

155. (c) The requirement is to determine whether the statements are applicable to type B reorganizations. In a type B reorganization, the acquiring corporation must use solely voting stock to acquire control of the target corporation immediately after the acquisition. The stock that is used to make the acquisition can be solely voting stock of the acquiring corporation, or solely voting stock of the parent corporation that is in control of the acquiring corporation, but not both. If a subsidiary uses its parent's stock to make the acquisition, the target corporation becomes a second-tier subsidiary of the parent corporation.

156. (d) The requirement is to determine Gow's recognized gain resulting from the exchange of Lad Corp. stock for Rook Corp. stock pursuant to a plan of corporate reorganization. No gain or loss is recognized to a shareholder if stock in one party to a reorganization (Lad Corp.) is exchanged **solely** for stock in another corporation (Rook Corp.) that is a party to the reorganization.

157. (a) The requirement is to determine the item that is defined in the Internal Revenue Code as a corporate reorganization. Corporate reorganizations generally receive nonrecognition treatment. Sec. 368 of the Internal Revenue Code defines seven types of reorganization, one of which is listed. An "F" reorganization is a mere change in identity, form, or place of organization of one corporation. A stock redemption is not a reorganization but instead results in dividend treatment or qualifies for exchange treatment. A change of depreciation method or inventory method is a change of an accounting method.

158. (c) The requirement is to determine the correct statement concerning corporate reorganizations. Answer (b) is incorrect because the reorganization provisions do provide for tax-free treatment for certain corporate transactions. Specifically, shareholders will not recognize gain or loss when they exchange stock or securities in a corporation that is a party to a reorganization solely for stock or securities in such corporation, or in another corporation that is also a party to the reorganization. Thus, securities in corporations not parties to the reorganization are always treated as "boot." Answer (d) is incorrect because the term "a party to the reorganization" includes a corporation resulting from the reorganization (i.e., the consolidated company). Answer (a) is incorrect because a mere change in identity, form, or place of organization of one corporation qualifies as a Type F reorganization.

159. (a) The requirement is to determine which is not a corporate reorganization. A corporate reorganization is specifically defined in Sec. 368 of the Internal Revenue Code. Sec. 368 defines seven types of reorganization, of which 3 are present in this item: Type A, a statutory merger; Type E, a recapitalization; and, Type F, a mere change in identity, form, or place of organization. Answer (a), a stock redemption, is the correct answer because it is not a reorganization as defined by Sec. 368 of the Code.

160. (a) The requirement is to determine the amount of Claudio's net operating loss (NOL) carryover that can be used to offset Stellar's 2009 taxable income. The amount of Claudio's NOL ($270,000) that can be utilized by Stellar for 2009 is limited by Sec. 381 to the taxable income of Stellar for its full taxable year (before a NOL deduction) multiplied by the fraction

$$\frac{\text{Days after acquisition date}}{\text{Total days in the tax table year}}$$

This limitation is 184/365 days × $360,000 = $181,479. Additionally, since there was a more than fifty percentage point change in the ownership of Claudio, Sec. 382 limits the amount of Claudio's NOL carryover that can be utilized by Stellar to the fair market value of Claudio multiplied by the federal long-term tax-exempt rate. $1,500,000 × 3% = $45,000. However, for purposes of applying this limitation for the year of acquisition, the limitation amount is only available to the extent allocable to the days in Stellar's taxable year after the acquisition date.

$$\$45,000 \times 184/365 \text{ days} = \$22,685$$

The remainder of Claudio's NOL ($270,000 – $22,685 = $247,315) can be carried forward and used to offset Stellar's taxable income (subject to the Sec. 382 limitation) in carryforward years.

161. (a) The requirement is to determine the recognized gain to be reported by Mueller on the exchange of her Disco bond for Disco preferred stock. The issuance by Disco Corporation of its preferred stock in exchange for its bonds is a nontaxable "Type E" reorganization (i.e., a recapitalization).

Since Mueller did not receive any boot, no part of her $400 realized gain is recognized.

162. (b) The requirement is to determine the amount of recognized gain in a recapitalization. Since a recapitalization is a reorganization, a realized gain will be recognized to the extent that consideration other than stock or securities is received, including the FMV of an excess principal amount of securities received over the principal amount of securities surrendered. Since no securities were surrendered, the entire $10,500 FMV of the securities received by Roberts is treated as boot. However, in this case, Roberts recognized gain is limited to her realized gain ($91,000 + $10,500) – $95,000 = $6,500.

SOLUTIONS TO SIMULATION PROBLEMS

Simulation Problem 1

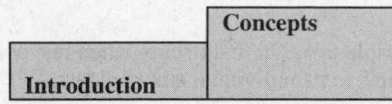

1. A corporation whose income was derived solely from dividends, interest, and royalties, and during the last six months of its year more than 50% of the value of its outstanding stock is owned by five or fewer individuals.

2. The basis used to determine gain on sale of property that was received as a gift.

3. The trade-in of production machinery for new production machinery by a corporation, when the corporation pays additional cash.

4. An unmarried individual whose filing status enables the taxpayer to use a set of income tax rates that are lower than those applicable to other unmarried individuals, but are higher than those applicable to married persons filing a joint return.

5. If income is unqualifiedly available, it will be subject to the income tax even though it is not physically in the taxpayer's possession.

6. A special tax imposed on corporations that accumulate their earnings beyond the reasonable needs of the business.

7. The classification of income from interest, dividends, annuities, and certain royalties.

8. The classification of depreciable assets and real estate used in a trade or business and held for more than one year.

9. This deduction attempts to mitigate the triple taxation that would occur if one corporation paid dividends to a corporate shareholder who, in turn, distributed such amounts to its individual shareholders.

10. Sale of property to a corporation by a shareholder for a selling price that is in excess of the property's fair market value.

	(A)	(B)	(C)	(D)	(E)	(F)	(G)	(H)	(I)	(J)	(K)	(L)	(M)	(N)	(O)	(P)	(Q)	(R)	(S)	(T)	(U)	(V)	(W)	(X)	(Y)	(Z)
1.	○	○	○	○	○	○	○	○	○	○	○	○	○	○	○	○	○	●	○	○	○	○	○	○	○	○
2.	○	○	○	○	○	○	○	○	○	○	○	○	○	○	○	○	○	○	○	○	○	○	○	○	○	●
3.	○	○	○	○	○	○	○	○	○	○	○	○	○	○	○	●	○	○	○	○	○	○	○	○	○	○
4.	○	○	○	○	○	○	○	○	○	○	○	○	○	○	●	○	○	○	○	○	○	○	○	○	○	○
5.	○	○	○	○	○	○	●	○	○	○	○	○	○	○	○	○	○	○	○	○	○	○	○	○	○	○
6.	●	○	○	○	○	○	○	○	○	○	○	○	○	○	○	○	○	○	○	○	○	○	○	○	○	○
7.	○	○	○	○	○	○	○	○	○	○	○	○	○	○	○	○	○	○	○	○	●	○	○	○	○	○
8.	○	○	○	○	○	○	○	○	○	○	○	○	○	○	○	○	○	○	○	○	○	○	●	○	○	○
9.	○	○	○	○	○	○	○	○	○	●	○	○	○	○	○	○	○	○	○	○	○	○	○	○	○	○
10.	○	○	○	○	○	●	○	○	○	○	○	○	○	○	○	○	○	○	○	○	○	○	○	○	○	○

Explanation of solutions

1. **(R)** To be classified as a personal holding company, a corporation must meet two requirements: (1) the corporation must receive at least 60% of its adjusted ordinary gross income as "personal holding company income" such as dividends, interest, rents, royalties, and other passive income; and (2) the corporation must have more than 50% of the value of its outstanding stock directly or indirectly owned by five or fewer individuals during any time in the last half of the tax year.

2. **(Z)** The transferred basis, equal to the basis of the donor plus any gift tax paid attributable to the net appreciation in the value of the gift, is the basis used to determine gain on sale of property that was received as a gift.

3. **(P)** A like-kind exchange, the exchange of business or investment property for property of a like-kind, qualifies as a non-taxable exchange. Thus, the exchange of production machinery for new production machinery when boot (money) is given is a nontaxable exchange.

4. **(O)** Head of household filing status applies to unmarried persons not qualifying for surviving spouse status who maintain a household for more than one-half of the taxable year for a dependent. The tax rates applicable to the head of household status are lower than those applicable to individuals filing as single, but are higher than rates applicable to married individuals filing a joint return.

5. **(G)** Under the doctrine of constructive receipt, income is includable in gross income and subject to income tax for the taxable year in which that income is made unqualifiedly available to the taxpayer without restriction, even though not physically in the taxpayer's possession.

6. **(A)** Corporations may be subject to an accumulated earnings tax, in addition to regular income tax, if a corporation accumulates earnings beyond reasonable business needs in order to avoid shareholder tax on dividend distributions.

7. **(U)** Portfolio income is defined as income from interest, dividends, annuities, and certain royalties.

8. **(W)** Section 1231 assets include depreciable assets and real estate used in a trade or business and held for more than one year.

9. **(J)** The dividends received deduction was enacted by Congress to mitigate the triple taxation that occurs when one corporation pays dividends to a corporate stockholder who, in turn, distributes such amounts to its individual stockholders.

10. **(F)** A constructive dividend results when a shareholder is considered to have received a dividend from a corporation, although the corporation did not specifically declare a dividend. This situation may occur when a shareholder/employee receives an excessive salary from a corporation, when there is a loan to a shareholder where there is no intent to repay the amount loaned, or when a corporation purchases shareholder property for an amount in excess of the property's fair market value. Constructive dividends often result when a transaction between a shareholder and corporation is not an arm's-length transaction.

Simulation Problem 2

	Tax Return Amount			
Situation		Schedule M-1	Research	Communication

1. **($20,000)** Interest on funds borrowed for working capital is deductible. However, interest incurred on borrowed funds to purchase municipal bonds is not deductible because the resulting income is exempt from tax.

2. **($20,000)** Interest earned on corporate bonds must be included in gross income. However, interest earned on municipal bonds is excluded.

3. **($8,000)** For organizational expenditures incurred or paid after October 22, 2004, a corporation may elect to deduct up to $5,000 for the tax year in which the corporation begins business. This $5,000 amount must be reduced by the amount by which organizational expenditures exceed $50,000. Remaining expenditures are deducted ratably over the 180-month period beginning with the month in which the corporation begins business. Aviator's qualifying expenditures include the legal fees and state incorporation fees, which total $50,000. However, the $15,000 commission for selling stock is neither deductible nor amortizable. The amount of Aviator's deduction for organizational expenditures for 2009 is $5,000 + ($45,000 × 12/180) = $8,000.

4. **($20,000)** All of the capital gains would be included in Aviator's gross income.

5. **($20,000)** Corporate capital losses can only be deducted to the extent of capital gains. Therefore, only $20,000 of capital losses can be deducted on the Aviator, Inc. tax return. Since this is Aviator's first year of existence, the excess of capital losses over capital gains ($10,000) will then be carried forward five years as a short-term capital loss, to offset capital gains.

6. **($35,000)** The dividends received deduction will be based on 70% of its dividends received, since Aviator, Inc. owns less than 20% of the dividend-paying corporation.

7. **($38,200)** A charitable contributions deduction is limited to a maximum of 10% of taxable income before the dividends received deduction and a charitable contributions deduction. Therefore, taxable income before these deductions needs to be calculated to determine the maximum allowable deduction. Taxable income is computed as follows:

Sales	$2,000,000
Dividends	50,000
Interest revenue	20,000
Gains on the sale of stock	20,000
Cost of goods sold	(1,000,000)
Salaries and wages	(400,000)
Depreciation	(260,000)
Losses on the sale of stock	(20,000)
Organizational expenditures	(8,000)
Interest expense	(20,000)
	$ 382,000

The charitable contributions deduction will be limited to $38,200 ($382,000 × 10%). The excess not allowed ($40,000 − $38,200 = $1,800) will be carried forward for up to five years.

		Schedule M-1		
Situation	Tax Return Amount		Research	Communication

Schedule M-1 of Form 1120 is used to reconcile a corporate taxpayer's income reported per books with income reported on the tax return. Generally, items of income or deduction whose book and tax treatment differ, result in Schedule M-1 items. However, since Schedule M-1 reconciles book income to taxable income before special deductions (line 28, page 1), the dividends received deduction and net operating loss deduction which are special deductions will never be reconciling items on Schedule M-1.

The beginning and ending balance of Retained Earnings and cash dividends paid to shareholders are neither deducted per books nor on the tax return and are not Schedule M-1 items. Instead they will be included on Schedule M-2 which provides an Analysis of Unappropriated Retained Earnings per books between the beginning and end of the year.

Schedule M-1	**Reconciliation of Income (Loss) per Books With Income per Return**					
	Note: Schedule M-3 required instead of Schedule M-1 if total assets are $10 million or more—see instructions					
1	Net income (loss) per books	310,000	**7**	Income recorded on books this year not included on this return (itemize):		
2	Federal income tax per books	104,150				
3	Excess of capital losses over capital gains	7,000		Tax-exempt interest $ 20,000		
4	Income subject to tax not recorded on books this year (itemize): _____			Insurance proceeds 100,000		
	_____			_____		120,000
5	Expenses recorded on books this year not deducted on this return (itemize):		**8**	Deductions on this return not charged against book income this year (itemize):		
a	Depreciation $ _____		**a**	Depreciation . . . . $ _____ 9,000		
b	Charitable contributions $ _____		**b**	Charitable contributions $ _____		
c	Travel and entertainment $ 3,000			_____		
	Insurance premiums 5,000	8,000	**9**	Add lines 7 and 8		9,000
						129,000
6	Add lines 1 through 5	429,150	**10**	Income (page 1, line 28)—line 6 less line 9		300,150

Line 2. The federal income taxes of $104,150 deducted per books is not deductible for tax purposes and is added back to book income.

Line 3. Since a corporation is not allowed to deduct a net capital loss, the $7,000 net capital loss deducted per books must be added back to book income.

Line 5c. Since only 50% of business meals and entertainment are deductible for tax purposes, 50% of the $6,000 of business entertainment expense deducted per books must be added back to book income. Additionally, the life insurance premiums of $5,000 on the president's life that were deducted per books represent an expense incurred in the production of tax-exempt income and are not deductible for tax purposes.

Line 7. The $20,000 of interest income from municipal bonds included per books is tax-exempt and must be subtracted from book income. Similarly, the $100,000 of life insurance proceeds received on the death of Aviator's president included in book income is not taxable and must be subtracted from book income.

Line 8a. Since Aviator's MACRS depreciation deductible for tax purposes exceeds the depreciation deducted for book purposes, the excess of $9,000 must be subtracted from book income.

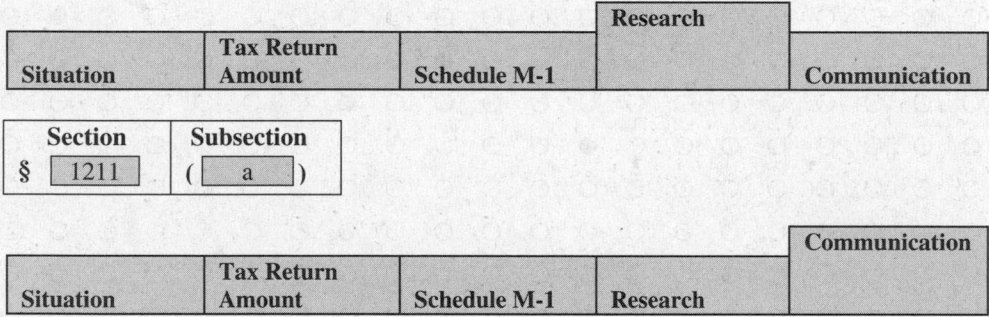

Situation	Tax Return Amount	Schedule M-1	Research	Communication

Section	Subsection
§ 1211	(a)

Situation	Tax Return Amount	Schedule M-1	Research	Communication

Dear Mr. Tyler,

This memorandum is designed to answer your questions about the deductibility of losses from the sale of stock by Aviator. In the case of a corporation, losses from the sale of capital assets, which include stock held as an investment, are allowed only to the extent of capital gains. As a result, a corporation is not allowed to deduct a net capital loss. However, the excess of capital losses over capital gains generally is treated as a capital loss carryback to each of the three preceding tax years and will offset capital gains in those years. If not fully used, the unused capital losses will be carried over to each of the five taxable years following the loss year, and will offset capital gains in those years. Since 2009 was Aviator's first tax year, no carryback is available for the 2009 and 2010 net capital losses. However, Aviator's net capital loss for 2009 and 2010 can provide a tax benefit by offsetting Aviator's capital gains in future years.

If you have any additional questions, please contact me.

Simulation Problem 3

Item for Ral's 2009 federal income tax

1. Amount of deduction for manager's $5,000 bonus for 2009.

2. Deduction for bad debts for 2009.

3. Deduction for keyman life insurance premiums for 2009.

4. Deduction for state income taxes for 2009.

5. Amount of interest to be included in gross income for 2009.

6. Dividends received deduction for dividends received from Clove Corp.

7. Dividends received deduction for dividends received from Ramo Corp.

8. Dividends received deduction for dividends received from Sol Corp.

9. Dividends received deduction for dividends received from Real Estate Investment Trust.

10. Dividends received deduction for dividends received from Mutual Fund Corp.

11. Dividends received deduction for dividends received from Money Market Fund.

12. Deduction for the $11,000 of dividends paid by Ral to its shareholders.

13. Deduction for net capital loss for 2009.

14. Ral's federal income tax for 2009 if taxable income were $100,000.

	(A)	(B)	(C)	(D)	(E)	(F)	(G)	(H)	(I)	(J)	(K)	(L)	(M)	(N)	(O)	(P)	(Q)	(R)	(S)	(T)	(U)	(V)	(W)	(X)	(Y)	(Z)
1.	○	○	○	○	○	○	○	○	○	○	○	○	○	○	○	●	○	○	○	○	○	○	○	○	○	○
2.	○	○	○	○	○	○	○	○	○	○	○	○	○	○	○	○	○	○	○	○	●	○	○	○	○	○
3.	●	○	○	○	○	○	○	○	○	○	○	○	○	○	○	○	○	○	○	○	○	○	○	○	○	○
4.	○	○	○	○	○	○	○	○	○	○	○	○	○	○	○	○	○	○	○	○	○	○	○	●	○	○
5.	○	○	○	○	○	○	○	○	○	○	○	○	○	○	○	●	○	○	○	○	○	○	○	○	○	○
6.	○	○	○	○	○	○	○	○	○	○	○	○	○	○	○	○	○	●	○	○	○	○	○	○	○	○
7.	○	○	○	○	○	○	○	○	○	○	○	○	●	○	○	○	○	○	○	○	○	○	○	○	○	○
8.	●	○	○	○	○	○	○	○	○	○	○	○	○	○	○	○	○	○	○	○	○	○	○	○	○	○
9.	●	○	○	○	○	○	○	○	○	○	○	○	○	○	○	○	○	○	○	○	○	○	○	○	○	○
10.	●	○	○	○	○	○	○	○	○	○	○	○	○	○	○	○	○	○	○	○	○	○	○	○	○	○
11.	●	○	○	○	○	○	○	○	○	○	○	○	○	○	○	○	○	○	○	○	○	○	○	○	○	○
12.	●	○	○	○	○	○	○	○	○	○	○	○	○	○	○	○	○	○	○	○	○	○	○	○	○	○
13.	●	○	○	○	○	○	○	○	○	○	○	○	○	○	○	○	○	○	○	○	○	○	○	○	○	○
14.	○	○	○	○	○	○	○	○	○	○	○	○	○	○	○	○	○	○	○	○	○	○	○	○	○	●

Explanation of solutions

1. **(P; $5,000)** Ral is an accrual method taxpayer, the payment was based on a formula in effect for 2009, and the sales manager had performed the services in 2009.

2. **(U; $8,000)** Since taxpayers are required to use the direct charge-off method in computing taxable income, only the $8,000 of actual bad debts for 2009 can be deducted.

3. **(A; $0)** Since Ral is the beneficiary of the policies and the eventual proceeds will be excluded from gross income, the premium cannot be deducted in computing taxable income.

4. **(X; $12,000)** State income taxes are deductible in computing federal taxable income.

5. **(P; $5,000)** The $3,000 interest on US Treasury notes and $2,000 interest on municipal arbitrage bonds is taxable, while the $200 interest on municipal bonds is nontaxable.

6. **(R; $5,600)** Since Clove is at least 20% owned, the $7,000 of dividends are eligible for an 80% dividends received deduction.

7. **(M; $4,200)** Since Ramo is less than 20% owned, the $6,000 of dividends are eligible for an 70% dividends received deduction.

8. **(A; $0)** No dividends received deduction is allowed because the stock was not held for more than forty-five days.

9. **(A; $0)** No dividends received deduction is allowed because a real estate investment trust (REIT) is a pass-through entity with only one level of tax paid (by its shareholders).

10. **(A; $0)** The $400 of capital gains dividends pass through as capital gains and are not eligible for a dividends received deduction.

11. **(A; $0)** No dividends received deduction is allowed because Money Market Fund derived all of its income from investments in "interest paying securities," not dividend paying stocks.

12. **(A; $0)** No federal income tax deduction is allowed for corporate dividend payments to its own shareholders.

13. **(A; $0)** Ral's net capital loss is $6,400 – $400 capital gains dividends = $6,000. However, a corporation cannot deduct a net capital loss. Instead, it is carried back three years and forward five years to offset capital gains in those years.

14. **(Z; $22,250)** The tax rate schedule indicates that the tax on $100,000 of taxable income is $22,250.

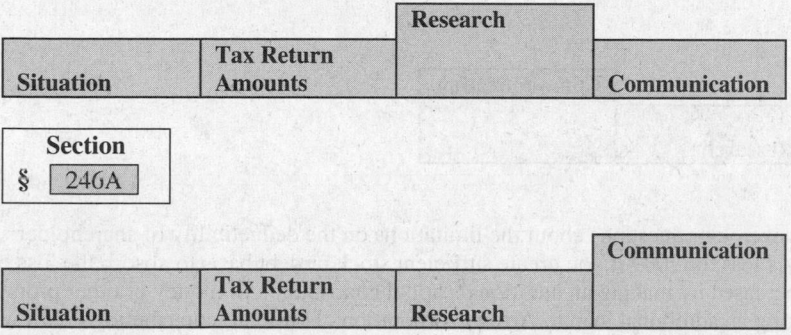

Dear Mr. Lathan,

    This memorandum is designed to answer your questions about the tax implications of your proposed investment in Diamond Corporation. The $23,000 of projected interest expense from the loan to purchase Diamond stock will be deductible for 2010. The dividends of $20,000 expected to be received from Diamond will have to be included in Ral's gross income and ordinarily would be eligible for a 70% dividends received deduction totaling $14,000. However, because 80% of Ral's investment in Diamond will be financed with debt for which Ral will receive an interest expense deduction, Sec. 246A requires that Ral's dividends received deduction percentage be reduced by 80%. As a result the dividends received deduction percentage will be 70% × (100% – 80%) = 14%. This means that the $20,000 dividend from Diamond will result in a dividends received deduction that will be limited to 14% × $20,000 = $2,800.

    If you have any additional questions about this tax issue, please contact me.

Simulation Problem 4

    For **items 1 through 4,** candidates were asked to determine the amount for Lan Corp. (an accrual-basis calendar-year S corporation), using the fact pattern for each item.

1. **($6,140)** The requirement is to determine the amount of net business income that Lan should report on Schedule K of Form 1120S. The term "net business income" corresponds to an S corporation's "ordinary income (loss) from trade or business activities." The computation of this amount excludes any item that must be separately stated and passed through to shareholders in order to retain the item's special tax characteristics. Here, the interest income on investments is portfolio income and must be separately stated and passed through to shareholders as interest income. Similarly, the charitable contributions must be separately stated and passed through to shareholders in order to apply the appropriate percentage limitations at the shareholder level. As a result, Lan's net business income consists of its $7,200 of gross receipts reduced by the $1,120 of supplies expense, or $6,140.

2. **($2,700)** The requirement it to determine the amount of net business income to be reported on Pike's 2009 Schedule K-1 from Lan. If there is no election to terminate the tax year following the sale of stock, the income of an S corporation for the entire taxable year is allocated per share, per day to anyone who was a shareholder during the year. Lan was formed on January 6, 2009, and its tax year consists of 360 days. So its net business income per share, per day would be $14,400 ÷ 200 shares ÷ 360 days = $.20. Since Pike purchased his forty shares on January 31, he is considered to own his stock for a total of 334 days during the year (counting February 1 as the first day). Thus, the amount of net business income to be reported on Pike's Schedule K-1 is (40 shares × 334 days × $.20) = $2,672. Since the instructions indicated that the answer should be rounded to the nearest hundred, the correct answer is $2,700.

3. ($3,150) The requirement is to determine Pike's basis for his Lan stock at December 31, 2009, assuming that he had purchased the stock for $4,000. An S corporation's items of income and deduction pass through to be reported on shareholder returns even though no distributions are made. As a result, a shareholder's S corporation stock basis is increased by the pass through of all income items (including tax-exempt income), and is decreased by all loss and deduction items (including nondeductible expenses). In this case, Pike's beginning basis of $4,000 would be increased by the $150 of municipal bond interest income, and decreased by the $1,000 of ordinary business loss.

4. ($9,000) The requirement is to determine Taylor's basis in Lan shares for determining gain or loss from the sale of stock to Pike. Taylor's beginning stock basis of $10,000 must be increased by his $2,000 share of the ordinary income from Lan prior to the sale, and must be decreased by the $3,000 nontaxable cash distribution that Taylor received. Recall that distributions by S corporations without accumulated earnings and profits are treated as a return of stock basis and are excluded from gross income.

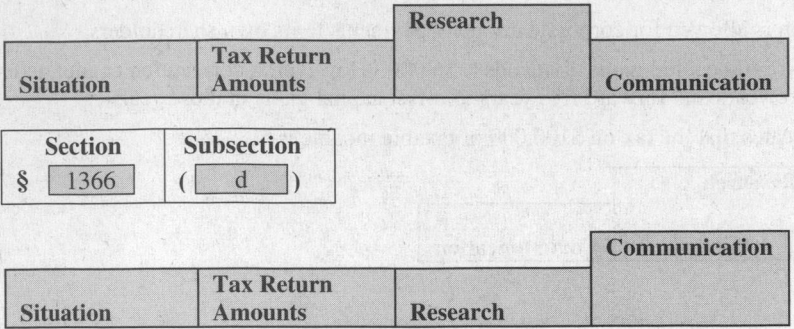

Dear Mr. Perry,

This memorandum is designed to answer your questions about the limitations on the deductibility of shareholder losses. You will be able to deduct Arrow's loss for 2009 if you create sufficient stock or debt basis to absorb the loss by the end of the year. Stock basis can be increased by making an additional capital contribution of money or other property, while debt basis can be increased by making an additional loan to Arrow Corporation. However, contributing your own note to Arrow will not create any additional stock basis because you have not incurred any cost in executing your own note and it has a zero basis to you. Similarly, guaranteeing Arrow's loan to the bank will not create any additional debt basis because your guarantee of the bank loan does not create any indebtedness that Arrow owes to you.

If you have any additional questions about this issue, please contact me.

Simulation Problem 5

Introduction	Schedule M-1 Adjustments	Deductibility	Taxability	Alternative Minimum Tax	Communication	Research

NOTE: Schedule M-1 is the schedule of the corporate income tax return that provides a reconciliation of net income (loss) per books with the corporation's taxable income before the net operating loss and dividends received deductions. If an item's treatment per books differs from its treatment for tax purposes, an M-1 adjustment will result.

	Schedule M-1 Adjustment	(I)	(D)	(N)
1. Reliant's disbursements included reimbursed employees' expenses in 2009 for travel of $100,000, and business meals of $30,000. The reimbursed expenses met the conditions of deductibility and were properly substantiated under an accountable plan. The reimbursement was not treated as employee compensation.	$15,000	●	○	○
2. Reliant's books expensed $7,000 in 2009 for the term life insurance premiums on the corporate officers. Reliant was the policy owner and beneficiary.	$ 7,000	●	○	○
3. Reliant's books indicated an $18,000 state franchise tax expense for 2009. Estimated state tax payments for 2009 were $15,000.	$0	○	○	●
4. Book depreciation on computers for 2009 was $10,000. These computers, which cost $50,000, were placed in service on January 2, 2008. Tax depreciation used MACRS with the half-year convention. No election was made to expense part of the computer cost and Reliant elected not to use bonus depreciation.	$ 6,000	○	●	○
5. For 2009, Reliant's books showed a $4,000 short-term capital gain distribution from a mutual fund corporation and a $5,000 loss on the sale of Retro stock that was purchased in 2007. The stock was an investment in an unrelated corporation. There were no other 2009 gains or losses and no loss carryovers from prior years.	$ 5,000	●	○	○

	Schedule M-1 Adjustment	(I) (D) (N)

6. Reliant's 2009 taxable income before the charitable contribution and the dividends received deductions was $500,000. Reliant's books expensed $15,000 in board of director authorized charitable contributions that were paid on January 5, 2010. Charitable contributions paid and expensed during 2009 were $35,000. All charitable contributions were properly substantiated. There were no net operating losses or charitable contributions that were carried forward.

○ ○ ●

$0

Explanation of solutions

1. ($15,000; I) The $100,000 reimbursement for employee travel is deductible for both book and tax purposes and no adjustment is necessary. However, since only 50% of the $30,000 of reimbursed business meals that was deducted per books is deductible for tax purposes, an M-1 increase adjustment results in the amount of $15,000 ($30,000 × 50%).

2. ($7,000; I) The $7,000 of term life insurance premiums on corporate officers that was deducted per books is not deductible for tax purposes because Reliant was the policy owner and beneficiary. As a result there is an M-1 increase adjustment of $7,000.

3. ($0; N) The $18,000 of state franchise taxes and $15,000 of estimated state tax payments are fully deductible for both book and tax purposes and no M-1 adjustment is necessary.

4. ($6,000; D) Since the computers are five-year recovery property and Reliant used MACRS and the half-year convention, depreciation would be computed using the 200% declining balance method (i.e., twice the straight-line rate) and the tax depreciation for 2008 would be ($50,000 × 40% × 1/2) = $10,000. The tax depreciation for 2009 would then be ($50,000 − $10,000) × 40% = $16,000. Since book depreciation was only $10,000, the book to tax difference in depreciation would result in an M-1 decrease adjustment of $6,000.

5. ($5,000; I) Since only **long-term capital gain distributions** from a mutual fund pass through as capital gain, the $4,000 of **short-term capital gain distribution** from a mutual fund corporation must be reported by Reliant as ordinary dividend income, and cannot be netted against the $5,000 capital loss from the sale of the Retro stock held as an investment. As a result, Reliant's sale of the Retro stock results in a net capital loss of $5,000 for 2009. Since a corporation cannot deduct a net capital loss for tax purposes, the $5,000 of net capital loss deducted per books results in a book to tax difference and an M-1 increase adjustment of $5,000.

6. ($0; N) Since Reliant had taxable income before the charitable contribution deduction of $500,000 for 2009, Reliant can deduct a maximum of ($500,000 × 10%) = $50,000 of charitable contributions for tax purposes. Reliant can deduct the $35,000 of contributions made during 2009, as well as the $15,000 paid on January 5, 2010, because Reliant is an accrual-basis taxpayer, the $15,000 contribution was authorized by Reliant's board of directors, and the $15,000 was paid within 2 1/2 months after the end of 2009. Since Reliant is deducting $50,000 of contributions for both book and tax purposes, there is no M-1 adjustment.

Introduction	Schedule M-1 Adjustments	Deductibility	Taxability	Alternative Minimum Tax	Communication	Research

(F) (P) (N)

1. Reliant purchased theater tickets for its out of town clients. The performances took place after Reliant's substantial and bona fide business negotiations with its clients.

○ ● ○

2. Reliant accrued advertising expenses to promote a new product line. Ten percent of the new product line remained in ending inventory.

● ○ ○

3. Reliant incurred interest expense on a loan to purchase municipal bonds.

○ ○ ●

4. Reliant paid a penalty for the underpayment of 2008 estimated taxes.

○ ○ ●

5. On December 9, 2009, Reliant's board of directors voted to pay a $500 bonus to each nonstockholder employee for 2009. The bonuses were paid on February 3, 2010.

● ○ ○

Explanation of solutions

1. (P) The cost of the theater tickets qualifies as a business entertainment expense which is only 50% deductible for 2009.

2. (F) Indirect costs that do not directly benefit a particular activity or are not incurred because of a particular activity may be currently deducted and are not required to be capitalized as part of the cost of inventory. Indirect costs that can be currently deducted include such costs as marketing, selling, advertising, distribution, and general and administrative expenses.

3. (N) Since the proceeds of the loan were used to purchase municipal bonds which generate tax-exempt income, the interest expense on the loan is not deductible.

4. (N) No deduction is allowed for the penalty that results from the underpayment of estimated income tax.

5. (F) An accrual method taxpayer can deduct compensation for nonstockholder employees when there is an obligation to make payment, economic performance has occurred, the amount is reasonable, and payment is made not later than 2 1/2 months after the end of the tax year. Here, the amount of bonus was determined on December 9, 2009, and was paid February 3, 2010.

Introduction	Schedule M-1 Adjustments	Deductibility	Taxability	Alternative Minimum Tax	Communication	Research

		(F)	(P)	(N)
1.	The portion of Reliant's refund that represented the overpayment of the 2007 federal taxes.	○	○	●
2.	The portion of Reliant's refund that is attributable to the interest on the overpayment of federal taxes.	●	○	○
3.	Reliant received dividend income from a mutual fund that solely invests in municipal bonds.	○	○	●
4.	Reliant, the lessor, benefited from the capital improvements made to its property by the lessee in 2009. The lease agreement is for one year ending December 31, 2009, and provides for a reduction in rental payments by the lessee in exchange for the improvements.	●	○	○
5.	Reliant collected the proceeds on the term life insurance policy on the life of a debtor who was not a shareholder. The policy was assigned to Reliant as collateral security for the debt. The proceeds exceeded the amount of the debt.	○	●	○

Explanation of solutions

1. (N) Since the payment of federal income tax does not result in a deduction, a subsequent refund of federal income tax will be nontaxable.

2. (F) Interest is generally fully included in gross income, including the interest on an overpayment of federal taxes.

3. (N) A mutual fund that invests in tax-exempt municipal bonds is permitted to pass the tax exemption on the bond interest on to its shareholders when the tax-exempt interest is distributed in the form of dividends. To qualify, the mutual fund has to have at least 50% of the value of its total assets invested in tax-exempt municipal bonds at the close of each quarter of its taxable year.

4. (F) Generally, a lessor will not recognize any income as a result of the capital improvements made by a lessee that revert to the lessor at the expiration of the lease. However, if the parties intend the improvements to be, in whole or in part, a substitute for rental payments, then the lessor must recognize the improvements as rental income equal in amount to the reduction in rental payments.

5. (P) Since Reliant was a collateral assignee as a result of the insured's indebtedness, Reliant received the insurance proceeds as payment on the debt, rather than as life insurance proceeds paid "by reason of death of the insured." Consequently, the insurance proceeds are tax-free only to the extent of the amount of unpaid debt, and any proceeds in excess of the debt repayment must be included in Reliant's gross income.

Introduction	Schedule M-1 Adjustments	Deductibility	Taxability	Alternative Minimum Tax	Communication	Research

		(I)	(D)	(N)
1.	Reliant used the 70% dividends received deduction for regular tax purposes.	○	○	●
2.	Reliant received interest from a state's general obligation bonds.	○	○	●
3.	Reliant used MACRS depreciation on seven-year personal property placed into service January 3, 2009, for regular tax purposes. No expense election was made, and Reliant elected not to use bonus depreciation.	●	○	○
4.	Depreciation on nonresidential real property placed into service on January 3, 2009, was under the general MACRS depreciation system for regular tax purposes.	○	○	●
5.	Reliant had only cash charitable contributions for 2009.	○	○	●

Explanation of solutions

1. (N) The dividends received deduction is not an adjustment in computing AMTI before the ACE adjustment. However, note that the 70% dividends received deduction is an increase adjustment in computing a corporation's ACE.

2. (N) The tax-exempt interest on a state's **general obligation** bonds is not an adjustment is computing AMTI before the ACE adjustment. However, note that the interest from state and local **private activity** bonds would be an increase adjustment in computing AMTI prior to the ACE adjustment for 2009.

3. **(I)** Generally for seven-year property, the 200% declining balance method would be used under MACRS for regular tax purposes, while the 150% declining balance method must be used for AMT purposes, resulting in an increase adjustment in computing AMTI prior to the ACE adjustment for the year placed in service.

4. **(N)** For real property placed in service after December 31, 1998, the AMT adjustment has been eliminated because for AMT purposes, the recovery period is the same as that used for regular tax MACRS depreciation (e.g., 39 years or 27 1/2 years). On the other hand, for real property that was placed in service before January 1, 1999, an AMT adjustment is necessary because for AMT purposes, real property must be depreciated using the straight-line method over a 40-year recovery period, rather than the 39-year or 27 1/2-year period used for regular tax purposes.

5. **(N)** Allowable charitable contributions do not result in an adjustment in computing AMTI or ACE.

Introduction	Schedule M-1 Adjustments	Deductibility	Taxability	Alternative Minimum Tax	Communication	Research

To: Ms. Evan
From: CPA Candidate

You have requested that I provide you with information regarding the deductibility of the costs of forming a corporation. A corporation may deduct up to $5,000 of organizational expenditures for the tax year in which the corporation begins business for organizational expenditures incurred or paid after October 22, 2004. The $5,000 amount must be reduced by the amount by which organizational expenditures exceed $50,000. Remaining expenditures are allowed as a deduction ratably over the 180-month period beginning with the month in which the corporation begins business. Organizational expenditures include fees for accounting and legal services incident to incorporation (e.g., fees for drafting the corporate chapter, bylaws, terms of stock certificates) expenses of organizational meetings and of temporary directors meetings, and fees paid to the state of incorporation. However, the costs incurred in issuing and selling stock and securities (e.g., professional fees to issue stock, printing costs, underwriting commissions) do not qualify as organizational expenditures and are not tax deductible.

If you have any additional questions about this issue, please contact me.

Introduction	Schedule M-1 Adjustments	Deductibility	Taxability	Alternative Minimum Tax	Communication	Research

Internal Revenue Code Section 170(b)(2) limits a corporation's deduction for charitable contributions to 10% of its taxable income before certain specified deductions.

Section	Subsection	Paragraph
§ 170	(b)	(2)

Simulation Problem 6

Situation	Schedule M-1 Adjustments	Taxability	Deductibility	Alternative Minimum Tax	Communication	Research

	Amount of Adjustment	(I)	(D)	(N)
1. At its corporate inception in 2007, Capital incurred and paid $40,100 in organizational costs for legal fees to draft the corporate charter. In 2007, Capital correctly elected, for book purposes, to expense the organizational costs and to amortize the organizational expenditures over the minimum allowable period on its federal income tax return. For 2009, no organizational costs were deducted on its books.	$ 2,340	○	●	○
2. Capital's 2009 disbursements included $10,000 for reimbursed employees' expenses for business meals and entertainment. The reimbursed expenses met the conditions of deductibility and were properly substantiated under an accountable plan. The reimbursement was not treated as employee compensation.	$ 5,000	●	○	○
3. Capital's 2009 disbursements included $15,000 for life insurance premium expense paid for its executives as part of their taxable compensation. Capital is neither the direct nor the indirect beneficiary of the policy, and the amount of the compensation is reasonable.	$0	○	○	●
4. In 2009, Capital increased its allowance for uncollectible accounts by $10,000. No bad debt was written off in 2009.	$10,000	●	○	○

Explanation of solutions

1. **($2,340; D)** $5,000 of capital's organizational costs of $40,100 would have been deducted in 2007 with remainder amortized over 180 months (15 years) for tax purposes. As a result, the tax amortization of organizational costs results in a tax deduction of $35,100 × 12/180 = $2,340 for 2009. Since no organizational costs were deducted per books for 2009, a Schedule M-1 decrease adjustment is necessary for the $2,340 difference.

2. **($5,000; I)** Only 50% of reimbursed employees' expenses for business meals and entertainment is deductible for tax purposes. As a result, an M-1 increase adjustment of $5,000 is necessary to reflect the fact that 50% of the $10,000 of reimbursed business meals and entertainment that was deducted for book purposes is not deductible for tax purposes.

3. **($0; N)** The $15,000 of life insurance premiums treated as reasonable compensation is fully deductible for both book and tax purposes and no M-1 adjustment is necessary.

4. **($10,000; I)** The reserve method of accounting for bad debts is not allowed for tax purposes. Instead, a bad debt deduction can be taken only when a specific debt is determined to be uncollectible. Since no bad debt was written off during 2009, an M-1 increase adjustment is necessary for the $10,000 addition to the allowance for uncollectible accounts for 2009.

Situation	Schedule M-1 Adjustments	Taxability	Deductibility	Alternative Minimum Tax	Communication	Research
						(F) (P) (N)
1. In 2009, Sunco received dividend income from a 35%-owned domestic corporation. The dividends were not from debt-financed portfolio stock, and the taxable income limitation did not apply.						○ ● ○
2. In 2009, Sunco received a $2,800 lease cancellation payment from a three-year lease tenant.						● ○ ○

Explanation of solutions

1. **(P)** Dividends received from a 35%-owned domestic corporation would be eligible for an 80% dividends received deduction. As a result, only 20% of the gross dividends received would be included in taxable income.

2. **(F)** A lease cancellation payment is treated as rent and must be fully included in income when received.

Situation	Schedule M-1 Adjustments	Taxability	Deductibility	Alternative Minimum Tax	Communication	Research
						(F) (P) (N)
1. Quest's 2009 taxable income before charitable contributions and dividends received deduction was $200,000. Quest's Board of Directors authorized a $38,000 contribution to a qualified charity on December 1, 2009. The payment was made on February 1, 2010. All charitable contributions were properly substantiated.						○ ● ○
2. During 2009 Quest was assessed and paid a $300 uncontested penalty for failure to pay its 2008 federal income taxes on time.						○ ○ ●

Explanation of solutions

1. **(P)** Since Quest is an accrual method corporation, it can elect to deduct contributions authorized by its board of directors during 2009, so long as the contribution is actually paid no later than 2 1/2 months after the end of the tax year. Thus, to maximize its deduction for 2009, Quest can elect to treat the $38,000 contribution as a deduction for 2009 subject to the 10% of taxable income limitation that applies for 2009. Since Quest had 2009 taxable income of $200,000 before the charitable contributions and dividends received deductions, Quest's 2009 deduction for the $38,000 charitable contribution is limited to $200,000 × 10% = $20,000.

2. **(N)** A penalty that is paid for a failure to pay federal income taxes on time is not deductible.

Situation	Schedule M-1 Adjustments	Taxability	Deductibility	Alternative Minimum Tax	Communication	Research
						(O) (U) (C)
1. For regular tax purposes, Gelco deducted the maximum MACRS depreciation on seven-year personal property placed in service on January 2, 2009. Gelco did not elect to expense any part of the cost of the property under Sec. 179, and elected not to take bonus depreciation.						○ ● ○
2. For regular income tax purposes, Gelco depreciated nonresidential real property placed in service on January 2, 1998, under the general MACRS depreciation system for a thirty-nine-year depreciable life.						○ ● ○

(O) (U) (C)

3. Gelco excluded state highway construction general obligation bond interest income earned in 2009 for regular income tax and alternative minimum tax (AMT) purposes.   ○ ○ ●

Explanation of solutions

1. (**U**) Generally for seven-year property, the 200% declining balance method would be used for MACRS, while the 150% declining balance method must be used for AMT purposes. Therefore, the use of MACRS would have the effect of understating AMTI before the ACE adjustment, and would necessitate an increase adjustment to convert 2009 regular taxable income to AMTI.

2. (**U**) MACRS depreciation for nonresidential real property placed in service during 1998 would be computed using the straight-line method and a thirty-nine-year recovery period. For AMT purposes depreciation would have to be computed using the straight-line method over a forty-year recovery period. Therefore, regular tax depreciation would have the effect of understating AMTI before the ACE adjustment, and would necessitate an increase adjustment to convert 2009 regular taxable income to AMTI. However, note that for real property placed in service after December 31, 1998, the AMT adjustment has been eliminated because for AMT purposes, the recovery period is the same as that used for regular tax MACRS depreciation (e.g., 39 years or 27 1/2 years). Thus, if the building had instead been placed in service **after** December 31, 1998, no AMT adjustment would be necessary and the correct answer would be (C).

3. (**C**)   Interest on a state's general obligation bonds is tax exempt for purposes of computing both regular taxable income, as well as for computing AMTI before the ACE adjustment, and would have the effect of correctly stating AMTI before the ACE adjustment. However, note that interest from a state's general obligation bonds is includible income for purposes of determining a corporation's ACE adjustment for 2009.

Situation	Schedule M-1 Adjustments	Taxability	Deductibility	Alternative Minimum Tax	Communication	Research

Dear Mr. King,

This memorandum is designed to answer your questions about the tax treatment of transfers of assets to a corporation in exchange for stock. Assuming the incorporation qualifies under Sec. 351 as a transfer to a corporation controlled by the transferor, your realized gain of $500,000 – $150,000 = $350,000 has to be recognized to the extent that the $180,000 recourse liability assumed by the corporation exceeds the $150,000 basis of the property transferred, or $30,000. Since this gain recognition rule compares total liabilities with the total basis of property transferred, you can avoid gain recognition by also transferring $30,000 cash or other assets with an adjusted basis of at least $30,000. Alternatively, since the liability is a recourse liability, you can avoid gain recognition by the corporation agreeing to assume only $150,000 of the liability, with you agreeing to satisfy the remaining $30,000 of liability.

If you have any additional questions about this issue, please contact me.

Situation	Schedule M-1 Adjustments	Taxability	Deductibility	Alternative Minimum Tax	Communication	Research

Internal Revenue Code Section 1223(1) provides that the holding period of the stock will include the holding period of the property transferred if the transferred property was either a capital asset or a Section 1231 asset.

Section	Paragraph
§ 1223	(1)

Simulation Problem 7

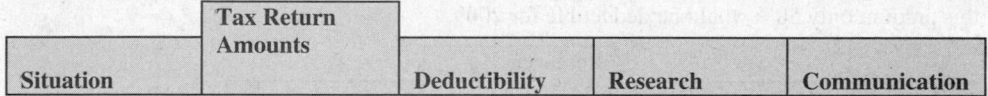

Situation	Tax Return Amounts	Deductibility	Research	Communication

For **items 1 through 5,** candidates were required to determine the amount that should be reported on Kimberly Corp.'s 2009 Federal income tax return.

1. (**$26,000**) All $26,000 of interest income from US Treasury bonds is taxable.

2. (**$8,000**) The furniture and fixtures are classified as seven-year recovery property. Under MACRS, their cost of $56,000 will be recovered using the 200% declining balance method of depreciation and the half-year convention. Thus, the amount of depreciation for the year of acquisition would be $56,000 × 2/7 × 1/2 = $8,000.

3. ($7,000) The bad debt deduction consists of the $7,000 of bad debts actually written off during the year. The reserve method, using the increase in the allowance for doubtful accounts based on an aging of accounts receivable, cannot be used for tax purposes.

4. ($25,000) Since the unimproved lot was used in the business and held for more than one year, the $20,000 gain on its sale is classified as a Sec. 1231 gain. Since Kimberly had no previous nonrecaptured Sec. 1231 losses, the net Sec. 1231 gain is treated as a LTCG. Combining this $20,000 LTCG with the $5,000 LTCG from the sale of XYZ stock results in a net LTCG of $25,000.

5. ($12,000) Deductible interest expense consists of the $10,000 interest on the mortgage loan and the $2,000 interest on the line of credit loan.. The $4,000 of interest expense on the loan obtained to purchase municipal bonds is not deductible because the municipal bonds produce tax-exempt income.

Situation	Tax Return Amounts	Deductibility		Research	Communication

		(F)	**(P)**	**(N)**
1. Organization expense incurred at corporate inception in 2007 to draft the corporate charter. No deduction was taken for the organization expense in 2007.		○	○	●
2. Life insurance premiums paid by the corporation for its executives as part of their compensation for services rendered. The corporation is neither the direct nor the indirect beneficiary of the policy and the amount of compensation is reasonable.		●	○	○
3. Vacation pay earned by employees which vested under a plan by December 31, 2009, and was paid February 1, 2010.		●	○	○
4. State franchise tax liability that has accrued during the year and was paid on March 15, 2010.		●	○	○
5. Entertainment expense to lease a luxury skybox during football season to entertain clients. A bona fide business discussion precedes each game. The cost of regular seats would have been one-half the amount paid.		○	●	○

Explanation of solutions

1. (N) Corporate organizational expenditures paid or incurred after October 22, 2004, may be amortized over a period of 180 months, beginning with the month that business begins, if a proper election statement is attached to the corporate return for the year that business begins. If no election is made, the expenditures must be capitalized and can only be de ducted when the corporation is liquidated. Here, the problem indicates that Kimberly was formed and commenced operations during 2007, and further states that no deduction was taken for the organization expense in 2007. Although not specifically stated, this would indicate that no election was made to amortize the organization expense for 2007 and, as a result, no amortization deduction would be available for 2009.

2. (F) The life insurance premiums are fully deductible because Kimberly is neither the direct nor indirect beneficiary of the policy. The life insurance premiums are deductible as part of the reasonable compensation paid to its executives.

3. (F) An accrual method taxpayer can deduct vacation pay for employees **in the year earned** if (1) it is paid during the year, or (2) the vacation pay is vested and paid no later than 2 1/2 months after the end of the year. Here, the vacation pay was vested and paid on February 1, 2010.

4. (F) Corporate franchise taxes are deductible as a business expense. An accrual method corporation can take a deduction for franchise taxes in the year it becomes legally liable to pay the tax regardless of the year that the tax is based on, or the year it is paid. The item indicates that the franchise tax liability accrued during the year (2009).

5. (P) The cost to lease a skybox is disallowed as an entertainment expense to the extent that the amount paid exceeds the cost of the highest-priced nonluxury box seat tickets multiplied by the number of seats in the skybox. Since the item indicates that the cost of regular seats would have been one half the amount paid, only 50% of the cost of the skybox would qualify as an entertainment expense. Of this amount only 50% would be deductible for 2009.

Situation	Tax Return Amounts	Deductibility	Research		Communication

In researching the item, "corporate dividend deduction" or "dividend income, corporations" are appropriate keywords for the search. The $10,000 dividend qualifies for an 80% dividends received deduction because the dividend was received from a "20-percent owned corporation." The appropriate excerpts from the IRC are presented below.

SEC. 243 Dividends Received by Corporations

243(a) General Rule—In the case of a corporation, there shall be allowed as a deduction an amount equal to the following percentages of the amount received as dividends from a domestic corporation which is subject to taxation under this chapter.

243(a)(1) 70 percent, in the case of dividends other than dividends described in paragraph (2) or (3);

243(a)(2) 100 percent, in the case of dividends received by a small business investment company operating under the Small Business Investment Act of 1958 (15 U.S.C. 661 and following); and

243(a)(3) 100 percent, in the case of qualifying dividends (as defined in subsection (b)(1)).

243(b) Qualifying Dividends—

243(b)(1) In General—For purposes of this section, the term "qualifying dividend" means any dividend received by a corporation—

243(b)(1)(A) if at the close of the day on which such dividend is received, such corporation is a member of the same affiliated group as the corporation distributing such dividend, and

243(b)(1)(B) if—

243(b)(1)(B)(i) such dividend is distributed out of the earnings and profits of a taxable year of the distributing corporation which ends after December 31, 1963, for which an election under section 1562 was not in effect, and on each day of which the distributing corporation and the corporation receiving the dividend were members of such affiliated group, or

243(b)(1)(B)(ii) such dividend is paid by a corporation with respect to which an election under section 936 is in effect for the taxable year in which such dividend is paid.

243(b)(2) Affiliated Group—For purposes of this subsection:

243(b)(2)(A) In General—The term "affiliated group" has the meaning given such term by section 1504(a), except that for such purposes sections 1504(b)(2), 1504(b)(4), and 1504(c) shall not apply.

243(c) Retention of 80-Percent Dividends Received Deduction for Dividends from 20-Percent Owned Corporations.

243(c)(1) In General—In the case of any dividend received from a 20-percent owned corporation—

243(c)(1)(A) subsection (a)(1) of this section, and

243(c)(1)(B) subsections (a)(3) and (b)(2) of section 244, shall be applied by substituting "80 percent" for "70 percent."

243(c)(2) 20-Percent Owned Corporation—For purposes of this section, the term "20-percent owned corporation" means any corporation is 20 percent or more of the stock of such corporation (by vote and value) is owned by the taxpayer. For purposes of the preceding sentence, stock described in section 1504(a)(4) shall not be taken into account.

1504(a) Affiliated Group Defined—For purposes of this subtitle—

1504(a)(1) In General—The term "affiliated group" means

1504(a)(1)(A) 1 or more chains of includible corporations connected through stock ownership with a common parent corporation which is an includible corporation, but only if—

1504(a)(1)(B)(i) the common parent owns directly stock meeting the requirements of paragraph (2) in at least 1 of the other includible corporations, and

1504(a)(1)(B)(ii) stock meeting the requirements of paragraph (2) in each of the includible corporations (except the common parent) is owned directly by 1 or more of the other includible corporations.

1504(a)(2) 80-Percent Voting and Value Test—The ownership of stock of any corporation meets the requirements of this paragraph if it—

1504(a)(2)(A) possesses at least 80 percent of the total voting power of the stock of such corporation, and

1504(a)(2)(B) has a value to at least 80 percent of the total value of the stock of such corporation.

Situation	Tax Return Amounts	Deductibility	Research	Communication

To: The files
From: CPA Candidate

This memorandum is designed to document the resolution of the tax issue regarding the dividends received deduction for Kimberly Corp. Kimberly Corp. received a $10,000 dividend from a 30% owned corporation. In accordance with Code Sec. 243(c), an 80% dividend received deduction is allowed for dividends received from corporations that are at least 20%, but less than 80%, owned. Accordingly, Kimberly Corp.'s dividends received deduction will be $10,000 × 80% = $8,000. Therefore, the corporation will pay taxes on only $2,000 of the dividend income.

MULTIPLE-CHOICE QUESTIONS (1-82)

1. Steve and Kay Briar, US citizens, were married for the entire 2009 calendar year. In 2009, Steve gave a $30,000 cash gift to his sister. The Briars made no other gifts in 2009. They each signed a timely election to treat the $30,000 gift as made one-half by each spouse. Disregarding the applicable credit and estate tax consequences, what amount of the 2009 gift is taxable to the Briars?

    a. $30,000
    b. $6,000
    c. $4,000
    d. $0

2. In 2009, Sayers, who is single, gave an outright gift of $50,000 to a friend, Johnson, who needed the money to pay medical expenses. In filing the 2009 gift tax return, Sayers was entitled to a maximum exclusion of

    a. $0
    b. $12,000
    c. $13,000
    d. $50,000

3. During 2010, Blake transferred a corporate bond with a face amount and fair market value of $20,000 to a trust for the benefit of her sixteen-year old child. Annual interest on this bond is $2,000, which is to be accumulated in the trust and distributed to the child on reaching the age of twenty-one. The bond is then to be distributed to the donor or her successor-in-interest in liquidation of the trust. Present value of the total interest to be received by the child is $8,710. The amount of the gift that is excludable from taxable gifts is

    a. $20,000
    b. $13,000
    c. $ 8,710
    d. $0

4. Under the unified rate schedule for 2009,

    a.   Lifetime taxable gifts are taxed on a noncumulative basis.
    b.   Transfers at death are taxed on a noncumulative basis.
    c.   Lifetime taxable gifts and transfers at death are taxed on a cumulative basis.
    d.   The gift tax rates are 5% higher than the estate tax rates.

5. Which of the following requires filing a gift tax return, if the transfer exceeds the available annual gift tax exclusion?

    a.   Medical expenses paid directly to a physician on behalf of an individual unrelated to the donor.
    b.   Tuition paid directly to an accredited university on behalf of an individual unrelated to the donor.
    c.   Payments for college books, supplies, and dormitory fees on behalf of an individual unrelated to the donor.
    d.   Campaign expenses paid to a political organization.

6. On July 1, 2009, Vega made a transfer by gift in an amount sufficient to require the filing of a gift tax return. Vega was still alive in 2010. If Vega did **not** request an extension of time for filing the 2009 gift tax return, the due date for filing was

    a.   March 15, 2010.
    b.   April 15, 2010.
    c.   June 15, 2010.
    d.   June 30, 2010.

7. Jan, an unmarried individual, gave the following outright gifts in 2010:

Donee	Amount	Use by donee
Jones	$15,000	Down payment on house
Craig	14,000	College tuition
Kande	5,000	Vacation trip

Jan's 2010 exclusions for gift tax purposes should total

    a. $32,000
    b. $31,000
    c. $29,000
    d. $18,000

8. When Jim and Nina became engaged in April 2010, Jim gave Nina a ring that had a fair market value of $50,000. After their wedding in July 2010, Jim gave Nina $75,000 in cash so that Nina could have her own bank account. Both Jim and Nina are US citizens. What was the amount of Jim's 2010 marital deduction?

    a. $ 63,000
    b. $ 75,000
    c. $113,000
    d. $125,000

9. Raff created a joint bank account for himself and his friend's son, Dave. There is a gift to Dave when

    a.   Raff creates the account.
    b.   Raff dies.
    c.   Dave draws on the account for his own benefit.
    d.   Dave is notified by Raff that the account has been created.

10. Fred and Ethel (brother and sister), residents of a non-community property state, own unimproved land that they hold in joint tenancy with rights of survivorship. The land cost $100,000 of which Ethel paid $80,000 and Fred paid $20,000. Ethel died during 2009 when the land was worth $300,000, and $240,000 was included in Ethel's gross estate. What is Fred's basis for the property after Ethel's death?

    a. $140,000
    b. $240,000
    c. $260,000
    d. $300,000

11. Bell, a cash-basis calendar-year taxpayer, died on June 1, 2009. In 2009, prior to her death, Bell incurred $2,000 in medical expenses. The executor of the estate paid the medical expenses, which were a claim against the estate, on July 1, 2009. If the executor files the appropriate waiver, the medical expenses are deductible on

    a.   The estate tax return.
    b.   Bell's final income tax return.
    c.   The estate income tax return.
    d.   The executor's income tax return.

12. If the executor of a decedent's estate elects the alternate valuation date and none of the property included in the gross estate has been sold or distributed, the estate assets must be valued as of how many months after the decedent's death?

    a.   12
    b.   9
    c.   6
    d.   3

13. What amount of a decedent's taxable estate is effectively tax-free if the maximum applicable estate tax credit is taken during 2009?
   a. $1,000,000
   b. $1,455,800
   c. $2,000,000
   d. $3,500,000

14. Which of the following credits may be offset against the gross estate tax to determine the net estate tax of a US citizen dying during 2009?

	Applicable credit	Credit for gift taxes paid on gifts made after 1976
a.	Yes	Yes
b.	No	No
c.	No	Yes
d.	Yes	No

15. Fred and Amy Kehl, both US citizens, are married. All of their real and personal property is owned by them as tenants by the entirety or as joint tenants with right of survivorship. The gross estate of the first spouse to die
   a.   Includes 50% of the value of all property owned by the couple, regardless of which spouse furnished the original consideration.
   b.   Includes only the property that had been acquired with the funds of the deceased spouse.
   c.   Is governed by the federal statutory provisions relating to jointly held property, rather than by the decedent's interest in community property vested by state law, if the Kehls reside in a community property state.
   d.   Includes one-third of the value of all real estate owned by the Kehls, as the dower right in the case of the wife or curtesy right in the case of the husband.

16. In connection with a "buy-sell" agreement funded by a cross-purchase insurance arrangement, business associate Adam bought a policy on Burr's life to finance the purchase of Burr's interest. Adam, the beneficiary, paid the premiums and retained all incidents of ownership. On the death of Burr, the insurance proceeds will be
   a.   Includible in Burr's gross estate, if Burr owns 50% or more of the stock of the corporation.
   b.   Includible in Burr's gross estate only if Burr had purchased a similar policy on Adam's life at the same time and for the same purpose.
   c.   Includible in Burr's gross estate, if Adam has the right to veto Burr's power to borrow on the policy that Burr owns on Adam's life.
   d.   Excludible from Burr's gross estate.

17. Following are the fair market values of Wald's assets at the date of death:

Personal effects and jewelry	$750,000
Land bought by Wald with Wald's funds five years prior to death and held with Wald's sister as joint tenants with right of survivorship	2,800,000

The executor of Wald's estate did not elect the alternate valuation date. The amount includible as Wald's gross estate in the federal estate tax return is
   a. $ 750,000
   b. $2,150,000
   c. $2,800,000
   d. $3,550,000

18. Which one of the following is a valid deduction from a decedent's gross estate?
   a.   Foreign death taxes.
   b.   Income tax paid on income earned and received after the decedent's death.
   c.   Federal estate taxes.
   d.   Unpaid income taxes on income received by the decedent before death.

19. Eng and Lew, both US citizens, died in 2009. Eng made taxable lifetime gifts of $100,000 that are **not** included in Eng's gross estate. Lew made no lifetime gifts. At the dates of death, Eng's gross estate was $2,600,000, and Lew's gross estate was $2,800,000. A federal estate tax return must be filed for

	Eng	Lew
a.	No	No
b.	No	Yes
c.	Yes	No
d.	Yes	Yes

20. With regard to the federal estate tax, the alternate valuation date
   a.   Is required to be used if the fair market value of the estate's assets has increased since the decedent's date of death.
   b.   If elected on the first return filed for the estate, may be revoked in an amended return provided that the first return was filed on time.
   c.   Must be used for valuation of the estate's liabilities if such date is used for valuation of the estate's assets.
   d.   Can be elected only if its use decreases both the value of the gross estate and the estate tax liability.

21. Proceeds of a life insurance policy payable to the estate's executor, as the estate's representative, are
   a.   Includible in the decedent's gross estate only if the premiums had been paid by the insured.
   b.   Includible in the decedent's gross estate only if the policy was taken out within three years of the insured's death under the "contemplation of death" rule.
   c.   Always includible in the decedent's gross estate.
   d.   Never includible in the decedent's gross estate.

22. Ross, a calendar-year, cash-basis taxpayer who died in June 2009, was entitled to receive a $10,000 accounting fee that had not been collected before the date of death. The executor of Ross' estate collected the full $10,000 in July 2009. This $10,000 should appear in
   a.   Only the decedent's final individual income tax return.
   b.   Only the estate's fiduciary income tax return.
   c.   Only the estate tax return.
   d.   Both the fiduciary income tax return and the estate tax return.

Items 23 and 24 are based on the following data:

   Alan Curtis, a US citizen, died on March 1, 2009, leaving an adjusted gross estate with a fair market value of $3,600,000 at the date of death. Under the terms of Alan's will, $900,000 was bequeathed outright to his widow, free of all estate and inheritance taxes. The remainder of Alan's estate was left to his mother. Alan made no taxable gifts during his lifetime.

23. Disregarding extensions of time for filing, within how many months after the date of Alan's death is the federal estate tax return due?

- a.   2 1/2
- b.   3 1/2
- c.   9
- d.   12

24. In computing the taxable estate, the executor of Alan's estate should claim a marital deduction of

- a. $ 450,000
- b. $ 780,800
- c. $ 900,000
- d. $1,455,800

25. In 2004, Edwin Ryan bought 100 shares of a listed stock for $5,000. In June 2009, when the stock's fair market value was $7,000, Edwin gave this stock to his sister, Lynn. No gift tax was paid. Lynn died in October 2009, bequeathing this stock to Edwin, when the stock's fair market value was $9,000. Lynn's executor did not elect the alternate valuation. What is Edwin's basis for this stock after he inherits it from Lynn's estate?

- a. $0
- b. $5,000
- c. $7,000
- d. $9,000

26. The generation-skipping transfer tax is imposed

- a.   Instead of the gift tax.
- b.   Instead of the estate tax.
- c.   At the highest tax rate under the unified transfer tax rate schedule.
- d.   When an individual makes a gift to a grandparent.

27. Under the terms of the will of Melvin Crane, $10,000 a year is to be paid to his widow and $5,000 a year is to be paid to his daughter out of the estate's income during the period of estate administration. No charitable contributions are made by the estate. During 2009, the estate made the required distributions to Crane's widow and daughter and for the entire year the estate's distributable net income was $12,000. What amount of the $10,000 distribution received from the estate must Crane's widow include in her gross income for 2009?

- a. $0
- b. $ 4,000
- c. $ 8,000
- d. $10,000

Items 28 and 29 are based on the following:

Lyon, a cash-basis taxpayer, died on January 15, 2009. In 2009, the estate executor made the required periodic distribution of $9,000 from estate income to Lyon's sole heir. The following pertains to the estate's income and disbursements in 2009:

2009 Estate Income
$20,000   Taxable interest
  10,000   Net long-term capital gains allocable to corpus

2009 Estate Disbursements
  $5,000   Administrative expenses attributable to taxable income

28. For the 2009 calendar year, what was the estate's distributable net income (DNI)?

- a. $15,000
- b. $20,000

- c. $25,000
- d. $30,000

29. Lyon's executor does not intend to file an extension request for the estate fiduciary income tax return. By what date must the executor file the Form 1041, US Fiduciary Income Tax Return, for the estate's 2010 calendar year?

- a.   March 15, 2011.
- b.   April 15, 2011.
- c.   June 15, 2011.
- d.   September 15, 2011.

30. A distribution from estate income, that was **currently** required, was made to the estate's sole beneficiary during its calendar year. The maximum amount of the distribution to be included in the beneficiary's gross income is limited to the estate's

- a.   Capital gain income.
- b.   Ordinary gross income.
- c.   Distributable net income.
- d.   Net investment income.

31. A distribution to an estate's sole beneficiary for the 2009 calendar year equaled $15,000, the amount currently required to be distributed by the will. The estate's 2009 records were as follows:

Estate income
$40,000   Taxable interest

Estate disbursements
$34,000   Expenses attributable to taxable interest

What amount of the distribution was taxable to the beneficiary?

- a. $40,000
- b. $15,000
- c. $ 6,000
- d. $0

32. With regard to estimated income tax, estates

- a.   Must make quarterly estimated tax payments starting no later than the second quarter following the one in which the estate was established.
- b.   Are exempt from paying estimated tax during the estate's first two taxable years.
- c.   Must make quarterly estimated tax payments only if the estate's income is required to be distributed currently.
- d.   Are not required to make payments of estimated tax.

33. A complex trust is a trust that

- a.   Must distribute income currently, but is prohibited from distributing principal during the taxable year.
- b.   Invests only in corporate securities and is prohibited from engaging in short-term transactions.
- c.   Permits accumulation of current income, provides for charitable contributions, or distributes principal during the taxable year.
- d.   Is exempt from payment of income tax since the tax is paid by the beneficiaries.

34. The 2010 standard deduction for a trust or an estate in the fiduciary income tax return is

- a. $0
- b. $650
- c. $750
- d. $800

35. Which of the following fiduciary entities are required to use the calendar year as their taxable period for income tax purposes?

	Estates	Trusts (except those that are tax exempt)
a.	Yes	Yes
b.	No	No
c.	Yes	No
d.	No	Yes

36. Ordinary and necessary administration expenses paid by the fiduciary of an estate are deductible
- a. Only on the fiduciary income tax return (Form 1041) and never on the federal estate tax return (Form 706).
- b. Only on the federal estate tax return and never on the fiduciary income tax return.
- c. On the fiduciary income tax return only if the estate tax deduction is waived for these expenses.
- d. On both the fiduciary income tax return and on the estate tax return by adding a tax computed on the proportionate rates attributable to both returns.

37. An executor of a decedent's estate that has only US citizens as beneficiaries is required to file a fiduciary income tax return, if the estate's gross income for the year is at least
- a. $ 400
- b. $ 500
- c. $ 600
- d. $1,000

38. The charitable contribution deduction on an estate's fiduciary income tax return is allowable
- a. If the decedent died intestate.
- b. To the extent of the same adjusted gross income limitation as that on an individual income tax return.
- c. Only if the decedent's will specifically provides for the contribution.
- d. Subject to the 2% threshold on miscellaneous itemized deductions.

39. On January 1, 2010, Carlt created a $300,000 trust that provided his mother with a lifetime income interest starting on January 1, 2010, with the remainder interest to go to his son. Carlt expressly retained the power to revoke both the income interest and the remainder interest at any time. Who will be taxed on the trust's 2010 income?
- a. Carlt's mother.
- b. Carlt's son.
- c. Carlt.
- d. The trust.

40. Astor, a cash-basis taxpayer, died on February 3. During the year, the estate's executor made a distribution of $12,000 from estate income to Astor's sole heir and adopted a calendar year to determine the estate's taxable income. The following additional information pertains to the estate's income and disbursements for the year:

Estate income	
Taxable interest	$65,000
Net long-term capital gains allocable to corpus	5,000

Estate disbursements	
Administrative expenses attributable to taxable income	14,000
Charitable contributions from gross income to a public charity, made under the terms of the will	9,000

For the calendar year, what was the estate's distributable net income (DNI)?
- a. $39,000
- b. $42,000
- c. $58,000
- d. $65,000

41. For income tax purposes, the estate's initial taxable period for a decedent who died on October 24
- a. May be either a calendar year, or a fiscal year beginning on the date of the decedent's death.
- b. Must be a fiscal year beginning on the date of the decedent's death.
- c. May be either a calendar year, or a fiscal year beginning on October 1 of the year of the decedent's death.
- d. Must be a calendar year beginning on January 1 of the year of the decedent's death.

42. The private foundation status of an exempt organization will terminate if it
- a. Becomes a public charity.
- b. Is a foreign corporation.
- c. Does **not** distribute all of its net assets to one or more public charities.
- d. Is governed by a charter that limits the organization's exempt purposes.

43. Which of the following exempt organizations must file annual information returns?
- a. Churches.
- b. Internally supported auxiliaries of churches.
- c. Private foundations.
- d. Those with gross receipts of less than $5,000 in each taxable year.

44. To qualify as an exempt organization other than a church or an employees' qualified pension or profit-sharing trust, the applicant
- a. Cannot operate under the "lodge system" under which payments are made to its members for sick benefits.
- b. Need **not** be specifically identified as one of the classes on which exemption is conferred by the Internal Revenue Code, provided that the organization's purposes and activities are of a nonprofit nature.
- c. Is barred from incorporating and issuing capital stock.
- d. Must file a written application with the Internal Revenue Service.

45. To qualify as an exempt organization, the applicant
- a. May be organized and operated for the primary purpose of carrying on a business for profit, provided that all of the organization's net earnings are turned over to one or more tax exempt organizations.
- b. Need **not** be specifically identified as one of the classes upon which exemption is conferred by the Internal Revenue Code, provided that the organization's purposes and activities are of a nonprofit nature.
- c. Must **not** be classified as a social club.

d.   Must **not** be a private foundation organized and operated exclusively to influence legislation pertaining to protection of the environment.

46. Carita Fund, organized and operated exclusively for charitable purposes, provides insurance coverage, at amounts substantially below cost, to exempt organizations involved in the prevention of cruelty to children. Carita's insurance activities are
a.   Exempt from tax.
b.   Treated as unrelated business income.
c.   Subject to the same tax provisions as those applicable to insurance companies.
d.   Considered "commercial-type" as defined by the Internal Revenue Code.

47. The filing of a return covering unrelated business income
a.   Is required of all exempt organizations having at least $1,000 of unrelated business taxable income for the year.
b.   Relieves the organization of having to file a separate annual information return.
c.   Is **not** necessary if all of the organization's income is used exclusively for charitable purposes.
d.   Must be accompanied by a minimum payment of 50% of the tax due as shown on the return, with the balance of tax payable six months later.

48. A condominium management association wishing to be treated as a homeowners association and to qualify as an exempt organization for a particular year
a.   Need **not** file a formal election.
b.   Must file an election as of the date the association was organized.
c.   Must file an election at the beginning of the association's first taxable year.
d.   Must file a separate election for each taxable year no later than the due date of the return for which the election is to apply.

49. An organization wishing to qualify as an exempt organization
a.   Is prohibited from issuing capital stock.
b.   Is limited to three prohibited transactions a year.
c.   Must **not** have non-US citizens on its governing board.
d.   Must be of a type specifically identified as one of the classes on which exemption is conferred by the Code.

50. Which one of the following statements is correct with regard to exempt organizations?
a.   An organization is automatically exempt from tax merely by meeting the statutory requirements for exemptions.
b.   Exempt organizations that are required to file annual information returns must disclose the identity of all substantial contributors, in addition to the amount of contributions received.
c.   An organization will automatically forfeit its exempt status if any executive or other employee of the organization is paid compensation in excess of $150,000 per year, even if such compensation is reasonable.

d.   Exempt status of an organization may **not** retroactively revoked.

51. To qualify as an exempt organization, the applicant
a.   Must fall into one of the specific classes upon which exemption is conferred by the Internal Revenue Code.
b.   **Cannot**, under any circumstances, be a foreign corporation.
c.   **Cannot**, under any circumstances, engage in lobbying activities.
d.   **Cannot** be exclusively a social club.

52. To qualify as an exempt organization,
a.   A written application need **not** be filed if no applicable official form is provided.
b.   No employee of the organization is permitted to receive compensation in excess of $100,000 per year.
c.   The applicant must be of a type specifically identified as one of the classes upon which exemption is conferred by the Code.
d.   The organization is prohibited from issuing capital stock.

53. Hope is a tax-exempt religious organization. Which of the following activities is(are) consistent with Hope's tax-exempt status?
I.   Conducting weekend retreats for business organizations.
II. Providing traditional burial services that maintain the religious beliefs of its members.
a.   I only.
b.   II only.
c.   Both I and II.
d.   Neither I nor II.

54. The organizational test to qualify a public service charitable entity as tax-exempt requires the articles of organization to
I. Limit the purpose of the entity to the charitable purpose.
II. State that an information return should be filed annually with the Internal Revenue Service.
a.   I only.
b.   II only.
c.   Both I and II.
d.   Neither I nor II.

55. Which of the following activities regularly conducted by a tax-exempt organization will result in unrelated business income?
I. Selling articles made by handicapped persons as part of their rehabilitation, when the organization is involved exclusively in their rehabilitation.
II. Operating a grocery store almost fully staffed by emotionally handicapped persons as part of a therapeutic program.
a.   I only.
b.   II only.
c.   Both I and II.
d.   Neither I nor II.

56. An organization that operates for the prevention of cruelty to animals will fail to meet the operational test to qualify as an exempt organization if

	The organization engages in insubstantial _nonexempt activities_	The organization directly participates in _any political campaign_
a.	Yes	Yes
b.	Yes	No
c.	No	Yes
d.	No	No

57. Which one of the following statements is correct with regard to unrelated business income of an exempt organization?

    a. An exempt organization that earns any unrelated business income in excess of $100,000 during a particular year will lose its exempt status for that particular year.

    b. An exempt organization is not taxed on unrelated business income of less than $1,000.

    c. The tax on unrelated business income can be imposed even if the unrelated business activity is intermittent and is carried on once a year.

    d. An unrelated trade or business activity that results in a loss is excluded from the definition of unrelated business.

58. Which of the following activities regularly carried out by an exempt organization will **not** result in unrelated business income?

    a. The sale of laundry services by an exempt hospital to other hospitals.

    b. The sale of heavy-duty appliances to senior citizens by an exempt senior citizen's center.

    c. Accounting and tax services performed by a local chapter of a labor union for its members.

    d. The sale by a trade association of publications used as course materials for the association's seminars that are oriented towards its members.

59. If an exempt organization is a corporation, the tax on unrelated business taxable income is

    a. Computed at corporate income tax rates.

    b. Computed at rates applicable to trusts.

    c. Credited against the tax on recognized capital gains.

    d. Abated.

60. During 2009, Help, Inc., an exempt organization, derived income of $15,000 from conducting bingo games. Conducting bingo games is legal in Help's locality and is confined to exempt organizations in Help's state. Which of the following statements is true regarding this income?

    a. The entire $15,000 is subject to tax at a lower rate than the corporation income tax rate.

    b. The entire $15,000 is exempt from tax on unrelated business income.

    c. Only the first $5,000 is exempt from tax on unrelated business income.

    d. Since Help has unrelated business income, Help automatically forfeits its exempt status for 2009.

61. Which of the following statements is correct regarding the unrelated business income of exempt organizations?

    a. If an exempt organization has any unrelated business income, it may result in the loss of the organization's exempt status.

    b. Unrelated business income relates to the performance of services, but **not** to the sale of goods.

    c. An unrelated business does **not** include any activity where all the work is performed for the organization by unpaid volunteers.

    d. Unrelated business income tax will **not** be imposed if profits from the unrelated business are used to support the exempt organization's charitable activities.

62. An incorporated exempt organization subject to tax on its 2009 unrelated business income

    a. Must make estimated tax payments if its tax can reasonably be expected to be $100 or more.

    b. Must comply with the Code provisions regarding installment payments of estimated income tax by corporations.

    c. Must pay at least 70% of the tax due as shown on the return when filed, with the balance of tax payable in the following quarter.

    d. May defer payment of the tax for up to nine months following the due date of the return.

63. If an exempt organization is a charitable trust, then unrelated business income is

    a. Not subject to tax.

    b. Taxed at rates applicable to corporations.

    c. Subject to tax even if such income is less than $1,000.

    d. Subject to tax only for the amount of such income in excess of $1,000.

64. With regard to unrelated business income of an exempt organization, which one of the following statements is true?

    a. If an exempt organization has any unrelated business income, such organization automatically forfeits its exempt status for the particular year in which such income was earned.

    b. When an unrelated trade or business activity results in a loss, such activity is excluded from the definition of unrelated business.

    c. If an exempt organization derives income from conducting bingo games, in a locality where such activity is legal, and in a state that confines such activity to nonprofit organizations, then such income is exempt from the tax on unrelated business income.

    d. Dividends and interest earned by all exempt organizations always are excluded from the definition of unrelated business income.

65. Which of the following acts constitute(s) grounds for a tax preparer penalty?

  I. Without the taxpayer's consent, the tax preparer disclosed taxpayer income tax return information under an order from a state court.

  II. At the taxpayer's suggestion, the tax preparer deducted the expenses of the taxpayers' personal domestic help as a business expense on the taxpayer's individual tax return.

    a. I only.

    b. II only.

    c. Both I and II.

    d. Neither I nor II.

66. Vee Corp. retained Water, CPA, to prepare its 2009 income tax return. During the engagement, Water discovered that Vee had failed to file its 2004 income tax return.

What is Water's professional responsibility regarding Vee's unfiled 2004 income tax return?

a. Prepare Vee's 2004 income tax return and submit it to the IRS.

b. Advise Vee that the 2004 income tax return has not been filed and recommend that Vee ignore filing its 2004 return since the statute of limitations has passed.

c. Advise the IRS that Vee's 2004 income tax return has not been filed.

d. Consider withdrawing from preparation of Vee's 2009 income tax return until the error is corrected.

67. To avoid tax return preparer penalties for a return's understated tax liability due to an intentional disregard of the regulations, which of the following actions must a tax preparer take?

a. Audit the taxpayer's corresponding business operations.

b. Review the accuracy of the taxpayer's books and records.

c. Make reasonable inquiries if the taxpayer's information is incomplete.

d. Examine the taxpayer's supporting documents.

68. Kopel was engaged to prepare Raff's 2009 federal income tax return. During the tax preparation interview, Raff told Kopel that he paid $3,000 in property taxes in 2009. Actually, Raff's property taxes amounted to only $600. Based on Raff's word, Kopel deducted the $3,000 on Raff's return, resulting in an understatement of Raff's tax liability. Kopel had no reason to believe that the information was incorrect. Kopel did not request underlying documentation and was reasonably satisfied by Raff's representation that Raff had adequate records to support the deduction. Which of the following statements is correct?

a. To avoid the preparer penalty for willful understatement of tax liability, Kopel was obligated to examine the underlying documentation for the deduction.

b. To avoid the preparer penalty for willful understatement of tax liability, Kopel would be required to obtain Raff's representation in writing.

c. Kopel is **not** subject to the preparer penalty for willful understatement of tax liability because the deduction that was claimed was more than 25% of the actual amount that should have been deducted.

d. Kopel is **not** subject to the preparer penalty for willful understatement of tax liability because Kopel was justified in relying on Raff's representation.

69. A penalty for understated corporate tax liability can be imposed on a tax preparer who fails to

a. Audit the corporate records.

b. Examine business operations.

c. Copy all underlying documents.

d. Make reasonable inquiries when taxpayer information appears incorrect.

70. A tax return preparer is subject to a penalty for knowingly or recklessly disclosing corporate tax return information, if the disclosure is made

a. To enable a third party to solicit business from the taxpayer.

b. To enable the tax processor to electronically compute the taxpayer's liability.

c. For peer review.

d. Under an administrative order by a state agency that registers tax return preparers.

71. A tax return preparer may disclose or use tax return information without the taxpayer's consent to

a. Facilitate a supplier's or lender's credit evaluation of the taxpayer.

b. Accommodate the request of a financial institution that needs to determine the amount of taxpayer's debt to it, to be forgiven.

c. Be evaluated by a quality or peer review.

d. Solicit additional nontax business.

72. Which, if any, of the following could result in penalties against an income tax return preparer?

I. Knowing or reckless disclosure or use of tax information obtained in preparing a return.

II. A willful attempt to understate any client's tax liability on a return or claim for refund.

a. Neither I nor II.

b. I only.

c. II only.

d. Both I and II.

73. Clark, a professional tax return preparer, prepared and signed a client's 2009 federal income tax return that resulted in a $600 refund. Which one of the following statements is correct with regard to an Internal Revenue Code penalty Clark may be subject to for endorsing and cashing the client's refund check?

a. Clark will be subject to the penalty if Clark endorses and cashes the check.

b. Clark may endorse and cash the check, without penalty, if Clark is enrolled to practice before the Internal Revenue Service.

c. Clark may endorse and cash the check, without penalty, because the check is for less than $1,000.

d. Clark may endorse and cash the check, without penalty, if the amount does **not** exceed Clark's fee for preparation of the return.

74. A CPA who prepares clients' federal income tax returns for a fee must

a. File certain required notices and powers of attorney with the IRS before preparing any returns.

b. Keep a completed copy of each return for a specified period of time.

c. Receive client documentation supporting all travel and entertainment expenses deducted on the return.

d. Indicate the CPA's federal identification number on a tax return only if the return reflects tax due from the taxpayer.

75. A CPA owes a duty to

a. Provide for a successor CPA in the event death or disability prevents completion of an audit.

b. Advise a client of errors contained in a previously filed tax return.

c. Disclose client fraud to third parties.

d. Perform an audit according to GAAP so that fraud will be uncovered.

76. In general, if the IRS issues a thirty-day letter to an individual taxpayer who wishes to dispute the assessment, the taxpayer

   a.   May, without paying any tax, immediately file a petition that would properly commence an action in Tax Court.
   b.   May ignore the thirty-day letter and wait to receive a ninety-day letter.
   c.   Must file a written protest within ten days of receiving the letter.
   d.   Must pay the taxes and then commence an action in federal district court.

77. A CPA will be liable to a tax client for damages resulting from all of the following actions **except**

   a.   Failing to timely file a client's return.
   b.   Failing to advise a client of certain tax elections.
   c.   Refusing to sign a client's request for a filing extension.
   d.   Neglecting to evaluate the option of preparing joint or separate returns that would have resulted in a substantial tax savings for a married client.

78. According to the AICPA Statement on Standards for Tax Services, which of the following statements is correct regarding the standards a CPA should follow when recommending tax return positions and preparing tax returns?

   a.   A CPA may recommend a position that the CPA concludes is frivolous as long as the position is adequately disclosed on the return.
   b.   A CPA may recommend a position in which the CPA has a good faith belief that the position has a realistic possibility of being sustained if challenged.
   c.   A CPA will usually **not** advise the client of the potential penalty consequences of the recommended tax return position.
   d.   A CPA may sign a tax return as preparer knowing that the return takes a position that will **not** be sustained if challenged.

79. According to the standards of the profession, which of the following statements is(are) correct regarding the action to be taken by a CPA who discovers an error in a client's previously filed tax return?

   I.   Advise the client of the error and recommend the measures to be taken.
   II. Withdraw from the professional relationship regardless of whether or not the client corrects the error.

   a.   I only.
   b.   II only.
   c.   Both I and II.
   d.   Neither I nor II.

80. According to the profession's ethical standards, a CPA preparing a client's tax return may rely on unsupported information furnished by the client, without examining underlying information, unless the information

   a.   Is derived from a pass-through entity.
   b.   Appears to be incomplete on its face.
   c.   Concerns dividends received.
   d.   Lists charitable contributions.

81. Which of the following acts by a CPA will **not** result in a CPA incurring an IRS penalty?

   a.   Failing, without reasonable cause, to provide the client with a copy of an income tax return.
   b.   Failing, without reasonable cause, to sign a client's tax return as preparer.
   c.   Understating a client's tax liability as a result of an error in calculation.
   d.   Negotiating a client's tax refund check when the CPA prepared the tax return.

82. According to the standards of the profession, which of the following sources of information should a CPA consider before signing a client's tax return?

   I.   Information actually known to the CPA from the tax return of another client.
   II. Information provided by the client that appears to be correct based on the client's returns from prior years.

   a.   I only.
   b.   II only.
   c.   Both I and II.
   d.   Neither I nor II.

SIMULATION PROBLEMS

Simulation Problem 1   (10 to 20 minutes)

Situation		
	Type of Gift	Generation-Skipping Tax

During 2010, various clients went to Rowe, CPA, for tax advice concerning possible gift tax liability on transfers they made throughout 2010.

	Type of Gift	
Situation		Generation-Skipping Tax

For each client, indicate whether the transfer of cash, the income interest, or the remainder interest is a gift of a present interest, a gift of a future interest, or not a completed gift.

Answer List

P.   Present Interest
F.   Future Interest
N.   Not Completed

Assume the following facts:

Cobb created a $500,000 trust that provided his mother with an income interest for her life and the remainder interest to go to his sister at the death of his mother. Cobb expressly retained the power to revoke both the income interest and the remainder interest at any time.

Items to be answered

                                                                     (P) (F) (N)

1. The income interest at the trust's creation.   ○ ○ ○

2. The remainder interest at the trust's creation.   ○ ○ ○

Kane created a $100,000 trust that provided her nephew with the income interest until he reached forty-five years of age. When the trust was created, Kane's nephew was twenty-five. The income distribution is to start when Kane's nephew is twenty-nine. After Kane's nephew reaches the age of forty-five, the remainder interest is to go to Kane's niece.

                                                                     (P) (F) (N)

3. The income interest.   ○ ○ ○

During 2010, Hall, an unmarried taxpayer, made a $10,000 cash gift to his son in May and a further $12,000 cash gift to him in August.

                                                                     (P) (F) (N)

4. The cash transfers.   ○ ○ ○

During 2010, Yeats transferred property worth $20,000 to a trust with the income to be paid to her twenty-two-year-old niece Jane. After Jane reaches the age of thirty, the remainder interest is to be distributed to Yeats' brother. The income interest is valued at $9,700 and the remainder interest at $10,300.

                                                                      (P) (F) (N)

5. The income interest.   ○ ○ ○

6. The remainder interest.   ○ ○ ○

Tom and Ann Curry, US citizens, were married for the entire 2010 calendar year. Tom gave a $40,000 cash gift to his uncle, Grant. The Currys made no other gifts to Grant in 2010. Tom and Ann each signed a timely election stating that each made one-half of the $40,000 gift.

                                                                     (P) (F) (N)

7. The cash transfers.   ○ ○ ○

Murry created a $1,000,000 trust that provided his brother with an income interest for ten years, after which the remainder interest passes to Murry's sister. Murry retained the power to revoke the remainder interest at any time. The income interest was valued at $600,000.

                                                                      (P) (F) (N)

8. The income interest.   ○ ○ ○

9. The remainder interest.   ○ ○ ○

Situation	Type of Gift	Generation-Skipping Tax

Determine whether the transfer is subject to the generation skipping tax, the gift tax, or both taxes. Disregard the use of any exclusions and the unified credit.

<u>Answer List</u>
A. Generation-Skipping Tax
B. Gift Tax
C. Both Taxes

                                                                          (A) (B) (C)

Martin's daughter, Kim, has one child, Dale. During 2010, Martin made an outright $5,000,000 gift to Dale.   ○   ○   ○

Simulation Problem 2   (5 to 10 minutes)

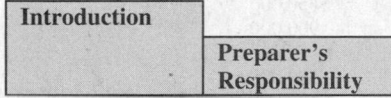

A CPA sole practitioner has tax preparers' responsibilities when preparing tax returns for clients.

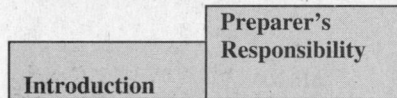

Items 1 through 9 each represent an independent factual situation in which a CPA sole practitioner has prepared and signed the taxpayer's income tax return. For each item, select from the following list the correct response regarding the tax preparer's responsibilities. A response may be selected once, more than once, or not at all.

<u>Answer List</u>
P. The tax preparer's action constitutes an act of tax preparer misconduct subject to the Internal Revenue Code penalty.
E. The Internal Revenue Service will examine the facts and circumstances to determine whether the reasonable cause exception applies; the good-faith exception applies; or both exceptions apply.
N. The tax preparer's action does **not** constitute an act of tax preparer misconduct.

                                                                          (P) (E) (N)

1. The tax preparer disclosed taxpayer income tax return information under an order from a state court, without the taxpayer's consent.   ○   ○   ○

2. The tax preparer relied on the advice of an advisory preparer to calculate the taxpayer's tax liability. The tax preparer believed that the advisory preparer was competent and that the advice was reasonable. Based on the advice, the taxpayer had understated income tax liability.   ○   ○   ○

3. The tax preparer did **not** charge a separate fee for the tax return preparation and paid the taxpayer the refund shown on the tax return less a discount. The tax preparer negotiated the actual refund check for the tax preparer's own account after receiving power of attorney from the taxpayer.   ○   ○   ○

4. The tax preparer relied on information provided by the taxpayer regarding deductible travel expenses. The tax preparer believed that the taxpayer's information was correct but inquired about the existence of the travel expense records. The tax preparer was satisfied by the taxpayer's representations that the taxpayer had adequate records for the deduction. Based on this information, the income tax liability was understated.   ○   ○   ○

5. The taxpayer provided the tax preparer with a detailed check register to compute business expenses. The tax preparer knowingly overstated the expenses on the income tax return.   ○   ○   ○

6. The tax preparer disclosed taxpayer income tax return information during a quality review conducted by CPAs. The tax preparer maintained a record of the review.   ○   ○   ○

7. The tax preparer relied on incorrect instructions on an IRS tax form that were contrary to the regulations. The tax preparer was **not** aware of the regulations or the IRS announcement pointing out the error. The understatement was immaterial as a result of the isolated error.   ○   ○   ○

	(P)	(E)	(N)

8. The tax preparer used income tax return information without the taxpayer's consent to solicit additional business.   ○ ○ ○

9. The tax preparer knowingly deducted the expenses of the taxpayer's personal domestic help as wages paid in the taxpayer's business on the taxpayer's income tax return.   ○ ○ ○

Simulation Problem 3   (10 to 20 minutes)

Situation		
	Estate Tax Treatment I	Estate Tax Treatment II

Before his death, Remsen, a US citizen, made cash gifts of $7,000 each to his four sisters. In 2009 Remsen also paid $2,000 in tuition directly to his grandchild's university on the grandchild's behalf. Remsen made no other lifetime transfers. Remsen died on January 9, 2009, and was survived by his wife and only child, both of whom were US citizens. The Remsens did not live in a community property state.

At his death Remsen owned

Cash	$650,000
Marketable securities (fair market value)	900,000
Life insurance policy with Remsen's wife named as the beneficiary (fair market value)	500,000

Under the provisions of Remsen's will, the net cash, after payment of executor's fees and medical and funeral expenses, was bequeathed to Remsen's son. The marketable securities were bequeathed to Remsen's spouse. During 2009 Remsen's estate paid

Executor fees to distribute the decedent's property (deducted on the fiduciary tax return)	$15,000
Decedent's funeral expenses	12,000

The estate's executor extended the time to file the estate tax return.

On December 3, 2009, the estate's executor paid the decedent's outstanding $10,000 medical expenses and filed the extended estate tax return.

	Estate Tax Treatment I	
Situation		Estate Tax Treatment II

For **items 1 through 5,** identify the federal estate tax treatment for each item. A response may be selected once, more than once, or not at all.

<u>Answer List</u>

F. Fully includible in Remsen's gross estate.
P. Partially includible in Remsen's gross estate.
N. Not includible in Remsen's gross estate.

	(F)	(P)	(N)

1. What is the estate tax treatment of the $7,000 cash gift to each sister?   ○ ○ ○

2. What is the estate tax treatment of the life insurance proceeds?   ○ ○ ○

3. What is the estate tax treatment of the marketable securities?   ○ ○ ○

4. What is the estate tax treatment of the $2,000 tuition payment?   ○ ○ ○

5. What is the estate tax treatment of the $650,000 cash?   ○ ○ ○

		Estate Tax Treatment II
Situation	Estate Tax Treatment I	

For **items 1 through 5,** identify the federal estate tax treatment for each item. A response may be selected once, more than once, or not at all.

<u>Answer List</u>

G. Deductible from Remsen's gross estate to arrive at Remsen's taxable estate.
I. Deductible on Remsen's 2009 individual income tax return.
E. Deductible on either Remsen's estate tax return or Remsen's 2009 individual income tax return.
N. Not deductible on either Remsen's estate tax return or Remsen's 2009 individual income tax return.

	(G)	(I)	(E)	(N)
1. What is the estate tax treatment of the executor's fees?	○	○	○	○
2. What is the estate tax treatment of the cash bequest to Remsen's son?	○	○	○	○
3. What is the estate tax treatment of the life insurance proceeds paid to Remsen's spouse?	○	○	○	○
4. What is the estate tax treatment of the funeral expenses?	○	○	○	○
5. What is the estate tax treatment of the $10,000 of medical expenses incurred before the decedent's death and paid by the executor on December 3, 2009?	○	○	○	○

Simulation Problem 4   (10 to 20 minutes)

Situation

Gift Tax Treatment

Scott Lane, an unmarried US citizen, made no lifetime transfers prior to 2010. During 2010, Lane made the following transfers:

- Gave a $13,000 cash gift to Kamp, a close friend.
- Made two separate $10,000 cash gifts to his only child.
- Created an **irrevocable** trust beginning in 2010 that provided his aunt with an income interest to be paid for the next five years. The remainder interest is to pass to Lane's sole cousin. The income interest is valued at $26,000 and the remainder interest is valued at $74,000.
- Paid $25,000 tuition directly to his grandchild's university on his grandchild's behalf.
- Created an **irrevocable** trust that provided his brother with a lifetime income interest beginning in 2012, after which a remainder interest passes to their sister.
- Created a **revocable** trust with his niece as the sole beneficiary. During 2010, the niece received $14,000 interest income from the trust.

Gift Tax Treatment

Situation

For **items 1 through 7,** determine whether the tax transactions are fully taxable, partially taxable, or not taxable to Lane in 2010 for gift tax purposes after considering the gift tax annual exclusion. Ignore the transfer tax credit when answering the items. An answer may be selected once, more than once, or not at all.

Gift Tax Treatments

F.   Fully taxable to Lane in 2010 for gift tax purposes.
P.   Partially taxable to Lane in 2010 for gift tax purposes.
N.   Not taxable to Lane in 2010 for gift tax purposes.

	(F)	(P)	(N)
1. What is the gift tax treatment of Lane's gift to Kamp?	○	○	○
2. What is the gift tax treatment of Lane's cash gifts to his child?	○	○	○
3. What is the gift tax treatment of the trust's income interest to Lane's aunt?	○	○	○
4. What is the gift tax treatment of the trust's remainder interest to Lane's cousin?	○	○	○
5. What is the gift tax treatment of the tuition payment to Lane's grandchild's university?	○	○	○
6. What is the gift tax treatment of the trust's income interest to Lane's brother?	○	○	○
7. What is the gift tax treatment of the $14,000 interest income that Lane's niece received from the revocable trust?	○	○	○

Simulation Problem 5   (25 to 30 minutes)

Situation
Research and Communication

Glen Moore inherited stock from his mother, Ruth. She had died on September 1, 2009, when the stock had a fair market value of $150,000. Ruth had acquired the stock on May 15, 2009, at a cost of $120,000. Ruth's estate was too small to require the filing of a federal estate tax return. Moore wants to know how much gross income he must report because of the receipt of his inheritance in 2009. Additionally, Glen would like to know how much gain he will have to report if he sells the stock for $165,000 in March 2010, and whether his gain will qualify as a long-term capital gain.

Research and Communication
Situation

Use the Internal Revenue Code to research the answer to Glen's questions, and prepare a memo for your firm's client files indicating the results of your research.

REMINDER: Your response will be graded for both technical content and writing skills. Technical content will be evaluated for information that is helpful to the intended reader and clearly relevant to the issues. Writing skills will be evaluated for development, organization, and the appropriate expression of ideas in professional correspondence. Use a standard business memo or letter format with a clear beginning, middle, and end. Do not convey information in the form of a table, bullet point list, or other abbreviated presentation.

To: Client Tax File
From: CPA Candidate

MULTIPLE-CHOICE ANSWERS

1. c	__ __	18. d	__ __	35. d	__ __	52. c	__ __	69. d	__ __
2. c	__ __	19. a	__ __	36. c	__ __	53. b	__ __	70. a	__ __
3. d	__ __	20. d	__ __	37. c	__ __	54. a	__ __	71. c	__ __
4. c	__ __	21. c	__ __	38. c	__ __	55. d	__ __	72. d	__ __
5. c	__ __	22. d	__ __	39. c	__ __	56. c	__ __	73. a	__ __
6. b	__ __	23. c	__ __	40. b	__ __	57. b	__ __	74. b	__ __
7. b	__ __	24. c	__ __	41. a	__ __	58. d	__ __	75. b	__ __
8. b	__ __	25. b	__ __	42. a	__ __	59. a	__ __	76. b	__ __
9. c	__ __	26. c	__ __	43. c	__ __	60. b	__ __	77. c	__ __
10. c	__ __	27. c	__ __	44. d	__ __	61. c	__ __	78. b	__ __
11. b	__ __	28. a	__ __	45. d	__ __	62. b	__ __	79. a	__ __
12. c	__ __	29. b	__ __	46. a	__ __	63. d	__ __	80. b	__ __
13. d	__ __	30. c	__ __	47. a	__ __	64. b	__ __	81. c	__ __
14. d	__ __	31. c	__ __	48. d	__ __	65. d	__ __	82. c	__ __
15. a	__ __	32. b	__ __	49. d	__ __	66. d	__ __		
16. d	__ __	33. c	__ __	50. b	__ __	67. c	__ __	1st: __/82 = __%
17. d	__ __	34. a	__ __	51. a	__ __	68. d	__ __	2nd: __/82 = __%

MULTIPLE-CHOICE ANSWER EXPLANATIONS

I.A. Gift Tax

1. (c) The requirement is to determine the amount of the $30,000 gift that is taxable to the Briars for 2009. Steve and Kay (his spouse) elected to split the gift made to Steve's sister, so each is treated as making a gift of $15,000. Since both Steve and Kay would be eligible for a $13,000 exclusion, each will have made a taxable gift of $15,000 − $13,000 exclusion = $2,000.

2. (c) The requirement is to determine the maximum exclusion available on Sayers' 2009 gift tax return for the $50,000 gift to Johnson who needed the money to pay medical expenses. The first $13,000 of gifts made to a donee during calendar year 2009 (except gifts of future interests) is excluded in determining the amount of the donor's taxable gifts for the year. Note that Sayers does not qualify for the unlimited exclusion for medical expenses paid on behalf of a donee, because Sayers did not pay the $50,000 to a medical care provider on Johnson's behalf.

3. (d) The requirement is to determine the amount of gift that is excludable from taxable gifts. Since the interest income resulting from the bond transferred to the trust will be accumulated and distributed to the child in the future upon reaching the age of twenty-one, the gift (represented by the $8,710 present value of the interest to be received by the child at age twenty-one) is a gift of a future interest and is not eligible to be offset by an annual exclusion.

4. (c) The requirement is to determine the correct statement regarding the unified transfer tax rate schedule. The unified transfer tax rate schedule applies on a cumulative basis to both life and death transfers. During a person's lifetime, a tax is first computed on cumulative lifetime taxable gifts, then is reduced by the tax on taxable gifts made in prior years in order to tax the current year's gifts at applicable marginal rates. At death, a unified transfer tax is computed on total life and death transfers, then is reduced by the tax already paid on post-1976 gifts, the unified transfer tax credit, state death taxes, foreign death taxes, and prior transfer taxes.

5. (c) The requirement is to determine which gift requires the filing of a gift tax return when the amount trans-

ferred exceeds the available annual gift tax exclusion. A gift in the form of payments for college books, supplies, and dormitory fees on behalf of an individual unrelated to the donor requires the filing of a gift tax return if the amount of payments exceeds the $12,000 ($13,000 for 2009) annual exclusion. In contrast, no gift tax return need be filed for medical expenses or college tuition paid on behalf of a donee, and campaign expenses paid to a political organization, because there are unlimited exclusions available for these types of gifts after the annual exclusion has been used.

6. (b) The requirement is to determine the due date for filing a 2009 gift tax return (Form 709). A gift tax return must be filed on a calendar-year basis, with the return due and tax paid on or before April 15th of the following year. If the donor subsequently dies, the gift tax return is due not later than the date for filing the federal estate tax return (generally nine months after date of death). Here, since Vega was still living in 2010, the due date for filing the 2009 gift tax return is April 15, 2010.

7. (b) The requirement is to determine Jan's total exclusions for gift tax purposes for 2010. In computing a donor's gift tax, the first $13,000 of gifts made to a donee during calendar year 2010 is excluded in determining the amount of the donor's taxable gifts. Thus, $13,000 of the $15,000 given to Jones, $13,000 of the $14,000 given to Craig, and all $5,000 given to Kande can be excluded, resulting in a total exclusion of $31,000. Jan's gift to Craig does not qualify for the unlimited exclusion of educational gifts paid on behalf of a donee because the amount was paid directly to Craig. All $14,000 could have been excluded if Jan had made the tuition payment directly to the college.

8. (b) The requirement is to determine the amount of Jim's gift tax marital deduction for 2010. An unlimited marital deduction is allowed for gift tax purposes for gifts to a donee, who at the time of the gift is the donor's spouse. Thus, Jim's gift of $75,000 to Nina made after their wedding is eligible for the marital deduction, whereas the gift of the $50,000 engagement ring does not qualify because Jim and Nina were not married at date of gift. The gift tax annual exclusion of $13,000 applies to multiple gifts to the same donee in chronological order, reducing the taxable gift of the engagement ring to $50,000 – $13,000 = $37,000. Since there is no remaining annual exclusion to reduce the gift of the $75,000 bank account, it would be completely offset by a marital deduction of $75,000.

9.   (c)   The requirement is to determine when a gift occurs in conjunction with Raff's creation of a joint bank account for himself and his friend's son, Dave. A gift does not occur when Raff opens the joint account and deposits money into it. Instead, a gift results when the noncontributing tenant (Dave) withdraws money from the account for his own benefit.

I.B. Estate Tax

10.   (c)   The requirement is to determine Fred's basis for the property after the death of the joint tenant (Ethel). When property is held in joint tenancy by other than spouses, the property's fair market value is included in a decedent's estate to the extent of the percentage that the decedent contributed toward the purchase. Since Ethel furnished 80% of the land's purchase price, 80% of its $300,000 fair market value, or $240,000 is included in Ethel's estate. Thus, Fred's basis is $240,000 plus the $20,000 of purchase price that he furnished, a total of $260,000.

11.   (b)   The requirement is to determine the correct treatment of medical expenses paid by the executor of Bell's estate if the executor files the appropriate waiver. The executor may elect to treat medical expenses paid by the decedent's estate for the decedent's medical care as paid by the decedent at the time the medical services were provided. To qualify for this election, the medical expenses must be paid within the one-year period after the decedent's death, and the executor must attach a waiver to the decedent's Form 1040 indicating that the expenses will not be claimed as a deduction on the decedent's estate tax return. Here, since Bell died during 2008, and the medical services were provided and paid for by Bell's estate during 2008, the medical expenses are deductible on Bell's final income tax return for 2008 provided that the executor attaches the appropriate waiver.

12.   (c)   If the executor of a decedent's estate elects the alternate valuation date and none of the assets have been sold or distributed, the estate assets must be included in the decedent's gross estate at their FMV as of six months after the decedent's death.

13.   (d)   The requirement is to determine the amount of a decedent's taxable estate that is effectively tax-free if the maximum applicable estate tax credit is taken for 2009. The maximum estate tax credit is $1,455,800 for 2009. Due to the graduated structure of the tax, this credit is the equivalent of an exemption of $3,500,000 and effectively permits $3,500,000 of taxable estate to be free of tax.

14.   (d)   The requirement is to determine which of the credits may be offset against the gross estate tax in determining the net estate tax of a US citizen for 2009. In computing the net estate tax of a US citizen, the gross estate tax may be offset by the applicable tax credit, and credits for foreign death taxes, and prior transfer taxes. For 2009, the applicable tax credit of $1,455,800 is allowed against estate taxes and is equivalent to an exemption of the first $3,500,000 of taxable gifts or taxable estate from the unified transfer tax. Only taxable gifts made after 1976 are added

back to a donor's taxable estate in arriving at the tax base for the application of the federal estate tax at death. To the extent these taxable gifts exceeded the exemption equivalent of the applicable credit and required the payment of a gift tax during the donor's lifetime, such tax is then subtracted from a donor's tentative estate tax at death in arriving at the gross estate tax. Thus, although post-1976 gift taxes reduce the net estate tax, they are not subtracted as a tax credit from the gross estate tax.

15.   (a)   The requirement is to determine the correct statement with regard to the gross estate of the first spouse to die when property is owned by them as tenants by the entirety or as joint tenants with right of survivorship. Under the general rule for joint tenancies, 100% of the value of jointly held property is included in a deceased tenant's gross estate except to the extent that the surviving tenants can prove that they contributed to the cost of the property. However, under a special rule applicable to spouses who own property as tenants by the entirety or as joint tenants with right of survivorship, the gross estate of the first spouse to die automatically includes 50% of the value of the jointly held property, regardless of which spouse furnished the original consideration for the purchase of the property.

16.   (d)   The requirement is to determine the amount of insurance proceeds included in Burr's gross estate with regard to a policy on Burr's life purchased by Adam in connection with a "buy-sell" agreement funded by a cross-purchase insurance arrangement. The gross estate of a decedent includes the proceeds of life insurance on the decedent's life if (1) the insurance proceeds are payable to the estate, (2) the proceeds are payable to another for the benefit of the estate, or (3) the decedent possessed an incident of ownership in the policy. An "incident of ownership" not only means ownership of the policy in a legal sense, but also includes the power to change beneficiaries, to revoke an assignment, to pledge the policy for a loan, or to surrender or cancel the policy. Here, since the policy owned by Adam on Burr's life was not payable to or for the benefit of Burr's estate, and Burr had no incident of ownership in the policy, the full amount of insurance proceeds would be excluded from Burr's gross estate.

17.   (d)   The requirement is to determine the amount includible as Wald's gross estate for federal estate tax purposes. If an executor does not elect the alternate valuation date, all property in which the decedent possessed an ownership interest at time of death is included in the decedent's gross estate at its fair market value at date of death. If property was held in joint tenancy and was acquired by purchase by other than spouses, the property's total fair market value will be included in the decedent's gross estate except to the extent that the surviving tenant can prove that he/she contributed toward the purchase. Since Wald purchased the land with his own funds, the land's total fair market value ($2,800,000) must be included in Wald's gross estate together with Wald's personal effects and jewelry ($750,000), resulting in a gross estate of $3,550,000.

18.   (d)   The requirement is to determine the item that is deductible from a decedent's gross estate. Unpaid income taxes on income received by the decedent before death would be a liability of the estate and would be deductible from the gross estate. Foreign death taxes, income tax paid on income earned and received after the decedent's death, and federal estate taxes are not deductible in computing a decedent's taxable estate. Note that although foreign death taxes are not deductible in computing a decedent's taxable estate, a limited tax credit is allowed for foreign death taxes in computing the net estate tax payable.

19.   (a)   The requirement is to determine whether federal estate tax returns must be filed for the estates of Eng and Lew. For a decedent dying during 2009, a federal estate tax return (Form 706) must be filed if the decedent's gross estate exceeds ($3,500,000). If a decedent made taxable lifetime gifts such that the decedent's applicable transfer tax credit was used to offset the gift tax, the ($3,500,000) exemption amount must be reduced by the amount of taxable lifetime gifts to determine whether a return is required to be filed.

Since Lew made no lifetime gifts and the value of Lew's gross estate was only $2,800,000, no federal estate tax return is required to be filed for Lew's estate. In Eng's case, the ($3,500,000) exemption is reduced by Eng's $100,000 of taxable lifetime gifts to $3,400,000. However, since Eng's gross estate totaled only $2,600,000, no federal estate tax return is required to be filed for Eng's estate.

20.   (d)   The requirement is to determine the correct statement regarding the use of the alternate valuation date in computing the federal estate tax. An executor of an estate can elect to use the alternate valuation date (the date six months after the decedent's death) to value the assets included in a decedent's gross estate only if its use decreases both the value of the gross estate and the amount of estate tax liability. Answer (a) is incorrect because the alternate valuation date cannot be used if its use increases the value of the gross estate. Answer (b) is incorrect because the use of the alternate valuation date is an irrevocable election. Answer (c) is incorrect because the alternate valuation date is only used to value an estate's assets, not its liabilities.

21.   (c)   The requirement is to determine when the proceeds of life insurance payable to the estate's executor, as the estate's representative, are includible in the decedent's gross estate. The proceeds of life insurance on the decedent's life are always included in the decedent's gross estate if (1) they are receivable by the estate, (2) the decedent possessed any incident of ownership in the policy, or (3) they are receivable by another (e.g., the estate's executor) for the benefit of the estate.

22.   (d)   The requirement is to determine the proper income and estate tax treatment of an accounting fee earned by Ross before death, that was subsequently collected by the executor of Ross' estate. Since Ross was a calendar-year, cash-method taxpayer, the income would not be included on Ross' final individual income tax return because payment had not been received. Since the accounting fee would not be included in Ross' final income tax return because of Ross' cash method of accounting, the accounting fee would be "income in respect of a decedent." For estate tax purposes, income in respect of a decedent will be included in the decedent's gross estate at its fair market value on the appropriate valuation date. For income tax purposes, the income tax basis of the decedent (zero) transfers over to the estate or beneficiary who collects the fee. The recipient of the income must classify it in the same manner (i.e., ordinary income) as would have the decedent. Thus, the accounting fee must be included in Ross' gross estate and must also be included in the estate's fiduciary income tax return

(Form 1041) because the fee was collected by the executor of Ross' estate.

23.   (c)   The requirement is to determine within how many months after the date of Alan's death his federal estate tax return should be filed. The federal estate tax return (Form 706) must be filed and the tax paid within nine months of the decedent's death, unless an extension of time has been granted.

24.   (c)   The requirement is to determine the amount of marital deduction that can be claimed in computing Alan's taxable estate. In computing the taxable estate of a decedent, an unlimited marital deduction is allowed for the portion of the decedent's estate that passes to the decedent's surviving spouse. Since $900,000 was bequeathed outright to Alan's widow, Alan's estate will receive a marital deduction of $900,000.

25.   (b)   The requirement is to determine Edwin's basis for the stock inherited from Lynn's estate. A special rule applies if a decedent (Lynn) acquires appreciated property as a gift within one year of death, and this property passes to the donor (Edwin) or donor's spouse. Then the donor's (Edwin's) basis is the basis of the property in the hands of the decedent (Lynn) before death. Since Lynn had received the stock as a gift, Lynn's basis before death ($5,000) becomes the basis of the stock to Edwin.

II.   Generation-Skipping Tax

26.   (c)   The requirement is to determine the correct statement regarding the generation-skipping transfer tax. The generation-skipping transfer tax is imposed as a separate tax in addition to the federal gift and estate taxes, and is designed to prevent an individual from escaping an entire generation of gift and estate taxes by transferring property to a person that is two or more generations *below* that of the transferor. The tax is imposed at the highest tax rate (45% for 2008) under the transfer tax rate schedule.

III. Income Taxation of Estates and Trusts

27.   (c)   The requirement is to determine the amount of the estate's $10,000 distribution that must be included in gross income by Crane's widow. The maximum amount that is taxable to beneficiaries is limited to the estate's distributable net income (DNI). Since distributions to multiple beneficiaries exceed DNI, the estate's $12,000 of DNI must be prorated to distributions to determine the portion of each distribution that must be included in gross income. Since distributions to the widow and daughter totaled $15,000, the portion of the $10,000 distribution that must be included in the widow's gross income equals ($10,000/$15,000) × $12,000 = $8,000.

28.   (a)   The requirement is to determine the estate's distributable net income (DNI). An estate's DNI generally is its taxable income before the income distribution deduction, increased by its personal exemption, any net capital loss deduction, and tax-exempt interest (reduced by related nondeductible expenses), and decreased by any net capital gains allocable to corpus. Here, the estate's DNI is the $20,000 of taxable interest reduced by the $5,000 of administrative expenses attributable to taxable income, or $15,000.

29.   (b)   The requirement is to determine the due date for the Fiduciary Income Tax Return (Form 1041) for the estate's 2010 calendar year. Form 1041 is due on the 15th day of the fourth month following the end of the tax year. Thus, an estate's calendar-year return is generally due on April 15th of the following year.

30.   (c)   The requirement is to determine the maximum amount to be included in the beneficiary's gross income for a distribution from estate income that was currently required. Distributable net income (DNI) is the maximum amount of distributions that can be taxed to beneficiaries as well as the maximum amount of distributions deduction for an estate.

31.   (c)   The requirement is to determine the amount of the estate's $15,000 distribution that is taxable to the sole beneficiary. The maximum amount that is taxable to the beneficiary is limited to the estate's distributable net income (DNI). An estate's DNI is generally its taxable income before the income distribution deduction, increased by its exemption, a net capital loss deduction, and tax-exempt interest (reduced by related nondeductible expenses), and decreased by any net capital gains allocable to corpus. Here, the estate's DNI is its taxable interest of $40,000, reduced by the $34,000 of expenses attributable to taxable interest, or $6,000.

32.   (b)   The requirement is to determine the correct statement regarding an estate's estimated income taxes. Trusts and estates must make quarterly estimated tax payments, except that an estate is exempt from making estimated tax payments for taxable years ending within two years of the decedent's death.

33.   (c)   The requirement is to determine the correct statement regarding a complex trust. A simple trust is one that (1) is required to distribute all of its income to designated beneficiaries every year, (2) has no beneficiaries that are qualifying charitable organizations, and (3) makes no distributions of trust corpus (i.e., principal) during the year. A complex trust is any trust that is not a simple trust. Answer (a) is incorrect because a complex trust is not required to distribute income currently, nor is it prohibited from distributing trust principal. Answer (b) is incorrect because there are no investment restrictions imposed on a complex trust. Answer (d) is incorrect because an income tax is imposed on a trust's taxable income.

34.   (a)   The requirement is to determine the amount of *standard deduction* for a trust or an estate in the fiduciary income tax return (Form 1041). No standard deduction is available for a trust or an estate on the fiduciary income tax return. On the other hand, a personal exemption is allowed for an estate or trust on the fiduciary income tax return. The personal exemption is $600 for an estate, $300 for a simple trust (i.e., a trust required to distribute all income currently), and $100 for a complex trust (i.e., a trust other than a simple trust).

35.   (d)   The requirement is to indicate whether estate and trusts are required to use the calendar year as their taxable year. All trusts (except those that are tax exempt) are generally required to use the calendar year for tax purposes. In contrast, an estate may adopt the calendar year, or any fiscal year as its taxable year.

36.   (c)   The requirement is to determine the proper treatment for ordinary and necessary administrative expenses paid by the fiduciary of an estate. Ordinary and necessary administrative expenses paid by the fiduciary of an estate can be deducted on either the estate's fiduciary income tax return, or on the estate's federal estate tax return. Although the expenses cannot be deducted twice, they can be allocated between the two returns in any manner that the fiduciary sees fit. If the administrative expenses are to be deducted on the fiduciary income tax return, the potential estate tax deduction must be waived for these expenses.

37.   (c)   The requirement is to determine when a fiduciary income tax return for a decedent's estate must be filed. The executor of a decedent's estate that has only US citizens as beneficiaries is required to file a fiduciary income tax return (Form 1041) if the estate's gross income is $600 or more. The return is due on or before the 15th day of the fourth month following the close of the estate's taxable year.

38.   (c)   The requirement is to determine the correct statement regarding the charitable contribution deduction on an estate's fiduciary income tax return (Form 1041). An estate is allowed a deduction for a contribution to a charitable organization if (1) the decedent's will specifically provides for the contribution, and (2) the recipient is a qualified charitable organization. The amount allowed as a charitable deduction is not subject to any percentage limitations, but must be paid from amounts included in the estate's gross income for the year of contribution.

39.   (c)   The requirement is to determine who will be taxed on the trust's 2010 income. During 2010, Carlt created a trust providing a lifetime income interest for his mother, with a remainder interest to go to his son, but he expressly retained the power to revoke both the income interest and remainder interest at any time. When the grantor of a trust retains substantial control over the trust, such as the power to revoke the income and remainder interests, the trust income will be taxed to the grantor and not to the trust or beneficiaries.

40.   (b)   The requirement is to determine the estate's distributable net income (DNI). An estate's DNI generally is its taxable income before the income distribution deduction, increased by its personal exemption, any net capital loss deduction, and tax-exempt income (reduced by related expenses), and decreased by any net capital gain allocable to corpus. Here, the estate's DNI is the $65,000 of taxable interest, reduced by the $14,000 of administrative expenses attributable to taxable income and the $9,000 of charitable contributions. Charitable contributions are allowed as a deduction if made under the terms of the decedent's will and are paid to qualified charitable organizations from amounts included in the estate's gross income.

41.   (a)   The requirement is to determine the correct statement for income tax purposes regarding the initial taxable period for the estate of a decedent who died on October 24. For income tax purposes, a decedent's estate is allowed to adopt a calendar year or any fiscal year beginning on the date of the decedent's death. Answer (b) is incorrect because an estate may adopt a calendar year and is not restricted to a fiscal year. Answer (c) is incorrect because the estate's first tax year would begin on October 24, not October 1. Answer (d) is incorrect because an estate is not restricted to a calendar year, and if it adopted a calendar year, its initial year would begin with the date of the decedent's death (October 24).

42. **(a)** The requirement is to determine what will terminate the private foundation status of an exempt organization. The private foundation status of an exempt organization will terminate if it becomes a public charity. Answer (b) is incorrect because a private foundation can be organized as a foreign corporation. Answer (c) is incorrect because private foundations are not required to distribute their assets to public charities. Answer (d) is incorrect because a private foundation's exempt purposes are already severely restricted by the Code.

43. **(c)** The requirement is to determine which exempt organizations must file annual information returns. Private foundations must file annual information returns specifically stating items of gross income, receipts, and disbursements, and such other information as may be required. In contrast, churches, religious groups, and exempt organizations other than private foundations are required to file an information return only if their gross receipts are more than $25,000.

44. **(d)** Organizations that can qualify as exempt organizations are listed in Sec. 501 of the Internal Revenue Code, and can take the form of a trust or corporation. To receive exempt status, the organization must file a written application with the IRS. In no event will exempt status be conferred upon an organization unless the organization is one of those types of organizations specifically listed in the Code. A fraternal benefit society must operate under the lodge system. An organization operating under the lodge system carries on its activities under a form of organization that comprises local branches chartered by a parent organization and can be established to provide its members with sick benefits.

45. **(d)** The requirement is to determine the correct statement regarding qualification as an exempt organization. To qualify as an exempt organization, the applicant must not be a private foundation organized and operated exclusively to influence legislation pertaining to protection of the environment. Exempt status is specifically denied to organizations if a substantial part of their activities consists of "carrying on propaganda, or otherwise attempting, to influence legislation," if expenditures exceed certain amounts. Answer (a) is incorrect because an exempt organization cannot be organized for the primary purpose of carrying on a business for profit. Answer (b) is incorrect because an organization must be one of those classes upon which exemption is specifically conferred by the Internal Revenue Code. Answer (c) is incorrect because a social club organized for recreation will qualify for exemption if substantially all of the activities of the club are for such purposes and none of the profits inure to the benefit of any shareholder.

46. **(a)** The requirement is to determine the proper tax treatment of Carita Fund's insurance activities. An otherwise qualifying exempt organization will instead be subject to tax if a substantial part of its activities consists of providing commercial-type insurance. Sec. 501(m)(3) provides that "commercial-type insurance" does not include insurance provided at substantially below cost to a class of charitable recipients. Since Carita Fund was organized and operated exclusively for charitable purposes, and provided below cost insurance coverage to exempt organizations involved in the

prevention of cruelty to children, its insurance activities are exempt from tax. The insurance activities do not constitute unrelated business income because the insurance activities were substantially related to the performance of the fund's exempt purpose. Answer (c) is incorrect because Carita Fund qualifies as an exempt organization.

47. **(a)** The filing of a return covering unrelated business income (Form 990-T) is required of all exempt organizations having at least $1,000 of unrelated business taxable income for the year. However, this does not relieve the organization of having to file a separate information return (Form 990) if it is otherwise required to file. Answer (c) is incorrect because in determining whether income is unrelated business income, the exempt organization's need for the income or the use it makes of the profits is irrelevant. Answer (d) is incorrect because the tax on unrelated business income of exempt organizations must be paid in full with the return.

48. **(d)** A condominium management association wishing to be treated as a homeowners association and thereby qualify as an exempt organization for a particular year must file a separate election for each taxable year no later than the due date of the tax return for which the election is to apply.

49. **(d)** An organization wishing to qualify as an exempt organization must be of a type specifically identified as one of the classes on which exemption is conferred by the Code. In no event will exempt status be conferred upon an organization unless the organization is one of those listed. Furthermore, in order to receive exempt status, the organization must file an application with the Internal Revenue Service. Answer (a) is incorrect since an exempt organization may be organized as a corporation. Answer (b) is incorrect because an exempt organization may lose its exempt status by engaging in any prohibited transaction. Answer (c) is incorrect because non-US citizens may be on an exempt organization's governing board.

50. **(b)** The requirement is to determine the correct statement regarding exempt organizations. With the exception chiefly of churches, an exempt organization (other than a private foundation) must nevertheless file an annual information return specifically stating items of gross income, receipts, and disbursements unless its gross receipts are normally not more than $25,000. An exempt organization required to file a return must annually report the total amount of contributions received as well as the identity of substantial contributors.

Answer (a) is incorrect because an organization can only achieve exempt status by filing an application for exemption with the Internal Revenue Service. Answer (c) is incorrect because there is no limitation on the amount of compensation that can be paid to an employee if the compensation is reasonable. Answer (d) is incorrect because exempt status can be retroactively revoked if an organization's character, purposes, or methods of operation are other than as stated in the application for exemption.

51. **(a)** The requirement is to determine the correct statement regarding qualification as an exempt organization. To qualify as an exempt organization, the applicant for exemption must fall into one of the specified classes of organizations that are listed in Sec. 501 as being exempt from tax. Answer (d) is incorrect because a social club can be an exempt organization as long as substantially all its activities are for such purposes and no part of its net earnings inures to the benefit of any private shareholder. Answer (c) is incorrect because most exempt organizations are permitted specified levels of lobbying expenditures, and can even elect to be subject to a tax equal to 25% of their excess lobbying expenditures to prevent loss of exempt status. Answer (b) is incorrect because foreign corporations can qualify as exempt organizations.

52. **(c)** Organizations that can qualify as exempt organizations are listed in Sec. 501 of the Internal Revenue Code. An exempt organization can take the form of a trust or a corporation. In order to receive exempt status, the organization must file an application with the Internal Revenue Service. In no event will exempt status be conferred upon an organization unless the organization is one of those listed in the Code. Answer (b) is incorrect because there is no limitation on the amount of salary that can be paid an employee.

IV.A.2. Sec. 501(c)(3) Organizations

53. **(b)** The requirement is to determine which of the activities is(are) consistent with Hope's tax-exempt status as a religious organization. An exempt organization must be operated exclusively for its exempt purpose, and other activities not in furtherance of its exempt purpose must be only an insubstantial part of its activities. A religious organization's providing traditional burial services that maintain the religious beliefs of its members would be consistent with its tax-exempt status as a religious organization. However, conducting recreational functions such as weekend retreats conducted for business organizations ordinarily would not be consistent with the tax-exempt status of a religious organization unless there were tightly scheduled religious activities and only limited free time for incidental recreation activities.

54. **(a)** The requirement is to determine which statements are correct in regard to the organizational test to qualify a public service charitable entity as tax-exempt. The term "articles of organization" includes the trust instrument, corporate charter, articles of association, or any other written instruments by which an organization is created. To satisfy the organizational test, the articles of organization (1) must limit the organization's purposes to one or more exempt purposes described in Sec. 501(c)(3); and, (2) must not expressly empower the organization to engage in activities that are not in furtherance of one or more exempt purposes, except as an insubstantial part of its activities.

55. **(d)** The requirement is to determine which of two activities (if any) will result in unrelated business income. Unrelated business income (UBI) is income derived from a trade or business, the conduct of which is not substantially related to the exercise or performance of an organization's exempt purpose. For a trade or business to be related, the conduct of the business activity must have a causal relationship to the achievement of the organization's exempt purpose. Selling articles made by handicapped persons as part of their rehabilitation would be substantially related to the exempt purpose of an organization exclusively involved in their rehabilitation. Similarly, operating a grocery store almost fully staffed by emotionally handicapped persons as part of a therapeutic program to allow the persons to become involved with society, assume responsibility, and to exercise

business judgment, would be substantially related to the rehabilitation purposes of the exempt organization.

56. **(c)** The operational test requires that an exempt organization be operated exclusively for an exempt purpose. An organization will be considered to be operated exclusively for an exempt purpose only if it engages primarily in activities that accomplish its exempt purpose. An organization will not be so regarded if more than an insubstantial part of its activities is not in furtherance of an exempt purpose. Thus, an organization that engages in insubstantial nonexempt activities will not fail the operational test. In contrast, an organization that operates for the prevention of cruelty to animals will fail the operational test if it directly participates in any political campaign.

IV.C.   Unrelated Business Income (UBI)

57. **(b)** The requirement is to determine the correct statement with regard to the unrelated business income of an exempt organization. An exempt organization is not taxed on unrelated business income of less than $1,000. Answer (a) is incorrect because the amount of unrelated business income will not cause the loss of exempt status. Answer (c) is incorrect because the tax will not apply to a business activity that is not regularly carried on. Answer (d) is incorrect because a loss from an unrelated trade or business activity is allowed in computing unrelated business taxable income.

58. **(d)** The requirement is to determine which one of the listed activities will not result in unrelated business income. Unrelated business income (UBI) is income derived from any trade or business, the conduct of which is not substantially related to the exercise or performance of an organization's exempt purpose. For a trade or business to be "related," the conduct of the business activity must have a causal relationship to the achievement of the exempt purpose. A business activity will be "substantially related" only if the causal relationship is a substantial one. Assuming that the development and improvement of its members is one of the purposes for which a trade association is granted an exemption, the sale of publications used as course materials for the association's seminars for its members would be substantially related.

Answer (a) is incorrect because even though a special rule permits an exempt hospital to perform services at cost for other hospitals with facilities to serve not more than 100 inpatients, the permitted services are limited to data processing, purchasing, warehousing, billing and collection, food, clinical, industrial engineering, laboratory, printing, communications, record center, and personnel services. Answer (b) is incorrect because even though an exempt senior citizen's center may operate a beauty parlor and barber shop for its members, selling major appliances to its members has been held to generate unrelated business income. Answer (c) is incorrect because the performance of accounting and tax services for its members would be unrelated to the exempt purpose of a labor union.

59. **(a)** The requirement is to determine the correct statement with regard to an exempt organization's unrelated business taxable income when the exempt organization is a corporation. An exempt organization's unrelated business income in excess of $1,000 is taxed at regular corporate income tax rates if the organization is a corporation. An exempt organization must be a trust in order for its unrelated business income to be taxed at the rates applicable to trusts.

60.   (b)   The requirement is to determine the correct statement regarding an exempt organization's income of $15,000 derived from conducting bingo games. If an exempt organization derives income from conducting bingo games, in a locality where such activity is legal, and in a state that confines such activity to nonprofit organizations, then such income is exempt from the tax on unrelated business income. Answer (d) is incorrect because unrelated business income will not cause the revocation or forfeiture of an organization's exempt status.

61.   (c)   The requirement is to determine the correct statement regarding the unrelated business income of exempt organizations. A tax-exempt organization may be subject to tax on its unrelated business income if the organization conducts a trade or business that is not substantially related to the exempt purpose of the organization, and the trade or business is regularly carried on by the organization. For an exempt organization, an unrelated business does not include any activity where all the work is performed for the organization by unpaid volunteers. Answer (a) is incorrect because although unrelated business income may result in a tax, it will not result in the loss of the organization's exempt status. Answer (b) is incorrect because the term "business" is broadly defined to include any activity conducted for the production of income through the sale of merchandise or the performance of services. Answer (d) is incorrect because using a trade or business to provide financial support for the organization's exempt purpose will not prevent an activity from being classified as an unrelated trade or business and being subject to the tax on unrelated business income.

62.   (b)   The requirement is to determine the correct statement regarding an exempt organization's payment of estimated taxes on its unrelated business income. An exempt organization subject to tax on its unrelated business income must comply with the Code provisions regarding installment payments of estimated income tax by corporations. This means that an exempt organization must make quarterly estimated tax payments if it expects its estimated tax on its unrelated business income to be $500 or more. Answers (c) and (d) are incorrect because any tax on unrelated business income must be paid in full by the due date of the exempt organization's return.

63.   (d)   The requirement is to determine the correct statement regarding the taxability of unrelated business income (UBI) to an exempt organization that is a charitable trust. Answer (c) is incorrect because an exempt organization that is a charitable trust is subject to tax on its UBI only to the extent that its UBI exceeds $1,000. Answers (a) and (b) are incorrect because an exempt organization with UBI in excess of $1,000 is subject to tax at rates applicable to trusts if it is organized as a charitable trust.

64.   (c)   Unrelated business income (UBI) is gross income derived from any trade or business the conduct of which is not substantially related to the exercise or performance of an organization's exempt purpose. Although dividends and interest are generally excluded from UBI, they will be included if they result from debt-financed investments. Answer (d) is incorrect because it states that dividends and interest are always **excluded** from UBI. An-

swer (a) is incorrect because the Code only imposes a tax on UBI, it does not revoke an organization's exempt status. Answer (b) is incorrect because a net operating loss is allowed in computing unrelated business taxable income. Answer (c) is correct because Code Sec. 513(f) specifically excludes from UBI an exempt organization's conducting bingo games where such activity is legal.

IV.   Tax Return Preparers

65.   (b)   The requirement is to determine which acts constitute(s) grounds for a tax preparer penalty. A return preparer will be subject to penalty if the preparer knowingly or recklessly discloses information furnished in connection with the preparation of a tax return, unless such information is furnished for quality or peer review, under an administrative order by a regulatory agency, or pursuant to an order of a court. Additionally, a return preparer will be subject to penalty if any part of an understatement of liability with respect to a return or refund claim is due to the preparer's willful attempt to understate tax liability, or to any reckless or intentional disregard of rules and regulations.

66.   (d)   The requirement is to determine Water's responsibility regarding Vee's unfiled 2004 income tax return. A CPA should promptly inform the client upon becoming aware of the client's failure to file a required return for a prior year. However, the CPA is not obligated to inform the IRS and the CPA may not do so without the client's permission, except where required by law. If the CPA is requested to prepare the current year's return (2009) and the client has not taken action to file the return for the earlier year (2004), the CPA should consider whether to withdraw from preparing the current year's return and whether to continue a professional relationship with the client. Also, note that the normal statue of limitations for the assessment of a tax deficiency is three years after the due date of the return or three years after the return is filed, whichever is later. Thus, the statute of limitations is still open with regard to 2004 since there is no time limit for the assessment of tax if no tax return was filed.

67.   (c)   The requirement is to determine which action a tax return preparer must take to avoid tax preparer penalties for a return's understated tax liability due to a taxpayer's intentional disregard of regulations. A return preparer may, in good faith, rely without verification upon information furnished by the client or by third parties, and is not required to audit, examine, or review books, records, or documents in order to independently verify the taxpayer's information. However, the preparer should not ignore the implications of information furnished and should make reasonable inquiries if the furnished information appears incorrect, incomplete, or inconsistent.

68.   (d)   According to the Statements on Standards for Tax Services, in preparing a tax return a CPA may in good faith rely upon information furnished by the client or third parties without further verification.

69.   (d)   The requirement is to determine the correct statement regarding the imposition of a preparer penalty for understated corporate tax liability. A return preparer may in good faith rely without verification upon information furnished, and is not required to audit, examine, or review books, records, or documents in order to independently verify a taxpayer's information. However, the preparer should not ignore the implications of information furnished and should make reasonable inquiries if information appears incorrect, incomplete, or inconsistent.

70. (a) A tax return preparer is subject to a penalty for knowingly or recklessly disclosing corporate tax return information, if the disclosure is made to enable a third party to solicit business from the taxpayer. Taxpayer return information can be disclosed by the preparer without penalty if the disclosure is made to enable the tax processor to electronically compute the taxpayer's liability, for purposes of the tax return preparer's peer review, or if the disclosure is made under an administrative order by a state agency that registers tax return preparers.

71. (c) The requirement is to determine the correct statement regarding a tax return preparer's disclosure or use of tax return information without the taxpayer's consent. Generally, a tax return preparer who knowingly or recklessly discloses **any** information furnished to him in connection with the preparation of a return, or uses any such information other than to prepare, or to assist in preparing a return, is guilty of a misdemeanor, and upon conviction may be subject to fine and/or imprisonment. A limited exception permits the disclosure or use of tax return information for purposes of being evaluated by quality or peer reviews.

72. (d) A penalty of up to $1,000 may be assessed against a tax return preparer who knowingly or recklessly discloses or uses any tax return information other than to prepare, or assist in preparing a return. Additionally, a penalty equal to the greater of $5,000, or 50% of the income to be derived by the return preparer from the return or refund claim will be assessed against a return preparer who willfully attempts to understate any client's tax liability on a return or claim for refund.

73. (a) Under Internal Revenue Code Section 6695(f) any person who is an income tax return preparer who endorses or otherwise negotiates any check which is issued to a taxpayer shall pay a penalty of $500.

74. (b) A CPA who prepares a federal income tax return for a fee must keep a completed copy of the return for a minimum of three years. Answer (a) is incorrect because prior to preparing a tax return the CPA would not be required to file certain notices and powers of attorney with the IRS. Answer (c) is incorrect because a CPA would only be required to ask the client if documentation of these expenses exists. The CPA would not have to actually receive and examine this documentation. Answer (d) is incorrect because the CPA's federal identification number would be required on any federal income tax return prepared for a fee.

75. (b) A CPA generally does owe a duty to inform a client that there are errors in a previously filed tax return so that the client may file an amended tax return. Answer (a) is incorrect because the client chooses his/her own CPA. Answer (c) is incorrect because CPAs are not required to disclose fraud by the client but are usually engaged to give an opinion on the fairness of the financial statements. Answer (d) is incorrect because although the CPA has a duty to perform an audit in accordance with GAAS and consistent with GAAP, the CPA is not under a duty to discover fraud in the audit unless the fraud would have been uncovered in the process of an ordinary audit or unless the CPA agreed to greater responsibility to uncover fraud.

76. (b) If the IRS issues a thirty-day letter to an individual taxpayer who wishes to dispute the assessment, the taxpayer may ignore the thirty-day letter and wait to receive a ninety-day letter. Answer (a) is incorrect because a taxpayer must receive a ninety-day letter before a petition can be filed in Tax Court. Answer (c) is incorrect because a taxpayer has a thirty-day period during which to file a written protest. Answer (d) is incorrect because a taxpayer is not required to pay the taxes and commence an action in federal district court.

Generally, upon the receipt of a thirty-day letter, a taxpayer who wishes to dispute the findings has thirty days to (1) request a conference with an appeals officer or file a written protest letter, or (2) may elect to do nothing during the thirty-day period and await a ninety-day letter. The taxpayer would then have ninety days to file a petition with the Tax Court. Alternatively, a taxpayer may choose to pay the additional taxes and file a claim for refund. When the refund claim is disallowed, the taxpayer could then commence an action in federal district court.

77. (c) A CPA will be liable to a tax client for damages resulting from the following activities: (1) failure to file a client's return on a timely basis, (2) gross negligence or fraudulent conduct resulting in client losses, (3) erroneous advice or failure to advise client of certain tax elections, and (4) wrongful disclosure or use of confidential information. A CPA will not be liable to a tax client for refusing to sign a client's request for a filing extension, therefore answer (c) is correct.

78. (b) According to the AICPA Statements on Standards for Tax Services, a CPA should not recommend a position unless there is a realistic possibility of it being sustained if it is challenged. Furthermore, a CPA should not prepare or sign an income tax return if the CPA knows that the return takes a position that will not be sustained if challenged. Therefore, answer (d) is incorrect. Also, a CPA should advise the client of the potential penalty consequences of any recommended tax position. Therefore, answer (c) is incorrect. Answer (a) is incorrect as a CPA may not recommend a position that is frivolous even if the position is adequately disclosed on the return.

79. (a) While performing services for a client, a CPA may become aware of an error in a previously filed return. The CPA should advise the client of the error (as required by the Statements on Standards for Tax Services) and the measures to be taken. It is the client's responsibility to decide whether to correct the error. In the event that the client does not correct an error, or agree to take the necessary steps to change from an erroneous method of accounting, the CPA should consider whether to continue a professional relationship with the client.

80. (b) A CPA may in good faith rely without verification upon information furnished by the client when preparing the client's tax return. However, the CPA should not ignore implications of information furnished and should make reasonable inquiries if information appears incorrect, incomplete, or inconsistent.

81. (c) Answer (a) is incorrect because IRC §6695(a) imposes a $50 penalty upon income tax return preparers who fail to furnish a copy of the return to the taxpayer. Answer (b) is incorrect because IRC §6695(b) imposes a $50 penalty upon income tax return preparers who fail to sign a return, unless the failure is due to reasonable cause. Answer (d) is incorrect because IRC §6695(f) imposes a $500 penalty upon income tax return preparers who endorse or otherwise negotiate a client's tax refund checks. There is no code section imposing a penalty for the understating of a client's tax liability due to an error in calculation.

82. (c) A CPA should consider both: (1) information actually known to the CPA from the tax return of another client; and (2) information provided by the client that appears to be correct based on the client's returns from prior years. In preparing or signing a return, a CPA may in good faith rely without verification upon information furnished by the client or by third parties. However, the CPA should not ignore the implications of information furnished and should make reasonable inquires if the information furnished appears to be incorrect, incomplete, or inconsistent either on its face or on the basis of other facts known to the CPA.

SOLUTIONS TO SIMULATION PROBLEMS

Simulation Problem 1

	Type of Gift	
Situation		Generation-Skipping Tax

For items 1 through 9, candidates were asked to determine whether the transfer of cash, an income interest, or a remainder interest represents a gift of a present interest (P), a gift of a future interest (F), or not a completed gift (N).

		(P)	(F)	(N)
1.	The income interest at the trust's creation.	○	○	●
2.	The remainder interest at the trust's creation.	○	○	●
3.	The income interest.	○	●	○
4.	The cash transfers.	●	○	○
5.	The income interest.	●	○	○
6.	The remainder interest.	○	●	○
7.	The cash transfers.	●	○	○
8.	The income interest.	●	○	○
9.	The remainder interest.	○	○	●

Explanation of solutions

1. **(N)** Since Cobb expressly retained the power to revoke the income interest transferred to his mother at any time, he has not relinquished dominion and control and the transfer of the income interest is not a completed gift.

2. **(N)** Since Cobb expressly retained the power to revoke the remainder interest transferred to his sister at any time, he has not relinquished dominion and control and the transfer of the remainder interest is not a completed gift.

3. **(F)** Kane's transfer of an income interest to a nephew and a remainder interest to a niece are completed gifts because Kane has relinquished dominion and control. Since Kane's nephew was twenty-five years of age when the trust was created, but income distributions will not begin until the nephew is age twenty-nine, the transfer of the income interest is a gift of future interest and does not qualify for the annual exclusion.

4. **(P)** Since Hall's gifts of cash to his son were outright gifts, they are gifts of a present interest and qualify for the annual exclusion.

5. **(P)** Yeats' gift of the income interest to her twenty-two-year-old niece is a gift of a present interest qualifying for the annual exclusion since Jane has the unrestricted right to immediate enjoyment of the income. The fact that the value of the income interest does not exceed $13,000 does not affect its nature (i.e., completed gift of a present interest).

6. **(F)** Yeats' gift of the remainder interest to her brother is a completed gift of a future interest since the brother cannot enjoy the property or any of the income until Jane reaches age thirty.

7. **(P)** Tom's gift of $40,000 cash to his uncle is an outright gift of a present interest and qualifies for the annual exclusion. Since gift-splitting was elected and Tom and Ann would each receive a $13,000 annual exclusion, Tom and Ann each made a taxable gift of $20,000 – $13,000 exclusion = $7,000.

8. **(P)** Murry's gift of the income interest to his brother is a completed gift because Murry has relinquished dominion and control. It is a gift of a present interest qualifying for the annual exclusion since his brother has the unrestricted right to immediate enjoyment of the income.

9. **(N)** Since Murry retained the right to revoke the remainder interest transferred to his sister at any time, the transfer of the remainder interest does not result in a completed gift.

		Generation-Skipping Tax
Situation	Type of Gift	

For this item, candidates were asked to determine whether the transfer is subject to the generation-skipping tax (A), the gift tax (B), or both taxes (C).

	(A)	(B)	(C)
Martin's daughter, Kim, has one child, Dale. During 2010, Martin made an outright $5,000,000 gift to Dale.	○	○	●

Explanation of solution

(**C**) Since Martin made an outright gift of $5,000,000 to Dale, the transfer is a gift of a present interest and is subject to the gift tax. Since Dale happens to be Martin's grandchild, the gift also is subject to the generation-skipping tax. The generation-skipping tax on the transfer of property is imposed in addition to federal gift and estates taxes and is designed to prevent individuals from escaping an entire generation of gift and estate taxes by transferring property to, or in trust for the benefit of, a person that is two or more generations younger than the donor or transferor. The tax approximates the transfer tax that would be imposed if the property were actually transferred to each successive generation.

Simulation Problem 2

Introduction	Preparer's Responsibility

For **items 1 through 9,** candidates were asked to determine for each item whether (P) the tax preparer's action constitutes an act of tax preparer misconduct subject to the Internal Revenue Code penalty; (E) the IRS will examine the facts and circumstances to determine whether the reasonable cause exception applies, the good faith exception applies, or both exceptions apply; or, (N) the tax preparer's action does not constitute an act of tax preparer misconduct.

		(P)	(E)	(N)
1.	The tax preparer disclosed taxpayer income tax return information under an order from a state court, without the taxpayer's consent.	○	○	●
2.	The tax preparer relied on the advice of an advisory preparer to calculate the taxpayer's tax liability. The tax preparer believed that the advisory preparer was competent and that the advice was reasonable. Based on the advice, the taxpayer had understated income tax liability.	○	●	○
3.	The tax preparer did **not** charge a separate fee for the tax return preparation and paid the taxpayer the refund shown on the tax return less a discount. The tax preparer negotiated the actual refund check for the tax preparer's own account after receiving power of attorney from the taxpayer.	●	○	○
4.	The tax preparer relied on information provided by the taxpayer regarding deductible travel expenses. The tax preparer believed that the taxpayer's information was correct but inquired about the existence of the travel expense records. The tax preparer was satisfied by the taxpayer's representations that the taxpayer had adequate records for the deduction. Based on this information, the income tax liability was understated.	○	○	●
5.	The taxpayer provided the tax preparer with a detailed check register to compute business expenses. The tax preparer knowingly overstated the expenses on the income tax return.	●	○	○
6.	The tax preparer disclosed taxpayer income tax return information during a quality review conducted by CPAs. The tax preparer maintained a record of the review.	○	○	●
7.	The tax preparer relied on incorrect instructions on an IRS tax form that were contrary to the regulations. The tax preparer was **not** aware of the regulations or the IRS announcement pointing out the error. The understatement was immaterial as a result of the isolated error.	○	●	○
8.	The tax preparer used income tax return information without the taxpayer's consent to solicit additional business.	●	○	○
9.	The tax preparer knowingly deducted the expenses of the taxpayer's personal domestic help as wages paid in the taxpayer's business on the taxpayer's income tax return.	●	○	○

Explanation of solutions

1. (**N**) A return preparer will be subject to penalty if the preparer knowingly or recklessly discloses information furnished in connection with the preparation of a tax return, unless such information is furnished for quality or peer review, under an administrative order by a regulatory agency, or pursuant to an order of a court.

2. (**E**) The reasonable cause and good faith exception applies if the return preparer relied in good faith on the advice of an advisory preparer who the return preparer had reason to believe was competent to render such advice.

3. (**P**) A return preparer will be subject to penalty if the preparer endorses or otherwise negotiates (directly or through an agent) any refund check issued to a taxpayer (other than the preparer) if the preparer was the preparer of the return or claim for refund which gave rise to the refund check.

4. (**N**) A return preparer may in good faith rely without verification upon information furnished by the client or third parties, and is not required to audit, examine, or review books, records, or documents in order to independently verify the taxpayer's information. If the IRS requires supporting documentation as a condition for deductibility, the return preparer should make appropriate inquiries to determine whether the condition has been met.

5. **(P)** A return preparer will be subject to penalty if there is a willful attempt in any manner to understate the tax liability of any taxpayer. A preparer is considered to have willfully attempted to understate liability if the preparer disregards information furnished by the taxpayer to wrongfully reduce the tax liability of the taxpayer.

6. **(N)** A return preparer will be subject to penalty if the preparer knowingly or recklessly discloses information furnished in connection with the preparation of a tax return, unless such information is furnished for quality or peer review, under an administrative order by a regulatory agency, or pursuant to an order of a court.

7. **(E)** Under these facts, a position taken on a return which is consistent with incorrect instructions does not satisfy the realistic possibility standard. However, if the preparer relied on the incorrect instructions and was not aware of the announcement or regulations, the reasonable cause and good faith exception may apply depending upon the facts and circumstances.

8. **(P)** A return preparer will be subject to penalty if the preparer knowingly or recklessly discloses information furnished in connection with the preparation of a tax return, unless such information is furnished for quality or peer review, under an administrative order by a regulatory agency, or pursuant to an order of a court.

9. **(P)** A return preparer will be subject to penalty if there is a willful attempt in any manner to understate the tax liability of any taxpayer or there is a reckless or intentional disregard of rules or regulations. The penalty will apply if a preparer knowingly deducts the expenses of the taxpayer's domestic help as wages paid in the taxpayer's business.

Simulation Problem 3

	Estate Tax Treatment I	
Situation		**Estate Tax Treatment II**

For **items 1 through 5,** candidates were asked to identify the federal tax treatment for each item by indicating whether the item was fully includible in Remsen's gross estate (F), partially includible in Remsen's gross estate (P), or not includible in Remsen's gross estate (N).

		(F)	(P)	(N)
1.	What is the estate tax treatment of the $7,000 cash gift to each sister?	○	○	●
2.	What is the estate tax treatment of the life insurance proceeds?	●	○	○
3.	What is the estate tax treatment of the marketable securities?	●	○	○
4.	What is the estate tax treatment of the $2,000 tuition payment?	○	○	●
5.	What is the estate tax treatment of the $650,000 cash?	●	○	○

Explanation of solutions

1. **(N)** Generally, gifts made before death are not includible in the decedent's gross estate, even though the gifts were made within three years of death.

2. **(F)** The gross estate includes the value of all property in which the decedent had a beneficial interest at time of death. Here, the life insurance proceeds must be included in Remsen's gross estate because the problem indicates that Remsen was the owner of the policy.

3. **(F)** The fair market value of the marketable securities must be included in Remsen's gross estate because Remsen was the owner of the securities at the time of his death.

4. **(N)** Generally, gifts made before death are not includible in the decedent's gross estate.

5. **(F)** The $650,000 cash that Remsen owned must be included in Remsen's gross estate.

		Estate Tax Treatment II	
Situation	**Estate Tax Treatment I**		

For **items 1 through 5,** candidates were asked to identify the federal tax treatment for each item by indicating whether the item was deductible from Remsen's gross estate to arrive at Remsen's taxable estate (G), deductible on Remsen's 2009 individual income tax return (I), deductible on either Remsen's estate tax return or Remsen's 2009 individual income tax return (E), or not deductible on either Remsen's estate tax return or Remsen's 2009 individual income tax return (N).

		(G)	(I)	(E)	(N)
1.	What is the estate tax treatment of the executor's fees?	○	○	○	●
2.	What is the estate tax treatment of the cash bequest to Remsen's son?	○	○	○	●
3.	What is the estate tax treatment of the life insurance proceeds paid to Remsen's spouse?	●	○	○	○

		(G)	(I)	(E)	(N)
4.	What is the estate tax treatment of the funeral expenses?	●	○	○	○
5.	What is the estate tax treatment of the $10,000 of medical expenses incurred before the decedent's death and paid by the executor on December 3, 2009?	○	○	●	○

Explanation of solutions

1.   (N) The $15,000 of executor's fees to distribute the decedent's property are deductible on **either** the federal estate tax return (Form 706) or the estate's fiduciary income tax return (Form 1041). Such expenses **cannot** be deducted twice. Since the problem indicates that these expenses were deducted on the fiduciary tax return (Form 1041), they cannot be deducted on the estate tax return.

2.   (N) A decedent's gross estate is reduced by funeral and administrative expenses, debts and mortgages, casualty and theft losses, charitable bequests, and a marital deduction for the value of property passing to the decedent's surviving spouse. There is no deduction for bequests to beneficiaries other than the decedent's surviving spouse.

3.   (G) Generally, property included in a decedent's gross estate will be eligible for an unlimited marital deduction if the property passes to the decedent's surviving spouse. Here, the life insurance proceeds paid to Remsen's spouse were included in Remsen's gross estate because Remsen owned the policy, and are deductible from Remsen's gross estate as part of the marital deduction in arriving at Remsen's taxable estate.

4.   (G) Funeral expenses are deductible only on the estate tax return and include a reasonable allowance for a tombstone, monument, mausoleum, or burial lot.

5.   (E) The executor of a decedent's estate may elect to treat medical expenses paid by the estate for the decedent's medical care as paid by the decedent at the time the medical services were provided. To qualify for this election, the medical expenses must be paid within the one-year period after the decedent's death, and the executor must attach a waiver to the decedent's Form 1040 indicating that the expenses will not be claimed as a deduction on the decedent's estate tax return. In this case, the medical expenses qualify for the election because Remsen died on January 9, 2009, and the expenses were paid on December 3, 2009.

Simulation Problem 4

Situation	Gift Tax Treatment

For **items 1 through 7,** candidates were asked to identify the federal gift tax treatment for each item by indicating whether the item is fully taxable (F), partially taxable (P), or not taxable (N) to Lane in 2010 for gift tax purposes after considering the gift tax annual exclusion.

		(F)	(P)	(N)
1.	What is the gift tax treatment of Lane's gift to Kamp?	○	○	●
2.	What is the gift tax treatment of Lane's cash gifts to his child?	○	●	○
3.	What is the gift tax treatment of the trust's income interest to Lane's aunt?	○	●	○
4.	What is the gift tax treatment of the trust's remainder interest to Lane's cousin?	●	○	○
5.	What is the gift tax treatment of the tuition payment to Lane's grandchild's university?	○	○	●
6.	What is the gift tax treatment of the trust's income interest to Lane's brother?	●	○	○
7.	What is the gift tax treatment of the $14,000 interest income that Lane's niece received from the revocable trust?	○	●	○

Explanation of solutions

1.   (N) There is no taxable gift because the $13,000 cash gift is a gift of a present interest and is fully offset by a $13,000 annual exclusion.

2.   (P) The $20,000 of cash gifts given to his child would be partially offset by a $13,000 annual exclusion, resulting in a tax-. able gift of $7,000.

3.   (P) The gift of the income interest valued at $26,000 to his aunt is a gift of a present interest and would be partially offset by a $13,000 annual exclusion, resulting in a taxable gift of $13,000.

4.   (F) Since the remainder interest will pass to Lane's cousin after the expiration of five years, the gift of the remainder interest is a gift of a future interest and is not eligible for an annual exclusion. As a result, the $74,000 value of the remainder interest is fully taxable.

5. **(N)** An unlimited exclusion is available for medical expenses and tuition paid on behalf of a donee. Since Lane paid the $25,000 of tuition directly to his grandchild's university on his grandchild's behalf, the gift is fully excluded and not subject to gift tax.

6. **(F)** Since Lane created the irrevocable trust in 2010 but his brother will not begin receiving the income until 2012, the gift of the income interest to his brother is a gift of a future interest and cannot be offset by an annual exclusion. As a result, the gift is fully taxable for gift tax purposes.

7. **(P)** The creation of a revocable trust is not a completed gift and trust income is taxable to the grantor (Lane). As a result, a gift occurs only as the trust income is actually paid to the beneficiary. Here, the $14,000 of interest income received by the niece during 2010 is a gift of a present interest and would be partially offset by a $13,000 annual exclusion.

Simulation Problem 5

Situation	Research and Communication

Keywords you might have used include, "inheritance," "basis," "holding period," and "capital gains and losses."

To: Client Tax File
From: CPA Candidate
Date: [*today's date*]

    This memorandum is designed to document my research regarding the tax implications of the sale of inherited stock. Glen Moore inherited stock when his mother, Ruth, died on September 1, 2009. The stock had cost Ruth $120,000 on May 15, 2009, and had a fair market value of $150,000 on the date of her death. Ruth's estate was too small to require the filing of a federal estate tax return. Moore may sell the stock for $165,000 in March 2010.

    The receipt of the stock will be excluded from Moore's gross income. The sale of the stock for $165,000 would result in a $15,000 long-term capital gain in 2010. Moore will be able to exclude the receipt of the stock from gross income since Code Sec. 102(a) provides that gross income does **not** include the value of property acquired by gift, bequest, devise, or inheritance. Sec. 1014(a)(1) provides that the basis of property acquired from a decedent shall be its fair market value at the date of decedent's death, which in this case is $150,000. Since the stock is being held as an investment and qualifies as a capital asset under Sec. 1221, a sale of the stock for $165,000 in March 2010 would result in a capital gain of $15,000. In regard to holding period, Sec. 1223(11) provides that if property is acquired from a decedent and its basis is determined under Sec. 1014, and the property is sold within one year after death, then the property shall be considered to have been held for more than one year. Finally, Sec. 1222 provides that the term "long-term capital gain" means gain from sale or exchange of a capital asset held for more than one year. As a result, Moore's gain of $165,000 – $150,000 = $15,000 would be reported as a long-term capital gain if the stock were sold in March 2010.

7 BUSINESS ENVIRONMENT AND CONCEPTS

The Business Environment and Concepts Exam is scheduled for two and one-half hours. Based on information released by the AICPA, candidates should expect three multiple-choice testlets of approximately twenty-five questions each.

The Uniform CPA Examination Content Specifications appear in *Volume 1, Outlines and Study Guides*.

MULTIPLE-CHOICE QUESTIONS (1-97)

1. Which of the following statements is not true of a sole proprietorship?
- a. Federal and state governments typically require a formal filing with the appropriate government officials whether or not the sole proprietorship uses a fictitious name.
- b. The sole proprietorship is not a separate legal entity apart from its owner.
- c. The capital to start the business is generally limited to the funds the sole proprietor either has or can borrow.
- d. It is generally considered to be the simplest type of business structure.

2. A general partnership must
- a. Pay federal income tax.
- b. Have two or more partners.
- c. Have written articles of partnership.
- d. Provide for apportionment of liability for partnership debts.

3. Which of the following can be a partnership?
- a. Karen and Sharon form a charitable organization in which they received donations to give to their favorite charities.
- b. Frank and Pablo are members of a union at work that has 150 members.
- c. Janice and Stanley form a club to encourage business contacts for computer programmers.
- d. None of the above.

4. A silent partner in a general partnership
- a. Helps manage the partnership without letting those outside the partnership know this.
- b. Retains unlimited liability for the debts of the partnership.
- c. Both of the above are correct.
- d. None of the above is correct.

5. Which of the following statements is correct with respect to a limited partnership?
- a. A limited partner may not be an unsecured creditor of the limited partnership.
- b. A general partner may not also be a limited partner at the same time.
- c. A general partner may be a secured creditor of the limited partnership.
- d. A limited partnership can be formed with limited liability for all partners.

6. A partnership agreement must be in writing if
- a. Any partner contributes more than $500 in capital.
- b. The partners reside in different states.
- c. The partnership intends to own real estate.
- d. The partnership's purpose **cannot** be completed within one year of formation.

7. Sydney, Bailey, and Calle form a partnership under the Revised Uniform Partnership Act. During the first year of operation, the partners have fundamental questions regarding the rights and obligations of the partnership as well as the individual partners. Which of the following questions can correctly be answered in the affirmative?

I. Is the partnership allowed legally to own property in the partnership's name?

II. Do the partners have joint and several liability for breaches of contract of the partnership?
III. Do the partners have joint and several liability for tort actions against the partnership?
- a. I only.
- b. I and II only.
- c. II and III only.
- d. I, II, and III.

8. Which of the following is not true of a general partnership?
- a. Ownership by the partners may be unequal.
- b. It is a separate legal entity.
- c. An important characteristic is that the partners share in the profits equally.
- d. Each partner has an equal right to participate in management.

9. The partnership agreement for Owen Associates, a general partnership, provided that profits be paid to the partners in the ratio of their financial contribution to the partnership. Moore contributed $10,000, Noon contributed $30,000, and Kale contributed $50,000. For the year ended December 31, 2008, Owen had losses of $180,000. What amount of the losses should be allocated to Kale?
- a. $ 40,000
- b. $ 60,000
- c. $ 90,000
- d. $100,000

10. Lark, a partner in DSJ, a general partnership, wishes to withdraw from the partnership and sell Lark's interest to Ward. All of the other partners in DSJ have agreed to admit Ward as a partner and to hold Lark harmless for the past, present, and future liabilities of DSJ. As a result of Lark's withdrawal and Ward's admission to the partnership, Ward
- a. Acquired only the right to receive Ward's share of DSJ profits.
- b. Has the right to participate in DSJ's management.
- c. Is personally liable for partnership liabilities arising before and after being admitted as a partner.
- d. Must contribute cash or property to DSJ to be admitted with the same rights as the other partners.

11. Cobb, Inc., a partner in TLC Partnership, assigns its partnership interest to Bean, who is not made a partner. After the assignment, Bean asserts the rights to

I. Participate in the management of TLC.
II. Cobb's share of TLC's partnership profits.

Bean is correct as to which of these rights?
- a. I only.
- b. II only.
- c. I and II.
- d. Neither I nor II.

12. The apparent authority of a partner to bind the partnership in dealing with third parties
- a. Will be effectively limited by a formal resolution of the partners of which third parties are aware.
- b. Will be effectively limited by a formal resolution of the partners of which third parties are unaware.
- c. Would permit a partner to submit a claim against the partnership to arbitration.
- d. Must be derived from the express powers and purposes contained in the partnership agreement.

13. In a general partnership, which of the following acts must be approved by all the partners?
    a. Dissolution of the partnership.
    b. Admission of a partner.
    c. Authorization of a partnership capital expenditure.
    d. Conveyance of real property owned by the partnership.

14. Under the Revised Uniform Partnership Act, partners have joint and several liability for
    a. Breaches of contract.
    b. Torts committed by one of the partners within the scope of the partnership.
    c. Both of the above.
    d. None of the above.

15. Which of the following actions require(s) unanimous consent of the partners under partnership law?

  I. Making partnership a surety.
  II. Admission of a new partner.

    a. I only.
    b. II only.
    c. Both I and II.
    d. Neither I nor II.

16. Which of the following statements best describes the effect of the assignment of an interest in a general partnership?
    a. The assignee becomes a partner.
    b. The assignee is responsible for a proportionate share of past and future partnership debts.
    c. The assignment automatically dissolves the partnership.
    d. The assignment transfers the assignor's interest in partnership profits and surplus.

17. Under the Revised Uniform Partnership Act, in which of the following cases will property be deemed to be partnership property?

  I. A partner acquires property in the partnership name.
  II. A partner acquires title to it in his/her own name using partnership funds.
  III. Property owned previously by a partner is used in the partnership business

    a. I only.
    b. I and II only.
    c. II only.
    d. I, II, and III.

18. Wind, who has been a partner in the PLW general partnership for four years, decides to withdraw from the partnership despite a written partnership agreement that states, "no partner may withdraw for a period of five years." Under the Uniform Partnership Act, what is the result of Wind's withdrawal?
    a. Wind's withdrawal causes a dissolution of the partnership by operation of law.
    b. Wind's withdrawal has **no** bearing on the continued operation of the partnership by the remaining partners.
    c. Wind's withdrawal is **not** effective until Wind obtains a court-ordered decree of dissolution.
    d. Wind's withdrawal causes a dissolution of the partnership despite being in violation of the partnership agreement.

19. Dowd, Elgar, Frost, and Grant formed a general partnership. Their written partnership agreement provided that the profits would be divided so that Dowd would receive 40%; Elgar, 30%; Frost, 20%; and Grant, 10%. There was no provision for allocating losses. At the end of its first year, the partnership had losses of $200,000. Before allocating losses, the partners' capital account balances were: Dowd, $120,000; Elgar, $100,000; Frost, $75,000; and Grant, $11,000. Grant refuses to make any further contributions to the partnership. Ignore the effects of federal partnership tax law.

    After losses were allocated to the partners' capital accounts and all liabilities were paid, the partnership's sole asset was $106,000 in cash. How much would Elgar receive on dissolution of the partnership?
    a. $37,000
    b. $40,000
    c. $47,500
    d. $50,000

20. Sharif, Hirsch, and Wolff formed a partnership with Sharif and Hirsch as general partners. Wolff was the limited partner. They failed to agree upon a profit-sharing plan but put in capital contributions of $120,000, $140,000, and $150,000, respectively. At the end of the first year how should they divide the profits?
    a. Sharif and Hirsch each receives half and Wolff receives none.
    b. Each of the three partners receives one-third.
    c. The profits are shared in proportion to their capital contribution.
    d. None of the above.

21. Which of the following is(are) true of a limited partnership?

  I. Limited partnerships must have at least one general partner.
  II. The death of a limited partner terminates the partnership.

    a. I only.
    b. II only.
    c. Neither I nor II.
    d. Both I and II.

22. Alchorn, Black, and Chan formed a limited partnership with Chan becoming the only limited partner. Capital contributions from these partners were $20,000, $40,000, and $50,000, respectively. Chan, however, helped in the management of the partnership and Ham, who had several contracts with the partnership, thought Chan was a general partner. Ham won several breach of contract actions against the partnership and the partnership does not have sufficient funds to pay these claims. What is the potential liability for Alchorn, Black, and Chan?
    a. Unlimited liability for all three partners.
    b. Unlimited liability for Alchorn and Black; $50,000 for Chan.
    c. Up to each partner's capital contribution.
    d. None of the above.

23. To create a limited partnership, a certificate of limited partnership must be filed with the Secretary of State. Which of the following must be included in this certificate under the Revised Uniform Limited Partnership Act?

  I. Names of all of the general partners.
  II. Names of the majority of the general partners.

III. Names of all of the limited partners.
IV. Names of the majority of the limited partners.

    a. I only.
    b. II only.
    c. I and III only.
    d. I and IV only.

24. Mandy is a limited partner in a limited partnership in which Strasburg and Hua are the general partners. Which of the following may Mandy do without losing limited liability protection?

  I. Mandy acts as an agent of the limited partnership.
  II. Mandy votes to remove Strasburg as a general partner.

    a. I only.
    b. II only.
    c. Both I and II.
    d. Neither I nor II.

25. In a limited partnership, the limited partners' capital contribution may be in which of the following forms?
    a. A promise to perform services in the future for the partnership.
    b. An agreement to pay cash.
    c. A promise to give property.
    d. All of the above.

26. Hart and Grant formed Hart Limited Partnership. Hart put in a capital contribution of $20,000 and became a general partner. Grant put in a capital contribution of $10,000 and became a limited partner. During the second year of operation, a third party filed a tort action against the partnership and both partners. What is the potential liability of Hart and Grant respectively?
    a. $20,000 and $0.
    b. $20,000 and $10,000.
    c. Unlimited liability and $0.
    d. Unlimited liability and $10,000.

27. The admission of a new general partner to a limited partnership requires approval by

  I. A majority of the general partners.
  II. All of the general partners.
  III. A majority of the limited partners.
  IV. All of the limited partners.

    a. I only.
    b. II only.
    c. I and III only.
    d. II and IV only.

28. The admission of a new limited partner to a limited partnership requires approval by

  I. A majority of the general partners.
  II. All of the general partners.
  III. A majority of the limited partners.
  IV. All of the limited partners.

    a. I only.
    b. II only.
    c. I and III only.
    d. II and IV only.

29. Riewerts, Morgar and Stonk form a limited partnership. Riewerts is the one general partner. Which of the following events will cause this limited partnership to be dissolved?

  I. Riewerts dies and is survived by the other two partners.
  II. Morgan dies leaving Riewerts and Stonk.

III. Riewerts takes out personal bankruptcy.
IV. Stonk takes out personal bankruptcy.

    a. I only.
    b. I and II only.
    c. I and III only.
    d. III and IV only.

30. Which of the following is **not** true of a joint venture?
    a. Each joint venturer is personally liable for the debts of a joint venture.
    b. Each joint venturer has the right to participate in the management of the joint venture.
    c. The joint venturers owe each other fiduciary duties.
    d. Death of a joint venturer dissolves the joint venture.

31. Which form(s) of a business organization can have characteristics common to both the corporation and the general partnership?

	Limited liability company	Subchapter S corporation
a.	Yes	Yes
b.	Yes	No
c.	No	Yes
d.	No	No

32. Which of the following is true of a limited liability company under the laws of the majority of states?
    a. At least one of the owners must have personal liability.
    b. The limited liability company is a separate legal entity apart from its owners.
    c. Limited liability of the owners is lost if they fail to follow the usual formalities in conducting the business.
    d. All of the above are true.

33. Which of the following is **not** characteristic of the typical limited liability company?
    a. Death of a member (owner) causes it to dissolve unless the remaining members decide to continue the business.
    b. All members (owners) are allowed by law to participate in the management of the firm.
    c. The company has, legally, a perpetual existence.
    d. All members (owners) have limited liability.

34. Owners and managers of a limited liability company (LLC) owe
    a. A duty of due care.
    b. A duty of loyalty.
    c. Both a duty of due care and a duty of loyalty.
    d. None of the above.

35. Which of the following is true of the typical limited liability company?
    a. It provides for limited liability for some of its members (owners), that is, those identified as limited members (owners).
    b. The members' (owners') interests are not freely transferable.
    c. Voting members (owners) but not all members can help choose the managers of the company.
    d. No formalities are required for its formation.

36. In which of the following respects do general partnerships and limited liability partnerships **differ**?

 I. In the level of liability of the partners for torts they themselves commit.
 II. In the level of liability of the partners for torts committed by other partners in the same firm.
 III. In the amount of liability of the partners for contracts signed by other partners on behalf of the partnership.
 IV. In the amount of liability of the partners for contracts they themselves signed on behalf of the firm.

    a. I only.
    b. II only.
    c. I and IV only.
    d. II and III only.

37. Under the federal Subchapter S Revision Act, all corporations are designated as
    a. Subchapter S corporations only.
    b. Either a Subchapter S corporation or a Subchapter C corporation.
    c. One of seven different types of corporations.
    d. Both a Subchapter S corporation and a Subchapter C corporation at the same time.

38. Under the federal Subchapter S Revision Act all corporations are
    a. Now treated as Subchapter S corporations.
    b. Divided into either a Subchapter C corporation or a Subchapter S corporation.
    c. Divided into either a Subchapter C corporation, a Subchapter E corporation, or a Subchapter S corporation.
    d. None of the above.

39. Which of the following statements is(are) true?
    a. Both Subchapter C corporations and Subchapter S corporations have limited liability for their shareholders.
    b. Both Subchapter C corporations and Subchapter S corporations are similar in their corporate management structure.
    c. All of the above are true.
    d. None of the above are true.

40. The main difference between Subchapter S corporations and Subchapter C corporations is
    a. Their tax treatment.
    b. That the federal Subchapter S Revision Act covers Subchapter S corporations but does not cover Subchapter C corporations.
    c. Their limited liability of their shareholders.
    d. Their structure of their corporate management.

41. Which of the following statements best describes an advantage of the corporate form of doing business?
    a. Day-to-day management is strictly the responsibility of the directors.
    b. Ownership is contractually restricted and is **not** transferable.
    c. The operation of the business may continue indefinitely.
    d. The business is free from state regulation.

42. Which of the following is not considered to be an advantage of the corporate form of doing business over the partnership form?

    a. A potential perpetual and continuous life.
    b. The interests in the corporation are typically easily transferable.
    c. The managers in the corporation and shareholders have limited liability.
    d. Persons who manage the corporation are not necessarily shareholders.

43. Which of the following is **not** a characteristic of a corporation?
    a. It has a continuous life.
    b. Shares in the corporation can normally be freely transferred.
    c. A corporation is treated as a legal entity separate from its shareholders.
    d. A corporation is automatically terminated upon the death of a majority of its shareholders.

44. A corporation as a separate legal entity can do which of the following?
    a. Contract in its own name with its own shareholders.
    b. Contract in its own name with its own shareholders only if a majority of its shareholders agree that such a contract can be made.
    c. Contract in its own name with third parties.
    d. Both a. and c. are correct.

45. Which of the following are characteristics of the corporate form of doing business?
    a. Persons who manage corporations need not be shareholders.
    b. The corporation may convey or hold property in its own name.
    c. The corporation can sue or be sued in its own name.
    d. All of the above are true.

46. Which of the following is a disadvantage of a Subchapter C corporation?
    a. It may face higher tax burdens than a Subchapter S corporation.
    b. The shareholders lose their limited liability when they switch from a general partnership to a corporation.
    c. A Subchapter C corporation is not well defined under the law.
    d. A Subchapter C corporation does not protect its shareholders from liability as well as a Subchapter S corporation does.

47. Bond Company is incorporated in Florida but not in Georgia. Bond has branch offices in both states. Which of the following is correct?

 I. Bond is a domestic corporation in Georgia.
 II. Bond is a domestic corporation in Florida.
 III. Bond needs to incorporate also in Georgia.

    a. I and II only.
    b. II only.
    c. II and III only.
    d. I, II, and III.

48. Colby formed a professional corporation along with two other attorneys. They took out loans in the name of the corporation. During the first year, Colby failed to file some papers on time for a client causing the client to lose a very

good case. For which does Colby have the corporate protection of limited liability?

    I. The negligence for failure to file the papers on time.
    II. The corporate loans.

      a.   I only.
      b.   II only.
      c.   Both I and II.
      d.   Neither I nor II.

49. Macro Corporation was incorporated and doing business in Illinois. It is doing business in various other states including Nevada. Which of the following statements is(are) true?

      a.   Macro must incorporate in Nevada.
      b.   Macro is a domestic corporation in Nevada.
      c.   Macro is a domestic corporation in Illinois.
      d.   All of the above are true.

50. Cleanit Corporation was incorporated in Colorado. Cleanit wishes to perform some transactions in other states but does not want to incorporate or obtain a certificate of authority to qualify to do business in those other states. Which of the following normally would require Cleanit to obtain a certificate of authority in other states?

      a.   Using the US mail to solicit orders in those states.
      b.   Holding bank accounts in those states.
      c.   Collecting debts in those states.
      d.   None of the above.

51. Which of the following statements is true of professional corporations under the various state laws?

    I. The professionals in the corporation have personal liability for their professional acts.
    II. Normally under state laws, only licensed professionals are permitted to own shares in professional corporations.

      a.   I only is true.
      b.   II only is true.
      c.   Both I and II are true.
      d.   Neither I nor II is true.

52. Which of the following statements is correct with respect to the differences and similarities between a corporation and a limited partnership?

      a.   Stockholders may be entitled to vote on corporate matters but limited partners are prohibited from voting on any partnership matters.
      b.   Stock of a corporation may be subject to the registration requirements of the federal securities laws but limited partnership interests are automatically exempt from those requirements.
      c.   Directors owe fiduciary duties to the corporation and limited partners owe such duties to the partnership.
      d.   A corporation and a limited partnership may be created only under a state statute and each must file a copy of its organizational document with the proper governmental body.

53. Under the Revised Model Business Corporation Act, which of the following must be contained in a corporation's articles of incorporation?

      a.   Quorum voting requirements.
      b.   Names of stockholders.
      c.   Provisions for issuance of par and nonpar shares.
      d.   The number of shares the corporation is authorized to issue.

54. Which of the following facts is(are) generally included in a corporation's articles of incorporation?

	Name of registered agent	Number of authorized shares
a.	Yes	Yes
b.	Yes	No
c.	No	Yes
d.	No	No

55. Absent a specific provision in its Articles of Incorporation, a corporation's board of directors has the power to do all of the following, **except**

      a.   Repeal the bylaws.
      b.   Declare dividends.
      c.   Fix compensation of directors.
      d.   Amend the Articles of Incorporation.

56. Which of the following statements is correct concerning the similarities between a limited partnership and a corporation?

      a.   Each is created under a statute and must file a copy of its certificate with the proper state authorities.
      b.   All corporate stockholders and all partners in a limited partnership have limited liability.
      c.   Both are recognized for federal income tax purposes as taxable entities.
      d.   Both are allowed statutorily to have perpetual existence.

57. Promoters of a corporation which is not yet in existence

      a.   Are persons that form the corporation and arrange for capitalization to help begin the corporation.
      b.   Are agents of the corporation.
      c.   Can bind the future corporation to presently made contracts they make for the future corporation.
      d.   Are shielded from personal liability on contracts they make with third parties on behalf of the future corporation.

58. Johns owns 400 shares of Abco Corp. cumulative preferred stock. In the absence of any specific contrary provisions in Abco's Articles of Incorporation, which of the following statements is correct?

      a.   Johns is entitled to convert the 400 shares of preferred stock to a like number of shares of common stock.
      b.   If Abco declares a cash dividend on its preferred stock, Johns becomes an unsecured creditor of Abco.
      c.   If Abco declares a dividend on its common stock, Johns will be entitled to participate with the common stock shareholders in any dividend distribution made after preferred dividends are paid.
      d.   Johns will be entitled to vote if dividend payments are in arrears.

59. Gallagher Corporation issued 100,000 shares of $40 par value stock for $50 per share to various investors. Subsequently, Gallagher purchased back 10,000 of those shares for $30 per share and held them as treasury stock. When the price of the stock recovered somewhat, Gallagher sold this treasury stock to Thomas for $35 per share. Which of the following statements is correct?

    I. Gallagher's purchase of the stock at below par value is illegal.
    II. Gallagher's purchase of the stock at below par value is void as an ultra vires act.

III. Gallagher's resale of the treasury stock at below par value is valid.

   a. I only.
   b. II only.
   c. III only.
   d. I and II only.

60. An owner of common stock will **not** have any liability beyond actual investment if the owner

   a. Paid less than par value for stock purchased in connection with an original issue of shares.
   b. Agreed to perform future services for the corporation in exchange for original issue par value shares.
   c. Purchased treasury shares for less than par value.
   d. Failed to pay the full amount owed on a subscription contract for no-par shares.

61. Which of the following securities are corporate debt securities?

	Convertible bonds	Debenture bonds	Warrants
a.	Yes	Yes	Yes
b.	Yes	No	Yes
c.	Yes	Yes	No
d.	No	Yes	Yes

62. All of the following distributions to stockholders are considered asset or capital distributions, **except**

   a. Liquidating dividends.
   b. Stock splits.
   c. Property distributions.
   d. Cash dividends.

63. Which of the following constitute(s) valid consideration or value to purchase shares of stock?

   a. Services performed.
   b. Intangible property.
   c. Services contracted to be performed in the future.
   d. All of the above.

64. Brawn subscribed to 1,000 shares of $1 par value stock of Caldo Corporation at the agreed amount of $20 per share. She paid $5,000 on April 1 and then paid $9,000 on August 1. Caldo Corporation filed for bankruptcy on December 1 and the creditors of the corporation sought to hold Brawn liable under her subscription agreement. Which of the following is true?

   a. Brawn has no liability to the creditors because subscription contract was with the corporation, not the creditors.
   b. Brawn has no liability to the creditors because she has paid more than $1,000 to the corporation which is the par value of the 1,000 shares.
   c. Brawn is liable for $6,000 to the creditors for the amount unpaid on the subscription price.
   d. Brawn is liable for $6,000 to the creditors based on the doctrine of ultra vires.

65. Pearl Corporation has some treasury stock on hand. Which of the following is(are) true?

   a. Pearl may not vote these shares of treasury stock.
   b. Pearl's treasury stock does not receive any dividends.
   c. Both of the above statements are true.
   d. None of the above statements are true.

66. Treasury stock of a corporation is stock that

   a. Has been issued by that corporation but is not outstanding.
   b. Was purchased from another corporation and is retained for a specified purpose.
   c. Has been cancelled.
   d. None of the above is true.

67. By law, a corporation

   a. Must issue both common stock and preferred stock.
   b. May issue more than one class of common stock as well as more than one class of preferred stock.
   c. Must issue dividends if it has earned a profit.
   d. Must issue at least some cumulative preferred stock.

68. Mesa Corporation is planning on issuing some debt securities. Which of the following statements is true?

   a. The holders of debt securities are owners of the corporation.
   b. A bond is an instrument for long-term secured debt.
   c. A debenture is an instrument for long-term secured debt.
   d. None of the above is true.

69. Stock of a corporation is called watered stock when the cash or property exchanged to acquire the stock is

   a. Less than the market value of the stock.
   b. More than the market value of the stock.
   c. Less than the par value or stated value of the stock.
   d. More than the par value or stated value of the stock.

70. Corporations generally have which of the following powers without shareholder approval?

  I. Power to acquire their own shares.
  II. Power to make charitable contributions.
  III. Power to make loans to directors.

   a. I only.
   b. I and II only.
   c. II and III only.
   d. I, II, and III.

71. Murphy is an employee of Landtry Corporation. Which of the following acts would make the corporation liable for Murphy's actions?

  I. Murphy deceived a customer to convince him to purchase one of Landtry's products.
  II. Murphy hit a customer with his fist breaking his jaw. The management had warned Murphy that he and not the corporation would be responsible for any aggression against customers.

   a. I only.
   b. II only.
   c. Both I and II.
   d. Neither I nor II.

72. Which of the following statements is(are) true?

  I. Corporations can be found liable for crimes.
  II. Directors can face prison sentences for crimes committed by their corporations.
  III. Employees can be found guilty of crimes they commit while working for their corporation.

   a. I only.
   b. I and II only.

c.   III only.

d.   I, II, and III.

73. Norwood was a promoter of Parker Corporation. On March 15, Norwood purchased some real estate from Burrows in Parker's name and signed the contract "Norwood, as agent of Parker Corporation." Parker Corporation, however, did not legally come into existence until June 10. Norwood never informed Burrows on or before March 15 that Parker Corporation was not yet formed. After the corporation was formed, the board of directors refused to adopt the preincorporation contract made by Norwood concerning the real estate deal with Burrows. Burrows sued Parker, Norwood, and the board of directors. Which of the following is correct?

a.   None of these parties can be held liable.

b.   Norwood only is liable.

c.   Norwood and Parker are liable but not the board of directors.

d.   Norwood, Parker, and the board of directors are all liable.

74. Under the Revised Model Business Corporation Act, which of the following statements is correct regarding corporate officers of a public corporation?

a.   An officer may **not** simultaneously serve as a director.

b.   A corporation may be authorized to indemnify its officers for liability incurred in a suit by stockholders.

c.   Stockholders always have the right to elect a corporation's officers.

d.   An officer of a corporation is required to own at least one share of the corporation's stock.

75. The officers of West Corporation wish to buy some used equipment for West Corporation. The used equipment is actually owned by Parks, a director of West Corporation. For this transaction to **not** be a conflict of interest for Parks, which of the following is (are) required to be true?

  I. Parks sells the used equipment to West Corporation in a contract that is fair and reasonable to the corporation.

 II. Parks' ownership of the used equipment is disclosed to the shareholders of West who approve it by majority vote.

III. Parks' ownership of the used equipment is disclosed to the board of directors, who approve it by a majority vote of the disinterested directors.

a.   Any one of I, II, or III.

b.   I and II are both required.

c.   I and III are both required.

d.   All three of I, II, and III are required.

76. The following are two statements concerning a fiduciary duty in a corporation.

  I. Officers and directors of a corporation owe a fiduciary duty to that corporation.

 II. Majority shareholders of a corporation can owe a fiduciary duty to the minority shareholders.

Which of the statements is(are) correct?

a.   I only.

b.   II only.

c.   Both I and II.

d.   Neither I nor II.

77. Hogan is a director of a large corporation. Hogan owns a piece of land that the corporation wishes to purchase and Hogan desires to sell this land at the fair market price. If he sells the land to the corporation, has he breached any fiduciary duty?

a.   No, a director does not owe a fiduciary duty to his corporation.

b.   No, since Hogan is selling the land to his corporation in a fair and reasonable contract.

c.   Yes, unless he discloses his conflict of interest to the shareholders who must then approve the sale of by a simple majority.

d.   Yes, unless he discloses his conflict of interest to the shareholders who must then approve the sale by a two-thirds vote.

78. Which of the following is **not** a power of the board of directors?

a.   May select the officers of the corporation.

b.   May declare the dividends to be paid to the shareholders.

c.   May amend the Articles of Incorporation.

d.   All of the above are powers of the board of directors.

79. Which of the following statements is(are) true under the law affecting corporations?

  I. A corporation may indemnify directors against lawsuits based on their good-faith actions for the corporation.

 II. A corporation may indemnify officers against lawsuits based on their good-faith actions for the corporation.

III. A corporation is allowed to purchase liability insurance for its directors.

a.   I only.

b.   I and II only.

c.   I and III only.

d.   I, II, and III.

80. Which of the following is(are) true concerning corporations?

a.   Directors owe a fiduciary duty to the corporation.

b.   Officers owe a fiduciary duty to the corporation.

c.   Both of the above are true.

d.   None of the above are true.

81. McGarry is an officer of Norton Corporation. McGarry has committed a tort while acting for Norton Corporation within the scope of her authority. Which of the following is(are) true?

a.   McGarry is liable for the tort committed.

b.   Norton Corporation is liable for the tort committed.

c.   Both McGarry and Norton are liable for the tort committed.

d.   Neither McGarry nor Norton are liable for the tort committed.

82. Acorn Corp. wants to acquire the entire business of Trend Corp. Which of the following methods of business combination will best satisfy Acorn's objectives without requiring the approval of the shareholders of either corporation?

a.   A merger of Trend into Acorn, whereby Trend shareholders receive cash or Acorn shares.

b.   A sale of all the assets of Trend, outside the regular course of business, to Acorn for cash.

c. An acquisition of all the shares of Trend through a compulsory share exchange for Acorn shares.

d. A cash tender offer, whereby Acorn acquires at least 90% of Trend's shares, followed by a short-form merger of Trend into Acorn.

83. Price owns 2,000 shares of Universal Corp.'s $10 cumulative preferred stock. During its first year of operations, cash dividends of $5 per share were declared on the preferred stock but were never paid. In the second year, dividends on the preferred stock were neither declared nor paid. If Universal is dissolved, which of the following statements is correct?

a. Universal will be liable to Price as an unsecured creditor for $10,000.

b. Universal will be liable to Price as a secured creditor for $20,000.

c. Price will have priority over the claims of Universal's bond owners.

d. Price will have priority over the claims of Universal's unsecured judgment creditors.

84. Under the Revised Model Business Corporation Act, when a corporation's Articles of Incorporation grant stockholders preemptive rights, which of the following rights is(are) included in that grant?

	The right to purchase a proportionate share of a newly issued stock	The right to a proportionate share of corporate assets remaining on corporate dissolution
a.	Yes	Yes
b.	Yes	No
c.	No	Yes
d.	No	No

85. Under the Revised Model Business Corporation Act, which of the following actions by a corporation would entitle a stockholder to dissent from the action and obtain payment of the fair value of his/her shares?

I. An amendment to the articles of incorporation that materially and adversely affects rights in respect of a dissenter's shares because it alters or abolishes a preferential right of the shares.

II. Consummation of a plan of share exchange to which the corporation is a party as the corporation whose shares will be acquired, if the stockholder is entitled to vote on the plan.

a. I only.

b. II only.

c. Both I and II.

d. Neither I nor II.

86. To which of the following rights is a stockholder of a public corporation entitled?

a. The right to have annual dividends declared and paid.

b. The right to vote for the election of officers.

c. The right to a reasonable inspection of corporate records.

d. The right to have the corporation issue a new class of stock.

87. Which of the following is correct pertaining to the rights of stockholders in a corporation?

a. Stockholders have no right to manage their corporation unless they are also directors or officers.

b. Stockholders have a right to receive dividends.

c. Stockholders have no right to inspect the books and records of their corporation.

d. Stockholders have a right to get a list of their corporation's customers to use for a business mailing list.

88. The limited liability of a stockholder in a closely held corporation may be challenged successfully if the stockholder

a. Undercapitalized the corporation when it was formed.

b. Formed the corporation solely to have limited personal liability.

c. Sold property to the corporation.

d. Was a corporate officer, director, or employee.

89. The corporate veil is most likely to be pierced and the shareholders held personally liable if

a. The corporation has elected S corporation status under the Internal Revenue Code.

b. The shareholders have commingled their personal funds with those of the corporation.

c. An ultra vires act has been committed.

d. A partnership incorporates its business solely to limit the liability of its partners.

90. Which of the following is correct about the law of corporations?

a. Each shareholder owes a fiduciary duty to his or her corporation.

b. Majority shareholders owe a fiduciary duty to their corporation.

c. Majority shareholders do not owe a fiduciary duty to minority shareholders.

d. All of the above are correct.

91. A parent corporation owned more than 90% of each class of the outstanding stock issued by a subsidiary corporation and decided to merge that subsidiary into itself. Under the Revised Model Business Corporation Act, which of the following actions must be taken?

a. The subsidiary corporation's board of directors must pass a merger resolution.

b. The subsidiary corporation's dissenting stockholders must be given an appraisal remedy.

c. The parent corporation's stockholders must approve the merger.

d. The parent corporation's dissenting stockholders must be given an appraisal remedy.

92. Under the Revised Model Business Corporation Act, a merger of two public corporations usually requires all of the following **except**

a. A formal plan of merger.

b. An affirmative vote by the holders of a majority of each corporation's voting shares.

c. Receipt of voting stock by all stockholders of the original corporations.

d. Approval by the board of directors of each corporation.

93. Which of the following statements is a general requirement for the merger of two corporations?

   a.   The merger plan must be approved unanimously by the stockholders of both corporations.

   b.   The merger plan must be approved unanimously by the boards of both corporations.

   c.   The absorbed corporation must amend its articles of incorporation.

   d.   The stockholders of both corporations must be given due notice of a special meeting, including a copy or summary of the merger plan.

94. Which of the following must take place for a corporation to be voluntarily dissolved?

   a.   Passage by the board of directors of a resolution to dissolve.

   b.   Approval by the officers of a resolution to dissolve.

   c.   Amendment of the certificate of incorporation.

   d.   Unanimous vote of the stockholders.

95. A corporate stockholder is entitled to which of the following rights?

   a.   Elect officers.

   b.   Receive annual dividends.

   c.   Approve dissolution.

   d.   Prevent corporate borrowing.

96. When a consolidation takes place under the law of corporations, which of the following is true?

   a.   Two or more corporations are joined into one new corporation.

   b.   All assets are acquired by the new corporation.

   c.   The new corporation is liable for the debts of each of the old corporations.

   d.   All of the above are true.

97. When a corporation elects to be a Subchapter S corporation, which of the following statements is(are) true regarding the federal tax treatment of the corporation's income or loss?

  I.   The corporation's income is taxed at the corporate level and not the shareholders' level.

  II.   The shareholders report the corporation's income on their tax returns when the income is distributed to them.

 III.   The shareholders report the corporation's income on their tax returns even if the income is not distributed to them.

 IV.   The shareholders generally report the corporation's loss on their tax returns.

   a.   I only is true.

   b.   II only is true.

   c.   III only is true.

   d.   III and IV only are true.

MULTIPLE-CHOICE ANSWERS*

1. a __ __	21. a __ __	41. c __ __	61. c __ __	81. c __ __
2. b __ __	22. a __ __	42. c __ __	62. b __ __	82. d __ __
3. d __ __	23. a __ __	43. d __ __	63. d __ __	83. a __ __
4. b __ __	24. c __ __	44. d __ __	64. c __ __	84. b __ __
5. c __ __	25. d __ __	45. d __ __	65. c __ __	85. c __ __
6. d __ __	26. d __ __	46. a __ __	66. a __ __	86. c __ __
7. d __ __	27. d __ __	47. b __ __	67. b __ __	87. a __ __
8. c __ __	28. d __ __	48. b __ __	68. b __ __	88. a __ __
9. d __ __	29. c __ __	49. c __ __	69. c __ __	89. b __ __
10. b __ __	30. d __ __	50. d __ __	70. b __ __	90. b __ __
11. b __ __	31. a __ __	51. c __ __	71. c __ __	91. b __ __
12. a __ __	32. b __ __	52. d __ __	72. d __ __	92. c __ __
13. b __ __	33. c __ __	53. d __ __	73. b __ __	93. d __ __
14. c __ __	34. c __ __	54. a __ __	74. b __ __	94. a __ __
15. c __ __	35. b __ __	55. d __ __	75. a __ __	95. c __ __
16. d __ __	36. b __ __	56. a __ __	76. c __ __	96. d __ __
17. b __ __	37. b __ __	57. a __ __	77. b __ __	97. d __ __
18. d __ __	38. b __ __	58. b __ __	78. c __ __	
19. a __ __	39. c __ __	59. c __ __	79. d __ __	1st: __/97 = __%
20. c __ __	40. a __ __	60. c __ __	80. c __ __	2nd: __/97 = __%

MULTIPLE-CHOICE ANSWER EXPLANATIONS

A. Nature of Sole Proprietorships

1.   (a)   Federal or state governments do not typically require any formal filing. If the business operates under a name different from that of the sole proprietor, most states require that a fictitious name statement be filed. Answer (b) is incorrect because the sole proprietorship and the sole proprietor are not separate legal entities. Answer (c) is incorrect because a sole proprietor does not have partners or shareholders from whom to obtain capital. Answer (d) is incorrect because the simplicity of this business structure is one of its advantages in its formation and operation.

B. Nature of Partnerships

2.   (b)   A general partnership is an association of two or more persons to carry on a business as co-owners for profit. There must be at least two partners involved in order for a partnership to exist. Answer (a) is incorrect because a general partnership is normally not recognized as a taxable entity under federal income tax laws. Answer (c) is incorrect because execution of written articles of partnership is not required to create a general partnership. A partnership agreement may be oral or in writing. Answer (d) is incorrect because a partnership does not have to provide for apportionment of liability for partnership debt. Note that even if the partners agreed to split partnership liability in a specified proportion, third parties can still hold each partner personally liable despite the agreement.

3.   (d)   A partnership involves two or more persons to carry on a business as co-owners for a profit. Partnerships do not include nonprofit associations such as charitable organizations, labor unions or clubs.

4.   (b)   A silent partner does not help manage the partnership but still has unlimited liability.

C. Types of Partnerships and Partners

5.   (c)   A general partner has a voice in management and has unlimited personal liability. Anyone, including a secured creditor of the limited partnership, may be a general partner if he/she takes on these responsibilities. Answer (a) is incorrect because an unsecured creditor of the limited partnership may also be a limited partner. A limited partner is defined as having no voice in management and his/her liability is limited to the extent of his/her capital contribution. Answer (b) is incorrect because a general partner may also be a limited partner at the same time. This partner would have the rights, powers, and liability of a general partner, and the rights against other partners with respect to his/her contribution as both a limited and a general partner. Answer (d) is incorrect because every limited partnership must have at least one general partner who will be liable for the partnership obligations.

D. Formation of Partnership

6.   (d)   A partnership agreement may be expressed or implied based upon the activities and conduct of the partners. The expressed agreement may be oral or in writing with, in general, one exception. A partnership agreement that cannot be completed within one year from the date on which it is entered into must be in writing. Answer (b) is incorrect because the partners may reside in different states without having to put the partnership agreement in writing. Answer (a) is incorrect because the $500 amount applies to the sale of goods which must be in writing, not partnerships. Answer (c) is incorrect because the purpose of the partnership is irrelevant. Agreements to buy and sell real estate must be in writing, while an agreement to form a partnership whose principal activity will involve the buying and selling of real estate normally need not be in writing unless the stated duration exceeds one year.

7. **(d)** Under RUPA, the partnership is a legal entity that can own property in its own name. The partners also have joint and several liability for all debts whether they are based in contract or tort.

8. **(c)** The partners may agree to share profits as well as losses unequally. Answer (a) is incorrect because the partners may agree that ownership in the partnership is unequal. Answer (b) is incorrect because under RUPA, the partnership is a separate legal entity. Answer (d) is incorrect because the partners may agree to unequal management rights.

E.   Partner's Rights

9. **(d)** Profits and losses in a general partnership are shared equally unless otherwise specified in the partnership agreement. If partners agree on unequal profit sharing but are silent on loss sharing, then losses are shared per the profit sharing proportions. The partnership agreement for Owen Associates provided that profits be paid to the partners in the ratio of their financial contribution to the partnership. The ratios are as follows:

Total contributed $10,000 + 30,000 + 50,000 = $90,000

Moore	$10,000 ÷ 90,000 = 1/9
Noon	$30,000 ÷ 90,000 = 1/3
Kale	$50,000 ÷ 90,000 = 5/9

For the year ended December 31, 2008, Owen had losses of $180,000. Therefore, Kale would be allocated $100,000 of the losses ($180,000 × 5/9).

10. **(b)** An incoming partner has the same rights as all of the existing partners. Thus, an incoming partner has the right to participate in the management of the partnership. Answer (c) is incorrect since a person admitted as a partner into an existing partnership is only liable for existing debts of the partnership to the extent of the incoming partner's capital contribution. Answer (d) is incorrect because a partner need not make a capital contribution to be admitted with the same rights as the other partners.

11. **(b)** A partner is free to assign his interest in any partnership to a third party. However, the assignee does not become a partner by virtue of this assignment, but merely succeeds to the assignor's rights as to profits and return of partner's capital contribution. The assignee does not receive the right to manage, to have an accounting, to inspect the books, or to possess or use any individual partnership property. Since Bean was not made a partner, he is entitled to Cobb's share of TLC's profits, but does not have the right to participate in the management of TLC.

F.   Relationship to Third Parties

12. **(a)** A partner's apparent authority is derived from the reasonable perceptions of third parties due to the manifestations or representations of the partnership concerning the authority each partner possesses to bind the partnership. However, if third parties are aware of a formal resolution which limits the partner's actual authority to bind the partnership, then that partner's apparent authority will also be limited. Answer (b) is incorrect because if third parties are unaware of such a resolution which limits the partner's actual authority, then the partner retains apparent authority to bind the partnership. Answer (c) is incorrect because third parties should be aware that in order for a partner to submit a claim against the partnership to arbitration, unanimous con-

sent of the partners is needed. Therefore, a partner has no apparent authority to take such an action. Answer (d) is incorrect because as stated above, the apparent authority of a partner to bind the partnership is not derived from the express powers and purposes contained in the partnership agreement.

13. **(b)** In a general partnership, unanimous consent is required of all of the partners to admit a new partner. Answer (a) is incorrect because any one partner can cause a dissolution by actions such as withdrawing. Answer (c) is incorrect because each partner is an agent of the general partnership and thus may purchase items for the business of the firm. Answer (d) is incorrect; an individual partner may sell real property on behalf of the partnership because s/he is an agent of the partnership.

14. **(c)** Under the Revised Uniform Partnership Act, partners have joint and several liability for not only torts but also breaches of contract. This is a change from previous law.

15. **(c)** Although individual partners normally have implied authority to buy and sell goods for the partnership, they do not have implied authority to do such things as making the partnership a surety or admitting a new partner. These require the consent of all partners.

16. **(d)** A partner's interest in a partnership is freely assignable without the other partners' consent. A partner's interest refers to the partners' right to share in profits and return of contribution. Answer (a) is incorrect because the assignee does not become a partner without the consent of all the other partners. Answer (b) is incorrect because the assignor remains liable as a partner. The assignee has only received the partner's right to share in profits and capital return. Answer (c) is incorrect because assignment of a partner's interest does not cause dissolution unless the assignor also withdraws.

G.   Termination of a Partnership

17. **(b)** Under RUPA, partnership property not only includes property purchased in the partnership name but also includes property purchased by a partner, who is an agent of the partnership, with partnership funds. Note that a partner may use property in the partnership business without it becoming partnership property.

18. **(d)** Even if a partner has agreed not to withdraw before a certain period of time, s/he has the power to do so anyway. That partner's withdrawal is a break of contract and causes a dissolution of the partnership. Answer (a) is incorrect because this dissolution is caused by an act of a partner rather than by operation of law. Answer (b) is incorrect because Wind's withdrawal does have an effect on the remaining partners because they must decide on what new terms they will operate or else wind up and terminate the partnership. Answer (c) is incorrect because the dissolution is effective once Wind does withdraw from the partnership. A court decree is not necessary.

19. (a)   The best approach to answer this question is to make a chart as follows:

	Dowd 40%	Elgar 30%	Frost 20%	Grant 10%
Capital Balance	$120,000	$100,000	$75,000	$11,000
Allocation of Loss $200,000	(80,000)	(60,000)	(40,000)	(20,000)
Remaining balance	40,000	40,000	35,000	(9,000)
Distribution of deficit of insolvent Partner:				9,000
40/90 × 9,000	(4,000)			
30/90 × 9,000		(3,000)		
20/90 × 9,000			(2,000)	
Balance	36,000	37,000	33,000	0
Cash distribution $106,000	(36,000)	(37,000)	(33,000)	0
	0	0	0	0

A capital deficit may be corrected by the partner investing more cash or assets to eliminate the deficit or by distributing the deficit to the other partners in their resulting profit and loss sharing ratio. The latter was done in this case, as the facts in the question indicated that Grant refuses to make any further contributions to the partnership. The remaining cash is then used to pay the three partners' capital balances.

H. Limited Partnerships

20. (c)   Under the Revised Uniform Limited Partnership Act, when the partners do not agree how to split profits, the split is made in proportion to their capital contributions. Note that this is different for general partners under the Revised Uniform Partnership Act.

21. (a)   Limited partnerships must have at least one general partner who has the unlimited personal liability of the firm. Unlike a general partner, the death of a limited partner does not cause a dissolution or termination of a partner.

22. (a)   Since Chan acted like a general partner and Ham thought he was a general partner, Chan has the liability of a general partner to Ham. Answers (b), (c), and (d) are incorrect because Ham believed Chan was a general partner based on Chan's actions. Therefore, Chan had the liability of a general partner, that is, unlimited liability.

23. (a)   Under the Revised Uniform Limited Partnership Act, none of the names of the limited partners need to be listed in the certificate of limited partnership that is filed with the Secretary of State. However, all of the general partners must be listed.

24. (c)   A limited partner is allowed, without losing the protection of limited liability, to act as an agent of the limited partnership. The limited partner may also vote on the removal of a general partner.

25. (d)   Partners' capital may not only be in cash, property, or services already performed, but also may be in the form of promises to give or perform these at a future date.

26. (d)   If the liability is more than the partnership can pay, each partner loses its capital contribution and then the general partner has personal, unlimited liability for the debt.

27. (d)   The admission of a new general partner to a limited partnership under the Revised Uniform Limited Partnership Act requires the approval of all partners.

28. (d)   Unlike the admission of a new general partner, the admission of a new limited partner requires the written approval of not only all of the general partners but also all of the limited partners.

29. (c)   Death or bankruptcy of a general partner in a limited partnership will cause dissolution of the limited partnership. However, this is not true if a limited partner dies or goes bankrupt.

I. Joint Ventures

30. (d)   The law of joint ventures is similar to the law of partnerships with some exceptions. One of these exceptions is that the death of a joint venturer does not automatically dissolve the joint venture. Answers (a), (b), and (c) are all incorrect because these are all examples in which joint venture law and partnership law are similar, involving liability, right to participate in management, and fiduciary duties.

J. Limited Liability Companies (LLC)

31. (a)   A limited liability company provides for limited liability of its members, similar to the limited liability of the shareholders of a corporation. However, it typically has a limited duration of existence, similar to that of a partnership in which the death or withdrawal of a member or partner causes the business to dissolve unless the remaining members or partners choose to continue the business. The limited liability company can also be taxed similar to a partnership if formed to do so. The Subchapter S corporation has the limited liability of the corporation but is taxed similar to a partnership.

32. (b)   The limited liability company statutes provide that it is a separate legal entity apart from its owners. Thus it may sue or be sued in its own name. Answer (a) is incorrect because all owners have limited rather than personal liability. Answer (c) is incorrect because limited liability is normally retained even if the owners fail to follow the formalities usual in conducting the business. Answer (d) is incorrect because (b) is correct.

33. (c)   Limited liability companies typically have a limited life. Provisions often provide that they exist for thirty years at most and dissolve if a member dies. Therefore (a) is an incorrect response. Answer (b) is also not chosen because members (owners) are permitted to participate in the management of the LLC or can choose the management. Answer (d) is an incorrect response because one of the main benefits of an LLC is the limited liability of its members (owners).

34. (c)   Owners and managers of an LLC owe a duty of due care to not be grossly negligent. They also owe a duty to be loyal to their LLC.

35. (b)   In the typical limited liability company (LLC), unlike the common corporation, the interests of the members are not freely transferable. The other members have to agree to admit new members. Answer (a) is incorrect because it provides for limited liability of all of its members. Answer (c) is incorrect because all members have a voice in the management of the LLC. Answer (d) is incorrect because a limited liability company must be formed pursuant to the filing requirements of the relevant state statute.

K.   Limited Liability Partnerships (LLP)

36.   (b)   In a limited liability partnership (LLP), where permitted by state statute, the basic difference between it and a general partnership is limited liability in some cases. In the LLP, partners have limited liability for the torts of the other partners. This is not true of a general partnership. Answer (a) is wrong because both in the LLP and the general partnership, the partners have unlimited liability for their own torts. Answers (c) and (d) are wrong because any contracts signed on behalf of the firm make all of the partners jointly liable in both the LLP and the general partnership.

L.   Subchapter C Corporations

37.   (b)   The federal Subchapter S Revision Act specifies that all corporations that do not meet the criteria of a Subchapter S corporation are categorized as a Subchapter C corporation. Answers (a), (c), and (d) are incorrect because the Act provides that a corporation is either a Subchapter S or Subchapter C corporation but not both at the same time.

38.   (b)   All corporations are divided under the federal Subchapter S Revision Act as being either a Subchapter C corporation or a Subchapter S corporation. Answer (a) is incorrect because the federal Subchapter S Revision Act provides that there are two categories of corporations: Subchapter C and Subchapter S corporations. Answer (c) is incorrect because this federal law provides for only two categories of corporations. A Subchapter E corporation is not one of these. Answer (d) is incorrect because answer (c) is correct.

39.   (c)   Both Subchapter C corporations and Subchapter S corporations are similar in their provisions for the limited liability of their shareholders and also in their corporate management structures. Answer (a) is incorrect because it does not include the similarity of the corporate management structures. Answer (b) is incorrect because it does not mention the similarity of the shareholders' limited liability. Answer (d) is incorrect for the reason that answer (c) is correct.

40.   (a)   Tax treatment is the main reason why Subchapter S corporations are formed instead of Subchapter C corporations. Answer (b) is incorrect because this federal Act covers both types of corporations. Answers (c) and (d) are incorrect because the provisions on the limited liability of shareholders and the provisions for the structure of corporate management are some of the ways that Subchapter C and Subchapter S corporations are generally similar.

M.   Characteristics and Advantages of Corporate Form

41.   (c)   One advantage of the corporate form of business is that it has a continuous life and is not terminated by the death of a shareholder or manager. Answer (a) is incorrect because although the power to manage the corporation is vested in the board of directors, they usually delegate the day-to-day management responsibilities to various managers. Answer (b) is incorrect because in most corporations, ownership is not contractually restricted. In fact, free transferability of the shares of stock is a major advantage of the corporate form of business. Answer (d) is incorrect because corporations are not free from state regulation.

42.   (c)   A major advantage is that shareholders have limited liability, that is, typically limited to what they paid for the stock. However, managers do not have limited liability for their actions as managers. If a manager is also a shareholder, that person has limited liability for the ownership in the stock but can still be sued for misdeeds as a manager. Answers (a), (b), and (d) are all considered to be advantages of a corporation. Note that since a person can manage a corporation without necessarily being an owner, this can encourage professional managers to get involved.

43.   (d)   The death of one or more of a corporation's shareholders does not automatically terminate it. Answer (a) is incorrect because a corporation continues to exist until it is dissolved, merged or otherwise terminated. Answer (b) is incorrect because shares in a corporation, represented by stocks, can be freely bought, sold, or assigned unless the shareholders have agreed to restrict this. Answer (c) is incorrect because a corporation is legally a separate entity apart from its shareholders.

44.   (d)   A corporation may make contracts in its own name with both its shareholders and third parties. Answer (a) is incorrect because it may also make contracts with third parties. Answer (b) is incorrect because corporations do not generally need the consent of other shareholders to contract with one shareholder. Answer (c) is incorrect because it may also contract with its shareholders.

45.   (d)   Persons who manage a corporation may be, but need not be, shareholders of that corporation. Also, a corporation as a separate legal entity may convey or hold property. It may also sue or be sued in its own name. Answers (a), (b), and (c) are not comprehensive enough.

N.   Disadvantages of Corporate Business Structure

46.   (a)   A Subchapter S corporation is often formed to help avoid the double taxation that a Subchapter C corporation may face. Answer (b) is incorrect because partners in a general partnership have unlimited personal liability. Shareholders of a corporation have limited liability with few exceptions. Answer (c) is incorrect because a Subchapter C corporation is any corporation that is not a Subchapter S corporation. Answer (d) is incorrect because both Subchapter C and Subchapter S corporations provide their shareholders with limited liability with few exceptions.

O.   Types of Corporations

47.   (b)   Bond is a domestic corporation in Florida since it incorporated there. It is a foreign corporation in Georgia since it did not incorporate there. Bond does not need to incorporate in Georgia but must qualify to do business there because it has branch offices in Georgia. This qualifying normally entails filing required documents with the state.

48.   (b)   In a professional corporation, the professional has most of the benefits of a corporation such as limited liability for corporate debts. However, the professional has personal liability for professional acts. Colby cannot avoid liability for the damage caused the client due to negligence in a professional act.

49.   (c)   A domestic corporation is one that operates and does business in the state in which it was incorporated. Answer (a) is incorrect because Macro, instead of incorporating in Nevada, may qualify to do business by obtaining a certificate of authority from Nevada. Answer (b) is incorrect because Macro is a foreign corporation in Nevada because it did not incorporate there. Answer (d) is incorrect because the statement in (c) is the only one that is true.

50.   (d)   None of the listed items are normally considered doing business in the other states such that Cleanit would be required to qualify to do business and thus have to obtain certificates of authority from those states. Therefore, answers (a), (b), and (c) are incorrect.

51.   (c)   Normally, under state laws, only licensed professionals may own shares in professional corporations. Furthermore, the licensed professionals retain personal liability for their professional acts in the professional corporation. Therefore (a), (b), and (d) are incorrect.

P.   Formation of Corporation

52.   (d)   Corporations and limited partnerships may only be created pursuant to state statutes. Normally, both the Articles of Incorporation and a Certificate of Limited Partnership must be filed with the Secretary of State. Answer (c) is incorrect since limited partners do not owe fiduciary duties to the partnership. Answer (a) is incorrect since limited partners have the right to vote on partnership matters such as the dissolution or winding up of the partnership, loans of the partnership, a change in the nature of the business of a partnership, and the removal of a general partner without jeopardizing their limited partner status. Answer (b) is incorrect since sale of limited partnership interests is not automatically exempted from the general securities laws' registration requirements.

53.   (d)   Under the Revised Model Business Corporation Act, a corporation's Articles of Incorporation generally must include the name of the corporation, the purpose of the corporation, the powers of the corporation, the name of the incorporators, the name of the registered agent of the corporation and the number of shares of stock the corporation is authorized to issue.

54.   (a)   The Articles of Incorporation are filed with the state and contain the names of the corporation, registered agent, and incorporators. This document also contains the purpose and powers of the corporation as well as a description of the types of stock and number of authorized shares.

55.   (d)   Normally, the board of directors of a corporation has the power to adopt, amend, and repeal the bylaws. It also has the power to declare dividends and fix the compensation of the directors. However, it does not have the power to amend the Articles of Incorporation.

56.   (a)   Corporations and limited partnerships may only be created pursuant to state statutes. Normally, both the Articles of Incorporation and a Certificate of Limited Partnership must be filed with the Secretary of State. Answer (b) is incorrect because a limited partnership requires at least one general partner who retains unlimited personal liability. Answer (c) is incorrect because a limited partnership is treated the same as a general partnership for tax purposes in that it is not recognized as a separate taxable entity. Answer (d) is incorrect because a limited partnership is not statutorily allowed perpetual existence.

57.   (a)   The basic concept of a promoter is one who forms a corporation with the goal of the corporation eventually coming into existence. Answer (b) is incorrect because for there to be an agent, there must be a principal. There is

no principal yet because the corporation is not yet formed. Answer (c) is incorrect because the promoters are not agents who can bind the future corporations to contracts. Answer (d) is incorrect because the promoters are not agents and thus cannot use agency law to protect them.

Q.   Corporate Financial Structure

58.   (b)   The Articles of Incorporation must include, among other things, the amount of capital stock authorized and the types of stock to be issued. Specific provisions applicable to stock must also be stated. Examples of stock provisions which must be authorized by the Articles of Incorporation include number of authorized shares, whether the stock is to be par value or no-par value, and classes of stock, including voting rights and dividend provisions. Preferred stock is given preferred status as to liquidations and dividends. This is part of the definition of preferred stock and need not be specifically included in the Articles of Incorporation in order to be enforceable. Therefore, Johns becomes an unsecured creditor upon Abco's declaration of preferred stock dividend. In order for Johns to be entitled to convert his/her preferred shares to common shares, to participate with common shareholders in any dividend distribution made after preferred dividends are paid, or to be entitled to vote if dividend payments are in arrears, it must be stated in the Articles of Incorporation.

59.   (c)   Gallagher originally sold the stock at above par value. It may buy back and resell the shares without regard to par value.

60.   (c)   A corporation may resell treasury shares without regard to par value. Therefore, an owner of common stock who purchased treasury shares for less than par value will not have any liability beyond actual investment. Answer (a) is incorrect because an owner of common stock who paid less than par value for stock purchased in connection with an original issue of shares is contingently liable in many states to creditors for the difference between the amount paid and par value. Answer (b) is incorrect because a promise to perform future services in exchange for original issue par value shares is an executory promise which is not considered valid consideration for shares. An owner of common stock who agreed to perform future services for the corporation in exchange for original issue par value shares is liable to creditors for the difference between any valid consideration (i.e., cash, property, or services performed) given and par value. Answer (d) is incorrect because once the corporation accepts an offer to buy stock subscriptions, the subscriber becomes liable for the purchase. Therefore, an owner of common stock who failed to pay the full amount owed on a subscription contract for no-par shares is liable for the difference between any amounts already paid and the full amount owed according to the contract.

61.   (c)   Corporate debt securities include the following: (1) registered bonds, (2) bearer bonds, (3) debenture bonds, (4) mortgage bonds, (5) redeemable bonds, and (6) convertible bonds. A warrant is not a corporate debt security, but rather is written evidence of a stock option which grants its owner the option to purchase a specified amount of shares of stock at a stated price within a specified period of time.

62.   (b)   A stock split increases the number of shares outstanding and proportionately decreases the par value per share. However, the total outstanding par value does not change and therefore no charge is made to retained earnings or capital. Liquidating dividends represent a return of the stockholders' capital and are considered a capital distribution. Both cash and property distributions are considered asset distributions. Property distributions are recorded at the fair market value of the asset at the date of transfer.

63. **(d)** Valid consideration or value to purchase shares of stock can be any benefit to the corporation including any services contracted for that are yet to be performed in the future.

64. **(c)** Since Brawn had a contract to purchase 1,000 shares at $20 per share, this is binding. Therefore, the creditors can recover in bankruptcy the remainder of the price not paid. Answer (a) is incorrect because the creditors have the right to see that the bankruptcy estate includes this amount owed the corporation. Answer (b) is incorrect because the contract required that the full $20,000 be paid, not just the par value. Answer (d) is incorrect because ultra vires acts are acts that are beyond the scope of the powers of the corporation. These do not apply to this fact pattern.

65. **(c)** Treasury stock are not votable nor do they receive dividends. Therefore, answers (a), (b), and (d) are incorrect.

66. **(a)** Treasury stock is stock that a corporation issued previously but is no longer outstanding because the corporation repurchased it back. Answer (b) is incorrect because treasury stock is a corporation's own stock that it has repurchased. Answer (c) is incorrect because canceled stock is no longer issued or outstanding. Answer (d) is incorrect because (a) is correct.

67. **(b)** A corporation by law may issue one or more classes of common stock. This is also true for preferred stock. Answer (a) is incorrect because a corporation is not required to issue preferred stock. Answer (c) is incorrect because it is at the discretion of the board of directors to declare a dividend. They may wish to keep the earnings in the corporation for expansion purposes, etc. Answer (d) is incorrect because if it issues preferred stock, it may be either cumulative preferred stock or noncumulative preferred stock.

68. **(b)** A bond represents long-term secured debt. Answer (a) is incorrect because holders of debt securities are creditors rather than owners of the corporation. Answer (c) is incorrect because a debenture represents long-term unsecured debt not long-term secured debt. Answer (d) is incorrect because there was one correct answer.

69. **(c)** The definition of watered stock refers to when the stock is acquired by exchanging cash or property worth less than the par or stated value of the stock.

R.   Powers and Liabilities of Corporation

70. **(b)** Corporations generally have the power to acquire or retire their own shares without shareholder approval. They can also make charitable contributions without such approval. Loans to directors require shareholder approval.

71. **(c)** A business is liable for the torts of its employees committed within the course and scope of employment. This is true even if management has warned the employee

that he and not the corporation will be liable. The injured third party can hold both the employee and the corporation liable in either case.

72. **(d)** All three statements are true in the interest of punishing all parties who commit crimes.

S.   Directors and Officers of Corporations

73. **(b)** Since the corporation never adopted the contract by words or actions, it is not liable. The board of directors is not personally liable either because they never agreed to the contract. However, Norwood is personally liable on the contract because he signed the contract and agency law will not protect him. This is true because he was not an agent, even though he claimed to be, because there was no principal to authorize him when the contract was made on March 15.

74. **(b)** Under the Revised Model Business Corporation Act, a corporation is authorized to indemnify its officers for expenses, attorney fees, judgments, fines and amounts paid in settlement incurred in a suit by stockholders when the liability is a result of the officer's good faith, nonnegligent actions on behalf of the best interest of the corporation. Answer (a) is incorrect because a corporate officer may also serve as a director. Answer (c) is incorrect because officers are appointed by the directors of a corporation who are in turn elected by the shareholders. Answer (d) is incorrect because there is no requirement that an officer must own any shares of the corporation's stock.

75. **(a)** The transaction the director wishes to have with the corporation is not a conflict of interest if any one of the following is true. (1) The transaction is fair and reasonable for the corporation. (2) The shareholders are given the relevant facts and they approve it by a majority vote. (3) The board of directors are given the relevant facts and they approve it by a majority vote of the disinterested members of the board of directors.

76. **(c)** Officers and directors are in important positions in a corporation. As such, they owe a fiduciary duty to the corporation to act in the best interests of the corporation. Courts have also recognized that because majority shareholders can exercise a lot of power in a corporation from their stockholdings and voting rights, they owe a fiduciary duty to the minority shareholders when these majority shareholders have de facto control over the corporation by virtue of their concentrated ownership.

77. **(b)** A contract between a director and his/her corporation is valid if it is reasonable to the corporation. Hogan has not breached his fiduciary duty with the corporation since he is selling the land at fair market value. Answer (a) is incorrect because a director does owe a fiduciary duty to his/her corporation to act in its best interests. Answers (c) and (d) are incorrect because since the transaction is fair and reasonable to the corporation, the shareholders need not approve it.

78. **(c)** The Articles of Incorporation may be amended by the shareholders' vote, not by the board of directors. Answer (a) is incorrect because one of the important powers of the directors is to select the officers of the corporation. Answer (b) is incorrect because it is up to the board of directors to declare any dividends to the shareholders. Answer (d) is incorrect because answer (c) is correct.

79. **(d)**   A corporation may indemnify both its directors as well as its officers against suits based on their duties for the corporation if they acted in good faith and in the best interests of the corporation. A corporation may also purchase insurance to cover the liability for lawsuits lost based on actions of its directors and also its officers.

80. **(c)**   Both directors as well as officers owe a fiduciary duty to their corporation.

81. **(c)**   McGarry is liable for the tort she committed. Because she was acting within the scope of her authority in the corporation, Norton corporation is also liable. Note that McGarry is not relieved of liability even though Norton Corporation is also liable because McGarry is the one who committed the tort. Therefore, answers (a), (b), and (d) are incorrect.

T.   Stockholder's Rights

82. **(d)**   When Acorn pays cash and buys 90% or more of Trend's shares, it has control of the Trend stock. It can then accomplish a short-form merger of Trend Corp. into Acorn Corp. Answer (a) is incorrect because this can require the approval of Acorn shareholders. Answer (b) is incorrect because this is not a regular sale of Trend's assets and will require shareholder approval. Answer (c) is incorrect because the entire compulsory exchange for Acorn shares to accomplish the acquisition does require shareholder approval.

83. **(a)**   Upon declaration, a cash dividend on preferred stock becomes a legal debt of the corporation, and the preferred shareholders become unsecured creditors of the corporation. However, any dividends not paid in any year concerning cumulative preferred stock are not a liability of the corporation until they are declared. Therefore, Universal will be liable to Price as an unsecured creditor for $10,000, which is the amount of the declared dividends. Answers (c) and (d) are incorrect because Price has become a general unsecured creditor for the declared dividends and will have the same priority as the debenture (unsecured) bond owners and the unsecured judgment creditors. Answer (b) is incorrect because the undeclared dividends did not become a legal liability to Universal.

84. **(b)**   The preemptive right gives the shareholder the right to purchase newly issued stock so as to keep the same overall percentage of ownership of the corporation. The Revised Model Business Corporation Act only provides this right if it is set forth in the Articles of Incorporation.

85. **(c)**   When the rights of individual shareholders may be adversely affected, the shareholder is given the right to dissent and receive payment of the fair value of his/her shares. This is true even if the dissenting shareholder has voting rights when s/he is being outvoted. In I., the shareholder has this right because his/her preference rights are being abolished. In II., the dissenting shareholder has this right because his/her shares being acquired by another corporation may affect the value and rights of the shares of stock.

86. **(c)**   Shareholders have the right to inspect the corporate records if done in good faith for a proper purpose. Answer (a) is incorrect because shareholders do not have a right to dividends. It is the decision of the board of directors whether or not to declare dividends. Answer (b) is incorrect

because although at least one class of stock must have voting rights to elect the **board of directors,** the **officers** may be selected by the board of directors. Answer (d) is incorrect because the shareholders cannot force an issuance of a new class of stock.

87. **(a)**   Stockholders do not have the right to manage their corporation. However, stockholders who are also directors or officers do have the right to manage as part of their rights as directors and officers. Answer (b) is incorrect because stockholders generally have no right to receive dividends unless the board of directors declares such dividends. Answer (c) is incorrect because stockholders are given the right to inspect the books and records of their corporation. Answer (d) is incorrect because the stockholders may demand a list of shareholders for a proper purpose such as to help wage a proxy fight; however, they may not require the corporation to give them a list of its customers to use for a mailing list.

U.   Stockholder's Liability

88. **(a)**   Normally, the liability of shareholders of corporations is limited to their capital contribution. However, the court will "pierce the corporate veil" and hold the shareholders personally liable for the debts of the corporation if the corporate entity is being used to defraud people or to achieve other injustices. Thus, if the shareholders establish a corporation, knowing that it would have less capital than required for it to pay its debts, then the court will "pierce the corporate veil" and hold the shareholders personally liable. Answer (c) is incorrect because a shareholder may sell property to the corporation without becoming personally liable for the debts of the corporation. Answer (d) is incorrect because shareholders may also be corporate officers, directors or employees without jeopardizing their limited liability status. Answer (b) is incorrect because the formation of a corporation solely to limit personal liability is a valid purpose so long as it is done without intent to defraud.

89. **(b)**   The court will disregard the corporate entity and hold the shareholders individually liable when the corporate form is used to perpetrate a fraud or is found to be merely an agent or instrument of its owners. An example of when the corporate veil is likely to be pierced is if the corporation and its shareholders commingle assets and financial records. In such a situation, the shareholders lose their limited liability and will be held personally liable for the corporation's legal obligations. Answer (a) is incorrect because the election of S corporation status is allowable under the law and is not, in itself, grounds for piercing the corporate veil. Answer (d) is incorrect because the desire of shareholders to limit their personal liability is a valid reason to form a corporation. Limited personal liability is one advantage of the corporate entity. Answer (c) is incorrect since the court will hold personally liable only those corporate officers responsible for the commission of an **ultra vires** act. The court will not pierce the corporate veil and hold the shareholders personally liable for such an act.

90. **(b)**   Majority shareholders now owe a fiduciary duty to their corporation. Answer (a) is incorrect because minority shareholders do not owe a fiduciary duty to their corporation. Their main purpose normally is to be investors. Answer (c) is incorrect because majority shareholders now not only owe a fiduciary duty to their corporation but also to the minority shareholders. Answer (d) is incorrect because answer (b) is correct.

V.   Substantial Change in Corporate Structure

91.   (b)   Under the Revised Model Business Corporation Act, a corporation that owns at least 90% of the outstanding shares of each class of stock of the subsidiary may merge the subsidiary into itself without approval by the shareholders of the parent or subsidiary. The approval of the shareholders or the subsidiary's board of directors is unnecessary since the parent owns 90% of the subsidiary. This ownership assures that the plan of the merger would be approved. The only requirement is a merger resolution by the board of directors of the parent corporation. Furthermore, the dissenting shareholders of the subsidiary must be given an appraisal remedy, that is the right to obtain payment from the parent for their shares. The shareholders of the parent do not have this appraisal remedy because the merger has not materially changed their rights.

92.   (c)   In order for a merger of two public corporations to be accomplished, it is required that a formal plan of merger be prepared and that the merger plan be approved by a majority of the board of directors and stockholders of both corporations.

93.   (d)   As one of the steps leading up to a merger of two corporations, the stockholders need to be given notice of the merger plan. This is true of the stockholders of both corporations, so a special meeting is called inviting both sets of stockholders. Answers (a) and (b) are incorrect because unanimous approval is not needed by either the stockholders or the boards of either corporation. Answer (c) is incorrect because the absorbed corporation will no longer exist after the merger plan is accomplished.

94.   (a)   A corporation voluntarily dissolves when its board of directors passes a resolution to dissolve and liquidate. Answer (d) is incorrect because this resolution must be ratified by a majority of stockholders who are entitled to vote. Following ratification, the corporation must file a certificate of dissolution with the proper state authority, cease business, wind up its affairs, and publish notice of its dissolution. Answers (b) and (c) are incorrect because they are not requirements of a voluntary dissolution.

95.   (c)   Shareholders have the right to vote on the dissolution of the corporation. Stockholders also have the right to elect the directors of the corporation, who in turn elect the officers. Answer (b) is incorrect as shareholders do not have the right to receive dividends unless they are declared by the board of directors. Answer (d) is incorrect as shareholders are not necessarily involved in the management of the corporation and cannot prevent corporate borrowing.

96.   (d)   Under corporate law when a consolidation takes place, one new corporation comes from the joining of two or more corporations. Also, the assets and liabilities of the old corporations are acquired by the new corporation and the new corporation is liable for the debts of the old corporations.

W.   Subchapter S Corporation

97.   (d)   When a corporation elects to be a Subchapter S corporation, the corporate income and loss flow through to the income tax returns of the individual shareholders even when the income is not distributed to them. Answer (a) is incorrect because the corporation's income is not taxed at the corporate level when the Subchapter S election is made. Answer (b) is incorrect because the income flows through to the stockholders' tax returns regardless of when the distribution takes place. Answer (c) is incorrect because statement IV as well as statement III are both correct as discussed above.

MULTIPLE-CHOICE QUESTIONS (1-135)

1. A software package that is used with a large set of organized data that presents the computer as an expert on a particular topic is referred to as a(n)
   a. Data mining.
   b. Expert system.
   c. Artificial intelligence.
   d. Virtual reality.

2. Computer memory which is used to store programs that must be accessed immediately by the central processing unit is
   a. Primary storage.
   b. Secondary storage.
   c. Tertiary storage.
   d. Tape storage.

3. The most common output device is a(n)
   a. Mouse.
   b. Printer.
   c. Expert system.
   d. Keyboard.

4. The part of the computer that does most of the data processing is referred to as the
   a. Analyter.
   b. Compiler.
   c. CPU
   d. Printer.

5. An "office suite" of software is least likely to include a(n)
   a. Databases.
   b. Operating system.
   c. Spreadsheet.
   d. Word processing.

6. Software that performs a variety of general technical computer-controlling operations is a(n)
   a. Integrated "suite."
   b. Shareware.
   c. Database.
   d. Operating system.

7. Which of the following is not a part of the central processing unit?
   a. Control unit.
   b. Arithmetic unit.
   c. Logic unit.
   d. Printer unit.

8. MIPS stands for
   a. Memory in protocol standards.
   b. Millions of instructions per second.
   c. Mitigating individualistic personnel standards.
   d. Multiple input physical savings.

9. Which of the following represents a type of applications software that a large client is most likely to use?
   a. Enterprise resource planning.
   b. Operating system.
   c. Central processing unit.
   d. Value-added network.

10. Which of the following characteristics distinguishes computer processing from manual processing?
   a. Computer processing virtually eliminates the occurrence of computational error normally associated with manual processing.
   b. Errors or fraud in computer processing will be detected soon after their occurrences.
   c. The potential for systematic error is ordinarily greater in manual processing than in computerized processing.
   d. Most computer systems are designed so that transaction trails useful for audit purposes do **not** exist.

11. Which computer application is most frequently used on mainframe computers?
   a. Databases.
   b. Graphics.
   c. Spreadsheets.
   d. Word processing.

12. Which computer application is most frequently used to analyze numbers and financial information?
   a. Computer graphics programs.
   b. WAN applications.
   c. Spreadsheets.
   d. Word processing programs.

13. Analysis of data in a database using tools which look for trends or anomalies without knowledge in advance of the meaning of the data is referred to as
   a. Artificial intelligence.
   b. Data mining.
   c. Virtual reality.
   d. Transitory analysis.

14. The most common type of primary storage in a computer is referred to as
   a. CMAN.
   b. RAM.
   c. ROM.
   d. Flash memory.

15. A set of step-by-step procedures used to accomplish a task is a(n)
   a. Algorithm.
   b. Compilation Master.
   c. Linux.
   d. Transitor.

16. Which of the following compiles a complete translation of a program in a high-level computer language before the program is run for the first time?
   a. Visual Basic.
   b. Java.
   c. Algorithm.
   d. Compiler.

17. GUI is the abbreviation for
   a. Grandfather, Uncle, Individual.
   b. Graphical User Interface.
   c. Graphics Utilization Institutes.
   d. Grand Union Internet.

18. Unix is a(n)
   a. Operating system.
   b. Singular disk drive.
   c. Central processing unit.
   d. Logic unit.

19. In a spreadsheet, each specific cell may be identified by a specific
- a. Address.
- b. Column.
- c. Row.
- d. Diagonal.

20. In a spreadsheet, which of the following is correct concerning rows and columns?

	Rows	Columns
a.	Numbered	Numbered
b.	Numbered	Lettered
c.	Lettered	Numbered
d.	Lettered	Lettered

21. Which of the following is **least** likely to be considered an advantage of a database?
- a. Easy to store large quantities of information.
- b. Easy to retrieve information quickly.
- c. Easy to organize and reorganize information.
- d. Easy to distribute information to every possible user.

22. Most current computers process data using which of the following formats?
- a. Analog.
- b. Digital.
- c. Memory enhanced.
- d. Organic.

23. A current day instruction to a computer such as "*Extract all Customers where 'Name' is Smith*" would most likely relate to a
- a. First generation programming language.
- b. Fourth generation programming language.
- c. Seventh generation programming language.
- d. Ninth generation programming language.

24. Several language interfaces exist in a database management system. These typically include a data definition language (DDL), a data control language (DCL), a data manipulation language (DML), and a database query language (DQL). What language interface would a database administrator use to establish the structure of database tables?
- a. DDL.
- b. DCL.
- c. DML.
- d. DQL.

25. Users making database queries often need to combine several tables to get the information they want. One approach to combining tables is known as
- a. Joining.
- b. Merging.
- c. Projecting.
- d. Pointing.

26. User acceptance testing is more important in an object-oriented development process than in a traditional environment because of the implications of the
- a. Absence of traditional design documents.
- b. Lack of a tracking system for changes.
- c. Potential for continuous monitoring.
- d. Inheritance of properties in hierarchies.

27. A company's management has expressed concern over the varied system architectures that the organization uses.

Potential security and control concerns would include all of the following **except:**
- a. Users may have different user ID codes and passwords to remember for the several systems that they use.
- b. There are difficulties in developing uniform security standards for the various platforms.
- c. Backup file storage administration is often decentralized.
- d. Having data distributed across many computers throughout the organization increases the risk that a single disaster would destroy large portions of the organization's data.

28. All of the following are methods for distributing a relational database across multiple servers **except:**
- a. Snapshot (making a copy of the database for distribution).
- b. Replication (creating and maintaining replica copies at multiple locations).
- c. Normalization (separating the database into logical tables for easier user processing).
- d. Fragmentation (separating the database into parts and distributing where they are needed).

29. Client/server architecture may potentially involve a variety of hardware, systems software, and application software from many vendors. The best way to protect a client/server system from unauthorized access is through
- a. A combination of application and general access control techniques.
- b. Use of a commercially available authentication system.
- c. Encryption of all network traffic.
- d. Thorough testing and evaluation of remote procedure calls.

30. What technology is needed in order to convert a paper document into a computer file?
- a. Optical character recognition.
- b. Electronic data interchange.
- c. Bar-coding scanning.
- d. Joining and merging.

31. Unauthorized alteration of online records can be prevented by employing
- a. Key verification.
- b. Computer sequence checks.
- c. Computer matching.
- d. Database access controls.

32. A manufacturer of complex electronic equipment such as oscilloscopes and microscopes has been shipping its products with thick paper manuals but wants to reduce the cost of producing and shipping this documentation. Of the following, the best medium for the manufacturer to use to accomplish this is
- a. Write-once-read-many.
- b. Digital audio tape.
- c. Compact disc/read-only memory.
- d. Computer-output-to-microform.

33. Misstatements in a batch computer system caused by incorrect programs or data may **not** be detected immediately because
- a. Errors in some transactions may cause rejection of other transactions in the batch.

b. The identification of errors in input data typically is **not** part of the program.

c. There are time delays in processing transactions in a batch system.

d. The processing of transactions in a batch system is **not** uniform.

34. Which of the following is **not** a characteristic of a batch processed computer system?

a. The collection of like transactions which are sorted and processed sequentially against a master file.

b. Keypunching of transactions, followed by machine processing.

c. The production of numerous printouts.

d. The posting of a transaction, as it occurs, to several files, without intermediate printouts.

35. Able Co. uses an online sales order processing system to process its sales transactions. Able's sales data are electronically sorted and subjected to edit checks. A direct output of the edit checks most likely would be a

a. Report of all missing sales invoices.

b. File of all rejected sales transactions.

c. Printout of all user code numbers and passwords.

d. List of all voided shipping documents.

36. First Federal S & L has an online real-time system, with terminals installed in all of its branches. This system will not accept a customer's cash withdrawal instructions in excess of $1,000 without the use of a "terminal audit key." After the transaction is authorized by a supervisor, the bank teller then processes the transaction with the audit key. This control can be strengthened by

a. Online recording of the transaction on an audit override sheet.

b. Increasing the dollar amount to $1,500.

c. Requiring manual, rather than online, recording of all such transactions.

d. Using parallel simulation.

37. Mill Co. uses a batch processing method to process its sales transactions. Data on Mill's sales transaction tape are electronically sorted by customer number and are subjected to programmed edit checks in preparing its invoices, sales journals, and updated customer account balances. One of the direct outputs of the creation of this tape most likely would be a

a. Report showing exceptions and control totals.

b. Printout of the updated inventory records.

c. Report showing overdue accounts receivable.

d. Printout of the sales price master file.

38. Where disk files are used, the grandfather-father-son updating backup concept is relatively difficult to implement because the

a. Location of information points on disks is an extremely time-consuming task.

b. Magnetic fields and other environmental factors cause off-site storage to be impractical.

c. Information must be dumped in the form of hard copy if it is to be reviewed before used in updating.

d. Process of updating old records is destructive.

39. In a computerized system, procedure or problem-oriented language is converted to machine language through a(n)

a. Interpreter.

b. Verifier.

c. Compiler.

d. Converter.

40. What type of computer system is characterized by data that are assembled from more than one location and records that are updated immediately?

a. Microcomputer system.

b. Minicomputer system.

c. Batch processing system.

d. Online real-time system.

41. Which of the following characteristics distinguishes electronic data interchange (EDI) from other forms of electronic commerce?

a. EDI transactions are formatted using the standards that are uniform worldwide.

b. EDI transactions need **not** comply with generally accepted accounting principles.

c. EDI transactions ordinarily are processed without the Internet.

d. EDI transactions are usually recorded without security and privacy concerns.

42. LAN is the abbreviation for

a. Large Area Network.

b. Local Area Network.

c. Longitudinal Analogue Network.

d. Low Analytical Nets.

43. A computer that is designed to provide software and other applications to other computers is referred to as a

a. Microcomputer.

b. Network computer.

c. Server.

d. Supercomputer.

44. Which is **least** likely to be considered a component of a computer network?

a. Applications programs.

b. Computers.

c. Software.

d. Routers.

45. The network most frequently used for private operations designed to link computers within widely separated portions of an organization is referred to as a(n)

a. Bulletin board service.

b. Local area network.

c. Wide area network.

d. Zero base network.

46. A set of rules for exchanging data between two computers is a

a. Communicator.

b. Operating system.

c. Protocol.

d. Transmission speed.

47. A web page is most frequently created using

a. Java or C++.

b. Visual Basic.

c. SQL.

d. HTML or XML.

48. Laptop computers provide automation outside of the normal office location. Which of the following would provide the **least** security for sensitive data stored on a laptop computer?

   a.   Encryption of data files on the laptop computer.
   b.   Setting up a password for the screensaver program on the laptop computer.
   c.   Using a laptop computer with a removable hard disk drive.
   d.   Using a locking device that can secure the laptop computer to an immovable object.

49. When developing a new computer system that will handle customer orders and process customer payments, a high-level systems design phase would include determination of which of the following?

   a.   How the new system will affect current inventory and general ledger systems.
   b.   How the file layouts will be structured for the customer order records.
   c.   Whether to purchase a turn-key system or modify an existing system.
   d.   Whether formal approval by top management is needed for the new system.

50. A company using EDI made it a practice to track the functional acknowledgments from trading partners and to issue warning messages if acknowledgments did not occur within a reasonable length of time. What risk was the company attempting to address by this practice?

   a.   Transactions that have not originated from a legitimate trading partner may be inserted into the EDI network.
   b.   Transmission of EDI transactions to trading partners may sometimes fail.
   c.   There may be disagreement between the parties as to whether the EDI transactions form a legal contract.
   d.   EDI data may not be accurately and completely processed by the EDI software.

51. Management is concerned that data uploaded from a microcomputer to the company's mainframe system in batch processing may be erroneous. Which of the following controls would best address this issue?

   a.   The mainframe computer should be backed up on a regular basis.
   b.   Two persons should be present at the microcomputer when it is uploading data.
   c.   The mainframe computer should subject the data to the same edits and validation routines that online data entry would require.
   d.   The users should be required to review a random sample of processed data.

Items 52 and 53 are based on the following information:

    One major category of computer viruses is programs that attach themselves to other programs, thus infecting the other programs. While many of these viruses are relatively harmless, some have the potential to cause significant damage.

52. Which of the following is an indication that a computer virus of this category is present?

   a.   Frequent power surges that harm computer equipment.

   b.   Unexplainable losses of or changes to data.
   c.   Inadequate backup, recovery, and contingency plans.
   d.   Numerous copyright violations due to unauthorized use of purchased software.

53. Which of the following operating procedures increases an organization's exposure to computer viruses?

   a.   Encryption of data files.
   b.   Frequent backup of files.
   c.   Downloading public-domain software from electronic bulletin boards.
   d.   Installing original copies of purchased software on hard disk drives.

54. Which of the following is a risk that is higher when an electronic funds transfer (EFT) system is used?

   a.   Improper change control procedures.
   b.   Unauthorized access and activity.
   c.   Insufficient online edit checks.
   d.   Inadequate backups and disaster recovery procedures.

55. The use of message encryption software

   a.   Guarantees the secrecy of data.
   b.   Requires manual distribution of keys.
   c.   Increases system overhead.
   d.   Reduces the need for periodic password changes.

**56. A company's management is concerned about computer data eavesdropping and wants to maintain the confidentiality of its information as it is transmitted. The company should utilize

   a.   Data encryption.
   b.   Dial-back systems.
   c.   Message acknowledgement procedures.
   d.   Password codes.

57. Which of the following is likely to be a benefit of electronic data interchange (EDI)?

   a.   Increased transmission speed of actual documents.
   b.   Improved business relationships with trading partners.
   c.   Decreased liability related to protection of proprietary business data.
   d.   Decreased requirements for backup and contingency planning.

58. The internal auditor is reviewing a new policy on electronic mail. Appropriate elements of such a policy would include all of the following **except:**

   a.   Erasing all employee's electronic mail immediately upon employment termination.
   b.   Encrypting electronic mail messages when transmitted over phone lines.
   c.   Limiting the number of electronic mail packages adopted by the organization.
   d.   Directing that personnel do not send highly sensitive or confidential messages using electronic mail.

59. Which of the following risks is more likely to be encountered in an end-user computing (EUC) environment as compared to a mainframe computer system?

   a.   Inability to afford adequate uninterruptible power supply systems.
   b.   User input screens without a graphical user interface (GUI).

** *CMA adapted*

c. Applications that are difficult to integrate with other information systems.

d. Lack of adequate utility programs.

60. Which of the following risks is **not** greater in an electronic funds transfer (EFT) environment than in a manual system using paper transactions?

a. Unauthorized access and activity.

b. Duplicate transaction processing.

c. Higher cost per transaction.

d. Inadequate backup and recovery capabilities.

61. Methods to minimize the installation of unlicensed microcomputer software include all of the following **except:**

a. Employee awareness programs.

b. Regular audits for unlicensed software.

c. Regular monitoring of network access and start-up scripts.

d. An organizational policy that includes software licensing requirements.

62. In traditional information systems, computer operators are generally responsible for backing up software and data files on a regular basis. In distributed or cooperative systems, ensuring that adequate backups are taken is the responsibility of

a. User management.

b. Systems programmers.

c. Data entry clerks.

d. Tape librarians.

63. An auditor is least likely to find that a client's data is input through

a. Magnetic tape reader.

b. Dynamic linking character reader.

c. Point-of-sale recorders.

d. Touch sensitive screens.

64. End-user computing is an example of which of the following?

a. Client/server processing.

b. A distributed system.

c. Data mining.

d. Decentralized processing.

65. End-user computing is most likely to occur on which of the following types of computers?

a. Mainframe.

b. Minicomputers.

c. Personal computers.

d. Personal reference assistants.

66. Which of the following statements is correct regarding the Internet as a commercially viable network?

a. Organizations must use firewalls if they wish to maintain security over internal data.

b. Companies must apply to the Internet to gain permission to create a homepage to engage in electronic commerce.

c. Companies that wish to engage in electronic commerce on the Internet must meet required security standards established by the coalition of Internet providers.

d. All of the above.

67. To reduce security exposure when transmitting proprietary data over communication lines, a company should use

a. Asynchronous modems.

b. Authentic techniques.

c. Call-back procedures.

d. Cryptographic devices.

68. Securing client/server systems is a complex task because of all of the following factors **except:**

a. The use of relational databases.

b. The number of access points.

c. Concurrent operation of multiple user sessions.

d. Widespread data access and update capabilities.

69. Which of the following would an auditor ordinarily consider the greatest risk regarding an entity's use of electronic data interchange (EDI)?

a. Authorization of EDI transactions.

b. Duplication of EDI transmissions.

c. Improper distribution of EDI transactions.

d. Elimination of paper documents.

70. Which of the following characteristics distinguish electronic data interchange (EDI) from other forms of electronic commerce?

a. The cost of sending EDI transactions using a value-added network (VAN) is less than the cost of using the Internet.

b. Software maintenance contracts are unnecessary because translation software for EDI transactions need not be updated.

c. EDI commerce is ordinarily conducted without establishing legally binding contracts between trading partners.

d. EDI transactions are formatted using strict standards that have been agreed to worldwide.

71. Which of the following is considered a component of a local area network?

a. Program flowchart.

b. Loop verification.

c. Transmission media.

d. Input routine.

72. Which of the following represents an additional cost of transmitting business transactions by means of electronic data interchange (EDI) rather than in a traditional paper environment?

a. Redundant data checks are needed to verify that individual EDI transactions are **not** recorded twice.

b. Internal audit work is needed because the potential for random data entry errors is increased.

c. Translation software is needed to convert transactions from the entity's internal format to a standard EDI format.

d. More supervisory personnel are needed because the amount of data entry is greater in an EDI system.

73. Many entities use the Internet as a network to transmit electronic data interchange (EDI) transactions. An advantage of using the Internet for electronic commerce rather than a traditional value-added network (VAN) is that the Internet

a. Permits EDI transactions to be sent to trading partners as transactions occur.

b. Automatically batches EDI transactions to multiple trading partners.

c.   Possesses superior characteristics regarding disaster recovery.

d.   Converts EDI transactions to a standard format without translation software.

74. Which of the following is not considered an exposure involved with electronic data interchange (EDI) systems as compared to other systems?

a.   Increased reliance upon computer systems.

b.   Delayed transaction processing time.

c.   Possible loss of confidentiality of information.

d.   Increased reliance upon third parties.

75. Which of the following statements is correct concerning internal control when a client is using an electronic data interchange system for its sales?

a.   Controls should be established over determining that all suppliers are included in the system.

b.   Encryption controls may help to assure that messages are unreadable to unauthorized persons.

c.   A value-added-network (VAN) must be used to assure proper control.

d.   Attention must be paid to both the electronic and "paper" versions of transactions.

76. Which of the following statements most likely represents a disadvantage for an entity that keeps microcomputer-prepared data files rather than manually prepared files?

a.   Random error associated with processing similar transactions in different ways is usually greater.

b.   It is usually more difficult to compare recorded accountability with physical count of assets.

c.   Attention is focused on the accuracy of the programming process rather than errors in individual transactions.

d.   It is usually easier for unauthorized persons to access and alter the files.

77. Which of the following is usually a benefit of transmitting transactions in an electronic data interchange (EDI) environment?

a.   A compressed business cycle with lower year-end receivables balances.

b.   A reduced need to test computer controls related to sales and collections transactions.

c.   An increased opportunity to apply statistical sampling techniques to account balances.

d.   No need to rely on third-party service providers to ensure security.

78. Which of the following is a network node that is used to improve network traffic and to set up as a boundary that prevents traffic from one segment to cross over to another?

a.   Router.

b.   Gateway.

c.   Firewall.

d.   Heuristic.

79. Which of the following is an example of how specific controls in a database environment may differ from controls in a nondatabase environment?

a.   Controls should exist to ensure that users have access to and can update only the data elements that they have been authorized to access.

b.   Controls over data sharing by diverse users within an entity should be the same for every user.

c.   The employee who manages the computer hardware should also develop and debug the computer programs.

d.   Controls can provide assurance that all processed transactions are authorized, but **cannot** verify that all authorized transactions are processed.

80. A retail entity uses electronic data interchange (EDI) in executing and recording most of its purchase transactions. The entity's auditor recognized that the documentation of the transactions will be retained for only a short period of time. To compensate for this limitation, the auditor most likely would

a.   Increase the sample of EDI transactions to be selected for cutoff tests.

b.   Perform tests several times during the year, rather than only at year-end.

c.   Plan to make a 100% count of the entity's inventory at or near the year-end.

d.   Decrease the assessed level of control risk for the existence or occurrence assertion.

81. Which of the following is an encryption feature that can be used to authenticate the originator of a document and ensure that the message is intact and has **not** been tampered with?

a.   Heuristic terminal.

b.   Perimeter switch.

c.   Default settings.

d.   Digital signatures.

82. In building an electronic data interchange (EDI) system, what process is used to determine which elements in the entity's computer system correspond to the standard data elements?

a.   Mapping.

b.   Translation.

c.   Encryption.

d.   Decoding.

83. Which of the following passwords would be most difficult to crack?

a.   OrCa!FlSi

b.   language

c.   12 HOUSE 24

d.   pass56word

84. Which of the following is a password security problem?

a.   Users are assigned passwords when accounts are created, but do **not** change them.

b.   Users have accounts on several systems with different passwords.

c.   Users copy their passwords on note paper, which is kept in their wallets.

d.   Users select passwords that are **not** listed in any online dictionary.

85. Which of the following procedures would an entity most likely include in its computer disaster recovery plan?

a.   Develop an auxiliary power supply to provide uninterrupted electricity.

b.   Store duplicate copies of critical files in a location away from the computer center.

c.   Maintain a listing of entity passwords with the network manager.

d.   Translate data for storage purposes with a cryptographic secret code.

86. A company is concerned that a power outage or disaster could impair the computer hardware's ability to function as designed. The company desires off-site backup hardware facilities that are fully configured and ready to operate within several hours. The company most likely should consider a

a.   Cold site.
b.   Cool site.
c.   Warm site.
d.   Hot site.

87. Which of the following procedures would an entity most likely include in its disaster recovery plan?

a.   Convert all data from EDI format to an internal company format.
b.   Maintain a Trojan horse program to prevent illicit activity.
c.   Develop an auxiliary power supply to provide uninterrupted electricity.
d.   Store duplicate copies of files in a location away from the computer center.

88. Almost all commercially marketed software is

	Copyrighted	*Copy protected*
a.	Yes	Yes
b.	Yes	No
c.	No	Yes
d.	No	No

89. A widely used disaster recovery approach includes

a.   Encryption.
b.   Firewalls.
c.   Regular backups.
d.   Surge protectors.

90. A "hot site" is most frequently associated with

a.   Disaster recovery.
b.   Online relational database design.
c.   Source programs.
d.   Temperature control for computer.

91. Output controls ensure that the results of computer processing are accurate, complete, and properly distributed. Which of the following is **not** a typical output control?

a.   Reviewing the computer processing logs to determine that all of the correct computer jobs executed properly.
b.   Matching input data with information on master files and placing unmatched items in a suspense file.
c.   Periodically reconciling output reports to make sure that totals, formats, and critical details are correct and agree with input.
d.   Maintaining formal procedures and documentation specifying authorized recipients of output reports, checks, or other critical documents.

92. Minimizing the likelihood of unauthorized editing of production programs, job control language, and operating system software can best be accomplished by

a.   Database access reviews.
b.   Compliance reviews.
c.   Good change-control procedures.
d.   Effective network security software.

93. Some companies have replaced mainframe computers with microcomputers and networks because the smaller computers could do the same work at less cost. Assuming that management of a company decided to launch a downsizing project, what should be done with respect to mainframe applications such as the general ledger system?

a.   Plan for rapid conversion of all mainframe applications to run on a microcomputer network.
b.   Consider the general ledger system as an initial candidate for conversion.
c.   Defer any modification of the general ledger system until it is clearly inadequate.
d.   Integrate downsized applications with stable mainframe applications.

94. A corporation receives the majority of its revenue from top-secret military contracts with the government. Which of the following would be of greatest concern to an auditor reviewing a policy about selling the company's used microcomputers to outside parties?

a.   Whether deleted files on the hard disk drive have been completely erased.
b.   Whether the computer has viruses.
c.   Whether all software on the computer is properly licensed.
d.   Whether the computer has terminal emulation software on it.

95. A manufacturer is considering using bar-code identification for recording information on parts used by the manufacturer. A reason to use bar codes rather than other means of identification is to ensure that

a.   The movement of all parts is recorded.
b.   The movement of parts is easily and quickly recorded.
c.   Vendors use the same part numbers.
d.   Vendors use the same identification methods.

96. A company often revises its production processes. The changes may entail revisions to processing programs. Ensuring that changes have a minimal impact on processing and result in minimal risk to the system is a function of

a.   Security administration.
b.   Change control.
c.   Problem tracking.
d.   Problem-escalation procedures.

97. Pirated software obtained through the Internet may lead to civil lawsuits or criminal prosecution. Of the following, which would reduce an organization's risk in this area?

  I. Maintain a log of all software purchases.
 II. Audit individual computers to identify software on the computers.
III. Establish a corporate software policy.
IV. Provide original software diskettes to each user.

a.   I and IV only.
b.   I, II, and III only.
c.   II and IV only.
d.   II and III only.

98. Good planning will help an organization restore computer operations after a processing outage. Good recovery planning should ensure that

a.   Backup/restart procedures have been built into job streams and programs.

b.   Change control procedures cannot be bypassed by operating personnel.
c.   Planned changes in equipment capacities are compatible with projected workloads.
d.   Service level agreements with owners of applications are documented.

99.   In a large organization, the biggest risk in not having an adequately staffed information center help desk is
a.   Increased difficulty in performing application audits.
b.   Inadequate documentation for application systems.
c.   Increased likelihood of use of unauthorized program code.
d.   Persistent errors in user interaction with systems.

100.   To properly control access to accounting database files, the database administrator should ensure that database system features are in place to permit
a.   Read-only access to the database files.
b.   Updating from privileged utilities.
c.   Access only to authorized logical views.
d.   User updates of their access profiles.

101.   When evaluating internal control of an entity that processes sales transactions on the Internet, an auditor would be most concerned about the
a.   Lack of sales invoice documents as an audit trail.
b.   Potential for computer disruptions in recording sales.
c.   Inability to establish an integrated test facility.
d.   Frequency of archiving and data retention.

102.   Which of the following statements is correct concerning internal control in an electronic data interchange (EDI) system?
a.   Preventive controls generally are more important than detective controls in EDI systems.
b.   Control objectives for EDI systems generally are different from the objectives for other information systems.
c.   Internal controls in EDI systems rarely permit control risk to be assessed at below the maximum.
d.   Internal controls related to the segregation of duties generally are the most important controls in EDI systems.

103.   Which of the following statements is correct concerning the security of messages in an electronic data interchange (EDI) system?
a.   When the confidentiality of data is the primary risk, message authentication is the preferred control rather than encryption.
b.   Encryption performed by physically secure hardware devices is more secure than encryption performed by software.
c.   Message authentication in EDI systems performs the same function as segregation of duties in other information systems.
d.   Security at the transaction phase in EDI systems is **not** necessary because problems at that level will usually be identified by the service provider.

104.   Which of the following is an essential element of the audit trail in an electronic data interchange (EDI) system?
a.   Disaster recovery plans that ensure proper backup of files.

b.   Encrypted hash totals that authenticate messages.
c.   Activity logs that indicate failed transactions.
d.   Hardware security modules that store sensitive data.

105.   Which of the following are essential elements of the audit trail in an electronic data interchange (EDI) system?
a.   Network and sender/recipient acknowledgments.
b.   Message directories and header segments.
c.   Contingency and disaster recovery plans.
d.   Trading partner security and mailbox codes.

106.   To avoid invalid data input, a bank added an extra number at the end of each account number and subjected the new number to an algorithm. This technique is known as
a.   Optical character recognition.
b.   A check digit.
c.   A dependency check.
d.   A format check.

107.   Preventing someone with sufficient technical skill from circumventing security procedures and making changes to production programs is best accomplished by
a.   Reviewing reports of jobs completed.
b.   Comparing production programs with independently controlled copies.
c.   Running test data periodically.
d.   Providing suitable segregation of duties.

108.   Computer program libraries can best be kept secure by
a.   Installing a logging system for program access.
b.   Monitoring physical access to program library media.
c.   Restricting physical and logical access.
d.   Denying access from remote terminals.

109.   Which of the following security controls would best prevent unauthorized access to sensitive data through an unattended data terminal directly connected to a mainframe?
a.   Use of a screen saver with a password.
b.   Use of workstation scripts.
c.   Encryption of data files.
d.   Automatic log-off of inactive users.

110.   An entity has the following invoices in a batch:

Invoice #	Product	Quantity	Unit price
201	F10	150	$ 5.00
202	G15	200	$10.00
203	H20	250	$25.00
204	K35	300	$30.00

Which of the following most likely represents a hash total?
a.   FGHK80
b.   4
c.   204
d.   810

111.   A customer intended to order 100 units of product Z96014, but incorrectly ordered nonexistent product Z96015. Which of the following controls most likely would detect this error?
a.   Check digit verification.
b.   Record count.
c.   Hash total.
d.   Redundant data check.

112. In entering the billing address for a new client in Emil Company's computerized database, a clerk erroneously entered a nonexistent zip code. As a result, the first month's bill mailed to the new client was returned to Emil Company. Which one of the following would **most likely have led to discovery of the error at the time of entry into Emil Company's computerized database?
    a. Limit test.
    b. Validity test.
    c. Parity test.
    d. Record count test.

113. Which of the following controls is a processing control designed to ensure the reliability and accuracy of data processing?

	Limit test	*Validity check test*
a.	Yes	Yes
b.	No	No
c.	No	Yes
d.	Yes	No

114. Which of the following activities would most likely be performed in the information systems department?
    a. Initiation of changes to master records.
    b. Conversion of information to machine-readable form.
    c. Correction of transactional errors.
    d. Initiation of changes to existing applications.

115. The use of a header label in conjunction with magnetic tape is **most** likely to prevent errors by the
    a. Computer operator.
    b. Keypunch operator.
    c. Computer programmer.
    d. Maintenance technician.

116. For the accounting system of Acme Company, the amounts of cash disbursements entered into a terminal are transmitted to the computer that immediately transmits the amounts back to the terminal for display on the terminal screen. This display enables the operator to
    a. Establish the validity of the account number.
    b. Verify the amount was entered accurately.
    c. Verify the authorization of the disbursement.
    d. Prevent the overpayment of the account.

117. When computer programs or files can be accessed from terminals, users should be required to enter a(n)
    a. Parity check.
    b. Personal identification code.
    c. Self-diagnosis test.
    d. Echo check.

118. The possibility of erasing a large amount of information stored on magnetic tape most likely would be reduced by the use of
    a. File protection rings.
    b. Check digits.
    c. Completeness tests.
    d. Conversion verification.

119. Which of the following controls most likely would assure that an entity can reconstruct its financial records?
    a. Hardware controls are built into the computer by the computer manufacturer.

    b. Backup diskettes or tapes of files are stored away from originals.
    c. Personnel who are independent of data input perform parallel simulations.
    d. System flowcharts provide accurate descriptions of input and output operations.

120. Which of the following input controls is a numeric value computed to provide assurance that the original value has **not** been altered in construction or transmission?
    a. Hash total.
    b. Parity check.
    c. Encryption.
    d. Check digit.

121. Which of the following is an example of a validity check?
    a. The computer ensures that a numerical amount in a record does **not** exceed some predetermined amount.
    b. As the computer corrects errors and data are successfully resubmitted to the system, the causes of the errors are printed out.
    c. The computer flags any transmission for which the control field value did **not** match that of an existing file record.
    d. After data for a transaction are entered, the computer sends certain data back to the terminal for comparison with data originally sent.

122. Which of the following is a computer test made to ascertain whether a given characteristic belongs to the group?
    a. Parity check.
    b. Validity check.
    c. Echo check.
    d. Limit check.

123. A control feature in an electronic data processing system requires the central processing unit (CPU) to send signals to the printer to activate the print mechanism for each character. The print mechanism, just prior to printing, sends a signal back to the CPU verifying that the proper print position has been activated. This type of hardware control is referred to as
    a. Echo control.
    b. Validity control.
    c. Signal control.
    d. Check digit control.

124. Which of the following is an example of a check digit?
    a. An agreement of the total number of employees to the total number of checks printed by the computer.
    b. An algebraically determined number produced by the other digits of the employee number.
    c. A logic test that ensures all employee numbers are nine digits.
    d. A limit check that an employee's hours do not exceed fifty hours per workweek.

125. Which of the following most likely represents a significant deficiency in internal control?
    a. The systems analyst reviews applications of data processing and maintains systems documentation.
    b. The systems programmer designs systems for computerized applications and maintains output controls.

    c.   The control clerk establishes control over data received by the information systems department and reconciles control totals after processing.

    d.   The accounts payable clerk prepares data for computer processing and enters the data into the computer.

126.   Internal control is ineffective when computer department personnel

    a.   Participate in computer software acquisition decisions.

    b.   Design documentation for computerized systems.

    c.   Originate changes in master files.

    d.   Provide physical security for program files.

127.   Which of the following activities most likely would detect whether payroll data were altered during processing?

    a.   Monitor authorized distribution of data control sheets.

    b.   Use test data to verify the performance of edit routines.

    c.   Examine source documents for approval by supervisors.

    d.   Segregate duties between approval of hardware and software specifications.

128.   Which of the following tools would best give a graphical representation of a sequence of activities and decisions?

    a.   Flowchart.

    b.   Control chart.

    c.   Histogram.

    d.   Run chart.

Items 129 and 130 are based on the following flowchart of a client's revenue cycle:

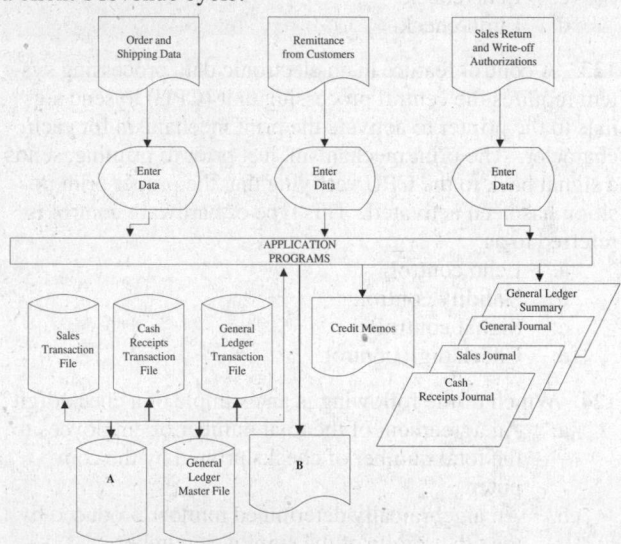

129.   Symbol A most likely represents

    a.   Remittance advice file.

    b.   Receiving report file.

    c.   Accounts receivable master file.

    d.   Cash disbursements transaction file.

130.   Symbol B most likely represents

    a.   Customer orders.

    b.   Receiving reports.

    c.   Customer checks.

    d.   Sales invoices.

131.   An auditor's flowchart of a client's accounting system is a diagrammatic representation that depicts the auditor's

    a.   Assessment of control risk.

    b.   Identification of weaknesses in the system.

    c.   Assessment of the control environment's effectiveness.

    d.   Understanding of the system.

Item 132 is based on the following flowchart:

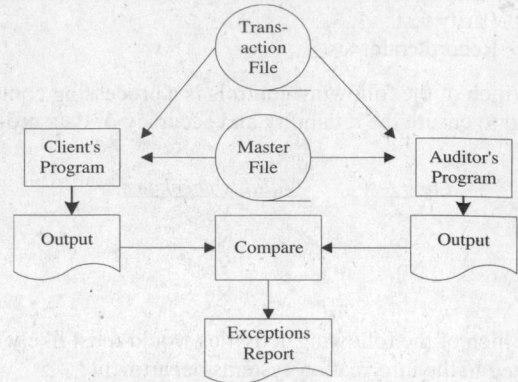

132.   The above flowchart depicts

    a.   Program code checking.

    b.   Parallel simulation.

    c.   Integrated test facility.

    d.   Controlled reprocessing.

Item 133 is based on the following flowchart:

133.   In a credit sales and cash receipts system flowchart, symbol X could represent

    a.   Auditor's test data.

    b.   Remittance advices.

    c.   Error reports.

    d.   Credit authorization forms.

134.   Which of the following symbolic representations indicate that a file has been consulted?

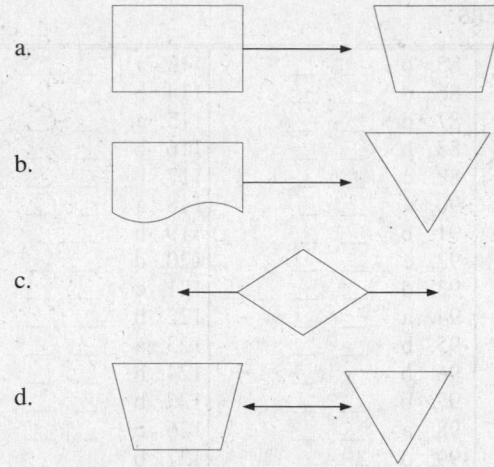

a.

b.

c.

d.

135. A well-prepared flowchart should make it easier for the auditor to

a. Prepare audit procedure manuals.
b. Prepare detailed job descriptions.
c. Trace the origin and disposition of documents.
d. Assess the degree of accuracy of financial data.

MULTIPLE-CHOICE ANSWERS

1. b		29. a		57. b		85. b		113. a	
2. a		30. a		58. a		86. d		114. b	
3. b		31. d		59. c		87. d		115. a	
4. c		32. c		60. c		88. b		116. b	
5. b		33. c		61. c		89. c		117. b	
6. d		34. d		62. a		90. a		118. a	
7. d		35. b		63. b		91. b		119. b	
8. b		36. a		64. d		92. c		120. d	
9. a		37. a		65. c		93. d		121. c	
10. a		38. d		66. a		94. a		122. b	
11. a		39. c		67. d		95. b		123. a	
12. c		40. d		68. a		96. b		124. b	
13. b		41. d		69. c		97. b		125. b	
14. b		42. b		70. d		98. a		126. c	
15. a		43. c		71. c		99. d		127. b	
16. d		44. a		72. c		100. c		128. a	
17. b		45. c		73. a		101. b		129. c	
18. a		46. c		74. b		102. a		130. d	
19. a		47. d		75. b		103. b		131. d	
20. b		48. b		76. d		104. c		132. b	
21. d		49. c		77. a		105. a		133. b	
22. b		50. b		78. c		106. b		134. d	
23. b		51. c		79. a		107. d		135. c	
24. a		52. b		80. b		108. c			
25. a		53. c		81. d		109. d			
26. d		54. b		82. a		110. d			
27. d		55. c		83. a		111. a		1st: __/135 __%	
28. c		56. a		84. a		112. b		2nd: __/135 __%	

MULTIPLE-CHOICE ANSWER EXPLANATIONS

A. Information Systems within a Business

1. **(b)** The requirement is to identify a type of software package that uses a large set of organized data that presents the computer as an expert on a particular topic. Answer (b) is correct because an expert system presents the computer as such an expert. Answer (a) is incorrect because data mining uses tools which look for trends or anomalies without advance knowledge of the meaning of the data. Answer (c) is incorrect because artificial intelligence is a branch of computer science that involves computer programs that can solve specific problems creatively. Answer (d) is incorrect because virtual reality involves computer creation of an artificial, three-dimension world that may be interacted with.

2. **(a)** The requirement is to identify the type of computer memory used to store programs that must be accessed immediately by the central processing unit. Answer (a) is correct because primary memory is quickly accessed and generally used to store programs that must be accessed immediately. Answer (b) is incorrect because secondary storage is accessed less quickly. Answer (c) is incorrect because the term tertiary storage has no meaning in information technology. Answer (d) is incorrect because tape storage requires relatively long access times.

3. **(b)** The requirement is to identify the most common output device. Answer (b) is correct because a printer is a common output device and because the other replies represent input, not output devices.

4. **(c)** The requirement is to identify the part of the computer that does most of the data processing. Answer (c) is correct because the CPU, the central processing unit, does

the primary processing for a computer. Answer (a) is incorrect because the word "analyter" has no meaning in information technology. Answer (b) is incorrect because a compiler is used to compile a particular type of computer program. Answer (d) is incorrect because a printer is an output device.

5. **(b)** The requirement is to identify the software least likely to be included in an "office suite" of software. Answer (b), operating systems (e.g., Windows, Linux, Unix) is not ordinarily included in an office suite. Answers (a), (c) and (d) are all incorrect because databases, spreadsheets, and word processing software are often included.

6. **(d)** The requirement is to identify the software that performs a variety of technical operations. Answer (d) is correct because an operating system controls the execution of computer programs and may provide various services. Answer (a) is incorrect because an integrated "suite" (e.g., Microsoft Office) is a series of applications such as a word processor, database, and spreadsheet. Answer (b) is incorrect because shareware is generally considered to be software made available at a low, or no, cost to users. Answer (c) is incorrect because a database system deals with more specific technical processing.

7. **(d)** The requirement is to identify the part listed that is not considered a part of the central processing unit. Answer (d) is correct because the printer is a separate output device. Answers (a), (b), and (c) are all incorrect because a computer includes control, arithmetic, and logic units.

8. **(b)** The requirement is to identify the meaning of MIPS. Answer (b) is correct because MIPS is an abbreviation for millions of instructions per second, a unit for measuring the execution speed of computers. Answers (a), (c), and (d) all include combinations of words with no particular meaning in information technology.

9. (a) The requirement is to identify the type of applications software that a large client is most likely to use. Answer (a) is correct because enterprise resource planning (ERP) software is a form of applications software that provides relatively complete information systems for large and medium size organizations. Answer (b) is incorrect because a computer operating system is considered systems software, not applications software. Answer (c) is incorrect because the central processing unit is the principal hardware component of a computer, not software. Answer (d) is incorrect because a value-added network is a privately owned network whose services are sold to the public.

10. (a) The requirement is to identify a characteristic that distinguishes computer processing from manual processing. Answer (a) is correct because the high degree of accuracy of computer computation virtually eliminates the occurrence of computational errors. Answer (b) is incorrect because errors or fraud in computer processing may or may not be detected, depending upon the effectiveness of an entity's internal control. Answer (c) is incorrect because a programming error will result in a high level of systematic error in a computerized system and therefore, such errors may occur in either a manual or a computerized system. Answer (d) is incorrect because most computer systems are designed to include transaction trails.

B. Characteristics of Computer Systems—General

11. (a) The requirement is to identify the most frequently used mainframe computer application. Answer (a) is correct because mainframe computers (the largest and most powerful computers available at a particular point in time) are generally used to store and process extremely large computer databases. Answers (b), (c), and (d) are all incorrect because they are less frequent mainframe computer applications.

12. (c) The requirement is to identify the computer application most frequently used to analyze numbers and financial information. Answer (c) is correct because the purpose of a spreadsheet is generally to process numbers and financial information; for example, spreadsheets are often used to perform "what if" analysis which makes various assumptions with respect to a particular situation. Answer (a) is incorrect because while computer graphics programs may present numbers and financial information, they do not in general process them to the extent of spreadsheets. Answer (b) is incorrect because a WAN is a wide area network, and not an application used to analyze numbers and financial information. Answer (d) is incorrect because the emphasis of word processing programs is not ordinarily on processing numbers and financial information.

13. (b) The requirement is to identify the type of analysis that uses a database and tools to look for trends or anomalies, without knowledge in advance of the meaning of the data. Answer (b) is correct because data mining uses tools which look for trends or anomalies without such advance knowledge. Answer (a) is incorrect because artificial intelligence is a branch of computer science that involves computer programs that can solve specific problems crea-

tively. Answer (c) is incorrect because virtual reality involves computer creation of an artificial, three-dimension world that may be interacted with. Answer (d) is incorrect because the term transitory analysis has no meaning relating to information technology.

14. (b) The requirement is to identify the most common type of primary storage in a computer. Answer (b) is correct because RAM (Random Access Memory) is the most common computer memory which can be used by programs to perform necessary tasks; RAM allows information to be stored or accessed in any order and all storage locations are equally accessible. Answer (a) is incorrect because CMAN has no meaning in information technology. Answer (c) is incorrect because ROM (Read Only Memory) is memory whose contents can be accessed and read but cannot be changed. Answer (d) is incorrect because it is a nonvolatile storage that can be electrically erased and programmed anew that is less common than RAM.

15. (a) The requirement is to identify a set of step-by-step procedures that are used to accomplish a task. Answer (a) is correct because an algorithm uses a step-by-step approach to accomplish a task. Answer (b) is incorrect because the term "compilation master" has no meaning in information technology. Answer (c) is incorrect because Linux is a form of operating system. Answer (d) is incorrect because the term "transitor" has no meaning in information technology.

16. (d) The requirement is to identify the item that compiles a complex translation of a program in a high-level computer language before the program is run for the first time. Answer (d) is correct because a compiler decodes instructions written in a higher order language and produces an assembly language program. Answers (a) and (b) are incorrect because Visual Basic and JAVA are programming languages. Answer (c) is incorrect because an algorithm is a "step-by-step" approach used to accomplish a particular task.

17. (b) The requirement is to identify the meaning of the abbreviation GUI. Answer (b), graphical user interface, is correct. The other replies all represent combinations of words with no meaning in information technology.

18. (a) The requirement is to identify the nature of Unix. Answer (a) is correct because Unix is a powerful operating system, originally developed by AT&T Bell Labs, that is used by many users of high-end computing hardware. Answers (b), (c), and (d) are all incorrect because Unix is not a singular disk drive, a central processing unit, or a logic unit.

19. (a) The requirement is to identify how each specific cell within a spreadsheet is identified. Answer (a) is correct because each cell has an address, composed of a combination of its column and row in the spreadsheet. Answer (b) is incorrect because the column portion of the address is not specific to the cell. Answer (c) is incorrect because the row portion of the address is not specific to the cell. Answer (d) is incorrect because no diagonal is ordinarily used to identify a particular cell.

20. (b) The requirement is to identify whether rows and columns of a spreadsheet are numbered or lettered. Answer (b) is correct because rows are numbered and columns are lettered. The other replies are all incorrect because they include incorrect combinations of "numbered" and "lettered."

21.   (d)   The requirement is to identify what is **least** likely to be considered an advantage of a database. Answer (d) is correct because a database itself does not make it easy to distribute information to every possible user— information must still be distributed either electronically or physically. Answer (a) is incorrect because a database is used to store large quantities of information. Answer (b) is incorrect because information may ordinarily be required quickly from a database. Answer (c) is incorrect because specific normalization rules have been identified for organizing information within a database.

22.   (b)   The requirement is to identify the most frequent current format for computer processing of data. Answer (b) is correct because most current computers process data using a digital approach in that they represent information by numerical (binary) digits. Answer (a) is incorrect because analog computers, which represent information by variable quantities (e.g., positions or voltages), are less frequent in practice than digital computers. Answer (c) is incorrect because "memory enhanced" is not a format for processing information. Answer (d) is incorrect because "organic" is not a format for processing information.

23.   (b)   The requirement is to identify the generation of programming language most likely to include an instruction such as "*Extract all Customers where 'Name' is Smith.*" Answer (b) is correct because fourth generation programs ordinarily include instructions relatively close to human languages—such as the instruction in this question. Answer (a) is incorrect because first generation instructions are in terms of "1's" and "0's." Answers (c) and (d) are incorrect because seventh and ninth generation programming languages have not yet been developed (a few fifth generation languages with extensive visual and graphic interfaces are currently in process).

24.   (a)   The requirement is to identify the language interface used to establish the structure of database tables. Answer (a) is correct because DDL is used to define (i.e., determine) the database. Answer (b) is incorrect because DCL is used to specify privileges and security rules. Answer (c) is incorrect because DML provides programmers with a facility to update the database. Answer (d) is incorrect because DQL is used for ad hoc queries.

25.   (a)   The requirement is to identify the function used in a database query to combine several tables. Answer (a) is correct because joining is the combining of one or more tables based on matching criteria. For example, if a supplier table contains information about suppliers and a parts table contains information about parts, the two tables could be joined on supplier number (assuming both tables contained this attribute) to give information about the supplier of particular parts. Answers (b), (c), and (d) are all incorrect.

26.   (d)   The requirement is to identify a reason that user acceptance testing is more important in an object-oriented development process than in a traditional environment. Answer (d) is correct because user acceptance testing is more important in object-oriented development because of the fact that all objects in a class inherit the properties of the hierarchy, which means that changes to one object may affect other objects, which increases the importance of user acceptance testing to verify correct functioning of the whole system. Answer (a) is incorrect because instead of traditional design documents, items such as the business model, narratives of process functions, iterative development screens, computer processes and reports, and product descriptions guides are produced in object-oriented development, but the existence of specific documents does not affect the importance of user acceptance testing. Answer (b) is incorrect because in general, object-oriented development systems do include tracking systems for changes made to objects and hierarchies. Answer (c) is incorrect; because object-oriented systems are usually developed in client/ server environments there is the potential for continuous monitoring of system use, but continuous monitoring typically occurs during system operation, not during development.

27.   (d)   The requirement is to identify the reply that does not represent a potential security and control concern. Answer (d) is correct because the distribution of data actually decreases this risk so this would not cause a control concern; it is a potential advantage to distributed systems of various architectures versus centralized data in a single mainframe computer. Answer (a) is incorrect because password proliferation is a considerable security concern because users will be tempted to write their passwords down or make them overly simplistic. Answer (b) is incorrect because consistent security across varied platforms is often challenging because of the different security features of the various systems and the decentralized nature of those controlling security administration. Answer (c) is incorrect because under centralized control, management can feel more confident that backup file storage is being uniformly controlled. Decentralization of this function may lead to lack of consistency and difficulty in monitoring compliance.

28.   (c)   The requirement is to determine which answer is not a method for distributing a relational database across multiple servers. Answer (c) is correct because normalization is a process of database design, not distribution. Answer (a) is incorrect because making a copy of the database for distribution is a viable method for the described distribution. Answer (b) is incorrect because creating and maintaining replica copies at multiple locations is a viable method for the described distribution. Answer (d) is incorrect because separating the database into parts and distributing where they are needed is a viable method for the described distribution.

29.   (a)   The requirement is to identify the best way to protect a client/server system from unauthorized access. Answer (a) is correct because since there is no perfect solution, this is the best way. Answer (b) is incorrect because authentication systems, such as Kerberos, are only a part of the solution. Answer (c) is incorrect because this only affects general access control techniques. Answer (d) is incorrect because testing and evaluation of remote procedure calls may be a small part of an overall security review.

30.   (a)   The requirement is to identify the technology needed to convert a paper document into a computer file. Answer (a) is correct because optical character recognition (OCR) software converts images of paper documents, as read by a scanning device, into text document computer files. Answer (b) is incorrect because electronic data interchange involves electronic transactions between trading partners. Answer (c) is incorrect because bar-code scanning reads price and item information, but does not convert a paper document into a computer file. Answer (d) is incorrect because joining and merging are processes applied to computer files.

31. **(d)** The requirement is to identify the best method for preventing unauthorized alteration of online records. Answer (d) is correct because users can gain access to databases from terminals only through established recognition and authorization procedures, thus unauthorized access is prevented. Answer (a) is incorrect because key verification ensures the accuracy of selected fields by requiring a second keying of them, ordinarily by another individual. Answer (b) is incorrect because sequence checks are used to ensure the completeness of input or update data by checking the use of preassigned document serial numbers. Answer (c) is incorrect because computer matching entails checking selected fields of input data with information held in a suspense master file.

32. **(c)** The requirement is to identify a way of eliminating thick paper manuals and reducing costs. Answer (c) is correct since a compact disc/read-only memory (CD-ROM) would be cheaper to produce and ship than the existing paper, yet would permit large volumes of text and images to be reproduced. Answer (a) is incorrect because write-once-read-many (WORM) is an optical storage technique often used as an archival medium. Answer (b) is incorrect because digital audio tape is primarily used as a backup medium in imaging systems and as a master for CD-ROM. Answer (d) is incorrect because computer-output-to-microform is used for frequent access to archived documents such as canceled checks in banking applications.

33. **(c)** The requirement is to identify a reason that misstatements in a batch computer system may **not** be detected immediately. Answer (c) is correct because batch programs are run periodically and thereby result in delays in processing; accordingly, detection of misstatements may be delayed. Answer (a) is incorrect because errors will be detected in the batch. Answer (b) is incorrect because the identification of errors in input data is typically included as a part of a batch program. Answer (d) is incorrect because a batch system will ordinarily process transactions in a uniform manner.

34. **(d)** The requirement is to determine which answer is **not** a characteristic of a batch processed computer system. Simultaneous posting to several files is most frequently related to an online real-time system, not a batch system. Answer (a) is incorrect since a batch system may process sequentially against a master file. Answer (b) is incorrect because keypunching is followed by machine processing in batch systems. Answer (c) is incorrect because the numerous batches ordinarily result in numerous printouts.

35. **(b)** The requirement is to identify the most likely direct output of an edit check included in an online sales order processing system. Edit checks are used to screen incoming data against established standards of validity, with data that pass all edit checks viewed as "valid" and then processed. Answer (b) is correct because an edit check will ordinarily create an output file of rejected transactions. Answer (a) is incorrect because sales invoices may not have

been prepared at the point of the sales order processing and because the answer is much less complete than answer (b). Answer (c) is incorrect because while periodic printouts of user code numbers and passwords should be prepared, this is not a primary purpose of an edit check. Answer (d) is incorrect because shipping documents will not ordinarily be prepared at this point and because the answer is much less complete than answer (b).

36. **(a)** The requirement is to determine a control which will strengthen an online real-time cash withdrawal system. Answer (a) is correct because documentation of all situations in which the "terminal audit key" has been used will improve the audit trail. Answer (b) is incorrect because increasing the dollar amount required for use of the key will simply reduce the number of times it is used (and allow larger withdrawals to be made without any required special authorization). Answer (c) is incorrect because there is no reason to believe that a manual system will be more effective than an online system. Answer (d) is incorrect because parallel simulation, running the data through alternate software, would seem to have no particular advantage for processing these large withdrawals.

37. **(a)** The requirement is to identify a direct output of a sorting, editing, and updating program. Answer (a) is correct because the program will output both exceptions and control totals to determine whether all transactions have been processed properly. Answers (b), (c), and (d) are all incorrect because while a program such as this may output such schedules, this will occur after exceptions are cleared and control totals are reconciled.

38. **(d)** The requirement is to determine why the grandfather-father-son updating backup concept is relatively difficult to implement for disk files. Answer (d) is correct because updating destroys the old records. Answer (a) is incorrect because the location of information points on disks is **not** an extremely time consuming task if the disks have been properly organized and maintained. Answer (b) is incorrect because off-site storage through disks is possible, though costly. Answer (c) is incorrect because information need not be dumped in the form of hard copy.

39. **(c)** The requirement is to determine the item which converts problem oriented language to machine language. A compiler produces a machine-language object program from a source-program (i.e., problem oriented) language. Answer (a) is incorrect because an interpreter is used to make punched cards easily readable to people. Answer (b) is incorrect because a verifier is used to test whether key punching errors exist on punched cards. Answer (d) is incorrect because a converter changes a program from one form of problem oriented language to another, related form (e.g., from one form of COBOL to another form of COBOL).

40. **(d)** The requirement is to determine the type of computer system characterized by more than one location and records that are updated immediately. Answer (d) is correct because online real-time systems typically allow access from multiple locations, and always have the immediate update of records. Answers (a) and (b) are incorrect because small computers often are limited to one location, and they may or may not allow immediate updating for particular applications. Answer (c) is incorrect because batch processing is a method which does not update records immediately (e.g., processing the "batch" of the firm's daily sales each evening, not at the moment they occur).

41. (a) The requirement is to identify a characteristic that distinguishes electronic data interchange (EDI) from other forms of electronic commerce. Answer (a) is correct because EDI transactions are ordinarily formatted using one of the available uniform worldwide sets of standards. Answer (b) is incorrect because, when financial statements are prepared, EDI transactions must follow generally accepted accounting principles. Answer (c) is incorrect because EDI transactions may or may not be processed using the Internet. Answer (d) is incorrect because security and privacy are considered when recording EDI transactions. See the Auditing Procedure Study *Audit Implications of EDI* for more information on electronic data interchange.

C. Characteristics of Computer Systems—Specific

42. (b) The requirement is to identify the meaning of the abbreviation LAN. Answer (b) is correct because LAN is the abbreviation for local area network. A local area network is a computer network for communication between computers. For example, a local area network may connect computers, word processors and other electronic office equipment to create a communication system within an office. Answers (a), (c) and (d) are all incorrect because they are combinations of words that have no specific meaning in information technology.

43. (c) The requirement is to identify the type of computer that is designed to provide software and other applications to other computers. Answer (c) is correct because a server provides other computers ("clients") with access to files and printers as shared resources to a computer network. Answer (a) is incorrect because a microcomputer is a small digital computer based on a microprocessor and designed to be used by one person at a time. Answer (b) is incorrect because a network computer is a low-cost personal computer for business networks that is configured with only essential equipment. Answer (d) is incorrect because a supercomputer is a mainframe computer that is one of the most powerful available at a given time.

44. (a) The requirement is to identify the item **least** likely to be considered a component of a computer network. Answer (a) is least likely because application program is a program that gives a computer instructions that provide the user with tools to accomplish a specific task (e.g., a word processing application) Answer (b) is incorrect because computers are an integral part of a computer network. Answer (c) is incorrect because software is required for operation of the network. Answer (d) is incorrect because routers are used to forward data within a computer network.

45. (c) The requirement is to identify the type of network used to link widely separated portions of an organization. Answer (c) is correct because a wide area network is used to span a wide geographical space to link together portions of an organization. Answer (a) is incorrect because a bulletin board is a computer that is running software that allows users to leave messages and access information of general interest. Answer (b) is incorrect because a local area network's coverage is restricted to a relatively small geographical area. Answer (d) is incorrect because the term "zero base network" has no meaning in information technology.

46. (c) The requirement is to identify a set of rules for exchanging data between two computers. Answer (c) is correct because a protocol is such a set of rules. Answer (a) is incorrect because the term "communicator" is very general and has no specific meaning in this context. Answer (b) is incorrect because while an operating system controls the execution of computer programs and may provide various services related to computers, it is not a set of rules for exchanging data. Answer (d) is incorrect because transmission speed is the speed at which computer processing occurs.

47. (d) The requirement is to identify the approach most frequently used to create a Web page. Answer (d) is correct because HTML (hypertext markup language) or XML (extensible markup language) are used to develop hypertext documents such as Web pages. Answers (a), (b), and (c) are all incorrect because while such tools may be used on Web page creation, they are not as fundamentally related as are HTML or XML.

48. (b) The requirement is to identify the reply that would provide the least security for sensitive data stored on a laptop computer. Answer (b) is correct because password protection for a screensaver program can be easily bypassed. Answer (a) is incorrect because data encryption provides adequate security for laptop computers. Answer (c) is incorrect because removable hard drives would provide adequate security. Answer (d) is incorrect because security is promoted by physically locking the laptop computer to an immovable object.

49. (c) The requirement is to identify the most likely procedure to be included in the high-level systems design phase of a computer system that will handle customer orders and process customer payments. Answer (c) is correct because the determination of what type of system to obtain is made during the high-level design phase. Answer (a) is incorrect because the effect of the new system would be part of the feasibility study. Answer (b) is incorrect because the file layouts are part of the detailed design phase. Answer (d) is incorrect because formal approval is made during the request for the systems design phase.

50. (b) The requirement is to identify the risk being controlled when a company using EDI makes it a practice to track the functional acknowledgments from trading partners. Answer (b) is correct because tracking of customers' functional acknowledgments, when required, will help to ensure successful transmission of EDI transactions. Answer (a) is incorrect because to address this issue, unauthorized access to the EDI system should be prevented, procedures should be in place to ensure the effective use of passwords, and data integrity and privacy should be maintained through the use of encryption and authentication measures. Answer (c) is incorrect because contractual agreements should exist between the company and the EDI trading partners. Answer (d) is incorrect because the risk that EDI data may not be completely and accurately processed is primarily controlled by the system.

51. (c) The requirement is to identify the best control to assure that data uploaded from a microcomputer to the company's mainframe system in batch processing is properly handled. Answer (c) is correct because this could help prevent data errors. Answer (a) is incorrect because while this practice is a wise control, it does not address the issue of upload-data integrity. Backups cannot prevent or detect data-upload problems, but can only help correct data errors that a poor upload caused. Answer (b) is incorrect because this control may be somewhat helpful in preventing fraud in data uploads, but it is of little use in preventing errors. Answer (d) is incorrect because this control is detective in nature, but the error could have already caused erroneous reports and management decisions. Having users try to find errors in uploaded data would be costly.

52. (b) The requirement is to identify the most likely indication that a computer virus is present. Answer (b) is correct because unexplainable losses of or changes to data files are symptomatic of a virus attack. Answer (a) is incorrect because power surges are symptomatic of hardware or environmental (power supply) problems. Answer (c) is incorrect because inadequate backup, recovery, and contingency plans are symptomatic of operating policy and/or compliance problems. Answer (d) is incorrect because copyright violations are symptomatic of operating policy and/or compliance problems.

53. (c) The requirement is to identify the operating procedure most likely to increase an organization's exposure to computer viruses. Answer (c) is correct because there is a risk that downloaded public-domain software may be contaminated with a virus. Answers (a) and (b) are incorrect because viruses are spread through the distribution of computer programs. Answer (d) is incorrect because original copies of purchased software should be virus-free and cannot legally be shared.

54. (b) The requirement is to identify the risk that increases when an EFT system is used. Answer (b) is correct because unauthorized access is a risk which is higher in an EFT environment. Answers (a), (c), and (d) are all incorrect because this is a risk which is common to each IT environment.

55. (c) The requirement is to identify the statement that is correct concerning message encryption software. Answer (c) is correct because the machine instructions necessary to encrypt and decrypt data constitute system overhead, which means that processing may be slowed down. Answer (a) is incorrect because no encryption approach absolutely guarantees the secrecy of data in transmission although encryption approaches are considered to be less amenable to being broken than others. Answer (b) is incorrect because keys may be distributed manually, but they may also be distributed electronically via secure key transporters. Answer (d) is incorrect because using encryption software does not reduce the need for periodic password changes because passwords are the typical means of validating users' access to unencrypted data.

56. (a) The requirement is to identify the method to prevent data eavesdropping. Answer (a) is correct because data encryption prevents eavesdropping by using codes to ensure that data transmissions are protected from unauthorized tampering or electronic eavesdropping. Answer (b) is incorrect because dial back systems ensure that data are received from a valid source. Answer (c) is incorrect because message acknowledgment procedures help ensure that data were received by the intended party. Answer (d) is incorrect because password codes are

designed to prevent unauthorized access to terminals or systems.

57. (b) The requirement is to identify a likely benefit of EDI. Answer (b) is correct because improved business relationships with trading partners is a benefit of EDI. Answer (a) is incorrect because EDI transmits document data, not the actual document. Answer (c) is incorrect because liability issues related to protection of proprietary business data are a major legal implication of EDI. Answer (d) is incorrect because EDI backup and contingency planning requirements are not diminished.

58. (a) The requirement is to identify the **least** likely part of a company's policy on electronic mail. Answer (a) is correct because the company should have access to the business-related e-mail that is left behind. Access to e-mail can also be critical in business or possible criminal investigations. The privacy concerns of the individual case must be mitigated by compelling business interests: the need to follow up on business e-mail and to assist in investigations. Answer (b) is incorrect because encryption helps prevent eavesdropping by unauthorized persons trying to compromise e-mail messages. Answer (c) is incorrect because limiting the number of packages would decrease the number of administrators who might have access to all messages. Answer (d) is incorrect because controlling the transmission of confidential information by e-mail will help avoid theft of information through intrusion by outsiders.

59. (c) The requirement is to identify the most likely risk relating to end-user computing as compared to a mainframe computer system. Answer (c) is correct because this risk is considered unique to end-user computing (EUC) system development. Answer (a) is incorrect because this risk relates to both traditional information systems and end-user computing (EUC) environments. Answer (b) is incorrect because this risk relates to both traditional information systems and end-user computing (EUC) environments. Answer (d) is incorrect because this risk relates to all computing environments.

60. (c) The requirement is to identify the risk that is not greater in an EFT environment as compared to a manual system using paper transactions. Answer (c) is correct because per transaction costs are lower with electronic funds transfer. Answer (a) is incorrect because this is a major risk factor inherent to electronic funds transfer (EFT). Answer (b) is incorrect because this is another inherent risk factor. Answer (d) is incorrect because this is a critical risk factor.

61. (c) The requirement is to identify the reply that is not a method to minimize the risk of installation of unlicensed microcomputer software. Answer (c) is correct because this technique will not affect introduction of unlicensed software. Answer (a) is incorrect because this technique works. Answer (b) is incorrect because such audits are a must to test the other controls that should be in place. Answer (d) is incorrect because the basis for all good controls is a written policy.

62. (a) The requirement is to determine whose responsibility it is to back up software and data files in distributed or cooperative systems. Answer (a) is correct because in distributed or cooperative systems, the responsibility for ensuring that adequate backups are taken is the responsibility of user management because the systems are under the control of users. Answer (b) is incorrect because in distributed environments, there will be no systems programmers comparable to those at central sites for traditional systems. Answer (c) is incorrect because in distributed environments, there may be no data entry clerks because users are typically performing their own data entry. Answer (d) is incorrect because in distributed environments, there are no tape librarians.

63. **(b)** The requirement is to identify the least likely way that a client's data will be input. Answer (b) is correct because the term "dynamic linking character reader" is a combination of terms that has no real meaning. The other three terms all represent methods of data input.

64. **(d)** The requirement is to identify what end-user computing is an example of. Answer (d) is correct because end-user computing involves individual users performing the development and execution of computer applications in a decentralized manner. Answer (a) is incorrect because client/server processing involves a networked model, rather than end-user approach. Answer (b) is incorrect because a distributed system involves networked computers processing transactions for a single (or related) database. Answer (c) is incorrect because using sophisticated techniques from statistics, artificial intelligence and computer graphics to explain, confirm and explore relationships among data may be performed in many environments.

65. **(c)** The requirement is to identify the type of computer that end-user computing is most likely to occur on. Answer (c) is correct because end-user computing involves individual users performing the development and execution of computer applications in a decentralized manner and these individuals are most likely to be using personal computers. Answers (a) and (b) are incorrect because they represent computers less frequently used by end users. Answer (d) is incorrect because "personal reference assistants" is a term not used in information technology.

66. **(a)** The requirement is to identify the correct statement regarding the Internet as a commercially viable network. Answer (a) is correct because companies that wish to maintain adequate security must use firewalls to protect data from being accessed by unauthorized users. Answer (b) is incorrect because anyone can establish a homepage on the Internet without obtaining permission. Answer (c) is incorrect because there are no such security standards for connecting to the Internet.

67. **(d)** The requirement is to identify a method of reducing security exposure when transmitting proprietary data over communication lines. Answer (d) is correct because cryptographic devices protect data in transmission over communication lines. Answer (a) is incorrect because asynchronous modems handle data streams from peripheral devices to a central processor. Answer (b) is incorrect because authentication techniques confirm that valid users have access to the system. Answer (c) is incorrect because callback procedures are used to ensure incoming calls are from authorized locations.

68. **(a)** The requirement is to identify the reply which is **not** a reason that securing client/server systems is a complex task. Answer (a) is correct because client/server implementation does not necessarily use relational databases. An-

swers (b), (c), and (d) are all incorrect because the number of access points, concurrent operation by multiple users, and widespread data access and update capabilities make securing such systems complex.

69. **(c)** The requirement is to identify what an auditor would ordinarily consider the greatest risk regarding an entity's use of electronic data interchange (EDI). Answer (c) is correct because an EDI system must include controls to make certain that EDI transactions are processed by the proper entity, using the proper accounts. Answers (a) and (b) are incorrect because authorization of EDI transactions and duplication of EDI transmissions ordinarily pose no greater risk than for other systems. Answer (d) is incorrect because the elimination of paper documents in and of itself does not propose a great risk.

70. **(d)** The requirement is to identify the characteristic that distinguishes electronic data interchange (EDI) from other forms of electronic commerce. Answer (d) is correct because standards for EDI transactions, within any one group of trading partners, have been agreed upon so as to allow the system to function efficiently. Answer (a) is incorrect because the cost of EDI transaction using a VAN will often exceed the cost of using the Internet. Answer (b) is incorrect because software maintenance contracts are often necessary. Answer (c) is incorrect because EDI commerce involves legally binding contracts between trading partners.

71. **(c)** The requirement is to identify a component of a local area network. Answer (c) is correct because a local area network requires that data be transmitted from one computer to another through some form of transmission media. Answers (a), (b), and (d) are all general replies that are not requirements of a local area network.

72. **(c)** The requirement is to identify an additional cost of transmitting business transactions by means of electronic data interchange (EDI) rather than in a traditional paper environment. Answer (c) is correct because such transactions must be translated to allow transmission. Answer (a) is incorrect because no particular controls are required for redundant data checks under EDI as compared to a traditional paper environment. Answer (b) is incorrect because there need be no increase in random data entry errors under EDI. Answer (d) is incorrect because since computer controls are ordinarily heavily relied upon under EDI, often fewer supervisory personnel are needed.

73. **(a)** The requirement is to identify an advantage of using the Internet for electronic commerce EDI transactions as compared to a value-added network (VAN). Answer (a) is correct because such simultaneous processing of transactions is more likely under an Internet system in which lines are often available at a fixed or nearly fixed rate. Answer (b) is incorrect because the Internet itself will not automatically prepare such batches. Answer (c) is incorrect because an Internet system will not ordinarily have superior characteristics regarding disaster recovery. Answer (d) is incorrect because translation software is needed both for Internet and VAN systems.

74. **(b)** The requirement is to identify the statement which does not represent an exposure involved with electronic data interchange (EDI) systems. Answer (b) is correct because EDI ordinarily decreases transaction processing time; it does not delay transaction processing time. Answer (a) is incorrect because increased reliance upon both one's own computers and those of other parties are involved in EDI. Answer (c) is incorrect because involvement with other parties in EDI systems may result in the loss of confidentiality of information. Answer (d) is incorrect because EDI systems involve third parties such as customers, suppliers, and those involved with the computer network, and accordingly result in increased reliance upon their proper performance of their functions.

75. (b) The requirement is to identify the correct statement concerning internal control when a client uses an electronic data interchange system for processing its sales. Answer (b) is correct because encryption controls are designed to assure that messages are unreadable to unauthorized persons and to thereby control the transactions. Answer (a) is incorrect because suppliers are not ordinarily included in a company's sales controls and because even in a purchasing EDI system all suppliers need not be included. Answer (c) is incorrect because a value-added-network that provides network services may or may not be used in an EDI system. Answer (d) is incorrect because "paper" versions of transactions typically disappear in an EDI system.

76. (d) The requirement is to identify the statement that represents a disadvantage for an entity that keeps microcomputer-prepared data files rather than manually prepared files. Answer (d) is correct because persons with computer skills may be able to improperly access and alter microcomputer files. When a system is prepared manually such manipulations may be more obvious. Answer (a) is incorrect because random error is more closely associated with manual processing than with computer processing. Answer (b) is incorrect because comparing recorded accountability with the physical count of assets should not be affected by whether a manual or a microcomputer system is being used. Answer (c) is incorrect because the accuracy of the programming process is not generally tested when microcomputers are used.

77. (a) The requirement is to identify a benefit of transmitting transactions in an electronic data interchange (EDI) environment. Answer (a) is correct because the speed at which transactions can occur and be processed electronically results in lower year-end receivables since payments occur so quickly. Answer (b) is incorrect because an EDI environment requires many controls related to sales and collections. Answer (c) is incorrect because sampling may or may not be used in such circumstances. Answer (d) is incorrect because third-party service providers are often involved in such transactions—accordingly they are relied upon. See Auditing Procedure Study *Audit Implications of EDI* for information on electronic data interchange systems.

78. (c) The requirement is to identify the network node that is used to improve network traffic and to set up as a boundary that prevents traffic from one segment to cross over to another. Answer (c) is correct because a firewall is a computer that provides a defense between one network (inside the firewall) and another network (outside the firewall) that could pose a threat to the inside network. Answer (a) is incorrect because a router is a computer that determines the best way for data to move forward to their destination. Answer (b) is incorrect because a gateway is a communications interface device that allows a local area network to be con-

nected to external networks and to communicate with external computers and databases. Answer (d) is incorrect because a heuristic is a simplified rule to help an individual make decisions.

79. (a) The requirement is to identify the best example of how specific controls in a database environment may differ from controls in a nondatabase environment. Answer (a) is correct because a primary control within a database environment is to appropriately control access and updating by the many users; in most nondatabase environments there are ordinarily far fewer users who are able to directly access and update data. Answer (b) is incorrect because controls over data sharing differ among users for both database and nondatabase environments. Answer (c) is incorrect because under both database and nondatabase systems, the programmer should debug the program. Answer (d) is incorrect because controls can verify that authorized transactions are processed under either a database or nondatabase environment.

80. (b) The requirement is to identify an effective audit approach in an EDI environment in which documentation of transactions will be retained for only a short period of time. Answer (b) is correct because performing tests throughout the year will allow the auditor to examine transaction documentation before the transactions are destroyed. Answer (a) is incorrect because if documentation relating to the transactions is not maintained, it will be impossible to perform such cutoff tests. Answer (d) is incorrect because such a situation need not lead to a 100% count of inventory at or near year-end. Answer (d) is incorrect because an increase in the assessed level of control risk rather than a decrease is more likely.

81. (d) The requirement is to identify the encryption feature that can be used to authenticate the originator of a document and to ensure that the message is intact and has not been tampered with. Answer (d) is correct because digital signatures are used in electronic commerce to authenticate the originator and to ensure that the message has not been tampered with. Answers (a), (b), and (c) are all incorrect because they do not directly deal with such authentication.

82. (a) The requirement is to identify the process used in building an electronic data interchange (EDI) system to determine that elements in the entity's computer system correspond to the standard data elements. Answer (a) is correct because mapping, or "data mapping," is the processes of selecting the appropriate data fields from the various application databases and passing them to the EDI translation software. Answer (b) is incorrect because translation involves the actual modification of the data into a standard format that is used by the EDI system. Answer (c) is incorrect because encryption is a technique for protecting information within a computer system in which an algorithm transforms that data to render it unintelligible; the process can be reversed to regenerate the original data for further processing. Answer (d) is incorrect because decoding is the process of making data intelligible. See the Auditing Procedure Study *Audit Implications of EDI* for more information on electronic data interchange.

83. (a) The requirement is to identify the password that would be most difficult to crack. A password is a secret series of characters that enables a user to access a file, computer, or program; ideally, the password should be something nobody could guess. Answer (a) is correct because OrCA!FlSi does not seem like a password that one would guess or even recall if seen briefly. Answers (b), (c), and (d) are all incorrect because they represent passwords that would be easier to identify.

84. (a) The requirement is to determine which reply represents a password security problem. A password is a secret series of characters that enables a user to access a file, computer, or program; ideally the password should be something that nobody could guess. Answer (a) is correct because individuals have a tendency to not change passwords, and over time, others may be able to identify them. Answer (b) is incorrect because using different passwords for different accounts on several systems represents a control (assuming the user can remember them). Answer (c) is incorrect because copying of passwords to a secure location (e.g., a wallet) does not ordinarily represent a security problem. Answer (d) is incorrect because passwords should be kept secret and not listed in an online dictionary.

D. Effect of IT on Internal Control

85. (b) The requirement is to identify the most likely procedure to be included in a computer disaster recovery plan. Answer (b) is correct because duplicate copies of critical files will allow an entity to reconstruct the data whose original files have been lost or damaged. Answer (a) is incorrect because an auxiliary power supply will provide uninterrupted electricity to avoid the need for a recovery since it may reduce the likelihood of such a disaster. Answer (c) is incorrect because simply maintaining passwords will not allow the entity to reconstruct data after a disaster has occurred. Answer (d) is incorrect because while cryptography will enhance the security of files from unintended uses, it is not a primary method to recover from a computer disaster.

86. (d) The requirement is to identify the type of backup site a company would most likely consider when there is concern about a power outage and desires for a fully configured and ready to operate system. Answer (d) is correct because a hot site is a site that is already configured to meet a user's requirements. Answer (a) is incorrect because a cold site is a facility that provides everything necessary to quickly install computer equipment but doesn't have the computers installed. Answers (b) and (c) are incorrect because they represent terms not frequently used in such circumstances.

87. (d) The requirement is to identify the procedure an entity would most likely include in its disaster recovery plan. Answer (d) is correct because storing duplicate copies of files in a different location will allow recovery of contaminated original files. Answer (a) is incorrect because converting all data from EDI format to an internal company format is ordinarily inefficient, and not a disaster recovery plan. Answer (b) is incorrect because a Trojan horse program (one which masquerades as a benign application but actually causes damage) ordinarily causes illicit activity, it does not prevent illicit activity. Answer (c) is incorrect because an auxiliary power supply is meant to prevent disaster, not recover from disaster.

88. (b) The requirement is to determine whether almost all commercially marketed software is copyrighted, copy protected, or both. Answer (b) is correct because while almost all such software is copyrighted, much of it is not copy protected. Answer (a) is incorrect because it suggests that almost all such software is copy protected. Answer (c) is incorrect both because it suggests that such software is not copyrighted and that it is copy protected. Answer (d) is incorrect because it suggests that such software is not copyrighted.

89. (c) The requirement is to identify a widely used disaster recovery approach. Answer (c) is correct because regular backups (copying) of data allows recovery when original records are damaged. Answer (a) is incorrect because encryption is used with a goal of making files impossible to read by those other than the intended users. Answer (b) is incorrect because firewalls are designed to control any possible inappropriate communication between computers within one system and those on the outside. Answer (d) is incorrect because surge protectors are electrical devices inserted in a power line to protect equipment from sudden fluctuations in current, and thereby prevent disasters, not recover from them.

90. (a) The requirement is to identify what a "hot site" is most frequently associated with. Answer (a) is correct because a hot site is a commercial disaster recovery service that allows a business to continue computer operations in the event of computer disaster. For example, if a company's data processing center become inoperable, that enterprise can move all processing to a hot site that has all the equipment needed to continue operation. Answer (b) is incorrect because a hot site is not frequently associated with online relational database design. Answer (c) is incorrect because source programs (programs written in a language from which statements are translated into machine language) are not directly related to a hot site. Answer (d) is incorrect because when used in information technology, the term hot site is not directly related to temperature control for computers.

91. (b) The requirement is to determine which reply is **not** a typical output control. Answer (b) is correct because matching the input data with information held on master or suspense files is a processing control, not an output control, to ensure that data are complete and accurate during updating. Answer (a) is incorrect because a review of the computer processing logs is an output control to ensure that data are accurate and complete. Answer (c) is incorrect because periodic reconciliation of output reports is an output control to ensure that data are accurate and complete. Answer (d) is incorrect because maintaining formal procedures and documentation specifying authorized recipients is an output control to ensure proper distribution.

92. (c) The requirement is to identify the best way to minimize the likelihood of unauthorized editing of production programs, job control language, and operating system software. Answer (c) is correct because program change control comprises: (1) maintaining records of change authorizations, code changes, and test results; (2) adhering to a systems development methodology (including documentation; (3) authorizing changeovers of subsidiary and headquarters' interfaces; and (4) restricting access to authorized source and executable codes. Answer (a) is incorrect because the purpose of database reviews is to determine if (1) users have gained access to database areas for which they have no authorization; and (2) authorized users can access the database using programs that provide them with unauthorized privileges to view and/or change information. Answer (b) is incorrect because the purpose of compliance reviews is to determine whether an organization has complied with applicable internal and external procedures and regulations. Answer (d) is incorrect because the purpose of network security software is to provide logical controls over the network.

93.   (d)   The requirement is to determine the most likely actions relating to mainframe applications when a company decides to launch a downsizing project. Answer (d) is correct because mainframe applications represent a significant investment and may still provide adequate service. The fact that mainframes can provide a stable platform for enterprise applications may be an advantage while exploring other nonmainframe options. Answer (a) is incorrect because the costs of converting mainframe applications to a microcomputer network and retraining the personnel who would rewrite and maintain them preclude any rapid transition. Answer (b) is incorrect because general ledger programs that aggregate business data on a regular basis will be among the last to be converted. Answer (c) is incorrect because incremental modifications may have high paybacks.

94.   (a)   The requirement is to identify the greatest concern relating to a client's setting of used microcomputers when that corporation receives the majority of its revenue from top-secret military contracts with the government. Answer (a) is correct because while most delete programs erase file pointers, they do not remove the underlying data. The company must use special utilities that fully erase the data; this is especially important because of the potential for top-secret data on the microcomputers. This risk is the largest because it could cause them to lose military contract business. Answer (b) is incorrect because while it could create a liability for the company if a virus destroyed the purchasing party's data or programs the purchasing party should use antiviral software to detect and eliminate any viruses. This concern, while important, is not as serious as the one in answer (a). Answer (c) is incorrect because the purchasing party has a responsibility to insure that all their software is properly licensed. If the company represented that all the software was properly licensed, this could create a liability. However, this liability is not as serious as the implication from answer (a). Answer (d) is incorrect because terminal emulation software is widely available.

95.   (b)   The requirement is to identify a reason to use bar codes rather than other means of identifying information on parts. Answer (b) is correct because a reason to use bar codes rather than other means of identification is to record the movement of parts with minimal labor costs. Answer (a) is incorrect because the movement of parts can escape being recorded with any identification method. Answer (c) is incorrect because each vendor has its own part-numbering scheme, which is unlikely to correspond to the buyer's scheme. Answer (d) is incorrect because each vendor has its own identification method, although vendors in the same industry often cooperate to minimize the number of bar code systems they use.

96.   (b)   The requirement is to identify the function that ensures that changes in processing programs have a minimal impact on processing and result in minimal risk to the system. Answer (b) is correct because change control is the process of authorizing, developing, testing, and installing coded changes so as to minimize the impact on processing and the risk to the system. Answer (a) is incorrect because security administration is not involved as directly applicable as is change control. Answer (c) is incorrect because problem tracking is the process of collecting operational data about processes so that they can be analyzed for corrective action. Answer (d) is incorrect because problem-escalation procedures are a means of categorizing problems or unusual circumstances so that the least skilled person can address them.

97.   (b)   The requirement is to identify the approach(es) that may reduce an organization's risk of civil lawsuit due to the use of pirated software. Answer (b) is correct because: (I) Maintaining a log protects an organization since a log documents software purchases. (II) Auditing individual computers will discourage illegal software usage. (III) Establishing a corporate software policy will discourage illegal software usage. (IV) Allowing users to keep original diskettes increases both the likelihood of illegal copies being made and the loss of diskettes. Answers (a), (c), and (d) are all incorrect.

98.   (a)   The requirement is to identify a benefit of good recovery planning. Answer (a) is correct because an essential component of a disaster recovery plan is that the need for backup/restart has been anticipated and provided for in the application systems. Answer (b) is incorrect because change control procedures should not be bypassed by operating personnel, but that is not generally a consideration in disaster recovery planning. Answer (c) is incorrect because planned changes in equipment capacities should be compatible with projected workloads, but that is not generally a consideration in disaster recovery planning. Answer (d) is incorrect because service level agreements with owners of critical applications should be adequate, but that is not generally a consideration in disaster recovery planning.

99.   (d)   The requirement is to identify the biggest risk in not having an adequately staffed information center help desk. Answer (d) is correct because not having such a help desk may lead to a situation in which users will unknowingly persist in making errors in their interaction with the information systems. Answer (a) is incorrect because application audits should be about the same difficulty with or without an adequately staffed help desk. Answer (b) is incorrect because the preparation of documentation is a development function, not a help desk function. Answer (c) is incorrect because the likelihood of use of unauthorized program code is a function of change control, not of a help desk.

100.   (c)   The requirement is to determine how a database administrator should ensure that the database system properly controls access to accounting database files. Answer (c) is correct because one security feature in database systems is their ability to let the database administrator restrict access on a logical view basis for each user. Answer (a) is incorrect because if the only access permitted is read-only, then there could no updating of database files Answer (b) is incorrect because permitting catalog updating from privileged software would be a breach of security, which might permit unauthorized access. Answer (d) is incorrect because updating of users' access profiles should be a function of a security officer, not the user.

101. (b) The requirement is to identify a major auditor concern when a client processes sales transactions on the Internet. Answer (b) is correct because computer disruptions may result in the incorrect recording of sales. Answer (a) is incorrect because electronic sales invoices may replace sales invoice documents in such an environment. Answer (c) is incorrect because there may or may not be a need to establish an integrated test facility in such circumstances. Answer (d) is incorrect because the frequency of archiving and data retention is not as important as is ensuring that such policies appropriately control system backup.

102. (a) The requirement is to identify the correct statement concerning internal control in an electronic data interchange (EDI) system. Answer (a) is correct because preventive controls are important and often cost-effective in an EDI environment so as to not allow the error to occur, and because detective controls may detect misstatements too late to allow proper correction. Answer (b) is incorrect because the control objectives under EDI systems generally remain the same as for other information systems. Answer (c) is incorrect because a well-controlled EDI system may allow control risk to be assessed below the maximum. Answer (d) is incorrect because the programmed nature of most EDI controls limits the possible segregation of duties within the system. See Auditing Procedure Study *Audit Implications of EDI* for information on electronic data interchange systems.

103. (b) The requirement is to identify the correct statement relating to the security of messages in an electronic data interchange (EDI) system. Answer (b) is correct because both the physical security of the hardware and the hardware itself create a situation in which the encryption is ordinarily more secure than encryption performed by software. Answer (a) is incorrect because message authentication deals with whether the message received is the same as that sent, and not as directly with confidentiality. Answer (c) is incorrect because message authentication deals most directly with whether changes have been made in the message sent, and not with the variety of other potential problems addressed by segregation of duties. Answer (d) is incorrect because security is necessary at the transaction phase in EDI systems. See Auditing Procedure Study *Audit Implications of EDI* for information on electronic data interchange systems.

104. (c) The requirement is to identify an essential element of the audit trail in an electronic data interchange (EDI) system. Answer (c) is correct because effective audit trails need to include activity logs, including processed and failed transactions, network and sender/recipient acknowledgments, and time sequence of processing. Answer (a) is incorrect because disaster recovery plans, while essential to the overall system, are not an essential element of the audit trail. Answer (b) is incorrect because encrypted hash totals deal less directly with the audit trail than do activity logs. Answer (d) is incorrect because hardware security modules that store sensitive data do not deal directly with the audit trail. See Auditing Procedure Study *Audit Implications of EDI* for information on electronic data interchange systems.

105. (a) The requirement is to identify an essential element of the audit trail in an electronic data interchange (EDI) system. Answer (a) is correct because effective audit trails need to include activity logs, including processed and failed transactions, network and sender/recipient acknowledgments, and time sequence of processing. Answer (b) is incorrect because neither message directories nor header segments directly affect the audit trial. Answer (c) is incorrect because contingency and disaster recovery plans, while important, are not as directly related to the audit trail as are the acknowledgments suggested in answer (a). Answer (d) is incorrect because while knowing trading partner security and mailbox codes is essential, it is more closely related to overall security than is answer (a). See Auditing Procedure Study *Audit Implications of EDI* for information on electronic data interchange systems.

106. (b) The requirement is to identify the type of control that involves adding an extra number at the end of an account number and subjecting the new number to an algorithm. Answer (b) is correct because a check digit is an extra reference number that follows an identification code and bears a mathematical relationship to the other digits. Answer (a) is incorrect because optical character recognition involves a computer being able to "read in" printed data. Answer (c) is incorrect because a dependency check involves some form of check between differing related pieces of data. Answer (d) is incorrect because a format check involves determining whether the proper type of data has been input or processed (e.g., numerical data input under account withdrawal amount).

107. (d) The requirement is to identify the best control for preventing someone with sufficient technical skill from circumventing security procedures and making changes to production programs. Answer (d) is correct because a suitable segregation of duties will make such alteration impossible since when duties are separated, users cannot obtain the detailed knowledge of programs and computer operators cannot gain unsupervised access to production programs. Answers (a), (b), and (c) are all incorrect because the reviews of jobs processed, comparing programs with copies, and running attest data will all potentially disclose such alteration, but will not prevent it.

108. (c) The requirement is to identify the best method of keeping computer program libraries secure. Answer (c) is correct because restricting physical and logical access secures program libraries from unauthorized use in person or remotely via terminals. Answers (a) and (b) are incorrect because installing a logging system for program access or monitoring physical access would permit detection of unauthorized access but would not prevent it. Answer (d) is incorrect because denying all remote access via terminals would likely be inefficient and would not secure program libraries against physical access.

109. (d) The requirement is to identify the security control that would best prevent unauthorized access to sensitive data through an unattended data terminal directly connected to a mainframe. Answer (d) is correct because automatic log-off of inactive users may prevent the viewing of sensitive data on an unattended data terminal. Answer (a) is incorrect because data terminals do not normally use screen-saver protection, and because a screen saver would not prevent access. Answer (b) is incorrect because scripting is the use of a program to automate a process such as startup. Answer (c) is incorrect because encryption of data files will not prevent viewing of data on an unattended data terminal.

110. (d)   The requirement is to identify the reply that most likely represents a hash total. A hash total is a control total where the total is meaningless for financial purposes, but has some meaning for processing purposes. Answer (d) is correct because 810 represents the sum of the invoice numbers. Answer (a) is incorrect because it appears to be an accumulation of all letters, plus a sum of the numbers. Answer (b) is more likely to be considered a record count. Answer (c) is incorrect because it is simply the invoice number of the last invoice in the batch.

111. (a)   The requirement is to determine the type of control that would detect a miscoding of a product number on an order from a customer. Answer (a) is correct because a check digit is an extra digit added to an identification number to verify that the number is authorized and to thereby detect such coding errors. Answer (b) is incorrect because a record count involves a count of the number of records processed which is not being considered here. Answer (c) is incorrect because the term "hash total" ordinarily relates to a total of items and is meaningless for financial purposes (e.g., the total of the invoice numbers for a particular day's sales), but has some meaning for processing purposes. Answer (d) is incorrect because a redundant data check uses two identifiers in each transaction record to confirm that the correct master file record has been updated (e.g., the client account number and first several letters of the customer's name can be used to retrieve the correct customer master record from the accounts receivable file).

112. (b)   The requirement is to identify the technique that would most likely detect a nonexistent zip code. Answer (b) is correct because a zip code that is nonexistent would not pass a validity test. It would not be a valid item. Answer (a) is incorrect because a limit test restricts the amount of a transaction that will be processed. Answer (c) is incorrect because a parity test prevents loss of digits in processing. Answer (d) is incorrect because a record count test helps prevent the loss of records.

113. (a)   The requirement is to determine whether limit tests and validity check tests are processing controls designed to ensure the reliability and accuracy of data processing. Answer (a) is correct because both a limit test and a validity check test may serve as a control over either inputs or processing in an accounting system. A limit test will establish an upper and/or lower limit as reasonable, with results outside of those limits indicated (e.g., after net pay is calculated, an "error message" is printed for any employee with a weekly salary in excess of a certain amount). A validity check test allows only "valid" transactions or data to be processed in the system (e.g., during the processing of payroll, a control determines whether a paycheck is improperly issued to an ex-employee).

114. (b)   The requirement is to identify the activity most likely to be performed in the information systems department. Answer (b) is correct because the conversion of information into machine-readable form is essential to the inputting of data; computer equipment is generally used to perform this function. Answer (a) is incorrect because under good internal control, the initiation of changes to master

records should be authorized by functions independent of those which process the records. Answer (c) is incorrect because a separate function should exist to correct transactional errors. Answer (d) is incorrect because changes to computer applications should be initiated by the appropriate user group.

115. (a)   The requirement is to determine the errors which a header label is likely to prevent. Since the header label is actually on the magnetic tape, it is the computer operator whose errors will be prevented. Answer (b) is incorrect because the keypunch operator deals with punch cards. Answer (c) is incorrect because the programmer will write the programs and not run them under good internal control. Answer (d) is incorrect because the maintenance technician will not run the magnetic tape.

116. (b)   The requirement is to determine the purpose of programming computer to immediately transmit back to the terminal for display information that has been input on cash disbursements. Answer (b) is correct because the entry of disbursement **amounts** and the subsequent display of the amounts on the terminal screen will allow the operator to visually verify that the data provided to be input was entered accurately. Answer (a) is incorrect because displaying on the screen the data entered does not ensure the validity of the data, only that the data was entered correctly. Answer (c) is incorrect because no evidence has been provided as to whether the disbursement was authorized. Answer (d) is incorrect because the display of the amount will not be compared to a "correct" amount—only to the amount that was to be input.

117. (b)   The requirement is to identify a useful control when computer programs or files can be accessed from terminals. Answer (b) is correct because use of personal identification codes (passwords) will limit access to the programs or files on the terminal to those who know the codes. Answers (a), (c), and (d) are all incorrect because while they list valid controls used in computer systems, none of them require entry of data by the user. A parity check control is a special bit added to each character stored in memory to help detect whether the hardware has lost a bit during the internal movement of that character. A self-diagnosis test is run on a computer to check the internal operations and devices within the computer system. An echo check is primarily used in telecommunications transmissions to determine whether the receiving hardware has received the information sent by the sending hardware.

118. (a)   The requirement is to identify the item which would reduce the possibility of erasing a large amount of information stored on magnetic tape. Answer (a) is correct because a file protection ring is a control that ensures that an operator does not erase important information on a magnetic tape. Answer (b) is incorrect because a check digit is a digit added to an identification number to detect entry errors. Answer (c) is incorrect because a completeness test would generally be used to test whether all data were processed. Answer (d) is incorrect because conversion verification would address whether the conversion of data from one form to another (e.g., disk to magnetic tape) was complete.

119. (b)   The requirement is to identify the controls most likely to assure that an entity can reconstruct its financial records. Answer (b) is correct because backup diskettes or tapes may be maintained that will provide the information needed to reconstruct financial records. Answer (a) is incorrect because while hardware controls are meant to assure the proper processing of data, when reconstruction is needed, hardware controls will not have the data necessary to reconstruct the financial records. Answer (c) is incorrect because parallel simulations will only occasionally be run and will not maintain adequate data to reconstruct records. Answer (d) is incorrect because while systems flowcharts will provide information on the design of the overall system, they will not assure the reconstruction of financial records.

120. (d)   The requirement is to identify the type of input control that is a numeric value computed to provide assurance that the original value has not been altered in construction or transmission. Answer (d) is correct because a check digit is an extra digit added to an identification number to detect such errors. Answer (a) is incorrect because the term "hash total" ordinarily relates to a total of items and is meaningless for financial purposes (e.g., the total of the invoice numbers for a particular day's sales), but has some meaning for processing purposes. Answer (b) is incorrect because a parity check is a process in which a computer reads or receives a set of characters and simultaneously sums the number of 1 bits in each character to verify that it is an even (or alternatively, odd) number. Answer (c) is incorrect because encryption involves a coding of data, ordinarily for purposes of ensuring privacy and accuracy of transmission.

121. (c)   The requirement is to identify the best example of a validity check. A validity test compares data (for example, employee, vendor, and other codes) against a master file for authenticity. Answer (c) is correct because the computer flagging of inappropriate transactions due to data in a control field that did not match that of an existing file record is such a test. Answer (a) is incorrect because a limit test ensures that a numerical amount in a record does not exceed some predetermined amount. Answer (b) is incorrect because the resubmission of data is not a validity check. Answer (d) is incorrect because the reading back of data to the terminal is an echo check.

122. (b)   The requirement is to identify type of computer test made to ascertain whether a given characteristic belongs to a group. Answer (b) is correct because a validity check determines whether a character is legitimate per the given character set. Note the validity check determines whether a given character is within the desired group. Answer (a) is incorrect because a parity check is a summation check in which the binary digits of a character are added to determine whether the sum is odd or even. Another bit, the parity bit, is turned on or off so the total number of bits will be odd or even as required. Answer (c) is incorrect because an echo check is a hardware control wherein data is transmitted back to its source and compared to the original data to verify the transmission correctness. Answer (d) is incorrect because a limit or reasonableness check is a programmed control based on specified limits. For example, a calendar month cannot be numbered higher than twelve, or a week cannot have more than 168 hours.

123. (a)   The requirement is to identify the type of hardware control that requires the CPU to send signals to the printer to activate the print mechanism for each character. Answer (a) is correct because an echo check or control consists of transmitting data back to the source unit for comparison with the original data that were transmitted. In this case, the print command is sent to the printer and then returned to the CPU to verify that the proper command was received. A validity check [answer (b)] consists of the examination of a bit pattern to determine that the combination is legitimate for the system character set (i.e., that the character represented by the bit combination is valid per the system). Answer (c), a signal control or signal check, appears to be a nonsense term. Answer (d), check digit control, is a programmed control wherein the last character or digit can be calculated from the previous digits.

124. (b)   The requirement is to identify an example of a check digit. Answer (b) is correct because a check digit is an extra digit in an identification number, algebraically determined, that detects specified types of data input, transmission, or conversion errors. Answer (a) is incorrect because the agreement of the total number of employees to the checks printed is an example of a control total. Answer (c) is incorrect because ensuring that all employee numbers are nine digits could be considered a logic check, a field size check, or a missing data check. Answer (d) is incorrect because determining that no employee has more than fifty hours per workweek is a limit check.

125. (b)   The requirement is to determine the most likely significant deficiency in internal control. Answer (b) is correct because the systems programmer should not maintain custody of output in a computerized system. At a minimum, the programming, operating, and library functions should be segregated in such computer systems.

126. (c)   The requirement is to identify the weakness in internal control relating to a function performed by computer department personnel. Answer (c) is correct because individuals outside of the computer department should originate changes in master files; this separates the authorization of changes from the actual processing of records. Answer (a) is incorrect because participation of computer department personnel in making computer software acquisition decisions is often appropriate and desirable given their expertise in the area. Answer (b) is incorrect for similar reasons as (a). In addition, computer department personnel will often be able to effectively design the required documentation for computerized systems. Answer (d) is incorrect because the physical security for program files may appropriately be assigned to a library function within the computer department.

127. (b)   The requirement is to identify the activity most likely to detect whether payroll data were altered during processing. Answer (b) is correct because test data may be used to provide evidence on whether edit routines (routines to check the validity and accuracy of input data) are operating and have not been altered. Answer (a) is incorrect because the distribution of any data control sheets will provide little information on altered data. Answer (c) is incorrect because the approval of source documents is not at issue—it is the alteration of payroll data. Answer (d) is incorrect because any segregation activities may eliminate future alterations, but would have little effect on prior alterations.

E. Flowcharting

128. (a)   The requirement is to identify the tool that would best give a graphical representation of a sequence of activities and decisions. Answer (a) is correct because a flowchart is a graphical representation of a sequence of activities and decisions. Answer (b) is incorrect because a control chart is used to monitor actual versus desired quality measurements during repetition operation. Answer (c) is incorrect because a histogram is a bar chart showing conformance to a standard bell curve. Answer (d) is incorrect because a run chart tracks the frequency or amount of a given variable over time.

129. (c) The requirement is to determine what the symbol A represents in the flowchart of a client's revenue cycle. Answer (c) is correct because the accounts receivable master file will be accessed during the revenue cycle and does not appear elsewhere on the flowchart. Answers (a), (b), and (d) are all incorrect because remittance advices, receiving reports, and cash disbursements transaction files are not a primary transaction file accessed during the revenue cycle.

130. (d) The requirement is to determine what the symbol B represents in the flowchart of a client's revenue cycle. Answer (d) is correct because it represents the only major document of the revenue cycle that is not presented elsewhere on the flowchart and because one would expect generation of a sales invoice in the cycle. Answer (a) is incorrect because the customer order appears in the top left portion of the flowchart. Answer (b) is incorrect because no receiving report is being generated during the revenue cycle. Answer (c) is incorrect because the customer's check (remittance) is represented on the top portion of the flowchart.

131. (d) The requirement is to identify the correct statement concerning an auditor's flowchart of a client's accounting system. Answer (d) is correct because a flowchart is a diagrammatic representation that depicts the auditor's understanding of the system. See AU 319 for various procedures auditors use to document their understanding of internal control. Answer (a) is incorrect because the flowchart depicts the auditor's understanding of the system, not the assessment of control risk. Answer (b) is incorrect because while the flowchart may be used to identify weaknesses, it depicts the entire system—strengths as well as weaknesses. Answer (c) is incorrect because the flowchart is of the accounting system, not of the control environment.

132. (b) The requirement is to determine the approach illustrated in the flowchart. Answer (b) is correct because parallel simulation involves processing actual client data through an auditor's program. Answer (a) is incorrect because program code checking involves an analysis of the client's actual program. Answer (c) is incorrect because an integrated test facility approach introduces dummy transactions into a system in the midst of live transaction processing and is usually built into the system during the original design. Answer (d) is incorrect because controlled reprocessing often includes using the auditor's copy of a client program, rather than the auditor's program.

133. (b) The requirement is to identify the item represented by the "X" on the flowchart. Answer (b) is correct because the existence of a credit memo, in addition to a sales invoice, would indicate that this portion of the flowchart deals with cash receipts; therefore, the "X" would represent the remittance advices. Thus, the receipt transactions are credited to the accounts receivable master file, and an updated master file, a register of receipts, and exception reports are generated. Answer (a) is incorrect because an auditor's

test data will not result in an input into the transactions file. Answer (c) is incorrect because since no processing has occurred at the point in question—an error report is unlikely. Answer (d) is incorrect because credit authorization will generally occur prior to the preparation of credit memos.

134. (d) The requirement is to determine the symbolic representations that indicate that a file has been consulted. Answer (d) indicates that a manual operation (the trapezoid symbol) is accessing data from a file and returning the data to the file (i.e., "consulting" the file). Answer (a) is incorrect because it represents a processing step (the rectangle) being followed by a manual operation. Answer (b) is incorrect because it represents a document being filed. Answer (c) is incorrect because the diamond symbol represents a decision process.

135. (c) The requirement is to determine a benefit of a well-prepared flowchart. A flowchart may be used to document the auditor's understanding of the flow of transactions and documents. Answer (a) is incorrect because while an audit procedures manual may suggest the use of flowcharts, flowcharts will not in general be used to prepare such a manual. Answer (b) is less accurate than (c) because while it may be possible to obtain general information on various jobs, the flowchart will not allow one to obtain a **detailed** job description. Answer (d) is incorrect because a flowchart does not directly address actual accuracy of financial data within a system.

MULTIPLE-CHOICE QUESTIONS (1-120)

**1. If both the supply and the demand for a good increase, the market price will
   a. Rise only in the case of an inelastic supply function.
   b. Fall only in the case of an inelastic supply function.
   c. Not be predictable with only these facts.
   d. Rise only in the case of an inelastic demand function.

**2. A supply curve illustrates the relationship between
   a. Price and quantity supplied.
   b. Price and consumer tastes.
   c. Price and quantity demanded.
   d. Supply and demand.

3. As a business owner you have determined that the demand for your product is inelastic. Based upon this assessment you understand that
   a. Increasing the price of your product will increase total revenue.
   b. Decreasing the price of your product will increase total revenue.
   c. Increasing the price of your product will have no effect on total revenue.
   d. Increasing the price of your product will increase competition.

Items 4 and 5 are based on the following information:

Assume that demand for a particular product changed as shown below from D1 to D2.

4. Which of the following could cause the change shown in the graph?
   a. A decrease in the price of the product.
   b. An increase in supply of the product.
   c. A change in consumer tastes.
   d. A decrease in the price of a substitute for the product.

5. What will be the result on the equilibrium price for the product?
   a. Increase.
   b. Decrease.
   c. Remain the same.
   d. Cannot be determined.

**6. Which one of the following has an inverse relationship with the demand for money?
   a. Aggregate income.
   b. Price levels.
   c. Interest rates.
   d. Flow of funds.

**7. An improvement in technology that in turn leads to improved worker productivity would most likely result in
   a. A shift to the right in the supply curve and a lowering of the price of the output.
   b. A shift to the left in the supply curve and a lowering of the price of the output.
   c. An increase in the price of the output if demand is unchanged.
   d. Wage increases.

8. Which of the following market features is likely to cause a surplus of a particular product?
   a. A monopoly.
   b. A price floor.
   c. A price ceiling.
   d. A perfect market.

**9. A decrease in the price of a complementary good will
   a. Shift the demand curve of the joint commodity to the left.
   b. Increase the price paid for a substitute good.
   c. Shift the supply curve of the joint commodity to the left.
   d. Shift the demand curve of the joint commodity to the right.

**10. Demand for a product tends to be price inelastic if
   a. The product is considered a luxury item.
   b. Few good complements for the product are available.
   c. The population in the market area is large.
   d. People spend a large share of their income on the product.

11. Which of the following has the highest price elasticity coefficient?
   a. Milk.
   b. Macaroni and cheese.
   c. Bread.
   d. Ski boats.

**12. The local video store's business increased by 12% after the movie theater raised its prices from $6.50 to $7.00. Thus, relative to movie theater admissions, videos are
   a. Substitute goods.
   b. Superior goods.
   c. Complementary goods.
   d. Public goods.

*13. An individual receives an income of $3,000 per month, and spends $2,500. An increase in income of $500 per month occurs, and the individual spends $2,800. The individual's marginal propensity to save is
   a. 0.2
   b. 0.4
   c. 0.6
   d. 0.8

**14. In any competitive market, an equal increase in both demand and supply can be expected to always
   a. Increase both price and market-clearing quantity.
   b. Decrease both price and market-clearing quantity.
   c. Increase market-clearing quantity.
   d. Increase price.

**15. Given the following data, what is the marginal propensity to consume?

---

  * *CIA adapted*
 ** *CMA adapted*

Level of	
Disposable income	Consumption
$40,000	$38,000
48,000	44,000

a. 1.33
b. 1.16
c. 0.95
d. 0.75

*16. Which of the following will cause a shift in the supply curve of a product?
a. Changes in the price of the product.
b. Changes in production taxes.
c. Changes in consumer tastes.
d. Changes in the number of buyers in the market.

**17. When the federal government imposes health and safety regulations on certain products, one of the most likely results is
a. Greater consumption of the product.
b. Lower prices for the product.
c. Greater tax revenues for the federal government.
d. Higher prices for the product.

18. In which of the following situations would there be inelastic demand?
a. A 5% price increase results in 3% decrease in the quantity demanded.
b. A 4% price increase results in a 6% decrease in the quantity demanded.
c. A 4% price increase results in a 4% decrease in the quantity demanded.
d. A 3% price decrease results in 5% increase in the quantity demanded.

**19. In a competitive market for labor in which demand is stable, if workers try to increase their wage
a. Employment must fall.
b. Government must set a maximum wage below the equilibrium wage.
c. Firms in the industry must become smaller.
d. Product supply must decrease.

*20. A polluting manufacturing firm tends, from the societal viewpoint, to
a. Price its products too low.
b. Produce too little output.
c. Report too little profitability.
d. Employ too little equity financing.

**21. If the federal government regulates a product or service in a competitive market by setting a maximum price below the equilibrium price, what is the long-run effect?
a. A surplus.
b. A shortage.
c. A decrease in demand.
d. No effect on the market.

**22. A valid reason for the government to intervene in the wholesale electrical power market would include which one of the following?
a. A price increase that is more than expected.
b. Electricity is an essential resource and the wholesale market is not competitive.

c. The electricity distribution companies are losing money.
d. Foreign power generators have contracts with the local government at very high prices.

23. If the income elasticity of demand coefficient for a particular product is 3.00, the good is likely
a. A luxury good.
b. A complementary good.
c. An inferior good.
d. A necessity.

**24. Long Lake Golf Course has raised greens fees for a nine-hole game due to an increase in demand.

	Previous rate	New rate	Average games played at previous rate	Average games played at new rate
Regular weekday	$10	$11	80	70
Senior citizen	6	8	150	82
Weekend	15	20	221	223

Which one of the following is correct?
a. The regular weekday and weekend demand is inelastic.
b. The regular weekday and weekend demand is elastic.
c. The senior citizen demand is elastic, and weekend demand is inelastic.
d. The regular weekday demand is inelastic, and weekend demand is elastic.

**25. Which one of the following would cause the demand curve for a commodity to shift to the left?
a. A rise in the price of a substitute product.
b. A rise in average household income.
c. A rise in the price of a complementary commodity.
d. A rise in the population.

**26. Price ceilings
a. Are illustrated by government price support programs in agriculture.
b. Create prices greater than equilibrium prices.
c. Create prices below equilibrium prices.
d. Result in persistent surpluses.

*27. X and Y are substitute products. If the price of product Y increases, the immediate impact on product X is
a. Price will increase.
b. Quantity demanded will increase.
c. Quantity supplied will increase.
d. Price, quantity demanded, and supply will increase.

28. Wilson Corporation has a major competitor that produces a product that is a close substitute for Wilson's good. If the coefficient of cross-elasticity of demand for Wilson's product with respect to the competitor's product is 2.00 and the competitor decreases its price by 5%, what is the expected effect on demand for Wilson's product?
a. A 5% increase in demand.
b. A 5% decrease in demand.
c. A 10% increase in demand.
d. A 10% decrease in demand.

**29. As the price for a particular product changes, the quantity of the product demanded changes according to the following schedule:

---

* CIA adapted
** CMA adapted

Total quantity demanded	Price per unit
100	$50
150	45
200	40
225	35
230	30
232	25

Using the arc method, the price elasticity of demand for this product when the price decreases from $50 to $45 is

- a. 0.20
- b. 10.00
- c. 0.10
- d. 3.80

30. As the price for a particular product changes, the quantity of the product demanded changes according to the following schedule:

Total quantity demanded	Price per unit
100	$50
150	45
200	40
225	35
230	30
232	25

Using the arc method, the price elasticity of demand for this product when the price decreases from $40 to $35 is

- a. 0.20
- b. 0.88
- c. 10.00
- d. 5.00

31. If a group of consumers decide to boycott a particular product, the expected result would be

- a. An increase in the product price to make up lost revenue.
- b. A decrease in the demand for the product.
- c. An increase in product supply because of increased availability.
- d. That demand for the product would become completely inelastic.

32. Which of the following is not likely to affect the supply of a particular good?

- a. Changes in government subsidies.
- b. Changes in technology.
- c. Changes in consumer income.
- d. Changes in production costs.

33. If a product's demand is elastic and there is a decrease in price, the effect will be

- a. A decrease in total revenue.
- b. No change in total revenue.
- c. A decrease in total revenue and the demand curve shifts to the left.
- d. An increase in total revenue.

34. All of the following are complementary goods except

- a. Margarine and butter.
- b. Cameras and rolls of film.
- c. VCRs and video cassettes.
- d. Razors and razor blades.

35. The law of diminishing marginal utility states that

- a. Marginal utility will decline as a consumer acquires additional units of a specific product.

- b. Total utility will decline as a consumer acquires additional units of a specific product.
- c. Declining utilities causes the demand curve to slope upward.
- d. Consumers' wants will diminish with the passage of time.

36. In the pharmaceutical industry where a diabetic must have insulin no matter the cost and where there is no other substitute, the diabetic's demand curve is **best** described as

- a. Perfectly elastic.
- b. Perfectly inelastic.
- c. Elastic.
- d. Inelastic.

37. Because of the existence of economies of scale, business firms may find that

- a. Each additional unit of labor is less efficient than the previous unit.
- b. As more labor is added to a factory, increases in output will diminish in the short run.
- c. Increasing the size of a factory will result in lower average costs.
- d. Increasing the size of a factory will result in lower total costs.

38. In the long run, a firm may experience increasing returns due to

- a. Law of diminishing returns.
- b. Opportunity costs.
- c. Comparative advantage.
- d. Economies of scale.

39. The measurement of the benefit lost by using resources for a given purpose is

- a. Economic efficiency.
- b. Opportunity cost.
- c. Comparative advantage.
- d. Absolute advantage.

Items 40 and 41 are based on the following information:

Total units of product	Average fixed cost	Average variable cost	Average total cost
6	$15.00	$25.00	$40.00
7	12.86	24.00	36.86
8	11.25	23.50	34.75
9	10.00	23.75	33.75

40. The total cost of producing seven units is

- a. $ 90.02
- b. $168.00
- c. $258.02
- d. $280.00

41. The marginal cost of producing the ninth unit is

- a. $23.50
- b. $23.75
- c. $25.75
- d. $33.75

42. Daily costs for Kelso Manufacturing include $1,000 of fixed costs and total variable costs are show below.

Unit output	10	11	12	13	14	15
Cost	$125	$250	$400	$525	$700	$825

The average total cost at an output level of 11 units is

- a. $113.64
- b. $125.00

c. $215.91
d. $250.00

Items 43 through 45 are based on the following information:

Number of workers	Total product units	Average selling price
10	20	$50.00
11	25	49.00
12	28	47.50

**43. The marginal physical product when one worker is added to a team of 10 workers is
   a. 1 unit.
   b. 8 units.
   c. 5 units.
   d. 25 units.

**44. The marginal revenue per unit when one worker is added to a team of 11 workers is
   a. $105.00
   b. $225.00
   c. $ 35.00
   d. $ 47.50

**45. The marginal revenue product when one worker is added to a team of 11 workers is
   a. $ 42.00
   b. $225.00
   c. $105.00
   d. $ 47.50

**46. Marginal revenue is
   a. Equal to price in monopolistic competition.
   b. The change in total revenue associated with increasing prices.
   c. Greater than price in pure competition.
   d. The change in total revenue associated with producing and selling one more unit.

**47. In microeconomics, the distinguishing characteristic of the long run on the supply side is that
   a. Only supply factors determine price and output.
   b. Only demand factors determine price and output.
   c. Firms are not allowed to enter or exit the industry.
   d. All inputs are variable.

48. What is the main factor that differentiates the short-run cost function from the long-run cost function?
   a. Nothing, the two functions are identical.
   b. The level of technology.
   c. Changes in government subsidies.
   d. The nature of the costs.

49. If consumer confidence falls, the impact upon the economy is
   a. A downturn.
   b. An upturn.
   c. No change.
   d. Consumer confidence does not have an impact upon the economy.

**50. If an increase in government purchases of goods and services of $20 billion causes equilibrium GDP to rise by $80 billion, and if total taxes and investment are constant, the marginal propensity to consume out of disposable income is

a. 0.75
b. 0.25
c. 1.25
d. 4.00

**51. During the recessionary phase of a business cycle
   a. The purchasing power of money is likely to decline rapidly.
   b. The natural rate of unemployment will increase dramatically.
   c. Potential national income will exceed actual national income.
   d. Actual national income will exceed potential national income.

*52. For a given level of tax collections, prices, and interest rates, a decrease in governmental purchases will result in a(n)
   a. Increase in aggregate demand.
   b. Increase in aggregate supply.
   c. Decrease in aggregate demand.
   d. Decrease in aggregate supply.

**53. In national income terms, aggregate demand is the
   a. Demand for money by the community in a period of full employment.
   b. Total expenditure on capital goods by entrepreneurs during a period of full employment.
   c. Demand that is needed if a country's economy is to operate at optimum level and the level of investment is to be raised.
   d. Total expenditures on consumer goods and investment, including government and foreign expenditures, during a given period.

*54. Which one of the following would not be included in the calculation of the gross domestic product (GDP)?
   a. Purchase of a new home.
   b. An automotive worker's wages.
   c. A doctor's fee.
   d. Purchase of common stock.

55. An upturn in economic activity is indicated by all of the following, except
   a. Increased housing starts.
   b. Reduction in the quantity of unemployment claims.
   c. Increase in personal travel.
   d. Reduction in the amount of luxury purchases.

56. Which of the following may provide a leading indicator of a future increase in gross domestic product?
   a. A reduction in the money supply.
   b. A decrease in the issuance of building permits.
   c. An increase in the timeliness of delivery by vendors.
   d. An increase in the average hours worked per week of production workers.

*57. Disposable income is calculated as
   a. Gross domestic product minus the capital cost allowance.
   b. Net domestic product minus indirect business taxes plus net income earned abroad.
   c. Personal income minus transfer payments.
   d. Personal income minus personal taxes.

---

* *CIA adapted*
** *CMA adapted*

*58. The primary reason for allowing legal immigration into industrial nations is the immigrants' potential for
    a. Reducing a trade deficit.
    b. Fulfilling a trade agreement.
    c. Contributing to economic growth.
    d. Fulfilling a political agreement.

*59. Some economic indicators lead the economy into a recovery or recession, and some lag it. An example of a lagging indicator is
    a. Chronic unemployment.
    b. Orders for consumer and producer goods.
    c. Housing starts.
    d. Consumer expectations.

**60. Government borrowing to finance large deficits increases the demand for lendable funds and
    a. Increases the supply of lendable funds.
    b. Exerts downward pressure on interest rates.
    c. Has no impact on interest rates.
    d. Puts upward pressure on interest rates.

**61. A period of rising inflation
    a. Increases the price level, which benefits those who are entitled to receive specific amounts of money.
    b. Enhances the positive relationship between the price level and the purchasing power of money.
    c. Will not be affected by contracts that include the indexing of payments.
    d. Increases the price level, which is negatively related to the purchasing power of money.

**62. The most effective fiscal policy program to help reduce demand-pull inflation would be to
    a. Decrease the rate of growth of the money supply.
    b. Increase both taxes and government spending.
    c. Decrease taxes and increase government spending.
    d. Increase taxes and decrease government spending.

*63. The money supply in a nation's economy will decrease following
    a. Open-market purchases by the nation's central bank.
    b. A decrease in the discount rate.
    c. An increase in the reserve ratio.
    d. A decrease in the margin requirement.

**64. The Federal Reserve Board most directly influences a corporation's decision of whether or not to issue debt or equity financing when it revises the
    a. Corporate income tax rate.
    b. Prime rate at which the Federal Reserve Bank lends money to member banks.
    c. Discount rate at which the Federal Reserve Bank lends money to member banks.
    d. Discount rate at which member banks lend money to their customers.

**65. According to fiscal policy principles, a tax increase will
    a. Increase spending and increase aggregate demand.
    b. Increase spending and reduce aggregate demand.
    c. Reduce spending and increase aggregate demand.
    d. Reduce spending and reduce aggregate demand.

**66. If the Federal Reserve Board wanted to implement an expansionary monetary policy, which one of the following actions would the Federal Reserve Board take?
    a. Raise the reserve requirement and the discount rate.
    b. Purchase additional US government securities and lower the discount rate.
    c. Reduce the reserve requirement and raise the discount rate.
    d. Raise the discount rate and sell US government securities.

**67. The Federal Reserve System's reserve ratio is
    a. The specified percentage of a commercial bank's deposit liabilities that must be deposited in the central bank.
    b. The rate that the central bank charges for loans granted to commercial banks.
    c. The ratio of excess reserves to legal reserves that are deposited in the central bank.
    d. The specified percentage of a commercial bank's demand deposits to total liabilities.

*68. Which of the following instruments of monetary policy is the most important means by which the money supply is controlled?
    a. Changing the reserve ratio.
    b. Open-market operations.
    c. Manipulation of government spending.
    d. Changing the discount rate.

*69. If a government were to use only fiscal policy to stimulate the economy from a recession, it would
    a. Raise consumer taxes and increase government spending.
    b. Lower business taxes and government spending.
    c. Increase the money supply and increase government spending.
    d. Lower consumer taxes and increase government spending.

**70. The federal budget deficit is the
    a. Total accumulation of the federal government's surpluses and deficits.
    b. Excess state, local, and federal spending over their revenues.
    c. Amount by which the federal government's expenditures exceed its revenues in a given year.
    d. Amount by which liabilities exceed assets on the federal government's balance sheet.

*71. Which of the following is a tool of monetary policy that a nation's central bank could use to stabilize the economy during an inflationary period?
    a. Selling government securities.
    b. Lowering bank reserve requirements.
    c. Lowering bank discount rates.
    d. Encouraging higher tax rates.

**72. Economists and economic policy makers are interested in the multiplier effect because the multiplier explains why
    a. A small change in investment can have a much larger impact on gross domestic product.
    b. Consumption is always a multiple of savings.

---

* CIA adapted
** CMA adapted

c. The money supply increases when deposits in the banking system increase.

d. The velocity of money is less than one.

73. Assume that the United States Congress passes a tax law that provides for a "rebate" to taxpayers. One of the goals of the rebate is

a. Increase consumer disposable income and expand the economy.

b. Increase consumer disposable income and contract the economy.

c. Decrease consumer disposable income and expand the economy.

d. Increase consumer disposable income and contract the economy.

74. The rate of unemployment caused by changes in the composition of unemployment opportunities over time is referred to as the

a. Frictional unemployment rate.

b. Cyclical unemployment rate.

c. Structural unemployment rate.

d. Full-employment unemployment rate.

75. The producer price index measures

a. The price of a basket of commodities at the point of the first commercial sale.

b. Price changes for all products sold by domestic producers to foreigners.

c. Price changes of goods purchased from other countries.

d. The price of a fixed market basket of goods and services purchased by a typical urban consumer.

76. The formula for calculating a price index for the year 2009, using the year 2004 as a reference period is

a. $\dfrac{\text{Price of 2009 market basket in 2009}}{\text{Price of 2009 market basket in 2004}} \times 100$

b. $\dfrac{\text{Price of 2004 market basket in 2009}}{\text{Price of 2004 market basket in 2004}} \times 100$

c. $\dfrac{\text{Price of 2009 market basket in 2004}}{\text{Price of 2004 market basket in 2004}} \times 100$

d. $\dfrac{\text{Price of 2004 market basket in 2004}}{\text{Price of 2004 market basket in 2009}} \times 100$

**77. The discount rate set by the Federal Reserve System is the

a. Required percentage of reserves deposited at the central bank.

b. Rate that commercial banks charge for loans to each other.

c. Rate that commercial banks charge for loans to the general public.

d. Rate that the central bank charges for loans to commercial banks.

78. Which of the following is true about deflation?

a. It motivates consumers to borrow money.

b. It motivates businesses to make investments.

c. It results in very low interest rates.

d. It results in economic expansion.

79. Economies often experience inflation but seldom experience long period of deflation. Which of the following is true about a deflationary economy?

a. Companies are hesitant to make investments.

b. The lower prices encourage consumers to make major purchases.

c. Interest rates tend to be high.

d. Actual GDP is above potential GDP.

80. What factor explains the difference between real and nominal interest rates?

a. Inflation risk.

b. Credit risk.

c. Default risk.

d. Market risk.

81. All of the following are true about international trade **except that

a. The gains from international trade depend on specialization with comparative advantage.

b. Absolute advantage without comparative advantage does not result in gains from international trade.

c. Absolute advantage is defined as the ability of one nation to produce a product at a relatively lower opportunity cost than another nation.

d. Where there is reciprocal absolute advantage between two countries, specialization will make it possible to produce more of each product.

82. If the central bank of a country raises interest rates sharply, the country's currency will **most likely

a. Increase in relative value.

b. Remain unchanged in value.

c. Decrease in relative value.

d. Decrease sharply in value at first and then return to its initial value.

83. Which one of the following groups would be the **primary beneficiary of a tariff?

a. Domestic producers of export goods.

b. Domestic producers of goods protected by the tariff.

c. Domestic consumers of goods protected by the tariff.

d. Foreign producers of goods protected by the tariff.

84. In the law of comparative advantage, the country which should produce a specific product is determined by

a. Opportunity costs.

b. Profit margins.

c. Economic order quantities.

d. Tariffs.

**85. Assuming exchange rates are allowed to fluctuate freely, which one of the following factors would likely cause a nation's currency to appreciate on the foreign exchange market?

a. A relatively rapid rate of growth in income that stimulates imports.

b. A high rate of inflation relative to other countries.

c. A slower rate of growth in income than in other countries, which causes imports to lag behind exports.

d. Domestic real interest rates that are lower than real interest rates abroad.

86. If the US dollar declines in value relative to the currencies of many of its trading partners, the likely result is that
     a. Foreign currencies will depreciate against the dollar.
     b. The US balance of payments deficit will become worse.
     c. US exports will tend to increase.
     d. US imports will tend to increase.

87. Exchange rates are determined by
     a. Each industrial country's government.
     b. The International Monetary Fund.
     c. Supply and demand in the foreign currency market.
     d. Exporters and importers of manufactured goods.

88. If the value of the US dollar in foreign currency markets changes from $1 = 6 marks to $1 = 4 marks
     a. The German mark has depreciated against the dollar.
     b. German imported products in the US will become more expensive.
     c. US tourists in Germany will find their dollars will buy more German products.
     d. US exports to Germany should decrease.

89. Which of the following measures creates the most restrictive barrier to exporting to a country?
     a. Tariffs.
     b. Quotas.
     c. Embargoes.
     d. Exchange controls.

90. When net exports are negative, there is a net flow of
     a. Goods from firms in foreign countries to the domestic country.
     b. Money from foreign countries to the firms of the domestic country.
     c. Goods from the firms of the domestic country to foreign countries.
     d. Goods and services which result in a trade surplus.

91. Which of the following factors is least likely to affect a country's currency foreign exchange rates?
     a. Interest rates in the country.
     b. Political stability in the country.
     c. Inflation in the country.
     d. The tax rate in the country.

92. Assume that the exchange rate of US dollars to euros is $1.80 to 1 euro. How much would a US company gain or lose if the company has a 10,000 euro receivable and the exchange rate went to $1.75 to 1 euro?
     a. $10,000 loss.
     b. $10,000 gain.
     c. $500 loss
     d. $500 gain.

93. Simon Corp., a US company, has made a large sale to a French company on a 120-day account payable in euros. If management of Simon wants to hedge the transaction risk related to a decline in the value of the euro, which of the following strategies would be appropriate?

     a. Lend euros to another company for payment in 120 days.
     b. Enter into a forward exchange contract to purchase euros for delivery in 120 days.
     c. Enter into a futures contract to sell euros for delivery in the future.
     d. Purchase euros on the spot market.

94. Which of the following is not a means by which a firm might hedge the political risk of an investment in another country?
     a. Insurance.
     b. Buy futures contracts for future delivery of the country's currency.
     c. Finance the operations with local-country capital.
     d. Enter into joint ventures with local-country firms.

Items 95 and 96 are based on the following information:

Karen Parker wants to establish an environmental testing company that would specialize in evaluating the quality of water found in rivers and streams. However, Parker has discovered that she needs either certification or approval from five separate local and state agencies before she can commence business. Also, the necessary equipment to begin would cost several million dollars. Nevertheless, Parker believes that if she is able to obtain capital resources, she can gain market share from the two major competitors.

95. The large capital outlay necessary for the equipment is an example of a(n)
     a. Entry barrier.
     b. Minimum efficient scale.
     c. Created barrier.
     d. Production possibility boundary.

96. The market structure Karen Parker is attempting to enter is best described as
     a. A natural monopoly.
     b. A cartel.
     c. An oligopoly.
     d. Monopolistic competition.

97. Patents are granted in order to encourage firms to invest in the research and development of new products. Patents are an example of
     a. Vertical integration.
     b. Market concentration.
     c. Entry barriers.
     d. Collusion.

98. The distinguishing characteristic of oligopolistic markets is
     a. A single seller of a homogeneous product with no close substitutes.
     b. A single seller of a heterogeneous product with no close substitutes.
     c. Lack of entry and exit barriers in the industry.
     d. Mutual interdependence of firm pricing and output decisions.

99. Economic markets that are characterized by monopolistic competition have all of the following characteristics except
     a. One seller of the product.
     b. Economies or diseconomies of scale.
     c. Advertising.
     d. Heterogeneous products.

---

  * *CIA adapted*
 ** *CMA adapted*

100. Which type of economic market structure is characterized by a few large sellers of a product or service, engaging primarily in nonprice competition?
    a. Monopoly.
    b. Oligopoly.
    c. Perfect competition.
    d. Monopolistic competition.

101. Which type of economic market structure is composed of a large number of sellers, each producing an identical product, and with no significant barriers to entry and exit?
    a. Monopoly.
    b. Oligopoly.
    c. Perfect competition
    d. Monopolistic competition.

102. The market for product RK-25 is perfectly competitive. The current market price is $30, and the quantity demanded is 4 million. Due to changes in consumer tastes, a permanent increase in demand for RK-25 is expected in the near term. If nothing else changes in this market, which of the following would be the **most feasible levels of short-term and long-term prices?

	Short-term	Long-term
a.	$39	$35
b.	$35	$39
c.	$35	$30
d.	$30	$35

**103. A natural monopoly exists because
    a. The firm owns natural resources.
    b. The firms holds patents.
    c. Economic and technical conditions permit only one efficient supplier.
    d. The government is the only supplier.

104. A market with many independent firms, low barriers to entry, and product differentiation is **best classified as
    a. A monopoly.
    b. A natural monopoly.
    c. Monopolistic competition.
    d. An oligopoly.

105. Which of the following is **not a key assumption of perfect competition?
    a. Firms sell a homogeneous product.
    b. Customers are indifferent about which firm they buy from.
    c. The level of a firm's output is small relative to the industry's total output.
    d. Each firm can price its product above the industry price.

106. The ultimate purpose of competitor analysis is to
    a. Identify the competition.
    b. Determine the competition's strength and weaknesses.
    c. Identify the competition's major customers.
    d. Understand and predict the behavior of the competition.

107. Which of the following is not an important aspect of supply chain management?
    a. Information technology.

    b. Accurate forecasts.
    c. Customer relations.
    d. Communications.

108. Which of the following types of organizations would more likely engage in public relations type advertising?
    a. An airline.
    b. A hotel chain.
    c. A toy manufacturer.
    d. An electric utility company.

109. Target marketing analysis involves
    a. Analyzing the firm's input markets.
    b. Understanding and segmenting the firm's customer markets.
    c. Analyzing the firm's market structure.
    d. Deciding on whether to offer a new product line.

110. If a firm's customers are businesses, market segmentation might be performed along all of the following dimensions, except
    a. Industry.
    b. Location.
    c. Lifestyle.
    d. Size.

Items 111 through 112 are based on the following information:

Yeager Corporation has used regression analysis to perform price elasticity analysis. In doing so management regressed the quantity demanded (y variable) against price (x variable) with the following results:

Multiple R	.86798
Adjusted R squared	.72458
Standard error	542.33
Intercept	56400.50
Price coefficient	–4598.20

111. What percentage of the variation in quantity demanded is explained by price?
    a. 86.798%
    b. 72.458%
    c. 56.4%
    d. 54.233%

112. Calculate the predicted quantity demanded if price is set at $7.00.
    a. 24,213
    b. 88,588
    c. 31,234
    d. 18,454

113. Which of the following is not one of the five forces in Porter's model for industry analysis?
    a. Competitors.
    b. Bargaining power of customers.
    c. Bargaining power of suppliers.
    d. General economic conditions.

114. Which of the following is a defining characteristic of supply chain management?
    a. Focuses on the sharing of information with suppliers and customers.
    b. Focuses on redesigning processes.
    c. Focuses on improving quality.
    d. Focuses on strategic alliances.

** CMA adapted

115. Which of the following is not a likely strategy for a firm in a purely competitive market?

a. Lean manufacturing.
b. Supply chain management.
c. Process reengineering.
d. Development of a brand name.

116. What is the purpose of a response profile in competitor analysis?

a. To develop an understanding of the firm's industry.
b. To analyze the firm's strengths in relation to its competitors.
c. To identify possible actions by competitors.
d. To understand the nature of the firm's major markets.

**117. The process of dividing all potential consumers into smaller groups of buyers with distinct needs, characteristics, or behaviors, who might require a similar product or service mix, is called

a. Strategic planning.
b. Market segmentation.
c. Product positioning.
d. Objective setting.

118. Which of the following measures of unemployment would be of least importance to management when trying to predict the future state of the economy?

a. Structural unemployment.
b. Cyclical unemployment.
c. Frictional unemployment.
d. Overall unemployment.

119. Which of the following best describes the steps involved in performing competitor analysis?

a. Gathering information about the competitor and using it to predict the competitor' behavior.
b. Determining the type of market structure and the number of competitors.
c. Assessing the general environment and determining how that affects competition.
d. Assessing the market structure to predict when new competitors will enter the market.

**120. An oligopolist faces a "kinked" demand curve. This terminology indicates that

a. When an oligopolist lowers its price, the other firms in the oligopoly will match the price reduction, but if the oligopolist raises its price, the other firms will ignore the price change.
b. An oligopolist faces a nonlinear demand for its product, and price changes will have little effect on demand for that product.
c. An oligopolist can sell its product at any price, but after the "saturation point" another oligopolist will lower its price and, therefore, shift the demand curve to the left.
d. Consumers have no effect on the demand curve, and an oligopolist can shape the curve to optimize its own efficiency.

** CMA adapted

MULTIPLE-CHOICE ANSWERS

1. c	__ __	26. c	__ __	51. c	__ __	76. a	__ __	101. c	__ __
2. a	__ __	27. b	__ __	52. c	__ __	77. d	__ __	102. c	__ __
3. a	__ __	28. d	__ __	53. d	__ __	78. c	__ __	103. c	__ __
4. c	__ __	29. d	__ __	54. d	__ __	79. a	__ __	104. c	__ __
5. a	__ __	30. b	__ __	55. d	__ __	80. a	__ __	105. d	__ __
6. c	__ __	31. b	__ __	56. d	__ __	81. c	__ __	106. d	__ __
7. a	__ __	32. c	__ __	57. d	__ __	82. a	__ __	107. c	__ __
8. b	__ __	33. d	__ __	58. c	__ __	83. b	__ __	108. d	__ __
9. d	__ __	34. a	__ __	59. a	__ __	84. a	__ __	109. b	__ __
10. d	__ __	35. a	__ __	60. d	__ __	85. c	__ __	110. c	__ __
11. d	__ __	36. b	__ __	61. d	__ __	86. c	__ __	111. b	__ __
12. a	__ __	37. c	__ __	62. d	__ __	87. c	__ __	112. a	__ __
13. b	__ __	38. d	__ __	63. c	__ __	88. b	__ __	113. d	__ __
14. c	__ __	39. b	__ __	64. c	__ __	89. c	__ __	114. a	__ __
15. d	__ __	40. c	__ __	65. d	__ __	90. a	__ __	115. d	__ __
16. b	__ __	41. c	__ __	66. b	__ __	91. d	__ __	116. c	__ __
17. d	__ __	42. a	__ __	67. a	__ __	92. c	__ __	117. b	__ __
18. a	__ __	43. c	__ __	68. b	__ __	93. c	__ __	118. c	__ __
19. a	__ __	44. c	__ __	69. d	__ __	94. d	__ __	119. a	__ __
20. a	__ __	45. c	__ __	70. c	__ __	95. a	__ __	120. a	__ __
21. b	__ __	46. d	__ __	71. a	__ __	96. c	__ __		
22. b	__ __	47. d	__ __	72. a	__ __	97. c	__ __		
23. a	__ __	48. d	__ __	73. a	__ __	98. d	__ __		
24. c	__ __	49. a	__ __	74. c	__ __	99. a	__ __	1st:	__/120 __%
25. c	__ __	50. a	__ __	75. a	__ __	100. b	__ __	2nd:	__/120 __%

MULTIPLE-CHOICE ANSWER EXPLANATIONS

Demand, Supply, and Market Equilibrium

1. (c) The requirement is to predict the market price based on an increase in both supply and demand. The correct answer is (c) because without additional information about the extent of the change, the effect on price is not determinable. Answer (a), (b), and (d) are incorrect because the price elasticity of the demand or supply function does not provide enough information to determine the effect.

2. (a) The requirement is to describe the relationship shown by a supply curve. A supply curve illustrates the quantity supplied at varying prices at a point in time. Therefore, the correct answer is (a). Answers (b) and (c) are incorrect because they deal with demand. Answer (d) is incorrect because it deals with demand-supply equilibrium.

3. (a) The requirement is to apply the concept of price-elasticity of demand. If demand is inelastic an increase in price will increase total revenue. Answer (a) is correct because it accurately states this rule. Answer (b) is incorrect because if demand is inelastic the quantity demanded will not be affected significantly by a change in price. Answer (c) is incorrect because if the quantity demanded is not significantly affected by an increase in price, total revenue will increase. Answer (d) is incorrect because an increase in price may, or may not, increase competition.

4. (c) The requirement is to identify the reason for the shift in demand. The correct answer is (c) because a shift demand could result from a change in consumer tastes. Answer (a) is incorrect because this would result in movement along the existing demand curve. Answer (b) is incorrect because a change in supply would not affect the demand function. Answer (d) is incorrect because a decrease in price of a substitute would result in a shift of the curve to the left.

5. (a) The requirement is to determine the effect of the shift in the demand function on the price of the product. The correct answer is (a) because the shift (increase) in demand will increase the price of the product. Answer (b) is incorrect because a shift of the demand curve to the left would have to occur to decrease price. Answers (c) and (d) are incorrect because the effect on price will not be to remain the same and it can be determined.

6. (c) The requirement is to identify the item that has an inverse relationship with the demand for money. The correct answer is (c) because as interest rates increase the demand for money decreases. Answers (a), (b), and (d) are incorrect because they do not have an inverse relationship with the demand for money.

7. (a) The requirement is to describe the effect of an improvement in technology that leads to increased worker productivity. If the cost of producing a good declines more will be supplied at a given price. Therefore, the supply curve will shift to the right and answer (a) is correct. Answer (b) is incorrect because a shift to the left would result in decreased supplies. Answer (c) is incorrect because price would not increase, and answer (d) is incorrect because wages would not necessarily increase.

8. (b) The requirement is to identify the market feature that is likely to cause a surplus of a particular product. Answer (b) is correct because a price floor, if it is above the equilibrium price, will cause excess production and a surplus. Answer (a) is incorrect because a monopoly market is likely to be characterized by underproduction of the product. Answer (c) is incorrect because a price ceiling, if it is below the equilibrium price, will cause underproduction and shortages. Answer (d) is incorrect because in a perfect market with no intervention demand and supply will be equal.

9. **(d)** The requirement is to describe the effect on demand for a good if a complementary good decreases in price. If the price of a complementary good decreases, demand for the joint commodity will increase. This is due to the fact that the total cost of using the two products decreases. If demand for a product increases the demand curve will shift to the right. Therefore, answer (d) is correct. Answer (a) is incorrect because a shift in the demand curve to the left depicts a decrease in demand. Answers (b) and (c) deal with supply and are not relevant.

10. **(d)** The requirement is to identify a characteristic of a product with price inelastic demand. The correct answer is (d) because price inelasticity means that the quantity demanded does not change much with price changes. This would be a characteristic of a good with few substitutes. Answers (a), (b), and (c) are characteristics of goods that have price elastic demand.

11. **(d)** The requirement is to apply the concept of price elasticity of demand. If substitutes for a good are readily available then the demand for the good is more elastic. Answer (d) is correct because there are many substitutes for luxury goods. Answers (a), (b), and (c) are all considered to be necessities and demand for them is less elastic.

12. **(a)** The requirement is to identify the relationship between two products for which one has increased demand when the other's price increases. Answer (a) is correct. Substitute goods are selected by a consumer based on price. When the price of one goes up, demand for the other increases. Answer (b) is incorrect because superior goods are those whose demand is directly influenced by income. Answer (c) is incorrect because complementary goods are used together and when the price of one goes up, demand for the other goes down. Answer (d) is incorrect because a public good is one for which it is difficult to restrict use, such as a national park.

13. **(b)** The requirement is to calculate the marginal propensity to save. Answer (b) is correct because the marginal propensity to save is the change in savings divided by the change in income [($700 − $500)/($3,500 − $3,000) = .4]. Answer (a) is incorrect because the average propensity to save would be calculated by dividing the new savings by the new income ($700/$3,500 = .2). Answer (c) is incorrect because the marginal propensity to consume is the change in spending divided by the change in income [($2,800 − $2,500)/($3,500 − $3,000) = .6]. Answer (d) is incorrect because the average propensity to consume would be calculated by dividing the new consumption by the new income ($2,800/$3,500 = .8).

14. **(c)** The requirement is to describe market conditions in a competitive market when both demand and supply increase. In a competitive market, the market will always clear at the equilibrium price. If there is an equal increase in both demand and supply, the equilibrium price may increase, decrease, or remain the same. However, there will be more units sold and, therefore, answer (c) is correct. Answers (a), (b), and (d) are incorrect because the equilibrium price may increase, decrease, or remain the same.

15. **(d)** The requirement is to calculate the marginal propensity to consume. Answer (d) is correct because the marginal propensity to consume is calculated by dividing the change in consumption by the change in disposable income.

Therefore, the marginal propensity to consume would be .75 [($44,000 − $38,000)/($48,000 − $40,000)].

16. **(b)** The requirement is to determine the item that will cause a shift in the supply curve. A shift in the supply curve may result from (1) changes in production technology, (2) changes or expected changes in resource prices, (3) changes in the prices of other goods, (4) changes in taxes or subsidies, (5) changes in the number of sellers in the market, and (6) expectations about the future price of the product. Answer (b) is correct because it identifies changes in production taxes, which will alter the supply curve. Answer (a) is incorrect because a change in the price of the product involves movement along the existing supply curve, not a shift in the supply curve. Answers (c) and (d) are incorrect because they identify changes that result in a shift in the demand curve.

17. **(d)** The requirement is to identify the effects of government regulation on a product. Government regulation increases the cost of the product and therefore will most likely result in higher prices. Thus answer (d) is correct. Answer (a) is incorrect because the regulation has no relationship to consumption. Answer (b) is incorrect because an increase in cost is not likely to result in a decrease in price. Answer (c) is incorrect because tax revenue will likely decline due to the added production costs and reduced sales.

18. **(a)** The requirement is to identify which of the situations indicate inelastic demand. Elasticity of demand is measured by the percentage change in the quantity demanded divided by the percentage change in price. If the quotient is greater than one, demand for product is price elastic, and if it less than one, demand for the product is price inelastic. A quotient of exactly one indicates unitary elasticity. Answer (a) is correct because the price elasticity quotient is equal to 0.6 (3%/5%). Answer (b) is incorrect because the quotient is 1.5 (6%/4%). Answer (c) is incorrect because the quotient is 1 (4%/4%). Answer (d) is incorrect because the quotient is equal to 1.67 (5%/3%).

19. **(a)** The requirement is to describe the effect of an increase in wages on demand for labor. Answer (a) is correct because, like any other good or service, if price is increased for labor, the demand will fall and employment will fall. Answer (b) is incorrect because setting a maximum wage will not allow workers to increase wages. Answer (c) is incorrect because firms may or may not change in size. Answer (d) is incorrect because supply will only decrease if the price of the product decreases.

20. **(a)** The requirement is to identify the market effects of a polluting manufacturer's actions. Answer (a) is correct because a polluting firm calculates its profits without considering the costs of environmental damage and, as a result, prices its products too low. Answer (b) is incorrect because the polluting manufacturer is producing too much, not too little output. Answer (c) is incorrect because the manufacturer reports too much, not too little profitability. Answer (d) is incorrect because there is no direct relationship between the use of equity versus debt financing and the externalities involved in the production activities of the firm.

21. **(b)** The requirement is to describe the effects of a government-mandated maximum price. If the government mandates a maximum price below the equilibrium price, the product will be selling at an artificially low price resulting in shortages. Thus the correct answer is (b). Answer (a) is incorrect because price floors result in surpluses. Answer (c) is incorrect because price ceilings would probably result in more demand. Answer (d) is incorrect because the market would be affected.

22.   (b)   The requirement is to identify a valid reason for government intervention in a wholesale market. Answer (b) is correct because a valid reason for government intervention is the lack of a competitive market. Answers (a), (c), and (d) are incorrect because they provide no indication that the market is not competitive.

23.   (a)   The requirement is to identify the type of good that is likely to have income elasticity coefficient of 3.00. Answer (a) is correct because an income elasticity coefficient of 3.00 indicates that demand for the good is very sensitive to income levels. This is a characteristic of a luxury good. Answer (b) is incorrect because while the good may be complementary, it would have to be complementary to a luxury good. Answer (c) is incorrect because an inferior good's coefficient will be negative. Answer (d) is incorrect because demand for a necessity is not sensitive to income levels.

24.   (c)   The requirement is to calculate the price elasticity of demand for golf. The price elasticity of demand is calculated as the percentage change in quantity divided by the percentage change in price. If the result is greater than one, demand is elastic; if it is less than one, it is inelastic; and if it is equal to one, it is unitary elastic. The regular weekday demand is elastic as calculated below.

$$\frac{(80 - 70) \div [(80 + 70) \div 2]}{(\$11 - \$10) \div [(\$11 + \$10) \div 2]} = 1.4$$

The weekend demand is inelastic as calculated below.

$$\frac{(223 - 221) \div [(223 + 221) \div 2]}{(\$20 - \$15) \div [(\$20 + \$15) \div 2]} = .03$$

The senior citizen demand is elastic as calculated below.

$$\frac{(150 - 82) \div [(150 + 82) \div 2]}{(\$8 - \$6) \div [(\$8 + \$6) \div 2]} = 2.05$$

The only statement that correctly defines these relationships is answer (c).

25.   (c)   The requirement is to identify the factor that would cause the demand curve for a product to shift to the left. Answer (c) is correct because a shift in the demand curve to the left would be indicative of a decrease in demand for the product, and an increase in the price of a complementary commodity would cause such a shift. Answers (a), (b), and (d) are incorrect because they would all potentially cause an increase in demand, causing the demand curve to shift to the right.

26.   (c)   The requirement is to describe the effect of price ceilings. Price ceilings cause the price of a product to be artificially low resulting in decreased supply. The price is below the equilibrium price as indicated by answer (c). Answer (a) is incorrect because government price support is an example of a price floor. Answer (b) is incorrect because price ceilings create prices less than equilibrium prices. Answer (d) is incorrect because price ceilings create shortages, not surpluses.

27.   (b)   The requirement is to determine the immediate effect upon one product of an increase in the price of a sub-

stitute good. The demand and price of substitute products are directly related. If the price of a good increases, the demand for its substitute will also increase. Answer (b) is correct because it depicts this relationship. Answer (a) is incorrect because the price of a product will not increase due to an increase in a substitute product's price. Answer (c) is incorrect because the quantity supplied will not be impacted by an increase in price of a substitute product. Answer (d) is incorrect because even though the quantity demanded will increase with an increase in price of a substitute product, the price and supply will not be directly affected.

28.   (d)   The requirement is to calculate the effect a decrease in the price of a substitute good has on demand for a good. Answer (d) is correct because if the coefficient of cross-elasticity is 2.00, a 5% decrease in price will result in a 10% (5% × 2.00) decrease in the demand for Wilson's product. Answers (a), (b), and (c) are incorrect because they misstate the relationship.

29.   (d)   The requirement is to calculate the price elasticity of demand for a product. Price elasticity using the arc method is calculated by dividing the percentage change in quantity demanded by the percentage change in price, using the average changes. In this case, price elasticity is calculated below.

$$\frac{(150 - 100) \div [(150 + 100) \div 2]}{(\$50 - \$45) \div [(\$50 + \$45) \div 2]} = 3.8$$

Therefore answer (d) is correct.

30.   (b)   The requirement is to calculate the price elasticity of demand. Answer (b) is correct because the formula for price elasticity is equal to the percentage change in quantity demanded divided by the percentage change in price. In this case, the percentage change in price is 0.88 as calculated below.

$$\frac{(225 - 200) \div [(225 + 200) \div 2]}{(\$40 - \$35) \div [(\$40 + \$35) \div 2]} = .088$$

31.   (b)   The requirement is to identify the effect of a boycott on demand for a good. Answer (b) is correct because a boycott means less people are purchasing the good. Therefore, demand is decreased. Answer (a) would not occur because, if anything, a decrease in demand would lead to a decrease in price. Answer (c) is incorrect because demand does not affect supply. Answer (d) is incorrect because the elasticity of demand for a good is determined by its nature.

32.   (c)   The requirement is to identify the factor that is not likely to affect the supply of a good. Answer (c) is correct because changes in consumer income could affect the demand for the good, but not its supply. Answer (a) is incorrect because government subsidies reduce the cost of producing a good, and therefore, affect supply. Answer (b) is incorrect because changes in technology can alter production costs, and therefore, affect supply. Answer (d) is incorrect because changes in production costs affect the supply of a good.

33.   (d)   The requirement is to identify the effect on total revenue of a decrease in price of a price-elastic product. Answer (d) is correct because if a product's demand is price-elastic, a decrease in price will lead to an even larger percentage increase in quantity demanded. Therefore, total revenue will increase. Answers (a), (b), and (c) are incorrect because they do not describe the appropriate effect.

34. (a) The requirement is to identify the goods that are not complementary goods. Complementary goods are those that are used together because they enhance each other's use. Margarine and butter are substitute goods, not complementary goods. Therefore, (a) is correct. Answers (b), (c), and (d) all are pairs of complementary goods.

35. (a) The requirement is to describe the law of diminishing marginal utility. The law states that marginal utility declines as consumers acquire more of a good. Therefore, answer (a) is correct. Answer (b) is incorrect because total utility will not decline as more of a good is acquired. Answer (c) is incorrect because the demand curve slopes downward.

36. (b) The requirement is to identify the price elasticity of an essential product with no substitutes. The correct answer is (b). Demand for the product is perfectly inelastic because the diabetic will purchase the product regardless of the price.

Costs of Production

37. (c) The requirement is to define the implications of economies of scale. In the long run firms may experience increasing returns because they operate more efficiently. With growth comes specialization of labor and related production efficiencies related to the law of diminishing returns. This phenomenon is called economies of scale. Answer (c) is correct because it accurately describes this concept. Answers (a) and (b) are incorrect because they describe inefficiencies. Answer (d) is incorrect because total costs do not decline but average costs do.

38. (d) The requirement is to identify the reason for increasing returns. In the long run firms may experience increasing returns because they operate more efficiently. With growth comes specialization of labor and related production efficiencies. This phenomenon is called economies of scale and, therefore, answer (d) is correct. Answer (a) is incorrect because the law of diminishing returns states that at some point firms get too large and diminishing returns occur. Answer (b) is incorrect because opportunity cost is the benefit foregone by the use of a particular resource. Answer (c) is incorrect because comparative advantage deals with the production choices of countries.

39. (b) The requirement is to identify the term used to describe the benefit lost by using resources for a given purpose. The correct answer is (b) because opportunity cost is the benefit given up from not using the resource for another purpose. Answer (a) is incorrect because economic efficiency is a comparison among uses of resources. Answers (c) and (d) are incorrect because they involve comparisons across countries.

40. (c) The requirement is to calculate the total cost of producing seven units. Total cost is equal to average total cost multiplied by the number of units produced. Therefore, the correct answer is (c) because $7 \times \$36.86 = \$258.02$.

41. (c) The requirement is to calculate marginal cost. Marginal cost is the additional cost of producing one additional item. To calculate the marginal cost of producing the ninth unit we take the total cost of producing nine units and deduct the total cost of producing eight units. Thus, the correct answer is (c) because $(9 \times \$33.75) - (8 \times \$34.75) = \$25.75$.

42. (a) The requirement is to calculate the average total cost at an output level of 11 units. Answer (a) is correct because the average total cost is calculated by dividing total cost by the number of units: $[(\$1,000 \text{ fixed cost} + \$250 \text{ variable cost})/11] = \$113.64$.

43. (c) The requirement is to calculate the marginal physical product. The marginal physical product is the additional output obtained by adding one additional worker. When one worker is added to a team of 10, five $(25 - 20)$ additional units are produced. Therefore, the correct answer is (c).

44. (c) The requirement is to calculate the marginal revenue per unit. The total revenue of adding one additional worker to a team of 11 is equal to the difference between total revenue at 12 workers and total revenue at 11 workers, or $\$105 [(25 \times \$49) - (28 \times \$47.50)]$. Answer (c) is correct because the marginal revenue per unit is $\$35 = \$105/3$. Answer (d) is incorrect because it is the average selling price for one unit.

45. (c) The requirement is to calculate the marginal revenue product when one worker is added. The marginal revenue product is the increase in total revenue received by the addition of one worker. The total revenue from adding one additional worker to a team of 11 is equal to the difference between total revenue at 12 workers and total revenue at 11 workers, or $\$105 [(25 \times \$49) - (28 \times \$47.50)]$. Therefore answer (c) is correct.

46. (d) The requirement is to define marginal revenue. The correct answer is (d) because marginal revenue is the change in total revenue associated with the sale of one more unit of output. Answer (a) is incorrect because in a monopolistic competitive market, price is greater than marginal cost. Answer (b) is incorrect because marginal revenue is the increase in revenue associated with the sale of one additional product. Answer (c) is incorrect because in a purely competitive market, marginal revenue is equal to price.

47. (d) The requirement is to identify the distinguishing characteristic of long-run supply. Answer (d) is correct because the distinguishing characteristic of the long-run production function is that all costs are variable. Answers (a) and (b) are incorrect because price and output are determined by demand and supply. Answer (c) is incorrect because firms can enter or exit the industry.

48. (d) The requirement is to identify the main factor that differentiates the short-run cost function from the long-run cost function. Answer (d) is correct because in the short run firms have fixed and variable costs, whereas in the long run all costs are variable. Answer (a) is incorrect because all costs are variable in the long run. Answer (b) is incorrect because the level of technology will affect short-run and long-run cost functions in a similar manner. Answer (c) is incorrect because changes in government subsidies will not affect an industry's cost functions.

Aggregate Demand and Business Cycles

49. (a) The requirement is to identify the impact of consumer confidence upon the economy. Answer (a) is correct because if consumer confidence falls then consumers will delay spending until the uncertainty is resolved. The end result is a downturn in the economy. Answers (b), (c), and

(d) are incorrect because they do not properly state the relationship between consumer confidence and the economy.

50. (a) The requirement is to determine the marginal propensity to consume given the multiplier. The multiplier refers to the fact that an increase in spending has a multiplied effect on GDP. The effect of the multiplier can be estimated using the economy's marginal propensity to consume, or vice versa. In this case, the multiplier is 4($80/20) and the marginal propensity to save is 25% (1.00/4). Therefore, answer (a) is correct because the marginal propensity to consume is one minus the marginal propensity to save, or 75% (100% – 25%).

51. (c) The requirement is to identify a characteristic of the trough of a business cycle. In the trough of a business cycle, actual output and income are below potential output and income. Therefore, the correct answer is (c). Answer (a) is incorrect because purchasing power is not directly related to business cycles. Answer (b) is incorrect because in a recession it is cyclical unemployment that is high, not natural unemployment. Answer (d) is incorrect because potential income will exceed actual income.

52. (c) The requirement is to describe the effect of a decrease in government spending on the economy. The government represents one segment of the economy that demands goods and services. If government spending decreases, aggregate demand decreases. Thus, answer (c) is correct. Answer (a) is incorrect because a decrease in government spending will result in a decrease in aggregate demand. Answers (b) and (d) are incorrect because a decrease in government spending will not immediately affect supply.

53. (d) The requirement is to define aggregate demand. The correct answer is (d) because aggregate demand is the total amount of expenditures for consumer goods and investment for a period of time. It includes purchases by consumers, businesses, government, and foreign entities.

54. (d) The requirement is to identify an item that would be included in GDP. Gross domestic product is the value of all final goods and services produced by the country by both domestic and foreign-owned sources. Answer (d) is correct because common stock is not a good or service; it is an ownership interest in a company. Answers (a), (b), and (c) are all incorrect because they all represent the value of goods or services produced.

55. (d) The requirement is to identify the indicator of an upturn in economic activity. Answer (d) is correct because a reduction in the amount of luxury purchases is an indicator of a downturn in economic activity. Answers (a), (b), and (c) are all indicators of positive economic changes.

56. (d) The requirement is to identify a leading indicator of economic expansion. Answer (d) is correct because an increase in weekly hours worked by production workers is a favorable leading indicator. Answer (a) is incorrect because a falling money supply is an indicator associated with falling GDP. Answer (b) is incorrect because a decline in the issuance of building permits signals lower expected building activity and a falling GDP. Answer (c) is incorrect because an increase in the timeliness of delivery by vendors indicates slacking business demand and potentially falling GDP.

57. (d) The requirement is to identify the definition of disposable income. Answer (d) is correct because disposable income equals personal income minus personal taxes. It is the portion of income that can be spent by the consumer. Answer (a) is incorrect because gross domestic product less the capital cost allowance is net domestic product. Answer (b) is incorrect because net domestic product minus indirect business taxes plus net income earned abroad is national income. Answer (c) is incorrect because disposable income is not measured by deducting transfer payments from personal income.

58. (c) The requirement is to identify the primary reason for allowing legal immigration into industrial nations. Answer (c) is correct because immigration will increase the supply of labor and lower its equilibrium price. This results in greater domestic and world output and increases income in the country to which workers migrate. Answer (a) is incorrect because the impact on trade deficit is less than that on growth. Answers (b) and (d) are incorrect because trade agreements and political agreements are not primary reasons.

59. (a) The requirement is to identify a lagging economic indicator. Lagging indicators include (1) average duration of unemployment in weeks, (2) the change in the index of labor cost per unit of output, (3) the average prime rate charged by banks, (4) the ratio of manufacturing and trade inventories to sales, (5) commercial and industrial loans outstanding, (6) the ratio of consumer installment credit outstanding to personal income, and (7) the change in the CPI for services. Answer (a) is correct because chronic unemployment is a lagging indicator. Answers (b), (c), and (d) are incorrect because they are all leading indicators.

Economic Measures and Policy

60. (d) The requirement is to identify the true statement about government borrowing to finance large deficits. The correct answer is (d) because increased borrowing by the government increases the demand for money, which puts upward pressure on interest rates. Answer (a) is incorrect because government borrowing reduces the amount of lendable funds; it does not increases them. Answer (b) is incorrect because government borrowing exerts upward pressure on interest rates not downward pressure. Answer (c) is incorrect because government borrowing puts upward pressure on interest rates.

61. (d) The requirement is to describe the effects of rising inflation. Answer (d) is correct because rising inflation increases the price level of goods, which means that individuals can purchase less. Answer (a) is incorrect because individuals that receive specific amounts of money lose purchasing power. Answer (b) is incorrect because there is an inverse relationship between price level and purchasing power. Answer (c) is incorrect because if the contracts have indexing provisions, the prices will increase.

62. (d) The requirement is to describe the most effective fiscal policy for reducing demand-pull inflation. Demand-pull inflation is caused by excess demand that bids up the cost of labor and other resources. The correct answer is (d) because the most effective government policy would involve reducing demand that could be done by taxation and reduced government spending. Answer (a) is incorrect because it involves monetary policy. Answers (b) and (c) are incorrect because increasing government spending would feed demand-pull inflation.

63. (c) The requirement is to identify an action that will cause a decrease in money supply. The correct answer is (c) because an increase in the reserve requirement will leave financial institutions with less money to lend and therefore decrease the money supply. Answers (a), (b), and (d) are incorrect because they would all result in an increase in the money supply.

64. (c) The requirement is to identify how the Federal Reserve Board most directly influences the decision of whether or not to issue debt or equity financing. Answer (c) is correct because the Board sets the discount rate at which the Federal Reserve Bank lends money to member banks, which directly influences the rates that commercial banks charge their customers. Answer (a) is incorrect because the Board does not affect the income tax rate. Answers (b) and (d) are incorrect because the Federal Reserve Bank charges member banks the discount rate.

65. (d) The requirement is to identify the effects of a tax increase. Answer (d) is correct because a tax increase reduces household income and, therefore, reduces spending and decreases aggregate demand.

66. (b) The requirement is to describe an expansionary monetary policy. The correct answer is (b) because purchasing US securities would increase the amount of money in the economy. Answer (a) is incorrect because raising the reserve requirement would decrease the amount of money in the economy. Answer (c) is incorrect because raising the discount rate would discourage borrowing by banks and therefore reduce the amount of money in the economy. Answer (d) is incorrect because both of the actions would tend to reduce the money supply.

67. (a) The requirement is to define the reserve ratio. The reserve ratio is the percentage of total checking deposits that a financial institution must hold on reserve in the central bank. Thus, the correct answer is (a). Answer is (b) is incorrect because it is the description of the discount rate.

68. (b) The requirement is to identify the most important way that the money supply is controlled. The correct answer is (b). The purchase and sale of government securities (open-market operations) is the most important way that the government controls the money supply. Answers (a) and (d) are incorrect because, while they are instruments of monetary policy, they are not the most important ways of controlling money supply. Answer (c) is incorrect because it describes an instrument of fiscal policy.

69. (d) The requirement is to define how the government uses fiscal policy to stimulate the economy. To stimulate the economy with fiscal policy, the government would lower taxes and/or increase spending. Therefore, the correct answer is (d). Answer (a) is incorrect because raising taxes does not stimulate the economy. Answer (b) is incorrect because decreasing government spending does not stimulate the economy. Answer (c) is incorrect because increasing the money supply involves monetary policy.

70. (c) The requirement is to define the federal budget deficit. The federal budget deficit is the amount by which the government's expenditures exceed its revenues in a given year. Thus, answer (c) is correct. Answer (a) is incorrect because it defines the government debt. Answer (b) is incorrect because state and local government amounts are not included in the federal budget deficit. Answer (d) is incorrect because the deficit does not deal with assets and liabilities of the government.

71. (a) The requirement is to identify the tool that would serve to control inflation. Answer (a) is correct because selling government securities serves to reduce capital available for other investments and, therefore, serves to contract the economy. Answer (b) is incorrect because lowering reserve requirements serves to increase the amount of funds available for investment. Answer (c) is incorrect because lowering the discount rate serves to decrease the cost of funds and increase investment. Answer (d) is incorrect because encouraging higher tax rates is a fiscal policy.

72. (a) The requirement is to determine the reason for the importance of the multiplier. The multiplier provides an indication of the impact of an increase in consumption or investment in GDP. An increase in spending ripples through the economy because individuals and business save only a portion of the increase in income. Therefore, the correct answer is (a).

73. (a) The requirement is to identify the purpose of a tax rebate. Answer (a) is correct because increasing the amount of funds available to the consumer increases disposable income that should stimulate economic activity. Consumers will spend the additional funds and correspondingly expand the economy. Answers (b), (c), and (d) are erroneous statements about the effects of the rebate.

74. (c) The requirement is to identify the definition of structural unemployment. Answer (c) is correct because structural unemployment exists when aggregate demand is sufficient to provide full employment, but the distribution of the demand does not correspond precisely to the composition of the labor force. This form of unemployment arises when the required job skills or the geographic distribution of jobs changes. Answer (a) is incorrect because frictional unemployment results from imperfections in the labor market. It occurs when both jobs and workers to fill them are available. Answer (b) is incorrect because cyclical unemployment is caused by contractions of the economy. Answer (d) is incorrect because the full-employment unemployment rate is the sum of frictional and structural unemployment.

75. (a) The requirement is to identify the nature of the producer price index. Answer (a) is correct because the price index measures the combined price of a selected group of goods and services for a specified period in comparison with the combined price of the same or similar goods for a base period. The US government's producer price index (PPI) is an example. It measures the price of a basket of 3,200 commodities at the point of their first sale by producers. Answer (b) is incorrect because the export price index measures price changes for all products sold by domestic producers to foreigners. Answer (c) is incorrect because the import price index measures price changes of goods purchased from other countries. Answer (d) is incorrect because the consumer price index measures the price of a fixed market basket of goods purchased by a typical urban consumer.

76. (a) The requirement is to identify the formula for calculating a price index. Answer (a) is correct because the 2009 price index using 2004 as a reference period is the price of the 2009 market basket in 2009 relative to the price of the same basket of goods in 2004. The correct formula is

$$\frac{\text{Price of market basket in a given year}}{\text{Price of same market basket in base year}} \times 100$$

Answer (b) is incorrect because the 2004 market basket is used. Answer (c) is incorrect because it uses two different market baskets. Answer (d) is incorrect because it uses the 2004 prices in the numerator and the denominator and different market baskets.

77. (d) The requirement is to describe the discount rate. The correct answer is (d) because the discount rate is the rate the central bank charges commercial banks for loans. Answer (a) is not correct because it describes the reserve requirement.

78. (c) The requirement is to identify which of the statements is true about deflation. Answer (c) is correct because deflation results in very low interest rates. They could even turn negative. Answer (a) is incorrect because consumers are not motivated to borrow money because they will be paying back the debt with money that has greater purchasing power. Answer (b) is incorrect because businesses are hesitant to make investments because prices for capital goods are declining. Answer (d) is incorrect because deflation typically stalls the economy.

79. (a) The requirement is to identify the characteristics of a deflationary economy. The correct answer is (a) because businesses are hesitant to make investments when the prices of assets are declining. Answer (b) is incorrect because consumers are hesitant to make major purchases when prices are declining. Answer (c) is incorrect because interest rates are very low in periods of deflation. Answer (d) is incorrect because when actual GDP exceeds potential GDP inflation will exist.

80. (a) The requirement is to identify the factor that explains the difference between real and nominal interest rates. Real interest rates are in terms of goods; they are adjusted for inflation. The difference between real and nominal rates is the inflation premium. Thus, answer (a) is correct. Answers (b) and (c) are incorrect because credit risk and default risk explain the difference between the nominal rate and the rate a particular borrower receives. Answer (d) is incorrect because market risk explains the difference between the nominal rate and the rate paid in a particular market.

International Economics

81. (c) The requirement is to identify the statement that is not true regarding international trade. Answer (c) is correct because absolute advantage is the ability to produce a product for less than other nations. Comparative advantage is the ability of one nation to produce at a relatively lower opportunity cost than another nation. Answers (a), (b), and (d) are all incorrect because they are true.

82. (a) The requirement is to describe the effect of an increase in the interest rate on a currency's value. The correct answer is (a) because if the interest rate is increased investors will be able to get a larger return on investment in the country. Therefore, demand for the currency will increase for investment purposes, and the relative value of the currency will increase.

83. (b) The requirement is to identify the group that would most benefit from a tariff. The correct answer is (b) because a tariff restricts the amount of imports of a specific good, and the group most benefiting would be the domestic producers of that good. Answers (a), (c), and (d) are incorrect because these groups would not benefit from the tariff.

84. (a) The requirement is to identify the description of comparative advantage. Answer (a) is correct because the respective opportunity costs determine which country will produce which product. Answer (b) is incorrect because profit margins do not enter into the decision. Answer (c) is incorrect because economic order quantity determines optimum inventory levels. Answer (d) is incorrect because tariffs would only come into play after each country produced its respective products.

85. (c) The requirement is to identify the scenario that would result in appreciation in the value of a country's currency. The correct answer is (c) because the lag in imports in relation to exports means that there will be more demand for the currency from other countries to pay for the country's exported goods. Answer (a) is incorrect because if the country is importing goods this will increase demand for other currencies and cause the country's currency to decline in relative value. Answer (b) is incorrect because a higher rate of inflation depresses a country's currency. Answer (d) is incorrect because lower interest rates means there will be less demand for the currency for investment.

86. (c) The requirement is to identify the effect of a decline in the US dollar. The correct answer is (c) because US goods will be cheaper in foreign countries and, therefore, US exports will increase. Answer (a) is incorrect because foreign currencies will appreciate if the dollar depreciates. Answer (b) is incorrect because the US balance of payments should improve due to the increase in exports. Answer (d) is incorrect because US imports will decline because of the increase in cost of foreign goods in dollars.

87. (c) The requirement is to describe how exchange rates are determined. The correct answer is (c) because exchange rates are determined in the same way price is determined for other goods, based on demand and supply. Answers (a), (b), and (d) are incorrect because while they can have a temporary influence on exchange rates, supply and demand is the major determining factor.

88. (b) The requirement is to determine the effect of changes in exchange rates. Answer (b) is correct because the dollar's value has declined against the mark and therefore German goods become more expensive. Answer (a) is incorrect because the German mark has appreciated against the dollar. Answer (c) is incorrect because the dollar will buy less in Germany. Answer (d) is incorrect because US exports to Germany should increase because they are less expensive in German marks.

89. (c) The requirement is to identify the most restrictive barrier to an exporting country. The correct answer is (c) because an embargo is a total ban on certain types of imports. Answer (a) is incorrect because a tariff is merely a tax on imports. Answer (b) is incorrect because quotas are merely restrictions on the amounts of imports. Answer (d) is incorrect because exchange controls are limits of the amount of foreign exchange that can be transacted or exchange rates.

90. **(a)** The requirement is to identify the effect of negative net exports. Answer (a) is correct because when a country has negative net exports, it imports more than it exports. Therefore, it results in a net flow of goods from firms in foreign countries to the domestic country.

91. **(d)** The requirement is to identify the factor that is least likely to affect a country's currency foreign exchange rate. Answer (d) is correct because the country's tax rate is least likely to affect the country's currency exchange rate. Answers (a), (b), and (c) are incorrect because they are all factors that affect the value of the country's currency.

92. **(c)** The requirement is to compute the foreign exchange loss or gain. The correct answer is (c) because before the decline in value, the receivable had a value of $18,000 (10,000 × $1.80), and after the decline in value, the receivable had a value of $17,500 (10,000 × $1.75). Therefore, the loss is equal to $500. Answers (a), (b), and (d) are incorrect because they inaccurately calculate the loss.

93. **(c)** The requirement is to identify the appropriate hedging strategy. The correct answer is (c) because by selling euros in the futures market, the firm has locked in the exchange rate today. Answer (a) is incorrect because lending euros puts the company at greater risk for changes in value of the euro. It would need to borrow euros to lock in the exchange rate. Answer (b) is incorrect because it involves the purchase of euros; the appropriate strategy would involve the sale of euros. Answer (d) is incorrect because the purchase of euros on the spot market would put the firm more at risk to losses from decline in the value of the euro.

94. **(b)** The requirement is to identify hedging strategies that are not appropriate for political risk. Political risk is the risk related to actions by a foreign government, such as enacting legislation that prevents the repatriation of a foreign subsidiary's profits or seizing a firm's assets. Answer (b) is correct because purchasing or selling futures contracts is designed to hedge transaction risks relating to foreign exchange rates. Answer (a) is incorrect because a firm can purchase insurance to mitigate political risk. Answer (c) is incorrect because if the firm finances the investment with local-country capital, it may not be forced to repay the loans if assets are seized by the government. Answer (d) is incorrect because by entering into joint ventures with local-country firms, the firm can reduce the risk of seizure of the investment by the government.

Economics and Strategy

95. **(a)** The requirement is to describe how a large required capital outlay affects a market. The correct answer is (a) because a large capital outlay constitutes a barrier to entry into the market. Answer (b) is incorrect because minimum efficient scale indicates that a company must be of sufficient size to compete. This is not indicated by the scenario. Answer (c) is incorrect because a created barrier is one created by the competing firms. Answer (d) is incorrect because the production possibility boundary shows the maximum combination of outputs that can be achieved with a given number of inputs.

96. **(c)** The requirement is to identify the type of economic market. The correct answer is (c) because an oligopoly is characterized by a few firms in the industry. Answer (a) is incorrect because a natural monopoly has only

one firm. Answer (b) is incorrect because a cartel is a group of firms that have joined together to fix prices. Answer (d) is incorrect because monopolistic competition is characterized by a large number of firms selling similar but differentiated products.

97. **(c)** The requirement is to describe how patents affect markets. The correct answer is (c) because a patent prevents another firm from coming into a market and selling the same or a very similar product. Therefore, it is a barrier to entry into the market. Answer (a) is incorrect because vertical integration refers to expansion into another phase of producing the same product. Answer (b) is incorrect because market concentration refers to how many firms compete in the market. Answer (d) is incorrect because collusion refers to firms acting collectively to control the market.

98. **(d)** The requirement is to identify the distinguishing characteristics of oligopolistic markets. The correct answer is (d) because of the small number of suppliers in an oligopolistic market, the actions of one affect the others; there is mutual interdependence with regard to pricing and output in an oligopolistic market. Answers (a) and (b) are incorrect because they describe monopolies. Answer (c) is incorrect because oligopolistic markets typically have barriers to entry.

99. **(a)** The requirement is to identify the characteristic that is not representative of monopolistic competition. The correct answer is (a) because monopolistic competition is a market that has numerous sellers of similar but differentiated products. Answers (b), (c), and (d) are incorrect because they are all characteristic of monopolistic competition.

100. **(b)** The requirement is to identify the market that is characterized by a few large sellers. Answer (b) is correct because it is the definition of an oligopoly. Answer (a) is incorrect because a monopoly has a single seller of a product or service for which there are no close substitutes. Answer (c) is incorrect because perfect competition is characterized by many firms selling an identical product or service. Answer (d) is incorrect because monopolistic competition is characterized by many firms selling a differentiated product or service.

101. **(c)** The requirement is to identify the different types of economic markets. Answer (c) is correct because it is the definition of perfect competition. Answer (a) is incorrect because a monopoly has a single seller of a product or service for which there are no close substitutes. Answer (b) is incorrect because an oligopoly is a form of market in which there are few large sellers of the product. Answer (d) is incorrect because monopolistic competition is characterized by many firms selling a differentiated product or service.

102. **(c)** The requirement is to estimate the short-term and long-term effects of an increase in demand in a perfectly competitive market. Answer (c) is correct because in the short term the price of the product will increase but in the long term it will return to the equilibrium price for the market. Answers (a), (b), and (d) are incorrect because the long-term price will not likely increase.

103. **(c)** The requirement is to identify the definition of a natural monopoly. The correct answer is (c) because a natural monopoly exists when, because of economic or technical conditions, only one firm can efficiently supply the product.

Answer (a) is incorrect because while owning natural resources may contribute to the establishment of a natural monopoly, the firm would still have to be the best possible producer of the product. Answer (b) is incorrect because a patent establishes a government-created monopoly. Answer (d) is incorrect because if the government is the only provider, the market is a government-created monopoly.

104. (c) The requirement is to identify the market described as one with low barriers to entry and product differentiation. The correct answer is (c) because monopolistic competition is a market that is characterized by a large number of small producers of a differentiated product. Answer (a) is incorrect because a monopoly has only one producer. Answer (b) is incorrect because a natural monopoly is an industry in which there is only one producer based on the economics of the industry. Answer (d) is incorrect because an oligopoly is an industry that has a few large producers with barriers to entry.

105. (d) The requirement is to identify the item that is not characteristic of perfect competition. In a perfectly competitive market there are a large number of small producers selling a standard product. Answer (d) is correct because all sellers must sell at the industry price. Answers (a), (b), and (c) are all characteristics of perfect competition.

106. (d) The requirement is to identify the ultimate purpose of competitor analysis. Answer (d) is correct because the ultimate purpose of competitor analysis is to understand and predict the behavior of a major competitor. Answer (a) is not a part of competitor analysis. Answers (b) and (c) are part of competitor analysis but not the ultimate purpose.

107. (c) The requirement is to identify the item that is not an important aspect of supply chain management. Supply chain management is primarily designed to manage the firm's relationships with suppliers by sharing key information all along the supply chain. The correct answer is (c) because the area of customer relations is not a primary focus of supply chain management. Answer (a) is incorrect because information technology is used extensively to share information electronically. Answer (b) is incorrect because accurate forecasts are essential to effective supply chain management. Answer (d) is incorrect because communication is the basis for supply chain management.

108. (d) The requirement is to identify the type of organization that would most likely engage in public relations-type advertising. Firms that have monopolies are more likely to engage in public relations-type advertising to forestall additional regulation. Therefore, the correct answer is (d).

109. (b) The requirement is to identify target market analysis. The correct answer is (b) because target market analysis involves obtaining a thorough understanding of the market in which the firm sells or plans to sell its product or services.

110. (c) The requirement is to identify an unlikely market segmentation dimension for business customers. Answer (c) is correct because lifestyle is a possible individual customer market segmentation dimension for individuals, not businesses. Answers (a), (b), and (d) are incorrect because they all represent possible dimensions for business customer segmentation.

111. (b) The requirement is to identify the percentage of variance in quantity demanded explained by price. Answer (b) is correct because the adjusted R squared (.72458) measures the percent of the variance in the dependent variable explained by the independent variable. Answer (a) is incorrect because it is the Multiple R that is the coefficient of correlation. Answer (c) is incorrect because it is the intercept that is used in the equation to predict quantity. Answer (d) is incorrect because it is the standard error that measures the standard deviation of the estimate of quantity.

112. (a) The requirement is to calculate the predicted quantity demanded. The correct answer is (a) because the formula is Quantity demanded = $a + bx = 56,400.50 + (7.00 \times -4,598.2) = 24,213$.

113. (d) The requirement is to identify the item that is not one of the forces in Porter's model for industry analysis. The correct answer is (d) because consideration of general economic conditions is not part of industry analysis. Answers (a), (b), and (c) are incorrect because the five forces include the threat of new entrants, the bargaining power of customers, the bargaining power of suppliers, the threat of substitute products or services, and the rivalry of the firms in the market.

114. (a) The requirement is to identify the defining characteristic of supply chain management. The correct answer is (a) because a key aspect of supply chain management is the sharing of key information from the point of sale to the consumer back to the manufacturer, the manufacturer's suppliers, and the supplier's suppliers. Answer (b) is incorrect because it is the focus of process reengineering. Answer (c) is incorrect because it is the focus of total quality management. Answer (d) is incorrect because strategic alliances involve joint ventures and partnerships.

115. (d) The requirement is to identify an unlikely strategy for a firm in a purely competitive market. The correct answer is (d) because in a purely competitive market firms compete based on price, and developing a brand name is a product differentiation strategy. Answers (a), (b), and (c) are all cost leadership strategies and appropriate for a firm in a purely competitive market.

116. (c) The requirement is to identify the purpose of a response profile. The correct answer is (c) because a response profile is a description of possible actions that may be taken by a competitor in varying circumstances. Answers (a), (b), and (d) all involve aspects of industry analysis.

117. (b) The requirement is to define the process of dividing all potential consumers into smaller groups of buyers with distinct needs, characteristics, or behaviors. Answer (b) is correct because this describes market segmentation. Answer (a) is incorrect because strategic planning involves deciding on the appropriate strategic initiatives for a period. Answer (c) is incorrect because product positioning involves deciding on a strategy for a particular product. Answer (d) is incorrect because objective setting involves establishing short-term goals.

118. (c) The requirement is to identify the least important measure of unemployment in predicting the future state of the economy. Answer (c) is the correct answer because frictional unemployment measures the temporary unemployment that always exists as workers change jobs or new workers enter the workforce. Answer (a) is incorrect because structural unemployment measures the workforce that is unemployed due to a mismatch in job skills. Significant amounts of structural unemployment can drag down the economy. Answer (b) is incorrect because cyclical unemployment measures the workforce that is unemployed due to economic conditions. Answer (d) is incorrect because overall unemployment includes the workforce that is unemployed for all reasons.

119.   (a)   The requirement is to identify the steps involved in performing competitor analysis. Answer (a) is correct because competitor analysis is designed to predict the behavior of major competitors. Answers (b) and (c) are incorrect because they describe aspects of industry analysis. Answer (d) is incorrect because it describes aspects of general environment and industry analyses.

120.   (a)   The requirement is to describe the reason for the kinked demand curve in an oligopolist market. An oligopolist faces a kinked demand curve because competitors will often match price decreases but are hesitant to match price increases. Therefore, answer (a) is correct. Answer (b) is incorrect because an oligopolist does not face a nonlinear demand for its product. Answer (c) is incorrect because an oligopolist cannot sell its product for any price. Answer (d) is incorrect because consumer demand determines the demand curve in all markets.

MULTIPLE-CHOICE QUESTIONS (1-137)

1. Which of the following is not a function of financial management?
- a. Financing.
- b. Risk-management.
- c. Internal control.
- d. Capital budgeting.

2. The inventory conversion period is calculated as follows:

a. $\dfrac{\text{Average inventory}}{\text{Cost of sales per day}}$

b. $\dfrac{\text{Year-end inventory}}{\text{Cost of sales per day}}$

c. $\dfrac{\text{Average inventory}}{\text{Accounts receivable}}$

d. $\dfrac{\text{Year-end inventory}}{\text{Cost of sales}}$

3. The payables deferral period is calculated as follows:

a. $\dfrac{\text{Average payables}}{\text{Sales per day}}$

b. $\dfrac{\text{Beginning payables}}{\text{Sales per day}}$

c. $\dfrac{\text{Average payables}}{\text{Purchases per day}}$

d. $\dfrac{\text{Average payables}}{\text{Cost of goods sold}}$

4. All of the following statements in regard to working capital are correct **except:
- a. Current liabilities are an important source of financing for many small firms.
- b. Profitability varies inversely with liquidity.
- c. The hedging approach to financing involves matching maturities of debt with specific financing needs.
- d. Financing permanent inventory buildup with long-term debt is an example of an aggressive working capital policy.

**5. Determining the appropriate level of working capital for a firm requires
- a. Evaluating the risks associated with various levels of fixed assets and the types of debt used to finance these assets.
- b. Changing the capital structure and dividend policy of the firm.
- c. Maintaining short-term debt at the lowest possible level because it is generally more expensive than long-term debt.
- d. Offsetting the benefit of current assets and current liabilities against the probability of technical insolvency.

6. Which of the following actions is likely to reduce the length of a firm's cash conversion cycle?
- a. Adopting a new inventory system that reduces the inventory conversion period.

- b. Adopting a new inventory system that increases the inventory conversion period.
- c. Increasing the average days sales outstanding on its accounts receivable.
- d. Reducing the amount of time the firm takes to pay its suppliers.

7. Eagle Sporting Goods has $2.5 million in inventory and $2 million in accounts receivable. Its average daily sales are $100,000. The firm's payables deferral period is 30 days and average daily cost of sales are $50,000. What is the length of the firm's cash conversion period?
- a. 100 days.
- b. 60 days.
- c. 50 days.
- d. 40 days.

8. Jones Company has $5,000,000 of average inventory and cost of sales of $30,000,000. Using a 365-day year, calculate the firm's inventory conversion period.
- a. 30.25 days.
- b. 60.83 days.
- c. 45.00 days.
- d. 72.44 days.

9. The length of time between the acquisition of inventory and payment for it is called the
- a. Operating cycle.
- b. Inventory conversion period.
- c. Accounts receivable period.
- d. Accounts payable deferral period.

10. If everything else remains constant and a firm increases its cash conversion cycle, its profitability will likely
- a. Increase.
- b. Increase if earnings are positive.
- c. Decrease.
- d. Not be affected.

*11. An organization offers its customers credit terms of 5/10 net 20. One-third of the customers take the cash discount and the remaining customers pay on day 20. On average, 20 units are sold per day, priced at $10,000 each. The rate of sales is uniform throughout the year. Using a 360-day year, the organization has days' sales outstanding in accounts receivable, to the nearest full day, of
- a. 13 days.
- b. 15 days.
- c. 17 days.
- d. 20 days.

**12. Troy Toys is a retailer operating in several cities. The individual store managers deposit daily collections at a local bank in a noninterest-bearing checking account. Twice per week, the local bank issues a depository transfer check (DTC) to the central bank at headquarters. The controller of the company is considering using a wire transfer instead. The additional cost of each transfer would be $25; collections would be accelerated by two days; and the annual interest rate paid by the central bank is 7.2% (0.02% per day). At what amount of dollars transferred would it be economically feasible to use a wire transfer instead of the DTC? Assume a 360-day year.
- a. It would never be economically feasible.
- b. $125,000 or above.
- c. Any amount greater than $173.
- d. Any amount greater than $62,500.

---

* *CIA adapted*

** *CMA adapted*

13. Which of the following is true about electronic funds transfer from a cash flow standpoint?
   a. It is always beneficial from a cash flow standpoint.
   b. It is never beneficial from a cash flow standpoint.
   c. It is beneficial from a cash receipts standpoint but not from a cash disbursements standpoint.
   d. It is beneficial from a cash disbursements standpoint but not from a cash receipts standpoint.

14. Management of Radker Corp. is considering a lockbox system. The bank will charge $10,000 annually for the service, which will save the firm approximately $5,000 in processing costs. The lockbox system will reduce the float for cash receipts by three days. Assuming that the average daily receipts are equal to $100,000, and short-term interest costs are 5%, calculate the benefit or loss from adopting the lockbox system.
   a. $5,000 loss.
   b. $10,000 loss.
   c. $10,000 benefit.
   d. $5,000 benefit.

15. Which of the following is true about a firm's float?
   a. A firm strives to minimize the float for both cash receipts and cash disbursements.
   b. A firm strives to maximize the float for both cash receipts and cash disbursements.
   c. A firm strives to maximize the float for cash receipts and minimize the float for cash disbursements.
   d. A firm strives to maximize the float for cash disbursements and minimize the float for cash receipts.

16. A firm is evaluating whether to establish a concentration banking system. The bank will charge $5,000 per year for maintenance and transfer fees. The firm estimates that the float will be reduced by two days if the concentration banking is put into place. Assuming that average daily receipts are $115,000 and short-term interest rates are 4%, what decision should the firm make regarding the concentration banking system?
   a. Do not establish the concentration banking system because the net cost is $5,000.
   b. Do not establish the concentration banking system because the net cost is $21,000.
   c. Establish the concentration banking system because the net benefit is $115,000.
   d. Establish the concentration banking system because the net benefit is $4,200.

17. A firm is evaluating whether to establish a lockbox system. The bank will charge $30,000 per year for the lockbox and the firm will save approximately $8,000 in internal processing costs. The firm estimates that the float will be reduced by three days if the lockbox system is put into place. Assuming that average daily cash receipts are $350,000 and short-term interest rates are 4%, what decision should the firm make regarding the lockbox system?
   a. Do not establish the lockbox system because the net cost is $30,000.
   b. Do not establish the lockbox system because the net cost is $22,000.

   c. Establish the lockbox system because the net benefit is $12,000.
   d. Establish the lockbox system because the net benefit is $20,000.

18. An organization has an opportunity to establish a zero balance account system using four different regional banks. The total amount of the maintenance and transfer fees is estimated to be $6,000 per annum. The organization believes that it will increase the float on its operating disbursements by an average of four days, and its cost of short-term funds is 4.5%. Assuming the organization estimates its average daily operating disbursements to be $40,000 what decision should the organization make regarding this opportunity?
   a. Do not establish the zero balance account system because it results in estimated additional net costs of $6,000.
   b. Do not establish the zero balance account system because it results in estimated additional net costs of $1,200.
   c. Establish the zero balance account system because it results in estimated net savings of $1,200.
   d. Establish the zero balance account system because it results in estimated net savings of $7,200.

**19. A working capital technique that increases the payable float and therefore delays the outflow of cash is
   a. Concentration banking.
   b. A draft.
   c. Electronic Data Interchange (EDI).
   d. A lockbox system.

**20. Newman Products has received proposals from several banks to establish a lockbox system to speed up receipts. Newman receives an average of 700 checks per day averaging $1,800 each, and its cost of short-term funds is 7% per year. Assuming that all proposals will produce equivalent processing results and using a 360-day year, which one of the following proposals is optimal for Newman?
   a. A $0.50 fee per check.
   b. A flat fee of $125,000 per year.
   c. A fee of 0.03% of the amount collected.
   d. A compensating balance of $1,750,000.

**21. A firm has daily cash receipts of $100,000. A bank has offered to reduce the collection time on the firm's deposits by two days for a monthly fee of $500. If money market rates are expected to average 6% during the year, the net annual benefit (loss) from having this service is
   a. $ 3,000
   b. $12,000
   c. $0
   d. $ 6,000

*22. A minimum checking account balance that a firm must maintain with a commercial bank is a
   a. Transaction balance.
   b. Compensating balance.
   c. Precautionary balance.
   d. Speculative balance.

**23. A firm has daily receipts of $100,000. A bank has offered to reduce the collection time on the firm's deposits by two days for a monthly fee of $500. If money market

---

* *CIA adapted*
** *CMA adapted*

rates are expected to average 6% during the year, the net annual benefit from having this service is

a. $0
b. $ 3,000
c. $ 6,000
d. $12,000

**24. Cleveland Masks and Costumes Inc. (CMC) has a majority of its customers located in the states of California and Nevada. Keystone National Bank, a major west coast bank, has agreed to provide a lockbox system to CMC at a fixed fee of $50,000 per year and a variable fee of $.50 for each payment processed by the bank. On average, CMC receives 50 payments per day, each averaging $20,000. With the lockbox system, the company's collection float will decrease by 2 days. The annual interest rate on money market securities is 6%. If CMC makes use of the lockbox system, what would be the net benefit to the company? Use 365 days per year.

a. $ 51,750
b. $ 60,875
c. $111,750
d. $120,875

25. The most important considerations with respect to short-term investments are

a. Return and value.
b. Risk and liquidity.
c. Return and risk.
d. Growth and value.

**26. All of the following are alternative marketable securities suitable for investment except:

a. US treasury bills.
b. Eurodollars.
c. Commercial paper.
d. Convertible bonds.

27. Which of the following investments generally pay the highest return?

a. Money market accounts.
b. Treasury bills.
c. Treasury notes.
d. Commercial paper.

**28. Which one of the following is not a characteristic of a negotiable certificate of deposit? Negotiable certificates of deposit

a. Have a secondary market for investors.
b. Are regulated by the Federal Reserve System.
c. Are usually sold in denominations of a minimum of $100,000.
d. Have yields considerably greater that bankers' acceptances and commercial paper.

29. Which changes in costs are most conducive to switching from a traditional inventory ordering system to a just-in-time ordering system?

	Cost per purchase order	Inventory unit carrying costs
a.	Increasing	Increasing
b.	Decreasing	Increasing
c.	Decreasing	Decreasing
d.	Increasing	Decreasing

30. To determine the inventory reorder point, calculations normally include the

a. Ordering cost.
b. Carrying cost.
c. Average daily usage.
d. Economic order quantity.

**31. Which of the following is not a correct comparison of a just-in-time system with a traditional system?

	Traditional	Just-in-time
a.	Longer lead times	Shorter lead times
b.	Inventory is an asset	Inventory is a liability
c.	Some scrap tolerated	Zero defects desired
d.	Lot size based on immediate need	Lot size based on formulas

32. The benefits of a just-in-time system for raw materials usually include

a. Elimination of non-value-added operations.
b. Increase in the number of suppliers, thereby ensuring competitive bidding.
c. Maximization of the standard delivery quantity, thereby lessening the paperwork for each delivery.
d. Decrease in the number of deliveries required to maintain production.

33. Bell Co. changed from a traditional manufacturing philosophy to a just-in-time philosophy. What are the expected effects of this change on Bell's inventory turnover and inventory as a percentage of total assets reported on Bell's balance sheet?

	Inventory turnover	Inventory percentage
a.	Decrease	Decrease
b.	Decrease	Increase
c.	Increase	Decrease
d.	Increase	Increase

34. As a consequence of finding a more dependable supplier, Dee Co. reduced its safety stock of raw materials by 80%. What is the effect of this safety stock reduction on Dee's economic order quantity?

a. 80% decrease.
b. 64% decrease.
c. 20% increase.
d. No effect.

35. The economic order quantity formula assumes that

a. Periodic demand for the good is known.
b. Carrying costs per unit vary with quantity ordered.
c. Costs of placing an order vary with quantity ordered.
d. Purchase costs per unit differ due to quantity discounts.

36. Ral Co. sells 20,000 radios evenly throughout the year. The cost of carrying one unit in inventory for one year is $8, and the purchase order cost per order is $32. What is the economic order quantity?

a. 625
b. 400
c. 283
d. 200

37. The following information pertains to material X that is used by Sage Co.:

Annual usage in units	20,000
Working days per year	250
Safety stock in units	800
Normal lead time in working days	30

Units of material X will be required evenly throughout the year. The order point is

a.   800
b.   1,600
c.   2,400
d.   3,200

38. Firms that maintain very low or no inventory levels

a.   Have higher ordering costs.
b.   Have higher carrying costs.
c.   Have higher ordering and carrying costs.
d.   Have lower ordering and carrying costs.

**39.   An example of a carrying cost is

a.   Disruption of production schedules.
b.   Quantity discounts lost.
c.   Handling costs.
d.   Obsolescence.

*40.   Which of the following is a characteristic of just-in-time (JIT) inventory management systems?

a.   JIT users determine the optimal level of safety stocks.
b.   JIT is applicable only to large companies.
c.   JIT does not really increase overall economic efficiency because it merely shifts inventory levels further up the supply chain.
d.   JIT relies heavily on good quality materials.

*41.   To evaluate the efficiency of purchase transactions, management decides to calculate the economic order quantity for a sample of the company's products. To calculate the economic order quantity, management would need data for all of the following **except:**

a.   The volume of product sales.
b.   The purchase prices of the products.
c.   The fixed cost of ordering products.
d.   The volume of products in inventory.

Items 42 and 43 are based on the following information:

Ethan, Inc. has seasonal demand for its products and management is considering whether level production or seasonal production should be implemented. The firms' short-term interest cost is 8%, and management has developed the following information to make the decision:

	Alternative 1 Level production	Alternative 2 Seasonal production
Average inventory	$2,000,000	$1,500,000
Production costs	$6,000,000	$6,050,000

42. Which alternative should be accepted and how much is saved over the other alternative?

a.   Alternative 1 with $500,000 in savings.
b.   Alternative 2 with $50,000 in savings.
c.   Alternative 2 with $10,000 in savings.
d.   Alternative 1 with $10,000 in savings.

43. At what rate of short-term interest rate would the two alternatives have the same cost?

a.   6%
b.   9%

c.   10%
d.   12%

**44.   The amount of inventory that a company would tend to hold in stock would increase as the

a.   Sales level falls to a permanently lower level.
b.   Cost of carrying inventory decreases.
c.   Variability of sales decreases.
d.   Cost of running out of stock decreases.

*45.   An appropriate technique for planning and controlling manufacturing inventories, such as raw materials, components, and subassemblies, whose demand depends on the level of production, is

a.   Materials requirements planning.
b.   Regression analysis.
c.   Capital budgeting.
d.   Linear programming.

46. The procedures followed by the firm for ensuring payment of its accounts receivables are called its

a.   Discount policy.
b.   Credit policy.
c.   Collection policy.
d.   Payables policy.

Items 47 and 48 are based on the following information:

Effective September 1, a company initiates seasonal dating as a component of its credit policy, allowing wholesale customers to make purchases early but not requiring payment until the retail selling season begins. Sales occur as follows:

Date of sale	Quantity sold
September 1	300 units
October 1	100 units
November 1	100 units
December 1	150 units
January 1	50 units

- Each unit has a selling price of $10, regardless of the date of sale.
- The terms of sale are 2/10 net 30, January 1 dating.
- All sales are on credit.
- All customers take the discount and abide by the terms of the discount policy.
- All customers take advantage of the new seasonal dating policy.
- The peak selling season for all customers is mid-November to late December.

47. For the selling firm, which of the following is **not** an expected advantage to initiating seasonal dating?

a.   Reduced storage costs.
b.   Reduced credit costs.
c.   Attractive credit terms for customers.
d.   Reduced uncertainty about sales volume.

48. For sales after the initiation of the seasonal dating policy on September 1, total collections on or before January 11 will be

a. $0
b. $6,370
c. $6,860
d. $7,000

49. Which of the following describes the appropriate formula for days' sales outstanding?

---

*   *CIA adapted*
**   *CMA adapted*

a. $\dfrac{\text{Average receivables}}{\text{Sales per day}}$

b. $\dfrac{\text{Receivables balance}}{\text{Sales per day}}$

c. $\dfrac{\text{Sales}}{\text{Average receivables}}$

d. $\dfrac{\text{Receivables balance}}{\text{Total sales}}$

50. Which of the following describes a firm's credit criteria?
   a. The length of time a buyer is given to pay for his/her purchases.
   b. The percentage of discount allowed for early payment.
   c. The diligence to collect slow-paying accounts.
   d. The required financial strength of acceptable customers.

Items 51 and 52 are based on the following information:

A company plans to tighten its credit policy. The new policy will decrease the average number of days in collection from 75 to 50 days and reduce the ratio of credit sales to total revenue from 70 to 60%. The company estimates that projected sales would be 5% less if the proposed new credit policy were implemented. The firm's short-term interest cost is 10%.

**51. Projected sales for the coming year are $50 million. Calculate the dollar impact on accounts receivable of this proposed change in credit policy. Assume a 360-day year.
   a. $ 3,819,445 decrease.
   b. $ 6,500,000 decrease.
   c. $ 3,333,334 decrease.
   d. $18,749,778 increase.

**52. What effect would the implementation of this new credit policy have on income before taxes?
   a. $2,500,000 decrease.
   b. $2,166,667 decrease.
   c. $ 83,334 increase.
   d. $ 33,334 increase.

**53. The sales manager at Ryan Company feels confident that if the credit policy at Ryan's were changed, sales would increase ancd consequently, the company would utilize excess capacity. The two credit proposals being considered are as follows:

	Proposal A	Proposal B
Increase in sales	$500,000	$600,000
Contribution margin	20%	20%
Bad debt percentage	5%	5%
Increase in operating profits	$ 75,000	$ 90,000
Desired return on sales	15%	15%

Currently, payment terms are net 30. The proposed payment terms for Proposal A and Proposal B are net 45 and net 90, respectively. An analysis to compare these two proposals for the change in credit policy would include all of the following factors except the
   a. Cost of funds for Ryan.
   b. Current bad debt experience.
   c. Impact on the current customer base of extending terms to only certain customers.

*   CIA adapted
** CMA adapted

   d. Bank loan covenants on days' sales outstanding.

**54. A company enters into an agreement with a firm who will factor the company's accounts receivable. The factor agrees to buy the company's receivables, which average $100,000 per month and have an average collection period of 30 days. The factor will advance up to 80% of the face value of receivables at an annual rate of 10% and charge a fee of 2% on all receivables purchased. The controller of the company estimates that the company would save $18,000 in collection expenses over the year. Fees and interest are not deducted in advance. Assuming a 360-day year, what is the annual cost of financing?
   a. 10.0%
   b. 14.0%
   c. 16.0%
   d. 17.5%

**55. A company with $4.8 million in credit sales per year plans to relax its credit standards, projecting that this will increase credit sales by $720,000. The company's average collection period for new customers is expected to be 75 days, and the payment behavior of the existing customers is not expected to change. Variable costs are 80% of sales. The firm's opportunity cost is 20% before taxes. Assuming a 360-day year, what is the company's benefit (loss) from the planned change in credit terms?
   a. $0
   b. $ 28,800
   c. $144,000
   d. $120,000

56. Gild Company has been offered credit terms of 3/10, net 30. Using a 365-day year, what is the nominal cost of not taking advantage of the discount if the firm pays on the 35th day after the purchase?
   a. 14.2%
   b. 32.2%
   c. 37.6%
   d. 45.2%

57. Newton Corporation is offered trade credit terms of 3/15, net 45. The firm does not take advantage of the discount, and it pays the account after 67 days. Using a 365-day year, what is the nominal annual cost of not taking the discount?
   a. 18.2%
   b. 21.71%
   c. 23.48%
   d. 26.45%

58. Assume that Williams Corp is financed with a heavy reliance on short-term debt and short-term rates have increased. How do these facts impact the interest expense, net income, and financial risk for Williams Corp?

	Interest expense	Net income	Financial risk
a.	Decreases	Decreases	Decreases
b.	Increases	Decreases	Increase
c.	Decrease	Increases	Increases
d.	Increases	Decreases	Decreases

59. If a firm is offered credit terms of 2/10, net 30 on its purchases. Sound cash management practices would mean that the firm would pay the account on which of the following days?
   a. Day 2 and 30.

b.   Day 2 and 10.
c.   Day 10.
d.   Day 30.

60. The following forms of short-term borrowings are available to a firm:

- Floating lien
- Factoring
- Revolving credit
- Chattel mortgages
- Bankers' acceptances
- Lines of credit
- Commercial paper

The forms of short-term borrowing that are unsecured credit are

a.   Floating lien, revolving credit, chattel mortgage, and commercial paper.
b.   Factoring, chattel mortgage, bankers' acceptances, and line of credit.
c.   Floating lien, chattel mortgage, bankers' acceptances, and line of credit.
d.   Revolving credit, bankers' acceptances, line of credit, and commercial paper.

*61.   A company obtaining short-term financing with trade credit will pay a higher percentage financing cost, everything else being equal, when

a.   The discount percentage is lower.
b.   The items purchased have a higher price.
c.   The items purchased have a lower price.
d.   The supplier offers a longer discount period.

62. If a firm borrows $500,000 at 10% and is required to maintain $50,000 as a minimum compensating balance at the bank, what is the effective interest rate on the loan?

a.   10.0%
b.   11.1%
c.   9.1%
d.   12.2%

63. If a retailer's terms of trade are 3/10, net 45 with a particular supplier, what is the cost on an annual basis of not taking the discount? Assume a 360-day year.

a.   24.00%
b.   37.11%
c.   36.00%
d.   31.81%

64.   Which of the following is not related to loans involving inventory?

a.   Factoring.
b.   Blanket liens.
c.   Trust receipts.
d.   Warehousing.

65.   The London Interbank Offered Rate (LIBOR) represents an example of a

a.   Risk-free rate.
b.   Nominal rate.
c.   Credit risk adjusted rate.
d.   Long-term rate

66.   An advantage of the use of long-term debt as opposed to short-term debt to finance current assets is

a.   It decreases the risk of the firm.
b.   It generally is less costly than short-term debt.
c.   It generally places fewer restrictions on the firm.
d.   It is easy to repay.

67. The chief financial officer of Smith Glass Inc. follows the policy of matching the maturity of assets with the maturity of financing. The implications of this policy include all of the following **except** that

a.   The seasonal expansion of cash, receivables, and inventory should be financed by short-term debt such as vendor payables and bank debt.
b.   The minimum level of cash, receivables, and inventory required to stay in business can be considered permanent, and financed with long-term debt or equity.
c.   Cash, receivables, and inventory should be financed with long-term debt or equity.
d.   Long-term assets, like plant and equipment, should be financed with long-term debt or equity.

68.   Which form of asset financing involves the public offering of debt collateralized by a firm's accounts receivables?

a.   Trust receipts.
b.   Warehousing.
c.   Blanket inventory liens.
d.   Securitization of assets.

69. Hagar Company's bank requires a compensating balance of 20% on a $100,000 loan. If the stated interest on the loan is 7%, what is the effective cost of the loan?

a.   5.83%
b.   7.00%
c.   8.40%
d.   8.75%

Items 70 and 71 are based on the following information:

CyberAge Outlet, a relatively new store, is a café that offers customers the opportunity to browse the Internet or play computer games at their tables while they drink coffee. The customer pays a fee based on the amount of time spent signed on to the computer. The store also sells books, tee shirts, and computer accessories. CyberAge has been paying all of its bills on the last day of the payment period, thus forfeiting all supplier discounts. Shown below are data on CyberAge's two major vendors, including average monthly purchases and credit terms.

Vendor	Average monthly purchases	Credit terms
Web Master	$25,000	2/10, net 30
Softidee	50,000	5/10, net 90

70. Assuming a 360-day year and that CyberAge continues paying on the last day of the credit period, the company's weighted-average annual interest rate for trade credit (ignoring the effects of compounding) for these two vendors is

a.   27.0%
b.   25.2%
c.   28.0%
d.   30.2%

71. Should CyberAge use trade credit and continue paying at the end of the credit period?

a.   Yes, if the cost of alternative short-term financing is less.

b.   Yes, if the firm's weighted-average cost of capital is equal to its weighted-average cost of trade credit.

c.   No, if the cost of alternative long-term financing is greater.

d.   Yes, if the cost of alternative short-term financing is greater.

72. With respect to the use of commercial paper by an industrial firm, which one of the following statements is **most likely to be true?

a.   The commercial paper is issued through a bank.

b.   The commercial paper has a maturity of 60-270 days.

c.   The commercial paper is secured by the issuer's assets.

d.   The commercial paper issuer is a small company.

**73. A company obtained a short-term bank loan of $250,000 at an annual interest rate of 6%. As a condition of the loan, the company is required to maintain a compensating balance of $50,000 in its checking account. The company's checking account earns interest at an annual rate of 2%. Ordinarily, the company maintains a balance of $25,000 in its checking account for transaction purposes. What is the effective interest rate of the loan?

a.   6.44%

b.   7.11%

c.   5.80%

d.   6.66%

*74. A manufacturing firm wants to obtain a short-term loan and has approached several lending institutions. All of the potential lenders are offering the same nominal interest rate, but the terms of the loans vary. Which of the following combinations of loan terms will be most attractive for the borrowing firm?

a.   Simple interest, no compensating balance.

b.   Discount interest, no compensating balance.

c.   Simple interest, 20% compensating balance required.

d.   Discount interest, 20% compensating balance required.

**75. Elan Corporation is considering borrowing $100,000 from a bank for one year at a stated interest rate of 9%. What is the effective interest rate to Elan if this borrowing is in the form of a discount note?

a.   8.10%

b.   9.00%

c.   9.81%

d.   9.89%

**76. The Red Company has a revolving line of credit of $300,000 with a one-year maturity. The terms call for a 6% interest rate and a 1/2% commitment fee on the unused portion of the line of credit. The average loan balance during the year was $100,000. The annual cost of this financing arrangement is

a. $6,000

b. $6,500

c. $7,000

d. $7,500

**77. Which of the following financial instruments generally provides the largest source of short-term credit for small firms?

a.   Installment loans.

b.   Commercial paper.

c.   Trade credit.

d.   Mortgage bonds.

**78. The prime rate is the

a.   Size of the commitment fee on a commercial bank loan.

b.   Effective cost of a commercial bank loan.

c.   Rate charged on business loans to borrowers with high credit ratings.

d.   Rate at which a bank borrows from the Federal Reserve central bank.

**79. A compensating balance

a.   Compensates a financial institution for services rendered by providing it with deposits of funds.

b.   Is used to compensate for possible losses on a marketable securities portfolio.

c.   Is a level of inventory held to compensate for variations in usage rate and lead time.

d.   Is an amount paid by financial institutions to compensate large depositors.

**80. On January 1, Scott Corporation received a $300,000 line of credit at an interest rate of 12% from Main Street Bank and drew down the entire amount on February 1. The line of credit agreement requires that an amount equal to 15% of the loan be deposited into a compensating balance account. What is the effective annual cost of credit for this loan arrangement?

a.   11.00%

b.   12.00%

c.   12.94%

d.   14.12%

81. Which of the following statements is correct when comparing bond-financing alternatives?

a.   A bond with a call provision typically has a lower yield to maturity than a similar bond without a call provision.

b.   A convertible bond must be converted to common stock prior to its maturity.

c.   A call provision is generally considered detrimental to the investor.

d.   A call premium requires the investor to pay an amount greater than par at the time of purchase.

82. Which of the following are characteristics of Euro-bonds?

a.   Are always denominated in Eurodollars.

b.   Are always sold in some country other than the one in whose currency the bond is denominated.

c.   Are sold outside the country of the borrower but are denominated in the currency of the county in which the issue is sold.

d.   Are generally issued as registered bonds.

83. At the inception of an operating lease how should the leased asset be accounted for on the lessee financial statements?

---

a. The present value of the future lease payments is recorded as an asset on the balance sheet.

b. The total amount of the lease payments is recorded as an asset on the balance sheet.

c. An asset is not recorded. The lease payments are expensed as rent as they are incurred.

d. The future value of the lease payments is recorded as an asset on the balance sheet.

84. Capital and operating leases differ in that the lessee

a. Obtains use of the asset only under a capital lease.

b. Is using the lease as a source of financing only under an operating lease.

c. Receives title to the asset in a capital lease.

d. Capitalizes the net investment in the lease.

85. Which of the following is an advantage of debt financing?

a. Interest and principal obligations must be paid regardless of the economic position of the firm.

b. Debt agreements contain covenants.

c. The obligation is generally fixed in terms of interest and principal payments.

d. Excessive debt increases the risk of equity holders and therefore depresses share prices.

86. All of the following are advantages of debt financing except

a. Interest is tax deductible.

b. The use of debt will assist in lowering the firm's cost of capital.

c. In periods of inflation, debt is paid back with dollars that are worth less than the ones borrowed.

d. The acquisition of debt decreases stockholders' risk.

87. If an investor is concerned about interest rate risk, the investor should consider investing in

a. Serial bonds.

b. Sinking fund bonds.

c. Convertible bonds.

d. Floating rate bonds.

88. Bonds in which the principal amount is paid as a series of installments over the life of the bond issue are called

a. Serial bonds.

b. Sinking fund bonds.

c. Convertible bonds.

d. Callable bonds.

89. Wilson Corporation issued bonds two years ago. If the _____ interest rate _____, the market value of the bond will decrease.

a. Coupon; increases.

b. Coupon; decreases.

c. Market; increases.

d. Market; decreases.

**90. DQZ Telecom is considering a project for the coming year that will cost $50 million. DQZ plans to use the following combination of debt and equity to finance the investment:

- Issue $15 million of 20-year bonds at a price of 101, with a coupon rate of 8%, and flotation costs of 2% of par.
- Use $35 million of funds generated from earnings.

The equity market is expected to earn 12%. US Treasury bonds are currently yielding 5%. The beta coefficient for DQZ is estimated to be .60. DQZ is subject to an effective corporate income tax rate of 40%.

The before-tax cost of DQZ's planned debt financing, net of flotation costs, in the first year is

a. 11.80%

b. 8.08%

c. 10.00%

d. 7.92%

**91. The best reason corporations issue Eurobonds rather than domestic bonds is that

a. These bonds are denominated in the currency of the country in which they are issued.

b. These bonds are normally a less expensive form of financing because of the absence of government regulation.

c. Foreign buyers more readily accept the issues of both large and small US corporations than do domestic investors.

d. Eurobonds carry no foreign exchange risk.

92. Which of the following provisions is generally considered detrimental to the investor?

a. Conversion.

b. Redeemable.

c. Callable.

d. Serial maturity.

93. Which of the following is not an advantage of leasing as a form of financing?

a. Up front costs may be less.

b. The provisions of the agreement may be less stringent than for other debt agreements.

c. The dollar cost.

d. The firm may be able to lease the asset when it does not have the credit capacity to purchase the asset.

94. Nerco has a bond issue that matures in fifteen years. Recently, the company's bond rating has gone from B to Baa. How would this affect the market price of the bonds?

a. Increase.

b. Decrease.

c. Remain the same.

d. The effect cannot be predicted.

Items 95 through 97 are based on the following information:

Watco, Inc. issued $1,000,000 in 8% bonds, maturing in ten years and paying interest semiannually. The bonds were issued at face value.

95. What can you assume about the interest rates at the time the bonds were issued?

a. The market rate for this bond was about 8%.

b. The nominal rate of interest was about 8%.

c. The coupon rate on the bond includes no premium for credit risk.

d. The risk-free interest rate is about 6%.

---

*   *CIA adapted*

** *CMA adapted*

96. If the market rate of interest for this type of bond increases to 9%, which of the following is true?
- a. The market value of Watco's bond will increase.
- b. The market value of Watco's bond will decrease.
- c. The effect will depend on the change in the LIBOR rate.
- d. The effect cannot be predicted.

97. Assume that one of Watco's bonds with $1,000 face is currently selling for $950. What is the current yield on the bond?
- a. 8.00%
- b. 9.00%
- c. 7.56%
- d. 8.42%

98. The market for outstanding, listed common stock is called the
- a. Primary market.
- b. New issue market.
- c. Over-the-counter market.
- d. Secondary market.

99. In capital markets, the primary market is concerned with
- a. New issues of bonds and stock securities.
- b. Exchanges of existing bond and stock securities.
- c. The sale of forward or future commodities contracts.
- d. New issues of bond and stock securities and exchanges of existing bond and stock securities.

*100. Which of the following is usually **not** a feature of cumulative preferred stock?
- a. Has priority over common stock with regard to earnings.
- b. Has priority over common stock with regard to assets.
- c. Has voting rights.
- d. Has the right to receive dividends in arrears before common stock dividends can be paid.

101. Which of the following is not an advantage of going public?
- a. Access to capital.
- b. Compliance.
- c. Use of stock options.
- d. Liquidity for owners' investments.

Items 102 and 103 are based on the following information:

The following information is available for Rothenberg, Inc.:

Balance sheet	
Current assets	$ 500,000
Property, plant, and equipment	4,000,000
Total assets	$4,500,000
Current liabilities	$ 30,000
Long-term debt	2,500,000
Common stock	200,000
Retained earnings	1,770,000
Total liabilities and stockholders' equity	$4,500,000

Budget income information	100,000 units	105,000 units
Sales	$3,000,000	$3,150,000
Expenses	(2,800,000)	(2,850,000)
Operating income (EBIT)	$ 200,000	$ 300,000
Earnings per share (EPS)	$0.20	$1.20

102. What is Rothenberg's degree of operating leverage?
- a. 1/5
- b. 10
- c. 5
- d. 2/3

103. What is the degree of financial leverage for Rothenberg, Inc.?
- a. 10
- b. 5
- c. 1/6
- d. 1/10

104. Which of the following is an advantage of equity financing in comparison to debt financing?
- a. Issuance costs are greater than for debt.
- b. Ownership is given up with respect to the issuance of common stock.
- c. Dividends are not tax deductible by the corporation whereas interest is tax deductible.
- d. The company has no firm obligation to pay dividends to common shareholders.

105. Assume that Company A and Company B are alike in all respects except that Company A utilizes more debt financing and less equity financing than does Company B. Which of the following statements is true?
- a. Company A has more net earnings variability than Company B.
- b. Company A has more operating earnings variability than Company B.
- c. Company A has less operating earnings variability than Company B.
- d. Company A has less financial leverage than Company B.

106. Which of the following is not a source of capital used to finance long-term projects?
- a. Common stock.
- b. Long-term debt.
- c. Preferred stock.
- d. Line of credit.

107. Which of the following factors generally does not impact management's capital structure strategy?
- a. Business risk.
- b. Tax position.
- c. Management aggressiveness.
- d. Expected return on assets.

**108. A firm with a higher degree of operating leverage when compared to the industry average implies that the
- a. Firm has higher variable costs.
- b. Firm's profits are more sensitive to changes in sales volume.
- c. Firm is more profitable.
- d. Firm is less risky.

*109. When a company increases its degree of financial leverage
- a. The equity beta of the company falls.
- b. The systematic risk of the company falls.

    c.   The unsystematic risk of the company falls.
    d.   The standard deviation of returns on the equity of the company rises.

*110.   A company has made the decision to finance next year's capital projects through debt rather than additional equity. The benchmark cost of capital for these projects should be
    a.   The before-tax cost of new-debt financing.
    b.   The after-tax cost of debt financing.
    c.   The cost of equity financing.
    d.   The weighted-average cost of capital.

Items 111 and 112 are based on the following information:

Management of Russell Corporation is considering the following two potential capital structures for a newly acquired business.

Alternative 1

Long-term debt, 6% interest	$3,000,000
Common equity	$3,000,000
Cost of common equity, 10%	
Marginal tax rate, 15%	

Alternative 2

Long-term debt, 7% interest	$5,000,000
Common equity	$1,000,000
Cost of common equity, 12%	
Marginal tax rate, 15%	

111.   Which of the following statements is not true if management decides to accept Alternative 1?
    a.   Alternative 1 is the more conservative capital structure.
    b.   Alternative 1 provides the greatest amount of financial leverage.
    c.   Net income will be less variable under Alternative 1.
    d.   Total interest expense will be less under Alternative 1.

112.   Which of the alternatives has the lowest weighted-average cost of capital and how much is the differential?
    a.   Alternative 1 by 1.5%
    b.   Alternative 2 by 0.59%
    c.   Alternative 1 by 0.167%
    d.   The alternatives have equal weighted-average cost of capital.

113.   Management of Kelly, Inc. uses CAPM to calculate the estimated cost of common equity. Which of the following would reduce the firm's estimated cost of common equity?
    a.   A reduction in the risk-free rate.
    b.   An increase in the firm's beta.
    c.   An increase in expected inflation.
    d.   An increase in the risk-free interest rate.

**114.   In general, it is more expensive for a company to finance with equity than with debt because
    a.   Long-term bonds have a maturity date and must, therefore, be repaid in the future.
    b.   Investors are exposed to greater risk with equity capital.
    c.   The interest on debt is a legal obligation.

    d.   Equity capital is in greater demand than debt capital.

115.   Which of the following is not a characteristic of the capital asset pricing model for estimating the cost of equity?
    a.   The model is simple to understand and implement.
    b.   The model can be applied to all firms.
    c.   The model does not rely on any dividend assumptions or growth of dividends.
    d.   It is based upon the stock's actual market price.

116.   Management of Terra Corp. is attempting to estimate the firm's cost of equity capital. Assuming that the firm has a constant growth rate of 5%, a forecasted dividend of $2.11, and a stock price of $23.12, what is the estimated cost of common equity using the dividend-yield-plus-growth approach?
    a.   9.1%
    b.   14.1%
    c.   15.6%
    d.   12.3%

117.   If nominal interest rates increase substantially but expected future earnings and dividend growth for a firm over the long run are not expected to change, the firm's stock price will
    a.   Increase.
    b.   Decrease.
    c.   Stay constant.
    d.   Change, but in no determinable direction.

118.   Assume that two companies, Company X and Company Y, are alike in all respects, except the market value of the outstanding common shares of Company X is greater than the market value of Company Y shares. This may indicate that
    a.   Company X's investors expect higher dividend growth than Company Y's investors.
    b.   Company X's investors expect lower dividend growth than Company Y's investors.
    c.   Company X's investors have longer expected holding periods than Company Y's investors.
    d.   Company X's investors have shorter expected holding periods than Company Y's investors.

119.   Which of the following methods explicitly recognizes a firm's risk when determining the estimated cost of equity?
    a.   Capital asset pricing model.
    b.   Dividend-yield-plus-growth model.
    c.   Bond-yield-plus model.
    d.   Return on equity.

120.   Assume a firm is expected to pay a dividend of $5.00 per share this year. The firm along with the dividend is expected to grow at a rate of 6%. If the current market price of the stock is $60 per share, what is the estimated cost of equity?
    a.   8.3%
    b.   6.0%
    c.   14.3%
    d.   12.0%

121.   The bond-yield-plus approach to estimating the cost of common equity involves adding a risk premium of 3% to 5% to the firm's
    a.   Cost of short-term debt.
    b.   Cost of long-term debt.

---

*   *CIA adapted*
**   *CMA adapted*

c. Return on assets.
d. Return on equity.

**122. In practice, dividends
a. Usually exhibit greater stability than earnings.
b. Fluctuate more widely than earnings.
c. Tend to be a lower percentage of earnings for mature firms.
d. Are usually changed every year to reflect earnings changes.

Items 123 and 124 are based on the following information:

Martin Corporation
STATEMENT OF FINANCIAL POSITION
December 31, 2009
(Dollars in millions)

Assets	
Current assets	$ 75
Plant and equipment	250
Total assets	$325
Liabilities and shareholders' equity	
Current liabilities	$ 46
Long-term debt (12%)	64
Common equity:	
Common stock, $1 par	10
Additional paid in capital	100
Retained earnings	105
Total liabilities and shareholders' equity	$325

Additional data

• The long-term debt was originally issued at par ($1,000/bond) and is currently trading at $1,250 per bond.
• Martin Corporation can now issue debt at 150 basis points over US Treasury bonds.
• The current risk-free rate (US Treasury bonds) is 7%.
• Martin's common stock is currently selling at $32 per share.
• The expected market return is currently 15%.
• The beta value for Martin is 1.25.
• Martin's effective corporate income tax rate is 40%

**123. Martin Corporation's current net cost of debt is
a. 5.5%
b. 7.0%
c. 5.1%
d. 8.5%

**124. Using the Capital Asset Pricing Model (CAPM), Martin Corporation's current cost of common equity is
a. 8.75%
b. 10.00%
c. 15.00%
d. 17.00%

Items 125 and 126 are based on the following information:

DQZ Telecom is considering a project for the coming year that will cost $50 million. DQZ plans to use the following combination of debt and equity to finance the investment.

• Issue $15 million of 20-year bonds at a price of 101, with a coupon rate of 8%, and flotation costs of 2% of par.
• Use $35 million of funds generated from earnings.

The equity market is expected to earn 12%. US Treasury bonds are currently yielding 5%. The beta coefficient for DQZ is estimated to be .60. DQZ is subject to an effective corporate income tax rate of 40%.

**125. Assume that the after-tax costs of debt is 7% and the cost of equity is 12%. Determine the weighted-average cost of capital.
a. 10.50%
b. 8.50%
c. 9.50%
d. 6.30%

**126. The Capital Asset Pricing Model (CAPM) computes the expected return on a security by adding the risk-free rate of return to the incremental yield of the expected market return that is adjusted by the company's beta. Compute DQZ's expected rate of return.
a. 9.20%
b. 12.20%
c. 7.20%
d. 12.00%

*127. When calculating the cost of capital, the cost assigned to retained earnings should be
a. Zero.
b. Lower than the cost of external common equity.
c. Equal to the cost of external common equity.
d. Higher than the cost of external common equity.

128. According to the Capital Asset Pricing Model (CAPM), the relevant risk of a security is its
a. Company-specific risk.
b. Diversifiable risk.
c. Systematic risk.
d. Total risk.

**129. Hi-Tech Inc. has determined that it can minimize its weighted-average cost of capital (WACC) by using a debt/equity ratio of 2/3. If the firm's cost of debt is 9% before taxes, the cost of equity is estimated to be 12% before taxes, and the tax rate is 40%, what is the firm's WACC?
a. 6.48%
b. 7.92%
c. 9.36%
d. 10.80%

Items 130 through 132 are based on the following information:

A new company requires $1 million of financing and is considering two arrangements as shown in the table below.

Arrangement	Amount of equity raised	Amount of debt financing	Before-tax cost of debt
#1	$700,000	$300,000	8% per annum
#2	$300,000	$700,000	10% per annum

In the first year of operations, the company is expected to have sales revenues of $500,000, cost of sales of $200,000, and general and administrative expenses of $100,000. The tax rate is 30%, and there are no other items on the income statement. All earnings are paid out as dividends at year-end.

130. If the cost of equity were 12%, then the weighted-average cost of capital under Arrangement #1, to the nearest full percentage point, would be
a. 8%
b. 10%

c.   11%
d.   12%

131. Which of the following statements comparing the two financing arrangements is true?
  a. The company will have a higher expected gross margin under Arrangement #1.
  b. The company will have a higher degree of operating leverage under Arrangement #2.
  c. The company will have higher interest expense under Arrangement #1.
  d. The company will have higher expected tax expense under Arrangement #1.

132. The return on equity will be \<List A\> and the debt ratio will be \<List B\> under Arrangement #2, as compared with Arrangement #1.

	List A	List B
a.	Higher	Higher
b.	Higher	Lower
c.	Lower	Higher
d.	Lower	Lower

*__133.__ A parent company sold a subsidiary to a group of managers of the subsidiary. The purchasing group invested $1 million and borrowed $49 million against the assets of the subsidiary. This is an example of a
  a. Spin-off.
  b. Leveraged buyout.
  c. Joint venture.
  d. Liquidation.

**__134.__ The acquisition of a retail shoe store by a shoe manufacturer is an example of
  a. Vertical integration.
  b. A conglomerate.
  c. Market extension.
  d. Horizontal integration.

**__135.__ A horizontal merger is a merger between
  a. Two or more firms from different and unrelated markets.
  b. Two or more firms at different stages of the production process.
  c. A producer and its supplier.
  d. Two or more firms in the same market.

136. A soft drink producer acquiring a bottle manufacturer is an example of a
  a. Horizontal merger.
  b. Vertical merger.
  c. Congeneric merger.
  d. Conglomerate merger.

137. A shoe manufacturing firm acquiring a brokerage house is an example of a
  a. Horizontal merger.
  b. Vertical merger.
  c. Congeneric merger.
  d. Conglomerate merger.

---

 *   CIA adapted
** CMA adapted

MULTIPLE-CHOICE ANSWERS

1.	c	__ __	30.	c	__ __	59.	c	__ __	88.	a	__ __	117.	b	__ __
2.	a	__ __	31.	d	__ __	60.	d	__ __	89.	c	__ __	118.	a	__ __
3.	c	__ __	32.	a	__ __	61.	d	__ __	90.	b	__ __	119.	a	__ __
4.	d	__ __	33.	c	__ __	62.	b	__ __	91.	b	__ __	120.	c	__ __
5.	d	__ __	34.	d	__ __	63.	d	__ __	92.	c	__ __	121.	b	__ __
6.	a	__ __	35.	d	__ __	64.	a	__ __	93.	c	__ __	122.	a	__ __
7.	d	__ __	36.	b	__ __	65.	b	__ __	94.	a	__ __	123.	c	__ __
8.	b	__ __	37.	d	__ __	66.	a	__ __	95.	a	__ __	124.	d	__ __
9.	d	__ __	38.	a	__ __	67.	c	__ __	96.	b	__ __	125.	a	__ __
10.	c	__ __	39.	d	__ __	68.	d	__ __	97.	d	__ __	126.	a	__ __
11.	c	__ __	40.	d	__ __	69.	d	__ __	98.	d	__ __	127.	b	__ __
12.	d	__ __	41.	d	__ __	70.	b	__ __	99.	a	__ __	128.	c	__ __
13.	c	__ __	42.	d	__ __	71.	d	__ __	100.	c	__ __	129.	c	__ __
14.	c	__ __	43.	c	__ __	72.	b	__ __	101.	b	__ __	130.	b	__ __
15.	d	__ __	44.	b	__ __	73.	a	__ __	102.	b	__ __	131.	d	__ __
16.	d	__ __	45.	a	__ __	74.	a	__ __	103.	a	__ __	132.	a	__ __
17.	d	__ __	46.	c	__ __	75.	d	__ __	104.	d	__ __	133.	b	__ __
18.	c	__ __	47.	b	__ __	76.	c	__ __	105.	a	__ __	134.	a	__ __
19.	b	__ __	48.	c	__ __	77.	c	__ __	106.	d	__ __	135.	d	__ __
20.	d	__ __	49.	b	__ __	78.	c	__ __	107.	d	__ __	136.	b	__ __
21.	d	__ __	50.	d	__ __	79.	a	__ __	108.	b	__ __	137.	d	__ __
22.	b	__ __	51.	c	__ __	80.	d	__ __	109.	d	__ __			
23.	c	__ __	52.	b	__ __	81.	c	__ __	110.	d	__ __			
24.	b	__ __	53.	b	__ __	82.	b	__ __	111.	b	__ __			
25.	b	__ __	54.	d	__ __	83.	c	__ __	112.	b	__ __			
26.	d	__ __	55.	d	__ __	84.	d	__ __	113.	a	__ __			
27.	d	__ __	56.	d	__ __	85.	c	__ __	114.	b	__ __			
28.	d	__ __	57.	b	__ __	86.	d	__ __	115.	d	__ __	1st:	__/137 = __%
29.	b	__ __	58.	b	__ __	87.	d	__ __	116.	b	__ __	2nd:	__/137 = __%

MULTIPLE-CHOICE ANSWER EXPLANATIONS

Working Capital Management

1. **(c)** The requirement is to identify the function that is not related to financial management. The correct answer is (c) because internal control is a function of the controller's office. Answers (a), (b), and (d) are incorrect because the functions of financial management include: financing, capital, budgeting, financial management, corporate governance, and risk management.

2. **(a)** The requirement is to identify the formula for the inventory conversion period. Answer (a) is correct because the inventory conversion period describes the average time required to convert materials into finished goods and sell those goods. Answers (b), (c), and (d) are all incorrect versions of the formula.

3. **(c)** The requirement is to identify the formula for the calculation of the payables deferral period. Answer (c) is correct because the payables deferral period is equal to the average length of time between the purchase of materials and the payment of cash for them. Answers (a), (b), and (d) are all incorrect because they illustrate inaccurate versions of the formula.

4. **(d)** The requirement is to determine the false statement regarding working capital management. Answer (d) is correct because financing permanent inventory buildup with long-term debt is an example of a conservative working capital policy. Answers (a), (b), and (c) are all accurate statements about working capital management.

5. **(d)** The requirement is to identify the factor considered in determining the appropriate level of working capital. Answer (d) is correct because the main reason to retain working capital is to meet the firm's financial obligations. Therefore, the amount is determined by offsetting the benefit of current assets and current liabilities against the probability of technical insolvency. Answer (a) is incorrect because it is a consideration regarding long-term financing. Answer (b) is incorrect because it is a consideration regarding capital structure. Answer (c) is incorrect because short-term debt is generally less expensive than long-term debt.

6. **(a)** The requirement is to identify the impact of decisions on the cash conversion cycle. The cash conversion cycle is equal to the Inventory conversion period + Receivables collection period – Payables deferral period. Answer (a) is correct because the impact of a decreased inventory conversion period is a reduction in the cash conversion cycle. Answers (b), (c), and (d) are incorrect because these actions would increase the length of a firm's cash conversion cycle.

7. **(d)** The requirement is to calculate the cash conversion cycle. The cash conversion period is calculated as the Inventory conversion period + Receivables collection period – Payables deferral period. Answer (d) is correct because the inventory conversion period is $2,500,000/$50,000 = 50 days, and the receivable conversion period is $2,000,000/$100,000 = 20 days. Therefore, the cash conversion cycle is equal to 50 days + 20 days – 30 days = 40 days. Answer (a) is incorrect because is erroneously adds the payable deferral period.

8. (b) The requirement is to calculate the inventory conversion period. The inventory conversion period is calculated as average inventory/(cost of sales per day). Answer (b) is correct because $5,000,000/($30,000,000/365) = 60.83 days.

9. (d) The requirement is to identify the definition of the payables deferral period. Answer (d) is correct because the payables deferral period is the average length of time between the purchase of materials and the payment of cash for them. Answer (a) is incorrect because the operating cycle is the period of time elapsing between the acquisition of goods and services involved in the manufacturing process and the final collection of cash from sale of the products. Answer (b) is incorrect because the inventory cycle is the average time required to convert materials into finished goods and sell those goods. Answer (c) is incorrect because the accounts receivable period is the length of time required to collect accounts receivable.

10. (c) The requirement is to identify the impact of the length of the cash conversion cycle on a firm's profitability. Answer (c) is correct because the longer the cash conversion cycle the greater the amount of time from when a firm pays its suppliers to the time it ultimately collects receivables. The greater the time frame the more likely the firm will have to borrow funds and incur interest expense which reduces profitability. Answers (a), (b), and (d) are incorrect because the incurrence of interest will reduce profitability.

11. (c) The requirement is to calculate the number of days' sales outstanding. Answer (c) is correct. One-third of the customers take advantage of the 5% cash discount and pay on day ten. The remaining two-thirds of the customers pay on day 20. Average days' sales outstanding is calculated as

Days' sales outstanding = (1/3) (10 days) + (2/3) (20 days) = 17 days

Answer (a) is incorrect because this inappropriately weights the two different types of customers. Answer (b) is incorrect because this uses a simple average of days rather than a weighted-average. Answer (d) is incorrect because this solution uses the 20-day collection period for customers not taking the cash discount as the days' sales outstanding, rather than the average days for payment by all customers.

Cash Management

12. (d) The requirement is to determine the effect of changing from using a depository transfer check to using a wire transfer. The change is feasible if the interest savings offsets the increased costs. For a fee of $25, the firm gets two extra days' interest on the average transfer amount. By dividing the $25 fee by the interest rate for two days, .04% (2 days × .02%), we get $62,500. Therefore, management should make the change if the average transfer is expected to be greater than $62,500. Answer (a) is incorrect because it is a calculating assuming there is only a one-day decrease in float.

13. (c) The requirement is to consider the cash flow implications of electronic funds transfer. Answer (c) is correct because electronic funds transfer takes the float out of both the cash receipts and disbursements processes. It is beneficial to take the float out of the cash receipts process but not the cash disbursements process.

14. (c) The requirement is to determine the benefit or loss from establishing the lockbox system. The firm saves money if the interest savings is greater than the increased cost of processing cash receipts. The increased cost of processing cash receipts is equal to $5,000 ($10,000 bank charge – $5,000 cost savings). The interest savings is measured by multiplying the increase in average funds by the short-term interest rate. The firm will have use of an additional $300,000 ($100,000 × 3 days) in average funds. Therefore, the interest savings is equal to $15,000 ($300,000 × 5%), and the overall benefit is equal to $10,000 ($15,000 – $5,000). Answer (a) is incorrect because it ignores the interest savings. Answer (b) is incorrect because it only considers the bank charge.

15. (d) The requirement is to describe how firms attempt to manage float. Float is the time that elapses relating to mailing, processing, and clearing checks. A firm strives to minimize its cash receipts float to get use of the receipts as soon as possible, and to maximize its cash disbursement float to get use of the funds for as long as possible. Therefore, the correct answer is (d).

16. (d) The requirement is to calculate the financial cost/benefit of establishing a concentration banking arrangement. The cost savings in interest from establishing the arrangement is equal to $9,200 [($115,000 × 2 days) × 4%]. Therefore, answer (d) is correct because implementing the concentration banking arrangement would result in a net savings of $4,200 ($9,200 – $5,000). Answer (a) is incorrect because it only considers the $5,000 cost. Answer (c) is incorrect because it considers the $115,000 in daily cash receipts the benefit.

17. (d) The requirement is to calculate the financial cost/benefit of establishing a lockbox system. Answer (d) is correct because the solution is found by comparing the cost in fees to the benefits in terms of reduced interest costs. Since the float is reduced by three days the firm gets the use of $1,050,000 ($350,000 × 3 days) in additional funds that results in interest savings of $42,000 ($1,050,000 × 4%). Therefore, the net benefit is equal to $20,000 ($42,000 – $22,000). Answer (a) is incorrect because it only considers the bank fee. Answer (b) is incorrect because it only considers the net change in processing costs.

18. (c) The requirement is to calculate the financial costs/benefit of establishing a zero balance account system. Answer (c) is correct because the solution is found by comparing the cost in fees to the benefit in terms of reduced interest costs. Since the float is reduced by four days then the firm gets the use of $160,000 ($40,000 × 4 days) additional funds which results in interest savings of $7,200 ($160,000 × 4.5%). The $1,200 savings is the excess of the interest savings of $7,200 over the costs of $6,000. Answer (a) is incorrect because it only considerers the cost without considering the interest savings. Answer (b) is incorrect because it is calculated by considering the $7,200 interest savings as a cost and the $6,000 in maintenance and transfer fees as a benefit. Answer (d) is incorrect because it only considers the interest savings.

19. (b) The requirement is to identify the working capital technique that increases the payable float. Answer (b) is the correct answer because payment by draft (e.g., a check) is slower than other methods of payment such as electronic cash transfers. Answers (a) and (d) are incorrect because they are techniques designed to speed the processing of cash receipts. Answer (c) is incorrect because EDI involves processing transactions electronically. This would speed up the payment of payables.

20. (d) The requirement is to determine the optimal agreement for a lockbox system. The number of checks issued during the year is determined by multiplying 700 times 360 days, which results in a total of 252,000 checks. The total amount of collections is equal to $453,600,000 (252,000 checks × $1,800 per check). Answer (d) is correct because it results in the lowest cost of $122,500 ($1,750,000 × 7%), which is the cost of maintaining the compensating balance. Answer (a) is incorrect because it results in a cost of $126,000 ($.50 × 252,000 checks). Answer (b) is incorrect because it results in a cost of $125,000. Answer (c) is incorrect because it results in a fee of $136,080 (3% × $453,600,000).

21. (d) The requirement is to calculate the annual benefit from accepting the bank's proposal. Answer (d) is correct because the net benefit from the reduction of the cash receipts float is $12,000 [($100,000 × 2) × 6%] minus the annual service fee, $6,000 ($500 × 12 months), which is equal to $6,000. Answer (b) is incorrect because it ignores the bank service charge. Answer (c) is incorrect because it assumes only a one-day reduction in float.

22. (b) The requirement is to identify the term used to describe a required minimum checking account balance. Answer (b) is correct because a compensating balance is a minimum balance required by the bank to compensate the bank for services. Answer (a) is incorrect because transactions balance is the amount of funds the firm needs on deposit to conduct day-to-day transactions. Answer (c) is incorrect because this precautionary balance represents the balance available for emergencies. Answer (d) is incorrect because this speculative balance represents the balance available for bargain purchases.

23. (c) The requirement is to calculate the net benefit from accepting the bank's proposal. The correct answer is (c) because the annual benefit is $6,000 which is equal to the interest income $12,000 ($100,000 × 2 days × 6%) – $6,000 ($500 × 12) cost.

24. (b) The requirement is to calculate the net benefit of using the lockbox system. Answer (b) is correct because the net benefit is equal to $60,875, which is equal to the interest savings of $120,000 ($20,000 average payment × 50 payments × 2 days × 6%) minus the cost of the service of $59,125 [$50,000 + (50 payments per day × 365 days × $0.50)].

Marketable Securities Management

25. (b) The requirement is to identify the most important consideration with respect to short-tem investments. Answer (b) is correct because short-term investments must be available to convert to cash when needed. Therefore, risk and liquidity are the most important considerations. Answers (a), (c), and (d) are incorrect because they are important considerations with respect to long-term investments.

26. (d) The requirement is to identify the security that is not suitable as a marketable investment. Answer (d) is correct because convertible bonds are long-term investments

that have more risk than securities that are typically used for short-term investment. The primary considerations regarding short-term investments are liquidity and safety. Answers (a), (b), and (c) are all appropriate as marketable investments. They are liquid and have a low degree of risk.

27. (d) The requirement is to identify the instrument with the highest return. Answer (d) is correct because commercial paper is issued by a corporation and, therefore, has more risk than Treasury notes, Treasury bonds, or money market accounts.

28. (d) The requirement is to identify the item that is not a characteristic of a negotiable certificate of deposit. The correct answer is (d) because negotiable certificates of deposit have lower yields than banker's acceptances and commercial paper—they have less risk. Answer (a) is incorrect because negotiable certificates of deposit do have a secondary market. Answer (b) is incorrect because negotiable certificates of deposit are regulated by the Federal Reserve System. Answer (c) is incorrect because they are usually sold in denominations of a minimum of $100,000.

Inventory Management

29. (b) In a just-in-time (JIT) purchasing system, orders are placed such that delivery of raw materials occurs just as they are needed for production. This system requires the placement of more frequent, smaller orders and ideally eliminates inventories. Conversely, in a traditional system large orders are placed less frequently and extra inventory is carried to avoid stockouts and the resulting production delays during order lead time. Certain cost changes would encourage managers to switch to a JIT system. One is **decreased** cost per purchase order, which would increase the attractiveness of placing the many more orders required. Another is **increased** inventory unit carrying costs, which would make the elimination of inventories desirable.

30. (c) Calculation of the reorder point includes consideration of the average daily usage, average delivery time, and stock-out costs. Answer (a) is incorrect because ordering costs are included in determining the economic order quantity but not the reorder point. Answer (b) is incorrect because carrying cost is considered in determining the economic order quantity but not the reorder point. Answer (d) is incorrect because the economic order quantity is not considered in determining the reorder point.

31. (d) The requirement is to identify the item that involves an incorrect comparison of a just-in-time system and a traditional system. Answer (d) is correct because in a just-in-time system the lot size is based on immediate need; a traditional system bases lot size on formulas. Answers (a), (b), and (c) are all incorrect because they express correct comparisons of just-in-time and traditional systems.

32. (a) The goal of a just-in-time system is to identify and eliminate all non-value-added activities. One of the major features of a just-in-time system is a decrease in the number of suppliers to build strong relations and ensure quality goods. In a just-in-time system raw material is purchased only as it is needed for production, thereby eliminating the need for costly storage. In a just-in-time system, vendors make more frequent deliveries of small quantities of materials that are placed into production immediately upon receipt.

33.   (c)   The purpose of a "just-in-time" production system is to decrease the size of production runs while increasing the number of lots processed during the year. This production philosophy requires that inventory be delivered as it is needed, rather than held in large quantities. Inventory turnover is computed as

$$\frac{\text{Cost of goods sold}}{\text{Average inventory}}$$

As average inventory decreases, inventory turnover increases. As average inventory levels decrease, inventory as a percentage of total assets will also decrease.

34.   (d)   The requirement is to determine the effect of a decrease in safety stock on Dee Co.'s economic order quantity (EOQ). The EOQ represents the optimal quantity of inventory to be ordered based on demand and various inventory costs. The formula for computing EOQ is

$$EOQ = \sqrt{\frac{2aD}{k}}, \text{ where}$$

D = Demand (in units) for a specified time period
a = Ordering costs per purchase order
k = Cost of carrying one unit in inventory for the specified time period

Safety stock is a buffer of excess inventory held to guard against stockouts. Safety stock is usually a multiple of demand and has no effect on a company's EOQ.

35.   (a)   The economic order quantity (EOQ) formula was developed on the basis of the following assumptions:

1.   Demand occurs at a constant rate throughout the year and is known with certainty.
2.   Lead-time on the receipt of orders is constant.
3.   The entire quantity ordered is received at one time.
4.   The unit costs of the items ordered are constant; thus, there can be no quantity discounts.
5.   There are no limitations on the size of the inventory.

Answer (a) is correct because it is assumption 1. Answer (b) is incorrect because it contradicts assumption 5. Answers (c) and (d) are incorrect because they are the opposite of assumption 4.

36.   (b)   The requirement is to calculate the economic order quantity (EOQ). The EOQ formula is

$$EOQ = \sqrt{\frac{2aD}{k}}$$

In the above equation, a = cost of placing one order, D = annual demand in units, and k = cost of carrying one unit in inventory for one year. Substituting the given information, the equation becomes

$$EOQ = \sqrt{\frac{(2)(32)(20,000)}{8}} = \sqrt{160,000} = 400 \text{ units}$$

37.   (d)   The requirement is to determine the order point for material X. When safety stock is maintained, the order point is computed as follows:

$$\frac{\text{Daily}}{\text{Demand}} \times \frac{\text{Lead time}}{\text{in days}} + \frac{\text{Safety}}{\text{stock}}$$

Daily demand is eighty units (20,000 units ÷ 250 days). Therefore, the order point is 3,200 units [(80 × 30) + 800].

38.   (a)   The requirement is to identify the impact of inventory levels on costs. Maintaining a low level of inventory requires that many smaller orders of inventory be made in order to satisfy customer demand. Answer (a) is correct because each order incurs ordering cost and as the quantity of orders increases the ordering costs will also increase. Answer (b) is incorrect because carrying costs are higher with a higher level of inventory. Answer (c) is incorrect because although the ordering costs are higher the carrying costs are lower. Answer (d) is incorrect because the ordering costs would be higher.

39.   (d)   The requirement is to identify an inventory carrying cost. The correct answer is (d). Part of the cost of holding inventory is the cost of obsolescence. Answer (a) is an example of a stockout cost. Answer (a) is a stock-out cost. Answer (b) and (c) are examples of ordering costs.

40.   (d)   The requirement is to identify the characteristic of JIT inventory systems. Answer (d) is correct because JIT systems rely on quality materials; otherwise production shutdowns will occur because no extra materials are available. Answer (a) is incorrect because there are no safety stocks in JIT systems. Answer (b) is incorrect because JIT is applicable to all size corporations. Answer (c) is incorrect because JIT generally is applied all along the supply chain.

41.   (d)   The requirement is to identify the factor not used in the economic order quantity formula. Answer (d) is correct because the volume of products in inventory is not a component of the economic order quantity formula. Answers (a), (b), and (c) are incorrect because they are all components of the EOQ formula.

42.   (d)   The requirement is to determine the cost savings from selecting one of the production alternatives. Under the level production alternative, the firm would incur an additional $40,000 [($1,500,000 − $2,000,000) × 8%] in inventory holding costs but it would save $50,000 in production costs. Therefore, answer (d) is the correct answer. Alternative 1 results in $10,000 ($50,000 − $40,000) in savings over Alternative 2.

43.   (c)   The requirement is to calculate the short-term interest rate that would cause the two alternatives to have equal costs. The cost of implementing Alternative 2 is the $50,000 in additional production costs. When the inventory holding costs related to Alternative 1 equals that amount the costs are equal. By dividing the $50,000 by the $500,000 in additional average inventory, we get 10% ($50,000 ÷ $500,000). Therefore, the correct answer is (c) because at a 10% interest rate the cost of holding the additional inventory under Alternative 1 is equal to the additional production costs under Alternative 2.

44.   (b)   The requirement is to determine the factor that would increase inventory levels. In answering this question, you should consider the components of the EOQ formula. The correct answer is (b) because if the cost of holding inventory decreases it would enable the firm to carry more inventory. Answer (a) is incorrect because a decrease in sales would result in a decrease in the required level of inventory. Answer (c) is incorrect because a decrease in sales variability decreases the required level of inventory. Answer (d) is incorrect because a decrease in the cost of running out of stock decreases the required level of inventory.

45. **(a)** The requirement is to identify the technique used to plan and control manufacturing inventories. Answer (a) is correct because materials requirements planning is an inventory planning technique. Answer (b) is incorrect because regression analysis is a technique used to estimate the relationship between variables. Answer (c) is incorrect because capital budgeting is a technique used to evaluate investments in capital assets. Answer (d) is incorrect because linear programming is a technique used to determine the optimal decision when resources are constrained.

Receivables Management

46. **(c)** The requirement is to identify the definition of collection policy. Answer (c) is correct because a firm's collection policy is the diligence used to collect slow paying accounts. Answer (a) is incorrect because the discount policy is the policy regarding the percentage discount given for early payment. Answer (b) is incorrect because the credit policy is a firm's requirements for customers in order to grant them credit. Answer (d) is incorrect because the payables policy is unrelated to accounts receivable.

47. **(b)** The requirement is to identify which item is not an advantage of initiating seasonal dating. Seasonal dating is a procedure for inducing customers to buy early by not requiring payment until the customers' selling season, regardless of when the merchandise is shipped. Under seasonal dating the selling firm incurs higher credit costs, as customers take longer to pay. Therefore, answer (b) is correct because this is not an advantage of seasonal dating. Answer (a) is incorrect because under seasonal dating, customers buy earlier and the selling firm incurs lower storage costs. This is an advantage of seasonal dating. Answer (c) is incorrect because providing attractive credit terms for customers is an advantage of a seasonal dating policy. Answer (d) is incorrect because reduced uncertainty about sales volume is an advantage of a seasonal dating policy.

48. **(c)** The requirement is to calculate the total collections on or before January 11. Answer (c) is correct because if all customers take advantage of seasonal dating and all customers take the discount, then collections on or before January 11 will be

= (Number of units sold) (Unit selling price) (1 – Discount percentage)
= (700 units) × $10 (1 – .02) × .98 = $6,860

Answer (a) is incorrect because all customers take the discount and abide by the terms of the discount policy, so they will pay on or before January 11. Answer (b) is incorrect because this solution omits the collection of the January 1 sales revenue. Answer (d) is incorrect because this solution does not take the discount into account.

49. **(b)** The requirement is to identify the formula for days' sales in accounts receivable. Answer (b) is correct because days' sales in receivables provides an overall measure of the accumulation of receivables. It is calculated by dividing the balance of receivables by sales per day. Answers (a), (c), and (d) are incorrect because they do not accurately illustrate the formula.

50. **(d)** The requirement is to describe a firm's credit criteria. Answer (d) is correct because the credit criteria are the policies used to decide whether a customer should be extended credit. Answer (a) is incorrect because it describes the credit period. Answer (b) is incorrect because it de-

scribes a portion of the discount policy. Answer (c) is incorrect because it describes the collection policy.

51. **(c)** The requirement is to calculate impact of this change in policy on accounts receivable. Under the existing policy, sales are equal to $50,000,000, 70% of which are on credit. Therefore, the average accounts receivable balance is equal to $7,291,667 [($35,000,000 credit sales ÷ 360 days) × 75 days]. Under the new policy credit sales are estimated to be $28,500,000 [($50,000,000 × 95%) × 60%]. Accordingly, the average accounts receivable balance under the new policy is estimated to be $3,958,333 [($28,500,000 credit sales ÷ 360) × 50 days]. Answer (c) is correct because the change in accounts receivable balance is estimated to be a decrease of $3,333,334 ($7,291,667 – $3,958,333).

52. **(b)** The requirement is to calculate the effect of the new policy on net income before taxes. Answer (b) is correct because the decrease in operating income is equal to $2,166,667 [$2,500,000 loss in sales – ($3,333,334 × 10%) interest savings]. Answer (a) is incorrect because it only considers the loss in sales. Answer (c) is incorrect because it treats the entire $3,333,334 change in average receivables as a benefit.

53. **(b)** The requirement is to determine the factor that is not considered in determining whether to change credit policy. Answer (b) is correct because the current bad debt experience is irrelevant to the decision. Management should consider only those factors that change based upon the alternative selected. Answer (a) is incorrect because the cost of funds is relevant to the decision. Answer (c) is incorrect because if there is any impact on the current customer base, this factor should be considered. Answer (d) is incorrect because the impact on bank loan covenants is obviously relevant.

54. **(d)** The requirement is to calculate the annual cost of the financing. Answer (d) is correct because the total amount paid to the factor would be ($100,000 × 80%) × 10% + ($100,000 × 12) × 2% = $32,000. The net cost is equal to $14,000 ($32,000 – $18,000 cost savings). Therefore, the annual interest cost is equal to $14,000/$80,000 = 17.5%.

55. **(d)** The requirement is to calculate the benefit or loss from changing credit policy. Answer (d) is correct because the benefit is equal to the contribution margin received from the additional sales minus the cost of having incremental funds tied up in accounts receivable. The benefit from an increase in sales is equal to $144,000 ($720,000 sales × 20% contribution margin). The interest opportunity cost is equal to 75 days' interest on the variable portion of sales, or ($720,000 × 80%)/360 × 75 × 20% interest = $24,000. Therefore, the net benefit is equal to $120,000 ($144,000 – $24,000).

Financing Current Assets

56. **(d)** The requirement is to calculate the cost of not taking a trade discount. The cost is calculated with the following formula:

$$\frac{\text{Discount percent}}{100\% - \text{Discount percent}} \times \frac{365 \text{ days}}{\text{Total pay period} - \text{Discount period}}$$

Answer (d) is correct because the discount percentage is 3%, the total pay period is 35 days, and the discount period is 15 days. Therefore, the nominal cost is calculated as follows:

$$\frac{3\%}{100\% - 3\%} \times \frac{365 \text{ days}}{35 \text{ days} - 10 \text{ days}} = 45.2\%$$

57. (b) The requirement is to calculate the cost of not taking a trade discount. The cost is calculated with the following formula:

$$\frac{\text{Discount percent}}{100\% - \text{Discount percent}} \times \frac{365 \text{ days}}{\text{Total pay period} - \text{Discount period}}$$

Answer (b) is correct because the discount percentage is 3%, the total pay period is 67 days, and the discount period is 15 days. Therefore, the nominal cost is calculated as follows:

$$\frac{3\%}{100\% - 3\%} \times \frac{365 \text{ days}}{67 \text{ days} - 15 \text{ days}} = 21.71\%$$

58. (b) The requirement is to analyze the impact upon a firm of rising short-term interest rates. A heavy reliance on short-term debt means that interest expense and the related net income will be variable and this increases the financial risk of the firm. Answer (b) is correct because if short-term interest rates increase then interest expense will increase which will cause a related decrease in net income.

59. (c) The requirement is to evaluate credit terms to made sound cash management decisions. Answer (c) is correct because a firm should take advantage of the cash discount and pay on the last day of the discount period, which is day 10. Answers (a) and (b) are incorrect because "2" is the amount of the percentage discount; not the discount period. Answer (d) is incorrect because if a firm pays bills on the final due date, it will not have taken advantage of cash discounts which are very lucrative.

60. (d) The requirement is to identify the forms of borrowing that are unsecured. Answer (d) is correct because revolving credit agreements, bankers' acceptances, lines of credit, and commercial paper all represent unsecured obligations. Answer (a) is incorrect because floating liens and chattel mortgages are secured. Answer (b) is incorrect because factoring agreements and chattel mortgages are secured. Answer (c) is incorrect because floating liens and chattel mortgages are secured.

61. (d) The requirement is to evaluate the cost of trade credit. Answer (d) is correct because if the discount period is longer, the days of extra credit obtained by foregoing the discount are fewer. This makes the trade credit more costly. Answer (a) is incorrect because the lower the discount percentage, the lower the opportunity cost of foregoing the discount and using the trade credit financing. Answers (b) and (c) are incorrect because percentage financing cost is unaffected by the purchase price of the items.

62. (b) The requirement is to calculate the effective interest rate on a loan with a compensating balance requirement. The interest rate is calculated with the following formula:

$$\frac{\text{Interest cost}}{\text{Funds available}} = \frac{10\% \times \$500,000}{\$500,000 - \$50,000} = 11.1\%$$

Therefore, answer (b) is correct.

63. (d) The requirement is to calculate the cost of not taking a trade discount. The formula for computing the interest is

$$\frac{\text{Discount percent}}{100\% - \text{Discount percent}} \times \frac{360 \text{ days}}{\text{Total pay period} - \text{Discount period}}$$

$$\frac{3\%}{100\% - 3\%} \times \frac{360 \text{ days}}{45 \text{ days} - 10 \text{ days}} = 31.81\%$$

Therefore, answer (d) is correct.

64. (a) The requirement is to identify the term that is not related to loans involving inventory. Answer (a) is correct because factoring involves the sale of accounts receivable. Answer (b) is incorrect because a blanket inventory lien involves a legal document that establishes inventory as collateral for a loan. Answer (c) is incorrect because a trust receipt is an instrument that acknowledges that the borrower holds the inventory and the proceeds from sale will be put in trust for the lender. Answer (d) is incorrect because warehousing involves storing inventory in a public warehouse under the control of the lender.

65. (b) The requirement is to identify the nature of LIBOR. Answer (b) is correct because LIBOR, like the prime rate, is an example of a nominal rate. It is adjusted for inflation risk, but not credit risk. Answer (a) is incorrect because the risk-free rate is a theoretical rate that is not quoted. Answer (c) is incorrect because LIBOR is not credit risk adjusted. Answer (d) is incorrect because LIBOR is a short-term rate.

66. (a) The requirement is to identify the advantage of using long-term debt as a source of financing current assets. Answer (a) is correct because financing with long-term as opposed to short-term debt reduces the risk of the firm. Long-term debt does not have to be repaid as soon as short-term debt. Answer (b) is incorrect because long-term debt is generally more costly than short-term debt. Answer (c) is incorrect because the debt covenants are usually more restrictive in long-term debt agreements. Answer (d) is incorrect because early payment of long-term debt can result in prepayment penalties.

67. (c) The requirement is to identify the item that is not an implication of the policy of matching maturity assets with the maturity of financing. Answer (c) is correct because under this policy current assets are financed with current liabilities. Answers (a), (b), and (d) are incorrect because they are all appropriate implications of the policy.

68. (d) The requirement is to identify the term used to describe asset-backed public offerings. Answer (d) is correct because securitization of assets is the offering of debt collateralized by a firm's accounts receivable. Answer (a) is incorrect because a trust receipt is an instrument that acknowledges that the borrower holds a collateralized inventory and that proceeds from the sale will be put in trust for the lender. Answer (b) is incorrect because warehousing is the storage of inventory in a public warehouse that can only be removed with the lender's permission. Answer (c) is incorrect because a blanket inventory lien is a document that establishes the inventory as collateral for the loan.

69. (d) The requirement is to calculate the effective cost of a loan with a compensating balance requirement. Answer (d) is correct because the effective interest rate is equal to the interest paid, $7,000 ($100,000 × 7%) divided by the funds that are available, $80,000 (80% × $100,000). Therefore, the effective interest rate is equal to 8.75% ($7,000 ÷ $80,000). Answer (a) is not reasonable because the amount is less than the stated interest rate. Answer (b) is incorrect because it is the stated rate. Answer (c) is incorrect because it is computed by adding 20% of the stated rate to the stated rate.

70. (b) The requirement is to calculate the weighted-average annual interest rate for trade credit. If the company does not pay Web Master within the discount period, it will incur interest costs of $500 ($25,000 × 2%). This results in an annualized interest rate of 36.7347% [($500 ÷ $24,500) × 360 days ÷ (30 − 10 days)]. If the company does not pay the Softidee account during the discount period, it will incur interest cost of $2,500 ($50,000 × 5%). This results in an annualized interest rate of 23.6842% [($2,500 ÷ $47,500) × 360 days ÷ (90 − 10 days)]. To determine the weighted-average interest rate, we must first determine the average amount borrowed. For Web Master, this is equal to $24,500 × (20 days ÷ 360 days) = $1,361.11, and for Softidee, it is equal to $47,500 × (80 days ÷ 360 days) = $10,555.56. Therefore, the weighted-average interest rate is equal to 25.2% {[(36.7347% × $1,361.11) + (23.6842% × $10,555.56)] ÷ ($1,361.11 + $10,555.56)}. Answer (a) is incorrect because it uses weights of $25,000 and $50,000. Answer (c) is incorrect because it is based on weights of $24,500 and $47,500. Answer (d) is incorrect because it is the unweighted-average of the two rates.

71. (d) The requirement is to identify the statement that determines whether CyberAge should continue to use the trade credit. Answer (d) is correct because the company should continue to use the trade credit as long as the alternative cost of other forms of financing is higher. Answer (a) is incorrect because if alternative sources are less, the alternative should be used. Answer (b) is incorrect because in considering short-term financing alternatives, it is the marginal cost of capital that is important, not the weighted-average cost of capital. Answer (c) is incorrect because if the cost of long-term financing is greater, the trade credit should be used.

72. (b) The requirement is to identify the statement that is most likely true about commercial paper. Answer (b) is correct because commercial paper is normally issued with a short maturity period, usually 2 to 9 months. Answer (a) is incorrect because commercial paper is issued by the corporation. Answer (c) is incorrect because commercial paper is unsecured. Answer (d) is incorrect because commercial paper is typically issued by large corporations.

73. (a) The requirement is to calculate the effective interest on the loan. Answer (a) is correct because the effective interest is 6.44%. The effective interest rate is determined by calculating the net interest expense, which is $15,000 ($250,000 × 6%) minus the interest income from the compensating balance $500 ($25,000 × 2%) equals $14,500. Then, this amount is divided by the amount of money that the firm has available, $250,000 − $25,000 compensating balance. Thus, the effective interest rate is 6.44% ($14,500/$225,000).

74. (a) The requirement is to identify the loan with the most favorable terms. Answer (a) is correct because simple interest with no compensating balance is the most favorable terms from an effective interest basis. Answers (b), (c), and (d) are incorrect because discount interest and/or a compensating balance increase the effective interest rate on the loan.

75. (d) The requirement is to calculate the effective interest rate when a loan is in the form of a discounted note. When a note is on a discounted basis, the interest is withheld from the proceeds. Answer (d) is correct because the effective interest rate is calculated by dividing the total amount of interest by the amount of funds available. In this case, the interest is equal to $9,000 ($100,000 × 9%) and the funds available are $91,000 ($100,000 − $9,000). Thus the interest rate is 9.89% ($9,000/$91,000). Answer (b) is incorrect because it represents the stated rate, not the effective rate.

76. (c) The requirement is to calculate the annual cost of the financing arrangement. Answer (c) is correct because the annual cost of the arrangement is calculated as $7,000 (6% × $100,000) + [($300,000 − $100,000) × 1/2%)]. Answers (a), (b), and (d) are incorrect because they represent inaccurate computations of the cost of the financing.

77. (c) The requirement is to identify the largest source of short-term financing. Answer (c) is correct because trade credit is the largest source of short-term financing for most small firms. It occurs automatically with the purchase of goods and services. Answers (a) and (b) are incorrect because they are not the largest source of short-term financing for most small firms. Answer (d) is incorrect because mortgage bonds are a source of long-term financing.

78. (c) The requirement is to define the prime rate of interest. Answer (c) is correct because the prime rate of interest is the rate financial institutions charge their customers with the highest credit rating. Answer (a) is incorrect because a commitment fee is not related to the rate of interest. Answer (b) is incorrect because the effective rate on the bank loans of most firms is greater than the prime rate. Answer (d) is incorrect because the rate at which a bank borrows from the Federal Reserve central bank is the discount rate.

79. (a) The requirement is to describe the purpose of a compensating balance. Answer (a) is correct because a compensating balance provides a form of additional compensation to financial institutions. Answers (b), (c), and (d) are incorrect because they do not describe the purpose of a compensating balance.

80. (d) The requirement is to calculate the effective annual interest rate of the credit arrangement. Answer (d) is correct because the effective interest rate is equal to the interest cost divided by the available funds. The interest cost is $36,000 ($300,000 × 12%), and the available funds is equal to $255,000 [$300,000 − (15% × $300,000)]. Therefore, the effective interest rate is 14.12% ($36,000/$255,000).

Long-Term Debt

81. (c) The requirement is to identify the correct statement about bond financing alternatives. Answer (c) is correct because a call provision is detrimental to the investor because he or she may be forced to redeem the bond. Answer (a) is incorrect because a bond with a call provision typically has a higher yield than a similar bond without a call provision. Answer (b) is incorrect because a convertible bond is convertible at the option of the holder. Answer (d) is incorrect because the relationship of the stated rate on the bond to the market rate determines whether or not the bond will sell for more than par value.

82. **(b)**   The requirement is to identify the definition of Eurobonds. Answer (b) is correct because Eurobonds are always sold in some country other than the one in whose currency the bond issue is denominated. The advantage of Eurobonds is that they are less regulated than other bonds and the transaction costs are lower. Answer (a) is incorrect because Eurobonds are not always denominated in Eurodollars, which are US dollars deposited outside the US. Answer (c) is incorrect because foreign bonds are denominated in the currency of the country in which they are sold. Answer (d) is incorrect because Eurobonds are usually issued not as registered bonds, but as bearer bonds.

83. **(c)**   The requirement is to identify the proper accounting for an operating lease. Answer (c) is correct because an operating lease is one that does not meet the criteria to be a capital lease. Operating leases are treated as rental agreements and the payments are expensed as rent as incurred. Answer (a) is incorrect because it describes the proper accounting for a capital lease. Answers (b) and (d) are incorrect because they describe accounting that is not proper for either type of lease.

84. **(d)**   The requirement is to identify the difference between a capital and an operating lease. Answer (d) is correct because in a capital lease, the risks and rewards of ownership are transferred to the lessee. If the risks/rewards are not transferred, the lease is a rental arrangement and is called an operating lease. In accounting for a capital lease, the lessee capitalizes the net investment in the lease. Answer (a) is incorrect because the lessee obtains use of the asset in all lease agreements. Answer (b) is incorrect because the lessee uses the lease as a source of financing under a capital lease. Answer (c) is incorrect because the lessee does not receive title to the asset in all cases.

85. **(c)**   The requirement is to identify the advantages/ disadvantages of debt versus equity financing. Answer (c) is correct because the fixed obligation of interest and principal is an advantage to debt financing. Answers (a), (b), and (d) are incorrect because they are all disadvantages of debt financing.

86. **(d)**   The requirement is to identify the advantages/ disadvantages of debt versus equity financing. Answer (d) is correct because debt actually increases stockholders' risk because the financial leverage of the firm is higher. Answers (a), (b), and (c) are incorrect because they are all advantages of debt financing.

87. **(d)**   The requirement is to identify what type of bond has less interest rate risk. Answer (d) is correct because a floating rate bond has a rate of interest that floats with changes in the market interest rate. Therefore, the market price of the bond does not fluctuate as widely. Answer (a) is incorrect because serial bonds are those that are paid off in installments over the life of the issue. Answer (b) is incorrect because sinking fund bonds are those for which the firm makes payments into a sinking fund to be used to retire the bonds by purchase. Answer (c) is incorrect because convertible bonds are those that may be converted into common stock.

88. **(a)**   The requirement is to identify the defining characteristic of serial bonds. Answer (a) is correct because serial bonds are those that are paid off in installments over the life of the issue. Answer (b) is incorrect because sinking fund bonds are those for which the firm makes payments into a sinking fund to be used to retire the bonds by purchase. Answer (c) is incorrect because convertible bonds are those that may be converted into common stock. Answer (d) is incorrect because callable bonds are those that have a call provision that allows the firm to force the bondholders to redeem the bonds before maturity.

89. **(c)**   The requirement is to identify the impact of changes in the market rate of interest on bond valuation. Answer (c) is correct because if the market rate of interest increases, the bond value will decrease (an inverse effect). Answers (a) and (b) are incorrect because the coupon rate does not change after issuance and determines the amount of the periodic interest payments, not changes in the bond valuation. Answer (d) is incorrect because if the market rate decreases, the value of the bond will increase.

90. **(b)**   The requirement is to calculate the first-year, before-tax cost of the planned debt financing, net of floatation costs. The first year cost would be calculated by dividing the interest rate by the amount of funds received after floatation costs. Therefore, the interest cost before tax is equal to 8% ÷ (101% issue price − 2% floatation costs) = 8.08%. Therefore, the correct answer is (b).

91. **(b)**   The requirement is to identify the reason for issuing Eurobonds rather than domestic bonds. Answer (b) is correct because Eurobonds are not subject to extensive regulation like US issued domestic bonds; therefore, they are less expensive to issue. Answer (a) is incorrect because Eurobonds are not denominated in the currency of the country in which they are issued. Answer (c) is incorrect because foreign buyers are not more readily accepting of the issues. Answer (d) is incorrect because Eurobonds do carry foreign exchange risk for the investor; they have losses if the US dollar declines relative to the country's currency.

92. **(c)**   The requirement is to identify the bond provision that is generally considered to be detrimental to the investor. Answer (c) is correct because a callable bond is one that can be redeemed at the option of the issuer. The investor has no choice but to redeem the bond. Answer (a) is incorrect because a conversion feature means the bond can be converted to common stock at the option of the investor. This is a favorable provision for the investor. Answer (b) is incorrect because redeemable bonds are redeemable at the option of the investor. Answer (d) is incorrect because bonds with serial maturity allow the investor to select the desired maturity date.

93. **(c)**   The requirement is to identify the statement that is not an advantage of leasing as a form of financing. Answer (c) is correct because the dollar cost to lease an asset is generally greater than the cost to purchase and finance though other means. Answer (a) is incorrect because leases often do not require down payments. Answer (b) is incorrect because the provisions of lease agreements are usually less stringent than for other forms of debt. Answer (d) is incorrect because firms may be able to lease when they do not have the credit capacity to buy an asset.

94. **(a)**   The requirement is to identify the effect of an increase in bond rating. Answer (a) is correct because going from a B rating to a Baa rating is an increase in the bond rating indicative of lower risk. Therefore, the market value of the bonds should increase. Answers (b), (c), and (d) are incorrect because the bond value should increase.

95. (a) The requirement is to identify the statement that can be assumed from the case scenario. Answer (a) is correct because if the bond sold at face value, then the coupon rate of 8% must have approximated the market rate for this bond. Answer (b) is incorrect because the nominal rate does not include credit risk. Answer (c) is incorrect because the coupon rate, if it was about equal to the market rate, includes a credit risk premium. Answer (d) is incorrect because the risk-free interest rate is always about 1 to 2%.

96. (b) The requirement is to identify the correct statement regarding the effect of a change in the market rate. Answer (b) is correct because an increase in the market rate will cause the bond to reduce in value until it sells at a price that will result in a yield to maturity equal to the current market rate. Answer (a) is incorrect because the market rate would have to decline for the bond to increase in value. Answer (c) is incorrect because LIBOR is only indirectly related to the long-term bond rate. Answer (d) is incorrect because the change in value can be predicted.

97. (d) The requirement is to calculate the current yield on a bond. The current yield is equal to the annual interest paid divided by the bond market price. Watco's $1,000 bond pays $80 per year in interest, the $1,000 face value × the 8% coupon rate. Answer (d) is correct because the current yield is equal to 8.42% ($80 ÷ $950). Answer (a) is incorrect because 8% is the coupon rate.

Equity

98. (d) The requirement is to identify the purpose of the secondary market. Answer (d) is correct because outstanding stocks of publicly owned companies are traded among investors in the secondary market. The original issuer receives no additional capital as a result of such trades. Answers (a) and (b) are incorrect because firms raise capital by issuing new securities in the primary market, and the initial public offering market is a frequently used term for the market in which previously privately owned firms issue new securities to the public. Answer (c) is incorrect because the over-the-counter market is the network of dealers that provides for trading in unlisted securities.

99. (a) The requirement is to identify the purpose of the primary market. Answer (a) is correct because the primary market is the market for new stocks and bonds. Answer (b) is incorrect because existing securities are traded on a secondary market. Answer (c) is incorrect because the futures market is where commodities contracts are sold, not the capital market. Answer (d) is incorrect because exchanges of existing securities do not occur in the primary market.

100. (c) The requirement is to identify the characteristic that is not usually a feature of cumulative preferred stock. Answer (c) is correct because preferred stock usually does not have voting rights. Preferred shareholders are generally given the right to vote for directors of the company only if the company has not paid the preferred dividend for a specified period of time, such as ten quarters. Answer (a) is incorrect because preferred stock does have priority over common stock with regard to earnings, so dividends must be paid on preferred stock before they can be paid on common stock. Answer (b) is incorrect because preferred stock does

have priority over common stock with regard to assets, so in the event of bankruptcy, the claims of preferred shareholders must be satisfied in full before the common shareholders receive anything. Answer (d) is incorrect because cumulative preferred stock does have the right to receive any dividends in arrears before common stock dividends are paid.

101. (b) The requirement is to identify the statement that describes an advantage of going public. Answer (b) is correct because the compliance cost of going public and complying with SEC regulations is substantial. Answer (a) is incorrect because going public does provide access to more capital. Answer (c) is incorrect because public companies can issue stock options to attract and retain management. Answer (d) is incorrect because owners obtain immediate liquidity for their investments when the firm goes public.

Optimal Capital Structure

102. (b) The requirement is to calculate the degree of operating leverage of the company. The formula for degree of operating leverage is

$$DOL = \frac{\text{Percent change in operating income}}{\text{Percent change in unit volume}}$$

In this case, the percent change in operating income is equal to 50% [($300,000 – $200,000) ÷ $200,000], and the percent change in unit volume is equal to 5% [(105,000 – 100,000 units) ÷ 100,000 units]. Therefore, the correct answer is (b) because DOL is equal to 10 (50% ÷ 5%).

103. (a) The requirement is to calculate the degree of financial leverage for the company. The formula for degree of financial leverage is

$$DFL = \frac{\text{Percent change in EPS}}{\text{Percent change in EBIT}}$$

In this case, the percent change in EPS is equal to 500% [($1.20 – $0.20) ÷ $0.20], and the percent change in EBIT is equal to 50% [($300,000 – $200,000) ÷ $200,000]. Therefore, the DFL is equal to 10 (500% ÷ 50%), and answer (a) is correct.

104. (d) The requirement is to identify the advantages/ disadvantages of equity financing. Answer (d) is correct because the lack of a firm obligation to pay dividends to common shareholders is an advantage of equity financing. Answers (a), (b), and (c) are incorrect because they are all disadvantages of equity financing.

105. (a) The requirement is to identify the impact of debt versus equity financing. Answer (a) is correct because Company A is more highly leveraged. It has greater fixed charges in the form of interest. Therefore, Company A will have more volatile net earnings than Company B. Answers (b) and (c) are incorrect because the level of fixed financing charges does not affect operating earnings variability. Operating income is computed before interest expense. Answer (d) is incorrect because Company A has greater, not less, financial leverage than Company B.

106. (d) The requirement is to identify the item that is not a potential long-term source of funding for a firm. Answer (d) is correct because a line of credit is a short-term financing source. Answers (a), (b), and (c) are incorrect because they are possible sources of financing for long-term projects.

107. (d)   The requirement is to identify the factor that does not affect management's judgment about the firm's capital structure.   Answer (d) is correct because the expected return on assets is not a factor that affects management's judgment about the firm's capital structure.   Answer (a) is incorrect because the greater the inherent risk of a business, the lower the optimal debt to equity ratio.   Answer (b) is incorrect because a major advantage of debt is the tax deductibility of interest payments.   Answer (c) is incorrect because a firm's target capital structure will be affected by the risk tolerance of management.   More aggressive management may take on more debt.

108. (b)   The requirement is to identify a characteristic of higher operating leverage.   Higher operating leverage involves more fixed costs, which results in more operating variability and more risk.   Answer (b) is correct because a firm's profits are more sensitive to changes in sales volume when the firm is more leveraged.   Answer (a) is incorrect because higher leveraged firms have less variable costs.   Answer (c) is incorrect because the firm may or may not be more profitable.   Answer (d) is incorrect because a highly leveraged firm is more risky.

109. (d)   The requirement is to identify the consequences of an increase in financial leverage.   Answer (d) is correct because when the degree of financial leverage rises, fixed interest charges rise.   This causes the standard deviation of returns to equity holders to increase.   Answers (a) and (b) are incorrect because an increase in the degree of financial leverage is associated with an increase in equity beta and an increase in the systematic risk of the company.   Equity beta is a measure of systematic risk of the company.   Answer (c) is incorrect because unsystematic risk of the company does not fall.

110. (d)   Answer (d) is correct because a weighted-average of the costs of all financing sources should be used, with the weights determined by the usual financing proportions.   Answer (a) is incorrect because the cost of funds for a particular project does not represent the cost of capital for the firm.   The cost of capital should also be calculated on an after-tax basis.   Answer (b) is incorrect because the cost of capital is a composite, or weighted-average, of all financing sources in their usual proportions.   Answer (c) is incorrect because the cost of capital is a composite, or weighted-average, of all financing sources in their usual proportions.   It includes both the after-tax cost of debt and the cost of equity financing.

111. (b)   The requirement is to identify the statement that is not true regarding the acceptance of Alternative 1.   Answer (b) is correct because Alternative 1 involves much less financial leverage than Alternative 2.   Answer (a) is incorrect because Alternative 1 is the more conservative capital structure because it involves less debt.   Answer (c) is incorrect because net income will be less variable under Alternative 1.   Answer (d) is incorrect because total interest expense will be less under Alternative 1.

112. (b)   The requirement is to compare the weighted-average cost of capital for the two alternatives.   Answer (b) is correct because the cost of debt after tax for is 5.1% [6% × (100% – 15% tax rate)] for Alternative 1 and 5.95% [7% × (100% – 15% tax rate)] for Alternative 2.   The weighted-average cost of capital for Alternative 1 is 7.55% [(5.1% ×

$3,000,000 ÷ $6,000,000) + (10% × $3,000,000 ÷ $6,000,000)], and the weighted-average cost of capital for Alternative 2 is 6.96% [(5.95% × $5,000,000 ÷ $6,000,000) + (12% × $1,000,000 ÷ $6,000,000)].   Therefore, the differential is 0.59% (7.55% – 6.96%).   Answer (a) is incorrect because it results from an unweighted computation.   Answer (c) is incorrect because it is the before-tax computation.

Cost of Capital

113. (a)   The requirement is to identify the factor that affects the calculation of the cost of equity using CAPM.   Answer (a) is correct because a reduction in the risk-free rate would reduce the required return demanded by stockholders.   Answers (b), (c), and (d) are incorrect because an increase in these items would cause the estimated cost of common equity to increase.

114. (b)   The requirement is to identify the reason why it is more expensive to finance with equity than with debt.   Answer (b) is correct because equity holders are subject to more risk than debt holders.   Therefore, they require a higher rate of return.

115. (d)   The requirement is to identify the item that does not describe a characteristic of the capital asset pricing model.   Answer (d) is correct because CAPM does not include the stock's market price in its computation.   Answers (a), (b), and (c) are incorrect because they are all characteristics of CAPM model.

116. (b)   The requirement is to apply the dividend-yield-plus-growth approach to calculate the cost of common equity.   The formula for estimated cost of common equity is equal to the expected dividend divided by the stock price plus the growth rate.   Therefore, the correct answer is (b) because the estimated cost of equity is 14.1% [(2.11/23.13) + 5%].

117. (b)   The requirement is to identify the impact of an increase in nominal interest rates on a company's share price.   Answer (b) is correct because an increase in the nominal interest rate would mean that investors would expect a higher return on all investments.   If the stock earnings and dividend growth is unchanged, the stock price will decrease.

118. (a)   The requirement is to identify the impact of investor expectations on stock price.   Answer (a) is correct because if investors expect a higher dividend growth rate, the market value of the common shares will be greater.   Answer (b) is incorrect because if investors expect a lower dividend growth rate, the market value of common shares will be lower.   Answers (c) and (d) are incorrect because holding periods are not related to the market value of common shares.

119. (a)   The requirement is to identify the technique that explicitly considers risk in calculating the firm's estimated cost of equity.   Answer (a) is correct because CAPM is the only technique that explicitly considers risk in the form of the firm's beta.   Beta measures the relationship between the price volatility of the market as a whole and the price volatility of the individual stock.   Answers (b) and (c) are incorrect because they do not directly incorporate the firm's risk in the calculation of the estimated cost of equity.   Answer (d) is incorrect because it is not utilized to determine the estimated cost of equity.

120. (c) The requirement is to use the dividend-yield-plus-growth-rate approach to calculate the estimated cost of equity. The estimated cost of equity is equal to the dividend divided by the price of the stock + the growth rate. Accordingly, answer (c) is correct because the estimated cost of equity is equal to 14.3% [($5 ÷ $60) + 6%].

121. (b) The requirement is to identify how the bond-yield-plus approach to estimating the cost of equity is applied. Answer (b) is correct because the bond-yield-plus approach involves adding a risk premium of 3% to 5% to the interest rate of the firm's long-term debt. Answers (a), (c), and (d) are incorrect because they involve items that are not components of the formula.

122. (a) The requirement is to identify the characteristic of typical dividend policies. Answer (a) is correct because management is hesitant to decrease dividends. Therefore, they are more stable than earnings. Answer (b) is incorrect because they do not fluctuate more widely than earnings. Answer (c) is incorrect because dividends tend to be higher for mature firms. Answer (d) is incorrect because dividends are usually not changed every year.

123. (c) The requirement is to calculate the current net cost of debt. The current cost of debt before tax is 8.5% (7% Treasury bond rate + 1.5%), and the cost of debt after tax is 5.1% [8.5% × (1 – 40% tax rate)]. Therefore, the correct answer is (c).

124. (d) The requirement is to calculate the cost of capital using CAPM. The CAPM formula is Cost of capital = Risk-free rate + (Market rate – Risk-free rate) × Beta. In this case, the estimated cost of equity is equal to 17% [7% + (15% – 7%) × 1.25]. Thus, the answer is (d).

125. (a) The requirement is to calculate the weighted-average cost of capital. The weighted-average cost of capital is determined by summing the cost of each funding source weighted by its percentage of the total. In this case, the funds received from the debt are equal to 99% (101% – 2%) × $15,000,000, or $14,850,000, and the funds from equity is $35 million, the amount of retained earnings. Therefore, total funding is $49,850,000. The weighted-average cost of capital is equal to ($14,850,000/$49,850,000) × 7% + ($35,000,000/$49,850,000) × 12% = 10.50%. Thus, the answer is (a).

126. (a) The requirement is to use the capital asset pricing model to compute the cost of equity (expected return of equity holders). The CAPM formula is: Cost of equity = Risk-free interest rate + (Market rate – Risk-free interest rate) × Beta. Therefore, the expected return = 9.2% [5% + (12% – 5%) × .60], or answer (a).

127. (b) The requirement is to specify the cost of capital assigned to retained earnings. Answer (b) is correct because newly issued or "external" common equity is more costly than retained earnings because the company incurs issuance costs when raising new funds. Answer (a) is incorrect because the cost of retained earnings is the rate of return stockholders require on retained equity capital. The opportunity cost of retained funds will be positive. Answer (c) is incorrect because retained earnings will always be less costly than external equity financing because earnings retention does not involve the payment of issuance costs. An-

swer (d) is incorrect because the cost is lower as described above.

128. (c) The requirement is to identify the relevant risk of a security according to CAPM. Answer (c) is correct because systematic risk is the component of the total risk of a security that cannot be eliminated through diversification and is relevant to valuation. Answer (a) is incorrect because "company-specific" risk can be eliminated through portfolio diversification and is not relevant to the valuation of the security. Answer (b) is incorrect because "diversifiable" risk can be eliminated through portfolio diversification and is not relevant to the valuation of the security. Answer (d) is incorrect because only the systematic component of total risk is relevant to security valuation.

129. (c) The requirement is to calculate the weighted-average cost of capital (WACC). Answer (c) is correct because the WACC is calculated as 9.36% {2/5 × [9% × (1 – 40%)]} + (3/5 × 12%). Answers (a), (b), and (d) are incorrect because they represent inaccurate computations of the cost of the financing.

130. (b) Answer (b) is correct because the weighted-average cost of capital is calculated as follows:

= (Weight of equity) × (Cost of equity) + (Weight of debt) × (Before-tax cost of debt) × (1 – Tax rate)
= (.7) × (.12) + (.3) × (.08) × (1 – .3) = .084 + .0168 = 10%

Answer (a) is incorrect because 8% is the cost of equity before tax. Answer (c) is incorrect because this solution uses the before-tax cost of debt rather than the after-tax cost of debt. Answer (d) is incorrect because 12% is the cost of equity.

131. (d) The requirement is to identify the true statement about the financing alternatives. Answer (d) is correct because taxes payable will be higher under Arrangement #1 because with lower interest expense, taxable income will be higher. Answer (a) is incorrect because expected gross margin is unaffected by the choice of financing arrangement. Answer (b) is incorrect because the degree of operating leverage is not affected by the method of financing. Answer (c) is incorrect because interest expense will be higher under Arrangement #2. Under Arrangement #1, interest expense will be $300,000 (.08) = $24,000, while under Arrangement #2, interest expense will be $700,000 (.10) = $70,000 per annum.

132. (a) The requirement is to calculate the return on equity and the debt ratio. Answer (a) is correct because return on equity is calculated as net income divided by the amount of equity invested. The debt ratio is the amount of debt financing divided by total assets. Calculations of the two ratios for both financing arrangements are as follows:

	#1	#2
Sales revenue	$500,000	$500,000
Cost of sales	200,000	200,000
General & admin. expense	100,000	100,000
Interest expense	24,000	70,000
Taxable income	$176,000	$130,000
Tax payable (30%)	52,800	39,000
Net income	$123,200	$91,000
Equity invested	700,000	300,000
Return on equity	123,200	91,000
	700,000	300,000
	17.6%	30.3%
Debt ratio	300,000	700,000
	1,000,000	1,000,000
	.3	.7

Mergers

133. (b)   The requirement is to identify the type of transaction described. Answer (b) is correct because a leveraged buyout is one that is financed primarily with debt using very little equity capital. Answer (a) is incorrect because a spinoff is a divestiture in which stock of a subsidiary are issued to existing shareholders of the parent. Answer (c) is incorrect because a joint venture is a project conducted jointly by two or more independent parties. Answer (d) is incorrect because liquidation involves the piecemeal sale of the assets of a firm.

134. (a)   The requirement is to identify the type of merger described. Answer (a) is correct because vertical integration is a merger involving companies in the same industry, but at different levels of the supply chain. Answer (b) is incorrect because a conglomerate merger is one involving firms from different industries. Answer (c) is incorrect because market extension involves moving into new market areas. Answer (d) is incorrect because a horizontal merger involves firms that are competitors in the same market.

135. (d)   The requirement is to identify a horizontal merger. Answer (d) is correct because a horizontal merger is one between competitors in the same market. Answer (a) is incorrect because it describes a conglomerate merger. Answers (b) and (c) are incorrect because they describe vertical mergers.

136. (b)   The requirement is to identify the type of merger. Answer (b) is correct because a vertical merger is a merger between a firm and one of its suppliers or customers. A bottle manufacturer can supply bottles to be used by a soft drink producer. Answer (a) is incorrect because a horizontal merger is a combination of two firms producing the same type of good or service. Answer (c) is incorrect because a congeneric merger is a merger of firms in the same industry, but the two firms do not have a customer or supplier relationship (as in vertical merger). Answer (d) is incorrect because a conglomerate merger is a merger of companies in totally different industries.

137. (d)   The requirement is to identify the type of merger. Answer (d) is correct because a conglomerate merger is a merger of companies in totally different industries. A shoe manufacturer and brokerage house are in totally different industries. Answer (a) is incorrect because a horizontal merger is a combination of two firms producing the same type of good or service. Answer (b) is incorrect because a vertical merger is a merger between a firm and

one of its suppliers or customers. Answer (c) is incorrect because a congeneric merger is a merger of firms in the same industry, but the two firms do not have a customer or supplier relationship (as in vertical merger).

MULTIPLE-CHOICE QUESTIONS (1-85)

1. If an investment is expected to be held for a long period of time the preferred method of calculating the expected return is
   a.   Arithmetic average.
   b.   Median.
   c.   Geometric average.
   d.   Subjective estimate.

2. Which of the following expresses the relationship between risk and return?
   a.   Inverse relationship.
   b.   Direct relationship.
   c.   Negative relationship.
   d.   No relationship.

3. The expected return of a portfolio is measured by the
   a.   Variance.
   b.   Weighted average.
   c.   Standard deviation.
   d.   Beta.

4. Russell Inc. is evaluating four independent investment proposals. The expected returns and standard deviations for each of these proposals are presented below.

Investment proposal	Expected returns	Standard deviation
I	16%	10%
II	14%	10%
III	20%	11%
IV	22%	15%

Which one of the investment proposals has the **least** relative level of risk?
   a.   Investment I.
   b.   Investment II.
   c.   Investment III.
   d.   Investment IV.

Items 5 and 6 are based on the following:

Natco has the following investment portfolio.

	Expected return	Investment	Beta
Investment A	15%	$100,000	1.2
Investment B	10%	$300,000	-0.5
Investment C	8%	$200,000	1.5
Investment D	8%	$100,000	-1.0

5. What is the expected return of the portfolio?
   a.   10.25%
   b.   9.86%
   c.   12.5%
   d.   11.35%

6. If management decided to sell one of the investments, which one should be selected?
   a.   Investment A.
   b.   Investment B.
   c.   Investment C.
   d.   Investment D.

7. A market analyst has estimated the equity beta of Modern Homes Inc. to be 1.4. This beta implies that the company's
   a.   Systematic risk is lower than that of the market portfolio.

   b.   Systematic risk is higher than that of the market portfolio.
   c.   Unsystematic risk is higher than that of the market portfolio.
   d.   Total risk is higher than that of the market portfolio.

*8. A measure that describes the risk of an investment project relative to other investments in general is the
   a.   Coefficient of variation.
   b.   Beta coefficient.
   c.   Standard deviation.
   d.   Expected return.

**9. The expected rate of return for the stock of Cornhusker Enterprises is 20%, with a standard deviation of 15%. The expected rate of return for the stock of Mustang Associates is 10%, with a standard deviation of 9%. The riskier stock is
   a.   Cornhusker because its return is higher.
   b.   Cornhusker because its standard deviation is higher.
   c.   Mustang because its standard deviation is higher.
   d.   Mustang because its coefficient of variation is higher.

**10. A US company currently has domestic operations only. It is considering an equal-size investment in either Canada or Britain. The data on expected rate of return and the risk associated with each of these proposed investments are given below.

Proposed investment	Mean return	Standard deviation
British Investment	22%	10%
Canadian Investment	28%	15%

The mean return on the company's current, domestic only, business is 20% with a standard deviation of 15%. Using the above data and the correlation coefficients, the company calculated the following portfolio risk and return (based on a ratio of 50% US domestic operations and 50% international operations).

Proposed investment	Mean return	Standard deviation
US and Britain	21%	3%
US and Canada	24%	15%

The company plans to select the optimal combination of countries based on risk and return for the domestic and international investments taken together. Because the company is new to the international business environment, it is relatively risk averse. Based on the above data, which one of the following alternatives provides the best risk-adjusted return to the firm?
   a.   Undertake the British investment.
   b.   Undertake the Canadian investment.
   c.   Do not undertake either investment.
   d.   Unable to determine based on data given.

11. According to market segmentation theory long-term interest rates are determined primarily by
   a.   Commercial banks.
   b.   Savings institutions.
   c.   Life insurance companies.
   d.   Individual investors.

12. Questo borrowed $100,000 from a bank on a one-year 8% term loan, with interest compounded quarterly. What is the effective annual interest on the loan?

---

* *CIA adapted*
** *CMA adapted*

a.   8%
b.   8.24%
c.   2%
d.   9.12%

13. The yield curve shown below implies that the

Interest
rate %

Years to maturity

a.   Credit risk premium of corporate bonds has increased.
b.   Credit risk premium of municipal bonds has increased.
c.   Long-term interest rates have a higher annualized yield than short-term rates.
d.   Short-term interest rates have a higher annualized yield than long-term rates.

14. Short-term interest rates are
a.   Usually lower than long-term rates.
b.   Usually higher than long-term rates.
c.   Lower than long-term rates during periods of high inflation only.
d.   Not significantly related to long-term rates.

*15. According to the expectations theory, if the yield curve on the New York money market is upward sloping while that on the Tokyo money market is downward sloping, then inflation in
a.   The United States is expected to decrease.
b.   The United States is expected to remain constant.
c.   Japan is expected to decrease.
d.   Japan is expected to remain constant.

*16. According to the expectations theory of the term structure of interest rates, if inflation is expected to increase, the yield curve is
a.   Humped, with an upward slope that peaks and then turns downward.
b.   Downward sloping.
c.   Upward sloping.
d.   Flat.

*17. A curve on a graph with the rate of return on the vertical axis and time on the horizontal axis depicts
a.   The internal rate of return on an investment.
b.   A yield curve showing the term structure of interest rates.
c.   The present value of future returns, discounted at the marginal cost of capital, minus the present value of the cost.
d.   A series of payments of a fixed amount for a specified number of years.

**18. The return paid for the use of borrowed capital is referred to as

a.   Cash dividends.
b.   Stock dividends.
c.   Interest.
d.   Principal payment.

19. Strobel Company has a large amount of variable rate financing due in one year. Management is concerned about the possibility of increases in short-term rates. Which of the following would be an effective way of hedging this risk?
a.   Buy Treasury notes in the futures market.
b.   Sell Treasury notes in the futures market.
c.   Buy an option to purchase Treasury bonds.
d.   Sell an option to purchase Treasury bonds.

20. In valuing interest rate swaps, the zero-coupon method uses all of the following variables except
a.   Discount rate.
b.   Timing of cash flows as specified by the contract.
c.   Estimated net settlement cash flows.
d.   Underlying assets.

21. Which of the following techniques is used to value stock options?
a.   Black-Scholes method.
b.   Zero-coupon method.
c.   Weighted-average method.
d.   Expected earnings method.

22. Which of the following risks relates to the possibility that a derivative might not be effective at hedging a particular asset?
a.   Credit risk.
b.   Legal risk.
c.   Market risk.
d.   Basis risk.

**23. An American importer of English clothing has contracted to pay an amount fixed in British pounds three months from now. If the importer worries that the US dollar may depreciate sharply against the British pound in the interim, it would be well advised to
a.   Buy pounds in the forward exchange market.
b.   Sell pounds in the forward exchange market.
c.   Buy dollars in the futures market.
d.   Sell dollars in the futures market.

**24. When a firm finances each asset with a financial instrument of the same approximate maturity as the life of the asset, it is applying
a.   Working capital management.
b.   Return maximization.
c.   Financial leverage.
d.   A hedging approach.

25. Banner Electronics has subsidiaries in several international locations and is concerned about its exposure to foreign exchange risk. In countries where currency values are likely to fall, Banner should encourage all of the following **except
a.   Granting trade credit wherever possible.
b.   Investing excess cash in inventory or other real assets.
c.   Purchasing materials and supplies on a trade credit basis.
d.   Borrowing local currency funds if an appropriate interest rate can be obtained.

_____

*   CIA adapted
** CMA adapted

*26. A company has recently purchased some stock of a competitor as part of a long-term plan to acquire the competitor. However, it is somewhat concerned that the market price of this stock could decrease over the short run. The company could hedge against the possible decline in the stock's market price by

a. Purchasing a call option on that stock.
b. Purchasing a put option on that stock.
c. Selling a put option on that stock.
d. Obtaining a warrant option on that stock.

*27. The risk of loss because of fluctuations in the relative value of foreign currencies is called

a. Expropriation risk.
b. Sovereign risk.
c. Multinational beta.
d. Exchange rate risk.

**28. If a $1,000 bond sells for $1,125, which of the following statements are correct?

I. The market rate of interest is greater than the coupon rate on the bond.
II. The coupon rate on the bond is greater than the market rate of interest.
III. The coupon rate and the market rate are equal.
IV. The bond sells at a premium.
V. The bond sells at a discount.

a. I and IV.
b. I and V.
c. II and IV.
d. II and V.

29. Para Co. is reviewing the following data relating to an energy saving investment proposal:

Cost	$50,000
Residual value at the end of 5 years	10,000
Present value of an annuity of 1 at 12% for 5 years	3.60
Present value of 1 due in 5 years at 12%	0.57

What would be the annual savings needed to make the investment realize a 12% yield?

a. $ 8,189
b. $11,111
c. $12,306
d. $13,889

30. On December 31, 2009, Jet Co. received a $10,000 note receivable from Maxx, Inc. in exchange for services rendered. Interest is calculated on the outstanding balance at the interest rate of 3% compounded annually and payable at maturity. The note from Maxx, Inc. is due in five years. The market interest rate for similar notes on December 31, 2009, was 8%. The compound interest factors are as follows:

Future value of $1 due in nine months at 3%	1.0225
Future value of $1 due in five years at 3%	1.1593
Present value of $1 due in nine months at 8%	.944
Present value of $1 due in five years at 8%	.680

At what amounts should this note receivable be reported in Jet's December 31, 2009 balance sheet?

a. $6,800
b. $7,820
c. $6,200
d. $7,883

---

* *CIA adapted*
** *CMA adapted*

31. The market price of a bond issued at a discount is the present value of its principal amount at the market (effective) rate of interest

a. Less the present value of all future interest payments at the market (effective) rate of interest.
b. Less the present value of all future interest payments at the rate of interest stated on the bond.
c. Plus the present value of all future interest payments at the market (effective) rate of interest.
d. Plus the present value of all future interest payments at the rate of interest stated on the bond.

32. At what stage of the capital budgeting process would management most likely apply present value techniques?

a. Identification stage.
b. Search stage.
c. Selection stage.
d. Financing stage.

33. How is the discounted payback method an improvement over the payback method in evaluating investment projects?

a. It involves better estimates of cash flows.
b. It considers the overall profitability of the investment.
c. It considers the time value of money.
d. It considers the variability of the return.

34. The capital budgeting technique known as payback period uses

	Depreciation expense	Time value of money
a.	Yes	Yes
b.	Yes	No
c.	No	No
d.	No	Yes

35. Which of the following is a strength of the payback method?

a. It considers cash flows for all years of the project.
b. It distinguishes the source of cash inflows.
c. It considers the time value of money.
d. It is easy to understand.

36. Tam Co. is negotiating for the purchase of equipment that would cost $100,000, with the expectation that $20,000 per year could be saved in after-tax cash costs if the equipment were acquired. The equipment's estimated useful life is ten years, with no residual value, and would be depreciated by the straight-line method. The payback period is

a. 4.0 years.
b. 4.4 years.
c. 4.5 years.
d. 5.0 years.

37. All of the following capital budgeting analysis techniques use cash flows as the primary basis for the calculation **except for the

a. Net present value.
b. Payback period.
c. Discounted payback period.
d. Accounting rate of return.

38. Which of the following is an advantage of the accounting rate of return method of evaluating investment returns?

a. The technique considers depreciation.
b. The technique corresponds to the measure that is often used to evaluate performance.

c.   The technique considers the time value of money.
d.   The technique considers the risk of the investment.

39. Tam Co. is negotiating for the purchase of equipment that would cost $100,000, with the expectation that $20,000 per year could be saved in after-tax cash costs if the equipment were acquired. The equipment's estimated useful life is ten years, with no residual value, and it would be depreciated by the straight-line method. Tam's predetermined minimum desired rate of return is 12%. The present value of an annuity of 1 at 12% for ten periods is 5.65. The present value of 1 due in ten periods at 12% is .322. Accrual accounting rate of return based on the initial investment is
    a.   30%
    b.   20%
    c.   12%
    d.   10%

40. Lin Co. is buying machinery it expects will increase average annual operating income by $40,000. The initial increase in the required investment is $60,000, and the average increase in required investment is $30,000. To compute the accrual accounting rate of return, what amount should be used as the numerator in the ratio?
    a. $20,000
    b. $30,000
    c. $40,000
    d. $60,000

41. The capital budgeting technique known as accounting rate of return uses

	Revenue over life of project	Depreciation expense
a.	No	Yes
b.	No	No
c.	Yes	No
d.	Yes	Yes

**42. If an investment project has a profitability index of 1.15, then the
    a.   Project's internal rate of return is 15%.
    b.   Project's cost of capital is greater than its internal rate of return.
    c.   Project's internal rate of return exceeds its net present value.
    d.   Net present value of the project is positive.

**43. The net present value (NPV) method of investment project analysis assumes that the project's cash flows are reinvested at the
    a.   Computed internal rate of return.
    b.   Risk-free interest rate.
    c.   Discount rate used in the NPV calculation.
    d.   Firm's accounting rate of return.

44. Kern Co. is planning to invest in a two-year project that is expected to yield cash flows from operations, net of income taxes, of $50,000 in the first year and $80,000 in the second year. Kern requires an internal rate of return of 15%. The present value of $1 for one period at 15% is 0.870 and for two periods at 15% is 0.756. The future value of $1 for one period at 15% is 1.150 and for two periods at 15% is 1.323. The maximum that Kern should invest immediately is

---

a. $ 81,670
b. $103,980
c. $130,000
d. $163,340

45. Pole Co. is investing in a machine with a three-year life. The machine is expected to reduce annual cash operating costs by $30,000 in each of the first two years and by $20,000 in year three. Present values of an annuity of $1 at 14% are

Period 1	0.88
2	1.65
3	2.32

Using a 14% cost of capital, what is the present value of these future savings?
    a. $59,600
    b. $60,800
    c. $62,900
    d. $69,500

46. For the next two years, a lease is estimated to have an operating net cash inflow of $7,500 per annum, before adjusting for $5,000 per annum tax basis lease amortization, and a 40% tax rate. The present value of an ordinary annuity of $1 per year at 10% for two years is 1.74. What is the lease's after-tax present value using a 10% discount factor?
    a. $ 2,610
    b. $ 4,350
    c. $ 9,570
    d. $11,310

47. A project's net present value, ignoring income tax considerations, is normally affected by the
    a.   Proceeds from the sale of the asset to be replaced.
    b.   Carrying amount of the asset to be replaced by the project.
    c.   Amount of annual depreciation on the asset to be replaced.
    d.   Amount of annual depreciation on fixed assets used directly on the project.

48. The discount rate (hurdle rate of return) must be determined in advance for the
    a.   Payback period method.
    b.   Time-adjusted rate of return method.
    c.   Net present value method.
    d.   Internal rate of return method.

**49. The internal rate of return is the
    a.   Rate of interest that equates the present value of cash outflows and the present value of cash inflows.
    b.   Minimum acceptable rate of return for a proposed investment.
    c.   Risk-adjusted rate of return.
    d.   Required rate of return.

**50. As used in capital budgeting analysis, the internal rate of return uses which of the following items in its computation?

	Net incremental investment	Incremental average operating income	Net annual cash flows
a.	Yes	No	Yes
b.	Yes	Yes	No
c.	No	No	Yes
d.	No	Yes	Yes

** *CMA adapted*

51. An organization is using capital budgeting techniques to compare two independent projects. It could accept one, both, or neither of the projects. Which of the following statements is true about the use of net present value (NPV) and internal rate of return (IRR) methods for evaluating these two projects?

   a. NPV and IRR criteria will always lead to the same accept or reject decision for two independent projects.

   b. If the first project's IRR is higher than the organization's cost or capital, the first project will be accepted but the second project will not.

   c. If the NPV criterion leads to accepting or rejecting the first project, one cannot predict whether the IRR criterion will lead to accepting or rejecting the first project.

   d. If the NPV criterion leads to accepting the first project, the IRR criterion will never lead to accepting the first project.

Items 52 and 53 are based on the following information:

A firm, with an 18% cost of capital, is considering the following projects (on January 1, 2009):

	Jan. 1, 2009, Cash outflow (000's omitted)	Dec. 31, 2013, Cash inflow (000's omitted)	Project internal rate of return
Project A	$3,500	$7,400	15%
Project B	4,000	9,950	?

Present Value of $1 Due at End of "N" Periods

N	12%	14%	15%	16%	18%	20%	22%
4	.6355	.5921	.5718	.5523	.5158	.4823	.4230
5	.5674	.5194	.4972	.4761	.4371	.4019	.3411
6	.5066	.4556	.4323	.4104	.3704	.3349	.2751

52. Using the net present value method, Project A's net present value is

   a. $316,920
   b. $0
   c. $(265,460)
   d. $(316,920)

53. Project B's internal rate of return is closest to

   a. 15%
   b. 18%
   c. 20%
   d. 22%

Items 54 thru 57 are based on the following information:

An organization has four investment proposals with the following costs and expected cash inflows:

Expected Cash Inflows

Project	Cost	End of year 1	End of year 2	End of year 3
A	Unknown	$10,000	$10,000	$10,000
B	$20,000	5,000	10,000	15,000
C	25,000	15,000	10,000	5,000
D	30,000	20,000	Unknown	20,000

Additional information

Discount rate	Number of periods	Present value of $1 due at the end of n periods [PVIF]	Present value of an annuity of $1 per period for n periods [PVIFA]
5%	1	0.9524	0.9524
5%	2	0.9070	1.8594
5%	3	0.8638	2.7232
10%	1	0.9091	0.9091
10%	2	0.8264	1.7355
10%	3	0.7513	2.4869
15%	1	0.8696	0.8696
15%	2	0.7561	1.6257
15%	3	0.6575	2.2832

54. If Project A has an internal rate of return (IRR) of 15%, then it has a cost of

   a. $ 8,696
   b. $22,832
   c. $24,869
   d. $27,232

55. If the discount rate is 10%, the net present value (NPV) of Project B is

   a. $ 4,079
   b. $ 6,789
   c. $ 9,869
   d. $39,204

56. The payback period of Project C is

   a. 0 years.
   b. 1 year.
   c. 2 years.
   d. 3 years.

57. If the discount rate is 5% and the discounted payback period of Project D is exactly two years, then the year two cash inflow for Project D is

   a. $ 5,890
   b. $10,000
   c. $12,075
   d. $14,301

58. Tam Co. is negotiating for the purchase of equipment that would cost $100,000, with the expectation that $20,000 per year could be saved in after-tax cash costs if the equipment were acquired. The equipment's estimated useful life is ten years, with no residual value, and would be depreciated by the straight-line method. Tam's predetermined minimum desired rate of return is 12%. Present value of an annuity of 1 at 12% for ten periods is 5.65. Present value of 1 due in ten periods at 12% is .322. In estimating the internal rate of return, the factors in the table of present values of an annuity should be taken from the columns closest to

   a. 0.65
   b. 1.30
   c. 5.00
   d. 5.65

59. How are the following used in the calculation of the internal rate of return of a proposed project? Ignore income tax considerations.

	Residual sales value of project	Depreciation expense
a.	Exclude	Include
b.	Include	Include
c.	Exclude	Exclude
d.	Include	Exclude

60. Neu Co. is considering the purchase of an investment that has a positive net present value based on Neu's 12% hurdle rate. The internal rate of return would be
a. 0
b. 12%
c. > 12%
d. < 12%

61. Bennet Inc. uses the net present value method to evaluate capital projects. Bennet's required rate of return is 10%. Bennet is considering two mutually exclusive projects for its manufacturing business. Both projects require an initial outlay of $120,000 and are expected to have a useful life of four years. The projected after-tax cash flows associated with these projects are as follows:

Year	Project X	Project Y
1	$40,000	$10,000
2	40,000	20,000
3	40,000	60,000
4	40,000	80,000
Total	$160,000	$170,000

Assuming adequate funds are available, which of the following project options would you recommend that Bennet's management undertake?

a. Project X only.
b. Project Y only.
c. Projects X and Y.
d. Neither project.

Items 62 thru 64 are based on the following information:

Capital Invest Inc. uses a 12% hurdle rate for all capital expenditures and has done the following analysis for four projects for the upcoming year.

	Project 1	Project 2	Project 3	Project 4
Initial capital outlay	$200,000	$298,000	$248,000	$272,000
Annual net cash inflows				
Year 1	$ 65,000	$100,000	$80,000	$ 95,000
Year 2	70,000	135,000	95,000	125,000
Year 3	80,000	90,000	90,000	90,000
Year 4	40,000	65,000	80,000	60,000
Net present value	(3,798)	4,276	14,064	14,662
Profitability index	98%	101%	106%	105%
Internal rate of return	11%	13%	14%	15%

**62. Which project(s) should Capital Invest Inc. undertake during the upcoming year assuming it has no budget restrictions?
a. All of the projects.
b. Projects 1, 2, and 3.
c. Projects 2, 3, and 4.
d. Projects 1, 3, and 4.

**63. Which project(s) should Capital Invest Inc. undertake during the upcoming year if it has only $600,000 of funds available?
a. Projects 1 and 3.
b. Projects 2, 3, and 4.
c. Projects 2 and 3.
d. Projects 3 and 4.

**64. Which project(s) should Capital Invest Inc. undertake during the upcoming year if it has only $300,000 of capital funds available?
a. Project 1.

b. Projects 2, 3, and 4.
c. Projects 3 and 4.
d. Project 3.

**65. A depreciation tax shield is
a. An after-tax cash outflow.
b. A reduction in income taxes.
c. The cash provided by recording depreciation.
d. The expense caused by depreciation.

**66. Andrew Corporation is evaluating a capital investment that would result in a $30,000 higher contribution margin benefit and increased annual personnel costs of $20,000. The effects of income taxes on the net present value computation on these benefits and costs for the project are to
a. Decrease both benefits and costs.
b. Have no net effect on either benefits or costs.
c. Decrease benefits but increase costs.
d. Increase benefits but decrease costs.

67. Buff Co. is considering replacing an old machine with a new machine. Which of the following items is economically relevant to Buff's decision? (Ignore income tax considerations.)

	Carrying amount of old machine	Disposal value of new machine
a.	Yes	No
b.	No	Yes
c.	No	No
d.	Yes	Yes

Items 68 and 69 are based on the following information:

Assume that Straper Industries is considering investing in a project with the following characteristics:

Initial investment	$500,000
Additional investment in working capital	10,000
Cash flows before income taxes for years 1 through 5	140,000
Yearly tax depreciation	90,000
Terminal value of investment	50,000
Cost of capital	10%
Present value of $1 received after 5 years discounted at 10%	.621
Present value of an ordinary annuity of $1 for 5 years at 10%	3.791
Marginal tax rate	30%
Investment life	5 years

Assume that all cash flows come at the end of the year.

68. What is the amount of the after-tax cash flows in year 2?
a. $140,000
b. $125,000
c. $ 98,000
d. $ 70,000

69. What is the net present value of the investment?
a. $175,000
b. $ 58,000
c. $ 1,135
d. $ (12,340)

**70. The Madison Company has decided to introduce a new product. The company estimates that there is a 30% probability that the product will contribute $700,000 to profits, a 30% probability that it will contribute $200,000, and a 40% probability that the contribution will be a nega-

---

* *CIA adapted*
** *CMA adapted*

tive $400,000. The expected contribution of the new product is

- a. $500,000
- b. $110,000
- c. $166,667
- d. $380,000

**71. Philip Enterprises, distributor of compact disks (CDs) is developing its budgeted cost of goods sold for 2010. Philip has developed the following range of sales estimates and associated probabilities for the year.

Sales Estimate	Probability
$ 60,000	25%
85,000	40%
100,000	35%

Philip's cost of goods sold averages 80% of sales. What is the expected value of Philip's 2010 budgeted cost of goods sold?

- a. $85,000
- b. $84,000
- c. $68,000
- d. $67,200

72. Which of the following capital budgeting techniques would allow management to justify investing in a project that could not be justified currently by using techniques that focus on expected cash flows?

- a. Real options.
- b. Net present value.
- c. Accounting rate of return.
- d. Internal rate of return.

Items 73 and 74 are based on the following information:

Assume that Reston Corp. is considering investing in a project. To evaluate the project, management has developed the following cash flow projections and related probabilities.

Present value of future cash flows	Probability of occurrence
$200,000	.4
$500,000	.3
$800,000	.3

73. What is the expected return for the project?

- a. $750,000
- b. $500,000
- c. $470,000
- d. $400,000

74. Assume that the standard deviation of the returns for the project is $150,000. What is the coefficient of variation for the project?

- a. .2345
- b. .3191
- c. .4256
- d. 1.10

75. Which of the following techniques recognizes that management often faces a series of decisions that may affect the value of an investment?

- a. Probability analysis.
- b. Risk-adjusted discount rate.
- c. Decision tree.
- d. Sensitivity analysis.

76. Which of the following is not a technique for considering the risk of an investment?

- a. Probability analysis.
- b. Risk-adjusted discount rate.
- c. Simulation techniques.
- d. Internal rate of return.

*77. The level of risk that concerns investors who supply capital to a diversified company is

- a. Project risk (beta).
- b. Pure play risk (beta).
- c. The standard deviation of project risk (betas).
- d. The weighted-average of project risk (betas).

*78. A company uses portfolio theory to develop its investment portfolio. If the company wishes to obtain optimal risk reduction through the portfolio effect, it should make its next investment in

- a. An investment that correlates negatively to the current portfolio holdings.
- b. An investment that is uncorrelated to the current portfolio holdings.
- c. An investment that is highly correlated to the current portfolio holdings.
- d. An investment that is perfectly correlated to the current portfolio holdings.

79. During 2008, Deet Corp. experienced the following power outages:

Number of outages per month	Number of months
0	3
1	2
2	4
3	3
	12

Each power outage results in out-of-pocket costs of $400. For $500 per month, Deet can lease an auxiliary generator to provide power during outages. If Deet leases an auxiliary generator in 2009 the estimated savings (or additional expenditures) for 2009 would be

- a. $(3,600)
- b. $(1,200)
- c. $ 1,600
- d. $ 1,900

80. Polo Co. requires higher rates of return for projects with a life span greater than five years. Projects extending beyond five years must earn a higher specified rate of return. Which of the following capital budgeting techniques can readily accommodate this requirement?

	Internal rate of return	Net present value
a.	Yes	No
b.	No	Yes
c.	No	No
d.	Yes	Yes

81. Under frost-free conditions, Cal Cultivators expects its strawberry crop to have a $60,000 market value. An unprotected crop subject to frost has an expected market value of $40,000. If Cal protects the strawberries against frost, then the market value of the crop is still expected to be $60,000 under frost-free conditions and $90,000 if there is a frost. What must be the probability of a frost for Cal to be indifferent to spending $10,000 for frost protection?

---

* CIA adapted
** CMA adapted

a. .167
b. .200
c. .250
d. .333

82. Dough Distributors has decided to increase its daily muffin purchases by 100 boxes. A box of muffins costs $2 and sells for $3 through regular stores. Any boxes not sold through regular stores are sold through Dough's thrift store for $1. Dough assigns the following probabilities to selling additional boxes:

Additional sales	Probability
60	.6
100	.4

What is the expected value of Dough's decision to buy 100 additional boxes of muffins?
a. $28
b. $40
c. $52
d. $68

83. Which tool would most likely be used to determine the best course of action under conditions of uncertainty?
a. Cost-volume-profit analysis.
b. Expected value (EV).
c. Program evaluation and review technique (PERT).
d. Scattergraph method.

84. To assist in an investment decision, Gift Co. selected the most likely sales volume from several possible outcomes. Which of the following attributes would that selected sales volume reflect?
a. The midpoint of the range.
b. The median.
c. The greatest probability.
d. The expected value.

85. Probability (risk) analysis is
a. Used only for situations involving five or fewer possible outcomes.
b. Used only for situations in which the summation of probability weights is greater than one.
c. An extension of sensitivity analysis.
d. Incompatible with sensitivity analysis.

MULTIPLE-CHOICE ANSWERS

1. c __ __	19. b __ __	37. d __ __	55. a __ __	73. c __ __
2. b __ __	20. d __ __	38. b __ __	56. c __ __	74. b __ __
3. b __ __	21. a __ __	39. d __ __	57. c __ __	75. c __ __
4. c __ __	22. d __ __	40. c __ __	58. c __ __	76. d __ __
5. b __ __	23. a __ __	41. d __ __	59. d __ __	77. d __ __
6. c __ __	24. c __ __	42. d __ __	60. c __ __	78. a __ __
7. b __ __	25. a __ __	43. c __ __	61. a __ __	79. c __ __
8. b __ __	26. b __ __	44. b __ __	62. c __ __	80. d __ __
9. d __ __	27. d __ __	45. c __ __	63. d __ __	81. b __ __
10. a __ __	28. c __ __	46. d __ __	64. d __ __	82. c __ __
11. c __ __	29. c __ __	47. a __ __	65. b __ __	83. b __ __
12. b __ __	30. d __ __	48. c __ __	66. a __ __	84. c __ __
13. c __ __	31. c __ __	49. a __ __	67. b __ __	85. c __ __
14. a __ __	32. c __ __	50. a __ __	68. b __ __	
15. c __ __	33. c __ __	51. a __ __	69. c __ __	
16. c __ __	34. c __ __	52. c __ __	70. b __ __	
17. b __ __	35. d __ __	53. c __ __	71. d __ __	1st: __/85 = __%
18. c __ __	36. d __ __	54. b __ __	72. a __ __	2nd: __/85 = __%

MULTIPLE-CHOICE ANSWER EXPLANATIONS

Risk and Return

1. **(c)** The requirement is to identify the preferred method of calculating the expected return for an investment that is expected to be held for a long period of time. Answer (c) is correct because the geometric average depicts the compound annual return earned by the investor. This method is preferred for evaluating long-term investments. Answer (a) is incorrect because the arithmetic average does not provide as good a measure as the geometric average especially when the returns vary through time. Answer (b) is incorrect because the median is a poor measure of return. Answer (d) is incorrect because a subjective estimate is not as good as a mathematical average.

2. **(b)** The requirement is to identify the relationship between risk and return. Answer (b) is correct because there is a direct (positive) relationship between risk and return. Higher returns are associated with higher degrees of risk. Answers (a) and (c) are incorrect because an inverse (negative) relationship would imply that higher returns are associated with less risk. Answer (d) is incorrect because there is a direct relationship between risk and returns.

Portfolio Returns and Risk

3. **(b)** The requirement is to identify the measure of the expected return of a portfolio. Answer (b) is correct because the weighted-average of the expected returns of the assets in the portfolio is equal to the expected return of the portfolio. Answers (a), (c), and (d) are incorrect because they are all measures of variability.

4. **(c)** The requirement is to identify the proposal that has the least amount of relative risk. Relative risk is measured as the ratio of the standard deviation of the return to the expected return. Therefore, answer (c) is correct because this investment's relative risk is .550 (11%/20%). Answers (a), (b), and (d) are incorrect because they have higher measures of relative risk.

5. **(b)** The requirement is to calculate the expected return of the portfolio. Answer (b) is correct because the expected return of the portfolio is the weighted-average of the individual investments. The expected return is equal to 9.68% = [15% × ($100,000 ÷ 700,000)] + [10% × ($300,000 ÷ 700,000)] + (8% × $200,000 ÷ 700,000)] + [8% × ($100,000 ÷ 700,000)]. Answer (a) is incorrect because this is the unweighted return for the portfolio.

6. **(c)** The requirement is to select the investment that should be sold. Answer (c) is correct because Investment C has a low return and the highest positive beta. The positive beta indicates that its return is highly correlated with the return of the portfolio and, therefore, it increases the risk of the portfolio. Answer (a) is incorrect because Investment A has the highest return and its beta is not as high as Investment C. Answer (b) is incorrect because it has a higher return than Investment C and its beta is negative. Therefore, Investment B reduces the overall risk of the portfolio. Answer (d) is incorrect because Investment D has a large negative beta and therefore, it reduces the overall risk of the portfolio.

7. **(b)** The requirement is to interpret an equity beta of 1.4. Beta is a measure of systematic risk of the investment. Answer (b) is correct because a beta of greater than 1 means the investment's systematic risk is higher than that of the market portfolio. Answer (a) is incorrect because the beta would have to be less than 1 for this relationship to exist. Answers (c) and (d) are incorrect because beta focuses on systematic risk.

8. **(b)** The requirement is to identify the measure of the risk of an investment relative to other investments in general. Answer (b) is correct because the beta coefficient of an individual stock is the correlation between the stock's price and the price of the overall market. As an example, if the market goes up 5% and the individual stock's price, on average, goes up 10%, the stock's beta coefficient is 2.0. Answer (a) is incorrect because the coefficient of variation compares the risk of the stock to its expected return. Answer (c) is incorrect because the standard deviation measures the dispersion of the individual stock's returns. Answer (d) is incorrect because the expected return does not measure risk.

9. **(d)** The requirement is to identify the riskier stock. Answer (d) is correct because the coefficient of variation of Mustang is higher. The coefficient of variation provides a measure of the relative variability of investments. It is calculated by dividing the standard deviation of the investment by its expected return. The coefficient of variation for Cornhusker is .75 (.15 ÷ .20) and the coefficient of variation for Mustang is .9 (0.09 ÷ .10). Answer (a) is incorrect because a higher return does not always mean higher risk. Answer (b) is incorrect because the higher standard deviation must be viewed relative to the expected return. Answer (c) is incorrect because Mustang's coefficient of variation is higher than Cornhusker's coefficient of variation.

10. (a) The requirement is to identify the alternative that provides the best risk-adjusted rate of return. The correct answer is (a) because expanding the investment into Britain would increase the portfolio return from 20% to 21%, and, at the same time, reduce risk as measured by the standard deviation. Answer (b) is incorrect because undertaking the Canadian investment would increase the return from 20% to 24% without any reduction in the risk. Answer (c) is incorrect because the investment into Britain increases portfolio return while reducing risk. Answer (d) is incorrect because the answer can be determined.

Interest Rates

11. (c) The requirement is to identify the determinate of long-term interest rates under market segmentation theory. Market segmentation theory states that the Treasury securities market is divided into market segments by the various financial institutions investing in the market. Answer (c) is correct because life insurance companies prefer long-term securities because of the nature of their commitments to policyholders. Answer (a) is incorrect because commercial banks prefer securities with short maturities. Answer (b) is incorrect because savings institutions prefer intermediate-term maturities. Answer (d) is incorrect because individual investors do not significantly affect the market.

12. (b) The requirement is to calculate the effective annual interest rate. Answer (b) is correct because the effective interest rate (EAR) is calculated as follows:

$$EAR = \left(1 + \frac{r}{m}\right)^m - 1$$
$$= \left(1 + \frac{.08}{4}\right)^4 - 1$$
$$= 8.24\%$$

Where

    r = Stated interest rate
    m = Compounding frequency

Answer (a) is incorrect because it is the stated interest rate. Answer (c) is incorrect because it is the interest rate for three months.

13. (c) The requirement is to interpret the yield curve. Answer (c) is correct because the term structure of interest rates is the relationship between yield to maturity and time to maturity. This relationship is depicted by a yield curve. The normal expectation is for long-term investments to pay higher rates because of their higher interest rate risk. Answers (a) and (b) are incorrect because the yield curve does not reflect the credit risk premium of bonds. Answer (d) is incorrect because long-term interest rates are normally higher than short-term rates.

14. (a) The requirement is to identify the true statement about short-term interest rates. Answer (a) is correct because there is less risk involved in the short run and investors are willing to accept lower rates on short-term investments because of their liquidity. Short-term rates have ordinarily been lower than long-term rates. Answer (b) is incorrect because short-term rates are typically lower than long-term rates. Answer (c) is incorrect because short-term rates are more likely to be greater than long-term rates if current levels of inflation are high. Answer (d) is incorrect because long-term rates may be viewed as short-term rates adjusted by a risk factor.

15. (c) The requirement is to predict the effect of inflation on the yield curve. The correct answer is (c) because a downward sloping yield curve indicates that long-term rates are lower than short-term rates. For this to be the case investors would have to be expecting a decline in the rate of inflation. Answers (a) and (b) are incorrect because an upward sloping yield curve would mean that investors are expecting an increase in inflation. Answer (d) is incorrect because a downward sloping yield curve would imply that investors are expecting inflation to decline.

16. (c) The requirement is to describe the effect on the yield curve of an expectation of an increase in inflation. Answer (c) is correct because if inflation is expected to increase, interest rates are expected to rise and therefore, intermediate-term and long-term rates will be higher than short-term rates. Answer (a) is incorrect because a humped yield curve is not consistent with expectations theory. Answer (b) is incorrect because a downward sloping curve would imply an expectation that inflation will decrease. Answer (d) is incorrect because a flat yield curve would imply inflation is expected to remain constant.

17. (b) The requirement is to identify a graph that depicts the rate of return on the vertical axis and time on the horizontal axis. Answer (b) is correct because such a graph presents a yield curve that shows the term structure of interest rates. The term structure of interest rates refers to how interest rates vary by time to maturity. Answer (a) is incorrect because internal rate of return is the interest rate that equates the present value of the future cash flows from an investment with its initial cost. Answer (c) is incorrect because it is the definition of net present value. Answer (d) is incorrect because it defines an annuity.

18. (c) The requirement is to identify the return paid for the use of borrowed capital. Answer (c) is correct because the return paid for the use of borrowed funds is called interest. Answers (a) and (b) are incorrect because dividends are paid to equity holders. Answer (d) is incorrect because the principal payment represents the return of capital.

Derivatives and Hedging

19. (b) The requirement is to identify the appropriate hedging strategy. Answer (b) is correct because by selling Treasury notes for delivery in the future, the company can hedge increases in short-term interest rates. If interest rates increase, the value of the Treasury notes will decline, resulting in a gain to the company. If the hedge is effective, the gain will offset the increase in the company's interest costs. Answer (a) is incorrect because buying Treasury notes would put the company at greater risk with respect to increases in interest rates. Answer (c) is incorrect because buying an option on Treasury bonds would hedge a decline in interest rates. Answer (d) is incorrect because an option allows the purchaser the option, but not the obligation, to purchase Treasury bonds. Therefore, selling options would not be effective at hedging increases in interest rates.

20.   (d)   The requirement is to identify the variable that is not used in valuing an interest rate swap. Answer (d) is correct because the underlying assets are not relevant. An interest rate swap involves an exchange of cash flows, usually the exchange of fixed cash flows for variable cash flows. Answer (a), (b), and (c) are all incorrect because they are all variables that are used in the zero-coupon method.

21.   (a)   The requirement is to identify the technique used to value stock options. Answer (a) is correct because the Black-Scholes option-pricing model is a commonly used option-pricing model. Answer (b) is incorrect because the zero-coupon method is used to value interest rate swaps. Answer (c) is incorrect because the weighted-average method is used to determine the expected return of a portfolio.

22.   (d)   The requirement is to identify the risk that relates to the possibility that a derivative might not be effective at hedging a particular asset. Answer (d) is correct because basis risk is the risk of loss from ineffective hedging activities. Answer (a) is incorrect because credit risk is the risk of loss as a result of the counterparty to the derivative agreement failing to meet its obligation. Answer (b) is incorrect because market risk is the risk of loss from adverse changes in market factors. Answer (c) is incorrect because legal risk is the risk of loss from a legal or regulatory action that invalidates the derivative agreement.

23.   (a)   The requirement is to identify how a company may hedge exchange risk. Answer (a) is the correct answer because by buying pounds today with a forward exchange contract, the firm protects itself against depreciation in the value of the dollar in relation to the pound. Answer (b) is incorrect because selling pounds would put the firm in greater risk with respect to appreciation of the pound. Answers (c) and (d) are incorrect because buying and selling dollars would do nothing to hedge the value of the pound.

24.   (d)   The requirement is to identify the strategy of matching maturities. Answer (d) is correct because the strategy of matching asset and liability maturities is referred to as a hedging approach. The strategy helps ensure that funds are generated from the assets when the related liabilities are due. Answer (a) is incorrect because working capital management involves managing current assets and current liabilities. Answer (b) is incorrect because return maximization is a more aggressive strategy than maturity matching. Answer (c) is incorrect because financial leverage is the relationship between debt and equity financing.

25.   (a)   The requirement is to identify the incorrect strategy when currency values are expected to fall. Answer (a) is correct because granting credit means that Banner will be paid back with currency that has less value. Answer (b) is incorrect because investing in assets will hedge a decrease in currency value. Answer (c) is incorrect because purchasing materials and supplies will hedge a decrease in currency value. Answer (d) is incorrect because if funds are borrowed they are paid back with currency with less value.

26.   (b)   The requirement is to identify a means of hedging a decline in the price of stock. Answer (b) is correct because purchasing a put option on the stock allows the purchaser the option to sell the stock at the specified price in the future. Thus, if the price of the stock declines, the value of the put option will increase by an equivalent amount. Answer (a) is incorrect because purchasing a call option on the stock provides the company with an option to purchase stock at a specified price. Answer (c) is incorrect because selling a put option provides the purchaser with an option to sell stock at a specified price. Answer (d) is incorrect because a warrant provides the purchaser with the option of obtaining additional stock at a specified price.

27.   (d)   The requirement is to identify the risk of loss because of fluctuations in the relative value of foreign currencies. Answer (d) is correct because the risk of fluctuations in the relative value of foreign currencies is referred to as exchange rate risk. Answers (a) and (b) are incorrect because expropriation and sovereign risks relate to the possibility that a country might seize a foreign investment. Answer (c) is incorrect because multinational beta would be risk of the individual investment relative to the multinational market as a whole.

Present Value

28.   (c)   The requirement is to identify characteristics of bonds that sell at a premium. Item I is not correct because if the bond sells at a premium the market rate is less than the coupon rate. Item III is not correct because the coupon rate is higher than the market rate. Item V is incorrect because the bond sells at a premium not a discount. Therefore, answer (c) is the only answer with two correct characteristics, II and IV.

29.   (c)   The requirement is to determine the annual savings needed for an investment to realize a 12% yield. The internal rate of return method of capital budgeting determines the rate of return at which the present value of the cash flows will exactly equal the investment outlay. In this problem, the desired IRR is given and the cash flows must be determined. The necessary annual savings can be computed as follows:

$$
\begin{aligned}
\text{TVMF} \times \text{Cash flows} &= \text{PV (investment today)} \\
3.60X + (.57 \times \$10,000) &= \$50,000 \\
3.60X &= \$50,000 - (.57 \times \$10,000) \\
3.60X &= \$44,300 \\
X &= \$12,306
\end{aligned}
$$

If the annual savings equals $12,306, the present value of the cash inflows will exactly equal the cash outflows.

30.   (d)   APB 21 states that receivables bearing an unreasonably low stated interest rate should be recorded at their present value. The Maxx receivable would be recorded at its present value, since it matures in five years. The Maxx receivable will result in a lump-sum collection of $11,593 ($10,000 × 1.1593), so its present value is $7,883 ($11,593 × .680).

31.   (c)   The market price of a bond issued at any amount (par, premium, or discount) is equal to the present value of all of its future cash flows, discounted at the current market (effective) interest rate. The market price of a bond issued at a discount is equal to the present value of both its principal and periodic future cash interest payments at the stated (cash) rate of interest, discounted at the current market (effective) rate.

Capital Budgeting

32. (c) The requirement is to identify the stage that management is most likely to use present value techniques. Answer (c) is correct because present value techniques will most likely be used in the selection stage in which management evaluates various alternatives. Commonly used present value techniques include net present value and the internal rate of return. Answer (a) is incorrect because the identification stage involves determining the types of capital projects that are necessary to achieve management's strategies. Answer (b) is incorrect because in the search stage management attempts to identify capital investments that will achieve management's objectives. Answer (d) is incorrect because in the financing stage management decides on the best source of funding for projects.

Capital Budgeting: Payback and Discounted Payback

33. (c) The requirement is to identify the difference between the payback method and the discounted payback method. Answer (c) is correct because the discounted payback method evaluates investments by discounting future cash flows and determining how many years it will take to recover the initial investment. Answer (a) is incorrect because the discounted payback method involves the same estimates of cash flows as the payback method. Answer (b) is incorrect because neither the payback method nor the discounted payback method considers the overall profitability of the investment. Answer (d) is incorrect because neither the payback method nor the discounted payback method considers variability of return.

34. (c) The payback period is computed by dividing the initial investment by the annual net cash inflow. Depreciation expense is not subtracted from cash inflow; only the income taxes that are affected by the depreciation deduction are subtracted. One of the weaknesses of the payback period is that it ignores the time value of money.

35. (d) The payback method is easy to understand but it is not very sophisticated. Answer (a) is incorrect because the payback method only considers cash flows until the cost is recovered. Answer (b) is incorrect because the payback method only considers net cash inflows from all sources. Answer (c) is incorrect because the payback method does not consider the time value of money.

36. (d) The payback method evaluates investments on the length of time until total dollars invested are recouped in the form of cash inflows or cash outflows avoided. It is calculated as Initial investment ÷ Annual cash inflow of a project. The payback period of the equipment under consideration by Tam is

$$\$100,000 \div \$20,000 = 5 \text{ years}$$

Capital Budgeting: Accounting Rate of Return

37. (d) The requirement is to identify the capital budgeting technique that does not use cash flows. Answer (d) is correct because the accounting rate of return uses accrual basis net income. Answers (a), (b), and (c) are incorrect because all of the other techniques use cash flows as the primary basis for the calculation.

38. (b) The requirement is to identify the advantage of the accounting rate of return method. Answer (b) is correct because accounting return is often used as a performance evaluation measure. Therefore, if it is also used as an evaluation technique, the consistency may lead to better decisions. Answer (a) is incorrect because the fact that results are affected by the depreciation method used is a disadvantage. Answer (c) is incorrect because the accounting rate of return method does not consider the time value of money. Answer (d) is incorrect because the accounting rate of return method does not consider the risk of the investment.

39. (d) The accounting rate of return (ARR) computes an approximate rate of return which ignores the time value of money. It is calculated as Expected increase in annual net income ÷ Initial (or Average) investment in a project. Tam's expected increase in annual income is as follows:

Annual savings in after-tax cash costs	$20,000
Annual depreciation on equipment	
($100,000 ÷ 10 years)	(10,000)
Increase in annual net income	$10,000

A $100,000 initial investment is required to purchase the equipment. Thus, the ARR of the equipment under consideration by Tam is

$$\$10,000 \div \$100,000 = 10\%$$

40. (c) The **accounting rate of return** method (ARR) computes an approximate rate of return which ignores the time value of money. It is computed as follows:

ARR = Expected increase in annual net income ÷ Average investment

Therefore, $40,000 (as stated in problem) is the numerator, the expected increase in annual income.

41. (d) The accounting rate of return (ARR) is based on financial statements prepared on the accrual basis. The formula to compute the ARR is

$$ARR = \frac{\text{Expected increase in annual net income}}{\text{Initial (or average) investment}}$$

Both the revenue over life of project and depreciation expense are used in the calculation of ARR. Depreciation expense over the project's life and other expenses directly associated with the project under consideration including income tax effects are subtracted from revenue over life of the project to determine net income over life of project. Net income over the project's life is then divided by the economic life to determine annual net income, the numerator of the ARR formula. This is a weakness of the ARR method because it does not consider actual cash flows or the time value of money.

Capital Budgeting: Net Present Value

42. (d) The requirement is to identify the implications of a profitability index of 1.15. Answer (d) is correct because the profitability index is the net present value of future cash flows divided by the amount of the initial investment. If the index is greater than 1.00, the net present value of the investment is positive.

43. (c) The requirement is to select the rate at which the NPV method assumes that the project's cash flows are reinvested. The correct answer is (c) because the NPV method assumes that cash flows can be reinvested at the discount rate used in the calculation. This is usually the cost of capital. Answer (a) is incorrect because the internal rate of return method assumes that cash flows are reinvested at that rate. Answer (b) is incorrect because the risk-free rate is never used to evaluate a project. Answer (d) is incorrect because the accounting rate of return is not relevant to the NPV method.

44. (b) The maximum amount that Kern Co. should invest now to obtain a 15% internal rate of return is the present value of the project's total net cash flows as computed below.

Year	Net cash flows	×	Present value of an ord. annuity	=	Present value of net cash flows
1	$50,000	×	.870	=	$ 43,500
2	$80,000	×	.756	=	$ 60,480
	Total present value				$103,980

45. (c) The requirement is to determine the present value of the future cash savings resulting from purchase of the new machine. The present value of the $30,000 savings per year for the first two years is calculated using the present value of an annuity for two periods. Since the amount of the cash savings drops to $20,000 in year three, this amount must be calculated separately. The PV of an annuity for three periods minus the PV of an annuity for two periods, equals the PV of an amount to be received three years in the future. The total present value of the cash savings is calculated as follows:

PV of $30,000 for 2 periods = $30,000 × 1.65 = $49,500
PV of $20,000 in period 3 = $20,000 × (2.32 – 1.65) = 13,400
Total present value of cash savings $62,900

Alternatively, $20,000 could have been treated as an annuity for three years and an additional $10,000 for two years.

46. (d) The net present value of a project equals

NPV = (PV future cash flows) – (Investment)

Since this problem involves a lease requiring only annual payments there is no initial investment in this case. Lease amortization must be subtracted from cash inflows to determine income tax expense.

$7,500	Annual cash inflow
– 5,000	Tax basis lease amortization
$2,500	Taxable lease income
× 40%	
$1,000	Tax expense per year

However, lease amortization is **not** a cash outflow and is thus excluded from the calculation of NPV. The after-tax present value of the lease equals:

$ 7,500	Annual cash inflow
– 1,000	Cash outflow for taxes
$6,500	
× 1.74	PV factor for two years at 10%
$11,310	

47. (a) A project's net present value is determined by considering the project's cash inflows and cash outflows discounted to their present values using the required rate of return. The initial outlay for the replacement asset is considered to be the cash outflow reduced by any proceeds from the sale of the asset to be replaced.

48. (c) The requirement is to determine when the discount rate (hurdle rate) must be determined before a capital budgeting method can be used. The payback method measures the time it will take to recoup, in the form of cash in-

flows from operations, the initial dollars invested in a project. The payback method does **not** consider the time value of money. The time-adjusted rate of return method is also called the internal rate of return method. This method computes the rate of interest at which the present value of expected cash inflows from a project equals the present value of expected cash outflows of the project. Here, the discount rate is not determined in advance but is the end result of the calculation. The net present value method is the correct answer because it calculates the expected net monetary gain or loss from a project by discounting all expected future cash inflows and outflows to the present using some predetermined minimum desired rate of return (hurdle rate).

Capital Budgeting: Internal Rate of Return

49. (a) The requirement is to identify a description of the application of the internal rate of return. Answer (a) is correct because the IRR is the interest rate that equates the present value of the future cash inflows with the present value of the future cash outflows.

50. (a) The requirement is to identify the items used in the computation of the internal rate of return. Answer (a) is correct because the IRR uses the net incremental investment and the net annual cash flows. However, it does not include the incremental average operating income.

51. (a) The requirement is to compare NPV and IRR. Answer (a) is correct because NPV and IRR criteria will always lead to the same accept or reject decision. Answer (b) is incorrect because if the second project's internal rate of return is higher than the first project's, the organization would accept the second project based on IRR.

52. (c) The requirement is to calculate the net present value of Project A. Answer (c) is correct. The December 31, 2013 cash inflow is five years from the present cash outflow, and the net present value method uses the firm's cost of capital of 18%. The present value factor for 18% for 5 years is .4371, and $7,400,000 times .4371 equals $3,234,540, which is $265,460 less than the present cash outflow of $3,500,000. Answer (a) is incorrect because this answer discounts the cash inflow at the correct discount rate (18%), but for four years instead of five. Answer (b) is incorrect because this answer discounts the cash inflow at 15% (the project's internal rate of return) instead of at 18% (the cost of capital), which the net present value method uses. Answer (d) is incorrect because this answer discounts the cash inflow at the correct discount rate (18%), but for four years instead of five, and also subtracts the cash outflow from the cash inflow, instead of vice versa.

53. (c) The requirement is to estimate Project B's internal rate of return. Answer (c) is correct because 20% is the rate of return that equates the cash inflows with the cash outflows. The present value of 20% for 5 years is .4019, which multiplied by $9,950,000 equals $3,998,905. Therefore, the net present value of the project approximates $0 using the 20% rate.

54. (b) The requirement is to calculate the cost of the project from its cash flow information. Answer (b) is correct. The internal rate of return is the discount rate that sets the net present value of the project to zero, so the present value of the costs equals the present value of the cash inflows. The cost of Project A can be calculated by determining the present value of the annual annuity of $10,000 cash flows discounted at 15%. Therefore, the cost of the investment is $22,832 ($10,000 × 2.2832). Answer (a) is incorrect because this solution uses the present value interest factor of 15%, one period rather than the present value interest factor for an annuity. Answer (c) is incorrect because this solution is obtained using a 10% rather than a 15% discount rate. Answer (d) is incorrect because this solution is obtained using a 5% rather than a 15% discount rate.

55. (a) The requirement is to calculate the net present value of Project B. Answer (a) is correct because the net present value is the present value of the cash inflows less the cost of the project. The net present value of the future inflows is $24,079 [($5,000 × .9091) + ($10,000 × .8264) + ($15,000 × .7513)]. Therefore, the net present value of the project is $4,079 ($24,079 – $20,000). Answer (b) is incorrect because this solution is obtained using a 5%, rather than a 10%, discount rate. Answer (c) is incorrect because this is the net present value of Project A at a 10% discount rate. Answer (d) is incorrect because this solution is obtained using the present value interest factor for annuities.

56. (c) The requirement is to calculate the payback period of Project C. Answer (c) is correct because after two years, the cumulative cash inflows for Project C are exactly equal to the initial investment outlay, $25,000 ($15,000 + 10,000). Answer (a) is incorrect because the payback period would be zero only if a project had no cost or provided immediate cash inflows in excess of the investment outlay. Project C does not provide an immediate payback of its investment cost. Answer (b) is incorrect because after one year, the cumulative cash inflows for Project C are only $15,000 versus an initial investment outlay of $25,000. The project has not yet recovered its costs. Answer (d) is incorrect because Project C pays back its initial investment outlay in only two years.

57. (c) The requirement is to calculate the year 2 cash inflow for Project D. Answer (c) is correct. The discounted payback period is the length of time required for discounted cash flows to recover the cost of the investment. The year two cash inflow for Project D that is consistent with a discounted payback period of 2 years can be calculated as follows:

Investment cost = present value of year 1 and 2 cash inflows
$30,000 = $20,000 × (.9524) + year 2 cash inflow × (0.9070)
Year 2 cash inflow = [$30,000 – ($20,000 × .9524)] ÷ 0.9070
= $12,075.

Answer (c) is incorrect because this solution is obtained using the present value interest factor for annuities. Answer (b) is incorrect because this solution is based on the regular payback period. Since the cash inflow in year 1 is $20,000, Project D pays back its $30,000 cost in two years if the cash inflow in year 2 is $10,000. Answer (d) is incorrect because this solution is obtained using a 10%, rather than a 5%, discount rate.

58. (c) The internal rate of return (IRR) determines the rate of discount at which the present value of the future cash flows will exactly equal the investment outlay. It is computed by setting up the following equation

Initial investment = TVMF × Cash flows

and solving for the time value of money factor (TVMF). The IRR can then be found by locating the TVMF for (n)

periods in the present value of an ordinary annuity table and tracing to the top of that column to find the rate of return. The problem asks for the TVMF for the IRR of the equipment, which is calculated as follows:

$$\$100,000 = TVMF \times \$20,000$$
$$5.00 = TVMF$$

In estimating the IRR, the factors in the table of present values of an annuity should be taken from the columns closest to 5.00.

59. (d) The internal rate of return of a proposed project includes the residual sales value of a project but not the depreciation expense. This is true because the residual sales value represents a future cash flow whereas depreciation expense (ignoring income tax considerations) provides no cash inflow or outflow.

60. (c) The relationship between the NPV method and the IRR method can be summarized as follows:

NPV	IRR
NPV > 0	IRR > Discount rate
NPV = 0	IRR = Discount rate
NPV < 0	IRR < Discount rate

Since the problem states that Neu Co. has a positive net present value on the investment, then the internal rate of return would be > 12%.

61. (a) The requirement is to determine which mutually exclusive investment should be accepted. Answer (a) is correct because Project X has the higher net present value as calculated below.

Net present value of Project X= $6,800= ($40,000 × 3.170) – $120,000

Net present value of Project Y= $5,310= [($10,000 × 0.909) +($20,000 × 0.826) + ($60,000 × 0.751) + ($80,000 × 0.683)] – $120,000

62. (c) The requirement is to select the projects that should be undertaken assuming no budget constraints. Answer (c) is correct because the company should undertake all projects with a positive net present value. This would include Projects 2, 3, and 4. Answers (a), (b), and (d) are incorrect because Project 1 has a negative net present value and should not be undertaken.

63. (d) The requirement is to select the projects that should be undertaken assuming the company has only $600,000 available. Answer (d) is correct because Projects 3 and 4 have the highest NPV, profitability indexes, and IRRs, so they are the most profitable projects. Answer (a) is incorrect because Project 1 has a negative net present value. Answer (b) is incorrect because it violates the $600,000 restriction. Answer (c) is incorrect because the combined NPV of Projects 2 and 3 is less than the combined NPV of Projects 3 and 4.

64. (d) The requirement is to identify the project(s) that should be undertaken assuming the company has only $300,000 available. Answer (d) is correct; because Project 3 has the highest profitability index and a positive NPV, it should be undertaken. The profitability index provides a good measure for comparing investments of different amounts because it provides an indication of the NPV per dollar invested. Answer (a) is incorrect because it has a negative NPV. Answers (b) and (c) are incorrect because they violate the $300,000 constraint.

Determining Future Cash Flows

65. (b) The requirement is to define the nature of a tax shield. Answer (b) is correct because the benefit of depreciation in cash flow analysis is the resulting tax savings (reduction in income taxes). Answers (a), (c), and (d) are incorrect because they do not describe the nature of the tax shield.

66. (a) The requirement is to identify the effects of income taxes on future cash flows. Answer (a) is correct because income taxes decrease both revenues and costs in projecting future cash flows. Answers (b), (c), and (d) are incorrect because income taxes decrease both benefits and costs.

67. (b) The requirement is to determine which costs are economically relevant to Buff Co.'s decision of whether to replace an old machine with a new machine. Costs that will not differ among alternatives are not relevant for decision-making purposes. Sunk costs are those that are not avoidable and are the result of a past decision. The original cost, accumulated depreciation, and therefore the carrying amount of Buff's old machine are not relevant to the decision because this is a past cost that cannot be changed. The costs associated with the new machine are avoidable. The disposal value of a new machine is relevant to Buff's decision because it represents a cash inflow that differs between the alternatives.

68. (b) The requirement is to calculate the after-tax cash flows in year 2. Answer (b) is correct. The after-tax cash flows are calculated by deducting tax expense from the before-tax cash flows. Since depreciation is deductible for tax purposes it provides a tax shield. Therefore, income taxes for year 2 are equal to $15,000 [($140,000 – 90,000) × 30%], and after-tax cash flows are $125,000 ($140,000 – 15,000). Answer (a) is incorrect because $140,000 is the before-tax cash flows. Answer (c) is incorrect because this solution fails to consider the deductibility of depreciation.

69. (c) The requirement is to calculate the net present value of the investment. Answer (c) is correct. The net present value is equal to the present value of the future after-tax cash flows minus the initial investment. The after-tax annual cash flows are calculated by taking the before-tax cash flows and deducting income taxes. Since depreciation is deductible for tax purposes, annual tax expense is equal to $15,000 [($140,000 – 90,000) × 30%]. Therefore, annual cash flows after taxes are $125,000 ($140,000 – 15,000). The present value of $125,000 received annually for 5 years discounted at 10% is $473,875 ($125,000 × 3.791). To properly evaluate the project, the investment in working capital ($10,000) must be considered a part of the initial investment, and its recovery at the end of year 5 must be discounted back to its present value, along with the terminal value of the investment of $50,000. The present value of $60,000 received at the end of 5 years is equal to $37,260 ($60,000 × .621). Therefore, the net present value is equal to $1,135 ($473,875 + 37,260 – 500,000 – 10,000). Answer (a) is incorrect because it is the result when amounts are not discounted. Answer (b) is incorrect because it is the result when taxes are not considered.

Considering Risk in Capital Budgeting

70. (b) The requirement is to calculate the expected contribution of a new product. Answer (b) is correct because the expected value of the contribution margin is equal to $110,000 [($700,000 × 30%) + ($200,000 × 30%) + (-$400,000 × 40%).

71. (d) The requirement is to determine the expected value of cost of goods sold. Answer (d) is correct because the estimated cost of goods sold is calculated by multiplying the cost of goods sold percentage by the expected value of sales. The expected value of sales is $84,000 [($60,000 × 25%) + (85,000 × 40%) + ($100,000 × 35%). Therefore, cost of goods sold is estimated to be $67,200 ($84,000 × 80%).

72. (a) The requirement is to identify the technique that would allow management to justify an investment based on considerations other than expected cash flows. Answer (a) is correct because the real options technique views an investment as purchasing an option. This may allow management to justify investments that do not currently have positive cash flows. Answers (b), (c), and (d) are all techniques that require expected return to exceed the initial investment.

73. (c) The requirement is to calculate the expected return for the project. Answer (c) is correct because the expected return is calculated by summing the outcomes weighted by their probability of occurrence. Therefore, the expected return is equal to $470,000 [($200,000 × .4) + ($500,000 × .3) + ($800,000 × .3)]. Answer (a) is incorrect because it is the simple average of the three potential outcomes. Answer (b) is incorrect because it is the median return.

74. (b) The requirement is to compute the coefficient of variation of the project. Answer (b) is correct because the coefficient of variation is equal to the standard deviation of returns divided by the amount of the expected return. The coefficient of variation is equal to .3191 ($150,000 ÷ 470,000).

75. (c) The requirement is to identify the technique that recognizes the series of decisions involved in an investment. Answer (c) is correct because decision tree provides management with a technique for evaluating investments that involve a series of decisions. Answer (a) is incorrect because probability analysis involves assigning probabilities to various outcomes. Answer (b) is incorrect because the risk-adjusted discount rate technique involves assigning different discount rates based on the risk involved. Answer (d) is incorrect because sensitivity analysis involves examining the sensitivity of results to changes in significant assumptions.

76. (d) The requirement is to identify the technique that is not used to consider risk. Answer (d) is correct because the traditional internal rate of return method does not explicitly include consideration of risk. Answer (a) is incorrect because probability analysis involves assigning probabilities to various outcomes. Therefore, it considers risk. Answer (b) is incorrect because the risk-adjusted discount rate method adjusts discount rates for risk. Answer (c) is incorrect because simulation techniques allow management to simulate results based on expected values and levels of risk.

77. (d) The requirement is to identify the type of risk that concerns investors in a diversified company. Answer (d) is correct because a diversified company can be thought of as an investment portfolio. The relevant risk for both management and investors is the weighted average of project risk. Answer (a) is incorrect because the firm has a diversified set of projects and, therefore, a single project risk is not relevant. Answer (b) is incorrect because pure play risk relates to a single project. Answer (c) is incorrect because the standard deviation of project risk does not adequately measure the risk of the portfolio.

78. (a) The requirement is to identify the nature of the next investment in a portfolio. Answer (a) is correct because to reduce the risk of a portfolio, the investor should select investments with negatively correlated returns. In that way, when one investment decreases in value others will increase. Therefore, the company should select an investment that correlates negatively to current portfolio holdings. Answer (b) is incorrect because an investment that is uncorrelated to the current holdings does not reduce risk as much as one that is negatively correlated. Answer (c) is incorrect because an investment that is highly correlated to the current holdings increases the risk of the portfolio. Answer (d) is incorrect because an investment that is perfectly correlated to the current holdings increases the risk of the portfolio.

79. (c) The requirement is to calculate Deet's estimated savings for 2009 if it leases an auxiliary generator for use during power outages. In 2008 Deet incurred the following costs due to power outages:

Number of outages per month		Number of months		Number of outages
0	×	3	=	0
1	×	2	=	2
2	×	4	=	8
3	×	3	=	9
		12		19

19 outages × $400/outage = $7,600

The cost of leasing an auxiliary generator is only $6,000 (12 mos. × $500/mo). Therefore, Deet would be expected to save $1,600 ($7,600 – $6,000) in 2009 by leasing the generator.

80. (d) The internal rate of return method determines the rate of return at which the present value of the cash flows will exactly equal the investment outlay. It will indicate the rate of return earned over the life of the project. The net present value method determines the present value of all future cash flows at a selected discount rate. If the NPV of the cash flows is positive, the return earned by the project is higher than the selected rate. Both methods will provide the information needed to decide if a project's rate of return will meet Polo Co.'s requirement.

81. (b) The requirement is to determine what the probability of frost must be for Cal to be indifferent to spending $10,000 for frost protection. In other words, you must find the point at which the cost of the frost protection equals the expected value of the loss from frost damage. The table below summarizes the possible outcomes.

	Frost	Frost-free
Protected	$90,000 Market value	$60,000 Market value
Unprotected	$40,000 Market value	$60,000 Market value

The difference between the market value of protected and unprotected strawberries if a frost were to occur is $50,000.

Since we want to determine the probability of a frost when the expected value of the loss from frost damage is $10,000, this probability can be calculated as follows:

Loss from damage	×	Probability of frost	=	Expected value of the loss
$50,000	×	P	=	$10,000
		P	=	$\frac{\$10,000}{\$50,000}$
		P	=	.200

82. (c) Expected values are calculated as the weighted-average of all possible outcomes using the probabilities of the outcomes as weights. The expected number of additional muffin sales is

Additional sales		Probability		Expected value
60	×	0.6	=	36
100	×	0.4	=	40
				76

Since Dough earns $1 profit per box ($3 sales price – $2 cost), this represents $76 (76 boxes × $1 profit) of additional profit. However, the twenty-four unsold boxes would have to be sold at a $1 loss per box ($1 sales price – $2 cost) through Dough's thrift store. Therefore, the expected value of the decision to purchase the additional muffins is $52 net profit ($76 profit – $24 loss).

83. (b) Because it is not always possible to make decisions under conditions of total certainty, decision makers must have a method of determining the best estimate or course of action where uncertainty exists. One method is probability analysis. Probabilities are used to calculate the expected value of each action. The expected value of an action is the weighted-average of the payoffs for that action, where the weights are the probabilities of the various mutually exclusive events that may occur. Cost-volume-profit analysis is used to predict profits at all levels of production in the relevant range. Program evaluation and review technique (PERT) is used to estimate, schedule, and manage a network of interdependent project activities. It is useful for managing large-scale, complex projects. The scattergraph method is a graphical approach to computing the relationship between two variables.

84. (c) A probability distribution describes the possible outcomes relating to a single action and the likelihood of occurrence of each possible outcome. Gift Co. selected the most likely sales volume from several possible outcomes, which was simply the sales volume with the greatest probability of occurring. Gift Co. did not calculate the weighted-average of the outcomes (the sum of the probability of each outcome occurring times the sales volume of that outcome) to find the expected value.

85. (c) Probability analysis is an extension of sensitivity analysis. There is no specified limit on the number of possible outcomes. The summation of the probability weights should always equal one. Probability analysis and sensitivity analysis are not incompatible.

MULTIPLE-CHOICE QUESTIONS (1-68)

1. What is the most important purpose of a balanced scorecard?
  a. Develop strategy.
  b. Measure performance.
  c. Develop cause-and-effect linkages.
  d. Set priorities.

2. Which of the following is not one of the four perspectives of the balanced scorecard?
  a. Investment in resources perspective.
  b. Customer perspective.
  c. Learning and growth perspective.
  d. Financial perspective.

3. The balanced scorecard generally uses performance measures with four different perspectives. Which of the following performance measures would be part of those used for the internal business processes perspective?
  a. Cycle time.
  b. Employee satisfaction.
  c. Hours of training per employee.
  d. Customer retention

4. The balanced scorecard has been adopted by many corporations. Which of the following best describes the balanced scorecard?
  a. A strategy that meets management's objectives.
  b. A diagram illustrating cause and effect relationships.
  c. A table of key actions to achieve strategic objectives.
  d. A strategic performance measurement and management framework.

5. The balanced scorecard and value-based management are techniques that are being used by a number of corporations. In comparison to the balanced scorecard, value-based management focuses on
  a. Nonfinancial measures.
  b. Financial measures.
  c. Both financial and nonfinancial measures.
  d. Quality measures.

6. Management has identified a relationship between customer satisfaction and return on investment. This relationship could be depicted in a
  a. Strategy map.
  b. Value chain.
  c. Customer perspectives chart.
  d. Strategic initiatives list.

7. Which of the following is not a component of the balanced scorecard?
  a. Strategic objectives.
  b. Targets.
  c. Strategy initiatives.
  d. Assessment of human resources.

8. Which of the following best describes a value chain in the balanced scorecard framework?
  a. The cause-and-effect linkages.
  b. The baseline level of performance.

  c. The sequence of business processes in which usefulness is added to products or services.
  d. The chain of financial and nonfinancial measures.

9. Which of the following is not a characteristic of the balanced scorecard?
  a. Both financial and nonfinancial performance measures are included.
  b. Cause-and-effect linkages between strategic objectives.
  c. Customer performance measures are excluded.
  d. Internal process performance measures are included.

10. In the balanced scorecard framework, a survey of employee satisfaction is a potential measure in which of the four perspectives?
  a. Financial.
  b. Customer.
  c. Internal business processes.
  d. Learning and growth.

*11. Which of the following is an example of an efficiency measure?
  a. The rate of absenteeism.
  b. The goal of becoming a leading manufacturer.
  c. The number of insurance claims processed per day.
  d. The rate of customer complaints.

12. A strategy objective in the balanced scorecard framework is
  a. A statement of what the strategy must achieve and what is critical to its success.
  b. Key action programs required to achieve strategic objectives.
  c. Diagrams of the cause-and-effect relationships between strategic objectives.
  d. The level of performance or rate of improvement needed in the performance measure.

13. A target in the balanced scorecard framework is
  a. A statement of what the strategy must achieve and what is critical to its success.
  b. A key action program required to achieve strategic objectives.
  c. A diagram of the cause-and-effect relationships between strategic objectives.
  d. The level of performance or rate of improvement needed in the performance measure.

Items 14 through 18 are based on the following information:

The following is selected data for the Consumer Products division of Arron Corporations for 200X:

Sales	$50,000,000
Average invested capital (assets)	20,000,000
Net income	2,000,000
Cost of capital	8%

14. What is the return on sales (ROS) for the division?
  a. 8%
  b. 4%
  c. 10%
  d. 20%

---

15. What is the asset turnover ratio for the division?
    a.   .25
    b.   10
    c.   2.5
    d.   8

16. What is the return on investment (ROI) for the division?
    a.   10%
    b.   8%
    c.   4%
    d.   2%

17. What is the amount of residual income (RI) for the division?
    a. $2,000,000
    b. $1,600,000
    c. $1,000,000
    d. $ 400,000

18. What is the amount of interest rate spread for the division?
    a.   8%
    b.   10%
    c.   2%
    d.   20%

Items 19 and 20 are based on the following information:

The following is available for Cara Corp. for 2009:

Sales	$2,000,000
Average invested capital	500,000
Net income	300,000
Required rate of return	18%

19. What is the return on investment at Cara Corp.?
    a.   60%
    b.   33%
    c.   18%
    d.   15%

20. What is the residual income for Cara Corp.?
    a. $0
    b. $200,000
    c. $210,000
    d. $246,000

Items 21 and 22 are based on the following information:

On the graph below, the line (A-B-C) illustrates residual income (measured on the vertical axis in dollars) at various interest rates. Point D is the cost of capital or the required rate of return. Point E is the residual income at the cost of capital.

21. What does point B represent?
    a.   Return on sales.
    b.   Return on investment.
    c.   Asset turnover.
    d.   Operating income.

22. What does point A represent?
    a.   Return on sales.
    b.   Return on investment.
    c.   Asset turnover.
    d.   Net income.

23. On the graph below, lines A-B-C and D-E-F illustrates residual income (measured on the vertical axis in dollars) at various interest rates. Point G is the firm's cost of capital. Line ABC represents the residual income of Division X at various interest rates. Line DEF represents the residual income of Division Y at various interest rates.

Based on the graph above, for Division X versus Division Y, is the residual income and ROI for Division X greater than or less than that of Division Y?

	Residual income of Division X is greater than the residual income for Division Y	Return on investment of Division X is greater than the ROI for Division Y
a.	Yes	Yes
b.	Yes	No
c.	No	Yes
d.	No	No

24. A company's rate of return on investment (ROI) is equal to the
    a.   Percentage of profit on sales divided by the capital employed turnover rate.
    b.   Percentage of profit on sales multiplied by the capital employed turnover rate.
    c.   Investment capital divided by the capital employed turnover rate.
    d.   Investment capital multiplied by the capital employed turnover rate.

25. Return on investment can be increased by
    a.   Increasing operating assets.
    b.   Decreasing operating assets.
    c.   Decreasing revenues.
    d.   Both b. and c.

26. The following information pertains to Bala Co. for the year ended December 31, 2009:

Sales	$600,000
Net income	100,000
Capital investment	400,000

Which of the following equations should be used to compute Bala's return on investment?
    a. $(4/6) \times (6/1) = ROI$
    b. $(6/4) \times (1/6) = ROI$
    c. $(4/6) \times (1/6) = ROI$
    d. $(6/4) \times (6/1) = ROI$

27. Select Co. had the following 2009 financial statement relationships:

Asset turnover	5
Profit margin on sales	0.02

What was Select's 2009 percentage return on assets?

- a.   0.1%
- b.   0.4%
- c.   2.5%
- d.   10.0%

28. The following selected data pertain to the Darwin Division of Beagle Co. for 2009:

Sales	$400,000
Net income	40,000
Capital turnover	4
Imputed interest rate	10%

What was Darwin's 2009 residual income?

- a. $0
- b. $ 4,000
- c. $10,000
- d. $30,000

29. Division A is considering a project that will earn a rate of return which is greater than the imputed interest charge for invested capital, but less than the division's historical return on invested capital. Division B is considering a project that will earn a rate of return that is greater than the division's historical return on invested capital, but less than the imputed interest charge for invested capital. If the objective is to maximize residual income, should these divisions accept or reject their projects?

	A	*B*
a.	Accept	Accept
b.	Reject	Accept
c.	Reject	Reject
d.	Accept	Reject

30. Which combination of changes in asset turnover and income as a percentage of sales will maximize the return on investment?

	Asset turnover	*Income as a percentage of sales*
a.	Increase	Decrease
b.	Increase	Increase
c.	Decrease	Increase
d.	Decrease	Decrease

*__31.__ Residual income is often preferred over return on investment (ROI) as a performance evaluation because

- a.   Residual income is a measure over time while ROI represents the results for a single time period.
- b.   Residual income concentrates on maximizing absolute dollars of income rather than a percentage return as with ROI.
- c.   The imputed interest rate used in calculating residual income is more easily derived than the target rate that is compared to the calculated ROI.
- d.   Average investment is employed with residual income while year-end investment is employed with ROI.

32. What is a major disadvantage of using economic value added (EVA) alone as a performance measure?

- a.   It fails to focus on creating shareholder value.

- b.   It promotes the acceptance of unprofitable projects.
- c.   It fails to reflect all of the ways that value may be created.
- d.   It discourages cost cutting.

Items 33 and 34 are based on the following information:

The following are selected data for Walkin Corporation for the year ended 20X1:

Net operating profit before taxes	$31,250,000
Inventory	5,000,000
Long-term debt	40,000,000
Depreciation expense	9,000,000
Change in net working capital	5,000,000
Capital expenditures	8,000,000
Invested capital (net assets)	80,000,000
Weighted average cost of capital	10%
Tax rate	20%

33. Which of the following measures economic value added for Walkin Corporation for the year?

- a. $ 3,000,000
- b. $ 7,000,000
- c. $15,000,000
- d. $17,000,000

34. Which of the following measures the amount of free cash flow for Walkin Corporation for the year?

- a. $ 7,000,000
- b. $ 8,000,000
- c. $21,000,000
- d. $25,000,000

35. The following information is available for the wholesale products division of Watco:

Net operating profit before interest and taxes	$30,000,000
Depreciation expense	10,000,000
Change in net working capital	5,000,000
Capital expenditures	4,000,000
Invested capital (total assets – current liabilities)	50,000,000
Weighted average cost of capital	10%
Tax rate	40%

What is the amount of economic value added (EVA) for the division?

- a. $30,000,000
- b. $13,000,000
- c. $25,000,000
- d. $ 5,000,000

Items 36 and 37 are based on the following information:

The following information is available for Armstrong Enterprises for 2009:

Net operating profit (income) after taxes	$36,000,000
Depreciation expense	15,000,000
Change in net working capital	10,000,000
Capital expenditures	12,000,000
Invested capital (total assets – current liabilities)	100,000,000
Weighted average cost of capital	10%

36. What is the amount of the economic value added (EVA)?

- a. $20,000,000
- b. $26,000,000
- c. $15,000,000
- d. $36,000,000

---

* *CIA adapted*

37. What is the free cash flow for 2009?
    a. $36,000,000
    b. $30,000,000
    c. $29,000,000
    d. $26,000,000

38. Which of the following is not a measure of asset utilization?
    a. Inventory turnover.
    b. Average accounts receivable collection period.
    c. Fixed asset turnover.
    d. Debt to total assets.

39. What financial analysis technique would imply benchmarking with other firms?
    a. Horizontal analysis.
    b. Vertical analysis.
    c. Cross-sectional analysis.
    d. Ratio analysis.

Items 40 and 41 are based on the following information:

The Dawson Corporation projects the following for the year 2009:

Earnings before interest and taxes	$35 million
Interest expense	5 million
Preferred stock dividends	4 million
Common stock dividend payout ratio	30%
Common shares outstanding	2 million
Effective corporate income tax rate	40%

**40. The expected common stock dividend per share for Dawson Corporation for 2009 is
    a. $2.34
    b. $2.70
    c. $3.90
    d. $2.10

**41. If Dawson Corporation's common stock is expected to trade at a price/earnings ratio of eight, the market price per share (to the nearest dollar) would be
    a. $125
    b. $ 56
    c. $ 72
    d. $ 68

Items 42 through 46 are based on the following information:

The data presented below show actual figures for selected accounts of McKeon Company for the fiscal year ended December 31, 2009. McKeon's controller is in the process of reviewing the 2009 results. McKeon Company monitors yield or return ratios using the average financial position of the company. (Round all calculations to three decimal places if necessary.)

	12/31/09	12/31/08
Current assets	$210,000	$180,000
Noncurrent assets	275,000	255,000
Current liabilities	78,000	85,000
Long-term debt	75,000	30,000
Common stock ($30 par value)	300,000	300,000
Retained earnings	32,000	20,000

2009 Operations	
Sales*	$350,000
Cost of goods sold	160,000
Interest expense	3,000
Income taxes (40% rate)	48,000
Dividends declared and paid in 2009	60,000
Administrative expense	67,000

* All sales are credit sales.

	Current Assets	
	12/31/09	12/31/08
Cash	$ 20,000	$10,000
Accounts receivable	100,000	70,000
Inventory	70,000	80,000
Other	20,000	20,000

**42. McKeon Company's debt-to-total-asset ratio at 12/31/09 is
    a. 0.352
    b. 0.315
    c. 0.264
    d. 0.237

**43. The 2009 accounts receivable turnover for McKeon company is
    a. 1.882
    b. 3.500
    c. 5.000
    d. 4.118

**44. Using a 365-day year, McKeon's inventory turnover is
    a. 2.133
    b. 2.281
    c. 1.995
    d. 4.615

**45. McKeon Company's total asset turnover for 2009 is
    a. 0.805
    b. 0.761
    c. 0.722
    d. 0.348

**46. The 2009 return on assets for McKeon Company is
    a. 0.261
    b. 0.148
    c. 0.157
    d. 0.166

Items 47 through 53 are based on the following information:

Depoole Company is a manufacturer of industrial products and employs a calendar year for financial reporting purposes. These questions present several of Depoole's transactions during the year. Assume that total quick assets exceeded total current liabilities both before and after each transaction described. Further assume that Depoole has positive profits during the year and a credit balance throughout the year in its retained earnings account.

**47. Payment of a trade account payable of $64,500 would
    a. Increase the current ratio but the quick ratio would not be affected.
    b. Increase the quick ratio but the current ratio would not be affected.
    c. Increase both the current and quick ratios.
    d. Decrease both the current and quick ratios.

**48. The purchase of raw materials for $85,000 on open account would
   a. Increase the current ratio.
   b. Decrease the current ratio.
   c. Increase net working capital.
   d. Decrease net working capital.

**49. The collection of a current accounts receivable of $29,000 would
   a. Increase the current ratio.
   b. Decrease the current ratio and the quick ratio.
   c. Increase the quick ratio.
   d. Not affect the current or quick ratios.

**50. Obsolete inventory of $125,000 was written off during the year. This transaction
   a. Decreased the quick ratio.
   b. Increased the quick ratio.
   c. Increased net working capital.
   d. Decreased the current ratio.

**51. The issuance of new shares in a five-for-one split of common stock
   a. Decreases the book value per share of common stock.
   b. Increases the book value per share of common stock.
   c. Increases total shareholders' equity.
   d. Decreases total shareholders' equity.

**52. The issuance of serial bonds in exchange for an office building, with the first installment of the bonds due late this year,
   a. Decreases net working capital.
   b. Decreases the current ratio.
   c. Decreases the quick ratio.
   d. Affects all of the answers as indicated.

**53. The early liquidation of a long-term note with cash affects the
   a. Current ratio to a greater degree than the quick ratio.
   b. Quick ratio to a greater degree than the current ratio.
   c. Current and quick ratio to the same degree.
   d. Current ratio but not the quick ratio.

54. Southwest Airlines benchmarked the process of turning around an airplane with the pit stop process for formula racecars. This is an example of
   a. Internal benchmarking.
   b. Generic benchmarking.
   c. Competitor benchmarking.
   d. Functional benchmarking.

55. Which measures would be useful in evaluating the performance of a manufacturing system?
   I. Throughput time.
   II. Total setup time for machines/Total production time.
   III. Number of rework units/Total number of units completed.

   a. I and II only.
   b. II and III only.
   c. I and III only.
   d. I, II, and III.

56. A tool which indicates how frequently each type of defect occurs is a
   a. Control chart.
   b. Pareto diagram.
   c. Cause-and-effect diagram.
   d. Fishbone diagram.

57. A tool which identifies potential causes for failures or defects is
   a. Control chart.
   b. Pareto diagram.
   c. Cause-and-effect diagram.
   d. Strategy map.

58. Which of the statements best describes the concept of six-sigma quality?
   a. 10 defects per million.
   b. 3.4 defects per million.
   c. 6.0 defects per million.
   d. 100 defects per million.

59. Which of the following quality tools is another term for continuous improvement?
   a. Theory of constraints.
   b. Kaizen.
   c. Six-sigma.
   d. Lean manufacturing.

60. In the theory of constraints, an operation or resource where the work performed approaches or exceeds the availability is referred to as
   a. A bottleneck.
   b. A time driver.
   c. Customer-response time.
   d. Manufacturing lead time.

**61. Antlers, Inc. produces a single product that sells for $150 per unit. The product is processed through the Cutting and Finishing departments. Additional data for these departments are as follows:

	Cutting	*Finishing*
Annual capacity (36,000 direct labor hours available in each department)	180,000 units	135,000 units
Current production rate (annualized)	108,000 units	108,000 units
Fixed manufacturing overhead	$1,296,000	$1,944,000
Fixed selling and administrative expense	$ 864,000	$1,296,000
Direct materials cost per unit	$ 45	$ 15

The current production rate is the budgeted rate for the entire year. Direct labor employees earn $20 per hour and the company has a "no layoff" policy in effect. What is the amount of the throughput contribution per unit as computed using the theory of constraints?
   a. $90.00
   b. $76.67
   c. $46.67
   d. $26.67

**62. Three of the basic measurements used by the Theory of Constraints (TOC) are

   a. Gross margin (or gross profit), return on assets, and total sales.
   b. Number of constraints (or subordinates), number of nonconstraints, and operating leverage.

**   *CMA adapted*

c. Throughput (or throughput contribution), inventory (or investments), and operational expense.

d. Fixed manufacturing overhead per unit, fixed general overhead per unit, and unit gross margin (or gross profit).

63. Which statement best describes the objective of the theory of constraints?

	Throughput contribution	Investment	Operating costs
a.	Increase	Decrease	Decrease
b.	Increase	Increase	Increase
c.	Decrease	Increase	Decrease
d.	Increase	Increase	Decrease

64. In considering cost of quality methodology, quality circles are associated with

a. Prevention.
b. Appraisal.
c. Internal failure.
d. External failure.

65. In the cost of quality, which of the following is an example of an "internal failure"?

a. Cost of inspecting products on the production line by quality inspectors.

b. Labor cost of product designers whose task is to design components that will not break under extreme temperature conditions.

c. Cost of reworking defective parts detected by the quality assurance group.

d. Cost of parts returned by customers.

66. In the cost of quality, which of the following is an example of a "prevention cost"?

a. Cost of inspecting products on the production line by quality inspectors.

b. Labor cost of product designers whose task is to design components that will not break under extreme temperature conditions.

c. Cost of reworking defective parts detected by the quality assurance group.

d. Cost of parts returned by customers.

67. Delta Manufacturing Co. has had a problem with its product quality. The company has had a large amount of costs related to product recalls. In considering cost of quality methodology, if the company wants to reduce these costs, the most likely place to incur costs would be for

a. Prevention.
b. Appraisal.
c. Internal failure.
d. External failure.

68. In the cost of quality, costs incurred in detecting individual units of product that do not conform to specifications are

a. Prevention costs.
b. Appraisal costs.
c. Internal failure costs.
d. External failure costs.

1. b			16. a			31. b			46. c
2. a			17. d			32. c			47. c
3. a			18. c			33. d			48. b
4. d			19. a			34. c			49. d
5. b			20. c			35. b			50. d
6. a			21. b			36. b			51. a
7. d			22. d			37. c			52. c
8. c			23. b			38. d			53. b
9. c			24. b			39. c			54. b
10. d			25. b			40. d			55. d
11. c			26. b			41. b			56. b
12. a			27. d			42. b			57. c
13. d			28. d			43. d			58. b
14. b			29. d			44. a			59. b
15. c			30. b			45. b			60. a

61. a	
62. c	
63. a	
64. a	
65. c	
66. b	
67. a	
68. b	
1st: __/68 = __%	
2nd: __/68 = __%	

MULTIPLE-CHOICE ANSWER EXPLANATIONS

Balanced Scorecard and Performance Measures

1. **(b)** The requirement is to identify the purpose of a balanced scorecard. Answer (b) is correct because the balanced scorecard uses financial and nonfinancial measures to measure performance. Answer (a) is incorrect because strategic planning is designed to develop strategy. Answer (c) is incorrect because developing cause-and-effect linkages is an important part of developing a balanced scorecard. Answer (d) is incorrect because setting priorities is a part of strategic planning.

2. **(a)** The requirement is to identify the item that is not one of the four perspectives of the balanced scorecard. Answer (a) is correct because investment in resources is not a perspective of the balanced scorecard. The balanced scorecard deals with performance measurement. Answer (b) is incorrect because customer perspective is used in the balanced scorecard. Answer (c) is incorrect because learning and growth perspective is used in the balanced scorecard. Answer (d) is incorrect because financial perspective is used in the balanced scorecard.

3. **(a)** The requirement is to identify the measure that is related to internal business processes. Answer (a) is correct because cycle time is the time it takes to manufacture a product and, therefore, is an important part of the business processes perspective. Answers (b) and (c) are incorrect because they are part of the learning and growth perspective. Answer (d) is incorrect because it is part of the customer perspective.

4. **(d)** The requirement is to define the balanced scorecard. Answer (d) is correct because the balanced scorecard is a strategic performance measurement and management framework. Answer (b) is incorrect because it is the definition of a strategy map. Answer (c) is incorrect because it is the definition of a list of strategic initiatives.

5. **(b)** The requirement is to identify the focus of value-based management. Answer (b) is correct because value-based management focuses on financial measures to measure performance. The balanced scorecard uses both financial and nonfinancial measures to measure performance.

6. **(a)** The requirement is to identify what illustrates cause-and-effect relationships. Answer (a) is correct be-

cause a strategy map displays cause-and-effect relationships within the balanced scorecard framework. Answer (b) is incorrect because the value chain is the sequence of business processes that add value to a good or service.

7. **(d)** The requirement is to identify the item that is not a component of the balanced scorecard. Answer (d) is correct because an assessment of human resources is not a component of a balanced scorecard. Answer (a) is incorrect because a statement of strategic objectives is a component of a balanced scorecard. Answer (b) is incorrect because targets for performance are part of a balanced scorecard. Answer (c) is incorrect because strategy initiatives are part of a balanced scorecard.

8. **(c)** The requirement is to identify the description of the value chain. Answer (c) is correct because the value chain is the sequence of business processes in which usefulness is added to the product or service. Answer (a) is incorrect because cause-and-effect linkages are used to develop the balanced scorecard. Answer (b) is incorrect because the baseline level of performance is the current level of performance. Answer (d) is incorrect because there is no chain of financial and nonfinancial measures.

9. **(c)** The requirement is to identify which item is not a characteristic of the balanced scorecard. Answer (c) is correct because customer performance is one of the four primary components of the balanced scorecard framework; therefore, it is not excluded. Answers (a), (b), and (d) are incorrect because they are all characteristics of the balanced scorecard.

10. **(d)** The requirement is to identify where in the balanced scorecard framework surveys of employee satisfaction should appear. Answer (d) is correct because surveys of employee satisfaction would appear in the learning and growth perspective which includes various employee measures including employee turnover. Answer (a) is incorrect because the financial perspective includes measures such as profitability and return on investment. Answer (b) is incorrect because the customer perspective includes measures like customer satisfaction. Answer (c) is incorrect because the internal business processes perspective includes measures related to cost, quality, and time.

11. **(c)** The requirement is to identify the efficiency measure. Answer (c) is correct because an efficiency measure relates output to a measure of input. Answer (a) is incorrect because it does not relate output to input. Answer (b) is incorrect because it is an effectiveness measure. Answer (d) is incorrect because it does not relate output to input.

12. (a)   The requirement is to identify the definition of a strategy objective. Answer (a) is correct because it is the definition of a strategy objective in the balanced scorecard framework. Answer (b) is incorrect because it describes a strategic initiative. Answer (c) is incorrect because it is the definition of a strategy map. Answer (d) is incorrect because it is the definition of a target.

13. (d)   The requirement is to identify the definition of a target. Answer (d) is correct because it is the definition of a target in the balanced scorecard framework. Answer (a) is incorrect because it is the definition of a strategic objective. Answer (b) is incorrect because it is the definition of strategy initiatives. Answer (c) is incorrect because it is the definition of a strategy map.

Value-Based Management: ROI and Residual Income

14. (b)   The requirement is to calculate the return on sales for the division. Answer (b) is correct because return on sales is calculated as net income/sales which is equal to 4% ($2,000,000/$50,000,000).

15. (c)   The requirement is to calculate the asset turnover ratio for the division. Answer (c) is correct because the asset turnover ratio is calculated by dividing sales by the average investment amount. Therefore, it is equal to 2.5 ($50,000,000/$20,000,000).

16. (a)   The requirement is to calculate ROI for the division. Answer (a) is correct because ROI is calculated by dividing net income by the amount of the average investment. Therefore, ROI is equal to 10% ($2,000,000/$20,000,000).

17. (d)   The requirement is to calculate RI for the division. Answer (d) is correct because RI is equal to net income minus interest on the investment. Therefore, RI is equal to $400,000 [$2,000,000 – ($20,000,000 × 8%)].

18. (c)   The requirement is to calculate the interest rate spread for the division. Answer (c) is correct because the interest rate spread is the difference between the return on investment and the required rate of return (cost of capital). In this case, the spread is equal to 2% [($2,000,000/$20,000,000) – 8%].

19. (a)   The requirement is to calculate the return on investment. Answer (a) is correct because the return on investment would be computed by dividing net income by average invested capital ($300,000/$500,000 = 60%).

20. (c)   The requirement is to calculate the residual income. Answer (c) is correct because the residual income would be computed as follows: Net income ($300,000) minus the interest on invested capital $90,000 (18% × $500,000) is equal to $210,000.

21. (b)   The requirement is to identify the graphical representation of ROI. Answer (b) is correct because point B is equal to ROI. Answer (a) is incorrect because return on sales (net income/sales) is not represented on this graph. Answer (c) is incorrect because asset turnover (sales/total assets) is not represented on this graph. Answer (d) is incorrect because operating income is located at point A.

22. (d)   The requirement is to identify the graphical representation of net income. Answer (d) is correct because point A is equal to net income. Answer (a) is incorrect because return on sales (net income/sales) is not represented on this graph. Answer (b) is incorrect because ROI is represented at point B. Answer (c) is incorrect because asset turnover (sales/total assets) is not represented on the graph.

23. (b)   The requirement is to identify the graphical representation of the relationship between residual income and ROI. Division X's residual income is located at point A and Division Y's residual income is located at point D. Division X has a larger residual income. Division X's ROI is located at point B and Division Y's ROI is located at point E. Thus Division Y's ROI is greater than Division X's ROI.

24. (b)   The requirement is to identify the formula for ROI. Answer (b) is correct because it describes the DuPont ROI analysis: ROI = Return on sales multiplied by the capital employed turnover rate (which can be measured as total asset turnover).

25. (b)   The requirement is to identify how ROI might be increased. One way of measuring ROI is return on assets (ROA). The formula is net income/total assets. Answer (b) is correct since if operating assets decrease (the denominator in ROI), then ROI would decrease. Answer (a) is incorrect because increasing operating assets would cause ROI to decrease. Answer (c) is incorrect because decreasing revenue would cause net income (the numerator) to decrease. A reduction in operating income would cause ROA to decrease.

26. (b)   Return on investment (ROI) may be calculated using the following equation:

$$\frac{\text{Sales}}{\text{Investment}} \times \frac{\text{Net income}}{\text{Sales}} = \text{ROI}$$

Thus, the equation that should be used to compute Bala's return on investment is (6/4) × (1/6) = ROI.

27. (d)   Return on assets, also referred to as return on investment (ROI), is calculated as follows:

ROI	=	Profit margin	×	Asset turnover
ROI	=	0.02	×	5
ROI	=	0.10, or 10%		

28. (d)   Residual income equals the net income of a division minus imputed interest on the division's assets. In this question, we are given Darwin's operating income and imputed interest rate, but Darwin's assets must be derived using sales and capital turnover, as shown below.

$$\text{Capital turnover} = \frac{\text{Sales of division}}{\text{Invested capital of division}}$$

$$4 = \frac{\$400,000}{x}$$

$$x = \frac{\$400,000}{4} = \$100,000$$

Since Darwin's invested capital is $100,000, its operating income is $40,000, and interest is imputed at 10%, residual income is calculated as follows:

$$\text{RI} = \frac{\text{Division}}{\text{net income}} - \frac{\text{Imputed interest on}}{\text{investment}}$$

RI = $40,000 – ($100,000 × 10%)
RI = $30,000

29. **(d)** Residual income is income minus an imputed interest charge for invested capital. Residual income will be maximized as long as the division earns a rate of return that exceeds the imputed charge. Division A's project will earn a rate of return **greater** than the imputed interest charge, so this project should be accepted. Division B's project will earn a rate of return **less** than the imputed interest charge, so this project should not be accepted.

30. **(b)** The DuPont formula is used to calculate return on investment.

$$\underset{\text{turnover}}{\text{Asset}} \times \underset{\text{sales}}{\begin{array}{c}\text{Income as a}\\ \text{percentage of}\end{array}} = \underset{\substack{\text{(ROI)}}}{\begin{array}{c}\text{Return on}\\ \text{investment}\end{array}}$$

$$\frac{\text{Revenue}}{\text{Invested capital}} \times \frac{\text{Income}}{\text{Revenue}} = \frac{\text{Income}}{\text{Invested capital}}$$

The combination of changes which will maximize return on investment are to increase both asset turnover and income as a percentage of sales, since multiplying two larger numbers will result in a larger product.

31. **(b)** The requirement is to identify why residual income is preferred over return on investment as a performance evaluation technique. Answer (b) is correct because the focus on return on investment can cause high-performing divisions not to invest in projects that are in the best interest of the overall organization. Answer (a) is incorrect because both techniques can measure results for a single period. Answer (c) is incorrect because the imputed interest rate and the target rate should be the same. Answer (d) is incorrect because the investment level should be computed on the same basis.

Value-Based Management: EVA

32. **(c)** The requirement is to identify the major disadvantage of using EVA alone. Answer (c) is correct because many times value creation activities do not immediately increase return, and EVA (in the short run) does not reflect the value of these activities. Answer (a) is incorrect because a major advantage of EVA is its focus on creating shareholder value. Answer (b) is incorrect because EVA does not promote the acceptance of unprofitable projects. Answer (d) is incorrect because EVA encourages cost cutting activities.

33. **(d)** The requirement is to calculate EVA. Answer (d) is correct because EVA is equal to Operating profit after taxes – Cost of invested capital. Net operating profit after taxes is equal to Net operating profit before taxes multiplied by one minus the tax rate, or $25,000,000 [$31,250,000 × (1 – .20)]. Accordingly, EVA is equal to $17,000,000 [$25,000,000 – ($80,000,000 × 10%)].

34. **(c)** The requirement is to calculate free cash flow. Answer (c) is correct because free cash flow is equal to Net operating profit after taxes + Depreciation expense – Change in net working capital – Capital expenditures. Therefore, free cash flow is equal to $21,000,000 ($25,000,000 + $9,000,000 – $5,000,000 – $8,000,000).

35. **(b)** The requirement is to calculate EVA for the division. Answer (b) is correct because EVA is calculated as net operating profit after taxes (NOPAT) minus the capital charge on invested capital. In this case, NOPAT is equal to net operating profit before interest and taxes ($30,000,000) minus taxes ($30,000,000 × 40%), which is

equal to $18,000,000. EVA is then equal to $13,000,000 [$18,000,000 – ($50,000,000 × 10%)].

36. **(b)** The requirement is to calculate economic value added. The formula for EVA is Net operating profit after taxes – Cost of invested capital.

EVA would be computed as follows:

Net operating profit after taxes	$36,000,000
– Capital charge on invested capital ($100,000,000 × 10%)	(10,000,000)
= Economic value added	$26,000,000

37. **(c)** The requirement is to calculate free cash flow. Free cash flow would be computed as follows:

Net operating profit after taxes	$36,000,000
+ Depreciation expense	15,000,000
– Change in net working capital	(10,000,000)
– Capital expenditures	(12,000,000)
Free cash flow	$29,000,000

Traditional Financial Statement Analysis

38. **(d)** The requirement is to identify the ratio that does not measure asset utilization. Answer (d) is correct because the debt to total assets ratio is a debt utilization (financial leverage) ratio. Answers (a), (b), and (c) are incorrect because they are asset utilization ratios.

39. **(c)** The requirement is to identify the nature of benchmarking with other firms. Answer (c) is correct because cross-sectional analysis involves comparing results and ratios to those of other firms in the same industry. Answer (a) is incorrect because horizontal analysis involves comparisons of results and ratios for the same firm over time. Answer (b) is incorrect because vertical analysis involves comparisons of relationships in a firm's financial statements for a single year. Answer (d) is incorrect because ratio analysis does not imply any particular comparison.

40. **(d)** The requirement is to calculate the expected dividend per share. Earnings after interest is equal to $30 million ($35 million – $5 million). Net earnings after taxes is equal to $18 million [$30 million × 1 – Tax rate (40%)]. The net earnings after dividends to preferred shareholders is equal to $14 million ($18 million – $4 million), and the dividend for common stockholders is equal to $4,200,000 ($14 million × 30%). The dividend per share is equal to $4,200,000/$2 million shares = $2.10. Therefore, the correct answer is (d).

41. **(b)** The requirement is to calculate the market price from the earnings per share and price/earnings ratio. Net earnings is equal to $18 million ($35 million – $5 million) × (1 – 40%). Net earnings available to common stockholders is equal to $14 million ($18 million – $4 million). Earnings per share is equal to $14 million/2 million shares, or $7.00. Therefore, the estimated market price would be $7.00 × 8 = $56, or answer (b).

42. **(b)** The requirement is to calculate the debt-to-total-asset ratio. Answer (b) is correct. The debt-to-total-asset ratio is calculated by dividing total debt by total assets. Therefore, the debt-to-total-asset ratio is equal to 0.315 ($78,000 current liabilities + $75,000 long-term debt) ÷ ($210,000 current assets + $275,000 noncurrent assets). Answers (a), (c), and (d) are incorrect because the computations are not correct.

43. **(d)** The requirement is to calculate accounts receivable turnover. Answer (d) is correct. Accounts receivable turnover is calculated by dividing total credit sales by the average balance of accounts receivable. The average balance of accounts receivable is $85,000 [($100,000 + $70,000) ÷ 2]. Therefore, accounts receivable turnover is equal to 4.118 ($350,000 credit sales ÷ $85,000 average accounts receivable).

44. **(a)** The requirement is to calculate inventory turnover. Answer (d) is correct. Inventory turnover is calculated by dividing cost of goods sold by average inventory. Average inventory is equal to $75,000 [($70,000 + $80,0000) ÷ 2]. Therefore, inventory turnover is equal to 2.133 ($160,000 ÷ $75,000).

45. **(b)** The requirement is to calculate total asset turnover. Answer (b) is correct. Total asset turnover is calculated by dividing sales by average total assets. Average total assets is equal to $460,000 = [($210,000 + $275,000) + ($180,000 + $255,000)] ÷ 2. Therefore, total asset turnover is equal to 0.761 ($350,000 ÷ $460,000).

46. **(c)** The requirement is to calculate return on total assets. Answer (c) is correct. Return on assets is calculated by dividing net income by average total assets. As determined in the previous question, average total assets is equal to $460,000. Net income is equal to $72,000 ($350,000 sales – $160,000 cost of goods sold – $3,000 interest expense – $48,000 income taxes – $67,000 administrative expense). Therefore, return on assets is equal to 0.157 ($72,000 ÷ $460,000), or 15.7%.

47. **(c)** The requirement is to determine the effect of payment of an account payable. Answer (c) is correct. The quick ratio is equal to quick assets divided by current liabilities and the current ratio is equal to current assets divided by current liabilities. Since we are told that quick assets exceed current liabilities, both ratios are greater than one. With a ratio greater than one if you reduce the numerator and denominator by an equal amount, the ratio will increase.

48. **(b)** The requirement is to determine the effect of a purchase of raw materials on account. The correct answer is (b). Since we know that the current ratio is greater than one, an increase in the numerator and the denominator by an equal amount will decrease the ratio. Answers (c) and (d) are incorrect because working capital will not change.

49. **(d)** The requirement is to determine the effect of the collection of accounts receivable. Answer (d) is correct. Collection of accounts receivable has no effect on the quick or current ratio because both cash and accounts receivable are part of the numerator of both ratios.

50. **(d)** The requirement is to determine the effect of writing off inventory. Answer (d) is correct because a write-off of inventory will decrease the current ratio. Answers (a) and (b) are incorrect because inventory is not used in computing the quick ratio. Answer (c) is incorrect because working capital will be decreased.

51. **(a)** The requirement is to determine the effect of a five-for-one stock split. Answer (a) is correct because a stock split increases the number of shares outstanding and, therefore, reduces the book value per share. Answers (c) and (d) are incorrect because the transaction does not affect total stockholders' equity.

52. **(d)** The requirement is to determine the effect of issuing serial bonds in exchange for an office building. Answer (d) is correct because the first installment is a current liability which affects the quick ratio, the current ratio, and working capital.

53. **(b)** The requirement is to determine the effect of liquidating a long-term note with cash. Answer (b) is correct. Cash is included in the numerator of both the quick and current ratios. However, a reduction in cash affects the quick ratio more than the current ratio because it is smaller.

Benchmarking and Best Practices

54. **(b)** The requirement is to identify the definition of benchmarking outside of the firm's industry. Answer (b) is correct because generic benchmarking involves benchmarking to the best practices regardless of the industry. Answer (a) is incorrect because internal benchmarking involves benchmarking within the firm. Answer (c) is incorrect because competitor benchmarking involves benchmarking against direct competitors. Answer (d) is incorrect because functional benchmarking involves benchmarking within the same broad industry.

55. **(d)** All of these nonfinancial measures would be useful in evaluating the performance of a manufacturing system. Throughput (cycle) time measures the total amount of production time required per unit. This measure is important to assess the timeliness of the production process, which is required for on-time delivery of goods. The proportion of total production time consumed by setup activities reflects one aspect of production efficiency. Setup time represents money spent on a non-value-adding activity, and thus should be minimized as much as possible. The proportion of total units completed which require rework is a useful measure of product quality. An excessive rate of rework alerts management that it needs to examine its quality control procedures.

Quality Control Principles

56. **(b)** The requirement is to identify which tool is used to identify frequency of defects. Answer (b) is correct because a Pareto chart ranks the causes of process variations by the degree of impact on quality. Answer (a) is incorrect because a control chart is a statistical plot that helps to detect deviations before they generate defects. Answer (c) is incorrect because a cause-and-effect diagram is used to identify the potential causes of defects. Answer (d) is incorrect because a fishbone diagram is an alternative name for cause-and-effect diagrams.

57. **(c)** The requirement is to select which tool identifies causes of failures or defects. Answer (c) is correct because cause-and-effect diagrams identify causes of failures/defects and can be used to identify the reasons why a process goes out of control. Answer (a) is incorrect because a control chart is a statistical plot that helps to detect deviations before they generate defects. Answer (b) is incorrect because a Pareto diagram indicates how frequently a type of defect may occur. Answer (d) is incorrect because a strategy map is a statement of what the strategy must achieve and what is critical to its success.

58. **(b)** The requirement is to identify the concept of six-sigma quality. Answer (b) is correct because six-sigma is a statistical measure expressing how close a product comes to its quality goal. Six-sigma is 99.999997% perfect with 3.4 defects per million parts.

59. **(b)** The requirement is to identify the terms used to identify continuous improvement. Answer (b), Kaizen, is correct because it is the Japanese art of continuous improvement. It underlies the total quality management and JIT business techniques. Answer (a) is incorrect because the theory of constraints is a method to maximize operating income when faced with some bottleneck operations. Answer (c) is incorrect because six-sigma is a statistical measure expressing how close a product comes to its quality goal. Six-sigma is 3.4 defects per million parts. Answer (d) is incorrect because lean manufacturing is an operational strategy focused on achieving the shortest possible cycle time by eliminating waste.

60. **(a)** The requirement is to identify a component of the theory of constraints. Answer (a) is correct because a bottleneck is any resource or operation where the capacity is less than the demand placed upon it. Answers (b), (c), and (d) are incorrect because they are not components of the theory of constraints.

61. **(a)** The requirement is to compute throughput contribution per unit. Answer (a) is correct because throughput contribution per unit is equal to revenue minus direct materials. Thus, throughput contribution per unit is equal to $150 (revenue per unit) – $45 (Cutting direct materials) – $15 (Finishing direct materials) = $90. Answers (b), (c), and (d) are incorrect because they represent incorrect computations of throughput contribution per unit.

62. **(c)** The requirement is to identify the three basic measurements used by the Theory of Constraints. Answer (c) is correct because the Theory of Constraints focuses on throughput contribution, investment (or inventory), and operational expense (operating costs). Answers (a), (b), and (d) are incorrect because they represent other types of performance measures.

63. **(a)** The requirement is to describe the objectives of the theory of constraints (TOC). The objective of TOC is to increase *throughput contribution* while decreasing *investment* and *operating costs*. **Throughput contribution** is revenues minus the direct materials cost of goods sold. **Investment** is the sum of materials cost in direct materials; work in process and finished goods inventories; research and development costs; and the costs of equipment and buildings. **Operating costs** include salaries and wages, rental expense, utilities, and depreciation.

Cost of Quality

64. **(a)** The requirement is to identify the nature of quality circles. Answer (a) is correct because quality circles are designed to develop ways to prevent defects. Answer (b) is incorrect because appraisal costs are related to inspecting and testing to ensure product acceptability. Answer (c) is incorrect because internal failure involves the costs of finding defective units before they are shipped to customers. Answer (d) is incorrect because external failure is the cost of defects that reach the customer.

65. **(c)** The requirement is to identify the item which reflects the internal failure component. An internal failure cost is a cost incurred when substandard products are produced but discovered before shipment to the customer. Reworking defective parts is an example of an internal failure. Answer (a) is incorrect because it is an example of an appraisal cost. Answer (b) is incorrect because it is an exam-

ple of a prevention cost. Answer (d) is incorrect because it is an example of an external failure cost.

66. **(b)** The requirement is to identify the item which reflects the prevention cost component. A prevention cost is a cost incurred to prevent defects. These costs include the cost to identify the cause of the defect, take corrective action to eliminate the cause, train people, and redesign the product or the production process. Answer (b) is correct because it is an example of a quality activity designed to do the job right the first time. Answer (a) is incorrect because it is an example of an appraisal cost. Answer (c) is incorrect because it is an example of an internal failure cost. Answer (d) is incorrect because it is an example of an external failure cost.

67. **(a)** The requirement is to identify where to incur costs to prevent product recalls. Answer (a) is correct because spending funds to prevent defects is generally most cost effective.

68. **(b)** The requirement is to identify how costs incurred to detect nonconforming units are classified. Answer (b) is correct because appraisal costs are costs associated with quality control and include testing and inspection. Answer (a) is incorrect because prevention costs involve any quality activity designed to do the job right the first time. Answer (c) is incorrect because internal failures occur when substandard products are produced but discovered before shipment to the customer. Answer (d) is incorrect because external failure costs are incurred for products that do not meet requirements of the customer and have been shipped to the customer.

MULTIPLE-CHOICE QUESTIONS (1-57)

1. The following information was taken from Kay Company's accounting records for the year ended December 31, 2009:

Increase in raw materials inventory	$ 15,000
Decrease in finished goods inventory	35,000
Raw materials purchased	430,000
Direct manufacturing labor payroll	200,000
Factory overhead	300,000
Freight-out	45,000

There was no work in process inventory at the beginning or end of the year. Kay's 2009 cost of goods sold is

- a. $950,000
- b. $965,000
- c. $975,000
- d. $995,000

Items 2 through 4 are based on the following information pertaining to Arp Co.'s manufacturing operations:

Inventories	3/1/09	3/31/09
Direct materials	$36,000	$30,000
Work in process	18,000	12,000
Finished goods	54,000	72,000

Additional information for the month of March 2009:

Direct materials purchased	$84,000
Direct manufacturing labor payroll	60,000
Direct manufacturing labor rate per hour	7.50
Factory overhead rate per direct labor hour	10.00

2. For the month of March 2009, prime cost was
- a. $ 90,000
- b. $120,000
- c. $144,000
- d. $150,000

3. For the month of March 2009, conversion cost was
- a. $ 90,000
- b. $140,000
- c. $144,000
- d. $170,000

4. For the month of March 2009, cost of goods manufactured was
- a. $218,000
- b. $224,000
- c. $230,000
- d. $236,000

5. During the month of March 2009, Nale Co. used $300,000 of direct material. At March 31, 2009, Nale's direct materials inventory was $50,000 more than it was at March 1, 2009. Direct material purchases during the month of March 2009 amounted to
- a. $0
- b. $250,000
- c. $300,000
- d. $350,000

6. Fab Co. manufactures textiles. Among Fab's 2009 manufacturing costs were the following salaries and wages:

Loom operators	$120,000
Factory foreman	45,000
Machine mechanics	30,000

What was the amount of Fab's 2009 direct manufacturing labor?

- a. $195,000
- b. $165,000
- c. $150,000
- d. $120,000

7. The fixed portion of the semivariable cost of electricity for a manufacturing plant is a

	Period cost	Product cost
a.	Yes	No
b.	Yes	Yes
c.	No	Yes
d.	No	No

8. Gram Co. develops computer programs to meet customers' special requirements. How should Gram categorize payments to employees who develop these programs?

	Direct costs	Value-added costs
a.	Yes	Yes
b.	Yes	No
c.	No	No
d.	No	Yes

9. In a job-costing system, issuing indirect materials to production increases which account?
- a. Materials control.
- b. Work in process control.
- c. Manufacturing overhead control.
- d. Manufacturing overhead allocated.

10. Costs are accumulated by responsibility center for control purposes when using

	Job order costing	Process costing
a.	Yes	Yes
b.	Yes	No
c.	No	No
d.	No	Yes

11. Birk Co. uses a job order cost system. The following debits (credit) appeared in Birk's work in process account for the month of April 2009:

April	Description	Amount
1	Balance	$ 4,000
30	Direct materials	24,000
30	Direct manufacturing labor	16,000
30	Factory overhead	12,800
30	To finished goods	(48,000)

Birk applies overhead to production at a predetermined rate of 80% of direct manufacturing labor costs. Job No. 5, the only job still in process on April 30, 2009, has been charged with direct manufacturing labor of $2,000. What was the amount of direct materials charged to Job No. 5?

- a. $ 3,000
- b. $ 5,200
- c. $ 8,800
- d. $24,000

12. In a job cost system, manufacturing overhead is

	An indirect cost of jobs	A necessary element in production
a.	No	Yes
b.	No	No
c.	Yes	Yes
d.	Yes	No

13. Under Pick Co.'s job order costing system manufacturing overhead is applied to work in process using a predetermined annual overhead rate. During January 2009, Pick's transactions included the following:

Direct materials issued to production	$ 90,000
Indirect materials issued to production	8,000
Manufacturing overhead incurred	125,000
Manufacturing overhead applied	113,000
Direct labor costs	107,000

Pick had neither beginning nor ending work in process inventory. What was the cost of jobs completed in January 2009?

a. $302,000
b. $310,000
c. $322,000
d. $330,000

14. A direct manufacturing labor overtime premium should be charged to a specific job when the overtime is caused by the

a. Increased overall level of activity.
b. Customer's requirement for early completion of job.
c. Management's failure to include the job in the production schedule.
d. Management's requirement that the job be completed before the annual factory vacation closure.

*15. A company services office equipment. Some customers bring their equipment to the company's service shop; other customers prefer to have the company's service personnel come to their offices to repair their equipment. The most appropriate costing method for the company is

a. A job order costing system.
b. An activity-based costing system.
c. A process costing system.
d. An operations costing system.

16. In developing a predetermined variable factory overhead application rate for use in a process costing system, which of the following could be used in the numerator and denominator?

	Numerator	*Denominator*
a.	Actual variable factory overhead	Actual machine hours
b.	Actual variable factory overhead	Estimated machine hours
c.	Estimated variable factory overhead	Actual machine hours
d.	Estimated variable factory overhead	Estimated machine hours

17. A job order cost system uses a predetermined fixed factory overhead rate based on normal activity and expected fixed cost. At the end of the year, underapplied fixed overhead might be explained by which of the following situations?

	Actual volume	*Actual fixed costs*
a.	Greater than normal	Greater than expected
b.	Greater than normal	Less than expected
c.	Less than normal	Greater than expected
d.	Less than normal	Less than expected

18. Worley Company has underapplied variable overhead of $45,000 for the year ended December 31, 2009. Before disposition of the underapplied overhead, selected December 31, 2009, balances from Worley's accounting records are as follows:

Sales	$1,200,000
Cost of goods sold	720,000
Inventories:	
Direct materials	36,000
Work in process	54,000
Finished goods	90,000

Under Worley's cost accounting system, over- or underapplied variable overhead is allocated to appropriate inventories and cost of goods sold based on year-end balances. There are no amounts of under or overapplied fixed overhead. In its 2009 income statement, Worley should report cost of goods sold of

a. $682,500
b. $684,000
c. $756,000
d. $757,500

19. Parat College allocates support department costs to its individual schools using the step method. Information for May 2009 is as follows:

	Support departments	
	Maintenance	*Power*
Costs incurred	$99,000	$54,000
Service percentages provided to:		
Maintenance	--	10%
Power	20%	--
School of Education	30%	20%
School of Technology	50%	70%
	100%	100%

What is the amount of May 2009 support department costs allocated to the School of Education?

a. $40,500
b. $42,120
c. $46,100
d. $49,125

20. Kerner Manufacturing uses a process cost system to manufacture laptop computers. The following information summarizes operations relating to laptop computer model #KJK20 during the quarter ending March 31:

	Units	*Direct Materials*
Work in process inventory, January 1	100	$70,000
Started during the quarter	500	
Completed during the quarter	400	
Work-in-process inventory, March 31	200	
Costs added during the quarter		$750,000

Beginning work in process inventory was 50% complete for direct materials. Ending work in process inventory was 75% complete for direct materials. What were the equivalent units of production with regard to materials for March using the FIFO unit cost, inventory valuation method?

a. 450
b. 500
c. 550
d. 600

21. Kerner Manufacturing uses a process cost system to manufacture laptop computers. The following information summarizes operations relating to laptop computer model #KJK20 during the quarter ending March 31:

---
* *CIA adapted*

	Units	Direct Materials
Work in process inventory, January 1	100	$50,000
Started during the quarter	500	
Completed during the quarter	400	
Work in process inventory, March 31	200	
Costs added during the quarter		$720,000

Beginning work in process inventory was 50% complete for direct materials. Ending work in process inventory was 75% complete for direct materials. What is the total value of material costs in ending work in process inventory using the FIFO unit cost, inventory valuation method?

a. $183,000
b. $194,000
c. $210,000
d. $216,000

22. In a process cost system, the application of factory overhead usually would be recorded as an increase in

a. Finished goods inventory control.
b. Factory overhead control.
c. Cost of goods sold.
d. Work in process inventory control.

23. The following information pertains to Lap Co.'s Palo Division for the month of April:

	Number of units	Cost of materials
Beginning work in process	15,000	$ 5,500
Started in April	40,000	18,000
Units completed	42,500	
Ending work in process	12,500	

All materials are added at the beginning of the process. Using the weighted-average method, the cost per equivalent unit for materials is

a. $0.59
b. $0.55
c. $0.45
d. $0.43

24. The Forming Department is the first of a two-stage production process. Spoilage is identified when the units have completed the Forming process. Costs of spoiled units are assigned to units completed and transferred to the second department in the period spoilage is identified. The following information concerns Forming's conversion costs in May 2009:

	Units	Conversion costs
Beginning work in process (50% complete)	2,000	$10,000
Units started during May	8,000	75,500
Spoilage—normal	500	
Units completed and transferred	7,000	
Ending work in process (80% complete)	2,500	

Using the weighted-average method, what was Forming's conversion cost transferred to the second production department?

a. $59,850
b. $64,125
c. $67,500
d. $71,250

25. In computing the current period's manufacturing cost per equivalent unit, the FIFO method of process costing considers current period costs

a. Only.
b. Plus cost of beginning work in process inventory.

c. Less cost of beginning work in process inventory.
d. Plus cost of ending work in process inventory.

26. In process 2, material G is added when a batch is 60% complete. Ending work in process units, which are 50% complete, would be included in the computation of equivalent units for

	Conversion costs	Material G
a.	Yes	No
b.	No	Yes
c.	No	No
d.	Yes	Yes

27. A process costing system was used for a department that began operations in January 2009. Approximately the same number of physical units, at the same degree of completion, were in work in process at the end of both January and February. Monthly conversion costs are allocated between ending work in process and units completed. Compared to the FIFO method, would the weighted-average method use the same or a greater number of equivalent units to calculate the monthly allocations?

Equivalent units for weighted-average compared to FIFO

	January	February
a.	Same	Same
b.	Greater number	Greater number
c.	Greater number	Same
d.	Same	Greater number

28. A department adds material at the beginning of a process and identifies defective units when the process is 40% complete. At the beginning of the period, there was no work in process. At the end of the period, the number of work in process units equaled the number of units transferred to finished goods. If all units in ending work in process were 66 2/3% complete, then ending work in process should be allocated

a. 50% of all normal defective unit costs.
b. 40% of all normal defective unit costs.
c. 50% of the material costs and 40% of the conversion costs of all normal defective unit costs.
d. None of the normal defective unit costs.

29. In its April 2009 production, Hern Corp., which does not use a standard cost system, incurred total production costs of $900,000, of which Hern attributed $60,000 to normal spoilage and $30,000 to abnormal spoilage. Hern should account for this spoilage as

a. Period cost of $90,000.
b. Inventoriable cost of $90,000.
c. Period cost of $60,000 and inventoriable cost of $30,000.
d. Inventoriable cost of $60,000 and period cost of $30,000.

Items 30 through 37 are based on the following:

Kimbeth Manufacturing uses a process cost system to manufacture Dust Density Sensors for the mining industry. The following information pertains to operations for the month of May 2009:

	Units
Beginning work in process inventory, May 1	16,000
Started in production during May	100,000
Completed production during May	92,000
Ending work in process inventory, May 31	24,000

The beginning inventory was 60% complete for materials and 20% complete for conversion costs. The ending inventory was 90% complete for materials and 40% complete for conversion costs.

Costs pertaining to the month of May are as follows:

- The beginning inventory costs are: materials, $54,560; direct labor, $20,320; and factory overhead, $15,240.
- Costs incurred during May are: materials used, $468,000; direct labor, $182,880; and factory overhead, $391,160.

**30. Using the first-in, first-out (FIFO) method, the equivalent units of production for materials are
- a.   97,600 units.
- b.   104,000 units.
- c.   107,200 units.
- d.   108,000 units.

**31. Using the FIFO method, the equivalent units of production for conversion costs are
- a.   85,600 units.
- b.   88,800 units.
- c.   95,200 units.
- d.   98,400 units.

**32. Using the FIFO method, the equivalent unit cost of materials for May is
- a. $4.12
- b. $4.50
- c. $4.60
- d. $4.80

**33. Using the FIFO method, the equivalent unit conversion cost for May is
- a. $5.65
- b. $5.83
- c. $6.00
- d. $6.20

**34. Using the FIFO method, the total cost of units in the ending work in process inventory at May 31 is
- a. $153,168
- b. $145,800
- c. $155,328
- d. $156,960

**35. Using the weighted-average method, the equivalent unit cost of materials for May is
- a. $4.12
- b. $4.50
- c. $4.60
- d. $5.03

**36. Using the weighted-average method, the equivalent unit conversion cost for May is
- a. $5.65
- b. $5.83
- c. $6.00
- d. $6.41

**37. Using the weighted-average method, the total cost of the units in the ending work in process inventory at May 31 is
- a. $ 86,400
- b. $154,800

- c. $155,328
- d. $156,960

*38. Which of the following would be a reasonable basis for allocating the material handling costs to the units produced in an activity-based costing system?
- a.   Number of production runs per year.
- b.   Number of components per completed unit.
- c.   Amount of time required to produce one unit.
- d.   Amount of overhead applied to each completed unit.

*39. An assembly plant accumulates its variable and fixed manufacturing overhead costs in a single cost pool which are then applied to work in process using a single application base. The assembly plant management wants to estimate the magnitude of the total manufacturing overhead costs for different volume levels of the application activity base using a flexible budget formula. If there is an increase in the application activity base that is within the relevant range of activity for the assembly plant, which one of the following relationships regarding variable and fixed costs is correct?
- a.   The variable cost per unit is constant, and the total fixed costs decrease.
- b.   The variable cost per unit is constant, and the total fixed costs increase.
- c.   The variable cost per unit and the total fixed costs remain constant.
- d.   The variable cost per unit increases, and the total fixed costs remain constant.

*40. In Belk Co.'s just-in-time production system, costs per setup were reduced from $28 to $2. In the process of reducing inventory levels, Belk found that there were fixed facility and administrative costs that previously had not been included in the carrying cost calculation. The result was an increase from $8 to $32 per unit per year. What were the effects of these changes on Belk's economic lot size and relevant costs?

	Lot size	Relevant costs
a.	Decrease	Increase
b.	Increase	Decrease
c.	Increase	Increase
d.	Decrease	Decrease

41. What is the normal effect on the numbers of cost pools and allocation bases when an activity-based cost (ABC) system replaces a traditional cost system?

	Cost pools	Allocation bases
a.	No effect	No effect
b.	Increase	No effect
c.	No effect	Increase
d.	Increase	Increase

42. Which of the following is true about activity-based costing?
- a.   It should not be used with process or job costing.
- b.   It can be used only with process costing.
- c.   It can be used only with job costing.
- d.   It can be used with either process or job costing.

43. In an activity-based costing system, what should be used to assign a department's manufacturing overhead costs to products produced in varying lot sizes?
- a.   A single cause-and-effect relationship.
- b.   Multiple cause-and-effect relationships.

---

* CIA adapted
** CMA adapted

c.   Relative net sales values of the products.
d.   A product's ability to bear cost allocations.

44. In an activity-based costing system, cost reduction is accomplished by identifying and eliminating

	All cost drivers	Non-value-adding activities
a.	No	No
b.	Yes	Yes
c.	No	Yes
d.	Yes	No

45. Nile Co.'s cost allocation and product costing procedures follow activity-based costing principles. Activities have been identified and classified as being either value-adding or non-value-adding as to each product. Which of the following activities, used in Nile production process, is non-value-adding?
a.   Design engineering activity.
b.   Heat treatment activity.
c.   Drill press activity.
d.   Raw materials storage activity.

46. Hoger Corporation accumulated the following cost information for its two products, A and B:

	A	B	Total
Production volume	2,000	1,000	
Total direct man. labor hrs.	5,000	20,000	25,000
Setup cost per batch	$ 1,000	$ 2,000	
Batch size	100	50	
Total setup costs incurred	$20,000	$40,000	$60,000
DMLH per unit	2	1	

A traditional costing system would allocate setup costs on the basis of DMLH. An ABC system would trace costs by spreading the costs per batch over the units in a batch. What is the setup cost per unit of product A under each costing system?

	Traditional	ABC
a.	$4.80	$10.00
b.	$2.40	$10.00
c.	$40.00	$200.00
d.	$4.80	$20.00

47. Lane Co. produces main products Kul and Wu. The process also yields by-product Zef. Net realizable value of by-product Zef is subtracted from joint production cost of Kul and Wu. The following information pertains to production in July 2009 at a joint cost of $54,000:

Product	Units produced	Market value	Additional cost after split-off
Kul	1,000	$40,000	$ 0
Wu	1,500	35,000	0
Zef	500	7,000	3,000

If Lane uses the net realizable value method for allocating joint cost, how much of the joint cost should be allocated to product Kul?
a. $18,800
b. $20,000
c. $26,667
d. $27,342

48. The diagram below represents the production and sales relationships of joint products P and Q. Joint costs are incurred until split-off, then separable costs are incurred in refining each product. Market values of P and Q at split-off are used to allocate joint costs.

If the market value of P at split-off increases and all other costs and selling prices remain unchanged, then the gross margin of

	P	Q
a.	Increases	Decreases
b.	Increases	Increases
c.	Decreases	Decreases
d.	Decreases	Increases

49. For purposes of allocating joint costs to joint products, the sales price at point of sale, reduced by cost to complete after split-off, is assumed to be equal to the
a.   Joint costs.
b.   Total costs.
c.   Net sales value at split-off.
d.   Sales price less a normal profit margin at point of sale.

50. Mig Co., which began operations in 2009, produces gasoline and a gasoline by-product. The following information is available pertaining to 2009 sales and production:

Total production costs to split-off point	$120,000
Gasoline sales	270,000
By-product sales	30,000
Gasoline inventory, 12/31/09	15,000
Additional by-product costs:	
Marketing	10,000
Production	15,000

Mig accounts for the by-product at the time of production. What are Mig's 2009 cost of sales for gasoline and the by-product?

	Gasoline	By-product
a.	$105,000	$25,000
b.	$115,000	$0
c.	$108,000	$37,000
d.	$100,000	$0

51. The following information pertains to a by-product called Moy:

Sales in 2009	5,000 units
Selling price per unit	$6
Selling costs per unit	2
Processing costs	0

Inventory of Moy was recorded at net realizable value when produced in 2008. No units of Moy were produced in 2009. What amount should be recognized as profit on Moy's 2009 sales?
a. $0
b. $10,000
c. $20,000
d. $30,000

52. Kode Co. manufactures a major product that gives rise to a by-product called May. May's only separable cost is a $1 selling cost when a unit is sold for $4. Kode accounts for May's sales by deducting the $3 net amount from the cost of goods sold of the major product. There are no inventories. If Kode were to change its method of accounting for May

from a by-product to a joint product, what would be the effect on Kode's overall gross margin?
- a. No effect.
- b. Gross margin increases by $1 for each unit of May sold.
- c. Gross margin increases by $3 for each unit of May sold.
- d. Gross margin increases by $4 for each unit of May sold.

53. In accounting for by-products, the value of the by-product may be recognized at the time of

	Production	Sale
a.	Yes	Yes
b.	Yes	No
c.	No	No
d.	No	Yes

54. Day Mail Order Co. applied the high-low method of cost estimation to customer order data for the first four months of 2009. What is the estimated variable order filling cost component per order?

Month	Orders	Cost
January	1,200	$ 3,120
February	1,300	3,185
March	1,800	4,320
April	1,700	3,895
	6,000	$14,520

- a. $2.00
- b. $2.42
- c. $2.48
- d. $2.50

55. Sender, Inc. estimates parcel mailing costs using data shown on the chart below.

What is Sender's estimated cost for mailing 12,000 parcels?
- a. $36,000
- b. $45,000
- c. $51,000
- d. $60,000

56. Which of the following may be used to estimate how inventory warehouse costs are affected by both the number of shipments and the weight of materials handled?
- a. Economic order quantity analysis.
- b. Probability analysis.
- c. Correlation analysis.
- d. Multiple regression analysis.

57. Sago Co. uses regression analysis to develop a model for predicting overhead costs. Two different cost drivers (machine hours and direct materials weight) are under consideration as the independent variable. Relevant data were run on a computer using one of the standard regression programs, with the following results:

	Coefficient
Machine hours	
Y Intercept	2,500
B	5.0
$R^2 = .70$	
Direct materials weight	
Y Intercept	4,600
B	2.6
$R^2 = .50$	

What regression equation should be used?
- a. $Y = 2,500 + 5.0X$
- b. $Y = 2,500 + 3.5X$
- c. $Y = 4,600 + 2.6X$
- d. $Y = 4,600 + 1.3X$

MULTIPLE-CHOICE ANSWERS

1. a __ __	13. b __ __	25. a __ __	37. d __ __	49. c __ __
2. d __ __	14. b __ __	26. a __ __	38. b __ __	50. d __ __
3. b __ __	15 a __ __	27. d __ __	39. c __ __	51. a __ __
4. d __ __	16. d __ __	28. a __ __	40. d __ __	52. b __ __
5. d __ __	17. c __ __	29. d __ __	41. d __ __	53. a __ __
6. d __ __	18. d __ __	30. b __ __	42. d __ __	54. a __ __
7. c __ __	19. c __ __	31. d __ __	43. b __ __	55. c __ __
8. a __ __	20. b __ __	32. b __ __	44. c __ __	56. d __ __
9. c __ __	21. d __ __	33. b __ __	45. d __ __	57. a __ __
10. a __ __	22. d __ __	34. a __ __	46. a __ __	
11. b __ __	23. d __ __	35. c __ __	47. c __ __	1st: __/57 = __%
12. c __ __	24. c __ __	36. c __ __	48. d __ __	2nd: __/57 = __%

MULTIPLE-CHOICE ANSWER EXPLANATIONS

A. Cost of Goods Manufactured

1.   (a)   Three computations must be performed: raw materials used, cost of goods manufactured, and cost of goods sold.

(1)	Raw materials purchased	$430,000
	Less: Increase in raw materials inventory	15,000
	Raw materials used	$415,000
(2)	Beginning WIP	--
	Raw materials used (from above)	415,000
	Direct manufacturing labor	200,000
	Factory overhead	300,000
	Cost to account for	$915,000
	Less: Ending WIP	--
	Cost of goods manufactured	$915,000
(3)	Cost of goods manufactured	$915,000
	Add: Decrease in finished goods inventory	35,000
	Cost of goods sold	$950,000

The increase in raw materials inventory represents the amount of inventory that was purchased but was not used. Therefore, this increase must be subtracted from raw materials purchased to determine the amount of raw materials used. Work in process inventory is an adjustment in arriving at cost of goods manufactured (as shown above). For this question no adjustment is necessary because Kay has no work in process inventory. The decrease in finished goods inventory represents the amount of inventory that was sold in excess of the inventory manufactured during the current period. Therefore, this amount must be added to cost of goods manufactured to determine cost of goods sold. The freight-out of $45,000 is irrelevant for this question because freight-out is a selling expense and thus, would not be used in computing cost of goods sold.

2.   (d)   Prime cost is the sum of direct materials and direct manufacturing labor. Direct manufacturing labor is $60,000. Direct materials used must be computed. The solutions approach is to enter the information given into the materials T-account and solve for the unknown:

Direct Materials Control		
3/1/09 bal.	36,000	
Purchases	84,000	? Materials used
3/30/09	30,000	

Using the T-account above, direct materials used are easily computed as $90,000. Thus, prime cost incurred was $150,000 ($90,000 + $60,000).

3.   (b)   Conversion cost is the sum of direct manufacturing labor ($60,000, as given) and applied factory overhead.

The factory overhead rate per direct manufacturing labor hour is $10.00. To compute the number of direct manufacturing labor hours worked, the direct manufacturing labor payroll ($60,000) is divided by the direct manufacturing labor rate per hour ($7.50), resulting in 8,000 direct manufacturing labor hours. Factory overhead applied is 8,000 hours at $10 per hour, or $80,000. Thus, conversion cost incurred was $140,000 ($60,000 of direct manufacturing labor plus $80,000 of applied factory overhead).

4.   (d)   Cost of goods manufactured (CGM) is the cost of goods completed **and** transferred to finished goods. It is the sum of direct materials used, direct manufacturing labor used, applied factory overhead, and any adjustment for work in process inventories. Direct manufacturing labor used ($60,000) is given. Direct materials used ($90,000) and applied factory overhead ($80,000) were computed in the answers to the two previous questions. Beginning work in process ($18,000) and ending work in process ($12,000) are given. Using this data, CGM can be computed as follows:

BWIP	$ 18,000
DM used	90,000
DML	60,000
OH applied	80,000
Costs to account for	$248,000
EWIP	(12,000)
CGM	$236,000

5.   (d)   To determine Nale's direct materials purchases for the month of March, trace the flow of costs through the direct materials account.

Direct materials			
Beg. bal.	x		
Purchased		$300,000	Used
End. bal.	x + $50,000		

The beginning balance was not given, but the problem states that the ending balance was $50,000 greater. Thus, we can label the beginning balance X and the ending balance X + $50,000. Purchases may be determined as follows:

$$(x + \$50,000) + \$300,000 - x = \$350,000$$

6.   (d)   Direct manufacturing labor costs include all labor costs which can be directly traced to the product in an economically feasible way. All other factory labor is considered indirect manufacturing labor. For Fab Co., the wages of loom operators can be directly traced to the textiles produced. However, the labor cost of factory foremen and machine mechanics are **not** direct manufacturing labor since these workers do not work directly on the product. Thus, answer (d) is correct because the amount of Fab's direct manufacturing labor is the loom operator cost of $120,000.

7.   (c)   Product costs are costs that can be associated with the production of specific revenues. These costs attach to a physical unit and become expenses in the period in which the unit to which they attach is sold. Product costs include direct labor, direct material, and factory overhead. Period costs, on the other hand, cannot be associated with specific revenues and, therefore, become expenses as time passes. Answer (c) is correct because the cost of electricity for a manufacturing plant, whether fixed or variable, is included in factory overhead and, therefore, is a product cost.

8.   (a)   The labor cost incurred to develop computer programs for sale to customers represents both a direct cost and a value-adding cost. The software is the cost object, and direct costs include any costs that are both related to it and which are easily traceable to specific units of production. Value-adding costs are those that cannot be eliminated without the customer perceiving a decline in product quality or performance. Obviously, the computer programmers cannot be eliminated from the software development process, so these payroll costs add value to the product.

9.   (c)   The requirement is to identify the account that is increased when indirect materials are issued to production. Answer (c) is correct because the cost of indirect materials used increases the Manufacturing Overhead Control account and decreases Materials Control. Answer (a) is incorrect because Materials Control is decreased with the transfer. Answer (b) is incorrect because Work in Process Control is increased by costs of direct materials and direct labor and the allocation of manufacturing overhead. Manufacturing Overhead Allocated is credited when overhead is allocated to work in process and debited when it is closed out at the end of the period.

B.   Cost Flows

10.   (a)   A responsibility center is any point within an organization where control exists over cost incurrence, revenue generation, and/or the use of investment funds. A responsibility center can be an operation, a department, a division, or even an individual. The key point to note for this question is that no matter what product costing method is used, the responsibility center is always used for control purposes. In job order costing, costs are accumulated by responsibility center and then assigned to specific jobs or orders through the use of a job cost sheet. Even though the job cost sheet will usually reflect the efforts of a number of responsibility centers, it will not be used for control purposes. Any needed cost control will be handled on the responsibility center level. In process costing, costs are accumulated by the responsibility center and recorded on a production cost report that will be used to develop a product's cost. Since the production cost report shows the efforts of only one responsibility center, it is used for both product costing and control purposes. Thus, for control purposes, costs are accumulated by responsibility center for both job-order and process costing.

C.   Job-Order Costing

11.   (b)   The requirement is to determine the amount of direct materials charged to Job No. 5. The problem states that Job 5 is the only job still in process on April 30, so the total costs charged to this job must equal the ending balance in work in process.

Work in Process Control			
Beg. bal.	4,000		
DM	24,000		
DML	16,000		
O/H	12,800	48,000	To FG
End. bal.	8,800		

The total costs charged to Job 5 are $8,800. Direct manufacturing labor accounts for $2,000 of this figure and overhead accounts for $1,600 ($2,000 DL × 80% O/H rate).

Direct manufacturing labor	$2,000
Factory overhead	1,600
Direct materials	--
Total cost of Job 5	$8,800

The remaining cost of $5,200 [$8,800 – ($2,000 + $1,600)] must be the amount of direct materials.

12.   (c)   Manufacturing overhead is considered an indirect cost because it is not directly traceable to specific jobs, although overhead is a necessary (inevitable) cost of production.

13.   (b)   The requirement is to determine the cost of jobs completed in January 2009. In a job order costing system, manufacturing overhead cannot be traced to specific jobs. Instead, overhead is accumulated in an overhead control account and applied to work performed based on some predetermined overhead rate. The difference between actual and applied overhead is normally either allocated to work in process, finished goods, and cost of goods sold or written off to cost of goods sold. In this case the cost of jobs completed is being determined for January only. Under- or overapplied overhead is not usually considered on a monthly basis. Therefore, the cost of jobs completed should include allocated overhead only. The amount of indirect materials issued to production has already been included in overhead applied. These costs do not need to be considered again in determining the cost of jobs completed. The cost of jobs completed can be computed as follows:

Direct materials issued to production	$ 90,000
Manufacturing overhead applied	113,000
Direct labor costs	107,000
Cost of jobs completed	$310,000

14.   (b)   The requirement is to determine which situation would cause a direct manufacturing labor overtime premium to be charged directly to a specific job. Answer (b) is correct because overtime resulting from a customer's requirement of early completion of a job would result in overtime directly traceable to that job. Answer (a) is incorrect because overtime incurred due to an overall high level of activity should be prorated over all jobs. Since production scheduling is generally at random, a specific job should not be penalized simply because it happened to be scheduled during overtime hours. Answers (c) and (d) are incorrect because the overtime is a result of management inefficiency.

15.   (a)   The requirement is to identify the appropriate type of costing system. Answer (a) is correct because job-order costing systems are designed to accumulate costs for tasks or projects that are unique and nonrepetitive. Service organizations are interested in identifying the costs applicable to each customer and/or each service call. Answer (b) is incorrect because the primary purpose of activity-based costing systems focuses on generating more accurate cost information by costing activities using cost drivers. Answer (c) is incorrect because process costing systems are designed for homogeneous products that are mass produced in continuous production runs. Answer (d) is incorrect because operations costing systems are designed for batches of homogeneous products; operations costing is a hybrid costing method between job-order and process costing.

D. Accounting for Overhead

16. (d)   A variable overhead application rate is commonly called a predetermined variable overhead rate and is computed as follows:

$$\frac{\text{Estimated variable overhead costs}}{\text{Estimated activity level}} = \text{Predetermined variable rate}$$

Estimated figures are used because actual figures are not known at the beginning of a period. Estimated variable overhead (the numerator) is estimated variable overhead costs, and estimated machine hours (the denominator) is an estimated activity level. Actual figures (either overhead costs or activity levels) are not known until the end of the period.

17. (c)   A predetermined factory overhead rate is developed by dividing estimated fixed overhead costs by the normal capacity based on a selected cost driver (DML, cost, machine hours, etc.). Overhead costs are then applied by multiplying the predetermined rate by the actual volume of the cost driver during the period. Overhead costs will be underapplied if (1) overhead costs are underestimated, making the application rate too small (actual costs are larger than expected), or (2) normal capacity is greater than actual activity, making the application rate too small (actual volume is less than normal).

E. Disposition of Under- and Overapplied Overhead

18. (d)   The requirement is to determine the amount of costs of goods sold to be reported on the 2009 income statement. The balance in the cost of goods sold account is $720,000. This amount must be increased by the portion of underapplied variable overhead allocated to cost of goods sold. The underapplied overhead is appropriately allocated to work in process, finished goods, and cost of goods sold. No overhead is allocated to direct materials inventory, since this account contains only the cost of unused materials. The other three accounts contain the cost of materials, labor, and overhead. The amounts to be allocated to work in process, finished goods, and cost of goods sold are determined by each account's relative balance as compared to the total balance in the accounts. The total balance of the three accounts is $864,000 ($720,000 + $54,000 + $90,000). Therefore, the amount allocable to cost of goods sold is [$720,000/$864,000 × ($45,000)] or $37,500. Since variable overhead was underapplied, not enough costs were applied to production during the year. Thus, cost of goods sold is increased to $757,500 ($720,000 + $37,500).

F. Service Department Cost Allocation

19. (c)   The step method of allocating support department costs uses a sequence of allocations which result in partial recognition of services rendered by one support department to another. Total costs of the support department that provides the greatest proportion of its services to other support departments are allocated first, followed by the department with the next highest proportion, and so forth. As

each "step" is allocated, each succeeding step involves one less department. Parat College's support department cost allocation is

	Support Departments		Operating Departments	
	Maintenance	Power	School of Education	School of Technology
Costs before allocation	$99,000	$54,000		
Allocation of maintenance $(\frac{2}{10},\frac{3}{10},\frac{5}{10})$	(99,000) $\underline{\$\qquad 0}$	19,800	$29,700	$49,500
Allocation of power $(\frac{2}{9},\frac{7}{9})$		(73,800) $\underline{\$\qquad 0}$	16,400 $\underline{\$46,100}$	57,400 $\underline{\$106,900}$

Therefore, $46,100 of May 2009 support department costs are allocated to the School of Education.

G. Process Costing

20. (b)   Equivalent units of production are calculated as follows:

Completed units	400
Plus: Equivalent units in ending inventory (200 × 75%)	150
Less: Equivalent units in beginning inventory (100 × 50%)	(50)
Equivalent units of production	500

21. (d)   Material costs in ending work in process inventory is calculated as $216,000 = 150 (equivalent units in ending inventory) × $1,440 ($720,000/500) per equivalent unit. Equivalent units of production are calculated as: 500 = 400 completed units + 150 (200 × 75%) equivalent units in ending inventory – 50 (100 × 50%) equivalent units in beginning inventory.

22. (d)   The application of factory overhead would increase the work in process inventory control account. In addition, the work in process account would be increased for other product costs (direct manufacturing labor and direct material). Only costs of completed products increase finished goods inventory control. Factory overhead control is increased by actual factory overhead costs incurred. Cost of goods sold is increased by the product costs of the finished units sold.

23. (d)   The requirement is to determine the cost per equivalent unit for materials using the weighted-average method. Under the weighted-average method, equivalent units of production and cost per unit are based on **all** work (this period's and last period's) done on units completed plus all work done to date on the units in ending work in process. Since materials are added at the beginning of the production process, both the units completed and the ending work in process are 100% complete with respect to materials. The cost per equivalent unit can be computed as follows:

Units completed	42,500
Ending WIP	12,500
Total equivalent units	55,000
Cost of materials:	
Beginning WIP	$ 5,500
Units started	18,000
Total costs incurred	$23,500
Divide by EUP	÷ 55,000
Cost per equivalent unit	$ .43

24.   (c)   The requirement is to calculate the amount of conversion cost transferred by Forming to the next production department. First, the physical flow of units must be determined.

Next, equivalent units of production (EUP) must be calculated, in this case using the weighted-average (WA) method. The WA computations of EUP and cost per equivalent unit include both work done **last** period on the current period's BWIP and all work done in the current period on units completed and on EWIP. Forming's EWIP is 80% complete.

Spoiled units must be accounted for separately because Forming adds their cost only to the cost of units transferred. To ignore spoiled units would result in the same total cost being allocated to 500 fewer units, thus spreading spoilage costs over all work done during the period, including EWIP.

	Total units	Equivalent units
Started and completed	7,000	7,000
Spoilage—normal	500	500
EWIP (80% complete)	2,500	2,000*
	10,000	9,500

*2,500 units x 80% completion

Since conversion costs total $85,500 for the period ($10,000 for BWIP + $75,500 for units started), Forming's conversion cost per equivalent unit is $9.00 ($85,500 ÷ 9,500 EUP). These costs are assigned as follows:

Good units completed (7,000 × $9)	$63,000
Spoiled units (500 × $9)	4,500
Conversion cost transferred	$67,500
EWIP (2,000 × $9)	18,000
Total costs accounted for	$85,500

Therefore, $67,500 was transferred to the second department.

25.   (a)   The FIFO method determines equivalent units of production (EUP) based on the work done in the current period only. The work done in the current period can be dichotomized as: (1) the work necessary to complete beginning work in process (BWIP), and (2) the work performed on the units started in the current period.

26.   (a)   Conversion costs consist of direct manufacturing labor and factory overhead. Because the EWIP units are 50% in process 2, some conversion costs have been incurred. These units would be included in the computation of equivalent units for conversion costs. However, because material G is added only when a batch is 60% complete, this material has not yet been added to this batch. These units would not be included in the computation of equivalent units for material G.

27.   (d)   The requirement is to compare the number of equivalent units of production (EUP) computed using the weighted-average method to the EUP computed using the FIFO method for two months. The weighted-average method determines EUP based on the work done on the units in all periods, while the FIFO method uses only the work done in the current period. Because the system began in January, there was no beginning inventory for the first

month of the comparison. Both methods would compute the same number of EUP for January because the only work done on these units was done in the period under consideration. Because there was ending inventory in January, however, February would have a beginning inventory. The weighted-average method would therefore compute a greater number of EUP than FIFO for February because it would include the work done in January while FIFO would not.

28.   (a)   The requirement is to determine the proper allocation of **normal** defective unit costs to the ending work in process. **Normal** defective unit costs are spread over the units of **good** output because the attaining of good units necessitates the appearance of normal spoiled units. The cost of the normal defective units is included in the total costs of the **good** equivalent units of output. Ending inventory comprised one-half of the total units of good output produced during the year; therefore, it will bear 50% of the normal defective unit costs incurred during the year.

29.   (d)   Normal spoilage is the cost of spoiled units which results due to the nature of the manufacturing process. Normal spoilage may be unavoidable under efficient operating conditions and is thus a necessary cost in the production process. Since it is treated as a product cost, the $60,000 normal spoilage should be inventoried. Conversely, units become abnormally spoiled as a result of some unnecessary act, event, or condition. Therefore, the $30,000 abnormal spoilage is treated as a period cost.

30.   (b)   The requirement is to calculate the equivalent units of production for materials using the FIFO method. Equivalent units of production are calculated as follows:

Completed units	92,000
Plus: Equivalent units in ending inventory (24,000 × 90%)	21,600
Less: Equivalent units in beginning inventory (16,000 × 60%)	(9,600)
Equivalent units of production	104,000

31.   (d)   The requirement is to calculate the equivalent units of production for conversion costs using the FIFO method. Equivalent units of production are calculated as follows:

Completed units	92,000
Plus: Equivalent units in ending inventory (24,000 × 40%)	9,600
Less: Equivalent units in beginning inventory (16,000 × 20%)	(3,200)
Equivalent units of production	98,400

32.   (b)   The requirement is to calculate the equivalent unit cost of materials using the FIFO method. The amount is determined by dividing the cost of materials used during the month by the number of equivalent units of production, which is equal to $4.50 ($468,000 ÷ 104,000).

33.   (b)   The requirement is to calculate the equivalent unit cost of conversion using the FIFO method. The amount is determined by dividing the conversion costs incurred during the month by the number of equivalent units of production, which is equal to $5.83 [($182,880 + $391,160) ÷ 98,400].

34.   (a)   The requirement is to calculate the cost of units in ending work in process inventory using the FIFO method. The amount is determined as follows:

Ending WIP:
Material costs (24,000 units × 90%) × $4.50	$ 97,200
Conversion costs (24,000 units × 40%) × $5.83	55,968
Total	$153,168

35. (c) The requirement is to calculate the equivalent unit cost of materials for the month using the weighted-average method. This amount is calculated as follows:

Units completed	92,000
Ending WIP (24,000 × 90%)	21,600
Total equivalent units	113,600
Cost of materials:	
Beginning WIP	$ 54,560
Units started	468,000
Total costs incurred	$522,560
Divide by EUP	÷ 113,600
Costs per equivalent unit	$4.60

36. (c) The requirement is to calculate the equivalent unit conversion cost for the month using the weighted-average method. This amount is calculated as follows:

Units completed	92,000
Ending WIP (24,000 × 40%)	9,600
Total equivalent units	101,600
Conversion costs:	
Beginning WIP	$ 35,560
Units started	574,040
Total costs incurred	$609,600
Divide by EUP	÷ 101,600
Costs per equivalent unit	$6.00

37. (d) The requirement is to calculate the total cost of the units in the ending work in process inventory using the weighted-average method. The amount is calculated as follows:

Ending WIP	
Material costs (24,000 units × 90%) × $4.60	$ 99,360
Conversion costs (24,000 units × 40%) × $6.00	57,600
Total	$156,960

J. Activity-Based Costing

38. (b) The requirement is to indicate the reasonable basis for allocating costs. Answer (b) is correct because there is a direct causal relationship between the number of components in a finished product and the amount of material handling costs incurred. Answer (a) is incorrect because this allocation basis is related to "batch" costs and not to individual unit costs. Answer (c) is incorrect because this allocation basis is the traditional basis for allocating overhead costs to the units produced when the production process is labor-intensive. Answer (d) is incorrect because this is not an allocation basis but rather the result of the allocation process when determining production costs.

39. (c) The requirement is to identify the valid cost relationship. Answer (c) is correct because both parts of the solution are stated correctly. Within the relevant range for the application activity base, the variable cost per unit and the total fixed cost would be constant. Answer (a) is incorrect because the second part of the solution is stated incorrectly. The fixed cost per unit of activity would decrease (cost is spread over more units), but total fixed cost in the flexible budget would be constant within the relevant range for the application activity base. The first part of the solution (variable cost per unit is constant) is correctly stated resulting in the total variable cost increasing with an increase in volume. Answer (b) is incorrect because the second part of the solution is stated incorrectly. The fixed cost

per unit of activity would decrease (cost is spread over more units), but total fixed costs in the flexible budget would be constant within the relevant range for the application activity base. The first part of the solution (variable cost per unit is constant) is correctly stated resulting in the total variable cost increasing with an increase in volume. Answer (d) is incorrect because the first part of the solution is stated incorrectly. The variable cost per unit does not increase (it is constant); rather, total variable cost would increase. The second part (the total fixed costs remain constant) of the solution is correctly stated because the total fixed costs in the flexible budget would be constant within the relevant range for the application activity base.

40. (d) The purpose of the just-in-time (JIT) production system is to decrease the size of production runs (and therefore inventory levels) by decreasing setup costs. Lot **sizes** would decrease as the **number** of lots processed during the year increases. Since inventory levels would decrease with JIT, relevant costs would also drop (i.e., capital invested in inventory could be invested in other assets—a cost savings). The **fixed** facility and administrative costs are irrelevant as fixed costs would remain the same regardless of changes for JIT. The unit costs will increase because fixed costs will be spread over fewer inventory units produced from JIT's eliminating effect on excess inventory production.

41. (d) An activity-based costing system allocates costs to products by determining which activities being performed by the entity are driving the costs. An activity-based costing approach differs from traditional costing methods that accumulate costs by department or function. Activity-based costing accumulates and allocates costs by the specific activities being performed. Since most entities perform a variety of activities, the number of cost pools and allocation bases greatly increases under activity-based costing.

42. (d) Activity-based costing can be used in conjunction with either process or job costing. Answer (a) is incorrect because activity-based costing can be used in conjunction with either process or job costing. Answer (b) is incorrect because activity-based costing can be used in conjunction with job costing. Answer (c) is incorrect because activity-based costing can be used in conjunction with process costing.

43. (b) In an activity-based costing (ABC) system, the activities which drive the manufacturing department's overhead costs would be analyzed. Overhead would then be allocated to products based on the resources consumed in their production. The effect of producing different products in different lot sizes is that some products incur more setup costs than others; products produced in small batches must be produced more often, and thus require more setups to achieve a given level of output. Therefore, setup costs bear a cause and effect relationship with and should be assigned to each production **batch** (and then spread over the units in the batch). However, setups are not the only activities driving overhead costs. Other overhead cost drivers identifiable in production systems may include materials handling, engineering changes to products, and rework costs. Therefore, manufacturing overhead should be assigned to products based on **multiple** cause and effect relationships [answer (b) is correct and answer (a) is incorrect]. Answers (c) and (d) are incorrect because allocation via these methods would wholly defeat the purpose of ABC, which is founded upon cause and effect allocation of costs to products.

44. (c) Activity-based costing (ABC) involves the allocation of overhead costs to products based on the cost driver that actually **caused** those costs to be incurred. In contrast to traditional costing methods which accumulate costs by department or function, ABC accumulates costs by the specific activity being performed. For example, costs related to the purchase of materials may be allocated according to the number of purchase transactions which occurred. Therefore, cost drivers comprise a necessary part of any ABC system. On the other hand, non-value-added activities represent expenditures for which no value is added to the product. Hence, costs can be reduced by eliminating non-value-added activities without affecting the salability of the product.

45. (d) Activity-based costing focuses on incorporating into product costs only those activities that provide value to the product. Design engineering is a fundamental activity needed to design a good product. Heat treatment activities would strengthen and protect the product being produced. A drill press activity alters the physical product as it moves on toward becoming a finished good. Raw materials storage activity does nothing to alter or improve the value of a product. It is a non-value-adding activity.

46. (a) Under a traditional costing system, setup costs are allocated using a cost driver, in this case, direct manufacturing labor hours. The first step is to calculate the setup costs per direct manufacturing labor hour ($60,000 incurred ÷ 25,000 total DMLH) of $2.40. Since two DMLH are needed to produce one unit of product A, the total setup cost per unit of A is ($2.40 × 2 DMLH) $4.80. Under ABC, one **batch** of product A creates the demand for setup activities that produce value. The setup cost per unit of A under ABC is calculated as the setup cost **per batch** of A ($1,000) divided by the number of units per batch (100), or, $10.00.

K. Joint Products

47. (c) The requirement is to determine how to allocate joint cost using the net realizable value (NRV) method when a by-product is involved. NRV is the predicted selling price in the ordinary course of business less reasonably predictable costs of completion and disposal. The joint cost of $54,000 is reduced by the NRV of the by-product ($4,000) to get the allocable joint cost ($50,000). The computation is

	Sales value at split-off	Weighting	Joint costs allocated
Kul	$40,000	40,000/75,000 × 50,000	$26,667
Wu	35,000	35,000/75,000 × 50,000	23,333
	$75,000		$50,000

Therefore, $26,667 of the joint cost should be allocated to product Kul.

48. (d) When using the relative sales value at split-off method for joint products, joint costs are allocated based on the ratio of each product's sales value at split-off to total sales value at split-off for all joint products. If the market value at split-off (sales value) of joint product P increases, then a larger proportion of the total joint costs will be allocated to that product. Because all other costs and selling prices remain unchanged, the gross margin of product P will, therefore, decrease. Product Q's gross margin will, how-

ever, increase because a smaller proportion of the total joint costs will be allocated to it.

49. (c) Joint costs may be allocated to joint products based on either sales price or some physical measure. Methods which use estimated sales price include relative sales value at split-off, estimated net realizable value (NRV), and constant gross margin percentage NRV. Under the sales value at split-off method, joint costs are allocated based on the ratio of each product's sales value at split-off to total sales value at split-off for all joint products. The estimated NRV method allocates joint costs at the split-off point based on net sales value (Estimated sales value of the joint products – Separable processing costs). Under the constant gross margin percentage NRV method, the overall gross margin (GM) percentage for all joint products combined (after deducting both joint and separable costs) is used to determine the GM for each joint product. This GM is deducted from the sales price of each joint product to determine total costs, and separable costs are then deducted from total costs to determine the joint cost allocation. However, this is not the same as answer (d), which uses a predetermined profit margin and ignores actual costs. The constant GM percentage NRV method does not use a preset GM, it uses the actual overall GM and spreads it uniformly among products so that all joint products yield the same GM percentage. The sales price cannot be based solely on costs. Conversely, costs must be based on sales price (or some physical measure) because joint costs can only be allocated arbitrarily.

L. By-Products

50. (d) The requirement is to find the cost of sales for both gasoline and the gasoline by-product. The value of the by-products may be recognized at two points in time: (1) at the time of production, or (2) at the time of sale. Under the production method (as given in the problem), the net realizable value of the by-products **produced** is deducted from the cost of the major products **produced**. The net realizable value of the by-product is as follows:

Sales value of by-product	$30,000	
Less: separable costs	25,000	(10,000 + 15,000)
	$ 5,000	

Therefore, cost of sales for gasoline is calculated as follows:

Total production (joint) costs	$120,000
Less: net realizable value of by-product	5,000
Net Production Cost	115,000
Less: costs in 12/31/09 inventory	15,000
	$100,000

Therefore, total cost of gasoline sales is $100,000, and no cost of sales is reported for the by-product.

51. (a) Because the inventory of by-product Moy was recorded at its net realizable value of $20,000 [($6 – $2) × 5,000] when produced in 2008, no profit will be recognized in 2009. When the units of Moy were sold in 2009, the proceeds equaled the inventory cost plus disposal costs, resulting in $0 profit for 2009. The following journal entries help to illustrate the situation:

2008	Main product(s) inventory	xxxx	
	By-product inventory	20,000	
	Work in process control		xxxx
2009	Cash or accounts receivable	30,000	
	Inventory		20,000
	Selling expenses		10,000

52.   (b)   The difference between treating the product named "May" as a joint product versus a by-product would be that under by-product treatment, the selling cost is netted against May's selling price thus reducing gross margin whereas under joint-product accounting, the selling cost would be deducting below the gross margin line as a selling expense. Thus, if the change to joint-product accounting were made, gross margin would increase.

53.   (a)   The value of the by-products may be recognized at two points in time: (1) at the time of production, or (2) at the time of sale. Under the production method, the net realizable value of the by-products **produced** is deducted from the cost of the major products **produced**. Under the sale method, net revenue from by-products **sold** (gross revenue from by-product sales minus separable costs incurred) is deducted from the cost of the major products **sold**.

M. Estimating Cost Functions

54.   (a)   The requirement is to determine the variable component of order filling cost per order. The high-low method of analysis should be used to separate the mixed cost into its fixed and variable components. The formula used in developing the variable rate is

$$\frac{\text{Cost at high point} - \text{Cost at low point}}{\text{High activity point} - \text{Low activity point}} = \text{Variable rate}$$

In this problem, order filling costs are given at four levels of activity because the number of orders was different in each month. Substituting the highest and lowest cost ($4,320 and $3,120) and activity (1,800 and 1,200) figures into the formula yields the variable cost of order filling per order.

$$\frac{\$4,320 - \$3,120}{1,800 - 1,200} = \$2.00/\text{order}$$

55.   (c)   The graph depicts Sender's fixed and variable parcel mailing costs. Fixed costs total $15,000, since this amount of cost is incurred even when zero parcels are mailed. Variable costs at a mailing volume of 20,000 parcels is $60,000 ($75,000 total cost – $15,000 fixed cost), resulting in a per unit variable cost of $3.00 ($60,000 VC / 20,000 units). Therefore, Sender's estimated cost of mailing 12,000 parcels is $51,000 [$15,000 FC + ($3 VC × 12,000 units)].

56.   (d)   Regression analysis determines the functional relationship between variables and provides a measure of probable error. Multiple regression analysis involves the use of two or more independent variables (such as the number of shipments and the weight of materials handled) to predict one dependent variable (inventory warehouse costs). Economic order quantity analysis determines the amount to be ordered while minimizing the sum of ordering and carrying costs. Probability analysis is an application of statistical decision theory that, under conditions of uncertainty, leads to more reliable decisions. Correlation analysis determines the relationship between only two variables.

57.   (a)   The determination that needs to be made is which of the cost drivers would be the best predictor of overhead costs (machine hours or direct materials weight). The information given regarding the coefficient of determination (R^2) measures the correlation between the cost driver and overhead costs. The higher the R^2, the better the correlation. Therefore, machine hours would be the more accurate cost driver.

MULTIPLE-CHOICE QUESTIONS (1-83)

1. At the breakeven point, the contribution margin equals total
   a.   Variable costs.
   b.   Sales revenues.
   c.   Selling and administrative costs.
   d.   Fixed costs.

2. The most likely strategy to reduce the breakeven point, would be to
   a.   Increase both the fixed costs and the contribution margin.
   b.   Decrease both the fixed costs and the contribution margin.
   c.   Decrease the fixed costs and increase the contribution margin.
   d.   Increase the fixed costs and decrease the contribution margin.

3. Del Co. has fixed costs of $100,000 and breakeven sales of $800,000. What is its projected profit at $1,200,000 sales?
   a. $ 50,000
   b. $150,000
   c. $200,000
   d. $400,000

**4. Associated Supply, Inc. is considering introducing a new product that will require a $250,000 investment of capital. The necessary funds would be raised through a bank loan at an interest rate of 8%. The fixed operating costs associated with the product would be $122,500 while the contribution margin percentage would be 42%. Assuming a selling price of $15 per unit, determine the number of units (rounded to the nearest whole unit) Associated would have to sell to generate earnings before interest and taxes (EBIT) of 32% of the amount of capital invested in the new product.
   a.   35,318 units.
   b.   32,143 units.
   c.   25,575 units.
   d.   23,276 units.

5. During 2008, Thor Lab supplied hospitals with a comprehensive diagnostic kit for $120. At a volume of 80,000 kits, Thor had fixed costs of $1,000,000 and a profit before income taxes of $200,000. Due to an adverse legal decision, Thor's 2009 liability insurance increased by $1,200,000 over 2008. Assuming the volume and other costs are unchanged, what should the 2009 price be if Thor is to make the same $200,000 profit before income taxes?
   a. $120.00
   b. $135.00
   c. $150.00
   d. $240.00

6. Breakeven analysis assumes that over the relevant range
   a.   Unit revenues are nonlinear.
   b.   Unit variable costs are unchanged.
   c.   Total costs are unchanged.
   d.   Total fixed costs are nonlinear.

7. Product Cott has sales of $200,000, a contribution margin of 20%, and a margin of safety of $80,000. What is Cott's fixed cost?

   a. $16,000
   b. $24,000
   c. $80,000
   d. $96,000

8. On January 1, 2009, Lake Co. increased its direct manufacturing labor wage rates. All other budgeted costs and revenues were unchanged. How did this increase affect Lake's budgeted breakeven point and budgeted margin of safety?

	Budgeted Breakeven point	*Budgeted margin of safety*
a.	Increase	Increase
b.	Increase	Decrease
c.	Decrease	Decrease
d.	Decrease	Increase

Items 9 and 10 are based on the following:

The diagram below is a cost-volume-profit chart.

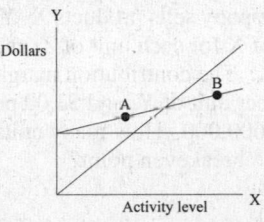

9. At point A compared to point B, as a percentage of sales revenues

	Variable costs are	*Fixed costs are*
a.	Greater	Greater
b.	Greater	The same
c.	The same	The same
d.	The same	Greater

10. If sales dollars are used to measure activity levels, total costs and total revenues may be read from the X and Y axis as follows:

	Total costs	*Total revenues*
a.	X or Y	X or Y
b.	X or Y	X only
c.	Y only	X or Y
d.	Y only	X only

**11. Which one of the following is and advantage of using variable costing?
   a.   Variable costing complies with the US Internal Revenue Code.
   b.   Variable costing complies with generally accepted accounting principles.
   c.   Variable costing makes cost-volume relationships more easily apparent.
   d.   Variable costing is most relevant to long-run pricing strategies.

12. In the profit-volume chart below, EF and GH represent the profit-volume graphs of a single-product company for 2007 and 2008, respectively.

If 2007 and 2008 unit sales prices are identical, how did total fixed costs and unit variable costs of 2008 change compared to 2007?

	2008 total fixed costs	2008 unit variable costs
a.	Decreased	Increased
b.	Decreased	Decreased
c.	Increased	Increased
d.	Increased	Decreased

13. Thomas Company sells products X, Y, and Z. Thomas sells three units of X for each unit of Z, and two units of Y for each unit of X. The contribution margins are $1.00 per unit of X, $1.50 per unit of Y, and $3.00 per unit of Z. Fixed costs are $600,000. How many units of X would Thomas sell at the breakeven point?

    a. 40,000
    b. 120,000
    c. 360,000
    d. 400,000

14. In calculating the breakeven point for a multi-product company, which of the following assumptions are commonly made when variable costing is used?

    I. Sales volume equals production volume.
    II. Variable costs are constant per unit.
    III. A given sales mix is maintained for all volume changes.

    a. I and II.
    b. I and III.
    c. II and III.
    d. I, II, and III.

15. In the budgeted profit/volume chart below, EG represents a two-product company's profit path. EH and HG represent the profit paths of products #1 and #2, respectively.

Budgeted profit/volume chart

Sales prices and cost behavior were as budgeted, actual total sales equaled budgeted sales, and there were no inventories. Actual profit was greater than budgeted profit. Which product had actual sales in excess of budget, and what margin does OE divided by OF represent?

	Product with excess sales	OE/OF
a.	#1	Contribution margin
b.	#1	Gross margin
c.	#2	Contribution margin
d.	#2	Gross margin

16. In its first year of operations, Magna Manufacturers had the following costs when it produced 100,000 and sold 80,000 units of its only product:

Manufacturing costs	Fixed	$180,000
	Variable	160,000
Selling and admin. costs	Fixed	90,000
	Variable	40,000

How much lower would Magna's net income be if it used variable costing instead of full absorption costing?

    a. $36,000
    b. $54,000
    c. $68,000
    d. $94,000

17. Using the variable costing method, which of the following costs are assigned to inventory?

	Variable selling and administrative costs	Variable factory overhead costs
a.	Yes	Yes
b.	Yes	No
c.	No	No
d.	No	Yes

18. At the end of Killo Co.'s first year of operations, 1,000 units of inventory remained on hand. Variable and fixed manufacturing costs per unit were $90 and $20, respectively. If Killo uses absorption costing rather than variable (direct) costing, the result would be a higher pretax income of

    a. $0
    b. $20,000
    c. $70,000
    d. $90,000

19. A manufacturing company prepares income statements using both absorption and variable costing methods. At the end of a period actual sales revenues, total gross profit, and total contribution margin approximated budgeted figures, whereas net income was substantially greater than the budgeted amount. There were no beginning or ending inventories. The most likely explanation of the net income increase is that, compared to budget, actual

    a. Manufacturing fixed costs had increased.
    b. Selling and administrative fixed expenses had decreased.
    c. Sales prices and variable costs had increased proportionately.
    d. Sales prices had declined proportionately less than variable costs.

20. A single-product company prepares income statements using both absorption and variable costing methods. Manufacturing overhead cost applied per unit produced in 2009 was the same as in 2008. The 2009 variable costing statement reported a profit whereas the 2009 absorption costing statement reported a loss. The difference in reported income could be explained by units produced in 2009 being

    a. Less than units sold in 2009.
    b. Less than the activity level used for allocating overhead to the product.
    c. In excess of the activity level used for allocating overhead to the product.
    d. In excess of units sold in 2009.

21. Which of the following is an output of a financial planning model?

    a. Strategic plan.

b. Actual financial results.
c. Projected financial statements.
d. Variance analysis.

22. Mien Co. is budgeting sales of 53,000 units of product Nous for October 2009. The manufacture of one unit of Nous requires four kilos of chemical Loire. During October 2009, Mien plans to reduce the inventory of Loire by 50,000 kilos and increase the finished goods inventory of Nous by 6,000 units. There is no Nous work in process inventory. How many kilos of Loire is Mien budgeting to purchase in October 2009?

a. 138,000
b. 162,000
c. 186,000
d. 238,000

23. The master budget

a. Shows forecasted and actual results.
b. Reflects controllable costs only.
c. Can be used to determine manufacturing cost variances.
d. Contains the operating budget.

Items 24 and 25 are based on the following information:

Operational budgets are used by a retail company for planning and controlling its business activities. Data regarding the company's monthly sales for the last 6 months of the year and its projected collection patterns are shown below.

The cost of merchandise averages 40% of its selling price. The company's policy is to maintain an inventory equal to 25% of the next month's forecasted sales. The inventory balance at cost is $80,000 as of June 30.

Forecasted Sales

July	$775,000
August	750,000
September	825,000
October	800,000
November	850,000
December	900,000

Types of Sales

Cash sales	20%
Credit sales	80%

Collection Pattern for Credit Sales

In the month of sale	40%
In the first month following the sale	57%
Uncollectible	3%

*24. The budgeted cost of the company's purchases for the month of August would be

a. $302,500
b. $305,000
c. $307,500
d. $318,750

*25. The company's total cash receipts from sales and collections on account that would be budgeted for the month of September would be

a. $757,500
b. $771,000
c. $793,800
d. $856,500

26. Which of the following **best describes tactical profit plans?

a. Detailed, short-term, broad responsibilities, qualitative.
b. Broad, short-term, responsibilites at all levels, quantitative.
c. Detailed, short-term, responsibilities at all levels, quantitative.
d. Broad, long-term, broad responsibilities, qualitative.

27. Which of the following budgeting systems focuses on improving operations?

a. Responsibility budgeting.
b. Activity-based budgeting.
c. Operational budgeting.
d. Kaizen budgeting.

28. Which of the following is included in a firm's financial budget?

a. Budgeted income statement.
b. Capital budget.
c. Production schedule.
d. Cost of goods sold budget.

29. Rolling Wheels purchases bicycle components in the month prior to assembling them into bicycles. Assembly is scheduled one month prior to budgeted sales. Rolling pays 75% of component costs in the month of purchase and 25% of the costs in the following month. Component cost included in budgeted cost of sales are

April	*May*	*June*	*July*	*August*
$5,000	$6,000	$7,000	$8,000	$8,000

What is Rolling's budgeted cash payment for components in May?

a. $5,750
b. $6,750
c. $7,750
d. $8,000

30. A 2009 cash budget is being prepared for the purchase of Toyi, a merchandise item. Budgeted data are

Cost of goods sold for 2009	$300,000
Accounts payable 1/1/09	20,000
Inventory—1/1/09	30,000
12/31/09	42,000

Purchases will be made in twelve equal monthly amounts and paid for in the following month. What is the 2009 budgeted cash payment for purchases of Toyi?

a. $295,000
b. $300,000
c. $306,000
d. $312,000

**31. Trumbull Company budgeted sales on account of $120,000 for July, $211,000 for August, and $198,000 for September. Collection experience indicates that 60% of the budgeted sales will be collected the month after the sale, 36% the second month, and 4% will be uncollectible. The cash from accounts receivable that should be budgeted for September would be

a. $169,800
b. $194,760
c. $197,880
d. $198,600

---

* *CIA adapted*
** *CMA adapted*

32. Cook Co.'s total costs of operating five sales offices last year were $500,000, of which $70,000 represented fixed costs. Cook has determined that total costs are significantly influenced by the number of sales offices operated. Last year's costs and number of sales offices can be used as the bases for predicting annual costs. What would be the budgeted costs for the coming year if Cook were to operate seven sales offices?

     a. $700,000
     b. $672,000
     c. $614,000
     d. $586,000

*33. In regression analysis, which of the following correlation coefficients represents the strongest relationship between the independent and dependent variables?

     a.   1.03
     b.   −.02
     c.   −.89
     d.   .75

*34. The internal auditor of a bank has developed a multiple regression model which has been used for a number of years to estimate the amount of interest income from commercial loans. During the current year, the auditor applies the model and discovers that the r^2 value has decreased dramatically, but the model otherwise seems to be working okay. Which of the following conclusions are justified by the change?

     a.   Changing to a cross-sectional regression analysis should cause r^2 to increase.
     b.   Regression analysis is no longer an appropriate technique to estimate interest income.
     c.   Some new factors, not included in the model, are causing interest income to change.
     d.   A linear regression analysis would increase the model's reliability.

*35. All of the following are useful for forecasting the needed level of inventory except:

     a.   Knowledge of the behavior of business cycles.
     b.   Internal accounting allocations of costs to different segments of the company.
     c.   Information about seasonal variations in demand.
     d.   Econometric modeling.

Items 36 thru 38 are based on the following information:

In preparing the annual profit plan for the coming year, Wilkens Company wants to determine the cost behavior pattern of the maintenance costs. Wilkens has decided to use linear regression by employing the equation $y = a + bx$ for maintenance costs. The prior year's data regarding maintenance hours and costs, and the result of the regression analysis are given below.

Average cost per hour	$9.00
a	684.65
b	7.2884
Standard error of a	49.515
Standard error of b	.12126
Standard error of the estimate	34.469
R^2	.99724

	Hours of activity	Maintenance costs
January	480	$ 4,200
February	320	3,000
March	400	3,600
April	300	2,820
May	500	4,350
June	310	2,960
July	320	3,030
August	520	4,470
September	490	4,260
October	470	4,050
November	350	3,300
December	340	3,160
Sum	4,800	$43,200
Average	400	$ 3,600

*36. In the standard regression equation $y = a + bx$, the letter b is best described as a(n)

     a.   Independent variable.
     b.   Dependent variable.
     c.   Constant coefficient.
     d.   Variable coefficient.

*37. The letter x in the standard regression equation is best described as a(n).

     a.   Independent variable.
     b.   Dependent variable.
     c.   Constant coefficient.
     d.   Coefficient of determination.

*38. Based upon the data derived from the regression analysis, 420 maintenance hours in a month would mean the maintenance costs (rounded to the nearest dollar) would be budgeted at

     a. $3,780
     b. $3,600
     c. $3,790
     d. $3,746

Items 39 thru 42 are based on the following information:

Lackland Ski Resort uses multiple regression to predict ski lift revenue for the next week based on the forecasted number of dates with temperatures above 10 degrees and predicted number of inches of snow. The following function has been developed:

Sales = 10,902 + (255 × no. of days predicted above 10 degrees) + (300 × no. of inches of snow predicted)

Other information generated from the analysis include

Coefficient of determination (Adjusted r squared)	.6789
Standard error	1,879
F-Statistic	6.279 with a significance of .049

39. Which variables(s) in this function is(are) the dependent variable(s)?

     a.   Predicted number of days above 10 degrees.
     b.   Predicted number of inches of snow.
     c.   Revenue.
     d.   Predicted number of days above 10 degrees and predicted number of inches of snow.

40. Assume that management predicts the number of days above 10 degrees for the next week to be 6 and the number of inches of snow to be 12. Calculate the predicted amount of revenue for the next week.

     a. $10,902
     b. $11,362

---

*   *CIA adapted*

c. $16,032
d. $20,547

41. Which of the following represents an accurate interpretation of the results of Lackland's regression analysis?

a.   6.279% of the variation in revenue is explained by the predicted number of days above 10 degrees and the number of inches of snow.
b.   The relationships are not significant.
c.   Predicted number of days above 10 degrees is a more significant variable than number of inches of snow.
d.   67.89% of the variation in revenue is explained by the predicted number of days above 10 degrees and the number of inches of snow.

42. Assume that Lackland's model predicts revenue for a week to be $13,400. Calculate the 95% confidence interval for the amount of revenue for the week. (The 95% confidence interval corresponds to the area representing 2.3436 deviations from the mean.)

a. $13,400 ± 6,279
b. $13,400 ± 4,404
c. $13,400 ± 6,786
d. $13,400 ± 8,564

43. Which of the following is a quantitative approach used to develop sales forecasts based on analysis of consumer behavior?

a.   Markov techniques.
b.   Regression analysis.
c.   Econometric models.
d.   Exponential smoothing.

44. Which of the following is a quantitative approach to developing a sales forecast?

a.   Delphi technique.
b.   Customer surveys.
c.   Moving average.
d.   Executive opinions.

**45. A forecasting technique that is a combination of the last forecast and the last observed value is called

a.   Delphi.
b.   Least squares.
c.   Regression.
d.   Exponential smoothing.

46. Using regression analysis, Fairfield Co. graphed the following relationship of its cheapest product line's sales with its customers' income levels:

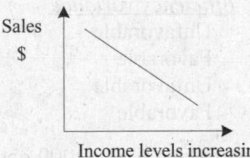

If there is a strong statistical relationship between the sales and customers' income levels, which of the following numbers best represents the correlation coefficient for this relationship?

a.   -9.00
b.   -0.93

c.   +0.93
d.   +9.00

47. The basic difference between a master budget and a flexible budget is that a master budget is

a.   Only used before and during the budget period and a flexible budget is only used after the budget period.
b.   For an entire production facility and a flexible budget is applicable to single departments only.
c.   Based on one specific level of production and a flexible budget can be prepared for any production level within a relevant range.
d.   Based on a fixed standard and a flexible budget allows management latitude in meeting goals.

48. A flexible budget is appropriate for a

	Marketing budget	Direct material usage budget
a.	No	No
b.	No	Yes
c.	Yes	Yes
d.	Yes	No

49. When production levels are expected to increase within a relevant range, and a flexible budget is used, what effect would be anticipated with respect to each of the following costs?

	Fixed costs per unit	Variable costs per unit
a.	Decrease	Decrease
b.	No change	No change
c.	No change	Decrease
d.	Decrease	No change

50. Controllable revenue would be included in a performance report for a

	Profit center	Cost center
a.	No	No
b.	No	Yes
c.	Yes	No
d.	Yes	Yes

51. The following is a summarized income statement of Carr Co.'s profit center No. 43 for March 2009:

Contribution margin		$70,000
Period expenses:		
Manager's salary	$20,000	
Facility depreciation	8,000	
Corporate expense allocation	5,000	33,000
Profit center income		$37,000

Which of the following amounts would most likely be subject to the control of the profit center's manager?

a. $70,000
b. $50,000
c. $37,000
d. $33,000

52. Wages earned by machine operators in producing the firm's product should be categorized as

	Direct labor	Controllable by the machine operators' foreman
a.	Yes	Yes
b.	Yes	No
c.	No	Yes
d.	No	No

53. Companies in what type of industry may use a standard cost system for cost control?

	Mass production industry	Service industry
a.	Yes	Yes
b.	Yes	No
c.	No	No
d.	No	Yes

54. In connection with a standard cost system being developed by Flint Co., the following information is being considered with regard to standard hours allowed for output of one unit of product:

	Hours
Average historical performance for the past three years	1.85
Production level to satisfy average consumer demand over a seasonal time span	1.60
Engineering estimates based on attainable performance	1.50
Engineering estimates based on ideal performance	1.25

To measure controllable production inefficiencies, what is the best basis for Flint to use in establishing standard hours allowed?

a. 1.25
b. 1.50
c. 1.60
d. 1.85

55. Which of the following standard costing variances would be **least** controllable by a production supervisor?

a. Overhead volume.
b. Overhead efficiency.
c. Labor efficiency.
d. Material usage.

56. The standard direct material cost to produce a unit of Lem is four meters of material at $2.50 per meter. During May 2009, 4,200 meters of material costing $10,080 were purchased and used to produce 1,000 units of Lem. What was the material price variance for May 2009?

a. $400 favorable.
b. $420 favorable.
c. $ 80 unfavorable.
d. $480 unfavorable.

57. Dahl Co. uses a standard costing system in connection with the manufacture of a "one size fits all" article of clothing. Each unit of finished product contains two yards of direct material. However, a 20% direct material spoilage calculated on input quantities occurs during the manufacturing process. The cost of the direct material is $3 per yard. The standard direct material cost per unit of finished product is

a. $4.80
b. $6.00
c. $7.20
d. $7.50

58. Carr Co. had an unfavorable materials usage variance of $900. What amounts of this variance should be charged to each department?

	Purchasing	Warehousing	Manufacturing
a.	$0	$0	$900
b.	$0	$900	$0
c.	$300	$300	$300
d.	$900	$0	$0

59. Yola Co. manufactures one product with a standard direct manufacturing labor cost of four hours at $12.00 per hour. During June, 1,000 units were produced using 4,100 hours at $12.20 per hour. The unfavorable direct labor efficiency variance was

a. $1,220
b. $1,200
c. $ 820
d. $ 400

60. The following direct manufacturing labor information pertains to the manufacture of product Glu:

Time required to make one unit	2 direct labor hours
Number of direct workers	50
Number of productive hours per week, per worker	40
Weekly wages per worker	$500
Workers' benefits treated as direct manufacturing labor costs	20% of wages

What is the standard direct manufacturing labor cost per unit of product Glu?

a. $30
b. $24
c. $15
d. $12

61. On the diagram below, the line OW represents the standard labor cost at any output volume expressed in direct labor hours. Point S indicates the actual output at standard cost, and Point A indicates the actual hours and actual cost required to produce S.

Which of the following variances are favorable or unfavorable?

	Rate variance	Efficiency variance
a.	Favorable	Unfavorable
b.	Favorable	Favorable
c.	Unfavorable	Unfavorable
d.	Unfavorable	Favorable

62. The following were among Gage Co.'s 2009 costs:

Normal spoilage	$ 5,000
Freight out	10,000
Excess of actual manufacturing costs over standard costs	20,000
Standard manufacturing costs	100,000
Actual prime manufacturing costs	80,000

Gage's 2009 actual manufacturing overhead was

a. $ 40,000
b. $ 45,000

c. $ 55,000
d. $120,000

63. Baby Frames, Inc. evaluates manufacturing overhead in its factory by using variance analysis. The following information applies to the month of May:

	Actual	Budgeted
Number of frames manufactured	19,000	20,000
Variable overhead costs	$4,100	$2 per direct labor hour
Fixed overhead costs	$22,000	$20,000
Direct labor hours	2,100	0.1 hour per frame

What is the fixed overhead spending variance?
a. $1,000 favorable.
b. $1,000 unfavorable.
c. $2,000 favorable.
d. $2,000 unfavorable.

64. Under the 2-variance method for analyzing overhead, which of the following variances consists of both variable and fixed overhead elements?

	Controllable (budget) variance	Volume variance
a.	Yes	Yes
b.	Yes	No
c.	No	No
d.	No	Yes

65. During 2009, a department's 3-variance overhead standard costing system reported unfavorable spending and volume variances. The activity level selected for allocating overhead to the product was based on 80% of practical capacity. If 100% of practical capacity had been selected instead, how would the reported unfavorable spending and volume variances be affected?

	Spending variance	Volume variance
a.	Increased	Unchanged
b.	Increased	Increased
c.	Unchanged	Increased
d.	Unchanged	Unchanged

66. The following information pertains to Roe Co.'s 2009 manufacturing operations:

Standard direct manufacturing labor hours per unit	2
Actual direct manufacturing labor hours	10,500
Number of units produced	5,000
Standard variable overhead per standard direct manufacturing labor hour	$3
Actual variable overhead	$28,000

Roe's 2009 unfavorable variable overhead efficiency variance was
a. $0
b. $1,500
c. $2,000
d. $3,500

67. Which of the following variances would be useful in calling attention to a possible short-term problem in the control of overhead costs?

	Spending variance	Volume variance
a.	No	No
b.	No	Yes
c.	Yes	No
d.	Yes	Yes

Items 68 and 69 are based on the following:

The diagram below depicts a factory overhead flexible budget line DB and standard overhead application line OA. Activity is expressed in machine hours with Point V indicating the standard hours required for the actual output in September 2009. Point S indicates the actual machine hours (inputs) and actual costs in September 2009.

68. Are the following overhead variances favorable or unfavorable?

	Volume (capacity) variance	Efficiency variance
a.	Favorable	Favorable
b.	Favorable	Unfavorable
c.	Unfavorable	Favorable
d.	Unfavorable	Unfavorable

69. The budgeted total variable overhead cost for C machine hours is
a. AB
b. BC
c. AC minus DO
d. BC minus DO

70. Lanta Restaurant compares monthly operating results with a static budget. When actual sales are less than budget, would Lanta usually report favorable variances on variable food costs and fixed supervisory salaries?

	Variable food costs	Fixed supervisory salaries
a.	Yes	Yes
b.	Yes	No
c.	No	Yes
d.	No	No

71. Cuff Caterers quotes a price of $60 per person for a dinner party. This price includes the 6% sales tax and the 15% service charge. Sales tax is computed on the food plus the service charge. The service charge is computed on the food only. At what amount does Cuff price the food?
a. $56.40
b. $51.00
c. $49.22
d. $47.40

72. Based on potential sales of 500 units per year, a new product has estimated traceable costs of $990,000. What is the target price to obtain a 15% profit margin on sales?
a. $2,329
b. $2,277
c. $1,980
d. $1,935

73. Briar Co. signed a government construction contract providing for a formula price of actual cost plus 10%. In addition, Briar was to receive one-half of any savings resulting from the formula price being less than the target price of $2,200,000. Briar's actual costs incurred were

$1,920,000. How much should Briar receive from the contract?

- a. $2,060,000
- b. $2,112,000
- c. $2,156,000
- d. $2,200,000

74. Vince, Inc. has developed and patented a new laser disc reading device that will be marketed internationally. Which of the following factors should Vince consider in pricing the device?

    I. Quality of the new device.
   II. Life of the new device.
  III. Customers' relative preference for quality compared to price.

- a. I and II only.
- b. I and III only.
- c. II and III only.
- d. I, II, and III.

75. The budget for Klunker Auto Repair Shop for the year is as follows:

Direct labor per hour	$ 30
Total labor hours	10,000
Overhead costs:	
Materials handling and storage	$ 10,000
Other (rent, utilities, depreciation, insurance)	$120,000
Direct materials cost	$500,000

Klunker allocates materials handling and storage costs per dollar of direct materials cost. Other overhead is allocated based on total labor hours. In addition, Klunker adds a charge of $8 per labor hour to cover profit margin. Tardy Trucking Co. has brought one of its trucks to Klunker for an engine overhaul. If the overhaul requires twelve labor hours and $800 parts, what price should Klunker charge Tardy for these repair services?

- a. $1,160
- b. $1,256
- c. $1,416
- d. $1,472

76. Ajax Division of Carlyle Corporation produces electric motors, 20% of which are sold to Bradley Division of Carlyle and the remainder to outside customers. Carlyle treats its divisions as profit centers and allows division managers to choose their sources of sale and supply. Corporate policy requires that all interdivisional sales and purchases be recorded at variable cost as a transfer price. Ajax Division's estimated sales and standard cost data for the year ending December 31, 2009, based on the full capacity of 100,000 units, are as follows:

	Bradley	Outsiders
Sales	$ 900,000	$ 8,000,000
Variable costs	(900,000)	(3,600,000)
Fixed costs	(300,000)	(1,200,000)
Gross margin	$(300,000)	$ 3,200,000
Unit sales	20,000	80,000

Ajax has an opportunity to sell the above 20,000 units to an outside customer at a price of $75 per unit during 2009 on a continuing basis. Bradley can purchase its requirements from an outside supplier at a price of $85 per unit.

    Assuming that Ajax Division desires to maximize its gross margin, should Ajax take on the new customer and drop its sales to Bradley for 2009, and why?

- a. No, because the gross margin of the corporation as a whole would decrease by $200,000.
- b. Yes, because Ajax Division's gross margin would increase by $300,000.
- c. Yes, because Ajax Division's gross margin would increase by $600,000.
- d. No, because Bradley Division's gross margin would decrease by $800,000.

77. The management of James Corporation has decided to implement a transfer pricing system. James' MIS department is currently negotiating a transfer price for its services with the four producing divisions of the company as well as the marketing department. Charges will be assessed based on number of reports (assume that all reports require the same amount of time and resources to produce). The cost to operate the MIS department at its full capacity of 1,000 reports per year is budgeted at $45,000. The user subunits expect to request 250 reports each this year. The cost of temporary labor and additional facilities used to produce reports beyond capacity is budgeted at $48.00 per report. James could purchase the same services from an external Information Services firm for $70,000. What amounts should be used as the ceiling and the floor in determining the negotiated transfer price?

- a. Floor, $36.00; Ceiling $56.00.
- b. Floor, $45.60; Ceiling $56.00.
- c. Floor, $48.00; Ceiling $70.00.
- d. Floor, $57.00; Ceiling $82.00.

**78. Systematic evaluation of the trade-offs between product functionality and product cost while still satisfying customer needs is the definition of

- a. Activity-based management.
- b. Theory of constraints.
- c. Total quality management.
- d. Value engineering.

79. Which of the following statements regarding transfer pricing is false?

- a. When idle capacity exists, there is no opportunity cost to producing intermediate products for another division.
- b. Market-based transfer prices should be reduced by any costs avoided by selling internally rather than externally.
- c. No contribution margin is generated by the transferring division when variable cost-based transfer prices are used.
- d. The goal of transfer pricing is to provide segment managers with incentive to maximize the profits of their divisions.

80. Clay Co. has considerable excess manufacturing capacity. A special job order's cost sheet includes the following applied manufacturing overhead costs:

Fixed costs	$21,000
Variable costs	33,000

The fixed costs include a normal $3,700 allocation for in-house design costs, although no in-house design will be done. Instead the job will require the use of external designers costing $7,750. What is the total amount to be included in the calculation to determine the minimum acceptable price for the job?

- a. $36,700
- b. $40,750

c. $54,000
d. $58,050

81. For the year ended December 31, 2009, Abel Co. incurred direct costs of $500,000 based on a particular course of action during the year. If a different course of action had been taken, direct costs would have been $400,000. In addition, Abel's 2009 fixed costs were $90,000. The incremental cost was

    a. $ 10,000
    b. $ 90,000
    c. $100,000
    d. $190,000

82. Mili Co. plans to discontinue a division with a $20,000 contribution margin. Overhead allocated to the division is $50,000, of which $5,000 cannot be eliminated. The effect of this discontinuance on Mili's pretax income would be an increase of

    a. $ 5,000
    b. $20,000
    c. $25,000
    d. $30,000

**83. Following are the operating results of the two segments of Parklin Corporation

	Segment A	Segment B	Total
Sales	$10,000	$15,000	$25,000
Variable cost of goods sold	4,000	8,500	12,500
Fixed cost of goods sold	1,500	2,500	4,000
Gross margin	4,500	4,000	8,500
Variable selling and administrative	2,000	3,000	5,000
Fixed selling and administrative	1,500	1,500	3,000
Operating income (loss)	$ 1,000	$ (500)	$ 500

Fixed costs of goods sold are allocated to each segment based on the number of employees. Fixed selling and administrative expenses are allocated equally. If Segment B is eliminated, $1,500 of fixed costs of goods sold would be eliminated. Assuming Segment B is closed, the effect on operating income would be

    a. An increase of $500.
    b. An increase of $2,000.
    c. A decrease of $2,000.
    d. A decrease of $2,500.

1. d __ __	19. b __ __	37. a __ __	55. a __ __	73. c __ __
2. c __ __	20. a __ __	38. d __ __	56. b __ __	74. d __ __
3. a __ __	21. c __ __	39. c __ __	57. d __ __	75. c __ __
4. b __ __	22. c __ __	40. c __ __	58. a __ __	76. c __ __
5. b __ __	23. d __ __	41. d __ __	59. b __ __	77. b __ __
6. b __ __	24. c __ __	42. b __ __	60. a __ __	78. d __ __
7. b __ __	25. b __ __	43. a __ __	61. d __ __	79. d __ __
8. b __ __	26. c __ __	44. c __ __	62. a __ __	80. b __ __
9. d __ __	27. d __ __	45. d __ __	63. d __ __	81. c __ __
10. c __ __	28. b __ __	46. b __ __	64. b __ __	82. c __ __
11. c __ __	29. c __ __	47. c __ __	65. c __ __	83. c __ __
12. a __ __	30. c __ __	48. c __ __	66. b __ __	
13. b __ __	31. a __ __	49. d __ __	67. c __ __	
14. c __ __	32. b __ __	50. c __ __	68. b __ __	
15. a __ __	33. c __ __	51. a __ __	69. d __ __	
16. a __ __	34. c __ __	52. a __ __	70. b __ __	
17. d __ __	35. b __ __	53. a __ __	71. c __ __	1st: __/83 = __%
18. b __ __	36. d __ __	54. b __ __	72. a __ __	2nd: __/83 = __%

MULTIPLE-CHOICE ANSWER EXPLANATIONS

A. Cost-Volume-Profit (CVP) Analysis

1.   (d)   Any income statement can be expressed as

Sales – Variable costs – Fixed costs = Operating income

At the breakeven point, operating income = $0. In addition, the Contribution margin = Sales – Variable costs. Therefore, the above equation may be restated as

Sales – Variable costs – Fixed costs = 0
Sales – Variable costs = Fixed costs
Contribution margin = Fixed costs

This makes sense because, by definition, the breakeven point is the point at which revenues equal expenses; after variable costs are subtracted from sales, the contribution margin remaining will be just enough to cover fixed costs.

2.   (c)   The short-cut breakeven point formula is calculated as follows:

$$\text{Breakeven (units)} = \frac{\text{Fixed costs}}{\text{Contribution margin}}$$

Thus, by decreasing the numerator (fixed costs) and increasing the denominator (contribution margin), the breakeven point will be reduced.

3.   (a)   The solutions approach is to work backward from breakeven sales to determine the contribution margin (CM) ratio. The CM ratio can then be used to determine Del's projected profit at $1,200,000 sales. This is accomplished by plugging fixed costs and breakeven sales into the breakeven equation.

$$\text{Breakeven sales} = \frac{\text{Fixed costs}}{\text{CM ratio}}$$

$$\$800,000 = \frac{\$100,000}{\text{CM ratio}}$$

$$\text{CM ratio} = 0.125, \text{ or } 12.5\%$$

Therefore, projected total contribution margin from $1,200,000 sales is $150,000 ($1,200,000 × 12.5%), and projected profit is $50,000 ($150,000 CM – $100,000 fixed costs).

4.   (b)   The requirement is to calculate the number of units that must be sold to generate earnings before interest and taxes (EBIT) in an amount equal to 32% of the amount of capital invested. Answer (b) is correct because the number of units is 32,143 as calculated below.

Desired return (EBIT)	= 32% × $250,000 (investment)
	= $80,000
Required number of units	= (Fixed costs + desired EBIT)/Contribution margin
	= ($122,500 + $80,000)/($15 × 42%)
	= 32,143

5.   (b)   The requirement is to determine the price that Thor Lab should charge to make the same profit with increased fixed costs. The first step in solving this problem is to calculate the variable cost per unit. The variable cost component is determined as follows:

Sales	–	VC	–	FC	=	Profit
(80,000 × $120)	–	(80,000x)	–	$1,000,000	=	$200,000
$9,600,000	–	80,000x	–	$1,000,000	=	$200,000
				$8,400,000	=	80,000x
				$105	=	x

The next step is to substitute the variable cost component and the increased fixed cost amount into the above equation to determine the necessary price. The price can be computed as follows:

$$80,000x - (80,000 \times \$105) - \$2,200,000 = \$ \ 200,000$$
$$80,000x = \$10,800,000$$
$$x = \$ \quad 135$$

6.   (b)   Breakeven analysis is based on several simplified assumptions. One assumption is that, over the relevant range, variable costs **per unit** remain unchanged. It is assumed that over the relevant range, selling price per unit remains constant. Thus, unit revenues are linear. Total variable costs increase with increases in production; therefore, total costs also increase. Over the relevant range, total fixed costs are always linear since they do not change.

7.   (b)   The requirement is to determine Cott's fixed cost using only sales, contribution margin, and margin of safety. First, Cott's breakeven sales should be determined. Since the margin of safety defines how far revenues can fall before the breakeven point is reached, breakeven sales equal $120,000 ($200,000 sales – $80,000 margin of safety). We also know that Cott's contribution margin is 20% of sales.

Contribution margin (CM) equals sales minus all related variable costs (VC), and the contribution margin percentage is calculated as

$$CM\% = \frac{\text{Total CM}}{\text{Revenues}}$$

Or, in this case,

$$20\% = \frac{\text{Total CM}}{\$120,000}$$

Total CM at breakeven = ($120,000) (20%) = $24,000

At the breakeven point, no profit exists and Sales – VC = FC. Therefore, the CM at the breakeven point equals fixed costs, and Cott's fixed costs total $24,000.

8. (b) The budgeted breakeven point is the volume at which total revenues equal total expenses. An increase in direct manufacturing labor wage rates would result in higher variable expenses and a lower contribution per unit. Accordingly, this **increases** the volume of sales necessary to breakeven. The budgeted margin of safety is the excess of budgeted total revenues minus total revenues at the breakeven point. As discussed above, the increase in direct manufacturing labor wages increased the breakeven point. This higher breakeven point **decreases** the budgeted margin of safety.

9. (d) To answer this question, an understanding of cost behavior patterns and CVP charts is needed. The CVP chart presented in the problem can be interpreted as follows:

Within a relevant range, **total** variable costs vary directly with the number of units produced and sold. Because these costs remain constant per unit, the variable costs associated with point A and point B will be the same percentage of total sales associated with each point. Total fixed costs remain constant in total at any activity level. Because these costs are allocated evenly to units produced and sold, they represent a higher percentage of lower sales than of higher sales. Point A is to the left of point B, indicating a lower sales level for point A. The fixed costs will, therefore, be a greater percentage of sales at point A than at point B.

10. (c) If sales dollars are used to measure activity levels, the various activity levels on the X axis would be expressed in terms of sales. Total costs could be read by comparing a point on the total cost line to the Y axis only, because total costs are a dependent variable, which are measured on the Y axis. Total revenues could be read by comparing a point on the total sales line to either the Y axis or the X axis.

11. (c) The requirement is to identify an advantage of using variable costing. Answer (c) is correct because a major advantage of the use of variable costing is that it makes cost-volume relationships more apparent. Answer (a) is incorrect because variable costing does not comply with the US Internal Revenue Code. Answer (b) is incorrect because

variable costing does not comply with generally accepted accounting principles. Answer (d) is incorrect because variable costing is not most relevant to long-run pricing strategies. In the long run all costs must be recovered.

12. (a) The profit-volume (P/V) chart provides a quick condensed comparison of how alternatives for pricing, variable costs, and/or fixed costs may affect net income as volume levels change. In this problem, sales prices remain constant and, therefore, are not relevant. In a P/V chart, the vertical (Y) axis represents net income/loss in dollars. The horizontal (X) axis represents volume in units or dollars. Points on the Y axis above the intersection with the X axis represent profits while points below the intersection represent losses. Total fixed costs are represented by the point at which a specific P/V line intersects the Y axis. This point is always below zero on the Y axis. Because point G (where the P/V line for 2008 intersects the Y axis) is closer to zero than point E (where the P/V line for 2007 intersects the Y axis), point G is less negative; therefore, total fixed costs decreased from 2007 levels. The effect of total variable costs on net income is represented by the positive slope of a P/V line. Variable costs stay the same per unit but change in total as volume levels change. Therefore, a higher per unit amount of variable costs causes a lower per unit amount of net income across various volume levels. Because the graph represents changes in levels of totals, a steeper P/V line slope indicates more profit per unit. Because the slope of line GH (the P/V line for 2008) is **less** steep than the slope of line EF (the P/V line for 2007), net income per unit is less in 2008 than in 2007. Variable costs, therefore, rose between 2007 and 2008.

A.2. Breakeven: Multiproduct Firm

13. (b) The requirement is to determine how many units of product X (one of three products) Thomas would sell at the breakeven point. The solutions approach is first to find the number of composite units to breakeven; a composite unit consists of the number of units of each of the three products in the mix. Since Thomas sells three units of X for each unit of Z and two units of Y for each unit of X, they are selling six units of Y for each unit of Z; therefore, a composite unit consists of 3X, 6Y, and 1Z. The total contribution margin for one composite unit is

X (3) ($1.00)	=	$ 3
Y (6) ($1.50)	=	$ 9
Z (1) ($3.00)	=	$ 3
		$15

The breakeven point in terms of units of the product mix group is

$600,000 ÷ $15 = 40,000 composite units

Since there are three units of X in each composite unit, (40,000) (3) or 120,000 units of X are sold at breakeven.

14. (c) Breakeven analysis is based upon several simplified assumptions. Included in these assumptions is that variable costs are constant per unit and, for a multiproduct company, that a given sales mix is maintained for all volume changes. When absorption costing is used, operating income is a function of **both** production volume and sales volume. This is because an increase in inventory levels causes fixed costs to be held in inventory while a decrease in inventory levels causes fixed costs to be charged to cost of goods sold. These fluctuations can dramatically affect income and the breakeven point. On the other hand, when variable costing is used the same amount of fixed costs will be deducted from income whether or not inventory levels fluctuate. As a result, the breakeven point will be the same even if production does not equal sales. Hence, operating income under variable costing is a function **only** of sales, and assumption I. is incorrect.

15. (a) If sales prices, cost behavior, and actual **total** sales were as budgeted, then the excess profit must have resulted from a departure from budget by the **individual** products. Since the slope of line EH is greater than that of line HG (the slope representing profit per unit), Product 1 had the excess sales. Line OE represents fixed costs and line OF represents quantity sold up to the breakeven point. OE/OF is the contribution margin that may offset fixed costs until the breakeven point, F, is reached.

B. Variable (Direct) and Absorption (Full) Costing

16. (a) The difference between net income under variable costing and net income under full absorption costing is $36,000, which is equal to 20,000 × $180,000/100,000. The difference between the two methods is the fixed cost of manufacturing in the ending inventory that would be capitalized under the full absorption costing method and expensed under the variable costing method. Answer (b) is incorrect because the fixed selling and administration costs would be expensed under either method.

17. (d) Under variable costing, both variable direct and variable indirect manufacturing costs are assigned to inventory. All fixed costs are considered sunk costs and thus are written off as an expense of the period. Additionally, variable selling and administrative costs are also treated as period costs and thus not assigned to inventory.

18. (b) The requirement is to determine the different results obtained using absorption and variable costing. Under absorption costing, fixed costs are applied to units produced and are inventoried as product costs. Variable costing considers fixed costs to be period rather than product costs. Killo Co.'s inventoried costs under both methods are as follows:

	Absorption	Variable
Variable costs	1,000 × $90 = $90,000	1,000 × $90 = $90,000
Fixed costs	1,000 × $20 = 20,000	
Total cost of inventory	$110,000	$90,000

Under the variable method, the $20,000 of fixed cost was charged to income, whereas with absorption costing the fixed costs were absorbed into inventory. Therefore, absorption costing results in a pretax income that is higher by $20,000.

19. (b) The solutions approach is to visualize each income statement as shown below.

Absorption costing IS

Sales
– Cost of goods sold
Gross profit (margin)
– Selling & Admin. Expenses
Operating income

Variable costing IS

Sales
– Variable expenses
Contribution margin
– Fixed expenses
Operating income

Because the question states that actual sales revenue, total gross profit, and total contribution margin approximated budgeted figures, CGS and variable expenses must have also approximated budgeted figures. Net income is substantially greater, therefore, because selling and administrative fixed expenses had decreased. If manufacturing fixed costs had increased, gross margin would have decreased. If sales prices and variable costs had increased proportionately, the contribution margin would have increased by the same percentage. If sales prices had declined proportionately less than variable costs, the contribution margin would have again increased.

20. (a) The requirement is to determine what situation would cause variable costing net income to be higher than absorption costing net income. Answer (a) is correct because this difference in reported income is explained if units produced in 2009 are less than units sold in 2009. This is true because under variable costing, the amount of overhead included in cost of goods sold is the amount applied in 2009 (since all units produced were sold), whereas under absorption costing the overhead released to cost of goods sold includes that applied in 2009 as well as overhead included in the 2008 year-end inventory. Answer (b) is incorrect since a level of production lower than the activity level used to allocate overhead would result in underapplied overhead. Answer (c) is incorrect because the opposite situation results in overapplied overhead. Answer (d) is incorrect because production in excess of units sold would produce a higher absorption costing income than the variable costing income.

C. Financial Planning

21. (c) The requirement is to identify the item that is an output from a strategic plan. Answer (c) is correct. A financial planning model is a mathematical model that attempts to forecast future financial results. Sets of projected financial statements are a major output from the model. Answer (a) is incorrect because strategic plans drive the financial planning process and must be developed before employing the financial planning model. Answers (b) and (d) are incorrect because the planning model does not provide outputs related to actual results.

D. Budgeting

22. (c) The requirement is to determine the number of kilos of chemical Loire that Mien is planning to purchase in October. The first step is to prepare a production budget for product Nous.

Sales	53,000
Increase in ending inventory	6,000
Total units needed	59,000

Next, a purchases budget for raw material Loire should be prepared.

Production needs (59,000 × 4)	236,000
Decrease in ending inventory	(50,000)
Total kilos needed	186,000

Note that the production needs for Loire equal the number of units of Nous to be produced times the number of kilos of Loire needed per unit (4).

23. (d) The requirement is to identify a characteristic of the master budget. Answer (d) is correct because the master budget is a comprehensive budget that includes both the operating and financial budgets. Answer (a) is incorrect because the master budget does not show actual results. Answer (b) is incorrect because the master budget shows all costs, controllable and uncontrollable. Answer (c) is incorrect because the master budget is not structured for the computation of variances.

24. (c) The requirement is to calculate the budgeted cost of purchases for the month of August. The cost of inventory needed to meet August forecasted sales is equal to $300,000 ($750,000 × 40%). The required ending inventory for August is equal to $82,500 ($825,000 September sales × 40% × 25%). The ending inventory for July is equal to $75,000 ($750,000 August sales × 40% × 25%). Budgeted cost of purchases for August would equal to $307,500 ($300,000 cost of goods sold + $82,500 required ending inventory – $75,000 beginning inventory). Therefore, answer (c) is correct. Answer (a) is incorrect because the June 30 inventory is deducted. Answer (b) is incorrect because it deducts what should be the ending inventory for June. Answer (d) is incorrect because it results from using sales prices for the beginning and ending inventories.

25. (b) The requirement is to calculate the budgeted amount of cash receipts from sales and collection for September. Forecasted sales for September are $825,000 of which $165,000 (20%) are cash sales. In addition, 40% of credit sales are collected in the month of sale, which is equal to $264,000 ($825,000) × 80% × 40%). Collections of August sales in September are equal to $342,000 ($750,000 × 80% × 57%). Accordingly, the projected collections for September are $771,000 ($165,00 + $264,000 + $342,000), and answer (b) is correct. Answer (a) is incorrect because $757,000 ignores cash sales. Answer (c) is incorrect because $793,800 assumes 57% of October sales are collected in September. Answer (d) is incorrect because $856,500 assumes the collections in September for August sales are 57% of total sales.

26. (c) The requirement is to define a tactical profit plan. Answer (c) is correct because tactical profit plans have the characteristics of being quantified, detailed and short-term, and assigning responsibilities at all levels. Answer (a) is incorrect because tactical profit plans are quantitative with detailed assigned responsibilities. Answer (b) is incorrect because tactical profit plans are detailed. Answer (d) is incorrect because tactical profit plans are detailed, short-term, quantitative, and include assigned responsibilities at all levels.

27. (d) The requirement is to identify the budgeting technique that focuses on improving operations. Answer (d) is correct because Kaizen budgeting projects costs on the basis of improvements to be implemented. Answer (a) is incorrect because responsibility budgeting focuses on the ability of the manager to control the cost. Answer (b) is incorrect because activity-based budgeting uses cost drivers to determine budgeted costs. Answer (c) is incorrect because operational budgeting focuses on budgeting operating costs.

28. (b) The requirement is to identify the item that is part of a financial budget. Answer (b) is correct. The financial budget includes the capital budget, cash budget, and the budgeted statement of cash flows. The operating budget includes the budgeted income statement and supporting budgets. Answers (a), (c), and (d) are incorrect because they are part of the operating budget.

29. (c) Calculation of the cash payments for components in May is shown below.

Payments for June sales	$1,750 ($7,000 × 25%)
Payment for July sales	$6,000 ($8,000 × 75%)
Total cash payments	$7,750

Answer (a) is incorrect because parts are ordered two months prior to sales. Therefore, costs of components for sales of June and July should be considered. Answer (b) is incorrect because parts are ordered two months prior to sales. Therefore, costs of components for sales of June and July should be considered. Answer (d) is incorrect because parts are ordered two months prior to sales. Therefore, costs of components for sales of June and July should be considered.

30. (c) The requirement is to determine budgeted cash disbursements for purchases for 2009. The solutions approach is to use T-accounts to trace the flow of budgeted costs through the accounts.

	Inventory		
Bal. 1/1/09	30,000		
Purchases	?	300,000	CGS
Bal. 12/31/09	42,000		

T-account analysis reveals that total purchases of inventory for the year must be $312,000.

Goods sold or on hand at 12/31	–	Beginning inventory	=	Purchases
($300,000 + $42,000)	–	$30,000	=	$312,000

Payments for purchases are made in the month following purchase. Thus, accounts payable at 1/1/09 will be paid in January 2009 and 1/12 of 2009 purchases (since Toyi is purchased in equal amounts each month) will be paid for in January 2010.

Accounts payable is depicted as follows:

	Accounts Payable		
Cash disbursements	306,000*	20,000	Bal. 1/1/09
		312,000	Purchases
		26,000**	Bal. 12/31/09

* ($312,000 purchases x 11/12) + $20,000 beg. AP
** $312,000 purchases x 1/12

Therefore, budgeted cash payments for Toyi for 2009 is $306,000.

31. (a) The requirement is to calculate the budgeted cash from collection of accounts receivable. Answer (a) is correct because the amount is equal to July's collections in September plus August's collections in September. This amount is $169,800 (36% × $120,000 + 60% × $211,000).

32. (b) The requirement is to find the total budgeted costs for the seven stores in the coming year. Fixed costs last year were $70,000, and therefore variable costs totaled $430,000. The key is to find the variable costs per store. This is calculated by dividing variable costs ($430,000) by the number of stores last year (five), or, $86,000. Therefore, total costs budgeted in the new year is calculated as follows:

Variable cost per store	$86,000
Number of stores	× 7
Total budgeted variable costs	602,000
Add: fixed costs	70,000
Total budgeted costs	$672,000

E. Forecasting Methods

33. (c) The requirement is to identify the correlation coefficient that represents the strongest relationship between the independent and dependent variables. Regression coefficients can range from -1.00 (perfect negative correlation to 1.00 (perfect positive correlation, and the closer to -1.00 or 1.00 the stronger the relationship. Answer (c) is correct because it is the coefficient closest to -1.00 or 1.00. Answer (a) is incorrect because it is not possible to have a correlation coefficient greater than 1.00. Answers (b) and (d) are incorrect because they are both further from -1.00 or 1.00.

34. (c) The requirement is to provide an explanation for a drop in r^2. The coefficient of determination (r^2) provides a measure of amount of variation in the dependent variable (interest income) explained by the independent variables. If there is a dramatic decrease in the coefficient of determination, the implication is that there are some new factors that are causing interest income to change. Therefore, answer (c) is correct. Answer (a) is incorrect because cross-sectional regression is not appropriate. Management is attempting to estimate interest income over time. Answer (b) is incorrect because regression analysis may still be appropriate. Answer (d) is incorrect because multiple regression is a linear model. Management may want to try other models such as nonlinear multiple regression.

35. (b) The requirement is to identify the factor that is not relevant to forecasting the needed level of inventory. Answer (b) is correct because knowledge of the internal accounting allocations is not relevant to determining the demand for the product. Answers (a), (c), and (d) are incorrect because they are all relevant to determining demand for the product and, therefore, the needed level of inventory.

36. (d) The requirement is to identify the meaning the of the letter *b* in the regression equation. Answer (d) is correct because *b* is the coefficient for the independent variable. The variable coefficient that describes the slope of the regression function. Answer (a) is incorrect because *x* is the independent variable. Answer (b) is incorrect because *y* is the dependent variable. Answer (c) is incorrect because *a* is the constant coefficient.

37. (a) The requirement is to identify the meaning of the letter *x* in the regression equation. Answer (a) is correct because *x* is the independent variable, the variable that is being used to predict the dependent variable. Answer (b) is incorrect because *y* is the dependent variable. Answer (c) is incorrect because *a* is the constant variable. Answer (d) is incorrect because r^2 is the coefficient of determination.

38. (d) The requirement is to use the regression equation to determine the amount of predicted maintenance costs. Substituting 420 maintenance hours into the equation results in a budgeted cost of $3,746.

$$y = a + bx$$
$$y = 684.65 + 7.2884 \ (420)$$
$$y = \$3,746$$

Therefore, (d) is the correct answer.

39. (c) The requirement is to identify the dependent variable. Answer (c) is correct because the dependent variable is the one being predicted, in this case revenue. Answers (a), (b), and (d) are incorrect because predicted number of days above 10 degrees and predicted number of inches of snow are both independent variables.

40. (c) The requirement is to calculate the predicted revenue for the next week. Answer (c) is correct because revenue is equal to $10,902 + (255 × 6) + (300 × 12) = 16,032. Answers (a), (b), and (d) are all incorrect computations of the prediction.

41. (d) The requirement is to identify the appropriate conclusion. Answer (d) is correct because the coefficient of determination indicates that 67.89% of revenue is explained by the predicted number of days above 10 degrees and the number of inches of snow. Answer (a) is incorrect because the *F*-Statistic measures the significance of the relationship. Answer (b) is incorrect because the *F*-Statistic indicates that the regression is significant. Answer (c) is incorrect because there is no information provided to make this determination.

42. (b) The requirement is to calculate the 95% confidence interval for the prediction of revenue. Answer (b) is correct because the 95% confidence interval is calculated by multiplying the standard error of the regression by 2.3436. Therefore, it is equal to 4,404 (1,879 × 2.3436).

43. (a) The requirement is to identify the sales forecasting technique that involves estimating sales based on analysis of consumer behavior. Answer (a) is correct because Markov techniques attempt to forecast consumer purchasing by considering factors such as brand loyalty and brand switching behavior. Answer (b) is incorrect because regression analysis forecasts sales based on the relationship between sales and one or more predictors. Answer (c) is incorrect because econometric models forecast sales based on the relationship between sales and economic data. Answer (d) is incorrect because exponential smoothing is used to forecast sales based on historical data.

44. (c) The requirement is to identify the quantitative technique to developing a sales forecast. Answer (c) is correct because the moving average technique uses the average of sales for the most recent periods to predict next period's sales. Answer (a) is incorrect because the Delphi technique is simply a structured approach to developing a subjective estimate from a group of people. Answers (b) and (d) are incorrect because they involve qualitative approaches to developing a sales forecast.

45. (d) The requirement is to identify the forecasting technique that is determined by a combination of the last forecast and the last observed value. Answer (d) is correct because exponential smoothing is a quantitative technique that forecasts sales based on prior data with the most recent observation being weighted more heavily. Answer (a) is incorrect because the Delphi technique forecasts with a consensus of opinion. Answers (b) and (d) are incorrect because least squares and regression forecast sales based on the correlation of sales with one or more independent variables.

46. (b) The correlation coefficient is a relative measure of the relationship between two variables. The range of the correlation coefficient is from -1 (perfect negative correlation) to +1 (perfect positive correlation). A correlation coefficient of zero means that there is **no** correlation between the two variables. Since the level of sales **increases** as the level of income **decreases,** this relationship represents a strong **negative** correlation. Answer (c) is incorrect because it represents a **positive** correlation. Answers (a) and (d) are incorrect because they lie outside of the range for correlation coefficients.

F. Flexible Budgets

47. (c) A flexible budget is simply a static budget adjusted for various possible volume levels within the relevant range. A master budget or a flexible budget may be used during both the planning phase, when the budget is prepared, and the controlling phase, when actual results are compared to the budget. A flexible budget may be prepared for any unit for which costs vary with changes in activity level. Flexible budgets provide as much cost control as do master budgets because they are based on costs **allowable** at different activity levels. In fact, flexible budgets may offer an even greater degree of control because valid guidelines are available to managers even if output deviates from expectations, whereas static budgets supply information regarding only the planned volume.

48. (c) The requirement is to determine whether a flexible budget is appropriate for a marketing and/or a direct material usage budget. Flexible budgets are used to analyze changes in costs and revenues as changes in activity levels take place. If no changes are expected to occur and thus all amounts in the flexible budget remain constant throughout the relevant range (i.e., all costs are fixed), there is no need for a flexible budget. A marketing budget includes expenses incurred for promotion and sales. Some of these items, such as sales commissions or sample promotional products change with activity level. Direct material usage is directly dependent on activity level. Since a flexible budget would be appropriate for both a marketing and a direct materials usage budget, answer (c) is correct.

49. (d) Within the relevant range, **total** fixed costs remain constant. As production levels increase, the same amount of fixed cost is spread over a greater number of units, and fixed costs **per unit** decrease. In contrast, variable costs **per unit** do not change within the relevant range.

G. Responsibility Accounting

50. (c) Responsibility accounting allocates to responsibility centers those costs, revenues, and/or assets which a manager can control. If a manager is only responsible for costs, the area of responsibility under his/her control is called a cost center. If the manager is responsible for both revenues and costs, his/her area of control is called a profit center. Thus, controllable revenue pertains to the profit center but not the cost center.

51. (a) A manager of a profit center is responsible for both the revenues and the costs of that center. Costs charged directly to a profit center, excluding fixed costs, are subject to the control of the profit center manager. As a result, the profit center's contribution margin (Sales – All variable costs) is controllable by the center manager. In this case, the manager of Carr Co.'s center No. 43 would be most likely to control the center's contribution margin of $70,000. The period expenses shown in the problem would not be subject to the manager's control and thus are irrelevant items.

52. (a) Direct manufacturing labor costs are labor costs that can be easily traced to the manufacture of a product. Wages earned by machine operators producing a firm's product are, therefore, direct manufacturing labor costs. Controllable costs are those which can be directly influenced by a given manager within a given time span. Wages earned by machine operators are controllable by the machine operators' foreman.

H. Standards and Variances

53. (a) Many service firms, nonprofit organizations, and governmental units, in addition to manufacturing firms, use standard cost systems. For example, a trucking company may set standards for fuel costs.

54. (b) Standard costs are predetermined target costs which should be attainable under **efficient** conditions. Currently attainable standards should be achieved under efficient operating conditions. Therefore, engineering estimates based on attainable performance would provide the best basis for Flint in establishing standard hours allowed.

55. (a) The requirement is to determine the standard costing variance which would be **least** controllable by a production supervisor. The overhead output level (volume) variance arises because the **actual** production volume level achieved usually does not coincide with the production level used as a denominator volume for calculating a budgeted overhead **application** rate. The overhead output level variance results from treating a **fixed cost** as if it were a **variable cost**. Answers (b), (c), and (d) are incorrect because all of these variances arise when the quantity of actual inputs used differs from the quantity of inputs that should have been used. A production manager would have more control over inputs to production than over the determination of the denominator volume.

56. (b) The requirement is to determine Lem's material price variance for May. The direct materials price variance is the difference between actual unit prices and standard unit prices multiplied by the actual quantity, as shown below.

AQ × AP	AQ × SP
$10,080	$10,500
	(4,200m × $2.50/m)

Material price variance, $420F

The $420 price variance is favorable because the actual purchase price of the material was lower than the standard price. Since the material was purchased for only $2.40 per meter ($10,080 cost ÷ 4,200m), Lem saved $.10 per meter compared to the standard price, for a total price savings of $420 (4,200m × $.10/m). Note that the standard quantity of materials is ignored in order to isolate these price differences; differences in quantity are addressed by the materials usage variance.

57. (d) Each unit of finished product contains two yards of direct material. However, the problem states that the 20% direct material spoilage is calculated on the quantity of direct material **input**. Although not mentioned, the facts in this question infer that the spoilage is normal and should be part of the product's standard cost. The solutions approach would be to set up the following formula:

Input quantity	–	Spoilage	=	Output amount
X	–	.2X	=	2 yds.
		.8X	=	2 yds.
		X	=	2.5 yds.

Thus, the standard direct material cost per unit of finished product is $7.50 (2.5 yds. × $3).

58. (a) The materials usage variance measures the **actual** amount of materials **used** versus the standard amount that should have been used given the level of output. Normally the only department with controls over usage of materials is the manufacturing department. The purchasing department normally controls the cost of materials **purchased,** and not the amounts used (materials price variance). The warehouse department has little or no control over the materials used.

59. (b) The solutions approach to compute the direct manufacturing labor efficiency variance is to set up a diagram as follows:

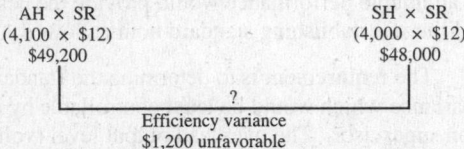

```
    AH × SR                    SH × SR
 (4,100 × $12)              (4,000 × $12)
    $49,200                    $48,000
         |_____|
                       ?
               Efficiency variance
               $1,200 unfavorable
```

NOTE: To compute the Standard Hours (SH), multiply the Standard Hours allowed per unit produced (4) by the number of units produced (1,000).

60. (a) Standard costs are predetermined target costs which should be attainable under efficient conditions. The standard direct manufacturing labor cost per unit of product Glu is calculated as follows:

Weekly wages per worker	$500
Benefits treated as DML cost	100
Total DML per week per worker	$600
Hours per week	÷40
DML cost per hour	$ 15
Hours required for each unit	× 2
Standard DML cost per unit	$ 30

61. (d) A labor rate variance is the difference between budgeted wage rates and the wage rates actually paid. The problem states that line OW represents the standard labor cost at any output volume. Because point A is **above** the line, the actual cost was higher than the standard. The rate variance is, therefore, unfavorable. A labor efficiency variance is the difference between actual hours worked and standard hours allowed for output. On the diagram, point S is further on the X axis (Direct manufacturing labor hours) than point A indicating that the standard hours allowed are higher than the actual hours worked. Because actual hours are less than standard hours, this variance would be favorable.

62. (a) To determine Gage's actual manufacturing overhead from the information given, total actual manufacturing costs must first be computed.

Standard manufacturing cost	$100,000
Excess of actual manufacturing cost over standard costs	20,000
Total actual costs	$120,000

Since prime costs consist of direct materials and direct manufacturing labor, these costs are deducted from total actual costs to derive the portion that are overhead costs. Ordinarily, normal spoilage is not added to actual manufac-

turing overhead. The cost of normal spoilage should be added to the cost of good units produced. Freight out is also excluded because it is a selling expense.

Total actual costs	$120,000
Prime costs	(80,000)
Actual manufacturing overhead	$ 40,000

63. (d) The fixed overhead spending variance is calculated as follows:

Budgeted fixed overhead	$20,000
Actual fixed overhead	22,000
Unfavorable fixed overhead spending variance	$ 2,000

64. (b) The requirement is to determine which of the variances given consist of both variable and fixed overhead elements under a two-variance method. As shown in the diagram below, the controllable or budget variance includes both variable and fixed overhead elements, because the actual overhead amount, the first vertical line, includes both elements as does the budgeted overhead amount, the middle vertical line.

```
                    Budget for
                 outputs achieved               Applied
  Actual         FOH + (SQ × SVR)              SQ × STR*
       |_____|_____|
            Budget var.           Volume var.
```

*   *STR = Standard variable rate (SVR) + Standard fixed rate (SFR)*

The output level (volume) variance includes only the variance of fixed overhead, because the SQ × SVR is common to both amounts (i.e., it is included in the STR) used to determine the output level variance. The difference in the two amounts is the output level variance. It arises because the middle vertical line includes the total amount of budgeted fixed overhead, whereas the third vertical line includes the amount of fixed overhead applied using a per unit amount based on normal volume or level of activity. Whenever the standard activity level based on good output (SQ) is different than the normal activity level, a volume variance will arise. Therefore, both variable and fixed overhead elements are included in the controllable variance but not in the output level variance.

65. (c) The requirement is to determine how unfavorable spending and output level (volume) variances computed using the three-variance method would be affected if the estimated activity level were increased. An increase in the activity level used to allocate overhead to the product will lower the standard fixed application rate (SFR). The formula for computing the SFR is

$$\frac{\text{Predetermined}}{\text{overhead rate}} = \frac{\text{Estimated fixed overhead cost}}{\text{Estimated activity level}}$$

If the denominator in this formula is raised, the SFR is lowered. However, an increase in activity level used to allocate overhead will not affect the standard variable application rate (SVR). This rate is computed using the high-low method or regression analysis. The diagram for the 3-variance method is

```
           Budget for              Budget for
          actual inputs          outputs achieved          Applied
 Actual   FOH + (AQ × SVR)       FOH + (SQ × SVR)        (SQ × STR)*
      |_____|_____|_____|
         Spending var.    Efficiency var.    Output level var.
      :_____Net (overall) overhead variance_____:
```

*STR = Standard variable rate (SVR) + Standard fixed rate (SFR)

When computing the standard variance, the SVR is used but the SFR is not. Therefore, this variance will not change with a change in activity level. The output level variance is computed by comparing the budgeted amount of total overhead costs for outputs achieved with the total amount of overhead applied. Both computations use SVR, but only the applied figure uses the SFR. In this problem, the output level variance is unfavorable indicating that the budgeted amount is more than the applied amount. When the SFR is lowered with the increase in activity level, less cost will be applied for every unit produced. The output level variance will therefore be increased and become more unfavorable.

66. **(b)** The solutions approach to compute the variable overhead efficiency variance is to set up a diagram as follows:

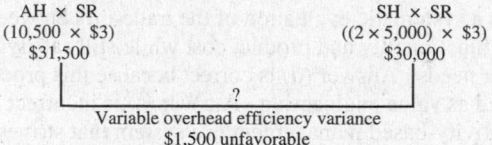

$$\begin{array}{cc} AH \times SR & SH \times SR \\ (10,500 \times \$3) & ((2 \times 5,000) \times \$3) \\ \$31,500 & \$30,000 \end{array}$$

Variable overhead efficiency variance
$1,500 unfavorable

67. **(c)** A spending variance is caused by differences between the actual amount spent on fixed and variable overhead items and the amounts budgeted based on actual inputs. An output level variance is the difference between budgeted fixed overhead and applied fixed overhead. It is caused by under- or overutilization of plant capacity. Differences between actual and budgeted amounts (spending variances) occur often and can be corrected by changing the accounting estimates used in the budgeting process or the purchasing policies used. A difference in under- or over-utilization of plant capacity is a complex problem not easily corrected. Spending variances indicate short-term problems dealing with amounts spent on overhead while output level variances indicate long-term problems dealing with plant capacity.

68. **(b)** The output level variance is solely a **fixed** overhead variance and is caused by under-/overutilization of capacity. This variance is computed by comparing the amount of fixed overhead budgeted with the amount of fixed overhead applied.

On the graph, line DB represents the flexible budget line for various outputs achieved and line OA represents the standard application line for various outputs achieved. Point V represents the standard quantity allowed for the output achieved. The dashed line extended vertically from V indicates the amount of overhead applied (where dashed line crosses OA) and the flexible budget amount (where dashed line crosses DB). Because the point on DB is below the point on OA, a larger amount was applied than the flexible budget amount. The output level variance is, therefore, favorable.

An overhead efficiency variance is solely a **variable** overhead variance and is caused by more (less) variable overhead being incurred due to inefficient (efficient) use of inputs. This variance is computed by comparing the flexible budget amount for actual inputs (Actual quantity of inputs × Standard variable application rate) with the amount applied (Standard quantity allowed for achieved output × Standard variable application rate). On the graph, Point S indicates the actual hours (inputs) used. Point V indicates the standard quantity allowed for the achieved outputs. Point S falls on the X axis further from zero than does Point V. Therefore, more hours were actually used than budgeted for the output achieved. The efficiency variance is unfavorable.

69. **(d)** On the graph, line DB represents the total factory overhead flexible budget line for various outputs achieved. Point D (the Y intercept) indicates the amount of fixed overhead included in the flexible budget. Line BC represents the total flexible budget amount estimated for the level of inputs used at Point C. Budgeted total variable overhead cost for C machine hours is total overhead budget (BC) less fixed overhead budgeted (DO).

70. **(b)** The requirement is to determine if favorable variances for variable food costs and fixed supervisory salaries would be reported by comparing actual results to amounts in a static budget. A static budget has only one planned volume level. The budget is not adjusted or altered to reflect changes in volume or other conditions during the budget period. In this problem, the actual level of sales was lower than the level used to make the static budget. Because variable costs remain the same per unit but change with levels of activity within the relevant range, actual variable costs would be lower than those in the budget. The variance reported for these costs would therefore be favorable. Fixed costs, however, are assumed to remain the same in total at all activity levels within the relevant range unless a change is specifically indicated. Because no such change is indicated in this problem concerning the fixed supervisory salaries, the actual amount for this cost would be the same as the amount in the static budget. There would be no variance reported for this fixed cost.

I. Product and Service Pricing

71. **(c)** The solutions approach is to algebraically reconstruct how Cuff Caterers determined the total price per person. Three components comprise the total price: the cost of the food, the service charge, and the sales tax. The 15% service charge is computed on the food (F) only. The 6% sales tax is computed on the food plus the service charge. The following equation is used to compute the price:

$$F + .15F + .06 \,(F + .15F) = \$60.00$$

Where

F	=	the cost of the food alone
$.15F$	=	the service charge
$.06\,(F + .15F)$	=	the sales tax

Solving algebraically

$1.219F$	=	\$60.00
F	=	\$49.22

72. **(a)** The target price is to be set at a budgeted ratio of operating income to revenue, or a profit margin on sales of 15%. This problem may be solved using the following equation:

Let x	=	Target price
Revenue – Cost	=	Profit
$500x - \$990,000$	=	$.15(500x)$
$.85(500x)$	=	\$990,000
$425x$	=	\$990,000
x	=	\$2,329

73. **(c)** The requirement is to determine the amount that Briar should receive from the contract. This amount can be computed as follows:

Actual costs incurred	\$1,920,000
Multiply by 110% (cost + 10%)	× 1.10
Formula price	\$2,112,000

The target price of $2,200,000 exceeds the formula price of $2,112,000 by $88,000. Briar is to receive 50% of this amount, or $44,000, in addition to the formula price. Therefore, Briar is to receive a total of $2,156,000 ($2,112,000 + $44,000).

74.　(d)　To determine the price at which expected product sales will yield the greatest profits, many factors such as customer preferences, competitors' reactions, cost structures, etc. must be considered. A customer's perception of the quality and durability (life) of a product affects how much s/he is willing to pay for that product. However, in some cases a customer may prefer to pay less money and receive a product of lesser quality. Therefore, Vince should consider the quality and life of the new device as well as customers' relative preference for quality compared to price.

75.　(c)　Klunker is using a "time and material" pricing approach. The charges for each are calculated below.

$$\text{Time:} \quad \begin{matrix}\text{Labor}\\\text{cost per}\\\text{hour}\end{matrix} + \frac{\text{Other overhead}}{\text{Total labor hours}} + \begin{matrix}\text{Profit}\\\text{margin}\\\text{per hour}\end{matrix}$$

$$\$30 + \frac{\$120,000}{10,000} + \$8 = \$50 \text{ per labor hour}$$

$$\text{Materials:} \quad \left(\begin{matrix}\text{Materials}\\\text{cost for job}\end{matrix}\right) + \left(\begin{matrix}\text{Materials}\\\text{cost for job}\end{matrix} \times \frac{\begin{matrix}\text{Materials}\\\text{handling \& storage}\end{matrix}}{\begin{matrix}\text{Total materials}\\\text{cost for year}\end{matrix}}\right)$$

$$\$800 + \left(\$800 \times \frac{\$10,000}{\$500,000}\right) = \$816$$

The total price for the overhaul should therefore be $1,416 [($50/hr. × 12 hrs) + $816)]. Note that materials handling and storage costs are allocated at $0.02 per dollar of materials, and other overhead is allocated at $12 per labor hour.

J.　Transfer Pricing

76.　(c)　The requirement is to determine whether Ajax should take on a new customer and end its sales to the Bradley division and why. As a profit center, Ajax will make the decision independent of the effects on the corporation as a whole. If Ajax sells to the new customer, its revenues will increase to $1,500,000 ($75 × 20,000), but its costs will remain the same at $1,200,000 ($900,000 + $300,000). This results in a positive gross margin of $300,000 ($1,500,000 – $1,200,000). The new gross margin is $600,000 [$300,000 – (–$300,000)] greater than the original gross margin. The shortcut (incremental) approach is to multiply 20,000 units times the $30 increase ($75 – $45) in Ajax's unit selling (transfer) price.

77.　(b)　Negotiated transfer prices should fall within a range limited by a ceiling and a floor. The ceiling is the lowest market price that could be obtained from an external supplier, and the floor equals the outlay costs plus opportunity cost of the transferring division. Since James' MIS department does not have to option to sell services to external customers, its opportunity cost is $0. Since all costs of service departments must be covered by the revenue-producing departments, the MIS department's outlay cost equals its total costs. The department's full capacity level is 1,000 reports per year. However, the user departments will be requesting 1,250 reports (5 user subunits × 250 reports each). Thus, the MIS department will incur costs of $12,000 [$48 × (1,250 – 1,000)] for the 250 reports above capacity,

in addition to the $45,000 budgeted costs for full capacity. The total cost of $57,000 ($45,000 + $12,000) is used to calculate the floor. The ceiling is based on the $70,000 that would be incurred to purchase MIS services externally. Since the MIS department will be producing 1,250 reports, the floor is $45.60 ($57,000 ÷ 1,250), and the ceiling is $56.00 ($70,000 ÷ 1,250). At full capacity, any differential costs of additional production are added to the floor. $48.00 represents only the differential cost of producing each report above full capacity, not cost per report for total production. Budgeted costs are based on production of 1,250 reports, not 1,000.

78.　(d)　The requirement is to identify the process that involves a systematic evaluation of the trade-offs between product functionality and product cost while still satisfying customer needs. Answer (d) is correct because this process is defined as value engineering. Answer (a) is incorrect because activity-based management is a system that strives for excellence through cost reduction, process improvement, and productivity gains. Answer (b) is incorrect because the Theory of Constraints refers to methods to maximize operating income when faced with some bottleneck operations. Answer (c) is incorrect because total quality management involves the application of quality principles to all company activities.

79.　(d)　The goal of transfer pricing is to encourage managers to make transfer decisions which maximize profits of the company as a **whole**. Some transfers may not be profitable to a particular division, but would effect a cost savings to the company by avoiding costs of purchasing externally. For example, when a division is already operating at full capacity and uses variable cost transfer prices, additional production for internal transfer would result in a loss for the transferring division because no contribution margin is earned to cover the differential fixed costs incurred. Conversely, internal production may be cheaper to the corporate entity than purchasing the product, in which case the division should accept the order. However, the division manager is likely to engage in suboptimization by rejecting the order to enhance the division's performance, while adversely affecting overall company performance.

K.　Short-Term Differential Cost Analysis

80.　(b)　When determining a price for a special order when there is idle capacity, only the differential manufacturing costs are considered. The underlying assumption is that acceptance of the order will not affect regular sales. In the short run, fixed costs are sunk costs and are irrelevant. Since regular sales will not be affected by the special order, fixed and variable costs incurred during normal operations are not considered. Clay Company should consider only the variable costs associated with the order and the differential cost of using the external designers. The costs to be considered total $40,750 ($33,000 + $7,750). The order is accepted if revenue from the order exceeds the differential costs.

81.　(c)　When deciding between alternatives, the only relevant costs or revenues are those expected future costs and revenues that differ across alternatives. In the short run, fixed costs are sunk costs and are irrelevant. Thus, Abel's 2009 fixed costs are ignored for purposes of short-term dif-

ferential cost analysis. The incremental cost was $100,000
($500,000 − $400,000).

82. (c)   The requirement is to evaluate the effect on pretax profit if a department is discontinued. The solutions
approach is to isolate those revenues and costs that would
differ if the department is discontinued. If the department is
discontinued, $20,000 of contribution margin would be lost.
The $5,000 of allocated overhead will continue regardless of
the decision made. Thus, $45,000 ($50,000 − $5,000) of
allocated overhead cost would be eliminated or avoided.
The net effect on pretax profit would be an increase of
$25,000 ($45,000 of cost avoided less $20,000 of contribu-
tion margin lost).

83. (c)   The requirement is to determine the effect on
operating income of closing Segment B. Answer (c) is correct because if Segment B is closed overall sales will be
reduced by $15,000, variable costs of goods sold will be
reduced by $8,500, fixed costs of goods sold will be reduced
by $1,500, and variable selling and administrative expenses
will be reduced by $3,000, resulting in a $2,000 ($15,000 −
8,500 − 1,500 − 3,000) decrease in operating income.

APPENDIX A: SIMULATIONS
AUDITING AND ATTESTATION

SIMULATION 1   (60 to 70 minutes)

Topics—Planning, Internal Control, and Evidence

Situation										
	Company Profile	Industry Information	Balance Sheet	Income Statement	Statement of Cash Flows	Risks	Financial Statement Analysis	Audit Procedures	Communication	Research

DietWeb Inc. (hereafter DietWeb) was incorporated and began business in March of 20X1, seven years ago. You are working on the 20X8 audit—your CPA firm's fifth audit of DietWeb.

	Company Profile									
Situation		Industry Information	Balance Sheet	Income Statement	Statement of Cash Flows	Risks	Financial Statement Analysis	Audit Procedures	Communication	Research

The company's mission is to provide solutions that help individuals to realize their full potential through better eating habits and lifestyles. Much of 20X1 and 20X2 was spent in developing a unique software platform that facilitates the production of individualized meal plans and shopping lists using a specific mathematical algorithm, which considers the user's physical condition, proclivity to exercise, food preferences, cooking preferences, desire to use prepackaged meals or dine out, among others. DietWeb sold its first online diet program in 20X2 and has continued to market memberships through increasing online advertising arrangements through the years. The company has continued to develop this program throughout the years and finally became profitable in 20X6.

DietWeb is executing a strategy to be a leading online provider of services, information and products related to nutrition, fitness and motivation. In 20X8, the company derived approximately 86% of its total revenues from the sale of approximately 203,000 personalized subscription-based online nutrition plans related to weight management, to dietary regimens such as vegetarianism and to specific medical conditions such as Type 2 diabetes. Given the personal nature of dieting, DietWeb assures customers of complete privacy of the information they provide. To this point DietWeb's management is proud of its success in assuring the privacy of information supplied by its customers—this is a constant battle given the variety of intrusion attempts by various Internet hackers.

DietWeb nutrition plans are paid in advance by customers and offered in increments of thirteen weeks with the customers having the ability to cancel and receive a refund of the unused portion of the subscription—this results in a significant level of "deferred revenue" each period. Although some DietWeb members are billed through use of the postal system, most DietWeb members currently purchase programs and products using credit cards, with renewals billed automatically, until cancellation. One week of a basic DietWeb membership costs less than one-half the cost of a weekly visit to the leading classroom-based diet program. The president, Mr. William Readings, suggests that in addition to its superior cost-effectiveness, the DietWeb online diet program is successful relative to classroom-based programs due to its customization, ease of use, expert support, privacy, constant availability, and breadth of choice. The basic DietWeb membership includes

- Customized meal plans and workout schedules and related tools such as shopping lists, journals, and weight and exercise tracking.
- Interactive online support and education including approximately 100 message boards on various topics of interest to members and a library of dozens of multimedia educational segments presented by experts including psychologists, mental health counselors, dietitians, fitness trainers, a spiritual advisor and a physician.
- 24/7/365 telephone support from a staff of approximately 30 customer service representatives, nutritionists and fitness personnel.

Throughout its nine-year history, Mr. William Readings has served as chief executive officer. The other three founders of the company are also officers. A fifth individual, Willingsley Williamson, also a founder, served as Chief Financial Officer until mid-20X8 when he left the company due to a difference of opinion with Mr. Readings. The four founders purchased Mr. Williamson's stock and invested an additional approximately $1.2 million in common stock during 20X8 so as to limit the use of long-term debt.

The company's board of directors is currently composed of the four individuals who remain active in the company; these four individuals also serve as the company's audit committee; Mr. Readings chairs both the board and the audit committee. Previously, Mr. Readings had also served on the board and the audit committee. With Mr. Williamson's departure, Ms. Jane Jennings, another of the founders, became the company's CFO.

		Industry Information								
Situation	Company Profile		Balance Sheet	Income Statement	Statement of Cash Flows	Risks	Financial Statement Analysis	Audit Procedures	Communication	Research

The nutrition and diet industry in many ways thrives because individuals are becoming more aware of the negative health and financial consequences of being overweight, and consider important both weight loss and healthy weight maintenance. A study by two respected researchers concluded that obesity was linked to higher rates of chronic illness than living in poverty, than smoking, or than drinking. In addition, the American Cancer Society reported that as many as 14% of cancer deaths in men and 20% of cancer deaths in women could be related to being overweight.

The financial costs of excess weight are also high. A 20X8 study based on data from a major automobile manufacturer's health care plan showed that an overweight adult has annual health care costs that are 7.3% higher than a person in a healthy weight range, while obese individuals have annual health care costs that are 69% higher than a person of a healthy weight. With health care cost inflation running in the double digits in the United States since 20X4, supporters of the industry believe that the implementation of effective weight management tools will attract more attention from insurers, employers, consumers, and the government. As of January 20X9 five nutrition- or fitness-related bills were being considered in Congress, and several states had enacted or were considering enacting legislation relating to the sale of "junk" food in public schools. In addition, the US Food and Drug Administration, Department of Health and Human Services, and Federal Trade Commission are contemplating new labeling requirements for packaged food and restaurant food, new educational and motivational programs related to healthy eating and exercise, and increased regulation of advertising claims for food.

In response to consumers' growing demand for more healthful eating options, quick-service and full-service restaurants have introduced new offerings including salads, sandwiches, burgers, and other food items designed for the weight-conscious person. At the retail level, sales of natural and organic foods have been growing more rapidly than the overall food and over-the-counter drug market for the last several years. Nutritional supplement sales in the US, for instance, are estimated to have grown 34% between 20X4 and 20X8, while natural and organic foods are estimated to be growing at a rate of approximately 15% annually. Also, the industry has a tendency to change quickly as "dicting fads" regularly are introduced; some remain popular for years, some for only months.

Approximately 60% of the US adult population, or 120 million adults, are overweight and, of those, the Calorie Control Council estimates only about 50 million are dieting in a given year. About 15% of these dieters are using a commercial weight loss center, generating revenues of approximately $1.5 billion annually. DietWeb targets dieters who are online, which represents about two-thirds of the total universe at current Internet penetration rates, or 34 million adults, about 5 million of whom are spending approximately $1 billion at weight loss centers.

At the same time, the online dieting segment of the market is growing rapidly. The online diet industry in the US generated in excess of $100 million in 20X8, compared to revenues of approximately $75 million in 20X2. The industry includes other online nutrition and diet-oriented Web sites.

Another group of competitors to DietWeb are commercial weight loss centers, an industry that has shown marked decline in the last decade. According to Market Analysis Enterprises, the number of commercial weight loss centers in the US declined approximately 50% between 20X2 and 20X8, from over 8,600 to approximately 4,400. DietWeb competes against this segment on the basis of lower price, superior value, convenience, availability, the ability to personalize a meal plan on an ongoing basis, its extensive support capabilities, and the breadth of its meal plan options.

Situation	Company Profile	Industry Information	Balance Sheet	Income Statement	Statement of Cash Flows	Risks	Financial Statement Analysis	Audit Procedures	Communication	Research

DietWeb, Inc.
BALANCE SHEET
December 31, 20X8 and 20X7
(in thousands)

	20X8	20X7
Assets		
Current assets		
Cash and cash equivalents	$3,032	$1,072
Trade receivables	485	450
Prepaid advertising expenses	59	609
Prepaid expenses and other current assets	175	230
Total current assets	3,751	2,361
Fixed assets, net	3,321	3,926
Total assets	$7,072	$6,287
Liabilities and shareholders' equity		
Current liabilities		
Accounts payable	$1,070	$ 909
Current maturities of notes payable	42	316
Deferred revenue	1,973	1,396
Other current liabilities	171	12
Total current liabilities	3,256	2,633
Long-term debt, less current maturity	34	176
Accrued liabilities	792	690
Deferred tax liability	15	145
Total liabilities	4,097	3,644
Shareholders' equity		
Common stock	6,040	4,854
Retained earnings	(3,065)	(2,211)
Total shareholders' equity	2,975	2,643
Total liabilities plus shareholders' equity	$7,072	$6,287

Situation	Company Profile	Industry Information	Balance Sheet	Income Statement	Statement of Cash Flows	Risks	Financial Statement Analysis	Audit Procedures	Communication	Research

DietWeb, Inc.
INCOME STATEMENT
Two Years Ended December 31, 20X8 and 20X7
(in thousands)

	20X8	20X7
Revenue	$19,166	$14,814
Costs and expenses		
Cost of revenue	2,326	1,528
Product development	725	653
Sales and marketing	13,903	8,710
General and administrative	2,531	2,575
Depreciation and amortization	629	661
Impairment of intangible assets	35	-
Total costs and expenses	20,149	14,127
Net income before taxes	(983)	687
Income tax benefit	129	125
Net income (loss)	$(854)	$812

Situation	Company Profile	Industry Information	Balance Sheet	Income Statement	Statement of Cash Flows	Risks	Financial Statement Analysis	Audit Procedures	Communication	Research

DietWeb, Inc.
STATEMENT OF CASH FLOWS
Year Ended December 31, 20X8

	20X8	20X7
Cash flows from operations		
Net income (loss)	$(854)	812
Adjustments to net income		
Depreciation	629	660
Increase in receivables	(35)	(47)
Decrease (Increase) in prepaid advertising	550	(650)
Decrease in other current assets	55	74
Increase (Decrease) in accounts payable	161	(540)
Increase in accrued liabilities	102	43
Increase (Decrease) in deferred revenue	432	(665)
Increase in common stock issued	1,186	-
Increase in other current liabilities	159	43
Net cash provided (used) by operations	2,385	(270)
Cash flows from investing activities		
Purchase of property and equipment	(320)	2,016
Cash flows from financing activities		
New debt	613	40
Debt payments	(718)	(918)
Net cash provided (used) by financing activities	(105)	(878)
Net increase in cash and cash equivalents	$1,960	868
Cash and equivalents at beginning of year	$1,072	204
Cash and equivalents at end of year	$3,032	1,072

Situation	Company Profile	Industry Information	Balance Sheet	Income Statement	Statement of Cash Flows	**Risks**	Financial Statement Analysis	Audit Procedures	Communication	Research

(A) (B) (C) (D)
○ ○ ○ ○

1. Of the following, which is likely to be one of DietWeb's major risks of doing business on the Internet in the future?

   A. Maintaining privacy of customer information.
   B. Maintaining the ability to pay Federal Communication Commission Internet use fees.
   C. Inability to provide 24/7/365 support.
   D. Inability to reach customers beyond the United States.

(A) (B) (C) (D)
○ ○ ○ ○

2. Which of the following is likely to be the most significant business risk for DietWeb?

   A. Internal control limitations due to the small size of the company.
   B. Inability of the Internet to provide adequate support for such a business due to its instability.
   C. Entrance of new competitors onto the Internet.
   D. Misstatements of revenues due to difficulties in determining appropriate year-end cutoffs.

Situation	Company Profile	Industry Information	Balance Sheet	Income Statement	Statement of Cash Flows	Risks	**Financial Statement Analysis**	Audit Procedures	Communication	Research

(A) (B) (C) (D)
○ ○ ○ ○

1. The most likely misstatement in the financial statements is

   A. The increase in cash in 20X8.
   B. Treatment of impaired intangible assets as an expense in 20X8.
   C. Treatment of common stock issued as an adjustment to net income.
   D. An income tax benefit on the income statement as contrasted to income tax expense.

(A) (B) (C) (D)
○ ○ ○ ○

2. Which of the following is the most unexpected change on the balance sheet, if one assumes the revenue increase in 20X8 is correct?

   A. Decrease in prepaid advertising expenses.
   B. Increase in accounts payable.
   C. Decrease in deferred revenues.
   D. Increase in common stock.

Situation	Company Profile	Industry Information	Balance Sheet	Income Statement	Statement of Cash Flows	Risks	Financial Statement Analysis	**Audit Procedures**	Communication	Research

The auditor determines that each of the following objectives will be part of DietWeb's audit. For each audit objective, select a substantive procedure that would help to achieve that objective. Each of the procedures may be used once, more than once, or not at all.

Substantive procedure
   A. Trace opening balances in the summary schedules to the prior year's audit working papers.
   B. Review the provision for deprecation expense and determine that depreciable lives and methods used in the current year are consistent with those used in the prior year.
   C. Determine that responsibility for maintaining the property and equipment records is segregated from the responsibility for custody of property and equipment.
   D. Examine deeds and title insurance certificates.
   E. Perform cutoff test to verify that property and equipment additions are recorded in the proper period.
   F. Determine that property and equipment is adequately insured.
   G. Physically examine all recorded major property and equipment additions.

(A) (B) (C) (D) (E) (F) (G)
○ ○ ○ ○ ○ ○ ○

1. DietWeb has legal rights to property and equipment acquired during the year.

○ ○ ○ ○ ○ ○ ○

2. DietWeb recorded property and equipment acquired during the year that did not actually exist at the balance sheet date.

Situation	Company Profile	Industry Information	Balance Sheet	Income Statement	Statement of Cash Flows	Risks	Financial Statement Analysis	Audit Procedures	Communication	Research

This is your firm's sixth audit of DietWeb. In a memorandum to the audit team (below) summarize your view of the audit committee's strengths, weaknesses, and any changes that have occurred relating to the audit committee this year.

REMINDER: Your response will be graded for both technical relevance and writing skills. Technical content will be evaluated for information that is helpful to the intended reader and clearly relevant to the issue. Writing skills will be evaluated for development, organization, and the appropriate expression of ideas in professional correspondence. Use a standard business memo or letter format with a clear beginning, middle, and end. Do not convey information in the form of a table, bullet point list, or other abbreviated presentation.

To: Audit Team
From: CPA Candidate
Re: DietWeb Audit Committee

Situation	Company Profile	Industry Information	Balance Sheet	Income Statement	Statement of Cash Flows	Risks	Financial Statement Analysis	Audit Procedures	Communication	Research

NOTE: This section is only possible to work in a meaningful way if you have the professional standards available—preferably in electronic form.

You are now working on the audit of DietWeb. Use the Professional Standards to identify risk factors that might indicate misstatements arising from misappropriation of assets. Do this by selecting the appropriate paragraph(s) of the Professional Standards.

SOLUTION TO SIMULATION 1

Situation	Company Profile	Industry Information	Balance Sheet	Income Statement	Statement of Cash Flows	Risks	Financial Statement Analysis	Audit Procedures	Communication	Research

                                           (A) (B) (C) (D)

1. Of the following, which is likely to be one of DietWeb's major risks of doing business on the Internet in the future?   ● ○ ○ ○

2. Which of the following is likely to be the most significant business risk for DietWeb?   ○ ○ ● ○

Explanation of solutions

1. **(A)** The requirement is to identify DietWeb's major listed risk of doing business on the Internet. Answer (A) is correct because DietWeb must carefully maintain the privacy of their customers' information—both due to law and due to DietWeb's assurance provided to its customers. Answer (B) is incorrect because there are no major Federal Communications Commission Internet use fees. Answer (C) is incorrect because the case indicates no particular problem in providing 24/7/365 support. Answer (D) is incorrect because the Internet is able to reach customers beyond the United States.

2. **(C)** The requirement is to identify the most significant business risk listed for DietWeb. Answer (C) is correct because barriers to entrance on the Internet are ordinarily not high. Another organization might develop similar (or more accepted) software, and/or charge lower prices than those charged by DietWeb. Answer (A) is incorrect because internal control limitations need not necessarily be a major problem, and because internal control relates to control risk more directly than to the company's business risk. Answer (B) is incorrect because while Internet instability may cause difficulties, few would consider it as significant a problem as new competitors. Answer (D) is incorrect because determining appropriate year-end cutoffs is not likely to create major difficulties.

Situation	Company Profile	Industry Information	Balance Sheet	Income Statement	Statement of Cash Flows	Risks	Financial Statement Analysis	Audit Procedures	Communication	Research

                                           (A) (B) (C) (D)

1. The most likely misstatement in the financial statements is   ○ ○ ● ○

2. Which of the following is the most unexpected change on the balance sheet, if one assumes the revenue increase in 20X8 is correct?   ● ○ ○ ○

Explanation of solutions

1. **(C)** The requirement is to identify a likely misstatement in the financial statements. Answer (C) is correct because common stock issued should be treated under financing rather than operations. Answer (A) is incorrect because an increase in cash may well occur—even during a year in which the company encounters a loss. Answer (B) is incorrect because there is no indication that the impairment expense is inappropriate. Answer (D) is incorrect because previous years' pattern of income and losses may create a situation in which a net income tax benefit occurs.

2. **(A)** The requirement is to identify, of the balance sheet changes listed, the most unexpected one. Answer (A) is unexpected in that prepaid advertising expenses decreased by more than ninety percent—at a time when the company increased its sales and marketing expenses so significantly. Answer (B) is incorrect because the relatively small increase in accounts payable may be expected given the increase in revenues. Answer (C) is incorrect because one would expect such an increase in deferred revenues as revenues increase. Answer (D) is incorrect since the company simply issued more stock—as indicated in the company profile.

Situation	Company Profile	Industry Information	Balance Sheet	Income Statement	Statement of Cash Flows	Risks	Financial Statement Analysis	Audit Procedures	Communication	Research

                              (A) (B) (C) (D) (E) (F) (G)

1. DietWeb has legal rights to property and equipment acquired during the year.   ○ ○ ○ ● ○ ○ ○

2. DietWeb recorded property and equipment acquired during the year that did not actually exist at the balance sheet date.   ○ ○ ○ ○ ○ ○ ●

Explanation of solutions

1. **(D)** The requirement is to identify the best substantive procedure to determine that DietWeb has legal rights to the property and equipment acquired during the year. Answer (D) is correct because the deeds and title insurance certificates will provide evidence that the company owns the property and equipment.

2. **(G)** The requirement is to identify the best substantive procedure to determine that DietWeb recorded property and equipment actually exists. Answer (G) is correct because physically examining the items will provide this evidence.

Situation	Company Profile	Industry Information	Balance Sheet	Income Statement	Statement of Cash Flows	Risks	Financial Statement Analysis	Audit Procedures	Communication	Research

To: Audit Team
From: CPA Candidate
Re: DietWeb Audit Committee

This memorandum is designed to describe certain issues with respect to DietWeb's audit committee. We have identified a number of concerns regarding the makeup of DietWeb's audit committee. The audit committee membership is identical to that of the board of directors. Accordingly, there are no independent members. Mr. Readings, the company's CEO, serves as chairman of both the board of directors and the audit committee. On the other hand, the committee members are competent and interested.

We will make a recommendation to the board of directors to correct this matter by bringing on independent board and audit committee members. In addition, we should consider the implications of this weakness in control environment on our audit.

Situation	Company Profile	Industry Information	Balance Sheet	Income Statement	Statement of Cash Flows	Risks	Financial Statement Analysis	Audit Procedures	Communication	Research

AU 316.85 presents the following examples of risk factors related to misstatements arising from misappropriation of assets:

Incentives/Pressures

    a.   Personal financial obligations may create pressure on management or employees with access to cash or other assets susceptible to theft to misappropriate those assets.

    b.   Adverse relationships between the entity and employees with access to cash or other assets susceptible to theft may motivate those employees to misappropriate those assets. For example, adverse relationships may be created by the following:

        - Known or anticipated future employee layoffs
        - Recent or anticipated changes to employee compensation or benefit plans
        - Promotions, compensation, or other rewards inconsistent with expectations

Opportunities

    a.   Certain characteristics or circumstances may increase the susceptibility of assets to misappropriation. For example, opportunities to misappropriate assets increase when there are the following:

        - Large amounts of cash on hand or processed
        - Inventory items that are small in size, of high value, or in high demand
        - Easily convertible assets, such as bearer bonds, diamonds, or computer chips
        - Fixed assets that are small in size, marketable, or lacking observable identification of ownership

    b.   Inadequate internal control over assets may increase the susceptibility of misappropriation of those assets. For example, misappropriation of assets may occur because there is the following:

        - Inadequate segregation of duties or independent checks
        - Inadequate management oversight of employees responsible for assets, for example, inadequate supervision or monitoring of remote locations
        - Inadequate job applicant screening of employees with access to assets
        - Inadequate recordkeeping with respect to assets
        - Inadequate system of authorization and approval of transactions (for example, in purchasing)
        - Lack of complete and timely reconciliations of assets
        - Lack of timely and appropriate documentation of transactions, for example, credits for merchandise returns
        - Lack of mandatory vacations for employees performing key control functions
        - Inadequate management understanding of information technology, which enables information technology employees to perpetrate a misappropriation
        - Inadequate access controls over automated records, including controls over and review of computer systems event logs.

Attitudes/Rationalizations

Risk factors reflective of employee attitudes/rationalizations that allow them to justify misappropriations of assets, are generally not susceptible to observation by the auditor. Nevertheless, the auditor who becomes aware of the existence of such information should consider it in identifying the risks of material misstatement arising from misappropriation of assets. For example, auditors may become aware of the following attitudes or behavior of employees who have access to assets susceptible to misappropriation:

        - Disregard for the need for monitoring or reducing risks related to misappropriations of assets
        - Disregard for internal control over misappropriation of assets by overriding existing controls or by failing to correct known internal control deficiencies
        - Behavior indicating displeasure or dissatisfaction with the company or its treatment of the employee
        - Changes in behavior or lifestyle that may indicate assets have been misappropriated

SIMULATION 2   (60 to 70 minutes)

Topics—Planning, Internal Control, Evidence, and Reporting

Situation										
	Company Profile	Industry Information	Balance Sheet	Income Statement	Statement of Cash Flows	Risks	Audit Findings	Audit Procedures	Communication	Research

Assume you are performing the 20X8 audit of Tommi Stone and Quarry.

	Company Profile									
Situation		Industry Information	Balance Sheet	Income Statement	Statement of Cash Flows	Risks	Audit Findings	Audit Procedures	Communication	Research

In 20X1 Jill Tommi founded Tommi Stone and Quarry (TSQ). Within its first year of existence, the company completed initial development of the extraction pit area and constructed an aggregate processing plant which is equipped to crush, screen, and wash aggregate products. By 20X3 the sand and gravel operation was profitable and growing market conditions justified modifications and expansion. Currently, at the conclusion of 20X8, TSQ produces a wide range of sand and stone products from its pit near Albuquerque, New Mexico. The materials it develops range from various sand and stone materials for residential and commercial construction and highway projects. TSQ sells to a wide variety of residential, commercial and governmental customers, with no one customer accounting for more than 5% of its total sales.

TSQ has worked closely with stucco manufacturers and plastering contractors in the Albuquerque plastering industry to produce a plaster sand ("Plasand") that exceeds normal specifications and produces a superior ingredient which improves stucco and plastering finished products. Plasand has been increasingly widely accepted as superior to products offered by competitors, and now accounts for approximately 10% of the company's sales, and 12% of its profits. TSQ is currently working closely with sport complexes and golf course architects in conjunction with test laboratories to develop a superior sand for use in the construction and top dressing of golf courses and sport complex playing fields.

The company experienced a level of profitability in 20X8 of about the same as that of 20X7—but this is well below the net incomes of the preceding several years. Jill suggested to you that, surprisingly, intense price competition from several smaller competitors in the Albuquerque area caused the somewhat low level of profitability. But, she added, she didn't expect the problem to last for long because she doubted that those companies could continue to operate selling at these lower prices. Jill had hoped for a more profitable year in 20X8 as a significant amount of the company's long-term debt is payable in 20X9. TSQ is currently involved in discussions with the bank on refinancing.

TSQ added significant additional crushing and washing plants and equipment during 20X8 to increase production in the future by more than 100% while expanding capabilities to produce custom specification materials.

Until 20X7 and 20X8, most of earnings were distributed through dividends to TSQ's five shareholders—CEO and Chair of the Board of Directors Jill Tommi, her husband Mort Tommi, CFO Googlo Permasi and two college friends of Jill's who invested in the company, Jian Zhang and Kendra Kovano. These five individuals make up the company's Board of Directors.

This year, in reaction to pressure from a bank that provides a significant portion of the financing, TSQ established an audit committee composed of Mort Tommi, Googlo Permasi, and Jian Zhang.

You are working on your firm's fifth audit of TSQ. The previous audits have all resulted in standard unqualified audit reports.

		Industry Information								
Situation	Company Profile		Balance Sheet	Income Statement	Statement of Cash Flows	Risks	Audit Findings	Audit Procedures	Communication	Research

The industry consists of preparation for the mining and extraction of sand and rock products. These include the activities of cleaning, separating and sorting of quarried sand and the crushing of rocks. The products are in the form of sand used in making concrete; sand used in laying bricks (contains little soil); sand used for fill (contains lots of soil, and quartz sand); and excluding the products of gravel quarrying (sandstone, gravel stone, and iron sand).

While sales within the industry are relatively unaffected by changes in technology, or obsolescence, sales rely heavily upon both the residential and commercial construction markets as well as government spending. During the past five years construction has performed well and that trend is expected to continue at least for the coming several years. Sand and gravel production has increased at approximately 3% per year during this time period, as has construction within the Albuquerque area.

The sand and gravel market in central New Mexico has been particularly healthy due in large part to the growth of Albuquerque into a major metropolitan area. The most significant question facing the industry is whether the strong construction will continue as expected. During the past two years the economy of the United States has been in a recovery period, yet unemployment remains high as compared to previous periods of recovery. Thus, the questions concerning the continuing construction demand.

Situation	Company Profile	Industry Information	Balance Sheet	Income Statement	Statement of Cash Flows	Risks	Audit Findings	Audit Procedures	Communication	Research

Tommi Stone and Quarry
BALANCE SHEET
December 31, 20X8 and 20X7

	20X8	20X7
Assets		
Current assets		
Cash and cash equivalents	$ 5,055	$ 3,822
Trade receivables	3,369,971	2,383,055
Inventory	1,713,118	1,810,361
Other current assets	17,140	10,200
Total current assets	5,105,284	4,207,438
Fixed assets, net	397,749	74,769
Total assets	$5,503,033	$4,282,207
Liabilities and shareholders' equity		
Current liabilities		
Accounts payable	$ 340,995	$ 316,164
Current maturities of notes payable	1,262,379	416,607
Accrued expenses	187,190	208,460
Other current liabilities	158,603	199,629
Total current liabilities	1,949,167	1,140,860
Long-term debt, less current maturity	3,249,934	2,959,200
Total liabilities	5,199,101	4,100,060
Shareholders' equity		
Common stock	57,333	57,333
Retained earnings	246,599	124,814
Total shareholders' equity	303,932	182,147
Total liabilities plus shareholders' equity	$5,503,033	$4,282,207

Situation	Company Profile	Industry Information	Balance Sheet	Income Statement	Statement of Cash Flows	Risks	Audit Findings	Audit Procedures	Communication	Research

Tommi Stone and Quarry
INCOME STATEMENT
Two Years Ended December 31, 20X8 and 20X7

	20X8	20X7
Revenue	$21,312,665	$17,261,974
Cost of goods sold	18,029,838	14,397,853
Gross profit on sales	3,282,827	2,864,121
Operating expenses	2,707,606	2,185,542
Repairs and maintenance	104,168	132,083
Depreciation	31,673	30,098
Interest expense	265,398	314,419
Total expenses	3,108,845	2,662,142
Net income before taxes	173,982	201,979
Provision for income taxes	52,197	80,792
Net income	$ 121,785	$ 121,187

Situation	Company Profile	Industry Information	Balance Sheet	Income Statement	Statement of Cash Flows	Risks	Audit Findings	Audit Procedures	Communication	Research

Tommi Stone and Quarry
STATEMENT OF CASH FLOWS
Year Ended December 31, 20X8

Cash flows from operations	
Net income (loss)	$121,785
Adjustments to net income	
Depreciation	31,673
Increase in receivables	(986,916)
Decrease in inventory	97,243
Increase in other current assets	(6,940)
Increase in accounts payable	24,831
Decrease in accrued expenses	(21,270)
Decrease in other current liabilities	(41,026)
Net cash provided (used) by operations	(780,620)
Cash flows from investing activities	
Purchase of property and equipment	(343,270)
Cash flows from financing activities	
New debt	1,682,666
Debt payments	(557,543)
Net cash provided (used) by financing activities	1,125,123
Net increase in cash and cash equivalents	$1,233
Cash and equivalents at beginning of year	$3,822
Cash and equivalents at end of year	$5,055

Situation	Company Profile	Industry Information	Balance Sheet	Income Statement	Statement of Cash Flows	Risks	Audit Findings	Audit Procedures	Communication	Research

(A) (B) (C) (D)

1. A risk factor relating to misstatements arising from fraudulent financial reporting is

   A. Earnings this year are lower than management had hoped.
   B. Fewer competitors exist than in the past, and this places the company in a position in which it is easier to manipulate earnings.
   C. Sales are made to residential, commercial, and governmental purchasers.
   D. The industry faces great technological changes in almost all of its products.

(A) (B) (C) (D)

2. Which of the following correctly identifies a risk facing TSQ that might adversely affect sales during the coming years?

   A. A general slowdown in the economy.
   B. Sales to many different types of customers.
   C. Increased attention to developing new products.
   D. A board of directors dominated by management.

Situation	Company Profile	Industry Information	Balance Sheet	Income Statement	Statement of Cash Flows	Risks	Audit Findings	Audit Procedures	Communication	Research

Ratio	20X8	20X7
Gross margin percentage	0.154	0.166
Current ratio	2.619	3.688

The above table presents two ratios that were identified as significant in the current and prior years' audits of TSQ. Compare the values of each ratio. Then select an audit finding that is consistent with these metrics. The finding need not explain the entire change. But, of the replies listed, it should potentially lead to the most significant change in the direction indicated by the change in the ratio. Each of the audit findings may be used once, more than once, or not at all.

Substantive procedure
A. Increases in costs of purchases were not completely passed on to customers through higher selling prices.
B. Increases in trade receivables.
C. Owners' equity increased due to retention of profits.
D. A larger percentage of sales occurred during the last month of 20X8, as compared to 20X7.
E. Interest expense decreased during 20X8.
F. The percentage tax included in the provision for income taxes for 20X8 was less than the percentage in 20X7.
G. A significant amount of long-term debt became current.

                                               (A) (B) (C) (D) (E) (F) (G)

1. An audit finding most consistent with the change in the gross margin percentage   O O O O O O O

2. An audit finding most consistent with the change in the current ratio   O O O O O O O

Situation	Company Profile	Industry Information	Balance Sheet	Income Statement	Statement of Cash Flows	Risks	Audit Findings	Audit Procedures	Communication	Research

The auditor determines that each of the following objectives will be part of TSQ's audit. For each audit objective, select a substantive procedure that would help to achieve that objective. Each of the procedures may be used once, more than once, or not at all.

Substantive procedure
A. Analyze the relationship of accounts receivable and purchases and compare it with relationships for preceding periods.
B. Analyze sales recorded in January to obtain assurance that sales transactions are recorded in the proper period.
C. Analyze sales recorded in December to obtain assurance that sales transactions are recorded in the proper period.
D. Review the aged trial balance for significant past due accounts.
E. Obtain an understanding of the business purpose of transactions that resulted in accounts receivable balances.
F. Review board of director minutes for information on sales of goods to officers.

                                               (A) (B) (C) (D) (E) (F)

1. Establish the completeness of receivables transactions.   O O O O O O

2. Determine that the valuation of receivables is at appropriate net realizable values.   O O O O O O

Situation	Company Profile	Industry Information	Balance Sheet	Income Statement	Statement of Cash Flows	Risks	Financial Statement Analysis	Audit Procedures	Communication	Research

This is your firm's fifth audit of TSQ. This year the company has formed an audit committee—composed of Mort Tommi, Jian Zhang, and Kendra Kovano. In a memorandum to the audit team (below) explain the likely effect of this change on audit risk. Mort is chairman of the audit committee.

REMINDER: Your response will be graded for both technical relevance and writing skills. Technical content will be evaluated for information that is helpful to the intended reader and clearly relevant to the issue. Writing skills will be evaluated for development, organization, and the appropriate expression of ideas in professional correspondence. Use a standard business memo or letter format with a clear beginning, middle, and end. Do not convey information in the form of a table, bullet point list, or other abbreviated presentation.

To: Audit Team
From: CPA Candidate
Re: TSQ Audit Committee

Situation	Company Profile	Industry Information	Balance Sheet	Income Statement	Statement of Cash Flows	Risks	Financial Statement Analysis	Audit Procedures	Communication	Research

You have now completed the audit work for the TSQ audit. Select the guidance from professional standards that provides a description of the items to be included in a standard audit report.

SOLUTION TO SIMULATION 2

Situation	Company Profile	Industry Information	Balance Sheet	Income Statement	Statement of Cash Flows	Risks	Audit Findings	Audit Procedures	Communication	Research

	(A)	(B)	(C)	(D)
1. A risk factor relating to misstatements arising from fraudulent financial reporting is	●	○	○	○
2. Which of the following correctly identifies a risk facing TSQ that might adversely affect sales during the coming years?	●	○	○	○

Explanation of solutions

1. (A) The requirement is to identify a risk factor relating to misstatements arising from fraudulent financial reporting. Answer (A) is correct because historically low levels of earnings may have created pressure on management to at least exceed the previous year's net income. Answer (B) is incorrect because there are not fewer competitors. Answer (C) is incorrect because selling to residential, commercial, and governmental purchasers presents no particular risk. Answer (D) is incorrect because there is no indication that the company is involved with overly complex transactions (maintaining lien rights on inventory is not complex) and the industry does not face great technological changes in products.

2. (A) The requirement is to identify the correct statement relating to a risk that might adversely affect TSQ's sales. Answer (A) is correct because the simulation emphasizes the fact that sales are dependent upon economic growth. Answer (B) is incorrect because selling to different types of customers diversifies away some of the risk of declining sales. Answer (C) is incorrect because increased attention to developing new products may help the company increase future sales. Answer (D) is incorrect because while the board of directors may be dominated by management, it is uncertain that such lack of independence would lead to a decline in sales.

Situation	Company Profile	Industry Information	Balance Sheet	Income Statement	Statement of Cash Flows	Risks	Audit Findings	Audit Procedures	Communication	Research

	(A)	(B)	(C)	(D)	(E)	(F)	(G)
1. An audit finding most consistent with the change in the gross margin percentage	●	○	○	○	○	○	○
2. An audit finding most consistent with the change in the current ratio	○	○	○	○	○	○	●

Explanation of solutions

1. (A) The requirement is to identify an audit finding most consistent with a decrease in the gross margin percentage—gross margin/sales. Answer (A) is correct because the inability to pass on increases in costs will decrease the gross margin because cost of goods sold as a percentage of sales will increase.

2. (G) The requirement is to identify an audit finding that is consistent with a decrease in the current ratio—current assets/current liabilities. Answer (G) is correct because the long-term debt becoming current increases the denominator of the current ratio, which decreases the ratio.

Situation	Company Profile	Industry Information	Balance Sheet	Income Statement	Statement of Cash Flows	Risks	Audit Findings	Audit Procedures	Communication	Research

	(A)	(B)	(C)	(D)	(E)	(F)
1. Establish the completeness of receivables transactions.	○	●	○	○	○	○
2. Determine that the valuation of receivables is at appropriate net realizable values.	○	○	○	●	○	○

Explanation of solutions

1. (B) The requirement is to identify a substantive procedure to establish the completeness of receivables transactions. Answer (B) is correct because analyzing sales recorded in January (performing cutoff tests) will reveal whether December sales were recorded in the wrong period.

2. (D) The requirement is to identify a procedure to determine the valuation of receivables at appropriate net realizable values. Answer (D) is correct because a review of the aged trial balance for significant past due accounts will provide evidence on how much is expected to be realized on receivables.

Situation	Company Profile	Industry Information	Balance Sheet	Income Statement	Statement of Cash Flows	Risks	Audit Findings	Audit Procedures	Communication		Research

To: Audit Team
Subject: TSQ Audit Committee

This memorandum describes issues related to TSQ's audit committee. As a reaction to pressure from its bank, TSQ has recently established an audit committee of the board of directors. The committee is made up of Mort Tommi, the CEO's husband, Googlo Permasi, the CFO, and Jian Zhang, a stockholder in the company. Mort Tommi is chairman of the committee. While this results in an independence issue with respect to the committee, we should remember that this is a closely held nonpublic company. These types of entities typically do not have audit committees. We should make inquiries of Jian Zhang to obtain information about the operation of the committee. If any issues arise related to the audit committee, please notify me immediately.

Situation	Company Profile	Industry Information	Balance Sheet	Income Statement	Statement of Cash Flows	Risks	Audit Findings	Audit Procedures	Communication	Research

The appropriate guidance regarding the content of the standard audit report is found in AU 508.08:

.08 The auditor's standard report identifies the financial statements audited in an opening (introductory) paragraph, describes the nature of an audit in a scope paragraph, and expresses the auditor's opinion in a separate opinion paragraph. The basic elements of the report are the following:

a. A title that includes the word *independent*
b. A statement that the financial statements identified in the report were audited
c. A statement that the financial statements are the responsibility of the Company's management and that the auditor's responsibility is to express an opinion on the financial statements based on his or her audit
d. A statement that the audit was conducted in accordance with generally accepted auditing standards and an identification of the United States of America as the country of origin of those standards (for example, auditing standards generally accepted in the United States of America or US generally accepted auditing standards)
e. A statement that those standards require that the auditor plan and perform the audit to obtain reasonable assurance about whether the financial statements are free of material misstatement
f. A statement that an audit includes—

   1) Examining, on a test basis, evidence supporting the amounts and disclosures in the financial statements
   2) Assessing the accounting principles used and significant estimates made by management
   3) Evaluating the overall financial statement presentation

g. A statement that the auditor believes that his or her audit provides a reasonable basis for his or her opinion
h. An opinion as to whether the financial statements present fairly, in all material respects, the financial position of the Company as of the balance sheet date and the results of its operations and its cash flows for the period then ended in conformity with generally accepted accounting principles. The opinion should include an identification of the United States of America as the country of origin of those accounting principles (for example, accounting principles generally accepted in the United States of America or US generally accepted accounting principles)
i. The manual or printed signature of the auditor's firm
j. The date of the audit report

The form of the auditor's standard report on financial statements covering a single year is as follows:

Independent Auditor's Report

We have audited the accompanying balance sheets of X Company as of December 31, 20XX, and the related statements of income, retained earnings, and cash flows for the years then ended. These financial statements are the responsibility of the Company's management. Our responsibility is to express an opinion on these financial statements based on our audit.

We conducted our audit in accordance with auditing standards generally accepted in the United States of America. Those standards require that we plan and perform the audit to obtain reasonable assurance about whether the financial statements are free of material misstatement. An audit includes examining, on a test basis, evidence supporting the amounts and disclosures in the financial statements. An audit also includes assessing the accounting principles used and significant estimates made by management, as well as evaluating the overall financial statement presentation. We believe that our audits provide a reasonable basis for our opinion.

In our opinion, the financial statements referred to above present fairly, in all material respects, the financial position of X Company as of [at] December 31, 20XX, and the results of its operations and its cash flows for the years then ended in conformity with accounting principles generally accepted in the United States of America.

[*Signature*]

[*Date*]

The form of the auditor's standard report on comparative financial statements is as follows:

Independent Auditor's Report

We have audited the accompanying balance sheets of X Company as of December 31, 20X2 and 20X1, and the related statements of income, retained earnings, and cash flows for the years then ended. These financial statements are the responsibility of the Company's management. Our responsibility is to express an opinion on these financial statements based on our audits.

We conducted our audits in accordance with auditing standards generally accepted in the United States of America. Those standards require that we plan and perform the audits to obtain reasonable assurance about whether the financial statements are free of material misstatement. An audit includes examining, on a test basis, evidence supporting the amounts and disclosures in the financial statements. An audit also includes assessing the accounting principles used and significant estimates made by management, as well as evaluating the overall financial statement presentation. We believe that our audits provide a reasonable basis for our opinion.

In our opinion, the financial statements referred to above present fairly, in all material respects, the financial position of X Company as of [at] December 31, 20X2 and 20X1, and the results of its operations and its cash flows for the years then ended in conformity with accounting principles generally accepted in the United States of America.

[*Signature*]

[*Date*]

SIMULATION 3

Topic—Audit Planning and Evidence

Situation			
	Risk Analysis	**Responding to Risk**	**Research and Communication**

You are working with William Bond, CPA, and you are considering the risk of material misstatement in planning the audit of Toxic Waste Disposal (TWD) Company's financial statements for the year ended December 31, 20X0. TWD is a privately owned entity that contracts with municipal governments to remove environmental waste.

	Risk Analysis		
Situation		**Responding to Risk**	**Research and Communication**

Based only on the information below, indicate whether each of the following factors would most likely increase (I), decrease (D), or have no effect on the risk of material misstatement (N).

	(I)	**(D)**	**(N)**
1. Because municipalities have received increased federal and state funding for environmental purposes, TWD returned to profitability for the first year following three years with losses.	O	O	O
2. TWD's Board of Directors is controlled by Mead, the majority stockholder, who also acts as the chief executive officer.	O	O	O
3. The internal auditor reports to the controller and the controller reports to Mead.	O	O	O
4. The accounting department has experienced a high rate of turnover of key personnel.	O	O	O
5. TWD's bank has a loan officer who meets regularly with TWD's CEO and controller to monitor TWD's financial performance.	O	O	O
6. TWD's employees are paid biweekly.	O	O	O
7. TWD has such a strong financial presence in its history so as to allow it often to dictate the terms or conditions of transactions with its suppliers.	O	O	O
8. During 20X1, TWD changed its method of preparing its financial statements from the cash basis to generally accepted accounting principles.	O	O	O
9. During 20X1, TWD sold one-half of its controlling interest in United Equipment Leasing (UEL) Co. TWD retained significant influence over UEL.	O	O	O
10. During 20X1, litigation filed against TWD from an action ten years ago that alleged that TWD discharged pollutants into state waterways was dropped by the state. Loss contingency disclosures that TWD included in prior years' financial statements are being removed from the 20X1 financial statements.	O	O	O
11. During December 20X1, TWD signed a contract to lease disposal equipment from an entity owned by Mead's parents. This related-party transaction is not disclosed in TWD's notes to the 20X1 financial statements.	O	O	O
12. During December 20X1, TWD completed a barter transaction with a municipality. TWD removed waste from the municipally owned site and acquired title to another contaminated site at below market price. TWD intends to service this new site in 20X2.	O	O	O
13. During December 20X1, TWD increased its casualty insurance coverage on several pieces of sophisticated machinery from historical cost to replacement cost.	O	O	O
14. Inquiries about the substantial increase in revenue TWD recorded in the fourth quarter of 20X1 disclosed a new policy. TWD guaranteed to several municipalities that it would refund the federal and state funding paid to TWD if any municipality fails a federal or state site clean-up inspection in 20X2.	O	O	O
15. An initial public offering of TWD's stock is planned for late 20X2.	O	O	O

Situation	Risk Analysis	Responding to Risk	Research and Communication

Assume that you have identified the following risks at the account level relating to TWD's property and equipment. Identify the most closely related financial statement assertion and the audit procedure that might be planned to most likely address the risk. Financial statement assertions and audit procedures may be used once, more than once, or not used at all.

Related financial statement assertion

A. Existence or occurrence
B. Completeness
C. Rights and obligations
D. Valuation or allocation
E. Presentation and disclosure

Audit procedures

F. Trace opening balances in the summary schedules to the prior year's audit working papers.
G. Review the provision for depreciation expense and determine that depreciable lives and methods used in the current year are consistent with those used in the prior year.
H. Determine that the responsibility for maintaining the property and equipment records is segregated from the responsibility for custody of property and equipment.
I. Examine deeds and title insurance certificates.
J. Perform cutoffs tests to verify that property and equipment additions are recorded in the proper period.
K. Determine that property and equipment are adequately insured.
L. Physically examine all major property and equipment additions.

	Risk identified	*Related financial statement assertion* (A) (B) (C) (D) (E)	*Audit procedures* (F) (G) (H) (I) (J) (K) (L)
1.	TWD may not have legal title to certain property and equipment recorded as acquired during the year.	O O O O O	O O O O O O O
2.	Recorded property and equipment acquisitions may include nonexistent assets.	O O O O O	O O O O O O O
3.	Recorded net property and equipment are for proper amounts.	O O O O O	O O O O O O O

Situation	Risk Analysis	Responding to Risk	Research and Communication

Because controls over accounts receivable appear to operate effectively, Bond is considering performing tests of controls and using negative confirmation requests rather than positive requests. He has asked you to research the conditions under which he would be able to use negative confirmation requests for the accounts (select the appropriate paragraph[s]) and to (1) prepare a summary, and (2) write a brief memo that provides the circumstances in which negative confirmations may appropriately be used.

NOTE: If you do not have access to professional standards indicate the keywords or section numbers that you would use to do your search.

SOLUTION TO SIMULATION 3

Situation	Risk Analysis	Responding to Risk	Research and Communication

AU 110, 312, and 316 all require that auditors consider factors influencing the risk of material misstatement and that the risk of material misstatement be considered during the planning phase of an audit engagement.

1. **(D)** Since TWD returned to profitable operation, its healthier financial condition leads to a decrease in the risk of material misstatement.

2. **(I)** The risk of material misstatement increases when management is dominated by a single person. Since Mead controls the Board of Directors, is a majority stockholder, and is the CEO, it would appear that Mead dominates management.

3. **(I)** The risk of material misstatement increases when the internal auditor reports to top management rather than to the audit committee because it is less likely that the internal auditor will be able to objectively perform the function.

4. **(I)** The risk of material misstatement increases when the key management positions (particularly senior accounting personnel) encounter turnover.

5. **(D)** The loan officer's continual monitoring of TWD decreases the risk of material misstatement.

6. **(N)** Timing of payroll cycles would normally have no impact on the risk of material misstatement.

7. **(I)** A strong financial presence or ability to dominate a certain industry sector that allows a company to dictate terms or conditions to suppliers or customers may result in inappropriate or non-arm's-length transactions.

8. **(I)** A change to generally accepted accounting principles will increase the risk of material misstatement because the change in basis requires management to prepare a number of entries that have not been made in the past; these entries may be made improperly. Also, difficulties in determining beginning accrual basis balances increases the risk of misstatement.

9. **(I)** The sale of one-half of the company's controlling interest in United Equipment Leasing is an entry that is out of the ordinary course of business, and accordingly, increases the risk of material misstatement.

10. **(D)** Litigation results in contentious and difficult accounting valuation issues because an accountant must attempt to determine the likelihood of loss and the amount.

11. **(I)** The risk of material misstatement increases when significant related-party transactions occur and management has an aggressive attitude towards reporting of the transactions.

12. **(I)** The risk of material misstatement increases in situations where there are unusual and difficult accounting issues present. It would appear that the barter transaction with a below market purchase would be considered an unusual transaction.

13. **(N)** The amount of insurance coverage would have little impact on the risk of material misstatement.

14. **(I)** The risk of material misstatement increases as it appears that management has taken an aggressive attitude toward reporting this transaction. In addition, this appears to be an unusual and difficult accounting issue involving revenue recognition.

15. **(I)** Experience has shown that a number of entities have intentionally misstated reported financial condition and operating results in situations in which a public (or private) placement of securities is planned. Accordingly, an initial public offering of stock increases the risk of material misstatement.

Situation	Risk Analysis	Responding to Risk	Research and Communication

Risk identified	Related financial statement assertion (A) (B) (C) (D) (E)	Audit procedures (F) (G) (H) (I) (J) (K) (L)
1. TWD may not have legal title to certain property and equipment recorded as acquired during the year.	○ ○ ● ○ ○	○ ○ ○ ● ○ ○ ○
2. Recorded property and equipment acquisitions may include nonexistent assets.	● ○ ○ ○ ○	○ ○ ○ ○ ○ ○ ●
3. Recorded net property and equipment are for proper amounts.	○ ○ ○ ● ○	○ ● ○ ○ ○ ○ ○

Explanation of solutions

1. **(C, I)** Legal titles relates most directly to the client having rights over the assets; an examination of deeds and title insurance certificates will provide assurance that the client has a legal right to the property and equipment acquired during the year.

2. **(A, L)** The recording of nonexistent assets relates most directly to existence of assets; physical examination of the major additions will address whether they exist.

3. (D, G) The proper recording of the net of property and equipment relates most directly to the valuation or allocation of the accounts; reviewing the provision for depreciation expense will address whether accumulated depreciation has been properly updated.

Situation	Risk Analysis	Responding to Risk	Research and Communication

The first step is to determine the manner in which the candidate wishes to identify the pertinent research in the area. If a keyword search is to be used, words such as "negative confirmation" or "negative confirmation requests" seem appropriate. Alternatively you may be able to use the index, or you may recall that guidance on confirmations is presented in AU 330. The following is included in AU 330:

.20 The negative form requests the recipient to respond only if he or she disagrees with the information stated on the request. Negative confirmation requests may be used to reduce the risk of material misstatement to an acceptable level when (1) the combined assessed level of inherent and control risk is low, (2) a large number of small balances is involved, and (3) the auditor has no reason to believe that the recipients of the requests are unlikely to give them consideration. For example, in the examination of demand deposit accounts in a financial institution, it may be appropriate for an auditor to include negative confirmation requests with the customer's regular statements when the combined assessed level of inherent risk is low and the auditor has no reason to believe that the recipients will not consider the requests. The auditor should consider performing other substantive procedures to supplement the use of negative confirmations.

A memo such as the following is appropriate:

To: Mr. William Bond
From: [*Your name*]
Re: Negative confirmation requests
Date: [*Today's date*]

You asked that I research the conditions in which the negative confirmation form is considered appropriate for accounts receivable. AU section 330 provides information on the confirmation process and paragraph 21 of that section states that the use of negative confirmation requests is appropriate when

a. The combined assessed level of inherent and control risk is low,
b. A large number of small balances is involved, and
c. The auditor has no reason to believe that the recipients of the requests are unlikely to give them consideration.

Attached are both paragraph 21 and the complete AU section 330. (*Alternatively you could choose to include paragraph 21 completely in your memo and/or simply tell Mr. Bond how AU 330 might be accessed.*)

Because TWD has receivables with large balances, it would seem that because of point b. above, the negative confirmation request is not appropriate for this client.

SIMULATION 4   (45 to 55 minutes)

Topic—Evidence and Reporting

Situation			
	Research	Reporting	Communication

On September 30, 20X2, White & Co. CPAs, was engaged to audit the consolidated financial statements of National Motors Inc. for the year ended December 31, 20X2. The consolidated financial statements of National had not been audited the prior year. National's inadequate inventory records precluded White from forming an opinion as to the proper application of generally accepted accounting principles to inventory balances on January 1, 20X2. Therefore, White decided not to express an opinion on the results of operations for the year ended December 31, 20X2. National decided not to present comparative financial statements.

Rapid Parts Company, a consolidated subsidiary of National, was audited for the year ended December 31, 20X2, by Green & Co. CPAs. Green completed its audit procedures on February 28, 20X3, and submitted an unqualified opinion on Rapid's financial statements on March 7, 20X3. Rapid's statements reflect total assets and revenues constituting $700,000 and $2,000,000, respectively, of the consolidated totals of National. White decided not to assume responsibility for the work of Green. Green's report on Rapid does not accompany National's consolidated statements.

White has completed its audit procedures on March 28, 20X3, and planned to submit its auditor's report to National on April 4, 20X3.

	Research		
Situation		Reporting	Communication

Before completing the audit work, White must perform certain audit procedures with respect to the period after the balance sheet date to consider the possible occurrence of subsequent events that might require financial statement adjustment or disclosure. Research the procedures an auditor must generally perform, and select the appropriate paragraph(s).

NOTE: If you do not have access to professional standards indicate the keywords or section numbers that you would use to do your search.

		Reporting	
Situation	Research		Communication

The following lists potential effects on White's audit report.

Effect on the Audit Report

A. Disclaim on balance sheet, income statement and statement of cash flows.
B. Disclaim only on results of operations.
C. Qualified audit opinion on results of operations.
D. Modification of report to set forth a division of responsibility for the audit.
E. Issuance of two separate reports.
F. Date the report March 28, 20X3.
G. Date the report April 4, 20X3.

For each circumstance described below select the most appropriate statement that reflects the effect on the audit report.

                                                                    (A) (B) (C) (D) (E) (F) (G)

1. National's inadequate inventory records precluded White from forming an opinion as to the proper application of generally accepted accounting principles to inventory balances on January 1, 20X2.   ○ ○ ○ ○ ○ ○ ○

2. Rapid Parts Company, a consolidated subsidiary of National, was audited for the year ended December 31, 20X2, by Green & Co. CPAs.   ○ ○ ○ ○ ○ ○ ○

3. White has completed its audit procedures on March 28, 20X3, and planned to submit its auditor's report to National on April 4, 20X3.   ○ ○ ○ ○ ○ ○ ○

Situation	Research	Reporting	Communication

Draft a memo to the audit workpapers explaining the circumstances that caused the issuance of a modified audit report for National Motors.

REMINDER: Your response will be graded for both technical relevance and writing skills. Technical content will be evaluated for information that is helpful to the intended reader and clearly relevant to the issue. Writing skills will be evaluated for development, organization, and the appropriate expression of ideas in professional correspondence. Use a standard business memo or letter format with a clear beginning, middle, and end. Do not convey information in the form of a table, bullet point list, or other abbreviated presentation.

To: Audit Files
From: CPA Candidate

SOLUTION TO SIMULATION 4

	Research		
Situation		Reporting	Communication

Because the requirement relates to subsequent events, that becomes an obvious term to search on. You might also add "auditing procedures" to the search. Paragraphs AU 560.10-.12 present the answer.

Auditing Procedures in the Subsequent Period

.10   There is a period after the balance sheet date with which the auditor must be concerned in completing various phases of his audit. This period is known as the "subsequent period" and is considered to extend to the date of the auditor's report. Its duration will depend upon the practical requirements of each audit and may vary from a relatively short period to one of several months. Also, all auditing procedures are not carried out as the same time and some phases of an audit will be performed during the subsequent period, whereas other phases will be substantially completed on or before the balance sheet date. As an audit approaches completion, the auditor will be concentrating on the unresolved auditing and reporting matters and he is not expected to be conducting a continuing review of those matters to which he has previously applied auditing procedures and reached satisfaction.

.11   Certain specific procedures are applied to transactions occurring after the balance sheet date such as (a) the examination of data to assure that proper cutoffs have been made and (b) the examination of data which provide information to aid the auditor in his evaluation of the assets and liabilities as of the balance sheet date.

.12   In addition, the independent auditor should perform other auditing procedures with respect to the period after the balance sheet date for the purpose of ascertaining the occurrence of subsequent events that may require adjustment or disclosure essential to a fair presentation of the financial statements in conformity with generally accepted accounting principles. These procedures should be performed at or near the completion of the audit work. The auditor generally should

    a.   Read the latest available interim financial statements; compare them with the financial statements being reported upon; and make any other comparisons considered appropriate in the circumstances. In order to make these procedures as meaningful as possible for the purpose expressed above, the auditor should inquire of officers and other executives having responsibility for financial and accounting matters as to whether the interim statements have been prepared on the same basis as that used for the statements under audit.

    b.   Inquire of and discuss with officers and other executives having responsibility for financial and accounting matters (limited where appropriate to major locations) as to

       (i)   Whether any substantial contingent liabilities or commitments existed at the date of the balance sheet being reported on or at the date of inquiry.

       (ii)   Whether there was any significant change in the capital stock, long-term debt, or working capital to the date of inquiry.

       (iii)   The current status of items, in the financial statements being reported on, that were accounted for on the basis of tentative, preliminary, or inconclusive data.

       (iv)   Whether any unusual adjustments had been made during the period from the balance sheet date to the date of inquiry.

    c.   Read the available minutes of meetings of stockholders, directors, and appropriate committees; as to meetings for which minutes are not available, inquire about matters dealt with at such meetings.

    d.   Inquire of client's legal counsel concerning litigation, claims, and assessments.

    e.   Obtain a letter of representations, dated as of the date of the auditor's report, from appropriate officials, generally the chief executive officer, chief financial officer, or others with equivalent positions in the entity, as to whether any events occurred subsequent to the date of the financial statements being reported on by the independent auditor that in the officer's opinion would require adjustment or disclosure in these statements. The auditor may elect to have the client include representations as to significant matters disclosed to the auditor in his performance of the procedures in subparagraphs (a) to (d) above and (f) below.

    f.   Make such additional inquiries or perform such procedures as he considers necessary and appropriate to dispose of questions that arise in carrying out the foregoing procedures, inquiries, and discussions.

		Reporting	
Situation	Research		Communication

	(A)	(B)	(C)	(D)	(E)	(F)	(G)
1. National's inadequate inventory records precluded White from forming an opinion as to the proper application of generally accepted accounting principles to inventory balances on January 1, 20X2.	○	●	○	○	○	○	○
2. Rapid Parts Company, a consolidated subsidiary of National, was audited for the year ended December 31, 20X2, by Green & Co. CPAs.	○	○	○	●	○	○	○

(A) (B) (C) (D) (E) (F) (G)

3. White has completed its audit procedures on March 28, 20X3, and planned to submit its auditor's report to National on April 4, 20X3.

○ ○ ○ ○ ○ ● ○

Explanation of solutions

1. **(B)** The lack of evidence about the beginning inventory affects only the results of operations (the income statement).

2. **(D)** The involvement of the other audit firm results in a division of responsibility because White does not want to take responsibility for the other auditor's work.

3. **(F)** The report should be dated as of the date that all substantive audit evidence has been obtained.

Situation	Research	Reporting	Communication

To: Audit Files
From: CPA Candidate

   This memorandum is designed to describe the implications of the issues related to the inadequate inventory records. We were engaged to audit the financial statements of National Motors Inc. for the year ended December 31, 20X2. The financial statements were not audited in the prior year. Due to a lack of adequate inventory records, we were unable to obtain sufficient evidence to form an opinion on the fairness of beginning inventories of the company. Accordingly, we will disclaim an opinion on the statements of income and cash flows. This disclaimer of opinion on the statement of income is necessary because the beginning inventories affect the cost of goods sold for the year. Similarly, the statement of cash flows is affected since both the beginning and ending level of inventories are used to measure the company's cash flows. The year-end balance sheet is unaffected since it reports only the ending inventory balances.

   If you have any additional questions, please ask the audit manager.

SIMULATION 5 (60 to 70 minutes)

Topic—Audit Evidence and Reporting

Company Profile									
	Industry Profile	Balance Sheet	Income Statement/Ratios	Statement of Cash Flows	Risks	Audit Findings	Audit Procedures	Communication	Research

You are beginning the 20X8 audit of Toastco, a nonissuer (nonpublic) company that manufactures various kitchen products. This is your firm's sixth annual audit of Toastco.

Toastco's most profitable product is a deluxe toaster that is designed for those who want "a truly outstanding toaster." The toaster was first marketed through *Sky Mall Magazine* which offers specialty-type products to airplane passengers. Demand has grown so that at this point the company advertises the product much more broadly through a variety of media. Sales have been outstanding from the start and continue to increase. The recorded level of sales for 20X8 indicates that the company now controls approximately 5% of the toaster market, which represents 55% of company sales. In addition to the toaster, the company manufactures other products, including toaster ovens, coffee makers, food blenders, and electric can openers. Most of the manufacturing process is performed in several plants in Asia.

The highly successful toaster is the product of Bill Williams who became Toastco's chief executive officer in 20X3. Bill and several other officers invested heavily in the company at that time with the intent of ultimately selling common stock to the public. He and those individuals' lives are centered about the firm and making it a success. Consistently, Toastco is of critical importance to each of these individuals financially.

Recently you discussed the coming audit with Bill. You quickly found that he was elated that the company had earned $1.21 per share, one cent more than he had assured the bank that had provided Toastco with extensive financing during 20X8. He suggested that some had feared that Toastco wouldn't make it after somewhat weak second and third quarters, but that he knew all along that a strong fourth quarter was ahead and that it would "bring us through." He also pointed out that sales are up about 38% compared to the previous year and income by 54%. Furthermore, he indicated that an initial public offering of securities was planned for approximately eighteen months from now.

Toastco's outstanding performance for the past several years is in large part due to the highly profitable toaster, with other products gaining sales at approximately the industry's growth rate. In fact, Bill indicated that the toaster has become even more profitable this year due to reengineering of its production process and components, which brought costs of production down and decreased sales returns and allowances.

Bill also suggested to you that the $42,216,000 bank loan received during the year has been primarily used to increase inventories and fixed assets to support the rapidly rising demand for the toaster, as well as Toastco's other products. He pointed out that the company could never have achieved its projected earnings per share goal without the bank's support. This bank support has also allowed Toastco to work on developing what Bill refers to as "our next super product... an improved can opener that works well with all sizes of cans and doesn't leave a mess."

Finally, Bill said that there was some sad news. The Chairman of the Board of Directors, John Whing, an independent director, had been forced to step down for health reasons. Bill had replaced Mr. Whing as Chairman of the Board, and Toastco Vice President Sam Adamson filled the empty seat on the board of directors. The seven-member board is now composed of Bill (who will begin serving as Chairman), Sam Adamson, two others from management, and the three independent directors. The audit committee has not been affected by the change, as the three independent directors continue to serve in that role.

Company Profile	Industry Profile	Balance Sheet	Income Statement/Ratios	Statement of Cash Flows	Risks	Audit Findings	Audit Procedures	Communication	Research

In the portions of the kitchen product industry in which Toastco operates, demand is influenced by economic trends such as increases or decreases in consumer disposable income, availability of credit, and housing construction. Competition is very active in all products and comes from a number of principal manufacturers and suppliers. An important factor is the degree of product differentiation achieved through innovation and new product features. Other significant factors include product quality and cost, brand recognition, customer responsiveness, and appliance service capability.

Overall, for the industry, sales have been and are expected to remain relatively stable with a slight increase—increases have approximated 3% industry-wide per year during the past five years, and are expected to continue at that rate of increase for the next five years. Much of the manufacturing of these products takes place in Asia, and to a lesser extent in South America. Increasingly, Asian companies are becoming directly involved in marketing their own household products.

Company Profile	Industry Profile	Balance Sheet	Income Statement/Ratios	Statement of Cash Flows	Risks	Audit Findings	Audit Procedures	Communication	Research

Toastco
BALANCE SHEET

Dollars (000s omitted)

	12/31/X8 Unaudited	12/31/X7 Audited
Assets		
Cash	885	514
Accounts receivable	51,076	27,801
Inventories	39,135	19,577
Other current assets	3,015	1,449
Total current assets	94,111	49,341
Fixed assets		
Land, property, plant, and equipment (net)	24,029	15,900
Total assets	118,140	65,241
Liabilities and equity		
Accounts payable	13,288	15,072
Accrued liabilities	4,710	5,468
Current portion long-term debt	1,250	900
Income taxes payable	3,782	2,619
Total current liabilities	23,030	24,059
Bank debt	62,057	19,841
Deferred income taxes	1,881	1,254
Total liabilities	86,968	45,154
Common stock	7,903	7,775
Retained earnings	23,269	12,312
Total liabilities and equity	118,140	65,241

Company Profile	Industry Profile	Balance Sheet	Income Statement/Ratios	Statement of Cash Flows	Risks	Audit Findings	Audit Procedures	Communication	Research

Toastco
INCOME STATEMENT

Dollars (000s omitted)

	12/31/X8 Unaudited	12/31/X7 Audited
Gross sales	183,767	133,504
Returns and allowances	2,644	5,270
Net sales	181,123	128,234
Cost of goods sold	94,934	70,756
Gross margin	86,189	57,478
Selling, advertising, research and development	64,285	42,600
Income from operations	21,904	14,878
Interest expense	3,189	1,584
Income before taxes	18,715	13,294
Income taxes	7,761	6,189
Net income	10,954	7,105
EPS	1.21	.78
Ratios*		
Current	4.1	2.1
Quick	2.3	1.2
Accounts receivable turnover	4.7	6.3
Days' sales in ending receivables	76.6	57.1
Inventory turnover	3.2	4.8
Days' sales in ending inventory	112.5	75.0
Interest expense/debt	0.05	0.08

* *Calculated using year-end data.*

Company Profile	Industry Profile	Balance Sheet	Income Statement/Ratios	Statement of Cash Flows		Risks	Audit Findings	Audit Procedures	Communication	Research

Toastco
STATEMENT OF CASH FLOWS
For the Year Ending 20X8

Dollars (000s omitted)

Cash flows from operation activities

Net income		10,954
Increase in accounts receivable	(23,275)	
Increase in inventories	(19,558)	
Increase in other current assets	(1,566)	
Decrease in accounts payable	(1,784)	
Increase in accrued liabilities	(758)	
Increase in income taxes payable	1,166	
Increase in deferred income taxes	627	(45,148)
Net cash flow from operating activities		(34,194)

Cash flows from investing activities

Increase in current long-term debt	350	
Payments for fixed assets	(8,129)	
Net cash flow from investing activities		(7,779)

Cash flows from financing activities

Proceeds from issuance of long-term debt	42,216	
Proceeds from issuance of stock	128	
Net cash flow from financing activities		42,344
Net cash inflow		371

Company Profile	Industry Profile	Balance Sheet	Income Statement/Ratios	Statement of Cash Flows	Risks		Audit Findings	Audit Procedures	Communication	Research

(A) (B) (C) (D)

1. Which of the following identifies an aspect of the company's business model, strategies, and/or business environment that is most likely to increase the risk of misstatement arising from fraudulent financial reporting?   ○ ○ ○ ○

A. Toastco sells more than one type of product.
B. The president's wealth is based on the success of Toastco.
C. The audit committee is composed entirely of independent directors.
D. Toastco continues to hire your firm for its fifth year.

Company Profile	Industry Profile	Balance Sheet	Income Statement/Ratios	Statement of Cash Flows	Risks	Audit Findings		Audit Procedures	Communication	Research

Change in inventory turnover

	20X8	20X7
Inventory turnover	3.2	4.8

(A) (B) (C) (D) (E) (F)

1. Which of the following is most consistent with such a decrease in inventory turnover?   ○ ○ ○ ○ ○ ○

A. A number of expense items were erroneously included in cost of goods sold (but not in ending inventory).
B. Sales have increased and a higher percentage of customers are paying their accounts on time.
C. Fourth quarter sales were higher than normal, thus inventory is lower than one would expect at year-end due to the increase in sales.
D. Inventory and cost of goods sold were adjusted to the year-end inventory count, a count that overcounted a number of significant items. A periodic inventory system is in use.
E. The new long-term debt agreement was achieved at a desirable rate of interest.
F. A number of receivables have been affected by an employee's lapping scheme.

Change in interest expense to debt ratio

	20X8	20X7
Interest expense/debt	0.05	0.08

(A) (B) (C) (D) (E) (F)

2. Which of the following is most consistent with such a decrease in the ratio of interest expense to debt?   ○ ○ ○ ○ ○ ○

   A. Short-term borrowing was refinanced on a long-term basis at the same interest rate.
   B. The company bought back shares of its common stock using proceeds from the new long-term loan.
   C. Sales increases have led to the need to expand production facilities, particularly for the popular toaster.
   D. While the significant increase in debt is at about the same interest rate as previous debt, it is at a rate well below the company's overall cost of capital.
   E. Interest expense for the year has not been accrued as of year-end.
   F. The new long-term debt was received early during 20X8, at a higher rate than existing debt.

Company Profile	Industry Profile	Balance Sheet	Income Statement/Ratios	Statement of Cash Flows	Risks	Audit Findings	Audit Procedures	Communication	Research

For each audit objective listed below select the most appropriate audit procedure for raw materials inventory, a significant portion of Toastco's total inventories. Audit procedures may be used once, more than once, or not at all.

List of audit procedures

   A. Compare standard costs of inventories with standardized market values.
   B. Determine that all direct labor and overhead has been expensed and not included in inventory valuation.
   C. Examine vendors' invoices.
   D. Perform analytical procedures comparing inventory to various industry averages.
   E. Review drafts of financial statement note disclosures.
   F. Select a sample of items during the physical count and determine that the client has included items on inventory count sheets.
   G. Select a sample of recorded items on count sheets and determine that the items are on hand.

(A) (B) (C) (D) (E) (F) (G)

1. Determine that company legally owns inventories.   ○ ○ ○ ○ ○ ○ ○

2. Establish the completeness of inventories.   ○ ○ ○ ○ ○ ○ ○

3. Determine that the cost of inventories is proper.   ○ ○ ○ ○ ○ ○ ○

Company Profile	Industry Profile	Balance Sheet	Income Statement/Ratios	Statement of Cash Flows	Risks	Audit Findings	Audit Procedures	Communication	Research

The following is one of the confirmation replies received from the confirmation process applied to accounts receivable:

Confirmation #22

The statement of our account showing a balance of $12,222 due Toastco, at December 31, 20X8, is correct except as noted below.

<u>Wilson Suppliers</u>

By <u>Kent Parry</u>

Date: 2/2/X9

Exceptions: *No way. Forget it. Toastco said we'd have these goods in 10 days on December 2. When we didn't receive them, I canceled the order on December 12th. Wilson Corp. shipped us similar goods overnight. We will never deal with Toastco again as long as I am around.*

In a memorandum to the audit team, explain any possible risks existing relating to this account and resulting additional audit procedures. Your response will be graded for both technical relevance and writing skills. For writing skills you should demonstrate an ability to develop your ideas, organize them, and express them clearly. Do not convey information in the form of a table, bullet point list, or other abbreviated presentation.

REMINDER: Your response will be graded for both technical relevance and writing skills. Technical content will be evaluated for information that is helpful to the intended reader and clearly relevant to the issue. Writing skills will be evaluated for development, organization, and the appropriate expression of ideas in professional correspondence. Use a standard business memo or letter format with a clear beginning, middle, and end. Do not convey information in the form of a table, bullet point list, or other abbreviated presentation.

To: Audit Team
Subject: Change in Board of Directors
Re: Confirmation #22

										Research
Company Profile	Industry Profile	Balance Sheet	Income Statement/Ratios	Statement of Cash Flows	Risks	Audit Findings	Audit Procedures	Communication		

Assume that you have completed the audit of Toastco and find that an unusually important subsequent event occurred after year-end, which Toastco has appropriately treated in the financial statements through a note disclosure. Using the research materials available to you by clicking the Standards button on the Title bar, identify any guidance available on emphasizing a matter in the audit report such as this large subsequent event. That is, while you believe that an unqualified report is appropriate, you also believe that it might be appropriate to emphasize this matter in your audit report. Select the professional guidance on examples of circumstances in which such emphasis may be appropriate and of any phrases that might be considered inappropriate in such a report.

SOLUTION TO SIMULATION 5

Company Profile	Industry Profile	Balance Sheet	Income Statement/Ratios	Statement of Cash Flows	**Risks**	Audit Findings	Audit Procedures	Communication	Research

                                                                                        (A) (B) (C) (D)

1. Which of the following identifies an aspect of the company's business model, strategies, and/or business environment that is most likely to increase the risk of misstatement arising from fraudulent financial reporting?   ○ ● ○ ○

Explanation of solution

1. **(B)** The requirement is to determine an aspect of a company that is most likely to increase the risk of misstatement arising from fraudulent financial reporting. Answer (B) is correct because the president's investment in Toastco creates a situation in which losses in value of the company will profoundly affect him—particularly given his desire to take the company public. Answer (A) is incorrect because selling more than one type of product may or may not affect the risk of misstatement. Answer (C) is incorrect because it is desirable to have the audit committee composed entirely of independent directors. Answer (D) is incorrect because the fact that this is a continuing engagement has no direct tie to the risk of misstatement.

Company Profile	Industry Profile	Balance Sheet	Income Statement/Ratios	Statement of Cash Flows	Risks	**Audit Findings**	Audit Procedures	Communication	Research

                                                                          (A) (B) (C) (D) (E) (F)

1. Which of the following is most consistent with such a decrease in inventory turnover?   ○ ○ ○ ● ○ ○

Explanation of solution

1. **(D)** The requirement is to identify a possible cause of a decrease in the inventory turnover ratio—cost of goods sold divided by inventories. Answer (D) is correct because an overstated ending inventory count will decrease cost of goods sold and increase inventory—both of these effects decrease the inventory turnover. Answer (A) is incorrect because an increase in cost of goods sold increases the inventory turnover. Answer (B) is incorrect because there is no direct tie to a change in the relationship between cost of goods sold and inventories when sales increase and customers pay more quickly. Answer (C) is incorrect because a lower inventory will increase the inventory turnover. Answer (E) and (F) are incorrect because neither the interest rate nor a receivable lapping scheme will directly affect the inventory turnover.

                                                                          (A) (B) (C) (D) (E) (F)

2. Which of the following is most consistent with such a decrease in the ratio of interest expense to debt?   ○ ○ ○ ○ ● ○

Explanation of solution

2. **(E)** The requirement is to identify a possible cause for a decrease in the ratio of interest expense to debt. Answer (E) is correct because lack of accrual of interest expense will decrease the ratio through understating interest expense. Answer (A), (B), (C), and (D) are all incorrect because refinancing at the same interest rate, buying back stock, increasing sales, and increasing the amount of debt (at a rate below the cost of capital) will not affect the ratio. Answer (F) is incorrect because the higher interest rate would increase the ratio.

Company Profile	Industry Profile	Balance Sheet	Income Statement/Ratios	Statement of Cash Flows	Risks	Audit Findings	**Audit Procedures**	Communication	Research

                                                                     (A) (B) (C) (D) (E) (F) (G)

1. Determine that company legally owns inventories.   ○ ○ ● ○ ○ ○ ○

2. Establish the completeness of inventories.   ○ ○ ○ ○ ○ ● ○

3. Determine that the cost of inventories is proper.   ○ ○ ● ○ ○ ○ ○

Explanations of solutions

1. **(C)** Because ownership information is included on invoices, examining vendors' invoices will provide evidence that the company legally owns inventory raw material items.

2. **(F)** Selecting a sample of items and agreeing to the physical count sheet will establish that those items have been included in the count, and this will address completeness of inventories.

3. **(C)** Examining vendors' invoices will provide evidence as to the cost of the inventory items.

Company Profile	Industry Profile	Balance Sheet	Income Statement/Ratios	Statement of Cash Flows	Risks	Audit Findings	Audit Procedures	Communication		Research

Memorandum

To: Audit Team
Subject: Change in Board of Directors
Re: Confirmation #22

This memorandum describes the implications of the exception on Confirmation #22. Confirmation #22 indicates that Wilson Suppliers did not receive the goods ordered from Toastco. The sale occurred on December 2 and Kent Parry of Wilson Suppliers states on the confirmation that his company canceled the purchase on December 12 when they had not received the goods.

Since this receivable was recorded and reflected in sales, we need to vouch it to determine whether the goods were shipped, and if so, their disposition. If we find that the goods were not shipped, it raises a questions as to whether Toastco has other receivables (and accordingly sales) for items not yet shipped. Therefore, if the item was never shipped, we must consider extending our procedures to determine whether this is a significant problem.

Company Profile	Industry Profile	Balance Sheet	Income Statement/Ratios	Statement of Cash Flows	Risks	Audit Findings	Audit Procedures	Communication	Research

The guidance is provided in AU 508.19

.19 In any report on financial statements, the auditor may emphasize a matter regarding the financial statements. Such explanatory information should be presented in a separate paragraph of the auditor's report. Phrases such as "with the foregoing [following] explanation" should not be used in the opinion paragraph if an emphasis paragraph is included in the auditor's report. Emphasis paragraphs are never required; they may be added solely at the auditor's discretion. Examples of matters the auditor may wish to emphasize are

- That the entity is a component of a larger business enterprise.
- That the entity has had significant transactions with related parties.
- Unusually important subsequent events.
- Accounting matters, other than those involving a change or changes in accounting principles, affecting the comparability of the financial statements with those of the preceding period.

[Paragraph renumbered and amended, effective for reports issued or reissued on or after February 29, 1996, by the issuance of Statement on Auditing Standards 79.]

SIMULATION 6   (50 to 55 minutes)

Topic—Audit Evidence and Reporting

Company Profile									
	Industry Profile	Balance Sheet	Income Statement/ Ratios	Statement of Cash Flows	Risks	Audit Findings	Audit Procedures	Communication	Research

You are beginning the 20X8 audit of Toastco, a nonissuer (nonpublic) company that manufactures various kitchen products. This is your firm's sixth annual audit of Toastco.

Toastco's most profitable product is a deluxe toaster that is designed for those who want "a truly outstanding toaster." The toaster was first marketed through *Sky Mall Magazine* which offers specialty-type products to airplane passengers. Demand has grown so that at this point the company advertises the product much more broadly through a variety of media. Sales have been outstanding from the start and continue to increase. The recorded level of sales for 20X8 indicates that the company now controls approximately 5% of the toaster market, which represents 55% of company sales. In addition to the toaster, the company manufactures other products, including toaster ovens, coffee makers, food blenders, and electric can openers. Most of the manufacturing process is performed in several plants in Asia.

The highly successful toaster is the product of Bill Williams who became Toastco's chief executive officer in 20X3. Bill and several other officers invested heavily in the company at that time with the intent of ultimately selling common stock to the public. He and those individuals' lives are centered about the firm and making it a success. Consistently, Toastco is of critical importance to each of these individuals financially.

Recently you discussed the coming audit with Bill. You quickly found that he was elated that the company had earned $1.21 per share, one cent more than he had assured the bank that had provided Toastco with extensive financing during 20X8. He suggested that some had feared that Toastco wouldn't make it after somewhat weak second and third quarters, but that he knew all along that a strong fourth quarter was ahead and that it would "bring us through." He also pointed out that sales are up about 38% compared to the previous year and income by 54%. Furthermore, he indicated that an initial public offering of securities was planned for approximately eighteen months from now.

Toastco's outstanding performance for the past several years is in large part due to the highly profitable toaster, with other products gaining sales at approximately the industry's growth rate. In fact, Bill indicated that the toaster has become even more profitable this year due to reengineering of its production process and components, which brought costs of production down and decreased sales returns and allowances.

Bill also suggested to you that the $42,216,000 bank loan received during the year has been primarily used to increase inventories and fixed assets to support the rapidly rising demand for the toaster, as well as Toastco's other products. He pointed out that the company could never have achieved its projected earnings per share goal without the bank's support. This bank support has also allowed Toastco to work on developing what Bill refers to as "our next super product... an improved can opener that works well with all sizes of cans and doesn't leave a mess."

Finally, Bill said that there was some sad news. The Chairman of the Board of Directors, John Whing, an independent director, had been forced to step down for health reasons. Bill had replaced Mr. Whing as Chairman of the Board, and Toastco Vice President Sam Adamson filled the empty seat on the board of directors. The seven-member board is now composed of Bill (who will begin serving as Chairman), Sam Adamson, two others from management, and the three independent directors. The audit committee has not been affected by the change, as the three independent directors continue to serve in that role.

Company Profile	Industry Profile	Balance Sheet	Income Statement/ Ratios	Statement of Cash Flows	Risks	Audit Findings	Audit Procedures	Communication	Research

In the portions of the kitchen product industry in which Toastco operates, demand is influenced by economic trends such as increases or decreases in consumer disposable income, availability of credit, and housing construction. Competition is very active in all products and comes from a number of principal manufacturers and suppliers. An important factor is the degree of product differentiation achieved through innovation and new product features. Other significant factors include product quality and cost, brand recognition, customer responsiveness, and appliance service capability.

Overall, for the industry, sales have been and are expected to remain relatively stable with a slight increase—increases have approximated 3% industry-wide per year during the past five years, and are expected to continue at that rate of increase for the next five years. Much of the manufacturing of these products takes place in Asia, and to a lesser extent in South America. Increasingly, Asian companies are becoming directly involved in marketing their own household products.

Company Profile	Industry Profile	Balance Sheet	Income Statement/ Ratios	Statement of Cash Flows	Risks	Audit Findings	Audit Procedures	Communication	Research

Toastco
BALANCE SHEET

	Dollars (000s omitted)	
	12/31/X8	12/31/X7
	Unaudited	*Audited*
Assets		
Cash	885	514
Accounts receivable	51,076	27,801
Inventories	39,135	19,577
Other current assets	3,015	1,449
Total current assets	94,111	49,341
Fixed assets		
Land, property, plant, and equipment (net)	24,029	15,900
Total assets	118,140	65,241
Liabilities and equity		
Accounts payable	13,288	15,072
Accrued liabilities	4,710	5,468
Current portion long-term debt	1,250	900
Income taxes payable	3,782	2,619
Total current liabilities	23,030	24,059
Bank debt	62,057	19,841
Deferred income taxes	1,881	1,254
Total liabilities	86,968	45,154
Common stock	7,903	7,775
Retained earnings	23,269	12,312
Total liabilities and equity	118,140	65,241

Company Profile	Industry Profile	Balance Sheet	Income Statement/ Ratios	Statement of Cash Flows	Risks	Audit Findings	Audit Procedures	Communication	Research

Toastco
INCOME STATEMENT

	Dollars (000s omitted)	
	12/31/X8	12/31/X7
	Unaudited	*Audited*
Gross sales	183,767	133,504
Returns and allowances	2,644	5,270
Net sales	181,123	128,234
Cost of goods sold	94,934	70,756
Gross margin	86,189	57,478
Selling, advertising, research and development	64,285	42,600
Income from operations	21,904	14,878
Interest expense	3,189	1,584
Income before taxes	18,715	13,294
Income taxes	7,761	6,189
Net income	10,954	7,105
EPS	1.21	.78
Ratios*		
Current	4.1	2.1
Quick	2.3	1.2
Accounts receivable turnover	4.7	6.3
Days' sales in ending receivables	76.6	57.1
Inventory turnover	3.2	4.8
Days' sales in ending inventory	112.5	75.0
Interest expense/debt	0.05	0.08

* Calculated using year-end data.

Company Profile	Industry Profile	Balance Sheet	Income Statement/ Ratios	Statement of Cash Flows		Risks	Audit Findings	Audit Procedures	Communication	Research

Toastco
STATEMENT OF CASH FLOWS
For the Year Ending 20X8

Dollars (000s omitted)

Cash flows from operation activities
Net income   10,954

Increase in accounts receivable   (23,275)
Increase in inventories   (19,558)
Increase in other current assets   (1,566)
Decrease in accounts payable   (1,784)
Increase in accrued liabilities   (758)
Increase in income taxes payable   1,166
Increase in deferred income taxes   627   (45,148)
    Net cash flow from operating activities   (34,194)

Cash flows from investing activities
Increase in current long-term debt   350
Payments for fixed assets   (8,129)
    Net cash flow from investing activities   (7,779)

Cash flows from financing activities
Proceeds from issuance of long-term debt   42,216
Proceeds from issuance of stock   128
    Net cash flow from financing activities   42,344
    Net cash inflow   371

Company Profile	Industry Profile	Balance Sheet	Income Statement/ Ratios	Statement of Cash Flows	Risks	Audit Findings	Audit Procedures	Communication	Research

(A) (B) (C) (D)

1. Which of the following identifies an aspect of the company's business model, strategies, and/or business environment that is most likely to increase the risk of misstatement arising from fraudulent financial reporting?   ○ ○ ○ ○

   A. The household products industry seems stable, and is not rapidly growing.
   B. Toastco reported a strong fourth quarter that brought it up to expectations for earnings per share.
   C. Toastco controls approximately 5% of the market for toasters.
   D. Toastco has one relatively profitable product, and a number of products that are not as profitable.

Company Profile	Industry Profile	Balance Sheet	Income Statement/ Ratios	Statement of Cash Flows	Risks	Audit Findings	Audit Procedures	Communication	Research

Change in accounts receivable turnover

	20X8	20X7
Accounts receivable turnover ratio	4.7	6.3

(A) (B) (C) (D)

1. Which of the following is most consistent with a decrease in the accounts receivable turnover ratio?   ○ ○ ○ ○

   A. A fraudulent transaction was recorded crediting sales and debiting property, plant, and equipment.
   B. An increasing amount of the company's sales are for cash—through cash transfers.
   C. Many items shipped on consignment during December were recorded as credit sales; no cash receipts have yet been received on those consignments.
   D. Toastco has increased sales by selling goods for lower prices, but shortened the length of credit terms from thirty days to twenty days.

Change in current ratio

	20X8	20X7
Current ratio	4.1	2.1

(A) (B) (C) (D)

2. Which of the following is most consistent with an increase in the current ratio?   ○ ○ ○ ○

A. Payments for fixed assets.
B. Proceeds obtained and used relating to long-term debt.
C. Decreased accounts payable.
D. Decreased sales returns and allowances.

Company Profile	Industry Profile	Balance Sheet	Income Statement/ Ratios	Statement of Cash Flows	Risks	Audit Findings	Audit Procedures	Communication	Research

For each audit objective select the most appropriate audit procedure for accounts receivable. Audit procedures may be used once, more than once, or not at all.

List of audit procedures

A. Analyze relationships between accounts receivable balances and changes in the current portion of long-term debt.
B. Compare accounts receivable on the accounts receivable lead schedule with those on supporting audit schedules.
C. Compare total 20X8 annual sales with those of 20X7.
D. Examine December 20X8 sales journal and determine that sales are properly recorded in December.
E. Examine January 20X9 sales journal and determine that sales are properly recorded in January.
F. Inquire of credit manager about the collectability of various receivables.
G. Review disclosure checklist for recommended and required accounts receivable disclosures.

	(A)	(B)	(C)	(D)	(E)	(F)	(G)
1. Determine that all accounts receivable are properly recorded as of year-end.	○	○	○	○	○	○	○
2. Determine that accounts receivable are properly valued at net realizable value.	○	○	○	○	○	○	○
3. Note disclosures related to accounts receivable are proper.	○	○	○	○	○	○	○

Company Profile	Industry Profile	Balance Sheet	Income Statement/ Ratios	Statement of Cash Flows	Risks	Audit Findings	Audit Procedures	Communication	Research

Your firm has been performing the audit of Toastco for five years. Since last year there has been a change in corporate governance in composition of the board of directors, although composition of the audit committee remains the same as in previous years. In a memorandum to the audit team, explain the impact of the change in audit risk. Your response will be graded for both technical relevance and writing skills. For writing skills you should demonstrate an ability to develop your ideas, organize them, and express them clearly. Do not convey information in the form of a table, bullet point list, or other abbreviated presentation.

REMINDER: Your response will be graded for both technical relevance and writing skills. Technical content will be evaluated for information that is helpful to the intended reader and clearly relevant to the issue. Writing skills will be evaluated for development, organization, and the appropriate expression of ideas in professional correspondence. Use a standard business memo or letter format with a clear beginning, middle, and end. Do not convey information in the form of a table, bullet point list, or other abbreviated presentation.

To: Audit Team
From: CPA Candidate
Subject: Change in Board of Directors

Company Profile	Industry Profile	Balance Sheet	Income Statement/ Ratios	Statement of Cash Flows	Risks	Audit Findings	Audit Procedures	Communication	Research

Assume that you have completed the audit of Toastco and find that you are able to issue a standard audit report on both 20X7 and 20X8, and that all the appropriate financial statements are presented. Assume that based on new information, you are considering changing your opinion on the prior year's financial statements. Using the research materials available to you select the paragraphs of professional standards that provide guidance regarding this situation.

SOLUTION TO SIMULATION 6

Company Profile	Industry Profile	Balance Sheet	Income Statement/ Ratios	Statement of Cash Flows	Risks	Audit Findings	Audit Procedures	Communication	Research

(A) (B) (C) (D)

1. Which of the following identifies an aspect of the company's business model, strategies, and/or business environment that is most likely to increase the risk of misstatement arising from fraudulent financial reporting?   ○ ● ○ ○

Explanation of solution

1.   **(B)** The requirement is to determine the aspect of Toastco that is most likely to increase the risk of misstatement arising from fraudulent financial reporting. Answer (B) is correct because the president, Bill Williams, felt pressure to meet the earnings per share number he had promised the bank due to weak second and third quarters. Therefore the high earnings in the fourth quarter represents a risk. Answer (A) is incorrect because the stability of the industry presents no particular risk. Answer (C) is incorrect because Toastco's market share by itself does not seem to pose a risk of misstatement. Answer (D) is incorrect because while Toastco would certainly be in a safer position with more profitable products, this is not as significant a fraud risk as is the pressure to achieve the earnings per share target.

Company Profile	Industry Profile	Balance Sheet	Income Statement/ Ratios	Statement of Cash Flows	Risks	Audit Findings	Audit Procedures	Communication	Research

(A) (B) (C) (D)

1. Which of the following is most consistent with a decrease in the accounts receivable turnover ratio?   ○ ○ ● ○

2. Which of the following is most consistent with an increase in the current ratio?   ○ ● ○ ○

Explanation of solutions

1.   **(C)** The requirement is to identify a possible cause of a decrease in the accounts receivable turnover—sales divided by accounts receivable. Answer (C) is correct because items on consignment, but recorded as sales, increase both the numerator and the denominator of the accounts receivable turnover ratio by the same amount (sales/accounts receivable); this will decrease the ratio. Answer (A) is incorrect because crediting sales increases the numerator of the ratio, and thereby increases the turnover ratio. Answer (B) is incorrect because sales for cash should increase sales which would increase the turnover ratio. Answer (D) is incorrect because shortening the credit terms should increase the turnover ratio.

2.   **(B)** The requirement is to identify a possible cause of an increase in the current ratio—current assets divided by current liabilities. Answer (B) is correct because the great amount of cash received from the bank loan of $42,216,000 creates a long-term debt, and a current asset of cash (most of which has already been used). Answer (A) is incorrect because payments for fixed assets decrease the current ratio through decreasing current assets. Answers (C) and (D) are incorrect because the decrease in accounts payable and in sales returns and allowances are much less than the amount of the proceeds from the loan.

Company Profile	Industry Profile	Balance Sheet	Income Statement/ Ratios	Statement of Cash Flows	Risks	Audit Findings	Audit Procedures	Communication	Research

(A) (B) (C) (D) (E) (F) (G)

1. Determine that all accounts receivable are properly recorded as of year-end.   ○ ○ ○ ○ ● ○ ○

2. Determine that accounts receivable are properly valued at net realizable value.   ○ ○ ○ ○ ○ ● ○

3. Note disclosures related to accounts receivable are proper.   ○ ○ ○ ○ ○ ○ ●

Explanations of solutions

1.   **(E)** When examining the January 20X9 sales journal the auditor may identify sales that should have been recorded in December of 20X8.

2.   **(F)** Auditors will generally inquire of the credit manager as to his or her beliefs concerning the collectability of various receivables, and thereby obtain evidence on the net realizable value of accounts receivable. Often one would expect an answer such as "analyze aging of receivables." Since that was not present here, (F) is the best reply.

3.   **(G)** A disclosure checklist is used to determine that the disclosure requirements of generally accepted accounting principles have been met.

Company Profile	Industry Profile	Balance Sheet	Income Statement/ Ratios	Statement of Cash Flows	Risks	Audit Findings	Audit Procedures	Communication		Research

Memorandum

To: Audit Team
Subject: Change in Board of Directors

 This memorandum describes the implication of the change in the Board of Directors. During the past year a significant change occurred on the Toastco Board of Directors. Sam Adamson, Vice President, replaced John Whing, one of the independent directors. Mr. Williams, President, informed me that Mr. Whing resigned for health reasons. Mr. Whing had also served as Chairman of the Board, a position assumed by Mr. Williams.

 The effect of this change is to decrease the independent directors to three, and increase inside directors to four. Also, the chairmanship of the board has changed from that of an independent director to that of Mr. Williams, President. This change tends to increase the power on the board of the management directors, and may adversely affect the overall independence of the board. The audit committee continues to be composed of the same three independent directors as in the past.

Company Profile	Industry Profile	Balance Sheet	Income Statement/ Ratios	Statement of Cash Flows	Risks	Audit Findings	Audit Procedures	Communication	Research

The appropriate guidance regarding this situation is contained in AU 508.68-69.

Opinion on Prior-Period Financial Statements Different from the Opinion Previously Expressed

.68 If, during the current audit, an auditor becomes aware of circumstances or events that affect the financial statements of a prior period, he or she should consider such matters when updating his or her report on the financial statements of the prior period. For example, if an auditor has previously qualified his or her opinion or expressed an adverse opinion on financial statements of a prior period because of a departure from generally accepted accounting principles, and the prior-period financial statements are restated in the current period to conform with generally accepted accounting principles, the auditor's updated report on the financial statements of the prior period should indicate that the statements have been restated and should express an unqualified opinion with respect to the restated financial statements. [Paragraph renumbered by the issuance of Statement on Auditing Standards No. 79, December 1995.]

.69 If, in an updated report, the opinion is different from the opinion previously expressed on the financial statements of a prior period, the auditor should disclose all the substantive reasons for the different opinion in a separate explanatory paragraph(s) preceding the opinion paragraph of his or her report. The explanatory paragraph(s) should disclose (a) the date of the auditor's previous report, (b) the type of opinion previously expressed, (c) the circumstances or events that caused the auditor to express a different opinion, and (d) that the auditor's updated opinion on the financial statements of the prior period is different from his or her previous opinion on those statements. The following is an example of an explanatory paragraph that may be appropriate when an auditor issues an updated report on the financial statements of a prior period that contains an opinion different from the opinion previously expressed:

Independent Auditor's Report

[*Same first and second paragraphs as the standard report.*]

 In our report dated March 1, 20X2, we expressed an opinion that the 20X1 financial statements did not fairly present financial position, results of operations, and cash flows in conformity with accounting principles generally accepted in the United States of America because of two departures from such principles: (1) the Company carried its property, plant, and equipment at appraisal values, and provided for depreciation on the basis of such values, and (2) the Company did not provide for deferred income taxes with respect to differences between income for financial reporting purposes and taxable income. As described in Note X, the Company has changed its method of accounting for these items and restated its 20X1 financial statements to conform with accounting principles generally accepted in the United States of America. Accordingly, our present opinion on the 20X1 financial statements, as presented herein, is different from that expressed in our previous report.

 In our opinion, the financial statements referred to above present fairly, in all material respects, the financial position of X Company as of [at] December 31, 20X2 and 20X1, and the results of its operations and its cash flows for the years then ended in conformity with accounting principles generally accepted in the United States of America.

[*Paragraph renumbered by the issuance of Statement on Auditing Standards No. 79, December 1995.*]

SIMULATION 7 (60 to 70 minutes)

Topic—Audit Evidence and Reporting

Company Profile	Balance Sheet	Income/ Cash Flow	Industry Info	Risks	Audit Findings	Audit Procedures	Analysis and Communication	Research

Enright Corporation is a **nonissuer (nonpublic)** manufacturer of golf balls, golf clubs, and other golf-related equipment. The company has been in business for over fifty years and has its headquarters in San Diego, California.

Enright is divided into two divisions, which represent the major markets for the company's products. One division focuses on new golf clubs and resorts, and providing them with all of the necessary golf equipment to begin operations. The other division focuses on new product development and helps existing golf clubs and resorts to upgrade their existing equipment. Currently, each division accounts for approximately equal amounts of Enright's revenues and net income.

The company experienced its second most profitable year in 2002. However, the financial results did not meet management's expectations. Total reported revenues for the year decreased three percent compared to the prior year. Management recognizes the fact that domestic sales growth has slowed significantly in recent years. As a result, the company is now adopting a global focus for marketing its products and is looking to open up new markets in Australia and Japan.

In order to be competitive in world markets, as well as to improve their domestic market share, management believes that they must strictly control costs and make their overall operations more efficient. At the end of 2002, Enright announced it would make a series of restructuring changes as part of its overall business plan for the future.

Senior management at the company has experienced a significant turnover in recent years. The CEO has been with the company for only two years. He was hired from a major competitor after the prior CEO left to take a position with a large manufacturing company in the Northeast. In addition, the company's long-time CFO retired after twenty-five years of service. The current CFO was hired six months ago. She is a former audit manager from the office that works on Enright's annual audit.

Enright has engaged the same auditing firm for its annual audits for the past decade. There have been no disagreements over accounting issues in any of the past three years.

Company Profile	Balance Sheet	Income/ Cash Flow	Industry Info	Risks	Audit Findings	Audit Procedures	Analysis and Communication	Research

Enright Corporation
BALANCE SHEET
December 31, 2002 and 2001

	12/31/02	12/31/01
Assets		
Current assets		
Cash and cash equivalents	$300,000	$235,000
Receivables—net	750,000	816,000
Investments	600,000	545,000
Inventory	1,000,000	1,171,000
Total current assets	2,650,000	2,767,000
Plant and equipment—net	850,000	876,000
Total assets	$3,500,000	$3,643,000
Liabilities and Stockholders' Equity		
Current liabilities		
Accounts payable	$390,000	$410,000
Current portion of long-term debt	620,000	620,000
Other current liabilities	315,000	298,000
Total current liabilities	1,325,000	1,328,000
Long-term debt	475,000	1,095,000
Total liabilities	1,800,000	2,423,000
Stockholders' equity		
Common stock	1,000,000	1,000,000
Retained earnings	700,000	220,000
Total stockholders' equity	1,700,000	1,220,000
Total liabilities and stockholders' equity	$3,500,000	$3,643,000

Company Profile	Balance Sheet	Income/ Cash Flow		Industry Info	Risks	Audit Findings	Audit Procedures	Analysis and Communication	Research

Enright Corporation
INCOME STATEMENT
For the Years Ended December 31, 2002 and 2001

	12/31/02	12/31/01
Sales	$5,250,000	$5,450,000
Cost of goods sold:	2,100,000	2,209,000
Gross profits on sales	3,150,000	3,241,000
Expenses		
Selling expenses	$1,050,000	$1,124,000
General and administrative	1,070,000	1,215,000
Other operating expenses		
Depreciation	30,000	35,000
Interest expense	200,000	227,000
Total expenses	$2,350,000	$2,601,000
Income before taxes	$800,000	$640,000
Provision for income taxes	320,000	256,000
Net income	$480,000	$384,000

Enright Corporation
STATEMENT OF CASH FLOWS
For the Year Ended December 31, 2002

Cash flows from operating activities:	
Net income (loss)	$480,000
Adjustments to reconcile net income (loss) to cash provided by (used for) operating activities	
Depreciation and amortization	30,000
Changes in certain assets and liabilities:	
Decrease (increase) in receivables	66,000
Decrease (increase) in inventory	171,000
Increase (decrease) in accounts payable	(20,000)
Increase (decrease) in other current liabilities	17,000
Net cash provided by (used for) operating activities	744,000
Cash flows from investing activities:	
Purchase of property, plant, and equipment	(4,000)
Change in short-term investments	(55,000)
Net cash provided by (used for) investing activities	(59,000)
Cash flows from financing activities:	
Principal payments on long-term debt	(620,000)
Net cash provided by (used for) financing activities	(620,000)
Net increase (decrease) in cash and cash equivalents	65,000
Cash and cash equivalents at beginning of year	235,000
Cash and cash equivalents at end of year	$300,000

			Industry Info						
Company Profile	Balance Sheet	Income/ Cash Flow		Risks		Audit Findings	Audit Procedures	Analysis and Communication	Research

Market Forecasts
USA Sports Equipment

In 2007, the USA sports equipment market is forecast to reach $47 million, an increase of 19.3% since 2002.

The compounded annual growth rate of the global sports equipment market over the period 2002-2007 is predicted to be 3.5%.

Table 4: USA Sports Equipment Market Value Forecasts: $Mn (2001 Prices), 2002-2007

Market value	$Mn (2001 prices)	% Growth
2002	$40,133.6	2.9%
2003	$41,398.3	3.2%
2004	$42,936.3	3.7%
2005	$44,389.8	3.4%
2006	$46,232.1	4.2%
2007	$46,892.1	3.6%
CAGR 2002-2007	3.5%	

Golf: Play Is Steadying While Sales Struggle[1]

With 1.02 billion participants aged six and over for the year 2001, golf is ranked number 15, compared to other sports.

In what proved to be a disappointing year, sale of golf clubs, balls, bags, gloves, and shoes declined about 6% in wholesale dollars, to about $2.375 billion in 2001. Sales of irons, which enjoyed strong growth in 2000, accounted for most of the decease in 2001.

Clearly, the weak economy was the root of the problem and the continuing weakness in 2002 is expected to result in further slight sales declines as players postpone the purchase of the big-ticket items such as clubs and bags.

The total number of golfers grew by 5%, from 28.9 million to 30.4 million, between 1990 and 2000. There are as many as 40 million people who would like to play or play more often. New course development was scaled back in 2001, with 314 construction projects completed through the first nine months, compared to 408 and 379 during the same periods in 2000 and 1999, respectively.

In what might be called a "Tiger Woods" effect, some experienced golfers are trying to open the game to very young players. A small national tournament for players aged four to twelve has been created. Some manufacturers are marketing youth-sized clubs and a few facilities are developing training programs for children once considered too young to play the game.

Company Profile	Balance Sheet	Income/ Cash Flow	Industry Info	**Risks**	Audit Findings	Audit Procedures	Analysis and Communication	Research

                                                                   (A) (B) (C) (D)

1. Which of the following correctly identifies an aspect of the company's business model, strategies, and operating environment that is most likely to increase audit risk?   ○ ○ ○ ○

    A. The lack of disagreements over accounting issues with the auditors.
    B. Difficulties in meeting management's financial results expectations for the year.
    C. The company is nonpublic.
    D. The large amount of net cash proceeds provided by operating activities.

Company Profile	Balance Sheet	Income/ Cash Flow	Industry Info	Risks	**Audit Findings**	Audit Procedures	Analysis and Communication	Research

The table below presents two ratios that were identified as significant in the current and prior years' audits of Enright. Compare the values of each ratio. Then select an audit finding that is consistent with these metrics.

Ratio	2002	2001
Quick ratio	1.25	1.20
Debt to equity	1.06	1.99

                                                                   (A) (B) (C) (D)

1. Audit finding consistent with the change in the quick ratio for Enright.   ○ ○ ○ ○

    A. Although the inventory was counted and included in the year-end total, a year-end inventory purchase (for credit) was not recorded.
    B. The company made common stock acquisitions of its own stock during the year.
    C. The company accumulated excess inventories that are physically deteriorating or are becoming obsolete.
    D. The company sold many short-term investments at year-end to increase its cash position.

                                                                   (A) (B) (C) (D)

2. Audit finding consistent with change in debt to equity for Enright.   ○ ○ ○ ○

    A. The company made principal payments on long-term debt.
    B. On an overall basis, the company sold short-term investments.
    C. The company recorded a significant increase in the amount of short-term debt.
    D. A dividend declared prior to the end of the year was recorded twice in the general ledger.

Company Profile	Balance Sheet	Income/ Cash Flow	Industry Info	Risks	Audit Findings	**Audit Procedures**	Analysis and Communication	Research

The auditor determines that each of the following objectives will be part of Enright's audit. For each audit objective, select a substantive procedure that would help to achieve the audit objectives. Each of the procedures may be used once, more than once, or not at all.

---

[1] *Source: Sporting Goods Manufacturers Association*

A. Review minutes of board of directors meetings and contracts, and make inquiries of management.
B. Test inventory transactions between a preliminary physical inventory date and the balance sheet date.
C. Obtain confirmation of inventories pledged under loan agreement.
D. Review perpetual inventory records, production records, and purchasing records for indication of current activity.
E. Reconcile physical counts to perpetual records and general ledger balances and investigate significant fluctuation.
F. Examine sales after year-end and open purchase order commitments.
G. Examine paid vendors' invoices, consignment agreements, and contracts.
H. Analytically review and compare the relationship of inventory balance to recent purchasing, production, and sales activity.

	(A)	(B)	(C)	(D)	(E)	(F)	(G)	(H)
1. Identify inventory transactions involving related parties.	○	○	○	○	○	○	○	○
2. Determine that items counted are included in the inventory listing.	○	○	○	○	○	○	○	○

Company Profile	Balance Sheet	Income/ Cash Flow	Industry Info	Risks	Audit Findings	Audit Procedures	Analysis and Communication	Research

Use the Excel Tool to calculate "common size" income statements (vertical analysis) for the two years. As indicated on the spreadsheet "solution," use each year's sales as "100%" and write a brief memo on whether any changes in **cost of goods sold** and **general administrative expense** seem consistent with the information provided by management in the company profile. Discuss how changes might affect audit procedures. Also, when considering changes, consider the fact that sales decreased by approximately 3% in 20X2.

REMINDER: Your response will be graded for both technical relevance and writing skills. Technical content will be evaluated for information that is helpful to the intended reader and clearly relevant to the issue. Writing skills will be evaluated for development, organization, and the appropriate expression of ideas in professional correspondence. Use a standard business memo or letter format with a clear beginning, middle, and end. Do not convey information in the form of a table, bullet point list, or other abbreviated presentation.

To: Audit Team
From: CPA Candidate
Re: Vertical Analysis—Changes in cost of goods sold and general and administrative expenses

Company Profile	Balance Sheet	Income/ Cash Flow	Industry Info	Risks	Audit Findings	Audit Procedures	Analysis and Communication	Research

Use the research material available to you by clicking the Standards button to select the guidance that describes the three purposes of analytical procedures during an audit.

SOLUTION TO SIMULATION 7

Company Profile	Balance Sheet	Income/ Cash Flow	Industry Info	Risks	Audit Findings	Audit Procedures	Analysis and Communication	Research

(A) (B) (C) (D)

1.   Which of the following correctly identifies an aspect of the company's business model, strategies, and operating environment that is most likely to increase audit risk?   ○ ● ○ ○

Explanation of solution

1.   **(B)** The requirement is to identify the aspect of a company that is most likely to increase audit risk. Answer (B) is correct because pressure to meet or come close to management's expectations may create a pressure to commit fraud, and thereby overstate income. This will increase audit risk. Answer (A) is incorrect because disagreements, not a lack of disagreements, are likely to indicate high audit risk. Answer (C) is incorrect because being a nonpublic company does not necessarily lead to an increase in audit risk. Answer (D) is incorrect because positive cash flow from operations may simply mean that the company generated a profit and the positive cash flow accompanied it.

Company Profile	Balance Sheet	Income/ Cash Flow	Industry Info	Risks	Audit Findings	Audit Procedures	Analysis and Communication	Research

(A) (B) (C) (D)

1.   Audit finding consistent with the change in the quick ratio for Enright.   ● ○ ○ ○

2.   Audit finding consistent with change in debt to equity for Enright.   ● ○ ○ ○

Explanation of solutions

1.   **(A)** The requirement is to identify the reply that is consistent with an increase in the quick ratio—(Cash + Short-term investments + Receivables)/ Current liabilities. Answer (A) is correct because not recording the payable portion of an inventory purchase will decrease the current liabilities, and thereby increase the quick ratio. Answer (B) is incorrect both because there does not seem to have been any common stock acquisitions, and because if there were, they would decrease the ratio, not increase it; the decrease would occur either due to an increase in accounts payable or a decrease in cash or accounts receivable. Answer (C) is incorrect because inventories are not included in the quick ratio and because inventory is lower at year-end rather than higher as might be suggested by obsolete inventories. Answer (D) is incorrect because the decrease in short-term investments is accompanied by an increase in cash or accounts receivable—accordingly, the transaction does not affect the quick ratio.

2.   **(A)** The requirement is to identify the audit finding consistent with a significant decrease in the debt to equity ratio—total debt/total equity. Answer (A) is correct because principal payments decrease the numerator of the ratio and because the financial statements reveal that such repayment of debt did occur. Answer (B) is incorrect because a sale of short-term investments does not directly affect the debt to equity ratio. Answer (C) is incorrect because an increase in short-term debt did not occur, and even if it had, it would have increased, not decreased the ratio. Answer (D) is incorrect because recording the dividend twice would increase the ratio in that total debt would increase and total equity would decrease.

Company Profile	Balance Sheet	Income/ Cash Flow	Industry Info	Risks	Audit Findings	Audit Procedures	Analysis and Communication	Research

(A) (B) (C) (D) (E) (F) (G) (H)

1.   Identify inventory transactions involving related parties.   ● ○ ○ ○ ○ ○ ○ ○

2.   Determine that items counted are included in the inventory listing.   ○ ○ ○ ○ ● ○ ○ ○

Explanation of solutions

1.   **(A)** The requirement is to identify a procedure for identifying inventory transactions involving related parties. The best procedure listed is review minutes of Board of Directors' meeting and contracts, and to make inquiries of management; these are all procedures used to identify related-party transactions.

2.   **(E)** The requirements is to identify a procedure for determining that items counted are included in the count sheet. The best procedure is to reconcile physical counts to perpetual records and general ledger balances and investigate significant fluctuations. This will allow the auditor to identify items not included.

Company Profile	Balance Sheet	Income/ Cash Flow	Industry Info	Risks	Audit Findings	Audit Procedures	Analysis and Communication	Research

Enright Corporation
VERTICAL ANALYSIS
For Years Ended 12/31/02 and 01

			Vertical analysis	
	12/31/02	*12/31/01*	*2002*	*2001*
Sales	5,250,000	5,450,000	100.0%	100.0%
Cost of goods sold	2,100,000	2,209,000	40.0%	40.5%
Gross profit on sales	3,150,000	3,241,000	60.0%	59.5%
Expenses				
Selling expenses	1,050,000	1,124,000	20.0%	20.6%
General and administrative	1,070,000	1,215,000	20.4%	22.3%
Other operating expenses				
Depreciation	30,000	35,000	0.6%	0.6%
Interest expense	200,000	227,000	3.8%	4.2%
Total expenses	2,350,000	2,601,000	44.8%	47.7%
Income before taxes	800,000	2,601,000	15.2%	11.8%
Provision of income taxes	320,000	256,000	6.1%	4.7%
Net income	560,000	448,000	9.1%	7.1%

To: Audit Team
Re: Vertical Analysis—Changes in cost of goods sold and general and administrative expenses

This memorandum describes the results of our analytical procedures related to cost of goods sold and general and administrative expenses. Sales decreased by approximately 3% in 20X2. Because of this, all things equal, one would expect expenses with fixed components to decrease by a somewhat smaller amount, while items composed largely of variable costs to retain the same percentage relationship to sales. At year-end, management announced a series of restructuring charges with the intent of making the company more profitable in the future.

The vertical analysis reveals that despite the decrease in sales, cost of goods sold as a percentage of sales decreased. This is consistent with economies due to the restructuring having been implemented, but is not consistent with a decrease in sales volume because of the fixed costs components in overhead included in cost of goods sold. Since management has indicated that the restructuring is just beginning, we should consider discussing the issue further with management.

General and administrative expenses also decreased during 20X2 as a percentage of sales. Since certain of these expenses may also be expected to have fixed components this is also not consistent with a decrease in sales, but may also indicate that Enright Corporation became more efficient during 20X2.

Our audit procedures should be aimed at determining that cost of goods sold and general and administrative expenses are properly valued. We primarily address cost of goods sold in our audit of inventories. Throughout our audit of asset accounts we must be aware of the possibility of capitalization of items that should be in expense accounts.

Company Profile	Balance Sheet	Income/ Cash Flow	Industry Info	Risks	Audit Findings	Audit Procedures	Analysis and Communication	Research

The guidance is provided in AU 329.04

.04 Analytical procedures are used for the following purposes:

a. To assist the auditor in planning the nature, timing, and extent of other auditing procedures.

b. As a substantive test to obtain evidential matter about particular assertions related to account balances or classes of transactions.

c. As an overall review of the financial information in the final review stage of the audit.

APPENDIX B: SAMPLE EXAMINATIONS
AUDITING AND ATTESTATION
TESTLET 1

1. Which of the following is ordinarily considered to be a fraud risk factor?
   a. The company's financial statements include a number of last minute material adjustments.
   b. Management regularly informs investors of forecast information.
   c. The company has experienced increasing earnings over the previous five years.
   d. The company's president is included as a member of the board of directors.

2. Which of the following statements **best** describes the primary purpose of Statements on Auditing Standards?
   a. They are guides intended to set forth auditing procedures that are applicable to a variety of situations.
   b. They are procedural outlines that are intended to narrow the areas of inconsistency and divergence of auditor opinion.
   c. They are authoritative statements, enforced through the Code of Professional Conduct.
   d. They are interpretive guidance.

3. The accountant who is not independent may perform which of the following types of engagements?
   a. Audit.
   b. Agreed-upon procedures.
   c. Compilation.
   d. Review.

4. Which of the following should an auditor obtain from the predecessor auditor prior to accepting an audit engagement?
   a. Analysis of balance sheet accounts.
   b. Analysis of income statement accounts.
   c. All matters of continuing accounting significance.
   d. Facts that might bear on the integrity of management.

5. Which of the following is correct concerning allowing additions and deletions to audit documentation after the documentation completion date under requirements of the Public Company Accounting Oversight Board?

	Additions	*Deletions*
a.	Allowed	Allowed
b.	Allowed	Not allowed
c.	Not allowed	Allowed
d.	Not allowed	Not allowed

6. One reason that an auditor only obtains reasonable, and not absolute, assurance that financial statements are free from material misstatement is
   a. Comprehensive basis reporting.
   b. Employee collusion.
   c. Material misstatements.
   d. Professional skepticism.

7. The auditors of a nonissuer (nonpublic) company must perform a test of the operating effectiveness of a significant control
   a. In all audits.
   b. When the control relates to a significant asset.
   c. When substantive procedures alone will not provide sufficient evidence about the related assertion.
   d. When the auditors believe that the control may not be effective.

8. The independent auditor selects several transactions in each functional area and traces them through the entire system, paying special attention to evidence about whether or not the controls are in operation. This is an example of a(n)
   a. Application test.
   b. Tests of a control.
   c. Substantive test.
   d. Test of a function.

9. In obtaining an understanding of a manufacturing entity's internal control over inventory balances, an auditor most likely would
   a. Review the entity's descriptions of inventory policies and procedures.
   b. Perform test counts of inventory during the entity's physical count.
   c. Analyze inventory turnover statistics to identify slow-moving and obsolete items.
   d. Analyze monthly production reports to identify variances and unusual transactions.

10. Further audit procedures consist of which of the following?

	Risk assessment procedures	*Substantive procedures*	*Test of controls*
a.	Yes	No	No
b.	Yes	Yes	No
c.	No	Yes	No
d.	No	Yes	Yes

11. The risk of material misstatement increases the acceptable level of
   a. Detection risk decreases.
   b. Business risk increases.
   c. Audit risk decreases.
   d. Materiality increases.

12. Which is **least** likely to be a question asked of client personnel during a walk-through in an audit of the internal control of an issuer (public) company?
   a. What do you do when you find an error?
   b. Who is most likely to commit fraud among your coworkers?
   c. What kind of errors have you found?
   d. Have you ever been asked to override the process or controls?

13. Which of the following matters is an auditor required to communicate to an entity's audit committee?

	Significant audit adjustments	*Changes in significant accounting policies*
a.	Yes	Yes
b.	Yes	No
c.	No	Yes
d.	No	No

14. An abnormal fluctuation in gross profit that might suggest the need for extended audit procedures for sales and inventories would most likely be identified in the planning phase of the audit by the use of
   a.   Tests of transactions and balances.
   b.   A preliminary review of internal control.
   c.   Specialized audit programs.
   d.   Analytical procedures.

15. When auditing merchandise inventory at year-end, the auditor performs a purchase cutoff test to obtain evidence that
   a.   All goods purchased before year-end are received before the physical inventory count.
   b.   No goods held on consignment for customers are included in the inventory balance.
   c.   No goods observed during the physical count are pledged or sold.
   d.   All goods owned at year-end are included in the inventory balance.

16. An auditor who uses the work of a specialist may refer to and identify the specialist in the auditor's report if the
   a.   Specialist is also considered to be a related party.
   b.   Auditor indicates a division of responsibility related to the work of the specialist.
   c.   Specialist's work provides the auditor greater assurance of reliability.
   d.   Auditor expresses an "except for" qualified opinion or an adverse opinion related to the work of the specialist.

17. Which of the following statements concerning evidential matter is correct?
   a.   Appropriate evidence supporting management's assertions should be convincing rather than merely persuasive.
   b.   Effective internal control contributes little to the reliability of the evidence created within the entity.
   c.   The cost of obtaining evidence is **not** an important consideration to an auditor in deciding what evidence should be obtained.
   d.   A client's accounting data **cannot** be considered sufficient audit evidence to support the financial statements.

18. The auditor is **most** likely to verify accrued commissions payable in conjunction with the
   a.   Sales cutoff review.
   b.   Verification of contingent liabilities.
   c.   Review of post balance sheet date disbursements.
   d.   Examination of trade accounts payable.

19. A note to the financial statements of the First Security Bank indicates that all of the records relating to the bank's business operations are stored on magnetic disks, and that there are no emergency back-up systems or duplicate disks stored since the First Security Bank and their auditors consider the occurrence of a catastrophe to be remote. Based upon this, one would expect the auditor's report to express
   a.   An adverse opinion.
   b.   An "except for" opinion.
   c.   An unqualified opinion.
   d.   A qualified opinion.

20. A company has changed its method of inventory valuation from an unacceptable one to one in conformity with generally accepted accounting principles. The auditor's report on the financial statements of the year of the change should include
   a.   No reference to consistency.
   b.   A reference to a prior period adjustment in the opinion paragraph.
   c.   An explanatory paragraph explaining the change.
   d.   A justification for making the change and the impact of the change on reported net income.

21. When an auditor reissues in 20X7 the auditor's report on the 20X5 financial statements at the request of the client without revising the 20X5 wording, the auditor should
   a.   Use the date of the original report.
   b.   Use the date of the client's request.
   c.   Use the date of the current period report.
   d.   Dual date the report.

22. Auditors who prefer statistical sampling to nonstatistical sampling may do so because statistical sampling helps the auditor
   a.   Measure the sufficiency of the evidential matter obtained.
   b.   Eliminate subjectivity in the evaluation of sampling results.
   c.   Reduce the level of tolerable misstatement (error) to a relatively low amount.
   d.   Minimize the failure to detect a material misstatement due to nonsampling risk.

23. Accounting control procedures within computer processing may leave no visible evidence indicating that the procedures were performed. In such instances, the auditor should test these accounting controls by
   a.   Making corroborative inquiries.
   b.   Observing the separation of duties of personnel.
   c.   Reviewing transactions submitted for processing and comparing them to related output.
   d.   Reviewing the run manual.

24. Which is **least** likely to be a response when an auditor has obtained evidence indicating a risk of material misstatement in the area of inventory?
   a.   Discuss questions of inventory valuation with any other auditors involved with the audit.
   b.   Make oral inquiries of major suppliers in addition to written confirmations.
   c.   Perform inventory observations on an unannounced basis.
   d.   Request inventory counts at the end of each month.

25. Confirmations of accounts receivable address which assertion most directly?
   a.   Completeness.
   b.   Existence.
   c.   Valuation.
   d.   Classification.

26. Which of the following is always present in an attestation engagement?
   a.   Assertion about the subject matter.
   b.   Generally accepted assurance principles.
   c.   Subject matter.
   d.   An examination report.

27. Which of the following is least likely to be a test of a control?

    a. Inquiries of appropriate personnel.

    b. Inspection of management's engagement letter.

    c. Observation of the application of a policy.

    d. Reperformance of the application of a policy

28. If information is for management's use only, which of the following forms of CPA association with financial information is most likely to result in no report being issued?

    a. An agreed-upon procedures engagement.

    b. An audit.

    c. A compilation.

    d. A review.

29. Which of the following examinations is most likely to result in a CPA issuing a "restricted use" report?

    a. Financial projection.

    b. Trust services.

    c. Management's discussion and analysis.

    d. Financial statements prepared following the tax basis of accounting.

30. Which of the following best illustrates the concept of sampling risk?

    a. A randomly chosen sample may not be representative of the population as a whole on the characteristic of interest.

    b. An auditor may select audit procedures that are not appropriate to achieve the specific objective.

    c. An auditor may fail to recognize misstatements in the documents examined for the chosen sample.

    d. The documents related to the chosen sample may not be available for inspection.

AUDITING AND ATTESTATION

ANSWERS TO TESTLET 1

1.	a	6.	b	11.	a	16.	d	21.	a	26.	c
2.	c	7.	c	12.	b	17.	d	22.	a	27.	b
3.	c	8.	b	13.	a	18.	a	23.	c	28.	c
4.	d	9.	a	14.	d	19.	c	24.	d	29.	a
5.	b	10.	d	15.	d	20.	c	25.	b	30.	a

Hints for Multiple-Choice Questions

1. Which factor deals most directly with expected intentional misstatements?

2. The SAS provide authoritative guidance.

3. Three of the services are always considered attest services

4. The auditor wants to minimize the likelihood of association with a client whose management lacks integrity.

5. Remember that audits may sometimes be affected by subsequent discovery of facts existing at the date of the audit report.

6. What real world difficulty makes detecting misstatements difficult?

7. For most assertions tests of controls are not required.

8. The auditor is trying to determine the effectiveness of internal control.

9. The auditor is not evaluating the effectiveness of internal control.

10. Which set of procedures is used to design the others?

11. Think about the audit risk components that vary inversely from one another.

12. Which question seems too aggressive?

13. The audit committee that has responsibility for the oversight of the client's financial reporting process, should be kept informed about the scope and results of the audit.

14. Which substantive test relies on the premise that plausible relationships among data may reasonably be expected to exist and continue in the absence of known conditions to the contrary?

15. The purchase cutoff test verifies that the purchasing transactions are recorded in the proper period.

16. The auditor refers to the specialist if the auditor issues a qualified, adverse, or disclaimer as a result of the specialist's work.

17. In addition to the accounting data, the auditor must obtain corroborating evidential matter.

18. The auditor wants to make sure that the liability is applied to the correct period.

19. The financial statements are presented fairly in conformity with GAAP.

20. The audit report should disclose the lack of consistency.

21. Nothing has changed with regard to the 20X5 report.

22. Statistical sampling provides the auditor with a mathematical model.

23. The auditor wants to see the effects of the controls on the transactions.

24. Think of procedures that are likely to provide additional evidence relating to the financial statements being reported upon.

25. Does a confirmation assure that the account will be collected?

26. A report may ordinarily be on two of these—but one of them is always present.

27. Which reply relates to an auditor prepared item?

28. Which situation is most likely to result in a report that only management will use?

29. Pick the reply that relies most directly upon a hypothetical assumption.

30. Sampling risk relates to not examining all of the items in the population.

Explanations

1. **(a)** Last minute material adjustments is a situation that has been found to be associated with fraudulent financial reporting.

2. **(c)** The Statements on Auditing Standards are authoritative statements that are enforced through the AICPA Code of Professional Conduct.

3. **(c)** Independence is required for audit and attest services. It is not required for a compilation.

4. **(d)** Prior to accepting the engagement, the successor auditor should obtain information to assist in deciding whether to accept the engagement, including facts that might bear on the integrity of management. All of the other items might be obtained but need not be obtained prior to acceptance.

5. **(b)** Under PCAOB standards, after the documentation completion date additions are allowed but deletions are not allowed.

6. **(b)** Employee collusion is a limitation of internal control. It may render internal control ineffective.

7. **(c)** Internal control must be tested when substantive procedures alone will not provide sufficient evidence.

8. **(b)** This describes a test of control using audit sampling.

9. **(a)** To obtain an understanding of internal control, the auditor would review the company's documentation of policies and procedures. Items (b), (c), and (d) are substantive tests of balances or transactions.

10.   (d)   After assessing risk by performing risk assessment procedures, the auditor designs further audit procedures, which include tests of controls and substantive procedures.

11.   (a)   If the risk of material misstatement increases, the auditor must compensate by decreasing detection risk.

12.   (b)   "Who is most likely to commit fraud among your coworkers?" is a confrontational question that is not likely to get a meaningful response.

13.   (a)   The audit committee should be informed about both significant audit adjustments and changes in significant accounting policies.

14.   (d)   Analytical procedures involve the use of comparisons of financial and nonfinancial information to identify fluctuations that increase risk or may need investigation.

15.   (d)   Cutoff tests are used to determine that items are recorded in the proper accounting period.

16.   (d)   The auditor may refer to the specialist only when the specialist's work affects the auditor's opinion.

17.   (d)   A client's accounting data cannot be considered sufficient audit evidence. Responses (a), (b) and (c) are not true.

18.   (a)   Since accrued commissions arise from sales, the amount payable would normally be verified in conjunction with the audit of sales.

19.   (c)   The lack of a back-up system does not affect the fairness of the financial statements. Therefore, an unqualified opinion would be appropriate.

20.   (c)   The auditors must refer to the change in an explanatory paragraph.

21.   (a)   If the auditor reissues a previously issued report at the request of the client, it would normally be dated its original date. To change the date would require the auditor to perform audit procedures up to the new date.

22.   (a)   The advantage of statistical sampling over nonstatistical sampling is that it allows quantitative measurement of the extent of the evidence obtained from the test.

23.   (c)   An approach to testing computer controls is comparing input to the computer output.

24.   (d)   Requesting inventory counts at the end of each month is least likely to be an effective procedure in this case.

25.   (b)   Conformation provides evidence of the existence of recorded transactions or balance sheet amounts.

26.   (c)   An attestation engagement always involves comparison of a subject matter to a set of criteria.

27.   (b)   The engagement letter has no relationship to internal control.

28.   (c)   If there is no need for any assurance to a third party, the information should most likely be compiled by the CPA.

29.   (a)   Reports on financial projections must be restricted to those who understand what the projection is designed to present.

30.   (a)   Sampling risk results from the chance that a sample might not be representative of the population from which it was drawn.

AUDITING AND ATTESTATION
TESTLET 2

1. Which of the following statements best describes an auditor's responsibility to detect misstatements due to errors and fraud?
   a. The auditor should study and evaluate the client's internal control, and design the audit to provide reasonable assurance of detecting all errors and fraud.
   b. The auditor should assess the risk that errors and fraud may cause the financial statements to contain material misstatements, and determine whether the necessary controls are prescribed and are being followed satisfactorily.
   c. The auditor should consider the types of errors and fraud that could occur, and determine whether the necessary controls are prescribed and are being followed.
   d. The auditor should assess the risk that errors and fraud may cause the financial statements to contain material misstatements, and design the audit to provide reasonable assurance of detecting material misstatements due to errors and fraud.

2. When one auditor succeeds another, the successor auditor should request the
   a. Client to instruct its attorney to send a letter of audit inquiry concerning the status of the prior year's litigation, claims, and assessments.
   b. Predecessor auditor to submit a list of internal control weaknesses that have **not** been corrected.
   c. Client to authorize the predecessor auditor to allow a review of the predecessor auditor's working papers.
   d. Predecessor auditor to update the prior year's report to the date of the change of auditors.

3. A difference of opinion concerning accounting and auditing matters relative to a particular phase of the audit arises between an assistant auditor and the auditor responsible for the engagement. After appropriate consultation, the assistant auditor asks to be disassociated from the resolution of the matter. The working papers would probably be
   a. Silent on the matter since it is an internal matter of the auditing firm.
   b. Expanded to note that the assistant auditor is completely disassociated from responsibility for the auditor's opinion.
   c. Expanded to document the additional work required, since all disagreements of this type will require expanded substantive testing.
   d. Expanded to document the assistant auditor's position, and how the difference of opinion was resolved.

4. On the audit of a nonissuer (nonpublic) company, the purpose of performing risk assessment procedures is to
   a. Obtain an understanding of the entity and its environment.
   b. Reduce detection risk.
   c. Evaluate management ability.
   d. Determine the operating effectiveness of controls.

5. When an auditor becomes aware of a possible client illegal act, the auditor should obtain an understanding of the nature of the act to
   a. Increase the assessed level of control risk.
   b. Recommend remedial actions to the audit committee.
   c. Evaluate the effect on the financial statements.
   d. Determine the reliability of management's representations.

6. Which of the following controls may prevent the failure to bill customers for some shipments?
   a. Each shipment should be supported by a prenumbered sales invoice that is accounted for.
   b. Each sales order should be approved by authorized personnel.
   c. Sales journal entries should be reconciled to daily sales summaries.
   d. Each sales invoice should be supported by a shipping document.

7. Which of the following is a control weakness for a company whose inventory of supplies consists of a large number of individual items?
   a. Supplies of relatively little value are expensed when purchased.
   b. The cycle basis is used for physical counts.
   c. The storekeeper is responsible for maintenance of perpetual inventory records.
   d. Perpetual inventory records are maintained only for items of significant value.

8. The accounts payable department receives the purchase order form to accomplish all of the following **except:**
   a. Compare invoice price to purchase order price.
   b. Ensure the purchase had been properly authorized.
   c. Ensure the goods had been received by the party requesting the goods.
   d. Compare quantity ordered to quantity purchased.

9. Before applying substantive tests to the details of asset and liability accounts at an interim date, the auditor should
   a. Assess the difficulty in controlling incremental audit risk.
   b. Investigate significant fluctuations that have occurred in the asset and liability accounts since the previous balance sheet date.
   c. Select only those accounts that can effectively be sampled during year-end audit work.
   d. Consider the tests of controls that must be applied at the balance-sheet date to extend the audit conclusions reached at the interim date.

10. Which of the following situations would **most** likely require special audit planning by the auditor?
   a. Some items of factory and office equipment do **not** bear identification numbers.
   b. Depreciation methods used on the client's tax return differ from those used on the books.
   c. Assets costing less than $500 are expensed even though the expected life exceeds one year.
   d. Inventory is comprised of precious stones.

11. After discovering that a related party transaction exists, the auditor should be aware that the
   a. Substance of the transaction could be significantly different from its form.
   b. Adequacy of disclosure of the transaction is secondary to its legal form.
   c. Transaction is assumed to be outside the ordinary course of business.
   d. Financial statements should recognize the legal form of the transaction rather than its substance.

12. Morgan, CPA, is the principal auditor for a multinational corporation. Another CPA has audited and reported on the financial statements of a significant subsidiary of the corporation. Morgan is satisfied with the independence and professional reputation of the other auditor, as well as the quality of the other auditor's examination. With respect to Morgan's report on the consolidated financial statements, taken as a whole, Morgan
   a. Must **not** refer to the audit of the other auditor.
   b. Must refer to the audit of the other auditor.
   c. May refer to the audit of the other auditor.
   d. May refer to the audit of the other auditor, in which case Morgan must include in the auditor's report on the consolidated financial statements a qualified opinion with respect to the examination of the other auditor.

13. If the objective of a test of details is to detect overstatements of sales, the auditor should trace transactions from the
   a. Cash receipts journal to the sales journal.
   b. Sales journal to the cash receipts journal.
   c. Source documents to the accounting records.
   d. Accounting records to the source documents.

14. The auditor's program for the examination of long-term debt should include steps that require the
   a. Verification of the existence of the bondholders.
   b. Examination of any bond trust indenture.
   c. Inspection of the accounts payable subsidiary ledger.
   d. Investigation of credits to the bond interest income account.

15. All corporate capital stock transactions should ultimately be traced to the
   a. Minutes of the Board of Directors.
   b. Cash receipts journal.
   c. Cash disbursements journal.
   d. Numbered stock certificates.

16. In testing plant and equipment balances, an auditor examines new additions listed on an analysis of plant and equipment. This procedure most likely obtains evidence concerning management's assertion of
   a. Completeness.
   b. Existence or occurrence.
   c. Presentation and disclosure.
   d. Valuation or allocation.

17. When the audited financial statements of the prior year are presented together with those of the current year, the continuing auditor's report should cover
   a. Both years.
   b. Only the current year.
   c. Only the current year, but the prior year's report should be presented.

   d. Only the current year, but the prior year's report should be referred to.

18. Information accompanying the basic financial statements in an auditor-submitted document should **not** include
   a. An analysis of inventory by location.
   b. A statement that the allowance for doubtful accounts is adequate.
   c. A statement that the depreciable life of a new asset is twenty years.
   d. An analysis of revenue by product line.

19. The objective of auditing procedures applied to segment information is to provide the auditor with a reasonable basis for concluding whether
   a. The information is useful for comparing a segment of one enterprise with a similar segment of another enterprise.
   b. Sufficient evidential matter has been obtained to allow the auditor to be associated with the segment information.
   c. A separate opinion on the segment information is necessary due to inconsistent application of accounting principles.
   d. The information is presented in conformity with the FASB Statement on segment information in relation to the financial statements taken as a whole.

20. An accountant has been asked to issue a review report on the balance sheet of a nonissuer (nonpublic) company but not to report on the other basic financial statements. The accountant may **not** do so
   a. Because compliance with this request would result in an incomplete review.
   b. Because compliance with this request would result in a violation of the ethical standards of the profession.
   c. If the scope of the inquiry and analytical procedures has been restricted.
   d. If the review of the balance sheet discloses material departures from generally accepted accounting principles.

21. An auditor was unable to obtain audited financial statements or other evidence supporting an entity's investment in a foreign subsidiary. Between which of the following opinions should the entity's auditor choose?
   a. Adverse and unqualified with an explanatory paragraph added.
   b. Disclaimer and unqualified with an explanatory paragraph added.
   c. Qualified and adverse.
   d. Qualified and disclaimer.

22. In which of the following cases would the auditor be most likely to conclude that all of the items in an account under consideration should be examined rather than tested on a sample basis?

	The measure of tolerable misstatement is	Misstatement frequency is expected to be
a.	Large	Low
b.	Small	High
c.	Large	High
d.	Small	Low

23. Which of the following factors is generally **not** considered in determining the sample size for a test of controls?
  a. Risk of incorrect acceptance.
  b. Tolerable rate.
  c. Risk of assessing control risk too low.
  d. Expected population deviation rate.

24. The most important function of generalized audit software is the capability to
  a. Access information stored on computer files.
  b. Select a sample of items for testing.
  c. Evaluate sample test results.
  d. Test the accuracy of the client's calculations.

25. A limitation on the scope of an auditor's procedures is likely to result in a report with a(n)

	Qualified opinion	*Adverse opinion*
a.	Yes	Yes
b.	Yes	No
c.	No	Yes
d.	No	No

26. Which of the following is least likely to be considered when assessing inherent risk?
  a. Nonroutine transactions.
  b. Estimation transactions.
  c. Susceptibility to theft.
  d. Expected effectiveness of controls.

27. In the audit risk model, the risk of misstatement is composed of

	Inherent risk	*Control risk*	*Detection risk*
a.	Yes	Yes	Yes
b.	Yes	Yes	No
c.	Yes	No	Yes
d.	Yes	No	No

28. Which of the following is most likely to result in modification of a compilation report?
  a. A departure from generally accepted accounting principles.
  b. A lack of consistency in application of generally accepted accounting principles.
  c. A question concerning an entity's ability to continue as a going concern.
  d. A major uncertainty facing the financial statements.

29. Analytical procedures are required

	Planning	*Substantive tests*	*Final review*
a.	Yes	Yes	Yes
b.	Yes	Yes	No
c.	Yes	No	Yes
d.	No	No	No

30. Which of the following is used to obtain evidence that the client's equipment accounts are **not** understated?
  a. Analyze repairs and maintenance expense accounts.
  b. Vouching purchases of plant and equipment.
  c. Recomputing depreciation expense.
  d. Analyzing the miscellaneous revenue account.

AUDITING AND ATTESTATION

ANSWERS TO TESTLET 2

1.	d	6.	a	11.	a	16.	b	21.	d	26.	d
2.	c	7.	c	12.	c	17.	a	22.	b	27.	b
3.	d	8.	c	13.	d	18.	b	23.	a	28.	a
4.	a	9.	a	14.	b	19.	d	24.	a	29.	c
5.	c	10.	d	15.	a	20.	c	25.	b	30.	a

Hints for Multiple-Choice Questions

1. AU 316 states that the auditor should design the audit to provide reasonable assurance of detecting material misstatement due to errors and fraud.

2. AU 315 states that the successor auditor should ask the prospective client to authorize the predecessor to respond fully to the successor's inquiries.

3. Working papers document the audit procedures applied, the information obtained and the conclusions reached during the engagement.

4. Audit risk often relates to business risk.

5. The auditor wants to obtain reasonable assurance that the financial statements contain no material misstatements.

6. A control should be present which readily shows a missing sales invoice.

7. Where is it most likely that control will be lost because of information overload?

8. The accounts payable department is responsible for the recordkeeping function.

9. The auditor needs to be assured that the assessed level of control risk is the same at the balance sheet date as it is at the interim date.

10. Which situation would require the auditor to use the work of a specialist?

11. The auditor wants to determine that there is a valid business purpose for the transactions.

12. The principal auditor must decide whether or not to assume responsibility for the work of the other auditor.

13. The auditor is testing for existence.

14. The audit program should include procedures to ensure that the debt is properly presented on the balance sheet.

15. Where does authorization for these transactions originate?

16. Are the new additions valid fixed assets?

17. The auditor's opinion regarding the financial statement should apply to the financial statements as a whole.

18. Which information is the auditor required to determine when auditing the financial statements?

19. The auditor normally considers segment information when performing an audit of financial statement in accordance with generally accepted auditing standards.

20. Limited reporting objectives is not the same as limiting the available procedures.

21. How does the auditor report a scope limitation?

22. Where does the auditor have the greatest risk of a material misstatement?

23. One reply deals with variables sampling, while three deal with attributes sampling.

24. Which item is not a responsibility of the auditor?

25. A scope limitation may lead to a situation in which an auditor does not know whether the financial statements follow GAAP.

26. Remember the auditor also assesses control risk.

27. Do not get mixed up, the question is not asking about the components of audit risk.

28. Reporting of which seems most essential to the CPA's role?

29. They are not required at all stages, at one stage the auditor may decide whether to use analytical procedures.

30. Which reply is most likely to find an equipment purchase that has not been capitalized?

Explanations

1. **(d)** Auditing standards require the auditor to design the audit to provide reasonable assurance of detecting material misstatements due to errors or fraud.

2. **(c)** The auditor should obtain permission from the client to communicate and get information from the predecessor auditor.

3. **(d)** In this situation, the documentation should be expanded to include the assistant's position and how the difference of opinion was resolved.

4. **(a)** Risk assessment procedures are performed to obtain an understanding of the entity and its environment to provide a basis to assess the risk of material misstatement and design further audit procedures.

5. **(c)** When the auditor determines that an illegal act has possibly occurred, he or she must obtain an understanding of the issue and assess its potential effect on the financial statements under audit.

6. **(a)** Requiring prenumbered sales invoices to support each shipment is an effective way to ensure that all shipments are billed.

7. **(c)** The individual with custody of an asset should not maintain the records.

8. **(c)** The purchase order would not have information about receipt of goods. A receiving report should also be obtained by accounts payable and would provide evidence of receipt of the goods.

9.   **(a)**   When a balance is audited at an interim date there is incremental audit risk that must be controlled by the auditor.

10.   **(d)**   The auditor normally does not have the requisite skills to determine the value of precious stones.

11.   **(a)**   The problem with related-party transactions is the possibility that the substance of the transactions may differ from their form.

12.   **(c)**   It is optional as to whether the principal auditor refers to the other auditor in the report.

13.   **(d)**   To detect overstatement the auditor would normally trace transactions from the accounting records to the source documents.

14.   **(b)**   In auditing long-term debt the auditor should examine the bond trust indenture to assure that covenants in the indenture are adequately disclosed in the financial statements.

15.   **(a)**   To determine that they are authorized, capital stock transactions should be traced to authorization in the minutes of board of director or shareholder meetings.

16.   **(b)**   By tracing from the accounting records to actual items, the auditor is testing the assertions of existence or occurrence.

17.   **(a)**   A continuing auditor's report should cover both years.

18.   **(b)**   If the allowance for doubtful accounts is inadequate, this fact should result in a qualification of the auditor's opinion.

19.   **(d)**   The procedures are performed to determine that the information is presented in conformity with the FASB requirements in relation to the financial statements taken as a whole.

20.   **(c)**   An accountant may review a balance sheet providing the scope of the procedures is not limited.

21.   **(d)**   If the auditor cannot obtain sufficient evidence, he or she must choose between a qualified opinion and a disclaimer, depending on the significance of the limitation.

22.   **(b)**   The auditor would most likely decide not to sample when the tolerable misstatement is small and the expected misstatement rate is high. In this case it would be more appropriate to examine all or most of the items in the population.

23.   **(a)**   The risk of incorrect acceptance is a consideration when sampling is used for a substantive procedure.

24.   **(a)**   The real value of generalized audit software is its ability to access data stored on various types of computer files.

25.   **(b)**   A significant limitation in the scope of audit procedures would result in a qualified opinion or a disclaimer of opinion depending on its significance.

26.   **(d)**   The effectiveness of internal control is a consideration regarding control risk.

27.   **(b)**   The risk of material misstatement is composed of inherent risk and control risk. The auditor controls audit-risk by adjusting detection risk.

28.   **(a)**   Compilation reports are modified for departures from generally accepted accounting principles. The other items do not affect compilation reports.

29.   **(c)**   Analytical procedures are required in the planning and final review stages of the audit.

30.   **(a)**   Analyzing repairs and maintenance expense may result in the discovery of property and plant expenditures that were erroneously expensed.

AUDITING AND ATTESTATION
TESTLET 3

1. The risk that an auditor's procedures will lead to the conclusion that a material misstatement does **not** exist in an account balance when, in fact, such misstatement does exist is referred to as
- a. Audit risk.
- b. Inherent risk.
- c. Control risk.
- d. Detection risk.

2. Which of the following types of fraud is an audit **least** likely to detect?
- a. Theft of cash received from collection of accounts receivable.
- b. Intentional omission of transactions relating to equipment purchases.
- c. Intentional violations of occupational safety and health laws.
- d. Misapplication of accounting principles relating to inventory.

3. Prior to beginning the fieldwork on a new audit engagement in which a CPA does **not** possess expertise in the industry in which the client operates, the CPA should
- a. Reduce audit risk by lowering the preliminary levels of materiality.
- b. Design special substantive tests to compensate for the lack of industry expertise.
- c. Engage financial experts familiar with the nature of the industry.
- d. Obtain a knowledge of matters that relate to the nature of the entity's business.

4. For purposes of an audit of internal control performed under Public Company Accounting Oversight Board standards, a significant deficiency is a control deficiency that
- a. Is at least as severe as a material weakness.
- b. Is probable of occurring in an amount that is material.
- c. Must be communicated to those responsible for oversight of the company's financial reporting.
- d. Remains unresolved at the date of completion of final internal control analysis procedures.

5. Which of the following controls would most likely be used to maintain accurate perpetual inventory records?
- a. Independent storeroom count of goods received.
- b. Periodic independent reconciliation of control and subsidiary records.
- c. Periodic independent comparison of records with goods on hand.
- d. Independent matching of purchase orders, receiving reports, and vendors' invoices.

6. Evidential matter concerning proper segregation of duties ordinarily is best obtained by
- a. Preparation of a flowchart of duties performed by available personnel.
- b. Inquiring whether control activities operated consistently throughout the period.
- c. Reviewing job descriptions prepared by the personnel department.
- d. Direct personal observation of the employees who apply control activities.

7. In considering internal control, the auditor is basically concerned that it provides reasonable assurance that
- a. Operational efficiency has been achieved in accordance with management plans.
- b. Material misstatements due to errors and fraud have been prevented or detected.
- c. Controls have **not** been circumvented by collusion.
- d. Management **cannot** override the system.

8. In properly designed internal control, the same employee should **not** be permitted to
- a. Sign checks and cancel supporting documents.
- b. Receive merchandise and prepare a receiving report.
- c. Prepare disbursement vouchers and sign checks.
- d. Initiate a request to order merchandise and approve merchandise received.

9. Which of the following is an effective control over cash payments?
- a. Signed checks should be mailed under the supervision of the check signer.
- b. Spoiled checks that have been voided should be disposed of immediately.
- c. Checks should be prepared only by persons responsible for cash receipts and cash disbursements.
- d. A check-signing machine with two signatures should be utilized.

10. Inquiries of warehouse personnel concerning possible obsolete or slow-moving inventory items provide assurance about management's assertion of
- a. Completeness.
- b. Existence.
- c. Presentation.
- d. Valuation.

11. The primary reason an auditor requests letters of inquiry be sent to a client's attorneys is to provide the auditor with
- a. A description and evaluation of litigation, claims, and assessments that existed at the date of the balance sheet.
- b. An expert opinion as to whether a loss is possible, probable, or remote.
- c. The opportunity to examine the documentation concerning litigation, claims, and assessments.
- d. Corroboration of the information furnished by management concerning litigation, claims, and assessments.

12. Which of the following ratios would an engagement partner most likely calculate when reviewing the balance sheet in the overall review stage of an audit?
- a. Quick assets/current assets.
- b. Accounts receivable/inventory.
- c. Interest payable/interest receivable.
- d. Total debt/total assets.

13. When providing limited assurance that the financial statements of a nonissuer (nonpublic) entity require **no** material modifications to be in accordance with generally accepted accounting principles, the accountant should

a. Understand internal control.

b. Test the accounting records that identify inconsistencies with the prior year's financial statements.

c. Understand the accounting principles of the industry in which the entity operates.

d. Develop audit programs to determine whether the entity's financial statements are fairly presented.

14. A written client representation letter most likely would be an auditor's best source of corroborative information of a client's plans to

a. Terminate an employee pension plan.

b. Make a public offering of its common stock.

c. Settle an outstanding lawsuit for an amount less than the accrued loss contingency.

d. Discontinue a line of business.

15. Which of the following procedures is **not** included in a review engagement of a nonissuer (nonpublic) entity?

a. Inquiries of management.

b. Inquiries regarding events subsequent to the balance sheet date.

c. Any procedures designed to identify relationships among data that appear to be unusual.

d. Tests of internal control.

16. Which of the following is not considered by the PCAOB as an indicator of the existence of a material weakness in internal control?

a. Identification of a material fraud committed by senior management in the areas of sales.

b. Restatement of previously issued financial statements to reflect correction of a material misstatement relating to improper inventory valuation.

c. Identification by the auditor of a material misstatement in cost of goods sold in circumstances that indicate that the misstatement would not have been detected by the company's internal control.

d. Lack of oversight by the audit committee of details of raw material purchases.

17. Kane, CPA, concludes that there is substantial doubt about Lima Co.'s ability to continue as a going concern for a reasonable period of time. If Lima's financial statements adequately disclose its financial difficulties, Kane's auditor's report is required to include an explanatory paragraph that specifically uses the phrase(s)

	"Possible discontinuance of operations"	"Reasonable period of time, **not** to exceed 1 year"
a.	Yes	Yes
b.	Yes	No
c.	No	Yes
d.	No	No

18. How are management's responsibility and the auditor's responsibility represented in the standard auditor's report?

	Management's responsibility	Auditor's responsibility
a.	Explicitly	Explicitly
b.	Implicitly	Implicitly
c.	Implicitly	Explicitly
d.	Explicitly	Implicitly

19. In estimation sampling for attributes, which one of the following must be known in order to appraise the results of the auditor's sample?

a. Estimated dollar value of the population.

b. Standard deviation of the values in the population.

c. Actual occurrence rate of the attribute in the population.

d. Sample size.

20. Processing data through the use of simulated files provides an auditor with information about the reliability of controls. One of the techniques involved in this approach makes use of

a. Controlled reprocessing.

b. Integrated test facility.

c. Input validation.

d. Program code checking

21. After the audit documentation completion date, the auditor

a. May not delete any audit documentation.

b. May not make changes in audit documentation.

c. May not add new information to audit documentation.

d. May make changes or deletions to audit documentation providing that the fact that alterations were made is documented.

22. Prior to or in conjunction with obtaining information to identify risks of fraud, which of the following is required?

a. A brainstorming session among team members about where financial statements may be susceptible to fraud.

b. A discussion with the client's legal counsel as to contingent liabilities likely to affect the financial statements.

c. Indirect verification of significant financial statement assertions.

d. Professional skepticism concerning indirect effect illegal acts.

23. Which of the following is **not** ordinarily performed in response to the risk of management override?

a. Evaluating the rationale for significant unusual transactions.

b. Observe counts of inventory at all locations.

c. Review accounting estimates for bias.

d. Test appropriateness of journal entries and adjustments.

24. When an auditor has a question concerning a client's ability to continue as a going concern, the auditor considers management's plans for dealing with the situation. That consideration is most likely to include consideration of management's plans to

a. Decrease ownership equity.

b. Dispose of assets.

c. Increase expenditures on key products.

d. Invest in derivative securities.

25. A change from one accounting principle to another with which the auditor concurs is likely to result in a report with a(n)

	Qualified opinion	*Adverse opinion*
a.	Yes	Yes
b.	Yes	No
c.	No	Yes
d.	No	No

26. A significant circumstance-caused scope limitation in a Sarbanes/Oxley 404 internal control audit is more likely to result in a(n)

    a.   Adverse opinion.
    b.   Qualified opinion.
    c.   Unqualified opinion with explanatory language.
    d.   Scope reduction opinion.

27. Which of the following statements regarding auditor documentation of the client's internal control is correct?

    a.   Documentation must include flowcharts.
    b.   Documentation must include procedural write-ups.
    c.   No documentation is necessary, although it is desirable.
    d.   No one particular form of documentation is required and the extent may vary.

28. Which of the following is least likely to be considered an attestation service?

    a.   Agreed-upon procedures.
    b.   Compilation.
    c.   Examinations.
    d.   Review.

29. Intentional misstatements of financial statements to deceive the financial statement users is considered by the AICPA to be

	Fraudulent financial reporting	*Misappropriation of assets*
a.	Yes	Yes
b.	Yes	No
c.	No	Yes
d.	No	No

30. Violation of which of the following is most likely to be considered a "direct effect" illegal act?

    a.   Environmental protection laws.
    b.   Occupational safety and health law violations.
    c.   Securities trading laws.
    d.   Tax law violations.

AUDITING AND ATTESTATION

ANSWERS TO TESTLET 3

1.	d	6.	d	11.	d	16.	d	21.	d	26.	b
2.	c	7.	b	12.	d	17.	d	22.	a	27.	d
3.	d	8.	c	13.	c	18.	a	23.	b	28.	b
4.	c	9.	a	14.	d	19.	d	24.	b	29.	b
5.	c	10.	d	15.	d	20.	b	25.	d	30.	d

Hints for Multiple-Choice Questions

1. The auditor performs audit procedures to detect material misstatements in the account balance.

2. Which type is least likely to misstate financial statement amounts?

3. The CPA must understand the business issues of the company and industry.

4. Think about control deficiencies, significant deficiencies, and material weaknesses.

5. Which independent check verifies the existence of the inventory?

6. Which control gives the auditor the best idea about the daily operation of the company?

7. Which area does the auditor have the most control over?

8. Segregate recordkeeping from authorization.

9. Which control helps the client maintain accountability for the cash payments?

10. Obsolete or slow moving inventory may never be sold and so the amount of inventory presented on the balance sheet may be overstated.

11. AU 337 states that a letter of audit inquiry to the client's lawyer is the auditor's primary means of obtaining corroboration of the information furnished by management concerning litigation, claims, and assessments.

12. The partner is looking at the big picture.

13. A requirement for any engagement is for the auditor to understand the environment they are working in.

14. Which situation would the client be the best source of information regarding future plans?

15. A review engagement provides only limited assurance.

16. Think carefully about the indicators provided by the PCAOB.

17. Mentally "write" an explanatory paragraph and consider whether it is likely that these items would be required.

18. The standard audit report should give the reader a clear understanding about responsibilities.

19. The auditor wants to determine a deviation rate for the sample.

20. Which technique places the simulated files into the midst of live transactions?

21. Documentation should be as accurate as possible.

22. Think about SAS 99s (AU 316) requirements.

23. Which procedure may not be practical in some situations?

24. Consider a reply that will provide resources to the company.

25. Client's are able to change accounting principles.

26. Scope limitations may result in two types of opinion—only one is listed.

27. Consider the great variation in the types of entities audited.

28. Reports on one of these engagements explicitly say that no assurance is being provided.

29. Consider the differences between fraudulent financial reporting and misappropriation of assets.

30. Which is most likely to result in direct misstatement of a financial statement account balance?

Explanations

1. **(d)** Detection risk is the risk that the auditor's procedures will fail to detect a material misstatement if it exists.

2. **(c)** Intentional violations of occupational safety and health laws are the most difficult to detect because they are not related to financial statement numbers and they are not within the auditor's expertise.

3. **(d)** If the auditor does not have an understanding of the client's industry, he or she should obtain that understanding.

4. **(c)** A significant deficiency is a matter that must be communicated to those responsible for oversight of the company's financial reporting process because it should be of interest to those individuals.

5. **(c)** Independent comparisons of records to goods on hand is an effective control to help ensure the accuracy of perpetual records.

6. **(d)** Direct personal observations of employees performing activities is the best test of segregation of duties.

7. **(b)** Internal control should be designed to provide reasonable assurance that material errors or fraud are prevented, or detected and corrected.

8. **(c)** In a properly designed system of internal control an individual should not have custody of assets (be able to sign checks) and also keep accounting records (prepare disbursement vouchers).

9. **(a)** For appropriate internal control the check signer should supervise the mailing of the checks.

10. **(d)** Inquiries of warehouse personnel about obsolete or slow-moving inventory items is designed to identify items that may be overvalued.

11. **(d)** The attorney's letter corroborates the information about litigation, claims, and assessments provided by management.

12. **(d)** The only ratio that is meaningful in the responses is total debt divided by total assets, which is a measure of leverage.

13. **(c)** Statement on Standards for Accounting and Review Services requires the accountant to understand the accounting principles of the industry in which the entity operates. All the other items are not required.

14. **(d)** The discontinuance of a line of business is a management decision. Therefore, the representation regarding plan to do so should be included in management representation letter. The other potential answers would be items that would be best verified in the minutes of board of directors meetings.

15. **(d)** A review of the financial statements of a nonissuer company does not involve tests of the effectiveness of internal control.

16. **(d)** The audit committee would not be expected to oversee the details of raw material purchases.

17. **(d)** Neither of these phrases is required in the auditor's explanatory paragraph.

18. **(a)** The auditor's report explicitly describes management's responsibility and the auditor's responsibility.

19. **(d)** The sample size and the occurrence rate in the sample are the items that must be known to evaluate the sample results.

20. **(b)** An integrated test facility introduces test (dummy) transactions with live transactions to test the effectiveness of IT controls.

21. **(d)** The auditor may make changes or deletions to audit documentation providing the fact that the changes were made is documented.

22. **(a)** Auditing standards require a brainstorming session among audit team members regarding where the financial statements may be susceptible to fraud.

23. **(b)** Observation of inventory is not ordinarily a procedure performed in response to the risk of management override of internal control.

24. **(b)** Management plans to deal with a going concern issue usually involves disposition of assets or obtaining additional financing.

25. **(d)** A change from one acceptable accounting principle to another acceptable principle does not result in either a qualified opinion or an adverse opinion. An unqualified opinion with explanatory language is appropriate.

26. **(b)** A circumstance-caused scope limitation would normally result in a qualified opinion.

27. **(d)** There is no prescribed form of documentation.

28. **(b)** Compilations provide no form of assurance. They are not attestation services.

29. **(b)** Intentional misstatements of financial statements to deceive users is considered to be fraudulent financial reporting.

30. **(d)** Direct-effect illegal acts affect the numbers in the financial statements. An important example is the violation of a tax law.

SIMULATION 1

Topics—Planning, Internal Control, Evidence, and Reporting

Situation	Company Profile	Industry Information	Balance Sheet	Income Statement	Statement of Cash Flows	Risks	Audit Findings	Audit Procedures	Communication	Research

Assume you are performing the 20X8 audit of Tommi Stone and Quarry.

Situation	Company Profile	Industry Information	Balance Sheet	Income Statement	Statement of Cash Flows	Risks	Audit Findings	Audit Procedures	Communication	Research

In 20X1 Jill Tommi founded Tommi Stone and Quarry (TSQ). Within its first year of existence, the company completed initial development of the extraction pit area and constructed an aggregate processing plant which is equipped to crush, screen, and wash aggregate products. By 20X3 the sand and gravel operation was profitable and growing market conditions justified modifications and expansion. Currently, at the conclusion of 20X8, TSQ produces a wide range of sand and stone products from its pit near Albuquerque, New Mexico. The materials it develops range from various sand and stone materials for residential and commercial construction and highway projects. TSQ sells to a wide variety of residential, commercial and governmental customers, with no one customer accounting for more than 5% of its total sales.

TSQ has worked closely with stucco manufacturers and plastering contractors in the Albuquerque plastering industry to produce a plaster sand ("Plasand") that exceeds normal specifications and produces a superior ingredient which improves stucco and plastering finished products. Plasand has been increasingly widely accepted as superior to products offered by competitors, and now accounts for approximately 10% of the company's sales, and 12% of its profits. TSQ is currently working closely with sport complexes and golf course architects in conjunction with test laboratories to develop a superior sand for use in the construction and top dressing of golf courses and sport complex playing fields.

The company experienced a level of profitability in 20X8 of about the same as that of 20X7—but this is well below the net incomes of the preceding several years. Jill suggested to you that, surprisingly, intense price competition from several smaller competitors in the Albuquerque area caused the somewhat low level of profitability. But, she added, she didn't expect the problem to last for long because she doubted that those companies could continue to operate selling at these lower prices. Jill had hoped for a more profitable year in 20X8 as a significant amount of the company's long-term debt is payable in 20X9. TSQ is currently involved in discussions with the bank on refinancing.

TSQ added significant additional crushing and washing plants and equipment during 20X8 to increase production in the future by more than 100% while expanding capabilities to produce custom specification materials.

Until 20X7 and 20X8, most of earnings were distributed through dividends to TSQ's five shareholders—CEO and Chair of the Board of Directors Jill Tommi, her husband Mort Tommi, CFO Googlo Permasi and two college friends of Jill's who invested in the company, Jian Zhang and Kendra Kovano. These five individuals make up the company's Board of Directors.

This year, in reaction to pressure from a bank that provides a significant portion of the financing, TSQ established an audit committee composed of Mort Tommi, Googlo Permasi, and Jian Zhang.

You are working on your firm's fifth audit of TSQ. The previous audits have all resulted in standard unqualified audit reports.

Situation	Company Profile	Industry Information	Balance Sheet	Income Statement	Statement of Cash Flows	Risks	Audit Findings	Audit Procedures	Communication	Research

The industry consists of preparation for the mining and extraction of sand and rock products. These include the activities of cleaning, separating and sorting of quarried sand, and the crushing of rocks. The products are in the form of sand used in making concrete; sand used in laying bricks (contains little soil); sand used for fill (contains lots of soil, and quartz sand); and excluding the products of gravel quarrying (sandstone, gravel stone, and iron sand).

While sales within the industry are relatively unaffected by changes in technology, or obsolescence, sales rely heavily upon both the residential and commercial construction markets as well as government spending. During the past five years construction has performed well and that trend is expected to continue at least for the coming several years. Sand and gravel production has increased at approximately 3% per year during this time period, as has construction within the central Ohio area.

The sand and gravel market in central New Mexico has been particularly healthy due in large part to the growth of Albuquerque into a major metropolitan area. The most significant question facing the industry is whether the strong construction will continue as expected. During the past two years the economy of the United States has been in a recovery period, yet unemployment remains high as compared to previous periods of recovery. Thus, the questions concerning the continuing construction demand.

Situation	Company Profile	Industry Information	Balance Sheet	Income Statement	Statement of Cash Flows	Risks	Audit Findings	Audit Procedures	Communication	Research

Tommi Stone and Quarry
BALANCE SHEET
December 31, 20X8 and 20X7

	20X8	20X7
Assets		
Current assets		
Cash and cash equivalents	$ 5,055	$ 3,822
Trade receivables	3,369,971	2,383,055
Inventory	1,713,118	1,810,361
Other current assets	17,140	10,200
Total current assets	5,105,284	4,207,438
Fixed assets, net	397,749	74,769
Total assets	$5,503,033	$4,282,207
Liabilities and shareholders' equity		
Current liabilities		
Accounts payable	$ 340,995	$ 316,164
Current maturities of notes payable	1,262,379	416,607
Accrued expenses	187,190	208,460
Other current liabilities	158,603	199,629
Total current liabilities	1,949,167	1,140,860
Long-term debt, less current maturity	3,249,934	2,959,200
Total liabilities	5,199,101	4,100,060
Shareholders' equity		
Common stock	57,333	57,333
Retained earnings	246,599	124,814
Total shareholders' equity	303,932	182,147
Total liabilities plus shareholders' equity	$5,503,033	$4,282,207

Situation	Company Profile	Industry Information	Balance Sheet	Income Statement	Statement of Cash Flows	Risks	Audit Findings	Audit Procedures	Communication	Research

Tommi Stone and Quarry
INCOME STATEMENT
Two Years Ended December 31, 20X8 and 20X7
(in thousands)

	20X8	20X7
Revenue	$21,312,665	$17,261,974
Cost of goods sold	18,029,838	14,397,853
Gross profit on sales	3,282,827	2,864,121
Operating expenses	2,707,606	2,185,542
Repairs and maintenance	104,168	132,083
Depreciation	31,673	30,098
Interest expense	265,398	314,419
Total expenses	3,108,845	2,662,142
Net income before taxes	173,982	201,979
Provision for income taxes	52,197	80,792
Net income	$ 121,785	$ 121,187

Situation	Company Profile	Industry Information	Balance Sheet	Income Statement	Statement of Cash Flows		Risks	Audit Findings	Audit Procedures	Communication	Research

Tommi Stone and Quarry
STATEMENT OF CASH FLOWS
Year Ended December 31, 20X8

Cash flows from operations	
Net income (loss)	$121,785
Adjustments to net income	
Depreciation	31,673
Increase in receivables	(986,916)
Decrease in inventory	97,243
Increase in other current assets	(6,940)
Increase in accounts payable	24,831
Decrease in accrued expenses	(21,270)
Decrease in other current liabilities	(41,026)
Net cash provided (used) by operations	(780,620)
Cash flows from investing activities	
Purchase of property and equipment	(343,270)
Cash flows from financing activities	
New debt	1,682,666
Debt payments	(557,543)
Net cash provided (used) by financing activities	1,125,123
Net increase in cash and cash equivalents	$1,233
Cash and equivalents at beginning of year	$3,822
Cash and equivalents at end of year	$5,055

Situation	Company Profile	Industry Information	Balance Sheet	Income Statement	Statement of Cash Flows	Risks	Audit Findings	Audit Procedures	Communication	Research

(A) (B) (C) (D)

○ ○ ○ ○

1. Which of the following correctly identifies a risk facing TSQ that might affect its ability to continue as a going concern over the long run?

    A. Competition from several competitors.
    B. Customer satisfaction with the quality of TSQ's current products.
    C. The nature of inventory items—small in size, high in value.
    D. Obsolescence of all major products due to rapid changes in technology in the industry.

(A) (B) (C) (D)

○ ○ ○ ○

2. The most significant risk factor relating to the to misstatement arising from fraudulent financial reporting for TSQ is that the company

    A. Operates in the Albuquerque area.
    B. Officers serve on the board of directors.
    C. Must refinance a significant portion of its debt.
    D. Paid no dividend this year.

Situation	Company Profile	Industry Information	Balance Sheet	Income Statement	Statement of Cash Flows	Risks	Audit Findings	Audit Procedures	Communication	Research

Ratio	20X8	20X7
Inventory turnover	10.52	7.95
Return on equity	0.40	0.67

The above table presents two ratios that were identified as significant in the current and prior years' audits of TSQ. Compare the values of each ratio. Then select an audit finding that is consistent with these metrics. The finding need not explain the entire change. But, of the replies listed, it should potentially lead to the most significant change in the direction indicated by the change in the ratio. Each of the audit findings may be used once, more than once, or not at all.

Audit findings

A. Increases in costs of purchases were not completely passed on to customers through higher selling prices.
B. Increases in trade receivables.
C. Owners' equity increased due to retention of profits.
D. A larger percentage of sales occurred during the last month of 20X8, as compared to 20X7.
E. Interest expense decreased during 20X8.
F. The percentage tax included in the provision for income taxes for 20X8 was less than the percentage in 20X7.

	(A)	(B)	(C)	(D)	(E)	(F)
1. An audit finding consistent with the change in inventory turnover for TSQ	○	○	○	○	○	○
2. An audit finding consistent with the change in the return on equity	○	○	○	○	○	○

Situation	Company Profile	Industry Information	Balance Sheet	Income Statement	Statement of Cash Flows	Risks	Audit Findings	Audit Procedures		Communication	Research

The auditor determines that each of the following objectives will be part of TSQ's audit. For each audit objective, select a substantive procedure that would help to achieve that objective. Each of the procedures may be used once, more than once, or not at all.

Substantive procedure

A. Examine current vendors' price lists.
B. Review drafts of the financial statements.
C. Select a sample of items during the physical inventory count and determine that they have been included on count sheets.
D. Select a sample of recorded items and examine supporting vendors' invoices and contracts.
E. Select a sample of recorded items on count sheets during the physical inventory count and determine that these items are on hand.
F. Test the reasonableness of general and administrative labor rates.

	(A)	(B)	(C)	(D)	(E)	(F)
1. Determine that the presentation and disclosure of inventories and cost of goods sold is adequate.	○	○	○	○	○	○
2. Establish that the client has rights to the recorded inventories.	○	○	○	○	○	○

Situation	Company Profile	Industry Information	Balance Sheet	Income Statement	Statement of Cash Flows	Risks	Audit Findings	Audit Procedures	Communication		Research

Your firm has performed the audit of TSQ for the past five years. The preceding materials describe the company's board of directors. Recent emphasis on corporate governance has caused your firm to increasingly document its understanding of the nature of the board of directors. In a memorandum to the audit team explain your view on the likely effectiveness of the board of directors as an oversight mechanism for TSQ.

REMINDER: Your response will be graded for both technical relevance and writing skills. Technical content will be evaluated for information that is helpful to the intended reader and clearly relevant to the issue. Writing skills will be evaluated for development, organization, and the appropriate expression of ideas in professional correspondence. Use a standard business memo or letter format with a clear beginning, middle, and end. Do not convey information in the form of a table, bullet point list, or other abbreviated presentation.

To: Audit Team
From: CPA Candidate
Re: TSQ Audit Committee

Situation	Company Profile	Industry Information	Balance Sheet	Income Statement	Statement of Cash Flows	Risks	Audit Findings	Audit Procedures	Communication	Research

You have now completed the fieldwork for the TSQ audit and find that due to a change in accounting principle mandated by the Financial Accounting Standards Board, you will need to add an explanatory paragraph for a lack of consistency for the year 20X6. Using the Professional Standards, find an example of an appropriate explanatory paragraph for a lack of consistency. Do this by selecting the appropriate guidance from the Professional Standards.

SOLUTION TO SIMULATION 1

Situation	Company Profile	Industry Information	Balance Sheet	Income Statement	Statement of Cash Flows	Risks	Audit Findings	Audit Procedures	Communication	Research

(A) (B) (C) (D)

1. Which of the following correctly identifies a risk facing TSQ that might affect its ability to continue as a going concern over the long run?   ● ○ ○ ○

2. The most significant risk factor relating to the to misstatement arising from fraudulent financial reporting for TSQ is that the company   ○ ○ ● ○

Explanation of solutions

1. **(A)** The requirement is to identify the risk facing TSQ that might affect its ability to continue as a going concern over the long run. Answer (A) is correct because the competition that has led to decreased sales prices may ultimately create a difficult situation for TSQ. Answer (B) is incorrect because customers are satisfied with the quality of TSQ's products. Answer (C) is incorrect because sand and gravel is not generally small in size and high in value in the quantities sold. Answer (D) is incorrect because obsolescence is not a problem.

2. **(C)** The requirement is to identify the most significant risk factor relating to misstatements arising from fraudulent financial reporting. Answer (C) is correct because the pressure to obtain the refinancing creates pressure on management. Answer (A) is incorrect because operating in the Albuquerque area presents no particular problem. Answer (B) is incorrect because company officers ordinarily serve on the board of directors. Answer (D) is incorrect because the lack of a dividend bears no particular relationship with fraudulent financial reporting.

Situation	Company Profile	Industry Information	Balance Sheet	Income Statement	Statement of Cash Flows	Risks	Audit Findings	Audit Procedures	Communication	Research

(A) (B) (C) (D) (E) (F)

1. An audit finding consistent with the change in inventory turnover for TSQ   ○ ○ ○ ● ○ ○

2. An audit consistent with the change in the return on equity   ○ ○ ● ○ ○ ○

Explanation of solutions

1. **(D)** The requirement is to identify the finding that is consistent with an increase in the inventory turnover ratio— cost of goods sold/inventory. Answer (D) is correct because a larger percentage of sales in the last month is likely to result in a lower ending inventory, thus increasing the inventory turnover ratio since the denominator of the fraction becomes smaller.

2. **(C)** The requirement is to identify the reply that is consistent with a decrease in the return on equity ratio—net income/shareholders' equity. Answer (C) is correct because retention of profits increases the shareholders' equity, thereby decreasing the ratio.

Situation	Company Profile	Industry Information	Balance Sheet	Income Statement	Statement of Cash Flows	Risks	Audit Findings	Audit Procedures	Communication	Research

(A) (B) (C) (D) (E) (F)

1. Determine that the presentation and disclosure of inventories and cost of goods sold is adequate.   ○ ● ○ ○ ○ ○

2. Establish that the client has rights to the recorded inventories.   ○ ○ ○ ● ○ ○

Explanation of solutions

1. **(B)** The requirement is to identify a substantive procedure that will help the auditor to determine that the presentation and disclosure of inventories and cost of goods sold is adequate. Answer (B) is correct because while reviewing drafts of the financial statements the auditor may discover presentation and disclosure omissions.

2. **(D)** The requirement is to identify a substantive procedure for establishing that the client has rights to the recorded inventories. Answer (D) is correct because examination of supporting vendors' invoices and contracts will reveal whether the transactions have been recorded properly.

Situation	Company Profile	Industry Information	Balance Sheet	Income Statement	Statement of Cash Flows	Risks	Audit Findings	Audit Procedures	Communication	Research

To: Audit Team
Subject: TSQ Board of Directors

This memorandum addresses the issues regarding the makeup of TSQ's Board of Directors. The makeup of the board of directors of TSQ may limit the effectiveness of this body in providing effective oversight of the organization. The board is composed of the company's CEO, Jill Tommi; her husband, Mort Tommi; the company's CFO, Googlo Permasi; and the company's other two stockholders, Jian Zhang and Kendra Kovano. Jill Tommi is chairman of the board, which brings into question the independence of the board.

This type of composition is not uncommon for small nonissuer (nonpublic) companies. However, we should consider the implications of the lack of independence in auditing the company's financial statements. We should also get additional background information on the two outside board members, Jian Zhang and Kendra Kovano.

Situation	Company Profile	Industry Information	Balance Sheet	Income Statement	Statement of Cash Flows	Risks	Audit Findings	Audit Procedures	Communication	Research

The proper terminology for a lack of consistency is presented in AU 508.17.

As discussed in Note X to the financial statements, the Company changed its method of computing depreciation in 20X2.

SIMULATION 2

Topic—Evidence

Background			
	Situation and Spreadsheet	Explanation for Analytical Results	Research

Analytical procedures are evaluations of financial information made by a study of plausible relationships among financial and nonfinancial data. Understanding and evaluating such relationships are essential to the audit process.

	Situation and Spreadsheet		
Background		Explanation for Analytical Results	Research

The following spreadsheet with the financial statements were prepared by Holiday Manufacturing Co. for the year ended December 31, 20X1. Also presented are various financial statement ratios for Holiday as calculated from the prior year's financial statements. Sales represent net credit sales. The total assets and the receivables and inventory balances at December 31, 20X1, were the same as at December 31, 20X0.

	A	B	C	D	E	F	G
1	**Holiday Manufacturing Co.**						
2	**Balance Sheet**						
3	**December 31, 20X1**						
4							
5	Cash		$240,000		Accounts Payable		$160,000
6	Receivables		400,000		Notes payable		100,000
7	Inventory		600,000		Other current liabilities		140,000
8	Total current assets		$1,240,000		Total current liabilities		400,000
9							
10	Plant and equipment—net		760,000		Long-term debt		350,000
11					Common stock		750,000
12					Retained earnings		500,000
13	Total assets		$2,000,000		Total liabilities and capital		$2,000,000
14							
15							
16	Income Statement						
17	Year ended December 31, 20X1						
18							
19	Sales				$3,000,000		
20	Cost of goods sold						
21	Materials		800,000				
22	Labor		700,000				
23	Overhead		300,000		1,800,000		
24	Gross margin				1,200,000		
25							
26	Selling expenses		240,000				
27	General and admin. exp.		300,000		540,000		
28	Operating income				660,000		
29	Less: interest expense				40,000		
30	Income before taxes				620,000		
31	Less: federal income taxes				220,000		
32	Net income				$400,000		
33							
34							
35							
36	Ratios		**12/31/X1**		**12/31/X0**		
37	Current ratio		(1)		2.5		
38	Quick ratio		(2)		1.3		
39	Accounts receivable turnover		(3)		5.5		
40	Inventory turnover		(4)		2.5		
41	Total asset turnover		(5)		1.2		
42	Gross margin %		(6)		35%		
43	Net operating margin %		(7)		25%		
44	Times interest earned		(8)		10.3		
45	Total debt to equity %		(9)		50%		

Insert spreadsheet formulas into the worksheet to allow the direct calculation of each ratio (1 through 9). Use cell location rather than amounts.

Background	Situation and Spreadsheet	Explanation for Analytical Results	Research

Items 1 through 6 represent an auditor's observed changes in certain financial statement ratios or amounts from the prior year's ratios or amounts. For each observed change, select the most likely explanation or explanations from List B. Select only the number of explanations as indicated. **The observed changes are not related to the calculations in requirement a. above, and are independent of each other.** Answers on the list may be selected once, more than once, or not at all.

List B

A. Items shipped on consignment during the last month of the year were recorded as sales.
B. A significant number of credit memos for returned merchandise that were issued during the last month of the year were not recorded.
C. Year-end purchases of inventory were overstated by incorrectly including items received in the first month of the subsequent year.
D. Year-end purchases of inventory were understated by incorrectly excluding items received before the year-end.
E. A larger percentage of sales occurred during the last month of the year, as compared to the prior year.
F. A smaller percentage of sales occurred during the last month of the year, as compared to the prior year.
G. The same percentage of sales occurred during the last month of the year, as compared to the prior year.
H. Sales increased at the same percentage as cost of goods sold, as compared to the prior year.
I. Sales increased at a greater percentage than cost of goods sold increased, as compared to the prior year.
J. Sales increased at a lower percentage than cost of goods sold increased, as compared to the prior year.
K. Interest expense decreased, as compared to the prior year.
L. The effective income tax rate increased, as compared to the prior year.
M. The effective income tax rate decreased, as compared to the prior year.
N. Short-term borrowing was refinanced on a long-term basis at the same interest rate.
O. Short-term borrowing was refinanced on a long-term basis at lower interest rates.
P. Short-term borrowing was refinanced on a long-term basis at higher interest rates.

Auditor's observed changes	(A)	(B)	(C)	(D)	(E)	(F)	(G)	(H)	(I)	(J)	(K)	(L)	(M)	(N)	(O)	(P)
1. Inventory turnover increased substantially from the prior year. (Select 3 explanations)	○	○	○	○	○	○	○	○	○	○	○	○	○	○	○	○
2. Accounts receivable turnover decreased substantially from the prior year. (Select 3 explanations)	○	○	○	○	○	○	○	○	○	○	○	○	○	○	○	○
3. Allowance for doubtful accounts increased from the prior year, but allowance for doubtful accounts as a percentage of accounts receivable decreased from the prior year. (Select 3 explanations)	○	○	○	○	○	○	○	○	○	○	○	○	○	○	○	○
4. Long-term debt increased from the prior year, but interest expense increased a larger-than-proportionate amount than long-term debt. (Select one explanation)	○	○	○	○	○	○	○	○	○	○	○	○	○	○	○	○
5. Operating income increased from the prior year although the entity was less profitable than in the prior year. (Select two explanations)	○	○	○	○	○	○	○	○	○	○	○	○	○	○	○	○
6. Gross margin percentage was unchanged from the prior year although gross margin increased from the prior year. (Select one explanation)	○	○	○	○	○	○	○	○	○	○	○	○	○	○	○	○

Background	Situation and Spreadsheet	Explanation for Analytical Results	Research

Research the professional standards and select the guidance that answers the following questions:

1. At what stages of the audit are analytical procedures required?
2. What is the purpose of analytical procedures performed in the planning stage of the audit?

SOLUTION TO SIMULATION 2

Background	Situation and Spreadsheet	Explanation for Analytical Results	Research

		Ratio	Spreadsheet Formula	Calculation
1.	(H)	Current ratio $= \dfrac{\text{Current assets}}{\text{Current liabilities}}$	=C8/G8	$\dfrac{\$1,240,000}{\$400,000} = 3.1$
2.	(E)	Quick ratio $= \dfrac{\text{Quick assets*}}{\text{Current liabilities}}$ *Cash + Accounts receivable. Also marketable securities would be included if the company owned any.*	=(C5+C6)/G8	$\dfrac{\$240,000 + \$400,000}{\$400,000} = \dfrac{\$640,000}{\$400,000} = 1.6$
3.	(K)	$\dfrac{\text{Accounts receivable}}{\text{turnover}} = \dfrac{\text{Sales}}{\text{Accounts receivable}}$	=E19/C6	$\dfrac{\$3,000,000}{\$400,000} = 7.5$
4.	(G)	$\dfrac{\text{Inventory}}{\text{turnover}} = \dfrac{\text{Cost of goods sold}}{\text{Inventory}}$	=E23/C7	$\dfrac{\$1,800,000}{\$600,000} = 3.0$
5.	(D)	$\dfrac{\text{Total asset}}{\text{turnover}} = \dfrac{\text{Sales}}{\text{Total assets}}$	=E19/C13	$\dfrac{\$3,000,000}{\$2,000,000} = 1.5$
6.	(T)	$\dfrac{\text{Gross margin}}{\text{percentage}} = \dfrac{\text{Gross margin}}{\text{Sales}}$	=E24/E19	$\dfrac{\$1,200,000}{\$3,000,000} = 40\%$
7.	(P)	$\dfrac{\text{Net operating}}{\text{margin \%}} = \dfrac{\text{Operating income}}{\text{Sales}}$	=E28/E19	$\dfrac{\$660,000}{\$3,000,000} = 22\%$
8.	(N)	$\dfrac{\text{Times interest}}{\text{earned}} = \dfrac{\text{Operating income}}{\text{Interest expense}}$	=E28/E29	$\dfrac{\$660,000}{\$40,000} = 16.5$
9.	(U)	$\dfrac{\text{Total debt to}}{\text{equity percentage}} = \dfrac{\text{Total debt*}}{\text{Owners' equity**}}$ * Total current liabilities + Long-term debt. ** Common stock + Retained earnings	=(G8+G10)/(G11+G12)	$\dfrac{\$400,000 + \$350,000}{\$750,000 + \$500,000} = \dfrac{\$750,000}{\$1,250,000} = 60\%$

Background	Situation and Spreadsheet	Explanation for Analytical Results	Research

	(A)	(B)	(C)	(D)	(E)	(F)	(G)	(H)	(I)	(J)	(K)	(L)	(M)	(N)	(O)	(P)
1. Inventory turnover increased substantially from the prior year. (Select 3 explanations)	●	●	○	●	○	○	○	○	○	○	○	○	○	○	○	○
2. Accounts receivable turnover decreased substantially from the prior year. (Select 3 explanations)	●	●	○	○	●	○	○	○	○	○	○	○	○	○	○	○
3. Allowance for doubtful accounts increased from the prior year, but allowance for doubtful accounts as a percentage of accounts receivable decreased from the prior year. (Select 3 explanations)	●	●	○	○	●	○	○	○	○	○	○	○	○	○	○	○
4. Long-term debt increased from the prior year, but interest expense increased a larger-than-proportionate amount than long-term debt. (Select one explanation)	○	○	○	○	○	○	○	○	○	○	○	○	○	○	○	●
5. Operating income increased from the prior year although the entity was less profitable than in the prior year. (Select two explanations)	○	○	○	○	○	○	○	○	○	○	○	○	●	○	○	●
6. Gross margin percentage was unchanged from the prior year although gross margin increased from the prior year. (Select one explanation)	○	○	○	○	○	○	○	●	○	○	○	○	○	○	○	○

Explanation of solutions

1.   (**A, B, D**) The requirement is to identify three explanations for an increase in the inventory turnover when compared to the prior year. The inventory turnover is calculated by dividing the cost of goods sold by the inventory. An increase may occur either through (1) an overstatement of the cost of goods sold (the numerator), (2) an understatement of inventory (the denominator), or (3) a combination of changes. Answer (A) is correct because the recording of the consignment shipment as a sale will overstate cost of goods sold and understate the ending inventory.   Answer (B) is correct because not recording the credit memos will result in understatement of inventory. Answer (D) is correct because the understatement of purchases of inventory will understate the ending inventory.

 Answer (C) is incorrect because overstating the year-end purchases will result in overstatement of inventory, and thereby decrease the inventory turnover. Answers (E) through (J) are all incorrect because such changes in sales will not affect the inventory turnover ratio. Answers (K) through (P) are all incorrect because the interest expense, income tax rate, and the short-term borrowing do not affect the inventory turnover. Note that this question relies upon an unstated assumption that the year-end inventory is not adjusted to a year-end physical count.

2.   (**A, B, E**) The requirement is to identify three explanations for a decrease in the accounts receivable turnover when compared to the prior year. The accounts receivable turnover is calculated by dividing sales by accounts receivable. A decrease may occur through (1) an understatement of sales (the numerator), (2) an overstatement of accounts receivable (the denominator), or (3) a combination of misstatements of sales and accounts receivable that decrease the ratio. Answer (A) is correct because recording the consignment as sales overstates both sales and accounts receivable by an identical amount, thus decreasing the ratio; the decrease is due to the entry debiting accounts receivable and crediting sales for the same amount. Answer (B) is correct because not recording the credit memo overstates both sales and accounts receivable by an identical amount, thus decreasing the ratio; this identical amount of decrease is due to the lack of a debit to sales returns and allowances and a credit to accounts receivable. Note that answers (A) and (B) are correct in any situation in which the ratio is greater than 1.0; when the ratio is less than 1.0 they result in an increase in the ratio.   Answer (E) is correct because while the sales for the year remain at the expected level, accounts receivable at year-end will be at a higher than average level due to the year-end sales.

 Answers (C) and (D) are incorrect because the level of inventory does not affect the ratio. Answers (F) and (G) are incorrect because a larger, not a smaller or the same, percentage of sales near year-end decreases the ratio. Answers (H), (I) and (J) are incorrect because one would expect accounts receivable to increase at the same rate as the increase in sales. Answers (K) through (P) are all incorrect because interest expense, income tax rate, and the short-term borrowing do not affect the accounts receivable turnover.

3.   (**A, B, E**) The requirement is to identify three explanations for an increase in the allowance for doubtful accounts, but a decrease in the allowance for doubtful accounts as a percentage of accounts receivable. The allowance for doubtful accounts as a percentage of accounts receivable is calculated by dividing the allowance for doubtful accounts by accounts receivable. The percentage may decrease due to (1) a decrease in the allowance for doubtful accounts, (2) an increase in the accounts receivable, or (3) a combination of misstatements that decrease the ratio; here, however, we are told that reason (1), a decrease in the allowance, has not occurred. Answer (A) is correct because recording the consignment as a sale results in an increase in accounts receivable which decreases the ratio. Answer (B) is correct because not recording the credit memos overstates accounts receivable, thereby decreasing the ratio. Answer (E) is correct because the larger percentage of sales occurring during the last month of the year results in accounts receivable at year-end that will be at a higher than average level due to the year-end sales.

 Answers (C) and (D) are incorrect because the level of inventory does not affect the ratio. Answers (F) and (G) are incorrect because a larger, not a smaller or the same, percentage of sales near year-end decreases the ratio. Answers (H), (I), and (J) are incorrect because one would expect accounts receivable and the allowance for doubtful accounts to increase at approximately the same rate as the increase in sales. Answers (K) through (P) are all incorrect because interest expense, income tax rate, and the short-term borrowing do not affect the accounts receivable turnover.

4.   (**P**) The requirement is to identify a reason why long-term debt increased, but interest expense increased a larger-than-proportionate amount than long-term debt. Answer (P) is correct because the higher interest rates on long-term debt will result in higher interest expense. Answers (A) through (M) are all incorrect because they relate neither to long-term debt nor interest expense. Answers (N) and (O) are incorrect because refinancing at the same or a lower interest rate will result in smaller-than-proportionate amounts of interest expense.

5.   (**L, P**) The requirement is to identify two reasons why operating income might increase, yet the company would be less profitable. Since operating income increased and net income decreased, the explanation must be items that are listed on the income statement between operating income and net income—interest expense and federal income taxes. The net of these two expenses must have increased to result in a situation in which the entity was less profitable. Answer (L) is correct because an increase in the effective income tax rate could decrease the profit when compared to the prior year. Answer (P) is correct because higher interest rates decrease profits. Answers (A) through (J) are all incorrect because they pertain to details of operating income. Answers (K) and (M) are incorrect because a decrease in interest expense or the income tax rate would increase net income. Answer (N) is incorrect because refinancing at the same rate will not affect net income. Answer (O) is incorrect because refinancing at a lower interest rate will increase profits.

6.   (**H**) The requirement is to identify one reason why the gross margin percentage may remain unchanged, despite an increase in gross margin from the prior year. Answer (H) is correct because when sales increase at the same percentage as cost of goods sold, the gross margin appenctage remains unchanged, and yet the increased sales will result in an increase in the gross margin. Answers (A) through (D) are all incorrect because they will result in a change in the gross margin percentage. Answers (E), (F), and (G) are all incorrect because no increase in sales is indicated and no information on the gross margin is provided. An-

swers (I) and (J) are incorrect because they suggest a decrease and an increase in the gross margin, respectively. Answers (K) through (P) are all incorrect because interest expense, income tax rate, and debt do not affect gross margin.

Background	Situation and Spreadsheet	Explanation for Analytical Results	Research

1. At what stages of the audit are analytical procedures required?

AU 329.04

.04 Analytical procedures are used for the following purposes:

a.   To assist the auditor in planning the nature, timing, and extent of other auditing procedures.

b.   As a substantive test to obtain evidential matter about particular assertions related to account balances or classes of transactions.

c.   As an overall review of the financial information in the final review stage of the audit.

Analytical procedures should be applied to some extent for the purposes referred to in (a) and (c) above for all audits of financial statements made in accordance with generally accepted auditing standards. In addition, in some cases, analytical procedures can be more effective or efficient than tests of details for achieving particular substantive testing objectives.

2. What is the purpose of analytical procedures performed in the planning stage of the audit?

AU 329.06

.06 The purpose of applying analytical procedures in planning the audit is to assist in planning the nature, timing, and extent of auditing procedures that will be used to obtain evidential matter for specific account balances or classes of transactions. To accomplish this, analytical procedures used in planning the audit should focus on (a) enhancing the auditor's understanding of the client's business and the transactions and events that have occurred since the last audit date, and (b) identifying areas that may represent specific risks relevant to the audit. Thus, the objective of the procedures is to identify such things as the existence of unusual transactions and events, and amounts, ratios and trends that might indicate matters that have financial statement and audit planning ramifications.

FINANCIAL ACCOUNTING AND REPORTING

TESTLET 1

Items 1 and 2 are based on the following:

The town of Silverton applies the provisions of GASB 34, *Basic Financial Statements—and Management's Discussion and Analysis—for State and Local Governments,* for its financial statements. As of December 31, 2009, Silverton compiled the information below for its capital assets, exclusive of infrastructure assets.

Cost of capital assets financed with general obligation debt and tax revenues	$5,000,000
Accumulated depreciation on the capital assets	1,000,000
Outstanding debt related to the capital assets	2,000,000

1. On the government-wide statement of net assets at December 31, 2009, under the governmental activities column, what amount should be reported for capital assets?
- a. $5,000,000
- b. $4,000,000
- c. $3,000,000
- d. $2,000,000

2. On the government-wide statement of net assets at December 31, 2009, under the governmental activities column, the information related to capital assets should be reported in the net assets section at which of the following amounts?
- a. $5,000,000
- b. $4,000,000
- c. $3,000,000
- d. $2,000,000

3. Tree City reported a $1,500 net increase in fund balance for governmental funds. During the year, Tree purchased general capital assets of $9,000 and recorded depreciation expense of $3,000. What amount should Tree report as the change in net assets for governmental activities?
- a. $ (4,500)
- b. $ 1,500
- c. $ 7,500
- d. $10,500

4. A not-for-profit voluntary health and welfare organization received a $500,000 permanent endowment. The donor stipulated that the income must be used for a mental health program. The endowment fund reported $60,000 net decrease in market value and $30,000 investment income. The organization spent $45,000 on the mental health program during the year. What amount of change in temporarily restricted net assets should the organization report?
- a. $75,000 decrease.
- b. $15,000 decrease.
- c. $0
- d. $425,000 increase.

5. Oz, a nongovernmental not-for-profit organization, received $50,000 from Ame Company to sponsor a play given by Oz at the local theater. Oz gave Ame 25 tickets, which generally cost $100 each. Ame received no other benefits. What amount of ticket sales revenue should Oz record?
- a. $0
- b. $2,500
- c. $47,500
- d. $50,000

6. Under Statement of Financial Accounting Concepts 2, the ability through consensus among measurers to ensure that information represents what it purports to represent is an example of the concept of
- a. Relevance.
- b. Verifiability.
- c. Comparability.
- d. Feedback value.

7. When a company changes the expected service life of an asset because additional information has been obtained, which of the following should be reported?

	Pro forma effects of retroactive application	Retrospective application
a.	Yes	Yes
b.	No	Yes
c.	Yes	No
d.	No	No

8. Gilbert Corporation issued a 40% stock split-up of its common stock that had a par value of $10 before and after the split-up. At what amount should retained earnings be capitalized for the additional shares issued?
- a. There should be no capitalization of retained earnings.
- b. Par value.
- c. Market value on the declaration date.
- d. Market value on the payment date.

9. A nonmonetary asset was received by Company Y in a nonreciprocal transfer from Company Z that has commercial substance. The asset should be recorded by Y at
- a. Z's recorded amount.
- b. Z's recorded amount or the fair value of the asset received, whichever is higher.
- c. Z's recorded amount or the fair value of the asset received, whichever is lower.
- d. The fair value of the asset received.

10. A development stage enterprise
- a. Does **not** issue an income statement.
- b. Issues an income statement that only shows cumulative amounts from the enterprise's inception.
- c. Issues an income statement that is the same as an established operating enterprise, but does **not** show cumulative amounts from the enterprise's inception as additional information.
- d. Issues an income statement that is the same as an established operating enterprise, and shows cumulative amounts from the enterprise's inception as additional information.

11. During a period of inflation, an account balance remains constant. With respect to this account, a purchasing power gain will be recognized if the account is a
- a. Monetary liability.
- b. Monetary asset.
- c. Nonmonetary liability.
- d. Nonmonetary asset.

12. The summary of significant accounting policies should disclose the

a. Pro forma effect of retroactive application of an accounting change.

b. Basis of profit recognition on long-term construction contracts.

c. Adequacy of pension plan assets in relation to vested benefits.

d. Future minimum lease payments in the aggregate and for each of the five succeeding fiscal years.

13. The following items relate to the preparation of a statement of cash flows:

	2009	2008		2009
Cash	$150,000	$100,000	Net sales	$3,200,000
AR--net	420,000	290,000	CGS	(2,500,000)
Merchandise inventory	330,000	210,000	Expenses	(500,000)
AP	265,000	220,000	Net income	$ 200,000

All accounts payable relate to trade merchandise. Accounts payable are recorded net and always are paid to take all of the discount allowed. The direct approach is used for operating activities. Under operating activities, cash payments during 2009 to suppliers amounted to

a. $2,575,000
b. $2,500,000
c. $2,455,000
d. $2,335,000

14. Boa Constructors, Inc. had an operating loss carryforward of $100,000 that arose from ordinary operations in 2009. There is no evidence that indicates the need for a valuation allowance. The income tax rate is 40%. For the year ended December 31, 2009, the tax benefit should be reported in the income statement as

a. A $40,000 reduction in income tax expense from continuing operations.
b. An extraordinary item of $40,000.
c. An operating gain of $40,000.
d. An extraordinary item of $100,000.

Items 15 through 17 are based on the following information:

The December 31, 2009 balance sheet of Ratio, Inc. is presented below. These are the only accounts in Ratio's balance sheet. Amounts indicated by a question mark (?) can be calculated from the additional information given.

Assets	
Cash	$ 25,000
Accounts receivable (trade)	?
Inventory	?
Property, plant and equipment (net)	294,000
	$432,000

Liabilities and stockholders' equity	
Accounts payable (trade)	?
Income taxes payable (current)	25,000
Long-term debt	100,000
Common stock	300,000
Retained earnings	?
	?

Additional information

Current ratio (at year-end)	1.5 to 1
Total liabilities divided by total stockholders' equity	.8
Inventory turnover based on sales and ending inventory	15 times
Inventory turnover based on cost of goods sold and ending inventory	10.5 times
Gross margin for 2009	$315,000

15. What was Ratio's December 31, 2009 balance in the inventory account?

a. $ 21,000
b. $ 30,000

c. $ 70,000
d. $135,000

16. What was Ratio's December 31, 2009 balance in trade accounts payable?

a. $ 67,000
b. $ 92,000
c. $182,000
d. $207,000

17. What was Ratio's December 31, 2009 balance in retained earnings?

a. $ 60,000 deficit.
b. $ 60,000
c. $132,000 deficit.
d. $132,000

18. Companies A and B have been operating separately for five years. Each company has a minimal amount of liabilities and a simple capital structure consisting solely of voting common stock. Company A, in exchange for 40% of its voting stock, acquires 80% of the common stock of Company B. This was a "tax free" stock for stock (type B) exchange for tax purposes. Company B identifiable assets have a total net fair market value of $800,000 and a total net book value of $580,000. The fair market value of the A stock used in the exchange was $700,000. The goodwill on this acquisition would be

a. Zero.
b. $ 60,000
c. $120,000
d. $236,000

19. Empire Corporation owns an office building and leases the offices under a variety of rental agreements involving rent paid monthly in advance and rent paid annually in advance. Not all tenants make timely payments of their rent. Empire's balance sheets contained the following information:

	2009	2008
Rentals receivable	$3,100	$2,400
Unearned rentals	6,000	8,000

During 2009, Empire received $20,000 cash from tenants. How much rental revenue should Empire record for 2009?

a. $17,300
b. $18,700
c. $21,300
d. $22,700

20. Moore Company carries product A in inventory on December 3, 2009, at its unit cost of $7.50. Because of a sharp decline in demand for the product, the selling price was reduced to $8.00 per unit. Moore's normal profit margin on product A is $1.60, disposal costs are $1.00 per unit, and the replacement cost is $5.30. Under the rule of cost or market, whichever is lower, Moore's December 31, 2009, inventory of product A should be valued at a unit cost of

a. $5.30
b. $5.40
c. $7.00
d. $7.50

21. On January 1, 2009, Richmond, Inc. signed a fixed-price contract to have Builder Associates construct a major plant facility at a cost of $4,000,000. It was estimated that it would take three years to complete the project. Also on January 1, 2009, to finance the construction cost, Richmond borrowed $4,000,000 payable in 10 annual installments of $400,000 plus interest at the rate of 11%. During 2009 Richmond made deposit and progress payments totaling $1,500,000 under the contract; the average amount of accumulated expenditures was $650,000 for the year. The excess borrowed funds were invested in short-term securities, from which Richmond realized investment income of $250,000. What amount should Richmond report as capitalized interest at December 31, 2009?

- a. $ 71,500
- b. $165,000
- c. $190,000
- d. $440,000

22. On May 1, 2009, Lane Corp. bought a parcel of land for $100,000. Seven months later, Lane sold this land to a triple-A rated company for $150,000, under the following terms: 25% at closing, and a first mortgage note (at the market rate of interest) for the balance. The first payment on the note, plus accrued interest, is due December 1, 2010. Lane reported this sale on the installment basis in its 2009 tax return. In its 2009 income statement, how much gain should Lane report from the sale of this land?

- a. $0
- b. $12,500
- c. $37,500
- d. $50,000

23. On January 1, 2009, Derby Company lent $20,000 cash to Elliott Company. The promissory note made by Elliott did not bear interest and was due on December 31, 2010. No other rights or privileges were exchanged. The prevailing interest for a loan of this type was 12%. The present value of $1 for two periods at 12% is 0.797. Derby should recognize interest income in 2009 of

- a. $0
- b. $1,913
- c. $2,030
- d. $2,400

24. Platt Co. has been forced into bankruptcy and liquidated. Unsecured claims will be paid at the rate of $.50 on the dollar. Maga Co. holds a noninterest-bearing note receivable from Platt in the amount of $50,000, collateralized by machinery with a liquidation value of $10,000. The total amount to be realized by Maga on this note receivable is

- a. $35,000
- b. $30,000
- c. $25,000
- d. $10,000

25. Included in W. Cody's assets at December 31, 2009, are the following:

2,000 shares of Dart Corporation common stock purchased in 2007 for $100,000. The market value of the stock was $80 per share at December 31, 2009.
A $500,000 whole life insurance policy having a cash value of $72,000 at December 31, 2009, subject to a $30,000 loan payable to the insurance company.

In Cody's December 31, 2009 personal statement of financial condition, the above assets should be reported at

- a. $232,000
- b. $202,000
- c. $172,000
- d. $142,000

26. Footnotes to the financial statements are beneficial in meeting the disclosure requirements of financial reporting. The footnotes should not be used to

- a. Describe significant accounting policies.
- b. Describe depreciation methods employed by the company.
- c. Describe the principles and methods peculiar to the industry in which the company operates, when these principles and methods are predominantly followed in that industry.
- d. Correct an improper presentation in the financial statements.

27. SFAS 95, *Statement of Cash Flows*, classifies cash receipts and cash payments as arising from operating, investing, and financing activities. All of the following should be classified as investing activities except

- a. Cash outflows to purchase manufacturing equipment.
- b. Cash inflows from the sale of bonds of other entities.
- c. Cash outflows to lenders for interest.
- d. Cash inflows from the sale of a manufacturing plant.

28. Initial direct costs incurred by the lessor under a sales-type lease should be

- a. Deferred and allocated over the economic life of the leased property.
- b. Expensed in the period incurred.
- c. Deferred and allocated over the term of the lease in proportion to the recognition of rental income.
- d. Added to the gross investment in the lease and amortized over the term of the lease as a yield adjustment.

29. An appropriation of retained earnings by the board of directors of a corporation for future plant expansion will result in

- a. The establishment of a fund to help finance future plant expansion.
- b. The setting aside of cash to be used for future plant expansions.
- c. A decrease in cash on the balance sheet with an equal increase in the investments and funds section of the balance sheet.
- d. The disclosure that management does not intend to distribute, in the form of dividends, assets equal to the amount of the appropriation.

30. An industry segment is a reportable segment if it is significant to the enterprise as a whole. An industry segment is considered significant when any of the following conditions are met **except** when the

- a. Segment revenue is 10% or more of the combined revenue of all of the company's segments.
- b. Segment identifiable assets are 10% or more of the combined identifiable assets of all segments.
- c. Segment identifiable liabilities are 10% or more of the combined identifiable liabilities of all segments.
- d. Absolute value of a segment's operating profit or operating loss is 10% or more of the combined operating profit of all segments that did not incur an operating loss.

FINANCIAL ACCOUNTING AND REPORTING

TESTLET 1 ANSWERS

1.	b	6.	b	11.	a	16.	a	21.	a	26.	d
2.	d	7.	d	12.	b	17.	a	22.	d	27.	c
3.	c	8.	b	13.	a	18.	b	23.	a	28.	b
4.	c	9.	d	14.	a	19.	d	24.	b	29.	d
5.	b	10.	d	15.	c	20.	b	25.	b	30.	c

Hints for Multiple-Choice Questions

1. Capital assets are presented net of accumulated depreciation.

2. In the net assets section capital assets are presented net of related debt.

3. Net assets is increased by increase in fund balance and increase in capital assets.

4. Endowment is a permanently restricted amount.

5. Ticket revenue is at fair value.

6. A characteristic of reliability.

7. This is a change in an accounting estimate.

8. This constitutes a large stock dividend. It is not a stock split because par value has not changed.

9. No tricks here.

10. Must follow GAAP.

11. Monetary items are fixed in amount.

12. Entity should disclose the accounting principles followed and methods of applying those principles.

13. Cash payments to suppliers is determined by adjusting **CGS** for changes in **inventory** and **AP**.

14. The operating loss reduces income from operations.

15. Calculate inventory algebraically—Sales = (10.5)

$$(INV) + \$315,000 = (15)(INV).$$

16. First calculate total current assets, then use current ratio.

17. Liabilities/SE = 0.8/1.0.

18. Measurement of GW.

19. Review Cash to accrual, Module 7, Section A.4.

20. Floor is NRV less normal profit.

21. Capitalized interest is avoidable interest.

22. Installment method can only be used under GAAP where collection is not reasonably assured.

23. $20,000 is both the PV and FV of this note.

24. Only $40,000 of the note is unsecured.

25. Present estimated current values of assets and current amounts of liabilities.

26. Footnotes provide additional information.

27. Investing activities relate to investments in property, plant, and equipment and securities.

28. Initial direct costs are part of cost of sales.

29. An appropriation simply informs users of the reason that dividends will not be declared.

30. Remember the test for segment reporting.

Explanations

1. **(b)** The assets under the governmental activities column would include the capital assets of $5,000,000 less the accumulated depreciation of $1,000,000.

2. **(d)** The amount of net assets is equal to assets minus liabilities. Therefore, the amount would be equal to $2,000,000 ($5,000,000 total assets – $1,000,000 accumulated depreciation – $2,000,000 liabilities).

3. **(c)** The changes in net assets is equal to $7,500 ($9,000 expenditures for capital assets – $1,500 increase in fund balances). The depreciation expense would not be included in the funds statement.

4. **(c)** The endowment would be a permanently restricted asset. The income would be initially recorded as temporarily restricted funds and the expenditures would be recorded as decreases in unrestricted assets. At the end of the period, the temporarily restricted income would be reclassified as unrestricted, resulting in $0 change in temporarily restricted assets. Note that if the entity had not spent all of the endowment income in this year there would have been a change in temporarily restricted assets.

5. **(b)** The ticket sales revenue should be equal to the fair market value of the tickets.

6. **(b)** Verifiability relates to the reliability of the measurement. The others related to relevance.

7. **(d)** A change in the expected service life of an asset because of new information is reported prospectively. Prior periods are not restated.

8. **(b)** In a large stock dividend, retained earnings should be charged for the par value of the additional shares issued.

9. **(d)** If the nonmonetary exchange has commercial substance, the asset received is recorded at its fair value.

10. **(d)** A development stage enterprise issues an income statement that is the same as an established operating enterprise and shows cumulative amounts from the enterprise's inception as additional information.

11. **(a)** In a period of inflation, a gain will be recognized on a monetary liability. The liability will be paid with dollars with less purchasing power.

12. **(b)** The summary of significant accounting policies should disclose the basis of profit recognition on long-term construction contracts.

13.   (a)   The cash payments to suppliers is equal to $2,575,000 ($2,500,000 CGS + $220,000 beg. AP – $265,000 end. AP – $210,000 beg. Inv. + $330,000 end. Inv.).

14.   (a)   The tax benefit is $40,000 ($100,000 × 40%).

15.   (c)   Inventory is equal to $70,000. To calculate this amount, inventory turnover based on cost of goods sold (10.5) is deducted from inventory turnover based on sales (15), which results in 4.5. Then , divide this amount into gross margin to get $70,000 ($315,000 ÷ 4.5).

16.   (a)   To calculate this amount, first calculate current assets by deducting the amount of property, plant, and equipment from total assets. Current assets is equal to $138,000 ($432,000 – $294,000). If the current ratio is equal to 1.5 to 1, then current liabilities are equal to $92,000 ($138,000 ÷ 1.5). Finally, accounts payable is equal to $67,000 ($93,000 CL – $25,000 income taxes payable).

17.   (a)   Retained earnings is equal to $60,000 deficit ($432,000 total assets – $67,000 AP – $25,000 income taxes payable – $100,000 long-term debt – $300,000 common stock).

18.   (b)   Because A Company acquired 80% of B Company, it acquired $640,000 ($800,000 × 80%) net identifiable assets. Goodwill is equal to $60,000 ($700,000 value of the stock – $640,000 value of the company's share of identifiable assets).

19.   (d)   Rent earned is equal to $22,700 ($20,000 cash received – $2,400 beg. rent receivable + $3,100 end. rent receivable + $8,000 beg. unearned rent – $6,000 end. unearned rent).

20.   (b)   The lower of cost or market value is the floor of $5.40 ($8.00 sales price – $1.00 disposal costs – $1.60 normal profit).

21.   (a)   Capitalized interest is equal to $71,500 ($650,000 average amount of accumulated expenditures × 11% interest rate).

22.   (d)   The total gain on the sales is $50,000 ($150,000 – $100,000). Under GAAP the total gain is recognized unless there is too much uncertainty about the amount to be collected.

23.   (a)   Since there were no other aspects to the transaction, no interest is implicit, and none should be imputed.

24.   (b)   The amount realized is equal to $10,000 (collateral value) + 50% of the remaining $40,000, or $30,000.

25.   (b)   The assets should be reported at their fair market values of $202,000 [(2,000 × $80) + ($72,000 – $30,000)]. Note that the insurance policy value is shown net of the loan.

26.   (d)   Footnotes should not correct errors in the financial statements.

27.   (c)   Cash outflows to lenders for interest are classified as financing activities.

28.   (b)   Initial direct costs incurred by a lessor should be expensed as incurred.

29.   (d)   An appropriation of retained earnings involves simply a reclassification of retained earnings and does not involve setting aside assets.

30.   (c)   Segment identifiable liabilities is not used as a base for identifying segments that must be presented.

FINANCIAL ACCOUNTING AND REPORTING
TESTLET 2

1. For which of the following governmental entities that use proprietary fund accounting should a statement of cash flows be presented?

	Swimming pool	Government utilities
a.	No	No
b.	No	Yes
c.	Yes	Yes
d.	Yes	No

2. The Williamsburg Zoo, a private not-for-profit organization, established a $1,000,000 quasi endowment on July 1, 2009. On the zoo's financial statement of financial position at December 31, 2009, the assets in this quasi endowment should be included in which of the following classifications?

- a. Temporarily restricted net assets.
- b. Unrestricted net assets.
- c. Permanently restricted net assets.
- d. Either temporarily or permanently restricted net assets, depending on the expected term of the endowment.

3. Chase City imposes a 2% tax on hotel charges. Revenues from this tax will be used to promote tourism in the city. Chase should record this tax as what type of nonexchange transaction?

- a. Derived tax revenue.
- b. Imposed nonexchange revenue.
- c. Government-mandated transaction.
- d. Voluntary nonexchange transaction.

4. Pica, a nongovernmental not-for-profit organization, received unconditional promises of $100,000 expected to be collected within one year. Pica received $10,000, prior to year-end. Pica anticipates collecting 90% of the contributions and has a June 30 fiscal year-end. What amount should Pica record as contribution revenue as of June 30?

- a. $ 10,000
- b. $ 80,000
- c. $ 90,000
- d. $100,000

5. Why is a reclassification adjustment used when reporting other comprehensive income?

- a. Adjustment made to reclassify an item of comprehensive income as another item of comprehensive income.
- b. Adjustment made to avoid double counting of items.
- c. Adjustment made to make net income equal to comprehensive income.
- d. Adjustment made to adjust for the income tax effect of reporting comprehensive income.

6. In a statement of cash flows, interest payments to lenders and other creditors should be classified as cash outflows for

- a. Operating activities.
- b. Borrowing activities.
- c. Lending activities.
- d. Financing activities.

7. When treasury stock is purchased for cash at more than its par value, what is the effect on total stockholders' equity under each of the following methods?

	Cost method	Par value method
a.	Increase	Increase
b.	Decrease	Decrease
c.	No effect	Decrease
d.	No effect	No effect

8. When the allowance method of recognizing bad debt expense is used, the allowance for doubtful accounts would decrease when a(n)

- a. Specified account receivable is collected.
- b. Account previously written off is collected.
- c. Account previously written off becomes collectible.
- d. Specific uncollectible account is written off.

9. In computing basic earnings per share, a company would include which of the following?

- a. Dividends on nonconvertible cumulative preferred stock.
- b. Dividends on common stock.
- c. Interest on convertible bonds.
- d. Number of shares of nonconvertible cumulative preferred stock.

10. On January 2, 2007, a company established a sinking fund in connection with an issue of bonds due in 2014. At December 31, 2009, the independent trustee held cash in the sinking fund account representing the annual deposits to the fund and the interest earned on those deposits. How should the sinking fund be reported in the company's classified balance sheet at December 31, 2009?

- a. The entire balance in the sinking fund account should appear as a noncurrent asset.
- b. The entire balance in the sinking fund account should appear as a current asset.
- c. The cash in the sinking fund should appear as a current asset.
- d. The accumulated deposits only should appear as a noncurrent asset.

11. For interim financial reporting, an inventory loss from a market decline in the second quarter that is **not** expected to be restored in the fiscal year should be recognized as a loss

- a. In the fourth quarter.
- b. Proportionately in each of the second, third, and fourth quarters.
- c. Proportionately in each of the first, second, third, and fourth quarters.
- d. In the second quarter.

12. A review of the December 31, 2009 financial statements of Rhur Corporation revealed that under the caption "extraordinary losses," Rhur reported a total of $260,000. Further analysis revealed that the $260,000 in losses was comprised of the following items:

- Rhur recorded a loss of $50,000 incurred in the abandonment of equipment formerly used in the business.
- In an unusual and infrequent occurrence, a loss of $75,000 was sustained as a result of hurricane damage to a warehouse.
- During 2009, several factories were shut down during a major strike by employees. Shutdown expenses totaled $120,000.
- Uncollectible accounts receivable of $15,000 were written off as uncollectible.

Ignoring income taxes, what amount of loss should Rhur report as extraordinary on its 2009 statement of income?

   a. $ 50,000
   b. $ 75,000
   c. $135,000
   d. $260,000

13. On December 30, 2008, Future, Incorporated paid $2,000,000 for land. At December 31, 2009, the current value of the land was $2,200,000. In January 2010, the land was sold for $2,250,000. Ignoring income taxes, by what amount should stockholders' equity be increased for 2009 and 2010 as a result of the above facts in current value financial statements?

	2009	2010
a.	$0	$ 50,000
b.	$0	$250,000
c.	$200,000	$0
d.	$200,000	$ 50,000

14. Kenny Company, a publicly traded company, adopted a defined benefit pension plan on January 1, 2008. The following data are available at December 31, 2009:

Pension expense 2009	$103,000
Pension funding 2009	90,000
Fair value of plan assets 12/31/09	225,000
Accumulated pension obligation12/31/09	208,000
Projected benefit obligation 12/31/09	290,000

At December 31, 2008, Kenny reported prepaid pension cost of $11,000. Kenny's pension liability to be reported in the December 31, 2009 balance sheet is

   a. $0
   b. $ 2,000
   c. $13,000
   d. $65,000

15. On May 1, 2009, the board of directors of Edgewood, Inc. approved a plan to sell its electronic component. The plan met the criteria to classify the component as "held for sale." During 2009 the component had a loss from operations of $500,000. In addition, the carrying value of the component's assets is estimated to be $700,000 greater than their fair value less costs to sell. Edgewood's effective tax rate for 2009 is 40%. For the year ended December 31, 2009, Edgewood should report a total loss (net of taxes) from discontinued operations of

   a. $240,000
   b. $400,000
   c. $480,000
   d. $720,000

16. Tapscott, Inc., is indebted to Bush Finance Company under a $600,000, 10%, five-year note dated January 1, 2007. Interest, payable annually on December 31, was paid on the December 31, 2007 and 2008 due dates. However, during 2009 Tapscott experienced severe financial difficulties and is likely to default on the note and interest unless some concessions are made. On December 31, 2009, Tapscott and Bush signed an agreement restructuring the debt as follows:

> Interest for 2009 was reduced to $30,000 payable March 31, 2010.
> Interest payments each year were reduced to $40,000 per year for 2010 and 2011.
> The principal amount was reduced to $400,000.

What is the amount of gain that Tapscott should report on the debt restructure in its income statement for the year ended December 31, 2009?

   a. $120,000
   b. $150,000
   c. $200,000
   d. $230,000

17. Included in Kerr Corporation's liability account balances at December 31, 2009, were the following:

14% note payable issued October 1, 2009, maturing September 30, 2010	$250,000
16% note payable issued April 1, 2007, payable in 6 equal annual installments of $100,000 beginning April 1, 2008	400,000

Kerr's December 31, 2009 financial statements were issued on March 31, 2010. On January 15, 2010, the entire $400,000 balance of the 16% note was refinanced by issuance of a long-term obligation payable in a lump sum. In addition, on March 10, 2010, Kerr consummated a noncancelable agreement with the lender to refinance the 14%, $250,000 note on a long-term basis, on readily determinable terms that have not yet been implemented. Both parties are financially capable of honoring the agreement, and there have been no violations of the agreement's provisions. On the December 31, 2009 balance sheet, the amount of the notes payable that Kerr should classify as short-term obligations is

   a. $0
   b. $100,000
   c. $250,000
   d. $350,000

18. On July 1, 2009, Diamond, Inc. paid $1,000,000 for 100,000 shares (40%) of the outstanding common stock of Ashley Corporation. At that date the net assets of Ashley totaled $2,500,000 and the fair values of all of Ashley's identifiable assets and liabilities were equal to their book values. Ashley reported net income of $500,000 for the year ended December 31, 2009, of which $300,000 was for the six months ended December 31, 2009. Ashley paid cash dividends of $250,000 on September 30, 2009. Diamond does not elect the fair value option for reporting its investment in Ashley. In its income statement for the year ended December 31, 2009, what amount of income should Diamond report from its investments in Ashley?

   a. $ 80,000
   b. $100,000
   c. $120,000
   d. $200,000

19. West Company determined that it has an obligation relating to employees' rights to receive compensation for future absences attributable to employees' services already rendered. The obligation relates to rights that vest, and payment of the compensation is probable. The amounts of West's obligations as of December 31, 2009, are reasonably estimated as follows:

Vacation pay	$110,000
Sick pay	80,000

In its December 31, 2009 balance sheet, what amount should West report as its liability for compensated absences?

   a. $0
   b. $ 80,000
   c. $110,000
   d. $190,000

20. The balance in Ashwood Company's accounts payable account at December 31, 2009, was $900,000 before any necessary year-end adjustment relating to the following:

- Goods were in transit from a vendor to Ashwood on December 31, 2009. The invoice cost was $50,000, and the goods were shipped FOB shipping point on December 29, 2009. The goods were received on January 4, 2010.
- Goods shipped FOB shipping point on December 20, 2009, from a vendor to Ashwood were lost in transit. The invoice cost was $25,000. On January 5, 2010, Ashwood filed a $25,000 claim against the common carrier.
- Goods shipped FOB destination on December 21, 2009, from a vendor to Ashwood were received on January 6, 2010. The invoice cost was $15,000.

What amount should Ashwood report as accounts payable on its December 31, 2009 balance sheet?

- a. $925,000
- b. $940,000
- c. $950,000
- d. $975,000

21. At December 31, 2009, Arno Beauticians had 1,000 gift certificates outstanding that had been sold to customers during 2009 for $75 each. Arno operates on a gross margin of 60%. How much revenue pertaining to the 1,000 outstanding gift certificates should be deferred at December 31, 2009?

- a. $0
- b. $30,000
- c. $45,000
- d. $75,000

22. On January 1, 2006, Green Company purchased a machine for $800,000 and established an annual depreciation charge of $100,000 over an eight-year life. During 2009, after issuance of the 2008 financial statements, Green applied the recoverability test to the machine and concluded that: (1) the machine suffered permanent impairment of its operational value, and (2) $200,000 is a reasonable estimate of the amount expected to be recovered through use of the machine for the period January 1, 2009, to December 31, 2013. The fair value of the machine is $160,000. In Green's December 31, 2009 balance sheet, the machine should be reported at a carrying amount of

- a. $0
- b. $100,000
- c. $160,000
- d. $400,000

23. On December 1, 2009, Poplar, Inc. purchased for cash at $18 per share all 200,000 shares of the outstanding common stock of Spruce Co. At December 1, 2009, Spruce's balance sheet showed a carrying amount of net assets of $3,200,000. The carrying amounts are equal to the fair values of all the identifiable assets except property, plant, and equipment. However, the fair value of Spruce's property, plant and equipment exceeded its carrying amount by $150,000. In its December 1, 2009 consolidated balance sheet, what amount should Poplar report as goodwill?

- a. $550,000
- b. $400,000
- c. $250,000
- d. $0

24. Cicci and Arias are partners who share profits and losses in the ratio of 7:3, respectively. On October 5, 2009, their respective capital accounts were as follows:

Cicci	$35,000
Arias	30,000
Total	$65,000

On that date they agreed to admit Soto as a partner with a one-third interest in the capital and profits and losses, upon

his investment of $25,000. The new partnership will begin with a total capital of $90,000. Immediately after Soto's admission, what are the capital balances of Cicci, Arias, and Soto, respectively?

- a. $30,000; $30,000; $30,000
- b. $31,500; $28,500; $30,000
- c. $31,667; $28,333; $30,000
- d. $35,000; $30,000; $25,000

25. A not-for-profit organization receives $1,000 from a donor. The donor receives two tickets to dinner with a fair market value of $150. What amount should be recorded as contribution revenue?

- a. $0
- b. $ 150
- c. $ 850
- d. $1,000

26. The impairment rules for long-lived assets apply to all of the following **except:**

- a. Buildings currently used in the business.
- b. Financial instruments.
- c. Land.
- d. Minicomputers used to run a production process.

27. A change from the sum-of-the-years' digits depreciation method to the straight-line depreciation method is accounted for as a(n)

- a. Accounting estimate change.
- b. Accounting principle change.
- c. Error correction.
- d. Prior period adjustment.

28. On December 1, Charles Company's board of directors declared a cash dividend of $1.00 per share on the 50,000 shares of common stock outstanding. The company also has 5,000 shares of treasury stock. Shareholders of record on December 15 are eligible for the dividend, which is to be paid on January 1. On December 1, the company should

- a. Make no accounting entry.
- b. Debit retained earnings for $45,000.
- c. Debit retained earnings for $55,000.
- d. Debit retained earnings for $50,000.

29. Depreciation of a plant asset is the process of

- a. Asset valuation for statement of financial position purposes.
- b. Allocating the cost of the asset to the periods of use.
- c. Accumulating a fund for the replacement of the asset.
- d. Asset valuation based on current replacement cost data.

30. When classifying assets as current and noncurrent for reporting purposes

- a. The amounts at which current assets are carried and reported must reflect realizable cash values.
- b. Prepayments for items such as insurance or rent are included in an "other assets" group rather than as current assets as they will ultimately be expensed.
- c. The time period by which current assets are distinguished from noncurrent assets is determined by the seasonal nature of the business.
- d. Assets are classified as current if they are reasonably expected to be realized in cash or consumed during the normal operating cycle.

FINANCIAL ACCOUNTING AND REPORTING

TESTLET 2 ANSWERS

1.	c	6.	a	11.	d	16.	b	21.	d	26.	b
2.	b	7.	b	12.	b	17.	a	22.	c	27.	a
3.	a	8.	d	13.	d	18.	c	23.	c	28.	d
4.	c	9.	a	14.	d	19.	d	24.	b	29.	b
5.	b	10.	a	15.	d	20.	d	25.	c	30.	d

Hints for Multiple-Choice Questions

1. Required for proprietary funds and governmental entities that use proprietary fund accounting.

2. Voluntarily established endowments are still part of unrestricted net assets.

3. Taxes on exchanges are derived tax revenue.

4. Contribution revenue is reported on accrual basis.

5. Reverse amounts that have been recognized.

6. Operating activities section of SCF parallels IS.

7. Cost—subtract from stockholders' equity; par value—subtract from shares issued.

8. Allowance increases when account previously written off becomes collectible.

9. Want to find income available to common stockholders.

10. These funds have been segregated for the company's long-term needs.

11. Defer if temporary.

12. A strike is not considered extraordinary.

13. Current cost accounting discards historical cost.

14. Pension liability = FV plan assets – PBO.

15. Loss on sale is estimated.

16. Gain = Prerestructure carrying amount (including unpaid interest) – Future cash flows.

17. Account for as short-term obligations expected to be refinanced.

18. The investment was held only for the last six months of the year. Equity method was used to account for the investment.

19. Recall the four conditions for accrual.

20. Under the terms "FOB shipping point," title is transferred when goods are delivered to the common carrier.

21. Review Module 10, Section C.1.h.

22. Depreciate over remaining useful life.

23. Purchase price minus fair market value of identifiable assets. $3,600,000 – $3,350,000 = $250,000.

24. Allocate bonus according to P & L ratio.

25. Contribution is amount above fair market value.

26. ASC Topic 360 on impairment applies to fixed assets.

27. Change in method and change in estimate may be related.

28. What entry is required on the day of declaration?

29. How are plant assets valued?

30. What is the definition of a current asset?

Explanations

1. (c) A statement of cash flows is required for proprietary funds, and proprietary funds include internal service funds and enterprise funds. Examples of enterprise funds include utilities, airports, and swimming pools.

2. (b) Quasi endowments are established voluntarily by the organization and may be rescinded at any time. Therefore, they are classified as part of unrestricted net assets.

3. (a) This is an example of derived tax revenue.

4. (c) The contributions revenue is $90,000 ($100,000 × 90 %), the amount expected to be collected.

5. (b) Reclassification adjustments are necessary to keep from double counting gains and losses that have been recognized in ordinary income during the period.

6. (a) Interest payments are classified as cash flows for operating activities.

7. (b) No matter what method is used, stockholders' equity is decreased as a result of the purchase of treasury stock.

8. (d) The only item that would decrease the allowance for doubtful accounts is the write-off of an uncollectible account.

9. (a) Basic earnings per share is calculated by dividing the number of shares of common stock outstanding by net income reduced by the amount of dividends to nonconvertible cumulative preferred stock.

10. (a) The amount should be reported as a noncurrent asset because it is committed to pay a noncurrent liability.

11. (d) A loss that is not expected to be recovered should be recognized in the quarter that it is incurred.

12. (b) Extraordinary items are unusual and infrequent in occurrence.

13. (d) On current value financial statements the increase in the value of $200,000 is reported in 2009 and the $50,000 additional gain on sale is recognized in 2010.

14. (d) The required minimum liability is $65,000 ($290,000 projected benefit obligation – $225,000 fair value of plan assets).

15. (d) The amount that should be presented as the total loss from discontinued operations is $720,000 [$1,200,000 – ($1,200,000 × 40%)]. Both the operating loss and the estimated loss on sale of assets is included, net of taxes.

16. **(b)** The amount of the gain is $150,000. The amount owed at the date of restructuring is $660,000 ($600,000 principle + $60,000 in accrued interest). The total future payments equal $510,000 ($400,000 + $30,000 + $40,000 + $40,000). The difference is equal to $150,000 ($660,000 – $510,000).

17. **(a)** Since the items were refinanced prior to issuance of the financial statements, both liabilities may be classified as noncurrent.

18. **(c)** Diamond should report $120,000 ($300,000 × 40%) in income from the investment. This investment should be accounted for using the equity method and Diamond should recognize its share of income earned.

19. **(d)** West should accrue the entire amount of the compensation for future absences earned by the employees.

20. **(d)** The amount of accounts payable that should be presented is $975,000 ($900,000 + $50,000 + $25,000). Where title had passed prior to year-end, the liability and asset should be included on Ashwood's financial statements.

21. **(d)** The certificates should be reported as a liability of $75,000 (1,000 × $75), the face value of the certificates.

22. **(c)** The machine should be written down to $200,000 in 2008 and depreciated over a 5-year period. Therefore, the carrying value of the machine at December 31, 2009 should be $160,000 [$200,000 – ($200,000 ÷ 5)].

23. **(c)** Goodwill should be recorded at $250,000 [($18 × 200,000) – $3,200,000 – $150,000].

24. **(b)** The capital balances should be $31,500; $28,500; $30,000. Since Soto is getting a 1/3 interest in the capital of the partnership, he should have 1/3 of the capital. The total capital after Soto's investment is $90,000 ($65,000 + $25,000) and, therefore, Soto's capital becomes $30,000 which is $5,000 more than his investment. This $5,000 should be distributed to the other two partners based on their profit and loss ratio. Cicci's capital would be reduced by $3,500 ($5,000 × 7/11), and Arias' capital would be reduced by $1,500 ($5,000 × 3/11).

25. **(c)** The contribution is the excess of the donation over the fair market value of the goods or services received by the donor, or $850 ($1,000 – $150).

26. **(b)** The standard does not apply to financial instruments.

27. **(a)** A change in estimate effected by a change in principle is accounted for as a change in estimate.

28. **(d)** Retained earnings is debited for the dividends on stock outstanding at the declaration date.

29. **(b)** Depreciation is simply the process of allocating the cost of an asset to the periods benefited by that asset.

30. **(d)** Current assets are those that are reasonably expected to be realized in cash or consumed during the normal operating cycle of the business.

FINANCIAL ACCOUNTING AND REPORTING
TESTLET 3

1. Wildlife Fund, a private not-for-profit organization, received contributions restricted for research totaling $1,000,000 in 2008. None of the contributions were spent in 2008. In 2009, $650,000 of the contributions were used to support the research activities of the organization. The net effect on the statement of activities for the year ended December 31, 2009, would be a

a. $350,000 increase in temporarily restricted net assets.
b. $650,000 decrease in temporarily restricted net assets.
c. $650,000 increase in unrestricted net assets.
d. $650,000 decrease in unrestricted net assets.

2. The statement of activities of the government-wide financial statements is designed primarily to provide information to assess which of the following?

a. Operational accountability.
b. Financial accountability.
c. Fiscal accountability.
d. Functional accountability.

3. According to GASB 34, *Basic Financial Statements—and Management's Discussion and Analysis—for State and Local Governments,* certain budgetary schedules are required supplementary information. What is the minimum budgetary information required to be reported in those schedules?

a. A schedule of unfavorable variances at the functional level.
b. A schedule showing the final appropriations budget and actual expenditures on a budgetary basis.
c. A schedule showing the original budget, the final appropriations budget, and actual inflows, outflows, and balances on a budgetary basis.
d. A schedule showing the proposed budget, the approved budget, the final amended budget, actual inflows and outflows on a budgetary basis, and variances between budget and actual.

4. Nox City reported a $25,000 net increase in the fund balances for total governmental funds. Nox also reported an increase in net assets for the following funds:

Motor pool internal service fund	$ 9,000
Water enterprise fund	12,000
Employee pension fund	7,000

The motor pool internal service fund provides service to the general fund departments. What amount should Nox report as the change in net assets for governmental activities?

a. $25,000
b. $34,000
c. $41,000
d. $46,000

5. Forkin Manor, a nongovernmental not-for-profit organization, is interested in having its financial statements reformatted using terminology that is more readily associated with for-profit entities. The director believes that the term "operating profit" and the practice of segregating recurring and nonrecurring items more accurately depict the organization's activities. Under what condition will Forkin be allowed to use "operating profit" and to segregate its recurring items from it nonrecurring items in its statement of activities?

a. The organization reports the change in unrestricted net assets for the period.
b. A parenthetical disclosure in the notes implies that the not-for-profit organization is seeking for-profit entity status.
c. Forkin receives special authorization from the Internal Revenue Service that this wording is appropriate.
d. At a minimum, the organizations reports the change in permanently restricted net assets for the period.

6. If inventory levels are stable or increasing, an argument that is not in favor of the LIFO method as compared to FIFO is

a. Income taxes tend to be reduced in periods of rising prices.
b. Cost of goods sold tends to be stated at approximately current cost in the income statement.
c. Cost assignments typically parallel the physical flow of the goods.
d. Income tends to be smoothed as prices change over time.

7. If financial assets are exchanged for cash or other consideration, but the transfer does not meet the criteria for a sale, the transferor should account for the transaction as a

	Secured borrowing	Pledge of collateral
a.	No	Yes
b.	Yes	Yes
c.	Yes	No
d.	No	No

8. In accounting for a long-term construction contract using the percentage-of-completion method, the amount of income recognized in any year would be added to

a. Deferred revenues.
b. Progress billings on contracts.
c. Construction in progress.
d. Property, plant, and equipment.

9. In calculating the carrying amount of a loan, the lender deducts from the principal

	Direct loan origination costs incurred by the lender	Loan origination fees charged to the borrower
a.	Yes	Yes
b.	Yes	No
c.	No	Yes
d.	No	No

10. How is compensation expense measured by public entities for share-based payments classified as equity-based payments?

a. Use the normal hourly rate of the employees.
b. Measure the intrinsic value of options difference between market price and exercise price at measurement date.
c. Measure the fair value of options using an option-pricing model.
d. Measure the difference between the market price and the fair value of the options.

11. A gain on the sale of a marketable equity security from the available-for-sale portfolio should be presented in a statement of cash flows in which the operating section is prepared using the direct method as a(n)
a. Inflow of cash under investing activities only.
b. Deduction from net income under operating activities and as an inflow of cash under investing activities.
c. Inflow of cash under operating activities only.
d. Deduction from net income only.

12. Lee Corporation's checkbook balance on December 31, 2009, was $4,000. In addition, Lee held the following items in its safe on December 31:

Check payable to Lee Corporation, dated January 2, 2010, not included in December 31 checkbook balance	$1,000
Check payable to Lee Corporation, deposited December 20, and included in December 31 checkbook balance, but returned by bank on December 30, stamped "NSF." The check was redeposited January 2, 2010, and cleared January 7	200
Postage stamps received from mail order customers	75
Check drawn on Lee Corporation's account, payable to a vendor, dated and recorded December 31, but not mailed until January 15, 2010	500

The proper amount to be shown as Cash on Lee's balance sheet at December 31, 2009, is
a. $3,800
b. $4,000
c. $4,300
d. $4,875

13. The books of Curtis Company for the year ended December 31, 2009, showed income of $360,000 before provision for income tax. In computing the taxable income for federal income tax purposes, the following differences were taken into account:

Depreciation deducted for tax purposes in excess of depreciation recorded on the books	$16,000
Royalty income reported for tax purposes in excess of royalty income recognized on the books	12,000

Assuming a corporate income tax rate of 40%, what should Curtis record as its current federal income tax liability at December 31, 2009?
a. $137,600
b. $142,400
c. $144,000
d. $145,600

14. Walker, Inc., a US corporation, ordered a machine from Nippon Corporation of Japan on July 15, 2009, for 1,000,000 yen when the spot rate for yen was 95 yen to the US dollar. Nippon shipped the machine on September 1, 2009, and billed Walker for 1,000,000 yen. The spot rate was 97 yen to the US dollar on this date. Walker bought 1,000,000 yen and paid the invoice on October 25, 2009, when the spot rate was 100 to the US dollar. In Walker's income statement for the year ended December 31, 2009, how much should be reported as foreign exchange gain?
a. $0
b. $217.04
c. $526.32
d. $743.36

15. On July 1, 2009, Jasmine Corporation borrowed $30,000 from the bank on a 5-year note. On July 5, Jasmine used the money as a down payment to buy equipment costing $50,000.

On the statement of cash flows for the year ending December 31, 2009, how should Jasmine disclose the July transactions?
a. Operating activities $20,000 decrease; investing activities $50,000 increase.
b. Investing activities $50,000 decrease; financing activities $50,000 increase.
c. Investing activities, $30,000 increase; financing activities $50,000 increase.
d. Investing activities $50,000 decrease; financing activities $30,000 increase.

16. Howard Co. incurred research and development costs in 2009 as follows:

Materials used in research and development projects	$ 400,000
Equipment acquired that will have alternate future uses in future research and development projects	2,000,000
Depreciation for 2009 on above equipment	500,000
Personnel costs of persons involved in research and development projects	1,000,000
Consulting fees paid to outsiders for research and development projects	100,000
Indirect costs reasonably allocable to research and development projects	200,000
	$4,200,000

The amount of research and development costs charged to Howard's 2009 income statement should be
a. $1,500,000
b. $1,700,000
c. $2,200,000
d. $3,500,000

17. Kay Company, a lessor of office machines, purchased a new machine for $600,000 on January 1, 2009, which was leased the same day to Lee. The machine will be depreciated $55,000 per year. The lease is for a four-year period expiring January 1, 2013, and provides for annual rental payments of $100,000 beginning January 1, 2009. Additionally, Lee paid $64,000 to Kay as a lease bonus. In its 2009 income statement, what amount of revenue and expense should Kay report on this leased asset?

	Revenue	*Expense*
a.	$100,000	$0
b.	$116,000	$0
c.	$116,000	$55,000
d.	$164,000	$55,000

18. In January 2009 Bell Company exchanged an old machine, with a book value of $39,000 and a fair value of $35,000, and paid $10,000 cash for a similar used machine having a list price of $50,000. The transaction has commercial substance. At what amount should the machine acquired in the exchange be recorded on the books of Bell?
a. $45,000
b. $46,000
c. $49,000
d. $50,000

19. During the course of your audit of the financial statements of H Co., a new client, for the year ended December 31, 2009, you discover the following:

- Inventory at January 1, 2009, had been overstated by $3,000.
- Inventory at December 31, 2009, was understated by $5,000.

• An insurance policy covering three years had been purchased on January 2, 2008, for $1,500. The entire amount was charged as an expense in 2008.

During 2009 the company received a $1,000 cash advance from a customer for merchandise to be manufactured and shipped during 2010. The $1,000 had been credited to sales revenues. The company's gross profit on sales is 50%.

Net income reported on the 2009 income statement (before reflecting any adjustments for the above items) is $20,000.

The proper net income for 2009 is
a. $26,500
b. $23,500
c. $16,500
d. $20,500

20. The following information is available for Cooke Company for 2009:

Net sales	$1,800,000
Freight-in	45,000
Purchase discounts	25,000
Ending inventory	120,000

The gross margin is 40% of net sales. What is an estimate of cost of goods available for sale?
a. $ 840,000
b. $ 960,000
c. $1,200,000
d. $1,220,000

21. Warrants exercisable at $20 each to obtain 10,000 shares of common stock were outstanding during a period when the average market price of the common stock was $25. Application of the treasury stock method for the assumed exercise of these warrants in computing diluted earnings per share will increase the weighted-average number of outstanding common stock shares by
a. 8,000
b. 8,333
c. 2,000
d. 1,667

22. Greg Corp. reported revenue of $1,250,000 in its accrual-basis income statement for the year ended June 30, 2009. Additional information was as follows:

Accounts receivable June 30, 2008	$400,000
Accounts receivable June 30, 2009	530,000
Uncollectible accounts written off during the fiscal year	15,000

Under the cash basis, Greg should report revenue of
a. $ 835,000
b. $ 850,000
c. $1,105,000
d. $1,135,000

23. On January 1, 2009, Mann Company's allowance for doubtful accounts had a credit balance of $30,000. During 2009 Mann charged $64,000 to doubtful accounts expense, wrote off $46,000 of uncollectible accounts receivable, and unexpectedly recovered $12,000 of bad debts written off in the prior year. The allowance for doubtful accounts balance at December 31, 2009, would be
a. $48,000
b. $60,000
c. $64,000
d. $94,000

24. Greene Company bought a patent from White Company on January 1, 2009, for $102,000. An independent research consultant retained by Greene estimated that the remaining useful life of the patent was four years. Its remaining legal life was six years. Its unamortized cost on White's books at January 1, 2009, was $30,000. How much should be amortized by Greene for the year ended December 31, 2009?
a. $ 5,000
b. $ 7,500
c. $17,000
d. $25,500

25. On January 1, 2009, Harry Corporation sold equipment costing $2,000,000 with accumulated depreciation of $500,000 to Anna Corporation, its wholly owned subsidiary, for $1,800,000. Harry was depreciating the equipment on the straight-line method over twenty years with no salvage value, which Anna continued. In consolidation at December 31, 2009, the cost and accumulated depreciation, respectively, should be
a. $1,500,000 and $100,000
b. $1,800,000 and $100,000
c. $2,000,000 and $100,000
d. $2,000,000 and $600,000

26. A loss that is material, unusual in nature, and infrequent in occurrence should be reported as
a. Part of continuing operations.
b. Part of discontinued operations.
c. An extraordinary item.
d. A prior period item.

27. According to ASC Topic 250, *Accounting Changes and Error Corrections* (SFAS 154), a change in the liability for warranty costs requires
a. Presenting prior period financial statements as previously reported.
b. Presenting the effect of pro forma data on income and earnings per share for all prior periods presented.
c. Restating the financial statements of all prior periods presented.
d. Reporting current and future financial statements on the new basis.

28. Items reported as prior period adjustments
a. Do not include the effect of a mistake in the application of accounting principles as this is accounted for as a change in accounting principle rather than as a prior period adjustment.
b. Do not affect the presentation of prior period comparative financial statements.
c. Do not require further disclosure in the body of the financial statements.
d. Are reflected as adjustments of the opening balance of the retained earnings of the earliest period presented.

Questions 29 and 30 are based on the following information. Patterson Company has the following information on one of its vehicles purchased on January 1, 2007:

Vehicle cost	$50,000
Useful life, years, estimated	5
Useful life, miles, estimated	100,000
Salvage value, estimated	$10,000
Actual miles driven, 2007	30,000
2008	20,000
2009	15,000

No estimates were changed during the life of the asset.

29. The 2009 depreciation expense for the vehicle using the sum-of-the-years' digits (SYD) method was

    a. $ 6,000
    b. $ 8,000
    c. $10,000
    d. $13,333

30. The fiscal 2008 year-end accumulated depreciation balance, using the double-declining balance method was

    a. $12,000
    b. $16,000
    c. $25,600
    d. $32,000

FINANCIAL ACCOUNTING AND REPORTING

TESTLET 3 ANSWERS

1. b	6. c	11. a	16. c	21. c	26. c
2. a	7. b	12. c	17. c	22. c	27. d
3. c	8. c	13. b	18. a	23. b	28. d
4. b	9. c	14. b	19. a	24. d	29. b
5. a	10. c	15. d	20. c	25. d	30. d

Hints for Multiple-Choice Questions

1. Spending of funds results in decrease in restricted assets.

2. Statement of activities focuses on operations.

3. Original budget, final budget, and actual inflows, outflows, and balances.

4. Water enterprise and pension fund are excluded.

5. Unrestricted net assets must be shown.

6. Most recent purchases go to CGS first, reducing income and matching current costs to revenues.

7. What is debt?

8. Recall the account to be debited.

9. How is lender's investment affected by these?

10. Recognize compensation for stock options.

11. The direct method is **not** based on net income, which includes gains and losses.

12. Postdated check should be excluded.

13. Deduct excess tax depreciation from book income.

14. Walker was billed at $.4875, but only had to pay $.4855.

15. Borrowing from the bank increases cash from financing activities by $30,000; purchasing equipment decreases cash by the amount of the purchase $50,000.

16. Only intangibles or fixed assets purchased from others having alternative future uses may be deferred.

17. The bonus is amortized over the lease term.

18. Losses are **always** recognized when FV is determinable.

19. The portion of the cash advance representing income = **unearned** revenues.

20. Freight-in and discounts are already included in cost of sales and ending inventory.

21. Calculate number of shares that could be reacquired with proceeds.

22. The entry to write off bad debts debits the allowance account (not expense).

23. A recovery is charged back to the allowance account.

24. Review Module 9, Sec. J.

25. Intercompany transactions must be eliminated.

26. What are unusual and infrequent items?

27. Warranty liabilities are estimated liabilities.

28. Prior period adjustments result in restatement.

29. Ratio is three-fifteenths.

30. DDB rate is equal to 40%.

Explanations

1. (b) The expenditure results in $650,000 being released from the temporarily restricted assets category.

2. (a) The statement of activities is designed to provide information to assess operational accountability.

3. (c) The minimum disclosure is the original budget, the final budget, and actual inflows, outflows and balances on a budgetary basis.

4. (b) The change in net assets for governmental activities would include the increase in the fund balances of governmental funds ($25,000) and the motor pool internal service fund. The amount for the water enterprise fund would be presented in business-type activities and the employee pension fund change would be presented in the fiduciary fund statement.

5. (a) This is allowed as long as the changes in net assets for each class are reported.

6. (c) FIFO cost assignment typically parallels the flow of goods, not LIFO.

7. (b) If the exchange of an asset does not meet the criteria for a sale, the transaction should be treated as a secured borrowing with pledged collateral.

8. (c) The amount of revenue recognized is added to construction in progress.

9. (c) In calculating the carrying amount of a loan, the lender deducts from the principle the loan origination fees charged to the borrower but not direct loan origination costs incurred by the lender.

10. (c) Compensation expense is measured at fair value, generally with the use of an option pricing model.

11. (a) The gain is included in the proceeds from the sale of the security in the investing activities section only. Since the operating section under the direct method does not start with net income, the gain would not be presented in the operating section.

12. (c) Cash is equal to $4,300 ($4,000 in the account – $200 NSF check + $500 postdated check).

13. (b) The current tax liability is equal to $142,400 ([$360,000 – $16,000 + $14,000] × 40%).

14. (b) The gain is the difference between the exchange rate when the machine title passed (shipping date) and the exchange rate when the liability is paid. Therefore the gain is equal to $309.28 [(1,000,000 yen ÷ 97 per dollar) – (1,000,000 yen ÷ 100 per dollar)].

15. (d) The transactions would be shown as investing activities ($50,000 decrease for the machine purchase) and financing activities ($30,000 for the loan from the bank).

16. (c) The total research and development costs would equal $2,200,000 ($400,000 materials + $500,000 depreciation + $1,000,000 personnel costs + $100,000 consulting fees + $200,000 indirect costs).

17. (c) Revenue is equal to $116,000 [$100,000 + ($64,000 ÷ 4 years)], and expense is equal to $55,000 depreciation.

18. (a) The machine should be recorded at the fair value of the consideration given or $45,000 ($35,000 + $10,000). The list price does not usually reflect the fair value of an item.

19. (a) The proper amount of income is equal to $26,500 ($20,000 + $3,000 overstatement of beginning inventory + $5,000 understatement of ending inventory – $500 insurance expense – $1,000 overstatement of revenue).

20. (c) Cost of goods available for sale is equal to cost of goods sold plus ending inventory. Cost of goods sold would be estimated to be $1,080,000 ($1,800,000 × 60%). Therefore, an estimate of cost of goods available for sale would be $1,2000,000 ($1,080,000 cost of goods sold + $120,000 ending inventory).

21. (c) The treasury stock method results in 2,000 additional shares [(10,000 × $20) ÷ $25].

22. (c) The cash basis revenue is equal to $1,105,000 ($1,250,000 + $400,000 – $530,000 – $15,000).

23. (b) The amount of the allowance for uncollectible accounts is $60,000 ($30,000 + $64,000 – $46,000 + $12,000).

24. (d) The amortization expense is equal to $25,500 ($102,000 ÷ 4 years).

25. (d) The cost and accumulated depreciation is equal to $2,000,000 and $600,000, respectively. On the consolidated financial statements the asset would have Harry's cost and accumulated depreciation.

26. (c) An extraordinary gain or loss is one that is unusual and infrequent in occurrence.

27. (d) A change in warranty liability is accounted for on a prospective basis.

28. (d) Prior period adjustments are reflected as adjustments to the opening balance of retained earnings of the earliest period presented.

29. (b) The depreciation expense under the sum-of-the-years' digits method is $8,000 [($50,000 – $10,000) × 3/15].

30. (d) The accumulated depreciation balance using the double-declining balance method is equal to $32,000 [($50,000 × 40%) + ($30,000 × 40%)].

SIMULATION PROBLEM 1   (50 to 55 minutes)

Situation				
	Property, Plant, and Equipment	Depreciation	Communication	Research

At December 31, 2008, Cord Company's plant asset and accumulated depreciation accounts had balances as follows:

Category	Plant assets	Accumulated depreciation
Land	$ 175,000	$ --
Building	1,500,000	328,900
Automobiles and trucks	172,000	100,325

Depreciation methods and useful lives

Buildings—150% declining balance; twenty-five years.
Automobiles and trucks—150% declining balance; five years, all acquired after 2002.
Depreciation is computed to the nearest month.
The salvage values of the depreciable assets are immaterial.

Transactions during 2009 and other information

On January 6, 2009, a plant facility consisting of land and building was acquired from King Corp. in exchange for 25,000 shares of Cord's common stock. On this date, Cord's stock has a market price of $50 a share. Current assessed values of land and building for property tax purposes are $187,500 and $562,500, respectively.

- On August 30, 2009, Cord purchased a new automobile for $12,500.
- On September 30, 2009, a truck with a cost of $24,000 and a carrying amount of $9,100 on date of sale was sold for $11,500. Depreciation for the nine months ended September 30, 2009, was $2,650.
- On November 4, 2009, Cord purchased for $350,000 a tract of land as a potential future building site.

Situation	Property, Plant, and Equipment			
		Depreciation	Communication	Research

Complete the following spreadsheet analyzing the changes in each of the plant asset accounts during 2009. Show supporting calculations in the space provided below the table.

	A	B	C	D	E	F	G
1	Cord Company						
2	ANALYSIS OF CHANGES IN PLANT ASSETS						
3	For the Year Ended December 31, 2009						
4							
5		Beginning				Ending	
6	Item	Balance	Additions		Disposals	Balance	
7							
8	Land	$175,000		[1]			
9	Buildings	$1,500,000		[1]			
10	Automobiles & Trucks	$172,000					
11		$1,847,000					
12							

Supporting Calculations:

	Situation	Property, Plant, and Equipment	Depreciation	Communication	Research

For each asset category, complete the following spreadsheet showing the amounts as indicated. **Round computations to the nearest whole dollar.** Show supporting calculations in the space provided.

	A	B	C	D	E	F	G
1	Cord Company						
2	ANALYSIS OF CHANGES IN PLANT ASSETS & DEPRECIATION						
3	For the Year Ended December 31, 2009						
4			Accumulated		Accumulated		
5			Depreciation	Current Year	Depreciation	Book	
6	Item	Cost	1/1/2009	Depreciation	12/31/2009	Value	
7							
8	Land						
9	Buildings						
10	Automobiles & Trucks						
11							
12							

Supporting Calculations:

	Situation	Property, Plant, and Equipment	Depreciation	Communication	Research

Cord Company's controller, Linda Heinz, wants a memorandum prepared providing the theoretical justification for use of accelerated methods of depreciation for presentation to the audit committee of the board of directors. Prepare the memorandum requested by Ms. Heinz.

REMINDER: Your response will be graded for both technical content and writing skills. Technical content will be evaluated for information that is helpful to the intended reader and clearly relevant to the issue. Writing skills will be evaluated for development, organization, and the appropriate expression of ideas in professional correspondence. Use a standard business memo or letter format with a clear beginning, middle, and end. Do not convey information in the form of a table, bullet point list, or other abbreviated presentation.

To: Ms. Linda Heinz
        Controller
From: CPA Candidate

	Situation	Property, Plant, and Equipment	Depreciation	Communication	Research

Research the issue of the capitalization of interest on self-constructed assets. Input the reference to professional standards that provides guidance on the type of assets that qualify.

SOLUTION TO SIMULATION PROBLEM 1

Situation	Property, Plant, and Equipment		Depreciation	Communication	Research

	A	B	C	D	E	F	G
1	Cord Company						
2	ANALYSIS OF CHANGES IN PLANT ASSETS						
3	For the Year Ended December 31, 2009						
4							
5		Beginning				Ending	
6	Item	Balance	Additions		Disposals	Balance	
7							
8	Land	$175,000	$312,500	[1]	$--	$487,500	
9	Buildings	1,500,000	937,500	[1]	--	2,437,500	
10	Automobiles & Trucks	172,000	12,500		24,000	160,500	
11		$1,847,000	$1,262,500		$24,000	$3,085,500	
12							

Explanation of amounts

[1]   Plant facility acquired from King 1/6/09—
          allocation to Land and Building

Fair value—25,000 shares of Cord common stock at $50 market price		$1,250,000

Allocation in proportion to appraised
values at the exchange date

	Amount	% to total
Land	$187,500	25
Building	562,500	75
	$750,000	100

Land	($1,250,000 × 25%)	$ 312,500
Building	($1,250,000 × 75%)	937,500
		$1,250,000

Situation	Property, Plant, and Equipment	Depreciation		Communication	Research

Cord Company
DEPRECIATION EXPENSE
For the Year Ended December 31, 2009

Building		
Carrying amount		$1,171,100
Building acquired 1/6/09		937,500
Total amount subject to depreciation		2,108,600
150% declining balance rate [(100% ÷ 25) × 1.5]		× ____6%
Depreciation on buildings for 2009		$126,516
Automobiles and trucks		
Carrying amount, 1/1/09 ($172,000 – $100,325)	$ 71,675	
Deduct carrying amount, 1/1/09 on		
truck sold 9/30/09 ($9,100 + $2,650)	11,750	
Amount subject to depreciation	59,925	
150% declining balance rate [(100% ÷ 5) × 1.5]	× ____30%	17,978
Automobile purchased 8/30/09	12,500	
Depreciation for 2009 (30% × 4/12)	× ____10%	1,250
Truck sold 9/30/09—depreciation		
for 2009 (1/1 to 9/30/09)		2,650
Depreciation on automobiles and trucks for 2009		$ 21,878
Total depreciation expense for 2009		$148,394

	A	B	C	D	E	F	G
1	Cord Company						
2	ANALYSIS OF PLANT ASSETS & DEPRECIATION						
3	For the Year Ended December 31, 2009						
4			Accumulated		Accumulated	Book	
5			Depreciation	Current Year	Depreciation	Value	
6	Item	Cost	1/1/2009	Depreciation	12/31/2009	12/31/2009	
7							
8	Land	$487,500	$0	$0	$0	$487,500	
9	Buildings	$2,437,500	$328,900	$126,516	$455,416	$1,982,084	
10	Automobiles & Trucks	$160,500	$100,325	$21,878	$122,203	$38,297	
11		$3,085,500	$429,225	$148,394	$577,619	$2,507,881	
12							

Situation	Property, Plant, and Equipment	Depreciation	Communication	Research

Ms. Linda Heinz
Controller
Cord Company

January 15, 2010

Dear Ms. Heinz:

This memorandum is in response to your request for a discussion of the theoretical justification for accelerated methods of depreciation. Accelerated methods of depreciation are justified based on the two assumptions. First, an asset is more efficient in the earlier years of its life. Therefore, larger depreciation charges in the earlier years would be matched with the larger revenues generated from that asset in those years. Second, repair expenses on an asset increase in the later years of its life. Therefore, smaller depreciation charges in the later years combined with the larger repair expenses in those years would result in a smooth or level pattern of total expenses of operating the asset over its useful life.

If you have any additional questions regarding this issue, please contact me.

Situation	Property, Plant, and Equipment	Depreciation	Communication	Research

ASC 835-20-15-5 through 8 (SFAS 34, paragraphs 9-11)

SIMULATION PROBLEM 2   (45 to 50 minutes)

Situation	Financial Statement Amounts	Stockholders' Equity	Per Share Amounts	Research and Communication

Moxley Co. is a publicly held company whose shares are traded in the over-the-counter market. The stockholders' equity accounts at December 31, 2008, had the following balances:

Preferred stock, $100 par value, 6% cumulative; 5,000 shares authorized; 2,000 issued and outstanding	$ 200,00
Common stock, $1 par value, 150,000 shares authorized; 100,000 issued and outstanding	100,00
Additional paid-in capital	800,000
Retained earnings	1,586,000
Total stockholders' equity	$2,686,000

Transactions during 2009 and other information relating to the stockholders' equity accounts were as follows:

- February 1, 2009—Issued 13,000 shares of common stock to Ram Co. in exchange for land. On the date issued, the stock had a market price of $11 per share. The land had a carrying value on Ram's books for $135,000, and an assessed value for property taxes of $90,000.

- March 1, 2009—Purchased 5,000 shares of its own commons stock to be held as treasury stock for $14 per share. Moxley uses the cost method to account for treasury stock. Transactions in treasury stock are legal in Moxley's state of incorporation.

- May 10, 2009—Declared a property dividend of marketable securities held by Moxley to common shareholders. The securities had a carrying value of $600,000; fair value on relevant dates were

Date of declaration (May 10, 2009)	$720,000
Date of record (May 25, 2009)	758,000
Date of distribution (June 1, 2009)	736,000

- October 1, 2009—Reissued 2,000 shares of treasury stock for $16 per share.

- November 4, 2009—Declared a cash dividend of $1.50 per share to all common shareholders of record November 15, 2009.

- December 20, 2009—Declared the required annual cash dividend on preferred stock for 2009. The dividend was paid on January 5, 2010.

- January 16, 2010—Before closing the accounting records for 2009, Moxley became aware that no amortization had been recorded for 2008 for a patent purchased on July 1, 2008. Amortization expense was properly recorded in 2009. The patent was properly capitalized at $320,000 and had an estimated useful life of eight year when purchased. Moxley's income tax rate is 30%. The appropriate correcting entry was recorded on the same day.

- Adjusted net income for 2009 was $838,000.

Items 1 through 8 represent amounts to be reported in Moxley's financial statements. **Items 9 and 10** represent other financial information. For all items, calculate the amounts requested. On the CPA exam, a list of numeric answers would be provided for the candidate to select from.

	Financial Statement Amounts	Stockholders' Equity	Per Share Amounts	Research and Communication
Situation				

Items 1 through 4 represent amounts to be reported on Moxley's 2009 statement of retained earnings.

1. Prior period adjustment.

2. Preferred dividends.

3. Common dividends—cash.

4. Common dividends—property.

	Financial Statement Amounts	Stockholders' Equity	Per Share Amounts	Research and Communication
Situation				

Items 1 through 4 represent amounts to be reported on Moxley's statement of stockholders' equity at December 31, 2009.

1. Number of common shares issued at December 31, 2009.

2. Amount of common stock issued.

3. Additional paid-in capital, including treasury stock transactions.

4. Treasury stock.

Situation	Financial Statement Amounts	Stockholders' Equity	Per Share Amounts	Research and Communication

Items 1 and 2 represent other financial information for 2008 and 2009.

1. Book value per share at December 31, 2008, before prior period adjustment.

2. Numerator used in calculation of 2009 basic earnings per share for the year.

Situation	Financial Statement Amounts	Stockholders' Equity	Per Share Amounts	Research and Communication

Research the professional standards and write a memo to the files describing the appropriate accounting for the issuance of a stock dividend.

REMINDER: Your response will be graded for both technical content and writing skills. Technical content will be evaluated for information that is helpful to the intended reader and clearly relevant to the issue. Writing skills will be evaluated for development, organization, and the appropriate expression of ideas in professional correspondence. Use a standard business memo or letter format with a clear beginning, middle, and end. Do not convey information in the form of a table, bullet point list, or other abbreviated presentation.

To: Client files
From: CPA Candidate

SOLUTION TO SIMULATION PROBLEM 2

Situation				
	Financial Statement Amounts	Stockholders' Equity	Per Share Amounts	Research and Communication

This problem is a collection of miscellaneous stockholders' equity problems. The candidate should start the problem by scanning the required information to determine the amounts to be calculated. While scanning, the candidate should recognize that some of the required items are related, such as 2 (preferred dividends) and 10 (numerator used in calculating EPS) and 5 (number of common shares issued) and 6 (amount of common stock issued); 7 (additional paid-in capital) and 8 (treasury stock). These relationships require that the candidate label each answer so that it will be possible to quickly find that answer when it is used in a subsequent problem.

Unlike many previous exam problems, the order of the information concerning the transactions does not coincide with the order of the required answers. This arrangement makes it necessary to read the required amount and then hunt for the transaction information needed to calculate that required amount.

	Financial Statement Amounts			
Situation		Stockholders' Equity	Per Share Amounts	Research and Communication

1.   **($14,000)** Prior period adjustment is the term generally applied to corrections of errors of prior periods. In this problem no amortization had been recorded in a prior year—an error. Since this is not a self-correcting error, it still existed in 2009. The calculation is cost ($320,000) ÷ useful life (eight years) for 1/2 year (purchased July 1). Prior period adjustments are disclosed net of tax (30%). $320,000/8 × 1/2 × (1 − .3) = $14,000. An adjustment is made to the opening balance of retained earnings in 2009. In addition, the financial statements of the prior period are restated to reflect the correct amounts of assets and liabilities at the beginning of the first period presented. Financial statements for each prior period are adjusted to reflect the correction of the period-specific effects of the error.

2.   **($12,000)** Preferred dividends are 6% and cumulative. They were declared during 2009 and paid in 2010. The declaration is sufficient to record and recognize the dividends legally; they do not have to be paid in the current year to be recognized during that time period. These dividends will be used in the numerator in question 10 when calculating the 2009 EPS. Since these dividends are cumulative, they would be used in the calculation of EPS even if they had not been declared. The amount of preferred dividends is derived by multiplying the par value of the stock by its rate. 6% × $200,000 par = $12,000 dividends.

3.   **($165,000)** Common dividends—cash is calculated by the formula: Common shares outstanding × Dividend per share. In this problem the number of shares outstanding is affected by the beginning shares (100,000), shares issued (13,000), and treasury shares purchased and sold (5,000 purchased, 2,000 sold) prior to the dividend date of November 4. 100,000 + 13,000 − 5,000 + 2,000 = 110,000 shares outstanding × dividend rate $1.50 = $165,000.

4.   **($720,000)** Common dividends—property differ from cash dividends because the property may be carried in the accounts at an amount which does not equal its fair value (cash is always at its fair value). Management intends to distribute the property at its fair value, therefore it is necessary to bring the property to fair value on the date management is legally forced to distribute it (the declaration date). Value fluctuations beyond that date are irrelevant.

		Stockholders' Equity		
Situation	Financial Statement Amounts		Per Share Amounts	Research and Communication

1.   **(113,000)** The number of shares issued differs from the number of shares outstanding which was used in question 3. Shares issued include those outstanding as well as those held in the treasury. Shares outstanding from question 3, 110,000 plus 3,000 treasury shares = 113,000 shares.

2.   **($113,000)** Amount of common stock issued—This question takes the answer from question 5 (113,000 shares) and multiplies that figure by the par value of each share, $1.

3.   **($934,000)** The additional paid-in capital, including treasury stock transactions, is derived by adding the beginning balance ($800,000) to the excess ($10) of issue price ($11) over par value ($1) for the shares issued (13,000) to acquire land on February 1, 2009. In addition, the sale of the treasury stock (2,000 shares) at an amount ($16) greater than cost ($14) gives rise to a nonoperating gain that cannot be included in net income since it was both not related to operations and is a transaction in the company's own stock. $800,000 + (13,000 × $10) + (2,000 × $16 − $14) = $934,000.

4.   **($42,000)** Treasury stock—Since the Moxley Co. follows the cost method of accounting for treasury stock, this answer is derived by multiplying the shares of treasury stock (3,000) by their cost ($14). 3,000 × $14 = $42,000.

Situation	Financial Statement Amounts	Stockholders' Equity	Per Share Amounts	Research and Communication

1. **($24.86)** Book value per share is a concept that relates common stockholders' equity to shares of common stock. The "per share" referred to is always the **common** shares unless the problem states some other type of shares. In this case it is to be calculated before the prior period adjustment. It is necessary to subtract preferred stock's total liquidating value ($100 × 2,000 sh = $200,000) from total stockholders' equity ($2,686,000) to obtain common stockholders' equity. In this problem no liquidating value is given, so par value is used. The resulting amount ($2,686,000 – $200,000 = $2,486,000) is divided by the common shares outstanding (100,000) to obtain book value per share ($24.86). ($2,686,000 – $200,000) ÷ 100,000 = $24.86.

2. **($826,000)** The formula for calculating earnings per share is (NI – Preferred dividends) ÷ Wtd-avg. shares outstanding. The numerator is income available to common stockholders. The problem states that adjusted net income for 2009 was $838,000. The word "adjusted" tells the candidate that net income includes all information concerning transactions in the problem and need not be changed in any way. Preferred dividends ($12,000) were calculated in question 2. $838,000 – $12,000 = $826,000.

Situation	Financial Statement Amounts	Stockholders' Equity	Per Share Amounts	Research and Communication

To: Client files
From: CPA Candidate

This memorandum is designed to document the appropriate accounting treatment for stock dividends. The proper accounting for a stock dividend depends on its size. Small stock dividends of less than 20 to 25% of the shares outstanding involve the capitalization of retained earnings in an amount equal to the fair value of the shares issued. A large stock dividend of more than 20 to 25% of the shares outstanding should involve a capitalization of retained earnings in an amount equal to the par value of the shares issued. Guidance for this issue is found in ASC Topic 505 (ARB 43, Chapter 7b).

REGULATION

TESTLET 1

1. Which of the following statements best describes the ethical standard of the profession pertaining to advertising and solicitation?

    a. All forms of advertising and solicitation are prohibited.

    b. There are **no** prohibitions regarding the manner in which CPAs may solicit new business.

    c. A CPA may advertise in any manner that is **not** false, misleading, or deceptive.

    d. A CPA may only solicit new clients through mass mailings.

2. Burrow & Co., CPAs, have provided annual audit and tax compliance services to Mare Corp. for several years. Mare has been unable to pay Burrow in full for services Burrow rendered nineteen months ago. Burrow is ready to begin fieldwork for the current year's audit. Under the ethical standards of the profession, which of the following arrangements will permit Burrow to begin the fieldwork on Mare's audit?

    a. Mare sets up a two-year payment plan with Burrow to settle the unpaid fee balance.

    b. Mare commits to pay the past due fee in full before the audit report is issued.

    c. Mare gives Burrow an eighteen-month note payable for the full amount of the past due fees before Burrow begins the audit.

    d. Mare engages another firm to perform the fieldwork, and Burrow is limited to reviewing the workpapers and issuing the audit report.

3. Which of the following is not a covered member for purposes of application of the independence requirements of the AICPA Code of Professional Conduct?

    a. A staff person on the attest team.

    b. A staff person that performs tax services for the attest client.

    c. The partner in charge of the firm office that performs the attest engagement.

    d. A partner that performs extensive consulting services for the attest client.

4. CPAs must be concerned with their responsibilities in the performance of professional services. In performing an audit, a CPA

    a. Is strictly liable for failure to exercise due professional care.

    b. Is strictly liable for failure to detect management fraud.

    c. Is **not** liable unless the CPA is found to be grossly negligent.

    d. Is strictly liable for failure to detect illegal acts.

5. The Apex Surety Company wrote a general fidelity bond covering defalcations by the employees of Watson, Inc. Thereafter, Grand, an employee of Watson, embezzled $18,900 of company funds. When his activities were discovered, Apex paid Watson the full amount in accordance with the terms of the fidelity bond, and then sought recovery against Watson's auditors, Kane & Dobbs, CPAs. Which of the following would be Kane & Dobbs' best defense?

    a. Apex is not in privity of contract.

    b. The shortages were the result of clever forgeries and collusive fraud that would not be detected by an examination made in accordance with generally accepted auditing standards.

    c. Kane & Dobbs were not guilty either of gross negligence or fraud.

    d. Kane & Dobbs were not aware of the Apex-Watson surety relationship.

6. If a stockholder sues a CPA for common law fraud based on false statements contained in the financial statements audited by the CPA, which of the following, if present, would be the CPA's best defense?

    a. The stockholder lacks privity to sue.

    b. The false statements were immaterial.

    c. The CPA did **not** financially benefit from the alleged fraud.

    d. The contributory negligence of the client.

7. Mathews is an agent for Sears with the express authority to solicit orders from customers in a geographic area assigned by Sears. Mathews has no authority to grant discounts or to collect payment on orders solicited. Mathews secured an order from Davidson for $1,000 less a 10% discount if Davidson makes immediate payment. Davidson had previously done business with Sears through Mathews but this was the first time that a discount-payment offer had been made. Davidson gave Mathews a check for $900 and, thereafter, Mathews turned in both the check and the order to Sears. The order clearly indicated that a 10% discount had been given by Mathews. Sears shipped the order and cashed the check. Later, Sears attempted to collect $100 as the balance owed on the order from Davidson. Which of the following is correct?

    a. Sears can collect the $100 from Davidson because Mathews contracted outside the scope of his express or implied authority.

    b. Sears **cannot** collect the $100 from Davidson because Mathews, as an agent with express authority to solicit orders, had implied authority to give discounts and collect.

    c. Sears **cannot** collect the $100 from Davidson as Sears has ratified the discount granted and made to Mathews.

    d. Sears **cannot** collect the $100 from Davidson because, although Mathews had **no** express or implied authority to grant a discount and collect, Mathews had apparent authority to do so.

8. Which of the following regarding workers' compensation is correct?

    a. A purpose of workers' compensation is for the employer to assume a definite liability in exchange for the employee giving up his common law rights.

    b. It applies to workers engaged in or affecting interstate commerce only.

    c. It is optional in most jurisdictions.

    d. Once workers' compensation has been adopted by the employer, the amount of damages recoverable is based upon comparative negligence.

9. Regulation D of the Securities Act of 1933 is available to issuers without regard to the dollar amount of an offering only when the
   a. Purchasers are all accredited investors.
   b. Number of purchasers who are nonaccredited is thirty-five or less.
   c. Issuer is **not** a reporting company under the Securities Exchange Act of 1934.
   d. Issuer is **not** an investment company.

10. During an audit of Actee Corporation, you examine the following:

- A check that is postdated and also says "Pay to Actee Corporation." You are concerned about these two issues but note that all other elements of negotiability are present in the check.
- A note that is payable on demand and says "Pay to Actee Corporation" on its face. You see that all other issues about negotiability are satisfied.

You question whether or not the issues raised above destroy negotiability of these two instruments. Which of the instruments is(are) negotiable instruments?

	The check	*The note*
a.	Yes	Yes
b.	Yes	No
c.	No	Yes
d.	No	No

11. Nat purchased a typewriter from Rob. Rob is not in the business of selling typewriters. Rob tendered delivery of the typewriter after receiving payment in full from Nat. Nat informed Rob that he was unable to take possession of the typewriter at that time, but would return later that day. Before Nat returned, the typewriter was destroyed by a fire. The risk of loss
   a. Passed to Nat upon Rob's tender of delivery.
   b. Remained with Rob, since Nat had not yet received the typewriter.
   c. Passed to Nat at the time the contract was formed and payment was made.
   d. Remained with Rob, since title had **not** yet passed to Nat.

12. Marco Auto Inc. made many untrue statements in the course of inducing Rockford to purchase a used auto for $3,500. The car in question turned out to have some serious faults. Which of the following untrue statements made by Marco should Rockford use in seeking recovery from Marco for breach of warranty?
   a. "I refused a $3,800 offer for this very same auto from another buyer last week."
   b. "This auto is one of the best autos we have for sale."
   c. "At this price the auto is a real steal."
   d. "I can guarantee that you will never regret this purchase."

13. On April 14, 2007, Seeley Corp. entered into a written agreement to sell to Boone Corp. 1,200 cartons of certain goods at $.40 per carton, delivery within thirty days. The agreement contained no other terms. On April 15, 2007, Boone and Seeley orally agreed to modify their April 14 agreement so that the new quantity specified was 1,500 cartons, same price and delivery terms. What is the status of this modification?

   a. Enforceable.
   b. Unenforceable under the statute of frauds.
   c. Unenforceable for lack of consideration.
   d. Unenforceable because the change is substantial.

14. Purdy purchased real property from Hart and received a warranty deed with full covenants. Recordation of this deed is
   a. Not necessary if the deed provides that recordation is not required.
   b. Necessary to vest the purchaser's legal title to the property conveyed.
   c. Required primarily for the purpose of providing the local taxing authorities with the information necessary to assess taxes.
   d. Irrelevant if the subsequent party claiming superior title had actual notice of the unrecorded deed.

15. Peters defaulted on a purchase money mortgage held by Fairmont Realty. Fairmont's attempts to obtain payment have been futile and the mortgage payments are several months in arrears. Consequently, Fairmont decided to resort to its rights against the property. Fairmont foreclosed on the mortgage. Peters has all of the following rights **except**
   a. To remain in possession as long as his equity in the property exceeds the amount of debt.
   b. An equity of redemption.
   c. To refinance the mortgage with another lender and repay the original mortgage.
   d. A statutory right of redemption.

16. Richard Brown, who retired on May 31, 2009, receives a monthly pension benefit of $700 payable for life. His life expectancy at the date of retirement is ten years. The first pension check was received on June 15, 2009. During his years of employment, Brown contributed $12,000 to the cost of his company's pension plan. How much of the pension amounts received may Brown exclude from taxable income for the years 2009, 2010, and 2011?

	2009	*2010*	*2011*
a.	$0	$0	$0
b.	$4,900	$4,900	$4,900
c.	$ 700	$1,200	$1,200
d.	$4,900	$8,400	$8,400

17. Lee, an attorney, uses the cash receipts and disbursements method of reporting. In 2009, a client gave Lee 500 shares of a listed corporation's stock in full satisfaction of a $10,000 legal fee the client owed to Lee. This stock had a fair market value of $8,000 on the date it was given to Lee. The client's basis for this stock was $6,000. Lee sold the stock for cash in January 2010. In Lee's 2009 income tax return, what amount of income should be reported in connection with the receipt of the stock?
   a. $10,000
   b. $ 8,000
   c. $ 6,000
   d. $0

18. Don Wolf became a general partner in Gata Associates on January 1, 2010, with a 5% interest in Gata's profits, losses, and capital. Gata is a distributor of auto parts. Wolf does not materially participate in the partnership business. For the year ended December 31, 2010, Gata had an operating loss of $100,000. In addition, Gata earned interest of $20,000 on a temporary investment. Gata has kept the principal temporarily invested while awaiting delivery of equipment that is presently on order. The principal will be used to pay for this equipment. Wolf's passive loss for 2010 is

- a. $0
- b. $4,000
- c. $5,000
- d. $6,000

19. In 2010, Don Mills, a single taxpayer, had $70,000 in taxable income before personal exemptions. Mills had no tax preferences. His itemized deductions were as follows:

State and local income taxes	$5,000
Home mortgage interest on loan to acquire residence	6,000
Miscellaneous deductions that exceed 2% of adjusted gross income	2,000

What amount did Mills report as alternative minimum taxable income before the AMT exemption?

- a. $72,000
- b. $75,000
- c. $77,000
- d. $83,000

20. An accuracy-related penalty applies to the portion of tax underpayment attributable to

I. Negligence or a disregard of the tax rules or regulations.
II. Any substantial understatement of income tax.

- a. I only.
- b. II only.
- c. Both I and II.
- d. Neither I nor II.

21. Smith, an individual calendar-year taxpayer, purchased 100 shares of Core Co. common stock for $15,000 on November 15, 2009, and an additional 100 shares for $13,000 on December 30, 2009. On January 3, 2010, Smith sold the shares purchased on November 15, 2009, for $13,000. What amount of loss from the sale of Core's stock is deductible on Smith's 2009 and 2010 income tax returns?

	2009	2010
a.	$0	$0
b.	$0	$2,000
c.	$1,000	$1,000
d.	$2,000	$0

22. Strom acquired a 25% interest in Ace Partnership by contributing land having an adjusted basis of $16,000 and a fair market value of $50,000. The land was subject to a $24,000 mortgage, which was assumed by Ace. No other liabilities existed at the time of the contribution. What was Strom's basis in Ace?

- a. $0
- b. $16,000
- c. $26,000
- d. $32,000

Items 23 and 24 are based on the following data:

Mike Reed, a partner in Post Co., received the following distribution from Post:

	Post's basis	Fair market value
Cash	$11,000	$11,000
Land	5,000	12,500

Before this distribution, Reed's basis in Post was $25,000.

23. If this distribution were nonliquidating, Reed's recognized gain or loss on the distribution would be

- a. $11,000 gain.
- b. $ 9,000 loss.
- c. $ 1,500 loss.
- d. $0.

24. If this distribution were in complete liquidation of Reed's interest in Post, Reed's basis for the land would be

- a. $14,000
- b. $12,500
- c. $ 5,000
- d. $ 1,500

25. Finbury Corporation's taxable income for the year ended December 31, 2009, was $2,000,000 on which its tax liability was $680,000. In order for Finbury to escape the estimated tax underpayment penalty for the year ending December 31, 2010, Finbury's 2010 estimated tax payments must equal at least

- a. 90% of the 2010 tax liability.
- b. 93% of the 2010 tax liability.
- c. 100% of the 2010 tax liability.
- d. The 2009 tax liability of $680,000.

26. Barbaro Corporation's retained earnings at January 1, 2009, was $600,000. During 2009 Barbaro paid cash dividends of $150,000 and received a federal income tax refund of $26,000 as a result of an IRS audit of Barbaro's 2006 tax return. Barbaro's net income per books for the year ended December 31, 2009, was $274,900 after deducting federal income tax of $183,300. How much should be shown in the reconciliation Schedule M-2, of Form 1120, as Barbaro's retained earnings at December 31, 2009?

- a. $443,600
- b. $600,900
- c. $626,900
- d. $750,900

27. Brooke, Inc., an S corporation, was organized on January 2, 2009, with two equal stockholders who materially participate in the S corporation's business. Each stockholder invested $5,000 in Brooke's capital stock, and each loaned $15,000 to the corporation. Brooke then borrowed $60,000 from a bank for working capital. Brooke sustained an operating loss of $90,000 for the year ended December 31, 2009. How much of this loss can each stockholder claim on his 2009 income tax return?

- a. $ 5,000
- b. $20,000
- c. $45,000
- d. $50,000

28. When Jim and Nina became engaged in April 2010, Jim gave Nina a ring that had a fair market value of $50,000. After their wedding in July 2010, Jim gave Nina $75,000 in cash so that Nina could have her own bank account. Both Jim and Nina are US citizens. What was the amount of Jim's 2010 marital deduction?

- a. $0
- b. $ 75,000
- c. $115,000
- d. $125,000

29. Ross, a calendar-year, cash-basis taxpayer who died in June 2010, was entitled to receive a $10,000 accounting fee that had not been collected before the date of death. The executor of Ross' estate collected the full $10,000 in July 2010. This $10,000 should appear in

    a. Only the decedent's final individual income tax return.

    b. Only the estate's fiduciary income tax return.

    c. Only the estate tax return.

    d. Both the fiduciary income tax return and the estate tax return.

30. Kopel was engaged to prepare Raff's 2009 federal income tax return. During the tax preparation interview, Raff told Kopel that he paid $3,000 in property taxes in 2009. Actually, Raff's property taxes amounted to only $600. Based on Raff's word, Kopel deducted the $3,000 on Raff's return, resulting in an understatement of Raff's tax liability. Kopel had no reason to believe that the information was incorrect. Kopel did not request underlying documentation and was reasonably satisfied by Raff's representation that Raff had adequate records to support the deduction. Which of the following statements is correct?

    a. To avoid the preparer penalty for willful understatement of tax liability, Kopel was obligated to examine the underlying documentation for the deduction.

    b. To avoid the preparer penalty for willful understatement of tax liability, Kopel would be required to obtain Raff's representation in writing.

    c. Kopel is **not** subject to the preparer penalty for willful understatement of tax liability because the deduction that was claimed was more than 25% of the actual amount that should have been deducted.

    d. Kopel is **not** subject to the preparer penalty for willful understatement of tax liability because Kopel was justified in relying on Raff's representation.

REGULATION

ANSWERS TO TESTLET 1

1. c	5. b	9. b	13. b	17. b	21. a	25. c	29. d
2. b	6. b	10. b	14. d	18. c	22. a	26. d	30. d
3. b	7. c	11. a	15. a	19. c	23. d	27. b	
4. a	8. a	12. a	16. c	20. c	24. a	28. b	

Hints for Multiple-Choice Questions

1. Advertising must be appropriate.

2. Prior year past due fees impair independence.

3. Only managers or partners performing nonattest services for an attest client may become covered members.

4. Professionals must exercise due professional care.

5. Compliance with GAAS indicates due care.

6. Recall proof requirements.

7. The principal accepted the benefits of the unauthorized act.

8. Employee gives up rights but receives automatic payment.

9. Recall the requirements for a private placement.

10. A note, unlike a draft or a check, is a two-party instrument.

11. Rob is **not** a merchant.

12. An **explicit** declaration of fact forms an express warranty; sales talk and predictions do not.

13. After modification, contract is for >$500.

14. Notice can be constructive or actual.

15. Foreclosure ends the mortgagor's rights in the property.

16. Each payment is part income and part a return of Brown's investment.

17. The amount of compensation is determined from the value of the property received.

18. Interest is generally considered portfolio income.

19. Qualified residence interest in the form of acquisition indebtedness is deductible for AMT purposes.

20. The items listed are two components of the accuracy-related penalty.

21. The acquisition of substantially identical stock within a thirty-day period before or after the date of the loss results in a wash sale.

22. The 75% net reduction in liability is treated as a deemed cash distribution.

23. No loss can be recognized in a nonliquidating distribution.

24. No loss can be recognized in a liquidating distribution if property other than cash, receivables, or inventory is received.

25. Because of taxable income in excess of $1 million, Finbury cannot use its tax for the preceding year as a safe estimate.

26. Schedule M-2 provides a reconciliation of unappropriated retained earnings per books.

27. Shareholders do not receive basis for the corporation's debts to third parties.

28. The taxpayer must be married on the date of gift to qualify for the marital deduction.

29. The fee qualifies as income in respect of a decedent.

30. A preparer is not required to audit or examine a client's books and records.

Explanations

1. **(c)** The AICPA Code of Professional Conduct allows advertising providing it is not false, misleading or deceptive.

2. **(b)** Independence is impaired when prior year fees for professional services remain unpaid for more than one year prior to the date of the report.

3. **(b)** Covered members include members of the attest engagement team, an individual in a position to influence the attest engagement, a partner who provides nonattest services to the attest client, a partner in the office in which the lead attest engagement partner practices, and the firm. A staff person that performs tax services for the attest client is not a covered member.

4. **(a)** CPAs are required ethically and legally to exercise due professional care in the performance of all services.

5. **(b)** The surety with respect to this loss is given the same rights as the client under common law and may sue for ordinary negligence. The CPAs' best defense is that an audit performed in accordance with professional standards would not have detected the fraud.

6. **(b)** Under common law, the shareholder has the right to sue for fraud on the part of the auditor. The auditor's best defense is to show that the false statements are not material.

7. **(c)** Sears cannot collect from Davidson because Sears ratified the discount granted by shipping the goods and cashing the check.

8. **(a)** The purpose of workers' compensation is for the employer to assume a definite liability with little degree of proof by the employee.

9. **(b)** Rule 506 allows private placement of unlimited amounts of securities if the number of unaccredited investors is no more than 35.

10. **(b)** To be negotiable the instrument must be payable to the order of the bearer, unless it is a check.

11. **(a)** Risk of loss passes to the buyer on tender of delivery unless the seller is a merchant.

12. **(a)** All of the statements are opinions except (a) which is a statement of fact.

13. **(b)** Modification of contract must be in writing if contract, as modified, is covered by the Statue of Frauds (i.e., sale of goods for $500 or more).

14. **(d)** Under a notice-type statute, a subsequent purchaser, whether he or she records or not, prevails over a previous purchaser who did not record before that subsequent purchase.

15. **(a)** The mortgagor has all of the rights except the right to remain in possession as long as his or her equity in the property exceeds the amount of debt.

16. **(c)** The amount that is not taxable is based on the ratio of contribution to total expected benefits. This ratio is $12,000/(120 months × $700), which is equal to $12,000/$84,000 or 1/7. In 2009, the nontaxable amount would equal $700 [1/7 × ($700 × 7 months)]. In 2010 and 2011, the nontaxable amount would equal $1,200 [1/7 × ($700 × 12)].

17. **(b)** The stock should be recognized as revenue at its fair market value when it is received.

18. **(c)** The interest income is portfolio income. Therefore, Wolf would have a passive loss of $5,000.

19. **(c)** The alternative minimum taxable income is $77,000 ($70,000 + $5,000 + $2,000). Since the mortgage interest was from a loan used to acquire a personal residence, it does not have to be added back.

20. **(c)** An accuracy-related penalty applies to both situations.

21. **(a)** The sale is a wash sale and the loss is not deductible.

22. **(a)** The basis of a partner's partnership interest is increased by the adjusted basis of the property contributed. Since the basis of the property ($16,000) is less than the amount of the mortgage assumed by the partnership ($24,000), the partner's basis is $0.

23. **(d)** A partner recognizes gain only to the extent that the money received exceeds the partner's partnership basis.

24. **(a)** The land assumes Reed's basis in the partnership after adjusting for the receipt of the cash, or $14,000 ($25,000 basis – $11,000 cash received).

25. **(c)** No penalty will be assessed if the estimated tax payments are equal to at least 100% of the current year's tax.

26. **(d)** Retained earnings at year end should be shown as $750,900 ($600,000 + $274,900 net income + $26,000 tax refund – $150,000 dividends).

27. **(b)** The shareholders are limited to their basis in the corporation ($5,000 cash contributed + $15,000 loan to the corporation).

28. **(b)** The marital deduction is generally unlimited. Therefore, the entire $75,000 is a deduction. The value of the ring is not considered because the individuals were not married when the gift was made.

29. **(d)** The amount would be included in both returns.

30. **(d)** The preparer is not required to audit the information and may accept the taxpayer's representation unless it is unreasonable.

REGULATION
TESTLET 2

1. Under the ethical standards of the profession, which of the following situations involving independent members of an auditor's family is most likely to impair the auditor's independence?

    a. A parent's immaterial investment in a client.

    b. A first cousin's loan from a client.

    c. A spouse's employment as CEO of a client.

    d. A sibling's loan to a director of a client.

2. What body has the responsibility for issuing auditing standards for auditors of issuer (public) companies?

    a. The AICPA's Auditing Standards Board.

    b. The Chief Accountant of the Securities and Exchange Commission.

    c. The Public Company Accounting Oversight Board.

    d. The Financial Accounting Standards Board.

3. According to the ethical standards for the profession, which of the following would impair the independence of an auditor in providing an audit for First State Bank, a nonpublic financial institution?

    a. The accountant has an automobile loan with the bank collateralized by the automobile.

    b. The accountant has a credit card with the bank with an outstanding balance of $12,000.

    c. The accountant has a $20,000 loan at the bank collateralized by a certificate of deposit.

    d. The accountant has a demand deposit account of $25,000 with the bank.

4. Hart, CPA, is concerned about the type of fee arrangements that are permissible under the profession's ethical standards. Which of the following professional services may be performed for a contingent fee?

    a. A review of financial statements.

    b. An examination of prospective financial statements.

    c. Preparation of a tax return.

    d. Information technology consulting.

5. Rhodes Corp. desired to acquire the common stock of Harris Corp. and engaged Johnson & Co., CPAs, to audit the financial statements of Harris Corp. Johnson failed to discover a significant liability in performing the audit. In a common law action against Johnson, Rhodes at a minimum must prove

    a. Gross negligence on the part of Johnson.

    b. Negligence on the part of Johnson.

    c. Fraud on the part of Johnson.

    d. Johnson knew that the liability existed.

6. A debtor will be denied a discharge in bankruptcy if the debtor

    a. Failed to timely list a portion of his debts.

    b. Unjustifiably failed to preserve his books and records which could have been used to ascertain the debtor's financial condition.

    c. Has negligently made preferential transfers to favored creditors within ninety days of the filing of the bankruptcy petition.

    d. Has committed several willful and malicious acts that resulted in bodily injury to others.

7. Which of the following is a part of the social security law?

    a. A self-employed person must contribute an annual amount that is equal to the combined contributions of an employee and his or her employer.

    b. Upon the death of an employee prior to his retirement, his estate is entitled to receive the amount attributable to his contributions as a death benefit.

    c. Social security benefits must be fully funded and payments, current and future, must constitutionally come only from social security taxes.

    d. Social security benefits are taxable as income when they exceed the individual's total contributions.

8. Duval Manufacturing Industries, Inc. orally engaged Harris as one of its district sales managers for an eighteen-month period commencing April 1, 2009. Harris commenced work on that date and performed his duties in a highly competent manner for several months. On October 1, 2009, the company gave Harris a notice of termination as of November 1, 2009, citing a downturn in the market for its products. Harris sues seeking either specific performance or damages for breach of contract. Duval pleads the Statute of Frauds and/or a justified dismissal due to the economic situation. What is the probable outcome of the lawsuit?

    a. Harris will prevail because he has partially performed under the terms of the contract.

    b. Harris will lose because his termination was caused by economic factors beyond Duval's control.

    c. Harris will lose because such a contract must be in writing and signed by a proper agent of Duval.

    d. Harris will prevail because the Statute of Frauds does **not** apply to contracts such as his.

9. Harp Corp. is offering to issue $450,000 of its securities pursuant to Regulation D of the Securities Act of 1933. Harp is not required to deliver a disclosure document in the states where the offering is being conducted. The exemption for small issues of $1,000,000 or less (Rule 504) under Regulation D

    a. Requires that the issuer be subject to the reporting requirements of the Securities Exchange Act of 1934.

    b. Does **not** require that any specific information be furnished to investors.

    c. Permits the use of general solicitation.

    d. Requires that each investor be a sophisticated investor or be represented by a purchaser representative.

10. Which of the following will **not** constitute value in determining whether a person is a holder in due course?

    a. The taking of a negotiable instrument for a future consideration.

    b. The taking of a negotiable instrument as security for a loan.

    c. The giving of one's own negotiable instrument in connection with the purchase of another negotiable instrument.

    d. The performance of services rendered the payee of a negotiable instrument who endorses it in payment for services.

11. Kent, a wholesale distributor of cameras, entered into a contract with Williams. Williams agreed to purchase 100 cameras with certain optional attachments. The contract was made on March 1, 2009, for delivery by March 15, 2009; terms: 2/10, net 30. Kent shipped the cameras on March 6, and they were delivered on March 10. The shipment did not conform to the contract, in that one of the attachments was not included. Williams immediately notified Kent that he was rejecting the goods. For maximum legal advantage Kent's most appropriate action is to
   a. Bring an action for the price less an allowance for the missing attachment.
   b. Notify Williams promptly of his intention to cure the defect and make a conforming delivery by March 15.
   c. Terminate his contract with Williams and recover for breach of contract.
   d. Sue Williams for specific performance.

12. If a seller repudiates his contract with a buyer for the sale of 100 radios, what recourse does the buyer have?
   a. He can "cover" (i.e., procure the goods elsewhere and recover the difference).
   b. He must await the seller's performance for a commercially reasonable time after repudiation.
   c. He can obtain specific performance by the seller.
   d. He can recover punitive damages.

13. Wilmont owned a tract of waterfront property on Big Lake. During Wilmont's ownership of the land, several frame bungalows were placed on the land by tenants who rented the land from Wilmont. In addition to paying rent, the tenants paid for the maintenance and insurance of the bungalows, repaired, altered and sold them, without permission or hindrance from Wilmont. The bungalows rested on surface cinderblock and were not bolted to the ground. The buildings could be removed without injury to either the buildings or the land. Wilmont sold the land to Marsh. The deed to Marsh recited that Wilmont sold the land, with buildings thereon, "subject to the rights of tenants, if any, ..." When the tenants attempted to remove the bungalows, Marsh claimed ownership of them. In deciding who owns the bungalows, which of the following is **least** significant?
   a. The leasehold agreement itself, to the extent it manifested the intent of the parties.
   b. The mode and degree of annexation of the buildings to the land.
   c. The degree to which removal would cause injury to the buildings or the land.
   d. The fact that the deed included a general clause relating to the buildings.

14. Smith purchased a tract of land. To protect himself, he ordered title insurance from Valor Title Insurance Company. The policy was the usual one issued by title companies. Accordingly
   a. Valor will not be permitted to take exceptions to its coverage if it agreed to insure and prepared the title abstract.
   b. The title policy is assignable in the event Smith subsequently sells the property.
   c. The title policy provides protection against defects in record title only.
   d. Valor will be liable for any title defect that arises, even though the defect could **not** have been discovered through the exercise of reasonable care.

15. Tremont Enterprises, Inc. needed some additional working capital to develop a new product line. It decided to obtain intermediate term financing by giving a second mortgage on its plant and warehouse. Which of the following is true with respect to the mortgages?
   a. If Tremont defaults on both mortgages and a bankruptcy proceeding is initiated, the second mortgagee has the status of general creditor.
   b. If the second mortgagee proceeds to foreclose on its mortgage, the first mortgagee must be satisfied completely before the second mortgagee is entitled to repayment.
   c. Default on payment to the second mortgagee will constitute default on the first mortgage.
   d. Tremont **cannot** prepay the second mortgage prior to its maturity without the consent of the first mortgagee.

16. Frank Lanier is a resident of a state that imposes a tax on income. The following information pertaining to Lanier's state income taxes is available:

Taxes withheld in 2009	$3,500
Refund received in 2009 of 2008 tax	400
Deficiency assessed and paid in 2009 for 2007:	
Tax	600
Interest	100

What amount should Lanier utilize as state and local income taxes in calculating itemized deductions for his 2009 federal tax return?
   a. $3,500
   b. $3,700
   c. $4,100
   d. $4,200

17. Ace Rentals, Inc., an accrual-basis taxpayer, reported rent receivable of $35,000 and $25,000 in its 2009 and 2008 balance sheets, respectively. During 2009, Ace received $50,000 in rent payments and $5,000 in nonrefundable rent deposits. In Ace's 2009 corporate income tax return, what amount should Ace include as rent revenue?
   a. $50,000
   b. $55,000
   c. $60,000
   d. $65,000

18. Sol and Julia Crane (both age 41) are married, and filed a joint return for 2009. Sol earned a salary of $110,000 in 2009 from his job at Troy Corp., where Sol is covered by his employer's pension plan. In addition, Sol and Julia earned interest of $3,000 in 2009 on their joint savings account. Julia is not employed, and the couple had no other income. On January 15, 2009, Sol contributed $4,000 to an IRA for himself, and $4,000 to an IRA for his spouse. The allowable IRA deduction in the Cranes' 2009 joint return is
   a. $0
   b. $4,000
   c. $6,000
   d. $8,000

19. Spencer, who itemizes deductions, had adjusted gross income of $60,000 in 2009. The following additional information is available for 2009:

Cash contribution to church	$4,000
Purchase of art object at church bazaar (with a fair market value of $800 on the date of purchase)	1,200
Donation of used clothing to Salvation Army (fair value evidenced by receipt received)	600

What is the maximum amount Spencer can claim as a deduction for charitable contributions in 2009?

- a. $5,400
- b. $5,200
- c. $5,000
- d. $4,400

20. The following information pertains to Wald Corp.'s operations for the year ended December 31, 2009:

Worldwide taxable income	$300,000
US source taxable income	180,000
US income tax before foreign tax credit	96,000
Foreign nonbusiness-related interest earned	30,000
Foreign income taxes paid on nonbusiness-related interest earned	12,000
Other foreign source taxable income	90,000
Foreign income taxes paid on other foreign source taxable income	27,000

What amount of foreign tax credit may Wald claim for 2009?

- a. $28,800
- b. $36,600
- c. $38,400
- d. $39,000

21. Platt owns land that is operated as a parking lot. A shed was erected on the lot for the related transactions with customers. With regard to capital assets and Section 1231 assets, how should these assets be classified?

	Land	Shed
a.	Capital	Capital
b.	Section 1231	Capital
c.	Capital	Section 1231
d.	Section 1231	Section 1231

22. At partnership inception, Black acquires a 50% interest in Decorators Partnership by contributing property with an adjusted basis of $80,000. Black recognizes a gain if

- I. The fair market value of the contributed property exceeds its adjusted basis.
- II. The property is encumbered by a mortgage with a balance of $100,000.

- a. I only.
- b. II only.
- c. Both I and II.
- d. Neither I nor II.

Items 23 and 24 are based on the following data:

The partnership of Hager, Mazer & Slagle had the following cash-basis balance sheet at December 31, 2009:

	Adjusted basis per books	Fair market value
Assets		
Cash	$51,000	$ 51,000
Accounts receivable	--	210,000
Totals	$51,000	$261,000
Liabilities and Capital		
Note payable	$30,000	$ 30,000
Capital accounts:		
Hager	7,000	77,000
Mazer	7,000	77,000
Slagle	7,000	77,000
Totals	$51,000	$261,000

Slagle, an equal partner, sold his partnership interest to Burns, an outsider, for $77,000 cash on January 1, 2010. In addition, Burns assumed Slagle's share of partnership liabilities.

23. What was the total amount realized by Slagle on the sale of his partnership interest?

- a. $67,000
- b. $70,000
- c. $77,000
- d. $87,000

24. How much ordinary income should Slagle report in his 2010 income tax return on the sale of his partnership interest?

- a. $0
- b. $10,000
- c. $70,000
- d. $77,000

25. Eastern Corp., a calendar-year corporation, was formed in 2009. On January 2, 2010, it placed five-year property in service. The property was depreciated under the general MACRS system. Eastern did not elect to use the straight-line method. The following information pertains to Eastern:

Eastern's 2010 taxable income	$300,000
Adjustment for the accelerated depreciation taken on 2010 five-year property	1,000
2010 tax-exempt interest from specified private activity bonds issued in 2006	5,000

What was Eastern's 2010 alternative minimum taxable income before the adjusted current earnings (ACE) adjustment?

- a. $306,000
- b. $305,000
- c. $304,000
- d. $301,000

26. Bank Corp. owns 80% of Shore Corp.'s outstanding capital stock. Shore's capital stock consists of 50,000 shares of common stock issued and outstanding. Shore's 2009 net income was $140,000. During 2009, Shore declared and paid dividends of $60,000. In conformity with generally accepted accounting principles, Bank recorded the following entries in 2009:

	Debit	Credit
Investment in Shore Corp.		
common stock	$112,000	
Equity in earnings of subsidiary		$112,000
Cash	48,000	
Investment in Shore Corp.		
common stock		48,000

In its 2009 consolidated tax return, Bank should report dividend revenue of

- a. $48,000
- b. $14,400
- c. $ 9,600
- d. $0

27. Kari Corp., a manufacturing company, was organized on January 2, 2009. Its 2009 federal taxable income was $400,000 and its federal income tax was $100,000. What is the maximum amount of accumulated taxable income that may be subject to the accumulated earnings tax for 2009 if Kari takes only the minimum accumulated earnings credit?

- a. $300,000
- b. $150,000
- c. $ 50,000
- d. $0

28. On February 10, 2010, Ace Corp., a calendar-year corporation, elected S corporation status and all shareholders consented to the election. There was no change in shareholders in 2010. Ace met all eligibility requirements for S status during the preelection portion of the year. What is the earliest date on which Ace can be recognized as an S corporation?

    a.   February 10, 2010.
    b.   February 10, 2011.
    c.   January 1, 2010.
    d.   January 1, 2011.

29. Lyon, a cash-basis taxpayer, died on January 15, 2009. In 2009, the estate executor made the required periodic distribution of $9,000 from estate income to Lyon's sole heir. The following pertains to the estate's income and disbursements in 2009:

<u>2009 Estate Income</u>

$20,000	Taxable interest
10,000	Net long-term capital gains allocable to corpus

<u>2009 Estate Disbursements</u>

$5,000	Administrative expenses attributable to taxable income

For the 2009 calendar year, what was the estate's distributable net income (DNI)?

    a. $15,000
    b. $20,000
    c. $25,000
    d. $30,000

30. A tax return preparer may disclose or use tax return information without the taxpayer's consent to

    a.   Facilitate a supplier's or lender's credit evaluation of the taxpayer.
    b.   Accommodate the request of a financial institution that needs to determine the amount of taxpayer's debt to it, to be forgiven.
    c.   Be evaluated by a quality or peer review.
    d.   Solicit additional nontax business.

REGULATION

ANSWERS TO TESTLET 2

1. c	5. b	9. b	13. d	17. d	21. d	25. a	29. a
2. c	6. b	10. a	14. d	18. b	22. d	26. d	30. c
3. b	7. a	11. b	15. b	19. c	23. d	27. c	
4. d	8. c	12. a	16. c	20. b	24. c	28. c	

Hints for Multiple-Choice Questions

1. Which is a close relative?

2. What body was created by the Sarbanes-Oxley Act of 2002?

3. Which loan is unsecured?

4. Which services are performed only for the client?

5. Rhodes Corp. is the client, not Harris Corp.

6. Preferential transfers will simply be set aside.

7. There is no other party to split the payments with.

8. The agreement cannot be performed within one year.

9. It is a small issue of securities.

10. An executory promise is not value until performed.

11. Kent is subject to the perfect tender rule.

12. Specific performance is not allowed if the buyer can cover.

13. Recall factors determining whether item is a fixture.

14. Insurer is liable for all defects not disclosed by survey and physical inspection.

15. First mortgage has priority.

16. Include amounts withheld or actually paid during the year.

17. Try setting up a "T" account and analyzing the journal entries that would have been made.

18. The deduction is subject to a special phaseout since Sol (but not Julia) is a participant in a qualified employer retirement plan.

19. The amount of contribution includes the excess of the amount paid over the value of the object received.

20. A separate FTC limitation applies to non-business-related interest.

21. The definition of capital assets excludes property used in a trade or business.

22. Generally no gain is recognized when property is transferred in exchange for a partnership interest.

23. The amount realized includes the buyer's assumption of the seller's share of partnership liabilities.

24. Ordinary income must be reported to the extent of the seller's share of unrealized receivables and appreciated inventory.

25. The 150% declining balance method of depreciation must be used for AMT purposes.

26. Intercompany dividends from affiliated group members are eliminated in the consolidation process.

27. The minimum accumulated earnings credit is $250,000 for nonservice corporations.

28. An election is effective at the beginning of a corporation's tax year.

29. The computation of DNI excludes capital gains allocable to corpus.

30. Only one answer choice merits disclosure.

Explanations

1.   (c)   The spouse is a member of the CPA's immediate family and is employed in a key position.

2.   (c)   The Public Company Accounting Oversight Board is the body responsible for issuing standards for auditors of public (issuer) companies.

3.   (b)   An interpretation of the independence rule prohibits credit card accounts in excess of $10,000.

4.   (d)   Rule 302 prohibits contingent fees for audits or reviews of financial statements, examinations of prospective financial information, and preparation of tax returns.

5.   (b)   Since Rhodes engaged Johnson, Rhodes is the client and in privity of contract. Therefore, Johnson could be held liable for ordinary negligence.

6.   (b)   Failing to keep books of account or records will bar the discharge of all debts.

7.   (a)   A self-employed individual must pay both halves of the required contribution.

8.   (c)   Agreements that cannot be performed within one year from the date of the agreement must be in writing to be enforceable under the Statute of Fraud.

9.   (b)   Regulation D does not require that any specific information be furnished to the investors.

10.   (a)   To be a holder in due course the individual must provide current value for the instrument.

11.   (b)   To get maximum legal advantage, the buyer must notify the seller of rejection of the goods on a timely basis.

12.   (a)   The buyer has the right to cover—to buy the goods from another seller and recover the difference paid.

13.   (d)   A general clause in the deed would have the least significance.

14.   (d)   Title insurance provides absolute assurance for all defects insured.

15. (b) The first mortgage has priority before repayment of any portion of the second mortgage.

16. (c) The taxes paid in 2009 are equal to $4,100 ($3,500 withheld and $600 for deficiency). The refund is included in income and the interest is not deductible.

17. (d) The amount of rent revenue is equal to $65,000 ($50,000 received – $25,000 beginning receivable + $35,000 ending receivable + $5,000 nonrefundable deposits).

18. (b) Julia's $4,000 contribution is allowable but Sol's is not because he is a participant in a pension plan and their combined compensation is greater than $105,000.

19. (c) The maximum is $5,000 ($4,000 cash contribution + $400 excess of purchase price over fair value of art object + $600 clothing contribution).

20. (b) The amount of credit that can be currently used cannot exceed the amount of US tax that is attributable to the foreign income. This foreign tax credit limitation can be expressed as follows:

$$\frac{\text{Foreign TI}}{\text{Worldwide TI}} \times (\text{US tax}) = \text{Foreign tax credit limitation}$$

One limitation must be computed for foreign source passive income (e.g., interest, dividends, royalties, rents, annuities), with a separate limitation computed for all other foreign source taxable income.

In this case, the foreign income taxes paid on other foreign source taxable income of $27,000 is fully usable as a credit in 2009 because it is less than the applicable limitation amount (i.e., the amount of US tax attributable to the income).

$$\frac{\$90,000}{\$300,000} \times (\$96,000) = \$28,000$$

On the other hand, the credit for the $12,000 of foreign income taxes paid on non-business-related interest is limited to the amount of US tax attributable to the foreign interest income, $9,600.

$$\frac{\$30,000}{\$300,000} \times (\$96,000) = \$9,600$$

Thus, Wald Corp.'s foreign tax credit for 2009 totals $27,000 + $9,600 = $36,600. The $12,000 – $9,600 = $2,400 of unused foreign tax credit resulting from the application of the limitation of foreign taxes attributable to foreign source interest income can be carried back one year and forward ten years to offset US income tax in those years.

21. (d) Both of the assets are Section 1231 property.

22. (d) No gain is recognized on the transfer. A gain would only be recognized if the decrease in the partner's liability exceeds his or her partnership basis.

23. (d) The amount realized is $87,000 ($77,000 cash received + $10,000 liability assumed).

24. (c) The ordinary income would be equal to his share of the unrealized receivables or $70,000 ($210,000 × 1/3). The remainder would be capital gain.

25. (a) The amount of alternative minimum taxable income before ACE adjustment is equal to $306,000 ($300,000 taxable income + $5,000 tax-exempt interest + $1,000 excess depreciation).

26. (d) On the consolidated tax return intercompany dividends are eliminated.

27. (c) The accumulated taxable income that may be subject to the accumulated earnings tax is $50,000 ($400,000 taxable income – $100,000 income tax – $250,000 accumulated earnings credit). The credit is equal to $250,000 ($250,000 – the accumulated earnings and profits at the end of the prior year which is $0).

28. (c) Since the election was filed on or before the fifteenth day of the third month of the year, it can become effective as of the beginning of that year.

29. (a) DNI would be net income $25,000 ($20,000 + $10,000 – $5,000) minus $10,000 net capital gains allocable to corpus, which equals $15,000.

30. (c) The only allowed use of the information is if the preparer is being evaluated under a quality or peer review.

REGULATION

TESTLET 3

1. Under the ethical standards of the profession, which of the following investments in a client is not considered to be a direct financial interest?

    a.   An investment held through a nonclient regulated mutual fund.

    b.   An investment held through a nonclient investment club.

    c.   An investment held in a blind trust.

    d.   An investment held by the trustee of a trust.

2. Lott and Lott, CPAs, recently acquired a public company as an audit client. With respect to this client, the Sarbanes-Oxley Act of 2002 requires

    a.   Rotation of accounting firms every five years.

    b.   Joint audits by two auditing firms.

    c.   Rotation of the partner in charge of the audit every five years.

    d.   Joint management of the audit by two or more partners.

3. According to the ethical standards for the profession, which of the following fee arrangements is prohibited?

    a.   A fee for a review of financial statements that is based on time spent on the engagement.

    b.   A fee for a review of financial statements that is based on time spent and a premium for the risk involved.

    c.   A fee for a review engagement that is based on a fixed fee of $5,000.

    d.   A fee for a review engagement that varies depending on the amount of financing that the company may obtain.

4. According to the ethical standards for the profession, which of the following is **not** acceptable advertising content?

    a.   The fees for services.

    b.   The qualifications of professional staff.

    c.   Implications regarding the ability to influence regulatory bodies.

    d.   Implications regarding the value of the services.

5. The CPA firm of Knox & Knox has been subpoenaed to testify and produce its correspondence and working papers in connection with a lawsuit brought against Johnson, one of its clients. Regarding the attempted resort to the privileged communication rule in seeking to avoid admission of such evidence in the lawsuit, which of the following is correct?

    a.   Federal law recognizes such a privilege if the accountant is a Certified Public Accountant.

    b.   The privilege is available regarding the working papers since the accountant is deemed to own them.

    c.   The privilege is as widely available as the attorney-client privilege.

    d.   In the absence of a specific statutory provision, the law does not recognize the existence of the privileged communication rule between an accountant and his client.

6. Which of the following is(are) true under the Americans with Disabilities Act?

    I.   The Act requires companies to make reasonable accommodations for disabled persons unless this results in undue hardship on the operations of the company.

    II.   The Act requires that companies with 100 or more employees set up a plan to hire Americans with disabilities.

    a.   Both I and II.

    b.   Neither I nor II.

    c.   I only.

    d.   II only.

7. The partnership of Maxim & Rose, CPAs, has been engaged by their largest client, a limited partnership, to examine the financial statements in connection with the offering of 2,000 limited-partnership interests to the public at $5,000 per subscription. Under these circumstances, which of the following is true?

    a.   Maxim & Rose may disclaim any liability under the Federal Securities Acts by an unambiguous, boldfaced disclaimer of liability on its audit report.

    b.   Under the Securities Act of 1933, Maxim & Rose has responsibility only for the financial statements as of the close of the fiscal year in question.

    c.   The dollar amount in question is sufficiently small so as to provide an exemption from the Securities Act of 1933.

    d.   The Securities Act of 1933 requires a registration despite the fact that the client is not selling stock or another traditional "security."

8. One of the major purposes of federal security regulation is to

    a.   Establish the qualifications for accountants who are members of the profession.

    b.   Eliminate incompetent attorneys and accountants who participate in the registration of securities to be offered to the public.

    c.   Provide a set of uniform standards and tests for accountants, attorneys, and others who practice before the Securities and Exchange Commission.

    d.   Provide sufficient information to the investing public who purchases securities in the marketplace.

9. Which of the following statements is(are) true of the National Environment Policy Act?

    I.   The Act provides tax breaks for those companies that help accomplish national environmental policy.

    II.   Enforcement of the Act is primarily accomplished by litigation of persons who decide to challenge federal government decisions.

    a.   I only.

    b.   II only.

    c.   Both I and II.

    d.   Neither I nor II.

10. Your client has in its possession the following instrument:

$700.000	Provo, Utah	May 1, 2002

Thirty days after date I promise to pay to the order of
<u>Cash</u>
<u>Seven hundred</u> Dollars
at <u>Boise, Idaho</u>

Value received with interest at the rate of 10% per annum.

This instrument is secured by a conditional sales contract.

No. 20   Due June 1, 2002   *Len Bowie*

This instrument is

   a. A negotiable time draft.

   b. A nonnegotiable note since it states that it is secured by a conditional sales contract.

   c. Not negotiable until June 1, 2002.

   d. A negotiable bearer note.

11. In which of the following situations would an oral agreement without any consideration be binding under the Uniform Commercial Code?

   a. A renunciation of a claim or right arising out of an alleged breach.

   b. A firm offer by a merchant to sell or buy goods which gives assurance that it will be held open.

   c. An agreement that is a requirements contract.

   d. An agreement that modifies an existing sales contract.

12. A dispute has arisen between two merchants over the question of who has the risk of loss in a given sales transaction. The contract does not specifically cover the point. The goods were shipped to the buyer who rightfully rejected them. Which of the following factors will be the most important factor in resolving their dispute?

   a. Who has title to the goods.

   b. The shipping terms.

   c. The credit terms.

   d. The fact that a breach has occurred.

13. Marcross and two business associates own real property as tenants in common that they have invested in as a speculation. The speculation proved to be highly successful, and the land is now worth substantially more than their investment. Which of the following is a correct legal incident of ownership of the property?

   a. Upon the death of any of the other tenants, the deceased's interest passes to the survivor(s) unless there is a will.

   b. Each of the cotenants owns an undivided interest in the whole.

   c. A cotenant cannot sell his interest in the property without the consent of the other tenants.

   d. Upon the death of a cotenant, his estate is entitled to the amount of the original investment, but not the appreciation.

14. Moch sold her farm to Watkins and took back a purchase money mortgage on the farm. Moch failed to record the mortgage. Moch's mortgage will be valid against all of the following parties **except**

   a. The heirs or estate of Watkins.

   b. A subsequent mortgagee who took a second mortgage since he had heard there was a prior mortgage.

   c. A subsequent bona fide purchaser from Watkins.

   d. A friend of Watkins to whom the farm was given as a gift and who took without knowledge of the mortgage.

15. Lake purchased a home from Walsh for $95,000. Lake obtained a $60,000 loan from Safe Bank to finance the purchase, executing a promissory note and mortgage. The recording of the mortgage by Safe

   a. Gives the world actual notice of Safe's interest.

   b. Protects Safe's interest against the claims of subsequent bona fide purchasers for value.

   c. Is necessary in order that Safe have rights against Lake under the promissory note.

   d. Is necessary in order to protect Safe's interest against the claim of a subsequent transferee who does **not** give value.

16. For the year ended December 31, 2009, Don Raff earned $1,000 interest at Ridge Savings Bank on a certificate of deposit scheduled to mature in 2010. In January 2010, before filing his 2009 income tax return, Raff incurred a forfeiture penalty of $500 for premature withdrawal of the funds. Raff should treat this $500 forfeiture penalty as a

   a. Reduction of interest earned in 2009, so that only $500 of such interest is taxable on Raff's 2009 return.

   b. Deduction from 2010 adjusted gross income, deductible only if Raff itemizes his deductions for 2010.

   c. Penalty **not** deductible for tax purposes.

   d. Deduction from gross income in arriving at 2010 adjusted gross income.

17. Axis Corp. is an accrual-basis calendar-year corporation. On December 13, 2009, the Board of Directors declared a 2% of profits bonus to all employees for services rendered during 2009 and notified them in writing. None of the employees own stock in Axis. The amount represents reasonable compensation for services rendered and was paid on March 13, 2010. Axis' bonus expense may

   a. Not be deducted on Axis' 2009 tax return because the per share employee amount **cannot** be determined with reasonable accuracy at the time of the declaration of the bonus.

   b. Be deducted on Axis' 2009 tax return.

   c. Be deducted on Axis' 2010 tax return.

   d. Not be deducted on Axis' tax return because payment is a disguised dividend.

18. On August 1, 2010, Graham purchased and placed into service an office building costing $264,000 including $30,000 for the land. What was Graham's MACRS deduction for the office building in 2010?

   a. $9,600

   b. $6,000

   c. $3,600

   d. $2,250

19. This item is based on the following selected 2010 information pertaining to Sam and Ann Hoyt, who filed a joint federal income tax return for the calendar year 2010. The Hoyts had adjusted gross income of $34,000 and itemized their deductions for 2010. Among the Hoyts' cash expenditures during 2010 were the following:

$2,500 repairs in connection with 2010 fire damage to the Hoyt residence. This property has a basis of $50,000. Fair market value was $60,000 before the fire and $55,000 after the fire. Insurance on the property had lapsed in 2009 for nonpayment of premium.

$800 appraisal fee to determine amount of fire loss.

What amount of fire loss were the Hoyts entitled to deduct as an itemized deduction on their 2010 return?

    a. $5,000
    b. $2,500
    c. $1,600
    d. $1,500

20. A calendar-year taxpayer files an individual tax return for 2009 on March 20, 2010. The taxpayer neither committed fraud nor omitted amounts in excess of 25% of gross income on the tax return. What is the latest date that the Internal Revenue Service can assess tax and assert a notice of deficiency?

    a.   March 20, 2013.
    b.   March 20, 2012.
    c.   April 15, 2013.
    d.   April 15, 2012.

21. On July 1, 2010, Riley exchanged investment real property, with an adjusted basis of $160,000 and subject to a mortgage of $70,000, and received from Wilson $30,000 cash and other investment real property having a fair market value of $250,000. Wilson assumed the mortgage. What is Riley's recognized gain in 2010 on the exchange?

    a. $ 30,000
    b. $ 70,000
    c. $ 90,000
    d. $100,000

22. In 2008, Martha received as a gift several shares of Good Corporation stock. The donor's basis of this stock was $2,800, and he paid gift tax of $50. On the date of the gift, the fair market value of the stock was $2,600. If Martha sells this stock in 2010 for $2,700, what amount and type of gain or loss should Martha report in her 2010 income tax return?

    a. $50 long-term capital gain.
    b. $100 long-term capital gain.
    c. $100 long-term capital loss.
    d.   No gain or loss.

23. Hall and Haig are equal partners in the firm of Arosa Associates. On January 1, 2009, each partner's adjusted basis in Arosa was $40,000. During 2009 Arosa borrowed $60,000, for which Hall and Haig are personally liable. Arosa sustained an operating loss of $10,000 for the year ended December 31, 2009. The basis of each partner's interest in Arosa at December 31, 2009, was

    a. $35,000
    b. $40,000
    c. $65,000
    d. $70,000

24. Clark and Hunt organized Jet Corp. with authorized voting common stock of $400,000. Clark contributed $60,000 cash. Both Clark and Hunt transferred other property in exchange for Jet stock as follows:

| | *Other property* | | |
	Adjusted basis	*Fair market value*	*Percentage of Jet stock acquired*
Clark	$ 50,000	$100,000	40%
Hunt	120,000	240,000	60%

What was Clark's basis in Jet stock?

    a. $0
    b. $100,000
    c. $110,000
    d. $160,000

25. Roberta Warner and Sally Rogers formed the Acme Corporation on October 1, 2010. On the same date Warner paid $75,000 cash to Acme for 750 shares of its common stock. Simultaneously, Rogers received 100 shares of Acme's common stock for services rendered. How much should Rogers include as taxable income for 2010 and what will be the basis of her stock?

	Taxable income	*Basis of stock*
a.	$0	$0
b.	$0	$10,000
c.	$10,000	$0
d.	$10,000	$10,000

26. The following information pertains to Hull, Inc., a personal holding company, for the year ended December 31, 2009:

Undistributed personal holding company income	$100,000
Dividends paid during 2009	20,000
Consent dividends reported in the 2009 individual income tax returns of the holders of Hull's common stock, but **not** paid by Hull to its stockholders	10,000

In computing its 2009 personal holding company tax, what amount should Hull deduct for dividends paid?

    a. $0
    b. $10,000
    c. $20,000
    d. $30,000

27. Bern Corp., an S corporation, had an ordinary loss of $36,500 for the year ended December 31, 2009. At January 1, 2009, Meyer owned 50% of Bern's stock. Meyer held the stock for forty days in 2009 before selling the entire 50% interest to an unrelated third party. Meyer's basis for the stock was $10,000. Meyer was a full-time employee of Bern until the stock was sold. Meyer's share of Bern's 2009 loss was

    a. $0
    b. $ 2,000
    c. $10,000
    d. $18,300

28. On July 1, 2010, in connection with a recapitalization of Yorktown Corporation, Robert Moore exchanged 1,000 shares of stock that cost him $95,000 for 1,000 shares of new stock worth $108,000 and bonds in the principal amount of $10,000 with a fair market value of $10,500. What is the amount of Moore's recognized gain during 2010?

    a. $0
    b. $10,500
    c. $23,000
    d. $23,500

29. Steve and Kay Briar, US citizens, were married for the entire 2009 calendar year. In 2009, Steve gave a $30,000 cash gift to his sister. The Briars made no other gifts in 2009. They each signed a timely election to treat the $30,000 gift as made one-half by each spouse. Disregarding the unified credit and estate tax consequences, what amount of the 2009 gift is taxable to the Briars?

    a. $18,000
    b. $ 6,000
    c. $ 4,000
    d. $0

30. Following are the fair market values of Wald's assets at the date of death:

Personal effects and jewelry	$650,000
Land bought by Wald with Wald's funds five years prior to death and held with Wald's sister as joint tenants with right of survivorship	2,900,000

The executor of Wald's estate did not elect the alternate valuation date. The amount includible as Wald's gross estate in the federal estate tax return is

    a. $ 650,000
    b. $2,600,000
    c. $2,900,000
    d. $3,550,000

REGULATION

ANSWERS TO TESTLET 3

1. a	5. d	9. b	13. b	17. b	21. d	25. d	29. c
2. c	6. c	10. d	14. c	18. d	22. d	26. d	30. d
3. d	7. d	11. d	15. b	19. d	23. c	27. b	
4. c	8. d	12. d	16. d	20. c	24. c	28. b	

Hints for Multiple-Choice Questions

1. What is an indirect financial interest?

2. Partner rotation helps assure independence.

3. Which fee is contingent?

4. Which is false, misleading, or deceptive?

5. Accountant-client privilege does not exist in common law.

6. ADA applies to employers with at least fifteen employees; forbidding discrimination.

7. Must comply with **all** requirements of the 1933 Act.

8. The goal is to help investors avoid fraudulent offerings.

9. The EPA ensures compliance with environmental protection laws.

10. A note is a two-party instrument.

11. Review Module 24, Section A.2.d.

12. Risk of loss is independent of title under UCC.

13. Each owns the whole.

14. To prevail, subsequent party must give value and must not have notice.

15. Recording gives constructive notice.

16. The interest forfeiture results in a deduction.

17. The amount must be fixed by a predetermined formula.

18. Remember to use the midmonth averaging convention.

19. Remember to subtract a $100 floor and 10% of AGI.

20. A return filed early is treated as filed on its due date for statute of limitations purposes.

21. The assumption of Riley's mortgage is treated as boot received.

22. The basis for gain is $2,800, and the basis for loss is $2,600.

23. An increase in partnership liabilities is treated as a deemed cash contribution.

24. Clark's basis must reflect his nonrecognition of gain.

25. The shares received as compensation are worth $100 per share.

26. Consent dividends are included as part of the corporation's dividends paid deduction.

27. S corporation items are allocated per share, per day to shareholders.

28. The definition of boot (other property) includes the FMV of an excess principal amount of security received.

29. The gift is treated as made one-half by each spouse.

30. In the case of jointly held property by other than spouses, the property is included in the gross estate except to the extent that the surviving tenant contributed toward the purchase.

Explanations

1. **(a)** An investment in a mutual fund that holds an investment in a client is considered to be an indirect financial interest.

2. **(c)** The Sarbanes-Oxley Act requires rotation of the partner in charge of the audit every five years.

3. **(d)** A fee that varies depending on the amount of financing obtained is a contingent fee that is not allowed for a review engagement.

4. **(c)** Advertising content that implies the ability to influence regulatory bodies would be considered false, misleading, or deceptive.

5. **(d)** In the absence of a specific statute, the law does not recognize the existence of privileged communication between an accountant and his client.

6. **(c)** The Americans with Disabilities Act requires companies to make reasonable accommodations for disabled persons. It also prohibits discrimination but does not require setting up plans to hire disabled persons.

7. **(d)** The Securities Act of 1933 covers sales of limited-partnership interests to the public.

8. **(d)** One of the major purposes of federal security regulation is to assure full and fair disclosure of information to the investing public.

9. **(b)** The National Environment Policy Act enforcement is primarily accomplished by litigation of persons who decide to challenge federal government decisions.

10. **(d)** The instrument is a negotiable bearer note because it is payable to the bearer (cash), unconditional, payable on a fixed date, and specifies a certain amount of cash.

11. **(d)** The only oral agreement that would be binding without consideration would be an agreement that modifies an existing sales contract.

12. **(d)** Risk of loss transfers when title passes unless there is a breach of contract.

13. **(b)** Tenants in common each own an undivided interest in the property. All of the other statements are false.

14. **(c)** A subsequent bona fide purchaser would take the property over a previous mortgage holder who fails to record.

15. **(b)** The purpose of recording is to obtain protection against future bona fide purchasers.

16. **(d)** The penalty may be deducted from adjusted gross income.

17. **(b)** The bonuses are deductible provided that they are paid within 2½ months of the close of the tax year.

18. **(d)** The depreciation allowed is $2,250 ($234,000 × 4.5 ÷ 468 months). Notice that the mid-month convention is used.

19. **(d)** The casualty loss is equal to $5,000 ($60,000 FMV before the casualty – $55,000 FMV after the casualty). The deductible loss is equal to $1,500 ($5,000 loss – $100 floor – $3,400 [10% of adjusted gross income]).

20. **(c)** The normal period for assessment of a tax deficiency is three years after the date of the return or three years after the return is filed, whichever is later.

21. **(d)** The gain is equal to $100,000, which is the amount of boot received in the like-kind exchange. The boot is equal to the $30,000 cash received plus the $70,000 liability assumed.

22. **(d)** Martha's basis for a gain is the basis of the donor increased by any gift tax paid, or $2,850. The basis for a loss is the lesser of gain basis ($2,850) or the FMV on the date of gift ($2,600). Therefore, no gain or loss is recognized.

23. **(c)** The basis of each partner's interest was $65,000 ($40,000 January 1 basis + $30,000 share of liability – $5,000 share of loss).

24. **(c)** Clark's basis is equal to $110,000 ($60,000 cash + $50,000 adjusted basis of property contributed).

25. **(d)** Rogers must include the FMV of the stock at the date of receipt in his taxable income. The basis of the investment in the stock also is the FMV of the stock at date of receipt.

26. **(d)** The corporation may deduct both regular and consent dividends.

27. **(b)** The amount of taxable income is $2,000 [$36,500 × 50% × (40 days/365 days)].

28. **(b)** The FMV of the bonds represents boot in the reorganization. Therefore, the recognized gain is $10,500.

29. **(c)** The amount taxable is $4,000 ($30,000 – $26,000 [two annual exclusions of $13,000 each]).

30. **(d)** The gross estate is equal to $3,550,000. The entire FMV of the property is included because it is held in joint tenancy and acquired by purchase by other than spouses.

SIMULATION PROBLEM 1   (30 to 35 minutes)

Sara Howley (social security #315-79-3579) works as a financial consultant and had a net profit from her sole proprietorship reported on Schedule C, line 31, of $70,000 for 2009. Sara also worked a second job as an employee and had social security wages of $50,000 for 2009.

Schedule SE			
Situation		Communication	Research

Complete the following 2009 Form 1040 Schedule SE to compute Sara's self-employment tax and her self-employment tax deduction.

		Communication	
Situation	Schedule SE		Research

Sara contacts you and indicates that she may start another business as a public relations consultant. Sara expects to incur a loss for the first two years in this new venture and wonders whether the loss from the public relations sole proprietorship will affect the amount of self-employment tax that she must pay as a financial consultant. Write a letter to Sara explaining the effect of the projected loss from her new venture on her self-employment tax.

REMINDER: Your response will be graded for both technical content and writing skills. Technical content will be evaluated for information that is helpful to the intended reader and clearly relevant to the issue. Writing skills will be evaluated for development, organization, and the appropriate expression of ideas in professional correspondence. Use a standard business memo or letter format with a clear beginning, middle, and end. Do not convey information in the form of a table, bullet point list, or other abbreviated presentation.

			Research
Situation	Schedule SE	Communication	

Sara may deduct a portion of her self-employment tax in arriving at her adjusted gross income for 2009. What Internal Revenue Code section and subsection provides for a deduction of self-employment taxes?

Section	Subsection
§	( )

Schedule SE (Form 1040) 2009   Attachment Sequence No. **17**   Page **2**

Name of person with **self-employment** income (as shown on Form 1040)	Social security number of person with **self-employment** income ▶

Section B—Long Schedule SE

Part I   Self-Employment Tax

Note. If your only income subject to self-employment tax is **church employee income**, skip lines 1 through 4b. Enter -0- on line 4c and go to line 5a. Income from services you performed as a minister or a member of a religious order **is not** church employee income. See page SE-1.

A   If you are a minister, member of a religious order, or Christian Science practitioner **and** you filed Form 4361, but you had $400 or more of **other** net earnings from self-employment, check here and continue with Part I . . . . ▶ ☐

1a	Net farm profit or (loss) from Schedule F, line 36, and farm partnerships, Schedule K-1 (Form 1065), box 14, code A. **Note.** Skip lines 1a and 1b if you use the farm optional method (see page SE-4)	**1a**	
b	If you received social security retirement or disability benefits, enter the amount of Conservation Reserve Program payments included on Schedule F, line 6b, or listed on Schedule K-1 (Form 1065), box 20, code Y	**1b**	( )
2	Net profit or (loss) from Schedule C, line 31; Schedule C-EZ, line 3; Schedule K-1 (Form 1065), box 14, code A (other than farming); and Schedule K-1 (Form 1065-B), box 9, code J1. Ministers and members of religious orders, see page SE-1 for types of income to report on this line. See page SE-3 for other income to report. **Note.** Skip this line if you use the nonfarm optional method (see page SE-4)	**2**	
3	Combine lines 1a, 1b, and 2	**3**	
4a	If line 3 is more than zero, multiply line 3 by 92.35% (.9235). Otherwise, enter amount from line 3	**4a**	
b	If you elect one or both of the optional methods, enter the total of lines 15 and 17 here . .	**4b**	
c	Combine lines 4a and 4b. If less than $400, **stop**; you do not owe self-employment tax. **Exception.** If less than $400 and you had **church employee income,** enter -0- and continue ▶	**4c**	
5a	Enter your **church employee income** from Form W-2. See page SE-1 for definition of church employee income. **5a**		
b	Multiply line 5a by 92.35% (.9235). If less than $100, enter -0-	**5b**	
6	**Net earnings from self-employment.** Add lines 4c and 5b . .	**6**	
7	Maximum amount of combined wages and self-employment earnings subject to social security tax or the 6.2% portion of the 7.65% railroad retirement (tier 1) tax for 2009	**7**	106,800 00
8a	Total social security wages and tips (total of boxes 3 and 7 on Form(s) W-2) and railroad retirement (tier 1) compensation. If $106,800 or more, skip lines 8b through 10, and go to line 11 **8a**		
b	Unreported tips subject to social security tax (from Form 4137, line 10) **8b**		
c	Wages subject to social security tax (from Form 8919, line 10) **8c**		
d	Add lines 8a, 8b, and 8c	**8d**	
9	Subtract line 8d from line 7. If zero or less, enter -0- here and on line 10 and go to line 11 . ▶	**9**	
10	Multiply the **smaller** of line 6 or line 9 by 12.4% (.124)	**10**	
11	Multiply line 6 by 2.9% (.029)	**11**	
12	**Self-employment tax.** Add lines 10 and 11. Enter here and on **Form 1040, line 56.** . . .	**12**	
13	**Deduction for one-half of self-employment tax.** Multiply line 12 by 50% (.50). Enter the result here and on **Form 1040, line 27** . **13**		

Part II   Optional Methods To Figure Net Earnings   (see page SE-4)

Farm Optional Method. You may use this method **only** if **(a)** your gross farm income[1] was not more than $6,540, **or (b)** your net farm profits[2] were less than $4,721.

14	Maximum income for optional methods	**14**	4,360 00
15	Enter the **smaller** of: two-thirds (2/3) of gross farm income[1] (not less than zero) or $4,360. Also include this amount on line 4b above	**15**	

Nonfarm Optional Method. You may use this method **only** if **(a)** your net nonfarm profits[3] were less than $4,721 and also less than 72.189% of your gross nonfarm income,[4] **and (b)** you had net earnings from self-employment of at least $400 in 2 of the prior 3 years. **Caution.** You may use this method no more than five times.

16	Subtract line 15 from line 14	**16**	
17	Enter the **smaller** of: two-thirds (2/3) of gross nonfarm income[4] (not less than zero) **or** the amount on line 16. Also include this amount on line 4b above	**17**	

[1] From Sch. F, line 11, and Sch. K-1 (Form 1065), box 14, code B.

[2] From Sch. F, line 36, and Sch. K-1 (Form 1065), box 14, code A— minus the amount you would have entered on line 1b had you not used the optional method.

[3] From Sch. C, line 31; Sch. C-EZ, line 3; Sch. K-1 (Form 1065), box 14, code A; and Sch. K-1 (Form 1065-B), box 9, code J1.

[4] From Sch. C, line 7; Sch. C-EZ, line 1; Sch. K-1 (Form 1065), box 14, code C; and Sch. K-1 (Form 1065-B), box 9, code J2.

Schedule SE (Form 1040) 2009

SOLUTION TO SIMULATION PROBLEM 1

Situation	Schedule SE	Communication	Research

Schedule SE (Form 1040) 2009   Attachment Sequence No. **17**   Page **2**

Name of person with **self-employment** income (as shown on Form 1040)	Social security number of person with **self-employment** income ▶
Sara Howley	315-79-3579

Section B—Long Schedule SE

Part I   Self-Employment Tax

Note. If your only income subject to self-employment tax is **church employee income,** skip lines 1 through 4b. Enter -0- on line 4c and go to line 5a. Income from services you performed as a minister or a member of a religious order **is not** church employee income. See page SE-1.

A	If you are a minister, member of a religious order, or Christian Science practitioner **and** you filed Form 4361, but you had $400 or more of **other** net earnings from self-employment, check here and continue with Part I . . . . ▶ ☐		
1a	Net farm profit or (loss) from Schedule F, line 36, and farm partnerships, Schedule K-1 (Form 1065), box 14, code A. **Note.** Skip lines 1a and 1b if you use the farm optional method (see page SE-4)	**1a**	
b	If you received social security retirement or disability benefits, enter the amount of Conservation Reserve Program payments included on Schedule F, line 6b, or listed on Schedule K-1 (Form 1065), box 20, code Y	**1b**	( )
2	Net profit or (loss) from Schedule C, line 31; Schedule C-EZ, line 3; Schedule K-1 (Form 1065), box 14, code A (other than farming); and Schedule K-1 (Form 1065-B), box 9, code J1. Ministers and members of religious orders, see page SE-1 for types of income to report on this line. See page SE-3 for other income to report. **Note.** Skip this line if you use the nonfarm optional method (see page SE-4)	**2**	70,000
3	Combine lines 1a, 1b, and 2	**3**	70,000
4a	If line 3 is more than zero, multiply line 3 by 92.35% (.9235). Otherwise, enter amount from line 3	**4a**	64,645
b	If you elect one or both of the optional methods, enter the total of lines 15 and 17 here . .	**4b**	
c	Combine lines 4a and 4b. If less than $400, **stop;** you do not owe self-employment tax. **Exception.** If less than $400 and you had **church employee income,** enter -0- and continue ▶	**4c**	64,645
5a	Enter your **church employee income** from Form W-2. See page SE-1 for definition of church employee income. **5a**		
b	Multiply line 5a by 92.35% (.9235). If less than $100, enter -0-	**5b**	
6	**Net earnings from self-employment.** Add lines 4c and 5b	**6**	64,645
7	Maximum amount of combined wages and self-employment earnings subject to social security tax or the 6.2% portion of the 7.65% railroad retirement (tier 1) tax for 2009	**7**	106,800 00
8a	Total social security wages and tips (total of boxes 3 and 7 on Form(s) W-2) and railroad retirement (tier 1) compensation. If $106,800 or more, skip lines 8b through 10, and go to line 11 **8a** 50,000		
b	Unreported tips subject to social security tax (from Form 4137, line 10) **8b**		
c	Wages subject to social security tax (from Form 8919, line 10) **8c**		
d	Add lines 8a, 8b, and 8c	**8d**	50,000
9	Subtract line 8d from line 7. If zero or less, enter -0- here and on line 10 and go to line 11 ▶	**9**	56,800
10	Multiply the **smaller** of line 6 or line 9 by 12.4% (.124)	**10**	7,043
11	Multiply line 6 by 2.9% (.029)	**11**	1,875
12	**Self-employment tax.** Add lines 10 and 11. Enter here and on **Form 1040, line 56.** . . .	**12**	8,918
13	**Deduction for one-half of self-employment tax.** Multiply line 12 by 50% (.50). Enter the result here and on **Form 1040, line 27** . **13** 4,459		

Part II   Optional Methods To Figure Net Earnings (see page SE-4)

Farm Optional Method. You may use this method **only if (a)** your gross farm income[1] was not more than $6,540, **or (b)** your net farm profits[2] were less than $4,721.

14	Maximum income for optional methods	**14**	4,360 00
15	Enter the **smaller** of: two-thirds (2/3) of gross farm income[1] (not less than zero) **or** $4,360. Also include this amount on line 4b above	**15**	

Nonfarm Optional Method. You may use this method **only if (a)** your net nonfarm profits[3] were less than $4,721 and also less than 72.189% of your gross nonfarm income,[4] **and (b)** you had net earnings from self-employment of at least $400 in 2 of the prior 3 years. **Caution.** You may use this method no more than five times.

16	Subtract line 15 from line 14	**16**	
17	Enter the **smaller** of: two-thirds (2/3) of gross nonfarm income[4] (not less than zero) **or** the amount on line 16. Also include this amount on line 4b above	**17**	

[1] From Sch. F, line 11, and Sch. K-1 (Form 1065), box 14, code B.

[2] From Sch. F, line 36, and Sch. K-1 (Form 1065), box 14, code A— minus the amount you would have entered on line 1b had you not used the optional method.

[3] From Sch. C, line 31; Sch. C-EZ, line 3; Sch. K-1 (Form 1065), box 14, code A; and Sch. K-1 (Form 1065-B), box 9, code J1.

[4] From Sch. C, line 7; Sch. C-EZ, line 1; Sch. K-1 (Form 1065), box 14, code C; and Sch. K-1 (Form 1065-B), box 9, code J2.

Schedule SE (Form 1040) 2009

To: Sara Howly
From: CPA Candidate
Re: Self-employment taxes

     This memorandum explains the effects of the operation of your two businesses on the amount of self-employment taxes you must pay.

     When an individual conducts two or more businesses as a sole proprietor, the net earnings from self-employment are the combined net earnings from all businesses. If there is a loss from one business, it reduces the income from another. The individual's self-employment tax is computed on one Schedule SE.

     If you have any questions, please contact me.

Situation	Schedule SE	Communication	Research

Internal Revenue Code Section 164(f) provides for a deduction equal to one-half of self-employment taxes paid.

Section	Subsection
§ 164	(f)

SIMULATION PROBLEM 2   (30 to 35 minutes)

Chris (social security #432-89-5567) and Robin Raulf were married and gainfully employed throughout 2009. Chris earned $24,000 and Robin earned $16,000 in wages during the year. The couple have a son. Colin (social security #343-04-3413), who is sent to an after-school child care center (Happy Times Child Care, 319 Fairway Drive, Superior, Colorado 80027, EIN #36-4567891) to enable the Raulfs to work. The Raulfs paid Happy Times $5,200 during the year for the care of Colin, but did not receive any employer-provided dependent care benefits. The Raulfs' adjusted gross income reported on Form 1040, line 38, was $41,600 for 2009, while the tax shown on the Raulfs' Form 1040, line 46, was $2,056. The Raulfs had no foreign tax credit on Form 1040, line 51.

Complete the following Form 2441 to determine the Raulfs' available credit for child and dependent care expenses for 2009.

Communication | Situation | Form 2441 | Research

The Raulfs contact you and indicate that although they know the amounts paid to Happy Times Child Care qualify for the child care credit, they wonder what other payments might also qualify. Write a letter to the Raulfs explaining what is included in "qualified expenses" for purposes of the child care credit.

REMINDER: Your response will be graded for both technical content and writing skills. Technical content will be evaluated for information that is helpful to the intended reader and clearly relevant to the issue. Writing skills will be evaluated for development, organization, and the appropriate expression of ideas in professional correspondence. Use a standard business memo or letter format with a clear beginning, middle, and end. Do not convey information in the form of a table, bullet point list, or other abbreviated presentation.

Research | Situation | Form 2441 | Communication

The credit for expenses for household and dependent care services necessary for gainful employment is allowed for expenses incurred for qualifying individuals. What Internal Revenue Code section and subsection defines a "qualified individual" for purposes of the child and dependent care credit?

Section	Subsection
§ [　　]	([　　])

Form **2441**	**Child and Dependent Care Expenses**		OMB No. 1545-0074
Department of the Treasury Internal Revenue Service (99)	▶ Attach to Form 1040, Form 1040A, or Form 1040NR. ▶ See separate instructions.	1040 / 1040A / 1040NR / 2441	**2009** Attachment Sequence No. **21**

Name(s) shown on return | Your social security number

Part I   **Persons or Organizations Who Provided the Care**—You **must** complete this part.
(If you have more than two care providers, see the instructions.)

1	(a) Care provider's name	(b) Address (number, street, apt. no., city, state, and ZIP code)	(c) Identifying number (SSN or EIN)	(d) Amount paid (see instructions)

Did you receive dependent care benefits?	**No** ▶	Complete only Part II below.
	Yes ▶	Complete Part III on the back next.

Caution. If the care was provided in your home, you may owe employment taxes. If you do, you cannot file Form 1040A. For details, see the instructions for Form 1040, line 59, or Form 1040NR, line 56.

Part II   **Credit for Child and Dependent Care Expenses**

2   Information about your **qualifying person(s)**. If you have more than two qualifying persons, see the instructions.

(a) Qualifying person's name		(b) Qualifying person's social security number	(c) Qualified expenses you incurred and paid in 2009 for the person listed in column (a)
First	Last		

3   Add the amounts in column (c) of line 2. **Do not** enter more than $3,000 for one qualifying person or $6,000 for two or more persons. If you completed Part III, enter the amount from line 34 . . . . **3**

4   Enter your **earned income**. See instructions **4**

5   If married filing jointly, enter your spouse's earned income (if your spouse was a student or was disabled, see the instructions); **all others**, enter the amount from line 4 . . . . **5**

6   Enter the **smallest** of line 3, 4, or 5 . . . . **6**

7   Enter the amount from Form 1040, line 38; Form 1040A, line 22; or Form 1040NR, line 36.   **7**

8   Enter on line 8 the decimal amount shown below that applies to the amount on line 7

If line 7 is:			If line 7 is:		
Over	But not over	Decimal amount is	Over	But not over	Decimal amount is
$0—15,000		.35	$29,000—31,000		.27
15,000—17,000		.34	31,000—33,000		.26
17,000—19,000		.33	33,000—35,000		.25
19,000—21,000		.32	35,000—37,000		.24
21,000—23,000		.31	37,000—39,000		.23
23,000—25,000		.30	39,000—41,000		.22
25,000—27,000		.29	41,000—43,000		.21
27,000—29,000		.28	43,000—No limit		.20

8   X.

9   Multiply line 6 by the decimal amount on line 8. If you paid 2008 expenses in 2009, see the instructions **9**

10   Enter the amount from Form 1040, line 46; Form 1040A, line 28; or Form 1040NR, line 43. . . . . **10**

11   Enter the amount from Form 1040, line 47; or Form 1040NR, line 44. Form 1040A filers, enter -0- **11**

12   Subtract line 11 from line 10. If zero or less, **stop.** You cannot take the credit **12**

13   **Credit for child and dependent care expenses.** Enter the **smaller** of line 9 or line 12 here and on Form 1040, line 48; Form 1040A, line 29; or Form 1040NR, line 45 . . . . **13**

For Paperwork Reduction Act Notice, see page 4 of the instructions.   Cat. No. 11862M   Form **2441** (2009)

SOLUTION TO SIMULATION PROBLEM 2

Situation	Form 2441	Communication	Research

Form **2441**	**Child and Dependent Care Expenses**	1040 / 1040A / 1040NR / 2441	OMB No. 1545-0074

Department of the Treasury
Internal Revenue Service (99)

▶ Attach to Form 1040, Form 1040A, or Form 1040NR.
▶ See separate instructions.

20**09**
Attachment Sequence No. **21**

Name(s) shown on return	Your social security number
Chris & Robin Raulf	432-89-5567

Part I   **Persons or Organizations Who Provided the Care**—You **must** complete this part.
(If you have more than two care providers, see the instructions.)

1	(a) Care provider's name	(b) Address (number, street, apt. no., city, state, and ZIP code)	(c) Identifying number (SSN or EIN)	(d) Amount paid (see instructions)
	Happy Times Child Care	319 Fairway Drive Superior, CO 80027	36-4567891	5,200

Did you receive dependent care benefits?	**No** ▶ Complete only Part II below. **Yes** ▶ Complete Part III on the back next.

Caution. If the care was provided in your home, you may owe employment taxes. If you do, you cannot file Form 1040A. For details, see the instructions for Form 1040, line 59, or Form 1040NR, line 56.

Part II   **Credit for Child and Dependent Care Expenses**

2   Information about your **qualifying person(s)**. If you have more than two qualifying persons, see the instructions.

(a) Qualifying person's name		(b) Qualifying person's social security number	(c) Qualified expenses you incurred and paid in 2009 for the person listed in column (a)
First	Last		
Colin	Raulf	343-04-3413	5,200

3	Add the amounts in column (c) of line 2. **Do not** enter more than $3,000 for one qualifying person or $6,000 for two or more persons. If you completed Part III, enter the amount from line 34	**3**	3,000
4	Enter your **earned income**. See instructions	**4**	24,000
5	If married filing jointly, enter your spouse's earned income (if your spouse was a student or was disabled, see the instructions); **all others**, enter the amount from line 4	**5**	16,000
6	Enter the **smallest** of line 3, 4, or 5	**6**	3,000
7	Enter the amount from Form 1040, line 38; Form 1040A, line 22; or Form 1040NR, line 36. . . . . **7** 41,600		

8   Enter on line 8 the decimal amount shown below that applies to the amount on line 7

If line 7 is:			If line 7 is:		
Over	But not over	Decimal amount is	Over	But not over	Decimal amount is
$0—15,000		.35	$29,000—31,000		.27
15,000—17,000		.34	31,000—33,000		.26
17,000—19,000		.33	33,000—35,000		.25
19,000—21,000		.32	35,000—37,000		.24
21,000—23,000		.31	37,000—39,000		.23
23,000—25,000		.30	39,000—41,000		.22
25,000—27,000		.29	41,000—43,000		.21
27,000—29,000		.28	43,000—No limit		.20

8	X . 21

9	Multiply line 6 by the decimal amount on line 8. If you paid 2008 expenses in 2009, see the instructions	**9**	630
10	Enter the amount from Form 1040, line 46; Form 1040A, line 28; or Form 1040NR, line 43. . . . . **10** 2,056		
11	Enter the amount from Form 1040, line 47; or Form 1040NR, line 44. Form 1040A filers, enter -0- . . . **11**		
12	Subtract line 11 from line 10. If zero or less, **stop.** You cannot take the credit	**12**	2,056
13	**Credit for child and dependent care expenses.** Enter the **smaller** of line 9 or line 12 here and on Form 1040, line 48; Form 1040A, line 29; or Form 1040NR, line 45	**13**	630

For Paperwork Reduction Act Notice, see page 4 of the instructions.   Cat. No. 11862M   Form **2441** (2009)

Situation	Form 2441	Communication		Research

This memorandum is designed to explain the nature of qualified expenses for the child care credit.

The term "qualified expenses" for purposes of the child care credit include amounts paid for household services and care of a qualifying person while you work or look for work. Household services are services needed to care for the qualifying person as well as to run the home. For example, they include the services of a cook, maid, babysitter, housekeeper, or cleaning person if the services were partly for the care of the qualifying person. Care of a qualifying person includes the cost of services for the qualifying person's well-being and protection. You can include the cost of care provided outside the home for a dependent under age 13 or any other qualifying person who regularly spends at least eight hours a day in your home. Care does not include the cost of schooling for a child in the first grade or above.

If you have any additional questions, please contact me.

Situation	Form 2441	Communication	Research

Internal Revenue Code Section 21(b) defines a qualifying individual for purposes of the child and dependent care credit.

Section	Subsection
§ 21	(b)

BUSINESS ENVIRONMENT AND CONCEPTS
TESTLET 1

1. Under the Revised Uniform Limited Partnership Act which of the following is required in the certificate of limited partnership filed with the Secretary of State?
    a. The names of all of the limited partners.
    b. The names of all of the general partners.
    c. The names of all of the partners.
    d. None of the above.

2. Which of the following is **not** considered to be an advantage of organizing a business as a sole proprietorship?
    a. Easy and inexpensive to organize.
    b. Allows freedom of action for the entrepreneur.
    c. Provides strong incentives to manage the business efficiently.
    d. Allows the proprietor to carry out all basic management functions.

3. Able, Bray, and Carry form a general partnership to produce and sell widgets. Able is a CPA, Bray has an MBA, and Carry has few skills. In their partnership agreement, they decide to split any profits they have in the following respective proportions: 45%, 45%, and 10%. They fail to agree on how they will share any losses. At the end of the first year of operations they have a large loss. Assuming each of the partners has sufficient assets to cover the loss of their partnership, how will they split the losses between Able, Bray, and Carry, respectively?
    a. 45%, 45%, and 10%.
    b. Equally.
    c. It cannot be determined yet until they agree upon a loss-sharing plan.
    d. A court of law will have to decide upon the way they will each share the loss.

4. Several individuals form a Limited Liability Company (LLC) under an LLC state statute that is like the statutes that the majority of states have passed. Which of the following characteristics will this LLC have?

I. All of the owners have limited liability.
II. Owners designated as limited partners have limited liability.
III. The LLC is a separate legal entity.

    a. I only.
    b. II only.
    c. I and III.
    d. II and III only.

5. Which of the following is not a fundamental characteristic of a Subchapter C corporation?
    a. The shareholders have limited liability.
    b. Those that manage the corporation must be shareholders.
    c. The shareholders generally elect the board of directors.
    d. The corporation is a legal entity in itself.

6. Which of the following is a part of the central processing unit?
    a. Analog translator converter.
    b. Arithmetic/logic unit.
    c. Optical disk.
    d. Printer unit.

7. A data model developed specifically for use in designing accounting information databases is
    a. REA data model.
    b. Data definition language.
    c. Entity-relationship model.
    d. Networked model.

8. The type of system most likely to be used to initially record the daily processing of transactions
    a. Transaction processing system.
    b. Management information system.
    c. Decision support system.
    d. Executive information system.

9. Which of the following is correct concerning the Internet?
    a. All communications are processed using URL—Uniform Resource Language.
    b. It is composed of an international collection of networks of independently owned computers.
    c. It requires the use of viruses, which invariably escape their proper primary use and infect user computers.
    d. The operating center of the Internet is headquartered in the New York World Wide Web Center.

10. A method to originally capture data to multiple magnetic disks is referred to as
    a. Analog approach.
    b. Parallel magnetic drums.
    c. RAID.
    d. Zip drive approach.

11. A system that stores transactions in a single database, but process them at various sites is referred to as
    a. Centralized system.
    b. Database management normalization system.
    c. Decentralized system.
    d. Distributed system.

Items 12 and 13 are based on the following information:

Total production costs of prior periods for a company are listed below. Assume that the same cost behavior patterns can be extended linearly over the range of 3,000 to 35,000 units and that the cost driver for each cost is the number of units produced.

Production in units per month	3,000	9,000	16,000	35,000
Cost X	$23,700	$52,680	$86,490	$178,260
Cost Y	47,280	141,840	252,160	551,600

12. What is the average cost per unit at a production level of 8,000 units for cost X?
    a. $5.98
    b. $5.85
    c. $7.90
    d. $4.83

13. Identify the cost curve for the average cost per unit for cost Y.

Curve 1

Quantity

Curve 2

Quantity

Curve 3

Quantity

Curve 4

Quantity

   a.   Curve 1.
   b.   Curve 2.
   c.   Curve 3.
   d.   Curve 4.

14. Layton Co. has an average accounts payable balance of $850,000 and its cost of goods sold for the year is $8,750,000. Using a 365-day year, calculate the firm's payables deferral period.
   a.   25.50 days.
   b.   30.50 days.
   c.   35.46 days.
   d.   42.33 days.

15. A strategy map in the balanced scorecard framework is
   a.   A statement of what the strategy must achieve and what is critical to its success.
   b.   Key action programs required to achieve strategic objectives.
   c.   Diagrams of the cause-and-effect relationships between strategic objectives.
   d.   The level of performance or rate of improvement needed in the performance measure.

Items 16 and 17 are based on the following information:

The following are selected data for Lenley Manufacturing Company for the year ended 20X1.

Sales	$30,000,000
Average invested capital (total assets)	10,000,000
Total fixed assets	6,000,000
Net income	3,000,000
Net cash flow	5,000,000
Imputed interest rate	10%

16. Which of the following measures the return on investments for Lenley Manufacturing Company for the year?
   a.   2%
   b.   8%
   c.   10%
   d.   30%

17. Which of the following measures residual income for Lenley Manufacturing Company for the year?
   a. $1,000,000
   b. $2,000,000
   c. $3,000,000
   d. $6,000,000

18. Which type of economic market structure is characterized by many firms selling a differentiated product with no significant barriers to entry?
   a.   Monopoly.
   b.   Oligopoly.
   c.   Perfect competition.
   d.   Monopolistic competition.

Items 19 and 20 are based on the following information:

The operating results in summarized form for a retail computer store for 2008 are

Revenue:	
Hardware sales	$4,800,000
Software sales	2,000,000
Maintenance contracts	1,200.00
Total revenue	$8,000,000
Costs and expenses	
Cost of hardware sales	$3,360,000
Cost of software sales	1,200,000
Marketing expenses	600,000
Customer maintenance costs	640,000
Administrative expenses	1,120,000
Total costs and expenses	$6,920,000
Operating income	$1,080,000

The computer store is in the process of formulating its operating budget for 2009 and has made the following assumptions:

- The selling prices of hardware are expected to increase 10% but there will be no selling price increases for software and maintenance contracts.
- Hardware unit sales are expected to increase 5% with a corresponding 5% growth in the number of maintenance contracts; growth in unit software sales is estimated at 8%.
- The cost of hardware and software is expected to increase 4%.
- Marketing expenses will be increased 5% in the coming year.
- Three technicians will be added to the customer maintenance operations in the coming year, increasing the customer maintenance costs by $120,000.
- Administrative costs will be held at the same level.

19. The retail computer store's budgeted total revenue for 2009 would be
   a. $8,804,000
   b. $8,460,000
   c. $8,904,000
   d. $8,964,000

20. The retail computer store's budgeted total costs and expenses for the coming year would be
   a. $7,252,400
   b. $7,526,960
   c. $7,558,960
   d. $7,893,872

21. The marginal cost of capital (MCC) curve for a company rises twice, first when the company has raised $75 million and again when $175 million of new funds have been raised. These increases in the MCC are caused by
   a.   Increases in the returns on the additional investments undertaken.
   b.   Decreases in the returns on the additional investments undertaken.

    c.   Decreases in the cost of at least one of the financing sources.

    d.   Increases in the cost of at least one of the financing sources.

22. Inventory turnover is calculated as follows:

    a. $\dfrac{\text{Net sales}}{\text{Year-end inventory}}$

    b. $\dfrac{\text{Year-end inventory}}{\text{Net sales}}$

    c. $\dfrac{\text{Cost of goods sold}}{\text{Average inventory}}$

    d. $\dfrac{\text{Net sales}}{\text{Average inventory}}$

23. Which one of the following is **not** a determinant in valuing a call option?

    a.   Exercise price.

    b.   Expiration date.

    c.   Forward contract price.

    d.   Interest rate.

24. A company obtaining short-term financing with trade credit will pay a higher percentage financing cost, everything else being equal, when

    a.   The discount percentage is lower.

    b.   The items purchased have a higher price.

    c.   The items purchased have a lower price.

    d.   The supplier offers a longer discount period.

25. An analyst covering Guilderland Mining Co. common stock estimates the following information for the next year.

Expected return on the market portfolio	12%
Expected return on Treasury securities	5%
Expected beta of Guilderland	2.2

Using the CAPM, the analyst's estimate of next year's risk premium for Guilderland's stock is closest to

    a.   7.0%

    b.   10.4%

    c.   15.4%

    d.   21.4%

BUSINESS ENVIRONMENT AND CONCEPTS

ANSWERS TO TESTLET 1

1. b	5. b	9. b	13. d	17. b	21. d	25. c
2. d	6. b	10. c	14. c	18. d	22. c	
3. a	7. a	11. d	15. c	19. d	23. c	
4. c	8. a	12. a	16. d	20. b	24. d	

Hints for Multiple-Choice Questions

1. Only general partners must be listed.

2. Professional management is desirable.

3. Losses are essentially negative profits.

4. All of the owners have no personal liability.

5. Ownership and management of the corporation can be kept separate.

6. Think of the type of processing the computer itself often performs.

7. One of these is less familiar terminology in general IT, but more familiar in the area of accounting information systems.

8. Nothing difficult here, "transactions" is the key.

9. Most of these replies are nonsense.

10. RAID means redundant array of independent (previously, inexpensive) disks.

11. Two of the replies would suggest various sites. One of those ordinarily includes a single database.

12. Cost X is a mixed cost.

13. Use the high-low method.

14. Deferral period is equal to payables divided by cost of goods sold per day.

15. Strategy maps associate strategies with measures.

16. ROI is equal to operating income divided by total fixed assets.

17. RI is equal to operating income minus a charge for the cost of capital.

18. No tricks here.

19. Be sure to consider all the changes in the variables.

20. Be sure to consider all the changes in the variables.

21. The marginal cost of capital is the weighted-average of the costs of different financing sources.

22. Inventory turnover is equal to CGS divided by average inventory.

23. Value is based on price, time, and interest rate.

24. Recall the formula for trade credit interest rate.

25. Risk premium = Beta × (Expected return of portfolio – Risk-free rate)

Explanations

1. **(b)** Under the Revised Uniform Limited Partnership Act the certificate of limited partnership must contain the names of all of the general partners.

2. **(d)** Allowing the proprietor to carry out all of the basic management functions is not an advantage because professional management is generally more qualified.

3. **(a)** If partners agree on unequal profit sharing but are silent on loss sharing, losses are shared based on the profit-sharing proportions.

4. **(c)** In limited liability corporations all partners have limited liability and they are separate legal entities.

5. **(b)** Subchapter C corporations have a separation of management and shareholders. Management is typically professional management who may or may not be shareholders.

6. **(b)** The central processing unit is made up of an arithmetic/logic unit, primary memory, and a control unit.

7. **(a)** An REA data model is designed for use in designing accounting information databases.

8. **(a)** A transaction processing system is used to process transactions.

9. **(b)** The internet is an international collection of networks made up of independently owned computers.

10. **(c)** RAID (redundant array of independent disks) is a way of storing the same data redundantly on multiple magnetic disks.

11. **(d)** In a distributed system, transactions for a single database are processed at various sites.

12. **(a)** Using the high-low method: ($178,260 – 23,700)/(35,000 – 3,000) = $4.83 variable cost. Fixed cost equals $23,700 – (3,000 × 4.83) = $9,210. Fixed cost per unit at 8,000 units is $1.15 (9,210 / 8,000). Average cost per unit is equal to $5.98 ($4.83 + $1.15).

13. **(d)** The average cost is constant because there are no fixed costs.

14. **(c)** The payables deferral period is equal to 35.46 [$850,000 / ($8,750,000 / 365)].

15. **(c)** Strategy maps are diagrams of the cause-and-effect relationships between strategic objectives.

16. **(d)** Return on investments is equal to 30% ($3,000,000 net income / $10,000,000 average investment).

17. **(b)** Residual income is equal to $2,000,000 [$3,000,000 net income – ($10,000,000 invested capital × 10% imputed interest rate)].

18. **(d)** Monopolistic competition is characterized by many firms selling a differentiated product with no significant barriers to entry.

19. (d) Budgeted revenue is equal to $8,964,000 [($4,800,000 × 1.05 × 1.10) + ($2,000,000 × 1.08) + ($1,200,000 × 1.05)].

20. (b) Budgeted total costs and expenses is equal to $7,526,960 [($3,360,000 × 1.05 (increase in unit sales) × 1.04 (increase in cost)] + [$1,200,000 × 1.08 (increase in unit sales) × 1.04 (increase in cost)] + [($600,000 × 1.05) + ($640,000 + $120,000) + $1,120,000].

21. (d) An increase in the cost of a financing source increases the marginal cost of capital.

22. (c) Inventory turnover is calculated as cost of goods sold divided by average inventory.

23. (c) A call option is valued by using the exercise price, the exercise date, and the interest rate.

24. (d) The cost of trade credit is measured by the [discount percent / (100% − discount percent) × 365 days / (total pay period − discount period)]. Therefore, if the discount period is increased, the interest rate increases.

25. (c) The risk premium is equal to about 15.4% [(12% − 5%) × 2.2]. Note that the risk premium is equal to CAPM–the risk free rate (20.5% − 5%).

BUSINESS ENVIRONMENT AND CONCEPTS
TESTLET 2

1. Apex, Bail, and Call formed a general partnership recently. Which of the following is not true concerning this partnership or these partners under the Revised Uniform Partnership Act?

- a. The partners each have limited liability similar to the liability of shareholders of a typical corporation.
- b. The partners have joint and several liability for any breaches of contract of their partnership.
- c. The partners have joint and several liability for any lawsuits against their partnership based on tort law.
- d. The partnership may legally own property in its own name.

2. Three partners have formed a general partnership that they desire to last for several years. They have not agreed to any specified time period. Which of the following is true under the Revised Uniform Partnership Act?

- a. The partnership agreement is required to be in writing.
- b. All three partners are required to share profits or losses equally.
- c. Each of the three partners has an equal right to participate in the management of the partnership.
- d. A partner may assign his or her interest in the partnership only if the other two agree.

3. Which of the following statements concerning the effect of an assignment of a general partnership interest is(are) true?

I. The assignment gives the assigner's interest in the partnership profits to the assignee.
II. The assignee becomes a partner in place of the assignor.

- a. I only.
- b. II only.
- c. Both I and II.
- d. Neither I nor II.

4. Which of the following is true concerning the rights of shareholders?

- a. Shareholders have the right to receive dividends when the corporation makes a profit.
- b. Shareholders have the right to manage the corporation.
- c. Shareholders have no right to inspect the books and records of the corporation.
- d. Shareholders can vote by proxy when they have voting rights.

5. A common input device is a(n)

- a. Compiler.
- b. Printer.
- c. Expert system.
- d. Point-of-sale recorder.

6. Which of the following is most likely to be considered an advantage of a sophisticated multiuser database?

- a. It may be operated and maintained without particular computer expertise.
- b. Information may be retrieved quickly.
- c. Conversion of traditional files to such a format is ordinarily extremely simple.

- d. It is easy to distribute information to every possible user.

7. Which of the following is not a widely used disaster recovery approach?

- a. Hot site.
- b. Firewall.
- c. Regular backups.
- d. Cold site.

8. Using sophisticated techniques from statistics, artificial intelligence, and computer graphics to explain, confirm, or explore relationships among data is referred to as

- a. Data mining.
- b. Data warehousing.
- c. Decision support.
- d. Distributed analysis.

9. The network most frequently used for private operations designed to link computers within a building in a research park is referred to as a(n)

- a. Bulletin board service.
- b. Local area network.
- c. Wide area network.
- d. Zero base network.

10. As used in information technology, a protocol is a set of rules for

- a. Exchanging data between two computers.
- b. Operating an operating system.
- c. Identifying proper computer technology needs.
- d. Measuring IT transmission speed.

Items 11 and 12 are based on the following information:

The power and maintenance departments of a manufacturing company are service departments that provide support to each other as well as to the organization's two production departments, plating and assembly. The manufacturing company employs separate departmental manufacturing overhead rates for the two production departments requiring the allocation of the service department costs to the two manufacturing departments. Square footage of area served is used to allocate the maintenance department costs while percentage of power usage is used to allocate the power department costs. Department costs and operation data are as follows:

	Service Departments		Production Departments	
Costs:	*Power*	*Maintenance*	*Plating*	*Assembly*
Labor	$60,000	$180,000		
Overhead	1,440,000	540,000		
Total costs	$1,500,000	$720,000		
Operating Data:				
Square feet	6,000	1,500	6,000	24,000
Percent of Usage:				
Long-run capacity	--	5%	60%	35%
Expected actual use	--	4%	70%	26%

11. The allocation method that would provide this manufacturer with the theoretically best allocation of service department costs would be

- a. A dual-rate allocation method allocating variable cost on expected actual usage and fixed costs on long-run capacity usage.

b. The step-down allocation method.
c. The direct allocation method.
d. The reciprocal (or linear algebra) allocation method.

12. Without prejudice to your answer in 11, assume that the manufacturing company employs the step-down allocation method to allocate service department costs. If it allocates the cost of the maintenance department first, then the amount of the maintenance department's costs that are directly allocated to the plating department would be
    a. $144,000
    b. $120,000
    c. $115,200
    d. $ 90,000

13. Economists generally agree that business cycles are caused by changes in
    a. Aggregate expenditures resulting from technological changes, political events, or government monetary policy.
    b. Stock prices resulting from the need for market corrections, inflation, or government intervention.
    c. Public expectations about the future direction of prices resulting from government policies.
    d. Federal government fiscal policy, particularly changes in effective income tax rates.

14. In the cost of quality, liability claims are examples of
    a. Prevention costs.
    b. Appraisal costs.
    c. Internal failure costs.
    d. External failure costs.

15. If the economy is facing demand-pull inflation, which of the following would be a logical action by the government?
    a. Decrease income taxes.
    b. Sell government securities.
    c. Lower the discount rate.
    d. Increase government spending.

Items 16 and 17 are based on the following information:

The following information is available for Lopinsky, Inc.:

Balance Sheet

Current assets	$ 500,000
Property, plant, & equipment	4,000,000
Total assets	$4,500,000
Current liabilities	$ 30,000
Long-term debt	2,500,000
Common stock	200,000
Retained earnings	1,770,000
Total liabilities and stockholders' equity	$4,500,000

Cost of debt before tax	7%
Cost of equity	12%
Tax rate	25%

16. What is Lopinsky's weighted-average cost of capital?
    a. 9.50%
    b. 8.75%
    c. 8.22%
    d. 6.10%

17. What is Lopinsky's debt-to-equity ratio?
    a. 1.28
    b. 0.56
    c. 1.20
    d. 2.10

18. What is the best measure of risk for a well-diversified portfolio?
    a. Beta.
    b. Standard deviation.
    c. Variance.
    d. Expected value.

19. An organization has an opportunity to establish a zero balance account system using four different regional banks. The total amount of the maintenance and transfer fees is estimated to be $8,000 per annum. The organization believes that it will increase the float on its operating disbursements by an average of two days, and its cost of short-term funds is 4%. Assuming the organization estimates its average daily operating disbursements to be $80,000, what decision should the organization make regarding this opportunity?
    a. Do not open the zero balance accounts due to the additional cost of $8,000.
    b. Do not open the zero balance accounts due to an excess of costs over benefits of $1,600.
    c. Open the zero balance accounts due to an estimated savings of $1,200.
    d. Open the zero balance accounts due to an estimated savings of $6,200.

20. The formula for calculating the times-interest-earned ratio is
    a. $\dfrac{\text{Earnings before interest and taxes}}{\text{Interest expense}}$
    b. $\dfrac{\text{Earnings before taxes}}{\text{Interest expense}}$
    c. $\dfrac{\text{Interest expense}}{\text{Earnings before interest and taxes}}$
    d. $\dfrac{\text{Interest expense}}{\text{Earnings before taxes}}$

21. A company expects to produce 100,000 units of a product at a total cost of $500,000. The selling price of the product that will provide the company with a 15% before-tax return, to the nearest cent, is
    a. $0.75
    b. $1.15
    c. $5.75
    d. $7.67

22. The economic order quantity for inventory is higher for an organization that has
    a. Lower annual unit sales.
    b. Higher fixed inventory ordering costs.
    c. Higher annual carrying costs as a percentage of inventory value.
    d. A higher purchase price per unit of inventory.

23. X and Y are complementary products. If the price of product Y increases, the immediate impact on product X is that its
    a. Price will decrease.
    b. Quantity demanded will decrease.

   c. Quantity supplied will decrease.

   d. Price, quantity demanded, and supplies will remain unchanged.

24. A consultant recommends that a company hold funds for the following two reasons.

Reason 1: Cash needs can fluctuate substantially throughout the year.

Reason 2: Opportunities for buying at a discount may appear during the year.

The cash balances used to address the reasons given above are correctly classified as

	Reason 1	*Reason 2*
a.	Speculative balances	Speculative balances
b.	Speculative balances	Precautionary balances
c.	Precautionary balances	Speculative balances
d.	Precautionary balances	Precautionary balances

25. Gild Company has been offered credit terms of 3/10, net 30. Using a 365-day year, what is the nominal cost of not taking advantage of the discount if the firm pays on the 35th day after the purchase?

   a. 14.2%

   b. 32.2%

   c. 37.6%

   d. 45.2%

BUSINESS ENVIRONMENT AND CONCEPTS
ANSWERS TO TESTLET 2

1. a	5. d	9. b	13. a	17. a	21. c	25. d
2. c	6. b	10. a	14. d	18. a	22. b	
3. a	7. b	11. d	15. b	19. b	23. b	
4. d	8. a	12. b	16. c	20. a	24. c	

Hints for Multiple-Choice Questions

1. Partners of a general partnership have unlimited liability.

2. Partners have many rights in a partnership unless they give up those rights.

3. The assignment transfers the right to receive the profits, but not the right to be a partner.

4. Shareholders may assign their voting rights.

5. Think carefully about ways you know that data may be input into a computer.

6. This is a "sophisticated, multiuser database"—not a database ordinarily used by one or two individuals.

7. One reply involves attempting to avoid a disaster, rather than help in the event of a disaster.

8. Exploring is the key.

9. This is within one building.

10. IT protocols ordinarily involve multiple computers.

11. Which method theoretically results in the best answer?

12. Plating has 6,000 square feet of the total allocation base of 36,000 square feet.

13. Business cycles are caused by changes in aggregate demand.

14. Liability claims result from defective products that are distributed to customers.

15. What action decreases demand?

16. Remember cost of debt is after tax.

17. Debt-to-equity is equal to total debt divided by total equity.

18. It is the covariance that is important.

19. Compare cost to interest savings.

20. No trick here.

21. Sales must equal 115% of cost.

22. EOQ balances order costs against holding costs.

23. Complementary products are used together.

24. Speculative balances are for investing.

25. Rate = [Discount percent/(100% – Discount)] × [365 days/(Total pay period – Discount period)].

Explanations

1. **(a)** General partners do not have limited liability under the Revised Uniform Partnership Act.

2. **(c)** In a general partnership all general partners have a right to participate in management.

3. **(a)** A partner in a general partnership may assign his or her rights to profits but cannot assign other partner rights. All general partners must agree to accepting another partner that participates in management.

4. **(d)** Shareholders have the right to vote by proxy at shareholder meetings. The other items are not rights and would require action by the board of directors.

5. **(d)** A point-of-sale recorder is a common input device used by businesses that sell items over the counter.

6. **(b)** In a sophisticated multiuser database, information may be retrieved quickly by the users. Databases require expertise, security, and data is not necessarily easy to convert.

7. **(b)** A firewall is designed to protect a system from unauthorized users, and is not a disaster recovery approach.

8. **(a)** Data mining involves using sophisticated techniques to explain, confirm, or explore relationships among data.

9. **(b)** A local area network is a privately owned network within a single building or campus of up to a few miles in size.

10. **(a)** A protocol is a set of rules for exchanging data between two or more computers.

11. **(d)** The reciprocal method provides the best answer when service departments provide services to each other.

12. **(b)** Cost allocated to the plating department is $120,000 {$720 × [$6,000 / ($6,000 + $6,000 + $24,000)]}.

13. **(a)** It is generally agreed that business cycles are caused by changes in aggregate economic output (or expenditures).

14. **(d)** Liability claims result when defective products get shipped and fail in use.

15. **(b)** Selling government securities would decrease funds available to purchase other items. All of the other items listed would make demand-pull inflation worse.

16. **(c)** The cost of capital is equal to 8.22% [(12% × $1,970,000 / $4,470,000) + 7% × (1 – 25%) × $2,500,000 / $4,470,000)]. The current liabilities are not included in the calculation.

17. **(a)** The debt-to-equity ratio is equal to 1.28 ($2,530,000 / $1,970,000).

18. (a) Beta is a standardized measure that has been developed to estimate investment risk.

19. (b) The cost of maintaining the zero balance accounts is $1,600 in excess of the benefits {$8,000 – [.04 × ($80,000 × 2)]}.

20. (a) The formula for calculating the times-interest-earned ratio is earnings before interest and taxes divided by the amount of interest expense.

21. (c) The selling price is equal to $5.75 {[$500,000 + (15% × $500,000)] / 100,000}.

22. (b) If a firm has higher fixed inventory ordering costs they should order less often and larger amounts.

23. (b) Complementary products move together in terms of demand. Therefore, if the price of Y increases, demand will decrease. The demand for X will also decrease.

24. (c) The first reason is precautionary (cash may be needed to pay bills), and the second is speculative (cash may be used to take advantage of a discount).

25. (d) The cost of not taking advantage of the discount is equal to 45.2% [3% discount / (100% – 3%)] × [365 / (35 – 10)].

BUSINESS ENVIRONMENT AND CONCEPTS
TESTLET 3

1. Which of the following is(are) true concerning the duty of due care by members and managers of a limited liability company?

    a. They owe a duty not to be grossly negligent so that the LLC is not injured.

    b. The duty of due care does not include negligence.

    c. Both of the above are true.

    d. None of the above are true.

2. Which of the following is(are) included in the Articles of Incorporation when a corporation is formed?

    a. The number of authorized shares of stock.

    b. The name of the registered agent of the corporation.

    c. The names and addresses of the incorporators.

    d. All of the above.

3. Which of the following actions of a corporation generally require the approval of its shareholders?

    a. Giving loans to its own employees when they benefit the corporation.

    b. Giving loans to its own directors.

    c. Making charitable contributions.

    d. Acquiring its own shares of stock.

4. Connect Corporation is going to sell additional shares of its stock. Which of the following would constitute valid consideration for the purchase of those additional shares?

    a. Services already performed.

    b. Services that are agreed to be performed later.

    c. Both of the above.

    d. None of the above.

5. Which of the following is **not** a control for limiting access to particular electronic information within the IT system?

    a. Database replication.

    b. Views.

    c. Passwords.

    d. Restricting privileges.

6. A combination of hardware and software that links to different types of networks is referred to as a

    a. Bridge.

    b. Gateway.

    c. Switch.

    d. Router.

7. In encryption, a value that must be placed into the algorithm to decode an encrypted message is referred to as a(n)

    a. Key.

    b. Algoret.

    c. Router.

    d. Alphanumeric.

8. One would most frequently expect a "help desk" to be a responsibility of

    a. Applications programming.

    b. Data library.

    c. Operations.

    d. Systems programming.

9. When using a "join" operation with SQL, one would most likely be

    a. Adding a new computed column to a table.

    b. Combining some or all of the information in two tables.

    c. Extending computer memory capability by combining two or more CPUs.

    d. Encrypting data.

10. A commercial disaster recovery service that allows a business to continue computer operations in the event of a computer disaster is a

    a. Hot site.

    b. Checkpoint.

    c. Rollback.

    d. DOS (Disaster Operating System).

11. In forecasting purchases of inventory for a firm, all of the following are useful **except**:

    a. Knowledge of the behavior of business cycles.

    b. Internal allocations of costs to different segments of the firm.

    c. Information on the seasonal variations in demand.

    d. Econometric modeling.

Items 12 and 13 are based on the following information:

	Total Cost	Unit Cost
Sales (40,000 units)	$1,000,000	$25
Raw materials	160,000	4
Direct labor	280,000	7
Factory overhead:		
Variable	80,000	2
Fixed	360,000	
Selling and general expenses:		
Variable	120,000	3
Fixed	225,000	

12. How many units does the company need to produce and sell to make a before-tax profit of 10% of sales?

    a. 65,000 units.

    b. 36,562 units.

    c. 90,000 units.

    d. 29,250 units.

13. Assuming that the company sells 80,000 units, what is the maximum that can be paid for an advertising campaign while still breaking even?

    a. $ 135,000

    b. $1,015,000

    c. $ 535,000

    d. $ 695,000

14. A reduction in economic activity will be displayed by all of the following except:

    a. Decreased housing starts.

    b. Increase in the quantity of unemployment claims.

    c. Reduction in the amount of luxury purchases.

    d. Increase in personal travel.

15. The primary reason for adopting TQM is to achieve

    a. Greater customer satisfaction.

    b. Reduced delivery time.

    c. Reduced delivery charges.

    d. Greater employee participation.

16. Deming Corporation utilizes the capital asset pricing model (CAPM) to estimate the cost of its common stockholder equity. Calculate CAPM given the following: the

risk-free rate of return is 5%, the expected rate of return is 10%, and firm's beta is 1.
- a. 11%
- b. 10%
- c. 5%
- d. 15%

17. The best reason corporations issue Eurobonds rather than domestic bonds is that
- a. These bonds are denominated in the currency of the country in which they are issued.
- b. These bonds are normally a less expensive form of financing because of the absence of government regulation.
- c. Foreign buyers more readily accept the issue of both large and small US corporations than do domestic investors.
- d. Eurobonds carry no foreign exchange risk.

18. From an investor's viewpoint, the **least** risky type of bond in which to invest is a(n)
- a. Debenture bond.
- b. Deep discount bond.
- c. Income bond.
- d. Secured bond.

19. If a movie theater increases ticket prices for the matinee shows by 10% and the quantity of tickets demanded decreases by 5% then the demand for matinee movie tickets is
- a. Inelastic.
- b. Elastic.
- c. Unitary.
- d. Not related to the change in price.

Items 20 and 21 are based on the following information:

The standard direct labor cost to produce one pound of output for a company is presented below. Related data regarding the planned and actual production activities for the current month for the company are also given below.

NOTE: DLH = Direct Labor Hours.

Direct Labor Standard:
.4 DLH @ $12.00 per DLH = $4.80

Planned production	15,000 pounds
Actual production	15,500 pounds
Actual direct labor costs (6,250 DLH)	$75,250

20. The company's direct labor rate variance for the current month would be
- a. $10 unfavorable.
- b. $240 unfavorable.
- c. $248 unfavorable.
- d. $250 unfavorable.

21. The company's direct labor efficiency variance for the current month would be
- a. $600 unfavorable.
- b. $602 unfavorable.
- c. $2,400 unfavorable.
- d. $3,000 unfavorable.

22. Davis Corp. is considering establishing a lockbox system. The bank will charge $30,000 annually for the service, which will save the firm approximately $15,000 in processing costs. The lockbox system will reduce the float for cash

receipts by 2 days. Assuming that the average daily cash receipts are equal to $400,000, and short-term interest costs are 4%, calculate the benefit or loss from adopting the lockbox system.
- a. $30,000 loss.
- b. $15,000 loss.
- c. $12,000 benefit.
- d. $17,000 benefit.

23. A call option on a share of common stock is more valuable when there is lower
- a. Market value of the underlying share.
- b. Exercise price on the option.
- c. Time to maturity on the option.
- d. Variability of market price on the underlying share.

Items 24 and 25 are based on the following information:

The financial management team of a company is assessing an investment proposal involving a $100,000 outlay today. Manager number one expects the project to provide cash inflows of $20,000 at the end of each year for six years. She considers the project to be of low risk, requiring only a 10% rate of return. Manager number two expects the project to provide cash inflows of $5,000 at the end of the first year, followed by $23,000 at the end of each year in years two through six. He considers the project to be of medium risk, requiring a 14% rate of return. Manager number three expects the project to be of high risk, providing one large cash inflow of $135,000 at the end of the sixth year. She proposes a 15% rate of return for the project.

Additional information

Number of years	Discount rate (percent)	Present value of $1 due at the end of n periods (PVIF)	Present value of an annuity of $1 per period for n periods (PVIFA)
1	10	.9091	.9091
1	14	.8772	.8772
1	15	.8696	.8696
5	10	.6209	3.7908
5	14	.5194	3.4331
5	15	.4972	3.3522
6	10	.5645	4.3553
6	14	.4556	3.8887
6	15	.4323	3.7845

24. According to the net present value criterion, which of the following is true?
- a. Manager one will recommend that the project be accepted.
- b. Manger two will recommend that the project be accepted.
- c. All three managers will recommend acceptance of the project.
- d. All three managers will recommend rejection of the project.

25. Which manager will assess the project as having the shortest payback period?
- a. Manager one.
- b. Manager two.
- c. Manager three.
- d. All three managers will agree on the payback period.

BUSINESS ENVIRONMENT AND CONCEPTS
ANSWERS TO TESTLET 3

1. c	5. a	9. b	13. a	17. b	21. a	25. a
2. d	6. b	10. a	14. d	18. d	22. d	
3. b	7. a	11. b	15. a	19. a	23. b	
4. c	8. c	12. c	16. b	20. d	24. d	

Hints for Multiple-Choice Questions

1. This duty of due care is more limited.

2. The Articles of Incorporation contain much important information.

3. Directors have a lot of power in a corporation.

4. Consideration for stock includes both services already performed as well as services contracted for the future.

5. One of these replies suggests "more," rather than less.

6. This one you need to understand the computer term.

7. To decode is similar to "unlocking" the code.

8. Which department deals with keeping the system functional on an hour-to-hour basis?

9. Which is most similar to joining a group?

10. Recovery operations often take place at another location.

11. Which item is arbitrary?

12. Calculate the contribution margin.

13. Calculate profit at 80,000 units.

14. Which item indicates improving conditions?

15. What is the ultimate value proposition for high-quality products?

16. CAPM = Risk-free rate + (Market rate – Risk-free rate) × Beta.

17. Eurobonds are denominated in US dollars.

18. What makes a bond less risky?

19. Elasticity of demand is equal to percentage of change in quantity divided by the percentage change in price.

20. DLRV is equal to direct labor hours times the difference between the standard rate and the actual rate.

21. DLEV is equal to the standard direct labor rate times the difference between the direct labor hours allowed and the actual hours worked.

22. The additional processing costs versus the interest savings.

23. An option value depends on option price, stock price, stock price variability, and maturity.

24. Calculate the NPV for each manager.

25. Payback period is equal to the number of years to recover initial investment.

Explanations

1. **(c)** Members and managers of a limited liability company owe a duty not to be grossly negligent, but the duty does not include a duty not to be ordinarily negligent.

2. **(d)** The Articles of Incorporation include the number of authorized shares of stock, the name of the registered agent, and the names and addresses of the incorporators, among other information.

3. **(b)** The only one of the items that require shareholder approval is providing loans to its own directors.

4. **(c)** Shares of stock may be issued for services already performed or those to be performed.

5. **(a)** Database replication is a backup procedure. All of the others are controls for limiting access.

6. **(b)** A gateway is a combination of hardware and software that links different networks.

7. **(a)** The key is the value that is used to decode the message.

8. **(c)** The operations department would normally have responsibility for the "help desk."

9. **(b)** The "join" operation in SQL is used to combine information in two different tables.

10. **(a)** A "hot site" is a disaster recovery service that allows a business to continue computer operations in the event of a disaster.

11. **(b)** Internal allocations of costs to different segments of the firm are irrelevant to forecasting purchases.

12. **(c)** The number of units that must be sold is 90,000 calculated as follows:

Sales	=	VC + FC + NI
$25X	=	$16X + $585,000 + .10($25X)
$6.5X	=	$585,000
X	=	90,000

13. **(a)** The amount can be calculated as follows:

Sales	=	VC + FC + NI
($25 × 80,000)	=	($16 × 80,000) + ($585,000 +Advertising) + $0
$2,000,000	=	$1,280,000 + $585,000 + Advertising
Advertising	=	$135,000

14. **(d)** A reduction in economic activity will not be displayed by an increase in personal travel.

15. **(a)** The primary reason to adopt TQM is to achieve greater customer satisfaction with higher quality products.

16. **(b)** CAPM is equal to 10% [5% risk free rate + (10% expected return – 5% risk free rate) /1].

17. **(b)** The registration and disclosure requirements for Eurobonds are less stringent. Therefore, the cost of issuance is less.

18. **(d)** Secured bonds are less risky because they include collateral.

19. (a) The demand is inelastic because the demand does not fall as much as the price increase.

20. (d) The direct labor rate variance is equal to $250 [$75,250 − ($12 per hour × 6,250 actual hours)].

21. (a) The direct labor efficiency variance is equal to $600 unfavorable [(6,250 actual hours × $12 standard rate) − (15,500 actual production × .4 standard hours × $12 standard rate)].

22. (d) The result is a $17,000 benefit [$15,000 reduction in processing costs + (4% × $400,000 × 2 days) − $30,000 bank charge].

23. (b) The option is more valuable when there is a lower exercise price on the option.

24. (d) The net present value is negative in all three cases.

25. (a) For manager one the payback period is 5 years ($20,000 × 5 = $100,000). For manager two the payback period is near the beginning of year 6 and for manager three the payback period is not until year 6.

1. Which of the following characteristics most likely would heighten an auditor's concern about the risk of material misstatements in an entity's financial statements?

    a. The entity's industry is experiencing declining customer demand.

    b. Employees who handle cash receipts are **not** bonded.

    c. Bank reconciliations usually include in-transit deposits.

    d. Equipment is often sold at a loss before being fully depreciated.

1. **(a)** The requirement is to identify the characteristic that would likely heighten an auditor's concern about the risk of material misstatements in an entity's financial statements. Answer (a) is correct because AU 316 states that a declining industry with increasing business failures and significant declines in customer demand is a risk factor relating to misstatements arising from fraudulent financial reporting. Answer (b) is incorrect because bonding will not necessarily affect the risk of material misstatements and is not included as a risk factor in AU 316. Answer (c) is incorrect because many bank reconciliations ordinarily include in-transit deposits and this does not necessarily increase the risk of material misstatement. Answer (d) is incorrect because equipment sold at a loss may often occur (as may gains) and not necessarily affect the risk of material misstatement.

2. Which of the following fraudulent activities most likely could be perpetrated due to the lack of effective internal controls in the revenue cycle?

    a. Fictitious transactions may be recorded that cause an understatement of revenues and an overstatement of receivables.

    b. Claims received from customers for goods returned may be intentionally recorded in other customers' accounts.

    c. Authorization of credit memos by personnel who receive cash may permit the misappropriation of cash.

    d. The failure to prepare shipping documents may cause an overstatement of inventory balances.

2. **(c)** The requirement is to identify the fraudulent activity most likely to be perpetrated due to the lack of effective internal control over the revenue cycle. Answer (c) is correct because the authorization of credit memos by personnel who receive cash presents a situation in which those individuals may issue fraudulent credit memos and misappropriate the cash. Answer (a) is incorrect because one would expect such fictitious transactions to overstate both revenues and receivables; note that the situation described in answer (a) with an understatement of revenues and an overstatement of receivables results in two debits and no credits. Answer (b) is incorrect because recording such claims in the wrong account is likely to be quickly detected when customers who have not received the credit complain. Answer (d) is incorrect because such an overstatement of inventory balances is likely to be detected through an inventory observation.

3. In planning an audit, the auditor's knowledge about the design of relevant controls should be used to

    a. Identify the types of potential misstatements that could occur.

    b. Assess the operational efficiency of internal control.

    c. Determine whether controls have been circumvented by collusion.

    d. Document the assessed level of control risk.

3. **(a)** The requirement is to determine how the auditor's knowledge about the design of relevant controls is used in planning an audit. Answer (a) is correct because such knowledge is used to (1) identify types of potential misstatements, (2) consider factors that affect the risk of material misstatements, and (3) design substantive tests. Answer (b) is incorrect because auditors are more concerned with identifying types of potential misstatements not detected by internal control rather than with assessing its operational efficiency. Answer (c) is incorrect because while auditors are concerned with whether controls are circumvented by collusion, this is not the primary emphasis during planning and is less complete than answer (a). Answer (d) is incorrect because documentation during planning emphasizes the auditor's understanding of the entity's internal control.

4. Which of the following information discovered during an audit most likely would raise a question concerning possible illegal acts?

    a. Related-party transactions, although properly disclosed, were pervasive during the year.

    b. The entity prepared several large checks payable to cash during the year.

    c. Material internal control weaknesses previously reported to management were **not** corrected.

    d. The entity was a campaign contributor to several local political candidates during the year.

4. **(b)** The requirement is to identify the information that most likely would raise a question concerning possible illegal acts. Answer (b) is correct because such large checks payable to cash raise a question as to their actual business purpose. Answer (a) is incorrect because the mere existence of **properly disclosed** related-party transactions is less likely to indicate an illegal act than are checks written to cash. Answer (c) is incorrect because management may, for valid reasons, choose to not correct material internal control weaknesses. Answer (d) is incorrect because such campaign contributions may well be legal. See AU 317 for information on illegal acts.

5. During an engagement to review the financial statements of a nonissuer (nonpublic) entity, an accountant becomes aware that several leases that should be capitalized are not capitalized. The accountant considers these leases to be material to the financial statements. The accountant decides to modify the standard review report because management will not capitalize the leases. Under these circumstances, the accountant should

    a.   Issue an adverse opinion because of the departure from GAAP.

    b.   Express **no** assurance of any kind on the entity's financial statements.

    c.   Emphasize that the financial statements are for limited use only.

    d.   Disclose the departure from GAAP in a separate paragraph of the accountant's report.

5.   **(d)**   The requirement is to determine an accountant's reporting responsibility when associated with a nonissuer (nonpublic) entity's **reviewed** statements which contain a material departure from generally accepted accounting principles. Answer (d) is correct because AR 100 requires the inclusion of a separate paragraph describing the departure. Answer (a) is incorrect because an adverse opinion may only be issued when an audit has been performed. Answer (b) is incorrect because a review report provides negative assurance, not **no** assurance. Answer (c) is incorrect because a review report is ordinarily available for general distribution, and need not emphasize that the financial statements are for limited use only.

SIMULATION 1 (50 to 60 minutes)

Company Profile	Balance Sheet	Income/ Cash Flow	Industry Info	Risks	Audit Findings	Audit Procedures	Analysis and Communication	Auditors Report

Enright Corporation is a **nonissuer (nonpublic)** manufacturer of golf balls, golf clubs, and other golf-related equipment. The company has been in business for over fifty years and has its headquarters in San Diego, California.

Enright is divided into two divisions, which represent the major markets for the company's products. One division focuses on new golf clubs and resorts, and providing them with all of the necessary golf equipment to begin operations. The other division focuses on new product development and helps existing golf clubs and resorts to upgrade their existing equipment. Currently, each division accounts for approximately equal amounts of Enright's revenues and net income.

The company experienced its second most profitable year in 2002. However, the financial results did not meet management's expectations. Total reported revenues for the year decreased three percent compared to the prior year. Management recognizes the fact that domestic sales growth has slowed significantly in recent years. As a result, the company is now adopting a global focus for marketing its products and is looking to open up new markets in Australia and Japan.

In order to be competitive in world markets, as well as to improve their domestic market share, management believes that they must strictly control costs and make their overall operations more efficient. At the end of 2002, Enright announced it would make a series of restructuring changes as part of its overall business plan for the future.

Senior management at the company has experienced a significant turnover in recent years. The CEO has been with the company for only two years. He was hired from a major competitor after the prior CEO left to take a position with a large manufacturing company in the Northeast. In addition, the company's long-time CFO retired after twenty-five years of service. The current CFO was hired six months ago. She is a former audit manager from the office that works on Enright's annual audit.

Enright has engaged the same auditing firm for its annual audits for the past decade. There have been no disagreements over accounting issues in any of the past three years.

Company Profile	Balance Sheet	Income/ Cash Flow	Industry Info	Risks	Audit Findings	Audit Procedures	Analysis and Communication	Auditors Report

Enright Corporation
BALANCE SHEET
December 31, 2002 and 2001

	12/31/02	12/31/01
Assets		
Current assets		
Cash and cash equivalents	$300,000	$235,000
Receivables—net	750,000	816,000
Investments	600,000	545,000
Inventory	1,000,000	1,171,000
Total current assets	2,650,000	2,767,000
Plant and equipment—net	850,000	876,000
Total assets	$3,500,000	$3,643,000
Liabilities and Stockholders' Equity		
Current liabilities		
Accounts payable	$390,000	$410,000
Current portion of long-term debt	620,000	620,000
Other current liabilities	315,000	298,000
Total current liabilities	1,325,000	1,328,000
Long-term debt	475,000	1,095,000
Total liabilities	1,800,000	2,423,000
Stockholders' equity		
Common stock	1,000,000	1,000,000
Retained earnings	700,000	220,000
Total stockholders' equity	1,700,000	1,220,000
Total liabilities and stockholders' equity	$3,500,000	$3,643,000

Company Profile	Balance Sheet	Income/ Cash Flow	Industry Info	Risks	Audit Findings	Audit Procedures	Analysis and Communication	Auditors Report

Enright Corporation
INCOME STATEMENT
For the Years Ended December 31, 2002 and 2001

	12/31/02	12/31/01
Sales	$5,250,000	$5,450,000
Cost of goods sold:	2,100,000	2,209,000
Gross profits on sales	3,150,000	3,241,000
Expenses		
Selling expenses	$1,050,000	$1,124,000
General and administrative	1,070,000	1,215,000
Other operating expenses		
Depreciation	30,000	35,000
Interest expense	200,000	227,000
Total expenses	$2,350,000	$2,601,000
Income before taxes	$800,000	$640,000
Provision for income taxes	320,000	256,000
Net income	$480,000	$384,000

Enright Corporation
STATEMENT OF CASH FLOWS
For the Year Ended December 31, 2002

Cash flows from operating activities:	
Net income (loss)	$480,000
Adjustments to reconcile net income (loss) to cash provided by (used for) operating activities	
Depreciation and amortization	30,000
Changes in certain assets and liabilities:	
Decrease (increase) in receivables	66,000
Decrease (increase) in inventory	171,000
Increase (decrease) in accounts payable	(20,000)
Increase (decrease) in other current liabilities	17,000
Net cash provided by (used for) operating activities	744,000
Cash flows from investing activities:	
Purchase of property, plant, and equipment	(4,000)
Change in short-term investments	(55,000)
Net cash provided by (used for) investing activities	(59,000)
Cash flows from financing activities:	
Principal payments on long-term debt	(620,000)
Net cash provided by (used for) financing activities	(620,000)
Net increase (decrease) in cash and cash equivalents	65,000
Cash and cash equivalents at beginning of year	235,000
Cash and cash equivalents at end of year	$300,000

Company Profile	Balance Sheet	Income/ Cash Flow	Industry Info	Risks	Audit Findings	Audit Procedures	Analysis and Communication	Auditors Report

Market Forecasts
USA Sports Equipment

In 2007, the USA sports equipment market is forecast to reach $47 million, an increase of 19.3% since 2002.

The compounded annual growth rate of the global sports equipment market over the period 2002-2007 is predicted to be 3.5%.

Table 4: USA Sports Equipment Market Value Forecasts: $Mn (2001 Prices), 2002-2007

Market value	$Mn (2001 prices)	% Growth
2002	$40,133.6	2.9%
2003	$41,398.3	3.2%
2004	$42,936.3	3.7%
2005	$44,389.8	3.4%
2006	$46,232.1	4.2%
2007	$46,892.1	3.6%
CAGR. 2002-2007	3.5%	

Golf: Play Is Steadying While Sales Struggle[1]

With 1.02 billion participants aged six and over for the year 2001, golf is ranked number 15, compared to other sports.

In what proved to be a disappointing year, sale of golf clubs, balls, bags, gloves, and shoes declined about 6% in wholesale dollars, to about $2.375 billion in 2001. Sales of irons, which enjoyed strong growth in 2000, accounted for most of the decease in 2001.

Clearly, the weak economy was the root of the problem and the continuing weakness in 2002 is expected to result in further slight sales declines as players postpone the purchase of the big-ticket items such ad clubs and bags.

The total number of golfers grew by 5%, from 28.9 million to 30.4 million, between 1990 and 2000. There are as many as 40 million people who would like to play or play more often. New course development was scaled back in 2001, with 314 construction projects completed through the first nine months, compared to 408 and 379 during the same periods in 2000 and 1999, respectively.

In what might be called a "Tiger Woods" effect, some experienced golfers are trying to open the game to very young players. A small national tournament for players aged four to twelve has been created. Some manufacturers are marketing youth-sized clubs and a few facilities are developing training programs for children once considered too young to play the game.

Company Profile	Balance Sheet	Income/ Cash Flow	Industry Info	Risks	Audit Findings	Audit Procedures	Analysis and Communication	Auditors Report

                                           (A) (B) (C) (D)

1. Which of the following correctly identifies an aspect of the company's business model, strategies, and operating environment that is most likely to increase audit risk?   ○ ○ ○ ○

A. The "Tiger Woods" effect.
B. The turnover of senior management in recent years.
C. The company's result in the current year of its second most profitable year in over fifty years of operations.
D. The company's organization into two divisions, which represent the major markets for the company's products.

Company Profile	Balance Sheet	Income/ Cash Flow	Industry Info	Risks	Audit Findings	Audit Procedures	Analysis and Communication	Auditors Report

The table below presents several ratios that were identified as significant in the current and prior year's audits of Enright. Compare the values for each ratio. Then double-click on each of the shaded spaces in the table and select a possible audit finding that could account for the 2002 value. For each ratio, you should select an audit finding that is consistent with these metrics. Each audit finding may be used once, more than once, or not at all. (Turnover ratios are based on year-end balances.)

Audit findings

A. The company uses a periodic inventory system for determining the balance sheet amount of inventory.
B. The company accumulated excess inventories that are physically deteriorating or are becoming obsolete.
C. Merchandise was received, placed in the stockroom, and counted, but not included in the year-end count.
D. A smaller percentage of sales occurred during the last month of the year, as compared to the prior year.
E. A dividend declared prior to the end of the year was not recorded in the general ledger.
F. A dividend declared prior to the end of the year was recorded twice in the general ledger.

	Ratio	2002	2001	(A)	(B)	(C)	(D)	(E)	(F)
1.	Inventory turnover	2.1	1.9	○	○	○	○	○	○
2.	Return on equity	28.2%	31.5%	○	○	○	○	○	○

Company Profile	Balance Sheet	Income/ Cash Flow	Industry Info	Risks	Audit Findings	Audit Procedures	Analysis and Communication	Auditors Report

The auditor determines that each of the following objectives will be part of Enright's audit. For each audit objective, select a substantive procedure that would help to achieve the audit objectives by double-clicking on each shaded space and selecting a procedure. Each of the procedures may be used once, more than once, or not at all.

Substantive procedures

A. Review minutes of board of director's meetings and contracts, and make inquiries of management.
B. Test inventory transactions between a preliminary physical inventory date and the balance sheet date.
C. Obtain confirmation of inventories pledged under loan agreement.
D. Review perpetual inventory records, production records, and purchasing records for indication of current activity.
E. Reconcile physical counts to perpetual records and general ledger balances and investigate significant fluctuation.
F. Examine sales after year-end and open purchase order commitments.
G. Examine paid vendors' invoices, consignment agreements, and contracts.
H. Analytically review and compare the relationship of inventory balance to recent purchasing, production, and sales activity.

---

[1] Source: *Sporting Goods Manufacturers Association*

	(A)	(B)	(C)	(D)	(E)	(F)	(G)	(H)
Objective								
1. Confirm that inventories represent items held for sale or use in the normal course of business.	○	○	○	○	○	○	○	○
2. Confirm that the inventory listing is accurately completed and the totals are properly included in the inventory accounts.	○	○	○	○	○	○	○	○

Company Profile	Balance Sheet	Income/ Cash Flow	Industry Info	Risks	Audit Findings	Audit Procedures	Analysis and Communication	Auditors Report

Your firm has been doing the audit of Enright Corporation for several years. Since last year, Enright changed the board of directors from family members owning stock in the company to independent executives with financial experience. In a memorandum to your audit team, explain the impact of the new board on audit risk.

REMINDER: Your response will be graded for both technical content and writing skills. Technical content will be evaluated for information that is helpful to the intended reader and clearly relevant to the issue. Writing skills will be evaluated for development, organization, and the appropriate expression of ideas in professional correspondence. Use a standard business memo or letter format with a clear beginning, middle, and end. Do not convey information in the form of a table, bullet point list, or other abbreviated presentation.

To: Audit Team
Re: New board and audit risk

Company Profile	Balance Sheet	Income/ Cash Flow	Industry Info	Risks	Audit Findings	Audit Procedures	Analysis and Communication	Auditors Report

During the fieldwork on Enright, the client asks that you perform a review of the financial statements for the current year only—and not a complete audit. You have now completed your fieldwork and find that you can issue a standard review report.

Using the research materials available to you by clicking the Standards button on the title bar, assemble model paragraphs that would be used to create the auditor's report that addresses this finding. In the reference, highlight and copy an appropriate paragraph. Click on the gray field below and paste the paragraph into the Auditor's Report form. Copy paragraphs as needed from the Standards, and click above, below, or in between paragraphs you have placed in the form to assemble the report. Use the controls provided to reorder or to delete paragraphs you highlight. **You should NOT edit the model paragraphs in any way.**

SOLUTION TO SIMULATION 1

Company Profile	Balance Sheet	Income/ Cash Flow	Industry Info	**Risks**	Audit Findings	Audit Procedures	Analysis and Communication	Auditors Report

                                                   (A) (B) (C) (D)

1. Which of the following correctly identifies an aspect of the company's business model, strategies, and operating environment that is most likely to increase audit risk?   ○ ● ○ ○

Explanation of solution

1. **(B)** The requirement is to identify the aspect of a company's business that is most likely to increase audit risk. Answer (B) is correct because turnover of senior management frequently signals a higher level of audit risk both because in some circumstances the reasons for turnover raise questions, and because of inexperience of new top management. Answer (A) is incorrect because the Tiger Woods effect is likely to increase sales through purchases made by young people and has no necessary tie to audit risk. Answer (C) is incorrect because simply having the second most profitable year doesn't make the information seem likely to indicate a misstatement. Answer (D) is incorrect because an organization with two divisions represents no major difficulty for the audit, and does not ordinarily increase audit risk.

Company Profile	Balance Sheet	Income/ Cash Flow	Industry Info	Risks	**Audit Findings**	Audit Procedures	Analysis and Communication	Auditors Report

	Ratio	2002	2001		(A) (B) (C) (D) (E) (F)
1.	Inventory turnover	2.1	1.9		○ ○ ● ○ ○ ○
2.	Return on equity	28.2%	31.5%		○ ○ ○ ○ ● ○

Explanation of solutions

1. **(C)** The requirement is to identify an explanation for an increase in the inventory turnover—the ratio of cost of goods sold to inventory. Answer (C) is correct because while the inventory was received, it was not included in the final inventory count and the purchase was not recorded. Thus, the denominator of the ratio decreases, increasing the overall turnover.

2. **(E)** The requirement is to identify a possible reason for a decrease in the return on equity—net income divided by stockholders' equity. Answer (E) is correct because not recording a dividend that has been declared has the effect of overstating the denominator (owner's equity) and thereby reducing the overall return rate.

Company Profile	Balance Sheet	Income/ Cash Flow	Industry Info	Risks	Audit Findings	**Audit Procedures**	Analysis and Communication	Auditors Report

                                       (A) (B) (C) (D) (E) (F) (G) (H)

1. Confirm that inventories represent items held for sale or use in the normal course of business.   ○ ○ ○ ● ○ ○ ○ ○

2. Confirm that the inventory listing is accurately completed and the totals are properly included in the inventory accounts.   ○ ○ ○ ○ ● ○ ○ ○

Explanation of solutions

1. **(D)** The requirement is to identify the best substantive procedure to confirm that inventories represent items held for sale or use in the normal course of business. Answer (D) is best because a review of perpetual inventory records, production records, and purchasing records for indication of current activity will reveal whether those items are being sold.

2. **(E)** The requirement is to identify the best substantive procedure to confirm that the inventory listing is accurately completed and the totals are properly included in the inventory counts. Answer (E) is correct because reconciling physical counts to perpetual records and general ledgers balances and investigating significant fluctuations will identify errors in totals.

Company Profile	Balance Sheet	Income/ Cash Flow	Industry Info	Risks	Audit Findings	Audit Procedures	Analysis and Communication	Auditors Report

Memorandum

To: Audit Team
Re: New board and audit risk

   This memorandum is designed to describe the effects of the new makeup of the board of directors on audit risk for the engagement. Enright changed the board of directors from family members owning stock in the company to independent executives with financial experience. This change increases the objectivity and competence of the board. With this structure in place there is less risk that financial statements will be misstated by management because of the new board's oversight. Therefore, audit risk for the engagement should be reduced.

Company Profile	Balance Sheet	Income/ Cash Flow	Industry Info	Risks	Audit Findings	Audit Procedures	Analysis and Communication	Auditors Report

Auditor's Review Report

[Addressee]

Source: AR§100.366 (SSARS)

I(we) have reviewed the accompanying balance sheet of XYZ Company as of December 31, 20X1, and the related statements of income, retained earnings, and cash flows for the year then ended, in accordance with Statements on Standards for Accounting and Review Services issued by the American Institute of Certified Public Accountants. All information included in these financial statements is the representation of the management (owners) of XYZ Company.

A review consists principally of inquiries of company personnel and analytical procedures applied to financial data. It is substantially less in scope than an audit in accordance with generally accepted auditing standards, the objective of which is the expression of an opinion regarding the financial statements taken as a whole. Accordingly, I(we) do not express such an opinion.

Based on my (our) review, I am (we are) not aware of any material modifications that should be made to the accompanying financial statements in order for them to be in conformity with generally accepted accounting principles.

FINANCIAL ACCOUNTING AND REPORTING TESTLETS RELEASED BY AICPA

1. For $50 a month, Rawl Co. visits its customers' premises and performs insect control services. If customers experience problems between regularly scheduled visits, Rawl makes service calls at no additional charge. Instead of paying monthly, customers may pay an annual fee of $540 in advance. For a customer who pays the annual fee in advance, Rawl should recognize the related revenue

    a. Evenly over the contract year as the services are performed.
    b. At the end of the contract year after all of the services have been performed.
    c. When the cash is collected.
    d. At the end of the fiscal year.

1. **(a)** Revenue is generally recognized when **realized or realizable** and **earned**. Revenues are considered earned when the entity has substantially accomplished what it must do to be entitled to the benefits represented by the revenues. Therefore, service revenue generally is earned as the work is performed, and it should be recognized evenly over the contract year as the monthly services are performed. Answer (c) is incorrect because accrual basis accounting is preferable; SFAC 6 explains that cash method provides little information about the results of operations. Answer (d) is incorrect because revenue should be recognized when earned. Answer (b) is incorrect because the completed-contract method should only be used when reasonable estimates of contract costs, revenues, and the extent of progress toward completion cannot be reasonably estimated.

2. Simm Co. has determined its December 31 inventory on a FIFO basis to be $400,000. Information pertaining to that inventory follows:

Estimated selling price	$403,000
Estimated cost of disposal	20,000
Normal profit margin	60,000
Current replacement cost	360,000

Simm records losses that result from applying the lower of cost or market rule. At December 31, what should be the amount of Simm's inventory?

    a. $400,000
    b. $388,000
    c. $360,000
    d. $328,000

2. **(c)** The lower of cost or market (LCM) is used for financial reporting of inventories. The market value of inventory is defined as the replacement cost (RC), as long as it is less than the ceiling (net realizable value, or NRV) and more than the floor (NRV less a normal profit, or NRV – NP). In this case, the amounts are

Ceiling: NRV = $408,000 est. sell. price –		
$20,000 dep. cost =		$388,000
Replacement cost		$360,000
Floor: NRV – NP = $388,000 – $60,000 =		$328,000

The designated market value is the replacement cost of $360,000 because it falls between the floor and the ceiling. Once market value is designated, LCM can be determined by simply picking the lower of cost ($400,000) or market ($360,000). Thus, the inventory should be reported at market.

3. A bond issued on June 1, 2010, has interest payment dates of April 1 and October 1. Bond interest expense for the year ended December 31, 2010, is for a period of

    a. Three months.
    b. Four months.
    c. Six months.
    d. Seven months.

3. **(d)** Under the accrual basis of accounting, expenses should be recognized when incurred, regardless of when cash is paid. Therefore, expense from the bond issue date (6/1/10) through year-end (12/31/10) should be recognized in 2011.

The seven months (6/1/10 - 12/31/10) of interest expense would be the net effect of entries prepared on the issuance date, the October 1 interest date, and December 31 (adjusting entry).

4. Governmental financial reporting should provide information to assist users in which situation(s)?

I. Making social and political decisions.
II. Assessing whether current-year citizens received services but shifted part of the payment burden to future-year citizens.

    a. I only.
    b. II only.
    c. Both I and II.
    d. Neither I nor II.

4. **(c)** Financial reporting by state and local governments is used in making economic, social, and political decisions and in assessing accountability. Additionally, current year citizens need information concerning when costs of current services are actually paid for. Thus, both items I and II are provided to the users of governmental reporting.

5. During the year, Jones Foundation received the following support:

- A cash contribution of $875,000 to be used at the board of directors' discretion;
- A promise to contribute $500,000 in the following year from a supporter who has made similar contributions in prior periods;
- Contributed legal services with a value of $100,000, which Jones would have otherwise purchased.

At what amounts would Jones classify and record these transactions?

	Unrestricted revenue	Temporarily restricted revenue
a.	$ 875,000	$500,000
b.	$ 975,000	$500,000
c.	$ 975,000	$0
d.	$1,375,000	$0

5.   (b)   Restricted revenues are recorded only when a restriction has been placed by the donor. One type of restricted revenue is a pledge that has not been received during the year. This is considered a time restriction; accordingly, the $500,000 would be considered a temporarily restricted revenue based on a time restriction. The $875,000 and the $100,000 would be considered unrestricted revenues. The $100,000 is considered contributed services and carries no restriction. Contributed services are recognized when the services received (1) create or enhance nonfinancial assets or (2) require specialized skills, are provided by individuals possessing those skills, and would typically need to be purchased if not provided by donation. The $100,000 contribution meets the second criterion.

SIMULATION 1

NOTE: This simulation has been modified to reflect the effects of SFAS 154.

(50 to 60 minutes)

Situation	Treatments	Cumulative Effect	Journal Entries	Financial Statement	Written Communication	Research

On January 1, 2006, Charleston Company purchased machinery at a cost of $150,000. The machinery was depreciated under the double-declining balance method, assuming a ten-year life and no salvage value. The company took full-year depreciation in the year of acquisition. During 2009, management decided to change depreciation methods to the straight-line method for financial reporting purposes, but it continued to use the accelerated method for tax purposes. Charleston has a 40% effective income tax rate.

Situation	Treatments	Cumulative Effect	Journal Entries	Financial Statement	Written Communication	Research

In the table below, determine which description applies to each event by double-clicking the shaded box in the Description column and selecting the appropriate description. Then determine the appropriate accounting treatment for each event by double-clicking the shaded box in the Accounting treatment column and selecting the appropriate accounting treatment. Assume that all events are material in amount. A selected item may be used once, more than once, or not at all.

Description	*Accounting treatment*
Change in accounting principle	Current income
Change in accounting estimate	Cumulative effect in current income
Correction of error	Prospective treatment
Neither a change nor an error correction	Retrospective adjustment
	Restatement of previous periods
	No impact

Event	*Description*	*Accounting treatment*
Change in long-term construction contract from percentage-of-completion method to completed-contract method		
Write-off of uncollectible receivables under the direct write-off method		
Write-off of uncollectible receivables under the reserve method		
Change in salvage value of a depreciable asset		
Change in useful life of a patent		

Situation	Treatments	Cumulative Effect	Journal Entries	Financial Statement	Written Communication	Research

Using the spreadsheet below, calculate the amount of the depreciation expense for Charleston for each year. You may record your entries as numbers or as formulas that produce the correct number. Be sure that the value of the change appears in the shaded cell at the bottom of the spreadsheet.

NOTE: To use a formula in the spreadsheet, it must be preceded by an equal sign (e.g., = B1 + B2).

A	B	C	D
		Depreciation expense	
Double-declining balance method			
	2006		
	2007		
	2008		
Straight-line method			
	2009		
Accumulated depreciation 12/31/2009			

Situation	Treatments	Cumulative Effect	Journal Entries	Financial Statement	Written Communication	Research

Use the form below to complete the journal entries required to record Charleston's accounting change in 2009 from the double-declining balance method to the straight-line method. Enter the appropriate account title in column A by clicking the shaded box and then selecting the desired account title from the list provided. Account titles may be used once, more than once, or not at all.

Use columns B and C to record the dollar value corresponding to each journal entry. Be sure your entries appear in the appropriate shaded spaces. Some of the shaded spaces may not be used.

<u>Column A</u>

Accounts payable   Deferred income taxes
Accounts receivable   Depreciation expense
Accumulated depreciation   Income tax expense
Cash   Prior period adjustment
Cumulative effect of change in accounting   Retained earnings
Retained earnings

A	B	C
	Debit	Credit

Situation	Treatments	Cumulative Effect	Journal Entries	Financial Statement	Written Communication	Research

Use your solutions to other parts of this simulation to complete the following excerpts from Charleston's balance sheet at December 31, 2009, and income statement for the year ending December 31, 2009. Insert the appropriate values in the shaded cells in column D below. Indicate in column F whether the net cumulative effect is income or expense by clicking the shaded box in column F and then selecting either "Income" or "Expense."

NOTE: To use a formula in the spreadsheet, if must be preceded by an equal sign (e.g., = B1 + B2).

A	B	C	D	E	F	H
Charleston Company						
Balance sheet						
December 31, 2009						
	Machinery					
	Accumulated depreciation					
	Net					
Charleston Company						
Income statement						
Year ending December 31, 2009						
	Depreciation expense					

Situation	Treatments	Cumulative Effect	Journal Entries	Financial Statement	Written Communication	Research

A junior staff accountant in your department seems to be confused about what constitutes an accounting change for financial reporting purposes. In a brief memorandum to the junior accountant, describe the three basic types of accounting changes. Type your description in the space below using the word processor provided.

Reminder: Your responses to this prompt will be graded for both technical content and writing skills. For writing skills, you should demonstrate the ability to develop your ideas, organize them, and express them clearly. Do not convey information in the form of a table, bullet point list, or other abbreviated presentation.

To: Junior Staff Accountant
Subject: Types of accounting change

Situation	Treatments	Cumulative Effect	Journal Entries	Financial Statement	Written Communication	Research

Use the resource materials available to you by clicking the Standards button to find the answer to the following question in either the Current Text or Original Pronouncements. Highlight and copy the appropriate citation in its entirety from the source you choose. Then click on the gray field below and paste the citation into the space provided below. Use only one source.

What constitutes the cumulative effect of an accounting change and how is it presented in an income statement?

SOLUTION TO SIMULATION 1

*NOTE: The solution to this testlet is based upon ASC Topic 250, **Accounting Changes and Error Corrections** (FAS 154). This question and solution are presented in its original form for you to see an actual simulation released by the AICPA.*

Situation	Treatments	Cumulative Effect	Journal Entries	Financial Statement	Written Communication	Research

Event	Description	Accounting treatment
Change in long-term construction contract from percentage-of-completion method to completed-contract method	Change in accounting principle	Retrospective application
Write-off of uncollectible receivables under the direct write-off method	Change in accounting estimate	Current income
Write-off of uncollectible receivables under the reserve method	Neither a change nor an error correction	No impact
Change in salvage value of a depreciable asset	Change in accounting estimate	Current income
Change in useful life of a patent	Change in accounting estimate	Current income

Situation	Treatments	Cumulative Effect	Journal Entries	Financial Statement	Written Communication	Research

A	B	C	D
		Depreciation expense	
Double-declining balance method			
	2006	$30,000	
	2007	$24,000	
	2008	$19,200	
Straight-line method			
	2009	$10,971	
Accumulated depreciation 12/31/2009			$84,171

There is no cumulative effect of change in method on the income statement for a change in depreciation method. The change is treated as a change in estimate effected by a change in accounting method. A change in estimate is accounted for in the period of the change and future periods.

The machinery was depreciated using the double-declining balance method assuming a ten-year life and no salvage. Assume the machinery was acquired on January 1, 2006, and the change in depreciation method to straight-line was made in 2009. To account for the change on a prospective basis, it is necessary to calculate the book value of the machinery as of December 31, 2009, at the end of Year 3.

Double-declining balance method

Year 1 (2006)	$30,000
Year 2 (2007)	24,000
Year 3 (2008)	19,200
Total depreciation 12/31/08	$73,200

To calculate book value at 12/31/08

Historical cost	$150,000
Less: Accum. depr.	(73,200)
Book value	$ 76,800

To calculate depreciation expense for 2009, straight-line depreciation is calculated using the book value at the beginning of the year in which the change is made and the remaining useful life of the asset.

($76,800 – $0 salvage) ÷ 7 years remaining life = $10,971

Situation	Treatments	Cumulative Effect	Journal Entries	Financial Statement	Written Communication	Research

There is no journal entry for a cumulative effect of change in accounting principle for a change in depreciation method. Since the accounting change is accounted for on a prospective basis, depreciation expense is calculated and recorded for the current year. The depreciation expense entry for Year 4 (2009) is

Depreciation expense	10,971	
Accumulated depreciation		10,971

Situation	Treatments	Cumulative Effect	Journal Entries	Financial Statement		Written Communication	Research

A	B	C	D	E	F	H
Charleston Company						
Balance sheet						
December 31, 2009 (End of Year 4)						
Machinery			$150,000			
Accumulated depreciation			$ (84,171)			
Net			$65,829			
Charleston Company						
Income statement						
Year ending December 31, 2009 (Year 4)						
Depreciation expense			$ (10,971)			

Situation	Treatments	Cumulative Effect	Journal Entries	Financial Statement	Written Communication		Research

To: Junior Staff Accountant

Subject: Types of accounting change

The technical points to be covered in this response should include. The three basic types of accounting change

- Change in accounting principal
- Change in accounting estimate
- Change in accounting entity

Situation	Treatments	Cumulative Effect	Journal Entries	Financial Statement	Written Communication	Research	

What constitutes a change in accounting principle and how is it presented in the financial statements?

FAS 154, Para 2(c)

2. The following terms are defined as used in this Statement:

c. Change in accounting principle—a change from one generally accepted accounting principle to another generally accepted accounting principle when there are two or more generally accepted accounting principles that apply or when the accounting principle formerly used is no longer generally accepted. A change in the method of applying an accounting principle also is considered a change in accounting principle.

FAS 154, Para 7

7. An entity shall report a change in accounting principle through retrospective application of the new accounting principle to all prior periods, unless it is impracticable to do so. Retrospective application requires the following:

a. The cumulative effect of the change to the new accounting principle on periods prior to those presented shall be reflected in the carrying amounts of assets and liabilities as of the beginning of the first period presented.

b. An offsetting adjustment, if any, shall be made to the opening balance of retained earnings (or other appropriate components of equity or net assets in the statement of financial position) for that period.

c. Financial statements for each individual prior period presented shall be adjusted to reflect the period-specific effects of applying the new accounting principle.

ASC 250-10-05-1 and 2, and ASC 250-10-45-1

REGULATION TESTLETS RELEASED BY AICPA

1. According to the profession's ethical standards, an auditor would be considered independent in which of the following instances?

    a.   The auditor is the officially appointed stock transfer agent of a client.

    b.   The auditor's checking account that is fully insured by a federal agency, is held at a client financial institution.

    c.   The client owes the auditor fees for more than two years prior to the issuance of the audit report.

    d.   The client is the only tenant in a commercial building owned by the auditor.

1. **(b)** The requirement is to identify the instance in which an auditor would be considered independent. Answer (b) is correct because per ET 191.140-.141 the auditor's independence would not be impaired, provided the checking accounts, etc. are fully insured by an appropriate deposit insurance agency. Answer (a) is incorrect because per ET 191.077-.078 an auditor's independence would be impaired since the function of a transfer agent is considered equivalent to that of a member of management. Answer (c) is incorrect because per ET 191.103-.104 an auditor's independence is considered to be impaired if, when the report on the client's current year is issued, fees remain unpaid, whether billed or unbilled, for professional services provided more than one year prior to the date of the report. Answer (d) is incorrect because per ET 191.58 leasing property to a client results in an indirect financial interest in that client. Therefore, an auditor's independence would be considered to be impaired if the indirect financial interest in a client is material to the auditor.

2. Which of the following rights is a holder of a public corporation's cumulative preferred stock always entitled to?

    a.   Conversion of the preferred stock into common stock.

    b.   Voting rights.

    c.   Dividend carryovers from years in which dividends were **not** paid, to future years.

    d.   Guaranteed dividends.

2. **(c)** Preferred shares of stock are shares that have a contractual preference over other classes of stock as to liquidations and dividends. If a preferred stock is cumulative, the shareholder would be entitled to dividend carryovers from years in which dividends were not paid, to future years and would receive all dividends in arrears before any dividend is paid to owners of common stock. Answers (a) and (b) are incorrect because in order for a shareholder to be entitled to convert preferred stock into common stock or to have voting rights, it must be stated in the articles of incorporation. These are not rights that a holder of preferred stock would always be entitled to. Answer (d) is incorrect because although a preferred stockholder has preference over other classes of stock as to declared dividends, the board of directors' power to declare dividends is discretionary and thus dividends are not guaranteed.

3. Leker exchanged a van that was used exclusively for business and had an adjusted tax basis of $20,000 for a new van. The new van had a fair market value of $10,000, and Leker also received $3,000 in cash. What was Leker's tax basis in the acquired van?

    a. $20,000

    b. $17,000

    c. $13,000

    d. $ 7,000

3. **(b)** The requirement is to determine the basis for Leker's new van. The exchange of Leker's old van with a basis of $20,000 that was used exclusively for business, for a new van worth $10,000 plus $3,000 cash qualified as a like-kind exchange. Since it is a like-kind exchange, Leker's realized loss of $20,000 – ($10,000 + $3,000) = $7,000 cannot be recognized, but instead is reflected in the basis of the new van. The new van's basis is the adjusted basis of Leker's old van of $20,000 reduced by the $3,000 of cash boot received, resulting in a basis of $17,000.

4. If a corporation's charitable contributions exceed the limitation for deductibility in a particular year, the excess

    a.   Is **not** deductible in any future or prior year.

    b.   May be carried back or forward for one year at the corporation's election.

    c.   May be carried forward to a maximum of five succeeding years.

    d.   May be carried back to the third preceding year.

4. **(c)** The requirement is to select the correct statement regarding a corporation's charitable contributions in excess of the limitation for deductibility in a particular year. Corporate charitable contributions in excess of the 10% of taxable income limitation may be carried forward to a maximum of five succeeding years, subject to a 10% limitation in those years.

5. Strom acquired a 25% interest in Ace Partnership by contributing land having an adjusted basis of $16,000 and a fair market value of $50,000. The land was subject to a $24,000 mortgage, which was assumed by Ace. No other liabilities existed at the time of the contribution. What was Strom's basis in Ace?

    a. $0

    b. $16,000

    c. $26,000

    d. $32,000

5. **(a)** The requirement is to determine Strom's initial basis for the 25% interest in Ace Partnership that was received in exchange for land, subject to a mortgage that was assumed by Ace. Strom's initial basis for the 25% partnership interest received consists of the $16,000 basis of the land contributed, less the net reduction in Strom's liabilities resulting from the partnership's assumption of the $24,000 mortgage. Since Strom received a 25% partnership interest, the **net** reduction in Strom's liability is $24,000 × 75% = $18,000. Since Strom cannot have a negative basis, his basis for his 25% interest in Ace is $16,000 – $18,000 = $0. Additionally, note that Strom must recognize a $2,000 gain because the liability reduction exceeded his basis in the transferred land.

SIMULATION 1 (35 to 40 minutes)

Directions							
	Situation	Gain/Basis	Depreciation Expense	Distributive Share	Liquidating Distributions	Written Communication	Research

In this problem, you will be asked to respond to various questions regarding the tax treatment of partnerships. The simulation will provide you with all the information necessary to do your work. For full credit, be sure to view and complete all work tabs.

Remember

- Information and data necessary to complete the simulation are found by clicking information tabs (i.e., those **without a pencil icon**).
- All tasks that you should complete before leaving the simulation are found on work tabs (i.e., those tabs **with** a pencil icon).
- An unshaded pencil icon means that you have not yet responded to anything on a particular work tab.
- A shaded pencil icon indicates that you have responded to some or all of the requirements on a work tab—it does **not** necessarily mean that you have completed the requirements on the tab.

To start this simulation, click on the Situation tab.
To respond to the tasks or questions, click on the work tabs.
Resources are available to you under the tab marked Resources. You may want to review what is included in the resources before beginning this simulation.

	Situation						
Directions		Gain/Basis	Depreciation Expense	Distributive Share	Liquidating Distributions	Written Communication	Research

Miller, Smith, and Tucker decided to form a partnership to perform engineering services. All of the partners have extensive experience in the engineering field and now wish to pool their resources and client contacts to begin their own firm. The new entity, Sabre Consulting, will begin operations on April 1, 2009, and will use the calendar year for reporting purposes.

All of the partners expect to work full time for Sabre and each will contribute cash and other property to the company sufficient to commence operations. The partners have agreed to share all income and losses of the partnership equally. A written partnership agreement, duly executed by the partners, memorializes this agreement among the partners.

The table below shows the estimated values for assets contributed to Sabre by each partner. None of the contributed assets' costs have been previously recovered for tax purposes.

Partner	Cash contribution	Estimated FMV of noncash property contributed	Basis in noncash property contributed
Miller	$15,000	$11,000	$10,000
Smith	10,000	17,000	15,000
Tucker	20,000	6,500	5,000
Totals	45,000	34,500	30,000

		Gain/Basis					
Directions	Situation		Depreciation Expense	Distributive Share	Liquidating Distributions	Written Communication	Research

Complete the shaded cells in the following table by entering the gain or loss recognized by each partner on the property contributed to Sabre Consulting, the partner's basis in the partnership interest, and Sabre's basis in the contributed property. Loss amounts should be recorded as a negative number.

NOTE: To use a formula in the spreadsheet, it must be preceded by an equal sign (e.g., = B1 + B2).

E16	▼	*fx*		
	A	B	C	D
1		Partner's gain or loss on property transferred	Partner's basis in partnership interest	Partnership's basis in property contributed
2	Miller			
3	Smith			
4	Tucker			

Directions	Situation	Gain/Basis	Depreciation Expense	Distributive Share	Liquidating Distributions	Written Communication	Research

Using the MACRS table (which can be found by clicking the Resources tab) and the partnership basis in the contributed assets calculated on the prior tab, complete the following table to determine Sabre's tax depreciation expense for 2009. Assume that none of the original cost of any asset was expensed by the partnership under the provisions of Section 179, and that the partnership elected not to take bonus depreciation.

NOTE: To use a formula in the spreadsheet, it must be preceded by an equal sign (e.g., =B1 + B2).

D15	▼	fx		
	A	B	C	D
1	**Partner**	**Asset type**	**Depreciable basis**	**2009 Depreciation expense**
2	Miller	Office furniture		
3	Smith	Pickup truck used 100% for business purposes		
4	Tucker	Computers and printers		

Directions	Situation	Gain/Basis	Depreciation Expense	Distributive Share	Liquidating Distributions	Written Communication	Research

Assume that Sabre had only the items of income and expense show in the following table for the 2009 tax year. Complete the remainder of the table by properly classifying each item of income and expense as ordinary business income that is reportable on page 1, Form 1065, or as a separately stated item that is reportable on Schedule K, Form 1065. Some entries may appear in both columns.

NOTE: To use a formula in the spreadsheet, it must be preceded by an equal sign (e.g., = B1 + B2).

G15	▼	fx		
	A	B	C	D
1			**Ordinary Income**	**Separately stated items**
2	Sales revenue	$500,000		
3	Interest income	$4,000		
4	Depreciation expense	$(7,500)		
5	Operating expenses	$(426,000)		
6	Charitable contributions	$(3,000)		
7				
8	Total net ordinary income			

Directions	Situation	Gain/Basis	Depreciation Expense	Distributive Share	Liquidating Distributions	Written Communication	Research

The partners have decided to liquidate Sabre Consulting at December 31, 2010. On that date, Tucker received the following asset as a liquidating distribution in exchange for his entire partnership interest. There were no partnership liabilities at the date of liquidation. Tucker's basis in the partnership interest at the date of liquidation was $3,000.

	Cost	Accumulated depreciation	Estimated FMV
Drafting equipment	$12,000	$8,000	$6,000

Based on the foregoing information, complete the following table. Loss amounts should be recorded as a negative number.

NOTE: To use a formula in the spreadsheet, it must be preceded by an equal sign (e.g., = B1 + B2).

D15	▼	*fx*		
		A		B
1		Gain or loss recognized by partnership on the liquidating distribution		
2		Gain or loss recognized by Tucker on the liquidating distribution		
3		Tucker's basis in the asset received as part of the liquidating distribution		

Directions	Situation	Gain/Basis	Depreciation Expense	Distributive Share	Liquidating Distributions	Written Communication	Research

You also handle Mr. Smith's personal taxes. He received dividends from foreign stocks during the year from which foreign taxes of $50 were withheld. He has requested your help in determining whether it would be more advantageous to claim these foreign taxes paid as an itemized deduction or as a credit against income taxes. For the current year, Mr. Smith is single, has adjusted gross income of $85,000, total itemized deductions of $8,000, and taxable income of $74,000. His marginal tax rate is 30%. Write a letter to Mr. Smith explaining which option would be more advantageous for the tax year based on the above information.

REMINDER: Your response will be graded for both technical content and writing skills. Technical content will be evaluated for information that is helpful to the intended reader and clearly relevant to the issue. Writing skills will be evaluated for development, organization, and the appropriate expression of ideas in professional correspondence. Use a standard business memo or letter format with a clear beginning, middle, and end. Do not convey information in the form of a table, bullet point list, or other abbreviated presentation.

Directions	Situation	Gain/Basis	Depreciation Expense	Distributive Share	Liquidating Distributions	Written Communication	Research

Use the research materials available to you by clicking the Code button to research the answer to the following questions. Find the code section that addresses the question, and enter the section citation in the shaded boxes below. Give the most precise a citation possible (i.e., both code section and subsection, if applicable). Do **not** copy the actual text of the citation.

During its initial tax year, Sabre Consulting incurred $2,000 of legal fees and $750 of accounting fees to organize the partnership. What code section and subsection permits the partnership to deduct these expenses for federal tax purposes?

Section	Subsection
§　[ ]	(　[ ]　)

SOLUTION TO SIMULATION 1

| Directions | Situation | Gain/Basis | Depreciation Expense | Distributive Share | Liquidating Distributions | Written Communication | Research |

E16	▼	fx			
	A	B	C	D
1	Partner	Partner's gain or loss on property transferred	Partner's basis in partnership interest	Partnership's basis in property contributed
2	Miller	$0	$25,000	$10,000
3	Smith	$0	$25,000	$15,000
4	Tucker	$0	$25,000	$5,000

Generally, no gain or loss is recognized on the contribution of property in exchange for a partnership interest. As a result, a partner's initial basis for a partnership interest consists of the amount of cash plus the adjusted basis of noncash property contributed. Similarly, a partnership receives a transferred basis for contributed noncash property equal to the partner's basis for the property prior to contribution. Miller's initial partnership basis consists of the $15,000 cash plus the $10,000 adjusted basis of noncash property contributed, or $25,000. Smith's partnership basis consists of the $10,000 cash plus the $15,000 basis of noncash property contributed, or $25,000. Tucker's partnership basis consists of the $20,000 cash plus the $5,000 basis of noncash property contributed, or $25,000.

| Directions | Situation | Gain/Basis | Depreciation Expense | Distributive Share | Liquidating Distributions | Written Communication | Research |

D15	▼	fx			
	A	B	C	D
1	**Partner**	**Asset type**	**Depreciable basis**	**2009 Depreciation expense**
2	Miller	Office furniture	$10,000	$1,429
3	Smith	Pickup truck used 100% for business purposes	$15,000	$3,000
4	Tucker	Computers and printers	$5,000	$1,000

The Sabre partnership's depreciable basis for the contributed property is a transferred basis equal to the contributing partner's basis for the property prior to contribution. The office furniture has a 7-year recovery period, while the pickup truck and computers and printers have a 5-year recovery period. The MACRS depreciation table that was provided is based on the 200% declining-balance method and already incorporates the half-year convention which permits just a half-year of depreciation for the year that depreciable personalty is placed in service. Thus, the 2009 depreciation expense for the office furniture is $10,000 × 14.29% = $1,429 (i.e., $10,000 × 2/7 × 1/2). The 2009 depreciation for the pickup truck is $15,000 × 20% = $3,000 (i.e., $15,000 × 2/5 × 1/2). The 2009 depreciation expense for the computers and printers is $5,000 × 20% = $1,000 (i.e., $5,000 × 2/5 × 1/2).

| Directions | Situation | Gain/Basis | Depreciation Expense | Distributive Share | Liquidating Distributions | Written Communication | Research |

G15	▼	fx			
	A	B	C	D
1			**Ordinary Income**	**Separately stated items**
2	Sales revenue	$500,000	$500,000	
3	Interest income	$4,000		$4,000
4	Depreciation expense	$(7,500)	$(7,500)	
5	Operating expenses	$(426,000)	$(426,000)	
6	Charitable contributions	$(3,000)		$(3,000)
7				
8	Total net ordinary income		$66,500	

Partnership items having special tax characteristics (e.g., passive activity losses, deductions subject to dollar or percentage limitations, etc.) must be separately stated and shown on Schedules K and K-1 so that their special characteristics are preserved when reported on partners' returns. In contrast, partnership ordinary income and deduction items having no special tax characteristics can be netted together in the computation of a partnership's ordinary income and deductions from trade or business activities on page 1 of Form 1065. Here, assuming the $4,000 of interest income is from investments, it represents portfolio income and must be separately stated on Schedule K. Similarly, the charitable contributions of $3,000 must be separately stated so that the appropriate percentage limitations can be applied when passed through to partners. Sales, depreciation, and operating expenses are ordinary items and result in net ordinary income of $66,500.

Directions	Situation	Gain/Basis	Depreciation Expense	Distributive Share	Liquidating Distributions	Written Communication	Research

D15	▼	fx		
		A		B
1		Gain or loss recognized by partnership on the liquidating distribution		$0
2		Gain or loss recognized by Tucker on the liquidating distribution		$0
3		Tucker's basis in the asset received as part of the liquidating distribution		$3,000

Generally, no gain or loss is recognized by a partnership on the distribution of noncash property in complete liquidation of the partnership. Similarly, no gain or loss is generally recognized by a distributee partner when noncash property is received in complete liquidation of the partner's partnership interest. Here, Sabre recognizes no gain when it distributes drafting equipment with a FMV of $6,000 and an adjusted basis of $4,000, and Tucker recognizes no gain when he receives the drafting equipment in liquidation of his partnership interest. Although distributed property generally has a transferred basis, the basis of the drafting equipment to Tucker is limited to his $3,000 basis for his partnership interest before the distribution.

Directions	Situation	Gain/Basis	Depreciation Expense	Distributive Share	Liquidating Distributions	Written Communication	Research

Mr. Harold Smith
232 Pine Street
Anytown, NB

Dear Mr. Smith:

This memorandum is designed to explain the best option regarding treatment of the foreign taxes paid by you. You have the option of deducting these taxes as an itemized deduction or receiving a tax credit. A tax credit is generally preferred over a deduction because one dollar of tax credit reduces a taxpayer's income tax by one dollar, while one dollar of deduction only reduces a taxpayer's income tax by the taxpayer's marginal tax rate (e.g., 30 cents if in the 30% marginal tax bracket). Therefore, I recommend that you take the tax credit.

If you need any further assistance, please call me.

Directions	Situation	Gain/Basis	Depreciation Expense	Distributive Share	Liquidating Distributions	Written Communication	Research

Section	Subsection
§ 709	(b)

Code Sec. 709(b) allows a partnership to deduct up to $5,000 of organizational expenditures for the tax year in which the partnership begins business. The $5,000 amount must be reduced by the amount by which organizational expenditures exceed $50,000. Remaining expenditures are deducted ratably over the 180-month period beginning with the month in which the partnership begins business.

BUSINESS ENVIRONMENT AND CONCEPTS TESTLETS RELEASED BY AICPA

1. Which of the following statements concerning the similarities between a general partnership and a corporation are correct?

    a.   Corporate stockholders and general partners have limited personal liability.

    b.   Corporations and general partnerships have perpetual existence.

    c.   Corporations and general partnerships can declare bankruptcy.

    d.   Corporations and general partnerships are recognized as taxpayers for federal income tax purposes.

2. Furl Corp., a corporation organized under the laws of Sate X, sued Row, a customer residing in State Y, for nonpayment for goods sold. Row attempted to dismiss the suit brought by Furl in State Y on the grounds that Furl was conducting business in State Y but had not obtained a certificate of authority from State Y to transact business therein. Which of the following actions by Furl would generally result in the court ruling that Furl was conducting business in State Y?

    a.   Maintaining bank accounts in State Y.

    b.   Shipping goods across state lines into State Y.

    c.   Owning and operating a small manufacturing plant in State Y.

    d.   Holding board of directors meetings in State Y.

3. In which of the following situations would there be inelastic demand?

    a.   A 5% price increase results in a 3% decrease in the quantity demanded.

    b.   A 4% price increase results in a 6% decrease in the quantity demanded.

    c.   A 4% price increase results in a 4% decrease in the quantity demanded.

    d.   A 3% decrease results in a 5% increase in the quantity demanded.

4. A project should be accepted if the present value of cash flows from the project is

    a.   Equal to the initial investment.

    b.   Less than the initial investment.

    c.   Greater than the initial investment.

    d.   Equal to zero.

1. **(c)** The requirement is to identify the similarity between a general partnership and a corporation. Answer (c) is correct because under the federal securities laws both a corporation and a general partnership may file for bankruptcy. Answer (a) is incorrect because general partners do not have limited liability for partnership debts. Answer (b) is incorrect because while corporations have perpetual existence general partnerships do not. Answer (d) is incorrect because while a corporation is a taxpaying entity, a partnership is a flow-through entity. The partners of the partnership pay the taxes.

2. **(c)** The requirement is to identify the actions that would result in Furl Corp. legally conducting business in a state. Furl Corp. is a domestic corporation in State X because Furl incorporated there. Furl is a foreign corporation in State Y because it was not incorporated in that state. When Furl is conducting business in State Y, Furl may be denied access to the courts to sue persons residing in State Y unless it qualified to do business in State Y by obtaining a certificate of authority from that state. Therefore, an important issue that the court examines is whether Furl was conducting business in State Y since Furl sued Row, a customer residing in this state. Generally a foreign corporation is ruled as conducting business in a state if the corporation's transactions are continuous rather than isolated. Owning and operating even a small manufacturing plant in the state would generally result in a ruling that Furl is conducting business in that state. Answer (a) is incorrect because merely maintaining a bank account in the state does not meet the definition of conducting business in that state. Answer (b) is incorrect because solely shipping goods across state lines into State Y does not meet the definition of conducting business in that state. Answer (d) is incorrect because Furl Corp. may hold its meetings for the board of directors in a state without meeting the definition of conducting business in that state.

3. **(a)** The requirement is to identify the situation in which there is inelastic demand. Demand elasticity is measured by the change in the quantity demanded divided by the change in the price. If the ratio is greater than one, demand is said to be elastic. If the ratio is less than one, demand is inelastic, and if the ratio is equal to one, demand is unitary. Accordingly, answer (a) is correct because it is the only situation that results in a ratio less than one, $3/5 = 0.60$. Answer (b) is incorrect because it indicates elastic demand, $6/4 = 1.5$. Answer (c) is incorrect because it indicates unitary demand, $4/4 = 1$. Answer (d) is incorrect because it indicates elastic demand, $5/3 = 1.67$.

4. **(c)** The requirement is to identify the decision rule for acceptance of a project. Answer (c) is correct because if a project's present value of cash flows is greater than the initial investment, the investment is expected to cover the cost of capital plus provide some additional return. Answer (a) is incorrect because it is not as desirable as answer (c). Answer (b) is incorrect because if management invests using this rule it will not cover the firm's cost of capital. Answer (d) is incorrect because acceptance of this project would result in losses.

5. Which of the following cash management techniques focuses on cash disbursements?
   a. Lockbox system.
   b. Zero-balance account.
   c. Preauthorized checks.
   d. Depository transfer checks.

5. (b) The requirement is to identify the cash management technique that focuses on cash disbursements. Answer (b) is correct because the zero-balance account technique involves establishing regional bank accounts to which just enough funds are transferred daily to pay the checks presented. It is a cash management technique for cash disbursements. Answer (a) is incorrect because a lockbox system is one in which customer payments are sent to a post office box that is maintained by the bank. Therefore, it involves cash receipts. Answer (c) is incorrect because use of preauthorized checks is not a cash management technique. Answer (d) is incorrect because depository transfer checks are used in conjunction with concentration banking which is a cash receipts management technique.

6. A customer intended to order 100 units of product Z96014, but incorrectly ordered nonexistent product Z96015. Which of the following controls would detect this error?
   a. Check digit verification.
   b. Record count.
   c. Hash total.
   d. Redundant data check.

6. (a) The requirement is to identify the control that would detect the error. Answer (a) is correct because check digit verification involves use of an extra (redundant) digit added to an identification number to detect errors in inputting or processing a transaction. The check digit allows the computer to detect and reject items that are not valid. Answer (b) is incorrect because a record count is simply a control total of the number of records processed. It would not detect an invalid part number. Answer (c) is incorrect because a hash total is a control total with a total that is meaningless. It would not detect an invalid part number. Answer (d) is incorrect because a redundant data check uses two identifiers in each transaction record (e.g., customer account number and the first five letters of the customer's name). While this control might be established to detect the error, it would not be as effective as a check digit.

7. The greatest financial threat to an organization that implemented the financial accounting module of an enterprise resource planning (ERP) system from a major vendor exists from errors detected during which of the following times?
   a. Project initiation.
   b. Requirements determination.
   c. Table configuration.
   d. Implementation.

7. (d) The requirement is to identify the phase in which there is the greatest financial threat to an organization that implemented an ERP system. Answer (d) is correct because in the implementation phase the system is operating with real data that could be corrupted by operation of the new system. Answers (a), (b), and (c) are incorrect because they all involve development phases where real data is not being used.

8. Which of the following procedures would an entity **most** likely include in its disaster recovery plan?
   a. Convert all data from EDI format to an internal company format.
   b. Maintain a Trojan horse program to prevent illicit activity.
   c. Develop an auxiliary power supply to provide uninterrupted electricity.
   d. Store duplicate copies of files in a location away from the computer center.

8. (d) The requirement is to identify the item most likely included in a disaster recovery plan. A disaster recovery plan should include priorities, insurance, backup approaches, specific assignments, periodic testing and updating, and documentation. As a part of backup approaches the plan would include procedures for storing backup files. Therefore, answer (d) is correct. Answer (a) is incorrect because conversion of data is not a part of disaster recovery. Answer (b) is incorrect because Trojan horses are not part of disaster recovery. Answer (c) is incorrect because developing an auxiliary power supply is not part of disaster recovery. Normal power interruption is not considered a disaster.

9. Which of the following definitions best characterizes benchmarking?
   a. A technique that examines product and process attributes to identify areas for improvements.
   b. The comparison of existing activities with the best levels of performance in other, similar organizations.
   c. The development of the most effective methods of completing tasks in a particular industry.
   d. The complete redesign of a process within an organization.

9. (b) The requirement is to identify the best characterization of benchmarking. Answer (b) is correct because benchmarking involves comparison of existing activities with the best levels of performance in other or similar organizations. Answer (a) is incorrect because it describes continuous improvement. Answer (c) is incorrect because it describes best practices. Answer (d) is incorrect because it describes process reengineering.

10. Which of the following is true about activity-based costing?

    a.   It should not be used with process or job costing.

    b.   It can be used only with process costing.

    c.   It can be used only with job costing.

    d.   It can be used with either process or job costing.

10.   **(d)**   The requirement is to identify the true statement about activity-based costing. Activity-based costing involves assigning costs to products or cost centers based on activities and cost drivers. Answer (d) is correct because it can be used in conjunction with either process or job order costing. Answer (a), (b), and (c) are incorrect because it can be used in conjunction with either process or job order costing.

APPENDIX D: 2010 RELEASED AICPA QUESTIONS

AUDITING AND ATTESTATION

1. Which of the following would be an appropriate title for a statement of revenue and expenses prepared using an other comprehensive basis of accounting (OCBOA)?
   a. Statement of operations.
   b. Statement of income—regulatory basis
   c. Income statement.
   d. Statement of activities.

2. An accountant has been engaged to review a nonissuer's financial statements that contain several departures from GAAP. Management is unwilling to revise the financial statements, and the accountant believes that modification of the standard review report is inadequate to communicate the deficiencies. Under these circumstances, the accountant should
   a. Determine the effects of the departures from GAAP and issue a special report on the financial statements.
   b. Express a disclaimer of opinion on the financial statements and advise the board of directors that the financial statements should **not** be relied on.
   c. Inform management that a review of the financial statements **cannot** be completed and request a change from a review to a compilation engagement.
   d. Withdraw from the engagement and provide **no** further services concerning these financial statements.

3. An independent auditor must have which of the following?
   a. A preexisting and well-informed point of view with respect to the audit.
   b. Technical training that is adequate to meet the requirements of a professional.
   c. A background in many different disciplines.
   d. Experience in taxation that is sufficient to comply with generally accepted auditing standards.

4. Which of the following conditions most likely would pose the greatest risk in accepting a new audit engagement?
   a. Staff will need to be rescheduled to cover this new client.
   b. There will be a client-imposed scope limitation.
   c. The firm will have to hire a specialist in one audit area.
   d. The client's financial reporting system has been in place for 10 years.

1. **(b)** The requirement is to identify an appropriate title for a statement of revenue and expenses prepared using an other comprehensive basis of accounting. Answer (b) is correct because AU 623 states that a title such as statement of income—regulatory basis is appropriate. Answers (a) and (c) are incorrect because titles such as *statement of operations* and *income statement* are generally understood to be applicable only to financial statements prepared following GAAP. Answer (d) is incorrect because the term *statement of activities* is a title used for financial statements of a not-for-profit organization prepared under GAAP.

2. **(d)** The requirement is to identify an accountant's responsibility when performing a review and departures from GAAP exist which management is unwilling to correct and the accountant does not believe that modification of the standard review report is adequate to communicate the deficiencies. Answer (d) is correct because AR 90 indicates that withdrawal is appropriate. Answer (a) is incorrect because the term "special report" does not relate to reviewed financial statements that use GAAP—see AU 623 for guidance on special reports. Answer (b) is incorrect because the accountant does not believe that modification of the standard review report is adequate to communicate the deficiencies and because the term "disclaimer of opinion" relates to audits, not reviews. Answer (c) is incorrect because the report should not be changed to a compilation in this type of situation.

3. **(b)** The requirement is to identify which attribute an independent auditor must have. Answer (b) is correct because GAAS require that an auditor have adequate technical training (AU 150). Answer (a) is incorrect because it is uncertain what is meant by this "point of view." Answer (c) is incorrect because an auditor need not have a background in many different disciplines. Answer (d) is incorrect because experience in taxation, while often helpful, is not required under GAAS.

4. **(b)** The requirement is to identify the condition that most likely would pose the greatest risk in accepting a new audit engagement. Answer (b) is correct because management is responsible for making all financial records and related information available to the auditor—a client-imposed scope limitation is likely to present significant problems in that it raises questions as to why management would restrict the scope of the audit. Answer (a) is incorrect because rescheduling staff can often be efficiently and effectively handled. Answer (c) is incorrect because a specialist is often needed on audits. Answer (d) is incorrect because simple existence of a financial reporting system for 10 years may not be indicative of a risk in accepting the audit engagement.

5. Which of the following information that comes to an auditor's attention most likely would raise a question about the occurrence of illegal acts?

    a. The exchange of property for similar property in a nonmonetary transaction.

    b. The discovery of unexplained payments made to government employees.

    c. The presence of several difficult-to-audit transactions affecting expense accounts.

    d. The failure to develop adequate procedures that detect unauthorized purchases.

6. Which of the following steps should an auditor perform first to determine the existence of related parties?

    a. Examine invoices, contracts, and purchasing orders.

    b. Request a list of all related parties from management.

    c. Review the company's business structure.

    d. Review proxy and other materials filed with the SEC.

7. Which of the following payroll control activities would most effectively ensure that payment is made only for work performed?

    a. Require all employees to record arrival and departure by using the time clock.

    b. Have a payroll clerk recalculate all time cards.

    c. Require all employees to sign their time cards.

    d. Require employees to have their direct supervisors approve their time cards.

8. Which of the following factors is most likely to affect the extent of the documentation of the auditor's understanding of a client's system of internal controls?

    a. The industry and the business and regulatory environments in which the client operates.

    b. The degree to which information technology is used in the accounting function.

    c. The relationship between management, the board of directors, and external stakeholders.

    d. The degree to which the auditor intends to use internal audit personnel to perform substantive tests.

5. **(b)** The requirement is to identify the information that most likely would raise a question about the occurrence of illegal acts. Answer (b) is correct because unexplained payments made to government employees may well not be legal (e.g., they may be illegal bribes). Answer (a) is incorrect because valid business reasons may exist for such nonmonetary exchanges (e.g., one piece of land may be traded for another). Answer (c) is incorrect because there are many difficult-to-audit transactions that may not be indicative of illegal acts (e.g., those related to accounting estimates). Answer (d) is incorrect because inadequate procedures relating to purchases may or may not result in illegal acts. See AU 317 for guidance on illegal acts.

6. **(b)** The requirement is to identify which of the procedures an auditor should *first* perform to determine the existence of related parties. Answer (b) is correct because AU 334 requires that auditors first evaluate the company's procedures for identifying such transactions and then ask management for a list of related parties. Answer (a) is incorrect because examining documentation such as invoices, contracts, and purchasing orders ordinarily occurs subsequently. Answer (c) is incorrect because while reviewing the company's business structure may reveal such transactions, it is not in AU 334's list of suggested specific audit procedures to determine the existence of related parties. Answer (d) is incorrect because it is considered a procedure for identifying related-party transactions as contrasted to determining the existence of related parties in AU 334.

7. **(d)** The requirement is to identify the payroll control activities that would most effectively ensure that payment is made only for work performed. Answer (d) is correct because supervisors should have the most direct knowledge of the hours worked by their subordinates. Answer (a) is incorrect because many schemes are available for overreporting time (e.g., record arrival and then depart for several hours rather than work). Answer (b) is incorrect because the payroll clerk ordinarily will only be able to identify miscalculations of recorded times. Answer (c) is incorrect because employees may sign time cards with incorrect times reported.

8. **(b)** The requirement is to identify the factor which is most likely to affect the extent of the documentation of the auditor's understanding of internal control. Answer (b) is correct because differences in information technology use will have a major effect. For example, documentation of the understanding of a complex information system with a large volume of transactions may include flowcharts, questionnaires, and/or decision tables; documentation for an information system with limited or no use of IT and few transactions may be in the form of a memorandum. Answer (a) is incorrect because the industry, business and regulatory environments ordinarily will have a lesser effect than IT. Answer (c) is incorrect because such relationships ordinarily will have a lesser effect than IT. Answer (d) is incorrect because the degree to which the auditor intends to use internal audit personnel to perform substantive procedures is likely to have only a small effect on the documentation of internal control. See AU 314 for guidance on documentation of the auditor's understanding of internal control.

9. Green, CPA, is auditing the financial statements of Ajax Co. Ajax uses the DP Service Center to process its payroll. DP's financial statements are audited by Blue, CPA, who recently issued a report on DP's policies and procedures regarding the processing of other entities' transactions. In considering whether Blue's report is satisfactory for Green's purposes, Green should
   a. Make inquiries concerning Blue's professional reputation.
   b. Assess control risk at the maximum level.
   c. Review the audit programs followed by Blue.
   d. Perform tests of controls at the DP Service Center.

10. Which of the following procedures is considered a test of controls?
   a. An auditor reviews the entity's check register for unrecorded liabilities.
   b. An auditor evaluates whether a general journal entry was recorded at the proper amount.
   c. An auditor interviews and observes appropriate personnel to determine segregation of duties.
   d. An author reviews the audit workpapers to ensure proper sign-off.

11. Which of the following would be a consideration in planning a sample for a test of subsequent cash receipts?
   a. Preliminary judgments about materiality levels.
   b. The amount of bad debt write-offs in the prior year.
   c. The size of the intercompany receivable balance.
   d. The auditor's allowable risk of assessing control risk is too low.

12. An auditor's analytical procedures indicate a lower than expected return on an equity method investment. This situation most likely could have been caused by
   a. An error in recording amortization of the excess of the investor's cost over the investment's underlying book value.
   b. The investee's decision to reduce cash dividends declared per share of its common stock.
   c. An error in recording the unrealized gain from an increase in the fair value of available-for-sale securities in the income account for trading securities.
   d. A substantial fluctuation in the price of the investee's common stock on a national stock exchange.

9. **(a)** The requirement is to identify the most relevant factor for deciding whether a service auditor's report (Blue's report) is satisfactory to be used by a user auditor (Green). Answer (a) is correct because in considering whether the service auditor's report is satisfactory, AU 324 requires that the user auditor make inquiries concerning the service auditor's professional reputation. Answer (b) is incorrect because use of a service auditor's report may result in an assessment of control risk below the maximum level. Answer (c) is incorrect because the user auditor will not in general review the audit programs followed by the service auditor. Answer (d) is incorrect because although an auditor may test controls at a service center, this is not ordinarily done as a step in determining whether the service auditor's report is satisfactory.

10. **(c)** The requirement is to identify the procedure most likely to be considered a test of controls. Answer (c) is correct because AU 314 points out that tests of controls involve inquiry (interviews), inspection, observation, and reperformance. Answers (a) and (b) are incorrect because reviewing the check register for unrecorded liabilities and reviewing details of journal entries are most likely to be considered substantive procedures. Answer (d) is incorrect because it relates to audit workpapers, not controls of the client.

11. **(a)** The requirement is to identify a consideration in planning a sample for a test of subsequent cash receipts. Answer (a) is correct because the auditor must determine which differences are material and which are not so to determine the size and nature of the sample. Answer (b) is incorrect because a consideration of bad debt write-offs in the prior year has no apparent benefit in planning a test of this year's subsequent cash receipts. Answer (c) is incorrect because the size of the intercompany receivable balance is not likely to affect the planning of a test of subsequent cash receipts which ordinarily will emphasize cash receipts of year-end receivables. Answer (d) is incorrect because testing subsequent cash receipts is often used as a substantive procedure and the risk of assessing control risk too low relates to internal control.

12. **(a)** The requirement is to identify the situation most likely to cause a lower than expected return on an equity method investment. Answer (a) is correct, because if the amortization is higher than proper, the return to the investment account will be lower than expected. Answer (b) is incorrect because the investee's cash dividend policy will not affect the return. Under the equity method dividends reduce the carrying value of the investment. Answer (c) is incorrect because such an error should not affect return on an investment accounted for on the equity basis. Answer (d) is incorrect because fluctuation in the price of the investee's common stock is not reflected by the equity method.

13. Under which of the following conditions may an auditor's observation procedure for inventory be performed during or after the end of the period under audit?

    a. When the client maintains periodic inventory records.

    b. When the auditor finds minimal variations in client records and test counts in prior periods.

    c. When total inventory has **not** varied more than 5% in the last five years.

    d. When well-kept perpetual inventory records are checked by the client periodically by comparisons with physical counts.

14. Which of the following is a computer-assisted audit technique that permits an auditor to use the auditor's version of a client's program to process data and compare the output with the client's output?

    a. Test data module.

    b. Frame relay protocol.

    c. Remote node router.

    d. Parallel simulation.

15. What is an auditor's primary method to corroborate information on litigation, claims, and assessments?

    a. Examining legal invoices sent by the client's attorney.

    b. Verifying attorney-client privilege through interviews.

    c. Reviewing the response from the client's lawyer to a letter of audit inquiry.

    d. Reviewing the written representation letter obtained from management.

16. Which of the following management roles would typically be acknowledged in a management representation letter?

    a. Management has the responsibility for the design of controls to detect fraud.

    b. Management communicates its views on ethical behavior to its employees.

    c. Management's knowledge of fraud is communicated to the audit committee.

    d. Management's compensation is contingent upon operating results.

13. **(d)** The requirement is to determine which situation may allow the auditor to observe a client's inventory either during the year or after year-end (as contrasted to at year-end). Answer (d) is correct because well-kept perpetual inventory records may result in a situation in which the auditor may observe a count at one of those times and then perform procedures to determine whether the year-end inventory is reasonable. Answer (a) is incorrect because perpetual, not periodic, inventory records are ordinarily needed. Answers (b) and (c) are incorrect because while such historical results are somewhat reassuring, it is the existence of controls during the current period that is more important.

14. **(d)** The requirement is to identify a computer-assisted audit technique that permits the auditors to use their program to process client data and compare it to the client's output. Answer (d) is correct because with parallel simulation client data is so processed using auditor software; if the client's program is operating properly, the client and auditor outputs should be equivalent. Answer (a) is incorrect because test data uses a set of dummy records and transactions developed to test a client's computer program or system. Answer (b) is incorrect because frame relay protocol is a standardized wide-area technology that specifies the physical and logical link layers of digital telecommunications channels. It is not typically used as a computer-assisted audit technique. Answer (c) is incorrect because routers allow multiple computers to use a communications channel and are not considered computer-assisted audit techniques.

15. **(c)** The requirement is to identify a primary method an auditor uses to corroborate information on litigation, claims and assessments. Answer (c) is correct because AU 337 outlines an approach in which auditors obtain information from a client's lawyer to corroborate client information on litigation, claims, and assessments. Answer (a) is incorrect because while legal invoices may reveal information on litigation, claims, and assessments, examining such invoices is not considered a primary method as compared to reviewing the lawyer's response. Answer (b) is incorrect because such attorney-client privilege is ordinarily a matter of law that is not verified on an audit. Answer (d) is incorrect because management does corroborate its earlier statements to the auditor in a representation letter. However, this is a much more limited corroboration than that provided by the client's lawyer, and it is not from an expert outside the company.

16. **(a)** The requirement is to identify the management role that would typically be acknowledged in a management representation letter. Answer (a) is correct because AU 333 indicates that auditors should obtain representations on management's acknowledgement of its responsibility for the design and implementation of programs and controls to prevent and detect fraud. Answer (b) is incorrect because while management may communicate its views on ethical behavior to employees (particularly those with relevance to the company), this is not required in a representation letter. Answer (c) is incorrect because while management's knowledge of fraud is obtained in a representation letter, its communication to the audit committee is not one of the representations obtained. Answer (d) is incorrect because such information on management compensation is not ordinarily included in a representation letter.

17. Before issuing a compilation report on the financial statements of a nonissuer for the prior year, the predecessor accountant is required to
   a. Make inquiries about actions taken at meetings of the board of directors during the current year.
   b. Verify that the reissued report will **not** be used to obtain credit from a financial institution.
   c. Review the successor accountant's working papers for matters affecting the prior year.
   d. Compare the prior year's financial statements with those of the current year.

17. **(d)** The requirement is to identify a predecessor accountant's responsibility when asked to reissue a compilation report for the prior year. Answer (d) is correct because AR 200 indicates that a predecessor should read the statements, compare them with those previously issued and those of the current period, and obtain a letter from the successor relating to the statements. Answer (a) is incorrect because such inquires are not required. Answer (b) is incorrect because the reissued report ordinarily may be used to obtain credit. Answer (c) is incorrect because the predecessor accountant need not review the successor accountant's working papers.

18. Which of the following procedures would a CPA ordinarily perform when reviewing the financial statements of a nonissuer in accordance with Statements on Standards for Accounting and Review Services (SSARS)?
   a. Apply year-end cutoff tests for the sales and purchasing functions.
   b. Compare the financial statements with budgets or forecasts.
   c. Obtain an understanding of the entity's internal control components.
   d. Document whether control risk is assessed at or below the maximum level.

18. **(b)** The requirement is to identify a procedure a CPA would perform when reviewing financial statements in accordance with SSARS. Answer (b) is correct because AR 80 suggests a comparison of the financial statements with budgets or forecasts. Answer (a) is incorrect because reviews ordinarily do not include such year-end cutoff tests. Answer (c) is incorrect because reviews performed under SSARS do not require an understanding of the entity's internal control (reviews performed under AU 722 do require such an understanding). Answer (d) is incorrect because no such documentation of control risk occurs in a SSARS review.

19. Wheat type of evidence would provide the highest level of assurance in an attestation engagement?
   a. Evidence secured solely from within the entity.
   b. Evidence obtained from independent sources.
   c. Evidence obtained indirectly.
   d. Evidence obtained from multiple internal inquiries.

19. **(b)** The requirement is to identify the type of evidence that would provide the highest level of assurance in an attestation engagement. Answer (b) is correct because AT 101 states that evidence from independent sources, from the attester's direct personal knowledge, and obtained under effective controls provide the highest level of assurance. Answer (a) is incorrect because evidence from independent sources (outside the entity) is considered to ordinarily provide more assurance. Answer (c) is incorrect because evidence obtained directly is considered to provide higher assurance. Answer (d) is incorrect because externally obtained evidence is considered to provide more assurance than internal inquiries, even multiple internal inquiries.

20. When performing a substantive test of a random sample of cash disbursements, an auditor is supplied with a photocopy of vendor invoices supporting the disbursements for one particular vendor rather than the original invoices. The auditor is told that the vendor's original invoices have been misplaced. What should the auditor do in response to this situation?
   a. Increase randomly the number of items in the substantive test to increase the reliance that may be placed on the overall test.
   b. Reevaluate the risk of fraud, and design alternate tests for the related transactions.
   c. Increase testing by agreeing more of the payments to this particular vendor to the photocopies of its invoices.
   d. Count the missing original documents as misstatements, and project the total amount of error based on the size of the population and the dollar amount of the errors.

20. **(b)** The requirement is to determine an auditor's proper response when told that original invoices have been misplaced. Answer (b) is correct because alternate tests should be designed, and because the unavailability of the documents may indicate a higher risk of fraud. Answer (a) is incorrect because in such a situation the auditor will often expand the sample to similar transactions as contrasted to using a random approach. Answer (c) is incorrect because it is the risk that the photocopies are improper that is being addressed. Answer (d) is incorrect because while this may be a partial solution, the auditor must consider the possibility that such a projection is inadequate in the situation. For example, if only a small dollar disbursement has been identified at this point, projecting based on this small amount may be inappropriate.

21. An auditor finds several errors in the financial statements that the client prefers not to correct. The auditor determines that the errors are not material in the aggregate. Which of the following actions by the auditor is most appropriate?

    a. Document the errors in the summary of uncorrected errors, and document the conclusion that the errors do **not** cause the financial statements to be misstated.

    b. Document the conclusion that the errors do **not** cause the financial statements to be misstated, but do **not** summarize uncorrected errors in the working papers.

    c. Summarize the uncorrected errors in the working papers, but do **not** document whether the errors cause the financial statements to be misstated.

    d. Do **not** summarize the uncorrected errors in the working papers, and do **not** document a conclusion about whether the uncorrected errors cause the financial statements to be misstated.

22. When qualifying an opinion because of an insufficiency of audit evidence, an auditor should refer to the situation in the

	Scope paragraph	Notes to the financial statements
a.	Yes	Yes
b.	Yes	No
c.	No	Yes
d.	No	No

23. An accountant compiled the financial statements of a nonissuer in accordance with Statements on Standards for Accounting and Review Services (SSARS). If the accountant has an ownership interest in the entity, which of the following statements is correct?

    a. The accountant should refuse the compilation engagement.

    b. A report need **not** be issued for a compilation of a nonissuer.

    c. The accountant should include the disclaimer "I am an owner of the entity" in the report.

    d. The accountant should include the statements "I am **not** independent with respect to the entity" in the compilation report.

24. Which of the following is correct about reporting on compliance with laws and regulations in a financial audit under *Government Auditing Standards* (the Yellow Book)?

    a. Auditors are **not** required to report fraud, illegal acts, and other material noncompliance in the audit report.

    b. In some circumstances, auditors are required to report fraud and illegal acts directly to parties external to the audited entity.

    c. The auditor's key findings of the audit of the financial statements should be communicated in a separate report.

    d. The reporting standards in a governmental audit modify the auditor's responsibilities under generally accepted auditing standards.

21. (a) The requirement is to determine an auditor's documentation responsibility when errors exist that are not material in the aggregate. Answer (a) is correct because AU 312 requires a summary of uncorrected misstatements (other than those considered trivial) and the auditor's conclusion about them. Answer (b) is incorrect because a summary is required. Answer (c) is incorrect because documentation of the effect on the financial statements is required. Answer (d) is incorrect because both a summary and conclusion are required.

22. (b) The requirement is to identify the proper method of qualifying an opinion because of an insufficiency of audit evidence (a scope limitation). Answer (b) is correct because the scope paragraph must refer to the limitation, and because the notes to the financial statements do not describe a scope limitation (or other matters related to details of the audit). Answer (a) is incorrect because the notes to the financial statements do not refer to the situation. Answer (c) is incorrect because the scope paragraph does refer to the situation and the notes do not. Answer (d) is incorrect because the scope limitation is referred to in the scope paragraph.

23. (d) The requirement is to identify an accountant's responsibility relating to performing a compilation when s/he is not independent. Answer (d) is correct because a compilation may be performed, but the report must indicate that the accountant is not independent (see AR 101). Answer (a) is incorrect because a compilation may be performed. Answer (b) is incorrect because a report must be issued when third-party reliance is anticipated. Answer (c) is incorrect because while the lack of independence must be indicated explicitly, the accountant may or may not choose to indicate the reason for the lack of independence.

24. (b) The requirement is to determine the correct statement relating to *Government Auditing Standards*. Answer (b) is correct because in certain circumstances auditors must report fraud and illegal acts to external parties (often regulatory agencies). Answer (a) is incorrect because such acts should be reported. Answer (c) is incorrect because key findings ordinarily are not in a separate report. Answer (d) is incorrect because governmental audit reporting standards do not modify auditor GAAS responsibilities.

25. Reports are considered special reports when issued in conjunction with

    a. Interim financial information reviewed to determine whether material modifications should be made to conform with GAAP.

    b. Feasibility studies presented to illustrate an entity's results of operations.

    c. Compliance with aspects of regulatory requirements related to audited financial statements.

    d. Pro forma financial presentations designed to demonstrate the effects of hypothetical transactions.

26. An accountant is required to comply with the provisions of Statements on Standards for Accounting and Review Services (SSARS) when

	Compiling financial statements generated through the use of computer software	Reproducing client-prepared financial statements, without modification, for client
a.	Yes	Yes
b.	Yes	No
c.	No	Yes
d.	No	No

27. How does Office of Management and Budget Circular A-133, *Audits of States, Local Governments, and Non-Profit Organizations*, define a subrecipient?

    a. As a nonfederal entity that provides a federal award to another entity to carry out a federal program.

    b. As an individual who receives and expends federal awards received from a pass-through entity.

    c. As a dealer, distributor, merchant, or other seller providing goods or services that are required for the conduct of a federal program.

    d. As a nonfederal entity that expends federal awards received from another entity to carry out a federal program.

28. Which of the following outcomes is a likely benefit of information technology used for internal control?

    a. Processing of unusual or nonrecurring transactions.

    b. Enhanced timeliness of information.

    c. Potential loss of data.

    d. Recording of unauthorized transactions.

29. Analytical procedures are most appropriate when testing which of the following types of transactions?

    a. Payroll and benefit liabilities.

    b. Acquisitions and disposals of fixed assets.

    c. Operating expense transactions.

    d. Long-term debt transactions.

25. (c) The requirement is to identify which listed report is considered a "special report." Answer (c) is correct because reports on compliance are considered special reports. AU 623 indicates that reports on comprehensive basis statements, specified element, compliance, financial presentations to comply with contractual agreements, and financial information on prescribed forms are special reports. Answers (a), (b), and (d) are all other reports not considered as "special reports."

26. (b) The requirement is to identify the circumstance(s) in which the provisions of SSARS apply. Answer (b) is correct because AR 80 states that when financial statements are compiled (regardless of the use of computer software) the provisions of SSARS apply, but they do not apply when reproducing client-prepared financial statements. Answer (a) is incorrect because SSARS do not apply when reproducing client-prepared financial statements. Answer (c) is incorrect because SSARS apply when compiling financial statements, and do not apply when reproducing client-prepared financial statements. Answer (d) is incorrect because SSARS apply when compiling financial statements.

27. (d) The requirement is to determine how OMB Circular A-133 defines a subrecipient. Answer (d) is correct because it defines a subrecipient as a nonfederal entity that expends federal funds received from another entity to carry out a federal program. Answer (a) is incorrect because the nonfederal entity does not provide a federal award to another entity. Answer (b) is incorrect because it does not involve an individual and a pass-through entity. Answer (c) is incorrect because a dealer, distributor, merchant or other seller providing goods or service is not a part of the definition.

28. (b) The requirements is to identify a likely benefit of information technology (IT) used for internal control. Answer (b) is correct because IT may result in enhanced timeliness of information due to the speed of electronic processing. Answer (a) is incorrect because IT has no particular benefit for unusual or nonrecurring transactions in that they are difficult to program and achieve a real benefit over other methods. Answer (c) is incorrect because both IT and other systems may result in loss of data. Answer (d) is incorrect because the recording of unauthorized transactions may occur using IT or other systems.

29. (c) The requirement is to determine the type of transaction for which analytical procedures are most appropriate. Answer (c) is correct because AU 329 indicates that analytical procedures are most effective when they are applied to plausible and predictable relationships, often involving income statement accounts. Answer (a) is incorrect because payroll and benefit liabilities may vary widely period to period and thus establishing a predictable relationship is difficult. Answer (b) is incorrect because acquisitions and disposals of fixed assets relate to the balance sheet and differ widely by period. Answer (d) is incorrect because long-term debt transactions relate to the balance sheet and may be expected to vary widely by period.

30. During the audit of a new client, the auditor determined that management had given illegal bribes to municipal officials during the year under audit and for several prior years. The auditor notified the client's board of directors, but the board decided to take no action because the amounts involved were immaterial to the financial statements. Under these circumstances, the auditor should

    a.   Add an explanatory paragraph emphasizing that certain matters, while **not** affecting the unqualified opinion, require disclosure.

    b.   Report the illegal bribes to the municipal official at least one level above those persons who received the bribes.

    c.   Consider withdrawing from the audit engagement and disassociating from future relationships with the client.

    d.   Issue an "except for" qualified opinion or an adverse opinion with a separate paragraph that explains the circumstances.

31. Which of the following procedures would be most appropriate for testing the completeness assertion as it applies to inventory?

    a.   Scanning perpetual inventory, production, and purchasing records.

    b.   Examining paid vendor invoices.

    c.   Tracing inventory items from the tag listing back to the physical inventory quantities.

    d.   Performing cutoff procedures for shipping and receiving.

32. Which of the following activities performed by a department supervisor most likely would help in the prevention or detection of a payroll fraud?

    a.   Distributing paychecks directly to department employees.

    b.   Setting the pay rate for departmental employees.

    c.   Hiring employees and authorizing them to be added to the payroll.

    d.   Approving a summary of hours each employee worked during the pay period.

33. An auditor is concerned about a policy of management override as a limitation of internal control. Which of the following tests would best assess the validity of the auditor's concern?

    a.   Matching purchase orders to accounts payable.

    b.   Verifying that approved spending limits are **not** exceeded.

    c.   Tracing sales orders to the revenue account.

    d.   Reviewing minutes of board meetings.

30. **(c)** The requirement is to determine an auditor's responsibility when a client's board of directors has decided to take no action for illegal bribes that are immaterial to the financial statements. Answer (c) is correct because AU 317 indicates that the auditor should consider the need to withdraw when the client does not take remedial action, even when the illegal act involved is immaterial. Answer (a) is incorrect because an explanatory paragraph would not ordinarily be added for such immaterial illegal acts. Answer (b) is incorrect because the auditor ordinarily need not communicate the illegal acts to an outside party. Answer (d) is incorrect because a material departure from GAAP is not involved.

31. **(d)** The requirement is to identify the procedure most appropriate for testing the completeness assertion for inventory. Answer (d) is correct because cutoff procedures applied to transactions recorded subsequent to year-end for shipping and receiving will address completeness—that is whether transactions that should have been recorded prior to year-end were so recorded. Answer (a) is incorrect because scanning perpetual inventory, production, and purchasing records are likely to address assertions other than completeness since with completeness one is addressing whether inventory transactions that should have been recorded were not. Answer (b) is incorrect because only paid vendor invoices recorded after year-end are likely to address completeness. Answer (c) is incorrect because tracing items from tag listing to physical inventory quantities addresses existence more directly than it addresses completeness.

32. **(d)** The requirement is to identify the activity performed by a department supervisor most likely to help prevent or detect a payroll fraud. Answer (d) is correct because the supervisor should know the actual or approximate number of hours worked by subordinates and be able to identify fraudulent reporting of hours. Answer (a) is incorrect because an individual independent of the function should distribute paychecks to make certain that all those being paid are actually present and working. Answer (b) is incorrect because while a department supervisor may recommend a pay rate, those above that individual should actually set the rate. Answer (c) is incorrect because a separate human resources department should be involved in hiring.

33. **(b)** The requirement is to identify the circumstance which will best address an auditor's concern about management override. Answer (b) is correct because management override often evidences itself through exceeding approved spending limits—thus, finding that those limits have not been exceeded provides some evidence that at least that form of management override did not occur. Answer (a) is incorrect because even if management override did occur, one would expect purchase orders related to the purchases. Answer (c) is incorrect for similar reasons to (a) in that one would expect a sale order even when management override occurred. Answer (d) is incorrect because it is unlikely that the board meeting minutes would provide indication of management override.

34. When an auditor plans to rely on controls that have changed since they were last tested, which of the following courses of action would be most appropriate?
- a. Test the operating effectiveness of such controls in the current audit.
- b. Document that reliance and proceed with the original audit strategy.
- c. Inquire of management as to the effectiveness of the controls.
- d. Report the reliance in the report on internal controls.

35. In which of the following circumstances would an auditor expect to find that an entity implemented automated controls to reduce risks of misstatement?
- a. When errors are difficult to predict.
- b. When misstatements are difficult to define.
- c. When large, unusual, or nonrecurring transactions require judgment.
- d. When transactions are high-volume and recurring.

36. Which of the following explanations best describes why an auditor may decide to reduce tests of details for a particular objective?
- a. The audit is being performed soon after the balance sheet date.
- b. Audit staff are experienced in performing the planned procedures.
- c. Analytical procedures have revealed **no** unusual or unexpected results.
- d. There were many transactions posted to the account during the period.

37. During the confirmation of accounts receivable, an auditor receives a confirmation via the client's fax machine. Which of the following actions should an auditor take?
- a. Not accept the confirmation and select another customer's balance to confirm.
- b. Not accept the confirmation and treat it as an exception.
- c. Accept the confirmation and file it in the working papers.
- d. Accept the confirmation but verify the source and content through a telephone call to the respondent.

34. **(a)** The requirement is to determine an auditor's proper course of action when s/he plans to rely on controls that have changed since they were last tested. Answer (a) is correct because AU 318 requires that when the auditor plans to rely on controls that have changed since they were last tested, the auditor should test the operating effectiveness of such controls in the current audit. Answer (b) is incorrect since the auditor must perform tests of controls, and not just document the strategy. Answer (c) is incorrect since inquiry of management alone is insufficient. Answer (d) is incorrect because tests of controls must be performed.

35. **(d)** The requirement is to identify the circumstance in which an auditor would expect to find that an entity has implemented automated controls to reduce the risks of misstatement. Answer (d) is correct because transactions that are high-volume and recurring are generally subject to automated controls due to their nature and volume. Answers (a) and (b) are incorrect because it is difficult to implement automated controls in areas in which errors are difficult to predict or define. Answer (c) is incorrect because automated controls are more effective for recurring transactions that do not involve a lot of judgment. Note that automated controls may be developed over all these options, but ordinarily they are easier to develop for high-volume and recurring type transactions.

36. **(c)** The requirement is to identify why an auditor may decide to reduce tests of details (a type of substantive procedure) for a particular audit objective. Answer (c) is correct because analytical procedures performed as substantive procedures which reveal no likely misstatements may reduce the needed extent of other substantive procedures. Answer (a) is incorrect because simply performing the audit soon after the balance sheet date does not reduce the need for tests of details. Answer (b) is incorrect because, even with an experienced audit staff, the need to obtain sufficient appropriate audit evidence remains. Answer (d) is incorrect because, if anything, the presence of many transactions, all things equal, may increase the need for tests of details.

37. **(d)** The requirement is to determine the most appropriate action to be taken when a confirmation reply is received via the client's fax machine. Answer (d) is correct because while the confirmation may be accepted, the auditor should verify the source and content in some manner, perhaps via a telephone call (AU 330). Answers (a) and (b) are incorrect because such a reply may be accepted. Answer (c) is incorrect because audit procedures must be performed on the confirmation—it should not simply be accepted and filed.

38. Which of the following tests of details most likely would help an auditor determine whether accounts payable have been misstated?

   a. Examining reported purchase returns that appear too low.
   b. Examining vendor statements for amounts **not** reported as purchases.
   c. Search for customer-returned goods that were **not** reported as returns.
   d. Reviewing bank transfers recorded as cash received from customers.

39. An audit client sells 15 to 20 units of product annually. A large portion of the annual sales occur in the last month of the fiscal year. Annual sales have not materially changed over the past five years. Which of the following approaches would be most effective concerning the timing of audit procedures for revenue?

   a. The auditor should perform analytical procedures at an interim date and discuss any changes in the level of sales with senior management.
   b. The auditor should inspect transactions occurring in the last month of the fiscal year and review the related sale contracts to determine that revenue was posted in the proper period.
   c. The auditor should perform tests of controls at an interim date to obtain audit evidence about the operational effectiveness of internal controls over sales.
   d. The auditor should review period-end compensation to determine if bonuses were paid to meet earnings goals.

40. An auditor should be aware of subsequent events that provide evidence concerning conditions that did not exist at year-end but arose after year-end. These events may be important to the auditor because they may

   a. Require adjustments to the financial statements as of the year-end.
   b. Have been recorded based on preliminary accounting estimates.
   c. Require disclosure to keep the financial statements from being misleading.
   d. Have been recorded based on year-end tests for asset obsolescence.

41. Which of the following disagreements between the auditor and management do **not** have to be communicated by the auditor to those charged with governance?

   a. Disagreements regarding management's judgment about accounting estimates for goodwill.
   b. Disagreements about the scope of the audit.
   c. Disagreements in the application of accounting principles relating to software development costs.
   d. Disagreement of the amount of LIFO inventory layer based on preliminary information.

38. **(b)** The requirement is to identify the test of details most likely to help the auditor to determine whether accounts payable have been misstated. Answer (b) is correct because examining vendor statements for amounts not reported as purchases is likely to reveal purchases that should have been recorded to increase accounts payable but were not. That is, the vendor may show a different balance due, leading the auditor to discover the accounts payable misstatement. Answer (a) is incorrect because while examining the reported returns themselves may reveal misstatements of payables, it is likely to be a less effective technique than examining vendor statements. Answer (c) is incorrect because customer returns relate to accounts receivables, not accounts payable. Answer (d) is incorrect because bank transfers recorded as cash received from customers relates to accounts receivable, not accounts payable.

39. **(b)** The requirement is to identify the most appropriate audit procedure concerning proper timing of audit procedures for revenue when most sales occur during the last month of the fiscal year. Answer (b) is correct because examining transactions occurring during the last month will reveal whether they have been recorded in the proper period. Answers (a) and (c) are incorrect because, since most sales occur during the final month, interim period testing will not address the last month sales very well. The interim period has different characteristics (at a minimum, lower sales) than sales in the last month. Answer (d) is incorrect as examining period-end compensation will not as directly address final month sales.

40. **(c)** The requirement is to determine why an auditor should be aware of subsequent events that provide evidence concerning conditions that did not exist at year-end but arose after year-end. Answer (c) is correct because these "type 2" subsequent events may require disclosure, but they do not result in adjustment of the financial statements. Answer (a) is incorrect because adjustments are not required for conditions that did not exist at year-end. Answer (b) is incorrect because the events may or may not relate to accounting estimates. Answer (d) is incorrect because the conditions did not exist at year-end.

41. **(d)** The requirement is to determine which disagreement between the auditor and management need not be communicated to those charged with governance. Answer (d) is correct because it is based only on preliminary information and may well be satisfactorily resolved. Answers (a), (b) and (c) are incorrect because AU 380 states that disagreements that should be communicated include those relating to estimates, the scope of the audit, application of accounting principles, the wording of the audit report, and other matters.

42. Which of the following is required of an accountant in reviewing a company's financial statements under Statements on Standards for Accounting and Review Services (SSARS)?

a. Obtain knowledge of the client's industry.
b. Send bank confirmations.
c. Confirm accounts receivable.
d. Observe client's physical inventory.

42. (a) The requirement is to identify what is required when reviewing a company's financial statements under SSARS. Answer (a) is correct because SSARS 90 requires that the accountant have knowledge of the client's industry. Answer (b) is incorrect because bank confirmations are not required on a review engagement. Answer (c) is incorrect because confirmation of accounts receivable is not required on a review engagement. Answer (d) is incorrect because observation of the client's physical inventory count is not required in a review engagement.

43. Which of the following procedures should an accountant perform during an engagement to compile prospective financial statements?

a. Test the entity's internal controls to determine if adequate controls exist so that financial projections can be reasonably achieved.
b. Make inquiries prior to the date of the report about possible future transactions that may impact the forecast once the report is issued.
c. Make inquiries about the accounting principles used in the preparation of the prospective financial statements.
d. Compare the prospective financial statements with the entity's historical results for the prior year.

43. (c) The requirement is to identify the procedure an accountant should perform during an engagement to compile prospective financial statements. Answer (c) is correct because AT 301 requires that accountants make inquiries about the accounting principles used in the preparation of the prospective financial statements. Answer (a) is incorrect because testing of internal control is not required in a compilation of prospective financial statements. Answer (b) is incorrect because no such inquiry about possible future transactions is required. Answer (d) is incorrect because the prospective financial statements need not be compared to historical results for the prior year.

44. When applying analytical procedures during an audit, which of the following is the best approach for developing and evaluating expectations?

a. Considering unaudited account balances and ratios to calculate what adjusted balances should be.
b. Identifying reasonable explanations for unexpected differences before talking to client management.
c. Considering the pattern of several unusual changes without trying to explain what caused them.
d. Comparing client data with client-determined expected results to reduce detailed test of account balances.

44. (b) The requirement is to identify the best approach for developing and evaluating expectations when applying analytical procedures during an audit. Answer (b) is correct because identifying reasonable explanations for unexpected differences before talking to client management will help the auditor to consider why the differences might have occurred and the reasonableness of management's replies. Answer (a) is incorrect because considering the unaudited balances does not involve developing and evaluating expectations. Answer (c) is incorrect because considering the pattern of several unusual changes occurs subsequent to developing expectations and because one should try to explain causes of differences. Answer (d) is incorrect because comparing client-expected results with actual results does not involve developing and evaluating independent expectations.

45. Which of the following statements is most accurate regarding sufficient and appropriate documentation?

a. Accounting estimates are **not** considered sufficient and appropriate documentation.
b. Sufficient and appropriate documentation should include evidence that the audit working papers have been reviewed.
c. If additional evidence is required to document significant findings or issues, the original evidence is **not** considered sufficient and appropriate and therefore should be deleted from the working papers.
d. Audit documentation is the property of the client, and sufficient and appropriate copies should be retained by the auditor for at least five years.

45. (b) The requirement is to identify the correct statement regarding sufficient and appropriate documentation. Answer (b) is correct because the review of audit working papers (and its documentation) are required. Answer (a) is incorrect because accounting estimates are made by management and are not in and of themselves audit documentation—although auditors may choose to document them in the working papers. Answer (c) is incorrect because original evidence need not be deleted from the working papers simply because it, by itself, is not sufficient and appropriate. Answer (d) is incorrect because audit documentation is the property of the auditor, not the client.

46. If **not** already performed during the overall review stage of the audit, the auditor should perform analytical procedures relating to which of the following transaction cycles?

a. Payroll.
b. Revenue.
c. Purchasing.
d. Inventory.

46. (b) The requirement is to determine the account to which analytical procedures should be applied during the overall review stage of an audit if not already performed. Answer (b) is correct because AU 316 suggests that there is a presumption that improper revenue recognition is a fraud risk. Answers (a), (c), and (d) all represent areas in which no such presumption exists.

47. Which of the following services, if any, may an accountant who is **not** independent provide?
    a. Compilations, but **not** reviews.
    b. Reviews, but **not** compilations.
    c. Both compilations and reviews.
    d. No services.

48. Which of the following situations would preclude an accountant from issuing a review report on a company's financial statements in accordance with Statements on Standards for Accounting and Review Services (SSARS)?
    a. The owner of a company is the accountant's father.
    b. The accountant was engaged to review only the balance sheet.
    c. Land has been recorded at appraisal value instead of historical cost.
    d. Finished-goods inventory does **not** include any overhead amounts.

49. Which of the following components is appropriate in a practitioner's report on the results of applying agreed-upon procedures?
    a. A list of procedures performed, as agreed to by the specified parties identified in the report.
    b. A statement that management is responsible for expressing an opinion.
    c. A title that includes the phrase "independent audit."
    d. A statement that the report is unrestricted in its use.

50. An auditor may report on condensed financial statements that are derived from a complete set of audited financial statements only if the auditor
    a. Expresses an unqualified opinion on the audited financial statements from which the condensed financial statements are derived.
    b. Indicates whether the information is fairly stated in all material respects in relation to the complete financial statements.
    c. Determines that the condensed financial statements include all the disclosures necessary for the complete set of financial statements.
    d. Presents the condensed financial statements in comparative form with the prior year's condensed financial statements.

47. **(a)** The requirement is to determine whether accountants must be independent when performing compilations, reviews, or both. Answer (a) is correct because AU 60 requires independence only for reviews. Answer (b) is incorrect because independence is required for reviews and not compilations. Answer (c) is incorrect because independence is required for reviews. Answer (d) is incorrect because independence is required for a number of services, including reviews and audits.

48. **(a)** The requirement is to identify the circumstance in which an accountant may not issue a review report. Answer (a) is correct because independence is required to perform a review, and if the owner of a client is the accountant's father, the accountant is not independent. Answer (b) is incorrect because an accountant may be engaged to review only one particular financial statement, here a balance sheet. Answer (c) is incorrect because a review may be performed, although it may reveal a departure from GAAP when land is recorded at appraisal value. Answer (d) is incorrect because while finished-goods inventory of a manufacturing client (not a nonmanufacturing client) should include overhead amounts, such a departure from GAAP does not result in a situation in which a review report may not be issued.

49. **(a)** The requirement is to identify the appropriate component of a practitioner's report on the results of applying agreed-upon procedures. Answer (a) is correct because agreed-upon procedure reports result in a list of procedures performed and findings—see AT 101. Answer (b) is incorrect because the auditor, not management, is responsible for expressing an opinion. Answer (c) is incorrect because while the title must include the word "independent," it should not include "audit." Answer (d) is incorrect because an agreed-upon procedures engagement results in a report that is restricted in its use.

50. **(b)** The requirement is to identify the proper statement regarding an auditor reporting on condensed financial statements derived from a complete set of audited financial statements. Answer (b) is correct because in such a report the auditor reports on whether the information is fairly stated in all material respects in relation to the complete financial statements (AU 552). Answer (a) is incorrect because an unqualified opinion on the audited financial statements is not necessary. Answer (c) is incorrect because the condensed financial statements need not include all such disclosures. Answer (d) is incorrect because there is no requirement that comparative form statements be presented.

SIMULATION 1

| Testlet 1 of 1 | Time Remaining 4 hours 14 minutes | Copy | Paste | Calculator | Sheet | Help | Unsplit | Split Horiz | Split Vert | Done |

Directions | Resources | ◫ Proposed Journal Entries | ◫ Type of Audit Procedures | ◫ Attorney Letters | ◫ Communication | ◫ Research / Authoritative Literature

In the following simulation, you will be asked to complete various tasks. You may use the content in the **Information Tabs** to complete the tasks in the **Work Tabs**.

Information Tabs:

| Directions | Resources |

FIG. 1

- Go through each of the **Information Tabs** to familiarize yourself with the simulation content
- The **Resources** tab will contain information, including formulas and definitions, that may help you to complete the tasks
- Your simulation may have more **Information Tabs** than those shown in Fig. 1

Work Tabs:

| ◫ Gain/Basis | ◫ Depreciation | ▌Communication |

FIG. 2

- **Work Tabs**, to the right of the **Information Tabs**, contain the tasks for you to complete
- **Work Tabs** contain directions for completing each task - be sure to read these directions carefully
- The tab names in Fig. 2 are for illustration only - yours may differ
- Once you complete any part of a task, the pencil for that tab will be shaded (see **Communication** in Fig. 2)
- The shaded pencil does **NOT** indicate that you have completed the entire task
- You must complete all of the tasks in the **Work Tabs** to receive full credit

Research / Authoritative Literature Tab:

| ◫ Research / Authoritative Literature |

FIG. 3

- This tab contains both the Research task and the Authoritative Literature
- Detailed instructions for completing the Research task, and for using the Authoritative Literature, appear on this tab
- You may use the Authoritative Literature as a resource for completing other tasks

Note: If you believe you have encountered a software malfunction, report it to the test center staff immediately.

You are the audit manager assigned to Joe's Office Supply. Based on substantive test work, the staff auditor has proposed the journal entries below, to be presented to the client. Assume all proposed journal entries are valid and material.

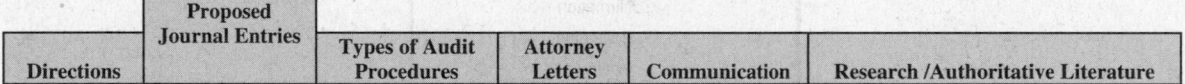

| Directions | Proposed Journal Entries | Types of Audit Procedures | Attorney Letters | Communication | Research /Authoritative Literature |

For each journal entry, determine the effect on the ratios below by double-clicking the associated shaded cells and selecting the effects from the drop-down list provided. A selection may be used once, more than once, or not at all.

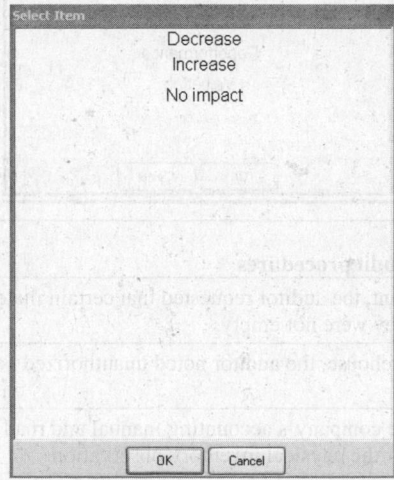

Select Item

Decrease
Increase
No impact

| OK | Cancel |

Proposed journal entry	Debit	Credit	Earnings per share	Days sales in accounts receivable	Gross profit
Sales reported after year-end that should have been reported before year-end:					
Cost of sales	90				
Accounts receivable	100				
Sales		100			
Inventory		90			
Error in adjusting entry:					
Cost of sales	45				
PP&E	45				
Utilities expense	12				
Cash	10				
Sales		45			
Accrued expenses		12			
Inventory		45			
Interest expense		10			
To record current and deferred income taxes:					
Income tax expense—current	50				
Deferred tax asset	15				
Income tax expense—deferred		10			
Deferred tax liability		5			
Income tax payable		50			

Directions	Proposed Journal Entries	Types of Audit Procedures	Attorney Letters	Communication	Research /Authoritative Literature

During Year 1 audit of Numbaro Co., the auditor performed various procedures.

For each of the audit procedures listed below, double-click on the associated shaded cell and select the type of audit procedure, if any, that the auditor performed. A type of audit procedure may be selected once, more than once, or not at all.

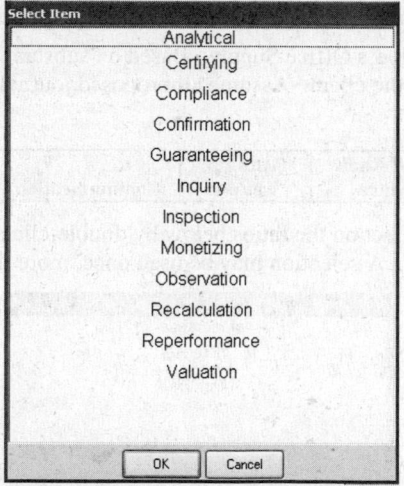

Select Item

- Analytical
- Certifying
- Compliance
- Confirmation
- Guaranteeing
- Inquiry
- Inspection
- Monetizing
- Observation
- Recalculation
- Reperformance
- Valuation

OK   Cancel

Audit procedures	Type of audit procedure
During the physical inventory count, the auditor requested that certain material containers by opened to ensure they were not empty.	
During a site visit to a branch warehouse, the auditor noted unauthorized personnel have access to the inventory.	
The auditor obtained a copy of the company's accounting manual and read the section on inventory to prepare for the physical inventory observation.	
The auditor sent a letter to the company's outside attorney accompanied by management's request for information concerning pending or threatened litigation, claims, and assessments.	

Audit procedures	Type of audit procedure
The auditing firm's computer assisted audit specialist obtained an electronic billing file from the company and checked the accuracy of the summarized billings file.	
The auditor obtained the company's aging of accounts receivable and independently created the aging of certain accounts.	
The auditor scanned the repairs and maintenance account for unusually large amounts.	

Directions	Proposed Journal Entries	Types of Audit Procedures	Attorney Letters	Communication	Research /Authoritative Literature

The following situations represent excerpts from the responses to audit inquiries of external legal counsel of XYZ Co. during the annual audit of year 1. For each excerpt, double-click the associated shaded cell and select the most appropriate audit response related to the financial statements in the audit response (financials) column. Then, in the audit response (report) column, double-click the associated shaded cell and select whether the auditor's report or the attorney's legal response letter needs to be updated. Each excerpt is independent. Responses may be used once, more than once, or not at all.

- The client's year-end is December 31, year 1
- The anticipated audit report date is February 15, year 2
- All amounts are material to the financial statements

Audit response (financials)

Audit response (report)

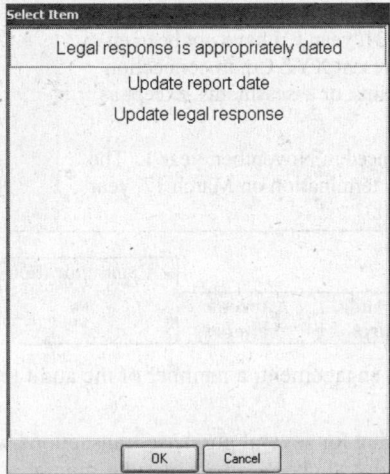

Situations	Audit response (financials)	Audit response (reported)
1. Letter dated February 14, year 2: "I advise you that at and since December 31, year 1, I have not been engaged to give substantive attention to, or represent XYZ Co. in connection with any pending or threatened litigation, claims, or assessments, nor am I aware of any loss contingencies. No amounts were due to this office for services provided at December 31, year 1."		
2. Letter dated January 21, year 2: "I advise you that at and since December 31, year 1, I have not been engaged to give substantive attention to, or represent XYZ Co. in connection with any pending or threatened litigation, claims, or assessments, nor am I aware of any loss contingencies. There were fees outstanding of $3,675 due to this office for services provided at December 31, year 1."		
3. Letter dated February 26, year 2: "I advise you that at and since December 31, year 1, I have not been engaged to give substantive attention to, or represent XYZ Co. in connection with any pending or threatened litigation, claims, or assessments, except as follows: K. Bowt v. XYZ Co.: This matter commenced in December, year 1. The plaintiff alleges discrimination relating to his termination on November 17, year 1. The company intends to defend this case vigorously. At this time, we are unable to evaluate the likelihood of an unfavorable outcome or estimate the amount or range of potential loss."		
4. Letter dated March 16, year 2: "I advise you that at and since December 31, year 1, I have not been engaged to give substantive attention to, or represent XYZ Co. in connection with any pending or threatened litigation, claims, or assessments, except as follows: J. Myers v. XYZ Co.: This matter commenced in March, year 2. The plaintiff alleges discrimination relating to his termination on November 17, year 1. The company intends to defend this case vigorously. At this time, we are unable to evaluate the likelihood of an unfavorable outcome. The plaintiff is demanding $50,000."		
5. Letter dated January 10, year 2: "I advise you that at and since December 31, year 1, I have not been engaged to give substantive attention to, or represent XYZ Co. in connection with any pending or threatened litigation, claims, or assessments, except as follows: R. Brown v. XYZ Co.: This matter commenced in November, year 1. The plaintiff alleges discrimination relating to his termination on March 17, year 1. The case was tentatively settled for $35,000, which will be covered by XYZ's insurance carrier."		
6. Letter dated January 20, year 2: "I advise you that at and since December 31, year 1, I have not been engaged to give substantive attention to, or represent XYZ Co. in connection with any pending or threatened litigation, claims, or assessments, except as follows: L. Peep v. XYZ Co.: This matter commenced in November, year 1. The plaintiff alleges discrimination relating to his termination on March 17, year 1. The case was tentatively settled for $35,000."		

				Communication	
Directions	Proposed Journal Entries	Types of Audit Procedures	Attorney Letters		Research /Authoritative Literature

During the preliminary fieldwork on this engagement, a member of the audit team brings to your attention the following suspicious activities:

- Supporting vendor invoices were missing for several purchase transactions with the same vendor.
- Second endorsements were found on several checks in a particular month.

As the engagement manager, it appears to you that these observations may be indicative of fraudulent activities. Write a memo to the engagement partner explaining why these observations may indicate fraudulent activities. In your response, you should assume that the suspicious events occurred at odd times of the month and were in amounts too high, too low, too consistent, or too different.

Type your communication in the response area below the horizontal line using the word processor provided.

REMINDER: Your response will be graded for both technical content and writing skills. Technical content will be evaluated for information that is helpful to the intended reader and clearly relevant to the issue. Writing skills will be evaluated for development, organization, and the appropriate expression of ideas in professional correspondence. Use a standard business memo or letter format with a clear beginning, middle, and end. Do not convey information in the form of a table, bullet point list, or other abbreviated presentation.

While preparing the auditor's report, the audit assistant believes the auditor's report can never reference the findings of a specialist. The audit manager disagrees. Which citation in the professional standards supports the audit manager's position?

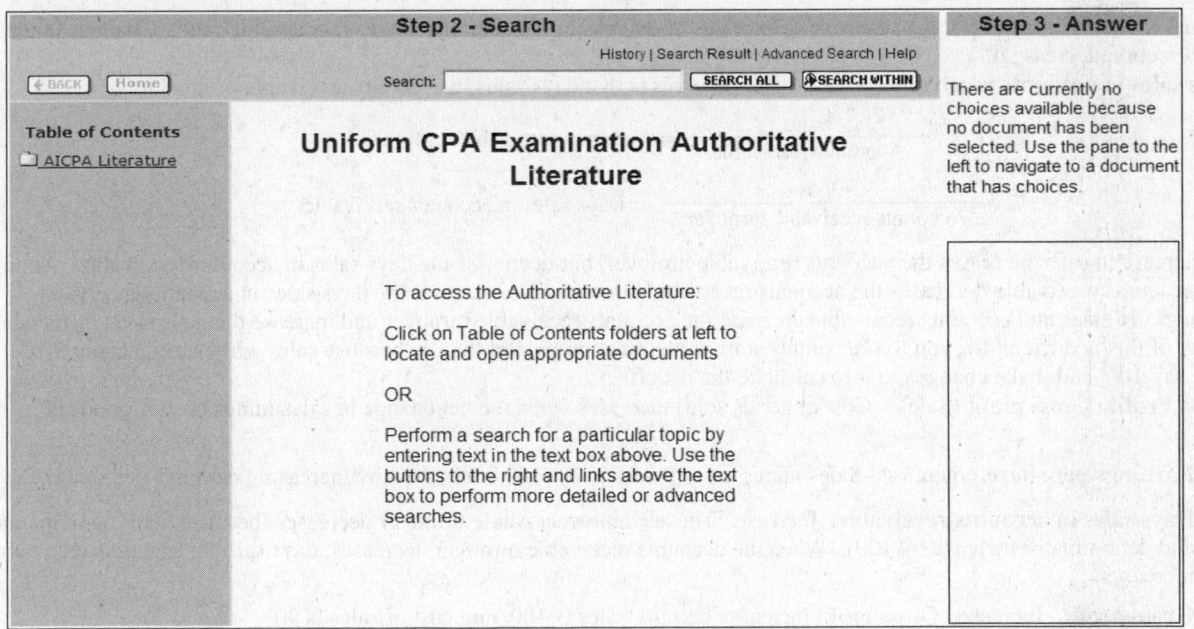

SOLUTION TO SIMULATION 1

Directions	Proposed Journal Entries	Types of Audit Procedures	Attorney Letters	Communication	Research /Authoritative Literature

Proposed journal entry	Debit	Credit	Earnings per share	Days sales in accounts receivable	Gross profit
Sales reported after year-end that should have been reported before year-end: Cost of sales Accounts receivable Sales Inventory	90 100	100 90	Increase	Increase	Increase
Error in adjusting entry: Cost of sales PP&E Utilities expense Cash Sales Accrued expenses Inventory Interest expense	45 45 12 10	45 12 45 10	Decrease	Decrease	No impact
To record current and deferred income taxes: Income tax expense—current Deferred tax asset Income tax expense—deferred Deferred tax liability Income tax payable	50 15	10 5 50	Decrease	No impact	No impact

To effectively address this question it is important to consider the factors that change ratios, and in which direction.

Earnings per share: Earnings per share is calculated as:

$$\frac{\text{Earnings}}{\text{Outstanding shares}}$$

Journal entries with a net effect of increasing earnings or decreasing outstanding shares increase the ratio. Changes in the opposite direction decrease it.

Days sales in accounts receivable. One way to view this is that days sales in accounts receivable is equal to

$$\frac{\text{Sales}}{\text{Accounts receivable}} = \text{Accounts receivable turnover}$$

$$\frac{365}{\text{Accounts receivable turnover}} = \text{Days sales in accounts receivable}$$

An increase in sales increases the accounts receivable turnover, but decreases the days sales in accounts receivable. An increase in accounts receivable decreases the accounts receivable turnover, but increases the days sales in accounts receivable. Equal changes in sales and accounts receivable decrease the accounts receivable turnover and increase the days sales in accounts receivable. If this is difficult for you to see, simply start with a fraction greater than 1 (because sales will exceed accounts receivable), say 10/3 and make changes to it to calculate the net effect.

Gross Profit. Gross profit (Sales – Cost of goods sold) increases when the net change in sales minus cost of goods is positive.

1. **Earnings per share.** Increase. Sales minus cost of sales is 10 (100 – 90), thereby increasing earnings per share.

    Days sales in accounts receivable. Increase. The accounts receivable turnover decreases (because both the numerator and denominator increase by 100). When the accounts receivable turnover decreases, days sales in accounts receivable increases.

    Gross profit. Increase. Gross profit increases because sales is 100, and cost of sales is 90.

2. **Earnings per share.** Decrease. The expenses here are 47 (increase in cost of sales 45 plus increase in utilities expense 12 minus decrease in interest expense 10), while the increase in sales is 45. Accordingly, earnings per share decreases due to a net decrease of 2.

    Days sales in accounts receivable. Decrease. Sales increases here with no corresponding change to accounts receivable. Therefore, the accounts receivable turnover increases—thus, days sales in accounts receivable decreases.

Gross profit. No impact. Because both sales and cost of sales increase by 45, there is no net impact on gross profit.

3. **Earnings per share.** Decrease. There are only increases in expenses here, and no change in sales. Accordingly, earnings per share decrease.

     Days sales in accounts receivable. No impact. There is no impact here since neither sales not accounts receivable is affected.

     Gross profit. No impact. There is no impact here since neither sales nor cost of sales is affected.

Directions	Proposed Journal Entries	Types of Audit Procedures	Attorney Letters	Communication	Research /Authoritative Literature

AU 326 provides the following types of audit procedures—inspection of documents or records, inspection of tangible assets, observation, inquiry, confirmation, recalculation, reperformance, and analytical procedures. Accordingly, one may rule out certifying, compliance, guaranteeing, and valuation as audit procedures.

Audit procedures	Type of audit procedure
During the physical inventory count, the auditor requested that certain material containers by opened to ensure they were not empty.	Inspection
During a site visit to a branch warehouse, the auditor noted unauthorized personnel have access to the inventory.	Observation
The auditor obtained a copy of the company's accounting manual and read the section on inventory to prepare for the physical inventory observation.	Inspection
The auditor sent a letter to the company's outside attorney accompanied by management's request for information concerning pending or threatened litigation, claims, and assessments.	Inquiry
The auditing firm's computer assisted audit specialist obtained an electronic billing file from the company and checked the accuracy of the summarized billings file.	Recalculation
The auditor obtained the company's aging of accounts receivable and independently created the aging of certain accounts.	Reperformance
The auditor scanned the repairs and maintenance account for unusually large amounts.	Analytical

Explanation of solutions

1. **Inspection (of tangible assets).** Inspection of tangible assets consists of physical examination of the assets, such as was done here with the material containers.

2. **Observation.** Observation consists of looking at a process or procedure being performed. Here the auditor is observing operations in the branch warehouse and notes unauthorized access to inventory.

3. **Inspection (of records or documents).** Inspection of records or documents consists of examining records or documents. Here the document is the accounting manual.

4. **Inquiry.** Inquiry consists of seeking information of knowledgeable persons, both inside or outside the entity. Here the inquiry is to the company's outside attorney.

5. **Recalculation.** Recalculation consists of checking the mathematical accuracy of documents or records. Here the accuracy of summarized billings is being recalculated.

6. **Reperformance.** Reperformance is the auditor's independent execution of procedures or controls that were originally performed as part of the entity's internal control Here the client already aged the receivables and the auditor is reperforming the calculation.

7. **Analytical.** Analytical procedures consist of evaluations of financial information made by a study of plausible relationships among both financial and nonfinancial data. Here the auditor is scanning repairs and maintenance to see if it seems reasonable.

Directions	Proposed Journal Entries	Types of Audit Procedures	Attorney Letters	Communication	Research /Authoritative Literature

Situations	Audit response (financials)	Audit response (reported)
1. Letter dated February 14, year 2: "I advise you that at and since December 31, year 1, I have not been engaged to give substantive attention to, or represent XYZ Co. in connection with any pending or threatened litigation, claims, or assessments, nor am I aware of any loss contingencies. No amounts were due to this office for services provided at December 31, year 1."	No impact on financial statement or footnotes	Legal response is appropriately dated
2. Letter dated January 21, year 2: "I advise you that at and since December 31, year 1, I have not been engaged to give substantive attention to, or represent XYZ Co. in connection with any pending or threatened litigation, claims, or assessments, nor am I aware of any loss contingencies. There were fees outstanding of $3,675 due to this office for services provided at December 31, year 1."	Verify amount due attorney is recorded in financial statements	Update legal response
3. Letter dated February 26, year 2: "I advise you that at and since December 31, year 1, I have not been engaged to give substantive attention to, or represent XYZ Co. in connection with any pending or threatened litigation, claims, or assessments, except as follows: K. Bowt v. XYZ Co.: This matter commenced in December, year 1. The plaintiff alleges discrimination relating to his termination on November 17, year 1. The company intends to defend this case vigorously. At this time, we are unable to evaluate the likelihood of an unfavorable outcome or estimate the amount or range of potential loss."	Disclosure in footnotes relating to nature of litigation, but no amount disclosed	Update report date
4. Letter dated March 16, year 2: "I advise you that at and since December 31, year 1, I have not been engaged to give substantive attention to, or represent XYZ Co. in connection with any pending or threatened litigation, claims, or assessments, except as follows: J. Myers v. XYZ Co.: This matter commenced in March, year 2. The plaintiff alleges discrimination relating to his termination on November 17, year 1. The company intends to defend this case vigorously. At this time, we are unable to evaluate the likelihood of an unfavorable outcome. The plaintiff is demanding $50,000."	Disclosure in footnotes relating to nature of litigation, but no amount disclosed	Update report date
5. Letter dated January 10, year 2: "I advise you that at and since December 31, year 1, I have not been engaged to give substantive attention to, or represent XYZ Co. in connection with any pending or threatened litigation, claims, or assessments, except as follows: R. Brown v XYZ Co.: This matter commenced in November, year 1. The plaintiff alleges discrimination relating to his termination on March 17, year 1. The case was tentatively settled for $35,000, which will e covered by XYZ's insurance carrier."	Potential litigation settlement not accrued in financial statements, amount disclosed in footnote	Update legal response
6. Letter dated January 20, year 2: "I advise you that at and since December 31, year 1, I have not been engaged to give substantive attention to, or represent XYZ Co. in connection with any pending or threatened litigation, claims, or assessments, except as follows: L. Peep v. XYZ This matter commenced in November, year 1. The plaintiff alleges discrimination relating to his termination on March 17, year 1. The case was tentatively settled for $35,000."	Potential litigation settlement accrued in financial statements	Update legal response

Explanation of solutions

1. **Financials:** No impact on financial statements or footnotes. There is no real issue here related to the financials.

   Report: Legal response is appropriately dated. AU 9337 requires that the effective date of the legal response approximate the expected date of the auditor's report. February 14 does approximate February 15.

2. **Financials:** Verify amount due attorney is recorded in financial statements. Because the services were provided at December 31, an adjusting journal entry is required as of year-end.

Report: Update legal response. January 21 does not approximate February 15; accordingly an updated legal response is necessary.

3. **Financials:** Disclosure in footnotes relating to nature of litigation, but no amount disclosed. Since determining the amount and likelihood is not possible, disclosure is required, but no amount is available. This presumes the likelihood of loss is greater than remote.

Report: Update report date. The date of the audit report must be updated since the report has not yet been issued, and the attorney's letter is dated February 26 (presumably, the auditor did not have sufficient appropriate audit evidence prior to that date).

4. **Financials:** Disclosure in footnotes relating to nature of litigation, but no amount disclosed. Because no likelihood of loss or reliable estimate of the amount is available, the amount need not be disclosed (although disclosure of such is acceptable).

Report: Update report date. The date of the audit report must be updated since the report has not yet been issued, and the attorney's letter is dated March 16 and refers to a subsequent event dated March 2. When a subsequent event requiring disclosure occurs after the date of the auditor's report but before issuance of the related financial statement, AU 530 requires that the auditor either dual date the audit report for that event, or change the report date to that later date.

5. **Financials:** Potential litigation settlement not accrued in financial statements, amount disclosed in footnote. No adjustment is necessary because it is the insurance carrier that will pay the settlement. Accordingly, there is no necessary accrual entry, although disclosure of the amount in the footnotes is appropriate.

Report: Update legal response. The date of the letter, January 10, does not approximate the date of the auditor's report (February 15).

6. **Financials:** Potential litigation settlement accrued in financial statements. Because the case was tentatively settled for $35,000, accrual is appropriate.

Report: Update legal response. The date of the letter, January 20, does not approximate the date of the auditor's report (February 15).

Directions	Proposed Journal Entries	Types of Audit Procedures	Attorney Letters	Communication	Research /Authoritative Literature

Although any number of issues might be brought up here, the following is an example of a memorandum.

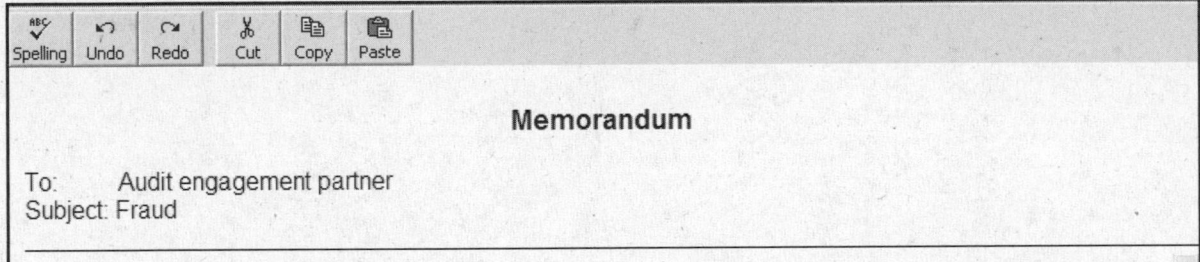

Memorandum

To: Audit engagement partner
Subject: Fraud

During our preliminary fieldwork on the XYZ engagement, Bill Wright, a member of the audit team, brought to my attention missing supporting vendor invoices for several purchase transactions with the same vendor and second endorsements on several checks in December. Both of these activities are consistent with possible fraud—most likely misappropriation of assets.

The missing invoices from Vendor A are consistent with a risk of misstatement arising from misappropriation of assets. The amounts involved are relatively high [*provide amounts*] and a questions arises as to whether goods were actually received relating to these invoices. Also, the fact that all of the invoices relate to Vendor A seems unlikely to have occurred by chance. In one extreme, the possibility exists that an employee (or associate of an employee) has developed a shell company which bills XYZ for products not received. Alternatively, a noncompliance vendor scheme may be occurring in which an employee abstracts the items purchased and/or the payment to the vendor. We have very limited information on this at this point and I suggest that we develop a plan to analyze these transactions in detail.

Second endorsements were noted on several checks written to vendors. Such second endorsements are a possible indication of a fraud scheme in which the first endorsement is fraudulently signed by an individual who abstracts the funds—the second endorser. The amounts here, again, are relatively high [*provide amounts*]. We have not analyzed them in detail at this point. They appear to be payable to a number of vendors, including Vendor A. The combination of missing invoices from Vendor A and second endorsements on the checks to Vendor A raises further suspicion of a nonaccomplice vendor scheme.

I bring these issues to your attention so we may meet and decide appropriate follow-up procedures. Please contact me at your earliest convenience on this matter.

Directions	Proposed Journal Entries	Types of Audit Procedures	Attorney Letters	Communication	Research /Authoritative Literature		

AU 336.16

This question may only be effectively answered through use of the authoritative literature. Yet, several hints are possible as the question itself suggests two possible approaches:

- Search table of contents.
- Perform keyword searches.

Searching the table of contents is relatively easy here since the problem refers to a specialist. The table of contents reveals that AU 336 relates to specialists. Paragraph 16 indicates that auditors may refer to the specialist when they believe that such reference will facilitate an understanding of the reason that an audit report has an explanatory paragraph or departs from the unqualified opinion form. Therefore, the answer is AU 336, paragraph 16.

When performing keyword searches using terms such as "specialist" and "specialist auditor's report" should be helpful in finding the appropriate portion of the standards.

FINANCIAL ACCOUNTING AND REPORTING

1. Ande Co. estimates uncollectible accounts expense using the ratio of past actual losses from uncollectible accounts to past net credit sales, adjusted for anticipated conditions. The practice follows the accounting concept of
  a. Consistency.
  b. Going concern.
  c. Matching.
  d. Substance over form.

2. In Dart Co.'s year 2 single-step income statement, as prepared by Dart's controller, the section titled "Revenues" consisted of the following:

Sales	$250,000
Purchase discounts	3,000
Recovery of accounts written off	10,000
Total revenues	$263,000

In its year 2 single-step income statement, what amount should Dart report as total revenues?
  a. $250,000
  b. $253,000
  c. $260,000
  d. $263,000

3. Which of the following would be reported as an investing activity in a company's statement of cash flows?
  a. Collection of proceeds from a note payable.
  b. Collection of a note receivable from a related party.
  c. Collection of an overdue account receivable from a customer.
  d. Collection of a tax refund from the government.

4. Young & Jamison's modified cash-basis financial statements indicate cash paid for operating expenses of $150,000, end-of-year prepaid expenses of $15,000, and accrued liabilities of $25,000. At the beginning of the year, Young & Jamison had prepaid expenses of $10,000, while accrued liabilities were $5,000. If cash paid for operating expenses is converted to accrual-basis operating expenses, what would be the amount of operating expenses?
  a. $125,000
  b. $135,000
  c. $165,000
  d. $175,000

1. **(c)** The requirement is to identify the accounting concept that the practice follows. Answer (c) is correct because estimating uncollectible accounts expense based on net credit sales is an example of application of the matching concept. The matching concept provides that expenses are recognized in the same period as the related revenues. Answer (a) is incorrect because the consistency concept requires use of the same accounting principle over time. Answer (b) is incorrect because the going concern concept assumes a business will continue in existence in the future. Answer (d) is incorrect because the substance over form concept provides that the accounting for a particular transaction should be based on the economic substance of the transaction and not merely its legal form.

2. **(a)** The requirement is to calculate total revenues. Total revenues recognized on an income statement are calculated as sales less sales returns and allowances, sales discounts, and estimated allowance for returns. The purchase discounts account is a contra account to purchases, and is not used in the calculation of net sales. Recovery of accounts written off requires an entry to reinstate the account receivable, and a second entry to record the payment. It does not affect total revenues. Therefore, total revenue is equal to the sales amount of $250,000.

3. **(b)** The requirement is to identify which item would be reported as an investing activity. Answer (b) is correct because collection of a note receivable is an investing activity. Answer (a) is incorrect because collection of proceeds from a note payable is reported as a financing activity. Answer (c) is incorrect because collection of an account receivable from a customer is an operating activity. Answer (d) is incorrect because collection of a tax refund is an operating activity.

4. **(c)** The requirement is to convert cash-basis operating expenses to accrual-basis operating expenses. The cash paid for operating expenses is $150,000. Because prepaid expenses increased by $5,000 (end of year of $15,000 less beginning of year $10,000), this amount is not included in accrual-basis expenses. The accrued liabilities increased from $5,000 at beginning of the year to $25,000 at the end of the year, indicating that an additional $20,000 of liabilities were incurred and not yet paid. To convert to accrual-basis operating expenses, the cash paid of $150,000 is adjusted by subtracting the increase in the prepaid expense account, and adding the increase in accrued liabilities. Therefore, answer (c) is correct because operating expenses are equal to $165,000 ($150,000 − 5,000 + 20,000).

5. Garson Co. recorded goods in transit purchased FOB shipping point at year-end as purchases. The goods were excluded from ending inventory. What effect does the omission have on Garson's assets and retained earnings at year end?

	Assets	Retained earnings
a.	No effect	Overstated
b.	No effect	Understated
c.	Understated	No effect
d.	Understated	Understated

6. Last year, Katt Co. reduced the carrying amount of its long-lived assets used in operations from $120,000 to $100,000, in connection with its annual impairment review. During the current year, Katt determined that the fair value of the same assets had increased to $130,000. What amount should Katt record as restoration of previously recognized impairment loss in the current year's financial statements?
- a. $0
- b. $10,000
- c. $20,000
- d. $30,000

7. Northstar Co. acquired a registered trademark for $600,000. The trademark has a remaining legal life of five years, but can be renewed every 10 years for a nominal fee. Northstar expects to renew the trademark indefinitely. What amount of amortization expense should Northstar record for the trademark in the current year?
- a. $0
- b. $ 15,000
- c. $ 40,000
- d. $120,000

8. Acme Co.'s accounts payable balance at December 31 was $850,000 before necessary year-end adjustments, if any, related to the following information:

- At December 31, Acme has a $50,000 debit balance in its accounts payable resulting from a payment to a supplier for goods to be manufactured to Acme's specifications
- Goods shipped FOB destination on December 20 were received and recorded by Acme on January 2; the invoice cost was $45,000.

In its December 31 balance sheet, what amount should Acme report as accounts payable?
- a. $850,000
- b. $895,000
- c. $900,000
- d. $945,000

9. On September 30, World Co. borrowed $1,000,000 on a 9% note payable. World paid the first of four quarterly payments of $264,200 when due on December 30. In its December 31 balance sheet, what amount should World report as note payable?
- a. $735,800
- b. $750,000
- c. $758,300
- d. $825,800

5. (d) The requirement is to determine the effect on assets and retained earnings. Goods shipped FOB shipping point should be included in Garson's ending inventory because title passed to Garson when the goods were shipped. Therefore, ending inventory is understated. If ending inventory is understated, cost of goods sold is overstated for the period, which results in net income being understated. If net income is understated for the period, the error causes retained earnings to be understated for the period. Therefore, answer (d) is correct because assets are understated and retained earnings is understated.

6. (a) The requirement is to identify the amount of restoration of impaired loss that should be recognized. For US GAAP reporting, previously recognized impairments of fixed assets may not be recovered or reversed. Therefore, answer (a) is the correct answer.

7. (a) The requirement is to determine the amount of amortization expense that should be recorded. For US GAAP purposes, assets with indefinite lives are not amortized. Instead, they are tested for impairment. Because the trademark is expected to be renewed indefinitely, it is treated as an asset with an indefinite life and is not amortized. Therefore, answer (a) is correct.

8. (c) The requirement is to compute the amount of accounts payable. Answer (c) is correct because accounts payable should be equal to $900,000 ($850,000 + $50,000 payment to supplier). The $50,000 payment to supplier represents a deposit (asset) for goods that had not yet been received. The goods shipped FOB destination were accounted for in an appropriate manner.

9. (c) The requirement is to calculate the carrying value of the note payable after the first quarterly payment is made. Interest expense is calculated as $1,000,000 × 9% × 3/12 months = $22,500. The payment of $264,200 less $22,500 in interest is equal to $241,700, which is the amount of the payment which is applied to the principal balance of the note. Therefore, answer (c) is correct because the carrying value of the note on December 31 is $758,300 ($1,000,000 − $241,700).

10. Finch Co. reported a total asset retirement obligation of $257,000 in last year's financial statements. This year, Finch acquired assets subject to unconditional retirement obligations measured at undiscounted cash flow estimates of $110,000 and discounted cash flow estimates of $68,000. Finch paid $87,000 toward the settlement of previously recorded asset retirement obligations and recorded an accretion expense of $26,000. What amount should Finch report for the asset retirement obligation in this year's balance sheet?

    a. $238,000
    b. $264,000
    c. $280,000
    d. $306,000

11. Falton Co. had the following first-year amounts related to its $9,000,000 construction contract:

Actual costs incurred and paid	$2,000,000
Estimated costs to complete	6,000,000
Progress billings	1,800,000
Cash collected	1,500,000

What amount should Falton recognize as a current liability at year-end, using the percentage-of-completion method?

    a. $0
    b. $200,000
    c. $250,000
    d. $300,000

12. Conlon Co. is the plaintiff in a patent-infringement case. Conlon has a high probability of a favorable outcome, and can reasonably estimate the amount of the settlement. What is the proper accounting treatment of the patent infringement case?

    a.   A gain contingency for the minimum estimated amount of the settlement.
    b.   A gain contingency for the estimated probable settlement.
    c.   Disclosure in the notes only.
    d.   No reporting is required at this time.

13. A firm has basic earnings per share of $1.29. If the tax rate is 30%, which of the following securities would be dilutive?

    a.   Cumulative 8%, $50 par preferred stock.
    b.   10% convertible bonds, issued at par, with each $1,000 bond convertible into 20 shares of common stock.
    c.   7% convertible bonds, issued at par, with each $1,000 bond convertible into 40 shares of common stock.
    d.   6%, $100 par cumulative convertible preferred stock, issued at par, with each preferred share convertible into four shares of common stock.

10. (b) The requirement is to determine the amount that should be reported for the asset retirement obligation. The asset retirement obligation (ARO) is recorded at its fair value in the period in which it is incurred. Subsequently, it is adjusted for revisions in estimates and the passage of time. The beginning balance in the asset retirement obligation account is $257,000. The fair value of the additional unconditional retirement obligations incurred during the year was $68,000 and will increase the ARO. The $87,000 paid toward the settlement of obligations will decrease the ARO. The $26,000 accretion expense is the expense recognized on the ARO due to the passage of time and will increase the ARO. Therefore, answer (b) is correct because the ending balance in the ARO is $264,000 ($257,000 + $68,000 − $87,000 + $26,000).

11. (a) The requirement is to calculate the current liability at year-end. The percentage-of-completion method uses a construction-in-progress account to record the costs accumulated during the period. A progress billings account is used to record the billings made on the long-term projects. At the end of the year, if the construction-in-progress account is greater than the progress billings, an asset is recognized. If the balance in the construction-in-progress account is less than the progress billings account, a liability is recognized. At the end of the year, Falton's construction-in-progress account was equal to $2,000,000 for the actual costs incurred and paid, and a balance of $1,800,000 was in the progress billings account for amounts billed to customers. Since the amount of costs incurred is greater than the amount billed, Falton would recognize as asset of $200,000 and no liability is recognized for the construction contract. Therefore, answer (a) is correct.

12. (c) The requirement is to identify the appropriate accounting treatment of the case. Conlon Co. is the plaintiff in this suit. US GAAP does not permit the recognition of contingency gains in the financial statements. Therefore, answer (c) is correct because the contingency gain would be reported only in the notes to the financial statements.

13. (c) The requirement is to determine which security is dilutive. Answer (c) is correct because the effect of assuming conversion of the 7% convertible bond would have the following effects on the numerator and denominator ($70 interest − $21 tax expense)/40 shares = $1.225 to 1 ratio, which would reduce the basic EPS of $1.29. Answer (a) is incorrect because the preferred stock is not convertible and would not be used to calculate diluted earnings per share. Answer (b) is incorrect because the 10% convertible bonds that can be converted into common stock would increase the numerator by $70 ($100 interest expense less $.30 tax expense) and would increase the denominator by 20. The ratio effect would be $70/20 = $3.5 to 1, which would be antidilutive. Answer (d) is incorrect, because the effect on the ratio would be ($100 × 6%)/4 = $1.5 to 1 ratio, which also is antidilutive.

14. On which of the following dates is a public entity required to measure the cost of employee services in exchange for an award of equity interests, based on the fair market value of the award?
    a.   Date of grant.
    b.   Date of restriction lapse.
    c.   Date of vesting.
    d.   Date of exercise.

14. (a) The requirement is to identify when a public entity must measure the cost of employee services in exchange for an award of equity interests. Answer (a) is correct because a share-based payment paid to employees in the form of equity is measured at the date of grant. Answers (b), (c), and (d) are incorrect.

15. An entity sponsors a defined benefit pension plan that is underfunded by $800,000. A $500,000 increase in the fair value of plan assets would have which of the following effects on the financial statements of the entity?
    a.   An increase in the assets of the entity.
    b.   An increase in accumulated other comprehensive income of the entity for the full amount of the increase in the value of the assets.
    c.   An decrease in accumulated other comprehensive income of the entity for the full amount of the increase in the value of the assets.
    d.   A decrease in the liabilities of the entity.

15. (d) The requirement is to determine the effect of an increase in the fair value of plan assets. For a defined benefit pension plan, the fair value of the plan assets is compared to the projected benefit obligation at the balance sheet date. If the fair value of plan assets is greater than the projected benefit obligation, a pension asset is recognized on the balance sheet. If the fair value of plan assets is less than the projected benefit obligation, a pension liability is recognized. If the defined benefit plan is underfunded by $800,000, and the plan assets increase in value by $500,000, the pension liability will decrease. Therefore, answer (d) is correct.

16. Neely Co. disclosed in the notes to its financial statements that a significant number of its unsecured trade account receivables are with companies that operate in the same industry. This disclosure is required to inform financial statement users of the existence of
    a.   Concentration of credit risk.
    b.   Concentration of market risk.
    c.   Risk of measurement uncertainty.
    d.   Off-balance-sheet risk of accounting loss.

16. (a) The requirement is to identify the reason for the disclosure. Credit risk is the risk of loss due to a particular borrower's nonpayment of a loan. Market risk is the risk that the value of an investment will change due to economic changes. Answer (a) is correct because the company has a concentration of credit risk in one industry.

17. Sun Co. was constructing fixed assets that qualified for interest capitalization. Sun had the following outstanding debt issuances during the entire year of construction:

$6,000,000 face value, 8% interest
$8,000,000 face value, 9% interest

None of the borrowings were specified for the construction of the qualified fixed asset. Average expenditures for the year were $1,000,000. What interest rate should Sun use to calculate capitalized interest on the construction?

    a.   8.00%
    b.   8.50%
    c.   8.57%
    d.   9.00%

17. (c) The requirement is to determine the interest rate that should be used to calculate capitalized interest on the construction. The interest rate used to capitalize interest on self-constructed assets is the user's interest on specific borrowings to construct the assets. However, if there are no specific borrowings for the self-constructed assets, the weighted-average interest rate on other borrowings is used to capitalize interest. In Sun's case, the total face value of the two borrowings is $14,000,000. The weighted-average interest rate is calculated as 8.57% ($6,000,000/14,000,000 × 8%) + ($8,000,000/14,000,000 × 9%). Therefore, answer (c) is correct.

18. Bard Co., a calendar-year corporation, reported income before income tax expense of $10,000 and income tax expense of $1,500 in its interim income statement for the first quarter of the year. Bard had income before income tax expense of $20,000 for the second quarter and an estimated effective annual rate of 25%. What amount should Bard report as income tax expense in its interim income statement for the second quarter?
    a. $3,500
    b. $5,000
    c. $6,000
    d. $7,500

18. (c) The requirement is to determine the income tax expense in the interim income statement. Tax expense for interim reporting purposes is calculated as year-to-date income times the estimated annual effective tax rate less the tax expense recognized in previous quarters. Therefore, the tax expense for the second quarter is calculated as $6,000 [($30,000 x 25%) - $1,500], and answer (c) is correct.

19. On January 2 of the current year, LTTI Co. entered into a three-year, noncancelable contract to buy up to 1 million units of a product each year at $.10 per unit with a minimum annual guarantee purchase of 200,000 units. At year-end, LTTI had only purchased 80,000 units and decided to cancel sales of the product. What amount should LTTI report as a loss related to the purchase commitment as of December 31 of the current year?

    a. $0
    b. $ 8,000
    c. $12,000
    d. $52,000

20. In Soan County's general fund statement of revenues, expenditures, and changes in fund balances, which of the following has an effect on the excess of revenues over expenditures?

    a.   Purchase of fixed assets.
    b.   Payment to a debt-service fund.
    c.   Special items.
    d.   Proceeds from the sale of capital assets.

21. How should state appropriations to a state university choosing to report as engaged only in business-type activities be reported in its statement of revenues, expenses, and changes in net assets?

    a.   Operating revenues.
    b.   Nonoperating revenues.
    c.   Capital contributions.
    d.   Other financing sources.

22. What is the major difference between an exchange transaction and a nonexchange transaction for governmental units?

    a.   The relationship between the amount of value given and received.
    b.   Time requirements and whether the transaction is required by law.
    c.   Purpose restrictions placed upon fund balances.
    d.   Whether resources acquired can be further exchanged.

23. A nongovernmental not-for-profit animal shelter receives contributed services from the following individuals valued at their normal billing rate:

Veterinarian provides volunteer animal care	$8,000
Board members volunteer to prepare books for audit	4,500
Registered nurse volunteers as receptionist	3,000
Teacher provides volunteer dog walking	2,000

What amount should the shelter record as contribution revenue?

    a. $ 8,000
    b. $11,000
    c. $12,500
    d. $14,500

19. (d) The requirement is to determine the loss to be reported. The cancellation of a firm purchase commitment to purchase goods requires recognition of the total liability when the contract is cancelled. Because LTTI purchased 80,000 units during year 1, it is liable for purchasing an additional 120,000 units in year 1, as well as 200,000 units in each of the next two years. Answer (d) is correct because the liability related to the canceled contract is equal to $52,000 {[120,000 (for year 1) + 400,000 (for years 2 and 3)] × $0.10 per unit}.

20. (a) The requirement is to identify the transaction that would impact the excess of revenues over expenditures. Answer (a) is correct because a purchase of fixed assets would be an expenditure of the general fund. Answer (b) is incorrect because a payment to a debt service fund would be a transfer out not affecting expenditures. Answer (c) is incorrect because special items should be presented at the bottom of the statement after the computation of the excess of revenues over expenditures. Answer (d) is incorrect because proceeds from the sale of a capital asset is a special item that would be presented at the bottom of the statement.

21. (b) The requirement is to identify how appropriations to a state university should be presented in its statement of changes in revenues, expenses, and changes in net assets. Answer (b) is correct because it should be presented as a part of nonoperating revenues. Answers (a), (c) and (d) are incorrect because the appropriations should be presented as a part of nonoperating revenues.

22. (a) The requirement is to identify the major difference between exchange and nonexchange transactions. Answer (a) is correct because the major difference is the relationship between the amount of value given and received. In an exchange transaction goods or services of equal value are exchanged. In a nonexchange transaction one party provides value for no direct benefit. An income tax is an example of a nonexchange transaction. The taxpayer pays the tax and receives no direct value in exchange.

23. (c) The requirement is to determine the amount of contributed services to be recognized. Answer (c) is correct because contributed services should be recognized only when the services (1) create or enhance nonfinancial assets, or (2) require specialized skills, are provided by individuals possessing those skills, and would typically be purchased if not provided by donation. This would include the veterinarian services ($8,000) and the services to prepare the books for audit ($4,500), or $12,500.

24. Whitestone, a nongovernmental not-for-profit organization, received a contribution in December, year 1. The donor restricted use of the contribution until March, year 2. How should Whitestone record the contribution?

    a. Footnote the contribution in year 1 and record as income when it becomes available in year 2.

    b. No entry required in year 1 and record as income in year 2 when it becomes available.

    c. Report as income in year 1.

    d. Report as deferred income in year 1.

25. A nongovernmental, not-for-profit organization received the following donations of corporate stock during the year:

	Donation 1	Donation 2
Number of shares	2,000	3,000
Adjusted basis	$ 8,000	$5,500
Fair market value at time of donation	8,500	6,000
Fair market value at year-end	10,000	4,000

What net value of investments will the organization report at the end of the year?

    a. $12,000

    b. $13,500

    c. $14,000

    d. $14,500

26. According to the FASB conceptual framework, which of the following correctly pairs a primary qualitative characteristic of accounting information with one of its components?

    a. Relevance and timeliness.

    b. Relevance and verifiability.

    c. Reliability and predictive value.

    d. Reliability and feedback value.

27. Which of the following is included in other comprehensive income?

    a. Unrealized holding gains and losses on trading securities.

    b. Unrealized holding gains and losses that result from a debt security being transferred into the held-to-maturity category from the available-for-sale category.

    c. Foreign currency translation adjustments.

    d. The difference between the accumulated benefit obligation and the fair value of pension plan assets.

28. Which of the following transactions should be classified as investing activities on an entity's statement of cash flows?

    a. Increase in accounts receivable.

    b. Sale of property, plant, and equipment.

    c. Payment of cash dividend to the shareholders.

    d. Issuance of common stock to the shareholders.

24. (c) The requirement is to identify how the contribution should be treated. Answer (c) is correct because contributions are accounted for on the accrual basis. Therefore the contribution would be recorded in year 1. If the time restriction was significantly into the future, the contribution would be recorded at its present value.

25. (c) The requirement is to determine the net value of investments to be reported by the organization in year-end financial statements. Answer (c) is correct because investments are reported at fair value. Therefore, the amount would be $14,000 ($10,000 + $4,000), the fair value at the end of the year.

26. (a) The requirement is to identify the accurate pairing of a qualitative characteristic with one of its components. Answer (a) is correct because the characteristic of relevance includes the components of predictive value, feedback value, and timeliness. Answer (b) is incorrect because verifiability relates to reliability. Answer (c) is incorrect because predictive value relates to relevance. Answer (d) is incorrect because feedback value is a component of relevance.

27. (c) The requirement is to identify the item that is included in other comprehensive income. Answer (c) is correct because the effects of foreign currency translation adjustments for the period are included in comprehensive income. Answer (a) is incorrect because unrealized holding gains and losses on trading securities are included in income of the period. Answer (b) is incorrect because unrealized holding gains and losses from the reclassification of a debt security from available-for-sale to held-to-maturity are included in accumulated other comprehensive income and amortized over the remaining holding period. Answer (d) is incorrect because the difference between the accumulated benefit obligation and the fair value of plan assets is no longer used to determine pension liability.

28. (b) The requirement is to identify the item that should be classified as investing activities. Answer (b) is correct because sale of property, plant, and equipment is an investing activity on the statement of cash flows. Answer (a) is incorrect because cash received from accounts receivable is an operating activity. Answer (c) is incorrect because payment of cash dividends to shareholders is a financing activity. Answer (d) is incorrect because issuance of stock to shareholders is a financing activity.

29. A company provides the following information:

	Year 1	Year 2	Year 3
Cash receipts from customers:			
From year 1 sales	$95,000	$120,000	
From year 2 sales		200,000	$ 75,000
From year 3 sales		50,000	225,000

What is the accrual-based revenue for year 2?
- a. $200,000
- b. $275,000
- c. $320,000
- d. $370,000

30. Milton Co. pledged some of its accounts receivable to Good Neighbor Financing Corporation in return for a loan. Which of the following statements is correct?
- a. Good Neighbor Financing cannot take title to the receivables if Milton does not repay the loan. Title can only be taken if the receivables are factored.
- b. Good Neighbor Financing will assume the responsibility of collecting the receivables.
- c. Milton will retain control of the receivables.
- d. Good Neighbor Financing will take title to the receivables and will return title to Milton after the loan is paid.

31. On April 1, Aloe, Inc. factored $80,000 of its accounts receivable without recourse. The factor retained 10% of the accounts receivable as an allowance for sales returns and charged a 5% commission on the gross amount of the factored receivables. What amount of cash did Aloe receive from the factored receivables?
- a. $68,000
- b. $68,400
- c. $72,000
- d. $76,000

32. What is the appropriate treatment for goods held on consignment?
- a. The goods should be included in ending inventory of the consignor.
- b. The goods should be included in ending inventory of the consignee.
- c. The goods should be included in cost of goods sold of the consignee only when sold.
- d. The goods should be included in cost of goods sold of the consignor when transferred to the consignee.

33. Talton Co. installed new assembly line production equipment at a cost of $185,000. Talton had to rearrange the assembly line and remove a wall to install the equipment. The rearrangement cost $12,000 and the wall removal cost $3,000. The rearrangement did not increase the life of the assembly line but it did make it more efficient. What amount of these costs should be capitalized by Talton?
- a. $185,000
- b. $188,000
- c. $197,000
- d. $200,000

29. **(b)** The requirement is to determine accrual basis revenues for year 2. Accrual based revenues would include all sales made during year 2. The cash received of $200,000 from year 2 sales and the cash received during year 3 of $75,000 for the year 2 sales are included in sales for year 2. Therefore, answer (b) is correct because revenue is equal to $275,000. Collection of year 1 sales would decrease the accounts receivable account. Collection of year 3 sales during year 2 would be recorded as unearned revenue.

30. **(c)** The requirement is to identify the correct statement about pledging accounts receivable. Answer (c) is correct because pledging accounts receivable is a borrowing with the accounts receivable used as collateral for the loan. Therefore, Milton retains control of the receivables. Answer (a) is incorrect because if Milton does not pay the loan, Good Neighbor Financing will take title to the receivables. Answer (b) is incorrect because Good Neighbor Financing will not assume responsibility for collecting the receivables. Answer (d) is incorrect because Milton retains title to the receivables.

31. **(a)** The requirement is to calculate the amount of cash received. The proceeds from the factored accounts receivable is $80,000 less the 10% factoring fee of $8,000, and less the 5% commission on the gross amount of receivables. Therefore, answer (a) is correct because the amount received from factoring the accounts receivable is $68,000 ($80,000 – $8,000 – $4,000).

32. **(a)** The requirement is to identify the appropriate treatment for goods held on consignment. The consignor is the individual or entity who owns the goods. The consignee is the individual or entity who is holding the goods to sell on behalf of the consignor. Therefore, the goods are included in the ending inventory of the consignor. The goods remain in the consignor's inventory until sold, and are included in cost of goods sold of the consignor when sold. The goods are not included in either the ending inventory or cost of goods sold of the consignee. Therefore answer (a) is correct, and answers (b), (c), and (d) are incorrect.

33. **(d)** The requirement is to determine the amount capitalized as the cost of equipment. All costs to place an asset in its intended and useful state should be capitalized. Therefore, Talton should include the cost of the equipment ($185,000), the rearrangement of the assembly line ($12,000) and the removal of the wall ($3,000) as costs to place the equipment into service. Therefore, answer (d) is correct because the total cost capitalized is equal to $200,000 ($185,000 + $12,000 + $3,000).

34. Newt Co. sold a warehouse and used the proceeds to acquire a new warehouse. The excess of the proceeds over the carrying amount of the warehouse sold should be reported as a(n)

    a.   Reduction of the cost of the new warehouse.

    b.   Gain from discontinued operations, net of income taxes.

    c.   Part of continuing operations.

    d.   Extraordinary gain, net of taxes.

35. When should a long-lived asset be tested for recoverability?

    a.   When external financial statements are being prepared.

    b.   When events or changes in circumstances indicate that its carrying amount may **not** be recoverable.

    c.   When the asset's carrying amount is **less** than its fair value.

    d.   When the asset's fair value has decreased, and the decrease is judged to be permanent.

36. A company recently acquired a copyright that now has a remaining legal life of 30 years. The copyright initially had a 38-year useful life assigned to it. An analysis of market trends and consumer habits indicated that the copyrighted material will generate positive cash flows for approximately 25 years. What is the remaining useful life, if any, over which the company can amortize the copyright for accounting purposes?

    a.   0 years.

    b.   25 years.

    c.   30 years.

    d.   38 years.

37. A company reported $6 million of goodwill in last year's statement of financial position. How should the company account for the reported goodwill in the current year?

    a.   Determine the current year's amortizable amount and report the current year's amortization expense.

    b.   Determine whether the fair value of the reporting unit is greater than the carrying amount and report a gain on goodwill in the income statement.

    c.   Determine whether fair value of the reporting unit is **less** than the carrying amount and report an impairment loss on goodwill in the income statement.

    d.   Determine whether the fair value of the reporting unit is greater than the carrying amount and report the recovery of any previous impairment in the income statement.

34. **(c)** The requirement is to identify how the excess proceeds should be reported. Answer (c) is correct because the excess of the proceeds from the sale of the warehouse over its carrying amount is a gain and should be reported as part of continuing operations. Answer (a) is incorrect because the transaction was a sale of the old warehouse; therefore, a gain or loss on disposal should be recognized. Answer (b) is incorrect because the sale of the warehouse does not qualify for discontinued operations treatment because it is not a component of the business. Answer (d) is incorrect because the sale of the warehouse does not qualify for extraordinary treatment because it is not infrequent and unusual.

35. **(b)** The requirement is to identify when a long-lived asset should be tested for recoverability. Answer (b) is correct because a long-lived asset is tested for recoverability when there are events or changes in circumstances that indicate its carrying amount may not be recoverable. Answer (a) is incorrect because it does not state the conditions that indicate that a long-lived asset must be tested for impairment. Answer (c) is incorrect because an asset is impaired if the fair value is less than the carrying value. Answer (d) is incorrect because it does not accurately describe the circumstances related to an asset impairment.

36. **(b)** The requirement is to determine the number of years over which the company should amortize the copyright. An intangible asset with a definite life is amortized over its useful life. Although the copyright has a remaining legal life of 30 years, its useful life is 25 years. The useful life is the remaining period of time the intangible asset will generate cash flows. Therefore, answer (b) is correct.

37. **(c)** The requirement is to identify the description that is accurate about accounting for goodwill. Answer (c) is correct because goodwill is tested for impairment by determining whether the fair value of the reporting unit is less than the carrying amount and, if so, an impairment loss is reported on the income statement. Answer (a) is incorrect because goodwill is not amortized. Answer (b) is incorrect because goodwill is not written up for increases in its value. Answer (d) is incorrect because a subsequent reversal of a previously recognized impairment loss is prohibited.

38. The senior accountant for Carlton Co., a public company with a complex capital structure, has just finished preparing Carlton's income statement for the current fiscal year. While reviewing the income statement, Carlton's finance director noticed that the earnings per share data has been omitted. What changes will have to be made to Carlton's income statement as a result of the omission of the earnings per share data?
   a. No changes will have to be made to Carlton's income statement. The income statement is complete without the earnings per share data.
   b. Carlton's income statement will have to be revised to include the earnings per share data.
   c. Carlton's income statement will only have to be revised to include the earnings per share data if Carlton's market capitalization is greater than $5,000,000.
   d. Carlton's income statement will only have to be revised to include the earnings per share data if Carlton's net income for the past two years was greater than $5,000,000.

39. A derivative financial instrument is best described as
   a. Evidence of an ownership interest in an entity such as shares of common stock.
   b. A contract that has its settlement value tied to an underlying notional amount.
   c. A contract that conveys to a second entity a right to receive cash from a first entity.
   d. A contract that conveys to a second entity a right to future collections on accounts receivable from a first entity.

40. In year 2, Ajax, Inc. reported taxable income of $400,000 and pretax financial statement income of $300,000. The difference resulted from $60,000 of nondeductible premiums on Ajax's officers' life insurance and $40,000 of rental income received in advance. Rental income is taxable when received. Ajax's effective tax rate is 30%. In its year 2 income statement, what amount should Ajax report as income tax expense—current portion?
   a. $ 90,000
   b. $102,000
   c. $108,000
   d. $120,000

41. When accounting for income taxes, a temporary difference occurs in which of the following scenarios?
   a. An item is included in the calculation of net income, but is neither taxable nor deductible.
   b. An item is included in the calculation of net income in one year and in taxable income in a different year.
   c. An item is **no** longer taxable due to a change in the tax law.
   d. The accrual method of accounting is used.

38. (b) The requirement is to identify the correct statement regarding omission of earnings per share data. Answer (b) is correct because earnings per share disclosures are required on the income statement for all public companies. Therefore, answers (a), (c), and (d) are incorrect.

39. (b) The requirement is to identify the best description of a derivative. Answer (b) is correct because a derivative is a contract that has its settlement value tied to an underlying notional amount. Answers (a), (c), and (d) are incorrect because they do not accurately state the definition of a derivative.

40. (d) The requirement is to determine the amount of income tax expense—current portion. The current portion of income tax is calculated as taxable income multiplied by the current tax rate. Therefore, answer (d) is correct because the income tax expense—current portion is $120,000 ($400,000 × 30%).

41. (b) The requirement is to determine which of the scenarios results in a temporary difference. Answer (b) is correct because a temporary difference, also referred to as a timing difference, occurs when an item is included in the calculation of net income in one year and in taxable income in a different year. Answer (a) is incorrect because it refers to a permanent difference. Answer (c) is incorrect because it refers to a permanent difference. Answer (d) is incorrect because a temporary difference is not caused by the accrual method of accounting.

42. How are discontinued operations and extraordinary items that occur at midyear initially reported?

    a. Disclosed only in the notes to the year-end financial statements.

    b. Included in net income and disclosed in the notes to the year-end financial statements.

    c. Included in net income and disclosed in the notes to interim financial statements.

    d. Disclosed only in the notes to interim financial statements.

43. Able Co. leased equipment to Baker under a noncancellable lease with a transfer of title. Will Able record depreciation expense on the leased asset and interest revenue related to the lease?

	Depreciation expense	Interest revenue
a.	Yes	Yes
b.	Yes	No
c.	No	No
d.	No	Yes

44. During the current year, Beta Motor Co. incurred the following costs related to a new solar-powered car:

Salaries of laboratory employees researching how to build the new car	$250,000
Legal fees for the patent application for the new car	20,000
Engineering follow-up during the early stages of commercial production (the follow-up occurred during the current year)	50,000
Marketing research to promote the new car	30,000
Design, testing, and construction of a prototype	400,000

What amount should Beta Motor report as research and development expense in its income statement for the current year?

    a. $250,000
    b. $650,000
    c. $720,000
    d. $750,000

45. An enterprise must separately report information about an operating segment when the segment's revenue meets what minimum percentage of the combined revenue of the reported operating segments?

    a. 5%
    b. 10%
    c. 20%
    d. 50%

46. King City Council will be establishing a library fund. Library fees are expected to cover 55% of the library's annual resource requirements. King has decided that an annual determination of net income is desirable in order to maintain management control and accountability over the library. What type of fund should King establish in order to meet their measurement objectives?

    a. Special revenue fund.
    b. General fund.
    c. Internal service fund.
    d. Enterprise fund.

42. (c) The requirement is to identify the statement that indicates how discontinued operations and extraordinary items that occur at midyear are initially reported. Answer (c) is correct because interim reporting standards require that discontinued operations and extraordinary items occurring during the year be included in interim net income and disclosed in the notes to the interim financial statements. Answers (a), (b), and (d) are incorrect.

43. (d) The requirement is to identify whether depreciation expense and interest revenue will be recorded. Able is the lessor, and the lease transfers title of the leased asset to the lessee. Therefore, the lease is recorded as a capital lease. Answer (d) is correct because as the lessor, Able will record interest revenue but not depreciation. The lessee will record depreciation expense on the equipment. Therefore, (a), (b), and (c) are incorrect.

44. (b) The requirement is to determine the amount of research and development expense. Research and development expenses include the salaries of laboratory employees researching how to build the new car (research), and the design, testing, and construction of a prototype (development). The Codification specifically excludes certain items from research and development, such as legal fees for the patent application and engineering follow-up during the early stages of commercial production. The cost of marketing research to promote the new car is a part of advertising expenses. Therefore, answer (b) is correct because the amount of research and development is $650,000 ($250,000 + $400,000).

45. (b) The requirement is to identify the minimum percentage of combined revenue threshold for segment reporting. Answer (b) is correct because the test to determine when an operating segment's revenue meets the percentage of the combined revenue of all reported operating segments uses a threshold of 10%.

46. (d) The requirement is to identify the type of fund that should be established. Answer (d) is correct because an enterprise fund is used to provide goods or services to external users for a fee. Answer (a) is incorrect because a special revenue fund is used to account for specific revenue sources that are legally restricted to expenditure for specific current purposes. Answer (b) is incorrect because the general fund accounts for all financial resources except those required to be accounted for in another fund. Answer (c) is incorrect because an internal service fund is used to report an activity that provides goods or services to other funds on a cost-reimbursement basis.

47. Which of the following statements are required to be presented for special-purpose governments engaged only in business-type activities (such as utilities)?
   a. Statement of net assets only.
   b. Management's Discussion and Analysis (MD&A) and Required Supplementary Information (RSI) only.
   c. The financial statements required for governmental funds including MD&A.
   d. The financial statements required for enterprise funds, including MD&A and RSI.

47. **(d)** The requirement is to identify the type of statements that are required. Answer (d) is correct because business-type units are accounted for in enterprise funds, which require presentation of enterprise fund statements with MD&A and RSI. Answer (a) is incorrect because a statement of net assets only is not acceptable. Answer (b) is incorrect because enterprise fund statements are also required. Answer (c) is correct because enterprise fund statements are required.

48. Brandon County's general fund had the following transactions during the year:

Transfer to a debt service fund	$100,000
Payment to a pension trust fund	500,000
Purchase of equipment	300,000

What amount should Brandon County report for the general fund as other financing uses in its governmental funds statement of revenues, expenditures, and changes in fund balances?
   a. $100,000
   b. $400,000
   c. $800,000
   d. $900,000

48. **(a)** The requirement is to determine the amount that should be presented as financing uses. Answer (a) is correct because the only use of funds for financing is the transfer to the debt service fund.

49. During the current year, the local humane society, a nongovernmental not-for-profit organization, received a $100,000 permanent endowment from Cobb. Cobb stipulated that the income must be used to care for older horses that can no longer race. The endowment reported income of $8,000 in the current year. What amount of unrestricted contribution revenue should the humane society report for the current year?
   a. $108,000
   b. $100,000
   c. $ 8,000
   d. $0

49. **(d)** The requirement is to determine the amount of unrestricted revenue that should be presented. Answer (d) is correct because the endowment and the income from the fund are both restricted.

50. How should operating expenses for a nongovernmental not-for-profit organization be reported?
   a. Change in temporarily restricted net assets.
   b. Change in unrestricted net assets.
   c. Change in permanently restricted net assets.
   d. Contra account to associated revenues.

50. **(b)** The requirement is to describe how operating expenses should be reported. Answer (b) is correct because operating expenses are presented as decreases in unrestricted net assets.

SIMULATION 1

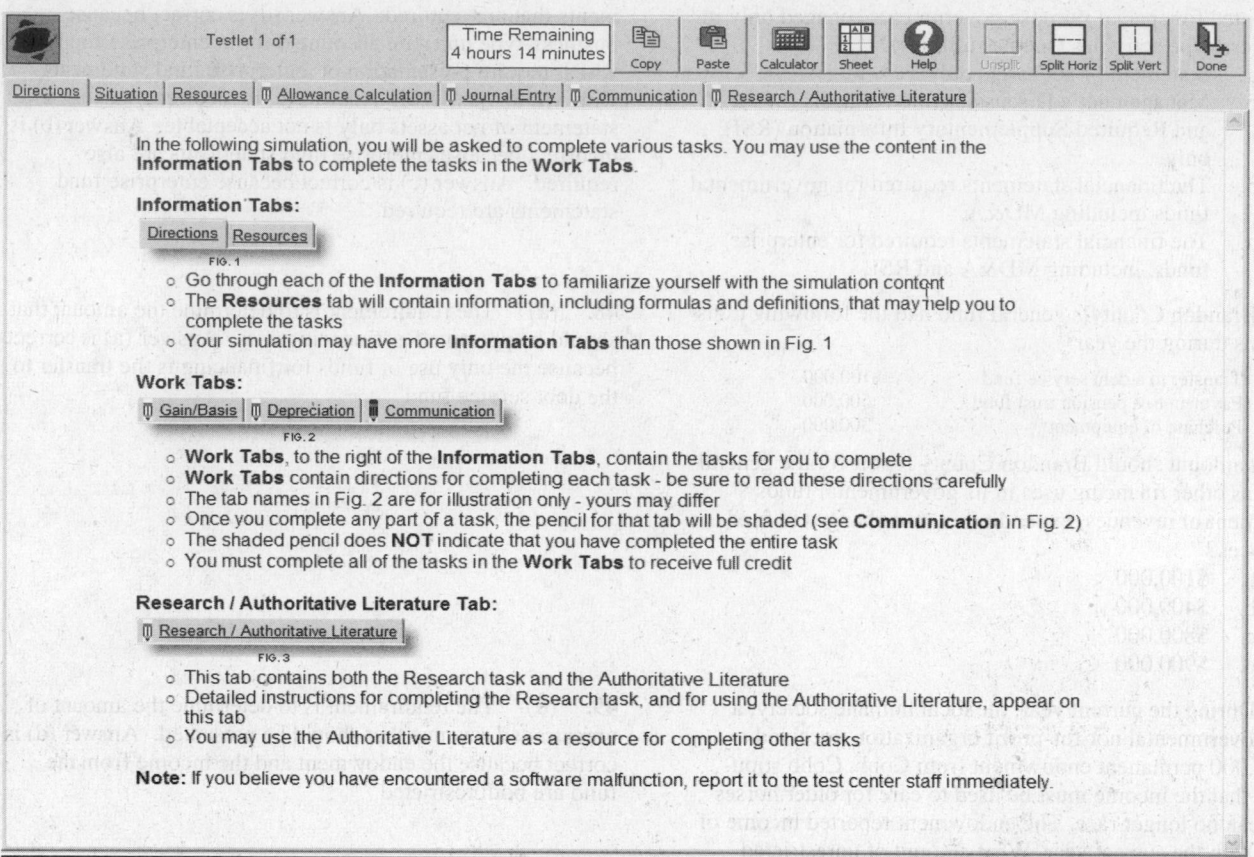

	Situation				
Directions		**Allowance Calculation**	**Journal Entry**	**Communication**	**Research /Authoritative Literature**

Lambert, Inc. is a manufacturer of men's casual clothing. The founder and CEO of the company retired on June 30, year 1, after 10 years of management. During this time, sales and net profits increased modestly, but the CEO was very conservative about taking credit risk.

On July 1, year 1, Lambert hired a new CEO with a strong marketing background. The company adopted a new business plan, which includes aggressive expansion into new markets and liberalization of the company's credit policy. This new business plan was implemented in the fourth quarter of year 1, and resulted in a significant increase in sales for the month of December.

Lambert uses the allowance method to record doubtful accounts for financial statement reporting. In prior years, Lambert estimated its uncollectible accounts receivable by applying an estimated percentage to each category reported on the accounts receivable aging analysis. This percentage is based on historical data. The following table summarizes the accounts receivable aging analysis at December 31, year 1, and the related estimated percentage uncollectible for each category.

Accounts receivable aging analysis at December 31, year 1

Aging category	Balance at December 31, year 1	Estimated percentage uncollectible
0-30 days	225,000	1%
31-60 days	240,000	9%
61-90 days	127,000	23%
Over 90 days	85,000	60%

The balance in the allowance for doubtful accounts at January 1, year 1, was $62,000. The activity in this account during year 1 consisted of the write-off of accounts valued at $19,000 and a recovery of $4,000 in accounts that were written off in previous years.

The Lambert accounting staff identified the following unrecorded adjustments while performing the year-end review of accounts receivable balances:

- An account receivable for $12,000 that was invoiced in February, year 1, was deemed uncollectible because the customer was declared bankrupt on November 30, year 1. The balance has not yet been written off.

- An account receivable for $5,000 that was invoiced in August, year 1, was collected. However, it was not properly removed from the accounts receivable subsidiary ledger and the aging analysis.

Directions	Situation	Allowance Calculation		Journal Entry	Communication	Research /Authoritative Literature

As a result of the change in the Lambert credit policy during year 1, the CFO believes that the estimated percentage uncollectible for each aging category should be increased by two percentage points.

Complete the following spreadsheet to calculate the allowance for doubtful accounts at December 31, year 1. For each shaded cell in columns C, D, E, and F, enter the appropriate values. The totals in column B will calculate automatically based on your entries. If there is nothing to enter in a particular cell, enter a zero (0).

NOTE: To use a formula in the spreadsheet, it must be preceded by an equal sign, e.g., =A1+B1.

	A	B	C	D	E	F
1		Total	0-30 days	31-60 days	61-90 days	Over 90 days
2	Accounts receivable					
3	Adjustments					
4	Adjusted accounts receivable					
5	Estimated percentage uncollectible					
6	Allowance for doubtful accounts					

NOTE: The "Total" column sums the values in columns C through F

Directions	Situation	Allowance Calculation	Journal Entry		Communication	Research /Authoritative Literature

Assume that the Lambert accounting staff has already made all necessary adjusting entries at December 31, year 1, with the exception of the adjustment to record the current year's bad debt expense. Use the information in the Situation tab and the values you calculated in the Allowance Calculation tab to prepare the journal entry that records the bad debt expense for year 1, if any.

- To enter an account, double-click the appropriate shaded area and choose the account title from the list provided.
- Insert the correct debit and credit values in the appropriate shaded cells in the form.
- Some shaded areas may not be used and certain accounts may be used more than once.

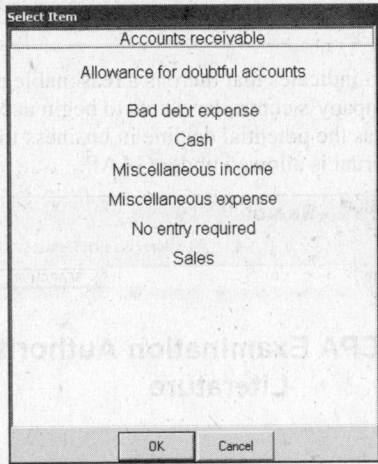

	A	B	C
1	Account	Dr.	Cr.
2			
3			
4			
5			
6			

Ocean Co. is considering purchasing a less than 100% interest in Malibu Corp. Ocean's CEO has asked for your guidance in understanding the requirements for preparing consolidated financial statements. In a memo to the CEO, explain the criteria for determining the conditions under which Ocean Co. would consolidate an ownership interest in Malibu Corp.

Type your communication in the response area below the horizontal line using the word processor provided.

REMINDER: Your response will be graded for both technical content and writing skills. Technical content will be evaluated for information that is helpful to the intended reader and clearly relevant to the issue. Writing skills will be evaluated for development, organization, and the appropriate expression of ideas in professional correspondence. Use a standard business memo or letter format with a clear beginning, middle, and end. Do not convey information in the form of a table, bullet point list, or other abbreviated presentation.

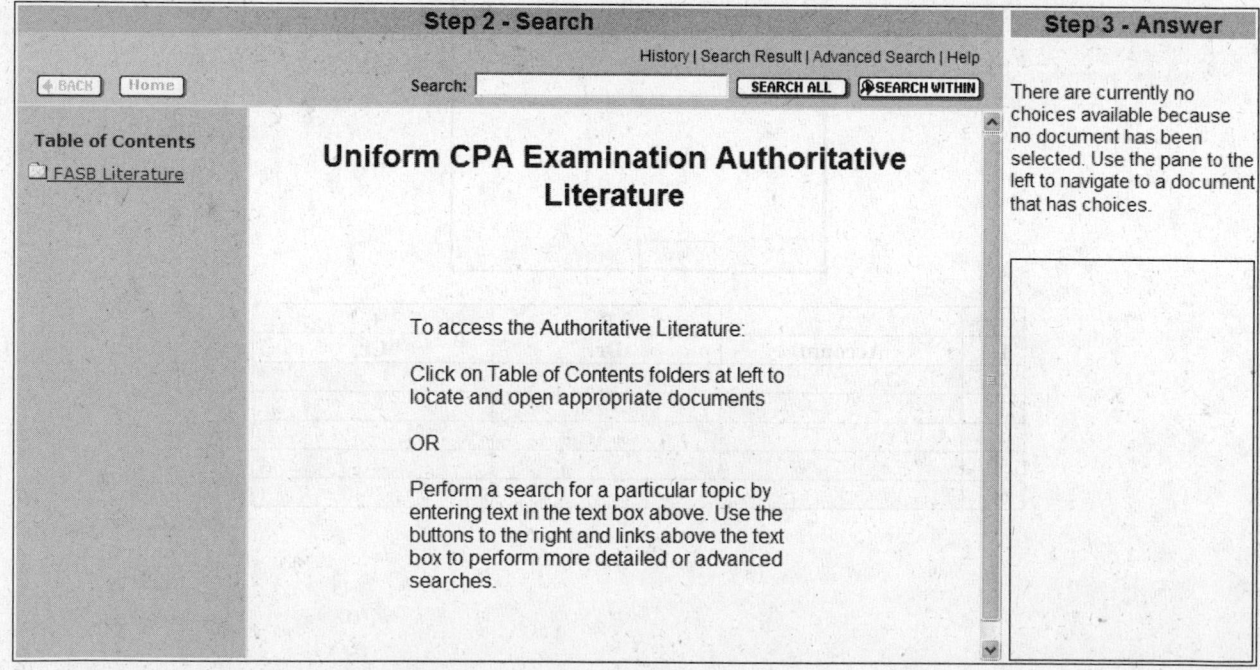

A recently issued demographic report indicates that there is a reasonable probability that Lambert's business may be adversely impacted in the future. The company's controller wants to begin accruing a general contingency reserve now for unspecified business contingencies, such as the potential decline in business that may occur in the future. Find authoritative guidance as to whether or not such an accrual is allowed under GAAP.

SOLUTION TO SIMULATION 1

Directions	Situation	Allowance Calculation	Journal Entry	Communication	Research /Authoritative Literature

	A	B	C	D	E	F
1		Total	0-30 days	31-60 days	61-90 days	Over 90 days
2	Accounts receivable	677,000	225,000	240,000	127,000	85,000
3	Adjustments	(17,000)	0	0	0	(17,000)
4	Adjusted accounts receivable	660,000	225,000	240,000	127,000	68,000
5	Estimated percentage uncollectible		0.03 or 3.00%	0.11 or 11.0%	0.25 or 25.00%	0.62 or 62.00%
6	Allowance for doubtful accounts	107,060	6,750	26,400	31,750	42,160

Explanation of solutions

Line 3 – Adjustments

The adjustment of $17,000 is made for two items: (1) the bankrupt customer invoice in February that is over 90 days old and not written off, and (2) the $5,000 of accounts receivable collected that were not credited to the accounts receivable account. Therefore, accounts receivable should be decreased by $17,000 ($12,000 + 5,000).

Line 4 – Adjusted accounts receivable

The adjusted accounts receivable balance is calculated as total accounts receivable plus or minus the required adjustments.

Line 5 – Estimated percentage uncollectible

The estimated percentage uncollectible is given in the table in the problem. Note that because management believes that the percentage point should be increased by 2% for each aging category, the new percentages used are 3%, 11%, 25%, and 62%.

Line 6 – Allowance for doubtful accounts

Allowance for doubtful accounts is determined by multiplying the ending balance of accounts receivable in each aging category by the appropriate percentage rate. The estimated amounts for each category are then added to arrive at a total allowance for uncollectible accounts of $107,060.

Directions	Situation	Allowance Calculation	Journal Entry	Communication	Research /Authoritative Literature

	A	B	C
1	Account	Dr.	Cr.
2	Bad debt expense	72,060	
3	Allowance for doubtful accounts		72,060
4			
5			
6			

Explanation of solutions

To calculate the bad debt expense for the year, an analysis is made of the allowance for doubtful accounts. The beginning balance in the allowance for doubtful accounts was $62,000. The journal entries required for allowance for doubtful accounts are

Allowance for doubtful accounts	19,000	
Accounts receivable		19,000

To write off uncollectible accounts during the year

Accounts receivable	4,000	
Allowance for doubtful accounts		4,000
Cash	4,000	
Accounts receivable		4,000

To reinstate account receivable for previously written off account and show payment

Allowance for doubtful accounts	12,000	
Accounts receivable		12,000

To adjust for account receivable at end of year due to customer bankruptcy

The aging schedule indicates that total allowance for doubtful accounts should be $107,060 at year-end. An analysis of the allowance for doubtful accounts is shown below.

Allowance for Doubtful Accounts

		62,000	Beg. bal.
Accounts written off	19,000		
		4,000	Recovery of write-off
Adjustment for write-off at year-end	12,000	72,060	Bad debt expense
		107,060	Desired ending balance

The journal entry required is to debit bad debt expense for $72,060 and credit allowance for doubtful accounts for $72,060.

Directions	Situation	Allowance Calculation	Journal Entry	Communication	Research /Authoritative Literature

Spelling	Undo	Redo	Cut	Copy	Paste

Memorandum

To: CEO, Ocean Co.
Subject: Consolidated Financial Statements

This memorandum is designed to answer your questions about the requirements regarding consolidated financial statements. Consolidated financial statements are required when a company acquires control of an acquiree. Control is presumed if the acquirer owns more than 50% of the acquiree. However, if the control is likely to be temporary, or control is not held by the majority owner, consolidated financial statements are not required.

Special situations may occur which indicate that control does not exist. For example, control may not exist when the acquiree is in legal reorganization or bankruptcy. Control may not be present if the acquiree operates in a foreign country that has restrictions of the financial transactions of the business firm or the acquiree is subject to political or economic uncertainty wherein the acquirer cannot control the subsidiary. In such situations, the facts and circumstances of each case must be considered.

In Ocean's case, if the company purchases more than 50% of Malibu, it will be presumed that Ocean gains control over Malibu. Ocean would be required to prepare consolidated financial statements unless special circumstances indicate that the company cannot exert such control.

Please contact me if you need additional assistance with the acquisition of Malibu.

Directions	Situation	Allowance Calculation	Journal Entry	Communication	Research /Authoritative Literature

ASC 450-20-25-8

Business Risks

25-8.   General or unspecified business risks do not meet the conditions for accrual in paragraph 450-20-25-2 and no accrual for loss shall be made.

REGULATION

1. According to the AICPA Code of Professional conduct, in which of the following circumstances may a CPA serve on a company's board of directors?

   a. The CPA audits a bank to which the company has applied for financing, and board approval is required for said financing to occur.

   b. The CPA is asked by the company to test the internal controls of the company and offers compensation to the CPA for said services.

   c. The CPA does **not** audit the company and has **no** other business connection with the company.

   d. The CPA performs attestation services for a nonpublic company.

2. How many audits of public companies per year does a CPA firm that is registered with the Public Company Accounting Oversight Board (PCAOB) have to perform before it receives an annual inspection from the PCAOB?

   a. One audit.

   b. More than 10 audits.

   c. More than 50 audits.

   d. More than 100 audits.

3. What defense must an accountant establish to be absolved from civil liability under Section 18 of the Securities Exchange Act of 1934 for false or misleading statements made in reports or documents filed under the Act?

   a. Lack of gross negligence.

   b. Exercise of due care.

   c. Good faith and lack of knowledge of the statement's falsity.

   d. Lack of privity with an injured party.

4. In which of the following situations is there a violation of client confidentiality under the AICPA Code of Professional Conduct?

   a. A member discloses confidential client information to a court in connection with arbitration proceedings relating to the client.

   b. A member discloses confidential client information to a professional liability insurance carrier after learning of a potential claim against the member.

   c. A member whose practice is in bankruptcy discloses a client's name.

   d. A member uses a records retention agency to store clients' records that contain confidential client information.

5. On December 1, Gem orally contracted with Mason for Mason to manage Gem's restaurant for one year starting the following January 1. They agreed that Gem would pay Mason $40,000 and that Mason would be allowed to continue to work for Gem if "everything worked out." On June 1, Mason quit to take a better paying job, alleging that the contract violated the statute of frauds. What will be the outcome of a suit by Gem for breach of contract?

   a. Gem will win because the contract was executory.

   b. Gem will win because the contract was for services, **not** goods.

   c. Gem will lose because the contract could **not** be performed within one year.

   d. Gem will lose because the contract required payment of more than $500.

1. **(c)** The requirement is to identify the circumstance in which the CPA may serve on a company's board of directors. Answer (c) is correct because if the CPA does not provide audit or attestation services for the client, there is no requirement for independence. Answer (a) is incorrect because the CPA is performing an audit of the bank and must be independent. Answer (b) is incorrect because testing controls is an attest service and the CPA must be independent to perform the service. Answer (d) is incorrect because if a CPA performs attestation services, he or she must be independent.

2. **(d)** The requirement is to identify when a CPA firm must have an annual inspection from the PCAOB. Answer (d) is correct because CPA firms that audit more than 100 issuers must have an annual inspection by the PCAOB. Answers (a), (b), and (c) are incorrect because a firm must have annual inspections only if they audit more than 100 issuers.

3. **(c)** The requirement is to identify the defense that must be established to absolve liability under Section 18 of the Securities Exchange Act of 1934. Answer (c) is correct because the auditor's required defense is that he or she acted in good faith and did not have knowledge of the statement's falsity. Answers (a), (b), and (d) are incorrect because they do not express the required defense under Section 18.

4. **(c)** The requirement is to identify the situation that would constitute a violation of client confidentiality. Answer (c) is correct because a member may not disclose client information in conjunction with a bankruptcy. Answer (a) is incorrect because a member may disclose client information in conjunction with arbitration proceedings relating to the client. Answer (b) is incorrect because a member may disclose client information to a professional liability carrier. Answer (d) is incorrect because a member may use a records retention agency.

5. **(c)** The requirement is to identify the likely outcome of the suit. Answer (c) is correct because Gem will lose the suit because contracts must be in writing if they cannot be performed within a year. Answers (a), (b), and (d) are incorrect because they do not accurately state the likely outcome.

6. Which of the following bonds are an obligation of a surety?

a. Convertible bonds.
b. Debenture bonds.
c. Municipal bonds.
d. Official bonds

6. **(d)** The requirement is to identify the bond that is an obligation of a surety. Answer (d) is correct because a surety insures performance by another party and an official bond insures compliance with laws and regulations. Answers (a), (b), and (c) are incorrect because these bonds are all primary obligations.

7. According to the Securities Act of 1933, which of the following statements is correct regarding an issuer of securities?

a. All securities issuers must provide potential investors with a prospectus containing specified information.
b. An issuer is permitted to advertise an initial offering of securities only through distribution of the prospectus.
c. All securities issuers must register the securities offering with the Securities and Exchange Commission (SEC).
d. If an issuer sells a security and fails to meet certain disclosure requirements, the purchaser may sell it back to the issuer and recover the price paid.

7. **(d)** The requirement is to identify the accurate statement regarding an issuer of securities. Answer (d) is correct because if an issuer fails to meet the disclosure requirements of the Securities Act of 1933, the buyer may ask for rescission of the sale. Answer (a) is incorrect because there are exemptions to the requirement to provide a prospectus. Answer (b) is incorrect because advertising may be done in other ways. Answer (c) is incorrect because there are exemptions to the registration requirements.

8. Which of the following circumstances best describes a landlord's constructive eviction of a tenant who has a written lease for the property?

a. The landlord changes the lock and refuses to give the tenant a new key.
b. The landlord starts a legal proceeding against the tenant for failure to pay rent.
c. The landlord sues the tenant because the tenant complained to a government agency about the condition of the premises.
d. The landlord refuses to provide utilities to the tenant.

8. **(d)** The requirement is identify the circumstance that best describes a landlord's constructive eviction. Answer (d) is correct because constructive eviction involves allowing conditions which make the property unusable when the lessor is liable for the condition of the premises. Answers (a), (b), and (c) are incorrect because they do not represent constructive eviction.

9. A calendar-year individual filed an income tax return on April 1. This return can be amended **no** later than

a. Four months and 15 days after the end of the calendar year.
b. Ten months and 15 days after the end of the calendar year.
c. Three years, three months, and 15 days after the end of the calendar year.
d. Three years after the return was filed.

9. **(c)** The requirement is to determine the last date that an individual calendar-year taxpayer can file an amended tax return. An individual taxpayer must file an amended return within three years from the date a return was filed, or two years from the date of payment of tax, whichever is later. If a return is filed before its due date, it is treated as filed on its due date. Thus, an individual's calendar-year return filed on April 1 is treated as filed on April 15. As a result, the last date an amended return can be filed would be three years, three months, and 15 days after the end of the calendar year (e.g., April 15, 2010, for a 2006 calendar-year return).

10. In the absence of an election to adopt an annual accounting period, the required tax year for a partnership is

a. A tax year that results in the greatest aggregate deferral of income.
b. A calendar year.
c. A tax year of one or more partners with a more than 50% interest in profits and capital.
d. A tax year of principal partner having a 10% or greater interest.

10. **(c)** The requirement is to determine the required tax year for a partnership if it does not make an election to adopt an annual accounting period. A partnership generally is restricted in choosing a tax year in order to prevent the deferral of income to partners that could otherwise occur. Thus, a newly formed partnership is required to adopt the same taxable year as its one or more partners owning a more than 50% interest in profits and capital. This insures that there will be no deferral of reporting for more than 50% of the partnership's income.

11. In the current year, Tatum exchanged farmland for an office building. The farmland had a basis of $250,000, a fair market value (FMV) of $400,000, and was encumbered by a $120,000 mortgage. The office building had an FMV of $350,000 and was encumbered by a $70,000 mortgage. Each party assumed the other's mortgage. What is the amount of Tatum's recognized gain?

    a. $0
    b. $ 50,000
    c. $100,000
    d. $150,000

11. (b) The requirement is to determine the amount of Tatum's recognized gain on the exchange. Generally, no gain or loss is recognized on the exchange of business or investment property for property of a like kind. Since like kind means the same class of property, an exchange of farmland for an office building qualifies as a like-kind exchange. However, in a like-kind exchange, a realized gain ($400,000 – $250,000 = $150,000 in this case) will be recognized to the extent of unlike property (i.e., boot) received. Here, Tatum's assumption of the $70,000 mortgage on the acquired office building is treated as boot paid, while the $120,000 mortgage on the farmland exchanged is treated as boot received. These mortgages are offset and result in Tatum receiving net boot and a recognized gain of $50,000.

12. Danielson invested $2,000,000 in DEC, a qualified small business corporation. Six years later, Danielson sold all of the DEC stock for $16,000,000 and purchased an office building with the proceeds. Danielson had not previously excluded any gain on the sale of small business stock. What is Danielson's taxable gain after the exclusion?

    a. $0
    b. $6,000,000
    c. $7,000,000
    d. $9,000,000

12. (c) The requirement is to determine Danielson's taxable gain after exclusion on the sale of qualified small business stock held for six years. A noncorporate taxpayer can exclude 50% of the capital gain resulting from the sale of qualified small business stock held more than five years. The amount of excludible gain is limited to the greater of $10 million, or 10 times the investor's stock basis. Here, the sale for $16,000,000 of qualified stock that was acquired for $2,000,000 results in a gain of $14,000,000. Since 50% of the gain can be excluded, Danielson's taxable gain after exclusion is $7,000,000.

13. Robbe, a cash-basis single taxpayer, reported $50,000 of adjusted gross income last year and claimed itemized deductions of $5,500, consisting solely of $5,500 of state income taxes paid last year. Robbe's itemized deduction amount, which exceeded the standard deduction available to single taxpayers for last year by $1,150, was fully deductible and it was not subject to any limitations or phaseouts. In the current year, Robbe received a $1,500 state tax refund relating to the prior year. What is the proper treatment of the state tax refund?

    a. Include none of the refund in income in the current year.
    b. Include $1,150 in income in the current year.
    c. Include $1,500 in income in the current year.
    d. Amend the prior year's return and reduce the claimed itemized deductions for that year.

13. (b) The requirement is to determine the proper treatment of the $1,500 state income tax refund relating to the prior year. A state income tax refund must be included in gross income for the current year under the *tax benefit rule* to the extent that the refunded amount was deducted in a prior year and the deduction provided a benefit by reducing the taxpayer's federal income tax for the prior year. Here, Robbe's $5,500 itemized deduction for state income tax provided a benefit only to the extent that it exceeded the standard deduction that was otherwise available to him. As a result, only $1,150 of the $1,500 refund must be included in gross income for the current year.

14. Lane, a single taxpayer, received $160,000 in salary, $15,000 in income from an S corporation in which Lane does not materially participate, and a $35,000 passive loss from a real estate rental activity in which Lane materially participated. Lane's modified adjusted gross income was $165,000. What amount of the real estate rental activity loss was deductible?

     a. $0
     b. $15,000
     c. $25,000
     d. $35,000

14. (b) The requirement is to determine the amount of the $35,000 rental real estate passive loss that is deductible by Lane. Generally, losses from passive activities can only be used to offset income from other passive activities. Here, since Lane did not materially participate in the S corporation, the S corporation income of $15,000 is treated as passive activity income and is offset by $15,000 of the rental real estate passive loss. Although a special rule permits up to $25,000 of income that is not from passive activities to be offset by losses from a rental real estate activity, that special $25,000 allowance is reduced by 50% of a taxpayer's modified AGI in excess of $100,000 and is fully phased out when modified AGI exceeds $150,000. Since Lane's modified AGI is $165,000, the $25,000 allowance is not available. As a result, Lane's rental real estate loss is deductible in the current year only to the extent that it offsets the $15,000 of passive activity income.

15. Which of the following disqualifies an individual from the earned income credit?

     a.   The taxpayer's qualifying child is a 17-year-old grandchild.
     b.   The taxpayer has earned income of $5,000.
     c.   The taxpayer's five-year-old child lived in the taxpayer's home for only eight months.
     d.   The taxpayer has a filing status of married filing separately.

15. (d) The requirement is to determine the statement that disqualifies an individual from the earned income credit. The earned income credit is a refundable tax credit for eligible low-income taxpayers. To be eligible, an individual must have earned income and generally must maintain a household for more than half the year for a qualifying child. A qualifying child includes the taxpayer's child or grandchild who lives with the taxpayer for more than half of the taxable year, and is under age 19, or a full-time student under age 24, or permanently or totally disabled. The earned income credit is not available to married taxpayers filing separately.

16. Which of the following can be an advantage of a limited liability company over an S corporation?

     a.   Double taxation of profits is avoided.
     b.   Owners receive limited liability protection.
     c.   Appreciated property can be distributed tax-free to an owner.
     d.   Incentive stock options can be used to compensate owners.

16. (c) The requirement is to determine the comparative advantage that a limited liability company (LLC) has over an S corporation. An LLC is a legal entity that combines the best features of a partnership and a corporation by being treated as a partnership for reporting purposes while providing the limited liability protection of a corporation. That is, similar to shareholders of an S corporation, LLC owners are subject to only a single level of taxation, and are *not* liable for the liabilities of the entity. Since an LLC is subject to partnership rules, it can distribute appreciated property tax-free to an owner. In contrast, an S corporation must recognize gain on the distribution of appreciated property to a shareholder. Since ownership in an S corporation is represented by stock, an S corporation can issue incentive stock options to shareholders who are employees. In contrast, LLC ownership interests are not "stock" and an LLC cannot issue incentive stock options.

17. Quigley, Roberk, and Storm form a corporation. Quigley exchanges $25,000 of legal fees for 30 shares of stock. Roberk exchanges land with a basis of $10,000 and a fair market value of $100,000 for 60 shares of stock. Storm exchanges $10,000 cash for 10 shares of stock. What amount of income should each shareholder recognize?

	Quigley	*Roberk*	*Storm*
a.	$0	$0	$0
b.	$25,000	$90,000	$0
c.	$25,000	$90,000	$10,000
d.	$0	$90,000	$0

17. (b) The requirement is to determine the income recognized by Quigley, Roberk, and Storm as a result of their formation of a corporation. No gain or loss is recognized if property is transferred to a corporation solely in exchange for stock if the transferors of property, in the aggregate, own at least 80% of the stock of the corporation after the exchange. Although the term *property* includes cash, it does not include services. Here, although Roberk and Storm transfer property, they own only 70 of the corporation's 100 outstanding shares after the exchange and fail the control test. As a result, the formation of the corporation is taxable and Roberk must recognize a gain of $100,000 − $10,000 = $90,000 on the transfer of land. Of course Storm doesn't recognize any gain on the transfer of cash, and Quigley must recognize compensation income of $25,000 on the receipt of stock in exchange for services.

18. Tap, a calendar-year S corporation, reported the following items of income and expense in the current year:

Revenue	$44,000
Operating expenses	20,000
Long-term capital loss	6,000
Charitable contributions	1,000
Interest expense	4,000

What is the amount of Tap's ordinary income?
- a. $13,000
- b. $19,000
- c. $20,000
- d. $24,000

18. **(c)** The requirement is to determine an S corporation's ordinary income. The computation of an S corporation's ordinary income excludes any item that must be separately stated and passed through to shareholders in order to retain the item's special tax characteristics. Here, the long-term capital loss must be separately stated and passed through as long-term capital loss to shareholders in order to be included in the netting of a shareholder's capital gains and losses. Similarly, charitable contributions must be separately stated and passed through to shareholders in order to apply the appropriate percentage limitations at the shareholder level. Tap's ordinary income consists of $44,000 of revenue, reduced by its $20,000 of operating expenses and $4,000 of interest expense, resulting in ordinary income of $20,000. This solution assumes that the interest expense of $4,000 is business interest expense.

19. During the current year, a trust reports the following information:

Dividends	$10,000
Interest from corporate bonds	12,000
Tax exempt interest from state bonds	4,000
Capital gain (allocated to corpus)	2,000
Trustee fee (allocated to corpus)	6,000

What is the trust's accounting income?
- a. $22,000
- b. $26,000
- c. $28,000
- d. $34,000

19. **(b)** The requirement is to determine a trust's accounting income. In fiduciary accounting, all receipts and disbursements are classified as either income or corpus (principal). For example, interest on state bonds may constitute accounting income even though not included in gross income for tax purposes. Other items, for example capital gain, would be included in gross income for tax purposes but may be classified as corpus (principal) for fiduciary accounting purposes. Any items allocated to corpus (principal) are not included in the computation of a trust's accounting income. Here, the trust's accounting income includes the $10,000 of dividends, $12,000 of interest from corporate bonds, and $4,000 of tax-exempt interest from state bonds, but excludes the capital gain and trustee fee which are allocated to corpus (principal).

20. Mackenzie is the grantor of a trust over which Mackenzie has retained a discretionary power to receive income. Kelly, Mackenzie's child, receives all taxable income from the trust unless Mackenzie exercises the discretionary power. To whom is the income earned by the trust taxable?
- a. To the trust to the extent it remains in the trust.
- b. To Mackenzie because he has retained a discretionary power.
- c. To Kelly as the beneficiary of the trust.
- d. To Kelly and Mackenzie in proportion to the distributions paid to them from the trust.

20. **(b)** The requirement is to determine to whom the trust's income is taxable when the grantor has retained a discretionary power to receive income. When the grantor of a trust retains substantial control over the trust, such as the power to revoke the trust or a discretionary power to have trust income distributed to the grantor or grantor's spouse, the income from the trust will be taxed to the grantor. In this case, because Mackenzie retained a discretionary power to receive the trust's income, all of the trust's income will be taxed to Mackenzie even though the income is retained by the trust or distributed to the trust's beneficiary (Kelly).

21. Smith, CPA, is a partner of Johnson Accounting Firm. Johnson audited the books of Hometown Bank. Smith's independence would be impaired under which of the following circumstances?
- a. Smith is a director of Hometown Bank.
- b. Smith has a collateralized automobile loan with Hometown Bank.
- c. Smith had an account with Hometown Bank two year ago.
- d. Smith and a Hometown Bank board member belong to the same church.

21. **(a)** The requirement is to identify the circumstance that would impair independence. Answer (a) is correct because serving as an officer, director, or employee of the bank impairs the auditor's independence. Answer (b) is incorrect because collateralized loans do not impair independence. Answer (c) is incorrect because having an account at the bank would not impair independence. Answer (d) is incorrect because being a member of the same church as a board member would not impair independence.

22. Which of the following is a correct statement about the circumstances under which a CPA firm may or may **not** disclose the names of its clients without the clients' express permission?

    a.   A CPA firm may disclose this information if the practice is limited to bankruptcy matters, so that prospective clients with similar concerns will be able to contact current clients.

    b.   A CPA firm may disclose this information if the practice is limited to performing asset valuations in anticipation of mergers and acquisitions.

    c.   A CPA firm may disclose this information **unless** disclosure would suggest that the client may be experiencing financial difficulties.

    d.   A CPA firm may **not** disclose this information because the identity of its clients is confidential information.

23. Lawson, a CPA, discovers material noncompliance with a specific Internal Revenue Code (IRC) requirement in the prior year return of a new client. Which of the following actions should Lawson take?

    a.   Wait for the statute of limitations to expire.

    b.   Discuss the requirements of the IRC with the client and recommend that client amend the return.

    c.   Contact the IRS and discuss courses of action.

    d.   Contact the prior CPA and discuss the client's exposure.

24. Able, CPA, was engaged by Wedge Corp. to audit Wedge's financial statements. Wedge intended to use the audit report to obtain a $10 million loan from Care Bank. Able and Wedge's president agreed that Able would give an unqualified opinion on Wedge's financial statements in the audit report even though there were material misstatements in the financial statements. Care refused to make the loan. Wedge then gave the audit report to Ranch to encourage Ranch to purchase $10 million worth of Wedge common stock. Ranch reviewed the audit report and relied on it to purchase the stock. After the purchase, Able's agreement with Wedge's president was revealed. As a result, Wedge stock lost half its value and Ranch sued Able for fraud. What will be the result of Ranch's suit?

    a.   Ranch will win because Able intentionally gave an unqualified opinion on Wedge's materially misstated financial statements.

    b.   Ranch will win because Able is strictly liable for errors made in auditing Wedge's financial statements.

    c.   Ranch will lose because Ranch is **not** a foreseen user of Able's audit report.

    d.   Ranch will lose because Ranch is **not** in privity with Able.

25. Which of the following terms best describes the relationship between a corporation and the CPA it hires to audit corporate books?

    a.   Employer and employee.

    b.   Employer and independent contractor.

    c.   Master and servant.

    d.   Employer and principal.

22. (c) The requirement is to identify the circumstances under which a CPA firm may disclose the names of its clients without their permission. Answer (c) is correct because a CPA may disclose client names unless disclosure releases confidential information, such as information that would suggest that the client may be experiencing financial difficulties. Answers (a), (b), and (d) are incorrect because names of clients may be disclosed unless such disclosure releases confidential information.

23. (b) The requirement is to identity the appropriate course of action regarding discovery of the material noncompliance. Answer (b) is correct because Lawson should discuss the matter with the new client and suggest that an amended tax return be filed. Answer (a) is incorrect because Lawson has a duty to notify the client. Answers (c) and (d) are incorrect because these actions would violate client confidentiality.

24. (a) The requirement is to identify the result of the suit. Answer (a) is correct because knowingly issuing an unqualified opinion on materially misstated financial statements is fraud. Answer (b) is incorrect because Able is not strictly liable for errors made in the financial statements. Answers (c) and (d) are incorrect because fraud on the part of Able was involved.

25. (b) The requirement is to identify the relationship between a corporation and the CPA. Answer (b) is correct because the relationship is that of employer and independent contractor. Answers (a), (c), and (d) are incorrect because the relationship is that of employer and independent contractor.

26. Card communicated an offer to sell Card's stereo to Bend for $250. Which of the following statements is correct regarding the effect of the communication of the offer?

    a. Bend should immediately accept or reject the offer to avoid liability to Card.

    b. Card is **not** obligated to sell the stereo to Bend until Bend accepts the offer.

    c. Card is required to mitigate any loss Card would sustain in the event Bend rejects the offer.

    d. Bend may **not** reject the offer for a reasonable period of time.

27. Worker's compensation benefits are available to which of the following parties?

    a. Only those employees injured while working on workplace premises.

    b. Only those employees injured while working within the scope of employment.

    c. All agents injured while commuting to and from work.

    d. All agents injured while using the employer's automobile for personal use.

28. Under the Negotiable Instruments Article of the UCC, which of the following statements is correct regarding a check?

    a. A check is a promise to pay money.

    b. A check is an order to pay money.

    c. A check does **not** need to be payable on demand.

    d. A check does **not** need to be drawn on a bank.

29. A tax preparer has advised a company to take a position on its tax return. The tax preparer believes that there is a 75% possibility that the position will be sustained if audited by the IRS. If the position is not sustained, an accuracy-related penalty and a late-payment penalty would apply. What is the tax preparer's responsibility regarding disclosure of the penalty to the company?

    a. The tax preparer is responsible for disclosing both penalties to the company.

    b. The tax preparer is responsible for disclosing only the accuracy-related penalty to the company.

    c. The tax preparer is responsible for disclosing only the late-payment penalty to the company.

    d. The tax preparer has **no** responsibility for disclosing any potential penalties to the company, because the position will probably be sustained on audit.

30. Sackett Corporation had a beginning inventory of 10,000 units, which were purchased in the prior year as follows:

	Units	Unit price
September	4,000	$2.00
October	4,000	$2.10
December	2,000	$2.30

In the current year, Sackett purchases an additional 12,000 units (7,000 in June at $2.50 and 5,000 in November at $2.70) and sells 16,000 units. Using the FIFO method, what is Sackett's ending inventory?

    a. $12,200 (4,000 @ $2.00 and 2,000 @ $2.10)

    b. $13,000 (4,000 @ $2.10 and 2,000 @ $2.30)

    c. $15,600 (6,000 @ $2.60 — average of $2.50 and $2.70)

    d. $16,000 (5,000 @ $2.70 and 1,000 @ $2.50)

26. **(b)** The requirement is to identify the statement that is correct about the offer. Answer (b) is correct because acceptance is required to have a contract. Answers (a), (c) and (d) are incorrect because acceptance is required to have a contract.

27. **(b)** The requirement is to identify the parties eligible for worker's compensation benefits. Answer (b) is correct because those injured while working within the scope of employment are eligible. Answers (a), (c), and (d) are incorrect because only those injured while working within the scope of employment are eligible.

28. **(b)** The requirement is to identify the correct statement regarding a check. Answer (b) is correct because a check is an order to pay money. Answer (a) is incorrect because a check is not a promise to pay money. Answer (c) is incorrect because a check is payable on demand. Answer (d) is incorrect because a check is drawn on a bank.

29. **(a)** The requirement is to determine a tax preparer's responsibility regarding the disclosure of potential penalties to a client. According to Statement on Standards for Tax Services 1, *Tax Return Positions*, when recommending a tax return position or when preparing or signing a tax return on which a tax return position is taken, a member should, when relevant, advise the taxpayer regarding potential penalty consequences of such tax return position and the opportunity, if any, to avoid such penalties through disclosure.

30. **(d)** The requirement is to determine Sackett's ending inventory using the FIFO method. FIFO (first-in, first-out) is an inventory costing method which assumes that the first items placed in inventory are the first sold. As a result, the inventory at the end of the year consists of the items most recently placed in inventory. Here, Sackett began with 10,000 units in inventory, acquired an additional 12,000 units during the year, and sold 16,000 units, resulting in an ending inventory of 6,000 units. Under FIFO, the units remaining in inventory are the 6,000 units most recently acquired which in this case would consist of the 5,000 units purchased at $2.70 each, plus 1,000 units purchased at $2.50 each, resulting in total inventory of $16,000.

31. Terry, a taxpayer, purchased stock for $12,000. Later, Terry sold the stock to a relative for $8,000. What amount is the relative's gain or loss?

a. $2,000 loss.
b. $0
c. $2,000 gain.
d. $4,000 gain.

32. Winkler, a CPA, provided accounting services to a client, Thompson. On December 15 of the same year, Thompson gave Winkler 100 shares of Foster Corp. as compensation for services. The adjusted basis of the stock was $4,000, and its fair market value at the time of transfer was $5,000. Two months later, Winkler sold the stock on February 15 for $7,500. What is the amount Winkler should recognize as gain on the sale of the stock?

a. $0
b. $1,000
c. $2,500
d. $5,000

33. Which of the following should be included when determining adjusted gross income?

a. Alimony received.
b. Compensation for injuries or sickness.
c. Rental value of parsonages.
d. Tuition scholarship.

34. An individual starts paying student loan interest in the current year. How many years may the individual deduct a portion of the student loan interest?

a. Current year only.
b. Five years.
c. Ten years.
d. Duration of time that interest is paid.

35. A taxpayer's spouse dies in August of the current year. Which of the following is the taxpayer's filing status for the current year?

a. Single.
b. Qualified widow(er).
c. Head of household.
d. Married filing jointly.

36. Which of the following entities must pay taxes for federal income tax purposes?

a. General partnership.
b. Limited partnership.
c. Joint venture.
d. C corporation.

31. **(b)** The requirement is to determine the relative's gain or loss as a result of the purchase of stock from Terry. Here, Terry purchased stock for $12,000 and later sold the stock for $8,000 to a relative. Since the value of the stock when sold to the relative is not given, and the relationship between Terry and the relative is not specified, it is impossible to determine whether Terry would be able to recognize a loss or whether Terry's transfer was in part a sale, and in part a gift to the relative. However, in any case, the relative would recognize no gain or loss on the purchase from Terry.

32. **(c)** The requirement is to determine Winkler's recognized gain from the sale of stock. Winkler received the stock as compensation for services rendered and would be taxed on the stock's $5,000 value when it was received in December. As a result, his tax basis for the stock would be its value of $5,000, so that the subsequent sale of the stock for $7,500 in February would result in a gain of $2,500.

33. **(a)** The requirement is to determine the item that should be included in determining an individual's adjusted gross income. The term gross income means income from whatever source derived and specifically includes alimony and separate maintenance payments. Compensation for injuries and sickness, the rental value of parsonages furnished to ministers of the gospel, and tuition scholarships are generally excluded from gross income as well as adjusted gross income.

34. **(d)** The requirement is to determine the number of years for which an individual may deduct a portion of student loan interest. An individual is allowed to annually deduct up to $2,500 for interest on qualified education loans. Qualified education expenses include tuition, fees, room, board, and related expenses. Although the deduction is subject to a phaseout based on income, there is no limitation on the number of years for which a deduction can be taken.

35. **(d)** The requirement is to determine a taxpayer's filing status for the current year if the taxpayer's spouse dies during the current year. A taxpayer may file a joint return with his or her deceased spouse for the year in which the spouse died, assuming that the surviving spouse does not remarry before the close of the tax year. When a joint return is filed, it is treated as if the tax years of both spouses ended on the closing date of the surviving spouse's tax year.

36. **(d)** The requirement is to determine the entity that must pay federal income taxes. A C corporation is a separate taxable entity subject to federal income taxes on its taxable income. In contrast, general partnerships, limited partnerships, and joint ventures are not taxable entities but instead are treated as pass-through entities with a single level of tax determined at the owner level.

37. Quail, Inc. manufactures consumer products and sells them to distributors. Quail advertises its products to increase sales and enhance the value of its trade name. What is the appropriate tax treatment of the advertising costs?
- a. Amortize the costs over 15 years.
- b. Amortize the costs over 36 months.
- c. Amortize the costs over 60 months.
- d. Deduct the costs currently as ordinary and necessary business expenses.

37. (d) The requirement is to determine the appropriate tax treatment for advertising costs. Advertising costs are deductible as an ordinary and necessary business expense if they are reasonable in amount and bear a reasonable relation to the business. Deductible expenses may be for the purpose of gaining immediate sales or developing goodwill. Advertising costs are deductible even though the advertising program is expected to result in benefits extending over a period of years.

38. On June 30, Gold and Silver are calendar-year C corporations. The corporations have merged, with Gold as a subsidiary of Silver. Silver owns 85% of Gold's voting stock and fair market value (FMV). Which of the following tax return filings would be appropriate for the two companies?
- a. Two separate returns, because Silver owns at least 80% of both the voting stock and FMV of Gold.
- b. Two separate returns, because the merger took place before the close of the second quarter.
- c. A consolidated return, because Silver owns at least 80% of both the voting stock and FMV of Gold.
- d. A consolidated return, because the merger took place before the close of the second quarter.

38. (c) The requirement is to determine the appropriate tax return filing for Silver and Gold. Because Silver Corporation directly owns at least 80% of the voting power and total value of all Gold Corporation stock, the corporations are affiliated and may elect to file a consolidated return. Although Silver and Gold may instead file separate tax returns, answer (a) is incorrect because Silver is not required to own at least 80% of Gold in order for Silver and Gold to file separate returns.

39. Stone Corp. has been an S corporation since inception. In each of year 1, year 2, and year 3, Stone made distributions in excess of each shareholder's basis. Which of the following statements is correct concerning these three years?
- a. In year 1 and year 2 only, the excess distributions are taxed as capital gain.
- b. In year 1 only, the excess distributions are tax-free.
- c. In year 3 only, the excess distributions are taxed as capital gain.
- d. In all three years, the excess distributions are taxed as capital gains.

39. (d) The requirement is to determine the correct statement regarding an S corporation's distributions that are in excess of each shareholder's stock basis. Because Stone has been an S corporation since inception, it does not have any earnings and profits and its distributions will not be taxed as dividends. Instead, all of Stone's distributions will be treated as a nontaxable return of stock basis for each shareholder until the shareholder's stock basis is fully recovered. Thereafter, distributions in excess of stock basis will be taxed as capital gains, just as if the shareholder had sold the stock.

40. Brown, a 50% partner in Brown & White, received a distribution of $12,500 in the current year. The partnership's income for the year was $25,000. What is the character of the payment that Brown received?
- a. Partial liquidation.
- b. Liquidating distribution.
- c. Disproportionate distribution.
- d. Current distribution.

40. (d) The requirement is to determine the character of the partnership's $12,500 payment made to partner Brown. Partnership distributions are categorized as either liquidating distributions or current (nonliquidating) distributions. A liquidating distribution completely terminates a partner's entire interest. All other distributions are current (nonliquidating) distributions. When a partnership makes a current distribution, the distribution is generally nontaxable to the partners because it generally represents the distribution of earnings that have already been taxed to partners and have already increased the basis for the partners' partnership interests. Answer (b) is incorrect because there is no indication that the distribution to Brown is in complete termination of Brown's interest. Answer (c) is incorrect because there is no indication that Brown's receipt of cash was in exchange for his share of unrealized receivables or inventory.

SIMULATION 1

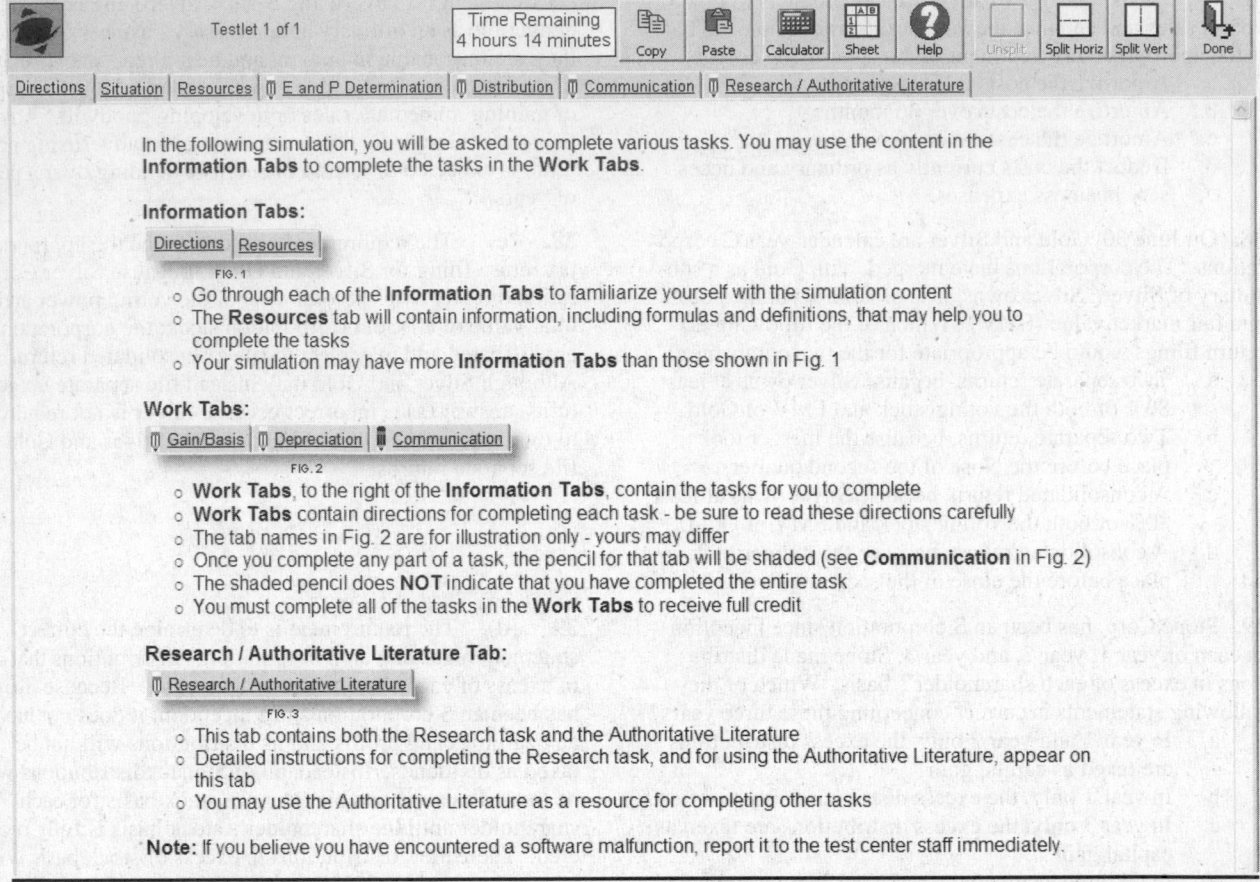

Alaska, Inc. is an accrual-basis C corporation that was incorporated on January 1, year 1. At the end of year 2, the corporation is considering converting to an S corporation. Alaska is required to determine its accumulated earnings and profits prior to conversion. The company has already calculated book net income, taxable income, and prior year accumulated earnings and profits, and is now attempting to calculate the company's current earnings and profits.

	E&P Determination			
Directions	**Situation**	**Distribution**	**Communication**	**Research /Authoritative Literature**

For purposes of this task, assume that all items of income and expense have been properly reported by Alaska on Form 1120, *US Corporation Income Tax Return*, for the appropriate years. Starting with taxable income as a benchmark, indicate the effect of each of the following items in the calculation of current year earnings and profits by placing a check in the correct column next to each item. Be sure a column is checked for each item.

Item	Add to taxable income (increase E&P)	Subtract from taxable income (decrease E&P)	No effect on E&P
Unrealized losses at the end of the year on securities owned.	○	○	○
Federal income taxes accrued and paid during the year.	○	○	○
Gain on prior year installment sale recognized in the current year.	○	○	○
Nondeductible portion of meals and entertainment expenses.	○	○	○
State tax refunds from prior year received in current year.	○	○	○
Increase in cash surrender value of life insurance policies owned by the company.	○	○	○

Directions	Situation	E&P Determination	Distribution		Communication	Research /Authoritative Literature

In year 4, Alaska is still a C corporation. Accumulated earnings and profits at the end of year 3 were $61,000. Current earnings and profits for year 4 are $24,000. During year 4, Alaska made two distributions on the dates indicated in column A of the table below. Allocate the distributions indicated in column B among columns C, D, and E. Round all answers to the nearest dollar.

Distribution dates	Distribution amounts	Current E&P	Accumulated E&P at 12/31/year 3	Excess distribution
3/31/year 4	58,000			
9/30/year 4	33,000			
Totals	91,000	24,000	61,000	6,000

Underwood, a 20% shareholder in Alaska, has a stock basis of $700 at the beginning of year 4. Complete the following table to indicate the characterization of the Alaska distributions to Underwood during year 4. Round all answers to the nearest dollar.

Underwood's total distribution	Dividend income	Return of capital	Capital gain

Directions	Situation	E&P Determination	Distribution	Communication		Research /Authoritative Literature

Alaska's controller, who has no tax background, was reviewing the corporate income tax return and does not understand why taxable income, as reported on the return, does not agree to net income before tax, as reported on the financial statements. Prepare a memo to the controller explaining the purpose of Schedule M-1, *Reconciliation of Income (Loss) per Books with Income per Return*, and provide an explanation for two items that would most likely appear on a corporation's Schedule M-1.

Type your communication in the response area below the horizontal line using the word processor provided.

REMINDER: Your response will be graded for both technical content and writing skills. Technical content will be evaluated for information that is helpful to the intended reader and clearly relevant to the issue. Writing skills will be evaluated for development, organization, and the appropriate expression of ideas in professional correspondence. Use a standard business memo or letter format with a clear beginning, middle, and end. Do not convey information in the form of a table, bullet point list, or other abbreviated presentation.

Spelling	Undo	Redo	Cut	Copy	Paste

Memorandum

To: Controller
Subject: Schedule M-1, *Reconciliation of Income (Loss) per Books with Income per Return*

Alaska, Inc. uses MACRS for income tax purposes. However, MACRS is not allowed in determining the company's current and accumulated earnings and profits. Which code section and subsection provides guidance on the effect of depreciation on earnings and profits?

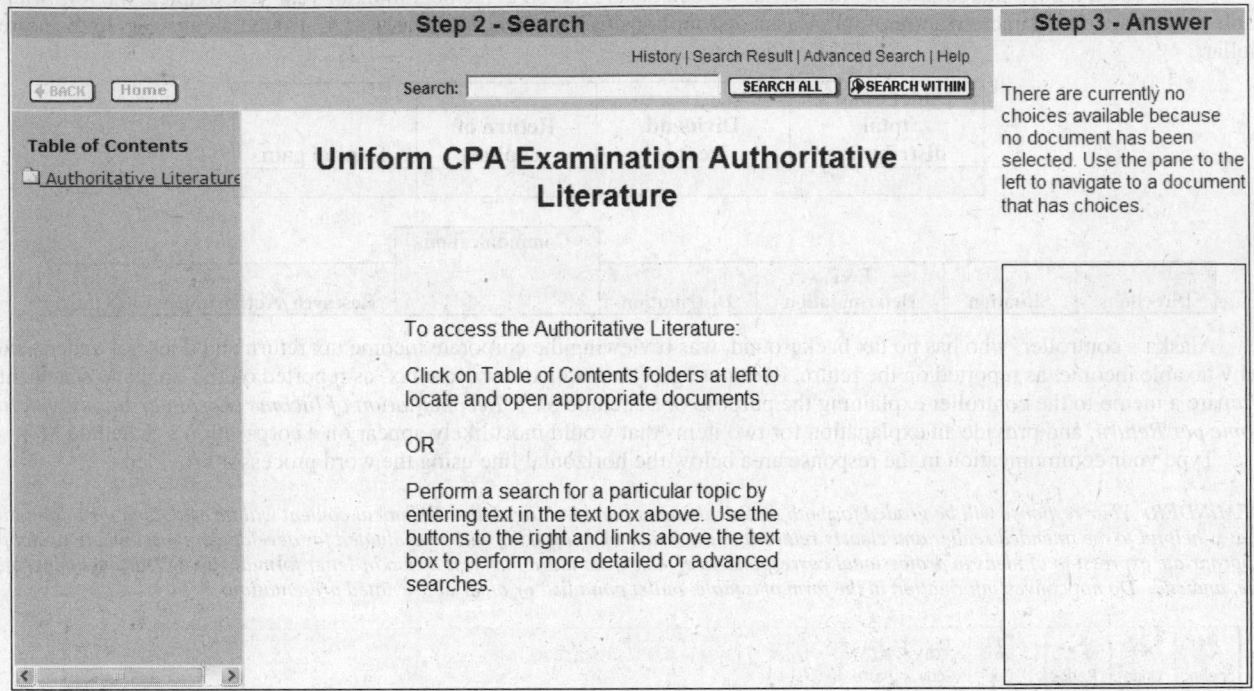

SOLUTION TO SIMULATION 1

Directions	Situation	E&P Determination	Distribution	Communication	Research /Authoritative Literature

A corporation's earnings and profits (E&P) generally represent its economic ability to pay dividends to shareholders without impairing its paid-in capital. E&P is an important concept because corporate distributions to shareholders are taxed as a dividend to the extent that distributions are made from earnings and profits for the current year (CEP) or from earnings and profits accumulated in prior years (AEP).

A corporation computes its earnings and profits on an annual basis, beginning with the corporation's taxable income (or NOL) for the year. Adjustments are then made to more appropriately reflect the corporation's economic ability to pay dividends. The CEP which results is somewhat similar to (but not identical with) book income.

In computing E&P, some adjustments result because income excluded from taxable income is included in E&P (e.g., tax-exempt interest). Other adjustments result because deductions allowed for taxable income purposes are not allowed in computing E&P (e.g., dividends-received deduction). Still other adjustments result because deductions not allowed for taxable income purposes are allowed in computing E&P (e.g., nondeductible fines and penalties).

Starting with taxable income as a benchmark, the requirement is to indicate the effect of each item on the calculation of current year earnings and profits by placing a check in the correct column next to each item either to (1) add to taxable income (increase E&P), (2) subtract from taxable income (decrease E&P), or (3) no effect on E&P.

Item	Add to taxable income (increase E&P)	Subtract from taxable income (decrease E&P)	No effect on E&P
Unrealized losses at the end of the year on securities owned.	○	○	●
Federal income taxes accrued and paid during the year.	○	●	○
Gain on prior year installment sale recognized in the current year.	○	●	○
Nondeductible portion of meals and entertainment expenses.	○	●	○
State tax refunds from prior year received in current year.	○	○	●
Increase in cash surrender value of life insurance policies owned by the company.	●	○	○

Explanation of solutions

1. Unrealized losses at the end of the year on securities owned have no effect on E&P. There is no effect because they are not deducted in computing taxable income and cannot be deducted in computing E&P.

2. Federal income taxes accrued and paid during the year are subtracted from taxable income (decreased E&P) because they are not allowed in computing taxable income but are allowed in computing E&P.

3. Gain on prior year installment sale recognized in the current year is subtracted from taxable income (decrease E&P). This adjustment results because the installment method cannot be used for purposes of computing E&P, but is being used in computing taxable income. That is, the installment gain included in taxable income this year was already included in E&P in the prior year, and so must be subtracted from this year's taxable income so that it is not double counted in computing E&P.

4. Nondeductible portion of meals and entertainment expenses are subtracted from taxable income (decrease E&P). This adjustment is necessary because only 50% of business meals and entertainment are deductible in computing taxable income while 100% is deductible in computing E&P.

5. State tax refunds from prior year received in current year have no effect on E&P. No adjustment results because the tax benefit rule would require the refunds to be included in current taxable income, and they similarly would be included in current year E&P.

6. Increase in cash surrender value of life insurance policies owned by the company would be added to taxable income (increase E&P). This adjustment is necessary because the increase in cash surrender value is excluded from taxable income but is included in E&P. It is included in E&P because the higher value increases the corporation's economic ability to pay a dividend.

Directions	Situation	E&P Determination	Distribution	Communication	Research /Authoritative Literature

Corporate distributions are deemed to be made first from current earnings and profits (CEP) and then from accumulated earnings and profits (AEP). If distributions during the year exceed CEP, CEP must be allocated on a pro rata basis to distributions regardless of when the distributions were made during the year. Distributions exceeding CEP are treated as made from AEP. Distributions from AEP are made in chronological order (i.e., allocated to distributions in the order that distributions are made). Distributions in excess of CEP and AEP are treated as a nontaxable return of capital and reduce the shareholder's stock basis, and to the extent in excess of stock basis are treated as capital gain.

Distribution dates	Distribution amounts	Current E&P	Accumulated E&P at 12/31/year 3	Excess distribution
3/31/year 4	58,000	115,297	42,703	0
9/30/year 4	33,000	8,703	18,297	6,000
Totals	91,000	24,000	61,000	6,000

Explanation of solutions

1. The requirement is to allocate the year 4 distributions indicated in column B among columns C (Current E&P), D (Accumulated E&P at 12/31/year3), and E (Excess distribution). Round all answers to the nearest dollar.

First, enter in column B the pro rata portion of each distribution that is deemed to come from Current E&P using the proportion

$$\frac{\text{Current E\&P}}{\text{Total distributions}}$$

$$\$58,000 \times (\$24,000 / \$91,000) = \$15,297$$
$$\$33,000 \times (\$24,000 / \$91,000) = \$8,703$$

Second, determine the portion of each distribution that comes from Accumulated E&P at 12/31/year 3.

$$\$58,000 - \$15,297 \text{ from CEP} = \$42,703 \text{ from AEP at } 12/31/\text{year 3}$$
$$\$33,000 - \$8,703 \text{ from CEP} = \$24,297, \text{ but limited to remaining balance of}$$
Accumulated E&P at 12/31/year 3 which is $61,000 - $42,703 = $18,297

Third, determine the excess distribution.

$$\$58,000 - (\$15,297 \text{ CEP} + \$42,703 \text{ AEP}) = \$0$$
$$\$33,000 - (\$8,703 \text{ CEP} + \$18,297 \text{ AEP}) = \$6,000$$

2. Underwood is a 20% shareholder of Alaska with a stock basis of $700. The requirement is to determine and enter in the table Underwood's total distribution, dividend income, return of capital, and capital gain.

Underwood's total distribution	Dividend income	Return of capital	Capital gain
18,200	17,000	700	500

Since Underwood is a 20% shareholder, his distributions would total $91,000 × 20% = $18,200. His dividend income would equal 20% of the dividends paid by Alaska which would be ($24,000 + $61,000) × 20% = $17,000. Underwood's return of capital would be limited to his $700 stock basis before the distribution. His distribution in excess of stock basis would be the total distribution of $18,200 – ($17,000 dividend + $700 return of basis) = $500 and would be treated as capital gain.

			Communication		
Directions	Situation	E&P Determination	Distribution		Research /Authoritative Literature

| Spelling | Undo | Redo | Cut | Copy | Paste |

Memorandum

To: Controller
Subject: Schedule M-1, *Reconciliation of Income (Loss) per Books with Income per Return*

    Schedule M-1 of Form 1120 is used to reconcile a corporation's income reported per books with its taxable income reported on its tax return Form 1120. Book income is calculated using generally accepted accounting principles, while taxable income is calculated according to tax rules. As a result, book income often differs from taxable income.

    Some differences are permanent in nature and result because income items reported per books are not taxed, or deductions taken per books might not be allowed as tax deductions. A common example would be the federal income taxes that are deducted per books are not allowed as a tax deduction and must be added back to book income in order to reconcile with taxable income. Other differences are temporary and result because income or deduction items impact book income and taxable income in different years. A common example would be the use of straight-line depreciation per books while accelerated depreciation is used for tax purposes. In this case, the excess of tax depreciation over book depreciation would have to be subtracted from book income in order to arrive at taxable income.

The above are just two examples of the many differences that might result because the rules for computing book income differ from the rules for computing taxable income. Please do not hesitate to contact me should you have any questions concerning this matter.

Sincerely,

CPA Candidate

Directions	Situation	E&P Determination	Distribution	Communication	Research /Authoritative Literature

IRC 312 (k)

Internal Revenue Code Section 312, subsection (k), provides for the effect of depreciation on earnings and profits and generally requires the use of the alternative depreciation system (ADS) for tangible property.

BUSINESS ENVIRONMENT AND CONCEPTS

1. Under the Revised Uniform Limited Partnership Act, which of the following is true regarding limited partnerships?

  a. A limited partnership has **no** general partners.
  b. General partnerships may **not** be converted to limited liability partnerships because they must be terminated first.
  c. The limited partners may **not** participate in the management of the company.
  d. Official formation is **not** necessary for a limited partnership other than two or more people carrying on as co-owners of a business for profit.

2. Terry recently started a new business and is trying to decide what type of entity to form. Terry is part-owner and is active in running the business. What type of entity would best protect Terry, as one of the owners, from personal liability?

  a. General ownership.
  b. Limited partnership.
  c. Joint venture.
  d. Limited liability company.

3. Which of the following is a characteristic of a C corporation?

  a. Includes most privately held businesses.
  b. Pays taxes on profits after paying dividends to shareholders.
  c. Subject to double taxation on profits if dividends are paid.
  d. Must have only one class of stock.

4. Which of the following is considered a corporate equity security?

  a. A shareholder's preemptive right.
  b. A shareholder's appraisal right.
  c. A callable bond.
  d. A share of callable preferred stock.

5. Which of the following statements generally is correct regarding a general partner in a general partnership as compared to a general partner in a limited partnership?

  a. A general partner in a general partnership has greater rights and powers than a general partner in a limited partnership.
  b. A general partner in a general partnership has greater liability than a general partner in a limited partnership.
  c. A general partner in a general partnership and a general partner in a limited partnership have the same rights and powers.
  d. A general partner in a general partnership has rights and powers provided by articles of partnership, while a general partner in a limited partnership has rights and powers provided by statute.

1. **(c)** The requirement is to identify the true statement regarding limited partnerships. Answer (c) is correct because the limited partners cannot participate in management of the partnership and maintain their limited liability status. Answer (a) is incorrect because a limited partnership must have at least one general partner and one limited partner. Answer (b) is incorrect because a general partnership can be converted to a limited partnership. Answer (d) is incorrect because limited partnerships must comply with state laws regarding formation.

2. **(d)** The requirement is to identify the form of business that would best protect an active, part-owner of a business. Answer (d) is correct because in a limited liability company all owner-managers have limited liability. Answer (a) is incorrect because in a general partnership no partners have limited liability. Answer (b) is incorrect because in a limited partnership only limited partners have limited liability and they cannot participate in management of the partnership. Answer (c) is incorrect because in a joint venture no members have limited liability

3. **(c)** The requirement is to identify the characteristic of a C corporation. Answer (c) is correct because the profits of a C corporation are taxable to the corporation and taxed again when distributed to the shareholders as dividends. Answer (a) is incorrect because most privately held businesses are partnerships or sole proprietorships. Answer (b) is incorrect because a C corporation pays taxes on profits when they are earned. Answer (d) is incorrect because a C corporation may have more than one class of stock.

4. **(d)** The requirement is to identify the item that is considered a corporate equity security. Answer (d) is correct because a share of stock is a corporate equity security even if it is callable. Answers (a) and (b) are incorrect because they are rights of a shareholder. Answer (c) is incorrect because a bond is a debt security.

5. **(c)** The requirement is to identify the statement that accurately contrasts a general partner in a general partnership with a general partner in a limited partnership. Answer (c) is correct because a general partner in either type of partnership has similar rights and powers. Answers (a) and (d) are incorrect because the rights and powers are the same. Answer (b) is incorrect because liability is identical.

6. Which of the following economic terms describes a general decline in prices for goods and services and in the level of interest rates?
- a. Expansion.
- b. Inflation.
- c. Deflation.
- d. Recession.

7. The primary purpose of the consumer price index (CPI) is to
- a. Establish a cost-of-living index.
- b. Identify the strength of an economic recovery.
- c. Help determine the Federal Reserve Bank's discount rate.
- d. Compare relative price changes over time.

8. Carter Co. paid $1,000,000 for land three years ago. Carter estimates it can sell the land for $1,200,000, net of selling costs. If the land is not sold, Carter plans to develop the land at a cost of $1,500,000. Carter estimates net cash flow from the development in the first year of operations would be $500,000. What is Carter's opportunity cost of the development?
- a. $1,500,000
- b. $1,200,000
- c. $1,000,000
- d. $ 500,000

9. What is the formula for calculating the profitability index of a project?
- a. Subtract actual after-tax net income from the minimum required return in dollars.
- b. Divide the present value of the annual after-tax cash flows by the original cash invested in the project.
- c. Divide the initial investment for the project by the net annual cash inflow.
- d. Multiply net profit margin by asset turnover.

10. Which of the following statements is correct regarding the weighted-average cost of capital (WACC)?
- a. One of a company's objectives is to minimize the WACC.
- b. A company with a high WACC is attractive to potential shareholders.
- c. An increase in the WACC increases the value of the company.
- d. WACC is always equal to the company's borrowing rate.

6. **(c)** The requirement is to identify the term that describes a general decline in prices of goods and services and in the level of interest rates. Answer (c) is correct because this is a description of deflation. Answer (a) is incorrect because expansion is a term used to describe growth in an economy. Answer (b) is incorrect because inflation is a term used to describe an increase in prices. Answer (d) is incorrect because recession is a term used to describe a contraction in an economy.

7. **(d)** The requirement is to identify the primary purpose of the consumer price index (CPI). Answer (d) is correct because the CPI compares relative prices of a basket of goods over time. Answer (a) is incorrect because establishing a cost-of-living index is not the primary purpose of the CPI. Answer (b) is incorrect because the CPI is not a good measure of the strength of an economic recovery. Answer (c) is incorrect because helping the Federal Reserve Bank set the discount rate is not the primary purpose of the CPI.

8. **(b)** The requirement is to identify the opportunity cost of the development. Answer (b) is correct because the opportunity cost is the value lost by not selecting the next best alternative for an investment. In this case the opportunity cost is the $1,200,000 that could be received from sale of the land. Answer (a) is incorrect because $1,500,000 is the cost of the investment alternative selected. Answer (c) is incorrect because $1,000,000 is the historical cost of the land and is irrelevant to deciding on an investment alternative. Answer (d) is incorrect because $500,000 is an element of the future returns from the investment.

9. **(b)** The requirement is to identify the formula for the profitability index. Answer (b) is correct because the profitability index is calculated by dividing the present value of the after-tax cash flows by the original cash invested. Answers (a), (c), and (d) are incorrect because these are not meaningful computations.

10. **(a)** The requirement is to identify the statement that is correct regarding the weighted-average cost of capital (WACC). Answer (a) is correct because all companies strive to minimize their WACC. Answer (b) is incorrect because a company with a low WACC is desirable to shareholders. Answer (c) is incorrect because an increase in the WACC decreases the value of the company. Answer (d) is incorrect because WACC is not equal to the company's borrowing rate. It is the average cost of all sources of capital.

11. An increase in which of the following should cause management to reduce the average inventory?
    a. The cost of placing an order.
    b. The cost of carrying inventory.
    c. The annual demand for the product.
    d. The lead time needed to acquire inventory.

12. Which of the following ratios would most likely be used by the management to evaluate short-term liquidity?
    a. Return on total assets.
    b. Sales to cash.
    c. Accounts receivable turnover.
    d. Acid test ratio.

13. Which of the following ratios would be used to evaluate a company's profitability?
    a. Current ratio.
    b. Inventory turnover ratio.
    c. Debt to total assets ratio.
    d. Gross margin ratio.

14. When a client's accounts payable computer system was relocated, the administrator provided support through a dial-up connection to a server. Subsequently, the administrator left the company. No changes were made to the accounts payable system at that time. Which of the following situations represents the greatest security risk?
    a. User passwords are **not** required to be in alphanumeric format.
    b. Management procedures for user accounts are **not** documented.
    c. User accounts are **not** removed upon termination of employees.
    d. Security logs are **not** periodically reviewed for violations.

15. An entity doing business on the Internet most likely could use any of the following methods to prevent unauthorized intruders from accessing proprietary information **except:**
    a. Password management.
    b. Data encryption.
    c. Digital certificates.
    d. Batch processing.

16. Which of the following information technology (IT) departmental responsibilities should be delegated to separate individuals?
    a. Network maintenance and wireless access.
    b. Data entry and antivirus management.
    c. Data entry and application programming.
    d. Data entry and quality assurance.

11. (b) The requirement is to identify which factor would cause management to reduce average inventory. Answer (b) is correct because if the cost of carrying inventory increases, management would carry less inventory. Answer (a) is incorrect because if the cost of placing an order increases, management would tend to place larger orders and, therefore, carry more inventory. Answer (c) is incorrect because if the annual demand for the product increases, management would not reduce the average inventory level. Answer (d) is incorrect because if the lead time needed to acquire inventory increases, management would not reduce the level of inventory.

12. (d) The requirement is to identify the ratio that would most likely be used to evaluate short-term liquidity. Answer (d) is correct because the acid test ratio is a measure of short-term liquidity. Answer (a) is incorrect because return on total assets is a measure of profitability. Answer (b) is incorrect because the ratio of sales to cash is not a meaningful ratio. Answer (c) is incorrect because accounts receivable turnover is a measure of efficiency of operations.

13. (d) The requirement is to identify the ratio that would be used to evaluate profitability. Answer (d) is correct because gross margin (gross profit divided by net sales) is a measure of profitability. Answer (a) is incorrect because the current ratio is a measure of liquidity. Answer (b) is incorrect because it is a measure of efficiency. Answer (c) is incorrect because debt to total assets is a measure of debt utilization.

14. (c) The requirement is to identify the greatest security risk. Answer (c) is correct because the greatest risk in this situation is that the ex-administrator would use his or her password to gain access to the system. Answers (a), (b), and (d) are incorrect because while they are all risks, they are not as significant as not removing passwords for terminated employees.

15. (d) The requirement is to identify the method that would not be used to prevent unauthorized intruders from accessing proprietary information. Answer (d) is correct because batch processing is a form of processing of transactions which does not relate to data access. Answers (a), (b), and (c) are incorrect because they are all methods to prevent unauthorized access to data.

16. (c) The requirement is to identify the responsibilities that should be segregated. Answer (c) is correct because data entry should be segregated from application programming. If these functions are not segregated, the programmer could cause unauthorized transactions to be processed. Answers (a), (b), and (d) are incorrect because none of the pairs of duties are incompatible.

17. Which of the following transaction processing modes provides the most accurate and complete information for decision making?
  a. Batch.
  b. Distributed.
  c. Online.
  d. Application.

18. Which of the following is considered an application input control?
  a. Run control total.
  b. Edit check.
  c. Report distribution log.
  d. Exception report.

19. Which of the following terms refers to a site that has been identified and maintained by the organization as a data processing disaster recovery site but has **not** been stocked with equipment?
  a. Hot.
  b. Cold.
  c. Warm.
  d. Flying start.

20. Relevant information for material A follows:

Actual quantity purchased	6,500 lbs.
Standard quantity allowed	6,000 lbs.
Actual price	$3.80
Standard price	$4.00

What was the direct material quantity variance for material A?
  a. $2,000 favorable.
  b. $1,900 favorable.
  c. $1,900 unfavorable.
  d. $2,000 unfavorable.

21. Smart Co. uses a static budget. When actual sales are **less** than budget, Smart would report favorable variances on which of the following expense categories?

	Sales commissions	*Building rent*
a.	Yes	Yes
b.	Yes	No
c.	No	Yes
d.	No	No

22. An increase in production levels within a relevant range most likely would result in
  a. Increasing the total cost.
  b. Increasing the variable cost per unit.
  c. Decreasing the total fixed cost.
  d. Decreasing the variable cost per unit.

17. (c) The requirement is to identify the transaction processing mode that provides the most accurate and complete information for decision making. Answer (c) is correct because in an online system data is readily available for decision making. Answer (a) is incorrect because in a batch system periodic reports are prepared for decision making which may not be timely or complete. Answer (b) is incorrect because the fact that the company uses a distributed system does not give us information about the availability of data. Answer (d) is incorrect because an application system has no implications for data availability.

18. (b) The requirement is to identify the application input control. Answer (b) is correct because an edit check is a check on the accuracy of data as it is inputted. Answer (a) is incorrect because a run control total is a processing control. Answer (c) is incorrect because a report distribution log is a distribution control. Answer (d) is incorrect because an exception report is a processing control.

19. (b) The requirement is to identify the term used to describe a disaster recovery site that has not been stocked with equipment. Answer (b) is correct because this describes a cold site. Answer (a) is incorrect because a hot site is one that is stocked and ready for operation. Answers (c) and (d) are incorrect because these terms are not used to describe backup sites.

20. (d) The requirement is to calculate the direct material quantity variance. Answer (d) is correct because the variance is $2,000 unfavorable [6,000 (std. quantity) × $4 (std. price) – 6,500 (act. quantity) × $4 (std. price)]. Answers (a), (b), and (c) are incorrect because they represent incorrect calculations of the variance.

21. (b) The requirement is to identify the variances that would be favorable. Answer (b) is correct because sales commissions would be lower than budgeted since sales are lower than budgeted. Rent would be budgeted at a fixed amount that would not change based on sales. Answers (a), (c), and (d) are incorrect because the variance in sales commissions would be favorable but rent would have no variance.

22. (a) The requirement is to identify the effect of an increase in production levels within a relevant range of activity. Answer (a) is correct because an increase in production levels would increase total costs. Answer (b) is incorrect because variable cost per unit is fixed within the relevant range. Answer (c) is incorrect because total fixed cost does not change over the relevant range. Answer (d) is incorrect because variable cost per unit is fixed over the relevant range.

23. A CPA would recommend implementing an activity-based costing system under which of the following circumstances?
   a. The client is a single-product manufacturer.
   b. Most of the client's costs currently are classified as direct costs.
   c. The client produced products that heterogeneously consume resources.
   d. The client produced many different products that homogeneously consume resources.

23. (c) The requirement is to identify the circumstances that would most likely justify recommending an activity-based costing system. Answer (c) is correct because an activity-based system captures costs based on cost drivers and is particularly appropriate when a company produces products that consume resources in various ways. Answer (a) is incorrect because with a single product a company would not benefit from adopting an activity-based system. Answer (c) is incorrect because activity-based systems are used to allocate indirect costs. If most costs are direct there is less benefit to adoption of an activity-based costing system. Answer (d) is incorrect because when products homogeneously consume resources, less benefit is derived from implementation of an activity-based costing system.

24. A company that produces 10,000 units has fixed costs of $300,000, variable costs of $50 per unit, and a sales price of $85 per unit. After learning that its variable costs will increase by 20%, the company is considering an increase in production to 12,000 units. Which of the following statements is correct regarding the company's next steps?
   a. If production in increased to 12,000 units, profits will increase by $50,000.
   b. If production in increased to 12,000 units, profits will increase by $100,000.
   c. If production remains at 10,000 units, profits will decrease by $50,000.
   d. If production remains at 10,000 units, profits will decrease by $100,000.

24. (d) The requirement is to identify the correct statement regarding the company's next steps. Answer (d) is correct because if production remains at 10,000 units, profits will decrease by $100,000 [10,000 units × (20% of $50 variable cost)]. Answers (a) and (b) are incorrect because current profits are $50,000 [($85 × 10,000 units) – ($50 variable cost × 10,000) - $300,000 fixed costs], and if variable costs increase by 20% and production is increased to 12,000 units, profits will be $0 [($85 x 12,000 units) – ($60 variable cost × 12,000 units) - $300,000 fixed costs]. Therefore, profits will decline by $50,000. Answer (c) is incorrect because if production remains at 10,000 units, profits will decrease by $100,000.

25. A delivery company is implementing a system to compare the costs of purchasing and operating different vehicles in its fleet. Truck 415 is driven 125,000 miles per year at a variable cost of $0.13 per mile. Truck 415 has a capacity of 28,000 pounds and delivers 250 full loads per year. What amount is the truck's delivery cost per pound?
   a. $0.00163 per pound.
   b. $0.00232 per pound.
   c. $0.58036 per pound.
   d. $1.72000 per pound.

25. (b) The requirement is to compute the delivery cost per pound. Answer (b) is correct because the cost per pound is $0.00232 per pound [(125,000 miles × $0.13 per mile)/(28,000 pounds per load × 250 loads)] . Answers (a), (c) and (d) are incorrect because they are all incorrect calculations of the cost per pound.

26. Which of the following disqualifies an entity from an S corporation election?
   a. Seventy-seven individual shareholders (including four married couples).
   b. An estate shareholder.
   c. A 501(c)(3) exempt organization shareholder.
   d. A nonresident alien shareholder.

26. (d) The requirement is to identify the factor that disqualifies an entity from an S corporation election. Answer (d) is correct because nonresident aliens cannot hold shares in an S corporation. Answer (a) is incorrect because an S corporation can have up to 75 shareholders, and a married couple is counted as one shareholder. Answer (b) is incorrect because shareholders can include estates. Answer (c) is incorrect because shareholders may be 501 (c) (3) exempt organizations.

27. Davis, an inventor, developed a new product but lacked money to get the product to the marketplace. Before creating a corporation to raise capital, Davis leased office space and equipment, entered into contracts with third parties, and identified investors. Who has liability for preincorporation debts?

    a.   Davis is liable until the corporation assumed the debts in novation.

    b.   Davis is liable until the articles of incorporation were filed.

    c.   If this corporation is **never** formed, Davis is **not** liable.

    d.   If this corporation is **never** formed, the unpaid third parties must write off the debt because **no** corporate entity existed at the time the debt was incurred.

27. **(a)** The requirement is to identify who has liability for preincorporation debts. Answer (a) is correct because the agreements made by the promoters are not binding on the future corporation until adopted after the corporation comes into existence. Answers (b), (c), and (d) are incorrect because the promoter is obligated until the corporation is formed and the obligations are formally adopted by the corporation.

28. Frey Corp. has 1,000 shares of issued and outstanding common stock. Frey's articles of incorporation permit a stockholder who owns 5% or more of the outstanding stock or who has owned the stock for longer than six months to inspect Frey's books and records. Ace, who has owned 25 shares of Frey stock for four months, wants to inspect the books and records. Under the Revised Model Business Corporation Act, which of the following statements is correct regarding Ace's right to inspect the books and records?

    a.   Ace must wait two months before being allowed to inspect the books and records.

    b.   Ace must purchase an additional 25 shares of Frey stock before being allowed to inspect the books and records.

    c.   Ace may, after giving five days' written notice, inspect the books and records to determine the value of Frey stock.

    d.   Ace may, after giving five days' written notice, inspect the books and records to provide a list of Frey stockholders to Ace's broker.

28. **(c)** The requirement is identify the correct statement regarding Ace's right to inspect the books and records. Answer (c) is correct because under the Revised Model Business Corporation Act a stockholder has the right to inspect the books and records with 5 days' notice. Answers (a) and (b) are correct because the articles of incorporation do not affect rights given by law. Answer (d) is incorrect because the shareholder may not get a list of shareholders or customers to use for a business mailing list.

29. Which of the following corporate shareholder rights is enforceable by means of a derivative suit?

    a.   Compelling payment of properly declared dividends.

    b.   Enforcing access to corporate records.

    c.   Recovering damages from a third party.

    d.   Protecting preemptive rights.

29. **(c)** The requirement is to identify the rights that are enforceable by means of a derivative suit. Answer (c) is correct because shareholders may sue on behalf of the corporation to recover damages from a third party if the corporation fails to do so. Answers (a), (b), and (d) are incorrect because in these cases the shareholder would sue on his or her own behalf. These cases would not involve derivative suits.

30. Toby invested $25,000 in a limited partnership with Connor and Blair. Toby was a general partner in the limited partnership. The partnership failed to pay Kelly $45,000 for services on behalf of the partnership. Which of the following statements is generally correct regarding Toby's liability under the Revised Uniform Limited Partnership Act?

    a.   Toby was liable for $25,000 because this was a limited partnership.

    b.   Toby was liable for zero because this was a partnership debt, **not** a personal debt.

    c.   Toby was liable for $45,000 because Toby was a general partner.

    d.   Toby was liable for $15,000 because this was a limited partnership.

30. **(c)** The requirement is to identify the correct statement regarding Toby's liability. Answer (c) is correct because Toby is liable for the $45,000. As a general partner he is personally liable for the debts of the corporation. Answers (a), (b), and (d) are incorrect because Toby is a general partner and personally liable for the total amount of the partnership debts.

31. Which of the following is an assumption in a perfectly competitive financial market?

    a.   No single trader or traders can have a significant impact on market prices.

    b.   Some traders can impact market prices more than others.

    c.   Trading prices vary based on supply only.

    d.   Information about borrowing/lending activities is only available to those willing to pay market prices.

32. A country's currency conversion value has recently changed from 1.5 to the US dollar to 1.7 to the US dollar. Which of the following statements about the country is correct?

    a.   Its exports are **less** expensive for the United States.

    b.   Its currency has appreciated.

    c.   Its imports of US goods are more affordable.

    d.   Its purchases of the US dollar will cost **less**.

33. Salem Co. is considering a project that yields annual net cash inflows of $420,000 for years 1 through 5, and a net cash inflow of $100,000 in year 6. The project will require an initial investment of $1,800,000. Salem's cost of capital is 10%. Present value information is presented below.

    Present value of $1 for 5 years at 10% is .62.
    Present value of $1 for 6 years at 10% is .56.
    Present value of an annuity of $1 for 5 years at 10% is 3.79.

What was Salem's expected net present value for this project?

    a. $ 83,000

    b. $(108,200)

    c. $(152,200)

    d. $(442,000)

34. SkBound Airlines provided the following information about its two operating divisions:

	Passenger	*Cargo*
Operating profit	$ 40,000	$ 50,000
Investment	250,000	500,000
External borrowing rate	6%	8%

Measuring performance using return on investment (ROI), which division performed better?

    a.   The Cargo division, with an ROI of 10%.

    b.   The Passenger division, with an ROI of 16%.

    c.   The Cargo division, with an ROI of 18%.

    d.   The Passenger division with an ROI of 22%.

35. Egan Co. owns land that could be developed in the future. Egan estimates it can sell the land for $1,200,000, net of all selling costs. If it is not sold, Egan will continue with its plans to develop the land. As Egan evaluates its options for development or sale of the property, what type of cost would the potential selling price represent in Egan's decision?

    a.   Sunk.

    b.   Opportunity.

    c.   Future.

    d.   Variable.

31. **(a)** The requirement is to identify the assumption involved in a perfectly competitive financial market. Answer (a) is correct because in a perfect market there are a large number of buyers and sellers and no single participant or group of participants can influence market prices. Answer (b) is incorrect because in a perfectly competitive market a single trader or groups of traders cannot impact market prices. Answer (c) is incorrect because prices vary based on both supply and demand. Answer (d) is incorrect because this is not an assumption involved in a perfectly competitive financial market.

32. **(a)** The requirement is to identify the correct statement about the country. Answer (a) is correct because when the value of the currency declines in relation to the dollar the country's exports are less expensive in the United States. Answer (b) is incorrect because the currency has depreciated, not appreciated. Answer (c) is incorrect because the imports of US goods are less affordable. Answer (d) is incorrect because purchases of the US dollar will cost more.

33. **(c)** The requirement is to determine the expected net present value for the project. Answer (c) is correct because the net present value is equal to negative $152,200 {$1,800,000 − [($420,000 x 3.79) + ($100,000 x .56)]}. Answers (a), (b), and (d) are incorrect because they represent inaccurate computations of the net present value.

34. **(b)** The requirement is to determine which division performed better. Answer (b) is correct because the Passenger division performed better with a return on investment of 16% ($40,000 operating profit / $250,000 investment). The Cargo division has a return on investment of 10% ($50,000/$500,000).

35. **(b)** The requirement is to identify what type of cost is the potential selling price of the land. Answer (b) is correct because the potential selling price of the land is the opportunity cost. It is the value foregone by selecting a particular alternative. Answer (a) is incorrect because a sunk cost is a cost that has been incurred in the past. Answer (c) is incorrect because a future cost is a cost expected to be incurred in the future. Answer (d) is incorrect because a variable cost varies directly with the level of activity.

36. Which of the following statements is correct regarding payback method as a capital budgeting technique?
  a. The payback method considers the time value of money.
  b. An advantage of the payback method is that it indicates if an investment will be profitable.
  c. The payback method provides the years needed to recoup the investment in a project.
  d. Payback is calculated by dividing the annual cash inflows by the net investment.

37. Larson Corp. issued $20 million of long-term debt in the current year. What is a major advantage to Larson with the debt issuance?

  a. The reduced earnings per share possible through financial leverage.
  b. The relatively low after-tax cost due to the interest deduction.
  c. The increased financial risk resulting from the use of the debt.
  d. The reduction of Larson's control over the company.

38. Green, Inc., a financial investment-consulting firm, was engaged by Maple Corp. to provide technical support for making investment decisions. Maple, a manufacturer of ceramic tiles, was in the process of buying Bay, Inc., its prime competitor. Green's financial analyst made an independent detailed analysis of Bay's average collection period to determine which of the following?
  a. Financing.
  b. Return on equity.
  c. Liquidity.
  d. Operating profitability.

39. Which of the following items would be most critical to include in a systems specification document for a financial report?

  a. Cost-benefit analysis.
  b. Data elements needed.
  c. Training requirements.
  d. Communication change management considerations.

40. An enterprise resource planning (ERP) system has which of the following advantages over multiple independent functional systems?
  a. Modifications can be made to each module without affecting other modules.
  b. Increased responsiveness and flexibility while aiding in the decision-making process.
  c. Increased amount of data redundancy since more than one module contains the same information.
  d. Reduction in costs for implementation and training.

41. Which of the following structures refers to the collection of data for all vendors in a relational data base?
  a. Record.
  b. Field.
  c. File.
  d. Byte.

36. **(c)** The requirement is to identify the correct statement regarding the payback method. Answer (c) is correct because the payback method calculates the years needed to recoup an investment. Answer (a) is incorrect because the payback method does not consider the time value of money. Answer (b) is incorrect because the payback method does not indicate whether an investment will be profitable because it does not consider the time value of money. Answer (d) is incorrect because the payback method calculates the number of years it takes to recover the initial investment.

37. **(b)** The requirement is to identify the major advantage to debt issuance. Answer (b) is correct because the tax deduction for interest reduces the cost of debt. Answer (a) is incorrect because appropriate use of debt increases earnings per share. Answer (c) is incorrect because increased financial risk is a disadvantage of the issuance of debt, not an advantage. Answer (d) is incorrect because issuance of debt does not dilute control.

38. **(c)** The requirement is to identify the purpose of a detailed analysis of average collection period. Answer (c) is correct because analysis of the average collection period is designed to evaluate liquidity. Answers (a), (b), and (d) are incorrect because the purpose of the calculation is to evaluate liquidity.

39. **(b)** The requirement is to identify the item that would be most critical to include in a systems specification document. Answer (b) is correct because a systems specification document should include a description of the data elements needed. Answers (a), (c), and (d) are incorrect because these are items that would be included in other documents related to system development.

40. **(b)** The requirement is to identify the advantage of an enterprise resource planning (ERP) system over multiple independent functional systems. Answer (b) is correct because an ERP system increases responsiveness and flexibility while aiding in the decision-making process. Answer (a) is incorrect because ERP systems are integrated and modifications in one module affect other modules. Answer (c) is incorrect because an ERP system has a reduced amount of data redundancy. Answer (d) is incorrect because ERP systems typically are more expensive to implement.

41. **(c)** The requirement is to identify the structure that refers to the collection of data for all vendors in a relational data base. Answer (c) is correct because the structure would be referred to as a vendor file. Answer (a) is incorrect because a record would refer to information about an individual vendor. Answer (b) is incorrect because a field is an element of a record. Answer (d) is incorrect because a byte is a piece of a field.

42. During the annual audit, it was learned from an interview with the controller that the accounting system was programmed to use a batch processing method and a detailed posting type. This would mean that individual transactions were
    a. Posted upon entry, and each transaction had its own line entry in the appropriate ledger.
    b. Assigned to groups before posting, and each transaction had its own line entry in the appropriate ledger.
    c. Posted upon entry, and each transaction group had a cumulative entry total in the appropriate ledger.
    d. Assigned to groups before posting, and each transaction group had a cumulative entry total in the appropriate ledger.

43. A company has a significant e-commerce presence and self-hosts its Web site. To assure continuity in the event of a natural disaster, the firm should adopt which of the following strategies?
    a. Backup the server database daily.
    b. Store records off-site.
    c. Purchase and implement RAID technology.
    d. Establish off-site mirrored Web server.

44. Which of the following is the primary advantage of using a value-added network (VAN)?
    a. It provides confidentiality for data transmitted over the Internet.
    b. It provides increased security for data transmissions.
    c. It is more cost effective for the company than transmitting data over the Internet.
    d. It enables the company to obtain trend information on data transmission.

45. Wexford Co. has a subunit that reported the following data for year 1:

Asset (investment) turnover	1.5 times
Sales	$750,000
Return on sales	8%

The imputed interest rate is 12%. What is the division residual income for year 1?
    a. $60,000
    b. $30,000
    c. $20,000
    d. $0

46. The target capital structure of Traggle Co. is 50% debt, 10% preferred equity, and 40% common equity. The interest rate on debt is 6%, the yield on the preferred is 7%, the cost of common equity is 11.5%, and the tax rate is 40%. Traggle does not anticipate issuing any new stock. What is Traggle's weighted-average cost of capital?
    a. 6.50%
    b. 6.77%
    c. 7.10%
    d. 8.30%

42. (b) The requirement is to identify the implications of the controller's comments. Answer (b) is correct because the described system is a batch processing system with each transaction having its own line entry in the appropriate ledger. Answers (a) and (c) are incorrect because posting upon entry describes an online processing system. Answer (d) is incorrect because the system is a detailed posting type.

43. (d) The requirement is to identify the strategy to assure continuity in the event of a natural disaster. Answer (d) is correct because establishing an off-site mirrored Web server would provide for continuous duplication of data in geographically separated locations. Answer (a) would not be effective because daily backup would be less effective and ineffective if the backup files were not stored off-site. Answer (b) is incorrect because it does not state that duplicate records are maintained at two different locations. Answer (c) is incorrect because RAID technology is designed to prevent loss of data in the event of equipment failure.

44. (b) The requirement is to identify the primary advantage of using a value-added network. Answer (b) is correct because value-added networks provided increased security over transactions. Answer (a) is incorrect because value-added networks use private networks. Answer (c) is incorrect because use of value-added networks cost more than transacting over the Internet. Answer (d) is incorrect because it is more difficult to collect data about transmissions.

45. (d) The requirement is to calculate the division's residual income for year 1. Residual income is equal to profit minus imputed interest on investment. If asset turnover is equal to 1.5 times, invested assets is equal to $500,000 ($1,500,000 sales ÷ 1.5 asset turnover). Answer (d) is correct because residual income is equal to $0 [($750,000 × 8%) − ($500,000 invested assets × 12%)].

46. (c) The requirement is to calculate Traggle's weighted-average cost of capital. Answer (c) is correct because the weighted-average cost of capital is equal to 7.10% {50% debt × [6% x (1 − .4 tax rate)] + (10% preferred stock × 7%) + (40% common stock × 11.5%)}.

47. Galax, Inc. had operating income of $5,000,000 before interest and taxes. Galax's net book value of plant assets at January 1 and December 31 were $22,000,000 and $18,000,000 respectively. Galax achieved a 25% return on investment for the year, with an investment turnover of 2.5. What were Galax's sales for the year?

  a. $55,000,000
  b. $50,000,000
  c. $45,000,000
  d. $20,000,000

48. Management has reviewed the standard cost variance analysis and is trying to explain an unfavorable labor efficiency variance of $8,000. Which of the following is the most likely cause of the variance?

  a. The new labor contract increased wages.
  b. The maintenance of machinery has been inadequate for the last few months.
  c. The department manager has chosen to use highly skilled workers.
  d. The quality of raw materials has improved greatly.

49. Boylc, Inc. makes two products, X and Y, that require allocation of indirect manufacturing costs. The following data was compiled by the accountant before making any allocations:

	Product X	Product Y
Quantity produced	10,000	20,000
Direct manufacturing labor hours	15,000	5,000
Setup hours	500	1,500

The total cost of setting up manufacturing processes and equipment is $400,000. The company uses a job-costing system with a single indirect cost rate. Under this system, allocated costs were $300,000 and $100,000 for X and Y, respectively. If an activity-based system is used, what would be the allocated costs for each product?

	Product X	Product Y
a.	$100,000	$300,000
b.	$150,000	$250,000
c.	$200,000	$200,000
d.	$250,000	$150,000

50. A company is offered a one-time special order for its product and has the capacity to take this order without losing current business. Variable costs per unit and fixed costs in total will be the same. The gross profit for the special order will be 10%, which is 15% less than the usual gross profit. What impact will this order have on total fixed costs and operating income?

  a. Total fixed costs increase and operating income increases.
  b. Total fixed costs do **not** change and operating income increases.
  c. Total fixed costs do **not** change and operating income does **not** change.
  d. Total fixed costs increase and operating income decreases.

47. (b) The requirement is to calculate Galax's sales for the year. Answer (b) is correct because sales is equal to $50,000,000, which can be calculated by multiplying investment turnover by the average investment, or 2.5 × [($22,000,000 + $18,000,000) ÷ 2] = $50,000,000.

48. (b) The requirement is to identify the most likely cause of the variance. Answer (b) is correct because if maintenance is inadequate, the machinery will break down more often resulting in less efficiency. Answer (a) is incorrect because this would affect the labor price variance. Answer (c) is incorrect because employing highly skilled workers would improve efficiency. Answer (d) is incorrect because improvement in the quality of raw materials would likely improve efficiency.

49. (a) The requirement is to determine the amount of costs allocated to each product. Answer (a) is correct because an activity-based system would allocate costs based on setup hours. Therefore, allocated costs to Product X would be $100,000 ($400,000 × 500 hrs. / 2,000 hrs.), and allocated costs to Product Y would be $300,000 ($400,000 × 1,500 hrs. / 2,000 hrs.).

50. (b) The requirement is to determine the impact of the special order on total fixed costs and operating income. Answer (b) is correct because total fixed costs do not change and operating income would increase. There is no change in fixed costs and the company makes a profit on the special order.

APPENDIX

Modifications to the CPA Exam after December 31, 2010

This appendix provides material for candidates that intend to take parts of the CPA exam after December 31, 2010. Beginning January 1, 2011, the AICPA will launch CBT-e, a new exam format. In addition, the subject matter of the various parts will change with the adoption of new Content and Skills Specifications.

CBT-e

The new CPA exam will have multiple-choice questions as it does now, but the multipart simulations that are included on the Auditing and Attestation (AUD), Financial Accounting and Reporting (FAR) and the Regulation (REG) parts are being replaced with short task-based simulations. These simulations are much like one part of the existing multipart simulations. In addition to the current multiple-choice questions, AUD, FAR, and REG will have 6 or 7 of these task-based simulations, one of which will involve a research task. Business Environment and Concepts (BEC) will have the current multiple-choice questions and three written communication tasks on BEC topics. No written communication tasks will appear on any other parts of the exam. In addition, the time allotment for AUD will be decreased by ½ hour and the time allotted to BEC will increase by ½ hour. Finally, the research questions will be in a slightly different format. All of these changes are summarized in the following tables.

Since the new task-based simulations are much like single parts of the simulations currently included on the exam, you should use the simulations in this manual to prepare you for the CBT-e exam.

Uniform CPA Examination Section Structure and Time Allocations

CBT-e Launch Date: January 1, 2011
Auditing and Attestation (AUD)

Current Structure	CBT-e Structure
• 3 Multiple-Choice Question (MCQ) testlets containing a total of 90 questions • 2 Simulations in current (long) format • 2 Written Communication tasks	• 3 Multiple-Choice Question (MCQ) testlets containing a total of 90 questions • 1 Testlet containing 7 short Task-Based Simulations (TBS) with the research question in a new format
Current Testing Time: 4.5 hours	**CBT-e Testing Time: 4 hours**

Business Environment and Concepts (BEC)

Current Structure	CBT-e Structure
• 3 Multiple-Choice Question (MCQ) testlets containing a total of 90 questions	• 3 Multiple-Choice Question (MCQ) testlets containing a total of 72 questions • 3 Written Communication tasks on BEC topics
Current Testing Time: 2.5 hours	**CBT-e Testing Time: 3 hours**

Financial Accounting and Reporting (FAR)

Current Structure	CBT-e Structure
• 3 Multiple-Choice Question (MCQ) testlets consisting of a total of 90 questions • 2 Simulations in current (long) format • 2 Written Communication tasks	• 3 Multiple-Choice Question (MCQ) testlets consisting of a total of 90 questions • 1 Testlet containing 7 short Task-Based Simulations (TBS) with the research question in a new format
Current Testing Time: 4 hours	**CBT-e Testing Time: 4 hours**

Regulation (REG)

Current Structure	CBT-e Structure
• 3 Multiple-Choice Question (MCQ) testlets consisting of 72 questions • 2 Simulations in current (long) format • 2 Written Communication tasks	• 3 Multiple-Choice Question (MCQ) testlets consisting of 72 questions • 1 Testlet containing 6 short Task-Based Simulations (TBS) with the research question in a new format
Current Testing Time: 3 hours	**CBT-e Testing Time: 3 hours**

Uniform CPA Examination Scoring Weights
CBT-e Launch Date: January 1, 2011

Auditing and Attestation (AUD)
Financial Accounting and Reporting (FAR)
Regulation (REG)

Item Format	Current Weight	CBT-e Weight
Multiple-Choice Questions (MCQ)	70%	60%
Simulations	20%	40%
Written Communication Tasks	10%	N/A

Business Environment and Concepts (BEC)

Item Format	Current Weight	CBT-e Weight
Multiple-Choice Questions (MCQ)	100%	85%
Simulations	N/A	N/A
Written Communication Tasks	N/A	15%

Task-Based Simulations

The new task-based simulations are answered much like the parts of the current multipart simulations, with pull-down menus, selections, and dollar entries. Below are a few that have currently been released by the AICPA.

Pull-Down Menu Example

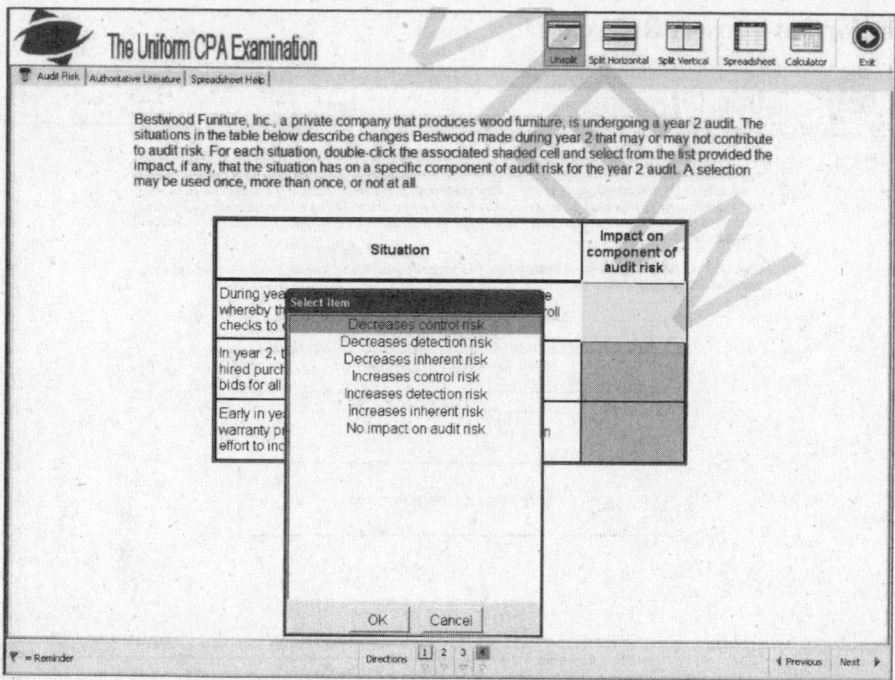

Pull-Down Menu for Account and Input Amount

New Research Format—Insert Reference

Written Communication—Only on BEC

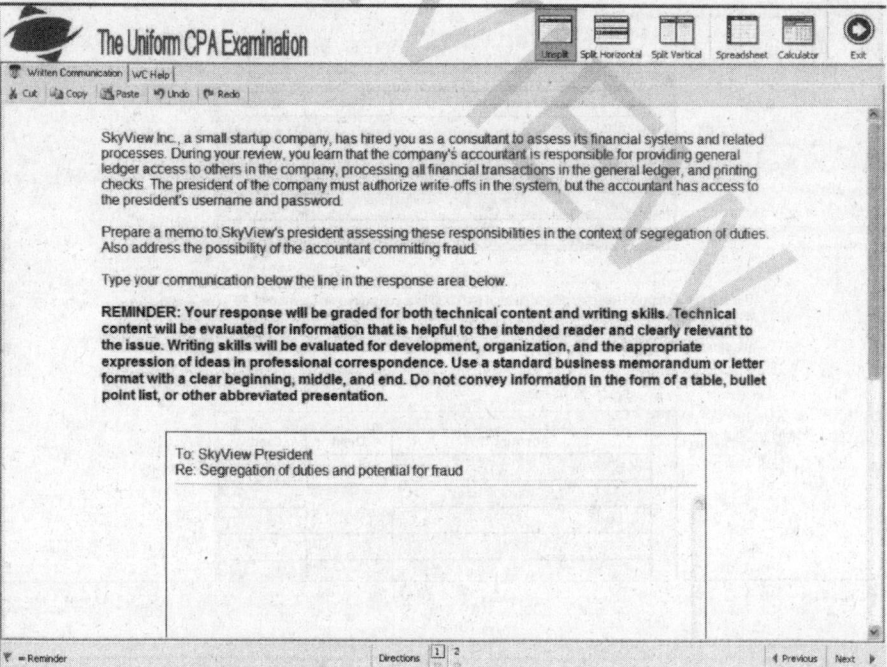

In about August of 2010 the AICPA will be posting tutorials and sample exams with the new CBT-e platform. You should continue to check for releases at www.cpa-exam.org.

New Content and Skills Specifications

The New Content and Skills Specifications cover new topics and shift some topics between parts. The New Content and Skills Specifications is currently available at www.cpa-exam.org. The remainder of this appendix will present guidance on what topics to study in the manuals for each part and provide summaries and questions for the new material to be included beginning after December 31, 2010.

AUDITING AND ATTESTATION SECTION

The Content and Skills Specifications for the Auditing and Attestation section of the CPA exam are similar to the current content specifications, with the following exceptions:

1. The topics of ethics and independence and responsibilities under the Sarbanes-Oxley Act have been moved from the Regulation section of the exam to the Auditing and Attestation section. Therefore, you should study the first part of Module 21, *Professional Responsibilities* (dealing with ethics), and the section of Module 22, *Securities Regulation,* related to the Sarbanes-Oxley Act, and the related questions.
2. Ethics and independence standards of the International Federation of Accountants, the Government Accountability Office, and the Department of Labor have been added to the specifications. These topics are summarized in this appendix.
3. Auditing standards of the International Federation of Accountants have been added to the specifications. This topic is summarized in this appendix.

NEW MATERIAL—AUDITING AND ATTESTATION SECTION

International Ethics Standards for Accountants

The International Ethics Standards Board for Accountants (IESBA) is a standard-setting body within the International Federation of Accountants (IFAC) that issues ethical standards for accountants throughout the world. This group has issued the *Code of Ethics for Professional Accountants,* which is similar to the *Code of Professional Conduct* issued by the AICPA for accountants in the US. The IESBA code is similar to the AICPA code, and has three parts.

- Part A—Framework applies to all professional accountants
- Part B—Applies to professional accountants in public practice
- Part C—Applies to professional accountants in business

Part A—Framework

Section 110—Integrity. Professional accountants should be straightforward and honest in all professional and business relationships. Integrity implies fair dealing and truthfulness. The accountant should not be associated with reports or other communications where the accountant believes the information contains a materially false or misleading statement, contains statements or information furnished recklessly, or omits or obscures information required to be included where such omission or obscurity would be misleading.

Section 120—Objectivity. Professional accountants should not compromise their professional or business judgment.

Section 130—Professional competence and due care. Professional accountants should maintain professional knowledge and skill at the level required to ensure that clients or employers receive competent professional service, and to act diligently in accordance with applicable technical and professional standards.

Section 140—Confidentiality. Professional accountants should refrain from disclosing confidential information unless there is a legal or professional obligation to do so, and using confidential information for personal advantage.

Section 150—Professional behavior. Professional accountants should comply with laws and regulations and avoid actions that would discredit the profession. In marketing services the professional accountant shall be honest and truthful.

Part B—Accountants in Public Practice

Section 200—Professional accountants in public practice. This section of the code begins with a framework that presents threats to ethical behavior and safeguards to help mitigate these threats.

Section 210—Professional appointment. Before accepting a new client, a professional accountant should determine whether acceptance would create any threats to compliance with fundamental principles.

Section 220—Conflicts of interest. A professional accountant should take reasonable steps to indentify circumstances that could pose a conflict of interest.

Section 230—Second opinions. When asked to provide a second opinion on applicable accounting, auditing, reporting or other standards to specific circumstances or transactions, a professional accountant should evaluate the significance of threats and apply necessary safeguards.

Section 240—Fees and other types of remuneration. Commissions, referral fees, fees that are not adequate, and contingent fees may create threats to compliance with professional standards. Therefore, the professional accountant should make sure that necessary safeguards are in effect around fee determination.

Section 250—Marketing professional services. Solicitation of new work through advertising or other forms of marketing may create a threat to compliance with fundamental principles. The accountant in public practice should not bring the profession in disrepute when marketing professional services. Assertions in marketing should be honest and truthful.

Section 260—Gifts and hospitality. Gifts and hospitality from a client may create a threat to independence. The accountant must evaluate the significance of the threat and apply necessary safeguards.

Section 270—Custody of client assets. A professional accountant in public practice shall not assume custody of client monies or other assets unless permitted by law.

Section 280—Objectivity—All services. A professional accountant shall determine when providing professional services whether there are threats to objectivity. If so, the accountant should apply necessary safeguards.

Section 290—Independence—Audit and review engagements. The international ethics rules regarding independence in audit and review engagements are similar to the AICPA rules. Both require the concepts of independence in mind and in appearance. However, the international ethics rules have fewer definitive prohibitions. Instead, the international standards rely on the conceptual framework approach of

1. Identify threats to independence;
2. Evaluate the significance of the threats identified; and
3. Apply safeguards, when necessary, to eliminate the threats or reduce them to an acceptable level.

When evaluating whether to accept or continue a particular engagement, or to assign a particular individual to the engagement team, the firm should identify any threats to independence. If the threats are not at an acceptable level, the firm should consider whether applying appropriate safeguards will reduce them to an acceptable level. If not, the firm should not accept or continue the engagement, or not assign the particular individual to the engagement team. The firm should document these considerations and the conclusion. Threats to independence arise from self interest, self review, advocacy, familiarity, or intimidation. Like the AICPA Code of Professional Conduct, the international ethics rules indicate these types of threats can arise from

- Financial interests in the client;
- Having certain business relationships with the client;
- Serving as a director, officer, or employee of the client; and
- Performing certain nonassurance services to the client.

Safeguards are of two categories: (1) those created by the profession, legislation, or regulation, and (2) those implemented by the firm in the work environment. An example of a safeguard in the first category is legislation that prohibits the performance of certain nonassurance services for audit clients. As an example in the second category, the audit firm may decide not to assign a particular individual to an audit engagement to mitigate a threat to independence.

Section 291—Independence for other assurance services. These requirements are similar to those established by the AICPA in the US They relate to maintaining independence from the parties making the assertion on which the accountant is providing assurance.

Part C—Professional Accountants in Business

The rules that apply to professional accountants in business relate to the following areas:

- Potential conflicts
- Preparation and reporting on information
- Acting with sufficient expertise
- Financial interests
- Inducements

Independence Standards of the Governmental Accountability Office (GAO)

The GAO has separate independence standards for audits performed in accordance with generally accepted government auditing standards (GAGAS). Overall the standards state

In all matters relating to the audit work, the audit organization and the individual auditor, whether government or public, must be free from personal, external, and organizational impairments to independence, and must avoid the appearance of such impairments of independence.

Impairments of independence are personal, external, and organizational.

1. Personal impairments result from relationships or beliefs that might bias the auditors in performing the audit work. Examples include

    a. Immediate family or close family member who is director or officer of the audited entity, or is an employee in a position to exert direct and significant influence over the entity or the program under audit.

    b. Financial interest that is direct, or is significant/material though indirect, in the audit entity or program.

    c. Responsibility for managing an entity or making decisions that could affect operations of the entity or program being audited (e.g., serving as a director, officer, or other senior position of the entity).

    d. Auditing an entity and program for which the auditors (1) maintained accounting records, (2) authorized, executed or consummated transactions, or (3) maintained bank accounts.

    e. Preconceived ideas toward individuals, groups, organizations, or objectives of a particular program that could bias the audit.

    f. Biases, including political, ideological, or social convictions.

    g. Seeking employment during the conduct of the audit with the organization being audited.

    Audit firms should have policies and procedures to identify such impairments and resolve them on a timely basis.

2. External impairments, which occur when auditors are deterred from acting objectively or performing an effective audit. Examples include external interference resulting from unreasonable restrictions on time for completion of the audit, restrictions on access to records, threats to replace the auditor, unreasonable pressure to reduce audit time to reduce audit costs.

3. Organizational impairments result from reporting responsibilities or other functions that the auditors perform that may affect their independence or performance of an effective audit. For external auditors such impairments may result from performing nonaudit services. Audit organizations that perform such services must evaluate whether providing the services creates impairment either in fact or appearance. The overreaching principles in making this evaluation are

    a. Auditors must not perform nonaudit services that involve performing management functions or making management decisions, and

    b. Auditors must not audit their own work or provide nonaudit services in situations in which the nonaudit services are significant or material to the subject matter of the audit.

Department of Labor Independence Requirements

Employee benefit plans must be audited in accordance with the Employee Retirement Security Act of 1974 (ERISA), as enforced by the Department of Labor (DOL). For purposes of auditing these plans, the DOL has issued guidelines to determine whether the accountant is independent.

An accountant is not independent with respect to the plan if

1. During the period of professional engagement, at the date of the opinion, or during the period covered by the financial statements, the accountant or his or her firm or a member thereof

    a. Had, or was committed to acquire, any direct financial interest or any material indirect financial interest in the plan or plan sponsor;

    b. Was connected as a promoter, underwriter, investment advisor, voting trustee, director, officer, or employee of the plan or plan sponsor except that a firm will not be deemed not independent if a former officer or employee of the plan or plan sponsor is employed by the firm and such individual has completely disassociated himself or herself from the plan or plan sponsor and does not participate in auditing financial statements of the plan covering any period of his or her employment by the plan or plan sponsor.

2. An accountant or a member of an accounting firm maintains financial records for the employee benefit plan.

However, an accountant may permissibly engage in or have members of his or her firm engage in certain activities that will not have the effect of removing recognition of independence. For example, an accountant will not fail to be recognized as independent if

1. At or during the period of his or her professional engagement the accountant or his or her firm is retained or engaged on a professional basis by the plan sponsor. However, the accountant must not violate the prohibitions in 1. and 2. preceding.
2. The rendering of services by an actuary associated with the accountant or his or her firm shall not impair the accountant's or the firm's independence.

International Auditing and Assurance Standards

International auditing standards are developed by the **International Auditing and Assurance Standards Board (IAASB)** of the **International Federation of Accountants (IFAC),** a worldwide organization of approximately 160 national accounting bodies (e.g., the AICPA). IFAC was established to help foster a coordinated worldwide accounting profession with harmonized standards. Its boards also establish ethical and quality control standards for accounting professionals and accounting firms. International auditing standards are issued as a series of statements referred to as *International Standards on Auditing.*

The pronouncements of the IAASB do not override the auditing standards of its members. Rather they are meant to help develop consistent worldwide professional standards. Members from countries that do not have their own standards may adopt IAASB standards as their own; members from countries that already have standards are encouraged to compare them to IAASB standards and to seek to eliminate any material inconsistencies. The following represent areas which a report commissioned by the European Commission (the executive organization of the European Union) suggests there are substantive differences between international and US PCAOB auditing standards:

1. International standards do not require an audit of internal control, while PCAOB standards do so require.
2. International standards do not allow reference to another audit firm involved in a portion of the audit, while PCAOB standards allow the principal auditor to so report (i.e., percentages or dollars audited by the other auditor are reported and the opinion is based in part upon the report of the other auditor).
3. International standards for documentation are less detailed than PCAOB standards, leaving more to professional judgment.
4. International standards in the area of going concern include a time horizon of at least, but not limited to twelve months, while PCAOB standards limit the foreseeable future for a going concern consideration to up to twelve months.
5. International standards are based on a risk assessment approach (obtaining a broad understanding of an entity and its environment in order to identify where there may be risks of material misstatements), while the PCAOB standards currently are not. This difference will soon disappear as the PCAOB is in the process of adopting such standards (as has the AICPA Auditing Standards Board).

Additional differences not included in the above report as substantive differences include

Topic	International	US Standards (both AIPCA and PCAOB)
Confirmation of accounts receivable.	Not required. In making a determination on whether to confirm, the auditor should consider the assessed risk of material misstatement at the assertion level and how the audit evidence from other planned audit procedures will reduce the risk of material misstatement at the assertion level to an acceptably low level.	Confirmation is presumptively required unless accounts receivable are immaterial, the use of confirmations would be ineffective, or the combined assessed level of inherent and control risk is low.
Fraud.	Auditors should obtain a written representation from management that it has disclosed to the auditor the results of its assessment of the risk of fraud.	Not required. However, various representations on fraud are obtained (management's knowledge of its responsibility, management's knowledge of fraud, allegations of fraud).
Illegal acts.	The auditor's concern is with whether laws and regulations may materially affect the financial statements. No explicit distinction is made between direct and indirect effect illegal acts.	The audit obtains reasonable assurance of detection of illegal acts that have a direct and material effect on financial statement amounts; if evidence about possible illegal acts with an indirect effect comes to the auditor's attention it is considered.

Topic	International	US Standards (both AIPCA and PCAOB)
Sending letter of audit inquiry to lawyers.	Only required when an auditor "assesses a risk of material misstatement."	Presumptively required.
Reviewing predecessor auditor's working papers for evidence on beginning balances.	The standard states that this may provide sufficient appropriate audit evidence on opening balances.	This statement is not included in standards.
Audit report modification for consistency related to changes in accounting principles.	Not required.	Audit reports are modified for changes with a material effect on the financial statements.
Inclusion of an emphasis of a matter paragraph in an audit report.	Preferably after the opinion paragraph.	No such statement (may be before or after opinion paragraph).
Providing location the auditor practices in an audit report.	Required.	Not required.
Dating the audit report for a subsequent event.	When management amends financial statements for a subsequent event, the auditor should perform necessary procedures and change the date of the audit report to no earlier than the date the financial statements were accepted as amended.	Auditors may "dual date" report (see Section A.2. of Reporting Module).

Switching from auditing standards to accounting standards, you should know that the International Financial Reporting Standards (IFRS) are developed by the International Accounting Standards Board (IASB). These standards represent an alternative financial reporting framework to United States GAAP. When a client follows IFRS it has an effect on the audit process because of the differences between IFRS and US GAAP. Apart from some specific differences in rules, IFRS are considered to be more principle-based than US GAAP. Therefore, IFRS generally require the application of more judgment.

QUESTIONS ON THE NEW AUDITING AND ATTESTATION MATERIAL

1.   In relation to the AICPA Code of Professional Conduct, the IFAC *Code of Ethics for Professional Accountants*
   a. Has more outright prohibitions.
   b. Has fewer outright prohibitions.
   c. Has no outright prohibitions.
   d. Applies only to professional accountants in business.

2.   Based on the IFAC *Code of Ethics for Professional Accountants,* threats to independence arise from all of the following except:
   a. Self interest.
   b. Advocacy.
   c. The audit relationship.
   d. Intimidation.

3.   If an audit firm discovers threats to independence with respect to an audit engagement, the IFAC *Code of Ethics for Professional Accountants* indicates that the firm should
   a. Immediately resign from the engagement.
   b. Notify the appropriate regulatory body.
   c. Document the issue.
   d. Evaluate the significance of the threats and apply appropriate safeguards to reduce them to an acceptable level.

4.   With respect to the acceptance of contingent fees for professional services, the IFAC *Code of Ethics for Professional Accountants* indicates that the accounting firm
   a. Should not accept contingent fees.
   b. Should establish appropriate safeguards around acceptance of a contingent fee.
   c. Should accept contingent fees only for assurance services other than audits of financial statements.
   d. Should accept contingent fees if it is customary in the country.

5.   With regard to marketing professional services, the IFAC *Code of Ethics for Professional Accountants* indicates that
   a. Direct marketing is prohibited.
   b. Marketing is allowed if lawful.
   c. Marketing should be honest and truthful.
   d. Marketing of audit services is prohibited.

6.   Independence standards of the GAO for audits in accordance with generally accepted government auditing standards describe three types of impairments of independence. Which of the following is not one of these types of impairments?
   a. Personal.
   b. Organizational.
   c. External.
   d. Unusual.

7.   In accordance with the independence standards of the GAO for performing audits in accordance with generally accepted government auditing standards, which of the following is not an example of an external impairment of independence?
   a. Reducing the extent of audit work due to pressure from management to reduce audit fees.
   b. Selecting audit items based on the wishes of an employee of the organization being audited.
   c. Bias in the items the auditors decide to select for testing.

   d. Influence by management on the personnel assigned to the audit.

8.   Under the independence standards of the GAO for performing audits in accordance with generally accepted government auditing standards, which of the following are overreaching principles for determining whether a nonaudit service impairs independence?
   I.   Auditors must not perform nonaudit services that involve performing management functions or making management decisions.
   II. Auditors must not audit their own work or provide nonaudit services in situations in which the nonaudit services are significant or material to the subject matter of the audit.
   III. Auditors must not perform nonaudit services which require independence.

   a. I only.
   b. I and II only.
   c. I, II and III.
   d. II and III only.

9.   Which of the following bodies enforce the audit requirements of the Employee Retirement Security Act of 1974 (ERISA) with respect to employee benefit plans?
   a. The Department of Labor.
   b. The Department of Pension Management.
   c. The Securities and Exchange Commission.
   d. The Public Company Accounting Oversight Board.

10. The requirement for independence by the auditor regarding audits of employee benefit plans apply to the plan as well as
   a. Investment companies doing business with the plan.
   b. Members of the plan.
   c. The plan sponsor.
   d. The actuary firm doing services for the plan.

11. What body establishes international auditing standards?
   a. The Public Company Accounting Oversight Board.
   b. The International Federation of Accountants.
   c. The World Bank.
   d. The International Assurance Body.

12. Which of the following is not true about international auditing standards?
   a. International auditing standards do not require an audit of internal control.
   b. International auditing standards do not allow reference to division of responsibilities in the audit report.
   c. International auditing standards require obtaining an attorney's letter.
   d. International auditing standards are based on a risk assessment approach.

13. Which of the following is not true about international auditing standards?
   a. Audit report modification for consistency in the application of accounting principles is required.
   b. Confirmation of accounts receivable is not required.
   c. The location in which the auditor practices must be disclosed in the audit report.
   d. International auditing standards do not require an audit of internal control.

ANSWER EXPLANATIONS FOR THE NEW AUDITING AND ATTESTATION MATERIAL

1. **(b)** The requirement is to identify the characteristic that differs between the two sets of ethical standards. Answer (b) is correct because the IFAC Code has fewer outright prohibitions than the AICPA Code. Answers (a) and (c) are incorrect because the IFAC Code has fewer outright prohibitions. Answer (d) is incorrect because the IFAC Code applies to all professional accountants.

2. **(c)** The requirement is to identify the item that is not a threat to independence. Answer (c) is correct because the audit relationship, in itself, is not a threat to independence. Answers (a), (b), and (d) are incorrect because they all represent types of threats to independence.

3. **(d)** The requirement is to identify the appropriate course of action when threats to independence are discovered. Answer (d) is correct because the firm should evaluate the significance of the threats and apply safeguards, if necessary, to reduce them to an acceptable level. Answer (a) is incorrect because the firm would only resign if appropriate safeguards could not reduce the threats to an acceptable level, or it is required based on a prohibition. Answer (b) is incorrect because the firm would not notify a regulatory body at this point. Answer (c) is incorrect because the firm would document the issue, but only after it is resolved.

4. **(b)** The requirement is to identify what the IFAC *Code of Ethics for Professional Accountants* provides with respect to contingent fees. Answer (b) is correct because the IFAC Code indicates that if the contingent fee presents a threat to apply fundamental principles, the firm should establish appropriate safeguards. Answer (a) is incorrect because a contingent fee may be accepted if threats can be reduced to an acceptable level. Answers (c) and (d) are incorrect because the IFAC Code does not contain these provisions.

5. **(c)** The requirement is to identify the IFAC Code provision regarding marketing. Answer (c) is correct because the IFAC Code indicates the marketing must be honest and truthful. Answers (a) and (d) are incorrect because no particular form of marketing is prohibited. Answer (b) is incorrect because marketing must be honest and truthful as well as legal.

6. **(d)** The requirement is to identify the impairment that is not one of the three types of impairments described in the GAO standards. Answer (d) is correct because an unusual impairment is not one of the types of impairments described in the GAO standards. Answers (a), (b) and (c) are incorrect because they are the three types of impairments described in the GAO standards.

7. **(c)** The requirement is to identify the example that does not represent an external impairment of independence. Answer (c) is correct because this item is an example of a personal impairment of independence. Answers (a), (b) and (d) are incorrect because they are all examples of external impairments of independence.

8. **(b)** The requirement is to identify the overreaching principles for identifying whether nonaudit services impair independence. Answer (b) is correct because I and II are the two principles. Answer (a) is incorrect because II is also an overreaching principle. Answer (c) is incorrect because III is not an overreaching principle. Answer (d) is incorrect because I is an overreaching principle and III is not.

9. **(a)** The requirement is to identify the body that enforces the audit requirements of ERISA. Answer (a) is correct because the Department of Labor is responsible for enforcing the audit requirements. Answer (b) is incorrect because the Department of Pension Management does not exist. Answers (c) and (d) are incorrect because the SEC and the PCAOB deal with auditing requirements for entities with publicly traded securities (issuers).

10. **(c)** The requirement is to identify the party that independence standards also apply to when performing an audit of an employee benefit plan. Answer (c) is correct because the Department of Labor rules also apply to independence from the plan and the plan sponsor. Answers (a), (b) and (d) are incorrect because the independence standards do not apply to these parties.

11. **(b)** The requirement is to identify the body that establishes international auditing standards. Answer (b) is correct because the International Auditing and Assurance Standards Board of the International Federation of Accountants establishes international auditing standards. Answer (a) is incorrect because the Public Company Accounting Oversight Board establishes standards for the audit of public companies in the US. Answers (c) and (d) are incorrect because these bodies do not establish auditing standards.

12. **(c)** The requirement is to identify the item that is not true about international auditing standards. Answer (c) is correct because international auditing standards require obtaining an attorney's letter only if the auditors assess a risk of material misstatement. Answers (a), (b) and (d) are incorrect because they are all true about international auditing standards.

13. **(a)** The requirement is to identify the item that is not true about international auditing standards. Answer (a) is correct because international auditing standards do not require a modification of the audit report for consistency in the application of accounting principles. Answers (b), (c), and (d) are incorrect because they are true about international auditing standards.

EXAMPLES OF THE NEW TASK-BASED SIMULATIONS— AUDITING AND ATTESTATION

The simulations in the Auditing and Assurance section of this manual will also help you review for the new smaller task-based simulations because many of the new task-based simulations are like single parts of the ones currently used.

Task-Based Simulation 1

Module 1

Green, CPA, is considering audit risk, including fraud risk, at the financial statement level in planning the audit of National Federal Bank (NFB) Company's financial statements for the year ended December 31, 2005. Audit risk at the financial statement level is influenced by the risk of material misstatements, which may be indicated by a combination of factors related to management, the industry, and the entity. In assessing such factors Green has gathered the following information concerning NFB's environment.

Company profile

NFB is a federally insured bank that has been consistently more profitable than the industry average by marketing mortgages on properties in a prosperous rural area, which has experienced considerable growth in recent years. NFB packages its mortgages and sells them to large mortgage investment trusts. Despite recent volatility of interest rates, NFB has been able to continue selling its mortgages as a source of new lendable funds.

NFB's board of directors is controlled by Smith, the majority stockholder, who also acts as the chief executive officer. Management at the bank's branch offices has authority for directing and controlling NFB's operations and is compensated based on branch profitability. The internal auditor reports directly to Harris, a minority shareholder, who also acts as chairman of the board's audit committee.

The accounting department has experienced little turnover in personnel during the five years Green has audited NFB. NFB's formula consistently underestimates the allowance for loan losses, but its controller has always been receptive to Green's suggestions to increase the allowance during each engagement.

Recent developments

During 2005, NFB opened a branch office in a suburban town thirty miles from its principal place of business. Although this branch is not yet profitable due to competition from several well-established regional banks, management believes that the branch will be profitable by 2007.

Also, during 2005, NFB increased the efficiency of its accounting operations by installing a new, sophisticated computer system.

Assume you are preparing for the audit personnel discussion of potential risks of material misstatement due to fraud for the NFB audit. While any matters below might be discussed, indicate by marking the appropriate **four** highest risks based on the information contained in the simulation description and requirements of professional standards.

Risk	*High-risk item*
1. Computer fraud risk	○
2. Risk related to management override of internal control	○
3. Fraud by branch management	○
4. Fraud by accounting personnel	○
5. Misstatement of accounting estimates	○
6. Fraud by loan processing clerks	○
7. Fraud by internal auditors	○
8. The risk of fraudulent misstatement of revenues	○

Task-Based Simulation 2

Module 2

Research

On the Adams audit your firm discovered certain immaterial audit adjustments that the client's management chose not to record. Management has now asked you not to communicate anything regarding these omitted entries to the audit committee— after all, they are immaterial.

1. Which section of the Professional Standards addresses this issue?

    a. AU
    b. PCAOB
    c. AT
    d. AR
    e. ET

    f. BL
    g. CS
    h. QC

2. Enter the exact section number and paragraphs that address communicating these uncorrected misstatements to the audit committee.

Task-Based Simulation 3

Module 3

Items 1 through 7 represent audit objectives for the investments and accounts receivable. To the right of each set of audit objectives is a listing of possible audit procedures for that account. For each audit objective, select the audit procedure that would primarily respond to the objective. Select only one procedure for each audit objective. A procedure may be selected only once, or not at all.

Audit procedures for investments

A. Trace opening balances in the subsidiary ledger to prior year's audit working papers.
B. Determine that employees who are authorized to sell investments do not have access to cash.
C. Examine supporting documents for a sample of investment transactions to verify that prenumbered documents are used.
D. Determine that any impairments in the price of investments have been properly recorded.
E. Verify that transfers from the current to the noncurrent investment portfolio have been properly recorded.
F. Obtain positive confirmations as of the balance sheet date of investments held by independent custodians.
G. Trace investment transactions to minutes of the Board of Directors meetings to determine that transactions were properly authorized.

Audit objectives for investments	(A)	(B)	(C)	(D)	(E)	(F)	(G)
1. Investments are properly described and classified in the financial statements.	○	○	○	○	○	○	○
2. Recorded investments represent investments actually owned at the balance sheet date.	○	○	○	○	○	○	○
3. Trading investments are properly valued at fair market value at the balance sheet date.	○	○	○	○	○	○	○

Audit procedures for accounts receivable

A. Analyze the relationship of accounts receivable and sales and compare it with relationships for preceding periods.
B. Perform sales cutoff tests to obtain assurance that sales transactions and corresponding entries for inventories and cost of goods sold are recorded in the same and proper period.
C. Review the aged trial balance for significant past due accounts.
D. Obtain an understanding of the business purpose of transactions that resulted in accounts receivable balances.
E. Review loan agreements for indications of whether accounts receivable have been factored or pledged.
F. Review the accounts receivable trial balance for amounts due from officers and employees.
G. Analyze unusual relationships between monthly accounts receivable balances and monthly accounts payable balances.

Audit objectives for accounts receivable	(A)	(B)	(C)	(D)	(E)	(F)	(G)
4. Accounts receivable represent all amounts owed to the entity at the balance sheet date.	○	○	○	○	○	○	○
5. The entity has legal right to all accounts receivable at the balance sheet date.	○	○	○	○	○	○	○
6. Accounts receivable are stated at net realizable value.	○	○	○	○	○	○	○
7. Accounts receivable are properly described and presented in the financial statements.	○	○	○	○	○	○	○

Solution to Task-Based Simulation 1

	Risk	*High-risk item*
1.	Computer fraud risk	○
2.	Risk related to management override of internal control	●
3.	Fraud by branch management	●
4.	Fraud by accounting personnel	○
5.	Misstatement of accounting estimates	●
6.	Fraud by loan processing clerks	○
7.	Fraud by internal auditors	○
8.	The risk of fraudulent misstatement of revenues	●

Solution to Task-Based Simulation 2

1. a

2.

AU	380	40-41

Solution to Task-Based Simulation 3

1. **(E)** The verification of transfers from the current to the noncurrent investment portfolio will provide assurance that the investments are properly classified in the financial statements.

2. **(F)** Positive confirmation replies as of the balance sheet date for investments held by independent custodians will provide assurance that the recorded investments are in fact owned by the audit client.

3. **(D)** Because trading investments should be valued at fair market value, determining whether any impairments in the price of investments have been recorded will provide assurance that investments are properly valued.

4. **(B)** Performance of sales cutoff tests will provide assurance that sales transactions and the related receivables are recorded in the proper period. Thus, sales cutoff tests will provide assurance that all amounts owed to the entity at the balance sheet date are recorded in that period.

5. **(E)** A review of loan agreements, paying special attention to accounts receivable that have been factored, will provide assurance as to whether the entity has a legal right to all accounts receivable at the balance sheet date.

6. **(C)** An analysis of the aged trial balance for significant past due accounts will provide evidence with respect to accounts that may be uncollectible. Accordingly, the procedure will address the net realizable value of accounts receivable.

7. **(F)** Because material amounts due from officers and employees should be segregated from other receivables, a review of the trial balance for amounts due from officers and employees will provide assurance that accounts receivable are properly described and presented in the financial statements.

FINANCIAL ACCOUNTING AND REPORTING SECTION

The Content and Skills Specifications for the Financial and Reporting section of the CPA exam are similar to the current content specifications, with the following exceptions:

1. International financial reporting standards are now included in the specifications. This material is summarized in this appendix.
2. SEC reporting requirements are now included in the specifications. This material is summarized in this appendix.

NEW MATERIAL—FINANCIAL ACCOUNTING AND REPORTING SECTION

International Financial Reporting Standards (IFRS)

A. Introduction

The International Accounting Standards Committee (IASC) issued International Accounting Standards (IAS) from 1973 to 2001. In addition, the IASC created a Standing Interpretations Committee (SIC) that provided further interpretive guidance on accounting issues not addressed in the standards. In 2001, the International Accounting Standards Board (IASB) replaced the IASC. The IASB adopted the existing International Accounting Standards (IAS) and interpretations issued by the Standing Interpretations Committee (SIC). Since 2001, the IASB is responsible for issuing International Financial Reporting Standards (IFRS), and the International Financial Reporting Interpretations Committee (IFRIC) is responsible for issuing interpretations of the standards. Therefore, the current international accounting guidelines are contained in the IAS and IFRS pronouncements, together with SIC and IFRIC interpretations.

It is often said that US GAAP employs a "rules" based approach. In other words, the standards are usually explicit as to precise rules that must be followed for recognition, measurement, and financial statement presentation. IFRS, on the other hand, is considered a "principles" based approach because it attempts to set general principles for recognition, measurement and reporting, and allows professional judgment in applying these principles. This principles-based approach should focus on a true and fair view or a fair representation of the financial information.

In 2002, the FASB and the IASB agreed to work toward convergence in the accounting standards. Therefore, you will find some IFRS accounting treatments identical, some similar, and others different from US GAAP. An effective study strategy is to study US GAAP and then learn the significant differences between US GAAP and IFRS. This compare/contrast strategy will help the candidate to remember which method is US GAAP and which method is IFRS. As you study this module, notice the differences in the following areas:

1. **Vocabulary or definition differences.** Although the concepts of US GAAP and IFRS are similar, vocabulary and definitions are often somewhat different.
2. **Recognition and measurement differences.** Differences may exist in when and how an item is recognized in the financial statements. Alternative methods may be acceptable in US GAAP, whereas only one method may be allowed for IFRS (or vice versa). In some instances, either IFRS or US GAAP may not require an item be recognized in the financial statements. In addition, the amount recognized (measurement of the item) may be different in the two sets of standards.
3. **Presentation and disclosure differences.** Presentation refers to the presentation of items on the financial statements, whereas disclosure refers to the additional information contained in the notes to financial statements. Again, differences exist as to whether an item must be presented in the financial statements or disclosed in the footnotes, as well as the types of information that must be disclosed.

The table below highlights the major accounting differences between US GAAP and IFRS.

Major Differences—IFRS versus US GAAP

US GAAP	*IFRS*
Financial Statement Presentation	
No specific requirement regarding comparative information.	Requires comparative information for prior year.
Comprehensive income may be presented within the statement of changes in shareholders' equity and changes in equity may be presented in the notes.	Requires a separate statement of comprehensive income and statement of changes in equity.
Presentation of certain items as extraordinary is required.	Extraordinary items are not allowed.
Revenue Recognition	
Construction contracts are accounted for using the percentage-of-completion method if certain criteria are met. Otherwise the completed contract method is used.	Construction contracts are accounted for using the percentage-of-completion method if certain criteria are met. Otherwise, revenue recognition is limited to the costs incurred. The completed contract method is not allowed.
Consolidated Financial Statements	
No exemption from consolidating subsidiaries in general purpose financial statements.	Under certain restrictive situations a subsidiary (normally required to be consolidated) may be exempt from the requirement.
Noncontrolling interest measured at fair value.	Noncontrolling interest may be measured either at fair value or the proportionate share of the value of the identifiable assets and liabilities of the acquiree.
Monetary Current Assets and Current Liabilities	
Short-term obligations expected to be refinanced can be classified as noncurrent if the entity has the intent and ability to refinance.	Short-term obligations expected to be refinanced can be classified as noncurrent only if the entity has entered into an agreement to refinance prior to the balance sheet date.
Contingencies that are probable and can be reasonably estimated are accrued.	Contingencies that are probable and measurable are considered provisions and accrued.
Inventory	
LIFO cost flow assumption is an acceptable method.	The LIFO cost flow assumption is not allowed.
Inventories are valued at lower of cost of market (between a floor and a ceiling).	Inventories are valued at lower of cost or net realizable value.
Any impairment write-downs create a new cost basis; previously recognized impairment losses are not reversed.	Previously recognized impairment losses are reversed.
Fixed Assets	
Revaluation not permitted.	Revaluation of assets is permitted as an election for an entire class of assets but must be done consistently.
No separate accounting for investment property.	Separate accounting is prescribed for investment property versus property, plant and equipment.
Unless the assets are "held for sale" they are valued using the cost model.	Investment property may be measured at fair value.
Biological assets are not a separate category.	Biological assets are a separate category and not included in property, plant and equipment.
There is no requirement to account for separate components of an asset.	If the major components of an asset have significantly different patterns of consumption or economic benefits, the entity must allocate the costs to the major components and depreciate them separately.
Impairment losses are not reversed.	Impairment losses may be reversed in future periods.
Financial Investments	
Compound (hybrid) financial instruments are not split into debt and equity components unless certain requirements are met but they may be bifurcated into debt and derivative components.	Compound financial interests (e.g., convertible bonds) are split into debt, equity and, if applicable, derivative components.
Declines in fair value below cost may result in impairment loss solely based on a change in interest rate unless entity has the ability and intent to hold the debt till maturity.	Generally, only evidence of a credit default results in impairment loss for an Available-for-Sale debt instrument.
When impairment is recognized through the income statement, a new cost basis is established and such losses cannot be reversed.	Impairment losses in Available-for-Sale investments may be reversed in future periods.
Unless the fair value option is elected, loans and receivables are classified as either (1) held for investment, which is measured at amortized cost, or (2) held for sale, which is measured at lower of cost or fair value.	Loans and receivables are measured at amortized cost unless classified into the Fair Value Through Profit or Loss category or the Available-for-Sale category, both of which are carried at fair value.

Leases

Operating leased assets are never recorded on the balance sheet.

Assets held by lessee under operating leases may be capitalized on the balance sheet if they meet certain requirements.

A lease for land and building that transfers ownership to the lessee or contains a bargain purchase option would be classified as a capital lease regardless of the relative value of the land. If the fair value of the land at inception represents 25% or more of the total fair value, the lessee must consider the components separately when evaluating the lease.

When land and buildings are leased, elements of the lease are considered separately when evaluating the lease unless the amount for the land element is immaterial.

Income Taxes

Deferred tax assets are recognized in full but valuation allowances reduce them to the amount that is more likely than not to be realized.

Deferred tax assets are recognized only to the extent it is probable that they will be realized.

B. Basic Concepts

The *IASB Framework for the Preparation and Presentation of Financial Statements* establishes the underlying concepts for preparing financial statements. This framework addresses the objectives of financial statements, underlying assumptions, qualitative characteristics of financial statement information, definitions, recognition, measurement, and capital maintenance concepts.

Although the IASB *Framework* contains information similar to the Statement of Financial Accounting Concepts by the US Financial Accounting Standards Board (FASB), several important differences exist. First, some terms and definitions are different. Second, the elements of financial statements are not identical. Third, the qualitative characteristics have several differences. Candidates should become familiar with these subtle differences in the two sets of concepts.

The IASB *Framework* is not considered an accounting standard and therefore does not override any accounting treatment required by the International Accounting Standards (IAS) or International Financial Reporting Standards (IFRS). The *Framework* exists to assist in the development of future international accounting standards and to assist preparers in accounting for topics that do not have guidance in an existing standard.

According to the IASB *Framework*, the objective of financial statements is to provide information about the financial position, performance, and changes in financial position of an entity that is useful to a wide range of users. Users of financial information include investors, employees, lenders, suppliers, creditors, customers, governments, and the public. The underlying assumptions in financial statements are that they are prepared using the accrual basis of accounting and that the entity is a going concern.

The *Framework* sets forth the following qualitative characteristics of financial statements:

1. Understandability
2. Relevance
3. Reliability
4. Comparability

Understandability. The concept of understandability requires that the information provided is readily understandable to users.

Relevance. Information has relevance when it can influence the user's economic decisions by helping them evaluate past, present, or future events. Relevance has certain attributes such as predictive value and a confirmatory role. (Note the change in vocabulary here: in US GAAP, relevance has predictive value and feedback value.) In addition, IFRS includes materiality under the characteristic of relevance. Relevance is affected by the nature and materiality of the information. Information is considered material if its omission or misstatement could make a difference in a user's decision.

Reliability. Information is reliable if it is free from material error and bias, and it faithfully represents what it purports to represent. The attributes for reliability include faithful representation, substance over form, neutrality, prudence, and completeness. Substance over form indicates that transactions and events should be accounted for and presented in accordance with their substance and economic reality and not merely the legal form. Neutrality means that the information should be free from bias and that the information should not influence the user as to a predetermined result or outcome. Prudence is the inclusion of caution in exercising judgments needed to make estimates when there is uncertainty. Prudence requires that if judgment is used, assets or income should not be overstated, and liabilities or expenses should not be understated. Prudence also requires that excessive provisions or reserves should not be used because in such cases, the financial statements would not be neutral. Completeness refers to not omitting information, because an omission would lead to false or misleading financial statements.

Comparability. The concept of comparability refers to the need for users to be able to compare financial statements of different entities to evaluate their financial position and performance. Comparability requires accounting policies to be disclosed, and financial statements have corresponding information for preceding periods (consistency).

The two constraints for relevant and reliable information are timeliness and the need to balance between cost and benefit. If information is not timely, it can lose relevance. The constraint of cost versus benefit provides that the benefits derived from the information should exceed the cost of providing it.

The most important distinctions in qualitative characteristics between the IASB *Framework* and FASB Concept Statements are the hierarchy of the characteristics and the terms used to describe them. Recall in the FASB Concept Statements the primary decision qualities were relevance and reliability. Relevance relied on predictive value, feedback value, and timeliness. With the IASB *Framework*, relevance relies on predictive and confirmatory value, as well as materiality. Under the FASB Concept Statements, reliability focused on verifiability, neutrality, and representational faithfulness. Under the IASB *Framework*, reliability focuses on faithful representation, substance over form, neutrality, prudence, and completeness. Finally, with the FASB Concept Statements, relevance and reliability were both impacted by comparability and consistency. With the IASB *Framework*, comparability focuses on identifying the accounting policies used and using the same policies in preceding periods. Although the term consistency is not overtly used in the IASB *Framework*, the concept of consistency is outlined under the heading "comparability."

Below is a chart to outline the subtle differences in the FASB Concept Statements and the IASB *Framework*:

FASB Conceptual Framework	IASB *Framework*
Understandability	**Understandability**
Decision usefulness	--

Relevance:
    Predictive value
    Feedback value
    Timeliness
	Relevance:
	    Predictive value
	    Confirmatory value
	    Materiality

Reliability:
    Verifiability
    Neutrality
    Representational faithfulness
	Reliability:
	    Faithful representation
	    Substance over form
	    Neutrality
	    Prudence
	    Completeness

Comparability
    Including Consistency
	Comparability
	    Corresponding information in previous periods

Constraints:
    Benefits > Cost
	Constraints:
	    Timeliness
	    Benefits > Cost
	    Balance between qualitative characteristics

Another difference between IFRS and US GAAP relates to the elements of financial statements. FASB SFAC 6 contains ten elements of financial statements: assets, liabilities, equity, investments by owners, distributions by owners, comprehensive income, revenues, expenses, gains, and losses. The IASB *Framework* contains only five elements: assets, liabilities, equity, income, and expense. Notice there are several significant vocabulary differences regarding the elements of financial statements. With US GAAP, the term "income" is not a financial statement element. In US GAAP, the term income is used to describe a calculation of some type (e.g., income from continuing operations, net income) or to designate a specific type of income such as interest income. However, with IFRS, the term income is a financial statement element, and the items that are considered "income" are revenues and gains. IFRS uses the term "profit" whereas US GAAP uses the term "net income."

The IASB *Framework*'s formal definitions of the five elements are shown below.

IASB *Framework*—Elements of Financial Statements

Asset	An asset is a resource controlled by the entity as a result of past events and from which future economic benefits are expected to flow to the entity.
Liability	A liability is a present obligation of the entity arising from past events, the settlement of which is expected to result in an outflow from the entity of resources embodying economic benefits.
Equity	Equity is the residual interest in the assets of the entity after deducting all its liabilities.
Income	Income is increases in economic benefits during the accounting period in the form of inflows or enhancements of assets or decreases of liabilities that result in increases in equity, other than those relating to contributions from equity participants.
Expenses	Expenses are decreases in economic benefits during the accounting period in the form of outflows or depletions of assets or incurrence of liabilities that result in decreases in equity, other than those relating to distributions to equity participants.

An important point to understand is that the definition of income includes both revenue and gains. Revenues arise in the normal course of business and are often referred to as sales, fees, interest, dividends, royalties and rent. Gains are other items that meet the definition of income, which may or may not arise in the normal course of business. The IASB *Framework* indicates that gains are increases in economic benefits and are no different in nature from revenues. Therefore, they are not regarded as a separate element in the *Framework*. The *Framework* treats losses in the same way, as no different in nature from other expenses. However, the *Framework* also indicates that when gains or losses are reported in the income statement, they are usually displayed separately because this knowledge may be useful to the decision maker. Gains may be reported net of their related expenses, and losses may be reported net of their related income.

The IASB *Framework* provides for capital maintenance adjustments. When assets or liabilities are revalued or restated, and there is a corresponding increase or decrease to equity, the definition of income or expense may not be met. Therefore, certain items may be included in equity as revaluation reserves.

The IASB *Framework* defines recognition as the process of incorporating into the balance sheet or income statement an item that meets the definition of an element and satisfies the criteria for recognition. The two criteria for recognition are (1) it is probable that a future economic benefit will flow to the entity, and (2) the item has a cost or value that can be measured reliably.

The *Framework* also outlines various bases of measurement such as historical cost, current cost, realizable (settlement) value, and present value. Current cost is the amount of cash or cash equivalent that would be paid if the same or equivalent asset was acquired currently. Realizable (settlement) value is the amount of cash that could be currently obtained by settling (e.g., selling) the asset in an orderly disposal. Although the measurement basis is commonly historical cost, certain accounts use different measurement methods.

1. Revenue Recognition

As indicated above, revenue is the gross inflow of economic benefits resulting from an entity's ordinary activities. These inflows must increase equity and not increase the contribution of owners or equity participants. Revenue is generated from the sale of goods, the rendering of services, and the use of an entity's assets by others. Various titles are used for revenue including sales, fees, interest, dividends, and royalties. Revenue is measured at the fair value of the consideration received or the receivable, net of trade discounts or rebates.

Revenue is recognized from the sale of goods if all five of the following criteria are met:

1. The significant risks and rewards of ownership of the goods are transferred to the buyer,
2. The entity does not retain either a continuing managerial involvement or control over the goods,
3. The amount of revenue can be measured reliably,
4. It is probable that economic benefits will flow to the entity from the transaction, and
5. The costs incurred can be measured reliably.

Revenue can be recognized from rendering services when the outcome of rendering services can be estimated reliably. This method is often referred to as the percentage-of-completion method. Note that progress payments or advances from customers are not used to determine the state of completion. The outcomes can be estimated reliably if all the following criteria are met:

1. The amount of revenue can be measured reliably,
2. It is probable that economic benefits will flow to the entity,
3. The stage of completion at the end of the reporting period can be measured reliably, and
4. The costs incurred and the costs to complete the transaction can be measured reliably.

If the outcomes cannot be estimated reliably, then revenue should be recognized using the cost recovery method. The cost recovery method recognizes revenue only to the extent that the expenses recognized are recoverable. Note that IFRS does not permit use of the completed contract method, which is allowed for US GAAP.

Barter transactions are not recognized if the exchanged goods are similar in nature and value. If the goods are dissimilar, revenue is recognized at fair value of the goods received. If the fair value of the goods received cannot be measured, revenue is recognized at the fair value of goods or services given up.

Interest income is recognized using the effective interest method. Royalties should be accrued as provided for in the contractual agreement. Dividends should be recognized when the shareholder has a right to receive the dividend payment.

2. **Error Correction**

Accounting for error correction is similar to US GAAP. A prior period error includes arithmetic mistakes, mistakes in applying accounting policies, and mistakes in recognition, measurement, presentation or disclosures in the financial statements. IFRS requires the entity to correct the error by restating the comparative amounts for prior periods. If the error occurred before the earliest period presented, then the opening balances of assets, liabilities, and equity should be restated for the earliest period presented. Similar to US GAAP, if it is impracticable to determine the periodic effects of the error, comparative information is restated from the earliest date practicable.

3. **Accounting Changes**

Change in accounting principle. The rules for accounting changes are also similar to US GAAP. Accounting changes may occur only when a change is required by an IFRS, or there is a voluntary change in accounting methods. In the case of a new IFRS pronouncement, the transition rules in the new IFRS statement should be followed. A voluntary change in accounting method may only be made if it provides reliable and more relevant information about the transactions, entity's financial position, performance, or cash flows. A voluntary change in accounting method is given retrospective application by applying the policy as if the new policy had always been applied. Retrospective application provides that the opening balances of equity is adjusted for the earliest period presented, and that other amounts are disclosed for each prior period as if the new accounting policy had always been applied. If it is impracticable to determine the effects of the change, then the change may be applied on a prospective basis. Disclosures include the title of the IFRS requiring the change, the nature of the change, the amount of the adjustments to each financial statement line item, and effects on earnings per share.

Change in accounting estimate. A change in accounting estimate occurs due to uncertainties in measuring items on the financial statements. Changes in estimates include changes in estimates for bad debts, inventory obsolescence, the fair value of financial assets or liabilities, the useful life of a depreciable asset, or warranty obligations. A change in estimates is accounted for on a prospective basis in the period of the change (current period) and future periods.

4. **Financial Statements**

IAS 1 provides that a complete set of financial statements must be prepared annually. A complete set of financial statements includes a statement of financial position, a statement of comprehensive income, a statement of changes in equity, a statement of cash flows, and notes containing significant accounting policies and explanations. The headings on the financial statements should include the name of the entity, the title of the statement, and the date of the statement. The financial statements should present a "true and fair view" of the company. IFRS must be used unless there is a rare circumstance where the use of IFRS would produce misleading financial statements. Whenever an entity retrospectively applies an accounting policy, retrospectively restates its financial statements, or reclassifies items, three years of statements of financial position are required for comparative purposes. Presentation and classification of items on the financial statements should be consistent for the periods presented.

The accrual basis of accounting is used to prepare the financial statements, with the assumption that the entity is a going concern. Assets and liabilities may not be offset against each other unless specifically permitted by an IFRS. Similarly, income and expenses may not be offset unless specifically permitted. Offsets may be used for valuation purposes, such as contra accounts (allowance for uncollectible accounts or accumulated depreciation). Items on the financial statements should be presented separately for each material class of similar items. If an item is not material, it may be aggregated with other items.

Statement of Financial Position. Assets are classified as current and noncurrent. An asset is current if it is expected to be realized or held for consumption in the normal course of the entity's operating cycle, held primarily for trading purposes, expected to be realized within 12 month of the end of the period, or is cash or a cash equivalent that is not restricted. Noncurrent assets include tangible, intangible, operating, and financial assets that are long-term, such as held-to-maturity investments, investment property, property and equipment, intangible assets, assets held for sale, and miscellaneous assets.

Liabilities are classified as current and noncurrent. A liability is current if it is expected to be settled in the normal course of business during the operating cycle, due to be settled within 12 months, held primarily for trading purposes, or does not have an unconditional right to defer settlement beyond 12 months. However, certain payables such as trade payables and accruals for operating costs are classified as current liabilities regardless of the settlement date.

Interest-bearing liabilities are classified based upon whether they are due within 12 months. However, if an agreement to refinance the liability on a long-term basis is executed prior to the financial statement date, the liability may be classified as noncurrent. Note that this is different from US GAAP, where if there is the intent and ability to refinance before the issuance of the financial statements, reclassification is permitted. An executed agreement prior to the balance sheet is not required. For IFRS, if the agreement to refinance is made after the balance sheet date, then the liability must be classified as current at the balance sheet date. Similar to US GAAP, if a long-term debt becomes callable due to violation of a loan covenant, the liability must be classified as a current liability.

For shareholders' equity the financial statements must disclose the number of shares of common stock authorized, issued, and outstanding. If there are preference shares (e.g., preferred stock), they must be reported separately including the number of shares authorized, issued, and outstanding. Preference shares that are redeemable at the option of the holder must be classified as liabilities. Treasury shares repurchased are stated at cost and shown as a reduction to shareholders' equity. Accumulated other comprehensive income is reported in the shareholders' equity section of the balance sheet, and noncontrolling interests are disclosed as a separate item in the equity section of the balance sheet.

Although IAS 1 does not require a specific format for the statement of financial position, the following categories should be displayed:

1. Property, plant, and equipment
2. Investment property
3. Intangible assets
4. Financial assets
5. Investments accounted for using the equity method
6. Biological assets
7. Inventories
8. Trade and other receivables
9. Cash and cash equivalents
10. The total assets classified as held for sale and assets included in disposal groups classified as held for sale under IFRS 5
11. Trade and other payables
12. Provisions
13. Financial liabilities
14. Liabilities and assets for current tax
15. Deferred tax liabilities and deferred tax assets
16. Liabilities included in disposal groups classified as held for sale
17. Noncontrolling interest
18. Issued capital and reserves attributable to owners of the parent

The Income Statement. IAS 1 requires that at a minimum, the following items should be included on an income statement:

1. Revenue (referred to as income)
2. Finance costs (interest expense)
3. Share of profits and losses of associates and joint ventures accounted for using equity method
4. Tax expense
5. Discontinued operations
6. Profit or loss
7. Noncontrolling interest in profit and loss
8. Net profit (loss) attributable to equity holders in the parent

If an entity acquires less than 100% of a subsidiary, the income statement should indicate the profit or loss attributable to the noncontrolling interest and the owners of the parent.

A significant difference between US GAAP and IFRS is that IFRS does not permit the classification of items as "extraordinary items" on the income statement. Any gains or losses should be reported as income or expense. In addition, operating expenses may be classified either by nature or by function. Classification by nature is based on the character of the expense, such as salaries and wages, raw materials used, interest expense, tax expense, and depreciation of assets. Classification by function is based on the purpose of the expenditure such as manufacturing, distribution, or administration. If the entity classifies expenses by function, cost of sales must be stated separately from other expenses. (Note that in US GAAP, expenses are classified by function, cost of goods sold, operating expenses, etc.). For IFRS, finance costs (interest expense) must be identified separately regardless of which classification scheme is used.

Operating expenses are normally classified as distribution costs (selling expenses) and general and administrative expenses. If an item is material in amount and of such a size, nature, or incidence that disclosure is important to understand the performance of the entity, then the item should be disclosed separately. Examples of those disclosures include write-downs of inventories, write-downs of plant, property, and equipment, restructuring costs, costs of litigation settlements, and reversals of provisions.

The treatment of discontinued operations is similar to US GAAP. If an asset is classified as held for sale or is part of a disposal group, it is valued at the lower of carrying value or fair value less costs to sell. The write-down net of tax is included in discontinued operations in the income statement. For discontinued operations, several calculations are required. First, the revenues, expenses, pretax profit or loss, and the related income tax expense are calculated. Second, the gain or loss on disposal or remeasurement is calculated with the related income tax expense. Finally, the total of these two amounts is determined (net of tax) and must be disclosed on the income statement. The footnote disclosures must include the pretax profit or loss, gain or loss on disposal, and tax effects, as well as the net cash flows from operating, investing, and financing activities.

Statement of Comprehensive Income. The statement of comprehensive income may be presented in either one statement or in two statements. The two-statement approach presents a separate income statement, and then presents a second statement, which begins with profit or loss and displays the components of comprehensive income. Items that are included in comprehensive income are changes in revaluation surplus for plant, property, and equipment, actuarial gains and losses on defined benefit plans, gains and losses from foreign currency translations, gains and losses on remeasuring available-for-sale financial assets, and the effective portion of gains and losses on hedging instruments in a cash flow hedge. Each component of comprehensive income should be stated separately on the statement of comprehensive income.

Statement of Cash Flows. The accounting rules for the Statement of Cash Flows are similar to US GAAP. For IFRS, cash flows include the inflows and outflows of both cash and cash equivalents. Cash equivalents include cash on hand, bank balances for immediate use, other demand deposits, and short-term investments with maturities of three months or less. Both the direct method and indirect method are acceptable methods for preparing the statement of cash flows. However, for the indirect method, operating activities may be presented using a modified approach. This modified indirect method shows revenues and expenses in operating activities, and then reports the changes in working capital accounts.

As in US GAAP, the statement of cash flows is divided into three parts: operating, investing, and financing activities. At the bottom of the statement of cash flows, a reconciliation must be made with the amounts in the statement of cash flows and the cash and cash equivalents reported in the statement of financial position.

The most significant difference between IFRS and US GAAP is where certain items are presented on the statement of cash flows. For example, interest and dividends received may be reported on the statement of cash flows as operating or investing activities. Interest and dividends paid may be reported either in the operating activities or the financing activities sections. Although the entity has discretion on where interest and dividends are reported, it must be reported on a consistent basis. Cash from the purchase and sale of trading securities are classified as operating activities. Cash advances and loans (bank overdrafts) are also usually classified as operating activities. Taxes paid on income must be disclosed separately in operating activities. However, cash flows from certain taxes may be classified elsewhere if they are related to investing or financing activities. In addition, the effects of noncash transactions are not reported on the statement of cash flows. Instead, significant noncash activities must be disclosed in the notes to the financial statements.

C. Inventory

IFRS accounting for inventory differs from US GAAP in three areas: cost flow assumption, valuation of inventory at year-end, and capitalization of interest.

With IFRS, the LIFO cost flow assumption is not permissible. Specific ID is required for inventory of goods that are not interchangeable, or goods that are produced and segregated for specific projects. FIFO and weighted-average methods are acceptable methods under IFRS for other types of inventory. The retail method may only be used for certain industries. In addition, the gross profit method can be used to estimate ending inventory when a physical count is not possible. Inventories are carried at the lower of cost or net realizable value (LCNRV). An exception to LCNRV rule applies to agricultural inventories (biological assets) which are carried at fair value less costs to sell at the point of harvest.

Recall that in US GAAP, lower of cost or market (LCM) is used to value inventories. Market is defined as replacement cost, subject to a ceiling and floor. The ceiling is net realizable value (NRV), and the floor is NRV less a less normal profit margin. Once inventory is written down, a loss may not be recovered. Although IFRS uses a similar valuation concept, IFRS values inventory at the lower of cost or net realizable value (LCNRV). Note that the calculations are different from US GAAP. NRV is calculated as estimated selling price less estimated costs of completion and sale. Generally, LCNRV is applied on an item-by-item basis. However, under IFRS if there are groups of items that have similar characteristics, they may be grouped for the application of LCNRV.

Assume the following facts for an inventory:

Historical cost	$100
Estimated selling price	90
Estimated costs to complete and sell	5
NRV	$ 85

To apply LCNRV to our example, you compare the cost of $100 to the estimated selling price less estimated costs to complete and sell ($90 – $5). NRV is $85. Therefore, the LCNRV is $85. The inventory would be written down to $85 with a corresponding expense on the income statement. If the inventory value at the end of Year 2 was $90, a recovery of the loss would be recorded by debiting Inventory and crediting an income account.

Note that if LCM were applied by US standards, additional information would be needed. Specifically, US GAAP would require the replacement cost, and the normal profit margin in order to arrive at the ceiling and the floor.

Rules for capitalization of interest are also different. US GAAP allows no capitalization of interest for inventories that are routinely manufactured or otherwise produced in quantities on a repetitive basis. Similar to US GAAP, IFRS does not allow interest or financing costs to be capitalized as an inventory cost if it is paid under normal credit terms. However, IFRS allows interest costs to be capitalized if there is a lengthy production period to prepare the goods for sale.

D. Fixed Assets

Some of the most significant differences between US GAAP and IFRS exist in the area of accounting for fixed assets. Items which are classified as noncurrent assets under US GAAP may be classified differently under IFRS. Specifically, noncurrent assets must be identified in categories such as plant, property, and equipment, investment property, intangible assets, and biological assets.

1. **Plant, Property, and Equipment**

   Plant, property, and equipment (PPE) are tangible items which are expected to be used during more than one period, and used in the production or supply of goods or services, for rental to others, or for administrative purposes. Plant, property, and equipment are recorded at cost. Cost includes the purchase price net of discounts and rebates, the expenditures to bring the asset to its required location and condition, delivery and handling, site preparation, installation, assembly costs, professional fees, and the estimate of the cost of obligations required for the asset's disposal (decommissioning or site restoration). Similar to US GAAP, costs of self-constructed assets include material, labor, and interest costs.

   After an asset is initially recognized at cost, it is subsequently measured using either the cost model (CM) or the revaluation model (RM). Long-lived assets are divided into classes, and a decision is made for each class on which valuation method is applied. Note that a different valuation model can be used for different classes of assets but not individual assets within a class. Examples of classes of assets include land, equipment, motor vehicles, land and buildings, ships, aircraft, and furniture and fixtures.

   The cost model (CM) provides that the asset is carried at cost less an accumulated depreciation and less any accumulated impairment loss. The depreciation method chosen should reflect the pattern of economic benefits expected to be consumed. The straight-line, declining balance, and units of production methods are acceptable depreciation methods. A change in depreciation method is considered a change in accounting estimate and is accounted for on a prospective basis.

   Under the revaluation model (RM), the carrying amount of the asset is the fair value at the date of revaluation less any subsequent accumulated depreciation and subsequent accumulated impairment loss. The revaluation model (RM) should be applied to assets whose value can be reliably measured. There is no rule regarding the frequency or date of revaluation; therefore, annual revaluations are not required. However, when revaluation is performed it must be performed for the entire class of assets. Revaluation to fair value usually involves obtaining appraisals. When a class of assets is revalued, the asset account is written up or down, and the adjustment is recorded to the revaluation surplus account which is reported in other comprehensive income for the period. If the revaluation model is used, accumulated depreciation can be adjusted proportionately, or the accumulated depreciation account can be eliminated and the asset shown net. When an asset is disposed of, a gain or loss is recognized and reported on the income statement. Any balance in the revaluation surplus account is transferred directly to retained earnings (not to profit or loss).

2. **Investment Property**

   Investment property is defined as property held to earn rentals, for capital appreciation, or both. To qualify as investment property, it may not be used in the production or supply of goods or services or for administrative purposes, nor can it be held for sale in the ordinary course of business. Investment property includes land or a building and can be held by the owner or by a lessee under a financing lease. Examples of investment property also include land held for long-term appreciation, land held for an undetermined future use, buildings owned by the entity, or a vacant building held to be leased under an operating lease.

   Investment property is recognized when it is probable that the future economic benefits of the property will flow to the entity and the cost of the property can be measured reliably. Investment property is measured at cost. After initial recognition, the investment property is measured under the fair value model (FVM) or the cost model (CM), with certain exceptions.

   The fair value model (FVM) requires investment property to be measured at fair value. Changes in fair value are recognized in profit or loss in the period of the change. Notice that this is different treatment than for plant, property, and equipment, wherein the revaluation is recorded in other comprehensive income. If the fair value model is used, no depreciation is recorded. The fair value is the price at which the property could be exchanged between knowledgeable parties in an arm's-length transaction.

   The cost model (CM) requires investment property to be carried on the balance sheet at cost less accumulated depreciation and less accumulated impairment losses. If an entity chooses the cost model, it must still disclose fair values in the notes to the financial statements.

   Another difference between IFRS and US GAAP involves investment property leased under operating leases. Under IFRS, an entity has the option to record investment property leased under an operating lease as an asset on the balance sheet if the lessee can reliably measure the fair value of the lease. Once this option is selected for one leased property, other investment property must also be accounted for using the fair value model.

Investment property does not include property used in the business, property being constructed or developed for others, property under construction that will be future investment property, and property held for sale in the normal course of business.

3. **Intangible Assets**

Intangible assets either have no physical substance or have a value that is not represented by its physical substance. Intangible assets are categorized as either identifiable or unidentifiable. An asset is identifiable if meets one of the two criteria: (1) it is based on contractual or legal rights, or (2) it can be separated from the entity, and sold, transferred, licensed, rented or exchanged. Notice this is similar to US GAAP where an identifiable intangible must meet the legal, contractual, or separability criteria. Identifiable intangibles include patents, copyrights, brand names, customer lists, trade names, computer software, formulae, licenses, and franchises.

Accounting for intangibles under IFRS depends upon whether the intangible assets were acquired or internally developed. If the intangible assets were acquired, the intangible asset is recorded at cost. If the intangible assets were acquired in a business combination, newly identified intangibles are recognized at fair value separately from goodwill.

Internally generated intangibles must meet the definition of an identifiable asset (i.e. it must have future economic benefits and can be measured reliably). Although internally generated goodwill may provide future economic benefits, it cannot be measured reliably. Therefore, internally generated goodwill is not recognized as an asset. Similarly, expenditures on research may not result in probable future economic benefits; therefore, research expenditures are treated as an expense of the period. Development is the application of research findings for the production of new products or technology. Development costs may be recognized as an intangible asset if the following six criteria are met: (1) technological feasibility of completing the asset for use or sale has been achieved; (2) the entity intends to complete and use or sell the asset; (3) the entity has the ability to use or sell the asset; (4) the entity understands how the asset will generate probable future economic benefits; (5) technical, financial, and other resources are available to complete development of the asset; (6) the entity has the ability to reliably measure the expenditures. If all six conditions are not met, development costs should be expensed in the current period. Once development costs are expensed, they cannot be capitalized in the future.

Intangible assets may use either the cost model (CM) or the revaluation model (RM). Similar to plant, property, and equipment, the cost model requires the asset to be recorded at its cost less any accumulated amortization or accumulated impairment losses. The revaluation model requires that the fair value must be determined in an active market. Therefore, only intangible assets that are traded with active market prices may be valued using the revaluation model. The revaluation model (RM) requires gains and losses on revaluation be recorded in other comprehensive income.

The useful life of an intangible asset is either finite or indefinite. Intangible assets with finite lives are amortized over the useful life; intangible assets with indefinite lives are not amortized, but tested for impairment annually (at the reporting date).

4. **Impairment of Assets**

An entity should determine at each reporting date if there are conditions that would cause an asset to be impaired. Asset impairment exists if the carrying value of the asset is greater than its recoverable amount. The recoverable amount is the greater of the net selling price or its value in use. An impairment loss for an asset accounted for at historical cost is recognized as an expense of the current period. The loss may be included with depreciation expense or identified separately on the income statement. If the revaluation model was used, an impairment adjustment may be treated as a reversal of an upward revaluation. Once the entire revaluation account is eliminated, the excess charge is recognized in expense of the period. Hence, the revaluation account cannot have a debit balance.

Intangible assets with finite lives are tested for impairment when the asset's carrying value is more than its recoverable amount. However, if an intangible asset has an indefinite life, a test for impairment must be made annually.

If an intangible asset's carrying value is more than its recoverable amount, the asset is considered impaired. The recoverable amount is the greater of the net selling price (fair value less costs of disposal) or its value in use. The value in use is determined by estimating the future cash flows expected from the continued use of the asset and its disposal. Impairments for intangible assets carried at historical cost are recognized as charges against the current period profit or loss. If the revaluation method was used for long-lived assets, any increase in value was recorded in a revaluation account in other comprehensive income. Therefore, the impairment adjustment is used to reverse any previous revaluation adjustment. Once the revaluation account is reduced to zero, the impairment is then charged to expense of the period.

An important difference between US GAAP and IFRS is that IFRS allows reversals of previously recognized impairments if the historical cost method is used. If the cost method is used, a reversal of impairment losses may be recognized in the income statement up to the amount of the impairments previously recognized. However, if the revaluation method is used, the recovery of impairments would be recognized in other comprehensive income.

5. **Biological Assets**

Biological assets (agricultural assets) are living animals or plants and must be disclosed as a separate item on the balance sheet. Biological assets are recognized when a future economic benefit is probable, the entity controls the asset as a result of past events, and the cost or fair value can be measured reliably. Agricultural produce should be measured as fair value less costs to sell at harvest.

E. Monetary Current Assets and Current Liabilities

Normally, assets are reported as current and noncurrent, and liabilities are reported as current and noncurrent on the balance sheet. If a liquidity presentation provides more relevant and reliable information, then balance sheet items may be reported based on their liquidity without segregation. In a balance sheet segregated between current and noncurrent items, an asset is classified as current when (1) the entity expects to realize the asset or to consume or sell it within 12 months or the normal operating cycle, or (2) it holds the asset primarily for the purpose of trading. A liability is classified as current when it expects to settle the liability within the normal operating cycle, the liability will be settled within 12 months after the reporting period, or it holds the liability for the purpose of trading.

IFRS defines the terms financial assets and financial liabilities. A financial asset is any asset that is cash, an equity instrument of another entity, a contractual right to receive cash or another financial asset, a contractual right to exchange a financial instrument, or a contract that will be settled in the reporting entity's own equity instruments. A financial liability is any liability that is a contractual obligation to deliver cash or another financial asset, a contractual obligation to exchange financial instruments under potentially unfavorable conditions, or a contract that may be settled in the entity's own equity instruments. Financial assets and liabilities are reported at cost, with an option to report them at fair value.

There are two important areas where IFRS differ from US GAAP. The first relates to short-term obligations expected to be refinanced. Under US GAAP, short-term obligations expected to be refinanced may be reported in the noncurrent liability section of the balance sheet if the company has the intent and ability to refinance. However, IFRS requires obligations expected to be refinanced to be reported as current liabilities unless there is an agreement to refinance in place prior to the balance sheet date.

The second area in which the terminology and rules are different are "provisions" and "contingencies." Under IFRS, a "provision" is a liability that is uncertain in timing or amount. Provisions are made for items such as taxes payable, compensated absences, bad debts, warranties, and other estimated liabilities. A "contingency," however, depends upon some future uncertainty or event.

A contingent asset is a possible asset that arises from past events that will be confirmed only by occurrence or nonoccurrence of uncertain future events that are not within the control of the reporting entity. As with US GAAP, a contingent asset is not recognized, but it is disclosed if the economic benefits are probable.

Under IFRS, a contingent liability does not have the same definition as in the US standards. Recall that under US GAAP, the accounting for a contingency depends on whether the outcome is probable, reasonably possible, or remote, and whether the contingency is measurable. In contrast, under IFRS if the outcome is probable and measurable, it is not considered a contingency. Instead, it classified as a "provision." Under IFRS, the term contingency is used to describe an event which is not recognized because it is not probable that an outflow will be required or the amount cannot be measured reliably. If an item qualifies as a contingency, the notes to the financial statements should include an estimate of the financial effect, an indication of the uncertainties, and the possibility of reimbursement. If the possibility of the event occurring is remote, no disclosure is required in the notes to the financial statements.

It should be noted that the "probable" threshold test for determining whether a provision should be made is "more likely than not" which is defined as a probability over 50%.

F. Borrowing Costs

IFRS 23 requires borrowing costs to be capitalized if they meet certain criteria. Borrowing costs must be capitalized if they are related to the acquisition, construction, or production of a qualifying asset. A qualifying asset is one that takes a substantial period of time to get ready for its intended use. Qualifying assets include inventory, plant, property, and equipment, intangible assets, or investment property. Borrowing costs that do not meet the rules for capitalization are expensed in the current period. Note that finance costs (interest expense) must be disclosed separately in the income statement.

G. Bonds

Similar to US accounting standards, IAS 39 provides that financial liabilities are initially measured at fair value, and subsequently measured at amortized cost using the effective interest method. An option can be made to value financial liabilities at fair value. Financial instruments with characteristics of both debt and equity are referred to as "compound instruments." Accounting for compound instruments is another area where IFRS differs from US GAAP. Convertible bonds, bonds with detachable warrants, and other compound instruments must be separated into their components of debt and equity. The liability component is initially recorded at fair value, and the residual value is assigned to the equity component. Each component is presented in the appropriate section of the balance sheet.

IFRS refers to the fair value option as "Fair Value through Profit or Loss" (FVTPL). If the fair value option is elected for a financial liability, then the liability is revalued at the end of the reporting period and the resulting gain or loss is recognized in profit or loss for the period.

H. Pensions

The area of employee benefits, and more specifically, pensions is where there are many similarities between US GAAP and IFRS.

In a defined contribution pension plan, the accounting is similar to US GAAP. The employer recognizes an expense for the period equal to the required contribution. If payment is made to the plan, then cash is credited. If the contribution is not made by the end of the accounting period, then the entity would recognize a liability for the accrued contributions.

With respect to defined benefit plans, some vocabulary is different. In US GAAP, the benefits-years-of-service method is used to calculate the projected benefit obligation (PBO). Under IFRS, the Projected Unit Credit Method is used to calculate the present value of the defined benefit obligation (PV-DBO). The concept is the same, but the terms are different. In addition, rather than the term "accumulated benefit obligation," IFRS uses the term "accrued benefit obligation."

In a defined benefit pension plan, the calculation of pension cost for the period is also similar to US GAAP. Under IFRS, net periodic pension cost is comprised of six components:

1. Current service cost,
2. Interest cost for the current period on the accrued benefit obligation,
3. Expected return on plan assets,
4. Actuarial gains and losses,
5. Past service costs, and
6. Effects of curtailments and settlements.

Under US GAAP, the discount rate used is the "settlement rate" (the rate at which the plans obligations could be settled). With IFRS the discount rate is determined by the market yields at the end of the reporting period for high-quality corporate bonds having a similar term or maturity. Another difference in accounting for pensions is that under IFRS, an entity may recognize a portion of the net accumulated actuarial gains or losses, or they may elect to recognize all of the actuarial gains and losses. If the entity wishes to recognize a portion, then the amount recognized is the excess of a "corridor" amount. The corridor amount is the greater of 10% of the present value of the defined benefit obligation, or 10% of the fair value of any plan assets. This excess gain or loss above the corridor amount is then amortized over the expected remaining working lives of the employees. Although the corridor rule is similar in US GAAP, the other option for recognizing all actuarial gains and losses is allowed only under IFRS.

Finally, IFRS has specific rules for netting the balances of pension plan assets and pension liabilities. Netting of plan assets and liability balances is only permissible when there is a legally enforceable right to use the assets of one plan to settle the obligations of another plan.

Termination benefits. When an entity provides voluntary termination benefits, a liability and expense are reported when the entity is demonstrably committed to a detailed formal plan that it cannot withdraw.

The plan should include information such as location, function, number of employees, benefits provided, and when the plan will be implemented.

I. Leases

Leasing is a topic where the IASB rules focus on substance over form. Unlike US GAAP, which uses certain thresholds to determine whether a lease should be classified as a capital lease, IAS 17 classifies leases based on whether substantially all the risks or benefits of ownership have been transferred. Leasing is also a topic where subtle terminology differences exist, for example, capital lease (US GAAP) versus finance lease (IFRS).

1. Criteria for Treatment of Leases

Under US GAAP, a lessee classifies a lease as either an operating lease or a capital lease. For the lessor, the lease is classified as an operating lease, a direct-financing lease, or a sales-type lease. However, under IAS 17 the lease is classified as either an operating lease or a finance lease for the lessee and the lessor. Of course, with a finance lease, the lessor is usually financing the item, or, if the lessor is a manufacturer or dealer, the lessor is selling the item through the leasing process.

Lease payments under an operating lease are recognized as expense on a straight-line basis over the lease term. The lessee must disclose in the footnotes the total future minimum payments for the next 12 months, payments due in Years 2-5, and payments due after five years, as well as a general description of the lease terms and restrictions imposed by the lease.

IFRS provides that a lease is a finance lease if substantially all of the risks or benefits of ownership have been transferred to the lessee. If any one of the four criteria is met, the lease is considered a finance lease.

1. The lease transfers ownership to the lessee by the end of the lease term or the lease contains a bargain purchase option, and it is reasonably certain that the option will be exercised.
2. The lease term is for the major part of the economic life of the asset (title may or may not pass to the lessee).
3. The present value of the minimum lease payments at the inception of the lease is at least equal to substantially all of the fair value of the leased asset.
4. The leased assets are of a specialized nature such that only the lessee can use them without modifications.

Although these four criteria are similar to the rules under US GAAP, notice that these rules do not carry specific thresholds such as a 75% of the economic life or 90% of the fair value of the leased asset. Therefore, the proper classification is determined based on judgments about the substance of the transaction.

In addition, the following three other circumstances may indicate that the lease should be treated as a finance lease:

1. If the lessee can cancel the lease, and the lessor's losses are borne by the lessee.
2. Gains or losses resulting from the fluctuations in fair value will accrue to the lessee.
3. The lessee has the ability to continue the lease for a supplemental term at a rent substantially lower than market value.

Under IFRS, a lease is classified as either an operating or finance lease at the inception of the lease. The inception of the lease is the earlier of the date of the lease agreement or the date of commitment to the lease agreement. The commencement date of the lease term is the date in which the lessee in entitled to use the leased asset. Although the lease must be classified as either an operating or finance lease on the date of inception, the lease is not recognized in the financial statements until the commencement date when the lessee is entitled to use the asset.

Another significant difference in classifying leases arises when land and buildings are leased together. Because land has an indefinite life, if title does not pass by the end of the lease term, the substantial risks and rewards of ownership do not transfer. Thus, in such cases the land lease cannot be classified as a finance lease. Under IFRS, the land and building would be treated as separate components; the land lease would be classified as an operating lease, and the building lease would be classified as a finance lease (assuming substantially all risks and rewards of ownership are transferred). The minimum lease payments would be allocated between the land and the buildings elements in proportion to the relative fair values of the leasehold interests of each element. If both elements of the lease are expected to pass to the lessee at the end of the lease term, then the entire lease is classified as a finance lease.

2. **Accounting by Lessees**

Under IFRS, the finance lease is recorded as an asset and as a liability by the lessee at the fair value of the leased property at the inception of the lease or the present value of the minimum lease payments. For the lessee, the minimum lease payments include the payments over the lease term that are required to be made, the bargain purchase option, and amounts guaranteed by the lessee. For the lessor, the minimum lease payments also include any residual value guaranteed by a third party not related to the lessor.

The interest rate used to calculate the present value of the minimum lease payments is the implicit rate. However, if the implicit rate cannot be determined, then the lessee's incremental borrowing rate is used. Any indirect costs incurred by the lessee in connection with negotiating and arranging the lease are added to the cost of the asset.

Each period the minimum lease payments are apportioned between the finance charge and the reduction of the principal outstanding. Any contingent rents are charged to expense as they are incurred. In addition, depreciation expense should be recognized for the leased asset. If ownership transfers at the end of the lease term, then the asset is depreciated over its useful life. If ownership does not transfer, then the finance lease is depreciated over the shorter of the lease term or the asset's useful life.

Disclosures required for leases include the net carrying amount at the end of the reporting period, the future minimum lease payments at the end of the reporting period, and the present value of the lease payment due within one year, due after one year and less than five years, and after five years. Disclosures should also indicate the contingent rents recognized as expense during the period, a description of the lease, and its terms and restrictions.

3. **Accounting by Lessors**

In a finance lease, the asset is removed from the lessor's balance sheet, and the net investment in the lease is recorded as an asset. The net investment in the lease is calculated as gross lease receivables less the unearned finance income (interest income).

Similar to US GAAP, a manufacturer or dealer will recognize the sale, cost of goods sold, lease receivable and unearned finance income.

4. **Sales and Leaseback**

A sale and leaseback transaction may be classified as either an operating lease or a finance lease. The same criteria (risk and benefits of ownership, substance over form) determine whether the sale and leaseback is an operating or a finance lease. If it is classified as a finance lease, the gain is deferred and amortized over the lease term. If it is classified as an operating lease, the profit or loss is recognized immediately. If it is an operating lease and the fair value at the time of the sale and leaseback transaction is less than the carrying amount of the asset, then a loss is recognized immediately.

J. Deferred Taxes

IFRS requires the use of the "liability method" to account for income taxes. Similar to US GAAP, its primary purpose is to focus on the statement of financial position and report deferred tax assets and deferred tax liabilities. IAS 12 prohibits deferred tax assets or deferred tax liabilities from being classified as current. Therefore, deferred taxes are classified as noncurrent items in the statement of financial position.

Current tax is the amount of income taxes payable or recoverable on the taxable profit or loss for the period. Deferred tax assets and liabilities arise due to temporary differences. Temporary differences are either taxable temporary differences or deductible temporary differences. A taxable temporary difference will result in an increase in taxable amounts in a future period. A deductible temporary difference will result in amounts that can be deducted in future periods.

A deferred tax asset arises when there is a deductible temporary difference. A deferred tax asset also arises when an entity has unused tax losses that can be deducted in the future or tax credits which can be used in the future. An entity can recognize a deferred tax asset if it is probable (more likely than not) that the tax benefit can be used. Deferred tax assets and liabilities are measured using the enacted rate or substantially enacted rate (unlike US GAAP which requires the use of the enacted tax rate).

The liability method requires an entity to identify all temporary differences. The differences are then classified as those giving rise to deferred tax liabilities, and those giving rise to deferred tax assets. This distinction is important because all deferred tax liabilities are reported, whereas deferred tax assets can only be recognized if it is probable (more likely than not) that the asset will be realized. Similar to US GAAP, tax expense is the sum of current tax expense and the deferred tax expense.

One of the significant differences in accounting for income taxes between US GAAP and IFRS is the classification of deferred taxes on the balance sheet. Recall that for US GAAP, the netting procedures involve netting current deferred tax assets (DTA) with current deferred tax liabilities (DTL) to present one amount, and netting noncurrent DTA with noncurrent DTL to present another amount. Under IFRS, deferred tax assets and liabilities may not be classified as current. The netting rules are also different. Netting of the components of deferred taxes is only permissible in certain situations. The rules for presentation and disclosure require that a current tax payable and a current tax recoverable (receivable) can be offset only if it relates to the same taxing authority. Likewise, the netting of deferred tax assets and deferred tax liabilities must relate to the same taxing authority. Therefore, in order to net these amounts, the entity must have a legal right to offset the amounts, and the amounts must relate to the same taxing authority.

K. Stockholders' Equity

Accounting for shareholders' equity may be influenced by the laws of a particular jurisdiction or country. Therefore, IFRS does not contain a comprehensive set of requirements for reporting shareholders' equity. Instead, IFRS provides some rules as to the minimum required disclosures. Note that in this area, there may be vocabulary differences when describing certain components of shareholders' equity.

IFRS requires disclosure of the issued share capital, retained earnings, and other components of equity. The par value and the number of authorized, issued, and outstanding shares must be disclosed. If shares were issued but not fully paid (referred to as subscribed stock in US and "calls" in other countries), the amount not collected is shown as a contra account in the equity section. A schedule must be presented that reconciles the number of shares of stock at the beginning and end of each period.

Additional items that are disclosed in the shareholders' equity section are the capital contributions in excess of par (also called additional paid-in capital, or "share premium"), the revaluation reserve, reserves for other items, and retained earnings. Mandatorily redeemable shares or puttable shares may not be treated as equity and should be classified as liabilities. Compound financial instruments that have the features of both debt and equity must be separated into a liability component and an equity component and recognized in the appropriate section of the balance sheet. Noncontrolling interest is included in the shareholders' equity section of the balance sheet.

Preferred shares that are convertible into ordinary shares are recorded in the preferred share account. Later, if the shares are converted, the book value method is used to account for the conversion of preferred stock into common stock.

Shares issued for services or property should be recorded at the fair value of the property or services. If the fair value of the property or services is not available, then the shares should be recorded at the fair value of the shares. However, if convertible debt is issued, the instrument is viewed as having a debt feature and an equity feature and should be allocated accordingly. The amount allocated to liabilities is the fair value of the liability component, and the residual amount is allocated to equity.

Notes to the financial statements should describe the rights, preferences, and restrictions with respect to dividends for each class of stock, cumulative dividends in arrears, reacquired shares, and shares reserved for future issuances under options and sales contracts.

Cash dividends are recorded in the same way as US GAAP. Although IFRS does not address share (stock) dividends, guidance is based on national accounting rules. If dividends have been proposed but not declared or formally approved, such dividends must be reported in the notes to the financial statements. In addition, information regarding dividends declared after the end of the period but prior to issuance of the financial statements should be disclosed in the notes to the financial statements.

If ordinary and preferred shares are issued to investors as a unit (referred to as share units), the proceeds are allocated in proportion to the relative market values of the securities issued. If only one security is publicly traded, that security is valued at market value, and the residual is allocated to the other security. If the market value of neither security is known, then an appraisal value may be used.

For share subscriptions, the accounting relies on the laws of the particular jurisdiction. In some instances, the subscription receivable is shown as either a current or noncurrent asset based upon the payment due date. However, in other instances, the subscription receivable is a contra account and reduces shareholders' equity.

For US GAAP, donated assets are recognized at fair value and as revenue when the contribution is received. IFRS does not currently address donated assets.

Treasury shares are the entity's shares that have been reacquired. There are three methods for accounting for treasury shares: cost method, par value method, and constructive retirement method. The cost method and par method entries are the same as US GAAP. The constructive retirement method is similar to the par value method except that the par value of the reacquired shares are charged to the share account instead of the treasury stock account. The constructive retirement method is used when management does not intend to reissue the shares or the jurisdiction of incorporation requires that reacquired shares be retired.

L. Share-Based Payments

IFRS accounting for share-based payments and US GAAP are similar due to the convergence project. However, some vocabulary differences exist. IFRS has three categories for share-based payments: equity-settled, cash-settled, or a choice to settle in either cash or equity. Equity-settled share-based payments to nonemployees are valued at fair value of goods or services received if it can be measured reliably. If the fair value of goods or services cannot be measured, then the fair value of the equity instrument is used. Equity-settled payments to employees are valued at the fair value of the security. A debit is made to either an expense or an asset, and a credit is made to equity. For cash-settled, share-based payments, such as stock appreciation rights or options, a liability is measured at the fair value at the measurement date. The liability is then remeasured at every reporting date, and additional income or expense is recognized in profit or loss.

M. Investments

As discussed earlier in fixed assets, the term investment is used in the area of investment property as well as investments in financial instruments of other entities. The accounting rules for investment property were covered under the section on fixed assets.

The term "investments" refers to investments that are held for trading (HFT), available for sale (AFS), and held to maturity (HTM), as well as investments accounted for using the equity method, and investments that require consolidated financial statements. The accounting for investments is covered by various IAS, depending upon the type of investment.

A financial instrument should be classified as either fair value through profit or loss (FVTPL), held to maturity (HTM), available for sale (AFS), or loans and receivables. The FVTPL category includes financial assets in the held-for-trading (HFT) category. HTM instruments have fixed and determinable payments and fixed maturity dates. Held-for-trading (HFT) securities are securities in which the entity has the intent to sell in the near term. Available-for-sale financial assets are those that are not classified as FVTPL, HTM, or loans and receivables.

If an asset is classified as fair value through profit or loss (FVTPL), it is remeasured to fair value at the end of each accounting period, and any profit or loss is recorded in that period. An election can be made to use the FVTPL method for accounting purposes for an asset normally classified as available for sale (AFS) or held to maturity (HTM). However, if an equity security has no active market in which to determine fair value, then the equity security may not be classified as FVTPL. Once the item is classified as FVTPL, it may not be subsequently reclassified. Any equity instrument that does not have a quoted market price or a determinable fair value should be accounted for using the cost method.

If FVTPL is not elected, different rules apply. If the investment is classified as held to maturity (HTM), the investment is recorded at cost, and is subsequently measured at amortized cost using the effective interest method. Similarly, if a financial asset is classified as loans or receivables, it is accounted for by using amortized cost and the effective interest method. If the investment is classified as available for sale (AFS), the asset is measured at fair value, and any income or loss is recognized in other comprehensive income for the period. Note that if a debt security is classified as available for sale, any premium or discount must be amortized using the effective interest method on the income statement, with the increase or decrease in fair value reported in other comprehensive income.

Investments in associates (affiliates) may also be accounted for using either the equity method or the FVTPL method. To qualify for the equity method, the entity must have significant influence over the investee. Significant influence is presumed when the investor owns between 20% and 50% of the voting power of another entity. Consistent with US GAAP, the equity method requires the investment to be recorded at cost, with the investor's share of profit or loss recognized at year-end in the investment account, and the investor's share of dividend distributions recognized as a reduction in the investment account. If the cost of the investment is greater than its share of the fair value of net assets, it is not recorded as goodwill. However, this portion of the cost of the investment over the carrying amount is amortized as the assets are realized. If the cost is less than the fair value of net assets, (goodwill is negative), this difference is recognized as income in the year of acquisition. An impairment of an investment is recognized if the carrying amount of the investment is greater than its recoverable amount.

N. Business Combinations

IFRS requires business combinations to be accounted for using the acquisition method. Although the accounting for business combinations is similar for US GAAP and IFRS, it is different in several respects.

Under US GAAP noncontrolling interest is recorded at its fair value. IFRS, on the other hand, allows noncontrolling interest to be valued either at fair value or the proportionate share of the value of the identifiable assets and liabilities of the acquiree. If the noncontrolling interest is valued at fair value, the noncontrolling interest is calculated by determining the market price for equity shares not held by the acquirer. If the market value is not available, other valuation techniques may be used to measure the fair value. The second method for valuing noncontrolling interest is to calculate the fair value of net assets acquired and multiply that amount times the percentage of shares owned by the noncontrolling interest. Note that these two methods may result in a different amount of goodwill being recognized by the acquirer.

The calculation of goodwill is

> Consideration transferred
> + Noncontrolling interest in acquiree (valued at % of FV or % share of net assets)
> + Fair value of previously held interests in acquiree
> <u>– Fair value of net assets acquired</u>
> Goodwill

If goodwill is negative, a gain from bargain purchase should be recognized in the current period on the income statement.

Consolidated financial statements are required for all parent and subsidiaries wherein the parent has control. Similar to US GAAP, control is presumed if the entity has more than 50% of the voting shares of another entity. However under IFRS, a parent may exclude a subsidiary only if three conditions are met: (1) it is wholly or partially owned and its other owners do not object to nonconsolidation; (2) it does not have any debt or equity instruments publicly traded; and (3) its parent prepares consolidated financial statements that comply with IFRS.

O. Derivatives and Hedging Instruments

A derivative is a financial instrument that (1) requires little or no initial investment, (2) changes in value in response to a change in the value of another instrument or index (called an underlying), and (3) is settled in the future. Examples of derivatives include options, futures, forward contracts, and swaps. Derivatives are recognized in the financial statements using the fair value through profit and loss method (FVTPL). Derivatives are remeasured at fair value, with gains and losses recorded in profit or loss for the period.

A hedging instrument is a type of derivative that is classified as a fair value hedge, a cash flow hedge, or a hedge of a net investment in operations. Hedge accounting allows the optional treatment to offset profits and losses on hedged items. If a company elects to use hedge accounting, the accounting treatment differs depending on the type of hedge. A fair value hedge is accounted for by recognizing the gains and losses in profit and loss of the period. A cash flow hedge and a hedge of a net investment are accounted for by reporting gains and losses in other comprehensive income for the period.

P. Interim Reporting

IFRS does not mandate interim reporting. However, when interim reports are required, four financial statements are required: the statement of financial position, the statement of comprehensive income, the statement of changes in equity, and the statement of cash flows. For consistency purposes, the entity must use the same accounting policies as used in year-end financial statements.

Q. Segment Reporting

IFRS 8 on segment reporting includes guidance very similar to US GAAP. It requires a management approach to identifying operating segments. An operating segment is a reportable segment if it meets one of the following defined quantitative thresholds:

1. The segment's revenue (including internal and external sales) is 10% or more of combined revenue of all segments,
2. The absolute value of the profit or loss is 10% or more than the greater (in absolute value) of the (1) combined reported profit of all segments that did not report a loss or (2) the combined reported loss of all segments that reported a loss, or
3. The assets are 10% or more of the combined assets of all segments.

In addition, the total external revenue by reportable segments must be at least 75% of the entity's revenue; otherwise additional segments must be identified and reported. Note that these thresholds are the same as for US GAAP.

R. Foreign Currency Transactions and Translations

Currencies are defined as either foreign, functional, or presentation currency. The functional currency is the currency of the primary economic environment in which the entity operates. A foreign currency is a currency other than the functional currency. The presentation currency is the currency in which financial statements are presented. Similar to US GAAP, the three-step process for translating financial statements is as follows:

1. Determine the functional currency.
2. Translate items into the functional currency.
3. Translate items into the presentation currency.

When translating financial statement items, the items are classified into two categories: monetary and nonmonetary items. Monetary items are translated at the year-end spot rate. Nonmonetary items measured at historical cost are translated at the historical exchange rate. Nonmonetary items measured at fair value are translated at the rate in effect when fair value was determined. If the functional currency is the same as the presentation currency, any gains and losses on translation are recognized in profit or loss in the period. However, there are several exceptions to this rule. Currency gains or losses on nonmonetary items for which gains and losses are recorded in other comprehensive income should also be reported in other comprehensive income.

If the functional currency is not the same as the presentation currency, then any translation gains and losses are recorded in other comprehensive income. In this case, assets and liabilities are recorded at the closing exchange rate, and income and expenses are recorded at the rate when the transaction occurred.

S. First-Time Adoption of IFRS

There are a number of options available upon first-time adoption of IFRS, as described below. Generally the adoption involves restating assets, liabilities and equity using IFRS principles. The "date of transition to IFRS" is defined as the beginning of the earliest period for which an entity presents full comparative information under IFRSs in its first IFRS financial statements. The "first IFRS reporting period" is defined as the latest reporting period covered by an entity's first IFRS financial statements.

Business combinations. With respect to business combinations, the first-time adopter has the option of retrospectively adopting IFRS 3 for all periods presented, or adjusting the assets and liabilities through retained earnings in the period of adoption.

Plant, property, and equipment. Unless an entity decides to use a fair value election, it will need to recalculate the life-to-date depreciation or amortization of any PPE or intangible assets under IFRS. This can be quite time consuming. Alternatively, the entity may use various methods to determine the fair value of the assets and use those amounts as the deemed cost at the time of adoption. IFRS would then be used going forward. The fair value election may be applied on an individual item basis.

SEC Reporting Requirements

Unless exempt by regulation, companies with assets of more than $10 million and 500 or more shareholders and securities that trade on a national securities exchange or an over-the-counter market must have the securities registered. Companies with registered securities (termed issuers) must file the following reports with the SEC:

1. Annual report (Form 10-K) provides a comprehensive picture of a company's performance, including audited financial statements. The 10-K includes the following sections:

   a. Business.
   b. Risk factors.
   c. Properties.
   d. Legal proceedings.
   e. Submission of matters to a vote of security holders.
   f. Market.
   g. Consolidated financial data.
   h. Management's discussion and analysis.
   i. Financial statements (two years of balance sheets and 3 years of income statements, statements of cash flows, and statements of comprehensive income.

2. The deadline for filing the Form 10-K is within 75 days after the close of the company's fiscal year for accelerated filers (companies with a market value of at least $75 million in equity held by nonaffiliates). Large accelerated filers (companies with a market value of at least $700 million in equity held

by nonaffiliates) must file within 60 days. Small reporting companies (less than $75 million in market value of equity) must file within 90 days.

3. Quarterly report (Form 10-Q) provides quarterly information similar to that in the 10-K but in less detail. It includes quarterly financial statements that are reviewed (not audited) by public accountants. The company files three Form 10-Qs every year and the Form 10-K contains the quarterly results for the fourth quarter. The Form 10-Q must include the following financial statements.

    a. An interim balance sheet as of the end of the most recent fiscal quarter and a balance sheet as of the end of the preceding fiscal year. An interim balance sheet as of the end of the corresponding fiscal quarter of the preceding fiscal year need not be provided unless necessary for an understanding of the impact of seasonal fluctuation on the company's financial condition.

    b. Interim statements of income for the most recent fiscal quarter, for the period between the end of the preceding fiscal year and the end of the most recent fiscal quarter, and for the corresponding periods of the preceding fiscal year.

    c. Interim statements of cash flows for the period between the end of the preceding fiscal year and the end of the most recent fiscal quarter, and for the corresponding period of the preceding fiscal year.

    Form 10-Qs are due 45 days after the end of the fiscal quarter for small reporting companies, and 40 days after the end of the fiscal quarter for accelerated and large accelerated filers.

4. Information statements (Form 8-K) provides information about material events that affect the company, such as mergers and acquisitions, changes in directors or CEO, other major changes in operations or status, changes in auditors, etc. The Form 8-K must be filed within 4 business days of the occurrence of the event.

5. Regulation S-X describes the form and content of financial statements filed with the SEC.

Financial Statements of Trusts

Trusts are entities that are formed to hold assets for the benefit of the beneficiaries. They are administered by trustees. Trusts generally present the following financial statements:

1. A statement of assets and liabilities.
2. A statement of operations.
3. A statement of changes in net assets.

The financial statements of a trust are generally presented on the accrual basis and the assets are generally presented at their fair values.

QUESTIONS ON THE NEW FINANCIAL ACCOUNTING AND REPORTING MATERIAL

1. Which of the following organizations is responsible for setting International Financial Reporting Standards?
   a. Financial Accounting Standards Board.
   b. International Accounting Standards Committee.
   c. Financial Accounting Committee.
   d. International Accounting Standards Board.

2. According to the *IASB Framework for the Preparation and Presentation of Financial Statements*, the qualitative characteristic of relevance includes
   a. Timeliness, predictive value, and feedback value.
   b. Verifiability, neutrality, and representational faithfulness.
   c. Predictive value, confirmatory value, and materiality.
   d. Comparability and consistency.

3. According to the IASB *Framework*, the financial statement element that is defined as increases in economic benefits during the accounting period in the form of inflows or enhancements of assets or decreases of liabilities that result in increases in equity, other than those relating to contributions from equity participants, is
   a. Revenue.
   b. Income.
   c. Profits.
   d. Gains.

4. According to the IASB *Framework*, the two criteria required for incorporating items into the income statement or statement of financial position are that
   a. It meets the definition of relevance and reliability.
   b. It meets the definition of an element and can be measured reliably.
   c. It satisfies the criteria of capital maintenance.
   d. It meets the requirements of comparability and consistency.

5. If the outcome of rendering services cannot be estimated reliably, IFRS requires the use of which revenue recognition method?
   a. Percentage-of-completion method.
   b. Completed-contract method.
   c. Cost recovery method.
   d. Installment method.

6. IFRS requires changes in accounting principles to be reported
   a. On a prospective basis.
   b. On a retrospective basis.
   c. By restating the financial statements.
   d. By a cumulative adjustment on the income statement.

7. Galaxy Corporation prepares its financial statements in accordance with IFRS. Galaxy intends to refinance a $10,000 note payable due on February 20, 2011. The company expects the note to be refinanced for a period of five years. Under what circumstances can Galaxy report the note payable as a noncurrent liability on its December 31, 2010 statement of financial position?
   a. If Galaxy has the intent and ability to refinance before December 31, 2010.
   b. If Galaxy has executed an agreement to refinance by December 31, 2010.

   c. If Galaxy has executed an agreement to refinance prior to the issuance of the financial statements in March, 2011.
   d. If Galaxy has the intent and ability to refinance before the issuance of the financial statements in March, 2011.

8. Largo Corporation prepares its financial statements in accordance with IFRS. Which of the following items is required disclosure on the income statement?
   a. Revenues, cost of goods sold, and advertising expense.
   b. Finance costs, tax expense, and income.
   c. Operating expenses, nonoperating expenses, and extraordinary items.
   d. Gross profit, operating profits, and net profits.

9. Which of the following may not be disclosed on the income statement for a company that prepares its financial statements in accordance with IFRS?
   a. Gain or loss.
   b. Tax expense.
   c. Gain or loss from extraordinary items.
   d. Gain or loss from discontinued operations.

10. Glenda Corporation prepares its financial statements in accordance with IFRS. Glenda must report finance costs on the statement of cash flows
   a. In operating activities.
   b. Either in operating activities or financing activities.
   c. In financing activities.
   d. In investing activities or financing activities.

11. Larimer Corporation prepares its financial statements in accordance with IFRS. Larimer acquired equipment by issuing 5,000 shares of its common stock. How should this transaction be reported on the statement of cash flows?
   a. As an outflow of cash from investing activities and an inflow of cash from financing activities.
   b. As an inflow of cash from financing activities and an outflow of cash from operating activities.
   c. At the bottom of the statement of cash flows as a significant noncash transaction.
   d. In the notes to the financial statements as a significant noncash transaction.

12. For IFRS purposes, cash advances and loans from bank overdrafts should be reported on the statement of cash flows as
   a. Operating activities.
   b. Investing activities.
   c. Financing activities.
   d. Other significant noncash activities.

13. Which of the following are acceptable methods for reporting comprehensive income under IFRS?
   I. One comprehensive income statement.
   II. Two statements: an income statement and a comprehensive income statement.
   III. In the statement of owners' equity.
   a. I only.
   b. I and II only.
   c. I, II, and III.
   d. I and II only.

14. Brady Corporation values its inventory at the lower of cost or net realizable value as required by IFRS. Brady has the following information regarding its inventory:

Historical cost	$1,000
Estimated selling price	900
Estimated costs to complete and sell	50
Replacement cost	800

What is the amount for inventory that Brady should report on the balance sheet under the lower of cost or net realizable value method?
   a. $1,000
   b. $ 900
   c. $ 850
   d. $ 750

15. For companies that prepare financial statements in accordance with IFRS, plant, property, and equipment should be valued using which models?
   a. The cost model or the revaluation model.
   b. The cost model or the fair value model.
   c. The cost model or the fair value through profit or loss model.
   d. The revaluation model or the fair value model.

16. Which is true about the revaluation model for valuing plant, property, and equipment?
   a. Revaluation of assets must be made on the last day of the fiscal year.
   b. Revaluation of assets must be made on the same date each year.
   c. There is no rule for the frequency or date of revaluation.
   d. Revaluation of assets must be made every two years.

17. When the revaluation model is used for reporting plant, property, and equipment, the gain or loss should be included in
   a. Income for the period.
   b. Gain from revaluation on the income statement.
   c. A revaluation surplus account in other comprehensive income.
   d. An extraordinary gain or loss on the income statement.

18. Linden Corporation has investment property that is held to earn rental income. Linden prepares its financial statements in accordance with IFRS. Linden uses the fair value model for reporting the investment property. Which of the following is true?
   a. Changes in fair value are reported as profit or loss in the current period.
   b. Changes in fair value are reported as other comprehensive income for the period.
   c. Changes in fair value are reported as an extraordinary gain on the income statement.
   d. Changes in fair value are reported as deferred revenue for the period.

19. Under IFRS, what valuation methods are used for intangible assets?
   a. The cost model or the fair value model.
   b. The cost model or the revaluation model.
   c. The cost model or the fair value through profit or loss model.
   d. The revaluation model or the fair value model.

20. Pinkerton Corp. uses the cost model for intangible assets. On April 10, 2009, Pinkerton acquired assets for $100,000. On December 31, 2009, it was determined that the recoverable amount for these intangible assets was $80,000. On December 31, 2010, it was determined that the intangible assets had a recoverable amount of $84,000. What is the impairment gain or loss recognized in 2009 and 2010 on the income statement?

	2009	*2010*
a.	$20,000 loss	$16,000 loss
b.	$20,000 loss	$0
c.	$20,000 loss	$4,000 gain
d.	$ 0	$0

21. On March 22, 2010, Cole Corporation received notification of legal action against the firm. Cole's attorneys determine that it is probable the company will lose the suit, and the loss is estimated at $2,000,000. Cole's accountants believe this amount is material and should be disclosed. Cole prepares its financial statements in accordance with IFRS. How should the estimated loss be disclosed in Cole's financial statements at December 31, 2010?
   a. As a loss recorded in other comprehensive income.
   b. As a contingent liability reported in the balance sheet and a loss on the income statement.
   c. As a provision for loss reported in the balance sheet and a loss on the income statement.
   d. In the footnotes to the financial statements as a contingency.

22. Roland Corp. signed an agreement with Linx, which requires that if Linx does not meet certain contractual obligations, Linx must forfeit land worth $40,000 to Roland. Roland's accountants believe that Linx will not meet its contractual obligations, and it is probable Roland will receive the land by the end 2011. Roland uses IFRS for reporting purposes. How should Roland report the land?
   a. As investment property in the asset section of the balance sheet.
   b. As a contingent asset in the current asset section of the balance sheet.
   c. In a footnote disclosure if the economic benefits are probable.
   d. As a contingent asset and other comprehensive income for the period.

23. On February 1, 2010, Blake Corporation issued bonds with a fair value of $1,000,000. Blake prepares its financial statements in accordance with IFRS. What methods may Blake use to report the bonds on its December 31, 2010 statement of financial position?

   I. Amortized cost.
   II. Fair value method.
   III. Fair value through profit or loss.

   a. I only.
   b. II only.
   c. I and III only.
   d. III only.

24. Which of the following methods is used in IFRS to account for defined benefit pension plans?
   a. Projected-unit-credit method.
   b. Benefit-years-of-service method.
   c. Accumulated benefits method.
   d. Vested years of service method.

25. Morgan Corp. signs a lease to rent equipment for ten years. The lease payments of $10,000 per year are due on January 2 each year. At the end of the lease term, Morgan may purchase the equipment for $50. The equipment is estimated to have a useful life of 12 years. Morgan prepares its financial statements in accordance with IFRS. Morgan should classify this lease as a(n)

    a. Operating lease.
    b. Capital lease.
    c. Finance lease.
    d. Sales-type lease.

26. Santiago Corp. signs an agreement to lease land and a building for 20 years. At the end of the lease, the property will not transfer to Santiago. The life of the building is estimated to be 20 years. Santiago prepares its financial statements in accordance with IFRS. How should Santiago account for the lease?

    a. The lease is recorded as a finance lease.
    b. The lease is recorded as an operating lease.
    c. The land is recorded as an operating lease and the building is recorded as a finance lease.
    d. The land is recorded as a finance lease, and the building is recorded as an operating lease.

27. Klaus Corporation prepares its financial statements in accordance with IFRS. Klaus locates its business in two jurisdictions, France and Germany. Assume that each country has the legal right to offset the taxes receivable and payable. Klaus prepares its taxes based on taxing authority and has the following information related to its deferred tax assets and liabilities:

Classification	Amount	Taxing jurisdiction
Deferred Tax Asset	$4,000	France
Deferred Tax Liability	$2,500	Germany
Deferred Tax Liability	$3,000	France

How should Klaus present its deferred taxes on its December 31, 2010 statement of financial position?

	Deferred tax asset	Deferred tax liability
a.	$4,000	$5,500
b.	$1,000	$2,500
c.	$0	$1,500
d.	$1,500	$3,000

28. Which of the following is true regarding reporting deferred taxes in financial statements prepared in accordance with IFRS?

    a. Deferred tax assets and liabilities are classified as current and noncurrent based on their expiration dates.
    b. Deferred tax assets and liabilities may only be classified as noncurrent.
    c. Deferred tax assets are netted with deferred tax liabilities to arrive at one amount presented on the balance sheet.
    d. Deferred taxes of one jurisdiction are offset against another jurisdiction in the netting process.

29. Logan Corporation issues convertible bonds for $500,000. At the date of issuance, it is determined that the fair value of the bonds is $480,000. Logan prepares its financial statements in accordance with IFRS. How should the issuance of the bonds be recognized?

    a. As a bond liability for $500,000.
    b. As a bond liability for $480,000 and other comprehensive income of $20,000.

    c. As a bond liability for $480,000 and an equity component of $20,000.
    d. As a bond liability for $500,000 and a contra liability of $20,000.

30. On March 1, 2010, Acadia purchased 1,000 shares of common stock of Marston Corp. for $50,000 and classified the investment as available-for-sale securities. On December 31, 2010, the Marston stock had a fair value of $53,000. Acadia Corp. prepares its financial statements in accordance with IFRS. Acadia elects to use the fair value through profit or loss to records its investments in available-for-sale securities. How is the gain on the investment in Marston stock reported in Acadia's 2010 financial statements?

    a. As a $3,000 gain in other comprehensive income.
    b. No gain or loss is reported in 2010.
    c. As a $3,000 prior period adjustment to retained earnings.
    d. As a $3,000 gain in current earnings of the period.

31. Which of the following is the SEC form used by issuer companies to file as an annual report with the SEC?

    a. Form 10-Q.
    b. Form 8-K.
    c. Form 10-K.
    d. Form S-1.

32. Which of the following best describes the content of the SEC Form 10-Q?

    a. Quarterly audited financial information and other information about the company.
    b. Annual audited financial information and nonfinancial information about the company.
    c. Disclosure of material events that affect the company.
    d. Quarterly reviewed financial information and other information about the company.

33. Under IFRS, changes in accounting policies are

    a. Permitted if the change will result in a more reliable and more relevant presentation of the financial statements.
    b. Permitted if the entity encounters new transactions, events, or conditions that are substantively different from existing or previous transactions.
    c. Required on material transactions, if the entity had previously accounted for similar, though immaterial, transactions under an unacceptable accounting method.
    d. Required if an alternate accounting policy gives rise to a material change in assets, liabilities, or the current year net income.

34. Under IFRS, an entity that acquires an intangible asset may use the revaluation model for subsequent measurement only if

    a. The useful life of the intangible asset can be reliably determined.
    b. An active market exists for the intangible asset.
    c. The cost of the intangible asset can be measured reliably.
    d. The intangible asset is a monetary asset.

35. Under IFRS, which of the following is a criterion that must be met in order for an item to be recognized as an intangible asset other than goodwill?

a. The item's fair value can be measured reliably.
b. The item is part of the entity's activities aimed at gaining new scientific or technical knowledge.
c. The item is expected to be used in the production or supply of goods or services.
d. The item is identifiable and lacks physical substance.

36. An entity purchases a trademark and incurs the following costs in connection with the trademark:

One-time trademark purchase price	$100,000
Nonrefundable VAT taxes	5,000
Training sales personnel on the use of the new trademark	7,000
Research expenditures associated with the purchase of the new trademark	24,000
Legal costs incurred to register the trademark	10,500
Salaries of the administrative personnel	12,000

Applying IFRS and assuming that the trademark meets all of the applicable initial asset recognition criteria, the entity should recognize an asset in the amount of
a. $100,000
b. $115,500
c. $146,500
d. $158,500

37. Under IFRS, when an entity chooses the revaluation model as its accounting policy for measuring property, plant, and equipment, which of the following statements is correct?
a. When an asset is revalued, the entire class of property, plant, and equipment to which that asset belongs must be revalued.
b. When an asset is revalued, individual assets within a class of property, plant, and equipment to which that asset belongs can be revalued.
c. Revaluations of property, plant, and equipment must be made at least every three years.
d. Increases in an asset's carrying value as a result of the first revaluation must be recognized as a component of profit or loss.

38. Upon first-time adoption of IFRS, an entity may elect to use fair value as deemed cost for
a. Biological assets related to agricultural activity for which there is **no** active market.
b. Intangible assets for which there is **no** active market.
c. Any individual item of property, plant, and equipment.
d. Financial liabilities that are **not** held for trading.

39. Under IFRS, which of the following is the first step within the hierarchy of guidance to which management refers, and whose applicability it considers, when selecting accounting policies?
a. Consider the most recent pronouncements of other standard-setting bodies to the extent they do **not** conflict with the IFRS or the IASB *Framework*.
b. Apply a standard from IFRS if it specifically relates to the transaction, other event, or condition.
c. Consider the applicability of the definitions, recognition criteria, and measurement concepts in the IASB *Framework*.
d. Apply the requirements in IFRS dealing with similar and related issues.

40. On January 1, year 1, an entity acquires for $100,000 a new piece of machinery with an estimated useful life of 10 years. The machine has a drum that must be replaced every five years and costs $20,000 to replace. Continued operation of the machine requires an inspection every four years after purchase; the inspection cost is $8,000. The company uses the straight-line method of depreciation. Under IFRS, what is the depreciation expense for year 1?
a. $10,000
b. $10,800
c. $12,000
d. $13,200

41. On July 1, year 2, a company decided to adopt IFRS. The company's first IFRS reporting period is as of and for the year ended December 31, year 2. The company will present one year of comparative information. What is the company's date of transition to IFRS?
a. January 1, year 1.
b. January 1, year 2.
c. July 1, year 2.
d. December 31, year 2.

42. A company determined the following values for its inventory as of the end of its fiscal year:

Historical cost	$100,000
Current replacement cost	70,000
Net realizable value	90,000
Net realizable value less a normal profit margin	85,000
Fair value	95,000

Under IFRS, what amount should the company report as inventory on its balance sheet?
a. $70,000
b. $85,000
c. $90,000
d. $95,000

43. Which of the following is the minimum reporting requirement for a company that is preparing its first IFRS financial statements?
a. Three statements of financial position.
b. Two statements of financial position.
c. One statement of comprehensive income.
d. One statement of cash flows.

44. How should a first-time adopter of IFRS recognize the adjustments required to present its opening IFRS statement of financial position?
a. All of the adjustment should be recognized in profit or loss.
b. Adjustments that are capital in nature should be recognized in retained earnings and adjustments that are revenue in nature should be recognized in profit or loss.
c. Current adjustments should be recognized in profit or loss and noncurrent adjustments should be recognized in retained earnings.
d. All of the adjustments should be recognized directly in retained earnings or, if appropriate, in another category of equity.

45. A company is required to file quarterly financial statements with the United States Securities and Exchange Commission on Form 10-Q. The company operates in an industry that is not subject to seasonal fluctuations that could have a significant impact on its financial condition. In addition to the most recent quarter-end, for which of the following periods is the company required to present balance sheets on Form 10-Q?

   a. The end of the corresponding fiscal quarter of the preceding fiscal year.

   b. The end of the preceding fiscal year and the end of the corresponding fiscal quarter of the preceding fiscal year.

   c. The end of the preceding fiscal year.

   d. The end of the preceding fiscal year and the end of the prior two fiscal years.

46. A company is an accelerated filer that is required to file Form 10-K with the United States Securities and Exchange Commission (SEC). What is the maximum number of days after the company's fiscal year-end that the company has to file Form 10-K with the SEC?

   a. 60 days.

   b. 75 days.

   c. 90 days.

   d. 120 days.

ANSWER EXPLANATIONS FOR THE NEW FINANCIAL ACCOUNTING AND REPORTING MATERIAL

1. (d) The requirement is to identify the body that sets international accounting standards. Answer (d) is correct because the International Accounting Standards Board (IASB) issues International Financial Reporting Standards.

2. (c) The requirement is to identify the qualitative characteristics of relevance. Answer (c) is correct because the IASB *Framework* provides that relevance includes the qualities of predictive value, confirmatory value, and materiality. Answer (a) is incorrect because these are the characteristics of relevance in the FASB Concept Statements. Answer (b) is incorrect because these qualities are the characteristics of reliability in the FASB Concept Statements. Answer (d) is incorrect because comparability and consistency are a part of relevance in the IASB *Framework*.

3. (b) The requirement is to identify the element that is defined as increases in economic benefits in the form of inflows or enhancements of assets or decreases of liabilities that result in increases in equity other than those resulting from contributions from equity participants. Answer (b) is correct because the IASB *Framework* has five elements: asset, liability, equity, income, and expense. The definition given is that of income. Note that income includes both revenues and gains.

4. (b) The requirement is to identify the criteria under IFRS that must be met for an item to be included in financial statements. Answer (b) is correct because in order for an item to be recognized in the financial statements, IFRS requires that it meet the definition of an element and can be measured reliably.

5. (c) The requirement is to identify the revenue recognition method that must be used if the outcome of rendering services cannot be estimated reliably. Answer (c) is correct because if the outcome of rendering services cannot be measured reliably, IFRS requires use of the cost recovery method. Answer (a) is incorrect because the percentage-of-completion method is used when reliable estimates can be made. Answer (b) is incorrect because the completed contract method is not permissible under IFRS. Answer (d) is incorrect because the installment method is a revenue recognition method used under US GAAP, not IFRS.

6. (b) The requirement is to identify the item that describes how changes in accounting principles are reported under IFRS. Answer (b) is correct because IFRS requires changes in accounting principles to be reported by giving retrospective application to the earliest period presented. Answer (a) is incorrect because a change in accounting estimate is accounted for on a prospective basis in the current and future periods. Answer (c) is incorrect because restatement is required for errors in the financial statements. Answer (d) is incorrect because cumulative adjustments on the income statement are not permitted.

7. (b) The requirement is to identify the circumstances in which Galaxy may present the note as a noncurrent liability. Answer (b) is correct because IFRS requires that Galaxy must have executed an agreement to refinance at the balance sheet date in order to classify the debt as a noncurrent liability. Inasmuch as no agreement existed at the balance sheet date, the note payable must be classified as a current liability. Therefore, answers (a), (c), and (d) are incorrect.

8. (b) The requirement is to identify the item required to be disclosed on the income statement. The correct answer is (b) because the income statement may be prepared by presenting expenses either by nature or by function. The minimum required disclosures on the income statement include income, finance costs, share of profits and losses using the equity method, tax expense, discontinued operations, profit or loss, noncontrolling interests in profits and losses, and the net profit (loss) attributable to equity holders of the parent. Therefore, answers (a), (c), and (d) are incorrect.

9. (c) The requirement is to identify the item that must be disclosed on the income statement under IFRS. Answer (c) is correct because gain or loss from extraordinary items is not allowed on an income statement prepared using IFRS. Answers (a), (b), and (d) are items that may be disclosed on the income statement.

10. (b) The requirement is to identify where finance costs are presented in the statement of cash flows. Answer (b) is correct because under IFRS finance costs (interest expense) may be reported in either the operating or financing section of the statement of cash flows. However, once it is disclosed in a particular section, it must be reported on a consistent basis. Therefore, answers (a), (c), and (d), are incorrect.

11. (d) The requirement is to identify how the transaction should be reported on the statement of cash flows. Answer (d) is correct because this transaction did not involve an exchange of cash; therefore, it is not included on the statement of cash flows. IFRS requires that significant noncash transactions be reported in the notes to the financial statements. (Note that for US GAAP, if there are only a few significant noncash transactions, they may be reported at the bottom of the statement of cash flows, or they may be reported in a separate schedule in the notes to the financial statements.)

12. (a) The requirement is to identify how cash advances and loans from bank overdrafts should be reported on the statement of cash flows. Answer (a) is correct because IFRS requires cash advances and loans from bank overdrafts to be classified as operating activities.

13. (b) The requirement is to identify the acceptable methods for presenting other comprehensive income. Answer (b) is correct because IFRS provides that comprehensive income may be presented in either one statement or in two statements. (US GAAP allows the presentation in all three ways.)

14. (c) The requirement is to calculate the amount that should be presented for inventory. Answer (c) is correct because the lower of cost or net realizable value method requires net realizable value to be calculated as the estimated selling price less estimated costs of completion and estimated costs to sell. Therefore, the NRV is $850 ($900 − $50). The lower of cost or net realizable value is determined by comparing the cost of $1,000 to the NRV of $850, and using the lower amount. Inventory should be reported at $850.

15. (a) The requirement is to identify the models that may be used to value plant, property, and equipment. Answer (a) is correct because IFRS allows the use of the cost model or the revaluation model for reporting plant, property, and equipment.

16. (c) The requirement is to identify the true statement about the revaluation model. Answer (c) is correct because IFRS does not provide requirements as to the frequency or date of revaluation of plant, property, and equipment.

17. (c) The requirement is to identify where the gain or loss should be presented. Answer (c) is correct because when the revaluation method is used for reporting plant, property, and equipment under IFRS, any gain or loss is recorded in a revaluation surplus account which is classified as other comprehensive income.

18. (a) The requirement is to identify the true statement regarding use of the fair value model. Answer (a) is correct because the fair value model requires that investment property be measured at fair value, and any changes in fair value are recognized in profit or loss of the period.

19. (b) The requirement is to identify the acceptable valuation methods for intangible assets. Answer (b) is correct because under IFRS, intangible assets can be measured using either the cost model or the revaluation model.

20. (c) The requirement is to determine the impairment gain or loss reported in the financial statements. Answer (c) is correct because if the cost model is used to record intangible assets, the impairment loss is recognized as a loss in the current period. If the cost model is used, a reversal of impairment losses may be recognized in the income statement up to the effects of the impairment loss previously recognized. Therefore, an impairment loss of $20,000 is recognized in 2009, and a gain is recognized in 2010 of $4,000.

21. (c) The requirement is to identify how the estimated loss should be disclosed in the financial statements. Answer (c) is correct because IFRS defines a provision as a liability that is uncertain in timing or amount. Provisions are made for estimated liabilities and recorded as a loss in earnings for the period if the outcome is probable and measurable. Answer (a) is incorrect because the loss should be recorded in the current period income statement. Answer (b) is incorrect because under IFRS, a contingency depends on some future uncertainty or event, is not probably that an outflow will be required to settle, or the amount cannot be measured with reliability. If an item qualifies as a contingency, it is disclosed in the notes to the financial statements. Answer (d) is incorrect because contingencies are disclosed in the footnotes.

22. (c) The requirement is to identify how Roland should report the land. Answer (c) is correct because IFRS provides that a contingent asset is a possible asset that arises from past events, and is confirmed only by the occurrence of uncertain future events that are not within the control of the reporting entity. A contingent asset is not recognized, but it is disclosed in the notes to the financial statements if the economic benefits are probable. Answer (a) is incorrect because it does not meet the definition of an asset. Answers (b) and (d) are incorrect because contingent assets are not recognized in the balance sheet.

23. (c) The requirement is to identify the method(s) that may be used to report the bonds. Answer (c) is correct because IFRS provides that financial liabilities may be re-

ported at amortized cost or at the fair value through profit or loss (FVTPL). If FVTPL is elected, the resulting gain or loss is recognized in profit or loss for the period.

24. (a) The requirement is to identify the method that is used for defined benefit pension plans. Answer (a) is correct because IFRS requires the use of the projected-unit-credit method to calculate the present value of the defined benefit obligation (PV-DBO). Answer (b) is incorrect because the benefit-years-of-service method is used in US GAAP. Answers (c) and (d) are incorrect because these are not methods for reporting pension benefits.

25. (c) The requirement is to identify how the lease should be classified. Answer (c) is correct because IFRS requires a lease to be classified as a finance lease if substantially all the risks or benefits of ownership have been transferred to the lessee. Because the lease contains a bargain purchase option, it meets the criteria for a finance lease. Answer (a) is incorrect because the lease does not qualify as an operating lease since the risks and benefits of ownership have been transferred. Answer (b) is incorrect because US GAAP uses the term capital lease, whereas IFRS uses the term "finance lease." Answer (d) is incorrect because IFRS does not use the term sales-type lease.

26. (c) The requirement is to identify how Santiago should account for the lease. Answer (c) is correct because IFRS provides that because land has an indefinite life, if title is not expected to pass by the end of the lease term, then the substantial risks and rewards of ownership do not transfer. Thus, the lease should be separated into two components. The land should be recorded as an operating lease and the building should be recorded as a finance lease.

27. (b) The requirement is to determine how deferred taxes should be presented. Answer (b) is correct because IFRS provides that the netting of deferred tax assets and liabilities may only occur if the accounts relate to the same taxing authority and the entity has a legal right to offset the taxes. Therefore, the deferred tax asset of $4,000 and the deferred tax liability of $3,000 related to France may be offset, which results in a $1,000 deferred tax asset. The deferred tax liability of $2,500 related to Germany may not be netted and is shown as a deferred tax liability of $2,500 on the balance sheet.

28. (b) The requirement is to identify the true statement about accounting for deferred taxes. Answer (b) correct because IFRS does not permit deferred tax assets or liabilities to be classified as current. Therefore, deferred tax assets and liabilities are reported in the noncurrent section of the statement of financial position. Answer (a) is incorrect because deferred taxes may not be classified as current. Answers (c) and (d) are incorrect because deferred tax assets and liabilities may only be netted if there is a legal right to offset the amounts and they relate to the same taxing authority.

29. (c) The requirement is to identify how Logan should recognize the issuance of the bonds. Answer (c) is correct because IFRS provides that financial instruments with characteristics of both debt and equity are compound instruments and must be separated into their respective components. The liability is valued at the fair value at the date of issuance and the residual value is assigned to the equity component. Therefore, the bond should be recorded at its fair value of

$480,000, and an equity component should be recorded for 20,000. Answers (a), (b), and (d) are incorrect.

30. (d) The requirement is to identify how the gain is reported. Answer (d) is correct because IFRS requires that if an asset is classified as fair value through profit or loss, it is remeasured to fair value and any profit or loss is recorded in the period. Therefore, Acadia should recognize a $3,000 gain in current earnings of the period. Answers (a), (b), and (c) are incorrect.

31. (c) The requirement is to identify the form used to file as an annual report with the SEC. Answer (c) is correct because the form 10-K is the title of the annual report required to be filed annually by issuer companies. Answer (a) is incorrect because this is the title of the quarterly financial report. Answer (b) is incorrect because Form 8-K is the information report that may be filed any time during the year. Answer (d) is incorrect because a Form S-1 is an initial registration form for securities under the Securities Act of 1933.

32. (d) The requirement is to identify the content of the SEC Form 10-Q. Answer (d) is correct because the Form 10-Q presents reviewed quarterly information and other information about the company. Answer (a) is incorrect because the information is reviewed, not audited. Answer (b) is incorrect because this describes the Form 10-K. Answer (c) is incorrect because this describes the Form 8-K.

33. (a) The requirement is to select the item that describes when changes in accounting policies are permitted or required. Answer (a) is correct because changes are permitted if it will result in a more reliable and more relevant presentation of the financial statements.

34. (b) The requirement is to identify the circumstances that allow the entity to use the revaluation model. Answer (b) is correct because the revaluation method can only be used if there is an active market for the intangible asset.

35. (d) The requirement is to identify the criterion that must be met in order for an item to be recognized as an intangible asset other than goodwill. Answer (d) is correct because the asset must be identifiable and lack physical substance.

36. (b) The requirement is to determine the amount that should be recognized in the financial statements for the trademark. Answer (b) is correct because the trademark amount should include the purchase price ($100,000) plus the VAT taxes ($5,000) plus the legal cost incurred to register the trademark ($10,500), which is equal to $115,500. The research expenditures, training costs, and salaries should be expensed.

37. (a) The requirement is to identify the correct statement regarding the use of the revaluation model. Answer (a) is correct because when an asset is revalued, the entire class must be revalued. Answer (b) is incorrect because the entire class must be revalued. Answer (c) is incorrect because there are no rules regarding the frequency of revaluation. Answer (d) is incorrect because the revaluation surplus is presented in other comprehensive income, not profit or loss.

38. (c) The requirement is to identify the assets for which the entity may use fair value as deemed cost upon adoption of IFRS. Answer (c) is correct because the entity may use fair value as deemed cost for any individual item of property, plant and equipment.

39. (b) The requirement is to identify the first step within the hierarchy of guidance to which management refers when selecting accounting policies. Answer (b) is correct because the highest level in the hierarchy is an IFRS standard applicable to the transaction. Answers (a), (c), and (d) are incorrect because they all represent lower levels in the hierarchy.

40. (d) The requirement is to calculate depreciation for the asset. Answer (d) is correct because IFRS requires each major component to be depreciated over its respective useful life. The machinery cost $72,000 ($100,000 – $20,000 – $8,000) would be depreciated over 10 years. The drum would be depreciated over 5 years, and the inspection would be depreciated over 4 years. Therefore, depreciation would be calculated as $13,200 (($72,000/10) + ($20,000/5) + ($8,000/4)).

41. (a) The requirement is to identify the transition date. Answer (a) is correct because the "date of transition to IFRS" is defined as the beginning of the earliest period for which an entity presents full comparative information under IFRS.

42. (c) The requirement is to determine the amount that should be reported as inventory. Answer (c) is correct because under IFRS inventory is reported at the lower of cost or net realizable value. Therefore, the amount is $90,000, which is the lower of $100,000 cost or $90,000 net realizable value.

43. (a) The requirement is to identify the minimum reporting requirement for a company that is preparing its first IFRS financial statements. Answer (a) is correct because IFRS requires three balance sheets, two income statements, two cash flow statements, and two statements of changes in equity for first-time adopters.

44. (d) The requirement is to identify how adjustments are reflected upon adoption of IFRS. Answer (d) is correct because upon first-time adoption of IFRS, any adjustments required to present the opening balances of the statement of financial position should be recognized directly in retained earnings or, if appropriate, in another category of equity.

45. (c) The requirement is to identify the balance sheet required in the Form 10-Q. Answer (c) is correct because the SEC requires that a Form 10-Q contain an interim balance sheet as of the end of the most recent fiscal quarter and a balance sheet as of the end of the preceding fiscal year. An interim balance sheet for the fiscal quarter of the preceding year does not need to be provided unless it is necessary for understanding the impact of seasonal fluctuations.

46. (b) The requirement is to identify the deadline for filing a Form 10-K for an accelerated filer. Answer (b) is correct because the maximum number of days for an accelerated filer to file a 10-K with the SEC is 75 days after the company's fiscal year-end. However, a large accelerated filer with $700 million of public float has a deadline of 60 days, and nonaccelerated filers have a deadline of 90 days.

EXAMPLES OF THE NEW TASK-BASED SIMULATIONS—
FINANCIAL ACCOUNTING AND REPORTING

The simulations in the Financial Accounting and Reporting section of this manual will also help you review for the new smaller task-based simulations because many of the new task-based simulations are like single parts of the ones currently used.

Task-Based Simulation 1

Module 12

Jasco Corporation is in its first year of operations. The company has pretax income of $400,000. The company has the following items recorded in its records. No estimated tax payments were made during 2009.

Premiums on life insurance of key officer	$10,000
Depreciation on tax return in excess of book depreciation	12,000
Interest on municipal bonds	5,300
Warranty expense	4,000
Actual warranty repairs	3,250
Bad debt expense	1,400
Beginning balance in allowance for uncollectible accounts	0
End balance for allowance for uncollectible accounts	800
Rent received in advance from clients that will be recognized evenly over the next three years	24,000
Tax rate for 2009 and future years	40%

Prepare the following schedule for the deferred tax amounts for the year. Choose items from the following list:

Items

Premium on life insurance	Warranties
Depreciation	Bad debts
Interest on municipal bonds	Rent received

Item	Difference between taxable amount and income statement amount	Classification: Deferred tax asset Deferred tax liability	Current or noncurrent	Deferred tax amount

Task-Based Simulation 2

Module 16

Presented below are selected amounts from the separate unconsolidated financial statements of Poe Corp. and its 90%-owned subsidiary, Shaw Co., at December 31, 2010. Additional information follows:

	Poe	*Shaw*
Selected income statement amounts		
Sales	$710,000	$530,000
Cost of goods sold	490,000	370,000
Gain on sale of equipment	--	21,000
Earnings from investment in subsidiary	63,000	--
Interest expense	--	16,000
Depreciation	25,000	20,000
Selected balance sheet amounts		
Cash	$ 50,000	$ 15,000
Inventories	229,000	150,000
Equipment	440,000	360,000
Accumulated depreciation	(200,000)	(120,000)
Investment in Shaw	191,000	--
Investment in Shaw bonds	100,000	--
Discount on bonds	(9,000)	--
Bonds payable	--	(200,000)
Common stock	(100,000)	(10,000)
Additional paid-in capital	(250,000)	(40,000)
Retained earnings	(404,000)	(140,000)
Selected statement of retained earnings amounts		
Beginning balance, December 31, 2009	$272,000	$100,000
Net income	212,000	70,000
Dividends paid	80,000	30,000

Additional information

- On January 2, 2010, Poe, Inc. purchased 90% of Shaw Co.'s 100,000 outstanding common stock for cash of $155,000. On that date the fair value of the noncontrolling interest was $1.70 per share. On that date, Shaw's stockholders' equity equaled $150,000 and the fair values of Shaw's identifiable assets and liabilities equaled their carrying amounts. Poe has accounted for the purchase as an acquisition.
- On January 3, 2010, Poe sold equipment with an original cost of $30,000 and a carrying value of $15,000 to Shaw for $36,000. The equipment had a remaining life of three years and was depreciated using the straight-line method by both companies.
- During 2010, Poe sold merchandise to Shaw for $60,000, which included a profit of $20,000. At December 31, 2010, half of this merchandise remained in Shaw's inventory.
- On December 31, 2010, Poe paid $91,000 to purchase 50% of the outstanding bonds issued by Shaw. The bonds mature on December 31, 2014, and were originally issued at par. The bonds pay interest annually on December 31 of each year, and the interest was paid to the prior investor immediately before Poe's purchase of the bonds.
- On September 4, 2010, Shaw paid cash dividends of $30,000.
- On December 31, 2010, Poe recorded its equity in Shaw's earnings.

1. On January 3, 2010, Poe sold equipment with an original cost of $30,000 and a carrying value of $15,000 to Shaw for $36,000. The equipment had a remaining life of three years and was depreciated using the straight-line method by both companies.

2. During 2010, Poe sold merchandise to Shaw for $60,000, which included a profit of $20,000. At December 31, 2010, half of this merchandise remained in Shaw's inventory.

3. On December 31, 2010, Poe paid $91,000 to purchase 50% of the outstanding bonds issued by Shaw. The bonds mature on December 31, 2014, and were originally issued at par. The bonds pay interest annually on December 31 of each year, and the interest was paid to the prior investor immediately before Poe's purchase of the bonds.

Task-Based Simulation 3

Module 12

Using the authoritative literature from the accounting standards, identify the appropriate paragraph that provides the definition for deferred tax expense. Enter the exact section number and paragraphs and subparagraphs in the following fields.

FAS ACS

Solution to Task-Based Simulation 1

Item	Difference between taxable amount and income statement amount	Classification: Deferred tax asset Deferred tax liability	Current or noncurrent	Deferred tax amount
Depreciation	12,000	Deferred tax liability	Noncurrent	4,800
Warranties	750	Deferred tax asset	Current	300
Bad debts	800	Deferred tax asset	Current	320
Rent received	8,000	Deferred tax asset	Current	3,200
Rent received	16,000	Deferred tax asset	Noncurrent	6,400

Explanation of solutions

The adjustment to warranties is the difference between warranty expense deducted on the income statement and the actual warranty work performed during the period ($4,000 – $3,250 = $750). The adjustment to bad debt is the difference between bad debt expense subtracted on the balance sheet, and the actual bad debts written off during the period ($1,400 – $600 = $800). Note that rent received is taxable in the period received, and for deferred tax purposes, it must be fragmented into two components, current and noncurrent.

Solution to Task-Based Simulation 2

1.

Gain on equipment	21,000	
Accumulated depreciation		15,000
Equipment		6,000
Accumulated depreciation	7,000	
Depreciation expense		7,000

2.

Sales	60,000	
Cost of goods sold		50,000
Ending inventory		10,000

3.

Bonds payable	100,000	
Discount on bonds	9,000	
Gain on retirement of bonds		9,000
Investment in bonds		100,000

Explanation of solutions

1.   (**$14,000**) When preparing consolidated financial statements, the objective is to restate the accounts as if the intercompany transactions had not occurred. Therefore, the 2010 gain on sale of equipment of $21,000 ($36,000 – $15,000) must be eliminated, since the consolidated entity has not realized any gain. In addition, for consolidated statement purposes, 2010 depreciation is based on the original cost of the equipment to Poe. This elimination entry can be made in two separate entries. The first entry eliminated the gain, and restores the accumulated depreciation and equipment accounts as if the intercompany sale were never made. The second entry adjusts the current year depreciation expense to the amount that would have been recorded if the sale were never made. New depreciation is $36,000 ÷ 3 years = $12,000 for Shaw. Poe's depreciation was book value $15,000 ÷ 3 years = $5,000 per year. Therefore, depreciation expense must be adjusted by $12,000 – $5,000 = $7,000.

2.   (**$10,000**) Unrealized profit in ending inventory arises when intercompany sales are made at prices above cost and the merchandise is not resold to third parties prior to year-end. The profit is unrealized because the inventory has not yet been sold outside the consolidated entity. In this case, one half of the merchandise was left in Shaw's inventory at year-end. For the consolidated entity, one half of the $20,000 profit has not been earned and must be eliminated.

3.   (**$9,000**) When Poe purchased the bonds from an investor outside the consolidated entity, the bonds are viewed as retired from a consolidated viewpoint since there is no longer any obligation to an outside party. Therefore, the consolidated entity would recognize an ordinary gain of $9,000 ($100,000 carrying value of the bonds – $91,000 purchase price) on the retirement of the debt.

Solution to Task-Based Simulation 3

FAS ACS	740	10	30	4

REGULATION SECTION

The Content and Skills Specifications for the Regulation section of the CPA exam are the same as the current content specifications, with the following exception:

1. The topics of ethics and independence and responsibilities under the Sarbanes-Oxley Act have been moved from the Regulation section of the exam to the Auditing and Attestation section. Therefore, you do not need to study the first part of Module 21, Professional Responsibilities (dealing with ethics), and the section of Module 22, Securities Regulation, related to the Sarbanes-Oxley Act, and the related questions.
2. The topic of Business Structure (Module 38) should be studied because it will now be tested in the Regulation section.

EXAMPLES OF THE NEW TASK-BASED SIMULATIONS—REGULATION

The simulations in the Regulation section of this manual will also help you review for the new smaller task-based simulations because many of the new task-based simulations are like single parts of the ones currently used.

Task-Based Simulation 1

Module 33

Frank and Dale Cumack are married and filing a joint 2009 income tax return. During 2009, Frank, sixty-five, was retired from government service and Dale, fifty-five, was employed as a university instructor. In 2009, the Cumacks contributed all of the support to Dale's father, Jacques, an unmarried French citizen and French resident who had no gross income.

For **items 1 through 10,** select the correct amount of income, loss, or adjustment to income that should be reported on page 1 of the Cumacks' 2009 Form 1040—Individual Income Tax Return to arrive at the adjusted gross income for each separate transaction. A tax treatment may be selected once, more than once, or not at all.

Any information contained in an item is unique to that item and is not to be incorporated in your calculations when answering other items.

Selections

A. $0	D. $3,000	F. $4,000	I. $10,000	K. $ 30,000
B. $1,000	E. $3,500	G. $5,000	J. $25,000	L. $125,000
C. $2,000		H. $9,000		M. $150,000

(A) (B) (C) (D) (E) (F) (G) (H) (I) (J) (K) (L) (M)

1. During 2009, Dale received a $30,000 cash gift from her aunt. O O O O O O O O O O O O O

2. Dale contributed $3,500 to her traditional Individual Retirement Account (IRA) on January 15, 2009. In 2009, she earned $60,000 as a university instructor. During 2009 the Cumacks were not active participants in an employer's qualified pension or annuity plan. O O O O O O O O O O O O O

3. In 2009, the Cumacks received a $1,000 federal income tax refund. O O O O O O O O O O O O O

4. During 2009, Frank, a 50% partner in Diske General Partnership, received a $4,000 guaranteed payment from Diske for services that he rendered to the partnership that year. O O O O O O O O O O O O O

5. In 2009, Frank received $10,000 as beneficiary of his deceased brother's life insurance policy. O O O O O O O O O O O O O

6. Dale's employer pays 100% of the cost of all employees' group-term life insurance under a qualified plan. Policy cost is $5 per $1,000 of coverage. Dale's group-term life insurance coverage equals $450,000. O O O O O O O O O O O O O

7. In 2009, Frank won $5,000 at a casino and had $2,000 in gambling losses. O O O O O O O O O O O O O

8. During 2009, the Cumacks received $1,000 interest income associated with a refund of their prior years' federal income tax. O O O O O O O O O O O O O

(A) (B) (C) (D) (E) (F) (G) (H) (I) (J) (K) (L) (M)

9. In 2009, the Cumacks sold their first and only residence for $400,000. They purchased their home in 1992 for $50,000 and have lived there since then. There were no other capital gains, losses, or capital loss carryovers. The Cumacks do not intend to buy another residence.

        O O O O O O O O O O O O O

10. In 2009, Zeno Corp. declared a stock dividend and Dale received one additional share of Zeno common stock for three shares of Zeno common stock that she held. The stock that Dale received had a fair market value of $9,000. There was no provision to receive cash instead of stock.

        O O O O O O O O O O O O O

Task-Based Simulation 2

Module 33

Research

Assume that the Cumacks' automobile was stolen in 2010. The automobile was uninsured for theft and had a fair market value of $7,000, and an adjusted basis of $10,000. Which code section and subsection provide the limitations that apply to the deductibility of the Cumacks' uninsured theft loss? Indicate the reference to that citation in the shaded boxes below.

Section	Subsection
§ [ ]	([ ])

Task Based Simulation 3

Module 36

Capital Corp., an accrual-basis calendar-year C corporation, began operations on January 2, 2007. Capital timely filed its 2009 federal income tax return on March 15, 2010.

The following items each require **two** responses:

- For each item below, determine the amount of Capital's 2009 Schedule M-1 adjustment necessary to reconcile book income to taxable income. On the CPA exam, a list of numeric answers would be presented for the candidate to select from.
- In addition, determine if the Schedule M-1 adjustment necessary to reconcile book income to taxable income increases, decreases, or has no effect on Capital's 2009 taxable income. An answer may be selected once, more than once, or not at all.

Selections
I.   Increases Capital's 2009 taxable income.
D.   Decreases Capital's 2009 taxable income.
N.   Has no effect on Capital's 2009 taxable income.

	Amount of Adjustment	(I) (D) (N)
1. At its corporate inception in 2007, Capital incurred and paid $40,100 in organizational costs for legal fees to draft the corporate charter. In 2007, Capital correctly elected, for book purposes, to expense the organizational costs and to amortize the organizational expenditures over the minimum allowable period on its federal income tax return. For 2009, no organizational costs were deducted on its books.	_____	O O O
2. Capital's 2009 disbursements included $10,000 for reimbursed employees' expenses for business meals and entertainment. The reimbursed expenses met the conditions of deductibility and were properly substantiated under an accountable plan. The reimbursement was not treated as employee compensation.	_____	O O O
3. Capital's 2009 disbursements included $15,000 for life insurance premium expense paid for its executives as part of their taxable compensation. Capital is neither the direct nor the indirect beneficiary of the policy, and the amount of the compensation is reasonable.	_____	O O O
4. In 2009, Capital increased its allowance for uncollectible accounts by $10,000. No bad debt was written off in 2009.	_____	O O O

Solution to Task-Based Simulation 1

	(A)	(B)	(C)	(D)	(E)	(F)	(G)	(H)	(I)	(J)	(K)	(L)	(M)
1. During 2009, Dale received a $30,000 cash gift from her aunt.	●	○	○	○	○	○	○	○	○	○	○	○	○
2. Dale contributed $3,500 to her traditional Individual Retirement Account (IRA) on January 15, 2009. In 2009, she earned $60,000 as a university instructor. During 2009 the Cumacks were not active participants in an employer's qualified pension or annuity plan.	○	○	○	○	●	○	○	○	○	○	○	○	○
3. In 2009, the Cumacks received a $1,000 federal income tax refund.	●	○	○	○	○	○	○	○	○	○	○	○	○
4. During 2009, Frank, a 50% partner in Diske General Partnership, received a $4,000 guaranteed payment from Diske for services that he rendered to the partnership that year.	○	○	○	○	○	○	●	○	○	○	○	○	○
5. In 2009, Frank received $10,000 as beneficiary of his deceased brother's life insurance policy.	●	○	○	○	○	○	○	○	○	○	○	○	○
6. Dale's employer pays 100% of the cost of all employees' group-term life insurance under a qualified plan. Policy cost is $5 per $1,000 of coverage. Dale's group-term life insurance coverage equals $450,000.	○	○	●	○	○	○	○	○	○	○	○	○	○
7. In 2009, Frank won $5,000 at a casino and had $2,000 in gambling losses.	○	○	○	○	○	○	●	○	○	○	○	○	○
8. During 2009, the Cumacks received $1,000 interest income associated with a refund of their prior years' federal income tax.	○	●	○	○	○	○	○	○	○	○	○	○	○
9. In 2009, the Cumacks sold their first and only residence for $400,000. They purchased their home in 1992 for $50,000 and have lived there since then. There were no other capital gains, losses, or capital loss carryovers. The Cumacks do not intend to buy another residence.	●	○	○	○	○	○	○	○	○	○	○	○	○
10. In 2009, Zeno Corp. declared a stock dividend and Dale received one additional share of Zeno common stock for three shares of Zeno common stock that she held. The stock that Dale received had a fair market value of $9,000. There was no provision to receive cash instead of stock.	●	○	○	○	○	○	○	○	○	○	○	○	○

Solution to Task-Based Simulation 2

Internal Revenue Code Section 165, subsection (h) provides that an individual's personal casualty loss is allowable to the extent that it exceeds $100, and that a net personal casualty loss is deductible to the extent that it exceeds 10% of adjusted gross income.

Section	Subsection
§ 165	(h)

Solution to Task Based Simulation 3

	Amount of Adjustment	(I)	(D)	(N)
1. At its corporate inception in 2007, Capital incurred and paid $40,100 in organizational costs for legal fees to draft the corporate charter. In 2007, Capital correctly elected, for book purposes, to expense the organizational costs and to amortize the organizational expenditures over the minimum allowable period on its federal income tax return. For 2009, no organizational costs were deducted on its books.	$ 2,340	○	●	○
2. Capital's 2009 disbursements included $10,000 for reimbursed employees' expenses for business meals and entertainment. The reimbursed expenses met the conditions of deductibility and were properly substantiated under an accountable plan. The reimbursement was not treated as employee compensation.	$ 5,000	●	○	○
3. Capital's 2009 disbursements included $15,000 for life insurance premium expense paid for its executives as part of their taxable compensation. Capital is neither the direct nor the indirect beneficiary of the policy, and the amount of the compensation is reasonable.	$0	○	○	●
4. In 2009, Capital increased its allowance for uncollectible accounts by $10,000. No bad		●	○	○

debt was written off in 2009. $10,000

Explanation of solutions

1. **($2,340; D)** $5,000 of Capital's organizational costs of $40,100 would have been deducted in 2007 with remainder amortized over 180 months (15 years) for tax purposes. As a result, the tax amortization of organizational costs results in a tax deduction of $35,100 × 12/180 = $2,340 for 2009. Since no organizational costs were deducted per books for 2009, a Schedule M-1 decrease adjustment is necessary for the $2,340 difference.

2. **($5,000; I)** Only 50% of reimbursed employees' expenses for business meals and entertainment is deductible for tax purposes. As a result, an M-1 increase adjustment of $5,000 is necessary to reflect the fact that 50% of the $10,000 of reimbursed business meals and entertainment that was deducted for book purposes is not deductible for tax purposes.

3. **($0; N)** The $15,000 of life insurance premiums treated as reasonable compensation is fully deductible for both book and tax purposes and no M-1 adjustment is necessary.

4. **($10,000; I)** The reserve method of accounting for bad debts is not allowed for tax purposes. Instead, a bad debt deduction can be taken only when a specific debt is determined to be uncollectible. Since no bad debt was written off during 2009, an M-1 increase adjustment is necessary for the $10,000 addition to the allowance for uncollectible accounts for 2009.

BUSINESS ENVIRONMENT AND CONCEPTS

The Content and Skills Specifications for the Business Environment and Concepts section of the CPA exam are somewhat similar to the current content specifications. However, a number of topics have been added, including

1. Corporate governance and internal controls.
2. Enterprise risk management.
3. Additional coverage of business process management and systems design.
4. Project management.
5. Additional coverage of valuation of assets and liabilities.
6. Additional coverage of economic globalization.

In addition, you should review section F., "New Responsibilities and Provisions under Sarbanes-Oxley Act," in Module 21. The topic of Business Structure (Module 38) will now be tested in Regulation and not BEC.

As discussed previously, you should be prepared for the written communication questions. As with the current written communication questions they will not be graded for technical accuracy providing they are on topic. However, the topics of the questions will now be Business Environment and Concepts topics.

NEW MATERIAL—BUSINESS ENVIRONMENT AND CONCEPTS SECTION

Corporate Governance and Internal Controls

Effective corporate governance and appropriately designed internal controls are essential to the appropriate operation of an organization and reliable financial reporting.

A. Corporate Governance

In the corporate form of organization, owners (shareholders) are separated from operations (management) of the firm. This creates an agency problem in that management (the agents) may not act in the best interest of the shareholders (the principals). Managers may be tempted to engage in self-serving activities, such as shirking, taking too little or too much risk, or consuming excessive perks. Effective corporate governance involves establishing incentives (i.e., forms of compensation) and monitoring devices to prevent this inappropriate activity.

1. **Forms of Executive Compensation**

Various types of compensation are used to attempt to align management behavior with the objectives of the shareholders. A key objective in setting executive compensation is to align management's decisions and actions with the long-term interests of shareholders (e.g., long-term stock price). If managers are given too much fixed compensation, they may become too complacent and not take appropriate risks to increase share price. If managers are given too much incentive compensation based on operating profit or short-term stock price, they have incentives to manage profit or take excessive risks to maximize their compensation. Common types of management compensation are described below.

a. Base salary and bonuses—Using this system, managers are compensated based on performance which is typically measured by accounting profit. Compensation systems based on accounting measures of profit are problematic because accounting profit can be manipulated or managed. For example, the timing of research and development and maintenance expenditures may be altered to manage profit and maximize bonuses. Managers may put too much focus on short-term profits instead of focusing on maximizing the long-term wealth of shareholders.

b. Stock options—The use of stock options as a form of compensation provides managers with an incentive to manage the corporation to increase the stock price, which is consistent with the goal of shareholders. A disadvantage of stock options is that managers may have an incentive to increase the stock price in the short-term at the expense of long-term stock value, even by manipulating accounting income to increase stock price. In addition, stock options may encourage management to take on risks that are that are in excess of shareholders' risk appetite. Finally, if the stock price falls substantially, the stock options may be so underwater that they no longer provide an incentive to management.

c. Stock grants—Stock grants involve issuing shares of stock as part of management's compensation. Two common types of stock grants are

(1) Restricted stock—The issuance of stock that cannot be sold by the manager for a specific period of time, usually about 10 years. This form of compensation is effective because it encourages managers to undertake operations that increase the long-term value of the corporation's stock price.

(2) Performance shares—The issuance of stock to management if certain levels of performance are met. If the price of the corporation's stock increases, the value of the manager's compensation increases.

d. Executive perquisites (perks)—Management also may get various perquisites such as retirement benefits, use of corporate assets, golden parachutes, and corporate loans.

e. The best forms of executive compensation—It is generally believed that the best compensation systems include a combination of fixed compensation and incentive compensation that is related to long-term stock price. For example, the incentive compensation may be in the form of stock options or stock that can be exercised or sold only after being held for a long period of time (e.g., 5 to 10 years). Bonuses are effective if they are based on a composite of performance measures in addition to net profit, such as the amount of research and development expenditures, the corporation's market share, the number of new products developed, and/or the percentage of stock held by institutional investors (who tend to hold the stock for the long term). Such performance systems are often referred to as a balanced scorecard.

2. **Monitoring Devices**

Various devices exist in the United States to monitor management behavior. Some of the devices are internal (e.g., the board of directors and internal auditors), while others are external (e.g., external auditors, analysts, credit agencies, attorneys, the SEC, and the IRS).

a. **Boards of directors.** The board of directors is charged with running the corporation on behalf of the shareholders and other stakeholders. It is responsible for providing strategic direction and guidance about the establishment of the key business objectives of the corporation. The board also provides governance oversight. To be effective, board members must be competent and a majority of the board members should be independent. Independence means the board member is not part of management of the corporation and does not receive significant benefit from the corporation other than compensation as a board member. Board members also must be adequately trained and be provided with complete and accurate information to carry out the board's functions.

Boards are responsible for representing the shareholders by (1) hiring and, in some cases, firing top management, (2) voting on major operating and financial proposals, (3) providing advice to management, and (4) ensuring accurate financial reporting by the corporation.

Boards should have a set of governance guidelines that are reviewed and revised annually. These guidelines will set forth the board organization, which will include its various committees and subcommittees. Those that are particularly important to effective corporate governance include (1) the nominating/corporate governance committee, (2) the compensation committee, and (3) the audit committee.

(1) The nominating/corporate governance committee (1) oversees board organization, including committee assignments, (2) determines director qualifications and training, (3) develops corporate governance principles, and (4) oversees CEO succession.

(2) The audit committee plays a critical role in corporate governance. The Sarbanes-Oxley Act defines the audit committee as a "committee established by and amongst the board of directors of an issuer for the purpose of overseeing the accounting and financial reporting processes of the issuer; and audits of the financial statements of the issuer." A major responsibility of the audit committee is the appointment, compensation and oversight of the corporation's external auditor, including the resolution of any disagreements between management and the external auditor. An independent audit committee is mandated by the Sarbanes-Oxley Act and regulations of the NYSE and NASDAQ. Other important characteristics of an audit committee include

(a) The Sarbanes-Oxley Act provides that at least one member should be a "financial expert." The names of the financial experts must be disclosed. If the firm does not have a financial expert, it must provide an explanation.

(b) The audit committee should appoint, determine compensation of, and oversee the work of the corporation's external auditor.

(c) External auditors must report directly to the audit committee.

(d) Internal auditors should have direct access to the audit committee.

(e) The audit committee should establish procedures for the receipt and treatment of complaints regarding accounting or auditing matters, including submission of concerns by employees (whistle-blowers).

(3) The compensation committee (1) reviews and approves CEO compensation based on meeting performance goals, (2) makes recommendations to the board with respect to incentive and equity-based compensation plans, and (3) attempts to align incentives with shareholder objectives and risk appetite.

b. **New York Stock Exchange (NYSE) & NASDAQ Rules Related to Corporate Governance and Director Independence**. Among other items, the NYSE and NASDAQ require listed corporations to

(1) Have a majority of independent directors on their boards.

(2) Make determination of independence of members and provide information to investors about the determination. Specific NYSE and NASDAQ rules that make a director not independent include

(a) A director is not independent if s/he has been an employee of the corporation or an affiliate in the last 5 years (3 years for NASDAQ).

(b) A director is not independent if a family member has been an officer of the corporation or affiliate in the last 5 years (3 years for NASDAQ).

(c) A director is not independent if s/he was a former partner or employee of the corporation's external auditor in the last 5 years (3 years for NASDAQ).

(d) A director is not independent if s/he or a family member in the last 3 years received more than $120,000 (for a twelve-month period) in payments from the corporation other than for director compensation.

(e) A director is not independent if s/he is an executive of another entity that receives significant amounts of revenue from the corporation.

(3) Identify certain relationships that automatically preclude a board member from being independent.

(4) Have nonmanagement directors meet at regularly scheduled executive sessions.

(5) Adopt and make publically available a code of conduct applicable to all directors, officers and employees, and disclose any waivers of the code for directors or executive officers.

(6) Have an independent audit committee. In addition, nominating/corporate governance and compensation decisions must be made by independent committees (or a majority of independent directors for NASDAQ).

It is important to remember that judgment must be used to determine whether a director is independent. For example, based on the facts and circumstances it may be concluded that a director is not independent even though s/he receives less than $120,000 in payments (other than director compensation).

c. **Internal auditors.** Internal auditors perform audits of the risk management activities, internal control, and other governance processes for the corporation. Such audits are often referred to as assurance services. The results of these audits should be communicated directly to the audit committee of the board of directors. To ensure the adequate performance of their activities, internal auditors should be independent and competent. For effective independence, the chief audit executive ideally should report functionally to the audit committee and administratively to the chief executive officer of the corporation. This helps to prevent their work from being influenced by management of the corporation. The chief audit executive should have direct communication with the audit committee to assist the committee in performance of its oversight activities. The internal auditors must be provided with access to all of the aspects of the corporation's operations. In addition, the internal auditors should not perform any functions that would impair their independence in auditing that function. For example it would be improper for the internal auditors to perform routine internal control procedures for the corporation because they are responsible for auditing for compliance with control procedures. The NYSE requires its listed companies to maintain an internal audit function to provide management and the audit committee with ongoing assessments of the company's risk management processes and system of internal control.

The Institute of Internal Auditors is a professional organization that issues professional standards for internal auditors. This organization also administers the Certified Internal Auditor (CIA) program. To become a CIA an individual must pass a multipart exam and have a minimum of two years of internal audit experience (or its equivalent). The CIA designation helps to demonstrate that the individual is competent to perform internal audits.

d. **External auditors.** The external auditor is responsible for performing an audit of the corporation's financial statements and internal control in accordance with standards of the Public Company Accounting Oversight Board (PCAOB). The external auditor is a major external corporate governance monitoring device for a corporation. The external audit helps assure that corporation financial reports are accurate and management is not engaging in fraudulent financial reporting. External auditors are required to communicate to the audit committee information that will help the committee perform its oversight function, including the following matters:

(1) Auditor responsibility to form and express an opinion.

(2) An audit does not relieve management or the audit committee with their responsibilities for governance.

(3) Planned scope and timing of the audit.

(4) Significant audit findings, including

   (a) Auditor views of qualitative aspects of significant accounting practices.
   (b) Significant difficulties encountered during the audit.
   (c) Disagreements with management.
   (d) Other findings or issues which the auditor believes are significant and relevant.
   (e) Uncorrected misstatements other than those that are trivial.

(5) Material corrected misstatements.

(6) Significant issues discussed with management.

(7) Auditor's views about significant matters on which management consulted with other accountants.

(8) Written representations the auditor is requesting.

(9) Significant deficiencies and material weaknesses in internal control.

e. **Investment banks and securities analysts.** Investment bankers help corporations issue equity and debt offerings. Therefore, they represent an external monitoring device because they must evaluate the company prior to becoming involved in selling the securities.

Securities analysts analyze companies to attempt to develop recommendations to "buy," "hold," or "sell" a particular corporation's stock. Therefore, securities analysts act as an external monitoring device because they use financial and nonfinancial information, including information about corporate management to make their recommendations. An issue with considering the recommendations of analysts is potential conflicts of interest. For example, analysts may be employed by firms that also perform investment banking activities, and the analyst's recommendations may be influenced by the fees received from the corporation for investment banking services.

f. **Creditors.** Creditors also act as an external monitoring device. Debt agreements contain covenants (requirements) that must be complied with to prevent the creditor from taking actions such as accelerating payment terms. Creditors monitor compliance by the corporation with the covenants of these agreements. One limitation of creditors as a monitoring device is that they monitor largely based on information provided by management. However, they do often engage external auditors to perform procedures to provide assurance about the corporation's compliance with certain covenants of the loan agreements.

g. **Credit rating agencies.** Credit rating agencies rate the creditworthiness of corporate bonds. Credit rating agencies are an external corporate monitoring device much like securities analysts. The biggest criticism of credit rating agencies is that they may improperly set the initial rating and are slow to downgrade the rating once the corporation gets in financial difficulty.

h. **Attorneys.** Corporate legal counsel provide another external monitoring device in that they review securities filings and provide management advice on legal matters.

i. **The Securities and Exchange Commission (SEC).** The SEC is responsible for protecting investors; maintaining fair, orderly, and efficient markets; and facilitating capital formation. In achieving these responsibilities, the SEC enforces the US securities laws. The SEC consists of five presidentially appointed Commissioners. The SEC's activities act as an important external monitoring device for corporate government. The divisions and offices of the SEC that are particularly relevant to corporate governance include

(1) Division of Corporate Finance—This division reviews documents of publicly held companies that are filed with the SEC. Through the review process, the Division checks to see if companies are meeting disclosure requirements and seeks to improve the quality of the disclosures by companies.

(2) Division of Enforcement—This division assists the SEC in executing its law enforcement function by recommending the commencement of investigations of securities law violations, recommending which cases to take to court, and prosecuting these cases on behalf of the Commission.

(3) The Office of the Chief Accountant—The Chief Accountant advises the Commission on accounting and auditing, oversees the development of accounting principles, and approves the auditing rules put forward by the Public Company Accounting Oversight Board (PCAOB).

Several provisions of the Sarbanes-Oxley Act improved the SEC's power as an external monitoring device, including

(1) The Sarbanes-Oxley Act requires the chief executive officer (CEO) and the chief financial officer (CFO) to certify the accuracy and truthfulness of periodic financial reports filed with the SEC. If the certification of the reports is later found to be inaccurate, the CEO and CFO can be found criminally liable and face imprisonment of 10 to 20 years. Also, civil penalties can involve fines of up to $5 million.

(2) Under Sarbanes-Oxley, any person who knowingly perpetrates or attempts a scheme to defraud any other person by misrepresenting or making false claims in connection with the purchase or sale of securities can be fined or imprisoned for up to 25 years, or both. While securities fraud has long been an offense under the other securities acts, Sarbanes-Oxley made prosecution much easier.

(3) The destruction, mutilation, alteration, concealment, or falsification of documentation with the intent to obstruct or influence an investigation that is ongoing or being considered can result in fines or imprisonment of up to 20 years.

(4) Sarbanes-Oxley prohibits any acts of retaliation against employees who alert the government to possible violations of securities laws (whistle-blowers). The punishment for a violation of this provision can include fines or imprisonment of up to 10 years or both.

j. **The Internal Revenue Service (IRS).** The IRS acts as an external governance device by requiring certain accounting information on the corporation's income tax return. The IRS also audits corporations' tax returns, and enforces penalties for filing false tax returns.

k. **Corporate takeovers.** Takeovers also act as a corporate governance device. If management is performing poorly, the corporation may be subject to takeover by a firm that believes it can more efficiently utilize the corporation's resources. This provides an incentive for management to operate the corporation consistent with the interests of the shareholders.

l. **Shareholder activism.** When management is not operating the corporation in the best interests of the shareholders, the shareholders may engage in activism. Large shareholders can be especially effective because they have the ability to elect board members.

B. Internal Controls

There are a number of internal control frameworks used as benchmarks. The most commonly used framework in the US is *Internal Control—Integrated Framework* developed by COSO. According to COSO internal control is

A process, effected by the entity's board of directors, management, and other personnel designed to provide reasonable assurance regarding the achievement of objectives in the categories of (1) reliability of financial reporting, (2) effectiveness and efficiency of operations, and (3) compliance with applicable laws and regulations.

Under COSO internal control can be viewed as including five components: (1) the control environment, (2) the risk assessment process, (3) control activities, (4) information and communication, and (5) monitoring.

1. **The Control Environment**

    The control environment sets the tone of an organization by influencing the control consciousness of people. It may be viewed as the foundation for the other components of internal control. Control environment factors include integrity and ethical values; commitment to competence; board of directors or audit committee; management's philosophy and operating style; organizational structure; assignment of authority and responsibility; and human resource policies and practices.

    a. Integrity and ethical values. The effectiveness of internal control depends on the communication and enforcement of integrity and ethical values. Management should establish a tone at the top of the organization that encourages appropriate behavior. Top management should communicate these values through a code of conduct, official policies, and by example.

    b. Commitment to competence. Effective internal control depends on having employees that possess the skills and knowledge essential to performing their jobs, especially when they are responsible for performing important control functions.

    c. Board of directors or audit committee. The control environment is significantly influenced by the effectiveness of the board of directors and its audit committee. The characteristics and requirements for an effective board and audit committee were discussed above in the section on corporate governance.

    d. Management's philosophy and operating style. The manner in which management runs the organization can have a significant effect on the control environment. Management that takes undue risks or stresses making profit goals by any means can create an environment where employees are motivated to engage in unethical or illegal activities.

    e. Organizational structure. An effective organizational structure provides a basis for planning, directing and controlling operations.

    f. Assignment of authority and responsibility. Personnel need a clear understanding of their responsibilities and the rules and regulations that govern their actions. Authority and responsibility is communicated through documents such as job descriptions and organizational charts.

    g. Human resource policies and procedures. The control environment is enhanced by effective policies and practices for hiring, training, evaluating, counseling, promoting, and compensating employees.

2. **Risk Assessment**

    Effective internal control requires that management have a system of risk assessment. Risk assessment is management's process for identifying, analyzing, and responding to risks. This process is described more fully in the section on enterprise risk management.

3. **Control Activities**

    Control activities are policies and procedures that help ensure that management directives are carried out. These policies and procedures promote actions that address the risks that face the organization. Typical controls include performance reviews, information processing controls, physical controls, and segregation of duties, which encompass the routine controls over processes and transaction cycles.

4. **Information and Communication**

    To make effective decisions, managers must have access to timely, reliable, and relevant information. Information systems should be implemented to capture information and process, summarize and report the information on an accurate and timely basis. Proper communication involves providing employees with an understanding of their roles and responsibilities. Open communication channels are essential to the proper functioning of internal control.

5. **Monitoring**

    Monitoring of controls is a process used to assess the quality of internal control performance over time. Monitoring may be achieved by performing ongoing activities or by separate evaluations. Ongoing monitoring activities include regularly performed supervisory and management activities, such as continuous monitoring of customer complaints, or reviewing the reasonableness of management reports. Separate evaluations are monitoring activities that are performed on a nonroutine basis, such as periodic audits by the internal auditors.

Technology has enhanced an organization's ability to monitor internal controls and risk. Information systems can have embedded modules that look for unusual or suspicious transactions or relationships. This allows management to monitor controls and risks on a much more effective basis. Internal auditors often use technology to perform continuous auditing of transactions and processes for the same purpose.

C. Controls over Business Processes

Organizations use various approaches to executing and controlling financial transactions. Some are still very manual in nature. However, more and more transactions are being processed completely by the technology through private links within and between companies, or over the Internet. All transactions have risks that must be controlled.

A fundamental control over transactions is segregation of duties. For each transaction cycle, the functions of authorization, approval (for certain types of transactions), execution (custody of assets), and recordkeeping should be segregated. In a manual accounting system, segregation of duties is achieved by having different individuals physically performing the functions. In a technology-based system, the computer performs many of these processes and segregation of duties is achieved by controlling access to terminals and through the use of passwords. Of course in a technology-based system control is achieved over processing and data by appropriate information technology controls as discussed in Module 39.

The table below presents two major processes (transaction cycles) including the risks and examples of controls that might be used to mitigate those risks.

Sales & Collections Business Process

Risk	Nature of the process	Example controls
Inaccurate or incomplete sales data and lack of security over sales order information	Sales orders inputted manually	Password control over terminals to assure that sales are authorized by sales department; accuracy and completeness controls over inputs*; physical controls over terminals and files
	Sales over the internet	Encryption of transmitted data; accuracy and completeness controls over inputs; password control over access to information to maintain a segregation of duties; data controls to ensure that sales prices are accurately inputted and updated
Sales to customers that are not creditworthy	Outsource credit to credit card company	Protect credit card information with password control and physical security over terminals and files
	Organization has credit department that extends credit	Credit department should be independent of sales function and approve credit limits; effective practices for collecting credit information to make evaluations to grant credit
Maintaining too much or too little inventory	Inventory control and management	Use of a perpetual inventory system; use of techniques such as just-in-time, economic order quantity, and reorder point as methods of managing inventory: heavy reliance on technology to determine when and how much to order
Inaccurate filling of orders	Manual filling of orders	Have an individual not involved in filling the order check it for accuracy
	Use technology to fill orders	Input controls to assure information is correct in computer fulfillment process; use technology such as bar code scanners to pack goods
Inaccurate billing of customers	Manual billing process	Individual doing billing match sales order to shipping document to assure the accuracy of billing invoice; use of prenumbered documents and accounting for all documents; invoice checked for clerical accuracy by an individual not involved in preparation; billing department is independent of individuals maintaining receivables records; account for numerical sequence of documents
	Technology used for billing	Accuracy and completeness input controls to assure billing information is accurate and based on accurate shipping information input by shipping personnel; accuracy and completeness controls to assure that pricing information is accurate and based on authorization from the sales department; password control over terminals to insure segregation of duties

Risk	Nature of the process	Example controls
Errors or fraud in processing and depositing cash receipts	Cash receipts received through the mail	Segregation of cash handling from accounts receivable records or use of a lockbox at a financial institution
	Electronic funds transfer system	Control over access to the system through the use of a password system; use of accuracy and completeness controls over input of cash receipt information
Accounts may be written off without authorization	Manual	Individual independent of sales and cash receipts should be authorized to write off accounts; use of prenumbered authorization forms; accounting for all forms
	Technology-based system	Access to terminal for authorization by independent individual should be restricted by password system

* *Accuracy and completeness controls include controls such as validity checks, missing data checks, logic checks, limit tests, etc.*

Acquisitions & Payments Process

Risk	Nature of the Process	Example Controls
Ordering un-needed goods	Manual or technology-based system	Use of a perpetual inventory system; ordering based on inventory management techniques, such as just-in-time, economic order quantity, and reorder points
Purchasing goods from unautho-rized vendors	Manual or technology-based system	Establish preferred vendor relationships; establish criteria for authorized vendors
		Creation of purchase orders; accuracy and completeness controls over inputting purchasing information into the computer; password control over terminals
Receiving goods that were not ordered	Manual system	Matching of purchase order to goods received
	Technology-based system	Computer comparison of purchase information input by the purchasing department with information on goods received inputted by the receiving department
Receiving goods that are damaged or inferior	Manual or technology-based system	Inspect goods received
Payment of goods not received	Manual system	Matching of purchase orders with receiving reports; accounting for all prenumbered documents; individual authorized to sign checks is independent of those maintaining records and receiving personnel; check signer cancels supporting documentation
	Computer generation of payments based on purchase and receiving information	Accuracy and completeness input controls for purchase and receiving information; segregation of those maintaining records and processing payments from those authorized to make payments; password control to ensure segregation of duties
Authorization of cash payments	Manual system	Segregation of duties of accounting and authorized check signers
	Technology-based system	Passwords and controls over terminals prevent issuance of unauthorized payments
Loss or theft of assets	Manual or technology-based system	Periodic reconciliations of physical assets to accounting records by individuals independent of individuals having custody of the assets and individuals maintaining the accounting records for the assets; examples include reconciliations of bank accounts, taking physical inventories, and inventories of supplies and equipment

D. Change Control Processes

Management must effectively control the inevitable changes that occur in processes, policies and procedures, and systems. An effective change control process enables management to control (1) change requests, (2) change analyses, (3) change decisions, and (4) change planning, implementation and tracking. When a change occurs in an organization, it often has an effect on other areas of the organization. It is important that the change control process considers these effects and incorporates them into the analysis, planning and implementation phases of the change. Also, a system of documentation should be established to ensure that changes are authorized, communicated, and documented. Finally, changes should be thoroughly tested before being implemented. If employees are not adequately trained on new processes, control may break down.

Enterprise Risk Management

In addition to an internal control framework, COSO has also developed a framework for enterprise risk management (ERM). The framework defines ERM as follows:

> *Enterprise risk management is a process, effected by an entity's board of directors, management and other personnel, applied in a strategy setting and across the enterprise, designed to identify potential events that may affect the entity, and manage risk to be within its risk appetite, to provide reasonable assurance regarding the achievement of entity objectives.*

ERM helps align the risk appetite of the organization with its strategy, enhances risk response decisions, reduces operational surprises and losses, identifies and manages cross-enterprise risks, provides integrated responses to multiple risks, helps the organization seize opportunities, and improves the deployment of capital.

A key aspect of ERM is the identification and management of events that have a negative impact, positive impact, or both. Events with negative impact represent risks. Events with positive impact may offset negative impacts or represent opportunities.

Everyone in the organization has some responsibility for ERM. The best run organizations have a culture of risk management that is understood by every employee. Many organizations assign a risk officer, financial officer, and/or internal auditor with key support responsibilities. The internal control of the organization is an integral part of the organization's ERM system.

A. Components of ERM

According to COSO, ERM consists of eight interrelated components, including (1) internal environment, (2) objective setting, (3) event identification, (4) risk assessment, (5) risk response, (6) control activities, (7) information and communication, and (8) monitoring.

1. Internal Environment

The internal environment is the basis for all other components of ERM, providing discipline and structure. It encompasses the tone of the organization, and sets the basis for how risk is viewed and addressed by an organization's people, including risk management philosophy and risk appetite, and integrity and ethical values.

The board of directors is a critical part of the internal environment. The board provides oversight over management's implementation of ERM, helping to make sure that it is effective.

Integrity and ethical values help insure that management and other individuals within the organization are not inclined to engage in unethical or illegal activities. Management sets an ethical tone by action and example, and communicates the tone through codes of conduct and established policies. Management also should avoid the use of incentives and temptations to engage in unethical behavior, unless effective controls are established to prevent such behavior.

Other factors that contribute to an effective internal environment include competent, well-trained employees, an appropriate organizational structure, properly assigned authority and responsibility, and effective human resource policies and procedures.

An important aspect of the organization's internal environment is its risk appetite. **Risk appetite** is the amount of risk an organization is willing to accept to achieve its goals. It reflects the organization's culture and operating style and is directly related to the organization's strategy. Some organizations consider risk appetite qualitatively (e.g., low, moderate, high) while others consider risk quantitatively (e.g. in percentages). **Risk tolerance** relate to the organization's objectives. It is the acceptable variation with respect to a particular objective. For example, a company may have an objective of 97% customer satisfaction rating but may tolerate as low as a 94% customer satisfaction rating.

2. Objective Setting

Objectives must exist before management can identify potential events affecting their achievement. Enterprise risk management ensures that management has in place a process to set objectives and that the chosen objectives support and align with the organization's mission and are consistent with its risk appetite. The organization's mission sets forth in broad terms what the organization aspires to achieve. Strategic objectives are high-level goals aligned with the organization's mission. These high-level objectives are linked and integrated with the specific objectives established for various activities. By setting objectives the organization can identify critical risk factors, which are the key things that must go right for the objectives to be met.

Objectives may be divided into three categories: (a) operations objectives, which relate to the effectiveness and efficiency of operations, (b) reporting objectives, which relate to reliable reporting of internal and external, financial and nonfinancial information, and (c) compliance objectives which relate to adherence to laws and regulations.

3. **Event Identification**

Potential internal and external events affecting achievement of an organization's objectives must be identified, distinguishing between risks and opportunities. An event is an incident that occurs or might occur that affects implementation of strategy or achievement of objectives. Events may be negative (risks), positive (opportunities) or both. Risks require a response while opportunities should be channeled back to management's strategy or objective-setting processes. Some events may be external in nature, such as those resulting from economic, natural environment, political, social, or technological factors. Other events result from internal factors such as the organization's infrastructure, personnel, processes, or technology.

Event identification techniques include

a. Event inventories. Developing a detailed listing of potential events.

b. Internal analysis. This may be done at regular staff meetings. It may involve using information from other stakeholders, such as customers, suppliers, etc.

c. Escalation or threshold triggers. Management predetermines limits that cause an event to be further assessed. For example, a pricing problem may be triggered when competitor sales prices change by a predetermined percentage.

d. Facilitated workshops or interviews. This technique involves soliciting information about events from management and staff. For example, a facilitator may lead a discussion of events that might affect achieving an organization's objectives.

e. Process flow analysis. Involves breaking processes down into inputs, tasks, responsibilities, and outputs to identify events that might adversely affect the process.

f. Leading event indicators. This technique involves monitoring data correlated to events, to identify when the event is likely to occur.

g. Loss event data methodologies. By developing repositories of data on past loss events, management can identify event trends and the root causes of events. Management can also perform **black swan analysis** which involves evaluating the occurrence of events that had negative effects and were unanticipated or viewed as highly unlikely.

4. **Risk Assessment**

Risks are analyzed, considering likelihood and impact, as a basis for determining how they should be managed. Management should assess both inherent risk and residual risk for an event. **Inherent risk** is the risk to the organization if management does nothing to alter its likelihood or impact. **Residual risk** is the risk of the event after considering management's response. Risks are assessed in terms of their likelihood of occurring and their impact (e.g., financial effect). Management often uses qualitative techniques to assess risk when risks do not lend themselves to quantification or when sufficient reliable data is not available to use a quantitative model. Probabilistic or nonprobabilistic models may be used to quantify risk. Probabilistic models associate a range of events and the resulting impact with the likelihood of those events based on certain assumptions. Examples of probabilistic models include value at risk, cash flow at risk, earnings at risk, and development of credit and operational loss distributions. Nonprobabilistic models use subjective assumptions in estimating the impact of events without quantifying an associated likelihood. Examples of nonprobabilistic models include sensitivity measures, stress tests, and scenario analysis.

5. **Risk Response**

In this aspect of ERM, management selects risk responses that are consistent with the risk appetite of the organization including

a. Avoidance. This response involves exiting the activity that gives rise to the risk.

b. Reduction. This response involves taking action to reduce risk likelihood or impact, or both. For example, this might involve managing the risk or adding additional controls to processes.

c. Sharing. This response involves reducing risk likelihood or impact by transferring or sharing a portion of the risk. Techniques for sharing include insurance, hedging, and outsourcing.

d. Acceptance. No action is taken because the risk is consistent with the risk appetite of the organization.

All risk responses must be assessed in terms of their costs and benefits to select the responses that should be implemented.

6. **Control Activities**

Policies and procedures should be established and implemented to help ensure the risk responses are effectively carried out.

7. **Information and Communication**

Relevant information is identified, captured, and communicated to enable people to carry out their responsibilities. Information is needed at all levels of the organization to identify, assess and respond to risks. Communication should effectively convey the importance and relevance of effective ERM, the organization's objectives, the organization's risk appetite and risk tolerances, a common risk language, and the roles and responsibilities of personnel in effecting and supporting the components of ERM.

8. **Monitoring**

The entire ERM process should be monitored to make needed modifications. Monitoring is accomplished by ongoing management activities, and separate evaluations, such as those internal auditors.

B. Limitations of ERM

In considering limitations of ERM, three distinct concepts must be recognized:

1. Risk relates to the future which is uncertain,

2. ERM provides information about risks of achieving objectives but it cannot provide even reasonable assurance that objectives will be achieved, and

3. ERM cannot provide absolute assurance with respect to any of the objective categories. Specific limitations include the following:

   a. The effectiveness of ERM is subject to the limitations of the ability of humans to make judgments about risk and impact.
   b. Well-designed ERM can break down.
   c. Collusion among two or more individuals can result in ERM failures.
   d. ERM systems can never be perfect due to cost-benefit constraints.
   e. ERM is subject to management override.

Business Process Management and Systems Design

A. Business Process Management

Business processes are the structured activities of an organization that produce a product or service. Business process management focuses on continuously improving processes to align all activities with the desires and needs of the customer. As a managerial approach, business process management views processes as strategic assets that must be understood, managed, and improved. To improve processes management focuses on both the human and technological aspect of processes, and the interaction of the two. Many organizations are finding it productive to improve processes by focusing on this human–technology interaction, as they try to develop technology that is designed for a task and the way the particular individual works.

The life-cycle of business process management includes design, modeling, execution, monitoring, and optimization.

1. **Design**

The design phase involves identification of existing processes and design of process improvements. Good process design is critical to preventing problems over the life of the process.

2. **Modeling**

In the modeling phase management simulates the process in a test environment and performs "what if" analysis to try to determine how it will work under varying conditions.

3. **Execution**

Execution involves installing software, training personnel, and implementing the new processes. It also involves testing the new processes.

4. **Monitoring**

The monitoring phase is continuous after the execution phase. It involves tracking the processes with performance statistics.

5. **Optimization**

   This phase of the life-cycle involves retrieving performance statistics from modeling or monitoring and identifying potential bottlenecks or other problems for additional improvement of the process.

   As processes are analyzed for improvement, it is sometime discovered that processes that were once performed by several departments should be centralized in one department. For example, employee training might become a centralized process to improve efficiency and effectiveness. Alternatively, management may decide to outsource a process to an external organization, or even outsource a process to an organization in another country (often referred to as off-shoring). There are a number of reasons that an organization may decide to outsource or off-shore, including costs saving, quality improvement, tax benefit, scalability, or to focus on core competencies. However, such strategy may present additional risks including

   - Quality risk. The company may have less control over the quality of outsourced or off-shored activities.
   - Language risk. Control over activities and customer service may be affected by language issues.
   - Information security risk. Control over confidential company or customer information may be put at risk.
   - Intellectual property risk. Information about the company's products and processes may be put at risk.
   - Public opinion risk. The company's reputation may be put at risk because it is off-shoring jobs.
   - Social responsibility risk. The company's reputation may be put at risk based on the practices of the organizations used in other countries.

   Obviously, the company can implement policies and controls, including requiring effective operating agreements, to mitigate these risks.

B. **Systems Design and Process Improvement**

   In the current environment, designing and implementing a new information and control system provides an opportunity to reexamine business processes, especially if the new system is an enterprise resource (ERP) system. Management can take advantage of the capabilities of the technology to redesign business processes making them more efficient and effective. The systems development life cycle includes the following steps: planning, analysis, design, development, testing, implementation, and maintenance.

1. **The Planning Phase**

   Major steps in the planning phase include

   a. Define the system to be developed. This involves identifying and selecting the system to be developed based on the strategic goals of the organization.
   b. Determine the project scope. In this step the high-level requirements are defined. A project scope document is used to describe the project scope. During the process of systems design, the scope of the project may be revisited and revised.
   c. Develop a project plan. The project plan defines the activities that will be performed, and the individuals and resources that will be used. A project manager is individual that develops the plan and tracks its progress. The plan establishes project milestones which set forth dates by which certain activities need to be performed.

2. **The Analysis Phase**

   This phase involves teams including end users, information technology specialists, and process design specialists to understand the requirements for the proposed system. During this phase a **needs assessment** may be performed. A needs assessment involves determining the requirements for the system in terms of processes, data capture, information and reporting. Next, an analysis is performed on the existing system along the same dimensions. Then, a gap analysis is performed to examine the differences (gaps) between the required system and the existing system. Finally, priorities will be established for the gaps (requirements) which will be documented in a requirements definition document, which will receive sign-off from the end users. It is during this phase that a company can take advantage of the processes inherent in the new system to improve existing processes.

3. **The Design Phase**

   The primary goal of the design phase is to build a technical blueprint of how the proposed system will work.

4. **The Development Phase**

During the development phase the documents from the design phase are transformed into the actual system. In the design phase the platform on which the system is to operate is built and the programs and databases are developed.

5. **The Testing Phase**

The testing phase involves verifying that the system works and meets the business requirements as set forth in the analysis phase. The testing phase is obviously critical. The following types of tests should be performed:

a. Unit testing. Unit testing involves testing the units or pieces of code.

b. System testing. System testing involves testing of the integration of the units or pieces of code into a system.

c. Integration testing. Integration testing involves testing whether the separate systems can work together.

d. User acceptance testing. User acceptance testing determines whether the system meets the business requirements and enables users to perform their jobs efficiently and effectively.

6. **The Implementation Phase**

The implementation phase involves putting the system in operation by the users. In order to effectively implement the system detailed user documentation must be provided to the users, and the users must be adequately trained. An organization may choose from a number of implementation methods including

a. Parallel implementation. This method uses both systems until it is determined that the new system is operating properly. This has the advantages of a full operational test of the new system with less risk of a system disaster. The disadvantage of this method is the additional work and cost during the period in which both systems are operating.

b. Plunge implementation. Using this method the organization ceases using the old system and begins using the new system immediately. This method is less costly than the parallel method but it has higher risk of a system breakdown.

c. Pilot implementation. This method involves having a small group of individuals using the new system until it is seen to be working properly. This has the advantage of providing a partial operational test of the new system at a lower cost than parallel implementation.

d. Phased implementation. This method involves installing the system in a series of phases.

7. **The Maintenance Phase**

This phase involves monitoring and supporting the new system. In this phase the organization provides ongoing training, help desk resources, and a system for making authorized and tested changes to the system.

Project Management

A project is a series of activities and tasks that

- Have specific definable objectives,
- Have defined start and end dates,
- Are subject to funding constraints,
- Consume resources, people, equipment, etc., and
- Cut across various functional areas of the organization.

Projects are usually planned and executed by multidisciplinary teams, consisting of individuals from different functional areas and led by a project manager. Team members must be knowledgeable and able to work together to plan and execute work in a team setting. Some projects are assigned a project oversight or steering group which takes responsibility for the business issues related to the project. These committees are responsible for approving budgetary strategy, defining and realizing benefits, and monitoring risks, quality and timeliness.

Effective project management involves efficiently achieving the project objectives within time and cost constraints. To achieve effective project management, the project leader must manage the four basic elements of a project, including

1. Resources—people, equipment, materials, etc.
2. Time—task durations, task interdependencies, the critical path, etc.

3. Money—costs, contingencies, profit, etc.
4. Scope—project size, goals, requirements, etc.

The processes involved in project management include project initiation, project planning, project execution, project monitoring and control, and project closure.

1. Project initiation includes

    a. Selection of the best project given resource constraints.
    b. Recognizing the benefits of the project.
    c. Authorizing the project. The project must have full support of management of the organization. Since projects often cross functional lines, a commitment by top management of the organization is critical to the success of any project.
    d. Assigning the project manager (leader). The project manager should be competent and have sufficient authority to get access to needed resources and people. The project manager should have planning skills, organizational skills, negotiating skills, administration skills, resource allocation skills, and entrepreneurial skills. A **project charter** authorizes the project, and sets forth the project manager's authority and responsibility.

2. Project planning involves determining the activities that need to be performed, who should perform them, and when the activities need to be completed. Planning includes

    a. Defining the work requirements.
    b. Defining the quality and quantity of the work.
    c. Indentifying the needed resources.
    d. Scheduling the activities and tasks.
    e. Indentifying and assessing risks.

    The planning process results in a number of documents. The scope of the work is often set forth in a **statement of work (SOW)** which is a narrative description of the work to be performed to complete the project, including the deliverables. One of the most common reasons for a scope change in a project is a poorly defined statement of work.

    The statement of work often includes the **project specifications** which is a detailed listing of the man-hour, equipment, and materials requirements. The **milestone schedule** sets forth the start date, the end date and other major milestones involved in completing the project. Finally, the **work breakdown structure (WBS)** breaks the project into manageable, independent, and measurable elements that can be budgeted and for which responsibility can be assigned. The WBS provides a basis for costing, risk analysis, control, and scheduling the project.

    Many companies use a **life-cycle approach** in planning, in which project planning is divided into defined phases, such as conceptualization, feasibility study, etc. At the end of each phase an assessment is done to evaluate the success of the phase, and determine whether the next phase should be undertaken.

    Many different techniques are used to schedule and control a project, including

    a. Gant chart—a type of bar chart that illustrates the scheduled start and finish of elements of a project over time.
    b. Milestone chart—a type of chart that illustrates the milestones for a project over time.
    c. Line of balance—a type of chart that illustrates the series of activities that are related. It is appropriate where a project has a series of repetitive activities.
    d. Network diagram—illustrates the logical representation of activities that defines the sequence of the work of a project. It illustrates the path of a project. A network diagram has advantages over other forms of techniques because it (1) illustrates the interdependencies between activities, (2) identifies critical paths in a project, (3) facilitates risk analysis for the activities in the project, and (4) enables management to evaluate the effect of an activity delay on the project completion date.
    e. Program Evaluation and Review Technique (PERT)—PERT is a network technique that formally focuses on the interdependency of activities and the time required to complete an activity to schedule and control the project. This technique focuses on the **critical path,** which is the shortest amount of time necessary to accomplish the project. Any slippage in the time of performing the activities along the critical path will result in a delay in completion of the project. Therefore, management knows which activities and events are most critical to timely

completion of the project. PERT uses three time estimates (optimistic, most likely, and pessimistic) to derive expected time to complete a particular task. In PERT analysis **slack time** is the difference between the expected time and the latest time the activity can be completed without delaying the project. PERT is probabilistic in nature which allows the calculation of the risk in completing the project. PERT is typically used where there is a high variability of completion time, such as research and development projects.

f. PERT cost—allows the addition of resource cost considerations to the schedule produced by the PERT technique. This allows the inclusion of cost uncertainty into the analysis.

g. Critical Path Method (CPM)—CPM is similar to PERT but it only uses one time estimate that represents the normal time to complete an activity. CPM is used for projects where there is less variability in time estimates. CPM includes a procedure for time/cost tradeoff to minimize the sum of direct and indirect project costs.

h. Graphical Evaluation and Review Technique (GERT)—GERT is similar to PERT but it has the advantage of allowing looping and branching based on the results of a particular activity. It is appropriate for projects that may be completed in number of ways.

i. **Project crashing** is a term used to describe the practice of adding resources to shorten selected activity time on the critical path of a project. In effect the manager is trading off money for time. Therefore, each activity may be viewed as having two types—a normal (planned) time and the crash time (the shortest possible time).

j. Another technique that is often used in conjunction with any of these scheduling techniques is **ABC analysis**. ABC analysis involves the categorization of tasks into groups. These groups are often marked A, B, and C—hence the name. Activities are ranked upon the following general criteria:

A – Tasks that are perceived as being urgent and important.
B – Tasks that are important but not urgent.
C – Tasks that are neither urgent nor important.

Then, each group is then rank-ordered in priority. This technique is particularly applicable to project management because it focuses attention on the critical activities or tasks.

Risk management is also applicable to project management. Project risks include those related to costs overruns, time slippage, inappropriately defined scope, and dissatisfaction with the deliverables. The steps in the risk management of a project include (1) identification of risks, (2) quantifying the risks, (3) prioritizing risks, and (4) developing a risk response. Like any type of risk management the response may involve such activities as developing controls or shifting the risk to another party.

3. Project execution includes

a. Negotiating for the team members.
b. Directing the work.
c. Managing team members to improve performance.

Management of a project requires much the same skills as managing any function. However, if the project crosses functional lines, the management process becomes complicated. Problems in project management typically arise from one of the following:

- Organizational uncertainty. The working relationship between the project manager and the functional managers has not been adequately defined by senior management.
- Unusual decision pressures. Project managers must make quick decisions in uncertain situations and with incomplete information. Senior management must recognize these difficulties and support the project manager's decisions.
- Inadequate senior management support. Delays in approval, inability to resolve reporting conflicts, and delays in providing resources can significantly delay or derail projects.

4. Project monitoring and control includes

a. Tracking progress of the project.
b. Comparing actual outcomes to predicted outcomes.
c. Analyzing variances and their effects.
d. Making adjustments.

Many of the typical management techniques are used to control projects, including budgets, variance analysis, and status analysis. The scheduling techniques discussed above also facilitate control of the project by allowing management to focus its attention on critical activities.

5. Project closure includes

   a. Determining that all work has been completed.
   b. Closure of the contract, financial charges, and paperwork.

Asset and Liability Valuation

An important part aspect of financial statements and finance is the valuation of assets and liabilities. Valuations are needed for a number of purposes including investment evaluation, capital budgeting, mergers and acquisitions, financial reporting, tax reporting, and litigation. The major types of valuation models include

1. Market values obtained from active markets for identical assets.
2. Market values derived from active markets for similar but not identical assets.
3. Valuation models.

1. **Using Active Markets for Identical Assets**

   The most straight forward method of valuing a financial instrument is using prices for identical instruments in an active market. The use of such markets is appropriate if they have sufficient volume of transactions to insure that the market price is reliable.

2. **Using Active Markets for Similar Assets**

   Another method for valuing instruments involves deriving values from the market prices of similar but not identical instruments. The key to this method of valuation is accurate adjustment for differences that exist between the instrument being valued and the instrument that is traded in the market. For example, the price might need to be adjusted for such factors as restrictions on sales, or differences in maturity dates, exercise dates, block sizes, credit risk, etc. Financial models are often used to adjust the value of the instrument for these differences.

3. **Valuation Models**

   A method that can be used in the absence of an active market is determining estimated fair value based on a valuation model, such as discounted cash flows. Such valuations generally rely on assumptions about future events and conditions that affect income and cash flows. These assumptions could materially affect the fair value estimate. Accordingly, they must be examined to determine whether they are reasonable and consistent with existing market information, the economic environment and past experience. For example, in determining the fair value of a rare asset for which market information is not available, consideration should be given to sales of similar assets, the general economic environment in which the asset is used and past experiences with similar assets. As another example, discount rates for calculating discounted cash flows must reflect market expectations of future rates and be consistent with the level of risk inherent in the future cash flows.

   In determining estimates of fair values it is also important that the model being used is appropriate based on the nature of the asset and current economic conditions.

Economic Globalization

Economic globalization refers to the increasing economic interdependence of national economies across the world through a rapid increase in cross-border movement of goods, service, technology and capital. It has led to a single world market in which developed economies have integrated with less developed countries by means of foreign direct investment, the reduction of trade barriers, and the modernization of the developing countries. The comparative advantages of natural resources or low-cost labor attract businesses and capital to developing (emerging) economies. Companies in developed countries are able to compete with companies in developing countries in a number of ways including

- Use of sophisticated technology to reduce costs.
- Effective process management.
- Innovation in products or services.
- Product quality.
- Customer service.
- Adopting a global strategy.

In operating in a global economy, it is important that executives understand the cultural differences among countries. Differences in customs, values, and behavior result in problems that can only be managed by cross-cultural communication and interaction. These cultural differences affect negotiations, personnel management, and commerce.

Multinational companies generally pursue a global strategy in which they locate and consolidate operations in countries with the greatest strategic advantages. Organizations that pursue a global strategy can benefit in a number of ways, including

- Pooling international production to one or a few locations can achieve increased economies of scale.
- Manufacturing costs can be cut by moving production to low-cost countries.
- A firm that can switch production among different countries has increased bargaining power over labor, suppliers, and host governments.
- Worldwide access to resources, labor, suppliers and customers.

QUESTIONS ON NEW BUSINESS ENVIRONMENT AND CONCEPTS MATERIAL

1. Which of the following best identifies the reason that effective corporate governance is important?
    a. The separation of ownership from management.
    b. The goal of profit maximization.
    c. Excess management compensation.
    d. Lack of oversight by Boards of Directors.

2. Which of the following forms of compensation would most likely align management's behavior with the interests of the shareholders?
    a. A fixed salary.
    b. A salary plus a bonus based on current period net income.
    c. A salary plus stock options that cannot be exercised for 10 years.
    d. A salary plus stock.

3. Which of the following forms of compensation would encourage management to take on excess risk?
    a. A fixed salary.
    b. A salary and bonuses based on current period net income.
    c. A salary plus stock options that cannot be exercised for 10 years.
    d. A salary plus restricted stock.

4. Which of the following is not a requirement of the New York Stock Exchange regarding corporate governance of companies listed on the exchange?
    a. Have a majority of independent directors of the corporate board.
    b. Adopt and make publically available a code of conduct.
    c. Prohibit the chief financial officer from serving on the board of directors.
    d. Have an independent audit committee

5. Which of the following does not act as an external corporate governance mechanism?
    a. External auditors.
    b. The SEC.
    c. Credit analysts.
    d. Independent boards of directors.

6. The Sarbanes-Oxley Act provides that at least one member of the audit committee should be
    a. Independent.
    b. The chief financial officer of the company.
    c. A financial expert.
    d. A CPA.

7. Which of the following is most effective as an external monitoring device for a publicly held corporation than the others?
    a. Internal auditors.
    b. External auditors.
    c. The SEC.
    d. Attorneys.

8. An important corporate governance mechanism is the internal audit function. For good corporate governance, the chief internal audit executive should have direct communication to the audit committee and report to
    a. The chief financial officer.
    b. The chief executive officer.
    c. The controller.
    d. The external auditors.

9. Securities analysts act as one form of monitoring device from a corporate governance standpoint. What is a limitation that is often identified when considering the effectiveness of securities analysts in this regard?
    a. Conflicts of interest.
    b. Lack of competence.
    c. Use of only nonfinancial information for analyses.
    d. They are employees of the company.

10. Which of the following divisions of the SEC reviews corporate filings?
    a. The Office of the Chief Accountant.
    b. The Division of Enforcement.
    c. The Division of Corporate Disclosure.
    d. The Division of Corporate Finance.

11. Which of the following components is considered the foundation of the internal controls established by an organization?
    a. Control activities.
    b. Monitoring.
    c. The control environment.
    d. The audit committee.

12. Which of the following is not a control environment factor?
    a. Integrity and ethical values.
    b. Board of directors or audit committee.
    c. Human resources policies and procedures.
    d. Control monitoring.

13. Which of the following components of internal control would encompass the routine controls over business processes and transactions?
    a. The control environment.
    b. Information and communication.
    c. Control activities.
    d. Risk assessment.

14. Which of the following is not a component in the COSO framework for internal control?
    a. Control environment.
    b. Segregation of duties.
    c. Risk assessment.
    d. Monitoring.

15. Management of Johnson Company is considering implementing technology to improve the monitoring component of internal control. Which of the following best describes how technology may be effective at improving monitoring?
    a. Technology can identify conditions and circumstances that indicate that controls have failed or risks are present.
    b. Technology can assure that items are processed accurately.
    c. Technology can provide information more quickly.
    d. Technology can control access to terminals and data.

16. Jarrett Corporation is considering establishing an enterprise risk management system. Which of the following is not a benefit of enterprise risk management?

a. Helps the organization seize opportunities.
b. Enhances risk response decisions.
c. Improves the deployment of capital.
d. Insures that the organization shares all major risks.

17. In the COSO enterprise risk management framework, the term risk tolerance refers to
a. The level of risk an organization is willing to accept.
b. The acceptable variation with respect to a particular objective.
c. The amount of risk of an event after considering management's response.
d. Events that require no risk response.

18. Management of Warren Company has decided to respond to a particular risk by hedging the risk with futures contracts. This is an example of risk
a. Avoidance.
b. Acceptance.
c. Reduction.
d. Sharing.

19. Which of the following is not a technique for identifying events in an enterprise risk management program?
a. Process flow analysis.
b. Facilitated workshops.
c. Probabilistic models.
d. Loss event data methodologies.

20. Devon Company is using an enterprise risk management system. Management of the company has set the company's objectives, identified events, and assessed risks. What is the next step in the enterprise risk management process?
a. Establish control activities to manage the risks.
b. Monitor the risks.
c. Determine a response to the risks.
d. Identify opportunities.

21. Which of the following is not an advantage of establishing an enterprise risk management system within an organization?
a. Reduces operational surprises.
b. Provides integrated responses to multiple risks.
c. Eliminates all risks.
d. Identifies opportunities.

22. Kelly, Inc. is considering establishing an enterprise risk management system. Which of the following is not a limitation of such a system?
a. Business objectives are not usually articulated.
b. The system may break down.
c. Collusion among two or more individuals can result in system failure.
d. Enterprise risk management is subject to management override.

23. In an attempt to improve operations, companies often go through analyses and redesign of the way processes are performed. Which of the following is not considered to be an aspect of a business process that may be focused on to achieve improvement?
a. Technology.
b. Human performance.
c. The interaction between technology and human performance.
d. Strategic goals.

24. Management of organizations that engage in business process management view business processes as:
a. Requirements for good control over the organization.
b. Systems that provide information for good management.
c. Strategic assets that must be understood, managed and improved.
d. Mechanisms that keep employees from shirking.

25. At which phase in the business process management life-cycle does management simulate performance of the process in a test environment?
a. Design.
b. Modeling.
c. Execution.
d. Optimization.

26. Which of the following is not a risk that is generally enhanced by a decision to off-shore business processes to a developing nation?
a. Language risk.
b. Technology risk.
c. Public opinion risk.
d. Social responsibility risk.

27. Samco Inc. is in the process of designing a new customer relations system. In which phase of the development life-cycle would a needs assessment most likely be performed?
a. Analysis.
b. Design.
c. Development.
d. Testing.

28. Which of the following system implementation models has the advantage of achieving a full operational test of the new system before it is implemented?
a. Parallel implementation.
b. Plunge implementation.
c. Pilot implementation.
d. Phased implementation.

29. Which of the following involves comparing measures of actual progress of a project to planned progress?
a. Project planning.
b. Project scheduling.
c. Project control.
d. Project closure.

30. Which of the following is a detailed listing of the man-hour, equipment, and materials requirements for a project?
a. Statement of work.
b. Work breakdown structure.
c. Project specifications.
d. Milestone schedule.

31. Which of the following is used to describe the practice of adding resources to shorten selected activity time on the critical path of a project?
a. Making adjustments.
b. Project crashing.
c. Slack time.
d. Reengineering.

32. When a project can be completed in a number of completely different ways that might involve branching after performing activities, the best schedule and control technique would be

    a.   Program Evaluation and Review Technique.
    b.   Gant chart.
    c.   Critical Path Method.
    d.   Graphical Evaluation and Review Technique.

33. A technique that is often used in project management to identify tasks where attention should be focused because they are the most critical is referred to as
    a.   ABC Analysis.
    b.   Milestone analysis.
    c.   Work breakdown analysis.
    d.   Tasking.

34. Which of the following methods of valuation provides the most reliable measure of fair value?
    a.   Use of a discounted cash flow method.
    b.   Market values obtained from active markets.
    c.   Combination of valuation models and active markets.
    d.   Sophisticated valuation models.

35. All of the following are ways that companies in developed countries generally may compete with companies in developing countries except
    a.   Technology.
    b.   Customer service.
    c.   Quality.
    d.   Low-cost resources.

36. According to the Sarbanes-Oxley Act of 2002, which of the following statements is correct regarding an issuer's audit committee financial expert?
    a.   The issuer's current outside CPA firm's audit partner must be the audit committee financial expert.
    b.   If an issuer does **not** have an audit committee financial expert, the issuer must disclose the reason why the role is **not** filled.
    c.   The issuer must fill the role with an individual who has experience in the issuer's industry.
    d.   The audit committee financial expert must be the issuer's audit committee chairperson to enhance internal control.

37. According to COSO, which of the following components of enterprise risk management addresses an entity's integrity and ethical values?
    a.   Information and communication.
    b.   Internal environment.
    c.   Risk assessment.
    d.   Control activities.

ANSWER EXPLANATIONS FOR NEW BUSINESS ENVIORNMENT AND CONCEPTS MATERIAL

1. **(a)** The requirement is to identify the reason that effective corporate governance is important. Answer (a) is correct because the separation of ownership and management creates an agency problem in that management may not act in the best interest of the shareholders. Answer (b) is incorrect because profit maximization is an appropriate goal of management. Answer (c) is incorrect because while corporate governance is designed to prevent excess management compensation that is not the only reason it is important. Answer (d) is incorrect because oversight by boards of directors is a part of corporate governance.

2. **(c)** The requirement is identify the form of compensation that would most likely align management's behavior with the interests of the shareholders. Answer (c) is correct because stock options that cannot be exercised for 10 years provide an incentive to manage the firm to maximize long-term stock value. Answer (a) is incorrect because a fixed salary does not provide an incentive to maximize shareholder value. Answers (b) and (d) are incorrect because they provide an incentive to maximize short-term profit of the firm. This may not be consistent with long-term profitability.

3. **(b)** The requirement is to identify the form of compensation that would encourage management to take on excess risk. Answer (b) is correct because with a bonus based on current period net income management has an incentive to take on excessive risk to maximize its bonuses. Answer (a) is incorrect because a fixed salary encourages management to take on little risk. Answers (c) and (d) are incorrect because stock options that cannot be exercised for 10 years and restricted stock encourage management to be concerned about the long-term viability of the firm.

4. **(c)** The requirement is to identify the item that is not a requirement of the NYSE regarding corporate governance of listed companies. Answer (c) is correct because the rules do not prohibit the CFO from serving on the board of directors. Answers (a), (b) and (d) are all requirements of the NYSE.

5. **(d)** The requirement is to identify the organization or group that does not act as an external corporate governance mechanism. Answer (d) is correct because directors are internal corporate governance mechanisms regardless of whether or not they are independent. Answers (a), (b), and (c) are incorrect because they all act as external corporate governance mechanisms.

6. **(c)** The requirement is to identify the characteristic that must apply to at least one member of the audit committee. Answer (c) is correct because Sarbanes-Oxley requires that at least one member of the audit committee be a financial expert. Answer (a) is incorrect because all audit committee members should be independent. Answer (b) is incorrect because the chief financial officer is not independent and should not be on the audit committee. Answer (d) is incorrect because while a CPA would generally qualify as a financial expert, it is not required that the financial expert be a CPA.

7. **(b)** The requirement is to identify the most effective external monitoring device. Answer (b) is correct because external auditors audit the financial statements and internal controls of a publicly held corporation. Answer (a) is in-

correct because internal auditors are an internal monitoring device. Answer (c) is incorrect because the SEC relies upon external auditors to audit the corporation's financial statements and internal controls. Answer (d) is incorrect because attorneys only advise management on legal issues. They cannot take action if management does not take their advice.

8. **(b)** The requirement is to identify to whom the chief audit executive should report. Answer (b) is correct because ideally the chief audit executive should report to the chief executive officer. Answers (a) and (c) are incorrect because reporting to financial personnel may compromise the internal auditor's effectiveness in assessing financial reporting and controls. Answer (d) is incorrect because the external auditors are not part of the organization.

9. **(a)** The requirement is to identify the limitation that is often attributed to securities analysts regarding their value as an external monitoring device. Answer (a) is correct because occasionally the analyst's firm has a vested interest in the welfare of the company. Answer (b) is incorrect because while some analysts my lack competence it is not a common trait. Answer (c) is incorrect because analysts use all types of information to make evaluations. Answer (d) is incorrect because analysts are not employees of the company.

10. **(d)** The requirement is to identify the division of the SEC that reviews corporate filings. Answer (d) is correct because the Division of Corporate Finance reviews filings. Answer (a) is incorrect because the Office of the Chief Accountant advises the SEC on accounting and auditing matters and approves the rules of the PCAOB. Answer (b) is incorrect because the Division of Enforcement assists the SEC in executing its law enforcement function. Answer (c) is incorrect because the Division of Corporate Disclosure is not a division of the SEC.

11. **(c)** The requirement is to identify the component that is considered the foundation of a company's internal control. Answer (c) is correct because the control environment is considered the foundation of all of the other components of internal control. Answers (a) and (b) are incorrect. While they are both components of internal control, neither is considered the foundation. Answer (d) is incorrect because the audit committee is one aspect of the control environment.

12. **(d)** The requirement is to identify the item that is not a control environment factor. Answer (d) is correct because control monitoring is a separate component of internal control. Answers (a), (b), and (c) are all incorrect because they are all aspects of the control environment.

13. **(c)** The requirement is to identify the component of internal control that encompasses the routine controls over processes and transaction cycles. Answer (c) is correct because control activities policies and procedures are designed to assure that management's directives are followed. Answer (a) is incorrect because the control environment is a high level control. Answer (b) is incorrect because information and communication encompass the controls to assure that management and employees have the information to perform their functions. Answer (d) is incorrect because risk assessment encompasses the organization's processes to identify, assess, and control risks.

14. (b) The requirement is to identify the item that is not a component of the COSO framework for internal controls. Answer (b) is correct because segregation of duties is an aspect of control activities, which is the component. Answers (a), (c) and (d) are all incorrect because they are components of internal control.

15. (a) The requirement is to identify the statement that best describes how technology can improve the monitoring component of internal control. Answer (a) is correct because monitoring involves collecting information to determine that controls are working. Answers (b), (c) and (d) are incorrect because while they represent control advantages to the use of technology, they do not relate as directly to the monitoring component.

16. (d) The requirement is to identify the item that is not a benefit of enterprise risk management. Answer (d) is correct because sharing risk is only one way of responding, and this technique cannot be used for all risks, nor should it be. Answer (a) is incorrect because ERM involves identifying events with positive effects (i.e., opportunities). Answer (b) is incorrect because ERM involves designing appropriate responses to risks. Answer (c) is incorrect because with ERM capital is deployed to opportunities that are consistent with the organization's risk appetite.

17. (b) The requirement is to identify the item that defines the term risk tolerance. Answer (b) is correct because the COSO ERM framework defines risk tolerance as the acceptable variation with respect to a particular organizational objective. Answer (a) is incorrect because it defines risk appetite. Answer (c) is incorrect because it defines residual risk. Answer (d) is incorrect because it defines risks that are accepted.

18. (d) The requirement is to decide what type of response is illustrated by hedging a risk. Answer (d) is correct because hedging involves sharing the risk with another party. Answer (a) is incorrect because avoidance involves exiting the activity that gives rise to the risk. Answer (b) is incorrect because acceptance involves no response to the risk. Answer (c) is incorrect because reduction involves managing the risk to reduce its likelihood or impact.

19. (c) The requirement is to identify the item that is not a technique for identifying risks. Answer (c) is correct because probabilistic models are used for risk assessment. Answers (a), (b) and (d) are incorrect because they are all methods used for event identification.

20. (c) The requirement is to identify the next step in the ERM process. Answer (c) is correct because the next step in the process is to determine the risk response to the assessed risks. Answers (a) and (b) are incorrect because they are subsequent steps in the process. Answer (d) is incorrect because it is part of the event identification process.

21. (c) The requirement is to identify the response that does not represent an advantage of enterprise risk management. Answer (c) is correct because an enterprise risk management system does not seek to eliminate all risks. Risks are avoided, reduced, shifted, or accepted based on the risk appetite of the organization. Answers (a), (b), and (d) are incorrect because they all represent advantages of an enterprise risk management.

22. (a) The requirement is to identify the item that is not a limitation of an enterprise risk management system. Answer (a) is correct because an enterprise risk management system assumes that objectives have been set as a part of the strategic planning process. Answers (b), (c), and (d) are incorrect because they all represent limitations of enterprise risk management systems.

23. (d) The requirement is to identify the aspect of business process improvement that is not generally a focus. Answer (d) is correct because examination of strategic goals is part of strategic planning, not part of business process management. Answers (a), (b) and (c) are incorrect because they all represent ways to improve business processes.

24. (c) The requirement is to identify how business process managers view business processes. Answer (c) is correct because business process managers view processes as strategic assets that can create value and competitive advantage. Answers (a), (b) and (d) are incorrect because they all describe very limited views of business processes.

25. (b) The requirement is to identify the phase that involves simulation of performance of the process in a test environment. Answer (b) is correct because this describes the modeling phase. Answer (a) is incorrect because the design phase involves design of the new process. Answer (c) is incorrect because the execution phase involves implementing the process. Answer (d) is incorrect because optimization involves identifying additional improvements in the process after it is implemented.

26. (b) The requirement is to identify the risk that is not enhanced by a decision to off-shore business processes. Answer (b) is correct because technology risk is not generally affected by the decision to off-shore processes. Answers (a), (c), and (d) are incorrect because these risks may be enhanced as a result of a decision to off-shore processes to a developing country.

27. (a) The requirement is to identify the phase that a needs assessment is most likely to be performed. Answer (a) is correct because in the analysis phase the team attempts to get an understanding of the requirements of the system. Answers (b), (c) and (d) are incorrect because these phases occur after the requirements have been determined.

28. (a) The requirement is to identify the implementation model that has the advantage of a full operational test of the system before it is implemented. Answer (a) is correct because with parallel implementation both systems are operated until it is determined that the new system is operating properly. Answer (b) is incorrect because with the plunge model the new system is put into operation without a full operational test. Answer (c) is incorrect because with pilot implementation the system is only tested with a pilot group. Answer (d) is incorrect with the phased implementation the system is phased in over time.

29. (c) The requirement is to identify the stage that involves comparing measures of actual progress to planned progress. Answer (c) is correct because this describes an aspect of project control. Answers (a), (b), and (d) are incorrect because they represent other stages of the project management life-cycle.

30. (c) The requirement is to identify which of the items is a detailed listing of the man-hour, equipment, and materials requirements for a project. Answer (c) is correct because this is a description of the project specifications. Answer (a) is incorrect because the statement of work is a narrative description of the work to be performed. Answer (b) is incorrect because the work breakdown structure breaks the project into manageable, independent, and measurable elements that can be budgeted and assigned. Answer (d) is incorrect because the milestone schedule sets forth the start date, the end date and other major milestones involved in completing the project.

31. (b) The requirement is to identify the term used to describe the practice of adding resources to shorten selected activity time on the critical path of a project. Answer (b) is correct because this describes project crashing. Answers (a), (c), and (d) are incorrect because they are not terms used to describe this process.

32. (d) The requirement is to identify the scheduling and control technique that would be most appropriate when a project can be completed in a number of completely different ways. Answer (d) is correct because the Graphical Evaluation and Review Technique is appropriate for these types of projects. Answers (a), (b), and (c) are incorrect because these scheduling and control techniques do not perform as well under these circumstances.

33. (a) The requirement is to identify the technique used to identify critical tasks. Answer (a) is correct because ABC Analysis involves categorizing tasks into groups from those that are urgent and important to those that are neither urgent nor important. Answers (b), (c), and (d) are incorrect because they are not terms used to describe a technique to identify critical tasks.

34. (b) The requirement is to identify the most reliable valuation method. Answer (b) is correct because the most reliable valuation comes from market values obtained from active markets. Answers (a), (c), and (d) are incorrect because these are all less reliable methods of determining fair value.

35. (d) The requirement is to identify the item that is not a way in which companies in developed countries can generally compete with companies in developing countries. Answer (d) is correct because developing countries typically have low-cost resources. Answers (a), (b) and (c) are incorrect because they all represent ways that a company in a developed country may compete with companies from developing countries.

36. (b) The requirement is to identify the correct statement regarding a financial expert. Answer (b) is correct because an issuer is required to disclose the names of the financial experts, or the reason that the issuer does not have a financial expert on the audit committee.

37. (b) The requirement is to identify the component that addresses an entity's integrity and ethical values. Answer (b) is correct because integrity and ethical values are part of the internal environment. Answer (a) is incorrect because information and communication is the way information is identified, captured, and communicated to enable people to carry out their responsibilities. Answer (c) is incorrect because risk assessment is the process of analyzing risks. Answer (d) is incorrect because control activities are policies and procedures to help ensure the risk responses are carried out.

EXAMPLE TASK-BASED SIMULATIONS—BUSINESS ECONOMICS AND CONCEPTS

Task-Based Simulation 1

Assume that you are a consultant providing services for Webster Corp. Webster is performing a significant project based implementation of a new enterprise resource system. The company is concerned about the difficulties in performing the project. Compose a memorandum to management describing the risks involved in executing a project that is cross-functional in nature.

REMINDER: Your response will be graded for both technical content and writing skills. Technical content will be evaluated for information that is helpful to the intended user and clearly relevant to the issue. Writing skills will be evaluated for development, organization, and the appropriate expression of ideas in professional correspondence. Use a standard business memorandum or letter format with a clear beginning, middle, and end. Do not convey the information in the form of table, bullet point list, or other abbreviated presentation.

> To: Webster Corp. President
> Re: ERP project management

Task-Based Simulation 2

Skyview, Inc., a small start-up company, has hired you as a consultant to assess its financial systems and related processes. During your review, you learned that the company accountant is responsible for providing general ledger access to others in the company, processing of transactions in the general ledger, and printing checks. The president of the company must authorize write-offs in the system, but the accountant has access to the president's user name and password.

Prepare a memorandum to Skyview's president assessing these responsibilities in the context of segregation of duties. Also assess the possibility of the accountant committing fraud.

REMINDER: Your response will be graded for both technical content and writing skills. Technical content will be evaluated for information that is helpful to the intended user and clearly relevant to the issue. Writing skills will be evaluated for development, organization, and the appropriate expression of ideas in professional correspondence. Use a standard business memorandum or letter format with a clear beginning, middle, and end. Do not convey the information in the form of table, bullet point list, or other abbreviated presentation.

> To: Skyview president
> Re: Segregation of duties and potential for fraud

Task-Based Simulation 3

Assume that you are acting as a consultant for Winston Co. The president of the company is considering implementing an enterprise risk management system. To evaluate whether to go forward with the project, the president has asked you to describe the limitations of an enterprise risk management system.

Prepare a memorandum to Winston's president describing the purpose and limitations of an enterprise risk management system.

REMINDER: Your response will be graded for both technical content and writing skills. Technical content will be evaluated for information that is helpful to the intended user and clearly relevant to the issue. Writing skills will be evaluated for development, organization, and the appropriate expression of ideas in professional correspondence. Use a standard business memorandum or letter format with a clear beginning, middle, and end. Do not convey the information in the form of table, bullet point list, or other abbreviated presentation.

> To: Winston Co. President
> Re: Limitations of an enterprise risk management system

Solution to Task-Based Simulation 1

To: Webster Corp. President
Re: ERP project management

You have requested that we provide information about the issues in executing a project to implement an enterprise resource management system. You should understand that the cross-functional nature of this project creates additional risk of failure that must be controlled. The most important requirement for success of a cross-functional project is full support by top management. The team must have this support to get adequate cooperation from the various function managers of the organization. This also means that the relationships between the project manger and various functional managers must be clearly defined to avoid conflict. Finally, senior management must support the project manager's decisions, recognizing that these decisions must be made quickly and with limited information to ensure that the project remains on schedule. If senior management recognizes and resolves these issues, the risk of failure will be significantly reduced.

If you have any additional questions about the issues regarding completing of the project, please contact me.

Solution to Task-Based Simulation 2

To: Skyview president
Re: Segregation of duties and potential for fraud

You have requested that I perform an independent assessment of Skyview's financial systems and related processes. In a properly controlled financial system the duties of authorization of transactions, approval of transactions, custody of assets, and record keeping should all be segregated. In other words, these functions should all be performed by different individuals. Your current financial system and processes do not include this proper segregation of duties. Skyview's accountant has incompatible duties that would allow him to make an error or perpetrate a fraud and prevent its detection. He processes transactions and has access to assets (printed checks). As an example, he could process fictitious purchase transactions to his own shell companies and cause payments to be made for goods or services that were not received by Skyview.

In addition, the fact that the accountant has access to your user name and password allows him to circumvent the control provided by your being the only individual authorized to write off accounts. This would allow the accountant to process an unauthorized sales transaction to his own shell company and use your user name and password to write off the account.

I would recommend that we develop a new financial system that would include appropriate segregation of duties to ensure that no individual in the organization has the ability to perpetrate errors or fraud without it being detected in the normal course of operations. In addition, we will establish polices regarding the maintenance and confidentiality of user names and passwords to ensure that the controls cannot be circumvented.

If you have any questions, please contact me.

Solution to Task-Based Simulation 3

To: Winston Co. President
Re: Limitations of an enterprise risk management system

You have requested that I provide you with information about an enterprise risk management system. You are particularly concerned with the limitations of such a system. The primary purpose of an enterprise risk management system is to provide processes to identify potential risks to achieving a company's objectives and to manage those risks to be within the company's risk appetite.

In considering implementation of an enterprise risk management system, it is important to recognize that these systems have limitations. All enterprise risk management systems rely on judgments about future events that may or may not occur. Also, while an enterprise risk management system provides information about risks to achieving the company's objectives, it does not even provide reasonable assurance that the objectives will be achieved. The company may have a well-established enterprise risk management system and still fail. Finally, as with all control systems, an enterprise risk management can break down for a number of reasons, including bad judgments about risks and their impact, collusion among two or more individuals, or override by management. Also, due to cost-benefit constraints, no enterprise risk management system can be perfect.

If you have any additional questions about enterprise risk management systems, please contact me.

The CPA Review Program is designed and taught by professors from DePaul University's College of Commerce; including the School of Accountancy and Management Information Systems, the Department of Finance, the Department of Economics, and the Department of Management. All faculty members come to the program with extensive teaching credentials and exemplary professional experience. The course is led by Kevin Stevens, Director of the School of Accountancy and Management Information Systems, under the guidance of O. Ray Whittington, author of *Wiley CPA Exam Review* and Dean of DePaul's College of Commerce.

Learn from the Best

CPA EXAM CREDIT

Candidates may earn up to 8 semester hours by taking the full CPA Review program for credit.
If you are taking the course for CPA exam credit, you connect online and work through the lecture content, complete the assignments and quizzes, as well as the final exam. Credit may only be earned for qualification toward the CPA exam and may not be applied toward any undergraduate or graduate degree program.

CPAREVIEW.DEPAUL.EDU

DEPAUL UNIVERSITY

World-Class CPA Review

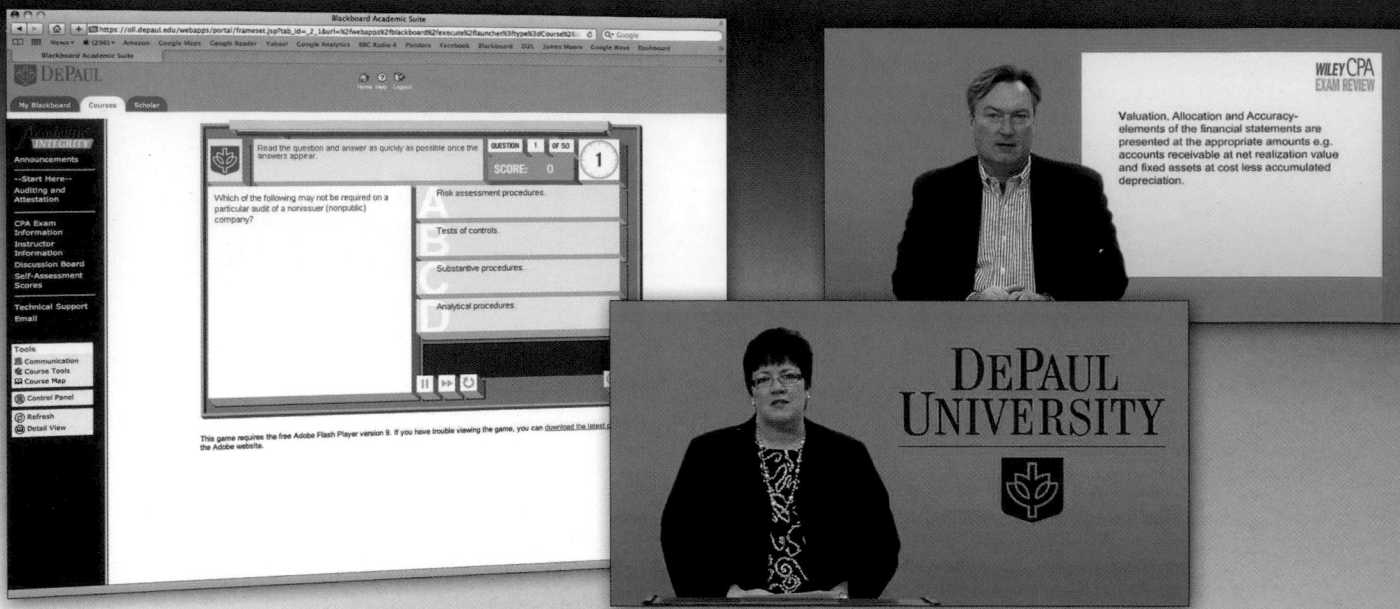

COURSE DESCRIPTIONS

Regulation (REG)

Topics include federal taxation, ethics, professional and legal responsibilities, and business law.

Auditing and Attestation (AUD)

Topics include generally accepted auditing procedures, generally accepted auditing standards and other standards related to attest engagements.

Financial Accounting and Reporting (FAR)

Topics include generally accepted accounting principles for business enterprises, not-for-profit organizations, and governmental entities.

Business Environment and Concepts (BEC)

Topics include general business environment and business concepts that candidates need to know in order to understand the underlying business reasons for and accounting implications of business transactions.

COURSE MODULES

REGULATION

Professional Responsibilities and Business Law
- Professional Responsibilities
- Federal Securities Acts
- Contracts
- Sales
- Commercial Paper
- Secured Transactions
- Bankruptcy
- Debtor-Creditor Relationships
- Agency
- Regulation of Employment and Environment
- Property
- Insurance

Federal Taxation
- Individual
- Transactions in Property
- Partnership
- Corporate
- Gift and Estate

AUDITING AND ATTESTATION
- Engagement Planning
- Internal Control
- Evidence
- Reporting
- Audit Sampling
- Auditing with Technology

BUSINESS ENVIRONMENT AND CONCEPTS
- Business Structure
- Information Technology
- Economics and Strategy
- Financial Management
- Risk Management and Capital Budgeting
- Performance Measures
- Cost Measurement
- Planning, Control, and Analysis

CPAREVIEW.DEPAUL.EDU

It's your choice!

You know your study plan better than anyone – and Wiley makes it easy to follow that plan. That's why we publish our industry-leading *CPA Exam Review* materials in two formats: the compact two-volume set, for candidates who want the whole package at once for less; and the four-volume set, for those who want to focus on one section of the Uniform CPA Exam at a time. Whichever study method suits you best, Wiley has the tools to help you pass the exam on the first try.

You can do it! *Wiley CPA Exam Review 2010* can help you get there.

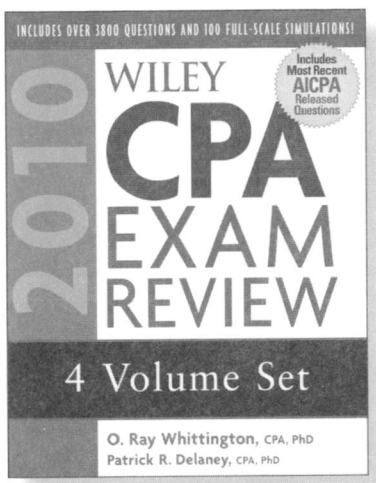

978-0-470-45353-7 • Paper • 2,880 pages
December 2009 • $220.00 US

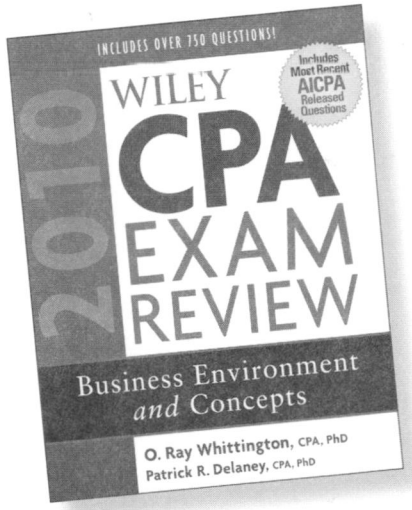

978-0-470-45350-6 • Paper • 408 pages
December 2009 • $55.00 US

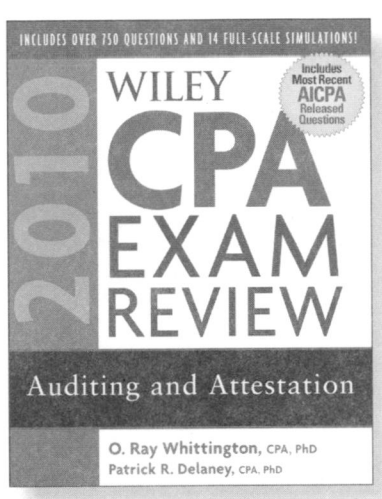

978-0-470-45349-0 • Paper • 672 pages
December 2009 • $55.00 US

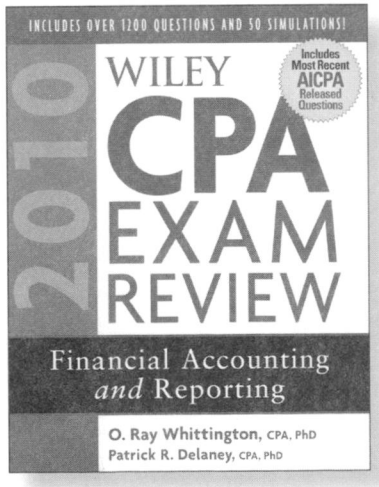

978-0-470-45351-3 • Paper • 1056 pages
December 2009 • $55.00 US

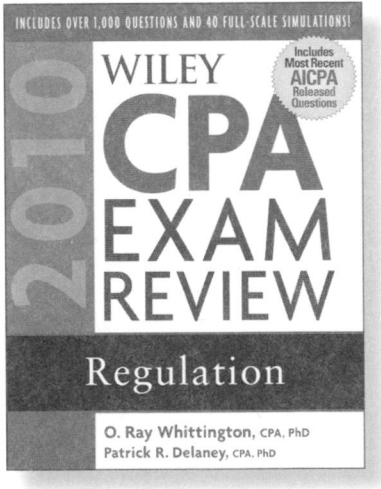

978-0-470-45352-0 • Paper • 744 pages
December 2009 • $55.00 US

Now you know.

Go to **www.wiley.com/cpa** for a complete list of Wiley CPA review products.